Welfare Benefits and Tax Credits Handbook

24th edition

Child Poverty Action Group

Child Poverty Action Group works on behalf of the more than one in four children in the UK growing up in poverty. It does not have to be like this. We use our understanding of what causes poverty and the impact it has on children's lives to campaign for policies that will prevent and solve poverty – for good. We provide training, advice and information to make sure hard-up families get the financial support they need. We also carry out high-profile legal work to establish and protect families' rights. If you are not already supporting us, please consider making a donation, or ask for details of our membership schemes, training courses and publications.

Published by Child Poverty Action Group
30 Micawber Street
London N1 7TB
Tel: 020 7837 7979
staff@cpag.org.uk
cpag.org.uk

A CIP record for this book is available from the British Library
ISBN: 978 1 910715 89 5
Child Poverty Action Group is a charity registered in England and Wales (registration number 294841) and in Scotland (registration number SC039339), and is a company limited by guarantee, registered in England (registration number 1993854). VAT number: 690 808117

Cover design by Colorido Studios
Internal design by Devious Designs
Typeset by DLxml, a division of RefineCatch Limited, Bungay, Suffolk
Content management system by Konnect Soft
Printed in the UK by CPI Group (UK) Ltd, Croydon CR0 4YY

The authors

Liam Bradford is a freelance writer on welfare rights.

Mark Brough is a freelance writer on welfare rights.

Barbara Donegan is a welfare rights worker at CPAG in Scotland.

Sabrina Dubash is a welfare rights worker at CPAG.

Moira Escreet is a welfare rights worker at CPAG in Scotland.

Carolyn George is a freelance writer on welfare rights.

Alison Gillies is a welfare rights worker at CPAG in Scotland.

Daphne Hall is an editor for *rightsnet*, and a freelance trainer and writer on welfare rights.

Will Hadwen is a freelance welfare rights worker for CPAG in Scotland and a freelance trainer.

Henri Krishna is a welfare rights worker at CPAG in Scotland.

Susan Mitchell is a welfare rights worker at CPAG.

Simon Osborne is a welfare rights worker at CPAG, based at CPAG in Scotland.

Judith Paterson is head of advice and rights at CPAG in Scotland.

Steph Pike is a freelance writer on welfare rights.

Frances Ryan is a welfare rights worker at CPAG in Scotland.

Jon Shaw is a welfare rights worker at CPAG in Scotland.

Jessica Strode is judicial review project worker at CPAG.

Carri Swann is a welfare rights worker at CPAG.

Angela Toal is a welfare rights worker at CPAG in Scotland.

Nick Turnill is a welfare rights worker at Oxfordshire Welfare Rights and a freelance welfare rights worker for CPAG.

Rebecca Walker is an advice worker at Sheffield Citizens Advice and Law Centre and a freelance trainer and writer on welfare rights.

Martin Williams is a welfare rights worker at CPAG.

Mark Willis is a welfare rights worker at CPAG in Scotland.

Acknowledgements

The authors would like to thank Lynsey Dalton, Adele Douse, Lizzie Flew, Barbara Gray, Claire Hall, Sophie Lawson, Alison Lord, David Malcolm, Paul Moorhouse, Daniel Norris, Owen Polley, Louise Ross, Kelly Smith, and Katie Wood at Maternity Action for their invaluable contribution.

Our thanks are also due to Simon Osborne, the book's content consultant.

We must acknowledge the efforts of the many authors of previous editions of the *National Welfare Benefits Handbook*, the *Rights Guide to Non-Means-Tested Benefits* and the *Jobseeker's Allowance Handbook*, on which this book is based.

Thanks are also due to Nicola Johnston, Pauline Phillips and Bridget Giles for editing and managing the production of the book, and to Kathleen Armstrong and Anne Ketley for proofreading the text. Particular thanks must go to Katherine Dawson and Anne Ketley for producing the index, Bryce Payton for the typesetting and Bridget Rendell for managing the digital edition on AskCPAG.

The law covered in this book was correct on 1 March 2022 and includes regulations laid up to this date.

Foreword

Welcome to the 2022/23 edition of the *Welfare Benefits and Tax Credits Handbook*, in a year set to be incredibly challenging for many. Following the upheaval of the pandemic, families now face very high inflation. Energy bills and supermarket costs are soaring, and financial support from the social security system is just not keeping pace. For many, the pandemic and current cost pressures are just the latest challenges – life on a low income was already very difficult before March 2020. Our social security system is simply not anywhere close to reflecting what people actually need to get by today.

Last autumn we saw the end of the furlough scheme, the self-employment income support scheme and the £20 increase to universal credit (UC) and working tax credit (WTC). These were all brought in at the beginning of the pandemic and, in practical terms, supported millions of people. But they also showed us that a different social security system is possible: a more generous system that relates to previous earnings in the case of the furlough and self-employment schemes. The £20 increase to UC and WTC were also very welcome, although still left benefit levels too low. Of course, these policies would not have been needed if the UK had a social security system worthy of the name – one that provided real security. The latest report from our Secure Futures project looks at how a combination of universal benefits, contribution-based benefits and 'light-touch' means-tested benefits could achieve income security and social solidarity, and prevent and reduce poverty. See more at cpag.org.uk/securefutures.

We campaigned, alongside many others, against the £20 cut to UC and WTC, and the Chancellor was forced to make some concessions at the Budget last October. We saw the taper rate in UC drop from 63p to 55p (the rate it was initially designed to be) and work allowances increased by £500 a year (although only some benefit from a work allowance). But these changes don't help people who cannot work or, in some cases, those who have only part-time work. For these families, the value of unemployment support is now at its lowest level in real terms since 1990/91. Many UC claimants are not even required to look for work because of their health, disability or caring responsibilities. And, of course, there was nothing in the Budget to support them or the legacy benefit claimants, who had already missed out on the £20 from the start.

The DWP is now ramping up plans to move everyone from legacy benefits on to UC by the end of 2024. It has three approaches to moving people over. First, as has been the case for some time, some changes in circumstances mean you have to apply for UC. Second, a new advertising campaign is encouraging people to look into whether they would be better off on UC and encouraging them to move voluntarily. We and other organisations have expressed concern about this: by DWP estimates just over 50 per cent of people will be better off on UC, but the benefit calculators it recommends are not always going to accurately determine if you will be among the 50 per cent (and you cannot go back once you've applied). And third, the DWP will start to move people over non-voluntarily. At the time of writing, details about how this will work are thin, but the speed at which it will have to happen, and the lack of apparent safeguards, gives us cause for alarm.

At the same time, the DWP is changing the rules about jobseekers claiming UC. As part of its 'Way to Work' campaign, the DWP is reducing the amount of time people will be able to limit their work search to their preferred field from three months to a meagre four weeks. After those four weeks, they will need to apply for and accept any job they can. Anyone deemed non-compliant will face sanctions and reduced income. This approach assumes that the only thing standing between a jobseeker and a job is a willingness to look to other sectors. We know that there is much more to it than that: will the job fit around school hours? Is suitable and affordable childcare available? Does it offer flexibility? Does it pay enough and provide guaranteed hours? Have people received the training and support they need? The government should be focusing its attention on these structural issues rather than making life harder for people already facing an uphill struggle.

Families need more support from the social security system. There is good news for some low-income families in Scotland, who will see a doubling of the Scottish child payment to £20 a week. But as we publish this latest edition of the *Handbook*, families across the UK are facing huge financial pressures. The support the government has put in place for rising energy costs will not go nearly far enough. The best way to support people is to invest in our social security system and support people with costs across the board. This includes lifting the benefit cap – otherwise those capped will not gain from any benefit increases and will face even greater pressures. We will continue to campaign on these issues, and we want to hear from you about problems your clients are facing with the social security system. Please get in touch through our Early Warning System so we can build our evidence and advocate for change: cpag.org.uk/policy-campaigns/early-warning-system.

We know the advice community will be there for families as they navigate these uncertain times. We in turn are here for you. Details of our advice line for advisers can be found at cpag.org.uk/advisers, and up-to-date information and resources are available at AskCPAG.org.uk and cpag.org.uk/shop.

Thank you for your support.

Alison Garnham
Chief Executive

Contents

Part 1 **Introduction**

Provides an overview of the benefits and tax credits system and explains how to use this book to identify which benefits, tax credits or statutory payments you can get and the amount you should receive. Read this part to understand how the information in the book is organised and how to find answers to specific questions about your entitlement.

Part 2 **Universal credit**

Covers the main rules for universal credit. Use this part if you are on a low income to check when you come under the universal credit system, whether you qualify for universal credit and to work out how much benefit you will get. It contains chapters on who can be included in your claim and on how your needs, housing costs, income and capital are calculated.

Part 3 **Other means-tested benefits and tax credits**

Contains chapters on all the means-tested benefits and tax credits, other than universal credit. Use this part if you are on a low income to check the main qualifying conditions.

Contents

Part 4   **General rules for other means-tested benefits**

Explains the general rules for means-tested benefits, including who can be included in your claim, how your needs, income and capital are calculated, and the help you can get for certain housing costs. Use this part to check how much benefit you should get.

Part 5   **Other benefits**

Contains chapters on other benefits, statutory payments and additional help you may be able to get. Use this part to check whether you qualify for any of these benefits or payments, and for information on how to claim, the amount you may receive and how you are paid.

Contents

Abbreviations

AA	attendance allowance	IS	income support
ADP	adult disability payment	ISA	individual savings account
ARAP	Afghan Relocation and Assistance Policy	JSA	jobseeker's allowance
		LES	scheme for locally employed staff in Afghanistan
BSL	British Sign Language		
CA	carer's allowance	MA	maternity allowance
CDP	child disability payment	MS	Medical Service
CFCD	Counter Fraud, Compliance and Debt Directorate	NI	national insurance
		PHSO	Parliamentary and Health Service Ombudsman
CJEU	Court of Justice of the European Union		
CRU	Compensation Recovery Unit	PAYE	pay as you earn
CTB	council tax benefit	PC	pension credit
CTC	child tax credit	PIP	personal independence payment
DLA	disability living allowance	REA	reduced earning allowance
DWP	Department for Work and Pensions	SAP	statutory adoption pay
ECtHR	European Court of Human Rights	SDA	severe disablement allowance
EEA	European Economic Area	SMP	statutory maternity pay
ESA	employment and support allowance	SPBP	statutory parental bereavement pay
EU	European Union	SPP	statutory paternity pay
EWC	expected week of childbirth	SSP	statutory sick pay
HB	housing benefit	SSPP	statutory shared parental pay
HMCTS	HM Courts and Tribunals Service	SSS	Social Security Scotland
HMRC	HM Revenue and Customs	UC	universal credit
IB	incapacity benefit	VINCYP	Visual Impairment Network for Children and Young People
ICE	Independent Case Examiner		
IIDB	industrial injuries disablement benefit	WTC	working tax credit

Universal credit rates

Standard allowance

		£pm
Single	Under 25	265.31
	25 or over	334.91
Couple	Both under 25	416.45
	One or both 25 or over	525.72

Elements

First child (if born before 6 April 2017)		290.00
First child (if born on or after 6 April 2017), second child and each subsequent child who qualifies		244.58
Disabled child addition	Lower rate	132.89
	Higher rate	414.88
Limited capability for work		132.89
Limited capability for work-related activity		354.28
Carer		168.81
Childcare costs	One child	up to 646.35
	Two or more children	up to 1,108.04
	Percentage covered	85%

Capital limits

Lower	Upper
6,000	16,000

Tariff income: £4.35 per £250 between lower and upper limits

Means-tested benefit rates

Income support/income-based jobseeker's allowance

Personal allowances

		£pw
Single	Under 25	61.05
	25 or over	77.00
Lone parent	Under 18	61.05
	18 or over	77.00
Couple	Both under 18	61.05
	Both under 18, certain cases	92.20
	One under 18, one 18–24	61.05
	One under 18, one 25 or over	77.00
	One under 18, certain cases	121.05
	Both 18 or over	121.05

Premiums

Carer		38.85
Disability	Single	36.20
	Couple	51.60
Enhanced disability	Single	17.75
	Couple	25.35
Severe disability	One qualifies	69.40
	Two qualify	138.80
Pensioner	Couple	157.65

Children

(Pre-6 April 2004 claims with no child tax credit)

Child under 20 personal allowance	70.80
Family premium	17.85
Disabled child premium	68.04
Enhanced disability premium (child)	27.44

Capital limits	Lower	Upper
Standard	6,000	16,000
Care homes	10,000	16,000

Tariff income: £1 per £250 between lower and upper limit

Income-related employment and support allowance

		Assessment phase	Main phase
Personal allowances			
Single	Under 25	61.05	77.00
	25 or over	77.00	77.00
Lone parent	Under 18	61.05	77.00
	18 or over	77.00	77.00
Couple	One or both under 18	61.05–121.05	77.00–121.05
	Both 18 or over	121.05	121.05
Components			
Work-related activity		–	30.60
Support		–	40.60
Premiums			
Carer		38.85	38.85
Severe disability (one qualifies)		69.40	69.40
Severe disability (two qualify)		138.80	138.80
Enhanced disability	Single	17.75	17.75
	Couple	25.35	25.35
Pensioner	Couple, no component	157.65	–
	Couple, work-related activity component	–	127.05
	Couple, support component	–	117.05

Capital limits
As for income support

Pension credit
Guarantee credit

Standard minimum guarantee	Single	182.60
	Couple	278.70
Severe disability addition	One qualifies	69.40
	Two qualify	138.80
Carer addition		38.85
Child addition	Standard amount	56.35
	Standard amount for eldest child born before 6 April 2017	66.85
	Disabled child increase	30.58
	Severely disabled child increase	95.48

Savings credit

Threshold	Single	158.47
	Couple	251.70
Maximum	Single	14.48
	Couple	16.20

Capital disregard

Standard/care homes	10,000
No upper limit	
Deemed income: £1 per £500 above disregard	

Housing benefit
Personal allowances

Single	Under 25	61.05
	Under 25 (on main phase ESA)	77.00
	25 or over	77.00
Lone parent	Under 18	61.05
	Under 18 (on main phase ESA)	77.00
	18 or over	77.00
Couple	Both under 18	92.20
	Both under 18 (claimant on main phase ESA)	121.05
	One or both 18 or over	121.05
Dependent children	Under 20	70.80
Pension age (and claimant/partner not on IS, income-based JSA, income-related ESA or UC)	Single (reached pension age before 1 April 2021)	197.10
	Single (reached pension age on or after 1 April 2021)	182.60
	Couple (one or both reached pension age before 1 April 2021)	294.90
	Couple (both reached pension age on or after 1 April 2021)	278.70

Components

Work-related activity	–	30.60
Support	–	40.60

Premiums

Carer		38.85
Disability	Single	36.20
	Couple	51.60
Disabled child		68.04
Enhanced disability	Single	17.75
	Couple	25.35
	Child	27.44

Severe disability	One qualifies	69.40
	Two qualify	138.80
Family	Ordinary rate	17.85
	Some lone parents	22.20

Capital limits	Lower	Upper
Standard	6,000	16,000
Care home or over pension age	10,000	16,000

Tariff income: £1 per £250 between lower and upper limits;
£1 per £500 for those over pension age
No upper limit or tariff income for those on pension credit guarantee credit

Social fund payments

Maternity grant		500.00
Cold weather payment		25.00
Winter fuel payment	Under 80	200.00
over pension age)	80 or over	300.00
	Care home (under 80)	100.00
	Care home (80 or over)	150.00

Scotland-only payments
Best Start grant
Pregnancy and baby payment

	First child	642.35
	Any subsequent child	321.20
Early learning payment		267.65
School-age payment		267.35
Scottish child payment		20.00

Non-means-tested benefit rates

Attendance allowance	£pw
Higher rate	92.40
Lower rate	61.85

Bereavement benefits
Widowed parent's allowance/widowed mother's allowance	126.35

Bereavement support payment
Higher rate

Lump sum	3,500
Monthly amount	350.00

Standard rate

Lump sum	2,500
Monthly amount	100.00

Carer's allowance
	69.70

Child benefit
Only/eldest child	21.80
Other child(ren)	14.45

Disability living allowance
Care component

Highest rate	92.40
Middle rate	61.85
Lowest rate	24.45

Mobility component

Higher rate	64.50
Lower rate	24.45

Contributory employment and support allowance
Assessment phase

Under 25	61.05
25 or over	77.00

Main phase

16 or over	77.00
Work-related activity component	30.60
Support component	40.60

• • • •

Guardian's allowance 18.55

Short-term incapacity benefit
Under pension age
Lower rate 89.25
Higher rate 105.55
Adult dependant 53.50
Over pension age
Lower rate 113.45
Higher rate 118.25
Adult dependant 66.10

Long-term incapacity benefit 118.25
Age addition (under 35) 12.55
Age addition (35–44) 6.95
Adult dependant 68.70
Industrial injuries disablement benefit 20%: £37.72 to 100%: £188.60

Contribution-based jobseeker's allowance
Under 25 61.05
25 or over 77.00

Maternity allowance
Standard rate 156.66

Personal independence payment
Daily living component
Standard rate 61.85
Enhanced rate 92.40

Mobility component
Standard rate 24.45
Enhanced rate 64.50

Retirement pensions
State pension (full rate) 185.15
Category A 141.85
Category B (widow(er)/surviving civil partner) 141.85
Category B (spouse/civil partner) 85.00
Category D 85.00

Severe disablement allowance 83.75
Age addition (under 40) 12.55
Age addition (40–49) 6.95
Age addition (50–59) 6.95
Adult dependant 41.20

Statutory maternity, adoption, paternity, shared parental and parental bereavement pay
Standard rate 156.66

Statutory sick pay 99.35

National insurance contributions
Lower earnings limit 123.00
Primary threshold 190 (242 from 6 July 2022)
Employee's class 1 rate 13.25% of £190 (£242 from 6 July 2022) to £967
Class 2 rate (self-employed) 3.25% above £967

Scotland-only payments
Adult disability payment
Daily living component
Standard rate 61.85
Enhanced rate 92.40

Mobility component
Standard rate 24.45
Enhanced rate 64.50

Child disability payment
Care component
Highest rate 92.40
Middle rate 61.85
Lowest rate 24.45

Mobility component
Higher rate 64.50
Lower rate 24.45

Carer's allowance supplement
245.70 (June 2022)
245.70 (December 2022)

Child winter heating assistance 214.10

Young carer grant 326.65

Tax credit rates

	£ per day	£ per year
Child tax credit		
Family element (child born before 6 April 2017)	1.50	545
Child element	8.05	2,935
Disabled child element		
Lower rate	9.72	3,545
Higher rate for a severely disabled child	13.64	4,975
Working tax credit		
Basic element	5.68	2,070
Lone parent element	5.83	2,125
Couple element	5.83	2,125
30-hour element	2.36	860
Disabled worker element	9.17	3,345
Severe disability element	3.96	1,445
Childcare element		
70% of eligible weekly childcare costs:		
One child		weekly maximum 175
Two or more children		weekly maximum 300
Thresholds		
Income threshold		
Working tax credit only or with child tax credit		6,770
Child tax credit only		17,005
Taper		41%
Income increase disregard		2,500

Part 1

· ·

Introduction

Chapter 1

How to use this book

This chapter covers:

1. **About this** *Handbook*

This *Handbook* is the definitive guide to benefits, tax credits and statutory payments, condensing a huge and complex area of law into a comprehensive and user-friendly book. It contains everything you need to know in order to understand your entitlement to benefits, tax credits and statutory payments, and aims to answer any questions you may have about your entitlement. The book explains how you claim and how much money you should get, how decisions are made and how to get them changed. It provides examples to illustrate how the rules work in practice and tactics to help you deal with common problems.

The book also helps you find the specific legislation, caselaw or official guidance relevant to the information contained in the text, should you need it. If you are an adviser, this *Handbook* is an essential tool, containing all you need to provide practical, effective and accurate advice.

Updates and digital access

This *Handbook* is published annually. The information in it is updated throughout the year to reflect changes in legislation and new caselaw. These updates are published in CPAG's bi-monthly *Welfare Rights Bulletin* and on AskCPAG, CPAG's digital service. Subscribing to AskCPAG gives you online access to this *Handbook*, as well as to other CPAG publications. It also gives you access to tools which help you solve difficult benefit queries and draft mandatory reconsideration letters or appeal submissions on commonly disputed matters. For further information, see AskCPAG.org.uk.

1

Scope of this *Handbook*

The information in this *Handbook* applies to Great Britain.

Scotland

If you live in Scotland, some benefits and payments are different from those in England and Wales, as are some limited aspects of universal credit. This is because the responsibility for certain benefits, and for certain aspects of universal credit, has been devolved to the Scottish Parliament. Social Security Scotland administers and pays benefits that come under the Scottish social security system, known in this *Handbook* as 'Scottish benefits'. Some Scottish benefits are already available, some new ones will be brought in during the course of 2022 and others after that. If you are resident in Scotland, see Chapter 72 for further information.

Northern Ireland

With some exceptions (such as tax credits, child benefit and guardian's allowance), responsibility for social security is devolved to Northern Ireland. However, a principle of 'parity' exists between Northern Ireland and Great Britain which ensures that, in most respects, the benefits described in this *Handbook* are available to people in Northern Ireland. Northern Ireland has its own benefits legislation but the rules largely correspond to those in Great Britain, although the administration and adjudicating bodies are often different, and sometimes particular provisions in Northern Ireland are different – eg, because a particular rule does not apply there or because certain provisions have been put in place in Northern Ireland to mitigate some of the effects of welfare reforms.

---

2. **Using this *Handbook***

There is a large amount of information in this *Handbook*, but you do not need to read it from cover to cover to find out about your benefit entitlement. If you are unfamiliar with the benefits system, a good place to start is the section in this chapter called 'Finding out which benefits and tax credits you can get' (see p8). This explains the best way to determine which benefits, tax credits or statutory payments you qualify for and to establish how they interact with each other.

If you want to find the answer to a particular question, or to understand the rules for a specific benefit, it should be easy to locate the information you need by using the detailed index or by using the individual benefit, tax credit and statutory payment chapters as your starting point.

Using the index

A simple way to find specific information in this book is to use the index. The index is designed to be detailed and intuitive to ensure you can easily locate the information you need.

- Use the entries in bold type, arranged alphabetically, to help you to find general information on a subject.
- Use the sub-entries under these, also arranged alphabetically, to find more specific information relevant to your search.
- Use the list at the start of the index to understand the abbreviations used.

For example, if you want to find information on how to claim attendance allowance, you can locate this either by looking up 'claims' and finding the 'AA' sub-heading underneath that, or by looking up 'attendance allowance' and finding the 'claims' sub-heading underneath that.

Using the individual benefit chapters

Another good starting point for finding specific information in this book is the chapter on the particular benefit, tax credit or statutory payment to which your search relates. These chapters follow a common structure to help you easily find the information contained in them, and they refer you to other relevant information that is elsewhere in the book.

- Find the chapter about the particular benefit, tax credit or statutory payment by using the contents list on pvii. Find the relevant part of the book and then locate the appropriate chapter in that part. To assist with this, tabs on the left-hand pages identify the number of the part you are in. The parts and chapters are also identified at the top of each page.
- Familiarise yourself with the standard way information is presented in these chapters (see p7). This will help you to locate information in the text easily. For example, if you want to know whether there are age limits for claiming a particular benefit, it is helpful to know that each chapter has a section called 'The rules about your age'.
- Alternatively, use the chapter contents at the start of each chapter to direct you to the likely section in the chapter to check. The section you are in within a chapter is identified at the top of the left-hand page.
- Follow any cross references in the text to find any other relevant information contained in the book.

Finding the law

To help you trace the source of the information given in the text, references to the law (both legislation and caselaw) and to guidance are given. It may be helpful to use these references, particularly if you are challenging a decision, as they provide the legal justification for the statements made in the text. For a useful introduction to legal sources, see pp1336–41.

- Find the information in the book relevant to the issue you want to check and find the note for that information.
- Check the relevant note at the end of the chapter for the legal reference.

Part 1: Introduction
Chapter 1: How to use this book
3. How this *Handbook* is organised

- Check Appendix 9 for an explanation of the abbreviations used in the references.
- See Appendices 1 and 2 for where to find the law and guidance online and for other useful sources of information.

The law referred to in this *Handbook* only applies in Great Britain. See p4 if you live in Northern Ireland.

3. **How this *Handbook* is organised**

The book is split into parts, and related chapters are grouped under these parts. A description of the information covered in each part, together with a list of chapters it contains, is included in the table of contents on pvii.

By developing a basic understanding of the purpose of each part, you can immediately identify where certain information will be in the book. For example, once you know that Part 11 covers the immigration and residence rules for benefits and tax credits, you know to use this part if you need to check whether your immigration status affects your right to a particular benefit.

Similarly, the common structure of many of the chapters is designed to make it easier to find information in them.

How the parts are organised

- **Part 1:** Introduction.
- **Part 2:** Universal credit. This contains chapters on the introduction of universal credit, the rules of entitlement, who is included in your claim and how your needs, income and capital affect your entitlement and the amount you receive. There is also a chapter that explains the help you can get within your universal credit for rent and certain other housing costs.
- **Part 3:** Other means-tested benefits and tax credits. This contains chapters on each of the other main means-tested benefits and tax credits.
- **Part 4:** General rules for other means-tested benefits. This part covers the general rules for means-tested benefits other than universal credit. It contains chapters explaining who is included in a claim for a means-tested benefit and how your needs, income and capital affect your entitlement, and chapters on the help you can get with your rent and certain other housing costs and when the amount of such help is restricted.
- **Part 5:** Other benefits. This contains chapters on non-means-tested benefits, statutory payments and other help you may get, in alphabetical order.
- **Part 6:** Special benefit rules. This contains chapters explaining the rules for particular groups of people: students, people in hospital or care homes, prisoners, and people leaving care or without accommodation.

1

- **Part 7**: National insurance, work and work-related rules. This contains chapters covering the national insurance (NI) contribution conditions for contributory benefits and the qualifying conditions for NI credits, how work affects your benefit entitlement, how limited capability for work is assessed, and the conditions you may have to meet to prepare for or find work, and what happens if you do not meet them.
- **Part 8**: Claiming benefits and getting paid. This contains chapters on claiming and backdating benefit, how and when you should be paid, whether you are entitled to hardship payments or are affected by the benefit cap, and information on overpayments and penalties.
- **Part 9**: Getting a benefit decision changed. This contains chapters on challenging decisions on benefits and statutory payments and how to complain.
- **Part 10**: General rules for tax credits. This contains chapters on the general rules for tax credits, including how your entitlement is worked out and how to challenge decisions.
- **Part 11**: Immigration and residence rules for benefits and tax credits. This contains chapters explaining your entitlement if you are a person subject to immigration control, if you are going to, or have come from, abroad or if you are covered by the European Union co-ordination rules.
- **Part 12**: Scottish social security benefits. This contains information on the Scottish social security system and gives details of the benefits and payments that are administered by Social Security Scotland, including how to claim Scottish benefits, how claims are administered and paid, and how to challenge determinations.
- **Appendices.** These contain further information, such as sources of information and advice, relevant dates for statutory payments for a birth and maternity allowance, and the legislation on particular assessments.

How the chapters are organised

To help you locate information easily, many of the *Handbook* chapters have a similar structure. Each chapter contains the following.
- **Chapter contents:** to help you find the section you need.
- **Key facts:** covering the key points about the information in the chapter. If the chapter is about a specific benefit, tax credit or statutory payment, these include standard information, such as how work affects your entitlement, whether the benefit is means tested or non-means tested, whether you must have paid NI contributions to qualify and who administers your claim.
- **Endnotes:** to the numbered references in the text. These are at the end of each chapter and, in most cases, cite the legal source of the information in the text.

The chapters on specific benefits, tax credits and statutory payments usually also contain information organised under the following standard headings.

Part 1: Introduction
Chapter 1: How to use this book
4. Finding out which benefits and tax credits you can get

1

- **Who can get the particular benefit, tax credit or statutory payment**: explains the qualifying conditions.
- **The rules about your age:** any age limits that are relevant.
- **People included in the claim:** who you can claim for, or whether you have to make a joint claim with someone else.
- **The amount of benefit:** the rules about how much money you should receive, with cross references to rules common to more than one benefit or tax credit.
- **Special benefit rules:** to alert you when there are additional rules that apply in particular circumstances – eg, if you are in hospital.
- **Claims and backdating:** how to claim, who should claim, the information you must provide, the date your claim is treated as having been made, whether your claim can be backdated, whether a claim for one benefit can be treated as a claim for another, and whether claims can be made in advance.
- **Getting paid:** how and when you are paid, and what to do if your circumstances change.
- **Tax, other benefits and the benefit cap:** whether the benefit, tax credit or statutory payment is taxable, how it interacts with other benefits or tax credits, and whether it is affected by rules on the benefit cap, plus information on other help you may get.

The text under these headings refers you to any other information in the book that is relevant. This is to ensure that not only is information easy to find within each chapter, but also that you can answer almost any question you have on your entitlement by using the individual benefit, tax credit or statutory payment chapter as a starting point.

4. **Finding out which benefits and tax credits you can get**

To find out about all the help you can get, it is important to check your entitlement in the following order.
- First check whether you qualify for any non-means-tested benefits or statutory payments.
- Next, check your entitlement to means-tested benefits.
- Finally, check whether there is any other help available to you.

Step one: do you qualify for any non-means-tested benefits or statutory payments?

What are non-means-tested benefits and statutory payments?

A non-means-tested benefit is a benefit for which it is not necessary to carry out a detailed assessment of your income or capital to work out your entitlement. You may need to meet national insurance contribution conditions to qualify for some non-means-tested benefits ('contributory benefits') and you may qualify for others just because of your circumstances. Certain non-means-tested benefits ('earnings-replacement benefits') are intended to compensate you for loss of earnings. Your entitlement to non-means-tested benefits is not affected by any savings that you have and only certain kinds of income affect your entitlement to some earnings-replacement benefits.

Statutory payments are payments an employer may be required to pay you if you are an employee and are unfit for work or off work on maternity, paternity, adoption, shared parental or parental bereavement leave. Your entitlement to statutory payments depends on the level of your past earnings (and, for statutory shared parental pay, the past earnings of your partner), but it is not affected by any other income or savings you have.

Both jobseeker's allowance (JSA) and employment and support allowance (ESA) may be made up of a non-means-tested, contributory element (contribution-based JSA and contributory ESA) and/or a means-tested element (income-based JSA and income-related ESA). However, income-based JSA and income-related ESA are being replaced by universal credit (UC), so new claims now can only be made for contribution-based JSA and contributory ESA (but see p23). If you qualify for both elements, in effect, the means-tested element tops up the contributory element.

- Use the table on p10 to see which non-means-tested benefits or statutory payments you might get. Check the benefits under all the circumstances that apply to you.
- Check which of these are 'earnings-replacement benefits' (these are marked with an * in the table).
- Turn to the chapter on the benefits you are interested in, looking at any earnings-replacement benefits or statutory payments first. The chapters are arranged in alphabetical order in Part 5 and, for people living in Scotland, in Part 12.
- Check whether you meet the qualifying conditions for the benefit by looking at the section explaining who can get that benefit. Cross references take you to further details you may need to check.
- Look in the section 'Tax, other benefits and the benefits cap' for details of how the benefit might be affected by other benefits you already get or want to claim. Because of the 'overlapping benefit' rules, certain non-means-tested benefits cannot be paid in full at the same time.
- If you think you qualify, use the section 'How to claim' for further information on what to do next.

Part 1: Introduction
Chapter 1: How to use this book
4. Finding out which benefits and tax credits you can get

1

Your circumstances	Benefits you might get	Chapter
Bereaved	Bereavement support payment* *or*	Chapter 25
	Widowed parent's allowance*	Chapter 25
	Statutory parental bereavement pay	Chapter 38
Carer	Carer's allowance*, *and,* if you live in	Chapter 26
	Scotland, carer's allowance	
	supplement	
Pregnant or have recently given birth	Statutory maternity pay	Chapter 38
	Maternity allowance*	Chapter 34
	Statutory shared parental pay	Chapter 38
	Child benefit	Chapter 27
Recently adopted a child	Statutory adoption pay	Chapter 38
	Statutory paternity pay	Chapter 38
	Statutory shared parental pay	Chapter 38
	Child benefit	Chapter 27
Father of a baby or partner of	Statutory paternity pay	Chapter 38
someone who has recently given	Statutory shared parental pay	Chapter 38
birth or adopted a child		
Responsible for a child	Child benefit	Chapter 27
	Guardian's allowance	Chapter 27
Disabled	Disability living allowance	Chapter 28
	In Scotland, child disability payment	Chapter 75
	Personal independence payment	Chapter 35
	In Scotland, adult disability payment	Chapter 73
	Attendance allowance	Chapter 24
	Industrial injuries benefits	Chapter 32
Unfit for work	Contributory employment and	Chapter 30
	support allowance*	
	Statutory sick pay	Chapter 39
	Industrial injuries benefits	Chapter 32
Pensioner	State pension*	Chapter 36
Unemployed and seeking work, or	Contribution-based jobseeker's	Chapter 33
working part time and seeking more	allowance*	
work		

* Earnings-replacement benefits

Step two: do you qualify for any means-tested benefits and tax credits?

UC is replacing other means-tested benefits and tax credits for people of working age. This means that you cannot make a new claim for the means-tested benefits: income support, income-based JSA, income-related ESA (but see p23), or (if you are under pension age) housing benefit (except in very limited circumstances), or for the tax credits: child tax credit or working tax credit (unless you already get one of them and are claiming the other). These means-tested benefits and tax credits are collectively known as 'legacy benefits'. Instead, if you are under pension age (or if your partner is), you can claim UC. If you are already getting a legacy benefit, provided you continue to satisfy the qualifying conditions, you can continue to receive it until you transfer to UC (see p26).

What are means-tested benefits and tax credits?

A means-tested benefit is one for which an assessment of your needs, income and capital is necessary to work out your entitlement. You only qualify for means-tested benefits if your (and your partner's) income and capital are not too high. Entitlement to tax credits, which are also means tested, depends on your assessed needs and the level of your (and your partner's) income. The assessment of the amount you need to live on for means-tested benefits and tax credits may increase if you get certain non-means-tested benefits. Depending on your circumstances and when you made your claim, you may be entitled to a combination of non-means-tested benefits, a statutory payment, means-tested benefits and/or tax credits. You cannot qualify for certain means-tested benefits at the same time.

- If you and, if you have a partner, your partner are pension age or over, check the table below.
- Otherwise, use Chapter 2 to see whether you come under the UC system as this affects the benefits you can get, then use the tables below to see which means-tested benefits and/or tax credits might be relevant to your circumstances.
- Turn to the chapter(s) on the relevant benefit(s).
- Follow the procedure explained for checking non-means-tested benefits, by looking at the sections on who can get the benefit, 'Tax, other benefits and the benefit cap' and 'How to claim' in any relevant chapters.

If you (and your partner, if you have a partner) are pension age or over*

Your circumstances	Benefit	Chapter
Pensioner	Pension credit**	Chapter 13
Tenant	Housing benefit	Chapter 10

* If you are a member of a couple, both you and your partner usually must be pension age or over for you to qualify for pension credit or to make a new claim for housing benefit. For further details and exceptions, see p174 and p257.

** If you are already getting child tax credit and/or working tax, you also may continue to qualify for them after reaching pension age.

Part 1: Introduction
Chapter 1: How to use this book
4. Finding out which benefits and tax credits you can get

1

If you come under the universal credit system

Your circumstance	Benefit	Chapter
Come under the UC system	Universal credit	Chapter 3

If you do not come under the universal credit system

Your circumstances	Benefits and tax credits	Chapter
Carer	Income support	Chapter 11
Pregnant or recently given birth	Income support	Chapter 11
	Income-related employment and support allowance	Chapter 9
	Child tax credit	Chapter 14
	Working tax credit (in limited circumstances)	Chapter 15
Recently adopted a child	Child tax credit	Chapter 14
	Working tax credit (in limited circumstances)	Chapter 15
	Income support (in some circumstances)	Chapter 11
Responsible for a child	Child tax credit	Chapter 14
	Income support (in some circumstances)	Chapter 11
Disabled or unfit for work	Income-related employment and support allowance	Chapter 9
	Income support (in limited circumstances)	Chapter 11
	Working tax credit (in limited circumstances)	Chapter 15
Tenant	Housing benefit	Chapter 10
Working	Working tax credit	Chapter 15
Unemployed and seeking work, or working part time and seeking more work	Income-based jobseeker's allowance	Chapter 12

Step three: can you get any other help?

What further help is there?

If you are entitled to certain benefits or tax credits, you may qualify for other benefits on
that basis. These are called 'passported benefits'. Some of these passported benefits can
also be awarded on the basis of your circumstances or age, or if you have a low income.

Other assistance may be available to people in certain circumstances and may be means tested – eg, council tax reduction.

Some types of passported benefits or other assistance are different in England, Wales and Scotland.

Entitlement to some of these payments is discretionary.

- Use the tables below to see the other help you may be able to get in your circumstances and to see whether the benefits or tax credits you get help you qualify for any additional 'passported benefits'.
- Use the relevant chapters to check whether you qualify for such help and how to apply.
- Check whether you qualify for council tax reduction (see p836).
- Check Chapter 40 to see whether there are any other payments or other kinds of help you might be able to get.

Your circumstances	Benefits and other help you might get	Chapter
Bereaved	In England and Wales, funeral expenses payment or,	Chapter 37
	in England, children's funeral fund payment	Chapter 37
	In Wales, help towards child funeral costs	Chapter 37
	In Scotland, funeral support payment	Chapter 76
Pregnant or recently given birth or adopted a child	In England and Wales, Sure Start maternity grant	Chapter 37
	In Scotland, Best Start grant pregnancy and baby payment	Chapter 74
	Health benefits	Chapter 31
	In England and Wales, Healthy Start food	Chapter 40
	In Scotland, Best Start foods	Chapter 40
	Healthy Start vitamins	Chapter 40
Responsible for a child	In England and Wales, Sure Start maternity grant (if child is no more than 12 months old)	Chapter 37
	In Scotland, Best Start grant pregnancy and baby payment, early learning payment or school-age payment	Chapter 74
	In Scotland, Scottish child payment	Chapter 77
	Free school lunches	Chapter 40

Part 1: Introduction
Chapter 1: How to use this book
4. Finding out which benefits and tax credits you can get

1

	Health benefits for child	Chapter 31
	In England and Wales, Healthy Start food	Chapter 40
	In Scotland, Best Start foods	Chapter 40
	Healthy Start vitamins	Chapter 40
	Cold weather payment (in some circumstances)	Chapter 37
	In Scotland, child winter heating assistance (in some circumstances)	Chapter 72
Disabled or unfit for work	Cold weather payment	Chapter 37
Carer	In Scotland, young carer grant	Chapter 78
Preparing for or starting work	Flexible Support Fund	Chapter 40
	For young people in Scotland, job start payment	Chapter 40
Pensioners	Winter fuel payment	Chapter 37
	Cold weather payment	Chapter 37
	Health benefits	Chapter 31
Aged 60 or over	Some health benefits	Chapter 31
Own a home	Council tax reduction	Chapter 40
	In England and Wales, discretionary reduction in council tax	Chapter 40
Have a mortgage	Loan for mortgage interest	Chapter 40
Tenant	Council tax reduction	Chapter 40
	Discretionary housing payment	Chapter 29
	In England and Wales, discretionary reduction in council tax	Chapter 40
Not enough money to meet certain needs	Budgeting loan	Chapter 37
	Budgeting advance of universal credit	Chapter 3
	Health benefits	Chapter 31
	Council tax reduction	Chapter 40
	Other payments	Chapter 40

Passported benefit	*Passports*
Free school lunches (p851)*	Some people on universal credit
	Income support
	Income-based jobseeker's allowance
	Income-related employment and support allowance
	Some people on child tax credit
	Guarantee credit of pension credit (England and Wales only)

Health benefits (Chapter 31)**	Some people on universal credit
	Income support
	Income-based jobseeker's allowance
	Income-related employment and support allowance
	Some people on child tax credit
	Some people on working tax credit
	Guarantee credit of pension credit
Sure Start maternity grant, in England and Wales (p782)	Universal credit
	Income support
	Income-based jobseeker's allowance
	Income-related employment and support allowance
	Some people on child tax credit
	Some people on working tax credit
	Pension credit
Best Start grants, in Scotland (Chapter 74)	Universal credit
	Income support
	Income-based jobseeker's allowance
	Income-related employment and support allowance
	Housing benefit
	Child tax credit
	Working tax credit
	Pension credit
Social fund funeral expenses payment, in England and Wales (p784)	Universal credit
	Income support
	Income-based jobseeker's allowance
Funeral support payment, in Scotland (Chapter 76)	Income-related employment and support allowance
	Housing benefit
	Child tax credit (in England and Wales, in some circumstances)
	Some people on working tax credit
	Pension credit
Social fund cold weather payment (p791)	Some people on universal credit
	Some people on income support
	Some people on income-based jobseeker's allowance
	Some people on income-related employment and support allowance
	Pension credit

Part 1: Introduction
Chapter 1: How to use this book
5. Working out how much benefit you should receive

1

Social fund budgeting loan (p778)	Income support
	Income-based jobseeker's allowance
	Income-related employment and support allowance
	Pension credit
Scottish child payment (Chapter 77)	Universal credit
	Income support
	Income-based jobseeker's allowance
	Income-related employment and support allowance
	Child tax credit
	Working tax credit
	Pension credit

*Additionally, in England and Scotland, all children in certain year groups are entitled to free school lunches and, in Scotland, pre-school children of parents getting certain benefits may qualify. In Scotland, if you get one of the benefits that qualifies your child for free school lunches, you may also get Scottish child payment bridging payment (see p1735). In Wales, children in local authority maintained primary schools are entitled to free school breakfasts. In England and Wales, children may continue to qualify for free school lunches after entitlement to the passporting benefit ends. See p851 for further information.

**Some health benefits are free for everyone in Scotland and Wales, and for people in England with certain conditions.

5. **Working out how much benefit you should receive**

How much benefit will you get?
The amount you get depends on which benefit you are claiming. Some non-means-tested benefits are paid at different rates depending on your circumstances. The amount of some contributory benefits may depend on your national insurance contribution record (or that of your spouse or civil partner), and some (but not all) non-means-tested earnings-replacement benefits are affected by certain types of income. The amount of means-tested benefits you get always depends on your circumstances and involves a detailed assessment of your needs, your income and your capital. Your entitlement to tax credits also depends on an assessment of your needs and income. Tables of benefit and tax credit rates for 2022/23 are on ppxiii–xxi.

• Look at the chapters dealing with the benefit(s) you are interested in, checking the non-means-tested benefits and statutory payments chapters first. This is

1

because any non-means-tested benefits you get may affect the amount of means-tested benefit to which you are entitled.

- If you are not already getting the benefit, check you meet the entitlement conditions and then look at the section 'The amount of benefit'. Follow any relevant cross references for more detailed information about different aspects of the calculation.
- Check the section 'Tax, other benefits and the benefit cap' for additional information on how the benefit or tax credit may be affected by other benefits or tax credits you receive.
- If in doubt, use Appendix 1 for details of where you can get further help.

---

6. Finding information on challenging a decision

Who makes decisions?

The Department for Work and Pensions (DWP) is responsible for administering most benefits. HM Revenue and Customs (HMRC) is responsible for administering tax credits, child benefit and guardian's allowance. HMRC also makes decisions on your national insurance (NI) contribution record and on your entitlement to statutory payments if you and your employer do not agree. Social Security Scotland administers Scottish benefits. Local authorities administer housing benefit, council tax reduction schemes, certain education benefits and local welfare assistance schemes. The Welsh government is responsible for the Discretionary Assistance Fund for Wales.

HM Courts and Tribunals Service, which is part of the Ministry of Justice, is responsible for administering benefit and tax credit appeals. The Scottish Courts and Tribunals Service administers appeals about Scottish benefits.

If you are unhappy with a decision that has been made on your claim, you can try to get it changed. The ways you can challenge a decision, and the procedures and time limits for doing so, depend on the benefit concerned and on whether the decision you want to challenge is an initial decision on your claim or a decision that has been made following a revision, supersession, redetermination or appeal. Use the following steps if you are considering challenging a decision.

- First check whether the decision is correct. See p4 for how to find answers to specific questions.
- If you think it is not correct, turn to the chapter on the benefit to which the decision relates and check the last bullet point in the key facts at the start of the chapter. This explains where to find information on challenging a decision relating to that benefit.

Part 1: Introduction
Chapter 1: How to use this book
6. Finding information on challenging a decision

1

- Check the chapters in Part 9, Chapter 67 for tax credits, or Chapter 80 for Scottish benefits, to find information on how you may be able to challenge the decision. For decisions relating to NI contributions, see p946. Check the information at the start of the chapter to be sure it is relevant to the benefit to which your challenge relates.
- Alternatively, look up 'challenging a decision' in the index. The sub-entries under it may help you to find the page number for the type of decision you want to challenge.

Part 2

Universal credit

Chapter 2

The introduction of universal credit

This chapter covers:
1. The introduction of universal credit (below)
2. The universal credit system (p22)
3. Transferring to universal credit (p26)
4. Change of circumstances (p31)

Key facts
- Universal credit (UC) has been introduced nationwide for new claimants.
- When you come under the UC system, UC replaces most other means-tested benefits and tax credits.
- Current claimants of means-tested benefits and tax credits do not automatically come under the UC system, but can transfer to UC via 'natural migration' – eg, by claiming UC after a change of circumstances, or otherwise deciding to claim UC.
- Current claimants of means-tested benefits and tax credits will be transferred to UC under the 'managed migration' process started by the DWP. The DWP began transferring a small number of cases under this process in early 2022. The number of people transferred is expected to increase during 2022.

1. The introduction of universal credit

Universal credit (UC) combines means-tested support for adults under pension age and children into one benefit.

When you come under the UC system (see p22), UC replaces the following means-tested benefits and tax credits (known as 'legacy benefits'):
- income support;
- income-based jobseeker's allowance (JSA);
- income-related employment and support allowance (ESA);
- housing benefit (HB) for people of working age, except for 'specified' and 'temporary' accommodation (see p173);

Part 2: Universal credit
Chapter 2: The introduction of universal credit
2. The universal credit system

- child tax credit;
- working tax credit.

UC does not replace pension credit (PC) or HB if you have reached pension age (see p257). However, if you are in a couple and you or your partner have reached pension age or are entitled to PC, you may come under the UC system in certain situations (see p24).

Even if you come under the UC system, you can still claim non-means-tested benefits. So, for example, you can still claim contribution-based JSA, contributory ESA, child benefit and carer's allowance, as well as UC.

UC has been introduced across Great Britain for most new claimants. New claims for legacy benefits are generally not possible (but see p23 for exceptions). Existing awards of the legacy benefits continue for the time being. You can transfer to UC by 'natural migration' if you claim UC (see p26). Under the government's official 'managed migration' transfer process, claimants with existing awards will be invited to claim UC and the existing legacy benefit awards closed (see p29).

2. The universal credit system

When you come under the universal credit system

This *Handbook* refers to you as coming 'under the UC system' when the universal credit (UC) rules apply to you. You come under the UC system when you make a claim for UC (if you are in a couple, you must usually claim UC jointly with your partner).[1] You are usually considered to have made a claim for UC at the point you submit your online UC claim form. See p43 for more details on claiming UC. Your entitlement to the legacy benefits (see p21) stops if you claim UC. See p24 for how these benefits and tax credits are affected.

You also come under the UC system if you make a new claim for jobseeker's allowance (JSA) or employment and support allowance (ESA) of any kind. You cannot then get income-based JSA or income-related ESA, but if you are entitled to contribution-based JSA or contributory ESA, you come under the UC system for these benefits (see p25). If you get JSA or ESA under the UC system, the DWP may refer to these as 'new-style' JSA and 'new-style' ESA. Your other legacy benefits and tax credits only stop if you claim UC. **Note**: if your claim for JSA or ESA was made before 12 December 2018 and UC had not then been introduced into your area, or you claimed before 27 January 2021 and were prevented by law from claiming UC as a severely disabled person (see below), your claim will not have brought you under the UC system.

You do not come under the UC system if you are prevented by law from claiming UC (see p23).

Once you have claimed and are entitled to UC, you remain under the UC system – you cannot go back to legacy benefits and tax credits.

People prevented from claiming universal credit

In very limited circumstances, you can be prevented by law from making a claim for UC. If this applies, you can make a new claim for the legacy means-tested benefits and tax credits instead (see below). Until 27 January 2021, this applied in particular to some severely disabled people (see Chapter 2 of the 2020/21 edition of this *Handbook*). Currently, people are prevented from claiming UC only in the following very limited circumstances:

- until 30 March 2022 (but not since), you (or, if you are in a couple, you and your partner) were a 'frontier worker' – ie, you worked in Great Britain or Northern Ireland but lived elsewhere;[2] *or*
- you come into another specified category of case from whom it has been decided not to accept claims, in order to safeguard or test the efficient administration of UC.[3] At the time of writing, no other category of case had been specified.

Who can make a new claim for means-tested benefits and tax credits

Even if you have not claimed UC, you cannot usually make a new claim for income support (IS), income-based JSA, income-related ESA, working-age housing benefit (HB – see p187), child tax credit (CTC) or working tax credit (WTC).[4]

However, you can make a new claim instead of claiming UC in the following circumstances.

- You can make a new claim for CTC if you are already entitled to WTC, and a new claim for WTC if you are already entitled to CTC.[5]
- You can make a new claim for HB if you are in a couple and only one of you has reached pension age (ie, you are in a 'mixed-age couple') in certain circumstances (see p172). If both of you have reached pension age, or you are single and have reached pension age, you can always make a new claim for pension-age HB.
- You can make a new claim for HB if you live in 'specified' or 'temporary' accommodation (see p172). You may still need to claim UC for your other basic needs.
- You can make a new claim for IS, income-based JSA, income-related ESA, HB, CTC or WTC if you are prevented by law from claiming UC because you (or, if you are in a couple, you and your partner) are a 'frontier worker', or because you are in a category from whom it has been decided not to accept claims for UC.[6]

Examples

Kelly-Ann is getting income-based JSA and HB. She then has a baby (her first child). Kelly-Ann cannot make a new claim for CTC. Instead, she claims and gets UC. Her entitlement to income-based JSA and HB comes to an end.

Part 2: Universal credit
Chapter 2: The introduction of universal credit
2. The universal credit system

Priya and Bobby are a couple getting WTC and HB. When they have their first child, they can start getting CTC, as well as staying on WTC and HB.

Ahmed is getting income-related ESA, which includes the severe disability premium. When he moves into standard rented accommodation in August 2022 and needs help with the rent, he cannot make a new claim for HB and must claim UC instead. Claiming UC ends Ahmed's entitlement to income-related ESA.

Anthony is getting income-related ESA and moves into 'specified' rented accommodation. He can make a new claim for HB (rather than UC) as that will help with the rent for that accommodation. As Anthony has not claimed UC, his income-related ESA can continue.

How your means-tested benefits and tax credits are affected

UC replaces means-tested benefits and tax credits, so the general rule is that if you claim UC you no longer qualify for:[7]

- IS. **Note:** your IS continues to be paid (as long as you would otherwise have remained entitled) for the first two weeks of your claim for UC;
- income-based JSA. This is 'abolished' (replaced by UC) if you come under the UC system and you submit a new claim for income-based or contribution-based JSA, income-related or contributory ESA or UC. **Note:** your income-based JSA continues to be paid (as long as you would otherwise have remained entitled) for the first two weeks of your claim for UC;[8]
- income-related ESA. This is 'abolished' (replaced by UC) if you come under the UC system and you submit a new claim for income-related or contributory ESA, income-based or contribution-based JSA or UC. **Note:** your income-related ESA continues to be paid (as long as you would otherwise have remained entitled) for the first two weeks of your claim for UC;[9]
- working-age HB, except for 'specified' and 'temporary' accommodation (see p173). Your HB continues to be paid (as long as you would otherwise have remained entitled) for the first two weeks of your claim for UC;
- CTC;
- WTC;
- PC. PC is not being replaced by UC, but you cannot get PC and UC at the same time. Single people must be under pension age (see p257) to get UC. A couple with only one partner who has has reached pension age (a 'mixed-age couple') can choose to claim PC instead of UC only in certain circumstances (see p257). If you come under the UC system as a single person, but later become a member of a couple and your partner is entitled to PC, see p31.

If you are already getting IS, income-based JSA, income-related ESA, HB, CTC or WTC and make a claim for UC, your award stops and you cannot reclaim – it does not matter whether or not you are actually entitled to UC. Although stopping your IS, HB, CTC or WTC requires the DWP to be satisfied that you meet all the basic conditions for UC on p35 (apart from having accepted a claimant commitment), this is done automatically, on the basis of the information in your online claim. So, for example, the DWP is not required at this stage to check whether you pass the right to reside test – it does that later, to decide if you are actually entitled to UC.[10] However, arguably that may be wrong, and may be reconsidered in a future case. Seek advice, and see AskCPAG and CPAG's *Welfare Rights Bulletin* for updates.

If you are already getting IS, income-based JSA, income-related ESA, HB, CTC or WTC and are prevented by law from claiming UC (see p23), your award should continue even if you try to claim UC. If you are prevented from claiming UC and you are a member of a mixed-age couple, your award of a legacy benefit can continue despite the rules about your age that apply to IS (see p237), income-based JSA (see p249), income-related ESA (see p164) and HB (see p187).

If you are entitled to UC, you cannot also be entitled to IS, income-based JSA, income-related ESA, HB (except for specified or temporary accommodation), CTC or WTC (or PC), even if you could make a new claim for them.[11]

Contribution-based jobseeker's allowance and contributory employment and support allowance

If you submit a new claim for JSA or ESA, in most cases you come under the UC system. You cannot get income-based JSA or income-related ESA because they are replaced by UC (see p23 for when this does not apply), but you can still get contribution-based JSA and contributory ESA.[12]

When contribution-based JSA and contributory ESA are paid under the UC system, the DWP refers to them as 'new-style' JSA and 'new-style' ESA. The rules about getting paid these benefits (eg, the rules on overpayments, claimant responsibilities and sanctions) are those that apply in the UC system.

If you come under the UC system and have a low income, usually you must claim UC if you need to 'top up' your new-style JSA or ESA. If you are prevented from making a claim from UC (see p23), you can instead top up your new-style JSA with income-based JSA and your new-style ESA with income-related ESA.[13]

If you do not come under the UC system, you can top up your contribution-based JSA with income-based JSA and your contributory ESA with income-related ESA. You do not need to make a new claim – your current award is adjusted.[14]

Example

John gets contributory ESA. When he claimed, he did not come under the UC system, so this is not new-style ESA. John's income has now decreased. He can top up his contributory ESA with income-related ESA. He does not need to make a new claim – his current ESA award can be adjusted. However, the DWP tells John that he must claim UC as a top-up. He refuses to do so and points out that his ESA is not 'new-style ESA'. The DWP checks this and adjusts his ESA award to include income-related ESA.

Part 2: Universal credit
Chapter 2: The introduction of universal credit
3. Transferring to universal credit

For some practical points about making a claim, see p697 for contribution-based JSA and p642 for contributory ESA.

3. **Transferring to universal credit**

Universal credit (UC) has been introduced for new claimants throughout the UK. If you are getting a legacy benefit (see p21), at some point you may transfer to UC. The process of transferring to UC is known as 'migration'. You can transfer to UC:

- at any time, under 'natural migration' (see below); *or*
- when invited, under the government's 'managed migration' process (see p29).

Natural migration

You can transfer to UC at any time if you submit a claim for UC (unless your claim for UC is under the 'managed migration' process instead – see p29). This is called 'natural migration'. Remember that when you claim UC any current awards of legacy benefits will stop (see p24), and you cannot return to them. It is your claim for UC that triggers these events – it does not matter if it turns out that you are not actually entitled to UC.

Natural migration can happen at any time, often after there has been a change in your circumstances and you decide to claim UC, or when you otherwise decide to make a claim for it. For example:

- you have your first child. You cannot usually make a new claim for child tax credit (CTC – but see p23 for when you can) and so may need to claim UC for means-tested support for your child;
- you move into a different local authority area and need help with your rent. Any previous housing benefit (HB) award will stop and you cannot usually make a new claim for HB (but see p23 for when you can), so you may need to claim UC. If you move within the same local authority area, your HB award continues;[15]
- you have a drop in your income due to work ending or reducing. You may need to claim UC to replace your lost income;
- you believe that you would be better off on UC and decide to make a claim for it. The DWP calls this 'voluntary migration', and is encouraging legacy benefit claimants to check whether they would be better off on UC and to claim if they would be. Be sure before you claim: remember that a claim for UC stops your legacy benefits and you cannot return to them.

If you are severely disabled and have transferred to UC, see p27.

Example
Gillian gets working tax credit (WTC) and HB. She moves to a different flat. Because this is in the same local authority area, she does not need to make a new HB claim and both her

HB and WTC continue. Gillian moves again, this time to a property in a different local authority area. Her current HB claim comes to an end. Gillian is not in 'specified' or 'temporary' accommodation, and is not prevented from claiming UC and so cannot make a new claim for HB. Instead, she claims UC. She has now transferred to UC via natural migration, and her entitlement to WTC comes to an end, whether or not she is actually entitled to UC.

Note:
- A change in your circumstances does not, in itself, mean you transfer to UC. You must make a claim for UC for this to happen. Some claimants have been wrongly told that they must claim UC, or had appointments arranged by their local job centre or local authority to arrange a transfer to UC following a change in their circumstances, even though the change does not require them to claim UC. If this happens to you, do not claim UC unless you are sure you want to.
- Depending on your circumstances, you can be worse off after you transfer to UC via natural migration. There is no guarantee that your UC will be worth as much as your legacy benefits. You may be particularly likely to be worse off if you or a member of your family have a disability, as UC does not include the same disability additions as the legacy benefits. Some claimants may be entitled to more on UC than they are on legacy benefits. This may be the case especially if you are working. But all will depend on your circumstances. Check your likely UC entitlement before claiming. Also remember to consider basic features of the UC system such as online claiming (see p43) and the UC work-related requirements (see Chapter 46). Seek advice if necessary. Transitional protection to ensure that you are not worse off on UC is only provided if you instead transfer under the managed migration process (see p29).
- The Court of Appeal held that two claimants who had their legacy benefit incorrectly terminated by the DWP, and who then claimed UC but were worse off, had been subject to a violation of their human rights. The court said it was up to the government to provide a remedy[16] but the government has not changed the rules. Instead, compensation is likely to be offered in appropriate cases. If you are severely disabled, see below. Further court decisions about the lack of transitional protection in other situations may follow. See AskCPAG and CPAG's *Welfare Rights Bulletin* for updates.

People who are severely disabled

If you transfer to UC via natural migration and you or your partner were entitled to the severe disability premium (see p330) in your (or your partner's) previous award of income support (IS), income-based jobseeker's allowance (JSA) or income-related employment and support allowance (ESA), you may be entitled to an additional amount of UC. This is called a 'transitional SDP element'.

Part 2: Universal credit
Chapter 2: The introduction of universal credit
3. Transferring to universal credit

2

Note: if your UC started before 27 January 2021, the additional amount of UC you may be entitled to is instead called a 'transitional SDP amount'. The rules are very similar to those for the transitional SDP element (and the amounts are the same), but you could not qualify unless you had yourself been the claimant of the IS, JSA or ESA: see Chapter 2 of the 2020/21 edition of this *Handbook* for details. However, between 16 January 2019 and 26 January 2021 inclusive, if you were entitled to the severe disability premium in your legacy benefit, you should have been prevented by law from claiming UC, and so from transferring to UC. The DWP has paid compensation in some cases in which claimants were wrongly allowed to claim UC: seek advice if necessary.

You are entitled to a transitional SDP element (ie, where your UC started on or after 27 January 2021) if:[17]

- you have not become part of a couple with someone already on UC; *and*
- within the month before your UC entitlement started, you were entitled (or you were part of a couple in which your partner was entitled) to IS, income-based JSA or income-related ESA, and that included the severe disability premium; *and*
- you continued to satisfy the conditions for getting the severe disability premium up to and including the first day of your UC entitlement.

Once you are entitled to a transitional SDP element under the rules above, it continues to be included in your UC even if you stop satisfying the conditions for the severe disability premium – eg, because someone becomes a carer for you. However, because your transitional SDP element is treated 'as if' it were a transitional element of UC, it can reduce or stop in the same way that the transitional element can – eg, if you start or stop being part of a couple (see p78).

You cannot get a transitional SDP element amount if you were only entitled to HB, even if this included a severe disability premium.

The amount for each UC monthly assessment period is:[18]

- if you are a single claimant, £120 if the limited capability for work-related activity element (see p71) is included in your UC, or £285 if it is not; *or*
- if you are in a joint claim, £405 if the severe disability premium was payable at the couple rate (see p331); *or*
- if you are in a joint claim, £120 if the £405 rate does not apply and a limited capability for work-related activity element is included in your UC; *or*
- if you are in a joint claim, £285 if the £405 rate does not apply and there is no limited capability for work-related activity element included in your UC.

Note:

- The transitonal SDP element is not treated as separate from your other entitlement to UC. Instead, it is treated 'as if' it were a 'transitional element' (which is the element that may be included in cases of transfer to UC under the managed migration process), and when working out your UC 'as if' it were part of your maximum amount of UC (see p39).[19] The transitional SDP element can be reduced or stopped in the same way that a transitional element can be (see p78).
- The payments may not fully protect you from being worse off under UC compared to the amount of your old legacy benefit and tax credit awards. A court has held that, in the case of a claimant entitled to the severe disability premium who was also entitled to the enhanced disability premium (see p327) and was worse off under UC because of the loss of that premium, the failure to protect the claimant against being worse off was unlawful.[20] Similarly, in the case of a claimant who, in addition to getting the severe disability premium, was also getting the low rate of the child disability element in CTC (see p1418) and was worse off on UC because that was replaced with the lower rate of the disabled child addition to the UC child element, the court also held that was unlawful. However, at the time of writing, the government's response to the court decision was not known and the rules had not changed. See AskCPAG and CPAG's *Welfare Rights Bulletin* for updates.

Managed migration

In early 2022, the DWP started transferring some people still getting the legacy benefits and tax credits to UC. This process is known as 'managed migration'. At first, this applied only to a small number of cases, but was expected to apply to more people during 2022. The official intent is to complete the managed migration process by the end of 2024.

Note: if you are transferred to UC under the managed migration process and the amount of your UC is less than the amount you were getting on your legacy benefits, you are entitled to a 'transitional element' in your UC (see p76). This transitional protection is intended to ensure that you are not worse off at the point you transfer to UC.

The main rules and procedures are as follows (these may be subject to change – see AskCPAG and CPAG's *Welfare Rights Bulletin* for updates).

- The DWP begins the managed migration process by sending you (and your partner, if you are in a couple) a 'migration notice'.[21] This tells you that your legacy benefit or tax credit award will end on your 'migration day', and invites you to make a claim for UC instead.
- When you are sent the migration notice, you become a 'notified person'.[22]
- You are given a date you must make your UC claim by. This is your 'deadline day'. This day must be at least three months from the date of your migration

Part 2: Universal credit
Chapter 2: The introduction of universal credit
3. Transferring to universal credit

2

notice. You can be given longer to make your claim if the DWP agrees that there is a good reason – eg, if you are unwell or need to arrange help in order to make your claim.[23]

- The DWP can cancel your migration notice – eg, if it was sent in error or if this is considered necessary to protect your interests.[24]
- If you have not claimed UC by your deadline day, but you do so within a month of that day (ie, by your 'final deadline'), you will still have claimed in time to get a transitional element in your UC.[25]

You have made your claim for UC when you submit it – ie, in most cases, when you have completed and submitted the online claim form. This establishes the date of your claim (see p46). After you claim, you are likely to be required to provide further information (eg, about your identity or income), usually at an interview (see p1140). If you do not provide the information within the time allowed (you should be given at least a month, but can be given longer), the DWP is likely to decide that you are not entitled to UC and say that your claim has been 'closed' (see p44). Although you can challenge this decision, unless it is changed, you are not entitled to a transitional element as you have been refused UC. If you make another claim before your final deadline and are awarded UC, the rules say that you cannot get a transitional element included, although it is not clear whether this is the official intention.[26]

Your entitlement to your legacy benefits ends when you claim UC or, if you do not claim, on the day before your deadline day.[27] Your IS, income-based JSA, income-related ESA and HB continue for the first two weeks of your UC claim, if you would otherwise have remained entitled (see p24) – ie, you get paid both your legacy benefits and UC for two weeks.

When you make your claim for UC, you are not automatically entitled – you must still satisfy the usual rules of entitlement (see Chapter 3). However, there are exceptions.[28]

- If you are a student when your legacy benefits end, you can get UC even if you are in full-time education – you do not have to satisfy the usual rule about not 'receiving education' (see p868).
- If you are entitled to tax credits when you claim UC and have capital of over £16,000, the capital above £16,000 is ignored when calculating your entitlement to UC. This is called a 'transitional capital disregard' and can apply for up to 12 months beginning with your first month on UC.

Have you been sent a migration notice?
If you have been sent a migration notice by the DWP, you are affected by managed migration. Note the following.
1. There is no choice about when you are affected. However, the DWP intends to apply the managed migration process gradually. Get advice if you are affected and you are worried or unsure.

2. If you need more time to claim UC than you have been given (eg, because you are unwell or need help with the online claim), contact the DWP and explain this.

3. If you are vulnerable because of your health, or have complex needs (eg, because you are homeless), the DWP should take account of that under its 'complex needs' procedures. If you think this has not happened, tell the DWP and ask that it does.

4. If you would be worse off on UC, you should be protected by a transitional element in your UC, provided you claim UC within the time allowed and later supply any further information required. If you claim UC outside the time limit, you will not have transferred to UC under the managed migration rules and are not entitled to this element.

5. If you submit your claim in time but then fail to supply any further information that is required, the DWP is likely to regard this as a 'failed claim' and then say that your claim is 'closed'. This means that you have been refused UC. You can challenge the decision to 'close' your claim (see p44). You could try making another claim before your final deadline, but the DWP may still refuse to award you a transitional element.

6. If you are awarded UC but are in financial difficulty while waiting to be paid, you can apply for an advance (see p1153).

4. Change of circumstances

Generally, once you have claimed and are entitled to universal credit (UC), you remain under the UC system. So, provided you continue to satisfy the rules of entitlement (see p35), you continue to get UC, even if your circumstances change – eg, you have a child or you become ill.[29] There are different rules for couples (see below).

If you stop being entitled to UC, you cannot usually make a new claim for any of the legacy benefits (see p23). If your UC ended but you may now be entitled again, to get it again you must reapply, unless the rules about couples apply. If it is less then six months since your award ended, you can reclaim by logging back into your UC online journal. This 'rapid reclaim' allows you to reclaim more quickly (see p43).

Couples

If you were getting UC as a single person but then become part of a couple, you must report this change. You continue to come under the UC system as a couple with your new partner without having to make a new claim, and you continue to get UC provided you still satisfy the basic rules.[30] If your new partner is getting pension credit (PC), see below.

If your partner was not entitled to UC as a single person, any award s/he has of income support (IS), income-based jobseeker's allowance, income-related employment and support allowance, housing benefit (HB) (except for 'specified'

NC21058

Part 2: Universal credit
Chapter 2: The introduction of universal credit
4. Change of circumstances

2

or 'temporary' accommodation – see p173), child tax credit (CTC) or working tax credit stops and you are treated as claiming UC as a couple.[31] If your partner was entitled to UC as a single person, you are entitled to UC as a couple without having to make a claim.[32]

> **Example**
> Rick has been entitled to UC as a single person since April 2020. He meets Kaye and moves in with her in August 2022. Kaye has a two-year-old son and has been getting IS as a lone parent, together with CTC and HB. She is severely disabled and is getting a severe disability premium in her benefit. Rick and Kaye now come under the UC system as a couple. They satisfy the basic rules of entitlement for UC as a couple, and are therefore entitled to UC without having to make a new claim. Kaye's awards of IS, CTC and HB end.

If your new partner is getting PC, you are treated as having made a joint claim for UC and your partner's PC stops.[33] The PC stops only from the date you became a couple, not the date of your joint claim for UC (the same applies regarding your partner's HB).[34] You do not need to make a new claim for UC. If only one of you is under pension age, you cannot usually make a new claim for PC (see p257).

If you were claiming UC as a couple but then separate from your partner, you must report the change. Both you and your ex-partner can stay on UC as single claimants without having to make new claims, and you both keep your existing UC assessment period (see p38 for what this is).[35]

> **Example**
> Olivia and Joshua were entitled to UC as joint claimants. They separate and Joshua notifies the DWP of the fact that they are no longer a couple. Both Olivia and Joshua can be entitled to UC as single people and do not need to make new claims. The date they are paid their UC remains as it was when they were a couple.

Notes

2. The universal credit system

1 Art 3(3) and Sch 5 WRA(No.9)O, as applied in UC areas by subsequent commencement orders
2 Art 4(11) WRA(No.32)O
3 Reg 4 UC(TP) Regs
4 The basic rules are in art 4 WRA(No.9)O, art 6 (11) WRA(No.21)O and art 7 WRA(No.23)O, as applied in subsequent commencement orders
5 Art 6(4) WRA(No.21)O and art 7(5) WRA(No.23)O, as applied in subsequent commencement orders
6 Art 5A WRA(No.9)O and art 7 WRA(No.23)O, as applied in subsequent commencement orders
7 Regs 5, 6, 8, 46 and 47 UC(TP) Regs
8 Art 4 WRA(No.9)O; regs 46 and 47 UC(TP) Regs
9 Art 4 WRA(No.9)O; regs 46 and 47 UC(TP) Regs
10 Reg 8 UC(TP) Regs; SK v HMRC [2022] UKUT 10 (AAC)
11 Reg 5 UC(TP) Regs
12 These benefits are not abolished under the UC system and can be claimed under the JSA Regs 2013 and the ESA Regs 2013.
13 Art 6 WRA(No.9)O; Vol V8 para V8100 ADM
14 LH v SSWP (ESA) [2014] UKUT 480 (AAC), reported as [2015] AACR 14

3. Transferring to universal credit

15 Housing Benefit Circular A7/2018
16 R (on the application of TD, AD and Reynolds) v SSWP [2020] EWCA Civ 618
17 Sch 2 UC(TP) Regs, as applied in awards from 27 January 2021, inserted by The Universal Credit (Transitional Provisions) (Claimants previously entitled to a severe disability premium) Amendment Regulations 2021 No.4
18 Sch 2 para 2 UC(TP) Regs
19 Sch 2 paras 4, 5 and 6 UC(TP) Regs
20 R (on the application of) TP and AR (TP and AR No.3) v SSWP [2022] EWHC 123 (Admin)
21 Reg 44 UC(TP) Regs
22 Reg 44(6) UC(TP) Regs
23 Regs 44(1)(b) and 45 UC(TP) Regs
24 Reg 44(5) UC(TP) Regs
25 Regs 46(4) and 48 UC(TP) Regs
26 Reg 57 UC(TP) Regs
27 Regs 46, 48 and 49 UC(TP) Regs
28 Regs 51 and 60 UC(TP) Regs

4. Change of circumstances

29 A change does not automatically bring UC entitlement to an end, and instead the award can be adjusted to reflect the new circumstances.
30 Reg 9(7) and (8) UC,PIP,JSA&ESA(C&P) Regs
31 Regs 5, 7 and 12A UC(TP) Regs; reg 9(8) UC,PIP,JSA&ESA(C&P) Regs
32 Reg 9(7) UC,PIP,JSA&ESA(C&P) Regs; paras M4051-60 ADM
33 Reg 9(8) UC,PIP,JSA&ESA(C&P) Regs; reg 5 UC(TP) Regs
34 Regs 5(2)(b)(ii) and (iv) and 7(5)(c) UC(TP) Regs
35 Reg 9(6) UC,PIP,JSA&ESA(C&P) Regs

Chapter 3

Universal credit

This chapter covers:

Key facts

- Universal credit (UC) is a benefit for people on a low income who are in or out of work.
- UC replaces income support, income-based jobseeker's allowance, income-related employment and support allowance, working-age housing benefit, child tax credit and working tax credit.
- UC has been introduced nationwide for new claimants.
- UC is a means-tested benefit.
- You do not have to have paid national insurance contributions to qualify.
- UC can be paid in addition to non-means-tested benefits, but some of these are taken into account as income when calculating your UC.
- A benefit cap may be applied if the total amount of certain benefits you receive exceeds a specified amount, and your UC can be reduced.
- UC is administered and paid by the DWP.
- If you disagree with a UC decision, you can apply for a revision or supersession (see Chapter 56), or appeal against it (see Chapter 57). You must apply for a mandatory reconsideration before you can appeal.

• •

1. Who can get universal credit

You qualify for universal credit (UC) if you (and your partner if you are in a couple):

• satisfy the **'basic conditions'** – ie:[1]
  – you are aged 18 or over and under pension age (see p765). **Note:** some 16/17 year olds can get UC (see p36); *and*
  – you are not 'receiving education', although there are some exceptions (see p36); *and*
  – you satisfy the 'habitual residence' and the 'right to reside' tests (see Chapter 69), and you are in, or treated as in, Great Britain (see Chapters 69 and 70); *and*
  – you are not a 'person subject to immigration control' (see p1524); *and*
  – usually, you have accepted a 'claimant commitment' (see p1024). This is an agreement that you will meet certain requirements.[2] In particular, the claimant commitment includes the work-related requirements you normally must meet, which may include attending work-focused interviews, work preparation, work search and work availability; *and*
• satisfy the **'financial conditions'** – ie:[3]
  – your income is not too high; *and*
  – your savings and other capital are £16,000 or less. If you transfer to UC from tax credits under the 'managed migration' process and have capital of over £16,000, that excess capital is ignored for UC for up to 12 months (see p26).

Couples

If you are a member of a couple (see p56), you must usually make a joint claim. Both of you must satisfy the above conditions of entitlement (and your income and capital are assessed jointly).[4]

Both of you do *not* need to meet all the basic conditions if one of you is:[5]
• over pension age; *or*
• 'receiving education' (but see below if one of you is aged 16 or 17).

If you are a member of a couple and one of you does not satisfy the conditions for UC, you may be able to claim as a single person. If so, your UC amounts are for a single person, but your income and capital are still assessed jointly. You can claim as a single person if your partner is:[6]
• aged 16 or 17 and is not someone who can get UC as an under-18 year old (see p36 for who can); *or*
• not in (or treated as in) Great Britain, including if s/he has failed the habitual residence or right to reside test (see Chapter 69); *or*
• a 'person subject to immigration control' (see p1524); *or*

- a prisoner or serving a sentence while detained in hospital, or is a member of a religious order and is fully maintained by the order.

You can also claim as a single person if you are in a polygamous marriage and:[7]
- your spouse is still married to someone else from an earlier marriage; *and*
- the other person in the earlier marriage is still living in the same household as your spouse.

Receiving education

In general, you cannot claim UC if you are 'receiving education'. The basic rule is that if you are a qualifying young person (see p61) or undertaking full-time education, study or training, you are regarded as 'receiving education'.[8] There are exceptions – eg, if you have a child or a disability, are on a traineeship, or are without parental support. For full details, see Chapter 41. **Note:** if you are transferred from a means-tested benefit or tax credits to UC under the 'managed migration' process (see p29), you can claim UC, even though you do not satisfy the basic rules because you are in full-time education (see p29).

If you are a member of a couple making a joint claim and one of you is receiving education (and so not eligible for UC) but the other is not, you may still be entitled to UC as a couple (see p35).

---

2. **The rules about your age**

In most cases, you (and your partner if you are making a joint claim) must be 18 or over to claim universal credit (UC). However, some 16/17 year olds can claim UC (see below).[9]

You must be under pension age (see p765).[10] If you are in a couple, at least one of you must be under pension age. If one of you has reached pension age, this is sometimes called being in a 'mixed-age couple'. **Note:** if you reach pension age while you are on UC, or you are in a mixed-age couple and the younger person also reaches pension age, your UC will 'run on' for the remainder of the monthly UC assessment period in which this change occurred.[11]

16/17 year olds

You must normally be at least 18 years old to qualify for UC. If you are aged 16 or 17, you can get UC if one of the following applies.[12]
- You have limited capability for work, or you have submitted and are covered by a medical certificate saying you are not fit for work and you are waiting for an assessment of your capability for work.
- You have 'regular and substantial caring responsibilities for a severely disabled person' – ie, you meet the conditions of entitlement to carer's allowance (CA)

(see Chapter 26), or would do but for the fact that your earnings are too high.[13] This does not apply if you receive earnings from those caring responsiblities. You do not have to claim CA. **Note:** you do not qualify under this rule if you were previously being looked after by a local authority (see p934).

- You are responsible for a child aged under 16 (see p62).
- You are a member of a couple and your partner satisfies the basic rules of entitlement for UC and is responsible for a child.
- You are pregnant and there are 11 weeks or less before the week your baby is due. **Note:** you do not qualify under this rule if you were previously being looked after by a local authority (see p934).
- You had a baby (or your baby was stillborn) not more than 15 weeks ago. **Note:** you do not qualify under this rule if you were previously being looked after by a local authority (see p934).
- You are without parental support (including support from someone acting in place of your parent – eg, a foster parent). For these purposes, you are treated as without parental support if you are not being looked after by a local authority, and:[14]
  - you are an orphan – ie, you do not have any parents; *or*
  - you have to live away from your parents because you are estranged from them (see p870 for the meaning) or there is a serious risk to your physical or mental health or you would experience significant harm if you lived with them; *or*
  - you are living away from your parents and they are unable to support you financially because they have a 'physical or mental impairment', or they are in custody, or they are prohibited from entering Great Britain – eg, because of the Immigration Rules.

  Note: you do not qualify under this rule if you were previously being looked after by a local authority (see p934).

If you are a member of a couple and one of you is either 18 or over or satisfies the rules above, but the other does not, the one who is 18 or over or who satisfies the above rules can claim UC as a single person, but the other partner's income and capital are taken into account.[15]

3. People included in the claim

If you are single, you claim universal credit (UC) for yourself. If you are a member of a couple, you and your partner must usually make a joint claim for UC (see p44).[16] See p56 for who counts as a couple.

Your maximum amount (see Chapter 5), which forms part of the calculation of your benefit, includes elements for a child(ren) for whom you are responsible.

2

Note: the number of children included in your maximum amount may be limited to two (see p66).

There are some situations in which you must show that you are 'responsible' for a child – eg:

- in order to take advantage of the special rules to help you meet the claimant responsibilities (see p1027 and p1111);
- so you can benefit from a 'work allowance' when calculating your UC entitlement (see p40);
- for some of the rules for the housing costs element (see Chapter 6).

You can count as responsible for any child under 16 and for any 'qualifying young person' (see p61 for who counts as a child).[17] You do not have to be the child's parent. For when you count as responsible for a child, see p62.

---

4. **The amount of benefit**

Universal credit (UC) is a means-tested benefit. The amount of UC you get depends on your needs (your 'maximum amount') and how much income and capital you (and your partner) have. If you are severely disabled and transferred to UC from your old means-tested benefit under the natural migration process, you may also get a transitional amount (known as a 'transitional SDP amount') included in your UC.

The amount you get is calculated over a monthly 'assessment period'. As your income increases, your UC award is reduced.

- -
Assessment period

The **'assessment period'** is one calendar month, beginning with the first date of entitlement to UC.[18] Each subsequent assessment period (ie, a calendar month) usually begins on the same day of the month, except if:

- the first day of entitlement to UC falls on the 31st of the month, in which case each assessment period begins on the last day of the month; *or*
- the first day of entitlement to UC falls on the 29th or 30th of the month, in which case each assessment period begins on the 29th or 30th. In February, it begins on the 27th (or in a leap year, on the 28th); *or*
- your entitlement has started before the actual date of claim because of the backdating rules, in which case the first assessment period begins on the first day of entitlement and ends on the day before the date of claim; *or*
- your first date of entitlement is changed, in which case the first assessment period is changed, but your other assessment periods still begin and end as they did originally.

Examples

Meera claims UC on 31 July. She is making a new claim as a single person. Her first monthly assessment period is from 31 July until 30 August inclusive. Her next assessment period begins on 31 August, and the one after that begins on 30 September.

Melvin claims UC on 2 November. His first assessment period is set to begin on 2 November, but he requests that his claim be backdated to 26 October as his disability meant he could not claim earlier, and this is accepted. Melvin's first assessment period now begins on 26 October and ends on 1 November, his second assessment period begins on 2 November, with all subsequent assessment periods beginning on the second day of the month.

Working out your universal credit

Your UC is worked out in the following way.
- **Step one:** calculate your maximum amount. See Chapter 5 for details of this.
- **Step two:** work out your earnings and check whether any can be ignored.
- **Step three:** work out your other income and how much can be ignored.
- **Step four:** calculate your total income.
- **Step five:** calculate your UC entitlement.

Step one: calculate your maximum amount

Your maximum monthly UC is made up of the total of:[19]
- a standard allowance – for a single claimant or a couple (see p65);
- a child element for each child, with an increase for a disabled or severely disabled child (see p66). **Note:** the number of children for whom you can get a child element may be limited to two;
- a limited capability for work element, if you can still get it (see p69), or a limited capability for work-related activity element (p71) for an adult with ill health or disability. The limited capability for work element was abolished for new claims made on or after 3 April 2017 (see p69);
- a carer element for someone looking after a severely disabled person (see p73);
- a housing costs element for people paying rent or service charges (see Chapter 6). **Note:** you cannot get UC for help with your mortgage or loan for repairs and improvements. Instead, the DWP may offer you a loan to help meet your mortgage interest payments (see p839);
- a childcare costs element (see p73);
- a transitional element – if you transfer to UC from the old means-tested benefits and tax credits under the 'managed migration' process (see p29) and your UC is worth less than your old benefits (see p76);
- any 'transitional SDP element' that you are entitled to after transferring to UC from your old means-tested benefits under the 'natural migration' process on

2

or after 27 January 2021 (see p27).[20] The payment is treated 'as if' it is part of your maximum amount. If you transferred before 27 January, you may be entitled instead to a 'transitional SDP amount'. This is very similar to the transitional SDP element and, in practice, is treated in the same way, although the rules are written slightly differently.[21]

Example
Kate and Toby are a couple both aged over 25. They claim UC in May 2021. They have two children born after 6 April 2017. Kate works; Toby is ill and has limited capability for work and work-related activity. They do not have housing or childcare costs.
Kate and Toby's maximum amount for UC is calculated as follows:

Standard allowance	£525.72
Child element (first child)	£244.58
Child element (second child)	£244.58
Limited capability for work-related activity element	£354.28
Total	**£1,369.16**

Step two: work out your earnings and how much can be ignored

See Chapter 7 for how to work out your earnings.

Once you have established your earnings, check whether any can be ignored when calculating your UC. This is done by comparing your earnings with a set amount, called a 'work allowance' (see below).

If your earnings do not exceed the work allowance, they are all ignored. If your earnings are more than your work allowance, 55 per cent of the excess is taken into account as income.[22] You are only entitled to a work allowance if certain circumstances apply. If no work allowance applies to you, 55 per cent of all your earnings are taken into account.

The way your earnings reduce the amount of your UC is sometimes called the '**taper**' – ie, the rate at which your UC tapers away as your earnings increase. As your earnings rise above any that are ignored, your UC reduces by 55 pence for every extra pound you earn.

The work allowance

A work allowance only applies if you (or your partner) are responsible for a child or have limited capability for work.[23]

The amount of the allowance depends on whether your UC includes a housing costs element. Only one work allowance can apply.

Note: if you are entitled to UC but also get housing benefit (HB) because you are in temporary accommodation (which is not also 'exempt accommodation' – see p387, the meaning is the same as for HB), your UC is treated as if it includes a housing costs element.[24]

Amount of the work allowance (per month)

UC includes a housing costs element	£344
UC does not include a housing costs element	£573

Examples

Maisey is a lone parent with a child aged six. She rents her home and is entitled to a housing costs element in her UC. She has a part-time job from which her earnings for UC over her assessment period are £400.

Because Maisey has a child, a work allowance applies and so some of her earnings can be ignored. Maisey's UC includes a housing costs element, so her work allowance is £344. Maisey's earnings exceed her work allowance by £56 (£400 – £344). Fifty-five per cent of this excess is £30.80. Therefore, £30.80 of Maisey's earnings is taken into account when calculating her UC.

Kate and Toby are a couple with two children. They are not entitled to a housing costs element in their UC. Kate has earnings from work. Toby is ill and has limited capability for work and work-related activity. Kate's earnings for UC over their assessment period are £1,200.

Because they have children and also because Toby has limited capability for work, a work allowance applies and some of Kate's earnings can be ignored. Their UC does not include a housing costs element, so the work allowance is £573. Kate's earnings exceed the work allowance by £627 (£1,200 – £573). Fifty-five per cent of this excess is £344.85. So £344.85 of Kate and Toby's earnings is taken into account when calculating their UC.

Step three: work out your other income and how much can be ignored

See Chapter 7 for how to work out your other income and how much can be ignored.

If you have other income (eg, other benefits), unless it is ignored, it affects your UC by reducing it pound for pound. This is in addition to any reductions from your earnings.

Income from capital

If you and your partner have more than £16,000 capital, you cannot get UC. An exception applies if you are transferred to UC from tax credits under the 'managed migration' process (see p26). If your capital is more than £6,000 but £16,000 or less, you count as having an income of £4.35 a month for every £250, or part of £250, over £6,000.[25] This assumed monthly income is sometimes referred to as 'tariff income'.

For how to calculate your capital, including assumed monthly income, see Chapter 8.

2

Step four: calculate your total income

Add together the income that is to be taken into account under Steps two and three.

Step five: calculate your universal credit entitlement

Deduct your total income to be taken into account (Step four) from your maximum UC (Step one).

Note: if you are not entitled to UC under these steps because your maximum UC does not yet include the limited capability for work-related activity element as you are still in the three-month waiting period (see p71), you are entitled to UC at the minimum amount of one pence.[26]

If you transferred from your old means-tested benefits and tax credits to UC under 'natural migration' on or after 27 January 2021 and are entitled to a 'transitional SDP element' (see p27), this is treated 'as if' it is part of your UC maximum amount. If you get a 'transitional SDP amount' because you transferred before 27 January 2021, this is an additional amount of UC (see p39).

Example

Kate and Toby are a couple both aged over 25, with two children. Kate works and earns £1,200 in their monthly assessment period. Toby is ill and has limited capability for work and work-related activity. He gets fortnightly payments of contributory employment and support allowance (ESA) of £235.20. For UC purposes, this is converted to a monthly figure of £509.60. They do not have housing costs or childcare costs included in their UC. They have savings of £5,000.

Their total income to be taken into account under Step four is £344.85 in earnings, plus £509.60 contributory ESA during their monthly assessment period = £854.45

Their maximum UC under Step one = £1,369.16

Their monthly UC entitlement = £1,369.16 – £854.45 = £514.71

Transitional protection

From some point, claimants with existing awards of legacy benefits (see p21) will begin to be transferred to UC under the DWP's 'managed migration' process (see p29). If you are transferred to UC in this way and your UC maximum amount would be less than the amount you were getting on your legacy benefit, a 'transitional element' is included in your UC maximum amount (see p76). This is intended to ensure that you are not worse off at the point of transfer to UC.

Transitional protection only applies if you transfer to UC under the 'managed migration' process. It does not apply if you claim UC after a transfer under the 'natural migration' process (see p26). So you could find that if you claim UC under the natural migration process, it is worth less than the legacy benefit you were getting previously (even if you qualify for the transitional SDP element).

5. Special benefit rules

Special rules may apply to:
- 16/17 year olds (see p36);
- people subject to immigration control (see Chapter 68);
- people who have come from or are going abroad (see Chapters 69 and 70);
- people who are studying (see Chapter 41);
- people in prison or detention (see Chapter 42).

6. Claims and backdating

The general rules about claims and backdating are covered in Chapter 50. This section explains the specific rules that apply to universal credit (UC).

You can usually make a new claim for UC whenever you want. Claiming UC brings you under the UC system (see p22).

Making a claim

Claims for UC must be made online at gov.uk/apply-universal-credit. You are asked to set up an online account and provide an email address, username, password and security questions. If you need help claiming online, you can call the UC helpline, free of charge, on 0800 328 5644 (textphone: 0800 328 1344; Welsh language: 0800 328 1744), Monday to Friday 8am to 6pm. There is also a British Sign Language video relay service for making a claim. The DWP adviser can complete an online form on your behalf or arrange for you to be helped at your local job centre. Alternatively, your local Citizens Advice office can help you make a claim via the 'Help to claim' service.

A claim can be made by telephone if the DWP allows it.[27] In exceptional circumstances, if you are unable to use either a computer or a telephone, the DWP may make a home visit to help you claim, but you should not rely on this.

You can amend or withdraw your claim before a decision is made (see p1135). If you are in financial need while waiting to be paid, you may be able to get an advance payment of UC (see p1153).

Forms

There are no paper claim forms for UC. The claim form is only available online.

If you were previously getting UC and it is less than six months since your award ended, you can reclaim by logging onto your online UC journal. This usually allows you to reclaim more quickly, and you have the same assessment payment as previously. If you are reclaiming after stopping work, you are only paid in full for the whole of the first assessment period if you reclaim within seven days of your job ending, although you can be allowed longer if you have a 'good reason' for not reclaiming within this time.[28]

Note: if you are transferring to UC from a legacy benefit under the 'managed migration' process, some special rules about claiming UC apply (see p29).

When you do not need to make a claim

You do not need to make a new claim (and you keep the same assessment period as before) if you have previously claimed UC and:[29]

- you were entitled to UC as a single claimant and you are now part of a couple and your partner was also entitled to UC as a single claimant. Although you do not need to make a new joint claim, you must tell the DWP that you are now part of a couple; *or*
- you are now a member of a couple and either you or your partner (but not both of you) were entitled to UC as a single claimant and that award has now been terminated; *or*
- you were a member of a couple making a joint claim but have now ceased to be a couple (but you must tell the DWP that you are now single or are a member of a new couple).

Also, where you have been refused UC or your award has been terminated, because (in either case) of having too much income, you can be treated as making a new claim, without actually making a new claim, if the DWP decides that it should do this – eg, where it has enough information to make an award without a claim.[30] This applies for up to the next five of what would have been your monthly UC assessment periods after you were refused UC or had your award terminated.

Who should claim

If you are single, you claim on your own behalf as a single person. If you are a member of a couple, you must normally make a joint claim with your partner.[31] For when you count as a couple, see p37. If you are a member of a couple and one of you does not satisfy the conditions for UC, you can claim as a single person (although your income and capital are assessed jointly with your partner) in certain circumstances (see p35). The DWP treats your joint claim as one made by a single person.[32]

If you are unable to manage your own affairs, another person can claim UC for you as your 'appointee' (see p1135).[33]

Information to support your claim

For the general information requirements that apply to all benefits, see p1136.

The DWP asks you to have certain information to hand when making your online claim. This includes:

- your bank, building society or credit union account details;
- the type of accommodation you have (eg, whether you are a private tenant, council tenant, housing association tenant or home owner) and your landlord's details, if you have one;
- an email address;
- your national insurance (NI) number (if you do not have an NI number, you will satisfy the NI number requirement if you have applied for one – see p1137);
- information about your housing – eg, how much rent you pay;
- details of your income – eg, recent payslips and any other benefits you are getting;
- details of savings and any investments – eg, shares or a property that you rent to others;
- details of how much you pay for childcare if you want help with your childcare costs included in your UC;
- proof of your identity – eg, a driving licence, passport, or a debit or credit card.

It is important that you provide any information required when you claim. Until you do, you may not count as having made a valid claim (see p1138). Your claim is valid if you provide the information requested on the online claim form.[34] In practice, in most cases if you have completed the online form and submitted it, you will have made a valid claim.

You are then usually asked to provide further information or evidence – eg, about your identity, or payslips, your rent agreement and bank statements. If you have a health condition that means that you cannot work, you are can self-certify this for the first seven days. After that you are normally asked to provide a medical certificate from your doctor. Where necessary, you should be able to verify your identity using the existing gov.uk verifying service or, if you have a Government Gateway online account, using your credentials from that. The DWP will contact you if it needs to check any of the information you have already submitted. You may be asked to attend an interview at your local job centre.

If you do not comply with a request for further information, the DWP is likely to say that you have made a 'failed claim' and that your claim has been 'closed'. You should therefore comply if you can. If you cannot, tell the DWP in advance. If your claim is closed, you should be given a decision about this saying that you are not entitled to UC.

Has your claim been closed?
If you are told that your claim has been closed, do the following.

1. If you can still access your online journal, use it to challenge the decision to close your claim – ie, that you are not entitled to UC. Download any documents and take screenshots of the decision to close your claim and of your challenge to that decision, then make a new

claim for UC as soon as possible. You will get a new online journal for your new claim, but may lose access to your old journal.

2. If you do not have access to your online journal, make a new claim for UC. You can then challenge the decision to close your claim on your new online journal.

3. There is nothing in the law about 'closing' a claim. What has actually happened is that the DWP has made a decision that you are not entitled to UC. The law does not say that you cannot be entitled to UC merely because you have not attended the interview.[35] So you may be able to argue that there is no basis for deciding that you were not entitled to UC. In any case, you must have been given at least a month to attend, or longer if considered reasonable.[36] If you have not attended an interview, the most common reason for a decision that you are not entitled to UC is because there is a doubt about your identity. If this is not in doubt (eg, if the DWP has accepted proof of your identity for your subsequent claim), you could argue that the decision to close your earlier claim should now be changed. See AskCPAG for a useful tool for challenging a decision to 'close' your claim.

If you are working for an employer, the DWP uses a 'real-time information system' to obtain information about your earnings. Your employer is required to send information to HM Revenue and Customs every time your wages are paid.

You may also be asked to provide information after you are awarded UC, and if you fail to do so, your UC could be suspended or even terminated (see p1162).

The date of your claim

The date of your claim is important as it determines when your entitlement to UC starts. This is not necessarily the date from when you are paid. For information about when payment of UC starts, see p48.

Your '**date of claim**' is usually the date on which your online claim is received by the DWP.[37] If you received help from the DWP (or someone providing services to the DWP) with making your claim before you claimed online, your date of claim is the date you notified the DWP that you needed help. **Note:** the DWP does not accept that this applies if you get help from a Citizens Advice office.

If you claim by telephone, your date of claim is the date on which the claim is 'properly completed', or earlier if you previously notified your intention to claim and the claim is made within a month of that. If you had to delay completing your online claim before submitting it (eg, in order to obtain some of the required information), you may be able to argue that your date of claim should be when you started completing the online form. See AskCPAG for a useful tool for challenging a decision about this.

Note: if a claim is considered 'defective', you are given a short time to correct the defects (see p1139). If you do, your claim is treated as having been made when you initially claimed.[38] In practice, however, very few UC claims are actually defective because without the required information on the online form, it is not possible to complete the claim. Instead, your claim is valid if you have been able to submit the online claim form, although you are also usually asked to provide further information or evidence in order to be entitled to UC (see p1140).

In some cases, you can claim in advance (see p48) and in some cases your claim can be backdated (see below). If you want this to be done, make this clear when you claim or the DWP might not consider it.

Backdating your claim

A claim for UC can be backdated for a maximum of one month, but only in certain circumstances. If you are making a joint claim, both you and your partner must satisfy one (or more) of these circumstances. Your claim can be backdated if you could not reasonably be expected to have claimed earlier because:[39]

- you were previously getting income support, jobseeker's allowance, employment and support allowance, housing benefit (HB), child tax credit or working tax credit, and you were not notified that your entitlement was going to end before it did; or
- you have a disability (the rules do not define this); or
- you were unwell and this meant you could not claim online or by telephone on time, and you have now supplied medical evidence showing that you were unwell; or
- you could not claim online because of a system failure or planned system maintenance, and you have now claimed on the first day that the system was working; or
- you made a joint claim for UC and this was either turned down or awarded but later terminated because your partner did not accept her/his claimant commitment, but you have now ceased to be a couple and you have reclaimed UC as a single person.

This could apply, for example, where you lost entitlement to HB having moved to a new local authority area (and so could not get HB again), but were not actually notified of that until later, when your new local authority told you that you had to claim UC instead.[40]

However, in practice the DWP says that you can only take advantage of these rules if you ask for backdating before a decision is made on your claim – ie, usually before the first payment statement on your UC online journal, which usually appears a month after you submit your claim. Arguably, that is wrong, because the rules do not actually say this. Ask for backdating as soon as you can and, if possible, before your claim is decided.[41] Failing that, you can still request backdating. If, the DWP does not agree, you can challenge that decision. The legal position may be clarified by a pending test case.[42] See AskCPAG and CPAG's *Welfare Rights Bulletin* for updates.

Note: if you are transferring to UC from a legacy benefit under the 'managed migration' process, but you have missed the 'deadline day' allowed for making a claim for UC, you are treated as having claimed on that day if you claim by your 'final deadline'. You do not have to satisfy the bullet points above. See p29 for more information about managed migration.

If you might have qualified for benefit earlier, but did not claim because you were given the wrong information by the DWP or were misled by it, you could ask for compensation (see p1403) or complain to the Ombudsman (see p1408).

If you claim the wrong benefit

There are no rules for when a claim for another benefit can be treated as a claim for UC. You should claim UC as soon as you can and, if necessary, ask for the claim to be backdated.

Claiming in advance

If you claim UC when you are not yet entitled, but the DWP thinks that you will be entitled within one month of the day you claimed, it can make an advance award. If this applies, your claim is treated as having been made on the first day on which you are entitled to UC.[43] However, the DWP only accepts advance claims in very limited circumstances: from prisoners who are to be released within a month and from care leavers who make their claim one month before their 18th birthday.[44]

7. **Getting paid**

The general rules on getting paid are covered in Chapter 51. This section explains the specific rules that apply to universal credit (UC).

When is universal credit paid?
You are normally paid within seven days of the end of an assessment period. UC is usually paid monthly, in arrears. If you live in Scotland, you can request that you be paid twice monthly.[45] If you find being paid monthly is difficult to budget for, you may be able to request more frequent payments under an 'alternative payment arrangement' (see p50).

Your award is assessed over an 'assessment period' of one calendar month, beginning from the date your entitlement starts (see p38).[46] UC should normally be paid direct into your account within seven days of the last day of the monthly assessment period or, if this is not possible, 'as soon as reasonably practicable' after that.[47] If you are getting UC as a single person and become a couple with someone else on UC, your new assessment period as a couple begins on the same day of each month as your old award ended, or that of your partner ended, whichever was earlier. If your new partner was not on UC, your new assessment period as a couple begins on the same day of the month as it did for your old award. If you were part of a couple on UC but are now single, your new assessment period begins on the same day of each month as it did for your old award.[48]

Your online UC journal should show when you will get your first payment of UC. In practice, you can expect to get your first payment about five weeks after claiming (although this may take longer in some cases). If you are in financial need in the meantime, or if there is a delay in subsequent payments, you may be able to get an advance payment of UC (see p1153). The advance must be repaid. Otherwise, you may be able to get help from your local authority (see p846).

Couples can decide which partner is paid. The DWP can decide that the other partner should be paid instead or can split the payments between you if it considers it to be in your interests, the interests of a child for whom you are responsible (see p62), or in the interests of a severely disabled person and your UC includes a carer element (see p73).[49] Couples with children making a new claim are guided to use the bank account of the main carer for their UC payments.

If you need a loan for an item you cannot afford, you can ask for a budgeting advance of UC (see p51).

Your UC can be paid in whole or in part to another person on your behalf, if the DWP considers this is necessary to protect your interests, or those of your partner, a child for whom you are responsible (see p62), or a severely disabled person and your UC includes a carer element (p73).[50]

The housing costs element to cover your rent is normally paid to you, rather than your landlord, unless paying your landlord would be in your interest. Official guidance says that your landlord can request that payment be made to her/him, and this will be granted automatically if your rent is over two months in arrears.[51] If you live in Scotland, you can request that payment be made direct to your landlord.[52] Otherwise, you may be able to request payment to your landlord under an 'alternative payment arrangement' (see below).

Note:

- Deductions can be made from your UC to pay third parties (see p1164).
- Your UC might be paid at a reduced rate if you have been sanctioned (see Chapter 47) or committed a benefit offence (see p1239).
- For information on missing payments, see p1150. If you cannot get your UC payments because you have lost your bank card or you have forgotten your PIN, see p1149. If your payment service card is lost or stolen, see p1150.
- If payment of your UC is delayed, see p1255. If you are waiting for a decision on your claim, or to be paid, you might be able to get an advance (p1153). If you wish to complain about how your claim has been dealt with, or claim compensation, see Chapter 61.
- If payment of your UC is suspended, see p1161.
- If you are overpaid UC, you might have to repay it (see Chapter 53) and, in some circumstances, you may have to pay a penalty (see p1229). If you have been accused of fraud, see Chapter 54.
- If you are owed arrears of UC, these can be paid in instalments (see p1148).

Alternative payment arrangements

If you find monthly payments difficult to budget for, or if having your UC housing costs element paid to you rather than to your landlord is leading to serious rent arrears, or if you need the payment of your UC to be split between you and your partner, it may be possible to have an alternative payment arrangement. This is discretionary and there is no right of appeal. You must show that you cannot manage the usual payment arrangement and, as a result, there is a risk of financial harm to you or to someone in your family. According to government guidance, the following applies.[53]

- The DWP must be satisfied that alternative payment arrangements should apply, based on your inability to cope with usual payment and on your circumstances. For example, are you managing to pay your bills on time? Can you manage a monthly budget? Are you used to managing money with your partner?

- Alternative payment arrangements are considered in the following order of priority:
  - paying rent direct to your landlord to safeguard your home;
  - more frequent payment – ie, two payments a month, rather than just one. Exceptionally, more frequent payments can be considered;
  - splitting payment between the partners in a couple in specific situations – eg, if one partner is mismanaging the UC award or if there is domestic abuse.

- The DWP splits claimants into two tiers: tier one for those with circumstances with a 'high likely need' for alternative payment arrangements and tier two those with 'less likely need'. **You are in tier one if you:**
  - have drug, alcohol and other addiction problems;
  - have learning difficulties;
  - have severe debt problems;
  - are living in temporary or supported accommodation;
  - are homeless;
  - have experienced domestic abuse;
  - have a mental health condition;
  - are currently in rent arrears or at threat of eviction or repossession;
  - are aged 16 or 17, or have left local authority care;
  - are a family with multiple and complex needs.

  You are in tier two if you:
  - have third-party deductions in place – eg, for utility arrears;
  - are a refugee or asylum seeker;
  - have a history of rent arrears;
  - were previously homeless or living in supported accommodation;
  - have a physical disability;
  - have just left prison or hospital;
  - are recently bereaved;

- have problems with language skills;
- are an ex-service person;
- are not in education, employment or training.

Budgeting advances

Budgeting advances are extra amounts of UC that are intended to help you with expenses – eg, buying essential furniture or household equipment, or expenses related to maternity or getting and keeping a job. Budgeting advances must be repaid, usually by deductions from future payments of your UC and usually over 12 months, although this can be extended by up to six months.[54] They are discretionary. If you are refused a budgeting advance, you do not have a right to appeal against this decision.

If you are awarded a budgeting advance, the DWP must send you notice in writing that you will have it deducted from subsequent payments of your UC and that, if it is not deducted, you must otherwise repay it. The same rules apply to deductions from your UC that apply to the recovery of overpayments on p1209.

To get a budgeting advance:[55]
- you must apply for one; *and*
- you (or your partner if you are a couple) must be getting UC and (unless the expense is 'necessarily related' to employment) have been getting UC or income support (IS), income-based jobseeker's allowance (JSA), income-related employment and support allowance (ESA) or pension credit (PC) for a continuous period of at least six months when the claim is made; *and*
- if you are not a member of a couple, your earnings from work must not exceed £2,600 in the period covered by the previous six complete monthly assessment periods. If you are a member of a couple, your joint earnings from work must not exceed £3,600 in this period. **Note:** if you are self-employed, your actual earned income is taken into account, not any assumed minimum income under the 'minimum income floor' (see p122); *and*
- there must be no outstanding budgeting advance (ie, which has not yet been recovered) paid to you (or your partner) and the DWP is satisfied that the budgeting advance can reasonably be expected to be recovered, taking into account all your debts and other liabilities.

The minimum amount of a budgeting advance is £100. The maximum payable is:
- if you are single and not responsible for a child, £348;
- if you are in a couple and not responsible for a child, £464;
- if you are responsible for a child and either single or in a couple, £812.

For when you are responsible for a child, see p307.

If your capital (or your joint capital if you are a couple) is over £1,000, the budgeting advance is reduced by the amount the capital exceeds £1,000. For how your capital is calculated, see Chapter 8.

Change of circumstances

You must report changes in your circumstances that you have been told you must report, as well as any that you might reasonably be expected to know might affect your right to, the amount of, or the payment of, your benefit. You should do this as soon as possible. You are usually expected to report a change on your online UC journal. Changes can be reported by telephoning the UC helpline on 0800 328 5644 (textphone: 0800 328 1344; Welsh language: 0800 328 1744), Monday to Friday 8am to 6pm. There is also a British Sign Language video relay service. However, it is advisable also to report the change on your online journal. See p1160 for further information.

If you become a member of a couple with someone who is not entitled to UC, her/his entitlement to IS, income-based JSA, income-related ESA, housing benefit (except for 'specified' or 'temporary' accommodation – see p173), child tax credit or working tax credit ends (see p31).

If you are working and being taxed through PAYE (pay as you earn), the DWP should get information about changes in your earnings automatically from HM Revenue and Customs through the 'real-time information system'. However, if your employer has not reported your earnings, you should report them yourself. The DWP may specifically require you to do this.[56] Check with your employer that your earnings are being reported as you are paid. If you are self-employed, you must report your earnings every month.

When you notify the DWP of a change of circumstances, the decision on your UC is changed by a supersession of your UC award. This usually takes effect from the first day of the monthly assessment period in which the change occurred, or is expected to occur.[57] So a change that occurs part way through a monthly assessment period can be treated as having occurred on the first day of the period. However, note the following important exceptions.

- If you are single and the change is that you have reached pension age, or you are in a mixed-age couple and the younger person has now also reached pension age, the change takes effect from the start of the assessment period that follows the assessment period in which you (or the younger person in the couple) reached pension age.[58]
- If you are required by the DWP to report your earnings, you reported them when you were required to do so and your earnings decrease, the supersession takes effect from the first day of the assessment period in which the decrease occurred.[59]
- A change of circumstances which is advantageous to you is only backdated to the start of the assessment period in which it occurred if you report it before the end of that assessment period, unless the time allowed is extended. Otherwise, the change applies from the start of the assessment period in which you reported it. For full details, see p1282.
- Other exceptions may apply (see p1279).

Examples

Gary, a lone parent aged 30 with one child (born before 6 April 2017), is entitled to maximum UC of £624.91 a month – ie, a standard allowance of £334.91, plus a child element of £290. His assessment period begins on 5 June. Halfway through this assessment period, Gary stops being responsible for a child as his son goes to live with his mother, and so Gary is no longer entitled to the child element. His maximum UC entitlement reduces to £334.91 a month. This change is not advantageous to Gary, but is backdated to the start of the assessment period – ie, to 5 June. This includes a period before he lost entitlement to the child element.

However, Gary is not overpaid UC as he does not get paid until seven days after the end of the assessment period on 4 July. So Gary gets paid just £334.91 for the whole of the assessment period in which the change occurred.

Marie, aged 26, is entitled to maximum UC of £334.91 a month (a standard allowance). Towards the end of her August monthly assessment period, she has a baby and her maximum UC entitlement increases by £244.58 as it now includes a child element. The change is advantageous to Marie. She reports the change before the end of the assessment period and it is backdated to the start of the assessment period – ie, including a period before she had her baby. When Marie gets paid (after the end of the assessment period in which the change occurred), she gets the additional £244.58 for the whole period. If Marie did not report the change until the start of her next assessment period, it may only have applied from the start of that period.

---

8. Tax, other benefits and the benefit cap

Tax

Universal credit (UC) is not taxable.

Means-tested benefits and tax credits

The general rule is that if you claim UC, you come under the UC system and can no longer get income support (IS), income-based jobseeker's allowance (JSA), income-related employment and support allowance (ESA), child tax credit (CTC) or working tax credit (WTC). You cannot qualify for housing benefit (HB), except if you are living in 'specified' or 'temporary' accommodation (see p173).

If you are in a couple and claim UC, your partner's IS, income-based JSA, income-related ESA, HB, WTC or CTC stops and you get UC as a couple instead (see p31). If one (but not both) of you has reached pension age so that you are in a 'mixed-age couple', you cannot usually make a new claim for pension credit (PC) and must claim UC instead. You may still be able to claim PC in certain circumstances (see p257).

In Scotland, UC is a qualifying benefit for Scottish child payment (see p1731).

2 Non-means-tested benefits

For the rules on entitlement to national insurance credits for people on UC, see p957.

When you come under the UC system (see p22):
- you can still claim contribution-based JSA or contributory ESA. These are taken into account in full as income for UC (and so reduce your UC entitlement);
- you can claim other non-means-tested benefits at the same time as UC – eg, carer's allowance, child benefit, personal independence payment, statutory sick pay and statutory maternity, adoption, paternity and shared parental pay;
- it can be worth claiming non-means-tested benefits. For example, if your child gets disability living allowance (or in Scotland child disability payment), you may be entitled to a disabled child addition (see p66).

For how non-means-tested benefits are treated when working out your income for UC, see Chapter 7.

The benefit cap

In some cases, there is a limit on the total amount of specified benefits you can receive (a 'benefit cap'). UC is one of the specified benefits. The benefit cap only applies if you are getting UC or HB. See p1156 for further information.

Passports and other sources of help

If you are entitled to UC, you may also qualify for health benefits such as free prescriptions (see Chapter 31) and education benefits such as free school lunches (see p851).[60] You may also qualify for social fund payments (see Chapter 37) or, in Scotland, a Best Start grant or funeral support payment (see Chapters 73 and 75), Healthy Start food and vitamins (see p847) or, in Scotland, Best Start foods (see p850), and help from your local welfare assistance scheme (see p846). You may be entitled to a council tax reduction (see p836).

Notes

Chapter 3

Universal credit

Chapter 4

People included in the claim

This chapter covers:
1. Couples (below)
2. Children (p61)

This chapter covers the rules for universal credit. For other means-tested benefits, see Chapter 16. For child tax credit, see Chapter 14 and for working tax credit, see Chapter 15.

Key facts
- Your partner and your children can be included in your universal credit (UC) claim.
- You count as a member of a couple if you are married or in a civil partnership and are living with your partner in the same household. You also count as a couple if you are not married or in a civil partnership, but are living with your partner as if you were living together as a married couple or civil partners.
- A child or 'qualifying young person' can be included as part of your family in your claim if you are responsible for her/him. S/he must normally live with you.
- You can continue to count as a couple, and children and young people can continue to be included in your UC, while you are living apart temporarily.

1. Couples

Your partner is included in your claim if you count as a 'couple'. You and your partner count as a couple if you are both aged 16 or over and you are:[1]
- married or civil partners and members of the same household; *or*
- not married or civil partners but 'living together as if' you are a married couple or civil partners.

Spouse or civil partner

You can still be treated as part of a couple, even if you are married to someone else or in a civil partnership with someone else.[2]

There are special rules if you are polygamously married. If your spouse has another spouse from an earlier marriage and you all live in the same household, you can get universal credit (UC) as a single person.[3] You count as polygamously married if you are part of a marriage in which one of you is married to more than one person and your marriages took place in a country that permits polygamy (see also p535).[4]

You count as someone's **civil partner** if you have been registered as her/his civil partner.

Living together as a married couple or civil partners

Even if you and your partner are not married or civil partners, you count as a couple if you are 'living together as if' you are a married couple or civil partners. This is referred to as 'cohabiting' in this *Handbook*. This applies to both different- and same-sex relationships.[5] The factors below are used as 'signposts' to determine whether or not you are cohabiting.[6] No one factor, in itself, is conclusive, as it is your overall relationship and your particular circumstances that are looked at.[7] The 'emotional aspect' of the relationship (your interdependence, devotion, love and affection) should also be considered.[8] This does not necessarily conflict with the factors below but, like your individual circumstances, should not be regarded as conclusive. For example, if your partner stays with you for three nights or more a week, you should not automatically be treated as living together as a couple.

Are you cohabiting?
1. Do you live in the same household? See below.
2. Do you have a sexual relationship? See below.
3. What are your financial arrangements? See p58.
4. Is your relationship stable? See p58.
5. Do you have children? See p58.
6. How do you appear in public? See p58.

Living in the same household

If you live in the same household, you may be treated as cohabiting. For what counts as a 'household', see p58.

Even if you *do* share a household, you may not be cohabiting. It is essential to look at *why* two people are in the same household.[9] For example, if you are living in the same household for 'care, companionship and mutual convenience', you can argue that you are not 'living together as husband and wife or civil partners'.[10]

Being in a sexual relationship

In practice, a decision maker may not ask you about the existence of a sexual relationship, in which case s/he only has the information if you volunteer it.

However, if you are appealing about whether you are a member of a couple, the First-tier Tribunal should consider this and may ask you about it.[11] If you do not have a sexual relationship, you should say so (and perhaps offer to show your separate sleeping arrangements).

Having a sexual relationship is not sufficient, by itself, to prove you are cohabiting. If you have never had a sexual relationship, there is a strong (but not necessarily conclusive) presumption that you are not cohabiting.[12] A couple who abstain from a sexual relationship before marriage should not be counted as cohabiting until they are formally married.[13]

Your financial arrangements

If one person is supported by the other or your household expenses are shared, this may be treated as evidence that you are cohabiting. However, it is important to consider how expenses are shared. There is a difference between, on the one hand, paying a fixed weekly contribution or rigidly sharing bills 50/50 (which does *not* suggest cohabitation) and, on the other hand, a common fund for income and expenditure (which might).

A stable relationship

Marriage and civil partnership are expected to be stable and lasting and so an occasional or brief association should not be regarded as cohabitation. However, the fact that your relationship is stable does not make it cohabitation – eg, you can have a stable relationship as a landlord and lodger, but not be cohabiting.

The way you spend your time together, the activities you undertake together and the things you do for each other are relevant, so questions about how you spend your holidays and how you organise the shopping, the laundry and cleaning may be important.

Children

If you have had a child together and live in the same household as the other parent, there is a strong (but not conclusive) presumption of cohabitation.

Your appearance in public

Decision makers may check the electoral roll and claims for other benefits to see whether you present yourselves as a couple. If you do not have a committed emotional loving relationship that is publicly acknowledged, you can argue that you are not living together as a married couple or civil partners.[14]

Households

The term '**household**' is not defined. Whether you and another person should be treated as members of the same household is decided on the particular facts of your case. In all cases, you must spend the major part of your time in the same household.

A house or flat can contain a number of separate households and if one person has exclusive occupation of separate accommodation from another, they are not considered to be living in the same household. Physical presence is not, in itself, conclusive. There must be a 'particular kind of tie' binding two people together in a domestic establishment. So, for example, a husband and wife may live in separate households in the same care or nursing home.[15] A household must also involve two or more people living together as a unit and having a reasonable level of independence and self-sufficiency. In one case, it was held that a married couple sharing a room in a residential home because they needed help organising their personal care and domestic activities were not self-sufficient and did not live in a domestic establishment, and therefore did not share a household.[16]

Is there a separate household?

If you think you should not be treated as a member of the same household as someone, check whether you can show that you maintain separate households. A separate household may exist if there are:

– independent arrangements for storing and cooking food or separate eating arrangements;
– independent financial arrangements or separate commitments for housing costs;
– no evidence of family life.

You cannot be a member of more than one household at the same time.[17] So if you are a member of one couple, you cannot also be treated as part of another. If two people maintain separate homes (ie, they each have a separate address where they usually live), they cannot share the same household.[18] Even if you have the right to occupy only part of a room, you may have your own household.[19]

If you are separated from your partner, but living under the same roof, you should not be treated as a couple if you are maintaining separate households. Any 'mere hope' of a reconciliation is not a 'reasonable expectation' if at least one partner has accepted that the relationship is at an end.[20]

Note: if you are still married or in a civil partnership, a shared attitude that the relationship is at an end may not be enough to show there is no shared household.[21]

Couples living apart

If you separate permanently (ie, you do not intend to resume living with your partner), you no longer count as a couple.[22] When deciding whether you intend to resume living together or not, your intention must be 'unqualified' – ie, it must not depend on something over which you have no control, such as the right of entry to the UK being granted by the Home Office[23] or the offer of a suitable job.[24]

2

If you and your partner are living apart temporarily, you continue to count as a couple because you are still treated as members of the same household. If you were not living together in the same household before your time apart, you should not be regarded as living apart temporarily.[25] Your former household need not have been in the UK.[26]

However, you no longer count as a couple (and therefore claim as a single person) if you have been separated (or expect to be separated) for more than six months.[27] Only your income and capital are taken into account.

If either you or your partner go abroad, see p1640.

If your partner is in hospital, see p907. If s/he is in a care home, see p918. If your partner is a prisoner or serving a sentence while in hospital, see p926.

In any situation in which you still count as a couple but claim UC as a single person (see p35), your income and capital is still assessed jointly (see p140).[28]

Challenging a decision that you are a couple

Your UC may be stopped or adjusted if the decision maker decides you are a member of a couple.

If you disagree with a decision that you are a couple, you can apply for a revision or supersession (see Chapter 56), or appeal (see Chapter 57).

How do you show that you are not a couple?

1. Consider carefully what evidence to submit:

– if you are married or in a civil partnership, to show that you are not living in the same household with your spouse or civil partner;

– if you are not married or in a civil partnership, in relation to each of the six questions on p57, the emotional aspect of your relationship and any other matters you consider relevant.

2. Provide evidence if the other person has another address (eg, a rent book and other household bills), receipts for board and lodging, statements from friends and relatives, or evidence of a formal separation, divorce proceedings or a dissolution application or order.

You do not have to prove that you are not a couple when you first claim, but you must provide any information that is reasonably required to decide your claim.[29] A decision should then be made on all the available evidence.[30] However, if your UC award as a single person is stopped because it is alleged that you are part of a couple, the onus is on the decision maker to prove that you are.[31]

Although UC can continue to be paid to you as a couple, it will be affected – eg, because your alleged partner must also satisfy the basic conditions for UC and your income and capital are assessed jointly.

2. Children

A child may count as part of your family and be included in your universal credit (UC) claim if you or your partner are 'responsible' for her/him – ie, s/he 'normally lives' with you (see p62).[32] You do not have to be the child's parent.

A child stops being included in your UC if you no longer fulfil these conditions or if s/he no longer counts as a child.

If you are responsible for a child, you can get an additional amount (a child element) included in your UC. However, in most cases, you can only get child elements for a maximum of two children (see p66).

Who counts as a child

A person usually counts as a child if:[33]
- s/he is aged under 16; or
- s/he is aged 16 or over but under 20 and counts as a 'qualifying young person' under the UC rules. This includes most young people studying for GCSEs or A levels or who are doing approved training. Specifically, it means someone who:[34]
  - is aged 16 but who has not reached 1 September following her/his 16th birthday; or
  - is aged 16–19 but who has not yet reached 1 September following her/his 19th birthday, and has been accepted for (or has enrolled on) approved training or non-advanced education at school or college, or another institution approved by the Secretary of State (see below). During term time there must be more than 12 hours, on average, of tuition, practical work, supervised study and examinations a week. Meal breaks and unsupervised study are not included.

Note: a 19 year old must have started (or been accepted for or enrolled on) the education or training before reaching 19 in order to count as a qualifying young person.

Approved training and non-advanced education for universal credit
'**Approved training**' is training that is approved by the DWP and provided under section 2(1) of the Employment and Training Act 1973 or section 2(3) of the Enterprise and New Towns (Scotland) Act 1990.

A course is '**non-advanced**' if it is below the level of 'advanced education'. Courses that count as advanced education include university degrees and other courses above GCSE, A level and Scottish National Qualifications above higher or advanced higher level.[35] See p564 for more examples of advanced and non-advanced courses.

Who does not count as a child

A person does not count as a child if s/he is getting UC, income support, income-based jobseeker's allowance (JSA), income-related employment and support allowance (ESA), working tax credit, child tax credit, contribution-based JSA under the UC system or contributory ESA under the UC system in her/his own right and so does not count as a qualifying young person (see p563).[36]

Responsibility for a child

A child is included in your UC claim if you are 'responsible' for her/him. You are treated as responsible for a child if s/he 'normally lives' with you.[37] When deciding whether a child lives with you, the DWP should consider the amount of time s/he spends with you, as well as the nature of the support you provide. **Note:** in practice, when deciding whether you are responsible for a child, the DWP checks to see whether you are entitled to child benefit for her/him. However, this is not the legal test of responsibility. In particular, the fact that you do not get child benefit for the child does *not* show that s/he is not 'normally living' with you.

If the child normally lives with two (or more) people who are not a couple (eg, if s/he lives in the homes of her/his separated parents), you are responsible if you have the main responsibility. In this situation, you can agree with the other person who this should be. The DWP can, however, decide otherwise or, if you cannot agree, decide which person has the main responsibility. Both the amount of time the child spends with you and the nature of the support you provide should be taken into account.[38] You cannot be treated as responsible for a child during any period in which s/he is:[39]

- being 'looked after by a local authority' (see below), except during planned short breaks in local authority care to provide respite care for the person who normally looks after her/him and except if the child is living with you and you are her/his parent or (unless you are a foster parent) someone with parental responsibility for her/him; *or*
- a prisoner; *or*
- temporarily absent from your household (see p58) and s/he has been, or is expected to be, absent for more than six months, including if this is for medical treatment abroad; *or*
- temporarily absent from your household and s/he has been, or is expected to be, absent from Great Britain for more than one month, unless it is under the same circumstances (medical treatment or death of a close relative) as those that apply to when you can get UC while absent (see p1639).

Being looked after by a local authority means being looked after by a local authority under specific legislation – ie, section 22 of the Children Act 1989, section 17(6) of the Children (Scotland) Act 1995 or section 74 of the Social Services and Well-being (Wales) Act 2014.[40]

2

If UC is paid for a child, it cannot be split between parents if a child spends her/his time equally between their two homes. The person who has main responsibility for the child has the child included in her/his UC.

Notes

1. Couples

1 s137(1) SSCBA 1992; CFC/7/1992; s39 WRA 2012
2 R(SB) 8/85
3 Reg 3(4) and (5) UC Regs
4 Reg 3(5) UC Regs
5 s39 WRA 2012
6 *Crake and Butterworth v SBC* [1982] 1 All ER 498; [1981] 2 FLR 264 (QBD)
7 R(SB) 17/81; R(G) 3/71; CIS/87/1993
8 *PP v Basildon DC (HB)* [2013] UKUT 505 (AAC)
9 *Crake and Butterworth v SBC* [1982] 1 All ER 498; [1981] 2 FLR 264 (QBD), quoted in R(SB) 35/85
10 R(SB) 35/85
11 CIS/87/1993; CIS/2559/2002; CIS/2074/2008
12 CIS/87/1993
13 CSB/150/1985
14 *JP v SSWP (IS)* [2014] UKUT 17 (AAC)
15 *Santos v Santos* [1972] 2 All ER 246; CIS/671/1992; CIS/81/1993
16 CIS/4935/1997
17 R(SB) 8/85
18 R(SB) 4/83
19 CSB/463/1986
20 CIS/72/1994
21 CIS/2900/1998
22 Reg 3(6) UC Regs
23 CIS/508/1992; CIS/13805/1996
24 CIS/484/1993
25 Reg 3(6) UC Regs; *Broxtowe BC v CS (HB)* [2014] UKUT 186 (AAC)
26 CIS/508/1992
27 Reg 3(6) UC Regs
28 Reg 3(3) UC Regs
29 Reg 37 UC, PIP, JSA&ESA(C&P) Regs
30 CIS/317/1994
31 R(I) 1/71

2. Children

32 s10 WRA 2012; reg 4(2) UC Regs
33 s40 WRA 2012; regs 2 and 5 UC Regs
34 Reg 5 UC Regs
35 Reg 12(3) UC Regs
36 Reg 5(5) UC Regs
37 Reg 4 UC Regs
38 Reg 4 UC Regs; *MC v SSWP (UC)* [2018] UKUT 44 (AAC)
39 Reg 4(6) and (7) UC Regs
40 Reg 2 UC Regs, definition of 'looked after by a local authority'

Chapter 5

The maximum amount

This chapter covers:
1. What is the maximum amount (below)
2. The standard allowance (p65)
3. Elements (p66)

Key facts

- Together with your income and capital, the maximum amount of universal credit (UC) is used to calculate the amount of UC to which you are entitled.
- The maximum amount is made up of a standard allowance plus, where applicable, one or more elements, depending on your circumstances.

1. What is the maximum amount

Your maximum universal credit (UC) is made up of the total of:
- a standard allowance, either for a single claimant or for a couple making a joint claim (see p65);
- a child element for each child, subject to a 'two-child limit' (exceptions may apply), with an increase for a disabled or severely disabled child (see p66);
- an element for an adult assessed as having limited capability for work and work-related activity (see p71). A separate element, abolished for new claimants, for someone assessed as just having limited capability for work can still be paid in some cases (see p69);
- a carer element for someone caring for a severely disabled person (see p73);
- a childcare costs element (see p73);
- a housing costs element for help with your rent or any service charges that you pay (see p76);
- a transitional element if you have transferred to UC under the 'managed migration' process and would otherwise be worse off than on legacy benefits (see p76). If you have transferred to UC under the 'natural migration' process and are entitled to a 'transitional SDP element' (or a 'transitional SDP amount') as a result, this is treated as if it is part of your maximum amount (see p76).

After a death

If any of the following people dies, your maximum amount of UC continues to be calculated as if that person had not died for the remainder of the monthly assessment period (see p38) in which the death occurs, and for the next two assessment periods:[1]

- your partner, if you have a joint UC claim with her/him (see p44);
- a child for whom you (or your partner in a joint claim) are responsible (see p66);
- a severely disabled person for whom you (or your partner in a joint claim) have regular and substantial caring responsibilities (see p73);
- someone who counts as a non-dependant for the purpose of the housing element (see p96).

For example, if you have a joint claim and your partner dies, your standard allowance (and any element paid in respect of your partner) continues at the couple rate for the remainder of the assessment period in which s/he died, and for the next two assessment periods.

2. The standard allowance

A standard allowance is always included in your universal credit (UC) maximum amount. The amount depends on your age and whether you are claiming as a single person or making a joint claim with your partner (see p44).[2] See p56 for who counts as a couple, including when one of you is temporarily absent.

If you are making a joint claim with your partner and your partner dies, see p64.

Note: if one member of a couple does not satisfy the rules of entitlement for UC, the other partner may be able to claim as a single person (see p44). In this case, the standard allowance for a single claimant applies.

Rates of standard allowance	
Single claimant	*per month*
Under 25	£265.31
25 or over	£334.91
Joint claimants	
Both under 25	£416.45
One or both 25 or over	£525.72

3. **Elements**

Child element

If you are responsible for a child or young person, you can get a child element included in your universal credit (UC) maximum amount. You are 'responsible' for a child if s/he is normally living with you (see p62).[3] The child must be aged under 16, or 16–19 and a 'qualifying young person' for UC purposes (see p61).[4]

Before 6 April 2017, you got a child element for each child or young person you or your partner were responsible for. From 6 April 2017, a 'two-child limit' applies (see below).

You may get a higher rate of the child element for the eldest or only child.[5] This was abolished from 6 April 2017, but continues to apply if your eldest or only child was born before that date.[6]

If a child is disabled, the child element is increased by a '**disabled child addition**'. You get the lower rate if the child is entitled to disability living allowance (DLA), child disability payment (CDP), personal independence payment (PIP) or adult disability payment (ADP). You get the higher rate instead if s/he is entitled to the DLA/CDP care component at the highest rate, the daily living component of PIP/ADP at the enhanced rate, or if s/he is certified as severely sight impaired or blind by a consultant ophthalmologist.[7] The disabled child addition is still paid for a child, even if you cannot get a child element for her/him because of the two-child limit.[8]

If your child dies, see p65.

Rates of child element

	per month
First child born before 6 April 2017	£290.00
Second child/all children born on or after 6 April 2017	£244.58
Disabled child addition	
Lower rate	£132.89
Higher rate	£414.88

The two-child limit

You cannot get an element for a child born on or after 6 April 2017 if you already have two or more other children included in your award, unless an exception applies (see p67). This is known as the 'two-child limit'.[9] You can always get an element for a child born before 6 April 2017.

When establishing the number of children you have for this purpose, a child who is covered by either of the first two exceptions starting below (ie, you have adopted her/him or s/he is living with you under a 'non-parental care arrangement') is ignored.

So you can get an element for:
- any child born before 6 April 2017; *and*
- a child born on or after 6 April 2017 who is not counted as your third or subsequent child; *and*
- a third or subsequent child born on or after 6 April 2017 to whom an exception applies.

Examples

Chloe has three children. One was born before 6 April 2017, the others were born on 6 May 2019 and 4 July 2021. No exceptions apply to the children. Chloe gets a child element for two children: the one born before 6 April 2017, and the one born on 6 May 2019.

Stevie and Alex have four children. Two were born before 6 April 2017, two (Elsie and Alfie) after that date. Elsie has been adopted by Stevie and Alex. They get child elements for three children: the two born before 6 April 2017, and one for Elsie, as she is covered by an exception. Although Elsie is not included when establishing how many children Stevie and Alex have, they still have three other children. One of these, Alfie, was born after 6 April 2017. He is not covered by any of the exceptions and so no child element is included for him.

The number and order of children (ie, whether a child is the first, second, third or subsequent child) is determined by allocating each child a date according to her/his date of birth, so that the eldest child is regarded as the first.[10]

The child element can become payable for a third child to whom the two-child limit would apply when an older child leaves the household (as you are no longer responsible for her/him), or when a young person leaves education (as s/he no longer qualifies). In these situations, you should report the change as soon as possible to ensure you continue to receive the maximum two child elements.

Exceptions

The two-child limit does not apply to the following children.[11]
- A child living with you under a 'non-parental caring arrangement'. This means either that s/he is a child whose parent is aged under 16 and you are responsible for the parent, *or* that the child is living with you on a long-term basis because s/he is unable to live with her/his parents and you are caring for her/him as a family member or friend. You or your partner must not be the child's parent or step-parent and you must:
  – be named in a child arrangements order under section 8 of the Children Act 1989 or a residence order under Article 8 of the Children (Northern Ireland) Order 1995 as a person with whom the child is to live; *or*

2

 - be the appointed or special guardian, or be entitled to guardian's allowance, for the child; *or*
 - have a kinship care order under section 72(1) of the Children and Young People (Scotland) Act 2014, or parental responsibilities or rights under section 80 of the Adoption and Children (Scotland) Act 2007; *or*
 - continue to be responsible for the child if any of the above bullet points applied immediately before the child's 16th birthday; *or*
 - be caring for the child because otherwise it is likely s/he would be taken into the care of the local authority.
- A child who is being adopted by you from local authority care or who has been placed with you for adoption. This exception does not apply if:
 - you or your partner were the child's step-parent immediately before the adoption; *or*
 - you or your partner have been the child's parent (other than by adoption) at any other time; *or*
 - the child is being adopted direct from abroad.
- A child born in a multiple birth, other than the first born if you already have two or more children. So, if you have:
 - no older children, you get the child element for all children in a multiple birth;
 - one older child, you get the child element for all children in a multiple birth;
 - two or more older children, you get the child element for all but one of the children in a multiple birth.
- A child who is likely to have been conceived as a result of rape, or in a controlling or coercive relationship (a 'non-consensual conception'). You must not be living at the same address as the alleged perpetrator for this exception to apply, even though you might have been living with that person at the time of conception. A 'controlling or coercive relationship' includes behaviour that causes you to fear, on at least two occasions, that violence will be used against you, or that causes you serious alarm or distress which has a substantial adverse effect on your day-to-day activities. You must provide evidence from an 'approved person' that you have had contact with her/him or another approved person about the rape or relationship. A list of 'approved persons' is in official guidance and includes healthcare professionals, social workers and approved organisations such as specialist rape charities.[12] Third-party evidence is not required if there has been a conviction for rape or coercive, controlling behaviour in the UK, or for a similar offence abroad, or if you have been awarded criminal injuries compensation after a sexual offence, physical abuse or mental injury, and it is likely that the offence or injury resulted in the conception. You can be treated as having provided evidence if you have already provided it to HM Revenue and Customs (HMRC) for child tax credit (CTC).

If you are the step-parent of the child but are no longer part of a couple with the child's parent, the exception can continue to apply if you are still responsible for the child, and the only reason for any breaks in your claim is your becoming single or part of a couple again. Get advice.

Limited capability for work element

The limited capability for work element was abolished for new claims from 3 April 2017.[13] You can no longer get the element if you are making a new claim for UC, unless you are covered by one of the exceptions in the bullet points below. If you (or your partner in a joint claim) are also entitled to the limited capability for work-related activity element (see p71), you receive that instead – you cannot get both elements. If you are also entitled to the carer element (see p73), usually the carer element is included instead of the limited capability for work element – but if you have a joint claim for UC, see below.

You can get the limited capability for work element if you (or your partner) are entitled to UC and have limited capability for work (see Chapter 45) and:[14]

- you were getting the element in your current award of UC (or had limited capability for work and were waiting for the element to be included in your UC) immediately before 3 April 2017; or
- you were getting the limited capability for work-related activity element in your current award of UC immediately before 3 April 2017 and on a reassessment it is decided that you are entitled to the limited capability for work element instead; or
- the decision that you had limited capability for work before 3 April 2017 is not made until after this date and you have supplied a medical certificate, including if the decision is made following a revision or an appeal; or
- you were entitled to employment and support allowance (ESA) or to national insurance (NI) credits for limited capability for work (see p956) immediately before 3 April 2017, and you remained entitled after this date until you claimed UC; or
- you claimed ESA before 3 April 2017 but the initial decision on your claim was changed following a revision or an appeal, and on or after 3 April 2017 your UC award needs to be changed to take account of this; or
- you were entitled to incapacity benefit, severe disablement allowance, income support 'on the grounds of disability' or NI contribution credits for incapacity for work (see p956) immediately before 3 April 2017, and you remained entitled after this date until you claimed UC. Certain other conditions apply. If you are in this situation, get specialist advice.

There may be a three-month waiting period before the element can be included in your UC for the first time.[15] In practice, it is usually included straight away, either under the same rules that allow the limited capability for work-related activity element to be included straight away (see p71) or because you are transferring to UC from ESA (see below).

Note: your entitlement to the element can continue if your UC stops and then starts again because you have become, or stopped being, a member of a couple, or if your UC stops because your income is too high but then starts again within six months. If you work and earn an amount at least equal to a certain earnings threshold, you may be treated as *not* having limited capability for work or you may be reassessed (see p992).

If your partner was entitled to the element, but dies, see p64.

Rate of limited capability for work element

	per month
Limited capability for work	£132.89

Transfers to universal credit

If you transfer to UC from ESA (under either the 'natural migration' or – when invited – the 'managed migration' process) and were entitled to the work-related activity component in your ESA (see p637) on the date you claimed UC, you are treated as having limited capability for work and the limited capability for work element can be included in your UC straight away.[16] However, in practice, the DWP has not always applied this rule, so challenge the failure to do this if necessary. See AskCPAG for a useful tool to help with such a challenge.

If you were still in the ESA 'assessment phase' (see p635) when you transferred, the time you spent in the assessment phase counts towards the three-month waiting period period that might otherwise apply before the element is included in your UC.[17]

Joint claims

If you are making a joint claim with your partner, only one limited capability for work element can be included, even if you both meet the conditions.[18]

If you were previously getting UC as a single person but then form a couple with someone who was not entitled to UC, but who was getting ESA that included the work-related activity component (see p637), the limited capability for work element is included in your joint UC award.[19]

If one of you satisfies the conditions for both the limited capability for work element and the carer element (see p73), usually the carer element is included in your maximum amount instead of the limited capability for work element. However, if you qualify for one of these elements and your partner qualifies for the other, both elements can be included.[20]

Example

Theo and Sally have a joint claim for UC, made before 3 April 2017. They have a disabled son, Zack. Theo has limited capability for work. Sally is Zack's carer and satisfies the conditions for the carer element. Both the limited capability for work element and the carer element were included in Theo and Sally's UC award before 3 April 2017, and continue for as long as they remain entitled.

If Theo were also a carer for Zack, they could nominate Sally as the main carer so that both the limited capability for work and carer elements can continue to be paid.

Limited capability for work-related activity element

A limited capability for work-related activity element is included in your maximum amount if you (or your partner in a joint claim) have been assessed as having limited capability for work-related activity.[21] If this applies to you, you are also regarded as having limited capability for work. For the assessment, see p1005. **Note:** in some claims by 'mixed-age' couples, the DWP has refused to carry out an assessment of the pension-age member of the couple, simply because s/he has reached pension age. That is wrong, as the basic rule is that any UC claimant can be assessed, and the limited situations in which an assessment may not be carried out do not include reference to the claimant's age.[22] A template for challenging a refusal to carry out an assessment on this basis by judicial review is available at cpag.org.uk/welfare-rights/judicial-review/judicial-review-pre-action-letters/work-capability-assessments.

If you are qualifying for the element for the first time, there is usually a three-month waiting period before it is included in your maximum amount. The three-month period begins on the day on which you provide a medical certificate (or, where it would have been unreasonable to require you to have provided one, other evidence sufficient to show you had limited capability for work). In practice, you may already have provided a medical certificate three months or more ago (ie, as evidence of having limited capability for work), in which case you will already have served the waiting period.[23] The element is then included from the beginning of the assessment period (see p38) that follows the assessment period in which the three months ended. The element can be included straight away if you (or your partner in a joint claim):[24]

- are terminally ill; *or*
- were entitled to the element (or the limited capability for work element) immediately before your current UC award started and your previous UC award ended because you became a member of a couple or you stopped being a member of a couple; *or*
- were entitled to the element (or the limited capability for work element) and your previous UC award ended within the six months before your current award started, because your income was too high; *or*
- are entitled to an award of ESA that includes the support component; *or*
- are entitled to the limited capability for work element in your UC, but are then assessed as entitled to the limited capability for work-related activity element.

If your award of UC immediately follows an 'extended period of sickness' on jobseeker's allowance (JSA) (see p692), the rules are not clear, but the intention seems to be that the element can be included from the beginning of the assessment period that follows the period in which the three months ended, beginning with the first day of your extended period of sickness.[25]

If you partner is entitled to the element but dies, see p65.

If you also satisfy the conditions for the carer element (see p73), the limited capability for work-related activity element is paid instead. However, if you are in a couple, if one of you can qualify for the limited capability for work-related activity element and the other qualifies for the carer element, both elements can be included.[26]

Rate of limited capability for work-related activity element

per month

Limited capability for work-related activity £354.28

Transfers to universal credit

If you transfer from ESA to UC (under either the 'natural migration' or – when invited – the 'managed migration' process) and were entitled to the support component in your ESA (see p636) on the date you claim UC, you are treated as having limited capability for work-related activity and the element is included in your UC straight away. The same applies if you were not entitled to ESA but, on the date you claim UC, were entitled to credits for limited capability for work and were assessed as having limited capability for work-related activity (see p1004). If you were still in the 'assessment phase' for ESA (see p635), but had been in it for less than 13 weeks, the time you spent in the assessment phase counts towards the three-month period. If you had already been in the assessment phase for at least 13 weeks and it is decided that you have limited capability for work-related activity for UC, the element is awarded from the beginning of your first assessment period.[27] In practice, the DWP has not always applied this rule, so point it out if necessary.

Joint claims

If you are making a joint claim with your partner, only one limited capability for work-related activity element can be included, even if you both meet the conditions.[28]

If you were previously getting UC as a single person but then form a couple with someone who was not entitled to UC but was getting ESA that included the support component (see p636), the limited capability for work-related activity element is included in your joint UC award.[29]

Carer element

A carer element is included in your maximum amount if you have 'regular and substantial' caring responsibilities for a severely disabled person. This means that you satisfy, or would satisfy were it not for the level of your earnings, the conditions for carer's allowance (CA) (see p546). You do not need to have claimed CA (however, if you live in Scotland and you do claim CA, it can be increased by a CA supplement – see p553). If you get the carer element, the severely disabled person cannot get a severe disability premium in her/his legacy means-tested benefit (see p330). **Note:** you do not qualify for the carer element if you have any earnings from your caring responsibilities.[30]

If you are claiming as a single person, only one carer element can be included, even if you care for more than one disabled person. If you are making a joint claim, you can get two carer elements if both you and your partner satisfy the conditions, provided you are not caring for the same person. If you are both caring for the same person, you get one carer element. You can decide between you which partner should be entitled – eg, if it is necessary for your partner to be entitled to the carer element so that you can also get the limited capability for work or limited capability for work-related activity element. If you do not decide which one of you should be entitled to the carer element, the DWP decides for you.[31] Similarly, if someone other than your partner is caring for the same person, only one of you can get CA or the carer element of UC for that care. You can decide between you who should be entitled.[32]

If the person you care for dies, the element should continue to be paid for a time (see p65). If the DWP fails to do this, see AskCPAG for a useful tool for challenging the decision.

Rate of carer element

	per month
Carer	£168.81

Childcare costs element

A childcare costs element is included in your maximum amount if you are working (or have an offer of work) and you have paid childcare costs for 'relevant childcare' (see below for what this covers).

The amount of the element is 85 per cent of your childcare costs, up to a maximum of £646.35 a month for one child and £1,108.04 a month for two or more children.[33]

Note:
- If you have upfront childcare costs (eg, a deposit, retainer or fees) in advance of the childcare starting and you have started work but not yet received your first wages, the government has said that your work coach can pay those costs

2

direct to the childcare provider using the Flexible Support Fund (see p858). You cannot get the costs covered by the childcare element. Once you have received your first wages, any further upfront childcare costs (eg, during the school holidays) can be met from a budgeting advance (see p51). If you get a budgeting advance, you can still get up to 85 per cent of the childcare costs (subject to the overall limits above) covered by the childcare costs element, once you have submitted a paid receipt.[34]

- If you are entitled to UC, you cannot also get tax-free childcare payments. In the future, if you register for the tax-free childcare scheme, all your UC could be terminated.[35] See p856 for more details.

To get the childcare costs element, you must be in paid work (there are no minimum hours) or have an offer of paid work that is due to start before the end of your next UC monthly assessment period (see p38).[36] If you are in a couple, your partner must also be in paid work, unless s/he cannot provide childcare her/himself because s/he has limited capability for work (see Chapter 45), or s/he is caring for a severely disabled person and gets (or would be entitled to) CA (see p545), or s/he is temporarily absent from your household. **Note:** you stop counting as a couple if your partner is (or is expected to be) absent from Great Britain for more than six months.[37] If your partner is temporarily absent abroad, see p1622.

You are treated as still in paid work if you are getting statutory sick pay, statutory maternity pay, statutory adoption pay, statutory paternity pay, statutory shared parental pay, statutory parental bereavement pay or maternity allowance. You are also treated as still in paid work if your work ended during your current assessment period or in the previous one.[38]

In addition, you must meet all the following conditions.[39]

- You have paid charges for 'relevant childcare' for a child for whom you are responsible – ie, s/he normally lives with you. The rules require you already to have paid the charges, rather than just be liable to pay them. **Note:** this requirement is currently the subject of a legal challenge.[40] See AskCPAG and CPAG's *Welfare Rights Bulletin* for updates.
- The child is aged under 16 or has not reached the 1 September following her/his 16th birthday.
- The childcare is to enable you to do paid work (or was to enable you to do paid work but that work has stopped).
- You report the charges to the DWP no later than the end of the monthly UC assessment period that follows the assessment period in which the charges were paid. The DWP may allow you to report them later than this, under the same rules that apply to late notification of a change in circumstances (see p1283).

Relevant childcare

'Relevant childcare' means care for a child provided by the following.

In England:[41]

– a registered childcare provider – ie, someone registered with Ofsted under Part 3 of the Childcare Act 2006; *or*

– a school on school premises out of school hours (or at any time if the child has not reached compulsory school age); *or*

– an official domiciliary care provider – ie, one registered with the Care Quality Commission.

In Scotland:[42]

– a registered childminder or similar provider of daycare – ie, registered as such under the Public Services Reform (Scotland) Act 2010; *or*

– a childcare agency under the Public Services Reform (Scotland) Act 2010; *or*

– a local authority registered to provide childminding or daycare under the Public Services Reform (Scotland) Act 2010.

In Wales:[43]

– a registered childminder or daycare provider – ie, registered under Part 2 of the Children and Families (Wales) Measure 2010; *or*

– someone providing daycare that would count for registration, were it not for the fact that it is provided in a care home, hospital, children's home, residential family centre or school; *or*

– someone providing childcare under a Welsh Assembly scheme for tax credit purposes or a home childcare approval scheme made by the Welsh Ministers; *or*

– out of school hours, a school on school premises or a local authority; *or*

– an official domiciliary care worker – ie, under the Domiciliary Care Agencies (Wales) Regulations 2004; *or*

– a foster parent (but not for the child who s/he is fostering) if, were it not for the fact that the child is too old, the childcare would count as registered childcare or daycare – ie, under Part 2 of the Children and Families (Wales) Measure 2010.

The following *does not count* as relevant childcare:[44]

– care provided by a 'close relative' of the child (ie, parent, parent-in-law, son, daughter, son-in-law, daughter-in-law, stepson, stepdaughter, stepbrother, stepsister and a partner of any of these) wholly or mainly in the child's home;[45]

– care provided by a foster parent, foster carer or kinship carer for a child who the person is fostering or looking after as a kinship carer.

Rates of childcare costs element

	per month
Maximum for one child	£646.35
Maximum for two or more children	£1,108.04

Housing costs element

A housing costs element is included in your maximum amount for qualifying housing costs. Housing costs can be either rent or service charges. See Chapter 6 for when you are entitled and the amount of your housing costs element. **Note:** you cannot get a housing costs element for your mortgage interest payments or for a loan for repairs and improvements. Instead, the DWP may offer you a loan (see p839).

Transitional element

If you transfer to UC under the 'managed migration' process (see p29) and the amount of your UC would be less than the total amount of your legacy benefits (see p21), a 'transitional element' is included in your UC. This is intended to ensure that you are not worse off at the point you transfer to UC.[46]

Note: you can only get a transitional element if you transfer to UC under the managed migration process (see p29). However, if you transfer to UC under the natural migration process, you may instead be entitled to a 'transitional SDP element' (or a 'transitional SDP amount').

Transitional SDP element
– If you transfer to UC under the 'natural migration' process on or after 27 January 2021, you may be entitled to an extra amount of UC called the 'transitional SDP element' (see p27). If you transferred before 27 January 2021, you may instead be entitled to a 'transitional SDP amount', which is very similar. These extra amounts of UC are intended to compensate you for not having a severe disability element in your UC, but are not intended to ensure that you are not worse off on UC overall.
– The transitional SDP element (and the transitional SDP amount) is treated 'as if' it were part of your maximum amount of UC in working out your UC (see p38). So it is included in your maximum amount.
– The transitional SDP element (and the transitional SDP amount) is also treated 'as if' it were a transitional element, so that it can be reduced or stopped in the same way that a transitional element can be (see p78).
– If you transfer to UC under the managed migration process, you can only get a transitional element: the transitional SDP element and the transitional SDP amount do not apply in such cases.

You *cannot* get a transitional element if:[47]
• you were claiming your legacy benefits (see p21) as a couple, you transfer to UC under the managed migration process, but you claim UC as a single person or as a member of a different couple; *or*

- you were claiming your legacy benefits as a member of a polygamous marriage, you transfer to UC under the managed migration process, but you claim UC as a single person or as a member of a couple; *or*
- it is decided that you are not entitled to UC at all, but you then reclaim and are awarded UC. You cannot usually get a transitional element included in your later claim, unless the reason you were not entitled to UC was because your earnings (or in a joint claim, your and your partner's combined earnings) were too high.[48] In this case, if you reclaim UC and it starts within three months of the end of what would have been your first UC monthly assessment period, you can be entitled to a transitional element in your UC.

To get a transitional element, you must transfer to UC under the managed migration process. This means the DWP must have sent you a 'migration notice' informing you that you are affected by the process. You must then have made a 'qualifying claim' for UC – ie, you claim before the 'final deadline'.[49] The final deadline is one month from the date you were told you must claim UC by (known as your 'deadline day').[50]

Even if you make your claim in time, you are usually required to provide further information at an interview. If you do not do so, the DWP regards this as a 'failed claim' and 'closes' your claim. This is actually a decision that you are not entitled to any UC at all, so you cannot get a transitional element. The rules say you cannot get a transitional element if you reclaim, even if you do so before your final deadline, although it is not clear that this is the official intention.[51] If your claim is 'closed', you can challenge this decision (see p44).

To decide whether you are entitled to a transitional element, the DWP compares:[52]

- your 'total legacy amount'. This is the total amount of your legacy benefits on the day before your first day of UC entitlement, converted to a monthly amount. If the benefit cap for UC would apply to you (see p1156) and your total legacy amount exceeds the level of the UC benefit cap, your total legacy amount is reduced by the level of the excess, minus your working tax credit (WTC) childcare costs; *and*
- your 'indicative UC amount'. This is the amount of UC you would get, based on your circumstances on the day before your first day of UC entitlement. The DWP assumes that if you get CTC for a child, you are responsible for that child, that if you get childcare costs in your WTC, these apply in the childcare costs element of your UC, and that your earnings are the same as those used to calculate your tax credits or (if you do not get tax credits) benefits. The DWP can use any further information and evidence if necessary. If the benefit cap for UC would apply to you (see p1156), your indicative UC amount is limited to the amount of the benefit cap plus your eligible childcare costs.

The weekly rate of your old means-tested benefits is converted to a monthly amount by multiplying it by 52 and dividing by 12. The daily rate of your tax credit award is converted to a monthly amount by multiplying it by 365 and dividing by 12.

If the amount of UC to which you are entitled is less than your total legacy benefit awards, the difference between the two is the amount of your transitional element. If the amount of UC is the same as, or more than, your total legacy benefit awards, you do not get a transitional element.

Example

Note: this example is to show how a transitional element is calculated; the actual figures used may differ.

Tilly is a single person aged 30. She gets income-related ESA (including the enhanced disability and severe disability premiums, and the support component) and HB. On the day before she makes her UC claim, she is entitled to income-related ESA at a weekly rate of £204.75 and HB at a weekly rate of £225.

Her income-related ESA is converted to a monthly amount of £887.25 (£204.75 x 52, divided by 12).

Her HB is converted to a monthly amount of £975 (£225 x 52, divided by 12).

So Tilly's total benefits (her 'total legacy amount') = £887.25 + £975 = £1,862.25

Tilly is entitled to UC:

Standard allowance £334.91

Limited capability for work-related activity element £354.28

Housing costs element £975

Tilly's 'indicative UC amount' is £334.91 + £354.28 + £975 = £1,664.19

The total amount of Tilly's legacy benefits is higher than the amount of UC she would get, so she gets the difference as a transitional element in her UC – ie, £1,862.25 – £1,664.19 = £198.06 per month. This will be reduced by future increases in her UC maximum amount. For example, if her housing costs element increases by £100 a month, the transitional element will be £198.06 – £100 = £98.06

When the transitional element reduces or stops

Note: the following also applies to the 'transitional SDP element' (or in cases where your severe disability premium began before 27 January 2021, your 'transitional SDP amount') (see p27).

The amount of your transitional element can be reduced over time. This is because, after your first monthly UC assessment period, the amount is reduced by any increase in the standard allowance or other elements included in your UC (including an element included for the first time), except for the childcare element.[53] See the example above. If these reductions reduce your element to nil, you do not get the transitional element again.

Your entitlement to a transitional element ends if:[54]

- at the time of your UC claim, your earnings from work (or in a joint claim, your and your partner's combined earnings) were at least the level at which you are not subject to work-search requirements (see p1050), but they have now been below this amount for three consecutive UC monthly assessment periods (your entitlement to the element ends in the UC assessment period after the third of the assessment periods); *or*
- you originally claimed UC as a couple, but you are now single, or you originally claimed UC as a single person, but you are now part of a couple (your entitlement to the element ends in the UC assessment period in which this occurs); *or*
- your UC comes to an end for any reason (note: the DWP may include in this where you stop being entitled to UC as part of a couple, or as a single person, although the law is not clear about this[55]). In this case, you cannot get a transitional element in any future award of UC, unless your previous UC award ended because your earnings (or in a joint claim, your and your partner's combined earnings) increased so that your income was too high and your new UC award starts within three months of the end of your last UC monthly assessment period. In these circumstances, your new UC award includes the same transitional element as in your previous award.

Changing a decision about the transitional element

The transitional element is part of the calculation of your UC. You can challenge the decision on your entitlement to the element by requesting a revision (see Chapter 56) or appealing against the decision on your UC entitlement – you must ask for a mandatory reconsideration first (see Chapter 57).

The decision about your UC can be revised or superseded if information used in the original calculation of your transitional element is now considered to be wrong because:[56]

- you (or your partner in a joint claim) misrepresented something; *or*
- you (or your partner in a joint claim) failed to report information you were required to report, and that failure was to your advantage; *or*
- there was an 'official error'. This means an error made by an officer of the DWP, HMRC, a local authority or a person employed by someone acting on behalf of these bodies. The rules on what counts as an official error are the same as what can count under the normal rules for revisions (see p1266).

If, since the date on which your UC entitlement started, a decision about your legacy benefit award has been revised or superseded, or has been the subject of an appeal decision, the decision about your UC can still be revised or superseded – ie, to take account of the effect of any change in your legacy benefit on your transitional element.[57]

Notes

2

1. What is the maximum amount
1 Reg 37 UC Regs

2. The standard allowance
2 Reg 36 UC Regs

3. Elements
3 Reg 4 UC Regs
4 Reg 24 UC Regs
5 Reg 36 UC Regs
6 House of Commons, *Hansard,* Written statement HCWS96, 20 July 2016, available at questions-statements.parliament.uk
7 Reg 24 UC Regs
8 s10(2) WRA 2012; reg 36 UC Regs
9 s10(1A) WRA 2012; reg 24A UC Regs
10 Reg 24B(1) UC Regs
11 Sch 12 UC Regs
12 gov.uk/government/publications/support-for-a-child-conceived-without-your-consent/approved-third-party-professionals-who-can-complete-these-forms
13 s16 WRWA 2016
14 Sch 2 Part 2 ESAUC(MA) Regs
15 Reg 28 UC Regs, as applied by Sch 2 Part 2 ESAUC(MA) Regs
16 Reg 19 UC(TP) Regs; Vol M6, para M6192 ADM
17 Regs 20 and 21 UC(TP) Regs
18 Reg 27(4) UC Regs
19 Reg 19(3) UC(TP) Regs
20 Reg 29(4) UC Regs
21 Reg 27 UC Regs
22 Regs 40 and 41 UC Regs
23 Reg 28 UC Regs; reg 2 SS(ME) Regs. See the official guidance and example in para F5046 ADM.
24 Reg 28 UC Regs
25 Reg 20A UC(TP) Regs
26 Reg 29(4) UC Regs
27 Regs 19, 20 and 21 UC(TP) Regs
28 Reg 27(4) UC Regs
29 Reg 19(4) UC Regs
30 Regs 29 and 30 UC Regs
31 Reg 29(2) and (3) UC Regs
32 Reg 29(3) UC Regs; s70(7) SSCBA 1992
33 Regs 34 and 36 UC Regs

34 House of Commons, *Hansard,* Written question 282562, answered 5 September 2019, available at questions-statements.parliament.uk
35 DWP, *Universal Credit: increasing the childcare offer,* December 2014
36 Reg 32 UC Regs
37 Reg 3(6) UC Regs
38 Reg 32(2) UC Regs
39 Reg 33 UC Regs
40 *Salvato v SSWP* [2021] EWCA Civ 1482
41 Reg 35(2) UC Regs
42 Reg 35(3) UC Regs
43 Reg 35(4) UC Regs
44 Reg 35(7) UC Regs
45 Reg 2, definition of 'close relative', UC Regs
46 Regs 50 and 52 UC(TP) Regs
47 Regs 50(2) and 57 UC(TP) Regs
48 Reg 57(2)(a) UC(TP) Regs
49 Regs 48 and 50 UC(TP) Regs
50 Reg 46(4) UC(TP) Regs
51 Reg 57(1)(b) UC(TP) Regs; *Draft Universal Credit (Managed Migration) Regulations 2018: SSAC report and government statement,* November 2018, p14. You cannot get a transitional element if you are not entitled to an award of UC.
52 Regs 52-54 UC(TP) Regs
53 Reg 55 UC(TP) Regs
54 Regs 56 and 57 UC(TP) Regs
55 There is no clear rule terminating a UC award in these circumstances, although reg 9(7) and (8) of the UC,PIP,JSA&ESA(C&P) Regs is written as if there were.
56 Reg 62(1)(a) UC(TP) Regs
57 Reg 62(1)(b) UC(TP) Regs

Chapter 6

The housing costs element

This chapter covers:

Key facts

- Your universal credit (UC) can include a housing costs element to help with your rent and/or service charges for which you are be liable.
- If you are a private tenant, the amount of rent used to calculate your housing costs element is based on a local housing allowance for a property with the number of bedrooms that you are entitled to under the rules. This amount may be lower than the rent you must pay.
- If you are a social rented sector tenant (eg, your landlord is a local authority or housing association) and your home has more bedrooms than you are entitled to under the rules, your housing costs element is usually reduced by a percentage deduction. This deduction is known as the 'bedroom tax'.
- If you are an owner-occupier (unless you have a shared ownership tenancy), you cannot get a housing costs element for your service charges if you (or your partner) have any earned income. Even if you have no earned income, you may not get a housing costs element during an initial 'qualifying period'.
- If your housing costs element does not cover your full housing costs, you may be able to get extra financial assistance by applying for discretionary housing payments from your local authority.

Future changes
In the future, the rules on UC housing costs may be different in Scotland.[1] See AskCPAG and CPAG's *Welfare Rights Bulletin* for updates.

Part 2: Universal credit
Chapter 6: The housing costs element
1. Who can get a housing costs element

1. Who can get a housing costs element

Your universal credit (UC) maximum amount (see p64) can include a housing costs element if:[2]

- your accommodation is in Great Britain; *and*
- your accommodation is residential – ie, not for a business. If your accommodation is partly for a business and partly residential, you can qualify for a housing costs element for the part that is residential; *and*
- you (or your partner, if you are a joint claimant) make rent payments (see p83) or service charge payments (see p84) that are eligible; *and*
- you (or your partner, if you are a joint claimant) are liable for the eligible rent or service charge payments, or are treated as liable (see p86); *and*
- you normally occupy the accommodation for which you make the eligible rent or service charge payments, as your home, or you are treated as doing so (see p90).

The accommodation can comprise the whole of a building or part of a building – eg, a flat in a block, a bedsit in a house or a room in a shared house. You can get a housing costs element whether or not the accommodation comprises separate and self-contained premises.[3]

A housing costs element can include any of the eligible payments that you make. If you have a shared ownership tenancy (ie, you are buying part of your home and renting the rest), your housing costs element can include rent, as well as the service charge payments you make.[4]

Make sure you tell the DWP that you pay rent or service charges when you claim UC, so a housing costs element is included. If you are already getting UC and want to get help with your housing costs, apply via your online journal and notify as a change of circumstances.

Note:

- You cannot get a housing costs element for help with your mortgage interest payments (or alternative finance payments). The DWP may offer you a loan for mortgage interest instead. See p839 for information and get independent financial advice before accepting a loan.
- If a housing costs element is included within your UC maximum amount and you qualify for a work allowance, the lower work allowance amount applies and more of your earnings are taken into account (see p40).
- Your housing costs element is normally paid to you, but see p49 for when it can be paid direct to your landlord.
- If you are getting housing benefit (HB) and make a new claim for UC, your HB entitlement continues for two weeks (called 'HB run-on' in this *Handbook* – see p219). You do not have to pay HB run-on back, even if you qualify for a UC housing costs element for your rent for the same period. If your HB is being

paid direct to your landlord, your HB run-on payments are usually also paid to her/him. If this applies to you, you can ask your landlord to pay you the HB run-on – eg, if you are up to date with your rent payments.

When you cannot get a housing costs element

Your UC maximum amount cannot include a housing costs element if you:

- rent your accommodation and you are 16 or 17 and are, or have been, looked after by a local authority (see p933);[5] *or*
- are an owner-occupier (unless you have a shared ownership tenancy), during an assessment period in which you (or your partner) have any earned income (see p117), however much your earnings are.[6] This includes earnings from work you can do while claiming contributory employment and support allowance (see p1019) or from work of less than 16 hours a week you can do while claiming contribution-based jobseeker's allowance (JSA – see p974). The nature and duration of the work is not relevant – eg, it does not matter if your job is part time or temporary; *or*
- live in 'specified' or 'temporary' accommodation (see p84 for what counts), for the rent you pay for that accommodation.[7] You *can* get HB for this.

Rent payments

Eligible rent payments include the rent you pay to your landlord and can also include other types of payment, such as payments as a licensee and for bed and breakfast or hostel accommodation. The eligible payments are:[8]

- rent; *and*
- payments for a licence or permission to occupy accommodation – eg, for bed and breakfast or a hostel. For houseboats, this can include continuous cruiser licence payments;[9] *and*
- mooring charges payable for a houseboat; *and*
- site rent for a caravan or mobile home (but not for a tent); *and*
- contributions made by a resident of a charity's almshouse towards its maintenance and the essential services in it. The almshouse must be provided by a housing association.

In this *Handbook*, we refer to any of these payments as 'rent'.

Payments that are not eligible

The following types of payments are *not* eligible rent payments:[10]

- ground rent; *and*
- payments for a tent or its pitch; *and*
- payments for approved premises – eg, a bail or probation hostel; *and*

Part 2: Universal credit
Chapter 6: The housing costs element
1. Who can get a housing costs element

2

- payments made for 'specified' or 'temporary' accommodation (see below for what counts). You *can* get HB for these (see Chapter 10); *and*
- payments made for a care home (see below for what counts).

> **Definitions**
> **'Specified accommodation'** is:[11]
> – accommodation provided by a relevant body to meet your need for, and where you get, care, support or supervision; *or*
> – temporary accommodation (eg, a refuge) provided by a local authority or a relevant body for people who have left home because of domestic abuse or violence; *or*
> – a local authority hostel for homeless people where you get care, support or supervision to assist you to be rehabilitated or resettled within the community; *or*
> – 'exempt accommodation', such as specified types of supported accommodation (see p387 – the meaning is the same as for HB).
>
> For these purposes, a 'relevant body' is a county council (in England) or a housing association, registered charity or voluntary organisation.
>
> Your accommodation is **'temporary accommodation'** if you live in a specified type of homeless accommodation that does not count as 'exempt accommodation' (see p387 – the meaning is the same as for HB) and your rent is payable to a local authority or a provider of social housing (see p91 for the meaning).[12]
>
> **'Care home'** means a care home (in England), a care home service (in Wales and Scotland) or an independent hospital.[13]

Service charge payments

Eligible service charge payments are those which are:[14]

- for the costs of, or charges for, services or facilities for the use or benefit of people occupying the accommodation – eg, communal cleaning or garden maintenance; *or*
- fairly attributable to the costs of, or charges for, services or facilities connected with the accommodation that are available for the use or benefit of people occupying the accommodation – eg, costs connected to providing laundry facilities.

The payments do not usually have to be separately identified – eg, in your tenancy agreement or lease. If you are renting in the private rented sector, it does not matter if they are paid in addition to, or as part of, your rent, or if they are made under the same or a different agreement to that under which you occupy your home. However, if you live in social rented sector accommodation (eg, your landlord is a local authority or housing association) or you are an owner-occupier, there are extra conditions and the rules specify the charges that are eligible.

Ineligible service charge payments

Payments are not eligible and cannot be included in your housing costs element if:[15]

- the services or facilities to which the payments relate are for someone occupying a tent, approved premises (eg, a bail or probation hostel), a care home (see p84) or 'exempt accommodation' (see p387 – you may instead qualify for HB); *or*
- you have taken out a loan to make the payments, which is secured on your home.

Extra conditions for social rented sector tenants and owner-occupiers

Social rented sector accommodation

Your accommodation is social rented sector accommodation if your landlord is a 'provider of social housing'. A provider of social housing is a local authority, a non-profit registered provider of social housing, a profit-making registered provider of social housing (if you have been housed in social housing) or a registered social landlord.[16]

If you live in social rented sector accommodation or you are an owner-occupier, service charge payments are only eligible if you must pay them as a condition of occupying your accommodation – eg, as part of your tenancy agreement or lease and not as an optional extra.[17] The costs and charges must be of a reasonable amount and for services and facilities that are reasonable to provide. They must fall into one or more of the following categories.[18]

- Category A: payments to maintain the general standard of accommodation – ie, for:
  - cleaning the outside of windows on the upper floors of a multi-storey building; *or*
  - if you have a shared ownership tenancy (ie, you are buying part of your home and renting the rest) or are an owner-occupier, internal or external maintenance or repair of the accommodation. The payments must be separately identifiable.
- Category B: payments for the general upkeep of communal areas – ie, for the ongoing maintenance of, and the supply of, water, fuel or any other commodity to internal or external areas – eg, communal gardens and children's play areas.
- Category C: payments for basic communal services. These are payments for the provision, ongoing maintenance, cleaning or repair of basic services generally available to everyone living in the accommodation – eg, refuse collection, communal lifts, secure building access, fire alarm systems or wireless or television aerials to receive a service free of charge. Payments for someone employed to provide an eligible service (eg, a groundskeeper or

Part 2: Universal credit
Chapter 6: The housing costs element
2. Liability for payments

caretaker), as well as the costs of managing and administering eligible services are also included.[19]

- Category D: accommodation-specific charges. These must be for the use of essential items specific to the particular accommodation you occupy – eg, for furniture or domestic appliances.

However, payments are *not* eligible and cannot be included in your housing costs element if they are:[20]

- for services or facilities for which public funding is available, whether or not you are entitled to such funding; *or*
- connected to the use of an asset which will result in the transfer of that asset, or any interest in it – eg, payments for furniture and equipment that will eventually become yours; *or*
- for food, medical services or personal services (including personal laundry, cleaning or personal care services).

2. **Liability for payments**

To qualify for a universal credit (UC) housing costs element, you (or your partner, if you are joint claimants) must be liable or *treated as* liable to make eligible payments on a commercial basis.[21] You count as liable if either you or your partner are liable. **Note:** you (or your partner) can be treated as not liable to make payments, even if you are (see p88).

In deciding whether your agreement is on a commercial basis, the DWP must look at the whole agreement and take all the circumstances into account. It is what you and your landlord have agreed, not what you or your landlord have later done or omitted to do that is relevant.[22] The DWP should consider, among other things, the following.[23]

- Whether your agreement includes terms that are not legally enforceable. This might arise, for example, if you do household chores. However, if you do chores in exchange for a lower rent, it could be considered commercial.
- The rent you have agreed to pay. However, the rent does not have to be a market rate rent. Your agreement can count as commercial even if your landlord is not collecting the full contractual rent from you – eg, if it is not being met in full because of the way your housing costs element is calculated.
- Your relationship to the person to whom you are liable to pay. However, just because s/he is a relative or close friend, or s/he provides you with care and support, does not mean that your agreement is non-commercial.

If you are jointly liable to make payments with someone, the way your housing costs element is calculated is adjusted accordingly. See p103 if you are a private tenant and p109 if you are a social rented sector tenant.

Liability to pay rent

For you to be liable to pay rent, your agreement must be legally enforceable.[24] It is not enough if you only have a moral obligation, such as a promise to pay something whenever you can afford to do so. You can be liable to pay rent even if someone else has been paying it on your behalf, or if your landlord has failed to provide you with his/her address and so your rent is treated as not being due.[25] You can be liable to pay rent by yourself (solely liable) or you can be jointly liable to do so.

Does your agreement have to be in writing?

If you have a written agreement with your landlord, this should establish that you are liable to pay rent, provided the liability is a genuine part of the agreement.[26]

Your agreement can be legally enforceable, even if it is not in writing. The fact that you have made a firm promise to pay money to your landlord in return for occupying the property should be sufficient to show you are liable to pay rent and so allow you to qualify for a housing costs element.[27] If the DWP refuses to accept that you have a legal liability, apply for a revision or appeal.

Even if the DWP accepts that your agreement is legally enforceable, it can still treat you as not liable to pay rent in specified situations (see p88).

Treated as liable to make payments

You (or your partner) are treated as liable to make payments:[28]
- if a child or qualifying young person for whom you (or your partner) are responsible (see p62) is liable to make the payments; *or*
- if you are a member of a couple but you are claiming UC as a single person (other than if you are in a polygamous marriage) and your partner is liable to make the payments. See p35 for when you can claim as a single person; *or*
- when someone else is liable to make the payments but is failing to do so so (see below); *or*
- if payments are waived by the person to whom you are liable (eg, your landlord) as reasonable compensation for your carrying out reasonable repairs or redecoration which s/he would otherwise have had to carry out; *or*
- during rent-free periods.

Failure to pay by the person who is liable

You (or your partner, if you are joint claimants) are treated as liable to make payments if someone else is liable to make them, but is not doing so and all of the following conditions are met:[29]
- the person who is liable for payments is not making payment; *and*

Part 2: Universal credit
Chapter 6: The housing costs element
2. Liability for payments

2

- you must make payments in order to continue to occupy the accommodation;[30] *and*
- it would be unreasonable to expect you to make other arrangements; *and*
- it is reasonable in all the circumstances to treat you as liable.

There are many situations where this may apply – including where:

- you have separated from your partner, who still remains on the tenancy agreement and you are only receiving half the amount of your housing costs element (the DWP refers to this as an 'untidy tenancy');
- you have given up your home to live with and care for someone and s/he has now gone into a care home (you can be treated as liable for the payments on her/his home);
- the liable person ceases to qualify for a housing costs element because s/he has become a full-time student.

It does not matter whether or not the landlord is prepared to transfer the tenancy to you or wants to evict you. If the DWP refuses to treat you as liable, highlight that the eligibility rules for the housing costs element and the rules for transferring tenancies are separate.[31] If you are refused the housing costs element, ask for a revision or appeal.

Treated as not liable to make payments

You (or your partner) can be treated as though you are *not* liable to make payments in the following situations.[32]

- You are liable to make the payments to someone who also lives in the accommodation, and who is:
  - your partner, or a child or qualifying young person for whom you (or your partner) are responsible (see p62); *or*
  - a close relative (see p89) of yours or your partner, or of a child or qualifying young person for whom you (or your partner) are responsible.

  For example, this applies if you are living with, and pay rent to, your parents. If you are liable to pay service charge payments to the same person, you are also treated as not liable for those payments.
- You are liable to make the payments to a trustee of a trust or a company. This only applies if the trustees or beneficiaries of the trust, or the owners or directors of the company, include you, your partner or a qualifying young person (or in the case of trusts, a child) for whom you (or your partner) are responsible, or a close relative of any of these if the close relative lives in the accommodation with you. If you are liable to pay service charge payments to a trustee of the same trust or same company (or of another trust whose trustees or beneficiaries include any of these people or a company whose owners or directors include any of these people), you are also treated as not liable for those payments.

- The payments are for any amount of arrears for your accommodation, or for accommodation you occupied previously, that increase what you would otherwise be required to pay. Also included are payments that are for any other unpaid payment or charge.
- The DWP considers your liability to be 'contrived' (see below).

You are treated as not liable to make service charge payments if you are liable to make them to someone who lives in your household (see p58 for the meaning), unless you also pay rent.[33]

Close relative

A '**close relative**' is a parent, parent-in-law (including a civil partner's parent), son, son-in-law (including a son's civil partner), daughter, daughter-in-law (including a daughter's civil partner), brother, sister, step-parent (including a parent's civil partner), stepson (including a civil partner's son), stepdaughter (including a civil partner's daughter), or the partners of any of these.[34] It also includes half-brothers and sisters.[35] Relations with in-laws or step-relatives are severed by divorce (or dissolution of a civil partnership) but arguably not by death – eg, a stepchild is still a stepchild after the death of her/his mother.

Contrived agreements

You can be treated as not liable to make payments if your liability was 'contrived' to get the housing costs element included in your UC, or to increase the amount of your housing costs element.[36] The DWP says this applies if either you or your landlord, or both of you, contrived the liability.[37] For your agreement to count as contrived, it must amount to an abuse of the UC scheme or to take improper advantage of it – ie, that the main reason you entered into the agreement to make payments was to obtain or increase your UC housing costs element.[38] All the circumstances should be taken into account when deciding whether this is the case, including what the person you are liable to pay says.[39] An agreement can count as contrived even if it was created from the best of motives.[40]

Have you been told your agreement is contrived?

The DWP may say that your agreement is contrived if you are in any of the situations described on pp177–179 for housing benefit. If this applies to you, get advice.

'Contrived' is not defined in the rules. You can argue the following.

1. Your agreement should not count as contrived just because the person you are liable to pay is your parent[41] or because you hope to be able to claim UC to help you with your rent – ie, if your main purpose is to get accommodation, not to obtain the UC housing costs element.[42]

2. You should not be regarded as having a contrived agreement just because you try to find out what payments can be covered by UC – eg, before moving in.

Part 2: Universal credit
Chapter 6: The housing costs element
3. Occupying accommodation as a home

3. If your landlord deliberately charges high rents in order to have them paid by UC, you may be affected by this provision, even though you had no such intention yourself. Argue that a high rent, in itself, does not mean that the liability is contrived.[43]

4. If your landlord says s/he will evict you if you cannot get the UC housing costs element, or get it increased, this suggests that the agreement is *not* contrived.[44]

Note: if the DWP says your agreement is contrived and does not include a housing costs element in your UC, you can request a mandatory reconsideration and, if needed, appeal.

3. **Occupying accommodation as a home**

To qualify for the universal credit (UC) housing costs element, you must normally occupy the accommodation for which you make eligible payments as your home.[45] You cannot usually qualify for a housing costs element for any other home. However, there are some exceptions if you:

- were delayed in moving into your new home due to adaptations for a disability (see below); *or*
- are liable to make payments for more than one dwelling (see p91); *or*
- are temporarily absent from home (see p92); *or*
- are in temporary accommodation while repairs are carried out on your home (see p92); *or*
- have left your previous home due to a fear of domestic abuse or violence (see p93).

Moving home

You can be treated as occupying accommodation for up to one month before you move in, provided you were liable (or treated as liable) for the eligible rent or service charges for the accommodation immediately before you moved in, and:[46]

- there was a reasonable and necessary delay in moving into your accommodation, to enable the accommodation to be adapted to **meet the disability needs** of you, your partner (if you are a joint claimant) or a child or qualifying young person for whom you (or your partner, if you are a joint claimant) are responsible (see p62). The adaptations do not need to involve a change to the fabric or structure of the accommodation, but must be reasonably required and be clearly connected to your disability needs.[47] The person with the disability must be getting the middle or highest rate of the disability living allowance or child disability payment care component, attendance allowance, armed forces independence payment or the daily living component of personal independence payment or adult disability payment.

Note: in these circumstances, you may also qualify for a housing costs element for your former home (see below), or for housing benefit (HB) for your former home (if it was 'specified' or 'temporary' accommodation – see p84); *or*

- you became liable to make payments on your new accommodation while you were a hospital inpatient or while you were living in a care home (see p84), or if you make a joint claim, while both of you were.

More than one home

You cannot usually be treated as occupying more than one dwelling.[48] If you are treated as occupying more than one dwelling, to decide which dwelling you normally occupy as your home, the DWP must consider all the circumstances. Note: different rules apply if you are living away from your normal home because of a fear of domestic abuse (see p93).

You *can* be treated as occupying more than one dwelling and get a housing costs element:

- for both your previous and your new home for up to one month if there was a delay in moving into your new home, due to reasonable and necessary adaptations to ensure your new accommodation meets your, your partner's (if your are a joint claimant) or a child or qualifying young person for whom you (or your partner, if you are joint claimants) are responsible disability needs.[49] The conditions are the same as those for moving home (see p90). This only applies if, immediately before you moved, you qualified for a housing costs element for your previous home and were also liable for the eligible rent or service charges (see p83, p84 and p86) for your new home. Note: if you are only liable to make payments for your new home, you may qualify for a housing costs element for that accommodation (see p90);
- for two homes indefinitely if you have been housed in two **dwellings** by a 'provider of social housing' because of the number of children and qualifying young people who live with you.[50] You must normally occupy both homes with the children or qualifying young people for whom you (or your partner, if you are a joint claimant) are responsible (see p62). You must be liable for the eligible rent or service charges (see p83, p84 and p86) for both dwellings.

Provider of social housing

A '**provider of social housing**' is a local authority, a non-profit registered provider of social housing, a profit-making registered provider of social housing (if you have been housed in social housing) or a registered social landlord.[51]

Part 2: Universal credit
Chapter 6: The housing costs element
3. Occupying accommodation as a home

Temporary absence from home

If you are only temporarily absent from your normal home, you continue to be treated as occupying it for up to six months, whatever the reason for your absence.[52]

You are no longer treated as occupying your normal home when your absence lasts, or is expected to last, longer than six months. The decision about whether or not your absence from home is expected to last longer than six months should initially be based on the circumstances on the date you leave your home.[53] If, at any time after that date, you no longer intend to return home, or it becomes likely that you will be away from home for more than six months, your entitlement can be reconsidered.[54] If you initially told the DWP you were going to be away from home for more than six months, but realise that your absence will be shorter, it should also reconsider your entitlement.

You can be treated as occupying your normal home for longer than six months if you have to live in other accommodation while repairs are being carried out on your normal home (see below) or you are living away from home because of a fear of domestic abuse (see p93).

You can be treated as temporarily absent from your home even if you have not yet stayed there – eg, you move your furniture and belongings in but then need to go into hospital.[55]

A new period of absence starts if you return home for even a short stay. A stay of at least 24 hours may be enough.[56]

If you are a prisoner (see p926 – including if you are on temporary release), you can get a housing costs element for up to six months under this rule while you are temporarily absent from home, provided you were entitled to UC as a single person immediately before you became a prisoner, your UC included a housing costs element and you are not expected to be in custody for more than six months.[57] If you are a member of a couple, your partner may instead be able to claim UC with a housing costs element in your absence.

Note:

- If you are temporarily absent from Great Britain for longer than a set period (from one to six months depending on the circumstances), your entitlement to UC may be affected. See p1639 for further information.
- If your partner, child or non-dependant is temporarily absent from your home, this may affect how many bedrooms you are entitled to when working out the amount of your housing costs element (see p100).

Temporary accommodation during repairs

If you move into temporary accommodation because essential repairs are being carried out on your normal home, but you intend to return to that home, the following applies. There is no limit to the amount of time you can qualify for a housing costs element under the following rules.[58]

- You can qualify for a housing costs element and are treated as occupying the home for which you are liable to pay eligible rent or service charges (if you are only liable to pay eligible rent or services charges for one home).
- If you are liable to pay eligible rent or service charges for both homes, you are only treated as occupying your normal home and can get a housing costs element for the payments you make in respect of it.

'**Essential repairs**' means basic works rather than luxuries, but they need not be necessary to make the house habitable.[59]

Domestic abuse or violence

Special rules apply if you are living in accommodation other than your normal home, and it is unreasonable to expect you to return to your normal home because of a reasonable fear of domestic abuse or violence. You must fear abuse or violence from someone in the home, or from a former partner against you or any child or qualifying young person for whom you are responsible. See p1039 for what counts as domestic abuse.[60] You must intend to return to your normal home. In these circumstances:[61]

- you are treated as occupying both the accommodation you are living in and your normal home for up to 12 months if:
  - you are liable to pay eligible rent or service charges for both your current accommodation and your normal home; *and*
  - it is reasonable to include an amount for the payments for both homes in your housing costs element; *or*
- if you are only liable to pay eligible rent or service charges for one of the homes, you are treated as occupying that home if it is reasonable to include an amount for the payments for that accommodation in your housing costs element. **Note:** if one of the homes is 'specified' or 'temporary' accommodation (eg, a refuge – see p84), you can qualify for HB for that accommodation and can get a housing costs element for your other home.

In both cases, you are no longer treated as occupying your normal home when your absence has lasted, or is expected to last, longer than 12 months.[62] The decision whether or not your absence from home is expected to last longer than 12 months should initially be based on the circumstances on the date you leave your home.[63] If, at any time after that date, you no longer intend to return, or it becomes likely that you will be away from home for more than 12 months, your entitlement can be reconsidered.[64]

Part 2: Universal credit
Chapter 6: The housing costs element
4. How the housing costs element is calculated: general rules

4. How the housing costs element is calculated: general rules

How your housing costs element is calculated depends on whether you live in private rented accommodation (see p103) or in social rented sector accommodation (see p107). For service charge payments, it depends on whether you rent your accommodation or are an owner-occupier (if you are an owner-occupier, see p110).

In all cases, to calculate your housing costs element you must first work out the monthly equivalent of your eligible rent or service charge payments (see p83 and p84), if these are paid other than calendar monthly. You must then work out:

- who counts as a member of your 'extended benefit unit' (broadly, the people who live with you – see p95); *and*
- the number of bedrooms you are entitled to under the rules (known as the 'size criteria' – see p97); *and*
- whether a deduction must be made for any non-dependant living with you (a 'housing costs contribution' – see p102).

How do you work out monthly equivalents?

If you pay your rent or service charges:[65]

– weekly, multiply by 52 and divide by 12;

– two-weekly, multiply by 26 and divide by 12;

– four-weekly, multiply by 13 and divide by 12;

– three-monthly, multiply by four and divide by 12;

– annually, divide by 12.

If you have a regular rent-free or service charge-free period, to work out the monthly equivalent divide the total payments you make over the year by 12 – eg, if you have four rent-free weeks each year and so only pay rent for 48 weeks, divide the total of the 48 weeks' payments by 12.

Note:

- If you are a joint tenant, the housing costs element calculation is adjusted accordingly (see p103 and p109).
- If a housing costs element is included in your universal credit (UC) maximum amount, only the lower work allowance applies and so more of your earnings are taken into account when calculating income within your assessment period (see p40).
- If you have a shared ownership tenancy (ie, you are buying part of your home and renting the rest), your housing costs element can include amounts for the rent and service charge payments you make.[66] Your service charge payments are calculated as they would be for rent payments.

If you have more than one home

Special rules apply when calculating your housing costs element while occupying, or being treated as occupying, more than one dwelling.

- If you have been **housed in two dwellings** by a provider of social housing (see p91 for the meaning) because of the number of your children, your housing costs element is worked out using a single calculation.[67] All the eligible payments for both dwellings are taken into account, and you are treated as having the combined total number of bedrooms in both dwellings. Your housing costs element is calculated under the rules for social rented sector tenancies (see p107) if you pay rent to a social sector landlord for both dwellings. Otherwise, your housing costs element is calculated under the rules for private sector tenancies (see p103), in which case there is a special rule for working out your 'cap rent' (see p104).

- If there was a delay in moving into your home because it was being **adapted for disability needs** and you qualify for a housing costs element for both your old and your new accommodation (see p91), amounts are calculated for each home under the rules for social rented sector or private sector tenancies (as appropriate) and your housing costs element is the total for both of these.[68] However, housing costs contributions for a non-dependant (see p102) are only deducted from the rent payments for your old home.

- If you are living away from your normal home because of a **fear of domestic abuse or violence** and are entitled to a housing costs element for both your current accommodation and your normal home (see p93), amounts are calculated for each home under the rules for social rented sector or private sector tenancies (as appropriate) and your housing costs element is the total of both of these. However, any housing costs contributions for non-dependants (see p102) are only deducted from the rent payments for the accommodation that you are determined as 'normally' occupying.[69]

Extended benefit unit

Your 'extended benefit unit' is relevant for working out how many bedrooms you are entitled to (see p97). The members of your 'extended benefit unit' are:[70]
- you; *and*
- your partner (if you are a joint claimant); *and*
- any child or qualifying young person for whom you (or your partner, if you are a joint claimant) are responsible (see p62); *and*
- any non-dependant (see below for who counts).

People can continue to be members of your extended benefit unit while absent from home for a temporary period (see p92) and while treated as occupying your home during a temporary absence (see p100). You can continue to be responsible

Part 2: Universal credit
Chapter 6: The housing costs element
4. How the housing costs element is calculated: general rules

for a child or qualifying young person while s/he is absent from your household for a period (see p62).

Who counts as a non-dependant

People who normally live in your accommodation with you (other than your partner and your children) are called 'non-dependants'.[71] Examples of non-dependants are adult sons or daughters (and their children), or friends or elderly relatives who share your home. If someone is only staying with you temporarily and has a home elsewhere, or is homeless and is only using your address as a postal address, s/he does not count as a non-dependant. If you think the DWP has wrongly assumed that a person is (or is not) your non-dependant, ask for a revision or appeal. **Note:** some people do not count as non-dependants even if they normally live with you (see below).

A person only 'lives in' your accommodation with you if s/he has her/his home with you and shares some accommodation with you.[72] This includes sharing the kitchen (unless it is only used by someone else to prepare food for her/him[73]).

A person only 'normally lives' in your accommodation with you if s/he has been there long enough to regard your home as her/his normal home.[74] **Note:** for these purposes, someone can only have one normal home at a time.[75]

A number of factors should be taken into account to decide whether a person normally lives in your accommodation with you, including:

- the relationship between you;
- how much time s/he spends at your address;
- where her/his post is sent;
- where s/he keeps her/his clothes and personal belongings;
- whether her/his stay or absence from your address is temporary or permanent and, if s/he is absent temporarily, how long the absence has lasted (see p100);
- whether s/he has other accommodation that could be regarded as home and if, for instance, s/he pays rent there or just travels around.

People who are not non-dependants

Even if they normally live with you, the following people do *not* count as non-dependants. When your housing costs element is calculated, you are not entitled to any bedrooms for them. No deduction for a housing costs contribution (see p102) is made from your housing costs element for them.[76]

- A child or qualifying young person for whom no one in your extended benefit unit (see p95) is responsible (p62).
- Your (or your partner's, if you are a joint claimant) foster child(ren).
- Someone to whom you (or your partner, if you are a joint claimant) are liable to pay rent or service charges, and any member of her/his household – eg, your resident landlord and her/his family.
- Someone who has already been treated as the non-dependant of another UC claimant, if the other claimant is also liable to pay rent or service charges for

the accommodation you occupy. The other claimant is allowed a bedroom for her/him, and a housing costs contribution (see p102) is only made from her/his housing costs element, not yours.

- Someone who is liable to pay rent or service charges on a commercial basis for the accommodation you occupy, whether this is to you (or your partner, if you are a joint claimant), or to another person – eg, s/he is your lodger or subtenant, or a joint tenant.

Note: your partner and any child or qualifying young person for whom you or your partner are responsible do not count as non-dependants.[77] However, you are allowed bedrooms for them if they count as members of your extended benefit unit.

The number of bedrooms you are entitled to

If you rent your home, to calculate your housing costs element you need to know how many bedrooms you are entitled to under the rules (known as the 'size criteria'). You are only allowed a bedroom for someone if s/he is a member of your 'extended benefit unit' (see p95). If your home has more bedrooms than you are permitted under the 'size criteria', your housing costs element may not meet your full rent. 'Bedroom' is not defined, but see p101 for what may count.

You are entitled to:[78]
- one bedroom for each of the following members of your 'extended benefit unit':
  - you (and your partner);
  - a qualifying young person for whom you (or your partner, if you are a joint claimant) are responsible (see p62);
  - each non-dependant aged at least 16 (see p96 for who counts). **Note:** you are entitled to one bedroom for each non-dependant, even if they are members of a couple;
  - two children under 16 of the same gender;
  - two children under 10;
  - any other child under 16.

Note: if someone fits into more than one category, s/he is treated as being in the category that results in the lowest number of bedrooms; *and*
- one or more additional bedrooms in specified situations.

Is there a limit to the number of bedrooms you are allowed?

If you are a private tenant, the maximum number of bedrooms you are allowed, including any additional bedrooms, is four.[79] If you are a social rented sector tenant, there is no maximum number of bedrooms.

Part 2: Universal credit
Chapter 6: The housing costs element
4. How the housing costs element is calculated: general rules

A bedroom can be included for a person in your extended benefit unit during her/his temporary absence from home (see p100). In some cases, this only applies for a period.

> **What if a member of your extended benefit unit dies?**
> If your partner (if you are a joint claimant), a child or qualifying young person for whom you (or s/he) were responsible (see p62), a non-dependant or a severely disabled person for whom you were caring dies, your UC continues to be calculated as if s/he had not died for the assessment period in which the death occurred and the following two assessment periods. So if you are no longer allowed as many bedrooms under the rules, this does not affect your housing costs element until after the three assessment periods.[80]

Additional bedrooms

In certain situations, in addition to the number of bedrooms you are entitled to under the rules above, you are also entitled to one or more additional bedrooms. If more than one situation applies, you are allowed the total number of additional bedrooms to which you are entitled.[81] 'Bedroom' is not defined, but see p101 for what may count.

- **Non-resident carers.** You are entitled to one additional bedroom for a non-resident carer, with whom you have an arrangement to provide regular, overnight care for you, any person in your extended benefit unit (see p95), or a child or young person in respect of whom you meet the 'foster parent condition' (see below). The person who receives the overnight care must receive attendance allowance (AA), the middle or highest rate of the disability living allowance (DLA) or child disability payment (CDP) care component, the daily living component of personal independence payment (PIP) or adult disability payment (ADP) or armed forces independence payment. Even if more than one person requires overnight care, only one additional bedroom is allowed.[82]
- **Member of a couple who cannot share a bedroom.** Unless you are a member of a couple claiming UC as a single person (see p35), you are entitled to one additional bedroom if you and your partner are not reasonably able to share a bedroom because of your (or her/his) disability. The disabled partner must be getting the higher rate of AA, the middle or highest rate of the DLA/CDP care component, the daily living component of PIP/ADP or armed forces independence payment.
- **Disabled child who cannot share a bedroom.** You are entitled to one additional bedroom if you or any other person in your extended benefit unit (see p95) are responsible for a child under 16 who would be expected to share a bedroom under the rules above, but cannot reasonably do so because of her/his disability. The child must be getting the middle or highest rate of the DLA/CDP care component. If more than one child qualifies, you are entitled to as

2

many additional bedrooms as you need to ensure that each child has her/his own bedroom.

• **Adoption, fostering and kinship carers.** You are entitled to one additional bedroom if you (or your partner, if you are a joint claimant) meet the 'foster parent condition'. Only one additional bedroom is permitted even if you have more than one foster child, or if both you and your partner are foster parents or adopters.

You meet the **'foster parent condition'** if you have a child placed with you for adoption or you are a foster parent (in Scotland, this includes kinship carers). If you are a foster parent, this applies even if you do not currently have a child placed with you, provided you have become an approved foster parent, or have fostered a child, within the last 12 months.

Examples

Mark and Mica have two daughters, aged 10 and 13, and two sons, aged 15 and 22. The 10-year-old daughter is severely disabled and is unable to share a bedroom because of this. Mark's parents live with them. They claim UC. They are entitled to one bedroom for Mark and Mica, one bedroom for the daughters, two bedrooms for their sons and two bedrooms for Mark's parents. They are entitled to one additional bedroom for their 10-year-old daughter due to her disability. This is a total of seven bedrooms. They are private tenants, so the housing costs element calculation is based on a four-bedroom property – the maximum allowed. If they had been social rented sector tenants, their housing costs element would have been calculated based on a seven-bedroom property.

Huw is the foster parent of two sisters, aged 10 and 16. He has two sons, aged 10 and 12, one of whom is getting the middle rate of the DLA care component and cannot share a bedroom because of his disability. Huw is entitled to one bedroom for himself, and would normally only be entitled to one bedroom for his two sons. However, he is entitled to one additional bedroom for his disabled son, and one additional bedroom because he is a foster parent. He is entitled to a total of four bedrooms.

Note:

• The rules that allow additional bedrooms were amended in the past following test cases. If you think you may have lost out, see pp98–99 of the 2020/21 edition of this *Handbook*.
• If you live in accommodation adapted for you under a 'sanctuary scheme' (see p108) and you are a social rented sector tenant, no deduction from your housing costs element can be made under the 'bedroom tax' rules (p107), no matter how many bedrooms there are in your home.[83]

Part 2: Universal credit
Chapter 6: The housing costs element
4. How the housing costs element is calculated: general rules

Temporary absence from home

When determining how many bedrooms you are entitled to, a person can continue to be included in your extended benefit unit (see p95) while temporarily absent from your home.

You (or your partner) continue to be included during:[84]

- the one- to six-month period in which you (or your partner) continue to qualify for UC while temporarily absent from Great Britain (see p1639); *or*
- the first six months you are a prisoner (see p926 – this includes if you are on temporary release), provided immediately before becoming a prisoner you were entitled to UC as a single person, you were getting a housing costs element and you are not expected to be in custody for more than six months.

Note: you (and your partner) can be treated as occupying your home during other periods when you are temporarily away (see p92 and p93).

Your child or qualifying young person continues to be included, if immediately before the start of the period of absence, s/he was included in your extended benefit unit and you were getting a housing costs element. S/he is included:[85]

- during the first six months of her/his absence if s/he is:
  - being looked after by a local authority; *or*
  - a prisoner (see p926 – this includes if s/he is on temporary release), provided s/he is not expected to be in custody for more than six months;
- in any other case, for the period you continue to be treated as responsible for her/him while s/he is absent from your household (see p62).

Your non-dependant continues to be included, if, immediately before the start of the absence, s/he was included in your extended benefit unit. S/he is included:[86]

- indefinitely, if s/he is your (or your partner's) son, daughter, stepson or stepdaughter who is a member of the armed forces deployed on operations;
- during the one- (or two-) month period in which s/he continues (or would have continued) to qualify for UC while temporarily absent from Great Britain (see p1639);
- during the first six months of her/his absence if s/he is:
  - temporarily absent from Great Britain to receive medical treatment or convalescence or to take her/his partner, child or a qualifying young person for medical treatment or convalescence (see p1639);
  - a prisoner (see p926 – this includes if s/he is on temporary release from prison), provided s/he is not expected to be in custody for more than six months;
- in any other case, for up to six months. However, s/he is no longer included if the absence lasts (or is expected to last) longer than six months.

Note: unless your non-dependant is a member of the armed forces deployed on operations, you must also have been getting a housing costs element immediately before the start of the period of absence.

What counts as a bedroom

When working out the number of bedrooms you are entitled to, you may need to consider what counts as a bedroom. For example, you may need to argue that a room is a bedroom; or it may be more advantageous for you to argue that a room is not a bedroom.

'Bedroom' is not defined in the rules. It is the ordinary meaning of the word that is relevant. It could be, for example, a lounge or living room, provided it contains a bed or is used for sleeping.[87]

The starting point is whether the room can be used as a bedroom – ie, a room is a bedroom if it is furnished and can be used for sleeping in. How a property is described by the landlord (eg, as a two- or three-bedroom house) or whether a room is designated as a bedroom may be relevant. However, the basis on which your rent is charged (eg, if your flat has two bedrooms but your landlord only charges the rent for a one-bedroom flat) is not relevant.[88]

You can try to argue that the DWP should not count a room in your home as a bedroom and therefore that your housing costs element should not be reduced (or reduced as much) under the rules on p103 (for private tenants) or p107 (for social rented sector tenants). The DWP should, for example, take into account:[89]

- the size of the room (the dimensions and height) – eg, whether it can accommodate a single bed and somewhere to store clothes, whether it has a flat surface on which to place things safely, such as a glass of water, and whether there is space to dress and undress. If a room is too small, provide a measured plan and photographs if you can; *and*
- access to the room and whether it has adequate natural and electric lighting, heating, ventilation and privacy; *and*
- whether the room is safe to sleep in – eg, if it is contaminated with asbestos.

Suggest your personal use of the room should also be taken into account (eg, if you have a disability and you use the room to store your equipment), as well as whether your home has been converted or adapted – eg, if two small bedrooms have been converted into one big bedroom, or if a bedroom has been redesignated. However, the DWP is likely to say that in deciding how many bedrooms there are in your home:

- it is the classification and description of the property when it is empty that is relevant and that this can only be changed if the property has been structurally altered with the approval of your landlord;[90]
- even if your home could be occupied in more than one way (eg, as either one- or two-bedroom), it can use the way your landlord designates the property to determine how many bedrooms it has.[91]

Part 2: Universal credit
Chapter 6: The housing costs element
4. How the housing costs element is calculated: general rules

2

Housing costs contributions

If your extended benefit unit includes a 'non-dependant' (see p96), a set deduction is usually made from your housing costs element.[92] This is because it is assumed that the non-dependant makes a contribution towards housing costs while living with you, whether or not s/he actually does so. The DWP calls these deductions 'housing costs contributions'. They are also known as 'non-dependant deductions'. In some circumstances, no deductions are made. **Note:**

- If you are an owner-occupier, no deduction is made from your service charge payments unless you have a shared ownership tenancy.
- A non-dependant can only be a member of the extended benefit unit of one UC claimant (or pair of joint claimants),[93] so a deduction is only made from that UC claimant's (or pair of joint claimants') housing costs element.

Exceptions to the housing costs contribution deduction

No housing costs contribution deduction is made for any of your non-dependants if you (or your partner, if you are a joint claimant):[94]

- get AA (or equivalent benefits paid because of an injury at work or a war injury), the middle or highest rate of the DLA/CDP care component, the daily living component of PIP/ADP or armed forces independence payment, or would receive one of these but for being in hospital; *or*
- are certified as severely sight impaired or blind by a consultant ophthalmologist.

No housing costs contribution deduction is made for any non-dependant who is:[95]

- getting AA, the middle or highest rate of the DLA care component, the daily living component of PIP/ADP or armed forces independence payment, or who would receive it but for being in hospital. This is also expected to apply to CDP; *or*
- getting carer's allowance; *or*
- getting pension credit; *or*
- a prisoner (see p926); *or*
- under 21 years old; *or*
- your (or your partner's, if you are a joint claimant) son, daughter, stepson or stepdaughter who is in the armed forces and is deployed on operations. **Note:** this only applies if s/he lived with you immediately before leaving, and intends to live with you at the end of the operations; *or*
- responsible for a child under five.

The amount of the housing costs contribution deduction

If a deduction must be made, it is made for every non-dependant who is a member of your extended benefit unit (see p95).[96] The deduction is a fixed amount of £77.87 for the assessment period, whether or not s/he is a member of a couple, irrespective of her/his income and what s/he pays you.[97]

5. The housing costs element for private rented sector tenants

If you are a private tenant, your housing costs element is calculated as follows.[98]
- **Step one:** work out the monthly equivalent of your 'core rent' (see below). This is broadly the amount of eligible rent and service charges you must pay.
- **Step two:** work out your 'cap rent'. This is the maximum amount of rent that can be included in your housing costs element (see p104). It may be lower than the rent you must pay.
- **Step three:** if your extended benefit unit (see p95) includes any non-dependants, deduct any housing costs contribution that applies (see p102) from the lowest of your core rent or your cap rent. This is the amount of your housing costs element. It can never be lower than nil – ie, no further reduction can be made to your universal credit (UC) award.[99]

If you qualify for a housing costs element for more than one dwelling, special rules apply (see p95).

Core rent

If you are solely liable to make payments, your 'core rent' is the total amount of all the eligible rent and service charge payments (see p83 and p84) that you are liable (or treated as liable) to make – ie, the amounts you actually pay using the monthly equivalent.[100]

Jointly liable for payments

If you are jointly liable to make payments with someone, different rules apply. Your core rent is worked out using the following steps.[101]
- **Step one:** work out the sum of all of the eligible rent and eligible service charge payments for which you and your joint tenant(s) are liable, for the whole of the accommodation, using the monthly equivalents.
- **Step two:**
  - if the only people who are jointly liable are in the list of 'relevant family members' below (eg, only you and your partner are liable), your core rent is the amount in Step one; *or*
  - if one or more people in the list of relevant family members below are jointly liable with one or more others who are not relevant family members (eg, you, your partner and a friend are joint tenants), divide the amount in Step one by the total number of people who are liable and multiply by the number of your relevant family members who are liable. This is your core rent. However, if the DWP is satisfied that it would be unreasonable to take this amount as your core rent, it must apportion the amount in a manner it considers appropriate, taking into account the number of people who are

Part 2: Universal credit
Chapter 6: The housing costs element
5. The housing costs element for private rented sector tenants

jointly liable and the amount of the rent and service charge payments for which each is liable.

Relevant family members

The '**relevant family members**' (the DWP calls them 'listed persons') are you, your partner and any child or qualifying young person for whom you (or your partner, if you are a joint claimant) are responsible (see p62).[102]

Example

Joanne and her partner Lisa are joint tenants of a two-bedroom private flat with a friend.
Step one: the rent is £120 a week. The monthly equivalent is £120 x 52 ÷ 12 = £520
Step two: Joanne and Lisa are jointly liable with a person who is not a 'relevant family member'. Their core rent is therefore £520 ÷ 3 (the number of joint tenants) x 2 (the number of relevant family members) = £346.67 a month.

Cap rent

Your cap rent is the maximum amount of rent that can be included in your housing costs element. It is normally the local housing allowance for the category of accommodation that applies to you, in the area where you live.[103] This depends on how many bedrooms you are entitled to (see p97), up to a maximum of four bedrooms. To work out which category of accommodation applies, see below. For information about the local housing allowance rates, see p106.

Note: your cap rent may be lower than the amount of rent you must pay. You may be able to get extra financial assistance by applying for discretionary housing payments from your local authority (see Chapter 29).

If you have been housed in two dwellings by a provider of social housing (see p91), and you pay rent to a social sector landlord for one of them and rent to a private landlord for the other, your housing costs element is calculated under the rules for private sector tenancies. In this case, if the cap rents for the two dwellings are different (eg, because they are in different areas), the lowest amount at the time your housing costs element is first calculated is used.[104] Your housing costs element continues to be calculated on the basis of the cap rent for that dwelling until you move to other accommodation.

Examples

Svetlana is a joint tenant of a four-bedroom private flat with Carol, a friend. Svetlana's son, aged 27, lives with them. The rent for the flat is £1,000 a month, including eligible service charge payments. Svetlana claims UC. Her extended benefit unit includes her and her son, who counts as a non-dependant; Carol does not count as a non-dependant.
Step one: Svetlana's core rent is £1,000 ÷ 2 x 1 = £500 a month.
Step two: Svetlana's cap rent is the local housing allowance for two-bedroom accommodation. In her area this is £400 a month. Her cap rent is lower than her core rent.

Step three: Svetlana's housing costs element is therefore £400 (the cap rent) – £77.87 (housing costs contribution) = £322.13

Note: if Carol also claims UC, her extended benefit unit does not include Svetlana's son as a non-dependant, so Carol's cap rent is the local housing allowance for one-bedroom shared accommodation. However, no housing costs contribution is deducted.

Abdur and Jahanara rent a two-bedroom private flat. They pay £150 a week. Their rent includes eligible service charges for the communal lift. Abdur's uncle Faisal and Faisal's 24-year-old son live with them. They are included in Abdur and Jahanara's extended benefit unit as non-dependants.

Step one: Abdur and Jahanara's core rent is £150 x 52 ÷ 12 = £650 a month.

Step two: their cap rent is the local housing allowance for three-bedroom accommodation (they are entitled to allowed one bedroom for themselves and one bedroom each for Faisal and his son). In their area, the local housing allowance rate for three-bedroom accommodation is £800 a month. Their core rent is lower than their cap rent.

Step three: Abdur and Jahanara's extended benefit unit includes two non-dependants. Housing costs contributions of £77.87 x 2 = £155.74 are deducted. Their housing costs element is £650 (the core rent) – £155.74 (housing costs contributions) = £494.26.

Categories of accommodation

The category of accommodation that applies to you depends on how many bedrooms you are entitled to under the rules (see p97) and whether or not the one-bedroom shared accommodation category applies.

One-bedroom shared accommodation

The one-bedroom shared accommodation category applies if you are a single person (or a member of a couple claiming as a single person – see p35), you are under 35 and you do not have any children for whom you are responsible or non-dependants. If you meet the conditions of this category, it applies even if you do not live in shared accommodation.[105]

However, there are exceptions and this category does *not* apply (even if you do live in shared accommodation) if:[106]

- you are under 35 and are getting attendance allowance, the middle or highest rate of the disability living allowance/child disability payment care component, the daily living component of personal independence payment/adult disability payment or armed forces independence payment; *or*
- you are under 35 and meet the 'foster parent condition' (see p99); *or*
- you are at least 18 but under 25 and were looked after by a local authority under specified provisions before you were 18 (see p934);[107] *or*
- you are under 35, a single claimant and are:
  - aged at least 16 and have lived in one or more hostels for homeless people for three months or more (this does not have to be continuous) and while

Part 2: Universal credit
Chapter 6: The housing costs element
5. The housing costs element for private rented sector tenants

living there you accepted support services to assist you in being rehabilitated or resettled in the community; *or*

- an offender subject to specific multi-agency public protection risk arrangements. It is understood that this applies if you are a level 2 or 3 offender.[108]

Note: the government says that, from October 2022, the one-bedroom shared accommodation category will not apply if you have experienced domestic abuse or modern slavery. See AskCPAG and CPAG's *Welfare Rights Bulletin* for updates.

One-bedroom self-contained accommodation

The one-bedroom self-contained accommodation category applies if you are only entitled to one bedroom under the rules (see p97) and the one-bedroom shared accommodation category (see p105) does not apply to you.[109] You must have the exclusive use of a kitchen, a bathroom, a toilet and a room suitable for living in. It must be reasonable for you to occupy this category of accommodation.

Note: if you are aged 35 and over (and you are single, not responsible for any children and have no non-dependants), it is understood that in practice the DWP applies this category of accommodation to you, even if you live in shared accommodation.

Accommodation with two or more bedrooms

If you are entitled to more than one bedroom under the rules, the category of accommodation that applies is the accommodation with the number of bedrooms you are entitled to (see p97), up to a maximum of four.[110] It must be reasonable for you to occupy this category of accommodation, taking into account the number of people in your 'extended benefit unit' (see p95).[111]

Local housing allowance rates

Local housing allowances for each category of accommodation are usually set by the rent officer annually on the last working day of January, to take effect the following April. From April 2022 to April 2023, the local housing allowance is the allowance set by the rent officer on 31 March 2020. This was the lowest of two figures:[112]

- the amount of rent at the 30th percentile point of local market rents for assured tenancies in what is known as a 'broad rental market area'; *or*
- for the specified categories of accommodation below, the amount listed.

Category of accommodation	Maximum local housing allowance
One-bedroom shared accommodation	£1,283.96
One-bedroom self-contained accommodation	£1,283.96
Two-bedroom accommodation	£1,589.99
Three-bedroom accommodation	£1,920.00
Four-bedroom accommodation	£2,579.98

See lha-direct.voa.gov.uk for the current local housing allowance rates in your area.

6. The housing costs element for social rented sector tenants

Social rented sector accommodation

Your accommodation is social rented sector accommodation if your landlord is a 'provider of social housing'. A provider of social housing is a local authority, a non-profit registered provider of social housing, a profit-making registered provider of social housing (if you have been housed in social housing) or a registered social landlord.[113]

For social rented sector tenants, your housing costs element is calculated depending on whether you are solely or jointly liable for your rent and service charges.

Note:

- If you qualify for a housing costs element for more than one accommodation, special rules apply (see p95).
- Your housing costs element may be lower than as calculated below if the DWP thinks your rent or service charges are higher than is reasonable for a housing costs element to meet.[114] In this case, the DWP can apply to the rent officer. If the rent officer thinks that your landlord could reasonably have expected to get a lower amount of rent than what you pay, the lower amount is used to calculate your housing costs element, unless the DWP is satisfied that this is not appropriate.
- Your housing costs element can *never* be lower than nil – ie, no further reduction can be made to your standard allowance and/or other elements within your universal credit (UC) award.[115]
- If your rent or service charge payments have been reduced by a provider of social housing under a government-approved tenant incentive scheme, your rent and service charges are worked out as per Steps one, two and three on p108 as if no reduction had been made.[116]

The 'bedroom tax'

If you are a social rented sector tenant, a deduction is usually made from your housing costs element when you have more bedrooms in your home than the number you are entitled to under the rules (see p97).[117] This is commonly referred to as the 'bedroom tax'. The DWP refers to this as the 'under-occupation deduction' or the 'removal of the spare room subsidy'. 'Bedroom' is not defined. See p101 for what may count.

Part 2: Universal credit
Chapter 6: The housing costs element
6. The housing costs element for social rented sector tenants

Exemptions to the 'bedroom tax'

No deduction can be made if:
- you have a shared ownership tenancy;[118] *or*
- you or a member of your 'extended benefit unit' (see p95) have experienced (including threats of) domestic abuse and/or violence by a partner, former partner or a relative (see p1040):[119] *and*
  - you are not living at the same address as the person who was abusive (or threatened you), unless that person is a qualifying young person and a dependant of a member of your extended benefit unit; *and*
  - your home has been adapted by a social housing provider under a 'sanctuary scheme'. A 'sanctuary scheme' is a scheme operated by a provider of social housing, whereby additional security to a property or the perimeters of property is installed, to enable people who have experienced domestic abuse to remain in their homes;[120] *and*
  - you provide relevant evidence from a person acting in an official capacity such as a healthcare professional, a police officer, a registered social worker, an employer or trade union representative or a public, voluntary or charitable body with which you have had direct contact in connection with domestic abuse.

Solely liable to make payments

If you are solely liable to make rent and service charge payments, your housing costs element is worked out as follows.[121]
- **Step one:** calculate the amount of your eligible rent payments (see p83), using the monthly equivalent (see p94).
- **Step two:** calculate the amount of your eligible service charge payments (see p84) using the monthly equivalent (see p94).
- **Step three:** total the payments in Step one and Step two. Deduct any amount that relates to the supply of a 'commodity' to your accommodation – eg, for water or fuel.
- **Step four:** add up the total number of bedrooms in your home and check that number does not exceed the total number of bedrooms you are entitled to (see p97). If you do not have more bedrooms than you are entitled to and Step six does not apply, then the amount in Step three is your housing costs element. If you have more bedrooms than you are entitled to, follow Step five.
- **Step five:** unless you have a shared ownership tenancy, if you have more bedrooms in your home than you are entitled to (see Step four), reduce the amount in Step three by:[122]
  - 14 per cent, if you have one bedroom too many; *or*
  - 25 per cent, if you have two or more bedrooms too many.
  Unless Step six applies, this is your housing costs element.

- **Step six:** if your 'extended benefit unit' includes any non-dependants, deduct any housing costs contribution that applies (see p102) from the amount in Step three or Step five as appropriate.[123] This is your housing costs element.

2

Example

Christina rents a four-bedroom house from the local authority. She lives there with her 14-year-old daughter. Her rent is £125 a week. She has four rent-free weeks every year. Her 'extended benefit unit' does not include any non-dependants.

Step one: the monthly equivalent of her rent payments is £125 x 48 ÷ 12 = £500

Step two: she does not have any service charge payments.

Step three: the total payment is £500 a month.

Step four: she has four bedrooms in her home. She is only entitled to two bedrooms under the rules: one bedroom for her and one bedroom for her daughter, therefore Step 5 applies.

Step five: she has two bedrooms too many. The amount in Step three must be reduced by 25 per cent. 25% x £500 = £125. £500 – £125 = £375

As Step six does not apply to Christina, her housing costs element is £375 a month.

Jointly liable to make payments

If you are jointly liable to make payments with someone (eg, you are a joint tenant), different rules apply.[124] Work out the total of the monthly equivalent of the eligible rent and service charge payments (see p83 and p84) for which you and your joint tenant(s) are liable, for the whole of the accommodation. Deduct any amount that relates to the supply of a 'commodity' to your accommodation – eg, for water or fuel. Then, if:

- the only people who are jointly liable are in the list of 'relevant family members' on p104 (eg, you and your partner are the only joint tenants), if applicable, a reduction is made as under Step five on p108 if you have more bedrooms in your home than you are entitled to under the rules (see p97). However, if you have a shared ownership tenancy (ie, you are buying part of your home and renting the rest), no reduction is made (see p108);[125] *or*
- one or more people in the list of 'relevant family members' on p104 are jointly liable with one or more others who are not relevant family members (eg, you and a friend are joint tenants), divide the total rent and service charge payments by the total number of people who are liable and multiply by the number of your relevant family members who are liable for eligible rent and/ or service charge payments. However, if the DWP is satisfied that it would be unreasonable to take this amount as your rent, it must apportion the amount in a manner it considers appropriate, taking into account the number of jointly liable people and the amount of the rent and service charge payments for

Part 2: Universal credit
Chapter 6: The housing costs element
7. The housing costs element for owner-occupiers

which each is liable. **Note:** no reduction due to the 'bedroom tax' is made for joint tenants as under Step five on p108.[126]

In all cases, if your extended benefit unit includes any non-dependants, deduct any housing costs contribution that applies (see p102).[127]

Example

Enzo and his partner are joint tenants of a three-bedroom housing association flat with a friend. The rent is £180 a week.

The monthly equivalent of the rent payments is £180 x 52 ÷ 12 = £780 a month.

They do not have any service charge payments.

The total payment is £780 a month.

Enzo and his partner are relevant family members. The amount that can be included in the housing costs element is therefore £780 ÷ 3 (the number of joint tenants) x 2 (the number of relevant family members) = £520 a month. No reduction is made as under Step five on p108.

Their 'extended benefit unit' does not include any non-dependants. The housing costs element is £520 a month.

7. **The housing costs element for owner-occupiers**

If you are an owner-occupier and you make payments for eligible service charges (see p84), you can get a housing costs element for these payments only.[128] You cannot get a housing costs element for any amount to cover mortgage interest, however you could get a loan for this instead (see p839).

The amount is calculated as follows.[129]

- **Step one:** work out the amount of each eligible service charge payment.
- **Step two:** work out the period for which each payment is payable, and if payments are made other than calendar monthly, work out the monthly equivalent (see p94).
- **Step three:** add all the monthly amounts together. This is the amount that can be included in your housing costs element.

Note:
- If you have a shared ownership tenancy (ie, you are buying part of your home and renting the rest), your housing costs element can also include an amount for your rent. In this case, your service charge payments are not calculated under these rules. They are calculated as for rented accommodation.[130] See

p103 if you live in private rented accommodation and p107 if you live in social rented sector accommodation.

- If you (or your partner) have any earned income, you cannot get a housing costs element (other than for rent and service charges if you have a shared ownership tenancy[131]) however much your earnings are.[132] This includes earnings from work you can do while claiming contributory employment and support allowance (ESA – see p1019) or from work of less than 16 hours a week you can do while claiming contribution-based jobseeker's allowance (JSA – see p974).
- You may only qualify for a housing costs element after a 'qualifying period'.

The qualifying period

If you are an owner-occupier, a housing costs element for service charge payments cannot usually be included until the beginning of the assessment period that follows the assessment period when a 'qualifying period' (also known as a 'waiting period') ends.[133] The qualifying period applies:[134]

- if you have a new award of universal credit (UC) (ie, you claim UC for the first time or claim after a break in your entitlement to UC), a housing costs element for service charge payments cannot be included until nine consecutive assessment periods have passed where you have been getting UC, and you would have qualified for a housing costs element, if the qualifying period rule did not apply, in each of those assessment periods;
- where a housing costs element for service charge payments ceases to be included in your UC award for any reason (eg, due to earnings from a temporary job), but your entitlement to UC continues, no housing costs element can be included again until there have been nine consecutive assessment periods in which you would otherwise qualify for a housing costs element were it not for the qualifying period rule.

If you cease to qualify for a housing costs element for service charge payments for any reason during a qualifying period, the qualifying period stops running. A new qualifying period starts when whichever of the above bullet points apply.[135]

Example

Zhen makes a claim for UC. She is unemployed at the time and has no income. She is an owner-occupier, pays eligible service charge payments for the cleaning of the common areas in her block of flats and for a concierge service and (but for having to serve a qualifying period) she qualifies for a housing costs element. She waits nine consecutive assessment periods and a housing costs element for service charge payments is then included in her UC. Zhen gets a part-time temporary job so she no longer qualifies for a housing costs element as she has earned income, although her entitlement to UC continues. When her job ends, a housing costs element will be included again, once she has been getting UC for a further nine consecutive assessment periods.

Part 2: Universal credit
Chapter 6: The housing costs element
7. The housing costs element for owner-occupiers

There are no qualifying period rules for rent payments. Therefore if you have a shared ownership tenancy (ie, you are buying part of your home and renting the rest), your housing costs element can include the rent and all service charge payments you make straight away, without a qualifying period.

Exceptions

There are limited exceptions to the general qualifying period rule.

- If you are entitled to 'new style' contribution-based JSA or contributory ESA, immediately before your award of UC starts, any period when you were only getting one of those benefits may be treated as an assessment period (or part of an assessment period) that counts towards your qualifying period.[136]
- If you (or your partner or a former partner) were entitled to income support (IS), income-based JSA or income-related ESA in the one month before the date you claimed (or were treated as claiming) UC (or you would have been entitled but for your entitlement ending because the benefit was abolished):[137]
  - if your (or your partner's or former partner's) IS/JSA/ESA included help with housing costs (see Chapter 18), the qualifying period does not apply and your UC award can include a housing costs element for service charge payments straight away; *or*
  - if your (or your partner's or your former partner's) IS/JSA/ESA did not yet include help with housing costs because you were serving a qualifying period (see p352), your UC qualifying period is 273 days, minus the number of days you were entitled to IS/JSA/ESA (including the time you were treated as entitled under the linking rules – see p358), as well as any time between the date the IS/JSA/ESA ended and the date you are awarded UC.
- If your joint UC award for joint owner-occupiers terminates as you cease to be a couple, if you occupy the same home and have been awarded UC as a single person:[138]
  - if a housing costs element *was not* included in your joint award of UC, any assessment period (or part of an assessment period) in respect of which you had been getting UC counts towards the qualifying period for your new UC award. For example, if you and your former partner had been getting UC for 45 days, a housing costs element can be included once you have been getting UC for nine assessment periods, minus 45 days;
  - if a housing costs element was included in your joint award of UC, you do not have to serve another qualifying period and a housing costs element is included in your UC award straight away.

  This can also apply to your former partner – ie, if s/he continues to occupy the same accommodation and claims and is awarded UC.

Notes

2

1. s35 and Sch 9 SS(S)A 2018, not yet in force

1. Who can get a housing costs element

2. s11 WRA 2012; regs 25 and 26 UC Regs
3. s11(2)(c) WRA 2012
4. Reg 26 (4)-(6) UC Regs
5. Reg 8(4) and Sch 4 para 4 UC Regs
6. Reg 26(5) and Sch 5 para 4 UC Regs
7. Sch 1 para 3(h) and (i) UC Regs
8. Reg 25(2)(a) and Sch 1 para 2 UC Regs
9. *AB v LB Camden (HB)* [2020] UKUT 158 (AAC)
10. Sch 1 paras 2 and 3 UC Regs
11. Sch 1 para 3A UC Regs
12. Sch 1 para 3B UC Regs
13. Sch 1 para 1 UC Regs
14. Reg 25(2)(c) and Sch 1 para 7(1), (2) and (4) UC Regs
15. Sch 1 para 7(1) and (3) UC Regs; reg 2 and Sch 1 para 5(2) LMI Regs
16. Schs 3 para 4(3) and 4 para 2 UC Regs
17. Sch 1 para 8(3) UC Regs
18. Sch 1 para 8(4) and (5) UC Regs
19. para F2074 ADM
20. Sch 1 para 8(6) UC Regs; para F2076-F2077 Chapter F2 ADM

2. Liability for payments

21. Reg 25(3) UC Regs
22. R(H) 1/03; *Warwick DC v SSWP and CH (HB)* [2020] UKUT 240 (AAC)
23. *R v Poole BC ex parte Ross* [1995] 28 HLR 351 (QBD); CH/1076/2002; CH/296/2004; CH/1097/2004
24. *R v Rugby BC HBRB ex parte Harrison* [1994] 28 HLR 36 (QBD); CH/2959/2006
25. s48 Landlord and Tenant Act 1987; CH/3579/2003; CH/257/2005
26. R(H) 3/03
27. *R v Poole BC ex parte Ross* [1995] 28 HLR 351 (QBD); *R v Warrington BC ex parte Williams* [1997] 29 HLR 872 (QBD)
28. Reg 25(3) and Sch 2 paras 1-4 UC Regs
29. Sch 2 para 2 UC Regs; *FK v Wandsworth BC (HB)* [2016] UKUT 570 (AAC); *Babergh DC v GW (HB)* [2017] UKUT 40 (AAC)

30. *ZD v LB Hillingdon (HB)* [2021] UKUT 305 (AAC)
31. para F2089 ADM; See DWP guidance to local authorities: paras A3/3.140-141 GM
32. Sch 2 paras 5-7, 9 and 10 UC Regs
33. Sch 2 para 8 UC Regs
34. Reg 2 UC Regs
35. R(SB) 27/87; *Bristol City Council v JKT* [2016] UKUT 517 (AAC)
36. Sch 2 para 10 UC Regs
37. para F2142 ADM
38. *R v Solihull MBC ex parte Simpson* [1995] 1 FLR 140 (CA); CH/39/2007
39. *R (Mackay) v Barking and Dagenham HBRB* [2001] EWHC Admin 234
40. CH/2258/2004
41. *R (Mackay) v Barking and Dagenham HBRB* [2001] EWHC Admin 234
42. *R v Sutton LBC HBRB ex parte Keegan* [1992] 27 HLR 92 (QBD)
43. *R v Manchester City Council ex parte Baragrove Properties Ltd* [1991] 23 HLR 337 (QBD); *R v Gloucestershire CC ex parte Dadds* [1997] 29 HLR 700 (QBD); CH/39/2007
44. *R v Poole BC ex parte Ross* [1995] 28 HLR 351 (QBD)

3. Occupying accommodation as a home

45. Reg 25(4) and Sch 3 paras 1(1) and 2 UC Regs
46. Sch 3 paras 7 and 8 UC Regs
47. *Bury MBC v DC (HB)* [2011] UKUT 43 (AAC); *R (Mahmoudi) v LB Lewisham and Another* [2014] EWCA Civ 284
48. Sch 3 para 1(2)-(4) UC Regs
49. Sch 3 para 5 UC Regs
50. Sch 3 para 4 UC Regs
51. Schs 3 para 4(3) and 4 para 2 UC Regs
52. Sch 3 para 9 UC Regs
53. CH/1237/2004
54. CH/3893/2004
55. R(H) 9/05
56. *R v Penwith DC ex parte Burt* [1988] 22 HLR 292 (QBD)
57. Regs 2 and 19(1)(b), (2) and (3) UC Regs; vol E3, para E3040-E3042 ADM
58. Sch 3 paras 3 and 9(2) UC Regs
59. R(SB) 10/81

60 The DWP is using the cross-governmental definition of domestic violence and abuse under the Domestic Abuse Act 2021. The UC Regs have not been amended at the time of writing. DWP, *Help available from the Department for Work and Pensions for people who are victims of domestic violence and abuse*, updated 1 October 2021, available on gov.uk; ss1 and 2 Domestic Abuse Act 2021
61 Schs 3 paras 6 and 9(3) UC Regs
62 Sch 3 para 9(3) UC Regs
63 CH/1237/2004
64 CH/3893/2004

4. **How the housing costs element is calculated: general rules**
65 Sch 4 para 7 and Sch 5 para 13 UC Regs
66 Reg 26(4)-(6) UC Regs
67 Sch 4 para 17 UC Regs
68 Sch 4 para 18 UC Regs
69 Sch 4 para 19 UC Regs
70 Sch 4 paras 1, definitions of 'renters' and 'joint renters', and 9(1) UC Regs
71 Sch 4 para 9(2) UC Regs
72 *AM v SSWP (IS)* [2011] UKUT 387 (AAC)
73 CSIS/185/1995
74 CIS/14850/1996
75 *JP v Bournemouth BC (HB)* [2018] UKUT 75 (AAC)
76 Sch 4 para 9(2) UC Regs
77 Sch 4 para 9(2)(a), (b) and (g) UC Regs
78 Sch 4 paras 2, 8 and 10 UC Regs
79 Sch 4 para 26 UC Regs
80 Reg 37 UC Regs
81 Reg 2 and Sch 4 paras 2 and 12 UC Regs
82 Reg 2, definition of 'attendance allowance', and Sch 4 para 12(3) UC Regs
83 *JD and A v the United Kingdom* [2019] ECHR 753; Sch 4 para 36 (6) UC Regs
84 Sch 4 para 11(3) UC Regs
85 Sch 4 para 11(2) UC Regs
86 Sch 4 para 11(4)-(6) UC Regs
87 *Bolton MBC v BF (HB)* [2014] UKUT 48 (AAC)
88 *CB v Manchester City Council and SSWP (HB)* [2015] UKUT 556 (AAC)
89 *SSWP v Nelson and Nelson* [2014] UKUT 525 (AAC), reported as [2015] AACR 21; *Stevenage BC v ML (HB)* [2016] UKUT 164 (AAC); *M v SSWP* [2017] UKUT 443 (AAC); *E v Bristol City Council* [2018] UKUT 287 (AAC)
90 *SSWP v the City of Glasgow Council and IB* [2017] CSIH 35, reported as [2017] AACR 29

91 *SSWP v RR (HB)* [2018] UKUT 180 (AAC)
92 Sch 4 paras 13, 22 and 33 UC Regs
93 Sch 4 para 9(2)(f) UC Regs
94 Sch 4 para 15 UC Regs
95 Sch 4 para 16 UC Regs
96 Sch 4 para 13 UC Regs
97 Sch 4 para 14(1) UC Regs

5. **The housing costs element for social rented sector tenants**
98 Reg 26(2) and Sch 4 para 22 UC Regs
99 Sch 4 para 14(3) UC Regs
100 Sch 4 paras 3(1), 6 and 23 UC Regs
101 Sch 4 paras 3(1), 6 and 24 UC Regs
102 Sch 4 para 2 UC Regs, definition of 'listed persons'
103 Sch 4 paras 25(1), (2) and (5) and 26 UC Regs
104 Sch 4 para 25(3) and (4) UC Regs
105 Sch 4 paras 27 and 28 UC Regs; Sch 1 para 1(a) RO(UCF)O
106 Sch 4 para 29 UC Regs
107 Sch 4 para 29(2) UC Regs
108 www.justice.gov.uk/downloads/offenders/mappa/mappa-guidance-2012-part1.pdf
109 Sch 4 paras 8 and 25(2) UC Regs; Sch 1 para 1(b) RO(UCF)O
110 Sch 4 paras 8, 25(2) and 26 UC Regs; Sch 1 para 1(c)-(e) RO(UC)O
111 Sch 4 para 8(1) UC Regs
112 Sch 4 para 25(2) and (5) UC Regs; arts 3 and 4 and Sch 1 RO(UCF)O; art 7 The Rent Officers (Housing Benefit and Universal Credit Functions) (Amendment and Modification) Order 2021 No.1380

6. **The housing costs element for social rented sector tenants**
113 Schs 3 para 4(3) and 4 para 2 UC Regs
114 Sch 4 para 32 UC Regs
115 Sch 4 para 14(3) UC Regs
116 Sch 4 para 32A UC Regs
117 Sch 4 paras 2 and 30 UC Regs
118 Sch 4 para 36 (5) UC Regs
119 Sch 4 para 36 (6) UC Regs
120 Sch 4 para 36 (6)(b) UC Regs
121 Sch 4 paras 3, 6, 30-34 and 36 UC Regs
122 Sch 4 paras 34 and 36 UC Regs
123 Sch 4 para 33 UC Regs
124 Sch 4 paras 3, 6, 30-32, 35 and 36 UC Regs
125 Sch 4 para 36 (5) UC Regs 2013

126 Sch 4 para 35(4) UC Regs;
data.parliament.uk/DepositedPapers/
Files/DEP2019-0980/108._Removal_of_
Spare_Room_Subsidy_v10.0.pdf
127 Sch 4 para 33 UC Regs

7. The housing costs element for owner-occupiers
128 Reg 26(3) UC Regs
129 Sch 5 para 13 UC Regs
130 Reg 26(4)-(6) UC Regs
131 Reg 26(4)-(6) and Sch 5 para 4(3) UC
Regs
132 Sch 5 para 4 UC Regs
133 Sch 5 para 5(1) UC Regs
134 Sch 5 para 5 (1) and (2) UC Regs
135 Sch 5 para 5(3) UC Regs
136 Reg 2, definitions of 'JSA' and 'ESA', and
Sch 5 para 6 UC Regs
137 Reg 29 UC(TP) Regs
138 Sch 5 paras 1(2) and 7 UC Regs

Chapter 7

Income

This chapter covers:
1. Whose income counts (below)
2. What counts as income (p117)
3. Earnings (p117)
4. Other income (p127)
5. Notional income (p133)
6. Working out monthly income (p135)

Key facts

- Your entitlement to universal credit (UC) and how much you get depends on your income.
- Your own income counts and, if you are a member of a couple, your partner's income also counts.
- Your earnings from employment and self-employment are taken into account on a monthly basis over each 'assessment period'.
- If earnings from self-employment are low, your UC award may be assessed on more earnings than you get, based on the number of hours the DWP expects you to work.
- Certain other kinds of income are also taken into account.

1. **Whose income counts**

If you are single, only your own income counts when working out your universal credit (UC) award.[1]

Couples usually make a joint claim, and your UC award is worked out using both your income and your partner's income.[2]

There are some situations in which one member of a couple qualifies for UC but the other does not – eg, in certain circumstances if your partner is under age 18, does not meet residence tests, is out of the country or is in prison (see p35). In these cases, you make a single claim. You do not get any amount for your partner in your UC award, but your partner's income (and capital) is still added to yours when working out how much UC you get.[3]

Children's income is ignored.[4]

2. **What counts as income**

The amount of universal credit (UC) you are entitled to depends on how much income you have.

'Income' for UC means:[5]

- earnings from employment (see p118) and self-employment (see p119);[6] *and*
- certain other income:[7]
  - certain benefits (see p127);
  - maintenance for you or your partner, but not for a child (see p128);
  - student loan and grants. See p871 for how much of the loan counts and which grants are ignored;
  - certain income from employment and training schemes (see p129);
  - occupational and personal pensions and annuities (see p129);
  - certain insurance payments (see p130);
  - income from a trust (see p130 for which types are ignored);
  - income you are assumed to have from savings and other capital (see p131);
  - sports awards from UK Sport (see p132);
  - miscellaneous income (see p132);
  - capital that is treated as income (see below).

In some situations, you may be treated as having income that you do not actually have. This is called 'notional income' (see p133). If a type of income is not specified in the rules as being included for UC, it is ignored and does not affect your award. See p132 for some examples of income that is ignored.

Income or capital?

Any amounts that are paid regularly and that refer to a specific period are treated as income and not as capital.[8] This is the case even if payments might otherwise be regarded as capital or as being part capital – eg, payments under an annuity are treated as income.

If you have a lump sum that is payable by instalments (eg, an investment bond that allows regular withdrawals), each instalment is treated as income while any instalments outstanding, together with any other capital you have, is above £16,000. Once the amount of any instalments outstanding, together with any other capital you have, is below this limit, each instalment is treated as capital.[9]

3. **Earnings**

How earnings are treated depends on whether you are employed (see p118) or self-employed (see p119).

Employed earnings

To work out the amount of earnings from employment to take into account in your universal credit (UC) assessment, do the following.

- Check whether the payment counts as earnings (see below).
- Work out your monthly earnings for the assessment period (see p135).
- Calculate your net earnings for the assessment period (see p119).

If you also have self-employed earnings, these are also worked out (see p119) and added to your monthly employed earnings to give your total earned income. To work out how your earnings affect your UC award, check whether you have a work allowance (see p40). The work allowance is deducted from your earnings and 55 per cent of what is left is taken into account as income in your UC award. If you do not have a work allowance, 55 per cent of your total earnings is taken into account. See p40 for more about how your earnings affect your UC award.

What counts as earnings

'**Earnings**' means 'remuneration or profits derived from... employment'. This includes:[10]

- wages and overtime pay;
- tips, bonuses and commission;
- fees;
- holiday pay;
- statutory sick pay or other sick pay from your employer;
- statutory maternity pay, statutory adoption pay, statutory paternity pay, statutory shared parental pay, statutory parental bereavement pay or other pay from your employer while you are on maternity, adoption, paternity or parental leave;
- any refund of income tax or national insurance (NI) contributions for a tax year when you were in paid work. This includes tax from unearned income but not from self-employment (see p120);
- an equal pay settlement – eg, through a 'single status' agreement.[11]

The DWP usually gets information on your earnings from the records your employer sends to HM Revenue and Customs (HMRC) each time you are paid (see p135). So what counts for earnings for UC is normally what is recorded on PAYE (pay as you earn) records and is defined in terms of what counts as taxable income. However, there are differences, and not all kinds of taxable income count for UC purposes.

What does not count as earnings

Types of income not taken into account as earnings for UC include the following (some of which are taxable):[12]

• •

- expenses incurred 'wholly, exclusively and necessarily' in the course of your employment;[13]
- certain taxable and tax-exempt expenses and allowances – eg, mileage allowance or homeworkers' additional expenses (eg, listed on HMRC Form P11D from your employer);[14]
- expenses if you are a service user being consulted about provision of services by certain public bodies;[15]
- benefits in kind – eg, a salary sacrifice scheme, non-cash vouchers (eg, for childcare), living accommodation connected with work, cars and car fuel benefits, parking or meals;[16]
- allowances for special types of employment – eg, certain armed forces allowances, free coal to miners or allowances in lieu of coal, and offshore oil and gas workers' travel, subsistence and accommodation allowances.[17]

Payments when you stop work

Your final earnings when you stop work are taken into account in the assessment period in which they are paid (even if they are paid late).[18] This includes arrears of pay, pay in lieu of notice and accrued holiday pay.[19] The following lump-sum payments are taken into account as capital:[20]

- statutory and contractual redundancy pay;
- employment tribunal awards for unfair dismissal.

Working out net earnings

From your monthly earnings for the assessment period, deduct the following payments you make in that period:[21]

- income tax; *and*
- class 1 NI contributions; *and*
- any contribution you make towards a personal or occupational pension scheme. If you pay contributions through your employer, your payslips should show your wages after the contributions have been deducted, so there is no further deduction to make.

Also deduct any charity payments made under a payroll giving scheme.

Self-employed earnings

To work out the amount of your self-employed earnings to take into account in the UC assessment, do the following.[22]

- Work out your actual receipts for the assessment period (see p120).
- Deduct any permitted expenses from your receipts (see p120).
- From the result (or your share of it, if you are in a business partnership), deduct any payment made in the assessment period for income tax and NI contributions. If the result is negative, there is a loss and the amount of your

self-employed earnings is nil (but set minimum earnings may apply – see p122).
- Deduct any contributions made by you to a personal or occupational pension (but not if these have already been deducted from your employed earnings). If the result is negative, the amount of your self-employed earnings is nil (but set minimum earnings may apply – see p122).
- Deduct any unused losses carried forward from earlier assessment periods, starting from the earliest (see p121).
- Check whether the amount worked out as above (adding any earnings from employment) is above a set minimum level of earnings (see p122).

Receipts from self-employment

The starting point to work out how much self-employed earnings are taken into account is the actual amount of receipts into the business in the assessment period – eg, sales, takings and payment for work.[23] Include:[24]
- any refund of income tax, VAT or NI contributions for the self-employment;
- receipts in kind – ie, the value of the goods or service you provided for which you accepted payment in kind;[25]
- sale of business assets (if previously deducted from earnings for UC as an expense). If you stop using an asset for the business but do not sell it, the market value counts as a receipt;
- any payment under the Self-Employment Income Support Scheme (a coronavirus support grant). Other government grants and loans to businesses impacted by coronavirus may be treated as capital and disregarded for 12 months.[26]

Permitted expenses

Expenses must be reasonable and 'wholly and exclusively' incurred for the purposes of your business.[27] Reasonable expenses may include:[28]
- regular costs – eg, rent, utilities, insurance and wages;
- stock purchase;
- stationery and advertising;
- repairs of business assets;
- transport (but see below for flat-rate deductions);
- equipment purchase and hire;
- up to £41 repayment of interest on a loan – eg, for an overdraft or credit card;
- VAT.

These are just examples. The deduction allowed is usually the actual amount of permitted expenses paid in the assessment period. However, there are flat-rate deductions for the use of a vehicle that you can choose to include instead of the actual expense of buying and using the vehicle:[29]
- for a motorcycle, 24 pence a mile;

• for a car, van or other vehicle, 45 pence a mile for the first 833 miles, then 25 pence a mile after that (for a car, you must use this rate rather than the actual expense).

If an expense has been incurred partly for business and partly for private purposes, it can be apportioned and the part that is identifiably for business deducted.[30] There are set deductions for the following.[31]

• If you use your own home for 'income-generating activities' for the business, instead of deducting actual expenses, there is a flat-rate deduction that depends on the number of hours completed in the assessment period. Income-generating activities include providing services to customers, business administration, sales and marketing, but do not include being on call.[32] The deduction is:
  – £10 for work of at least 25 hours, but no more than 50 hours in the month; or
  – £18 for work of more than 50 hours, but no more than 100 hours in the month; or
  – £26 for more than 100 hours' work in the month.
• If you live in premises that you use mainly for your business, deduct an amount from the expenses relating to the premises, depending on the number of people living there:
  – £350 if you live alone; or
  – £500 if you live with one other person; or
  – £650 if you live with two or more other people.

Example
Madeleine runs a guest house. She and her partner, Thierry, live in the guest house. Madeleine works out her expenses as £1,500 for the monthly assessment period for the whole house. She finds it difficult to say which expenses are for the business. Instead of apportioning expenses for business and personal use, she deducts £500 from the £1,500 for the whole house. The expenses allowed are £1,000.

Offsetting losses

If your receipts in an assessment period are less than your expenses, income tax and NI contributions (but not adding pension contributions), this amount is a loss. A loss from a previous assessment period is deducted from the next assessment period in which there is a profit. The loss is deducted from your self-employed earnings worked out as above after tax, NI contributions and pension contributions are deducted. If there is not enough profit to use up the whole loss, the amount left over (the 'unused loss') is carried forward.[33] If there are unused losses to apply from more than one assessment period, these are deducted in order starting with the earliest. Losses from a previous UC award are offset against profits in a new award if the break in your claims is no more than six months. However, losses from months between awards cannot be offset unless you have made a UC claim for those months.

Example

Vanessa is a self-employed gardener. Business is slow in the winter. For the assessment periods ending:

– 28 February, she receives £300 cash from customers, pays £600 for new equipment, has travel expenses of £100, pays no tax or NI and pays £50 into her pension. Her self-employed earnings are nil and she has a loss of £400 (£300 – £600 – £100);

– 28 March, she receives £300 cash from customers, has travel expenses of £100, pays no tax or NI and pays £50 into her pension. Before offsetting her losses, her self-employed earnings are £150 (£300 – £100 – £50). She uses up £150 of her £400 loss from the previous month, giving self-employed earnings of nil and leaving £250 unused losses to carry forward;

– 28 April, she receives £1,700 cash from customers, has travel expenses of £200, pays no tax or NI and pays £50 into her pension. Before offsetting her losses, her self-employed earnings are £1,450 (£1,700 – £200 – £50). She uses up the remaining £250 unused losses, giving self-employed earnings of £1,200.

(In February and March, Vanessa's earnings are below the set minimum, so are treated as being at the 'minimum income floor'.)

Minimum level of earnings

Note: due to the coronavirus pandemic, the DWP suspended (ie, did not apply) this rule (the 'minimum income floor') between 13 March 2020 and 31 July 2021. From August 2021, if it was suspended in your case, it applies again when the DWP decides that you are still in gainful self-employment, or at the end of any remaining 'start-up period' (see p125) that was still to run when the minimum income floor was suspended in March 2021. If your business is not affected by the pandemic, the minimum income floor now applies as normal. However, until the end of July 2022, if you can show that your business is affected by the pandemic, your work coach can suspend the minimum income floor for up to two months at a time and six months in total.[34]

If your main work is self-employment but your earnings are low, your UC may be assessed on higher earnings than you have. This is called the '**minimum income floor**' and is generally at the level of the national minimum wage for the number of hours the DWP expects you to work – usually 35 hours a week. This applies if:[35]

- you are in 'gainful self-employment' (see p124); *and*
- you are not in a 'start-up' period (see p125); *and*
- you would be subject to all work-related requirements were it not for having the minimum income floor applied. (Having the minimum income floor

applied means no work-related requirements can be imposed on you.) If you are not subject to any work-related requirements (for a reason other than having the minimum income floor applied), or just subject to work-focused interviews or work preparation, your actual earnings from self-employment are taken into account, however low they are.

If you are single and the minimum income floor applies to you, your earnings are treated as being at the individual earnings threshold in any assessed income period in which your earned income from self-employment, together with any earnings from employment, is below this level.[36] The individual earnings threshold is the same threshold used to decide your work-related requirements (see p1043), with a notional amount for tax and NI contributions deducted.

Example

Lukasz has a window cleaning business. He is single. For the current assessment period, he declares earnings of £300. The DWP works out Lukasz's minimum income floor to be £1,280 a month (35 hours a week x £9.50 x 52 ÷ 12 rounded down, less £160 for notional tax and NI contributions). Lukasz's UC award for the assessment period is worked out on earnings of £1,280.

If you are in a couple and the minimum income floor applies to you, your combined earnings for the UC assessment are usually your partner's earnings added to the minimum income floor for you. However, you cannot be treated as having combined earnings of more than a certain amount. This amount is the same as the joint earnings threshold for couples used to decide if there are any work-related requirements to fulfil (see p1043), but with a notional amount for tax and NI contributions deducted.[37]

- If your actual combined earnings are above the joint earnings threshold, your actual earnings count in the UC assessment, with no minimum income floor.
- If your actual combined earnings (ie, ignoring the minimum income floor) are below the joint earnings threshold in any assessed income period, your earnings are treated as being the individual earnings threshold (see p1043) less:
  – a notional amount for tax and NI contributions; *and*
  – an amount to ensure that, when added to your partner's earnings, you are not treated as having more than the joint earnings threshold.

If you are a couple but claiming as a single person (eg, because your partner is a 'person subject to immigration control'), the minimum income floor does not apply to your partner's self-employed earnings. Instead, her/his actual earnings are combined with yours.

2

Example

Sara and André are a couple. André is a self-employed builder and Sara works part time in a shop. They have a two-year-old child and Sara is the 'responsible carer'. André declares earnings of £500 and Sara £700. The DWP works out André's minimum income floor to be £1,280 a month (35 hours a week x £9.50 x 52 ÷ 12 rounded down, less £160 for tax and NI contributions).

André and Sara's actual combined earnings are £1,200 (£500 + £700).

This is below their joint earnings threshold of £1,938 (£1,280 for André plus £658 for Sara (16 hours a week x £9.50 x 52 ÷ 12 rounded down with no tax or NI contribution deduction at this earnings level)).

Adding André's minimum income floor to Sara's actual earnings gives £1,980 (£1,280 + £700). This is £42 above their joint earnings threshold of £1,938, so André is treated as having earnings of £1,238 (£1,280 – £42).

Gainful self-employment

When you claim UC or when you tell the DWP that you are self-employed, you are asked to attend a 'gateway' interview if you are someone who must meet all the work-related requirements. You are asked to bring evidence that you are in 'gainful self-employment'. This means that:[38]

- the self-employment is your main employment – ie, it is your only employment or, if you also work for an employer, you normally spend more hours on, or have more earnings from, your self-employment; *and*
- your earnings count as self-employed earnings – ie, they are not employed earnings and are from carrying out a 'trade, profession or vocation'.[39] If it is not clear whether you are employed or self-employed, the DWP may look at a number of factors including whether you pay your own tax, whether your work is supervised and whether you can decide your own hours;[40] *and*
- your self-employment is 'organised, developed, regular and carried on in expectation of profit' – eg, whether you work for financial gain, how many hours you do, whether you have a business plan or have taken steps to get work, what work is arranged, whether you are registered as self-employed with HMRC and whether you advertise your business.[41]

The DWP may decide that you are in gainful self-employment even though you are off sick and not able to do any work, or you currently have no income at all from your business. If you disagree with a decision to apply a minimum income floor, you can ask for a revision and then appeal. You may be able to argue, for example, that your self-employment is no longer organised or regular and you no longer have an expectation of profit. Bear in mind that business assets can only be disregarded for a limited time (see p481). If you are off sick and your weekly earnings are below 16 times the hourly rate of the minimum wage (see Appendix 7), send the DWP medical certificates so that it can assess whether you have limited capability for work. See p992 for how your earnings affect this assessment. If so, only your actual earnings should be taken into account, because you should no longer be subject to all the work-related requirements (see p122).

Once the DWP decides you are in gainful self-employment, you normally have a start-up period before the minimum income floor applies (see below).

If you are not in gainful self-employment, you must still report your earnings and these are taken into account in your UC award, but no minimum income floor is applied.

Start-up period

If you are self-employed, you may have 12 months, called the 'start-up period', in which the minimum income floor does not apply and your UC is worked out on your actual earnings, however low they are.[42]

The start-up period runs from the beginning of the assessment period in which the DWP decides you are in gainful self-employment, irrespective of when your self-employment began. (Before 23 September 2020, it only applied to new businesses.) However, if you have ever had the minimum income floor applied to that self-employment before, it applies again without a start-up period. You are expected to take active steps to increase your earnings to the level of your individual earnings threshold – ie, the level that means you no longer have to meet work-related requirements (see p1043). The DWP can end the start-up period if it decides you are not doing this, or are no longer in gainful self-employment.

The start-up period continues to run even if your UC stops and starts during the year.[43] Although you can only have one start-up period for the same self-employment, if you begin different self-employment, you can have a new start-up period provided more than five years have passed since the start of the earlier period. See p122 if the start-up period was interrupted by the minimum income floor being suspended in March 2020.

Surplus earnings from employment and self-employment

If you earn above a certain threshold and your UC stops, an amount of 'surplus earnings' may be carried over to a new UC claim if you claim again within six months. This applies if:[44]

- your earnings (and your partner's earnings, if you are a couple) in the assessment period in which your UC ended were above the 'relevant threshold'. Your actual self-employed earnings are included, not the minimum income floor; *and*
- you make a new claim, or the DWP treats you as claiming,[45] within six months of your previous UC entitlement – ie, the start of the new assessment period is within six months of the end of the previous one; *and*
- you have not been entitled to UC since the end of your previous award, and neither has your partner in a joint claim; *and*

- you have not recently experienced domestic abuse (either now or when your previous UC ended – see p1039).

The 'relevant threshold' is:
- £2,500; *plus*
- any work allowance to which you are entitled; *plus*
- maximum UC (see p64) less any income you have other than earnings, multiplied by 100 and divided by 55.

The amount above this threshold is your surplus earnings. **Note:** the £2,500 figure may decrease to £300 from April 2023.[46] See AskCPAG and CPAG's *Welfare Rights Bulletin* for updates.

If you have surplus earnings included in a new claim for UC, the amount of your award may be reduced in the first month or you may get no UC. The amount of surplus earnings is recalculated each time you claim over the six months by adding your actual earnings to the surplus from the last claim. Any amount above the relevant threshold becomes the new surplus which is again added to your actual earnings the next time you claim. This means that if your actual earnings drop below the relevant threshold and you make a new claim, the surplus goes down. If the first reclaim is unsuccessful, you can claim again in the following month(s) until you become entitled. Once the six-month period is over, any remaining surplus is ignored.

Normally to become entitled to UC again without delay, you should claim as soon as your earnings are below the relevant threshold because the surplus does not decrease until a claim is actually made. However, the DWP may treat you as making a claim on the first day of each assessment period after your entitlement ended, for up to five months so that surplus earnings can decrease each month until your UC award can start again automatically.[47] Bear in mind that the surplus can also increase if you claim again when your earnings are still above the threshold. In this case, consider waiting until your earnings decrease before you make a new claim.

If you separate from your partner, any surplus earnings from a previous joint claim are normally shared equally in a new single claim, but if an equal share is not reasonable ask the DWP to change it.

Examples
Sonia and Leighton have claimed UC jointly since Sonia's self-employed earnings stopped. Leighton works part time and earns £600 a month. Their maximum UC is £1,000 a month. Sonia gets some temporary work and in May, she earns £8,000 and their UC award ends.
– The relevant threshold is £4,318.18 (£2,500 plus £1,000 maximum UC x 100 ÷ 55).
   Surplus earnings are therefore £4,281.82 (£8,600 actual earnings minus the relevant threshold of £4,318.18).

– In June, their income is still above maximum UC so is too high for an award of UC (£4,281.82 surplus earnings plus £600 Leighton's earnings = £4,881.82 x 55 per cent = £2,685). Surplus earnings of £563.64 (£4,881.82 minus the relevant threshold of £4,318.18) are carried forward.

– In July, Sonia is still not earning and their income is now below their maximum UC of £1,000 (£563.64 surplus earnings plus £600 Leighton's earnings = £1,163.64 x 55 per cent = £640). They are awarded UC of £360 (£1,000 maximum UC minus £640 earnings). There are no more surplus earnings to carry forward.

Asha's UC stops in December when she gets a bonus on top of her earnings. She has surplus earnings of £500. In January her earnings are back to normal. However, she does not claim again until February. The claim is turned down because her earnings are too high once the £500 surplus is added to February's earnings. She claims again in March and is awarded UC. If Asha had started claiming again in January, the £500 surplus would have been used up in January and she would have got UC again from her second claim in February instead of having to wait until March.

4. Other income

Only certain specified types of income, other than earnings, are taken into account for universal credit (UC). These are listed on p117 and explained in more detail below. This kind of income reduces your UC pound for pound. Any other income is ignored.

Benefits

Some benefits are taken into account as income; others are disregarded.

Benefits that are taken into account

The following benefits count in full:[48]

- carer's allowance (CA) – but not CA supplement in Scotland;
- employment and support allowance (ESA);
- industrial injuries benefit, except constant attendance allowance and exceptionally severe disablement allowance, which are disregarded;
- jobseeker's allowance (JSA);
- maternity allowance;
- retirement pensions;
- severe disablement allowance;
- widow's pension and widowed parent's allowance;
- foreign social security benefits and state retirement pensions that are similar to those listed above;

2

- an overpayment of income support (IS), income-based JSA (not joint-claim JSA), income-related ESA or housing benefit if you are not entitled to that benefit and the overpayment falls within a UC assessment period.[49]

Statutory sick pay, statutory maternity pay, statutory adoption pay, statutory paternity pay, statutory shared parental pay and statutory parental bereavement pay are treated as earnings and so may benefit from the work allowance.

Benefits that are not taken into account

All other benefits are ignored – eg:
- adult disability payment (in Scotland);
- armed forces independence payment;
- attendance allowance;
- bereavement support payment;
- Best Start grant (in Scotland);
- CA supplement (in Scotland);
- child benefit;
- child disability payment (in Scotland);
- child winter heating assistance (in Scotland);
- disability living allowance;
- funeral support payment (in Scotland);
- guaranteed income payment and surviving guaranteed income payment under the Armed Forces Compensation Scheme;
- guardian's allowance;
- industrial injuries constant attendance allowance and exceptionally severe disablement allowance;
- personal independence payment;
- Scottish child payment;
- social fund payments;
- two-week run-on of IS, income-based JSA and income-related ESA (see p241);
- war disablement pension;
- war widow's, widower's or surviving civil partner's pensions;
- young carer grant (in Scotland).

Maintenance payments

Maintenance for a child is ignored completely.

Any maintenance for you or your partner made by your or your partner's spouse/civil partner or former spouse/civil partner under a court order or under a maintenance agreement counts in full as income.

If a former partner makes payments direct to a third party (eg, your mortgage lender), this should not count as your income.[50] However, if there is income available to you which you choose not to access, you may be treated as having it under the 'notional income' rules (see p133).

If you *pay* maintenance to a former partner or a child not living with you, your payments are not disregarded when working out your income for UC.

Student loans and grants

For the special rules on the treatment of student loans, grants and other types of student support, see Chapter 41.

Employment and training schemes

The following payments from employment or training programmes under section 2 of the Employment and Training Act 1973 or section 2 of the Enterprise and New Towns (Scotland) Act 1990 are taken into account:[51]
- those made as a substitute for UC – eg, a training allowance;
- those intended for certain living costs. Payments for food, ordinary clothing or footwear, fuel, rent or other housing costs, including council tax, are all taken into account.

All other payments are disregarded – eg:
- travel expenses;
- training premium;
- childcare expenses;
- special needs payments.

Occupational and personal pensions and annuities

The following income is taken into account:[52]
- an occupational pension;
- income from a personal pension;
- income from a retirement annuity contract (including an annuity purchased for you or transferred to you on divorce);
- payments from a former employer for early retirement on the grounds of ill health or disability, unless this was under a court order or settlement of a claim;
- an overseas pension;
- a Civil List Act pension;
- payment under an equity release scheme. This provides regular payments from a loan secured on your home;
- payments from the Financial Assistance Scheme and periodic payments from the Pension Protection Fund (these help some people with underfunded occupational schemes whose employer has gone out of business).

See p134 if you are over pension age and have not drawn your pension. If you are under pension age, UC is not affected if you choose not to draw a pension.

DWP guidance says that the full amount should be taken into account before any deduction for income tax.[53] Income from an annuity is taken into account, except income from an annuity bought from personal injury compensation, which is ignored.[54] An annuity is usually when you pay a lump sum to an insurance company, often on retirement, with the capital built up in your personal pension, which then pays you an income for the rest of your life. It may also be through a home income plan where the annuity is bought with a loan secured on the home.

Insurance payments

Payments under a policy to insure against the risk of losing income due to illness, accident or redundancy are taken into account in full.[55]

Trusts, personal injury payments and special compensation schemes

If you get an amount awarded to you because of a personal injury (see p148), it can be disregarded in certain circumstances.[56]
- If you receive the compensation in regular payments, they are disregarded as income.
- If the compensation is in a trust, both the capital value of the trust and any income from it are ignored. For more about how payments from personal injury trusts or other trusts are treated, see p142 and p148.
- If the compensation was used to buy an annuity, payments under the annuity are ignored.
- If the compensation is administered by the court on your behalf or can only be used by direction of the court, the capital is ignored and regular payments are disregarded as income.
- If the compensation is not used in one of the above ways, it is disregarded as capital for 12 months. This gives you a chance to spend some or all of it, or to put it in a trust or buy an annuity.

Personal injury payments include compensation from the Criminal Injuries Compensation Scheme.[57] Victims payments to people injured in a Northern Ireland 'Troubles-related incident' are disregarded as income or capital indefinitely.[58]

Income from a trust that is not set up from personal injury compensation is taken into account, whether it is a discretionary trust or other type of trust.

Special compensation schemes

Payments of income (or capital) are ignored from specific schemes and certain schemes approved by the government, including:[59]
- the National Emergencies Trust;

* the Windrush Compensation Scheme;
* the Child Migrants Trust (for children subjected to migration programmes before 1971);
* schemes to make child abuse payments for historic institutional child abuse in the UK;
* for people infected from contaminated blood products;
* for people affected by the 2017 fire at Grenfell Tower.

Income from capital

If you have capital over £16,000, you are not entitled to UC. If your capital is below this level, it can affect the amount of income that is taken into account. This is either because you have actual income from the capital, such as income from a trust, or because it is assumed that the capital gives you a certain amount of income.

Assumed monthly income from capital

If your capital is over £6,000 but not more than £16,000, you are treated as having some income from it. This 'assumed monthly income', often called 'tariff income', is set at the rate of £4.35 a month for every £250, or part of £250, between £6,000.01 and £16,000.[60]

Example
Victoria and Frazer have savings of £7,000. This is above the £6,000 limit, so they are treated as having an income of £17.40 a month from their savings (4 x £4.35).

When working out how much capital you have, some capital is disregarded (see p143). You are not treated as having an assumed monthly income from disregarded capital.[61]

Rental and other income from capital

If your capital is treated as giving you tariff income, any actual income you have from the same capital is treated as part of your capital from the day it is due to be paid to you.[62] For example, if you own a property, other than the home in which you live, rent is taken into account not as income but as capital and added to the capital value of the property itself (see also p133). However, if the value of the property can be disregarded (see p477), there is no tariff income, which means that the rental income is also ignored.[63] If you are running a property business, rental income counts as self-employed earnings (see p119).

Example

Khaled owns a flat that he rents out for £1,000 a month, which he uses to pay the mortgage. He does not live in the flat himself and is not running a property business, so the rent he gets does not count as income for UC but is added to his capital. The flat is valued at £100,000 but only £7,000 counts as capital once his outstanding mortgage is deducted. He has an assumed income of £34.80 (£7,000 + £1,000 = £8,000, £4.35 for each £250 above £6,000 is 8 x £4.35 = £34.80).

Actual income from from an annuity and from a trust is taken into account, unless the income is disregarded because the annuity or trust is from personal injury compensation (see p129 and p130). In these two cases, the capital is not treated as giving you any assumed monthly income.[64] See p130 for more about how trusts are treated.

Sports awards

A sports award from UK Sport out of National Lottery funds for living expenses is taken into account. This covers food, ordinary clothing and footwear, fuel, rent, housing costs and council tax for you, your partner or dependent child.[65] Amounts for anything else are ignored – eg, sportswear.

Specified miscellaneous income

Miscellaneous income taken into account is unearned income that is taxable under the HM Revenue and Customs 'sweep-up' provisions in Part 5 of the Income Tax (Trading and Other Income) Act 2005 – eg:[66]

- copyright royalties;
- income from films and sound recordings;
- income from estates in administration.

Other income

Only income specified in the rules and described above can affect your UC. Any other kind of income is ignored – eg:

- adoption allowances, fostering allowances, child arrangement order payments and kinship care payments;
- support from a charity;
- voluntary payments – eg, if a relative gives you regular money. However, if it is voluntary maintenance for you (rather than for a child, which is always ignored) from a separated or former spouse or civil partner, this is taken into account;
- payments to third parties – eg, if a relative pays your phone bill for you;
- mortgage protection policy payments;

- rental income from a room you let in your own home.[67] This is because actual income that comes from capital that is disregarded (the value of the home you live in is disregarded) is not in the list of income that is taken into account. However, if you rent out a property that you do not live in, the capital value of that property is taken into account and the rent is treated as capital, not as income (see p131);
- test and trace payments (in England), self-isolation support grants (in Scotland) and self-isolation support scheme payments (in Wales);[68]
- payments to people approved to provide accommodation under the Homes for Ukraine scheme are expected to be ignored.

---

5. Notional income

In some circumstances, you can be treated as having income that you do not actually have. This is called 'notional income'. You may be treated as having notional income if:
- you deliberately reduce your earnings in order to claim, or increase the amount of, universal credit (UC); or
- you work free of charge or for less than the going rate; or
- you fail to apply for available income.

Deliberately getting rid of income

If you deliberately reduce your earnings from employment or self-employment in order to claim UC or increase the amount you get, you are treated as though you still have that income.[69] In particular, this applies if you got UC, or more UC, and the DWP believes this was a foreseeable result and was what you intended. Even if your employer has arranged for you to lose income, you may still be treated as though you had the income if you or your employer intended you to get UC, or more UC, by doing so.

Cheap or unpaid labour

If you are doing work free of charge or for less than the going rate (eg, you are working for a relative), you are treated as though you had earnings that would be reasonable for that work.[70] The comparison is with what the pay would be for similar work in the same location.

You are not treated as having more income than you receive for that work if:[71]
- the person cannot afford to pay you, or pay you more than s/he does; or
- you work for a charitable or voluntary organisation or as a volunteer and it is accepted that it is reasonable for you to give your services free of charge or at less than the going rate; or
- you are on a government-approved employment or training programme; or

• you are a service user who is being consulted about provision of services by certain public bodies.

2 Failing to apply for income

If you fail to apply for income that would be available to you if you applied for it, you are treated as having that income.[72]

However, you cannot be treated as having another benefit that you have not applied for, with the exception of retirement pension.

If you are over pension age, you may be treated as having pension income even though you have not applied for it. If you are under pension age, you can choose not to apply for pension income without your UC award being affected (see below).

This rule does not apply to earnings from employment or self-employment.

Deferring a state pension

If you are over pension age and you defer your state pension, retirement pension, graduated retirement benefit or any shared additional pension paid on divorce, you are treated as having that income for UC.

The amount that counts is the pension to which you would expect to be entitled, less any overlapping benefit you get – eg, carer's allowance. To take account of the time it can take to process claims, you are only treated as having this income from the date you could expect to get it were you to make a claim.

Leaving funds in an occupational or personal pension

Although you can usually choose to take some, or all, of your occupational or personal pension from age 55, your UC is not affected if you do not, unless you are over pension age.

If you are over pension age, the following applies.

• You are treated as having income from an occupational pension you have elected to defer beyond the scheme's retirement age,[73] as though you had claimed it. The time it might take to process it is taken into account and any overlapping benefit is deducted.

• If you have a defined contribution occupational or personal pension, you are generally expected to buy an annuity or take the equivalent income that would be payable through an annuity.[74] If you leave funds in your pension pot, you are treated as having notional income based on the annuity those funds could yield. If you take one or more lump sums from your pension pot, these count as capital and notional income is worked out on what is left in your pension pot.

See p129 for how pension payments are treated.

6. **Working out monthly income**

Universal credit (UC) is paid in arrears for the previous monthly assessment period (see p38). Awards are worked out month by month. Your award is then adjusted as your earnings or other income increase or decrease, but always for a whole assessment period.[75] UC awards are not adjusted for income changes part way through the monthly assessment period. See p52 for reporting changes in your earnings and when this affects your award.

Earnings

When you first claim, the DWP can make a decision on whether you qualify for UC based on an estimate of your earnings.[76] At the end of the first assessment period, your award is based on your actual earnings instead.[77]

The amount of earnings used to work out your UC award for each assessment period is based on the actual amount you received in that assessment period.[78] There is no averaging from one month to the next.

Wage cycles

You may find that two lots of monthly wages fall into one assessment period – eg, in a month when you are paid early because the usual payday falls on a weekend. To avoid your UC payments changing, the two payments of wages can be allocated over two assessment periods.[79] This should happen automatically.

However, if you are paid weekly, fortnightly or four-weekly, your regular pay is not reallocated when an 'extra' payday falls in an assessment period. Your UC will reduce or end in these months. If your UC ends, reclaim in the following month if your UC award does not start up again automatically.

Note: cases about four-weekly payments that were appealed have held that the DWP is correct to take pay into account when it is actually paid, even if that means counting two lots of pay in one assessment period or that wages are too low in other months to be exempt from the benefit cap.[80]

See cpag.org.uk/welfare-rights/legal-test-cases for more information and updates.

See also AskCPAG and CPAG's *Welfare Rights Bulletin* for updates.

If you are employed, your employer is required to report your earnings to HM Revenue and Customs (HMRC) every time you are paid. This is called 'real-time information'. Usually, the employed earnings figure used in the UC assessment is taken from the amount in the report(s) received by the DWP in that assessment period.[81] If your employer is late in paying you, the payment counts when it is reported, not when it was due to be paid to you.[82] However, if your employer is late in reporting earnings to HMRC, the DWP can take the payment into account in the assessment period in which you received it instead of when it was reported.[83]

Instead of using a real-time information report, the DWP must decide the amount of earnings using other evidence if:[84]

- the DWP thinks your employer is unlikely to provide an accurate report on time;
- no information is received from HMRC in an assessment period – eg, because your employer has not sent a report to HMRC or HMRC has not passed it on;
- the information in the report is wrong.

If you think the DWP has used the wrong earnings figure or the real-time information report is wrong, send any evidence you have of the correct amount (eg, wage slips, bank statements) and ask for a formal decision. You can then ask for a revision and appeal.[85] However, unless the DWP thinks it is a failure or mistake, if no real-time information report is received, you are simply treated as having no earnings for that assessment period.

If you are self-employed, you must report your earnings every month. Your UC award is based on the actual amount received in the assessment period and the actual amounts paid – eg, tax and expenses. The way you work out your earnings for the assessment period is explained on p119.

If you are asked to self-report, you must act quickly in order for your earnings to be taken into account in the same assessment period as you received them. If you report late, the DWP can treat your earnings as received in that later period. If you fail to provide information or evidence, payment of your UC may be suspended (see p1161).

Other income

Any other income you have that is not earnings is worked out as a monthly amount – eg:[86]

- multiply weekly payments by 52 and divide by 12;
- multiply fortnightly payments by 26 and divide by 12;
- multiply payments for four weeks by 13 and divide by 12;
- multiply payments for three months by four and divide by 12;
- a payment of income for a whole year is divided by 12.

If your income varies and there is a cycle that can be identified, take one cycle and convert this into a monthly amount. If there is no cycle to the income, it is worked out by taking three months of income, or another period if that would give a more accurate picture, and calculating an average monthly amount.

Note: there are different rules for working out student income (see p871).

Example

Kai gets contributory employment and support allowance (ESA) of £154 every two weeks. The amount of ESA taken into account in his UC award is £333.67 (£154 x 26 ÷ 12).

If you start or stop getting any unearned income, the amount taken into account is worked out over the number of days for which the income is paid in that assessment period. For example, if ESA of £154 a fortnight is awarded from 18 November (giving a monthly amount of £333.67) and your assessment period runs from 29 October to 28 November, the amount taken into account for that period is £120.67 (£333.67 x 12 ÷ 365 x 11 days).

Notes

1. Whose income counts
1 s8(4)(a) WRA 2012
2 s8(4)(b) and Sch 1 para 4(5) WRA 2012; reg 22(1) UC Regs
3 Regs 3(3) and (6) and 22(3) UC Regs
4 Because ss5 and 8 WRA 2012 only count income of a 'claimant' or 'joint claimants'.

2. What counts as income
5 s8(3) WRA 2012
6 Reg 52 UC Regs
7 Reg 66 UC Regs
8 Reg 46(3) UC Regs
9 Reg 46(4) UC Regs; para H5102 ADM

3. Earnings
10 Reg 55(2), (4) and (4A) UC Regs; HMRC, *Employment Income Manual*, para 00520
11 *Minter v Kingston upon Hull City Council and Potter v SSWP* [2011] EWCA Civ 1155; HMRC, *Employment Income Manual*, para 02530
12 Reg 55(2) and (3)(a) UC Regs
13 Part 5 Ch 2 and s336 IT(EP)A 2003
14 Part 4 IT(EP)A 2003
15 Regs 53(2) and 55(3)(b) UC Regs
16 Part 3 Chs 2-11 and Part 4 Ch 6 IT(EP)A 2003
17 Part 4 Ch 8 IT(EP)A 2003
18 Reg 54(1) UC Regs; *NM v SSWP* [2021] UKUT 46 (AAC)

19 Reg 55(2) UC Regs; *RMcE v Department for Communities (UC)* [2021] NICom 59. These are 'general earnings' under s7(3) IT(EP)A 2003 – see HMRC, *Employment Income Manual*, paras 12850 and 13874 for non-contractual pay in lieu of notice.
20 Reg 55(2) UC Regs. These come under s401 IT(EP)A 2003 and are therefore not 'general earnings' under s7(3) – see HMRC, *Employment Income Manual*, paras 12960 and 13005.
21 Reg 55(5) UC Regs
22 Reg 57 UC Regs
23 Regs 54 and 57(3) UC Regs
24 Reg 57(4) and (5) UC Regs
25 para H4184 ADM
26 Reg 2 The Universal Credit (Coronavirus) (Self-employed Claimants and Reclaims) (Amendment) Regulations 2020 No.522
27 Reg 58(1) UC Regs
28 Reg 58(2) and (3) UC Regs; para H4214 ADM
29 Reg 59(2) UC Regs
30 Reg 58(1)(b) UC Regs
31 Reg 59(3) and (4) UC Regs
32 para H4241 ADM
33 Reg 57A UC Regs; reg 4 The Universal Credit (Surpluses and Self-employed Losses) (Digital Service) Amendment Regulations 2015 No.345

34 The Universal Credit (Coronavirus) (Restoration of the Minimum Income Floor) Regulations 2021 No.807
35 Reg 62(1) and (5) UC Regs
36 Reg 62(2) and (4) UC Regs
37 Reg 62(3) and (4) UC Regs
38 Reg 64 UC Regs
39 Reg 57(1) UC Regs
40 para H4016 ADM
41 para H4050 ADM
42 Reg 63 UC Regs
43 para H4102 (Example 2) ADM
44 Reg 54A UC Regs
45 Reg 32A UC,PIP,JSA&ESA(C&P) Regs
46 Secretary of State determination under reg 5 The Universal Credit (Surpluses and Self-employed Losses) (Digital Service) Amendment Regulations 2015 No.345
47 Reg 32A UC,PIP,JSA&ESA(C&P) Regs

4. Other income
48 Reg 66(1)(a) and (b) UC Regs; reg 25(1) UC(TP) Regs
49 Reg 10 UC(TP) Regs
50 Because there is no rule to treat payments to a third party as yours.
51 Reg 66(1)(f) UC Regs
52 Regs 66(1)(la) and 67 UC Regs; reg 16 SPC Regs
53 para H5004 ADM
54 Reg 66(1)(i) UC Regs
55 Reg 66(1)(h) UC Regs
56 Reg 75 UC Regs
57 para H2028 ADM
58 Reg 26 VP Regs
59 Reg 76 UC Regs; para H2051 ADM; Memo ADM 21/21
60 Reg 72(1) UC Regs
61 Reg 72(2) UC Regs
62 Reg 72(3) UC Regs
63 Regs 66 and 72 UC Regs
64 Reg 72(2) UC Regs
65 Reg 66(1)(g) UC Regs
66 Reg 66(1)(m) UC Regs; Part 5 IT(TOI)A 2005
67 para H5112 ADM
68 Memo ADM 20/20

5. Notional income
69 Reg 60(1) and (2) UC Regs
70 Reg 60(3) UC Regs
71 Reg 60(4) UC Regs
72 Reg 74 UC Regs
73 para H5170 ADM; *BRG v SSWP (SPC)* [2014] UKUT 246 (AAC)
74 para H5172 ADM

6. Working out monthly income
75 Sch 1 paras 20-30 UC,PIP,JSA&ESA(DA) Regs
76 Reg 54(2)(a) UC Regs
77 para H3011 ADM
78 Reg 54 UC Regs
79 Reg 61(6) UC Regs
80 *LG v SSWP (UC)* [2021] UKUT 121 (AAC); *Pantellerisco and others v SSWP* [2021] EWCA Civ 1454
81 Reg 61(2)(a) UC Regs
82 *NM v SSWP* [2021] UKUT 46 (AAC)
83 Reg 61(5) UC Regs
84 Reg 61 UC Regs
85 Reg 41 UC,PIP,JSA&ESA(DA) Regs
86 Reg 73 UC Regs

Chapter 8

Capital

This chapter covers:
1. The capital limits (below)
2. Whose capital counts (p140)
3. What counts as capital (p140)
4. Disregarded capital (p143)
5. Notional capital (p149)
6. How capital is valued (p152)

Key facts
- Capital includes savings, investments, property and lump-sum payments.
- Some kinds of capital are ignored when working out your universal credit (UC) – eg, the value of the home in which you live.
- If you have more than £16,000 capital, you are not entitled to UC.
- If you have capital above a certain amount, your UC is affected, because this is assumed to give you a certain monthly income.
- If you deliberately get rid of capital in order to get more UC, you are treated as still having it. This is called 'notional capital'.

1. The capital limits

There is a lower and upper capital limit.[1]
- The lower limit is £6,000.
- The upper limit is £16,000.

If you have over £16,000 of capital, you are not entitled to universal credit (UC). The first £6,000 is ignored and does not affect your benefit. If you have between £6,000.01 and £16,000, you may be entitled to benefit, but it is assumed that you have some income from your capital.

This assumed monthly income, often called 'tariff income' (see p131), is £4.35 a month for every £250, or part of £250, of your capital between £6,000.01 and £16,000.

When working out the value of your capital, some is disregarded (see p143). You may be treated as having capital which you do not actually have (see p149).

> *Example*
> Naia has £7,100 savings. She is assumed to have £21.75 a month income from her savings (5 x £4.35).

Any amount of capital above £16,000 is ignored for up to 12 monthly assessment periods if you were entitled to tax credits and had over £16,000 immediately before becoming entitled to UC on a claim made through the 'managed migration' process (see p29). This is referred to as the **'transitional capital disregard'**. The disregard ends if your capital drops below £16,000 and also in any of the circumstances in which someone loses a UC transitional element (see p78).[2]

2. **Whose capital counts**

If you are a member of a couple (see p303), you must usually make a joint claim for universal credit (UC) and your partner's capital is added to yours when working out your entitlement (see p35).[3]

In the limited circumstances when you must make a single claim for UC despite being a member of a couple (see p35), your partner's capital (and income) is still added to yours.[4]

Your child's capital is not taken into account and does not affect your benefit.

3. **What counts as capital**

All your capital is taken into account, unless it is disregarded (see p143) or is treated as income (see p117).

The term 'capital' is not defined. In general, it means lump-sum or one-off payments, rather than a series of payments – eg, it includes savings, property and statutory redundancy payments.[5]

Capital payments can normally be distinguished from income because they are not payable for any specified period and are not part of a regular series of payments (although capital can be paid by instalments).[6]

Note: some capital is treated as income (see p117) and some income is treated as capital (see p142).

Savings

Your savings generally count as capital – eg, cash you have at home, premium bonds, shares, unit trusts and money in a bank or building society account.

If you have put aside money to pay bills, this is still counted as your capital.[7] If your savings are just below the capital limit, you could pay bills by monthly direct debit or use a budget account to keep your capital below the limit.

Income not spent by the end of the assessment period after the one in which you received it is treated as your capital.[8]

Fixed-term investments

Fixed-term investments count as capital. However, if an investment is currently unobtainable, it may have little or no value. If you can convert the investment into a form that lets you access it or sell your interest, or raise a loan through a reputable bank using the asset as security, the amount you can get for it counts.

Property and land

Any property or land you own counts as capital. Many types of property are disregarded (see p143). If there is doubt about who owns the property, see below.

Loans and ownership of capital

Usually it is clear when capital belongs to you and should be taken into account. However, it may be less clear if you are holding money for someone else or if you have been given a loan which you are expected to repay.

A loan to you usually counts as money you possess and therefore counts as capital. However, you can argue that a loan, money or other assets you hold for someone else should be disregarded if it is:
- a loan granted on condition that you only use the interest, but do not touch the capital because the capital element has never been at your disposal;[9] or
- money you have been given to be used for a particular purpose on condition that it must be returned if not used in that way;[10] or
- property you have bought on behalf of someone else who is paying the mortgage;[11] or
- money held in your bank account on behalf of another person, which is to be returned to her/him at a future date;[12] or
- savings from someone else's benefit paid to you as an 'appointee' – eg, your child's disability living allowance;[13] or
- a loan, which you are under an immediate obligation to repay;[14] or
- your asset but you have expressed a clear intention that it is for someone else's benefit and renounced its use for yourself;[15] or
- some property and you lead someone to believe that you are transferring your interest in it to her/him but fail to do so (eg, it is never properly conveyed) and

2

that person acts on the belief that s/he owns it (eg, spends money on repairs). You can argue the asset has been transferred and you are like a trustee.[16] This is called '**proprietary estoppel**'.

If you lend money to someone, it could still count as your 'notional capital' (see p149), depending on your reasons for lending it. You usually have a legal right to be repaid and this, in itself, could have a capital value (although the value would normally be less than the amount loaned, and could be nil if you have no expectation of getting the money back).[17]

Trusts

Capital in a non-discretionary trust is taken into account because you can obtain the capital at any time. If this takes you over the £16,000 capital limit, you are not entitled to UC. However, if your capital is between £6,000.01 and £16,000, you are not treated as having an assumed monthly income from the capital.[18] Capital in a discretionary trust does not normally count as your capital because payments are at the discretion of the trustee and you cannot demand payment.[19]

There is no difference between a discretionary and non-discretionary trust in the way that payments to you from the trust are treated. In either case, they are taken into account. Generally, regular payments for a particular period are treated as income, and a lump sum is treated as capital.[20] If trustees of a discretionary trust choose to pay your bills direct or buy you something that is disregarded (eg, because it is a personal possession), this should not affect your benefit.

If the trust is from money for a personal injury to you or your partner, the rules are more generous (see p148).

Note: putting money in a discretionary trust has the advantage of the value of the trust itself being disregarded. However, if you transfer money into a trust in order to get more benefit, it can still count as yours under the notional capital rules (see p149).

Money held by your solicitor

Money held by your solicitor normally counts as your capital. This includes compensation payments (but see p148 for when payments for personal injury are disregarded).[21] If you have had legal aid and your solicitor is holding money back while working out the statutory charge to be deducted for legal costs, it does not count as your capital.[22]

Income treated as capital

Unless the capital is disregarded (see p143) or does not give you an assumed monthly income, actual income from capital (eg, interest on your savings, share dividends or rent from a property that is not your home) is treated as capital from the day it is due to be paid.[23] This avoids any double counting of income from capital that is also treated as giving you an assumed monthly income (see p131).

Example

Roman has £6,800 savings, which gives him interest of £8 a month. His UC assessment takes into account an assumed monthly income from his savings of £17.40 (£4.35 a month for each £250, or part of £250, above the £6,000 lower capital limit). The actual £8 interest is added to his capital.

4. Disregarded capital

Your home

If you own the home in which you live, its value is ignored.[24] This disregard can continue to apply if you are temporarily away from home.[25]

If you own more than one property, only the one you occupy is disregarded under this rule.[26]

Exceptionally, two separate properties can be regarded as a single home, as though one were an annexe of the other, if you personally (rather than a member of your family) normally occupy both properties.[27] This is more likely if you have a large family, but you could argue that it should apply if neither property on its own meets your family's needs – eg, if you are a carer living between two properties.[28]

Your home can include croft land and smallholdings if they cannot be sold separately.[29]

When the value of the property is disregarded

The value of the property can be disregarded, even if you do not normally live in it, in the following circumstances.

- **If you have left your former home following a relationship breakdown**, the value of the property is ignored for six months from the date you left. It may also be disregarded for longer if any of the steps listed below are taken. If it is occupied by your former partner and s/he is a lone parent, its value is ignored for as long as s/he lives there.[30]
- **If you have sought legal advice or have started legal proceedings in order to occupy property as your home**, its value is ignored for six months from the date you first took either of these steps.[31] The six months can be extended if it is reasonable to do so, if you need longer to move in.
- **If you are taking reasonable steps to dispose of a property**, its value is ignored for six months from the date you first took such steps (which may be before you claim benefit).[32] Advertising at an unrealistic sale price does not

count as 'reasonable', but placing the property with an estate agent or contacting a possible buyer should,[33] as might taking ancillary proceedings to resolve financial issues in a divorce.[34] The disregard can continue beyond six months, even for years – eg, if a court orders that a former matrimonial home should not be sold until the children are grown up.[35] Taking a property off the market and putting it on again does not necessarily begin a new six-month period, but it may do if the second attempt to sell is quite separate.[36]

- **If you are carrying out essential repairs or alterations which are needed so that you can occupy a property as your home**, the value of the property is ignored for six months from the date you began the repairs.[37] 'Steps' may include applying for planning permission or a grant or loan to make the property habitable, employing an architect or finding someone to do the work.[38] If you cannot move into the property within that period because the work is not finished, its value can be disregarded for as long as is necessary to allow the work to be carried out.

- **If you have acquired a property and intend to live in it as your home but have not yet moved in,** its value is ignored for six months from the date you acquired it, or for longer if that is reasonable.[39]

- **If you sell your home and intend to use the money from the sale to buy another home**, the capital is ignored for six months from the date you received the money.[40] This also applies even if you do not own your home but, for a price, you surrender your tenancy rights to a landlord.[41] If you need longer to complete a purchase, your capital can continue to be ignored if it is reasonable to do so. You do not need to have decided within the six months to buy a particular property. It is sufficient if you intend to use the proceeds to buy some other home within the six-month (or extended) period,[42] although your 'intention' must involve more than a mere 'hope' or 'aspiration'.[43] There must be an element of 'certainty' which you may be able to show by evidence of a practical commitment to another purchase, although this need not involve any binding obligation.[44] If you intend to use only part of the proceeds of sale to buy another home, only that part is disregarded even if, for example, you have put the rest of the money aside to renovate your new home.[45]

- **If your home is damaged or you lose it altogether**, an insurance policy payment is ignored for six months from the date it is received, or longer if it is reasonable to do so.[46]

- **If you have taken out a loan or been given money for the express purpose of essential repairs or alterations to your home**, it is ignored for six months, or longer if it is reasonable to do so.[47] If it is a condition of the loan that it must be returned if the improvements are not carried out, you could argue that it should be ignored altogether.[48]

- **If you have deposited money with a housing association as a condition of occupying your home**, this is ignored indefinitely.[49] If money which was deposited for this purpose is now to be used to buy another home, this is ignored for six months, or longer if reasonable, in order to allow you to complete the purchase.[50]

- **Grants made to buy a home** are ignored for six months, or longer if it is reasonable to do so.[51]

When considering whether it is reasonable to extend the disregard period, all the circumstances should be considered – eg, your personal circumstances, any efforts made by you to use, or dispose of, the home[52] and the general state of the property market. In practice, periods of around 18 months are not considered unusual.

Note: it is possible for property to be ignored under more than one of the above paragraphs in succession.[53]

Rent that you receive from property which is disregarded is ignored, unless the rent counts as self-employed earnings from a property business (see p131).

The home of a partner, former partner or relative

The value of a home is ignored if it is occupied as her/his home by:[54]

- a close relative who is over pension age or has limited capability for work; *or*
- your former partner from whom you are not estranged but you are living apart (so are not treated as still living together or living in the same household for universal credit (UC) purposes) – eg, if one of you is living in a care home; *or*
- your former partner from whom you are estranged and who is a lone parent. If your former partner is not a lone parent, the value of the home is ignored for six months for UC from the date you ceased to live in the home.

Definitions

'**Close relative**' includes a parent, son, daughter, step-parent, stepson, stepdaughter, parent-in-law, son-in-law, daughter-in-law, brother or sister, or a partner of any of these people.[55] It also includes half-brothers and -sisters and adopted children.[56]

You are '**estranged**' if you are living apart because your relationship has broken down, even if the separation is amicable.[57]

'**Lone parent**' is not defined. You could argue for a broad definition – eg, including shared care arrangements and irrespective of which parent receives child benefit.

Personal possessions

All personal possessions, including jewellery, furniture or cars, are ignored.[58] A personal possession has been defined as any physical asset not used for business purposes, other than land.[59] However, a home that you own but do not live in is not normally considered a personal possession and counts as capital (see p143). Personal possessions are not ignored if you have bought them in order to be able to claim or get more benefit. In this case, the sale value, rather than the purchase price, is counted as actual capital and the difference is treated as notional capital (see p149).[60]

An insurance payment for damage to, or the loss of, any personal possessions, which is to be used for their repair or replacement, is ignored for six months, or longer if reasonable.[61]

Business assets

If you are self-employed, your business assets are ignored for as long as you continue to work in that business.[62]

If you cannot work because you are sick or incapacitated, the assets are disregarded for six months from when you stopped work if you can reasonably expect to work in the business again when you recover, or for longer if reasonable in the circumstances.[63]

If you stop working in the business, you are allowed six months (or longer if reasonable) to sell these assets without their value affecting your UC, provided you are taking reasonable steps to sell them.[64]

If the purchase value of an asset was deducted as an expense from your earnings and you later sell or stop using the asset for the business, the sale price (or market value if you were to sell) is treated as a receipt when working out your earnings (see p120).[65]

If not otherwise ignored, grants or loans to meet business expenses or losses relating to coronavirus are ignored for 12 months from the date received (see p120 for rules about the Self-Employment Income Support Scheme).[66]

It is sometimes difficult to distinguish between personal and business assets. The test is whether the assets are 'part of the fund employed and risked in the business'.[67] If the assets of a business partnership (eg, plant and machinery) have been sold but the partnership has not yet been dissolved, the proceeds of sale can still count as business assets.[68] **Note:** letting a single house is not likely to constitute a business.[69]

Personal pension schemes

The value of the right to receive an occupational or personal pension is ignored.[70] The value of a fund held in a personal pension scheme is also ignored as capital.[71] However, if you are over pension age, you are expected to take your pension and are treated as having a notional income if you do not take it all (see p134).

Insurance policy and annuity surrender values

The surrender value of a life assurance policy is ignored.[72] Some investments include an element of life insurance – eg, endowment policies. If the policy terms include how the payment on death is calculated, the whole investment is ignored.[73] However, you cannot choose to put money in such an investment in order to increase your benefit entitlement, because you are likely to be caught by the notional capital rule if you do (see p150).

Benefits and tax credits

Arrears of benefits and tax credits

Arrears of the following benefits and tax credits, and any compensation you get for late payment of these, are ignored for 12 months from when you receive them, or longer in some cases of arrears of £5,000 or more (see below):[74]

- UC;
- any benefit that is ignored as income for UC (see p127);
- income support (IS), income-based jobseeker's allowance (JSA), income-related employment and support allowance (ESA), housing benefit (HB), council tax benefit, child tax credit (CTC) and working tax credit (WTC);
- compensation for lost or delayed ('new-style') contributory ESA because of a DWP error;
- maternity allowance if you received the arrears either during the current UC award or while you were getting IS, income-based JSA, income-related ESA, HB, pension credit (PC), CTC or WTC, they were disregarded in that award and you became entitled to UC within a month of that award ending.

Arrears of £5,000 or more continue to be ignored beyond 12 months to the end of the UC award in which you received them if they are:

- paid to compensate for an official error or error of law and they would be disregarded from an award of another means-tested benefit under the rules described on p482 or p507;
- compensation for lost or delayed (new-style) contributory ESA because of a DWP error.[75]

In either of the two bullets above, if the arrears were ignored in an earlier award of IS, income-based JSA, income-related ESA, HB, PC, CTC or WTC, they continue to be ignored in a UC award that starts within a month of the earlier award ending.

Example

Harry is on income-related ESA. On 1 November 2021 he gets a payment of £12,000 arrears of ESA due to him because of an official error. In December 2021, he claims UC and his ESA ends. The £12,000 arrears continue to be disregarded in his UC for as long as the award continues.

Note: although arrears are ignored as capital, you may have been paid more UC or other means-tested benefit than you would have been entitled to if benefit had been paid on time. The DWP may deduct the difference from the arrears of the delayed benefit. Otherwise, if the arrears are not reduced, the overpayment is recoverable (see p1198).

Other benefits and payments

- The initial lump sum of bereavement support payment is ignored for 12 months from the date you receive it.[76]
- Social fund payments and, in Scotland, Best Start grant and funeral support payment, are ignored for 12 months from the date you receive them.[77]
- Young carer grant and child winter heating assistance (in Scotland) are ignored for 52 weeks from the date you receive them.[78]
- Any 'transitional SDP amount' of UC (see p27) paid as a lump sum in a UC award that started before 27 January 2021 is ignored for 12 months from the date of payment or until your award ends if this is longer.[79]

Personal injury and other compensation payments

If you have money in a trust or annuity from a personal injury to you, the value of the trust and any income from the trust or annuity is disregarded. A lump sum from the trust or annuity is, however, taken into account as capital.[80] It should not affect your UC if the trustees give you regular, or even annual, payments, pay your bills instead of giving you a lump sum or buy you something that would be disregarded because it is a personal possession – eg, furniture or a car. If an award is administered by a court (eg, the Court of Protection), its value and income from it is also disregarded. A payment for personal injury to you that is not in a trust is disregarded for 12 months from the date it is paid to you. If the personal injury is to your partner and s/he has since died, you cannot carry over the remainder of the 12-month disregard, or if the payment is in a trust, it is no longer ignored.[81]

> *Definitions*
>
> **'Personal injury'** includes not only accidental and criminal injuries, but also any disease and injury as a result of a disease.[82]
>
> **'Sum awarded'** includes any amounts as a result of personal injury – eg, for loss of earnings.[83]
>
> **'Trust'**. Any money in a trust 'derived from' compensation for personal injury to you is disregarded irrespective of the type of trust.[84]

Personal injury payments include compensation from the Criminal Injuries Compensation Scheme.[85] Victims payments to people injured in a Northern Ireland 'Troubles-related incident' are disregarded as income or capital indefinitely.[86]

Payments of capital (or income) are ignored from specific schemes and certain schemes approved by the government, including:[87]

- the National Emergencies Trust;
- the Windrush Compensation Scheme;
- the Child Migrants Trust (for children subjected to migration programmes before 1971);
- schemes to make child abuse payments for historic institutional child abuse in the UK;
- for people infected from contaminated blood products;
- for people affected by the 2017 fire at Grenfell Tower.

Funeral plan payments

The value of any funeral plan contract is ignored indefinitely.[88] A funeral plan contract is a contract under which:
- you make payments to another person to ensure you are provided with a funeral; *and*
- the sole purpose of the plan is to provide a funeral.

Social services and community care payments

The following payments from a local authority are ignored for 12 months:[89]
- payments for children, young people and families made under: sections 17, 23B, 23C or 24A of the Children Act 1989; section 12 of the Social Work (Scotland) Act 1968; sections 29 or 30 of the Children (Scotland) Act 1995; or sections 37, 38, 109, 110, 114 or 115 of the Social Services and Well-being (Wales) Act 2014;
- payments to meet welfare needs related to old age or disability, unless they are for certain living expenses (eg, food, fuel, clothing, footwear, rent, housing costs or council tax) for you, your partner or dependent child.

Miscellaneous payments

The following payments are disregarded:
- 20 per cent of money in a tax-free childcare account (see p856);[90]
- any payments made to holders of the Victoria or George Cross;[91]
- £150 energy rebate paymennt paid by the local authority (eg, to households in council tax bands A to D) is disregarded for 12 months from when you receive it.

5. Notional capital

In certain circumstances, you are treated as having capital that you do not have. This is called **'notional capital'**.[92] Notional capital counts in the same way as the capital you do have.

2

You may be treated as having notional capital if:

- you deliberately deprive yourself of capital in order to claim or increase the amount of your universal credit (UC) (see below); *or*
- you are a sole trader or a partner in a business (see p152).

Note: if you are treated as having notional capital because you have deliberately deprived yourself of capital in order to claim or increase benefit, a 'diminishing notional capital rule' (see p151) may be applied so that the value of the notional capital you are treated as having is considered to reduce over time.

Deliberately getting rid of capital

If you deliberately get rid of capital in order to claim or increase your UC, you are treated as still having it.[93] You are not treated as having deprived yourself of capital if:[94]

- you pay off or reduce a debt which you owe; *or*
- you pay for goods or services if the purchase was reasonable in the circumstances of your case.

Paying off debts and bankruptcy

You are not treated as having deprived yourself of capital if you repay or reduce a debt that you owe – eg, you could repay a credit card debt, mortgage, overdraft or loan. It does not matter if the terms of the debt allow you to repay later. However, you may be asked for evidence that you owed the debt, so if you repay a loan from a family member, it may be harder to show that the debt existed.

If you are declared bankrupt, you cannot spend your capital without court approval and cannot usually be considered to have deprived yourself of it if you do. Capital you have (but cannot spend) does not count for benefit purposes from the date of the bankruptcy order.[95] However, if you deliberately go bankrupt or do not take reasonable steps to discharge the bankruptcy in order to get benefit, your capital can still count as notional capital.

Paying for goods and services

If you spend money on goods and services, you are not treated as having deprived yourself of capital if the purchase was reasonable. There is no list of items that are allowed or excluded – it depends on the circumstances. However, you are less likely to be caught by this rule if you spend money on day-to-day necessities or replacing household goods, and more likely to be caught if you choose to buy something like an expensive holiday.

Intention to claim or increase universal credit

If you have spent your capital in some way other than paying off a debt or paying for goods and services that are regarded as reasonable, you are only treated as having deprived yourself of capital if you intended to claim UC or increase the amount of UC.

Relevant factors include the following.

- At the time you used your capital, how much choice did you have in spending the money in the way you did?[96]
- How long was it before you needed to claim UC? The longer it was, the less likely it is that you spent the capital in order to get UC. However, there is no set safe period after which you can claim UC without the DWP considering whether you have deliberately deprived yourself of capital.[97]
- Were you mentally capable at the time?[98]

You should not be treated as having deprived yourself of capital if:

- you did not know about the capital limit for UC – you cannot have an intention to get more UC if you do not know about the capital rules. If you are already familiar with the benefit system (eg, you have claimed benefit before and had official information about the capital rules), this is evidence that you did know about the capital limits;[99] *or*
- you told the DWP what you planned to do with your capital and were told that it would not affect your UC. If you went ahead and spent the money the way you said you would, you cannot be said to have intended to get more UC by doing so.[100]

If you use up your resources, you may have more than one motive for doing so. Even if qualifying for benefit is only a less significant motive for your actions and the main motive is something different (eg, ensuring your home is in good condition by spending capital on repairs and improvements), you may still be considered to have deprived yourself of a resource in order to get benefit.[101]

You can deprive yourself of capital, even if you receive another resource in return.[102] For example, if you buy a car so that you can get more benefit, your actual capital includes the value of the car, and the difference between that and the purchase price is treated as notional capital.[103]

The diminishing notional capital rule

If you have deliberately deprived yourself of capital, the value of your notional capital is assumed to reduce over time. This is known as the 'diminishing notional capital rule'.

The notional capital amount is not fixed, but reduces over time at a set rate, as follows.

If you are treated as having notional capital of:[104]

- over £16,000 and your UC entitlement stops, in the following month the amount of UC you would have received but for the notional capital is deducted from the amount of notional capital;

- between £6,000 and £16,000, in the following assessment period the amount of the assumed income from that notional capital is deducted from the amount of notional capital.

Notional capital is reduced in the same way in each subsequent month.

Notional capital is added to any actual capital you may have. This may reduce your UC award because of the amount of assumed monthly income from capital included in the assessment (see p131), or end it altogether.

If your UC stops altogether, make a fresh claim when you think you might become entitled. Ask the DWP to tell you how long it will be before a new claim might succeed. If you have both actual and notional capital, you may need to spend your actual capital to meet your living expenses.

Companies run by sole traders or a few partners

Normally, if you hold shares in a company, their value is taken into account as capital.[105] If, however, your influence in the company is such that you are like a sole trader or like a partner in a small partnership, you are treated accordingly. The value of your shareholding is ignored but you are treated as having a proportionate share of the capital of the company.[106] However, these company assets are not taken into account while you are doing any work on the company's business,[107] even if you only do a little work for the company – eg, taking messages.[108] It has, however, been held that a 'sleeping partner' in a business managed and worked exclusively by others cannot benefit from this disregard. As well as having a financial commitment to the business, you must also be involved or engaged in it in some practical sense as an earner.[109]

Note: income from the company, or your share of it, is regarded as your self-employed earnings. If this is your main employment, it counts as 'gainful employment', so you can be treated as having a minimum level of earnings from that employment if your actual earnings are low (see p122).[110] You may also have employed earnings as a director or employee.

As the value of your shareholding is ignored, dividends are also ignored as income (because actual income that comes from disregarded capital is not in the list of income taken into account for UC – see p131 and p142). Exceptionally, dividends could in reality be earnings and counted as such.[111]

6. **How capital is valued**

Market value

Your capital is valued at its current market or surrender value.[112] This means the amount of money you could raise by selling it or raising a loan against it. This is the price that would be paid by a willing buyer to a willing seller on a particular date.[113] So if an asset is difficult or impossible to realise, its market value should be heavily discounted or even nil.[114]

If you cannot legally dispose of capital (eg, because of a restraint order), the market value is nil.[115]

In the case of a house, an estate agent's figure for a quick sale is a more appropriate valuation than the district valuer's figure for a sale within three months.[116]

It is not uncommon for an unrealistic assessment to be made of the value of your capital. If you disagree with the decision, you could ask for a revision or appeal (see Chapters 56 and 57).

Expenses of sale

If there would be expenses involved in selling your capital, 10 per cent is deducted from its value (before any debts are deducted) for the cost of sale.[117]

Debts

Deductions are made from the gross value of your capital for any debt or mortgage secured on it.[118] If a creditor (eg, a bank) holds the land certificate to your property as security for a loan and has registered notice of its deposit at the Land Registry, this counts as a debt secured on your property.[119] If a single mortgage is secured on a house and land, and the value of the house is disregarded for benefit purposes, the whole of the mortgage can be deducted when calculating the value of the land.[120]

If you have debts that are not secured against your capital (eg, tax liabilities), these cannot be offset against the value of your capital.[121] However, once you have repaid your debts, your capital may be reduced. **Note:** you can still be treated as having the capital if you deliberately get rid of it in order to get benefit (see p150).

If you have an overdrawn bank account and have savings in another account with the same bank, the amount of the overdraft should be deducted from your savings if the terms of the accounts allow the bank to make these transfers.[122]

Jointly owned capital

If you own any capital asset (except as a partner in a company – see p152) with someone else under a 'joint tenancy', you are treated as owning an equal share of the asset with the other owner(s) – eg, if you own the asset with one other person, you are each treated as having a 50 per cent share of it.[123] This applies regardless of whether the capital asset is in the UK or abroad. See p155 for the rules that apply to assets abroad.[124]

This does not apply if you jointly own the capital asset as 'tenants in common'.[125] In this case, your actual share in the asset is valued.

2

Joint tenancies and tenancies in common

With a '**joint tenancy**', each co-owner owns the whole of the capital asset 'jointly and severally'. If one of the joint tenants were to die, her/his interest in the asset would pass automatically to the other joint tenant(s).

With a '**tenancy in common**', each co-owner owns a discrete share in the asset. This share can be passed on by the person who has died to whoever s/he wishes.

If you have a joint tenancy, the value of your deemed share is calculated in the same way as your actual capital. However, it is only the value of your deemed share looked at in isolation that counts, and this will usually be worth less than the same proportion of the value of the whole asset. For example, if the asset is a house, the value of any deemed share may be very small or even worthless, particularly if the house is occupied and there is a possibility that the sale of the property cannot be forced. This is because even a willing buyer could not be expected to pay much for an asset s/he would have difficulty making use of.[126] Whether a sale can be forced depends on individual circumstances, and valuations should take into account legal costs and the length of time it could take to gain possession of the property.[127] A valuation should set out details of the valuer's expertise (where relevant), describe the property in sufficient detail to show that all factors relevant to its value have been taken into account, state any assumptions on which it is based and explain what the market is for that type of sale.[128] You may need to challenge any decision (see Chapters 56 and 57) based on an inadequate valuation.

Treatment of assets after a relationship breakdown

When partners separate, assets, such as a former home or bank account, may be in joint or sole names. If, for instance, a bank account is in joint names, you and your former partner are treated as having a 50 per cent share each under the rules on jointly held capital (see p153). On the other hand, a former partner may have a right to some, or all, of an asset that is in your sole name – eg, s/he may have deposited most of the money in a bank account in your name. If this is established, you may be treated as not entitled to the whole of the account but as holding part of it as trustee for your former partner.[129] If an asset such as the matrimonial home belongs to your former partner and you have no share in it, you cannot be treated as having any interest in it under the Matrimonial Causes Act 1973 unless you take divorce or separation proceedings and get a property order.[130]

Shares

Shares are valued at their current market value less 10 per cent for the cost of sale, and after deducting any 'lien' held by brokers for sums owed for purchase or commission.[131] Market value can be worked out from the listed share price. If a more exact value is needed (eg, because your capital is close to the limit), it should be calculated using HM Revenue and Customs guidance, by taking the lowest and highest share prices for the day and using the lowest price plus a quarter of the difference between the two.[132] Fluctuations in price between routine reviews of your award are normally ignored.

Unit trusts

Unit trusts are valued on the basis of the 'bid' price quoted in newspapers. No deduction is allowed for the cost of sale because this is already included in the 'bid' price.[133]

The right to receive a payment in the future

The value of any such right is its market value – what a willing buyer will pay to a willing seller.[134] For something which is not yet realisable, this may be very small.

Overseas assets

If you have assets abroad and there are no exchange controls or other prohibitions to prevent you transferring your capital to the UK, your assets are valued at their current market or surrender value in that country.[135]

If you are not allowed to transfer your capital, you are treated as having capital equal to the amount that a willing buyer in this country would give for those assets (which might not be very much).[136]

Deduct 10 per cent for any expenses of sale, any debts or mortgage secured on the assets and any charges for converting the payment into sterling.[137]

Notes

2

1. The capital limits
1 Regs 18 and 72 UC Regs
2 Reg 51 UC(TP) Regs

2. Whose capital counts
3 s5(2) WRA 2012
4 Reg 18(2) UC Regs

3. What counts as capital
5 para H1020 ADM
6 *R v SBC ex parte Singer* [1973] 1 WLR 713; reg 46(3) UC Regs
7 R(IS) 3/93
8 para H1050 ADM
9 R(SB) 12/86
10 *Barclays Bank v Quistclose Investments Ltd* [1970] AC 567; R(SB) 49/83; R(SB) 53/83; R(SB) 1/85; *MW v SSWP (JSA)* [2016] UKUT 469 (AAC), reported as [2017] AACR 15
11 R(SB) 49/83
12 R(SB) 12/86; for how this works in Scotland, see *JK v SSWP (JSA)* [2010] UKUT 437 (AAC), reported as [2011] AACR 26; *DF v SSWP* [2015] UKUT 611 (AAC)
13 *MC v SSWP (IS)* [2015] UKUT 600 (AAC)
14 CIS/2287/2008
15 R(IS) 1/90; CSIS/639/2006
16 R(SB) 23/85; CSIS/639/2006
17 *JC v SSWP* [2009] UKUT 22 (AAC)
18 Reg 72(2) UC Regs
19 *Gartside v Inland Revenue Commissioners* [1968] 1 All ER 121; [1968] AC 553; *LG v SSWP (ESA)* [2019] UKUT 220 (AAC)
20 Regs 46, 48 and 66(1)(j) UC Regs
21 *Thomas v CAO*, appendix to R(SB) 17/87
22 CIS/984/2002
23 Reg 72(3) UC Regs

4. Disregarded capital
24 Sch 10 para 1 UC Regs
25 para H2038 ADM
26 Schs 3 para 1(1) and 10 para 1(2) UC Regs
27 R(JSA) 9/03; R(SB) 10/89
28 *MM v SSWP (IS)* [2012] UKUT 358 (AAC); para H2040 ADM
29 Sch 3 paras 1(4) and 2 UC Regs; para H2039 ADM

30 Reg 48(2) and Sch 10 para 5 UC Regs
31 Reg 48(2) and Sch 10 para 4(1)(b) and (2) UC Regs
32 Sch 10 para 6 UC Regs
33 R(SB) 32/83
34 R(IS) 5/05
35 Reg 48(2) UC Regs
36 *SP v SSWP* [2009] UKUT 255 (AAC)
37 Reg 48(2) and Sch 10 para 4(1)(c) UC Regs
38 *R v LB Tower Hamlets Review Board ex parte Kapur*, 12 June 2000, unreported
39 Reg 48(2) and Sch 10 para 4(1)(a) UC Regs
40 Reg 48(2) and Sch 10 para 13(a) UC Regs
41 R(IS) 6/95
42 R(IS) 7/01
43 CIS/685/1992
44 CIS/8475/1995; CIS/15984/1996
45 R(SB) 14/85
46 Reg 48(2) and Sch 10 para 14 UC Regs
47 Reg 48(2) and Sch 10 para 15 UC Regs
48 *Barclays Bank v Quistclose Investments Ltd* [1970] AC 567; CSB/975/1985
49 Sch 10 para 12 UC Regs
50 Reg 48(2) and Sch 10 para 13(b) UC Regs
51 Reg 48(2) and Sch 10 para 13(c) UC Regs
52 CIS/4757/2003
53 CIS/6908/1995
54 Sch 10 paras 2, 3 and 5 UC Regs
55 Reg 2 UC Regs
56 CSB/209/1986; CSB/1149/1986; R(SB) 22/87
57 R(IS) 5/05; CH/3777/2007
58 Reg 46(2) UC Regs
59 R(H) 7/08
60 CIS/494/1990 and R(IS) 8/04; para H1895 ADM
61 Reg 48(2) and Sch 10 para 14 UC Regs
62 Sch 10 para 7 UC Regs
63 Reg 48(2) and Sch 10 para 8(b) UC Regs
64 Reg 48(2) and Sch 10 para 8(a) UC Regs
65 Reg 57(5) UC Regs
66 The Universal Credit (Coronavirus) (Self-employed Claimants and Reclaims) (Amendment) Regulations 2020 No.522

67 R(SB) 4/85
68 CIS/5481/1997
69 CFC/15/1990; R(FC) 2/92; *RM v Sefton Council (HB)* [2016] UKUT 357 (AAC), reported as [2017] AACR 5
70 Sch 10 para 10 UC Regs
71 para H5174 ADM
72 Sch 10 para 9 UC Regs
73 R(IS) 7/98
74 Sch 10 para 18 UC Regs; regs 10B and 10C UC(TP) Regs
75 Regs 10A and 10C UC(TP) Regs
76 Sch 10 para 20 UC Regs
77 Sch 10 paras 16, 21 and 22 UC Regs
78 Sch 10 paras 23 and 24 UC Regs
79 Sch 2 para 7 UC(TP) Regs; reg 3 The Universal Credit (Transitional Provisions) (Claimants previously entitled to a severe disability premium) Amendment Regulations 2021 No.4
80 Reg 75 UC Regs
81 R(IS) 3/03
82 R(SB) 2/89; *KQ v SSWP (IS)* [2011] UKUT 102 (AAC), reported as [2011] AACR 43
83 R(IS) 15/96
84 *Q v SSWP (JSA)* 2020 UKUT 49 (AAC)
85 para H2028 ADM
86 Reg 26 VP Regs
87 Reg 76 UC Regs; para H2051 ADM; Memo ADM 21/21
88 Sch 10 para 11 UC Regs
89 Sch 10 para 17 UC Regs
90 para H1156 ADM
91 Sch 10 para 19 UC Regs

5. Notional capital

92 Regs 50(1) and 77(2) UC Regs
93 Reg 50(1) and (2) UC Regs
94 Reg 50(2) UC Regs
95 *KS v SSWP* [2009] UKUT 122 (AAC), reported as [2010] AACR 3
96 R(SB) 12/91; para H1832 ADM
97 CIS/264/1989; R(IS) 7/98
98 para H1830 ADM
99 R(SB) 9/91; R(SB) 12/91
100 *LH v SSWP (IS)* [2014] UKUT 60 (AAC); para H1842 ADM
101 R(SB) 38/85; R(IS) 1/91; R(H) 1/06
102 R(SB) 40/85
103 R(IS) 8/04
104 Reg 50(3) UC Regs
105 para H1020 ADM
106 Reg 77(1) and (2) UC Regs
107 Reg 77(3)(a) UC Regs
108 Vol 5 Ch 29, para 29879 DMG; see also R(IS) 13/93
109 R(IS) 14/98

110 Reg 77(3) UC Regs
111 *HMRC v PA Holdings Ltd* [2011] EWCA Civ 1414

6. How capital is valued

112 Reg 49(1) UC Regs
113 R(SB) 57/83; R(SB) 6/84
114 R(SB) 18/83
115 *CS v SSWP* [2014] UKUT 518 (AAC)
116 R(SB) 6/84
117 Reg 49(1) UC Regs
118 Reg 49(1)(b) UC Regs
119 CIS/255/1989
120 R(SB) 27/84
121 R(SB) 2/83; R(SB) 31/83
122 *JRL v SSWP (JSA)* [2011] UKUT 63 (AAC), reported as [2011] AACR 30
123 Reg 47 UC Regs
124 CIS/2575/1997
125 *Hourigan v SSWP* [2002] EWCA 1890, reported as R(IS) 4/03
126 CIS/15936/1996; CIS/263/1997; CIS/3283/1997 (joint decision); R(IS) 26/95
127 R(IS) 3/96
128 R(JSA) 1/02; *Reigate and Banstead BC v GB (HB)* [2018] UKUT 225 (AAC)
129 R(IS) 2/93
130 R(IS) 1/03
131 Reg 49 UC Regs
132 paras H1660-65 ADM
133 para H1673 ADM
134 *Peters v CAO*, appendix to R(SB) 3/89
135 Reg 49(2)(a) UC Regs
136 Reg 49(2)(b) UC Regs
137 Reg 49(3) UC Regs

Part 3

Other means-tested benefits and tax credits

Chapter 9

Income-related employment and support allowance

3

This chapter covers:
1. Who can get income-related employment and support allowance (p162)
2. The rules about your age (p164)
3. People included in the claim (p164)
4. The amount of benefit (p164)
5. Special benefit rules (p167)
6. Claims and backdating (p167)
7. Getting paid (p167)
8. Tax, other benefits and the benefit cap (p168)

Key facts
- You can only make a new claim for income-related employment and support allowance (ESA) in very limited circumstances.
- ESA is a benefit for people who are unable to work because of illness or disability (known as having 'limited capability for work') and who are not entitled to statutory sick pay.
- Entitlement to ESA is assessed by a test called the work capability assessment.
- There are two types of ESA: **contributory ESA**, which is not means tested (but can be affected by certain pensions), and **income-related ESA**, which is means tested.
- You do not have to have paid national insurance contributions to qualify for income-related ESA.
- ESA is administered and paid by the DWP.
- If you disagree with an ESA decision, you can apply for a revision or supersession (see Chapter 56), or appeal against it (see Chapter 57). You must apply for a mandatory reconsideration before you can appeal. All parts of the decision may be looked at.

Part 3: Other means-tested benefits and tax credits
Chapter 9: Income-related employment and support allowance
1. Who can get income-related employment and support allowance

New claims for, and continuing entitlement to, income-related ESA

Until 30 March 2022, you could make a new claim for income-related ESA if you were prevented from claiming universal credit (UC) because you were (or if you are a member of a couple, each of you were) a 'frontier worker' – ie, you are in Great Britain to work, but do not live there or in Northern Ireland.[1] This is no longer the case.

If the DWP wants to safeguard or test the efficient administration of UC, it can designate categories of case that are prevented from claiming UC.[2]

If you are already entitled to income-related ESA, you can continue to qualify until:

– you claim UC. **Note:** when you make a new claim for UC, your income-related ESA entitlement can continue for two weeks. See p168 for information about income-related ESA run-on; *or*

– you become a member of a couple and your partner is getting UC; *or*

– you and your partner are affected by the 'managed migration' transfer to UC process, that is, you are told by the DWP that your income-related ESA will end and are invited to claim UC. See p29 for further information, and AskCPAG and CPAG's *Welfare Rights Bulletin* for updates (see p29).

1. **Who can get income-related employment and support allowance**

You qualify for employment and support allowance (ESA) if you:[3]

• have 'limited capability for work' (see p987); *and*
• are aged 16 or over but under pension age (see p257); *and*
• are in Great Britain (see p167 if you go abroad); *and*
• are not entitled in your own right to statutory sick pay, income support (IS) or jobseeker's allowance (JSA), and are not in a couple entitled to joint-claim JSA (see p247); *and*
• are not doing any work (except work you can do while claiming – see p1019).

The above conditions apply to both types of ESA. To qualify for income-related ESA, you must also satisfy extra rules (see p163).

You cannot usually qualify for income-related ESA if you are pension age or over. However, if you are already getting income-related ESA and you are or become a member of a 'mixed-age couple' (ie, you have reached pension age but your partner has not), in some circumstances your income-related ESA can continue even though you have reached pension age (see p164).

You may qualify for income-related ESA even if you do not qualify for contributory ESA. You may qualify for both income-related ESA and contributory ESA.

Note: if you are already entitled to contributory ESA and do not come under the universal credit (UC) system, you may be able to top this up with income-related ESA without having to make a new claim (see p25).

Some claimants of ESA (but not those in the 'support group' – see p636) must take part in work-focused interviews (see p1110) and some of those can also be required to undertake 'work-related activity' (see p1111).

Extra rules for income-related employment and support allowance

You qualify for income-related ESA if, in addition to satisfying the basic rules of entitlement to ESA on p162:[4]

- your income (see Chapter 20) is less than your applicable amount (see Chapter 17); *and*
- your capital (see Chapter 22) is not over £16,000;[5] *and*
- you are not entitled to pension credit (PC); *and*
- your partner, if you are in a couple (see p303), is not engaged in full-time paid work (p974) or treated as being in full-time paid work (p977); *and*
- your partner is not entitled to income-related ESA, income-based JSA, IS or PC in her/his own right; *and*
- you are not 'receiving education', unless you are entitled to disability living allowance, personal independence payment or armed forces independence payment, in which case you can still qualify for income-related ESA;[6] *and*
- you are not a 'person subject to immigration control' (see p1524);[7] *and*
- you satisfy the 'right to reside' and 'habitual residence' tests (see Chapter 69).[8]

Education

You are in **'education'** if you are a 'qualifying young person' (eg, you are aged under 20 and in full-time, non-advanced education or approved training – see p563) or if you are on a course that is classed as full time.[9] The rules are very similar to those that apply to the definition of full-time courses for IS (see p874). Get advice if you are unsure.

Disqualification from benefit

You can be disqualified from receiving ESA for up to six weeks (or have your benefit paid at a reduced rate if you are a 'person in hardship') in the circumstances described on p633. The rules are the same for both income-related ESA and contributory ESA.

However, the rules for income-related ESA are different from those for contributory ESA if you are:

- absent from Great Britain (see p1627); *or*
- a prisoner or detained in legal custody (see p927).

Part 3: Other means-tested benefits and tax credits
Chapter 9: Income-related employment and support allowance
4. The amount of benefit

2. The rules about your age

To satisfy the basic rules for employment and support allowance (ESA), you must be aged at least 16, but under pension age (see p766). It is your age as the claimant that is relevant, not the age of your partner. However, if you are already getting income-related ESA and are, or become, a member of a 'mixed-age couple' (ie, you have reached pension age but your partner has not) and you are both 'frontier workers', you are prevented from claiming universal credit (see p23), and your income-related ESA continues even though you have reached pension age.[10]

For the rules about housing benefit if you are a member of a mixed-aged couple, see p188.

3. People included in the claim

If you are single, you get income-related employment and support allowance (ESA) for yourself.

If you are a member of a couple (see p303 for who counts), one of you can get income-related ESA for both of you. The applicable amount that forms part of the calculation of your benefit includes a personal allowance for a couple and can include premiums based on both your and your partner's circumstances. When your benefit is worked out, your partner's income and capital are usually added to yours. Whichever one of you gets ESA, the other may qualify for national insurance (NI) credits in order to protect her/his NI record. See Chapter 43 for more details.

ESA does not include amounts for children. However, there are some situations in which you must show that you are 'responsible' for a child who is living in your household – eg:

- to be exempt from compulsory work-focused interviews and work-related activity (see p1110 and p1111);
- for help with your housing costs if you are an owner-occupier (see p347 and p353).

You do not have to be the child's parent. For who counts as a child, see p308. For when you count as responsible for a child and when s/he counts as living in your household, see pp309–311.

4. The amount of benefit

The amount of income-related employment and support allowance (ESA) you get depends on your needs (your 'applicable amount') and how much income and capital you have.

You are paid a limited amount of ESA during an initial **'assessment phase'**. See p635 for more information (the rules on when the assessment phase applies are the same as for contributory ESA). After this, there is a **'main phase'**. During the main phase you may get an additional component included in your applicable amount. For the calculation, see below.

Note:

- You are not entitled during the first seven 'waiting days' of your period of limited capability for work, unless an exception applies (see p634 – the rules are the same as for contributory ESA). You may be able to get a short-term advance before your first payment of ESA is due (see p1153).

- If you are appealing against a decision that you do not have limited capability for work and you get ESA pending the outcome of your appeal (see p1015), you are only paid at the assessment phase rate – ie, you do not get an additional component.

- You are entitled to just one award of ESA, but this may be made up of both contributory ESA and income-related ESA.[11] If you are entitled to both types of ESA, the total amount of ESA payable is the same amount as your income-related ESA, but is made up of contributory ESA topped up with income-related ESA.

Calculating income-related employment and support allowance

Income-related ESA is worked out as follows.

Step one: calculate your applicable amount

Your applicable amount consists of:

- in both the assessment phase (see p635) and the main phase:
  - **a personal allowance** (see p317). Your personal allowance is paid at a lower rate if you are under 25 or, in some cases, if you are under 18, and while you are in the assessment phase (see p635); *and*
  - **premiums** for any special needs (see p323);
- usually in the main phase only: **a support component** (see p636 – the rules are the same as for contributory ESA) or (if you can still get it) **a work-related activity component** (see p637 – the rules are the same as for contributory ESA). **Note:** the work-related activity component was abolished for new claimants from April 2017. In some circumstances (eg, if you are terminally ill), you can be entitled to one of these components during the assessment phase;
- **a 'transitional addition'** if you were transferred from incapacity benefit, severe disablement allowance or income support (IS) on grounds of disability to ESA, and were entitled to income-related ESA as part of the transfer (eg, because your ESA would have been less than your IS, or on transfer your

Part 3: Other means-tested benefits and tax credits
Chapter 9: Income-related employment and support allowance
4. The amount of benefit

contributory ESA should have been topped up with income-related ESA). See p26 for more on the transfer process. Although your ESA can continue to include a transitional addition, it is reduced by increases in your ESA.

You cannot get help with your mortgage interest costs in your income-related ESA applicable amount. Instead, you may be able to get a loan from the DWP (see p839).

For more details on applicable amounts, see Chapter 17.

Step two: calculate your income

This is the amount you have coming in each week from, for instance, other benefits, part-time earnings, working tax credit and maintenance (see Chapter 20). If you have capital over £6,000 (£10,000 if you live in a care home), it also includes your tariff income (see p427).

Step three: deduct income from applicable amount

If your income is less than your applicable amount, your income-related ESA equals the difference between the two. If your income is the same as or more than your applicable amount, you are not entitled to ESA.

Example

Luke is aged 35 and is getting ESA. He lives with his wife, Maeve, and six-year-old son. They get child benefit and child tax credit (CTC). Maeve works 10 hours a week and earns £100 a week. Luke is assessed as being entitled to a support component. He has not paid enough national insurance contributions to get contributory ESA.

Assessment phase

In practice, this phase will already have been served in Luke's case. There would have been an applicable amount consisting just of a personal allowance for a couple aged 18 or over, but no additional component, and on the facts of his case no premiums applied in the assessment phase.

Income taken into account: £80 (child benefit and CTC ignored; £20 earnings disregard applied)

Main phase

Applicable amount = £187 (personal allowance of £121.05 for couple both aged 18 or over *plus* an enhanced disability premium (at the couple rate) of £25.35 *plus* a support component of £40.60)

Income to be taken into account (child benefit and CTC ignored; £20 earnings disregard applies) = £80

Luke's income-related ESA during the main phase is £187 *minus* £80 = £107

Note:
- If you are not currently entitled to ESA because of the level of your income, but will be when a component is included in your applicable amount, you may be given an **'advance award'**. Under this, you are entitled from the point the additional component is awarded, provided you still satisfy the other conditions, without needing to claim again.[12]
- Earnings you receive for 'permitted work' (see p1019) are disregarded when calculating the amount of your income-related ESA.

Your ESA may be reduced if:
- you do not comply with a requirement to attend work-focused interviews and work-related activity (see p1110 and p1111). **Note:** these requirements do not apply if you are entitled to a support component; *or*
- you are disqualified from ESA but are a person in 'hardship' (see p633 – the rules are the same as for contributory ESA); *or*
- you have committed a benefit offence (see p1239).

5. Special benefit rules

Special rules may apply to:
- people subject to immigration control (see Chapter 68);
- people who have come from abroad (see Chapter 69) or are going abroad (see Chapter 70);
- people who are living in a care home or similar accommodation, or people in prison or detention (see Chapter 42).

6. Claims and backdating

There are now very few people who can make a new claim for income-related ESA (see p161). If you can make a new claim, the general rules about claims and backdating are covered in Chapter 50. For the specific rules that apply to income-related ESA, see pp166–68 of the 2020/21 edition of this *Handbook*.

7. Getting paid

As income-related and contributory employment and support allowance (ESA) are two types of the same benefit, the rules described on p645 on getting paid contributory ESA also apply to income-related ESA.

Part 3: Other means-tested benefits and tax credits
Chapter 9: Income-related employment and support allowance
8. Tax, other benefits and the benefit cap

You may be asked to provide information after you are awarded ESA and if you fail to do so, your ESA could be suspended or even terminated (see p1162).

For details of when your income-related ESA might be paid at a reduced rate, see p166.

Income-related employment and support allowance run-on

If you are getting income-related ESA and make a new claim for universal credit (UC), your income-related ESA entitlement continues for two weeks (called a 'run-on payment' or a 'transitional income-related ESA payment'), as long as you would otherwise have remained entitled.[13] You do not have to make a claim for a run-on payment. It should be made automatically. You do not have to pay a run-on payment back and it does not count as a specified benefit for the purposes of the benefit cap (see p1156).[14]

Change of circumstances

You must report changes in your circumstances that you have been told to report, as well as any that you might reasonably be expected to know might affect your right to, the amount of or the payment of your benefit. You should do this as soon as possible, preferably in writing. See p1160 for further information.

Note: if you become a member of a couple with someone entitled to UC, your entitlement to income-related ESA ends (see p31).

8. Tax, other benefits and the benefit cap

Tax

Income-related employment and support allowance (ESA) is not taxable.[15]

Means-tested benefits and tax credits

If you are entitled to income-related ESA:
- it is an automatic passport to maximum housing benefit (HB). If you are not entitled to HB already, you must make a separate claim (if you still can). It is also an automatic passport to maximum child tax credit (CTC) and usually to maximum working tax credit (WTC). In Scotland, income-related ESA is a qualifying benefit for Scottish child payment (see p1731);
- you and your partner may be able to claim WTC if your partner works at least 16 hours but less than 24 hours a week, and you can still make a new claim (see p284). You and your partner may be able to claim WTC as well as, or instead of, income-related ESA. Get advice about whether you can still make a new claim and, if so, how you would be better off financially;

- WTC is taken into account as income when working out your income-related ESA, but CTC is not.

If you or your partner have just stopped work or reduced your hours, you may be able to get 'WTC run-on' for a four-week period (see p289).

Non-means-tested benefits

You can be entitled to income-related ESA and contributory ESA at the same time.

While you are on income-related ESA, you get national insurance credits for limited capability for work (see p954).

You are not entitled to ESA if you are entitled to statutory sick pay.[16]

Most non-means-tested benefits are taken into account as income when working out the amount of income-related ESA you get. However:

- attendance allowance, disability living allowance, child disability payment, personal independence payment, adult disability payment, guardian's allowance and child benefit are not taken into account;
- it can still be worth claiming non-means-tested benefits. If you or your partner qualify for certain of these, you also qualify for certain premiums and therefore a higher rate of income-related ESA.

You cannot get ESA and jobseeker's allowance (JSA) in your own right at the same time. If your partner is entitled to contribution-based JSA, you can get ESA (but note that you can only make a new claim for income-related ESA in very limited circumstances – see p161). Your partner's JSA is taken into account when assessing your income for income-related ESA.

The benefit cap

In some cases, there is a limit on the total amount of specified benefits you can receive (a 'benefit cap'). ESA is one of the specified benefits. However, the benefit cap does *not* apply if you or your partner receive ESA which includes a support component. In other cases, it only applies if you are getting universal credit or HB. See p1156 for further information.

Passports and other sources of help

If you are entitled to income-related ESA, you also qualify for health benefits such as free prescriptions (see Chapter 31) and education benefits such as free school lunches (see p851). You may also qualify for social fund payments (see Chapter 37) or, in Scotland, a Best Start grant (see Chapter 74) or a funeral support payment (see Chapter 76). You may be entitled to a council tax reduction (see p836).

Part 3: Other means-tested benefits and tax credits
Chapter 9: Income-related employment and support allowance
Notes

Financial help on starting work

If you stop getting income-related ESA because you or your partner start work, or your partner's earnings or hours in her/his existing job increase, you might be able to get housing costs run-on if you have had those included (see p359) or a mortgage interest run-on if you have been getting a loan for your mortgage interest payments (see p845), or extended payments of HB if you pay rent (see p217). Your local authority may also provide extended help with council tax. See p858 for information about other financial help you might get.

Notes

1 Art 5A WRA(No.9)O
2 Reg 4 UC(TP) Regs

1. Who can get income-related employment and support allowance
3 ss1 and 20(1) WRA 2007; reg 40(1) ESA Regs
4 Sch 1 para 6 WRA 2007
5 Reg 110 ESA Regs
6 Reg 18 ESA Regs; Schs 1 para 2 and 2 para 2 ESA(TP)(EA)(No.2) Regs
7 s115 IAA 1999
8 Reg 70 and Sch 5 para 11 ESA Regs
9 Regs 14-17 ESA Regs

2. The rules about your age
10 Art 8 WRA(No.31)O; HB Circular A9/2019

4. The amount of benefit
11 s6 WRA 2007
12 s5 WRA 2007; reg 146 ESA Regs

7. Getting paid
13 Reg 5 UC(MMP&MA) Regs
14 Reg 8B UC(TP) Regs

8. Tax, other benefits and the benefit cap
15 s677 IT(EP)A 2003
16 s20 WRA 2007

Chapter 10

• •

Housing benefit

This chapter covers:

Key facts

- You can only make a new claim for housing benefit (HB) in limited circumstances.
- HB is a benefit for people on a low income who pay rent.
- You may qualify for HB under two separate sets of rules – what is known as 'working-age HB' or 'pension-age HB'.
- The amount of rent used to calculate the HB you get may be restricted, so HB does not necessarily meet the full amount of rent you must pay.
- HB is a means-tested benefit.
- You do not need to have paid national insurance contributions to qualify.
- You can qualify for HB whether you are in or out of work.
- If you need extra financial assistance to meet your housing costs, you can claim discretionary housing payments to top up your HB.
- A benefit cap may be applied if the total amount of certain benefits you receive exceeds a specified amount and your HB can be reduced.
- HB is administered and paid by local authorities, although it is a national scheme and the rules are mainly determined by DWP regulations.
- If you disagree with an HB decision, you can apply for a revision or a supersession (see Chapter 56), or appeal against it (see Chapter 57). You do *not* have to apply for a mandatory reconsideration before you can appeal.

Part 3: Getting a benefit decision changed
Chapter 10: Housing benefit
1. Who can get housing benefit

New claims for, and continuing entitlement to, housing benefit

You can now only make a **new claim** for HB in limited circumstances (see p173).

If you are already entitled to HB, you can continue to qualify:

– until you claim universal credit (UC) or you become a member of a couple with a partner who is getting UC (see p24 and p31). **Note:** in both cases, you continue to qualify for HB, even if you are entitled to UC, if the HB is for 'specified accommodation' or 'temporary accommodation' (see p173 for what counts); *or*

– until you and your partner are affected by the 'managed migration' transfer process, that is, you are told by the DWP that your HB will end and are invited to claim UC. See p29 for further information, and AskCPAG and CPAG's *Welfare Rights Bulletin* for updates; *or*

– for two weeks after you become entitled to UC (called 'HB run-on' – see p219).

Note: at some point, the DWP will begin to transfer existing 'pension-age HB' claims to pension credit. At the time of writing, this was not due to start until 2025.

1. **Who can get housing benefit**

You qualify for housing benefit (HB) if:[1]

• your income is low enough (see p189 and Chapter 20 (for 'working-age HB') or Chapter 21 (for 'pension-age HB')); *and*

• your capital is worth £16,000 or less (unless you or your partner are getting the guarantee credit of pension credit (PC) – see Chapter 22 (for 'working-age HB') or Chapter 23 (for 'pension-age HB');[2] *and*

• the payments you make can be met by HB (see p175); *and*

• you or your partner count as liable to pay rent (see p176); *and*

• the payments you make are for the home in which you normally live (see p180) or you are only temporarily absent from it; *and*

• you satisfy the 'right to reside' and the 'habitual residence' tests (see Chapter 69); *and*

• you are not a 'person subject to immigration control' (see p1524). There are exceptions to this rule.

Which housing benefit rules apply?

There are two sets of HB rules, and so two different ways you can qualify for HB. You can qualify for what is known as 'working-age HB' or for 'pension-age HB'. See p187 to find out which rules apply to you. **Note:** if you are a member of a 'mixed-age couple' (ie, one of you is at least pension age – see p766 – but not the other), you may qualify for working-age HB instead of pension-age HB, even though one of you is at least pension age. In some cases, if you are, or become, a mixed-age couple, your entitlement to HB can end and you need to claim universal credit (UC) for help with your rent (see p188).

Who can make a new claim for housing benefit

You can only make a new claim for HB in limited circumstances. You can make a new claim for HB if it is for 'specified accommodation' or 'temporary accommodation'; you can get HB for the rent you pay even if you are getting UC.[3] In addition, you can make a new claim for HB if either of the following apply.[4]

- You (and if you are in a couple, you and your partner) are at least pension age (see p766). The DWP intention is that you can make a new claim for pension-age HB in this situation.[5] **Note:** if you are a member of a 'mixed-age couple' (ie, one of you is at least pension age but not the other), you cannot normally make a new claim for HB, but see p174 for the exceptions. If you cannot make a new claim under this rule, check whether you can under any of the other rules in this section.
- Until 30 March 2022, you were prevented from claiming UC because you (or if you are in a couple, you and your partner) were a 'frontier worker' – ie, you are in Great Britain to work but do not live there or in Northern Ireland.

If you cannot make a new claim for HB under any of these rules, or the rules for mixed-age couples on p174, you can make a claim for UC.

Specified and temporary accommodation
'Specified accommodation' is:[6]
– accommodation provided by a relevant body to meet your need for, and where you get, care, support or supervision – eg, supported accommodation for vulnerable young people or for those affected by mental ill health or substance abuse; *or*
– temporary accommodation provided by a local authority or a relevant body because you have left your home because of domestic abuse – eg, a refuge; *or*
– a local authority hostel for homeless people where you get care, support or supervision to assist you to be rehabilitated or resettled within the community; *or*
– 'exempt accommodation' (certain types of supported accommodation – see p387).
For these purposes, a 'relevant body' is a county council in England, housing association, registered charity or voluntary organisation.
Your accommodation is **'temporary accommodation'** if you live in a defined type of homeless accommodation that does not count as 'exempt accommodation' (see p387) and your rent is payable to a local authority or a provider of social housing.[7]

Note:
- If there is a break in your entitlement to HB (eg, you move to a new home in a different local authority area), you can only make a new claim for HB if the rules above, or the rules below that allow claims by mixed-age couples, apply.

Part 3: Getting a benefit decision changed
Chapter 10: Housing benefit
1. Who can get housing benefit

- Although you cannot usually make a claim for HB if you are a UC claimant, you can make a new claim in limited cases for a period before your entitlement to UC starts. You must notify the local authority of your intention to claim HB before the date of your UC claim.[8]
- If you are a UC claimant and reach pension age (see p766), you can make a new claim for HB (and for PC) during your last UC assessment period. Your entitlement to HB can then start from the date you reach pension age, even if you are still getting UC.[9] See below if you are a member of couple and your partner is not yet pension age – ie, you are a mixed-age couple.
- If the DWP wants to safeguard or test the efficient administration of UC, it can designate other categories of case that are prevented from claiming UC.[10]

Mixed-age couples

You cannot normally make a new claim for HB if you are a member of a mixed-age couple – ie, if one of you is at least pension age but not the other. If you cannot claim HB under these rules, check whether you can claim under any of the rules on p173. If you cannot make a new claim for HB under any of the rules, you can make a claim for UC.

There are exceptions and you *can* make a new claim for HB if:[11]

- you were at least pension age on 14 May 2019, you were entitled to pension-age HB (see p187) or PC (or both) on that date and have continued to be entitled to some pension-age HB or PC on each day since that date as part of the same mixed-age couple. **Note:** claims for pension-age HB can be backdated by up to three months, so if you claimed backdated pension-age HB by 13 August 2019, you could have been entitled to it on 14 May 2019; *or*
- you are a member of a couple and you are at least pension age and are not entitled to UC either as a single claimant or jointly with your partner because:
    – your partner:
        – has been temporarily absent from home for more than six months; *or*
        – is aged 16 or 17 and is not someone who can get UC as an under-18-year-old (see p36 for who can); *or*
        – is a 'person subject to immigration control' (see Chapter 68); *or*
        – is not in (or treated as in) Great Britain, including if s/he has failed the habitual residence test or right to reside test (see Chapter 69); *or*
        – is a prisoner or serving a sentence while detained in hospital; *or*
        – is a member of a religious order and is fully maintained by the order; *or*
    – you are in a polygamous marriage in specified circumstances.
    In this case, you can claim pension-age HB as a single person; *or*
- you are in a polygamous marriage but are treated as a couple with one of your partners and both of you are at least pension age. In this case, you or the other member of the couple can claim pension-age HB; *or*
- you are at least pension age and are no longer treated as a couple for UC purposes because your partner is expected to be, or has been, absent from your

household for more than six months. In this case, you can claim pension-age HB as a single person.

Note:
- If you become a member of a mixed-age couple while you are entitled to HB, in some situations your entitlement to HB can end and in some it can continue (see p188).
- If you were getting UC jointly with your partner as a member of a mixed-age couple, you are no longer a couple and you are at least pension age, you can claim and qualify for 'pension-age' HB from the first day of the UC assessment period in which you stopped being a couple.[12]

Payments that can be met by housing benefit

HB can meet any of the following types of payment.[13]
- Rent paid in respect of a tenancy. This can include rent or ground rent payable in respect of a lease of 21 years or less.[14] If your lease is for longer than 21 years, the rent or ground rent may be met by PC (or income support (IS), income-based jobseeker's allowance (JSA) or income-related employment and support allowance (ESA)) (see p344).
- Payments in respect of a licence or other permission to occupy premises – eg, if you are a lodger or live in bed and breakfast accommodation. **Note:** for houseboats, this can include continuous cruiser licence payments.[15]
- 'Mesne profits' (in Scotland, 'violent profits'), including payments made if you remain in occupation when a tenancy has been ended.
- Other payments for the use and occupation of premises. This does not include boat licence and mooring permit fees if you live in a houseboat, but see above.[16]
- Payments for eligible service charges (see p196).
- Rent, including mooring charges, for a houseboat.
- Site rent for a caravan or mobile home (but not a tent, although this may be met by PC (or IS, income-based JSA or income-related ESA) – see p344).
- Rent paid on a garage or land (unless used for business purposes). Either you must be making a reasonable effort to end your liability for it, or you must have been unable to rent your home without it.[17]
- Contributions made by a resident of a charity's almshouse.
- Payments made under a rental purchase agreement under which the purchase price is paid in more than one instalment and you do not finally own your home until all, or an agreed part of, the purchase price has been paid.
- In Scotland, payments in respect of croft land.

In this *Handbook*, we refer to any of these payments as 'rent'. The payment must be in return for your occupation of the home. This usually means that the payments must be made to the person who has the right to let you occupy it, or someone acting on her/his behalf, but payments to someone else might qualify.

Part 3: Getting a benefit decision changed
Chapter 10: Housing benefit
1. Who can get housing benefit

This depends on, for example, whether you have a valid tenancy agreement with that person.[18]

Payments that cannot be met by housing benefit

HB cannot meet any of the following types of payments – ie, payments made:[19]

- by an owner or under a long tenancy (ie, you own your accommodation or have a lease of more than 21 years), unless you have a shared ownership tenancy – ie, you are only buying a share of your home. In this case, you can get HB for the rent or eligible service charges you pay. You are treated as the owner of the property if you have the right to sell it, even though you may not be able to do so without the consent of other joint owners;[20]
- for a dwelling owned (or part-owned) by your partner;
- by a Crown tenant;
- for a dwelling let by a housing association under a co-ownership scheme under which you receive a payment related to the value of the accommodation when you leave;
- under a hire purchase (eg, for the purchase of a mobile home), credit sale or a conditional sale agreement except to the extent that it is in respect of land.

In some of the above situations, the payments may be met by PC (or IS, income-based JSA or income-related ESA) instead. See Chapter 18 for further information.

Note:

- HB cannot meet payments if you are getting IS, income-based JSA or income-related ESA for these.[21]
- If you live in a care home, you cannot usually get HB for the rent you pay to the home (see p919).

Liability to pay rent

To qualify for HB you must count as liable to pay rent. You count as liable if either you or your partner are liable.[22] You can be treated as liable even if you are not (see p177). You can be treated as not liable even if you are (or can be treated as) liable (see p177). If you pay your rent in advance, you are treated as liable to pay it, even if you paid it before claiming HB.[23] You can be liable to pay rent by yourself or you can be jointly liable to do so (see p180).

For you to be liable to pay rent, your agreement must be legally enforceable.[24] It is not enough if you only have a moral obligation, such as a promise to pay something whenever you can afford to do so. You can count as liable to pay rent even if someone else has been paying it on your behalf, or if your landlord has failed to provide notice of an address so rent is treated as not being due.[25]

Does your agreement have to be in writing?

If you have a written agreement with your landlord, this should establish that you are liable to pay rent, provided the liability is a genuine part of the agreement.[26]

Your agreement can be legally enforceable even if it is not in writing. The fact that you have made a firm promise to pay money to your landlord in return for your occupation of the property should be sufficient to show you are liable to pay rent and so allow you to qualify for HB.[27] If the local authority refuses to accept that you have a legal liability, apply for a revision or appeal.

Note: if you are under 18 years old, you can be liable to pay rent and can qualify for HB (if you can still make a new claim). If you are under 16, there may be a question about whether you have a legally enforceable liability for rent. See p187 of the 2021/22 edition of this *Handbook* for further information.

People treated as liable to pay rent

You are treated as liable to pay rent if:[28]

- you have to pay rent in order to continue to live in your home because the liable person is not doing so; *and*
  - you are the former partner of the liable person; *or*
  - you are not the former partner of the liable person and it is reasonable to treat you as liable.[29] It must be reasonable in all of the circumstances, and in light of the overall purpose of the HB scheme.[30]

  It does not matter whether or not the landlord is prepared to transfer the tenancy to you or wants to evict you.[31] If the local authority refuses your HB claim, point out that the eligibility rules for HB and for transferring tenancies are separate, and apply for a revision or appeal; *or*
- your landlord allows you a rent-free period as compensation for carrying out repairs or redecoration which s/he would otherwise have had to carry out (for a maximum of eight benefit weeks in a rent-free period). If you expect the work to last longer, arrange with your landlord to schedule the work in periods of eight weeks or less, separated by at least one complete benefit week in which you resume paying rent; *or*
- you are the partner of a full-time student who is treated as not liable to pay rent. This means that you can qualify for HB even if your partner cannot.

Even if you fall into one of these categories, in certain circumstances you can still be treated as not liable to pay rent, and so not entitled to HB.

People treated as not liable to pay rent

Even if you or your partner are liable to pay rent, you can be treated as though you are not liable. In this case, you cannot qualify for HB. This applies if you are in any of the following situations.[32]

Part 3: Getting a benefit decision changed
Chapter 10: Housing benefit
1. Who can get housing benefit

- You are a full-time student. This does *not* apply if you are getting pension-age HB (see p187) or if you are a student who can qualify for HB (see p883) and you are getting working-age HB (see p187).
- You do not satisfy the habitual residence test (see p1550).
- You are a member of, and are fully maintained by, a religious order.[33]
- You are living in a care home or an independent hospital (but see p919).[34]
- You pay rent to someone who also lives in the dwelling and who is your (or your partner's) close relative (see p179 for who counts).[35] Your landlord might be regarded as living in your dwelling if you share some accommodation with her/him, other than a bathroom, toilet or a hall or passageway.[36] It does not matter if you use the accommodation at different times or if you pay to use it.[37]
- Your agreement to pay rent is not on a commercial basis.[38] It is what you and your landlord have agreed, not what you or your landlord have later done or omitted to do that is relevant.[39] In deciding whether or not your agreement is commercial, the local authority must look at the whole agreement, taking all the circumstances into account. It must consider, among other things:[40]
  - whether your agreement includes terms that are not legally enforceable;
  - the rent you must pay under the agreement. It does not have to be a market rent. Paying a low rent does not necessarily mean your agreement is not commercial – eg, if you do chores in exchange for a lower rent. Your agreement can count as commercial even if your landlord is not collecting the full contractual rent from you;
  - your relationship to your landlord. However, just because you are a relative of, or have a close friendship with, her/him, or s/he provides you with care and support, does not mean that your agreement is non-commercial.
- You are renting from:[41]
  - any ex-partner of yours and the home is your former joint home with that ex-partner; *or*
  - any ex-partner of your partner and the home is your partner's former joint home with that ex-partner.
- You or your partner are responsible for a child (under 16) of a person who is your landlord.[42] This only applies if the child is included in your HB claim.
- You or your partner, or an ex-partner or close relative of either of you, who lives with you, is either:[43]
  - a director or employee of a company which is your landlord; *or*
  - a trustee or beneficiary of a trust which is your landlord.
  This rule does not apply if you can show the arrangement was not intended to take advantage of the HB scheme (see p179).
- You are renting accommodation from a trustee of a trust, of which your (or your partner's) child (under 16) is a beneficiary.
- You were previously the non-dependant (see p198) of someone who lived, and continues to live, in the accommodation. This rule does not apply if you can

show that the agreement was not created to take advantage of the HB scheme (see below).[44]

- You or your current partner previously owned, or had a long tenancy in (ie, a lease of more than 21 years), the accommodation and less than five years have passed since you last owned it (or the tenancy ceased).[45]

  This rule does not apply if you can show that you could not have continued to occupy the accommodation without giving up ownership (or the tenancy) – eg, the lender was seeking possession of your home. Whether you were legally or practically compelled to give up ownership or the tenancy is relevant, but your motivation for doing so is not.[46] You do not have to be in immediate danger of having to leave your home for this exception to apply.[47] You may need to show that you have taken steps to explore alternatives.[48]

- You or your partner are employed by your landlord and are occupying your accommodation as a condition of employment. This should not apply if you continue to live in the accommodation after ceasing employment.

- If none of the above apply, the local authority considers that your liability to pay rent has been created to take advantage of the HB scheme (see below).

Close relatives

A '**close relative**' is a parent, parent-in-law (including a civil partner's parent), son, son-in-law (including a son's civil partner), daughter, daughter-in-law (including a daughter's civil partner), brother, sister, step-parent (including a parent's civil partner), stepson (including a civil partner's son), stepdaughter (including a civil partner's daughter), or the partners of any of these.[49] It also includes half-brothers and half-sisters.[50] Relations with in-laws or steprelatives are severed by divorce (or dissolution of a civil partnership) but arguably not by death – eg, a stepchild is still a stepchild after the death of her/his mother.[51]

Agreements taking advantage of the housing benefit scheme

For your agreement to count as 'taking advantage of the HB scheme', it must amount to an abuse of the scheme or to taking improper advantage of it. It must be shown that the main reason you entered into the agreement was to obtain HB.[52] All the circumstances should be taken into account, including what your landlord has to say.[53] An agreement can count as taking advantage of the HB scheme even if it was created from the best of motives.[54] Bear the following in mind.

- You should *not* be seen as taking advantage of the HB scheme just because:
  - your landlord is your parent;[55] *or*
  - you hope to be able to claim HB to help you with your rent – ie, if your main purpose is to get accommodation, not to obtain HB;[56] *or*
  - you seek to find out what rent can be covered by HB before moving in.

Part 3: Getting a benefit decision changed
Chapter 10: Housing benefit
1. Who can get housing benefit

3

- If you are a tenant of a landlord who deliberately charges high rents in order to have them paid by HB, you may be affected by this provision, even though you had no such intention yourself. Argue that a high rent, in itself, does not mean that the liability takes advantage of the HB scheme.[57]
- If your landlord says s/he will evict you if you cannot get HB, this suggests that the agreement does *not* take advantage of the HB scheme.[58]

If the local authority says your agreement is taking advantage of the HB scheme and that you are therefore not entitled to HB, you can appeal.

Joint liability

If you are a member of a couple (see p303) and are jointly liable for the rent, only one of you can claim HB.[59]

The way a group of single people living together and paying rent to their landlord is treated depends on how many of you are liable under the agreement. If all, or some, of you have joint liability for the rent, you can each make a separate claim and be paid HB on your share (unless the local authority thinks the joint tenancy has been created to take advantage of the HB scheme – see p179).

If you live in shared accommodation with people other than your partner and children included in your claim, and are jointly liable for the rent with them, see p194 for how this affects the calculation of your benefit – ie, how your eligible rent is apportioned between you.

Occupying accommodation as your home

HB is paid for the home in which you and your partner and any children included in your claim (see p307) normally live.[60] You cannot usually be paid for any other home. However, there are special rules if you:

- have just moved into your home (see p181);
- are temporarily absent from home (see p181);
- are liable to pay rent on more than one home (see p185);
- are in certain other situations (see p186).

If you occupy more than one property or room as your home (eg, because you have a large family and rent adjacent flats, or have a live-in carer and rent two adjacent rooms in shared accommodation), you can argue that both properties or rooms count as part of your home – ie, that you only have one home.[61]

If you have to live in an approved bail or probation hostel or are a prisoner on temporary release, you are treated as not occupying the accommodation in which you are staying.[62] You cannot qualify for HB for any rent you pay for the hostel, but you may be able to qualify for HB for your normal home. See p181 for the rules on temporary absence from home.

Moving home

If you have just moved into your home but were liable to pay rent before moving in, you can get HB on your new home for up to four weeks before you moved in. If you must pay rent for your old home as well as your new accommodation, you can only get HB for one of these unless you are covered by the rules described on p185.[63] You only qualify if the delay in moving was reasonable and:[64]

- you were waiting for a payment from a local welfare assistance scheme or the Scottish Welfare Fund or a social fund payment for a need connected with the move – eg, removal expenses or to help you set up home. This only applies if:
  - you have a child aged five or under living with you; or
  - you are getting pension-age HB; or
  - you are getting working-age HB and you qualify for a disability, severe disability or disabled child premium, or a support component, or you or your partner are a member of the work-related activity group (see p638); or
- you were waiting for adaptations to be finished to meet needs you, your partner or a child included in your claim (see p307) have because of a disability. The adaptations do not have to involve a change to the fabric or structure of the dwelling, but must be reasonably required and have a clear connection to the disability needs;[65] or
- you became liable to make payments on your new home while you were a hospital patient or in residential accommodation (see p184 for the meaning).

Before moving, you must either have claimed HB or have notified the local authority of the move. If you have given up your previous home and have no other home, you can argue that the date you move in is the date you move your furniture and belongings in.[66] Your HB is not paid until you move in. If an earlier claim for HB you made before you moved in was turned down, you must claim again within four weeks of moving to qualify.

If you are not liable to pay rent for your new accommodation

If you move and are not liable to pay rent in your new accommodation (eg, if you are now staying with a relative or are in prison or hospital and you cannot get HB while temporarily absent from home), you can get HB for up to four weeks for your former home if you:[67]

- were liable for rent on it immediately before moving and continue to be liable – eg, because you have to give notice to your landlord; and
- could not reasonably have avoided liability for rent on your former home.

Temporary absence from home

If you are temporarily absent from your normal home, you can qualify for HB for a period, provided you have not rented out your home and you intend to return to it.[68] The length of time you can be away depends on the circumstances and on whether you are absent from home in or outside Great Britain. You can argue that

Part 3: Getting a benefit decision changed
Chapter 10: Housing benefit
1. Who can get housing benefit

you count as temporarily absent from your home even if you have not yet stayed there – eg, you move your furniture and belongings in, but then have to go into hospital.[69] **Note:** you can claim and qualify for HB while you are temporarily absent from home, even if you were not getting HB before you left.

You can get HB while you are absent from your normal home for up to:

- **13 weeks**, whatever the reason for your absence (see below); *or*
- **52 weeks**, if you are in any of the situations described on p183.

The period can be shorter if you are, or have been, absent from Great Britain (see p184).

The number of weeks runs from the date you leave home.[70] The day you leave home is included, but not the day you return home.[71] If, for example, you have been away from home for 10 weeks and then have grounds to continue to get HB for 52 weeks, you only get HB for the balance: 42 weeks. A new period of absence starts if you return home for even a short stay. A stay of at least 24 hours may be enough.[72] **Note:** if you are a prisoner on temporary release, you continue to be treated as absent from home.[73]

The local authority may use these rules to decide:

- if someone living with you who is temporarily absent from home (eg, s/he is a student who is away during term time) is a non-dependant (see p198);[74] *or*
- whether your partner, or a child or young person included in your claim, counts as occupying your home.

Will you be away from home temporarily?

1. Let the local authority know that you are going to be absent from your normal home and the reason for this, as well as if you will be absent from Great Britain, preferably before you go away. Make it clear that your absence will be temporary and that you are unlikely to be away for longer than the period allowed.

2. Your intention to return, and whether or not you are unlikely to be away for longer than the period allowed, should be based initially on the circumstances on the date you leave your home, unless you are in residential accommodation for a trial period.[75]

3. If, at any time after the date you leave your home, you no longer intend to return or it becomes likely that you will be away from home (or absent from Great Britain) for longer than the period allowed, inform the local authority of this change in your circumstances to avoid an overpayment. In this case, the local authority can reconsider your entitlement.[76] If you initially told the local authority you were going to be away from home for more than the period allowed, but realise that your absence will now be shorter, it should also reconsider your entitlement.

Housing benefit for up to 13 weeks

You can get HB for up to 13 weeks while you are absent from your normal home and you are in Great Britain.[77] It does not matter why you are away from home.

You must be unlikely to be away for more than 13 weeks. Within the 13-week period, you can be absent from Great Britain for up to four weeks. The four-week period can be extended by up to another four weeks in limited cases (see p184).

Housing benefit for up to 52 weeks

You can get HB while you are in Great Britain in residential accommodation (see p184 for the meaning) for a trial period to see whether it suits your needs.[78] On the date you enter the accommodation, you must intend to return home if it is not suitable.[79] You get HB for up to 13 weeks. If the accommodation does not suit your needs, you can have further 13-week trial periods in other accommodation and get HB for further 13-week periods, provided you are not away from home for more than 52 weeks in total.

You can get HB for up to 52 weeks if you are absent from your normal home within Great Britain if you are unlikely to be away for longer than this (or, in exceptional circumstances, unlikely to be away for substantially longer than this) in the situations listed below.[80] Within the 52-week period, you can be absent from Great Britain for up to four or 26 weeks at a time as the case may be (see below and p184). The four-week period can be extended by up to another four weeks in limited cases.

You can get HB for up to 52 weeks if you are absent from home within Great Britain in the following circumstances.[81] Within the 52-week period, you can get HB while you are temporarily absent from Great Britain for up to 26 weeks (see p184).

- You are **resident in a hospital or similar institution** as a patient. You cannot get HB after you have been resident in hospital for 52 weeks, even if this is because you are seriously mentally ill. **Note:** a new period of absence starts if you return home for even a short stay.[82]
- You, your partner or a 'dependent child' under 16 are **undergoing medical treatment or medically approved convalescence**, other than in residential accommodation (see below for the meaning). 'Dependent child' is not defined in the rules, so could include children who are not included in your claim.
- You are **receiving 'medically approved' care** (ie, certified by a medical practitioner), other than in residential accommodation (see p184 for the meaning).
- You are away from home because of a **fear of violence**. Argue that fear of controlling behaviour or of psychological, physical, sexual, financial and emotional abuse should count.[83] You need not have experienced actual violence, but you must be in fear of violence in your home or from a former partner, or a child or qualifying young person previously included in your claim. Violence in your home includes violence by neighbours and hate crimes directed at your home. See p185 if you need to claim for two homes and p186 if you do not intend to return to your former home.

Part 3: Getting a benefit decision changed
Chapter 10: Housing benefit
1. Who can get housing benefit

You can also get HB for up to 52 weeks if you are absent from home within Great Britain in the following circumstances.[84] Within the 52-week period, you can get HB while you are temporarily absent from Great Britain for up to four weeks (see below).

- You are a **remand prisoner** held in custody pending trial or sentence. Once you are sentenced, you no longer qualify for HB under this rule, but might still qualify under the 13-week rule on p182. The 13 weeks run from the date you were first in prison, so any time you spend in prison awaiting trial or sentence counts towards the 13 weeks. **Note:** you are treated as still in custody if you are on temporary release.[85]
- You are required to live in an approved hostel or at an address away from your normal home as a **condition of bail**.
- You are **providing 'medically approved' care** – ie, certified by a medical practitioner.
- You are **caring for a child** under 16 whose parent or guardian is away from home receiving medically approved care or medical treatment.
- You are **undertaking a training course** (see below).
- You are a **student**. You must not come into the first category under 'Other situations' on p186, or be entitled to HB on two homes (see p185).
- You are in residential accommodation for **short-term or respite care**.

Definitions[86]
'Residential accommodation' means a care home, an independent hospital or an Abbeyfield home. It also means an establishment managed or provided by a body incorporated by Royal Charter or constituted by an Act of Parliament, other than a local social services authority.

A **'training course'** is a course of training or instruction provided by or on behalf of, or approved by, a government department, the Secretary of State, Skills Development Scotland, Scottish Enterprise or Highlands and Islands Enterprise.

Absence from Great Britain
You can get HB while you are temporarily absent from Great Britain for up to:
- **four weeks**, whatever the reason.[87] You must be unlikely to be away for longer than four weeks; *or*
- **eight weeks**, if you are temporarily absent from Great Britain in connection with the death of your partner or a child or young person included in your claim (see p307), or the death of your or your partner's or child's or young person's close relative and the local authority thinks it is unreasonable to expect you to return to Great Britain within four weeks; *or*
- **four or 26 weeks**, in the situations in which you can get HB while absent from home for up to 52 weeks (see p183). You must be unlikely to be away for longer

than this (or, in exceptional circumstances, unlikely to be away for substantially longer than this);[88]

- **26 weeks**, while you are absent from Great Britain as a member of the armed forces posted overseas, a mariner or a continental shelf worker. You must be unlikely to be away for longer than 26 weeks.[89]

The number of weeks runs from the first day of absence from Great Britain.[90] The 13 or 52 weeks you are allowed to be absent from home *in* Great Britain continue to run during any period you are absent from Great Britain.[91] When you return to Great Britain, if you are still away from your normal home, you can continue to get HB for the remainder (if any) of the 13- or 52-week period allowed. However, if your HB ceased because you were no longer treated as occupying your normal home (eg, because you had been absent from Great Britain too long), you cannot qualify for HB until you return home.[92] **Note:** if you are a European Economic Area (EEA) national and have a right to reside in the UK and go abroad to an EEA state, see p1629.

Examples

Jason visits his mother in London for a week before going on a three-week holiday to France. He lets the local authority know this and also that he plans to visit his sister in Manchester for two weeks on the way home. He can be absent from home for up to 13 weeks and absent from Great Britain for up to four weeks within that period. He gets HB for 1 + 3 + 2 = 6 weeks while he is temporarily absent from home.

Molly travels to Canada to visit her grandmother for two weeks. At the end of the second week, she notifies the local authority that she intends to stay a further three weeks. She is no longer treated as occupying her normal home because she is going to be absent from Great Britain for longer than four weeks. She therefore only gets HB for two weeks.

Kim goes on a training course in York. She notifies the local authority that she will be away from home for 20 weeks. During the 20-week course, she will be on a placement in France for two weeks. Kim therefore continues to get HB for the 20-week period she is away from home (18 weeks in Great Britain and two weeks outside Great Britain).

Housing benefit for more than one home

You can usually only get HB for one home. **Note:** if you occupy more than one property as a home (eg, you rent adjacent flats because you have a large family or two adjacent rooms in shared accommodation because you have a live-in carer), you can argue that you only have one home.[93]

If you occupy two homes, you can get HB:

- **for up to four weeks** for your new and your old home, if:[94]
  - you have moved into the new home and you could not reasonably avoid having to pay rent on your old home.[95] The local authority must consider

Part 3: Getting a benefit decision changed
Chapter 10: Housing benefit
1. Who can get housing benefit

the reasons why you had to move quickly – eg, if you were forced to move quickly to take advantage of better accommodation, you may not have been able to avoid leaving without giving notice; *or*
- a move was delayed while you were adapting your new home to meet needs you, your partner or a child included in your claim have because of disability. You can get HB on both homes for the four weeks prior to the date you move. The adaptations do not have to involve a change to the fabric or structure of the dwelling, but must be reasonably required and have a clear connection to the disability needs;[96]
- **for up to 52 weeks** for a temporary home and your normal home, if you have left your home because of a fear of violence (see p183 for the meaning). You must intend to return to your normal home, and it must be reasonable for you to receive payments for both homes. The payments can be either HB or UC. For example, if your temporary home counts as 'specified accommodation' or 'temporary accommodation' (see p173), you can get HB for it, and HB (or a UC housing costs element) for the rent you pay for your normal home;[97]
- **indefinitely** for your two normal homes, if:[98]
  - you are a member of a couple and you or your partner are a student eligible for HB (see p883) or are on a training course (see p184 for the meaning), it is necessary for you to live apart and it is reasonable for you to receive HB for both homes; *or*
  - the local authority has housed you in more than one home because your family is large.

Other situations

If you have left your home because of a **fear of violence** (see p183 for the meaning) and you do not intend to return, you can get HB for four weeks for your former home.[99] You can only get HB for your former home if your liability to pay rent was unavoidable – eg, you should have given your landlord notice, but had to leave in a hurry.

If you have two homes, and you are only liable to pay for one of them, you are treated as occupying the home for which you pay and therefore get HB for that home, even when you are not there. This only applies if:[100]
- you are a single claimant or a lone parent, and you are either a student eligible for HB (see p883) or are on a training course (see p184), and you live in one home during periods of study or training and another home at other times – eg, for vacations; *or*
- you had to move into temporary accommodation because essential repairs are being carried out on your main home. 'Essential repairs' means basic works rather than luxuries, but they need not be crucial to making the house habitable.[101]

Note: you cannot get HB under this rule if you pay rent for both homes, or if you pay rent for one and a mortgage on the other.

2. **The rules about your age**

There are no lower or upper age limits for claiming housing benefit (HB). However, if you are:

- under 16, there may be a question about whether you have a legally enforceable liability for rent (see p176);
- 16 or 17 and are being, or have been, looked after by a local authority, you cannot usually qualify for HB. See p933 for further information;
- a single claimant under 35 and are living in private rented accommodation, the amount of your rent is usually restricted – ie, the amount of rent that can be met by HB is based on that for shared accommodation (see Chapter 19).

Working-age or pension-age housing benefit

You can qualify for HB under two different sets of rules – ie, for 'working-age HB' or 'pension-age HB'.[102] Which rules apply usually depends on your (and your partner's) age. See below if you are a member of a mixed-age couple – ie, if one of you is at least pension age but not the other.

You can qualify for **working-age HB** if:[103]

- you are not yet pension age; *or*
- you are at least pension age but you or your partner are on income support (IS), income-based jobseeker's allowance (JSA), income-related employment and support allowance (ESA) or universal credit (UC).

You can qualify for **pension-age HB** if:[104]

- you are at least pension age; *and*
- neither you nor your partner are on IS, income-based JSA, income-related ESA or UC.

You do *not* have to be getting pension credit (PC) to qualify for pension-age HB.

Most of the rules are the same, but there are some differences. For example, if you get pension-age HB, your applicable amount is higher than for working-age HB and the income and capital rules are more generous. Pension-age HB can be backdated for up to three months, but working-age HB can only be backdated for up to one month.

Mixed-age couples

If you are a member of a 'mixed-age couple' (ie, one of you is at least pension age but not the other):

- since 15 May 2019, you can only make a new claim for HB and for PC in limited circumstances (see p173 and p257). You may have to claim UC or working-age HB (if you still can) instead of pension-age HB, even though one of you is at least pension age;

Part 3: Getting a benefit decision changed
Chapter 10: Housing benefit
2. The rules about your age

- in some situations, your HB entitlement can end (see below). If your entitlement to both HB and PC ends, you can claim UC.

When housing benefit ends if you are in a 'mixed-age couple'

If you were entitled to pension-age HB before 15 May 2019, your entitlement can continue and, in limited cases, you can make a new claim (see p173). However, your entitlement to HB can end if you are, or become, a member of a 'mixed-age couple', if your entitlement to pension-age HB as a member of that couple would otherwise start on or after 15 May 2019.

Your entitlement to HB ends:[105]

- when you become a member of a mixed-age couple. This applies if you were not in a mixed-age couple when you were awarded HB – eg, because you were getting pension-age HB as a single person; *or*
- when you reach pension age so you are now a member of a mixed-age couple, if you were getting working-age HB while you and your partner were both under pension age; *or*
- if you are pension age, are a member of a mixed-age couple and are getting working-age HB because you (or your partner) are on IS, income-based JSA, income-related ESA or UC, when entitlement to that benefit ends.

Your HB entitlement ends on the date the change takes effect under under the HB rules (see p222).

Note: your entitlement to HB does *not* end, even if you are a member of a mixed-age couple, if:

- the HB is for 'specified accommodation' or 'temporary accommodation' (see p173 for what counts);[106] *or*
- you are not yet pension age, are getting working-age HB and are on IS, income-based JSA or income-related ESA when your partner reaches pension age; *or*
- you are at least pension age and are prevented from claiming UC (see p173) and, in addition, you cannot qualify for PC or pension-age HB because you are a member of a mixed-age couple. In this case, you are treated as not yet pension age so your award of working-age HB can continue.[107] If you are also getting IS, income-based JSA or income-related ESA, your entitlement to that benefit can also continue under this rule.

Examples
Femi and Lisa are a couple, both under pension age. Femi has been getting working-age HB while in low-paid work. When he reaches pension age, his HB entitlement ends. He cannot make a new claim for pension-age HB because he is now a member of a mixed-age couple. He and Lisa can make a joint claim for UC.

Seren is getting pension-age HB. She and her partner Gareth decide to live together. Gareth is not yet pension age. Seren's HB entitlement ends. She and Gareth can make a joint claim for UC.

Dot and Elsa are a couple. Dot gets working-age HB and income-based JSA. When Elsa reaches pension age, Dot's entitlement to HB and income-based JSA continues, even though she is now a member of a mixed-age couple. Dot gets a full-time job and her entitlement to income-based JSA ends. Her entitlement to working-age HB therefore also ends. She and Elsa can make a joint claim for UC.

3. People included in the claim

You get housing benefit (HB) for yourself. However, if you are a member of a couple, only one of you can qualify for HB; you or your partner get HB for you both. Your applicable amount includes a personal allowance for a couple and can include premiums and components based on both your and your partner's circumstances. When your benefit is worked out, your partner's income and capital are usually added to yours. See p303 for who counts as a couple.

There are some situations in which you must show that you are 'responsible' for a child who is living in your household – eg:

- so your applicable amount can include allowances and premiums for a child(ren);
- to show you are a lone parent so you can benefit from a higher earnings disregard (see p414 and p456);
- to qualify for a disregard of earnings for childcare costs (see p416 and p458);
- for some of the rules about the size of accommodation or the number of bedrooms you are allowed that affect your maximum HB (see Chapter 19).

See p308 for who counts as a child (this includes some qualifying young people). You do not have to be the child's parent. For when you count as responsible for a child, and when s/he counts as living in your household, see pp309–312.

4. The amount of benefit

The amount of housing benefit (HB) you get depends on:

- your 'applicable amount' (see Chapter 17). This is made up of personal allowances, as well as premiums and components based on your circumstances. It may include a transitional addition if you or your partner were transferred to contributory employment and support allowance (ESA), or appealed a decision not to transfer you to ESA. For more information about the transitional addition, see p356 of the 2019/20 edition of this *Handbook*;
- your 'maximum HB' (see p192);

Part 3: Getting a benefit decision changed
Chapter 10: Housing benefit
4. The amount of benefit

• if you are not on the guarantee credit of pension credit (PC) (or income support (IS), income-based jobseeker's allowance (JSA), income-related ESA or universal credit (UC)), how much:
  – capital you have (see p191 and Chapter 22 (for working-age HB) or Chapter 23 (for pension-age HB)); *and*
  – income you have (see p191 and Chapter 20 (for working-age HB) or Chapter 21 (for pension-age HB)).

For how to calculate HB, if you are on a means-tested benefit, see below, and if you are *not* on a means-tested benefit, see p191.

If you do not qualify for HB currently, you may qualify if you can still make a new claim for HB (see p173) and:

• the benefit rates go up; *or*
• you (or your partner or a child included in your claim) become entitled to another benefit (a 'qualifying benefit' – see p210); *or*
• you or your partner reach pension age (see p766). If you qualify for pension-age HB (see p187), your applicable amount is higher and the income and capital rules are also more generous.

If you need help with the costs of your housing in addition to the HB you get, you may qualify for discretionary housing payments (see Chapter 29).

Note: you might get a reduced amount of HB if:

• you are affected by the benefit cap (see p1156); *or*
• your HB is restricted because of a benefit offence (see p1239).

If you are on a means-tested benefit

Being on the guarantee credit of PC (or IS, income-based JSA, income-related ESA or UC) is an automatic passport to maximum HB because all of your income and capital are ignored.[108] The amount of HB you get is always your 'maximum HB' (see p192 for how to work this out).

For these purposes, you are treated as being on:[109]

• income-based JSA when it is payable to you and also:
  – when you satisfy the conditions of entitlement but are not being paid it because of a sanction (see p1116); *and*
  – on your waiting days (see p253); *and*
  – when it is not paid because of the benefit offence rules (see p1239);
• income-related ESA when it is payable to you and also:
  – when you satisfy the conditions of entitlement but are not being paid it because you are disqualified for the reasons on p163; *and*

Chapter 10

- on your waiting days (see p646). The rules are the same as for contributory ESA;
- UC on any day you are entitled to it, whether or not it is being paid to you.

Example

Rory and his partner are the joint housing association tenants of a two-bedroom flat. Rory's aunt lives with them and counts as a non-dependant. They pay rent of £150 a week. Rory gets income-related ESA. Rory's aunt gets UC. Rory gets working-age HB. None of the rent restriction rules apply so no reduction to the rent is made and the amount of rent that can be covered (the 'eligible rent' – see p193) is £150 a week. Rory's maximum HB is therefore £133.55 a week (£150 *minus* a non-dependant deduction of £16.45).
Because he gets income-related ESA, Rory's HB is £133.55 a week.

If you are not on a means-tested benefit

If you are not on the guarantee credit of PC (or IS, income-based JSA or income-related ESA or UC), follow the steps below to calculate your HB.[110]
- **Step one:** check that your capital is not too high (see Chapter 22 for working-age HB or Chapter 23 for pension-age HB).
- **Step two:** work out your 'maximum HB' (see p192).
- **Step three:** work out your applicable amount (see Chapter 17).
- **Step four:** work out your income (see Chapter 20 (for working-age HB) or Chapter 21 (for pension-age HB), but also p887 if you are a student and p452 if you are getting the savings credit of PC).
- **Step five:** calculate HB.
  - **If your income is less than or equal to your applicable amount**, HB equals your 'maximum HB'.
  - **If your income is greater than your applicable amount**, work out the difference. HB equals your 'maximum HB' minus 65 per cent of the difference between your income and your applicable amount.

Examples

Ben and Jenny are a couple who are joint private tenants. They pay £160 rent a week. Ben is aged 45. He is unemployed. Jenny is aged 46 and works 21 hours a week. She is paid £201.75 a week after deductions of tax and national insurance (NI) contributions. Jenny gets working-age HB. A rent restriction is applied and so the amount of rent that can be covered (her 'eligible rent' – see p193) is £120 a week.
The couple have no non-dependants. Therefore, Jenny's maximum HB (see p192) is £120 a week. Her applicable amount is £121.05 (the standard rate for a couple if one member is at least 18).
Income to be taken into account is £191.75 of Jenny's earnings a week (because £10 of her earnings are disregarded – see p415).

Part 3: Getting a benefit decision changed
Chapter 10: Housing benefit
4. The amount of benefit

The difference between her income and her applicable amount is £70.70 a week (£191.75 – £121.05).

65% x £70.70 = £45.95 a week.

Jenny's HB is therefore £120 (maximum HB) – £45.95 = £74.05 a week.

Ken is 70 years old. He lives alone. He gets pension-age HB. He receives an 'old' retirement pension (see Chapter 36) of £141.85 a week. His weekly income from his private pension is £60. His total weekly income is therefore £201.85 (£141.85 + £60). He is a sole tenant of his one-bedroom council flat. His rent of £125 a week includes his heating and hot water. No reduction is made under any rent restriction rules, but deductions are made for heating and hot water so his 'eligible rent' (see p193) is £85.65 a week (£125 – £35.25 and £4.10). Therefore, his maximum HB is £85.65 because he does not have any non-dependants.

His applicable amount is £197.10 (adult personal allowance for a single person who reached pension age before 1 April 2021).

The difference between his income and his applicable amount is £4.75 (£201.85 – £197.10).

65% x £4.75 = £3.09 a week.

Ken's HB is therefore £85.65 – £3.09 = £82.56 a week.

Maximum housing benefit

In order to calculate your HB, you need to know the maximum amount of HB you can get. Your maximum HB is worked out as follows.[111]

- **Step one:** work out the amount of your rent that can be covered by HB (your 'eligible rent') on a weekly basis. Unless you have any non-dependants for whom a deduction must be made (see p198), this is your maximum HB.
- **Step two:** if you have any non-dependants for whom a deduction must be made, your maximum HB is the figure in Step one, minus the non-dependant deduction(s) (see p198). This is because it is assumed a non-dependant makes a contribution towards your outgoings, whether or not s/he does so.

Example

Stephen and Jody and their adult son live together in a two-bedroom flat rented from the local authority. Stephen is the sole tenant. The rent is £100 a week. This does not include any service charges. Their son earns £150 a week gross.

The amount of rent that can be covered (eligible rent)	£100
Minus non-dependant deduction (see p200)	£37.80
Maximum HB	**£62.20**

Eligible rent

The amount of your rent that can be covered by HB is called your 'eligible rent'. This is not necessarily the rent you pay to your landlord. You need to know your 'eligible rent' to work out your 'maximum HB' (see p192).

Your 'eligible rent' is:[112]

- if any of the rent restriction schemes apply to you, the amount to which your rent is restricted under those rules (known as your 'maximum rent'). See Chapter 19 for details of all the schemes, which one (if any) applies to you and how your rent may be restricted; *or*

- if none of the rent restriction rules apply to you, the amount of rent you must pay your landlord (your contractual rent) minus any ineligible charges (see p194). The local authority has general powers to decrease your eligible rent to an amount it considers appropriate (but see p368).

If your rent has been reduced by a 'provider of social housing' under a government-approved tenant incentive scheme, your eligible rent is worked out as if no reduction had been made.[113] A provider of social housing is a local authority, a non-profit registered provider of social housing, a profit-making registered provider of social housing (if you have been housed in social housing) or a registered social landlord.

Note:

- If you are in shared accommodation and are jointly liable for the rent, your eligible rent might be apportioned between you and the people with whom you share (see p194).

- If the rent you pay covers both residential and other accommodation (eg, for business use), your HB only covers the rent you pay for the residential accommodation.[114] You cannot get HB for any part of your accommodation that is used exclusively for business purposes.

- You cannot get HB for rent supplements charged to clear your rent arrears.[115]

Calculating your weekly eligible rent

HB is always paid for a specific benefit week – a period of seven consecutive days beginning with a Monday and ending on a Sunday.[116] If you pay rent at different intervals (eg, monthly or daily), the amount must be converted to a weekly figure before HB can be calculated.[117]

Rent-free periods

If you have a regular rent-free period (eg, you only pay rent 48 weeks a year), you get no HB during your rent-free period. Your applicable amount, weekly income, non-dependant deductions, the set deductions for meals and fuel charges and the minimum amount payable (but not your eligible rent) are adjusted.[118] This is to ensure that you do not lose or gain benefit by ignoring your circumstances in the weeks that you do not pay rent.

Part 3: Getting a benefit decision changed
Chapter 10: Housing benefit
4. The amount of benefit

This does not apply if your landlord has temporarily waived the rent in return for your doing repairs (see p177).

If you live in shared accommodation

Unless the local housing allowance or social sector rent restriction rules apply to you (see p368 and p375), if you share accommodation with people other than your partner and children included in your claim and are jointly liable for the rent with them (see p180), the local authority apportions your eligible rent between you. If the rent includes any ineligible service charges, these are apportioned between you on the same basis. If only one of you is liable for the rent, that person is treated as the tenant and the other(s) might count as a non-dependant(s) (see p198).

To work out how to apportion your eligible rent, the local authority considers:[119]

- the number of jointly liable people in the property (including any students who are treated as not liable to pay rent);[120] *and*
- the proportion of the rent actually paid by each liable person; *and*
- any other relevant circumstances, such as:
  - the number of rooms occupied by each jointly liable person; *and*
  - whether any formal or informal agreement exists between you regarding the use and occupation of the home; *and*
  - if one of the jointly liable people has left the accommodation, the demands being made by the landlord on those who remain, or the possibility of finding other accommodation.

In some circumstances, it could be appropriate to apportion the whole of the rent to you, even if you are jointly liable.[121]

Example
Chidinma and her sister rent a two-bedroom housing association flat. They are joint tenants and pay rent of £100 a week and this is the 'eligible rent'. Chidinma claims pension-age HB. The eligible rent is apportioned between her and her sister. Chidinma's HB is based on £50 (£100 divided by two).

Note: if the local housing allowance or social sector rules apply to you, it is not necessary to apportion the eligible rent in this way, but the local authority does apportion the rent when looking at whether a restriction applies. See Chapter 19 for details.

Ineligible charges

The local authority normally deducts ineligible charges when it works out the amount of your eligible rent. **Note:** if your rent is restricted under the local housing allowance rules (see p368), or the rules for hostels, houseboats, mobile homes, caravans and boarders (see p381), an adjustment for ineligible charges is made in this process.

Ineligible charges include:

- water charges for your personal use. Water charges in respect of communal areas (eg, in supported or sheltered accommodation) are eligible;[122] *and*
- most fuel charges; *and*
- some service charges (see p197), including charges for meals.

Communal areas

'**Communal areas**' include access areas like halls and passageways, but not rooms in common use, except those in sheltered accommodation – eg, a shared TV lounge or dining room.[123]

Fuel charges

Fuel charges are ineligible unless they are for communal areas (see p196).[124] If your fuel charge is:

- specified on your rent book or is readily identifiable from your agreement with your landlord, the full amount of the charge is ineligible.[125] However, if your fuel charge is considered to be unrealistically low, a flat-rate amount is ineligible instead (see below). This is also the case if your total fuel charge is specified but contains an unknown amount for communal areas;
- not readily identifiable, a flat-rate amount is ineligible. The amounts are:[126]

If you and your family occupy more than one room:

For heating (other than hot water)	£35.25
For hot water	£4.10
For lighting	£2.85
For cooking	£4.10

If you and your family occupy one room only:

For heating alone, or heating combined with either hot water or lighting or both	£21.10
For cooking	£4.10

The above amounts are added together if fuel is supplied for more than one purpose. If you live in shared accommodation and are a joint tenant with people other than your partner and children included in your claim, all the amounts may be apportioned according to your share of the rent (see p194).

The local authority must notify you if flat-rate fuel amounts have been used in calculating your HB. It must explain that if you can produce evidence from which

Part 3: Getting a benefit decision changed
Chapter 10: Housing benefit
4. The amount of benefit

the actual or approximate amount of your fuel charge can be estimated, the flat-rate amounts may be varied accordingly.

Do you occupy one room only?

The lower amounts apply if the accommodation you and your partner and children occupy comprises one room only. This is not defined, but the decision maker may say this means that if you only occupy one room but share the use of other rooms (such as a communal lounge), the higher amounts apply.[127] Argue that bathrooms, toilets and shared kitchens are not rooms you occupy. If you are forced to live in one room because the other room(s) in your accommodation are, in practice, unfit to live in (eg, because of severe mould or dampness), argue that the lower amounts apply.

Fuel for communal areas

If you pay a service charge for the use of fuel in communal areas and that charge is separately identified from any other charge for fuel used within your accommodation, it may be included as part of your eligible rent.[128] If you pay a charge for the provision of a heating system (eg, regular boiler maintenance), this is also eligible if the amount is separately identified from any other fuel charge you pay.[129]

Service charges

Service charges are only covered by HB if payment is a condition of occupying the accommodation rather than an optional extra. Eligible and ineligible charges are listed below. If the local authority regards any of the eligible charges as excessive, it estimates a reasonable amount given the cost of comparable services. If you are in supported accommodation, see below.

Eligible services

The following services are eligible for HB:

- services for the provision of adequate accommodation. These include some warden and caretaker services, and water charges in respect of communal areas (see p195) – eg, in supported or sheltered accommodation, gardens, children's play areas, lifts, for entryphones, communal telephone costs, portering and rubbish removal.[130] TV and radio relay charges are covered – eg, satellite or cable, including free-to-view UK channels;[131] *and*
- laundry facilities (eg, a laundry room in an apartment block), but not charges for the provision of personal laundry;[132] *and*
- furniture and household equipment, but not if there is an agreement that the furniture will eventually become yours;[133] *and*
- cleaning of the outside of windows if you or a member of your household cannot clean them yourself, and cleaning of rooms and windows in communal

areas, unless your local authority, a county council in England or the Welsh Ministers pays for these.[134]

Ineligible services

The following services are not eligible for HB:[135]

- food, including prepared meals (see below);
- sports facilities;
- TV rental, licence and subscription fees (but see above);
- transport;
- personal laundry service;
- provision of an emergency alarm system;
- medical expenses;
- nursing and personal care;
- counselling and other support services;
- any other charge not connected with the provision of adequate accommodation and not specifically included in the list of eligible charges above.

It is the amount of the charge specified in your rent agreement that is not eligible for HB, although local authorities can substitute their own estimate if they consider the amount to be unreasonably low.[136] If the amount is not specified in your rent agreement, the local authority estimates how much is fairly attributable to the service, given the cost of comparable services.[137]

If your housing costs include an amount for meals, set amounts are ineligible regardless of the actual cost.[138] The amounts are:

If at least three meals a day are provided:

For the claimant, partner and each child aged 16 or over included in the claim	£30.10
For each child aged under 16 included in the claim	£15.25

If breakfast only is provided:

For the claimant, partner and each child included in the claim	£3.70

In all other cases (part board):

For the claimant, partner and each child aged 16 or over included in the claim	£20.05
For each child aged under 16 included in the claim	£10.05

A child only counts as having reached the age of 16 on the first Monday in September following her/his 16th birthday.

The standard amounts are also ineligible for everyone who has meals paid for by you – eg, a non-dependant.[139]

Part 3: Getting a benefit decision changed
Chapter 10: Housing benefit
4. The amount of benefit

Support services in supported accommodation

If you live in supported accommodation, HB can help with your rent. However, HB is not available for the support services provided with your accommodation. Instead, the local authority funds these (eg, via your landlord or a voluntary organisation) and you may be charged for them.

Deductions for non-dependants

If other people normally live with you in your home, other than your partner and children included in your claim (called 'non-dependants'), a set deduction is usually made from your eligible rent when your 'maximum HB' is calculated (see p192).[140] This is because it is assumed the non-dependant makes a contribution towards your outgoings, whether or not s/he does so. Examples of non-dependants are adult sons or daughters, elderly relatives or friends who share your home.

Non-dependant deductions: checklist

1. Do you have a non-dependant – ie, someone who normally lives with you? If not, no deduction can be made.

2. Even if you have a non-dependant, must a deduction be made?

3. If a non-dependant deduction must be made, what is the correct amount of the deduction?

Who counts as a non-dependant

A person only counts as your non-dependant if s/he normally lives with you.[141] So, for example, if someone is only staying with you temporarily but normally lives elsewhere, or is homeless and is only using your address as a postal address, s/he should not count as a non-dependant. If you think the local authority has wrongly assumed that a person is your non-dependant, ask for a revision or appeal. **Note:** some people do not count as non-dependants even if they normally live with you (see p199).

A person only 'lives with you' if s/he has her/his home with you and shares some accommodation with you.[142] If s/he only shares a bathroom, toilet or a communal area such as a hall, passageway or a room in common use in sheltered accommodation, s/he does not count as living with you. If other areas of the house are shared (including the kitchen, unless it is only used by someone else to prepare food for her/him[143]), the person counts as living with you. This is the case even if you only use them at different times, provided you have a shared right to use them and are living in the same household (see p312 for the meaning of 'household').[144] A person who is separately liable to pay rent to your landlord does not count as living with you for these purposes.

A person should only count as 'normally' living with you if s/he has been there long enough to regard your home as her/his normal home.[145] Factors to be taken into account include:[146]

- the relationship between you;
- how much time s/he spends at your address;
- where s/he has her/his post sent;
- where s/he keeps her/his clothes and personal belongings;
- whether her/his stay or absence from your address is temporary or permanent. The temporary absence rules on p181 may be used to work this out;[147]
- whether s/he has another place that could be regarded as home and if, for instance, s/he pays rent or water charges there, or s/he just travels around.

People who do not count as non-dependants

The following people do *not* count as non-dependants, and no non-dependant deduction is made for them, even if they normally live with you:[148]

- your partner;
- a child or qualifying young person included in your claim;
- a child or qualifying young person living with you who does not count as a member of your household (see p311) – eg, a foster child;
- someone who is staying with you but whose normal home is elsewhere. **Note:** for these purposes, someone can only have one normal home at a time;[149]
- someone who is a resident carer for you or your partner, who is employed by a charitable or voluntary organisation. This applies where a charge is made for her/his services, paid by you or a public body on your behalf;
- any person, or a member of her/his household, to whom you or your partner are liable to pay rent on a commercial basis – eg, a resident landlord;
- someone who jointly occupies your home and is either the joint owner with you or your partner or is liable with you or your partner to make payments in respect of occupying it. You do not jointly occupy the home with someone unless you made a joint agreement with your landlord to do so. The mere fact that you live in the same home does not make you joint occupiers;[150]
- someone who is liable to pay rent on a commercial basis to you or your partner – eg, your tenants or lodgers. However, although no non-dependant deduction can be made for her/him, the rent s/he pays can count as your income (see p426 and p461).

Note: if the person comes within the last three categories above, s/he *does* count as a non-dependant if s/he is treated as not liable for rent under the rules explained on pp177–79 (other than if s/he is a student or a person who has failed the 'habitual residence test').[151]

When a non-dependant deduction is not made

A deduction is not made for any of your non-dependants if either you or your partner:[152]

Part 3: Getting a benefit decision changed
Chapter 10: Housing benefit
4. The amount of benefit

- are certified as severely sight impaired or blind by a consultant ophthalmologist (or are within 28 weeks of ceasing to be certified); *or*
- receive attendance allowance (AA) (or equivalent benefits paid because of injury at work or a war injury), the care component of disability living allowance (DLA) or child disability payment (CDP), the daily living component of personal independence payment (PIP) or adult disability payment (ADP) or armed forces independence payment.

If deductions must be made, no deduction is made for any non-dependant who is:[153]

- staying with you temporarily, but whose normal home is elsewhere;
- receiving a training allowance in connection with youth training under specified provisions;[154]
- a full-time student, if you are getting pension-age HB (see p187). This includes those getting JSA who count as full-time students while on a specified scheme for assisting people to obtain employment (see p1122);
- a full-time student during her/his period of study, if you are getting working-age HB (see p187). This includes those getting JSA who count as full-time students while on a specified scheme for assisting people to obtain employment (see p1122). In addition, no deduction is made during the summer vacation, unless the student is in full-time paid work;
- a member of the armed or reserved forces who usually lives with you and is away on operations, irrespective of how long s/he has been away;
- in hospital for more than 52 weeks. Separate stays in hospital which are not more than 28 days apart are added together when calculating the 52 weeks;
- in prison;
- under 18 years old;[155]
- under 25 and:
  - entitled to UC, provided s/he does not have any earned income; *or*
  - on IS; *or*
  - on income-based JSA; *or*
  - on income-related ESA, unless s/he receives the support component or s/he has been placed in the work-related activity group (see p638).

  S/he can be treated as being on income-based JSA or income-related ESA for these purposes (see p190);
- on PC.

The amount of deductions

If you have a non-dependant living with you who is 18 or over, and for whom a deduction must be made, when working out your maximum HB a fixed amount is deducted from your eligible rent (see p192), whatever s/he pays you. A deduction is made for every non-dependant living in your household, except in the case of a non-dependant couple (see p201).

Unless your non-dependant is in full-time paid work, a £16.45 deduction is made each week. If your non-dependant is in full-time paid work, the amount of the deduction depends on her/his gross weekly income as follows.[156]

Income bands	Deduction
Aged 18 or over and in full-time paid work with a weekly gross income of:	
£484 or more	£106.05
£389–£483.99	£96.60
£292–£388.99	£84.85
£224–£291.99	£51.85
£154–£223.99	£37.80
All others (for whom a deduction is made)	£16.45

The rules on full-time paid work are in Chapter 44. **Note:**

- A non-dependant who is not in (or is treated as not being in) full-time paid work does not attract the higher levels of deduction even if her/his weekly gross income is £154 or more.
- If someone is on IS, or is on (or treated as being on) income-based JSA or income-related ESA (see p190) for more than three days in a benefit week, s/he does not count as being in full-time paid work in that week.[157] This means the lower deduction (£16.45) is made (or, in some cases, no deduction).

Gross income includes wages before tax and NI are deducted, plus any other income the non-dependant has (apart from AA (or equivalent benefits paid because of injury at work or a war injury), DLA/CDP, PIP/ADP, and armed forces independence payment). Also ignored are payments from specified trusts and schemes established to compensate people, including victims of medical and other errors, institutional child abuse, emergencies, disasters and acts of terrorism.[158]

Do you know your non-dependant's income?

If you do not know your non-dependant's income, ask the local authority to consider the circumstances – eg, if your non-dependant is doing a job which is normally very low paid. The local authority should not assume the worst – eg, that your non-dependant is earning the highest amount. It should assess the likely level of her/his income on the evidence available.[159]

Non-dependant couples

Only one deduction is made for a couple (or the members of a polygamous marriage) who are non-dependants. The deduction made is the highest that

Part 3: Getting a benefit decision changed
Chapter 10: Housing benefit
5. Special benefit rules

would have been made if they were treated as individuals.[160] For the purpose of deciding which income band applies (see p200), their joint income counts, even if only one of them is in full-time work.[161]

Non-dependants of joint occupiers

If you share a non-dependant with any other joint occupiers, the deduction is divided between you, taking into account the proportion of housing costs paid by each of you.[162] If the person is a non-dependant of only one of you, the full deduction is made from that person's benefit. No apportionment is made between the members of a couple (or polygamous marriage).

If you are getting pension-age HB

If you are getting pension-age HB (see p187), if a non-dependant moves in with you so a deduction should be made, or there has been a change of circumstances in respect of a non-dependant so a higher deduction should be made, the effect of this can be delayed for 26 weeks.[163]

Your non-dependant's income or capital is more than yours

Normally, the income and capital of any non-dependant is only relevant when deciding which non-dependant deduction applies. However, unless you are on the guarantee credit of PC or IS, or are on or treated as on income-based JSA or income-related ESA (see p190), your HB entitlement is assessed on the basis of your non-dependant's income and capital rather than your own if:[164]

- her/his income and capital are both greater than yours; *and*
- the local authority is satisfied you have made an arrangement with your non-dependant to take advantage of the HB scheme (see p179).

Any income and capital normally treated as belonging to you is completely ignored, but the rest of the HB calculation proceeds as normal.

5. **Special benefit rules**

Special rules may apply to:

- 16/17 year olds previously looked after by a local authority (see p933);
- people who have come from or are going abroad (see Chapters 68, 69 and 70);
- people who are studying (see Chapter 41);
- people who are in hospital, living in a care home or similar accommodation, or people in prison (see Chapter 42).

6. Claims and backdating

To be entitled to housing benefit (HB), you must make a claim for it.[165] Claim HB as soon as you think you might be entitled to it or you may lose benefit. The rules about backdating are explained on p208. To find out when your entitlement to HB starts, see p212.

If you want to claim discretionary housing payments, you must make a separate claim for these from the local authority (see Chapter 29).

Making a claim

A claim for HB must normally be made in writing on a properly completed claim form.[166] See p205 for information about where to claim. **Note:** if you are claiming another benefit (ie, pension credit (PC), or if you can still make a new claim, income support (IS), income-based jobseeker's allowance (JSA) or employment and support allowance (ESA)), you can claim HB at the same time (see below).

It is always best to claim in writing if you can. However, you may also be able to claim:

- by telephone if:
  - your local authority has published a number for this purpose.[167] If the local authority provides a written statement of your circumstances, you must approve this statement for your telephone claim to be valid. **Note:** even if you cannot claim by telephone, if you telephone to ask to be sent a claim form and you return it within one month, your written claim is backdated to the date of your call (see p207); *or*
  - you claim PC (or IS, JSA or ESA) by telephone (see below);
- by electronic communication (eg, online or by email), if your local authority has authorised it.[168]

If you claim in writing, keep a copy in case queries arise. **Note:** the local authority can treat any written document (eg, a letter) as a claim for benefit, provided the written information and evidence you provide is sufficient.[169]

You must provide any information and evidence required (see p206). You can amend or withdraw your claim before a decision is made (see p205).

Forms

Claim forms are available free of charge from your local authority.[170] Check your local authority's website to find out where to get a claim form. To find your local authority, see gov.uk/apply-housing-benefit-from-council.

If you are claiming another benefit

If you are claiming PC by telephone, or if you are still able to make a new claim for IS, JSA or ESA and you are claiming by telephone, your HB claim is usually

Part 3: Getting a benefit decision changed
Chapter 10: Housing benefit
6. Claims and backdating

completed at the same time.[171] The DWP takes your details and sends you a statement of your circumstances to check, sign and return to the Jobcentre Plus office, along with evidence to support your claim. It forwards your HB claim to the local authority. You can claim HB by phoning the DWP (using the number specified for this purpose) at any time before a decision is made on your claim for PC (or for IS, JSA or ESA). If the local authority or DWP provides a written statement of your circumstances, you must approve this for your claim to be valid.

If you are providing evidence or information that is required or notifying a change of circumstances to the DWP in connection with your PC, IS, JSA or ESA award (eg, by telephone), then you can claim HB in the same manner as you reported the change to the DWP if it agrees. You must claim HB before a decision is made on the award of benefit to which the evidence, information or change of circumstances relates.[172]

You may be asked for further information and evidence (see p206).

Making sure your claim is valid

Where possible, your claim for HB should be accompanied by all the information and evidence needed to assess it.[173] Your claim is 'defective' if you:

- do not complete your claim form properly or you claim in writing, but not on the claim form (eg, by letter or email), and do not provide sufficient information and evidence; or
- claim by telephone and do not provide all the information required during the telephone call.

It is very important that you provide any information or evidence required. Until you do, your claim may be defective and you may not count as having made a valid claim. However, you should not delay your claim just because you do not have all the evidence ready to send.

Correcting a defective claim

If your claim is defective, you are given the opportunity to correct it. If you have:[174]

- not completed the claim form properly, the local authority can return it to you to do so. However, if you sent or gave your claim form to the DWP, it can ask you to provide the local authority with information needed to complete the form; or
- claimed in writing, but not on the claim form (eg, by letter or email), the local authority can send you a claim form to complete properly; or
- claimed by telephone to:
  - the local authority, the local authority must give you an opportunity to provide the information required; or

– the DWP, it can give you an opportunity to provide the information required. However, if the DWP does not do so, the local authority *must* give you an opportunity to provide the information, unless it thinks it already has sufficient information. If it does, your claim is treated as though it was received on the date of your original claim.

If you return the form completed properly or provide the information or evidence within one month of the last time you were told your claim is defective, your claim is treated as though it was received on the date of your original claim.[175] The local authority can allow you longer than one month if it thinks this reasonable.

Note: if you are told your claim is defective and it is not accepted as valid, you should be given a decision saying so. You can appeal against the decision.

Amending or withdrawing your claim

You may amend your claim (this includes asking for your claim to be backdated) at any time before a decision is made. You can do this by writing to the local authority, by telephone to the local authority or the DWP on the specified number or by any other manner the local authority or DWP decides or accepts.[176] Amendments are treated as though they were part of your original claim.

You may withdraw your claim at any time before a decision is made.[177] You must do this by writing to the local authority or, if you made your claim by telephone to the local authority, by telephone to the local authority. A notice to withdraw your claim takes effect from the day it is received.

Where to claim

If you claim in writing, you must usually send or give your HB claim to the local authority's designated office for the receipt of HB claims.[178] The address is usually on the claim form or a notice accompanying it. You can check for the address on your local authority's website. It is always best to send or give your claim direct to the local authority and it may speed up your claim if you do so. However, you can also send or give your claim to:[179]

- if you or your partner are also claiming PC (or IS, JSA or, ESA), either your DWP office or the local authority's designated office for HB claims. If you send your HB claim to the DWP, the DWP must usually forward it to the local authority within two working days of receiving it, or as soon as practicable after;[180] *or*
- a county council office, if your local authority has arranged for claims to be received there; *or*
- if you are at least pension age, any 'authorised office' – ie, an office nominated by the DWP and authorised by the local authority for receiving HB claims.

Keep a copy of your claim form wherever possible. Ask for confirmation that you have delivered it to the relevant office.

Part 3: Getting a benefit decision changed
Chapter 10: Housing benefit
6. Claims and backdating

Who should claim

If you are a single person or a lone parent, you claim HB on your own behalf. If you are a member of a couple only one of you can claim; you can decide between you who should do so. If you cannot agree, the local authority decides.[181]

- -

Who should you choose to make the claim?

If you are a member of a couple, the choice of claimant may affect the amount of HB you receive – eg, if one of you is a full-time student and not eligible for HB (see p882) or if one of you is getting ESA and the other is getting personal independence payment. In addition, if you are considering changing the claim to your partner's name, check whether s/he can make a new claim (see p173) and whether this could result in your becoming subject to harsher rent restriction rules (see Chapter 19) or losing entitlement to any premiums or components (see Chapter 17).

- -

Appointees

If a person is either temporarily or permanently unable to manage her/his own affairs, the local authority must accept a claim made by someone formally appointed to act legally on her/his behalf.[182] If no one has been formally appointed to look after a claimant's affairs, the local authority can decide to make someone aged over 18 an appointee who can act on her/his behalf. For the purpose of the claim, an appointee has the same rights and is responsible for carrying out the same duties as though s/he were the claimant.

You can write to ask to be an appointee. If you no longer want to be an appointee, you can resign after giving four weeks' notice. The local authority may terminate any appointment at any time.[183] If someone is given a formal legal appointment, that person automatically takes over from the person appointed by the local authority.[184]

Information to support your claim

When you claim HB, you must:
- satisfy the national insurance (NI) number requirement (see below), unless you are living in a hostel.[185] If you are a member of a couple, your partner must also usually satisfy this requirement; *and*
- provide proof of your identity, if required; *and*
- provide information and evidence required with the claim. Until you do, you may not count as having made a valid claim (see p204). Correct any defects as soon as possible or your date of claim may be affected.

If you or your partner are getting JSA or (if you are getting working-age HB) IS, and have notified the DWP that you (or your partner) have started work, the DWP can ask you to provide the local authority with any information or evidence it needs to decide whether you continue to be entitled to HB.[186] This only applies if, as a result of the change, entitlement to IS or JSA will end or the amount of contribution-based JSA will reduce.

The local authority may ask you to provide information *after* you are awarded HB if this is needed to determine whether you are still entitled to HB. You must then supply this within one month, or longer if the local authority thinks this is reasonable.[187] If you fail to do so, your HB could be suspended or even terminated (see p1162). **Note:** you must actually have been notified; proof of posting to your last known address is not sufficient.[188]

The national insurance number requirement

For how you (and your partner) can satisfy the NI number requirement, and for when your partner is exempt, see p1137. The rules are the same as for other benefits. However, note the following.

- You do not have to satisfy the NI number requirement if you live in a hostel.[189]
- If you have claimed HB in association with a claim for PC (or IS or income-based JSA) and the DWP has accepted that you satisfy the NI number requirement, the local authority can accept that you also satisfy it for HB purposes.[190]

The date of your claim

The date of your claim is important because it determines when your entitlement to HB starts. This is not necessarily the date from when you are paid. For information about when entitlement to HB starts, see p213.

Your date of claim is not necessarily the date it is received by the local authority. It can be an earlier date.

Your **'date of claim'** is usually the earliest of:[191]

- the date you first notify a designated office, DWP office or authorised office (see p205) (or county council office, if the local authority has arranged for claims to be received there) that you want to claim HB, provided a properly completed claim is received in one of those offices within one month. The one-month period can be extended if the local authority thinks it is reasonable; *or*
- the date your valid claim is received by the designated office, DWP office or authorised office (or county council office, if the local authority has arranged for claims to be received there).

There are exceptions to the above rules.[192]

- If you or your partner have successfully claimed the guarantee credit of PC and your HB claim is made within one month of that claim being received by the DWP, your claim is treated as having been made on the first day of entitlement to that benefit. For example, if your claim for the guarantee credit of PC is backdated, your date of claim for HB purposes is the date to which your PC

Part 3: Getting a benefit decision changed
Chapter 10: Housing benefit
6. Claims and backdating

claim is backdated. **Note:** if you can make a new claim for IS, income-based JSA or income-related ESA, this rule also applies. For these purposes, you are treated as entitled to JSA or ESA on your 'waiting days'.[193]

- If you are awarded universal credit (UC) and you claim HB within one month of your UC claim or, if you are someone who does not have to make a claim for UC, within one month of being notified that you were awarded UC, your HB claim is treated as having been made on the first day of entitlement to UC.
- If you or your partner are on the guarantee credit of PC or UC (or IS, income-based JSA or income-related ESA), have just become liable to pay rent for your home and your HB claim reaches the local authority's designated office or DWP office within one month of your becoming liable, your claim is treated as having been made on the date that you first became liable to pay rent.
- If you have separated from your partner or s/he has died and s/he was claiming HB for you on the date this happened and you claim within one month of this, your claim is treated as having been made on the date you separated or your partner died.

You must make sure your claim is valid. If it is 'defective', you are given a short time to correct the defects (see p204). If you do, your claim is treated as having been made when you initially claimed.

In some cases, you can claim in advance (see p210) and in some cases your claim can be backdated (see below).

Backdating your claim

It is very important to claim in time. Even if your claim is backdated, the arrears of HB that you can get are limited. Your claim can be backdated:

- for up to three months if you claim pension-age HB. In this case, you do not have to show a good reason for your late claim (see p209);
- for up to one month if you claim working-age HB. In this case, you must show a good reason for your late claim (called 'good cause' – see p209).

For backdated HB to be considered, you must ask for HB for a past period. Do this as soon as possible, preferably at the same time as your claim for HB. Any backdated HB is calculated on the basis of your circumstances and the HB rules as they were over the backdating period.

If you would have been entitled to HB for an earlier period than the backdating rules allow, you could:

- ask for an 'any time' revision if there are grounds (see p1265);
- ask for compensation from the local authority if you were given wrong information or misled by it (see p1403);
- complain to the Ombudsman (see p1409).

If you only qualify for HB when a qualifying benefit is awarded, see p210 for when your claim might be backdated further.

Three months' backdating

If you claim pension-age HB (see p187), your claim can be backdated for up to three months.[194] This applies whatever the reasons were for your delay in claiming and, even if you do not ask for HB for a past period, until some time after you make your claim for HB. You only need to show that you qualified for HB during that period.

You can get backdated HB for the three months before the date of your HB claim (see p207) – eg, the date your claim was received or the date you notified the local authority that you wanted to claim HB.[195] However, if you or your partner successfully claimed the guarantee credit of PC and your claim for HB is received within one month of your PC claim being received by the DWP, your entitlement to HB cannot begin earlier than three months before your claim for PC was made (or treated as having been made).

One month's backdating

If you claim working-age HB (see p187), your claim can be backdated for up to one month.[196]

You must show that you qualified for HB during the period *and* prove you had a continuous good reason (called 'good cause') for failing to claim or to ask for backdated HB (see below). You can only get backdated HB from the latest of:[197]

- **date one:** the day from which you had continuous good cause for your late claim; *or*
- **date two:** the day one month before your date of claim. Your date of claim is not necessarily the date it is received by the local authority. It can be an earlier date (see p207); *or*
- **date three:** the day one month before you asked for backdated HB.

> *Example*
> Chrissy, aged 41, claimed working-age HB on 7 May 2021. After getting advice, she asked for backdated HB on 18 May 2021.
> The local authority accepts that she had a continuous good cause for her late claim from 24 February 2021.
> Date one = 24 February 2021.
> Date two = 8 April 2021. This is the day one month before her date of claim for HB.
> Date three = 18 April 2021. This is the day one month before she asked for backdated HB.
> Chrissy gets backdated HB from 18 April 2021, the latest of the three relevant dates.

If you are claiming HB after a previous entitlement ended, as well as asking for backdated HB, you should see whether you can challenge the local authority's decision to end your entitlement to HB (see Chapters 56 and 57).

You count as having **'good cause'** for your late claim if you can show there is something that would probably have caused a reasonable person of your age and

Part 3: Getting a benefit decision changed
Chapter 10: Housing benefit
6. Claims and backdating

experience to act (or fail to act) as you did, taking all the circumstances into account (including your state of health and the information which you received and which you might have obtained).[198] The more reasonable your behaviour in not claiming earlier given your circumstances, the more likely it is that you have a good cause.[199] If you have a mental health problem that makes you act unreasonably, this must be borne in mind.[200] If you have difficulty communicating in English or understanding documents, or have little knowledge of the benefits system, this should be taken into account, but these are not usually considered a good cause in themselves.[201] For some examples of what might count as good cause for a late claim, see p210 of the 2020/21 edition of this *Handbook*.

> **What if you choose not to claim HB?**
>
> If you choose not to claim but later change your mind, you must still show that you have a good cause for your late claim. The longer you have delayed in claiming, the harder this may be.[202] However, you may be able to show that you have a good cause – eg, if the reason you did not claim earlier was because you were making real efforts to find work to avoid relying on benefits, and you only chose not to claim for a limited period.

If you claim the wrong benefit

There are no rules that allow a claim for another benefit to be treated as a claim for HB.

Claiming in advance

You can claim HB in advance if you become liable for rent for the first time but cannot move into your accommodation until after your liability begins. You must claim HB as soon as you are liable for rent. Once you move in, you may be able to receive HB for the four weeks before moving in (see p181).

If you are not entitled to HB now, the local authority can treat your claim as having been made in the benefit week immediately before you are first entitled, unless the reason you do not qualify straight away is because you fail the 'habitual residence test' (see p1550). This applies if you will become entitled:[203]

- within 13 weeks of claiming working-age HB or 17 weeks of claiming pension-age HB; *or*
- within 17 weeks of claiming either type of HB if you or your partner will be pension age (see p766) within 17 weeks.

If this happens, you do not need to make a further claim later.

Housing benefit after an award of a qualifying benefit

You may not be entitled to HB currently, but would be once you, your partner or a child or qualifying young person included in your claim become entitled to another 'qualifying benefit' (eg, a disability benefit or carer's allowance), because you then qualify for premiums or components. Alternatively, you might be entitled to a higher rate of benefit once the qualifying benefit is awarded. If you are already entitled to HB when the qualifying benefit is awarded, see p1268, p1278 and p1287.

Do you only qualify for housing benefit when a qualifying benefit is awarded?
If you only qualify for HB when a qualifying benefit is awarded, the rules operate in an unfair way so you should do the following.
1. Claim HB (if you still can) while waiting to hear about the claim for a qualifying benefit.
2. If you do not qualify for HB, ask the local authority to wait to make a decision on your claim until the award of the qualifying benefit is made (known as 'stockpiling' your claim). You may have to persuade the local authority that it can do so. If the local authority refuses, argue that its failure to delay making a decision on your claim was an 'error of law' and that there are grounds for an 'any time' revision (see p1265).[204]
3. If you are refused HB but are then awarded a qualifying benefit, claim again and ask for your claim to be backdated. If you need to, argue that you have a good cause for your late claim (see p209).
4. If you lose benefit because of the way the rules operate, ask your local authority for compensation to cover the period before your fresh HB claim.

Notice of the decision

Once the local authority has all the information and evidence required, it must make a decision on your claim for HB within 14 days or as soon as 'reasonably practicable'.[205] If you are a person affected by the decision, you must be notified of it by the local authority without delay or as soon as 'reasonably practicable'.[206] In all other cases (eg, if a decision is made following a change in your circumstances), you (and other people affected by the decision) must be notified within 14 days or as soon as reasonably practicable. You can request reasons for a decision. Your request must be in writing and it must be signed by you.[207]

Person affected by a decision
You are a **'person affected by a decision'** if you are:[208]
– a claimant; or
– someone acting for a claimant who is unable to act for her/himself – eg, an appointee; or
– someone from whom the local authority decides to recover an overpayment (including a landlord); or
– a landlord or agent if the decision concerns whether or not to make a direct payment of HB to you.[209]

Part 3: Getting a benefit decision changed
Chapter 10: Housing benefit
6. Claims and backdating

Information a decision notice should contain

If the decision is one you can appeal (see p1303), you must be informed of:[210]

- your right to appeal against the decision; *and*
- your right to a written statement of reasons for the decision (if this is not already included – see p1256. The rules are the same as for other benefits.)

The other information that must be provided varies with the particular circumstances of your case and includes the following.[211]

- The normal weekly amount of HB to which you are entitled, including the amount of any deductions for non-dependants and fuel. You must be told why fuel deductions have been made and that they can be varied if you provide evidence of the actual amount involved.
- The amount of your rent that can be covered by HB (your weekly 'eligible rent' – see p193).
- If you are a private tenant, the day your HB will be paid and whether payment will be made weekly or monthly.
- The date on which your entitlement starts (see below).
- In some cases, how your applicable amount is calculated, how your income has been assessed and the amount of capital the local authority has taken into account. If the income and capital of a non-dependant has been used instead of yours to calculate your HB (see p202), you must be informed of this and the reasons why.
- If your claim was:
  - successful, your duty to notify the local authority of any change in circumstances which might affect your entitlement and the kinds of changes that should be reported;
  - unsuccessful, a statement explaining exactly why you are not entitled.
- If it has been decided to pay your HB direct to your landlord, information saying how much is to be paid to her/him and when payments will start.

When your entitlement starts

Your entitlement to HB starts:[212]

- if you became liable for rent for the first time (for a home you have moved into) in the week your claim is made or is treated as having been made, from the Monday of that week. This includes if you become liable for daily payments in a hostel or accommodation provided by the local authority on a short-term lease or because you are homeless. This means that your HB starts on the same day your liability to pay rent actually begins;[213] *or*
- in all other cases, from the Monday following your date of claim, or following the date from when you are treated as claiming if your claim is backdated.

7. **Getting paid**

How payment of housing benefit (HB) is made depends on whether you are the tenant of the local authority responsible for paying HB or a private or housing association tenant. If you are unable to act for yourself, payment can be made to someone acting on your behalf (see p214). In some circumstances, payment can be made direct to your landlord (see p214). No HB is payable if the amount would be less than 50 pence a week.[214]

When is housing benefit paid?

You are normally paid in arrears at intervals of a week, two weeks, four weeks or a month, depending on when your rent is usually due. HB can also be paid at longer intervals if you agree.[215] If you are a private or housing association tenant, the local authority can pay your HB weekly to avoid an overpayment or if you are liable to pay rent weekly and it is in your interests for HB to be paid weekly.

Different rules apply if HB is paid direct to your landlord.[216]

Note:

- Your HB might be paid at a reduced rate if you have been sanctioned for a benefit offence (see p1239).
- If payment of your HB is delayed, see p220. You might be able to get a 'payment on account'. If you wish to complain about how your claim has been dealt with or claim compensation, see Chapter 61.
- If payment of your HB is suspended, see p1161.
- If you are overpaid HB, you might have to repay it (see Chapter 53) and, in some circumstances, you may have to pay a penalty (see p1229). If you have been accused of fraud, see Chapter 54.

How your benefit is paid

If your landlord is the local authority responsible for paying HB, your HB is paid in the form of a reduction in your rent. This is called a 'rent rebate'.[217]

If you are a private or housing association tenant, you receive HB in the form of a 'rent allowance'.[218] If you live in a caravan, mobile home or houseboat, this applies even if you are also liable to make payments to a local authority – eg, for site or mooring fees. HB is normally paid to you although, in some cases, it may be paid direct to your landlord or to someone acting on your behalf.

Note: if your rent allowance is:

- less than £1 a week, the local authority can pay your HB up to six months in arrears;[219]
- more than £2 a week, you can insist on two-weekly payments, unless HB is paid direct to your landlord.[220]

The local authority has the discretion to pay you by whatever method it chooses, but, in doing so, it must consider your 'reasonable needs and convenience'.[221] It should not insist on paying your HB into a bank account if you do not have one (but it may encourage you to open one), nor should it make you collect it if it is difficult to reach the office by public transport.[222] If it does, complain to your local councillor. If that has no effect, ask your MP to take up the matter (see p1408) and also complain to the Ombudsman (see p1409).

If the local authority refuses to replace a payment which has never arrived, you could write to the local authority and threaten to sue in the County Court (sheriff court in Scotland).

Payment to someone acting on your behalf

If an appointee or some other person legally empowered to act for you has claimed HB on your behalf, that person can also receive the HB payments.[223]

If you are able to claim HB for yourself, you can still nominate an agent to receive or collect it for you. To do this, you must make a written request to the local authority. Anyone you nominate must be aged 18 or over.[224]

If a claimant dies, any unpaid HB may be paid to her/his personal representative or, if there is none, to her/his next of kin aged 16 or over.[225] A written application must be received by the local authority within 12 months of the claimant's death. The local authority may allow longer. If HB was being paid to the landlord before the claimant's death, the local authority can pay any outstanding HB to her/him to clear remaining rent due.

Payment direct to a landlord

Your HB can be paid direct to your landlord (or the person to whom you pay rent) but only in specified circumstances. Your landlord could contact the local authority about this.[226] The local authority can suspend payment while it makes enquiries about who should be paid your HB.[227] If the local authority has concerns about your landlord, see p216.

If you have just claimed HB or the local authority has carried out a supersession of your award, and the local authority thinks you have not already paid your rent and that it would be in the interests of the 'efficient administration' of HB, it can make the first payment to your landlord.[228]

Both you and your landlord should be notified if HB is to be paid to your landlord. If it is *not* in your interests to have HB paid direct to your landlord, it is worth trying to persuade the local authority to withhold it rather than paying it to your landlord. Get advice before you do so.

When payment must be made to your landlord

The local authority *must* pay your HB, including payments on account (see p220), direct to your landlord (or the person to whom you pay rent) if:[229]

- you or your partner are getting pension credit (PC), income support (IS), jobseeker's allowance (JSA) or employment and support allowance (ESA) and the DWP has decided to pay part of that benefit to your landlord for arrears (see p1166). **Note:** this does not apply if you are getting universal credit (UC); *or*
- you have rent arrears equivalent to eight weeks' rent or more, unless you can show that it is in your overriding interest not to make direct payments.[230] Once your arrears have been reduced to less than eight weeks' rent, compulsory direct payments stop. The local authority may then choose to continue direct payments on a discretionary basis.

Payment to your landlord on a discretionary basis

The local authority may pay your HB direct to your landlord (or the person to whom you pay rent):

- if the local housing allowance rent restriction rules do *not* apply to you (see p368):[231]
  - if you have requested or agreed to direct payments; *or*
  - without your agreement, if it decides that direct payments are in your or your family's best interests. You do not have to have any of your family living with you for payment to be made to your landlord under this rule;[232]
- if the local housing allowance rent restriction rules apply to you (see p368), if the local authority:[233]
  - thinks you are likely to have difficulty managing your own financial affairs or that it is improbable that you will pay your rent. The local authority can make direct payments (for a maximum of eight weeks) while it considers the situation; *or*
  - thinks it will help you to secure or to keep accommodation. **Note:** the government's intention is that this should only apply if the rent is at a level you can afford; *or*
  - has already made direct payments to your landlord during your current award of HB in any of the situations when direct payments must be made;
- whether or not the local housing allowance rent restriction rules apply to you, without your agreement if you have left the address for which you were getting HB and there are rent arrears. In this case, direct payments of any unpaid HB due in respect of that accommodation can be made, up to the total of the outstanding arrears.[234] If your landlord retained your tenancy deposit to cover any of the rent arrears, the local authority should take this into account when working out how much HB to pay to her/him. It should also deduct any amounts you would be able to offset against what you would owe if your landlord were to take you to court to recover the rent arrears – eg, an amount you paid for repairs that were your landlord's responsibility.[235]

When the local authority has concerns about a landlord

The local authority may refuse to make direct payments if it is not satisfied that your landlord is a 'fit and proper person'.[236] However, direct payments may still be made if the local authority is satisfied it is in your or your family's best interests.[237]

If the local authority decides not to make payments to your landlord, it can make payments to you (including sending you a cheque payable to the landlord, or paying you in the presence of your landlord) or to a trusted third party, such as a social worker or solicitor.[238]

Continuing payments

Your HB can continue to be paid at the same rate, even though your entitlement might otherwise have changed:

- when you stop claiming:
  - IS, income-based JSA or income-related ESA because you or your partner are moving onto PC. You may be able to continue to receive HB at the same rate for four weeks (see below); or
  - IS, income-based JSA, income-related or contributory ESA or severe disablement allowance (SDA) because you or your partner start work or increase your hours or earnings. You may be entitled to extended payments of HB (see p217);
- if you are getting HB when you make a new claim for UC. Your HB may continue for two weeks (called HB run-on – see p219).

Continuing payments on claiming pension credit

To avoid problems caused by delays in reassessing your HB when you move from IS, income-based JSA or income-related ESA onto PC, you can receive pension-age HB for a period, normally at the same rate as the HB you were getting before. Your maximum HB (see p192) is recalculated if your rent increases or there is a change in the non-dependant deductions (see p198) that should be made.[239] **Note:** although this rule does not apply if you transfer to PC from UC, instead you can claim pension-age HB during your last UC assessment period, and qualify for HB from the date you reach pension age.[240]

You qualify for continuing payments if:[241]
- your partner has claimed PC and the DWP has certified this; or
- your IS, income-based JSA or income-related ESA ceased because you reached pension age (see p766). The DWP must certify this and that you are required to claim, or have claimed, PC (or are treated as having done so).

You get continuing payments for:[242]
- a period of four weeks from the day after your IS, income-based JSA or income-related ESA ceases; or
- if the four-week period ends other than on a Sunday, until the Sunday after the end of the four-week period.

Extended payments of housing benefit

If you or your partner are on IS, income-based JSA, income-related or contributory ESA or SDA and your entitlement ends because you (or your partner) start work or increase your hours or pay, you may be entitled to continue to receive the same amount of HB as you did before your entitlement to one of those benefits ended, for up to four weeks. These are called extended payments of HB.

You do not have to make a claim for extended payments of HB. They should be paid automatically.[243] However, your local authority needs to know that your or your partner's entitlement to IS, income-based JSA, ESA or SDA has ceased, so you must notify it.

If you want to get an extended payments decision changed, you can apply for a revision or supersession or appeal (see Chapters 56 and 57).

Who can get extended payments

You qualify for extended payments of HB if you are getting HB, you (or your partner) started work (including self-employed work) or increased your hours or pay, and:[244]

- you are getting working-age HB (see p187) and your (or your partner's) entitlement to IS, income-based JSA or income-related ESA ended.[245] You (or your partner) must have been entitled to, and in receipt of, either IS, contribution-based, income-based or joint-claim JSA or income-related ESA, or a combination of these, for at least 26 weeks. **Note:** you cannot qualify if, immediately before your entitlement to IS ended, you qualified for housing costs run-on (see p359); *or*
- your (or your partner's) entitlement to contributory ESA or SDA ended, and:[246]
    - you (or your partner) were not entitled to or in receipt of IS, income-based JSA or income-related ESA; *and*
    - if you are getting pension-age HB, you are not in receipt of PC; *and*
    - you (or your partner) had been continuously entitled to, and in receipt of, contributory ESA or SDA, or a combination of these, for at least 26 weeks.

In all cases, the work, or increase in earnings or hours, must be expected to last at least five weeks.

Do you need to report the change in your circumstances?

1. If you are getting IS, JSA, ESA or SDA and you start work or your hours or pay change, you must report this to the DWP. The end of your entitlement to these benefits is also a change in your circumstances that you must report to the local authority (see p220).

2. If you do not report the end of your entitlement to IS/JSA/ESA/SDA to the local authority, your entitlement to extended payments of HB is not affected, but this could result in an overpayment of HB after the extended payment period.

3. You could be entitled to a higher rate of HB than you were before your entitlement to IS/JSA/ESA/SDA ended. Report the change as soon as possible so it can be taken into account.

If you move home, you can still qualify for extended payments of HB, provided the day you moved was in the same week, or the week before, you or your partner started work or increased your hours or pay.[247] See below for how the amount of the extended payments can be affected.

The amount of the extended payments and how long they last

Extended payments of HB are paid for four weeks unless:[248]
- any of the weeks count as rent-free periods (see p193); *or*
- your liability to pay rent ceases altogether within the four weeks.

If you claim UC during the four-week period, your entitlement to HB can still continue for two weeks (called HB run-on – see p219). However, your entitlement can end at the end of the four-week period, if this is sooner, if you would no longer have been entitled to HB after the end of that period.

The weekly amount of your extended payments (unless you move into local authority accommodation in a different local authority area – see below) is the higher of the amount of HB:[249]
- you got in the last (non-rent-free) week before your entitlement to IS/JSA/ESA/ SDA ended; *or*
- to which you would be entitled based on your new circumstances; *or*
- to which your partner would be entitled if s/he claimed based on her/his circumstances.

However, if the benefit cap is, or was, applied (see p1156), it is the amount of HB you would have got – ie, the amount before any reduction.[250]

Always report any changes in your circumstances during the four-week period. This is because the weekly amount you get is then the highest of the above amounts.[251]

Example

Jess is a local authority tenant with a non-dependant. She gets working-age HB. Her rent is £102 a week. She was getting HB of £66.15 in the week before her entitlement to IS ceased, because a non-dependant deduction of £37.80 was made. Her weekly HB entitlement based on her circumstances is £54.37. Her extended payments are therefore £66.15 a week. In the second week of the four-week period, Jess's non-dependant moves out. Her weekly entitlement based on her circumstances is now £92.17 (£54.37 + £37.80), because a non-dependant deduction is no longer made. Her extended payments are now £92.17 for the remainder of the four-week period. This is also Jess's HB entitlement from the end of the period.

You may qualify for extended payments of HB for two homes (see p185). However, if your liability to pay rent for either of these ceases within the four-week period, the amount of your extended payments is reduced by the amount of HB payable for that home.[252]

If you were being paid discretionary housing payments (see Chapter 29), ask for these to continue for the extended payment period.

If you move into local authority accommodation in a different local authority area, the weekly amount of your extended payments of HB is the amount of HB you got in the last (non-rent-free) week before your entitlement to IS/JSA/ESA/SDA ended – ie, the amount you got at your old address.[253] The extended payments can be paid to you or to the new local authority landlord. If you or your partner claim HB at your new address, the amount you or your partner get is reduced by the weekly amount of the extended payments. The effect of this is that, if your new HB entitlement is higher, your extended payments are 'topped up'.

If you move house in any other circumstances (eg, to privately rented or housing association accommodation, or within the same local authority area), your extended payments are worked out under the normal rules. If you also qualify for HB at your new address, it does not appear that the local authority can reduce the amount of HB you get by the weekly amount of your extended payments.[254] It is not clear if this was the intention.

Ongoing entitlement to housing benefit

Your entitlement to HB continues until at least the end of the extended payment period.[255] It can continue after that if you qualify under the normal HB rules, but at the weekly rate based on your new circumstances. You do not have to make a fresh claim. Your HB entitlement is continuous.

Note: unless you move to local authority accommodation in a different local authority area, if your partner claims HB, this cannot be paid to her/him while you are getting extended payments of HB.[256]

Housing benefit run-on

If you are getting HB and make a new claim for UC, your HB entitlement continues for two weeks (called a 'run-on' or transitional HB payment), as long as you would otherwise remain entitled.[257] You do not have to make a claim for a run-on payment. It should be made automatically. You do not have to pay a run-on payment back, even if you qualify for a UC housing costs element for your rent for the same period. HB run-on counts as a specified benefit for the purposes of the benefit cap.

If your HB is being paid direct to your landlord, your run-on payment is usually also paid to her/him. If this happens, you should ask your landlord to pay you the HB run-on – eg, if you are up to date with your rent payments.

Note:

- You are treated as entitled to UC during the two-week run-on period, even if no decision has been made on your UC claim.[258] UC is a passport to maximum

HB (see p190). However, if you claimed UC because you were sent a 'migration notice' under the managed migration process (see p29), the amount of your HB run-on is the amount of HB to which you were entitled on the first day of the two-week run-on period.[259]

- Your entitlement to HB can continue indefinitely if this is for 'specified accommodation' or 'temporary accommodation' (see p173 for what counts).
- A benefit cap is not applied to your HB if you are getting UC.[260]

Delays and complaints

The local authority must make a decision on your claim, tell you in writing what the decision is, and pay you any HB to which you are entitled within 14 days or, if that is not reasonably practicable, as soon as possible after that.[261] If you consider a delay to be unreasonable, make a complaint (see p1407). In serious cases, you may want to obtain advice on whether you have grounds for a judicial review (see Chapter 59).

Payments on account

If you are a private or housing association tenant and the local authority has not been able to assess your HB within the required period, the local authority must normally make a 'payment on account' (sometimes called an interim payment) while your claim is being sorted out.[262] The local authority should automatically do this. You should not have to request a payment on account.[263] Bear the following in mind.

- Payments on account are not discretionary. The local authority *must* pay you an amount that it considers reasonable, given what it knows about your circumstances.
- Payments on account can only be refused if it is clear that you will not be entitled to HB, or the reason for the delay is that you have been asked for information or evidence in support of your claim and you have failed, without a good reason, to provide it (see p206).[264] If the delay has been caused by a third party (eg, the rent officer, your bank or employer), this does not affect your right to a payment on account.
- The local authority must notify you of the amount of a payment on account and that it can recover any overpayment which occurs if your actual HB entitlement is different from the payment.[265]
- If your payment on account is less than your actual entitlement, your future HB can be adjusted to take account of the underpayment.[266]
- If the local authority has not made a payment on account, complain.

Change of circumstances

It is your duty to report any change in your circumstances which you might reasonably be expected to know might affect your right to, the amount of or payment of your HB.[267] You should do this promptly to the office handling your claim. The local authority must tell you in writing about the changes you must report.[268] There may be a number of changes which the local authority requires you to report, depending on the particular circumstances of your case. **Note:** if you are getting PC, you only have to report specified changes (see p222).

If you do not report a change promptly, any resulting overpayment may be recoverable from you (see Chapter 53) and, in some circumstances, you may have to pay a penalty (see p1229). If you are considered to have acted knowingly or dishonestly, you may also be guilty of an offence (see Chapter 54). **Note:**

- It is important to report changes to the right department, not to other parts of the local authority such as social services. Your duty to notify changes is to the HB department, not to the local authority as a whole.[269]
- If your benefit is paid to someone else on your behalf, the duty to report any relevant changes also extends to her/him.[270]

If in doubt, always report changes in circumstances. If you think that the local authority might not have taken a change into account, you should check with it.

How to report a change of circumstances

It is always best to report a change in your circumstances in writing (eg, in a letter) and keep a copy. However, you can also report a change to the local authority:[271]

- by telephone (unless the local authority says you must report it in writing), if your local authority has published a telephone number for this purpose or allows you to claim HB by telephone (see p203); *or*
- electronically (eg, by email), if your local authority authorises it.[272]

You may report a change in your circumstances to the DWP, instead of the local authority, if the DWP has provided a telephone number for this purpose and:[273]

- you or your partner are getting JSA or (if you are on working-age HB) IS; *and*
- the change of circumstances is that you or your partner have started work; *and*
- as a result of the change, entitlement to IS or JSA will end or, if you or your partner are getting contribution-based JSA, the amount will reduce.

If the change is a a death, there is a special rule (sometimes called 'Tell Us Once'). You can report such a change in person at a local authority (and, in England, a county council) office, if such an office has been specified.[274] You can notify it to the DWP electronically, or by telephone if a number has been specified for that purpose. Check with your local authority to see whether it provides this service. More information is available at gov.uk/after-a-death/organisations-you-need-to-contact-and-tell-us-once.

Changes you must report if you get pension credit

If you get PC, the only changes you must report to the local authority are:[275]

- any change to your tenancy, apart from changes in your rent if you are a local authority tenant; *and*
- any changes affecting the residence or income of a non-dependant who normally lives with you; *and*
- any absence from your home which is, or is likely to be, for more than 13 weeks (more than four weeks if you are absent from Great Britain); *and*
- if you are only getting the savings credit of PC:[276]
  - changes affecting a child under 16 who lives with you that could affect how much HB you get. You need not report changes in the child's age; *and*
  - any changes to your capital that do, or could, take it above £16,000; *and*
  - any changes in the income or capital of a non-dependant of yours, if your HB has been assessed on the basis of this instead of your own (see p202), and whether s/he has stopped, or resumed, living with you; *and*
  - any changes in the income or capital of your partner that have not been taken into account since the determination of your PC award, and whether your partner has stopped, or resumed, living with you.

You must report other changes in connection with your PC claim to the DWP. Relevant changes in your circumstances should then be passed to the local authority by the DWP.

Changes you must report if you do not get pension credit

The changes you must report if you are getting PC, listed above, are all changes that could affect your right to, the amount of or payment of your HB. So they are also changes you must report if you are *not* getting PC. Examples of other types of change you must report if you do not get PC include changes to:

- your family income or capital;
- the number of boarders you have or the payments made by them;
- your status – eg, marriage, civil partnership, cohabitation or separation.

However, you do *not* have to report:[277]

- any change in your age, or that of your partner or child(ren) or your non-dependant(s). **Note:** you *do* have to report any change that results in a child or young person no longer being included in your claim (see p307);
- if you are on IS, income-based JSA or income-related ESA, any changes that affect the amount of those benefits. **Note:** you *do* have to report entitlement to IS, income-based JSA or income-related ESA ending. Do not assume that the DWP does this on your behalf.

When changes in circumstances take effect

In most cases, a change takes effect from the Monday after it occurred.[278] This applies whether or not a decision is advantageous to you. However, if you are liable to pay rent on a daily basis (eg, in a hostel) and the change means you are no longer entitled to HB, it takes effect on the day it occurs.[279]

Exceptions

There are a number of exceptions to the general rule described above, which include the following.

- If the change is one you are required to notify to the local authority, it is advantageous to you and you fail to notify the change within the one-month time limit (or any longer period allowed by the local authority – see p1283), the date of notification is usually treated as if this is the date the change occurred. This means you lose out if you reported the change late.
- If you are getting pension-age HB and either a non-dependant comes to live with you or there is a change so that a higher non-dependant deduction should be made, the effect of this can be delayed for 26 weeks.[280]
- If you are entitled to HB (but not UC) when you become a member of a couple with someone getting UC and s/he moves in with you, unless your HB is for 'specified accommodation' or 'temporary accommodation' (see p173 for what counts) or you are at least pension age and are getting pension-age HB, your entitlement to HB ends on the day before the date you are jointly entitled to UC with your new partner, or the day before the date you would have been entitled had you met all the financial conditions for UC. [281] **Note:** if you move in with your new partner, or you are at least pension age and are getting pension-age HB, your HB entitlement ends under the normal HB rules.[282]

There are additional exceptions to the rules described above:

- if you are being paid PC, the amount of this changes because of a change in your circumstances or a correction of an official error (see p1266), and so the amount of HB you can be paid changes;[283]
- if there is a change in your rent, if you move to a new home or if you become (or cease to be) entitled to HB for more than one home, and if you or your partner become entitled to ESA which includes a support component or you (or s/he) are put in the work-related activity group.[284]

---

8. Tax, other benefits and the benefit cap

Tax

Housing benefit (HB) is not taxable.

Means-tested benefits and tax credits

If you are entitled to HB:

- entitlement to the guarantee credit of pension credit (PC), universal credit (UC), income support (IS), income-based jobseeker's allowance (JSA) or

Part 3: Getting a benefit decision changed
Chapter 10: Housing benefit
8. Tax, other benefits and the benefit cap

income-related employment and support allowance (ESA) acts as an automatic passport to maximum HB (see p192) because all your income and capital are ignored;
- working tax credit counts as income when working out your HB;
- child tax credit counts as income unless you are getting pension-age HB (see p187).

Non-means-tested benefits

Most non-means-tested benefits are taken into account as income when working out the amount of HB you get. However:
- attendance allowance, disability living allowance, personal independence payment, guardian's allowance and child benefit and certain Scottish benefits (ie, adult disability payment, child disability payment, carer's allowance supplement, child winter heating assistance, young carer grant and Scottish child payment) are not taken into account;
- it can still be worth claiming non-means-tested benefits, even if they are taken into account. If you, your partner or your child(ren) qualify for certain of these, you also qualify for certain premiums and components (see Chapter 17) and, potentially, a higher rate of HB. If you think you might qualify, get advice to see whether you would be better off.

You may only qualify for HB once you or your partner, or a child or qualifying young person included in your claim, are awarded another benefit (known as a 'qualifying benefit'). You may be entitled to a higher rate of HB once the qualifying benefit is awarded (see p210).

The benefit cap

In some cases, there is a limit on the total amount of specified benefits you can receive (a 'benefit cap'). HB is one of the specified benefits (but HB for 'specified accommodation' – see p173 for what counts – is ignored). The benefit cap only applies if you are getting HB or UC. See p1156 for further information.

Passports and other sources of help

If you have been awarded HB, you may qualify for a Best Start grant in Scotland (see Chapter 74), a social fund funeral expenses payment (see p784) or, in Scotland, a funeral support payment (see Chapter 76). You may be entitled to a council tax reduction (see p836).

Financial help on starting work

You may be entitled to extended payments of HB (see p217). Your local authority may also offer extended help with council tax. See p858 for information about other financial help you might get.

Notes

1. Who can get housing benefit

1 s130 SSCBA 1992; s115 IAA 1999; reg 10 HB Regs; reg 10 HB(SPC) Regs
2 Reg 26 HB(SPC) Regs
3 Reg 6(8) UC(TP) Regs; art 6(2) WRA(No.21)O; art 7(3) WRA(No.23)O
4 Reg 6 UC(TP) Regs; art 6 WRA(No.21)O; art 7 WRA(No.23)O; art 4 WRA(No.31)O; art 4(11) WRA(No.32)O
5 Email to CPAG, 30 January 2019
6 Reg 2(1) UC(TP) Regs; Sch 1 para 3A UC Regs
7 Reg 2(1) UC(TP) Regs; Sch 1 para 3B UC Regs
8 Reg 6(6) UC(TP) Regs
9 Regs 5(2)(c) and 6(8A) UC(TP) Regs
10 Reg 4 UC(TP) Regs
11 Art 6(3)(a) WRA(No.21)O; art 7(4)(a) WRA(No.23)O; arts 2(3), 4 and 7 WRA(No.31)O
12 Art 7(2)(b) and (3)(b) WRA(No.31)O
13 Regs 11(1) and 12(1) HB Regs; regs 11(1) and 12(1) HB(SPC) Regs
14 CH/3110/2003; R(H) 3/07
15 *AB v LB Camden (HB)* [2020] UKUT 158 (AAC)
16 R(H) 9/08; *Kirklees MBC v JM (HB)* [2018] UKUT 219 (AAC)
17 Reg 2(4)(a) HB Regs; reg 2(4)(a) HB(SPC) Regs
18 *R v Cambridge CC ex parte Thomas,* 10 February 1995 (QBD); CH/2959/2006
19 Regs 11(2) and 12(2) HB Regs; reg 12(2) HB(SPC) Regs
20 Reg 2(1) HB Regs and reg 2(1) HB(SPC) Regs, definition of 'long tenancy' and 'owner'; CH/2258/2004; *Burton v New Forest DC* [2004] EWCA Civ 1510, reported as R(H) 7/05; R(H) 3/07; CH/3586/2005; R(H) 8/07; *CR v Wycombe DC* [2009] UKUT 19 (AAC); *GN v Sevenoaks BC (HB)* [2016] UKUT 271 (AAC); *BC v (1) Liverpool City Council (2) SSWP* [2020] UKUT 28 (AAC)
21 Reg 11(2) HB Regs
22 Reg 8(1)(a) and (b) HB Regs; reg 8(1)(a) and (b) HB(SPC) Regs
23 Reg 8(2) HB Regs; reg 8(2) HB(SPC) Regs
24 *R v Rugby BC HBRB ex parte Harrison* [1994] 28 HLR 36 (QBD); CH/2959/2006
25 s48 Landlord and Tenant Act 1987; CH/3579/2003; CH/257/2005
26 R(H) 3/03
27 *R v Poole BC ex parte Ross* [1995] 28 HLR 351 (QBD); *R v Warrington BC ex parte Williams* [1997] 29 HLR 872 (QBD)
28 Reg 8(1)(c)-(e) HB Regs; reg 8(1)(c)-(e) HB(SPC) Regs; *ZD v LB of Hillingdon (HB)* [2021] UKUT 305 (AAC)
29 CSHB/606/2005
30 *FK v Wandsworth BC (HB)* [2016] UKUT 570 (AAC); *Babergh DC v GW (HB)* [2017] UKUT 40 (AAC)
31 paras A3/3.140-141 GM
32 Regs 9, 10 and 56 HB Regs; regs 9 and 10 HB(SPC) Regs
33 *Scott v SSWP* [2011] EWCA Civ 103
34 Reg 9(4) HB Regs; reg 9(4) HB(SPC) Regs; CH/1326/2004; CH/1328/2004
35 CH/542/2006; R(H) 5/06 decided that the rule did not conflict with the Human Rights Act.
36 Reg 3(4) HB Regs; reg 3(4) HB(SPC) Regs; R(H) 5/06; CPC/1446/2008; *RK v SSWP* [2008] UKUT 34 (AAC)
37 *Thamesdown BC v Goonery* [1995] 1 CLY 2600
38 R(H) 1/03; CH/1171/2002; CH/2899/2005
39 R(H) 1/03; *Warwick DC v SSWP and CH (HB)* [2020] UKUT 240 (AAC)
40 Reg 9(2) HB Regs; reg 9(2) HB(SPC) Regs; *R v Poole BC ex parte Ross* [1995] 28 HLR 351 (QBD); CH/1076/2002; CH/296/2004; CH/1097/2004; paras A3/3.258-65 GM
41 *DH v Kirklees MBC and SSWP (HB)* [2011] UKUT 301 (AAC), reported as [2012] AACR 16; *LB Bexley v KM* [2017] UKUT 354 (AAC)
42 *R (Tucker) v Secretary of State* [2001] EWCA Civ 1646. The court decided that the rule did not conflict with the Human Rights Act; *South Lanarkshire Council v DG* [2018] UKUT 417 (AAC); para A3/3.269 GM.

• •

43 Reg 9(3) HB Regs; reg 9(3) HB(SPC) Regs; *SD v LB Brent* [2009] UKUT 7 (AAC)

44 Reg 9(3) HB Regs; reg 9(3) HB(SPC) Regs

45 Reg 2(1) HB Regs; reg 2(1), definition of 'owner' and 'long tenancy', HB(SPC) Regs; CH/1278/2002; CH/0296/2003; *MH v Wirral MBC* [2009] UKUT 60 (AAC); *Bradford MDC v MRC (HB)* [2010] UKUT 315 (AAC); *Nottingham CC v CJ (HB)* [2011] UKUT 392 (AAC); *GN v Sevenoaks BC (HB)* [2016] UKUT 271 (AAC)

46 CH/3853/2001; CH/396/2002; R(H) 6/07; *KH v Sheffield CC* [2008] UKUT 11 (AAC)

47 *RS v Fife Council and SSWP* [2018] UKUT 322 (AAC)

48 *CH v Wakefield DC* [2009] UKUT 20 (AAC)

49 Reg 2(1) HB Regs; reg 2(1) HB(SPC) Regs

50 R(SB) 22/87; *Bristol City Council v JKT (HB)* [2016] UKUT 517 (AAC)

51 paras A3/3.243-45 GM

52 *R v Solihull MBC ex parte Simpson* [1995] 1 FLR 140 (CA); CH/39/2007

53 *R (Mackay) v Barking and Dagenham HBRB* [2001] EWHC Admin 234

54 CH/2258/2004

55 *R (Mackay) v Barking and Dagenham HBRB* [2001] EWHC Admin 234

56 *R v Sutton LBC HBRB ex parte Keegan* [1992] 27 HLR 92 (QBD)

57 *R v Manchester CC ex parte Baragrove Properties Ltd* [1991] 23 HLR 337 (QBD); *R v Gloucestershire CC ex parte Dadds* [1997] 29 HLR 700 (QBD); CH/39/2007

58 *R v Poole BC ex parte Ross* [1995] 28 HLR 351 (QBD)

59 s134(2) SSCBA 1992; reg 82(1) HB Regs; reg 63(1) HB(SPC) Regs

60 s130(1) SSCBA 1992; reg 7(1) and (2) HB Regs; reg 7(1) and (2) HB(SPC) Regs

61 R(H) 5/09; *Birmingham City Council v IB* [2009] UKUT 116 (AAC)

62 Reg 7(5), (14) and (15)(c) HB Regs; reg 7(5), (14) and (15)(c) HB(SPC) Regs

63 CH/2201/2002

64 Regs 2(1) and 7(8) HB Regs; regs 2(1) and 7(8) HB(SPC) Regs

65 *Bury MBC v DC (HB)* [2011] UKUT 43 (AAC); *R (Mahmoudi) v LB Lewisham and Another* [2014] EWCA Civ 284

66 R(H) 9/05

67 Reg 7(7) HB Regs; reg 7(7) HB(SPC) Regs; para A3/3.430 GM

68 Reg 7(11)(b) and (c), (13)(a) and (b), (13D)(a) and (b), (13G)(a) and (b), (16)(a)-(c) and (18) HB Regs; reg 7(11)(b) and (c), (13)(a) and (b), (13D)(a) and (b), (13G)(a) and (b), (16)(a)-(c) and (18) HB(SPC) Regs

69 R(H) 9/05

70 Reg 7(13) and (17) HB Regs; reg 7(13) and (17) HB(SPC) Regs

71 *KdeS v Camden LB (HB)* [2011] UKUT 457 (AAC)

72 *R v Penwith DC ex parte Burt* [1988] 22 HLR 292 (QBD); para A3/3.460 GM

73 Reg 7(14) and (15)(a) HB Regs; reg 7(14) and (15)(a) HB(SPC) Regs

74 R(H) 8/09; *SK v South Hams DC (HB)* [2010] UKUT 129 (AAC), reported as [2010] AACR 40

75 CH/1237/2004

76 CH/3893/2004

77 Reg 13 HB Regs; reg 13 HB(SPC) Regs

78 Reg 7(11) and (12) HB Regs; reg 7(11) and (12) HB(SPC) Regs

79 *SSWP v Selby DC and Bowman* [2006] EWCA Civ 271, reported as R(H) 4/06

80 Reg 7(16)(d)(i) and (17) HB Regs; reg 7(16)(d)(i) and (17) HB(SPC) Regs

81 Reg 7(16)(c)(ii), (iii), (vii) and (x) HB Regs; reg 7(16)(c)(ii), (iii), (vii) and (x) HB(SPC) Regs

82 *Obrey and Others v SSWP* [2013] EWCA Civ 1584

83 gov.uk/government/publications/domestic-violence-and-abuse-help-from-dwp

84 Reg 7(16)(c)(i), (iv)-(vi), (viii)-(ix) and (16A) HB Regs; reg 7(16)(c)(i), (iv)-(vi), (viii)-(ix) and (16A) HB(SPC) Regs

85 Reg 7(14) and (15)(b) HB Regs; reg 7(14) and (15)(b) HB(SPC) Regs; CSH/499/2006

86 Reg 7(18) HB Regs; reg 7(18) HB(SPC) Regs

87 Reg 7(13C)-(13E) HB Regs; reg 7(13C)-(13E) HB(SPC) Regs

88 Reg 7(16)(d)(ii) and (iii), (17C) and (17D) HB Regs; reg 7(16)(d)(ii) and (iii), (17C) and (17D) HB(SPC) Regs

89 Reg 7(13F), (13G) and (18) HB Regs; reg 7(13F), (13G) and (18) HB(SPC) Regs

90 Reg 7(13D), (13G), (17C) and (17D) HB Regs; reg 7(13D), (13G), (17C) and (17D) HB(SPC) Regs; *Slough BC v PK* [2019] UKUT 128 (AAC)

91 Reg 7(13A) and (17A) HB Regs; reg 7(13A) and (17A) HB(SPC) Regs

92 Reg 7(13B) and (17B) HB Regs; reg 7(13B) and (17B) HB(SPC) Regs

93 R(H) 5/09; *Birmingham City Council v IB* [2009] UKUT 116 (AAC)

94 Reg 7(6)(d) and (e) HB Regs; reg 7(6)(d) and (e) HB(SPC) Regs

95 CH/1911/2006

96 *R (Mahmoudi) v LB Lewisham and Another* [2014] EWCA Civ 284

97 Reg 7(6)(a) HB Regs; reg 7(6)(a) HB(SPC) Regs

98 Reg 7(6)(b) and (c) HB Regs; reg 7(6)(b) and (c) HB(SPC) Regs

99 Reg 7(10) HB Regs; reg 7(10) HB(SPC) Regs

100 Reg 7(3) and (4) HB Regs; reg 7(3) and (4) HB(SPC) Regs

101 R(SB) 10/81

2. The rules about your age

102 For working-age HB, see the HB Regs. For pension-age HB, see the HB(SPC) Regs.

103 Reg 5 HB Regs

104 Reg 5 HB(SPC) Regs

105 Art 6 WRA(No.31)O

106 Art 6(4) WRA(No.31)O

107 Art 8 WRA(No.31)O

4. The amount of benefit

108 s130(3) SSCBA 1992; Schs 4 para 12, 5 para 4, and 6 para 5 HB Regs; reg 26 HB(SPC) Regs; *R v Penwith DC ex parte Menear* [1991] 24 HLR 120 (QBD); *R v South Ribble DC HBRB ex parte Hamilton* [2000] 33 HLR 104 (CA); *DF v LB Waltham Forest (HB)* [2017] UKUT 306 (AAC)

109 Reg 2(3), (3A) and (3B) HB Regs; reg 2(3) and (3A) HB(SPC) Regs; *SMcH v Perth and Kinross Council (HB)* [2015] UKUT 126 (AAC)

110 s130(3) SSCBA 1992; reg 71 HB Regs; reg 51 HB(SPC) Regs

111 Reg 70 HB Regs; reg 50 HB(SPC) Regs

112 Reg 12B(2) HB Regs; reg 12B(2) HB(SPC) Regs

113 Reg 12(2A) and (2B) HB Regs; reg 12(2A) and (2B) HB(SPC) Regs; reg 12(6A) and (6B) HB Regs, as set out in Sch 3 para 5(1) HB&CTB(CP) Regs

114 Regs 12B(3) and 12C(2) HB Regs; regs 12B(3) and 12C(2) HB(SPC) Regs; reg 12(4) HB Regs and reg 12(4) HB(SPC) Regs, as set out in Sch 3 para 5 HB&CTB(CP) Regs

115 Reg 11(3) HB Regs; reg 11(2) HB(SPC) Regs

116 Reg 2(1) HB Regs; reg 2(1) HB(SPC) Regs

117 Reg 80 HB Regs; reg 61 HB(SPC) Regs

118 Reg 81(3) and Sch 1 para 7(2) HB Regs; reg 62(3) and Sch 1 para 7(2) HB(SPC) Regs

119 Regs 12B(4) and 12C(2) HB Regs; regs 12B(4) and 12C(2) HB(SPC) Regs; reg 12(5) HB Regs and reg 12(5) HB(SPC) Regs, as set out in Sch 3 para 5 HB&CTB(CP) Regs; CH/3376/2002

120 *R (Naghshbandi) v Camden LBC* [2002] EWCA Civ 1038

121 CH/3376/2002

122 Reg 12B(2) HB Regs; reg 12B(2) HB(SPC) Regs; reg 12(3) HB Regs and reg 12(3) HB(SPC) Regs, as set out in Sch 3 para 5 HB&CTB(CP) Regs; *R v Bristol City Council ex parte Jacobs* [1999] 32 HLR 82 (QBD); *Liverpool City Council v (1) NM, (2) WD (HB)* [2015] UKUT 532 (AAC), reported as [2016] AACR 19

123 Sch 1 para 8 HB Regs; Sch 1 para 8 HB(SPC) Regs. For the meaning of 'sheltered accommodation', see *Oxford City Council v Basey* [2012] EWCA Civ 115, reported as [2012] AACR 38.

124 Sch 1 para 5 HB Regs; Sch 1 para 5 HB(SPC) Regs

125 Sch 1 para 6(1) HB Regs; Sch 1 para 6(1) HB(SPC) Regs

126 Sch 1 para 6(2) and (3) HB Regs; Sch 1 para 6(2) and (3) HB(SPC) Regs

127 paras A4/4.912-13 GM

128 Sch 1 paras 5 and 6(1)(b) HB Regs; Sch 1 paras 5 and 6(1)(b) HB(SPC) Regs

129 Sch 1 para 8 HB Regs; Sch 1 para 8 HB(SPC) Regs

130 para A4/4.730 GM; *CP and Others v Aylesbury Vale DC v SSWP (HB)* [2011] UKUT 22 (AAC); *Liverpool City Council v (1) NM, (2) WD (HB)* [2015] UKUT 532 (AAC), reported as [2016] AACR 19

131 Sch 1 para 1(a)(iii) HB Regs; Sch 1 para 1(a)(iii) HB(SPC) Regs

132 Sch 1 para 1(a)(ii) HB Regs; Sch 1 para 1(a)(ii) HB(SPC) Regs

133 Sch 1 para 1(b) HB Regs; Sch 1 para 1(b) HB(SPC) Regs

134 Sch 1 para 1(a)(iv) HB Regs; Sch 1 para 1(a)(iv) HB(SPC) Regs

135 Reg 12B(2)(b) and Sch 1 para 1 HB Regs; reg 12B(2)(b) and Sch 1 para 1 HB(SPC) Regs; reg 12(3)(b) HB Regs and reg 12(3)(b) HB(SPC) Regs, as set out in Sch 3 para 5 HB&CTB(CP) Regs

136 Reg 12B(2)(c) and Sch 1 para 3(2) HB Regs; reg 12B(2)(c) and Sch 1 para 3(2) HB(SPC) Regs; reg 12(3)(c) HB Regs and reg 12(3)(c) HB(SPC) Regs, as set out in Sch 3 para 5 HB&CTB(CP) Regs
137 Sch 1 para 3 HB Regs; Sch 1 para 3 HB(SPC) Regs
138 Sch 1 paras 1(a)(i) and 2(1) HB Regs; Sch 1 paras 1(a)(i) and 2(1) HB(SPC) Regs
139 Sch 1 para 2(6) and (7) HB Regs; Sch 1 para 2(6) and (7) HB(SPC) Regs
140 Reg 70 HB Regs; reg 50 HB(SPC) Regs
141 Reg 3(1) HB Regs; reg 3(1) HB(SPC) Regs
142 Reg 3(4) and Sch 1 para 8 HB Regs; reg 3(4) and Sch 1 para 8 HB(SPC) Regs; CPC/1446/2008; *AM v SSWP (IS)* [2011] UKUT 387 (AAC)
143 CSIS/185/1995
144 *Thamesdown BC v Goonery* [1995] 1 CLY 2600 (CA); *RK v SSWP* [2008] UKUT 34 (AAC)
145 CIS/14850/1996
146 para A5/5.521 GM
147 R(H) 8/09; *SK v South Hams DC (HB)* [2010] UKUT 129 (AAC), reported as [2010] AACR 40
148 Reg 3(2) HB Regs; reg 3(2) HB(SPC) Regs
149 *JP v Bournemouth BC (HB)* [2018] UKUT 75 (AAC), reported as [2018] AACR 30
150 *R v Chesterfield BC ex parte Fullwood* [1993] 26 HLR 126
151 Reg 3(3) HB Regs; reg 3(3) HB(SPC) Regs
152 Regs 2(1), definition of 'attendance allowance', and 74(6) HB Regs; regs 2(1), definition of 'attendance allowance', and 55(6) HB(SPC) Regs
153 Reg 74(7) and (10) HB Regs; reg 55(7) and (9) HB(SPC) Regs
154 s2 ETA 1973; s2 Enterprise and New Towns (Scotland) Act 1990
155 Reg 74(1) HB Regs; reg 55(1) HB(SPC) Regs
156 Reg 74(1) and (2) HB Regs; reg 55(1) and (2) HB(SPC) Regs
157 Reg 6(6) HB Regs; reg 6(6) HB(SPC) Regs
158 Reg 74(9) HB Regs; reg 55(10) HB(SPC) Regs
159 CH/48/2006
160 Reg 74(3) HB Regs; reg 55(3) HB(SPC) Regs
161 Reg 74(4) HB Regs; reg 55(4) HB(SPC) Regs

162 Reg 74(5) HB Regs; reg 55(5) HB(SPC) Regs
163 Reg 59(10)-(13) HB(SPC) Regs
164 Reg 26 HB Regs; reg 24 HB(SPC) Regs

6. Claims and backdating
165 s1 SSAA 1992
166 Reg 83(1) and (9) HB Regs; reg 64(2) and (10) HB(SPC) Regs
167 Reg 83(4A) and (4B) HB Regs; reg 64(5A) and (5C) HB(SPC) Regs
168 Reg 83A and Sch 11 HB Regs; reg 64A and Sch 10 HB(SPC) Regs
169 Reg 83(1) HB Regs; reg 64(2) HB(SPC) Regs
170 Reg 83(2) HB Regs; reg 64(3) HB(SPC) Regs
171 Reg 83(4AA), (4AB) and (4BA) HB Regs; reg 64(5B), (5BA) and (5CA) HB(SPC) Regs
172 Reg 83(4AC)-(4AE) HB Regs; reg 64(5BB)-(5BD) HB(SPC) Regs; Explanatory Memorandum to SI 2008 No.2299
173 Reg 83(1), (4C), (6) and (9) HB Regs; reg 64(2), (5D), (7) and (10) HB(SPC) Regs
174 Reg 83(4D), (4DA), (7) and (7A) HB Regs; reg 64(5E), (5EA), (8) and (8A) HB(SPC) Regs
175 Reg 83(4E), (4F), (8) and (8A) HB Regs; reg 64(5F), (5G), (9) and (9A) HB(SPC) Regs
176 Reg 87(1) and (3) HB Regs; reg 68(1) and (3) HB(SPC) Regs
177 Reg 87(4)-(6) HB Regs; reg 68(4)-(6) HB(SPC) Regs
178 Reg 83(4)(b) HB Regs; reg 64(5)(b) HB(SPC) Regs
179 Regs 2, definition of 'appropriate DWP office', and 83(4)(a), (f) and (g) and (13) HB Regs; regs 2, definition of 'appropriate DWP office', and 64(5)(a), (f) and (g) and (14) HB(SPC) Regs
180 Reg 83(4)(c) HB Regs; reg 64(5)(c) HB(SPC) Regs
181 Reg 82(1) HB Regs; reg 63(1) HB(SPC) Regs; CH/2995/2006
182 Reg 82(2), (3), (5) and (6) HB Regs; reg 63(2), (3), (5) and (6) HB(SPC) Regs
183 Reg 82(4) HB Regs; reg 63(4) HB(SPC) Regs
184 Reg 82(4)(c) HB Regs; reg 63(4)(c) HB(SPC) Regs
185 s1(1A)-(1C) SSAA 1992
186 Reg 86(1A) HB Regs; reg 67(1A) HB(SPC) Regs; *CH v Plymouth City Council and DE* [2018] UKUT 215 (AAC)

187 Reg 86(1) HB Regs; reg 67(1) HB(SPC) Regs
188 *AA v LB Hounslow* [2008] UKUT 13 (AAC)
189 Reg 4(1)(a) HB Regs; reg 4(1)(a) HB(SPC) Regs
190 para A1/1.300 GM
191 Reg 83(5)(d) and (e) HB Regs; reg 64(6)(d) and (e) HB(SPC) Regs
192 Reg 83(5)(a)-(c) and (5A) HB Regs; reg 64(6)(a)-(c) HB(SPC) Regs
193 *Leicester City Council v LG* [2009] UKUT 155 (AAC)
194 Reg 64(1) HB(SPC) Regs
195 Regs 57 and 64(1), (1A) and (6) HB(SPC) Regs; *Leicester City Council v LG* [2009] UKUT 155 (AAC)
196 Reg 83(12) HB Regs
197 Reg 83(12A) HB Regs
198 R(S) 2/63 (T); CH/2659/2002; CH/474/2002; CH/393/2003; A2/Annex A GM
199 *UH v LB Islington (HB)* [2010] UKUT 64 (AAC)
200 CH/474/2002
201 R(G) 1/75
202 *FR v Broadband DC* [2012] UKUT 449 (AAC)
203 Reg 83(10) and (11) HB Regs; reg 64(11) and (12) HB(SPC) Regs
204 CG/1479/1999; CIS/217/1999
205 Reg 89 HB Regs; reg 70 HB(SPC) Regs
206 Reg 90 HB Regs; reg 71 HB(SPC) Regs; reg 10 HB&CTB(DA) Regs
207 Reg 90(2) HB Regs; reg 71(2) HB(SPC) Regs; reg 10 HB&CTB(DA) Regs
208 Reg 3 HB&CTB(DA) Regs
209 CH/180/2006
210 Reg 10(1) HB&CTB(DA) Regs
211 Sch 9 paras 9-15 HB Regs; Sch 8 paras 9-15 HB(SPC) Regs; reg 10(1) HB&CTB(DA) Regs
212 Reg 76 HB Regs; reg 57 HB(SPC) Regs; R(H) 9/07; *SL v Renfrewshire Council (HB)* [2014] UKUT 411 (AAC)
213 Regs 2(1), definition of 'benefit week', and 80(2), (3)(a), (4) and (8) HB Regs; regs 2(1), definition of 'benefit week', and 61(2), (3)(a), (4) and (8) HB(SPC) Regs

7. Getting paid
214 Reg 75 HB Regs; reg 56 HB(SPC) Regs
215 Reg 92(1) and (6) HB Regs; reg 73(1) and (6) HB(SPC) Regs
216 Reg 92(3) and (4) HB Regs; reg 73(3) and (4) HB(SPC) Regs
217 s134(1A) SSAA 1992

218 s134(1B) SSAA 1992; regs 91A and 94(1) HB Regs; regs 72A and 75(1) HB(SPC) Regs
219 Reg 91(2) HB Regs; reg 72(2) HB(SPC) Regs
220 Reg 92(5) HB Regs; reg 73(5) HB(SPC) Regs
221 Reg 91(1)(b) HB Regs; reg 72(1)(b) HB(SPC) Regs
222 para A6/6.120 GM
223 Reg 94(2) HB Regs; reg 75(2) HB(SPC) Regs
224 Reg 94(3) HB Regs; reg 75(3) HB(SPC) Regs
225 Reg 97 HB Regs; reg 78 HB(SPC) Regs
226 *R v Haringey LBC ex parte Azad Ayub* [1992] 25 HLR 566 (QBD)
227 R(H) 1/08
228 Reg 96(2) HB Regs; reg 77(2) HB(SPC) Regs
229 Reg 95 HB Regs; reg 76 HB(SPC) Regs; Sch 9 SS(C&P) Regs; *R v Haringey LBC ex parte Azad Ayub* [1992] 25 HLR 566 (QBD)
230 CH 3244/2007; *ST v Sunderland City Council (HB)* [2019] UKUT 33 (AAC), reported as [2019] AACR 20
231 Reg 96(1)(a) and (b) and (3A)(a) HB Regs; reg 77(1)(a) and (b) and (3A)(a) HB(SPC) Regs
232 *DLT v Eastleigh BC (HB)* [2014] UKUT 242 (AAC)
233 Regs 95(2A) and 96(3A)(b) HB Regs; regs 76(2A) and 77(3A)(b) HB(SPC) Regs
234 Regs 95(2A) and 96(1)(c) HB Regs; regs 76(2A) and 77(1)(c) HB(SPC) Regs
235 *E v Dacorum BC & M* [2017] UKUT 93 (AAC)
236 Regs 95(3) and 96(3) HB Regs; regs 76(3) and 77(3) HB(SPC) Regs
237 Reg 96(3) HB Regs; reg 77(3) HB(SPC) Regs
238 para A6/6.212 GM
239 Reg 54(6) HB(SPC) Regs
240 Reg 5(2)(c) UC(TP) Regs
241 Reg 54(1) and (2) HB(SPC) Regs
242 Regs 2(1), definition of 'benefit week', and 54(3)-(5) HB(SPC) Regs
243 s32(4) WRA 2007
244 ss32-34 WRA 2007
245 Reg 72 HB Regs
246 Reg 73 HB Regs; reg 53 HB(SPC) Regs
247 Regs 72(4) and 73(2) HB Regs; reg 53(2) HB(SPC) Regs; CH/1762/2004
248 Regs 72A, 72B(6), 73A and 73B(6) HB Regs; regs 53A and 53B(6) HB(SPC) Regs

. . . .

3

249 Regs 72B and 73B HB Regs; regs 52 and 53B HB(SPC) Regs
250 Regs 72E and 73E HB Regs
251 Regs 72D(2) and 73D(2) HB Regs; regs 52 and 53D(2) HB(SPC) Regs
252 Regs 72B(5) and 73B(5) HB Regs; reg 53B(5) HB(SPC) Regs
253 Regs 72C and 73C HB Regs; regs 52 and 53C HB(SPC) Regs
254 s34(3) WRA 2007; reg 2(1) HB Regs; reg 2(1), definitions of 'mover' and 'second authority', HB(SPC) Regs
255 s32(1), (2) and (13) WRA 2007; regs 72D and 73D HB Regs; reg 53D HB(SPC) Regs
256 Regs 72B(7) and 73B(7) HB Regs; regs 52(3) and 53B(7) HB(SPC) Regs
257 Regs 8(2A), 8A, 44, 46(1)(a) and 47(2)(a) UC(TP) Regs
258 Reg 8A(a) UC(TP) Regs
259 Reg 8A(c) UC(TP) Regs
260 Reg 75F(1)(g) HB Regs
261 Regs 89(2), 90(1) and 91(3) HB Regs; regs 70(2), 71(1) and 72(3) HB(SPC) Regs
262 Reg 93(1) HB Regs; reg 74(1) HB(SPC) Regs
263 *R v Haringey LBC ex parte Azad Ayub* [1992] 25 HLR 566 (QBD)
264 Reg 93(1) HB Regs; reg 74(1) HB(SPC) Regs; *R v Haringey LBC ex parte Azad Ayub* [1992] 25 HLR 566 (QBD)
265 Reg 93(2) HB Regs; reg 74(2) HB(SPC) Regs
266 Reg 93(3) HB Regs; reg 74(3) HB(SPC) Regs
267 Reg 88(1) HB Regs; reg 69(1) HB(SPC) Regs; reg 4 SS(NCC) Regs
268 Regs 86(3) and 90 and Sch 9 paras 9(1)(g) and 10(a) HB Regs; regs 67(3) and 71 and Sch 8 paras 9(1)(g) and 10(a) HB(SPC) Regs
269 Regs 2(1), 86(3) and 88(1) HB Regs; regs 2(1), 67(3) and 69(1) HB(SPC) Regs
270 Reg 88(1) HB Regs; reg 69(1) HB(SPC) Regs
271 Reg 88(1) HB Regs; reg 69(1) HB(SPC) Regs
272 Reg 88A and Sch 11 HB Regs; reg 69A and Sch 10 HB(SPC) Regs
273 Reg 88(6) HB Regs; reg 69(9) HB(SPC) Regs
274 Reg 88ZA HB Regs; reg 69ZA HB(SPC) Regs
275 Reg 69(6)-(8) HB(SPC) Regs
276 Reg 69(7) HB(SPC) Regs
277 Reg 88(1), (3) and (4) HB Regs; reg 69(1), (3) and (4) HB(SPC) Regs

278 Regs 2(1), definition of 'benefit week', and 79(1) HB Regs; regs 2(1), definition of 'benefit week', and 59(1) HB(SPC) Regs; reg 8(2) HB&CTB(DA) Regs
279 Reg 79(8) HB Regs; reg 59(8) HB(SPC) Regs
280 Reg 59(10)-(13) HB(SPC) Regs
281 Regs 5(2)(a) and 7 UC(TP) Regs
282 Regs 5(2) and 7(5)(b) and (c) UC(TP) Regs
283 Reg 60 HB(SPC) Regs
284 Regs 7(2)(o) and 8(14D) HB&CTB(DA) Regs; reg 79(2), (2A), (2B), (8) and (9) HB Regs; reg 59(2), (2A), (2B), (8) and (9) HB(SPC) Regs

Chapter 11

Income support

Key facts

- You can only make a new claim for income support (IS) in very limited circumstances.
- IS is a means-tested benefit for which only specific groups of people can qualify.
- You do not have to have paid national insurance contributions to qualify.
- You cannot qualify for IS if you (or your partner) count as being in full-time paid work.
- IS is administered and paid by the DWP.
- If you disagree with an IS decision, you can apply for a revision or a supersession (see Chapter 56), or appeal against it (see Chapter 57). You must apply for a mandatory reconsideration before you can appeal.

New claims for, and continuing entitlement to, income support

Until 30 March 2022, you could make a **new claim** for IS if you were prevented from claiming universal credit (UC) because you were (or if you are a member of a couple, each of you were) a 'frontier worker' – ie, you are in Great Britain to work, but do not live there or in Northern Ireland.[1] This is no longer the case.

If the DWP wants to safeguard or test the efficient administration of UC, it can designate categories of case that are prevented from claiming UC.[2]

If you are already entitled to IS, you can **continue to qualify** until:

– you claim UC. **Note:** when you make a new claim for UC, your IS entitlement can continue for two weeks. See p241 for information about IS run-on; *or*

– you become a member of a couple and your partner is getting UC; *or*

Part 3: Getting a benefit decision changed
Chapter 11: Income support
1. Who can get income support

– you and your partner are affected by the 'managed migration' transfer process, that is, you are told by the DWP that your IS will end and are invited to claim UC. See p29 for further information, and AskCPAG and CPAG's *Welfare Rights Bulletin* for updates.

1. **Who can get income support**

You qualify for income support (IS) if:[3]
- you are in at least one of the specified groups on pp233–37; *and*
- neither you nor your partner count as being in full-time paid work (see p237); *and*
- you are not studying full time. There are exceptions to this rule (see p876). See p878 if you are studying part time and p873 if you are at school or college in 'relevant education'; *and*
- you are not entitled to jobseeker's allowance (JSA) or employment and support allowance (ESA); *and*
- your partner is not entitled to income-based JSA, joint-claim JSA, income-related ESA or pension credit (PC); *and*
- you are at least 16 and are under pension age (see p766). **Note:** if you are already getting IS and you are or become a member of a 'mixed-age' couple (ie, you have reached pension age but your partner has not), in some circumstances, your IS can continue even though you have reached pension age (see p237); *and*
- your income is less than your applicable amount (see p238); *and*
- your savings and other capital are worth £16,000 or less. Some capital (including your home) is ignored (see Chapter 22); *and*
- you are not a 'person subject to immigration control' (see p1524). There are exceptions to this rule; *and*
- you satisfy the 'habitual residence' and 'right to reside' tests, and are present in Great Britain. To find out whether you are exempt from the tests, see Chapter 69. To see whether you can claim IS during a temporary absence abroad, see p1629.

In some cases, in order to get IS, you (and your partner) may be required to attend a work-focused interview. If the only reason you are getting IS is because you are a lone parent and you do not have any children under the age of three, you may also be required to undertake work-related activity (see p1111).

Note: you can only make a new claim for IS in limited circumstances (see p231).

Groups of people who can qualify for income support

Only certain groups of people can qualify for IS. Broadly these are:
- people who are sick or disabled (see below);
- pregnant women and certain people who are looking after children (see below);
- carers (see p235);
- certain pupils, students and people on training courses (see p235);
- other groups – eg, people in custody pending trial or sentence, refugees learning English and some people involved in a trade dispute (see p236).

Even if you are in one of the above groups, you must also satisfy the other rules for getting IS described on p232.[4]

Note:
- Because very few people can make a new claim for IS, the groups are now mainly relevant for enabling you to continue to be entitled to IS.
- If you come into one of the groups on any day in a benefit week (see p438), you count as doing so for the whole week.
- If your circumstances change and you no longer come into a particular group, check whether you are in any of the other groups. If so, your entitlement to IS continues.[5]
- If you are a member of a couple and you are not in one of the groups, but your partner is, s/he could be the claimant if s/he can make a new claim for IS (see p231). Whichever one of you gets IS, the other may qualify for national insurance (NI) credits to protect her/his NI record (see Chapter 43).
- In the past, there were additional groups of people who could qualify for IS. If you are getting IS on the basis of being in one of these 'transitional groups' (see p236), you may continue to qualify on this basis.

People who are sick or disabled

You come into one of the groups of people who can qualify for IS if either of the following applies to you.[6]
- You are entitled to statutory sick pay.
- You are receiving the enhanced rate of the daily living component of personal independence payment (PIP). This only applies if, immediately before you started getting PIP, you were entitled to and in receipt of IS because you were receiving disability living allowance (DLA) highest rate care component and were therefore treated as incapable of work.

Pregnant women and certain people looking after children

You come into one of the groups of people who can qualify for IS if any of the following apply to you.[7]
- You are pregnant and:
  - incapable of work because of your pregnancy;[8] *or*

Part 3: Getting a benefit decision changed
Chapter 11: Income support
1. Who can get income support

– there are 11 weeks or less before the week your baby is due.
- You were pregnant and your pregnancy ended not more than 15 weeks ago – ie, when your baby was born or you had a miscarriage.
- You are a lone parent aged 18 or over and have at least one child under five, or you are a lone parent under the age of 18 and have a child of any age. The child must be included in your claim (see p307).[9] You do not have to be the child's parent – eg, you could be a grandparent or sibling.
- You are on 'parental leave' from work under specific provisions (this does *not* include shared parental leave) and:
  – during the period for which you are claiming IS, you are not entitled to any kind of payment from your employer; *and*
  – you and your child(ren) live in the same household (see p311); *and*
  – you were entitled to housing benefit (HB) (or to child tax credit (CTC) of more than the family element (see p277) or working tax credit (WTC)) on the day before your parental leave began.
- You are on paternity leave[10] and:
  – you are not entitled to statutory paternity pay or to any kind of payment from your employer during the period for which you are claiming IS; *or*
  – you were entitled to HB (or to CTC of more than the family element (see p277) or WTC) on the day before your paternity leave began.
- You are a lone foster parent – ie, a child under 16 has been placed with you by a local authority or voluntary organisation, or because of an order or warrant under the Children's Hearings (Scotland) Act 2011, and you are not a member of a couple. The child must be living with you or accommodated by you.[11]
- A child has been placed with you for adoption by an adoption agency and you are not a member of a couple.

What happens when you no longer qualify for income support as a lone parent?
1. Unless you are under 18, once your only or youngest child turns five, you cannot qualify for IS unless you are in one of the other groups of people who can qualify – eg, if you are a carer. You can continue to qualify for IS on that basis, even if you can no longer qualify as a lone parent.[12]
2. If you no longer qualify for IS, you may be able to qualify for universal credit (UC) (or JSA or ESA if you can still make a new claim). If you qualify for UC or JSA, there are special rules that may help you satisfy the work-related requirements or jobseeking conditions (see Chapters 46 and 48).

You can qualify for IS for a temporary period while any of the following apply to you.[13]
- You are looking after a child under 16 because her/his parent or the person who usually looks after her/him is temporarily ill or temporarily away.[14]

- A child under 16 is included in your claim (see p307) and your partner is temporarily out of the UK.
- You are looking after your partner, or a child (this includes a 'qualifying young person') who is included in your claim (see p307), who is temporarily ill.[15]

Carers

You come into one of the groups of people who can qualify for IS if you are a carer and either of the following applies to you.[16]

- You receive carer's allowance (CA), or you would receive it had you not been given a sanction for a benefit offence (see p1239).
- The person you care for:
  - receives attendance allowance (AA), the highest or middle rate care component of DLA or child disability payment (CDP), the daily living component of PIP, or armed forces independence payment; or
  - has been awarded AA, the highest or middle rate care component of DLA or CDP or the daily living component of PIP on an advance claim, but payments have not yet been made; or
  - has claimed AA, DLA, CDP, PIP or armed forces independence payment. You can qualify for IS for up to 26 weeks from the date of that claim or until the claim is decided, whichever comes first.

You must be 'regularly and substantially engaged' in providing care. If you do not receive CA, the decision maker must look at the quality and quantity of care you provide. This could be less than the 35 hours a week needed to qualify for CA.[17]

If you stop meeting these conditions or stop being a carer, you can continue to qualify for IS for a further eight weeks.[18] After that, you cannot get IS unless you come into one of the other groups of people who can qualify for IS.

Pupils, students and people on training courses

You come into one of the groups of people who can qualify for IS if any of the following apply to you.[19]

- You are in 'relevant education' (see p873) or you are a full-time student who can qualify for IS while studying (see p876).
- You are on a course of full-time, non-advanced education (or were accepted or enrolled on it) and you are under 21, or you are 21 but turned 21 while on such a course. This only applies if:
  - you are an orphan and have no one acting as your parent; or
  - you have to live away from your parents and any person acting in their place because you are estranged from them, are in physical or moral danger or there is a serious risk to your physical or mental health; or
  - you live away from your parents and any person acting in their place, they are unable to support you financially and:

Part 3: Getting a benefit decision changed
Chapter 11: Income support
1. Who can get income support

- they are chronically sick, or are mentally or physically disabled – ie, they could get a disability premium, or they are entitled to ESA including a work-related activity or support component (or would be but for their one-year's entitlement to contributory ESA expiring), or they are 'substantially and permanently disabled'; *or*
- they are detained in custody under a sentence from the court or while they are awaiting trial or sentence; *or*
- they are not allowed to come to Great Britain because they do not have leave to enter under the Immigration Rules.
- You are aged 16 to 24 and on a training course provided by the Secretary of State, the Welsh Ministers or, in Scotland, by a local enterprise company. This does not apply if you count as a child or qualifying young person for child benefit purposes (see p563), or if you count as being in full-time paid work.

Others

You come into one of the groups of people who can qualify for IS if any of the following apply to you.[20]

- You are on parental bereavement leave from work and:
  - you are not entitled to statutory parental bereavement pay or to any kind of payment from your employer during the period for which you are on leave and claiming IS; *or*
  - you were entitled to HB (or to CTC of more than the family element (see p277) or WTC) on the day before your parental bereavement leave began.
- You have to go to a court or tribunal as a justice of the peace, juror, witness or party to the proceedings.
- You have been remanded in custody, or committed in custody, but only until your trial or until you have been sentenced. You can only get IS for certain housing costs – eg, for your ground rent or service charges (see Chapter 18).
- You are a refugee who is learning English in order to obtain employment. You must be on a course for more than 15 hours a week and, at the time the course started, you must have been in Great Britain for a year or less. You can only get IS for up to nine months under this rule.
- You qualify for 'housing costs run-on' – eg, for ground rent or service charges (see p359).
- You are involved in a trade dispute or you have been back at work for 15 days or less following a trade dispute (see p982).

Transitional groups

In the past, there were additional groups of people who could qualify for IS – eg, if you were claiming IS 'on the grounds of disability', as a disabled worker, or as a lone parent aged 18 or over of a child aged five or over. If you came into a 'transitional group', you could continue to qualify for IS on this basis even though a new claim could no longer be made by someone in these circumstances. See previous editions of this *Handbook* for further information.

Full-time paid work

You cannot usually qualify for IS if you or your partner are in, or are treated as being in, full-time paid work. If you are the IS claimant, this means 16 hours or more each week. For your partner, this means 24 hours or more each week. If you and your partner work fewer hours than these limits, you may be able to get IS. See Chapter 44 for the rules on work and how your hours are calculated. **Note:** in some situations you are treated as *not* being in full-time work even if you work 16/24 hours or more (see p977).

If you or your partner have just taken up full-time paid work, you may be able to qualify for IS for help with some of your housing costs (eg, for ground rent or service charges) for the first four weeks (called 'housing costs run-on' in this *Handbook* – see p359). If you do, you do not count as being in full-time paid work. You must notify the DWP that you are starting full-time paid work in order to get the run-on.

---

2. The rules about your age

You must be at least 16 to qualify for income support (IS). If you are aged 16 or 17, see below.

You cannot usually qualify for IS if you are pension age or over (see p766). It is your age as the claimant that is relevant, not the age of your partner. If you are at least pension age, you may be able to claim pension credit (see Chapter 13). However, if you are getting IS and you are, or become, a member of a 'mixed-age couple' (ie, you have reached pension age but your partner has not) and you are prevented from claiming universal credit (see p231), you are treated as not yet pension age and your IS continues.[21]

16/17 year olds

If you are 16 or 17, you can qualify for IS in your own right if you satisfy the rules of entitlement described in this chapter.[22] If you can make a new claim (see p231), you should not have it refused or be turned away by the DWP simply because of your age or because you have been included in someone else's benefit or tax credit claim.

Note: if you have been, or are being, looked after by a local authority, your local authority should support and accommodate you.

Part 3: Getting a benefit decision changed
Chapter 11: Income support
4. The amount of benefit

3

3. **People included in the claim**

If you are single, you get income support (IS) for yourself. If you are a member of a couple, one of you can get IS for both of you. If you are in a couple, your applicable amount includes a personal allowance for a couple and can include premiums based on both your and your partner's circumstances. When your benefit is worked out, your partner's income and capital are usually added to yours.

IS does not normally include amounts for your child(ren). However, there are some situations when you must show that you are responsible for a child who is living in your household – eg, to show you are a lone parent so you can benefit from a higher earnings disregard (see p414).

You do not have to be the child's parent. For who counts as a child, see p308. For when you count as responsible for a child and when s/he counts as living in your household, see pp309–312.

4. **The amount of benefit**

Income support (IS) tops up your income to a level that is set by the government. The amount you get depends on your needs (your 'applicable amount') and on how much income and capital you (and your partner) have.[23] There are three steps involved in working out your IS.

Step one: calculate your applicable amount

Your applicable amount consists of:

- a personal allowance (see p317); *plus*
- premiums (see p323) for any special needs; *plus*
- certain housing costs – eg, for your ground rent or service charges (see Chapter 18). You cannot get IS for help with your mortgage or a loan for repairs and improvements. Instead, the DWP may offer you a loan (see p839). You cannot get help with your rent. Instead, you may qualify for housing benefit.

Note: if it is not possible to assess your housing costs accurately or confirm your entitlement to the severe disability premium (see p330), the DWP can exclude these from your IS until they can be calculated.[24]

Do you have children?

IS does not normally include allowances and premiums for your children, but they may be included if your claim began before 6 April 2004 (see p317). If you *do* get allowances and premiums for your children, there are special rules for how their income and capital are treated (see p404 and p474).

Step two: calculate your income

This is the amount you (and your partner) have coming in each week from, for instance, certain other benefits, part-time earnings and maintenance (see Chapter 20). If you have capital over £6,000 (£10,000 if you live in a care home) but under £16,000, it also includes your 'tariff income' (see p427).

Step three: deduct income from applicable amount

Example

Michael and Mia, aged 27 and 29, have a daughter, Evie, aged 10. Michael has been caring for Evie, who is severely disabled. He gets carer's allowance (CA) of £69.70. Mia gets child benefit and child tax credit (CTC), as well as disability living allowance (DLA) for Evie. The couple live in rented accommodation. Their applicable amount is:

Personal allowance	£121.05
Carer premium	£38.85
Total	£159.90

Their income (CA) to be taken into account is £69.70. Child benefit, CTC and DLA are all ignored.

Their IS is £159.90 (applicable amount) *minus* £69.70 (income) = £90.20

You might be entitled to more IS than you get currently, once you, your partner or a child included in your claim become entitled to another benefit (a 'qualifying benefit') because you are then entitled to additional premiums.

You might get a reduced amount of IS if:
- you (or, in some cases, your partner) were required to take part in a work-focused interview and you failed to do so without good cause; *or*
- you are a lone parent without any children under three, you were required to undertake work-related activity and you failed to do so without good cause; *or*
- you have committed a benefit offence (see p1239).

5. **Special benefit rules**

Special rules may apply to:
- 16/17 year olds who have been, or are being, looked after by a local authority (see p933);
- people who have come from or are going abroad (see Chapters 68, 69 and 70);
- people who are studying (see Chapter 41);
- people involved in a trade dispute (see p982);
- people without accommodation, people who (or whose partner or children) are in hospital or living in a care home or similar accommodation, and people in prison or detention (see Chapter 42).

6. **Claims and backdating**

There are now very few people who can make a new claim for income support (IS) – see p231. If you can make a new claim, the general rules about claims and backdating are covered in Chapter 50. For the specific rules that apply to IS, see pp241–45 of the 2020/21 edition of this *Handbook*.

7. **Getting paid**

The general rules on getting paid are covered in Chapter 51. This section explains the specific rules that apply to income support (IS).

When is income support paid?

You are normally paid fortnightly in arrears.[25] The day you are paid depends on your national insurance number (see p1150).

You are paid in advance if you are returning to work after a trade dispute.[26]

IS is a weekly benefit. However, if you are only entitled to IS for part of a week, you are only paid for the part week.[27]

If you are entitled to less than 10 pence a week (£5 a week if you are getting IS while involved in a trade dispute), you are not paid IS at all, unless you are receiving another social security benefit which can be paid with IS.[28] If you are entitled to less than £1 a week, the DWP can decide to pay you at 13-week intervals in arrears.[29]

Your entitlement to IS usually starts from the date of your claim (see p1141, and p243 of the 2020/21 edition of this *Handbook*).[30]

Note:

- Deductions can be made from your IS to pay to third parties (see p1164).
- Your IS might be paid at a reduced rate if you have been given a sanction for:
  - failing to take part in a work-focused interview or, if you are a lone parent and do not have any children aged under three, to undertake work-related activity; *or*
  - a benefit offence (see p1239).
- If payment of your IS is suspended, see p1161.
- For information on missing payments, see p1150. If you cannot get your IS payments because you have lost your bank card or have forgotten your PIN, see p1149. If your payment service card has been lost or stolen, see p1150.
- If payment of your IS is delayed, see p1255. If you are waiting for a decision on your claim, or to be paid, you may be able to get a short-term advance (see

p1153). If you wish to complain about how your claim has been dealt with or to claim compensation, see Chapter 61.

- If you are overpaid IS, you might have to repay it (see Chapter 53) and, in some circumstances, you may have to pay a penalty (see p1229). If you have been accused of fraud, see Chapter 54.
- If you are owed arrears of IS, these can be paid in instalments (see p1148).

Income support run-on

If you are getting IS and make a new claim for universal credit, your IS entitlement continues for two weeks (called a 'run-on payment' or 'transitional IS payment'), as long as you would otherwise remain entitled.[31] You do not have to make a claim for a run-on payment. It should be made automatically. You do not have to pay a run-on payment back and it does not count as a specified benefit for the purposes of the benefit cap (see p1158).[32]

Change of circumstances

You must report changes in your circumstances that you have been told you must report, as well as any that you might reasonably be expected to know might affect your right to, the amount of, or the payment of, your benefit. You should do this as soon as possible, preferably in writing. See p1160 for further information.

When there has been a relevant change of circumstances, a decision maker looks at your claim again and makes a new decision. To see when your IS is then adjusted, see below.

Note: if you become a member of a couple with someone entitled to UC, your entitlement to IS ends (see p31).

When your income support is adjusted

As a general rule, if you are paid IS in arrears, your IS is adjusted from the beginning of the week in which the change of circumstances takes effect.[33] There are a number of exceptions, including the following.[34]

- If a decision is to your advantage (eg, it means you are entitled to more IS), but you failed to notify the DWP of a change within the time limit (normally one month, but this can be extended – see p1283), your IS is adjusted:
  - if you are paid in arrears, from the beginning of the week in which you notified the change; *or*
  - if you are paid in advance, from the day on which you notified the change if this is the day you are paid benefit or, if it is not, your IS is adjusted from the next week.
- Your IS is adjusted from the date of the change of circumstances (or the day on which this is expected to take place) if:
  - you are paid IS in arrears and the change of circumstances means you no longer qualify for IS, unless this is because your income is too high; *or*

Part 3: Getting a benefit decision changed
Chapter 11: Income support
8. Tax, other benefits and the benefit cap

- you live in a care home for part of the week and are entitled to disability living allowance or personal independence payment when you are staying elsewhere. This means that you can be paid, for example, the severe disability and enhanced disability premiums (see p330 and p327) when you are staying away from the care home.

8. **Tax, other benefits and the benefit cap**

Tax

Income support (IS) is normally not taxable. However, it is taxable if you are a member of a couple and you are involved in a trade dispute but your partner is not.[35]

Means-tested benefits and tax credits

If you are entitled to IS:
- IS is an automatic passport to maximum housing benefit (HB), maximum child tax credit (CTC) and usually to maximum working tax credit (WTC), but if you are not already entitled you may be unable to make a new claim. In Scotland, IS is a qualifying benefit for Scottish child payment (see p1731);
- if you work less than 16 hours a week and your partner works at least 16 hours but less than 24 hours a week, if you still can, you and your partner may be able to claim WTC as well as, or instead of, IS. Get advice to see whether you can still make a new claim and, if so, whether you would be better off financially;
- WTC is taken into account as income when working out your IS, but CTC is not.

Non-means-tested benefits

In some situations, while you are on IS you get national insurance credits (see p954).

Most non-means-tested benefits are taken into account as income when working out the amount of IS you get. However:
- attendance allowance, disability living allowance, personal independence payment, armed forces independence payment, monthly payments of bereavement support payment, guardian's allowance, child benefit (if you are getting CTC) and certain Scottish benefits (ie, adult disability payment, child disability payment, child winter heating assistance, Scottish child payment and young carer grant) are not taken into account;
- it can still be worth claiming non-means-tested benefits, even if they are taken into account. If you or your partner qualify for certain non-means-tested

benefits, you also qualify for certain premiums (see p323) and therefore a higher rate of IS.

The benefit cap

In some cases, there is a limit on the total amount of specified benefits you can receive (a 'benefit cap'). IS is one of the specified benefits. However, the benefit cap only applies if you are getting universal credit or HB. See p1156 for further information. **Note:** IS run-on (see p241) does not count as a specified benefit.

Passports and other sources of help

If you are entitled to IS, you also qualify for health benefits such as free prescriptions (see Chapter 31) and education benefits such as free school lunches (see p851). You may also qualify for help from your local welfare assistance scheme (see p846), for a council tax reduction (see p836), for social fund payments (see Chapter 37), in Scotland for a Best Start grant (see Chapter 74) or funeral support payment (see Chapter 76), and for Healthy Start food and vitamins (see p847) or, in Scotland, Best Start foods (see p850). In Scotland, you may also qualify for Scottish child payment (see Chapter 77).

Financial help on starting work

If you stop getting IS because you or your partner start work, or your earnings or hours in your existing job increase, you may be able to continue to get IS for help with certain housing costs (eg, ground rent or service charges) for a further four weeks (called 'housing costs run-on' in this *Handbook* – see p359) or extended payments of HB (if you pay rent – see p217). Your local authority may also provide extended help with council tax. If you have a DWP loan for your mortgage interest, this may continue for four weeks (see p845). See p858 for information about other financial help you might get.

Notes

1 Art 5A WRA(No.9)O; art 4(11) WRA(No.32)O
2 Reg 4 UC(TP) Regs

1. Who can get income support
3 s124 SSCBA 1992
4 Reg 4ZA and Sch 1B IS Regs
5 R(IS) 10/05
6 Sch 1B paras 7(d) and 7A IS Regs
7 Sch 1B paras 1-2A, 14, 14A and 14B IS Regs
8 CIS/0542/2001
9 CIS/2260/2002
10 The rules on paternity leave are in Part 2 PAL Regs.
11 *JS v SSWP (IS)* [2015] UKUT 306 (AAC), reported as [2016] AACR 13
12 R(IS) 10/05
13 Sch 1B paras 3 and 23 IS Regs
14 CIS/866/2004
15 CIS/4312/2007
16 Sch 1B para 4 IS Regs
17 R(IS) 8/02
18 Sch 1B paras 5 and 6 IS Regs
19 Sch 1B paras 11, 15, 15A and 28 IS Regs
20 Sch 1B paras 9A, 14C and 18-22 and Sch 7 para 8(b) IS Regs

2. The rules about your age
21 Art 8 WRA(No.31)O; HB Circular A9/2019
22 s124(1)(a) SSCBA 1992

4. The amount of benefit
23 s124(4) SSCBA 1992
24 Reg 13 SS&CS(DA) Regs

7. Getting paid
25 Sch 7 para 1 SS(C&P) Regs
26 Sch 7 paras 2(d) and 6(2) SS(C&P) Regs
27 s124(5) and (6) SSCBA 1992; reg 73 IS Regs
28 Reg 26(4) SS(C&P) Regs
29 Sch 7 para 5 SS(C&P) Regs
30 Sch 7 paras 3 and 6 SS(C&P) Regs
31 Regs 8(2A), 46(1) and 47(2) UC(TP) Regs

32 Reg 8B UC(TP) Regs
33 Reg 7 and Sch 3A para 1(a) SS&CS(DA) Regs
34 Reg 7 and Sch 3A paras 1(b) and 2-6 SS&CS(DA) Regs

8. Tax, other benefits and the benefit cap
35 s665 IT(EP)A 2003

Chapter 12

Income-based jobseeker's allowance

3

This chapter covers:
1. Who can get income-based jobseeker's allowance (p246)
2. The rules about your age (p249)
3. People included in the claim (p250)
4. The amount of benefit (p251)
5. Special benefit rules (p251)
6. Claims and backdating (p252)
7. Getting paid (p252)
8. Tax, other benefits and the benefit cap (p253)

Key facts

- You can only make a new claim for income-based jobseeker's allowance (JSA) in very limited circumstances.
- JSA is a benefit for people who are looking for work.
- There are three types of JSA. **Contribution-based JSA** is a non-means-tested benefit. **Income-based JSA** and **joint-claim JSA** are means-tested benefits.
- You do not have to have paid national insurance contributions to qualify for income-based JSA or joint-claim JSA.
- You cannot qualify for any type of JSA if you count as being in full-time paid work or, for income-based JSA or joint-claim JSA, if your partner counts as being in full-time paid work.
- You must normally be fit for work and satisfy the 'jobseeking conditions'.
- In a number of situations (eg, if you refuse to take up a job or a place on an employment programme), you may be given a sanction and your JSA may be paid at a reduced (or nil) rate.
- JSA is administered and paid by the DWP. It sometimes calls income-based JSA 'old-style' JSA.
- If you disagree with a JSA decision, you can apply for a revision or a supersession (see Chapter 56), or appeal against it (see Chapter 57). You must apply for a mandatory reconsideration before you can appeal.

Part 3: Getting a benefit decision changed
Chapter 12: Income-based jobseeker's allowance
1. Who can get income-based jobseeker's allowance

3

Note: unless otherwise stated, references to income-based JSA in this chapter also refer to joint-claim JSA.

New claims for, and continuing entitlement to, income-based jobseeker's allowance

Until 30 March 2022, you could make a **new claim** for income-based JSA if you were prevented from claiming universal credit (UC) because you were (or if you are a member of a couple, each of you were) a 'frontier worker' – ie, you are in Great Britain to work, but do not live there or in Northern Ireland.[1] This is no longer the case.

If the DWP wants to safeguard or test the efficient administration of UC, it can designate categories of case that are prevented from claiming UC.[2]

If you are already entitled to income-based JSA, you can **continue to qualify** until:

– you claim UC. **Note:** when you make a new claim for UC, your income-based JSA entitlement can continue for two weeks. See p253 for information about income-based JSA run-on; *or*

– you become a member of a couple and your partner is getting UC; *or*

– you and your partner are affected by the 'managed migration' transfer process, that is, you are told by the DWP that your income-based JSA will end and are invited to claim UC. See p29 for further information, and AskCPAG and CPAG's *Welfare Rights Bulletin* for updates.

---

1. **Who can get income-based jobseeker's allowance**

You qualify for jobseeker's allowance (JSA) if you:[3]

- are not in full-time paid work (see p248); *and*
- do not have limited capability for work. However, in certain circumstances, people who are sick, or who have gone abroad for NHS hospital treatment can get JSA (see p249); *and*
- are not in 'relevant education' (see p873). In addition, if you are a full-time student, you usually cannot get JSA (see p874); *and*
- satisfy 'jobseeking conditions' (see p1092) – ie, you must:
  - be (or be treated as) available for work; *and*
  - be (or be treated as) actively seeking work; *and*
  - have a current jobseeker's agreement with the DWP. The DWP may call this a 'claimant commitment'; *and*
- are below pension age (see p766). **Note:** if you are already getting income-based JSA and you are or become a member of a 'mixed-age' couple (ie, you have reached pension age but your partner has not), in some circumstances,

your income-based JSA can continue even though you have reached pension age (see p249); *and*

- are in Great Britain. JSA can continue to be paid in limited circumstances while you are temporarily away (see p1631).

The above conditions apply to all types of JSA. To qualify for income-based JSA, you must also satisfy extra rules below.

You may qualify for income-based JSA even if you do not qualify for contribution-based JSA. You may qualify for both income-based JSA and contribution-based JSA.

Extra rules for income-based jobseeker's allowance

You qualify for income-based JSA if, in addition to satisfying the rules that apply to all types of JSA (see p246):[4]

- your income is less than your applicable amount (see p251); *and*
- your savings and other capital are worth £16,000 or less. Some capital (including your home) is ignored (see Chapter 22); *and*
- your partner does not count as being in full-time paid work (see p248); *and*
- you are aged 18 or over. If you are a 16/17 year old, you might get income-based JSA if you satisfy special rules (see p249); *and*
- if you are a joint-claim couple (see below), at least one of you is aged 18 or over. If one of you is a 16/17 year old, you can get income-based JSA if the member of the couple who is 16/17 satisfies special rules (see p249); *and*
- neither you nor your partner are entitled to IS, income-related ESA or pension credit (PC), and, if you are not a joint-claim couple, your partner is not entitled to income-based JSA; *and*
- you are not included as a child in someone else's IS or income-based JSA claim (see p307). However, you may qualify for JSA in your own right and you cannot be included in someone's claim for income-based JSA if you are (or would be) entitled to JSA;[5] *and*
- you satisfy the 'habitual residence' and the 'right to reside' tests. To find out if you are exempt from these tests, see Chapter 69; *and*
- you are not a 'person subject to immigration control' (see p1524). There are exceptions to this rule.

Joint-claim couples

If you are a 'joint-claim couple', both you and your partner must usually make a joint claim for JSA and satisfy all the rules for getting income-based JSA. You are a 'joint-claim couple' if you are a member of a couple (see p303) and:[6]

- at least one of you is 18 or over. **Note:** if one of you is 16 or 17, special rules apply (see p249); *and*
- neither of you is responsible for a child in specified circumstances.

Part 3: Getting a benefit decision changed
Chapter 12: Income-based jobseeker's allowance
1. Who can get income-based jobseeker's allowance

Because these rules now apply to very few claimants, they are not described in detail here. See the 2019/20 edition of this *Handbook* for further information. To find out:

- when you count as responsible for a child and what happens if you stop or start being responsible, see pp245–46 of that edition;
- whether one of you does not have to satisfy all the conditions for getting JSA, see pp246–47 of that edition. This might apply, for example, if one of you is studying full time, is a carer or is unable to work because of sickness;
- what happens if one of you does not qualify for JSA and how this affects the way your benefit is calculated, see pp247–48 of that edition.

Jobseeking periods

A 'jobseeking period' is the period during which you:[7]
- meet the conditions that apply to all types of JSA (see p246); *or*
- do not satisfy the jobseeking conditions, but receive hardship payments (see Chapter 52).

You are not usually entitled to JSA for the first seven days of your jobseeking period. These are known as 'waiting days' (see p253).

Certain days do not count as part of a jobseeking period.[8] The rules are broadly the same as for contribution-based JSA (see p689). In addition, days for which you lost your entitlement to JSA because you failed to participate in an interview when required or to 'sign on' and days for which you have been refused JSA because you did not provide your partner's national insurance number do not count.

In some cases, two or more jobseeking periods can be linked together and treated as if they were one. Also, certain periods in which you satisfy other conditions can be linked to a jobseeking period (see p689 – the rules are broadly the same as for contribution-based JSA).[9]

Full-time paid work

You cannot usually qualify for income-based JSA if you or your partner are in, or are treated as being in, full-time paid work. If you are the JSA claimant, this means 16 hours or more each week.[10] For your partner, this means 24 hours or more each week.

If you are a joint-claim couple, you cannot get joint-claim JSA if either one of you is in, or treated as being in, full-time paid work. If one of you is not working or is working fewer than 16 hours a week, the other can then work up to 24 hours a week. In this situation, you do not have to make a joint claim.[11] The person working fewer than 16 hours can qualify for income-based JSA.

All the rules on work are covered in Chapter 44. **Note:** in some situations you are treated as not being in full-time paid work even if you work 16/24 hours a week or more (see p977).

If you or your partner have just taken up full-time paid work, you may be able to qualify for help with certain housing costs for the first four weeks ('housing costs run-on' – see p359). You must notify the DWP that you are starting full-time paid work in order to get the run-on.

Limited capability for work

Usually, to qualify for JSA you must not have 'limited capability for work'.[12] If a decision maker has decided that you have (or do not have) limited capability for work for ESA purposes, you are automatically treated as having (or not having) limited capability for work for JSA.[13] See Chapter 45 for details about the test that decides this for ESA purposes.

If your health improves and you move on to JSA from ESA, you may be asked to provide medical evidence that you no longer have limited capability for work. In all cases, you must still show that you are available for work if you are ill or have a disability. However, there are rules that may allow you to restrict your availability (see p1098).

Even if you have limited capability for work, you can continue to qualify for JSA:

- for certain short periods of up to 13 weeks; *or*
- if you are temporarily absent from Great Britain to obtain NHS hospital treatment under certain provisions.

See p691 for further information. The rules are the same as for contribution-based JSA.

2. The rules about your age

You cannot usually qualify for:

- **income-based jobseeker's allowance** (JSA) until you are 18. There are special rules that can help you qualify if you are 16 or 17. If you do not qualify, check whether you qualify for universal credit (UC) instead;
- **joint-claim JSA** unless you and your partner are both 18. If only one of you is 18 or over, the other must satisfy the conditions for income-based JSA in her/his own right as a 16/17 year old.[14] If both of you are under 18, you do not count as a joint-claim couple and so one of you may be able to qualify for income-based JSA for the other.[15]

Part 3: Getting a benefit decision changed
Chapter 12: Income-based jobseeker's allowance
3. People included in the claim

Because very few people can now make a new claim for income-based JSA, the additional rules for 16 and 17 year olds are not described in detail here. See pp250–55 of the 2019/20 edition of this *Handbook* for further information.

You cannot qualify for any type of JSA if you are pension age or over (see p766). It is your age as the claimant that is relevant, not the age of your partner. However, if you are getting income-based JSA and you are, or become, a member of a 'mixed-age couple' (ie, you have reached pension age but your partner has not) and you are prevented from claiming UC (see p246), you are treated as not yet pension age and your income-based JSA continues.[16]

---

3. **People included in the claim**

If you are single, you get income-based jobseeker's allowance (JSA) for yourself.

If you are a 'joint-claim couple' (see p247), you and your partner must usually both qualify for joint-claim JSA. If you are not a joint-claim couple, one of you can get income-based JSA for both of you. Whichever one of you qualifies for JSA, the other may qualify for national insurance (NI) credits in order to protect her/his NI record. See Chapter 43 for more details about NI credits.

If you are in a couple, your applicable amount includes a personal allowance for a couple and can include premiums based on both your and your partner's circumstances. When your benefit is worked out, your partner's income and capital are usually added to yours.

Income-based JSA does not normally include amounts for your children. However, there are some situations in which you must show that you are responsible for a child who is living in your household – eg:

- in order to take advantage of the special rules to help you meet the jobseeking conditions (see p1092);
- to show you are a lone parent so you can benefit from a higher earnings disregard (see p414);
- for some of the rules for help with housing costs – eg, ground rent or service charges (see Chapter 18).

You do not have to be the child's parent. See p308 for who counts as a child. For when you count as responsible for a child and when s/he counts as living in your household, see pp309–312.

Note: there are different rules about children for deciding whether you must claim joint-claim JSA (see p247).

4. The amount of benefit

Income-based jobseeker's allowance (JSA) tops up your income to a level set by the government. The amount you get depends on your needs (your 'applicable amount') and on how much income and capital you and your partner have.[17]

Your applicable amount consists of:
- a personal allowance (see p317); *and*
- premiums (see p323) for any special needs; *and*
- certain housing costs (see Chapter 18). **Note:** you cannot get income-based JSA for help with your mortgage interest or a loan for repairs and improvements. Instead, the DWP may offer you a loan (see p839). You cannot get help with your rent. Instead, you may qualify for housing benefit (see Chapter 10).

Income-based JSA is calculated in the same way as for income support (IS) (see p238).

You may be able to get a short-term advance if you are waiting for a payment of JSA (see p1153).

Do you have children?

Income-based JSA does not normally include allowances and premiums for your children, but they may be included if your claim began before 6 April 2004 (see p317). If you *do* get allowances and premiums for your children, there are special rules for how their income and capital are treated (see p404 and p474).

You might get a reduced amount of JSA if:
- you have been given a sanction (see p1116); *or*
- you are in a joint-claim couple and your partner has not made a joint claim with you (see p247 and pp245–48 of the 2019/20 edition of this *Handbook*); *or*
- you are not in a joint-claim couple, you have a partner and s/he has failed to attend a work-focused interview without good cause; *or*
- you are receiving a hardship payment of income-based JSA (see Chapter 52); *or*
- you have committed a benefit offence (see p1239).

5. Special benefit rules

Special rules may apply to:
- 16/17 year olds (see pp250–55 of the 2019/20 edition of this *Handbook*). This includes those who have been, or are being, looked after by a local authority (see p933);
- workers who are laid off or working short time;

Part 3: Getting a benefit decision changed
Chapter 12: Income-based jobseeker's allowance
7. Getting paid

- people who have come from or are going abroad (see Chapters 68, 69, 70 and 71);
- people who are studying (see Chapter 41);
- people involved in a trade dispute (see p982);
- people without accommodation, people who are (or whose partner or children are) in hospital or living in a care home or similar accommodation, and people in prison (see Chapter 42).

6. **Claims and backdating**

There are now very few people who can make a new claim for income-based jobseeker's allowance (JSA) – see p246. If you *can* make a new claim, the general rules about claims and backdating are covered in Chapter 50. For the specific rules that apply to income-based JSA, see pp259–65 of the 2020/21 edition of this *Handbook*.

7. **Getting paid**

Information about payment of your jobseeker's allowance (JSA) is on p703. The rules are the same as for contribution-based JSA.

If you and your partner are a joint-claim couple, you must nominate which one of you receives payment for both of you. If you cannot agree, a decision maker decides.[18] If your JSA is being paid at a reduced rate because one of you has been given a sanction, it is paid to the other member of the couple.[19] Even if you are not the person nominated to receive the JSA, if you separate from your partner and s/he cannot be traced, you can be paid any arrears of JSA that are due.[20]

After you are awarded jobseeker's allowance

Once you have been awarded JSA, you are expected to verify your claim for income-based JSA annually by completing a questionnaire and signing a declaration. There are also other requirements that you (and in some cases your partner) must meet. See p1106 for further information about the requirements after you are awarded JSA and p1140 for information and evidence you can be required to provide.

In some cases, if you fail to meet requirements, you may be given a sanction (see p1116) or your entitlement to JSA can end (see p1109 and p1109). If you fail to provide information and evidence when required to do so, your JSA could be suspended or even terminated (see p1162).

Income-based jobseeker's allowance run-on

If you are getting income-based JSA and make a new claim for universal credit (UC), your income-based JSA entitlement continues for two weeks (called a 'run-on payment' or 'transitional income-based JSA payment'), as long as you would otherwise remain entitled.[21] You do not have to make a claim for a run-on payment. It should be made automatically. You do not have to pay back a run-on payment and it does not count as a specified benefit for the purposes of the benefit cap (see p1158).[22]

Change of circumstances

You must report changes in your circumstances that you have been told you must report, as well as any that you might reasonably be expected to know might affect your right to, the amount of, or the payment of, your benefit, including any that are likely to occur. You should do this as soon as possible, preferably in writing. See p1160 for further information.

If there has been a relevant change of circumstances, a decision maker looks at your claim again and makes a new decision. To see when your JSA is then adjusted, see p704. The rules are the same as for contribution-based JSA.

Note: if you become a member of a couple with someone entitled to UC, your entitlement to income-based JSA ends (see p31).

Waiting days

You are not entitled to JSA for the first seven 'waiting days' of any jobseeking period (see p248). There are exceptions to this rule.[23] See p257 of the 2021/22 edition of this *Handbook* for further information.

8. Tax, other benefits and the benefit cap

Tax

Jobseeker's allowance (JSA) is taxable.[24] The maximum amount of JSA that is taxable is:
- if you are claiming for yourself, an amount equal to the appropriate personal allowance for a person of your age (see p317); *or*
- if you are a member of a couple, an amount equal to the income-based JSA personal allowance for a couple (half this amount if your partner is prevented from entitlement to JSA because s/he is involved in a trade dispute – see p982).

The tax is not deducted while JSA is being paid but reduces the refund you would otherwise receive through PAYE (pay as you earn) when you return to work.

Part 3: Getting a benefit decision changed
Chapter 12: Income-based jobseeker's allowance
8. Tax, other benefits and the benefit cap

Any refunds of PAYE payments are paid to you at the end of the tax year to which they relate. Any other tax refund is paid only when you stop getting JSA.

Means-tested benefits and tax credits

If you are entitled to income-based JSA:

- it is an automatic passport to maximum housing benefit (HB), child tax credit (CTC) and usually to maximum working tax credit (WTC), but if you are not already entitled, you must be able to make a new claim. In Scotland, income-based JSA is a qualifying benefit for Scottish child payment (see p1731);
- if you work less than 16 hours a week and your partner works at least 16 hours but less than 24 hours a week, you and your partner may be able to qualify for WTC as well as, or instead of, income-based JSA. Get advice to see whether you can still make a new claim, and if so, how you would be better off financially;
- WTC is taken into account as income when working out your income-based JSA, but CTC is not.

Non-means-tested benefits

While you are on JSA you are entitled to national insurance credits (see p955).
Most non-means-tested benefits are taken into account when working out the amount of income-based JSA you can get. However:

- attendance allowance, disability living allowance, personal independence payment, armed forces independence payment, monthly payments of bereavement support payment, guardian's allowance and child benefit (if you are getting CTC), and certain Scottish benefits (ie, adult disability payment, child disability payment, child winter heating assistance, young carer grant and Scottish child payment), are not taken into account;
- it can still be worth claiming non-means-tested benefits even if they are taken into account. If you or your partner qualify for certain ones of these, you also qualify for certain premiums (see p323) and therefore a higher rate of income-based JSA.

The benefit cap

In some cases, there is a limit on the total amount of specified benefits you can receive (a 'benefit cap'). JSA is one of the specified benefits. However, the benefit cap only applies if you are getting universal credit or HB. See p1156 for further information. **Note:** income-based JSA run-on (see p253) does not count as a specified benefit.

Passports and other sources of help

If you are entitled to income-based JSA, you also qualify for health benefits such as free prescriptions (see Chapter 31) and education benefits such as free school lunches (see p851). You may also qualify for help from your local welfare assistance scheme (see p846), for a council tax reduction (see p836), for social fund payments (see Chapter 37) or, in Scotland, a Best Start grant (see Chapter 74) or funeral support payment (see Chapter 76), and for Healthy Start food and vitamins (see p847) or, in Scotland, Best Start foods (see p850). In Scotland, you may also qualify for Scottish child payment (see Chapter 77).

Financial help on starting work

If you stop getting JSA because you or your partner start work, or your earnings or your hours in your existing job increase, you may be able to continue to get help with your housing costs (eg, ground rent or service charges) for a further four weeks (see p359) or extended payments of HB if you pay rent (see p217). Your local authority may also provide extended help with council tax. If you have a DWP loan for your mortgage interest, this may continue for four weeks (see p845). See p858 for information about other financial help you might get.

Notes

1 Art 5A WRA(No.9)O; art 4(11) WRA(No.32)O
2 Reg 4 UC(TP) Regs

1. Who can get income-based jobseeker's allowance
3 s1 JSA 1995
4 ss3, 3A and 13 JSA 1995
5 Reg 76(2)(b) JSA Regs
6 s1(2B)-(2D) and (4) and Sch 1 paras 8A and 9A-9D JSA 1995; regs 3A-(3G) and Sch A1 JSA Regs; CJSA/2633/2004
7 Reg 47(1) and (2) JSA Regs
8 Reg 47(3) JSA Regs
9 Sch 1 para 3 JSA 1995; reg 48 JSA Regs
10 Reg 51 JSA Regs
11 Reg 3E(2)(g) JSA Regs
12 s1(2)(f) JSA 1995
13 Sch 1 para 2 JSA 1995; reg 10 SS&CS(DA) Regs

2. The rules about your age
14 s3A(1)(d) and (e) JSA 1995; reg 58 JSA Regs
15 Reg 3A JSA Regs
16 Art 8 WRA(No.31)O; HB Circular A9/2019

4. The amount of benefit
17 ss4(3) and (3A) and 13 JSA 1995

7. Getting paid
18 s3B JSA 1995
19 ss19(7), 19A(10) and 19B(8) JSA 1995
20 Reg 30A SS(C&P) Regs
21 Regs 46(1) and 47(2) UC(TP) Regs; reg 5 The Universal Credit (Managed Migration Pilot and Miscellaneous Amendments) Regulations 2019 No.1152
22 Reg 8B UC(TP) Regs
23 Sch 1 para 4 JSA 1995; reg 46 JSA Regs; arts 12 and 13 WRA(No.9)O; art 11(2) WRA(No.11)O

8. Tax, other benefits and the benefit cap
24 ss671-75 IT(EP)A 2003

Chapter 13

Pension credit

This chapter covers:
1. Who can get pension credit (p257)
2. The rules about your age (p257)
3. People included in the claim (p258)
4. The amount of pension credit (p259)
5. Special benefit rules (p262)
6. Claims and backdating (p263)
7. Getting paid (p265)
8. Tax, other benefits and the benefit cap (p267)

Key facts

- Pension credit (PC) is a benefit for people on a low income who are at least pension age.
- There are two types of PC: **guarantee credit**, which ensures a minimum level of income, and **savings credit**, which is intended to 'reward' you for making provision for your retirement, such as through savings or an occupational pension. You can be entitled to either guarantee credit, savings credit or both.
- PC is a means-tested benefit.
- PC can include additional amounts for severe disability, carers and for a child or qualifying young person for whom you are responsible.
- You do not have to have paid national insurance contributions to qualify.
- You can qualify for PC whether you are in or out of work.
- PC is administered and paid by the Pension Service, which is part of the DWP.
- If you disagree with a PC decision, you can apply for a revision or supersession (see Chapter 56), or appeal against it (see Chapter 57). You must apply for a mandatory reconsideration before you can appeal.

1. Who can get pension credit

Guarantee credit

You qualify for the guarantee credit of pension credit (PC) if:[1]

- you are at least pension age (see p766). If you have a partner and make a new claim for PC, both of you must usually be pension age. There are exceptions (see p258);[2] *and*
- you are not a 'person subject to immigration control' (see p1524), although there are exceptions to this rule (see p1530); *and*[3]
- you are in Great Britain (except for periods of temporary absence – see p1635) and satisfy the 'habitual residence' and 'right to reside' tests (see Chapter 69);[4] *and*
- your partner (if you have one) is not entitled to PC;[5] *and*
- you have no income, or your income is below a certain amount (known as the 'appropriate minimum guarantee' – see p259).[6]

Savings credit

You qualify for the savings credit of PC if:[7]

- either:
  - you and your partner (if you have one) reached pension age (see p766) before 6 April 2016; *or*
  - either you or your partner reached pension age before 6 April 2016, you were entitled to savings credit on 6 April 2016 and you have remained entitled to it;[8] *and*
- you or your partner are 65 or over;[9] *and*
- you are in Great Britain (except for periods of temporary absence – see p1635) and satisfy the 'habitual residence' and 'right to reside' tests (see Chapter 69);[10] *and*
- your partner (if you have one) is not entitled to PC;[11] *and*
- you are not a 'person subject to immigration control', although there are exceptions to this rule (see p1530);[12] *and*
- your 'qualifying income' exceeds the 'savings credit threshold', but is not so high that it produces a nil award (see p262).[13]

2. The rules about your age

You must have reached pension age – ie, the minimum qualifying age for state retirement pension.[14] The pension age for both men and women is currently 66 years.[15] When you reach pension age depends on your date of birth.

To check your pension age, see gov.uk/state-pension-age.

Part 3: Getting a benefit decision changed
Chapter 13: Pension credit
3. People included in the claim

If you are a member of a couple and you are at least pension age but your partner is not (called a 'mixed-age couple' in this *Handbook*), you cannot usually qualify for PC.[16] You and your partner may be able to claim universal credit (UC) instead.

There are exceptions to this rule. If you are a member of a mixed-aged couple, you can continue to qualify for PC if, on 14 May 2019 as part of the same couple, you were entitled to:[17]

- PC; *or*
- pension-age housing benefit (HB); *or*
- both PC and pension-age HB.

You continue to qualify for PC provided you have been continuously entitled to PC or pension-age HB or both, as part of the same mixed-age couple. You can make a new claim for PC, provided you are entitled to HB on this basis and have been since 14 May 2019.

If you are in a mixed-age couple, you have reached pension age and your partner cannot claim UC because s/he does not satisfy certain UC conditions, you can instead get PC (and pension-age HB) as a single person, either until the reason your partner cannot claim UC no longer applies, or s/he reaches pension age.[18] This situation can arise if s/he:

- does not satisfy the habitual residence test (see Chapter 69), or is a person subject to immigration control (see Chapter 68); *or*
- is a prisoner, or is detained in hospital serving a prison sentence (see p923); *or*
- is a member of a religious order and fully maintained by it; *or*
- is absent from Great Britain for more than the permitted period (normally one month although there are exceptions – see p1640); *or*
- is under 18, and not someone who is able to claim UC when 16/17 (see p36).

If the partner under pension age is temporarily absent from the household and is, or is expected to be, absent for more than six months, the person who has reached pension age can claim PC (and HB) as a single person until the end of the absence, as you are no longer treated as a couple for UC (see p60).

3. **People included in the claim**

If you are single, you claim pension credit (PC) for yourself. If you are a member of a couple and both you and your partner are pension age (see p257), either of you can claim PC for you both. If only one of you is pension age, see above. See p303 for who counts as a couple.

The 'appropriate minimum guarantee' that forms part of the calculation of your PC includes an allowance for a couple and can include additional amounts based on your and your partner's circumstances. When the amount of your PC is worked out, your partner's income and capital are usually added to yours.

If you are claiming PC but your partner has not yet reached pension age, s/he may qualify for national insurance (NI) credits in order to protect her/his NI record. See Chapter 43 for more details about NI credits.

You can get amounts for a child or qualifying young person for whom you are responsible included in your PC if you are not entitled to tax credits.[19]

4. The amount of pension credit

The amount of pension credit (PC) you get depends on whether you claim as a single person or as a member of a couple, whether you are responsible for any children or qualifying young people, and whether you have a severe disability, caring responsibilities or eligible housing costs. The maximum amount of guarantee credit you could receive is reduced by your income (subject to any applicable disregards). Your savings credit entitlement is based on the amount of your pension(s) and certain other income (see p262). For general information on income and capital, see Chapters 21 (income) and 23 (capital). For information on qualifying income for savings credit, see p262.

Guarantee credit

Your maximum amount of guarantee credit is known as the 'appropriate minimum guarantee'[20] and is made up of:
- the standard minimum guarantee; *and*
- where applicable, additional amounts.

Standard minimum guarantee

If you do not have any additional needs, you receive an award of PC which ensures that your weekly income is brought up to a standard minimum guarantee level, depending on your circumstances.

Amount of standard minimum guarantee

Single person[21]	£182.60
Couple[22]	£278.70
Each additional spouse in a polygamous marriage[23]	£96.10

Additional amounts

If you have certain additional needs, an additional amount(s) is added to the standard minimum guarantee. There is also a transitional additional amount to ensure you are not worse off as a result of moving on to PC from income support

Part 3: Getting a benefit decision changed
Chapter 13: Pension credit
4. The amount of pension credit

(IS), income-based jobseeker's allowance (JSA) or income-related employment and support allowance (ESA).

Note: you cannot get an amount in your PC for the cost of your mortgage interest payments or for a loan for repairs and improvements. Instead, the DWP may offer you a loan (see p839).

Additional amounts		
Severe disability[24]	£69.40	£138.88
The qualifying rules are broadly the same as for the severe disability premium (see p330).		(if both partners qualify)
Carer[25]	£38.85	£38.85
The qualifying rules are the same as for the carer premium (see p334).		(for each partner who qualifies)
Children (see p307).[26]	£66.85	Additional £30.58
First child born before 6 April 2017	£56.35	for disability, or £95.48
Each subsequent child		for severe disability
Transitional[27]	See below	

Transitional amount

If you were in receipt of IS, income-based JSA or income-related ESA immediately before you first became entitled to PC, in order to ensure you are not worse off by moving onto PC, your appropriate minimum guarantee may include a transitional amount.[28] The transitional amount reduces over time by any increase in your appropriate minimum guarantee and stops when you or your partner are no longer entitled to PC (disregarding any break in entitlement of less than eight weeks).[29]

When your appropriate minimum guarantee may be reduced

Your appropriate minimum guarantee may be reduced in certain circumstances. The most important of these are if:[30]

- you are a couple and one of you is a 'person subject to immigration control' (see p1535);
- you are a prisoner (see p927);
- your partner is abroad (see p1635);
- you are a member of and fully maintained by a religious order. In this case, your appropriate amount is nil.

The guarantee credit calculation

Step one: calculate your appropriate minimum guarantee

Your appropriate minimum guarantee comprises:

- the standard minimum guarantee for you and your partner, if you have one; *plus*
- additional amounts for any special needs and/or certain housing costs.

Step two: calculate your income

This is the amount you have coming in each week – eg, from benefits (including state retirement pensions), private pensions and earnings.[31] Not all income counts (eg, personal independence payment (PIP), disability living allowance/child disability payment, attendance allowance (AA), child tax credit and child benefit are disregarded in full) and some income can be disregarded. See Chapter 21 for details. If you have more than £10,000 capital, you are treated as having income of £1 for every £500 (or part thereof) over £10,000.[32]

Step three: deduct income from appropriate minimum guarantee

The amount of your guarantee credit is your appropriate minimum guarantee less any relevant income you have.[33] If your income is above the appropriate minimum guarantee, you do not qualify for any guarantee credit. You may qualify for guarantee credit if you or your partner become entitled to a qualifying benefit, like AA, which may increase the amount of your appropriate minimum guarantee.

Examples

Jahinda is single and aged 70. She gets AA. She lives alone and no one gets carer's allowance for looking after her. She lives in rented accommodation.

Her appropriate minimum guarantee is:

Standard minimum guarantee (single person rate)	£182.60
Severe disability additional amount	£69.40
Total	**£252.00**

Her weekly income is her basic state pension of £141.85. AA is ignored as income.

She is therefore entitled to £110.15 guarantee credit to bring her total income up to £252. She is also entitled to maximum housing benefit and any other passported benefits that may apply.

Ann and Vinnie are a couple. Ann is 70 and Vinnie is 72. Claire, their 44-year-old daughter, lives with them and she gets universal credit. Ann gets the enhanced rate of the daily living component of PIP and Vinnie gets AA.

Their appropriate minimum guarantee is £278.70.

Their joint weekly income for calculating PC is £324.85, made up of basic state pension of £226.85 (Ann £85.00, Vinnie £141.85), occupational pension of £95 and £3 deemed income from £11,500 savings. PIP and AA are ignored as income.

They are not entitled to any guarantee credit because their income exceeds their appropriate minimum guarantee of £278.70. Their appropriate minimum guarantee does not include a severe disability addition because Claire lives with them.

Part 3: Getting a benefit decision changed
Chapter 13: Pension credit
5. Special benefit rules

Savings credit

Savings credit is currently being phased out. You can only get savings credit if:

- you or your partner (if you have one) are 65 or over and you both reached pension age (see p766) before 6 April 2016; *or*
- either you or your partner reached pension age before 6 April 2016, and on that date you had an existing award of savings credit and you have remained entitled to it since then.[34]

In addition, the amount of your 'qualifying income' must be above the savings credit threshold.[35]

Savings credit threshold

Single person	£158.47
Couple	£251.70

'**Qualifying income**' for this purpose is all the income that counts for guarantee credit (see Chapter 21) except:[36]

- working tax credit;
- incapacity benefit;
- contributory ESA;
- contribution-based JSA;
- severe disablement allowance;
- maternity allowance;
- maintenance payments for you, or your partner, from a spouse or former spouse.

The amount of savings credit to which you are entitled is subject to a maximum figure, known as the '**maximum savings credit**'.[37]

Maximum savings credit

Single person	£14.48
Couple	£16.20

For details of how to calculate the amount of savings credit, see pp138–39 of the 2016/17 edition of this *Handbook*.

5. Special benefit rules

Special rules may apply to:

- people subject to immigration control (see Chapter 68);

- people who have come from or are going abroad (see Chapters 69 and 70);
- people who are in hospital or living in a care home or similar accommodation, and people in prison or detention (see Chapter 42).

---

6. Claims and backdating

The general rules about claims and backdating are covered in Chapter 50. This section explains the specific rules that apply to pension credit (PC).

Making a claim

A claim can be made:[38]
- if you have already claimed your state pension and have no children to include in your claim, online at gov.uk/pension-credit/how-to-claim; *or*
- by telephone. Call the Pension Service on 0800 99 1234 (textphone: 0800 169 0133; Relay UK and BSL video services are available) from 8am to 6pm, Monday to Friday; *or*
- in writing on the approved form (Form PC1), although the Pension Service usually prefers you to claim online or by telephone if you can. You ask for the form by telephoning the number above or print a copy from gov.uk/pension-credit/how-to-claim. Local authority housing benefit (HB) offices and some other 'alternative offices' (see p1134) can provide the form.

You must provide any information or evidence required (see below). In certain circumstances, the DWP may accept a written application not on the approved form. You can amend or withdraw your claim before a decision is made (see p1135). If there is a delay in dealing with your claim, you may be able to get a short-term advance of benefit (see p1153).

Who should claim

If you are a single person, you must claim on your own behalf. If you are a member of a couple, you must choose which one of you claims for you both (see p303). If you cannot agree who should claim, a decision maker decides.[39]

You can swap who claims, provided you both agree. It may be worthwhile doing so – eg, if one of you is about to go abroad.

If you are unable to manage your own affairs, another person can claim PC for you as your 'appointee' (see p1135).

Information to support your claim

For the general information requirements that apply to all benefits, see p1136.

It is important you provide any information required when you claim. Until you do, you may not count as having made a valid claim (see p1138). Correct any defects as soon as possible or your date of claim may be affected.

Part 3: Getting a benefit decision changed
Chapter 13: Pension credit
6. Claims and backdating

When you claim, you are asked about your circumstances, including details of any income and savings and any housing costs you or your partner have. You must include details of any personal pension scheme to which you belong. If further information or evidence is needed, see below for when your claim begins.[40]

Once your claim has been decided, you are sent a letter detailing the amount of any award, and the information on which it was based. You are asked to check this and report any omissions or changes.

Even if your claim is valid, you may be asked to supply further information to support your claim (see p1140). You may also be asked to provide further information after you are awarded PC. If you fail to do so, your benefit may be suspended or even terminated (see p1162).

The date of your claim

The date of your claim is important as it determines when your entitlement to PC starts. This is not necessarily the date from when you are paid. For information about when payment of PC starts, see p265.

Your '**date of claim**' (unless the backdating rules apply) is:[41]

- the date your claim, properly completed with all the required information and evidence, is received at the appropriate office (the DWP, local authority HB office or county council office); *or*
- the date you notify the appropriate office of your intention to claim, and you submit a properly completed claim with all the required information and evidence within one month of this date.

You must make sure your claim is valid. If it is 'defective', you are given one month (or longer if considered reasonable) to correct the defects (see p1138). If you do, your claim is treated as having been made when you initially claimed.[42] If you are making an advance claim for PC before you have reached pension age and your claim is defective, you may correct it at any time before the end of the advance period.[43] The one-month time limit runs from the day following the end of the advance period.[44]

In some cases, you can claim in advance (see p265) and in some cases your claim can be backdated (see below). If you want this to be done, make this clear when you claim or the DWP might not consider it.

Backdating your claim

It is important that you claim in time because PC can only be backdated for up to three months. Your claim can be backdated if you satisfy the qualifying conditions over the period for which you require backdating – you do not have to show why your claim was late.[45] If you want your claim to be backdated, it is important that you ask – claims are not automatically backdated. When you make a telephone claim, you should be asked about the date from when you want your claim to start.

If you claim backdated PC within three months of being awarded a qualifying benefit and an earlier PC claim was refused because you did not get a qualifying benefit (see p1143) at that time, your PC can be backdated to the date of your earlier PC claim or the date when the qualifying benefit was first payable, whichever is later.[46]

For general rules on backdating, see p1142.

Claiming in advance

You can make an advance claim for PC to give the DWP time to ensure you receive your benefit as soon as you become entitled. PC can be claimed up to four months before you qualify, whether this is before you reach pension age and you know you will be entitled then *or* after you reach pension age when you know you will have a future entitlement – eg, because of a drop in income.[47] The date of your claim is the date on which you qualify. You cannot make an advance claim if the reason you do not qualify straight away is because you fail the habitual residence test (see p1551).

If you were claiming universal credit (UC) immediately before becoming entitled to PC, you should receive a full month's UC for the assessment period during which you reach pension age. Any PC or HB you receive should be ignored for the UC payment. Similarly, any UC payment should be ignored for the new PC award.[48]

7. Getting paid

The general rules on getting paid are in Chapter 51. This section explains the specific rules that apply to pension credit (PC).

When is pension credit paid?

	Qualifying age on or after 6 April 2010	Qualifying age before 6 April 2010
When is PC paid?	The day you are paid depends on your national insurance number (see p1150).[49]	Monday, or the same day as your retirement pension is paid.[50]
How often is PC paid?	Weekly, fortnightly or four-weekly in arrears.	Weekly in advance. If you were entitled to income support immediately before 6 October 2003 and paid in arrears, PC is also paid in arrears.[51]

If you are entitled to less than 10 pence a week, you are not paid PC, unless you are receiving another social security benefit that can be paid with PC.[52] You still have an underlying entitlement. If your entitlement is less than £1 a week, a decision maker can decide to pay you quarterly in arrears.

There may be a delay between the date of your claim and the date PC becomes payable. This is because payment does not normally start until the first payday following the claim.[53] There are exceptions to this rule.[54]

Note:
- Deductions can be made from your PC to pay to third parties (see p1164).
- Your PC might be paid at a reduced rate if you have been sanctioned for a benefit offence (see p1239).
- For information on missing payments, see p1150. If you cannot get your PC payments because you have lost your bank card or have forgotten your PIN, see p1149. If your payment service card has been lost or stolen, or if you have forgotten your memorable date, see p1150.
- If payment of your PC is delayed, see p1255. If you are waiting for a decision on your claim, or to be paid, you may be able to get a short-term advance (see p1153). If you wish to complain about how your claim has been dealt with, or claim compensation, see Chapter 61.
- If payment of your PC is suspended, see p1161.
- If you are overpaid PC, you might have to repay it (see Chapter 53) and, in some circumstances, you may have to pay a penalty (see p1229). If you have been accused of fraud, see Chapter 54.
- If you are owed arrears of PC, these can be paid in instalments (see p1148).

Change of circumstances

You must report changes in your circumstances you have been told to report, as well as any that you might reasonably be expected to know might affect your right to, the amount of, or the payment of your benefit. You should do this as soon as possible, preferably in writing. See p1160 for further information.

See below for the circumstances that do not need to be reported during the assessed income period.

If there has been a relevant change of circumstances, a decision maker looks at your claim again and makes a new decision. To find out when the new decision takes effect, see p1279.

If you become a member of a 'mixed-age couple' (see p258), your entitlement to PC stops (see p32). Your partner may be able to claim universal credit instead.

When your pension credit is adjusted

Generally, your PC is adjusted from the day the change occurs or is expected to occur, if this is the day you are paid benefit. If it is not, your PC is adjusted from the start of the next benefit week. However, there are a few exceptions to this general rule.[55]

Assessed income period

If you were already getting PC before 6 April 2016, an assessed income period may have been set. From 6 April 2016, no new assessed income periods have been set.

An 'assessed income period' is a set period during which you are not required to report any changes in certain types of your income, known as 'retirement provision'.[56] 'Retirement provision' means income from:[57]

- a retirement pension (other than state retirement pensions);
- an annuity (other than retirement pension income);
- capital;
- periodic payments from the Pension Protection Fund or the Financial Assistance Scheme.

The effect of this is that if you have an increase in, or subsequently start to receive, retirement provision during your assessed income period, you do not have to report this to the DWP. All other changes in your income that affect your PC entitlement must be reported to the DWP as soon as they occur. During the assessed income period, your PC entitlement may change as a result of 'deemed increases in retirement provision' – eg, periodic increases in an occupational pension. See the 2015/16 edition of this *Handbook* for details.

Before 6 April 2016 an assessed income period could be set for a fixed period, usually five years or, if you were 75 or over, for an indefinite period.[58] All fixed-period assessed income periods have now ended. If an assessed income period has been set for an indefinite period, it continues unless you have a change of circumstances.

Your assessed income period comes to an end if:[59]

- you become a member of a couple; *or*
- you cease to be a member of a couple; *or*
- you or your partner reach the age of 65; *or*
- you are no longer entitled to PC; *or*
- you are single and go to live in a care home on a permanent basis; *or*
- payments of retirement provision due to you stop temporarily or are less than the amount due, and your PC award is superseded as a result.

8. Tax, other benefits and the benefit cap

Tax

Pension credit (PC) is not taxable.

Part 3: Getting a benefit decision changed
Chapter 13: Pension credit
8. Tax, other benefits and the benefit cap

Means-tested benefits and tax credits

If you are entitled to PC, the following applies.

- An award of guarantee credit is an automatic passport to maximum housing benefit (HB), but if you are not already entitled to HB, you must make a separate claim (if you still can). If you are only entitled to savings credit, your HB claim is calculated in the usual way. The Pension Service provides the local authority with its assessment of your income.
- If you get guarantee credit, the £16,000 limit on your capital does not apply for HB. It does apply if you only receive savings credit.
- PC is a passport to maximum working tax credit (WTC) and child tax credit (CTC). If you had an award of WTC and/or CTC on 31 January 2019, this can continue. You can claim amounts for a child in your PC, if you are not already getting tax credits. If you are getting an amount for a child(ren) in your PC and are then awarded WTC or CTC retrospectively (eg, following an appeal), entitlement to the amount for a child(ren) in your PC ends.
- In Scotland, PC is a qualifying benefit for Scottish child payment (see p1731).

Non-means-tested benefits

Some non-means-tested benefits are taken into account as income when calculating entitlement to PC. Others have a £10 disregard and some are disregarded entirely. See Chapter 21 for details.

Qualifying for certain non-means-tested benefits can help you qualify for more PC. For example, if you get carer's allowance, you may be entitled to a carer addition with your appropriate minimum guarantee.

The benefit cap

In some cases, there is a limit on the total amount of specified benefits you can receive (a 'benefit cap'). PC is *not* one of the specified benefits. The benefit cap only applies if you are getting working-age HB or universal credit.

Passports and other sources of help

If you are entitled to PC, you may also be eligible for:
- a Christmas bonus (see p861);
- health benefits, if you are getting the guarantee credit (see Chapter 31);
- free school lunches, if you are getting the guarantee credit. This only applies in England and Wales – in Scotland, you can qualify via CTC (see p851);
- social fund payments (see Chapter 37) or, in Scotland, a Best Start grant (see Chapter 74) or funeral support payment (see Chapter 76);
- council tax reduction from your local authority (see p836);
- home insulation grants and discretionary grants from the local authority towards the cost of home improvements (see p860).

Notes

1. Who can get pension credit
1   s2 SPCA 2002
2   ss1(6) and 4(1A) SPCA 2002
3   s4(2) SPCA 2002
4   s1(2)(a) SPCA 2002; regs 2 and 3 SPC Regs
5   s4(1) SPCA 2002
6   s2(2) SPCA 2002; reg 6 SPC Regs
7   s3 SPCA 2002
8   s3 SPCA 2002, as amended by PA 2014; reg 7A SPC Regs
9   s3(1) SPCA 2002
10 s1(2)(a) SPCA 2002; regs 2-4 SPC Regs
11 s4(1) SPCA 2002
12 s4(2) SPCA 2002
13 s3(2)-(4) SPCA 2002

2. The rules about your age
14 s1(6) SPCA 2002
15 s126 and Sch 4 PA 1995
16 s4(1A) SPCA 2002
17 Art 4 WRA(No.31)O; HB Circular A9/2019 (10 July 2019)
18 Art 7 WRA(No.31)O; Vol 13, para 77035 DMG; HB Circular A9/2019, paras 15-17

3. People included in the claim
19 Reg 6(6)(d) and Sch IIA SPC Regs

4. The amount of pension credit
20 s2(3) SPCA 2002
21 Reg 6(1)(b) SPC Regs
22 Reg 6(1)(a) SPC Regs
23 Reg 6 and Sch 3 para 1(5) SPC Regs
24 Reg 6(4) and (5) SPC Regs
25 Reg 6(6)(a) SPC Regs
26 Reg 6(6)(d) and Sch IIA SPC Regs
27 Reg 6(6)(b) SPC Regs
28 Reg 6(6)(b) and Sch 1 para 6 SPC Regs
29 Sch 1 para 6(8) and (9) SPC Regs
30 Regs 5 and 6(2)(b) and (3) SPC Regs
31 s15 SPCA 2002; regs 14-24 SPC Regs
32 Reg 15(6) SPC Regs
33 s2(2) SPCA 2002
34 s3 SPCA 2002, as amended by PA 2014; reg 7A SPC Regs
35 Reg 7(2) SPC Regs
36 Reg 9 SPC Regs
37 s3(7) SPCA 2002; reg 7(1)(a) SPC Regs

6. Claims and backdating
38 Reg 4D SS(C&P) Regs
39 Reg 4D(7) SS(C&P) Regs
40 Reg 7(4) SS(C&P) Regs
41 Reg 4F SS(C&P) Regs
42 Reg 4D(6E) SS(C&P) Regs
43 Regs 4D(12) and 4E(3) SS(C&P) Regs
44 Reg 7(1C) SS(C&P) Regs
45 Reg 19(2) and (3) SS(C&P) Regs
46 Reg 6(16) and (18) SS(C&P) Regs
47 Regs 4E and 13D SS(C&P) Regs
48 Explanatory Memorandum to the Universal Credit (Persons who have attained state pension credit qualifying age) (Amendment) Regulations 2020 No.655

7. Getting paid
49 Reg 26BA SS(C&P) Regs
50 Reg 26B SS(C&P) Regs
51 Reg 36(6) SPC(CTMP) Regs
52 Reg 13 SPC Regs
53 Reg 16A(1) and (4) SS(C&P) Regs
54 Reg 16A(2) SS(C&P) Regs
55 Reg 7 and Sch 3B SS&CS(DA) Regs
56 ss6-10 SPCA 2002; regs 10-12 SPC Regs
57 s7(6) SPCA 2002
58 s9(1) SPCA 2002
59 s9(4) SPCA 2002; reg 12 SPC Regs

Chapter 14

Child tax credit

3

This chapter covers:

1. Who can get child tax credit (p271)
2. The rules about your age (p277)
3. People included in the claim (p277)
4. The amount of child tax credit (p277)
5. Claims and renewals (p278)
6. Getting paid (p279)
7. Tax, other benefits and the benefit cap (p280)

Key facts

- You cannot usually make a new claim for child tax credit.
- Child tax credit (CTC) is paid to families with children or qualifying young people who have not claimed universal credit (UC).
- You do not have to have paid national insurance contributions to qualify.
- CTC is paid whether or not you or your partner are working.
- CTC does not count as income for income support, income-based jobseeker's allowance, income-related employment and support allowance or pension credit purposes, and can be paid in addition to these benefits.
- CTC is administered and paid by HM Revenue and Customs.
- If you disagree with a CTC decision, you can apply for a mandatory reconsideration and then appeal if you are unhappy with the outcome (see Chapter 67).
- If you claim UC, your entitlement to CTC ends.

New claims for, and continuing entitlement to, child tax credit

You can now only make a new claim for CTC in very limited circumstances (see p271). If you are already entitled to CTC, you can continue to qualify until:

– you claim UC;[1] *or*

– you become a member of a couple and your partner is getting UC; *or*

– you and your partner are affected by the 'managed migration' transfer process, that is, you are told by the DWP that your CTC will end and are invited to claim UC. See p29 for further information, and AskCPAG and CPAG's *Welfare Rights Bulletin* for updates.

1. Who can get child tax credit

You qualify for child tax credit (CTC) if:[2]
- you (or your partner) are 'responsible' for a child or qualifying young person (see below); *and*
- your income is sufficiently low (see Chapter 63); *and*
- you are not a 'person subject to immigration control' (see Chapter 68); *and*
- you are 'present' and 'ordinarily resident' in the UK. You can be treated as present and ordinarily resident in the UK in some circumstances – eg, if you are temporarily away. You can be treated as not being in the UK if you claim CTC and do not have a 'right to reside'. You must usually have been living in the UK for at least three months, although there are exceptions to this rule. See Chapter 69 for further information.

Although full-time paid work does not affect your entitlement to CTC, income from work affects the amount you can be paid.

Who can make a new claim for child tax credit

You can only make a new claim for CTC if any of the following apply.[3]
- You already have an award of working tax credit (WTC). If you then become entitled to CTC because you are responsible for a child, this is treated as a change in circumstances and a new claim is not formally required.
- You were entitled to CTC in 2021/22 and are making a claim for 2022/23. This includes renewals, but could also apply in other situations. It does not apply if you have already renewed your claim and then attempt to reclaim later in the year after a gap in entitlement.[4]
- You are prevented from claiming universal credit (UC) because you (or if you are in a couple, you and your partner) are in a category from which it has been decided not to accept claims for UC.[5]
- You are a refugee who applied for asylum in the UK on or before 31 January 2019, and you claim CTC within one month of being granted refugee status (see p1540).[6]

If you cannot make a new claim for CTC under these rules, you can make a claim for UC or for pension credit, including an additional amount for a child.

Children

To qualify for CTC, you must be 'responsible' for at least one child or qualifying young person.[7] The terms 'child' or 'children' in this chapter also refer to qualifying young people. You do not have to be the child's parent – eg, you could be a grandparent, sister or brother. See p273 for when you count as responsible for a child and p275 for when you do not count as responsible.

Part 3: Getting a benefit decision changed
Chapter 14: Child tax credit
1. Who can get child tax credit

If you are entitled to CTC for a child and the child dies, you continue to be entitled to CTC for the child for eight weeks immediately following her/his death (or up to the date your child would have turned 20, if this is earlier).[8]

Who counts as a child

Someone counts as a child until her/his 16th birthday.[9] In some circumstances, a young person aged under 20 also counts as a child. HM Revenue and Customs (HMRC) refers to her/him as a **'qualifying young person'**.

A young person counts as a child during any period:[10]

- from her/his 16th birthday until 31 August following that birthday, whether or not s/he is in full-time, non-advanced education or 'approved training' (but see p273 for when s/he may not count as a child); or
- from 1 September following her/his 16th birthday (or from 31 August if s/he turns 16 on that date), while s/he is under 20 and in:
  - full-time, non-advanced education (see p564) or in appropriate full-time education (in England only). This does not apply if s/he is getting the education because of her/his employment. A young person counts as being in full-time education during any gaps between the ending of one course and the start of another, if s/he is enrolled on and commences the other course; or
  - approved training (see p565 for what counts) or has been enrolled on or accepted to undertake approved training. This does not apply if s/he is getting the training through a contract of employment.

  The course or approved training must have begun before s/he reached 19, or s/he must have been enrolled on or accepted to undertake the course or approved training before that age. **Note:** there is no equivalent to the child benefit 'terminal date rule' (see p566) so, unless the young person is under 18 and the rule in the next bullet point applies, s/he cannot count as a child once the course or training ends. However, HMRC guidance states that if s/he intends to continue full-time education but at an advanced level, payment can continue until the last day of the academic year (31 August) or, if earlier, the date s/he changes her/his mind and decides not to continue in education.[11] Therefore, ensure you notify HMRC when the course or training ends and of what your child intends to do next; or
- from 1 September following her/his 16th birthday (or from 31 August if s/he turns 16 on that date), while s/he is under 18, has ceased full-time education or approved training and it is not more than 20 weeks since s/he did so. S/he must notify HMRC within three months of ceasing full-time education or approved training that s/he has registered for work or training with a qualifying body – eg, the place where the local authority provides careers advice for young people or the Ministry of Defence. This rule can apply again if s/he goes back into full-time education or approved training and ceases again.

* *

What should you do when your child turns 16?

Notify HMRC in the September after your child's 16th birthday if s/he is staying on in non-advanced education, appropriate full-time education (in England only), or approved training. In England, this applies even though the school participation age is 17. To be sure that your CTC continues, you should also notify HMRC in the September after your child's 17th, 18th and 19th birthdays that s/he is continuing in education.

* *

When working out whether a young person counts as being in full-time education or approved training, HMRC ignores:[12]

- an interruption of up to six months, whether it began before or after the young person turned 16; *and*
- an interruption of any length which is due to the young person's physical or mental illness or disability.

The interruption is only ignored if HMRC thinks it is reasonable to do so. You should notify HMRC if the above applies.

When a young person does not count as a child

A young person cannot count as a child during any period following her/his 16th birthday in which:[13]

- having ceased full-time education or approved training, s/he is in full-time paid work. This means work of 24 hours or more per week. For information about:
  - what counts as paid work, see p284;
  - how the hours are calculated, see p285;
  - situations when the young person is not treated as being in full-time paid work, see p291.

  The rules are the same as for WTC.

  Remember that, even if a young person has *not* started full-time paid work, s/he cannot count as a child from 1 September after her/his 16th birthday if s/he has ceased full-time education or 'approved training' and has not registered for work or training with a qualifying body; *or*
- s/he gets UC, income support (IS), income-based jobseeker's allowance (JSA) or income-related employment and support allowance (ESA) in her/his own right. **Note:** you do not count as responsible for a child aged 16 or over if s/he gets CTC, WTC or contributory ESA in her/his own right (see p275).

Being responsible for a child

For tax credit purposes, a child can only count as the responsibility of one claimant (or joint-claim couple).[14] You are treated as 'responsible' for a child if:[15]

- s/he normally lives with you (see below); *or*

Part 3: Getting a benefit decision changed
Chapter 14: Child tax credit
1. Who can get child tax credit

- s/he normally lives with you and also with someone else, but you have the main responsibility for her/him (see below).

If a child for whom you are treated as being responsible has a child of her/his own (eg, your grandchild) who normally lives with her/him, you also count as being responsible for that child, but not if your child is 16 or over and is awarded CTC in her/his own right.[16]

Entitlement to child benefit is not a specific factor in working out who is responsible for a child for CTC purposes.

Does the child normally live with you?

The rules do not define when a child counts as normally living with you. HMRC says it means that your child 'regularly, usually, typically' lives with you and that this allows for temporary or occasional absences.[17] So if your child counts as normally living with you, s/he should also count as doing so even if s/he is away from home – eg, because s/he is away at school or for a temporary period on holiday or in hospital. You can argue that a child is normally living with you if s/he spends more time with you than with anyone else.[18]

Your child can count as normally living with you even if s/he also lives with someone else, or only lives with you for part of the week and lives for part of the week with someone else – eg, her/his other parent. However, CTC can only be paid to one claimant (or joint-claim couple) – see below. If you are seeking to rely on European Union co-ordination rules to qualify for CTC for a child in another member state, see p1661 for more information.

Do you have main responsibility?

If you (and your partner) and at least one other person (or couple) with whom the child also normally lives claim CTC for the same child, you only qualify for CTC for the child if you can show you have the 'main responsibility' for her/him. This applies if:[19]

- your child normally lives with both you and:
  - at least one other person in another household – eg, with you and with the child's other parent from whom you have separated; *or*
  - someone who is not your partner in the same household – eg, with you and with the child's grandparent where you live together.

  It also applies if it is a combination of these situations. 'Household' is not defined. See p312 for ideas about what might count as a household; *and*
- you and at least one of the other people with whom your child normally lives claim CTC.

You and the other CTC claimant(s) can decide which of you should count as having main responsibility. If you cannot agree, a decision maker decides.[20] You can challenge the decision (see p276).

'**Main responsibility**' is not defined in the rules. The approach for tax credits is different from that for child benefit, housing benefit or child support maintenance, and does not refer to the legal concept of 'parental responsibility'.[21] The decision maker is likely to consider things like:[22]

- whether any court orders exist that set out where your child is to live or who is to care for her/him (although the terms of a court order are not conclusive – what matters is what happens in practice[23]);
- who pays for your child's food and clothes and who is responsible for giving her/him pocket money (but this does not mean that the claimant who spends most on the child always has main responsibility);
- how much of the time the child is living with you (but there is no set threshold of days/nights per week or year);
- where the majority of her/his clothes and belongings are kept and who does her/his laundry;
- who is the main contact or registered address for the school or college, nursery or childcare provider, and who takes most responsibility for your child when s/he is at school;[24]
- who arranges appointments to see a doctor/dentist.

Even though you may be sharing responsibility for a child and s/he normally lives with you for part of the week, HMRC might not treat you as having the main responsibility. There is no provision for allowing CTC to be split between parents if a child divides her/his time between their homes.

Do you share responsibility for a child?
If you share responsibility for your child(ren) equally with other CTC claimant(s), it may be difficult to decide who has the main responsibility. If you and another claimant have more than one child, you can each get CTC for different children – eg, if you have two children, you could get CTC for one child and the other claimant could get CTC for the other.

When you do not count as responsible for a child
Even if a child normally lives with you, you do *not* count as responsible for the child and cannot qualify for CTC for her/him during any period when s/he is:[25]
- provided with, or placed in, accommodation and the accommodation or the child's maintenance is funded wholly or partly by the local authority under specified provisions or out of other public funds. This includes children staying with foster carers who get foster payments for them from the local authority. This does not apply if your child is staying in certain forms of residential accommodation and this is only necessary because your child has a disability or because her/his health would be significantly impaired or further impaired if s/he were not staying in the accommodation. You must have been treated as

Part 3: Getting a benefit decision changed
Chapter 14: Child tax credit
1. Who can get child tax credit

responsible for her/him immediately before s/he went into the accommodation;[26] *or*
- being looked after by a local authority and has been placed with you because you want to adopt her/him. This only applies if the local authority is paying for the child's accommodation or maintenance or both under specified provisions; *or*
- in custody. This only applies if your child:
  - is serving a life or unlimited sentence; *or*
  - is serving a term of more than four months; *or*
  - has been detained 'at Her Majesty's pleasure'; *or*
- at least 16 and:
  - is awarded CTC in her/his own right for a child for whom s/he is responsible; *or*
  - receives WTC in her/his own right (including in a joint claim); *or*
  - is entitled to and receiving contributory ESA in her/his own right; *or*
  - is married, in a civil partnership or living with someone as a couple and her/his partner is not in full-time, non-advanced education or approved training; *or*
  - is your partner and and you are living with her/him.

Note: a young person does not count as a child if s/he gets IS, income-based JSA, income-related ESA or UC in her/his own right (see p273).

Challenging a decision

HMRC may decide that your child does not normally live with you or that you are not the person with main responsibility for her/him, so you are not entitled to CTC. It may also decide that someone else has claimed CTC for your child(ren) and s/he has the main responsibility. In this case, your entitlement to CTC ends and you may have been overpaid, but from no earlier than the date of the competing claim, which should not be backdated.[27]

If you think a decision is wrong and it affects your tax credits, you can request a mandatory reconsideration and then appeal if you are unhappy with the outcome (see Chapter 67). If as a result of a decision or following the outcome of an appeal HMRC says you have been overpaid, you can dispute recovery (see p1485). **Note:** if HMRC has paid two claimants for the same period for the same child who normally lives with both claimants, this is likely to be an official error and so any overpayment should not be recovered.[28]

It is possible that the DWP, the local authority, the Tax Credit Office and the Child Benefit Office might reach different conclusions about whether your child(ren) can be included in your claims. If so, you should appeal *all* the decisions with which you disagree.

2. The rules about your age

You (and your partner) must be aged at least 16 to qualify for child tax credit (CTC).[29] There is no upper age limit. If you are under 16, someone else (eg, your parent or the adult with whom you normally live) may be able to claim CTC for you *and* your child.

3. People included in the claim

You can only qualify for child tax credit (CTC) if you are responsible for one or more children. Some qualifying young people continue to count as children until they are 20. See pp271–76 for who counts as a child and when you count as responsible for her/him.

If you are single, you get CTC yourself.[30] If you are a member of a couple, you get CTC jointly with your partner.[31] For who counts as a couple for tax credit purposes, see p1460. **Note:** if you get tax credits jointly with your partner, but then cease to count as a couple (or you get tax credits as a single person, but then become a member of a couple), your entitlement to CTC ends. You should therefore report this change in your circumstances and you will usually then have to claim universal credit as a single person (or a couple).

If you are a couple:
- when working out how much CTC you get, your partner's income is added to yours (see Chapter 63);
- CTC is paid to the person who is the main carer of your children (see p1467).

4. The amount of child tax credit

The amount of child tax credit (CTC) you get depends on:
- your maximum CTC. This is made up of a combination of 'elements':
  - family element (£545 a year) if the claim includes a child born before 6 April 2017; *and*
  - child element (£2,935 a year) – one for each child. **Note:** a child element is not payable for a child born on or after 6 April 2017 if you already have two or more children included in your award. There are exceptions (see p1415); *and*
  - disabled child element lower rate (£3,545 a year) – one for each child who qualifies; *or*
  - higher rate for a severely disabled child (£4,975 a year) – one for each child who qualifies.

For details of how you qualify for the above elements, see Chapter 62; *and*

Part 3: Getting a benefit decision changed
Chapter 14: Child tax credit
5. Claims and renewals

- how much income you have; *and*
- the 'income threshold figure' that applies to you.

If you are on a means-tested benefit

Being on income support (IS), income-based jobseeker's allowance (JSA), income-related employment and support allowance (ESA) or pension credit (PC) is an automatic passport to maximum CTC.[32] You do not need to work out your income or capital. In these circumstances, your CTC award equals maximum CTC.

If you are not on a means-tested benefit

If you are not on IS, income-based JSA, income-related ESA or PC, follow the steps below to calculate your CTC.
- **Step one:** work out your 'relevant period' (see p1413).
- **Step two:** work out your maximum entitlement (your maximum CTC) for the relevant period (see p1414).
- **Step three:** work out your 'relevant income' (see p1428 and p1436).
- **Step four:** compare your income with the 'income threshold figure' for the relevant period. This is £17,005 a year if you are entitled to CTC only, or £6,770 a year if you are entitled to CTC and your maximum amount of tax credits includes working tax credit (WTC) elements.[33] See p1429 for further information.
- **Step five:** calculate your CTC entitlement for the relevant period (see p1429). If your income is less than the income threshold figure, CTC equals your maximum CTC. If your income exceeds the income threshold figure, your maximum CTC is reduced by 41 per cent of the excess.

You may also be entitled to WTC. Full details of both calculations are in Chapter 62.

5. **Claims and renewals**

The general rules on claiming, backdating and how your claim can be renewed at the end of the year are in Chapter 64. This section gives an outline of the rules on claims for child tax credit (CTC).

You can only reclaim CTC if you were entitled to CTC in 2021/22, or you are already entitled to working tax credit, or you are prevented from claiming universal credit (see p23). Claim by telephoning the Tax Credit Helpline on 0345 300 3900 (textphone: 0345 300 3909; Relay UK service available). Your claim ends if you were claiming as a couple and are now single, or if you were claiming as a single person and are now part of a couple.[34]

Renewal awards

After the end of the tax year in which you claimed CTC, you (and your partner), receive an 'annual review' from HMRC asking you to confirm or declare your income and your household circumstances for the previous tax year (see p1475). If required, you must reply within a strict time limit. HMRC then makes a final decision, based on your actual income during the tax year. It decides whether you were entitled to CTC and, if so, the amount of your award. HMRC also uses the information about your income and household circumstances for the previous tax year to renew your award for the next tax year.[35] Some awards are finalised and renewed automatically on the information held by HMRC, as shown on your annual review, but you must check this and report any errors or changes. Your tax credit claim can continue to be renewed even though you cannot make a new claim for tax credits anymore because of the introduction of universal credit. **Note:** if you have a 'nil award', you may be given notice that your claim will not be renewed unless you specifically request this.

---

6. Getting paid

This section gives an outline of the rules about payment of child tax credit (CTC). For more information about getting paid, see p1467.

Payment of CTC is normally made in arrears into the bank (or similar) account of whoever you nominate as the main carer of your children (see p1467). If you are unable to act for yourself, payment can be made to someone else on your behalf – called your 'appointee' (see p1462).[36]

When is child tax credit paid?

You are paid every week or every four weeks, whichever you choose, although HM Revenue and Customs (HMRC) can decide how often.[37]

You can be paid by a Post Office Payout voucher while your account arrangements are being finalised. HMRC no longer issues cheques.

Note:

- Even if you have been sanctioned for a benefit offence, your CTC cannot be paid at a reduced rate.
- If you have forgotten your PIN, see p1149. The issues are the same as for benefits.
- If payment of your CTC is delayed and this is causing hardship, ask HMRC to make an urgent next day/same day payment (see p1469). If you wish to complain about how your claim has been dealt with, see p1405. You might be able to claim compensation (see p1403).

Part 3: Getting a benefit decision changed
Chapter 14: Child tax credit
7. Tax, other benefits and the benefit cap

- If payment of your CTC is suspended or postponed, see p1469.
- If you are overpaid CTC, you might have to repay it (see Chapter 65). In some cases, interest can be added to the overpayment. In some circumstances, you may have to pay a penalty (see p1498). If you have been accused of fraud, see Chapter 66.

Change of circumstances

Your initial award of CTC is made on the basis of your (and your partner's) previous year's income and your personal circumstances at the start of the tax year. If your current year's income or your personal circumstances change, your award of CTC can be amended. **Note:**

- There are some changes you *must* report to HMRC (see p1470). If you fail to do so within one month, you might be given a financial penalty. Some changes end your entitlement to CTC and you will usually have to claim universal credit (UC) instead.
- Other changes that affect your maximum entitlement to CTC are not compulsory to report, so you cannot be given a penalty, but they should still be reported to avoid an overpayment or underpayment – eg, when you have a baby or if one of your children stops getting disability living allowance (see p1472). Changes that increase your maximum entitlement to CTC can generally only be backdated one month from when you notify HMRC. Changes that decrease your entitlement generally take effect from the date of change, so may result in an overpayment.
- It is optional to report an estimated change in your current year income (see p1473). Your actual income is always taken into account at the end of the tax year, but you may want to consider reporting an estimate sooner in order to avoid an overpayment or underpayment of CTC.
- Report if you become a member of a couple with someone entitled to UC. Your entitlement to CTC will end (see p31).

7. **Tax, other benefits and the benefit cap**

Tax

Child tax credit (CTC) is not taxable.

Means-tested benefits and tax credits

If you are entitled to CTC:

- CTC is not taken into account as income for income support (IS), income-based jobseeker's allowance (JSA), income-related employment and support allowance (ESA) or pension credit (PC);

- CTC is not counted as income for universal credit (UC), but there are very limited circumstances when you can be entitled to CTC during an assessment period for UC.[38] This can happen if you become the new partner of a UC claimant (see p31), in which case her/his assessment period continues so that you may receive your last payment of CTC during the first assessment period of your joint UC claim;[39]
- unless you are on IS, income-based JSA or income-related ESA or are at least pension age, the amount of CTC you are paid *is* taken into account as income for housing benefit (HB);
- in Scotland, CTC is a qualifying benefit for Scottish child payment (see p1731).

If you get arrears of CTC, these count as capital for means-tested benefits and can be disregarded in some circumstances (see p482 and p507).

If you are in full-time paid work, you may qualify for working tax credit (WTC) in addition to CTC.

Non-means-tested benefits

CTC can be paid in addition to any non-means-tested benefits to which you (or your partner) are entitled, including child benefit, but see Chapter 63 for which of these benefits may be taken into account as income for CTC. If your child qualifies for disability living allowance (DLA), child disability payment (CDP), personal independence payment (PIP) or armed forces independence payment, you qualify for the disabled child or severely disabled child elements of CTC and the income from DLA, CDP, PIP or armed forces independence payment is ignored.

The benefit cap

In some cases, there is a limit on the total amount of specified benefits you can receive (a 'benefit cap'). CTC is one of the specified benefits. However, the benefit cap only applies if you are getting UC or HB. See p1156 for further information.

Passports and other sources of help

If you are entitled to CTC, you may also qualify for health benefits such as free prescriptions (see Chapter 31) and education benefits such as free school lunches (see p851). You may also qualify for a Sure Start maternity grant (Best Start grant in Scotland) or a funeral expenses payment (funeral support payment in Scotland). You may be entitled to a council tax reduction (see p836).

Note: if you apply for, and are entitled to, payments under the tax-free childcare scheme, your CTC award is terminated, as you cannot get both at the same time. See p856 for more details.

Part 3: Getting a benefit decision changed
Chapter 14: Child tax credit
Notes

Notes

1 Reg 8 UC(TP) Regs; *HMRC v LD (TC)* [2018] UKUT 306 (AAC)

1. Who can get child tax credit

2 ss3(3) and (7), 8 and 42 TCA 2002; regs 3-5 CTC Regs; reg 3 TC(R) Regs; reg 3 TC(Imm) Regs
3 Art 7(1), (2), (5) and (6) WRA(No.23)O
4 *HMRC v RS* [2021] UKUT310 (AAC)
5 Art 4(11) WRA(No.32)O
6 *R (on the application of) DK vHMRC and SSWP* [2022] EWCA Civ 120
7 s8(1) TCA 2002
8 s8(5) TCA 2002; reg 6 CTC Regs
9 s8(3) TCA 2002; reg 2(1), definition of 'child', CTC Regs
10 s8(4) TCA 2002; regs 2, definition of 'qualifying young person' and 'full-time education', 4 and 5(1)-(3A) CTC Regs
11 TCTM 02230 and TCM 0114100
12 Reg 5(7) CTC Regs
13 Regs 2, definition of 'remunerative work', and 5(4) CTC Regs
14 Reg 3(1) rule 2.2 CTC Regs
15 s8(2) TCA 2002; reg 3(1) rules 1 and 2 CTC Regs
16 Reg 3(1) rule 4 Case D and (2) CTC Regs
17 TCTM 02202
18 CFC/1537/1995
19 Reg 3(1) rule 2 CTC Regs
20 Reg 3 rule 3 CTC Regs
21 *PG v HMRC (TC)* [2016] UKUT 216 (AAC)
22 TCTM 02204; *PG v HMRC (TC)* [2016] UKUT 216 (AAC)
23 *GJ v HMRC (TC)* [2013] UKUT 561 (AAC)
24 *KN v HMRC (TC)* [2009] UKUT 79 (AAC)
25 Reg 3(1) rule 4.1 CTC Regs
26 Reg 3(1) rule 4.2 CTC Regs; reg 9 CB Regs
27 *LP v HMRC (TC)* [2014] UKUT 533 (AAC)
28 *SH v HMRC and SC (TC)* [2013] UKUT 297 (AAC); *AG v HMRC and AG (TC)* [2018] UKUT 318 (AAC)

2. The rules about your age

29 s3(3) TCA 2002

3. People included in the claim

30 s3(3)(b) TCA 2002
31 s3(3)(a) and (5A) TCA 2002; reg 2(1) CTC Regs; CTC/3864/2004; R(TC) 1/07

4. The amount of child tax credit

32 ss7(2) and 13 TCA 2002; reg 4 TC(ITDR) Regs
33 Reg 3(2) and (3) TC(ITDR) Regs

5. Claims and renewals

34 s3(4) TCA 2002
35 Regs 11 and 12 TC(CN) Regs

6. Getting paid

36 s24(3) TCA 2002; reg 6 TC(PC) Regs
37 Regs 8 and 13 TC(PC) Regs

7. Tax, other benefits and the benefit cap

38 Reg 66 UC Regs
39 Reg 5(2)(b)(iii) UC(TP) Regs; reg 21(3B) UC Regs

Chapter 15

Working tax credit

Key facts

- You cannot usually make a new claim for working tax credit (WTC).
- WTC is paid to some low-paid workers who have not claimed universal credit (UC).
- You do not have to have paid national insurance contributions to qualify.
- WTC is administered and paid by HM Revenue and Customs.
- If you disagree with a WTC decision, you can apply for a mandatory reconsideration and then appeal if you are unhappy with the outcome (see Chapter 67).
- If you claim UC, your entitlement to WTC ends.

New claims for, and continuing entitlement to, working tax credit

You can now only make a new claim for WTC in very limited circumstances (see p284). If you are already entitled to WTC, you can continue to qualify until:

– you claim UC;[1] or

– you become a member of a couple and your partner is getting UC; or

– you and your partner are affected by the 'managed migration' transfer process, that is, you are told by the DWP that your WTC will end and are invited to claim UC. See p29 for further information, and AskCPAG and CPAG's *Welfare Rights Bulletin* for updates.

Part 3: Getting a benefit decision changed
Chapter 15: Working tax credit
1. Who can get working tax credit

1. Who can get working tax credit

You qualify for working tax credit (WTC) if:[2]
- you (or your partner) are in paid work (see below); *and*
- your income is sufficiently low (see Chapter 63); *and*
- you are not a 'person subject to immigration control' (see Chapter 68); *and*
- you are 'present' and 'ordinarily resident' in the UK. You can be treated as present and ordinarily resident in the UK in some circumstances – eg, if you are away temporarily. See Chapter 69 for further information.

Who can make a new claim for working tax credit

You can only make a new claim for WTC if any of the following apply.[3]
- You already have an award of child tax credit (CTC). If you then become entitled to WTC because you are working sufficient hours, this is treated as a change in circumstances and a new claim is not formally required.
- You were entitled to WTC in 2021/22 and are making a claim for 2022/23. This includes renewals but could also apply in other situations. It does not apply if you have already renewed your claim and then attempt to reclaim later in the year after a gap in entitlement.[4]
- You are prevented from claiming universal credit (UC) because you (or if you are a couple, you and your partner) are in a category from which it has been decided not to accept claims for UC.[5]

If you cannot make a new claim for WTC under these rules, you can make a claim for UC.

Paid work

To qualify for WTC, you or your partner must be in paid work for which you are paid or expect to be paid. HM Revenue and Customs (HMRC) calls this 'remunerative work'.[6] Payment of a benefit (eg, carer's allowance – CA) does not count as paid work. The number of hours required for tax credits purposes depends on your circumstances. 'Work' includes self-employment and work which is done from home.

In some circumstances, you may be treated as not being in work (see p291). In others, you may be treated as if you are in work when you are not actually working (see p288).

Income from work affects your entitlement to WTC. This means that, although your (or your partner's) hours of work are high enough for you to qualify, you might not satisfy the means test.

How many hours you need to work

You qualify for WTC if any of the following apply.[7]
- You normally work at least **30 hours** a week and you are aged 25 or over.

- You normally work at least **16 hours** a week and:
  - you qualify for a disabled worker element (see p1420); *or*
  - you are aged 60 or over; *or*
  - you are a single claimant and are responsible for at least one child or qualifying young person (see p273); *or*
  - you are a member of a couple, you (or your partner) are responsible for at least one child or qualifying young person (see p273) and your partner either counts as incapacitated for the purposes of the childcare element (see p1423) or s/he is entitled to CA, or s/he is a hospital inpatient or is in prison.
- You and your partner's combined hours of work are normally at least **24 hours** a week, and you (or your partner) are responsible for at least one child or qualifying young person (see p273). One of you must normally work at least 16 hours a week. If only one of you works, that person must work at least 24 hours a week.

If you are under 25, you can only qualify for WTC if you work at least 16 hours a week and qualify for a disabled worker element, or you are responsible for a child in the circumstances above.

If your circumstances change and you are no longer responsible for a child or qualifying young person, or no longer qualify for a disabled worker element, unless you are 60 or over, you may have to increase your weekly hours to at least 30 to continue to qualify for WTC. See Chapter 64 for more information on changes of circumstances and when you must report them.

The work must be expected to continue for at least four weeks.[8]

Note:

- You can continue to count as being in work for four weeks after you leave work, or your hours reduce to less than the number you (or your partner) need to do. See p289 for information about this 'WTC run-on'.
- If you normally work sufficient hours a week, but are off sick or on maternity, paternity, parental bereavement or adoption leave, you may be able to continue to get WTC as you can be treated as working your normal hours (see p288).

How your hours are calculated

How you calculate your hours depends on whether you are employed or self-employed.[9]

- If you are employed, include all the hours:
  - you normally work under your contract, if you are an apprentice or employee; *or*
  - you normally perform in the office in which you are employed, if you are an office holder. This includes if you are in an elective office or are a company director; *or*
  - for which you are normally paid by the employment agency with whom you have a contract, if you are an agency worker.

Part 3: Getting a benefit decision changed
Chapter 15: Working tax credit
1. Who can get working tax credit

• If you are self-employed, include all the hours you normally do for payment or for which you expect to be paid, and on activities which are necessary to the employment.

Paid meal and refreshment breaks count towards the total hours you work.[10] Also included is any time allowed for medical appointments, but only if this is to treat or monitor your disability and if you are paid, or expect to be paid, for the time.[11] Your total hours from more than one job are added together.

Periods when you are on a customary or paid holiday from work are ignored when calculating your hours.[12] Unpaid meal and refreshment breaks are also ignored.

Employed and self-employed[13]

You count as **'employed'** if you are employed under a contract of service or apprenticeship and your earnings are taxable as employment income under certain provisions of the Income Tax (Earnings and Pensions) Act 2003.

You count as **'self-employed'** if you are carrying out a trade, profession or vocation that is organised and regular, on a commercial basis and with a view to making a profit. A business plan may help to demonstrate this, but the absence of one does not mean you are not self-employed.[14] There is no requirement of actual profitability, and no minimum income floor.[15]

Hours you normally work

Whether you are employed or self-employed, the measure for WTC purposes is the number of hours you normally work.[16] 'Normally' is not defined in the WTC rules. HMRC says you should calculate your hours based on what you 'regularly, usually or typically' do and that the number of hours you normally work might not be the number of hours specified in your contract of employment.[17] The hours that are relevant are those you *actually* work. If you routinely do paid overtime, argue that these are hours you normally work and that they should be included. See below if your hours fluctuate.

Example

Joy is a cashier in a supermarket. Her partner stays at home to look after their children. She is contracted to work 21 hours a week over a three-day week but she does 3.5 hours overtime almost every week. She gets an unpaid half-hour lunch break. When Joy and her partner claim WTC, she has just returned from two weeks' paid holiday.

Joy normally works 21 + 3.5 = 24.5 hours a week. Unpaid lunch breaks and the time she was on paid holiday are not taken into account. As Joy and her partner are responsible for children, one of them needs to work at least 16 hours a week and, between them, they need to work at least 24 hours a week. Joy therefore counts as being in full-time paid work.

Chapter 15

Working tax credit

When working out your normal hours if you are self-employed, HMRC says you can include not only the hours you spend providing orders or services but also those that are necessary to your self-employment – eg, trips to wholesalers and retailers, visits to potential clients, advertising or canvassing, cleaning the business or vehicles used as part of the business, bookkeeping and research work.[18]

If your hours fluctuate

Working out the number of hours you normally work is straightforward if you do the same number of hours each and every week, or if your hours vary but you always do at least enough hours each week to qualify for WTC.

However, if your weekly hours fluctuate, it can be more complicated. Unless you are a term-time only worker (see below), there is no rule on how to average your hours. There is no requirement to work the necessary number of hours each and every week, and a common sense approach should be taken.[19] If you have a regular pattern of work (a recognised work cycle), HMRC says the hours you normally work are those that reflect an overall view of the pattern of your hours over a representative period, or over a year.[20] For example, if you always work two weeks on and two weeks off, you could argue that your hours should be averaged over a four-week period.

If you are in any doubt about what your normal hours are, contact HMRC and get advice. To avoid a potential overpayment, it is advisable to report your actual hours every four weeks.

Examples

Joel works in a residential project. He works three weeks on and one week off. When he is on, he works 40 hours a week. His average hours are 40 x 3 ÷ 4 = 30 hours a week. Joel can try to argue that he normally works 30 hours or more a week. As Joel is aged 45, does not have a physical or mental disability and has no children, he must work at least 30 hours a week to be entitled to WTC.

Meya is contracted to do 15 hours a week. However, she gets regular overtime of three hours every other week. Her average hours are 15 + 18 ÷ 2 = 16.5 hours. Meya can try to argue that she normally works 16 hours or more a week. As Meya is a lone parent, she need only work 16 hours or more a week to be entitled to WTC.

If you think your average hours have been calculated unfairly, you can request a mandatory reconsideration and then appeal. You should first work out whether you would be better off claiming UC rather than WTC.

Term-time and seasonal workers

If you only work in school term times or similar, periods when you are not working are ignored when deciding whether you are in full-time paid work if:[21]

Part 3: Getting a benefit decision changed
Chapter 15: Working tax credit
1. Who can get working tax credit

- you work in a school, an educational establishment or other place of employment; *and*
- you have a recognisable 'work cycle' that lasts for a year; *and*
- your 'work cycle' includes periods of school holidays or similar vacations during which you do not work.

3

In practice, if the hours of work you do during term time mean they are enough to qualify for WTC during term time, you also qualify over the holidays. You can get WTC during this period if your normal hours of work each week are sufficient during term time.

Example
Gayle is 35 years old and is a lone parent with two children. She is a cleaner at a local college and works 16 hours a week, 36 weeks of the year. She does not work (and is not paid) when the students are on study leave and on holiday. The periods when Gayle does not work are ignored. She qualifies for WTC during term time because she works at least 16 hours a week. She therefore counts as being in paid work throughout the year and can get WTC for the whole year.

Note:
- It may not be clear whether you have a work cycle that lasts a year – eg, if you have only started your job recently or have a fixed-term contract that finishes at the end of the school term, or are employed on a casual or relief basis.[22] If you have an indefinite contract to work in term time only, you can argue that you have a yearly work cycle from the start.[23]
- If you work casually or intermittently (eg, you are a seasonal worker who only works in the summer but you are unemployed the rest of the year), HMRC is likely to say your work cycle is that part of the year in which you are working and that you do not count as being in work when you are unemployed.[24]

People treated as being in paid work

You or your partner are treated as still working your normal hours in a number of situations.

Maternity, adoption, paternity, parental bereavement or shared parental leave

You or your partner are treated as still working your normal hours when:[25]
- you are being paid statutory maternity pay (SMP), statutory adoption pay (SAP), statutory paternity pay (SPP), statutory shared parental pay (SSPP), statutory parental bereavement pay (SPBP) or maternity allowance (MA); *or*
- you are absent from work during the first 39 weeks of maternity leave, or adoption leave or two weeks of paternity leave; *or*

- you are absent from work during a period of statutory shared parental leave or parental bereavement leave, but only during the period in which you would have been paid SSPP or SPBP had you qualified.

If you are an employee, you are treated as still being in work from the start of the period above, provided you were working sufficient hours for WTC purposes immediately before the period begins.[26]

If you are self-employed, you count as being in work during any period when the above would have applied had the work done in the week before the period began been as an employee.

If you do not return to work when your SMP, SAP, SPP, SSPP, SPBP or MA ends, or after the allowed number of weeks of leave, you must notify HMRC, as you are no longer treated as being in work under this rule. The statutory entitlement to maternity or adoption leave is 52 weeks, but you are only treated as working for tax credit purposes for the first 39 weeks.

Note: notify HMRC if you are in any of the above situations and provide an estimate of your current year's income. This is because any MA and the first £100 a week of any SMP, SAP, SPP, SPBP and SSPP is ignored as income for WTC.

Periods of ill health

You or your partner are treated as still working your normal hours work when:[27]
- you are being paid statutory sick pay (SSP); *or*
- you are:
  - being paid employment and support allowance (ESA); *or*
  - getting national insurance (NI) credits because you are incapable of work or have limited capability for work (including where you are getting NI credits because you are treated as having limited capability for work).
  The period treated as 'in work' while on income support (IS), ESA or NI credits only applies for 28 weeks.

You must have been working sufficient hours for WTC purposes immediately before the period began.

If you are self-employed, you count as being in work during any period when the above would have applied had the work done in the week before the period began been as an employee.

If you do not return to work when your SSP ceases (or after 28 weeks on IS, ESA or NI credits), you no longer count as being in full-time paid work under this rule.

Working tax credit run-on

If you or your partner stop work or reduce your hours, you can get 'WTC run-on'. You are treated as still working your normal hours for the four weeks immediately after you stop work, or your hours reduce to fewer than the number you (or your

Part 3: Getting a benefit decision changed
Chapter 15: Working tax credit
1. Who can get working tax credit

partner) must do to count as being in full-time paid work.[28] This means you continue to qualify for:

- WTC for the four-week period, even if you are no longer working sufficient hours;
- all the elements you were previously getting for that period (eg, the 30-hour element and the childcare element), even if the reduction in hours means you would otherwise lose entitlement to these.

You must report the change in your circumstances to HMRC within one month.

Your tax credits award, including the four-week run-on, is terminated if you claim UC and entitlement ends from the date you claim.

During the coronavirus pandemic

You could remain entitled to WTC if you were on furlough or reduced working hours due to coronavirus. These rules only applied when the government's Coronavirus Job Retention Scheme was open – ie, up to but not including 1 October 2021. For full details, see the 2021/22 edition of this *Handbook*.

Other situations

You or your partner are treated as being in work:

- if you were working sufficient hours within the past seven days.[29] This means you can make a new claim or continue to qualify for WTC – eg, during a short period between jobs or when you are on jury service for no more than one week; *or*
- during any period when you are on strike or are suspended from work while complaints or allegations against you are investigated, provided you were in full-time paid work for WTC purposes immediately before the start of the period. You must not be on strike for longer than 10 consecutive days when you should be working.[30]

Moving between situations in which you are treated as being in work

The rules allow you to be treated as being in work for WTC purposes for certain periods in the situations described on p288. If you move from one situation to another (eg, maternity leave followed by sickness leave), HMRC has previously stated that you can continue to be treated as being in work throughout the second period, provided you were treated as being in work immediately before it began.[31] However, the Upper Tribunal has held that you cannot continue to be treated as being in work if you move from a period on SSP to a period on ESA, or if you move from the four-week 'run-on' period (see p289) to a period on MA.[32]

You continue to be treated as being in work if you moved from a period treated as in work due to the coronavirus pandemic to a period of maternity, adoption or parental bereavement leave or ill health.[33]

People treated as not being in work

You or your partner are treated as *not* being in work if:[34]

- you are receiving pay in lieu of notice for more than four weeks after you stop work (you continue to qualify for four weeks under the four-week 'run-on' rule) (see p289);[35]
- you are a volunteer (except for emergency volunteering leave from your usual job during the coronavirus pandemic), or are working for a charity or voluntary organisation and are giving your services free (except for your expenses);
- you are providing care for someone who is staying with you temporarily but who is not normally a member of your household and:
  - the only payment you receive is from a health authority, a local authority, a voluntary organisation, a clinical commissioning group or the person her/ himself for caring for her/him; *and*
  - the payment is disregarded as a tax-free payment under HMRC's 'rent-a-room' scheme (see p1450).

  Note: if you are an adult placement (sometimes known as 'shared lives') carer who has *not* opted for the 'rent-a-room' scheme, you *can* count as being in full-time paid work;[36]
- you are working on a training scheme and are being paid a training allowance (see below), unless the training allowance or the money you are being paid by the DWP is subject to income tax as a profit from work;[37]
- the only payment you receive, or expect to receive, is a sports award from a sports council;
- you are working while you are a sentenced or remand prisoner. This means you cannot qualify for WTC even if the work you do is outside the prison – eg, while you are on temporary release.

Training allowance

A **'training allowance'** is an allowance paid to maintain you or a member of your family:[38]

- by a government department or by or on behalf of the Secretary of State, Scottish Enterprise or the Highlands and Islands Enterprise; *and*
- for the period, or part of a period, during which you are on a course provided or approved by, or under arrangements made by, any of the above.

Allowances paid to, or in respect of, you by a government department or by the Scottish government are not included if these are paid because you are a trainee teacher or on a full-time course of education, unless this is under arrangements made under section 2 of the Employment and Training Act 1973.

Part 3: Getting a benefit decision changed
Chapter 15: Working tax credit
3. People included in the claim

Students

You are not excluded from getting WTC simply because you are a student. However, you must do sufficient hours of paid work in addition to your studies and the work must be expected to last for four weeks.

Is the work part of your course?

1. If you are paid in return for the work you do (eg, you are paid by an employer during a work placement), you can argue that you are in paid work.

2. Any work you do in studying for a degree or other qualification does not count as paid work – any grant or loan you receive is not paid in return for work done on the course.

3. You are not considered to be in paid work if you are a student nurse, because the grants or loans you get are not payments for work done on the course and do not count as income for tax credit purposes.[39]

When calculating how much WTC you can get, student loans and most other student income are disregarded. See p1447 for what income counts.

Foster carers

If you are working sufficient hours as a foster carer (or approved kinship carer, in Scotland), you can qualify for WTC. HMRC generally accepts that foster carers come under the definition of self-employed (see p285), even if you have no profits and no loss for income tax purposes, and the hours of work you declare should be accepted.[40] If you do more than one job, the total hours are added together. So, if you are doing work in addition to foster caring, the hours from the other work can be added to those spent foster caring.

Fostering allowances (and kinship care allowances, in Scotland) that qualify for tax relief are generally ignored when calculating your WTC (see p1452).

2. The rules about your age

You (and your partner) must be aged at least 16 to get working tax credit (WTC).[41] There is no upper age limit.

If you are under 25, you can only qualify for WTC if you work at least 16 hours a week and you are a disabled worker or are responsible for a child in the circumstances described on p285.

3. People included in the claim

If you are a single person, you get working tax credit (WTC) for yourself.[42] If you are a member of a couple (see p1460), you get WTC jointly with your partner.[43]

WTC includes elements for you and your partner and for any special needs either of you have (see Chapter 62). When working out how much WTC you get, your partner's income is added to yours (see Chapter 63). **Note:** if you get tax credits jointly with your partner but then no longer count as a couple (or you get tax credits as a single person but then become a member of a couple), your entitlement to WTC ends. You should report this change in your circumstances and you usually have to claim universal credit as a single person (or a couple) instead.

If you are responsible for at least one child or qualifying young person:
- you (or your partner) must work at least 16 hours a week to qualify for WTC (although if you are a member of a couple, in most cases your combined hours must be at least 24 a week);
- and you are a couple and one of you works at least 16 hours a week, your hours of work can be added to those of your partner to enable you to qualify for the 30-hour element (see p1420);
- you (and your partner) might qualify for the childcare element in your WTC if you pay for childcare.

See p272 for who counts as a child or qualifying young person. For when you count as responsible for a child, see p273. The rules are the same as for child tax credit.[44]

---

4. The amount of working tax credit

The amount of working tax credit (WTC) you get depends on:
- your maximum WTC. This is made up of a combination of 'elements' (see Chapter 62 for how you qualify for these):
  - basic element (£2,070 a year);
  - lone parent/couple element (£2,125 a year);
  - 30-hour element (£860 a year);
  - disabled worker element (£3,345 a year). More than one can be included if you are a member of a couple and you both qualify;
  - severe disability element (£1,445 a year). More than one can be included if you are a member of a couple and you both qualify;
  - childcare element;
- how much income you have (see Chapter 63); *and*
- the 'income threshold figure'.

If you are on a means-tested benefit

Being on income support (IS), income-based jobseeker's allowance (JSA), income-related employment and support allowance (ESA) or pension credit (PC) is an automatic passport to maximum WTC.[45] You therefore do not need to work out

Part 3: Getting a benefit decision changed
Chapter 15: Working tax credit
5. Claims and renewals

your income. In these circumstances, WTC equals maximum WTC. **Note:** this does not apply while you are getting 'WTC run-on' (see p289).

If you are not on a means-tested benefit

If you are not on IS, income-based JSA, income-related ESA or PC, follow the steps below to calculate your WTC.

- **Step one:** work out your 'relevant period' (see p1413).
- **Step two:** work out your maximum entitlement (your maximum WTC) for the relevant period (see p1428).
- **Step three:** work out your 'relevant income' (see p1428 and p1436).
- **Step four:** compare your income with the 'income threshold figure' for the relevant period – £6,770 a year for WTC if you are not entitled to child tax credit (CTC).[46]
- **Step five:** calculate your WTC entitlement for the relevant period (see p1429). If your income is less than the 'income threshold figure', WTC equals your maximum WTC. If your income exceeds the 'income threshold figure', your maximum WTC is reduced by 41 per cent of the excess.

You may also be entitled to CTC. Full details of both calculations are in Chapter 62.

5. Claims and renewals

The general rules on claiming, backdating and how your claim can be renewed at the end of the year are in Chapter 64.

You can only reclaim working tax credit (WTC) if you were entitled to WTC in 2021/22, or you are already entitled to child tax credit, or you are prevented from claiming universal credit (UC – see p23). Claim by telephoning the Tax Credit Helpline on 0345 300 3900 (textphone: 0345 300 3909; Relay UK service available).

Your claim ends if you were claiming as a couple and are now single, or if you were claiming as a single person and are now part of a couple.[47]

Renewal awards

At the end of the tax year in which you claimed WTC, you (and your partner if you are a member of a couple) receive an 'annual review' from HM Revenue and Customs (HMRC) asking you to confirm or declare your income and your household circumstances for the previous tax year (see p1475). If required, you must reply within a strict time limit. HMRC then makes a final decision, based on your actual income during the tax year. It decides whether you were entitled to WTC and, if so, the amount of your award. HMRC also uses the information about your income and household circumstances for the previous tax year to renew your award for the next tax year.[48] Some awards are finalised and renewed automatically on the information held by HMRC, as shown on your annual review, but you must check this and report any errors or changes. Your tax credits claim can continue to be renewed even though you cannot usually make a new claim for tax credits because of the introduction of UC. **Note:** if you have a 'nil award', you may be given notice that your claim will not be renewed unless you specifically request this.

6. Getting paid

This section gives an outline of the rules on payment of working tax credit (WTC). For more information about getting paid, see p1467.

Payment of WTC is normally made in arrears into your bank (or similar) account. If you make a joint claim, any WTC to which you are entitled towards your childcare expenses is paid to whoever you nominated as the main carer of your child(ren) (see p1467), but cannot be paid direct to the childcare provider. If you are unable to act for yourself, payment can be made to someone on your behalf – called your 'appointee' (see p1462).[49]

When is working tax credit paid?
You are paid every week or every four weeks, whichever you choose, although HM Revenue and Customs (HMRC) can decide how often.[50]

You can be paid by Post Office Payout voucher while your account arrangements are finalised. HMRC no longer issues cheques.
Note:
- You can be disqualified from being paid WTC if you have committed a benefit offence (see p1242).
- If you have forgotten your PIN, see p1149. The issues are the same as for benefits.
- If payment of your WTC is delayed and this is causing hardship, ask HMRC to make a next day/same day payment. If you wish to complain about how your claim has been dealt with, see p1405. You may be able to claim compensation (see p1403).
- If payment of your WTC is suspended or postponed, see p1469.
- If you are overpaid WTC, you might have to repay it (see Chapter 65). In some cases, interest can be added to the overpayment. In some circumstances, you may have to pay a penalty (see p1498). If you have been accused of fraud, see Chapter 66.

Part 3: Getting a benefit decision changed
Chapter 15: Working tax credit
7. Tax, other benefits and the benefit cap

Change of circumstances

Your award of WTC is made on the basis of your (and your partner's) previous year's income and your personal circumstances at the start of the tax year. If your current year's income or your personal circumstances change, your award of WTC can be amended. **Note:**

- There are some changes you *must* report to HMRC (see p1470). If you fail to do so within one month, you might be given a financial penalty. Some changes end your entitlement to WTC and you will then usually have to claim universal credit (UC) instead.
- Other changes that affect your maximum entitlement to WTC are not compulsory to report, so you cannot be given a penalty, but they should still be reported to avoid an underpayment or overpayment – eg, when your hours increase to 30 or more so you would qualify for a 30-hour element, or the rate of your partner's personal independence payment award is reduced so you no longer qualify for the severe disability element (see p1472). Changes that increase your maximum entitlement to WTC can generally only be backdated one month from when you notify HMRC. Changes that decrease entitlement generally take effect from the date of change, so may result in an overpayment.
- It is optional to report an estimated change in your current year's income (see p1473). Your actual income is always taken into account at the end of the tax year, but you may want to consider reporting an estimate sooner to avoid an overpayment or underpayment of WTC.

If you are getting WTC and you only qualify for the lone parent or childcare element because you (or your partner) are responsible for a child and the child dies, you are paid WTC for a further eight weeks (or up to the date your child would have turned 20, if this is earlier) as if this had not happened.[51] This is only the case if you would have continued to qualify for the element but for the child's death. After this period, you may continue to qualify for WTC – eg, if you still satisfy the means test and work sufficient hours.

Note: if you become a member of a couple with someone entitled to UC, your entitlement to WTC ends (see p31).

7. **Tax, other benefits and the benefit cap**

Tax

Working tax credit (WTC) is not taxable.

Means-tested benefits and tax credits

If you are entitled to WTC:
- WTC counts as income for income support, income-based jobseeker's allowance, income-related employment and support allowance, pension credit (PC) and housing benefit (HB);
- you can get WTC at the same time as PC because there is no rule that prevents you or your partner doing full-time paid work while claiming PC;
- if you get HB, you might get an additional earnings disregard (see p415 and p458);
- WTC does not count as income for universal credit (UC), but there are very limited circumstances when you can be entitled to WTC during an assessment period for UC.[52] This can happen if you become a new partner of a UC claimant (see p31), in which case her/his assessment period continues so that you may receive your last payment of WTC during the first assessment period of your joint UC claim;[53]
- in Scotland, WTC is a qualifying benefit for Scottish child payment (see p1731).

If you get arrears of WTC, these count as capital for means-tested benefits and can be disregarded in some circumstances (see p482 and p507).

If you have dependent children (including a 'qualifying young person'), you may qualify for child tax credit (CTC) in addition to WTC.

Non-means-tested benefits

In some situations, while you are receiving WTC you get national insurance credits (see p962).

WTC can be paid in addition to any non-means-tested benefits to which you (or your partner) are entitled, but see Chapter 63 for which of these benefits may be taken into account as income for WTC. Qualifying for certain non-means-tested benefits means you may also qualify for the disabled worker element or severe disability element of WTC.

The benefit cap

In some cases, there is a limit on the total amount of specified benefits you can receive (a 'benefit cap'). WTC is *not* one of the specified benefits. The benefit cap does *not* apply if you or your partner are entitled to WTC. See p1156 for further information.

Passports and other sources of help

If you are entitled to WTC, you may qualify for health benefits, such as free prescriptions (see Chapter 31). You do not have to satisfy the means test if your gross annual income is below a set amount and you are getting WTC which

Part 3: Getting a benefit decision changed
Chapter 15: Working tax credit
Notes

includes a disabled worker element or a severe disability element, or CTC with your WTC.

You may qualify for a Sure Start maternity grant (a Best Start grant in Scotland) or a social fund funeral expenses payment (funeral support payment in Scotland). You may be entitled to a council tax reduction (see p836).

Note: if you apply for, and are entitled to, payments under the tax-free childcare scheme, your WTC award is terminated, as you cannot get both at the same time. See p856 for more details.

Notes

1 Reg 8 UC(TP) Regs; *HMRC v LD (TC)* [2018] UKUT 306 (AAC)

1. Who can get working tax credit
2 ss3(3) and (7), 10 and 42 TCA 2002; regs 4-8 WTC(EMR) Regs; reg 3 TC(R) Regs; reg 3 TC(Imm) Regs
3 Art 7(1), (2), (5) and (6) WRA(No.23)O
4 *HMRC v RS* [2021] UKUT 310 (AAC)
5 Art 4(11) WRA(No.32)O
6 s10(1) TCA 2002
7 Reg 4(1) (second condition) WTC(EMR) Regs
8 Reg 4(1) (third condition) WTC(EMR) Regs
9 Reg 4(3) WTC(EMR) Regs
10 Reg 4(4)(b) WTC(EMR) Regs
11 Reg 4(5) WTC(EMR) Regs
12 Reg 4(4)(a) WTC(EMR) Regs
13 Reg 2(1) WTC(EMR) Regs
14 *JF v HMRC (TC)* [2017] UKUT 334 (AAC)
15 *JW v HMRC (TC)* [2019] UKUT 114 (AAC)
16 Reg 4(3) WTC(EMR) Regs
17 TCTM 02451-52
18 TCTM 02453
19 CTC/2103/2006
20 TCTM 02457
21 Reg 7 WTC(EMR) Regs; *Stafford and Banks v CAO (TC)* [2001] UKHL 33 (HL), reported as R(IS) 15/01
22 R(JSA) 8/03; CIS/914/1997; CJSA/2759/1998
23 R(JSA) 5/02
24 R(JSA) 1/07; *Saunderson v SSWP* [2012] ScotCS CSIH 10; TCTM 02458

25 Reg 5 WTC(EMR) Regs
26 Reg 5A WTC(EMR) Regs
27 Reg 6 WTC(EMR) Regs
28 Reg 7D WTC(EMR) Regs
29 Reg 8 WTC(EMR) Regs
30 Regs 7A and 7B WTC(EMR) Regs
31 HMRC Benefits and Credits Consultation Group email to CPAG, 20 December 2007
32 *TK v HMRC (TC)* [2016] UKUT 45 (AAC); *AG v HMRC (TC)* [2017] UKUT 67 (AAC)
33 Regs 5(3) and 6(3) WTC(EMR) Regs
34 Reg 4(2) WTC(EMR) Regs
35 Reg 7C WTC(EMR) Regs
36 TCTM 02440
37 Reg 4(2)(c) and (d) and (2A) WTC(EMR) Regs
38 Reg 2(1) WTC(EMR) Regs
39 R(FIS) 1/83; R(FIS) 1/86; TCTM 02431
40 TCTM 02440

2. The rules about your age
41 s3(3) TCA 2002

3. People included in the claim
42 s3(3)(b) TCA 2002
43 s3(3)(a) and (5A) TCA 2002; CTC/3864/2004; R(TC) 1/07
44 Reg 2, definition of 'child' and 'qualifying young person', WTC(EMR) Regs

4. The amount of working tax credit
45 ss7(2) and 13 TCA 2002; reg 4 TC(ITDR) Regs
46 Reg 3(2) TC(ITDR) Regs

5. **Claims and renewals**
   47 s3(4) TCA 2002
   48 Regs 11 and 12 TC(CN) Regs

6. **Getting paid**
   49 s24(3) TCA 2002; reg 6 TC(PC) Regs
   50 Regs 8 and 13 TC(PC) Regs
   51 Reg 19 WTC(EMR) Regs; reg 6 CTC Regs

7. **Tax, other benefits and the benefit cap**
   52 Reg 66 UC Regs
   53 Reg 5(2)(b)(iii) UC(TP) Regs; reg 21(3B)
       UC Regs

Part 4

General rules for other means-tested benefits

Chapter 16

People included in the claim

This chapter covers:
1. Couples (below)
2. Children (p307)
3. Households (p312)

This chapter covers the rules for means-tested benefits other than universal credit (UC). For UC, see Chapter 4. For child tax credit, see Chapter 14, and for working tax credit, see Chapter 15.

Key facts
- Your partner and, in some cases, your children can be included in your means-tested benefit claim.
- You count as a member of a couple if you are married or in a civil partnership and are living with your partner in the same household. You also count as a couple if you are not married or in a civil partnership, but are living with your partner as if you were living together as a married couple or civil partners.
- A child or 'qualifying young person' can be included as part of your family if you are responsible for her/him. S/he must also live in your household.
- You can continue to count as a couple, and children and young people can continue to be included in your means-tested benefit claim, while you are living apart temporarily.

1. Couples

Your partner is included in your means-tested benefit claim if you count as a 'couple'. You and your partner count as a 'couple' for means-tested benefit purposes if you are both 16 or over and you are:[1]
- married or civil partners and members of the same household; *or*
- not married or civil partners but 'living together as if' you are a married couple or civil partners.

For when you count as living in the same 'household', see p312. **Note:** for pension credit (PC) only, if your partner is a 'person subject to immigration control' (see

Part 4: General rules for other means-tested benefits
Chapter 16: People included in the claim
1. Couples

p1524), you are treated as *not* being members of the same household and so do not count as a couple.[2]

Spouse or civil partner

You can still be treated as part of a couple, even if you are married to someone else or in a civil partnership with someone else.[3]

There are special rules if you are polygamously married.[4] You count as **polygamously married** if you are part of a marriage in which one of you is married to more than one person and your marriages took place in a country that permits polygamy (see also p535).[5] For employment and support allowance (ESA) only, you and all your partners must also be living in the same household (see p312).

You count as someone's **civil partner** if you have been registered as her/his civil partner.

Living together as a married couple or civil partners

Even if you and your partner are not married or civil partners, you count as a couple if you are 'living together as if' you are a married couple or civil partners. This is referred to as 'cohabiting' in this *Handbook*. This applies to both different- and same-sex relationships.[6]

If you are awarded income support (IS), income-based jobseeker's allowance (JSA) or income-related ESA, usually the local authority should not make a separate decision about whether you are cohabiting when considering your claim for housing benefit (HB).[7] However, if the local authority thinks that the benefit claim on which your HB claim is based is fraudulent, it can decide that you are not entitled to HB.[8] If you have not been awarded IS, income-based JSA, income-related ESA or PC, the local authority must consider whether you are cohabiting and may reach a different conclusion from that of the DWP.[9]

The factors below are used as 'signposts' to determine whether or not you are cohabiting.[10] No one factor, in itself, is conclusive, as it is your overall relationship and your particular circumstances that are looked at.[11] The 'emotional aspect' of the relationship (your interdependence, devotion, love and affection) should also be considered.[12] This does not necessarily conflict with the factors below but, like your individual circumstances, should not be regarded as conclusive. For example, if your partner stays with you for three nights or more a week, you should not automatically be treated as living together as a couple.

Are you cohabiting?

1. Do you live in the same household? See p305.

2. Do you have a sexual relationship? See p305.

3. What are your financial arrangements? See p305.

4. Is your relationship stable? See p305.

5. Do you have children? See p305.

6. How do you appear in public? See p306.

Living in the same household

If you live in the same household, you may be treated as cohabiting. For what counts as a 'household', see p312.

Even if you *do* share a household, you may not be cohabiting. It is essential to look at *why* two people are in the same household.[13] For example, if you are living in the same household for 'care, companionship and mutual convenience', you can argue that you are not living together as a husband and wife or civil partners.[14]

Being in a sexual relationship

In practice, a decision maker may not ask you about the existence of a sexual relationship, in which case s/he only has the information if you volunteer it. However, if you are appealing about whether you are a member of a couple, the First-tier Tribunal should consider this and may ask you about it.[15] If you do not have a sexual relationship, you should say so (and perhaps offer to show your separate sleeping arrangements).

Having a sexual relationship is not sufficient, by itself, to prove you are cohabiting. If you have never had a sexual relationship, there is a strong (but not necessarily conclusive) presumption that you are not cohabiting.[16] A couple who abstain from a sexual relationship before marriage should not be counted as cohabiting until they are formally married.[17]

Your financial arrangements

If one person is supported by the other or your household expenses are shared, this may be treated as evidence that you are cohabiting. However, it is important to consider how expenses are shared. There is a difference between, on the one hand, paying a fixed weekly contribution or rigidly sharing bills 50/50 (which does *not* suggest cohabitation) and, on the other hand, a common fund for income and expenditure (which might).

A stable relationship

Marriage and civil partnership are expected to be stable and lasting and so an occasional or brief association should not be regarded as cohabitation. However, the fact that your relationship is stable does not make it cohabitation – eg, you can have a stable relationship as a landlord and lodger, but not be cohabiting.

The way you spend your time together, the activities you undertake together and the things you do for each other are relevant, so questions about how you spend your holidays and how you organise the shopping, the laundry and cleaning may be important.

Children

If you have had a child together and live in the same household as the other parent, there is a strong (but not conclusive) presumption of cohabitation.

Part 4: General rules for other means-tested benefits
Chapter 16: People included in the claim
1. Couples

Your appearance in public

Decision makers may check the electoral roll and awards of other benefits to see whether you present yourselves as a couple. If you do not have a committed emotional loving relationship that is publicly acknowledged, you can argue that you are not living together as a married couple.[18]

Couples living apart

If you separate permanently (ie, you do not intend to resume living with your partner), you no longer count as a couple.[19] When deciding whether you intend to resume living together or not, your intention must be 'unqualified' – ie, it must not depend on something over which you have no control, such as the right of entry to the UK being granted by the Home Office[20] or the offer of a suitable job.[21]

If you and your partner are living apart temporarily, you continue to count as a couple because you are still treated as members of the same household (but see below). If you were not living together in the same household before your time apart, you should not be regarded as living apart temporarily.[22] Your former household need not have been in this country.[23]

However, even if you and your partner are only living apart temporarily, **you no longer count as a couple if:**
- **for IS, income-based JSA, income-related ESA, PC and HB,** you are likely to be separated for more than 52 weeks. However, you still count as a couple if you are unlikely to be separated for 'substantially' longer than 52 weeks and there are exceptional circumstances, such as a stay in hospital, or having no control over the length of the absence;[24]
- **for IS, income-based JSA, income-related ESA and PC:**[25]
  - either of you are in custody;
  - either of you are released on temporary licence from prison;
  - either of you are detained in a high security psychiatric hospital (in Scotland, a 'state hospital') under the mental health provisions;
  - either of you are staying permanently in a care home, an Abbeyfield Home or an independent hospital;
  - you are abroad and do not qualify for benefit while temporarily absent from Great Britain. For when you qualify while temporarily absent and for when your partner is abroad, see p1629 (for IS), p1631 (for income-based JSA), p1627 (for income-related ESA) and p1635 (for PC).

If you and your partner continue to count as a couple while you are temporarily living apart, your partner's income and capital continue to be taken into account. However, in certain situations, your benefit is calculated in a different way (see p920 for care homes and p929 for approved bail or probation hostels).

Challenging a decision that you are a couple

Your benefit may be stopped or adjusted if the decision maker decides you are a member of a couple. If you disagree with a decision that you are a couple, you can apply for a revision or supersession (see Chapter 56), or appeal to the First-tier Tribunal (see Chapter 57).

How do you show that you are not a couple?

1. Consider carefully what evidence to submit:
   - if you are married or in a civil partnership, to show that you are not living in the same household with your spouse or civil partner;
   - if you are not married or in a civil partnership, in relation to each of the six questions on p304, the emotional aspect of your relationship and any other matters you consider relevant.

2. Provide evidence if the other person has another address (eg, a rent book and other household bills), receipts for board and lodging, statements from friends and relatives, or evidence of a formal separation, divorce proceedings or a dissolution application or order.

If your benefit as a single person is stopped because it is alleged that you are a couple, the burden of proof is on the decision maker to prove that you are.[26]

If your benefit is stopped because it is decided that you are a couple, challenge the decision.

2. Children

A child may count as part of your family for your means-tested benefit. However, you can only get additional amounts in your benefit for her/him in certain circumstances. You do not have to be the child's parent.

For income support (IS), income-based jobseeker's allowance (JSA), income-related employment and support allowance (ESA) and housing benefit (HB), a child is part of your family for benefit purposes (although you do not necessarily get additional amounts for her/him) if:

- you or your partner are 'responsible' for her/him (see p309); *and*
- s/he is living in your 'household' (see p311).[27]

For the guarantee credit of pension credit (PC), a child is part of your family if:[28]

- you are 'responsible' for her/him (see p309); *and*
- you do not have an award of either child tax credit (CTC) or working tax credit (and you are not treated as having such an award because you are renewing your award and awaiting a decision).

Part 4: General rules for other means-tested benefits
Chapter 16: People included in the claim
2. Children

A child stops being part of your family for your benefit if you no longer fulfil the above conditions or if s/he no longer counts as a child (see below).

If a child is part of your family for benefit purposes, you can get an additional amount for her/him included in your HB and your PC. But you can only get an additional amount in your IS or income-based JSA if:

- you already have a current claim for IS or income-based JSA that began before 6 April 2004; *and*
- you had a child included in that claim before 6 April 2004 and you have not been awarded CTC.

Note: usually, you only get additional amounts in your benefit for a maximum of two children. For more information, see p321. However, this does not apply to PC. If an amount for children can be included in your PC, you get an additional amount for each child that qualifies.

ESA does not include additional amounts for children.[29]

Who counts as a child

For IS, income-based JSA, income-related ESA and HB, a person usually counts as a child if:[30]

- s/he is aged under 16; *or*
- s/he is aged 16 or over but under 20 and counts as a 'qualifying young person' for child benefit purposes . This includes, for example, most young people who are at school or college full time studying for GCSEs or A levels (or equivalent), or who are doing approved training. See p563 for who counts as a qualifying young person. A young person can continue to count as a child after s/he has left school or training until the 'terminal date' (see p566) or the end of the child benefit 'extension period' (see p565).

A 19 year old must have started (or been accepted for or enrolled on) the education or training before reaching 19 in order to count as a qualifying young person.

For PC, a person usually counts as a child if:[31]

- s/he is aged under 16; *or*
- s/he is 16 or over but under 20 and is a 'qualifying young person' for PC.

A 'qualifying young person' for PC includes most young people studying for GCSEs or A levels or who are doing approved training. Specifically, it means someone who:[32]

- is aged 16 but who has not reached 1 September following her/his 16th birthday; *or*
- is aged 16–19 but who has not yet reached 1 September following her/his 19th birthday, and has been accepted for (or has enrolled on) approved training or non-advanced education at school or college, or another institution approved by the Secretary of State (see below). During term time there must be more

than 12 hours, on average, of tuition, practical work, supervised study and examinations a week. Meal breaks and unsupervised study are not included.

Approved training and non-advanced education for pension credit

'**Approved training**' is training that is approved by the DWP and provided under section 2(1) of the Employment and Training Act 1973 or section 2(3) of the Enterprise and New Towns (Scotland) Act 1990.

A course is '**non-advanced**' if it is below the level of 'advanced education'. Courses that count as advanced education include university degrees and other courses above GCSE, A level and Scottish National Qualifications above higher or advanced higher level.[33] See p564 for more examples of advanced and non-advanced courses.

Who does not count as a child

For **IS, income-based JSA, income-related ESA and HB**, a person does *not* count as a child if:[34]

- s/he is getting certain benefits or tax credits in her/his own right and so does not count as a qualifying young person (see p570). For IS and income-based JSA, s/he may not count as a child if s/he is entitled to one of these benefits but is not getting it – eg, because it has been suspended; *or*
- s/he is excluded from entitlement to IS, income-based JSA and HB because s/he is aged 16 or 17, has left local authority care on or after 1 October 2001, and certain other conditions apply (see p933).

For **PC**, a person does not count as a child if s/he is getting universal credit, ESA (contributory or income-related), JSA (contribution-based or income-based) or IS in her/his own right.[35]

Responsibility for a child

For **IS, income-based JSA, income-related ESA and HB**, a child is included in your benefit if you are 'responsible' for her/him and s/he is living in your 'household'.

- **You are treated as responsible for a child for IS** if you get child benefit for her/him (see Chapter 27).[36] If no one gets child benefit, you are responsible if you are the only one who has applied for it. In all other cases, the person responsible is the person with whom the child usually lives.[37] If a child for whom you are responsible gets child benefit for another child, you are also responsible for that child.[38]
- **You are treated as responsible for a child for JSA** if either you get child benefit for her/him or, if no one gets child benefit for her/him, the child 'usually lives' with you or you are the only person who has applied for child benefit.[39] If you share responsibility for the child, even if you do not get child

Part 4: General rules for other means-tested benefits
Chapter 16: People included in the claim
2. Children

benefit for her/him, you might be regarded as responsible for her/him if you are the 'substantial minority carer' – ie, you have the child with you for at least 104 nights a year.[40] If a child for whom you are responsible gets child benefit for another child, you are also responsible for that child. **Note:** the rules for when you count as responsible for a child for the purposes of deciding whether you must claim joint-claim JSA are different.[41]

- **You are treated as responsible for a child for ESA** if s/he 'usually lives' with you. This is not defined in the rules.[42]
- **You are treated as responsible for a child for HB** if the child is 'normally living' with you.[43] This means that s/he spends more time with you than with anyone else.[44] If it is unclear in whose household the child lives, or if s/he spends an equal amount of time with two parents in different homes (this may not mean literally three and a half days with each parent[45]), you are treated as having responsibility if:[46]
  - you get child benefit for her/him (see Chapter 27); *or*
  - no one gets child benefit, but you have applied for it; *or*
  - no one has applied for child benefit, or both of you have applied, but you appear to have the most responsibility.

Note: substantial minority carers cannot be regarded as responsible for a child for HB.[47]

For HB, it is only necessary to look at who gets child benefit when it is unclear in whose household the child *normally* lives. **For IS**, it is essential to look first at who gets child benefit, and only if this is not decisive is it relevant to look at where the child *usually* lives.

A child can only be the responsibility of one person in any week for IS, income-based JSA and HB.[48] The rules for ESA do not expressly say this but, in any case, a person can only be responsible for a child if s/he usually lives with her/him.

If benefit is paid for a child, it cannot be split between parents if a child spends her/his time equally between their two homes.

For PC, a child is included if you are 'responsible' for her/him. You are responsible for a child if s/he 'normally lives with' you.[49] This includes considering the amount of time s/he spends with you, but is not limited to this and should also take into account the nature of the support you provide. If the child normally lives with two (or more) people who are not a couple (eg, if s/he lives in the homes of her/his separated parents), you are responsible if you have the main responsibility. In this situation, you can agree with the other person who this should be. The DWP can, however, decide otherwise or, if you cannot agree, decide which person has the main responsibility. Both the amount of time the child spends with you and the nature of the support you provide should be taken into account.[50] You cannot be treated as responsible for a child during any period in which s/he is:[51]

- looked after by a local authority (including being placed with a foster parent), except during planned short breaks in local authority care to provide respite care for the person who normally looks after her/him, or where s/he is placed with someone who has parental responsibility for her/him; *or*
- a prisoner; *or*
- temporarily absent but in Great Britain, and s/he has been, or is expected to be, absent for more than 52 weeks, unless there are 'exceptional circumstances' (eg, s/he is in hospital) and the absence is unlikely to be substantially more than 52 weeks; *or*
- temporarily absent from Great Britain and s/he has been, or is expected to be, absent from Great Britain for more than four weeks, unless it is for the death of a close relative or medical treatment, when the period of absence may be, respectively, eight weeks or 26 weeks (see p1635).

Living in the same household

In addition to being responsible for her/him, for IS, JSA, ESA and HB a child is only included if s/he is a member of the same household. If you count as responsible for a child, s/he is usually treated as a member of your household, despite any temporary absence. For exceptions to the rule, see below. For what 'household' means, see p312. The requirement for the child to be a member of your household does not apply to PC (but the child must normally be living with you).

When a child does not count as a member of your household

A child does *not* count as a member of your household if:[52]

- **for IS, JSA, ESA and HB,** s/he is not living with you and:
  - s/he has no intention of resuming living with you; *or*
  - s/he is likely to be absent for more than 52 weeks, unless there are exceptional circumstances, such as being in hospital, or if you have no control over the length of absence and the absence is unlikely to be substantially longer than 52 weeks;
- **for IS, JSA, ESA and HB:**
  - s/he is being fostered by you or your partner following a formal placement by social services. This does not apply if you are fostering privately or if social services has made a less formal arrangement for the child to live with you; *or*
  - s/he is living with you or your partner prior to adoption and has been placed by social services or an adoption agency; *or*
  - s/he is boarded out with you or your partner, whether or not with a view to adoption (for JSA, ESA and HB only); *or*
  - s/he has been placed with someone else prior to adoption; *or*
  - s/he is in the care of, or being looked after by, the local authority and not living with you. However, s/he counts as a member of your household on

Part 4: General rules for other means-tested benefits
Chapter 16: People included in the claim
3. Households

the days when s/he comes home – eg, for the weekend or a holiday.[53] Make sure you tell the decision maker in good time. For HB, your child counts as a member of the household for all that week whether s/he returns for all or only part of it;[54]

- **for IS, JSA and ESA**, s/he is not living with you and:
  - s/he has been in hospital or in a local authority home for more than 12 weeks and has not been in regular contact with you or other members of your household. The 12 weeks run from the date s/he went into hospital or the home, or from the date you claim IS/JSA/ESA, if later.[55] However, the 12 weeks run from the date s/he went into the hospital or home if:[56]
    - you were getting income-based JSA immediately before your claim for IS; *or*
    - you were getting IS or income-related ESA immediately before your claim for JSA; *or*
    - you were getting IS or income-based JSA immediately before your claim for ESA;
  - s/he is in custody. **Note:** s/he can still be included in your claim for any periods s/he spends at home;[57] *or*
  - s/he has been abroad for more than four weeks, or for more than eight weeks (26 weeks for ESA) to get medical treatment.[58] The four-/eight-/26-week period runs from the day s/he went abroad, or from the day you claim IS/JSA/ESA, if later. However, the four-/eight-/26-week period is calculated from the day after the child went abroad if:[59]
    - you were getting income-based JSA immediately before your claim for IS; *or*
    - you were getting IS or income-related ESA immediately before your claim for JSA; *or*
    - you were getting IS or income-based JSA immediately before your claim for ESA;
- **for IS and income-based JSA**, s/he is living with you and away from her/his parental or usual home in order to attend school. The child is not included in your claim, but remains a member of her/his parent's household.[60]

3. Households

The term **'household'** is not defined. Whether you and another person should be treated as members of the same household is decided on the particular facts of your case. In all cases, you must spend the major part of your time in the same household. For pension credit only, if your partner is a 'person subject to immigration control' (see p1524), you are treated as *not* being members of the same household and so do not count as a couple.[61]

A house or flat can contain a number of separate households and if one person has exclusive occupation of separate accommodation from another, they are not considered to be living in the same household. Physical presence is not, in itself, conclusive. There must be a 'particular kind of tie' binding two people together in a domestic establishment. So, for example, a husband and wife may live in separate households in the same care or nursing home.[62] A household must also involve two or more people living together as a unit and having a reasonable level of independence and self-sufficiency. In one case, it was held that a married couple sharing a room in a residential home because they needed help organising their personal care and domestic activities were not self-sufficient and did not live in a domestic establishment, and therefore did not share a household.[63]

Is there a separate household?

If you think you should not be treated as a member of the same household as someone, check whether you can show that you maintain separate households. A separate household may exist if there are:

- independent arrangements for storing and cooking food or separate eating arrangements;
- independent financial arrangements or separate commitments for housing costs;
- no evidence of family life.

You cannot be a member of more than one household at the same time.[64] So if you are a member of one couple, you cannot also be treated as part of another. If two people maintain separate homes (ie, they each have separate addresses where they usually live), they cannot share the same household.[65] Even if you have the right to occupy only part of a room, you may have your own household.[66]

If you are separated from your partner, but living under the same roof, you should not be treated as a couple if you are maintaining separate households. Any 'mere hope' of a reconciliation is not a 'reasonable expectation' if at least one partner has accepted that the relationship is at an end.[67]

If you are still married or in a civil partnership, a shared attitude that the relationship is at an end may not be enough to show there is no shared household.[68]

Part 4: General rules for other means-tested benefits
Chapter 16: People included in the claim
Notes

Notes

1. Couples

1 s137(1) SSCBA 1992; CFC/7/1992
   IS Reg 2(1) IS Regs
   JSA s35(1) JSA 1995; reg 1(3) JSA Regs
   ESA Sch 1 para 6(5) WRA 2007; reg 2(1) ESA Regs
   PC s17(1) SPCA 2002; reg 1(2) SPC Regs
   HB Reg 2(1) HB Regs; reg 2(1) HB(SPC) Regs
2 Reg 5(1)(h) SPC Regs
3 R(SB) 8/85
4 **IS** Regs 18 and 23 IS Regs
   JSA Regs 84 and 88(4) and (5) JSA Regs
   ESA Regs 68 and 83 ESA Regs
   PC Reg 8 and Sch 3 SPC Regs
   HB Regs 23 and 25 HB Regs; regs 22 and 23 HB(SPC) Regs
5 **IS** Reg 2(1) IS Regs
   JSA Reg 1(3) JSA Regs
   ESA Reg 2(1) ESA Regs
   PC s12 SPCA 2002
   HB Reg 2(1) HB Regs; reg 2(1) HB(SPC) Regs
6 **IS** Reg 2(1) IS Regs
   JSA s35(1A) JSA 1995; reg 1(3) JSA Regs
   ESA Sch 1 para 6(6) WRA 2007; reg 2(1) ESA Regs
   PC s17(1A) SPCA 2002; reg 1(2) SPC Regs
   HB Reg 2(1) HB Regs; reg 2(1) HB(SPC) Regs
   IS/HB s137(1A) SSCBA 1992
7 *R v Penwith DC HBRB ex parte Menear* [1991] 24 HLR 115 (QBD). However, *AM v Chelmsford BC (HB)* [2013] UKUT 245 (AAC) suggests that this only applies to the assessment of income and capital, and not to cohabitation questions.
8 *R v South Ribble BC HBRB ex parte Hamilton* [2000] 33 HLR 102 (CA)
9 CH/4014/2007
10 *Crake and Butterworth v SBC* [1982] 1 All ER 498; [1981] 2 FLR 264 (QBD)
11 R(SB) 17/81; R(G) 3/71; CIS/87/1993
12 *PP v Basildon DC (HB)* [2013] UKUT 505 (AAC)
13 *Crake and Butterworth v SBC* [1982] 1 All ER 498; [1981] 2 FLR 264 (QBD), quoted in R(SB) 35/85

14 R(SB) 35/85
15 CIS/87/1993; CIS/2559/2002; CIS/2074/2008
16 CIS/87/1993
17 CSB/150/1985
18 *JP v SSWP (IS)* [2014] UKUT 17 (AAC)
19 **IS** Reg 16(2)(a) IS Regs
   JSA Reg 78(2)(a) JSA Regs
   ESA Reg 156(3)(a) ESA Regs
   PC Reg 5(1)(a)(i) SPC Regs
   HB Reg 21(2)(a) HB Regs; reg 21(2)(a) HB(SPC) Regs
20 CIS/508/1992; CIS/13805/1996
21 CIS/484/1993
22 **IS** Reg 16(1) IS Regs
   JSA Reg 78(1) JSA Regs
   ESA Reg 156(2) ESA Regs
   PC Reg 5(2) SPC Regs
   HB Reg 21(1) HB Regs; reg 21(1) HB(SPC) Regs
   All *Broxtowe BC v CS (HB)* [2014] UKUT 186 (AAC)
23 CIS/508/1992
24 **IS** Reg 16(2) IS Regs
   JSA Reg 78(2) JSA Regs
   ESA Reg 156(3) ESA Regs
   PC Reg 5(1)(a) SPC Regs
   HB Reg 21(2) HB Regs; reg 21(2) HB(SPC) Regs
25 **IS** Reg 16(3) IS Regs
   JSA Reg 78(3) JSA Regs
   ESA Reg 156(4) ESA Regs. This wrongly refers to Chapter 4, but correctly refers to the rules on temporary absence from Great Britain.
   PC Reg 5(1)(b)-(d) and (f) SPC Regs
26 R(I) 1/71

2. Children

27 s137 SSCBA 1992
   JSA s35 JSA 1995; reg 77 JSA Regs
   ESA Reg 2(1), definition of 'family', ESA Regs
28 Reg 6 and Sch IIA SPC Regs
29 Reg 1 SS(WTCCTC)(CA) Regs

30 **IS** Reg 14 IS Regs
JSA s35 JSA 1995; regs 1(3) and 76 JSA Regs
ESA Reg 2(1) ESA Regs
HB Reg 19 HB Regs; reg 19 HB(SPC) Regs
IS/HB s137 SSCBA 1992
31 Reg 4A and Sch IIA SPC Regs
32 Reg 4A and Sch IIA SPC Regs
33 Reg 4A SPC Regs
34 **IS** Reg 14(2) IS Regs
JSA Reg 76(2) JSA Regs
ESA Reg 2(1), definition of 'young person', ESA Regs
HB Reg 19(2) HB Regs; reg 19(2) HB(SPC) Regs
35 Reg 4A SPC Regs
36 Reg 15(1) IS Regs
37 Reg 15(2) IS Regs
38 Reg 15(1A) IS Regs
39 Reg 77(1)-(3) JSA Regs
40 Reg 77 JSA Regs, as applied in *Hockenjos v Secretary of State for Social Security* [2004] EWCA Civ 1749, reported as R(JSA) 2/05. However, see also CJSA/2507/2002.
41 Reg 77(2) JSA Regs
42 Reg 156(10) ESA Regs
43 Reg 20(1) HB Regs; reg 20(1) HB(SPC) Regs
44 CFC/1537/1995
45 CFC/1537/1995
46 Reg 20(2) HB Regs; reg 20(2) HB(SPC) Regs
47 *JD v SSWP and LB Richmond upon Thames (HB)* [2013] UKUT 642 (AAC); *JB v SSWP and Basingstoke and Deane BC (HB)* [2014] UKUT 223 (AAC)
48 **IS** Reg 15(4) IS Regs
JSA s3(1)(d) JSA 1995; reg 77(5) JSA Regs
HB Reg 20(3) HB Regs; reg 20(3) HB(SPC) Regs
49 Sch IIA para 3 SPC Regs
50 Sch IIA para 3(3) and (4) SPC Regs; reg 4 UC Regs; *MC v SSWP (UC)* [2018] UKUT 44 (AAC) was about UC but arguably should also apply to PC
51 Sch IIA paras 4-8 SPC Regs
52 **IS** Reg 16 IS Regs
JSA Reg 78 JSA Regs
ESA Reg 156 ESA Regs
HB Reg 21 HB Regs; reg 21 HB(SPC) Regs
53 **IS** Regs 15(3) and 16(6) IS Regs
JSA Regs 77(4) and 78(7) JSA Regs
ESA Reg 156(8) ESA Regs

54 Reg 21(5) HB Regs; reg 21(5) HB(SPC) Regs
55 **IS** Reg 16(5)(b) IS Regs
JSA Reg 78(5)(c) JSA Regs
ESA Reg 156(6)(c) ESA Regs
56 **IS** Reg 16(5A) IS Regs
JSA Reg 78(6) JSA Regs
ESA Reg 156(7) ESA Regs
57 **IS** Regs 15(3) and 16(6) IS Regs
JSA Regs 77(4) and 78(5)(i) and (7) JSA Regs
ESA Reg 156(6)(h) and (8) ESA Regs
58 **IS** Reg 16(5)(a) and (aa) IS Regs
JSA Reg 78(5)(a) and (b) JSA Regs
ESA Reg 156(6)(a) and (b) ESA Regs
59 **IS** Reg 16(5A) IS Regs
JSA Reg 78(6) JSA Regs
ESA Reg 156(7) ESA Regs
60 **IS** Reg 16(7) IS Regs
JSA Reg 78(8) JSA Regs

3. Households

61 Reg 5(1)(h) SPC Regs
62 *Santos v Santos* [1972] 2 All ER 246; CIS/671/1992; CIS/81/1993
63 CIS/4935/1997
64 R(SB) 8/85
65 R(SB) 4/83
66 CSB/463/1986
67 CIS/72/1994
68 CIS/2900/1998

Chapter 17

Applicable amounts

Key facts
- Applicable amounts are used in some means-tested benefits to help calculate the amount of benefit to which you are entitled.
- Applicable amounts apply in income support, income-based jobseeker's allowance, income-related employment and support allowance and housing benefit. There are additional amounts in the guarantee credit of pension credit for people who are severely disabled, carers or people who have a child, which are similar to applicable amounts.
- Applicable amounts are made up of personal allowances, premiums, certain housing costs and, in some cases, components. You may have one or more of these included.

1. What are applicable amounts

Your applicable amount for income support (IS), income-based jobseeker's allowance (JSA) and income-related employment and support allowance (ESA) is the amount you are expected to live on each week. Your applicable amount for housing benefit (HB) is the amount used to calculate how much help you need with your rent. This chapter explains how to work out your applicable amount for these benefits. For the way your benefit is calculated, see p238 for IS, p693 for income-based JSA, p165 for income-related ESA and p189 for HB.

What is included in your applicable amount

Your applicable amount is made up of:
- **personal allowances:** the amount the law says you need for living expenses (see p317);

- **premiums:** the amount given for certain extra needs you, your partner or children may have (see p323);
- **a support or work-related activity component** in income-related ESA and, in some circumstances, in HB (see p336);
- certain **housing costs** in IS, income-based JSA and income-related ESA (see p344). **Note:** you cannot get benefit to help with the cost of your mortgage or loan for repairs and improvements. Instead, the DWP may offer you a loan to help meet your interest payments (see p839);
- **a transitional addition** in income-related ESA and HB if you have been transferred to ESA from incapacity benefit, severe disablement allowance or IS on the grounds of disability (see p339).

Can you get allowances and premiums for children?

You can get allowances and premiums for children in your HB (see p321 and p323). You can get an additional amount for children as part of the guarantee credit of pension credit (see p323).

IS and income-based JSA have not included allowances and premiums for children since 6 April 2004. However, you may continue to have these included if:[1]

– you have an award which began before 6 April 2004; *and*

– you had a child included in the award before 6 April 2004; *and*

– you have not been awarded child tax credit (CTC).

In these circumstances, personal allowances and premiums for children continue to be included in your award (and amounts for a new child can be added) unless you are awarded CTC.

2. Personal allowances

The amount of your personal allowance in income support (IS), income-based jobseeker's allowance (JSA), income-related employment and support allowance (ESA) and housing benefit (HB) depends on your age and whether you are claiming as a single person or a couple. You also get an allowance for each child included in your HB and, in some circumstances, in IS and income-based JSA.

If you are polygamously married (see p303), you receive an extra amount for each additional spouse in your household.[2] However, unless you are entitled to joint-claim JSA (see p247), if any additional spouse is under the age of 18, you only receive an extra amount for her/him if:[3]

- for IS, income-based JSA and income-related ESA, s/he is either responsible for a child (see p309) or would otherwise meet the special conditions for qualifying for JSA as a 16/17 year old; *or*
- for IS and income-related ESA, s/he would qualify for that benefit in her/his own right were s/he not a member of a polygamous marriage.

Rates of personal allowances for people aged 18 or over

Note: some 16/17 year olds may also be entitled to these rates (see p319).

If you have been getting working-age HB (see p187) and this continues even though you are now a member of a 'mixed-age couple ' (ie, if one of you is at least pension age, but not the other) (see p188), your personal allowance remains as for working-age HB, even though one of you has reached pension age.

	IS/JSA/ESA/ working-age HB	Pension-age HB only
Single claimant:		
Aged 18–24	£61.05	
Aged 25 or over	£77.00	
Aged 18 or over and ESA includes (or would include) a support component or claimant in work-related activity group (ESA/working-age HB only)	£77.00	
Pension age or over (reached pension age before 1 April 2021)		£197.10
Pension age or over (reached pension age on or after 1 April 2021)		£182.60
Lone parent:		
Aged 18 or over	£77.00	
Pension age or over		£197.10
Couple:		
Both aged 18 or over	£121.05	
One or both pension age or over (one or both reached pension age before 1 April 2021)		£294.90
Both pension age or over (both reached pension age on or after 1 April 2021)		£278.70
One aged under 18 (some IS/JSA/ESA cases only and all HB cases)	£121.05	
One aged under 18 (other IS/JSA/ESA cases):		
either	£77.00	
or	£61.00	
Polygamous marriages (each additional qualifying spouse):		
Partner aged 18 or over, or under 18 in certain circumstances (see p317)	£44.05	
One or more spouse pension age or over (one or more reached pension age before 1 April 2021)		£97.80
All spouses pension age or over (all reached pension age on or after 1 April 2021)		£96.10

Rates of personal allowances for 16/17 year olds

- For IS and income-based JSA:
  - if you are single and aged 16 or 17 (including if you are a lone parent), you get the same rate as single 18–24 year olds – ie, £61.05; or
  - if you are in a couple (unless one of the circumstances below applies) and your partner is also aged under 18, you get £61.05. If your partner is aged 18 or over, see the table on p318.
- For income-related ESA:
  - you get £59.20; or
  - if your ESA includes the support component or if you are in the work-related activity group, you get £77.00; or
  - if you are in a couple (unless one of the circumstances below applies) and your partner is also under 18, the same amounts as above (£61.05 or £77.00) apply.
- For HB:
  - if you are single (including if you are a lone parent), you get the same rate as 18–24 year olds – ie, £61.05; or
  - if you are entitled to ESA and qualify for the support component or you are in the work-related activity group (see p336), you get £77.00; or
  - if you are in a couple and your partner is also under 18, you get £92.20. If your partner is aged 18 or over, or if you are entitled to ESA and either get the support component or are in the work-related activity group, you get £121.05.

For this purpose, you count as qualifying for an ESA component even if your actual award of ESA is nil – eg, because you are only entitled to national insurance contribution credits.

Most 16/17 year olds who have previously been looked after by a local authority cannot claim IS/JSA or HB (see p933).

Young couples in special circumstances

Note: the following rules apply to IS, income-based JSA and income-related ESA only.[4]

If you are a young couple, the amount of personal allowance paid depends on your ages and whether one or both of you are entitled to IS, income-based JSA (including JSA severe hardship payments) or income-related ESA, or you would be if you were a single person. The amount of your ESA personal allowance depends on whether you are in the ESA assessment phase or the ESA main phase, and on whether you qualify for the support component or are in the work-related activity group (see p336). For some couples, the personal allowance may be no more than that for a single person.

Age	£pw
Both aged 16–17, higher rate:	
ESA assessment phase	92.20
ESA main phase	121.05
IS/JSA	92.20
Both aged 16–17, lower rate:	
ESA assessment phase	61.05
ESA main phase	77.00
IS/JSA	61.05
One aged 16–17, one 18 or over, higher rate:	
ESA assessment phase	121.05
ESA main phase	121.05
IS/JSA	121.05
One aged 16–17, one 18–24, lower rate:	
ESA assessment phase	61.05
ESA main phase	77.00
IS/JSA	61.05
One aged 16–17, one 25 or over, lower rate:	
ESA assessment phase	77.00
ESA main phase	77.00
IS/JSA	77.00

If both of you are aged 16 or 17, you get the higher rate personal allowance in the following circumstances.

- For IS:
  - one of you is responsible for a child; *or*
  - both of you would qualify for IS or income-related ESA if you were not a couple; *or*
  - the claimant's partner would qualify for income-based JSA or JSA severe hardship payments if s/he were single.
- For JSA:
  - one of you is responsible for a child; *or*
  - both of you would qualify for income-based JSA if you were not a couple; *or*
  - the claimant would qualify for income-based JSA and her/his partner would qualify for IS or income-related ESA if you were not a couple, or you would both qualify for JSA severe hardship payments if you were single; *or*
  - one of you would qualify for JSA severe hardship payments if you were single and the other for income-based JSA, IS or income-related ESA if s/he were single; *or*
  - you are married or civil partners and you both qualify for income-based JSA, or one does and the other is registered for work or training.

- For ESA:
  - one of you is responsible for a child; *or*
  - both of you would qualify for income-related ESA if you were not a couple; *or*
  - the claimant's partner would qualify for IS if s/he were single; *or*
  - the claimant's partner would qualify for income-based JSA or JSA severe hardship payments as a single person.

The higher rate is paid at the main phase rate if the claimant qualifies for a support or work-related activity component (see pp636–37). Otherwise, it is paid at the assessment phase rate.

If one of you is aged 16 or 17 and the other is 18 or over, you get the higher rate personal allowance in the following circumstances.

- For IS, the younger partner qualifies for IS or income-related ESA (or s/he would do so if s/he were not a member of a couple) or income-based JSA or JSA severe hardship payments.
- For JSA, the younger partner is treated as responsible for a child, or qualifies for income-based JSA or JSA severe hardship payments, or either IS (or s/he would do so were s/he not a member of a couple) or income-related ESA (were s/he to make a claim).
- For ESA, the younger partner would either qualify for IS or income-related ESA (were s/he not a member of a couple), or for income-based JSA or JSA severe hardship payments. It is paid at the same rate in the assessment phase and main phase.

Personal allowances for children

Personal allowances for children are included in your HB applicable amount. IS, income-based JSA and income-related ESA do *not* usually include personal allowances for children. However, if you have been claiming IS or income-based JSA since before 6 April 2004, these can sometimes be included (see p317). You cannot get personal allowances for children in joint-claim JSA, as you cannot claim this type of JSA if you have children. Although there is no personal allowance for a child as part of pension credit (PC), you may be entitled to an additional amount in your guarantee credit of PC (see p323).

For when children are included in your claim and for who counts as a child, see p307.

Note: your child's income and capital do not affect the amount of HB to which you are entitled. However, if you are still entitled to a personal allowance for your child in your IS or income-based JSA, you do not get an allowance for a child in your IS or income-based JSA if s/he has over £3,000 capital. See p404 for how a child's income may affect IS or income-based JSA.

The two-child limit

You get one personal allowance for each child. However, you cannot get a personal allowance for a third or subsequent child born on or after 6 April 2017, unless an exception applies (see below). Also, for HB only, you do not get a personal allowance for a third or subsequent child who becomes part of your claim (eg, s/he is the child of a new partner) on or after 6 April 2017 or is in a new claim made on or after that date, unless an exception applies. This is known as the 'two-child limit'. The limit applies to children for whom you or your partner are responsible and who are living in your household (see p62).[5]

If you already had a personal allowance for a third or subsequent child included in your HB on 5 April 2017, you continue to get a personal allowance for her/him while that award continues. Also, if you get an element for a child in your child tax credit (CTC), you get a personal allowance for her/him in your HB.

A personal allowance can become payable for a third child who is born on or after 6 April 2017 and to whom this limit applies if an older child leaves the household (so that you are no longer responsible for her/him), or if a young person leaves education (so that s/he no longer qualifies). In these situations, you should report the change as soon as possible so that you continue to get the maximum two personal allowances.

An exception applies, and so a personal allowance is payable, to any child who is living with you and who is being adopted by you from local authority care, or who is living with you under a 'non-parental caring arrangement'. For HB, this means the same as it does for CTC (see p1416). For IS and income-based JSA, this means the same as it does for universal credit (UC) (see p67). In addition, when establishing how many children you have for the two-child limit, such children are ignored. So you can get an element for any such child, plus up to two more children, plus any further (third or subsequent) child to whom an exception also applies.

An exception also applies to a third or subsequent child who is:[6]
- born in a multiple birth, other than the first born if you already have two or more children;
- likely to have been conceived as a result of rape or in a controlling or coercive relationship and you are not living with the alleged perpetrator. For HB, this means the same as it does for CTC (see p1416). For IS and income-based JSA, this means the same as it does for UC (see p67).

For an exception to apply to a child in your HB claim, you must have applied for CTC and have had an exception applied for her/him. See p1416 for more details.

Rate of personal allowance for children

For HB (and for IS and income-based JSA if still included), there is one rate of personal allowance for children who are included in your claim – £70.80. You get one personal allowance for each child.

3. Premiums and additional amounts

Premiums are added to your personal allowance and are intended to help with the extra expenses you have as a result of your age, having a disability and, in some circumstances, children. Some premiums are not included in some of the means-tested benefits. Pension credit (PC) has additional amounts for severe disability, carers and children.

Note: if you or your partner are entitled to 'pension-age' housing benefit (HB) (see p187), your HB can only include the family, disabled child, enhanced disability for a child, severe disability and carer premiums.[7] In these circumstances, your HB cannot include a disability premium. If you (or your partner) are entitled to 'working-age' HB (see p187), that can include the disability premium. If you are in a 'mixed-age' couple (ie, one of you has reached pension age but the other has not), and you are prevented from claiming universal credit (UC) (see p23), you may be entitled to HB – either pension-age HB or working-age HB, depending on your circumstances (see p187). There are no pensioner premiums in either pension-age or working-age HB.

See p336 for information about backdating premiums. See p335 for the premium rates and for which premiums can be paid in addition to other premiums.

Premiums and additional amount for children

Certain premiums can be included in your HB applicable amount if you have children included in your claim. These are the family premium, disabled child premium and the child rate of the enhanced disability premium. Income support (IS), income-based jobseeker's allowance (JSA) and income-related employment and support allowance (ESA) do not usually include these premiums. However, if you have been claiming IS or income-based JSA since before 6 April 2004, see p317.

For who counts as a child and when children are included in your claim, see p307.

Note: your child's income and capital do not affect the amount of your HB. However, if you are still entitled to premiums for children in your IS or income-based JSA, you do not get a premium (except a family premium) for a child who has over £3,000 capital. See p404 for how a child's income may affect IS or income-based JSA.

You can qualify for an additional amount for a child in the guarantee credit of PC if you are not entitled, or treated as entitled, to tax credits, and are responsible for the child (see p307).[8] You get an additional amount for each child who qualifies. The weekly standard amount of the addition is £56.35 for each child born on or after 6 April 2017, or £66.85 for your eldest child if s/he was born before that date. If the child is entitled to disability living allowance (DLA), child

Part 4: General rules for other means-tested benefits
Chapter 17: Applicable amounts
3. Premiums and additional amounts

disability payment (CDP), personal independence payment (PIP) or adult disability payment (ADP), the standard amount is increased by £30.58. If s/he is entitled to the highest rate of the care component of DLA/CDP or the enhanced rate of the daily living component of PIP/ADP, or s/he is certified as severely sight impaired or blind by a consultant opthalmologist, the standard rate is increased by £95.48.

If your child dies, you can continue to get the additional amount for up to eight weeks after her/his death (or until s/he would have reached 20 years old, if that is earlier).

4 Family premium

You cannot get a family premium in any new HB award if you claimed on or after 1 May 2016, or any new IS or income-based JSA award if you claimed on or after 6 April 2004. The family premium cannot be included in any income-related ESA.

Otherwise, you may be entitled to a family premium in your HB, IS or income-based JSA if at least one child is included (see p307). Only one family premium can be included, irrespective of how many children you have.[9]

The premium can be paid even if you are not the parent of the child.

For HB, if you had a child included before 1 May 2016, you continue to get the premium, provided you still have a child included and you do not make a new claim for HB on or after that date.[10]

For IS and income-based JSA, you are only entitled to a family premium in certain circumstances (see p316). If you are entitled, a family premium is included even if you do not receive a personal allowance in your IS or income-based JSA for any child because s/he has capital over £3,000.

If a child who is being looked after by a local authority or who is in custody comes home for part of a week, your IS or income-based JSA includes a proportion of the weekly premium, based on the number of days the child is with you.[11] You can be paid the full premium in your HB if your child who is being looked after by a local authority is part of your household for any part of the week, provided the local authority thinks this is reasonable, given how often and for how long the child is at home with you.[12]

Disabled child premium

You are entitled to a disabled child premium in your HB and, if applicable, your IS and income-based JSA (see p317), for each child included who gets DLA, CDP, PIP, ADP (where s/he counts as a 'qualifying young person' for child benefit purposes – see p563 – and is still part of your family for benefit purposes – see p307) or armed forces independence payment if s/he is at least 16, or extra-statutory payments to compensate for non-payment of DLA/CDP or PIP/ADP, or who is blind.[13] A disabled child premium can still be included for a third or subsequent child, even if you do not get a personal allowance for her/him because of the 'two-child limit' (see p321). Income-related ESA does not include a disabled child premium.

A child is treated as blind if s/he is certified as severely sight impaired or blind by a consultant ophthalmologist, and for the first 28 weeks after s/he has ceased to be certified as such on regaining her/his sight.[14] If DLA/CDP or PIP/ADP stops because the child has gone into hospital, see p910.

If your child is looked after by a local authority or is in custody for part of the week, the disabled child premium is affected in the same way as the family premium (see above).

Your child's capital does not affect the amount of your HB.[15] For IS and income-based JSA, if your child has over £3,000 capital or has been in hospital for more than 52 weeks, you do not get this premium.[16]

If your child dies

If your child dies, you may be able to continue receiving the disabled child premium for eight weeks.[17] This applies if:

- you get child benefit for the child following her/his death (see p581); *and*
- you were getting the disabled child premium for that child in your applicable amount immediately before her/his death.

Disability premium

Income-related ESA does not include a disability premium.

You qualify for a disability premium if one of the following qualifying conditions apply, and none of the exclusions apply (see p327).[18] The person who satisfies the qualifying condition must be under pension age (see p765).

For IS and income-based JSA, if you or your partner have reached pension age, you may get the higher pensioner premium instead (see p329). There is a single rate or (if you are in a couple, as long as at least one of you qualifies) a couple rate.

- You (or your partner) are getting a qualifying benefit. These are:[19]
  - attendance allowance (AA) (see Chapter 24), DLA (see Chapter 28), PIP (see Chapter 35), ADP (see Chapter 73), armed forces independence payment or an equivalent benefit paid to meet attendance needs because of an injury at work (see Chapter 32) or a war injury;[20] *or*
  - AA, DLA, PIP or ADP if you (or your partner) were getting one of these benefits, but payment was suspended when one of you became a hospital patient.[21] In the case of IS and income-based JSA only, you or your partner must previously have qualified for a disability premium; *or*
  - for IS and income-based JSA, your partner or, for joint-claim JSA, you or your partner, were getting incapacity benefit paid at the long-term rate which stopped at pension age for income-based JSA (including joint-claim JSA)[22] or when retirement pension/state pension became payable for IS. For IS, you must have been continuously entitled to IS or income-based JSA since that

Part 4: General rules for other means-tested benefits
Chapter 17: Applicable amounts
3. Premiums and additional amounts

time.[23] If it was your partner who reached pension age or began receiving a retirement pension/state pension, s/he must still be alive.[24] You or your partner must have previously qualified for a disability premium;[25] *or*

- war pensioner's mobility supplement; *or*
- the disabled worker element or severe disability element of working tax credit (WTC); *or*
- severe disablement allowance (SDA). For IS and HB, you must be getting SDA. For income-based JSA, your partner must be getting it. For joint-claim JSA, either you or your partner must be getting it; *or*
- an NHS mobility scooter or private car (for you or your partner) because of a disability;[26] *or*
- extra-statutory payments to compensate you or your partner for not getting any of the above benefits.[27]

Once you qualify for the disability premium, you or your partner are treated as still getting a qualifying benefit if you no longer receive it because of the overlapping benefit rules (see p1151).[28]

- You (or your partner) are certified as severely sight impaired or blind by a consultant opthalmologist. If you (or your partner) regain your sight, you still qualify for 28 weeks after you stop being certified.
- You have incapacity for work (see p683 of the 2013/14 edition of this *Handbook*) and have been incapable of work, or treated as incapable of work (or, for IS and joint-claim JSA only, entitled to statutory sick pay (SSP)) for 364 days or 196 days if you are terminally ill. Your incapacity for work must have started before 27 October 2008. If you become entitled to benefit on the basis of limited capability for work instead of incapacity for work (see Chapter 45), the premium stops.
- For joint-claim JSA only, either you or your partner have (or are treated as having) 'limited capability for work' (see p987) for a continuous qualifying period of:
  - 196 days if you or s/he are 'terminally ill'; *or*
  - 364 days in all other cases.

For this purpose, gaps in your periods of limited capability for work that last no more than 12 weeks are ignored.[29]

If you undertake training

If you go on a government training course or receive a training allowance for any period, you keep the disability premium even though you may stop receiving one of the qualifying benefits, or cease to be entitled to SSP during the course, provided you continue to be entitled to IS, income-based JSA or HB. After the course, the premium continues if you are getting a qualifying benefit, remain entitled to SSP (for IS only), or remain incapable of work.[30]

Exclusions

You may not be entitled to the disability premium in your IS or income-based JSA once you or your partner have been receiving free treatment as a hospital inpatient for more than 52 weeks (see p903).

You cannot get a disability premium in your HB if:

- you have, or are treated as having, limited capability for work.[31] This applies even if you would otherwise qualify for the premium – eg, if you (or your partner) get DLA, PIP or are certified as blind or severely sight impaired. If your partner is the HB claimant and s/he does not have (and is not treated as having) limited capability for work, the disability premium can be included;[32] *or*
- you get pension-age HB (see p187).

4

Do you have limited capability for work?

1. If you claim ESA or national insurance credits on the basis of limited capability for work and you are a member of a couple, it may be beneficial for your partner to be the HB claimant instead of you in order for the disability premium to be be included in your applicable amount.

2. If you have (or are treated as having) limited capability for work, although you cannot qualify for a disability premium, you may qualify for either the support or work-related activity component in your applicable amount, although this is not normally until after the ESA 'assessment phase' has ended. **Note:** the work-related activity component was abolished for new claims from 3 April 2017.

3. If your partner has limited capability for work but you do not, you can still qualify for the disability premium, which is paid at the couple rate. However, if the disability premium is awarded, you cannot qualify for a support or work-related activity component in your applicable amount.

Enhanced disability premium

The enhanced disability premium can be included in respect of disabled adults and disabled children.[33]

Regarding **disabled adults**, you are entitled to an enhanced disability premium (at the single rate, or if you are in a couple, the couple rate) in your IS, income-based JSA, income-related ESA and HB if:

- you or your partner receive the highest rate of the DLA care component, the enhanced rate of the daily living component of PIP/ADP or armed forces independence payment. If it is your partner who satisfies this, s/he must be under pension age; *or*
- for income-related ESA, you qualify for the support component (see p636); *or*
- for HB, the decision maker has determined that you have, or can be treated as having, limited capability for work-related activity (see p1005).

Part 4: General rules for other means-tested benefits
Chapter 17: Applicable amounts
3. Premiums and additional amounts

This premium can be paid in addition to both the disability and severe disability premiums (see p335). For more details of the premiums with which the enhanced disability premium can be paid, see p335.

The person who qualifies for the premium must usually be under pension age (p765). For HB, if you are single and you reach pension age, you are paid the higher personal allowance (as part of pension-age HB) instead. If you are in a mixed-age couple (ie, one of you has reached pension age and the other has not) and you continue getting working-age HB (see p187), you are treated as both still under pension age and can continue to get the premium. For IS, income-based JSA and income-related ESA, if you are in a mixed-age couple and you remain entitled to the benefit, you are paid a pensioner premium instead.

Regarding **disabled children**, for HB, you qualify for one enhanced disability premium for each child included in your claim who gets the highest rate of the DLA/CDP care component, the enhanced rate of the daily living component of PIP/ADP, or armed forces independence payment.

For IS and income-based JSA, you are only entitled to the child rate of this premium in certain circumstances (see p317). If your child dies, the premium continues for eight weeks if you or your partner continue to get child benefit for her/him (see p581).

An enhanced disability premium can still be included for a third or subsequent child, even if you do not get a personal allowance for her/him because of the 'two-child limit' (see p321).

Income-related ESA does not include the child rate of this premium (although you can qualify for the adult rate).

In most cases, you (or your partner or child) are treated as receiving the highest rate of the DLA/CDP care component or the enhanced rate of the daily living component of PIP/ADP during any period when DLA, CDP, PIP or ADP is suspended while you/they are in hospital. However, the following people cannot qualify:

- for the child rate, for IS and income-based JSA only, children who have been in hospital for more than 52 weeks, or who have more than £3,000 in capital;[34] *and*
- some people who have been in hospital for more than 52 weeks or, in some cases, if their partner has (see p909).

Pensioner premiums

There is a pensioner premium and a higher pensioner premium. They are paid at the same rate.[35]

In most cases, you qualify for a pensioner premium if your partner has reached pension age (see p765). This applies to IS, income-based JSA and income-related ESA only.

You qualify for a higher pensioner premium instead of a pensioner premium in IS or income-based JSA if:
- your partner is aged 80 or over; *or*
- you or your partner are sick or disabled and certain conditions are satisfied.

Note: if you are a member of a mixed-age couple and your IS has continued when you have reached pension age but your partner has not (see p237), you can be entitled to either pensioner premium on the basis of your age, rather than your partner's age.[36]

There are no pensioner premiums in HB. You get a higher personal allowance instead.

Although paid at the same rate as the pensioner premium, qualifying for the higher pensioner premium may be important – eg, because it qualifies you for a £20 earnings disregard (see p414) or because it meets one of the qualifying conditions for the disabled worker element in WTC (see p1420). For joint-claim JSA, there is no pensioner premium or higher pensioner premium on age grounds if your partner is aged 75 or over.

Pensioner premiums are paid at a single or couple rate. The couple rate of the premium is included in your applicable amount even if only one partner fulfils the condition. The rate of the pensioner premium in income-related ESA depends on whether or not you are entitled to the support component or are in the work-related activity group (see p337) and whether you are a member of a couple.

Higher pensioner premium

You qualify for the higher pensioner premium in IS or income-based JSA if:[37]
- your partner is aged 80 or over; *or*
- your partner has reached pension age (see p765) and receives a qualifying benefit (eg, AA, DLA, PIP or SDA), is certified as severely sight impaired or blind, or has an NHS mobility scooter or a private car allowance.
  If your AA, DLA, PIP or ADP stops because you go into hospital, see p905. If you are getting SDA, see below; *or*
- for IS, you were getting a disability premium as part of your IS or income-based JSA at some time in the eight weeks before your partner reached pension age and have continued to get IS since then. You are treated as being continuously entitled to benefit if there is a break in your entitlement of eight weeks or less, including the day your partner reached pension age.[38]

Note: if you are a member of a mixed-age couple and your IS has continued when you have reached pension age but your partner has not (see p237), you can be entitled to the higher pensioner premium on the basis of your age, rather than your partner's age.[39]

Part 4: General rules for other means-tested benefits
Chapter 17: Applicable amounts
3. Premiums and additional amounts

In the case of couples, the person who was the benefit claimant before s/he reached pension age must continue to claim after that, but the claimant does not need to have been the person who qualified for the disability premium.

Note:

- If you get SDA when you reach 65, you are awarded it for life.[40] This also applies even if it ceases to be paid because you get retirement pension at a higher rate.[41]
- You may not be entitled to the higher pensioner premium once you or your partner have been receiving free treatment as a hospital inpatient for more than 52 weeks (see p909).

4. Severe disability premium and severe disability addition

You qualify for a severe disability premium (or for a severe disability addition in the guarantee credit of PC) if *all* the following apply to you.[42]

- You receive a 'qualifying benefit' (see p331). If you are a couple for IS, income-based JSA, income-related ESA or HB, your partner must also be getting a qualifying benefit, or be certified as severely sight impaired or blind by a consultant ophthalmologist (or treated as certified because it is no more than 28 weeks since s/he stopped being certified).[43] For PC, both of you must be getting a qualifying benefit or one must be getting a qualifying benefit and the other certified as severely sight impaired or blind or treated as certified. For PC only, either partner can be the claimant.[44] If you are a member of a couple, you and your partner are treated as getting any of these benefits while one or both of you are in hospital, but only if you are not claiming the premium or additional amount for severe disability on the basis that your partner (or you, for PC) is certified as severely sight impaired or blind or treated as certified.[45] For IS, income-based JSA, income-related ESA and HB, the benefit must be paid for you or your partner. Receipt of benefit for someone else (eg, a child) does not count.[46] It is probably intended that the same rule should apply to PC.
- You do not have a non-dependant aged 18 or over (eg, an adult son or daughter) 'normally residing with you' (see p332). It does not matter whose house it is.[47] Someone is only counted as residing with you if you share accommodation, apart from a bathroom, lavatory or a communal area such as a hall, passageway or a room in common use in sheltered accommodation. If s/he is separately liable to pay for the accommodation, s/he does not count as residing with you.[48]
- No one gets carer's allowance (CA) or the UC carer element for looking after you or, if you are a couple, no one gets CA or the UC carer element for both of you (but see p907 if you and/or your partner go into hospital). If you are a member of a couple and someone gets CA or the carer element for one (but not both) of you, but you are both disabled, you can get the severe disability premium at the single person's rate. Only actual receipt of CA counts (except if it is not paid because of the loss of benefit rules – see p1239).[49] No account is

taken of any underlying entitlement to CA if it is awarded but not paid because of the overlapping benefit rules, or of any extra-statutory payments to compensate for its not being paid. Similarly, no account is taken of any backdated payments or arrears of CA or of the carer element.[50] Also argue that no account should be taken of any overpaid CA or carer element and that, if you have been denied the premium because of a CA or carer element overpayment, it should be repaid to you (see p334).

Receiving a qualifying benefit

A 'qualifying benefit' is either AA, the middle or highest rate of the DLA care component, the daily living component of PIP, ADP, armed forces independence payment, constant attendance allowance or exceptionally severe disablement allowance (or the equivalent war pension).

You are 'treated as receiving' a qualifying benefit if you receive an extra-statutory payment to compensate you for not receiving that benefit.[51]

Couples

You get the couple rate if both you and your partner get a qualifying benefit and no one gets CA or the carer element of UC for either of you. If CA or the carer element of UC is paid for one of you, or if your partner does not get a qualifying benefit but is certified as severely sight impaired or blind by a consultant ophthalmologist (or treated as certified), you get the single person's rate. In polygamous marriages, the single person's rate is awarded for each eligible spouse who gets a qualifying benefit while CA or the carer element of UC is not paid.

Note:
- You and/or your partner are treated as getting a qualifying benefit, even though it has stopped because you/your partner have been in hospital for more than four weeks, but the severe disability premium is paid at the single person's rate only. Similarly, for IS, income-based JSA, income-related ESA and HB, if you are a couple, a person who is caring for you or your partner is treated as receiving CA or the carer element of UC even though s/he is no longer getting it because the person for whom s/he cares has been in hospital for more than four weeks.[52]
- For couples on IS, JSA and income-related ESA only, if you or your partner temporarily move into a care home, you still count as a couple but your applicable amount is calculated in a different way (see p920).[53] If your applicable amount is calculated as if you and your partner were single claimants, this means that if the person who stays at home gets a qualifying benefit, a severe disability premium is included in the applicable amount of that person.
- For PC, if you or your partner temporarily move into a care home, you still count as a couple if you have not been apart for substantially more than 52

Part 4: General rules for other means-tested benefits
Chapter 17: Applicable amounts
3. Premiums and additional amounts

weeks (see p919). So, once the partner in the care home loses her/his AA or DLA care component, no severe disability premium can be paid for either of you, even if the partner at home gets a qualifying benefit, unless the partner in the care home is certified as severely sight impaired or blind (or treated as certified).

Who is not a non-dependant

Non-dependants are adults living with you who are not included in your benefit claim (eg, an adult son or daughter, or a parent), but who are regarded as being able to contribute towards your household costs.

The following people who live with you do *not* count as non-dependants.[54]

For IS, income-based JSA, income-related ESA, HB and PC:
- anyone aged under 18;
- anyone else who receives a qualifying benefit for the severe disability premium (see p330);[55]
- anyone who is certified as severely sight impaired or blind by a consultant ophthalmologist (or treated as certified);[56]
- anyone staying in your home who normally lives elsewhere. In deciding whether someone normally lives with you or elsewhere, it may be relevant to consider things like why the residence started, how long it has continued and your relationship;[57]
- any person (and, for IS, income-based JSA, income-related ESA and PC only, her/his partner) employed by a charitable or voluntary body as a resident carer for you or your partner if you pay a charge for that service (even if the charge is only nominal).[58] **Note:** these rules do not apply to a live-in carer employed directly by you (even if, for example, you are paying her/him from direct payments made to you by social services for that purpose).

For IS, income-based JSA, income-related ESA and HB:
- any member of your 'family' (see below for who counts). This may include any child under the age of 20 (see p307) as well as your partner, although your partner must be getting a qualifying benefit (or would be if s/he were not in hospital) or be certified as severely sight impaired or blind, for you to get the severe disability premium (see p330);
- any child or qualifying young person who is living with you but who is not a member of your household (see p311).[59]

For IS, income-based JSA, income-related ESA and PC:
- any person (or her/his partner) who jointly occupies (see p334) your home and is either the co-owner with you or your partner, or jointly liable with you or your partner to make payments to a landlord for occupying it. If this person is a close relative (see p333), however, s/he *does* count as a non-dependant *unless*

the co-ownership or joint liability to make payments to a landlord existed either before 11 April 1988 or by the time you or your partner first moved in;
- any person (or any member of her/his household) who is liable to pay you or your partner on a commercial basis (see p334) for occupying the dwelling (eg, tenants or licensees), unless s/he is a close relative of you or your partner;
- any person (or any member of her/his household) to whom you or your partner are liable to make payments on a commercial basis for occupying the dwelling, unless s/he is a close relative of you or your partner.

For PC:
- any child or qualifying young person.[60] This is defined in the same way as for UC (see p308).

Note: for IS, income-based JSA, income-related ESA and PC, if someone comes to live with you in order to look after you (or your partner) and has not lived with you before, your severe disability premium or amount for severe disability remains in payment for the first 12 weeks after the carer moves in, even if s/he would otherwise count as a non-dependant.[61] After that, you lose the premium or the amount for severe disability. The carer should then consider claiming CA (see Chapter 26).

For HB:[62]
- any person who jointly occupies your home and is either the co-owner with you or your partner, or liable with you or your partner to make payments for occupying it. A joint occupier who was a non-dependant at any time within the previous eight weeks counts as a non-dependant if the local authority thinks that the change of arrangements was created to take advantage of the HB scheme;
- any person who is liable to pay you or your partner on a commercial basis for occupying the dwelling unless s/he is a close relative of yours or your partner, or if the local authority thinks that the rent or other agreement has been created to take advantage of the HB scheme (but this cannot apply if the person was otherwise liable to pay rent for the accommodation at any time during the eight weeks before the agreement was made);
- any person, or any member of her/his household, to whom you or your partner are liable to make payments for your accommodation on a commercial basis unless s/he is a close relative of you or your partner.

Definitions
'Close relative' is a parent, parent-in-law (including a civil partner's parent), son, son-in-law (including a son's civil partner), daughter, daughter-in-law (including a daughter's civil partner), brother, sister, step-parent (including a parent's civil partner), stepson (including a civil partner's son), stepdaughter (including a civil partner's daughter), or the partners of any of these.[63]

Part 4: General rules for other means-tested benefits
Chapter 17: Applicable amounts
3. Premiums and additional amounts

'**Member of the family**' means your partner and any child who lives in your household and for whom you or your partner count as 'responsible' (see p307).[64]

'**Jointly occupies**' is a legal relationship involving occupation by two or more people (whether as owner-occupiers, tenants or licensees) with one and the same legal right.[65] It does not exist if people merely have equal access to different parts of the premises.

'**Commercial basis**' has no legal meaning, and there is no requirement for there to be an intention to make a profit.[66] It may be sufficient if a 'reasonable' charge is made, even if this does not fully cover the cost of the accommodation and meals being provided.[67] The reasonableness of the charge should be judged just against the cost of occupying the dwelling, not taking into account the additional costs of providing food, clothing and care.[68] A useful, but not conclusive, test to apply is to consider whether the same arrangement might have been entered into with a lodger.[69]

'**Liability**' means a legal or contractual liability. The arrangements need not be in writing.[70]

Carer premium and carer addition

You qualify for a carer premium, or a carer addition in PC, if you or your partner are entitled to CA (see Chapter 26).[71]

You are entitled to CA even if (having claimed it) you do not receive it because of the overlapping benefit rules (see p1151) – eg, you get contributory ESA or retirement pension instead.

If the person you or your partner are getting CA for dies, or you or your partner stop being entitled to CA for another reason, your entitlement to a carer premium or carer addition continues for a further eight weeks. The eight-week period runs from the Sunday after the death (or from the date of the death, if the death occurs on a Sunday). In other cases, it runs from the date entitlement to CA stops.[72]

A double-rate premium is awarded if both you and your partner satisfy the conditions for it.

Should you claim carer's allowance?

1. Before claiming CA, consider how your claim might affect the entitlement to the severe disability premium or severe disability addition of the disabled person for whom you care – particularly if the only financial advantage to you as the carer is the amount of the carer premium/addition, which may be worth considerably less than the severe disability premium (but see p330 for the rules on notional income).

2. Any backdated award of CA does not affect a disabled person's entitlement to the severe disability premium or severe disability addition.[73] You may be able to take advantage of this rule so that you are paid CA or the carer premium/addition for the same period in which the disabled person has already received a severe disability premium or a severe disability addition.

3. Although the severe disability premium or severe disability addition is not payable throughout any period during which a carer is receiving CA, if you are a carer and it is later decided that you have been overpaid CA, the disabled person should ask for the decision refusing her/him the severe disability premium or addition to be revised. You must be both

entitled to *and* in receipt of CA for the severe disability premium/addition not to be payable.[74]

4. Other than for HB, if payment of CA stops, the severe disability premium/addition can be backdated to the date the CA stopped.[75]

5. Even if you do not claim CA, if you get UC and your award includes a carer element (see p73), the disabled person for whom you care cannot get the severe disability premium or severe disability addition.

Rates of premiums

Rates of premiums

The following premiums can be paid in addition to any other premium, except that the enhanced disability premium cannot be paid in addition to the pensioner or higher pensioner premium.[76]

Family premium	£17.85
Disabled child premium	£68.04
(for each qualifying child)	
Severe disability premium	
Single (or one partner qualifies)	£69.40
Couple (both partners qualify)	£138.80
Carer premium	
Single (or one partner qualifies)	£38.85
Couple (both partners qualify)	£77.70
Enhanced disability premium	
Child (for each qualifying child)	£27.44
Single	£17.75
Couple (one or both partners qualify)	£25.35

Only one of the following premiums can be paid. If you qualify for more than one, you get the highest.[77]

Disability premium	
Single	£36.20
Couple	£51.60
Pensioner and higher pensioner premium for IS/income-based JSA	
Couple	£157.65
Pensioner premium for income-related ESA	
Entitled to support component, couple	£117.05
Entitled to work-related activity component, couple	£127.05
Not entitled to either component, couple	£157.65

Note: you may be entitled to a lone parent increase (£4.35) in the HB family premium if you were entitled to it on 5 April 1998.[78] See p793 of the 2011/12 edition of this *Handbook*.

Backdating premiums

To qualify for the disability, enhanced disability, higher pensioner, severe disability, disabled child or carer premium, you or your partner or child must usually have been awarded a 'qualifying benefit' that applies to each premium. The date you can begin to get your premium may, therefore, depend on the date from when your qualifying benefit is awarded. However, because of the time it may take to deal with your claim for the qualifying benefit, or if your claim is backdated (see p1142) or initially refused but awarded some time later after a revision (see p1261), supersession (see p1274) or appeal (see p1297), you may not get your premium straight away and you may have to apply for it to be backdated.

If you are already getting benefit

If you are already getting IS, JSA, ESA, HB or PC, you should ask for your award of this benefit either to be revised or superseded and for your premium to be backdated to the date from which the qualifying benefit is awarded, or to when you first got (or claimed) IS, JSA, ESA, HB or PC, if that is later. There is no limit to the period for which arrears can be paid to you.[79]

If you were refused benefit or lost entitlement

If you were refused or lost your entitlement to IS, income-based JSA, income-related ESA or HB and you are later awarded a qualifying benefit, in most cases, you can no longer make a new claim for IS, income-based JSA, income-related ESA or HB (but see below) and must now claim UC instead. If you lost entitlement, but should have been entitled to a premium while you were entitled, you may still be able to get arrears for the period before your entitlement ended. For when you may still be able to make a new claim, see p23. **Note:** unless you are prevented from claiming UC (see p23), making a new claim for JSA or ESA will bring you under the UC system (see p22).

New claims for PC can still be made after the award of a qualifying benefit. See p264 for the rules on backdating.

If you lose your HB because you lose entitlement to a qualifying benefit, the decision ending your HB can be revised if the qualifying benefit is reinstated. Your HB can be fully backdated in this situation. You must tell the local authority that you have had your qualifying benefit reinstated, but you do not need to make a fresh claim for HB.[80]

4. Components

Your applicable amount for income-related employment and support allowance (ESA) and, in certain circumstances, housing benefit (HB) may include either:[81]

- a support component (see p337); *or*
- if you can still get it, a work-related activity component (see p337).

You cannot be awarded both components at the same time.

You can qualify for one of these components in your HB if either you or your partner meet the conditions for it and have limited capability for work. If you qualify for one component and your partner qualifies for the other, the component for which *you* qualify is awarded.[82]

To qualify for a component in income-related ESA, you must meet the conditions yourself – ie, as the claimant. You cannot qualify on the basis of your partner's limited capability for work alone.

Note:

- You cannot start to qualify for a component in your HB applicable amount if you have reached pension age (see p765), unless you or your partner are on income support, income-based jobseeker's allowance, income-related ESA or universal credit (UC).

- For HB, provided either you or your partner satisfy the conditions for the component and have limited capability for work, it does not matter if ESA is not paid, or if your entitlement to ESA has stopped because of the rules on how long you can be paid contributory ESA.

- For income-related ESA, if you or your partner have been receiving free treatment as a hospital inpatient for a continuous period of more than 52 weeks, you cannot qualify for either component.[83]

Support component

In order to qualify for a support component in income-related ESA, you must meet the conditions described on p636.

You qualify for a support component in your HB if:[84]

- you or your partner have claimed ESA and you are entitled to the support component (see p636), or you have been refused ESA but you would have been entitled to the component had you been entitled to ESA; *and*
- you are not entitled to a disability premium (p325); *and*
- either you or your partner have limited capability for work-related activity (see p1005).

Work-related activity component

The work-related activity component was abolished for new claims from 3 April 2017. For details of who can still get a work-related activity component in ESA, see p637.

You can still get a work-related activity component in your HB if:[85]

- you or your partner have claimed ESA and are entitled to the work-related activity component (see p637), or you have been refused ESA but you would have been entitled to the component had you been entitled to ESA; *and*
- you are not entitled to a disability premium (p325); *and*

- the decision maker has determined that you or your partner have, or can be treated as having, limited capability for work (see p987).

Note: you keep the maximum work-related activity component in your HB even if you lose it in ESA because of a sanction.[86] The full amount of ESA continues to be taken into account as your income.

Rates of components

Rates of components[87]

Support component	£40.60
Work-related activity component	£30.60

There is no higher rate of the support or work-related activity component paid for couples.

Backdating components

Your entitlement to either the support or work-related activity component in your ESA normally starts once the 'assessment phase' has ended (see p635). If your assessment phase ends later than 13 weeks after you claim, your entitlement to a component can be backdated to the beginning of the 14th week of your claim.[88] If you make a claim, or request a revision or supersession of your entitlement expressly on the grounds of being terminally ill (see p638 – the rules are the same as for contributory ESA), you do not have to wait for the assessment phase to end to qualify for the support component, but can qualify either from the date of your claim, or from the date on which you became terminally ill if that is later.[89]

If you are getting HB and you become entitled to a support or work-related activity component, you qualify for that component in your applicable amount from the Monday on or after your entitlement to the component began. If your HB entitlement starts after the date your entitlement to the component began, you qualify for the component in your HB applicable amount from the date your entitlement to HB began.[90]

If you only become entitled to HB once a component is awarded to you, you should claim (or reclaim) HB as promptly as you can, as you can only get a maximum of one month's backdating (see p208). **Note:** in most cases, you cannot now make a new claim for HB and will need to claim UC instead. See p172 for when you can make a new claim for HB. Claiming UC brings you under the UC system (see p22).

5. Transitional addition

All awards of incapacity benefit, severe disablement allowance and income support 'on the grounds of disability' have been transferred to employment and support allowance (ESA) (see p640).

When you transferred, you may have been entitled to a transitional addition included in your income-related ESA or housing benefit applicable amount. For more information, see p356 of the 2019/20 edition of this *Handbook*.

4

Notes

1. What are applicable amounts
1   Reg 1(3) and (7) SS(WTCCTC)(CA) Regs

2. Personal allowances
2   **IS** Reg 18(1)(b) IS Regs
JSA Regs 84(1)(b) and 86B(b) JSA Regs
ESA Reg 68(1)(b) ESA Regs
HB Reg 23(b) HB Regs; Sch 3 para 1 HB(SPC) Regs
3   **IS** Reg 18(2) IS Regs
JSA Reg 84(2) JSA Regs
ESA Reg 68(2) ESA Regs
4   **IS** Sch 2 para 1(3) IS Regs
JSA Sch 1 para 1(3) JSA Regs
ESA Sch 4 para 1(3) ESA Regs
5   Regs 5, 6 and 9 The Social Security (Restrictions on Amounts for Children and Qualifying Young Persons) (Amendment) Regulations 2017 No.376; reg 22 HB Regs; reg 22 HB(SPC) Regs
6   Regs 5, 6 and 9 The Social Security (Restrictions on Amounts for Children and Qualifying Young Persons) (Amendment) Regulations 2017 No.376; reg 22 HB Regs; reg 22 HB(SPC) Regs

3. Premiums and additional amounts
7   Sch 3 paras 3 and 6-9 HB(SPC) Regs
8   Reg 6(6)(d) and Sch IIA SPC Regs

9   **IS** Sch 2 para 3 IS Regs
JSA Sch 1 para 4 JSA Regs
HB Sch 3 para 3 HB Regs; Sch 3 para 3 HB(SPC) Regs
10   Reg 4 The Housing Benefit (Abolition of the Family Premium and date of claim) (Amendment) Regulations 2015 No.1857
11   **IS** Regs 15(3) and 16(6) IS Regs
JSA Regs 74(4) and 78(7) JSA Regs
12   Reg 21(4) and (5) HB Regs; reg 21(4) and (5) HB(SPC) Regs
13   **IS** Sch 2 paras 14 and 15(6) IS Regs
JSA Sch 1 para 16 JSA Regs
HB Sch 3 paras 16 and 20(7) HB Regs; Sch 3 paras 8 and 12(3) HB(SPC) Regs
14   **IS** Sch 2 paras 12(1)(a)(iii) and (2) and 14(c) IS Regs
JSA Sch 1 para 14(1)(h) and (2) JSA Regs
HB Sch 3 paras 13(1)(a)(v) and (2) and 16(c) HB Regs; Sch 3 para 8(b) HB(SPC) Regs
15   Reg 25(3) HB Regs; reg 23(3) HB(SPC) Regs
16   **IS** Sch 2 para 14(2)(a) IS Regs
JSA Sch 1 para 16(2)(a) JSA Regs
17   **IS** Sch 2 para 14 IS Regs
JSA Sch 1 para 16 JSA Regs
HB Sch 3 para 16 HB Regs; Sch 3 para 8 HB(SPC) Regs
18   **IS** Sch 2 para 11 IS Regs
JSA Sch 1 paras 13, 14, 20G and 20H JSA Regs
HB Sch 3 para 12 HB Regs

⬤ ⬤

19 **IS** Sch 2 para 12(1)(a)(i) IS Regs
  JSA Sch 1 paras 14(1)(a)-(d) and
  20H(1)(a)-(d) JSA Regs
  HB Sch 3 para 13(1)(a)(i) HB Regs
20 **IS** Reg 2(1), definition of 'attendance
  allowance', IS Regs
  JSA Reg 1(3), definition of 'attendance
  allowance', JSA Regs
  HB Reg 2(1), definition of 'attendance
  allowance', HB Regs
21 **IS** Sch 2 para 12(1)(d) IS Regs
  JSA Sch 1 paras 14(1)(g)(ii) and
  20H(1)(h)(ii) JSA Regs
  HB Sch 3 para 13(1)(a)(iii) HB Regs
22 R(IS) 7/02
23 **IS** Sch 2 para 12(1)(c)(i) IS Regs
  JSA Sch 1 paras 14(1)(g)(i) and
  20H(1)(h)(i) JSA Regs
  HB Sch 3 para 13(1)(a)(ii) HB Regs
24 **IS** Sch 2 para 12(1)(c)(i) IS Regs
  JSA Sch 1 paras 14(1)(g)(i) and
  20H(1)(h)(i) JSA Regs
25 **IS** Sch 2 para 12(1)(c) IS Regs
  JSA Sch 1 paras 14(1)(g) and 20H(1)(h)
  JSA Regs
26 **IS** Sch 2 para 12(1)(a)(ii) IS Regs
  JSA Sch 1 paras 14(1)(e) and (f) and
  20H(1)(f) and (g) JSA Regs
  HB Sch 3 para 13(1)(a)(iv) HB Regs
27 **IS** Sch 2 para 14A IS Regs
  JSA Sch 1 paras 18 and 20K JSA Regs
  HB Sch 3 para 18 HB Regs
28 **IS** Sch 2 para 7(1)(a) IS Regs
  JSA Sch 1 paras 8(1)(a) and 20D(1)(a)
  JSA Regs
  HB Sch 3 para 7(1)(a) HB Regs
29 Sch 1 para 20H(1)(ee) JSA Regs
30 **IS** Sch 2 paras 7(1)(b) and 12(5) IS Regs
  JSA Sch 1 paras 8(1)(b) and 20D(b) JSA
  Regs
  HB Sch 3 paras 7(1)(b) and 13(5) HB
  Regs
31 The rules only refer to the 'claimant'.
32 Sch 3 para 13(9) HB Regs
33 **IS** Sch 2 para 13A IS Regs
  JSA Sch 1 paras 15A and 20IA JSA Regs
  ESA Sch 4 para 7 ESA Regs
  HB Sch 3 para 15 HB Regs; Sch 3 para 7
  HB(SPC) Regs
34 **IS** Sch 2 para 13A IS Regs
  JSA Sch 1 para 15A JSA Regs
35 **IS** Sch 2 paras 9 and 9A IS Regs
  JSA Sch 1 paras 10, 11, 20E and 20F JSA
  Regs
  ESA Sch 4 para 5 ESA Regs
36 Art 8(4) WRA(No.31)O
37 **IS** Sch 2 para 10 IS Regs
  JSA Sch 1 paras 12 and 20F JSA Regs

38 Sch 2 para 10(1)(b)(ii), (3) and (4) IS
  Regs; reg 32 IS(JSACA) Regs
39 Art 8(4) WRA(No.31)O
40 CIS/458/1992
41 **IS** Sch 2 para 7(1)(a) IS Regs
  JSA Sch 1 paras 8(1)(a) and 20D(1)(a)
  JSA Regs
42 **IS** Sch 2 para 13 IS Regs
  JSA Sch 1 paras 15 and 20I JSA Regs
  ESA Sch 4 para 6 ESA Regs
  PC Reg 6(4) and Sch 1 paras 1 and 2
  SPC Regs
  HB Sch 3 para 14 HB Regs; Sch 3 para 6
  HB(SPC) Regs
43 **IS** Sch 2 para 13(2A) IS Regs
  JSA Sch 1 paras 15(3) and 20I(2) JSA
  Regs
  ESA Sch 4 para 6(3) and (9) ESA Regs
  HB Sch 3 para 14(3) HB Regs; Sch 3 para
  6(3) HB(SPC) Regs
44 Sch 1 para 11(b) and (c) SPC Regs
45 **IS** Sch 2 para 13(3A)(a) IS Regs
  JSA Sch 1 paras 15(5)(a) and 20I(4)(a)
  JSA Regs
  ESA Sch 4 para 6(5)(a) ESA Regs
  PC Sch 1 para 1(2)(b) SPC Regs
  HB Sch 3 para 14(5) HB Regs; Sch 3 para
  6(7) HB(SPC) Regs
46 **IS** Sch 2 para 14B IS Regs
  JSA Sch 1 paras 19 and 20L JSA Regs
  ESA Sch 4 para 10 ESA Regs
  HB Sch 3 para 19 HB Regs; Sch 3 para
  11 HB(SPC) Regs
  See also R(IS) 10/94, upheld in *Rider v
  CAO* [1996] *The Times*, 30 January (CA).
47 *Bate v CAO* [1996] 2 All ER 790, reported
  as R(IS) 12/96
48 **IS** Reg 3(4) and (5) IS Regs
  JSA Reg 2(6) and (7) JSA Regs
  ESA Reg 71(6) ESA Regs
  HB Reg 3(4) HB Regs; Sch 3 para 6(7)
  HB(SPC) Regs
49 **IS** Sch 2 para 13(2)(a)(iii) and (b) IS Regs
  JSA Sch 1 paras 15(1)(c) and (2)(d) and
  20I(1)(d) JSA Regs
  ESA Sch 4 para 6(2)(a)(iii) and (b) ESA
  Regs
  PC Sch 1 para 1(1)(a)(iii) SPC Regs
  HB Sch 3 para 14(2)(a)(iii) and (b) HB
  Regs; Sch 3 para 6(2)(a)(iii) and (b)
  HB(SPC) Regs
50 **IS** Sch 2 para 13(3ZA) IS Regs
  JSA Sch 1 paras 15(7) and 20I(6) JSA
  Regs
  ESA Sch 4 para 6(6) ESA Regs
  PC Sch 1 para 2(c) SPC Regs
  HB Sch 3 para 14(6) HB Regs; Sch 3 para
  6(8) HB(SPC) Regs

51 **IS** Sch 2 para 14A IS Regs
JSA Sch 1 paras 18 and 20K JSA Regs
ESA Sch 4 para 9 ESA Regs
PC Sch 1 para 1(2)(a)(ii) SPC Regs
HB Sch 3 para 18 HB Regs; Sch 3 para 10 HB(SPC) Regs

52 **IS** Sch 2 para 13(3A) IS Regs
JSA Sch 1 paras 15(5) and 20I(4) JSA Regs
ESA Sch 4 para 6(5) ESA Regs
PC Reg 6(5) and Sch 1 para 1(2)(b) SPC Regs
HB Sch 3 para 14(5) HB Regs; Sch 3 para 6(7) HB(SPC) Regs

53 **IS** Reg 16(1) and Sch 7 para 9 IS Regs
JSA Reg 78(1) and Sch 5 para 5 JSA Regs
ESA Reg 156 and Sch 5 para 4 ESA Regs

54 **IS** Reg 3 and Sch 2 para 13 IS Regs
JSA Reg 2 and Sch 1 paras 15 and 20I JSA Regs
ESA Reg 71 and Sch 4 para 6 ESA Regs
PC Sch 1 para 2 SPC Regs
HB Reg 3 HB Regs; reg 3 HB(SPC) Regs

55 **IS** Sch 2 para 13(3)(a) IS Regs
JSA Sch 1 paras 15(4)(a) and 20I(3)(a) JSA Regs
ESA Sch 4 para 6(4)(a) ESA Regs
PC Sch 1 para 2(2)(a) SPC Regs
HB Sch 3 para 13(4) HB Regs; Sch 3 para 6(6) HB(SPC) Regs

56 **IS** Sch 2 para 13(3)(d) IS Regs
JSA Sch 1 paras 14(1)(h) and (2), 15(4)(c), 20H(1)(i) and (3) and 20I(3)(c) JSA Regs
ESA Sch 4 para 6(4)(c) and (9) ESA Regs
PC Sch 1 para 2(2)(b) and (c) SPC Regs
HB Sch 3 para 14(4)(b) HB Regs; Sch 3 para 6(6)(b) HB(SPC) Regs

57 CIS/14850/1996, para 10

58 **IS** Reg 3(2)(c) and (d) IS Regs
JSA Reg 2(2)(c) and (d) JSA Regs
ESA Reg 71(2)(c) and (d) ESA Regs
PC Sch 1 para 2(d) and (e) SPC Regs
HB Reg 3(2)(f) HB Regs; reg 3(2)(f) HB(SPC) Regs

59 **IS** Reg 3(2)(b) IS Regs
JSA Reg 2(2)(b) JSA Regs
ESA Reg 71(2)(b) ESA Regs
HB Reg 3(2)(c) HB Regs; reg 3(2)(c) HB(SPC) Regs

60 Sch 1 para 2(2)(f) SPC Regs

61 **IS** Sch 2 para 13(3)(c) and (4) IS Regs
JSA Sch 1 paras 15(4)(b) and (6) and 20I(3)(b) and (5) JSA Regs
ESA Sch 4 para 6(4)(b) and (7) ESA Regs
PC Sch 1 para 2(3) and (4) SPC Regs

62 Regs 3 and 9(1) HB Regs; regs 3 and 9(1) HB(SPC) Regs

63 **IS** Reg 2(1) IS Regs
JSA Reg 1(3) JSA Regs
ESA Reg 2(1) ESA Regs
HB Reg 2(1) HB Regs; reg 2(1) HB(SPC) Regs
All Definition of 'close relative'

64 **IS/HB** s137(1) SSCBA 1992
JSA s35(1) JSA 1995
ESA Reg 2(1) ESA Regs

65 *Bate v CAO* [1996] 2 All ER 790 (HL)

66 R(IS) 11/98, tribunal of commissioners

67 CSIS/43/1989

68 CIS/754/1991; R(IS) 11/98, para 12

69 R(IS) 11/98, para 8

70 CIS/754/1991

71 **IS** Sch 2 para 14ZA IS Regs
JSA Sch 1 paras 17 and 20J JSA Regs
ESA Sch 4 para 8 ESA Regs
PC Reg 6(6)(a) and Sch 1 para 4 SPC Regs
HB Sch 3 para 17 HB Regs; Sch 3 para 9 HB(SPC) Regs

72 **IS** Sch 2 paras 7 and 14ZA(3) and (4) IS Regs
JSA Sch 1 paras 8, 17(3) and (4) and 20J(3) and (3A) JSA Regs
ESA Sch 4 para 8(2)-(4) ESA Regs
PC Sch 1 para 4(2) and (3) SPC Regs
HB Sch 3 paras 7 and 17(3) and (4) HB Regs; Sch 3 paras 5 and 9(3) HB(SPC) Regs

73 **IS** Sch 2 para 13(3ZA) IS Regs
JSA Sch 1 paras 15(7) and 20I(6) JSA Regs
ESA Sch 4 para 6(6) ESA Regs
PC Sch 1 para 1(2)(c) SPC Regs
HB Sch 3 para 14(6) HB Regs; Sch 3 para 6(8) HB(SPC) Regs

74 **IS** Sch 2 para 13(2)(a)(iii) and (b) IS Regs
JSA Sch 1 paras 15(1)(c) and (2)(d) and 20I(1)(d) JSA Regs
ESA Sch 4 para 6(2)(a)(iii) and (b) ESA Regs
PC Sch 1 para 1(1)(ii), (b) and (c)(iv) SPC Regs
HB Sch 3 para 14(2)(a)(iii) and (b) HB Regs; Sch 3 para 6(2)(a)(iii) and (b) HB(SPC) Regs

75 Reg 7(2)(bc) SS&CS(DA) Regs

76 **IS** Sch 2 para 6(2) IS Regs
JSA Sch 1 paras 7(2) and 20C(2) JSA Regs
ESA Sch 4 para 3 ESA Regs
HB Sch 3 para 6 HB Regs

77 **IS** Sch 2 para 5 IS Regs
JSA Sch 1 paras 6 and 20B JSA Regs
HB Sch 3 para 5 HB Regs

78 Sch 3 para 3 HB Regs

79 **IS/JSA/ESA** Regs 3(7) and 6(2)(e)
SS&CS(DA) Regs
HB Regs 4(7B) and 7(2)(i) HB&CTB(DA)
Regs
80 Reg 4(7C) HB&CTB(DA) Regs

4. Components
81 **ESA** s4(2), (4) and (5) WRA 2007
HB Reg 22 and Sch 3 paras 21-24 HB
Regs
82 Sch 3 para 22(2) HB Regs
83 Reg 69(2) and Sch 5 para 13 ESA Regs
84 Sch 3 paras 22 and 24 HB Regs
85 Sch 3 para 23 HB Regs; Sch 2 Part 1
ESAUC(MA) Regs
86 Because there is no provision to remove
it in these circumstances.
87 **ESA** Sch 4 paras 12 and 13 ESA Regs
HB Sch 3 paras 25 and 26 HB Regs
88 Regs 6(2)(r) and 7(38) SS&CS(DA) Regs
89 Reg 7(1)(a) ESA Regs; regs 3(9)(c),
6(2)(a) and 7(2)(be) SS&CS(DA) Regs
90 Regs 4(7B), 7(2)(o) and 8(14D)
HB&CTB(DA) Regs

Chapter 18

Help with ground rent, service charges and other housing costs

4

This chapter covers:
1. Who can get help with housing costs (p344)
2. Which housing costs can be met (p344)
3. The amount of housing costs (p346)
4. Waiting periods (p352)
5. Liability to pay housing costs (p352)
6. Occupying accommodation as your home (p353)
7. Linking rules (p358)
8. Housing costs run-on (p359)

If you are an owner-occupier or a long leaseholder, this chapter covers the rules for help with ground rent, service charges and certain other housing costs that can be included in your pension credit (or in your income support, income-based jobseeker's allowance or income-related employment and support allowance, if you still qualify for these). It does not cover the rules on help with these costs or your rent for universal credit (see Chapter 6) or for help with your rent with housing benefit (see Chapter 10). It does not cover DWP loans for mortgage interest (see p839).

Key facts
- If you are entitled to pension credit, income support (IS), income-based jobseeker's allowance (JSA) or income-related employment and support allowance (ESA) and you own or are buying your home or you are a long leaseholder, your benefit can include help with a variety of housing costs, such as ground rent and service charges.
- Your benefit cannot include help with your mortgage or other loans – eg, for repairs or improvements. Instead, the DWP may offer you a loan.
- If you make a new claim for IS, JSA or ESA (if you still can), you might not get help with your housing costs during an initial 'waiting period'.

Part 4: General rules for other means-tested benefits
Chapter 18: Help with ground rent, service charges and other housing costs
2. Which housing costs can be met

1. **Who can get help with housing costs**

If you are entitled to pension credit, help with some of your housing costs can be included in your appropriate minimum guarantee (see p259). If you are entitled to income support, income-based jobseeker's allowance or income-related employment and support allowance, help with these costs can be included in your applicable amount (see Chapter 17).[1] To qualify:

- the housing costs must be a type that can be met (see below) – eg, ground rent or service charges; *and*
- you or your partner must count as liable to pay the housing costs, or be treated as liable (see p352); *and*
- the housing costs must be for the home in which you normally live (see p353).

Note: if you have a mortgage, the DWP may offer you a loan to help you with your mortgage interest payments (see p839). Get independent financial advice before you accept this.

2. **Which housing costs can be met**

Your pension credit (PC), income support (IS), income-based jobseeker's allowance (JSA) or income-related employment and support allowance (ESA) can include any of the following housing costs:[2]

- service charges (see p345). **Note:** some service charges are excluded;
- rent or ground rent if you have a lease of more than 21 years. If your lease is of 21 years or less, the rent or ground rent may be met by housing benefit (HB) instead (see p175);[3]
- rentcharge payments (payments by freeholders, similar to ground rent);
- payments under a co-ownership scheme – a type of scheme where the home is let by a housing association, does not involve buying a share in the home and any payment made to a former member is based on the value of the home;[4]
- rent if you are a Crown tenant (in England and Wales, minus any water charges[5]);
- payments for a tent and its pitch if that is your home.

If your home is used for both business and residential purposes, you can only get help with your housing costs for the part in which you live.[6]

Deductions for fuel charges

Charges for fuel (if they are included in the housing costs listed above) cannot be met.[7] If the charge for fuel is not specified, the set deductions below are made.

Heating	£35.25	Lighting	£2.85
Hot water	£4.10	Cooking	£4.10

Service charges

Your PC, IS, income-based JSA or income-related ESA can include charges for services. Some service charges are ineligible (see p197 – the rules are the same as for HB).[8] Some service charges can only be met if they relate to the provision of 'adequate accommodation'.[9]

> **Services**
>
> A '**service**' is something that is agreed and arranged on your behalf and for which you are required to pay – eg, if you own a flat and the freeholder arranges for the exterior of the building to be painted, for which you have to pay a share of the cost.

Bear the following in mind.
- Service charges to cover minor repairs and maintenance are eligible. However, those for any of the types of excluded repairs and improvements listed below are not.
- Payments for support services are not eligible. Instead, you may get help with these through your local authority.
- House insurance paid under the terms of your lease can be a service charge, but insurance required by a bank as a condition of your mortgage is not.[10]
- Services provided by an authority that you arrange yourself are not covered. So, charges for water and sewerage paid to a water company are not met.[11]

Excluded repairs and improvements

You cannot get help with a service charge for specified repairs and improvements undertaken to maintain the fitness of your dwelling, or the building it is in, for human habitation, that is:[12]
- providing a bath, shower, toilet, wash basin and the necessary plumbing for these, and the provision of hot water not connected to a central heating system;[13]
- repairs to your heating system;
- damp-proof measures;
- providing:

Part 4: General rules for other means-tested benefits
Chapter 18: Help with ground rent, service charges and other housing costs
3. The amount of housing costs

- ventilation and natural lighting;
- drainage facilities;
- facilities for preparing and cooking food;
- home insulation;
- electric lighting and sockets;
- storage facilities for fuel or refuse;
- repairing unsafe structural defects;
- adaptations for a 'disabled person';[14]
- providing separate sleeping accommodation for a boy and a girl aged 10 or over but under 20 for whom you or your partner are responsible and who live with you.

Note: if you have (or take out) a loan to pay for any of the types of repairs and improvements above, you may be offered a loan by the DWP to help with the interest (see p839). Get independent financial advice before you accept this.

3. **The amount of housing costs**

Once you have worked out which housing costs your pension credit (PC), income support (IS), income-based jobseeker's allowance (JSA) or income-related employment and support allowance (ESA) can meet, you can calculate the amount that is included in your appropriate minimum guarantee (see p259) or applicable amount (see Chapter 17). This is the normal weekly charge for the housing costs that can be included in your benefit.[15] If your home is used for both business and residential purposes, only the housing costs for the part in which you live are included.[16]

- **Step one:** work out the weekly equivalent of all your qualifying housing costs. Remember to deduct any charges that are not eligible – eg, fuel charges.
- **Step two:** deduct any amounts for other people living in your home (known as non-dependants – see p347).

How do you work out weekly equivalents?

If you pay your housing costs annually or irregularly or over 53 weeks, the weekly amount is worked out by dividing what is payable for the year by 52.[17]

Example

Peter is the owner-occupier of a two-bedroom flat. He does not have a mortgage. His brother, who is on contributory ESA, lives with him. Peter is getting PC. He pays ground rent of £936 a year and a qualifying service charge for caretaker services of £8.50 a week.

Step one: £936 ÷ 52 = £18 a week for ground rent + £8.50 a week for service charges = £26.50 a week housing costs.

Step two: the weekly non-dependant deduction (see below) for Peter's brother is £16.45. £26.50 – £16.45 = £10.05 a week help with housing costs.

Even if your housing costs have been waived because you or your partner (or, for IS, JSA or ESA only, a child or qualifying young person included in your claim) have paid for repairs or redecoration that are not your responsibility, you can still get PC, IS, income-based JSA or income-related ESA for them for up to eight weeks.[18]

Note: you may only get a share of the housing costs if you share liability, or are treated as liable because you share the costs with someone (see p352).

Deductions for non-dependants

If other people normally live with you in your home who are not part of your family for benefit purposes (called 'non-dependants'), a set deduction is usually made from the amount of benefit you get for housing costs.[19] This is because it is assumed the non-dependant makes a contribution towards your outgoings, whether or not s/he does so. Examples of non-dependants are adult sons or daughters or elderly relatives who share your home. For who counts as a non-dependant, see p198 – the rules are the same as for housing benefit (HB).

The DWP may use the rules on p354 to decide that someone is only temporarily absent from your home.[20] If you think the DWP has wrongly assumed that a person is normally living with you, ask for a revision or appeal (see Chapters 56 and 57).

People who are not non-dependants

The following people do not count as non-dependants, even if they normally live with you, and no deduction is made (although any rent or lodging charges paid to you affect the amount of your PC (see p461) or your IS, income-based JSA or income-related ESA (see p426)).[21]

* Your partner and:
  – for PC only, anyone under 20 for whom you or your partner are responsible ('responsible' is not defined in the rules);
  – for IS, JSA and ESA only, any child or qualifying young person included in your claim (see p307) and any child or qualifying young person living with you who does not count as a member of your household (see p311) – eg, a foster child or a child placed with you prior to adoption.
* Someone who is liable to pay you or your partner on a commercial basis in order to live in your home (eg, a subtenant, licensee or boarder), along with other members of her/his household. This does not apply if the person is your or your partner's close relative (see p353 for who counts). A low charge does not necessarily mean that the arrangement is not commercial. You do not have to make a profit. An arrangement between friends can be commercial.[22]
* For IS, JSA and ESA only, someone other than a close relative (see p353 for who counts) to whom you, or your partner, are liable to make payments on a commercial basis (ie, as a subtenant, licensee or boarder) in order to live in

Part 4: General rules for other means-tested benefits
Chapter 18: Help with ground rent, service charges and other housing costs
3. The amount of housing costs

her/his property. Other members of her/his household also do not count as non-dependants.

- Someone who jointly occupies your home and is a co-owner or joint tenant with you or your partner. Your joint occupier's partner is also not a non-dependant. For IS, JSA and ESA only, close relatives (see p353 for who counts) who jointly occupy your home are treated as non-dependants unless they had joint liability before 11 April 1988 or joint liability existed on or before the date you first lived in the property (or your partner did, if s/he is the joint owner/tenant). However, a non-dependant deduction is not made for them even though they are non-dependants (see below).
- Someone who is employed by a charitable or voluntary organisation as a resident carer for you, or your partner, and who you pay for that service (even if the charge is nominal). If the carer's partner lives in your home, s/he also does not count as a non-dependant.

When a deduction is not made

No non-dependant deduction is made for any of your non-dependants if either you or your partner:[23]

- are certified as severely sight impaired or blind by a consultant ophthalmologist (or are within 28 weeks of ceasing to be certified); or
- get attendance allowance (AA) (or equivalent benefits paid because of injury at work or a war injury), the care component of disability living allowance (DLA), the daily living component of personal independence payment (PIP) or armed forces independence payment, or for IS, income-based JSA and income-related ESA, the care component of child disability payment (CDP).

If a deduction must be made, no deduction is made for a non-dependant:[24]

- who is staying with you but whose normal home is elsewhere. **Note:** for these purposes, someone can only have one normal home at a time;[25] or
- for whom a deduction is already being made from your HB; or
- who is 16 or 17 years old; or
- who is under 25 years old and:
  - getting IS or income-based JSA; or
  - if s/he is someone who can still get a work-related activity component after 3 April 2017 (see p637), is getting income-related ESA which does not include a work-related activity or support component; or
  - if s/he is someone who cannot get a work-related activity component after 3 April 2017 (see p637), s/he is getting income-related ESA and:
    - for PC and JSA, her/his income-related ESA does not include a support component and s/he is not in the 'work-related activity group' (see p638);
    - for ESA, is still in the assessment phase (see p635);
    - for IS, is not in the 'work-related activity group' (see p638) or the 'support group' (see p637); or

- – entitled to universal credit, provided s/he does not have any earned income; *or*
- who is getting PC; *or*
- who gets a training allowance in connection with youth training under specific provisions;[26] *or*
- for IS, JSA and ESA, who is a full-time student during her/his period of study (see p874). This includes those getting JSA who count as full-time students while on a specified government scheme for assisting people to obtain employment (see p1122).[27] **Note:** no deduction is made during the summer vacation unless the student is in full-time paid work; *or*
- for PC, who is a full-time student. This includes those getting JSA who count as full-time students while on a specified government scheme for assisting people to obtain employment (see p1122);[28] *or*
- who is not living with you at present because s/he:
  - – has been in hospital for more than 52 weeks. Separate stays in hospital which are not more than 28 days apart are added together when calculating the 52 weeks;
  - – is a prisoner (see p927 for who counts); *or*
- for IS, JSA and ESA only, who is a close relative (see p353 for who counts) and a co-owner or joint tenant with you, or your partner. For PC, no deduction is made because co-owners and joint tenants do not count as non-dependants, even if they are close relatives.

The amount of the deduction

If you have a non-dependant living with you for whom a deduction must be made, a fixed amount is deducted from the housing costs included in your benefit, whatever s/he pays you. A deduction is usually made for each non-dependant in your home. If you also have a loan for mortgage interest from the DWP (see p839), the deduction is apportioned between the help you get with housing costs and your loan payments. **Note:** if the amount that must be deducted is higher than the amount of housing costs that can be included, no housing costs are included in your benefit.

The deduction is calculated as follows.[29]

- **Step one:** work out the weekly amount of housing costs that can be included in your benefit (see p346). If you have a loan for mortgage interest from the DWP (see p839), add the weekly amount of your loan payments to the amount of housing costs included in your benefit.
- **Step two:** work out the total amount of non-dependant deductions (see p350). Remember that a deduction is generally made for each of your non-dependants. If you do *not* have a loan for mortgage interest from the DWP, the amount in this step is the non-dependant deduction made from your housing costs and you do not need to go on to Steps three and four.

Part 4: General rules for other means-tested benefits
Chapter 18: Help with ground rent, service charges and other housing costs
3. The amount of housing costs

- **Step three:** if you have a loan for mortgage interest from the DWP, divide the weekly amount of your loan payments by the total from Step one. Multiply the result by the total amount of non-dependant deductions in Step two.
- **Step four:** work out the difference between the amount in Step two and the amount in Step three. If you have a loan for mortgage interest from the DWP, this is the non-dependant deduction made from your housing costs.

Examples
Meena is getting PC. She owns her flat and pays ground rent of £2,002 a year and a service charge of £30 a week. Her sister, aged 45, lives with her and earns £250 a week. Meena does not have a loan for mortgage interest from the DWP.
Step one: the weekly amount of housing costs that can be included in Meena's PC is £38.50 (£2,002 ÷ 52) + £30 = £68.50
Step two: the weekly non-dependant deduction for her sister is £51.85. As Meena does not have a loan for mortgage interest, this is the non-dependant deduction. Her PC housing costs are therefore £16.65 (£68.50 – £51.85).

Ewan is the owner-occupier of a three-bedroom flat. He has been getting income-based JSA for 50 weeks. He pays a mortgage, has a loan for mortgage interest and gets weekly loan payments of £121.90 a week. He pays ground rent of £18 a week and qualifying service charges of £10 a week. Two friends live with him. One is on contributory ESA. The other is in low-paid full-time work and earns £157 a week (gross).
Step one: the weekly amount of housing costs is £28 (£18 + £10).
£28 + £121.90 (weekly loan payment) = £149.90
Step two: the weekly non-dependant deduction for the friend on contributory ESA is £16.45 and for the friend in low-paid work is £37.80. The total amount of non-dependant deductions is £54.25 (£16.45 + £37.80).
Step three: £121.90 (loan payment) divided by £149.90 (the total in Step one) x £54.25 (the total non-dependant deductions) = £44.12
Step four: the non-dependant deduction to be made from Ewan's housing costs is £10.13 (£54.25 – £44.12).
So Ewan's income-based JSA includes housing costs of £17.87 a week (£28 – £10.13). A non-dependant deduction of £44.12 is made from his loan payments.

The deductions

Unless your non-dependant is in full-time paid work, a deduction of £16.45 is made for her/him each week. If your non-dependant is in full-time paid work, the amount of the deduction depends on her/his gross weekly income.[30]

Gross weekly income	Weekly non-dependant deduction
£484 or more	£106.05
£389–£483.99	£96.60
£292–£388.99	£84.85
£224–£291.99	£51.85
£154–£223.99	£37.80
Less than £154	£16.45

The rules on full-time paid work are covered in Chapter 44. **Note:**

- A non-dependant who is not in (or is treated as not in) full-time paid work does not attract the higher level of deduction even if her/his gross weekly income is £154 or more.

- For PC, if the non-dependant is getting IS or income-based JSA for more than three days in a benefit week, s/he does not count as being in full-time paid work in that week.[31] This means the lower deduction (£16.45) is made (or, in some cases, no deduction is made).

Gross income includes wages before tax and national insurance are deducted, plus any other income the non-dependant has, but not AA (or equivalent benefits paid because of injury at work or a war injury), DLA, PIP and armed forces independence payment. Also ignored are payments from specified trusts and schemes established to compensate people, including victims of medical and other errors, of institutional child abuse, emergencies, disasters and acts of terrorism and, for PC only, payments in kind, or for IS, income-based JSA and income-related ESA, CDP.[32]

Do you know your non-dependant's income?

You should try to provide information to show which deduction applies. However, if you do not know your non-dependant's income, explain fully why you are unable to get this information. Ask the DWP to consider the circumstances – eg, if your non-dependant is doing a job which is normally very poorly paid. **Note:** the DWP should not assume that your non-dependant is earning the highest amount. It should assess the likely level of your non-dependant's earnings on the evidence available.[33]

A deduction is made for each non-dependant in your home. However, if you have a non-dependant couple and a non-dependant deduction applies to both members, only one deduction is made – the highest applicable.[34] The couple's joint income counts.

If you are a joint occupier with someone other than your partner, any deductions are shared proportionally between you and the other joint occupier(s).[35]

Part 4: General rules for other means-tested benefits
Chapter 18: Help with ground rent, service charges and other housing costs
5. Liability to pay housing costs

4. **Waiting periods**

When you make a claim for income support (IS), income-based jobseeker's allowance (JSA) or income-related employment and support allowance (ESA) (if you still can), your housing costs are not usually included in your benefit calculation until you have been entitled (or treated as entitled) to IS, JSA or ESA for 39 weeks.[36] This is known as a 'waiting period'.[37] **Note:** there is no waiting period if:[38]

- you claim and qualify for pension credit; *or*
- you have already been entitled to IS, JSA or ESA for sufficient weeks when you agree to pay housing costs; *or*
- in some other situations (eg, your partner is at least pension age or the housing costs are for payments under a co-ownership scheme or for a tent.

There are now very few people who can make a new claim for IS, income-based JSA or income-related ESA so the detailed rules for waiting periods are not covered here. If you are currently a serving a waiting period, or you can, and do, make a new claim for one of these benefits, see pp368–69 of the 2020/2021 edition of this *Handbook*.

5. **Liability to pay housing costs**

You count as liable to pay housing costs if:[39]

- either you, or your partner, are liable to pay them. However, you do not count as liable to pay housing costs if you pay these to someone who is a member of your household (see p312 for the meaning of 'household'). If you or your partner share liability, you might only get help with your share (see below); *or*
- you share the costs with other members of your household and are treated as liable to pay them. You might only get help with your share; *or*
- someone else is liable to pay them but is not paying, so you have to meet the cost yourself in order to continue to live in your home. You must show that it is reasonable in all the circumstances for you to pay instead – eg, if you have given up your home to live with and care for someone and s/he has now gone into a care home, or if you have separated from your partner (even if you have not lived in the home continuously since your partner left[40]).

Shared liability

If you or your partner share liability with someone else, you might only get help with your share. However, if the other person is not paying her/his share, you can argue that you should get help with the full amount.

You are treated as liable to pay housing costs (even if you are not legally liable) if:[41]
- you share the costs with other members of your household; *and*
- at least one of those with whom you share is liable.

You can be paid for your share, provided the people with whom you share are not your or your partner's 'close relatives' and it is reasonable in all the circumstances to treat you as sharing responsibility for the costs.[42]

Close relative

'**Close relative**' means a parent, parent-in-law (including a civil partner's parent), son, son-in-law (including a son's civil partner), daughter, daughter-in-law (including a daughter's civil partner), brother, sister, step-parent (including a parent's civil partner), stepson (including a civil partner's son) or stepdaughter (including a civil partner's daughter), or the partners of any of these. 'Sister' or 'brother' includes a half-sister or half-brother. An adopted child ceases to be related to her/his birth family on adoption and becomes the relative of her/his adoptive family.[43]

6. Occupying accommodation as your home

You can get help with housing costs for the home in which you normally live.[44] You cannot usually be paid for any other home. Even if you are liable to pay housing costs for a property, if you have no immediate intention of living there, you cannot get help with the costs.[45] You can argue that a home can consist of more than one building if you occupy more than one dwelling – eg, because your family is too large for one.[46]

Your home

Your '**home**' is defined as the building, or part of the building, in which you live. This includes any garage, garden, outbuildings and other premises and land which it is not reasonable or practicable to sell separately.[47]

There are special rules if you:
- have just moved into your home (see below); *or*
- are temporarily absent from home (see p354); *or*
- are liable to pay housing costs on more than one home (see p357).

Moving home

If you have just moved into your home but were liable to pay housing costs before moving in, your pension credit (PC), income support (IS), income-based

Part 4: General rules for other means-tested benefits
Chapter 18: Help with ground rent, service charges and other housing costs
6. Occupying accommodation as your home

jobseeker's allowance (JSA) or income-related employment and support allowance (ESA) can include help with the costs for up to four weeks before you moved in if your delay in moving was reasonable. You must have claimed PC (or if you still can, IS, JSA or income-related ESA) before moving in.

You must satisfy one of the following conditions.[48]

- You were waiting for adaptations to be finished to meet your or your partner's disability needs or those of:
  - for PC, someone under 20 for whom you or your partner are responsible ('responsible' is not defined in the rules); or
  - for IS, JSA and ESA, a child or qualifying young person included in your claim (see p307).

  The adaptations do not need to involve a change to the fabric or structure of the dwelling, but must be reasonably required and have a clear connection to the disability.[49]

- You became responsible for the housing costs while you were in hospital or a similar institution, or you were in a care home or an independent hospital (or, for IS, JSA and ESA only, in an Abbeyfield home).

- You were waiting for local welfare assistance, a payment from the Scottish Welfare Fund or a social fund payment for a need connected with the move – eg, for removal expenses or items to help you set up home.[50] In addition, for IS, JSA and ESA you must:
  - have a child aged five or under living with you, or be getting child tax credit which includes an element for a disabled or severely disabled child; or
  - qualify for a severe disability or pensioner premium; or
  - for IS and JSA only, qualify for a disability or disabled child premium; or
  - for ESA only, be getting main phase ESA – ie, after the assessment phase has ended.

Note: the amount for housing costs is not actually included in your benefit until you move in. If the earlier PC (or IS, JSA or ESA) claim you made before you moved was turned down, you must claim again within four weeks of moving in to qualify.

Temporary absence from home

If you are temporarily absent from home but are still entitled to PC, IS, income-based JSA or income-related ESA, have not rented out your home and intend to return, help with your housing costs continues to be paid for a period. You can argue that you count as temporarily absent even if you have not yet stayed there – eg, you move your furniture and belongings in but then have to go into hospital.[51]
Note: your entitlement to benefit may be affected if you are absent from home outside Great Britain (see Chapter 70).

You can get help with housing costs for up to:

- **13 weeks** while you are away, whatever the reason. You must be unlikely to be away for longer than this;[52]
- **52 weeks** if you are in one of the groups on pp356–357. You must be unlikely to be away for longer than this (or, in exceptional circumstances, unlikely to be away for substantially longer than this).[53]

The 13 and 52 weeks both run from the date you leave home. The day you leave home is included, but not the day you return home.[54] If, for example, you have been away from home for 10 weeks and then have grounds to continue to get help with housing costs for 52 weeks, you only get this for the balance: 42 weeks. However, a new period of absence starts if you return home even for a short stay – eg, a day or a weekend.[55]

Are you going to be away from home for a period?

1. You must let the DWP know about your absence from home, preferably before you go away.

2. Make it clear that your absence is going to be temporary and how long you are likely to be away.

3. Your intention to return, and whether or not you are unlikely to be away for longer than 13/52 weeks, is considered initially based on the circumstances on the date you leave your home, unless you are in a care home, independent hospital (or, for IS, JSA or ESA, an Abbeyfield home) for a trial period (see below).[56] If at any time after that date, you no longer intend to return or it becomes likely that you will be away from home for more than the 13/52 weeks, your entitlement can be reconsidered.[57] If you initially told the DWP you were going to be away from home for more than six months, but realise that your absence will now be shorter, it should also reconsider your entitlement.

Note: if you have someone living with you who is temporarily absent (eg, a student who is away during term time), the DWP may use these rules to decide whether s/he is a non-dependant (see p347).[58]

If you have to live in temporary accommodation while essential repairs are done to your normal home and you only have to pay housing costs for one of the homes, your PC, IS, income-based JSA or income-related ESA includes help with the housing costs for that home.[59] This is not subject to the normal limits on temporary absence from home.[60] If you have to pay for both homes, you may be able to get help with housing costs for both for up to four weeks (see p357). However, after the four weeks, you are only paid for one home – your normal home if you are unlikely to be away for more than 13/52 weeks, or your temporary home if you will be away for longer.

Part 4: General rules for other means-tested benefits
Chapter 18: Help with ground rent, service charges and other housing costs
6. Occupying accommodation as your home

Housing costs for up to 52 weeks

You can get help with your housing costs if you are in a care home or an independent hospital (or, for IS, JSA and ESA only, an Abbeyfield home) for a trial period to see if it suits your needs. On the date you enter the accommodation, you must intend to return home if it is not suitable.[61] You can only get your housing costs met for up to 13 weeks.[62] If the accommodation does not suit your needs, you can have further trial periods in other homes and your housing costs met for further 13 week periods, as long as you are not away from home for more than 52 weeks in total.

You can get help with your housing costs for up to 52 weeks if you are unlikely to be away for longer than this (or, in exceptional circumstances, unlikely to be away for substantially longer than this) in the following situations.[63]

- You are resident in a hospital or a similar institution. You cannot get help with housing costs after you have been resident in hospital for 52 weeks even if this is because you are seriously mentally ill. However, a new period of absence starts if you return home even for a short stay.[64]

  Note: if you are getting JSA, this only applies during a two-week period of sickness when you are treated as capable of work for JSA purposes (see p691 – the rules are the same as for contribution-based JSA). If you are sick for longer than you are allowed, you can claim universal credit (UC).

- You are receiving care (approved by a doctor) in the UK or abroad, or you, your partner or a dependent child (for PC, a dependant under 20) are receiving medical treatment or convalescing in the UK or abroad (approved by a doctor). This must not be in a care home or an independent hospital (or, for IS, JSA and ESA only, an Abbeyfield home).

- You are attending a specified 'training course' in the UK or abroad.

- You are required to live in an approved hostel or an address away from your normal home as a condition of bail.

- For PC, IS and ESA only, you are in prison on remand pending trial or sentence. You can argue that this applies even if you are simultaneously serving another sentence.[65] If you were getting JSA before going into prison, you can only get help with your housing costs if you can claim IS or income-related ESA. Once you are sentenced, you are no longer entitled to help with housing costs in PC, IS or ESA.

- You are in a care home or an independent hospital (or, for IS, JSA and ESA only, an Abbeyfield home) for short-term or respite care.

- You are providing care for someone living in the UK or abroad (approved by a doctor).

- You are caring for a child under 16 (or, for PC only, someone under 20) whose parent or guardian is receiving medical treatment or care (approved by a doctor) away from home.

- You are away from home because of a fear of violence (see below if you need to claim for two homes and for what counts as violence).

- You are a full-time student (see p874) and:
  - living apart from your partner but cannot get help with housing costs for two homes (see p358); *or*
  - a single claimant or a lone parent who is liable to pay housing costs on both a term-time and a home address.

There must be some causal link between your absence from home and being in one of the situations above.[66]

Housing costs for more than one home

In most cases, you can only get help with the housing costs for one home. If you occupy more than one dwelling as a home (eg, because you have a large family), you can argue that you only have one home.[67]

If you have to pay housing costs for two homes, you *can* get PC, IS, income-based JSA or income-related ESA for both:[68]

- **for up to four weeks** if you have moved into a new home and cannot avoid having to pay for the other one as well;[69]
- **indefinitely** if you left your home because of a fear of violence. Argue that fear of controlling behaviour or of psychological, physical, sexual, financial and emotional abuse should count.[70] Provided you left home because of this and are still away from home because of this, it does not matter if you were away from home for some other reason during this period – eg, because you were in prison.[71] You must show that it is reasonable for you to get payment for two homes. So, if you do not intend to return home or someone else is paying the housing costs, you might not get PC, IS, income-based JSA or income-related ESA for both homes.

  'Violence' means violence against you and not caused by you.[72] For the purpose of these rules, it must be fear of violence:[73]
  - in your home. Fear of a racist attack should be covered, provided the attack would take place in your home. Remember that your garden and garage, for example, count (see p353); *or*
  - from a former partner; *or*
  - for PC, from a close relative (see p353 for who counts); *or*
  - for IS, JSA and ESA, from a child or qualifying young person who is no longer included in your claim;
- **indefinitely** if you are one of a couple and you or your partner are a full-time student or on a training course and living away from your home (see below). You have to show that it is reasonable for you to get payment for two homes.

If you have to live in temporary accommodation while essential repairs are done to your normal home and you only have to pay for housing costs for one of the homes, see p355.

Part 4: General rules for other means-tested benefits
Chapter 18: Help with ground rent, service charges and other housing costs
7. Linking rules

If you have to live away from your normal home because you or your partner are a full-time student (see p874) or on a specified training course:[74]
- if you are one of a couple and have to live apart, you can get help with housing costs for both of your homes if it is reasonable for you to get help with both;
- if you are a single person or lone parent and must pay housing costs for *either* your normal home *or* your term-time accommodation but not both, you can get help with housing costs for the home for which you pay.

If neither of the above applies, you may only get help with your usual home for up to 52 weeks during a temporary absence (see p354).[75]

If you have been getting help with housing costs for your term-time accommodation and you stop living there during a vacation, you cannot continue to get this unless you are away because you are in hospital.[76]

7. **Linking rules**

You are treated as entitled to, or receiving, income support (IS), income-based jobseeker's allowance (JSA) or income-related employment and support allowance (ESA) for certain periods, even though you were not actually entitled to or receiving it. These are known as 'linking rules'. **Note:** periods when you are treated as entitled to IS, income-based JSA or income-related ESA can count towards your waiting period (see p352), so you can get help with housing costs earlier.

You are treated as entitled to and receiving:[77]
- IS for any period when you were entitled to or receiving income-based JSA or income-related ESA;
- JSA for any period when you were entitled to or receiving IS or income-related ESA;
- income-related ESA for any period when you were entitled to or receiving IS, income-based JSA or pension credit (PC);
- IS or JSA for any period when you were receiving JSA as a 'joint-claim couple' (see p247);
- IS, JSA or income-related ESA during a period of no more than 12 weeks between two periods when:
  - for IS and JSA, you were entitled to, receiving or treated as receiving IS, JSA or income-related ESA, or were treated as entitled to one of these while your income or capital was too high in specified circumstances; *or*
  - for ESA, you were entitled to, receiving or treated as receiving IS, income-based JSA, income-related ESA or PC, or were treated as entitled to one of these while your income or capital was too high in specified circumstances.

  The 12 weeks is extended to 104 weeks if you or your partner are a 'work or training beneficiary' (see p365 of the 2018/19 edition of this *Handbook*) or to

52 weeks if you qualify for a longer linking period (see p368 of the 2018/19 edition of this *Handbook*);

- IS or JSA during any period for which you are awarded IS, JSA or income-related ESA after a revision, supersession or appeal;
- income-related ESA during any period for which you are awarded IS, income-based JSA, income-related ESA or PC after a revision, supersession or appeal.

There are other linking rules for periods when:[78]

- you were not entitled to IS, income-based JSA or income-related ESA (or for ESA only, PC) when you claimed because your income was too high or your capital was over £16,000; *or*
- your partner or former partner was receiving or treated as receiving IS, income-based JSA or income-related ESA; *or*
- you stopped getting IS, income-based JSA or income-related ESA (or for ESA only, PC) because you or your partner were on training under specified provisions or were on an employment training rehabilitation course; *or*
- you and a child or young person who is a member of your family counted as the member of a former claimant's family.

For full details of these linking rules, see pp366–67 of the 2018/19 edition of this *Handbook*.

8. Housing costs run-on

When you (or your partner) return to work or increase your hours and so count as being in full-time paid work, you no longer qualify for income support (IS), income-based jobseeker's allowance (JSA) or income-related employment and support allowance (ESA). However, if you qualify for housing costs run-on, you are paid IS for your housing costs for the first four weeks after you go into full-time paid work, even if the benefit you were claiming was income-based JSA or income-related ESA. **Note:**

- You do not have to make a claim to qualify for housing costs run-on; it is paid automatically.[79] However, you must let the DWP know you are starting full-time paid work.
- Housing costs run-on is a payment of IS. Therefore:
  - it is not taxable; *and*
  - it is included in the benefit cap (see p1156); *and*
  - you might get health benefits (see Chapter 31) and education benefits, such as free school lunches (see p851).

Part 4: General rules for other means-tested benefits
Chapter 18: Help with ground rent, service charges and other housing costs
8. Housing costs run-on

Who can get housing costs run-on

You qualify for housing costs run-on if:[80]
- you or your partner take up a new job or increase your weekly hours of work and so count as being in full-time paid work for IS purposes (see p974). You must expect the work to last for at least five weeks; *and*
- throughout the 26 weeks before the day you count as being in full-time paid work, you or your partner were receiving IS, income-based JSA or income-related ESA. Periods when you were receiving housing costs run-on do not count towards the 26 weeks;[81] *and*
- on the day before you or your partner started the work, your IS, income-based JSA or income-related ESA applicable amount included help with any of the types of housing costs that can be met (see p344) and you or your partner are still liable (or treated as liable) to pay them.

If you qualify, you are paid IS for the housing costs for the first four weeks of full-time paid work.[82] If you claim universal credit during that period, your entitlement to IS can still continue for two weeks (called 'IS run-on' – see p241), or if sooner, until the end of the four-week period.

The amount of housing costs run-on

You are paid the lowest of:[83]
- the weekly amount of IS, income-based JSA or income-related ESA for housing costs that you were getting immediately before you or your partner took up full-time paid work; *or*
- your or your partner's IS, income-based JSA or income-related ESA entitlement in the week before you took up full-time paid work (or the amount to which you would have been entitled had you not been getting a training allowance).

Your earnings from the full-time paid work and any other income you get are disregarded.[84] All of your capital is also disregarded.[85]

Your housing costs run-on can be adjusted if specified changes occur.[86]

Chapter 18

Help with ground rent, service charges and other housing costs

Notes

1. Who can get help with housing costs

1. **IS** Regs 17(1)(e) and 18(1)(f) and Sch 3 para 1 IS Regs
JSA Regs 83(7), 84(1)(g) and 86A(d) and Sch 2 para 1 JSA Regs
ESA Regs 67(1)(c) and 69(1)(d) and Sch 6 para 1 ESA Regs
PC Reg 6(6)(c) and Sch 2 para 1 SPC Regs

2. Which housing costs can be met

2. **IS** Sch 3 para 17(1) IS Regs
JSA Sch 2 para 16(1) JSA Regs
ESA Sch 6 para 18(1) ESA Regs
PC Sch 2 para 13(1) SPC Regs
All s1 Rentcharges Act 1977
3. CH/3110/2003; R(H) 3/07
4. **IS** Reg 2(1) IS Regs
JSA Reg 1(4) JSA Regs
ESA Reg 2(1) ESA Regs
PC Sch 2 para 13(6)(a) SPC Regs
All paras 23601-3 DMG
5. **IS** Sch 3 para 17(5) IS Regs
JSA Sch 2 para 16(5) JSA Regs
ESA Sch 6 para 18(5) ESA Regs
PC Sch 2 para 13(5) SPC Regs
6. **IS** Sch 3 para 5 IS Regs
JSA Sch 2 para 5 JSA Regs
ESA Sch 6 para 7 ESA Regs
PC Sch 2 para 6 SPC Regs
7. **IS** Sch 3 para 17(2) IS Regs
JSA Sch 2 para 16(2) JSA Regs
ESA Sch 6 para 18(2) ESA Regs
PC Sch 2 para 13(2) SPC Regs
8. **IS** Sch 3 para 17(2)(b) IS Regs
JSA Sch 2 para 16(2)(b) JSA Regs
ESA Sch 6 para 18(2)(b) ESA Regs
PC Sch 2 para 13(2)(b) SPC Regs
9. R(IS) 4/91; CIS/1460/1995; CIS/15036/1996
10. R(IS) 4/92; R(IS) 19/93
11. CIS/4/1988
12. **IS** Sch 3 para 17(2)(c) and (6) IS Regs
JSA Sch 2 para 16(2)(c) and (6) JSA Regs
ESA Sch 6 para 18(2)(c) and (6) ESA Regs
PC Sch 2 para 13(2)(c) and (7) SPC Regs
All CIS/15036/1996; CIS/488/2008

13. *KW v SSWP (IS)* [2012] UKUT 180 (AAC)
14. **IS** Sch 3 para 1(3) and (4) IS Regs
JSA Sch 2 para 1(3) and (4) JSA Regs
ESA Sch 6 para 1(3) and (4) ESA Regs
PC Sch 2 para 1(2)(a) and (3) SPC Regs

3. The amount of housing costs

15. **IS** Sch 3 para 17(1) IS Regs
JSA Sch 2 para 16(1) JSA Regs
ESA Sch 6 para 18(1) ESA Regs
PC Sch 2 para 13(1) SPC Regs
16. **IS** Sch 3 para 5 IS Regs
JSA Sch 2 para 5 JSA Regs
ESA Sch 6 para 7 ESA Regs
PC Sch 2 para 6 SPC Regs
17. **IS** Sch 3 para 17(3) IS Regs
JSA Sch 2 para 16(3) JSA Regs
ESA Sch 6 para 18(3) ESA Regs
PC Sch 2 para 13(3) SPC Regs
18. **IS** Sch 3 para 17(4) IS Regs
JSA Sch 2 para 16(4) JSA Regs
ESA Sch 6 para 18(4) ESA Regs
PC Sch 2 para 13(4) SPC Regs
19. **IS** Reg 3 and Sch 3 para 18 IS Regs
JSA Reg 2 and Sch 2 para 17 JSA Regs
ESA Reg 71 and Sch 6 para 19 ESA Regs
PC Sch 2 paras 1(4)-(9) and 14 SPC Regs
20. R(H) 8/09; *SK v South Hams DC (HB)* [2010] UKUT 129 (AAC), reported as [2010] AACR 40
21. **IS** Reg 3 IS Regs
JSA Reg 2 JSA Regs
ESA Reg 71 ESA Regs
PC Sch 2 para 1(4)-(7) SPC Regs
22. CSB/1163/1988
23. **IS** Sch 3 para 18(6) IS Regs
JSA Sch 2 para 17(6) JSA Regs
ESA Sch 6 para 19(6) ESA Regs
PC Sch 2 para 14(6) SPC Regs
24. **IS** Sch 3 para 18(7) IS Regs
JSA Sch 2 para 17(7) JSA Regs
ESA Sch 6 para 19(7) ESA Regs
PC Sch 2 para 14(7) SPC Regs
25. *JP v Bournemouth BC (HB)* [2018] UKUT 75 (AAC)

Part 4: General rules for other means-tested benefits
Chapter 18: Help with ground rent, service charges and other housing costs
Notes

- -

26 Made under s2 ETA 1973 or s2
   Enterprise and New Towns (Scotland)
   Act 1990 or by the Secretary of State for
   people enlisted in HM forces for any
   special term of service specified in
   regulations
27 Reg 3 JSA(SAPOE) Regs
28 Reg 3 JSA(SAPOE) Regs
29 **IS** Sch 3 para 18(2A) IS Regs
   JSA Sch 2 para 17(2A) JSA Regs
   ESA Sch 6 para 19(2A) ESA Regs
   PC Sch 2 para 14(2A) SPC Regs
   All Reg 14 LMI Regs
30 **IS** Sch 3 para 18(1) and (2) IS Regs
   JSA Sch 2 para 17(1) and (2) JSA Regs
   ESA Sch 6 para 19(1) and (2) ESA Regs
   PC Sch 2 para 14(1) and (2) SPC Regs
   All Reg 14 LMI Regs
31 Sch 2 para 2(6) SPC Regs
32 **IS** Sch 3 para 18(8) IS Regs
   JSA Sch 2 para 17(8) JSA Regs
   ESA Sch 6 para 19(8) ESA Regs
   PC Sch 2 para 14(8) SPC Regs
33 CH/48/2006
34 **IS** Sch 3 para 18(3) and(4) IS Regs
   JSA Sch 2 para 17(3) and (4) JSA Regs
   ESA Sch 6 para 19(3) and (4) ESA Regs
   PC Sch 2 para 14(3) and (4) SPC Regs
35 **IS** Sch 3 para 18(5) IS Regs
   JSA Sch 2 para 17(5) JSA Regs
   ESA Sch 6 para 19(5) ESA Regs
   PC Sch 2 para 14(5) SPC Regs

4. Waiting periods
36 **IS** Sch 3 paras 1(2) and 8 IS Regs
   JSA Sch 2 paras 1(2) and 7 JSA Regs
   ESA Sch 6 paras 1(2) and 9 ESA Regs
   All CJSA/2028/2000
37 **IS** Sch 3 para 8 IS Regs
   JSA Sch 2 para 7 JSA Regs
   ESA Sch 6 para 9 ESA Regs
38 **IS** Sch 3 para 9 IS Regs
   JSA Sch 2 para 8 JSA Regs
   ESA Sch 6 para 10 ESA Regs

5. Liability to pay housing costs
39 **IS** Sch 3 para 2 IS Regs
   JSA Sch 2 para 2 JSA Regs
   ESA Sch 6 para 4 ESA Regs
   PC Sch 2 para 3 SPC Regs
40 *Ewens v Secretary of State for Social
   Security,* reported as R(IS) 8/01

41 **IS** Sch 3 para 5(5) IS Regs
   JSA Sch 2 para 5(5) JSA Regs
   ESA Sch 6 para 7(5) ESA Regs
   PC Sch 2 para 6(5) SPC Regs
   All R(SB) 22/87; *FK v Wandsworth BC
   (HB)* [2016] UKUT 570 (AAC); *Babergh
   DC v GW (HB)* [2017] UKUT 40 (AAC)
42 R(IS) 4/95
43 **IS** Reg 2(1) IS Regs
   JSA Reg 1(3) JSA Regs
   ESA Reg 2(1) ESA Regs
   PC Reg 1(2) SPC Regs
   All R(SB) 22/87

6. Occupying accommodation as your home
44 **IS** Sch 3 para 3(1) IS Regs
   JSA Sch 2 para 3(1) JSA Regs
   ESA Sch 6 para 5(1) ESA Regs
   PC Sch 2 para 4(1) SPC Regs
45 CIS/297/1994; *PJ v SSWP (SPC)* [2014]
   UKUT 152 (AAC)
46 *SSWP v Mohamed Miah,* reported as
   R(JSA) 9/03; R(H) 5/09
47 **IS** Reg 2(1) IS Regs
   JSA Reg 1(3) JSA Regs
   ESA Reg 2(1) ESA Regs
   PC Reg 1(2) SPC Regs
   All Definition of 'dwelling occupied as
   the home', s137(1) SSCBA 1992 and reg
   2(1), definition of 'dwelling', ESA Regs
48 **IS** Sch 3 para 3(7) and (13) IS Regs
   JSA Sch 2 para 3(7) and (13) JSA Regs
   ESA Sch 6 para 5(7) and (13) ESA Regs
   PC Sch 2 para 4(7) SPC Regs
49 *R (Mahmoudi) v LB Lewisham and
   Another* [2014] EWCA Civ 284, reported
   as [2014] AACR 14
50 **IS** Reg 2(1) IS Regs
   JSA Reg 1(3) JSA Regs
   ESA Reg 2(1) ESA Regs
   PC Reg 1(2) SPC Regs
   All Definition of 'local welfare provision'
51 R(H) 9/05
52 **IS** Sch 3 para 3(10) IS Regs
   JSA Sch 2 para 3(10) JSA Regs
   ESA Sch 6 para 5(10) ESA Regs
   PC Sch 2 para 4(10) SPC Regs
53 **IS** Sch 3 para 3(11)-(13) IS Regs
   JSA Sch 2 para 3(11)-(13) JSA Regs
   ESA Sch 6 para 5(11)-(13) ESA Regs
   PC Sch 2 para 4(11)-(13) SPC Regs
54 *KdeS v Camden LB (HB)* [2011] UKUT 457
   (AAC)
55 *R v Penwith DC ex parte Burt* [1990] 22
   HLR 292 (QBD)
56 CH/1237/2004
57 CH/3893/2004

58 R(H) 8/09; *SK v South Hams DC (HB)* [2010] UKUT 129 (AAC), reported as [2010] AACR 40

59 **IS** Sch 3 para 3(5) IS Regs
JSA Sch 2 para 3(5) JSA Regs
ESA Sch 6 para 5(5) ESA Regs
PC Sch 2 para 4(5) SPC Regs

60 CIS/719/1994

61 *SSWP v Selby DC and Bowman* [2006] EWCA Civ 271, reported as R(H) 4/06

62 **IS** Sch 3 para 3(8) and (9) IS Regs
JSA Sch 2 para 3(8) and (9) JSA Regs
ESA Sch 6 para 5(8) and (9) ESA Regs
PC Sch 2 para 4(8) and (9) SPC Regs

63 **IS** Sch 3 para 3(11)-(13) IS Regs
JSA Sch 2 para 3(11)-(13) JSA Regs
ESA Sch 6 para 5(11)-(13) ESA Regs
PC Sch 2 para 4(11)-(13) SPC Regs

64 *Obrey and Others v SSWP* [2013] EWCA Civ 1584

65 *MR v Bournemouth BC (HB)* [2011] UKUT 284 (AAC)

66 *Torbay BC v RF* [2010] UKUT 7 (AAC), reported as [2010] AACR 26

67 R(H) 5/09

68 **IS** Sch 3 para 3(6) IS Regs
JSA Sch 2 para 3(6) JSA Regs
ESA Sch 6 para 5(6) ESA Regs
PC Sch 2 para 4(6) SPC Regs

69 CH/1911/2006

70 gov.uk/government/publications/domestic-violence-and-abuse-help-from-dwp

71 CIS/543/1993

72 CIS/339/1993

73 **IS** Sch 3 para 3(6)(a) IS Regs
JSA Sch 2 para 3(6)(a) JSA Regs
ESA Sch 6 para 5(6)(a) ESA Regs
PC Sch 2 para 4(6)(a) SPC Regs

74 **IS** Sch 3 para 3(3), (6)(b) and (13) IS Regs
JSA Sch 2 para 3(3), (6)(b) and (13) JSA Regs
ESA Sch 6 para 5(6)(b) ESA Regs
PC Sch 2 para 4(6)(b) SPC Regs

75 **IS** Sch 3 para 3(11)(c)(viii) IS Regs
JSA Sch 2 para 3(11)(c)(viii) JSA Regs
ESA Sch 6 para 5(11)(c)(viii) ESA Regs
PC Sch 2 para 4(11)(c)(viii) SPC Regs

76 **IS** Sch 3 para 3(4) IS Regs
JSA Sch 2 para 3(4) JSA Regs
ESA Sch 6 para 5(4) ESA Regs
PC Sch 2 para 4(4) SPC Regs

7. Linking rules

77 **IS** Sch 3 para 14(1)(a), (3A) and (15) IS Regs; reg 32 IS(JSACA) Regs
JSA Sch 2 paras 13(1)(a), (2A) and (4) and 18(1)(c) JSA Regs
ESA Sch 6 paras 15(1)(a), (5), (15) and (16) and 20(1)(c) ESA Regs

78 **IS** Sch 3 para 14(1)(c), (d), (e) and (f), (3), (3A), (4), (5), (5A), (5B), (6), (14) and (15) IS Regs; reg 32 IS(JSACA) Regs
JSA Sch 2 paras 13(1)(c), (d), (dd), (e) and (f), (3), (4), (5), (6), (7), (8), (9), (16) and 18(1)(c) JSA Regs; reg 32 IS(JSACA) Regs
ESA Sch 6 paras 2(9), 15(1)(c), (d), (e), (g), (3), (5), (8), (9), (10), (11), (12), (15), (19) and 20(1)(c) ESA Regs

8. Housing costs run-on

79 Reg 3(h) SS(C&P) Regs

80 Reg 6(5) and (8) IS Regs

81 Reg 6(7) IS Regs

82 Reg 6(6) IS Regs; Sch 9A para 3(9) SS(C&P) Regs

83 Sch 7 para 19A(1) IS Regs

84 Schs 8 para 15C and 9 para 74 IS Regs

85 Sch 10 para 62 IS Regs

86 Sch 7 para 19A(2) and (3) IS Regs

Housing benefit rent restrictions

This chapter covers:
1. How to use this chapter (below)
2. The local housing allowance rules (p368)
3. The social sector rules: the 'bedroom tax' (p375)
4. Hostels, houseboats, mobile homes, caravans and boarders (p381)
5. Exempt accommodation and claimants: the old scheme rules (p387)
6. Common rules (p392)
7. Delaying a rent restriction (p396)
8. Challenging a rent restriction (p397)

This chapter covers the rent restriction rules for housing benefit. The rent restriction rules for the universal credit housing costs element are covered in Chapter 6.

Key facts
- If you are a private tenant, your housing benefit (HB) may be based on a rent lower than the one you are liable to pay if it is restricted under one of three rent restriction schemes.
- If you are a local authority or housing association tenant and your home has more bedrooms than the rules allow, the rent used to calculate your HB may be restricted under the social sector rent restriction rules (often called the 'bedroom tax'). In exceptional cases, some housing association tenants have their rent restricted under one of the schemes that apply to private tenants.
- If you are entitled to HB and your rent is restricted, you may be able to get discretionary housing payments from your local authority to help with any shortfall.

1. How to use this chapter

Your housing benefit (HB) might not cover the full amount of rent you have to pay. This is because, in many cases, the local authority must reduce the rent it uses to calculate your HB by applying what is known as a 'rent restriction'. The result is referred to in this *Handbook* as your 'maximum rent'.

> **How does 'maximum rent' affect your housing benefit calculation?**
> The maximum amount of HB you can get (your 'maximum HB') is your 'eligible rent', minus any non-dependant deductions that must be made. If any of the rent restriction schemes apply, your 'eligible rent' is your 'maximum rent'. See p192 for further information.

There are four possible rent restriction schemes:
- the local housing allowance rules;
- the social sector rules, sometimes called the 'bedroom tax';
- the rules for those living in hostels, houseboats, mobile homes or caravans or who are boarders;
- the rules that apply if you live in what is known as 'exempt accommodation' or you are an 'exempt claimant'.

The scheme that applies to you depends on the type of tenancy you have and the type of accommodation you occupy. You should therefore do the following.
- **Step one:** work out which rent restriction scheme, if any, applies to you. **Note:** your tenancy may be excluded from some or all of the schemes (see below);
- **Step two:** go to the relevant section in this chapter for the rules that affect your HB award.

For the common rules that apply to more than one scheme, see p392. To find out if you can get a rent restriction delayed, see p396, or challenge a rent restriction decision, see p397.

Which rent restriction rules apply

There are four possible rent restriction schemes, depending on the type of tenancy you have and the type of accommodation you occupy.

To check which scheme applies to you, if:
- you are a private tenant, see p367;
- you are a housing association tenant, see p367
- you are a local authority tenant, see p368.

Note: if you are a private or housing association tenant, your tenancy may be excluded from some or all of the rent restriction schemes (see p366). If none of the rent restriction schemes apply to you, see p368.

Part 4: General rules for other means-tested benefits
Chapter 19: Housing benefit rent restrictions
1. How to use this chapter

> *Are you thinking of moving home or will there be a break in your claim?*
> If you are getting HB and are considering a move, or there will be a break in your claim and
> you can still claim HB (see p173), check whether the rent restriction rules that will apply in
> your new situation will be more or less favourable to you. In some cases, you can check the
> rent figure that will be used to calculate your HB. **Note:** if there is a break in your claim,
> you may have to claim universal credit instead of HB for help with your rent.

When your tenancy is excluded

If you are a private or housing association tenant, you may have what is known as
an 'excluded tenancy'. If you have one and you are:

- a private tenant, none of the rent restriction schemes apply to you;
- a housing association tenant, none of the rent restriction schemes apply to
  you unless your landlord is a registered housing association (see below for
  what counts). If this is the case, the social sector rules on p375 may apply.

The following are excluded tenancies.[1]

- A regulated or protected tenancy – ie, a tenancy entered into before 15 January
  1989 or, in Scotland, 2 January 1989.
- A tenancy in an approved bail or probation hostel. However, if you are required
  to live in such a hostel, you cannot qualify for HB towards the rent you pay to
  the hostel (see p180).
- A former local authority or new town letting which has been transferred to a
  new owner. Your tenancy is *not* excluded if there has been a rent increase since
  the transfer and:
  - the local authority considers your rent to be unreasonably high; *or*
  - if the transfer took place before 7 October 2002, the local authority considers
    your accommodation to be unreasonably large.
  If your tenancy is not excluded, the rules that apply to hostels, houseboats,
  mobile homes, caravans and boarders on p381 apply, even if you do not live in
  one of those types of accommodation.
- A shared ownership tenancy – ie, you are buying part of your home and renting
  the rest. However, your tenancy is *not* excluded if your shared ownership
  tenancy is with a private landlord, in which case the local housing allowance
  rules on p368 apply.
- A letting by a registered housing association (see p367), by a county council (if
  you live in a caravan or mobile home provided on a travellers' site[2]) or in a
  caravan, mobile home or houseboat (if you are also liable to make payments to
  a local authority – eg, for site or mooring fees). Your tenancy is *not* excluded if:
  - the local authority considers your rent to be unreasonably high; *or*
  - you are getting pension-age HB (see p187) and the local authority considers
    your accommodation to be unreasonably large.

If your tenancy is not excluded, the rules that apply to hostels, houseboats, mobile homes, caravans and boarders on p381 apply, even if you do not live in one of those types of accommodation.

Registered housing association

A 'registered housing association' is a private registered provider of social housing (in England), a housing association registered in a register maintained by the Welsh Ministers (in Wales), a housing association registered by the Scottish Ministers (in Scotland) or a registered social landlord (in Wales or Scotland).[3] **Note:** in England, if the provider is profit making, a tenancy is only an excluded tenancy if the housing is available at a rent below the market rate.

If you are a private tenant

If you are a private tenant, and your tenancy is not excluded (see p366), in most cases, the local housing allowance rules on p368 apply. However, there are exceptions. If:

- you live in a specified type of temporary or supported accommodation (called 'exempt accommodation' – see p387) or you have you been getting HB since 1 January 1996 usually for the same property, the old scheme rules on p387 apply; *or*
- your rent includes board and attendance, or you live in a hostel, houseboat, mobile home or caravan, the rules that use rent officer determinations on p381 apply. These rules *may* also apply in other situations if the local authority considers your rent to be unreasonably high or your accommodation to be unreasonably large.

If you are a housing association tenant

If you are a housing association tenant, and your tenancy is not excluded (see p366), in most cases, if neither you nor your partner are at least pension age (see p766), the social sector rules (often called the 'bedroom tax') on p375 apply. However, there are exceptions. If:

- you live in a specified type of temporary or supported accommodation (called 'exempt accommodation' – see p387) or you have been getting HB since 1 January 1996 usually for the same property, the old scheme rules on p387 apply; *or*
- your rent includes board and attendance, or you live in a hostel, houseboat, mobile home or caravan, the rules that use rent officer determinations on p381 apply. These rules *may* also apply in other situations if the local authority considers your rent to be unreasonably high or your accommodation to be unreasonably large; *or*
- if your landlord is not a registered social landlord (in Wales or Scotland) or a registered provider of social housing (in England), the local housing allowance

Part 4: General rules for other means-tested benefits
Chapter 19: Housing benefit rent restrictions
2. The local housing allowance rules

rules apply (see below). For information about registered providers of social housing in England, see gov.uk/guidance/lists-of-registered-social-housing-providers-and-regulatory-judgements. For information about registered social landlords in Wales, see gov.wales/registered-social-landlords and in Scotland, see housingregulator.gov.scot.

If you are a local authority tenant

If you are a local authority tenant, and you are getting working-age HB, not pension-age HB (see p187), the social sector rules on p375 (often called the 'bedroom tax') usually apply. This is the case if both you and your partner are below pension age (see p766). If only one of you is below that age (ie, you are a member of a mixed-age couple), see p375. **Note:** if you are at least pension age and you have been getting HB since 1 January 1996 usually for the same property, in exceptional cases, the old scheme rules on p387 may apply.

If none of the rent restriction rules apply

Even if none of the rent restriction rules apply to you, the local authority still has discretion to decrease the amount of rent it uses to calculate your HB to an amount it considers 'appropriate'.[4] It should have evidence which justifies doing so and must use its discretion properly. All the circumstances should be taken into account, including your health and financial circumstances, the special housing-related needs of anyone occupying your home and whether alternative accommodation is available to HB claimants.[5] Local authorities should rarely use their powers to decrease your HB in this way. If your HB is reduced under this rule, apply for a revision or appeal (see Chapters 56 and 57).

Has the local authority used rent officer determinations to calculate your HB?
The local authority may say that it can use its discretion to decrease the amount of rent used to calculate your HB, even though it has already restricted your rent under the rules that use rent officer determinations (see p381).[6] If this happens, argue that the local authority should only use its discretion in this way if none of the rent restriction rules apply.[7]

2. **The local housing allowance rules**

If the local housing allowance rules apply, they determine the amount of rent used to calculate your housing benefit (HB) – called your 'maximum rent' in this *Handbook*.[8] Your maximum rent may be lower than the rent you must pay to your landlord. **Note:** these rules do *not* apply if you have an excluded tenancy (see p366).

The local housing allowance rules apply if you move to a new home while you are entitled to HB or you make a new claim for HB (if you still can), and you are:[9]

- a private tenant. This includes if you have a shared ownership tenancy with a private landlord. **Note:** there are exceptions and other rules may instead apply (see p367);

- a housing association tenant, but only if your landlord is *not* a registered social landlord (in Wales or Scotland) or a registered provider of social housing (in England). **Note:** if this is not the case, other rules may instead apply (see p367).

Note: if your dwelling has been adapted under a 'sanctuary scheme' and the social sector rules apply, your rent cannot be restricted (see p376). There is no similar exclusion if the local housing allowance rules apply.

How your rent is restricted

The local housing allowance rules restrict your rent for HB purposes. This is your **'maximum rent'** and is the amount of rent used to calculate your HB. Your maximum rent is the lower of:[10]

- the local housing allowance that applies to you (see p370); *or*
- your 'cap rent'.

Cap rent

Your **'cap rent'** is the rent you are liable (or treated as liable) to pay for your home (including service charges).[11] If you share your accommodation with anyone other than your partner and you are jointly liable for the rent with her/him, the local authority apportions the cap rent between you. **Note:** the local authority may say it has general discretion to decrease your cap rent to an amount it considers appropriate under the rules for those where none of the rent restriction rules apply (see p368).[12]

Note:
- If you share accommodation and are jointly liable for the rent (eg, you are joint tenants) with someone other than your partner (or a child included in your claim), and you are not members of the same household, your maximum rent is based on the local housing allowance that applies to you personally, subject to the cap rent rule – ie, it is based on your share of the rent.
- A rent restriction can be delayed in specified circumstances (see p396).
- You may be able to challenge a rent restriction (see p397).

Examples
Osian, aged 28, shares a privately rented house with four friends. Osian gets HB. The appropriate local housing allowance for him is that for one-bedroom shared accommodation: £80 a week. The rent for the house is £300 a week. His cap rent is £60 (£300 ÷ 5). This is lower than the local housing allowance, so Osian's maximum rent is £60 a week.

Part 4: General rules for other means-tested benefits
Chapter 19: Housing benefit rent restrictions
2. The local housing allowance rules

> Sasha and her partner have a joint tenancy of a private flat. Sasha's cousin lodges with them. Sasha gets HB. The appropriate local housing allowance for her is that for two-bedroom accommodation: £150 a week. The rent for the flat is £210 a week. This is her cap rent. This is higher than the local housing allowance, so Sasha's maximum rent is £150 a week.

Which local housing allowance applies

The local housing allowance that applies to you depends on the area in which you live and the category of dwelling that applies to you (see p372). The category of dwelling is based on the number of bedrooms you are allowed under the rules, known as the '**size criteria**'.

The number of bedrooms you are allowed

You are allowed (up to a maximum of four bedrooms):[13]
*   one bedroom for each of the following 'occupiers', each coming only into the first category that is applicable:
    *   a couple (see p303 for who counts);
    *   a 'member of a couple who cannot share a bedroom' (see p394 for who counts);
    *   the partner of a 'member of a couple who cannot share a bedroom';[14]
    *   a person aged 16 or over;
    *   a 'child who cannot share a bedroom' (see p395 for who counts);
    *   two children under 16 of the same sex;
    *   two children under 10;
    *   a child under 16; *and*
*   one or two additional bedrooms in specified situations (see p371).

Note: you are only allowed a bedroom for a 'child who cannot share a bedroom' or a 'member of a couple who cannot share a bedroom' if you have a bedroom in your home that is additional to those you would be allowed if the child or the member of the couple *were* able to share a bedroom. 'Bedroom' is not defined, but see p393 for what may count.

You cannot argue that a category is not applicable if there is no room in your home large enough to accommodate the people in that category.[15]

Occupiers

For the local housing allowance rules, an '**occupier**' is:[16]
*   you and anyone else living in the dwelling who the local authority is satisfied occupies your dwelling as a home (other than a joint tenant who is not a member of your household – see p312); *and*

- your (or your partner's) son, daughter, stepson or stepdaughter who is in the armed forces deployed on operations who was your non-dependant (see p198) before being deployed, provided s/he intends to return home.

'Occupiers' therefore include not only your partner and children, but also other people – eg, a joint tenant who is a member of your household, a non-dependant or a live-in carer.[17] A foster child or child placed with you for adoption under specified provisions does not count as an occupier.[18] However, you may qualify for an additional bedroom if you or your partner are a 'qualifying parent or carer' or if the child is a 'person who requires overnight care' (see below).

You can argue that someone is an 'occupier' if s/he normally lives with you, but is temporarily away.[19] However, if you share the care of a child, the child is considered to be occupying the home of the person with whom s/he normally lives.[20] **Note:** the local authority may use the temporary absence rules described on p181 to decide whether someone counts as occupying your home.

Examples

Kevin and Ally have two sons, both under age 10. Ally's nephew, aged 20, lives with them. Kevin gets HB. He is allowed three bedrooms under the rules: one for Kevin and Ally, one for the two sons and one for the nephew.

Julian, aged 40, lives with his father in the same household. They are joint tenants. He is allowed two bedrooms under the rules, even though he is getting HB as a single person.

Additional bedrooms

You are allowed one additional bedroom in the following situations. If both apply, you are allowed two additional bedrooms.[21]

- **Non-resident carers.** If you (or your partner), a person who occupies your dwelling as a home (eg, your child or a non-dependant) or a child or young person in respect of whom you or your partner are a 'qualifying parent or carer' (eg, your foster child) are a 'person who requires overnight care' (see p395 for who counts), you are allowed one additional bedroom for a non-resident carer. Even if more than one person requires overnight care, only one additional bedroom is allowed.
- **Fostering, adoption and kinship carers.** If you (or your partner) are a 'qualifying parent or carer' (ie, certain foster parents and people with whom a child has been placed for adoption – see p396 for who counts), you are allowed one additional bedroom. Even if you (or your partner) have more than one foster child or child placed with you for adoption, only one additional bedroom is allowed.

Part 4: General rules for other means-tested benefits
Chapter 19: Housing benefit rent restrictions
2. The local housing allowance rules

4

Note:
- The rules that allow additional bedrooms were amended in the past following test cases. If you think you may have lost out, see pp98–99 of the 2020/21 edition of this *Handbook*.
- If you need more bedrooms than are allowed under the rules above, seek advice.
- Even if your dwelling has been adapted under a 'sanctuary scheme', you are not allowed additional rooms under the local housing allowance rules. However, if the social sector rules apply, your rent cannot be restricted (see p376).

Example
Lewis is the foster parent of two children. His non-dependent son, aged 24, lives with him. He is allowed three bedrooms under the rules: one for Lewis, one for his son and one additional room because he is a 'qualifying parent or carer'.

Categories of dwelling

The category of dwelling that applies to you depends on how many bedrooms you are allowed under the rules (see p370) and whether or not you are living in shared accommodation.

One-bedroom shared accommodation

Unless you (or your partner) qualify for a severe disability premium, the one-bedroom shared accommodation category of dwelling applies if you are only allowed one bedroom under the rules and:[22]
- you are under 35 and are a 'young individual' — see p393 for who counts (even if you do not live in shared accommodation). This category does not apply if you have a non-dependant living with you (see p198); *or*
- you (and your partner) live in shared accommodation. You count as living in shared accommodation if you do not have the exclusive use of at least two rooms, or the exclusive use of one room as well as the exclusive use of a bathroom, a toilet and a kitchen or facilities for cooking. This category does not apply if:[23]
  – you (or your partner) are under the age of 25 and:
    – were provided with accommodation by the local authority under specified provisions.[24] Note: in some cases, you cannot qualify for HB if you are being, or were previously, looked after by a local authority (see p934); *or*
    – were looked after by (in the care of), or under the supervision of, a local authority under specific legal provisions after you turned 16; *or*
    – ceased to be subject to a compulsory supervision order under section 83 of the Children's Hearings (Scotland) Act 2011 which had continued after you turned 16. **Note:** there are exceptions.

Note:

- If you are only allowed one bedroom under the rules and the shared accommodation category of dwelling does not apply to you, the DWP says that your HB should be based on the local housing allowance for one-bedroom self-contained accommodation.[25] This applies even if you live in shared accommodation.
- The government says that, from October 2022, this category of dwelling will also not apply to people who have experienced domestic abuse or modern slavery. See AskCPAG and CPAG's *Welfare Rights Bulletin* for updates.

One-bedroom self-contained accommodation

The one-bedroom self-contained accommodation category of dwelling applies if you are allowed one bedroom under the rules (see p370).[26] You must have:

- the exclusive use of at least two rooms; *or*
- the exclusive use of one room as well as the exclusive use of a bathroom, a toilet and a kitchen or facilities for cooking.

Note: this category does not apply to you if you are a 'young individual' (see p393 for who counts), you do not have a non-dependant living with you and you do not qualify for the severe disability premium. Instead, the one-bedroom shared accommodation category applies.

You have the 'exclusive use' of a room if you have the legal right to exclude others from the room.[27]

> **Room**
>
> '**Room**' means a bedroom or a 'room suitable for living in', other than one you share with someone who is not a member of your household, a non-dependant or someone who pays rent to you or your partner.[28]

Dwellings with two or more bedrooms

If you are allowed more than one bedroom under the rules, the category of dwelling that applies is that for a dwelling with the number of bedrooms you are allowed (see p370), up to a maximum of four.[29] So this category applies, for example, if you are a lone parent or a member of a couple with children, you have a non-dependant living with you, you are a 'person who requires overnight care', someone who lives with you is a 'member of a couple who cannot share a bedroom', you are a 'qualifying parent or carer', or you are a joint tenant with someone who is a member of your household.

Local housing allowance rates

Local housing allowances for each category of dwelling are usually set by the rent officer annually on the last working day of January, to take effect the following

Part 4: General rules for other means-tested benefits
Chapter 19: Housing benefit rent restrictions
2. The local housing allowance rules

April. From April 2022 to April 2023, the local housing allowance is the allowance set by the rent officer on 31 March 2020. This was the lowest of two figures:[30]

- the amount of rent at the 30th percentile point of local market rents for assured tenancies for each category of dwelling in what is known as a 'broad rental market area'; or
- for the specified categories of dwelling below, the amount listed.

Category of dwelling	Maximum local housing allowance
One-bedroom shared accommodation	£295.49
One-bedroom self-contained accommodation	£295.49
Two-bedroom accommodation	£365.92
Three-bedroom accommodation	£441.86
Four-bedroom accommodation	£593.75

See lha-direct.voa.gov.uk for the current rates in your area.

How long the restriction applies

The amount of your restricted rent (your 'maximum rent') is based on the local housing allowance that applies to you at the time your award of HB is assessed. Your HB is based on this amount until the next time the local authority assesses your award.[31] This is usually only annually (on 1 April), even if the amount of the local housing allowance changes. When the local authority reassesses your award, it uses the local housing allowance that then applies. Some changes of circumstance can lead to an earlier reassessment – ie, if:[32]

- there is a change in the category of dwelling that applies to you (see p372) – ie, you are allowed more or fewer bedrooms because, for instance, someone has moved in with you or has moved out, or your child has reached age 16 and is allowed her/his own bedroom; or
- your partner or a child included in your claim (see p307) (or a relative of yours or your partner who lives in the same accommodation as you without a separate right to do so) dies. **Note:** see p396 to find out if a restriction can be delayed; or
- there is a change that affects the amount of your cap rent (see p369) – eg, the rent you pay goes up or down; or
- you move to a new home.

Your maximum rent is then based on the local housing allowance that applies on the date of the change.[33]

Example

Nala rents a three-bedroom house from a private landlord. She pays £170 a week rent. This is her cap rent. She has one son, aged seven. The local housing allowance that applies is that for a dwelling with two bedrooms. When her HB award is assessed, this is £105. Nala's maximum rent is £105 because this is lower than her cap rent.

Nala's sister comes to live with her. As there has been a change in the category of dwelling that applies to Nala (this is now a dwelling with three bedrooms), the local authority reassesses her HB award. The local housing allowance for a dwelling with three bedrooms is now £158. Nala's maximum rent is now £158 because this is still lower than her cap rent.

If you are considering renting accommodation

If you are renting accommodation privately, you are getting HB and the local housing allowance rules apply, you may wish to find out the rent figure that will be used when your HB award is reassessed (usually annually). If you are considering renting accommodation privately, and you can still make a new claim for HB (see p173), you may want to find out the rent figure that will be used to calculate it.

Check which category of dwelling applies to you (see p372) and work out the local housing allowance that applies to you. Then check the amount of that local housing allowance in your area at lha-direct.voa.gov.uk.

3. The social sector rules: the 'bedroom tax'

If the social sector rules apply, they determine the amount of rent used to calculate your housing benefit (HB) – called your 'maximum rent' in this *Handbook*.[34] Your maximum rent may be lower than the rent you must pay.

The social sector rules usually apply if you are a local authority or housing association tenant and you are living in accommodation that has more bedrooms than you are allowed under the rules (known as the 'size criteria' – see p378).[35] The social sector rules are commonly referred to as the 'bedroom tax', or by the DWP as the 'removal of the spare room subsidy' or the 'under-occupation charge'.

Note: there are exceptions. Your rent *cannot* be restricted under the social sector rules if:[36]

- you are getting pension-age HB (see p187); *or*
- you are getting working-age HB (see p187), and if you are a member of a couple, you or your partner are at least pension age – ie, you are a member of a mixed-age couple (but see below); *or*
- any of the other rent restriction rules described in this chapter apply. See p368, p381 and p387; *or*

Part 4: General rules for other means-tested benefits
Chapter 19: Housing benefit rent restrictions
3. The social sector rules: the 'bedroom tax'

- you are a housing association tenant and your tenancy is one of the excluded tenancies listed on p366 (other than the last one), unless your landlord is a registered housing association (see p367); or
- you live in a dwelling adapted for you under a 'sanctuary scheme' (see below); or
- you have a shared ownership tenancy – ie, you are buying part of your home and renting the rest; or
- your rent is for mooring charges for a houseboat or for identifiable payments for caravan or mobile home site fees;[37] or
- you live in specified types of temporary accommodation for homeless people provided by a local authority or a registered housing association (see p367).

Are you a member of a mixed-age couple?

The local authority may say that your rent can be restricted under the social sector rules if:[38]

– you are getting working-age HB (see p187) as a member of a mixed-age couple and you are at least pension age; and

– you are prevented from claiming universal credit (UC) because you (or your partner) are a frontier worker (see p173); and

– you would usually be unable to qualify for HB but are treated as being under pension age for the assessment of your award of HB.

Try to argue that this rule simply allows your award of HB to continue – ie, that you are only treated as under pension age for this purpose, and that, because you are actually at least pension age, the exception from the social sector rules applies.

Your rent *cannot* be restricted under the social sector rules if you live in a dwelling adapted for you under a **'sanctuary scheme'** – ie, a scheme that provides enhanced security measures to enable households at risk of domestic abuse to remain safely in their homes. This applies if:[39]

- the scheme is operated by a local authority, a registered social landlord (in Wales or Scotland) or a registered provider of social housing (in England). For information about registered providers of social housing in England, see gov.uk/guidance/lists-of-registered-social-housing-providers-and-regulatory-judgements. For details about registered social landlords in Wales, see gov.wales/registered-social-landlords and, for the details in Scotland, see housingregulator.gov.scot; and
- you or a member of your household have experienced domestic abuse (including threats of domestic abuse) by a partner, a former partner or a relative; and
- you (or the member of your household) are not living at the same address as the partner, former partner or relative unless that person is a dependant of a member of your household; and

• you provide relevant evidence from a healthcare professional, a police officer, a registered social worker, an employer or trade union representative or a public, voluntary or charitable body.

For these purposes, 'relative' means the victim's (or her/his partner's or former partner's) father, mother, stepfather, stepmother, son, daughter, stepson, stepdaughter, grandmother, grandfather, grandson or granddaughter. It also includes the victim's (or the victim's partner's or former partner's) brother, sister, uncle, aunt, niece, nephew or first cousin (whether of the full blood or of the half blood or by marriage or civil partnership).

How your rent is restricted

If you are the only person liable for the rent for your home (or you are jointly liable, but only with your partner), your 'maximum rent' is determined under the following steps.[40] **Note:** if you are jointly liable for your rent with someone other than your partner (ie, with a joint tenant) the rules are different (see p378).

• **Step one:** establish the number of bedrooms in your home. 'Bedroom' is not defined, but see p393 for what may count.
• **Step two:** work out how many bedrooms you are allowed under the rules for all the people who occupy your home (see p378).
• **Step three:** calculate the amount of rent that can be covered by HB. This is known as your 'eligible rent' (see p193) and is the contractual rent for the whole dwelling minus any ineligible charges – eg, for fuel or services. If the number of bedrooms in Step one is the same as or lower than the number in Step two, this is your maximum rent – ie, your rent is *not* restricted.
• **Step four:** if the number of bedrooms in Step one is more than the number in Step two, reduce the amount in Step three by:
  – 14 per cent if you have one too many bedrooms; *or*
  – 25 per cent if you have at least two too many bedrooms.
  This is your maximum rent. If it appears to the local authority that the amount in Step four is still too high to be met by HB, it has a general discretion to restrict your maximum rent further.[41]

Note:
• No matter how many bedrooms you have, if you live in a dwelling adapted for you under a 'sanctuary scheme' (see p376), your rent *cannot* be restricted under the social sector rules.
• A restriction can be delayed in specified circumstances (see p396).
• You may be able to challenge a rent restriction (see p397).

Part 4: General rules for other means-tested benefits
Chapter 19: Housing benefit rent restrictions
3. The social sector rules: the 'bedroom tax'

Example

Dawn and her partner rent a two-bedroom flat from a housing association. Their rent is £140 a week. Dawn gets HB.

Step one: there are two bedrooms in their home.

Step two: they are only allowed one bedroom under the rules (see below).

Step three: the amount of the rent that can be covered by HB (the 'eligible rent') is £140 a week.

Step four: because they have one more bedroom than the number allowed in Step two, the amount in Step three is reduced by 14 per cent.

14% x £140 = £19.60. Dawn's maximum rent is restricted to £120.40 (£140 – £19.60).

If you are a joint tenant

If you (and your partner) are liable for the rent with at least one other person (eg, you are a joint tenant with someone other than your partner), the local authority apportions the amount in Step three or Step four (as the case may be) between you, taking all the circumstances into account, including the number of people and the proportion of rent each pays.[42]

Example

Bella and Jake are joint tenants of a four-bedroom council house. They are not a couple. Their rent is £210 a week. Bella pays £140 and Jake pays £70. Bella is an approved foster parent. Jake gets HB.

Step one: the number of bedrooms in Jake's home is four.

Step two: he is allowed three bedrooms under the rules (see below): one for himself, one for Bella and an additional room because Bella counts as a 'qualifying parent or carer'.

Step three: the amount of the rent that can be covered by HB (the 'eligible rent') is £210.

Step four: because Jake has one more bedroom than the number allowed in Step two, the amount in Step three is reduced by 14 per cent. 14% x £210 = £29.40

£210 – £29.40 = £180.60

Jake pays one-third of the rent, and the local authority apportions the maximum rent accordingly. One-third of £180.60 = £60.20

Jake's maximum rent is £60.20.

Note: if Bella is also getting HB, her maximum rent would be two-thirds of £180.60 = £120.40. If Bella is getting UC, see p109.

The number of bedrooms you are allowed

Under the rules (the 'size criteria'), you are allowed:[43]

* one bedroom for each of the following 'occupiers', each coming only into the first category that is applicable:
  - a couple (see p303 for who counts);

- a 'member of a couple who cannot share a bedroom' (see p394 for who counts);
- the partner of a 'member of a couple who cannot share a bedroom';[44]
- a person aged 16 or over;
- a 'child who cannot share a bedroom' (see p395 for who counts);
- two children under 16 of the same sex;
- two children under 10;
- a child under 16; *and*
- one or more additional bedrooms in specified circumstances (see below).

You cannot argue that a category is not applicable if there is no room in your home large enough to accommodate the people in that category.[45]

Unlike the local housing allowance rules, there is no maximum number of bedrooms.

Occupiers

For the social sector rules, an **'occupier'** is anyone who the local authority is satisfied occupies your dwelling as a home.[46] 'Occupiers' therefore include not only you and your partner or children included in your claim but also other people – eg, a joint tenant, a non-dependant or a live-in carer. However, a foster child or child placed with you for adoption under specified provisions does not count as an occupier, but you may qualify for an additional bedroom if you or your partner (or another person jointly liable for the rent with you) are a 'qualifying parent or carer' or if the child is a 'person who requires overnight care' (see below).[47]

Note:

- The local authority must include a member of the armed forces deployed on operations as an occupier if s/he is your (or your partner's) son, daughter, stepson or stepdaughter who was your non-dependant (see p198) before being deployed and s/he intends to return home.[48]
- You can argue that someone counts as occupying your home if s/he normally lives with you but is temporarily away.[49] However, if you share the care of a child, the child is considered to be occupying the home of only one person – the person with whom the child normally lives.[50] **Note:** the local authority may use the temporary absence rules described on p181 to decide whether someone counts as occupying your home.

Additional bedrooms

You are allowed one additional bedroom in the following situations. If both apply, you are allowed two additional bedrooms.[51]

- **Non-resident carers.** If you (or your partner), a person who occupies your dwelling as a home (eg, your child or a non-dependant) or a child or young person in respect of whom you or your partner are a 'qualifying parent or carer'

Part 4: General rules for other means-tested benefits
Chapter 19: Housing benefit rent restrictions
3. The social sector rules: the 'bedroom tax'

(eg, your foster child) are a 'person who requires overnight care' (see p395 for who counts), you are entitled to one additional bedroom for a non-resident carer. Even if more than one person requires overnight care, only one additional bedroom is allowed.

- **Fostering, adoption and kinship carers.** If you (or your partner) are a 'qualifying parent or carer' (ie, certain foster parents and people with whom a child has been placed for adoption – see p396 for who counts), you are allowed one additional bedroom. Even if, for example, you (or your partner) have more than one foster child, only one additional bedroom is allowed.

In addition, if you are jointly liable for the rent with someone other than your partner (eg, a joint tenant), you are allowed an additional bedroom for her/him if s/he (or her/his partner) is a 'person who requires overnight care' or a 'qualifying parent or carer'.[52] You are allowed two additional bedrooms if both conditions are satisfied.

Note: the rules that allow additional bedrooms were amended in the past following test cases. If you think you may have lost out, see pp98–99 of the 2020/21 edition of this *Handbook*.

If you need more bedrooms than are allowed under the rules above, seek advice.

Examples

Jordan lives with his wife and child in a four-bedroom council house. He gets HB. Jordan gets the daily living component of personal independence payment and needs a carer to stay with him overnight. He is therefore a 'person who requires overnight care'. Jordan is allowed three bedrooms under the rules: one for himself and his wife, one for his child and one for a non-resident carer. He has one too many bedrooms and his rent is restricted.

Jin, an approved foster parent, shares a four-bedroom council house with his mother and father. His foster daughter lives with them. Jin's mother is severely disabled and requires, and receives, overnight care. Jin and his father are joint tenants. Jin gets HB. Jin is allowed two bedrooms under the rules: one for him and one for his mother and father. However, he is allowed one additional bedroom because he is a 'qualifying parent or carer' and one additional bedroom because his mother is a 'person who requires overnight care'. So he is allowed a total of four bedrooms. For the purposes of the social sector rules, he does not have too many bedrooms and his rent is not restricted.

4. Hostels, houseboats, mobile homes, caravans and boarders

If you live in certain types of accommodation, the local authority uses 'determinations' made by the rent officer (see p383) to restrict the amount of rent it uses to calculate your housing benefit (HB) – called your 'maximum rent' in this *Handbook*. These are sometimes called the local reference rent rules. Your 'maximum rent' is usually the lowest of the rent officer's determinations, even if the rent you pay is higher.[53] **Note:** these rules do not apply if you have an excluded tenancy (see p366).

These rules apply if:[54]

- you live in a hostel, houseboat, mobile home or caravan; *or*
- your rent includes board and attendance – eg, you are a boarder or live in a hotel or guest house.

In rare cases, these rules also apply if:

- your landlord is a registered housing association (see p367), or is a county council (if you live in a caravan or mobile home provided on a travellers' site[55]), or you are renting a caravan, mobile home or houseboat (and you are also liable to make payments to a local authority – eg, for the site or mooring fees). However, they only apply if the local authority considers your rent to be unreasonably high (or, in some cases, your accommodation to be unreasonably large). Otherwise, you have an 'excluded tenancy' (see p366); *or*
- your tenancy was a local authority or new town letting, but it has been transferred to a new owner. However, they only apply if there has been a rent increase since the transfer; *and*
  - the local authority considers your rent to be unreasonably high; *or*
  - if the transfer took place before 7 October 2002, the local authority considers your accommodation to be unreasonably large.

  Otherwise, you have an 'excluded tenancy' (see p366).

Note: if you have been getting HB continuously since before 7 April 2008, these rules may still apply if you live in other types of accommodation – eg, if you rent a private house or flat. See p398 of the 2019/20 edition of this *Handbook*.

How your rent is restricted

Under these rules, the local authority asks the rent officer to make determinations about the rent for your home and uses these to establish the amount of rent used to calculate your HB – called your '**maximum rent**' in this *Handbook*. The determinations include:

- a 'claim-related rent', based on the size of your accommodation and the rent you pay (see p384); *and*

Part 4: General rules for other means-tested benefits
Chapter 19: Housing benefit rent restrictions
4. Hostels, houseboats, mobile homes, caravans and boarders

- a 'local reference rent', based on average rents for specific types of accommodation in the area in which you live (see p386); *and*
- a 'single room rent', based on average rents for shared accommodation in your area (see p386).

Your maximum rent is then either:[56]
- the lowest of the claim-related rent (see p384) or the local reference rent (see p386); *or*
- if you are a 'young individual' (see p393) and it is relevant, the lowest of the single room rent (see p386) or the claim-related rent (minus any payments for meals).

Example

Meshach and Otis are a couple who rent a three-bedroom mobile home with a living room and separate dining room. They pay rent of £120 a week. The rent officer decides that the accommodation is too big and that the rent is too high, so determines a claim-related rent of £90 and a local reference rent of £80. Their maximum rent is therefore £80 a week.

Note:
- Your maximum rent only covers the rent you pay for residential accommodation.
- If you are in shared accommodation, your maximum rent can be apportioned between you and the people with whom you share.[57]
- A rent restriction can be delayed in specified circumstances (see p396).
- If you have been continuously entitled to, and in receipt of, HB for the same property since 5 October 1997, your maximum rent is the local reference rent plus half the difference between the local reference rent and the claim-related rent.[58]
- If you are considering renting accommodation, the local reference rent rules apply and you are likely to claim HB, you can apply to the local authority for a pre-tenancy determination to find out the rent that will be used to calculate it (see p387).
- The local authority is likely to say it has general discretion to decrease your maximum rent to an amount it considers appropriate (but see p368).[59]
- You may be able to challenge a rent restriction (see p397).

How long the restriction applies

Once your maximum rent is set, your HB is paid on the basis of this until the next time the local authority applies to the rent officer for determinations about the rent for your home (usually annually). However, if you negotiate with your landlord and s/he agrees a new rent which is lower than the maximum rent, your HB is recalculated using your new rent.[60]

The rent officer's determinations about your rent

In most cases, the local authority must apply to the rent officer and ask her/him to make 'determinations'. The rent officer then makes determinations about the rent for your home (see p384), comparing it with the rent for other private sector tenancies in the area. S/he also makes determinations that indicate the average rents for specific types of accommodation (see p386). **Note:** the local authority *cannot* apply to the rent officer in specified situations.[61] This means that in some cases a determination made for a previous tenant may be valid for your HB award.

When the local authority must apply to the rent officer

The local authority must apply to the rent officer if you move to a new home while you are entitled to HB, or if the last reference to the rent officer was made in respect of your home at least 52 weeks ago.[62] It must also apply if:

- there has been a specified change in circumstances since the rent officer's last determinations (see below); *or*
- you make a new claim for HB (if you still can); *or*
- your HB was being restricted under the local housing allowance rules on p368, but these no longer apply – eg, if the home you rent was sold to a housing association and the rules that use rent officer determinations now apply instead.

Specified changes in circumstances

The local authority must apply to the rent officer if there has been one of the following changes in circumstances since a rent officer's determination.[63]

- The number of occupiers has changed (except in a hostel). Argue that this should *not* apply if someone who normally lives with you is only away temporarily.[64]
- There has been a substantial change in the condition of the dwelling or the terms of the tenancy (other than a term relating to the rent).
- There has been an increase in the rent under a term of the tenancy, unless the previous determination was a significantly high, size-related or exceptionally high rent determination (see p384).[65]
- A size-related rent determination was made and a child living with you has reached the age of 10 or 16, or there has since been a change in the composition of the household – eg, someone has moved in or moved out, but not if the person is your (or your partner's) son, daughter, stepson or stepdaughter who usually lives with you, who is in the armed forces away on (or who has returned home from) operations.
- The size of accommodation you are allowed under the rules (see p384) is affected because:
  - you or your partner, a person who occupies your dwelling as a home, or a child or young person in respect of whom you or your partner are a

Part 4: General rules for other means-tested benefits
Chapter 19: Housing benefit rent restrictions
4. Hostels, houseboats, mobile homes, caravans and boarders

'qualifying parent or carer' (eg, your foster child) become, or cease to be, a 'person who requires overnight care' (see p395); *or*
- you or your partner become or cease to be a 'qualifying parent or carer' (see p396); *or*
- a child becomes, or stops being, a 'child who cannot share a bedroom' (see p395); *or*
- a person occupying your dwelling as a home becomes, or stops being, a 'member of a couple who cannot share a bedroom' (see p394).

4. The claim-related rent

The '**claim-related rent**' is the lowest of the determinations below or, if no such determination is made, the rent you are supposed to pay.[66]
- A '**significantly high rent determination**' is made if your rent is significantly higher than that paid for similar tenancies and dwellings in the immediate area around your home. It is the amount your landlord might reasonably be paid for your tenancy.[67]
- An '**exceptionally high rent determination**' is made if the rent officer considers the 'rent payable' for your home to be exceptionally high. It is the highest amount your landlord might reasonably be paid for an assured tenancy in the neighbourhood for a home that is the same size as yours (or the size you are allowed under the rules).[68]
- A '**size-related rent determination**' is made if your accommodation is larger than you are allowed under the rules. It is the amount your landlord might reasonably be paid for a similar tenancy of an appropriate size for you in the vicinity.[69] **Note:** if you are a single person under 35 and are a 'young individual' (see p393), the rent officer must also identify a single room rent (see p386).

The size of accommodation you are allowed

To work out the size of accommodation you are allowed under the rules (known as the 'size criteria'), the rent officer allows you one bedroom or 'room suitable for living in' for each of the following 'occupiers' (see p385 for who counts), each coming only into the first category for which s/he is eligible:[70]
- a couple (see p303 for who counts);
- a 'member of a couple who cannot share a bedroom' (see p394 for who counts);
- the partner of a 'member of a couple who cannot share a bedroom';[71]
- a person aged 16 or over;
- a 'child who cannot share a bedroom' (see p395 for who counts);
- two children under 16 of the same sex;
- two children under 10;
- a child under 16.

Note: you are only allowed a bedroom for a 'child who cannot share a bedroom' or a 'member of a couple who cannot share a bedroom' if you have a bedroom in your home that is additional to those you would be allowed if the child or the member of the couple *were* able to share a bedroom. 'Bedroom' is not defined, but see p393 for what may count.

You are allowed an **additional bedroom** (or 'room suitable for living in') in the following situations. If both apply, you are allowed two additional bedrooms (or rooms suitable for living in).[72]

- **Non-resident carers.** If you (or your partner), a person who occupies your dwelling as a home (eg, your child or a non-dependant) or a child or young person in respect of whom you or your partner are a 'qualifying parent or carer' (eg, your foster child) are a 'person who requires overnight care' (see p395 for who counts), you are allowed one additional room for a non-resident carer. Even if more than one person requires overnight care, only one additional room is allowed.

- **Fostering, adoption and kinship carers.** If you (or your partner) are a 'qualifying parent or carer' (see p396 for who counts), you are allowed one additional bedroom. Even if, for example, you (or your partner) have more than one foster child, only one additional room is allowed.

Note: unlike the local housing allowance rules, there is no maximum number of bedrooms.

You are also allowed the following number of **'rooms suitable for living in'** – eg, a living room or dining room.

Number of occupiers	Number of rooms
Fewer than four	One
Four to six	Two
Seven or more	Three

If any of the rooms in your home are not suitable for living in (eg, because of their size or lack of ventilation), argue that they should be ignored.

A person counts as an **'occupier'** if the local authority includes her/him on the form used to refer your tenancy to the rent officer.[73] This can include people in addition to your partner or children included in your claim – eg, a non-dependant or a live-in carer. It does not include a foster child or a child placed with you for adoption under specified provisions, but you may be entitled to an additional bedroom if you (or your partner) are a 'qualifying parent or carer' (see p396) or if the child is a 'person who requires overnight care' (see p395).[74]

Note:
- Someone also counts as an occupier if s/he is your (or your partner's) son, daughter, stepson or stepdaughter who usually lives with you and who is in the armed forces, even when s/he is deployed on operations, provided s/he intends to return home.[75]

Part 4: General rules for other means-tested benefits
Chapter 19: Housing benefit rent restrictions
4. Hostels, houseboats, mobile homes, caravans and boarders

- You can argue that someone is an occupier if s/he normally lives with you, but is temporarily away.[76] However, if you share the care of a child, the child is considered to be occupying the home of only one person – the person with whom s/he normally lives.[77] **Note:** the local authority may use the temporary absence rules described on p181 to decide whether someone counts as occupying your home.

Example
Abbie and Bradley have three children: two sons, aged 12 and 14, and a daughter, aged 17. Under the rules, they are allowed one room for themselves, one for their sons and one for their daughter – three bedrooms, as well as two other 'rooms suitable for living in'. They are therefore allowed five rooms, as well as a kitchen, bathroom and toilet.

The local reference rent and single room rent

The rent officer makes determinations that indicate the average rents for specific types of accommodation in a 'broad rental market area'. These are the following.

- The **'local reference rent'** is the mid-point of 'reasonable market rents' for assured tenancies in the broad rental market area appropriate to the size of property in which you live (or the size you are allowed – see p384).[78]
- The **'single room rent'** is the midpoint of 'reasonable market rents' for assured tenancies in the broad rental market area in which the tenant has exclusive use of one bedroom only, and other than that only shares a living room, kitchen, toilet and bathroom, and makes no payment for board and attendance.[79] **Note:** it is only used to calculate your HB if you are under 35 and are a 'young individual' (see p393 for who counts). Your 'maximum rent' (see p381) is based on the single room rent unless you qualify for a severe disability premium as part of your applicable amount or you have a non-dependant living with you (see p198).[80]

Note: the government says that, from October 2022, the shared accommodation category of dwelling under other rent restriction schemes will not apply to people who have experienced domestic abuse or modern slavery. It is not clear if this will also apply to the single room rent rules. See AskCPAG and CPAG's *Welfare Rights Bulletin* for updates.

Service charges

The local authority notifies the rent officer of the amount of rent you are supposed to pay, whether this includes service charges and the amount of the charges that can and cannot be met by HB (see p196).[81] The claim-related rent (see p384) does not include ineligible charges unless you live in one-room accommodation and the landlord provides substantial board and attendance. In this case, the claim-related rent and local reference rent (though not the single room rent) include charges for meals.[82]

If you are considering renting accommodation

If you are considering renting accommodation, the rules that use rent officer determinations apply and you are likely to claim HB, you might want to find out the rent figure that will be used to calculate it. In this case, you can apply for a **pre-tenancy determination**.[83] You can also apply if you are already receiving HB and your tenancy is due for renewal, but your tenancy agreement must have started at least 11 months before you apply.[84]

Note:

- You must apply in writing on the form approved by your local authority. Both you and your prospective landlord must sign it.[85]
- A pre-tenancy determination is usually valid for a year.[86] So, if someone else applied for a pre-tenancy determination for your accommodation in the previous 12 months, it also applies to you.
- You cannot appeal against a pre-tenancy determination. However, if you accept the tenancy and claim HB, you can ask for it to be redetermined. If you subsequently negotiate a lower rent with your landlord which is lower than your 'maximum rent', your HB is recalculated using your new rent.[87]

5. Exempt accommodation and claimants: the old scheme rules

More generous rent restriction rules (called the 'old scheme' rules in this *Handbook*) apply if you are getting housing benefit (HB) and you live in specified types of temporary or supported accommodation, known as 'exempt accommodation'. These rules can also apply if you have been getting HB since 1 January 1996, usually for the same property – ie, if you are an 'exempt claimant'. These rules are sometimes called the 'pre-January 1996 rules'.

Note: you cannot usually qualify for HB if you come under the universal credit (UC) system (see p22). However, if you live in 'exempt accommodation', the help you get with your rent for this is not provided in UC. Instead, you can claim HB for the rent you pay and the old scheme rules apply.

Exempt accommodation

The old scheme rules apply to you if you live in what is known as 'exempt accommodation', whenever you started living there – eg, even if this was recently. Your accommodation is exempt accommodation if it is:[88]

Part 4: General rules for other means-tested benefits
Chapter 19: Housing benefit rent restrictions
5. Exempt accommodation and claimants: the old scheme rules

- temporary accommodation (resettlement places) for people without a settled way of life, funded by the government; *or*
- accommodation provided by a housing association, non-metropolitan county council, registered charity or voluntary organisation and that body, or a person acting on its behalf, also provides you with care, support or supervision.[89] You must need the care, support or supervision and it must be more than a token or minimal amount.[90] Even if the care, support or supervision provided by your landlord duplicates other provisions (eg, in a local authority care plan), you can still count as living in exempt accommodation.[91] **Note:** if the person (or body) providing the care, support or supervision has a contract with the local authority to provide these, but is not providing the accommodation, the decision maker is likely to say it is not exempt accommodation.[92]

Exempt claimants: getting housing benefit since 1 January 1996

The old scheme rules also apply to you if you are what is known as an 'exempt claimant' – ie, you are a private tenant (or, in exceptional cases, a local authority or housing association tenant – see p389) and you:[93]
- have been continuously entitled to and in receipt of HB since 1 January 1996; *and*
- continue to occupy the same property as your home (except if you are forced to move because fire, flood or natural catastrophe makes it uninhabitable).

If you can still make a new claim for HB (see p173), provided that, when you make it, you are *not* someone to whom the local housing allowance rules would now apply (see p368):[94]
- breaks in your HB claim of up to four weeks are ignored; *and*
- an exemption can be transferred to you if you claim HB because:
  - an exempt claimant dies and you are a member of her/his family, or her/his relative (see p397 for who counts) occupying the same accommodation without a separate right to do so. You must continue to occupy the same property and claim within four weeks of the death; *or*
  - your partner (who was exempt) has been detained in custody and is not entitled to HB under the temporary absence rules (see p181). You must continue to occupy the same property and claim within four weeks of her/his detention; *or*
  - your partner (who was exempt) has left the dwelling and you claim within four weeks of the date s/he left.

The exemption can only be transferred if the exempt claimant was in receipt of HB at the time s/he died (or left the dwelling).[95] If it cannot be transferred, other rent restriction rules may apply when you make a new claim.

Note: if you are thinking of making any changes to your claim, check whether this would mean these rules no longer apply. They are usually more generous than the other rent restriction rules.

If you are a local authority or housing association tenant

You cannot count as an exempt claimant if you are a local authority or registered housing association tenant (see p367) unless:[96]

- you (or your partner) are at least pension age (see p766); *or*
- the old scheme rules applied to you on or before 31 March 2013 – ie, using these rules, the local authority:
  - restricted your rent; *or*
  - decided that your accommodation was too large or your rent was too high, but did not restrict your rent because the rules for those in a protected group applied (see p390), or the restriction was delayed for either of the reasons on p396.

How your rent is restricted

If the old scheme rules apply, they determine the amount of rent used to calculate your HB – called your 'maximum rent' in this *Handbook*. This amount may be lower than the rent you must pay. Your **maximum rent** is either:

- your contractual rent minus ineligible charges (see p194). It only covers the rent you pay for residential accommodation. If you are in shared accommodation, the rent is apportioned between you and the people with whom you share;[97] *or*
- if the local authority decides your rent should be restricted because your accommodation is unreasonably large (see p390) or your rent is unreasonably high (see p390), the amount it considers appropriate.[98]

If the local authority restricts your rent, it must take into account the cost of suitable alternative accommodation (see p391 for what counts) and other circumstances that are reasonably relevant to the decision – eg, pregnancy, the difficulty of finding other suitable accommodation and whether it would have to rehouse you if you had to move.[99] It should not be unduly influenced by the amount of subsidy it is paid by the government, but can take this into account when deciding on a reasonable level of rent. Your maximum rent cannot be reduced below the amount of rent payable for suitable alternative accommodation.[100]

Note:

- If you are in a protected group (see p390), your rent cannot be restricted unless suitable cheaper alternative accommodation is available and it is reasonable to expect you to move.
- A rent restriction can be delayed in some circumstances (see p396).
- You may be able to challenge a rent restriction (see p397).

Part 4: General rules for other means-tested benefits
Chapter 19: Housing benefit rent restrictions
5. Exempt accommodation and claimants: the old scheme rules

Is your accommodation unreasonably large?

Your accommodation counts as unreasonably large if it is larger than what is reasonably needed for you and anyone else who occupies the accommodation.[101] This should include whether you need additional space – eg, because you or someone who lives with you has a disability, or someone who lives elsewhere visits you regularly. When deciding whether your home is unreasonably large, the local authority must take account of suitable alternative accommodation (see p391) occupied by other households of the same size.[102]

Is your rent unreasonably high?

Your rent (including service charges and licence fees) counts as too high if it is unreasonably high for you to have to pay compared with that for suitable alternative accommodation (see p391) elsewhere.[103] In making the comparison, the local authority:

- must consider the full range of rents that could be paid for such accommodation and not just the cheapest;[104] *and*
- can consider subsidised rents (eg, by public funding) even if your rent is not subsidised.[105]

If your rent is within the range or just above it, the local authority may find it difficult to justify finding your rent to be unreasonably high.[106]

Note: when deciding whether your rent is unreasonably high, the local authority may ask a rent officer to assess what a reasonable rent for your property would be, but the figures are not binding. The local authority (not the rent officer) must decide whether your rent is unreasonably high, using different criteria from that used by the rent officer.[107]

Are you in a protected group?

Even if the local authority decides that your rent or the size of your accommodation is unreasonable, if you are in a 'protected group', your rent can only be restricted if:[108]

- suitable cheaper alternative accommodation is available to you (see p391); *and*
- it is reasonable to expect you to move (see p392).

You are in a protected group if any of the people the local authority must take into account:[109]

- are at least pension age (see p766); *or*
- satisfy any of the tests for having limited capability for work or being incapable of work (see Chapter 45);[110] *or*
- have a child (including a 'qualifying young person') living with them for whom they are responsible (see p309).

Who must the local authority take into account?

The local authority must take into account:[111]
– you; and
– your partner; and
– any child(ren), including qualifying young people, included in your claim (see p307); and
– any of your (or your partner's) relatives (see p397 for who counts) who live in the same dwelling as you without a separate right to do so.

4

Suitable alternative accommodation

'Suitable alternative accommodation' must be suitable for the age and health of all the people that the local authority must take into account, having regard to the nature of the accommodation and the facilities available.[112] The local authority must consider these factors, even if you do not raise your housing needs yourself.[113]

Your home must be compared with 'alternative accommodation'.

- It is not sufficient for the local authority simply to show that cheaper or smaller alternative accommodation exists.
- It cannot just compare homes with the same number of bedrooms. It must try to establish what other facilities are available.[114]
- It must compare your home with other properties offering the same security of tenure – eg, if you have an assured tenancy, the local authority cannot rely on comparisons with accommodation that is let on an assured shorthold tenancy, or with council or housing association properties.[115]
- It does not have to exclude properties which you cannot take because the landlord wants a deposit that you cannot afford.[116] However, if you are in a 'protected group', you might be able to argue that the accommodation is not available to you (see p390).
- It should not make comparisons with other parts of the country where accommodation costs differ widely from local ones, but it may compare your property with one in a less expensive area within the same city.[117]

Is suitable cheaper alternative accommodation available?

Suitable cheaper alternative accommodation is only 'available' if the local authority proves that it exists and is available to you. It must:

- have sufficient evidence to show there is an active housing market with accommodation of a suitable type, rent and location for you, but it does not need to refer to specific properties;[118] and
- take into account personal factors, such as whether you can afford to pay a deposit.[119] The local authority may produce a list of properties that it says are available to you. If they are not available because of your personal circumstances, try to show why.[120]

Part 4: General rules for other means-tested benefits
Chapter 19: Housing benefit rent restrictions
6. Common rules

Is it reasonable to expect you to move?

In deciding whether it is reasonable to expect you to move, the local authority must take into account the effects of a move on:[121]

- your ability to retain your job; *and*
- the education of any child or young person living with you. In considering this, the local authority must justify any decision that it is reasonable to make the child travel to, or move, school.[122]

The local authority may say that it does not need to consider any other factors, such as your health.[123] However, if there are good reasons why you cannot move other than those listed above, try to argue that alternative accommodation cannot be suitable.[124]

If your rent increases

If your landlord increases your rent while you are entitled to HB, the local authority cannot increase the amount of your rent that can be covered by HB (your 'eligible rent' – see p193) by the full amount of the increase if it decides that the increase is:[125]

- unreasonably high compared with increases in suitable alternative accommodation (see p391 for what counts). The local authority must consider the amount of the increase, as well as the amount of your previous rent and what your rent will be, and compare it with the rent in the suitable alternative accommodation.[126] It should also consider, for example, the quality of the accommodation, your age and state of health, whether you would have to move if the increase is not met and how a move would affect you;[127] *or*
- unreasonable because there has been an increase within the preceding 12 months.

If the local authority considers a rent increase to be unreasonable, it may refuse to meet all of that increase or meet only so much of it as it considers appropriate. If your rent has been increased for the second time in under 12 months, but is still below the market level for suitable alternative accommodation, or the increase reflects improvements made to your accommodation, argue for the full amount to be allowed.

6. **Common rules**

There are some terms that are the same for some or all of the rent restriction rules. These are covered in this section and are referred to above where relevant.

Young individuals

If you are a 'young individual', your maximum rent is based on the local housing allowance for one-bedroom shared accommodation (under the local housing allowance rules) or the single room rent (under the rules for hostels, houseboats, mobile homes, caravans and boarders). In general, you count as a 'young individual' if you are a single claimant under 35, but there are exceptions. You do *not* count as a young individual if:[128]

- your landlord is a registered housing association (see p367); *or*
- you are under the age of 25 and:
  - were looked after by (in the care of), or under the supervision of, a local authority under specific legal provisions after you turned 16 or were provided with accommodation by the local authority under specific provisions; *or*
  - ceased to be subject to a compulsory supervision order under section 83 of the Children's Hearings (Scotland) Act 2011 which had continued after you turned 16. **Note:** there are exceptions; *or*
- you are a 'person who requires overnight care' (see p395 for who counts); *or*
- you are a 'qualifying parent or carer' (see p396 for who counts); *or*
- you are at least 16 but under 35 and have lived in one or more hostels for homeless people for three months or more (this does not have to be continuous) and while living in such a hostel accepted support services to assist you in being rehabilitated or resettled in the community; *or*
- you are at least 25 but under 35 and are an offender subject to specific multi-agency public protection management arrangements. It is understood that this applies if you are a level 2 or 3 offender.[129]

Note: the government says that, from October 2022, the shared accommodation category of dwelling under the local housing allowance rules will not apply to people who have experienced domestic abuse or modern slavery. It is not clear if this will also apply to the single room rent rules. See AskCPAG and CPAG's *Welfare Rights Bulletin* for updates.

What counts as a bedroom

When working out the number of bedrooms you are allowed under the rules, you may need to consider what counts as a bedroom. For example, you may need to argue that a room is a bedroom, or it may be more advantageous for you to argue that a room is not a bedroom.

'Bedroom' is not defined in the rules. It is the ordinary meaning of the word that is relevant. It could be, for example, a lounge or living room, provided it contains a bed or is used for sleeping.[130]

The starting point is whether the room can be used as a bedroom – ie, a room is a bedroom if it is furnished and can be used for sleeping in. How a property is described by the landlord (eg, as a two- or three-bedroom house) or whether a

Part 4: General rules for other means-tested benefits
Chapter 19: Housing benefit rent restrictions
6. Common rules

room is designated as a bedroom may be relevant. However, the basis on which your rent is charged (eg, if your flat has two bedrooms but your landlord only charges the rent for a one-bedroom flat) is not relevant.[131]

You may want to argue that the local authority should not count a room in your home as a bedroom and therefore that your housing benefit should not be reduced (or reduced as much) under the rent restriction rules. In deciding whether a room is a bedroom, the local authority should, for example, take into account:[132]

- the size of the room (the dimensions and height) – eg, whether it can accommodate a single bed and somewhere to store clothes and whether it has a flat surface on which to place things safely, such as a glass of water, and whether there is space to dress and undress. If a room is too small, provide a measured plan and photographs if you can; *and*
- access to the room and whether it has adequate natural and electric lighting, heating, ventilation and privacy; *and*
- whether the room is safe to sleep in – eg, if it is contaminated with asbestos.

Suggest your personal use of the room should also be taken into account (eg, if you use the room to store equipment you need because of a severe disability), as well as whether your home has been converted or adapted – eg, if two small bedrooms have been converted into one big bedroom, or if a bedroom has been redesignated. However, the local authority is likely to say that in deciding how many bedrooms there are in your home:

- it is the classification and description of the property when it is empty that is relevant and that the classification can only be changed if the property has been structurally altered with the approval of your landlord;[133]
- even if your home could be used in more than one way (eg, as either a one- or two-bedroom property), the local authority can use the way your landlord designates the property to determine how many bedrooms it has.[134]

Couples who cannot share a bedroom

If you and your partner, or the members of any couple occupying your dwelling as a home (eg, your non-dependants), cannot share a bedroom, you are allowed an additional room under the size criteria. To count as a 'couple who cannot share a bedroom':[135]

- the person who cannot share must be getting the higher rate of attendance allowance (AA), the middle or highest rate of disability living allowance (DLA)/ child disability payment (CDP) care component, the daily living component of personal independence payment (PIP)/adult disability payment (ADP) or armed forces independence payment; *and*
- the local authority must be satisfied that because of her/his disability, the person cannot reasonably share a bedroom with the other member of the couple.

Note:
- Under the local housing allowance rules and the rules that use rent officer determinations, you are only allowed an additional room if you have a bedroom in your home additional to those you would be allowed if the couple were able to share a bedroom (see p370 and p384).
- Before 1 April 2017, a bedroom might not have been allowed (when it should have been) for a disabled member of a couple who cannot share a bedroom. You can still apply for a revision on grounds of official error if you were affected and think you should have been allowed an additional bedroom.[136]

Child who cannot share a bedroom

If a child who cannot share a bedroom is living in your home, you are allowed an additional room for her/him under the size criteria. To count as a 'child who cannot share a bedroom':[137]
- the child must be under 16 and must be entitled to the middle or highest rate of DLA/CDP care component, whether or not it is being paid; *and*
- the local authority must be satisfied that because of her/his disability, the child cannot reasonably share a bedroom with another child under 16.

Note:
- Under the local housing allowance rules and the rules that use rent officer determinations, you are only allowed an additional room if you have a bedroom in your home additional to those you would be allowed if the child were able to share a bedroom (see p370 and p384).
- Before 4 December 2013, a bedroom might not have been allowed (when it should have been) for a severely disabled child who cannot share a bedroom. You can still apply for a revision on grounds of official error if you were affected and think you should have been allowed a bedroom for a disabled child.[138]

Person who requires overnight care

If you (or your partner), a person who occupies your dwelling as a home (eg, your child or a non-dependant) or a child or young person in respect of whom you or your partner are a 'qualifying parent or carer' (eg, your foster child) are a 'person who requires overnight care', you are allowed an additional room under the size criteria. Under the social sector rules, you are also allowed an additional bedroom for someone who is jointly liable for the rent with you if s/he (or her/his partner) is a 'person who requires overnight care' (see p380).

A person counts as a 'person who requires overnight care' if:[139]
- s/he is getting AA, the middle or highest rate of DLA/CDP care component, the daily living component of PIP/ADP or armed forces independence payment; *or*

Part 4: General rules for other means-tested benefits
Chapter 19: Housing benefit rent restrictions
7. Delaying a rent restriction

• s/he has (or if the person is a child, you have) provided the local authority with sufficient certificates, documents, information or evidence to satisfy it that overnight care is required.

In addition, arrangements must have been made for one or more people who do not live with you to provide overnight care and to stay overnight regularly in your home for this purpose. You must satisfy the local authority that this care is reasonably required. The carer does not necessarily have to stay overnight on the majority of nights, but the care must be needed often and steadily enough that a bedroom has to be available for the carer.[140] The carer must be provided with the use of a bedroom additional to those used by other people who live with you. 'Bedroom' is not defined, but see p393 for what might count.

Note: a person can count as a 'person who requires overnight care' while away from your home, provided s/he can be treated as occupying it – eg, while temporarily absent (see p181).

Qualifying parent or carer

If you (or your partner) are a 'qualifying parent or carer', you are allowed one additional bedroom under the size criteria. Under the social sector rules, you are also allowed an additional bedroom for someone who is jointly liable for the rent with you if s/he (or her/his partner) is a 'qualifying parent or carer' (see p380).

You count as a 'qualifying parent or carer' if:[141]
• a child has been placed (or in Scotland, boarded out) with you under specified provisions – eg, prior to adoption or as a foster parent; *or*
• you are an approved foster parent (in Scotland, this includes foster and kinship carers). This applies even if you do not currently have a child placed with you, provided you have become an approved foster parent, or have fostered a child, within the last 52 weeks.

To come within the definition, you must have a bedroom in your home that is additional to those used by the other people living in your home. 'Bedroom' is not defined, but see p393 for what might count.

Note: you do not count as a qualifying parent or carer if you provide accommodation for a disabled person under an adult placement scheme. However, you can argue that you should still be allowed an additional bedroom.[142]

7. **Delaying a rent restriction**

A rent restriction can be delayed:
• for up to 12 months, if a member of your family (or any of your or your partner's relatives who lived in the same accommodation as you without a

separate right to do so) dies and you still live there (temporary absences of up to 13 weeks are allowed);[143] *or*

- for up to 13 weeks, if you, or a member of your family (or any of your or your partner's relatives who live in the same dwelling as you without a separate right to do so) could meet the costs of the dwelling when you took them on (this could include other bills as well as the rent). This only applies if neither you nor your partner were entitled to housing benefit (HB) in the 52 weeks before your current award of HB.[144]

Under the local housing allowance and social sector rent restriction rules, the amount of your rent that can be covered by your HB (your 'eligible rent' – see p193) can change before the end of the 12-month/13-week period if, as calculated under these rules, it is now the same or higher, or you move to a new home or another member of your family (or relative) dies.[145]

Family members and relatives[146]
'**Family**' means you, your partner and any child or qualifying young person for whom you or your partner are responsible and who lives in your household.
'**Relative**' means a close relative (see p179 for who counts) or a grandparent, grandchild, uncle, aunt, nephew or niece.

Example
Dylan lives in a private three-bedroom flat with his wife and their four-year-old son. They pay rent of £225 a week. Until her recent death, Dylan's mother lived with them. Dylan's rent was being restricted to the local housing allowance for a three-bedroom property (£190).
When he notifies the local authority of the death of his mother, his rent is restricted to the local housing allowance for a two-bedroom property (£150). However, the decrease is delayed for 12 months from the date of his mother's death.
Dylan gets income support. Before his mother's death, his HB was £173.55 a week (£190 *minus* a non-dependant deduction of £16.45).
For 12 months from his mother's date of death, his HB is £190 a week.

8. Challenging a rent restriction

If you disagree with the local authority's decision to apply a rent restriction (eg, if you think the rules do not apply in your case, or the wrong rules have been applied) or with the factual basis on which the decision was made (eg, you are a 'person who requires overnight care' or a 'member of a couple who cannot share a bedroom' and you should have been allowed more bedrooms under the rules or a room in your home should not count as a bedroom), you can ask for a revision

Part 4: General rules for other means-tested benefits
Chapter 19: Housing benefit rent restrictions
Notes

or appeal (see Chapters 56 and 57).[147] However, if the local housing allowance rules apply, you cannot appeal against the amount of the local housing allowance.

If the rules that use rent officer determinations apply

If the rules that use rent officer determinations apply (see p381), you cannot appeal against a rent officer's determination, but the local authority can ask for it to be redetermined.[148] The rent officer's redetermination might reduce your maximum rent (and the local authority might restrict your rent further), so consider your position carefully before requesting one – you could end up with less housing benefit. For details of the rules, see p414 of the 2019/20 edition of this *Handbook*.

You *can* appeal against local authority decisions about your award of housing benefit which involve rent officer determinations – ie, you can challenge the factual basis on which the rent officer made a determination, such as whether you are a 'young individual' or whether someone occupies accommodation with you.[149] If you are in doubt, you may want to appeal *and* ask for a redetermination.

Notes

1. How to use this chapter
1 Regs 13C(5)(a) and (c) and 14(2)(b) and Sch 2 paras 3-13 HB Regs; regs 13C(5)(a) and (c) and 14(2)(b) and Sch 2 paras 3-13 HB(SPC) Regs
2 The law refers to 'gypsies and travellers': Sch 2 para 3 HB Regs; Sch 2 para 3 HB(SPC) Regs.
3 Reg 2(1) and Sch 2 para 3(1A) HB Regs; reg 2(1) and Sch 2 para 3(1A) HB(SPC) Regs
4 Reg 12B(6) HB Regs; reg 12B(6) HB(SPC) Regs
5 R on the application of Laali v Westminster City Council [2002] HLR 179; R v Macclesfield BC HBRB ex parte Temsamani [1999] unreported (QBD); A4 Annex B GM
6 Reg 12C(2) and (3) HB Regs; reg 12C(2) HB(SPC) Regs; DC v LB Bromley (HB) [2018] UKUT 416 (AAC)
7 AA v Chesterfield BC [2011] UKUT 156 (AAC)

2. The local housing allowance rules
8 Reg 12D(2)(a) HB Regs; reg 12D(2)(a) HB(SPC) Regs
9 Reg 13C(1), (2)(a)-(c) and (5) HB Regs; reg 13C(1), (2)(a)-(c) and (5) HB(SPC) Regs
10 Reg 13D(1) and (5) HB Regs; reg 13D(1) and (5) HB(SPC) Regs
11 Reg 13D(4) and (12) HB Regs; reg 13D(4) and (12) HB(SPC) Regs
12 DC v LB Bromley (HB) [2018] UKUT 416 (AAC)
13 Reg 13D(2)(c) and (3) HB Regs; reg 13D(2)(c) and (3) HB(SPC) Regs
14 Reg 2(6) HB Regs; reg 2(7) HB(SPC) Regs
15 SSWP v Hockley and Nuneaton and Bedworth BC [2019] EWCA Civ 1080
16 Reg 13D(12), definition of 'occupiers', HB Regs; reg 13D(12), definition of 'occupiers', HB(SPC) Regs
17 AA v Chesterfield BC and SSWP (HB) [2011] UKUT 156 (AAC)

18 Reg 21(3) HB Regs; reg 21(3) HB(SPC) Regs

19 R(H) 8/09; *SK v South Hams DC (HB)* [2010] UKUT 129 (AAC), reported as [2010] AACR 40

20 *R v Swale BC HBRB ex parte Marchant* [1999] 1 FLR 1087 (QBD); [2000] 1 FLR 246; *R (Cotton and Others) v SSWP and New Forest DC and Others* [2014] EWHC 3437 (Admin); *PC v SSWP (HB)* [2014] UKUT 467 (AAC); *MR v North Tyneside Council and SSWP* [2015] UKUT 34 (AAC); *SSWP v MM and Northumberland CC* [2015] UKUT 624 (AAC)

21 Reg 13D(3A) and (3B) HB Regs; reg 13D(3A) and (3B) HB(SPC) Regs

22 Reg 13D(2)(a) HB Regs; reg 13D(2)(a) HB(SPC) Regs

23 Regs 2(1), definition of 'young individual', (b)-(f) and (i) and (1A)-(1C), and 13D(2)(a) HB Regs; reg 13D(2)(a) and (12) HB(SPC) Regs

24 Regs 2(1), definition of 'young individual', (c) and (f) and 13D(2)(a) HB Regs; reg 13D(2)(a) and (12) HB(SPC) Regs

25 Ch 2 paras 2.054 and 2.080 *Local Housing Allowance Guidance Manual*

26 Reg 13D(2)(b) HB Regs; reg 13D(2)(b) HB(SPC) Regs

27 *JS v SSWP and Cheshire West and Chester BC (HB)* [2014] UKUT 36 (AAC), reported as [2014] AACR 26

28 Reg 13D(2)(b) HB Regs; reg 13D(2)(b) HB(SPC) Regs

29 Reg 13D(2)(c) HB Regs; reg 13D(2)(c) HB(SPC) Regs

30 Reg 13D(1) HB Regs; reg 13D(1) HB(SPC) Regs; Art 4B(2A) and (2B) and Sch 3B RO(HBF)O; Art 4B(2A) and (2B) and Sch 3B RO(HBF)(S)O; The Rent Officers (Housing Benefit and Universal Credit Functions) (Amendment and Modification) Order 2021 No.1380

31 Regs 12D(2) and 13C(3) HB Regs; regs 12D(2) and 13C(3) HB(SPC) Regs

32 Regs 2, definition of 'linked person', 12D(2)(b) and 13C(2)(d) HB Regs; regs 2, definition of 'linked person', 12D(2)(b) and 13C(2)(d) HB(SPC) Regs

33 Reg 13D(1) and (12), definition of 'relevant date', HB Regs; reg 13D(1) and (12), definition of 'relevant date', HB(SPC) Regs

3. **The social sector rules: the 'bedroom tax'**

34 Reg 12BA HB Regs

35 Reg A13(1) HB Regs

36 Regs 2(1), definition of 'registered housing association', and A13(1)-(5) HB Regs

37 *FT v Perth and Kinross Council and SSWP (HB)* [2019] UKUT 43 (AAC)

38 Art 8 WRA(No.31)O; HB Circular A9/2019, *Mixed-age Couples: further guidance (revised)*, 10 July 2019, para 14, Example 2

39 Regs 12(2B), A13(2)(f) and (5) and 75H HB Regs

40 Reg B13(2) HB Regs

41 Reg B13(4) HB Regs

42 Reg B13(2)(c) HB Regs

43 Reg B13(5) and (8) HB Regs

44 Reg 2(6) HB Regs

45 *SSWP v Hockley and Nuneaton and Bedworth BC* [2019] EWCA Civ 1080

46 Reg B13(5) HB Regs

47 Reg 21(3) HB Regs

48 Reg B13(8) HB Regs

49 R(H) 8/09; *SK v South Hams DC (HB)* [2010] UKUT 129 (AAC), reported as [2010] AACR 40

50 *R v Swale BC HBRB ex parte Marchant* [1999] 1 FLR 1087 (QBD); [2000] 1 FLR 246; *R (Cotton and Others) v SSWP and New Forest DC and Others* [2014] EWHC 3437 (Admin); *PC v SSWP (HB)* [2014] UKUT 467 (AAC); *MR v North Tyneside Council and SSWP* [2015] UKUT 34 (AAC)

51 Reg B13(6)(a) and (b), (7)(a) and (9)(a), (b) and (e) HB Regs

52 Reg B13(6)(ab) and (b), (7) and (9)(c) and (d) HB Regs

4. **Hostels, houseboats, mobile homes, caravans and boarders**

53 Reg 12C HB Regs; reg 12C HB(SPC) Regs

54 Regs 13(1), 13C(5)(a)-(e) and (6) and 14(1) HB Regs; regs 13(1), 13C(5)(a)-(e) and (6) and 14(1) HB(SPC) Regs

55 The law refers to 'gypsies and travellers': Sch 2 para 3 HB Regs; Sch 2 para 3 HB(SPC) Regs

56 Reg 13(2), (3) and (5) HB Regs; reg 13(2), (3) and (5) HB(SPC) Regs

57 Reg 12C(2) and (3) HB Regs; reg 12C(2) HB (SPC) Regs

58 Reg 13(4) HB Regs; reg 13(4) HB(SPC) Regs; Sch 3 para 8 HB&CTB(CP) Regs

Part 4: General rules for other means-tested benefits
Chapter 19: Housing benefit rent restrictions
Notes

● ●

4

59 *DC v LB Bromley (HB)* [2018] UKUT 416 (AAC)
60 Reg 13ZB(1) HB Regs; reg 13ZB(1) HB(SPC) Regs
61 Reg 14(2)(a) and (7) and Sch 2 para 2(1) and (2) HB Regs; reg 14(2)(a) and (7) and Sch 2 para 2(1) and (2) HB(SPC) Regs
62 Reg 14(1) and (8) HB Regs; reg 14(1) and (8) HB(SPC) Regs
63 Reg 14(1) and (8) and Sch 2 para 2(3)(a)-(d) and (f)-(h) and (4) HB Regs; reg 14(1) and (8) and Sch 2 para 2(3)(a)-(g) and (4) HB(SPC) Regs
64 R(H) 8/09; *SK v South Hams DC (HB)* [2010] UKUT 129 (AAC), reported as [2010] AACR 40
65 CH/1556/2006; CH/3590/2007
66 Sch 1 para 6 RO(HBF)O; Sch 1 para 6 RO(HBF)(S)O
67 Sch 1 para 1 RO(HBF)O; Sch 1 para 1 RO(HBF)(S)O
68 Sch 1 para 3 RO(HBF)O; Sch 1 para 3 RO(HBF)(S)O
69 Sch 1 paras 1(4) and 2 RO(HBF)O; Sch 1 paras 1(4) and 2 RO(HBF)(S)O
70 Sch 2 para 1 RO(HBF)O; Sch 2 para 1 RO(HBF)(S)O
71 Reg 2(6) HB Regs; reg 2(7) HB(SPC) Regs
72 Sch 2 paras 1A and 1B RO(HBF)O; Sch 2 paras 1A and 1B RO(HBF)(S)O
73 Art 2(1) RO(HBF)O; Art 2(1) RO(HBF)(S)O. Both, definition of 'occupier'.
74 Reg 21(3) HB Regs; reg 21(3) HB(SPC) Regs
75 Sch 2 para 2(4) HB Regs; Sch 2 para 2(4) HB(SPC) Regs
76 R(H) 8/09; *SK v South Hams DC (HB)* [2010] UKUT 129 (AAC), reported as [2010] AACR 40
77 *R v Swale BC HBRB ex parte Marchant* [1999] 1 FLR 1087 (QBD); [2000] 1 FLR 246; *R (Cotton and Others) v SSWP and New Forest DC and Others* [2014] EWHC 3437 (Admin); *PC v SSWP (HB)* [2014] UKUT 467 (AAC); *MR v North Tyneside Council and SSWP* [2015] UKUT 34 (AAC); *SSWP v MM and Northumberland CC* [2015] UKUT 624 (AAC)
78 Sch 1 paras 4 and 9(2) RO(HBF)O; Sch 1 paras 4 and 9(2) RO(HBF)(S)O
79 Sch 1 para 5 RO(HBF)O; Sch 1 para 5 RO(HBF)(S)O
80 Reg 13(5) and (6) HB Regs
81 Reg 114A(6) and (8)(a) HB Regs; reg 95A(6) and (8)(a) HB(SPC) Regs

82 Sch 1 paras 5(2)(c) and 7(1) RO(HBF)O; Sch 1 paras 5(2)(c) and 7(1) RO(HBF)(S)O
83 Reg 14(1)(e) and (2) HB Regs; reg 14(1)(e) and (2) HB(SPC) Regs
84 Reg 14(8), definition of 'prospective occupier', HB Regs; reg 14(8), definition of 'prospective occupier', HB(SPC) Regs
85 Reg 14(1)(e) and (8), definition of 'specified matters', HB Regs; reg 14(1)(e) and (8), definition of 'specified matters', HB(SPC) Regs
86 Sch 2 para 2(2)(b) HB Regs; Sch 2 para 2(2)(b) HB(SPC) Regs
87 Reg 13ZB(2)-(4) HB Regs; reg 13ZB(2)-(4) HB(SPC) Regs

5. Exempt accommodation and claimants: the old scheme rules
88 Reg 13C(5)(b) HB Regs; reg 13C(5)(b) HB(SPC) Regs; Sch 3 para 4(1)(b) and (10) HB&CTB(CP) Regs; CH/1289/2007
89 R(H) 7/07; R(H) 4/09; CH/3900/2005; CH/2726/2008; *East Hertfordshire DC v KT* [2009] UKUT 12 (AAC); *Bristol City Council v AW* [2009] UKUT 109 (AAC)
90 R(H) 7/07; CH/1289/2007; *Salford CC v PF* [2009] UKUT 150 (AAC)
91 *MMcF v Sefton BC (HB)* [2016] UKUT 403 (AAC)
92 R(H) 2/07
93 Sch 3 para 4(1)(a), (2), (3) and (4) HB&CTB(CP) Regs
94 Reg 13C HB Regs; reg 13C HB(SPC) Regs; Sch 3 para 4(2)(a) and (b), (5), (6), (9) and (10) HB&CTB(CP) Regs
95 Sch 3 para 4(10), definition of 'previous beneficiary', HB&CTB(CP) Regs
96 Reg 2(1), definition of 'registered housing association', HB Regs; Sch 3 para 4(2)(aa) HB&CTB(CP) Regs
97 Reg 12(3)-(5) HB Regs and reg 12(3)-(5) HB(SPC) Regs, as set out in Sch 3 para 5(1) HB&CTB(CP) Regs
98 Reg 13(3) HB Regs and reg 13(3) HB(SPC) Regs, as set out in Sch 3 para 5(2) HB&CTB(CP) Regs
99 *R v City of Westminster HBRB ex parte Mehanne* [1992] 2 All ER 317
100 *R v Brent LBC HBRB ex parte Connery* [1989] 22 HLR 40 (QBD)
101 *R v Kensington and Chelsea RBC HBRB ex parte Pirie*, 26 March 1997, unreported (QBD)
102 Reg 13(3)(a) HB Regs and reg 13(3)(a) HB(SPC) Regs, as set out in Sch 3 para 5(2) HB&CTB(CP) Regs

103 Reg 13(3)(b) HB Regs and reg 13(3)(b) HB(SPC) Regs, as set out in Sch 3 para 5(2) HB&CTB(CP) Regs; *R v Beverley DC HBRB ex parte Hare* [1995] 27 HLR 637 (QBD); *R v Kensington and Chelsea RBC ex parte Abou-Jaoude*, 10 May 1996, unreported (QBD)

104 *Macleod v Banff and Buchan District HBRB* [1988] SLT 753 (CS); *Malcolm v Tweedale District HBRB* [1994] SLT 1212 (CS); CH/4970/2002

105 *Birmingham City Council v SSWP and Others* [2016] EWCA Civ 1211

106 *R v Kensington and Chelsea RBC ex parte Abou-Jaoude*, 10 May 1996, ureported (QBD); *R v Coventry City Council ex parte Waite*, 7 July 1995, unreported (QBD)

107 *R v Kensington and Chelsea RBC HBRB ex parte Sheikh*, 14 January 1997, unreported (QBD)

108 Reg 13(4) HB Regs and reg 13(4) HB(SPC) Regs, as set out in Sch 3 para 5(2) HB&CTB(CP) Regs

109 Reg 13(4) HB Regs and reg 13(4) HB(SPC) Regs, as set out in Sch 3 para 5(2) HB&CTB(CP) Regs

110 R(H) 3/06

111 Reg 13(10) and (11) HB Regs and reg 13(10) and (11) HB(SPC) Regs, as set out in Sch 3 para 5(2) HB&CTB(CP) Regs

112 Reg 13(9) HB Regs and reg 13(9) HB(SPC) Regs, as set out in Sch 3 para 5(2) HB&CTB(CP) Regs

113 R(H) 2/05

114 *R v Lambeth LBC HBRB ex parte Harrington*, 22 November 1996, unreported (QBD)

115 Reg 13(9)(a) HB Regs and reg 13(9)(a) HB(SPC) Regs as set out in Sch 3 para 5(2) HB&CTB(CP) Regs; *R v Kensington and Chelsea RBC ex parte Pirie*, 26 March 1997, unreported (QBD); *R v Coventry CC ex parte Waite*, 7 July 1995, unreported (QBD)

116 *R v Waltham Forest LBC ex parte Holder* [1996] 29 HLR 71 (QBD); *R v Slough BC ex parte Green*, 15 November 1996, unreported (QBD)

117 *R v Waltham Forest LBC ex parte Holder* [1996] 29 HLR 71 (QBD); *R v Kensington and Chelsea RBC HBRB ex parte Sheikh*, 14 January 1997, unreported (QBD)

118 *R v East Devon DC HBRB ex parte Gibson* [1993] 25 HLR 487 (QBD); CH/4306/2003

119 *R v Waltham Forest LBC ex parte Holder* [1996] 29 HLR 71 (QBD)

120 *R v Oadby and Wigston DC ex parte Dickman* [1995] 28 HLR 806 (QBD)

121 Reg 13(9)(b) HB Regs and reg 13(9)(b) HB(SPC) Regs, as set out in Sch 3 para 5(2) HB&CTB(CP) Regs

122 *R v Kensington and Chelsea RBC HBRB ex parte Sheikh*, 14 January 1997, unreported (QBD)

123 *R v Kensington and Chelsea RBC HBRB ex parte Carney* [1997] *Crown Office Digest* 124 (QBD)

124 *R v Camden LBC HBRB ex parte W* [1999] unreported (QBD); *R v Westminster CC HBRB ex parte Pallas* [1997] unreported (QBD)

125 Reg 13ZA HB Regs and reg 13ZA HB(SPC) Regs, as set out in Sch 3 para 5(3) HB&CTB(CP) Regs

126 *BM v Cheshire West and Cheshire Council* [2009] UKUT 162 (AAC)

127 CH/2214/2003

6. Common rules

128 Regs 2(1) and (1A)-(1C), definition of 'young individual', HB Regs

129 gov.uk/government/publications/multi-agency-public-protection-arrangements-mappa-guidance

130 *Bolton MBC v BF (HB)* [2014] UKUT 48 (AAC)

131 *CB v Manchester City Council and SSWP (HB)* [2015] UKUT 556 (AAC)

132 *SSWP v Nelson and Nelson* [2014] UKUT 525 (AAC), reported as [2015] AACR 21; *Stevenage BC v ML (HB)* [2016] UKUT 164 (AAC); *M v SSWP* [2017] UKUT 443 (AAC); *Nuneaton and Bedworth BC v RH and SSWP* [2017] UKUT 471 (AAC); *E v Bristol City Council* [2018] UKUT 287 (AAC)

133 *SSWP v the City of Glasgow Council and IB* [2017] CSIH 35, reported as [2017] AACR 2

134 *SSWP v RR (HB)* [2018] UKUT 180 (AAC)

135 Reg 2(1) HB Regs; reg 2(1) HB(SPC) Regs

136 *R (Carmichael) v SSWP and R (Rutherford) v SSWP* [2016] UKSC 58

137 Reg 2(1) HB Regs; reg 2(1) HB(SPC) Regs

138 *Burnip v Birmingham City Council and Others* [2012] EWCA Civ 629

139 Reg 2(1) HB Regs; reg 2(1) HB(SPC) Regs

140 *SD v Eastleigh BC (HB)* [2014] UKUT 325 (AAC)

4

Part 4: General rules for other means-tested benefits
Chapter 19: Housing benefit rent restrictions
Notes

• •

141 Reg 2(1) HB Regs; reg 2(1) HB(SPC)
     Regs
142 *SSWP v PE and Bolton MBC* [2017] UKUT
     393 (AAC)

7. Delaying a rent restriction

143 Regs 2(1), definitions of 'reckonable
     rent' and 'linked person', 12BA(3)-(5),
     12D(3), (4) and (8) and 13ZA(1) and (2)
     HB Regs; regs 2(1), definitions of
     'reckonable rent' and 'linked person',
     12D(3), (4) and (8) and 13ZA(1) and (2)
     HB(SPC) Regs; reg 13(5) HB Regs and
     reg 13(5) HB(SPC) Regs, as set out in
     Sch 3 para 5(2) HB&CTB(CP) Regs
144 Regs 12BA(6)-(8), 12D(5), (6) and (8)
     and 13ZA(3) and (4) HB Regs; regs
     12D(5), (6) and (8) and 13|ZA(3) and
     (4) HB(SPC) Regs; reg 13(7) and (8) HB
     Regs and reg 13(7) and (8) HB(SPC)
     Regs, as set out in Sch 3 para 5(2)
     HB&CTB(CP) Regs
145 Regs 12BA(5) and (8) and 12D(7) HB
     Regs; reg 12D(7) HB(SPC) Regs
146 Reg 2(1) HB Regs; reg 2(1) HB(SPC)
     Regs

8. Challenging a rent restriction

147 *LB Bexley v LD (HB)* [2010] UKUT 79
     (AAC); *SK v South Hams DC (HB)* [2010]
     UKUT 129 (AAC), reported as [2010]
     AACR 40
148 Regs 15, 16 and 17 HB Regs; regs 15, 16
     and 17 HB(SPC) Regs
149 *SK v South Hams DC (HB)* [2010] UKUT
     129 (AAC), reported as [2010] AACR 40;
     LB Bexley v LD (HB) [2010] UKUT 79
     (AAC)

Chapter 20

Income: under pension age

This chapter covers:
1. Whose income counts (p404)
2. What counts as income (p404)
3. Earnings (p405)
4. Other income (p419)
5. Notional income (p433)
6. Working out weekly income (p437)

This chapter explains the rules for working out your weekly income for income support, income-based jobseeker's allowance and income-related employment and support allowance. It also covers working-age housing benefit (HB) rules if you and your partner are under pension age. For pension credit and pension-age HB rules if you and your partner are over pension age, see Chapter 21. If you are in a couple and one of you is over pension age but not the other, see p187 for whether the working-age or pension-age HB rules apply. For universal credit, see Chapter 7; for tax credits, see Chapter 63; for carer's allowance, see Chapter 26; and for health benefits, see Chapter 31.

Key facts
- Your entitlement to income support (IS), income-based jobseeker's allowance (JSA), income-related employment and support allowance (ESA) and working-age housing benefit (HB) and the amount you get depend on how much income you have.
- Your own income counts and, if you are a member of a couple, your partner's income also counts.
- Some income may be completely or partly ignored, or it may count in full.
- Some income may be treated as capital and some capital treated as income.
- If you get IS, income-based JSA or income-related ESA (or universal credit), you are entitled to maximum HB, so you do not need to work out your income again for HB.

Part 4: General rules for other means-tested benefits
Chapter 20: Income: under pension age
2. What counts as income

1. **Whose income counts**

Your income counts and, if you are a member of a couple, your partner's income also counts. The income of your dependent children does not count except in the limited circumstances below.

Note: if you or your partner are getting income support (IS), income-based jobseeker's allowance (JSA) or income-related employment and support allowance (ESA) (or universal credit), all your (and your partner's) income is ignored for housing benefit.[1]

Your partner's income

If you are a member of a couple (see p303), your partner's income is added to yours.[2]

If you or your partner are under 18 and so the rate of the IS, income-based JSA or income-related ESA personal allowance for a couple (£121.05) is reduced to £77.00 or £61.05 (see p319), an amount of income equivalent to the reduction is ignored.[3]

A dependent child's income

Maintenance paid to, or for, a child is usually disregarded (see p422).

The income of a dependent child does not affect your means-tested benefits. However, for IS and income-based JSA, if you have been getting benefit since before 6 April 2004 with a child included in your claim and you do not yet have an award of child tax credit, her/his income is counted as yours if s/he does not have capital of over £3,000.[4] Some income may be disregarded.

See p903, p927 and p935 of the 2012/13 edition of this *Handbook* for details.[5]

2. **What counts as income**

All income is taken into account for income support (IS), income-based jobseeker's allowance (JSA) and income-related employment and support allowance (ESA) unless it is specifically ignored (or 'disregarded').

If you get IS, income-based JSA or income-related ESA (or universal credit), all your income is ignored for housing benefit (HB).[6] Otherwise, all income is taken into account for HB, other than income that is specifically disregarded.

Income only counts if it is paid to you for your own use. It may not count if you cannot prevent it being paid to a third party (eg, paying maintenance under an attachment of earnings order), although other payments for you made to a third party might count (see p435).[7]

Income is converted into a weekly amount (see p437).

Income or capital?

The difference between income and capital is not defined. Payments of income are normally made in respect of a specified period and form part of a regular series of payments.[8] However, sometimes a one-off payment can be income depending on what it is paid for – eg, a settlement for underpaid wages under equal pay legislation.[9] Some income is treated as capital (see p477) and some capital is treated as income (see p428).

3. Earnings

How earnings are treated depends on whether you are employed (see below) or self-employed (see p411). In both cases, some of your earnings can be disregarded (see p413).

Employed earnings

This section explains how any earnings received by you or your partner and, in some cases, a dependent child (see p404) are treated. The same rules apply to your (but not your partner's or child's) earnings if you are claiming contribution-based jobseeker's allowance (JSA – see p694).

To work out how earnings are taken into account, do the following.
- Check whether the payments count as earnings (see below). In some cases, payments are treated as capital, as income other than earnings, or ignored altogether.
- Calculate your net earnings (see p407 and p411).
- Work out your weekly net earnings (see p437).
- Deduct the appropriate weekly earnings disregard (see p413).
- Work out the date from when earnings are taken into account (see p440). For income support (IS), income-based JSA and income-related employment and support allowance (ESA), also work out the period covered by the earnings (see p437). Normally, a payment counts from the date it is due to be paid and for the length of time it has been paid – eg, a month's wages count for a month, starting from the day they are due, at the weekly rate as calculated.

There are special rules for how payments affect benefit when you leave a job (see p408).

What counts as earnings

'Earnings' means 'any remuneration or profit derived from ... employment'. This includes:[10]
- wages and overtime pay;
- any bonus or commission (including tips);

Part 4: General rules for other means-tested benefits
Chapter 20: Income: under pension age
3. Earnings

- holiday pay (but see p408 if your job ends or you are off work);
- for housing benefit (HB), any statutory sick pay (SSP) or contractual sick pay.[11] For IS, income-based JSA and income-related ESA, all sick pay is treated as 'other income' rather than earnings (and therefore does not attract an earnings disregard) and is counted in full, less any tax, class 1 national insurance (NI) contributions and half of any pension contributions;[12]
- for HB, any statutory maternity pay (SMP), statutory adoption pay (SAP), statutory paternity pay (SPP), statutory shared parental pay (SSPP) or statutory parental bereavement pay (SPBP) or any other payment made to you by your employer while you are on maternity, adoption, paternity, shared parental or parental bereavement leave.[13] For IS, income-based JSA and income-related ESA, all such pay is treated as 'other income' rather than earnings (and, therefore, does not attract an earnings disregard) and is counted in full less any tax that is payable, class 1 NI contributions and half of any pension contributions;[14]
- any payments made by your employer for expenses not 'wholly, exclusively and necessarily' incurred in carrying out your job, including any travel expenses to and from work, and any payments made to you for looking after members of your family. The latter can apply if you are looking after your child, even if s/he cannot be included in your claim;
- a retainer (eg, payments during the school holidays if you work for the school meals service[15]) or a guarantee payment – eg, if you are working short time or laid off;[16]
- certain compensation payments in respect of the termination of your employment, including employment tribunal awards and pay in lieu of notice. See p408 for the way these are treated when you stop work. For IS, JSA and income-related ESA, compensatory refunds of contributions to an occupational scheme[17] are not treated as earnings;
- an equal pay settlement – eg, through a 'single-status agreement';[18]
- any payment of a non-cash voucher which is liable for class 1 NI contributions.[19] Non-cash vouchers that are not liable for contributions are classed as payments in kind (see below).[20]

What does not count as earnings

Examples of payments not counted as earnings include the following.

- Payments in kind (eg, petrol) are ignored,[21] unless you are on IS or income-based JSA and involved in a trade dispute (see p982), although they may be counted as 'notional income' (see p436).[22] Non-cash vouchers which are not liable for class 1 NI contributions (eg, certain childcare and charitable vouchers) are treated as payments in kind and are disregarded.[23]
- The value of any free accommodation provided as part of your job should be ignored.[24]

- An advance of earnings or a loan from your employer is treated as capital.[25] However, it is treated as earnings for IS or income-based JSA if you or your partner are involved in, or have returned to work after, a trade dispute.
- Payments towards expenses that are 'wholly, exclusively and necessarily' incurred during the course of your work, such as travelling expenses, are ignored.[26] For example, deductions could be made for:
  - tools or work equipment;
  - special clothing or uniforms;[27]
  - postage and telephone costs (including rental);[28]
  - fuel costs (including standing charges);
  - secretarial expenses;[29]
  - running a car (including petrol, tax, insurance, repairs and maintenance, and rental on a leased car).[30]

  If any expenditure is for both business and private use, it should be apportioned as appropriate (and any determination by HM Revenue and Customs normally followed).[31]
- If you are a local councillor, travelling expenses and subsistence payments are (and basic allowances may be[32]) ignored as expenses 'wholly, exclusively and necessarily' incurred in your work.
- Earnings payable abroad which cannot be brought into the UK (eg, because of exchange control regulations) are ignored.[33] **Note:** if your earnings are paid in another currency, any bank charges for converting them into sterling are deducted before taking them into account.[34]
- Any occupational pension[35] counts as 'other income', not earnings, and the net amount is taken into account in full.[36] See p695 (and p639) for the occupational pension rules for contribution-based JSA (and contributory ESA).
- If you are a member of the reserve forces, earnings while on training are disregarded for up to 43 days in your first year of training and 15 days thereafter, to allow you to keep a minimum 10 pence a week IS, JSA or income-related ESA entitlement.[37]

Calculating net earnings from employment

Both your 'gross' earnings and 'net' earnings must be calculated.

Gross and net earnings

'**Gross earnings**' means the amount of earnings received from your employer less deductions for any expenses wholly, necessarily and exclusively incurred by you in order to carry out the duties of your employment.[38] See p405 for what counts as earnings and p406 for examples of expenses that can be deducted.

'**Net earnings**' means your gross earnings less any deductions made for:[39]

- income tax; *and*
- class 1 NI contributions; *and*
- half of any contribution you make towards a personal or occupational pension scheme.

Part 4: General rules for other means-tested benefits
Chapter 20: Income: under pension age
3. Earnings

For HB, if your earnings are estimated, the amount of tax and NI contributions you would expect to pay on those earnings is also estimated. This amount, plus half of any pension contribution you are paying, is then deducted.[40]

For HB, the local authority has the discretion to ignore changes in tax or NI contributions for up to 30 benefit weeks. This can be used, for example, if April tax changes are not reflected in your actual income until several months later. When the changes are eventually taken into account and your benefit entitlement is either increased or reduced accordingly, you are not treated as having been underpaid or overpaid benefit during the period of the delay.[41]

4. Payments when you stop work

If you were getting benefit while working, your final earnings are generally taken into account. If you stop work and are not already getting benefit, see p409.

You were getting benefit when working

If your job ends and you were getting benefit while you were in work, any payments made to you when that job ends are taken into account as earnings as follows.[42]

- Final earnings are taken into account as normal (including wages, bonuses and expenses that count as earnings).
- For IS, income-related ESA and HB, pay in lieu of notice is taken into account; for IS and income-related ESA, final earnings are taken into account first, followed by pay in lieu of notice.
- Contractual redundancy pay, ex gratia payments and other types of compensation (other than employment tribunal awards) above the level of entitlement to statutory redundancy pay:
  - are treated as capital for IS and income-related ESA, if you work out your notice or get full pay in lieu of notice. Otherwise, they are taken into account as earnings for one week only;
  - together with pay in lieu of notice, are treated as earnings for JSA, up until the end of the fixed-term contract, if you had one, or until the end of the notice period (sometimes longer if the employer says it covers a longer period). For JSA, if none of the payment covers pay in lieu of notice or early termination of a fixed-term contract, the total of these payments covers a standard number of weeks arrived at by dividing the payment by the weekly maximum statutory redundancy payment (£571) if this is shorter than the notice period;
  - are treated as capital for HB, except any amount representing loss of income, which is taken into account as earnings.
  The weeks the payments count for start after the period covered by final earnings and any pay in lieu of notice.
- Holiday pay normally counts as earnings. However, it counts as capital if your contract provides for it to be payable more than four weeks after employment

ends. For IS, JSA and income-related ESA, it counts for the number of weeks covered by the holiday pay (not the number of working weeks[43]) starting after the period covered by other payments listed in the above three bullet points.

- An employment tribunal award (eg, for unfair dismissal) is taken into account as earnings.
- Arrears of sick, maternity, adoption, paternity, shared parental and parental bereavement pay count as earnings for HB, and as 'other income', rather than earnings, for IS, JSA and income-related ESA.[44]
- Statutory redundancy payments are treated as capital.

Example
Sundus has been getting HB while working part time. She earned £50 a week. She finishes work on 16 July and on that day is given £60, made up of £30 final wages and £30 holiday pay. The £60 wages and holiday pay are taken into account as normal for HB, deducting the earnings disregard.

Note: you cannot make a new claim for IS, income-based JSA, income-related ESA and only for HB in certain circumstances (see p23). Instead, you can claim universal credit (UC). Claiming UC means that awards of any of these benefits (or tax credits) will end (see p24 for exceptions).

Your job ends before benefit starts

If your employment ends before your entitlement to JSA or HB begins, any payments that count as earnings (see p405), including wages, holiday pay (but see below) and pay in lieu of notice, are ignored as income for that benefit, except for the payments below.[45] For IS and income-related ESA, see p415 of the 2018/19 edition of this *Handbook*.

Note: you cannot make a new claim for IS, income-based JSA, income-related ESA and only for HB in certain circumstances (see p23 for exceptions). Instead you can claim UC. Claiming UC means that awards of any of these benefits (or tax credits) will end (see p24 for exceptions).

The following payments are taken into account.
- A retainer counts as earnings.
- If you were in full-time paid work (see p974), certain employment tribunal awards (and 'out-of-court' settlements) count as earnings, including:
  - compensation because of unfair dismissal;[46]
  - a 'protective' award when an employer fails to comply with redundancy procedures and, for JSA, a compensatory award in respect of trade union activity;[47]
  - for HB, pay under a continuation of contract award or for arrears of pay in respect of a reinstatement or re-engagement order.[48]

Part 4: General rules for other means-tested benefits
Chapter 20: Income: under pension age
3. Earnings

If you were in part-time work, the above are all ignored for HB, but count for JSA.

- Guarantee payments for workless days or while suspended on medical or maternity grounds count as earnings, including when awarded by an employment tribunal.[49]
- Arrears of statutory or contractual sick, maternity, adoption, paternity, shared parental and parental bereavement pay and lump-sum advance payments are taken into account for JSA as income, without any earnings disregard, from when they are paid for the same length of time covered by the arrears. They are ignored for HB.[50]
- Statutory redundancy pay counts as capital.[51]
- Contractual redundancy pay (deducting an amount for your statutory entitlement) is ignored completely for JSA.[52] For HB, it counts as capital.[53]
- Some redundancy schemes make periodic payments after leaving work. These are treated as income other than earnings.[54]
- Ex gratia payments and other kinds of compensation (other than employment tribunal awards) are treated in the same way as contractual redundancy pay.
- Holiday pay is usually ignored. However, if your job ends, it counts as capital if your contract provides for it to be payable more than four weeks after termination of employment.[55]

If you stop work before your benefit begins but your employment has not ended (eg, you go on sick leave or maternity leave), statutory and contractual sick, maternity, adoption, paternity, shared parental and parental bereavement pay are taken into account as income without any earnings disregard for JSA.[56] For HB, they count as earnings with the usual disregard.[57] If holiday pay is due to be paid more than four weeks after you stopped work, it is treated as capital (unless, for JSA, you are involved in a trade dispute). If it is due to be paid less than four weeks after you stopped work, it is ignored.[58] All other payments that count as earnings are ignored, except for a retainer or guarantee payments for workless days or for medical or maternity suspension.[59] If you are suspended from work, any earnings are taken into account as normal.

> *Example*
> Kerry has had to leave her home and her job because of domestic abuse. She leaves her full-time job on 31 May with one month's wages, and three days' holiday pay. Both are due to be paid on 31 May. She moves into temporary accommodation and claims HB after her job ends. Her final wages and holiday pay are ignored. She is entitled to HB from 1 June.

Note: if you were getting HB while working and after your job has ended you made a fresh claim for JSA, your final earnings are taken into account for HB (see p408), but disregarded for JSA.

Self-employed earnings

This section explains how any earnings from self-employment received by you or your partner and, in some cases, a dependent child (see p404) are treated. The same rules apply to your (but not your partner's or child's) earnings if you are claiming contribution-based JSA (see p694).

To work out how earnings are taken into account, do the following.

- Calculate net earnings (see below).
- Work out your average earnings (see p412).
- Deduct the appropriate weekly earnings disregard (see p413).

Calculating net earnings

Your 'net profit'must be worked out. This is your self-employed earnings minus:[60]

- reasonable expenses (see below); *and*
- income tax and NI contributions; *and*
- half of any premium paid in respect of a personal pension scheme which is eligible for tax relief.

Payments from the Self-Employment Income Support Scheme (a coronavirus support grant) count as earnings.[61] Drawings from capital do not count as income, whether or not the business is in profit.[62] If you receive payments for board and lodging, these do not count as earnings,[63] but as other income (less any disregards – see p426).

If you are getting help with your business through the DWP scheme New Enterprise Allowance, income and expenses are treated differently (see p428).

Reasonable expenses

Expenses must be reasonable and 'wholly and exclusively' incurred for the purposes of your business.[64] This involves similar considerations to those that apply to the allowances permitted in assessing gross earnings of employed earners. If a car or telephone, for example, is used partly for business and partly for private purposes, the costs of it can be apportioned and the amount attributable to business use can be deducted.[65]

Reasonable expenses include:[66]

- repayments of capital on loans for replacing equipment and machinery;
- repayments of capital on loans for, and income spent on, the repair of a business asset, unless this is covered by insurance;
- interest on a loan taken out for the purposes of the business;
- excess of VAT paid over VAT received.

Reasonable expenses do not include:[67]

- any capital expenditure;
- depreciation;[68]

Part 4: General rules for other means-tested benefits
Chapter 20: Income: under pension age
3. Earnings

- money for setting up or expanding the business – eg, the cost of adapting the business premises;
- any loss incurred before the beginning of the current period being used to work out average earnings (see below). If the business makes a loss, the net profit is nil. The losses of one business cannot be offset against the profit of any other business in which you are engaged, or against your earnings as an employee[69] (although if two businesses or employments share expenses, these may be apportioned and offset);[70]
- capital repayments on loans taken out for business purposes;
- business entertainment expenses;
- for HB, debts (other than proven bad debts) – but the expenses of recovering a debt can be deducted.

Working out average earnings from self-employment

For IS, income-based JSA and income-related ESA, the weekly amount is the average of earnings:[71]
- over a period of one year (in practice, normally the last year for which accounts are available);[72] *or*
- over a more appropriate period if you have recently taken up self-employment, there has been a change that will affect your business, or for any other reason if a different period may enable your income and expenditure to be calculated more accurately.

For example, a payment from the Self-Employment Income Support Scheme is averaged over three months and counted from the date of payment.[73] For HB, the amount of your weekly earnings is averaged over an 'appropriate' period (usually based on your last year's trading accounts), which must not be longer than a year.[74]

For all benefits, if your earnings are royalties, copyright payments or payments under the Public Lending Right scheme, the amount of earnings is divided by the weekly amount of benefit that would be payable if you had not received this income plus the amount that would be disregarded from those earnings (for income-related ESA, the amount of benefit that would be payable includes any contributory ESA).[75] For IS, income-based JSA and income-related ESA, you are not entitled to benefit for the resulting number of weeks. For HB, earnings are taken into account for the resulting number of weeks.

If you stop doing self-employed work, any earnings from that work are disregarded except for royalties and copyright and Public Lending Right scheme payments.[76]

Childminders

In practice, childminders are always treated as self-employed. Your net profit is deemed to be one-third of your earnings less income tax, your NI contributions and half of personal pension scheme contributions (see p411).[77] The rest of your earnings are completely ignored.

Disregarded earnings

Some of your earnings from employment or self-employment are disregarded and do not affect your benefit. The amount of the disregard depends on your circumstances. For the amount of disregarded earnings for contribution-based JSA, see p694.

- For HB, there is an additional disregard depending on the hours you work, a childcare costs disregard and a permitted work disregard.
- For income-related ESA, usually £20 a week is disregarded. However, different rules apply if you are doing 'permitted work'.

Disregards for income-related employment and support allowance

Permitted work disregard

- All your earnings from 'permitted work' (see p1020) are disregarded up to whichever earnings limit applies: £20 or £152. (Only £20 can be disregarded from self-employed earnings from royalties, copyright payments or Public Lending Right scheme payments.)[78]
- If your earnings are less than the £20 or £152 limit, up to £20 of what is left can be disregarded from your partner's earnings.[79]

Note: your earnings from any permitted work (for both contributory and income-related ESA) are assessed in the same way as that described in this chapter.[80]

£20 disregard

Twenty pounds of your earnings (including those of your partner) is disregarded if:[81]

- you are doing work you may do while claiming ESA (see p1019), but only if it is:
  - as a councillor; *or*
  - as a disability member of the First-tier Tribunal. If you are also doing 'permitted work', instead of the £20 disregard, any unused permitted work disregard up to £20 can be deducted from these tribunal earnings; *or*
  - during an emergency to protect someone or to prevent serious damage to property or livestock; *or*
  - while receiving assistance in pursuing self-employment under a government scheme; *or*
- your partner is in part-time employment of under 24 hours a week (but if you are doing permitted work, see above); *or*
- your partner would be treated as not being in full-time paid work for IS purposes, other than if this is because of qualifying for housing costs run-on (see p977); *or*

Part 4: General rules for other means-tested benefits
Chapter 20: Income: under pension age
3. Earnings

- your partner is working, but does not count as being in full-time paid work because s/he:
  - is childminding in her/his home; *or*
  - is a carer under the rules for who can qualify for IS (see p235); *or*
  - is receiving assistance under the 'self-employment route' – eg, New Enterprise Allowance; *or*
  - is an auxiliary coastguard, part-time firefighter, part-time member of a lifeboat crew or member of the reserve forces; *or*
  - is working as a councillor; *or*
  - would not qualify for JSA on the grounds that s/he has been involved in a trade dispute (see p982), or it is the first 15 days following her/his return to work after having been involved in a trade dispute.

Disregards for income support, income-based jobseeker's allowance and housing benefit

£25 disregard

Lone parents on HB have £25 of their earnings ignored.[82] **Note:** if you get IS, income-based JSA or income-related ESA (or UC), all your earnings are disregarded for HB, so this £25 disregard does not apply.

£20 disregard

Twenty pounds of your earnings (including those of your partner) is disregarded if:

- for IS or income-based JSA, you are a lone parent;[83] *or*
- you or your partner qualify for a disability premium (see p325).[84] For IS and income-based JSA, you are treated as qualifying for the premium if you would do so but for the fact that you are in hospital; *or*
- for HB, you or your partner qualify for a severe disability premium (see p330), the support component or work-related activity component (see p337), or you are in the 'work-related activity group' (see p638);[85] *or*
- you or your partner qualify for a carer premium (see p334). The disregard applies to the carer's earnings. If both partners in a couple get the carer premium, £20 is disregarded from their combined earnings. If you are the carer and the claimant, and your earnings are less than £20, up to £5 (£10 for HB) of the disregard can be used on your partner's earnings (or all of what is left of it if your partner's earnings are from one of the services listed in the next bullet point) – but the total disregard cannot be more than £20;[86] *or*
- you or your partner are an auxiliary coastguard, part-time firefighter, part-time member of a lifeboat crew or member of the reserve forces.[87] If you earn less than £20 for doing any of these services, you can use up to £5 (up to £10 for HB, if you have a partner) of the disregard on another job[88] or on a partner's earnings from another job;[89] *or*

- for IS and income-based JSA only, you are a member of a couple, your benefit would include a disability premium but for the fact that one of you qualifies for the higher pensioner premium (see p329), and one of you is under pension age (see p257) and either of you are in employment;[90] *or*
- for IS and income-based JSA only, you or your partner qualify for the higher pensioner premium (see p329) and, immediately before reaching pension age (see p257), you or your partner were in part-time employment and you were entitled to a £20 disregard because of qualifying for a disability premium. Since reaching the pension age, you or your partner must have continued in part-time employment, although breaks of up to eight weeks when you were not getting IS, income-based JSA or income-related ESA are ignored.[91]

If you qualify under more than one category, you still have a maximum of only £20 of your earnings disregarded.

Basic £5 or £10 disregard

If you do not qualify for a £25 or £20 disregard (or, for HB, the permitted work disregard – see below), £5 of your earnings is disregarded if you are single. If you claim as a member of a couple, £10 of your total earnings is disregarded – whether or not you are both working.[92]

Permitted work disregard for housing benefit

If you or your partner are doing 'permitted work' (see p1020 for what this means) and getting contributory ESA, severe disablement allowance (SDA) or NI credits for limited capability for work or incapacity, the permitted work earnings limit for that benefit or credit (either £20 or £152) is also disregarded from earnings for HB.[93] This is instead of the usual disregard of £5, £10, £20 or £25.

If your earnings from permitted work are less than the limit, you can use up the rest:

- on your partner's earnings, up to a maximum of £20 or up to the limit if s/he is also doing permitted work, but there is only one disregard between you; *or*
- on your own earnings from other work. See p1019 for other work you may do while claiming one of these benefits. If you are a lone parent, you can also top up the disregard on earnings from other work to £25.

Additional disregard for housing benefit

For HB only, whichever earnings disregard applies is increased by £17.10 if:[94]

- you or your partner receive the 30-hour element as part of your (or your partner's) working tax credit (WTC – see p1420); *or*
- you or your partner are aged 25 or over and work 30 hours or more a week on average; *or*
- you or your partner work 16 hours or more a week on average and you have a child who is part of your family for benefit purposes (see p307), or your HB includes the family premium (see p324); *or*

Part 4: General rules for other means-tested benefits
Chapter 20: Income: under pension age
3. Earnings

- you are a lone parent and work 16 hours or more a week on average; *or*
- you or your partner work 16 hours or more a week on average and your HB includes a disability premium (see p325), the support component or work-related activity component (see p336), or you are in the 'work-related activity group' (see p638). For couples, the partner for whom the premium/component is awarded or who is in the work-related activity group must be working 16 hours or more a week on average.

The additional earnings disregard does not apply if your total earnings are less than the total of £17.10 plus any earnings disregard and childcare costs disregard (see below). In this case, £17.10 is disregarded from any WTC awarded to you or your partner, but the earnings disregard is not increased.

Note: only one additional disregard is allowed from your (or your partner's) earnings.

Example
Ella and Megan are a couple with one child aged eight. Ella gets contributory ESA and HB. Megan works part time for 16 hours a week, earning £160.
The amount of Megan's earnings taken into account for HB is £122.90 a week. From her £160 wages, £20 is disregarded because Ella is in the work-related activity group, and £17.10 is disregarded because they have a child and Megan works sufficient hours for the additional disregard.

Childcare costs disregard for housing benefit

For HB, up to £175 a week for one child, or up to £300 a week for two or more children, can be deducted from your (or your partner's) earnings (from employment or self-employment) for childcare costs if you are:[95]

- a lone parent working 16 hours or more a week; *or*
- a couple and both of you work 16 hours or more a week, or one of you works 16 hours or more a week and the other is 'incapacitated' (see p418), or is in hospital or prison.

The most that can be deducted for one child is £175, even if you pay more. For more than one child, £300 is the maximum even if you pay more or have to pay for more than two children.

It is not necessary for the childcare to be provided only while you are at work, nor for it to be work-related, and there is no requirement for the charges to be reasonable.

You can still get this disregard for childcare costs if you are off work sick, although for lone parents it stops after 28 weeks (see p418).

If you also get WTC or child tax credit (CTC) and your earnings, once other HB disregards have been allowed, are less than the deduction for childcare costs, your earnings and the WTC/CTC are added together before the deduction for childcare costs is made.[96]

The childcare costs disregard only applies to charges you pay for certain types of childcare provided for any child(ren) in your family under the age of 15 (or 16 if s/he is disabled – see below). A child is not treated as having reached the age of 15/16 until the day before the first Monday in September following her/his 15th/16th birthday.[97]

Disabled child

A child is defined as '**disabled**' if s/he is:[98]

– in receipt of disability living allowance (DLA), child disability payment (CDP), personal independence payment (PIP), adult disability payment (ADP) or armed forces independence payment; or

– certified as severely sight impaired or blind by a consultant ophthalmologist, or stopped being certified before the first Monday in September following her/his 16th birthday, but no more than one year and 28 weeks before then.

The childcare must be provided:[99]

- by a registered childminder or other registered childcare provider (such as a nursery or local authority daycare service); or
- out of school hours for children between the ages of eight and 15/16, by a school on school premises or a local authority – eg, an out-of-hours or holiday play scheme; or
- by another relevant childcare provider (see p1424 – these are the same as for WTC).

You cannot include charges for care provided by a relative of the child in the child's own home even if s/he is a registered childminder, nor charges paid by you to your partner or by your partner to you for a child in your family. You can include charges for childcare outside the child's home provided by a relative, provided s/he is not your partner and is a registered childminder. The registered childminder could be a former partner who may even be the child's parent. Charges for compulsory education do not count.

If you or your partner are on maternity, adoption, paternity, shared parental or parental bereavement leave, you are treated as working, and so can get the childcare disregard if you (or your partner):[100]

- were working in the week immediately before the leave began; and
- are entitled to SMP, SAP, SPP, SSPP, SPBP (see Chapter 38) or maternity allowance (MA) (see Chapter 34), or are getting IS because you are on paternity leave.

Part 4: General rules for other means-tested benefits
Chapter 20: Income: under pension age
3. Earnings

You are no longer treated as working and so cannot get the childcare costs disregard when:

- the maternity, adoption, paternity, shared parental or parental bereavement leave ends; *or*
- if you are not receiving the childcare element of WTC, you or your partner stop getting SMP, SAP, SPP, SSPP, SPBP or MA, or IS because you are on paternity leave; *or*
- if you are receiving the childcare element of WTC when you stop getting SMP, SAP, SPP, SSPP, SPBP or MA or IS because you are on paternity leave, you stop getting the childcare element of WTC.

You can get the childcare costs disregard for the new child in your family while you are still on maternity, adoption, paternity, shared parental or parental bereavement leave.

Childcare costs and ill health or disability

You can still have a childcare costs disregard while off work sick for the first 28 weeks while you are getting SSP, ESA or NI credits for limited capability for work, provided you were working at least 16 hours a week immediately before you started getting one of these benefits.[101]

After 28 weeks, lone parents who are off work sick can no longer get a childcare costs disregard, but couples can do so (before or after 28 weeks) if one of them works 16 hours or more a week and the other is treated as 'incapacitated'.

Incapacitated

You (or your partner) are treated as **'incapacitated'** if:[102]

– you get ESA which includes a support or work-related activity component, or SDA; *or*
– you get attendance allowance, DLA/CDP, PIP/ADP, armed forces independence payment or constant attendance allowance (or an equivalent award under the war pensions or industrial injuries schemes) or you would receive one of these benefits but for the fact that you (or your partner) are in hospital; *or*
– you have an NHS-provided wheelchair or mobility scooter or similar vehicle; *or*
– your HB includes a disability premium, support component or work-related activity component for the incapacitated person's incapacity or limited capability for work, or that person is in the 'work-related activity group' (see p638); *or*
– you (but not your partner) have been treated either as having limited capability for work or as being incapable of work for a continuous period of 196 days or more (disregarding any break of up to 84 or 56 days respectively).

Calculating childcare costs

The costs to be taken into account are estimated over whatever period, not exceeding a year, that will give the best estimate of the average weekly charge based on information provided by the childminder or care provider.

4. Other income

As well as income from earnings, most other forms of income are taken into account in full, less any tax due. To work out the weekly income to take into account, check whether the payment can be disregarded (in part or in full), deduct any tax due and work out the weekly amount (see p437). Where a taxable benefit or other unearned income is not taxed at source and you have not yet had a tax assessment, ask HM Revenue and Customs for a forecast of the tax due on that income. Otherwise, the DWP calculates how much tax to deduct.[103] For housing benefit (HB), the local authority has discretion to ignore changes in tax rates and in the maximum rate of child tax credit (CTC) and working tax credit (WTC) for up to 30 weeks – eg, where April changes are not reflected in your income until later.[104]

Benefits and tax credits

Benefits and tax credits that are taken into account

The following count in full:

- carer's allowance (CA) – but not CA supplement in Scotland;[105]
- for HB only, CTC. See p421 if your CTC is reduced to recover a tax credit overpayment;
- child's payment under the Armed Forces Compensation Scheme (but if it is paid for a dependent child, it is usually ignored – see p404);
- contribution-based jobseeker's allowance (JSA);
- contributory employment and support allowance (ESA). If ESA is paid at a reduced rate because of a sanction, it is still the full rate that counts;[106]
- severe disablement allowance;
- industrial injuries benefits, except constant attendance allowance and exceptionally severe disablement allowance, which are disregarded;
- maternity allowance;
- retirement pensions;
- statutory sick pay, statutory maternity pay, statutory adoption pay, statutory paternity pay, statutory shared parental pay and statutory parental bereavement pay count for income support (IS), income-based JSA and income-related ESA only, less any class 1 national insurance contributions and half of any pension contributions and any tax.[107] These are treated as earnings for HB and, therefore, may benefit from an earnings disregard (see p413);[108]
- widow's pension;
- WTC:
  - for IS, income-based JSA and income-related ESA;
  - for HB, except if earnings are too low to use the whole £17.10 additional full-time earnings disregard (see p415). In this case, £17.10 is disregarded from your WTC instead of your earnings. You must satisfy the conditions for the

Part 4: General rules for other means-tested benefits
Chapter 20: Income: under pension age
4. Other income

additional earnings disregard and have earnings of less than £17.10 plus whichever other earnings disregard applies plus any childcare costs disregard.[109] If earnings are too low to use the full childcare costs disregard, see p416.

See p421 if a tax credit overpayment is being deducted.

Benefits and tax credits that are not taken into account

The following are ignored completely:
- adult disability payment (ADP - in Scotland);[110]
- armed forces independence payment;[111]
- attendance allowance (AA);[112]
- bereavement support payment;[113]
- Best Start grants (in Scotland);[114]
- CA supplement (in Scotland);[115]
- child benefit.[116] However, for IS and income-based JSA, it is taken into account if you have been getting IS or income-based JSA since before 6 April 2004 and have an amount for that child in your claim (and do not get CTC);[117]
- child disability payment (in Scotland);[118]
- Christmas bonus;[119]
- constant attendance allowance, exceptionally severe disablement allowance or severe disablement occupational allowance paid because of an injury at work or a war injury;[120]
- CTC is ignored for IS, income-based JSA and income-related ESA;[121]
- disability living allowance (DLA);[122]
- funeral support payment (in Scotland);[123]
- guardian's allowance;[124]
- HB;[125]
- universal credit (UC), IS, income-based JSA and income-related ESA are ignored for HB.[126] There are special HB rules for these (see p190);
- mobility supplement under the War Pension Scheme;[127]
- personal independence payment (PIP);[128]
- Scottish child payment;[129]
- any extra-statutory payment made to you to compensate for non-payment of IS, income-based JSA, income-related ESA, UC, mobility supplement, AA, DLA or PIP/ADP;[130]
- social fund payments.[131] They are also disregarded as capital indefinitely;[132]
- any supplementary payments to war widows, widowers or surviving civil partners for pre-1973 service;[133]
- any payment made by the DWP to compensate for the loss of HB;[134]
- any payment in consequence of a reduction in liability for council tax, including from a council tax reduction scheme.[135]

Benefits that are partly taken into account

For HB only, widowed parent's allowance has £15 ignored.[136]

The following benefits have £10 ignored (or more for HB – see below):[137]

- for IS, income-based JSA and income-related ESA only, widowed parent's allowance;
- war disablement pension;
- guaranteed income payment and survivor's guaranteed income payment under the Armed Forces Compensation Scheme (or if another pension reduces the payment to below £10, ignore the remainder from the pension);
- war widow's, widower's or surviving civil partner's pension;
- an extra-statutory payment made instead of the above pensions;
- similar payments made by another country;
- a pension from any government paid to the victims of Nazi persecution.[138]

Even if you have more than two payments which attract a £10 disregard, only £20 in all can be ignored.[139] However, the £10 disregard allowed on the above payments is in addition to the total disregard of any mobility supplement or attendance allowance (ie, constant attendance allowance, exceptionally severe disablement allowance and severe disablement occupational allowance) paid as part of a war disablement pension.

The £10 disregard may overlap with other disregards, such as on student loans and access funds (see p891 and p894), when a combined maximum of £20 is allowed.

Local authorities may have discretionary local schemes to increase the £10 disregard on war disablement pension, war widow's or widower's pension, and the guaranteed income payment and survivor's guaranteed income payment in your HB. Most increase the disregard or ignore the full amount, so check your local scheme.[140]

Benefit delays

Problems can arise if a decision maker tries to take into account a benefit you are not receiving (such as CA) because it has been delayed. In such a case, the benefit should not be treated as income you have. For IS, income-based JSA and income-related ESA, you should get your full benefit and the DWP deducts the difference from the arrears of the delayed benefit when it is eventually awarded.[141]

For the treatment of payments of arrears of certain benefits and tax credits, see p482.

Benefit deductions and overpayments

Usually, if any deductions are being taken from your benefit (eg, for an overpayment, rent or bills), the full amount of benefit is taken into account before the deduction is taken off.[142] However, if an overpayment of tax credits is being deducted from a tax credits award, it is the amount you actually receive that is

Part 4: General rules for other means-tested benefits
Chapter 20: Income: under pension age
4. Other income

taken into account after the deduction to recover the overpayment has been taken off.[143]

Maintenance payments

If you get **child maintenance** for a child who is a member of your family, it is all ignored if it is made by the child's parent (who is not your partner) or by another 'liable relative' (see below).[144] Child maintenance payments include:

- any payment made voluntarily;
- payments under a court order or consent order;
- child support maintenance (assessed by the Child Maintenance Service);
- in Scotland, payments under a registered maintenance agreement.

Note: arrears of regular child support maintenance should be treated as income for a past period. Arrears are ignored as income if, for HB, they cover a period since 27 October 2008 or, for other benefits, since 12 April 2010. Before that, arrears may mean that you have been overpaid benefit, although some overpaid benefits can be deducted from arrears before you get them.[145]

Other kinds of maintenance

If you get another kind of maintenance payment from a former partner (eg, maintenance for yourself):[146]

- £15 is ignored for HB if you have a child who is part of your family for benefit purposes (see p307) or a family premium included in your HB. If you get maintenance from more than one person, only £15 of the total is ignored;
- for other benefits, it is regarded as a 'liable relative' payment and usually counts in full.

Liable relative
A **'liable relative'** is:[147]
– a spouse, civil partner, former spouse or civil partner; *or*
– a parent of a child who is a member of your family; *or*
– someone who can reasonably be treated as the child's father because of the financial support he makes.

For IS, income-based JSA and income-related ESA, any payment from a liable relative other than child maintenance is taken into account in full as income, whether it is paid regularly or as a lump sum, with some exceptions as follows.[148]

- Payments made direct to someone else and not to you (ie, to a third party) are taken into account as maintenance if they are for certain normal living expenses (food, clothing, footwear), for certain bills (fuel, council tax, water charges), for rent met by HB or for housing costs met by IS, JSA or ESA (such as service charges). Payments for other kinds of expenses, such as mortgage repayments paid direct to the mortgage lender or TV licence payments paid direct, are ignored.[149] This means it can be better for you if your ex-partner pays these other kinds of expenses direct rather than to you. If you use your maintenance payments to pay the mortgage yourself, it is taken into account as your income, so you will get less benefit.

- Payments in kind, such as food, holidays and clothing, are ignored (except if you are involved in a trade dispute).
- Gifts (eg, birthday and Christmas presents) of up to £250 in total in any period of 52 weeks are not taken into account as maintenance, but may count as capital.
- If you have already spent a payment before the DWP makes its decision about the effect on your benefit, the payment is ignored, provided you did not deliberately get rid of the money in order to claim or increase your benefit. The issues are the same as the deprivation of income/capital rule on p487.
- A payment from a 'disposition of property' because of divorce, separation, nullity or dissolution of a civil partnership is not taken into account as maintenance (so is not treated as income), but usually counts as capital. This applies, for example, if your former partner buys out your interest in a home so you get a lump-sum settlement instead of a share of the property itself.[150]
- Payments for a child who is not a member of your household (eg, a child looked after by a local authority and not living with you, or a child in custody) do not count as maintenance. They should be ignored if you spend the money on the child, but count as income if you keep the money or spend it on yourself.[151]
- A payment made after the liable relative has died no longer counts as maintenance (so is not automatically treated as income), but is still taken into account as income or capital under the normal rules.

If you get payments towards maintenance from someone who is not a liable relative (eg, a grandparent), this normally counts as a voluntary payment and is ignored (see p425).

If you pay maintenance

If you *pay* maintenance to a former partner or a child not living with you, your payments are not disregarded for the purpose of calculating your income for any benefits.[152] See p491 if part of a personal or occupational pension is paid to a former partner.

Student loans and grants

For the special rules on the treatment of student loans, grants and other types of student support, see Chapter 41.

Part 4: General rules for other means-tested benefits
Chapter 20: Income: under pension age
4. Other income

Adoption, fostering and similar payments

Adoption allowance

An adoption allowance is disregarded in full, except in the following circumstances.[153]

- If the adoption allowance is paid for a child who is not a member of your family (eg, because the adoption order has not yet been granted), it is fully disregarded in England.[154] In Scotland and Wales, any amount you spend on the child is disregarded and any you keep for yourself is taken into account.[155]

- For IS and income-based JSA, if you have been getting benefit since before 6 April 2004 with a child included in your claim and do not have an award of CTC, the adoption allowance is taken into account in full up to the level of the adopted child's personal allowance and any disabled child premium.[156] Above that level it is ignored. Get advice to check whether you would be better off claiming UC instead.

Fostering allowance

The way a fostering allowance is treated depends on whether the arrangement is official or private. If a child is placed or boarded out with you by a local authority directly or through an independent fostering agency[157] or a voluntary organisation under specific legal provisions,[158] the child is not counted as a member of your family (see p311) and any fostering allowances you receive while the child is placed with you should be ignored.[159] If the fostering arrangement is a private one, any money you receive from the child's parent(s) is counted as maintenance (see p422).

Child arrangements order allowance and similar payments

If you are paid a child arrangements order allowance by a local authority (in England and Wales), this is treated in the same way as an adoption allowance (see above).[160] Any payments made by the birth parents count as maintenance (see p422). In Scotland, kinship care payments made under section 73 of the Children and Young People (Scotland) Act 2014, section 22 of the Children (Scotland) Act 1995 or regulation 33 of the Looked After Children (Scotland) Regulations 2009 are ignored altogether, but if made under section 50 of the Children Act 1975, they are treated in the same way as an adoption allowance.[161]

Special guardianship allowance

The law treats a special guardianship allowance, payable in England and Wales for a child who is a member of your family, in the same way as an adoption allowance (see above), but official guidance advises that it should be fully disregarded for IS and income-based JSA.[162]

Charitable, voluntary and personal injury payments

Payments from special compensation schemes

Any payments are ignored indefinitely from specified schemes including:[163]
- the National Emergencies Trust;
- the Windrush Compensation Scheme;
- schemes to make child abuse payments for historic institutional child abuse in the UK;
- for people infected from contaminated blood products;
- for people affected by the 2017 fire at Grenfell Tower.

Money from your partner's payments is ignored indefinitely, and from your child's payments for two years if s/he has no partner or dependent child.

Any income or capital that derives from any such payments is also disregarded.

Other payments

Most other charitable or voluntary payments that are made irregularly and are intended to be made irregularly are treated as capital and are unlikely to affect your benefit claim unless they take your capital above the limit.[164] However, if you are on IS or income-based JSA, they count as income if you are involved in a trade dispute and, for IS only, for the first 15 days following your return to work after a dispute (see p982).[165]

Payments made on a regular basis

Charitable and voluntary payments and certain personal injury payments are ignored if they are made, or are due to be made, regularly.[166]

A **'voluntary payment'** is one given without getting anything back in return.[167]

For IS and income-based JSA, these payments are not disregarded if you are involved in a trade dispute and, for IS only, for the first 15 days following your return to work after a trade dispute (see p982).

Payments from a former partner, or the parent of your child, are treated as maintenance (see p422).

Personal injury payments

'Personal injury payments' are:[168]
- payments from a trust fund set up out of money paid because of any personal injury to you;
- payments under an annuity purchased either under an agreement or court order set up because of any personal injury to you, or from money paid because of any personal injury to you;
- payments you get under an agreement or court order because of any personal injury to you. This does not include an occupational pension – eg, if you have retired early because of personal injury.[169]

Part 4: General rules for other means-tested benefits
Chapter 20: Income: under pension age
4. Other income

See also p435 for payments made to someone else on your behalf, p432 for payments disregarded under miscellaneous income and p484 for lump sum personal injury payments.

Victims payments to people injured in a Northern Ireland 'Troubles-related incident' are ignored as income (or capital).[170]

Concessionary coal to former British Coal workers and their surviving partners is ignored (except to strikers). Cash in lieu of coal counts in full.[171]

Income from tenants and lodgers

How income from tenants is treated depends on whether or not you live in the same property.

Lettings without board

If you let out a room(s) in your home to tenants, subtenants or licensees under a formal contractual arrangement, £20 of your weekly charge for each tenant, subtenant or licensee (and her/his family) is ignored.[172] The balance counts as income.

If someone shares your home under an informal arrangement, any payment s/he makes to you for living and accommodation costs is ignored,[173] but a non-dependant deduction may be made from any HB or housing costs paid with IS/income-based JSA/income-related ESA (see p198 and p347).

Boarders

If you have a boarder(s) on a commercial basis in your own home, and the boarder or any member of her/his family is not a close relative of yours, the first £20 of the weekly charge is ignored and half of any balance remaining is then taken into account as your income.[174] For HB, this applies even if the boarder is a close relative and it is not a commercial arrangement. However, a non-dependant deduction may be made for her/him (see p198). This disregard applies for each boarder you have. The charge must normally include at least some meals.[175] If you have a business partner, even though your gross income includes just your share of the weekly charge to boarders, you still get the full disregard of £20 plus half the excess for each boarder.[176]

Note: if you let part of your home, any income left after applying the above disregards which is intended to be used to meet any housing costs of your own which are not met by IS, income-based JSA, income-related ESA or HB, may also be disregarded (see p430).[177]

Tenants in other properties

If you have a freehold interest in a property other than your home and you let it out, the rent is normally treated as capital.[178] This rule also applies if you have a leasehold interest in another property which you are subletting. The full rent counts initially (as well as the capital value of the property itself) but, if you spend some on a debt that is immediately repayable (eg, a monthly mortgage payment) after a period (eg, a month for monthly paid rent), only what remains continues to count as capital. If you spend it on something else to deliberately increase your benefit, the notional capital rules could treat you as still having the money (see p486).[179]

The rent is treated as income if the property you let is in one of the categories where the capital value is disregarded (see p478). In this case, the expenses listed below are deducted from the income.

Income from capital

In general, actual income generated from capital (eg, interest on savings) is ignored as income.[180] It counts as capital from the date you are due to receive it.[181] However, income derived from the following categories of disregarded capital (see p477) is treated as income:[182]

- your home;
- your former home, if you are estranged, divorced or your civil partnership has ended;
- property which you have acquired for occupation as your home, but you have not yet been able to move into;
- property which you intend to occupy as your home, but which needs essential repairs or alterations;
- property occupied wholly or partly by a partner or relative of any member of your family who has reached pension age or who is incapacitated;
- property occupied by your former partner, unless you are estranged, divorced or your civil partnership has ended;
- property for sale;
- property which you are taking legal steps to obtain to occupy as your home;
- your business assets;
- a trust of personal injury compensation.

Some expenses are deducted from this income. Income from property (other than your current home) is ignored up to the amount of the total mortgage repayments (ie, capital and interest, and any payments that are a condition of the mortgage, such as insurance or an endowment policy),[183] council tax and water charges paid in respect of the property for the same period over which the income is received.[184]

Tariff income from capital

If your capital is over a certain level, you are treated as having an assumed income from it, called your '**tariff income**'. You are assumed to have an income of £1 a week for every £250, or part of £250, by which your capital exceeds £6,000 but does not exceed £16,000.[185]

If you are in a care home or similar accommodation (see p473), tariff income applies between £10,000 and £16,000.

Part 4: General rules for other means-tested benefits
Chapter 20: Income: under pension age
4. Other income

Capital that counts as income

The following capital is treated as income:

- instalments of capital outstanding when you claim benefit, if they would bring you over the capital limit. For IS, income-based JSA and income-related ESA, the instalments to be counted are any outstanding, either when your benefit claim is decided or when you are first due to be paid benefit, whichever is earlier, or at the date of any subsequent supersession.[186] For HB, it is any instalments outstanding when your claim is made or treated as made, or when your benefit is revised or superseded.[187] The outstanding instalments count as income by spreading them over the number of weeks between each instalment;[188]
- any payment from an annuity[189] (see p429 for when this is disregarded);
- any professional and career development loan (see p893);[190]
- for IS only, a tax refund if you or your partner have returned to work after a trade dispute (see p982);[191]
- periodic payments made under an agreement or court order for any personal injury to you (see p425 for when these are disregarded);[192]
- some lump sums from liable relatives (see p422).

Note: capital counted as income cannot also be treated as producing a tariff income (see p427).[193]

Sometimes, you may find that withdrawals from a capital sum are treated as income.[194] This is most likely if the sum was intended to help cover living expenses over a particular period – eg, a bank loan taken out by a student. If this is not the intended use of any capital sum, dispute the decision. Even if the sum is intended for living expenses, argue that, unless it is actually paid in instalments, it should be treated as capital.[195] A loan that you have an obligation to repay immediately should not be treated as your income (or capital), however it is paid.[196]

Income tax refunds

Pay as you earn (PAYE) refunds and self-employment tax refunds are treated as capital.[197]

For IS and JSA, tax refunds paid during a trade dispute are treated as income and taken into account.[198] For IS only, if you or your partner have returned to work after a trade dispute (see p982), tax refunds are treated as income and are taken into account in full.[199]

Income from employment and training programmes

Payments from employment or training programmes under section 2 of the Employment and Training Act 1973 or section 2 of the Enterprise and New Towns (Scotland) Act 1990 are treated as follows.[200]

The following payments are taken into account:
- for ESA, those made as a substitute for ESA or JSA; for other benefits, payments made as a substitute for IS, JSA or ESA – eg, a training allowance; *and*
- those intended for certain living costs while you are participating in a scheme to enhance your employment prospects. Payments for food, ordinary clothing or footwear, fuel, rent met by HB, housing costs met by IS, JSA or income-related ESA, council tax or water charges are all taken into account.

All other payments are disregarded – eg:
- travel expenses;
- training premium;
- childcare expenses;
- special needs payments;
- expenses for participating in a specified scheme for assisting people to obtain employment (see p1122);[201]
- New Enterprise Allowance weekly allowance.

For ESA, any payment for expenses incurred in complying with a requirement to undertake work-related activity (see p1111) is ignored.[202]

If you have been getting help under the New Enterprise Allowance, any payments to meet expenses 'wholly and necessarily' incurred while trading, or used to repay a loan necessary for the business, are also disregarded if they are from a special account set up for this programme.[203] Income built up in your special account while you are getting this help is treated as capital for HB.[204] At the end of the programme, this is treated as income for IS/JSA/ESA and spread over the same number of weeks in the future for which you have been receiving assistance, less any income tax due on the profits and an earnings disregard appropriate to your circumstances (see p413).[205]

Occupational and personal pensions and annuities

Although you can usually choose to take some, or all, of your occupational or personal pension from age 55, your benefit is not affected if you do not – ie, there is no notional income or capital assumed. Any regular withdrawals from your pension pot or pension income you take count in full as income. If you take a lump sum, this counts as capital, and notional capital rules can apply to how you spend it (see p486).[206] If your partner has reached pension age and chooses not to take income from an occupational or personal pension, you are treated as having notional income. If you (or your partner) have reached pension age, see also p463.

Discretionary payments from a hardship fund are not regarded as an occupational pension, but are treated as charitable or voluntary payments (see p425).[207]

Part 4: General rules for other means-tested benefits
Chapter 20: Income: under pension age
4. Other income

Payments from an annuity count in full unless:
- the annuity is set up with money paid because of personal injury to you, or under an agreement or court order because of personal injury to you (see p425); *or*
- the annuity is set up with money from a home income plan, in which case income from the annuity equal to the interest payable on the loan with which the annuity was bought is ignored if:[208]
  - you used at least 90 per cent of the loan made to you to buy the annuity; *and*
  - the annuity will end when you and your partner die; *and*
  - you or your partner are responsible for paying the interest on the loan; *and*
  - you (if you took out the loan), or your partner (if s/he did), were at least 65 at the time the loan was made; *and*
  - the loan is secured on a property which you or your partner own or in which you have an interest, and the property on which the loan is secured is your home, or that of your partner.

If the interest on the loan is payable after income tax has been deducted, it is an amount equal to the net interest payment that is disregarded. Otherwise, it is the gross amount of the interest payment.

Mortgage and insurance payments

For IS, income-based JSA and income-related ESA only, ignore:
- payments you receive under a mortgage insurance policy which you use to maintain mortgage payments;[209]
- provided you have not already used mortgage protection insurance payments for the same purpose, any money you receive which is given, and which you use, to make the following payments:[210]
  - payments due on a secured loan that does not qualify for a DWP loan for mortgage interest (see p839);
  - capital payments and interest payments on a loan that qualifies for a DWP loan for mortgage interest, but which are not met by the DWP loan;
  - service charges and other eligible housing costs that are not met by the help you get with housing costs in your benefit (see Chapter 18);
- payments of premiums on an insurance policy which you took out to insure against the risk of not being able to make the payments in the above three categories, and premiums on a buildings insurance policy;
- payment of any rent that is not covered by HB (see Chapter 10);
- payment of the part of your accommodation charge in a care home that exceeds that payable by a local authority.

Example

Asim is on income-based JSA. He is an owner-occupier with a mortgage. He gets a DWP loan for mortgage interest, which pays £70 a month towards his interest payments of £100 a month. He still has to pay £30 a month mortgage interest, £90 a month capital repayments and £20 a month premiums on his buildings insurance, which totals £140. He receives £170 a month from an income protection insurance policy. Of this, £140 is ignored and £30 a month counts as his income.

If you are using maintenance from a former partner or parent of your child (but not child maintenance, which is disregarded whatever you use it for) to pay these costs, it may be taken into account as a 'liable relative payment', unless it is paid direct to someone else – eg, a lender (see p422).

For HB only, payments you receive under an insurance policy to insure against the risk of being unable to maintain payments on a loan secured on your home are ignored. However, anything you get above the total of the following counts as your income:[211]

- the amount you use to maintain your payments; *and*
- any premium you pay for the policy; *and*
- any premium for an insurance policy to insure against loss or damage to your home.

Payments you receive under an insurance policy to insure against the risk of being unable to maintain hire purchase or similar payments or other loan payments (eg, credit card debts) are also ignored. However, anything you get above the amount you use to make your payments and the premium for the policy counts as your income.[212]

Social services, community care and other payments

The following payments are ignored:

- local welfare assistance to meet an immediate short-term need or establish or maintain a settled home in certain circumstances (see p846). These include test and trace support payments (in England), self-isolation support grants (in Scotland) and self-isolation support scheme payments (in Wales);[213] *and*
- payments from a local authority for children, families and people in need, made under section 17 of the Children Act 1989, section 12 of the Social Work (Scotland) Act 1968, section 22 of the Children (Scotland) Act 1995 or sections 37 or 38 of the Social Services and Well-being (Wales) Act 2014.[214] See p982 if you or your partner are involved in a trade dispute; *and*
- payments from a local authority for young people who were previously looked after by the local authority, paid under sections 23B or 24A of the Children Act 1989, section 30 of the Children (Scotland) Act 1995 or sections 109, 110, 114

Part 4: General rules for other means-tested benefits
Chapter 20: Income: under pension age
4. Other income

or 115 of the Social Services and Well-being (Wales) Act 2014. A payment under section 23C is also ignored as the young person's income and as yours if s/he passes it to you, s/he was in your care, is still living with you and is aged 18 or over – eg, under 'staying put' arrangements. In Scotland, this applies to payments under sections 26A and 29 of the Children (Scotland) Act 1995 and includes young people aged 16 or over in 'continuing care'. See p982 if you or your partner are involved in a trade dispute;[215] *and*

- direct payments to you under an education, health and care plan for a child with special educational needs (paid in England);[216] *and*
- any community care or healthcare direct payments. Local authorities or the NHS pay these to disabled people or carers to buy their own services instead of providing services direct. A direct payment is not ignored as the income of the person you pay for services, even if this is your partner;[217] *and*
- any payment you or your partner receive for looking after someone who is temporarily in your care if it is paid under community care arrangements by the NHS, local authority, voluntary organisation or the person being looked after.[218] Any HB paid to you by a local authority for that person is not ignored, although see p426 for other possible disregards; *and*
- payments from a local authority for support services to help you live independently (eg, under the Supporting People programme, often called 'housing-related support') are ignored indefinitely;[219] *and*
- if you live in a care home and a local authority arranged your place, local authority payments towards your fees are ignored for IS, JSA and income-related ESA. If a local authority did not arrange your place, any payment intended and used for your maintenance is fully disregarded if it is a voluntary or charitable payment, and partly disregarded if not – up to the difference between the care home fees and your applicable amount;[220] *and*
- a lump-sum payment from a local authority to enable you to make adaptations to your home for a disabled child. This is treated as capital and ignored.[221]

Miscellaneous income

The following income is ignored:
- any discretionary housing payments paid by a local authority;[222] *and*
- education maintenance allowances (paid in Scotland and Wales) and 16 to 19 bursary fund payments (paid in England).[223] These are paid to some young people staying on at school or other non-advanced education; *and*
- any payment to cover your expenses if you are working as an unpaid volunteer, or working unpaid for a charity or voluntary organisation;[224] *and*
- payments in kind (except for IS or income-based JSA, if you or your partner are involved in a trade dispute – see p982).[225] These may include food, fuel, cigarettes,[226] clothing, holidays, gifts, accommodation, transport or nursery education vouchers. However, see p433 for the rules on notional income and

p405 for the rules on non-cash vouchers paid as earnings. Items for essential living needs provided by the Home Office to an asylum-seeking partner are ignored for IS, income-based JSA and income-related ESA; *and*

- a payment (other than a training allowance) to a disabled person under the Disabled Persons (Employment) Act 1944 to assist her/him to obtain or retain employment;[227] *and*
- any payments, other than for loss of earnings or a benefit, made to jurors or witnesses for attending court;[228] *and*
- Victoria Cross or George Cross payments or similar awards;[229] *and*
- income paid outside the UK which cannot be transferred here;[230] *and*
- if income is paid in another currency, any bank charges for converting the payment into sterling;[231] *and*

- fares to hospital and refunds for prescription or dental charges;[232] *and*
- payments instead of milk tokens and vitamins, or instead of Healthy Start food vouchers;[233] *and*
- payments to assist prison visits;[234] *and*
- for HB, if you make a parental contribution to a student's grant or loan, an equal amount of any 'unearned' income you have for the period the grant or loan is paid. If your 'unearned' income does not cover the contribution, the balance can be disregarded from your earnings. If you are a parent of a student under 25 in advanced education who does not get a grant or loan (or who only gets a smaller discretionary award), up to £61.05 of your contribution to her/his living expenses is ignored from your 'unearned' income (less the weekly amount of any discretionary award the student has). This is only ignored during the student's term. Any balance can be disregarded from your earnings;[235] *and*
- a sports award made by UK Sport from National Lottery funds for living expenses is taken into account. This covers food, ordinary clothing or footwear, fuel, council tax, water charges and rent (less any non-dependant deductions) for which HB could be payable or housing costs that could be met by IS, income-based JSA or income-related ESA. Payments for anything else are ignored – eg, sportswear and dietary supplements to enhance performance;[236] *and*
- any payment for expenses if you are being consulted as a service user by the DWP or a health, care or housing body that provides statutory services (expenses do not count as earnings either).[237]

5. Notional income

In certain circumstances, you may be treated as having income, even if you do not possess it or if you have used it up.

Part 4: General rules for other means-tested benefits
Chapter 20: Income: under pension age
5. Notional income

Deliberately getting rid of income

If you deliberately get rid of income in order to claim or increase your benefit, you are treated as though you still receive that income.[238] The basic issues involved are the same as those for deliberately getting rid of capital (see p487). **Note:** the rule only applies if your intention was to gain benefit for yourself or your partner. It should not apply if, for example, you stop claiming carer's allowance (CA) solely to allow the cared-for person to get a severe disability premium unless s/he is your partner (see p330).[239] However, if you do not claim a benefit which would clearly be paid if you did, it may be argued that you have failed to apply for income (see below).

The rule still applies if you move from one benefit to another in the case of income support (IS), jobseeker's allowance (JSA) and employment and support allowance (ESA). For example, if you got rid of income to increase the amount of your ESA and then claimed JSA instead, you are still treated as having the income for your JSA claim. However, you are not automatically treated as having the income if you claim universal credit (UC) instead, although the income could be considered under the UC rules (see p133).

Failing to apply for income

If you fail to apply for income to which you are entitled without having to fulfil further conditions, you are treated as having it from the date you could have obtained it.[240]

This does not include, for example, income from:
- a discretionary trust;
- a trust set up from money paid as a result of a personal injury;
- funds administered by a court as a result of a personal injury;
- a rehabilitation allowance made under the Employment and Training Act 1973;
- JSA (for IS, JSA and ESA) or ESA (for ESA only);
- if you are under pension age (see p257), a personal or occupational pension scheme or payments from the Pension Protection Fund. However, if you or your partner have reached that age and choose not to take your full pension, you are treated as having an income;[241]
- working tax credit and child tax credit.[242]

It must be certain that the income or benefits would be paid if you were to apply. For example, it may be difficult for the DWP to establish that there was 'no doubt' that CA would be paid to you if you have chosen not to claim it because of the effect on the benefit of the person you are caring for (see p330).[243]

As soon as you apply or make a claim, the rule ceases to apply.[244]

Income due to you that has not been paid

For IS, income-based JSA and income-related ESA only, you are treated as possessing any income that is owing to you – eg:[245]
- wages that are legally due to you, but are not paid;
- an occupational pension payment that is due but has not been received, unless the pension scheme has insufficient funds.[246]

This rule should not apply if:
- any social security benefit has been delayed; *or*
- you are waiting for a late payment of a government training allowance or a benefit from a European Economic Area country; *or*
- money is due to you from a discretionary trust or a trust set up from money paid as a result of a personal injury; *or*
- you are owed earnings when your job has ended because of redundancy but these have not been paid to you.[247]

The income must be due to *you* (or your family) and for your own benefit.[248]

Unpaid wages

For IS, income-based JSA and income-related ESA only, if you have wages due to you, but you do not yet know the exact amount or you have no proof of what they will be, you are treated as having a wage similar to that normally paid for that type of work in that area.[249] If your wages cannot be estimated, you may qualify for a short-term advance (see p1153).[250] For how wages are estimated for housing benefit, see p439.

Income paid to someone else on your behalf

If money is paid to someone on your behalf (eg, a landlord for your rent), this can count as notional income.[251] If so, it is still subject to the usual disregards that would apply if it were actual income – eg, a voluntary or charitable payment of income is ignored whether it is paid direct to you or to someone else on your behalf. See p490 for a description of these third-party rules – they are the same as those for notional capital.

Income in kind given to a third party for you is ignored (eg, a food parcel used to prepare meals for you) unless, for IS or income-based JSA, you or your partner are involved in a trade dispute. However, money given to someone who uses it to buy you goods or services counts as notional income under the usual rules.

Income paid to you for someone else

If you or your partner get a payment for someone not in the 'family' (eg, a relative living with you), it counts as your income if you keep any of it yourself or spend it on yourself or your partner unless it is, for example:[252]

Part 4: General rules for other means-tested benefits
Chapter 20: Income: under pension age
5. Notional income

- from a specified infected blood payment scheme (see p425);
- concessionary coal under the Coal Industry Act 1994;
- a payment for an approved employment-related course of education or a specified scheme for assisting people to obtain employment (see p1122);
- income in kind (eg, a food parcel given to you to make meals for someone else), unless, for IS or income-based JSA, you or your partner are involved in a trade dispute.

Cheap or unpaid labour

If you are helping another person or an organisation by doing work that would normally be paid, or be paid a higher wage, you are deemed to receive a wage similar to that normally paid for that kind of job in that area.[253]

The burden of proving that your work is something for which an employer would pay, and what the comparable wages are, lies with the decision maker in the DWP or local authority.[254]

The rule does not apply if:[255]

- you are on an unpaid approved work placement or work experience; or
- you are on a government employment or training programme with no training allowance, or only travel or meals expenses; or
- you can show that the person (including a limited company[256]) cannot, in fact, afford to pay, or afford to pay more; or
- you work for a charitable or voluntary organisation or as a volunteer, and it is accepted that it is reasonable for you to give your services free of charge.[257]

Sometimes it may also be reasonable to do a job free of charge from a sense of community duty, particularly if the job would otherwise remain undone and there would be no financial profit to an employer.[258]

If you are caring for a sick or disabled relative, it is usually accepted that it is reasonable to do this free of charge rather than expecting her/him to pay you from benefits. However, if you need to show that it is reasonable, you should take into account, for instance:[259]

- how much care you give and what other care options there are;
- your housing arrangements;
- whether you gave up work to care;
- the risk of your losing entitlement to CA if you were paid, or to a social services assessment of your needs;
- whether your relative would actually pay you.

6. Working out weekly income

Income support, income-based jobseeker's allowance and income-related employment and support allowance

To work out your weekly income for income support (IS), income-based jobseeker's allowance (JSA) and income-related employment and support allowance (ESA), you should do the following.

- Work out the period covered by the income (see below).
- Establish the date from when to start taking the income into account (see below).
- Convert the income into a weekly amount if necessary (see p438). There are special rules on variable income, payments for less than a week and overlapping payments.

These rules apply to earnings from employment and to income other than earnings. See p412 for how self-employed earnings are assessed.

Period covered by a payment

- If a payment of income is made for an identifiable period, it is taken into account for a period of equal length.[260] For example, a week's part-time earnings are taken into account for a week. If you are paid monthly, the payments are taken into account for the number of weeks between the date you are treated as having been paid and the date you are next due to be paid.
- If the payment does not relate to a particular period, the amount of the payment is divided by the amount of the weekly IS, income-based JSA or income-related ESA to which you would otherwise be entitled. If part of the payment should be disregarded, the amount of IS, income-based JSA or income-related ESA is increased by the appropriate disregard. The result of this calculation is the number of weeks that you are not entitled to IS, income-based JSA or income-related ESA.[261] **Note:** if your benefit is stopped, you cannot make a new claim for any of these benefits (see p23 for exceptions). If you claim universal credit (UC) instead, the payment is assessed under UC rules.
- Payments made on leaving a job, if not ignored, are taken into account for a forward period (see p408).

Date from when a payment counts

For IS, income-based JSA and income-related ESA, the date from when a payment of earnings and/or other income counts depends on when it was due to be paid. If it was due to be paid before you claimed IS, income-based JSA or income-related ESA, it counts from the date on which it was due to be paid.[262] Otherwise, it is treated as having been paid on the first day of the benefit week in which it is due,

Part 4: General rules for other means-tested benefits
Chapter 20: Income: under pension age
6. Working out weekly income

or on the first day of the first benefit week after that in which it is practicable to take it into account.[263]

Payments of UC, IS, JSA, ESA and maternity allowance (MA) are treated as paid on a daily basis for each day for which they are paid.[264]

Benefit week

The 'benefit week' for JSA, and usually also for IS and ESA, although this may vary, is normally the seven days ending with the day allocated to you according to your national insurance number (also your payday).[265] The benefit week for HB is the seven days starting on a Monday.[266]

The date a payment is due may be different from the date of actual payment. Earnings are due on the employee's normal payday. If the contract of employment does not reveal the date of due payment and there is no evidence to indicate otherwise, the date the payment was received should be taken as the date it was due.[267] If your contract of employment is terminated without proper notice, outstanding wages, wages in hand, holiday pay and any pay in lieu of notice are due on the last day of employment and are treated as having been paid on that day, even if this does not happen (although these are usually disregarded).[268]

If you receive compensation (eg, in a sex discrimination equal pay case), there is disagreement as to whether the relevant date is the date when the earnings in question were due to be paid[269] or when the compensation was awarded.[270]

For the treatment of payments at the end of a job, see p408.

Converting income into a weekly amount

To convert income to a weekly amount:
- if the payment is for less than a week, it is treated as the weekly amount;
- if the payment is for a month, multiply by 12 and divide by 52;
- multiply a payment for three months by four and divide by 52;
- divide a payment for a year by 52 (unless it is a working tax credit (WTC) payment, in which case divide by 365 and multiply by seven);
- for any other period, divide the payment by the number of days in the period then multiply by seven.

If you work on certain days but are paid monthly, it is necessary to decide whether the payment is for the days worked or for the whole month. This generally depends on the terms of your contract of employment,[271] but may depend on how your employer has arranged to make payments to you.[272]

Variable income

If your income fluctuates or your earnings vary because you do not work every week, your weekly income may be averaged over the cycle if there is an identifiable one or, if there is not, over five weeks, or over another period if this would be more accurate.[273] If the cycle involves periods when you do no work, those periods are included in the cycle, but not other absences – eg, holidays or sickness.

Part weeks

- If income covering a period up to a week is paid before your first 'benefit week' (see p438) and part of it is counted for that week or if, in any case, you are paid for a period of a week or more and only part of it is counted in a particular benefit week, multiply the whole payment by the number of days it covers in the benefit week, then divide the result by the total number of days covered by the payment.[274]
- If any payment of MA falls partly into the benefit week, only the amount paid for those days is taken into account. For any payment of IS, JSA or ESA, the amount taken into account is the weekly amount multiplied by the number of days in the part week and divided by seven.[275]

Overlapping payments

If you have regularly received a certain kind of payment of income from one source and in a particular 'benefit week' (see p438) you receive that payment and another of the same kind from the same source (eg, if your employer first pays you sick pay in arrears and this then overlaps with a payment in advance), the maximum amount to be taken into account is the one paid first.[276]

This does not apply if the second payment was due to be taken into account in another week but the overlapping week is the first in which it could practically be counted (see p437).

Housing benefit

To assess your current normal weekly income for HB, you should do the following.
- Average your earnings over a past period (see p440 for earnings from employment and p412 for self-employed earnings).
- Estimate income other than earnings (see p419 for what income counts) by looking at an appropriate period of up to 52 weeks. The period chosen must give an accurate assessment of your income.[277]
- Convert earnings from employment and income other than earnings into a weekly amount if necessary:
  – count a payment for less than a week as the weekly amount;
  – multiply a monthly payment by 12 and divide by 52;
  – for other periods, divide the payment by the number of days in the period then multiply by seven.
- Deduct the appropriate earnings disregard(s) (see p413).
- Work out the date from when the income is taken into account (see p440).

Part 4: General rules for other means-tested benefits
Chapter 20: Income: under pension age
6. Working out weekly income

Averaging earnings

For HB, earnings as an employee are usually averaged out over the previous:
- five weeks if you are paid weekly; *or*
- two months if you are paid monthly.[278]

If your earnings vary, or if there is likely to be, or has recently been, a change (eg, you usually do overtime but have not done so recently, or you are about to get a pay rise), the local authority may average them over a different period if this is likely to give a more accurate picture of what you are going to earn.[279]

If you are on strike, the local authority should not take into account your pre-strike earnings and average them out over the strike period.[280]

If you have only just started work and your earnings cannot be averaged over the normal period (ie, five weeks or two months), an estimate is made, based on any earnings you have been paid so far if these are likely to reflect your future average wage. If you have not yet been paid or your initial earnings do not represent what you will normally earn, your employer must provide an estimate of your average weekly earnings.[281] If you start work after having been on certain benefits, you may get four weeks' extended payments of HB at the same amount (see p217). If your earnings change during your award, your new weekly average figure is estimated on the basis of what you are likely to earn over whatever period (up to 52 weeks) best allows an accurate estimate.[282] If averaging does not result in a weekly figure, the amount is converted (see above).

Date from when a payment counts

The average weekly earnings from employment are taken into account for HB from the start of a new claim or from the first day of the 'benefit week' (see p438) after you start work if you are already getting HB. If average weekly earnings change, the new amount counts from the date of change, even if you are not paid until later.[283]

Child tax credit and WTC are taken into account instalment by instalment – eg, if paid weekly or four-weekly, each instalment counts for the seven or 28 days ending on the day it is due to be paid.[284] Other benefits are taken into account for the period they are paid for.[285]

Notes

1. Whose income counts

1 Schs 4 para 12 and 5 para 4 HB Regs
2 **IS/HB** s136(1) SSCBA 1992
  JSA s13(2) JSA 1995
  ESA Sch 1 para 6(2) WRA 2007; reg 83 ESA Regs
3 **IS** Reg 23(4) IS Regs
  JSA Reg 88(3) JSA Regs
  ESA Reg 83(4) ESA Regs
4 **IS** Reg 23(2) IS Regs
  JSA Reg 88(2) JSA Regs
  ESA Reg 83(2) ESA Regs
  HB Reg 25(3) HB Regs
5 **IS** Reg 44(4) and Sch 8 para 15 IS Regs
  JSA Reg 106(4) and Sch 6 para 18 JSA Regs
  Both Reg 1 SS(WTCCTC)(CA) Regs

2. What counts as income

6 Schs 4 para 12 and 5 para 4 HB Regs
7 R(IS) 4/01; see *BL v SSWP (SPC)* [2018] UKUT 4 (AAC) for the meaning of 'income'
8 *R v SBC ex parte Singer* [1973] 1 WLR 713
9 *Minter v Kingston Upon Hull City Council and Potter v SSWP* [2011] EWCA Civ 1155

3. Earnings

10 **IS** Reg 35(1) IS Regs
  JSA Reg 98(1) JSA Regs; reg 58(1) JSA Regs 2013
  ESA Reg 95(1) ESA Regs; reg 80(1) ESA Regs 2013
  HB Reg 35(1) HB Regs
  All R(SB) 21/86
11 Reg 35(1)(i)-(j) HB Regs
12 **IS** Regs 35(2)(b) and 40(4) and Sch 9 paras 1, 4 and 4A IS Regs
  JSA Regs 98(2)(c) and 103(6) and Sch 7 paras 1, 4 and 5 JSA Regs; reg 58(2)(c) JSA Regs 2013
  ESA Regs 95(2)(b) and 104(8) and Sch 8 paras 1, 4 and 5 ESA Regs; reg 80(2)(b) ESA Regs 2013
13 Reg 35(1)(i)-(j) HB Regs
14 **IS** Regs 35(2)(b) and 40(4) and Sch 9 paras 1 and 4 IS Regs
  JSA Regs 98(2)(c) and 103(6) and Sch 7 paras 1 and 4 JSA Regs; reg 58(2)(c) JSA Regs 2013
  ESA Regs 95(2)(b) and 104(8) and Sch 8 paras 1 and 4 ESA Regs; reg 80(2)(b) ESA Regs 2013
15 **IS** Reg 35(1)(e) IS Regs
  JSA Reg 98(1)(d) JSA Regs; reg 58(1)(d) JSA Regs 2013
  ESA Reg 95(1)(e) ESA Regs; reg 80(1)(e) ESA Regs 2013
  HB Reg 35(1)(e) HB Regs
16 R(IS) 9/95
17 **IS** Reg 35(3)(a)(iv) IS Regs
  JSA Reg 98(3)(d) JSA Regs; reg 67(4)(d) JSA Regs 2013
  ESA Reg 95(4), definition of 'compensation', ESA Regs; reg 80(4) ESA Regs 2013
18 *Minter v Kingston Upon Hull City Council and Potter v SSWP* [2011] EWCA Civ 1155
19 **IS** Reg 35(1)(j) IS Regs
  JSA Reg 98(1)(h) JSA Regs; reg 58(1)(i) JSA Regs 2013
  ESA Reg 95(1)(k) ESA Regs; reg 80(1)(k) ESA Regs 2013
  HB Reg 35(1)(k) HB Regs
20 **IS** Reg 35(2A) IS Regs
  JSA Reg 98(2A) JSA Regs; reg 58(3) JSA Regs 2013
  ESA Reg 95(3) ESA Regs; reg 80(3) ESA Regs 2013
  HB Reg 35(3) HB Regs
21 **IS** Reg 35(2)(a) and Sch 9 para 21 IS Regs
  JSA Reg 98(2)(a) and Sch 7 para 22 JSA Regs; reg 58(2)(a) JSA Regs 2013
  ESA Reg 95(2)(a) and Sch 8 para 22 ESA Regs; reg 80(2)(a) ESA Regs 2013
  HB Reg 35(2)(a) and Sch 5 para 23 HB Regs
22 CIS/11482/1995
23 Vol 5 Ch 26, para 26096 DMG

Part 4: General rules for other means-tested benefits
Chapter 20: Income: under pension age
Notes

• •

24 **IS** Reg 35(2)(a) IS Regs
    JSA Reg 98(2)(a) JSA Regs; reg 58(2)(a) JSA Regs 2013
    ESA Reg 95(2)(a) ESA Regs; reg 80(2)(a) ESA Regs 2013
    HB Reg 35(2)(a) HB Regs
    All Vol 5 Ch 26, para 26040 DMG
25 **IS** Reg 48(5) IS Regs
    JSA Reg 110(5) JSA Regs
    ESA Reg 112(5) ESA Regs
    HB Reg 46(5) HB Regs
26 **IS** Reg 35(2)(c) IS Regs
    JSA Reg 98(2)(d) JSA Regs; reg 58(2)(d) JSA Regs 2013
    ESA Reg 95(2)(c) ESA Regs; reg 80(2)(c) ESA Regs 2013
    HB Reg 35(2)(b) HB Regs
27 R(FC) 1/90
28 CFC/26/1989
29 R(FIS) 4/85
30 R(IS) 13/91; R(IS) 16/93; CFC/26/1989
31 R(FIS) 4/85; R(FC) 1/91; R(IS) 13/91
32 CIS/77/1993; CIS/89/1989
33 **IS** Sch 8 para 11 IS Regs
    JSA Sch 6 para 14 JSA Regs; Sch para 9 JSA Regs 2013
    ESA Sch 7 para 9 ESA Regs
    HB Sch 4 para 13 HB Regs
34 **IS** Sch 8 para 12 IS Regs
    JSA Sch 6 para 15 JSA Regs; Sch para 10 JSA Regs 2013
    ESA Sch 7 para 10 ESA Regs
    HB Sch 4 para 14 HB Regs
35 **IS** Reg 35(2)(d) IS Regs
    JSA Reg 98(2)(e) JSA Regs; reg 58(2)(e) JSA Regs 2013
    ESA Reg 95(2)(d) ESA Regs; reg 80(2)(d) ESA Regs 2013
    HB Reg 35(2)(c) HB Regs
36 **IS** Reg 40(4) and Sch 9 para 1 IS Regs
    JSA Reg 103(6) and Sch 7 para 1 JSA Regs
    ESA Reg 104(8) and Sch 8 para 1 ESA Regs
    HB Reg 40(10) and Sch 5 para 1 HB Regs
37 **IS** Sch 8 para 15A IS Regs
    JSA Sch 6 para 19 JSA Regs
    ESA Sch 7 para 11A ESA Regs
38 *Parsons v Hogg* [1985] 2 All ER 897 (CA), appendix to R(FIS) 4/85
39 **IS** Reg 36(3) IS Regs
    JSA Reg 99(1) and (4) JSA Regs; reg 59(1) and (3) JSA Regs 2013
    ESA Reg 96(3) ESA Regs; reg 81(2) ESA Regs 2013
    HB Reg 36(3) HB Regs
40 Regs 29(2) and 36(6) HB Regs

41 Reg 34 HB Regs; para BW2.34 GM
42 **IS** Reg 35 IS Regs
    JSA Reg 98 JSA Regs; reg 58 JSA Regs 2013
    ESA Reg 95 ESA Regs
    HB Reg 35 HB Regs
43 R(JSA) 1/06
44 **IS** Regs 35(2)(b) and 40(4) IS Regs
    JSA Regs 98(2)(c) and 103(6) JSA Regs; reg 58(2)(c) JSA Regs 2013
    ESA Regs 95(2)(b) and 104(8) ESA Regs
45 **JSA** Sch 6 paras 1(1)(a) and (2) and 2 JSA Regs; Sch paras 1(1)(a) and (2) and 2 JSA Regs 2013
    HB Sch 4 paras 1(b) and 2(b)(i) HB Regs
46 **JSA** Reg 98(1)(f) JSA Regs; reg 58(1)(f) JSA Regs 2013
    HB Reg 35(1)(g) HB Regs
47 **JSA** Reg 98(1)(g) JSA Regs; reg 58(1)(h) JSA Regs 2013
    HB Reg 35(1)(h) HB Regs
48 **HB** Reg 35(1)(h) HB Regs
49 **JSA** Sch 6 paras 1(1)(a), (2)(a)(ii), (2)(b)(ii) and 2 JSA Regs; Sch paras 1(1)(a), (2)(a)(ii), (2)(b)(ii) and 2 JSA Regs 2013
    HB Sch 4 paras 1(b)(i)(bb), (b)(ii)(bb) and 2 HB Regs
50 **JSA** Regs 98(2)(c) and 103(6) and Sch 7 paras 4 and 5 JSA Regs; reg 58(2)(c) JSA Regs 2013
    HB Reg 35(1)(i) to (j) HB Regs
51 **JSA** Reg 98(2)(f) JSA Regs; reg 58(2)(f) JSA Regs 2013
    HB Because not listed as earnings in reg 35 HB Regs
52 Regs 98(1)(b), (3) and 104(4) and Sch 6 para 1(1) JSA Regs
53 **JSA** Reg 98(1)(b) and Sch 6 paras 1(1)(a) and 2 JSA Regs; reg 58(1)(b) and Sch paras 1(1)(a) and 2 JSA Regs 2013
    HB Reg 35 HB Regs
    Both CJSA/82/98
54 **JSA** Regs 98(2)(b) and 103(6)(a) JSA Regs; reg 58(2)(b) JSA Regs 2013
    HB Reg 35(1)(b) HB Regs
55 **JSA** Regs 98(1)(c) and 110(3) JSA Regs; reg 58(1)(c) JSA Regs 2013
    HB Regs 35(1)(d) and 46(3) HB Regs
56 **IS** Regs 35(2)(b) and 40(4) IS Regs
    JSA Regs 98(2)(c) and 103(6) JSA Regs; reg 58(2)(c) JSA Regs 2013
    ESA Regs 95(2)(b) and 104(8) ESA Regs
57 Reg 35(1)(i)-(j) and Sch 4 paras 1(c) and 2(b)(ii) HB Regs

58 **IS** Regs 35(1)(d) and 48(3) and Sch 8 paras 1(1)(b) and 2 IS Regs
JSA Regs 98(1)(c) and 110(3) and Sch 6 paras 1(1)(b) and 2 JSA Regs; reg 58(1)(c) and Sch paras 1(1)(b) and 2 JSA Regs 2013
ESA Regs 95(1)(d) and 112(3) and Sch 7 paras 1(1)(b) and 2 ESA Regs
HB Regs 35(1)(d) and 46(3) and Sch 4 paras 1(c) and 2(b)(ii) HB Regs

59 **IS** Sch 8 paras 1(1)(b) and 2 IS Regs
JSA Sch 6 paras 1(1)(b) and 2 JSA Regs; Sch paras 1(1)(b) and 2 JSA Regs 2013
ESA Sch 7 paras 1(1)(b) and 2 ESA Regs
HB Sch 4 paras 1(c) and 2(b)(ii) HB Regs

60 **IS** Regs 37(1) and 38(3) IS Regs
JSA Regs 100(1) and 101(4) JSA Regs; regs 60(1) and 61(3) JSA Regs 2013
ESA Regs 97(1) and 98(3) ESA Regs; regs 82(1) and 83(2) ESA Regs 2013
HB Regs 37 and 38(3) HB Regs

61 Memo DMG 13/20

62 *AR v Bradford MDC* [2008] UKUT 30 (AAC), reported as R(H) 6/09

63 **IS** Reg 37(2)(a) IS Regs
JSA Reg 100(2)(a) JSA Regs; reg 60(2)(a) JSA Regs 2013
ESA Reg 97(2)(a) ESA Regs; reg 82(2)(a) ESA Regs 2013
HB Sch 5 para 42 HB Regs

64 **IS** Reg 38(3)(a), (4), (7) and (8)(a) IS Regs
JSA Reg 101(4) and (8) JSA Regs; reg 61(3) and (7) JSA Regs 2013
ESA Reg 98(3)(a), (4), (7) and (8)(a) ESA Regs; reg 83(2)(a), (3), (6) and (7)(a) ESA Regs 2013
HB Reg 38(3)(a), (4), (7) and (8)(a) HB Regs

65 R(IS) 13/91; R(FC) 1/91; CFC/26/1989

66 **IS** Reg 38(6) and (8)(b) IS Regs
JSA Reg 101(7) and (9) JSA Regs; reg 61(6) and (8) JSA Regs 2013
ESA Reg 98(6) and (8)(b) ESA Regs; reg 83(5) and (7)(b) ESA Regs 2013
HB Reg 38(6) and (8)(b) HB Regs

67 **IS** Reg 38(5) IS Regs
JSA Reg 101(6) and (8) JSA Regs; reg 61(5) and (7) JSA Regs 2013
ESA Reg 98(5) ESA Regs; reg 83(4) ESA Regs 2013
HB Reg 38(5) HB Regs

68 *SSWP v SK (CA)* [2013] UKUT 12 (AAC), reported as [2014] AACR 24

69 **IS** Reg 38(11) IS Regs
JSA Reg 101(12) JSA Regs; reg 61(11) JSA Regs 2013
ESA Reg 98(11) ESA Regs; reg 83(10) ESA Regs 2013
HB Reg 38(10) HB Regs
All R(FC) 1/93

70 CFC/836/1995

71 **IS** Regs 30 and 38(10) IS Regs; R(JSA) 1/09
JSA Regs 95 and 101(11) JSA Regs; regs 55 and 61(10) JSA Regs 2013
ESA Regs 92 and 98(10) ESA Regs; regs 77 and 83(9) ESA Regs 2013

72 Vol 5 Ch 27, para 27054 DMG, but see *GM v SSWP (JSA)* [2010] UKUT 221 (AAC), reported as [2011] AACR 9

73 Memo DMG 13/20

74 Regs 30(1) and 33(2) HB Regs

75 **IS** Reg 30(2) IS Regs
JSA Reg 95(2) JSA Regs; reg 55(2) JSA Regs 2013
ESA Reg 92(2) ESA Regs
HB Reg 37(3) and (4) HB Regs

76 **IS** Sch 8 para 3 IS Regs
JSA Sch 6 para 4 JSA Regs; Sch para 4 JSA Regs 2013
ESA Sch 7 para 4 ESA Regs
HB Sch 4 para 2A HB Regs

77 **IS** Reg 38(9) IS Regs
JSA Reg 101(10) JSA Regs; reg 61(9) JSA Regs 2013
ESA Reg 98(9) ESA Regs; reg 83(8) ESA Regs 2013
HB Reg 38(9) HB Regs

78 Sch 7 paras 5 and 5A ESA Regs

79 Sch 7 para 6 ESA Regs

80 Reg 88 ESA Regs; reg 39(5) ESA Regs 2013

81 Sch 7 paras 7 and 14 ESA Regs

82 Sch 4 para 4 HB Regs

83 **IS** Sch 8 para 5 IS Regs
JSA Sch 6 para 6 JSA Regs

84 **IS** Sch 8 para 4(2) IS Regs
JSA Schs 6 para 5(1) and (2) and 6A para 1(1) and (2) JSA Regs
HB Sch 4 para 3(2) HB Regs

85 Sch 4 para 3(2) HB Regs

86 **IS** Sch 8 paras 6A and 6B IS Regs
JSA Schs 6 paras 7 and 8 and 6A para 2 JSA Regs
HB Sch 4 paras 5 and 6 HB Regs

87 **IS** Sch 8 para 7(1) IS Regs
JSA Schs 6 para 9(1) and 6A para 3 JSA Regs
HB Sch 4 para 8(1) HB Regs

Part 4: General rules for other means-tested benefits
Chapter 20: Income: under pension age
Notes

. . . .

4

88 **IS** Sch 8 para 8 IS Regs
    JSA Schs 6 para 10 and 6A para 4 JSA
    Regs
    HB Sch 4 para 9 HB Regs
89 **IS** Sch 8 para 7(2) IS Regs
    JSA Schs 6 paras 9 and 10 and 6A paras
    3 and 4 JSA Regs
    HB Sch 4 para 8(2)(b) HB Regs
90 **IS** Sch 8 para 4(3) IS Regs
    JSA Schs 6 para 5(3) and 6A para 1(3)
    JSA Regs
91 **IS** Sch 8 para 4(4) and (7) IS Regs
    JSA Schs 6 para 5(4) and (7) and 6A
    para 1(4) and (5) JSA Regs
92 **IS** Sch 8 paras 6 and 9 IS Regs
    JSA Schs 6 paras 11 and 12 and 6A para
    6 JSA Regs
    HB Sch 4 paras 7 and 10 HB Regs
93 Sch 4 para 10A HB Regs
94 Sch 4 para 17 HB Regs
95 Regs 27(1)(c) and 28 HB Regs; reg
    30(1)(c) HB(SPC) Regs
96 Reg 27(2) HB Regs; reg 30(2) HB(SPC)
    Regs
97 Reg 28(6) HB Regs; reg 31(6) HB(SPC)
    Regs
98 Reg 28(13) HB Regs; reg 31(13)
    HB(SPC) Regs
99 Reg 28(6)-(8) HB Regs; reg 31(6)-(8)
    HB(SPC) Regs
100 Reg 28(14) HB Regs; reg 31(14)
    HB(SPC) Regs
101 Reg 28(2)-(4) HB Regs; reg 31(2)-(4)
    HB(SPC) Regs
102 Reg 28(11), (12) and (12A) HB Regs; reg
    31(11), (12) and (12A) HB(SPC) Regs

4. Other income
103 R(IS) 4/05
104 Reg 34 HB Regs; BW2.34 GM
105 **IS** Sch 9 para 81 IS Regs
    JSA Sch 7 para 77 JSA Regs
    ESA Sch 8 para 69 ESA Regs
    HB Sch 5 para 68 HB Regs
106 **IS** Reg 40(6) IS Regs
    JSA Reg 103(5B) JSA Regs
    HB Reg 40(5A) HB Regs
107 **IS** Reg 35(2) and Sch 9 para 4 IS Regs
    JSA Sch 7 para 4 JSA Regs
    ESA Reg 95(2) and Sch 8 para 4 ESA
    Regs
108 Reg 35(1)(i) HB Regs
109 Sch 5 para 56 HB Regs
110 **IS** Sch 9 paras 6 and 9 IS Regs
    JSA Sch 7 paras 7 and 10 JSA Regs
    ESA Sch 8 paras 8 and 11 ESA Regs
    HB Sch 5 para 73 HB Regs

111 **IS** Sch 9 para 76A IS Regs
    JSA Sch 7 para 72A JSA Regs
    ESA Sch 8 para 66 ESA Regs
    HB Sch 5 para 6 HB Regs
112 **IS** Sch 9 para 9 IS Regs
    JSA Sch 7 para 10 JSA Regs
    ESA Sch 8 para 11 ESA Regs
    HB Sch 5 para 9 HB Regs
113 **IS** Sch 9 para 80 IS Regs
    JSA Sch 7 para 76 JSA Regs
    ESA Sch 8 para 68 ESA Regs
    HB Sch 5 para 67 HB Regs
114 **IS** Sch 9 para 82 IS Regs
    JSA Sch 7 para 78 JSA Regs
    ESA Sch 8 para 70 ESA Regs
    HB Sch 5 para 69 HB Regs
115 **IS** Sch 9 para 81 IS Regs
    JSA Sch 7 para 77 JSA Regs
    ESA Sch 8 para 69 ESA Regs
    HB Sch 5 para 68 HB Regs
116 **IS** Sch 9 para 5B(2) IS Regs
    JSA Sch 7 para 6B(2) JSA Regs
    ESA Sch 8 para 7(2) ESA Regs
    HB Sch 5 para 65 HB Regs
117 **IS** Reg 7(4)-(6) SS(WTCCTC)(CA) Regs
    JSA Reg 8(3)-(5) SS(WTCCTC)(CA) Regs
118 **IS** Sch 9 para 86 IS Regs
    JSA Sch 7 para 82 JSA Regs
    ESA Sch 8 para 74 ESA Regs
    HB Sch 5 para 73 HB Regs
119 **IS** Sch 9 para 33 IS Regs
    JSA Sch 7 para 35 JSA Regs
    ESA Sch 8 para 37 ESA Regs
    HB Sch 5 para 32 HB Regs
120 **IS** Sch 9 para 9 IS Regs
    JSA Sch 7 para 10 JSA Regs
    ESA Sch 8 para 11 ESA Regs
    HB Sch 5 paras 6 and 9 HB Regs
121 **IS** Sch 9 para 5B(1) IS Regs
    JSA Sch 7 para 6B(1) JSA Regs
    ESA Sch 8 para 7(1) ESA Regs
122 **IS** Sch 9 paras 6 and 9 IS Regs
    JSA Sch 7 paras 7 and 10 JSA Regs
    ESA Sch 8 paras 8 and 11 ESA Regs
    HB Sch 5 para 6 HB Regs
123 **IS** Sch 9 para 83 IS Regs
    JSA Sch 7 para 79 JSA Regs
    ESA Sch 8 para 71 ESA Regs
    HB Sch 5 para 70 HB Regs
124 **IS** Sch 9 para 5A(1) IS Regs
    JSA Sch 7 para 6A(1) JSA Regs
    ESA Sch 8 para 6 ESA Regs
    HB Sch 5 para 50 HB Regs
125 **IS** Sch 9 paras 5 and 52 IS Regs
    JSA Sch 7 paras 6 and 51 JSA Regs
    ESA Sch 8 paras 64 and 65 ESA Regs
    HB Sch 5 para 51 HB Regs
126 Sch 5 para 4 HB Regs

127 **IS** Sch 9 para 8 IS Regs
   JSA Sch 7 para 9 JSA Regs
   ESA Sch 8 para 10 ESA Regs
   HB Sch 5 para 8 HB Regs
128 **IS** Sch 9 paras 6 and 9 IS Regs
   JSA Sch 7 paras 7 and 10 JSA Regs
   ESA Sch 8 paras 8 and 11 ESA Regs
   HB Sch 5 para 6 HB Regs
129 **IS** Sch 9 para 84 IS Regs
   JSA Sch 7 para 80 JSA Regs
   ESA Sch 8 para 72 ESA Regs
   HB Sch 5 para 71 HB Regs
130 **IS** Sch 9 paras 7 and 8 IS Regs
   JSA Sch 7 paras 8 and 9 JSA Regs
   ESA Sch 8 paras 9 and 10 ESA Regs
   HB Sch 5 paras 7 and 8 HB Regs
131 **IS** Sch 9 para 31 IS Regs
   JSA Sch 7 para 33 JSA Regs
   ESA Sch 8 para 35 ESA Regs
   HB Sch 5 para 31 HB Regs
132 **IS** Sch 10 para 18 IS Regs
   JSA Sch 8 para 23 JSA Regs
   ESA Sch 9 para 23 ESA Regs
   HB Sch 6 para 20 HB Regs
133 **IS** Sch 9 paras 54-56 IS Regs
   JSA Sch 7 paras 53-55 JSA Regs
   ESA Sch 8 paras 49, 51 and 52 ESA Regs
   HB Sch 5 paras 53-55 HB Regs
134 **IS** Sch 9 para 40 IS Regs
   JSA Sch 7 para 42 JSA Regs
   ESA Sch 8 para 42 ESA Regs
   HB Sch 5 para 36 HB Regs
135 **IS** Sch 9 para 46 IS Regs
   JSA Sch 7 para 45 JSA Regs
   ESA Sch 8 para 44 ESA Regs
   HB Sch 5 para 41 HB Regs
136 Sch 5 para 16 HB Regs
137 **IS** Sch 9 para 16 IS Regs
   JSA Sch 7 para 17 JSA Regs
   ESA Sch 8 para 17 ESA Regs
   HB Sch 5 para 15 HB Regs; Sch Part 2 HB&CTB(WPD) Regs
138 *MN v (1) Bury Council (2) SSWP (HB)* [2014] UKUT 187 (AAC)
139 **IS** Sch 9 para 36 IS Regs
   JSA Sch 7 para 38 JSA Regs
   ESA Sch 8 para 39 ESA Regs
   HB Sch 5 para 34 HB Regs
140 s134(8) SSAA 1992; HB&CTB(WPD) Regs
141 s74(2) SSAA 1992
142 **IS** Reg 40(1) and (3) IS Regs
   JSA Reg 103(1) and (3) JSA Regs
   ESA Reg 104(1) and (3) ESA Regs
   HB Reg 40(1) and (5) HB Regs
143 R(IS) 5/99; Vol 5 Ch 28, para 28008 DMG

144 **IS** Sch 9 para 73 IS Regs
   JSA Sch 7 para 70 JSA Regs
   ESA Sch 8 para 60 ESA Regs
   HB Sch 5 para 47A HB Regs
145 *KW v Lancaster City Council v SSWP (HB)* [2011] UKUT 266 (AAC); s74A SSAA 1992
146 Sch 5 para 47 HB Regs
147 **IS** Reg 54 IS Regs
   JSA Reg 117 JSA Regs
   ESA Reg 119 ESA Regs
148 **IS** Regs 54 and 55 IS Regs
   JSA Regs 117 and 118 JSA Regs
   ESA Regs 119 and 120 ESA Regs
149 **IS** Reg 42(4)(a) IS Regs
   JSA Reg 105(10)(a) JSA Regs
   ESA Reg 107(3)(c) ESA Regs
150 R(SB) 1/89
151 **IS** Reg 42(4)(b) IS Regs
   JSA Reg 105(10)(b) JSA Regs
   ESA Reg 107(4) ESA Regs
152 CIS/683/1993
153 **IS** Sch 9 para 25(1)(a) and (1A) IS Regs
   JSA Sch 7 para 26(1)(a) and (1A) JSA Regs
   ESA Sch 8 para 26(1)(a) and (2) ESA Regs
   HB Sch 5 para 25(1)(a) and (2) HB Regs
154 **IS** Sch 9 para 25(1A) IS Regs
   JSA Sch 7 para 26(1A) JSA Regs
   ESA Sch 8 para 26(2) ESA Regs
   HB Sch 5 para 25(2) HB Regs
155 **IS** Reg 42(4)(b) IS Regs
   JSA Reg 105(10)(b) JSA Regs
   ESA Reg 107(4) ESA Regs
   HB Reg 42(6)(c) HB Regs
   All Vol 5 Ch 28, para 28174 DMG
156 **IS** Sch 9 para 25(1)(a) and (2)(b) IS Regs
   JSA Sch 7 para 26(1)(a) and (2)(b) JSA Regs
157 *Hillingdon LBC v EB* [2021] UKUT 208 (AAC)
158 That is, under ss22C(2) or 59(1)(a) Children Act 1989, s81(2) Social Services and Well-being (Wales) Act 2014 or s26 Children (Scotland) Act 1995 or regs 33 or 51 Looked After Children (Scotland) Regulations 2009 No.210.
159 **IS** Sch 9 para 26 IS Regs
   JSA Sch 7 para 27 JSA Regs
   ESA Sch 8 para 28 ESA Regs
   HB Sch 5 para 26 HB Regs
160 **IS** Sch 9 para 25(1)(c) and (2) IS Regs
   JSA Sch 7 para 26(1)(c) and (2) JSA Regs
   ESA Sch 8 para 26(1)(b) ESA Regs
   HB Sch 5 para 25(1)(ba) HB Regs

Part 4: General rules for other means-tested benefits
Chapter 20: Income: under pension age
Notes

161 **IS** Sch 9 paras 25(1)(ba), 26(a)(iii) and
28(1)(c) IS Regs
JSA Sch 7 paras 26(1)(ba), 27(a)(iii) and
29(1)(c) JSA Regs
ESA Sch 8 paras 26(1)(b), 28(a)(iii) and
30(1)(c) ESA Regs
HB Sch 5 paras 25(1)(ba), 26(a)(iii) and
28 HB Regs
162 **IS** Sch 9 para 25(1)(e) IS Regs; Vol 5 Ch
28, para 28402 DMG
JSA Sch 7 para 26(1)(e) JSA Regs; Vol 5
Ch 28, para 28402 DMG
ESA Sch 8 para 26(1)(d) ESA Regs
HB Sch 5 para 25(1)(d) HB Regs
163 **IS** Sch 9 para 39 IS Regs
JSA Sch 7 para 41(1) JSA Regs
ESA Sch 8 para 41 ESA Regs
HB Sch 5 para 35 HB Regs
All Vol 5 Ch 28, para 28450 DMG
164 **IS** Reg 48(9) IS Regs
JSA Reg 110(9) JSA Regs
ESA Reg 112(7) ESA Regs
HB Reg 46(6) HB Regs
165 **IS** Reg 48(10)(a) IS Regs
JSA Reg 110(10) JSA Regs
166 **IS** Sch 9 para 15 IS Regs
JSA Sch 7 para 15 JSA Regs
ESA Sch 8 para 16 ESA Regs
HB Sch 5 para 14 HB Regs
167 R(H) 5/05 explains the difference
between a loan and a voluntary
payment
168 **IS** Sch 9 para 15(5A) IS Regs
JSA Sch 7 para 15(5A) JSA Regs
ESA Sch 8 para 16(3) ESA Regs
HB Sch 5 para 14 HB Regs
169 *Malekout v SSWP* [2010] EWCA Civ 162,
reported as [2010] AACR 28
170 Reg 26 VP Regs
171 Vol 5 Ch 28, para 28102 DMG
172 **IS** Sch 9 para 19 IS Regs
JSA Sch 7 para 20 JSA Regs
ESA Sch 8 para 20 ESA Regs
HB Sch 5 para 22 HB Regs
173 **IS** Sch 9 para 18 IS Regs
JSA Sch 7 para 19 JSA Regs
ESA Sch 8 para 19 ESA Regs
HB Sch 5 para 21 HB Regs
174 **IS** Sch 9 para 20 IS Regs
JSA Sch 7 para 21 JSA Regs
ESA Sch 8 para 21 ESA Regs
HB Sch 5 para 42 HB Regs

175 **IS** Reg 2(1) IS Regs
JSA Reg 1(3) JSA Regs
ESA Reg 2(1), definition of 'board and
lodging', ESA Regs
HB Sch 5 para 42(2) HB Regs
IS/JSA/HB definition of 'board and
lodging accommodation'
176 CIS/521/2002
177 CIS/13059/1996
178 **IS** Reg 48(4) IS Regs
JSA Reg 110(4) JSA Regs
ESA Reg 112(4) ESA Regs
HB Reg 46(4) HB Regs
All *CAO v Palfrey and Others, The Times,*
17 February 1995; R(IS) 26/95
179 CIS/563/1991
180 **IS** Sch 9 para 22(1) IS Regs
JSA Sch 7 para 23 JSA Regs
ESA Sch 8 para 23(1) ESA Regs
HB Sch 5 para 17(1) HB Regs
181 **IS** Reg 48(4) IS Regs
JSA Reg 110(4) JSA Regs
ESA Reg 112(4) ESA Regs
HB Reg 46(4) HB Regs
182 **IS** Sch 9 para 22(1) IS Regs
JSA Sch 7 para 23(2) JSA Regs
ESA Sch 8 para 23(2) ESA Regs
HB Sch 5 para 17(1) HB Regs
183 CFC/13/1993
184 **IS** Sch 9 para 22(2) IS Regs
JSA Sch 7 para 23(2) and (3) JSA Regs
ESA Sch 8 para 23(2) and (3) ESA Regs
HB Sch 5 para 17(2) HB Regs
185 **IS** Reg 53 IS Regs
JSA Reg 116 JSA Regs
ESA Reg 118 ESA Regs
HB Reg 52 HB Regs
186 **IS** Reg 41(1) IS Regs
JSA Reg 104(1) JSA Regs
ESA Reg 105(1) ESA Regs
187 Reg 41(1) HB Regs
188 **IS** Reg 29(2) IS Regs
JSA Reg 94(2) JSA Regs
ESA Reg 91(2) ESA Regs
HB Reg 33 HB Regs
189 **IS** Reg 41(2) IS Regs
JSA Reg 104(2) JSA Regs
ESA Reg 105(2) ESA Regs
HB Reg 41(2) HB Regs
190 **IS** Reg 41(6) IS Regs
JSA Reg 104(5) JSA Regs
ESA Reg 105(4) ESA Regs
HB Reg 41(4) HB Regs
191 Regs 41(4) and 48(2) IS Regs
192 **IS** Reg 41(7) IS Regs
JSA Reg 104(6) JSA Regs
ESA Reg 105(5) ESA Regs
HB Reg 41(5) HB Regs

193 **IS** Sch 10 para 20 IS Regs
JSA Sch 8 para 25 JSA Regs
ESA Sch 9 para 25 ESA Regs
HB Sch 6 para 22 HB Regs
194 *R v SBC ex parte Singer* [1973] 1 All ER
931; *R v Oxford County Council ex parte
Jack* [1984] 17 HLR 419; *R v West Dorset
DC ex parte Poupard* [1988] 20 HLR 295
195 R(H) 8/08
196 *Leeves v Chief Adjudication Officer* [1998]
EWCA 1706, reported as R(IS) 5/99; CIS/
2287/2008
197 **IS** Reg 48(2) IS Regs
JSA Reg 110(2) JSA Regs
ESA Reg 112(2) ESA Regs
HB Reg 46(2) HB Regs
198 **IS** s126(5) SSCBA 1992
JSA s5(2)(c) JSA 1995
199 Regs 41(4) and 48(2) IS Regs
200 **IS** Sch 9 para 13 IS Regs
JSA Sch 7 para 14 JSA Regs
ESA Sch 8 para 15 ESA Regs
HB Sch 5 para 13 HB Regs
201 **IS** Sch 9 para 1A IS Regs
JSA Sch 7 paras A2 and A3 JSA Regs
ESA Sch 8 para 1A ESA Regs
HB Sch 5 paras A2 and A3 HB Regs
202 Sch 8 para 15A ESA Regs
203 **IS** Sch 9 para 64 IS Regs
JSA Sch 7 para 62 JSA Regs
ESA Sch 8 para 55 ESA Regs
HB Sch 5 para 58 HB Regs
204 Reg 46(7) HB Regs
205 **IS** Regs 39C and 39D IS Regs
JSA Regs 102C and 102D JSA Regs
ESA Regs 102 and 103 ESA Regs
206 Vol 5 Ch 28, para 28627 DMG
207 Vol 5 Ch 28, para 28090 DMG
208 **IS** Reg 41(2) and Sch 9 para 17 IS Regs
JSA Reg 104(2) and Sch 7 para 18 JSA
Regs
ESA Reg 105(2) and Sch 8 para 18 ESA
Regs
HB Reg 41(2) HB Regs
209 **IS** Sch 9 para 29 IS Regs; Vol 5 Ch 28,
para 28240 DMG
JSA Sch 7 para 30 JSA Regs
ESA Sch 8 para 31 ESA Regs
210 **IS** Sch 9 para 30 IS Regs
JSA Sch 7 para 31 JSA Regs
ESA Sch 8 para 32 ESA Regs
All R(IS) 13/01
211 Sch 5 para 29 HB Regs
212 **IS** Sch 9 para 30ZA IS Regs
JSA Sch 7 para 31A JSA Regs
ESA Sch 8 para 33 ESA Regs
HB Sch 5 para 29 HB Regs

213 **IS** Sch 9 para 31A IS Regs
JSA Sch 7 para 33A JSA Regs
ESA Sch 8 para 35A ESA Regs
HB Sch 5 para 31A HB Regs; LA Welfare
Direct 12/2020
All Memo DMG 18/20
214 **IS** Sch 9 para 28 IS Regs
JSA Sch 7 para 29 JSA Regs
ESA Sch 8 para 30 ESA Regs
HB Sch 5 para 28 HB Regs
215 **IS** Sch 9 para 28(2) and (5) IS Regs
JSA Sch 7 para 29(2) and (5) JSA Regs
ESA Sch 8 para 30(2) and (3) ESA Regs
HB Sch 5 para 28A HB Regs
216 **IS** Sch 9 para 79 IS Regs
JSA Sch 7 para 75 JSA Regs
ESA Sch 8 para 67 ESA Regs
HB Sch 5 para 66 HB Regs
217 **IS** Sch 9 para 58 IS Regs
JSA Sch 7 para 56 JSA Regs
ESA Sch 8 para 53 ESA Regs
HB Sch 5 para 57 HB Regs
All *Casewell v SSWP* [2008] EWCA Civ
524, reported as R(IS) 7/08
218 **IS** Sch 9 para 27 IS Regs
JSA Sch 7 para 28 JSA Regs
ESA Sch 8 para 29 ESA Regs
HB Sch 5 para 27 HB Regs
219 **IS** Sch 9 para 76 IS Regs
JSA Sch 7 para 72 JSA Regs
ESA Sch 8 para 63 ESA Regs
HB Sch 5 para 63 HB Regs
220 **IS** Sch 9 paras 15, 30A and 66 IS Regs
JSA Sch 7 paras 15, 32 and 64 JSA Regs
ESA Sch 8 paras 16, 34 and 56 ESA Regs
221 **IS** Sch 10 para 8(b) IS Regs
JSA Sch 8 para 13(b) JSA Regs
ESA Sch 9 para 12(b) ESA Regs
HB Sch 6 para 10(b) HB Regs
222 **IS** Sch 9 para 75 IS Regs
JSA Sch 7 para 71 JSA Regs
ESA Sch 8 para 62 ESA Regs
HB Sch 5 para 62 HB Regs
223 **IS** Sch 9 para 11 IS Regs
JSA Sch 7 para 12 JSA Regs
ESA Sch 8 para 13 ESA Regs
HB Sch 5 para 11 HB Regs
224 **IS** Sch 9 para 2 IS Regs
JSA Sch 7 para 2 JSA Regs
ESA Sch 8 para 2 ESA Regs
HB Sch 5 para 2 HB Regs
225 **IS** Sch 9 para 21 IS Regs
JSA Sch 7 para 22 JSA Regs
ESA Sch 8 para 22 ESA Regs
HB Sch 5 para 23 HB Regs
226 BW2 Annex B para 13 GM

Part 4: General rules for other means-tested benefits
Chapter 20: Income: under pension age
Notes

227 **IS** Sch 9 para 51 IS Regs
JSA Sch 7 para 50 JSA Regs
ESA Sch 8 para 48 ESA Regs
HB Sch 5 para 49 HB Regs
228 **IS** Sch 9 para 43 IS Regs
JSA Sch 7 para 43 JSA Regs
ESA Sch 8 para 43 ESA Regs
HB Sch 5 para 39 HB Regs
229 **IS** Sch 9 para 10 IS Regs
JSA Sch 7 para 11 JSA Regs
ESA Sch 8 para 12 ESA Regs
HB Sch 5 para 10 HB Regs
230 **IS** Sch 9 para 23 IS Regs
JSA Sch 7 para 24 JSA Regs
ESA Sch 8 para 24 ESA Regs
HB Sch 5 para 24 HB Regs
231 **IS** Sch 9 para 24 IS Regs
JSA Sch 7 para 25 JSA Regs
ESA Sch 8 para 25 ESA Regs
HB Sch 5 para 33 HB Regs
232 **IS** Sch 9 para 48 IS Regs
JSA Sch 7 para 47 JSA Regs
ESA Sch 8 para 45 ESA Regs
HB Sch 5 para 44 HB Regs
233 **IS** Sch 9 para 49 IS Regs
JSA Sch 7 para 48 JSA Regs
ESA Sch 8 para 46 ESA Regs
HB Sch 5 para 45 HB Regs
234 **IS** Sch 9 para 50 IS Regs
JSA Sch 7 para 49 JSA Regs
ESA Sch 8 para 47 ESA Regs
HB Sch 5 para 46 HB Regs
235 Schs 4 para 11 and 5 paras 19 and 20 HB Regs
236 **IS** Sch 9 para 69 IS Regs
JSA Sch 7 para 67 JSA Regs
ESA Sch 8 para 57 ESA Regs
HB Sch 5 para 59 HB Regs
237 **IS** Sch 9 para 2A IS Regs
JSA Sch 7 para 2A JSA Regs
ESA Sch 8 para 2A ESA Regs
HB Sch 5 para 2A HB Regs

5. Notional income
238 **IS** Reg 42(1) IS Regs
JSA Reg 105(1) JSA Regs
ESA Reg 106(1) ESA Regs
HB Reg 42(1) HB Regs
239 Vol 5 Ch 28, paras 28608-16 DMG; see also CIS/15052/1996
240 **IS** Reg 42(2) IS Regs
JSA Reg 105(2) JSA Regs
ESA Reg 106(2) ESA Regs
HB Reg 42(2) HB Regs
241 **IS** Reg 42(2ZA) and (2A) IS Regs
JSA Reg 105(2B) and (3) JSA Regs
ESA Reg 106(3) and (4) ESA Regs

242 **IS** Reg 42(2)(e) and (f) IS Regs
JSA Reg 105(2)(d) JSA Regs
ESA Reg 106(2)(e) and (f) ESA Regs
HB Reg 42(2)(f) and (g) HB Regs
243 Vol 5 Ch 28, paras 28608-16 DMG
244 CIS/16271/1996
245 **IS** Reg 42(3) IS Regs
JSA Reg 105(6) JSA Regs
ESA Reg 107(1) ESA Regs
246 **IS** Reg 42(3A) and (3B) IS Regs
JSA Reg 105(7)(a), (8) and (9) JSA Regs
ESA Reg 107(2)(a) and (b) ESA Regs
247 **IS** Reg 42(3C) IS Regs
JSA Reg 105(7)(d) JSA Regs
ESA Reg 107(2)(c) ESA Regs
248 CIS/15052/1996, para 10
249 **IS** Reg 42(5) IS Regs
JSA Reg 105(12) JSA Regs
ESA Reg 108(1) ESA Regs
250 Reg 2 SS(PAOR) Regs
251 **IS** Reg 42(4)(a) IS Regs
JSA Reg 105(10)(a) JSA Regs
ESA Reg 107(3) ESA Regs
HB Reg 42(6)(b) HB Regs
252 **IS** Reg 42(4)(b) and (4ZA) IS Regs
JSA Reg 105(10)(b) and (10A) JSA Regs
ESA Reg 107(4) and (5) ESA Regs
HB Reg 42(6)(c) and (7) HB Regs
253 **IS** Reg 42(6) IS Regs; CIS/191/1991
JSA Reg 105(13) JSA Regs
ESA Reg 108(3) ESA Regs
HB Reg 42(9) HB Regs
254 R(SB) 13/86
255 **IS** Reg 42(6A) IS Regs
JSA Reg 105(13A) JSA Regs
ESA Reg 108(4) ESA Regs
HB Reg 42(10) HB Regs
256 R(SB) 13/86
257 **IS** Reg 42(6A)(a) IS Regs
JSA Reg 105(13A)(a) JSA Regs
ESA Reg 108(4)(a) ESA Regs
HB Reg 42(10)(a) HB Regs
258 CIS/147/1993
259 *Sharrock v CAO*, 26 March 1991 (CA); CIS/93/1991; CIS/422/1992; CIS/701/1994

6. Working out weekly income
260 **IS** Reg 29(2) IS Regs
JSA Reg 94(2) JSA Regs; reg 54(2) JSA Regs 2013
ESA Reg 91(2) ESA Regs; reg 76(2) ESA Regs 2013
261 **IS** Reg 29(2)(b) IS Regs
JSA Reg 94(2)(b) JSA Regs; reg 54(2)(c) JSA Regs 2013
ESA Reg 91(2)(c) ESA Regs; reg 76(2)(c) ESA Regs 2013

262 **IS** Reg 31(1)(a) IS Regs
JSA Reg 96(1)(a) JSA Regs; reg 56(a) JSA
Regs 2013
ESA Reg 93(1)(a) ESA Regs; reg 78(a)
ESA Regs 2013
263 **IS** Reg 31(1)(b) IS Regs
JSA Reg 96(1)(b) JSA Regs; reg 56(b) JSA
Regs 2013
ESA Reg 93(1)(b) ESA Regs; reg 78(b)
ESA Regs 2013
264 **IS** Reg 31(2) IS Regs
JSA Reg 96(2) JSA Regs
ESA Reg 93(2) ESA Regs
265 **IS** Reg 2(1) IS Regs
JSA Reg 1(3) JSA Regs; reg 2(2) JSA Regs
2013
ESA Reg 2(1) ESA Regs; reg 2 ESA Regs
2013
266 Reg 2 HB Regs
267 R(SB) 33/83
268 R(SB) 22/84; R(SB) 11/85
269 CIS/590/1993
270 *SSWP v JP (JSA)* [2010] UKUT 90 (AAC)
271 R(IS) 3/93
272 R(IS) 10/95
273 **IS** Reg 32(6) IS Regs
JSA Reg 97(6) JSA Regs; reg 57(5) JSA
Regs 2013
ESA Reg 94(6) ESA Regs; reg 79(5)(b)
ESA Regs 2013
274 **IS** Reg 32(2) and (3) IS Regs
JSA Reg 97(2) and (3) JSA Regs; reg
57(2) and (3) JSA Regs 2013
ESA Reg 94(2) and (3) ESA Regs; reg
79(2) and (3) ESA Regs 2013
275 **IS** Reg 32(4) IS Regs
JSA Reg 97(4) JSA Regs
ESA Reg 94(4) ESA Regs
276 **IS** Reg 32(5) and Sch 8 para 10 IS Regs
JSA Reg 97(5) and Sch 6 para 13 JSA
Regs; reg 57(4) and Sch para 8 JSA Regs
2013
ESA Reg 94(5) and Sch 7 para 8 ESA
Regs; reg 79(4) ESA Regs 2013
277 Reg 31 HB Regs
278 Reg 29(1)(a) HB Regs
279 Reg 29(1)(b) HB Regs; para BW2/W2.53
GM
280 *R v HBRB of LB Ealing ex parte Saville*
[1986] 18 HLR 349
281 Reg 29(2) HB Regs
282 Reg 29(3) HB Regs
283 Reg 29A HB Regs
284 Reg 32 HB Regs
285 Reg 31(2) HB Regs

4

Chapter 21

Income: over pension age

This chapter covers:
1. Whose income counts (p451)
2. What counts as income (p451)
3. Earnings (p453)
4. Income other than earnings (p458)
5. Notional income (p465)
6. Working out weekly income (p467)

This chapter explains the rules for working out your weekly income for pension credit (PC) and for pension-age housing benefit (HB) if you and your partner are over pension age and neither of you are on income support (IS), income-based jobseeker's allowance (JSA), income-related employment and support allowance (ESA) or universal credit (UC). See Chapter 20 for the rules for IS, income-based JSA and income-related ESA and for working-age HB if you and your partner are under pension age. See Chapter 7 for the rules for UC. If you are in a couple and one of you is over pension age but not the other, see p187 for whether the working-age or pension-age HB rules apply.

Note: whenever HB is referred to in this chapter, this only applies to the pension-age rules. The law refers to the qualifying age for PC rather than pension age, but since December 2018 this has been the same as pension age.

Key facts
- Your entitlement to pension credit (PC) and pension-age housing benefit (HB) and the amount you get depends on how much income you have.
- Your own income counts and, if you are a member of a couple, your partner's income also counts.
- Some income may be completely or partly ignored, or it may count in full.
- If you get the guarantee credit of PC, you are entitled to maximum HB, so you do not need to work out your income again for HB.

1. **Whose income counts**

If you are a member of a couple (see p303), your partner's income is added to yours.[1]

The income of a dependent child does *not* affect pension credit or housing benefit.[2]

2. **What counts as income**

Pension credit

For pension credit (PC), '**income**' means:[3]
- earnings (see p453 and p455);
- certain benefits and tax credits, including state retirement pensions and war pensions (see p458);
- maintenance (see p461);
- income from tenants and lodgers (see p461);
- income from capital (see p462);
- other specified miscellaneous income, including occupational and personal pensions (see p463);
- notional income (see p465);
- any income paid in lieu of the above.

For each type of income, some income is taken into account and some is ignored (or 'disregarded') in the assessment of PC. If the rules do not specify a type of income as being included in the assessment, it is ignored and does not affect your benefit.

For the rules on qualifying income for the savings credit and the 'assessed income period', see Chapter 13.

Housing benefit

How your income affects your entitlement to housing benefit (HB) depends on whether you are getting PC and, if so, which type of PC.

If you get pension credit guarantee credit

If you (or your partner) get the guarantee credit of PC, all your (and your partner's) income is ignored.[4] This is because entitlement to guarantee credit of PC acts as a passport to maximum HB.

Part 4: General rules for other means-tested benefits
Chapter 21: Income: over pension age
2. What counts as income

If you get pension credit savings credit

If you (or your partner) only get the savings credit of PC, your income for HB purposes is the income (and capital) figure used by the DWP to work out your PC, plus:[5]

- the amount of savings credit of PC; *and*
- any income (and capital) of your partner which was not taken into account in the PC calculation;

minus:[6]

- an amount disregarded from your earnings for childcare charges (see p458);
- the higher amount disregarded from your earnings if you:
  - are a lone parent (see p457);
  - pay maintenance (see p461);
- any additional full-time earnings disregard (see p458);
- any earnings disregarded from 'permitted work' (see p457);
- any discretionary increase to the £10 disregard for war pensions, and war widows' and widowers' pensions (see p460).

If you do not get pension credit

If you or your partner are over pension age (see p257) and do not get the guarantee or savings credit of PC (or universal credit, income support, income-based jobseeker's allowance or income-related employment and support allowance), income is defined in the same way as for PC (see p451).[7] Some income is taken into account and some disregarded, but the rules are not always the same as for PC. The differences are explained in the relevant sections below.

Net weekly income

The income that is taken into account is the amount after deducting any tax or national insurance (NI) contributions.[8]

For HB, the local authority may ignore changes (eg, Budget changes) in tax or NI contributions and the maximum rate of tax credits for up to 30 benefit weeks. When the changes are eventually taken into account, you are not treated as having been underpaid or overpaid benefit during the period of the delay.[9]

Once you have worked out what income should be taken into account, this is converted into a weekly amount (see p467) and the total taken into account in the benefit assessment. See p468 for the date from which a payment is counted. Chapters 10 and 13 explain how income affects the amount of HB or PC you get.

3. Earnings

How earnings are treated depends on whether you are an employed earner (see below) or are self-employed (see p455). In both cases, some of your earnings can be disregarded (see p456).

Employed earnings

What counts as earnings

'Earnings' means 'any remuneration or profit derived from... employment'. This includes:[10]

- wages and overtime pay;
- any bonus or commission (including tips);
- holiday pay – but this is ignored if your employment ends before your pension credit (PC) or housing benefit (HB) entitlement starts;
- statutory sick pay and contractual sick pay,[11] statutory maternity pay, statutory adoption pay, statutory paternity pay, statutory shared parental pay or statutory parental bereavement pay or any other payment made to you by your employer while you are on maternity leave;[12]
- any payments made by your employer for expenses not 'wholly, exclusively and necessarily' incurred in carrying out your job, such as travel expenses to and from work, and payments made to you for looking after members of your family;
- pay in lieu of notice, or pay in lieu of remuneration except for periodic payments following redundancy. However, all earnings, including pay in lieu, are ignored if your employment ends before your PC or HB entitlement starts;
- a retainer fee (eg, payment during the school holidays if you work for the school meals service[13]) or a guarantee payment;[14]
- an equal pay settlement – eg, through a 'single status agreement';[15]
- any payment of a non-cash voucher which is liable for class 1 national insurance (NI) contributions.[16] Non-cash vouchers that are not liable for contributions (eg, certain childcare and charitable vouchers) are classed as payments in kind and ignored.[17]

What does not count as earnings

Examples of payments not counted as earnings include the following.

- Payments in kind (eg, petrol) are ignored.[18]
- An advance of earnings or a loan from your employer is treated as capital.[19]
- The value of free accommodation provided as part of your job is ignored.[20]
- Payments towards expenses that are 'wholly, exclusively and necessarily' incurred, such as travelling expenses during the course of your work, are ignored.[21]

Part 4: General rules for other means-tested benefits
Chapter 21: Income: over pension age
3. Earnings

- If you are a local councillor, travelling expenses and subsistence payments are (and basic allowances may be[22]) ignored as expenses 'wholly, exclusively and necessarily' incurred in your work.
- If your earnings are paid in another currency, any bank charges for converting them into sterling are deducted before taking them into account.[23]
- The net amount of any occupational pension,[24] although not counted as earnings, counts as other income and is taken into account in full.[25]
- Any compensation payments made by an employment tribunal for unfair dismissal or unlawful discrimination do not count as earnings.[26]

Calculating net earnings from employment

Both your 'gross' earnings and 'net' earnings must be calculated. It is your 'net earnings' that are taken into account in the assessment. See p467 for how earnings are converted into a weekly amount.

Gross and net earnings

'**Gross earnings**' means the amount of earnings received from your employer less deductions for any expenses wholly, necessarily and exclusively incurred by you in order to carry out the duties of your employment.[27] See p453 for what counts as earnings and examples of expenses that can be deducted.

'**Net earnings**' means your gross earnings less any deductions made for:[28]

– income tax; *and*

– class 1 NI contributions; *and*

– half of any contribution you make towards a personal or occupational pension scheme.

If your earnings are estimated for HB, the amount of tax and NI you would expect to pay on those earnings is estimated and deducted, together with half of any pension contributions you are paying.[29]

Payments when you stop work

Redundancy payments are treated as capital.[30]

If you leave a job before you claim HB or PC, any earnings should be disregarded as income except certain copyright royalties, and payments for patents, trademarks or under the Public Lending Right scheme.[31]

If you are already getting HB or PC when you leave your job, your earnings are not disregarded for that benefit.

For PC, any final payment is treated as having been paid on the date your next regular payment of earnings would have been paid and taken into account for the same period, unless the final payment is higher than the normal amount. If it is higher, work out over how many normal payment periods it counts – eg, if the final payment is between two and three times as much as normal, it counts over three payment periods.[32]

Example

Nancy has been getting PC and working part time. She earns £90 a week, paid on a Friday. She finishes work on Wednesday 3 August and on that day is given £100, made up of £60 final wages and £40 holiday pay. This £100 is treated as having been paid on Friday 5 August and taken into account for two benefit weeks: £90 in the first week and the remaining £10 in the second week.

Self-employed earnings

Calculating net earnings

Your '**net profit**' over the period before your claim must be worked out. This is your self-employed earnings minus:[33]

- reasonable expenses (see p411 – the rules are the same as those for people under pension age, except that expenses relating to debts are not excluded); *and*
- income tax and NI contributions; *and*
- half of any premium paid in respect of a personal pension scheme which is eligible for tax relief.[34] You must supply certain information about the scheme or annuity contract to the DWP or local authority, if requested.[35]

Payments from the Self-Employment Income Support Scheme (a coronavirus support grant) count as earnings.[36] If you receive payments for board and lodging charges, these do not count as earnings, but as other income (less any disregards – see p461).[37]

Working out average earnings from self-employment

The weekly amount is the average of earnings:[38]

- over a period of one year (in practice, normally the last year for which accounts are available); *or*
- over a more appropriate period if you have recently taken up self-employment or there has been a change which will affect your business. For example, a payment from the Self-Employment Income Support Scheme is averaged over three months and counted from the date of payment.[39]

Childminders

In practice, childminders are always treated as self-employed. Your net profit is deemed to be one-third of your earnings less income tax, NI contributions and half of certain pension contributions.[40] The rest of your earnings are completely ignored.

Part 4: General rules for other means-tested benefits
Chapter 21: Income: over pension age
3. Earnings

Disregarded earnings

Some of your earnings from employment or self-employment are disregarded and do not affect your PC or HB. The amount depends on your circumstances. For HB, there is also an additional disregard depending on the hours you work, a childcare costs disregard and a permitted work disregard.

Pension credit

£20 disregard

Twenty pounds of your earnings (including those of your partner) is disregarded if:

- you are a lone parent;[41] *or*
- you or your partner qualify for an additional amount of PC for being a carer (see p334). If both of you qualify, only £20 is disregarded in total;[42] *or*
- you or your partner are in receipt of:[43]
  - employment and support allowance (ESA) or severe disablement allowance (SDA); *or*
  - attendance allowance (AA), disability living allowance (DLA), personal independence payment (PIP), adult disability payment (ADP), armed forces independence payment or a mobility supplement; *or*
  - the disabled worker or severe disability element of working tax credit (WTC); *or*
- you or your partner are certified as severely sight impaired or blind by a consultant ophthalmologist;[44] *or*
- you or your partner previously had a £20 earnings disregard in your income support, income-based jobseeker's allowance or income-related ESA and that benefit ended no more than eight weeks before PC entitlement began (the disregard ends if you have a break in employment of more than eight weeks) or, immediately before reaching pension age, there was a £20 disregard in your PC because you or your partner were getting incapacity benefit or SDA. You cannot get this disregard if you have more than an eight-week break in your PC claim;[45] *or*
- you or your partner are an auxiliary coastguard, a part-time firefighter, part-time member of a lifeboat crew or member of the reserve forces.[46] If your earnings are less than £20 a week, what is left over can be disregarded from your, or your partner's, earnings from any other employment.

Note: if you qualify under more than one category, you still have a maximum of £20 of your earnings disregarded.

Basic £5 or £10 disregard

If you do not qualify for a £20 disregard, £5 of your earnings is disregarded if you are single. If you claim as a member of a couple, £10 of your total income is disregarded, whether or not you are both working.[47]

Housing benefit

Permitted work disregard

For HB only, £20 or £152 is disregarded from earnings if you or your partner are doing 'permitted work' in the circumstances described on p415.[48]

£25 disregard

Lone parents on HB have £25 of their earnings ignored.[49]

£20 disregard

Twenty pounds of your earnings is disregarded if:

- you or your partner qualify for a carer premium. If both of you qualify, only £20 is disregarded in total;[50] *or*
- you or your partner are in receipt of:[51]
  - ESA with a work-related activity or support component or SDA; *or*
  - AA, DLA, PIP, ADP (in practice[52]), armed forces independence payment or a mobility supplement; *or*
  - the disabled worker or severe disability element of WTC; *or*
- you or your partner are certified as severely sight impaired or blind by a consultant ophthalmologist;[53] *or*
- you or your partner have (or are treated as having) limited capability for work and the assessment phase has ended;[54] *or*
- you or your partner are (or are treated as) incapable of work and have been for a continuous period of 364 days (196 days if you are terminally ill);[55] *or*
- you or your partner had a £20 earnings disregard in your HB or council tax benefit (CTB) in the eight weeks before you or your partner reached pension age. You cannot get this disregard if you have more than an eight-week break in your employment or in your HB claim (or previously, CTB claim);[56] *or*
- you or your partner are an auxiliary coastguard, a part-time firefighter, part-time member of a lifeboat crew or in the reserve forces. If your earnings are less than £20 a week, what is left can be disregarded from your or your partner's earnings from other employment.[57]

Note: if you qualify under more than one category, you still have a maximum of £20 of your earnings disregarded.

Basic £5 or £10 disregard

If you do not qualify for a £25 or £20 disregard, or a permitted work disregard, £5 of your earnings is disregarded if you are single. If you claim as a member of a couple, £10 of your total income is disregarded, whether or not you are both working.[58]

Part 4: General rules for other means-tested benefits
Chapter 21: Income: over pension age
4. Income other than earnings

Additional disregard

For HB only, whichever earnings disregard applies is increased by £17.10 if:[59]
- you or your partner receive the 30-hour element as part of your (or your partner's) WTC (see p1420); *or*
- you or your partner work 30 hours or more a week on average; *or*
- you or your partner work 16 hours or more a week on average and you have a child who is part of your family for benefit purposes (see p307) or your HB includes the family premium (see p324); *or*
- you are a lone parent and work 16 hours or more a week on average; *or*
- you or your partner work 16 hours or more a week on average and one or both of you get ESA which includes a support or work-related activity component, SDA, AA, DLA, PIP, ADP (in practice[60]) armed forces independence payment, a mobility supplement or the disabled worker or severe disability element in your WTC, or you are certified as severely sight impaired or blind by a consultant ophthalmologist or have been incapable of work for 364 days (196 days if terminally ill). For couples, the partner who is disabled is the one who must be working 16 hours or more a week on average.

The additional earnings disregard does not apply if your total earnings are less than the total of £17.10, plus any earnings disregard and childcare costs disregard (see below). In this case, £17.10 is disregarded from any WTC awarded to you or your partner, but the earnings disregard is not increased.

Note: only one additional disregard is allowed from your (or your partner's) earnings.

Childcare costs disregard

For HB only, up to £175 a week for one child, or up to £300 a week for two or more children, can be deducted from your (or your partner's) earnings (from employment or self-employment) for childcare costs in certain circumstances.[61] The rules are the same as those for people under pension age (see p416), except you can also have a childcare costs disregard if you are a couple and one of you works 16 hours or more a week and the other is aged 80 or over. There is no childcare costs disregard for PC.

4. **Income other than earnings**

Benefits and tax credits

Some benefits and tax credits are taken into account as income; others are disregarded, either in full or partly.

Benefits and tax credits that are taken into account

The following benefits and tax credits are taken into account:[62]

- widow's pension;
- carer's allowance (CA) – but not CA supplement in Scotland;
- a war orphan's pension, dependant's allowance or payment under the Armed Forces Compensation Scheme for someone whose parent died and who is still eligible as an adult because of disability;[63]
- contribution-based jobseeker's allowance;
- severe disablement allowance;
- contributory employment and support allowance (ESA). If ESA is paid at a reduced rate because of a sanction, the full rate still counts;[64]
- industrial injuries benefits, except constant attendance allowance and exceptionally severe disablement allowance, which are disregarded;
- maternity allowance;
- retirement pensions;
- statutory sick pay, statutory maternity pay, statutory adoption pay, statutory paternity pay, statutory shared parental pay and statutory parental bereavement pay. These are treated as earnings and may benefit from an earnings disregard (see p456);[65]
- working tax credit (WTC). However, for housing benefit (HB), if your earnings are too low to use the whole £17.10 additional full-time earnings disregard (see p458), £17.10 is disregarded from your WTC instead.[66] If earnings are too low to use the full childcare costs disregard, see p416;
- foreign social security benefits which are similar to the benefits listed above.[67]

Benefits and tax credits that are not taken into account

The following benefits and tax credits are ignored completely:[68]

- adult disability payment (in Scotland);
- armed forces independence payment;
- attendance allowance (AA);
- bereavement support payment;
- Best Start grant (in Scotland);
- CA supplement (in Scotland);
- child benefit;
- child disability payment (in Scotland);
- child tax credit;[69]
- child winter heating assistance (in Scotland);
- Christmas bonus (see p861);
- constant attendance allowance, exceptionally severe disablement allowance or severe disablement occupational allowance paid because of an injury at work or a war injury;
- disability living allowance;
- funeral support payment (in Scotland);

Part 4: General rules for other means-tested benefits
Chapter 21: Income: over pension age
4. Income other than earnings

- guardian's allowance;
- HB;
- mobility supplement under the War Pension Scheme;
- personal independence payment;
- Scottish child payment;
- social fund payments;
- supplementary payments to pre-1973 war widows or widowers;
- universal credit;
- young carer grant (in Scotland).

Benefits that are partly taken into account

For HB only, £15 of widowed parent's allowance is ignored.[70]

The following benefits have £10 ignored (or more for HB – see below):

- for PC only, widowed parent's allowance;[71]
- war disablement pension;[72]
- guaranteed income payment and survivor's guaranteed income payment under the Armed Forces Compensation Scheme (if reduced to under £10 by another pension, the remainder is disregarded from the pension);[73]
- war widow's, widower's or surviving civil partner's pension;[74]
- an extra-statutory payment made instead of the above pensions;[75]
- similar payments made by another country;[76]
- a pension from any government paid to the victims of Nazi persecution.[77]

The £10 disregard allowed on the above war pensions is in addition to the total disregard of any mobility supplement or attendance allowance (ie, constant attendance allowance, exceptionally severe disablement allowance and severe disablement occupational allowance) paid as part of a war disablement pension.

Local authorities may have discretionary local schemes to increase the £10 disregard on a war disablement, war widow's, widower's or surviving civil partner's pension and on the guaranteed income payment and survivor's guaranteed income payment in your HB.[78] Most increase the disregard or ignore the full amount, so check your local scheme.

Benefit delays

If you have made a claim for benefit but have not yet been paid, the benefit should not be treated as income you have. For PC, you should get your full benefit and the DWP deducts the difference from arrears of the delayed benefit when it is awarded.[79]

For the treatment of payments of arrears of certain benefits and tax credits, see p507.

Benefit deductions and overpayments

Usually, if any deductions are being taken from a benefit (eg, for an overpayment, rent or bills), the full amount of benefit is taken into account before taking off the deduction.[80] However, if an overpayment of tax credits is being deducted from a tax credits award, it is the amount of WTC you actually receive that is taken into account for PC and HB, after the deduction to recover the overpayment has been taken off.[81]

Maintenance payments

For PC, any maintenance payments for you or your partner made by your (or your partner's) spouse/civil partner or former spouse/civil partner count in full as income. Maintenance for a child is ignored completely.[82]

For HB, if you have a child who is part of your family for benefit purposes (see p307) or have a family premium included in your HB, £15 of any maintenance payments for you or your partner made by your (or your partner's) spouse/civil partner or former spouse/civil partner is disregarded.[83] If you receive maintenance from more than one person, only £15 of the total is disregarded. Other kinds of maintenance (eg, for a child) do not count as income and are ignored completely.[84]

If you *pay* maintenance to a former partner or a child not living with you, your payments are not disregarded for the purpose of calculating your income for PC or HB.[85] See p466 if part of a personal or occupational pension is paid to a former partner.

Income from tenants and lodgers

How income from tenants is treated depends on whether or not you live in the same property.

Lettings without board

If you own or are the tenant of your home, and you rent out a room(s) under an agreement, £20 of your weekly charge for each person is ignored. The balance is taken into account.[86]

If someone shares your home under an informal arrangement and is not paying rent under an agreement, any money s/he pays is ignored,[87] but a non-dependant deduction may be made from any HB or housing costs paid with PC (see p198 and p347).

Boarders

If you have a boarder in your own home, the first £20 a week of the amount s/he pays you is ignored and half of any balance remaining is taken into account as your income.[88] For PC, this does not apply if the boarder is a close relative (see p353) or the arrangement is not commercial.[89] Instead, the whole payment is ignored but there could be a non-dependant deduction from any housing costs paid with PC.[90] For HB, a non-dependant deduction could apply on top of this disregard if the boarder is a close relative or the arrangement is not commercial.[91]

Part 4: General rules for other means-tested benefits
Chapter 21: Income: over pension age
4. Income other than earnings

This disregard applies for each boarder you have. The charge must normally include at least some meals.[92] If you have a business partner, even though your gross income includes just your share of the weekly charge to boarders, you still get the full disregard of £20 plus half the excess for each boarder.[93]

Tenants in other properties

Rent from a property other than your home is not taken into account as income.[94] Instead, the value of the property counts as capital and is treated as producing a 'tariff income' (see below). If the value of the property can be disregarded (see p504), both the rent and the capital value are ignored (there is no tariff income).[95]

Income from capital

The general rule is that capital (unless it is disregarded) is assumed to provide a set rate of income – called 'deemed income' (often called 'tariff income') (see below). *Actual* income generated from capital is ignored as income, except from the types of capital listed below.[96] In these cases, any actual income (but no deemed income) is taken into account.[97] **Note:** for HB, it is only taken into account if the total capital listed below is worth more than £10,000.[98]

Actual income from the following capital is taken into account:
- the value of the right to receive a payment in the future of:
  - income under a life interest or life rent;
  - rent, unless you only have a reversionary (ie, future) interest in the property. For the way the actual rent is treated, see p461;
  - the surrender value or income under an annuity;
- property held in a trust, but not charitable trusts or, for PC, trusts set up out of payments from personal injury to you or your partner or, for HB, from specified infected blood payment schemes, the Child Migrants Trust or specified emergency and disaster funds (see p509). Income from a discretionary trust can be ignored in some circumstances (see p464).

There are no rules that treat capital of any kind as though it were income.

Deemed income from capital

For PC, if you have capital above £10,000, you are treated as having an assumed income of £1 a week for every £500, or part of £500, by which your capital exceeds £10,000.[99] This is called 'deemed income'. There is no upper capital limit.

For HB, the following applies.
- If you or your partner are getting the guarantee credit of PC, all your (and your partner's) capital is ignored.[100]
- In any other case, there is a capital limit of £16,000.[101] If you have capital above £10,000, you are treated as having an assumed income of £1 a week for every £500, or part of £500, of capital between £10,000.01 and £16,000.[102]

For **PC and HB**, you are not treated as having any deemed income on capital that is disregarded (see p504).

Example

Rhodri, aged 72, has savings of £12,000. Deemed income of £4 a week is taken into account. Any interest from the savings is ignored as income.

Occupational and personal pensions

The following income is taken into account:[103]
- an occupational pension;
- income from a personal pension;
- income from a retirement annuity contract, including an annuity purchased for you or transferred to you on divorce;
- payments from a former employer for early retirement on the grounds of ill health or disability, unless this was under a court order or settlement of a claim;[104]
- an overseas pension;
- a Civil List Act pension;[105]
- payment under an equity release scheme.[106] This provides regular payments from a loan secured on your home. For some home income plans where you buy an annuity, interest on the loan can be disregarded (see p464);
- payments from the Financial Assistance Scheme and periodic payments from the Pension Protection Fund (these help some people with underfunded occupational schemes whose employer has gone out of business).

Some charitable trusts provide discretionary income to people retired from specific occupations. This is ignored for PC and HB.[107]

Occupational and personal pension options

If you have a defined contribution occupational or personal pension (a 'money purchase' pension), for benefit purposes you are generally expected to buy an annuity or take the equivalent income that would be payable through an annuity. Income from an annuity is taken into account. Income that you draw direct from your pension pot is compared to the amount you could get from an annuity and whichever amount is higher is taken into account.[108]

If you also take a lump sum, this counts as your capital.[109] **Note:** if you choose to take a lump sum and spend it in the hope of increasing benefit entitlement, you are likely to be caught by the rules on deprivation of capital (see p487).

If you leave some, or all, of the funds in your pension pot, you are treated as having notional income, usually based on the annuity those funds could yield (see p466).

If you are below pension age, the rules are different (see p429).

Part 4: General rules for other means-tested benefits
Chapter 21: Income: over pension age
4. Income other than earnings

Specified miscellaneous income

Any income from copyright royalties and payments for patents, trademarks or under the Public Lending Right scheme are counted in full. Add the payments to your earnings (if any), if you are the first owner of the copyright or patent or author of the book, and deduct the appropriate earnings disregards on p456.[110]

The following income is ignored:

- income paid outside the UK which cannot be transferred here;[111]
- if income is paid in another currency, any bank charges for converting the payment into sterling;[112]
- income from an annuity is normally taken into account. However, an amount equal to the interest payable on the loan with which the annuity was bought is ignored if:[113]
  - you used at least 90 per cent of the loan made to you to buy the annuity; *and*
  - the annuity will end when you and your partner die; *and*
  - you or your partner are responsible for paying the interest on the loan; *and*
  - you (if you took out the loan) or your partner (if s/he did) were at least 65 at the time the loan was made; *and*
  - the loan is secured on a property which you or your partner own or have an interest in, and the property on which the loan is secured is your home or your partner's home.

  If the interest on the loan is payable after income tax has been deducted, it is an amount equal to the net interest payment that is disregarded, otherwise it is the gross amount of the interest payment;
- any discretionary payment made to you by trustees is ignored altogether, except if the payment is for the purpose of:
  - obtaining food, ordinary clothing or footwear, or household fuel. School uniforms and sportswear are examples of clothing and footwear that are not ordinary; *or*
  - paying rent, council tax or water charges for which you or your partner (if any) are liable. 'Rent' means eligible rent for HB purposes, less any non-dependant deductions; *or*
  - meeting housing costs which could be met by PC.

  In this case, £20 of the payment is disregarded or, if the payment is less than £20, the whole of the payment is disregarded.[114] If this disregard overlaps with certain other disregards (eg, certain war pensions), a combined maximum of £20 is allowed.[115] **Note:** this is a weekly disregard, so payments spread over different or successive benefit weeks attract a £20 disregard for each week;
- periodic payments made to you or your partner under an agreement entered into in settlement of a claim for any injury to you or your partner;[116]
- any payment ordered by a court to be made to you or your partner because of an accident, injury or disease you or your partner (or, for HB only, your child) have.[117]

Other income

Only income that is specified in the rules can affect your benefit (see p451). Any other kind of income is ignored – eg:

- local welfare assistance payments. These include test and trace support payments (in England), self-isolation support grants (in Scotland) and self-isolation support scheme payments (in Wales);[118]
- student loans and grants.[119] For HB only, see p433 if you make a parental contribution to a student's grant or loan or towards your under-25-year-old child's expenses in advanced education;
- adoption allowances, fostering allowances, child arrangements order payments and kinship care payments;[120]
- charitable and voluntary payments are not taken into account as income, so if a charity or a person gives you voluntary payments, these do not reduce your benefit. **Note:** maintenance payments can affect your benefit (see p461);
- payments for expenses if you are being consulted as a service user by certain public bodies. Other payments count as earnings but, if you choose not to take them or have them paid to someone else on your behalf, they do not count as your notional income;[121]
- victims' payments to people injured in a 'Troubles-related incident'.[122]

5. Notional income

In certain circumstances, you may be treated as having income that you do not possess.

Note: if you are working but earning less than the going rate, you are not treated as though your wages are higher than those you get, as you are for other means-tested benefits (see p436).

Deliberately getting rid of income

If you deliberately get rid of income in order to claim or increase your benefit, you are treated as though you were still in receipt of that income.[123] The basic issues involved are the same as those for deliberately getting rid of capital (see p511). **Note:** this rule can only apply if your intention was to gain benefit for *yourself* (or your partner). It should not apply if, for example, you stop claiming carer's allowance (CA) solely to allow the cared-for person to get a severe disability premium in her/his benefit (see p330).[124]

If you give up income you get from a small occupational or personal pension to take a lump sum instead, you could be caught by this rule. However, if this is a 'trivial commutation lump sum', you are not treated as still having that income (although the capital counts). There are similar sounding lump sums (eg, 'trivial

Part 4: General rules for other means-tested benefits
Chapter 21: Income: over pension age
5. Notional income

commutation lump-sum death benefit' which is paid to a dependant), which do not have this protection, so get advice from your pension provider.[125]

Failing to apply for pension income

Sometimes you can be treated as having pension income, even though you have not applied for it.[126]

Deferring a state pension

If you defer your state pension, category A or B pension, graduated retirement benefit or any shared additional pension paid on divorce, you are *not* treated as having that income for housing benefit (HB) before you claim it. However, you are treated as having that income for pension credit (PC).

The amount that counts for PC is the pension to which you would expect to be entitled were you to claim, less any overlapping benefit you get – eg, CA. If you have a choice of taking a lump sum instead of extra pension income, the amount is based on your taking the lump-sum option (there is no lump-sum choice when claiming a deferred post-April 2016 state pension). To take account of the time it can take to process claims, you are only treated as having this income from the date you could expect to get it were you to make a claim.

For both PC and HB, you are treated as having any amount of category C or D pension and age addition to which you might expect to be entitled if you were to claim. For PC, any overlapping benefit you get is deducted.

Leaving funds in an occupational or personal pension

You are treated as having any income from an occupational pension you have elected to defer beyond the scheme's retirement age,[127] as though you had claimed it. For PC, the time it might take to process it is taken into account and any overlapping benefit is deducted. If you have a defined contribution occupational or personal pension, for benefit purposes you are generally expected to buy an annuity or take the equivalent income that would be payable through an annuity.

If you leave funds in your pension pot, this is disregarded as capital but you are treated as having notional income based on the annuity those funds could yield.[128] If you take one or more lump sums from your pension pot, these count as capital and notional income is worked out on what is left in your pension pot. See p463 for how pension payments are treated.

Income paid to someone else on your behalf

Any money that counts as income and is paid to someone on your behalf is normally treated as being yours and is then either taken into account or ignored as income under the rules described in this chapter. The exception is for payments of income made under an occupational or personal pension scheme (or, for HB only, from the Pension Protection Fund) if you or your partner are bankrupt (or, in Scotland, the subject of a sequestration order). In this case, if the payment is made to the trustee or other person acting on your creditors' behalf and you (and your partner) have no income other than the payment made, it is not treated as being yours.[129]

If you have had a judicial separation rather than a divorce so that usual pension-splitting arrangements are not available, and a court has ordered you to pay part of your pension to your former partner, you could argue this does not count as yours.[130] However, if you pay maintenance from your pension under an agreement out of court, this income is likely to still count as yours.[131]

6. Working out weekly income

To work out your weekly income, you should do the following.
- Work out whether income is taken into account, or fully or partly disregarded (see p451).
- If income varies, work out an average income (see below).
- Convert the income into a weekly amount if necessary (see p468).
- Add any deemed weekly income from capital (see p462).

Averaging income

If your earnings vary because you do not work the same hours every week, your weekly income may be averaged over the cycle, if there is an identifiable one.[132] If you do not work a recognisable cycle or your income fluctuates, your income is worked out on the basis of:[133]
- the last two payments before your claim was made or treated as made (or, where applicable, before your claim was superseded) if those payments are at least one month apart; or
- the last four payments before your claim was made or treated as made (or, where applicable, before your claim was superseded) if the last two payments are less than a month apart; or
- calculating (or estimating for housing benefit – HB) any other payments that would give a more accurate figure for your average weekly income.

In all cases, if the cycle involves periods when you do no work, these are included in the cycle, but not other absences – eg, holidays or sickness.

The payment is treated as if made for a period of a year if you are entitled to:[134]
- royalties or other sums for the use of any copyright, patent or trademark; or
- payments for any book registered under the Public Lending Right 1982 scheme; or
- payments made on an occasional basis.

Part 4: General rules for other means-tested benefits
Chapter 21: Income: over pension age
6. Working out weekly income

Converting income into a weekly amount

Pension credit (PC) and HB are calculated on a weekly basis, so your earnings and other income have to be converted into a weekly amount if necessary. The following rules apply to income from employment and other income.[135] For income from self-employment, see p455.

- If the payment is for less than a week, it is treated as the weekly amount.
- If the payment is for a month, multiply by 12 and divide by 52.
- Multiply a payment for three months by four and divide by 52.
- Divide a payment for a year by 52.
- Multiply payments for any other periods by seven and divide by the number of days in the period.

Date from when a payment counts

The general rule for PC is that benefits are treated as having been paid on the last day of the PC 'benefit week' in which the benefit is payable, but on the first day if the benefit is paid in advance.[136] Some benefits are treated slightly differently. Contribution-based jobseeker's allowance, contributory employment and support allowance and maternity allowance are treated as having been paid on the day that benefit is payable. For HB, benefits are taken into account over the period for which they are payable.[137]

For other types of income, for PC the general rule is that income counts from the date it is paid for the length of time it has been paid – eg, a month's occupational pension paid on 10 November counts from 10 November to 9 December.[138]

For HB, weekly earnings are taken into account from the start of a new claim or from the first day of the 'benefit week' after you start work. If average weekly earnings change, the new amount counts from the date of change, even if you are not paid until later.[139]

Benefit week

For PC, a **'benefit week'** is the seven days ending on the day PC is payable if paid in arrears, or starting on that day if paid in advance.[140]

For HB, a **'benefit week'** is the seven days starting on a Monday.[141]

Notes

1. Whose income counts

1 **PC** s5 SPCA 2002
  HB s136(1) SSCBA 1992
2 Reg 23(3) HB(SPC) Regs

2. What counts as income

3 s15 SPCA 2002; reg 15 SPC Regs
4 Regs 25 and 26 HB(SPC) Regs
5 Reg 27(4) HB(SPC) Regs
6 Reg 27(4) HB(SPC) Regs
7 Reg 29 HB(SPC) Regs
8 **PC** Reg 17(10) SPC Regs
  HB Reg 33(12) HB(SPC) Regs
9 Reg 34 HB(SPC) Regs

3. Earnings

10 **PC** Reg 17A(2) SPC Regs
   HB Reg 35(1) HB(SPC) Regs
11 **PC** Reg 17A(h) and (k) SPC Regs
   HB Reg 35(1)(h) and (k) HB(SPC) Regs
12 **PC** Reg 17A(h)-(k) SPC Regs
   HB Reg 35(1)(h)-(k) HB(SPC) Regs
13 **PC** Reg 17A(2)(e) SPC Regs
   HB Reg 35(1)(e) HB(SPC) Regs
14 R(IS) 9/95
15 *Minter v Kingston Upon Hull City Council and Potter v SSWP* [2011] EWCA Civ 1155
16 **PC** Reg 17A(2)(g) SPC Regs
   HB Reg 35(1)(g) HB(SPC) Regs
17 **PC** Reg 17A(4) SPC Regs
   HB Reg 35(3) HB(SPC) Regs
18 **PC** Reg 17A(3)(a) SPC Regs
   HB Reg 35(2)(a) HB(SPC) Regs
19 Vol 14 Ch 86, para 86058 DMG
20 Vol 14 Ch 86, para 86054 DMG
21 **PC** Reg 17A(3)(b) SPC Regs
   HB Reg 35(2)(b) HB(SPC) Regs
22 CIS/77/1993; CIS/89/1989
23 **PC** Sch 6 para 7 SPC Regs
   HB Sch 4 para 10 HB(SPC) Regs
24 **PC** Reg 17A(3)(c) SPC Regs
   HB Reg 35(2)(c) HB(SPC) Regs
25 **PC** s15(1)(c) SPCA 2002
   HB Reg 29(1)(c) HB(SPC) Regs
26 **PC** Reg 17A(3)(e) SPC Regs
   HB Reg 35(2)(e) HB(SPC) Regs
27 *Parsons v Hogg* [1985] 2 All ER 897 (CA), appendix to R(FIS) 4/85

28 **PC** Regs 17(10) and 17A(4A) SPC Regs
   HB Reg 36(2) and (4) HB(SPC) Regs
29 Reg 36(5) HB(SPC) Regs
30 Vol 14 Ch 86, para 86162 DMG
31 **PC** Sch 6 para 6 SPC Regs
   HB Sch 4 para 8 HB(SPC) Regs
32 Reg 17ZA SPC Regs
33 **PC** Reg 17B(5) SPC Regs; reg 13(1) and (4) SSB(CE) Regs
   HB Reg 39(1)-(3) HB(SPC) Regs
34 **PC** Reg 17B(1) SPC Regs; regs 2 and 13(4) SSB(CE) Regs
   HB Regs 2(1) and 39(2) and (11) HB(SPC) Regs
35 **PC** Reg 32(3) SS(C&P) Regs
   HB Reg 67(5) HB(SPC) Regs
36 Memo DMG 13/20
37 **PC** Reg 17B(4)(b) SPC Regs; reg 12(2) SSB(CE) Regs
   HB Reg 38(2)(a) HB(SPC) Regs
38 **PC** Reg 17B SPC Regs; reg 11(1) SSB(CE) Regs
   HB Reg 37(1) HB(SPC) Regs
39 Memo DMG 13/20
40 **PC** Reg 17B(5)(b) SPC Regs; reg 13(10) SSB(CE) Regs
   HB Reg 39(8) HB(SPC) Regs
41 Sch 6 para 1 SPC Regs
42 Sch 6 paras 3 and 4A SPC Regs
43 Sch 6 para 4(1)(a) SPC Regs
44 Sch 6 para 4(1)(b) SPC Regs
45 Sch 6 para 4(2)-(4) SPC Regs
46 Sch 6 para 2 SPC Regs
47 **PC** Sch 6 para 5 SPC Regs
   HB Sch 4 para 7 HB(SPC) Regs
48 Sch 4 para 5A HB(SPC) Regs
49 Sch 4 para 2 HB(SPC) Regs
50 Sch 4 para 4 HB(SPC) Regs
51 Sch 4 para 5(1)(a) HB(SPC) Regs
52 ADP is not listed in regulations but the official intention is generally to treat ADP the same as PIP; LA Welfare Direct 2/22
53 Sch 4 para 5(1)(b) HB(SPC) Regs
54 Sch 4 para 5(1)(d) HB(SPC) Regs
55 Sch 4 para 5(1)(c) HB(SPC) Regs
56 Sch 4 para 5(2) HB(SPC) Regs
57 Sch 4 para 3 HB(SPC) Regs
58 **PC** Sch 6 para 5 SPC Regs
   HB Sch 4 para 7 HB(SPC) Regs
59 Sch 4 para 9 HB(SPC) Regs

Part 4: General rules for other means-tested benefits
Chapter 21: Income: over pension age
Notes

60 ADP is not listed in regulations but the official intention is generally to treat ADP the same as PIP; LA Welfare Direct 2/22
61 Reg 30(1)(c) HB(SPC) Regs

4. Income other than earnings
62 **PC** s15(1)(b) and (e) SPCA 2002; reg 15(1) SPC Regs
    HB Reg 29(1)(b) and (j) HB(SPC) Regs
63 **PC** Reg 15(5)(a) and (ab) SPC Regs
    HB Reg 29(1)(h) and (l) HB(SPC) Regs
64 **PC** Reg 15(3) SPC Regs
    HB Reg 29(3) HB(SPC) Regs
65 **PC** Reg 17A(2)(h)-(j) SPC Regs
    HB Reg 35(1)(h)-(j) HB(SPC) Regs
66 **PC** s15(1)(b) SPCA 2002
    HB Sch 5 para 21 HB(SPC) Regs
67 **PC** Reg 15(2) SPC Regs
    HB Reg 29(1)(k) HB(SPC) Regs
68 **PC** s15 SPCA; reg 15(1) and Sch 4 paras 2-6 SPC Regs
    HB Reg 29(1) and Sch 5 paras 2-6 HB(SPC) Regs
69 s15 SPCA 2002
70 Sch 5 paras 7 and 8 HB(SPC) Regs
71 Sch 4 paras 7 and 7A SPC Regs
72 **PC** Sch 4 para 1(a) SPC Regs
    HB Sch 5 para 1(a) HB(SPC) Regs; Sch Part 1 HB&CTB(WPD) Regs
73 **PC** Sch 4 para 1(cc) SPC Regs
    HB Sch 5 para 1(d) HB(SPC) Regs
74 **PC** Sch 4 para 1(b), (ba) and (c) SPC Regs
    HB Sch 5 para 1(b) and (c) HB(SPC) Regs; Sch Part 1 HB&CTB(WPD) Regs
75 **PC** Sch 4 para 1(d) SPC Regs
    HB Sch 5 para 1(e) HB(SPC) Regs
76 **PC** Sch 4 para 1(e) SPC Regs
    HB Sch 5 para 1(f) HB(SPC) Regs
77 **PC** Sch 4 para 1(f) SPC Regs
    HB Sch 5 para 1(g) HB(SPC) Regs
    Both MN v (1) Bury Council (2) SSWP (HB) [2014] UKUT 187 (AAC)
78 ss134(8) and 139(6) SSAA 1992; R v South Hams District Council ex parte Ash [1999] EWHC Admin 418
79 s74(2) SSAA 1992
80 **PC** Reg 15(3) SPC Regs
    HB Reg 29(3) HB(SPC) Regs
81 **PC** Vol 14 Ch 85, para 85022 DMG
    HB Reg 29(5) HB(SPC) Regs
    Both R(IS) 5/99
82 Reg 15(5)(d) SPC Regs
83 Sch 5 para 20 HB(SPC) Regs
84 Reg 29(1)(o) HB(SPC) Regs
85 CIS/683/1993
86 **PC** Sch 4 para 9 SPC Regs
    HB Sch 5 para 10 HB(SPC) Regs

87 **PC** Income from capital under s15(1)(i) SPCA 2002 would count, but is ignored under regs 15(6) and 17(8), Sch 5 para 1A and Sch 4 para 18 SPC Regs
    HB Reg 29(1)(i) HB(SPC) Regs
88 **PC** Sch 4 para 8 SPC Regs
    HB Sch 5 para 9 HB(SPC) Regs
89 Reg 1(2), definition of 'board and lodging accommodation', SPC Regs
90 Sch 4 para 18 SPC Regs
91 Reg 2(1), definition of 'board and lodging accommodation', HB(SPC) Regs
92 **PC** Reg 1(2), definition of 'board and lodging accommodation', SPC Regs
    HB Reg 2(1), definition of 'board and lodging accommodation', HB(SPC) Regs
93 CIS/521/2002
94 **PC** s15(1)(i) SPCA 2002; Sch 4 para 18 SPC Regs
    HB Reg 29(1)(i) and Sch 5 para 22 HB(SPC) Regs
95 **PC** Reg 17(8) SPC Regs
    HB Regs 29(1)(i) and 44(2) HB(SPC) Regs
96 **PC** Sch 4 para 18 SPC Regs
    HB Sch 5 para 22 HB(SPC) Regs
97 **PC** s15(1)(i) SPCA 2002; reg 15(6) and Sch 4 para 18 SPC Regs
    HB Reg 29(1)(i) HB(SPC) Regs
98 Sch 5 para 24 HB(SPC) Regs
99 s15(2) SPCA 2002; reg 15(6) SPC Regs
100 Regs 25 and 26 HB(SPC) Regs
101 Reg 43 HB(SPC) Regs
102 Reg 29(2) HB(SPC) Regs
103 **PC** ss15(1)(c) and 16(1) SPCA 2002; reg 16 SPC Regs
    HB Reg 29(1)(c) HB(SPC) Regs
104 **PC** Reg 16 SPC Regs
    HB Reg 29(1)(s) HB(SPC) Regs
105 **PC** Reg 16 SPC Regs
    HB Reg 29(1)(t) HB(SPC) Regs
106 **PC** Reg 16 SPC Regs
    HB Reg 29(1)(w) HB(SPC) Regs
107 Vol 14 Ch 85, para 85139 DMG
108 **PC** Reg 18(2)-(10) SPC Regs; Vol 14 Ch 85, para 85460 DMG
    HB Reg 41(4)-(8) HB(SPC) Regs
109 Vol 14 Ch 85, para 85457 DMG
110 **PC** Reg 17(9) SPC Regs
    HB Reg 33(8) HB(SPC) Regs
111 **PC** Sch 4 para 15 SPC Regs
    HB Sch 5 para 16 HB(SPC) Regs
112 **PC** Sch 4 para 16 SPC Regs
    HB Sch 5 para 17 HB(SPC) Regs
113 **PC** Sch 4 para 10 SPC Regs
    HB Sch 5 para 11 HB(SPC) Regs

114　**PC** Sch 4 para 11 SPC Regs
　　　HB Sch 5 para 12 HB(SPC) Regs
115　**PC** Sch 4 para 11(3)(b) SPC Regs
　　　HB Sch 5 para 12(3) HB(SPC) Regs
116　**PC** Sch 4 para 14 SPC Regs
　　　HB Sch 5 para 15 HB(SPC) Regs
117　**PC** Sch 4 para 13 SPC Regs
　　　HB Sch 5 para 14 HB(SPC) Regs
118　Memo DMG 18/20; LA Welfare Direct
　　　12/2020
119　The rules do not include grants and
　　　loans in the definition of 'income'
120　**PC** s15 SPCA 2002; regs 15 and 17B(4)
　　　SPC Regs
　　　HB Regs 29 and 38(2) HB(SPC) Regs
121　**PC** Regs 17A(3)(f), 18(7A) and 24(2)
　　　SPC Regs
　　　HB Regs 35(2)(f), 41(8C) and 42(3)
　　　HB(SPC) Regs
122　Reg 26 VP Regs

5. Notional income
123　**PC** Reg 18(6)-(8B) SPC Regs
　　　HB Reg 41(8)-(8BD) HB(SPC) Regs
124　Vol 5 Ch 28, paras 28608-16 DMG; see
　　　also CIS/15052/1996
125　**PC** Reg 18(9) SPC Regs
　　　HB Reg 41(11) HB(SPC) Regs
126　**PC** Reg 18(1)-(5) SPC Regs
　　　HB Reg 41(1)-(7) HB(SPC) Regs
127　Vol 14 Ch 85, para 85453 DMG; *BRG v
　　　SSWP (SPC)* [2014] UKUT 246 (AAC)
128　**PC** Reg 18(2)-(5) SPC Regs; Vol 14 Ch
　　　85, para 85456 DMG; *SSWP v Goulding*
　　　[2019] EWCA Civ 839
　　　HB Reg 41(4)-(8) HB(SPC) Regs
129　**PC** Reg 24 SPC Regs
　　　HB Reg 42 HB(SPC) Regs
130　CH/1672/2007
131　*BL v SSWP (SPC)* [2018] UKUT 4 (AAC)

6. Working out weekly income
132　**PC** Reg 17(2)(b)(i) SPC Regs
　　　HB Reg 33(2)(b)(i) HB(SPC) Regs
133　**PC** Reg 17(2)(b)(ii) SPC Regs
　　　HB Reg 33(2)(b)(ii) HB(SPC) Regs
134　**PC** Reg 17(4) SPC Regs
　　　HB Reg 33(4) HB(SPC) Regs
135　**PC** Reg 17(1) SPC Regs
　　　HB Reg 33(1) HB(SPC) Regs
136　Reg 13B SPC Regs
137　Reg 33(6) HB(SPC) Regs
138　R(PC) 3/08; *PS v SSWP (SPC)* [2016]
　　　UKUT 21 (AAC)
139　Reg 33(2A) and (3A) HB(SPC) Regs
140　Reg 1(2) SPC Regs
141　Reg 2 HB(SPC) Regs

Chapter 22

• •

Capital: under pension age

This chapter explains how capital affects your entitlement to income support, income-based jobseeker's allowance and income-related employment and support allowance. It also applies to working-age housing benefit (HB) rules if you and your partner are under pension age. Chapter 23 explains the rules for pension credit and for pension-age HB rules if you and your partner are over pension age. If you are in a couple and one of you is over pension age but not the other, see p187 for whether the working-age or pension-age HB rules apply. For universal credit, see Chapter 8. For the capital limits for health benefits, see Chapter 31. There are no capital rules for non-means-tested benefits.

Key facts

- If you have more than £16,000 capital, you are not entitled to income support (IS), income-based jobseeker's allowance (JSA), income-related employment and support allowance (ESA) or working-age housing benefit (HB).
- If you have capital above a lower limit of £6,000 (higher if you live in a care home), your benefit is affected because it is assumed that your capital gives you some income – often called 'tariff income'.
- Some kinds of capital are ignored when working out your benefit – eg, the value of the home in which you live.
- Getting IS, income-based JSA or income-related ESA means you always get the maximum amount of HB, so there is no need to work out your capital again for HB.
- If you deliberately get rid of capital in order to get more benefit, you are treated as still having it. This is called 'notional capital'.

1. The capital limits

There is a lower and upper limit.[1]
- The lower limit is £6,000.
- The upper limit is £16,000.

If you have over £16,000 of capital, you are not entitled to benefit. The first £6,000 is ignored and does not affect your weekly benefit. If you have between £6,000.01 and £16,000, you may be entitled to benefit, but it is assumed that you have some income from your capital. This is known as 'tariff income'.

This 'tariff income' (see p427) is assumed to be £1 a week for every £250, or part of £250, of your capital between £6,000.01 and £16,000.

If you live in a care home, see below.

When working out the value of your capital, some capital is disregarded (see p477). You may also be treated as having some capital which you do not actually have (see p486).

Example
Neil gets income-based jobseeker's allowance. He has £6,900 in savings. He is assumed to have tariff income of £4 a week.

Care homes

If you live permanently in a care home (see p919):
- the lower limit is £10,000;
- the upper limit is £16,000.

Tariff income starts above £10,000.

Example
Richard gets income-related employment and support allowance (ESA). He has £8,100 in savings. He is assumed to have tariff income of £9 a week. Richard moves permanently into a care home. Because his savings are below the £10,000 limit, they are now disregarded entirely. A few months later he sells his home and gets £80,000. As a result, he is no longer entitled to income-related ESA.

2. Whose capital counts

Your partner's capital

If you are a member of a couple (see p303), your partner's capital is added to yours.[2]

Part 4: General rules for other means-tested benefits
Chapter 22: Capital: under pension age
3. What counts as capital

Your child's capital

Your child's capital is not added to yours and does not affect your benefit.[3] However, if you still have amounts for children included in your income support or income-based jobseeker's allowance (see p317), although your child's capital is not added to yours, if it is over £3,000 you cannot get benefit included for her/him other than the family premium (see p324).[4] If this applies, any income of the child is not counted as yours.[5]

4

3. **What counts as capital**

All your capital is taken into account, unless it is specifically ignored (or 'disregarded') (see p477) or is treated as income (see p428).

The term 'capital' is not defined. In general, it means lump-sum or one-off payments rather than a series of payments – eg, it includes savings, property and statutory redundancy payments.[6]

Capital payments can normally be distinguished from income because they are not payable for any specified period and are not part of a regular series of payments (although capital can be paid by instalments).[7]

Note: some capital is treated as income (see p428) and some income is treated as capital (see p477).

Savings

Your savings generally count as capital – eg, cash you have at home, premium bonds, shares, unit trusts and money in a bank account or building society.

If you have put aside money to pay bills, this is still counted as your capital.[8] If your savings are just below the capital limit, you could pay bills by monthly direct debit or use a budget account to keep your capital below the limit.

Savings from past employed earnings and other income (including benefits – see p482) are treated as capital after the period for which the income was paid has lapsed – eg, a weekly payment of child benefit becomes capital a week after it is paid and a monthly occupational pension becomes capital after a month.[9] Beyond that, employed earnings continue to be treated as income until deductions for tax, national insurance and pension contributions have been made.[10]

Fixed-term investments

Capital held in fixed-term investments counts. However, if it is currently unobtainable, it may have little or no value. If you can convert the investment into a form that lets you access it or sell your interest, or raise a loan through a reputable bank using the asset as security, the amount you can get for it counts.

Property and land

Any property or land that you own counts as capital. Many types of property are disregarded (see p477). If there is doubt about who owns the property, see below.

Loans and ownership of capital

Usually it is clear when capital belongs to you and should be taken into account. However, it may be less clear if you are holding money for someone else or if you have been given a loan which you are expected to repay.

A loan to you usually counts as money you possess and therefore counts as capital. However, you can argue that a loan, money or other asset you hold for someone else should be disregarded if it is:

- a loan granted on condition that you only use the interest, but do not touch the capital because the capital element has never been at your disposal;[11]
- money you have been paid to be used for a particular purpose on condition that the money must be returned if not used in that way;[12]
- property you have bought on behalf of someone else who is paying the mortgage;[13]
- money held in your bank account on behalf of another person, which is to be returned to her/him at a future date;[14]
- savings from someone else's benefit paid to you as an appointee – eg, your child's disability living allowance;[15]
- a loan and when you get it, you are under an immediate obligation to repay it;[16]
- your own asset but you have expressed a clear intention that it is for someone else's benefit and renounced its use for yourself;[17]
- your interest in a property and you lead someone to believe that you are transferring it to her/him but fail to do so (eg, it is never properly conveyed) and that person acts on the belief that s/he owns it (eg, s/he spends money on repairs). You can argue the asset has been transferred and you are like a trustee.[18] This is called '**proprietary estoppel**'.

See p428 if you find that a loan is taken into account as income even though it is paid as a lump sum.

If you lend money to someone, it could still count as your 'notional capital' (see p486), depending on your reasons for lending it. You usually have a legal right to be repaid and this, in itself, could have a capital value, although the value would normally be less than the amount loaned, and could be nil if you have no expectation of getting the money back.[19]

Trusts

A trust is a way of owning any asset such as money, a house or shares. A 'trustee' looks after the capital and owns the legal title. The trustee uses the capital for the

Part 4: General rules for other means-tested benefits
Chapter 22: Capital: under pension age
3. What counts as capital

benefit of someone else (the 'beneficiary'). If you are a trustee, the capital is not yours to use for yourself unless you are also a beneficiary.

Whether your money is in a discretionary or non-discretionary trust can make a difference to how your benefits are affected.

Payments made from:

- a discretionary trust count as income or capital depending on the nature of the payment.[20] Capital payments are taken into account in full, but income from the trust is generally treated as a voluntary payment and is ignored.[21] The trust asset itself does not normally count as your capital because payments are at the discretion of the trustees and you cannot demand payment (of either income or capital).[22] To be a discretionary trust, the terms of the trust must give trustees discretion over not just when to pay but also whether to make payments at all;[23]
- a non-discretionary trust count in full as capital, whatever the nature of the payment.[24] The trust asset itself also counts as your capital, because in a non-discretionary trust you can obtain the asset from the trustee at any time. For under-18 year olds who have no right to payment (16 in Scotland, or older if the trust specifies), the value of the trust asset may have a current value which is less than the whole amount;
- a trust set up from money for a personal injury to you or your partner are treated more generously (see p484).

Trustees may have a discretion to use such funds to purchase items that would normally be disregarded as capital, such as personal possessions (eg, a wheelchair, car or new furniture) or to arrange payments that would normally be disregarded as income – eg, ineligible housing costs. Similarly, they may have discretion to clear debts or pay for a holiday, leisure items or educational or medical needs. See p425 for the treatment of voluntary payments, and p425 and p435 for the treatment of payments made to third parties.

Note:

- Putting money in a discretionary trust has the advantage of the value of the trust itself being disregarded. However, if you transfer money into a trust in order to get more benefit, it can still count as yours under the notional capital rules (see p486).
- Capital in a non-discretionary trust is taken into account. If this takes you over the £16,000 capital limit, you are not entitled to benefit.

Money held by your solicitor

Money held by your solicitor normally counts as your capital. This includes compensation payments (but see p484 for when payments for personal injury are disregarded).[25] If you have had legal aid and your solicitor is holding money back while working out the statutory charge to be deducted for legal costs, it does not count as your capital.[26]

Income treated as capital

Certain payments that appear to be income are treated as capital. These are:[27]

- income from capital (eg, interest on a bank account, share dividends and income from property let to tenants (see p426). However, the following count as income, not capital:
  - income from the first five disregarded property bullet points on p478;
  - trust funds administered by a court (see p484);
  - income from the home of a partner, former partner or relative in the circumstances described on p480;
  - income from the home in which you normally live;
  - income from business assets or personal injury trusts;
- a lump sum or 'bounty' paid to you not more than once a year as a part-time firefighter, part-time member of a lifeboat crew, auxiliary coastguard or member of the reserve forces. If paid more often, it counts as earnings;
- the following payments:
  - an advance of earnings or loan from your employer;
  - holiday pay which is not payable until more than four weeks after your employment ends or is interrupted;
  - income tax refunds;
  - irregular (one-off) charitable or voluntary payments.

  This does not apply to income support (IS) or income-based jobseeker's allowance (JSA) if you are involved in a trade dispute, or to IS if you are returning to work after a dispute (see p982);
- for IS, income-based JSA and income-related employment and support allowance only, a discharge grant paid on release from prison;
- for housing benefit (HB) only, any arrears of child tax credit or working tax credit;[28]
- for HB only, the gross receipts from work carried out under the New Enterprise Allowance.

4. Disregarded capital

Your home

If you own the home in which you normally live, its value is ignored.[29]

Your home

Your '**home**' includes any garage, garden, outbuildings and land belonging to the property, together with any premises that you do not occupy as your home but which it is impractical or unreasonable to sell separately – eg, croft land.[30]

Part 4: General rules for other means-tested benefits
Chapter 22: Capital: under pension age
4. Disregarded capital

This disregard applies to any home in which you are treated as normally living – eg, because you are only temporarily living away from it (see p354). If you own more than one property, only the one that you normally occupy is disregarded under this rule.[31]

Exceptionally, two separate properties can be regarded as a single home as though one was an annexe of the other, if you personally (rather than a member of your family) normally occupy both properties.[32] This is most likely to be the case for a large family, but other situations are possible where neither property on its own caters for a family's needs – eg, if there is a carer living between two properties.[33]

When the value of the property is disregarded

The value of the property can be disregarded, even if you do not normally live in it, in the following circumstances.

- **If you have left your former home following a relationship breakdown,** the value of the property is ignored for 26 weeks from the date you left. It may also be disregarded for longer if any of the steps below are taken. If it is occupied by your former partner who is a lone parent, its value is ignored for as long as s/he lives there.[34]
- **If you have sought legal advice or have started legal proceedings in order to occupy the property as your home,** its value is ignored for 26 weeks from the date you first took either of these steps.[35] The 26 weeks can be extended if it is reasonable to do so, if you need longer to move in.
- **If you are taking reasonable steps to dispose of a property,** its value is ignored for 26 weeks from the date you first took such steps (which may be before you claim benefit).[36] The steps you take must be 'reasonable'. Advertising at an unrealistic sale price does not count, but placing the property with an estate agent or contacting a possible buyer should,[37] as might taking ancillary proceedings to resolve financial issues in a divorce.[38] The disregard can continue beyond 26 weeks, even for years if it is reasonable – eg, if a court orders that the former matrimonial home should not be sold until the children are grown up. Taking a property off the market and putting it on again does not necessarily begin a new 26-week period, but it may do if the second attempt to sell is quite separate.[39]
- **If you are carrying out essential repairs or alterations which are needed so that you can occupy a property as your home,** the value of the property is ignored for 26 weeks from the date you first began to take steps to carry them out.[40] 'Steps' may include applying for planning permission or a grant or loan to make the property habitable, employing an architect or finding someone to do the work.[41] If you cannot move into the property within that period because the work is not finished, its value can be disregarded for as long as is necessary to allow the work to be carried out.

- **If you have acquired a property and intend to live there as your home but have not yet moved in**, its value is ignored if you intend to live there within 26 weeks of acquiring it.[42] If you cannot move in by then, the value of the property can be ignored for as long as seems reasonable.
- **If you sell your home and intend to use the money from the sale to buy another home**, the capital is ignored for 26 weeks from the date of the sale.[43] This also applies even if you do not own your home but, for a price, you surrender your tenancy rights to a landlord.[44] If you need longer to complete a purchase, your capital can continue to be ignored if it is reasonable to do so. You do not need to have decided within the 26 weeks to buy a particular property. It is sufficient if you intend to use the proceeds to buy some other home within the 26-week (or extended) period,[45] although your 'intention' must involve more than a mere 'hope' or 'aspiration'.[46] There must be an element of 'certainty' which you may be able to show by evidence of a practical commitment to another purchase, although this need not involve any binding obligation.[47] If you intend to use only part of the proceeds of sale to buy another home, only that part is disregarded even if, for example, you have put the rest of the money aside to renovate your new home.[48]
- **If your home is damaged or you lose it altogether**, any payment in consequence of that, including compensation, which is to be used for its repair, or for acquiring another home, is ignored for 26 weeks, or longer if it is reasonable to do so.
- **If you have taken out a loan or been given money for the express purpose of essential repairs or improvements to your home**, it is ignored for 26 weeks, or longer if it is reasonable to do so.[49] If it is a condition of the loan that it must be returned if the improvements are not carried out, you should argue that it should be ignored altogether.[50]
- **If you have deposited money with a housing association as a condition of occupying your home**, this is ignored indefinitely.[51] If money which was deposited for this purpose is now to be used to buy another home, this is ignored for 26 weeks, or longer if reasonable, in order to allow you to complete the purchase.[52]
- **Grants made to buy a home** are ignored for up to 26 weeks if made to local authority tenants to buy a home or do repairs or alterations to it. They can be ignored for longer, if reasonable, to allow completion of the purchase or the repairs/alterations. **Note:** the repairs or alterations must be required to make the property fit for occupation as your home.[53]

When considering whether it is reasonable to extend the period during which time the value of your property is disregarded, all the circumstances should be considered – eg, your personal circumstances, any efforts made by you to use or dispose of the home[54] and the general state of the property market. In practice, periods of around 18 months are not considered unusual.

Part 4: General rules for other means-tested benefits
Chapter 22: Capital: under pension age
4. Disregarded capital

Note: it is possible for property to be ignored under more than one of the above paragraphs in succession.[55]

Some income generated from property which is disregarded is ignored (see p427).

The home of a partner, former partner or relative

The value of a home (see p477) is ignored if it is occupied as her/his home by:[56]
- someone over pension age (see p257), or who has limited capability for work or is incapacitated (see below), who is:
  - a relative of yours or of your partner or dependent child; *or*
  - your spouse or civil partner, provided you are still treated as living in the same household (see p303), or your cohabitee, provided you are still treated as living together as a married couple (see p304); *or*
- your former partner from whom you are not estranged but you are living apart (and are therefore not treated as still living together or as living in the same household) – eg, if one of you is living in a care home; *or*
- your former partner from whom you are estranged and who is a lone parent. If your former partner is not a lone parent, the value of the home is ignored for 26 weeks from the date you ceased to live in the home.

Definitions

'Incapacitated' is not defined, but guidance suggests it includes anyone who is getting employment and support allowance (ESA), statutory sick pay, attendance allowance (AA) or disability living allowance (DLA) or who would qualify because of her/his health condition or disability.[57] It may also include anyone who is getting personal independence payment (PIP), adult disability payment (ADP) or universal credit (UC) who has limited capability for work or limited capability for work-related activity. However, you should argue for a broader interpretation, if necessary.

'Relative' is a parent, son, daughter, step-parent, stepson, stepdaughter, parent-in-law, son-in-law, daughter-in-law, brother or sister, or a partner of any of these people, half-brother or half-sister, adopted child, grandparent or grandchild, uncle, aunt, nephew or niece.[58]

You are **'estranged'** if you are living apart because your relationship has broken down, even if the separation is amicable.[59]

Personal possessions

All personal possessions, including jewellery, furniture or a car, are ignored.[60] A personal possession has been defined as any physical asset not used for business purposes, other than land.[61] For example, in one case, a static caravan on a non-residential site was treated as a personal possession. However, a home that you own but do not live in is not normally a personal possession and does count as capital (see p478). Personal possessions are not ignored if you have bought them in order to be able to claim or get more benefit. In this case, the sale value, rather than the purchase price, is counted as actual capital and the difference is treated as notional capital (see p486).[62]

Compensation for damage to, or the loss of, any personal possessions, which is to be used for their repair or replacement, is ignored for six months, or longer if reasonable.[63]

Business assets

If you are self-employed, your business assets are ignored for as long as you continue to work in that business.[64] These include grants and loans intended to support the business during the coronavirus pandemic.[65] Payments from the Self-Employment Income Support Scheme count as earnings (see p411).

If you cannot work because you are sick or incapacitated, the assets are disregarded for 26 weeks from the date of claim if you intend to work in the business again when you are able, or for longer if reasonable in the circumstances.[66]

If you stop working in the business, you are allowed a reasonable time to sell these assets without their value affecting your benefit.

It is sometimes difficult to distinguish between personal and business assets. The test is whether the assets are 'part of the fund employed and risked in the business'.[67] If the assets of a business partnership (eg, plant and machinery) have been sold but the partnership has not yet been dissolved, the proceeds of sale can still count as business assets.[68] **Note:** letting a single house is not likely to constitute a business.[69]

For the treatment of business assets if you are taking part in the New Enterprise Allowance, see p486.

Personal pension schemes

The value of a fund held in a personal pension scheme is ignored as capital.[70] The value of the right to receive an occupational or personal pension is also ignored. However, if your partner is over pension age and chooses not to take income from the pension, you are treated as having notional income (see p429).

Insurance policy and annuity surrender values

The surrender value of a life assurance policy is ignored.[71] Some investments include an element of life insurance – eg, endowment policies. If the policy terms include how the payment on death is calculated, the whole investment is ignored.[72] However, you cannot choose to put money into such an investment in order to increase your benefit entitlement, because you are likely to be caught by the notional capital rule if you do (see p487).

Part 4: General rules for other means-tested benefits
Chapter 22: Capital: under pension age
4. Disregarded capital

The surrender value of any annuity is also ignored (see p427 and p473),[73] as is the value of the right to receive any payment under an annuity. Any payment under the annuity counts as income[74] (but see p429 for when this is ignored).

Future interest in property

A future interest in most kinds of property is ignored.[75] A **'future interest'** is one which will only revert to you, or become yours for the first time, when some future event occurs – eg, where someone else has a life interest in a fund and you are only entitled to it after that person has died.

However, this does not include a freehold or leasehold interest in property which has been let *by you* to tenants. If you did not let the property to the tenant (eg, because the tenancy was entered into before you bought the property), your interest in the property should be ignored as a future interest in the normal way.

The right to receive a payment in the future

If you know that you will receive a payment in the future and you could sell your right to it at any time, it has a market value and therefore constitutes an actual capital resource. The value of this is ignored if it is a right to receive:[76]

- income under a life interest or, in Scotland, a life rent; *or*
- an occupational or personal pension; *or*
- any rent if you are not the freeholder or leaseholder. Any actual income which this right generates for you and which is not disregarded as income can be taken into account as income; *or*
- any payment under an annuity (see p432). Any actual income generated by this right and which is not disregarded as income can be taken into account as income; *or*
- any earnings or income that is ignored because it is frozen abroad; *or*
- any outstanding instalments if capital is being paid by instalments; *or*
- any payment under a trust fund set up with money paid because of a personal injury to you or your partner.

Benefits and tax credits

Arrears of benefits and tax credits

Arrears of the following are ignored for 52 weeks after you receive them, or longer in some cases where there has been official error or an error of law (see below):[77]

- AA;
- ADP (in Scotland);
- armed forces independence payment;
- bereavement support payment;
- child disability payment (in Scotland);
- child tax credit;
- council tax benefit;

- DLA;
- discretionary housing payments;
- income-related ESA;
- housing benefit (HB);
- income support (IS);
- income-based jobseeker's allowance (JSA);
- maternity allowance;
- mobility supplement;
- PIP;
- Scottish child payment;
- UC;
- working tax credit (WTC);
- concessionary payments instead of any of the above;
- for HB only, compensation for lost or delayed (new-style) contributory ESA because of a DWP error.

If the arrears are £5,000 or more and are paid to compensate for an official error (see p1266) or an error of law, they are ignored until the end of your (or your partner's) award. If you or your partner then reclaim the same benefit, or move from UC, IS, income-based JSA or income-related ESA to another of these four benefits, they continue to be ignored for the whole of this next and any subsequent award(s) if there is no gap between awards.[78]

Note: although arrears are ignored as capital, you may have been paid more IS, income-based JSA, income-related ESA or HB than you would have been entitled to if benefit had been paid on time. Usually, the DWP deducts the difference from the arrears of the delayed benefit. Otherwise, if the arrears are not reduced, the overpayment is recoverable from you (see p1198). For HB, the overpayment is not deducted from the arrears but may be recoverable (see p1214).

Other benefits and payments

The following are ignored for 52 weeks from the date you receive them, or indefinitely where specified:

- initial lump sum of bereavement support payment;[79]
- social fund payments (ignored indefinitely);[80]
- Best Start grant in Scotland (ignored indefinitely);[81]
- child winter heating assistance in Scotland (ignored indefinitely);[82]
- fares to hospital, and payments for prescriptions and dental charges;[83]
- funeral support payment in Scotland (ignored indefinitely);[84]
- payments in lieu of milk tokens, vitamins or Healthy Start food vouchers;[85]
- payments to assist prison visits;[86]
- certain payments to war widows, widowers and surviving civil partners;[87]
- young carer grant in Scotland (ignored indefinitely);[88]
- any payments by the Secretary of State to compensate for the loss of entitlement to HB (ignored indefinitely).[89]

Part 4: General rules for other means-tested benefits
Chapter 22: Capital: under pension age
4. Disregarded capital

Charitable, personal injury and other compensation payments

- **Charitable payments.** Any payment in kind by a charity is ignored.[90]
- **Personal injury payments.** If you have money in a trust from a personal injury to you, the value of the trust and any income from it is disregarded.[91] A lump sum from the trust is taken into account as capital. It should not affect your benefit if the trustees give you regular or even annual payments, pay your bills or, instead of giving you a lump sum, buy you something that would be disregarded because it is a personal possession – eg furniture or a car.

  If an award for damages for personal injury to you is administered by a court (eg, the Court of Protection), its value and income from it is also disregarded.[92] This also applies if the court-administered fund is for children to compensate for the death of a parent.

  If you have just received a payment for personal injury to you, it is disregarded for 52 weeks from when you receive it.[93] This gives you time to spend it or put it into a trust or annuity before your benefit is affected. There is no 52-week disregard for another payment for the same injury, but it is disregarded as soon as it is in a trust.

  If the personal injury is to your partner, there is a 52-week disregard for the initial payment and the value of a trust is disregarded, but not income from the trust or annuity. If your partner has since died, you cannot carry over the remainder of the 52-week disregard, or if the payment is in a trust, it is no longer ignored.[94]

  Personal injury payments include compensation from the Criminal Injuries Compensation Scheme.[95] Victims payments to people injured in a Northern Ireland 'Troubles-related incident' are disregarded as income or capital indefinitely.[96]

Definitions

'Personal injury' includes not only accidental and criminal injuries, but also any disease and injury as a result of a disease.[97]

Payments include any amounts in consequence of personal injury – eg, for loss of earnings.[98]

'Trust'. Any money in a trust 'derived from' compensation for personal injury to you is disregarded irrespective of the type of trust.[99]

- **Special compensation schemes.** Any payment of capital from certain special schemes is ignored including:
  - the National Emergencies Trust;
  - the Windrush Compensation Scheme;
  - the Child Migrants Trust (for children subjected to migration programmes before 1971);

- schemes to make child abuse payments for historic institutional child abuse in the UK;
- for people infected from contaminated blood products;
- for people affected by the 2017 fire at Grenfell Tower.

For most of the schemes, money from your partner's payments is ignored indefinitely, or for two years from your child's payments if s/he has no partner or dependent child.

Social services, community care and other payments

The following payments from a local authority are ignored indefinitely:[100]
- payments for children and families made under section 17 of the Children Act 1989, section 12 of the Social Work (Scotland) Act 1968 or, for HB, section 22 of the Children (Scotland) Act 1995 and sections 37 and 38 of the Social Services and Well-being (Wales) Act 2014;
- payments to young people who have previously been looked after by the local authority made under sections 23B or 24A of the Children Act 1989, section 30 of the Children (Scotland) Act 1995 or sections 109, 110, 114 or 115 of the Social Services and Well-being (Wales) Act 2014. A payment under section 23C of the Children Act 1989 is also ignored as the young person's capital, and as yours if s/he passes it to you and s/he was in your care, is still living with you and is aged 18 or over – eg, under 'staying put' arrangements. In Scotland, this applies to payments under sections 26A and 29 of the Children (Scotland) Act 1995 and includes young people aged 16 or over in 'continuing care'.

See p982 if you or your partner are involved in a trade dispute.

Also ignored indefinitely are:
- local welfare assistance to meet an immediate short-term need or establish or maintain a settled home in certain circumstances. These include £150 energy rebate payments paid by the local authority (eg, to households in council tax bands A to D), test and trace support payments (in England), self-isolation support grants (in Scotland), self-isolation support scheme payments (in Wales) and Scottish child payment bridging payments;[101]
- community care or healthcare direct payments;[102]
- education, health and care plan payments, paid in England for a child with special educational needs;[103]
- payments from a local authority for support services to help you live independently (eg, under the Supporting People programme, often called 'housing-related support');[104]
- special guardianship allowances, payable in England and Wales;[105]
- kinship care payments, payable in Scotland;[106]
- payments under sections 2, 3 or 4 of the Adoption and Children Act 2002.[107]

Part 4: General rules for other means-tested benefits
Chapter 22: Capital: under pension age
5. Notional capital

Employment and training programme payments

Some payments are ignored for 52 weeks from the date they are received:[108]
- payment for travel or other expenses from a specified scheme for assisting people to obtain employment (see p1122);
- for income-related ESA, payment for travel or other expenses for undertaking required work-related activity;
- payment under section 2 of the Employment and Training Act 1973 or section 2 of the Enterprise and New Towns (Scotland) Act 1990;
- capital acquired for the purpose of participating in the New Enterprise Allowance.[109] Any capital acquired is ignored for as long as you are receiving assistance for taking part in the programme and, after you have ceased trading, for as long as is reasonable in order to dispose of the assets.[110]

Payments to disabled people under the Disabled Persons (Employment) Act 1944 (other than a training allowance) to assist with employment, or local authority payments to assist blind homeworkers, are ignored indefinitely.[111]

For when employment and training programme payments are treated as income, notional income and notional capital, see p428, p435 and p490.

Miscellaneous payments

The following payments are disregarded:
- a sports award made by the UK Sport National Lottery funds, except for any part of the award which is made for ordinary living expenses (see p433). It is disregarded for 26 weeks;[112]
- an education maintenance allowance or a 16 to 19 bursary fund payment are ignored indefinitely;[113]
- for IS, income-based JSA and income-related ESA, any payments made to jurors or witnesses for attending at court, except for payments for loss of earnings or benefit;[114]
- refunds of council tax liability (ignored for 52 weeks from the date you receive the arrears);[115]
- 20 per cent of money in a tax-free childcare account (see p856);[116]
- any payments made to holders of the Victoria or George Cross.[117]

5. **Notional capital**

In certain circumstances, you are treated as having capital that you do not have. This is called '**notional capital**'.[118] There is a similar rule for notional income (see p433 and p133). Notional capital counts in the same way as the capital you do have.

You may be treated as having notional capital if:

- you deliberately deprive yourself of capital in order to claim or increase benefit (see below); *or*
- you fail to apply for capital which is available to you (see p490); *or*
- someone makes a payment of capital to a third party on your behalf or on behalf of a member of your family (see p490); *or*
- you (or a member of your family) receive a payment of capital on behalf of a third party and you (or the member of your family) use or keep the capital (see p491); *or*
- you are a sole trader or a partner in a business which is a limited company (see p492).

Note: if you are treated as having notional capital because you have deliberately deprived yourself of capital in order to claim or increase benefit, a 'diminishing notional capital rule' (see p489) may be applied so that the value of the notional capital you are treated as having is considered to reduce over time.

Deliberately getting rid of capital

If you deliberately get rid of capital in order to claim or increase your benefit, you are treated as still having it.[119] The same applies if your partner got rid of capital, even if s/he did so before you became a couple.[120] You are likely to be affected by this rule if, at the time of using up your money, you knew that you might qualify for benefit (or more benefit), or qualify more quickly as a result. You should not be affected if you knew nothing about the effect of using up your capital (eg, you did not know about the capital limit for claiming benefit)[121] or if you have been using up your capital at a rate which is reasonable in the circumstances. This is because you cannot have the intention if you do not know about the capital rules.[122] Knowledge of capital limits can be inferred from a reasonable familiarity with the benefit system as a claimant,[123] but if you fail to make enquiries about the capital limit, this does not constitute an intention to secure benefit.

In practice, arguing successfully that you have not deprived yourself of capital to get or increase benefit may depend on whether you can show that you would have spent the money in the way you did (eg, to pay off debts or reduce your mortgage) regardless of the effect on your benefit entitlement. If this is unclear, the burden of proving that you did it to get benefit lies with the decision maker.

Your intentions

Even if you did know about the capital limits, it still has to be shown that you intended to obtain, retain or increase your benefit.[124] For example, in one case, a claimant faced repossession of his home and transferred ownership to his daughter (who he feared would otherwise be made homeless), despite having been warned by DWP staff that he would be disqualified from benefit if he did so. It was held that, under the circumstances, he had not disposed of the property

Part 4: General rules for other means-tested benefits
Chapter 22: Capital: under pension age
5. Notional capital

with the intention of gaining benefit.[125] The longer the period that has elapsed since the disposal of the capital, the less likely it is for the purpose of obtaining benefit.[126] However, no matter how long it has been since you may have disposed of an asset, there is no set 'safe' period after which benefit can be claimed without the need for further enquiry.[127]

If you use up your resources, you may have more than one motive for doing so. Even if qualifying for benefit is only a lesser motive for your actions and the main motive is something different (eg, ensuring your home is in good condition by spending capital on repairs and improvements), you may still be considered to have deprived yourself of a resource in order to gain benefit.[128]

The test is not what the money has been spent on, but your intention behind the expenditure. However, examples of the kinds of expenditure that could be caught by this rule are expensive holidays and putting money in trust.[129] **Note:** for income support (IS), income-based jobseeker's allowance (JSA) and income-related employment and support allowance (ESA), putting money in trust for yourself does not constitute deprivation if the capital came from compensation paid for a personal injury.[130]

You can deprive yourself of capital, even if you receive another resource in return.[131] For example, if you buy a car so that you can get more benefit, your actual capital includes the value of the car, and the difference between that and the purchase price is treated as notional capital.[132]

Paying off debts and bankruptcy

If you pay off a debt that you are legally required to repay immediately, you may not be counted as having deprived yourself of capital in order to gain benefit.[133] It is the facts of your case that are important: if you paid off an immediately repayable debt when you thought it would not be recalled for some time, you might be considered to have deprived yourself of money in order to get benefit. However, even if you pay off a debt that you are not legally required to repay immediately, the decision maker must still prove that you did so in order to get benefit.[134]

If you are declared bankrupt, you cannot spend your capital without court approval and cannot usually be held to have deprived yourself of it if you do. Capital you have (but cannot spend) does not count for benefit purposes from the date of the bankruptcy order.[135] However, if you deliberately go bankrupt or do not take reasonable steps to discharge the bankruptcy in order to get benefit, your capital can still count as notional capital.

How notional capital is calculated

Notional capital is generally calculated in the same way as actual capital and the same disregards usually apply (see p477).[136] However, you may not be able to rely on the 26-week (or longer) disregard you would otherwise be allowed to take steps to dispose of a property (see p478), even if the new owner is trying to sell it (but there is conflicting caselaw on this).[137]

If more than one benefit is involved

If you have intentionally deprived yourself of capital in order to get IS, it does not necessarily follow that you also intended to get housing benefit (HB). Similarly, deprivation of capital to get income-based JSA cannot be treated as a deprivation for IS, although deprivation for IS can be treated as deprivation for income-based JSA, and deprivation for IS or income-based JSA can be treated as deprivation for income-related ESA. Each decision maker must reach her/his own decision on each benefit. This may result in different conclusions being drawn for each benefit. Even if intent is found in two different benefits, there may be different views about the amount of capital that has been intentionally disposed of.

However, if you are considered to have deprived yourself of capital for the purposes of claiming HB and you then make a successful claim for IS, income-based JSA or income-related ESA, the local authority should put the notional capital rules for HB on hold for as long as the other benefit remains in payment.[138]

The diminishing notional capital rule

The 'diminishing notional capital rule' provides a way of working out how the value of your notional capital may be treated as reducing over time. It only applies if you have deliberately deprived yourself of capital.[139]

It applies from the first week after the week in which it is decided that notional capital is to be taken into account.

- If your benefit is reduced because of tariff income from your notional capital, that capital is diminished by the amount of the reduction each week. For example, if your notional capital is £6,750 (and you have no other capital), giving a tariff income of £3 a week, the reduction is £3 a week until it reaches £6,500, when it will be £2 and so on. For HB, the amount of your notional capital is also reduced by the amount of IS, income-based JSA or income-related ESA you would have had if no notional capital had been taken into account.
- If you have both actual and notional capital, you may have to use your actual capital to meet your living expenses. There is no reason why this should affect the amount by which your notional capital is diminished, even if this effectively results in double counting. Any reduction in your actual capital should be taken into account in calculating any tariff income arising from your combined actual and notional capital, unless you have spent it at such a rate and in such a way that it raises questions of intent, when you may find that the notional capital rules are applied all over again.
- If your benefit award has ended because of notional capital, the amount of notional capital reduces over time. Once it has reduced to a point when a fresh claim might succeed, you cannot usually make a new claim for IS, income-

Part 4: General rules for other means-tested benefits
Chapter 22: Capital: under pension age
5. Notional capital

based JSA, income-related ESA or HB (see p23 for exceptions). Instead, you can claim universal credit (UC). See p494 of the 2018/19 edition of this *Handbook* for the way notional capital is reduced for these benefits. **Note:** you are not automatically treated as having the notional capital in a UC claim. If you wish to claim UC, you should do so without delay in order to have the capital considered again under the UC rules (see p150).

Failing to apply for capital

You are expected to apply for any capital that is due to you – eg, if money is held by a court which could be released if you applied, or an unclaimed premium bond win. If you would get capital if you applied for it, you are treated as having that capital.[140]

You are only treated as having such capital from the date you could obtain it. This rule does not apply if you do not apply for:

- capital from a discretionary trust; *or*
- capital from a trust (or fund administered by a court) set up from money paid as a result of a personal injury; *or*
- capital from a personal pension scheme or, if you are under pension age (see p257), from an occupational pension scheme or a payment from the Pension Protection Fund; *or*
- a loan which you could only get if you gave your home or other disregarded capital (see p477) as security; *or*
- for HB only, child tax credit or working tax credit.[141]

Capital payments made to a third party on your behalf

If someone pays an amount to a third party (eg, a fuel company or a building society) for you or your partner (or a child for HB, or for IS or income-based JSA if children are still included in your claim – see p474), this may count as your capital. It counts if the payment is to cover:[142]

- certain normal living expenses – ie, food, household fuel, council tax, water charges or ordinary clothing or footwear. School uniforms and sportswear are not ordinary clothing,[143] nor are special shoes needed because of a disability.[144] Payments made, for instance, for food or clothes for you or your partner count as yours. However, since a child's capital is not counted as belonging to you, a payment to, for example, a clothes shop for your child should count as the child's notional capital and not yours, and, in most cases, is ignored; *or*
- rent which could be met by HB (less any non-dependant deductions); *or*
- for IS, income-based JSA and income-related ESA only, housing costs which could be met by IS, income-based JSA or income-related ESA.

Payments to a third party do *not* count as yours if they are:[145]
- for other kinds of expenses (eg, a TV licence or mortgage repayments), unless they come from a benefit or pension (see below); *or*
- from a specified infected blood payment scheme or emergency funds (see p484); *or*
- for participating in a specified scheme for assisting people to obtain employment (see p1122).

Payments from an occupational or personal pension scheme or from the Pension Protection Fund to a third party count as yours regardless of whether or not the payments are used, or intended to be used, for ordinary living expenses.[146] They are disregarded if:

- you (or your partner) are bankrupt (or in Scotland, the subject of a sequestration order), the payment is made to the trustee or other person acting on your creditors' behalf and you and your partner (or your family for HB, and for IS or income-based JSA if amounts for children are still included in your claim) have no income other than the payment made;[147] *or*
- the payments do not support you financially and therefore do not reduce or remove your need to be supported by IS, income-based JSA, income-related ESA or HB – eg, deductions from an occupational pension made under an attachment of earnings order to a former partner.[148] If you have had a judicial separation, rather than divorce, so the usual pension-splitting arrangements are not available, and a court has ordered you to pay part of your pension to your former partner, you could argue that this does not count as yours.[149]

For IS, income-based JSA and income-related ESA only, payments *derived* from certain social security benefits (including war disablement pensions, war widows' pensions and Armed Forces Compensation Scheme payments) and paid to a third party count:[150]
- as yours, if you are entitled to the benefit; *and*
- as your partner's, if s/he is entitled to the benefit.

For IS, income-based JSA and income-related ESA, there are different rules if you could be liable to pay maintenance (see p422).

Capital payments made to you for a third party

If you or your partner get a payment for someone not in your family (eg, a relative), it only counts as yours if it is kept or used by you.[151] For HB (and for IS or income-based JSA if amounts for children are still included in your claim – see p474), the same also applies to payments received by a member of your family for someone not in the family. Payments from a specified infected blood payment scheme or emergency funds (see p484), or a specified scheme for assisting people to obtain employment (see p1122), do not count at all. Payments from pension

Part 4: General rules for other means-tested benefits
Chapter 22: Capital: under pension age
6. How capital is valued

schemes paid for a third party are disregarded in the same circumstances as described on p490.

Companies run by sole traders or a few partners

Normally, if you hold shares in a company, their value is taken into account as capital. If, however, your influence in the company is such that you are like a sole trader or like a partner in a small partnership, you are treated accordingly. For IS, income-based JSA and income-related ESA, the value of your shareholding is ignored but you are treated as having a proportionate share of the capital of the company.[152] However, these company assets are not taken into account while you are doing any work on the company's business,[153] even if you only do a little work for the company – eg, taking messages.[154] It has, however, been held that a 'sleeping partner' in a business managed and worked exclusively by others may not benefit from this disregard. As well as having a financial commitment to the business, you must also be involved or engaged in it in some practical sense as an earner.[155]

For HB, the local authority has discretion about whether to apply the same rules as for IS. If it decides to, it must apply them all.[156]

6. How capital is valued

Market value

Your capital is valued at its current market or surrender value.[157] This means the amount of money you could raise by selling it or raising a loan against it. This is the price that would be paid by a willing buyer to a willing seller on a particular date.[158] So if an asset is difficult or impossible to realise, its market value should be heavily discounted or even nil.[159]

If you cannot legally dispose of capital (eg, because of a restraint order), the market value is nil.[160]

In the case of a house, an estate agent's figure for a quick sale is a more appropriate valuation than the district valuer's figure for a sale within three months.[161]

It is not uncommon for an unrealistic assessment to be made of the value of your capital. If you disagree with the decision, you could ask for a revision or appeal (see Chapters 56 and 57).

Expenses of sale

If there would be expenses involved in selling your capital, 10 per cent is deducted from its value (before any debts are deducted) for the cost of sale.[162]

Debts

Deductions are made from the gross value of your capital for any debt or mortgage secured on it.[163] If a creditor (eg, a bank) holds the land certificate to your property as security for a loan and has registered notice of its deposit at the Land Registry, this counts as a debt secured on your property.[164] If a single mortgage is secured on a house and land, and the value of the house is disregarded for benefit purposes, the whole of the mortgage can be deducted when calculating the value of the land.[165]

If you have debts that are not secured against your capital (eg, tax liabilities), these cannot be offset against the value of your capital.[166] However, once you have repaid your debts, your capital may be reduced. **Note:** you can still be treated as having the capital if you deliberately get rid of it in order to get benefit (see p487).

If you have an overdrawn bank account and have savings in another account with the same bank, the amount of the overdraft should be deducted from your savings if the terms of the accounts allow the bank to make these transfers.[167]

Jointly owned capital

If you own any capital asset (except as a partner in a company – see p492) with someone else under a 'joint tenancy', you are treated as owning an equal share of the asset with the other owner(s) – eg, if you own the asset with one other person, you are each treated as having a 50 per cent share of it.[168] This applies regardless of whether the capital asset is in the UK or abroad. See p495 for the rules that apply to assets abroad.[169]

This does not apply if you jointly own the capital asset as 'tenants in common'.[170] In this case, your actual share in the asset is valued.

Joint tenancies and tenancies in common

With a '**joint tenancy**', each co-owner owns the whole of the capital asset 'jointly and severally'. If one of the joint tenants were to die, her/his interest in the asset would pass automatically to the other joint tenant(s).

With a '**tenancy in common**', each co-owner owns a discrete share in the asset. This share can be passed on by the person who has died to whoever s/he wishes.

If you have a joint tenancy, the value of your deemed share is calculated in the same way as your actual capital. However, it is only the value of your deemed share looked at in isolation that counts, and this will usually be worth less than the same proportion of the value of the whole asset. For example, if the asset is a house, the value of any deemed share may be very small or even worthless, particularly if the house is occupied and there is a possibility that the sale of the property cannot be forced. This is because even a willing buyer could not be

Part 4: General rules for other means-tested benefits
Chapter 22: Capital: under pension age
6. How capital is valued

expected to pay much for an asset s/he would have difficulty making use of.[171] Whether a sale can be forced depends on individual circumstances, and valuations should take into account legal costs and the length of time it could take to gain possession of the property.[172] A valuation should set out details of the valuer's expertise (where relevant), describe the property in sufficient detail to show that all factors relevant to its value have been taken into account, state any assumptions on which it is based and explain what the market is for that type of sale.[173] You may need to challenge any decision (see Chapters 56 and 57) based on an inadequate valuation.

Treatment of assets after a relationship breakdown

When partners separate, assets, such as a former home or bank account, may be in joint or sole names. If, for instance, a bank account is in joint names, you and your former partner are treated as having a 50 per cent share each under the rules on jointly held capital (see above). On the other hand, a former partner may have a right to some, or all, of an asset that is in your sole name – eg, s/he may have deposited most of the money in a bank account in your name. If this is established, you may be treated as not entitled to the whole of the account but as holding part of it as trustee for your former partner.[174] If an asset such as the matrimonial home belongs to your former partner and you have no share in it, you cannot be treated as having any interest in it under the Matrimonial Causes Act 1973 unless you take divorce or separation proceedings and get a property order.[175]

Shares

Shares are valued at their current market value less 10 per cent for the cost of sale, and after deducting any 'lien' held by brokers for sums owed for purchase or commission.[176] Market value can be worked out from the listed share price. If a more exact value is needed (eg, because your capital is close to the limit), it should be calculated using HM Revenue and Customs guidance, by taking the lowest and highest share prices for the day and using the lowest price plus a quarter of the difference between the two.[177] Fluctuations in price between routine reviews of your award are normally ignored. If you have a minority holding of shares in a company, the value of the shares should be based on what you could realise on them, and not by valuing the entire share capital of the company and attributing to you an amount calculated according to the proportion of shares held.[178]

Unit trusts

Unit trusts are valued on the basis of the 'bid' price quoted in newspapers. No deduction is allowed for the cost of sale because this is already included in the 'bid' price.[179]

The right to receive a payment in the future

The value of any such right that is not ignored (see p482) is its market value – what a willing buyer will pay to a willing seller.[180] For something which is not yet realisable, this may be very small.

Overseas assets

If you have assets abroad and there are no exchange controls or other prohibitions to prevent you transferring your capital to the UK, your assets are valued at their current market or surrender value in that country.[181]

If you are not allowed to transfer your capital, you are treated as having capital equal to the amount that a willing buyer in this country would give (which might not be very much).[182] Deduct 10 per cent for any expenses of sale, any debts or mortgage secured on the assets and any charges for converting the payment into sterling.[183]

Notes

1. The capital limits
1 **IS** Regs 45 and 53 IS Regs
   JSA Regs 107 and 116 JSA Regs
   ESA Regs 110 and 118 ESA Regs
   HB Regs 43 and 52 HB Regs

2. Whose capital counts
2 **IS/HB** s136(1) SSCBA 1992
   JSA s13(2) JSA 1995
   ESA Sch 1 para 6(2) WRA 2007
3 **IS** Reg 23(2) IS Regs
   JSA Reg 88(2) JSA Regs
   ESA Reg 83(2) ESA Regs
   HB Reg 25(3) HB Regs
4 **IS** Reg 17(1)(b) IS Regs
   JSA Reg 83(b) JSA Regs
5 **IS** Reg 44(5) IS Regs
   JSA Reg 106(5) JSA Regs

3. What counts as capital
6 para BW1.71 GM; Vol 5 Ch 29, para 29020 DMG
7 *R v SBC ex parte Singer* [1973] 1 WLR 713
8 R(IS) 3/93
9 R(IS) 3/93 para 22
10 R(SB) 2/83; R(SB) 35/83; R(IS) 3/93
11 R(SB) 12/86

12 *Barclays Bank v Quistclose Investments Ltd* [1970] AC 567; R(SB) 49/83; R(SB) 53/83; R(SB) 1/85; *MW v SSWP (JSA)* [2016] UKUT 469 (AAC), reported as [2017] AACR 15
13 R(SB) 49/83
14 R(SB) 12/86; for how this works in Scotland, see *JK v SSWP (JSA)* [2010] UKUT 437 (AAC), reported as [2011] AACR 26; *DF v SSWP* [2015] UKUT 611 (AAC)
15 *MC v SSWP (IS)* [2015] UKUT 600 (AAC)
16 CIS/2287/2008
17 R(IS) 1/90; CSIS/639/2006
18 R(SB) 23/85; CSIS/639/2006
19 *JC v SSWP* [2009] UKUT 22 (AAC)
20 CIS/25/1989
21 **IS** Sch 9 para 15 IS Regs
   JSA Sch 7 para 15 JSA Regs
   ESA Sch 8 para 16 ESA Regs
   HB Sch 5 para 14 HB Regs
   All Vol 5 Ch 29, para 29239 DMG; *SM v SSWP* [2020] UKUT 265 (AAC)
22 *Gartside v Inland Revenue Commissioners* [1968] 1 All ER 121; [1968] AC 553

Part 4: General rules for other means-tested benefits
Chapter 22: Capital: under pension age
Notes

● ●

23 *LG v SSWP (ESA)* [2019] UKUT 220
   (AAC), reported as [2020] AACR 5
24 **IS** Reg 48(4) IS Regs
   JSA Reg 110(4) JSA Regs
   ESA Reg 112(4) ESA Regs
   HB Reg 46(4) HB Regs
25 *Thomas v CAO,* appendix to R(SB) 17/87
26 CIS/984/2002
27 **IS** Reg 48 IS Regs
   JSA Reg 110 JSA Regs
   ESA Reg 112 ESA Regs
   HB Reg 46 HB Regs
28 Reg 46(9) HB Regs

4. Disregarded capital
29 **IS** Sch 10 para 1 IS Regs
   JSA Sch 8 para 1 JSA Regs
   ESA Sch 9 para 1 ESA Regs
   HB Sch 6 para 1 HB Regs
30 **IS** Reg 2(1), definition of 'dwelling
   occupied as the home', IS Regs; R(SB) 3/
   84; CIS/427/1991 and R(IS) 3/96
   JSA Reg 1(3), definition of 'dwelling
   occupied as the home', JSA Regs
   ESA Reg 2(1), definition of 'dwelling
   occupied as the home', ESA Regs
   HB Sch 6 para 11 HB Regs
31 **IS** Sch 10 para 1 IS Regs
   JSA Sch 8 para 1 JSA Regs
   ESA Sch 9 para 1 ESA Regs
   HB Sch 6 para 1 HB Regs
32 R(JSA) 9/03; R(SB) 10/89
33 *MM v SSWP (IS)* [2012] UKUT 358 (AAC)
34 **IS** Sch 10 para 25 IS Regs
   JSA Sch 8 para 5 JSA Regs
   ESA Sch 9 para 5 ESA Regs
   HB Sch 6 para 25 HB Regs
35 **IS** Sch 10 para 27 IS Regs
   JSA Sch 8 para 7 JSA Regs
   ESA Sch 9 para 7 ESA Regs
   HB Sch 6 para 27 HB Regs
36 **IS** Sch 10 para 26 IS Regs
   JSA Sch 8 para 6 JSA Regs
   ESA Sch 9 para 6 ESA Regs
   HB Sch 6 para 26 HB Regs
   All CIS/6908/1995; R(IS) 4/97
37 R(SB) 32/83
38 R(IS) 5/05
39 *SP v SSWP* [2009] UKUT 255 (AAC)
40 **IS** Sch 10 para 28 IS Regs
   JSA Sch 8 para 8 JSA Regs
   ESA Sch 9 para 8 ESA Regs
   HB Sch 6 para 28 HB Regs
41 *R v LB Tower Hamlets Review Board ex
   parte Kapur,* 12 June 2000, unreported

42 **IS** Sch 10 para 2 IS Regs
   JSA Sch 8 para 2 JSA Regs
   ESA Sch 9 para 2 ESA Regs
   HB Sch 6 para 2 HB Regs
43 **IS** Sch 10 para 3 IS Regs
   JSA Sch 8 para 3 JSA Regs
   ESA Sch 9 para 3 ESA Regs
   HB Sch 6 para 3 HB Regs
44 R(IS) 6/95
45 R(IS) 7/01
46 CIS/685/1992
47 CIS/8475/1995; CIS/15984/1996
48 R(SB) 14/85
49 **IS** Sch 10 para 8(b) IS Regs
   JSA Sch 8 para 13(b) JSA Regs
   ESA Sch 9 para 12(b) ESA Regs
   HB Sch 6 para 10(b) HB Regs
50 *Barclays Bank v Quistclose Investments Ltd*
   [1970] AC 567; CSB/975/1985
51 **IS** Sch 10 para 9(a) IS Regs
   JSA Sch 8 para 14(a) JSA Regs
   ESA Sch 9 para 13(a) ESA Regs
   HB Sch 6 para 11(a) HB Regs
52 **IS** Sch 10 para 9(b) IS Regs
   JSA Sch 8 para 14(b) JSA Regs
   ESA Sch 9 para 13(b) ESA Regs
   HB Sch 6 para 11(b) HB Regs
53 **IS** Sch 10 para 37 IS Regs
   JSA Sch 8 para 9 JSA Regs
   ESA Sch 9 para 36 ESA Regs
   HB Sch 6 para 38 HB Regs
54 CIS/4757/2003
55 CIS/6908/1995
56 **IS** Sch 10 paras 4 and 25 IS Regs
   JSA Sch 8 paras 4 and 5 JSA Regs
   ESA Sch 9 paras 4 and 5 ESA Regs
   HB Sch 6 paras 4 and 25 HB Regs
57 **HB** BW1/Annex A/A1.01 GM
   Other benefits Vol 5 Ch 29, para
   29434 DMG
58 **IS** Reg 2(1) IS Regs
   JSA Reg 1(3) JSA Regs
   ESA Reg 2(1) ESA Regs
   HB Reg 2(1) HB Regs
   All CSB/209/1986; CSB/1149/1986;
   R(SB) 22/87
59 R(IS) 5/05; CH/3777/2007; *Bristol City
   Council v SJP (HB)* [2019] UKUT 360
   (AAC)
60 **IS** Sch 10 para 10 IS Regs
   JSA Sch 8 para 15 JSA Regs
   ESA Sch 9 para 14 ESA Regs
   HB Sch 6 para 12 HB Regs
61 R(H) 7/08
62 CIS/494/1990 and R(IS) 8/04

63 **IS** Sch 10 para 8(a) IS Regs
JSA Sch 8 para 13(a) JSA Regs
ESA Sch 9 para 12(a) ESA Regs
HB Sch 6 para 10(a) HB Regs
64 **IS** Sch 10 para 6(1) IS Regs
JSA Sch 8 para 11(1) JSA Regs
ESA Sch 9 para 10(1) ESA Regs
HB Sch 6 para 8(1) HB Regs
65 Memo DMG 13/20
66 **IS** Sch 10 para 6(2) IS Regs
JSA Sch 8 para 11(2) JSA Regs
ESA Sch 9 para 10(2) ESA Regs
HB Sch 6 para 8(2) HB Regs
67 R(SB) 4/85
68 CIS/5481/1997
69 CFC/15/1990; R(FC) 2/92; *RM v Sefton
Council (HB)* [2016] UKUT 357 (AAC),
reported as [2017] AACR 5
70 **IS** Sch 10 para 23A IS Regs
JSA Sch 8 paras 28 and 29 JSA Regs
ESA Sch 9 paras 28 and 29 ESA Regs
HB Sch 6 para 32 HB Regs
71 **IS** Sch 10 para 15 IS Regs
JSA Sch 8 para 20 JSA Regs
ESA Sch 9 para 20 ESA Regs
HB Sch 6 para 17 HB Regs
72 R(IS) 7/98
73 **IS** Sch 10 para 11 IS Regs
JSA Sch 8 para 16 JSA Regs
ESA Sch 9 para 15 ESA Regs
HB Sch 6 para 13 HB Regs
74 **IS** Reg 41(2) IS Regs
JSA Reg 104(2) JSA Regs
ESA Reg 105(2) ESA Regs
HB Reg 41(2) HB Regs
All *Beattie v Secretary of State for Social
Security* [2001] EWCA Civ 498,
upholding CIS/114/1999, reported as
R(IS) 10/01
75 **IS** Sch 10 para 5 IS Regs
JSA Sch 8 para 10 JSA Regs
ESA Sch 9 para 9 ESA Regs
HB Sch 6 para 7 HB Regs
76 **IS** Sch 10 paras 11-14, 16, 23 and 24 IS
Regs
JSA Sch 8 paras 16-19, 21, 28 and 30
JSA Regs
ESA Sch 9 paras 15, 16, 18, 19, 21, 28
and 30 ESA Regs
HB Sch 6 paras 13-16, 18, 31 and 33 HB
Regs
77 **IS** Sch 10 para 7 IS Regs
JSA Sch 8 para 12 JSA Regs
ESA Sch 9 para 11 ESA Regs
HB Sch 6 paras 9 and 9A HB Regs

78 **IS** Sch 10 para 7(2) IS Regs
JSA Sch 8 para 12(2) JSA Regs
ESA Sch 9 para 11(2) ESA Regs
HB Sch 6 para 9(2) HB Regs
79 **IS** Sch 10 para 72 IS Regs
JSA Sch 8 para 65 JSA Regs
ESA Sch 9 para 60 ESA Regs
HB Sch 6 para 62 HB Regs
80 **IS** Sch 10 para 18 IS Regs
JSA Sch 8 para 23 JSA Regs
ESA Sch 9 para 23 ESA Regs
HB Sch 6 para 20 HB Regs
81 **IS** Sch 10 para 75 IS Regs
JSA Sch 8 para 68 JSA Regs
ESA Sch 9 para 63 ESA Regs
HB Sch 6 para 65 HB Regs
82 **IS** Sch 10 para 78 IS Regs
JSA Sch 8 para 71 JSA Regs
ESA Sch 9 para 66 ESA Regs
HB Sch 6 para 68 HB Regs
83 **IS** Sch 10 para 38 IS Regs
JSA Sch 8 para 36 JSA Regs
ESA Sch 9 para 37 ESA Regs
HB Sch 6 para 40 HB Regs
84 **IS** Sch 10 para 76 IS Regs
JSA Sch 8 para 69 JSA Regs
ESA Sch 9 para 64 ESA Regs
HB Sch 6 para 66 HB Regs
85 **IS** Sch 10 para 39 IS Regs
JSA Sch 8 para 37 JSA Regs
ESA Sch 9 para 38 ESA Regs
HB Sch 6 para 41 HB Regs
86 **IS** Sch 10 para 40 IS Regs
JSA Sch 8 para 38 JSA Regs
ESA Sch 9 para 39 ESA Regs
HB Sch 6 para 42 HB Regs
87 **IS** Sch 10 para 41 IS Regs
JSA Sch 8 para 39 JSA Regs
ESA Sch 9 para 40 ESA Regs
HB Sch 6 para 39 HB Regs
88 **IS** Sch 10 para 77 IS Regs
JSA Sch 8 para 70 JSA Regs
ESA Sch 9 para 65 ESA Regs
HB Sch 6 para 67 HB Regs
89 **IS** Sch 10 para 31 IS Regs
JSA Sch 8 para 33 JSA Regs
ESA Sch 9 para 33 ESA Regs
HB Sch 6 para 30 HB Regs
90 **IS** Sch 10 para 29 IS Regs
JSA Sch 8 para 31 JSA Regs
ESA Sch 9 para 31 ESA Regs
HB Sch 6 para 34 HB Regs

4

Part 4: General rules for other means-tested benefits
Chapter 22: Capital: under pension age
Notes

• •

91 **IS** Schs 9 para 15 and 10 para 12 IS Regs
JSA Schs 7 para 15 and 8 para 18 JSA Regs
ESA Schs 8 para 16 and 9 para 16 ESA Regs
HB Schs 5 para 14 and 6 para 14 HB Regs
All *R v ex parte Singer* [1973] 1 WLR 713

92 **IS** Schs 9 paras 15 and 22, and 10 paras 44 and 45 IS Regs
JSA Schs 7 paras 15 and 23, and 8 paras 42 and 43 JSA Regs
ESA Schs 8 paras 16 and 23, and 9 paras 43 and 44 ESA Regs
HB Schs 5 paras 14 and 17, and 6 paras 45 and 46 HB Regs

93 **IS** Sch 10 para 12A IS Regs
JSA Sch 8 para 17A JSA Regs
ESA Sch 9 para 17 ESA Regs
HB Sch 6 para 14A HB Regs

94 R(IS) 3/03

95 Vol 5 Ch 29, para 29414 DMG

96 Reg 26 VP Regs

97 R(SB) 2/89; *KQ v SSWP (IS)* [2011] UKUT 102 (AAC), reported as [2011] AACR 43

98 R(IS) 15/96

99 *Q v SSWP (JSA)* 2020 UKUT 49 (AAC)

100 **IS** Sch 10 para 17 IS Regs
JSA Sch 8 para 22 JSA Regs
ESA Sch 9 para 22 ESA Regs
HB Sch 6 para 19 HB Regs

101 **IS** Sch 10 para 18A IS Regs
JSA Sch 8 para 23A JSA Regs
ESA Sch 9 para 23A ESA Regs
HB Sch 6 para 20A HB Regs; LA Welfare Direct 12/20
All UC(ERSD) Regs; Memo DMG 18/20; Scottish government, *Guidance to local authorities – pandemic support payments*, August 2021

102 **IS** Sch 10 para 67 IS Regs
JSA Sch 8 para 60 JSA Regs
ESA Sch 9 para 56 ESA Regs
HB Sch 6 para 58 HB Regs

103 **IS** Sch 10 para 71 IS Regs
JSA Sch 8 para 64 JSA Regs
ESA Sch 9 para 59 ESA Regs
HB Sch 6 para 61 HB Regs

104 **IS** Sch 10 para 66 IS Regs
JSA Sch 8 para 59 JSA Regs
ESA Sch 9 para 55 ESA Regs
HB Sch 6 para 57 HB Regs

105 **IS** Sch 10 para 68A IS Regs
JSA Sch 8 para 61A JSA Regs
ESA Sch 9 para 58 ESA Regs
HB Sch 6 para 60 HB Regs

106 **IS** Sch 10 para 74 IS Regs
JSA Sch 8 para 67 JSA Regs
ESA Sch 9 para 62 ESA Regs
HB Sch 6 para 64 HB Regs

107 **IS** Sch 10 para 68 IS Regs
JSA Sch 8 para 61 JSA Regs
ESA Sch 9 para 57 ESA Regs
HB Sch 6 para 59 HB Regs

108 **IS** Sch 10 paras 1A and 30 IS Regs
JSA Sch 8 paras A2, A3 and 32 JSA Regs
ESA Sch 9 paras 1A, 32 and 32A ESA Regs
HB Sch 6 paras A2, A3 and 35 HB Regs

109 **IS** Sch 10 para 52 IS Regs
JSA Sch 8 para 47 JSA Regs
ESA Sch 9 para 46 ESA Regs
HB Sch 6 para 49 HB Regs

110 **IS** Sch 10 para 6(3) and (4) IS Regs
JSA Sch 8 para 11(3) and (4) JSA Regs
ESA Sch 9 para 10(3) and (4) ESA Regs
HB Sch 6 para 8(3) and (4) HB Regs

111 **IS** Sch 10 paras 42 and 43 IS Regs
JSA Sch 8 paras 40 and 41 JSA Regs
ESA Sch 9 paras 41 and 42 ESA Regs
HB Sch 6 paras 43 and 44 HB Regs

112 **IS** Sch 10 para 56 IS Regs
JSA Sch 8 para 51 JSA Regs
ESA Sch 9 para 47 ESA Regs
HB Sch 6 para 50 HB Regs

113 **IS** Sch 10 para 63 IS Regs
JSA Sch 8 para 52 JSA Regs
ESA Sch 9 para 52 ESA Regs
HB Sch 6 para 51 HB Regs

114 **IS** Sch 10 para 34 IS Regs
JSA Sch 8 para 34 JSA Regs
ESA Sch 9 para 34 ESA Regs

115 **IS** Sch 10 para 36 IS Regs
JSA Sch 8 para 35 JSA Regs
ESA Sch 9 para 35 ESA Regs
HB Sch 6 para 37 HB Regs

116 H1156 ADM

117 **IS** Sch 10 para 46 IS Regs
JSA Sch 8 para 44 JSA Regs
ESA Sch 9 para 45 ESA Regs
HB Sch 6 para 47 HB Regs

5. Notional capital

118 **IS** Reg 51(6) IS Regs
JSA Reg 113(6) JSA Regs
ESA Reg 115(8) ESA Regs
HB Reg 49(6) HB Regs

119 **IS** Reg 51(1) IS Regs
JSA Reg 113(1) JSA Regs
ESA Reg 115(1) ESA Regs
HB Reg 49(1) HB Regs

120 R(IS) 7/07

121 CIS/124/1990; CSB/1198/1989

122 CIS/124/1990

Chapter 22

123 R(SB) 9/91
124 CIS/40/1989
125 CIS/621/1991. See also CJSA/3937/
2002 and *LH v SSWP (IS)* [2014] UKUT
60 (AAC).
126 CIS/264/1989
127 R(IS) 7/98, para 12(3)
128 R(SB) 38/85; R(IS) 1/91; R(H) 1/06
129 para BW1.714 GM
130 **IS** Reg 51(1)(a) IS Regs
JSA Reg 113(1)(a) JSA Regs
ESA Reg 115(1)(a) ESA Regs
131 R(SB) 40/85
132 R(IS) 8/04
133 R(SB) 12/91; *Verna Jones v SSWP* [2003]
EWCA Civ 964; *VW v SSWP (IS)* [2015]
UKUT 51 (AAC), reported as [2015]
AACR 39
134 CIS/2627/1995; *Verna Jones v SSWP*
[2003] EWCA Civ 964
135 *KS v SSWP* [2009] UKUT 122 (AAC),
reported as [2010] AACR 3
136 **IS** Reg 51(6) IS Regs
JSA Reg 113(6) JSA Regs
ESA Reg 115(8) ESA Regs
HB Reg 49(7) HB Regs
137 CIS/30/1993, but other commissioners
have taken a different view (see, for
example, CIS/25/1990 and CIS/81/
1991)
138 para BW1.831 GM
139 **IS** Reg 51A(1) IS Regs
JSA Reg 114(1) JSA Regs
ESA Reg 116(1) ESA Regs
HB Reg 49(1) HB Regs
140 **IS** Reg 51(2) IS Regs
JSA Reg 113(2) JSA Regs
ESA Reg 115(2) ESA Regs
HB Reg 49(2) HB Regs
141 Reg 49(2) HB Regs
142 **IS** Reg 51(3)(a)(ii) and (8) IS Regs
JSA Reg 113(3)(a)(ii) and (8) JSA Regs
ESA Regs 2(1) and 115(3)(c) ESA Regs
HB Reg 49(3)(a) and (7) HB Regs
143 **IS** Reg 51(8) IS Regs
JSA Reg 113(8) JSA Regs
ESA Reg 2(1) ESA Regs
HB Reg 49(7)(b) HB Regs
144 Vol 5 Ch 29, para 29867 DMG
145 **IS** Reg 51(3)(a)(ii), (3A)(a) and (ba) IS
Regs
JSA Reg 113(3)(a)(ii), (3A)(a), (bb) and
(bc) JSA Regs
ESA Reg 115(3)(c), (5)(a) and (ba) ESA
Regs
HB Reg 49(3)(b), (4)(a), (bb) and (bc)
HB Regs

146 **IS** Reg 51(3)(a)(ia) IS Regs
JSA Reg 113(3)(a)(ia) JSA Regs
ESA Reg 115(3)(b) ESA Regs
HB Reg 49(3)(a) HB Regs
147 **IS** Reg 51(3A)(c) IS Regs
JSA Reg 113(3A)(c) JSA Regs
ESA Reg 115(5)(c) ESA Regs
HB Reg 49(4)(c) HB Regs
148 R(IS) 4/01
149 CH/1672/2007
150 **IS** Reg 51(3)(a)(i) IS Regs
JSA Reg 113(3)(a)(i) JSA Regs
ESA Reg 115(3)(a) ESA Regs
151 **IS** Reg 51(3)(b) IS Regs
JSA Reg 113(3)(b) JSA Regs
ESA Reg 115(4) ESA Regs
HB Reg 49(3)(c) HB Regs
152 **IS** Reg 51(4) IS Regs
JSA Reg 113(4) JSA Regs
ESA Reg 115(6) ESA Regs
HB Reg 49(5) HB Regs
153 **IS** Reg 51(5) IS Regs
JSA Reg 113(5) JSA Regs
ESA Reg 115(7) ESA Regs
HB Reg 49(6) HB Regs
154 Vol 5 Ch 29, para 29879 DMG; see also
R(IS) 13/93
155 R(IS) 14/98
156 Reg 49(5) HB Regs

6. How capital is valued

157 **IS** Reg 49(a) IS Regs
JSA Reg 111(a) JSA Regs
ESA Reg 113 ESA Regs
HB Reg 47(a) HB Regs
158 R(SB) 57/83; R(SB) 6/84
159 R(SB) 18/83
160 *CS v SSWP* [2014] UKUT 518 (AAC)
161 R(SB) 6/84
162 **IS** Reg 49(a) IS Regs
JSA Reg 111(a) JSA Regs
ESA Reg 113(a) ESA Regs
HB Reg 47(a) HB Regs
163 **IS** Reg 49(b) IS Regs
JSA Reg 111(b) JSA Regs
ESA Reg 113(b) ESA Regs
HB Reg 47(b) HB Regs
164 CIS/255/1989
165 R(SB) 27/84
166 R(SB) 2/83; R(SB) 31/83
167 *JRL v SSWP (JSA)* [2011] UKUT 63 (AAC),
reported as [2011] AACR 30
168 **IS** Reg 52 IS Regs
JSA Reg 115 JSA Regs
ESA Reg 117 ESA Regs
HB Reg 51 HB Regs
169 CIS/2575/1997

Part 4: General rules for other means-tested benefits
Chapter 22: Capital: under pension age
Notes

• •

170 *Hourigan v SSWP* [2002] EWCA 1890,
     reported as R(IS) 4/03
171 CIS/15936/1996; CIS/263/1997; CIS/
     3283/1997 (joint decision); R(IS) 26/95
172 R(IS) 3/96
173 R(JSA) 1/02; CH/1953/2003; *Reigate
     and Banstead BC v GB* [2018] UKUT 225
     (AAC)
174 R(IS) 2/93
175 R(IS) 1/03
176 **IS** Reg 49(a) IS Regs
     JSA Reg 111(a) JSA Regs
     ESA Reg 113 ESA Regs
     HB Reg 47(a) HB Regs
177 R(IS) 18/95; Vol 5 Ch 29, paras 29666-
     71 DMG
178 R(SB) 18/83; R(IS) 2/90
179 **IS/JSA** Vol 5 Ch 29, para 29681 DMG
     HB BW1/1.530 GM
180 *Peters v CAO* (appendix to R(SB) 3/89)
181 **IS** Reg 50(a) IS Regs
     JSA Reg 112(a) JSA Regs
     ESA Reg 114(a) ESA Regs
     HB Reg 48(a) HB Regs
182 **IS** Reg 50(b) IS Regs
     JSA Reg 112(b) JSA Regs
     ESA Reg 114(b) ESA Regs
     HB Reg 48(b) HB Regs
183 **IS** Sch 10 para 21 IS Regs
     JSA Sch 8 para 26 JSA Regs
     ESA Sch 9 para 26 ESA Regs
     HB Sch 6 para 23 HB Regs

Chapter 23

Capital: over pension age

This chapter covers:

4

This chapter explains how capital affects your entitlement to pension credit (PC). It also applies to pension-age housing benefit (HB) if you and your partner are over pension age and neither of you are on income support (IS), income-based jobseeker's allowance (JSA), income-related employment and support allowance (ESA) or universal credit (UC). If you get IS, income-based JSA, income-related ESA or UC, your capital is ignored for HB. Chapter 22 explains the rules for IS, income-based JSA, income-related ESA and for working-age HB if you and your partner are under pension age. If you are in a couple and one of you is over pension age but not the other, see p187 for whether the working-age or pension-age HB rules apply. Chapter 8 explains the rules for UC.

Note: whenever HB is referred to in this chapter, this only applies to the rules for people over pension age. The law refers to the qualifying age for PC rather than pension age, but since December 2018 this has been the same as pension age.

Key facts

- There is no upper capital limit for pension credit (PC).
- Generally, you are not eligible for pension-age housing benefit (HB) if your total capital is over £16,000. However, if you get the guarantee credit of PC, there is no capital limit for HB because all your capital is ignored.
- If you have capital over £10,000, this affects the amount of PC or HB you get because it is assumed that your capital gives you some income – called 'deemed income'.
- Capital includes your and your partner's savings, investments and property. Some kinds of capital are ignored when working out your PC or HB – eg, the value of the home in which you live.

Part 4: General rules for other means-tested benefits
Chapter 23: Capital: over pension age
1. The capital limits

- If you deliberately get rid of capital in order to get more benefit, you are treated as still having it. This is called 'notional capital'.

1. **The capital limits**

Pension credit

There is no upper capital limit for pension credit (PC) beyond which you are excluded from benefit. There is, however, a lower limit of £10,000.

Capital of £10,000 or less is ignored. If you have capital above £10,000, you are treated as having a deemed income (sometimes called 'tariff income') of £1 for every £500, or part of £500, by which your capital exceeds £10,000.[1]

Housing benefit

There is a lower and upper limit.[2]
- The lower capital limit is £10,000.
- The upper limit is £16,000.

The first £10,000 of your capital is ignored. If you have capital above £10,000, you are treated as having a deemed income of £1 for every £500, or part of £500, by which your capital exceeds that amount.[3] If you have over £16,000, you are not entitled to housing benefit (HB) unless you get the guarantee credit of PC, in which case all your and your partner's capital (and income) is ignored for HB.[4] This is because entitlement to PC guarantee credit acts as a passport to maximum HB. Because PC has no upper capital limit, you can get maximum HB even with capital above £16,000.

If you get the savings credit of PC, but not the guarantee credit, the following applies.[5]
- Your capital for HB purposes is the capital figure worked out by the DWP for your PC. This is modified to include any capital belonging to your partner which was not taken into account in the PC calculation.
- During an 'assessed income period' (see p267), an increase in your capital does not affect your PC savings credit, but may affect HB. If capital increases above £16,000 (worked out by the local authority under the HB rules), you are no longer entitled to HB. If your capital increases but is still less than £16,000, the local authority must continue to use the DWP's capital figure.

Example
Eileen is 80 and a widow. She has a state pension and a personal pension. She gets HB and the savings credit of PC, but not the guarantee credit. Her PC award letter shows that she has an assessed income period. When she inherits £20,000 her HB stops, but her PC is not affected unless the assessed income period ends because of a change in her circumstances.

2. Whose capital counts

If you are a member of a couple, your partner's capital is added to yours.

3. What counts as capital

All your capital is taken into account, unless it is specifically ignored (or 'disregarded') (see p504).

The term 'capital' is not defined. In general, it means lump-sum or one-off payments rather than a series of payments – eg, savings, investments and property.[6] Capital payments can normally be distinguished from income because they are not payable for any specified period and are not part of a regular series of payments (although capital can be paid by instalments).[7]

Savings

Your savings generally count as capital – eg, cash you have at home, premium bonds, stocks and shares, unit trusts and money in a bank account.

Savings from past income (including benefits – see p507) are treated as capital after the period for which the income was paid has lapsed. If you have put aside money to pay bills, this is still counted as your capital.[8] If your savings are just below the capital limit, you could pay bills by monthly direct debit or use a budget account to keep your capital below the limit.

Fixed-term investments

Capital held in fixed-term investments counts. However, if it is currently unobtainable, it may have little or no value. If you can convert the investment into a form that lets you access it or sell your interest, or raise a loan through a reputable bank using the asset as security, the amount you can get for it counts. If it takes time to produce evidence about the nature and value of the investment, you may be able to get a short-term advance of pension credit (see p1153) or a 'payment on account' of housing benefit (see p220).[9]

Property and land

Any property or land that you own counts as capital. Many types of property are disregarded (see p505). If there is doubt about who owns the property, see p475.

Loans

A loan to you usually counts as money you possess and counts as capital. However, in some limited circumstances you can argue that a loan should be disregarded (see p475). If you lend someone money, see p475.

Part 4: General rules for other means-tested benefits
Chapter 23: Capital: over pension age
4. Disregarded capital

Trusts

Money or property held in a trust for you or your partner is ignored when working out whether you have any deemed income from capital (see p462). You are not assumed to have a fixed income from the trust.[10] This applies to both discretionary and non-discretionary trusts. However, payments actually made from the trust can be taken into account. If made regularly, payments are treated as income. For discretionary trusts, regular payments are either disregarded in full or in part (see p464). If payments are not made regularly, they are taken into account as capital.

The rules are different if the trust is set up from personal injury payments (see p509). Payments made from certain charitable trusts are specifically ignored (see p509).

Money held by your solicitor

Money held by your solicitor normally counts as your capital. This includes compensation payments (but see p509 for when payments for personal injury are disregarded).[11] If you have had legal aid and your solicitor is holding money back while working out the statutory charge to be deducted for legal costs, it does not count as your capital.[12]

4. Disregarded capital

Your home

If you own the home you normally live in, its value is ignored.[13]

Your home
Your **'home'** includes any garage, garden, outbuildings and land belonging to the property, together with any premises that you do not occupy as your home but which it is impractical or unreasonable to sell separately – eg, croft land.[14]

This disregard applies to any home in which you are treated as normally living – eg, because you are only temporarily living away from it (see p354). However, if you own more than one property, only the value of the one normally occupied is disregarded under this rule.[15] Exceptionally, two separate properties can be regarded as a single home, as though one was an annexe of the other, if you personally (rather than a member of your family) normally occupy both.[16] This is most likely to be the case for a large family, but other situations are possible where neither property on its own caters for a family's needs – eg, if there is a carer living between two properties.[17]

When the value of the property is disregarded

The value of the property can be disregarded, even if you do not normally live in it, in the following circumstances.

- **If you have left your former home following a relationship breakdown,** the value of the property is ignored for 26 weeks from the date you left. It may also be disregarded for longer if any of the steps below are taken. If it is occupied by your former partner who is a lone parent, its value is ignored for as long as s/he lives there.[18]

- **If you have sought legal advice or have started legal proceedings in order to occupy the property as your home,** its value is ignored for 26 weeks from the date you first took either of these steps.[19] The 26 weeks can be extended, if it is reasonable to do so, if you need longer to move into the property.

- **If you are taking reasonable steps to dispose of any property,** its value is ignored for 26 weeks from the date you first took such steps (which may start before you claimed benefit).[20] See p478 for more details.

- **If you are carrying out essential repairs or alterations which are needed so that you can occupy a property as your home,** the value of the property is ignored for 26 weeks from the date you first began to take steps to carry them out.[21] See p478 for more details.

- **If you have acquired a property to occupy as your home but have not yet moved in,** its value is ignored if you intend to live there within 26 weeks of acquiring it.[22] If you cannot move in by then, the value of the property can be ignored for as long as seems reasonable.

- **Any amounts paid to you or deposited in your name for the sole purpose of buying a home for you to live in or carrying out essential repairs or alterations to your home or the home you intend to occupy** are ignored for a year from the date you were paid them.[23] This includes money from the sale of a home that you earmark to buy another place to live in.[24] For pension credit (PC), if there is an assessed income period (p267) that extends beyond the year's disregard, the rules provide for the disregard to last until the end of that period. However, it is not clear how this applies in all cases. For example, it would not apply if your PC entitlement or assessed income period began only after the year's disregard had expired. Arguably, it should apply in other cases where there is an assessed income period.[25]

- **Any compensation paid under an insurance policy because of loss or damage to your home** is ignored for a year from the date it is paid to you.[26] For PC, if there is an assessed income period, it can be disregarded until the end of that period in the same way as explained in the bullet point above.

When considering whether it is reasonable to increase the period during which time the value of your property is disregarded, all the circumstances should be considered – eg, your personal circumstances, any efforts made by you to use or

Part 4: General rules for other means-tested benefits
Chapter 23: Capital: over pension age
4. Disregarded capital

dispose of the home[27] and the general state of the property market. In practice, periods of around 18 months are not considered unusual.

Note: it is possible for the value of the property to be ignored under more than one of the above paragraphs in succession.[28]

The home of a former partner or relative

The value of a home (see p504) is ignored if it is occupied wholly or partly as her/his home by:[29]

- a relative of yours or of your partner (see p480 for who this includes) who is over pension age (see p257) or who is incapacitated (see below);[30] *or*
- your former partner from whom you are not estranged, divorced or out of a civil partnership – eg, if one of you is living in a care home; *or*
- your former partner from whom you are estranged, divorced or out of a civil partnership if s/he is a lone parent. If s/he is not a lone parent, the value of the home is ignored for 26 weeks from the date you ceased to live in the home.[31]

Definitions

'**Incapacitated**' is not defined, but guidance suggests it includes anyone who is getting employment and support allowance (ESA), statutory sick pay (SSP), attendance allowance (AA) or disability living allowance (DLA), or who would qualify because of her/his health condition or disability.[32]

It may also include anyone getting personal independence payment (PIP), adult disability payment (ADP) or universal credit (UC) who has limited capability for work or limited capability for work-related activity. However, you should argue for a broader interpretation, if necessary.

You are '**estranged**' if you are living apart because your relationship has broken down, even if the separation is amicable.[33]

Personal possessions

All personal possessions, including items such as jewellery, furniture or a car, are ignored.[34] A personal possession has been defined as any physical asset not used for business purposes, other than land.[35] A home that you own but do not live in is not a personal possession, but counts as capital (see p462).

Compensation paid under an insurance policy for damage to, or loss of, your personal possessions is ignored for a year from the date you were paid the compensation or, for PC only, until the end of the assessed income period (if there is one) if that is longer.[36]

Business assets

If you are self-employed, your business assets are ignored for as long as you continue to work in that business.[37] If you cannot work because of physical or mental illness, but intend to work in the business when you are able, the disregard operates for 26 weeks from the date of claim, or for longer if reasonable in the circumstances.[38] For more about this, see p481.

Insurance policy and annuity surrender values

The surrender value of any life assurance policy is ignored.[39] Some investments include an element of life insurance – eg, endowment policies. If the policy terms include how the payment on death is calculated, the whole investment is ignored.[40] However, you cannot choose to put money into such an investment in order to increase your benefit entitlement, because you are likely to be caught by the notional capital rule if you do (see p510).

The surrender value of any annuity is also ignored for the purposes of the deemed income rule (see p462). Any actual income the surrender value generates for you, and which is not disregarded as income, can be taken into account as income.[41] Any payment under the annuity counts as income (but see p464 for when this is ignored).[42]

Future interests in property

A future interest in most kinds of property is ignored.[43] A **'future interest'** is one which will only revert to you, or become yours for the first time, when some future event occurs. However, this does not include a freehold or leasehold interest in property which has been let by you to tenants. If you did not let the property to the tenant (eg, because the tenancy was entered into before you bought the property), your interest should be ignored as a future interest.

The right to receive a payment in the future

If you know you will receive a payment in the future and you could sell your right to that payment at any time, it has a market value and therefore constitutes an actual capital resource. The value of this is ignored if it is a right to receive:[44]
- income under a life interest or, in Scotland, a life rent; *or*
- an occupational or personal pension; *or*
- any rent if you are not the freeholder or leaseholder; *or*
- any payment under an annuity.

Benefits and tax credits

Arrears of benefits and tax credits
Arrears of specified benefits are ignored as capital:[45]
- for one year after they are received by you; *or*
- for PC, if there is an assessed income period that extends beyond the year's disregard (p267), the rules provide for the disregard to last until the end of that period. However, it is not clear how this applies in all cases. For example, it

Part 4: General rules for other means-tested benefits
Chapter 23: Capital: over pension age
4. Disregarded capital

does not apply if your PC entitlement or assessed income period began only after the year's disregard had expired.[46] Arguably, it should apply in other cases where there is an assessed income period;[47] *or*

- for the remainder of the PC or housing benefit (HB) award if the arrears are £5,000 or more and are paid to compensate for an official error or an error of law, and which you received in full since becoming entitled to PC or HB. If you got the compensation before then, it is still disregarded if your current award follows immediately from a previous award of income support (IS), income-based jobseeker's allowance (JSA), income-related ESA, UC, HB or council tax benefit (CTB) (or PC, for current awards of HB) in which the compensation was disregarded, or it is still being disregarded in an award of one of those benefits.

The **'specified benefits'** are:
- armed forces independence payment;
- AA, constant attendance allowance and exceptionally severe disablement allowance;
- ADP (in Scotland);
- bereavement support payment;
- Best Start grant (in Scotland);
- child disability payment (in Scotland);
- child tax credit;
- child winter heating assistance in Scotland (for HB, it is ignored indefinitely);
- CTB;
- DLA;
- funeral support payment (in Scotland);
- income-related ESA;
- HB;
- IS;
- income-based JSA;
- maternity allowance;
- PC;
- PIP;
- Scottish child payment;
- UC;
- young carer grant in Scotland (for HB, it is ignored indefinitely);
- for PC only, child benefit and social fund payments;
- for HB only, working tax credit and discretionary housing payments;
- concessionary payments (ie, compensation) made instead of any of the above benefits or payments made in lieu of any of these benefits;
- compensation for lost or delayed (new-style) contributory ESA because of a DWP error.

Note: although arrears are ignored as capital, you may have been paid more PC or HB than you would have been entitled to if benefit had been paid on time. For PC, the DWP usually deducts the difference from the arrears of the delayed benefit. Otherwise, if the arrears are not reduced, the overpayment is recoverable from you (see p1198). For HB, the overpayment may be recoverable (see p1214).

Other benefits and payments

The following payments are ignored for one year (or, for PC, to the end of the assessed income period) from when you get them:[48]
- refunds of council tax liability, including from a council tax reduction scheme;
- arrears of a supplementary pension to war widows, widowers or surviving civil partners for pre-1973 service.

The initial lump sum of bereavement support payment is ignored for 52 weeks from when you get the payment.[49] Lump-sum state retirement pension, if you deferred your pension and chose a lump sum rather than increased income, is ignored indefinitely.[50]

Personal injury and other compensation payments

- **Personal injury payments.** Any money paid because of a personal injury to you or your partner is ignored, whether or not it has been placed in a trust.[51] Neither deemed income (see p462) nor actual income from the fund is taken into account. If the personal injury was to your partner and s/he has since died, the capital value is no longer ignored.[52] If an award for damages for personal injury to you or your partner is administered by a court (eg, the Court of Protection), its value, and income and capital from it, are disregarded.[53] 'Personal injury' includes not only accidental and criminal injury (including from the Criminal Injuries Compensation Scheme[54]) but also any disease and injury as a result of a disease.[55] Victims payments to people injured in a Northern Ireland 'Troubles-related incident' are disregarded indefinitely.[56]
- **Special compensation schemes.** Any payment of capital (or income) from specific schemes is ignored including:[57]
  - the National Emergencies Trust;
  - the Windrush Compensation Scheme;
  - the Child Migrants Trust (for children subjected to migration programmes before 1971);
  - schemes to make child abuse payments for historic institutional child abuse in the UK;
  - for people infected from contaminated blood products;
  - for people affected by the 2017 fire at Grenfell Tower.

For most of the schemes, money from your partner's payments is ignored indefinitely, or for two years from your child's payments if s/he has no partner or dependent child.

Part 4: General rules for other means-tested benefits
Chapter 23: Capital: over pension age
5. Notional capital

Funeral plan payments

The value of any funeral plan contract is ignored indefinitely.[58]
A funeral plan contract is a contract under which:
- you make at least one payment to another person; *and*
- that person undertakes to ensure you are provided with a funeral; *and*
- the sole purpose of the plan is to ensure you are provided with a funeral.

Social services, community care and other payments

The following payments are ignored for one year (or for PC, to the end of the assessed income period) from when you get the payments £150 energy rebate payment paid by the local authority:[59]
- local welfare assistance payments. These include £150 energy rebate payments paid by the local authority, test and trace support payments (in England), self-isolation support grants (in Scotland), self-isolation support scheme payments (in Wales) and Scottish child payment bridging payments;
- payments from a local authority for support services to help you live independently (eg, under the Supporting People programme, sometimes called 'housing-related support').

Ignored indefinitely are:[60]
- community care or healthcare direct payments;
- payments from a local authority to a young person in Scotland aged 16 or over in 'continuing care' or passed to you by the young person if s/he still lives with you and was in your care;
- for HB, direct payments under an education, health and care plan, paid in England for a child with special educational needs.

5. Notional capital

In certain circumstances, you are treated as having capital which you do not have. This is called **'notional capital'**.[61] There is a similar rule for notional income (see p465).
You are treated as having notional capital if:
- you deliberately deprive yourself of capital in order to claim or increase benefit (see p511);
- you are a sole trader or a partner in a business (see p511).

Notional capital counts in the same way as capital you do have, except that a 'diminishing notional capital rule' (see p489) may be applied so that the value of the notional capital you are treated as having is considered to reduce over time.

Deliberately getting rid of capital

If you deliberately get rid of capital in order to claim or increase your benefit, you are treated as still having it (see p487).[62] You are not treated as having deprived yourself of capital if:

- you pay off or reduce a debt which you owe; *or*
- you pay for goods or services if the purchase of those goods or services was reasonable in the circumstances of your case.

The diminishing notional capital rule

The diminishing notional capital rule applies if you are treated as having notional capital because of depriving yourself of capital.

If you are getting pension credit (PC), the amount of the notional capital goes down each week by the extra PC you are losing because of the notional capital – eg, through having 'deemed income' taken into account.[63] For example, if your notional capital is £11,000, you have £2 a week less PC because of deemed income (see p462), so £2 a week is deducted from the notional capital until it reaches £10,500 when it will be £1 a week.

If you are not getting any PC, notional capital goes down, not just by the amount of PC you would have had, but also by any additional housing benefit (HB) you would have had if notional capital had not been taken into account. Ask the DWP for a forecast of when it is worth claiming again. If in doubt, you can claim every 26 weeks (but not more often).

For HB, the same rule applies to reduce your notional capital except that, not only is it reduced by the amount of HB you are losing because of the notional capital, but it is also reduced by any PC you would have been entitled to (or income-based jobseeker's allowance or income-related employment and support allowance), whether or not you are currently getting HB.[64]

Companies run by sole traders or a few partners

The value of shares you hold is normally taken into account as capital, but not if you are treated as a sole owner or partner in the business. Instead, your share of the value of the company itself counts. See p492 – the rules for people over pension age are the same except that local authorities have no discretion but are obliged to follow these rules.[65]

---

6. How capital is valued

There are a number of issues to consider when valuing capital.
- **Market value.** Capital is valued at its current market or surrender value,[66] which could be very low if it is difficult to sell. See p492 for more information.

Part 4: General rules for other means-tested benefits
Chapter 23: Capital: over pension age
6. How capital is valued

- **Expenses of sale.** If there would be expenses involved in selling your capital, 10 per cent is deducted from its value for the cost of sale.[67]
- **Debts.** Deductions are made from the 'gross' value of your capital for any debt or mortgage secured on it.[68] For more information, see p493.
- **Capital that is jointly owned under a joint tenancy.** If you jointly own any capital asset (except as a partner in a company, when the rules explained on p511 apply instead) under a joint tenancy, you are treated as owning an equal share of the asset with all other owners.[69] For example, if two of you own the asset, you are each treated as having a 50 per cent share of it. This rule does not apply, however, if you jointly own the capital asset as 'tenants in common'.[70] For more information, see p493.
- **Treatment of assets after a relationship breakdown.** There are no specific rules about this, but there is some guidance and caselaw (see p494).
- **Shares** are valued at their current market value, less 10 per cent for the cost of sale and after deducting any 'lien' held by brokers for sums owed for the cost of their acquisition and any commission.[71] See p494 for more details.
- **Unit trusts** are valued on the basis of the 'bid' price quoted in newspapers. No deduction is allowed for the cost of sale because this is already included in the 'bid' price.[72]
- **The right to receive a payment in the future.** The value that is not ignored (see p507) is its market value – ie, what a willing buyer would pay to a willing seller.[73] For something which is not yet realisable, this may be very small.
- **Overseas assets.** If you have assets abroad, and there are no exchange controls or other prohibitions that would prevent you transferring your capital to this country, your assets are valued at their current market or surrender value in that country.[74] If you are not allowed to transfer your capital, you are treated as having capital equal to the amount that a willing buyer in this country would give (which might not be very much).[75] Deduct 10 per cent for any expenses of sale, any debts or mortgage secured on the assets and any charges for converting the payment into sterling.[76]
- **Payments in other currencies.** Any payment in a currency other than sterling is taken into account after deducting banking charges or commission payable on conversion.[77]

Notes

1. The capital limits
1 s15(2) SPCA 2002; reg 15(6) SPC Regs
2 Reg 43 HB(SPC) Regs
3 Reg 29(2) HB(SPC) Regs
4 Reg 26 HB(SPC) Regs
5 Reg 27 HB(SPC) Regs

3. What counts as capital
6 BP1/P1.71 GM
7 *R v SBC ex parte Singer* [1973] 1 WLR 713
8 R(IS) 3/93; R(PC) 3/08
9 **PC** Reg 2 SS(PAOR) Regs
   HB Reg 74(1) HB(SPC) Regs
10 **PC** Sch 5 para 28 SPC Regs
   HB Sch 6 para 30 HB(SPC) Regs
11 *Thomas v CAO*, appendix to R(SB) 17/87
12 CIS/984/2002

4. Disregarded capital
13 **PC** Sch 5 para 1A SPC Regs
   HB Sch 6 para 26 HB(SPC) Regs
14 **PC** Reg 1(2), definition of 'dwelling occupied as the home', SPC Regs
   HB Reg 2(1), definition of 'dwelling occupied as the home', HB(SPC) Regs
15 **PC** Sch 5 para 1A SPC Regs
   HB Sch 6 para 26 HB(SPC) Regs
16 R(JSA) 9/03; R(SB) 10/89
17 *MM v SSWP (IS)* [2012] UKUT 358 (AAC)
18 **PC** Sch 5 para 6(1) SPC Regs
   HB Sch 6 para 6(1) HB(SPC) Regs
19 **PC** Sch 5 para 2 SPC Regs
   HB Sch 6 para 2 HB(SPC) Regs
20 **PC** Sch 5 para 7 SPC Regs
   HB Sch 6 para 7 HB(SPC) Regs
   Both CIS/6908/1995; R(IS) 4/97
21 **PC** Sch 5 para 3 SPC Regs
   HB Sch 6 para 3 HB(SPC) Regs
22 **PC** Sch 5 para 1 SPC Regs
   HB Sch 6 para 1 HB(SPC) Regs
23 **PC** Sch 5 paras 17 and 19 SPC Regs
   HB Sch 6 paras 18 and 20 HB(SPC) Regs
24 *DG v SSWP (SPC)* [2010] UKUT 241 (AAC); DWP, *A detailed guide to pension credit for advisers PC10S*, p38
25 *DG v SSWP (SPC)* [2010] UKUT 241 (AAC). But see CPC/206/2005 and CPC/1928/2005, which suggest an assessed income period could be reduced on revision in some cases.

26 **PC** Sch 5 paras 17 and 18 SPC Regs
   HB Sch 6 paras 18 and 19 HB(SPC) Regs
27 CIS/4757/2003
28 CIS/6908/1995
29 **PC** Sch 5 para 4 SPC Regs
   HB Sch 6 para 4 HB(SPC) Regs
30 **PC** Reg 1(2), definition of 'close relative', SPC Regs
   HB Reg 2(1), definition of 'close relative', HB(SPC) Regs
31 **PC** Sch 5 para 6 SPC Regs
   HB Sch 6 para 6 HB(SPC) Regs
32 **PC** para 84444 DMG
   HB para BP1, Annex A1.01 GM
33 R(IS) 5/05; CPC/683/2007; *Bristol City Council v SJP (HB)* [2019] UKUT 360 (AAC)
34 **PC** Sch 5 para 8 SPC Regs
   HB Sch 6 para 8 HB(SPC) Regs
35 R(H) 7/08
36 **PC** Sch 5 paras 17 and 18 SPC Regs
   HB Sch 6 paras 18 and 19 HB(SPC) Regs
37 **PC** Sch 5 para 9 SPC Regs
   HB Sch 6 para 9 HB(SPC) Regs
38 **PC** Sch 5 para 9A SPC Regs
   HB Sch 6 para 10 HB(SPC) Regs
39 **PC** Sch 5 para 10 SPC Regs
   HB Sch 6 para 11 HB(SPC) Regs
40 R(IS) 7/98
41 **PC** Sch 5 para 26 SPC Regs
   HB Sch 6 para 29 HB Regs
42 **PC** s15(1)(d) SPCA 2002
   HB Reg 29(1)(d) HB(SPC) Regs
   Both R(IS) 10/01
43 **PC** Sch 5 para 5 SPC Regs
   HB Sch 6 para 5 HB(SPC) Regs
44 **PC** Sch 5 paras 22 and 24-26 SPC Regs
   HB Sch 6 paras 24 and 27-29 HB(SPC) Regs
45 **PC** Sch 5 paras 17, 20 and 20A SPC Regs
   HB Sch 6 paras 18, 21, 22, 26J and 26K HB(SPC) Regs
46 *DG v SSWP (SPC)* [2010] UKUT 241 (AAC)
47 But see CPC/206/2005 and CPC/1928/2005, which suggest that an assessed income period could be reduced on revision in some cases

Part 4: General rules for other means-tested benefits
Chapter 23: Capital: over pension age
Notes

48 **PC** Sch 5 paras 20(1)(f) and 20B SPC
Regs
HB Sch 6 paras 26B and 26E HB(SPC)
Regs
49 **PC** Sch 5 para 23E SPC Regs
HB Sch 6 para 26H HB(SPC) Regs
50 **PC** Sch 5 paras 23A and 23AA SPC Regs
HB Sch 6 paras 26A and 26AA HB(SPC)
Regs
51 **PC** Sch 5 para 16(1) SPC Regs
HB Sch 6 para 17(1) HB(SPC) Regs
52 R(IS) 3/03
53 **PC** Schs 4 paras 13 and 14, and 5 para
16(2) SPC Regs
HB Schs 5 paras 14 and 15, and 6 para
17(2) HB(SPC) Regs
54 Para BP1.160 GM; Vol 5 Ch 29, para
29414 DMG
55 R(SB) 2/89
56 Reg 26 VP Regs
57 **PC** Sch 5 paras 12-15 SPC Regs
HB Sch 6 paras 13-16 HB(SPC) Regs
Both Vol 14 Ch 84, para 84475 DMG;
Memo DMG 15/21
58 **PC** Sch 5 para 11 SPC Regs
HB Sch 6 para 12 HB(SPC) Regs
59 **PC** Sch 5 paras 17 and 20(1)(d) and (e)
SPC Regs; Memo DMG 18/20
HB Sch 6 paras 18 and 21(1)(e) and (f)
HB(SPC) Regs; LA Welfare Direct 12/
2020
Both UC(ERSD) Regs; Scottish
government, *Guidance to local
authorities – pandemic support payments,*
August 2021
60 **PC** Sch 5 paras 23C and 23D SPC Regs
HB Sch 6 paras 26D, 26F and 26G
HB(SPC) Regs

5. Notional capital
61 **PC** Reg 21 SPC Regs
HB Reg 47 HB(SPC) Regs
62 **PC** Reg 21(1) SPC Regs
HB Reg 47(1) HB(SPC) Regs
63 Reg 22 SPC Regs
64 Reg 48 HB(SPC) Regs
65 **PC** Reg 21(3) and (4) SPC Regs
HB Reg 47(3) and (4) HB(SPC) Regs

6. How capital is valued
66 **PC** Reg 19(a) SPC Regs
HB Reg 45(a) HB(SPC) Regs
67 **PC** Reg 19(a) SPC Regs
HB Reg 45(a) HB(SPC) Regs
68 **PC** Reg 19(b) SPC Regs
HB Reg 45(b) HB(SPC) Regs
69 **PC** Reg 23 SPC Regs
HB Reg 49 HB(SPC) Regs

70 R(IS) 4/03
71 **PC** Reg 19(a) SPC Regs
HB Reg 45(a) HB(SPC) Regs
72 **PC** Vol 14 Ch 84, para 84772 DMG
HB BP1/P1.530 GM
73 *Peters v CAO* (appendix to R(SB) 3/89)
74 **PC** Reg 20(a) SPC Regs
HB Reg 46(a) HB(SPC) Regs
75 **PC** Reg 20 SPC Regs
HB Reg 46(b) HB(SPC) Regs
76 **PC** Sch 5 para 21 SPC Regs
HB Sch 6 para 23 HB(SPC) Regs
77 **PC** Sch 5 para 21 SPC Regs
HB Sch 6 para 23 HB(SPC) Regs

Part 5

Other benefits

Chapter 24

Attendance allowance

This chapter covers:
1. Who can get attendance allowance (p518)
2. The rules about your age (p519)
3. People included in the claim (p519)
4. The amount of benefit (p519)
5. Special benefit rules (p520)
6. Claims and backdating (p521)
7. Getting paid (p524)
8. Tax, other benefits and the benefit cap (p526)

Key facts

- Attendance allowance (AA) is a benefit for people with disabilities or long-term health problems who have attention or supervision needs and who are pension age or over when they claim.
- AA is a non-means-tested benefit.
- You do not have to have paid national insurance contributions to qualify.
- You can get AA whether or not you work.
- AA can be paid in addition to other benefits and is disregarded as income for means-tested benefits and tax credits.
- AA is administered and paid by the DWP.
- If you disagree with an AA decision, you can apply for a revision or supersession (see Chapter 56), or appeal against it (see Chapter 57). You must apply for a mandatory reconsideration before you can appeal.

Future changes

At some point in the future, new claims for AA in Scotland will be replaced by claims for pension age disability payment (see Chapter 72). The rules for who can get pension age disability payment and the rates of payment are expected to be similar to AA. Social Security Scotland will be responsible for administering and paying pension age disability payment. See AskCPAG and CPAG's *Welfare Rights Bulletin* for updates.

1. **Who can get attendance allowance**

You can get attendance allowance (AA) if:[1]
- you satisfy the residence conditions (see p1601); *and*
- you are not a 'person subject to immigration control', although there are exceptions to this (see p1524); *and*
- you are pension age or over when you first claim (see p519); *and*
- you satisfy the disability conditions (see below); *and*
- you are not entitled to the care component of disability living allowance (DLA) (see Chapter 28), personal independence payment (see Chapter 35) or adult disability payment (see Chapter 73).

The disability conditions

AA is paid at a lower or higher rate, depending on your care and supervision needs. You get the lower rate of AA if you satisfy one of the daytime disability conditions *or* one of the night-time disability conditions.[2] You may also get the lower rate of AA if you undergo renal dialysis (see p520). You get the higher rate of AA if you satisfy one of the daytime disability conditions *and* one of the night-time disability conditions.[3] You also get the higher rate of AA if you are terminally ill (see p520).

The daytime disability conditions are that you are so severely disabled, physically or mentally, that throughout the day you need:[4]
- frequent attention from another person in connection with your bodily functions; *or*
- continual supervision in order to avoid substantial danger to yourself or others.

The night-time disability conditions are that you are so severely disabled, physically or mentally, that at night you need:[5]
- prolonged or repeated attention from another person in connection with your bodily functions; *or*
- another person to be awake for a prolonged period or at frequent intervals to watch over you in order to avoid substantial danger to yourself or others.

The daytime and night-time disability conditions are the same as those for the middle and highest rates of the care component of DLA (see p594).

Unless you are terminally ill, you must have satisfied the disability conditions for six months before the first day of entitlement.[6]

2. The rules about your age

You can only claim attendance allowance (AA) if you have reached pension age.[7] Your pension age will be after you turn 65 if you reached 65 on or after 6 December 2018, and is 66 from October 2020 (see p766).

If you are approaching pension age and have problems with daily living or mobility, it may be better to claim personal independence payment (PIP) or adult disability payment (ADP) if you can rather than AA, since PIP/ADP has a mobility component in addition to a daily living component. Because the disability tests for PIP/ADP are different from those for AA, it may be worth making a claim for AA after you reach pension age if your claim for PIP/ADP is refused. Get specialist advice if this applies to you.

Your award continues if you are getting:
- PIP/ADP when you reach pension age; *or*
- disability living allowance (DLA) and you turned 65 on or before 8 April 2013.

In these circumstances, you can renew your award of either benefit after you reach pension age instead of having to claim AA. This also means that you can claim, or continue to receive, the mobility component after you reach pension age in certain circumstances if you continue to satisfy the relevant disability conditions (see p605 for DLA, p744 for PIP and p1683 for ADP). You cannot get AA at the same time as PIP/ADP or the care component of DLA. If you are over pension age and have an award of only the mobility component of DLA, you can claim AA in addition to it.

If you have reached pension age and need to renew or change a DLA or PIP/ADP award, or have received DLA or PIP/ADP within the last 12 months, see p605 for DLA, p743 for PIP and p1682 for ADP.

3. People included in the claim

You claim attendance allowance for yourself.

4. The amount of benefit

Attendance allowance is paid at one of two weekly rates:[8]
- the lower rate is £61.85;
- the higher rate is £92.40.

5. **Special benefit rules**

Special rules may apply to:
- people on renal dialysis (see below);
- people who are terminally ill (see below);
- people subject to immigration control (see Chapter 68);
- people who have come from or are going abroad (see Chapters 69, 70 and 71);
- people who are in hospital or a hospice, living in a care home or similar accommodation, or people in prison or detention (see Chapter 42).

Renal dialysis

If you are undergoing renal dialysis on a kidney machine, special rules may apply that entitle you to the lower rate of attendance allowance (AA).[9]

You must have treatment regularly for two or more sessions a week. The dialysis must normally require the attendance or supervision of another person.

If you dialyse in hospital as an outpatient, you must not have help from any member of staff. Others who dialyse in hospital do not qualify by this special route but can count these spells of hospital dialysis towards the qualifying period. This can help you get AA more quickly for the times you dialyse at home, if you alternate between dialysis in hospital and at home. Even if you do not qualify under this route, you may qualify under the ordinary conditions.

Terminal illness

You are regarded as 'terminally ill' if you have a progressive disease and can reasonably be expected to die within six months as a result.[10] This does not mean that it must be more likely than not that you will die within this period. It simply means that your doctor would not be surprised were you to die within six months. Doctors are expected to take a flexible approach to interpreting this in practice.[11] **Note:** the 'six-month rule' is expected to change, although the timescale for this is not yet known. See AskCPAG and CPAG's *Welfare Rights Bulletin* for updates.

If you are terminally ill, you are automatically treated as satisfying the conditions for the higher rate of AA. This is paid straight away without you having to serve the six-month qualifying period.[12] These claims are referred to as 'claims under the special rules'. See p522 for how to make a special rules claim. The special rules only apply if your claim, or a request for a revision or supersession of an existing claim, expressly states that you are terminally ill.[13] The DWP can supersede your award if your condition or prognosis improves so that you are no longer regarded as 'terminally ill'.

6. **Claims and backdating**

The general rules about claims and backdating are covered in Chapter 50. This section explains the specific rules that apply to attendance allowance (AA).

Making a claim

A claim for AA must be in writing. To secure your date of claim (see p522), you should request the approved form (AA1) from the AA helpline. It is usually best to send the completed form to Freepost DWP Attendance Allowance (all on one line; you do not need a postcode or a stamp). You can also take or send it to any other DWP office, and may be able to take or send it to an 'alternative office' (see p1134).

5

> ### Forms
>
> Form AA1 is available from the AA helpline on 0800 731 0122 (textphone: 0800 731 0317; Relay UK and BSL video relay services are available).

The form should have a date stamped on it. Keep a record of the date you asked for the form. The DWP may complete a checklist to assess your 'potential benefit entitlement'. This is not part of the claim process and you should always be sent a claim pack.

Claim packs are also available from Citizens Advice and other advice agencies. A version of the form that can be filled in online and then printed is available at gov.uk/attendance-allowance/how-to-claim.

These packs are not date stamped. Send the completed form as soon as possible to secure your date of claim (see p522).

Note: the success of an AA claim can often depend on how well you have completed the claim form, so try to include all the relevant information and use extra pages if necessary. Keep a copy of your claim form in case queries arise. There are useful tips on completing the form in the disability living allowance (DLA) chapter (see pp611–15). Although those pages focus on DLA for children, the disability conditions for the middle and highest rate care component of DLA are the same as the conditions for AA. As there is no mobility component for AA, problems you have with walking outdoors may only be relevant to your AA claim if you need attention or supervision while walking. Some difficulties with walking *are* important when claiming AA – eg, if you need help to avoid falling when moving indoors because you are unsteady walking.

You must provide any information or evidence required (see p522). In certain circumstances, the DWP may accept a written application which is not on the approved form.[14] You can amend or withdraw your claim before a decision is made (see p1135).

Claims for terminally ill people are made in a different way (see p522).

Who should claim

You normally claim AA for yourself. If you are unable to manage your own affairs, another person can claim AA for you as your 'appointee' (see p1135).

Claiming for terminally ill people

To claim under the special rules for terminal illness (see p520), you must provide Form DS1500, completed by your GP, consultant or specialist nurse, detailing your medical condition. You do not need to fill in the parts of the AA claim form relating to your need for personal care.

When the DWP receives Form DS1500, it decides whether you meet the special rules. The DWP may contact your healthcare professionals for further information. (If you send in the DS1500 form separately from the claim form, it is helpful if you include your national insurance number so that the DS1500 form can easily be linked to your claim.) If the DWP decides you do not meet the special rules, you can claim AA in the normal way or request a mandatory reconsideration of the decision.

Someone else can make a claim, apply for a revision or supersession or appeal, on behalf of a terminally ill person without her/his knowledge or permission.[15]

Information to support your claim

For the general information requirements that apply to all benefits, see p1136.

It is important that you provide any information required when you claim. Until you do, you may not count as having made a valid claim (see p1138). Correct any defects as soon as possible or your date of claim may be affected. See p614 for the evidence you might want to provide to help support your claim.

Even if you have provided all that was required when you claimed, you may be asked to provide further information to support your claim (see p1140). You may also be asked to provide information after you are awarded AA and, if you fail to do so, your AA could be suspended, or even terminated (see p1162).

The date of your claim

The date of your claim is important as it determines when your entitlement to AA starts. This is not necessarily the date from when you are paid. For information about when payment of AA starts, see p524.

The '**date of your claim**' is the date your request for a claim pack is received by the DWP or 'alternative office' (see p1134), provided you return the properly completed form within six weeks of the date of your request.[16] If the DWP has issued a form without date stamping it, write and explain when and where it was issued and ask to be paid from that date or six weeks before you sent it in.[17] The DWP can extend the six-week deadline if it considers that it is reasonable, so if you return the form late explain why.[18] **Note:** if you are delayed in returning the form for a reason relating to coronavirus (eg, you have had to self-isolate or you could not get advice), say this on the form and ask for the deadline to be extended.

If your claim form was issued by an advice agency or downloaded from the internet, it will not have a date stamp on it and your date of claim is the date the completed form is received by the DWP.

You must make sure your claim is valid. If it is 'defective', you are given a short time to correct the defects (see p1139). If you do, your claim is treated as having been made when you initially claimed.[19]

In some cases, you can claim in advance (see below). If you want to do this, make this clear when you claim or the DWP might not consider it. If you claimed DLA or personal independence payment (PIP) or adult disability payment (ADP) when you should have claimed AA, or if you claimed industrial injuries disablement benefit, see below.

5

Backdating your claim

It is very important to claim as soon as you think you might qualify. A claim for AA *cannot* be backdated.[20]

If you might have qualified for benefit earlier but did not claim because you were given the wrong information or were misled by the DWP, you could ask for a compensation payment (see p1403) or complain to the Ombudsman (see p1408).

If you claim the wrong benefit

A claim for DLA or PIP/ADP can be treated as a claim for AA and vice versa, but only if it appears to the DWP that you are not entitled to the benefit you claimed. A claim for an increase of industrial injuries disablement benefit where constant attendance is needed can be treated as a claim for AA and vice versa (see p1144).[21]

Claiming in advance

A claim for AA can be made before you have satisfied the six-month qualifying period (see p518),[22] or any other qualifying condition. Provided you claim no more than six months before you would qualify for AA, a decision can be made on your claim in advance of your date of entitlement. The date of your claim is the date on which you qualify – ie, the date from which you can be paid is the date you complete the six-month qualifying period.

Renewal claims

AA can be awarded for fixed periods (see p525). Renewal claims can be invited up to six months before your old award expires. It is important that you return your completed renewal claim form before your old award expires as no backdating is possible.

The DWP normally treats a renewal claim as a new claim, beginning on the day after your old award ends.[23] However, it may use the information you give in the renewal claim to revise or supersede your existing award, in which case your entitlement may be changed earlier.[24]

If your AA award has ended, you can reclaim the same rate within two years without having to serve the standard six-month qualifying period again.[25]

How your claim is dealt with

The DWP can award AA on the basis of your claim form alone, but may choose to contact someone you have named on the form for more information. It is a good idea to include details of all the medical professionals and other people who know and understand your needs and, if possible, enclose evidence from them. If the DWP cannot obtain sufficient information, it may also arrange for you to be given a medical examination by a healthcare professional acting on behalf of the DWP, who may visit you at home.

If you refuse a medical examination without good cause, the DWP must decide your claim against you.[26]

The DWP may telephone you to ask for further information. If you do not want to be telephoned, state this clearly on the claim form.

The DWP aims to deal with new claims for AA within 40 working days. Claims made under the special rules for terminal illness (see p520) should be decided more quickly.

7. Getting paid

The general rules on getting paid are covered in Chapter 51. This section explains the specific rules that apply to attendance allowance (AA).

When is attendance allowance paid?
You are normally paid on a Monday, but the DWP can vary the payday.[27] AA is normally paid every four weeks in arrears. However, AA can be paid:
– at shorter intervals in individual cases;[28]
– weekly in advance.
If you leave hospital or a care home and expect to return within 28 days, AA can be paid at a daily rate for days at home.[29]

Note:
- If you get other DWP benefits, AA may be paid in a single payment with them instead (usually with retirement pension).
- Even if you have been sanctioned for a benefit offence (see p1239), you must be paid your AA.

- For information on missing payments, see p1150. If you cannot get your AA payments because you have lost your bank card or have forgotten your PIN, see p1149. If your payment service card has been lost or stolen, see p1150.
- If payment of your AA is delayed, see p1255. If you wish to complain about how your claim has been dealt with, or claim compensation, see Chapter 61.
- If payment of your AA is suspended, see p1161.
- If you have been overpaid AA, you might have to repay it (see Chapter 53) and, in some circumstances, you may have to pay a penalty (see p1229). If you have been accused of fraud, see Chapter 54.
- If you are owed arrears of AA, these can be paid in instalments (see p1148).

Length of awards

Awards of AA can be made for either fixed or indefinite periods.[30] The length of an award depends on how long the DWP estimates your current needs may last. If you have an indefinite award, you will not have to make a renewal claim at any stage, but the DWP can reduce or stop your award if it has grounds to revise or supersede it.

There is no legal minimum length for an award.[31] If you think benefit should be awarded for longer, perhaps because your condition is such that your care needs will not decrease, you can consider asking for a revision (see p1261). However, if you challenge the length of your award, the rate of your award may also be reconsidered.

Awards under the special rules for terminal illness (see p520) are normally made for a fixed period of three years.

Change of circumstances

You must report changes in your circumstances that you have been told to report, as well as any that you might reasonably be expected to know might affect your right to, the amount of or payment of your benefit. You should do this as soon as possible, preferably in writing. See p1160 for further information.

If your condition deteriorates so that you become eligible for the higher rate, benefit can be backdated to the day you become eligible, provided you tell the DWP no later than a month after completing the six-month qualifying period. If payment of (but not entitlement to) AA has stopped (eg, while you are in hospital or a care home), still notify the DWP so that the correct rate is paid when payment resumes. If you do not report a change of circumstances within the month, benefit can still be backdated if you do so within 13 months and there were special circumstances that meant it was not practical to report the change earlier.[32]

If your condition improves so that you do not qualify for the higher rate or you lose benefit altogether, the new decision usually takes effect from the date you tell the DWP of the improvement, or from the date of the decision if the DWP changed it without your asking.[33] It only takes effect from an earlier date (and causes an overpayment) if you should have realised earlier that the change should have been reported. It is accepted that it is difficult for claimants to realise when a gradual improvement begins to affect benefit entitlement.[34]

---

8. Tax, other benefits and the benefit cap

Tax

Attendance allowance (AA) is not taxable.[35]

Means-tested benefits and tax credits

AA is not taken into account as income when calculating any of the means-tested benefits. AA is paid on top of these, and if you or your partner get AA, this can increase the amount you get (or mean that you qualify for means-tested benefits for the first time, if your income was previously too high). AA is also ignored when calculating child tax credit and working tax credit (WTC).

You may qualify for one or more of the following extra amounts:

- a limited capability for work-related activity element (see p71) included in your universal credit (UC) if you are entitled to AA, as you are treated as having limited capability for work-related activity (see p1008);
- a higher pensioner premium (see p329) included in your income support (IS) or income-based jobseeker's allowance (JSA) if you have a partner who gets AA;
- a severe disability premium (see p330) included in your IS, income-based JSA or income-related employment and support allowance (ESA) if your partner gets AA and you meet the other conditions for this premium;
- a severe disability premium included in your housing benefit (HB), or an addition for severe disability included in the guarantee credit of pension credit (PC) if you get AA and meet the other conditions for this premium or addition (see p330);
- a disabled worker element in your WTC if you get AA. If you or your partner get the higher rate of AA, a severe disability element is included in WTC (see Chapter 62).

No housing costs contributions from a non-dependant are taken into account when calculating your UC housing costs element if you, your partner or the non-dependant get AA, or would get it but for being in hospital (see p102). If you or your partner get AA, non-dependant deductions are not made from your HB (see p199), or from any housing costs included in your IS, income-based JSA, income-related ESA or the guarantee credit of PC (see p348).

Non-means-tested benefits

AA may be paid in addition to any other non-means-tested benefits, except that it 'overlaps' with armed forces independence payment (see p857) and constant attendance allowance under the industrial injuries scheme (see p678) or war pensions scheme.[36] See p1151 for details of the overlapping benefits rules. You cannot claim AA if you are entitled to personal independence payment or the care component of disability living allowance.[37] It is also likely that you will not be able to claim AA if you are also entitled to adult disability payment in Scotland (see Chapter 73).

If you get AA and someone regularly looks after you, that person may be entitled to carer's allowance (CA) (see Chapter 26), and s/he (or her/his partner if claiming as a couple) may also get a carer element in UC (see p73), a carer premium in IS, income-based JSA, income-related ESA or HB, or a carer addition in the guarantee credit of PC (see p334). However, your entitlement to a severe disability premium (or severe disability additional amount) can be affected if s/he gets CA or a carer element in UC, so always get advice.

A young person aged 16, 17 or 18 living in Scotland who cannot get CA may be able to get a young carer grant for looking after you (see Chapter 78).

The benefit cap

In some cases, there is a limit on the total amount of specified benefits you can receive (a 'benefit cap'). AA is *not* one of the specified benefits. The benefit cap does *not* apply if you or your partner get AA (even if it is not paid because you (or s/he) are in hospital or a care home). In other cases, it only applies if you are getting UC or HB. See p1156 for further information.

Passports and other sources of help

You qualify for a Christmas bonus if you get AA at any rate (see p861). You may qualify for council tax reduction (see p836).

If any member of your household gets AA at any rate, you may get a grant for help with insulation and other energy efficiency measures in your home (see p860).

Notes

1. Who can get attendance allowance
1 ss64, 65 and 66 SSCBA 1992; reg 2 SS(AA) Regs
2 s65(3) SSCBA 1992
3 s65(3) SSCBA 1992
4 s64(2) SSCBA 1992
5 s64(3) SSCBA 1992
6 ss65(1)(b) and 66(1)(a)(ii) SSCBA 1992

2. The rules about your age
7 s64(1) SSCBA 1992

4. The amount of benefit
8 Sch 4 Part III SSCBA 1992

5. Special benefit rules
9 s65(2) SSCBA 1992; reg 5 SS(AA) Regs
10 s66(2)(a) SSCBA 1992
11 DWP, *DWP Medical (Factual) Reports: a guide to completion,* August 2019
12 s66(1) SSCBA 1992
13 Regs 3(9)(b) and 6(6)(c) SS&CS(DA) Regs

6. Claims and backdating
14 Reg 4(1) SS(C&P) Regs
15 s66(2)(b) SSCBA 1992; regs 3(9)(b), 6(6)(c) and 25(b) SS&CS(DA) Regs
16 Reg 6(8), (8A) and (9) SS(C&P) Regs
17 Reg 6(8A) SS(C&P) Regs
18 Reg 6(9) SS(C&P) Regs; *SNN v SSWP (PIP)* [2018] UKUT 210 (AAC) – although decided on similar rules for PIP, this case considers circumstances that may be reasonable and the discussion is relevant for AA claims
19 Reg 6(1)(b) SS(C&P) Regs
20 s65(4) SSCBA 1992
21 Reg 9(1) and Sch 1 SS(C&P) Regs; reg 25(3) and (4) UC,PIP,JSA&ESA(C&P) Regs
22 s65(6) SSCBA 1992
23 Reg 13C SS(C&P) Regs
24 CDLA/14895/1996
25 s65(1)(b) SSCBA 1992; reg 3 SS(AA) Regs
26 s19(3) SSA 1998

7. Getting paid
27 Reg 22(3) and Sch 6 SS(C&P) Regs
28 Reg 22 SS(C&P) Regs

29 Reg 25 SS(C&P) Regs
30 s65(1)(a) SSCBA 1992
31 R(DLA) 11/02
32 Regs 7(9)(b) and 8 SS&CS(DA) Regs
33 s10(5) SSA 1998
34 Reg 7(2)(c) SS&CS(DA) Regs; *RD v SSWP (DLA)* [2011] UKUT 95 (AAC); *DC v SSWP (DLA)* [2011] UKUT 336 (AAC)

8. Tax, other benefits and the benefit cap
35 s677 IT(EP)A 2003
36 Sch 1 paras 5 and 5a SS(OB) Regs
37 s64(1) and (1A) SSCBA 1992

Chapter 25

∙ ∙

Bereavement benefits

This chapter covers:
1. Bereavement support payment (below)
2. Widowed parent's allowance (p531)
3. Definitions (p533)
4. Special benefit rules (p536)
5. Claims and backdating (p537)
6. Getting paid (p540)
7. Tax, other benefits and the benefit cap (p541)

Key facts

- Bereavement benefits are paid to widows, widowers and surviving civil partners. If your spouse or civil partner died on or after 6 April 2017, the relevant bereavement benefit is **bereavement support payment**. If s/he died before this date, and you have dependent children, you may be able to get **widowed parent's allowance**.
- To qualify for all bereavement benefits, your late spouse or civil partner must have either satisfied the national insurance contribution conditions, or been an 'employed earner' and died as a result of an industrial accident or disease.
- You must be under pension age to qualify for bereavement benefits.
- Bereavement benefits are non-means-tested benefits.
- You can get bereavement benefits whether you are in or out of work.
- Beginning a new relationship may affect your entitlement.
- Bereavement benefits are administered and paid by the DWP.
- If you disagree with a bereavement benefit decision, you can apply for a revision or a supersession (see Chapter 56), or appeal against it (see Chapter 57). You must apply for a mandatory reconsideration before you can appeal.

---

1. Bereavement support payment

Bereavement support payment is a benefit for people whose spouse or civil partner dies on or after 6 April 2017. It comprises monthly payments, payable for a maximum period of 18 months, and a lump-sum payment in the first month.

Who can get bereavement support payment

You can get bereavement support payment if:[1]
- you are a widow, widower or surviving civil partner; *and*
- your spouse or civil partner died on or after 6 April 2017; *and*
- your late spouse or civil partner either:
  - satisfied the national insurance (NI) contribution conditions (see p968); *or*
  - was an 'employed earner' and died as a result of an industrial injury or disease (see p536); *and*
- you are under pension age; *and*
- you satisfy the residence condition (see p1598).

Note: arguably, due to a court decision, the requirement that your late spouse or civil partner satisfied the NI conditions is unlawful if, because of disability, s/he could not work (and so could never make NI contributions) throughout her/his working life.[2]

Time limits

To get bereavement support payment for the maximum 18-month period, you must make a claim within three months of the date your spouse or civil partner died (see p538).

To get the initial lump-sum payment, you must claim within 12 months of your spouse or civil partner's death.[3]

The rules about your age

There is no lower age limit for bereavement support payment. Anyone who is legally old enough to marry or form a civil partnership may qualify.

Bereavement support payment cannot be paid if you are pension age or over, but you may qualify for state pension (see p764) or a survivor's inherited state pension instead (see p769).

People included in the claim

You claim bereavement support payment for yourself. You cannot get an increase for a new partner, or for your child(ren). If you have a dependent child, you are, however, paid the higher rate of bereavement support payment.[4]

The amount of bereavement support payment

There are two rates of bereavement support payment – a standard rate and a higher rate. You get the higher rate if:[5]
- you were pregnant when your spouse or civil partner died; *or*
- you were entitled to child benefit when your spouse or civil partner died; *or*
- since your spouse or civil partner died, you have become entitled to child benefit for a child or qualifying young person who was residing with you or

your late spouse/civil partner immediately before s/he died. This applies even if you subsequently cease to be entitled to child benefit for that child or qualifying young person.

Rates of bereavement support payment[6]

	Standard rate	Higher rate
Initial lump sum	£2,500	£3,500
Monthly amount	£100	£350

Starting a new relationship

If you start cohabiting with a new partner, enter into a new civil partnership or remarry, this does not affect your entitlement to bereavement support payment.[7]

2. Widowed parent's allowance

Widowed parent's allowance is a benefit for people whose spouse or civil partner died before 6 April 2017. It comprises fortnightly payments, payable for as long as the conditions of entitlement are met.

Who can get widowed parent's allowance

You can get widowed parent's allowance if:[8]
- you are a widow, widower or surviving civil partner; *and*
- your spouse or civil partner died before 6 April 2017; *and*
- your late spouse or civil partner either:
  - satisfied the national insurance (NI) contribution conditions (see p969); *or*
  - was an 'employed earner' and died as the result of an industrial injury or disease (see p536); *and*
- you are under pension age; *and*
- you are entitled to child benefit for at least one 'eligible child'.

Eligible child

A 'child' means both a 'child' and a 'qualifying young person' (see p563 for the definitions). A child counts as an 'eligible child' if:[9]
- s/he is your and your late spouse's/civil partner's child; *or*
- you were residing with your late spouse or civil partner immediately before s/he died and *you* were entitled to child benefit for the child at that time – ie, even if the child is not your late spouse's/civil partner's child; *or*
- immediately before s/he died, your late spouse or civil partner was entitled to child benefit for the child – ie, even if the child is not your child.

Treated as entitled to child benefit
- You still count as entitled to child benefit if it has been awarded to you, but you have elected for it not to be paid to avoid the high-income child benefit charge (see p581).
- If you were residing together, you are treated as entitled to any child benefit to which your late spouse or civil partner was entitled, and vice versa.[10]
- You or your late spouse or civil partner can be treated as entitled to child benefit if you would have been entitled to it had you claimed it, and had the child in question not been abroad.[11]

Treated as residing with your spouse or civil partner
- If you and your spouse or civil partner were living apart at the time of her/his death, you can still be considered to have been residing with her/him if your separation was only intended to be temporary.[12] This depends on the facts of your case.[13]
- If you have been widowed before, or survived a previous civil partner, and this meant that you were left to care for a dependent child(ren), you can qualify for widowed parent's allowance on the basis of the death of your most recent spouse or civil partner, even if you were not residing with her/him when s/he died.[14]

Time limit
Provided you meet all the conditions of entitlement on p531, there is no time limit for claiming widowed parent's allowance after the death of your spouse or civil partner. It then remains payable until you no longer meet one of these conditions – eg, your child is no longer an eligible child because of her/his age.

The rules about your age
There is no lower age limit for widowed parent's allowance. Anyone who is legally old enough to marry or form a civil partnership may qualify.

Widowed parent's allowance cannot be paid if you are pension age or over, but you may qualify for state pension (see p764) or a survivor's inherited state pension instead (see p769).

People included in the claim
You claim widowed parent's allowance for yourself. You cannot claim widowed parent's allowance if you have a new partner (see p533). New claims do not include an increase for your child(ren), although if you have been in receipt of widowed parent's allowance since 5 April 2003, it may still include an addition for a child.

The amount of widowed parent's allowance

Widowed parent's allowance is made up of:

- a basic allowance. The full weekly rate of this is £126.35, but it may be paid at a reduced rate if your late spouse's or civil partner's NI contribution record was incomplete (see below); *and*
- an additional earnings-related payment based on your late spouse's or civil partner's earnings under the additional state pension scheme, if her/his NI contribution record qualifies you for this (see p969). You may be entitled to this even if her/his contribution record is not sufficient for you to qualify for basic widowed parent's allowance.[15]

Reduction if your late spouse or civil partner had an incomplete contribution record

If your late spouse or civil partner had an incomplete NI contribution record, the amount of widowed parent's allowance you receive is reduced proportionately.[16] You may be able to increase your entitlement to widowed parent's allowance by paying voluntary NI contributions on your spouse's or civil partner's behalf, even though s/he has died. Contact the HM Revenue and Customs helpline (tel: 0300 200 3500; textphone: 0300 200 3519) about this. See p952 for further details and for the time limits for making such payments.

Starting a new relationship

Entitlement to widowed parent's allowance ends if you remarry or enter into a new civil partnership. You cannot requalify for it, even if you subsequently get divorced or if your civil partnership is dissolved. It is suspended if you begin cohabiting (see p536), but can be reinstated if you stop cohabiting.[17]

3. Definitions

Widows, widowers and surviving civil partners

To get bereavement benefits, you must be a widow, widower or surviving civil partner. For this to apply, you must have been married to your spouse (in either a same-sex or opposite-sex marriage), or in a civil partnership with your partner, at the date of her/his death (but see the note on p534). The marriage or civil partnership must have been valid under UK law.

Two court cases have successfully challenged the lawfulness of refusing bereavement benefits to surviving cohabiting partners with children.[18] As a result, the law is due to change[19] to include surviving cohabitees with children who were living with their partner at the time of their partner's death. At the time of writing, the law had not been changed, though this is expected by summer 2022. See AskCPAG and CPAG's *Welfare Rights Bulletin* for updates.

Note: it is expected that if your partner died prior to the planned change in the law, to get the maximum amount of higher rate bereavement support payment (or widowed parent's allowance in limited circumstances), you must have been entitled to the relevant bereavement benefit on or after 30 August 2018 *and* you must claim within 12 months of the law being changed. Payments are not made automatically.

Marriage 'by cohabitation with habit and repute'

In Scotland,[20] you can count as a widow or widower if you were married by 'cohabitation with habit and repute', even if you did not go through a wedding ceremony, provided your cohabitation began before 4 May 2006.[21] For this to apply, your relationship must have been like that of a husband and wife and more than simply living together – there must have been something about it which meant it could be inferred that you and your partner consented to marriage and that nothing existed that would have prevented a valid marriage taking place – eg, one of you being married to someone else.[22] In addition, your relationship must have been such that other people generally believed that you were married.[23]

If you have more than one bereavement

If, following the death of your spouse or civil partner, you remarry or form a new civil partnership and your new spouse or civil partner then dies, your entitlement to bereavement benefits depends on the national insurance contribution record of your most recent spouse or civil partner.

Invalid marriages

A **void** marriage or civil partnership (ie, one in which at least one of the partners was not eligible to marry or form a civil partnership) is invalid. From a legal point of view, it is treated as if it never existed.[24] In England and Wales, a **voidable** marriage or civil partnership is treated as having been valid until a decree absolute of annulment is pronounced.[25] Questions about the validity of marriages or civil partnerships are decided by a special unit at the DWP. If a question arises over the validity of your marriage or civil partnership, get advice from a family law specialist.

Separation, divorce and dissolution

If you were divorced when your former spouse died, or if your civil partnership had been dissolved when your former civil partner died, you are not a widow, widower or surviving civil partner.

A divorce only becomes effective when the decree absolute is pronounced (a decree of divorce, in Scotland), and a civil partnership is dissolved when a final dissolution order is issued (a decree of dissolution, in Scotland). If you were in the process of obtaining a divorce or of dissolving your civil partnership but your spouse or civil partner died before it was finalised, you are still a widow, widower or surviving civil partner (and so may be entitled to bereavement benefits). This is the case even if you were judicially separated.

Polygamous marriages

If your marriage was polygamous, you are not usually entitled to bereavement benefits following the death of your spouse because, generally, the law in England, Wales and Scotland does not treat you as legally married unless your marriage is a monogamous one.[26]

Note:

- If your marriage was *previously* polygamous rather than actually polygamous when your spouse died (eg, if any other spouse had already died), you can qualify.
- A marriage is only considered polygamous if the law of the country where the marriage takes place permits either party to have another wife or husband.[27]
- Whether your marriage is considered polygamous depends on whether you were your spouse's first wife or husband, and on where you and your spouse were 'domiciled' at the time of your marriage and any subsequent marriage. In general terms, 'domicile' means the country in which you have chosen to make your permanent home.[28] In particular, no one who is domiciled in England or Wales is allowed to contract a polygamous marriage anywhere in the world even if the local law allows it.[29]
- If you are the surviving partner but your marriage is considered to have been polygamous and you are refused benefit, depending on the facts of your case (in particular, where the facts suggest that your marriage was actually monogamous), you may be able to argue that you should still be entitled under human rights rules.[30] Seek advice.

Example
At the time of their wedding, Maryam and her husband were domiciled in Pakistan and were married under Islamic law. After the wedding they came to live in England, made their permanent home here and had no intention of returning to live in Pakistan at any time. Later, Maryam's husband returned temporarily to Pakistan and married a second wife. As her husband was domiciled in England rather than Pakistan at the time of the second marriage, English law does not recognise the second marriage and therefore regards Maryam as her late husband's only wife. Provided she meets the other conditions of entitlement, she is entitled to bereavement benefits.[31] If her husband had reacquired domicile in Pakistan at the time of his second marriage, and his second wife was still alive, both marriages would be polygamous, and neither wife could claim bereavement benefits.[32]

Cohabitation

'**Cohabiting**' means living with someone as if you are a married couple. Deciding whether or not you are cohabiting may not be straightforward. For further information, see p304.

If the DWP refuses you widowed parent's allowance because it believes you are cohabiting with a new partner and you do not agree, you can challenge its decision (see Chapters 56 and 57).

Industrial accident or disease

The meaning of 'industrial accident or disease' is discussed on p666 and p670. To qualify for bereavement benefits, the industrial accident or disease must have been a cause of your late spouse or civil partner's death, but it need not have been a direct cause or the only cause.[33] Your late spouse or civil partner must have been an 'employed earner' – ie, an employee, not self-employed (see p947).[34]

4. **Special benefit rules**

Special rules may apply to:
- widows whose husbands died before 9 April 2001 (see below);
- people who have obtained a gender recognition certificate (see below);
- people who are going abroad (see Chapter 70);
- people in prison or detention (see Chapter 42).

Widows whose husbands died before 9 April 2001

If you are a widow whose husband died before 9 April 2001, you are not entitled to bereavement benefits, but you may still be getting widowed mother's allowance or widow's pension.

For an explanation of the main qualifying conditions for these widows' benefits, see the 2000/01 edition of this *Handbook*.

If your entitlement to widowed mother's allowance ends because you no longer have an eligible child, you may qualify for a widow's pension. This can be paid until you reach 65, provided you satisfy the qualifying conditions.

Once you reach pension age, you may be entitled to both state pension and either widow's pension or widowed mother's allowance. Because of the overlapping benefit rules, you cannot receive both in full at the same time. It is likely to be preferable to claim a state pension, as you are then free to remarry, cohabit or form a new civil partnership, without losing any entitlement.

People who have obtained a gender recognition certificate

If you annulled or dissolved an existing marriage or civil partnership in order to obtain a full gender recognition certificate (which, before 10 December 2014 in

England and Wales and 16 December 2014 in Scotland, you had to do),[35] you are not entitled to bereavement benefits on the basis of your ex-spouse's or ex-civil partner's national insurance contribution record, if s/he subsequently dies.

If you are getting widow's pension when a full gender recognition certificate is issued, any entitlement ends. Widowed mother's allowance also ends, but you can qualify for widowed parent's allowance instead.[36]

5. Claims and backdating

The general rules about claims and backdating are covered in Chapter 50. This section explains the specific rules that apply to bereavement benefits.

Making a claim

A claim for bereavement support payment or widowed parent's allowance can be made:

- by telephoning the DWP's Bereavement Service on 0800 731 0469 (Welsh language: 0800 731 0453; textphone: 0800 731 0464; Relay UK and BSL relay services are available). After giving information on the telephone, you are sent a statement to approve, sign and return; *or*
- in writing, normally on the approved form.

Forms

Form BSP1 is the approved form for bereavement support payment.

Form BB1 is the approved form for widowed parent's allowance.

When you register the death, you are normally given a Certificate of Registration of Death. If you complete the form on the certificate and send it to the DWP, you should be sent the correct bereavement benefit form. Alternatively, you can request a form from DWP's Bereavement Service on the telephone number above or apply online at gov.uk.

You must provide any information or evidence required (see p538).

If there is a delay in dealing with your claim, you may be able to get a short-term advance of benefit (see p1153).

Who should claim

You must normally claim bereavement benefits yourself. If you are unable to manage your own affairs, another person can claim bereavement benefits for you as your 'appointee' (see p1135).

Information to support your claim

For the general information requirements that apply to all benefits, see p1136.

It is important that you provide any information required when you claim. Until you do, you may not count as having made a valid claim (see p1138). Correct any defects as soon as possible or your date of claim may be affected.

You are normally also expected to provide proof of your spouse's or civil partner's death. If you have reported the death to a local DWP office under the 'Tell Us Once' arrangements (see p1161), you are given a reference number, which you can use as proof of death when you make a claim through the Bereavement Service.

Alternatively, when you register the death you get a death certificate, which can be provided as proof. If you do not have proof that your spouse or civil partner has died, see p539.

You are also usually expected to provide your marriage or civil partnership certificate.[37] Caselaw has provided guidance on assessing evidence from countries where reliable documentary proof of life events, such as marriage, may not be available.[38]

Even if you have provided all that was required when you claimed, you may be asked to provide further information to support your claim (see p1140). You may be asked to provide information after you are awarded bereavement benefits. If you fail to do so, your benefit may be suspended or even terminated (see p1162).

The date of your claim

The date of your claim is important as it determines:
- when your entitlement to bereavement support payment or widowed parent's allowance starts. This is not necessarily the date from when you are paid. For information about when payment of a bereavement benefit starts, see p540; *and*
- whether you qualify for an initial lump sum of bereavement support payment.

The '**date of your claim**' is normally the date of your call, if you claim by telephone, or the date your written claim is received.[39]

You must make sure your claim is valid. If it is 'defective', you are given a short time to correct the defects (see p1139). If you do, your claim is treated as having been made when you initially claimed.[40]

Backdating your claim

Bereavement support payment is automatically backdated to the date of your spouse's or civil partner's death, provided you claim within three months of the date of her/his death.[41]

Your bereavement support payment award ends 18 months after your spouse or civil partner died,[42] so you should claim within three months of the date of her/his death to receive the maximum 18-month award.

If you claim more than three months after the date of her/his death, your claim is automatically backdated for three months.[43] Because of this, you can make a claim for bereavement support payment up until 21 months after your spouse or civil partner dies, but you will not receive the maximum award.[44]

Examples

Roger's wife died on 6 May 2021. He claimed bereavement support payment on 10 July 2021. It is paid for the period 6 May 2021 to 6 November 2022 – ie, he receives the maximum 18-month award.

Carol's civil partner died on 20 August 2021. She claimed bereavement support payment on 4 February 2022. It is paid for the period 4 November 2021 to 20 February 2023. The length of her award is therefore limited to approximately 15.5 months.

Esther's husband died on 10 July 2020. She claimed bereavement support payment on 28 March 2022. It is paid for the period 28 December 2021 to 10 January 2022. The length of her award is therefore limited to two weeks. She also misses out on the initial lump-sum payment.

Payment of **widowed parent's allowance** can be backdated for up to three months before the date you make your claim, provided you satisfy the qualifying conditions over that period. You do not need to show reasons why your claim is late.

If you might have qualified for benefit earlier but did not claim because you were given the wrong information or were misled by the DWP, you could make a complaint and seek compensation (see Chapter 61).

If there is a delay in hearing or uncertainty about a death

If you did not find out straight away that your spouse or civil partner had died, but you find out within 12 months of the death, you can apply for bereavement support payment within 12 months of becoming aware of the death, and request that it be backdated to the date of death.[45]

If it is presumed that your spouse or civil partner has died, but this has not been established for certain, you can ask the DWP to make a decision that s/he has died (or is likely to have died) on a particular date. You should provide the information and evidence that has led you to presume s/he has died.

If the DWP decides s/he died *before 6 April 2017*, you can then claim widowed parent's allowance within 12 months of the date of that decision, and have it backdated to the date the DWP has decided your late spouse or civil partner died.[46]

Note: these are also the only circumstances in which you may still qualify for the other two 'old' bereavement benefits (bereavement allowance and/or a bereavement payment). See Chapter 24 of the 2017/18 edition of this *Handbook* for more information about these benefits.

If the DWP decides s/he died *on or after 6 April 2017*, you can claim bereavement support payment within 12 months of the date of that decision, and have it backdated to the presumed date of death.

If you claim the wrong benefit

The decision maker can treat a claim for state pension as a claim for bereavement benefits (but not bereavement support payment) and vice versa.[47] A claim for bereavement support payment can be treated as a claim for widowed parent's allowance and vice versa. See p1144 for details of interchanging claims in this way.

Claiming in advance

You can claim bereavement benefits up to three months before you expect to qualify. In most circumstances, you will not know of your need to claim benefit in advance, but this may be relevant if, for example, you know that you will no longer be cohabiting.[48] The date of your claim is the date on which you qualify.

6. Getting paid

The general rules on getting paid are covered in Chapter 51. This section explains the specific rules that apply to bereavement benefits.

When are bereavement benefits paid?

Bereavement support payment is paid monthly in arrears, on the same day of the month as the date of death of your spouse or civil partner. In months when it cannot be paid on this day because it falls on the 29th, 30th or 31st, it is paid on the last day of the month.[49]

Widowed parent's allowance is normally paid fortnightly, in arrears.

Bereavement support payment and widowed parent's allowance are daily benefits. Payments can be made for part periods at the beginning and end of claims. Part payments are calculated using the daily rate.

Note:
• Your widowed parent's allowance might be paid at a reduced rate in certain circumstances (see p533).
• You may not be paid bereavement benefit if you have received a sanction for a benefit offence (see p1239).
• For information on missing payments, see p1150.

- For what to do if you lose your bank card or forget your PIN, see p1149. If you lose your payment service card, see p1150.
- If payment of your bereavement benefit is delayed, see p1255. If you are waiting for a decision on your claim, or to be paid, you might be able to get a short-term advance (see p1153). If you wish to complain about how your claim has been dealt with, or claim compensation, see Chapter 61.
- If payment of your bereavement benefit is suspended, see p1161.
- If you are overpaid a bereavement benefit, you might have to repay it (see Chapter 53) and, in some circumstances, you may have to pay a penalty (see p1229). If you have been accused of fraud, see Chapter 54.
- If you are owed arrears of a bereavement benefit, these can be paid in instalments (see p1148).

Change of circumstances

You must report changes in your circumstances that you have been told to report, as well as any that you might reasonably be expected to know might affect your right to, the amount of, or the payment of, your benefit. You should do this as soon as possible, preferably in writing. See p1160 for further information.

If a change of circumstances affects your entitlement to widowed parent's allowance, before your benefit can be stopped or adjusted, the decision maker should first revise or supersede the earlier decision on your entitlement (see Chapter 56).[50] The date from when a new decision takes effect following a supersession normally depends on whether or not it is advantageous to you and whether you reported the change in time (see p1280).

---

7. Tax, other benefits and the benefit cap

Tax

Bereavement support payment is not taxable.[51] **Widowed parent's allowance** is taxable (except for any increase to widowed parent's allowance for children, which you may still receive, if you have been in receipt of it since 5 April 2003).[52]

Means-tested benefits and tax credits

The initial lump sum of bereavement support payment counts as capital for all means-tested benefits, but it is disregarded for up to 52 weeks. The monthly payments count as income, but are disregarded for all means-tested benefits, including universal credit (UC).[53] Bereavement support payment is ignored when calculating your entitlement to tax credits, as it is not taxable.

Widowed parent's allowance counts as income for means-tested benefits. However:

- £10 of your weekly widowed parent's allowance is disregarded when calculating your entitlement to income support (IS),[54] income-based jobseeker's allowance (JSA),[55] income-related employment and support allowance (ESA)[56] and pension credit (PC);[57]
- an increase in your widowed parent's allowance for a child is disregarded when calculating your entitlement to income-related ESA and PC, and may be ignored when calculating your entitlement to IS and income-based JSA;
- £15 of your weekly widowed parent's allowance is disregarded when calculating your entitlement to housing benefit (HB).[58] However, if you are getting the savings credit (and not the guarantee credit) of PC, the income used to calculate your HB is that used by the DWP to calculate your entitlement to PC (which includes only a £10 disregard from your widowed parent's allowance – see p452).

There are no equivalent widowed parent's allowance disregards for UC.[59]

For tax credits, widowed parent's allowance counts as pension income.

If your partner was entitled to HB when s/he died, this will end. You can now only make a new claim for HB in limited circumstances (see p173). If you can make a new HB claim and you claim within a month of your partner's death, your HB claim can be treated as having been made on the date your partner died (see p207). In some circumstances, it can be backdated further (see p208). If you cannot make a new HB claim, you can claim UC (see Chapter 3).

Non-means-tested benefits

Bereavement support payment does not overlap with contribution-based JSA or contributory ESA – you can be paid bereavement support payment at the same time. However, widowed parent's allowance is affected by the overlapping benefit rules (see p1151).

If you receive an increase in your widowed parent's allowance for a child, the overlapping benefit rules may also affect you. If you get child benefit or guardian's allowance for the same child, see p1153.

Once you reach pension age, your entitlement to bereavement benefits stops. However, you may qualify for state pension (see p764) or a survivor's inherited state pension instead (see p769).

If your bereavement benefit stops before you reach pension age, you may qualify for national insurance credits following bereavement for contributory ESA and contribution-based JSA (see p962).[60]

The benefit cap

In some cases, there is a limit on the total amount of specified benefits you can receive (a 'benefit cap'). Bereavement support payment is not a specified benefit –

payments do not count towards the benefit cap.[61] However, widowed parent's allowance is a specified benefit.[62] The benefit cap only applies if you are getting UC or HB. Fifteen pounds of your weekly widowed parent's allowance is ignored if the cap is applied through your HB. See p1156 for further information.

Passports and other sources of help

If you are entitled to widowed parent's allowance, you are also entitled to a Christmas bonus (see p861).

In some circumstances, you may qualify for a social fund funeral expenses payment (see p784). In Scotland, you may qualify for a funeral support payment (see Chapter 76).

If your child has died, you may qualify for a payment from the children's funeral fund in England or a £500 payment towards funeral costs in Wales (see p785).

If your child has died and you are an employee, you may be entitled to statutory parental bereavement pay (see p801).

If you have low income and capital, you may be entitled to UC (see Chapter 3) and/or council tax reduction (see p836). In limited circumstances, you may be entitled to HB (see Chapter 10).

For advice about what to do after someone dies, see gov.uk. In Scotland, see also the online Scottish government leaflet 'What to Do After a Death in Scotland', available at gov.scot.

Notes

1. Bereavement support payment

1 s30 PA 2014
2 O'Donnell v Department for Communities [2020] NICA 36. However, this Northern Ireland case is not formally binding in Great Britain, and the law is structured differently so could lead to a different result.
3 Reg 3(2) and (5) BSP Regs
4 Reg 4 BSP Regs
5 Reg 4 BSP Regs
6 Reg 3(1)-(6) BSP Regs
7 House of Commons, Hansard, Written statement HCWS409, 12 January 2017, para 5, available at questions-statements.parliament.uk

2. Widowed parent's allowance

8 ss39A and 60(2) and (3) SSCBA 1992
9 s39A(3) SSCBA 1992
10 s122(4) SSCBA 1992
11 Reg 16ZA(1)(a) SS(WB&RP) Regs
12 Reg 2(4) SSB(PRT) Regs
13 CIS/1059/2014
14 Reg 16ZA(2) SS(WB&RP) Regs
15 Reg 6(2) SS(WB&RP) Regs
16 Reg 6 SS(WB&RP) Regs
17 s39A(4), (4A) and (5) SSCBA 1992

3. Definitions

18 *McLaughlin, Re Judicial Review (Northern Ireland)* [2018] UKSC 48; *Jackson and others v SSWP* [2020] EWHC 183
19 The Bereavement Benefits (Remedial) Order 2021
20 But see *CAO v Bath* [1999] (CA), reported as R(G) 1/00; R(G) 2/70
21 R(G) 5/83; s3 Family Law (Scotland) Act 2006; The Family Law (Scotland) Act 2006 (Commencement, Transitional Provisions and Savings) Order 2006 No.212
22 R(G) 1/71
23 CSG/7/1995; CSG/681/2003; but see also CSG/648/2007
24 R(G) 2/63
25 R(G) 1/73
26 *Hyde v Hyde* [1866]; reg 2 SSFA(PM) Regs
27 Reg 1(2) SSFA(PM) Regs
28 R(S) 2/92
29 s11(3) MCA 1973
30 *NA v SSWP (BB)* [2019] UKUT 144 (AAC). The facts included a religious marriage recognised in Pakistan but not recognised in England and Wales, where the late spouse had only ever lived with one other spouse.
31 R(G) 1/95
32 R(G) 1/93; R(P) 2/06
33 CI/142/1949; R(I) 14/51
34 ss2(a) and 60(2) SSCBA 1992

4. Special benefit rules

35 s4 GRA 2004
36 Sch 5 paras 3-5 GRA 2004

5. Claims and backdating

37 Reg 7(1) SS(C&P) Regs
38 CP/4062/2004; see also CP/891/2008 and *AR v SSWP* [2012] UKUT 467 (AAC)
39 Reg 6(1) and (1ZA) SS(C&P) Regs
40 Regs 4(7), (7ZA), (8), (12) and (13) and 6(1) SS(C&P) Regs
41 Reg 2(2)(a) BSP Regs
42 Reg 2(3) BSP Regs
43 Reg 2(2)(b) BSP Regs
44 Reg 2(2)(b)(ii) BSP Regs
45 ss1(2) and 3(1)(b)(ii) and (2)(b) SSAA 1992; s8 SSA 1998; CG/7235/95, para 13
46 ss1(2) and 3(1)(b)(i), (2)(a) and (3) SSAA 1992; s8 SSA 1998; CG/7235/95, para 14
47 Reg 9(1) and Sch 1 Part 1 SS(C&P) Regs
48 Reg 13 SS(C&P) Regs

6. Getting paid

49 Reg 3 BSP Regs
50 Reg 17 SS(C&P) Regs

7. Tax, other benefits and the benefit cap

51 s677 IT(EP)A 2003
52 ss577-79 and 676 IT(EP)A 2003
53 **UC** Reg 66 UC Regs
   IS Sch 9 para 80 IS Regs
   JSA Sch 7 para 76 JSA Regs
   ESA Sch 8 para 68 ESA Regs
   HB Sch 5 para 67 HB Regs
54 Reg 40 and Sch 9 para 16(h) IS Regs
55 Reg 103 and Sch 7 para 17(i) JSA Regs
56 Sch 8 para 17(i) ESA Regs
57 Sch IV para 7 SPC Regs
58 Reg 40 and Sch 5 para 16 HB Regs; reg 29 and Sch 5 para 7 HB(SPC) Regs
59 Regs 22 and 66 UC Regs
60 Reg 8C SS(Cr) Regs
61 s96 WRA 2012
62 Reg 79 UC Regs; regs 75A, 75C and 75G HB Regs

Chapter 26

Carer's allowance

This chapter covers:
1. Who can get carer's allowance (p546)
2. The rules about your age (p552)
3. People included in the claim (p553)
4. The amount of benefit (p553)
5. Special benefit rules (p554)
6. Claims and backdating (p554)
7. Getting paid (p557)
8. Tax, other benefits and the benefit cap (p558)

Key facts
- Carer's allowance (CA) is paid to people who care for someone who is severely disabled. A supplement may also be paid if you live in Scotland.
- CA is a non-means-tested benefit.
- You do not have to have paid national insurance contributions to qualify.
- You can qualify for CA whether you are in or out of work, but you must not earn more than £132 a week.
- CA can be paid in addition to other benefits and tax credits, but the overlapping benefit rules may apply. CA counts as income for means-tested benefits, but you may be entitled to more benefit if you get CA.
- CA is administered and paid by the DWP's Carer's Allowance Unit.
- If you disagree with a CA decision, you can apply for a revision or a supersession (see Chapter 56), or appeal against it (see Chapter 57). You must apply for a mandatory reconsideration before you can appeal.
- A young carer grant has been introduced in Scotland (see Chapter 78).

Future changes
CA in Scotland will be replaced by claims for carer's assistance. The Scottish government plans to transfer existing CA claimants in Scotland to the new benefit, and also to make increased payments to CA claimants caring for more than one disabled child. At the time of writing, details of these plans were awaited. See Chapter 72, and AskCPAG and CPAG's *Welfare Rights Bulletin* for updates.

Part 5: Other benefits
Chapter 26: Carer's allowance
1. Who can get carer's allowance

1. **Who can get carer's allowance**

You qualify for carer's allowance (CA) if:[1]

- you are caring for a 'severely disabled person' (see below). You do not have to be the person's relative, nor do you have to live with her/him; *and*
- the care you give is regular and substantial (see below); *and*
- you are not gainfully employed, which means you earn £132 or less a week (see p547); *and*
- you are not in full-time education (see p886); *and*
- you are aged 16 or over; *and*
- you are not a 'person subject to immigration control' (see p1524); *and*
- you satisfy the residence conditions (see p1601).

Severely disabled person
In this chapter, a **'severely disabled person'** is someone who is paid either attendance allowance (AA), the highest or middle rate of the care component of disability living allowance (DLA) or child disability payment (CDP), either rate of the daily living component of personal independence payment (PIP) or adult disability payment (ADP), armed forces independence payment or constant attendance allowance of £75.50 a week or more paid with an industrial injuries benefit or war disablement pension (see p678).[2]

Note:[3]
- Only one person can qualify for CA and/or the carer's element in universal credit for caring for the same disabled person. If you cannot agree on who this should be, the DWP decides.
- Even if you care for two or more disabled people, you can only qualify for one award of CA for the same day.

Regularly and substantially caring

To qualify for CA, you must be 'regularly and substantially' caring for a severely disabled person. You satisfy this requirement during any week in which you are (or are likely to be) engaged and regularly engaged in caring for her/him for 35 hours or more.[4] A week runs from Sunday to Saturday.[5] Caring can include supervision as well as assistance. If some of the time is spent preparing for the disabled person to come to stay with you or clearing up after her/his visit, this can also count towards the 35 hours.[6]

Note:
- You cannot average the hours if you provide care for more than 35 hours in some weeks and fewer than 35 in others.[7] You must be caring for at least 35 hours in each week of your claim.

- If you are caring for two or more disabled people, you can only qualify for CA if you are caring for at least one of them for 35 hours or more a week.[8] You cannot add together the hours you are caring for both/all of them to make up the 35.

Breaks from caring

You can take a temporary break from caring and continue to qualify for CA. This applies if you have been providing care for at least 35 hours a week in 22 of the last 26 weeks, or for at least 14 of the last 26 weeks if the reason you did not provide care for 22 weeks was that either you or the disabled person were in hospital (or in a similar institution). Weeks before you claimed CA can be counted. This means you can have a four-week break from caring in any period of six months, or a 12-week break if one of you was in hospital or in a similar institution (see p904 for what counts) for at least eight of those weeks.[9]

CA stops if the AA, DLA/CDP, PIP/ADP or constant attendance allowance of the person for whom you are caring stops because s/he is in hospital or in a similar institution (see p905).[10]

If the person receiving care dies

If the person you care for dies, you continue to be entitled to CA for a further eight weeks, provided you satisfy the other qualifying conditions. This means that you are not entitled if payment of the person's PIP/ADP, DLA/CDP or AA had stopped because s/he had been in hospital or a care home for more than 28 days when s/he died (see p905 and p914). The eight weeks run from the Sunday following the death, or from the day of the death if this was a Sunday.[11]

Gainfully employed

You cannot qualify for CA if you are 'gainfully employed'. You count as gainfully employed in a week (and cannot qualify for CA in that week) if your earnings from employment and/or self-employment in the previous week were more than £132.[12] Your earnings are ignored if you are working during a period when you are not actually caring for the severely disabled person – eg, because s/he is in hospital or you are on a four-week break from caring (see above).[13]

Earnings from employment

To work out how earnings from employment affect your entitlement to CA:
- check whether the payment counts as earnings (see below) and whether it can be disregarded (see p551);
- work out your weekly net earnings (see p549);
- work out the date from when your earnings count and the period they cover (see p549).

Part 5: Other benefits
Chapter 26: Carer's allowance
1. Who can get carer's allowance

What counts as earnings

For employees, '**earnings**' mean 'any remuneration or profit derived from... employment'. The main type of income which counts as earnings is therefore your wages. The following are also included:[14]

- any bonus or commission (including tips);
- holiday pay (but not if it is payable more than four weeks after a job ends or is interrupted);
- compensation for unfair dismissal and certain other types of compensation under the Employment Rights Act 1996 or under trade union legislation;
- an equal pay settlement;[15]
- any payments made by an employer for expenses not 'wholly, exclusively and necessarily' incurred in carrying out the job, including any travel expenses to and from work, and any payments made to you for the cost of arranging care for members of your family;
- a retainer (eg, paid during the school holidays to people who work for the school meals service) or a guarantee payment;
- statutory and/or contractual sick, maternity, adoption, paternity, shared parental and parental bereavement pay;
- certain payments at the end of a job (see below).

This list is not exhaustive and other payments from employment may also count as earnings.[16]

It is the pay you actually receive that is taken into account, rather than what you are legally entitled to,[17] so if you receive less than the minimum wage, it is this lesser amount that counts as 'earnings'.

What does not count as earnings

The following are examples of payments that *do not* count as earnings:

- periodic payments made as part of a redundancy scheme;[18]
- occupational pension payments;[19]
- payments towards expenses that are 'wholly, exclusively and necessarily' incurred in the performance of employment, such as travelling expenses during the course of work;[20]
- payments relating to expenses incurred for participating in a service user consultation.[21]

See p551 for information on earnings disregards.

Payments when you stop work

If you stop work before you claim CA, your final earnings generally do not affect your benefit. Provided your entitlement begins after the employment ends, the following are disregarded:[22]

- final wages, paid or due, including bonuses, commission, tips and expenses that count as earnings;
- holiday pay;
- pay in lieu of notice;
- pay in lieu of remuneration – eg, a loss of earnings payment to a councillor;
- statutory or contractual redundancy pay and other compensation payments (other than from an employment tribunal complaint).

Certain final payments *are* taken into account (unless you are over pension age and they are paid on retirement):[23]
- statutory or contractual maternity, adoption, paternity, shared parental, parental bereavement and sick pay;
- an employment tribunal award or settlement of a complaint to a tribunal or court – eg, compensation for unfair dismissal;
- a retainer.

If you are already entitled to CA when a job ends, any final earnings at the end of that employment are not disregarded.

Calculating net earnings from employment

'Earnings' are net earnings. '**Net earnings**' are gross earnings less any deductions made for income tax, class 1 national insurance (NI) contributions (but not class 3 voluntary contributions[24]) and half of any contribution made towards a personal or occupational pension scheme.[25] It is the amount of weekly earnings that is important; monthly earnings are multiplied by 12 and divided by 52 to arrive at a weekly figure.[26] If payment is for a period of less than a week, it is treated as a payment for a week.[27]

If your earnings fluctuate, your weekly earnings may be averaged as follows.[28]
- If you have a regular pattern of work, your weekly earnings are averaged over one complete 'cycle' of work. This includes periods when no work is done if this forms part of your regular pattern of work – eg, if you regularly work three weeks on and one week off, your earnings are averaged over four weeks.
- In any other case, your earnings are averaged over five weeks, or whatever other period enables the average weekly earnings to be assessed more accurately.[29]

The date from when earnings from employment are counted

Earnings are usually treated as having been received on the first day of the benefit week in which they are due to be paid.[30] If the payment is made on a different date to that on which it is due, see p875 of the 2014/15 edition of this *Handbook*.

Benefit week
The '**benefit week**' is the seven days corresponding to the week for which CA is paid.[31]

Part 5: Other benefits
Chapter 26: Carer's allowance
1. Who can get carer's allowance

The period covered by earnings from employment

Earnings count for a future period starting from the above date. The length of that period is worked out as follows.[32]

- If a payment is made for a particular period, it is taken into account for the number of benefit weeks corresponding to that period. For example, a week's part-time earnings are taken into account for a week. For monthly payments, earnings are taken into account for the number of weeks between the date they are treated as paid and the date the next monthly earnings are treated as paid. If a payment is for a particular period but is a one-off payment (eg, holiday pay on leaving a job if the final payments count – see p548), it is taken into account for the number of weeks from the date it is due to the date the next normal monthly earnings would be treated as paid.[33]
- One-off payments that are not for a specific period are divided by the relevant earnings limit (£132 in 2022/23) plus one penny and any disregard that applies to your earnings to work out the number of weeks for which you will not get benefit.
- If two payments of different types of earnings are made (eg, wages and holiday pay) and the periods worked out as above overlap, they are taken into account consecutively.[34]

Earnings from self-employment

Weekly earnings from self-employment (including any allowance from a DWP scheme to assist with a business[35]) are averaged over a year unless:[36]
- you have recently become self-employed; *or*
- there has been a change that is likely to affect the normal pattern of the business.

In either case, earnings are averaged over whatever other period the decision maker considers will give the most accurate figure. This means that when you first claim CA, you should provide an up-to-date set of accounts.

For royalties or similar payments (eg, from copyrights), the period for which these payments count is calculated in a similar way to that for payments made for unspecified periods to employees.[37]

See below for the way earnings of childminders, members of a partnership or share fishermen are calculated. Otherwise, the net profit from self-employment is used.

'Net profit' is calculated by taking the earnings from self-employment over the period and deducting:[38]
- expenses incurred during the period wholly and exclusively for the purposes of the business. For example, if a car or telephone is used partly for business and partly for private purposes, the costs of it can be apportioned and the amount attributable to business use can be deducted.[39] Certain expenses cannot be deducted, including business entertainment, repayment of capital

on a business loan, capital expenditure and depreciation, and providing board and lodging or renting a room in your home; *and*

- income tax and NI contributions;[40] *and*
- half of any contributions made during the period towards a personal pension scheme or retirement annuity contract.

Childminders are always treated as self-employed and your net profit is deemed to be one-third of your earnings from childminding less income tax, NI contributions and half of certain pension contributions.[41] The rest of your earnings are completely ignored.

For members of a partnership or share fishermen, the relevant share of the 'net profit' is used, and expenses incurred wholly and exclusively for the business are deducted before calculating the share of the profits. After that, income tax, NI contributions and half of any premiums paid into a personal pension or under a retirement annuity contract are deducted from the share.[42]

Notional earnings

You are treated as having 'notional earnings' if it is not possible to work out your actual earnings from employment or self-employment when your claim is decided.[43] This may apply if, for example, the job is new and pay depends on performance, or it is a new business and there is no way of calculating what the profits of that business will be. If so, the 'notional earnings' are an amount that is considered reasonable, taking into account the number of hours worked and the earnings paid for comparable work in the area.

Estimates of the appropriate deductions for income tax and NI contributions and half of any occupational or personal pension contributions are deducted from notional earnings, as are any earnings disregards or, where relevant, allowances for childcare or care costs.

Disregarded earnings

Some income, which might otherwise be classed as earnings, is specifically disregarded and does not affect your CA entitlement. The same earnings disregards apply whether the earnings are from employment or self-employment.

When calculating earnings, the cost of looking after the person you care for, up to a maximum amount, can be deducted from your earnings. If you are getting CA and, because of your work, you have to pay for someone (other than a close relative) to look after the severely disabled person for whom you care (or to look after a child under 16 for whom you or your partner are getting child benefit), these care costs can be deducted when your earnings are calculated (in addition to any disregarded earnings).[44] The maximum deduction is 50 per cent of the

Part 5: Other benefits
Chapter 26: Carer's allowance
2. The rules about your age

figure which would otherwise be your net earnings. Any disregarded income is deducted from your net earnings before calculating the 50 per cent figure.

Close relative

'**Close relative**' means a parent, son, daughter, brother, sister or partner (see p303) of you or the severely disabled person for whom you care.

In addition, the following amounts can be disregarded from your earnings:[45]
- any payment made to you by someone who normally lives with you on an informal or non-contractual basis as part of her/his contribution towards shared living expenses;
- the first £20 a week of any income for renting out room(s) in your home;
- the first £20 of any income you receive each week for providing board and lodging in your home. If you get more than £20 a week, 50 per cent of the excess is also disregarded. This disregard applies to each person who lodges with you;
- payments from a local authority or voluntary organisation for fostering or accommodating a child under formal arrangements;
- payments from a health authority, clinical commissioning group, local authority or voluntary organisation for providing temporary care. There is no set time after which care is no longer temporary;[46]
- income tax refunds;
- if you are an employee, any loan or advance of earnings from your employer;
- certain 'bounty' payments made to part-time firefighters, auxiliary coastguards, members of the reserve armed forces and part-time lifeboat crews;
- unless you are abroad yourself, earnings payable abroad which cannot be brought into Great Britain and any bank charges for converting earnings paid in another currency into sterling.

2. **The rules about your age**

You can claim carer's allowance (CA) if you are aged 16 or over.[47] There is no upper age limit. However, because of the overlapping benefit rules, if you receive retirement pension you may not be paid CA, even if you qualify (see p1151). Even if you are not paid CA, you may qualify for a carer element in your universal credit (see p73), a carer premium in your means-tested benefits or a carer addition in pension credit (see p334). If you are aged 16 to 18 and live in Scotland, you may be able to get a young carer grant (see Chapter 78).

3. People included in the claim

You claim carer's allowance (CA) for yourself. You cannot claim any increase in your CA for an adult dependant, or normally claim for a child. Some claimants who received increases for children before 6 April 2003 can continue to receive them. See p559 of the 2021/22 edition of this *Handbook* for further details.

4. The amount of benefit

Carer's allowance (CA) is paid at a weekly rate of £69.70.[48]

Note: if you are a member of a couple, your CA might be paid at a reduced rate if your partner fails to take part in a work-focused interview.

Carer's allowance in Scotland

CA is due to be replaced in Scotland by carer's assistance. When it is introduced, it will be paid at the same rate as jobseeker's allowance (JSA). Until carer's assistance is introduced, a CA supplement is paid to people resident in Scotland who are in receipt of CA to increase their amount of CA to the level of JSA.[49]

CA supplement is paid in two lump-sum payments each year and is adjusted annually to take account of inflation. The payments in 2022 will be made in June and December at £245.29 each.

To qualify, you must be resident in Scotland and be receiving CA on the qualifying date for each payment. The qualifying dates in 2022 are 11 April and 10 October. Anyone getting CA and living in Scotland on these dates will receive a payment. If you are not getting CA on a qualifying date, but are later awarded CA backdated to include the qualifying date, you can get a supplement for that period. You do not get CA supplement if you do not receive CA – eg, if you have an underlying entitlement only, or if you get the carer element of universal credit (UC) without claiming CA. If you get a carer element in your UC, you should claim CA in order to qualify for the supplement, provided your earnings are not too high to prevent this.

You do not need to get CA or live in Scotland for the whole of a six-month period to qualify; it is enough to be in receipt of CA and resident on the qualifying date. You should not need to make a separate claim for the supplement. Social Security Scotland (SSS) should pay you automatically using information shared by the DWP. If you have problems with the payment, call SSS on 0800 182 2222.

CA supplement is disregarded as income for means-tested benefits and tax credits.

Part 5: Other benefits
Chapter 26: Carer's allowance
6. Claims and backdating

5. **Special benefit rules**

Special rules may apply if:
- you are subject to immigration control (see Chapter 68);
- you have come from or are going abroad (see Chapters 69, 70 and 71);
- you or the person you are caring for are in hospital or in prison, or the person you are caring for is in a care home or similar accommodation (see Chapter 42).

6. **Claims and backdating**

The general rules on claims and backdating are covered in Chapter 50. This section explains the specific rules that apply to carer's allowance (CA).

If you are claiming a means-tested benefit, see p558 before claiming CA. It is not always advisable for you to claim CA because of the effect it has on your other benefits (and possibly those of the person for whom you care). You do not have to claim CA in order to get the carer element in universal credit (see p73).

Making a claim

A claim for CA must be made in writing. You can do this by completing:
- an online application form at gov.uk/carers-allowance; *or*
- the approved form. Send it to the Carer's Allowance Unit, Mail Handling Site A, Wolverhampton WV98 2AB. You may also be able to make your claim by taking or sending it to an 'alternative office' (see p1134).

Forms
Get Form DS700 (DS700(SP) if you get retirement pension) from gov.uk/government/publications/carers-allowance-claim-form or the Carer's Allowance Unit by telephone (0800 731 0297; textphone: 0800 731 0317; Relay UK and BSL relay services are available).

Keep a copy of your claim form in case queries arise.

You must provide any information or evidence required (see p555). In certain circumstances, the DWP may accept a written application not on the approved form.[50] You can amend or withdraw your claim before a decision is made (see p1135). If there is a delay in making a claim, you may be able to get a short-term advance of benefit (see p1153).

Who should claim

You must normally claim CA on your own behalf. However, if you are unable to manage your own affairs, another person can claim CA for you as your 'appointee' (see p1135).

Before claiming, you should be aware of how CA affects your entitlement to means-tested benefits and the means-tested benefit entitlement of the person for whom you care (see p558).

Information to support your claim

For the general information requirements that apply to all benefits, see p1136.

It is important that you provide any information required when you claim. Until you do, you may not count as having made a valid claim (see p1138). Correct any defects as soon as possible or your date of claim may be affected.

Even if your claim is valid, you may be asked to provide further information to support your claim (see p1140). You may also be asked to provide information after you are awarded CA and if you fail to do so, your CA could be suspended, or even terminated (see p1162).

The date of your claim

The date of your claim is important as it determines when your entitlement to CA starts. This is not necessarily the date from when you are paid. For information about when payment of CA starts, see p557.

Your **'date of claim'** is usually the date on which your completed claim form is received by the DWP or a designated 'alternative office' (see p1134).[51] If you submit your claim online, your date of claim is usually the date it is received, although a decision maker has the discretion to treat it as having been received on an earlier or later date than this.[52]

You must make sure your claim is valid. If it is 'defective', you are given a short time to correct the defects (see p1139). If you do, your claim is treated as having been made when you initially claimed.[53]

In some cases, you can claim in advance (see p556) and, in some cases, your claim can be backdated (see below). If you want this to be done, make this clear when you claim or the DWP may not consider it.

Backdating your claim

It is very important to claim in time. A claim for CA can usually only be backdated for a maximum of three months.[54] You must satisfy the qualifying conditions over that period. You do not have to show any reasons why your claim was late. The claim form asks you the date from which you want the claim to start.

Your claim can be backdated for more than three months in the following situations.[55]

Part 5: Other benefits
Chapter 26: Carer's allowance
6. Claims and backdating

- If you claim CA within three months of a decision to award a 'qualifying benefit' to the person for whom you care (including a decision made by the First-tier Tribunal, the Upper Tribunal or a court), your CA is backdated to the first day of the benefit week in which the qualifying benefit is payable. However, if the decision awarding the qualifying benefit was made following a renewal claim where a fixed period award has ended or is due to end, your CA is only backdated to the first day of the benefit week in which the renewal award became payable.

- Your CA stopped because the 'qualifying benefit' of the person for whom you care was reduced or stopped. This includes if a fixed-term award for the qualifying benefit came to an end or if payment of attendance allowance (AA), disability living allowance (DLA), child disability payment (CDP), personal independence payment (PIP) or adult disability payment (ADP) stopped because the person for whom you care went into hospital, a care home or other similar accommodation. If you make a further claim within three months of the decision to reinstate the qualifying benefit, or of payment starting again, your CA is backdated to the date your earlier claim ended or the date from when the qualifying benefit was re-awarded or became payable again, whichever is later.

Qualifying benefit

A **'qualifying benefit'** is either AA, the middle or highest rate of the DLA/CDP care component, either rate of the daily living component of PIP/ADP, armed forces independence payment or constant attendance allowance.

If you might have qualified for benefit earlier but did not claim because you were given the wrong information or were misled by the DWP, you could ask for compensation (see p1403) or complain to the Ombudsman (see p1408).

Claiming in advance

You can claim CA up to three months before you qualify.[56] This gives the DWP time to ensure you receive benefit as soon as you are entitled. The date of your claim is the date on which you qualify. The decision maker can award benefit from a future date if s/he believes you will satisfy all the CA qualifying conditions on that date. You should consider claiming in advance – eg, if you are currently earning more than £132 a week, but you plan to stop work or reduce your hours.

7. **Getting paid**

The general rules on getting paid are covered in Chapter 51. This section explains the specific rules that apply to carer's allowance (CA).

When is carer's allowance paid?

You are paid on a Monday (or Wednesday if the person for whom you care receives constant attendance allowance with an industrial injuries benefit or war pension).[57] CA is paid weekly in advance or four-weekly in arrears (13-weekly in arrears if you agree).[58]

Payments normally run from the first payday after the date of your claim, unless the date of your claim is on your payday, when they run from that day.

Note:

- CA awards are usually made for an indefinite period, but can be made for a fixed period – eg, if a change of circumstances is expected.[59]

- Deductions can be made from your CA to repay certain loans (see p1169) and, in some cases, to pay child support maintenance (see p1168).

- You may not be paid CA if you have been sanctioned for a benefit offence (see p1239).

- For information on missing payments, see p1150. If you cannot get your CA payments because you have lost your bank card or you have forgotten your PIN, see p1149. If you have lost your payment service card, see p1150.

- If payment of your CA is delayed, see p1255. If you are waiting for a decision on your claim, or to be paid, you may be able to get a short-term advance (see p1153). If you wish to complain about how your claim has been dealt with, or claim compensation, see Chapter 61.

- If payment of your CA is suspended, see p1161.

- If you are overpaid CA, you may have to repay it (see Chapter 53) and, in some circumstances, you may have to pay a penalty (see p1229). If you have been accused of fraud, see Chapter 54.

- If you owed arrears of CA, these can be paid in instalments (see p1148).

Change of circumstances

You must report changes in your circumstances that you have been told to report, as well as any that you might reasonably be expected to know might affect your right to, the amount of, or the payment of, your benefit. You should do this as soon as possible, preferably in writing. See p1160 for further information. You can also notify your change of circumstances at gov.uk/carers-allowance.[60]

When there has been a relevant change of circumstances, a decision maker looks at your claim again and makes a new decision. To find out the date from which the new decision takes effect, see p1280.

Part 5: Other benefits
Chapter 26: Carer's allowance
8. Tax, other benefits and the benefit cap

8. Tax, other benefits and the benefit cap

Tax

Carer's allowance (CA) (including an increase for your spouse, civil partner or someone who cares for your child, if you still receive this) is taxable.[61] However, increases for children (if you still receive these) are not taxable.

Means-tested benefits and tax credits

Before you claim CA, consider how your claim might affect your entitlement to means-tested benefits and tax credits. If in doubt, obtain advice.

If you are entitled to CA:
- you may get a carer element included in your universal credit (UC) (see p73) or a carer premium or carer addition included in your other means-tested benefit (see p334);
- you come within one of the groups of people who can claim income support (IS) (see p235) if you receive CA – however, you cannot usually make a new claim for IS;
- if you are a member of a couple with at least one child or qualifying young person, the other member of the couple only has to work 16 hours a week to qualify for working tax credit (WTC) (see p284). You may also qualify for the childcare element in WTC (see p1422);
- if you are getting UC, you do not have to meet any of the work-related requirements (see p1039). This also applies if you would qualify for CA but for the fact that your earnings are higher than £132 a week;
- if you are a member of a 'joint-claim couple' getting income-based jobseeker's allowance (JSA), you are not required to satisfy the jobseeking conditions.

Note: if the person for whom you care has a severe disability premium/additional amount included in her/his IS, income-based JSA, income-related employment and support allowance (ESA), pension credit (PC) or housing benefit (HB), her/his entitlement to that premium/additional amount can be affected (see p334). Bear in mind that the severe disability premium/additional amount is worth more than the carer premium/additional amount.

Income

CA counts in full as income for all means-tested benefits.

CA counts as qualifying income for the savings credit of PC (see p262).

CA counts in full as income for WTC and child tax credit (CTC). Remember, however, that you cannot get CA if you are in 'gainful employment' (see p547).

Note:
- For IS, income-based JSA, income-related ESA and working-age HB, if you choose not to claim CA and the DWP decides that you failed to apply for it deliberately, you may be treated as if you receive it (see p434).
- For all means-tested benefits other than UC, if you give up your claim for CA, you can be treated as if you receive it if the DWP decides that you deliberately deprived yourself of it in order to qualify for, or increase your entitlement to, benefit for yourself or your family (but see p434 and p465).

The amount of means-tested benefits

If you are getting UC and:
- you are a member of a couple, you can get a childcare costs element in your UC if one of you is in paid work and the other is not in paid work, is unable to provide childcare and qualifies for CA;
- you (or your partner) qualify for CA, or would do but for the fact that your (or her/his) earnings are higher than £132 a week, a carer element is included in your UC maximum amount. However, if you:
  - have limited capability for work and are a carer, your UC cannot include both a limited capability for work element and a carer element for the same person;
  - are a single claimant with limited capability for work-related activity, your UC includes a limited capability for work-related activity element instead of a carer element;
  - are a member of a couple, your UC includes the limited capability for work-related activity element if one has not already been included for your partner. However, if a limited capability for work-related activity element has been included for you, a carer element can be included for your partner if s/he satisfies the conditions, whether or not s/he would also qualify for a limited capability for work-related activity element.

You may need to work out how you would be better off financially.

If you receive CA (or are entitled to it but do not receive it because of the overlapping benefit rules – see p1151), a carer premium/additional amount is included in your IS, income-based JSA, income-related ESA, PC and HB.

Non-means-tested benefits

For each week you receive CA, you can get national insurance credits (see p960).

CA is subject to the overlapping benefit rules, which means that you may not be paid CA in full if another earnings-replacement benefit (eg, retirement pension) is paid to you (see p1151).

The benefit cap

In some cases, there is a limit on the total amount of specified benefits you can receive (a 'benefit cap'). CA is not one of these specified benefits.[62] If you receive CA (or you would receive it but for the overlapping benefit rules), you are exempt from the cap. See p1156 for further information.

Passports and other sources of help

If you get CA (or would get it but for the overlapping benefit rules), you are entitled to a Christmas bonus (see p861). You may be able to get help, support and services from your local authority – ask for a carer's assessment. If you have a low income, you may be entitled to council tax reduction (see p836).

Notes

1. Who can get carer's allowance
1 s70 SSCBA 1992; reg 9(1) SS(ICA) Regs
2 s70(2) SSCBA 1992; reg 3 SS(ICA) Regs
3 s70(7) SSCBA 1992
4 Reg 4(1) SS(ICA) Regs
5 s122 SSCBA 1992
6 CG/6/1990
7 R(G) 3/91
8 Reg 4(1A) SS(ICA) Regs
9 Reg 4(2) SS(ICA) Regs
10 SSWP v Pridding [2002] EWCA Civ 306
11 s70(1A) SSCBA 1992
12 Reg 8(1) SS(ICA) Regs
13 Reg 8(2) SS(ICA) Regs
14 Reg 9 SSB(CE) Regs
15 Minter v Kingston Upon Hull CC and Potter v SSWP [2011] EWCA Civ 1155
16 R(IS) 9/95; CIS/743/1992
17 R(IB) 7/03
18 Reg 9(1)(b) SSB(CE) Regs
19 Reg 2(1) SSB(CE) Regs
20 Reg 9(3) SSB(CE) Regs; Parsons v Hogg [1985] 2 All ER 897 (CA), appendix to R(FIS) 4/85
21 Reg 9(3)(b) SSB(CE) Regs
22 Sch 1 para 12 SSB(CE) Regs
23 Sch 1 para 12(2) SSB(CE) Regs
24 CIS/521/1990
25 Reg 10(4) SSB(CE) Regs
26 Regs 6(1) and 8(1)(b)(i) SSB(CE) Regs
27 Reg 8(1)(a) SSB(CE) Regs
28 Reg 8(3) SSB(CE) Regs
29 CG/4941/2003
30 Reg 7(b) SSB(CE) Regs
31 Reg 2(1) SSB(CE) Regs
32 Reg 6(2) SSB(CE) Regs
33 Cotton v SSWP [2009] EWCA Civ 1333, reported as [2010] AACR 17
34 Reg 6(3) SSB(CE) Regs; Cotton v SSWP [2009] EWCA Civ 1333, reported as [2010] AACR 17
35 Reg 12(1) SSB(CE) Regs
36 Reg 11(1) SSB(CE) Regs
37 Reg 11(2) SSB(CE) Regs
38 Reg 13(1)(a) and (b), (4) and (5) SSB(CE) Regs
39 R(IS) 13/91; R(FC) 1/91; CTC/26/1989
40 See also reg 14 SSB(CE) Regs
41 Regs 13(10) and 14 SSB(CE) Regs
42 Reg 13(5) SSB(CE) Regs
43 Reg 4(1) and (3) SSB(CE) Regs and R(IB) 7/03, disapplying reg 4(2) of these Regs
44 Regs 10(3) and 13(3) and Sch 3 SSB(CE) Regs
45 Sch 1 SSB(CE) Regs
46 CG/1752/2006

2. The rules about your age
47 s70(3) SSCBA 1992

- -

5

Chapter 27

. . . .

Child benefit and guardian's allowance

This chapter covers:

Key facts

- You may be entitled to child benefit if you are responsible for a child or 'qualifying young person'. You need not be the child's parent.
- You may be entitled to guardian's allowance if you are responsible for a child or qualifying young person and one or both of her/his parents have died. Usually, you must *not* be the child's parent.
- Child benefit and guardian's allowance are non-means-tested benefits.
- You do not need to have paid national insurance contributions to qualify.
- You can qualify whether you are in or out of work.
- If your or your partner's income is over £50,000 a year, one of you may be liable to pay more tax if you get child benefit. Guardian's allowance is not taxable.
- Child benefit and guardian's allowance are administered and paid by HM Revenue and Customs.
- If you disagree with a decision, you can apply for a revision or a supersession (see Chapter 56), or appeal against it (see Chapter 57). You must apply for a mandatory reconsideration before you can appeal.

1. Who can get child benefit

Note: in this chapter the term 'child' is generally used to refer to both a child and a 'qualifying young person'.

You qualify for child benefit for a child if:[1]
* s/he is a 'child' or 'qualifying young person' (see below); *and*
* you are 'responsible' for the child (see p567); *and*
* you have priority over other claimants (see p568); *and*
* you are not a 'person subject to immigration control' (see Chapter 68); *and*
* you and the child satisfy the residence conditions (see p1599).

In some circumstances, even if you meet these conditions, you cannot get child benefit (see p570). If a child you get child benefit for dies, see p581.

Note: guardian's allowance is a separate benefit, but to qualify you must usually get child benefit. For who can get guardian's allowance, see p571.

Who counts as a child

Anyone aged under 16 counts as a **'child'**.[2] You can also get child benefit for a child aged 16 or over if s/he counts as a 'qualifying young person'.

Who is a qualifying young person

A **'qualifying young person'** is someone aged 16, 17, 18 or 19 who is:[3]
* not in 'relevant education' or training, but only until 31 August (or, if s/he was born on 31 August, 1 September)[4] after her/his 16th birthday; *or*
* 16 or 17, not in *any* education or training, and is in an 'extension period' (see p565); *or*
* undertaking, or enrolled or accepted on, a qualifying type of education (see p564) or 'approved training' (see p565); *or*
* not in relevant education or approved training and it is before the 'terminal date' (see p566).

See p570 for when you cannot get child benefit for a qualifying young person.

Relevant education
'Relevant education' is defined as education which is full time and not advanced, so any 'full-time, non-advanced education' (see p564) counts as relevant education. HM Revenue and Customs (HMRC) says that 'appropriate full-time education' in England (see p565) is treated as relevant education.[5]

A child counts as a qualifying young person until none of the above situations apply.[6] If child benefit for a child stops because s/he is not a qualifying young

Part 5: Other benefits
Chapter 27: Child benefit and guardian's allowance
1. Who can get child benefit

person, but s/he later meets the conditions again, you can make a new claim. See p566 if there is a temporary interruption in meeting the conditions.

Education

A child under 20 counts as a qualifying young person if s/he:[7]

- is in 'full-time, non-advanced education' (see below), which s/he started, or was enrolled or accepted on, before turning 19; *or*
- receives 'appropriate full-time education' in England (see p565), which s/he started, or was enrolled or accepted on, before turning 19; *or*
- was previously in one of these types of education, and is enrolled or accepted on another such course.

The education must not be provided as a result of the child's employment or because of an office s/he holds. See p566 if your child's education is interrupted.
Note:

- If a child leaves education before s/he is 20, s/he may still count as a qualifying young person (see p563).
- HMRC sometimes treats a child who starts a course of full-time, non-advanced education while s/he is 19 as having begun the course before turning 19 if s/he has been in full-time, non-advanced education *continuously* since before turning 19. This means s/he counts as a qualifying young person during the course, even if s/he was not enrolled or accepted on it before turning 19.

Examples of non-advanced and advanced courses of education[8]

Non-advanced courses	Advanced courses
GCSEs, AS and A levels	A university degree
NVQ and SVQ level 3 and below	NVQ or SVQ level 4 or above
Scottish National Qualifications (up to Higher or Advanced Higher level)	HND or HNC
International Baccalaureate	Diploma of Higher Education
BTEC and OCR Nationals	A teaching qualification

Full-time, non-advanced education

To count as 'full-time, non-advanced education', a child's course must normally be provided at a school or college.[9] If a child is educated elsewhere (eg, at home), this also counts if either s/he was being educated in this way before the age of 16 or s/he has a statement of special educational needs that assesses home education as suitable for her/his needs.[10] HMRC must approve these kinds of education.[11]

To count as full time, the course must be for an average of over 12 hours a week during term time, including tuition, supervised study,[12] exams and practical work, but not meal breaks and unsupervised study.[13]

Appropriate full-time education

To count as 'appropriate full-time education', the education must be suitable for the child, taking into account her/his age, ability and aptitude and any special educational needs s/he has. It cannot be an advanced course.[14]

It does not matter where the education takes place, provided it is in England. If the education is provided at home, it is treated as full time. Education which is not provided at a school is treated as full time if it is tailored activity designed to enable the child to stay in education or training, or if it lasts at least 540 hours a year and was developed by a college, higher education institution or training provider to meet the child's needs.[15]

Approved training

Note: in England, there is no approved training. Check whether a child's training counts as 'appropriate full-time education' (see above).

A child under 20 counts as a qualifying young person if s/he:[16]

- is doing approved training, which s/he started, or was enrolled or accepted on, before turning 19; *or*
- was in full-time, non-advanced education or approved training, and is now enrolled or accepted on approved training.

Approved training

'Approved training' includes:[17]

– in Scotland, Employability Fund activity or No One Left Behind;

– in Wales, Traineeships or Foundation Apprenticeships.

The training must not be paid or provided under a contract of employment (but see p566).

See p566 if a child's training is interrupted. If a child leaves approved training before turning 20, s/he may still count as a qualifying young person (see p563).

The extension period

If a child is 16 or 17, s/he continues to count as a qualifying young person during an 'extension period' if:[18]

- s/he is not in any kind of education or training; *and*
- s/he is registered as available for work, education or training with a careers service or a specified body; *and*
- s/he is not in remunerative work (see p571); *and*
- you were entitled to child benefit for her/him immediately before the extension period started; *and*
- you apply in writing (or by another method if HMRC accepts this) within three months of the date your child's education or training finished.

Part 5: Other benefits
Chapter 27: Child benefit and guardian's allowance
1. Who can get child benefit

The extension period begins on the Monday after the child's course of education or training ends and lasts for 20 weeks. If a child turns 18 during the extension period, child benefit ends unless s/he counts as a qualifying young person on another ground (see p563).

If a child's extension period is interrupted, see below.

The 'terminal date rule'

If a child leaves qualifying education (see p564) or approved training (see p565) before reaching 20, s/he counts as a qualifying young person until:[19]

- the 'terminal date' if this is a Sunday, or the Sunday after the 'terminal date' (see below); or
- if earlier, the Sunday of the week in which s/he turns 20, or the day before her/his 20th birthday if s/he turns 20 on a Monday.

A child does not count as a qualifying young person under this rule if s/he is in remunerative work (see p571).

Terminal date

The **'terminal date'** is the first of the following dates that falls after the date a child left education or training:

– the last day in February; or

– 31 May; or

– 31 August; or

– 30 November.

Note:
- If a child has left education, but returns to sit an exam for her/his previous course, s/he is treated as still being in education until the date of the last exam for which s/he was entered before leaving education.[20]
- A child who has completed her/his Highers or Advanced Highers in Scotland is treated as being in education until a comparable course in England or Wales ends, if this is later.[21]
- A child cannot count as a qualifying young person while in education or training that is provided as a part of her/his job. If s/he is under 20, it is arguable that s/he counts as a qualifying young person from the date s/he leaves such a course until the terminal date, as this rule does not exclude people whose course is provided as part of a job.

Interruptions

If there is a break in a child's satisfying the conditions to be a qualifying young person, this is ignored:[22]

- for up to six months (whether the interruption began before or after the child turned 16) if it is 'reasonable' in the circumstances; *or*
- indefinitely if it is caused by the child's physical or mental illness or disability, and the length of the interruption is 'reasonable' in the circumstances.

This means that a child still counts as a qualifying young person during the interruption. HMRC states that this only applies if there is an interruption during a course of education or training, but it arguably also applies to 16/17 year olds during the extension period.

However, an interruption cannot be ignored if, immediately afterwards, the child starts or is likely to start:[23]

- a training course which is not 'approved training'; *or*
- a course of advanced education; *or*
- education connected to her/his employment.

Responsible for a child

You are only entitled to child benefit for a child you are 'responsible' for. You count as responsible for a child in any week in which:[24]

- the child is living with you (see below); *or*
- you contribute to the cost of supporting the child (see p568).

A child 'living with' you

To count as living with a child, you must share both a home and 'a settled course of daily living'.[25] This is not the same as 'residing together' or 'presence under the same roof'.[26] A child may be 'living with' you even while s/he is away. There are special rules if a child is looked after by a local authority (see p574).

Living apart

If a child used to live with you, but is now absent, s/he is treated as still living with you if you have not lived apart for more than 56 days in the last 16 weeks.[27] Days a child is absent are ignored if s/he is away *only* to:[28]

- receive education or training (HMRC states that this must be full-time education or approved training); *or*
- stay in certain types of residential accommodation because of her/his disability, or because her/his health would be 'significantly impaired or further impaired' if s/he did not stay there (but see below); *or*
- receive inpatient treatment in a hospital or similar institution (but see below).

In the latter two situations above, a maximum of 12 consecutive weeks' absence can be ignored, unless you regularly incur expenditure in respect of the child, in which case the absence can be ignored indefinitely.[29] If you make visits, or give the child pocket money, this rule should be satisfied. Periods in hospital or

Part 5: Other benefits
Chapter 27: Child benefit and guardian's allowance
1. Who can get child benefit

residential accommodation separated by 28 days or less are treated as one when calculating the 12-week period.

Even if a child is not living with you, you may still qualify for child benefit for her/him if you contribute to the cost of supporting her/him.

See p1623 if your child is abroad.

Example

Mae's son was in hospital for 18 weeks. She regularly took him food and comics. On being discharged, he stayed with his aunt for a month, then returned home. Mae is entitled to child benefit while her son was away from home. He is treated as still living with her while in hospital as she regularly incurred expenditure for him. He also counts as still living with her while staying with his aunt, as he was not absent from home for more than 56 days in the previous 16 weeks – the period in hospital is ignored when calculating the 56 days.

Contributing to the cost of supporting a child

If a child does not live with you, you can still qualify for child benefit if you contribute to the cost of supporting her/him. You must contribute at least the amount of child benefit that would be paid for the child (see p574).[30]

Note:

- Contributions need not be regular, but must total the amount of child benefit that you would qualify for during the period that is being considered.[31]
- Payments in kind, rather than cash, may be counted.[32]
- If you live with your spouse or civil partner, any contribution made by one of you can be treated as a contribution by the other.[33]
- If you and another person(s) each contribute less than the amount of child benefit for the child, but your total contributions are at least the amount of child benefit payable, one of you is treated as contributing the whole sum. If you do not agree who this should be, HMRC decides. If you are awarded child benefit on this basis, you alone must then contribute at least the amount of child benefit paid for the child to remain entitled.[34]

Priority between claimants

More than one person can potentially qualify for child benefit for the same child – eg, if s/he lives with one parent and is maintained by the other. Only one person can be awarded child benefit for a child, so there is an order of priority for who gets child benefit if two or more people make a claim.[35]

If two or more people have claimed child benefit for the same child and would qualify for it, the following order of priority applies.[36]

- If you live with the child, you have priority over someone who is contributing to the cost of supporting her/him.
- If you are a woman, you have priority over your *male* spouse or civil partner if you reside together (see p570).

- If you are the child's parent (including a step-parent, adoptive parent and someone who has legal parental responsibility),[37] you have priority over a non-parent.
- If you are the child's mother or stepmother and are *not* married or in a civil partnership with a man, you have priority over the other parent if you reside together (see p570).
- In any other case, the person agreed between you and the other claimant has priority. If there is no agreement, HMRC chooses who has priority. You cannot appeal against HMRC's choice (but see p1304).[38]

If your claim takes priority over an existing claim, child benefit continues to be paid on the existing claim for the three weeks following the week in which you claim, unless the other claimant withdraws her/his claim or her/his child benefit entitlement ends.[39] Even if your claim has priority, you cannot usually receive child benefit for a period before you made your claim if it has already been paid to someone else for the same child (but see p580).

If you have claimed child benefit and want someone who has equal or lower priority to you to receive it, contact the Child Benefit Office (see p576).[40]

Consider conceding priority to your partner if you spend time abroad, as child benefit normally ends if you have been abroad for more than eight (or sometimes 12) weeks (see p1623).

Separation and the priority rules

Problems can arise if there are competing child benefit claims from recently separated parents. Even if a child only lives with one parent, s/he may also be treated as still living with the other parent for a period (usually 56 days) under the rules described on p567. If you are in this situation and a child lives with you, but is still treated as living with her/his other parent, both of you are potentially entitled to child benefit for the child. If neither of you withdraws your claim, the priority rules apply (see p568). In practice, this means that if you are the child's mother, your claim normally takes priority for 56 days after you separate permanently, whoever the child lives with. However, if you are the child's father and you got child benefit before you separated, your claim has priority for three weeks after the week in which the mother claims.[41]

Note: if your ex-partner was getting child benefit when you made your competing claim, see p580.

Do you share your child's care with her/his other parent?

Separated parents may both potentially be entitled to child benefit. If you do not agree who should receive it, HMRC decides who should be paid. This usually involves looking at who has the greater responsibility of care. In deciding how best to present your case to HMRC, consider the following questions.

1. How many hours each week do you each care for the child?

Part 5: Other benefits
Chapter 27: Child benefit and guardian's allowance
1. Who can get child benefit

2. What are the terms of any court orders? Do they reflect the actual care arrangements, and does the other parent pay you child support maintenance?

3. Where are the child's possessions kept?

4. At which address is the child registered with services, such as school and her/his doctor?

5. What contributions do each of you make to the cost of bringing up the child? (This may not be conclusive if the resources of one parent are greater than the other.)

6. What impact might the decision have on each parent?

7. Are there other children of the same relationship? In one case involving two parents with almost equal responsibility for their two children, the High Court held that it was reasonable for HMRC to decide that each parent should get child benefit for one child.[42]

These are just examples of the issues to consider – each case depends on its circumstances.

Residing together

It may be important to decide whether you and another person are treated as 'residing together'[43] if you both claim child benefit for the same child (see p568). If you are married, in a civil partnership or a child's parent, you and your spouse/ civil partner/the other parent are treated as residing together if your absence from each other:[44]

- is not likely to be permanent (even if you have never lived together);[45] *or*
- is solely because one of you is in hospital, or in a similar institution for people with mental health problems, whether this is temporary or permanent.

It is also possible to be absent from one another while you are living under the same roof – eg, if you are maintaining separate households.[46]

When you cannot get child benefit

Even if you meet all the entitlement conditions, you cannot get child benefit if:[47]

- you are the child's spouse, civil partner or partner; *or*
- the child is married, in a civil partnership or living with her/his partner as if they were married or civil partners[48] unless:
  - the child's spouse, civil partner or partner is in full-time, non-advanced education or approved training; *or*
  - the child and her/his spouse or civil partner are not 'residing together' (see above – the definition is the same); *or*
- in some circumstances, the child is in 'remunerative work' (see p571); *or*
- the child is aged 16 or over and receiving universal credit, income support, income-based jobseeker's allowance, employment and support allowance, working tax credit or child tax credit; *or*
- the child has spent more than eight consecutive weeks (but see p574):
  - in prison or other custody; *or*
  - being looked after by a local authority.

16–19 year olds who work

If a child is aged 16 or over and counts as a 'qualifying young person' under the terminal date rule (see p566) or is in an extension period (see p565), you cannot get child benefit for her/him if s/he is in 'remunerative work' – ie, s/he works for 24 hours or more a week in expectation of payment.[49]

If a child is under 16 or a qualifying young person on any other ground (see p563), any work s/he does should not affect your child benefit.

---

2. Who can get guardian's allowance

You qualify for guardian's allowance for a 'child' or 'qualifying young person' (see p563 for who counts – the rules are the same as for child benefit) if:[50]
- you are entitled to, or treated as entitled to, child benefit for her/him (see below); *and*
- s/he is an 'eligible child' (see below) and either:
  – s/he lives with you, or is treated as living with you (see p567); *or*
  – you contribute to the cost of providing for her/him (see p573); *and*
- the residence conditions are satisfied (see p1600); *and*
- you are not the child's parent (but see p573).

If a child for whom you get guardian's allowance dies, see p581.

Entitled to child benefit

To get guardian's allowance for a child, you must normally be entitled to child benefit for her/him (see p563). You are treated as entitled to child benefit if:[51]
- you elect not to be paid your entitlement to avoid the 'high-income child benefit charge' (see p581); *or*
- you live with your spouse and s/he is entitled to child benefit for the child; *or*
- you live in Great Britain and you would be entitled to child benefit for the child were you (or your spouse or civil partner, if you live with her/him) not getting a family benefit from another country.

You are treated as entitled to child benefit in the week before your entitlement begins, so guardian's allowance can start on the same day as child benefit.[52]

Eligible child

A child is an **'eligible child'** if her/his parents (or if s/he was adopted, adoptive parents):[53]
- have both died (or the child was adopted by one person who has now died); *or*
- were not married or in a civil partnership, the mother has died and the father is unknown (but see p573 if the child has been adopted); *or*

Part 5: Other benefits
Chapter 27: Child benefit and guardian's allowance
2. Who can get guardian's allowance

- are divorced or their civil partnership has been dissolved, one parent has died and when s/he died, the other parent did not have custody of, and was not maintaining, the child and neither arrangement was required by a court order or child support calculation.

A child is also an eligible child if one of her/his parents (or adoptive parents) has died, and:[54]

- when s/he died the other parent was missing and cannot be found; *or*
- the other parent is in prison or detained in hospital by a court order (but see below).

Missing parents

If one of a child's parents has died, you may qualify for guardian's allowance if, at the date of the death, you did not know the whereabouts of the other parent. Since then, you must have been unable to discover her/his whereabouts, despite making all reasonable efforts to do so – eg, by asking known relatives and friends and checking old addresses.[55] You may not have to make such efforts if there is a risk that you or the child might experience harm or undue distress if you try to trace the missing parent – eg, if s/he is a threat to your, or the child's, physical safety or emotional wellbeing.[56]

If you have had contact with the other parent since the death (but before the decision on the claim), you cannot get guardian's allowance, as her/his whereabouts are known.[57] This may apply even if the contact was only brief (eg, at the funeral), and even if the surviving parent later disappears.

If there has been no contact, but you can communicate with the surviving parent in some way, this is probably sufficient to show that her/his whereabouts are known.[58] 'Whereabouts' is not the same as an address, so showing that you do not know her/his address may not be enough to qualify for guardian's allowance if you have some details of where s/he lives, works or can often be found. However, if all that you know is that the surviving parent is in a large urban area, you can argue that her/his whereabouts are unknown.

Prison sentences

If one of a child's parents has died and the other is in prison, you are only entitled to guardian's allowance if the surviving parent is:[59]

- serving a sentence of imprisonment or detention of at least two years (whether that sentence started before or after the date of death); *or*
- detained in hospital by order of a court under specified legislation.

There are detailed rules about what counts as imprisonment or detention, and for calculating whether the length of a sentence amounts to two years, so get advice if you are affected.[60] Guardian's allowance is reduced if the parent in prison contributes to the cost of providing for the child.[61]

Contributing to the cost of providing for a child

To qualify for guardian's allowance for a child who does not live with you, you must contribute at least £18.55 a week to the cost of providing for her/him. This must be in addition to any contribution you make in order to qualify for child benefit for the child (see p568).[62]

When calculating whether you contribute at least £18.55 a week, include contributions made by your spouse or civil partner if you live together. If you do not currently make contributions, you are treated as doing so if you state in writing that you will once you are awarded guardian's allowance. Any decision to award you guardian's allowance on this basis is revised if you do not make the contributions.[63]

Parents, adoptive parents and step-parents

You cannot qualify for guardian's allowance for a child if you are her/his parent, unless one of the following exceptions applies.[64]

- If a child is adopted, her/his adoptive parents count as parents, so if you are her/his biological parent you can claim guardian's allowance (if the qualifying conditions are met).
- If you have adopted a child, you can continue to get guardian's allowance if you were entitled to it immediately before the adoption.
- HM Revenue and Customs says that if you are a child's step-parent, you do not count as a parent for guardian's allowance and so can get guardian's allowance for your stepchild.[65]

5

3. The rules about your age

If you claim child benefit or guardian's allowance, there is no upper or lower age limit to be entitled.

4. People included in the claim

You claim child benefit for each child for whom you are responsible. You claim guardian's allowance for each eligible child (see p571).

Part 5: Other benefits
Chapter 27: Child benefit and guardian's allowance
6. Special benefit rules

5. **The amount of benefit**

Child benefit and guardian's allowance are paid at the following weekly rates.[66]

	£pw
Child benefit – eldest eligible child	21.80
Child benefit – other children (each)	14.45
Guardian's allowance	18.55

The higher rate of child benefit is normally paid for the eldest (or only) child in a family.[67] If you live with your partner and both of you receive child benefit for a child from a previous relationship, the higher rate is only paid to the person who has the eldest child.[68]

6. **Special benefit rules**

Special rules may apply to your child benefit or guardian's allowance if:
- a child is being looked after by a local authority, or is in prison or detention;
- you or the child have come from, or are going, abroad (see Chapters 68, 69, 70 and 71);
- you are in prison or detention (see Chapter 42).

Your child is being looked after by a local authority, or is in prison or detention

Note: the rules in this section prevent you from getting guardian's allowance for an 'eligible child' (see p571) if your child benefit for that child stops.
Special rules apply if a child is:[69]
- looked after by a local authority, is provided with or placed in accommodation under certain legislation and some of the cost of the child's accommodation or maintenance is met by local authority or public funds (but see below); *or*
- subject to a compulsory supervision order and lives in residential accommodation under certain legislation; *or*
- in prison or other detention (such as a detention centre or young offenders' institution) as a result of criminal proceedings or non-payment of a penalty imposed on conviction.

If any of these circumstances apply to a child and have done so for at least one day a week in the last eight consecutive weeks, your child benefit entitlement for her/him ends, unless the child 'ordinarily' lives with you throughout at least one whole day each week (even if s/he is not actually at home in that particular week).[70] A 'day' runs from midnight to midnight, so, in practice, s/he must 'ordinarily' stay with you for two nights during a week for you to qualify.[71] A 'week' means seven days beginning with a Monday.[72]

After the first eight weeks' absence, even if the child does not 'ordinarily' live with you for at least one day a week, you can still get child benefit when the child comes to stay with you for a week or more.[73]

Note:

- Even if a child ordinarily lives with you or comes to stay with you for over a week, if the local authority is making certain payments you may still not qualify for child benefit (see below).

- If a child stops being looked after by a local authority, stops being subject to a supervision order or stops being in prison for at least a week (ie, from Monday to Sunday), but is later in one of those situations again, the eight-week period restarts.

- You can still get child benefit for a child who is looked after by a local authority if s/he is placed in residential accommodation because s/he has a disability or because her/his health would be impaired were s/he not in the accommodation (see p567).[74]

- If a child is detained in a hospital or similar institution because of mental health problems, s/he is only treated as being in prison if s/he was moved there from prison or detention and the expected release date under her/his sentence has not passed. Otherwise, you can continue to get child benefit, provided you meet the normal qualifying conditions.[75]

- If a child was in custody, but is not sentenced to imprisonment or detention, you should be paid child benefit for her/him for the period of her/his detention.[76]

Fostering, adoption and kinship care

If you are a foster carer, a kinship carer or are adopting a child, payments you get from the local authority may affect your child benefit. In many situations, child benefit entitlement is not affected, but it is in the following circumstances.

- *You* cannot get child benefit for a child if a local authority has arranged for her/him to be placed with you under a placement, or a looking-after or fostering arrangement and the local authority pays for her/his accommodation or maintenance under section 22C(10) of the Children Act 1989, regulation 33 of the Looked After Children (Scotland) Regulations 2009 or section 81(13) of the Social Services and Well-being (Wales) Act 2014.[77]

- *No one* can get child benefit for a child if s/he has been placed with her/his prospective adopters and a local authority pays for the child's accommodation or maintenance under the above provisions.[78]

Part 5: Other benefits
Chapter 27: Child benefit and guardian's allowance
7. Claims and backdating

If the situations above do not apply, the normal rules on entitlement apply, including the rules on children who are being looked after by a local authority described on p574 (and the exceptions to these rules described on p575).

Your entitlement to child benefit is not affected if you look after a child under private fostering arrangements.

7. Claims and backdating

The general rules about claims and backdating are covered in Chapter 50. This section explains the specific rules for child benefit and guardian's allowance.

Making a claim

A claim for child benefit must normally be made in writing to the Child Benefit Office. However, you can make a claim by telephoning the child benefit helpline if you already get child benefit, you are claiming for an additional child who is aged under six months, that child was born in the UK and the birth has been registered in England, Wales or Scotland.[79]

Note: if you are unable to get an appointment to register the birth before the child is three months old, you can apply for child benefit, but you will not receive the payments until you inform HM Revenue and Customs (HMRC) that the birth has been registered.

You must usually get child benefit to be able to get guardian's allowance, but you must make a separate claim. A claim for guardian's allowance should be made in writing to the Guardian's Allowance Unit at the Child Benefit Office.

Forms
The approved child benefit form is Form CH2, which you can get by telephoning the Child Benefit Office. The approved guardian's allowance form is Form BG1, which you can get by telephoning the Guardian's Allowance Unit (part of the Child Benefit Office). Both forms are also available from gov.uk. They can be completed online, but must be printed, signed and sent by post.[80]

The postal address for enquiries is: HMRC – Child Benefit Office, PO Box 1, Newcastle upon Tyne NE88 1AA. If your letter is about guardian's allowance, you should write 'Guardian's Allowance Unit' at the start of the address. The address is slightly different if you are sending a claim by post, and is written on the claim form. You can also contact HMRC by telephone:
- child benefit helpline: 0300 200 3100; Welsh language,: 0300 200 1900; textphone: 0300 200 3103 (Relay UK service available);
- child benefit intermediaries' helpline (for advisers only): 0300 322 9078;
- guardian's allowance helpline: 0300 322 9080 (textphone: 0300 200 3103).

Keep a copy of your claim form in case queries arise. HMRC has the discretion to accept claims made in another way in individual cases.

You must provide any information or evidence required (see below). You can amend or withdraw your claim before a decision is made (see p1135). If there is a delay in deciding your claim, you can ask for an interim payment (see p580).

Who should claim

You must normally make your own claim for child benefit and guardian's allowance. If you are unable to manage your own affairs, another person can claim for you as your 'appointee' (see p1135).

If someone else also claims child benefit for the same child, you can only get child benefit for that child if your claim has priority (see p568).

If you are a woman and live with your *male* spouse or civil partner, you are entitled to guardian's allowance rather than him.[81] However, it can be paid to either of you unless you ask for him not to be paid, using the approved form.[82]

Information to support your claim

For the general information requirements that apply to all benefits, see p1136.

It is important that you provide any information required when you claim. Until you do, you may not count as having made a valid claim (see p1138). Correct any defects as soon as possible or your date of claim may be affected.

HMRC must normally see your child's original birth or adoption certificate when you claim child benefit, unless:

- child benefit has already been paid for the child (to you or someone else); *or*
- the child was born in Great Britain and the birth has been registered. In this case, you must give details from the birth certificate – the system number in England and Wales or the district, year and entry number in Scotland.

Note: if you are unable to register the birth before the child is three months old, you can apply for child benefit and then inform HMRC when the birth has been registered in order to start being paid.

If your child was born abroad, HMRC requires her/his original passport or travel documents used to enter the UK.

If you claim guardian's allowance, you must normally provide the child's original birth certificate, together with the original death certificates of her/his parent(s) and an adoption certificate, if relevant to your claim.

You can send any original documents that you must provide to the Child Benefit Office. You should also be able to take them to your local Jobcentre Plus office, where a certified copy can be made and sent to the Child Benefit Office.[83]

Even if you have provided all that was required when you claimed, you may be asked to provide further information to support your claim (see p1140). You may

Part 5: Other benefits
Chapter 27: Child benefit and guardian's allowance
7. Claims and backdating

also be asked to provide information after you are awarded benefit. If you fail to do so, your benefit could be suspended, or even terminated (see p1162).

The date of your claim

The date of your claim is important as it determines when your entitlement to child benefit and guardian's allowance starts. This is not necessarily the date from which you are paid. For information about when payment starts, see p579.

Your '**date of claim**' is normally the date on which your claim form is received at the Child Benefit Office.[84]

You must make sure your claim is valid. If it is 'defective', you are given a short time to correct the defect (see p1139). If you do, your claim is treated as having been made when you initially claimed.[85]

In some cases, you can claim in advance (see below), and in some cases your claim can be backdated (see below). If you want this to be done, make this clear when you claim or HMRC might not consider it. If you initially claimed the wrong benefit, see below.

Backdating your claim

It is very important to claim in time. A claim for child benefit or guardian's allowance can normally only be backdated for up to three months.[86] If you are unable to register the birth before the child is three months old, you can apply before registering in order to be paid from the date of birth. Payments start once you have informed HMRC that the registration has taken place. There are special rules if you are getting benefit and move between Great Britain and Northern Ireland, or if you have been recognised as a refugee (see p1540). You do not have to show any reason why your claim was late, but you should explain when you want your claim to start from. However, if someone else has an award of child benefit for the same child, see p580.

If you might have been entitled to child benefit or guardian's allowance earlier but did not claim as you were given the wrong information or misled by the DWP or HMRC, you could ask for compensation or complain to the Ombudsman (see Chapter 61).

If you claim the wrong benefit

A claim for guardian's allowance can also be treated as a claim for child benefit for the same child and vice versa.[87] See p1144 for further information.

Claiming in advance

If you do not qualify for child benefit or guardian's allowance when you claim but will do within three months of that date, the decision maker can make an advance award and treat your date of claim as the date on which you first qualify.[88]

8. Getting paid

The general rules on getting paid are covered in Chapter 51. This section explains the specific rules for child benefit and guardian's allowance.

When is your benefit paid?

You are normally paid on a Monday (or on a Tuesday), although HM Revenue and Customs (HMRC) can choose any day of the week as your normal payday. Benefit is usually paid four-weekly for three weeks in arrears and one week in advance.

Child benefit and guardian's allowance are weekly benefits. You must normally meet the entitlement conditions at the start of a week (ie, midnight between Sunday and Monday) to be entitled to benefit for that week.[89] Payment begins from the Monday after the date of your claim (see p578) or, if the date of your claim is a Monday, from that date.[90] See p580 if someone else has been getting child benefit for the child.

You can be paid weekly if:[91]

- you are a lone parent; *or*
- you or your partner get universal credit, income support, income-based jobseeker's allowance, income-related employment and support allowance or pension credit; *or*
- HMRC is satisfied that a four-weekly payment 'is causing hardship'.

Your guardian's allowance is always paid at the same time as your child benefit, if you are entitled to both.[92]

Child benefit and guardian's allowance cannot be paid for periods of less than a week. If your entitlement ends, payment normally continues up to the end of that week.

Your benefit is awarded for an indefinite period unless this would be inappropriate – eg, if a change is expected in the near future.[93]

Note:

- Your benefit can be paid to someone else if this is needed to protect your interests or the interests of the child.[94]
- Even if you have been sanctioned for a benefit offence (see p1239), you must be paid child benefit and guardian's allowance.
- If you have forgotten your PIN, see p1149. If a payment voucher is lost or stolen, see p1150.
- If your payment of child benefit or guardian's allowance is delayed (see p1255), you might be able to get an interim payment (see p580). If you want to complain about how your claim has been dealt with, or claim compensation, see Chapter 61.
- If payment of child benefit or guardian's allowance is suspended, see p1161.

• If you are overpaid benefit, you might have to repay it (see Chapter 53) and, in some circumstances, you may have to pay a penalty (see p1229). If you have been accused of fraud, see Chapter 54.

Interim payments

If your claim for child benefit or guardian's allowance is delayed, you can ask HMRC for an interim payment. HMRC does not make an interim payment if you have an appeal pending. An interim payment can be made if it seems that you may be entitled to benefit and:[95]
• there is a delay in your making a claim; *or*
• you have claimed, but not in the correct way – eg, you have filled in the form incorrectly; *or*
• you have claimed correctly, but it is not possible for the claim to be dealt with immediately; *or*
• you have been awarded benefit, but it cannot be paid immediately, other than by an interim payment.

Note:
• There is no right of appeal against a refusal of an interim payment. See the note on p1155 – but it is HMRC that must change the decision, not the DWP.
• An interim payment can be deducted from any later payment of benefit. If it is more than your actual entitlement, the overpayment can be recovered. You should be notified of this in advance.[96]

If someone else has been getting child benefit for the child

If you claim child benefit for a child and someone else is already getting child benefit for her/him, you are only entitled if your claim has priority over the existing claimant's claim (see p568). If so, your benefit starts from the fourth week after the week in which you claim, unless the existing claimant withdraws her/his claim before then or stops getting child benefit for another reason.

Even if your claim has priority, if child benefit has already been paid to someone else for the same child for a period before you claimed, you can only get child benefit for the period before you claimed if:[97]
• a decision maker (or the First-tier or Upper Tribunal) has decided that the child benefit paid is recoverable because the other person failed to disclose, or misrepresented, a material fact (see p1200) and no appeal against that decision has been made within the time limit. **Note:** if you appeal against a decision refusing your claim under this rule, the tribunal cannot decide that the other person was not entitled for a period before you claimed;[98] *or*
• a decision has been made that the other person was not entitled to child benefit, and s/he has voluntarily repaid the child benefit for that period.

These rules usually prevent you from getting guardian's allowance for a child if someone else gets child benefit for her/him (as you must usually be entitled to child benefit to qualify for guardian's allowance – see p571).

Change of circumstances

You must report any change in your circumstances that you are told to report, as well as any that you might reasonably be expected to know might affect your right to, the amount of, or the payment of your benefit. You should do this as soon as possible, preferably in writing.

You can also report changes of circumstances at gov.uk. See p1160 for further information.

If there has been a relevant change of circumstances, HMRC looks at your claim again and makes a new decision. For when the new decision takes effect, see p1280.

If a child dies

If you were getting child benefit for a child who then dies, your benefit is paid for the next eight weeks, or until the Monday after s/he would have turned 20, if that is sooner. If your partner got child benefit for the child and s/he also dies, you are entitled to benefit for the eight-week period if you were living together when s/he died.[99]

If a child is born and dies in the same week, you can also get child benefit for this eight-week period if you satisfied the conditions of entitlement during that week.[100]

These rules allow you to also get guardian's allowance for a child during a period after s/he dies, provided s/he continues to count as an 'eligible child'. You do not need to satisfy the conditions about living together or providing for her/his needs (see p571).[101]

9. Tax, other benefits and the benefit cap

Tax

Guardian's allowance is not taxable.[102]

If your (or your partner's) 'adjusted net income' in a tax year is over £50,000, you are liable to pay tax on your 'taxable child benefit' for that year. This is called the 'high-income child benefit charge'. For this rule, income is counted on an individual basis – ie, it is *not* the combined income of you and your partner.

Your 'taxable child benefit' includes child benefit for any week that starts in the tax year which is paid to:[103]

- you; *or*
- your partner (but only for weeks when you were partners); *or*

Part 5: Other benefits
Chapter 27: Child benefit and guardian's allowance
9. Tax, other benefits and the benefit cap

- someone who gets child benefit for a child who lives with you, but not with her/him (but only if neither that person nor her/his partner is liable for the charge themselves).

If both you and your partner have income over £50,000, whoever has the highest income is liable for the charge for weeks throughout which you were partners. If you are liable for the charge, you must declare this to HM Revenue and Customs (HMRC) by giving details of your income on a self-assessment tax form within the time limit to do so. See p582 of the 2013/14 edition of this *Handbook* and gov.uk/child-benefit-tax-charge for further details.

Note:[104]

- The high-income child benefit charge is 1 per cent of your taxable child benefit for each complete £100 of income you have over £50,000 in a tax year. If your income is over £60,000, the charge equals the total amount of taxable child benefit.
- Child benefit awarded for the period after a child dies is not included in your taxable child benefit.

Electing not to be paid child benefit

You (or your partner, if s/he is the claimant) can ask HMRC not to pay child benefit, in order to avoid liability for the high-income child benefit charge. HMRC may not agree to this – eg, if deductions are being made from child benefit to recover an overpayment.[105]

If you elect not to be paid (rather than not claiming child benefit, or ending your claim), your entitlement to child benefit continues. This means that you (or someone with whom you live or who cares for your child) may still qualify for national insurance (NI) credits (see p957 and p959). You can also qualify for guardian's allowance if the child is an 'eligible child' (see p571), or other benefits, such as more generous bereavement benefits (see Chapter 25). For these reasons, consider claiming child benefit, even if you do not want it to be paid.

Note: after electing not to receive child benefit, you have up to two years after the end of the tax year to ask for child benefit to be paid for that year, if you realise that your child benefit would have been more than the charge.

Means-tested benefits and tax credits

If you get child benefit or guardian's allowance:

- means-tested benefits and tax credits can be paid in addition to them;
- they are ignored when calculating your entitlement to universal credit (UC), income-related employment and support allowance, pension credit, housing benefit (HB), working tax credit and child tax credit.[106] They are usually ignored when calculating your entitlement to income support and income-based jobseeker's allowance[107] (but see p420 for when child benefit is taken into account).

Non-means-tested benefits

Increases in non-means-tested benefits for dependent children were abolished in 2003, but some people still get them. You cannot get both guardian's allowance and an increase for the same child.[108] If you still get an increase for a child, it is reduced if you also get the higher rate of child benefit (£21.80) for that child (see p1153).[109]

If you get child benefit for a child aged under 12, you (or, in some circumstances, someone who resides with you or cares for the child) can qualify for NI credits (see p957 and p959).

Your entitlement to any other non-means-tested benefit is not affected by getting child benefit or guardian's allowance.

The benefit cap

In some cases, there is a limit on the total amount of specified benefits you can receive (a 'benefit cap'). Child benefit is one of the specified benefits. However, the benefit cap only applies if you are getting UC or HB. You are exempt from the benefit cap if you get guardian's allowance.[110] See p1156 for further information.

Other sources of help

If your income is low, you may be entitled to a council tax reduction (see p836). You may be eligible for free school lunches for your child (see p851).

In Scotland, you may be entitled to Scottish child payment (see Chapter 77).

Children and young people under 19 may qualify for health benefits (see Chapter 31). Young people aged 16 to 19 who are in non-advanced education may qualify for financial help with their studies (see p853).

Notes

1. Who can get child benefit
1 ss141-47 SSCBA 1992; s115 IAA 1999
2 s142(1) SSCBA 1992
3 s142(2) SSCBA 1992; regs 2-7 CB Regs
4 If a child turns 16 on 31 August, HMRC states that s/he is only a qualifying young person up to and including that day but, arguably, this is not correct: compare para 07030 CBTM with reg 4(3) CB Regs.
5 para 07020 CBTM
6 Reg 2(2) CB Regs
7 Reg 3 CB Regs
8 Reg 1(3) CB Regs
9 Reg 3(2)(a)(i) CB Regs
10 Reg 3(3) CB Regs
11 Reg 3(2)(a)(ii) CB Regs

• •

12 'Supervised' study requires the close proximity of a teacher or tutor to enforce discipline, and provide encouragement and help: R(F) 1/93, but see also *Flemming v SSWP* [2002] EWCA Civ 641 (reported as R(G) 2/02) and *SSWP v Deane* [2010] EWCA Civ 699.

13 Reg 1(3) CB Regs

14 Reg 3(2)(ab) CB Regs; s4 Education and Skills Act 2008

15 s4 Education and Skills Act 2008; reg 3 The Duty to Participate in Education or Training (Miscellaneous Provisions) Regulations 2013 No.1205

16 Reg 3(2)(c), (d) and (4) CB Regs

17 Reg 1(3) CB Regs

18 Reg 5 CB Regs

19 Reg 7 CB Regs

20 Reg 7(2)2.1 CB Regs

21 Reg 7(2)1.3 CB Regs

22 Reg 6(2) and (3) CB Regs

23 Reg 6(4) CB Regs

24 s143 SSCBA 1992

25 R(F) 2/81

26 R(F) 2/79

27 s143(2) SSCBA 1992

28 s143(3) SSCBA 1992; reg 9 CB Regs; para 06040 CBTM

29 s143(3)(b) and (c) and (4) SSCBA 1992; reg 10 CB Regs

30 s143(1)(b) SSCBA 1992

31 *RK v HMRC (CHB)* [2015] UKUT 357 (AAC), reported as [2016] AACR 4

32 R(U) 3/66

33 Reg 11(4) CB Regs

34 Reg 11 CB Regs

35 s144(3) and Sch 10 SSCBA 1992

36 s13(1) SSAA 1992 and Sch 10 SSCBA 1992

37 s147(3) SSCBA 1992; R(F) 1/08

38 Sch 2 para 4 SSA 1998

39 Sch 10 para 1 SSCBA 1992

40 Regs 14 and 15 CB Regs

41 CF/1771/2003

42 *R (on the application of Ford) v Board of Inland Revenue* [2005] EWHC 1109 (Admin); see also *R (Chester) v Secretary of State for Social Security* [2001] EWHC Admin 1119

43 Or 'residing with' each other – see *Grove v Insurance Officer*, reported as an appendix to R(F) 4/85

44 s147(4) SSCBA 1992; regs 1(3) and 34 CB Regs

45 R(F) 4/85

46 R(F) 3/81

47 Sch 9 SSCBA 1992; regs 8, 12, 13 and 16 CB Regs

48 But see *KW v HMRC (CB)* [2011] UKUT 489 (AAC)

49 Regs 1(3), 5(2)(c) and 7(3) CB Regs

2. **Who can get guardian's allowance**

50 ss77 and 122(5) SSCBA 1992

51 s122(4) and (5) SSCBA 1992; reg 4A SSB(Dep) Regs

52 Reg 4A(1)(b) and (3) SSB(Dep) Regs

53 s77(2)(a) and (8)(a) SSCBA 1992; regs 3-6 GA(Gen) Regs

54 s77(2)(b) and (c) and (8) SSCBA 1992; reg 7 GA(Gen) Regs

55 s77(2)(b) SSCBA 1992

56 para 12090 CBTM

57 CG/60/1992; R(G) 2/83

58 CG/60/1992; CF/2735/2003

59 Reg 7 GA(Gen) Regs

60 Reg 7 GA(Gen) Regs; para 12050 CBTM

61 s77(8)(c) SSCBA 1992; reg 8 GA(Gen) Regs

62 s77(6)(b) SSCBA 1992

63 Reg 5 SSB(Dep) Regs

64 s77(10) and (11) SSCBA 1992; regs 4 and 6(2) GA(Gen) Regs; R(G) 4/83 (appendix)

65 para 12010 CBTM; and s147(3) SSCBA 1992 only treats a step-parent as a parent for child benefit purposes, but see also R(F) 1/08 which suggests that anyone with parental responsibility is likely to count as a parent.

5. **The amount of benefit**

66 Reg 2(1) CB(R) Regs; Sch 4 Part III para 5 SSCBA 1992

67 Reg 2(1) CB(R) Regs

68 Reg 2(2) CB(R) Regs

6. **Special benefit rules**

69 s147(2) and Sch 9 para 1 SSCBA 1992; regs 16-19 CB Regs

70 Reg 16(1)(b)(iv) and (2) CB Regs

71 R(F) 3/85

72 s147(1) SSCBA 1992

73 Reg 16(1)(b)(i)-(iii) CB Regs

74 Regs 9 and 18(b) CB Regs

75 Reg 17(2)-(5) CB Regs

76 Regs 1(3) and 17(1) CB Regs

77 Reg 16(3) CB Regs

78 Reg 16(4) and (5) CB Regs

7. **Claims and backdating**

79 Reg 5 CB&GA(Admin) Regs; HMRC, *Claim Child Benefit*, undated, available at gov.uk/child-benefit/how-to-claim

80 Reg 5 CB&GA(Admin) Regs

81 s77(9) SSCBA 1992

* *

82 Reg 10 GA(Gen) Regs; para 12080 CBTM
83 Regs 3(2) and 5(5) CB&GA(AA) Regs
84 Reg 5 CB&GA(Admin) Regs
85 Reg 10 CB&GA(Admin) Regs
86 Reg 6 CB&GA(Admin) Regs
87 Reg 11 CB&GA(Admin) Regs
88 Reg 12 CB&GA(Admin) Regs

8. Getting paid
89 s147(2) SSCBA 1992
90 Reg 13 CB&GA(Admin) Regs
91 Regs 18 and 19 CB&GA(Admin) Regs
92 Reg 18(4) CB&GA(Admin) Regs
93 Reg 15 CB&GA(Admin) Regs
94 Reg 33 CB&GA(Admin) Regs
95 Reg 22 CB&GA(Admin) Regs
96 Regs 22(3), 41 and 42 CB&GA(Admin) Regs
97 Sch 10 para 1 SSCBA 1992; s13(2) SSAA 1992; reg 38 CB Regs; CF/2826/2007
98 *CB v HMRC and AE (CHB)* [2016] UKUT 506 (AAC)
99 s145A SSCBA 1992; reg 20 CB Regs
100 s145A(3) SSCBA 1992
101 s145A(4) SSCBA 1992

9. Tax, other benefits and the benefit cap
102 s677 IT(EP)A 2003
103 ss681B, 681D and 681H IT(EP)A 2003
104 ss681C, 681E and 681H IT(EP)A 2003
105 s13A SSAA 1992; see also HMRC, *Elections Not to Receive Child Benefit,* 2012, available at gov.uk/government/publications/elections-not-to-receive-child-benefit
106 **UC** Reg 66 UC Regs
    ESA Sch 8 para 7(2) ESA Regs
    PC Regs 9 and 15(1)(j) SPC Regs
    HB Sch 5 para 65 HB Regs; regs 27 and 29 HB(SPC) Regs
    TC Reg 7 TC(DCI) Regs
107 Sch 9 para 5B IS Regs; Sch 7 para 6B JSA Regs
108 Reg 7(4) SS(OB) Regs
109 Reg 8 SS(OB) Regs
110 **UC** Reg 83(1)(k) UC Regs
    HB Reg 75F(1)(i) HB Regs

Chapter 28

Disability living allowance

This chapter covers:

New claims for disability living allowance (DLA) can only be made for children under 16. Disabled people aged between 16 and pension age can claim personal independence payment (PIP) (see Chapter 35). When a child who gets DLA turns 16, s/he is usually invited to claim PIP (see p602).

If you are aged 16 or over but were under 65 on 8 April 2013 and were already getting DLA, you will be invited to claim PIP (see p602).

Key facts
- Disability living allowance (DLA) is a benefit for disabled people or people with long-term health problems who need help getting around and/or who need supervision or attention.
- You must be under 16 to make a new claim. Note that the rules are different for children living in Scotland (see p587).
- DLA has a care component and a mobility component. You can get either one or both of the components. Each component has different rates.
- DLA is a non-means-tested benefit.
- You can get DLA whether you are in or out of work.
- You do not have to have paid national insurance contributions to get DLA.
- DLA can be paid in addition to other benefits and is disregarded as income for means-tested benefits and tax credits.
- DLA is administered and paid by the DWP.

- If you disagree with a DLA decision, you can apply for a revision or a supersession (see Chapter 56), or appeal against it (see Chapter 57). You must apply for a mandatory reconsideration before you can appeal.

Scotland

Children under 16 who live in Scotland cannot make a new claim for DLA. Instead, they should claim child disability payment (CDP) (see Chapter 75). The rules for who can get CDP and the rates of payment are very similar to those for DLA. Social Security Scotland is responsible for administering and paying CDP. The Scottish government has started transferring children and young people in Scotland who are existing DLA claimants to CDP. It aims to complete this process by spring 2023 (see p1717). See AskCPAG and CPAG's *Welfare Rights Bulletin* for updates.

Children in Scotland who currently get DLA can continue to make renewal claims (see p610), or apply for their DLA award to be revised or superseded, until they are transferred to CDP (see Chapter 75).

---

1. Disability living allowance mobility component

Disability living allowance (DLA) mobility component is for children under 16 who have difficulties when walking. It can be paid at a lower or higher rate.

See p612 for tips on answering the mobility questions on the DLA claim form.

Who can get the mobility component

A child can get DLA mobility component if s/he:[1]
- satisfies the residence conditions (see p1601); *and*
- is not a 'person subject to immigration control', although there are some exceptions (see p1524); *and*
- is under 16 when you first claim (see p601); *and*
- satisfies the 'disability conditions' for either the higher rate (see p588) or the lower rate (see p592); *and*
- unless terminally ill (see p607), has satisfied the disability conditions throughout the three months immediately before the award begins (see p610 if reclaiming) and is likely to continue to satisfy them for the next six months; *and*
- is likely to be able to 'benefit from enhanced facilities for locomotion'.

Part 5: Other benefits
Chapter 28: Disability living allowance
1. Disability living allowance mobility component

To benefit from enhanced facilities for locomotion
To get the DLA mobility component, a child must be able to '**benefit from enhanced facilities for locomotion**': s/he must be able to make outdoor journeys from time to time, even if s/he has to be carried to a car for a ride.[2] It is not essential that s/he is interested in or enjoys going out, provided it would be beneficial for her/him to do so.

Disability conditions for the higher rate mobility component

A child can get the higher rate mobility component if s/he:[3]
- has a disability from a physical cause that means s/he is unable, or virtually unable, to walk (see below); *or*
- is both blind and deaf (see p590); *or*
- is blind or severely visually impaired (see p590); *or*
- was born without feet or is a double amputee (see p591); *or*
- has a 'severe mental impairment', has 'severe behavioural problems' and qualifies for the highest rate of DLA care component (see p591).

'Unable or virtually unable to walk'

A child can get the higher rate if s/he has a disability from a physical cause that means:[4]
- s/he is unable to walk; *or*
- her/his ability to walk outdoors is so limited in terms of the distance, speed, length of time, or the manner in which s/he can make progress on foot without severe discomfort that s/he is virtually unable to walk; *or*
- the exertion required to walk would constitute a danger to her/his life or be likely to lead to a serious deterioration in her/his health.

Personal circumstances, such as the location of the child's home, should not be taken into account. It is not, for instance, relevant if s/he lives a long way from the nearest bus stop,[5] or if s/he cannot use public transport.

Physical disability

A child's inability, or virtual inability, to walk must arise from her/his physical condition.[6] There can be a physical cause, (eg, pain or dizziness) even without a medically diagnosed origin. It does not matter if the original cause was mental, provided a current physical impairment affects her/his walking. If a child's walking is impaired by weakness due to anorexia nervosa, the cause is physical.[7] Myalgic encephalomyelitis (ME), or chronic fatigue syndrome, should be accepted as having a physical origin unless there is evidence that any mobility restrictions are purely psychological.[8] A child's discomfort from chronic diarrhoea might make her/him virtually unable to walk.[9] Inability to make progress on foot because of behavioural problems may qualify if the cause is physical – eg, Down's syndrome or autism are both accepted as physical disorders of development of the brain.[10]

Unable to walk

A child is unable to walk if s/he cannot move her/his body along by alternate, weight-bearing steps of the feet.[11]

Prostheses, aids and medication

A child's ability to walk takes into account any prosthesis or artificial aid s/he uses, or that would be suitable for her/him.[12] S/he may not qualify if s/he is able to walk with crutches. However, if s/he has one leg and no artificial limb suitable to use, s/he is regarded as 'unable to walk', even if s/he can get around on crutches.[13] If s/he has no feet, s/he qualifies automatically (see p591).[14]

Any medication the child normally and reasonably uses is taken into account – eg, it may not be practical to carry a bulky nebuliser.[15] Her/his walking should be assessed as s/he is now, not how s/he might be after any treatment.[16]

Outdoors

The test is how a child copes with the terrain and environment normally encountered outdoors. Take into account any problems s/he has with balance on uneven pavements/roads, or if her/his condition is made worse by wind or rain.[17] Walking indoors is not necessarily an indication of ability to walk outdoors.[18]

Distance

The law does not specify a distance to be used when determining a child's inability to walk. In practice, s/he may be refused benefit if you tick on the claim form that s/he can walk more than 50 metres. However, her/his walking speed, the time it takes to cover the distance and the manner of walking are also relevant, so give details about these on the form. Taking more than a minute to walk 50 metres is slow, so if an older child cannot walk this fast without severe discomfort, say so.[19]

Without severe discomfort

Any walking that a child can do only with severe discomfort should be ignored when considering whether s/he is virtually unable to walk.[20] This is a lesser test than 'severe pain or distress'.[21] If, when walking, s/he feels severe discomfort (eg, pain or breathlessness brought on by walking), make this clear.[22] S/he may be able to walk a distance without severe discomfort, a further distance that causes severe discomfort, and then have to stop altogether. The test is how far s/he can walk before going any further causes severe discomfort. You should state this distance on the claim form, rather than how far s/he can walk before actually having to stop. If s/he can walk further without severe discomfort after a brief rest, this could be taken into account.[23]

If a child is in severe discomfort before s/he starts to walk, even if the pain gets no worse, s/he should count as being virtually unable to walk, provided her/his

Part 5: Other benefits
Chapter 28: Disability living allowance
1. Disability living allowance mobility component

disability affects the physical act of walking.[24] S/he does not count as being virtually unable to walk if something unconnected with walking (eg, a skin condition affected by sunlight) causes the discomfort.[25]

The exertion required to walk

A child can get the higher rate mobility component if the exertion required to walk endangers her/his health. If the deterioration in health is sudden, you must show that s/he would never recover, or recovery would take a significant period of time (eg, 12 months) or would require some form of medical intervention. So, a child with ME who needs a few days' rest after walking would not satisfy this test.[26] The fact that walking may cause a child stress, or lead to a deterioration in mental health, does not count.[27]

Blind and deaf

A child can get the higher rate mobility component if:
- the degree of disablement resulting from her/his loss of vision is 100 per cent; *and*
- the degree of disablement resulting from her/his loss of hearing is 80 per cent on a scale where 100 per cent represents absolute deafness;[28] *and*
- the combined effect of the blindness and deafness means that s/he is unable to walk to any intended or required destination while outdoors without the help of another person.[29]

The regulations do not specify how to assess the degree of disablement, but caselaw suggests that the industrial injury provisions should be used (see p672).[30] So 100 per cent disablement through 'loss of vision' means 'loss of sight to such an extent as to render the claimant unable to perform any work for which eyesight is essential'.[31] This is the definition used when someone is registered as severely sight impaired (blind). However, whether or not a child is registered, or the outcome of visual acuity and visual fields tests, is not conclusive of whether s/he satisfies this condition. All evidence of how a child's sight difficulties might affect her/his ability to carry out a real paid job in practice should be considered.[32]

If a child's level of hearing loss, averaged between both ears at 1, 2 and 3 kHz, is at least 87 decibels, s/he satisfies the 80 per cent disablement test.[33] S/he may have to undertake a hearing test. The test takes into account any hearing aid s/he uses or could reasonably be expected to use.[34]

Blind or severely visually impaired

A child must have been certified blind or severely sight impaired and have combined visual acuity, in both eyes, on the 'Snellen scale', while using appropriate corrective lenses if necessary, of:[35]
- less than 3/60; *or*

• 3/60 or more, but less than 6/60, if s/he has a complete loss of peripheral vision and a central visual field of no more than 10 degrees.

'Appropriate' corrective lenses are ones that s/he can wear without discomfort.[36] The test has to be met by both eyes – an average cannot be used if her/his level of vision in one eye is worse than the other.[37]

The Snellen test is taken indoors. This may be discriminatory.[38] If a child does not qualify according to the Snellen scale but her/his vision is significantly worse outdoors, get specialist advice.

Note: the system of certifying a person as blind or severely sight impaired no longer applies to children under 16 in Scotland. If this affects a child's ability to get the higher rate mobility component under this rule, seek advice.

People without feet

If a child does not have feet or legs (missing from the ankle or above), s/he is automatically treated as being unable to walk,[39] even if s/he can walk with prostheses.

Severe mental impairment and behavioural problems

A child can get the higher rate mobility component if s/he:[40]
• has a 'severe mental impairment' – ie, arrested development, or incomplete physical development, of the brain, which results in severe impairment of intelligence and social functioning; *and*
• displays severe behavioural problems – ie, the child:
    – exhibits extreme disruptive behaviour; *and*
    – regularly requires someone else to intervene and physically restrain her/him to prevent her/him causing injury to her/himself or others or damage to property; *and*
    – is so unpredictable that another person has to be present and watching over her/him whenever s/he is awake;[41] *and*
• qualifies for the highest rate of the DLA care component (see p594).

If a child does not meet all the above conditions, s/he might still get the higher rate mobility component because a disability prevents her/him from walking effectively, so that s/he is virtually unable to walk (see p588).[42]

Arrested or incomplete development

'Arrested or incomplete development' must occur before the brain reaches its final development. This is during the thirties or early forties for most people, so any condition that affects a child should be accepted as occurring before this.[43] As a result of this arrested or incomplete brain development, s/he must also have a severe impairment of intelligence and of social functioning (see p592).[44]

Part 5: Other benefits
Chapter 28: Disability living allowance
1. Disability living allowance mobility component

Severe impairment of intelligence and social functioning

An IQ of 55 or less is generally accepted as a 'severe impairment of intelligence'. However, using a crude measure of intelligence based on IQ alone is not appropriate. Some children may have a higher IQ but be unable to apply it practically.[45] A child's 'useful intelligence' (eg, her/his 'degree of judgement in relation to everyday living', including factors such as sense of danger) should be taken into account.[46] For example, an autistic child with no awareness of danger may have severely impaired intelligence even if her/his IQ is over 55, and language and communication skills assessment may be particularly important in considering a child's social functioning.[47] Whether a child has 'severe impairment of intelligence and social functioning' should, therefore, be treated as a single test and all the evidence considered as a whole.

Physical restraint

Physical restraint may involve as little as a hand on the arm. You do not need to show that any force is used.[48] If the presence of someone who watches over a child is enough to prevent her/him from being disruptive, or a specially adapted environment allows her/him to be safely left alone, s/he may not pass the test. However, the DWP should not focus only on how s/he is outdoors or in a structured safe environment, and must consider her/his need for, and the nature of, intervention in all environments.[49] There is no definition in the law of how often intervention has to be needed before it can be said to be 'regularly' required. The DWP should consider the facts as a whole and decide if the behaviour occurs regularly according to the ordinary meaning of the word. Behaviour does not have to be violent to be classed as 'disruptive'.[50] Involuntary behaviour, such as falls due to seizures, can be classed as 'disruptive'.[51]

Disability condition for the lower rate mobility component

A child can get the lower rate mobility component if s/he can walk but is 'so severely disabled physically or mentally' that s/he cannot get around outdoors 'without guidance or supervision from another person most of the time'.[52] S/he must also satisfy the 'additional requirements' test (see below).

Any ability s/he may have to use familar routes without guidance or supervision should be ignored.[53] Getting the lower rate mobility component is based on the child's need for supervision or guidance, rather than any physical difficulty s/he has walking that may mean s/he can get the higher rate.[54]

The 'additional requirements' test

You must show that a child requires guidance or supervision and also that either:[55]
- s/he requires substantially more guidance or supervision than children of her/his age in 'normal' physical and mental health; *or*
- children of the same age in 'normal' physical and mental health would not require such guidance or supervision.

The fact that all young children require some guidance or supervision outdoors is not the point. If a child needs a substantially greater amount or a different type of guidance or supervision, compared to what is normally needed by children of a similar age, s/he should qualify.[56] For example, a child with a visual impairment or learning disability may need an adult to hold, guide or watch over her/him in situations in which most children of a similar age would only require someone to accompany them. Similarly, a young deaf child may need someone to stay within touching distance, whereas a hearing child would not.[57]

See p611 for tips on how to describe a child's needs on the claim form.

Supervision

'Supervision' can be precautionary. For example, it can be monitoring a child's physical, mental or emotional state in case s/he needs more assistance to continue walking, or monitoring the route ahead for obstacles/dangers or places/situations which might upset her/him. Supervision can also be active, such as encouraging or cajoling a child, or distracting her/him from fears[58] or possibly alarming situations.[59]

Unlike the 'continual supervision' condition for the DLA care component, the child does not need to require supervision to prevent 'substantial danger'.[60] If s/he gets the care component because s/he requires continual supervision, s/he may also get the lower rate mobility component.[61] However, this is not automatic; her/his eligibility must be assessed on the mobility criteria alone.[62]

The supervision does not need to improve the child's walking ability, but should enable her/him to 'take advantage of the faculty of walking'. It is enough that supervision helps, even if it does not remove risks completely or if s/he may not always respond well to the person providing it.[63] If s/he needs to have supervision (eg, to provide help in the event of seizures),[64] even though s/he has no difficulty getting about, s/he can get the lower rate mobility component.[65]

Guidance

'Guidance' can mean physically leading or directing a child, giving oral suggestions or persuasion, helping to avoid obstacles or places that upset her/him, or leading or persuading a child when s/he becomes disorientated or is anxious. Even if a companion only intervenes occasionally, s/he could still be guiding 'most of the time' if a child would otherwise not know when to change direction. If a child has a visual impairment, s/he may need guidance to follow directions, avoid obstacles or cross roads (even if s/he uses a guide dog or cane). If s/he is deaf and her/his main method of communication is sign language, s/he may require guidance in unfamiliar places if s/he is unable to ask for or follow directions. However, an older child may not qualify if s/he can study maps, read street signs or communicate with passers by.[66]

Part 5: Other benefits
Chapter 28: Disability living allowance
2. Disability living allowance care component

Fear and anxiety

A child can get the lower rate mobility component because of a mental as well as a physical disablement. If s/he has an anxiety disorder and needs an escort's help to overcome fear of going outside, s/he is likely to satisfy the 'guidance or supervision' requirement.[67] There is conflicting caselaw, but if no amount of reassurance can persuade her/him to go outside, s/he may not qualify.[68] If s/he can just manage a walk into her/his garden, this could be enough to qualify.[69]

Any fear or anxiety that stops a child going out alone must be a symptom of mental disability in order to count. Fear and anxiety arising from a physical disability, such as a fear of having to cope with incontinence while alone, is not sufficient, although s/he may still have a physical need for supervision.[70] If her/his physical disability causes such fear or anxiety that s/he can be said to be mentally disabled, s/he may qualify.

2. **Disability living allowance care component**

Disability living allowance (DLA) care component is for children under 16 who have attention or supervision needs. It can be paid at a lowest, middle or highest rate.

See p611 for tips on completing the DLA claim form.

Who can get the care component

A child can get the DLA care component if s/he:[71]
- satisfies the residence conditions (see p1601); *and*
- is not a 'person subject to immigration control', although there are some exceptions (see p1524); *and*
- is under 16 when you first claim (see p601); *and*
- is not in residential care (see p913); *and*
- satisfies the disability conditions for the lowest, middle or highest rate of the care component (see below) and, unless s/he is terminally ill, satisfies the 'additional requirements' test (see p595); *and*
- unless terminally ill (see p607), has satisfied the disability conditions throughout the three months immediately before the award begins (see p610 if reclaiming) and is likely to continue to satisfy them for the next six months.

The disability conditions

A child can get the **lowest rate care component** if s/he is so severely disabled, physically or mentally, that s/he requires (see p596) attention from another person for a significant portion of the day (whether during a single period or a number of periods) in connection with her/his bodily functions (see p597 and p599).[72]

A child can get the **middle rate care component** if s/he:
- satisfies one of the daytime disability conditions *or* one of the night-time disability conditions;[73] *or*
- undergoes renal dialysis in certain circumstances (see p607).[74]

A child can get the **highest rate care component** if s/he:
- satisfies one of the daytime disability conditions *and* one of the night-time disability conditions;[75] *or*
- is terminally ill (see p607).[76]

The daytime disability conditions are that a child is so severely disabled, physically or mentally, that s/he requires (see p596):[77]
- frequent attention from another person throughout the day in connection with her/his bodily functions (see p597); *or*
- continual supervision throughout the day in order to avoid substantial danger to her/himself or others (see p600).

The night-time disability conditions are that a child is so severely disabled, physically or mentally, that s/he requires (see p596):[78]
- prolonged or repeated attention from another person at night (see p600) in connection with her/his bodily functions (see p597); *or*
- another person to be awake at night for a prolonged period or at frequent intervals to watch over her/him (see p601) in order to avoid substantial danger to her/himself or others.

The 'additional requirements' test

You must show not only that a child requires attention or supervision, but also that either:[79]
- the child has attention or supervision requirements 'substantially in excess of the normal requirements' of a child of the same age; *or*
- the child has substantial attention or supervision requirements which younger children in 'normal' physical and mental health may also have, but which children of the same age and in 'normal' physical and mental health would not have. If this is due to 'developmental delay', see p596.

This extra test does not apply if you are claiming DLA care component for a child who is terminally ill (see p607).[80]

The fact that all young children require assistance throughout the day is not the point. If a child needs substantially more, or a diferent type of, assistance, compared to that normally required by a child of the same age, s/he should qualify.[81] See p611 for tips on how to describe a child's needs on the claim form.

Part 5: Other benefits
Chapter 28: Disability living allowance
2. Disability living allowance care component

'So severely disabled physically or mentally'

To get the care component, a child must be 'so severely disabled physically or mentally' that s/he needs attention or supervision. S/he does not need to have a specific medical condition. What is important is that s/he is so disabled that s/he has care needs.[82] However, medical evidence can still be important to establish that s/he is disabled and what her/his care needs are.[83]

Problems sometimes arise if, for example, a child has behavioural problems or a developmental delay that have not been attributed to a disability. The test is whether a child has the physical or mental power to control the behaviour.[84]

Attention and supervision

'Requires'

You must show that a child 'requires' attention or supervision from another person. It must be 'reasonably required' rather than 'medically required'.[85] For example, if an incontinent child needs help changing bedding, this help should count as 'reasonably required', even if not actually required to protect her/his skin. All younger children may be incontinent from time to time, so the attention a child requires must be substantially more than, or different from, the attention normally needed by children of the same age (see p595).

Reasonably requires attention

Attention must be 'reasonably required to enable' a child 'as far as reasonably possible to live a normal life'. Having a social life, recreation and cultural activities are part of normal life. If a child is blind, it is reasonable for you to read to her/him, describe television pictures, or guide her/him during social outings. Similarly, if a child has learning disabilities, it is reasonable to help her/him to travel to, or take part in, social and recreational pursuits. A child's age and interests should be taken into account when deciding what is reasonable.[86]

Reasonably requires supervision

The requirement for supervision need only be reasonable. Most risks can be avoided by staying in a chair all day, but that may be totally unreasonable.[87] A child cannot be expected to avoid every risk of harm (eg, any situation in which s/he might fall) in order to avoid the need for her/him to have supervision.[88]

When considering a child's need for continual supervision (see p600), you can argue that the fact that supervision is provided shows it is needed. Bear in mind that the supervision must be substantially more than, or different from, the supervision a child the same age might normally require (see p595).

Refusing medical treatment

Refusing medical treatment for a child may affect whether or not s/he can get the care component. If treatment offered by her/his doctor would remove the need for help, the attention or supervision a child gets may not be reasonably required. However, it may not be 'reasonably appropriate' for you to agree to the treatment – eg, because of the risks or side effects.[89] Attention or supervision should be accepted as reasonable if you refuse invasive surgery for a child.[90]

Attention

The attention a child requires must be in connection with 'bodily functions' – ie, the normal action of any organ of the body, or a number of organs acting together.

The attention is in connection with bodily functions if it is a substitute way of providing what the function would, were it not impaired.[91] For example, guiding a visually impaired child so that s/he is able to walk outside should be treated as attention with the bodily function of 'seeing' rather than 'walking'. A guide assists with 'seeing' by acting 'as the eyes'. Similarly, help to push a child who uses a wheelchair should be treated as attention.[92]

'Attention' is 'a service of a close and intimate nature... involving personal contact carried out in the presence of the disabled person'.[93] So helping a child to drink counts; carrying the drinks to where s/he is sitting does not.[94] Although attention must usually involve personal contact, it need not be *physical* contact. Contact established by spoken word may count if, for example, a child is blind.[95] Thus, reading, describing or giving verbal instructions can be attention.

Similarly, if a child needs to be cajoled or stimulated to do routine tasks, s/he may require attention in the form of active stimulation.[96] Spoken reassurance can count if it must be given in the physical presence of a child. Bear in mind that the attention must be substantially more than, or different from, the attention a child the same age might normally require (see p595).

Attention or supervision?

'Attention' involves a service of an 'active nature'.[97] 'Supervision' is passive and 'may be precautionary or anticipatory, yet never result in intervention'.[98] Where supervision does lead to intervention, it becomes attention, so the two categories can overlap. If a child needs to be supervised because s/he is likely to fall and injure her/himself, s/he receives attention when a carer gives her/him a steadying hand or warns of an obstacle.[99] If attention is frequent, a child can get the middle rate care component, even if the supervision is not 'continual' throughout the day. Sometimes an act can be both supervision and attention. It is, therefore, important to emphasise the full extent of a child's needs without trying to fit them neatly into either category at the expense of leaving things out.

Communication

Communication involves several bodily functions, including functions of the brain (eg, language processing or comprehension) or senses (eg, hearing). You need to identify which bodily function is impaired and what attention is needed from another person in connection with that function.[100] If a child is profoundly

Part 5: Other benefits
Chapter 28: Disability living allowance
2. Disability living allowance care component

deaf, s/he may need an interpreter,[101] or extra effort may be required to initiate a two-way conversation.[102]

Explaining written information to a child with poor literacy skills as a result of deafness[103] or a learning disability may also qualify.[104]

Domestic duties

Although attention must normally be given in a child's presence, a period of attention can include incidental activities that could be done without her/him. If a carer strips a soiled bed at night, the extra tasks of wringing out the sheets or hanging them up to dry could count as attention if done on the spot, as would cleaning a soiled carpet in the event of incontinence.[105] Taking the washing away or doing the cleaning at a different time does not qualify as attention.

Domestic tasks performed by a carer outside a child's presence do not normally count as attention. There is conflicting caselaw on whether helping an older child do domestic tasks that children of the same age might normally do for themselves is attention that is reasonably required.[106] Helping a child who has a visual impairment to tidy up around the house is assistance with the bodily function of 'seeing' and can count as attention.[107] Similarly, helping a child with a learning disability to go shopping for clothes may include attention to help her/him communicate her/his requirements. Argue that if an older child can learn to tidy up at home or shop for her/himself, this is part of what constitutes a 'normal life' (see the definition of 'requires' on p596).[108]

Childcare

If an older child is a parent, help to enable her/him to look after her/his children can also count as attention.[109] For example, lifting or holding a baby for feeding is a sufficiently intimate service.[110] It will help if you can identify the bodily function in connection with which the child needs attention. Similarly, assistance to take part in outdoor activities with her/his children allows a young parent to lead a normal social life.[111] However, while help provided to a disabled young parent may count as attention, help given directly to her/his child does not.[112]

Special diets

Attention only counts if it needs to be given in a child's physical presence, so it is often difficult to include help with food preparation. Arguably, this type of help may count if it is part of a broader sequence of care tasks. For example, the various parts of the process of regulating a younger diabetic child's blood sugar levels, some of which require personal contact and some not, should all be treated as attention because they are integral elements of an overall regime.[113] A child with a learning disability or an eating disorder might need similar help to eat properly.

Night and day

A child who needs help using the toilet at 3am, when most people are asleep, clearly needs that help at night. Depending on the age of a child and the amount and type of help required, this may be help that children of the same age do not normally need. Problems showing that help is needed at night can arise when a child needs supervision or attention in the late evening or early morning.

'**Night**' is 'that period of inactivity' which begins when 'the household... closes down for the night'.[114] 'Night' is normally assumed to be the period beginning at around 11pm and ending around 7am.[115] The pattern of activities of each household needs to be taken into account. If a carer stays up late to help a child but would otherwise go to bed earlier, that should count as night care.[116] Similarly, if a carer gets up early in the morning to help her/him rather than rise later with the rest of the household, that should count as night care.[117] The definition of 'night' for a child is the same as for an adult, so that help given to a child in the evening before the adults have gone to bed counts only towards satisfying the day condition even if the child is in bed.[118]

'Attention... for a significant portion of the day'

If a child needs attention for a 'significant portion of the day', s/he can get the lowest rate care component.[119] This can be attention for either one period or a number of periods – eg, s/he could need help with activities connected with getting up at the beginning of the day and with activities connected with going to bed at the end of the day, but otherwise not need extra help. Help at night does not count for the lowest rate.[120]

'A significant portion of the day' is often taken to mean an hour or thereabouts.[121] However, if a child's carer spends less time than that in total but has to give help for a number of short periods, that might qualify.[122]

If a carer has little time available or the help s/he gives is in spells of particularly concentrated activity, less than an hour's help may be enough. Factors like the amount, importance or effect of the attention may be taken into account.[123]

Frequent attention throughout the day

To satisfy the day attention condition, you must show that a child needs frequent attention throughout the day.[124] Frequency refers to the number and pattern of times attention is needed over a period of time, and should be considered as a whole.[125] A child may still qualify even if the times when attention is needed are not spread evenly throughout the day.[126] The aggregate amount of time taken up is not relevant. So it is possible for a child to need help frequently for a short period each time, and so get the middle rate care component, even if the total amount of time may not be regarded as a 'significant portion of the day', and so s/he might not get the lowest rate.[127]

If a child only needs help at the beginning and end of the day, this is unlikely to be accepted as frequent. Help with toileting (eg, to reach the toilet, use a commode or deal with zips) or help to walk inside the house are both examples of activities that most children usually engage in frequently. Most children who satisfy this condition do so by virtue of a range of different types of care needs.

Part 5: Other benefits
Chapter 28: Disability living allowance
2. Disability living allowance care component

Prolonged or repeated attention at night

The attention a child needs during the night must be either prolonged or repeated.[128] There is no clear definition of 'prolonged'. An assumption that 20 minutes is prolonged has been accepted as a reasonable starting point, but shorter periods should also be considered.[129] 'Repeated' simply means twice or more.[130] There is no requirement that attention should be needed 'most of the time' – eg, on more than half the nights in a week. A broad overall judgement of a child's needs should be made.[131]

Sleeping is a 'bodily function', so soothing a child back to sleep is attention.[132] The fact that difficulty sleeping or being soothed back to sleep may not be a direct result of the child's disability does not matter. It is the attention the child reasonably requires that must be considered. Attention may also be needed with communication or other bodily functions to help a child get back to sleep.[133]

Continual supervision

A child satisfies the daytime supervision condition if s/he requires another person to provide 'continual supervision' throughout the day to avoid the risk of substantial danger to the child or to others.[134] Supervision can be precautionary and anticipatory. It does not necessarily involve direct intervention. The supervision test has four aspects.[135]

- **There must be a substantial danger to a child or someone else as a result of her/his medical condition.** What is a 'substantial danger' must be decided on the facts of each case. For example, if a child falls and loses consciousness (eg, due to seizures), s/he would not be able to do anything to save her/himself from injury and so this is more likely to be a 'substantial danger' than if other children fall but only sustain minor bruises.

- **The substantial danger must be one against which it is reasonable to guard.** The test is not whether harm is more likely than not to occur, but whether there is a real possibility that cannot be ignored of harm occurring.[136] This involves weighing the remoteness of the risk and the seriousness of the consequences should it arise. For example, the consequences of allowing a child to run out onto the road could be dire, even though such an incident may be isolated.[137] So, it can be argued that the child reasonably requires continual supervision.[138] In assessing the likelihood of danger, the DWP must look at what has happened in the past as well as what may happen.[139]

- **There must be a need for the supervision.** What counts is the level of supervision a child 'reasonably requires' (see p596). If s/he has mental health problems and is at risk of harming her/himself, it would be wrong to suggest that no amount of supervision would prevent a determined child from doing this and supervision is, therefore, not required. The correct approach is to decide whether supervision would result in 'a real reduction in the risk of harm' to her/him.[140]

• **The supervision must be continual.** This is less than 'continuous', but supervision which is required only occasionally or spasmodically is insufficient.[141] However, the fact that, for example, a child may need less supervision in a safe structured environment, such as school, does not mean that continual supervision is not required.[142] If it is unavoidable that a child is left alone for a period, s/he can still qualify if you can show that s/he is at risk during this time. A child who is liable to seizures without warning may need continual supervision, although attention for the period between the seizures is not required.[143] Even if s/he has warning of seizures and can prevent her/himself from falling, s/he may require continual supervision if s/he suffers from prolonged periods of confusion, or needs monitoring to make sure s/he comes out of the seizure safely.[144]

Bear in mind that the supervision a child requires must be substantially more than, or different from, the supervision normally needed by children of the same age (see p595).

Watching over

A child satisfies the night-time supervision condition if s/he needs someone to be awake to watch over her/him at night to avoid the risk of substantial danger to her/him or others.[145] The person watching over must be awake for a 'prolonged period' or 'at frequent intervals'. A 'prolonged period' may mean 20 minutes or more.[146] 'At frequent intervals' is more than twice. The frequent intervals need not be spread throughout the night, but can be concentrated in one part of it.[147]

3. **The rules about your age**

New claims for disability living allowance (DLA) can only be made for children under 16. **Note:** children in Scotland making a new claim must claim child disability payment rather than DLA (see p587).

The higher rate mobility component can be paid from age three onwards and the lower rate mobility component from age five.[148] The three months before the child reaches this age can form the qualifying period (see p587), enabling payment to be made from her/his birthday.

There is no lower age limit for DLA care component. However, a baby must still meet the qualifying conditions for three months before DLA becomes payable, unless s/he is terminally ill.[149]

See p602 for how the introduction of personal independence payment (PIP) affects a child's DLA when s/he turns 16.

Part 5: Other benefits
Chapter 28: Disability living allowance
3. The rules about your age

Transferring from disability living allowance to personal independence payment

PIP (see Chapter 35) has replaced DLA for working-age people.

Note: if you get DLA and live in Scotland, you may not be transferred to PIP as part of this process, unless your award is coming to an end or you report a relevant change in your circumstances (see p1670).[150] In Scotland, adult disability payment (ADP) is being introduced to replace PIP for working-age people. From August 2022, people in Scotland who are working age and who get DLA (or PIP – see Chapter 35) will begin to have their claims transferred to ADP. See Chapter 73 for details of ADP and the transfer process.

Anyone who is 16 or over, was under 65 on 8 April 2013 and still gets DLA will be invited to claim PIP at some point (see p603 for what happens when a child who gets DLA reaches age 16). This process is expected to be completed by 2025. You do not need to do anything until you are notified in writing by the DWP. You will also be invited to claim PIP if your DLA award expires or you report a relevant change in your circumstances (unless the change is that you are leaving Great Britain).[151] Always check letters about your DLA carefully to see whether you have been told to claim PIP.

If you are over pension age when you are told to claim, you are assessed for PIP as if you were under pension age and so you will have access to all the components and rates of PIP.[152] If you are not awarded any rate of PIP, your claim should be treated as a claim for attendance allowance (AA – see Chapter 24).[153]

If you are 16 or over (and were under 65 on 8 April 2013), you can choose to claim PIP, even if you have not been sent a letter telling you to do so.[154]

Should you claim personal independence payment?

1. If you have received a letter saying that you must claim PIP, you should do so straight away or you risk your DLA award ending (see p604).

2. If you have *not* been told to claim PIP, get specialist advice before claiming PIP, to help you decide whether it is a good idea. This is because the entitlement conditions are completely different and you may not qualify for PIP at all. If you claim PIP, your DLA award ends. Once you have claimed PIP, usually you cannot change your mind.[155]

3. If you already get the higher rate mobility component and highest rate care component of DLA and have not been told to claim PIP, the DWP will advise you not to proceed with a claim for PIP unless your condition has improved.[156]

Note: if you get DLA and you turned 65 on or before 8 April 2013, you can continue to receive DLA for as long as you meet the qualifying conditions.[157] See p605 for how you can make a renewal claim for DLA or seek a different rate.

Transferring to personal independence payment on reaching age 16

If you are claiming DLA for a child, s/he will normally be invited to claim PIP when s/he reaches 16 and her/his DLA will end.[158] The DWP will normally write to explain this to you when the child is 15 years and seven months old. It will send a further letter when the child is 15 years and 10 months old, and will write again when the child is 16 to invite her/him to claim PIP. If a child gets DLA while a hospital inpatient, s/he is exempt from the transfer to PIP while in hospital. This exemption applies even if you report a relevant change in her/his circumstances (eg, her/his care needs have changed) while s/he is in hospital.[159]

If your child is about to turn 16 and her/his award of DLA for either component is for a fixed term that is due to end on the day before her/his 16th birthday or within the following six months, the DWP will extend the award until the day before s/he turns 17 or, if earlier, the day her/his DLA ends under the rules on transferring to PIP.[160] These extensions are to give her/him time to claim PIP and have a decision made on entitlement.

If your child gets DLA under the 'special rules' on the basis of terminal illness (see p607), s/he will only be invited to claim PIP when her/his current award expires.[161]

Always check letters about your DLA carefully to see whether you have been asked to claim PIP.

Note: if you are claiming DLA for a child who lives in Scotland and who turned 16 on or after 1 September 2020, s/he will not be invited to claim PIP until s/he is 18, and if the award of DLA is for a fixed term, it will not expire until s/he is aged 18 years and six months in order to give you time to make the claim for PIP.[162] This process for a young person living in Scotland is now also likely to be affected by the introduction of ADP in Scotland (see Chapter 73). You can still choose to claim PIP for a child who has turned 16 if you think s/he may be better off by doing so (but note that, if you withdraw the claim for PIP, her/his DLA award will still end). It is understood that you can also report a relevant change of circumstances for a child in Scotland who has turned 16, and her/his DLA award can be superseded rather than requiring to the child to claim PIP. Get advice before either choosing to claim PIP or requesting a supersession of a DLA award.

Note also: these rules will also apply if the child was getting DLA and living in England and Wales when s/he turned 16 on or after 1 September 2020 and was invited to claim PIP, but subsequently moves to live in Scotland. In this situation only, if s/he claimed PIP after being invited, the claim will continue to be treated as having been made even though s/he now lives in Scotland. However, unless that claim has actually been decided, you can withdraw the claim without her/him losing the DLA, if you wish.

Claims for personal independence payment

If you are sent a written invitation to claim PIP, it must state that you have 28 days to make a claim and tell you how to do so. The time limit can be extended if the

Part 5: Other benefits
Chapter 28: Disability living allowance
3. The rules about your age

DWP thinks it reasonable to do so.[163] The letter must also tell you that, if you do not claim PIP, your DLA award will end and when this will happen.[164]

You should claim PIP, following the instructions in the letter, as soon as possible, because your DLA award will end whether you claim PIP or not.[165] If you do not claim PIP within the time allowed, your DLA award is suspended from your next payment day.[166] You must be sent a letter explaining that your award has been suspended and will be terminated if you do not claim PIP within 28 days of the date on which it was suspended.[167] If you do so, your award of DLA is reinstated. If you still do not claim PIP, your DLA award ends from the date it was suspended.[168] You should make a new claim for PIP if you satisfy the rules of entitlement (see p723).

If you get DLA and have been invited to claim PIP or are in the process of claiming PIP and notify the DWP of a change of circumstances that may affect your entitlement to DLA, this is treated as a change of circumstances affecting your entitlement to PIP.[169]

See p747 for details of the assessment process once you claim PIP.

If you do not provide information needed to assess your entitlement to PIP (see p747) and do not have a good reason (see p751), your PIP claim will be refused. If this happens, your DLA award ends 14 days after the first DLA payday following the decision refusing your PIP claim.[170] If you win an appeal against the decision that you do not have good reason, your DLA award should be reinstated until a decision on your PIP claim is made.[171] If you are subsequently awarded PIP, it starts from the day after your DLA award ends (see below).[172]

These rules apply if you choose to claim PIP as well as if you are notified that your DLA will stop and you are invited to claim PIP.[173]

The qualifying conditions for PIP have some similarities to those for DLA, but are also significantly different. See Chapter 35 for details. It is possible that a young person claiming PIP on turning 16 will be awarded a different rate of PIP from the rate of DLA s/he previously received. If this applies to you, get advice and consider seeking a revision and then appealing. Although the qualifying conditions are different, the evidence used to make the previous DLA award may address the same needs for help with daily living and mobility as are relevant to the PIP conditions. The DWP (and the First-tier Tribunal on appeal) should consider this evidence where relevant.[174]

If you have a car through the Motability scheme (see p621) and are not awarded the enhanced rate mobility component of PIP when you transfer from DLA, you will no longer be able to continue in the Motability scheme. Contact Motability for details of support and transitional payments available.

When your disability living allowance ends

If you claim PIP, your DLA award continues until a decision is made on your PIP claim. Your DLA award ends:[175]

- if you are terminally ill (see p607) and your payment of PIP is higher than your payment of DLA was, on either the Tuesday after your PIP claim is decided or the day before your next normal DLA payday, whichever is earlier; *or*
- in any other case, four weeks after the next DLA payday after the decision is made on your PIP claim (whether or not you are awarded PIP).

Your entitlement to PIP starts from the day after your DLA award ends. The rules above also apply if your claim for DLA is refused and you then claim PIP, but the refusal is then overturned following a revision or appeal before your PIP claim is decided.[176] If your PIP claim is decided before the decision on your DLA refusal is changed, any DLA award that is later made to you ends on:[177]

- the day before your PIP award started; *or*
- four weeks after the next DLA payday following the decision to refuse you PIP.

If you withdraw your claim, or notify the DWP that you do not wish to claim PIP when invited to do so, your DLA award ends 14 days after the first DLA payday following the date you notified the DWP.[178]

You must be notified in writing of the date your DLA award ends and the start date of any PIP award.[179]

If you get disability living allowance and turned 65 on or before 8 April 2013

If you get DLA and turned 65 on or before 8 April 2013, you can continue to receive it and are unaffected by the introduction of PIP.

You can make a renewal claim if your DLA award expires, provided you reclaim within a year of the previous award ending.[180] If you are awarded the same rate, you can be paid without having to serve the standard qualifying period again.

If your condition has changed since you turned 65 so that you need more assistance, your award can be increased to the middle or highest rate of the care component. This applies regardless of which component or rate you previously had. You must show that you have met the qualifying conditions for the increased rate for six months (not three months) before it can be awarded, unless you had already completed a three-month qualifying period before you turned 65.[181] This is because the rules about qualifying periods for people in receipt of DLA care component at the age of 65 or over are the same as for AA.[182] This applies both when a renewal claim is made and when an award is revised or superseded.

If you have an existing award of DLA that was made before you turned 65 (ie, not an award made on a renewal claim, or on a revision or supersession decision, after you turned 65), you can be awarded any rate of either component if you request a revision or supersession of your award after you are 65, provided you show that you have satisfied the disability conditions for the new rate or component since before you turned 65.[183] Otherwise, you cannot qualify for

Part 5: Other benefits
Chapter 28: Disability living allowance
4. People included in the claim

either rate of the mobility component or the lowest rate of the care component for the first time after you turned 65.

If your award was made after you turned 65 (either on a renewal claim or on a revision or supersession of a decision) and you have an award of the mobility component lower rate, it cannot be increased to the higher rate after you have turned 65. If you have an award of either rate of the mobility component, you can be awarded the middle or highest rate of the care component on a renewal claim or a revision or supersession, but not the lowest rate.[184]

Examples

Tom turned 65 in 2010, and is now 76. Tom has multiple sclerosis, and has received the DLA care component middle rate and mobility component higher rate since he was 64. Tom's award expires when he turns 77. Because he was 65 before 8 April 2013, Tom can make a renewal claim for DLA. His mobility has not changed, but the DWP accepts that he now needs sufficient care at night to qualify for the highest rate care component. An indefinite award of the care component highest rate and the mobility component higher rate is made on the renewal claim. The DWP accepts that Tom's night-time needs have existed for six months, and so the new rate is paid from the date his renewal award starts.

Shirley turned 65 on 8 March 2013, and is now 74. Shirley has an indefinite award of the care component middle rate, made in 2001, and her condition has deteriorated steadily since then. For several years she has been able to walk only very short distances, and only with severe discomfort. She requests a supersession. The DWP accepts that Shirley has been virtually unable to walk since before she turned 65. Her award is superseded to include the mobility component higher rate from the date of her supersession request.

If it has been over a year since your last DLA award ended, you must claim AA (see Chapter 24) instead of DLA. If you make a renewal claim for DLA in these circumstances, it will be treated as a claim for AA.

Differences in the rules for adults

There are some important differences between the rules for DLA for adults and those for children that are described in this chapter. See Chapter 27 of the 2015/16 edition of this *Handbook* for full details of the rules for adults.

4. **People included in the claim**

You claim disability living allowance for a child under 16.

5. The amount of benefit

Disability living allowance (DLA) mobility component is paid at one of two weekly rates:[185]
- the lower rate is £24.45;
- the higher rate is £64.50.

DLA care component is paid at one of three weekly rates:[186]
- the lowest rate is £24.45;
- the middle rate is £61.85;
- the highest rate is £92.40.

6. Special benefit rules

Special rules may apply to children:
- on renal dialysis (see below);
- who are terminally ill (see below);
- subject to immigration control (see Chapter 68);
- who have come from or are going abroad (see Chapters 69, 70 and 71);
- in hospital or a hospice or living in a care home or similar accommodation, or in a young offenders' institution or other form of detention (see Chapter 42).

Renal dialysis

If a child has renal dialysis on a kidney machine, special rules may allow her/him to get the middle rate of disability living allowance (DLA) care component.[187] The rules are the same as for attendance allowance (AA) (see p520).

Terminal illness

If a child is terminally ill, s/he is automatically treated as satisfying the conditions for the highest rate of the DLA care component and does not need to satisfy the three-month qualifying period.[188] Claims for children who are terminally ill are referred to as 'claims under the special rules' (see p609). The rules are the same as for AA (see p520).[189]

S/he does not automatically get DLA mobility component. S/he must satisfy the usual disability conditions (except the three-month qualifying period) and be likely to continue to satisfy them for the next six months until the anticipated date of death.[190]

Part 5: Other benefits
Chapter 28: Disability living allowance
7. Claims and backdating

7. **Claims and backdating**

The general rules about claims and backdating are covered in Chapter 50. This section explains the specific rules that apply to disability living allowance (DLA).

Making a claim

A claim for DLA must be in writing. You should do this by completing the approved claim form (DLA1A Child). It is best to request a form by telephone from the DLA helpline. The DWP may complete a checklist to assess a child's 'potential benefit entitlement'. This is not part of the claim process and you should always be sent a claim form. It is best to send the completed form to the address on it (Disability Benefit Centre 4, Post Handling Site B, Wolverhampton WV99 1BY). You can also take or send it to any other DWP office, and may be able to take or send it to an 'alternative office' (see p1134).

Forms

Form DLA1A Child is available from the DLA helpline on 0800 121 4600, textphone: 0800 121 4523 (Relay UK and BSL video services available).

The form should be date stamped. You have six weeks from the date of your request to return it. If you return it within this time, the date you requested it will be treated as your date of claim.[191] Keep a record of the date you asked for it.

Claim forms are also available from Citizens Advice or other advice agencies. A version of the form that can be filled in online and then printed is available at gov.uk. These forms are not date stamped. Send in the completed form as soon as possible. Your date of claim is the date your completed form is received by the DWP (see p609 for details).

Note: the success of a DLA claim can often depend on how well you have completed the form. Include all the relevant information and use extra pages if necessary. Keep a copy of the form in case queries arise. For tips on completing the form, see p611.

You must provide any information or evidence required. In certain circumstances, the DWP may accept a written application which is not on the approved form (see p1139).[192] You can amend or withdraw the claim before a decision is made (see p1135).

Claims for terminally ill children are made in a different way (see p609).

Who should claim

A claim for a child under 16 is made by an appointee (see p1135). This is usually the child's parent. We use 'you' throughout this chapter to refer to the appointee who is claiming on behalf of a child.

Before a child reaches 16, the DWP should ask whether s/he will continue to need an appointee or will be able to handle her/his own benefits affairs.[193] See p602 for how the introduction of personal independence payment (PIP) affects DLA for a child when s/he turns 16.

Claiming for a child who is terminally ill

If you are claiming on the basis of a child's terminal illness (see p607), you must tick the box on the claim form to say you are claiming under the 'special rules'.[194] In addition to the claim form you must provide Form DS1500, completed by the child's GP, consultant or specialist nurse, detailing her/his medical condition. However, you do not need to fill in the parts of the claim form relating to her/his need for personal care. If you also wish to claim the mobility component for the child, you must answer all the relevant questions on the claim form. If the DWP decides that the child does not meet the special rules, you can claim in the normal way or request a mandatory reconsideration of the decision.

Information to support your claim

For the general information requirements that apply to all benefits, see p1136.

It is important that you provide any information required when you claim. Until you do, you may not count as having made a valid claim (see p1138). Correct any defects as soon as possible or your date of claim may be affected. **Note:** for DLA, there is no requirement to provide a national insurance number for a child under 16.

For suggestions about evidence you might want to provide when completing the claim form, see p611.

Even if you have provided all that was required when you claimed, you may be asked to provide further information to support the claim (see p1140). You may be asked to provide information after DLA is awarded, and if you fail to do so, DLA could be suspended or even terminated (see p1162).

The date of your claim

The date of your child's claim is important as it determines when her/his entitlement to DLA starts. This is not necessarily the date from when DLA is paid. For information about when payment of DLA starts, see p616.

The date of claim is not necessarily the date it is received by the DWP. The **'date of claim'** is the date your request for a claim pack is received by the DWP or an 'alternative office' (see p1134), provided you return the properly completed form within six weeks of the date of your request.[195]

If the DWP has issued a form without date stamping it, write and explain when and where it was issued and ask to be paid from that date or six weeks before you sent it in.[196] The DWP can extend the six-week deadline if it considers that it is reasonable, so if you return the form late, explain why.[197] **Note:** if you are delayed

Part 5: Other benefits
Chapter 28: Disability living allowance
7. Claims and backdating

in returning the form for a reason relating to coronavirus (eg, you have had to self-isolate), say this on the form and ask for the deadline to be extended.

If you are using a downloaded claim form or one issued by an advice agency, your date of claim is the date the DWP receives your completed form.

You must make sure the claim is valid. If it is 'defective', you are given a short time to correct the defects (see p1139). If you do, the claim is treated as having been made when you initially claimed.[198]

In some cases, a claim can be made in advance (see below). If you want to do this, make this clear when you claim or the DWP might not consider it. If a claim was made for attendance allowance (AA) or PIP instead of DLA, see below.

Backdating your claim

It is very important to claim in time. A claim for DLA *cannot* be backdated.[199]

If a child might have qualified for benefit earlier but you did not claim because you were given the wrong information or were misled by the DWP, you could ask for a compensation payment (see p1403) or complain to the Ombudsman (see p1408).

If you claim the wrong benefit

If you claim AA or PIP by mistake for a child under 16 instead of DLA, the claim for AA or PIP can be treated as a claim for DLA, and vice versa (see p1144).[200]

Claiming in advance

A claim for DLA can be made before a child has satisfied the three-month qualifying period[201] or any other qualifying condition. Provided you claim no more than three months before s/he would qualify for DLA, a decision can be made on the claim in advance of her/his date of entitlement. The date of the claim is the date on which the child qualifies.

Renewal claims

DLA can be awarded for fixed periods (see p617). Renewal claims can be invited up to six months before an old award expires. It is important that you send back your completed renewal claim form well before the award expires, as no backdating is possible.

The DWP normally treats a renewal claim as a new claim beginning on the day after an award ends.[202] However, the information you give in the renewal claim may be used to revise or supersede the child's existing award, in which case her/his entitlement may be changed earlier.[203]

On a renewal claim, a child does not have to serve the three-month qualifying period again, provided s/he meets all the other qualifying conditions for the rate previously received. The last three months of the previous award is treated as the qualifying period.[204] If s/he qualifies for a different rate when you reclaim, s/he *does* have to show s/he has met the qualifying conditions for three months.

When a child approaches age 16, s/he will normally be required to claim PIP, rather than make a renewal claim for DLA. See p603 for details.

See p602 for how the introduction of PIP affects adults who get DLA (including those who turned 65 after 8 April 2013) and p605 for how adults who receive DLA and turned 65 on or before 8 April 2013 can make a renewal claim for DLA.

Note: although a child under 16 who lives in Scotland cannot make a new claim for DLA, if s/he has a fixed-term award of either component that is coming to an end, s/he can make a renewal claim if invited to do so in order to continue to receive DLA.[205]

Completing the claim form

The DLA claim form is long and asks about different aspects of a child's mobility problems and supervision and attention needs. If you find it difficult to complete the form, the DWP can help you by telephone or, in some circumstances, can send a visiting officer to your home. Most advice agencies can also help. The following advice should help you fill in the form as fully as possible.

- **Give as much detail as you can.** Fill in all the relevant pages. If the same difficulties apply on more than one page, repeat the information or refer back to earlier in the form. The same help may count towards both the care component and the mobility component – eg, if a child needs attention to deal safely with seizures, this may help satisfy the conditions for the care component and may also mean s/he needs guidance and supervision when walking outdoors.[206] If you need extra space to explain the child's situation, use a separate piece of paper. Do not worry if a lot of the questions do not apply to the child. The information you give in just one section could be enough for her/him to get DLA. There is space to include details of people who know about her/his difficulties – include carers and support workers, as well as medical professionals. There is also a statement to be completed by someone who knows the child. If her/his doctor or hospital fills this in, they should not charge for this.[207] If you do not have anyone who can complete it, leave it blank.

- **Aids and adaptions.** The form asks about aids and adaptations the child uses or has been assessed for. If the DWP thinks that a child can use a particular aid or adaptation, it may decide the child does not need attention or supervision. Therefore, try to explain how useful any equipment actually is, the help the child needs to use it and whether s/he still needs extra help from another person in spite of the equipment. If, for instance, you have had a bath rail fitted, but s/he still finds it very difficult to climb in or out of a bath, explain this. If a child uses picture cards to communicate, explain the amount of help s/he needs to use them, and how long this takes to communicate effectively compared to communication with a non-disabled child.

Part 5: Other benefits
Chapter 28: Disability living allowance
7. Claims and backdating

- **Frequency, variability and duration.** You are asked throughout the form to estimate how long the child needs help for, and how often. Explain:
  - how long s/he needs help for, to show that s/he needs attention for a 'significant portion of the day' (see p599) or 'prolonged' attention at night (see p600);
  - how often s/he needs help, to show that s/he needs 'frequent attention throughout the day' (see p599) or watching over 'repeatedly' during the night (see p601);
  - how many days a week s/he needs help, to establish her/his overall needs, particularly if s/he has a variable or fluctuating condition. If the child's condition does not vary but s/he only receives all the help s/he needs on certain days, say that s/he needs help seven days a week. It is the help needed, not the help s/he gets, that counts. If s/he only has problems a few days a week, s/he may still get DLA. It is not simply comparing the number of 'good' versus 'bad' days.[208] Explain fully the help s/he needs on 'bad' days, but include the help needed on 'good' days for an overall picture.

- **Mobility.** See p588 and p592 and the tactics on p614 for how to describe a child's walking ability or the help s/he needs getting about outdoors. Children can only qualify for DLA mobility component from the age of three, but problems with getting around may also indicate care or supervision needs, so explain these even if the child is younger than three. It can be difficult to explain how a disabled child requires 'substantially more' guidance or supervision outdoors in order to qualify for the lower rate mobility component (see p592). Most young children do not go out, at least in unfamiliar places, on their own. However, a child with a sensory impairment or learning disability may require much more direct or close supervision than a non-disabled child.[209] A child may normally be allowed to walk in the presence of an adult, but a disabled child may require an adult to hold or guide her/him. Also, even a familiar route may be hazardous to a child whose sight is impaired. It may help to make comparisons with siblings or classmates. A child with attention deficit disorder may need to be accompanied to school or to local shops, whereas other children might be allowed to go alone.[210]

- **Extra attention, supervision or guidance.** When explaining a child's 'extra' requirements, bear in mind that they must be 'substantially in excess' of those required by a child of the same age who does not have a disability (see p592 and p595). It may be either the extra time you devote or the degree of attention, supervision or guidance a child requires.[211] The fact that it may not be unusual for some children of the same age to require similar assistance is irrelevant. The comparison should be with an 'average child' the same age – ie, a child of average intelligence whose behaviour is neither particularly good nor bad.[212] Disabled children may need extra help to develop daily living skills, language and social skills. For example, babies with sensory impairments may require more physical stimulation to aid parental bonding and develop communication skills. A child with a disability might need intensive help with eating, rather than be expected to eat unaided or only need certain foods cut up. Similarly, a child with a disability may need supervision to avoid dangers that children would usually be expected to deal with themselves by her/his age. A child with a disability may need help to use toys, may need to be coaxed to explore her/his environment and may develop these skills later than other children. Similarly, you may let a non-disabled child play outdoors and instruct her/him not to cross roads; you may be able to supervise indirectly without having to watch her/him all the time. However, you may have to supervise directly a child with sensory impairments or behavioural problems, or keep her/him indoors. Consider also whether certain activities are more difficult for the child than usual – eg, if they cause her/him pain, or make her/him dizzy, tired or breathless. If s/he takes a long time to perform particular tasks, explain this. Also say if s/he is not able to perform a particular activity adequately – eg, if s/he cannot bend to reach her/his feet when washing.

- **Sensory impairments**. There are sections on help with seeing, hearing, speaking and communication. The specific needs of deaf children or blind children can be described here. Blind children may need additional help with lots of daily activities. Explain the help required throughout the form. For example, they may need someone to tell them if they have stains on their clothes or if their hands are clean – you should explain these problems in the 'dressing' and 'washing' sections and not just in the 'seeing' section. The help a child with a sensory impairment needs to undertake social and leisure activities should also be explained.

- **Communicating**. Prelingual deaf children whose first language is British Sign Language may need help to understand or communicate in written or spoken English. Blind children will not only need help to understand written information, but may also need help to learn Braille. Children with learning difficulties may need help to express themselves, understand other people or follow instructions or warnings.

- **Mental disabilities.** In the sections on help with communication and on supervision during the day, mention any problems caused by anxiety, intrusive thoughts or anger, or learning difficulties. Remember that a child who needs encouraging or prompting to do things can get DLA, as well as a child who needs physical help with them. If s/he needs assistance to undertake social or leisure activities, information about that help may also fit in the form's mobility section. At the end of the form is a page to 'tell us anything else you think we should know'. It often helps to summarise mental health problems here and explain any other attention or supervision needs the child has.

- **About the child's development.** Describing the extra care or supervision that a child needs compared to others is extremely important. If you are not sure when a child should normally be crawling, walking, speaking, playing with others, understanding instructions, using the toilet independently, feeding

Part 5: Other benefits
Chapter 28: Disability living allowance
7. Claims and backdating

her/himself, and so on, ask your health visitor or paediatrician. For example, most children pick up and eat food by 8–12 months. Therefore, if you are still feeding a child after 12 months, you are providing attention that a non-disabled child of the same age would not need. It often helps to make comparisons with other children you know. When completing renewal forms, always describe all the child's needs. Bear in mind that, if you do not mention something, the DWP may suppose that the child no longer needs the same help as s/he did when s/he was younger. However, it is wrong for the DWP to assume that all disabled children develop in the same way.

• **Children of nursery or school age.** Children who have a disability, particularly those with sensory impairments or learning disabilities, usually require extra help with learning and school work. This should be explained, as well as other help (eg, help going to the toilet) that they may need at school or nursery. Extra help in the classroom or with homework due to special educational needs can count towards a child's attention needs, as cognition is a bodily function of the brain (see p597).[213] Straightforward teaching would probably not be sufficiently intimate to qualify,[214] but additional help (eg, because of dyslexia) may count.[215]

• **When the child is in bed at night.** Only the needs the child has after the rest of the household has gone to bed count as night-time needs (see p598).

What evidence should you provide?

When making a claim, and especially when preparing for an appeal, ensure that you have as much evidence as possible to support what you say about the child in the claim pack. This can include any of the following.

Evidence that you provide about your knowledge of the child

About her/his care needs. Often the easiest way for the DWP or First-tier Tribunal to get a picture of a child's care needs and their pattern is for you to keep a diary for a week or a month, to record variations in her/his condition and the help s/he needs. This can be particularly useful if s/he has unpredictable care needs or experiences irregular events, such as seizures or falls, which mean that s/he needs extra supervision. Usually this is best presented as a table. The DLA claim form shows an example. You can also ask other carers, friends or family members to keep a diary or write letters in support of the claim or appeal.

About her/his walking ability. Walk outdoors with the child to measure the distance s/he can walk without severe discomfort, then write a description of the time it takes to walk this far. It may help to give an example of the distance – eg, 'S/he can walk past five houses – about 40 metres.'

Describe the terrain. Is it rough or uneven? Are there steps or slopes which present her/him with problems?

Explain what sort of discomfort s/he experiences (eg, pain or breathlessness) and how it changes as s/he walks.

Describe her/his manner of walking – eg, s/he may have problems with balance, or may walk with a limp, drag her/his feet or shuffle.

Say if the child needs to stop to rest. Try to explain how far s/he can walk before s/he needs to stop, and for how long s/he needs to rest. Bear in mind that if s/he can walk a further distance without severe discomfort after a brief rest, it is the total distance that counts.

You can use the 'Directions' function on Google Maps to measure distances.

Go somewhere unfamiliar with the child and describe all the difficulty s/he has and the guidance s/he needs.

Evidence from third parties

You can send photocopies of any reports with the claim form.

Doctors' reports. These could be reports already provided by specialists to the child's GP. Often hospital doctors will send copies of reports they write to the child's parent/guardian. Ask the GP for copies of any reports you do not have from the child's medical records. Alternatively, ask the GP or specialist to write a specific letter for the child's claim or appeal. The doctor may charge for writing reports and providing copies from the child's records. It is not usually worth providing hospital appointment letters and other routine documents which do not comment on the child's diagnosis, treatment or disability. The DWP may request a specific report from the child's GP. It can help to make an appointment to discuss with the GP beforehand the child's day-to-day problems.

Reports from other medical professionals. Reports from health visitors, physiotherapists, psychiatric and other specialist nurses and occupational therapists can often provide more detailed information about a child's disability and how it affects her/his day-to-day life than reports from doctors, who only discuss symptoms and treatment.

Social services and educational reports. If a child has had a social care needs assessment, statement of special educational needs or other care or support plan, this may provide useful supporting evidence of the extra help s/he needs.

DWP medical services assessments. The DWP's decisions can be based on reports by doctors or other healthcare professionals acting on behalf of the DWP. These should not necessarily be preferred to your own or your GP's evidence. You should examine any report carefully and explain why any unhelpful findings or assessments are wrong. If, however, the assessment report supports your claim, you should highlight this.

How your claim is dealt with

DLA can be awarded on the basis of the claim form alone, but the DWP may contact someone you named on the form for more information. It is a good idea to include details of all the medical professionals and other people who know and understand the child's needs and, if possible, enclose evidence from them.

The DWP may telephone you to ask for further information. If you do not want to be telephoned, write this clearly on the claim form.

If the DWP cannot get sufficient information, it may also arrange for the child to be given a medical examination by a healthcare professional acting on behalf of the DWP, who will sometimes visit her/him at home.

If you (or an older child) refuse a medical examination 'without good cause', the claim is likely to be refused.[216]

The DWP aims to deal with new claims for DLA within 40 working days. Claims made under the special rules for terminal illness (see p607) should be decided more quickly. If you disagree with the decision, you can ask for a revision and then appeal (see Chapters 56 and 57) on behalf of the child. See p614 for suggestions about the evidence you can use to support a claim, revision or appeal.

8. **Getting paid**

The general rules on getting paid are covered in Chapter 51. This section explains the specific rules that apply to disability living allowance (DLA).

As DLA is claimed for a child under the age of 16, it is usually paid to an adult with whom s/he is living. The DWP appoints the adult (an 'appointee') to act on the child's behalf. The appointee is normally the child's parent.[217]

DLA can continue to be paid to the appointee in some circumstances when the child and appointee are not living together, including during a temporary separation of up to 12 weeks, or when the child is absent at a boarding school or in residential care (although other rules may mean that payment stops in such circumstances – see Chapter 42). DLA ceases to be paid to the appointee immediately when the child is in the care of a local authority or any similar arrangement, unless it is not intended to last for more than 12 weeks.[218]

When is disability living allowance paid?
You are normally paid on a Wednesday, but the DWP can vary the payday.[219] DLA is usually paid every four weeks in arrears. However:
- DLA can be paid at shorter intervals in individual cases;[220]
- DLA under the special rules for terminal illness can be paid weekly.
If the child leaves a care home and expects to return within 28 days, DLA can be paid at a daily rate for days at home.[221]

Note:
- If you get other DWP benefits, DLA may be paid in a single payment with them.
- The higher rate of the DLA mobility component can be paid direct to Motability if you are buying a car through the scheme (see p621).
- Even if you have been sanctioned for a benefit offence (see p1239), you must be paid DLA.
- For information on missing payments, see p1150. If you cannot get payments because you have lost your bank card or forgotten your PIN, see p1149. If you have lost your payment service card, see p1150.

- If payment of DLA is delayed, see p1255. If you wish to complain about how your claim has been dealt with, or claim compensation, see Chapter 61.
- If payment of a child's DLA is suspended, see p1161. If you have been overpaid DLA, you might have to repay it (see Chapter 53) and, in some circumstances, you may have to pay a penalty (see p1229). If you have been accused of fraud, see Chapter 54.
- If you are owed arrears of DLA, these can be paid in instalments (see p1148).

Length of awards

Awards of DLA can be made for fixed or indefinite periods.[222] An award's length depends on how long the DWP estimates the child's current needs may last.

Awards are usually made for at least six months because of the requirement that a child should satisfy the disability conditions for the next six months. However, there is no legal minimum length for an award.[223] If you think benefit should be awarded for longer, perhaps because the child's condition is such that her/his care or mobility needs will not decrease, consider asking for a revision (see p1261). Bear in mind that if you challenge the length of an award, the rate of the award may also be reconsidered. Even if a child has a longer term award, the DWP can reduce or stop the award if it has grounds to revise or supersede it.

If an award is for a limited period, you will be invited to make a renewal claim up to six months before the award runs out (see p610).

A 'special rules' award (see p607) on the basis of terminal illness is normally made for three years. If there is already a mobility award, the length of the special rules award may be adjusted to finish at the same time as the mobility award.

Although DLA has two components, there can only be a single DLA award, consisting of one or both components. If a child has an award of both components, they must be aligned to end on the same day (even if they started at different times).[224]

See p603 for how the introduction of personal independence payment affects DLA when a child reaches 16 (even if s/he currently has an indefinite award of DLA).

Change of circumstances

You must report any change in a child's circumstances that you have been told you must report, as well as any that you might reasonably be expected to know might affect her/his right to, the amount of, or payment of DLA. You should do this as soon as possible, preferably in writing. See p1160 for further information.

If a child's condition deteriorates so that s/he becomes eligible for a higher rate or another component, benefit can be backdated to the day s/he becomes eligible, provided you tell the DWP no later than a month after s/he completes the three-month qualifying period. If payment of (but not entitlement to) DLA has stopped

Part 5: Other benefits
Chapter 28: Disability living allowance
9. Tax, other benefits and the benefit cap

(eg, while a child is in a care home), still notify the DWP of any change so that the correct rate is paid when payment resumes.

If you do not report a change of circumstances within the month, benefit can still be backdated if you do so within 13 months and there were 'special circumstances' that meant it was not practical to report the change earlier.[225]

If a child's condition improves so that s/he should drop down a rate, lose a component or lose benefit altogether, the new decision normally takes effect from the date you tell the DWP of the improvement, or from the date of the decision if the DWP changed it without your asking.[226] It only takes effect from an earlier date (and causes an overpayment) if you should have realised earlier that the change should have been reported. It is accepted that it may be difficult to realise when a gradual improvement begins to affect benefit entitlement.[227]

If a child who gets DLA and lives in another part of the UK moves to Scotland, s/he should notify Social Security Scotland. S/he will be transferred to child disability payment (CDP – see Chapter 75) automatically without having to make a claim. If a child who lives in Scotland and gets CDP moves to another part of the UK, s/he will continue to be treated as resident in Scotland and entitled to CDP for 13 weeks to allow her/him time to claim DLA.[228] The DLA claim form includes questions to identify anyone who has recently moved from Scotland to England or Wales and who gets, or is waiting on a decision on a claim for, CDP.

9. **Tax, other benefits and the benefit cap**

Tax

Disability living allowance (DLA) is not taxable.[229]

Means-tested benefits and tax credits

DLA for a child is not taken into account as income when calculating any of the means-tested benefits or tax credits for a person who has responsibility for the child. DLA is paid on top of these benefits and tax credits, and getting DLA can increase the amount of them (or mean that the person qualifies for them for the first time, if her/his income was previously too high).

If your child is entitled to DLA, you may qualify for one or more of the following extra amounts:

- a disabled child addition in your universal credit (UC) if you come under the UC system (see p22). This is paid at the higher rate if s/he is entitled to the highest rate care component. **Note:** the disabled child addition is included for the child even if the child element is not received because of the 'two-child limit' (see p66);
- a disabled child premium (see p324) in your housing benefit (HB). If s/he gets the highest rate care component, your HB also includes an enhanced disability

premium (see p327). These premiums are also included in your income support (IS) and income-based jobseeker's allowance (JSA) if you do not get child tax credit (CTC). **Note:** these premiums are included for the child even if a personal allowance is not received for the child because of the 'two-child limit' (see p66);

- a disabled child element in your CTC for each child who gets DLA (at any rate). If s/he gets the highest rate care component, a severely disabled child element is included in CTC (see p1418). If one or both of these elements should have been included in your CTC but has not been, get advice. **Note:** these elements are included for the child even if the child element is not received because of the 'two-child limit' (see p66).

If you or your partner receive DLA, you may qualify for one or more of the following extra amounts:

- the disabled worker element in working tax credit (WTC). If you or your partner get the highest rate care component, a severe disability element is included in WTC (two elements are included if you both get the highest rate). See Chapter 62 for further information;
- a disability premium (see p325) in your IS, income-based JSA and, unless you have reached pension age, HB (or for IS and JSA only, higher pensioner premium (see p329) if either of you have reached pension age). If you or your partner are entitled to the highest rate care component and aged under pension age, you also get an enhanced disability premium (see p327). This is also paid with income-related employment and support allowance (ESA);
- a severe disability premium/addition is included in your IS, income-based JSA, income-related ESA, the guarantee credit of pension credit (PC) and HB, if you receive the highest or middle rate care component and meet the other conditions for that premium/addition (see p330).

No housing costs contributions from a non-dependant are taken into account when calculating your UC housing costs element if you, your partner or the non-dependant get the DLA middle or highest rate care component, or would get it but for being in hospital (see p102). If you or your partner get any rate of the care component, non-dependant deductions are *not* made from any housing costs covered by your HB (see p199), or from any housing costs included in your IS, income-based JSA, income-related ESA or the guarantee credit of PC (see p348).

If you or your partner have reached pension age but you claim UC because the other person has not yet reached this age, and the person over pension age is entitled to DLA, you may still qualify for the limited capability for work element in your UC award (see p69). If the person over pension age is entitled to the highest rate care component, you get the limited capability for work-related activity element in your UC award instead (see p71).

Part 5: Other benefits
Chapter 28: Disability living allowance
9. Tax, other benefits and the benefit cap

Non-means-tested benefits

You can get DLA in addition to any other non-means-tested benefits, except that:
- DLA overlaps with armed forces independence payment;[230]
- DLA care component overlaps with attendance allowance and constant attendance allowance under the industrial injuries scheme (see p678) or war pensions scheme (see p857);[231] *and*
- DLA mobility component overlaps with the war pensioners' mobility supplement payable under the war pensions scheme (see p857).[232]

See p1151 for details of the overlapping benefits rules.

You cannot be paid both DLA and personal independence payment (see Chapter 35). You cannot be entitled to both DLA and child disability payment (see Chapter 75) at the same time.[233]

A person who regularly looks after a child or adult who gets the highest or middle rate care component may be entitled to carer's allowance (CA) (see Chapter 26), and s/he (or her/his partner if claiming as a couple) may also get a carer element in UC (see p73), a carer premium in IS, income-based JSA, income-related ESA or HB, or a carer addition in the guarantee credit of PC (see p334). However, if you are an adult and your carer gets CA or a carer element in UC, it may affect your entitlement to a severe disability premium (or additional amount), so always get advice.

A young person aged 16, 17 or 18 living in Scotland who cannot get CA may be able to get a young carer grant for looking after you (see Chapter 78).

A child in Scotland who gets the DLA highest rate care component is eligible for a child winter heating assistance payment (see p1673).

The benefit cap

In some cases, there is a limit on the total amount of specified benefits you can get (a 'benefit cap'). DLA is *not* one of the specified benefits. The benefit cap does *not* apply if you, your partner or child get DLA (even if it is not paid because the person entitled is in hospital or a care home). In other cases, it only applies if you are getting UC or HB. See p1156 for further information.

Passports and other sources of help

You qualify for a Christmas bonus if you receive DLA at any rate (see p861). If you are on a low income, you may be entitled to council tax reduction (see p836).

If you get the higher rate mobility component, you or your carer can be exempt from paying road tax on a car used solely by, or for, you. Contact the Disability Benefit Centre (see p608) for an exemption certificate. You may be able to get a provisional driving licence from age 16 instead of 17. You can apply online at gov.uk.

If you get the higher rate mobility component, you should qualify for the blue badge scheme of parking concessions. Contact your local authority for further information.

If any member of your household receives DLA at any rate, you can get a grant for help with insulation and other energy efficiency measures in your home (see p860) and may be entitled to other benefits, such as concessionary travel.

Motability

Motability is a charity that runs a scheme to help you lease or buy a car if you receive (or a child for whom you are responsible receives) the higher rate of DLA mobility component for 12 months or more (see p587). DLA mobility component is paid direct to Motability.[234] You may also have to make extra payments. For further details, telephone 0300 456 4566 or visit motability.co.uk.

Notes

1. **Disability living allowance mobility component**
   1 ss71(6) and 73 SSCBA 1992
   2 CM/5/1986; *BP v SSWP* [2009] UKUT 90 (AAC)
   3 s73 SSCBA 1992; reg 12(1)(b) SS(DLA) Regs
   4 Reg 12(1)(a) SS(DLA) Regs
   5 R(M) 3/78
   6 Reg 12(1)(a) SS(DLA) Regs; R(M) 2/78; R(DLA) 4/06
   7 CDLA/1525/2008
   8 CDLA/2822/1999; CDLA/4329/2001
   9 *MMF v SSWP (DLA)* [2012] UKUT 312 (AAC)
   10 R(M) 3/86; CSDLA/202/2007; CDLA/3839/2007; *DM v SSWP (DLA)* [2010] UKUT 375 (AAC)
   11 R(M) 2/89; CDLA/97/2001; *Sandhu v SSWP* [2010] EWCA Civ 962
   12 Reg 12(4) SS(DLA) Regs
   13 R(M) 2/89
   14 Reg 12(1)(b) SS(DLA) Regs
   15 CDLA/3188/2002; *HJ v SSWP (DLA)* [2010] UKUT 307 (AAC)
   16 R(M) 1/95; CSDLA/171/1998
   17 CM/208/1989
   18 *JK v SSWP (DLA)* [2010] UKUT 197 (AAC)
   19 CDLA/1389/1997; CDLA/2195/2008
   20 R(M) 1/81
   21 R(M) 2/92
   22 R(M) 1/83
   23 CM/267/93; CDLA/608/1994; R(DLA) 4/03
   24 R(DLA) 4/04
   25 *Hewitt and Diment v CAO*, 29 June 1998, reported as R(DLA) 6/99
   26 R(M) 1/98; CDLA/3941/2005 interpreted 'exertion' to mean the activity of walking 'however slight the exertion'.
   27 *KS v SSWP (DLA)* [2013] UKUT 390 (AAC)
   28 Reg 12(2) SS(DLA) Regs
   29 Reg 12(3) SS(DLA) Regs
   30 R(DLA) 3/95
   31 Sch 2 SS(GB) Regs
   32 *GB v SSWP (DLA)* [2016] UKUT 566 (AAC)
   33 Reg 34(2) and Sch 3 Parts II and III SS(IIPD) Regs
   34 Reg 12(2)(b) SS(DLA) Regs
   35 s73(1AB) SSCBA 1992; reg 12(1A) SS(DLA) Regs
   36 *NC v SSWP (DLA)* [2012] UKUT 384 (AAC)
   37 *SSWP v IK (DLA)* [2014] UKUT 174 (AAC)

38 *SSWP v YR (DLA)* [2014] UKUT 80 (AAC)
39 Reg 12(1)(b) SS(DLA) Regs
40 s73(3) SSCBA 1992; reg 12(5) and (6) SS(DLA) Regs
41 *JH v SSWP (DLA)* [2010] UKUT 456 (AAC); *AH v SSWP (DLA)* [2012] UKUT 387 (AAC); *SSWP v MG (DLA)* [2012] UKUT 429 (AAC)
42 R(M) 3/86; CSDLA/202/2007
43 *N McM v SSWP (DLA)* [2014] UKUT 312 (AAC)
44 R(DLA) 3/98; *MP v SSWP (DLA)* [2014] UKUT 426 (AAC)
45 *M (a child) v CAO* 29 October 1999, reported as R(DLA) 1/00
46 CDLA/95/1995; *DM v SSWP (DLA)* [2015] UKUT 87 (AAC); *EC (by SC) v SSWP (DLA)* [2017] UKUT 391 (AAC)
47 CDLA/3215/2001; *CD v SSWP (DLA)* [2013] UKUT 68 (AAC); *MP v SSWP (DLA)* [2014] UKUT 426 (AAC)
48 CDLA/2054/1998
49 R(DLA) 7/02; R(DLA) 9/02; CDLA/3244/2001; CDLA/2955/2008; *SSWP v DM (DLA)* [2010] UKUT 318 (AAC); *SSWP v MG (DLA)* [2012] UKUT 429 (AAC)
50 *XTC v SSWP (DLA)* [2020] UKUT 342 (AAC)
51 *TV v SSWP (DLA)* [2013] UKUT 364 (AAC)
52 s73(1)(d) SSCBA 1992
53 R(DLA) 6/03
54 CDLA/42/1994
55 s73(4A) SSCBA 1992
56 *BM v SSWP (DLA)* [2015] UKUT 18 (AAC); *KC-M S (by EC) v SSWP (DLA)* [2015] UKUT 284 (AAC)
57 CDLA/2268/1999
58 R(DLA) 3/04
59 CDLA/42/1994
60 CDLA/42/1994
61 CDLA/42/1994; CDLA/3360/1995; CSDLA/591/1997; CDLA/2643/1998
62 R(DLA) 4/01
63 *IN v SSWP (DLA)* [2013] UKUT 249 (AAC)
64 R(DLA) 6/05
65 R(DLA) 4/01
66 R(DLA) 4/01
67 CDLA/42/1994; R(DLA) 3/04
68 CDLA/2364/1995 and *KH v SSWP (DLA)* [2015] UKUT 8 (AAC), but see CDLA/42/1994
69 CDLA/2142/2005
70 Reg 12(7) and (8) SS(DLA) Regs; R(DLA) 3/04; CDLA/2409/2003; R(DLA) 6/05; *SSWP v DC (DLA)* [2011] UKUT 235 (AAC)

2. **Disability living allowance care component**
71 ss71(6) and 72 SSCBA 1992
72 s72(1)(a) and (4)(c) SSCBA 1992
73 s72(4)(b) SSCBA 1992
74 Reg 7 SS(DLA) Regs
75 s72(4)(a) SSCBA 1992
76 s72(5) SSCBA 1992
77 s72(1)(b) SSCBA 1992
78 s72(1)(c) SSCBA 1992
79 s72(1A)(b) SSCBA 1992
80 s72(5) SSCBA 1992
81 R(DLA) 1/05; *BM v SSWP (DLA)* [2015] UKUT 18 (AAC), reported as [2015] AACR 29
82 R(DLA) 3/06, tribunal of commissioners
83 CDLA/4475/04
84 R(DLA) 3/06, tribunal of commissioners
85 R(A) 3/86; *Mallinson v Secretary of State for Social Security*, 21 April 1994 (HL), reported as R(A) 3/94
86 *Secretary of State for Social Security v Fairey (aka Halliday)*, 21 May 1997 (HL), reported as R(A) 2/98
87 R(A) 3/89
88 R(A) 5/90
89 CDLA/3925/1997; *HJ v SSWP (DLA)* [2010] UKUT 307 (AAC)
90 R(DLA) 10/02
91 *Mallinson v Secretary of State for Social Security*, 21 April 1994 (HL), reported as R(A) 3/94
92 *SJ v SSWP (DLA)* [2014] UKUT 222 (AAC)
93 Reg 10C SS(DLA) Regs; *R v National Insurance Commissioner ex parte Secretary of State for Social Services* [1981] 1 WLR 1017 (CA), also reported as R(A) 2/80
94 R(A) 1/06
95 *Mallinson v Secretary of State for Social Security*, 21 April 1994 (HL), reported as R(A) 3/94
96 CA/177/1988; CDLA/14696/1996; R(DLA) 1/07, tribunal of commissioners
97 R(A) 3/74
98 R(A) 2/75
99 CA/86/1987
100 R(DLA) 1/07, tribunal of commissioners
101 *R v Social Security Commissioner ex parte Butler*, February 1984, unreported; *Secretary of State for Social Security v Fairey (aka Halliday)*, 21 May 1997 (HL), reported as R(A) 2/98
102 *Secretary of State for Social Security v Fairey (aka Halliday)*, 21 May 1997 (HL), reported as R(A) 2/98; R(DLA) 1/02; R(DLA) 2/02; R(DLA) 3/02; *SSWP v PV (DLA)* [2010] UKUT 33 (AAC)

103 R(DLA) 2/02
104 CDLA/3607/2001
105 *Cockburn v CAO and Another*, 21 May 1997 (HL), reported as R(A) 2/98; *Ramsden v SSWP*, 31 January 2003 (CA), reported as R(DLA) 2/03
106 CDLA/267/1994, CDLA/11652/1995, CDLA/3711/1995, CDLA/12381/1996, CDLA/16996/1996, CDLA/16129/1996 and CDLA/4352/1999 are useful, but conflict with CSDLA/281/1996 and CSDLA/314/1997
107 CDLA/267/1994
108 *Secretary of State for Social Security v Fairey (aka Halliday)*, 21 May 1997 (HL), reported as R(A) 2/98
109 CDLA/16129/1996, CDLA/16996/1996 and CDLA/4352/1999 are helpful, but conflict with CSDLA/314/1997
110 CDLA/4352/1999 and CDLA/5216/1998, the latter being more restrictive
111 CDLA/4352/1999
112 CDLA/5216/1998
113 R(DLA) 1/98
114 *R v National Insurance Commissioner ex parte Secretary of State for Social Services* [1974] 1 WLR 1290 (DC), also reported as R(A) 4/74
115 R(A) 1/04
116 CDLA/2852/2002
117 CDLA/997/2003; *LB v SSWP (DLA)* [2018] UKUT 445 (AAC)
118 R(A) 1/78
119 s72(1)(a)(i) SSCBA 1992
120 R(DLA) 8/02
121 CDLA/58/1993
122 CSDLA/29/1994
123 *Ramsden v SSWP*, 31 January 2003 (CA), reported as R(DLA) 2/03; *SO v SSWP (DLA)* [2019] UKUT 272 (AAC)
124 s72(1)(b)(i) SSCBA 1992
125 R(DLA) 5/05
126 CA/140/1985
127 *AB v SSWP (DLA)* [2015] UKUT 522 (AAC)
128 s72(1)(c)(i) SSCBA 1992
129 R(DLA) 5/05
130 R(DLA) 5/05
131 *AD v SSWP (DLA)* [2017] UKUT 29 (AAC)
132 R(A) 3/78
133 *ES (by CS, appointee) v SSWP (DLA)* [2020] UKUT 10 (AAC)
134 s72(1)(b)(ii) SSCBA 1992
135 R(A) 1/83

136 *RJ, GMcL and CS v SSWP (PIP)* [2017] UKUT 105 (AAC), reported as [2017] AACR 32. Although this case relates to PIP, the same arguments about the likelihood of harm occurring and the need for supervision to prevent it also apply to DLA.
137 CA/15/1979, approved in R(A) 1/83
138 R(A) 2/89
139 CA/33/1984
140 R(A) 3/92
141 R(A) 1/73
142 *CP v SSWP (DLA)* [2013] UKUT 230 (AAC)
143 *Moran v Secretary of State for Social Services, The Times,* 14 March 1987 (CA), reported as R(A) 1/88
144 R(A) 5/81
145 s72(1)(c)(ii) SSCBA 1992
146 Vol 10 Ch 61, para 61165 DMG
147 Vol 10 Ch 61, para 61164 DMG

3. The rules about your age

148 s73(1A) SSCBA 1992
149 s72(2) and (5) SSCBA 1992
150 gov.scot/publications/joint-ministerial-working-group-on-welfare-minutes-june-2019
151 Reg 3(5) and (6) PIP(TP) Regs
152 Reg 27 PIP(TP) Regs
153 DWP, *Personal Independence Payment Handbook*, December 2018, p22, available at gov.uk
154 Reg 4 PIP(TP) Regs
155 Regs 12, 13 and 15 PIP(TP) Regs
156 DWP, *Personal Independence Payment Handbook*, December 2018, p22, available at gov.uk
157 Reg 4(1)(a) PIP(TP) Regs
158 Reg 3(3) PIP(TP) Regs
159 Reg 3(4A) and (5B) PIP(TP) Regs
160 Reg 18 PIP(TP) Regs
161 Reg 3(4) PIP(TP) Regs; DWP, *Personal Independence Payment Handbook*, December 2018, p43, available at gov.uk
162 Regs 3(3ZA), 4A and 18A PIP(TP) Regs, as inserted by The Personal Independence Payment (Transitional Provisions) Amendment (Scotland) Regulations 2020 No.218
163 Reg 8(4) PIP(TP) Regs
164 Regs 3 and 7 PIP(TP) Regs
165 Regs 9, 11 and 17 PIP(TP) Regs
166 Reg 9 PIP(TP) Regs
167 Reg 10 PIP(TP) Regs
168 Reg 11 PIP(TP) Regs
169 Reg 20 PIP(TP) Regs

170 Reg 13(1) PIP(TP) Regs
171 *OM v SSWP (PIP)* [2017] UKUT 458 (AAC)
172 Regs 13(2) and 17(2)(b) PIP(TP) Regs
173 Reg 12 PIP(TP) Regs
174 R(M) 1/96; *CH and KN v SSWP (PIP)* [2018] UKUT 330 (AAC); *CH (by TH) v SSWP (PIP)* [2020] UKUT 70 (AAC)
175 Reg 17 PIP(TP) Regs
176 Reg 30 PIP(TP) Regs
177 Reg 17(4) and (5) PIP(TP) Regs
178 Regs 14 and 15 PIP(TP) Regs
179 Reg 17(1) and (3) PIP(TP) Regs
180 Sch 1 paras 3(3), 5(3), 6 and 7 SS(DLA) Regs; see also CSDLA/388/2000
181 Reg 6(3) and (4) SS(DLA) Regs
182 Sch 1 para 3(2) SS(DLA) Regs
183 Sch 1 para 1(3) SS(DLA) Regs
184 Sch 1 paras 2, 6 and 7 SS(DLA) Regs; *DB v SSWP (DLA)* [2016] UKUT 205 (AAC)

5. The amount of benefit
185 Reg 4(2) SS(DLA) Regs
186 Reg 4(1) SS(DLA) Regs

6. Special benefit rules
187 Reg 7 SS(DLA) Regs
188 s72(5) SSCBA 1992
189 ss66(1) and (2) and 72(5) SSCBA 1992
190 s73(9)(b)(ii) and (12) SSCBA 1992

7. Claims and backdating
191 Reg 6(8), (8A) and (9) SS(C&P) Regs
192 Reg 4(1) SS(C&P) Regs
193 For the process of moving from an appointee for a child getting DLA to one for a person aged 16 or over claiming PIP, see regs 28 and 29 PIP(TP) Regs and *P v SSWP (PIP)* [2018] UKUT 359 (AAC).
194 ss72(5) and 73(12) SSCBA 1992; regs 3(9)(b) and 6(6)(c) SS&CS(DA) Regs
195 Reg 6(8), (8A) and (9) SS(C&P) Regs
196 Reg 6(8A) SS(C&P) Regs
197 Reg 6(9) SS(C&P) Regs; *SNN v SSWP (PIP)* [2018] UKUT 210 (AAC) - although decided on similar rules for PIP, this case considers circumstances that may be reasonable and the discussion is relevant for DLA claims.
198 Reg 6(1)(b) SS(C&P) Regs
199 s76(1) SSCBA 1992
200 Reg 9(1) and Sch 1 SS(C&P) Regs; reg 25(3) and (4) UC,PIP,JSA&ESA (C&P) Regs
201 Reg 13A(1) SS(C&P) Regs
202 Reg 13C SS(C&P) Regs
203 CDLA/14895/1996
204 Regs 6 and 11 SS(DLA) Regs

205 Reg 19 Disability Assistance for Children and Young People (Consequential Amendment and Transitional Provision) (Scotland) Regulations 2021 No.73
206 R(DLA)4/01; CDLA/333/2005; *DN v SSWP (DLA)* [2016] UKUT 233 (AAC)
207 DWP, *DWP Medical (Factual) Reports: a guide to completion,* October 2020
208 R(A) 2/74; see also *Moyna v SSWP,* 31 July 2003 (HL), reported as R(DLA) 7/03; *DJ v SSWP (DLA)* [2016] UKUT 169 (AAC)
209 CDLA/2268/1999
210 CDLA/4806/2002
211 CSDLA/76/1998
212 CA/92/1992; *DJ v SSWP (DLA)* [2016] UKUT 169 (AAC)
213 *SSWP v Hughes (a minor),* reported as R(DLA) 1/04
214 CDLA/1983/2006
215 *KM v SSWP (DLA)* [2013] UKUT 159 (AAC), reported as [2014] AACR 2
216 s19(3) SSA 1998

8. Getting paid
217 Reg 43 SS(C&P) Regs
218 Reg 43 SS(C&P) Regs
219 Reg 22(3) and Sch 6 SS(C&P) Regs
220 Reg 22 SS(C&P) Regs
221 Reg 25 SS(C&P) Regs
222 s71(3) SSCBA 1992
223 R(DLA) 11/02
224 s71(3) SSCBA 1992; CDLA/2887/2008
225 Regs 7(9) and 8 SS&CS(DA) Regs
226 s10(5) SSA 1998
227 Reg 7(2)(c) SS&CS(DA) Regs; *RD v SSWP (DLA)* [2011] UKUT 95 (AAC); *DC v SSWP (DLA)* [2011] UKUT 336 (AAC)
228 Regs 35 and 36 DACYP(S) Regs

9. Tax, other benefits and the benefit cap
229 s677 IT(EP)A 2003
230 Art 24C The Armed Forces and Reserve Forces (Compensation Scheme) Order 2011 No.517
231 Sch 1 para 5 SS(OB) Regs
232 Reg 42(1)(b)(ii) SS(C&P) Regs
233 s71(7) SSCBA 1992
234 Regs 44, 45 and 46 SS(C&P) Regs

Chapter 29

Discretionary housing payments

This chapter covers:
1. Who can get discretionary housing payments (p626)
2. The rules about your age (p627)
3. People included in the claim (p627)
4. The amount of discretionary housing payments (p627)
5. Claims, decisions and getting paid (p628)
6. Tax, other benefits and the benefit cap (p629)

Key facts

- Discretionary housing payments are extra payments that can be made by your local authority if you need help to meet your housing costs – eg, because deductions are being made for non-dependants living with you, you are affected by the benefit cap, or your universal credit (UC) or housing benefit (HB) does not cover your full rent because it has been restricted.
- Discretionary housing payments can also be made for lump-sum payments – eg, if you need rent in advance or a deposit for a new home, or if you have removal expenses.
- You must be entitled to help with your rent in UC or to HB to get discretionary housing payments.
- Payments are discretionary. They are paid from a cash-limited budget allocated to your local authority.
- You cannot appeal to the First-tier Tribunal against a discretionary housing payment decision, but you can ask the local authority for a review.

Future changes

The Scottish parliament is responsible for making rules on discretionary housing payments in Scotland. The legal basis for paying discretionary housing payments in Scotland will eventually change. It is not expected that the rules will change significantly when this happens. See AskCPAG and CPAG's *Welfare Rights Bulletin* for updates.

Part 5: Other benefits
Chapter 29: Discretionary housing payments
1. Who can get discretionary housing payments

1. Who can get discretionary housing payments

A local authority can pay you discretionary housing payments if you are entitled to:[1]

- universal credit (UC) and your maximum amount includes a housing costs element for rent (see Chapter 6), or would include one but for the fact that you live in 'specified' or 'temporary' accommodation (see p84 for what counts); *or*
- housing benefit (HB) (see Chapter 10).

You must also appear to the local authority to require financial assistance, in addition to the benefit to which you are entitled, in order to meet your housing costs. 'Housing costs' are not defined in the rules. You can get discretionary housing payments even if your benefit is being paid direct to your landlord.[2]

> **When can discretionary housing payments be made?**
> Examples of when discretionary housing payments can be made include:[3]
> – if your UC or HB is being paid at a reduced rate because non-dependant deductions are being made, because of the policy to limit benefit to two children, because of the benefit cap, or under any of the rent restriction rules in Chapter 6 or Chapter 19;
> – if you were getting HB with a severe disability premium and are now getting UC;
> – lump-sum payments for rent in advance, deposits or removal expenses.[4]
> **Note:** it is understood that the government in Scotland funds local authorities fully to use discretionary housing payments to mitigate the effects of the social sector rent restriction rules (the 'bedroom tax'). So, if you apply for a discretionary housing payment in Scotland for a loss due to the bedroom tax, you should receive one.

The local authority has discretion on whether to pay you, on the amount to pay you (within certain limits) and what period to pay you, even if your UC housing costs element or HB is being paid in full direct to your landlord on your behalf.[5] The rules do not limit the length of time you can be paid discretionary housing payments. These can be paid indefinitely.

DWP guidance to local authorities in England and Wales is at gov.uk/government/publications/discretionary-housing-payments-guidance-manual. Local authorities in Scotland can consider and use this guidance, but the Scottish government has the power to issue its own guidance and is expected to do so at some point in the future.

When discretionary housing payments cannot be made

Discretionary housing payments cannot be made to you if you need financial assistance as a consequence of any of the following:[6]

- ineligible service charges under the UC or HB schemes (see p85 and p194);
- water and sewerage charges;
- liability for council tax. However, you may be able to get help from your local authority's council tax reduction scheme (see p836);
- your rent payments increasing to cover arrears of rent, service charges or other unpaid charges;
- your benefit (eg, income support or employment and support allowance) being reduced because you refused to take part in a work-focused interview;
- your UC or jobseeker's allowance (JSA) being paid at a reduced (or nil) rate because you have been sanctioned under specified rules;
- if you are 16 or 17 and are getting income-based JSA on a discretionary basis (known as 'severe hardship payments') and this is reduced because you gave up a place on a training scheme or failed to attend without a good reason;
- any of your benefits being suspended;
- a reduction in your benefit because an overpayment of UC, HB or council tax benefit is being recovered;
- your benefit being restricted because of a benefit offence (see p1239). **Note:** DWP guidance to local authorities in England and Wales wrongly suggests this applies if you are in breach of a community service order.

2. The rules about your age

There are no lower or upper age limits for discretionary housing payments. However, you must be entitled to universal credit (UC) that includes (or would include) a housing costs element for rent, or to housing benefit (HB), to qualify for discretionary housing payments and there *are* age rules for UC and HB (see p36 and p187).

3. People included in the claim

You claim discretionary housing payments for yourself. However, your circumstances and needs as well as those of your child(ren) and your partner should be taken into account in deciding whether you can be paid and how much you can get.

4. The amount of discretionary housing payments

Discretionary housing payments are normally paid in weekly amounts. The local authority can decide how much you can be paid, how long you can be paid and

Part 5: Other benefits
Chapter 29: Discretionary housing payments
5. Claims, decisions and getting paid

how far your payments can be backdated.[7] However, it can only pay discretionary housing payments for periods during which you are (or were) entitled to universal credit (UC) and your maximum amount includes (or would include) a housing costs element for rent, or you are (or were) entitled to housing benefit (HB).

You cannot be paid more than:[8]

- if you are entitled to UC and your discretionary housing payments are calculated as a monthly amount, the amount of housing costs element for rent as calculated for your maximum amount (see Chapter 6), or if you are in 'specified' or 'temporary' accommodation (see p84 for what counts), the amount of your rent (other than that for your specified or temporary accommodation) and service charges; or

- if you are entitled to HB and your discretionary housing payments are calculated as a weekly amount, the amount of your rent and other payments that can be met by HB (see p175), not including any amounts paid for ineligible service charges and rent-free periods.

Any UC or HB you have already received (or will receive) for the period may be deducted.[9]

There is no restriction on the amount of one-off payments.[10] Larger amounts (eg, for rent in advance, a rent deposit or removal expenses) can therefore be paid by a lump sum.

Note:

- In deciding whether to pay you discretionary housing payments and, if so, how much to pay you, the local authority can look at what income and capital you have. However, it cannot take disability living allowance into account.[11] You should argue that it also cannot take attendance allowance, personal independence payment, adult disability payment or child disability payment into account.[12]

- If you need additional help with housing costs because there is a shortfall between your UC or HB and the rent you are liable to pay, ensure the local authority knows this, in particular if you are getting UC as it may not already have this information.

---

5. **Claims, decisions and getting paid**

Ask your local authority how to make a claim for discretionary housing payments. It can accept a claim from you, or from someone acting on your behalf, provided you are entitled to universal credit that includes (or would include) a housing costs element for rent, or to housing benefit.[13] Your local authority decides what 'form or manner' your claim should take – eg, in writing or by other means.[14]

You must provide grounds for your claim and provide any other information that the local authority specifies.[15] Provide any evidence that shows why you

need discretionary housing payments – eg, a financial statement and evidence of any disability or medical condition affecting you or the people who live with you.
Note:

- If you want your claim to be backdated, tell the local authority.
- You must be given written notice of the local authority's decision on your claim and the reasons for its decision as soon as is 'reasonably practicable'.[16]
- The local authority can pay you or, if reasonable, someone else (eg, your landlord) where appropriate.[17]
- It is your duty to report to the local authority any change in your circumstances that may be relevant to payment of your discretionary housing payments continuing.[18]

Getting a decision changed

You do not have a right to appeal to the First-tier Tribunal against a discretionary housing payment decision. However, you can ask the local authority for a review of its decision.[19] You are entitled to written notice of, and reasons for, the review decision as soon as is 'reasonably practicable'.[20] If you are unhappy with a review decision, you can make a complaint (see p1407). You may be able to challenge a review decision by judicial review (see Chapter 59). If the local authority's decision involves maladministration (error or wrongdoing) which results in injustice to you, you can also complain to the Ombudsman (see p1409).

6. Tax, other benefits and the benefit cap

Discretionary housing payments are not taxable.
If you get discretionary housing payments:

- they are disregarded as income and capital for the purposes of all the means-tested benefits and tax credits;[21]
- in England and Wales, you may also qualify for a discretionary reduction in your council tax bill (see p836).[22] Ensure you claim both this and discretionary housing payments, if relevant, to avoid missing out.

In some cases there is a limit on the total amount of specified benefits you can receive (a 'benefit cap' – see p1156). Discretionary housing payments are *not* one of the specified benefits.

Notes

1. Who can get discretionary housing payments

1 s69 CSPSSA 2000; reg 2(1) DFA Regs
2 *Discretionary Housing Payments Guidance Manual*, 1 February 2021, para 2.10
3 *Discretionary Housing Payments Guidance Manual*, 1 February 2021, para 2.8
4 *Discretionary Housing Payments Guidance Manual*, 1 February 2021, para 1.16
5 Reg 2(2) DFA Regs
6 Reg 3 DFA Regs

4. The amount of discretionary housing payments

7 Reg 5 DFA Regs
8 Reg 4 DFA Regs
9 *R (Gargett) v Lambeth LB* [2008] EWCA Civ 1450
10 *Discretionary Housing Payments Guidance Manual*, 1 February 2021, paras 4.12 and 4.13
11 *R (Hardy) v Sandwell MBC* [2015] EWHC 890 (Admin)
12 *Discretionary Housing Payments Guidance Manual*, 1 February 2021, para 5.11

5. Claims, decisions and getting paid

13 Reg 6 DFA Regs
14 Reg 6(1)(a) DFA Regs
15 Reg 7 DFA Regs
16 Reg 6(3) DFA Regs
17 Reg 6(2) DFA Regs
18 Reg 7(b) DFA Regs
19 Reg 8 DFA Regs
20 Reg 6(3) DFA Regs

6. Tax, other benefits and the benefit cap

21 **UC** Reg 66 UC Regs
IS Schs 9 para 75 and 10 para 7(1)(d) IS Regs
JSA Schs 7 para 71 and 8 para 12(1)(d) JSA Regs
ESA Schs 8 para 62 and 9 para 11(1)(c) ESA Regs
PC Reg 15 SPC Regs
HB Schs 5 para 62 and 6 para 9(1)(d) HB Regs; reg 29 HB(SPC) Regs
22 s13A(1)(c) LGFA 1992

Chapter 30

Contributory employment and support allowance

This chapter covers:
1. Who can get contributory employment and support allowance (p632)
2. The rules about your age (p634)
3. People included in the claim (p634)
4. The amount of benefit (p634)
5. Special benefit rules (p641)
6. Claims and backdating (p642)
7. Getting paid (p645)
8. Tax, other benefits and the benefit cap (p646)

Key facts

- Employment and support allowance (ESA) is a benefit for people who have 'limited capability for work' (ie, they are unable to work because of illness or disability) and who are not entitled to statutory sick pay.
- Entitlement to ESA is assessed by a test called the 'work capability assessment'.
- There are two types of ESA: **contributory ESA**, which is not means tested (but can be affected by certain pensions), and **income-related ESA**, which is means tested. Contributory ESA paid under the universal credit (UC) system is sometimes referred to as 'new-style' ESA; contributory ESA paid outside the UC system is sometimes referred to as 'old-style' ESA.
- To qualify for contributory ESA, you must have paid sufficient national insurance contributions.
- In some cases, contributory ESA is paid for a maximum of 365 days.
- You may be able to get your contributory ESA topped up with UC or (if you do not come under the UC system) with income-related ESA.
- ESA is administered and paid by the DWP.
- If you disagree with an ESA decision, you can apply for a revision or supersession (see Chapter 56), or appeal against it (see Chapter 57). You must apply for a mandatory reconsideration before you can appeal. All parts of the decision may be looked at.

Part 5: Other benefits
Chapter 30: Contributory employment and support allowance
1. Who can get contributory employment and support allowance

1. Who can get contributory employment and support allowance

You qualify for employment and support allowance (ESA) if you:[1]
- have 'limited capability for work' (see p987); *and*
- are aged 16 or over, but under pension age (see p766); *and*
- are in Great Britain (see Chapters 70 and 71 if you go abroad); *and*
- are not entitled in your own right to income support or jobseeker's allowance (JSA), and are not in a couple entitled to joint-claim JSA (see p247). However, you can get contributory ESA if you are entitled to joint-claim JSA and do not have to satisfy all the JSA conditions; *and*
- are not entitled to statutory sick pay; *and*
- are not engaged in any work, whether it is paid or unpaid, unless it is work you are allowed to do while claiming (called 'permitted work' – see p1020).

In addition to the above, you must satisfy the extra rules that apply to contributory ESA on p633.

Do you come under the universal credit system?

New claims for contributory ESA are usually only possible under the universal credit (UC) system. The DWP calls this **'new-style' ESA**. If you make a new claim, you will come under the UC system (see p25). You will usually have to accept a 'claimant commitment' (see p1024). However, if you claimed ESA before 12 December 2018 and have not come under the UC system, or (in rare cases) you make a new claim for contributory ESA and are prevented from claiming UC (see p23), you do not come under the UC system and your claim is dealt with under the old rules. In this situation, the DWP calls your ESA **'old-style' ESA**.

You are not usually entitled to ESA for the first seven days of your claim (see p1018). However, you may be able to get a short-term advance of ESA paid to you during this waiting period (p1153). You cannot get ESA and certain other benefits at the same time (see p646).

Incapacity benefit and severe disablement allowance

Contributory ESA has, in most cases, replaced awards of two older non-means-tested benefits paid for people unable to work because of ill health. These benefits were incapacity benefit (IB) and severe disablement allowance (SDA). If you were already entitled to SDA and reached pension age before 6 April 2014, you can continue to receive it. In other cases, existing awards of IB and SDA have been transferred to claims for ESA. For more details, see p640.

Extra rules for contributory employment and support allowance

As well as satisfying the basic rules for ESA on p632, you qualify for contributory ESA if:[2]
- you satisfy the national insurance (NI) contribution conditions (see p964); *or*
- you were getting IB or SDA and you have been transferred to contributory ESA (see p640); *or*
- you satisfied the conditions for ESA in youth and you remain entitled (see below).

Employment and support allowance in youth

ESA in youth was abolished for new claimants from 1 May 2012.[3] For details of the rules, see Chapter 10 of the 2012/13 edition of this *Handbook*.

If you lose entitlement to ESA in youth because you have received it for a year, but have still got limited capability for work and are put in the 'support group' (see p637) because your condition has worsened, you can requalify for contributory ESA without having to satisfy the NI contribution conditions.[4]

Disqualification from benefit

You can be disqualified from receiving ESA for up to six weeks if you:[5]
- have 'limited capability for work' because of your own misconduct (but not, for example, if this is due to pregnancy or a sexually transmitted disease); *or*
- have failed without 'good cause' to accept medical treatment (excluding vaccination, inoculation or major surgery) recommended by a doctor treating you and which would be likely to overcome your limited capability for work; *or*
- have failed without 'good cause' to stop engaging in behaviour that would 'retard' your recovery; *or*
- are absent from your home without telling the DWP where you may be found without 'good cause'.

'Good cause' is not defined.

You are not disqualified if you inform the DWP of your circumstances and you are considered to be in hardship – ie, if you are:[6]
- pregnant, or a member of your family is pregnant; *or*
- a single claimant aged under 18, or a member of a couple and both of you are under 18; *or*
- responsible (or your partner is responsible) for a child who lives with you. This does not apply to contributory ESA if you come under the UC system (see p22); *or*
- entitled (or your partner is entitled) to attendance allowance (AA), the middle or highest rate of the care component of disability living allowance (DLA) or of

Part 5: Other benefits
Chapter 30: Contributory employment and support allowance
4. The amount of benefit

child disability payment (CDP), the daily living component of personal independence payment (PIP) or of adult disability payment (ADP) or armed forces independence payment; *or*

- waiting (or your partner is waiting) for a decision on a claim for AA, DLA, CDP, PIP, ADP or armed forces independence payment; *or*
- caring (or your partner is caring) for someone who is entitled to AA, the middle or highest rate care component of DLA/CDP, the daily living component of PIP/ADP or armed forces independence payment (or who is waiting for a decision on a claim for AA, DLA/CDP, PIP/ADP or armed forces independence payment); *or*
- at least pension age (see p765), or your partner is at least pension age; *or*
- at risk of hardship (or a member of your family is at risk) if ESA is not paid to you, including if there is a 'substantial risk' that you will not have sufficient essential items such as food, clothing and heating.

In any of the above situations, your ESA is paid at a reduced rate. You get 80 per cent of your basic allowance in contributory ESA, or 80 per cent of your personal allowance in income-related ESA (see p317).[7]

You can also be disqualified from receiving contributory ESA during any period in which you are:

- absent from Great Britain (see p1627); *or*
- a prisoner or detained in legal custody (see Chapter 42).

2. The rules about your age

To be entitled to employment and support allowance, you must be aged at least 16 but under pension age (see p766).

3. People included in the claim

You claim contributory employment and support allowance for yourself. You cannot claim any increases for your partner or children.

4. The amount of benefit

During an initial 'assessment phase' (see p635), you are usually paid just a basic allowance of contibutory employment and support allowance (ESA). After the assessment phase has ended and the 'main phase' has started, you may also get an additional component of ESA. You can get either a 'support component' (see p636) or (in certain cases only) a 'work-related activity component' (see p637). **Note:** the work-related activity component was abolished for new claimants from 3 April 2017. For who can still get the component, see p637.

There are no increases in contributory ESA for other adults or children.

Your contributory ESA may be reduced if:

- you get a pension or a councillor's allowance (see p639); *or*
- the work-related activity component (see p637) applies to you and you do not comply with requirements to attend work-focused interviews and carry out work-related activity (see Chapter 48 or, if you come under the universal credit (UC) system, Chapter 46); *or*
- you have been given a sanction because you have committed a benefit offence (see p1239).

Note:

- If you are appealing against a decision that you do not have limited capability for work and get ESA pending your appeal being heard (see p1015), you are paid at the assessment phase rate – ie, you get the basic allowance only.
- You may also be entitled to UC, if you come under the UC system (see p22). If you are, your contributory ESA is topped up by your UC. If you do not come under the UC system, your contributory ESA may be topped up by income-related ESA.

The assessment phase

When you are first entitled to ESA, you are in an 'assessment phase' until a decision is made on your limited capability for work. This applies to both contributory and income-related ESA. You usually just get a basic allowance of contributory ESA, the amount of which depends on your age. Your ESA does not usually include an additional component (but see p638 for when a component can be included in the assessment phase).

The assessment phase lasts for at least 13 weeks. If after 13 weeks the DWP has not decided whether you have limited capability for work (eg, because it has not yet completed the work capability assessment – see Chapter 45), the assessment phase continues until the DWP has made its decision.[8] In practice, delays of longer than 13 weeks in completing assessments are common. If you are claiming immediately after an 'extended period of sickness' on jobseeker's allowance (JSA – see p692), the 13-week period starts on the first day of the period of sickness.

If the assessment phase lasts longer than 13 weeks, the additional component is backdated to the 14th week of your claim.[9]

If you are appealing against a decision that you do not have limited capability for work and are getting ESA pending your appeal (see p1015), the assessment phase does not usually end until the First-tier Tribunal has made its decision. However, if you experience a new condition or your condition significantly

Part 5: Other benefits
Chapter 30: Contributory employment and support allowance
4. The amount of benefit

worsens before your appeal is heard, a new determination on your limited capability for work can be made and it is possible for the assessment phase to end.[10]

It is possible for your assessment phase to begin on the first day of a period of previous entitlement to ESA (of either kind), so that some, or all, of the 13 weeks are treated as already served.[11] This happens if your current period of limited capability for work is linked to a previous one (see p1018) in which you were entitled to ESA for less than 13 weeks. In these circumstances, your assessment phase ends when your combined entitlement from the previous and current ESA awards amounts to 13 weeks, unless the DWP has not yet completed your assessment, in which case it does not end until the DWP has made its decision.

If you were on JSA during an 'extended period of sickness' (see p692), this counts as time when you had a previous entitlement to ESA.

Calculating your contributory employment and support allowance

Contributory ESA is worked out as follows.
- Add together the basic allowance and the amount of any component to which you are entitled.
  - In the 'assessment phase', you are normally only entitled to a basic allowance.[12] This is £61.05 if you are under 25 or £77.00 if you are 25 or over. In some circumstances, such as if you are terminally ill, you may also be entitled to either a support component (see below) or a work-related activity component (see p637).
  - After the assessment phase is over, you are entitled to a basic allowance of £77.00, irrespective of your age. If you qualify, you can also get a support component of £40.60 a week or (if you can still get it) a work-related activity component of £30.60 a week.
- Deduct from this sum an amount for certain pension payments or for a councillor's allowance, if applicable (see p639).
- Add any transitional addition to which you are entitled if you have been transferred to ESA from incapacity benefit (IB) or severe disablement allowance (SDA) (see p640).[13]

Support component

The support component can be included in your entitlement to both contributory and income-related ESA.[14]

In most cases, you are entitled to the support component if:
- the assessment phase (see p635) has ended (but see p638); *and*

- as well as having limited capability for work, you are also assessed as having 'limited capability for work-related activity' (see p1004).

The support group

If you are assessed as having, or are treated as having, limited capability for work-related activity, the DWP describes you as being in the **'support group'**.

The DWP decides whether or not you have limited capability for work-related activity as part of the work capability assessment (see p987). You can appeal if you do not agree with the DWP's decision, although usually you must apply for a mandatory reconsideration first. But if the DWP has decided that you do not have limited capability for work (ie, you have 'failed' the work capability assessment) and so are not entitled to ESA at all, you may be able to appeal straight away, without first applying for a mandatory reconsideration (see p1014). If you appeal and the First-tier Tribunal finds that you have limited capability for work, it should also consider whether you have limited capability for work-related activity.[15]

If you are in the support group, you do not have to take part in work-focused interviews or associated activity as a condition of getting benefit.[16]

Work-related activity component

The work-related activity component was abolished for new claimants of both contributory and income-related ESA from 3 April 2017.[17] You can no longer get the component if you are making a new claim for ESA (but see below). You may still be able to get the support component.

You can still get the work-related activity component after 3 April 2017 if:[18]

- your current ESA entitlement started before 3 April 2017 (this includes if you only became entitled to ESA after a mandatory reconsideration or appeal that was after that date);
- you claimed ESA before 3 April 2017 and had limited capability for work (see Chapter 45), you have had a break in your period of limited capability for work, but you have reclaimed ESA within 12 weeks of your previous period ending;
- you were entitled to ESA before 3 April 2017 and then became entitled to maternity allowance (MA), and you have reclaimed ESA within 12 weeks of your MA ending;
- your assessment phase (see p635) for a previous ESA claim began before 3 April 2017, but you were entitled to ESA for no more than 13 weeks and you have reclaimed it within 12 weeks of your previous entitlement ending. **Note:** if you were getting JSA in an 'extended period of sickness' (see p692), this counts as a previous ESA claim;

Part 5: Other benefits
Chapter 30: Contributory employment and support allowance
4. The amount of benefit

- you claimed ESA on or after 3 April 2017, but your claim was backdated to before this date, and it is decided that you are in the 'work-related activity group';
- you were transferred from IB or SDA to contributory ESA, or from income support (IS) to income-related ESA.

The work-related activity group

If you are assessed under the work capability assessment as having limited capability for work, but not for work-related activity (see Chapter 45), the DWP describes you as being in the '**work-related activity group**'. This is the case even if you cannot get the work-related activity component. The DWP also describes you as being in the work-related activity group if you are treated as having limited capability for work (see p988), except if you are waiting for your work capability assessment to be carried out or if you are appealing.[19]

If you can get it, the work-related activity component can be included in both contributory and income-related ESA if:[20]
- the assessment phase (see p635) has ended (but see below); *and*
- you are not assessed as having 'limited capability for work-related activity' (see p1004) – ie, you are not entitled to the support component; *and*
- you comply with the requirement to attend work-focused interviews and associated activity. If you do not, your ESA may be reduced.

You may be required to take part in work-focused interviews and undertake work-related activity (see Chapter 48 or, if you come under the UC system, Chapter 46).

Who can get a component in the assessment phase

You are entitled to the support component (or the work-related activity component, if you can still get it) during the assessment phase if:[21]
- you have requalified for contributory ESA after having previously lost it because of the rules on how long it can be paid (see p640) and now satisfy the conditions for the support component; *or*
- you are terminally ill (ie, you have a progressive disease, as a result of which your death can reasonably be expected within six months) and have either claimed ESA on these grounds, or asked for a revision or supersession and have said that you are terminally ill. In this case, you qualify for the support component automatically and it is included straight away; *or*
- your period of limited capability for work is linked under the 12-week linking rule (see p1018) to an earlier period in which you were entitled to ESA, you were entitled to a component in this earlier claim and it did not end because you were found to be fit for work – ie, you did not fail the work capability assessment. In this case, the component can be included straight away; *or*

- your period of limited capability for work is linked under the 12-week linking rule (see p1018) to an earlier period in which you were entitled to ESA, you were entitled to a component or that award lasted 13 weeks or longer, and it ended either because you failed the work capability asssessment or before you could be assessed. In this case, you can only get the component again once you have been assessed as passing the work capability assessment, although it is dated from the start of your second award; *or*
- your ESA entitlement started within 12 weeks of your losing entitlement to IS, when your IS ended it included the disability premium and the sole reason for your losing entitlement to IS was that you were a lone parent and your youngest child no longer met the age rules (see p233).

Deductions for pension payments and councillor's allowance

A deduction is made from your contributory ESA if you receive certain pension payments of over £85 a week and/or if you are a local councillor and your net allowances are more than £152 a week.[22]

Pension payments taken into account for contributory ESA are periodic payments made under:[23]
- any personal, occupational or public service pension scheme;
- any permanent health insurance policy arranged by your employer that provides payments in connection with ill health or disability after your employment ends. However, if you contributed more than 50 per cent of the pension premiums, the amount you receive from this kind of pension is ignored;
- the Pension Protection Fund and the Financial Assistance Scheme.

If the total amount of the gross pension payments you receive is more than £85 a week, your contributory ESA is reduced by half the pension payments above £85.

Other types of pension payments (including one-off lump-sum payments) are ignored. The following types of payment are also ignored:[24]
- any part of your pension paid direct to an ex-spouse or ex-civil partner by the pension scheme trustees under a court order (although the DWP may not accept this);[25]
- any payments you receive as a result of the death of the pension holder;
- any shortfall in your pension if it cannot be paid in full because the pension scheme is in deficit or has insufficient funds;
- payments under a pension scheme for death as a result of military or war service under section 639(2) of the Income Tax (Earnings and Pensions) Act 2003, or a guaranteed income payment.

Note: if you were transferred from IB to ESA (see p640) and your pension payment was ignored immediately before the transfer, it continues to be ignored in your ESA.[26]

Part 5: Other benefits
Chapter 30: Contributory employment and support allowance
4. The amount of benefit

If you are a local councillor and your net allowances are more than £152 a week, your contributory ESA is reduced by the amount by which the net allowances exceed £152.[27]

Transfers to employment and support allowance

Most people who were getting IB, SDA or IS on the grounds of disability on 27 October 2008 have had their claim transferred to a claim for ESA. If you were transferred from IB or SDA but your contributory ESA would have been less, you were entitled to the difference as a transitional addition to your contributory ESA. But, as ESA is a single benefit, you may also have been entitled to income-related ESA if your income and capital were low enough. Those getting IS had their award automatically converted to a claim for income-related ESA. If you get a transitional addition, it is reduced by subsequent increases in your ESA. For more details, see Chapter 31 of the 2016/17 edition of this *Handbook*.

The transfer process did not apply to people who reached pension age before 6 April 2014. If you were getting SDA and reached pension age before 6 April 2014, you can continue to get SDA as long as you continue to meet the qualifying conditions. See Chapter 4 of the 2000/01 edition of this *Handbook* for the qualifying conditions for SDA.

Duration of contributory employment and support allowance

Contributory ESA is only paid for a maximum of 365 days. However, when calculating this 365-day period, any time when you have limited capability for work-related activity (p1004) and are in in the 'support group' is ignored. So you can be entitled for longer than 365 days if you are in the support group. Once you have received contributory ESA for a year and have not been entitled to the support component for that time, you lose your entitlement to contributory ESA. The following applies.[28]

- Time spent in the assessment phase is taken into account when calculating the 365-day period, except if you were assessed as having limited capability for work-related activity (p1004) and put in the support group.
- If you are appealing about not being in the support group, days when you get ESA while you are appealing are taken into account when calculating the 365-day period. This time is then ignored if your appeal is successful.
- If you were transferred from IB or SDA to contributory ESA, your 365-day period is calculated from the date your award was converted to contributory ESA.

You can requalify for contributory ESA again if:[29]
- you remain assessed or treated as having limited capability for work, and you are also assessed as having limited capability for work-related activity for the support component (see p1004); *or*

- the tax years used to decide whether you satisfy the national insurance (NI) contribution conditions (see p964) include at least one year which is later than the last of the relevant tax years which applied to your previous entitlement, and you satisfy the NI contribution conditions again. If you continue to have limited capability for work and still get income-related ESA, under the linking rules (p1018) the tax years remain the same as those that applied to your previous entitlement, so you cannot requalify in this way. However, if you have a break in your ESA entitlement altogether (ie, of both contributory and income-related ESA) of more than 12 weeks (including if you get UC during the break), you start a new period of limited capability for work and the linking rules do not apply.[30]

Example

Femi is aged 24. He has worked since leaving school and has a full NI contribution record, but in July 2021 had to leave his job because of ill health. He gets the standard rate of the daily living component of personal independence payment. He is not assessed as being in the ESA support group. As Femi comes under the UC system, he is not entitled to any income-related ESA.

ESA during assessment phase = £61.05 (basic allowance for someone aged under 25)

ESA during main phase = £77.00

Because Femi is not in the support group, his award of contributory ESA, which began in July 2021, is limited to 365 days.

The relevant tax years for the NI contribution conditions for the July 2021 claim are 2018/19 and 2019/20.

After a year of payment, Femi's contributory ESA stops on 1 July 2022. His condition has not changed and he still does not qualify for the support component. He still has limited capability for work. As his ESA has stopped completely (ie, he is not entitled to income-related ESA either), after 12 weeks Femi may requalify for contributory ESA. This is because when he makes a new claim for ESA he starts a new period of limited capability for work which does not link to his previous one. One of the relevant tax years that applies to the new claim (2020/21) is later than the years that applied to Femi's previous claim. However, he must still satisfy the NI contribution conditions again using the new relevant tax years.

5. **Special benefit rules**

Special rules may apply to:
- 'people subject to immigration control' (employment and support allowance in youth only) (see Chapter 68);
- people going abroad (see Chapters 70 and 71);
- people in prison or detention (see Chapter 42).

Part 5: Other benefits
Chapter 30: Contributory employment and support allowance
6. Claims and backdating

6. **Claims and backdating**

The general rules about claims and backdating are covered in Chapter 50. This section explains the specific rules that apply to contributory and income-related employment and support allowance (ESA). The rules may be different depending on whether or not you come under the universal credit (UC) system.

Sometimes, you must attend a medical examination to assess whether you have limited capability for work (p987) or limited capability for work-related activity (p1004). Also, unless you are in the 'support group' (see p636), you may be required to attend compulsory work-focused interviews and, in some cases, carry out work-related activity. These interviews can include a 'health and work conversation' (see p1027 if you come under the UC system, or p1111 if you do not).

If you are appealing against a decision that you do not have limited capability for work, you do not need to make a claim for ESA in order to get ESA pending your appeal, although you must submit a medical certificate.[31] For when ESA can be paid pending an appeal, see p1015.

Note: if you are refused contributory ESA because you do not meet the national insurance (NI) contribution conditions, in some cases it may be worth claiming at a later date that falls in a different benefit year (see p964).

Making a claim

The DWP refers to contributory ESA paid under the UC system as 'new-style' ESA. This applies to most new claims. For when you come under the UC system (which includes where you make a new claim for ESA), see p22.

You can start a claim for new-style ESA:[32]

- online at gov.uk/how-to-claim-new-style-esa; *or*
- if you cannot claim online, by telephone on 0800 328 5644 (textphone: 0800 328 1344; Relay UK and BSL relay services available).[33] Say that you wish to claim 'new-style' contributory ESA.

If you do not come under the UC system, you may be able to get 'old-style' contributory ESA instead. However, unless you are prevented by law from claiming UC (see p23), you cannot make a new claim for old-style ESA (if you do, that will bring you under the UC system). Instead, you need to be getting income-related ESA already and then satisfy the NI contribution conditions for having that award changed so as also to include contributory ESA, without the need for a new claim. Contact Jobcentre Plus about this.

If you want to claim UC to top up your contributory ESA (such a claim will bring you under the UC system if you are not already), you must do this separately.

> **Are you prevented from claiming universal credit?**
> In rare cases, you might be prevented by law from claiming UC (see p23). If that applies,
> you do not come under the UC system and can get income-related ESA as well as old-style
> contributory ESA. Contact Jobcentre Plus.

You provide information or evidence as required (see p698). You can amend or withdraw your claim before a decision is made (see p1135). If there is a delay in deciding your claim, you may be able to get a short-term advance (see p1153).

Who should claim

You claim contributory ESA on your own behalf. However, if you are unable to manage your own affairs, another person can claim ESA for you as your 'appointee' (see p1135).

If you are employed

If you are employed, you should normally be paid statutory sick pay (SSP) (see Chapter 39) for the first 28 weeks of your limited capability for work. If your employer thinks that you are not entitled to SSP, or if your entitlement to SSP has run out, it should complete and give you Form SSP1. To get contributory ESA, you then need to claim ESA. **Note:** claiming ESA will mean that you come under the UC system (see p22). You are normally expected to include Form SSP1 and a medical certificate with your claim. If your employer refuses you SSP on the grounds that you are not entitled to it, your claim for ESA can be backdated to the date of your SSP claim (see p644). If you disagree with your employer's decision not to pay SSP, you can refer the matter to HM Revenue and Customs (HMRC – see Chapter 60), but do not delay claiming ESA. If you have asked HMRC to decide whether you are entitled to SSP, tell the DWP this when you claim ESA.

Information to support your claim

For the general information requirements that apply to all benefits, see p1136.

It is important that you provide any information required when you claim. Until you do, you may not count as having made a valid claim (see p1138). Correct any defects as soon as possible or your date of claim may be affected.

The DWP may ask you to provide information, including:

- your NI number;
- a medical certificate from your doctor, sometimes called a 'fit note' or 'sick note';
- your GP's address and telephone number;
- your contact telephone number (if you have one);
- your bank account details;
- details of your employer (if you have one);

Part 5: Other benefits
Chapter 30: Contributory employment and support allowance
6. Claims and backdating

- details of other money you are getting, such as benefits, pensions or health insurance payments.

For the first seven days of your limited capability for work, the DWP should accept a self-certificate as medical evidence. After seven days, usually you must provide a medical certificate from your doctor. If it is unreasonable to expect you to provide this, the DWP can accept other evidence if that is sufficient.[34]

You may be referred by the DWP for a medical assessment. If you do not attend the medical without good cause, your claim can be refused.[35]

Even if you have provided all that was required when you claimed, you may be asked to provide further information to support your claim (see p1140). You may also be asked to provide information after you are awarded ESA and, if you fail to do so, your ESA could be suspended, or even terminated (see p1162).

The date of your claim

The date of your claim is important as it determines when your entitlement to ESA starts (subject to the rules on waiting days – see p646). This is not necessarily the date from when you are paid. For information about when payment of ESA starts, see p645.

Unless it is backdated, the **'date of your claim'** is usually the date of your telephone call, or the date your claim form is received at a DWP office (or a local authority office – see p642).[36] However, if you notify the DWP that you intend to send a claim form and you send a properly completed form within one month, your date of claim is the date you notified the DWP that you intended to claim.

You must make sure your claim is valid. If it is 'defective', you are given a short time to correct the defects (see p1139). If you do, your claim is treated as having been made when you initially claimed.[37]

In some cases, you can claim in advance (see p645) and in some cases your claim can be backdated (see below). If you want this to be done, make this clear when you claim or the DWP might not consider it. If you claimed SSP or maternity allowance (MA) when you should have claimed ESA, see below.

Backdating your claim

Your claim can be backdated for up to three months before the day you actually claim – ie, for time during this period when you were entitled to ESA. You should state from which date you are claiming in that period and ask for it to be backdated. You do not need special reasons for backdating.[38]

If you claim the wrong benefit

If your employer has decided that you are not entitled to SSP and you claim ESA within three months of being notified in writing of this, your ESA claim is treated as having been made on the date of your SSP claim.[39]

A claim for MA can be treated as a claim for ESA and vice versa.[40] If your MA claim is accepted as a claim for ESA, your ESA can be backdated for up to three months before the date you claimed MA if you satisfy the qualifying conditions during that period (see p1144).

Claiming in advance

You can claim ESA up to three months before the date on which you qualify for it.[41] The date of your claim is the date on which you qualify.

Starting work when your claim ends

If you start work, you may be able to benefit from the rules for linking periods of limited capability for work should you fall sick again later (see p1018). If this is the case, provided you claim ESA again within a 12-week linking period, you get the same amount of ESA that you previously received.

---

7. Getting paid

The general rules on getting paid are covered in Chapter 51. This section explains the specific rules that apply to both contributory and income-related employment and support allowance (ESA).

When is employment and support allowance paid?

The day you are paid depends on your national insurance number (see p1150).[42] ESA is usually paid fortnightly in arrears, although it can be paid at different intervals, including at a daily rate of one-seventh of the weekly amount.[43]

ESA is a weekly benefit, although in some cases it can be paid for a part week.[44]

Note:
- Your contributory ESA might be paid at a reduced rate in some circumstances (see p635).
- Deductions can be made from your ESA to pay to third parties (see p1164).
- You might not be paid ESA, or it might be paid at a reduced rate, if you have been sanctioned for a benefit offence (see p1239). You may also be sanctioned for other reasons (see Chapter 49).
- For information on missing payments, see p1150. If you cannot get your ESA payments because you have lost your bank card or you have forgotten your PIN, see p1149. If you have lost your payment service card, see p1150.
- If payment of your ESA is delayed, see p1255. If you are waiting for a decision on your claim, or to be paid, you might be able to get a short-term advance (see p1153). If you wish to complain about how your claim has been dealt with, or claim compensation, see Chapter 61.

Part 5: Other benefits
Chapter 30: Contributory employment and support allowance
8. Tax, other benefits and the benefit cap

- If payment of your ESA is suspended, see p1161. This includes if you have failed to supply evidence of your limited capability for work.
- If you are overpaid ESA, you might have to repay it (see Chapter 53) and, in some circumstances, you may have to pay a penalty (see p1229). If you have been accused of fraud, see Chapter 54.
- If you are owed arrears of ESA, these can be paid in instalments (see p1148).

Change of circumstances

You must report changes in your circumstances that you have been told you must report, as well as any that you might reasonably be expected to know might affect your right to, the amount of, or the payment of your benefit. You should do this as soon as possible, preferably in writing. See p1160 for further information.

Your ESA is usually adjusted from the beginning of the week in which the change of circumstances takes effect.[45] However, there are exceptions – eg, if you have notified the DWP that you are terminally ill or if you have failed to notify it of a change about your limited capability for work (see p1279).[46]

Waiting days

You are not entitled to ESA for a period of seven '**waiting days**' at the beginning of your period of limited capability for work (see p1018).[47] This does not apply if:
- your entitlement to ESA starts within 12 weeks of your entitlement to income support, incapacity benefit, severe disablement allowance, pension credit, jobseeker's allowance, carer's allowance, statutory sick pay or maternity allowance coming to an end; or
- you have requalified for contributory ESA on the basis of being put in the support group (see p637), having previously lost entitlement because of the rules on how long you can be paid contributory ESA (see p640); or
- you are terminally ill; or
- you have been discharged from the armed forces and three or more days before the discharge were days of sickness absence.

You may be able to get a short-term advance before your first payment is due (see p1153).

8. Tax, other benefits and the benefit cap

Tax

Contributory employment and support allowance (ESA), including ESA in youth, is taxable.[48] If you were transferred from incapacity benefit (IB) or severe disablement allowance (SDA) to contributory ESA (see p640), your contributory ESA is still taxable, even if your IB/SDA was not.

Means-tested benefits and tax credits

If you are entitled to contributory ESA:

- your contributory ESA counts as income for the purposes of means-tested benefits if you do not get income-related ESA;
- if you come under the universal credit (UC) system (see p22), you may be entitled to UC to top up your new-style contributory ESA;
- if you do not come under the UC system, you may be entitled to income-related ESA to top up your old-style contributory ESA, without making a new claim (see p25);
- you may be entitled to an additional component as part of your housing benefit (HB) (see p336).

You cannot get ESA at the same time as:

- income support (IS) in your own right;[49]
- income-related jobseeker's allowance (JSA) in your own right, including as part of a joint-claim couple. However, you can get contributory ESA if you are part of a JSA joint-claim couple and you do not have to satisfy all the JSA conditions.[50] If your partner is entitled in her/his own right to income-based JSA (and it is not joint-claim JSA – eg, because you have a dependent child), you can get contributory ESA at the same time.

Non-means-tested benefits

While you are on contributory ESA, you may be entitled to national insurance credits for limited capability for work (see p954).

Contributory ESA is affected by the rules on overlapping benefits (see p1151), which means that you may not be paid it in full if another earnings-replacement benefit is paid to you.

You are not entitled to ESA if you are entitled to statutory sick pay.[51] You can continue to get contributory ESA if you then get statutory maternity pay (SMP) or statutory adoption pay (SAP). You can get contributory ESA and statutory paternity pay (SPP) or statutory parental bereavement pay (SPBP). You can get contributory ESA and statutory shared parental pay (SSPP) if the amount of the SSPP is less than the amount of ESA. Your ESA is reduced by the amount of the SMP, SAP or SSPP you get.[52]

You cannot claim ESA and contribution-based JSA in your own right at the same time. If your partner is entitled to contribution-based JSA, you can claim ESA.

The benefit cap

In some cases, there is a limit on the total amount of specified benefits you can receive (a 'benefit cap'). ESA is one of the specified benefits. However, the benefit cap does not apply if you or your partner receive ESA which includes a support component. In other cases, it only applies if you are getting UC or HB. See p1156 for further information.

Passports and other sources of help

If you receive contributory ESA, you may be eligible for a Christmas bonus (see p861). You may also qualify for health benefits such as free prescriptions (see Chapter 31), and education benefits such as free school lunches (see p851). You may be entitled to council tax reduction (see p836).

Financial help on starting work

If you stop getting contributory ESA because you start work, you may be able to get extended payments of HB if you pay rent (see p217). Your local authority may provide extended help with council tax. See p858 for information about other financial help you may get.

Notes

1. **Who can get contributory employment and support allowance**
   1 ss1 and 20(1) WRA 2007; reg 40(1) and (7) ESA Regs; reg 37(1) and (8) ESA Regs 2013
   2 Sch 1 paras 1-4 WRA 2007
   3 s53 WRA 2012; s1(3A) WRA 2007
   4 s52 WRA 2012
   5 s18 WRA 2007; reg 157 ESA Regs; reg 93 ESA Regs 2013
   6 Regs 157(3) and 158 ESA Regs; reg 94 ESA Regs 2013
   7 Sch 5 para 14 ESA Regs; reg 63 ESA Regs 2013

4. **The amount of benefit**
   8 s24(2) WRA 2007; reg 4 ESA Regs; reg 5 ESA Regs 2013
   9 Reg 7(38) SS&CS(DA) Regs; reg 35(7) UC,PIP,JSA&ESA(DA) Regs
   10 Regs 4, 5 and 147A ESA Regs; regs 5, 6 and 87 ESA Regs 2013
   11 Reg 5 ESA Regs; reg 6 ESA Regs 2013
   12 s2(1)(a) WRA 2007; regs 7 and 67(2) and Sch 4 para 1(1)(b) and (c) ESA Regs; regs 7 and 62(1) ESA Regs 2013

   13 s2(2) and (3) WRA 2007; reg 67(2) and (3) and Sch 4 paras 1(a), 12 and 13 ESA Regs; Sch 2 para 12 ESA(TP)(EA)(No.2) Regs
   14 ss2(2) and 4(4) WRA 2007
   15 *PM v SSWP (ESA)* [2012] UKUT 188 (AAC)
   16 Reg 54 ESA Regs; ss11 and 11D WRA 2007
   17 s15 WRWA 2016
   18 Sch 1 Part 1 ESAUC(MA) Regs
   19 Reg 2 IS Regs; reg 1 JSA Regs; reg 1 SPC Regs; reg 2 HB Regs; reg 2 HB(SPC) Regs; reg 1 SFCWP Regs
   20 ss2(3) and 4(5) WRA 2007
   21 Reg 7 ESA Regs; reg 7 ESA Regs 2013
   22 Regs 72-79 ESA Regs; regs 64-72 ESA Regs 2013
   23 s3 WRA 2007; regs 72, 72A and 74 ESA Regs; regs 64, 65 and 67 ESA Regs 2013
   24 Reg 75 ESA Regs; reg 68 ESA Regs 2013
   25 R(IB) 1/04 applied this to IB, but it is not followed by the DWP for ESA.
   26 Schs 1 para 11 and 2 para 14 ESA(TP)(EA)(No.2) Regs

27 Regs 76(1), 79 and 94(1) ESA Regs; regs
69, 72 and 79 ESA Regs 2013
28 ss51 and 52 WRA 2012; ss1A and 1B
WRA 2007
29 ss1A and 1B WRA 2007
30 Vol 8 Ch 41, para 41847 DMG; Ch V2,
para 045 ADM

6. Claims and backdating
31 Reg 3(j) SS(C&P) Regs; reg 7 ESA Regs
2013
32 Regs 13 and 15 UC,PIP,JSA&ESA(C&P)
Regs
33 gov.uk/employment-support-
allowance/how-to-claim
34 Regs 2 and 5 SS(ME) Regs
35 s19 SSA 1998; reg 23 ESA Regs
36 Reg 6(1F) SS(C&P) Regs; regs 14 and 16
UC,PIP,JSA&ESA(C&P) Regs
37 Regs 4G(5) and 4H(6) and (7) SS(C&P)
Regs; regs 13(5) and 15(4)
UC,PIP,JSA&ESA(C&P) Regs
38 Reg 19 and Sch 4 para 16 SS(C&P) Regs;
reg 28 UC,PIP,JSA&ESA(C&P) Regs
39 Reg 10(1A) SS(C&P) Regs; reg 17
UC,PIP,JSA&ESA(C&P) Regs
40 Reg 9 and Sch 1 SS(C&P) Regs; reg 25
UC,PIP,JSA&ESA(C&P) Regs
41 Reg 13(9) SS(C&P) Regs; reg 34
UC,PIP,JSA&ESA(C&P) Regs

7. Getting paid
42 Reg 26C(2) SS(C&P) Regs; reg 51
UC,PIP,JSA&ESA(C&P) Regs
43 Reg 26C SS(C&P) Regs; reg 51(5)
UC,PIP,JSA&ESA(C&P) Regs
44 Vol 8 Ch 46, para 46011 DMG
45 Reg 7(2)(a) and Sch 3C SS&CS(DA)
Regs; reg 35 and Sch 1 para 1
UC,PIP,JSA&ESA(C&P) Regs
46 Reg 7(2) and (25) and Sch 3C
SS&CS(DA) Regs; reg 35 and Sch 1
paras 6 and 9 UC,PIP,JSA&ESA(C&P)
Regs
47 Reg 144 ESA Regs; reg 85 ESA Regs
2013

8. Tax, other benefits and the benefit cap
48 ss658(4) and 661(1) IT(EP)A 2003
49 s1(3)(e) WRA 2007
50 s1(3)(f) WRA 2007
51 s20 WRA 2007
52 Regs 80-82A ESA Regs; regs 73-75 ESA
Regs 2013

Chapter 31

Health benefits

Key facts

- Health benefits provide help with the costs of NHS prescriptions, dental treatment, sight tests and glasses, and wigs and fabric supports, as well as fares to receive NHS treatment.
- Some people are exempt from charges and can get full help with NHS costs and fares. Others qualify for full or partial help in specific situations or if their income and capital are below a certain amount (known as the low income scheme).
- Health benefits are administered by the NHS Business Services Authority.

1. Who can get health benefits

Although the NHS generally provides free healthcare, there are fixed charges for some items and services such as prescriptions, dental treatment, sight tests and glasses, and wigs and fabric supports. You may also have fares to pay to get to hospital or another establishment for NHS treatment. However, you may qualify for full help with the charges and fares (ie, you may get the items or services free of charge) or you may get partial help (ie, you get a reduction).

In some cases, you must make a claim (see p660). If you pay for an item or service that you could have received free, or at a reduced cost, you can apply for a refund (see p662).

Full help

You get full help with charges and fares if you:
- are in an exempt group; *or*
- satisfy specific conditions, depending on the item or service. See p656 for prescriptions, p657 for dental treatment and dentures, p657 for sight tests and glasses, p659 for wigs and fabric supports and p659 for fares to receive NHS treatment; *or*
- get full help with health costs under the low income scheme (see p652). If you do not qualify for full help with health costs, you may qualify for partial help under the low income scheme.

Exempt groups

You qualify for full help with charges and fares if you are in an exempt group. You are in an exempt group if:[1]
- you, or a member of your family (see p652 for who counts), get any of the following qualifying benefits:
  - universal credit (UC). In the assessment period (see p38) before the health cost was incurred, you (or you and your partner together) must either have:
    - no earnings; *or*
    - earnings no greater than £435 (or £935, if you have a limited capability for work, or if the child element is included in your UC);
  - income support (IS), income-based jobseeker's allowance, income-related employment and support allowance (ESA) or the guarantee credit of pension credit (PC); *or*
  - child tax credit (CTC), or both CTC and working tax credit (WTC), or WTC that includes a disabled worker or severe disability element. Your gross annual income for tax credits must not exceed £15,276;
- you, or a member of your family, are an asylum seeker who gets asylum support (see p1538). Dependants for whom you are claiming asylum support count as members of your family;
- you are aged 16 or 17 and you get support from a local authority after being looked after (in Scotland, getting support under section 29(1) of the Children (Scotland) Act 1995 after leaving care). This does not appear in the regulations for sight tests in England and Wales or for vouchers for glasses and contact lenses in England, but NHS booklet *Help with Health Costs* (HC11) states you are entitled to full help with health costs.

Even if you are not in one of the exempt groups, note the following.
- If you are a war disablement pensioner, you may qualify for free prescriptions and wigs and fabric supports. You may also be able to claim money back for dental treatment, sight tests, glasses or contact lenses or fares to hospital. You must have a valid war pension exemption certificate, and you must need the

items or treatment, or to travel, because of your war disability. See p660 for where to claim.

- If you are a hospital inpatient, all medication and NHS treatment is provided free of charge (including glasses and contact lenses if prescribed through the hospital eye service). If you are an outpatient or are at a walk-in centre, medication taken and treatment given while you are in the hospital or walk-in centre is also provided without charge (but you may be charged for dentures and bridges).

Member of the family

'**Family**' means you and your partner and any child or qualifying young person included in your claim for the qualifying benefit or tax credit (see p307 for means-tested benefits and p271 for tax credits).

Partial help

If you do not qualify for full help with charges and fares, you may still qualify for partial help under the low income scheme.

The low income scheme

You and members of your family (see above for who counts) may be entitled to full or partial help with NHS charges under the low income scheme, even if you do not qualify for full help on other grounds. You must make a claim (see p660). The low income scheme is administered by the NHS Business Services Authority.

You (and members of your family) qualify for full help under the low income scheme if:

- you have capital of less than £16,000 (or if you live permanently in a care home, less than £23,250 in England and Scotland, or £24,000 in Wales).[2] Your capital is calculated as for IS (see Chapter 22); *and*
- your income (see p655) does not exceed your 'requirements' (see p653) by more than 50 per cent of the current cost of an English prescription (currently 50 per cent of £9.35 = £4.67).[3] If your income exceeds your requirements by more than this amount, see below to find out whether you qualify for partial help with charges.

If you are entitled to full help, you are issued with an HC2 certificate. If you are entitled to partial help, you are issued with an HC3 certificate. See p661 for more information.

Partial help with items and services

If you do not qualify for full help with NHS charges, you (and members of your family) may qualify for partial help with these under the low income scheme. You may get:[4]

- reduced-cost dental treatment (including check-ups) and appliances (including dentures); *and*
- reduced-cost sight tests. There is no set charge for sight tests, so it is worth shopping around if you are not entitled to a free test; *and*
- vouchers towards the cost of glasses and contact lenses; *and*
- in England, reduced-cost wigs and fabric supports (these are free in Wales and Scotland); *and*
- partial help with fares to receive NHS treatment.

Note: in England, you cannot qualify for reduced-cost prescriptions under the low income scheme, only free prescriptions. If you cannot qualify for free prescriptions, see p657 for information about prepayment certificates. In Wales and Scotland, prescriptions are free of charge.

You are expected to pay up to a set amount towards the charges. The set amount is:[5]

- for dental charges and charges for wigs and fabric supports, three times the amount by which your income exceeds your requirements (your 'excess income');
- for glasses or lenses, twice the amount of your excess income;
- for a sight test or fares to receive NHS treatment, the amount of your excess income.

Example

Duncan's income exceeds his requirements by £6 so he cannot qualify for full help under the low income scheme. However, he may get partial help. He has to pay the first £18 of dental charges and charges for wigs and fabric supports, the first £6 of the cost of a sight test, the first £12 towards the cost of glasses and lenses and the first £6 of his fares to receive NHS treatment. If he lives in England, he must pay the full cost of prescriptions.

Calculating your requirements

Your 'requirements' are similar to the IS 'applicable amount' (see Chapter 17). The most significant elements and differences are set out on p654. There are no reductions in the applicable amounts of people who are subject to immigration control or who are not habitually resident in the UK, or for students, people engaged in a trade dispute or people without accommodation.

Your requirements are made up of the following elements.[6]
- **Personal allowance(s):**

Single person aged under 25	£61.05
Single person aged under 25, entitled to ESA work-related activity or support component, or incapable of work for at least 28 weeks starting on or after 27 October 2008	£77.00
Single person aged 25–59 or lone parent aged under 60	£77.00
Single person or lone parent aged 60 or over	£182.60
Couples, both partners aged under 60	£121.05
Couples, one or both partners aged 60 or over	£278.70

- **Premiums:** the disability, enhanced disability, severe disability and carer premiums are added to your requirements if you would qualify for them under the IS rules (see p323).

  A disability premium can also be included if you or your partner have been incapable of work for 28 weeks. It can also be included if you (or your partner) have been awarded ESA which includes a work-related activity or support component, or if you (or s/he) have been getting ESA for at least 28 weeks. You (and your partner) must be under 60.

  If you are a single claimant or a lone parent, the amount of the disability premium is increased to £40.60 if you qualify for an ESA support component or if you are getting the middle or highest rate care component of disability living allowance (DLA), either rate of the daily living component of personal independence payment (PIP) or adult disability payment (ADP), or armed forces independence payment, and have been getting ESA or have been incapable of work, for at least 28 weeks.

  An enhanced disability premium can be included if you (or your partner) are getting the DLA highest rate care component, the enhanced rate of the daily living component of PIP/ADP, armed forces independence payment or ESA which includes a support component. You (and your partner) must be under 60.
- **Weekly council tax.**
- **Weekly rent** *less* **any housing benefit** (HB) and any non-dependant deductions, applied broadly in the same way as the deductions under the rules on IS housing costs (see p347). Deductions for fuel and ineligible service charges are made in accordance with the HB rules.
- **Weekly mortgage interest and capital payments on loans** secured on a home, to buy a home or to adapt a home for the special needs of a disabled person, and payments on an endowment policy relating to the purchase of a home. Some other housing costs can be included. Deductions are made for non-dependants.

If you live permanently in a care home, your requirements are your weekly accommodation charge, including meals and services, and a personal expenses allowance. If your place is being funded by a local authority (fully or in part), you are exempt from some charges.

Calculating your income

Your income is calculated as for IS (see Chapter 20), with modifications. These include the following.[7]

- Your income is normally taken into account in the week in which it is paid. If you are affected by a trade dispute, your normal earnings are taken into account.
- You are entitled to an earnings disregard of £20 if you get a disability premium (see p325), or if you or your partner are aged 60 or over.
- If you (or your partner) are doing permitted work while claiming ESA (see p1020), the amount of earnings that can be disregarded is the same as for income-related ESA (see p413). If you *and* your partner are both doing permitted work, the disregard is applied to your joint income.
- The full amount of your (or your partner's) contributory ESA is taken into account, even if it is paid at a reduced rate because you failed to take part in a work-focused interview. This does not appear to apply to 'new-style' ESA (see p631), so the amount received should be taken into account.
- Regular liable relative payments (see p422) count as weekly income. Irregular payments are averaged over the 13 weeks prior to your claim. Lump-sum payments are treated as capital.
- Student loans and grants are divided by 52, unless you are in your final year or are doing a one-year course, in which case the loan is divided by the number of weeks you are studying. The £10 disregard from student loans only applies if you are eligible for a premium, you receive an allowance because of deafness, or you are not a student but your partner is. In addition, in England and Wales, sums in excess of a specified amount of a maintenance grant and certain loans paid to Scottish students studying in England or Wales are disregarded. Also, if a voluntary payment is taken into account, up to £20 of it is disregarded.
- Insurance policy payments for housing costs that cannot be met by IS count as income, but payments for unsecured loans for repairs and improvements (including premiums) are ignored.
- If you live permanently in residential or nursing care:
  - in Wales, no tariff income from any capital is taken into account;
  - in England and Scotland, the lower threshold for tariff income is £14,250.
  Remember that if your place is being funded by a local authority (in full or in part), you are exempt from some charges.
- The savings credit of PC is ignored as income.

2. **Prescriptions**

Prescriptions are free in Wales and Scotland. You qualify for free prescriptions in England (and you can get an English prescription free of charge in Wales and Scotland) if:[8]

- you are in one of the exempt groups listed on p651; *or*
- you qualify under the low income scheme (see p652); *or*
- you are aged 60 or over; *or*
- you are aged under 16, or you are under 19 and in full-time education; *or*
- you are pregnant or have given birth in the last 12 months; *or*
- you are a permanent resident in a care home and your place is partly or wholly funded by a local authority; *or*
- you are prescribed or given specific medicines for a pandemic disease; *or*
- you are in prison or a young offenders' institution or other secure accommodation (or were given the prescription while you were); *or*
- you are detained under the Immigration Act 1971 or section 62 of the Nationality, Immigration and Asylum Act 2002; *or*
- you have:
  - a continuing physical disability, which prevents you going out without the help of another person;
  - epilepsy requiring continuous anticonvulsive therapy;
  - a permanent fistula, including a caecostomy, ileostomy, laryngostomy or colostomy, needing continuous surgical dressing or an appliance;
  - diabetes mellitus (except where treatment is by diet alone);
  - diabetes insipidus and other forms of hypopituitarism;
  - myxoedema;
  - hypoparathyroidism;
  - forms of hypoadrenalism (including Addison's disease), for which specific substitution therapy is essential;
  - myasthenia gravis;
  - cancer, for which you are undergoing treatment, or for the effects of cancer or cancer treatment.

If you have any of the conditions listed in the last bullet point, ask your GP for Form FP92A to apply for a medical exemption certificate which you should present when you collect your prescription. Medical exemption certificates are valid for no more than five years.

If you are exempt from NHS charges on the basis that you are pregnant or have given birth in the last 12 months, ask your midwife, health visitor or GP for a maternity exemption form, which can be issued online straight away or by post.

Prepayment certificates

In England, if you are not exempt from charges and you need more than three prescription items in three months or 12 items in a year, you can save money by buying a prepayment certificate.

Apply on Form FP95, online at nhsbsa.nhs.uk/help-nhs-prescription-costs/prescription-prepayment-certificates, at registered chemists, by telephone (0300 330 1341) or by post.

A refund can be claimed in certain circumstances – eg, if you buy a prepayment certificate and then qualify for free prescriptions.

3. Dental treatment and dentures

NHS dental check-ups are free in Scotland. In England, Wales and Scotland, you qualify for free NHS dental treatment (including check-ups) and appliances (including dentures) if, when your treatment is arranged or charges are made:[9]

- you are in one of the exempt groups listed on p651; *or*
- you qualify under the low income scheme (see p652); *or*
- you are under 18, or you are under 19 and in full-time education; *or*
- in Wales, for free check-ups only, you are under 25 or are 60 or over; *or*
- you are pregnant or have given birth within the last 12 months; *or*
- you are a permanent resident in a care home and your place is being partly or wholly funded by a local authority; *or*
- in England and Wales, you are in prison or a young offenders' institution; *or*
- you are a patient of the community dental service (available if you have difficulty getting treatment because of a disability or for other reasons – contact your health authority for details) or an NHS hospital dental service. **Note:** there may be a charge for dentures and bridges.

4. Sight tests and glasses

Free sight tests

NHS sight tests are free in Scotland. In England and Wales you qualify for a free NHS sight test if:[10]

- you are in one of the exempt groups listed on p651; *or*
- you qualify under the low income scheme (see p652); *or*
- you are aged 60 or over; *or*
- you are under 16, or you are under 19 and in full-time education; *or*
- you are registered blind or partially sighted; *or*
- you have been prescribed complex or powerful lenses; *or*

- you have been diagnosed as having diabetes or glaucoma or are at risk of getting glaucoma; *or*
- you are aged 40 or over and are the parent, brother, sister or child of someone with glaucoma; *or*
- you are a patient of the hospital eye service; *or*
- in England, you are on leave from prison or a young offenders' institution.

Vouchers for glasses and contact lenses

If you are given a prescription for glasses following an eye test, you may be entitled to a voucher that you can use to buy glasses or contact lenses if you need these for the first time, or because your previous ones have worn out through fair wear and tear, or your new prescription differs from your old one. You qualify if:[11]

- you are in one of the exempt groups listed on p651; *or*
- you qualify under the low income scheme (see p652); *or*
- you are under 16, or under 19 and in full-time education; *or*
- you are a hospital eye service patient needing frequent changes of glasses or contact lenses; *or*
- you have been prescribed complex or powerful lenses; *or*
- in England, you are on leave from prison or a young offenders' institution.

In addition, you may be entitled to a voucher when your glasses or lenses need to be replaced or repaired if, because of illness (illness or disability in Scotland), you have lost or damaged them and the cost of repair or replacement is not covered by insurance or warranty. This only applies if:[12]

- you are under 16, or under 19 and in full-time education. **Note:** the requirement for the loss or damage to have been caused by illness (illness or disability in Scotland) does not apply to children under 16 and, in England, to young people under 18 who were previously looked after by a local authority;[13] *or*
- you or a member of your family (see p652 for who counts) are covered by the first bullet point listed under 'Exempt groups' on p651; *or*
- you qualify under the low income scheme (see p652); *or*
- you have been prescribed complex or powerful lenses.

You can redeem the voucher at any supplier when you buy your glasses or contact lenses (or have glasses repaired). Vouchers are, however, only valid for two years.[14] Vouchers might not cover the full cost of the glasses or lenses you choose to buy. Prices vary; you may need to shop around if you do not want to pay the extra cost.

- -

5. **Wigs and fabric supports**

Wigs and fabric supports are free in Scotland and Wales. You qualify for free wigs and fabric supports in England if:[15]

- you are in one of the exempt groups listed on p651; *or*
- you qualify under the low income scheme (see p652); *or*
- you are a hospital inpatient; *or*
- you are aged under 16, or under 19 and in full-time education; *or*
- you are a permanent resident in a care home and your place is being partly or wholly funded by a local authority; *or*
- you are in prison or a young offenders' institution or are detained under the Immigration Act 1971 or section 62 of the Nationality, Immigration and Asylum Act 2002.

6. **Fares to receive NHS treatment**

You qualify for full help with your fares to attend a hospital or any other establishment for NHS treatment or services if:[16]

- you are in one of the exempt groups listed on p651; *or*
- you qualify under the low income scheme (see p652); *or*
- you are a permanent resident in a care home and your place is being partly or wholly funded by a local authority; *or*
- you live in the Isles of Scilly or the Scottish Islands or Highlands and have to travel more than a specified distance. Special rules, including maximum costs, apply.[17]

The travel expenses of a companion can also be covered – eg, if your child is attending a hospital and you need to accompany her/him, or if you need to be accompanied for medical reasons. You get help with the cost of travelling by the cheapest means of transport that is reasonable and, in Scotland, if necessary, the cost of overnight accommodation. This usually means standard-class public transport. If you have to travel by car or taxi, you should be paid a mileage allowance and road and toll charges, or taxi fares.

Claim at the place where you receive NHS treatment. You may be able to request payment in advance of travelling if this is necessary.

Travel expenses can be covered if you are travelling abroad to receive NHS treatment if the means and cost of travel, as well as any requirements for a companion, have been agreed in advance with the health service body that has arranged the treatment. In England and Wales, you are entitled to payment for the cost of travel to and from the airport, ferry port or international train station if you are in one of the above groups. You are also entitled to payment or repayment of onward travelling expenses to the treatment centre, whether or not you come into one of the above groups. In Scotland, the rules do not specify what can be covered.

7. Claims and refunds

In some situations, you do not have to make a claim for help with charges.

- If you are exempt on the grounds of your age, receipt of a qualifying benefit or because you are a full-time student aged under 19, complete the back of the prescription form (if required), or complete the appropriate form at your dentist, optician or hospital. See below if you get universal credit (UC).
- If you are an asylum seeker receiving asylum support, an HC2 certificate is issued by the Home Office. For further advice, call Migrant Help (0808 801 0503).
- If you are exempt because you receive tax credits, HM Revenue and Customs automatically sends you an exemption certificate. If you do not receive your certificate, present your letter of entitlement to tax credits.
- If you are exempt because you are pregnant or have given birth in the last 12 months, you need an exemption certificate. Ask your doctor, midwife or health visitor for a form.
- If you are entitled to free prescriptions because you have one of the conditions listed on p656, you need an exemption certificate. Apply on Form FP92A, which you can get from your GP.

In other cases, you must make a claim.

Note: if you are a war disablement pensioner, contact the Veterans UK helpline on 0808 191 4218 or see gov.uk/guidance/war-pension-scheme-wps.

Claiming if you get universal credit

Not all help with health costs claim forms have a tick box for UC. In this situation, the official NHS information suggests that you tick the box for income-based jobseeker's allowance instead.[18] If you are unsure whether you are entitled to help with health costs because you do not know how much you earned in your last complete assessment period before the day you apply for help with health costs, check your online journal or call the UC helpline (tel: 0800 328 5644). If you cannot get a figure for your last month's earned income and you think it might exceed the threshold, you should pay the relevant charge and ask for a refund form at the same time. For prescription charges, you will not be able to get the refund form (Form FP57) at a later stage.

Claiming under the low income scheme

To get full or partial help with charges and fares under the low income scheme, you must make a claim. This includes if you are an asylum seeker but you are not receiving asylum support. If you *are* receiving asylum support, see p660. This also includes if you are exempt because you live in a care home or you are aged 16 or 17 and were previously looked after by a local authority.

Claim on Form HC1. If you have less than £6,000 capital, you can claim online at nhsbsa.nhs.uk/nhs-low-income-scheme. You can download a form via nhsbsa.nhs.uk/nhs-low-income-scheme or by phoning 0300 330 1343 (England), 0345 603 1108 (Wales) or 0131 275 6386 (Scotland). Another person can apply on your behalf if you are unable to act for yourself.

If you live in a care home or you are aged 16 or 17 and were previously looked after by a local authority, you can use a shorter Form HC1(SC).

Getting a certificate and when it expires

If you qualify for:
- full help, you are sent an HC2 certificate;
- partial help, you are sent an HC3 certificate which tells you the contribution you must make towards the charges.

Certificates are normally valid for 12 months. However, they are valid for:[19]
- five years if you are a single person aged 65 or over, or one of a couple, one aged 60 or over and the other aged 65 or over. This only applies if you do not receive earnings, or payments from an occupational pension, a personal pension or an annuity, and you do not have a dependent child or young person as a member of your household; *or*
- six months from the date of claim if you are receiving asylum support; *or*
- until the end of your course or the start of the next academic year if you are a full-time student.

Make a repeat claim on Form HC1 shortly before the expiry date. If you have a five-year certificate, you must notify the issuing authority of any changes in the composition of your family or household. In other cases, changes of circumstances (eg, starting work and increases in income) do not affect the validity of a certificate. However, if the change could result in increased help (eg, your income has *decreased*), you can reapply for a fresh assessment before the certificate expires.

Overpayments and fraud

If you receive help to which you were not entitled, you can be issued with a penalty notice requiring you to pay the charge you should have paid plus a penalty, unless you can show that you did not act 'wrongfully' or with 'any lack of care'. The penalty can be increased if you do not pay it within 28 days, and court proceedings can be taken to recover the debt. Anyone wrongly claiming help with charges on your behalf can be liable to pay a penalty charge. You can also be prosecuted if you obtain help wrongly, on the basis of a false statement or representation.[20]

Delays and complaints

For general queries or to make an informal complaint, telephone 0300 330 1343. If you are unhappy with the decision on your claim or how it has been dealt with, or there are delays in obtaining a certificate, you can make a formal complaint by telephone, in writing or email to the head of the relevant service at the NHS Business Services Authority. See nhsbsa.nhs.uk/contact-us/complaints for more details. If necessary, you could pay for the treatment or items you need and, after the outcome of your complaint, try to obtain a refund.

Refunds

If you pay for an item or service that you could have got free, or at reduced cost, you can apply for a refund. Do this within three months of paying the charge, although the time limit can, in some cases, be extended if you can show good cause for applying late – eg, you were ill.[21]

Apply for a refund of a prescription charge (in England) on Form FP57, which you must obtain when you pay as one cannot be supplied later. For other items and services, apply on the relevant Form HC5 specific to that item/service, available to download at nhsbsa.nhs.uk or by phoning 0300 330 1343 (England), 0345 603 1108 (Wales) or 0131 275 6386 (Scotland). You must submit a receipt or other documents to show that you have paid the charge. If you need an HC2 or HC3 certificate and have not applied for one, send a Form HC1 with your application for a refund.

Notes

1. Who can get health benefits
 1 **E** Regs 2-5 NHS(TERC) Regs; reg 3 POS Regs; reg 8 NHS(OCP) Regs 2013
 S Regs 2 and 4 NHS(TERC)(S) Regs; regs 3 and 8 NHS(OCP)(S) Regs
 W Regs 2-5 NHS(TERC)(W) Regs; reg 13 NHS(GOS) Regs; regs 3 and 8 NHS(OCP) Regs
 2 **E** Sch 1 Table A NHS(TERC) Regs
 S Sch Part 1 NHS(TERC)(S) Regs
 W Sch 1 Table A NHS(TERC)(W) Regs

 3 **E** Reg 5(2)(e) and (f) NHS(TERC) Regs; reg 3(2)(c) and (d) POS Regs; regs 3(2) and 8(3)(b) and (c) NHS(OCP) Regs 2013
 S Reg 4(2)(c) and (d) NHS(TERC)(S) Regs; regs 3(2) and 8(3)(e) and (f) NHS(OCP)(S) Regs
 W Reg 5(2)(e) NHS(TERC)(W) Regs; reg 13(2)(e) and (f) NHS(GOS) Regs; regs 3(2) and 8(3)(e) and (f) NHS(OCP) Regs

Chapter 31

Health benefits

4 **E** Reg 6 NHS(TERC) Regs; regs 3 and 8 NHS(OCP) Regs 2013
   S Reg 5 NHS(TERC)(S) Regs; regs 3 and 8 NHS(OCP)(S) Regs
   W Reg 6 NHS(TERC)(W) Regs; regs 3 and 8 NHS(OCP) Regs
5 **E** Reg 6 NHS(TERC) Regs; regs 7, 15 and 20 NHS(OCP) Regs 2013
   S Reg 5 NHS(TERC)(S) Regs; regs 14 and 19 NHS(OCP)(S) Regs
   W Reg 6 NHS(TERC)(W) Regs; regs 7, 14 and 19 NHS(OCP) Regs
6 **E** Reg 17 and Sch 1 Table B NHS(TERC) Regs
   S Reg 8 and Sch Part 2 NHS(TERC)(S) Regs
   W Reg 16 and Sch 1 Table B NHS(TERC)(W) Regs
7 **E** Reg 16 and Sch 1 Table A NHS(TERC) Regs
   S Reg 8 and Sch Part 1 NHS(TERC)(S) Regs
   W Reg 15 and Sch 1 Table A NHS(TERC)(W) Regs

2. Prescriptions
8 **E** Regs 10-13 NHS(CDA) Regs; regs 4 and 5 NHS(TERC) Regs
   S Regs 3 and 4 NHS(FP&CDA)(S) Regs
   W Regs 3, 4 and 8 NHS(FP&CDA)(W) Regs; regs 4 and 5 NHS(TERC)(W) Regs

3. Dental treatment and dentures
9 **E** s177 NHSA 2006; regs 3 and 7 and Sch 5 NHS(DC) Regs; regs 4 and 5 NHS(TERC) Regs
   S Sch 11 NHS(S)A 1978; reg 5 and Sch 2 NHS(DC)(S) Regs; regs 3 and 4 NHS(TERC)(S) Regs
   W s126 NHS(W)A 2006; regs 3 and 7 and Sch 5 NHS(DC)(W) Regs; regs 4 and 5 NHS(TERC)(W) Regs

4. Sight tests and glasses
10 **E** Reg 3 POS Regs; regs 3 and 8 NHS(OCP) Regs 2013
   W Reg 13 NHS(GOS) Regs; regs 3 and 8 NHS(OCP) Regs
11 **E** Regs 8 and 9 NHS(OCP) Regs 2013
   S Regs 8 and 9 NHS(OCP)(S) Regs
   W Regs 8 and 9 NHS(OCP) Regs
12 **E** Regs 8 and 16 NHS(OCP) Regs 2013
   S Regs 8 and 15 NHS(OCP)(S) Regs
   W Regs 8 and 15 NHS(OCP) Regs

13 **E** Reg 16(3) NHS(OCP) Regs 2013
   S Reg 15(1) NHS(OCP)(S) Regs
   W Reg 15(1) NHS(OCP) Regs
14 **E** Reg 12(1) NHS(OCP) Regs 2013
   S Reg 12(1) NHS(OCP)(S) Regs
   W Reg 12(1) NHS(OCP) Regs

5. Wigs and fabric supports
15 **E** Regs 10,11 and 12 NHS(CDA) Regs; regs 4 and 5 NHS(TERC) Regs
   S Regs 3 and 4 NHS(FP&CDA)(S) Regs
   W Regs 3, 4 and 8 NHS(FP&CDA)(W) Regs

6. Fares to receive NHS treatment
16 **E** s183(a) NHSA 2006; regs 3 and 5 NHS(TERC) Regs
   S s75A(1)(b) NHS(S)A 1978; regs 3 and 4 NHS(TERC)(S) Regs
   W s131(a) NHS(W)A 2006; regs 3 and 5 NHS(TERC)(W) Regs
17 **E** Reg 9 NHS(TERC) Regs
   S Reg 7 NHS(TERC)(S) Regs

7. Claims and refunds
18 nhs.uk/nhs-services/help-with-health-costs/help-with-health-costs-for-people-getting-universal-credit
19 **E** Reg 8 NHS(TERC) Regs
   S Reg 10 NHS(TERC)(S) Regs
   W Reg 8 NHS(TERC)(W) Regs
20 **E** ss193 and 194 NHSA 2006
   S ss99ZA and 99ZB NHS(S)A 1978
   W ss141 and 142 NHS(W)A 2006
21 **E** Reg 11 NHS(TERC) Regs; reg 18 NHS(CDA) Regs; regs 6 and 24 NHS(OCP) Regs 2013
   S Reg 11 NHS(TERC)(S) Regs; reg 5 NHS(FP&CDA)(S) Regs; reg 20 NHS(OCP)(S) Regs
   W Reg 10 NHS(TERC)(W) Regs; regs 3(10) and 11A NHS(FP&CDA)(W) Regs; regs 6 and 20 NHS(OCP) Regs

Chapter 32

Industrial injuries benefits

This chapter covers:
1. Who can get industrial injuries benefits (p665)
2. Industrial injuries disablement benefit (p676)
3. Reduced earnings allowance (p678)
4. Retirement allowance (p680)
5. Special benefit rules (p680)
6. Claims and backdating (p681)
7. Getting paid (p683)
8. Tax, other benefits and the benefit cap (p684)

Key facts

- Industrial injuries benefits are paid if you are disabled as a result of an accident at work or a disease caused by your job (but not if this is self-employment).
- The main industrial injuries benefit is **disablement benefit**, but you may also qualify for **reduced earnings allowance** or **retirement allowance**.
- All industrial injuries benefits are non-means-tested benefits.
- You do not have to have paid national insurance contributions to qualify.
- You can qualify whether you are in or out of work.
- Industrial injuries benefits are administered and paid by the DWP.
- If you disagree with an industrial injuries benefit decision, you can apply for a revision or a supersession (see Chapter 56), or appeal against it (see Chapter 57). You must apply for a mandatory reconsideration before you can appeal.

Future changes

In Scotland, industrial injuries benefits will be replaced by employment injury assistance. Social Security Scotland will be responsible for administering and paying this and existing industrial injuries disablement benefits in Scotland. See Chapter 72 and AskCPAG and CPAG's *Welfare Rights Bulletin* for updates.

1. Who can get industrial injuries benefits

You can qualify for industrial injuries benefits if you satisfy the **'industrial injury condition'** – ie:[1]

* you have had a 'personal injury' in an 'industrial accident' (see p666) or you have a 'prescribed industrial disease' (see p670); *and*
* at the time of the injury you were an employed earner (see below); *and*
* as a result of that accident or disease, you have had a 'loss of faculty' (see p672); *and*
* as a result of that 'loss of faculty', you are 'disabled'.

Industrial injuries benefits include industrial injuries disablement benefit, reduced earnings allowance (REA) and retirement allowance. You can only qualify for REA or retirement allowance if, in the case of a claim resulting from an accident, your accident occurred before 1 October 1990.[2] If your claim for REA or retirement allowance results from a prescribed industrial disease, the date of onset must have been before this date (see p679).[3]

If you have been injured by your work, you may also have the right to sue your employer. Legal help may be available and you may be able to get a free consultation with a solicitor. Your right to compensation from your employer is separate from your rights to benefit under the industrial injuries scheme (although your compensation may be reduced if you have received benefits from the DWP – see p1174).

Employed earners

You can only get industrial injuries benefits if you were an 'employed earner' (see p947) and your accident or disease was caused by your employment.[4] If you are self-employed, you are excluded from the scheme.

If you pay, or ought to pay, class 1 national insurance (NI) contributions (see p948) as an employed earner, you can qualify for industrial injuries benefits. This includes if you pay class 1 (and, in the case of volunteer development workers, class 2 – see p949) contributions while abroad.[5] You can also qualify if your earnings are too low to pay contributions.

Certain workers are treated as employed earners – eg, apprentices, agency workers, taxi drivers, office cleaners and various others.[6] You can also be treated as an employed earner if you are participating in a government course or training scheme which forms part of a mandatory work scheme. The person or organisation providing the training is treated as the employer for the purposes of making a claim.[7] If you are uncertain whether you can be treated as an employed earner, seek advice.

Part 5: Other benefits
Chapter 32: Industrial injuries benefits
1. Who can get industrial injuries benefits

You are treated as *not* being an employed earner if:[8]

- you are employed by your spouse or civil partner and either your employment is not for the purpose of her/his business or profession (eg, if your partner employs you as her/his carer) or your earnings are normally below the lower earnings limit (see p948); *or*
- you are employed by a close relative (parent, step-parent, grandparent, son, daughter, stepchild, grandchild, brother, sister, half-brother or half-sister) in a private house where you both live, and your employment is not for your relative's trade or business carried out there; *or*
- you are a member of, or a civilian employed by, visiting armed forces, unless (in the case of a civilian employee) you are normally resident in the UK.

If you were not lawfully employed in the work in which you had the accident or contracted the disease that gave rise to your claim for benefit, you can still be treated as an employed earner. This is at the DWP's discretion.[9]

Personal injury

Personal injury includes the obvious, such as broken legs or arms, but also covers the less obvious, such as strains and psychological injury.[10] An assault at work causing slight physical injury may cause a far greater psychological injury resulting in agoraphobia, for example. The question is whether or not you have experienced a physiological or psychological change for the worse. It is not enough just to be in pain if the pain is merely a symptom of an existing condition and does not make that condition substantially worse.[11] The damage must be to you or part of you. Dislocation of an artificial hip joint counts as a personal injury,[12] but damage to a pair of spectacles does not.[13]

Accident

The term 'accident' has been defined as an unlooked-for mishap or occurrence.[14] However, an accident need only be unexpected from your point of view.[15] It does not matter if it could have been predicted by an expert. If you do a heavy or dangerous job where accidents are common, a resulting injury is just as much an accident as if your job is sedentary and comparatively safe. A heart attack can be an injury but there needs to be some external event or series of events causing it, such as heavy lifting or work-related stress.[16] Deliberate acts by third parties can be accidents – eg, assaults on security workers or on staff in shops and hospitals.[17]

An accident is 'industrial' if you can show a connection with your work. This connection is established if the accident arose 'out of and in the course of your employment'.[18] It is not only industrial workers who can have 'industrial accidents'; all employees can. For example, if you are an office worker and you trip over boxes of office supplies left in front of a door and injure yourself, this should count as an 'industrial accident'. There need not be a dramatic event; any accident sustained while you are doing your job can qualify – eg, spilling a hot drink and scalding yourself. Mental trauma following an interview could count as an industrial accident.[19]

Accident or process?

Benefit is payable for an 'accident', but not for a 'process' (unless it causes a 'prescribed disease' – see p670). Falling from a ladder and breaking your leg is an accident, but developing back pain as the result of years of heavy manual work is a process, as is breathing in dust over many years.[20] However, sometimes a series of events, over a period of time, can be treated as an accident for benefit purposes.[21] The cumulative effect of a series of incidents can also result in an accident.[22] Your claim for benefit should not be refused simply because you cannot identify which incidents caused the injury.[23]

Example

Kobe's job is trimming excess plastic from electrical cables with a pair of clippers. A particularly rigid batch comes through and each cut requires greater strength. Over two or three days he suffers a strain injury in his hand. The series of cuts constitutes a series of accidents that meets the definition.

It is easier to establish the series of events as an accident if the period of time is fairly short,[24] or if it is noticed at an identifiable moment.[25] An accident is proved if you can establish that an identifiable occurrence must have happened, even if it is impossible to prove when.[26]

In the course of employment

The accident must arise 'in the course of employment'.

Generally, when you arrive at your employer's workplace and are on its private property, you are 'in the course of your employment'. You do not have to have clocked in or have reported to your workplace. If you arrive early (eg, to get ready for work or to have a meal in the canteen),[27] you are covered, unless you arrive early for your own convenience.[28] You are probably covered during breaks from working if you remain on the employer's property,[29] but probably not if you go elsewhere. So if, during a tea break, you go to a local shop to buy a snack, you are outside the course of your employment.[30] If you are allowed to have a snack either at home or at work while still on duty, you are covered.[31]

While at work, most activities are considered to be in the course of employment.[32] Chatting[33] or attending union meetings,[34] for example, are 'reasonably incidental' to the employment, provided they are not done in breach

Part 5: Other benefits
Chapter 32: Industrial injuries benefits
1. Who can get industrial injuries benefits

of instructions.[35] Even if you were doing something in breach of instructions, you may still be covered if:

- the accident would have been taken as arising out of, and in the course of, your employment if you had not been acting in breach of those instructions; *and*
- what you were doing was for the purposes of, or in connection with, your employment.[36]

Example

Naomi works in a paper factory where there is an absolute ban on riding on the load of a forklift truck. She is seen riding on the load, falls off and is injured. Usually she would not be covered, but she saw the load was slipping and rode on the truck in order to hold it on. This was done for the purposes of her employment and so on this occasion she is covered.

Even if you are at home, depending on your contract, you may be covered.[37] You may be covered when you are off on sick leave, if you are engaged in contractual duties.[38]

Example

While on sick leave with stress, Ricky is seen relaxing in the park by a former colleague he had reported for theft. He is assaulted and his jaw is broken. This is an industrial accident arising *out of* his employment (see p669) but not in the course of it, as he was not engaged in any contractual duties, or any activities related to his work, at the time of the assault.

In making your claim (see p681) or arguing your case at an appeal (see Chapter 57), consider all aspects of your employment, including the wording of your contract and the degree of flexibility in the arrangements between you and your employer.[39]

Accidents while travelling

You are not in the course of your employment (see p667) during ordinary journeys to and from work, unless you are travelling on transport operated by or on behalf of your employer, or arranged by your employer, and not being operated in the ordinary course of a public transport service.[40]

Many employees have no set place of work – eg, lorry drivers, home helps, fuel company employees. Lorry drivers are at work when driving their lorries, but gas company workers travelling directly from home to their first job of the day are not always in the course of employment (see p667), even if driving a company van. It depends on the circumstances, including the rules for the use of the van.[41] In one case, a home help was found to be in the course of her employment travelling between jobs, but not going to the first job or from the last. This is because she became engaged in her employment once she started at the first job and remained engaged until the end of the day.[42]

Some employees with no fixed hours of work may be regarded as covered from the moment of leaving home.[43] Caselaw has eased the rules on travelling – eg, to conferences or meetings. So, you can be treated as being at your place of work while attending a meeting at a site where you do not work.[44] You must look at all the factors when deciding whether or not you were in the course of your employment. For example, a police officer who had to travel about 40 miles from home to a training course was in the course of his employment while travelling.[45] Provided you go reasonably directly, with no marked deviation from a proper route, and do not embark on activities unrelated to the journey, you may be covered.

One important factor in deciding whether you are in the course of your employment is whether you receive wages for travelling.[46] However, if you receive a flat-rate travelling allowance as compensation for having to work at a workplace other than your normal base, this may not be enough to make your journey to your alternative workplace part of your work.[47]

Out of employment

As well as arising in the course of your employment (see p667), the accident (see p666) must arise 'out of' your employment, so that in some way the employment contributed to it. For example, the fact that you suffered a detached retina at work is not sufficient to show it arose 'out of' the employment, but medical evidence which shows that it was caused by sudden head movements while inspecting a production line enables you to establish that an industrial accident (see p666) took place. An unexplained fracture while walking at work is not an industrial accident,[48] but it is if you slip and the fracture occurs while you are falling. You are covered even if you are more susceptible to injury because, for example, your bones are brittle[49] or your eyesight is poor.

Example

Evan, a farm worker, suffers sudden pain in the groin while doing his normal job of digging. It is found that a previous hernia, which had been surgically repaired, has given way again. The DWP says that this could have happened at any time and so did not arise 'out of' the employment. Evan's doctor says it could have happened at any time but probably did so at that time because of the heavy digging. The First-tier Tribunal awards him benefit.

An accident also arises out of your employment if it arises in the course of employment (see p667) and it is caused by:[50]
- another's misconduct, 'skylarking' or negligence; *or*
- the behaviour or presence of an animal (including a bird, fish or insect); *or*
- your being struck by any object or by lightning.

Part 5: Other benefits
Chapter 32: Industrial injuries benefits
1. Who can get industrial injuries benefits

In all cases, you must not have contributed to the accident by your conduct, either outside your employment or by any act 'not incidental to' the employment. (This involves looking at what you are employed to do, then at whether you were discharging a duty when the accident occurred, or whether what you were doing was reasonably incidental to that duty.) If you are skylarking at work and are injured as a result, for example, this is not incidental to your employment. If you act to deter someone else from doing so, however, this does not take you out of the course of your employment.[51]

An accident is deemed to arise out of, and in the course of, your employment if you are helping people in an emergency, or trying to save property at or near where you are employed.[52]

Prescribed industrial disease

It is necessary for the disease to be a 'prescribed industrial disease'. This means it is on a list,[53] set out in regulations, of diseases that are known to have a link to a particular 'prescribed' occupation (see below).[54] Each prescribed disease has a statutory definition and you must fit within that. It is not sufficient simply to have a medical diagnosis that you have a particular condition.[55] From time to time new diseases are added to the list and the definitions of existing diseases are amended or 'extended'. For example, the definition of prescribed disease C34 (extrinsic allergic alveolitis) was extended to cover cases resulting from exposure to 'any chemical' causing the condition in prescribed occupations.[56] However, you cannot claim for a disease for any period before it was added to the list.[57] Each prescribed industrial disease has a letter and number to identify it – eg, prescribed disease A12 is carpal tunnel syndrome and prescribed disease D1 is pneumoconiosis. The complete list is in Appendix 5.

If the DWP accepts that you have a prescribed industrial disease, other diseases which result from it are included when assessing your 'loss of faculty' and disablement.[58] See p672 for how your disablement is assessed.

Prescribed occupations

Different diseases are 'prescribed' for specific types of jobs because particular jobs have different health risks. To qualify for benefit on grounds of a prescribed industrial disease, you must have a disease which is on the list and prove that:

- you have worked in one or more of the jobs for which that disease is prescribed ('prescribed occupations'); *and*
- your job caused the disease.

If the DWP refuses to accept that you have worked in a prescribed occupation, you should obtain advice, preferably from your trade union or an advice agency. An expert's report may help to prove your case.

Time limits

For most prescribed diseases, you do not have to have worked in a prescribed occupation for any minimum length of time. You can also claim at any time, even if it is many years since you worked in that occupation. However, there are exceptions to these general rules. For example, if you have occupational deafness (prescribed disease A10), you must have worked in a prescribed occupation for 10 years and claim within five years of having done so.[59] If you have occupational asthma (prescribed disease D7), you must claim within 10 years of working in a prescribed occupation.[60] If you have cataracts (prescribed disease A2), you must have worked in a prescribed occupation for five years or more in aggregate.[61] Appendix 5 lists relevant time limits or qualifying periods for other prescribed diseases.

Cause

For some diseases, unless the contrary can be proved, it is assumed that, if you have the disease within a particular interval (one, two, six or 12 months, depending on the disease) of working in the prescribed occupation (see p670), the occupation caused it.[62] With other diseases, there is a presumption that a specific type of occupation caused them, regardless of when you last worked in that occupation.[63] There are also diseases where no assumed link exists (eg, dermatitis – prescribed disease D5), and you must establish the link 'on a balance of probabilities' – ie, that it is more likely than not that there is a connection.[64] The DWP investigates the connection issue, and you may need to ask your GP or consultant for a report linking the disease to your occupation. DWP guidance says that, for some prescribed diseases, barring exceptional circumstances, the presumption that the disease was caused by the occupation should be automatic.[65]

There are different time conditions for carpal tunnel syndrome (prescribed disease A12[66]) in respect of some prescribed occupations, tuberculosis (prescribed disease B5[67]), pneumoconiosis (prescribed disease D1[68]) and, for some prescribed occupations, certain cancers of the urinary tract (prescribed disease C23[69]).

Examples

Holly has been a farm worker for 10 years and has developed osteoarthritis of the hip (prescribed disease A13). She also broke her hip on a climbing holiday three years ago. The climbing accident does not alter the presumption that her prescribed disease was caused by her occupation.

Stefan is a legal clerk who spends several hours a day at work typing on a computer keyboard. He develops typist's cramp (task-specific focal dystonia: prescribed disease A4) and is unable to continue using keyboards. His claim for benefit is rejected on the basis that he has not shown, on the balance of probabilities, that his work caused the condition. The decision maker points out that he has a computer at home which he uses every evening and at weekends for online gaming. Stefan successfully appeals the decision: he produces evidence that he uses a virtual reality headset and controllers at home along with a report from his physiotherapist stating that this activity would be unlikely to cause his symptoms.

Part 5: Other benefits
Chapter 32: Industrial injuries benefits
1. Who can get industrial injuries benefits

Onset and recrudescence

The '**onset**' (date of starting) of a prescribed disease is taken as the date you first had a relevant 'loss of faculty' (see below). In deafness cases, it is the later of either the date you first experienced the loss of faculty or the date you successfully claimed benefit.[70] For Dupuytren's contracture (prescribed disease A15), the date of onset is the date that the contracture stage of the disease is reached.[71]

In diseases other than deafness, asthma and respiratory conditions, you can improve and then worsen again. It is important to know whether it is a '**recrudescence**' (fresh outbreak of the existing disease) or a completely new attack. The first is deemed to be a continuation of the existing prescribed disease;[72] with the second, you have to wait 15 weeks before disablement benefit can be claimed. If a further attack starts during a current period of assessment, it is assumed to be a recrudescence unless proved otherwise.

Loss of faculty and disablement

In addition to showing the link between your injury or disease and your occupation, you must also establish that you have had a 'loss of faculty' and are 'disabled'.

'**Loss of faculty**' is the damage or impairment of part of the body or mind caused by the industrial accident or disease. '**Disability**' is the inability to do something as a result of that damage or impairment. The total of all of your disabilities, taken together, amount to a '**disablement**'. This disablement is expressed as a percentage.

In assessing your disablement, the DWP considers three questions.
* Has the relevant industrial accident (see p666) or prescribed disease (see p670) resulted in a loss of faculty (see below)?
* What is the extent of disablement resulting from a loss of faculty (this is expressed as a percentage – see below)?
* What period is to be taken into account by the assessment (see p675)?

A loss of faculty

A 'loss of faculty' is an 'impairment of the proper functioning of part of the body or mind'[73] caused by an accident or disease. A 'loss of faculty' is not the same as disablement. It includes disfigurement, even if the disfigurement is not accompanied by a loss of physical faculty.[74] A decision that there has been a personal injury resulting from an industrial accident (see p666) does not prevent the DWP or the First-tier Tribunal from finding that there is no loss of faculty.[75]

The extent of disablement

The extent of your disablement is assessed on a percentage basis. In order to qualify for disablement benefit (see p676), generally you must reach a threshold of at least 14 per cent disablement. However, a finding of at least 1 per cent may permit a claim for REA (see p678).

Any assessment between 14 and 19 per cent is treated as being 20 per cent.[76] If the total disablement from all industrial accidents and diseases is more than 20 per cent, it is rounded to the nearest multiple of 10 per cent, with multiples of 5 per cent being rounded upwards.[77] For example, an assessment of 22 per cent is rounded down to 20 per cent and an assessment of 25 per cent is rounded up to 30 per cent, as is an assessment of 26 per cent.

Some assessments of disablement are set out in regulations.[78] These are known as 'prescribed degrees of disablement' and include various amputations (eg, loss of a hand or a leg) and degrees of hearing loss (see Appendix 4). However, even in these cases, the DWP must take into account the real disablement resulting from an injury and increase or decrease the figure to arrive at a reasonable assessment[79] – eg, the loss of a right hand is more disabling for a right-handed person than for a left-handed person. The full extent of your disablement caused by the injury must be taken into account. A further disablement or condition which arises at a later date, but which can be shown to be caused by the industrial accident or disease, must be included in the assessment.[80]

Diffuse mesothelioma causing impaired functioning of the pleura, pericardium or peritoneum automatically has an assessment of 100 per cent disablement.[81]

Apart from age, sex and physical and mental condition, your personal circumstances must be ignored, so that particular problems you may have, like the location of your office or the distance to the nearest bus stop, are not taken into account.

Your disablement should be assessed by comparing you with a person of the same age and sex whose physical and mental condition is 'normal'.[82]

When there is no prescribed degree of disablement, reference may be made to the prescribed percentages to help with the assessment.[83] Although you may suggest that your assessment should be a particular percentage, the DWP makes its own judgement.[84]

What happens at the assessment?
It is important that you are straightforward with the examining healthcare professional. There are checks to establish that your symptoms are consistent with the injury, and that your movements are consistent with the disablement you claim you have. Therefore, how you walk, sit and how you undress (if relevant) are also considered. Make sure that the person examining you is aware of all the things that you now cannot do as a result of your injury or disease.

Offsets if your disability has more than one cause
If a disability is congenital or arose before an industrial one, it is deducted from the total disablement.[85] The reduction is often called the 'offset'. Mistakes are sometimes made because the DWP incorrectly offsets for medical conditions that have not caused any disability.

Part 5: Other benefits
Chapter 32: Industrial injuries benefits
1. Who can get industrial injuries benefits

Examples

Nasim loses a hand, which would normally be 60 per cent, but he had previously lost the index finger. So 14 per cent is deducted, leaving 46 per cent (rounded up to 50 per cent).

Clara has a back injury as a result of an industrial accident. The DWP has reduced her assessment by 5 per cent on the grounds of a pre-existing disability of which she knew nothing. Many people have spines that are slightly curved as a result of lifting things. The DWP may have looked at an x-ray, correctly considered that her curved spine was not due to the relevant accident and then incorrectly reduced her assessment.

In the second example, the DWP should have considered whether the pre-existing loss of faculty (see p672), the curved spine, really had (or would have) led to disablement that would have occurred regardless of the industrial accident. It should have considered, among other things, whether the loss of faculty led to disablement before the industrial accident occurred. There is no physical disablement if you do not have any pain or restriction of movement and it is, therefore, wrong to reduce your assessment unless there is a good reason for deciding that disablement would have arisen during the period of assessment even if the industrial accident had not occurred.

In the second example, depending on the medical opinion:
- there may be no offset; *or*
- it may be appropriate to make a life award (see p675) with some uniform offset over the whole period in respect of any future back problems Clara is likely to have; *or*
- it may be appropriate to make a stepped assessment, making no offset initially but bringing one in at some future date, or applying different levels of offset for different parts of the period covered by the award.[86]

No reduction is made if your injury is one for which the regulations award 100 per cent and this is considered a reasonable assessment for the industrial accident.[87]

The DWP should also bear in mind that, even if you had a pre-existing problem which caused a disability, the accident may worsen the effects of it, as well as cause a new problem. In such a case, the assessment should reflect the increase in the original problem as well as the new disability.[88]

If another disability arose after an industrial accident, the DWP first has to assess the disablement arising from the industrial injury. If it is less than 11 per cent, any disability from the other cause is ignored. If it is more than 11 per cent, any extra disablement caused by the effect of the industrial injury on the other disability is added.[89]

Examples

Rocco loses a little finger in an industrial accident and is assessed as 7 per cent disabled as a result. He then loses the other fingers of that hand in a non-industrial accident. He continues to be assessed as 7 per cent disabled because of the industrial accident.

Jorge loses the middle, ring and little fingers of one hand in an industrial accident and is assessed as 30 per cent disabled as a result. He then loses the index finger of that hand in a non-industrial accident. His total disablement is now 50 per cent. But loss of the index finger only would have been 14 per cent. The disablement resulting from his industrial accident may, therefore, be reassessed at 36 per cent (50 per cent *minus* 14 per cent), which is rounded up to 40 per cent.

Two or more industrial accidents or diseases

If you have more than one industrial accident, the percentages of disablement (see p672 and Appendix 4) can be added together and may entitle you to benefit, even if neither accident would do so on its own. If you have two or more industrial accidents, you may end up in a situation where the second or later accident is made worse by the interaction with the effect of the previous accident(s). Your most recent assessment should include an increase for any such interaction.[90] This also applies if an industrial disease (see p670) interacts with the effects of an industrial accident.

Example

Atiyah has a fall at work and seriously injures her left leg. She receives a life assessment of 10 per cent. Years later, she has a further fall and seriously injures the other leg. She is assessed as 10 per cent disabled for that accident, with a further 5 per cent for the extra disability she has as a result of the interaction between the two injuries. The total of 25 per cent is rounded up, resulting in payment of a 30 per cent pension.

There are special rules if you have pneumoconiosis. They allow for certain conditions to be taken into account in order to increase the assessment, even though these conditions did not arise from the pneumoconiosis. Any effect of tuberculosis is assessed with the effects of the pneumoconiosis.[91] If your disability is assessed at 50 per cent because of the pneumoconiosis, any additional disability because of chronic obstructive pulmonary disease is added.[92] If you have made such a claim for pneumoconiosis, you cannot then make a separate claim for chronic obstructive pulmonary disease.[93]

The period covered by the assessment

The DWP or the First-tier Tribunal decides how long you are likely to be affected by a relevant loss of faculty and how long you have already been affected (see

Part 5: Other benefits
Chapter 32: Industrial injuries benefits
2. Industrial injuries disablement benefit

p672). Percentage assessments are usually made for six months, or for one or two years, or are given for life,[94] but definite dates must be given.

An assessment is either final or provisional.[95] You get a provisional assessment when there is doubt about what will happen in the future, and you are automatically called for another assessment at the end of the period.[96] Life assessments are final.

If you are given a final assessment for a fixed period, this means that the DWP believes you will no longer be affected by your accident or disease by the end of that period. If you think that the effects of the accident or disease will last for longer, consider an appeal against that assessment (see Chapter 57).

If your condition deteriorates during a period of assessment, or if you still have a disability at the end of a period for which you have been given a final assessment, you should apply for a supersession (see p1274).

An assessment of disablement for occupational deafness is for life.[97]

2. **Industrial injuries disablement benefit**

The main benefit linked to industrial accidents and diseases is industrial injuries disablement benefit (IIDB). You may qualify for additional amounts of benefit paid along with or as increases to IIDB. These are:

- constant attendance allowance (see p678);
- exceptionally severe disablement allowance (see p678);
- reduced earnings allowance (see p678).[98]

Who can get industrial injuries disablement benefit

You can qualify for IIDB if:[99]

- you satisfy the industrial injury condition (see p665) as a result of one or more industrial accidents (see p666) or prescribed diseases (see p670); *and*
- your resulting disablement is assessed as being at least 14 per cent (1 per cent in the case of pneumoconiosis, byssinosis and diffuse mesothelioma) (see p672 and Appendix 4); *and*
- 90 days (excluding Sundays) have elapsed since the date of the accident or of the onset of the prescribed disease or injury (if you have mesothelioma, you can be paid without serving this waiting period).

Disqualification

You may be disqualified for up to six weeks if you do not provide the required information or notify changes in your circumstances, or do not have a medical examination or treatment. You cannot, however, be disqualified for refusing to have an operation, unless it is a minor one.[100]

The rules about your age

There are no specific age rules or requirement to have paid national insurance contributions. You must simply be under a contract of employment. Therefore, a child who is working is covered, as well as a person over pension age.

People included in the claim

You claim IIDB for yourself. You cannot claim any increases for an adult or your child(ren) unless you are getting unemployability supplement (abolished for new claims after 5 April 1987).

The amount of benefit

The amount of benefit you get depends on the extent of your disablement.[101] See p672 for how this is assessed.

Extent of disablement	£ per week
100%	188.60
90%	169.74
80%	150.88
70%	132.02
60%	113.16
50%	94.30
40%	75.44
30%	56.58
11% – 20%	37.72

IIDB can be paid if the assessment of your disablement is at least 14 per cent,[102] except in the cases of pneumoconiosis, byssinosis and diffuse mesothelioma, when it must be at least 1 per cent.[103] Before 1 October 1986, IIDB was paid for an assessment of disablement of at least 1 per cent. The old rules are still in force for claims made before this date.[104] If you are getting a payment as a result of such a small percentage assessment, see p176 of the 17th edition of CPAG's *Rights Guide to Non-Means-Tested Benefits*.

You may be able to get an increase of benefit.

Increases of industrial injuries disablement benefit

You get increased IIDB if you qualify for constant attendance allowance or exceptionally severe disablement allowance.

Part 5: Other benefits
Chapter 32: Industrial injuries benefits
3. Reduced earnings allowance

Constant attendance allowance

You qualify for constant attendance allowance if:[105]

- you are entitled to IIDB based on a degree of disablement assessed at 100 per cent; *and*
- you require constant attendance as a result of the relevant loss of faculty (see p672).

Disablement as a result of pre-1948 industrial accidents and diseases, war injuries and injuries incurred while on police or fire duty, may be taken into account in considering the degree of your disablement.

The amount you get depends on your disability and the amount of attendance you need.[106]

- The higher weekly rate of £151.00 is paid if you are 'so exceptionally severely disabled as to be entirely, or almost entirely dependent on (constant) attendance for the necessities of life and [are] likely to remain so dependent for a prolonged period and the attendance so required is whole-time'.
- The lower weekly rate of £75.50 is paid if you are 'to a substantial extent dependent on (constant) attendance for the necessities of life, and [are] likely to remain so dependent for a prolonged period'. This amount can be increased to as much as £113.25 a week if 'the extent of such attendance is greater by reason of the beneficiary's exceptionally severe disablement'. If attendance is part time only, the amount payable is 'such sum as may be reasonable in the circumstances' (usually £37.75 a week).

Some people will be better off claiming disability living allowance, personal independence payment or attendance allowance instead, where this is paid at a higher rate.

Exceptionally severe disablement allowance

This is paid at the weekly rate of £75.50 if you are entitled to constant attendance allowance (or would be if you were not in hospital) at the higher or intermediate rate and you are likely to remain so permanently.[107]

3. **Reduced earnings allowance**

Reduced earnings allowance (REA) is available if you had an accident or started to have a disease before 1 October 1990. A successful first claim can still be made now if you had an accident or disease before this date.

The amount of REA you get depends on whether your current earnings, or earnings in a job which it is considered you could do, are less than the current earnings in your previous 'regular occupation'. This involves looking at your work history and the content of your job, rather than at your job title.

See Chapter 31 of the 2015/16 edition of this *Handbook* for the qualifying conditions for REA.

Who is still entitled to reduced earnings allowance

You qualify for REA if:[108]
- you satisfy the industrial injury condition (see p665) because of an industrial accident (see p666) before 1 October 1990 or an industrial disease (see p670), the onset of which was before that date (see p672); *and*
- your resulting disablement is assessed as being at least 1 per cent (see p672 and Appendix 4); *and*
- as a result of a relevant loss of faculty, either:
  - you are incapable and likely to remain permanently incapable of following your regular occupation and are incapable of following employment of an equivalent standard which is suitable in your case; *or*
  - you are, and have been at all times since the end of the 90-day qualifying period for industrial injuries disablement benefit (IIDB), incapable of following your regular occupation or employment of an equivalent standard which is suitable in your case. (If you did return to your former, regular occupation – eg, to see whether you were capable of carrying on – this will not necessarily prevent a later claim for REA from succeeding.[109])

Date of onset before October 1990?

If the disease you suffer from was added to the list of prescribed industrial diseases on or after 10 October 1990, you will not qualify for REA in respect of it, even if the date of onset was before this date. In some cases, the definition of a prescribed disease on the list of industrial diseases can be 'extended', meaning that the qualifying criteria have been widened since it was first added to the list. If you suffer from a disease which is classified as a prescribed industrial disease on the basis of such extended criteria, and the extension occurred on or after 10 October 1994, then you cannot get REA in respect of that disease, regardless of the date of onset.[110]

For more details, see p695 of the 2015/16 edition of this *Handbook*.

The amount of benefit

The amount of REA you get is the amount by which your current earnings, or earnings in a job which it is considered you could do, are less than the current earnings in your previous regular occupation (see p697 of the 2015/16 edition of this *Handbook*).[111]

If you are unemployed, the DWP's healthcare professional is asked for your limitations, a DWP disability employment adviser is asked what job s/he thinks

Part 5: Other benefits
Chapter 32: Industrial injuries benefits
5. Special benefit rules

you could do and Jobcentre Plus is asked to quote a wage that such a job would pay in your area.

Once the first assessment has been made, the amount is usually increased in line with earnings in that industry or workplace, unless that regular occupation has ceased to exist.[112] In this case, it is calculated as rising in line with the nearest 'occupational group' as defined by the DWP. You can ask for a fresh assessment to take into account your prospects of advancement, but you must show that promotion would have happened (eg, at the end of a period of employment or training), not just that it might have happened had you been particularly diligent.[113]

The maximum amount you can receive for any one award is £75.44 a week.[114] The total you can receive from IIDB and REA (whether for one or more awards) is 140 per cent of the standard rate of IIDB.[115] If you were over pension age and retired before 6 April 1987, your allowance is reduced if it would otherwise mean you would be receiving more than 100 per cent of the standard rate of IIDB.[116] If you qualified for REA and were retired or treated as retired on either 10 April 1988 or 9 April 1989, you continue to receive the allowance at the same 'frozen' rate. Its value therefore erodes over time.

4. Retirement allowance

Retirement allowance is a reduced rate of reduced earnings allowance (REA – see p678) for people over pension age, paid for life.

You qualify for retirement allowance if:[117]
- you are over pension age (see p766);
- you have given up regular employment;
- you were entitled to REA at a rate of at least £2 a week (in total, if you had more than one award) immediately before you gave up regular employment;
- you are not entitled to REA.

You can only get one award of retirement allowance, even if you had more than one award of REA.[118]

The amount of retirement allowance you get is £18.86 a week or 25 per cent of the amount of REA you were receiving, whichever is the lower. There are no increases for dependants.

5. Special benefit rules

Special rules may apply to:
- people who are going abroad (see Chapters 70 and 71);
- people in prison or detention (see Chapter 42).

6. Claims and backdating

The general rules about claims and backdating are covered in Chapter 50. This section explains the specific rules that apply to industrial injuries benefits.

Making a claim

Claims for industrial injuries benefits should normally be made in writing.[119] You do not have to make a claim for retirement allowance.[120] A video relay service for British Sign Language users is available at gov.uk/industrial-injuries-disablement-benefit/how-to-claim.

The notes you get with the claim form tell you the address to which you should send your completed claim form. Keep a copy of your claim in case queries arise.

Forms

There are different forms depending on the benefit claimed and whether you are claiming for an accident or a disease. You can download the IIDB form from gov.uk/industrial-injuries-disablement-benefit/how-to-claim or telephone to request a form (0800 121 8379; textphone: 0800 169 0314; Relay UK service available).[121] You need to request the REA form by telephone (0800 121 8379; textphone: 0800 169 0314; Relay UK service available).

You must provide any information or evidence required. In certain circumstances, the DWP may accept a written application not on the approved form.[122] You can amend or withdraw your claim before a decision is made (see p1135). If there is a delay in making a claim, you may be able to get a short-term advance of benefit (see p1153).

Who should claim

You claim for yourself. If you are unable to manage your own affairs, another person can claim industrial injuries benefits for you as your 'appointee' (see p1135).

Information to support your claim

For the general information requirements that apply to all benefits, see p1136.

It is important that you provide any information required when you claim. Until you do, you may not count as having made a valid claim (see p1138). Correct any defects as soon as possible or your date of claim may be affected.

Even if your claim is valid, you may be asked to provide further information to support your claim (see p1140). You may also be asked to provide information

Part 5: Other benefits
Chapter 32: Industrial injuries benefits
6. Claims and backdating

after you are awarded industrial injuries benefits, and if you fail to do so, your benefit could be suspended, or even terminated (see p1162).

The date of your claim

The date of your claim is important, as it determines when your entitlement to industrial injuries benefits starts. This is not necessarily the date from when you are paid. For information about when payment of benefit starts, see p683.

The 'date of your claim' is the date it is received at the industrial injuries disablement benefit (IIDB) centre.

You must make sure your claim is valid. If it is 'defective', you are given a short time to correct the defects (see p1139). If you do, your claim is treated as having been made when you initially claimed.[123]

In some cases, you can claim in advance (see below) and in some cases, your claim can be backdated (see below). If you want this to be done, make this clear when you claim or the DWP may not consider it. If you claimed disability living allowance (DLA), personal independence payment (PIP) or attendance allowance (AA) instead of constant attendance allowance, see below.

Backdating your claim

It is important to claim in time. Your claim can be backdated for up to three months if you satisfy the qualifying conditions over that period. You do not have to show any reasons why your claim was late. The rules on backdating are covered on p1142.

If you might have qualified for benefit earlier but did not claim because you were given the wrong information or were misled by the DWP, ask for compensation (see p1403) or complain to the Ombudsman (see p1408).

If you claim the wrong benefit

In some circumstances, it is possible for a claim for one benefit to be treated as a claim for a different benefit (see p1144). However, for industrial injuries benefits it is only possible to 'interchange' constant attendance allowance with DLA, PIP and AA.

Claiming in advance

An advance claim can be made for IIDB if you have had an accident or have a prescribed disease and you are within the 90-day waiting period. The date of your claim is the date on which you qualify. Otherwise it is not possible to claim industrial injuries benefits in advance.

Renewal claims

Assessments can be provisional or final, and for a limited period or for life. A provisional assessment means that the DWP considers that your medical condition has not yet settled down, and may get worse or better. At the end of a provisional assessment, you are invited to be re-examined. A final assessment means that the DWP believes that your condition has settled down and your case is dealt with once and for all. At the end of a period of award, you must therefore apply for a renewal of benefit.

If you get IIDB for a particular disease, you may recover at some point but subsequently have a further attack. If there is a continuation (or recrudescence) of the old disease, you do not have to wait 90 days before becoming entitled to IIDB.

7. Getting paid

The general rules on getting paid are covered in Chapter 51. This section explains the specific rules that apply to industrial injuries benefits.

When are industrial injuries benefits paid?
You are paid on a Wednesday,[124] weekly in advance or four weeks in arrears.[125]

Note:
- You might not be paid your industrial injuries benefit if you have been sanctioned for a benefit offence (see p1239).
- For information on missing payments, see p1150. If you cannot get your payments because you have lost your bank card or you have forgotten your PIN, see p1149. If you have lost your payment service card, see p1150.
- If payment of your industrial injuries benefit is delayed, see p1255. If you are waiting for a decision on your claim, or to be paid, you may be able to get a short-term advance (see p1153). If you wish to complain about how your claim has been dealt with, or claim compensation, see Chapter 61.
- If payment of your industrial injuries benefit is suspended, see p1161.
- If you are overpaid industrial injuries benefit, you may have to repay it (see Chapter 53) and, in some circumstances, you may have to pay a penalty (see p1229). If you have been accused of fraud, see Chapter 54.
- If you are owed arrears of industrial injuries benefit, these can be paid in instalments (see p1148).

Change of circumstances

You must report any change of circumstances that you have been told you must report, as well as any that you might reasonably be expected to know might affect your right to, the amount of, or the payment of your benefit. You should do this as soon as possible, preferably in writing. See p1160 for further information.

Part 5: Other benefits
Chapter 32: Industrial injuries benefits
8. Tax, other benefits and the benefit cap

8. **Tax, other benefits and the benefit cap**

Tax

Industrial injuries benefits are not taxable.[126]

Means-tested benefits and tax credits

Industrial injuries disablement benefit (IIDB), reduced earnings allowance (REA) and retirement allowance are taken into account in full for all the means-tested benefits. Constant attendance allowance and exceptionally severe disablement allowance are disregarded. Industrial injuries benefits are ignored as income for tax credits.

Non-means-tested benefits

In general, the overlapping benefits rule does not apply to industrial injuries benefits. It is possible, for example, to get full disablement benefit as well as full employment and support allowance.

Carer's allowance (see Chapter 26) may be paid to someone who is 'regularly and substantially caring' for you while you are getting constant attendance allowance (see p678).[127]

If your spouse or civil partner died as a result of an industrial accident or disease, you may qualify for a bereavement benefit even though the national insurance contribution conditions are not satisfied (see Chapter 25).[128]

The benefit cap

In some cases, there is a limit on the total amount of specified benefits you can receive (a 'benefit cap'). Industrial injuries benefits are *not* specified benefits. The benefit cap only applies if you are getting universal credit or housing benefit. It does *not* apply if you or your partner get IIDB, REA or retirement allowance. See p1156 for further information.

Passports and other sources of help

You qualify for a Christmas bonus if you get disablement benefit, but only if it includes unemployability supplement or constant attendance allowance (see p861).

If you have (or are a dependant of someone who has died and who had) pneumoconiosis (including asbestosis, silicosis and kaolinosis), byssinosis, diffuse mesothelioma, diffuse pleural thickening, or primary carcinoma of the lung if accompanied by asbestosis or diffuse pleural thickening, and you cannot get compensation from your employer (eg, because it has ceased trading), or you do not have a realistic chance of obtaining damages from that employer, you may be able to get a one-off lump-sum payment from the DWP in addition to any industrial injuries benefit. You must make a claim within 12 months of the decision awarding IIDB.[129] Similarly, you can be entitled to a one-off lump-sum payment from the DWP for diffuse mesothelioma (including if you are a dependant of someone who had that condition immediately before s/he died), without the need to have worked.[130] The time limit for claiming is 12 months (from the date of diagnosis or death). The time limit may be extended if there is good cause. All these lump-sum payments may be recovered (ie, deducted) from compensation (see p1174).

Notes

1. Who can get industrial injuries benefits

1 ss94 and 103 SSCBA 1992
2 Sch 7 para 11(1) SSCBA 1992
3 Sch 7 para 11(1) SSCBA 92; reg 14A SS(IIPD) Regs
4 ss94(1) and 108(1) SSCBA 1992
5 Reg 10C(5) and (6) SSB(PA) Regs
6 Regs 2, 4 and 6 SS(EEEIIP) Regs; *Uber BV and others (Appellants) v Aslam and others (Respondents)* [2021] UKSC 5; *Addison Lee Ltd v Lange and others* [2021] EWCA Civ 594
7 Regs 2 and 3 IIB(ETSC) Regs; s95A SSCBA 1992
8 Reg 3 SS(EEEIIP) Regs
9 s97 SSCBA 1992
10 R(I) 49/52
11 R(I) 1/76
12 R(I) 5/81
13 R(I) 1/82
14 *Fenton v Thorley* [1903] AC 443 (HL)
15 CI/123/1949
16 *Jones v Secretary of State for Social Services* [1972] AC 944 (HL), also reported as an appendix to R(I) 3/69; *SSWP v Scullion* [2010] EWCA Civ 310
17 *Trim Joint District School Board of Management v Kelly* [1914] AC 667 (HL)
18 s94(1) SSCBA 1992
19 CI/105/1998; CI/142/2006
20 *Roberts v Dorothea Slate Quarries Co Ltd* [1948] 2 All ER 201 (HL)
21 R(I) 24/54; R(I) 43/55

22 CI/3370/1999
23 *Mullen v SSWP* [2002] Session Case 251; SLT 149; SCLR 475; *Greens Weekly Digest* 3-121, IH (2DIV)
24 R(I) 43/61; R(I) 4/62
25 R(I) 18/54
26 CI/159/1950
27 *R v National Insurance Commissioner ex parte East* [1976] ICR 206 (DC), also reported as an appendix to R(I) 16/75
28 R(I) 1/59; R(I) 45/55
29 *R v Industrial Injuries Commissioner ex parte AEU* [1966] 2 QB 31 (CA), also reported as an appendix to R(I) 4/66
30 R(I) 10/81
31 *R v National Insurance Commissioner ex parte Reed* (DC), reported as an appendix to R(I) 7/80
32 s94(3) SSCBA 1992
33 R(I) 46/53
34 R(I) 9/57
35 *R v Industrial Injuries Commissioner ex parte AEU* [1966] 2 QB 31 (CA), also reported as an appendix to R(I) 4/66
36 s29(6)(b) SSA 1998; CI/210/1950
37 R(I) 64/51
38 R(I) 1/99
39 *Nancollas v Insurance Officer* [1985] 1 All ER 833 (CA), also reported as an appendix to R(I) 7/85
40 s99 SSCBA 1992
41 R(I) 1/88
42 R(I) 12/75

● ●

43 R(I) 4/70
44 R(I) 1/93
45 *Nancollas v Insurance Officer* [1985] 1 All ER 833 (CA); *Ball v Insurance Officer* [1985] 1 All ER 833 (CA); both also reported as an appendix to R(I) 7/85
46 *Smith v Stages* [1989] 2 WLR 529 (HL)
47 R(I) 1/91
48 R(I) 6/82
49 R(I) 12/52
50 s101 SSCBA 1992
51 R(I) 3/67
52 s100 SSCBA 1992
53 Sch 1 SS(IIPD) Regs
54 Reg 2 SS(IIPD) Regs
55 R(I) 3/03
56 SS(IIPD)(A) Regs
57 R(I) 2/03; R(I) 4/96
58 Reg 3 SS(IIPD) Regs
59 Regs 2(c) and 25 SS(IIPD) Regs
60 Reg 36 SS(IIPD) Regs
61 Reg 2(e) SS(IIPD) Regs
62 Reg 4(1), (4) and (5) SS(IIPD) Regs
63 Reg 4(2) and (6) SS(IIPD) Regs
64 Reg 4(1) SS(IIPD) Regs
65 Appendix 7 Ch 67 DMG
66 Reg 4(5) SS(IIPD) Regs
67 Reg 4(3) SS(IIPD) Regs
68 Reg 4(7) SS(IIPD) Regs
69 Reg 4(6) SS(IIPD) Regs
70 Reg 6(2)(c) SS(IIPD) Regs
71 *DR v SSWP (II)* [2021] UKUT 191 (AAC)
72 Reg 7 SS(IIPD) Regs
73 *Jones v Secretary of State for Social Services* [1972] AC 944 (HL), also reported as an appendix to R(I) 3/69
74 CI/499/2000; s122(1) SSCBA 1992
75 s30 SSA 1998
76 s103(3) SSCBA 1992
77 s103(2) and (3) SSCBA 1992; regs 15A and 15B SS(IIPD) Regs
78 Sch 2 SS(GB) Regs; Sch 3 SS(IIPD) Regs
79 Reg 11(6) SS(GB) Regs
80 *JL and DO v SSWP (II)* [2011] UKUT 294 (AAC), reported as [2012] AACR 15
81 Reg 20A SS(IIPD) Regs
82 Sch 6 para 1 SSCBA 1992
83 Reg 11(8) SS(GB) Regs; R(I) 5/95; R(I) 1/04
84 CI/636/1993. In some cases, it may be an error of law to arrive at a different figure without giving reasons for this (para 10).
85 Reg 11(3) SS(GB) Regs
86 CI/34/1993
87 Reg 11(7) SS(GB) Regs
88 R(I) 3/91
89 Reg 11(4) SS(GB) Regs
90 R(I) 3/91
91 Reg 21 SS(IIPD) Regs
92 Reg 22 SS(IIPD) Regs
93 Reg 2(d) SS(IIPD) Regs; para 67943 DMG
94 Sch 6 para 6 SSCBA 1992
95 Sch 6 para 7 SSCBA 1992
96 Sch 6 para 6(2)(b) SSCBA 1992
97 Reg 29 SS(IIPD) Regs

2. Industrial injuries disablement benefit
98 s94(2) SSCBA 1992
99 ss94, 103 and 108 SSCBA 1992
100 Reg 40 SS(GB) Regs
101 Sch 4 SSCBA 1992
102 s103(1) SSCBA 1992
103 Reg 20(1) SS (IIPD) Regs
104 Sch 7 para 9(1)(a) SSCBA 1992; reg 14 SS(II&D)MP Regs
105 s104 SSCBA 1992
106 s104 SSCBA 1992; reg 19 SS(GB) Regs
107 s105 SSCBA 1992

3. Reduced earnings allowance
108 Sch 7 paras 11 and 12(1), (2) and (7) SSCBA 1992
109 *SSWP v RD (II)* [2017] UKUT 481 (AAC)
110 Reg 14A SS(IIPD)Regs
111 Sch 7 para 11(10) SSCBA 1992
112 Sch 7 para 11(14) SSCBA 1992
113 Sch 7 para 11(6) SSCBA 1992
114 Regs 2 and 3 SS(II)(REA) Regs; Sch 7 para 11(13) SSCBA 1992
115 Sch 7 para 11(10) SSCBA 1992
116 Sch 7 para 11(11) SSCBA 1992

4. Retirement allowance
117 Sch 7 para 13 SSCBA 1992
118 *TA v SSWP (II)* [2010] UKUT 101 (AAC)

6. Claims and backdating
119 Reg 4(1) SS(C&P) Regs
120 Reg 3(e) SS(C&P) Regs
121 s68(1) WRA 2012
122 Reg 4(1) SS(C&P) Regs
123 Reg 6(1)(b) SS(C&P) Regs

7. Getting paid
124 Sch 6 para 3 SS(C&P) Regs
125 Reg 22 SS(C&P) Regs

8. Tax, other benefits and the benefit cap
126 s667 IT(EP)A 2003
127 Regs 14, 17 and 21 SS(IB)(T) Regs
128 s60(2) and (3) SSCBA 1992
129 DWP, *Industrial Injuries Disablement Benefits: technical guidance*, section 11.5
130 Part 4 CMOPA 2008; Vol 11 DMG

Chapter 33

Contribution-based jobseeker's allowance

This chapter covers:
1. Who can get contribution-based jobseeker's allowance (p688)
2. The rules about your age (p693)
3. People included in the claim (p693)
4. The amount of benefit (p693)
5. Special benefit rules (p697)
6. Claims and backdating (p697)
7. Getting paid (p703)
8. Tax, other benefits and the benefit cap (p704)

Key facts
- Jobseeker's allowance (JSA) is a benefit for people who are looking for work.
- There are three types of JSA. **Contribution-based JSA** is a non-means-tested benefit, but it can be affected by earnings and certain pension payments. **Income-based JSA** and **joint-claim JSA** are means-tested benefits.
- You may be able to get your contribution-based JSA topped up with universal credit (UC), or if you can still make a new claim, income-based JSA or joint-claim JSA.
- To qualify for contribution-based JSA, you must have paid sufficient national insurance contributions.
- You cannot qualify for any type of JSA if you count as being in full-time paid work.
- You must normally be fit for work and meet work-related requirements.
- In a number of situations (eg, if you refuse to attend a job interview or to take up a job or a place on an employment programme), you may be given a sanction and your JSA may be paid at a reduced or nil rate.
- JSA is administered and paid by the DWP. It sometimes calls contribution-based JSA 'new-style' JSA.
- If you disagree with a JSA decision, you can apply for a revision or a supersession (see Chapter 56), or appeal against it (see Chapter 57). You must apply for a mandatory reconsideration before you can appeal.

Part 5: Other benefits
Chapter 33: Contribution-based jobseeker's allowance
1. Who can get contribution-based jobseeker's allowance

1. Who can get contribution-based jobseeker's allowance

You qualify for jobseeker's allowance (JSA) if you:[1]

- are not in full-time paid work (see p690); *and*
- do not have limited capability for work. However, in certain circumstances, people who are sick or who have gone abroad for NHS hospital treatment can get JSA (see p690); *and*
- are not in 'relevant education'. In addition, if you are a full-time student you usually cannot get JSA (see p886); *and*
- are below pension age (see p766); *and*
- accept a 'claimant commitment' (see p1024); *and*
- are in Great Britain. JSA can continue to be paid in limited circumstances while you are temporarily away (see p1631). For changes due to the UK leaving the European Union, see p1645.

In addition to the rules above, you must satisfy the extra rules on p689. You can be required to meet work-related requirements, as well as some requirements connected to these – ie:[2]

- work-focused interviews;
- work preparation;
- work search;
- work availability.

You can be given a sanction if you fail to do so. See Chapter 46 for full details of these requirements.

If you do not come under the universal credit system

New claims for contribution-based JSA are usually only possible under the universal credit (UC) system (see p25). However, until 30 March 2022, if you were prevented from claiming UC because you were a frontier worker (see p246 – the rules are the same as for income-based JSA), you did not come under the UC system. In this case, if you made a new claim for contribution-based JSA, your claim was dealt with under old rules. The DWP may call this 'old-style' JSA. This is no longer the case.

Many of the rules for contribution-based JSA for those who do not come under the UC system are the same as the rules for income-based JSA. For this reason and because very few, if any, people can now make a new claim for 'old-style' contribution-based JSA, these rules are not explained in this chapter. For details of these rules, see Chapter 12 and the 2020/21 edition of this *Handbook*.

Extra rules for contribution-based jobseeker's allowance

In addition to satisfying the rules that apply to all types of JSA, you must:[3]
- satisfy the contribution conditions (see p964). This depends on your record of national insurance (NI) contributions and credits in the two tax years (6 April to 5 April) immediately before the benefit year (the calendar year) in which your jobseeking period begins (or in which a period linked to a jobseeking period begins, if earlier). For example, if you claim JSA immediately after a period of limited capability for work, the contribution test is applied using the date on which you first had limited capability for work; *and*
- not have earnings from part-time work above a prescribed amount (see p694).

Example
Raj was working full time until he was injured in a car accident on 5 November 2021 and claimed employment and support allowance (ESA). On 28 April 2022, he is fit for work and claims contribution-based JSA. Because the period during which he had limited capability for work links to his current jobseeking period (see the rules for linked periods on p690), he must have sufficient NI contributions in the two tax years before 2021 (the relevant benefit year) – ie, 2018/2019 and 2019/2020.

Jobseeking periods

A 'jobseeking period' is the period during which you meet the conditions that apply to all types of JSA (see p688).[4] Your jobseeking period is relevant for a number of reasons, including for whether you satisfy the contribution conditions for JSA. You are not usually entitled to JSA for the first seven days of your jobseeking period. These are known as 'waiting days' (see p704).

What does not count as part of a jobseeking period
The following do not count as part of a jobseeking period:[5]
- days for which you do not claim (or are not treated as claiming) JSA;
- a period for which you claimed backdated benefit which has been refused;
- any week (Sunday to Saturday) for which you are not entitled to JSA because you were involved in a trade dispute (see p982) for all or part of that week;
- days on which you are not entitled to JSA because you have not provided your NI number (see p1137).

How jobseeking periods link
In some cases, two or more jobseeking periods can be linked together and treated as if they were one period. Also, certain periods in which you satisfy other conditions ('linked periods' – see p690) can be linked to a jobseeking period. This means, for example, that:

Part 5: Other benefits
Chapter 33: Contribution-based jobseeker's allowance
1. Who can get contribution-based jobseeker's allowance

- the question of whether you satisfy the NI contribution conditions for contribution-based JSA is decided by looking at your situation at the beginning of the first jobseeking period (or the beginning of a period linked to a jobseeking period, if earlier) and not at the beginning of your current claim;[6]
- if you make a fresh claim for JSA but your jobseeking period links with a previous one, you do not have to serve any waiting days (see p704) to get JSA;
- if the jobseeking periods together are longer than 182 days, you cannot get any more contribution-based JSA (see p696).

Two jobseeking periods are treated as linked if they are separated by one or any combination of the following:[7]

- any period of no more than 12 weeks; *or*
- a period during which you are doing jury service; *or*
- a 'linked period' (see below); *or*
- any period of no more than 12 weeks which comes between two linked periods or between a jobseeking period and a 'linked period'.

Linked periods

A **'linked period'** is any period during which you:[8]

– are entitled to carer's allowance, but only if this allows you to get contribution-based JSA when you would not otherwise satisfy the contribution conditions; *or*

– have, or are treated as having, limited capability for work (see Chapter 45); *or*

– are incapable of work or treated as incapable of work; *or*

– are entitled to maternity allowance; *or*

– are undergoing training for which a training allowance is payable.

You cannot argue that a period spent taking time out of work to look after children is a linked period for these purposes.[9]

Full-time paid work

You cannot usually qualify for contribution-based JSA if you are in full-time paid work. This means 16 hours or more each week.[10] All the rules on work are covered in Chapter 44.

In some situations, you are treated as *not* being in full-time work even if you work 16 hours or more (see p977). In others, you are treated as being in full-time work when you are not (see p977). See p975 for how your hours are calculated and p974 for what counts as paid work.

Limited capability for work

To qualify for JSA, usually you must not have 'limited capability for work'.[11] See Chapter 45 for details about the test that decides this. If your health improves and you move onto JSA (eg, from ESA), you may be asked to provide medical evidence that you no longer have limited capability for work. In all cases, you must still show that you are available for work if you are ill or have a disability. However, there are special rules that may help you meet the work-related requirements (see p1035).

Periods of sickness when you can claim jobseeker's allowance

Even if you have limited capability for work, you can be treated as not having limited capability for work:

- during a short period of up to two weeks (see below); *or*
- during an extended period of up to 13 weeks (see p692); *or*
- while you are temporarily absent from Great Britain to obtain NHS hospital treatment under certain provisions (see p693).

In all cases, you can continue to claim JSA if the *only* reason why you would not otherwise qualify is that you are unable to work because of ill health.[12]

Note: before 21 August 2021, you could be treated as not having limited capability for work indefinitely if you (or a child for whom you were caring) had COVID-19 or were self-isolating.

You do not have to continue to claim JSA during these periods and can instead claim ESA, and UC, to top this up if relevant. If you are only going to be unable to work for a short time, it may be better to continue to claim JSA. Get advice if you are unsure. Take the following into account.

- Switching from JSA to ESA and then back again when you are no longer sick means you must make a succession of benefit claims. You could be without income while these are being processed. You will start to come under the UC system if you do not do so already.
- If you qualify for contribution-based JSA, you can only receive this for 182 days in any jobseeking period (see p696). If you qualify for contributory ESA, it is paid indefinitely if you are in the support group. Otherwise, it is paid for 365 days (see p640).

Two-week periods of sickness

You are allowed up to two two-week periods of sickness in a jobseeking period (see p689) or, if your jobseeking period has lasted more than 12 months, in any successive 12-month period.[13] You must make a written declaration that you have been unfit for work from a specific date or for a specific period on a form available from the Jobcentre Plus office.[14] You are *not* allowed a two-week period of sickness if you state in writing that you are going to claim (or have claimed) UC or ESA.

If you are sick more often than this, or for a longer period, you may be able to claim JSA during an 'extended period of sickness' (see p692). Otherwise, you must claim ESA instead of JSA for the time you are unable to work, and UC to top this up if relevant.

Part 5: Other benefits
Chapter 33: Contribution-based jobseeker's allowance
1. Who can get contribution-based jobseeker's allowance

Note:
- The two-week periods do not include any period when you qualify for an 'extended period of sickness'.[15]
- You are *not* allowed a two-week period of sickness if you were getting statutory sick pay (SSP) in the eight weeks before you were sick, or if the period of sickness follows immediately after an 'extended period of sickness' under the rules on below.[16] Instead, you can claim benefit on the basis of having limited capability for work without having to serve any 'waiting days' (see p646).

You do not normally have to meet a work search requirement and a special rule helps you meet the work availability requirement (see p1048).[17] If you are sick for more than seven days, you must provide a medical certificate from a doctor.

Note: before 21 August 2021, the two-week periods did not include any period when you (or a child for whom you were caring) had COVID-19 or were self-isolating.

Extended periods of sickness

You are allowed an 'extended period of sickness' if you state that you:[18]
- have been, or expect to be, unable to work for more than two weeks, but not for more than 13 weeks; *or*
- have already been unable to work for two two-week periods of sickness under the rules described on p691 and you have been, or expect to be, unable to work for two weeks or less.

You are not allowed an extended period of sickness if you state in writing that you are going to claim (or have claimed) UC or ESA.

You must satisfy the DWP that you are unable to work by providing evidence as required. This includes a medical certificate from a doctor.

You are treated as not having limited capability for work for up to 13 weeks from the first day you are sick, or until you are no longer sick if this is sooner.[19] You are only allowed one extended period of sickness in the 12 months that start on the first day of sickness.[20] Before 21 August 2021, this did not include any period when you (or a child for whom you were caring) had COVID-19 or were self-isolating.

If you are sick more often than this or for a longer period, you must claim UC or ESA instead of JSA for the time you are unable to work.

You are not allowed an extended period of sickness if you were getting SSP in the eight weeks before you were sick.[21] Instead, you can claim benefit on the basis of having limited capability for work without having to serve any waiting days (see p646).

You do not have to meet a work search requirement if the DWP is satisfied that it would be unreasonable to require you to comply with one, and special rules help you meet the work availability requirement if the DWP is satisfied it would be unreasonable to apply the normal rules.[22]

NHS treatment abroad

You are treated as not having limited capability for work if you are temporarily absent from Great Britain for the purpose of getting NHS hospital treatment under certain provisions.[23] You can claim for an indefinite period. This does not apply if you stated in writing before the period of absence began that you claimed ESA immediately before the beginning of the period.

You must make a written declaration that you will be unfit for work from a specific date or for a specific period on a form available from the Jobcentre Plus office.[24]

You do not have to meet a work search requirement and a special rule helps you meet the work availability requirement.[25]

2. The rules about your age

There is no minimum age for entitlement to contribution-based jobseeker's allowance (JSA). However, in practice, because you can only qualify if you satisfy the national insurance contribution conditions, you are unlikely to qualify before you are 18. You cannot claim any type of JSA if you are pension age or over (see p766).

3. People included in the claim

You claim contribution-based jobseeker's allowance for yourself. You cannot claim any increases for your partner or child(ren).

4. The amount of benefit

Contribution-based jobseeker's allowance (JSA) is paid at the following weekly rates.[26]

Age of claimant	£pw
Under 25	61.05
25 or over	77.00

Part 5: Other benefits
Chapter 33: Contribution-based jobseeker's allowance
4. The amount of benefit

These amounts are reduced penny for penny if you receive certain pension payments of more than £50 in any week or any part-time earnings. For more on how these types of income affect contribution-based JSA, see below. Other types of income and any capital, including any earnings and capital of your partner, do not affect your contribution-based JSA.

Note:
- Contribution-based JSA is only paid for a limited period (see p696).
- You may qualify for universal credit (UC) to top up your contribution-based JSA if you satisfy the means test – eg, if you have a partner or a child, if you, your partner or child have a disability so you qualify for elements, or if you pay rent, service charges or ground rent, or for childcare.
- Your JSA might be paid at a reduced (or nil) rate if you are given a sanction (see Chapter 47) or if you have committed a benefit offence (see p1239).

Deductions for earnings and pension payments

Earnings and pension payments you receive can affect your entitlement to contribution-based JSA.[27] Any other income you receive does *not* affect your contribution-based JSA (but see p1151 for the rules on overlapping benefits).

Note:
- You cannot qualify for JSA if you are in full-time paid work (see p690), so it is earnings from part-time work that are taken into account.
- Any savings you have and the income and savings of your partner and children do not affect your contribution-based JSA, but may affect your means-tested benefits.

Earnings

Your earnings from part-time work can affect your entitlement to contribution-based JSA. The rules on the following are the same as for income-based JSA:
- what counts as earnings (p405);
- calculating net earnings from employment (p407);
- payments when you stop work (p408);
- calculating net earnings from self-employment (p411);
- working out average earnings from self-employment (p412);
- childminders (p412);
- how weekly earnings from employment are assessed (p437).

There are different rules on how your earnings affect your contribution-based JSA.

How earnings affect your contribution-based jobseeker's allowance

Your contribution-based JSA is reduced by the full amount of any earnings you receive over a disregarded amount.[28] For contribution-based JSA, normally £5 a week of your earnings is disregarded. However, if you are an auxiliary coastguard, a part-time firefighter, a part-time member of a lifeboat crew or a member of the reserve forces, £20 a week is disregarded.[29] If you earn less than £20 for doing any of these services, you can use up to £5 of the disregard on earnings from another job.

You are not entitled to contribution-based JSA for any week in which your earnings exceed a prescribed amount.[30] However, the days in any week when your earnings exceed this amount do not count towards your maximum 182 days of contribution-based JSA (see p696). The prescribed amount is not the same for everyone. It is calculated by adding together the amount of the relevant earnings disregard and the rate of contribution-based JSA paid to someone your age (see p693), and then deducting one penny.

Example
Melissa, aged 35, is entitled to contribution-based JSA of £77 a week. She works part time and her net earnings are £45 a week. Her earnings disregard is £5 a week. Melissa therefore gets £37 contribution-based JSA a week (£77 – £40). Applying the formula: (£77 + £5) – £0.01 = £81.99. So if Melissa were to earn more than £81.99 a week, she would not be entitled to contribution-based JSA.

Pension payments
Certain pension payments you receive may affect your contribution-based JSA.[31] The gross amount of your pension payments is taken into account (ie, the amount before tax is deducted), and this is converted into a weekly amount.[32]

Any pension payments you receive because of the death of a person who was a member of a pension scheme are ignored.[33] For example, if your late partner was a member of a scheme, any payment made to you following her/his death does not affect your contribution-based JSA.

Fifty pounds of your weekly pension payments (or if you get more than one pension, of the total of your weekly pensions) is disregarded, and your contribution-based JSA is reduced by the remainder.[34]

Any pension payment you receive is counted from the first day of the benefit week in which the payment is made to you.[35]

Example
Jaden claims JSA and is entitled to contribution-based JSA from Wednesday 20 April 2022. His benefit week begins on a Friday. He starts receiving a personal pension of £68 a week from Monday 25 April 2022. £18 a week (£68 – £50) is deducted from his contribution-based JSA from the benefit week starting Friday 22 April 2022.

If your pension increases while you are on contribution-based JSA, the change should be taken into account from the first day of the benefit week in which the increase is paid.[36]

Part 5: Other benefits
Chapter 33: Contribution-based jobseeker's allowance
4. The amount of benefit

Note:
- The amount of your pension payments may mean that you are not paid any JSA. However, unless your earnings also exceed the prescribed amount (see p694), you remain *entitled* to contribution-based JSA (provided you also satisfy the other conditions for getting JSA).
- Any day on which you are entitled to JSA (even if it is not paid) counts towards your 182 days' entitlement to contribution-based JSA (see below).
- A combination of earnings and pension payments may mean that you are not paid any JSA, even though you may remain entitled to it.

Duration of contribution-based jobseeker's allowance

You cannot receive more than 182 days of contribution-based JSA in any jobseeking period (see p689) or in two or more jobseeking periods if your entitlement is based on national insurance (NI) contributions in the same two contribution years.[37]

You can have another 182 days of contribution-based JSA for a later claim if:[38]
- you satisfy the contribution conditions; *and*
- at least one of the two contribution years used to decide whether you satisfy the contribution conditions is later than the second contribution year used to decide your previous entitlement. This can only apply if you are in a later jobseeking period than the one during which you exhausted your entitlement to contribution-based JSA.

Days that count towards the 182-day total

Each day for which you are entitled to contribution-based JSA, even if you are not paid, counts, including days when the amount of JSA you are paid has been reduced to nil because you have been given a sanction, or because you are getting a pension or a combination of pension and earnings.

Days on which you are *not* entitled to contribution-based JSA can also count. This applies to days within a jobseeking period on which you are not entitled to contribution-based JSA because it is not payable either because you have been given a sanction (see Chapter 47) or because you have committed a benefit offence, so long as you satisfy the contribution conditions for JSA.

Days on which you are not entitled to JSA and which do *not* count include:
- waiting days (see p704); *and*
- days in any benefit week in which you are not entitled to JSA because you earn more than the prescribed amount (see p694) – but see above if you have been given a sanction.

5. Special benefit rules

Special rules may apply to:
- people who have come from or are going abroad (see Chapters 68, 69, 70 and 71);
- people who are studying (see Chapter 41);
- people involved in a trade dispute (see p982).

6. Claims and backdating

The general rules about claims and backdating are covered in Chapter 50. This section explains the specific rules that apply to contribution-based jobseeker's allowance (JSA).

Note: in rare cases, it may be beneficial for you to delay your claim for contribution-based JSA so that you can draw on a different year's record of national insurance (NI) contributions.

JSA claims are dealt with by DWP decision makers (see p1248) and work coaches (see p1025).

Making a claim

You can start your claim for contribution-based JSA (the DWP sometimes calls it 'new-style' JSA):[39]
- online at gov.uk/guidance/new-style-jobseekers-allowance#how-to-claim (if you are aged 18 or over); or
- if you cannot claim online, by telephone on 0800 055 6688 (Welsh language: 0800 012 1888; textphone: 0800 023 4888; Relay UK and BSL relay services available. Say that you want to claim 'new-style' JSA. You may be sent Form UCJSA 1 to complete.

If you cannot do either, you can claim by completing a paper claim form approved by the DWP, or you may be asked to attend the Jobcentre Plus office to make your claim in person.[40] There is no rule that says you must claim online or by telephone, so get advice if you are unable to do so, or find this difficult, and the Jobcentre Plus office tells you that you cannot start your claim in any other way. **Note:** you can make initial contact with the DWP by telephone or letter to say you want to claim. The date of your initial contact is important because it usually determines the date on which your claim is treated as having been made (see p699).

If you claim online, you get a text to confirm your claim has been submitted. The DWP then contacts you within ten days of your claim to arrange for you to complete your claim at an initial interview.[41] At the time of writing, this is a

Part 5: Other benefits
Chapter 33: Contribution-based jobseeker's allowance
6. Claims and backdating

telephone interview. See below for further information and for what you must bring with you.

You may be sent or given a form to complete about the work you will be looking for and how you intend to go about getting it. The information you give forms the basis of your claimant commitment.

If you want to claim universal credit to top up your contribution-based JSA, you must do this separately.

You must provide any information or evidence required. You can amend or withdraw your claim before a decision is made (see p1135). If there is a delay in deciding your claim, you may be able to get a short-term advance (see p1153).

Claiming national insurance credits

If you do not get JSA but want to claim NI credits for unemployment, see p955.

Who should claim

You claim contribution-based JSA on your own behalf. If you are unable to manage your own affairs, another person can claim JSA for you as your 'appointee' (see p1135).

Information to support your claim

For the general information requirements that apply to all benefits, see p1136. In addition, for JSA, the DWP asks you to provide details of your bank or building society account or those of a family member or trusted friend, employment details for the past six months including your employer's contact details and the dates you worked for her/him, and if you have a private pension, a statement letter.

It is important that you provide any information required when you claim. Until you do, you may not count as having made a valid claim (see p1138).

Correct any defects as soon as possible or your date of claim may be affected.

Even if you have provided all that was required when you claimed, you may be asked to provide further information to support your claim (see p1140). You may also be asked to provide information after you are awarded JSA, and if you fail to do so, your JSA could be suspended, or even terminated (see p1162).

The initial interview

In order for your JSA claim to be valid, you must usually attend and participate in an initial interview. At the time of writing, this is a telephone interview with a work coach at a Jobcentre Plus office. The DWP contacts you within ten days of your claim to arrange this.[42] If you do not attend the interview at the right time or place, your date of claim is affected (see p700). If you do not attend the interview at all (and the DWP does not waive the requirement to do so), you have not made a valid claim and so do not qualify for JSA.

If you are required to attend the Jobcentre Plus office and this would mean that you would have to be away from home for too long, arrangements can be made for your interview to be carried out elsewhere.

If you are asked to provide any documents for the initial interview, make sure you do so.

If you have been sent a claim form, complete it before your interview. If you do not provide all the evidence and information required, your interview might not go ahead.

At the interview:

- you are told what is expected from you while you are receiving JSA;
- you and your work coach discuss what work you are looking for and what you intend to do to find it;
- a claimant commitment is drawn up for you to sign;
- you may be referred to a job vacancy immediately. However, a claimant commitment should still be completed to establish your entitlement in case you do not get the job.

The interview also covers what you were doing before you became unemployed and, in particular, why you left your previous job. If the person who interviews you thinks that you may have left voluntarily or been dismissed for misconduct, your case is referred to a decision maker who will probably make further enquiries to decide whether to give you a sanction.

The date of your claim

The date of your claim is important as it determines when your entitlement to JSA starts (subject to the rules on waiting days – see p704).[43] This is not necessarily the date from when you are paid.

Your date of claim is not necessarily the date it is received by the DWP. It can be an earlier date (see below).

Your '**date of claim**' depends on whether or not you are required to attend an initial interview.

- If you are required to attend an initial interview (see p698), your date of claim is the date you first contact the Jobcentre Plus office if you attend your initial interview at the time specified by the DWP and by that time a properly completed claim is, or has been, provided (on a form, online or by telephone). The DWP can extend the time you have to provide or make a properly completed claim up to the date one month after the date of first contact. This is discretionary, so provide your claim as required wherever possible. If you fail to attend your initial interview, see p700.[44]
- If you are not required to attend an initial interview, your date of claim is the earliest of:[45]
  - the date you first contact the Jobcentre Plus office, so long as a properly completed claim (on a form, online or by telephone) with all the information

Part 5: Other benefits
Chapter 33: Contribution-based jobseeker's allowance
6. Claims and backdating

and evidence required is provided within one month of your first contact or a longer period that the DWP thinks is reasonable; *or*

- the date on which a properly completed claim (on a form, online or by telephone) with all the information and evidence required is received at the Jobcentre Plus office; *or*
- if you are notified that your claim is defective and you supply all the information required within one month of this, or a longer period that the DWP thinks is reasonable, the date your claim is received.

In some cases, you can claim in advance (see p702) and in some cases your claim can be backdated (see below). If you want this to be done, make this clear when you claim or the DWP might not consider it.

If you fail to attend the initial interview

If you fail to attend your initial interview at the time specified by the DWP, or you fail to provide a properly completed claim by the date of the interview and cannot show a good reason for this (called 'good cause'), the rules above do not apply. Instead, so long as a properly completed claim is provided, your date of claim is the date you eventually go to the Jobcentre Plus office. Your entitlement to JSA cannot start until that date.[46]

'**Good cause'** is not defined. All relevant circumstances must be considered. These may relate to your abilities, or to external factors. The general test is whether there is some factor that would probably cause a reasonable person of your age and experience to act, or fail to act, as you did.[47]

Backdating your claim

It is very important to claim in time. A claim for JSA can only be backdated for up to one or three months in limited circumstances, and only if these circumstances mean you could not reasonably claim sooner. For the circumstances that allow your claim to be backdated one month and for three months, see p701.

If you want your JSA claim to be backdated:
- state this clearly when you claim. Explain why you are claiming late and provide evidence or information that backs this up if you can;
- explain why there was no one else who could have helped you to claim, if relevant. However, if a person has been formally appointed by a court or the DWP to act on your behalf, your appointee (see p1135), not you, must show that it was not reasonable to expect her/him to claim sooner than s/he did.[48] If someone is informally acting on your behalf, you must show that s/he was acting for you, that it was reasonable for you to delegate responsibility for your claim and that you took care to ensure that the person helping you claimed properly.[49]

Note: if you might have qualified for JSA earlier but did not claim because you were given the wrong information or were misled by the DWP, you could ask for compensation (see p1403) or complain to the Ombudsman (see p1408).

One month's backdating

The decision maker must backdate your claim for up to one month if one or more of the following applies (or has applied), and because of this you could not reasonably have been expected to make your claim any earlier.[50]

- The office where you were supposed to claim was closed (eg, because of a strike) and there were no other arrangements for claims to be made.
- You could not get to the DWP office because there were difficulties with the type of transport you normally use and there was no reasonable alternative.
- There were adverse postal conditions – eg, bad weather, a postal strike, or the post office failed to act under its agreement to deliver under-stamped mail to the DWP.[51]
- You could not make an online claim for JSA because the DWP's computer system was not working.
- You stopped getting contributory employment and support allowance, but were not informed before your entitlement ceased, so you could not claim JSA in time.
- In the month before you claimed JSA:
  - you separated from your partner; or
  - a close relative of yours died. 'Close relative' means your partner, parent, son, daughter, brother or sister.
- You were unable to notify the DWP by telephone of your intention to claim because the telephone lines to the office were busy or not working.

Three months' backdating

The decision maker must backdate your claim for up to three months if one or more of the following applies (or has applied), and because of this you could not reasonably have been expected to make your claim any earlier.[52] If more than one reason applies, the combined effect of all of them must be considered in deciding whether it was reasonable for you to claim earlier.[53]

- You were given information by an officer of the DWP and, as a result, thought your claim would not succeed. 'Information' includes general information produced by the DWP and placed on government websites. It does not have to be tailored to your circumstances or involve personal communication between you and an officer.[54] The information that is relevant includes if:
  - you were given incorrect information or the wrong claim form and this led you to claim the wrong benefit;
  - someone with authority to act on your behalf was given incorrect information;[55]
  - you were told your claim would not be accepted;[56]
  - you were told you did not have to fill in a claim form;[57]
  - the refusal of, or failure to respond to, an earlier claim for the same or a different benefit led you to believe that you were not entitled;[58]

Part 5: Other benefits
Chapter 33: Contribution-based jobseeker's allowance
6. Claims and backdating

- the information was incomplete and had not included advice on claiming when it should have done.[59]

'**Officer**' includes anyone carrying out public functions at the benefit office – eg, a security guard.[60] It does not matter if the information you received was correct or reasonable on the basis of any information that you gave to the officer about your circumstances, provided the officer's advice caused you to think that a claim would fail.[61] If you have been misled, misinformed or given insufficient advice by an officer of the DWP, explain how and when this happened and, where possible, give the name and a description of the officer concerned.

- You were given advice in writing by Citizens Advice or another advice service, a solicitor or other professional adviser (eg, an accountant), a doctor or a local authority and, as a result, thought your claim would not succeed. 'Advice in writing' includes leaflets, emails or information on a website, provided it is directed at claimants in your position.[62] It is not enough for your adviser to record a note of verbal advice unless you are provided with a copy.[63] However, your claim should be backdated if you are given written confirmation of advice that was originally given to you orally, provided this is done before the decision maker decides whether you are entitled to backdating.[64]
- You could not get to the DWP office because of bad weather.
- It was not 'reasonably practicable' for you to seek help from anyone else to make your claim, and:
  - you have learning, language or literacy difficulties, or you are deaf or blind; or
  - you were caring for someone who is sick or disabled; or
  - you were dealing with a domestic emergency that affected you.

It is whether it is reasonably practicable for you to seek help, not whether it is reasonably practicable for another person to proactively offer help to you.[65] The DWP should consider all the circumstances. If you are mentally ill, this does not automatically mean you are unable to seek assistance.[66]

If you claim the wrong benefit

There are no rules that allow a claim for another benefit to be treated as a claim for JSA.

Claiming in advance

If you do not qualify for JSA from the date of your claim, but will do so within the next three months, you can be awarded JSA from the first date on which you qualify.[67] This gives the DWP time to ensure you receive benefit as soon as you are entitled. Let the DWP know you want to claim in advance when you claim and at your initial interview. You might have to persuade the DWP that it can accept a claim in advance.

7. Getting paid

The general rules on getting paid are covered in Chapter 51. This section explains the specific rules that apply to jobseeker's allowance (JSA). **Note:** the rules in this section apply to all types of JSA.

When is jobseeker's allowance paid?
JSA is normally paid fortnightly in arrears.[68]

JSA is a weekly benefit, although in some cases it can be paid for part weeks.[69] Most questions about entitlement and payment are decided in relation to a particular 'benefit week' – ie, the period of seven days ending on the day of the week allocated to you according to your national insurance (NI) number.[70]

If you are entitled to less than 10 pence a week, you are not paid JSA at all,[71] but you are still eligible for NI credits (see p955). If you are entitled to less than £1 a week, the DWP can decide to pay you at longer intervals of not more than 13 weeks.[72]

Note:
- Deductions can sometimes be made from your JSA to pay to third parties (see p1164).
- Your JSA might be paid at a reduced (or nil) rate if you have been sanctioned for a benefit offence (see p1239). You may also be given a sanction for other reasons – see Chapter 47 (see p1116 for income-based JSA).
- For information on missing payments, see p1150. If you cannot get your JSA payments because you have lost your bank card or you have forgotten your PIN, see p1149. If you have lost your payment service card, see p1150.
- If payment of your JSA is delayed, see p1255. If you are waiting for a decision on your claim, or to be paid, you may be able to get a short-term advance (see p1153). If you wish to complain about how your claim has been dealt with, or claim compensation, see Chapter 61.
- If payment of your JSA is suspended, see p1161.
- If you are overpaid JSA, you might have to repay it (see Chapter 53) and, in some circumstances, you may have to pay a penalty (see p1229). If you have been accused of fraud, see Chapter 54.
- If you are owed arrears of JSA, these can be paid in instalments (see p1148).

After you are awarded jobseeker's allowance

Once you have been awarded JSA, in order to continue to receive it you must provide any evidence and information required by the DWP. If you do not do so, your JSA could be suspended or even terminated (see p1162). In addition, you must:

Part 5: Other benefits
Chapter 33: Contribution-based jobseeker's allowance
8. Tax, other benefits and the benefit cap

- attend and participate in regular interviews; *and*
- confirm that you continue to qualify for JSA – eg, by signing on.

In some cases, if you fail to participate in interviews, you may be given a sanction (see p1066). You are required to meet work-related requirements and you can be given a sanction if you fail to do so. See Chapter 46 for the requirements after you are awarded JSA, and Chapter 47 for information about sanctions.

Change of circumstances

You must report changes in your circumstances that you have been told you must report, as well as any that you might reasonably be expected to know might affect your right to, the amount of, or the payment of, your benefit, including any that are likely to occur. You should do this as soon as possible, preferably in writing. See p1160 for further information.

When there has been a relevant change of circumstances, a decision maker looks at your claim again and makes a new decision.

As a general rule, your JSA is adjusted from the first day of the benefit week in which the change occurs or is expected to do so.[73] There are a number of exceptions to this rule.[74] In particular, if a decision is to your advantage, but you failed to notify the DWP of a change within the time limit (normally one month, but this can be extended – see p1283), your JSA is adjusted from the first day of the benefit week in which you notified the change.

Waiting days

You are not entitled to JSA for the first seven 'waiting days' in any jobseeking period (see p689) unless:[75]
- your claim is linked to a previous claim for JSA, so both are treated as part of the same jobseeking period; *or*
- you were entitled to income support (IS), employment and support allowance (ESA) or carer's allowance in the 12 weeks before you became entitled to JSA.

In addition, you do not have to serve any waiting days if you swap from claiming IS or ESA to claiming JSA.[76]

You may be able to get a short-term advance before your first payment of JSA is due (see p1153).

8. **Tax, other benefits and the benefit cap**

Tax

Jobseeker's allowance (JSA) is taxable.[77] The maximum amount of JSA that is taxable is:

- an amount equal to the weekly rate of JSA for a person of your age (see p693); or
- if you are a member of a couple, an amount equal to the income-based JSA applicable amount for a couple which would be included if you were getting income-based JSA.

The tax is not deducted while JSA is being paid, but reduces the refund you would otherwise receive through pay as you earn (PAYE) when you return to work.

Any tax refunds of PAYE payments are paid to you at the end of the tax year to which they relate. Any other tax refund is paid only when you stop getting JSA.

Means-tested benefits and tax credits

If you are entitled to contribution-based JSA, it counts as income for the purposes of means-tested benefits and tax credits. However, if you (or your partner) get universal credit (UC), pension credit (PC), income support (IS), income-based JSA or income-related employment and support allowance (ESA), it is ignored for housing benefit (HB) purposes.

If you need more income, you (and your partner) may be able to claim UC to top up your contribution-based JSA. If you have a partner, s/he may be able to claim other benefits (see p8).

Non-means-tested benefits

While you are on JSA, you are entitled to national insurance credits (see p955). Contribution-based JSA is affected by the overlapping benefit rules (see p1151).

The benefit cap

In some cases, there is a limit on the total amount of specified benefits you can receive (a 'benefit cap'). JSA is one of the specified benefits. The benefit cap only applies if you are getting UC or HB. See p1156 for further information. **Note:** income-based JSA run-on (see p253) does *not* count as a specified benefit.

Passports and other sources of help

If you (or your partner) are entitled to UC (or IS, income-based JSA or income-related ESA) in addition to contribution-based JSA, you may also qualify for other sources of help. See the chapters on those benefits for further information. If you are not entitled to one of those benefits, you may qualify for health benefits under the low income scheme (see p652). Whether or not you are entitled to one of those benefits, you may qualify for council tax reduction (see p836). You may also qualify for help from your local welfare assistance scheme (see p846).

Financial help on starting work

See p858 for information about other financial help you might get.

Notes

5

1. Who can get contribution-based jobseeker's allowance

1 s1 JSA 1995
2 ss60-6I JSA 1995
3 s2 JSA 1995
4 Reg 37(1) JSA Regs 2013
5 Reg 37(2) JSA Regs 2013
6 s2(1) and (4) JSA 1995
7 Reg 39 JSA Regs 2013; reg 48 JSA Regs
8 Reg 39(2) and (4) JSA Regs 2013; reg 48(2) and (3) JSA Regs
9 *LE v SSWP* [2009] UKUT 166 (AAC). The judge decided that the rule indirectly discriminated against women but that the discrimination was justified.
10 Reg 42 JSA Regs 2013
11 s1(2)(f) JSA 1995
12 Regs 46(1), 46A(1) and 47(1) JSA Regs 2013; regs 55(1), 55ZA(1) and 55A(1) JSA Regs
13 Reg 46(1) and (3) JSA Regs 2013; reg 55(1) and (3) JSA Regs
14 Reg 46(2) JSA Regs 2013; reg 55(2) JSA Regs
15 Reg 46(7) JSA Regs 2013; reg 55(7) JSA Regs
16 Reg 46(4) and (6) JSA Regs 2013; reg 55(4) and (6) JSA Regs
17 Reg 16(5) JSA Regs 2013
18 Reg 46A(1), (3) and (3A) JSA Regs 2013; reg 55ZA(1), (3) and (3A) JSA Regs
19 Reg 46A(4) JSA Regs 2013; reg 55ZA(4) JSA Regs
20 Reg 46A(5) JSA Regs 2013; reg 55ZA(5) JSA Regs
21 Reg 46A(6) JSA Regs 2013; reg 55ZA(6) JSA Regs
22 Reg 16A JSA Regs 2013
23 Reg 47 JSA Regs 2013; reg 55A JSA Regs
24 Reg 47(2) JSA Regs 2013; reg 55A(2) JSA Regs
25 Reg 16(3)(b)(iii) JSA Regs 2013

4. The amount of benefit

26 s4(1) and (2) JSA 1995; reg 49 JSA Regs 2013
27 s4(1) JSA 1995
28 s4(1)(b) JSA 1995; reg 50 JSA Regs 2013
29 Regs 59(2) and 61(2) and Sch JSA Regs 2013

30 s2(1)(c) JSA 1995; reg 48 JSA Regs 2013
31 ss4(1) and 35(1) JSA 1995; R(JSA) 1/01
32 Reg 51 JSA Regs 2013; R(U) 8/83
33 Reg 51(4) JSA Regs 2013
34 Reg 51(1) JSA Regs 2013
35 Reg 51(2) JSA Regs 2013
36 Reg 51(3) JSA Regs 2013
37 s5(1) JSA 1995
38 s5(2) JSA 1995

6. Claims and backdating

39 Regs 3 and 23 and Sch 2 UC,PIP,JSA&ESA(C&P) Regs; gov.uk/guidance/new-style-jobseekers-allowance
40 Reg 21 UC,PIP,JSA&ESA(C&P) Regs
41 Reg 19 UC,PIP,JSA&ESA(C&P) Regs
42 Reg 19 UC,PIP,JSA&ESA(C&P) Regs
43 Reg 29(1) UC,PIP,JSA&ESA(C&P) Regs
44 Reg 20 UC,PIP,JSA&ESA(C&P) Regs
45 Regs 21, 22 and 24 UC,PIP,JSA&ESA(C&P) Regs
46 Reg 20(2) UC,PIP,JSA&ESA(C&P) Regs
47 CS/371/1949
48 R(SB) 17/83; CIS/812/1992
49 R(P) 2/85
50 Reg 29(4) and (5) UC,PIP,JSA&ESA(C&P) Regs
51 CIS/4901/2002; CJSA/3960/2006
52 Reg 29(2) and (3) UC,PIP,JSA&ESA(C&P) Regs
53 CIS/2484/1999
54 *SSWP v PG (JSA)* [2015] UKUT 616 (AAC), but see also *S K-G v SSWP (JSA)* [2014] UKUT 430 (AAC), which earlier came to the opposite conclusion, holding that 'information' must be tailored to your circumstances in some way
55 CJSA/4573/1999
56 CJSA/4066/1998
57 CIS/610/1998
58 R(IS) 3/01; CIS/4490/1998
59 CJSA/0580/2003
60 CIS/610/1998
61 CIS/3994/1998; CSIS/815/2004
62 CIS/5430/1999
63 CIS/5430/1999
64 CJSA/1136/1998; CIS/5430/1999
65 CIS/2057/1998

- -

66 C12/98 (IS)
67 Reg 34 UC,PIP,JSA&ESA(C&P) Regs

7. Getting paid
68 Reg 52 UC,PIP,JSA&ESA(C&P) Regs; reg 26A SS(C&P) Regs
69 s1(3) and Sch 1 para 5 JSA 1995; reg 64 JSA Regs 2013; reg 150 JSA Regs
70 Reg 2(2) JSA Regs 2013; reg 1(3) JSA Regs
71 Reg 52 JSA Regs 2013; reg 87A JSA Regs
72 Reg 52(3) UC,PIP,JSA&ESA(C&P) Regs; reg 26A(3) SS(C&P) Regs
73 Reg 35 and Sch 1 UC,PIP,JSA&ESA(DA) Regs; reg 7 and Sch 3A para 7 SS&CS(DA) Regs
74 Reg 35 and Sch 1 Part 1 UC,PIP,JSA&ESA(DA) Regs; reg 7 and Sch 3A paras 8-13 SS&CS(DA) Regs
75 Sch 1 para 4 JSA 1995; reg 36 JSA Regs 2013; reg 46 JSA Regs
76 Reg 48(5) UC,PIP,JSA&ESA(DA) Regs

8. Tax, other benefits and the benefit cap
77 ss671-75 IT(EP)A 2003

Chapter 34

Maternity allowance

This chapter covers:

Key facts

- If you are pregnant or have recently given birth and are not entitled to statutory maternity pay, you may qualify for maternity allowance (MA).
- MA is a non-means-tested benefit.
- You can qualify for MA whether you are in or out of work, but to qualify you must have recently been employed or self-employed or have helped your spouse or civil partner with her/his business.
- You do not need to have paid national insurance (NI) contributions to qualify although, in some circumstances, your entitlement may depend on your spouse's or civil partner's NI contribution record and if you are self-employed, your NI contribution record may affect the amount of MA you receive.
- MA is affected by the overlapping benefit rules, so you may not be able to get MA and another earnings-replacement benefit at the same time.
- If you work while claiming MA, you may be disqualified from getting MA for a period.
- MA is administered and paid by the DWP.
- If you disagree with a decision on MA, you can apply for a revision or supersession (see Chapter 56), or appeal against it (see Chapter 57). You must apply for a mandatory reconsideration before you can appeal.

1. **Who can get maternity allowance**

You qualify for maternity allowance (MA) if:[1]

- you are pregnant or have recently given birth; *and*
- you are not entitled to statutory maternity pay (SMP) for the same pregnancy or birth; *and either*
- you qualify on the basis of your own employment or self-employment – ie:
  - you have been employed or self-employed in at least 26 weeks in your 'test period' (see p710). This is called the 'employment condition' (see p710); *and*
  - your average weekly earnings in 13 weeks of your test period (or, if you are self-employed, the average weekly earnings you are treated as having) are at least £30 a week. This is called the 'earnings condition' (see p711); *and*
  - you are within your 39-week 'maternity allowance period' (MA period – see p711); *or*
- you qualify on the basis of having helped your spouse or civil partner with her/his self-employment – ie:
  - your spouse or civil partner was a self-employed earner in at least 26 weeks in your test period and s/he has paid class 2 national insurance (NI) contributions for those 26 weeks (s/he can pay class 2 contributions early to help you meet this condition – see p949);[2] *and*
  - for at least part of each of those 26 weeks you took part in, or assisted, your spouse or civil partner with her/his self-employment, but you were not employed by, or in partnership with, her/him; *and*
  - you are within your 14-week 'qualifying period' (see p713); *and*
  - you do not qualify for MA on the basis of your own employment or self-employment.

If you qualify for MA on the basis of your own employment or self-employment, your MA can be paid over a longer period and may be paid at a higher weekly rate than if you qualify for MA on the basis of having helped your spouse or civil partner with her/his self-employment.

Provided you meet the above conditions, you do not currently need to be employed or self-employed to get MA.

In certain circumstances, you may be disqualified from receiving MA if you work or fail to attend a medical examination (see p713).

Note:
- Even if you do not qualify for MA, you may qualify for employment and support allowance (see p720).
- If you get SMP (or if you would have got SMP but for having reduced your maternity pay period in connection with a claim for shared parental leave or statutory shared parental pay (SSPP – see Chapter 38)), you cannot receive MA for the same week for the same baby, even if you have more than one job or have been self-employed as well as employed.[3]

Definitions

Your '**expected week of childbirth**' (EWC) is the week, starting on a Sunday, in which your baby is due to be born.

Your '**test period**' is the 66 weeks immediately before your EWC. For the date on which your test period starts, see Appendix 8.

Employment condition

To qualify for MA on the basis of your employment or self-employment, you must have been employed or self-employed for at least 26 weeks in your test period.[4] If you are employed or self-employed for part of a week, the whole of that week counts. The 26 weeks do not need to be consecutive and you do not need to have been in the same job for the whole period. You need only show that you have been employed and/or self-employed for any part of each of the 26 weeks. For MA, a week starts on a Sunday and to count as employed or self-employed you must be an employed or self-employed earner (see p947).

See p716 if you have worked abroad.

Note:

- If you are an agency worker or have a zero-hours contract and you have a contract of employment, or a contract to provide services, you count as an employed earner whether or not you are provided with work in a particular week.[5]
- When you become self-employed, you are normally required to register with HM Revenue and Customs (HMRC) for NI and tax purposes. If you delay registering, the DWP may consider the date on which you registered as the date your self-employment started, rather than the date you became a self-employed earner. If, as a consequence, the DWP decides you do not meet the employment condition for MA, get advice.
- Even if you do not meet this employment condition, you may still qualify for MA if you have helped your spouse or civil partner with her/his self-employment (see p709).

Example

Fay's baby is due on Saturday 2 July 2022.

Fay's EWC begins on Sunday 26 June 2022 and her 66-week 'test period' runs from Sunday 21 March 2021 to Saturday 25 June 2022. In this period, Fay was a self-employed earner from Tuesday 11 May 2021 until Thursday 29 July 2021 and was employed from Monday 3 January 2022 until Friday 8 April 2022. As the weeks in which she is employed or self-employed for part of a week count as a full week, the weeks in which she started and ended her self-employment and employment count, and Fay meets the 26-week employment condition.

Earnings condition

To qualify for MA on the basis of your employment or self-employment, your average weekly earnings in 13 weeks of your test period (or, if you are self-employed, the average weekly earnings you are treated as having – see below) must be at least £30 a week. This is known as the 'MA threshold'. For how earnings are averaged, see p715.[6]

Note: even if you do not meet this earnings condition, you may still qualify for MA if you have helped your spouse or civil partner with her/his self-employment (see p709).

Earnings from employment

If you are employed, your gross earnings are used to calculate your average weekly earnings. What counts as earnings is the same as for SMP (see p805).[7] If you get a backdated pay rise for the period over which your earnings are averaged, this is included in the calculation.[8]

For any weeks that you were furloughed during the coronavirus pandemic and for which your furlough pay was less than you would otherwise have earned for the week, your average weekly earnings are calculated using the wages you would have been paid had you not been furloughed.[9]

Earnings from self-employment

The amount you actually earn from self-employment is not taken into account. Instead, you are treated as earning a certain amount based on whether or not you have paid class 2 NI contributions, and this figure is used to calculate your average weekly earnings. For each week:[10]

- for which you have paid a class 2 NI contribution, you are treated as having earnings of an amount 90 per cent of which is equal to the maximum amount of MA that can be paid for that week. In 2022/23, this is £174.07;[11]
- for which you could have paid a class 2 contribution but have not done so, you are treated as having earnings of £30 a week – ie, equal to the MA threshold.

Note: if you are self-employed, your liability to pay class 2 contributions is calculated after the end of the tax year through the income tax self-assessment procedure. To help you meet the condition in the first bullet point (which qualifies you for a higher rate of MA – see p715), you can pay class 2 contributions early, on a voluntary basis (see p949).[12] If you would benefit from this, after you have claimed MA you normally get a letter from HMRC telling you the amount to pay and how to pay it, should you want to pay early.

Maternity allowance period

MA awarded on the basis of your employment or self-employment can only be paid for weeks in your MA period.[13] This is a period of 39 consecutive weeks that normally starts on the day your maternity pay period would have begun had you been entitled to SMP (see p797). However:[14]

- if you are not employed or self-employed at the beginning of the 11th week before your EWC (see p710), your MA period starts from the beginning of that week (but if your baby was born before this, it starts from the day after the birth); *and*

- if you are not entitled to MA during the 11th week before your EWC, but you become entitled to it before your baby is born (perhaps because you then meet the earnings or employment condition), provided you have stopped work, the earliest day on which your MA period can start is the day you become entitled to MA, and the latest it can start is the day after the birth.

To calculate the 11th week before your EWC, see Appendix 8.

Reducing your maternity allowance period and statutory shared parental pay

If you get MA on the basis of your own employment or self-employment (rather than on the basis that you help your spouse or civil partner with her/his self-employment), you can end your MA period early, relinquishing up to 37 weeks of your MA, so that the father of your child or your partner can qualify for SSPP from her/his employer (see p800) and/or shared parental leave from work. If s/he meets the qualifying conditions, s/he can then get SSPP for the number of weeks of MA that you have chosen to give up.

To reduce your MA period in this way, you must give the DWP office dealing with your claim a 'curtailment notification' stating the date you want your MA period to end (called your 'curtailment date'). This should be submitted at least eight weeks before your curtailment date (although the DWP has discretion to accept less notice than this).[15] Your curtailment date must fall at least two weeks after the birth of your baby (or four weeks after it, if you are employed in a factory or workshop) and at least one week before what would have been the last day of your MA period. It is advisable to give a curtailment notification in writing, although the DWP cannot insist on this.

Think carefully before giving up your MA in this way as it is only possible to cancel a curtailment notification if:[16]

- you do so before your curtailment date; and either:
  - you gave the curtailment notification before your child was born, and inform the DWP that you want to cancel it within six weeks of the birth. (Note: you can subsequently give another curtailment notification); *or*
  - your partner has died and you inform the DWP within a reasonable time after the death and provide the date of death.

14-week qualifying period

MA awarded on the basis that you have helped your spouse or civil partner with her/his self-employment can be paid for a maximum of 14 consecutive weeks, called the 'qualifying period'. Your qualifying period starts:[17]

- if you stopped working with your spouse or civil partner before the beginning of the 11th week before your EWC, on the first day of the 11th week before your EWC;
- if you stopped working with your spouse or civil partner during or after the 11th week before your EWC (but before the day your baby is born), on the day after you stop work. Once you have reached the fourth week before your EWC, this applies even if you just refrain from working with your spouse or civil partner (eg, because you are unwell), if this is at least in part because of your pregnancy or childbirth;
- otherwise, on the day after you have your baby.

'Stopping work' means either stopping permanently or until after the birth. To calculate the 11th week before your EWC, see Appendix 8.

Note: if you are not entitled to MA during the 11th week before your EWC but you become entitled to it before your baby is born, provided you have stopped working with your spouse or civil partner, the earliest day your 14-week qualifying period can start is the day you become entitled to MA and the latest is the day after the birth.[18]

Disqualification from maternity allowance

In some circumstances, you can be disqualified from MA if you work or if you fail to attend a medical examination. You can challenge the DWP's decision that you should be disqualified from MA, including its decision on the length of the disqualification period (see Chapters 56 and 57).

If you work

It is important to tell the DWP of any work that you do. This is because the DWP can disqualify you from receiving MA if:[19]

- you are entitled to MA on the basis of your own employment or self-employment (see p709) and you work for more than 10 days during your MA period. The disqualification must be for no longer than is reasonable given the circumstances, but must be for at least the number of days you worked in excess of these 10 days. Both employed and self-employed work counts and the 10 days do not need to be consecutive. If you work for part of a day, it counts as a full day. If you work for 10 days or less, your MA is unaffected, even if you are paid for that work; or
- you are entitled to MA on the basis of helping with your spouse or civil partner's self-employment (see p709) and you do *any* work during your 14-

week qualifying period. This applies if the work is helping your spouse or partner with her/his business or work you do as an employee or as a self-employed earner. The disqualification must be for no longer than is reasonable given the circumstances, but must be for at least the number of days you worked.

Example

Before going on maternity leave, Saira, who is self-employed, worked full time. She qualifies for MA of £156.66 a week (because she paid class 2 NI contributions for 13 weeks in her test period) but while on maternity leave still does small amounts of administrative work, such as responding to enquiries with information about when she will return to work after her maternity leave. She also took on a contract that meant she worked for three hours a day over an 11-day period. The DWP decides that the small amounts of administrative work she does, which are minimal and necessary to maintain her business while she is on leave, can be ignored. However, each of the days on which she worked for three hours count as a full day of work. Although the first 10 such days do not affect her entitlement to MA, the 11th does. The DWP decides that it is reasonable to disqualify her from MA for one day and deducts £22.38 from her weekly MA (one-seventh of £156.66).[20]

If you are employed and on maternity leave, working for your employer for more than 10 days may affect your continued entitlement to leave. If you do not want your maternity leave to end, get employment advice before agreeing to such work.

If you have been disqualified from MA because you have returned to work and have worked for more than 10 days, provided you have not brought your MA period to an end by submitting a curtailment notification (see p712), you may be able to get MA again if you stop work and are still within your MA period. If you are employed and your maternity leave has ended because of your return to work, this could be during a period when you are on sick leave or when you take shared parental leave. It is not necessary for you to end your MA period in order to qualify for shared parental leave (but it may be necessary to submit a curtailment notification for your partner to qualify for SSPP and/or shared parental leave).

If you fail to attend a medical

You are disqualified from receiving MA if, before the birth of your baby, you fail to attend a medical examination without good cause. For this to apply, you must have been given written notice of the examination at least three days beforehand by the DWP or someone acting on its behalf. The DWP can disqualify you for as long as is reasonable given the circumstances, but the disqualification cannot start until the day of the missed examination and cannot continue once you have given birth.[21]

Whether or not you have good cause for failing to attend depends on your circumstances.

2. The rules about your age

There are no upper or lower age limits for receiving maternity allowance.

3. People included in the claim

You claim maternity allowance for yourself. You cannot claim any increase for your partner or child(ren).

4. The amount of benefit

Type of maternity allowance	Maximum period of payment	Weekly amount
Entitlement arising from your own employment or self-employment (see p709)	39 weeks	£156.66 or 90 per cent of your average weekly earnings, whichever is less.[22]
Entitlement arising from helping your spouse or civil partner with her/his self-employment (see p709)	14 weeks	£27[23]

Calculating average weekly earnings

If you qualify for maternity allowance (MA) on the basis of your own employment or self-employment, your average weekly earnings are used to determine both whether you meet the earnings condition (see p711) and the amount of MA you get. They are calculated as follows.[24]

- If you have paid class 2 national insurance contributions as a self-employed person (see p949) for at least 13 weeks in your 66-week test period, no calculation is needed – you automatically qualify for the maximum weekly amount of MA of £156.66 a week.
- Otherwise, add together your earnings (this includes your earnings from employment (see p711) and/or the earnings you are treated as having from self-employment – see p711) in the 13 weeks in your 66-week test period when your earnings are highest and divide the total by 13. If you have more than one

job, the earnings from all your jobs, including earnings you are treated as having from self-employment, are counted.

In both cases, the 13 weeks do not need to be consecutive. If you are not paid weekly, work out your weekly earnings by dividing the payments you receive by the nearest number of weeks in the period for which they are paid.[25]

5. **Special benefit rules**

Special rules may apply to:
- people who are going abroad (see Chapters 70 and 71);
- people in prison or detention (see Chapter 42).

There are also special rules if you have been employed abroad.
- If, following a period of employment abroad, you have returned to Great Britain and you remained ordinarily resident in Great Britain while you were away, you may be able to rely on your employment abroad to satisfy the employment and earnings condition for maternity allowance (MA).[26]
- In some circumstances, you may be able to rely on periods you have worked in a European Economic Area country to qualify for MA (see p1606).

6. **Claims and backdating**

The general rules about claims and backdating are covered in Chapter 50. This section explains the specific rules that apply to maternity allowance (MA).

If you are (or have recently been) employed, you may be entitled to statutory maternity pay (SMP) (see Chapter 38) from your employer (or ex-employer) instead of MA. If you were employed in the 15th week before your expected week of childbirth (EWC), the DWP expects you to have applied for SMP. If your employer has decided you are not entitled to SMP, it should give you Form SMP1 explaining why and you should send this to the DWP to support your claim for MA. If you disagree with your employer's decision, or your employer fails to give you a decision, also ask HM Revenue and Customs to make a decision on your entitlement to SMP (see Chapter 60).

Making a claim

A claim for MA must be made in writing, normally on the approved form.

Forms

The approved form is Form MA1, which you can get from gov.uk/maternity-allowance/how-to-claim or from the Jobcentre Plus national contact centre by telephone (0800 055 6688; textphone: 0800 023 4888; Relay UK and BSL video relay services available).

Keep a copy of your claim in case queries arise. Your claim will not be accepted unless it is received after the 15th week before your EWC.[27]

The decision maker at the DWP may accept a written application not on the approved form.[28] You must provide any information or evidence required (see below). You can amend or withdraw your claim before a decision is made (see p1135). If there is a delay in deciding your claim or you are waiting to be paid, you may be able to get a short-term advance of benefit (see p1153).

Who should claim

You must normally claim MA for yourself. If you are unable to manage your own affairs, another person can claim MA for you as your 'appointee' (see p1135).

Information to support your claim

For the general information requirements that apply to all benefits, see p1136.

It is important that you provide any information required when you claim. Until you do, you may not count as having made a valid claim (see p1138). Correct any defects as soon as possible as your date of claim may be affected.

The DWP also expects you to provide:

- Form MAT B1 from your doctor or a registered midwife, giving the expected date of birth of your child and, if you are claiming MA after your baby is born, giving the date of the baby's birth.[29] Form MAT B1 is not accepted as evidence of your EWC if it is issued before the 20th week before your EWC. If you cannot obtain Form MAT B1, other evidence can be accepted, if it is sufficient;
- if you have been employed, pay slips or other written proof of your earnings and Form SMP1 from any employer for whom you worked during the 15th week before your EWC. Do not delay claiming MA because you are waiting for your SMP1 or evidence of your earnings; you can send these in later;
- if you are claiming MA on the basis that you help your spouse or civil partner with her/his self-employment, your marriage or civil partnership certificate.

Even if you have provided all that was required when you claimed, you may be asked to provide further information to support your claim (see p1140). You may also be asked to provide information after you are awarded MA. If you fail to do so, your MA could be suspended, or even terminated (see p1162).

The date of your claim

The date of your claim is important as it can determine when your entitlement to MA starts. This is not necessarily the date from when you are paid. For information about when payment of MA starts, see p718.

The '**date of your claim**' is normally the date it is received at a DWP office.[30]

You must make sure your claim is valid. If it is 'defective', you are given a short time to correct the defect (see p1139). If you do, your claim is treated as having been made when you initially claimed.[31]

In some cases, you can claim in advance (see below) and in some cases your claim can be backdated (see below). If you want to claim in advance or to have your claim backdated, make this clear when you claim or the DWP may not consider it. If you claimed employment and support allowance (ESA) instead of MA, or if you have been refused SMP, see below.

Backdating your claim

A claim for MA can be backdated for up to three months if you satisfy the qualifying conditions over that period. You do not have to show any reasons why your claim was late.[32]

If you might have qualified for benefit earlier but did not claim because you were given the wrong information or were misled by the DWP, you could ask for compensation (see p1403) or complain to the Independent Case Examiner or to the Ombudsman (see p1404 and p1408).

If you claimed ESA instead of MA, or if you have been refused SMP, see below.

If you claim the wrong benefit

A claim for ESA may also be treated as a claim for MA and vice versa (see p1144).[33]

If your employer (or former employer) has decided that you are not entitled to SMP and you claim MA within three months of being notified of your employer's decision in writing, your claim for MA is treated as having been made either on the date you gave your employer notice of when you wanted the maternity pay period to start or at the beginning of the 14th week before your EWC, whichever is later.[34]

Claiming in advance

You cannot make a claim for MA until after the 15th week before your EWC (ie, until week 26 of pregnancy), but you should claim as soon as possible after that.[35] However, if you qualify on the basis of your own employment or self-employment, it may be worth waiting a few weeks before claiming if this means you will have higher average earnings, and these would increase the amount of your MA.

7. Getting paid

The general rules on getting paid are covered in Chapter 51. This section explains the specific rules that apply to maternity allowance (MA).

When is maternity allowance paid?
The day you are paid depends on your national insurance number (see p1150). MA is normally paid fortnightly or four-weekly in arrears.[36]

If you have claimed in time and are entitled to MA, payment normally runs from the first day of your MA period (see p711) or 14-week qualifying period (see p713) until that period ends. To calculate the amount of MA due for a period of less than a week, use the daily rate of MA, which is one-seventh of the weekly amount.[37]

Note:

- In some circumstances, you can be disqualified from receiving MA (see p713).
- Even if you have been sanctioned for a benefit offence (see p1239), you must be paid your MA.
- For information on missing payments, see p1150. If you cannot get your MA payments because you have lost your bank card or you have forgotten your PIN, see p1149. If you have lost your payment service card, see p1150.
- If payment of your MA is delayed, see p1255. If you are waiting for a decision on your claim, or to be paid, you might be able to get a short-term advance (see p1153). If you wish to complain about how your claim has been dealt with, or claim compensation, see Chapter 61.
- If payment of your MA is suspended, see p1161.
- If you are overpaid MA, you might have to repay it (see Chapter 53) and, in some circumstances, you may have to pay a penalty (see p1229). If you have been accused of fraud, see Chapter 54.
- If you are owed arrears of MA, these can be paid in instalments (see p1148).

Change of circumstances

You must report any change in your circumstances that you have been told you must report, as well as any that you might reasonably be expected to know might affect your right to, the amount of, or the payment of, your benefit. You should do this as soon as possible, preferably in writing. See p1160 for further information.

If the change affects your entitlement to MA, a decision maker looks at your claim again and makes a new decision (see p1274). The date from which the new decision takes effect depends on whether or not it is advantageous to you and whether you reported the change in time (see p1280).

---

8. Tax, other benefits and the benefit cap

Tax

Maternity allowance (MA) is not taxable.[38]

Means-tested benefits and tax credits

If you are entitled to MA:

- you may also qualify for universal credit (UC) (see Chapter 3). If you or you partner are getting a 'legacy benefit' (see p21), seek advice before claiming UC because claiming UC is likely to end your entitlement to any legacy benefits and it is advisable first to check whether you will be better off on UC;

- the MA you get is taken into account in full as income when calculating your entitlement to UC, income support, income-based jobseeker's allowance, income-related employment and support allowance (ESA), the guarantee credit of pension credit and housing benefit (HB). However, any arrears of MA paid on the basis of your employment or self-employment may be ignored as capital for these benefits for a certain period (see p147, p482 and p507);
- MA is ignored when calculating your entitlement to working tax credit (WTC) and child tax credit, and sometimes you can be treated as being in full-time work for WTC purposes while getting MA (see p288).

5 Non-means-tested benefits

MA is affected by the overlapping benefit rules (see p1151).

For details of how your entitlement to MA affects your entitlement to statutory sick pay, see p828.

If you get MA on the basis of your own employment or self-employment, reducing your MA period may allow the father of your baby or your partner to get statutory shared parental pay and/or shared parental leave (see Chapter 38).

You can get national insurance credits for each week for which you get MA (because you are treated as having limited capability for work in those weeks – see p956).

Because a claim for MA can be treated as a claim for ESA (see p1144), if you claim MA but do not qualify for it, the DWP also considers your entitlement to ESA. You can be treated as having limited capability for work for a period before and after the birth if you have submitted a MAT B1 (or similar evidence of your expected week of childbirth) to the DWP, or if, because of your pregnancy, there is a serious risk to your or your baby's health if you work (see p990).

If you qualify for both MA and contributory ESA (because you can be treated as having limited capability for work during the period when you are entitled to MA), you cannot receive both benefits in full because of the overlapping benefit rules. If you qualify for both, you normally get the higher benefit. In some circumstances, contributory ESA may be more than your MA entitlement.

The benefit cap

In some cases, there is a limit on the total amount of specified benefits you can receive (a 'benefit cap'). MA is one of the specified benefits. However, the benefit cap only applies if you are getting UC or HB. See p1156 for further information.

Other sources of help

For details of whether you may qualify for:
- a Sure Start maternity grant if you live in England or Wales, see p782, or, if you live in Scotland, a Best Start grant pregnancy and baby payment, see p1697;
- Scottish child payment if you live in Scotland, see Chapter 77;
- certain health benefits, see Chapter 31;
- Healthy Start food and vitamins, see p847, or, if you live in Scotland, Best Start foods, see p850;
- council tax reduction, see p836;
- help with childcare costs, see p854.

5

Notes

1. Who can get maternity allowance
1 ss35(1) and (2) and 35B(1), (2) and (4) SSCBA 1992
2 Reg 90ZA SS(Con) Regs
3 ss35(1)(d) and (3E) and 35B(1)(d) SSCBA 1992
4 s35(1)(b) SSCBA 1992
5 para 62516 DMG
6 ss35(1)(c) and (6A) and 35A(4) SSCBA 1992
7 s35A(4)(a) SSCBA 1992; reg 2 SS(MatA)(E) Regs
8 Reg 6(2) SS(MatA)(E) Regs
9 Reg 6(4)-(6) SS(MatA)(E) Regs
10 Reg 3 SS(MatA)(E) Regs
11 s35A(5)(c), (5A) and (5B) SSCBA 1992; reg 5 SS(MatA)(E) Regs
12 Reg 90ZA SS(Con) Regs
13 ss35(2) and 165 SSCBA 1992; reg 2(2) SMP Regs
14 ss35(2) and 165 SSCBA 1992; reg 2 SMP Regs; reg 3 SS(MatA) Regs
15 Regs 3-5 MA(C) Regs
16 Reg 6 MA(C) Regs
17 s35B(4)-(8) SSCBA 1992
18 Reg 3(2B) and (2C) SS(MatA) Regs
19 Reg 2(1)-(4) SS(MatA) Regs
20 paras 62592-9 DMG
21 Reg 2(7) and (8) SS(MatA) Regs

4. The amount of benefit
22 ss35(1) and 35A SSCBA 1992
23 ss35(6A) and 35B(3) and (10) SSCBA 1992
24 Regs 4 and 6 SS(MatA)(E) Regs
25 Reg 6(3) SS(MatA)(E) Regs

5. Special benefit rules
26 SS(MatA)(WA) Regs

6. Claims and backdating
27 Reg 14(1) SS(C&P) Regs
28 Reg 4(1) SS(C&P) Regs
29 Reg 2(3) SS(ME) Regs
30 Reg 6(1) SS(C&P) Regs
31 Regs 4(7) and (7ZA) and 6(1) SS(C&P) Regs
32 Reg 19(2) SS(C&P) Regs
33 Regs 9 and 11 and Sch 1 Part I SS(C&P) Regs; regs 18 and 25 UC,PIP,JSA&ESA(C&P) Regs
34 Reg 10(3) and (4) SS(C&P) Regs
35 Reg 14 SS(C&P) Regs

7. Getting paid
36 Reg 24 SS(C&P) Regs
37 s35(5) SSCBA 1992

8. Tax, other benefits and the benefit cap
38 s677 IT(EP)A 2003

Personal independence payment

This chapter covers:
1. Who can get personal independence payment (p723)
2. The rules about your age (p743)
3. People included in the claim (p745)
4. The amount of benefit (p745)
5. Special benefit rules (p745)
6. Claims and backdating (p746)
7. Getting paid (p752)
8. Tax, other benefits and the benefit cap (p755)

Key facts
- Personal independence payment (PIP) is a benefit for working age adults with a disability or long-term health problem who have difficulty with getting around or daily living activities.
- PIP has daily living and mobility components. You can qualify for one or both components.
- PIP is a non-means-tested benefit.
- You do not have to have paid national insurance contributions to qualify.
- You can get PIP whether or not you work.
- PIP is administered and paid by the DWP.
- If you disagree with a PIP decision, you can apply for a revision or a supersession (see Chapter 56), or appeal against it (see Chapter 57). You must apply for a mandatory reconsideration before you can appeal.

Note: PIP in Scotland is starting to be replaced by adult disability payment (ADP) from March 2022 (see p1687). The Scottish government plans to transfer PIP claimants in Scotland to ADP by 2025. See Chapter 73 for more information.

1. Who can get personal independence payment

You can get personal independence payment (PIP) if you:
- meet the age rules (see p743); *and*
- are not a 'person subject to immigration control' (see Chapter 68); *and*
- meet the residence conditions (see p1601); *and*
- meet the disability conditions for the daily living component, the mobility component or both (see below); *and*
- meet the required period condition (see p742), unless you are terminally ill.

If you meet these criteria, but live in Scotland, see Chapter 73.

If you are entitled to disability living allowance (DLA), see p602 to help you decide whether to claim PIP.

The disability conditions

A points-based test is used to assess how your physical or mental condition affects your ability to undertake specific daily living activities (see p724) and mobility activities (see p737).[1] Each activity has a list of statements ('descriptors') which describe different difficulties with the activity or types of help you might need to manage it.

The test is what help you reasonably need, not what help you have available.[2] You should be assessed for your ability to perform activities while living a 'normal' daily life, and should not lose points if you can manage to perform certain activities, but only by adopting a significantly sheltered or altered lifestyle – eg, going out only at certain times, or avoiding all noisy environments.[3] However, the fact that you do not need, or choose not, to do some activities cannot help you to score points. For example, if you have never learned to cook, the assessment considers whether you *would* have difficulty preparing and cooking food due to your condition.

Each descriptor has a points score, and you get points for one descriptor for each activity – the one which best describes the difficulties you have with that activity. See p741 if your difficulties with the activities vary on different days, or if more than one descriptor in an activity applies to you.

The points you score for each activity relevant to a component are added together. You qualify for a component at:[4]
- the standard rate if you score eight points or more; *or*
- the enhanced rate if you score 12 points or more.

You automatically qualify for the enhanced rate of the daily living component if you are terminally ill (see p745).

Part 5: Other benefits
Chapter 35: Personal independence payment
1. Who can get personal independence payment

Physical or mental condition

Your difficulties must be due to your 'physical or mental condition'.[5] This does not require an additional test of whether you have a specific medical diagnosis.[6] However, there must be a physical or mental cause of your difficulty with carrying out a particular activity.[7] For example, if you are illiterate, you cannot score points for this reason unless you have a condition that affects your ability to learn to read.[8] Drug or alcohol dependency counts as a mental condition.[9]

The daily living activities

There are 10 daily living activities. This section does not cover every kind of disability or health problem, so think carefully about how your condition affects your ability to undertake each activity.

The assessment of your ability to manage an activity distinguishes between different kinds of help you may need. You do not score any points if you can manage it 'unaided'. This means without 'supervision', 'prompting' or 'assistance', and without using an 'aid or appliance' (see p725).[10]

The highest scoring descriptor for most activities applies if you cannot undertake the activity at all, even with these kinds of help. If you need so much help with an activity that someone else is effectively doing it for you, any contribution that you can make should arguably be ignored – and the 'cannot' descriptor applied.[11]

Assistance, supervision and prompting[12]

'**Assistance**' means 'physical intervention by another person and does not include speech'. It is help to carry out an activity and does not include someone doing the whole activity for you.[13] It does not include giving verbal instructions, which counts as 'prompting'.

'**Supervision**' means 'the continuous presence of another person for the purpose of ensuring [your] safety'. You must need supervision throughout the activity. You need supervision if there is a 'real risk' of harm while carrying out the activity, considering both the likelihood and seriousness of the harm.[14] This means that you may score points even if you would not come to any harm most days if left unsupervised. This interpretation was not previously accepted. The DWP is looking again at PIP decisions made since 9 March 2017 to check they are in line with this interpretation.[15] Get advice if you think that you should have scored more points.

The risk does not need to be caused by doing the activity; it is enough that you need continuous supervision to carry it out (see p740).[16] If someone is also supervising other people at the same time, you can still satisfy a supervision descriptor.[17]

'**Prompting**' means 'reminding, encouraging or explaining by another person'. You can score points for needing prompting even if you can sometimes manage unaided when there is a specific or urgent need to undertake the activity. Whether you can manage the activity on a day when there is not such an urgent need must also be considered.[18] The person prompting you does not always need to be in your presence, so prompting by telephone (or, arguably, someone leaving you notes or reminders)[19] can allow you to score points, if you need this to be able to carry out an activity.

For how your ability to carry out the activities with these kinds of help is assessed, see p740.

For how to decide which descriptor you satisfy if your difficulties vary, see p741.

You qualify for the enhanced rate of the daily living component if you are terminally ill (see p745), even if you have no problems with any of the activities.

Aids and appliances

You score points for most of the daily living activities if you do not need help from another person, but need an 'aid or appliance' to carry out the activity. An aid or appliance means 'any device which improves, provides or replaces [your] impaired mental or physical function; and includes a prosthesis'.[20] Some examples are an artificial leg, walking stick, wheelchair, modified cutlery needed because of your disability, or adaptations to your home like grab rails in the bathroom or a shower seat. It is unlikely to include surgical implants like hip replacements, retinal implants and heart valves.[21] If you have such an implant, think carefully about whether the effects of your condition with it in place mean that you should still score points in the assessment.

An aid or appliance that you do not use is still taken into account if you could 'reasonably be expected' to use it to manage the activity.[22]

Could you use an aid or appliance?

When you could reasonably be expected to use an aid or appliance is not set out in the regulations. Some factors that may be relevant to whether it is reasonable for you to use an aid or appliance include whether:

– you have been advised to use it by a medical professional;
– it is available to you (this might include affordability if the NHS does not provide it); *and*
– it is practical for you to use it – eg, whether you can store it in your home.

If you are assessed as needing an aid or appliance to manage an activity and you think this is not reasonable, try to get evidence to show that you cannot use it, it is not affordable or practical, or you still need help from someone, despite using it.

To score points in the assessment for needing an aid or appliance, you must need to use it because of your physical or mental condition. The aid need not be something that only disabled people use,[23] or designed to help with the task that you need it for. However, it must improve, provide or replace a function that is vital to managing the specific activity, not just to managing it in a particular way.[24] For example, many people sit down to dress, so you will not score points for needing to do this if you are otherwise able to dress unaided (see p732). However, if you need an aid to perform an essential part of the activity (eg, a crutch to stand up while dressing), you should still score points.[25] Something that

Part 5: Other benefits
Chapter 35: Personal independence payment
1. Who can get personal independence payment

you must use before you can manage an activity (eg, to warm up your hands, improving your manual dexterity) can also count as an aid.[26]

Your ability to use reasonable alternatives may mean that you are assessed as managing an activity 'unaided'. However, any alternatives that significantly restrict your choices arguably still count as aids.[27]

Examples

Gordon wears slip-on shoes because he has arthritis and it takes him more than twice as long to tie his shoelaces as it used to. He can manage all his other clothing unaided. As slip-on shoes are a reasonable adjustment, Gordon can dress and undress unaided.

Ed has severely restricted motor function following a stroke. He must wear slip-on shoes to manage alone. He must also wear loose-fitting clothing, cardigans without buttons and trousers with elasticated waistbands to dress within a reasonable time. The clothes that Ed must wear in order to dress without help amount to using aids to dress, even though someone without Ed's difficulties may also choose to wear them.

Activity one: preparing food

Descriptors	Points
a. Can prepare and cook a simple meal unaided.	0
b. Needs to use an aid or appliance to be able to either prepare or cook a simple meal.	2
c. Cannot cook a simple meal using a conventional cooker but is able to do so using a microwave.	2
d. Needs prompting to be able to either prepare or cook a simple meal.	2
e. Needs supervision or assistance to either prepare or cook a simple meal.	4
f. Cannot prepare and cook food.	8

Definitions[28]

'**Simple meal**' means a cooked one-course meal for one using fresh ingredients.
'**Prepare**', in the context of food, means make food ready for cooking or eating.
'**Cook**' means heat food at or above waist height. (This means that difficulty bending down to use a low oven is not relevant.)[29]
See also the definitions common to all the daily living activities on p724. For what counts as being able to carry out an activity, see p740.

This is an objective test of your ability to manage the tasks involved in preparing ingredients and cooking a reasonable range of simple meals, so takes no account of your specific dietary needs,[30] religious beliefs or cultural preferences.[31] Similarly, the impact of things such as childcare responsibilities or family size on your ability to prepare a meal is not relevant.[32]

Descriptor 1c only looks at whether you can *cook* using a microwave – your ability to *prepare* the ingredients for a simple meal must also be considered.[33] To 'prepare' food, you must be able to peel and chop vegetables.[34] If you must use pre-prepared vegetables, you score points for needing assistance to prepare or cook a meal, unless you could prepare them with an aid or appliance. Aids to help you prepare and cook food could include specialist cooking utensils or a spiked chopping board. Lever arm taps and lightweight pans are less likely to be accepted as aids,[35] and a perching stool arguably does not count as an aid unless your condition means that you are only able to stand for very short periods.[36]

If you cannot read, tell the time or use timers because of your condition, this is relevant to whether you score points for this activity. However, you do not automatically score any points due to reading difficulties, as it is possible to cook without being able to read.[37]

It is arguable that you satisfy descriptor 1f if you are completely unable to either prepare or cook food, no matter how much help you get, even though you can manage the other task unaided.[38]

Activity two: taking nutrition

Descriptors	Points
a. Can take nutrition unaided.	0
b. Needs:	2
(i) to use an aid or appliance to be able to take nutrition; *or*	
(ii) supervision to be able to take nutrition; *or*	
(iii) assistance to be able to cut up food.	
c. Needs a therapeutic source to be able to take nutrition.	2
d. Needs prompting to be able to take nutrition.	4
e. Needs assistance to be able to manage a therapeutic source to take nutrition.	6
f. Cannot convey food and drink to their mouth and needs another person to do so.	10

Definitions[39]
'**Take nutrition**' means cut food into pieces, convey food and drink to one's mouth and chew and swallow food and drink, or take nutrition by using a therapeutic source.
'**Therapeutic source**' means parenteral or enteral tube feeding, using a rate-limiting device such as a delivery system or feed pump.
See also the definitions common to all the daily living activities on p724. For what counts as being able to carry out an activity, see p740.

This activity focuses on the mechanical actions involved in eating and drinking (or using a therapeutic source), so the nutritious quality of what you consume is

Part 5: Other benefits
Chapter 35: Personal independence payment
1. Who can get personal independence payment

not relevant.[40] However, if your condition means that you need prompting to eat at all,[41] or your condition means that you need to eat lots of calories and you need prompting to eat enough, you can satisfy descriptor 2d.[42] You must be able to manage every aspect of taking nutrition without a therapeutic source to manage this activity unaided, so difficulty swallowing solid foods can potentially allow you to score points for this activity.[43]

If you spill so much food that you need to change your clothes after eating, this is arguably not taking nutrition to an acceptable standard. Unless an aid or appliance (eg, adapted cup or cutlery), help to cut up your food or prompting from someone else means you can manage this, you should satisfy descriptor 2f.

Specially designed cutlery (eg, which is easier to grip) counts as an aid for this activity.

If you need help to set up or put away therapeutic feeding equipment due to your condition, you should satisfy descriptor 2e, even if you do not need help to use it once it has been set up. If you use such equipment overnight, you count as using it on two days for the purpose of deciding how many points you score, if your needs vary on different days (see p741).[44]

Activity three: managing therapy or monitoring a health condition

Descriptors	Points
a. Either:	0
(i) does not receive medication or therapy or need to monitor a health condition; or	
(ii) can manage medication or therapy or monitor a health condition unaided.	
b. Needs any one or more of the following:	1
(i) to use an aid or appliance to be able to manage medication;	
(ii) supervision, prompting or assistance to be able to manage medication;	
(iii) supervision, prompting or assistance to be able to monitor a health condition.	
c. Needs supervision, prompting or assistance to be able to manage therapy that takes no more than 3.5 hours a week.	2
d. Needs supervision, prompting or assistance to be able to manage therapy that takes more than 3.5 but no more than 7 hours a week.	4
e. Needs supervision, prompting or assistance to be able to manage therapy that takes more than 7 but no more than 14 hours a week.	6
f. Needs supervision, prompting or assistance to be able to manage therapy that takes more than 14 hours a week.	8

Definitions[45]

'Manage medication' means take medication, where a failure to do so is likely to result in a deterioration in your health.

'**Medication**' means medication to be taken at home, which is prescribed or recommended by a registered doctor, nurse or pharmacist.

'**Monitor a health condition**' means detect significant changes in your condition which are likely to lead to a deterioration in your health, and take action advised by a registered doctor, registered nurse, or health professional who is regulated by the Health Professions Council,[46] without which your health is likely to deteriorate.

'**Manage therapy**' means undertake therapy, where a failure to do so is likely to result in a deterioration in your health.

'**Therapy**' means therapy to be undertaken at home which is prescribed or recommended by a registered doctor, nurse or pharmacist, or health professional regulated by the Health Professions Council, but does not include taking or applying, or otherwise receiving or administering, medication (whether orally, topically or by any other means), or any action which, in your case, falls within the definition of 'monitor a health condition'.

See also the definitions common to all the daily living activities on p724. For what counts as being able to carry out an activity, see p740.

Examples of 'therapy' include needing help with dialysis, to fit prescribed bandages,[47] to undertake specialist massage treatment at home or to manage a special diet.[48] You cannot score points for help with therapy if there is a specific descriptor in another activity that describes exactly the same kind of help.[49] For example, needing assistance to self-catheterise scores points under Activity 5 (see p731),[50] and needing assistance to take nutrition using a therapeutic device scores points under Activity 2 (see p727).[51]

Note: needing supervision or prompting with these things may arguably score you points for Activity 3.[52] General supervision provided in supported accommodation is not 'therapy'.[53] Smoking cessation treatment and weight loss counselling do not count as therapy if there is no evidence that smoking or obesity are making your condition worse.[54] It is arguable that if you need help with exercises to *improve* some aspect of how your condition affects you or to make you more comfortable, your health would deteriorate without it and so it counts as 'therapy'.[55]

As your need for therapy will itself result from your condition, you do not need to show that your condition is connected to the specific help that you need with it, just that you need help.[56] When deciding which descriptor is satisfied, the amount of time you need help with therapy is relevant, not the length of time the therapy takes.[57] The help you need to set up a machine you use for therapy (eg, a TENS machine) counts, even if you can manage unaided once it has been set up.[58]

As the descriptors about therapy refer to the amount of help you need during 'a week', you should not be excluded by the rule on fluctuating conditions (see p741) if you only need help with therapy on a minority of days.

Part 5: Other benefits
Chapter 35: Personal independence payment
1. Who can get personal independence payment

Monitoring your health condition could include someone checking on how you are – eg, if you have schizophrenia which is normally controlled by medication.

Aids and appliances to help you manage medication could include a dosette box to organise pills if you are forgetful due to your condition, or a specialist device to help you to inject yourself, if you have difficulty with manual dexterity. However, an inhaler or syringe does not count as an aid, as it is a way of delivering medication, not something you need to use to help you manage your medication independently.[59]

Note: the DWP is looking again at decisions made after 28 November 2016 which concern medication and monitoring, or diet as therapy.[60] Get advice if you think you should have scored more points for this activity.

Activity four: washing and bathing

Descriptors	Points
a. Can wash and bathe unaided.	0
b. Needs to use an aid or appliance to be able to wash or bathe.	2
c. Needs supervision or prompting to be able to wash or bathe.	2
d. Needs assistance to be able to wash either their hair or body below the waist.	2
e. Needs assistance to be able to get in or out of a bath or shower.	3
f. Needs assistance to be able to wash their body between the shoulders and waist.	4
g. Cannot wash and bathe at all and needs another person to wash their entire body.	8

Definitions[61]
'**Bathe**' includes get into or out of an unadapted bath or shower.
See also the definitions common to all the daily living activities on p724. For what counts as being able to carry out an activity, see p740.

If you cannot get into an unadapted bath without help, you satisfy descriptor 4e, even if you have a wet room at home so never need to do this.[62] A bath seat counts as an aid for this activity.[63]

If you are at risk if you bathe alone, whether you need supervision depends on the seriousness of the harm and how likely it is (see p724). You should not be expected to reduce the time you spend in the bath or shower to avoid the risk.[64] If you have to remove your hearing aid to shower or bathe and could not hear a standard fire or smoke alarm or someone breaking into your home without it, you should satisfy either descriptor 4b or 4c.[65]

To wash to an acceptable standard, you should be clean (and, arguably, dry)[66] when you have finished. If it takes you a long time to wash and bathe without help, you can argue that you need assistance to do so.

If you can only motivate yourself to have a bath or shower if you have something important to do that day, it is arguable that you still need prompting to wash or bathe if you would not manage this unprompted on a normal day.[67]

Activity five: managing toilet needs or incontinence

Descriptors	Points
a. Can manage toilet needs or incontinence unaided.	0
b. Needs to use an aid or appliance to be able to manage toilet needs or incontinence.	2
c. Needs supervision or prompting to be able to manage toilet needs.	2
d. Needs assistance to be able to manage toilet needs.	4
e. Needs assistance to be able to manage incontinence of either bladder or bowel.	6
f. Needs assistance to be able to manage incontinence of both bladder and bowel.	8

Definitions[68]

'**Manage incontinence**' means manage involuntary evacuation of the bowel or bladder, including use a collecting device or self-catheterisation, and clean oneself afterwards.

'**Toilet needs**' means getting on and off an unadapted toilet, evacuating the bladder and bowel, and cleaning oneself afterwards.

See also the definitions common to all the daily living activities on p724. For what counts as being able to carry out an activity, see p740.

Even if you only have difficulty with one of the three things included in the definition of 'toilet needs' above, you can still score points for this activity.[69] However, you must have difficulty with an aspect of the activity as defined, so following a strict hygiene regime to avoid infections does not mean that you score points, unless your ability to do one of these three things is affected by your condition.[70]

Examples of aids and appliances include a raised toilet seat, grab rails near the toilet,[71] a stoma and colostomy bag,[72] incontinence pads,[73] or a shower head used to clean yourself.[74] If it is *reasonable* for you to use incontinence pads most days (this includes using pads overnight) as a precaution, you satisfy descriptor 5b, even if you are only actually incontinent on a minority of days,[75] or do not actually use pads.[76] A commode can count as an aid for this activity, but only if part of the reason you must use it is that your condition means you have difficulty with toilet needs or incontinence (not if you only use it because of problems

Part 5: Other benefits
Chapter 35: Personal independence payment
1. Who can get personal independence payment

managing the stairs at home, for example).[77] You score more points if you need help from someone else to use one of these things.

Difficulty dressing and undressing to use the toilet does not allow you to score points for this activity.[78]

Activity six: dressing and undressing

Descriptors	Points
a. Can dress and undress unaided.	0
b. Needs to use an aid or appliance to be able to dress or undress.	2
c. Needs either:	2
(i) prompting to be able to dress, undress or determine appropriate circumstances for remaining clothed; *or*	
(ii) prompting or assistance to be able to select appropriate clothing.	
d. Needs assistance to be able to dress or undress their lower body.	2
e. Needs assistance to be able to dress or undress their upper body.	4
f. Cannot dress or undress at all.	8

Definitions[79]

'Dress and undress' includes put on and take off socks and shoes.

See also the definitions common to all the daily living activities on p724. For what counts as being able to carry out an activity, see p740.

You can score points if you only have difficulty with either dressing or undressing. Similarly, you can score points if you have difficulty with either socks or shoes.[80]

If you must wear them due to your condition, clothes that are easier to manage, such as slip-on shoes, cardigans rather than jumpers, or items with zips rather than buttons, may count as aids to help you dress, depending on how much your choices are restricted by your condition(s).[81] If you only need one of these things (eg, your only difficulty is with tying shoelaces), you may still be able to dress and undress unaided.[82]

If you must sit down to dress or undress, this does not count as needing an aid or appliance.[83] However, if you then need to use an aid (eg, a crutch) to get up and finish dressing (eg, to pull trousers fully into position and do them up), you may satisfy descriptor 6b.[84]

Selecting appropriate clothing includes choosing the right clothes for the weather, and also not reusing dirty clothes.[85] If you take a long time to choose clothes due to your condition, you may satisfy descriptor 6c.[86]

Activity seven: communicating verbally

Descriptors	Points
a. Can express and understand verbal information unaided.	0
b. Needs to use an aid or appliance to be able to speak or hear.	2
c. Needs communication support to be able to express or understand complex verbal information.	4
d. Needs communication support to be able to express or understand basic verbal information.	8
e. Cannot express or understand verbal information at all even with communication support.	12

Definitions[87]

'**Basic verbal information**' means information in your native language conveyed verbally in a simple sentence.

'**Complex verbal information**' means information in your native language conveyed verbally in either more than one sentence or one complicated sentence.

'**Communication support**' means support from a person trained or experienced in communicating with people with specific communication needs, including interpreting verbal information into a non-verbal form and vice versa.

See also the definitions common to all the daily living activities on p724. For what counts as being able to carry out an activity, see p740.

If you have problems speaking English because you have never learned the language, this does not count. If strangers find it hard to understand you (due to your condition affecting your speech rather than your accent), you may need help to communicate to an acceptable standard and within a reasonable time.

Your ability to read, write or send text messages is not relevant, but if you use writing to communicate in the absence of speech (eg, pen and paper or a text-to-audio device) you may satisfy descriptor 7b.[88] The ability to lip read is not used to conclude that you can understand speech (ie, your lip-reading ability will be disregarded and you can still score points).[89] If you have difficulty using a phone or understanding speech in a noisy environment due to your condition, you may score points.[90]

The definition of 'communication support' includes both someone with specialist training, like a British Sign Language interpreter, and someone who knows you and is experienced in helping you to communicate.[91] How many points you score depends on whether you need help with even a single simple sentence, or whether you can manage this but need help with anything more complicated. If you have problems speaking or understanding speech because of a mental health problem or cognitive impairment, you can score points for this activity if your problems are with the act of speaking, hearing or understanding speech – ie, not a reluctance to speak because you are shy in social situations.[92]

Part 5: Other benefits
Chapter 35: Personal independence payment
1. Who can get personal independence payment

Activity eight: reading and understanding signs, symbols and words

Descriptors	Points
a. Can read and understand basic and complex written information either unaided or using spectacles or contact lenses.	0
b. Needs to use an aid or appliance, other than spectacles or contact lenses, to be able to read or understand either basic or complex written information.	2
c. Needs prompting to be able to read or understand complex written information.	2
d. Needs prompting to be able to read or understand basic written information.	4
e. Cannot read or understand signs, symbols or words at all.	8

Definitions[93]

'**Basic written information**' means signs, symbols and dates written or printed in standard size text in your native language.

'**Complex written information**' means more than one sentence of written or printed standard size text in your native language.

'**Read**' includes read signs, symbols and words, but does not include read Braille. (The exclusion of Braille from the definition means that if you have no effective sight at all, you are treated as unable to read.)

See also the definitions common to all the daily living activities on p724. For what counts as being able to carry out an activity, see p740.

If your ability to read is affected so that you satisfy a descriptor at certain times of the day, you should score points even if you can read unaided at other times of the day.[94] Similarly, it is arguable that you should be assessed as needing an aid or appliance to read (rather than someone to help) only if you can read both outside and inside using aids.

If you can read to the standard required with one eye (including using glasses), then a problem with your other eye does not mean you score points.[95]

If you have a mental or cognitive impairment and, because of this, need help to understand the meaning of written information, you should score points for this activity. If you have never learned to read in English, you only score points for this activity if this is because of a physical or mental condition.[96] While the standard of reading required is low, to satisfy descriptor 8d (rather than 8e) you must be able to quickly read and understand some words without any help.[97]

Activity nine: engaging with other people face to face

Descriptors	Points
a. Can engage with other people unaided.	0
b. Needs prompting to be able to engage with other people.	2
c. Needs social support to be able to engage with other people.	4
d. Cannot engage with other people due to such engagement causing either:	8
(i) overwhelming psychological distress to the claimant; *or*	
(ii) the claimant to exhibit behaviour which would result in a substantial risk of harm to the claimant or another person.	

Definitions[98]
'**Psychological distress**' means distress related to an enduring mental health condition or an intellectual or cognitive impairment.
'**Social support**' means support from a person trained or experienced in assisting people to engage in social situations.
See also the definitions common to all the daily living activities on p724. For what counts as being able to carry out an activity, see p740.

This activity looks at your ability to interact with individuals or small groups,[99] and in social situations.[100] 'Engage with other people' means to 'interact with others in a contextually and socially appropriate manner', 'understand body language' and 'establish relationships'.[101] All three factors should be considered.[102] Your ability to interact with strangers, as well as people you know, should be considered. The test is whether you can engage with adults generally, not just with particular groups of people, such as women or young people.[103]

'Establish relationships' does not refer to any particular type of relationship, but means something more than just the ability to respond to questions.[104] Both mental and physical conditions are relevant to this activity, so a visual impairment may affect your ability to understand body language, for example.[105] Even if you undertake social activities (eg, going to a pub), you may still score points for this activity if you cannot engage with other people without help,[106] or if the social activities you can cope with alone are very specific and limited by your condition.[107]

The person helping you does not always need to be physically present.[108] While the descriptors distinguish between 'prompting' and 'social support', there is some overlap between them. To satisfy descriptor 9c, you must show that the prompting (or other social support) must be provided by someone trained or experienced to be effective. This could include a family member or friend who is experienced in helping you.[109]

If you cannot engage with other people at all, this must be for one of the reasons mentioned in descriptor 9d for you to satisfy it.[110]

Part 5: Other benefits
Chapter 35: Personal independence payment
1. Who can get personal independence payment

Note: the DWP's interpretation of this activity used to be less generous. It is contacting claimants who get PIP (or who have been refused it since 6 April 2016) who might score more points for this activity. Get advice if you think you would have scored more points for this activity or been entitled to PIP, but your need for social support was not properly taken into account.

Activity 10: making budgeting decisions

Descriptors	Points
a. Can manage complex budgeting decisions unaided.	0
b. Needs prompting or assistance to be able to make complex budgeting decisions.	2
c. Needs prompting or assistance to be able to make simple budgeting decisions.	4
d. Cannot make any budgeting decisions at all.	6

Definitions[111]
'Complex budgeting decisions' means decisions involving calculating household and personal budgets, managing and paying bills and planning future purchases.
'Simple budgeting decisions' means decisions involving calculating the cost of goods and calculating change required after a purchase.
See also the definitions common to all the daily living activities on p724. For what counts as being able to carry out an activity, see p740.

The descriptors assess difficulty making decisions because of your physical or mental condition, not poor money management skills. But if your condition means that you are very impulsive, you can satisfy descriptor 10b if this prevents you from budgeting effectively.[112] Similarly, if your condition (eg, a mental health problem or an autism spectrum disorder) means that you cannot manage your own finances, you can score points for descriptor 10b regardless of your level of intelligence.[113] You only satisfy a descriptor (as opposed to a higher scoring one) if you can make all of the types of decision described with help from someone else. So, even if you can pay bills by yourself or with some help, if you cannot manage a household budget at all due to your condition, you should satisfy descriptor 10c.[114]

It is unlikely that you will be awarded points for this activity based solely on a physical condition.[115] However, if you have difficulty *making decisions* due to a physical condition (eg, you have a visual impairment and need someone to read information repeatedly to be able to make a decision), you may arguably satisfy descriptor 10b.[116]

The mobility activities

There are two mobility activities in the assessment. Remember that your difficulties with the activities must be caused by a physical or mental condition (see p724) for you to score points. This section does not cover every kind of disability or health problem, so think carefully about how your condition affects your ability to manage each of the activities.

For how your ability to carry out an activity as described by a descriptor is assessed, see p740.

For which descriptor you satisfy if your difficulties vary, see p741.

Activity one: planning and following journeys

Descriptors[117]	Points
a. Can plan and follow the route of a journey unaided.	0
b. Needs prompting to be able to undertake any journey to avoid overwhelming psychological distress to the claimant.	4
c. Cannot plan the route of a journey.	8
d. Cannot follow the route of an unfamiliar journey without another person, assistance dog or orientation aid.	10
e. Cannot undertake any journey because it would cause overwhelming psychological distress to the claimant.	10
f. Cannot follow the route of a familiar journey without another person, an assistance dog or an orientation aid.	12

Definitions[118]

'Assistance dog' means a dog trained to guide or assist a person with a sensory impairment.

'Orientation aid' means a specialist aid designed to assist disabled people to follow a route safely. (This means that a standard satnav does not count as an orientation aid, although one designed or modified for disabled people might.)[119]

'Prompting' means reminding, encouraging or explaining by another person.

'Psychological distress' means distress related to an enduring mental health condition or an intellectual or cognitive impairment.

'Unaided' means without the use of an aid or appliance, or supervision, prompting or assistance.

If you need prompting to leave the house as the thought of going out causes overwhelming psychological distress, you can satisfy descriptor 1b even if once you start a journey you do not need to be accompanied by someone else.[120] Prompting by telephone is arguably sufficient, if it is needed for you to leave the house.[121] It is arguable that you can satisfy descriptor 1b or 1e if you need

Part 5: Other benefits
Chapter 35: Personal independence payment
1. Who can get personal independence payment

prompting to, or cannot, go out during part of a day, if your 'lifestyle is restricted to more than a trivial extent'.[122]

The use of the words 'follow the route' means that you can satisfy descriptors 1d and 1f if you need someone to help you get to your destination (this could include help to navigate, supervision to keep you safe, or help to deal with unexpected diversions), but not if you only need help to communicate with people you meet during a journey.[123] It is possible to satisfy descriptor 1d or 1f if you sometimes manage a specific journey alone, as long as you generally need one of the kinds of help described.[124]

If you can manage part of a journey (eg, in your car) by yourself, you can still score points if you need someone else with you at the start or end of the journey.[125] Your ability to manage a range of journeys using different types of transport (and not just a short or local journey) should be considered.[126] However, to score points for this activity, your difficulties must be due to a mental, cognitive or sensory impairment, and not purely physical difficulties with managing different kinds of transport.[127]

You can only satisfy descriptors 1d and 1f due to anxiety if you need someone with you to avoid *overwhelming* psychological distress.[128] That person does not need to be taking action to help you if their presence alone is enough to relieve the distress.[129]

DWP guidance suggests that if you satisfy descriptor 1e as you cannot leave the house at all on the majority of days, you cannot also satisfy descriptor 1f.[130] This is arguably not correct (eg, if you also have a visual impairment and would need a guide dog if you were able to go out), but the Upper Tribunal has held that if you satisfy descriptor 1e, whether you also satisfy descriptor 1f should be decided without taking account of any psychological distress that you experience.[131]

Note: the DWP is contacting claimants who get PIP (or who have been refused it since 28 November 2016) who might score more points for this activity.[132] Get advice if you think you would have scored more points for this activity or been entitled to PIP, but the effects of psychological distress were not taken into account.

Activity two: moving around

Descriptors	Points
a. Can stand and then move more than 200 metres, either aided or unaided.	0
b. Can stand and then move more than 50 metres but no more than 200 metres, either aided or unaided.	4
c. Can stand and then move unaided more than 20 metres but no more than 50 metres.	8
d. Can stand and then move using an aid or appliance more than 20 metres but no more than 50 metres.	10
e. Can stand and then move more than one metre but no more than 20 metres, either aided or unaided.	12
f. Cannot, either aided or unaided: (i) stand; or (ii) move more than one metre.	12

Definitions[133]
'Aided' means with the use of an aid or appliance, or supervision, prompting or assistance. (See also the definitions of these terms on p724 and p725.)
'Stand' means stand upright with at least one biological foot on the ground. (This means that double amputees are treated as unable to stand and satisfy descriptor 2f.)
'Unaided' means without the use of an aid or appliance, or supervision, prompting or assistance.

This activity looks at your ability to 'stand and then move', so any movement you can manage using a wheelchair is ignored. The descriptors assess your ability on the usual type of surfaces you might encounter outdoors, including your ability to manage kerbs, but not flights of steps or steep slopes.[134]

The points you score for this activity should take account of how often you want to go out, but cannot, due to your condition (as long as this is reasonable).[135]

If you can manage more than 50 metres using an aid or appliance or with help, you can only satisfy descriptors 2a and 2b, even if you can only manage less than 50 metres unaided.[136]

It is not necessary for you to be able to manage the distance mentioned in one go, as brief stops do not mean that you cannot move this distance.[137] However, the length and duration of any stops are relevant to whether you can move that distance repeatedly and within a reasonable time period (see p740). If you can move a particular distance 'within a reasonable time period', the fact that you can only move slowly is not relevant to whether you are managing the activity to an acceptable standard.[138] However, pain,[139] dizziness, breathlessness, and any risk to your health if you walk too far[140] are all relevant to whether you are able to move to an acceptable standard (or safely).

Part 5: Other benefits
Chapter 35: Personal independence payment
1. Who can get personal independence payment

If moving around causes you significant pain, its impact on how far you can walk can be considered, even if the pain has no known physical cause.[141] However, if your physical difficulties walking are caused by psychological distress, this is considered under Activity 1 (see p737), and not this activity.[142]

Can you carry out an activity?

If a descriptor describes help you need to carry out an activity, unless you can manage an activity in the way described by a descriptor in *all* of the following ways, you must be awarded a higher scoring descriptor.[143]

- **Safely.** This means 'in a manner unlikely to cause harm to [you] or to another person, either during or after completion of the activity'. This means that there is 'a real possibility that cannot be ignored of harm occurring'. This involves considering both the likelihood of any harm occurring, and the severity of the consequences if it did occur.[144] You should not be expected to restrict the way in which you carry out an activity (eg, how long you shower for) in order to do it safely.[145] The way that 'safely' is understood has changed as the result of an Upper Tribunal decision and the DWP is looking again at decisions made since 9 March 2017.[146] Get advice if you think that your ability to perform activities 'safely' has not been properly assessed.
- **To an acceptable standard.** This is not defined in the regulations, and what it means is closely linked to the activity in question. What is an acceptable standard will depend to an extent on your experience of doing the activity, making the test a subjective one.[147] The level of pain you experience when managing an activity is one factor that should be considered.[148]
- **Repeatedly.** This means 'as often as the activity being assessed is reasonably required to be completed'. This means that if you have problems with an activity at some point during a day, you should satisfy a scoring descriptor on that day.[149] In considering how often you 'reasonably' need to undertake an activity, your own choices should generally be respected, so think carefully about what you would want to do if you did not have your condition.[150]
- **Within a reasonable time period.** This means 'no more than twice as long as the maximum period that a person without a physical or mental condition which limits that person's ability to carry out the activity in question would normally take to complete that activity'. Time you spend thinking about the activity (eg, choosing clothes) can be taken into account if the hesitation is due to your condition.[151]

These four factors should be considered separately. For example, if you can manage the activity within a reasonable time period as defined, the fact that you are doing it slowly is not relevant to the question of whether you can manage to an acceptable standard.[152]

These definitions still leave a lot of discretion to the DWP. If you think you have not been given enough points because of this rule, you can ask for a mandatory reconsideration and then appeal. Explain which factor means you cannot carry out the activity as described by the descriptor you were awarded, and which descriptor you think you should satisfy.

Example

Lola has a condition that means she is impatient and has limited perception of danger. Having a friend prompt her while she prepares and cooks food does not allow her to manage this activity safely. Even using a microwave leaves her at risk of harm from preparing vegetables with knives or eating undercooked food. As she can manage some of the other tasks involved in preparing food safely, she satisfies descriptor 1e (see p726).

5

Fluctuating conditions

If a scoring descriptor applies to you at some point in a day (ie, 24 hours, starting from midnight), you should be accepted as satisfying it on that day, unless the amount of help you need is so minimal that it can be ignored.[153]

Example

Archie has a visual impairment, which causes him difficulty in poor light. After dark he needs another person with him to be able to follow the route of an unfamiliar journey. During daylight hours he can often follow journeys by himself. He should satisfy descriptor 1d in the planning and following journeys activity (see p737).

Which descriptor you are awarded for an activity also depends on how your condition affects you on different days. You are normally assessed over a one-year period starting from three months before you claim PIP, or starting from the date your condition starts to affect you if that is later.[154] If you reclaim PIP after a gap and the 'special rule' on p743 applies, the assessment looks at the last three months of your previous award and the nine months from the date of your new claim.[155]

The descriptor you score points for is decided as follows.[156]

- If only one descriptor in the activity applies to you on over 50 per cent of the days in the one-year period described above, that descriptor is used.
- If two or more descriptors each apply to you on over 50 per cent of the days in the period, the one that scores the most points is used.
- If neither of the above bullet points apply, but the number of days on which you satisfy two or more scoring descriptors totals more than 50 per cent of the days, the scoring descriptor that applies most often is used. If two descriptors apply on the same number of days, the highest scoring one is used.

Part 5: Other benefits
Chapter 35: Personal independence payment
1. Who can get personal independence payment

Example

Aisha makes a new claim for PIP on 5 May 2022. She has arthritis, which has affected her ability to dress for more than three months, so the period considered is from 5 February 2022 to 4 February 2023 (three months before the date she claimed and nine months after that date). Her condition is not deteriorating, but affects her differently on different days. On about two days a week (or 104 days a year), she can dress and undress unaided. Three days a week (or 156 days a year), she manages to dress using loose clothes with no buttons, slip-on shoes and a grabber to help with her socks. On a further two days a week (104 days a year), she also needs assistance from a family member to dress her upper body. The third bullet point above applies, as no single descriptor is satisfied on over half the days. Aisha satisfies descriptor 6b (see p732) as she meets one or other of the scoring descriptors on over half of the days, and this descriptor applies most often.

It can be very difficult to decide which descriptors you satisfy if your condition fluctuates. It may be helpful for you to keep a diary over several weeks to help explain how your condition affects you.

When calculating which descriptor you should satisfy under this rule, it is important to think about how the effects of your condition vary, bearing in mind that you may not need to attempt some activities every day. For example, if your mental health condition means you can only go out or make budgeting decisions on good days, a couple of times a week, you can score points for these activities even if you do all your shopping and pay your bills on good days as you have no one to help you on bad days. Similarly, the fact that you can sometimes manage activities if there is a specific reason you must do so does not mean that you do not need prompting to manage them on other days.[157]

Note: if you have more than one fluctuating condition and these affect your ability to manage a particular activity independently of each other, you may be affected on more than half of the days in the period considered, even if each condition only affects you on a minority of days.[158]

The required period condition

Unless you are terminally ill (see p745), you cannot get PIP unless you satisfy the 'required period condition'.[159] This normally means that you must be expected to meet the disability conditions for over one year in total. The required period condition is made up of two separate periods.[160]

If it is likely that you have met the disability conditions for three months ('the past period') when you claim PIP, it can be awarded from the date you claim. You must also be likely to continue to meet them for at least another nine months from that date ('the prospective period').

If you do not satisfy the past period condition when you claim, a PIP award can be made starting up to three months after the date your claim is decided, if you will satisfy both parts of the required period condition by then.[161]

For how the required period condition affects an ongoing award of PIP, see p754.

Note:
- A special rule applies if:
  - you used to get PIP; *and*
  - your award ended less than two years ago (one year if you are aged 66 or over); *and*
  - you make a new claim on the basis of the same condition(s) or a new condition that developed as a result of a previous one.

  In this situation, if you met the disability conditions for a component at a particular rate during the last three months of your previous award, you qualify for the same component from the date of your new claim, if your needs are expected to last for at least nine months from that date.[162]
- If you claim PIP and either you get DLA and are being transferred to PIP (see p602) or your DLA award ended under two years ago (one year if you are 66 or over), you do not have to satisfy the past period test. You must still satisfy the prospective period test.[163]

---

2. **The rules about your age**

You must be aged 16 or over to claim personal independence payment (PIP).[164]

The upper age limit for making a new PIP claim is normally the day before you turn 66.[165]

Future changes

The upper age limit to claim PIP will increase to 67 as the pension age rises between 2026 and 2028 (see p766).

There are several qualifications to the upper age limit.
- If you were under 65 on 8 April 2013 and either you are entitled to disability living allowance (DLA) or your entitlement ended less than a year ago, you can claim PIP even if you are 66 or over.[166] See p602 if you get DLA and are thinking about claiming PIP.
- If you claimed PIP when you were under 66, an award can be made to you.[167]
- If you are entitled to PIP when you turn 66, your award continues to its end date, if you still meet the entitlement conditions.[168]
- Your PIP award can be revised or superseded after you turn 66 (see Chapter 56).[169]

Part 5: Other benefits
Chapter 35: Personal independence payment
2. The rules about your age

- If your PIP award has a fixed end date, you can make a renewal claim up to six months before this date, even if you are 66 or over (see p753). Also, if you have been entitled to PIP, you can reclaim it within one year of your previous award ending, even if you are now 66 or over. Your new claim must be on the basis of the same disability or health condition(s) as your former award, or a new condition that has developed as a result of the original one(s).

Note: in the latter two situations above, your entitlement to the mobility component is restricted (see below).[170]

Mobility component for older people

If you are entitled to the mobility component when you turn 66, you continue to get it, provided you still meet the entitlement conditions. However, if you make a PIP claim (including a renewal claim) after turning 66, your entitlement to the mobility component must be due to the same condition(s) as your previous award, or a new condition that has developed as a result of the original one(s).[171] Special rules restrict the rate you can get.[172]

- You only get the enhanced rate of the mobility component if you meet the normal entitlement conditions and you got the enhanced rate in an award which ended less than one year before you claim.
- You can get the standard rate if you meet the entitlement conditions and you got either rate of the mobility component in an award which ended less than one year before you claim.

There are also restrictions if your existing award of PIP is superseded due to:[173]
- a change in your circumstances that happened after you turned 66; *or*
- receipt of further medical evidence, if you turned 66 before you asked for a supersession or the DWP first considered superseding your award.

If your PIP award is superseded in one of these situations, you can only get the mobility component if you currently get it, or it stopped less than a year before the date on which the decision takes effect.[174] In Scotland, this also applies where your existing award is superseded due to receipt of a new official medical report after you reach pension age.[175] Also, to get the mobility component at the same rate, your entitlement must be due to substantially the same condition(s) as your previous award.[176] You can move from the enhanced rate to the standard rate (even if your mobility needs result from a new condition),[177] but you cannot get the mobility component for the first time or move from the standard rate to the enhanced rate.[178]

Note: there may be other grounds to supersede your PIP award (see p1274). It is only if your award is superseded for one of the reasons above that your entitlement to the mobility component is restricted.[179]

There are no restrictions on your entitlement to the mobility component due to your age if:[180]
- you make a claim for PIP; *and*
- you were under 65 on 8 April 2013; *and*
- either you are entitled to DLA and claiming PIP as part of the transfer process (see p602), or your entitlement to DLA ended less than a year ago.

3. People included in the claim

You claim personal independence payment as an individual.

4. The amount of benefit

The daily living component of personal independence payment (PIP) is paid at one of two weekly rates:[181]
- the standard rate is £61.85;
- the enhanced rate is £92.40.

The mobility component of PIP is paid at one of two weekly rates:[182]
- the standard rate is £24.45;
- the enhanced rate is £64.50.

5. Special benefit rules

Special rules may apply if you:
- are terminally ill (see below);
- have come from, or are going, abroad (see Chapters 68, 69, 70 and 71);
- are in hospital or living in a care home or similar accommodation, or in prison or detention (see Chapter 42).

Terminal illness

Note: the UK government has stated that the definition of a terminal illness for personal independence payment (PIP) will be changed. It is not clear when this will happen. See AskCPAG and CPAG's *Welfare Rights Bulletin* for updates.

You are regarded as 'terminally ill' if you have a progressive disease from which your death can reasonably be expected within six months.[183] If you claim PIP and you are terminally ill, you are automatically entitled to the enhanced rate of the daily living component.[184] You must still satisfy the disability conditions in order to get the mobility component (see p737), but you do not need to satisfy the

Part 5: Other benefits
Chapter 35: Personal independence payment
6. Claims and backdating

required period condition (see p742).[185] If you claim PIP and are terminally ill, it does not matter how long you have lived in Great Britain.[186] However, there are other residence tests that you must satisfy (see p1601).

Claims from terminally ill people are referred to as 'special rules' claims. If you want to claim PIP, or you are requesting a revision or supersession, on the basis of being terminally ill, you should expressly state this.[187] Someone else can claim PIP on behalf of a terminally ill person without her/his knowledge or authority.[188]

Note: the process of claiming PIP is different if you are terminally ill (see p747).

6. **Claims and backdating**

The general rules about claims are covered in Chapter 50. This section explains the specific rules that apply to personal independence payment (PIP).

Note: if you get disability living allowance (DLA) and have received a letter telling you to claim PIP, you should do so straight away, as your DLA award will end. If you get DLA and have *not* been sent a letter telling you to claim PIP, get specialist advice to help you decide whether it is a good idea to do so. See p602 for further details.

Making a claim

It is usually best to claim PIP by telephone. Contact the PIP claims line on 0800 917 2222 (textphone: 0800 917 7777; Relay UK and BSL video relay services available, see gov.uk/pip/how-to-claim). If you are unable to claim by these methods, you can ask for form PIP1 to be sent to you.[189]

- -
Forms

Form PIP1 is available from the PIP claims line.

If you cannot use the telephone and there is no one to help you, write asking for a claim form to Personal Independence Payment New Claims, Post Handling Site B, Wolverhampton WV99 1AH. This will delay your date of claim.
- -

If you need to submit your claim form via email as your condition means that you cannot claim by telephone or in writing, you should be able to request an email address to send your claim to.[190]

Note: the DWP is testing a fully digital claims process. At the time of writing, a six-month pilot with small numbers of new claimants is due to run until the end of July 2022.[191]

Note: if you have a query about an *existing* PIP claim, there is a different telephone number. Contact the PIP helpline on 0800 121 4433 (textphone: 0800

121 4493; Relay UK and BSL video relay available, see gov.uk/disability-benefits-helpline).

You must provide any information or evidence required (see below). You can amend or withdraw your claim before a decision is made (see p1135).

If you get PIP already and your award ends within the next year, see p753.

If your entitlement to PIP ended because you were abroad (see p1601), but you return to Great Britain less than 12 months later, a new PIP claim can be assessed on the basis of information held about your claim if your needs have not changed.[192] The DWP refers to this as a 'rapid reclaim'.

People who are terminally ill

The PIP claims process is different if you are terminally ill. You should explain that the claim is on the grounds of terminal illness when making it. Your GP, consultant or specialist nurse should complete Form DS1500, giving details of your condition and prognosis.

You are asked questions about mobility needs as part of the claim. If you are accepted as terminally ill, you are not asked to complete a separate questionnaire or attend a consultation.[193]

Someone else can claim PIP on behalf of a terminally ill person without her/his knowledge or authority.[194] If you have claimed PIP on someone else's behalf, you can also ask for a revision or supersession (see p1259) and appeal against a decision without her/his knowledge or authority.[195]

Who should claim

You must normally make a claim for PIP yourself. If you are unable to manage your affairs, another person can claim PIP for you as your 'appointee' (see p1135). Someone else can also claim PIP for a person who is terminally ill (see above).

Information to support your claim

For the general information requirements that apply to all benefits, see p1136.

It is important that you provide any information required when you claim. Until you do, you may not count as having made a valid claim (see p1138). Correct any defects as soon as possible or your date of claim may be affected.

You do not need to have a national insurance number to start a claim for PIP.[196]

Once you have claimed, there is a separate assessment process (see below).

Even if your claim is valid, you may be asked to provide further information to support your claim (see p1140). You may also be asked to provide information after you are awarded PIP and, if you fail to do so, your PIP could be suspended, or even terminated (see p1162).

The assessment process

Note: this assessment process does not apply if you are terminally ill, and you claim PIP on that basis (see above).

Part 5: Other benefits
Chapter 35: Personal independence payment
6. Claims and backdating

If you claim PIP and meet the basic entitlement conditions (see p723), you are assessed to see whether you meet the disability conditions (see p723) and the required period condition (see p742). You are also assessed if your PIP award is being reviewed (see p753) or you report a change in your circumstances (see p754). The assessment process can include requirements to:[197]

- provide information or evidence (normally in the form of a questionnaire about how you manage daily living and mobility activities); *and*
- attend and participate in a consultation with a health professional.

The questionnaire

You are sent a questionnaire about your condition(s), any treatment that you get, and the daily living and mobility activities. Your completed questionnaire must be received by the DWP within one month of the day it was sent to you. You may be allowed longer, if this is considered reasonable.[198] If you do not return the questionnaire (or other information requested about the disability conditions) without good reason (see p751), a 'negative determination' is made, and your claim is refused (or your existing award ends).[199]

If you need to ask for extra time to complete your questionnaire, contact the DWP as soon as possible. If your request is refused, and a negative determination made, see p751.

You can request the questionnaire in an alternative format – eg, an electronic version, large print, Braille or British Sign Language. If you need an alternative format, contact the PIP helpline (see p747). If your request is refused, you can complain (see p1402), but you should try to return the questionnaire you have if you can, as otherwise your claim may be refused.

The questionnaire asks for contact details of the best health professional to contact about how your condition affects you. **Note:** it is your responsibility to provide any supporting evidence you have, as the DWP does not normally contact this person.

If you have made a new claim, the questionnaire (PIP2) also asks for details of all of the other professionals who help you, and any help you will need if you have to attend a face-to-face assessment.

If your award is being reviewed or you have reported a change in your circumstances, you are sent a different questionnaire (AR1). It asks if anything has changed since you were awarded PIP, when this happened and how you are affected now.

How you should complete the questionnaire

1. Read the notes with the questionnaire before answering the questions. It may help to draft your answers on a sheet of paper first.

2. Many advice agencies can help you to complete the questionnaire. If you have difficulties with English, reading or writing, you should get help.

3. If someone else has to fill in the questionnaire for you, or you are only able to do so slowly, or with pain, explain this.

4. Compare your answers with the information on pp724–40 to work out your likely score. Your answers should not be exaggerated, but check that you have not underestimated any of your problems and have given all the details you can.

5. Remember that many of the terms in the assessment have special definitions. For example, 'cook' means heat food at or above waist height.

6. Explain whether you have better and worse days. You may need different help with an activity on different days or at different times of day. If so, try to explain how often you need each kind of help, as this is also relevant to the points that you score (see p741).

7. List any aids or appliances (see p725) that you need to help you complete an activity, and any problems you have using them.

8. Explain if an activity takes you a long time or puts you at risk, or if you cannot complete it as often as you need to, only to a low standard or with pain (see p740).

9. If you can, ask someone who knows you well to check that your answers fully explain your difficulties with the activities.

10. If you have other information that is relevant to your difficulties with daily living or mobility activities, send a copy of it with the questionnaire. This could include a report from an occupational therapist or consultant, or information from your doctor, a support worker or carer. You could also send a statement from a friend or family member. If you are unsure whether evidence is helpful, check how closely it relates to the activities in the assessment. Evidence that confirms the severity of your condition may also be useful – eg, x-rays, test results or a Certificate of Vision Impairment.

11. If you have had a previous award of DLA, ask the DWP to consider evidence from your DLA claim when making a decision on your PIP claim. You might also ask the DWP to look at evidence from a work capability assessment (see Chapter 45).

12. If you can, make a copy of the completed questionnaire before returning it to the DWP, and keep a copy of any additional information that you send with it.

The DWP sends your completed questionnaire to a health professional, who decides what other evidence s/he thinks is needed. This may include requiring you to take part in a consultation.

The consultation

You can be required to take part in a consultation with a health professional to assess whether you satisfy the disability conditions (even if you already have a PIP award). Independent Assessment Services or Capita will carry out the consultation on behalf of the DWP.[200] They will contact you to explain what you need to do. You can find more information in letters they send to you, or on their websites.[201] The DWP also publishes a guide to carrying out assessments for health professionals.[202]

Part 5: Other benefits
Chapter 35: Personal independence payment
6. Claims and backdating

Before arranging a consultation, the health professional decides whether to ask for evidence from someone who knows you. It is possible that a health professional will prepare a report without a consultation.[203]

You must normally be sent written notice of the date and time of the consultation (and, if face to face, where it will be) at least seven days in advance.[204] This rule does *not* apply if you accept less notice or notice by telephone.[205]

You should not be asked to travel for more than 90 minutes on public transport to get to a face-to-face consultation.[206]

Note: face-to-face consultations had been suspended due to the coronavirus pandemic but, from May 2021, have begun to be used again in some cases. Consultations may still be carried out by telephone or video. See AskCPAG and CPAG's *Welfare Rights Bulletin* for updates.

Recordings of consultations

The assessment provider can make an audio recording of your telephone, video or face-to-face assessment. You must request this in advance.[207]

If you want to make your own audio recording, you will be asked to give express agreement not to use it for unlawful purposes.

Video recordings are not permitted.[208]

You can ask for someone else to take part in the consultation to support you, and s/he can also give information to the health professional. In order to produce a report for the decision maker, the health professional asks you questions about how you manage the different daily living and mobility activities.

What you should do at the consultation

1. Explain as much as possible about how you are affected by your condition(s).

2. If you need to take additional medication to take part in the consultation, explain this, and also what you can and cannot do taking your normal dose.

3. If you have good and bad days, make sure that you explain this, and how your needs are different on a bad day. This is especially important if you are assessed on a better day.

4. If you are not fluent in English, it is vital that someone who can interpret for you takes part. Contact the assessment provider as soon as possible if you need an interpreter.

5. The assessment report can also include informal observations of your behaviour – eg, whether you can take part without support, and (for face-to-face consultations) how far you appear to be able to walk and whether you travelled to the assessment centre alone.

If you are required to take part in a face-to-face consultation, you can ask for it to take place at your home or a local healthcare centre. You should try to provide medical evidence explaining why you cannot attend an assessment centre (but should not be required to pay for evidence).[209] If your request is refused and you do not attend, your claim may be refused (see below).

If you fail to complete part of the assessment process

If you do not return a questionnaire on time or do not take part in a consultation, and the DWP does not accept that you had good reason for the failure, it makes a 'negative determination'. This results in a new PIP claim being refused,[210] or an existing award being superseded and removed from the date of the decision (see p1275).[211]

If the DWP makes a negative determination, you can ask for a mandatory reconsideration (see p1299), and appeal if the decision is not changed. You should also get advice about making a new claim, in case your challenge is not successful.

Check carefully any letters that you received about the assessment process. It may be arguable that the information sent to you was not sufficient to make you aware of the requirement to return the questionnaire or take part in the consultation.[212]

Good reason

In deciding whether you have '**good reason**', the DWP must consider the state of your health and the nature of your disability, along with any other reasons why you did not do what was required.[213] Guidance suggests a number of other things *may* amount to good reason, including domestic emergencies and not having received notifications.[214] The guidance suggests that telling the assessment provider what has happened as soon as possible is relevant to whether you have good reason or not. You should contact the assessment provider as soon as you can to explain why you will not be able to (or did not) take part in a consultation. Guidance to health professionals suggests that a negative determination should not be made if you have a mental or cognitive impairment and do not return a questionnaire, so if you have this kind of condition you should explain any effect it had on your ability to return it.[215]

You should try to get supporting evidence – eg, confirmation of postal problems at your address, or medical evidence of the impact of the request to take part in a consultation on your condition. The unsuitability of the location at which you were required to take part in a consultation can be a good reason for not attending it.[216]

The date of your claim

The date of your claim is important as it determines when your entitlement to PIP starts. For information about when *payment* of PIP starts, see p752.

If you claim by telephone or online, your '**date of claim**' is usually the date of your call to the PIP claims line.[217] If you request a paper claim form, your date of claim is the date the DWP receives your request, as long as it receives your properly completed form within one month (or longer if reasonable).[218]

You must make sure your claim is valid. If it is 'defective', you are given a short time to correct the defects (see p1138). If you do, your claim is treated as having been made when you initially claimed.[219]

In some cases, you can claim in advance (see below). If you claimed DLA or attendance allowance (AA) when you should have claimed PIP, see below.

Backdating your claim

You cannot backdate a claim for PIP.[220]

If you might have qualified for PIP sooner but did not claim because you were given the wrong information or misled by the DWP, you could pursue a complaint, asking for compensation (see Chapter 61).

If you claim the wrong benefit

A claim for DLA or AA can be treated as a claim for PIP and vice versa.[221] In both cases, this only applies if the DWP thinks you are not entitled to the benefit you actually claimed. See p1144 for further information.

Claiming in advance

You can claim PIP in advance if you do not satisfy the entitlement conditions, but will do so within three months of the date your claim is decided.[222] This may be relevant if you do not satisfy the required period condition (see p742) when you first claim. In this situation, the date you first qualify is your date of claim.

If you already get PIP, you can make a renewal claim up to six months before your award ends (see p753).

7. Getting paid

The general rules on getting paid are in Chapter 51. This section explains the specific rules that apply to personal independence payment (PIP).

> **When is personal independence payment paid?**
>
> PIP is usually paid on the same day of the week as the decision was made on your claim, but this can be changed by the DWP.[223] PIP is usually paid every four weeks in arrears, or if you are terminally ill, weekly in advance.[224]
>
> Payment of PIP starts after a decision has been made on your claim.

Note: the enhanced rate of the mobility component can be paid direct to Motability (see p757) if you are buying or leasing a car through the scheme.[225]

- Payment of PIP may be made to someone else on your behalf, if this is needed to protect your interests.[226]

- Payment of a lump sum of PIP (ie, back pay) may be made to you in instalments, with your consent, if receiving a large sum of money would put you at risk.[227]

- Even if you have been sanctioned for a benefit offence (see p1239), you must be paid PIP.

- For information on missing payments, see p1150. If you have lost your bank card or you have forgotten your PIN, see p1149. If you have lost your payment service card, see p1150.

- If payment of your PIP is delayed, see p1255. If you wish to complain about how your claim has been dealt with, or claim compensation, see Chapter 61.

- If payment of your PIP is suspended, see p1161.

- If you are overpaid PIP, you may have to repay it (see Chapter 53) and, in some circumstances, you may have to pay a penalty (see p1229). If you have been accused of fraud, see Chapter 54.

- If you are owed arrears of PIP, these can be paid in instalments (see p1148).

Length of awards

PIP is normally awarded for a fixed period – eg, two or five years. The length of award depends on how likely it is that your needs will change over time. You are normally awarded PIP for three years if you are terminally ill.[228]

An indefinite award can be made if a fixed-term award would be inappropriate.[229] Most indefinite awards are reviewed every 10 years, to check they are still correct.[230]

If you think that you should have been given a longer award, you can ask for a mandatory reconsideration (see p1261), and appeal if the decision is not changed.[231] If you do this, the amount of your benefit may also be reconsidered.

Note: your entitlement to PIP can be reassessed at any time after it has been awarded.[232] For what happens if your award is coming to an end, see below.

Reviews and renewal claims

If you already get PIP, you can make a renewal claim up to six months before your award ends.[233] However, you may not need to do this, as your award may be reviewed by the DWP one year before it ends.[234]

If your award is not reviewed, the DWP should contact you around three months before it ends, to remind you to make a new claim. You do *not* need to wait to be contacted to make a new claim.

Note: if no decision is made on a renewal claim or review before the end of your award, your PIP will stop and other benefits may also be affected.

Is your personal independence payment award ending?

If you are awarded PIP for a fixed period, you may be referred for a review a year before your award ends. Your award letter should say whether your award will be reviewed,[235] or you can contact the PIP helpline to check (see p747).

The process of reviewing your award is similar to the assessment process for new claims (see p747). Return the questionnaire as soon as possible and take part in any consultation, as otherwise a negative determination may be made, ending your PIP award (see p751). A decision maker then decides whether to carry out a supersession (see p1274). A supersession decision could extend, change or remove your PIP award.

If your award is due to end in less than six months and the DWP has not contacted you, you should either make a renewal claim or request a supersession (see p1274) as soon as possible, to make sure you get a decision before your award ends. Get advice about the possible impact on your current award.

If there is a delay in getting a decision, or you are not sure what is happening, contact the PIP helpline (see p747). If you are told that your award is likely to end before an assessment can be carried out, make a complaint (see Chapter 61).

'LEAP exercises'

The DWP is undertaking several PIP administrative review exercises, also called legal entitlements and administrative practices (LEAP) reviews. These reviews involve PIP decisions being looked at again because there has been a new understanding of the law after an Upper Tribunal or higher court decision. See p730, p736, p738 and p740. Get advice if you receive a letter saying that an earlier decision about your entitlement to PIP has been looked at again, or if you have not heard from the DWP but think you should be included in a LEAP exercise.

Change of circumstances

Note: a change of circumstances can include that your needs are now expected to last beyond the end date of your award, even if the *level* of your needs is still the same.[236] If your award is due to end in less than one year, see p753.

You must report any changes in your circumstances that you have been told you must report, as well as any that you might reasonably be expected to know might affect your right to, the amount of, or the payment of, PIP. To continue to qualify for PIP, your needs must be expected to last for a further nine months on any day of your award.[237] So, if a change means that your needs are no longer expected to last at least this long, you should report it. Get advice if you think that your condition has improved so much that your entitlement to PIP might be affected.

Get advice before reporting a change of circumstances if you think that, due to a change in health, you should be entitled to a higher award of PIP.

You should report any changes in your circumstances as soon as possible, preferably in writing. See p1160 for further information.

If payment of (but not entitlement to) PIP has stopped (because you are in hospital, a care home or prison – see Chapter 42), still notify the DWP of any changes so the correct rate is paid when payment resumes.

If there has been a relevant change of circumstances, a decision maker looks at your award again and makes a new decision. To find out the date from which the new decision takes effect, see p1279.

Note: if you get PIP, already live in Scotland, and plan to report a change of circumstances, see p1692. If you get PIP and are planning to move to Scotland, see p1692.

---

8. Tax, other benefits and the benefit cap

Tax

Personal independence payment (PIP) is not taxable.[238]

Means-tested benefits and tax credits

PIP is not taken into account as income when calculating means-tested benefits and tax credits, and is paid in addition to them. Getting PIP can increase the amount you get, or can mean that you qualify for means-tested benefits or tax credits for the first time, if your income was previously too high.

If you or your partner are entitled to PIP, you may qualify for:

- a limited capability for work-related activity element in your universal credit (UC) if you or your partner are entitled to the enhanced rate of the PIP daily living component and are aged 66 or over (see p71). Alternatively, a limited capability for work element is included in your UC if you or your partner are entitled to PIP, but not the enhanced rate of the daily living component, and are 66 or over, in some circumstances (see p69);
- a disability premium in income support (IS), income-based jobseeker's allowance (JSA) or housing benefit (HB) if you are under 66 (see p325);
- a higher pensioner premium in IS or income-based JSA if you have a partner and either of you have reached 66 (see p329);
- an enhanced disability premium in IS, income-based JSA, income-related employment and support allowance (ESA) or HB if you or your partner are entitled to the enhanced rate of the daily living component and are under 66 (see p327);
- a severe disability premium/addition in IS, income-based JSA, income-related ESA, the guarantee credit of pension credit (PC) or HB if you or your partner receive the daily living component and meet other conditions (see p330);
- a disabled worker element in working tax credit (WTC) if you or your partner receive PIP, work 16 hours a week or more and meet other conditions (see p1420);
- a severe disability element in WTC if you or your partner are entitled to the enhanced rate of the daily living component (see p1422).

Part 5: Other benefits
Chapter 35: Personal independence payment
8. Tax, other benefits and the benefit cap

If your child is entitled to PIP and still counts as part of your household (even if you do not get a basic amount for her/him because of the 'two-child limit'), you may qualify for:

- a disabled child addition in UC, paid at a higher rate if s/he is entitled to the enhanced rate of the daily living component (see p66);
- a disabled child premium in HB and, if you do not get child tax credit (CTC), in IS or income-based JSA (see p324);
- an enhanced disability premium in HB if s/he is entitled to the enhanced rate of the daily living component and (if you do not get CTC) in IS or income-based JSA (see p327);
- a disabled child element in CTC (see p1418), or a severely disabled child element instead if s/he is entitled to the enhanced rate of the daily living component (see p1418);
- an additional amount in your PC (if you do not get CTC), paid at a higher rate if s/he is entitled to the enhanced rate of the daily living component (see p323).

If you or your partner receive the daily living component, non-dependant deductions are not made from your HB (see p198), or from any housing costs included in your IS, income-based JSA, income-related ESA or the guarantee credit of PC (see p347).

No housing costs contributions from a non-dependant are taken into account when calculating your UC housing costs element if you, your partner or the non-dependant receive the PIP daily living component, or are entitled to it but payment is suspended as you are in hospital (see p102).

Non-means-tested benefits

PIP may be paid in addition to any other non-means-tested benefits, except that:

- you are not entitled to PIP while you are entitled to adult disability payment or child disability payment;[239]
- if you are entitled to PIP, you cannot claim disability living allowance[240] or attendance allowance;[241]
- PIP overlaps with some war pension payments for constant attendance or mobility, and armed forces independence payment (see p857);[242]
- PIP daily living component overlaps with constant attendance allowance under the industrial injuries scheme (see p678);[243]
- PIP mobility component is not paid if you get a grant for the use of a vehicle from the NHS.[244]

If you get the daily living component of PIP and someone regularly looks after you, that person may be entitled to carer's allowance (CA) (see Chapter 26) and the carer element of UC (see p73). However, any severe disability premium/

addition you get will stop if s/he gets CA or the carer element, so always get advice.

If you get the daily living component, a young person living in Scotland may be able to get a young carer grant for looking after you (see Chapter 78).

The benefit cap

In some cases, there is a limit on the total amount of specified benefits you can receive (a 'benefit cap'). PIP is *not* one of the specified benefits. The benefit cap does *not* apply if you, your partner or child get PIP (even it is not paid because the person entitled is in hospital or a care home). In other cases, it only applies if you are getting UC or HB. See p1156 for further information.

Passports and other sources of help

You qualify for a Christmas bonus if you get PIP (see p861).

If you get PIP, you may be entitled to other 'passported' benefits such as a blue badge parking concession or a concessionary travel card. Contact your local authority for more information.

If you receive the PIP mobility component and you or your carer have a car used only by you or for you, your vehicle excise duty (road tax) may be reduced. There are details at gov.uk/financial-help-disabled/vehicles-and-transport.

If you have a low income, you may be entitled to council tax reduction (see p836).

Motability

Motability is a charity that runs a scheme to help you lease or buy a car, scooter or powered wheelchair. You are eligible if you get the enhanced rate of the PIP mobility component and have 12 months or more left to run on your award.

If you use the scheme, your PIP mobility component is paid direct to Motability.[245] You may also have to make extra payments. For further information, telephone 0300 456 4566 (textphone: 0300 037 0100) or see motability.co.uk. If you use British Sign Language, see motability.co.uk/contact/british-sign-language-service.

Notes

1. Who can get personal independence payment

1 ss77-80 WRA 2012; Part 2 and Sch 1 SS(PIP) Regs
2 *MB v SSWP (PIP)* [2016] UKUT 250 (AAC)
3 *PM v SSWP (PIP)* [2017] UKUT 154 (AAC); *EG v SSWP (PIP)* [2017] UKUT 101 (AAC)
4 Regs 5 and 6 SS(PIP) Regs
5 ss78-9 WRA 2012
6 *MR v SSWP (PIP)* [2017] UKUT 86 (AAC)
7 *TK v SSWP (PIP)* [2020] UKUT 22 (AAC), reported as [2020] AACR 18
8 *KP v SSWP (PIP)* [2017] UKUT 30 (AAC)
9 *SD v SSWP (PIP)* [2017] UKUT 310 (AAC); *DE v SSWP (PIP)* [2021] UKUT 226 (AAC)
10 Sch 1 Part 1 SS(PIP) Regs
11 *JT v SSWP (PIP)* [2018] UKUT 101 (AAC); *CP v SSWP (PIP)* [2018] UKUT 5 (AAC)
12 Sch 1 Part 1 SS(PIP) Regs
13 *SSWP v GM (PIP)* [2017] UKUT 268 (AAC)
14 *RJ, GMcL and CS v SSWP v RJ (PIP)* [2017] UKUT 105 (AAC), reported as [2017] AACR 32
15 DWP, *Safety and Supervision: changes to PIP law from 9 March 2017*, 20 September 2021, gov.uk/government/publications/personal-independence-payment-changes/safety-and-supervision-changes-to-pip-law-from-9-march-2017
16 *SSWP v IM (PIP)* [2015] UKUT 680 (AAC)
17 *LB v SSWP (PIP)* [2017] UKUT 436 (AAC)
18 *GG v SSWP (PIP)* [2016] UKUT 194 (AAC); *PM v SSWP (PIP)* [2017] UKUT 502 (AAC)
19 *SSWP v MMcK* [2017] CSIH 57. The Supreme Court made no comment on this suggestion in the appeal against this decision (*SSWP v MM (Scotland)* [2019] UKSC 34, reported as [2019] AACR 26).
20 Reg 2 SS(PIP) Regs
21 *MR v SSWP (PIP)* [2017] UKUT 86 (AAC), although the comments were not strictly necessary to the decision in that case
22 Reg 4(2) SS(PIP) Regs

23 *CW v SSWP (PIP)* [2016] UKUT 197 (AAC), reported as [2016] AACR 44; *NA v SSWP (PIP)* [2015] UKUT 572 (AAC)
24 *CW v SSWP (PIP)* [2016] UKUT 197 (AAC), reported as [2016] AACR 44; *AP v SSWP (PIP)* [2016] UKUT 501 (AAC)
25 *MR v SSWP (PIP)* [2019] UKUT 293 (AAC)
26 *RB v SSWP (PIP)* [2019] UKUT 186 (AAC)
27 *PE v SSWP (PIP)* [2015] UKUT 309 (AAC), reported as [2016] AACR 10; *JM v SSWP (PIP)* [2016] UKUT 542 (AAC)
28 Sch 1 Part 1 SS(PIP) Regs
29 *RH v SSWP (PIP)* [2015] UKUT 281 (AAC)
30 *SSWP v KJ (PIP)* [2017] UKUT 358 (AAC)
31 *ZI v SSWP (PIP)* [2016] UKUT 572 (AAC), reported as [2018] AACR 1
32 *SC v SSWP (PIP)* [2017] UKUT 317 (AAC)
33 *AI v SSWP (PIP)* [2016] UKUT 322 (AAC)
34 *LC v SSWP (PIP)* [2016] UKUT 150 (AAC)
35 *GB v SSWP (PIP)* [2015] UKUT 546 (AAC) accepted that lever arm taps were an aid, but the DWP no longer believes that this decision is correct, so this may not be accepted: see *AP v SSWP (PIP)* [2016] UKUT 501 (AAC). *YW (deceased) by MM v SSWP (PIP)* [2017] UKUT 42 (AAC) suggested that lightweight pans are not aids, but note that this view was not necessary to the decision.
36 *DR v SSWP (PIP)* [2018] UKUT 209 (AAC), but see also *EG v SSWP (PIP)* [2015] 275 UKUT (AAC), which came to the opposite view
37 *SSWP v DT (PIP)* [2017] UKUT 272 (AAC)
38 *AI v SSWP (PIP)* [2016] UKUT 322 (AAC)
39 Sch 1 Part 1 SS(PIP) Regs
40 *MM and BJ v SSWP (PIP)* [2016] UKUT 490 (AAC), reported as [2017] AACR 17
41 *JW v SSWP (PIP)* [2018] UKUT 169 (AAC)
42 *TW v SSWP (PIP)* [2020] UKUT 22 (AAC)
43 *PA v SSWP (PIP)* [2019] UKUT 270 (AAC)
44 *SSWP v KS (PIP)* [2018] UKUT 102 (AAC)
45 Sch 1 Part 1 SS(PIP) Regs
46 Now called the Health and Care Professions Council
47 *PM v SSWP (PIP)* [2018] UKUT 138 (AAC)

48 *SSWP v LB (PIP)* [2016] UKUT 530 (AAC). The DWP interprets this aspect of the decision as still applying to the current definition of 'therapy' - see DWP, *Special Diet as Therapy: changes to PIP law from 28 November 2016*, 7 October 2020, available at gov.uk/government/publications/personal-independence-payment-changes/special-diet-as-therapy-changes-to-pip-law-from-28-november-2016.

49 *KM v SSWP (PIP)* [2018] UKUT 296 (AAC)

50 *AS v SSWP (PIP)* [2017] UKUT 104 (AAC), reported as [2017] AACR 31

51 *SSWP v TMcI (PIP)* [2016] UKUT 574 (AAC)

52 *SSWP v KS (PIP)* [2018] UKUT 102 (AAC)

53 *DC v SSWP (PIP)* [2016] UKUT 11 (AAC)

54 *AH v SSWP (PIP)* [2016] UKUT 276 (AAC). While this case was the subject of a further appeal to the Court of Appeal (*Hickey v SSWP* [2018] EWCA Civ 851), this aspect of the Upper Tribunal's decision was not considered in the court's judgment.

55 *MM v SSWP (PIP)* [2018] UKUT 193 (AAC), but note that the point was not finally decided

56 *TK v SSWP (PIP)* [2020] UKUT 22 (AAC), reported as [2020] AACR 18

57 *MF v SSWP (PIP)* [2015] UKUT 554 (AAC), reported as [2016] AACR 20

58 *RH v SSWP (PIP)* [2015] UKUT 281 (AAC)

59 *RB v SSWP (PIP)* [2016] UKUT 556 (AAC)

60 ADM memo 17/19: *PIP Daily Living Activity 3 – Effect of UT Decision*

61 Sch 1 Part 1 SS(PIP) Regs

62 *SP v SSWP (PIP)* [2016] UKUT 190 (AAC), reported as [2016] AACR 43

63 *AP v SSWP (PIP)* [2016] UKUT 501 (AAC)

64 *SH v SSWP (PIP)* [2018] UKUT 251 (AAC); *RJ, GMcL and CS v SSWP v RJ (PIP)* [2017] UKUT 105 (AAC), reported as [2017] AACR 32

65 *KT and SH v SSWP (PIP)* [2020] UKUT 252 (AAC)

66 *MB v SSWP (PIP)* [2018] UKUT 139 (AAC)

67 *GG v SSWP (PIP)* [2016] UKUT 194 (AAC)

68 Sch 1 Part 1 SS(PIP) Regs

69 *GW v SSWP (PIP)* [2015] UKUT 570 (AAC)

70 *DA v SSWP (PIP)* [2019] UKUT 320 (AAC)

71 *FK v SSWP (PIP)* [2017] UKUT 375 (AAC)

72 *JM v SSWP (PIP)* [2016] UKUT 296 (AAC)

73 *BS v SSWP (PIP)* [2016] UKUT 456 (AAC)

74 *GW v SSWP (PIP)* [2015] UKUT 570 (AAC)

75 *SSWP v NH (PIP)* [2017] UKUT 258 (AAC)

76 *KO v SSP (PIP)* [2018] UKUT 78 (AAC)

77 *KW v SSWP (PIP)* [2017] UKUT 54 (AAC)

78 *GP v SSWP (PIP)* [2015] UKUT 498 (AAC)

79 Sch 1 Part 1 SS(PIP) Regs

80 *JM v SSWP (PIP)* [2016] UKUT 542 (AAC)

81 *PE v SSWP (PIP)* [2015] UKUT 309 (AAC), reported as [2016] AACR 10

82 *JM v SSWP (PIP)* [2016] UKUT 542 (AAC)

83 *CW v SSWP (PIP)* [2016] UKUT 197 (AAC), reported as [2016] AACR 44; *AP v SSWP (PIP)* [2016] UKUT 501 (AAC)

84 *MR v SSWP (PIP)* [2019] UKUT 293 (AAC)

85 *DP v SSWP (PIP)* [2017] UKUT 156 (AAC)

86 *ML v SSWP (PIP)* [2017] UKUT 171 (AAC)

87 Sch 1 Part 1 SS(PIP) Regs

88 *BM v DfC (PIP)* [2019] NICom 33, reported as [2020] AACR 15 and therefore persuasive while not binding outside of Northern Ireland

89 *P v SSWP (PIP)* [2018] UKUT 376 (AAC)

90 *EG v SSWP (PIP)* [2017] UKUT 101 (AAC)

91 *TC v SSWP (PIP)* [2016] UKUT 550 (AAC)

92 *SSWP v AS (PIP)* [2017] UKUT 454 (AAC); *GJ v SSWP (PIP)* [2016] UKUT 8 (AAC)

93 Sch 1 Part 1 SS(PIP) Regs

94 *TR v SSWP (PIP)* [2015] UKUT 626 (AAC), reported as [2016] AACR 23

95 *MR v SSWP (PIP)* [2017] UKUT 86 (AAC)

96 *KP v SSWP (PIP)* [2017] UKUT 30 (AAC)

97 *SE v SSWP (PIP)* [2021] UKUT 1 (AAC)

98 Sch 1 Part 1 SS(PIP) Regs

99 *SM v SSWP (PIP)* [2019] UKUT 292 (AAC); *AM v SSWP (PIP)* [2017] UKUT 7 (AAC)

100 *DV v SSWP (PIP)* [2017] UKUT 244 (AAC); *SF v SSWP (PIP)* [2016] UKUT 543 (AAC)

101 Sch 1 Part 1 SS(PIP) Regs; *SF v SSWP (PIP)* [2016] UKUT 543 (AAC); *SSWP v AM (PIP)* [2015] UKUT 215 (AAC). Both decisions held that the definition of 'engage socially' applies to the words 'engage with other people' in the descriptors.

102 *HA v SSWP (PIP)* [2018] UKUT 56 (AAC)

103 *HA v SSWP (PIP)* [2018] UKUT 56 (AAC); *RC v SSWP (PIP)* [2017] UKUT 352 (AAC)

104 *RC v SSWP (PIP)* [2017] UKUT 352 (AAC)

105 *DV v SSWP (PIP)* [2017] UKUT 244 (AAC)

106 *HJ v SSWP (PIP)* [2016] UKUT 487 (AAC)

107 *AC v SSWP (PIP)* [2021] UKUT 216 (AAC)

108 *SSWP v MM (Scotland)* [2019] UKSC 34, reported as [2019] AACR 26

109 *SSWP v MM (Scotland)* [2019] UKSC 34, reported as [2019] AACR 26; *SL v SSWP (PIP)* [2016] UKUT 147 (AAC)

110 *JT v SSWP (PIP)* [2020] UKUT 186 (AAC)

111 Sch 1 Part 1 SS(PIP) Regs

• •

112 *DP v SSWP (PIP)* [2017] UKUT 156 (AAC)
113 *PR v SSWP (PIP)* [2015] UKUT 584 (AAC); *JW v SSWP (PIP)* [2018] UKUT 169 (AAC)
114 *SE v SSWP (PIP)* [2021] UKUT 1 (AAC)
115 *RB v SSWP (PIP)* [2016] UKUT 393 (AAC)
116 *SSWP v LB (PIP)* [2016] UKUT 530 (AAC)
117 In 2017, the DWP amended the wording of some descriptors in this activity, but the High Court quashed the changes in *R (RF) v SSWP* [2017] EWHC 3375 (Admin), reported as [2018] AACR 13. The changes are not included in the descriptors, as they never had any effect (see *AH v SSWP (PIP)* [2018] UKUT 262 (AAC)).
118 Sch 1 Part 1 SS(PIP) Regs
119 *SSWP v NF (PIP)* [2017] UKUT 480 (AAC)
120 *AA v SSWP (PIP)* [2018] UKUT 339 (AAC)
121 The definition of 'prompting' does not require the physical presence of the person who is prompting you
122 *TR v SSWP (PIP)* [2015] UKUT 626 (AAC), reported as [2016] AACR 23; *PM v SSWP (PIP)* [2017] UKUT 154 (AAC); *AA v SSWP (PIP)* [2018] UKUT 339 (AAC). Note that PIP AG Part 2 suggests that this argument may not be accepted, although it does suggest that only being able to go out in darkness is not managing this activity to an acceptable standard.
123 *MH v SSWP (PIP)* [2016] UKUT 531 (AAC), reported as [2018] AACR 12
124 *AA v SSWP (PIP)* [2018] UKUT 339 (AAC)
125 *JB v SSWP (PIP)* [2019] UKUT 203 (AAC); *SB v SSWP (PIP)* [2019] UKUT 274 (AAC)
126 *MC v SSWP (PIP)* [2019] UKUT 264 (AAC); *SSWP v IV (PIP)* [2016] UKUT 420 (AAC)
127 *HO'H v SSWP (PIP)* [2020] UKUT 135 (AAC)
128 *MH v SSWP (PIP)* [2016] UKUT 531 (AAC), reported as [2018] AACR 12
129 *AA v SSWP (PIP)* [2018] UKUT 339 (AAC)
130 PIP AG Part 2
131 *MH v SSWP (PIP)* [2016] UKUT 531 (AAC), reported as [2018] AACR 12
132 ADM Memo 16-18; DWP, *Overwhelming Psychological Distress and Journeys: changes to PIP law from 28 November 2016*, 7 October 2020, available at gov.uk/government/publications/ personal-independence-payment- changes/overwhelming-psychological- distress-and-journeys-changes-to- pip-law-from-28-november-2016
133 Sch 1 Part 1 SS(PIP) Regs
134 *DT v SSWP (PIP)* [2016] UKUT 240 (AAC)

135 *PM v SSWP (PIP)* [2017] UKUT 154 (AAC); *BM v SSWP (PIP)* [2017] UKUT 486 (AAC)
136 *AP v SSWP (PIP)* [2016] UKUT 501 (AAC), but note that *KL v SSWP (PIP)* [2015] UKUT 612 (AAC) came to a different conclusion and interprets the law more generously
137 *KN v SSWP (PIP)* [2016] UKUT 261 (AAC); *TF v SSWP (PIP)* [2015] UKUT 661 (AAC)
138 *KL v SSWP (PIP)* [2016] UKUT 545 (AAC)
139 *LH v SSWP (PIP)* [2018] UKUT 57 (AAC); *PS v SSWP (PIP)* [2016] UKUT 536 (AAC)
140 *CM v SSWP (PIP)* [2020] UKUT 259 (AAC)
141 *NK v SSWP (PIP)* [2016] UKUT 146 (AAC)
142 *MH v SSWP (PIP)* [2016] UKUT 531 (AAC), reported as [2018] AACR 12
143 Reg 4(2A) and (4) SS(PIP) Regs; *TF v SSWP (PIP)* [2015] UKUT 661 (AAC)
144 *RJ, GMcL and CS v SSWP v RJ (PIP)* [2017] UKUT 105 (AAC), reported as [2017] AACR 32
145 *SH v SSWP (PIP)* [2018] UKUT 251 (AAC)
146 ADM memo 15/18: *PIP – the meaning of 'safely' – amended version*
147 *PA v SSWP (PIP)* [2019] UKUT 270 (AAC); *PM v SSWP (PIP)* [2017] UKUT 154 (AAC)
148 *PS v SSWP (PIP)* [2016] UKUT 326 (AAC)
149 *TR v SSWP (PIP)* [2015] UKUT 626 (AAC), reported as [2016] AACR 23
150 *PM v SSWP (PIP)* [2017] UKUT 154 (AAC)
151 *ML v SSWP (PIP)* [2017] UKUT 171 (AAC)
152 *KL v SSWP (PIP)* [2016] UKUT 545 (AAC)
153 *TR v SSWP (PIP)* [2015] UKUT 626 (AAC), reported as [2016] AACR 23. This is essentially a question of whether an activity can be undertaken 'repeatedly'.
154 Regs 2, 7(3) and 14 SS(PIP) Regs; reg 24 PIP(TP) Regs; *AB v SSWP (PIP)* [2017] UKUT 217 (AAC)
155 Regs 2, 7(3) and 15 SS(PIP) Regs
156 Reg 7 SS(PIP) Regs
157 *GG v SSWP (PIP)* [2016] UKUT 194 (AAC)
158 *AK v SSWP (PIP)* [2015] UKUT 620 (AAC)
159 ss81 and 82 WRA 2012; regs 12-14 SS(PIP) Regs
160 *AH v SSWP (PIP)* [2016] UKUT 541 (AAC)
161 Reg 33(1) UC,PIP,JSA&ESA(C&P) Regs

162 Regs 15 and 26 SS(PIP) Regs
163 Reg 23 PIP(TP) Regs; *AH v SSWP (PIP)* [2016] UKUT 541 (AAC). Note that *EB v SSWP (PIP)* [2017] UKUT 311 (AAC) came to a different conclusion – that this rule can only apply to the effects of a condition that existed when you were last awarded DLA. Arguably, this is not correct, as Sch 10 para 5(b) and (c) WRA 2012 permits regulations to take account of periods of entitlement to DLA in deciding whether the required period condition is satisfied. This provision was not mentioned in *EB*, and it is arguably a more natural reading of the regulations that current or recent DLA entitlement means that the 'past period test' is automatically satisfied.

2. The rules about your age
164 Reg 5 PIP(TP) Regs
165 s83 WRA 2012
166 Reg 27 PIP(TP) Regs
167 Reg 25(b) SS(PIP) Regs
168 Reg 25(a) SS(PIP) Regs
169 Reg 27 SS(PIP) Regs
170 Regs 15 and 26 SS(PIP) Regs
171 Regs 15 and 26 SS(PIP) Regs
172 Reg 26(2)(c) SS(PIP) Regs
173 Reg 27(2) SS(PIP) Regs
174 Reg 27(3) SS(PIP) Regs
175 The Social Security (Personal Independence Payment) Amendment (Scotland) Regulations 2020 No.340
176 Reg 27(3)(a)(ii) and (3)(b) SS(PIP) Regs
177 Reg 27(3) SS(PIP) Regs
178 Reg 27(3)(a)(i) and (4) SS(PIP) Regs
179 *MH v SSWP (PIP)* [2020] UKUT 185 (AAC)
180 Reg 27 PIP(TP) Regs. The definitions of 'previous award' and 'component' in reg 2 SS(PIP) Regs mean that regs 15 and 26 of those regulations only apply to people who have had a previous PIP award.

4. The amount of benefit
181 Reg 24(1) SS(PIP) Regs
182 Reg 24(2) SS(PIP) Regs

5. Special benefit rules
183 s82(4) WRA 2012
184 s82(2) WRA 2012
185 s82(3) WRA 2012
186 Reg 21 SS(PIP) Regs
187 s82(1)(b) WRA 2012; regs 5(2)(c) and 23(2) UC,PIP,JSA&ESA(DA) Regs
188 s82(5) WRA 2012

6. Claims and backdating
189 Reg 11(1) UC,PIP,JSA&ESA(C&P) Regs; DWP, *Personal Independence Payment Handbook,* December 2021, available at gov.uk/government/publications/ personal-independence-payment-fact-sheets/pip-handbook
190 House of Commons, *Hansard,* Written question 121453, answered 18 January 2018, available at questions-statements.parliament.uk
191 DWP, *Touchbase* e-newsletter, 28 January 2022
192 House of Commons, *Hansard,* Written statement HCWS603, 20 April 2017, available at questions-statements.parliament.uk. The DWP confirmed the introduction of this process by email to CPAG on 5 January 2018.
193 DWP, *Personal Independence Payment Handbook,* December 2021, available at gov.uk/government/publications/ personal-independence-payment-fact-sheets/pip-handbook
194 s82(5) WRA 2012
195 Reg 49(c) UC,PIP,JSA&ESA(DA) Regs
196 para A2148 ADM
197 s80 WRA 2012; regs 8 and 9 SS(PIP) Regs
198 Reg 8(1) and (2) SS(PIP) Regs
199 Reg 8(3) SS(PIP) Regs
200 Broadly speaking, if you live in Scotland, northern England or southern England, the contractor is Independent Assessment Services. If you live in the Midlands or Wales, it is Capita. There is a map showing postcode areas covered by each contractor at gov.uk/ government/publications/pip-postcode-map-uk.
201 capita-pip.co.uk or mypipassessment.co.uk
202 DWP, *Personal Independence Payment (PIP) Assessment Guide for Assessment Providers,* 24 January 2022, available at gov.uk/government/publications/ personal-independence-payment-assessment-guide-for-assessment-providers (abbreviated here as PIP AG)
203 Reg 9(1) SS(PIP) Regs says that you 'may' be required to attend a consultation.
204 Reg 9(3)(a) and (4) SS(PIP) Regs
205 Reg 9(3)(b) SS(PIP) Regs

206 DWP, *Personal Independence Payment Handbook*, December 2021, available at gov.uk/government/publications/personal-independence-payment-factsheets/pip-handbook
207 PIP AG, paras 1.6.58-62
208 PIP AG, paras 1.6.60-64
209 PIP AG, paras 1.6.72-76
210 s80(4)-(6) WRA 2012; regs 8(3) and 9(2) SS(PIP) Regs
211 Reg 26(2) UC,PIP,JSA&ESA(DA) Regs; *KB v SSWP (PIP)* [2016] UKUT 537 (AAC)
212 *IR v SSWP (PIP)* [2019] UKUT 374 (AAC)
213 Reg 10 SS(PIP) Regs
214 Ch P6 ADM
215 PIP AG para 1.1.7
216 *OM v SSWP (PIP)* [2017] UKUT 458 (AAC); *TC v SSWP (PIP) (No.2)* [2018] UKUT 286 (AAC)
217 Reg 12(1)(b) UC,PIP,JSA&ESA(C&P) Regs
218 Reg 12(1)(c) UC,PIP,JSA&ESA(C&P) Regs
219 Regs 11(6) and 12 UC,PIP,JSA&ESA(C&P) Regs
220 Reg 27 UC,PIP,JSA&ESA(C&P) Regs
221 Reg 25(3) and (4) UC,PIP,JSA&ESA(C&P) Regs
222 Reg 33(1) UC,PIP,JSA&ESA(C&P) Regs

7. Getting paid
223 Reg 49 UC,PIP,JSA&ESA(C&P) Regs
224 Reg 48 UC,PIP,JSA&ESA(C&P) Regs
225 Reg 62 UC,PIP,JSA&ESA(C&P) Regs
226 Reg 58(2) UC,PIP,JSA&ESA(C&P) Regs
227 The Social Security Benefits (Claims and Payments) (Amendment) Regulations 2021 No.1065
228 para P2079 ADM
229 s88(2) and (3) WRA 2012
230 para P2062 ADM
231 *RS v SSWP (PIP)* [2016] UKUT 85 (AAC); *GT v SSWP (PIP)* [2019] UKUT 30 (AAC)
232 Reg 11 SS(PIP) Regs
233 Reg 33(2) UC,PIP,JSA&ESA(C&P) Regs
234 para P2063 ADM
235 DWP, *If your PIP claim is reviewed* (undated), available at gov.uk/pip/when-your-pip-claim-is-reviewed
236 *PH v SSWP (DLA)* [2013] UKUT 268 (AAC). While this was a DLA case, it is strongly arguable that the reasoning also applies to fixed-term awards of PIP.
237 Reg 14(b) SS(PIP) Regs; *BM v SSWP (PIP)* [2017] UKUT 486 (AAC)

8. Tax, other benefits and the benefit cap
238 s677(1) IT(EP)A 2003
239 s77(4)(5) WRA 2012
240 Reg 22(1) PIP(TP) Regs
241 s64(1) and (1A) SSCBA 1992
242 Sch 1 paras 5 and 5a SS(OB) Regs; reg 61 UC,PIP,JSA&ESA(C&P) Regs
243 Sch 1 para 5 SS(OB) Regs
244 Reg 61 UC,PIP,JSA&ESA(C&P) Regs
245 Regs 62, 63 and 64 UC,PIP,JSA&ESA(C&P) Regs

Chapter 36

Retirement pensions

This chapter covers:
1. Who can get state pension (p764)
2. The rules about your age (p765)
3. People included in the claim (p766)
4. The amount of benefit (p766)
5. Special benefit rules (p771)
6. Claims and backdating (p772)
7. Getting paid (p775)
8. Tax, other benefits and the benefit cap (p776)

This chapter covers the rules that apply to people who reach pension age on or after 6 April 2016 and who are eligible for the new state retirement pension, known as 'state pension'. People who reached pension age before 6 April 2016, including those who had already claimed their state retirement pension and those who had deferred claiming it, continue on the previous retirement pension scheme. In this chapter, these pensions are referred to as 'old' retirement pensions. For more details about these, see the 2015/16 edition of this *Handbook*.

Key facts
- State pension is a non-means-tested, contributory benefit, paid to people who reach pension age on or after 6 April 2016.
- State pension is an individual pension based solely on your own national insurance contributions (although there are some limited exceptions).
- You can qualify whether you are in or out of work.
- State pension is affected by the overlapping benefit rules.
- State pension is administered and paid by the Pension Service, which is part of the DWP.
- If you reached pension age before 6 April 2016, you cannot get state pension, but you may be entitled to an 'old' retirement pension instead.
- If you disagree with a decision on your state pension, you can apply for a revision or a supersession (see Chapter 56), or appeal against it (see Chapter 57). You must apply for a mandatory reconsideration before you can appeal.

1. **Who can get state pension**

You can get state pension if you reach pension age (see p766) on or after 6 April 2016. Whether you qualify, and the amount you receive, depends on your national insurance (NI) contribution record. Your NI record contributions and credits before 6 April 2016 form your 'starting amount'. The starting amount will be either the amount you would have got under the old retirement pension rules, or the amount you would have got if the new state pension rules had always existed, whichever is higher. If your starting amount is less than the current full state pension, the Pension Service will also look at your NI record after 5 April 2016 to see if you had any qualifying years from this point. If you do, each year will increase your state pension payment but you cannot be paid more than the full rate.[1] If you have qualifying years from before 6 April 2016, your state pension is paid at the transitional rate (see p768). This may be more or less than, or the same as, the full rate. You normally need at least 10 qualifying years to receive any state pension. See Chapter 43 for full details of the contribution conditions for state pension.

Did you reach pension age before 6 April 2016?

If you reached pension age before 6 April 2016, you cannot claim state pension. However, you may be entitled to an 'old' retirement pension – ie, a category A, category B or category D retirement pension. This applies even if you reached pension age before 6 April 2016 but deferred claiming your retirement pension until after that date.

The rules for 'old' retirement pensions are not explained in detail in this chapter. See Chapter 36 of the 2015/16 edition of this *Handbook* for full details.

You do not automatically become entitled to state pension just by reaching pension age. You must make a claim, unless you are a widow in certain situations (see p773). If you do not claim, you are treated as having deferred your state pension (see below).

You do not have to retire from work if you reach pension age and claim state pension. If you decide to carry on working, your earnings do not reduce the state pension you receive and you no longer pay NI contributions. However, the amount of tax you pay may increase because state pension is taxable.

There are some groups of claimants to whom special rules apply (see p771).

Deferring your state pension

Once you reach pension age, you can choose to defer your entitlement to state pension. In return, you later become entitled to a higher rate of pension. **Note:** you do not have the option of taking a taxable lump-sum payment plus interest.

You can defer your state pension by simply not claiming it when you reach pension age. If you are already claiming, you can choose to stop getting it in order to get more later on, but you can only do this once. To stop claiming, you must notify the Pension Service by telephone or in writing.[2] You can specify a future date on which you want to stop claiming, provided this is within four weeks of your notifying the Pension Service.[3] You can cancel the deferment at any time by making a claim for state pension, and can backdate that cancellation by up to 12 months.[4]

Your state pension is increased by one-ninth of 1 per cent for each week of deferment.[5] For example, if you defer your pension for one year, it increases by approximately 5.8 per cent, which increases a full state pension by approximately £10.74 a week. You are not entitled to any increase unless you defer your pension for long enough to earn an increase of at least 1 per cent.[6]

The increase is calculated on the amount you would have received immediately before the end of the deferral period if you had not deferred claiming. If your entitlement changes during the deferral period (eg, because you become entitled to an inherited amount on the death of your spouse or civil partner – see p769), the calculation takes this into account so that it is based on the rates of pension to which you would have been entitled throughout the deferral period.[7]

You do not receive an increase in state pension for any whole week in the period of deferral in which:[8]

- you get severe disablement allowance, incapacity benefit, carer's allowance, widow's pension, widowed mother's allowance or unemployability supplement, or your spouse, civil partner or anyone you are residing with is getting an increase in any of these benefits for you; *or*
- you would have been disqualified from receiving state pension because you were a prisoner; *or*
- you or your partner gets pension credit, universal credit, income support, income-based jobseeker's allowance or income-related employment and support allowance.

If you die either while you are deferring your state pension or after you have started to receive your state pension, your deferral increase is not inheritable.

If you are going to live abroad and have deferred your state pension, see p771.

2. The rules about your age

State pension can be claimed when you reach pension age if this is on or after 6 April 2016. If you reached pension age before this date, you may be entitled to an 'old' retirement pension instead (see Chapter 36 of the 2015/16 edition of this *Handbook*). You can claim state pension from your 66th birthday.

Pension age

Pension age for men and women has been the same since November 2018.

From December 2018, the pension age for men and women increased by one month every two months, reaching 66 by October 2020. Between 2026 and 2028 it will rise to 67.[9] A person born after 5 October 1954 but before 6 April 1960 will reach pension age at 66. A person born between 6 April 1960 and 5 March 1961 will reach pension age at up to 66 years and 11 months, depending on her/his date of birth. Someone born after 5 March 1961 but before 6 April 1977 will reach pension age at 67.[10] The government announced an increase in pension age to 68 will take place between 2037 and 2039. Men and women born after 5 April 1977 are affected.[11]

You can check when you will reach pension age using the official calculator at gov.uk/ state-pension-age.

5

3. **People included in the claim**

You claim state pension for yourself. You do not get an increase in your state pension for an adult dependant or your child(ren).

If you are entitled to an 'old' retirement pension and already have an increase included for a child, you can continue to be paid the increase in certain circumstances. See Chapter 33 of the 2012/13 edition of this *Handbook* for details of who continues to qualify for an increase. You do not get the increase for your child if your partner's earnings are at or above the earnings limit. In 2022/23, this is £255 a week for the first child, increased by £34 for each subsequent child. If you qualify, you are paid £8 a week for the eldest child for whom child benefit is also paid, and £11.35 a week for each subsequent child. Adult dependency increases were abolished from April 2020.

4. **The amount of benefit**

The full weekly rate of state pension is £185.15. In addition, you may receive a higher pension if you deferred your entitlement to state pension (see p764). Some people may receive a transitional rate of state pension that is higher than £185.15 (see p768). You can request a statement estimating your state pension entitlement from the Future Pension Centre by telephone on 0800 731 0175 (textphone: 0800 731 0176), by writing to the Pension Service or at gov.uk/check-state-pension.

You are not entitled to any increase in state pension for an adult or child dependant.

The amount of 'old' retirement pensions

If you reached pension age before 6 April 2016, you cannot get state pension but may instead be entitled to an 'old' retirement pension.

Category A retirement pension is paid at a weekly rate of £141.85.

Category B retirement pension for a spouse or civil partner is paid at a weekly rate of £85.

Category B retirement pension for a widow, widower or surviving civil partner is paid at a weekly rate of £141.85.

Category D retirement pension is paid at a weekly rate of £85.

The above amounts are the full rates. If you have not paid or been credited with sufficient national insurance (NI) contributions to qualify for the full rate, you get a reduced rate.

If you receive one of these retirement pensions, you receive an age addition of 25 pence a week if you are over 80.

Depending on which pension you are entitled to, you may also receive:

– graduated retirement benefit, based on earnings between 1961 and 1975;
– an additional state pension, based on earnings after 5 April 1978;
– a higher pension if entitlement was deferred;
– an amount equivalent to the age-related addition to long-term incapacity benefit if you were receiving this within eight weeks of reaching pension age (see p766). If you have an additional state pension, this amount is offset against it;
– an increase for a child (see p766).

See Chapter 36 of the 2015/16 edition of this *Handbook* for full details of when you may be entitled to these additional amounts.

State pension is an individual pension based solely on your own contributions (except in the circumstances described on p768) – ie, you cannot count the contributions of your spouse or civil partner towards your pension. State pension is based on your starting amount for contributions before 2016/17 and, if necessary to increase your payment, NI contributions from 2016/17 onwards. If your spouse or civil partner reached pension age before 6 April 2016, s/he may be entitled to an 'old' retirement pension based on your NI contributions up to 5 April 2016.

If you do not have the required qualifying years (see p964) for the full rate of state pension, you get a reduced rate. This is calculated by multiplying 1/35th of the full rate by the number of qualifying years (which must be at least 10 to receive any state pension).[12] For example, if you have 17 qualifying years, you receive a state pension of £89.93 a week (17 x £185.15/35). Only people whose qualifying years are all from 2016/17 onwards have their state pension calculated this way.

For many years, people are likely to have a mix of contributions made before and after 6 April 2016. NI contributions and credits for years before 6 April 2016 count towards your state pension. There are transitional rules that aim to ensure that anyone reaching pension age after this date receives at least the same level of entitlement as they would have done under the 'old' retirement pension scheme based on their own NI contributions.

There are transitional provisions for:

- people who have paid, been treated as having paid, or been credited with contributions for tax years before the introduction of state pension (see below); *and*
- women who, before 1977, elected to pay a reduced rate of contributions (see p769); *and*
- inheriting entitlement from a late spouse or civil partner who had made contributions for tax years before the introduction of state pension (see p769).

5 Transitional rate of state pension

If you have qualifying years (see p964) before 6 April 2016, the amount of your state pension is worked out to ensure that your 'starting amount' is at least as much as you would have received under the 'old' retirement pension rules.[13] You must have at least 10 qualifying years to receive a transitional rate of state pension.[14]

Your 'starting amount' is the higher of:

- your entitlement to 'old' retirement pension. This takes account of your entitlement to basic category A retirement pension, additional pension and graduated retirement benefit. See Chapter 36 of the 2015/16 edition of this *Handbook*; *and*
- your entitlement under the new state pension rules as if they had applied throughout your working life.

In each case, a deduction is made if you were contracted out from the additional state pension scheme.

If you are entitled to a substantial amount of additional pension, your starting amount may be higher than the full rate of state pension. If so, the difference between your starting amount and the full rate is called your 'protected payment'. Your protected payment is paid on top of your full state pension and is increased each year in line with inflation. Your transitional rate of state pension up to the level of the full state pension is increased each year at the same rate as the state pension.[15] Any further qualifying years you have do not add more to your state pension.

If your starting amount is lower than the full state pension, you can add additional qualifying years up to the amount needed to qualify for a full-rate state pension or until you reach pension age, whichever is first. You may wish to do this even if you already have more than 35 qualifying years – eg, if, despite having more than 35 qualifying years, you do not qualify for the full rate because a deduction has been applied to reflect contracting out.[16] You may be able to pay NI contributions to fill in gaps in your record (see Chapter 43). Each qualifying year on your NI record adds 1/35th of the full amount (about £5.29 a week) to your state pension.

Women who paid reduced-rate contributions

Before 1977, married women and widows could opt out of gaining entitlement to retirement pension in their own right by electing to pay reduced-rate NI contributions (see Chapter 43). Their entitlement to retirement pension was based on the contributions of their spouse.

State pension is based on an individual's own contribution record, but there are special transitional rules for women who reach pension age on or after 6 April 2016 and who have paid reduced-rate contributions. These apply if you still had the right to pay reduced-rate NI contributions at the start of the period of 35 years ending in the tax year before you reach pension age – ie, if you reached pension age in May 2016, you had a 'reduced-rate election' in force at the beginning of the 1981/82 tax year.

If you have any qualifying years from having paid or been credited with sufficient NI contributions in some tax years before 2016/17, there is an alternative calculation if this would be more beneficial than the transitional rate to which you would otherwise be entitled. This is at least equivalent to the combination of:[17]

- the standard rate of basic 'old' retirement pension based on the NI contributions of a spouse or civil partner (£85 if you are married or in a civil partnership and your spouse or civil partner has also reached state pension age, or £141.85 if you are widowed, divorced or if your civil partnership is dissolved); *and*
- any additional pension to which you are entitled based on your own contribution record.

If you have no qualifying years from before 6 April 2016, you receive a transitional rate of state pension equivalent to the full category B retirement pension if both you and your spouse have reached pension age, or to the full category A retirement pension if you are no longer married or in a civil partnership.[18]

Note: the DWP is contacting some married women, widows and women aged over 80 who were underpaid state pension. See gov.uk/government/publications/ state-pension-underpayments-progress-on-cases-reviewed-to-30-september-2021 for more information.

Widows, widowers and surviving civil partners

If you reach pension age on or after 6 April 2016, there are transitional rules that may allow you to qualify for an amount of state pension (known as a 'survivor's inherited state pension') based on the additional pension that your late spouse or civil partner would have been entitled to under the 'old' retirement pension scheme. This only applies if you were married or in a civil partnership before 6 April 2016 and your spouse or civil partner died while you were married or civil partners. If you were under pension age when s/he died and you remarry or enter a new civil partnership before you reach pension age, you do not qualify.[19]

If your spouse or civil partner reached pension age, or died below pension age, before 6 April 2016, you may be entitled to an inherited amount based on the amount of additional pension you would have been entitled to under the 'old' category B retirement pension rules.[20]

You may be entitled to an inherited amount of half of the difference between your spouse or civil partner's transitional rate and the full rate of state pension, if:[21]

- s/he reached pension age, or died below pension age, on or after 6 April 2016; *and*
- s/he was entitled to the transitional rate of state pension immediately before s/he died (or would have been if s/he had reached pension age before s/he died or on the same day as you reached pension age); *and*
- her/his transitional rate was, or would have been, more than the full rate of state pension.

Your survivor's pension is paid in addition to any state pension or transitional rate of state pension (including one paid to women who elected to pay reduced-rate NI contributions – see p769).

You do not lose this amount if you marry or form a civil partnership again after reaching pension age. However, as this new marriage or civil partnership takes place after 6 April 2016, you cannot get an inherited amount from your new spouse/civil partner if s/he subsequently dies, even if this would have been a higher amount.

Note: if you reached pension age before 6 April 2016 and your spouse or civil partner dies after this date, you may still be able to qualify for a category B retirement pension based on her/his contributions in the tax years before the tax year beginning 6 April 2016. See Chapter 36 of the 2015/16 edition of this *Handbook* for more details. This applies whether or not s/he reached pension age before 6 April 2016.

For how your entitlement to bereavement benefits affects entitlement to state pension, see Chapter 25.

Inheriting a deferred 'old' retirement pension

You may inherit an amount of state pension equivalent to an inherited deferred amount of 'old' retirement pension if:[22]

- your spouse or civil partner reached pension age before 6 April 2016; *and*
- s/he had either claimed her/his 'old' retirement pension and was receiving a weekly increase from having deferred it, or was still deferring her/his 'old' retirement pension when s/he died; *and*

- at the time of her/his death you were over pension age or, if you were under pension age, you had not remarried or entered a new civil partnership before reaching pension age.

If your spouse or civil partner was deferring her/his 'old' retirement pension when s/he died and had deferred it for at least 12 months, you can choose to claim this amount as a lump sum or as a weekly state pension (a 'widowed person's or surviving civil partner's lump sum or pension'). If you do not make a choice within three months of being notified by the DWP of your right to do so (or a longer period if the DWP allows this), you are paid a lump sum. In certain circumstances, you can change your mind, provided you do so within three months of making a choice.[23] If your spouse or civil partner was already getting her/his 'old' retirement pension or s/he had deferred it for less than 12 months, you receive the inherited deferral payment as an extra weekly amount.

These rules mean that you have the same options as you would have had under the old retirement pension system, so it applies regardless of when you reach pension age.

Inherited graduated retirement benefit

You may be entitled to an amount of inherited survivor's state pension based on the graduated retirement benefit entitlement of your late spouse or civil partner. This is based on graduated contributions s/he may have paid between 1961 and 1975. You have the option of choosing a lump sum or a weekly amount if s/he had deferred her/his entitlement to graduated retirement benefit for at least 12 months at the time of her/his death.[24]

5. Special benefit rules

Special rules may apply to:
- people who have come from or are going abroad (see below);
- people in prison or detention (see Chapter 42).

People coming from or going abroad

If you have lived elsewhere than the UK during your working life, your state pension may be affected – eg, it may be paid at a reduced rate. However, there are reciprocal arrangements with many countries that may help you qualify for a full pension. If you have worked in a European Economic Area (EEA) state, you may benefit from the European Union (EU) co-ordination rules (see Chapter 71). If you are covered by these, your employment in an EEA state and contributions paid there can count towards your overall national insurance contribution record used to determine your entitlement to state pension (see p1659). If you are not covered by the EU co-ordination rules, you may be able to benefit from a reciprocal agreement or an association or co-operation agreement (see p1546).

If you go to live abroad, your pension can be paid in any other country. However, unless you move to live in an EEA state, Switzerland, Gibraltar or a country with which the UK has a reciprocal agreement for pensions, you are not entitled to uprating increases, so the amount of pension you receive is frozen at the rate at which it was paid when you went abroad. Similarly, if you claim a deferred pension abroad, the uprating increases that occurred while you were abroad are ignored when calculating both the deferral increase and rate payable.[25]

6. **Claims and backdating**

The general rules about claims and backdating are covered in Chapter 50. This section explains the specific rules that apply to state pension.

Making a claim

You must usually make a claim for state pension (but see below if you are a widow). You should get a letter no later than two months before you reach pension age, telling you to make a claim online or call for a claim form. If you do not receive this before reaching pension age, call the helpline.

A claim for state pension can be made:[26]
- online at gov.uk/get-state-pension;
- by telephone (0800 731 7898; textphone: 0800 731 7339; Relay UK and BSL relay services are available). You can ask for a claim form to be sent to you, or claim during the call; *or*
- in writing by completing the approved form. Send it to the Pension Service 8, Post Handling Site B, Wolverhampton WV98 1AF. You may be able to make your claim by taking or sending it to an alternative office (see p1134).

Keep a copy of your claim in case queries arise.

You must provide any information or evidence required (see p773). In certain circumstances, the DWP may accept a written application not on the approved form.[27] You can amend or withdraw your claim before a decision is made (see p1135). If there is a delay in making a claim, you may be able to get a short-term advance of benefit (see p1153).

Forms
Form BR1NSP is normally sent to you by the DWP about four months before you reach pension age. Otherwise, you can get it from the state pension claim line on 0800 731 7898 (textphone: 0800 731 7339).

If you are a widow

If you are a widow, you do not need to make a claim for state pension if either:[28]
- you are over 65 when you stop getting widowed mother's allowance; *or*
- you are getting a widow's pension immediately before your 65th birthday.

You must make a claim for state pension if you want to start receiving it before your widow's pension or widowed mother's allowance stops. If your widow's pension or widowed mother's allowance includes additional state pension, you receive this as an extra amount on top of your state pension, provided you do not remarry or form a new civil partnership before you reach pension age. If your state pension, plus any inherited amount, is less than your widow's pension or widowed mother's allowance, you are paid the difference until those benefits come to an end.

If you make a claim for state pension, your pension should be calculated under the rules (including the various transitional rules) as they apply to you. You do not need to identify and claim for the different elements that apply to you.[29]

Who should claim

You must normally claim state pension on your own behalf. However, if you are unable to manage your own affairs, another person can claim state pension for you as your 'appointee' (see p1135).

Information to support your claim

For the general information requirements that apply to all benefits, see p1136.

It is important to provide any information required when you claim. Until you do, you may not count as having made a valid claim (see p1138). Correct any defects as soon as possible or your date of claim may be affected.

When you claim state pension, you must prove you have reached pension age. For most people, it is sufficient to produce your birth certificate, but problems can occur if you were born in a country which did not have a formal system of registering births. Other evidence that can prove your birth date includes:
- passport or identity card; *or*
- school or health records; *or*
- army records; *or*
- statements from people who know you.

Even if you have provided all that was required when you claimed, you may be asked to provide further information to support your claim (see p1140). You may also be asked to provide information after you are awarded state pension and if you fail to do so, your state pension could be suspended, or even terminated (see p1162).

The date of your claim

The date of your claim is important as it determines when your entitlement to state pension starts. This is not necessarily the date from when you are paid. For information about when payment of state pension starts, see p775.

The **'date of your claim'** is the date your written or online claim, properly completed with all the required evidence and information, is received at the Pension Service or other designated office.

You must make sure your claim is valid. If it is not, you are given a short time to correct the defects (see p1138). Your claim is then treated as having been made when you initially claimed.[30]

In some cases, you can claim in advance (see p775) and in some cases your claim can be backdated (see below). If you want this to be done, make this clear when you claim or the DWP might not consider it. If you claimed the wrong benefit when you should have claimed state pension, see below.

Backdating your claim

It is very important to claim in time, because the maximum period for backdating is 12 months. You cannot backdate your claim for any period before the date you would have first become entitled to state pension.[31] You do not have to show any reason why your claim is late. The rules on backdating are covered on p1142.

If you claim more than 12 months after you became entitled to state pension, you are treated as having deferred your entitlement. You can still request that your claim is backdated but you should consider the impact on your deferral amount when requesting backdating. If you backdate your claim, it reduces the amount of time you deferred claiming your pension, which reduces the amount of your weekly increase. Weigh up the financial implications of your options when considering backdating – if necessary, get advice.

If you might have qualified for state pension earlier but did not claim because you were given the wrong information or were misled by the DWP, you could ask for compensation (see p1403) or complain to the Ombudsman (see p1408).

If you claim the wrong benefit

If you have claimed the wrong benefit, in certain circumstances it is possible for your claim to be interchanged with another benefit.[32] For state pension, this interchange is only possible with bereavement allowance. If you make a claim for state pension, your pension should be calculated under the rules (including the various transitional rules) as they apply to you. You do not need to identify and claim for the different elements that apply to you. If you claim state pension on the wrong form (eg, you complete a claim form for 'old' retirement pension), it is likely to be treated as a valid claim if the form is properly completed.[33]

Claiming in advance

Claims for state pension (including a claim where you have deferred your entitlement – see p764) can be made up to, but no more than, four months in advance.[34] You should take advantage of this, as it can take a long time to sort out your contribution record. The date of your claim is the date on which you qualify.

7. **Getting paid**

The general rules on getting paid are covered in Chapter 51. This section explains the specific rules that apply to state pension. **Note:** rules on payment of 'old' retirement pension are very similar to rules on payment of state pension. See p781 of the 2015/16 edition of this *Handbook*.

When is state pension paid?

The day you are paid depends on your national insurance number (see p1150).[35] State pension is normally paid weekly, fortnightly or four-weekly in arrears. It can be paid every 13 weeks if you agree, or at longer intervals of up to a year if the DWP directs and you are entitled to less than £5 a week.[36]

State pension is payable from the date on which you reach pension age. If this is a day other than your payday, part-week payments are made.

Note:

- Deductions can be made from your state pension to pay third parties (see p1164).
- Even if you have been sanctioned for a benefit offence (see p1239), you must be paid your state pension.
- For information on missing payments, see p1150. If you cannot get your pension payments because you have lost your bank card or have forgotten your PIN, see p1149. If your payment service card has been lost or stolen, see p1150.
- If payment of your state pension is delayed, see p1255. If you are waiting for a decision on your claim, or to be paid, you may be able to get a short-term advance (see p1153). If you wish to complain about how your claim has been dealt with, or claim compensation, see Chapter 61.
- If payment of your state pension is suspended, see p1161.
- If you are overpaid state pension, you may have to repay it (see Chapter 53) and, in some circumstances, you may have to pay a penalty (see p1229). If you have been accused of fraud, see Chapter 54.
- If you are owed arrears of state pension, these can be paid in instalments (see p1148).

Change of circumstances

You must report changes in your circumstances that you have been told you must report, as well as any that you might reasonably be expected to know might affect your right to, the amount of, or the payment of, your state pension. You should do this as soon as possible, preferably in writing. See p1160 for further information.

8. **Tax, other benefits and the benefit cap**

Tax

State pension (and 'old' retirement pension) is taxable.[37] This includes inheritable lump-sum payments of deferred 'old' retirement pension and graduated retirement benefit.[38]

Means-tested benefits and tax credits

State pension (and 'old' retirement pension) is taken fully into account for the purposes of means-tested benefits, but pensioners receive a higher rate of some means-tested benefits. They are partially taken into account as income for tax credits (see Chapter 63).

You may qualify for pension credit to top up your state pension income (see p257).

Non-means-tested benefits

State pension (and 'old' retirement pension) is affected by the overlapping benefit rules (see p1151).

The benefit cap

In some cases, there is a limit on the total amount of specified benefits you can receive (a 'benefit cap'). State pension (and 'old' retirement pension) is *not* a specified benefit.[39] The benefit cap only applies if you are getting universal credit or housing benefit (HB). If you are getting HB, the benefit cap normally only applies if you are below pension age. See p1156 for further information.

Passports and other sources of help

You qualify for a Christmas bonus (see p861) if you receive state pension (or 'old' retirement pension).[40] People aged 60 or over qualify for free prescriptions and eye tests regardless of their income. You may be able to get a winter fuel payment from the social fund (see Chapter 37). If you are on a low income, you may be entitled to council tax reduction (see p836).

Notes

1. **Who can get state pension**
   1 s2(1)-(3) PA 2014; reg 13(1) SP Regs
   2 Reg 7 SP Regs
   3 Reg 8 SP Regs
   4 Reg 9 SP Regs
   5 s17(4) PA 2014; reg 10 SP Regs
   6 s17(2) PA 2014
   7 Reg 12A SP Regs
   8 Regs 11 and 12 SP Regs

2. **The rules about your age**
   9 s126 and Sch 4 PA 1995; s26 PA 2014
   10 Memo DMG 18/14
   11 'New timetable for state pension
   changes to maintain fair and sustainable
   pension', DWP press release, 19 July
   2017; 'Second state pension age review
   launches', DWP press release, 14
   December 2021

4. **The amount of benefit**
   12 s3(2) PA 2014
   13 s5 and Sch 1 PA 2014
   14 s4 PA 2014; reg 13(2) SP Regs
   15 Sch 2 PA 2014; ss148AC and 151A SSAA
   1992
   16 PA 2014, Explanatory Notes, para 61
   17 s11 and Sch 6 PA 2014
   18 s12 and Sch 7 PA 2014
   19 s7 and Schs 3 and 4 PA 2014
   20 Sch 3 paras 2-4 PA 2014
   21 Sch 3 paras 5-8 PA 2014
   22 s8 PA 2014
   23 ss8 and 9 PA 2014; regs 4-6 SP Regs
   24 s10 PA 2014; regs 15-20 SP Regs

5. **Special benefit rules**
   25 ss18(3) and 20 PA 2014; s179 SSAA
   1992; regs 21-23 SP Regs

6. **Claims and backdating**
   26 Regs 4 and 4ZC SS(C&P) Regs
   27 Reg 4(1) SS(C&P) Regs
   28 Reg 3(d) SS(C&P) Regs
   29 Reg 3(ja) SS(C&P) Regs
   30 Reg 6(1)(b) SS(C&P) Regs
   31 Reg 19(1) and Sch 4 SS(C&P) Regs
   32 Reg 9(1) and Sch 1 SS(C&P) Regs
   33 Reg 4(1) SS(C&P) Regs
   34 Regs 15 and 15B(2) SS(C&P) Regs

7. **Getting paid**
   35 Reg 22CA(4) SS(C&P) Regs
   36 Reg 22CA(2) and (3) SS(C&P) Regs

8. **Tax, other benefits and the benefit cap**
   37 s577(2)(za) IT(EP)A 2003
   38 s8(4B) Finance (No.2) Act 2005
   39 s96(11)(za) WRA 2012
   40 s150(2) SSCBA 1992

5

Chapter 37

....

Social fund payments

This chapter covers:
1. Budgeting loans (below)
2. Sure Start maternity grants (p782)
3. Funeral expenses payments (p784)
4. Cold weather payments (p791)
5. Winter fuel payments (p792)
6. Tax, other benefits and the benefit cap (p794)

Key facts
- The social fund provides one-off loans and payments for specific expenses or circumstances.
- **Budgeting loans** are interest-free loans. **Sure Start maternity grants, funeral expenses payments, cold weather payments and winter fuel payments** are non-repayable.
- Social fund loans and payments are administered and paid by the DWP.
- If you disagree with a budgeting loan decision, there is an internal review system and then a further review to the Independent Case Examiner.
- If you disagree with a decision on a Sure Start maternity grant, funeral expenses payment, cold weather payment or winter fuel payment, you can apply for a revision (see Chapter 56) or appeal against it (see Chapter 57). You must apply for a mandatory reconsideration before you can appeal.

1. Budgeting loans

Budgeting loans are available in England, Wales and Scotland. To be eligible, you must satisfy all the following conditions. **Note:** if you come under the universal credit (UC) system (see p22), you cannot apply for a budgeting loan and must apply for a budgeting advance of your UC payments instead (see p51).

- **You must be in receipt of a 'qualifying benefit'** when your budgeting loan application is determined.[1] Qualifying benefits are: income support (IS), income-based jobseeker's allowance (JSA), income-related employment and support allowance (ESA) and pension credit (PC) (guarantee or savings credit). Payments on account and hardship payments are included. You are treated as being in receipt of a qualifying benefit if it is being paid to you, or to an appointee on your behalf. You are eligible if you receive a backdated award of a qualifying benefit, covering the date your application is determined. **Note:** you are not 'in receipt of' a qualifying benefit if your partner or another member of your family is the claimant.[2] If you are a member of a 'joint-claim couple' for JSA, you are only eligible for a budgeting loan if you are the partner being paid JSA.

- **You and/or your partner, between you, must have been receiving a qualifying benefit throughout the 26 weeks before the date on which your application is determined**, disregarding any number of breaks of 28 days or less.[3] If you are in receipt of PC, any time when you were in receipt of UC can count when calculating the 26 weeks and any breaks of up to one calendar month are ignored. A period covered by a payment of arrears should count, as should any benefit received while in Northern Ireland. The waiting days at the start of a claim for JSA or ESA (see p704 and p646) do not count. More than one partner could help you satisfy the qualifying period.

- **You must not have too much capital.**[4] Any budgeting loan award is reduced by the amount of capital you have in excess of £1,000 (£2,000 if you or your partner are aged 63 or over). Capital is calculated as for the qualifying benefit that you are receiving (see Chapters 22 and 23). Payments made from the Family Fund to you, your partner or child, and refugee integration loans are ignored. Capital held by your child(ren) should be disregarded.

- **You, or your partner, must not be involved in a trade dispute** (see p982).[5]

- **You must not be a 'person subject to immigration control'** (there are exceptions to this rule) – see p1524.

- **The loan must be for one or more of the following categories of allowable expenses**, the need for which occurs in the UK:[6]
  - furniture and household equipment;
  - clothing and footwear;
  - maternity expenses;
  - funeral expenses;
  - rent in advance and/or removal expenses to secure accommodation;
  - improvement, maintenance and security of the home;
  - travelling expenses;
  - expenses associated with seeking or re-entering work;
  - hire purchase and other debts for any of the above items.

  You are required to tick the category of expense for which you need the loan on the application form. You do not have to specify the particular items you need – eg, a bed or a winter coat.

- **The loan must be a minimum of £100.**[7] You must state how much you are asking for on your application form. You cannot be awarded more than the maximum amount.

- **You must be likely to be able to repay the loan** (see p781).[8]

The maximum amount you can be awarded is:
- £348 if you are a single person; *or*
- £464 if you have a partner; *or*
- £812 if you or your partner claim child benefit.

You may get less, depending on the amount you requested and the capital rules. Any loan may also be reduced by the amount of any other social fund debt you or your partner have. You cannot be liable to repay more than £1,500 in total.

Applying and getting paid

Apply online at gov.uk/budgeting-help-benefits, or in writing on Form SF500, available from gov.uk or your local job centre, or in any other written form accepted by the Secretary of State. An application can be made on your behalf by your appointee, or by another person, provided you give your written consent.[9]

If you apply by post, you should receive a written decision within 21 days. If you apply online, you can choose to receive the decision by text or email, which should be received within seven days. If you take this option, you can accept the loan online and payment will be made more quickly.

Your application is treated as having been made on the day it is received by the DWP.[10] If your application was incomplete and you comply with a request for additional information, it is treated as having been made on the day it was originally received.

Loans are generally paid in the same way as your qualifying benefit.

Challenging a decision

You should receive a written decision within seven days (if you applied online) or 21 days (if you applied by post), with an explanation if it has been refused or partly refused, together with a notification of your right to request a review.

If you want to challenge the decision, you can ask for a review which is carried out by a different decision maker. However, a decision is only likely to be changed if it was based on incorrect information about your circumstances, or if the amount you are allowed to borrow has increased.

You must apply for a review of a decision by writing to the office where the decision was made within 28 days of the date the decision was issued to you.[11] Your application must include your grounds for requesting a review.[12] If someone is making an application on your behalf, it must be accompanied by your written permission (unless the person is your appointee – see p1135).[13]

Late applications can be accepted for 'special reasons'.[14] Special reasons are not defined, but if you cannot apply in time, it may be quicker to submit a new application.

If a decision is not wholly revised in your favour, the reviewing officer must either telephone or write to you to explain why and ask further questions if necessary.

If you are still unhappy with the decision, you can ask the Independent Case Examiner (see p1404) to carry out a second-tier review.[15] Do this in writing within 28 days, although the time limit may be extended if there are special reasons.

Repayments

All loans must be repaid to the DWP.[16]

The decision maker may give you more than one option for repaying a loan, depending on whether you have any other outstanding social fund loans and your other financial commitments. S/he may offer an option of a higher loan with an increased repayment rate, but you cannot be asked to repay at a rate higher than 20 per cent of your IS, income-based JSA or income-related ESA applicable amount or PC appropriate minimum guarantee plus any child tax credit or child benefit you receive. The loan must be repaid within 104 weeks.

The details of the loan offer and repayment terms are included in the decision. You have 14 days from the date the decision was sent to return the declaration agreeing to one of the offers made to you. This time limit can be extended for 'special reasons'.[17]

Methods of repayment

Budgeting loans are usually recovered by direct deductions from your benefit, although you can make a payment at any time to pay off all, or part, of the debt. Deductions can only be made from the following benefits:[18]

- bereavement benefits (except bereavement support payment);
- carer's allowance;
- disablement benefit, reduced earnings allowance and industrial death benefit;
- ESA (contributory or income-related);
- incapacity benefit;
- IS;
- JSA;
- maternity allowance;
- PC;
- retirement pensions;
- severe disablement allowance;
- UC.

A loan can be recovered from:[19]

- you (the applicant) or the person who the loan was for;
- your partner, if you are living together as a couple (see p303);
- a person who is liable to maintain either the person who made the application or the person on whose behalf it was made.

Part 5: Other benefits
Chapter 37: Social fund payments
2. Sure Start maternity grants

Rescheduling repayment terms

You cannot request a review of a decision relating to repayment terms or recovery. If you have accepted a loan, however, and the repayment terms are causing hardship (eg, because your financial situation has deteriorated), you can ask the DWP to reschedule the loan so that the weekly repayment rate is reduced.

2. **Sure Start maternity grants**

Sure Start maternity grants are available in England and Wales. If you live in Scotland, you may qualify for a Best Start grant (see Chapter 74).

You qualify for a Sure Start maternity grant if you satisfy all the following conditions.

- **You or your partner have been awarded one of the following qualifying benefits** (including payments on account and hardship payments) in respect of the day you claim a maternity grant:[20]
  - universal credit;
  - income support (IS);
  - income-based jobseeker's allowance;
  - income-related employment and support allowance;
  - child tax credit, which includes a child, disabled child or severely disabled child element (see p1414);
  - working tax credit, including the disabled worker or severe disability element (see p1420);
  - pension credit (guarantee or savings credit).

  You are treated as receiving one of these benefits if you are entitled to a DWP loan for help with your mortgage interest (see p839), even if you are not actually entitled to the benefit. You are eligible if you receive a backdated award of a qualifying benefit covering the date you claim a maternity grant. If you are waiting for a decision on a claim for a qualifying benefit, the DWP may defer making a decision on your maternity grant claim until the qualifying benefit claim has been decided. If your maternity grant claim is refused while you are waiting for a decision on a qualifying benefit, you should reclaim a maternity grant within three months of being awarded the qualifying benefit. **Note:** if you do not claim a maternity grant within the time limits (see p784), a backdated award of a qualifying benefit does not qualify you for a grant. If you are not entitled to a qualifying benefit in your own right because you are under 16 (or under 20 and in 'relevant education' – see p873), a member of your family can claim a maternity grant for you if s/he is getting a qualifying benefit in respect of you.

- **You live in England or Wales.**[21]
- **One of the following applies:**[22]

- you or a member of your family are pregnant or have given birth in the last six months (including stillbirth after 24 weeks of pregnancy);
- you are the parent (but not the mother and not the mother's partner) of a child who is less than 12 months old, or you are responsible for that parent, and you are responsible for the child;
- you are the guardian of a child who is less than 12 months old;
- you or your partner have a child who is less than 12 months old placed with you for adoption and you are responsible for the child;
- you have adopted a child who is less than 12 months old under a recognised adoption which takes place outside the UK;
- you or your partner have been granted a child arrangements order, parental order (following a surrogate pregnancy) or adoption order for a child who is less than 12 months old.

In the last five cases, you are entitled to a payment even if one has already been made to the birth mother or a member of her family.[23]

- **There is no other member of your family who is under 16 at the time of claim** (excluding any child you adopted or became responsible for as a kinship carer or foster carer, provided s/he was over 12 months old when you became responsible for her/him). However, a grant can be awarded for each child of a multiple birth, but the number of grants is reduced if there are other children in the family who are under 16. For example, if you give birth to triplets and already have one or more children under 16 in the family (and none of them are multiple births) two grants are awarded, or if you already have twins you are awarded one grant. If you are under 20 and another member of your family claims for you, the grant is payable, provided you do not have other children under 16.[24] If you are a refugee, you can be entitled in respect of your first child born in the UK, even if you have another child or children from before you came to the UK.[25]
- **You or your partner are not involved in a trade dispute** (see p982), unless specified circumstances apply.[26]
- **You claim within the time limits** (see p784).
- **You have received advice from a healthcare professional** (see p784).[27]
- **You are not a 'person subject to immigration control'** (there are exceptions to this rule) – see p1524.

The terms 'partner' and 'family' in the above rules have almost the same meanings as they do for IS purposes (see Chapter 16).[28]

The amount

You are entitled to a grant of £500 for each qualifying child or expected qualifying child.[29] The payment is not affected by any capital you have and is not repayable.

Part 5: Other benefits
Chapter 37: Social fund payments
3. Funeral expenses payments

Claiming and getting paid

Claim on Form SF100, which you can get from your local Jobcentre Plus office or from gov.uk or by telephone (0800 169 0140). At the time of writing, it is not possible to submit an online claim for a maternity grant through gov.uk, although it was expected that this method of claiming is going to be introduced. Check gov.uk/sure-start-maternity-grant/how-to-claim for updates.

There are strict time limits for claiming. You can claim a maternity grant at any time from 11 weeks before the first day of your expected week of childbirth until six months after the actual date of the birth. If you adopt a child, have a child arrangements order for a child or have a child by a surrogate mother, you can claim up to six months following the date of the adoption, child arrangements order or parental order, provided the child is under 12 months when the claim is made. You cannot make a successful claim outside these time limits.[30]

The back of your claim form must be signed by a healthcare professional (eg, a midwife, health visitor or doctor) to confirm that you have received health and welfare advice about your baby or your maternal health. If you are close to the deadline, you can send the form without this being signed and get a statement at a later date.

Your date of claim is normally the date your form is received by the DWP.[31] If you make a written claim in some other way, you should be sent the appropriate form to complete. If you return it within one month, or a longer period if the DWP considers this reasonable, your date of claim is the date the DWP received your initial application.[32] See p782 for when your claim can be backdated if you are subsequently awarded a qualifying benefit.

If you are overpaid a maternity grant, you may have to repay it (see Chapter 53) and, in some circumstances, you may have to pay a penalty (see p1229).

---

3. Funeral expenses payments

Funeral expenses payments are available in England and Wales. If you live in Scotland, you may qualify for a funeral support payment (see Chapter 76).

You qualify for a funeral expenses payment if you satisfy all the following conditions.

- **You or your partner have been awarded one of the following qualifying benefits** (including payments on account and hardship payments) in respect of the day you claim a funeral expenses payment:[33]
  - universal credit;
  - income support (IS);
  - income-based jobseeker's allowance;
  - income-related employment and support allowance;
  - housing benefit (HB);

- child tax credit, which includes a child, disabled child or severely disabled child element (see p1414);
- working tax credit, which includes the disabled worker or severe disability element (see p1419);
- pension credit (guarantee or savings credit).

You are treated as receiving one of these benefits if you are entitled to a DWP loan for help with your mortgage interest (see p839), even if you are not actually entitled to the benefit. You are eligible if you receive a backdated award of a qualifying benefit which covers the date you claim a funeral expenses payment. If you are waiting for a decision on a claim for a qualifying benefit, the DWP may defer making a decision on a claim for a funeral expenses payment until the qualifying benefit claim has been decided. If your claim for a funeral expenses payment is refused while you are waiting for a decision on a qualifying benefit claim, reclaim within three months of being awarded the qualifying benefit. **Note:** if you do not claim a funeral expenses payment within the time limit, a backdated award of a qualifying benefit does not qualify you for a grant.

- **You live in England or Wales.**[34]
- **You or your partner are in one of the categories of eligible people** listed below who can be treated as responsible for the funeral expenses.
- **You or your partner accept responsibility for funeral expenses** (see p788).[35] If you are claiming as a 'close relative' or 'close friend', it must also be reasonable for you to accept responsibility.
- **The funeral takes place in the UK**[36] – see p788 for exceptions for European Economic Area (EEA) nationals.[37]
- **A social fund funeral payment has not already been made in respect of the person who has died** (but the amount of a previous award can be revised up to the maximum allowed under the rules).[38]
- **The person who died was 'ordinarily resident' in the UK** (see p1550).[39]
- **You are not a 'person subject to immigration control'** (there are exceptions to this rule) – see p1524.
- **You claim within the time limits** (see p790).

In addition in England, there is a **children's funeral fund payment**.[40] This is available for the funeral of a child aged under 18 or a stillborn child born after the 24th week of pregnancy. The payment covers 'reasonable' burial or cremation fees and 'reasonable' associated expenses, including a coffin or casket, but not costs exclusively related to religious requirements. The payment is available for all such funerals, and does not depend on low income, entitlement to benefit or on satisfying residence conditions. No children's funeral fund payment can be made if a funeral expenses payment has already been paid to cover the same items. In most cases, the application is made by the person providing the funeral – eg, the funeral director. In Wales, there is a £500 payment towards the cost of a

Part 5: Other benefits
Chapter 37: Social fund payments
3. Funeral expenses payments

child's funeral (also local and community council burial and cremation fees for children under the age of 18 are waived). This is understood to be in addition to the funeral expenses payment from the social fund.

Eligible people

You are only eligible for a funeral expenses payment if you or your partner are in one of the following groups of people who can be treated as responsible for the funeral costs.[41]

- You were the 'partner' of the person when s/he died.
- The deceased was a 'child' for whom you were responsible when s/he died and there is no 'absent parent', or there is an absent parent but s/he (or her/his partner) was getting a qualifying benefit (see p784) when the child died. If there is an absent parent who was not getting a qualifying benefit when the child died, you may qualify for a payment as a close relative of the child. If the deceased was a stillborn child, you are eligible for a funeral expenses payment if you were the parent or the parent's partner – it does not matter whether there is an absent parent.
- You were a parent, son or daughter of the person who died and it is reasonable for you to accept responsibility for the funeral expenses (see p788), and you are not excluded by the rules on p787.
- You were a 'close relative' or a 'close friend' of the person who died and it is reasonable for you to accept responsibility for the funeral expenses (see p788), and you are not excluded by the rules on p787.

Definitions[42]

'**Child**' is defined as for IS purposes (see p307). You are 'responsible' for a child if you get, or could get, child benefit for her/him (see p309).

'**Stillborn child**' means a child born dead after 24 weeks of pregnancy.

'**Absent parent**' means a parent of a deceased child, where the child:
– was not living in that parent's household at the date of death; *and*
– was living with another person who was responsible for her/him.

'**Close relative**' means parent, parent-in-law, son, son-in-law, daughter, daughter-in-law, step-parent, stepson, stepson-in-law, stepdaughter, stepdaughter-in-law, brother, brother-in-law, sister, sister-in-law.

'**Close friend**' is not defined in the law. It can include a relative who is not a close relative – eg, a grandparent or grandchild.[43]

'**Partner**' has the same meaning as for IS (see p303). You also count as a partner, however, if you were living in a care home when the person died and:[44]
– you and your spouse or civil partner were living in the same home; *or*
– you were a member of a couple before one or both of you moved into the home.
This rule is designed to enable a surviving partner to claim a funeral expenses payment if one or both partners were in a home at the date of death.

Exclusion of certain close relatives and friends

If you claim as a close relative or close friend of the person who died (see p788), you cannot get a funeral expenses payment if:

- the person who died had a partner (unless that partner died before the funeral without making a claim for a funeral payment);[45] *or*
- the deceased was a child or stillborn child and a responsible person or parent is able to claim a funeral payment under the above rules;[46] *or*
- there is (other than you) a parent, son or daughter of the person who died, unless s/he is:[47]
  - under the age of 18; *or*
  - aged 18 or 19 and counts as a qualifying young person for child benefit purposes (see p563); *or*
  - getting (or her/his partner gets) a qualifying benefit (see p784); *or*
  - estranged from the deceased when s/he died ('estranged' is not defined); *or*
  - a student aged 18 on a full-time course of advanced education (see p874), or aged 19 to pension age on any full-time course; *or*
  - a member of a religious order which fully maintains her/him; *or*
  - a prisoner (including in youth custody or a remand centre) who (or whose partner) was getting a qualifying benefit immediately before being detained; *or*
  - resident in a care establishment and the costs are met in whole or in part by a local authority; *or*
  - an inpatient receiving free treatment in a hospital or similar institution and s/he (or her/his partner) received a qualifying benefit immediately before becoming a patient; *or*
  - an asylum seeker receiving asylum support from the Home Office or a local authority; *or*
  - ordinarily resident (see p1550) outside the UK; *or*
- there is a close relative of the deceased who was in *closer contact* with the deceased than you were, taking into account the nature and extent of such contact;[48] *or*
- there is a close relative of the deceased who was in *equally close contact* with the deceased as you were and who (or whose partner) is not getting a qualifying benefit (see p784).[49]

Note: the last two bullet points do not apply if the close relative was under the age of 18 when the person died, or was a student, member of a religious order, prisoner, inpatient or asylum seeker as set out above, or was ordinarily resident outside the UK.[50]

If you are refused a payment on this ground, the DWP (not you) must establish whether there is another close relative who is not getting a qualifying benefit.[51]

Part 5: Other benefits
Chapter 37: Social fund payments
3. Funeral expenses payments

Examples

Siobhan is not entitled to a funeral expenses payment because, although she looked after her brother for many years before he died, he had a son who is not getting a qualifying benefit (see p784). Although the son rarely saw his father, they were not estranged.

Micah is entitled to a funeral expenses payment when his close friend Felix dies because, although Felix had two surviving close relatives, a son and a sister-in-law, the son is getting HB and Micah was in closer contact with Felix than either of them were.

Accepting responsibility for funeral costs

To qualify for a funeral payment, you or your partner must 'accept responsibility' for funeral expenses.[52] This means you must be liable to pay the costs of a funeral, even if you do not make the arrangements.[53]

If the funeral director's account or contract is in your name, you should normally be treated as having accepted responsibility. If it is in someone else's name (or another person has paid the bill), you can still be 'responsible' if:

- s/he is acting as your agent – eg, because you are too distressed to act on your own behalf;[54] *or*
- s/he transfers liability to you, prior to full payment, with the consent of the funeral director.[55]

If you are a close relative (see p786) or close friend of the person who died, it must also be 'reasonable' for you to accept responsibility for the funeral expenses, in the light of the nature and extent of your contact with her/him.[56] In one case, it was held reasonable for a person to have accepted responsibility for his father's funeral even though he had not seen him for 24 years.[57]

European Economic Area nationals

Note: these rules only apply if you have protected rights from 1 January 2021 (see p1645).

You can get a funeral expenses payment for a funeral that takes place in any member state of the EEA or Switzerland (see p1644) if:[58]

- you are a 'worker' or self-employed, or you retain that status; *or*
- you are a member of the family of a worker – ie:
  - her/his spouse or civil partner; *or*
  - the worker's/spouse's/civil partner's child, grandchild or other descendant who is either under 21 or dependent; *or*
  - a dependent relative of the worker, spouse or civil partner in the ascending line – eg, a parent or grandparent; *or*
- you have a permanent right to reside in the UK.

If you have been refused a payment for a funeral that took place in an EEA state and you satisfied the above rules, you should ask for a revision (see p1265).

The amount

You are entitled to a payment that is sufficient to cover:[59]
- the necessary costs of purchasing a new burial plot and necessary burial fees, including any medical references or other required documents. The burial of ashes following cremation is not, however, covered; *and*
- the necessary cremation fees, including medical references, certificates and removing a pacemaker (restricted to £20 if not carried out by a doctor); *and*
- the costs of documentation necessary for the release of the assets of the person who died; *and*
- the reasonable cost of transport for the portion of journeys in excess of 80 kilometres (50 miles), undertaken to:
  - transport the body within the UK to a funeral director's premises or to a place of rest; *and*
  - transport the coffin and bearers in a hearse and the mourners in another vehicle from the funeral director's premises or place of rest to the funeral. The cost of this plus burial in an existing plot cannot exceed the cost of such transport plus the purchase and burial costs of a new plot;[60] *and*
- the necessary expenses of one return journey for the responsible person to arrange or attend the funeral. The maximum allowed is the cost of a return journey from home to where the burial or cremation costs are incurred; *and*
- up to £1,000 for any other funeral expenses – eg, funeral director's fees, religious costs, flowers and other transport costs.

Note:
- The cost of any items or services provided under a prepaid funeral plan or equivalent arrangement cannot be met. Expenses not covered by the plan can be met if they fall into the above categories, but the maximum allowed under the last category is restricted to £120.[61]
- Costs relating to religious requirements cannot be included in the amount allowed for burial and transport.[62]
- Where there is more than one ceremony for the deceased, a payment can only be awarded for the event that encompasses final disposal of the body.[63] Where a body has not been recovered, a payment can be made for a service that is equivalent to a burial or cremation.

If the amount awarded does not cover your funeral expenses, you may be able to claim a budgeting loan (see p778).

Part 5: Other benefits
Chapter 37: Social fund payments
3. Funeral expenses payments

Deductions from awards

The following are deducted from an award of a funeral expenses payment:[64]

- the assets of the person who died, which are available to you or a member of your family (defined as for IS purposes) without probate or letters of administration. However, if you have a joint account with the person who died, those assets become yours at the point of death and cannot be deducted.[65] Assets at the date of death count, even if you have spent or distributed them before your claim for a funeral payment.[66] However, arrears of most benefits and tax credits payable to the deceased at the date of death are excluded from the assets;[67]
- a lump sum legally due to you or a member of your family from an insurance policy, occupational pension scheme, burial club or equivalent source on the person's death;
- a funeral grant paid by the government for a war disablement pensioner;
- an amount paid or payable under a prepaid funeral plan or equivalent arrangement (whether or not the plan was fully paid).

Any capital you have apart from the above does not affect the amount of the funeral payment.

Claiming and getting paid

Claim on Form SF200, available from your local Jobcentre Plus office or from gov.uk or by telephone (Bereavement Service: 0800 731 0469; textphone 0800 731 0464; or the Social Fund helpline: 0800 169 0140; textphone 0800 169 286; Relay UK and BSL relay services are available). At the time of writing, it was not possible to submit an online claim for a funeral expenses payment through gov.uk, although it is expected that this method of claiming is going to be introduced. Check gov.uk/funeral-payments/how-to-claim for updates.

There are strict time limits for claiming. You can claim at any time from the date of death to up to six months after the date of the funeral.[68] There is no provision for late claims.

When completing the form, bear in mind the rules about accepting responsibility for the funeral expenses and your contact with the person who died.

Your date of claim is normally the date the form is received by the DWP or the date you make your telephone claim.[69] If you do not complete Form SF200 properly or apply in writing but not on the form, you should be sent the form to complete or correct. If you submit it within one month (or a longer period if the DWP considers this reasonable), your claim is treated as having been made on the date you originally applied.[70] See p785 for when your claim can be backdated if you are subsequently awarded a qualifying benefit.

Payment is normally made direct to the funeral director, unless you have already paid the bill.[71]

If you are overpaid a funeral expenses payment, you may have to repay it (see Chapter 53) and, in some circumstances, you may have to pay a penalty (see p1229). However, see below for recovery from the estate of the person who died.

Recovery from the estate

The DWP is entitled to recover funeral expenses payments from the estate of the person who died and usually attempts to do so.[72] Funeral expenses are a first charge on the estate and have priority over anything else (although there may be insufficient assets for full repayment).[73]

4. Cold weather payments

Cold weather payments are available in England, Wales and Scotland. **Note:** it is expected that cold weather payments will be replaced by low income winter heating assistance for some claimants in Scotland from winter 2022 (see p1671).

You qualify for a cold weather payment if you satisfy all the following conditions.

- **There is a period of cold weather** in the area where you have your usual home. This is defined as seven consecutive days during which your designated local weather site either forecasts or records a temperature at or below zero degrees celsius.[74]
- **You have been awarded pension credit** (guarantee or savings credit) for at least one day during the period of cold weather. **You also qualify if you have been awarded universal credit (UC), income support (IS), income-based jobseeker's allowance (JSA), or income-related employment and support allowance (ESA)** for at least one day during the period of cold weather[75] and:
  - your UC includes an increase for a disabled or severely disabled child, or you have been assessed as having, or are treated as having, limited capability for work or limited capability for work and work-related activity, and you are not in employment or gainful self-employment during the period of cold weather or on the day it is forecast; *or*
  - your IS or income-based JSA applicable amount includes a disability, severe disability, enhanced disability, disabled child, pensioner or higher pensioner premium (see p323); *or*
  - your income-related ESA applicable amount includes the pensioner premium, severe disability premium or enhanced disability premium, or you have been assessed as having, or are treated as having, limited capability for work or limited capability for work-related activity; *or*
  - you are responsible for a child under five (if you get UC, this only applies if you are not in work or self-employment during the period of cold weather or on the day it is forecast); *or*

Part 5: Other benefits
Chapter 37: Social fund payments
5. Winter fuel payments

– you are getting child tax credit (CTC) which includes a disabled child or severely disabled child element (see p1414).

You are treated as receiving one of the above benefits if you are entitled to a DWP loan for help with your mortgage interest (see p839), even if you are not actually entitled to the benefit.

- **You are not living in a care home, independent hospital or Abbeyfield Home** unless you are responsible for a child under five or getting CTC which includes a disabled child or a severely disabled child element.[76]
- **You are not a 'person subject to immigration control'** (there are exceptions to this rule) – see p1524.

The amount

£25 is paid for each week of cold weather.[77]

Claiming and getting paid

You do not need to make a claim for a cold weather payment. The DWP should automatically pay you if you qualify. However, if you are in receipt of IS, JSA or ESA and have a baby, or a child under five comes to live with you, you should notify the DWP to ensure you get a payment automatically. Your district DWP should publicise when there are periods of cold weather in your area. If you do not receive payment and you think you are entitled, submit a written claim and ask for a written decision. A payment cannot be made more than 26 weeks from the last day of the winter period (1 November to 31 March) in which the cold weather period fell.[78] If you are overpaid a cold weather payment, you might have to repay it (see Chapter 53) and, in some circumstances, you may have to pay a penalty (see p1229).

5. **Winter fuel payments**

Winter fuel payments are available in England, Wales and Scotland. In Scotland, child winter heating assistance is also payable for some disabled children and young people (see p1673).

Future changes

It is expected that winter fuel payments will be replaced by winter heating assistance for some claimants in Scotland. The Scottish government plans to transfer existing winter fuel payment claimants in Scotland to the new benefit by 2024 (see p1670).

You qualify for a winter fuel payment if you satisfy all the following conditions.[79]
- **You have reached pension age** in the 'qualifying week'.
- **You are ordinarily resident in Great Britain** (see p1550) **or you can benefit from the European Union co-ordination rules** (see p1609).
- **You claim in time** (see p794), if a claim is required.
- **You are not excluded from a payment under the rules below.**

The qualifying week
The '**qualifying week**' is the week beginning on the third Monday in September.

Who cannot get a winter fuel payment

You are excluded from entitlement to a payment if, throughout the qualifying week (see above):[80]
- you are serving a custodial sentence; *or*
- you have been receiving free inpatient treatment for more than 52 weeks in a hospital or similar institution (see p904); *or*
- you are receiving pension credit (PC), income-based jobseeker's allowance (JSA) or income-related employment and support allowance (ESA) and you are living in residential care (see below);[81] *or*
- you are a 'person subject to immigration control' (there are exceptions) – see p1524.

Living in residential care
You count as '**living in residential care**' if you are living in a care home (ie, an independent home which is registered or exempt from registration, or a local authority home which provides board) or independent hospital throughout the qualifying week and the 12 preceding weeks, disregarding temporary absences.

The amount

Subject to the rules below, you are entitled to a winter fuel payment of:[82]
- £200 if you are aged between pension age and 79 (inclusive) in the qualifying week (see p792); *or*
- £300 if you are aged 80 or over in the qualifying week.

If you do not get PC, income-based JSA or income-related ESA and you share your accommodation with another qualifying person (whether as a partner or friend), you get £100 if you are both between pension age and 79 or £150 if you are both aged 80 or over. If only one of you is aged 80 or over, s/he gets £200 and the other person gets £100.

Part 5: Other benefits
Chapter 37: Social fund payments
6. Tax, other benefits and the benefit cap

If you get PC, income-based JSA or income-related ESA, you (and your partner if you have one) get £200 if one or both of you is between pension age and 79, or £300 if one or both of you is aged 80 or over, regardless of whether there is anyone else in your household who qualifies.

If you are living in residential care (see p793) in the qualifying week and are not getting PC, income-based JSA or income-related ESA, you are entitled to a payment of £100 if you are aged between pension age and 79, or £150 if you are aged 80 or over.

Claiming and getting paid

You should automatically receive a payment without having to make a claim if you received a payment the previous year, or if you are getting retirement pension or any other social security benefit (except universal credit, child benefit, council tax reduction and housing benefit) in the qualifying week.[83]

Otherwise, you must claim a winter fuel payment on or before 31 March following the qualifying week.[84] To ensure you receive your payment before Christmas, submit your claim before the qualifying week. You can claim via the winter fuel payment helpline on 0800 731 0160 (textphone: 0800 731 0176; Relay UK and BSL relay services are available), or download a claim form from gov.uk/winter-fuel-payment.

You should get a written decision.

If you are a member of a couple and your partner is receiving income support, the payment can be made to either of you (even though your partner is under pension age).[85]

The government aims to make payments between mid-November and Christmas.

6. Tax, other benefits and the benefit cap

Social fund loans and payments are not taxable.

They are disregarded as income and capital for the purposes of means-tested benefits and tax credits, and do not affect entitlement to any non-means-tested benefits.

In some cases, there is a limit on the total amount of specified benefits you can receive (a 'benefit cap'). Social fund loans and payments are *not* one of the specified benefits. The benefit cap only applies if you are getting universal credit or housing benefit.

Notes

1. **Budgeting loans**
   1 Dir 8 BLG
   2 *R v SFI ex parte Davey,* 19 October 1998 (HC), unreported
   3 Dir 8 BLG
   4 Dir 9 BLG
   5 Dir 8 BLG
   6 Dir 2 BLG
   7 Dir 53 BLG
   8 Dir 11 BLG
   9 Reg 4 SF(AM) Regs
   10 Reg 5 SF(AM) Regs
   11 Reg 2(1)(a) and (2)(a) SF(AR) Regs
   12 Reg 2(4) SF(AR) Regs
   13 Reg 2(6) SF(AR) Regs
   14 Reg 2(3) SF(AR) Regs
   15 para 132 Part 4 BLG
   16 s78(1) SSAA 1992
   17 Reg 6(3) and (4) SF(AM) Regs
   18 Reg 3 SF(RDB) Regs
   19 s78(3) SSAA 1992

2. **Sure Start maternity grants**
   20 Reg 5(2) SFM&FE Regs
   21 Reg 5(6) SFM&FE Regs
   22 Reg 5(3) SFM&FE Regs
   23 Reg 3A SFM&FE Regs
   24 Reg 5A SFM&FE Regs
   25 *SK and LL v SSWP* [2020] UKUT 145 (AAC)
   26 Reg 6 SFM&FE Regs
   27 Reg 5(4) SFM&FE Regs
   28 Reg 3(1) and (2) SFM&FE Regs
   29 Reg 5(1) SFM&FE Regs
   30 Reg 19 and Sch 4 para 8 SS(C&P) Regs
   31 Reg 6(1)(a) SS(C&P) Regs
   32 Regs 4(7) and 6(1)(b) SS(C&P) Regs

3. **Funeral expenses payments**
   33 Reg 7(3) and (4) SFM&FE Regs
   34 Reg 7(9A) SFM&FE Regs
   35 Reg 7(7) SFM&FE Regs
   36 Reg 7(9)(b) SFM&FE Regs
   37 Reg 7(9)(a) SFM&FE Regs
   38 Reg 4(1) and (2) SFM&FE Regs
   39 Reg 7(5) SFM&FE Regs
   40 The Social Fund (Children's Funeral Fund for England) Regulations 2019 No.1064
   41 Reg 7(8)(a)-(e) SFM&FE Regs
   42 Reg 3(1) SFM&FE Regs

43 CIS/788/2003
44 Reg 3(2) SFM&FE Regs
45 Regs 7(8)(e) and 8(4) SFM&FE Regs
46 Reg 7(8)(e) SFM&FE Regs; R(IS) 7/04
47 Reg 8(1) and (2) SFM&FE Regs
48 Reg 8(7)(a) SFM&FE Regs
49 Reg 8(7)(b) SFM&FE Regs
50 Reg 8(8) SFM&FE Regs
51 *Kerr v Department for Social Development (NI)* [2004] All ER(D) 65, reported as [2004] UKHL 23
52 Reg 7(7) SFM&FE Regs
53 CSB/488/1982
54 CIS/12344/1996; R(IS) 6/98
55 CIS/85/1991
56 Reg 7(8)(e) SFM&FE Regs
57 CIS/12783/1996
58 Reg 7(10) SFM&FE Regs
59 Reg 9(1), (2) and (3) SFM&FE Regs
60 Reg 9(8) SFM&FE Regs
61 Reg 9(10) SFM&FE Regs
62 Reg 9(7) SFM&FE Regs
63 *JEC v SSWP* [2021] UKUT 243 (AAC); ADM Memo 17/21; DMG Memo 12/21
64 Reg 10(1) SFM&FE Regs
65 Vol 7 Ch 39, para 39404 DMG
66 R(IS) 14/91
67 Reg 10(1A) SFM&FE Regs
68 Sch 4 para 9 SS(C&P) Regs
69 Reg 6(1)(a) SS(C&P) Regs
70 Regs 4(7) and 6(1)(b) SS(C&P) Regs
71 Reg 35(2) SS(C&P) Regs
72 s78(4) SSAA 1992; CIS/616/1990
73 R(SB) 18/84

4. **Cold weather payments**
   74 Reg 2(1) and (2) SFCWP Regs
   75 Regs 1A(2), (3) and (6) SFCWP Regs
   76 Reg 1A(4) SFCWP Regs
   77 Reg 3 SFCWP Regs
   78 Reg 2(6) SFCWP Regs

5. **Winter fuel payments**
   79 Reg 2 SFWFP Regs
   80 Reg 3 SFWFP Regs
   81 Reg 1(2) and (3) SFWFP Regs
   82 Reg 2 SFWFP Regs
   83 Reg 4 SFWFP Regs
   84 Reg 3(1)(b) and (2) SFWFP Regs
   85 Reg 36(2) SS(C&P) Regs

Chapter 38

Statutory maternity, adoption, paternity and other parental pay

This chapter covers:
1. Who can get a payment (p797)
2. The rules about your age (p808)
3. People included in the claim (p808)
4. The amount of benefit (p809)
5. Special benefit rules (p809)
6. Claims (p812)
7. Getting paid (p813)
8. Tax, other benefits and the benefit cap (p814)

Key facts
- Statutory maternity pay (SMP), statutory adoption pay (SAP), statutory paternity pay (SPP) and statutory shared parental pay (SSPP) are payments made to certain employees by their employers for the birth or adoption of a child.
- Statutory parental bereavement pay (SPBP) is a payment made to certain employees by their employers following the death of a child or a stillbirth.
- SMP, SAP, SPP, SSPP and SPBP are not means tested, although they have employment and earnings conditions.
- You do not need to intend to return to work to qualify for SMP, SAP, SPP, SSPP or SPBP, and you do not have to repay any of these payments if you do not return.
- You may be entitled to more maternity, adoption, paternity, shared parental pay or pay in connection with a bereavement under your employment contract.
- If you disagree with your employer's decision on your entitlement, or if your employer has failed to make a decision, you can challenge this (see Chapter 60).

1. Who can get a payment

Statutory maternity pay

You qualify for statutory maternity pay (SMP) from your employer if you are pregnant or have recently given birth and:

- you have been continuously employed by the same employer for at least 26 weeks (see p803) by the end of the week which is 15 weeks before the week in which your baby is due (the 'expected week of childbirth');[1] *and*
- your average gross weekly earnings are at least the 'lower earnings limit' (£123 a week in 2022/23). Your earnings are looked at over a 'relevant period' which depends on the expected week of childbirth (see p805);[2] *and*
- you are in the 'maternity pay period' (see below);[3] *and*
- you give your employer at least 28 days' notice of the date you want payment of your SMP to start,[4] and Form MAT B1 from your doctor or midwife, confirming the expected date of birth.[5]

If you do not qualify for SMP, you may be able to get maternity allowance (MA) instead (see Chapter 34).

The maternity pay period

SMP is paid for 39 consecutive weeks. You can usually choose to start to receive SMP at any point between 11 weeks before your baby is due and the day after your baby is born. However, if you have to stop work earlier than planned, your maternity pay period may begin earlier than the date given in your notice to your employer.[6]

- If your baby is born early, your maternity pay period begins on the day after the birth. You should let your employer know about the birth as soon as you can (if possible, within 28 days). Your employer can ask you to confirm this in writing.[7]
- If you are off work because of your pregnancy on a day within four weeks of your due date, your SMP starts the day after.
- If you leave your job, see p809.

You may decide to reduce your maternity pay period – eg, if this would allow the father of the child/your partner to claim statutory shared parental leave and/or pay (see p800). The earliest your maternity pay period can end is two weeks after the birth (four weeks if you are employed in a factory).

Statutory adoption pay

You qualify for statutory adoption pay (SAP) from your employer if you are adopting a child under UK law and:

Part 5: Other benefits
Chapter 38: Statutory maternity, adoption, paternity and other parental pay
1. Who can get a payment

- you have been continuously employed by the same employer for at least 26 weeks (see p803) when you are notified that you have been matched with a child for adoption;[8] *and*
- your average gross weekly earnings are at least the 'lower earnings limit' (£123 a week in 2022/23). Your earnings are looked at over a 'relevant period' which depends on the date you are matched with a child – see p805;[9] *and*
- you are in the 'adoption pay period' (see below);[10] *and*
- you give your employer at least 28 days' notice of when you want payments of SAP to start (you can give a start date which relates to the day of placement – ie, without specifying an actual date), the 'matching certificate' from the adoption agency confirming the placement date and the date you were notified of it, and a written declaration that you want to receive SAP rather than statutory paternity pay (SPP).[11]

Note: you will usually be better off claiming SAP rather than SPP, as it is paid for longer.

If you are jointly adopting a child, only one of you can claim SAP. It may be preferable for the person whose average earnings are higher to apply, as this determines the amount paid (see p809). The person who is not claiming SAP may be able to claim SPP (adoption), see below.

See p811 if you are adopting a child from abroad.

The adoption pay period

SAP is paid for 39 consecutive weeks. You can choose to start to receive SAP at the earliest 14 days before the day you expect the child to be placed with you and, at the latest, on the date of placement (or the day after if you are at work that day). When giving notice, you can choose a date which relates to the expected placement date. You need to inform your employer when the child is actually placed with you if you asked for your SAP to start on that day or the following day.[12]

The adoption pay period ends early if the child is not placed with you, or if the adoption ends because the child dies or s/he is returned to the adoption agency.[13] In these circumstances, payment of SAP continues for eight weeks, then stops.

You may decide to reduce the adoption pay period yourself – eg, if this would allow your partner to claim statutory shared parental leave and/or pay (see p800). The earliest date your adoption pay period can end is two weeks after it started.

Statutory paternity pay

You qualify for SPP from your employer if you are taking time off work to care for a child or to support your partner, and you satisfy the conditions below. You can be:

- the child's father, if you expect to have responsibility for her/his upbringing; *or*

- the partner of the child's mother, if you expect to share the main responsibility for the child's upbringing with her;[14] *or*
- the person adopting a child; *or*
- the adopter's partner, if you expect to share the main responsibility for the child's upbringing with her/him.[15]

Note: you may have a choice between SAP and SPP if you are adopting with your partner. Bear in mind that SAP can be worth more to begin with, depending on your earnings, and has a longer maximum pay period (see p809).

You qualify for SPP if:

- you have been continuously employed by the same employer for at least 26 weeks (see p803):
  - by the end of the week which is 15 weeks before the week the baby is due (the 'expected week of childbirth');[16] *or*
  - by the end of the week in which you (and/or your partner) are notified that you have been matched with a child for adoption;[17] *and*
- your average gross weekly earnings are at least the 'lower earnings limit' (£123 a week in 2022/23). Your earnings are looked at over a 'relevant period' which depends on the expected week of childbirth or the date you are matched with a child for adoption (see p805);[18] *and*
- you are in the 'paternity pay period' (see below);[19] *and either*
- at least 15 weeks in advance of the date the baby is due, you notify your employer of this due date and of the date you want payment of your SPP to start (see below), and provide a declaration that you are entitled to claim;[20] *or*
- within seven days of notification of the adoption match, you notify your employer of the date you expect the child to be placed for adoption and of the date you want payment of your SPP to start (you can give a date which relates to the day of placement – ie, without specifying an actual date), and provide a declaration that you are entitled to claim.[21]

You cannot be paid SPP at the same time as statutory shared parental pay (SSPP), nor if you have already taken SSPP for the same birth/adoption.

The paternity pay period

SPP is paid for two consecutive weeks. The earliest SPP can be paid is the child's date of birth or the date of the child's placement for adoption, and the latest is eight weeks after that date. For SPP for a birth, you can choose whether you want it to start on the day the child is born, the following day, or a specified number of days after the birth. In this case, you must inform your employer of the date the child is born as soon as you can after the birth. Alternatively, you can request that SPP start on a specific date so long as this is after the first day of the week in which the child is expected. In this case, you only need to let the employer know if the

Part 5: Other benefits
Chapter 38: Statutory maternity, adoption, paternity and other parental pay
1. Who can get a payment

child has not arrived by the date you specified for your SPP to begin, as this will have to be changed.[22]

For SPP for an adoption, you can choose whether you want SPP to start on the day the child is placed with you and your partner, the following day, or a specified number of days after the placement. In this case, you must inform your employer when the child is placed with you as soon as you can. Alternatively, you can request that SPP start on a specific date as long as this is later than the expected date of placement. In this case, you only need to let your employer know if the child has not been placed with you by the date you have asked SPP to start, as this will have to be changed.[23]

Statutory shared parental pay

You may qualify for SSPP from your employer if your partner has chosen to give up her SMP or MA, or her/his SAP, early.

You may also qualify if you have recently given birth or adopted a child and you choose to give up your SMP or SAP early. You might choose to do this because the rules on when SSPP can be paid are more flexible and it could allow you to return to work for a longer period than would otherwise be possible without losing your right to more paid leave. If you are doing this as a mother/adopter, bear in mind that SMP/SAP is worth more than SSPP for the first six weeks.

Note:
- SMP, SAP or MA must have been paid for at least two weeks before it can be given up early.[24]
- If you or your partner change your mind about swapping to SSPP, any 'curtailment' (ie, early ending) of SMP, SAP or MA can be cancelled if the curtailment notice was given before the birth and it is cancelled within six weeks of the birth or (for birth or adoption) your partner dies and you cancel the curtailment of your SMP, SAP or MA within a reasonable period after the death.[25]

You qualify for SSPP if:
- you have been continuously employed by the same employer for at least 26 weeks (see p803) by the end of either the week that is 15 weeks before the week the baby is due (the 'expected week of childbirth')[26] or when you (and/or your partner) are notified that you have been matched with a child for adoption.[27] You also need to continue in this employment at least until the week before your SSPP starts; *and*
- your average gross weekly earnings are at least the 'lower earnings limit' (£123 a week in 2022/23). Your earnings are looked at over a relevant period which depends on the expected week of childbirth or the date you are matched with a child for adoption (see p805);[28] *and*
- you are in the 'shared parental pay period' (see p801);[29] *and*

- your partner has sent a 'curtailment notice' to her/his employer at least eight weeks before s/he wants payment of her/his SMP, SAP or MA to stop,[30] or you have sent your employer a curtailment notice if you want your own SMP or SAP to stop[31] and you have given your employer:
    - at least eight weeks' notice of the date you want payments of SSPP to start; *and*
    - notification of the baby's due date, the date of birth or the date of the adoption placement; *and*
    - confirmation of the total number of weeks and the period(s) for which you intend to claim SSPP; *and*
    - declaration from your partner confirming that s/he consents to your claiming SSPP and that you will share the main responsibility for the care of the child with her/him, and a declaration from you, confirming that you are entitled to claim.[32]

If you are the mother or the SAP claimant and you want to claim SSPP, your partner in the application (this can be the father of the child, your spouse, civil partner or your partner who lives with you and the child) must:[33]

- have the main responsibility of the child (apart from you); *and*
- have been employed for 26 weeks in the 66 weeks before the expected week of childbirth or before the week you are notified that you have been matched with a child for adoption; *and*
- have average weekly earnings of at least £30 in 13 of those 66 weeks.

The shared parental pay period

When you or your partner give notice that you wish to 'curtail' your SMP, SAP or MA (after it has been paid for at least two weeks), SSPP is payable for the remaining number of weeks in the 39-week period. If both you and your partner qualify for SSPP, and you both intend to claim it, you can share the available weeks of SSPP between you in whatever proportion you choose. If you are going to do this, you must both give at least eight weeks' notice of your intention to take SSPP. You can get SSPP for the same or different weeks. Alternatively, either one of you can get all the available weeks of SSPP. The weeks of SSPP can be paid over one continuous period, or over a number of shorter periods (if your employer agrees to this). It cannot be paid for any day falling after the child's first birthday, or after the first anniversary of her/his adoption placement. You can give your employer notice of your intention to take SSPP and then follow this up with notice of specific periods of SSPP (and leave) you wish to book, or do both these at the same time (see p812), but you must usually give at least eight weeks' notice before any period of SSPP.

Statutory parental bereavement pay

Statutory parental bereavement pay (SPBP) is paid for up to two weeks to employees who meet certain conditions in respect of the death of a child or a

Part 5: Other benefits
Chapter 38: Statutory maternity, adoption, paternity and other parental pay
1. Who can get a payment

stillbirth. It applies only where the death or stillbirth happens on or after 6 April 2020.[34] You qualify for SPBP if a child under 18 dies or is stillborn after 24 weeks of pregnancy (see p810) and you:[35]

- are a bereaved parent; *and*
- have been continuously employed by the same employer for at least 26 weeks (see p803) ending with the week immediately before the week in which the child died, and continue to be employed by that employer from that point to the day of the child's death; *and*
- your average gross weekly earnings are at least the 'lower earnings limit' (£123 in 2022/23). Your earnings are looked at over a 'relevant period' which depends on the week in which the death occurred (see p805); *and*
- you give your employer notice of the week or weeks you want the payment to be made.

A bereaved parent includes all legal parents (including adoptive parents), natural (biological) parents whose children have been adopted where the adopter was required to allow them to be in contact with the child, legal parents, and intended parents (who have applied for, or intend to apply for, a parental order in respect of a child under a surrogacy arrangement).[36]

You are also a bereaved parent if you had day to day responsibility for the child, and s/he was living in your own home for at least four weeks ending with the day the child died. However, you are not a parent if an actual parent of the child, or someone else who had responsibility for the child, is also living in the premises where the child is cared for. You are also not a parent if you are entitled to receive any remuneration in respect of the care of the child. Remuneration means payment for work that you do, whether in cash or kind, but some payments do not count – eg, a fostering allowance paid by a local authority. Remuneration also does not include benefits you may receive for the child such as child benefit, child tax credit or universal credit.

The partner of a bereaved parent is also entitled to SPBP if s/he meets the other conditions. A partner means someone who lives with the parent and the child in an enduring family relationship and is not a close relative of the parent.[37]

You must give your employer notice of the SPBP you want to take. The maximum number of weeks of SPBP for the death of one child is two (however, you can be entitled to SPBP in respect of more than one child[38]). You can choose to be paid for either one week or two, or you can take two separate weeks at different times. SPBP can only be paid within 56 weeks beginning with the date of the child's death.[39] You are supposed to give notice of at least 28 days before the first day for which you want to receive SPBP, but if this is not reasonably practicable, you should give it as soon as you can do so.[40]

With your notice, you should include the following in writing:[41]

- the name of the person claiming SPBP; *and*
- the date of the child's death; *and*

- a declaration that you meet one of the conditions for being a bereaved parent – eg, you are the child's parent or the partner of a bereaved parent.

If you later change your mind about your weeks of SPBP, you can withdraw your notice. You must give notice to withdraw no later than the first day of a week of SPBP if you were going to be taking it within 56 days of the child's death, and at least a week before a week of SPBP if you were going to be taking it later than that.[42]

Continuous employment

To satisfy the continuous employment rule, you must have been employed by an employer who was liable to pay employer's national insurance (NI) contributions for you, or would have been if your earnings had been high enough (see p948) or you had been older (if you are under 16).[43] For all statutory payments in this chapter, you need to have been employed for 26 weeks by the end of the week which is 15 weeks before the expected week of childbirth (see p797), for adoption, by the date you (and/or your partner) are notified that you have been matched with a child, or for the death of a child, by the end of the week before the week in which your child died. Any work, even for only part of a week, counts as a week of work. A week for SMP, SAP, SPP, SSPP or SPBP usually runs from Sunday to Saturday, so you need to check which week the date falls into and count backwards. Tables to help you do this for SMP, SPP for a birth and SSPP for a birth are in Appendix 8.

For SPBP, if you have been employed in each of the 26 weeks (but no more) ending with the week before the week of the child's death, the first week of your employment for counting the 26 weeks starts on the first day you were employed by your employer, even if this is not a Sunday. For any subsequent weeks, as with the other statutory payments, you do not have to work full time, as work in all or part of a week counts as a week of work.

If you are an 'employed earner' for NI purposes (see p947), you normally count as an employee.[44] If you are employed under a contract of apprenticeship, you count as an employee.[45] Agency workers count, if someone is liable to pay employer's NI contributions, as do company directors who are paid a salary.

You do not need to have a written contract of employment to count as an employee.

Periods of employment in a European Economic Area country may count towards your period of continuous employment if you were employed by the same employer in Great Britain in the 15th week before your baby was due, the week you were notified that you had been matched with a child for adoption, or, for the death of a child, the week immediately before the week in which your child died.[46] In addition, if you were working outside Great Britain but your employer was liable to pay class 1 NI on your earnings, then your period of employment may count.

Part 5: Other benefits
Chapter 38: Statutory maternity, adoption, paternity and other parental pay
1. Who can get a payment

Even if you are an employee, you may not be entitled to SMP, SAP, SPP or SSPP if your employer is based outside Great Britain (see p1637). See p1637 if you are employed abroad.

If the baby is born early (in or before the 15th week before your expected week of childbirth), you satisfy the continuous employment rule if you would have done so (for SMP or SPP for a birth) had the baby been born on the expected date or (for SSPP for a birth) if the baby had been born after the 15th week before the expected week of childbirth. For SSPP, you must also continue to be employed by the same employer from the date of the baby's birth until the week before your first period of SSPP begins.[47]

For SMP, if you are employed for only part of the 15th week before your expected week of childbirth, the whole week still counts towards your continuous employment. For SAP, the same applies if you are employed for only part of the week in which you received notification that you have been matched with a child. For SMP, SAP, SPP, SSPP and SPBP, if you have been employed for each of the 26 weeks needed (but no more), the first of those 26 weeks does not need to be a complete week. For the purposes of counting the weeks, the first week starts on the first day of your employment and ends at midnight on the following Saturday (or ends at midnight on the start date if you started employment on a Saturday).[48]

Breaks in employment

If you return to work for the same employer following a break in your employment, certain weeks when you were not employed can still count towards your 26 weeks' continuous employment. These include weeks in which you were:[49]

- incapable of work because of sickness or injury; *or*
- absent because your employer temporarily had no work to offer you – eg, you are an agency worker and the agency is unable to find you work in any particular week; *or*
- absent from work, but because of an arrangement or custom, you are regarded as continuing in employment – eg, if you are a teacher employed on a term-by-term contract.

Note: the above rules are only relevant when there is a *break* in your employment with your employer. So, for example, sickness absence should count towards your continuous employment if you remain employed by your employer while off sick, as should absence because of adoption, paternity, shared parental, parental bereavement or parental leave.

For SMP only, if you have gaps between contracts with the same employer of no more than 26 weeks during which you are absent from work wholly or partly because of pregnancy, and you are employed both before and after your baby is born but not while you are off work due to childbirth, the weeks in between the contracts can still count towards your continuous employment.[50]

If your employer offers contracts of up to 26 weeks, at least twice a year, to people who have worked there before, and you are absent from work due to pregnancy (for SMP), disease or disability, you do not need to return to work to benefit from these rules.[51]

If your employment is legally transferred from one employer to another, your employment is unbroken.[52] If you have been reinstated or re-engaged following an unfair dismissal claim, any period between your dismissal and your reinstatement or re-engagement counts towards your 26 weeks' continuous employment.[53] If you have been dismissed without being reinstated or re-engaged, see p809.

If being on strike has affected the weeks which count towards your continuous employment, see p984.

Earnings

What counts as earnings

As well as your gross wages, bonuses and any overtime pay you receive during the relevant period, your earnings include payments such as:[54]

- other statutory payments;
- arrears of pay following reinstatement or re-engagement in your job or a continuation of your contract of employment under the Employment Rights Act 1996.

Certain payments (eg, some payments in kind) are ignored.[55]

How earnings are averaged

For births, earnings are averaged over a 'relevant period' ending with the last normal payday which falls either in or before the 15th week before the expected week of childbirth, and going back to the day after the last normal payday which fell at least eight weeks before that (ie, roughly 23 weeks before the baby is due). See Appendix 8 for help working out dates. For adoptions, the relevant period ends with the last normal payday that falls in or before the week you are notified of being matched with a child for adoption, and goes back to the day after the last normal payday which falls at least eight weeks before that. For the death of a child, the relevant period ends with the last normal payday which falls before the first day of the week in which the child dies, and goes back to the day after the last normal payday which falls at least eight weeks before that. In the case of a stillbirth, you may also be entitled to SMP (see p810).

A week for SMP, SPP, SAP, SSPP and SPBP runs from a Sunday to Saturday. If you are paid at intervals of one or more calendar months, weekly earnings are calculated by dividing earnings received in the relevant period by the number of calendar months in that period (to the nearest whole number), multiplying by 12 and dividing by 52.[56] If you are not paid monthly or weekly, or there is not an exact number of weeks in the relevant period that applies to you, your weekly

Part 5: Other benefits
Chapter 38: Statutory maternity, adoption, paternity and other parental pay
1. Who can get a payment

earnings are calculated by taking the total of your earnings in the relevant period, dividing by the number of days in the relevant period and multiplying by seven.

Pay rises

For SMP, if you are awarded a pay rise that affects your wages for any part of the period from the first day of your 'relevant period' until the last day of your statutory maternity leave, your employer should reassess your average earnings during the relevant period as if your earnings for each of the weeks in that period had included the pay increase, and pay any arrears of SMP due to you. This is the case, even if the pay rise did not happen until after the relevant period.[57] If you become entitled to SMP as a result of the pay rise, your employer should deduct any payments of MA that you may have received for the same period from the SMP you are owed.[58]

For SAP, SPP, SSPP and SPBP, only a backdated pay rise that is paid in respect of the relevant period used to calculate your SAP, SPP or SSPP will lead to your employer recalculating the average and paying any arrears of SAP, SPP or SSPP due to you.[59]

The lower earnings limit

For births, the lower earnings limit used is the one in force at the end of the 15th week before the expected week of childbirth. For adoptions, the lower earnings limit used is the one in force at the end of the week in which you or the adopter are notified of being matched with the child for adoption. For deaths, the lower earnings limit is the one in force at the end of the week immediately before the week in which the child dies. For the tax year 2022/23, the lower earnings limit is £123 a week. See Appendix 6 for the amounts for other years.

Working while getting statutory payments for the birth, adoption or death of a child

Your entitlement to SMP, SAP, SPP, SSPP or SPBP is not affected by any work you do on a self-employed basis. However, your entitlement may be affected if you work for an employer.

Working for the employer who is paying you

You can do up to 10 'keeping in touch' days' work for the employer who pays you SMP or SAP, and up to 20 for SSPP, without your entitlement to these payments being affected. However, if you do any work for that employer in excess of these 10/20 days, you lose a week's payment for every week in which you do that further work.[60] **Note:** HM Revenue and Customs seems to interpret the rules about 'keeping in touch' days for SSPP as meaning that, if you work for 20 days or more, your SSPP ends altogether. Arguably, this is incorrect and can be challenged. Seek specialist advice if you are affected.

If you do any work during the paternity pay period for an employer who is paying you SPP, that employer is not liable to pay you SPP for the week in which you work.[61] If you do any work during the parental bereavement pay period for an employer who is paying you SPBP, that employer is not liable to pay you SPBP for the week in which you work.[62]

These rules apply even if you are working for the employer under a new contract which did not exist before your maternity, paternity, shared parental, parental bereavement or adoption pay period began.

For SMP, if you return to work for your employer but you are then off sick during what would otherwise be your maternity pay period, you are not entitled to statutory sick pay (SSP). Instead, you can get SMP for each week in which you are off for a whole week. This does not apply if you have curtailed your maternity pay period and you are past the curtailment date (see p801), when you would be able to get SSP as usual. If you had returned to work before giving a curtailment notice, any additional weeks' SMP you are paid while off work sick are ignored when calculating the number of weeks for which SSPP can be paid.[63] This may allow you or your partner to book SSPP.

Working for more than one employer who is liable to pay you

If you work for more than one employer and you meet the conditions of entitlement to SMP (see p797), SAP (see p797), SPP (see p798) or SPBP (see p801) in respect of the work you do for each, you can get SMP, SAP, SPP or SPBP from each job. However, if your earnings from any of your jobs are aggregated when calculating your liability to pay NI contributions, the jobs are counted as one and the amount of SMP, SAP or SPP your employers must pay is apportioned between them.

If more than one employer is liable to pay you SMP, SAP, SPP or SPBP, unless the payments are just one award apportioned between them, any work you do for one of them does not affect your entitlement to SMP, SAP SPP or SPBP from the other.

If more than one employer is liable to pay you SSPP, you do not need to be on shared parental leave from all your jobs at the same time. The number of weeks of SSPP you can get from each employer is calculated without looking at how many weeks of SSPP you get from any other employer. However, *all* the weeks you get SSPP, from any employer, are counted when calculating the number of weeks of SSPP which would be left for your partner to take. There is no double counting of the same week(s) though, so if you get SSPP from more than one employer for one week, that week is only counted once, meaning you may be better off claiming SSPP from all your liable employers for the same weeks if your partner intends to take some SSPP as well.[64]

Part 5: Other benefits
Chapter 38: Statutory maternity, adoption, paternity and other parental pay
3. People included in the claim

Working for another employer

If you work for another employer who is not liable to pay you SMP, SAP, SPP, SSPP or SPBP, this usually brings your statutory payments to an end early. You also cannot get SMP, SAP and SPP for the remainder of your maternity, paternity or adoption pay period.[65] This means that if you start working for a new employer, your SMP, SAP, SPP or SSPP comes to an end. However, there are two exceptions.

- For SMP, if the work is done before your baby is born, your entitlement to SMP is unaffected.[66]
- Your SMP, SAP, SPP, SSPP or SPBP is not affected by any work you do for an employer who is not liable to pay you SMP, SAP, SPP, SSPP or SPBP if you also worked for that employer in the:
  - 15th week before the expected week of confinement, for SMP, SPP (birth) and SSPP (birth); *or*
  - week in which you or the adopter were notified that you had been matched with a child for adoption, for SAP and SPP (adoption); *or*
  - 15th week before the expected week of the child's placement for adoption, for SSPP (adoption); *or*
  - week immediately before the week of the child's death.[67]

If you work for an employer who is not liable to pay you, and for whom you did not work in the relevant week, you must notify the employer who is paying you within seven days of the first day on which you do the work. It is advisable to inform your employer in writing and for SAP, SPP, SSPP and SPBP, your employer has the right to request the information in writing.[68]

2. The rules about your age

There are no upper or lower age limits for statutory maternity pay, statutory adoption pay, statutory paternity pay, statutory shared parental pay or statutory parental bereavement pay.

3. People included in the claim

You claim statutory maternity pay, statutory adoption pay, statutory paternity pay, statutory shared parental pay or statutory parental bereavement pay for yourself. You cannot claim any increase for your partner or child(ren).

4. The amount of benefit

	Maximum period of payment	Gross amount
Statutory maternity pay and statutory adoption pay	39 weeks	First six weeks: 90% of average weekly earnings Remaining 33 weeks: Lesser of £156.66 or 90% of average weekly earnings
Statutory paternity pay	Two weeks	Lesser of £156.66 or 90% of average weekly earnings
Statutory shared parental pay	37 weeks	Lesser of £156.66 or 90% of average weekly earnings
Statutory parental bereavement pay	Two weeks	Lesser of £156.66 or 90% of average weekly earnings

If you meet the conditions of entitlement with more than one employer, see p807.

5. Special benefit rules

Special rules may apply to:
- people who give up their job or who have been dismissed (see below);
- stillbirths, multiple births or adoption (see p810);
- people who have adopted a child from abroad (see p811);
- foster parents approved as adopters (see p811);
- people whose baby is born with the help of a surrogate (see p812);
- people in prison or detention (see p923);
- people who are abroad or going abroad (see Chapter 70);
- people involved in a trade dispute (see p984).

If you give up your job or are dismissed

Your employer is still liable to pay you statutory maternity pay (SMP), statutory adoption pay (SAP), statutory paternity pay (SPP), statutory shared parental pay (SSPP) or statutory parental bereavement pay (SPBP) if:
- you give up your job or are dismissed after you start receiving your statutory payments (but see p1400 if your employer is insolvent);[69] or

Part 5: Other benefits
Chapter 38: Statutory maternity, adoption, paternity and other parental pay
5. Special benefit rules

- your employer dismisses you at any time, provided HM Revenue and Customs or an employment tribunal finds this was 'solely or mainly' to avoid paying SMP, SAP, SPP, SSPP or SPBP, and you had been employed by that employer for at least eight continuous weeks. In this situation, the amount you are paid for SMP, SAP, SPP or SPBP is calculated using your average earnings during the eight-week period ending with the last day in respect of which you are paid.[70] For the amount of SSPP, your average earnings are calculated over the period ending on the last day you are paid and going back to the day after the last payday which falls at least eight weeks before that;[71] *or*
- you satisfy the qualifying conditions and your job ends for any reason at any time after:
  - **for SMP,** the beginning of the 15th week before your baby is due;[72] *or*
  - **for SAP,** the beginning of the week in which you were notified of being matched with a child for adoption;[73] *or*
  - **for SPP,** the day on which the child is born,[74] or placed for adoption;[75] *or*
  - **for SSPP,** the beginning of the week in which your first period of SSPP starts;[76] *or*
  - **for SPBP,** the day on which the child dies.[77]

If you qualify for SMP but your job ends before your maternity pay period was due to start, your SMP starts at the beginning of the 11th week before the date your baby is due or, if your job ends after this, on the day after you finish work, unless your baby is born before these dates (in which case it begins the day after the birth).[78]

If you qualify for SAP but your job ends before your adoption pay period was due to start, it starts 14 days before the expected date of placement or, if your job ends after this, on the day after you finish work, unless your child is placed with you before this (in which case it begins on the date of placement).[79]

If you are dismissed while pregnant or in connection with maternity, adoption, paternity, shared parental or parental bereavement leave or pay, get advice about your employment rights urgently.

Stillbirths, multiple births and adoptions

If your baby is stillborn after 24 weeks' pregnancy, SMP and SPP are payable in the same way as for a live birth, so if you have a stillbirth certificate, you can qualify.[80] If the baby is stillborn before you have completed 24 full weeks of pregnancy, this is treated as a miscarriage, and SMP and SPP are not payable. You may, however, qualify for statutory sick pay (SSP), employment and support allowance or universal credit. It may be possible to argue that a week for the purposes of this rule means seven days and not the Sunday to Saturday definition used for the employment or earnings conditions (see p805).[81] You should get advice if you are close to 24 weeks and miss out due to the way the weeks are counted.

If the baby is born alive but then dies (even after only a moment), this is a live birth and you can get SMP or SPP, even if it happens before 24 weeks' of pregnancy. Even if SMP has been awarded for the birth, SSPP can only be paid if the child's death occurs after you have given notice to your employer of your intention to claim SSPP.

You may be entitled to SPBP as well as SMP, SPP or SSPP. You can take this in addition as long as you do so within 56 weeks of the stillbirth, and give the required notice (see p802). The 'relevant period' for averaging earnings is different for the death of a child (see p805), but if you are already on SMP when your baby is stillborn, you will usually qualify for SPBP as well, unless your SMP is very low. If you were on SSP in the period before a stillbirth you may not qualify for SPBP but could still qualify for SMP.

If you do qualify for both SMP and SPBP, remember that SMP has to be taken immediately after the stillbirth (unless SMP has already started). SPBP will need to be taken at some point after the SMP ends, but this does not have to be immediately afterwards (as long as it is within the 56-week period), and you will need to give your employer separate notice for this.

No additional SMP, SAP, SPP or SSPP is payable if you or your partner give birth to more than one baby, or have more than one child placed with you for adoption, unless this happens as part of a different adoption arrangement.[82] You are entitled to SPBP in respect of each child if you satisfy the conditions in respect of the death of more than one child.[83]

If you are adopting a child from abroad

If you are adopting a child from abroad, you may be entitled to SAP, SPP or SSPP. To qualify, you must still satisfy the usual rules of entitlement (see p797 and p800), but with certain modifications.[84] Although you must have 'official notification' that you have been approved for adoption from the UK authorities (sometimes called a 'certificate of eligibility and suitability to adopt'), you will not have been matched with a child for adoption by UK authorities under UK law, and so you will not be able to provide the date of placement or the date of notification of being matched for adoption. You should therefore use Form SC6 (for SAP) or Form SC5 (for SPP), available from gov.uk, to apply for SAP or SPP from your employer for an overseas adoption. At the time of writing, there is no official form for SSPP.

Foster parents approved as adopters

In England, if you are a local authority foster parent who has been approved as a prospective adopter and you are fostering the child in the meantime (sometimes called a 'fostering for adoption' placement), you may qualify for SAP, SPP or SSPP before the actual adoption.[85]

If your baby is born with the help of a surrogate

If you have had a child with the help of a surrogate mother, you may qualify for SAP, SPP or SSPP if:[86]

- you have obtained a parental order from the court; *or*
- on the date of the child's birth you intend to apply for a parental order from the court within six months of the baby's birth, and you expect your application to be successful.

If this applies, your entitlement to SAP, SPP and SSPP can start from the due date or the date of birth of the child, instead of the date of the adoption match or adoption placement. If a child born with the help of a surrogate dies, you may be entitled to SPBP (see p802).

6. **Claims**

Making a claim

It is not necessary for you to complete a claim form to qualify for statutory maternity pay (SMP), statutory adoption pay (SAP), statutory paternity pay (SPP), statutory shared parental pay (SSPP) or statutory parental bereavement pay (SPBP), but you must give your employer the required notice and evidence within the relevant time limit.

> *Forms*
>
> For SPP, you may use Form SC3 to provide the information and notice to your employer for a birth, or Form SC4 for an adoption. They are available from gov.uk/paternity-pay-leave.
>
> Forms for SSPP and leave are available from gov.uk/shared-parental-leave-and-pay.
>
> It is advisable to use these forms to ensure all the information and notice requirements are met.

Notification sent to your employer in a properly addressed and prepaid letter is treated as having been given on the day it is posted.[87] For SMP, SAP, SPP and SPBP, you should provide notice in writing and supply evidence at the same time, if you are able to do so, or as soon as possible afterwards. For SSPP, you can send notice and information to your employer electronically, if your employer has agreed to this.

Time limits

You must give your employer notice of when you want your SMP, SAP, SPP, SSPP or SPBP to start within a certain period of time 'or as soon as reasonably practicable after that'. There is also a time limit for providing the required evidence (which may sometimes be required at the same time as the notice) and this can be extended if there is a 'good cause' for the delay. These terms are not defined – you must show that any delay was reasonable, given your circumstances. If time limits are missed, your employer may not pay you. If you think your employer's decision is wrong, you can challenge it (see Chapter 60).

If your employer has its own maternity, adoption, paternity, shared parental or parental bereavement pay scheme, the notice requirements for this scheme may be different. Check this with your employer.

Who should claim

If you are entitled to SMP, SAP, SPP, SSPP or SPBP but are not well enough to deal with your own affairs, HM Revenue and Customs (HMRC) can appoint someone else to act for you.[88] This person must apply in writing to be your 'appointee' (see p1135). For further information, contact the HMRC national insurance helpline (tel: 0300 200 3500; textphone: 0300 200 3519).

If you claim the wrong benefit

In some circumstances where you claim statutory sick pay but you are close to your due date, your employer may be able to start your maternity leave and pay you SMP instead (see p815).

You may get a claim for maternity allowance backdated if your employer has informed you that you are not entitled to SMP (see p718).

7. Getting paid

Statutory maternity pay (SMP), statutory adoption pay (SAP), statutory paternity pay (SPP), statutory shared parental pay (SSPP) and statutory parental bereavement pay (SPBP) are usually paid by your employer in the same way and at the same intervals as your normal wages or salary.[89]

Note:
- If you are also entitled to contractual maternity, adoption, paternity, shared parental or parental bereavement pay (or any other contractual remuneration) from your employer, SMP, SAP, SPP, SSPP or SPBP forms part of your payments. Your employer can offset any payment of SMP, SAP, SPP, SSPP or SPBP from its contractual liability to pay you for the same period.[90]

Part 5: Other benefits
Chapter 38: Statutory maternity, adoption, paternity and other parental pay
8. Tax, other benefits and the benefit cap

- Your employer cannot pay you SMP, SAP, SPP, SSPP or SPBP by making a payment in kind, or by providing board and lodging, or by providing a service or some other facility.[91]
- If you become entitled to SMP because of a pay rise, your employer can deduct any maternity allowance (MA) you received for the same period from the SMP you are owed.[92]
- If your entitlement has been decided by a decision maker from HM Revenue and Customs (HMRC), or by the First-tier or Upper Tribunal, your employer may be required to pay you within a certain time limit (see p1399). If your employer cannot or will not pay you, see p1400 for when payment can be made by HMRC.[93]
- The rules on overpayments described in Chapter 53 do not apply to SMP, SAP, SPP, SSPP or SPBP. If your employer tells you that you have been overpaid SMP, SAP, SPP, SSPP or SPBP, get advice on your entitlement. You may also need debt advice. If your employer decides you have been paid SMP in error, consider claiming MA. You may be able to get this backdated (see p718).
- If your employer becomes insolvent, see p1400.
- For SAP, SSPP and SPBP, HMRC, not your employer, pays you if you are entitled for a period after you were imprisoned or detained, or if you were subsequently released without charge, found not guilty or given a non-custodial sentence (see p924).[94]

Change of circumstances

You must keep your employer informed of any change of circumstances that may affect your entitlement, such as if you start work for someone else while your employer is paying you SMP, SAP, SPP, SSPP or SPBP. For SSPP, you must inform your employer if the person getting SMP, MA or SAP decides to revoke the agreement to end these payments early and continue to receive SMP, MA or SAP, as this means you will not qualify for SSPP.

If you qualify for SMP, SAP, SPP, SSPP or SPBP, your entitlement is not affected if you go abroad.

8. **Tax, other benefits and the benefit cap**

Tax

Statutory maternity pay (SMP), statutory adoption pay (SAP), statutory paternity pay (SPP), statutory shared parental pay (SSPP) and statutory parental bereavement pay (SPBP) are treated as earnings, and you pay tax and national insurance (NI) contributions as appropriate.[95]

Means-tested benefits and tax credits

If you come under the universal credit (UC) system (see p22), you may qualify for UC as well as SMP, SAP, SPP, SSPP and SPBP.

For UC and contributory employment and support allowance (ESA), in some circumstances you can be treated as having limited capability for work-related activity while pregnant (see p1008).

If you do not come under the UC system, in some circumstances, you can be treated as being in full-time work for working tax credit (WTC) (see Chapter 15) while you are getting SMP, SAP, SPP, SSPP or SPBP (or for some periods when you are on maternity, adoption, paternity or shared parental leave – see p288). You may also qualify for child tax credit (CTC) (see Chapter 14). If you are entitled to WTC, you may be able to get help with the cost of childcare, even before you return to work (see p1422). You cannot make a completely new claim for tax credits (see p284), but you can start to get CTC if you already get WTC, or WTC if you already get CTC, and you can add children to your tax credit award.

When calculating your entitlement to means-tested benefits and tax credits, SMP, SAP, SPP, SSPP and SPBP are:

- treated as employed earnings for UC;
- treated in full as income for income support, income-based jobseeker's allowance (JSA) and income-related ESA;
- treated as earnings for housing benefit (HB) and pension credit. You may be able to get an allowance for certain childcare charges deducted from your earnings when calculating your entitlement to HB;
- treated as employment income for CTC and WTC. The first £100 of your weekly SMP, SAP, SPP, SSPP or SPBP is disregarded.

Non-means-tested benefits

Provided you do not have limited capability for work and are not treated as having limited capability for work (but see p688), you may qualify for contribution-based JSA while getting SMP, SAP, SPP, SSPP or SPBP. As you must accept a claimant commitment to qualify for JSA, get advice before claiming if you are still employed – the DWP may contact your employer and this may jeopardise your employment.

You cannot get statutory sick pay (SSP) when you are receiving SMP. If you are sick with a pregnancy-related illness (or an existing condition made worse by your pregnancy) in the four weeks before the week your baby is due, your employer can start your maternity leave (even if it is sooner than you had planned) and pay you SMP rather than SSP. It cannot do this if your illness is *not* pregnancy related.

You cannot receive SAP, SPP, SSPP or SPBP for any week in which you are entitled to SSP.[96]

If you get SMP, you cannot also get maternity allowance (MA) for the same period in respect of the same pregnancy.[97]

Part 5: Other benefits
Chapter 38: Statutory maternity, adoption, paternity and other parental pay
8. Tax, other benefits and the benefit cap

If you are getting SMP, SAP, SSPP or SPBP, you may qualify for NI credits (see p961). It may be important to claim credits in order to protect your future entitlement to contributory benefits, such as state pension. However, you will not need them if your SMP, SAP, SSPP or SPBP is at least the lower earnings limit.

Contributory employment and support allowance

You can qualify for contributory ESA as well as SPP if you satisfy the conditions for contributory ESA during your paternity pay period.

You can also qualify for contributory ESA while you are getting SMP, SAP or SSPP if you satisfy the NI contribution conditions and had limited capability for work (or you could be treated as having limited capability for work) on the day before your statutory payments started.[98] However, your contributory ESA is reduced by the amount of SMP, SAP or SSPP you receive for the same week.

In some circumstances, if you are pregnant or have recently given birth, you can be treated as having limited capability for work or as having limited capability for work-related activity if you are pregnant (see p988 and p1008).

The benefit cap

In some cases, there is a limit on the total amount of specified benefits you can receive (a 'benefit cap'). SMP, SAP, SPP, SSPP and SPBP are *not* specified benefits. The benefit cap only applies if you are getting UC or HB. See p1156 for further information.

Other sources of help

For details of:
- a Sure Start maternity grant if you live in England or Wales, see p782, or, if you live in Scotland, a Best Start grant pregnancy and baby payment, see p1697. In some circumstances, you may qualify for a maternity grant even if you are not the mother of the child. You do not have to be a person who has given birth to a child to qualify for these grants;
- funeral expenses payments and other financial help specific to the cost of children's funerals if you live in England or Wales, see p784, or if you live in Scotland, a funeral support payment, see Chapter 76;
- free prescriptions and free NHS dental treatment, see Chapter 31;
- Healthy Start food vouchers and vitamins if you live in England or Wales, see p847, or, in Scotland, the Best Start foods scheme, see p850;
- council tax reduction, see p836;
- tax-free childcare, see p856.

Notes

1. **Who can get a payment**
   1 s164(2)(a) SSCBA 1992
   2 s164(2)(b) SSCBA 1992
   3 s165 SSCBA 1992; reg 2 SMP Regs
   4 s164(4) and (5) SSCBA 1992
   5 Reg 22 SMP Regs
   6 Reg 2 SMP Regs
   7 Reg 23 SMP Regs
   8 s171ZL(2)(b) and (3) SSCBA 1992
   9 ss171ZL(2)(d) and 171ZS(6)-(8) SSCBA 1992
   10 s171ZN(2) SSCBA 1992; reg 21 SPPSAP(G) Regs
   11 s171ZL(6) and (7) SSCBA 1992; regs 23 and 24 SPPSAP(G) Regs
   12 Regs 21 and 23 SPPSAP(G) Regs
   13 Reg 22 SPPSAP(G) Regs
   14 s171ZA(2)(a) SSCBA 1992; reg 4 SPPSAP(G) Regs
   15 s171ZB(2)(a) SSCBA 1992; reg 11 SPPSAP(G) Regs
   16 s171ZA(2)(b) and (3) SSCBA 1992
   17 s171ZB(2)(b) and (3) SSCBA 1992
   18 **Father/mother's partner**
      ss171ZA(2)(c) and 171ZJ(6)-(8) SSCBA 1992
      Adopter/adopter's partner
      ss171ZB(2)(c) and 171ZJ(6)-(8) SSCBA 1992
   19 **Father/mother's partner** s171ZE(2) SSCBA 1992; reg 6 SPPSAP(G) Regs
      Adopter/adopter's partner
      s171ZE(2) SSCBA 1992; reg 12 SPPSAP(G) Regs
   20 s171ZC(1) and (3)(c) SSCBA 1992; reg 9 SPPSAP(G) Regs
   21 s171ZC(1) and (3)(c) SSCBA 1992; reg 15 SPPSAP(G) Regs
   22 Regs 6 and 7 SPPSAP(G) Regs
   23 Regs 12 and 13 SPPSAP(G) Regs
   24 Regs 7(2)(b), (3) and (6) and 12(2)(c) and (5) SMP&SAP(C) Regs
   25 **SMP and SAP** Regs 8 and 13 SMP&SAP(C) Regs
      MA Reg 6 MA(C) Regs
   26 **Father/mother's partner**
      s171ZU(4)(d) and (g) SSCBA 1992; reg 30 SSPP(G) Regs
      Mother s171ZU(2)(c) and (f) SSCBA 1992; reg 30 SSPP(G) Regs

   27 **Adopter** s171ZV(2)(c) and (f) SSCBA 1992; reg 31 SSPP(G) Regs
      Adopter's partner s171ZV(4)(d) and (g) SSCBA 1992; reg 31 SSPP(G) Regs
   28 **Father/mother's partner**
      ss171ZU(4)(f) and 171ZZ4(6)-(8) SSCBA 1992; reg 30 SSPP(G) Regs
      Mother ss171ZU(2)(e) and 171ZZ4(6)-(8) SSCBA 1992; reg 30 SSPP(G) Regs
      Adopter ss171ZV(2)(e) and 171ZZ4(6)-(8) SSCBA 1992; reg 31 SSPP(G) Regs
      Adopter's partner ss171ZV(4)(f) and 171ZZ4(6)-(8) SSCBA 1992; reg 31 SSPP(G) Regs
   29 **Father/mother's partner/mother**
      Reg 10 SSPP(G) Regs
      Adopter/adopter's partner Reg 22 SSPP(G) Regs
   30 **Father/mother's partner** Regs 5 and 7 SMP&SAP(C) Regs
      Adopter's partner Regs 10 and 12 SMP&SAP(C) Regs
   31 **Mother** Regs 4 and 7 SMP&SAP(C) Regs
      Adopter Regs 9 and 12 SMP&SAP(C) Regs
   32 **Father/mother's partner**
      ss171ZU(4)(j)-(p) and 171ZW(1)(b) SSCBA 1992; reg 7 SSPP(G) Regs
      Adopter's partner ss171ZV(4)(j)-(p) and 171ZW(1)(b) SSCBA 1992; reg 20 SSPP(G) Regs
      Mother ss171ZU(2)(i)-(o) and 171ZW(1)(b) SSCBA 1992; reg 6 SSPP(G) Regs
      Adopter ss171ZV(2)(i)-(o) and 171ZW(1)(b) SSCBA 1992; reg 19 SSPP(G) Regs
   33 Regs 4(1) and (3), 17(1) and (3) and 29 SSPP(G) Regs
   34 Reg 2 SPBP(G) Regs
   35 ss171ZZ6 and 171ZZ7 SSCBA 1992
   36 Reg 4 SPBP(G) Regs
   37 Reg 4(1)(g) and (8)(b), (c) and (d) SPBP(G) Regs
   38 s171ZZ6(6) SSCBA 1992
   39 Reg 7 SPBP(G) Regs
   40 Reg 8(1) SPBP(G) Regs
   41 Reg 8(2), (3), (4) and (5) SPBP(G) Regs

42 Reg 8(6), (7), (8) and (9) SPBP(G) Regs

43 **SMP** s171(1) SSCBA 1992; reg 17 SMP Regs
    SAP&SPP ss171ZJ(1) and (2) and 171ZS(1) and (2) SSCBA 1992; reg 32 SPPSAP(G) Regs
    SSPP s171ZZ4(1) SSCBA 1992; reg 33 SSPP(G) Regs
    SPBP s171ZZ8(1) SSCBA 1992; reg 11 SPBP(G) Regs

44 **SMP** Reg 17 SMP Regs
    SAP&SPP Reg 32 SPPSAP(G) Regs
    SSPP Reg 33 SSPP(G) Regs
    SPBP Reg 11 SPBP(G) Regs

45 **SMP** Reg 17(2) SMP Regs
    SAP&SPP Reg 32 SPPSAP(G) Regs
    SSPP Reg 33(4) SSPP(G) Regs
    SPBP Reg 114) SPBP(G) Regs

46 **SMP** Regs 2 and 5 SMP(PAM) Regs
    SAP&SPP Regs 3, 5 and 6 SPPSAP(PAM) Regs
    SSPP Regs 5 and 7 SSPP(PAM) Regs
    SPBP Regs 5 and 7 SPBP(PAM) Regs

47 **SMP** Reg 4(2)(a) SMP Regs
    SAP&SPP Reg 5(a) SPPSAP(G) Regs
    SSPP Reg 30(2) and (3) SSPP(G) Regs

48 **SMP** 16A SMP(G) Regs
    SAP&SPP Reg 35A(2) SPPSAP(G) Regs
    SSPP Reg 30(1B) SSPP (G) Regs
    SPBP Reg 15 SPBP(G) Regs

49 **SMP** Reg 11 SMP Regs
    SAP&SPP Reg 33 SPPSAP(G) Regs
    SSPP Reg 34 SSPP(G) Regs
    SPBP Reg 12 SPBP(G) Regs

50 Reg 11(1)(d) and (3) SMP Regs

51 **SMP** Reg 11(3A) SMP Regs
    SAP&SPP Reg 33(3) SPPSAP(G) Regs
    SSPP Reg 34(4) SSPP(G) Regs
    SPBP Reg 11(4) SPBP(G) Regs

52 **SMP** Reg 14 SMP Regs
    SAP&SPP Reg 36 SPPSAP(G) Regs
    SSPP Reg 37 SSPP(G) Regs
    SPBP Reg 16 SPBP(G) Regs

53 **SMP** Reg 12 SMP Regs
    SAP&SPP Reg 34 SPPSAP(G) Regs
    SSPP Reg 35 SSPP(G) Regs
    SPBP Reg 13 SPBP(G) Regs

54 **SMP** Reg 20 SMP Regs
    SAP&SPP Reg 39 SPPSAP(G) Regs
    SSPP Reg 32(7) and (8) SSPP(G) Regs
    SPBP Reg 19 SPBP(G) Regs

55 **SMP** Reg 20(2)(a) SMP Regs
    SAP&SPP Reg 39(2)(a) SPPSAP(G) Regs
    SSPP Reg 32(7)(a) SSPP(G) Regs
    SPBP Reg 19(2) SPBP(G) Regs

56 **SMP** Reg 21(5) SMP Regs
    SAP&SPP Reg 40(5) SPPSAP(G) Regs
    SSPP Reg 32(4) SSPP(G) Regs
    SPBP Reg 19(6) SPBP(G) Regs

57 Reg 21(7) SMP Regs

58 Reg 21B SMP Regs

59 **SAP&SPP** Reg 40(7) SPPSAP(G) Regs
    SSPP Reg 32(6) SSPP(G) Regs
    SPBP Reg 19(8) SPBP(G) Regs

60 **SMP** s165(4) and (5) SSCBA 1992; reg 9A SMP Regs
    SAP s171ZN(3) and (4) SSCBA 1992; reg 27A SPPSAP(G) Regs
    SSPP Regs 4(2)(g), 5(2)(e), 12, 15, 17(2)(g), 18(2)(e), 24 and 27 SSPP(G) Regs

61 s171ZE(5) and (6) SSCBA 1992

62 s171ZZ9(6) SSCBA 1992

63 Regs 10(1)(a)(i) and 22(1)(a)(i) SSPP(G) Regs

64 ss171ZU(2)(n) and (o) and (4)(o) and (p) and 171ZV(2)(n) and (o) and (4)(o) and (p) SSCBA 1992; regs 10(7) and (8) and 22(5) and (6) SSPP(G) Regs

65 **SMP** s165(6) SSCBA 1992; reg 8(2) SMP Regs
    SAP s171ZN(5) SSCBA 1992; reg 26(1) SPPSAP(G) Regs
    SPP s171ZE(7) SSCBA 1992; reg 17(1) SPPSAP(G) Regs
    SSPP ss171ZU(2)(n) and (4)(o), 171ZV(2)(n) and (4)(o) and 171ZY(4) SSCBA 1992; regs 12, 15, 24 and 27 SSPP(G) Regs

66 s165(6) SSCBA 1992

67 **SMP** Reg 8(1) SMP Regs
    SAP Reg 25 SPPSAP(G) Regs
    SPP Regs 10 and 16 SPPSAP(G) Regs
    SPP Regs 12, 15, 24 and 27 SSPP(G) Regs
    SPBP Reg 10 SPBP(G) Regs

68 **SMP** Reg 24 SMP Regs
    SAP Reg 26(2) and (3) SPPSAP(G) Regs
    SPP Reg 17(2) and (3) SPPSAP(G) Regs
    SSPP Regs 12(2) and (3) and 24(2) and (3) SSPP(G) Regs
    SPBP Reg 10 (2) and (3) SPBP(G) Regs

- -

5. Special benefit rules
69 **SMP** s164(2)(a) and (3) SSCBA 1992
SAP s171ZM SSCBA 1992
SPP s171ZD SSCBA 1992
SSPP s171ZX SSCBA 1992
70 **SMP** s164(8) SSCBA 1992; reg 3(1)
SMP Regs
SAP s171ZM(2) SSCBA 1992; reg 30
SPPSAP(G) Regs
SPP s171ZD(2) SSCBA 1992; reg 20
SPPSAP(G) Regs
SPBP Reg 22 SPBP(G) Regs
71 s171ZX(2) SSCBA 1992; reg 42 SSPP(G)
Regs
72 s164(2)(a) SSCBA 1992
73 s171ZL(2)(b) and (3) SSCBA 1992
74 s171ZA(2)(b) and (d) SSCBA 1992
75 s171ZB(2)(b) and (d) SSCBA 1992
76 Regs 30(2)(a) and (c) and 31(2)(a) and
(c) SSPP(G) Regs
77 s171ZZ6(2)(e) SSCBA 1992
78 s165(2) SSCBA 1992; reg 2(3) and (5)
SMP Regs
79 Reg 29 SPPSAP(G) Regs
80 ss171(1) and 171ZA(5) SSCBA 1992
81 para 62025 DMG. This guidance relates
to MA but it is arguable that a similar
approach could be taken for SMP.
82 **SMP** s171(1) SSCBA 1992
SAP s171ZL(5) SSCBA 1992
SPP ss171ZA(4) and 171ZB(6) SSCBA
1992
SSPP ss171ZU(16) and 171ZV(16)
SSCBA 1992
83 s171ZZ6(6) SSCBA 1992
84 SSCBA(AAO) Regs;
SPP(A)&SAP(AO)(No.2) Regs; Statutory
Paternity Pay (Adoption) and Statutory
Adoption Pay (Adoptions from
Overseas) (Administration) Regulations
2003 No.1192; Statutory Shared
Parental Pay (Adoption from Overseas)
Regulations 2014 No.3093
85 Reg 2(2)(c) and (d), (3) and (4)
SPPSAP(G) Regs; reg 2 SSPP(G) Regs
86 **SPP** ss171ZA, 171ZB and 171ZE SSCBA
1992; SPPSAP(G) Regs
SAP ss171ZL and 171ZN SSCBA 1992;
SPPSAP(G) Regs
SSPP s171ZV SSCBA 1992; SSPP(G)
Regs

6. Claims
87 **SMP** Regs 22(4) and 23(3) SMP Regs
SAP&SPP Reg 47 SPPSAP(G) Regs
SSPP Reg 49(3)(b) SSPP(G) Regs
88 **SMP** Reg 31 SMP Regs
SAP&SPP Reg 46 SPPSAP(G) Regs
SSPP Reg 48 SSPP(G) Regs
SPBP Reg 28 SPBP(G) Regs

7. Getting paid
89 **SMP** Reg 27 SMP Regs
SAP&SPP Reg 41 SPPSAP(G) Regs
SSPP Reg 43 SSPP(G) Regs
SPBP Reg 23 SPBP(G) Regs
90 **SMP** Sch 13 para 3 SSCBA 1992
SAP s171ZP(5) SSCBA 1992
SPP s171ZG(2) SSCBA 1992
SSPP s171ZZ1 SSCBA 1992
SPBP s171ZZ11 SSCBA 1992 and reg
21 SPBP(G) Regs
91 **SMP** Reg 27 SMP Regs
SAP&SPP Reg 41 SPPSAP(G) Regs
SSPP Reg 43 SSPP(G) Regs
SPBP Reg 23 SPBP(G) Regs
92 Reg 21B SMP Regs
93 **SAP** Reg 44 SPPSAP(G) Regs
SSPP Reg 46 SSPP(G) Regs
SPBP Reg 24 SPBP(G) Regs
94 **SAP** Reg 44 SPPSAP(G) Regs
SSPP Reg 46 SSPP(G) Regs
SPBP Reg 26 SPBP(G) Regs

8. Tax, other benefits and the benefit cap
95 s4(1)(a)(ii)-(vii) SSCBA 1992
96 **SAP** Reg 27(1)(a) SPPSAP(G) Regs
SPP Reg 18(a) SPPSAP(G) Regs
SSPP Regs 14(1)(a) and 26(1)(a)
SSPP(G) Regs
SPBP Reg 9(1)(a) SPBP(G) Regs
97 s35(1)(d) SSCBA 1992
98 s20(2)-(5), (6) and (7) WRA 2007; regs
80, 81, 82A ESA Regs; regs 73, 74 and
75A ESA Regs 2013

Chapter 39

● ●

Statutory sick pay

This chapter covers:

Key facts

- Statutory sick pay (SSP) is paid by employers to certain employees who are unfit for work.
- SSP can be paid for up to 28 weeks.
- SSP is a non-means-tested benefit.
- Your entitlement to SSP is not based on your national insurance contribution record, but your usual earnings must be above a certain amount to qualify.
- If you qualify, SSP is the minimum amount your employer should pay while you are sick. You may also be entitled to occupational sick pay under your contract.
- If you disagree with your employer's decision on your entitlement to SSP, or if your employer has failed to make a decision, you can challenge this (see Chapter 60).

---

1. Who can get statutory sick pay

You qualify for statutory sick pay (SSP) if:[1]

- you are an employee (see p821); *and*
- you are incapable of work (see p821); *and*
- you are within a period of incapacity for work (see p823); *and*
- you are within your period of entitlement to SSP (see p823); *and*
- the day is a qualifying day (see p825); *and*

● ● ● ●

- your normal earnings are at least the lower earnings limit for national insurance (NI) contributions (see p824).

There are some groups of people to whom special rules apply (see p828). Certain people do not qualify for SSP (see p824). See below if your employer has dismissed you solely or mainly to avoid paying SSP.

Employees

To be entitled to SSP you must be an employee. If you count as an 'employed earner' for NI purposes (see p947), or you would do so but for being under 16, you normally count as an employee for SSP purposes – eg, you may count as an employee if you are an agency worker.

You do not have to have a written contract of employment. It is the fact that you are employed that matters. Your right to SSP cannot be taken away by any agreement, whether you sign it or not.[2] If your employer dismisses you to avoid paying SSP, see below.

Even if you are an employee, you are treated as if you are not (and so your employer does not have to pay you SSP) if your employer is:[3]

- not resident and not present in Great Britain, and does not have a place of business in Great Britain (and is not treated as having one); *or*
- exempt from social security legislation because of an international treaty.

Dismissal from work

If your employer dismisses you during your period of entitlement to SSP solely or mainly to avoid paying you SSP, it is still liable to pay you SSP. In these circumstances, your employer should continue to pay you SSP until either your period of entitlement to SSP ends or until your contract would have ended had you not been dismissed, whichever occurs first.[4] If your employer dismisses you for another reason (ie, not solely or mainly to avoid paying you SSP), you are not normally entitled to SSP from that employer once your contract ends.

Incapable of work

To qualify for SSP, you must be 'incapable of work'. This has a specific meaning for SSP. Other tests, such as that of 'limited capability for work' described in Chapter 45, do not apply to SSP.

To be 'incapable of work' for SSP purposes, you must be:[5]

- incapable of doing work that you could reasonably be expected to do under the terms of your contract because you have a specific disease, or a physical or mental disability; *or*
- treated as incapable of such work (see p822).

Part 5: Other benefits
Chapter 39: Statutory sick pay
1. Who can get statutory sick pay

Usually, after seven days of absence you need to provide evidence of your incapacity for work (see p830).

Does your employer doubt your incapacity for work?

1. It is up to your employer to decide whether it accepts that you are incapable of work. If it does not, it does not pay you SSP, although you can challenge its decision.

2. Your employer can get further advice. It may consult its own medical officer (if it has one), your doctor (with your permission) or HM Revenue and Customs (HMRC).

3. If the matter is not resolved and your employer consults HMRC, HMRC may involve its Medical Service (MS) and, with your permission, the MS may contact your doctor to arrange for you to have a medical examination with an MS doctor (or other healthcare professional). Your employer is then given only the MS's view on whether you are fit for work in the job you do. It is still your employer's decision whether or not to pay you SSP.

4. If your employer refuses to pay you SSP, you can ask HMRC to make a decision (see Chapter 60).

Treated as incapable of work

Even if you are not actually incapable of work, your employer may treat you as incapable of work if:[6]

- you have been officially excluded or prevented from working because you have (or it is suspected that you have) an infection, disease or contamination detailed under public health legislation, or you have been in contact with someone who has; *or*
- you are under medical care in connection with a specific disease or physical or mental disability; *and*
  - a doctor has stated that you should not work as a precautionary measure or in order to convalesce; *and*
  - you do not go in to work for your employer.

Note: before 25 March 2022, you could be treated as incapable of work in some situations involving coronavirus – eg, if self-isolating for a required period because you had tested positive. These special rules no longer apply.[7] For details of when you could be treated as incapable of work due to coronavirus, see the 2021/22 edition of this *Handbook*. You may still be actually incapable of work because of the effects of coronavirus, as with any other illness.

If you are incapable of work for just part of a day, you must be treated as incapable of work for the whole day provided you do not do any work on that day. If you are a shift worker and you are incapable of work for part of a day but you do some work on that day, you should still be treated as incapable of work for the whole day if you only finish a shift that began the day before and you do not do any work on a shift that starts on that day and ends the next.

Period of incapacity for work

For SSP to be paid, you must be within a 'period of incapacity for work'.[8] This is defined as four or more consecutive days of incapacity for work. This means that you can only qualify for SSP if you are incapable of work for at least four days in a row. Every day of the week (including Sunday) counts, even if it is not a day on which you would normally work. Days of incapacity for work that fall before or after the period covered by your contract can still be included in your period of incapacity for work (but see p825 if you have not yet started work).

Two or more periods of incapacity for work are 'linked' and treated as a single period if they are separated by eight weeks or less.

Period of entitlement to statutory sick pay

You only qualify for SSP if you are within 'a period of entitlement'. In certain circumstances, a period of entitlement cannot arise and so you do not qualify for SSP (see p824).

When entitlement to statutory sick pay starts

A period of entitlement normally starts on the first day of your period of incapacity for work, unless your contract of employment starts either during your period of incapacity for work or between two linked periods (see below).[9]

When entitlement to statutory sick pay ends

A period of entitlement to SSP ends (and so your SSP stops) if:[10]
* your period of incapacity for work ends; or
* you reach your maximum 28 weeks' entitlement to SSP from a particular employer (see p827); or
* your contract of employment ends, including where you leave your job (unless it has been brought to an end by your employer solely or mainly to avoid paying SSP – see p821); or
* in some circumstances, you are pregnant or have just had a baby (see p828); or
* you reach the third anniversary of the start of the period of entitlement; or
* you are in prison or detained in legal custody (see p924).

Two or more periods of incapacity for work that are separated by eight weeks or less are linked and treated as a single period.[11] It may therefore be possible for you to have a period of entitlement which lasts for three years and not to have exhausted your 28 weeks' entitlement to SSP over that period.

If you have received your maximum 28 weeks' entitlement to SSP from a particular employer and you are still incapable of work, see p827.

If your employer stops paying you SSP because it decides your period of entitlement has ended, see p831.

Part 5: Other benefits
Chapter 39: Statutory sick pay
1. Who can get statutory sick pay

When statutory sick pay is not paid

In certain circumstances, a period of entitlement to SSP cannot arise. As a result, you do not qualify for any SSP during your period of incapacity for work.

A period of entitlement cannot arise if:[12]

- your normal weekly earnings are below the lower earnings limit (see below); *or*
- at some time in the 85 days before the date on which your period of entitlement would have begun you were entitled to employment and support allowance (ESA) or, in some circumstances, you would have been entitled. For this to apply, you must have claimed ESA (or made a claim for another benefit that was treated as a claim for ESA). If you have limited capability for work, you may qualify for universal credit (UC) and/or ESA instead of SSP; *or*
- at the time when your period of entitlement would have begun there is a strike at your workplace (but see p983); *or*
- you have not yet started work under your contract of employment (but see p825 if you had an earlier contract with the same employer); *or*
- you are in prison or legal custody (see p924); *or*
- at the time when your period of entitlement would have begun, you were entitled to statutory maternity pay (SMP) or, in some circumstances, maternity allowance (see p828); *or*
- you are within the period immediately before or after you give birth (see p828).

If your employer decides not to pay you SSP on any of the above grounds, see p831.

People with low earnings

You cannot get SSP if your 'normal weekly earnings' are less than the lower earnings limit for NI contributions (£123 a week in 2022/23 – see p948).

Your '**normal weekly earnings**' are calculated by averaging your gross earnings from your employer (ie, before tax and NI contributions are deducted) over the period between:[13]

- your last normal payday before your period of entitlement to SSP began (see below); *and*
- the day after the last normal payday that falls at least eight weeks before this.

Only payments actually made in this period (including the last normal payday before entitlement began, but not including the one at least eight weeks before that) count, even if, in theory, you should have been paid more.[14] However, if your employer has unlawfully withheld *all* of your wages for the period over which your earnings are averaged, you should not be excluded from entitlement to SSP on the basis that you have low earnings if you otherwise would have qualified.[15]

If you are paid every one or more calendar months, your average earnings are calculated by dividing your earnings over the above period by the number of calendar months in the period (to the nearest whole number), multiplying by 12 and dividing by 52. If you are paid at other intervals and the period is not an exact number of weeks, the average is calculated by dividing your earnings by the number of days in the above period and multiplying by seven.

As well as your wages, your gross earnings include payments such as:[16]

- SSP, SMP, statutory adoption pay, statutory paternity pay, statutory shared parental pay and statutory parental bereavement pay;
- contractual or occupational maternity pay;
- arrears of pay following reinstatement or re-engagement in your job or a continuation of a contract of employment under particular legislation.

Certain payments (eg, some payments in kind) are ignored.[17]

There are special rules to calculate your earnings if you have not been employed sufficiently long to have been paid wages over this eight-week period.[18] The rules allow your normal weekly earnings to be calculated in reference to the period for which you have actually received earnings, or the earnings you are entitled to for a week's work.

See p827 if you have more than one job.

People who have not yet started work

If you have agreed to work for an employer but have not started work when your period of incapacity for work begins, you are not entitled to SSP from that employer for any day during your period of incapacity for work, unless your current contract of employment can be linked to a previous one with the same employer. Your employment is linked if there are eight weeks or less between the date your new contract starts and the date your last contract with the employer ended.[19] You do not have to have written contracts for this to apply.

Qualifying days

You can only be entitled to SSP for 'qualifying days'. SSP is generally not paid for your first three qualifying days, which are known as 'waiting days' (see p826).[20]

Qualifying days are usually those days of the week on which you normally work. Other days may be selected as qualifying days by agreement between you and your employer if they would better reflect your contract of employment – eg, if you work a complicated shift pattern. For this purpose, a week begins on Sunday and there must be a minimum of one qualifying day in each week.[21]

If you and your employer cannot agree which days are qualifying days, they are presumed to be:[22]

- the days on which it is agreed that you are required to work; *or*
- Wednesday, if it is agreed that you are not required to work on any day in that week – eg, offshore oil workers, who may work two weeks 'on' and then two weeks 'off'; *or*

Part 5: Other benefits
Chapter 39: Statutory sick pay
4. The amount of benefit

* if you cannot agree about which days you are or are not required to work, every day in the week, except days on which you and your employer agree that no employee works.

Required to work
'Required to work' means required by the terms of your contract of employment.[23] Days when you can choose whether or not to work do not count – eg, voluntary overtime shifts.

Waiting days

SSP is not paid for the first three qualifying days in a period of entitlement.[24] These are called '**waiting days**' and, as they must be qualifying days, they are not necessarily the first three days of your sickness.

Waiting days did not apply to periods of incapacity for work related to COVID-19 which started before 24 March 2022. For periods of incapacity for work after that date, waiting days apply in the normal way in all cases, even if your illness is COVID-19 (see p822).[25]

If your period of incapacity for work can be linked to an earlier one in your period of entitlement with the same employer (see p823), any waiting days you served in the earlier linked period(s) do not have to be served again and you can get SSP from your first qualifying day in your present one.

2. The rules about your age

There are no lower or upper age limits for entitlement to statutory sick pay.

3. People included in the claim

You claim statutory sick pay for yourself. You cannot claim any increases for your partner or child(ren).

4. The amount of benefit

Statutory sick pay (SSP) is generally not paid for the first three qualifying days in a period of entitlement, known as waiting days (see above for when they do and do not apply). After that, it is payable at a rate of £99.35 a week. If you qualify, the weekly amount of SSP is the same irrespective of the number of hours you normally work for your employer each week when you are not sick.[26]

SSP is a daily benefit, so it can be paid for periods of less than a week. The daily rate is calculated by dividing the weekly amount by the number of qualifying days you have in that week. A week for these purposes runs from Sunday to Saturday.

Example

Britney is employed in a shop and works four days a week (Wednesday to Saturday). These are her qualifying days. After injuring her hand, she is incapable of work for just over two weeks. In the week of her injury, she works on Wednesday and is off sick for the rest of the week. Her period of entitlement to SSP begins on Thursday, the first day of her absence, but she is not entitled to SSP for that week as the first three qualifying days in her period of entitlement (Thursday to Saturday) are waiting days. As she is incapable of work for all her qualifying days in the next week she gets £99.35 SSP. In the following week, she is off sick on Wednesday, Thursday and Friday and returns to work on Saturday. She receives £72.26 SSP (£99.35 divided by her four qualifying days to give a daily rate paid for three days).

People with more than one job

If you cannot work, you are entitled to SSP from any job for which you fulfil the qualifying conditions. So, you can get payments of SSP from two different employers or payments for more than one contract with the same employer – eg, if you are both a daytime teacher and an evening tutor with a local authority. However, if your earnings from any of your different jobs are added together when calculating your liability to pay class 1 national insurance contributions (which usually means you contribute less than if they had been treated separately), you can only receive a total of £99.35 a week from those jobs. In these circumstances, your employers' liability to pay you SSP is apportioned by agreement between them or, if they cannot agree, in proportion to their share of your combined earnings.[27]

It is possible for you to be unable to work on one contract and be entitled to SSP, but be able to work on a different contract – eg, if you perform different tasks for each.

Maximum entitlement to statutory sick pay

You are entitled to a maximum of 28 weeks of SSP from a particular employer in any one period of entitlement (see p823) – ie, 28 times the weekly rate of SSP.[28]

Once you have reached your maximum 28 weeks' entitlement with a particular employer, you cannot qualify for SSP again from that employer for the same contract until your current period of incapacity for work ends and a new one arises. Previous periods of incapacity for work are linked to your current one if

Part 5: Other benefits
Chapter 39: Statutory sick pay
5. Special benefit rules

they are separated by eight weeks or less.[29] However, see p824 if you got employment and support allowance (ESA) in the intervening period.

If you are still incapable of work after you have received your 28-week entitlement to SSP, consider claiming ESA and/or universal credit if you are not already claiming it (see Chapters 3 and 30).

5. **Special benefit rules**

Special rules may apply to:
- people who are going abroad (see p1637);
- women who are pregnant or who have recently given birth (see below);
- people involved in a trade dispute (see p982) and people in prison or detention (see p923).

Women who are pregnant or who have recently given birth

If you are entitled to statutory maternity pay (SMP – see p797), you cannot get statutory sick pay (SSP) during the maternity pay period. If you are entitled to maternity allowance (MA) on the basis of your own employment or self-employment (see p709), you cannot get SSP during the MA period.[30] Within the limits set out on p711 and p797 (and unless your baby is born early), you can choose when your maternity pay or MA period begins. So, for example, your employer cannot insist that you claim SMP or MA at the earliest possible date in order to limit the period for which it has to pay SSP.

Even if you are not entitled to SMP or MA, or if you are entitled to MA on the basis that you have helped your spouse or civil partner with her/his self-employment (see p709):[31]
- you cannot get SSP (because a period of entitlement cannot arise) if your period of incapacity for work started at some time during the 18 weeks which run from the first of the following dates:
  - the beginning of the week in which you had your baby (but see below); or
  - if you are incapable of work either wholly or partly because of your pregnancy on a day that falls in the four weeks before your 'expected week of childbirth', the beginning of the week that contains the first such day;
- if SSP is already being paid to you (because your period of entitlement started before the above period, or because your incapacity for work was not initially linked to your pregnancy), it stops from the first of the following dates:[32]
  - the first day falling on or after the beginning of the fourth week before your expected week of childbirth when you are incapable of work wholly or partly because of your pregnancy; or
  - the date on which you have your baby.

For the above purposes, a week begins on a Sunday. If your baby is stillborn before you have completed 24 weeks of pregnancy, you qualify for SSP if you satisfy the other conditions of entitlement.

6. Claims and backdating

To qualify for statutory sick pay (SSP), you must notify your employer of your incapacity for work, rather than notifying the DWP or HM Revenue and Customs (HMRC).

Making a claim

You do not need to complete a claim form to qualify for SSP – just inform your employer that you are sick. Your employer should then decide whether you are entitled to SSP.

Telling your employer that you are sick

Your employer can decide the time limit within which you should report your sickness absence and how you should report it. Your employer must take reasonable steps to inform you of what you need to do when you are absent due to sickness. However, for SSP purposes, your employer cannot insist that you report your sickness:[33]

- earlier than the first qualifying day (which is not necessarily your first day of sickness – see p825), or by a specific time on the first qualifying day; *or*
- personally; *or*
- by providing medical evidence; *or*
- more than once a week; *or*
- on a printed form or other document provided by your employer.

Time limits

The following time limits apply for notifying your employer.[34]

- You must report your incapacity for work within the time limit set by your employer, if it has taken reasonable steps to inform you of this (unless it requires you to give notice earlier than the first qualifying day).
- If your employer has not taken reasonable steps to inform you, or it has made no arrangements about the notification required, you must report your incapacity for work in writing on or before the seventh day after your first qualifying day (see p825).
- This seven-day time limit, or your employer's time limit, can be extended by one month if you have good cause for the delay. What is 'good cause' is not defined in the regulations, but you must show that your delay was reasonable given the circumstances.

Part 5: Other benefits
Chapter 39: Statutory sick pay
6. Claims and backdating

- If it is not practical for you to inform your employer within that time, the time limit can be extended further, provided you have notified it as soon as is reasonably practicable and at the latest on or before the 91st day after your first qualifying day.

Notice sent in a properly addressed pre-paid letter is treated as having been given on the day it was posted. If you do not notify your employer of your absence within the above time limits, you can still be entitled to SSP (and qualify for a total of 28 weeks' payment in your period of entitlement if you are off work for that long), but your entitlement starts from a later date.[35]

Information to support your claim

Your employer can require you to provide 'such information as may reasonably be required' to determine your claim for SSP.[36]

Medical evidence

For the first seven days of your incapacity for work you are only required to provide a self-certificate as evidence of your incapacity for work. Your employer cannot insist on your obtaining a medical certificate.[37] After the first seven days, employers usually expect you to provide a medical certificate from a doctor. On the medical certificate your doctor can state either that you are not fit for work, or that you 'may be fit for work taking account of the following advice'. These statements are not related to your specific job. If your doctor thinks you may be fit for some work, s/he can include a description of the effects of your condition on your ability to work and specify whether s/he thinks you may benefit from a phased return to work, altered hours, amended duties or workplace adaptations to facilitate your return to work.[38] If you provide a certificate from someone else, such as an osteopath or chiropractor, this can be accepted if your employer considers it sufficient.[39] Whatever type of medical evidence you provide, it is up to your employer to decide whether or not to accept it. See Chapter 60 if you want to challenge your employer's decision.

Who should claim

As your employer cannot insist that you personally notify it of your incapacity for work, someone else can notify your employer on your behalf.

If you are not well enough to be able to deal with your own affairs, HMRC can appoint someone else to act for you (an 'appointee' – see p1135). For further information, contact the HMRC helpline (tel: 0300 200 3500; textphone: 0300 200 3519).

If you claim the wrong benefit

A claim for another benefit cannot be treated as a claim for SSP. However, if you have notified your employer of your sickness, but you are not entitled to SSP, you may be able to get a claim for employment and support allowance (ESA) backdated more than the usual three months (see p644).

Backdating your entitlement

To qualify for SSP, you must notify your employer of your sickness (see p829). Even if you have not notified your employer promptly, your entitlement can still be backdated if you do so within the time limits on p829.

If statutory sick pay ends or is refused

If your employer decides that you are not entitled to SSP or stops paying you, it should provide you with a statement (usually on Form SSP1) within certain time limits, giving you the reasons for its decision.[40] If you do not agree with your employer's decision, see Chapter 60 for how to challenge it.

Whether or not you agree with your employer's decision, you should consider claiming other benefits. If you are not well enough to work, consider claiming ESA and/or universal credit (UC) (see Chapters 3 and 30). You should seek advice before claiming UC if you are getting any of the benefits which it replaces (see p21). The DWP usually asks HMRC to make a decision on your entitlement to SSP before it makes a decision on your claim for ESA.

7. Getting paid

Statutory sick pay (SSP) is usually paid in the same way and at the same intervals as your wages or salary.

SSP is a daily benefit, so if you qualify for it, it can be paid for periods of less than a week. See p826 for the way the daily rate is calculated.

Note:

- If you are entitled to contractual sick pay from your employer, SSP forms part of your pay. Your employer can deduct the amount of SSP you are entitled to from the contractual sick pay it is liable to pay you for the same period.[41]
- Your employer cannot pay you SSP by making a payment in kind or by providing board and lodging, a service or other facilities.[42]
- Deductions that can be made from your wages (eg, union subscriptions) can also be made from your SSP.[43]
- If your entitlement to SSP has been decided by HM Revenue and Customs (HMRC) or by the First-tier Tribunal or Upper Tribunal, your employer may be required to pay your SSP within a certain time limit (see p1399).
- If your employer cannot or will not pay you, see p1400 for details of when payment of SSP can be made by HMRC.
- The rules on overpayments and recovery of overpaid benefit described in Chapter 53 do not apply to SSP. If your employer pays you SSP and later decides

Part 5: Other benefits
Chapter 39: Statutory sick pay
8. Tax, other benefits and the benefit cap

that you were not entitled to it, it may attempt to recover the sum it considers overpaid by making a deduction from your wages. If this happens, get advice. If your employer decides that you have been overpaid SSP in error, consider claiming employment and support allowance. You may be able to get your claim backdated (see p644).

Change of circumstances

Notify your employer of any change in your circumstances that may affect your entitlement to SSP.

8. **Tax, other benefits and the benefit cap**

Tax

Statutory sick pay (SSP) is treated like any other earnings. You pay tax and, depending on the amount of your earnings in the same week, national insurance (NI) contributions by pay as you earn (PAYE) in the normal way.[44]

Means-tested benefits and tax credits

You (and your partner) may be able to claim universal credit (UC) as well as SSP or, if you are already getting UC, you may be entitled to more.

For the purpose of qualifying for help with the cost of childcare in your UC, you can be treated as still in paid work while getting SSP (see p73).

In some circumstances, you can be treated as being in full-time work for working tax credit (WTC) while you are getting SSP (see p289). Entitlement to SSP can help you qualify for the disabled worker element (see p1420) and/or a childcare element (see p1422) in your WTC.[45] However, if you are not already claiming tax credits, you cannot make a new claim. You may be able to claim UC instead.

When calculating your entitlement to means-tested benefits and tax credits, SSP is:
- treated as employed earnings for UC. When calculating your entitlement to UC, it is your net earnings that are taken into account, so certain amounts may be deducted first (see p119);
- treated as earnings for pension credit and housing benefit (HB) (see Chapters 20 and 21). If you get SSP, an allowance for certain childcare charges may be deducted from your earnings when calculating your entitlement to HB (see p416);
- treated as employment income for WTC and child tax credit (see p1443).

Non-means-tested benefits

If you are getting SSP, you cannot get:
- employment and support allowance; *or*
- statutory adoption pay (SAP); *or*
- statutory paternity pay (SPP); *or*
- statutory shared parental pay (SSPP); *or*,
- statutory parental bereavement pay (SPBP).[46]

You cannot qualify for SSP during your maternity pay period or, if your entitlement is based on your own employment or self-employment, during your maternity allowance (MA) period (see p711).[47] If you get MA on the basis of your spouse's or partner's employment or self-employment, see p828.

SSP may affect your entitlement to some non-means-tested benefits.
- SSP counts towards the earnings condition for MA, statutory maternity pay, SAP, SPP, SSPP and SPBP.
- SSP counts as earnings for carer's allowance and reduced earnings allowance.

SSP does not affect your entitlement to other non-means-tested benefits.

Unless you have other earnings, such as occupational sick pay, you do not have to pay NI contributions while on SSP as the weekly rate of SSP is below the NI lower earnings limit. Instead, you are entitled to class 1 NI credits (see p956).[48]

The benefit cap

In some cases, there is a limit on the total amount of specified benefits you can receive (a 'benefit cap'). SSP is *not* a specified benefit. The benefit cap only applies if you are getting UC or HB. The benefit cap may not apply if you or your partner have worked recently. For HB, you may count as in work while receiving SSP, but for UC, this depends on your earnings per assessment period (including SSP). See p1156 for further information.

Other sources of help

If you are on a low income, you may be entitled to certain health benefits (see Chapter 31). You may be entitled to council tax reduction (see p836).

If you are asked to self-isolate due to COVID-19 under guidance for your area, and you live in Scotland, then you may be able to get a self-isolation support grant from your local authority. You can find out more on your local authority's website. These grants cease to be available in Wales from the end of June 2022. These grants are no longer available in England.

Notes

1. Who can get statutory sick pay
1   ss151-154 SSCBA 1992
2   s151(2) SSCBA 1992
3   Reg 16(2) SSP Regs
4   Reg 4 SSP Regs
5   s151(4) SSCBA 1992
6   Reg 2 and Sch 1 SSP Regs
7   See s89 Coronavirus Act 2020 and para 129 of *COVID-19 Response: living with COVID-19*, February 2022 available at assets.publishing.service.gov.uk/government/uploads/system/uploads/attachment_data/file/1056229/COVID-19_Response_-_Living_with_COVID-19.pdf
8   s152 SSCBA 1992
9   s153(2), (7) and (8) SSCBA 1992
10 ss153(2) and (12) and 155 SSCBA 1992; reg 3(1), (3) and (4) SSP Regs
11 s152(3) SSCBA 1992
12 s153(3) and Sch 11 SSCBA 1992; reg 3 SSP Regs
13 s163(2) SSCBA 1992; regs 17 and 19 SSP Regs
14 CSSP/2/1984; CSSP/3/1984
15 *Seaton v HMRC* [2011] UKUT 297 (TCC)
16 Reg 17 SSP Regs
17 Reg 17(2) SSP Regs
18 Reg 19(7) and (8) SSP Regs
19 Sch 11 para 6 SSCBA 1992
20 ss154 and 155(1) SSCBA 1992
21 s154(3) SSCBA 1992
22 Reg 5(2) and (3) SSP Regs
23 R(SSP) 1/85
24 s155(1) SSCBA 1992
25 *COVID-19 Response: living with COVID-19*, February 2022 available at assets.publishing.service.gov.uk/government/uploads/system/uploads/attachment_data/file/1056229/COVID-19_Response_-_Living_with_COVID-19.pdf

4. The amount of benefit
26 s157 SSCBA 1992
27 Regs 20 and 21 SSP Regs
28 s155(2)-(4) SSCBA 1992
29 s152(3) SSCBA 1992

5. Special benefit rules
30 s153(2)(d) and (12) SSCBA 1992
31 Reg 3(5) SSP Regs
32 Reg 3(4) SSP Regs

6. Claims and backdating
33 Reg 7(1), (4) and (5) SSP Regs
34 Reg 7(1)-(3) SSP Regs
35 s156 SSCBA 1992
36 s14(1) SSAA 1992
37 Reg 2(2) SSP(ME) Regs
38 Sch 1 SSP(ME) Regs
39 Reg 2(1) SSP(ME) Regs
40 Reg 15 SSP Regs

7. Getting paid
41 Sch 12 para 2 SSCBA 1992
42 Reg 8 SSP Regs
43 s151(3) SSCBA 1992

8. Tax, other benefits and the benefit cap
44 s4(1) SSCBA 1992
45 Regs 6, 9 and 13 WTC(EMR) Regs
46 s20(1) WRA 2007; regs 18 and 27 SPPSAP(G) Regs; regs 14(1)(a) and 26(1)(a) SSPP(G) Regs; reg 9(1)(a) SPBP(G) Regs
47 s153(2)(d) and (12) SSCBA 1992
48 Reg 8B(2)(a)(iii) SS(Cr) Regs

Chapter 40

Other payments and support

This chapter covers:
1. Council tax reduction (p836)
2. Loans for mortgage interest (p839)
3. Local welfare assistance schemes (p846)
4. Healthy Start food and vitamins (p847)
5. Education benefits (p851)
6. Help with childcare costs (p854)
7. Payments for former members of the armed forces (p857)
8. Financial help when preparing for and starting work (p858)
9. Other financial help (p859)

Key facts

- There are a number of payments and other support you may be able to get in addition to your benefits. For some of these you must be receiving a 'qualifying benefit'.
- You may be able to get financial help from your local authority – eg, your council tax may be reduced, you may qualify for help under its welfare assistance scheme or your child may be able to get help with certain costs of education, such as free school lunches.
- If you are an owner-occupier and getting universal credit or another means-tested benefit, you may be offered a loan from the DWP to help with your mortgage interest payments.
- Under the Healthy Start scheme, you can get vouchers for milk, fruit and vegetables, and coupons for free vitamins. A similar scheme, Best Start foods, operates in Scotland. Free milk is also available to children in daycare under the welfare food scheme.
- You can get free childcare, or help with childcare costs, in certain circumstances.
- You may qualify for payments if you have an illness or disability due to serving in the armed forces.
- You can get payments to help you start work in certain circumstances.
- Other sources of financial help are available – eg, if you are on a low income, have children, are an older person, have an illness or disability, need help with home improvements or have other special needs.

Part 5: Other benefits
Chapter 40: Other payments and support
1. Council tax reduction

1. **Council tax reduction**

If you need help to pay your council tax, you may be able to get a reduction under your local authority's council tax reduction scheme. In some areas, this is known as council tax support or rebate. **Note:** a council tax reduction is *not* a social security benefit or a tax credit and the rules for benefits and tax credits in this *Handbook* do not apply.

In:[1]

* England and Wales, local authorities may devise their own local schemes which must meet minimum requirements. In Wales, if a local authority does not adopt its own scheme, a default scheme applies. Check with your local authority whether it has its own local scheme or the default scheme applies;
* Scotland, there is a national scheme, administered by local authorities.

Check with your local authority whether you qualify for a council tax reduction. Ensure the rules are being applied correctly in your case. If your local authority has adopted its own scheme, check that it meets the minimum requirements. **Note:**

* You may be able to get extended help for a period if you take up paid work, more paid work or better paid work.
* In England and Scotland, but not in Wales, there is an alternative maximum council tax reduction (known as 'second adult rebate') designed to help you if you share your home with anyone on a low income.
* In Scotland, if your property is in one of the Bands E to H, you may be entitled to additional council tax reduction if your income is below a certain level.

* *

Can you get a discretionary reduction from your local authority?

In England and Wales, in addition to its council tax reduction scheme, your local authority has a discretionary power to reduce your council tax bill.[2] Local authorities can reduce the council tax payable in individual circumstances (eg, if you are in financial hardship) and in group cases (eg, during a local emergency, such as flooding). You should apply for a discretionary reduction in writing, stating that you are applying for a reduction under section 13A of the Local Government Finance Act 1992, and provide any supporting evidence. If the local authority refuses, you can appeal against its decision to a valuation tribunal.

* *

You may also qualify for a council tax discount (eg, a 25 per cent discount if you are the only resident) or exemption (eg, if only students occupy the dwelling), which is not means tested and depends on your circumstances. For further information, see CPAG's *Council Tax Handbook*.

Common rules for all applicants

The following basic conditions apply in England, Wales and Scotland for all applicants, whether you are under or over pension age.

- You must be liable for council tax on the dwelling in which you are a resident.[3]
- You must not be a 'person subject to immigration control' (see p1524) and you must satisfy the habitual residence test (see p1551).[4]
- You must make an application for council tax reduction.[5] You can apply in writing. You can also apply by telephone or online if your local authority allows this. If your claim is 'defective', you must be notified and given at least one month to correct it.
  - If you or your partner have been awarded universal credit (UC) or pension credit (PC) and apply for council tax reduction within one month of applying for that benefit, the date of your application is the date of your benefit claim.
  - If you or your partner are on UC, income support (IS), income-based jobseeker's allowance (JSA), income-related employment and support allowance (ESA) or PC and apply for council tax reduction within one month of becoming liable to pay council tax for the first time, the date of your application is the date you became liable for council tax.
- Your council tax reduction is generally applied by reducing your council tax bill.
- If you disagree with a council tax reduction decision, you can appeal, initially to the local authority. Appeals must be in writing and made within one month of your being sent the decision in Wales or within two months in Scotland. There are no formal time limits for appeals in England.
- If you are not satisfied with the outcome of the appeal, you can make a further appeal to a valuation tribunal (in England and Wales) or the council tax reduction review panel (in Scotland). In England and Wales, you must appeal within two months of the date of the local authority's response. In Scotland, you must appeal within 42 days of the date of the response.[6]

Common rules for applicants over pension age

The following rules apply in England, Wales and Scotland for applicants of pension age or over. These rules apply if your partner is under pension age, but they do not apply if you or your partner are entitled to UC, IS, income-based JSA or income-related ESA.[7]

- If you or your partner are getting the guarantee credit of PC, you are entitled to the maximum council tax reduction, which is 100 per cent of your council tax liability less any non-dependant deductions.
- You cannot qualify for council tax reduction if you have capital over £16,000, unless you are getting the guarantee credit of PC. Capital under £10,000 is

Part 5: Other benefits
Chapter 40: Other payments and support
1. Council tax reduction

ignored. If you have capital between £10,000 and £16,000, a tariff income is counted of £1 a week for every £500, or part of £500, over £10,000.

- If you are not getting PC, your applicable amount, income and capital are calculated in a broadly equivalent way to housing benefit (HB) (see Chapters 17, 21 and 23).
- If your income is below your applicable amount, you are entitled to the maximum council tax reduction, which is 100 per cent of your council tax liability less any non-dependant deductions.
- If your income is above your applicable amount, your maximum council tax reduction is reduced by 20 per cent of your excess income.
- A non-dependant deduction may be made for another adult living in your home. The rules for who counts as a non-dependant and when a deduction is made are the same as for HB (see p198), but the amounts are different.
- Your application can be backdated for three months.

If you are under pension age

England

In England, the support available for working-age people varies from one local authority to another. Some of the main features or the minimum requirements of council tax reduction schemes for people under pension age in England are as follows.[8]

- The capital limit may be less than £16,000.
- If you get IS, income-based JSA or income-related ESA, you are entitled to the maximum council tax reduction, but this may be less than 100 per cent of your council tax liability, so you may be required to make a minimum payment.
- Your local authority may set rules to allow your application to be backdated, but is not obliged to do so.
- Your local authority must make a decision within 14 days of receiving your properly completed application, or as soon as is reasonable.

Wales

Some of the main features of the minimum requirements and the default scheme in Wales are as follows.[9]

- You cannot qualify for council tax reduction if you have capital over £16,000. Capital under £6,000 is ignored. If you have capital between £6,000 and £16,000, a tariff income is counted of £1 a week for every £250, or part of £250, over £6,000.
- If you get IS, income-based JSA or income-related ESA, you are entitled to maximum council tax reduction, which is 100 per cent of your council tax liability less any non-dependant deductions.
- If you get UC, your applicable amount is your maximum UC, and your income is the figure used by the DWP plus the amount of UC payable. Monthly

amounts are converted to weekly amounts by multiplying by 12 and dividing by 52.

- If you do not get UC, your applicable amount is calculated in a similar way as for means-tested benefits, but all personal allowances and premiums have increased in line with inflation since 2013, even if the equivalent allowances in social security payments have been frozen.
- If your income is below your applicable amount, you are entitled to maximum council tax reduction, which is 100 per cent of your council tax liability less any non-dependant deductions.
- If your income is more than your applicable amount, your maximum council tax reduction is reduced by 20 per cent of your excess income.
- Your application may be backdated for up to three months if you had continuous good cause for not applying earlier.

Scotland

Some of the main features of the council tax reduction scheme in Scotland are as follows.[10]

- You cannot qualify for council tax reduction if you have capital over £16,000. Capital under £6,000 is ignored. If you have capital between £6,000 and £16,000, a tariff income is counted of £1 a week for every £250, or part of £250, over £6,000.
- There is no two-child limit, and the amount for each child is higher than the child element in UC.
- If your income is below your applicable amount, you are entitled to maximum council tax reduction, which is 100 per cent of your council tax liability.
- If your income is more than your applicable amount, your maximum council tax reduction is reduced by 20 per cent of your excess income.
- Your application may be backdated for up to six months if you had continuous good cause for not applying earlier.
- Arrears of council tax are not recoverable if they are due to an official error that overpaid your council tax reduction.

2. Loans for mortgage interest

If you have a mortgage, the DWP may offer you loan payments to help with the interest payments. You are only eligible for the offer of a loan if you are entitled to universal credit (UC), income support (IS), income-based jobseeker's allowance (JSA), income-related employment and support allowance (ESA) or pension credit (PC). The DWP calls these loans 'support for mortgage interest loans'.

If you accept a loan for your mortgage interest, regular payments are made, usually direct to your lender.[11] Payments are made monthly (for UC) or four-weekly (for IS, income-based JSA, income-related ESA or PC). The amount of each

Part 5: Other benefits
Chapter 40: Other payments and support
2. Loans for mortgage interest

loan payment is calculated with a formula and is not necessarily what you have to pay (see p842).

Getting advice

It is vital to get independent legal and financial advice (eg, from a financial adviser or solicitor) before accepting a loan for mortgage interest from the DWP. **Note:** the information about the loan you get from the DWP or its agent (currently in a telephone call from Serco) is *not* independent advice.

Note:
- A loan for mortgage interest is *not* a social security benefit.
- You normally have to repay the loan (see p845). There are exceptions.
- A charge on your property (a standard security in Scotland) is made in favour of the DWP. This enables the DWP to recover what you owe it, if there is sufficient equity in your property.
- The DWP adds interest to the total amount you owe until the earliest of the date the loan is paid back (or written off), or you have died (or until both you and your partner have died) or, in some cases, you are sent a statement of what you owe the DWP so you can repay in full.[12] The rate of interest charged by the DWP is set out in the rules and is currently 0.8 per cent.[13]

Even though a loan for mortgage interest is not a benefit, if you disagree with a decision about a loan, you can apply for a revision or a supersession, or appeal against the decision under the rules that apply to benefits.[14] You must apply for a mandatory reconsideration before you can appeal. See Chapters 56 and 57.

Note: if you have other housing costs (eg, ground rent or service charges), help with these *can* be included in your UC, IS, income-based JSA, income-related ESA or PC. See Chapter 6 for UC and Chapter 18 for the other means-tested benefits.

Who can get a loan for mortgage interest

You can get a loan for mortgage interest if:[15]
- you are entitled to UC, and you (and your partner) do not have any earned income (see p117).[16] This includes earnings from work you can do while claiming contributory ESA (see p1019) or work of fewer than 16 hours a week you can do while claiming contribution-based JSA (see p974). The nature and duration of the work is not relevant – eg, it does not matter if your job is part time or temporary; *or*
- you are entitled (or treated as entitled – see below) to IS, income-based JSA, income-related ESA or PC.

In either case, you must also meet the following conditions:
- your loan qualifies (see below); *and*
- you (or your partner) count as liable to pay your loan (see p842); *and*
- your loan is for the home in which you normally live (see p842); *and*
- the DWP offers you a loan for mortgage interest and you accept the offer. You (and your partner) must sign and return the loan agreement. You must also create a legal charge (in England and Wales) or a standard security (in Scotland) in favour of the DWP. If you have a partner and both of you are the legal owners of your home, you must both do this. If only one of you is the legal owner, the other must give her/his written consent.

The DWP must provide you with specified information within six months of your accepting the offer of a loan for mortgage interest.[17] This includes a summary of the terms and conditions of the DWP loan agreement and information about where you and your partner can get further information and independent legal and financial advice about the loan. The information may be provided by a third party on the DWP's behalf. Currently, the third party is Serco. The DWP says this information will be provided by telephone. **Note:** this information is *not* independent advice.

Note: you are treated as entitled to IS, JSA, ESA or PC if you have claimed it and you are not entitled solely because your income is the same as, or more than, your applicable amount (your standard minimum guarantee for PC), but is less than this amount plus the weekly loan payments you would receive if you were entitled.[18] You cannot be treated as entitled to UC in this way – you must actually be entitled to UC.

Which loans qualify

Depending on which benefit you are entitled to, the loan for mortgage interest can cover:[19]
- for UC, interest payments on a loan that is secured on the accommodation you occupy, or are treated as occupying, as a home (see p90), whatever the purpose of the loan; *and*
- for IS, JSA, ESA or PC, mortgages and other loans for house purchase and loans used to pay for specified repairs and improvements or to meet a service charge for these. The types of repairs and improvements are those on p345 that are excluded from help with housing costs; *and*
- for UC or PC, 'alternative finance payments' – ie, payments made under alternative finance arrangements to enable you to acquire an interest in the accommodation you occupy, or are treated as occupying, as a home (see p842), such as a Sharia-compliant mortgage.

The rules for the type of loans that qualify are broadly the same as for the housing costs rules before 6 April 2018. See the 2017/18 edition of this *Handbook* for

Part 5: Other benefits
Chapter 40: Other payments and support
2. Loans for mortgage interest

details. For UC, see pp488–89 and for IS, JSA, ESA and PC, see pp46–52. For IS, JSA, ESA and PC, restrictions might be made if you took out or increased your home loan or loan for repairs and improvements while entitled to IS, income-based JSA, income-related ESA or PC, or in a period between claims.[20]

Liability for payments

To get a loan for mortgage interest, you (or your partner) must be liable to make payments on a loan that qualifies, or you (or s/he) must be treated as liable.[21] **Note:** you (or your partner) can be treated as *not* liable to make payments even if you are, in specified situations, or if you are entitled to UC, if the DWP considers the liability to be contrived.[22]

For UC, the rules for who counts as liable for payments are broadly the same as for the housing costs rules before 6 April 2018. See pp490–94 of the 2017/18 edition of this *Handbook*. For IS, JSA, ESA and PC, the rules for who counts as liable are broadly the same as for the housing costs rules in Chapter 18 (see p352).

Note: if you are jointly liable to make payments with someone other than your partner, you are only treated as liable for the proportion of the payments for which you (and your partner) are responsible.[23]

Occupying the accommodation as a home

To get a loan for mortgage interest, you must normally occupy the accommodation as your home.[24] You cannot usually get a loan for mortgage interest for any other home. However, there are special rules if you:[25]
- have just moved into your home;
- are liable to make payments for more than one dwelling, including if you have left your home because of a fear of domestic violence;
- are temporarily absent from home, including if you are away from home because of a fear of domestic violence;
- are a student or on a training course;
- are in temporary accommodation while repairs are carried out on your home.

For UC, the rules on occupying accommodation are broadly the same as for the housing costs rules before 6 April 2018. See pp494–98 of the 2017/18 edition of this *Handbook*. For IS, JSA, ESA and PC, the rules on occupying accommodation are broadly the same as for the housing costs rules in Chapter 18 (see p353).

The amount of loan payments

If you accept a loan, regular payments are made usually direct to your lender. Your monthly (for UC) or weekly (for IS, income-based JSA, income-related ESA or PC) loan payments are worked out by applying a standard percentage rate to the amount you owe to your lender, subject to an upper limit, and dividing by 12 or 52 as the case may be.[26] Any income above your applicable amount (for IS/ESA/JSA) or above your appropriate minimum guarantee (for PC) or any unearned income above your maximum amount (for UC) is deducted. Also deducted is the amount of any payment you get under a mortgage protection insurance policy. The standard rate is the average mortgage rate published by the Bank of England and changes when this differs by 0.5 percentage points or more.[27] The current rate is at gov.uk/support-for-mortgage-interest and is 2.09 per cent.

Example

Eileen is an owner-occupier with a mortgage. The amount she owes her mortage lender is £175,000. She is unemployed and her only income is UC. She accepts a loan for mortgage interest from the DWP. Her loan payments are worked out as follows.

£175,000 x 2.09% = £3,657.50

£3,657.50 ÷ 12 = £304.79

Eileen's monthly loan payments are therefore £304.79. Her debt to the DWP comprises each loan payment she gets, along with the interest that accrues on that debt. So, for example, if Eileen gets loan payments for 10 months, she will owe the DWP £3,047.90 plus interest (this is different from the average mortgage rate and is currently 0.8 per cent).

Note: even if there is a reduction in the amount you owe your lender, your regular loan payments are usually only recalculated annually, on the anniversary of the date you started getting them.[28]

If the amount you owe your lender is more than an upper limit, the amount of your loan payments is usually calculated using the upper limit.[29] The upper limit is usually £200,000 if you are entitled to UC, IS, JSA or ESA.

If you are entitled to PC, the upper limit is usually £100,000. However, if you are entitled to IS, JSA or ESA with an upper limit of £200,000, but you then claim PC within 12 weeks, this higher upper limit continues to apply.[30]

Deductions for non-dependants

If you are entitled to IS, income-based JSA, income-related ESA or PC, a set deduction is made from your weekly loan payments for people who normally live with you in your home who are not part of your family for benefit purposes (called 'non-dependants').[31] The rules for who counts as a non-dependant, and when a deduction is made, are broadly the same as for the housing costs rules in Chapter 18 (see pp347–349). To calculate the amount of the deduction, see p349. If you have other housing costs (eg, ground rent or service charges, see p345) and help with these is included in your benefit, the non-dependant deduction is apportioned between the help you get with housing costs and your loan payments. There are no non-dependant deductions or housing costs contributions deducted from loan payments if you get UC.

Part 5: Other benefits
Chapter 40: Other payments and support
2. Loans for mortgage interest

When loan payments start and end

Once you have accepted a loan for mortgage interest, your regular loan payments start:[32]

- if you are entitled to PC, from the first day of the first benefit week after your first date of entitlement (there is no 'waiting period' for PC); or
- if you are entitled to UC, from the first day of the first assessment period after an initial 'waiting period' of nine consecutive assessment periods in which you are entitled to UC. If you were getting loan payments while entitled to (or treated as entitled to) IS, income-based JSA or income-related ESA and claim UC within one month of that claim ending, you do not have to serve the waiting period again for UC; or
- if you are entitled to (or treated as entitled to) IS, income-based JSA or income-related ESA, after an initial 'waiting period' of 39 consecutive weeks in which you are entitled to (or treated as entitled to) one of those benefits; or
- if you were entitled to (or treated as entitled to) IS, income-based JSA or income-related ESA but had not completed the waiting period, and claim UC within one month of that claim ending, from the first day of the first assessment period after a waiting period of 273 days when you were entitled to (or treated as entitled to) those benefits or UC; or
- a later start date if you request.

Loan payments are always made in arrears.

Once loan payments start, you can ask to stop getting them at any time. Loan payments end if:[33]

- you are no longer entitled to UC. If you become entitled to UC again, you will only be eligible for loan payments after the waiting period of nine consecutive months in which you are entitled to UC; or
- you are entitled to UC and you (or you partner) have any earned income – eg, if you start a job. If you are still entitled to UC and in a subsequent assessment period you have no earnings, you should qualify for loan payments without having to serve the nine-month waiting period again. The rules do not stipulate that you must have no earnings during the waiting period. DWP guidance is not clear on this point – you can request a mandatory reconsideration of a decision that you are not eligible for an offer of a loan in this situation; or
- you are no longer entitled (or treated as entitled) to IS, income-based JSA, income-related ESA or PC. However, if you have been getting IS, JSA or ESA, check whether you qualify for mortgage interest run-on (see p845). If you become entitled to IS, income-based JSA or income-related ESA again within 52 weeks (although you will only be able to make a new claim for these benefits in very limited circumstances), you can be offered loan payments without having to serve the 39-week waiting period again (there is no 'waiting period' for PC); or

- you are no longer liable (or treated as liable) to pay your loan; *or*
- you are no longer occupying (or treated as occupying) your home; *or*
- your loan for mortgage interest agreement ends in accordance with its terms.

Check whether you have to repay your loan for mortgage interest (see below).

Are you moving onto universal credit?

If you have been getting loan payments in IS, income-based JSA or income-related ESA and move onto UC, you can only get loan payments in UC if you have no earned income. So, for example, if you have been working within the 'permitted work' limits for ESA and are still working when you move onto UC, your loan payments will stop.

Mortgage interest run-on

When you (or your partner) return to work or increase your hours and so count as being in full-time paid work, you no longer qualify for IS, income-based JSA or income-related ESA and therefore no longer qualify for a loan for mortgage interest. However, if you qualify for mortgage interest run-on, your weekly loan payments continue to be paid for the first four weeks after you go into full-time paid work.[34] **Note:** you do not have to make a claim to qualify for mortgage interest run-on; it is paid automatically. However, you must let the DWP know you are starting full-time paid work. The rules are broadly the same as they were before 6 April 2018. See pp474–75 of the 2017/18 edition of this *Handbook* for details.

Repaying the loan

The amount of your loan (ie, the total of all the loan payments you have received) and any interest you owe the DWP must normally be repaid in full in any of the following situations.[35]

- You sell your home (although if you have bought a new home, you can request that a loan balance can be transferred to your new home).[36]
- Ownership of your home is transferred, assigned or otherwise disposed of. This does not apply if this is to:
  - you, following your partner's death, or your partner, following your death, provided you or your partner live in the home; *or*
  - you, from a former spouse or civil partner under a court order or an agreement for maintenance, provided you live in the home.
- You die, or, if you have a partner s/he is the owner and s/he dies, or if you are both owners, both of you die.

In the first two situations, repayment is made from the proceeds of the sale, transfer or assignment. In the third situation, repayment is made from the person's estate.

Part 5: Other benefits
Chapter 40: Other payments and support
3. Local welfare assistance schemes

Interest is charged on the amount of loan payments at the average gilt rate published by the Office for Budget Responsibility (at the time of writing, 0.8 per cent) and is set for six-month periods starting on 1 January and 1 July.[37] You can repay some, or all, of what you owe before any of the above situations occur, provided you pay at least £100 at a time. **Note:** if your home is transferred, assigned or otherwise disposed of at less than the market value, it is treated as if this happened at market value for the purposes of the repayment rules.[38]

Note: if the DWP has a legal charge (in England or Wales) or a standard security (in Scotland) on your home and there is not enough equity to cover the amount you owe, repayment is limited to the amount that is available after other prior ranking charges or securities (eg, your outstanding mortgage) have been paid.[39] This means that if there is insufficient left, or nothing left, after repayment of the prior rankings, any remaining loan for mortgage interest and any interest you owe the DWP are written off and are considered to be fully repaid.

3. **Local welfare assistance schemes**

Help may be available under local welfare assistance schemes set up by your local authority (in England) or by the devolved administrations (the Discretionary Assistance Fund in Wales and the Scottish Welfare Fund in Scotland). The DWP may refer to this as 'local welfare provision'.

You may qualify if you need help, for example:
- with immediate short-term needs in a crisis – eg, if you do not have sufficient resources, or you need help with expenses in an emergency or as a result of a disaster, such as a fire or flood in your home;
- to establish yourself in the community following a stay in institutional or residential accommodation, or to help you remain in the community;
- to set up a home in the community as part of a planned resettlement programme;
- to ease exceptional pressure on your family;
- to enable you to care for a prisoner or young offender on temporary release;
- with certain travel expenses – eg, to visit someone in hospital, to attend a funeral, to ease a domestic crisis, to visit a child living with her/his other parent or to move to suitable accommodation;

In England, the local scheme is at your local authority's discretion. Check with your local authority to find out what help is available, whether you qualify and how to apply.

In Wales, the Discretionary Assistance Fund offers non-repayable emergency assistance payments and individual assistance payments.

The Scottish Welfare Fund provides community care grants and crisis grants. The basic rules for the scheme are set by the Scottish government, with each local authority having some discretion. You should apply to your local authority.[40]

---

4. Healthy Start food and vitamins

In England and Wales, if you qualify for Healthy Start food and vitamins, you get free vitamins as well as vouchers that can be used to buy specified types of food. In Scotland, Healthy Start has been replaced by Best Start foods (see p850).

Healthy Start food vouchers

If you qualify for Healthy Start food, you:[41]
- get fixed-value vouchers (worth £4.25 a week each) that can be exchanged for 'Healthy Start food' at registered food outlets; *or*
- are paid an amount equal to the value of the vouchers, if there is no registered food outlet within a reasonable distance of your home.

Healthy Start food
'Healthy Start food' means liquid cow's milk and cow's milk-based infant formula, fresh, frozen or canned fruit, vegetables and pulses including loose, pre-packed, whole, sliced, chopped or mixed fruit or vegetables (but not to which fat, salt, sugar, flavouring or any other ingredients have been added).[42]

Who can claim

You qualify for Healthy Start food vouchers if:[43]
- **you are at least 10 weeks pregnant** and you are:
  - 18 or over and are entitled to (or are a partner or member of the family of someone who is entitled to) a 'qualifying benefit' (see p849);
  - under 18, whether or not you are entitled to a qualifying benefit (but not if you are excluded from these because you are a 'person subject to immigration control' – see p1524); *or*
- **you are a mother** who has 'parental responsibility' for a child under one and:
  - you are 16 or over and entitled to (or you are a partner or member of the family of someone who is entitled to) a qualifying benefit. If you are entitled to universal credit (UC) or pension credit (PC), your child must be under one year old. For other benefits, your child must be under one or it is less than a year since her/his expected date of birth. This means you can continue to qualify for vouchers for a period after your child is one – ie, if s/he was born prematurely; *or*
  - it is less than four months since your baby's expected date of birth and you have not yet notified Healthy Start that s/he was born. You must have been

Part 5: Other benefits
Chapter 40: Other payments and support
4. Healthy Start food and vitamins

entitled to a qualifying benefit before your baby was born. This allows your entitlement to vouchers to continue until you notify the birth. Once you do, you can then qualify under the rule above (if you are 18 or over). **Note:** as long as you provided the notification within the four-month period, you can also get extra vouchers for your child from her/his date of birth.

If you qualify for vouchers for more than one child under this rule (eg, you have twins), you get a voucher for each. If you do not have 'parental responsibility' but would otherwise qualify for vouchers, your child qualifies instead of you;[44]

- **you are responsible for a child under four** who is a member of your family. You or a member of the family must be entitled to a qualifying benefit; *or*
- **you are responsible for a child under four** who is a British citizen, you have no recourse to public funds due to your immigration status (see p1527) and your monthly earned income is no more than £408.[45]

If this applies to you, you should start your claim by emailing Healthystart-claim@dhsc.gov.uk.

In practical terms, this means that each week you get one voucher for each of your children aged between one and four, two vouchers for each of your children under one (or within one year of their expected date of birth), plus one voucher if you are pregnant.

The **'qualifying benefits'** are:[46]

- UC, if during the last complete assessment period or the assessment period before that you (and your partner) have no earnings, or earned no more than £408. If you subsequently cease to be entitled to UC or your earnings exceed the £408 threshold, you continue to qualify for Healthy Start food vouchers for a further eight weeks after the last complete assessment period;
- child tax credit (CTC), provided that gross income for CTC purposes does not exceed £16,190 and there is no entitlement to working tax credit (WTC), other than if this is during the four-week WTC run-on period (see p289);
- income support (IS);
- income-based jobseeker's allowance (JSA);
- PC;
- income-related employment and support allowance (ESA) – a qualifying benefit during pregnancy only.

Example

Rhea is 17 weeks pregnant. She has three children: twin girls aged two and a boy aged seven. She is getting IS and CTC. She qualifies for a voucher because she is more than 10 weeks pregnant. Her twins each qualify for a voucher as they are under four. Her son does not qualify for a voucher. Rhea gets three vouchers each week totalling £12.75. When the baby is born, Rhea will be entitled to two vouchers for a child under one, plus one voucher for each of the twins aged under four. She will get four vouchers each week, totalling £17.

Definitions

'Parental responsibility' means parental responsibility as defined in section 3(1) of the Children Act 1989 (in England or Wales).[47]

'Family' means a person and her/his partner and any child or qualifying young person who is a member of her/his household and for whom s/he or her/his partner counts as being responsible.[48] So, for example, if you are not entitled to a qualifying benefit but are included in your mother's or father's claim for one of these, you can qualify for Healthy Start food vouchers.

To count as the member of a family of someone entitled to UC, s/he must be 'responsible' for you under the UC rules (see p309) and must also satisfy the £408 earnings rule described above.

If you are an asylum seeker receiving asylum support, you get an extra amount to help you buy healthy food if you are pregnant or have a child under three.

Claims

You must make an initial claim for Healthy Start food vouchers in writing and must provide specified information and evidence.[49] You can:

- complete the form in the Healthy Start leaflet (HS01), available from midwives, health visitors, maternity clinics and some doctors' surgeries or from 0345 607 6823;
- download a form or complete it online and print it off, or email yourself a form at healthystart.nhs.uk.

If you are under 16, your claim must also be signed by your parent or carer. Send the completed form to: Healthy Start Issuing Unit, Freepost RRTY-SYAE-JKCR, PO Box 1067, Warrington WA55 1EG.

If you are getting Healthy Start food vouchers while you are pregnant and then inform Healthy Start of your baby's birth by telephone while s/he is under four months old, you can get extra vouchers for her/him from her/his date of birth.[50] You may need to make a claim for UC for her/him (or add her/him to your existing UC or tax credits claim) to ensure that you continue to get the vouchers. You are still entitled to Healthy Start vouchers for a child even if a child element is not payable in UC/CTC/IS/JSA because of the 'two-child limit'.

If you do not get vouchers to which you think you are entitled, or have any other problems with these, contact the Healthy Start Issuing Unit on 0345 607 6823.

Note: paper vouchers may be replaced with a prepayment card in the future.

Part 5: Other benefits
Chapter 40: Other payments and support
4. Healthy Start food and vitamins

Healthy Start vitamins

If you qualify for Healthy Start food vouchers, you also qualify for Healthy Start vitamins.[51] Ask your local health professional what the local arrangements are for getting these.

You do not have to make a separate claim for Healthy Start vitamins. You are sent Healthy Start vitamin coupons with your Healthy Start food vouchers. However, you must show evidence to the vitamin supplier that you are entitled (ie, the letter to which your most recent Healthy Start vouchers were attached) and, if requested, proof of your child's age.[52] In Scotland, all pregnant women are eligible for free vitamins, regardless of income.[53] If you are entitled to Best Start foods in Scotland, you can also get free vitamins from your health board.

5 Best Start foods in Scotland

The Best Start foods payment card has replaced the Healthy Start voucher scheme in Scotland.[54] If you qualify, you will get a payment of £4.50 for yourself if you are pregnant, £9.00 for a child aged under one and £4.50 for each child aged one or two. Payments are made by credits to a payment card.

Best Start foods are administered by Social Security Scotland. Best Start foods include cow's milk, first infant formula milk, fresh, frozen or tinned fruit and vegetables, fresh or tinned pulses and eggs.

You qualify for Best Start foods if you are pregnant or responsible for a child under three and you are:[55]
- 18 or over and are entitled to (or are a member of the family of someone who is entitled to) a 'qualifying benefit'; *or*
- under 18, whether or not you are entitled to a 'qualifying benefit'. You continue to qualify until the end of your pregnancy if you turn 18 during pregnancy, or until your child's first birthday if you turn 18 while responsible for her/him; *or*
- responsible for a child aged under three who is a British citizen, you have no recourse to public funds due to your immigration status (see p1527) and your income is £625 a month or less.[56]

The qualifying benefits for Best Start foods are:[57]
- UC if you, or you and your partner together, have an earned income of £660 or less in either of the last two complete monthly assessment periods. If you stop getting UC, or your earned income exceeds this limit, you continue to be entitled to Best Start foods for eight weeks after the end of the most recent assessment period;
- IS, income-based JSA, income-related ESA or PC;
- CTC (if not entitled to WTC) if you have an annual income of £17,005 or less;
- CTC and WTC if you have an annual income of £7,920 or less;
- housing benefit if your weekly income is £328 or less.

If you are pregnant, you can apply from the start of your pregnancy. You will usually only be asked for evidence when around 24 weeks' pregnant. You must report the child's birth within four months to get the payment from the child's date of birth.[58] Responsibility for a child is defined in the same way as for Best Start grants (see p1699). You are still entitled to Best Start foods for a child even if a child element is not payable in UC/CTC/IS/JSA because of the 'two-child limit'.

You can apply for Best Start foods:
- online at mygov.scot/best-start-grant-best-start-foods; *or*
- by telephone on 0800 182 2222; *or*
- in writing on the approved form, which you can download or request by telephone to be sent to you.

You can apply for a Best Start grant (see Chapter 74) and Scottish child payment (see Chapter 77) on the same form.

If you were previously entitled to Best Start foods within 12 weeks, and you think you are eligible again, you can contact Social Security Scotland and become entitled again without having to make a new claim.[59]

5. Education benefits

Financial help is available from your local authority if you are in school or are a student, or if you have children in school or college.

Free school lunches

School children are entitled to free school lunches if their families get:[60]
- universal credit (UC). In Scotland, your earnings (and those of your partner, if you make a joint claim) must not be more than £625 (from the UC assessment period before your application. In England and Wales, your earnings (and those of your partner, if you make a joint claim) must not exceed:
  - £616.67 in the UC assessment period immediately before the date you claim free school lunches; *or*
  - £1,233.34 in the two UC assessment periods immediately before the date you claim free school lunches; *or*
  - £1,850 in the three UC assessment periods immediately before the date you claim free school lunches;
- income support (IS), income-based jobseeker's allowance or income-related employment and support allowance (ESA);
- child tax credit and have annual taxable income of £16,190 (in England and Wales) or £17,005 (in Scotland), or less. However, this does not apply if the family is entitled to working tax credit (WTC) unless:
  - this is during the four-week 'WTC run-on' period (see p289); *or*

– in Scotland only, the WTC award is based on annual taxable income of £7,500 or less;
• in England and Wales only, guarantee credit of pension credit (PC).

Note: pupils eligible for free school lunches in England on 31 March 2018 or in Wales on 31 March 2019, and those who become eligible after this date, remain so until 31 March 2022 in England or 31 December 2023 in Wales, whether or not they (or their parents) continue to be entitled to a qualifying benefit. Those entitled to free school lunches on 31 March 2022 in England or on 31 December 2023 in Wales continue to be entitled until they finish their current stage of education – eg, primary or secondary school.[61]
Also entitled are:
• 16–18-year-olds getting the above benefits or tax credits in their own right;[62]
• asylum seekers in receipt of asylum support. Free school meals are also temporarily extended to some families with no recourse to public funds in England, and at the local authority's discretion in Wales and Scotland;[63]
• in Scotland, a child attending pre-school nursery (or similar) who is entitled under any of the first three bullet points above, or if her/his family gets PC, incapacity benefit or severe disablement allowance, or if since the age of two the child is being, or has been, looked after by a local authority or is the subject of a kinship care or guardianship order (and may also be entitled when of school age at the local authority's discretion).[64]

Note: free school lunches are provided to all children during the first three years of primary school in England, and Primary 1–5 in Scotland. In Wales, free school breakfasts are provided to all children in primary schools maintained by the local authority.[65]

School transport and school clothes

Local authorities must provide **free transport to school** for pupils aged five to 16 if it is considered necessary to enable the pupil to get to the 'nearest suitable school'. This applies if the pupil lives more than a set distance from that school. However, if there is no safe walking route, a pupil must be given free transport no matter how far away s/he lives from the nearest suitable school. Free school transport must also be provided to pupils with special educational needs and to those whose parents are on a low income – ie, if they qualify for free school lunches or their parents are on the maximum rate of WTC.
Local authorities can give **grants for school uniforms and other school clothes**. Each authority determines its own eligibility rules. Some school governing bodies or parents' associations also provide help with school clothing.

Free milk for children

Children under five are entitled to 189–200 millilitres of free milk on each day they are looked after for two hours or more:[66]
* in local authority daycare; *or*
* by a registered childminder or daycare provider; *or*
* in a school, playcentre or workplace nursery which is exempt from registration.

Children under one are allowed fresh or dried milk. This is provided by the welfare food scheme. In Scotland a non-dairy alternative and a healthy snack are also included, although parts of this scheme have been ruled unlawful.[67]

Schoolchildren may also be provided with free milk, and where it is provided in England and Wales, it should be free for children entitled to free school meals due to low income.[68]

Free period products

Free period products are available in schools and colleges. In England, if you are in school or aged under 19 in non-advanced education, you should be able to access free period products when you need them. If you are aged 19 or over, you can access free period products if you are continuing on a course you began before 19 or have an education, health and care plan.[69] In Wales, every school and college provides free period products.[70] In Scotland, education authorities are required to make period products available to all school pupils.[71]

Education maintenance allowance and 16 to 19 bursaries

An **education maintenance allowance** is a means-tested payment for young people who stay on in non-advanced education and who live in Wales or Scotland. Payments are made direct to the young person and are conditional on regular course attendance. The young person gets a weekly allowance during term time. The amount depends on the household income. For further details, see studentfinancewales.co.uk or mygov.scot/ema.

16 to 19 bursaries are payments for young people aged 16 to 19 who stay on in further education or training in England. These are available through the school, college or training provider. Certain young people in need (eg, young people in care, care leavers, young people without parental support who get UC or IS, or who get UC or ESA and either disability living allowance or personal independence payment) can get the maximum bursary. Discretionary bursaries are available to those in financial difficulty. See gov.uk/1619-bursary-fund for further information.

Neither payment counts as income for any benefits or tax credits the parent may be getting. They are also not affected by any income the young person has from part-time work.

Part 5: Other benefits
Chapter 40: Other payments and support
6. Help with childcare costs

Note: if you are a student, to find out what help is available to finance your studies, contact your local authority or college or university, or see gov.uk/student-finance. Also see CPAG's *Student Support and Benefits Handbook* and *Benefits for Students in Scotland Handbook* – both are open access on AskCPAG.

6. **Help with childcare costs**

Free early education and childcare

Pre-school children are entitled to a certain number of free hours of registered childcare, depending on their age and circumstances. You may also be able to get help with childcare costs through universal credit (UC) (see p73) or working tax credit (WTC) (see p1422) for extra hours that are not funded by this free provision, and for childcare for other age groups. The free childcare available differs in each country of the UK.

England

At the age of two, your child is entitled to 570 hours a year of free childcare (equal to 15 hours a week for 38 weeks) if you get:[72]
- UC, and your (and your partner's combined) earnings are no more than:
  - £1,283.34 in the previous assessment period; *or*
  - £2,556.67 in the previous two assessment periods; *or*
  - £3,850 in the previous three assessment periods; *or*
- child tax credit (CTC) (not entitled to WTC) and your annual income is no more than £16,190; *or*
- income support (IS); *or*
- income-based jobseeker's allowance (JSA); *or*
- income-related employment and support allowance (ESA); *or*
- the guarantee credit of pension credit (PC); *or*
- asylum support from the Home Office.

Your child is also entitled to this free childcare place at the age of two (regardless of your income or benefits) if s/he:[73]
- is looked after by a local authority;
- has left care under an adoption order, special guardianship order or child arrangements order;
- has a statement of special educational needs or an education, health and care plan; *or*
- gets disability living allowance.

At the ages of three and four, your child is entitled to 570 hours a year of free childcare (equal to 15 hours a week for 38 weeks), regardless of your income and whether you are in work or not.[74]

Your child is entitled to 1,140 hours a year of free childcare (equal to 30 hours a week for 38 weeks) at the ages of three and four if you are in work and earning within set limits. You must usually expect to earn at least the amount of the minimum wage at 16 hours a week over the next three months, and no more than £100,000 a year. If you have a partner, you must usually both be working within these individual limits. You can still qualify if one of you works and the other gets carer's allowance or the carer element of UC, ESA or has limited capability for work. You are still treated as in work while you are on maternity, paternity, shared parental, adoption or parental bereavement leave or getting associated statutory payments.

For more information and how to apply, see childcarechoices.gov.uk.

Wales

Your child may be entitled to free childcare and other support at the age of two or three under the 'Flying Start' scheme in some areas of Wales. See your local council's Family Information Service for more information.[75]

At the ages of three and four, your child is entitled to 10 hours a week free early education for 48 weeks of the year, known as Foundation Phase nursery. Your child may also be entitled to up to 20 hours a week childcare for 48 weeks of the year at the ages of three and four if you are in work and earning within set limits. You must usually be earning at least the amount of the minimum wage at 16 hours a week and less than £100,000 a year. If you have a partner, you must usually both be working within these individual limits. You are still treated as in work if you are on statutory leave.[76] The Childcare Offer for Wales is made up of a minimum of 10 hours a week of early education and up to 20 hours a week of childcare. The exact amount of childcare you can get depends on your local authority.

Scotland

At the age of two, your child is entitled to 1,140 hours a year of free early education and childcare (around 30 hours a week during term time) if you get:[77]

- UC with earnings no more than £660 in the assessment period before you apply;[78] *or*
- CTC and WTC with an annual income no more than £7,920;[79] *or*
- CTC (not entitled to WTC) with an annual income no more than £17,005 ; *or*
- IS; *or*
- income-based JSA; *or*
- income-related ESA; *or*
- incapacity benefit or severe disablement allowance; *or*
- PC.

Once s/he is eligible, your child remains entitled to free childcare even if you stop receiving these benefits. Your child also qualifies for 600 hours of free childcare

Part 5: Other benefits
Chapter 40: Other payments and support
6. Help with childcare costs

from the age of two if s/he is looked after by the local authority or the subject of a kinship care order.

At the ages of three and four, your child is entitled to 1,140 hours a year of free childcare, regardless of your income and whether you are in work or not.[80]

Tax-free childcare

Tax-free childcare is a government scheme to help middle and higher income parents with the cost of childcare. Parents of children aged under 12 (under 17, if they are disabled) can apply.[81]

The government tops up each payment of 80 pence you make into an online childcare account by 20 pence. The maximum annual top-up for each child in qualifying childcare is £2,000 (£4,000 for each disabled child). Payments from the account are debited to a registered childcare provider.

Payments can be made up until 1 September after the child's 11th birthday (16th birthday, if s/he is disabled). There is no limit on the number of children for whom you can make payments.

You (and your partner) must usually both be working and each earning at least 16 times the minimum wage for your age, and your individual earnings are not expected to exceed £100,000 a year each. One of a couple does not have to be in work if s/he is entitled to carer's allowance or contributory ESA or credits for limited capability for work.[82]

Note: you cannot be in the tax-free childcare scheme and still get UC or tax credits.[83] If you are entitled to UC, you are not eligible for the scheme. If you are getting tax credits, your award stops once you register for tax-free childcare – ie, you lose all your entitlement, not just the childcare element. The government may introduce rules that mean you lose all your UC entitlement if you register for the scheme.

If you are considering tax-free childcare, you should therefore check whether or not you will be better off. In most cases, you will be better off continuing to claim UC or tax credits. If you are in any doubt, get advice. **Note:**
- The maximum amount of top-up payments in the tax-free childcare scheme may be considerably less than what you can get in UC or tax credits.
- Tax-free childcare does not include any other amounts, and must be spent on childcare. UC and tax credits include amounts for adults, children and disability as well as a childcare element (in UC and WTC), and UC may include an amount for your housing costs.
- You must reconfirm your circumstances with the tax-free childcare scheme every three months, whereas UC uses a monthly assessment period and tax credits are assessed on annual income and finalised annually.
- If you leave the tax-free childcare scheme and claim UC again, you may be disqualified from applying for tax-free childcare again for up to three years, unless there has been a relevant change of circumstances – eg, a change in the make-up of your household or a change in your work.[84]

For more information, see childcarechoices.gov.uk and guidance available at depositedpapers.parliament.uk/depositedpaper/2283669/files?page=8.

7. Payments for former members of the armed forces

If you are a former member of the armed forces, you can claim under the following schemes, administered by the Ministry of Defence.

You can qualify for **war pension disablement benefits** if you have ill health or a disablement caused by service before 6 April 2005. The degree of your disablement is assessed on a percentage scale, with 100 per cent being the level of disablement that qualifies for the maximum award. If you are assessed at 20 per cent or more, you receive a pension, and if you are assessed at under 20 per cent, you get a lump sum (gratuity). You can also qualify for a number of supplementary allowances. Two of these are particularly important.

- **Constant attendance allowance.** You qualify for this if your disablement is assessed at 80 per cent or more, and because of your disablement you require 'constant attendance'. This has the same meaning as either 'attention' or 'supervision' for attendance allowance (AA) or disability living allowance (DLA) care component (see p596). The allowance is paid at four different rates depending on the number of hours for which you require constant attendance and whether this is in the daytime or at night. If you claim AA, DLA care component or the daily living component of personal independence payment (PIP), any constant attendance allowance to which are entitled is deducted from these benefits. **Note:** the top two rates of constant attendance allowance are considerably more than the highest rates of AA, DLA care component or PIP daily living component.

- **Mobility supplement.** You qualify for this if your disablement is assessed at 40 per cent or more, and because of your disablement your ability to walk is 'of little or no practical use'. This is, in effect, the same test as for the higher rate of the mobility component of DLA. There is a single rate of benefit currently worth £68.35 a week. If you claim DLA mobility component or PIP mobility component, any mobility supplement to which you are entitled is deducted from your DLA or PIP entitlement. **Note:** unlike DLA and PIP, there is no upper age limit for claiming mobility supplement.

You can qualify for help under the **Armed Forces Compensation Scheme** if you have ill health or a disablement caused by service on or after 6 April 2005. The main benefit is a lump-sum payment. To qualify, you must have had an injury or ill health that comes within one of the specified 'descriptors'. Each descriptor is assigned to a 'tariff level', running from 1 (the most severe) to 15, which

Part 5: Other benefits
Chapter 40: Other payments and support
8. Financial help when preparing for and starting work

determines the amount payable. If you receive an award within tariff levels 1-11, you also qualify for a 'guaranteed income payment', calculated as a percentage of your salary on the day your service in the armed forces ended. Awards are at 30, 50, 75 or 100 per cent, depending on your tariff level.

Armed forces independence payment is payable to those entitled to a guaranteed income payment under the Armed Forces Compensation Scheme at the 50 per cent rate or more. It is payable at a rate equivalent to the total of the enhanced rates of both the daily living and mobility components of PIP.

For more information, see gov.uk/government/organisations/veterans-uk or call Veterans UK on 0808 1914 2 18.

8. Financial help when preparing for and starting work

Flexible Support Fund

If you are attending training/education, a job interview or starting work, you may be able to get some financial support from the Flexible Support Fund, administered by Jobcentre Plus, to help your transition into work after a period of time on benefit – eg, for childcare costs, travel expenses and new clothes for interviews, and training course fees. You are expected to fund travel costs for fortnightly work search interviews yourself, but travelling expenses for additional appointments can be refunded.[85] Payments are discretionary. The government has said that the Flexible Support Fund can be used more widely for upfront childcare costs before you receive your first wage.[86] You cannot claim the universal credit (UC) childcare element for childcare costs that have been met by a Flexible Support Fund payment. Check with your Jobcentre Plus office or employment scheme or programme provider to see what is available. Do this before you start work, because you may have to apply before your job starts or within a short period of starting it.

New Enterprise Allowance

If you are aged at least 18 and starting or developing your own business, you may be eligible for the New Enterprise Allowance. You may be able to get mentoring to help set up a business plan, a weekly allowance worth up to £1,274 over 26 weeks and be able to apply for a start-up loan. You or your partner must be getting UC, jobseeker's allowance (JSA) or employment and support allowance (ESA), or you must be getting income support (IS) as a lone parent. Ask your Jobcentre Plus work coach for more information. **Note:** this scheme is closed to new applicants.

Job Start Payment (Scotland)

In Scotland, you may be able to get a Job Start Payment if you are a young person starting work averaging at least 12 hours a week over a four-week period. You qualify if you are aged 16 to 24 and have been out of work and claiming UC, IS, income-based JSA or income-related ESA for six months, or if you are a care leaver aged 16 to 25 and getting one of those benefits when you are offered the job. The Job Start Payment is a one-off grant of £260.35, or £416.50 if you are responsible for a child. You cannot receive another Job Start Payment within two years of getting one. The Job Start Payment is administered by Social Security Scotland. See mygov.scot/job-start-payment for more information and how to apply.

Travel discount card

If you are looking for work, you may be eligible for a Jobcentre Plus travel discount card, which entitles you to a 50 per cent reduction on selected rail fares, and on other public transport in some areas. This is available if you have been unemployed and claiming UC or JSA for three to nine months if you are aged under 25, or three to 12 months if you are aged 25 or over. You may also qualify if you are claiming other benefits and are 'actively engaged' with a Jobcentre Plus adviser.[87] Some information is available at gov.uk/government/publications/support-to-help-with-the-cost-of-transport.

9. Other financial help

This *Handbook* focuses on information about social security benefits and tax credits. However, there is other financial help, or help in kind, to which you may be entitled, especially if you are on a low income, have children, have an illness, disability or other special needs, or are an older person.

See the *Disability Rights Handbook*, published by Disability Rights UK, for help for those with care needs.

Food banks

If you are experiencing severe financial hardship (eg, caused by debt or benefit delays), you may be able to get vouchers for food which can be redeemed at a food bank. Vouchers are available from front-line care professionals such as doctors and social workers. Jobcentre Plus staff may also give out vouchers. You can find further information and contact details for many food banks at trusselltrust.org or by contacting your local authority.

You may be able to get help with food or meals through local community groups which are part of the FareShare network. See more information at fareshare.org.uk.

Part 5: Other benefits
Chapter 40: Other payments and support
9. Other financial help

Help to Save

Help to Save is a UK-wide government scheme offering a top-up to working people on low incomes who open a new type of savings account and pay into it regularly. To be eligible, you must be getting either:[88]

- universal credit (UC) with earnings of at least £658.66 a month (the monthly equivalent of 16 hours a week at the 'national living wage'); *or*
- working tax credit (WTC). You must either get WTC at more than a nil rate, or be eligible for WTC and get child tax credit at more than a nil rate.

Help to Save accounts last for four years. You can pay in up to £50 a month. After two years, the government will pay in a bonus of 50 per cent of your highest balance, and again at the end of the four years. The government bonus is disregarded as capital for UC, other means-tested benefits and tax credits. Your account can remain open, and you can keep paying into it and receive bonuses, even if you are no longer entitled to the benefit or tax credit that made you eligible to open it. Help to Save is administered by HM Revenue and Customs. See gov.uk/get-help-savings-low-income for more information. You can withdraw money at any time, but it will affect the amount of bonus you can get. You can close your account at any time, but if you close your account early, you will not get a bonus and will not be able to open another account.

Repairs, improvements and energy efficiency

Your local authority may be able to provide you with a grant to help with the cost of improving your home. The main types of grants available are:
- home improvement grants; *and*
- disabled facilities grants.

You may also be able to get:
- assistance from a home improvement agency (a local not-for-profit organisation) to repair, improve, maintain or adapt your home, sometimes called 'care and repair' or 'staying put' schemes, or with small repairs, safety checks and odd jobs from a handyperson service. For information see, in England, foundations.uk.com, in Wales, careandrepair.org.uk and in Scotland, careandrepairscotland.co.uk;
- a one-off discount of £140 on your energy bill under the Warm Home Discount scheme if you get the guarantee credit of pension credit (PC), or you are on a low income and get other qualifying means-tested benefits and meet your energy supplier's criteria. This does not affect your entitlement to a cold weather payment (see p791) or winter fuel payment (see p792). For further information, visit gov.uk/the-warm-home-discount-scheme;
- a grant for help with insulation and other energy efficiency measures in your home. Different schemes operate in England, Wales and Scotland. For further

information, visit energysavingtrust.org.uk. For more details, see CPAG's *Fuel Rights Handbook*.

Special funds for sick or disabled people

A range of help is available for people with an illness or disability to assist with things like paying for care services in their own home, equipment, holidays, furniture and transport needs, and for people with haemophilia or HIV contracted via haemophilia treatment. Grants are also available for practical support to help people do their jobs – eg, to pay for specialist equipment and travel.

For more information, see the *Disability Rights Handbook*, published by Disability Rights UK.

Help from social services

Local authority social services departments have statutory duties to provide a range of practical and financial help to families, children, young people, older people, people with disabilities, carers and asylum seekers. Contact your local authority.

Charities

There are many charities that provide various types of help to people in need. Your local authority social services department or local advice centre may know of appropriate charities that could assist you, or you can consult publications, such as *A Guide to Grants for Individuals in Need* and the *Charities Digest*, in your local library. Turn2us has details of charities that can provide financial help on its website turn2us.org.uk. In many cases, you can apply for support direct from the website. Information on grants available for individuals can also be found at fundsonline.org.uk.

Christmas bonus

You qualify for a Christmas bonus of £10 if you are entitled (or treated as being entitled) to any of the qualifying benefits for at least part of the 'relevant week' (even if the benefit is paid later).[89] The relevant week is usually the week beginning with the first Monday in December.[90]

Qualifying benefits[91]

Armed forces independence payment; attendance allowance; carer's allowance; disability living allowance; contributory employment and support allowance which includes either the support or the work-related activity component; long-term incapacity benefit; industrial death benefit for widows or widowers; industrial injuries disablement benefit (if it includes unemployability supplement or constant attendance allowance); PC; personal independence payment; severe disablement allowance; state pension or retirement pensions; war disablement pension (if it includes the mobility supplement, constant attendance allowance or unemployability supplement, or if you are at least pension age – see p766);[92] war widow's or surviving civil partner's pension; and widowed parent's allowance.

You may also qualify for an extra bonus for your partner (a further £10) if s/he has not received a bonus in her/his own right, and:[93]

- you are both at least pension age (see p766) and you are entitled, or may be treated as entitled, to an increase in one of the qualifying benefits in respect of her/him; *or*
- you are both at least pension age and the only qualifying benefit you get is PC.

The bonus is not taxable and has no effect on other benefits or tax credits.

It is paid automatically. However, you should contact the DWP within a year if you have not obtained your bonus, otherwise your right is lost.[94]

Notes

1. Council tax reduction

1 s13A LGFA 1992
   E CTRS(DS)E Regs; CTRS(PR)E Regs
   W CTRS(DS)W Regs; CTRSPR(W) Regs
   S CTR(S) Regs; CTR(SPC)S Regs
2 s13A(1)(c) LGFA 1992
3 ss13A(1) and 80 LGFA 1992
4 **E** Regs 12 and 13 CTRS(PR)(E) Regs
   W Regs 28 and 29 CTRSPR(W) Regs
   S Regs 16 and 17 CTR(S) Regs; regs 16 and 17 CTR(SPC)S Regs
5 **E** Sch 7 para 1 CTRS(PR)(E) Regs
   W Sch 12 paras 1-7 CTRSPR(W) Regs
   S Regs 82-88 CTR(S) Regs; regs 61-68 CTR(SPC)S Regs
6 **E** Sch 7 para 2 CTRS(PR)E Regs
   W Sch 12 paras 8-10 CTRSPR(W) Regs
   S Regs 90A-90D CTR(S) Regs; regs 70A-70C CTR(SPC)S Regs
7 **E** Reg 3 CTRS(PR)(E) Regs
   W Reg 3 CTRSPR(W) Regs
   S Reg 12 CTR(SPC)S Regs
8 CTRS(PR)(E) Regs
9 CTRSPR(W) Regs
10 CTR(S) Regs

2. Loans for mortgage interest

11 Reg 17 LMI Regs
12 Reg 15 LMI Regs
13 Reg 15(5) and (6) LMI Regs
14 s8(3)(bc) SSA 1998
15 Regs 2(1), 3, 4 and 5 LMI Regs
16 Reg 3(4) LMI Regs
17 Regs 5(2)(d) and 6 LMI Regs
18 Reg 2(1), definition of 'claimant', 'joint claimant' and 'single claimant', and (2)(aa) LMI Regs
19 Regs 2 and 3(2)(a) and Sch 1 LMI Regs
20 Reg 2(2)(aa) and Sch 1 para 3 LMI Regs; *Saleem v Secretary of State for Social Security*, reported as R(IS) 5/01; *SSWP v Mohammed* [2011] EWCA Civ 1358, reported as [2012] AACR 29
21 Reg 3(2)(b) and Sch 2 LMI Regs
22 Sch 2 paras 3 and 6 LMI Regs
23 Reg 3(3) LMI Regs
24 Reg 3(2)(c) and Sch 3 LMI Regs

25 Sch 3 paras 4-10 and 13-18 LMI Regs
26 Regs 2(1), 7, 11, 12, 13 and 14A LMI Regs
27 Reg 13 LMI Regs
28 Regs 2(1), 11(4) and (5) and 12(4) and (5) LMI Regs; reg 7(12B) SS&CS(DA) Regs
29 Regs 11(1), (2) and (3) and 12(1) and (2) LMI Regs
30 Reg 11(2) LMI Regs; 'modified rules' is defined in Reg 2 by reference to the Social Security (Housing Costs Special Arrangements) (Amendment and Modification) Regulations 2008 No.3195. These do not specify UC but the information on gov.uk/support-for-mortgage-interest/what-youll-get says that the higher limit applies when moving from other benefits to PC.
31 Reg 14 LMI Regs
32 Regs 2, definition of 'qualifying period', 8 and 9(7) LMI Regs
33 Reg 9(1)-(3) LMI Regs
34 Reg 9(4)-(6) LMI Regs
35 Reg 16 LMI Regs
36 Reg 16A LMI Regs
37 Reg 15 LMI Regs
38 Reg 16(7) LMI Regs
39 Reg 16(4), (5) and (6) LMI Regs

3. Local welfare assistance schemes
40 Welfare Funds (Scotland) Act 2015; The Welfare Funds (Scotland) Regulations 2016 No.107

4. Healthy Start food and vitamins
41 Regs 5(2) and 8 HSS&WF(A) Regs
42 Regs 2(1) and 5(1) and Sch 3 HSS&WF(A) Regs; HSS(DHSF)(W) Regs
43 Reg 3 HSS&WF(A) Regs
44 Reg 3(5) HSS&WF(A) Regs
45 healthystart.nhs.uk/how-to-apply/
46 Reg 3(8)-(11) HSS&WF(A) Regs
47 Reg 2(1) HSS&WF(A) Regs
48 Reg 2(1) HSS&WF(A) Regs
49 Reg 4 and Sch 2 HSS&WF(A) Regs
50 Reg 4(2) HSS&WF(A) Regs
51 Reg 3 HSS&WF(A) Regs
52 Reg 8A HSS&WF(A) Regs
53 gov.scot/policies/maternal-and-child-health/free-vitamins-for-all-pregnant-women
54 WF(BSF)(S) Regs
55 Regs 6, 7 and 8 WF(BSF)(S) Regs
56 mygov.scot/best-start-grant-best-start-foods/public-funds-access
57 Reg 10 WF(BSF)(S) Regs
58 Reg 11 WF(BSF)(S) Regs
59 Reg 11 WF(BSF)(S) Regs

5. Education benefits
60 **E** s512ZB Education Act 1996; The Education (Free School Lunches) (Prescribed Tax Credits) (England) Order 2003 No.383; Free School Lunches and Milk, and School and Early Years Finance (Amendments Relating to Universal Credit) (England) Regulations 2018 No.148
    W s512ZB Education Act 1996; The Education (Free School Lunches) (Prescribed Tax Credits) (Wales) Order 2003 No.879 (W.110); The Free School Lunches and Milk (Universal Credit) (Wales) Order 2019 No.187 (W.47)
    S s53(7) and (8) Education (Scotland) Act 1980; Reg 4A The Education (School Lunches) (Scotland) Regulations 2009 No.178
61 Art 3 Welfare Reform Act 2012 (Commencement No.30 and Transitory Provisions) Order 2018 No.145; Art 3 The Free School Lunches and Milk (Universal Credit) (Wales) Order 2019 No.187 (W.47)
62 For CTC, the legislation only provides for this in Scotland
63 **E** gov.uk/government/publications/covid-19-free-school-meals-guidance/guidance-for-the-temporary-extension-of-free-school-meals-eligibility-to-nrpf-groups
    W gov.wales/free-school-meals-coronavirusguidance-schools#section-40902
    S mygov.scot/school-meals
64 The Education (School Lunches) (Scotland) Regulations 2015 No.269; mygov.scot/school-meals
65 s88 School Standards and Organisation (Wales) Act 2013
66 Reg 18 WF Regs
67 [2022] CSOH 11, School and Nursery Milk Alliance Limited for Judicial Review
68 **E&W** s512ZB Education Act 1996
    S s53 Education (Scotland) Act 1980
69 Department of Education, *Period product scheme for schools and colleges in England*, 16 December 2020, gov.uk/government/publications/period-products-in-schools-and-colleges/period-product-scheme-for-schools-and-colleges-in-England

70 Welsh Government press release, 3 January 2020, gov.wales/its-just-ensuring-girls-period-isnt-barrier-her-succeeding-life
71 The Period Products in Schools (Scotland) Regulations 2020 No.183

6. **Help with childcare costs**
72 The Local Authority (Duty to Secure Early Years Provision Free of Charge) (Amendment) Regulations 2018 No.146
73 Reg 1(2), definition of 'eligible child', The Local Authority (Duty to Secure Early Years Provision Free of Charge) Regulations 2014 No.2147
74 Reg 3 The Local Authority (Duty to Secure Early Years Provision Free of Charge) Regulations 2014 No.2147
75 gov.wales/get-help-flying-start
76 gov.wales/childcare-3-and-4-year-olds
77 The Provision of Early Learning and Childcare (Specified Children) (Scotland) Order 2014 No.196
78 The Welfare Reform (Consequential Amendments) (Scotland) Regulations 2017 No.182
79 The Provision of Early Learning and Childcare (Specified Children) (Scotland) Amendment Order 2019 No.359
80 The Provision of Early Learning and Childcare (Specified Children) (Scotland) Order 2014 No.196
81 childcarechoices.gov.uk
82 Reg 15 Childcare Payments (Eligibility) Regulations 2015 No.448
83 ss30 and 31 Childcare Payments Act 2014
84 s33 Childcare Payments Act 2014

8. **Financial help when preparing for and starting work**
85 See researchbriefings.parliament.uk/ResearchBriefing/Summary/SN06079 and data.parliament.uk/DepositedPapers/Files/DEP2019-0980/52._Flexible_Support_Fund_v5.0.pdf
86 Parliamentary Written Question 275211 answered on 17 July 2019
87 See response to Freedom of Information request 'Job Centre Discount Card', 2 August 2015 on whatdotheyknow.com

9. **Other financial help**
88 The Savings (Government Contributions) Act 2017; The Help-to-Save Accounts Regulations 2018 No.87
89 ss148(1) and 149(1) SSCBA 1992

90 s150(4) SSCBA 1992
91 s150(1) SSCBA 1992
92 s149(4) SSCBA 1992
93 ss148(2) and (5) and 150(2) SSCBA 1992
94 Reg 38 SS(C&P) Regs

Part 6

Special benefit rules

Chapter 41

Benefits for students

This chapter covers:
1. Universal credit (p868)
2. Income support and jobseeker's allowance (p873)
3. Employment and support allowance (p880)
4. Housing benefit (p882)
5. Other benefits (p886)
6. Student income and means-tested benefits (p887)
7. Giving up, changing or taking time out from your course (p895)

England, Scotland and Wales have separate education systems with different student funding.

This chapter covers only those benefits which are potentially affected if you are studying.

Key facts

- If you are a part-time student, your benefits are not usually affected by your studying, although there are extra conditions to meet for jobseeker's allowance and, for some students, universal credit.
- Most full-time students are excluded from claiming means-tested benefits. There are some exceptions, including for parents, disabled students and some young people on further education courses.
- Even if you can claim means-tested benefits, most student funding for living costs counts as income and reduces or stops your benefit.
- If you are a full-time student and are taking time out from your course but have not abandoned it completely, you still count as a student and cannot usually claim benefits, but there are some exceptions.
- Child tax credit, working tax credit and certain benefits, including maternity allowance, statutory sick pay, child benefit, disability living allowance, child disability payment, personal independence payment and adult disability payment, have no special eligibility rules for full-time students, so you can claim these in the same way as anyone else, although your student income may affect your entitlement to tax credits in some cases.

Part 6: Special benefit rules
Chapter 41: Benefits for students
1. Universal credit

1. **Universal credit**

Universal credit (UC) is being introduced gradually over the next few years. For more information about when you come under the UC system, see p22.

Undertaking a course of study (the law refers to this as 'receiving education') may mean that you are not eligible for UC, unless you are in one of the groups of people for whom an exception is made (see p869). In general, these are students with children, some disabled students and young students in non-advanced education who have no parental support.

Receiving education

If you are 'receiving education', in most cases you are not eligible for UC.[1] There are exceptions (see p869).

You are 'receiving education' if you are:[2]

- undertaking a full-time course of advanced education. This is education above the level of advanced NVQ, AS/A level or a Scottish national qualification (higher or advanced higher), and includes degree-level or postgraduate-level courses, and HNDs; *or*
- undertaking another full-time course of study or training for which a loan or grant is provided for your maintenance.

In addition, you are treated as receiving education if:

- you are a 'qualifying young person'. You must be enrolled on, or accepted on, a course of non-advanced education or approved training of more than 12 hours a week, and you must have been enrolled on, accepted on or have started the course before you turned 19. You can continue to be a qualifying young person until 31 August after your 19th birthday (see p61).[3] A qualifying young person on a 'relevant training scheme' is not treated as receiving education. This includes someone on a traineeship,[4] or on certain courses or schemes of work or voluntary work preparation. If you have left education, you are still a qualifying young person until 31 August after your 16th birthday; *or*
- none of the above three bullet points apply, but you are on a course that is not compatible with your work-related requirements (see p870).[5]

You count as receiving education from the day you start, to the last day of your course, or sooner if you abandon it or are dismissed from it.[6]

If you are undertaking a part of a modular course (one that consists of two or more modules, and your college or university requires you to complete successfully a specific number of modules before it considers you to have completed the course), you count as undertaking it for the period beginning on the day that part of the course starts, and ending on the last day on which you are registered with your college or university as attending or undertaking that part of your course. This includes any vacations, unless that vacation follows the last day on which you are required to attend or undertake your course, or on such earlier date that you finally abandon or are dismissed from that part of the course.[7]

If you have failed examinations or failed to complete a module, any period in which you undertake the course in order to retake those examinations or modules is classed as part of the course and you are treated as undertaking a course (even if your college or university registers you as a part-time student during your re-sit period).

Who is entitled to universal credit while receiving education

You are eligible for UC while receiving education (although at least some of your student funding may count as income) if you are:[8]

- under 21 on a non-advanced course (or you are aged 21 and turned 21 on the course) and are 'without parental support' (see below);
- responsible for a child or qualifying young person (p61);
- a single foster parent;
- a member of a couple, both of you are full-time students and one of you is responsible for a child or is a foster parent;
- assessed as having or treated as having limited capability for work for UC (see p987) and you also get attendance allowance, disability living allowance, child disability payment, personal independence payment or adult disability payment (it must have been decided that you have limited capability for work before the date you start receiving education);
- over pension age (see p257);
- a student with a partner who is not a student, or who is a student but would be entitled to UC her/himself while receiving education;[9]
- waiting to return to your course after taking time out because of illness or caring responsibilities (see p872).[10]

Without parental support
'**Without parental support**' means you are not looked after by a local authority and you:[11]
– have no parent; *or*
– cannot live with your parents because you are estranged from them, or because there is a serious risk to your physical or mental health, or you would suffer significant harm if you lived with them; *or*
– are living away from your parents, and they cannot support you financially because they are ill or disabled, in prison or not allowed to enter Britain.
'**Parent**' includes a person acting in place of a parent.
A '**person acting in place of a parent**' can include a local authority or voluntary organisation if you are being cared for by them, or foster carers, but only until you leave care.[12] It does not include a person who is your sponsor under the Immigration Rules.[13]

Part 6: Special benefit rules
Chapter 41: Benefits for students
1. Universal credit

This depends on the facts, but for example, living with a friend's parents does not necessarily mean they are acting as your parent.[14]

'**Estrangement**' implies emotional disharmony,[15] where you have no desire to have any prolonged contact with your parents or they feel similarly towards you. It is possible to be estranged even though your parents are providing some financial support or you still have some contact with them. If you are being cared for by a local authority, it is also possible to be estranged from the local authority. If you are, you could qualify for UC if you have to live away from accommodation provided by a local authority.[16]

When someone else can claim for you

If you cannot get UC yourself, someone may be able to claim for you if you are a 'qualifying young person' – ie, generally, if you are under 20 and in non-advanced education (see p61 and p308).

Your work-related requirements

Most people claiming UC have work-related requirements as a condition of getting benefit, which may involve undertaking work-related activity or looking for work (see p1027). You have no work-related requirements if you are receiving education and are eligible for UC (unless you are only eligible under the last bullet point on p868 – waiting to return to your course) and you are:[17]

- under 21 (or 21 and you turned 21 on your course) in non-advanced education and 'without parental support' (see p869); *or*
- in receipt of student income which is taken into account for UC – ie, a student loan or a maintenance grant (see p871). For English or Welsh-funded students, if your student income is a postgraduate loan, this only applies if your course is full time. **Note:** over the summer vacation, when student income is ignored, you may have work-related requirements.

Note: even if you do not fit into one of the above groups, you may have no work-related requirements under the general rules – eg, if you are responsible for a child under one, or if you are severely disabled (see p1039).

If you are receiving education but do not get a loan or grant, you may therefore be subject to all work-related requirements, and must be available for and actively seeking work (see p1047). This is more likely to be the case if you are in non-advanced education or on some postgraduate courses.

Studying part time

If you are on a part-time course, you may still be treated as 'receiving education' if the course is not compatible with your work-related requirements.[18] So if you are subject to all work-related requirements, you must show that you meet these despite being on a part-time course. In some cases, it may be possible to argue that the course should be seen as 'voluntary work preparation' and therefore reduce your work search requirements (see p1030).[19]

If you are on a part-time course that is accepted as being compatible with your work-related requirements, you can get UC.

How student income affects universal credit

If you (or your partner) have any student income, it may count as income for UC.[20]

You are counted as having student income if you are undertaking a course and have a student loan or grant in respect of that course.[21]

Grants

The term 'grant' means an educational grant or award. It does not include a grant paid to someone under 21 in non-advanced education to enable them to finish a course.[22] This means that education maintenance allowance payments and 16 to 19 bursary fund payments do not count as student income. Access or discretionary fund payments are likely to count as student income (as an 'educational grant'), unless they can be disregarded under the rules below (although note that one-off payments count as capital rather than income).

If you get a grant but do not get a loan, the grant income is taken into account for UC. Certain amounts of your grant are disregarded as your income if they are:[23]

- for tuition fees or exams;
- in respect of your disability;
- for extra costs of residential study away from your usual place of study during term time;
- to pay for the costs of your normal home (if you live somewhere else during your course), unless these are met by your UC;
- for the maintenance of someone who is not included in your UC claim;
- for books, equipment, course travel costs or childcare costs.

If you get a grant and also get a loan and your grant is paid for the same period, it is completely disregarded unless it is for the maintenance of someone who is part of your UC claim (eg, a partner or a child) or for rent payments that are met by UC.[24]

Student loans

Student loans for maintenance count as income if you could get a loan by taking 'reasonable steps', even if you choose not to apply for one.[25] The maximum loan you could be entitled to (or 30 per cent of the maximum, for a postgraduate master's degree or doctoral loan in England or Wales[26]) is taken into account as income.

Part 6: Special benefit rules
Chapter 41: Benefits for students
1. Universal credit

This is the case even if the loan is reduced by an assessed parental (or partner) contribution, or if part of the loan is replaced by a grant. However, if you are eligible for a special support element as part of your maintenance loan in England, this is disregarded, as it is paid for books, travel, equipment and childcare.[27] You may need to get a statement from Student Finance England explaining your entitlement. Welsh students may have any grant in excess of the special support element taken into account, but it is arguable the whole grant should be disregarded. In Scotland, a student loan includes a young student's bursary.[28]

Calculating student income

UC is paid for an 'assessment period' of one month (see p48). Student income counts as income in assessment periods that fall during the course, as well as in the assessment period in which the course, and any subsequent year of the course, begins.[29] Student income is ignored in the assessment period in which the end of the course or the start of the long vacation falls. The long vacation is the longest holiday, lasting at least a month, in a course which is at least two years long. Student income is also ignored in any other assessment period that falls completely within the long vacation.[30]

In each assessment period, £110 of student income is disregarded.

To work out how much of your student income is taken into account:

- **Step one:** calculate your annual loan or grant or, if the course lasts for less than a year, the amount of loan or grant for the course.
- **Step two:** work out how many assessment periods apply for that year, or for the course if it is less than a year long.
- **Step three:** divide the amount from Step one by the number of assessment periods in Step two.
- **Step four:** deduct £110.

Example
Holly gets a student loan of £10,815 in total. This includes a special support element of £4,014, which is disregarded, leaving £6,801. Year one of her course runs from 27 September 2021 to 13 May 2022. Her assessment periods run from the 20th of the month to the 19th of the following month. Her loan counts as income for seven assessment periods.
£6,801 ÷ 7 = £971.57
£971.57 – £110 = £861.57
Holly's UC is calculated on student income of £861.57 a month from 20 September 2021 to 19 April 2022.

Taking time out from your course

During a period of temporary absence from your course, you usually still count as receiving education, so the student rules apply. Therefore, if you take time out because you have to re-sit exams or because you are ill, you still count as receiving education and are only eligible for UC if you are in one of the eligible groups (see p869) – eg, you are a parent.

You do not count as 'receiving education' and can claim UC if you have taken time out from your course because of illness or caring responsibilities, you have now recovered or your caring responsibilities have ended, you are not eligible for a grant or student loan, and you are waiting to return to your course.[31] Your institution must have agreed to your taking time out, and you must have recovered from your illness or your caring responsibilities must have ended within the last year.

If you leave your course completely, you no longer count as receiving education, so the normal UC rules apply. Student income is taken into account up to the end of the assessment period before the one in which you leave the course.

If you take time out of a modular course, which amounts to time out of 'a part' of such a course, it may be argued that you do not count as undertaking a course during that period.[32]

2. Income support and jobseeker's allowance

You cannot make a new claim for income support (IS) or income-based jobseeker's allowance (JSA) (see p23). If you are already entitled to IS or income-based JSA, you can continue to get it if you remain eligible, although you may have to claim universal credit (UC) at some point. The rules below apply, therefore, to people who already get IS or income-based JSA.

If you are studying, you may count as being in 'relevant education' (see below), or as a 'full-time student' (see p874). You cannot usually qualify for IS or JSA (either contribution-based or income-based). There are some exceptions, however, which are outlined in this section. You may also be able to qualify if you are studying part time (see p878).

Note: this section deals with the rules for income-based JSA, and for contribution-based JSA if claiming under the legacy benefit system. The rules are different for 'new style' contribution-based JSA if you come under the UC system (see p886).

Relevant education

If you are in relevant education, you can only get IS in some circumstances and you cannot usually get JSA.[33] **Note:** for JSA, a young person on a traineeship does not count as being in relevant education. For this purpose, traineeship is a course of up to six months which helps 16–24 year olds to prepare for work and is funded or arranged by the Secretary of State under section 14 of the Education Act 2002.[34]

Part 6: Special benefit rules
Chapter 41: Benefits for students
2. Income support and jobseeker's allowance

You count as being in 'relevant education' if you are a 'qualifying young person' for child benefit purposes (see p563) – ie, you are under 20 and in full-time, non-advanced education or approved training on which you were accepted, enrolled or started when you were under 19.[35] For these purposes, 'full time' means more than 12 hours a week in term time, not including meal breaks and unsupervised study. 'Non-advanced' means anything below degree, HNC or HND level.

Very few people aged under 20 will be on IS or income-based JSA. If this does apply to you, see Chapter 41 of the 2021/22 edition of this *Handbook*.

Full-time students

If you are a full-time student, you cannot usually qualify for IS or JSA for the duration of your course, including vacations.[36] See p876 for exceptions to this rule. See p895 if you give up, change or take time out from your course and p878 if you are studying part time.

You count as a full-time student if you are not in relevant education (see p873), you are not getting a training allowance, and:[37]

- you are under 19 and attending or undertaking a full-time course of 'advanced education'. '**Advanced education**' means degree- or postgraduate-level qualifications, teaching courses, diplomas of higher education, HND or HNC and all other courses above advanced GNVQ or equivalent, OND, A levels or a Scottish national qualification (higher or advanced level); *or*
- you are 19 or over but under pension age (see p766) and attending or undertaking a full-time course of study. If your course is full time, you are treated as a full-time student regardless of the level of the course, unless you are aged under 20 and can still be treated as being in 'relevant education' (see p873); *or*
- you are on a sandwich course (see p875).

You are treated as a student until either the last day of your course or until you abandon or are dismissed from it.[38] The 'last day of the course' is the date on which the last day of the final academic year is officially scheduled to fall.[39]

For JSA, the period of study includes periods during which you are doing work connected to the course, even if this is after the normal end of your study.[40]

Full-time courses

In England and Wales, your course counts as full time and you are treated as a full-time student if:[41]

- it is fully or partly funded by the Secretary of State under section 14 of the Education Act 2002, section 100 of the Apprenticeships, Skills, Children and Learning Act 2009 or the Welsh government, and your personal 'learning agreement' involves more than 16 hours of 'guided learning' each week. Courses include academic or vocational courses leading to a recognised qualification. The Secretary of State and the Welsh government also fund basic literacy and numeracy courses, English as a Second or Other Language (ESOL) programmes, Access and similar courses that prepare you to move on to qualification-bearing courses, and courses developing independent living skills for people with learning difficulties. The number of guided learning hours you do each week is set out in your learning agreement. This is signed by you and the college. The DWP uses this agreement to decide whether or not you are on a full-time course;[42] *or*

- it is not funded by the Secretary of State under section 14 of the Education Act 2002, section 100 of the Apprenticeships, Skills, Children and Learning Act 2009 or the Welsh government and is a 'full-time course of study'.

In Scotland, your course counts as full time and you are treated as being a full-time student if:[43]

- it is totally or partly funded by the Scottish Ministers at a college of further education, is not higher education *and* your personal learning document states that your course:
  - involves more than 16 hours a week of classroom-based or workshop-based programmed learning under the guidance of a teacher; *or*
  - involves more than 21 hours' study a week, 16 hours or less of which involve classroom-based or workshop-based programmed learning, and the rest of which involve using structured learning packages with the help of a teacher.
  The number of hours of 'learning' you do each week is set out in your learning document. This is signed by you and the college. The DWP uses this document to decide whether or not you are on a full-time course; *or*
- it is a course of higher education which is funded wholly or in part by the Scottish Ministers and is a full-time course of study; *or*
- it is not funded by the Scottish Ministers and is a full-time course of study.

Sandwich courses

A course is a 'sandwich course' if it consists of alternate periods of full-time study at your educational institution and periods of industrial, professional or work experience organised so that, taking the course as a whole, you attend the periods of full-time study for an average of at least 18 weeks in each year.[44] This does not apply if it is a course of initial teacher training. If your periods of full-time study and work experience alternate within any week of your course, the days of full-time study are aggregated with each other and with any weeks of full-time study to determine the number of weeks of full-time study in each year.

Work experience includes periods of employment abroad for modern language students whose course is at least half composed of modern language study.

Health-related courses

If you attend a health-related course for which you are entitled to receive an NHS bursary, you are treated as a full-time or part-time student as appropriate, and not an employee.[45]

Part 6: Special benefit rules
Chapter 41: Benefits for students
2. Income support and jobseeker's allowance

Modular courses

A modular course consists of two or more modules, and your college or university requires you to complete successfully a specific number of modules before it considers you to have completed the course.[46] You are treated as a full-time student if you are currently attending part of a modular course that would be classed as a full-time course.[47] You are treated as a full-time student for the period beginning on the day your course is defined as a full-time course and ending on the last day on which you are registered with your college or university as attending or undertaking that part of your course. This includes any vacations, unless that vacation follows the last day on which you are required to attend or undertake your course, or on such earlier date that you finally abandon or are dismissed from that part of the course.[48]

If you have failed examinations or failed to complete a module, any period in which you attend or undertake the course in order to retake those examinations or modules is classed as part of the full-time course and you are treated as a full-time student (even if your college or university registers you as a part-time student during your re-sit period).[49]

Because the rules do not define what is a full-time course, unless funded by the Secretary of State under section 14 of the Education Act 2002, section 100 of the Apprenticeships, Skills, Children and Learning Act 2009 or Scottish Ministers (see p875), you may be able to argue that you are not attending a full-time course, regardless of your attendance, if your course is not defined as full time or part time by your college or university.[50]

Note: if you take time out of a complete 'part' of a modular course, you may not count as undertaking a course during this time.[51]

Other courses

If your course does not automatically count as full time under the rules above, whether it counts as a 'full-time course of study' depends on the college or university. Definitions are often based on local custom and practice within educational institutions. The college or university's definition is not absolutely final, but if you want to challenge it, you will have to produce a good argument showing why it should not be accepted.[52] If your course is only for a few hours each week, argue that it is not full time. However, a course could be full time even though you only have to attend a few lectures a week.[53]

Full-time students who are entitled to income support

Even if you are a full-time student, you can qualify for IS (although new claims cannot be made, and most student funding counts as income) if you are:[54]

- a lone parent under age 18 (regardless of the age of your child/ren), or a lone parent of a child under five; *or*
- a lone foster carer of a child under 16; *or*
- single, or are one of a couple and both of you are full-time students and:

- you fit into one of the groups of people who can claim IS (see Chapter 11); *and*
- you (or, if you are one of a couple, either one or both of you) are responsible for a child or young person (see p567); *and*
- it is the summer vacation;
- a refugee who is learning English to obtain employment (see p236); *or*
- in, enrolled on or accepted for full-time non-advanced education and you are aged under 21, or you are 21 and you reached that age while in such education. In addition, you must:
  - have no parents (or anyone acting in their place); *or*
  - have to live away from your parents (or anyone acting in their place) because you are estranged from them, or are in physical or moral danger or there is a serious risk to your physical or mental health; *or*
  - be living away from your parents (or anyone acting in their place) and they cannot support you financially and they are:
    - chronically sick or mentally or physically disabled; *or*
    - in prison; *or*
    - prohibited from entering or re-entering Great Britain.

Full-time students who are entitled to jobseeker's allowance

Even if you are a full-time student, you can qualify for JSA (although new claims cannot be made, and most student funding counts as income) if you are:

- single and responsible for a child or, if you are one of a couple, both of you are full-time students and either one or both of you is responsible for a child (see p567). This exception only applies during the summer vacation and if you are available for work, or treated as available because you are on either of the courses in the next bullet point;[55] *or*
- on an employment-related course of up to two weeks that has been approved in advance by the DWP,[56] or a Venture Trust training programme of up to four weeks.[57] In either case, only one course is allowed in any 12-month period; *or*
- participating in a scheme for assisting people to obtain employment (eg, Skills Conditionality – see p1122) – ie, you have been required to attend full-time training under it;[58] *or*
- aged 25 or over and on a qualifying course;[59] *or*
- waiting to go back to your course, having taken approved time out because of an illness or caring responsibility and that has now come to an end (see p895).

Maintaining two homes

In some cases, if you qualify for IS or income-based JSA, you may be entitled to help with the costs of more than one home if you have to live away from your normal home to attend a course. For further details, see p357.

Part 6: Special benefit rules
Chapter 41: Benefits for students
2. Income support and jobseeker's allowance

Part-time students

If you are studying but are not in relevant education (see p873) or attending a full-time course (see p874), you are treated as attending a part-time course and classed as a part-time student.

Who is entitled to income support while studying part time

You can get IS while studying part time if you are not on a full-time course and you satisfy the other rules for getting IS (see Chapter 11).

If you are currently studying part time on a course you previously attended full time, the DWP may argue that you are attending a full-time course and should therefore be treated as a full-time student. It may be possible to challenge this interpretation.[60] Get specialist advice if you are in this situation.

Who is entitled to jobseeker's allowance while studying part time

You count as a part-time student if your course is not full time.[61] You can get JSA while studying part time if you meet the jobseeking conditions – ie, you are available for work, actively seeking work and you have a valid jobseeker's agreement (see p1092). If you have agreed restrictions with the DWP on the hours that you are available for work, there are special rules that can help you claim JSA and study part time (see p879).

When you claim JSA you may be asked to fill in a 'student questionnaire'. Your answers are taken into account when deciding whether you are available for and actively seeking work. The DWP must be satisfied that you are genuinely available for and actively seeking work while you are studying part time.

Availability for work and part-time study

Your availability for work should not be affected by your part-time course if your hours of study or training are at times outside your agreed pattern of availability (see p1099) – ie, they do not clash with the times you are willing and able to work. If the hours of your course *do* clash with the times you say you are available for work (as set out in your jobseeker's agreement – see p1104), you are only accepted as available for work if either:[62]

- you are able to rearrange the hours of the course or study to fit around your job; *or*
- you are willing and able to give up the course should a job become available.

Deciding whether you are available for work

A number of factors should be considered when deciding whether you are available for work while you are studying part time. If, for example, it appears you are not willing or able to give up your course or that you cannot confine your study to times that would fit in with employment, you are treated as not being available for work. The factors that may be relevant include:[63]

- if you are studying or training away from home, whether you can be contacted if a job becomes available;
- the extent of your efforts to find employment;
- how important the successful completion of the course is to your future career, including whether it will enhance your chances of finding employment;
- whether you gave up a job or training to do the course;
- the days and hours you are required to attend the course;
- whether the times of attendance could be changed to fit in with any job you might obtain or whether successful completion of the course is possible if you miss some of the scheduled attendances;
- the duration of the study or training;
- whether a fee was paid and, if so, the amount and whether any of the fee could be refunded or transferred if you abandoned or interrupted your studies. If you have paid a fee, it may be more difficult (depending on the amount) to convince the DWP that you are prepared to abandon the course;
- whether you received a grant and, if so, the source, the amount and whether you would have to repay any or all of it if you interrupted or abandoned the course.

The guidance for decision makers states that where a number of claimants are following the same course, some may be able to show that they are available, but others may not.[64] The DWP should consider each claim individually and not operate a blanket policy. The DWP assumes that you may be less willing to leave a course if you are near its end or as the chance of obtaining a qualification approaches.[65]

Restricting your availability for work

There are special rules that can help you qualify for JSA if you are a part-time student. These say that, in certain circumstances, the fact that you are on your course is ignored when deciding whether you are available for work if the hours of your course fall wholly or partly within the times you say you are available for work. However, you still have to be available for and actively seeking work during the rest of the week when you are not on your course.

These rules apply to you if you are a part-time student, and you are willing and able to rearrange the hours of your course to take up a job and the restrictions on your hours of availability have been agreed with the DWP because:[66]

- of your physical or mental condition (see p1099); *or*
- of your caring responsibilities (see p1100); *or*
- you are working 'short time'; *or*
- they leave you available for work for at least 40 hours a week (see p1099).

Part 6: Special benefit rules
Chapter 41: Benefits for students
3. Employment and support allowance

You must also satisfy one of two conditions.

- For the three months immediately before the date you started the course, you were unemployed and getting JSA, or you were incapable of work and getting IS, incapacity benefit (IB) or ESA, or you were on a course of 'training'.
- In the six months immediately before you started the course, you were unemployed and getting JSA, or you were incapable of work and getting IS, IB or ESA, or you were on a course of training for a total of at least three months and, for any remaining part of the six months, you were working full time or earning too much to qualify for benefit.

The three-month and six-month periods can only begin after you have reached your terminal date (see p566) and are treated as having ceased to be in relevant education (see p566).

Training

'Training' means training for which young people aged under 18 are eligible, or for which a person aged 18–24 may be eligible, provided or arranged by the Secretary of State under section 14 of the Education Act 2002, the Welsh government or Skills Development Scotland.[67]

How student income affects income support and jobseeker's allowance

There are special rules for assessing your income from your student grant, loan or other types of student support (see p887), including for people claiming IS while in 'relevant education'.[68] These rules do not apply if you are receiving a training allowance.

The normal rules for assessing your other income and capital apply (see Chapters 20 and 22).

3. Employment and support allowance

Whether you can qualify for employment and support allowance (ESA) while studying full time depends on the type of ESA.

You can qualify for contributory ESA as a full-time or part-time student (see p633).

You cannot qualify for income-related ESA if you are 'receiving education' unless you are getting disability living allowance (DLA), child disability payment (CDP), personal independence payment (PIP), adult disability payment (ADP) or armed forces independence payment (see p881). You may be able to qualify if you are studying part time (see p882).

Note: in certain circumstances, if you are attending a training course and are paid a training allowance, you cannot qualify for ESA because you do not count as having limited capability for work (see p992).[69]

Who is entitled to income-related employment and support allowance

You cannot make a new claim for income-related ESA (see p23).

However, if you currently get contributory ESA and do not come under the UC system (see p22) (sometimes referred to as 'new-style' ESA), you can also qualify for income-related ESA if your income is low enough.

If you are 'receiving education', you can only qualify for income-related ESA if you are getting DLA, CDP, PIP, ADP or armed forces independence payment.[70] This usually applies for the duration of your course, including vacations. See p882 if you have finished studying and p895 if you give up, change or take time out from your course.

For income-related ESA purposes, you count as 'receiving education' if you are:

- a 'qualifying young person' for child benefit purposes (see p563), but not if you are on a traineeship;[71] *or*
- undertaking a 'course of study'.[72] The DWP may refer to you as a 'full-time student'. The definition is the same as the definition of full-time student for income support (IS) and jobseeker's allowance (JSA) (see p874). A course of study is similar to a full-time course for IS and JSA, except, for ESA, it also includes a sandwich course (see p874) and does not include a traineeship. Note that if you take time out of a complete part of a modular course, you may not count as undertaking a course during that time.[73]

Note:

- The term 'full-time student' is used in the rest of this section to refer to someone who is receiving education for income-related ESA purposes.
- Unless you are a 'qualifying young person' for child benefit purposes, if you qualify for income-related ESA as a full-time student because you are getting DLA, CDP, PIP, ADP or armed forces independence payment, you automatically count as having limited capability for work (see p988).[74]

Maintaining two homes

In some cases, if you are a full-time student and you qualify for income-related ESA, you may be entitled to help with the costs of more than one home if you have to live away from your normal home to attend a course. For further details, see p357.

Part 6: Special benefit rules
Chapter 41: Benefits for students
4. Housing benefit

When you stop being a full-time student

Once you stop being a full-time student, you may be able to get income-related ESA (see Chapter 9). However, bear the following in mind.

- If you were a 'qualifying young person' for child benefit purposes (eg, you were under 20 and on a full-time course of non-advanced education – see p563), you continue to count as a qualifying young person for a period after your education or training ends – eg, if you have enrolled on another course or during the child benefit 'extension period' (see p565). While you continue to be treated as a qualifying young person, you can only qualify for income-related ESA if you are receiving DLA, CDP, PIP, ADP or armed forces independence payment. If you cannot qualify for ESA in your own right, your parents may be able to continue to claim child benefit and tax credits for you.

- If you counted as a full-time student other than because you were a 'qualifying young person' for child benefit purposes (see p563), you continue to be treated as a full-time student until the last day of your course, or until you abandon the course or are dismissed from it (see p895).

Studying part time

You can qualify for income-related ESA if you do not count as a full-time student under the rules described on p881.

When someone else can claim for you

If you are under 20, a 'qualifying young person' for child benefit purposes (see p563) and cannot qualify for ESA because you are 'receiving full-time education' (see p880) or are a full-time student (see p881), someone else may be able to qualify for child benefit, and UC or child tax credit and working tax credit if s/he is treated as 'responsible' for you.

How student income affects employment and support allowance

There are special rules for assessing your income from your student grant, loan or other types of student support (see p887).

The normal rules for assessing your other income and capital apply (see Chapters 20 and 22).

4. Housing benefit

You cannot usually make a new claim for housing benefit (HB) (but see p23 for the exceptions).

Note: if you are eligible for HB, have reached pension age and neither you nor your partner are in receipt of income support (IS), income-based jobseeker's allowance (JSA) or income-related employment and support allowance (ESA), the student rules for HB do not apply and there are no restrictions on your studying and qualifying for HB.[75]

Whether you can get HB depends on whether you are classed as a full-time or a part-time student.

The rules for deciding whether you are a full-time student are similar to the rules for IS and JSA (see p874), except that there is no separate rule in HB if you are in 'relevant education' (see p873).

If you are a full-time student (see p874), you cannot usually qualify for HB, but there are some exceptions (see below).

Full-time students who are entitled to housing benefit

You can qualify for HB (although most student funding counts as income) if:[76]

- you are on IS, income-based JSA, income-related ESA or universal credit (UC) except if your UC includes an amount for housing costs (see Chapter 6); *or*
- you are under 21, not following a course of higher education (higher education includes degree courses, teacher training, HND, HNC and postgraduate courses), or are aged 21 and you reached that age while on such a course and are still on it, or you are a child or a 'qualifying young person' for child benefit purposes (see p563); *or*
- you and your partner are both full-time students and either or both of you are responsible for a child or qualifying young person (see p563). **Note:** unlike for IS and JSA, this provision applies throughout the year; *or*
- you are a lone parent responsible for a dependent child or qualifying young person aged under 20 (see p563); *or*
- you are a lone foster carer and the child has been formally placed with you; *or*
- you meet the conditions for the disability premium (see p325). **Note:** you cannot qualify for a disability premium if you have limited capability for work; *or*
- you have been (or have been treated as) incapable of work (see p683 of the 2013/14 edition of this *Handbook*) for 196 days (28 weeks); *or*
- you have had (or have been treated as having) limited capability for work (see p987) for 196 days (28 weeks) and you continue to have it. Two or more periods are joined to form a single period if they are separated by 12 weeks or less. **Note:** claims from 27 October 2008 are assessed under these rules rather than the incapacity for work rules in the bullet point above, unless, broadly, you already get incapacity benefit or IS because of incapacity for work; *or*
- you meet the conditions for the severe disability premium (see p330); *or*
- you qualify for a disabled students' allowance because you are deaf; *or*

Part 6: Special benefit rules
Chapter 41: Benefits for students
4. Housing benefit

- you are waiting to go back to your course, having taken approved time out because of an illness or caring responsibility and this has now come to an end (see p896).

Note: even if you are a full-time student who comes into one of the above groups, you cannot qualify for HB if the circumstances under either of the two headings below apply to you.

Being away from your term-time accommodation

Even if you are a full-time student who can qualify for HB (see p883), if your main reason for occupying your home is to enable you to attend your course, you cannot qualify for HB on that home for any full week when you are absent from it outside your period of study (see p888).[77]

This rule does not apply if:

- you are away from home because you are in hospital;[78]
- the main reason for occupying your home is *not* to enable you to attend your course but for some other purpose – eg, to provide a home for your children or for yourself because you do not have a home elsewhere to live when you are not attending your course. If this applies, any absences outside your period of study are dealt with under the temporary absence rules (see p181).

Accommodation rented from an educational establishment

If you are a full-time student who can qualify for HB (see p883), you can usually get HB even if you rent your accommodation from your educational establishment.[79] If you are a part-time student, this rule applies if you would be able to qualify for HB if you were treated as a full-time student.

You cannot, however, get HB if you are a:

- full-time student waiting to go back to your course, having taken approved time out because of illness or caring responsibilities (see p896) and your illness or caring responsibilities have not yet ended; *or*
- part-time student whose only basis of entitlement to HB if you were a full-time student would be that you are receiving IS, income-based JSA or income-related ESA.

The above two exceptions do not apply if:

- your educational establishment itself rents the accommodation from a third party other than on a long lease or where the third party is an education authority providing the accommodation as part of its functions; *or*
- the accommodation is owned by a separate legal body – eg, a company established to build halls of residence.

You cannot get HB if the local authority decides that your educational establishment has arranged for your accommodation to be provided by a person or body other than itself in order to take advantage of the HB scheme.

Maintaining two homes

The rules about claiming HB for two homes are explained on p185. If you are one of a couple and receive HB for two homes, the assessment of HB for each home is based on your joint income and your applicable amount as a couple.

Part-time students

You may be able to qualify for HB if you are studying part time. The rules for deciding whether you are a part-time student are similar to the rules for IS and JSA (see p878), except that there is no separate rule in HB if you are in 'relevant education' (see p873).

Partners of students

If your partner is not a student, s/he can qualify for HB if s/he meets the qualifying conditions.[80] The claim is assessed in the normal way, except that the rules about being away from term-time accommodation (see p884) apply to your partner's claim.[81] Additionally, the special rules for assessing any income you receive from a grant, loan and other types of student support for students apply (see p887).

How student income affects housing benefit

If you or your partner are on IS, income-based JSA, income-related ESA or UC, you are entitled to maximum HB (see Chapter 10).

If you are not on UC, IS, income-based JSA or income-related ESA but you or your partner are eligible for HB, your entitlement is calculated in the same way as for other claimants (see Chapters 20 and 22), except that there are special rules for assessing the amount of your income from grants, loans and other types of student support (see p887). **Note:** for courses lasting more than one year, in many cases loans and grants are not counted as income over the summer vacation. You may find therefore that your HB entitlement is higher over this period, and that you need to check that your entitlement is reviewed at that time.

Payments

Students are covered by all the normal rules on the administration and payment of HB (see Chapter 10). However, there is a provision that can apply specifically to students. The local authority may decide to pay a rent allowance once each term, although students have the same right as other claimants to insist on fortnightly payments if their entitlement is more than £2 a week.[82]

Part 6: Special benefit rules
Chapter 41: Benefits for students
5. Other benefits

5. **Other benefits**

Carer's allowance

You cannot qualify for carer's allowance (CA) (see Chapter 26) if you are in full-time education.[83] Usually, if the course you are attending is described by the university, college or school as full time, you are regarded as being in full-time education, although there may be exceptions – eg, if you are exempted from parts of the course.[84] So the actual hours you attend may not be crucial. However, if you are attending for 21 hours a week or more (as specified by the institution), you are treated as being in full-time education. When calculating the 21 hours, include only hours spent in 'supervised study' (see below). Ignore any time spent on meal breaks or unsupervised study undertaken on or off the premises of the educational establishment.[85]

You are treated as still being in full-time education during vacations and any temporary interruption of the course, but not if you have abandoned the course or been dismissed from it. If an interruption is not temporary (eg, if you have agreed with your institution to take a whole year out of your course), you may be able to claim CA.[86]

Supervised study

'**Supervised study**' does not depend on whether your supervisor (ie, teacher, tutor, lecturer) is present with you.[87] If your study is directed to your course of education and the curriculum of your course and it is undertaken to meet the reasonable requirements of your course, it normally counts as supervised study. It counts regardless of whether that study is undertaken on or off the premises of the educational institution you attend.

'**Unsupervised study**' means work beyond the reasonable requirements of your course. In assessing your hours of attendance, evidence from your educational institution about the amount of time you are expected to study to complete your course is important.

Contribution-based jobseeker's allowance

If you come under the universal credit (UC) system (see p22) and are claiming contribution-based jobseeker's allowance (JSA) (sometimes referred to as 'new-style' JSA), the rules in this section apply. If you do not come under the UC system and are claiming contribution-based JSA, the rules on p874 apply.

Students who are in 'relevant education' cannot claim contribution-based JSA. You are in relevant education if you are:[88]

- a qualifying young person (see p563);
- on a full-time course of advanced education;
- on another full-time course for which a loan or grant is provided for your maintenance;
- on a course which is not compatible with your work-related requirements.

Note: if you are in relevant education, you can only claim contribution-based JSA if you took time out because of illness or caring responsibilities, you have now recovered or the caring responsibilities have ended, and you are waiting to rejoin your course.

National insurance credits

You may be able to receive national insurance credits (see Chapter 43) for a tax year in which you were on a full-time course.

6. Student income and means-tested benefits

The rules in this section apply to income support (IS), income-based jobseeker's allowance (JSA), income-related employment and support allowance (ESA) and housing benefit (HB). They apply if you are a part-time or a full-time student. If you are claiming universal credit (UC), see p871.

There are many types of financial support available for students, paid as either grants or loans. Some types of grant or loan are available to all students who meet the conditions of entitlement. Others are available on a discretionary basis. The support varies depending on whether you live in England, Wales or Scotland. For more information, see gov.uk/student-finance, studentfinancewales.co.uk, saas.gov.uk or CPAG's *Student Support and Benefits Handbook* and *Benefits for Students in Scotland Handbook* (both available free on AskCPAG).

If you (or your partner) are a student, some of your (or your partner's) income from your grant, loan and certain other forms of student support is taken into account when calculating the amount of your benefit.[89] Your other income and capital are dealt with under the normal rules (see Chapters 20 and 22).

Note: the DWP has issued guidance to decision makers on how student support should be treated. Often this guidance only covers some of the benefits to which this section refers. For example, guidance may have been issued for HB purposes, but no equivalent guidance has been issued for IS, JSA or ESA. In addition, the legislation and guidance may not cover all sources of student support across the UK, particularly as new sources of support are introduced.

- The information in this section applies to support available to new students for the 2021/22 academic year. For how grants and loans are treated for students who started their course in previous academic years, see the previous editions of this *Handbook*.
- Grant and loan income do not affect your contribution-based JSA or contributory ESA.
- Any student income you have from a grant or loan is not taken into account as income if you are claiming HB and you are getting IS, income-based JSA, income-related ESA or UC.[90]

Part 6: Special benefit rules
Chapter 41: Benefits for students
6. Student income and means-tested benefits

Grants

Student grants include any kind of educational grant or award, bursary (such as those paid by the NHS for certain health-related courses), scholarship, studentship, exhibition or supplementary allowance.[91] Payments from access funds (see p893), education maintenance allowances or similar payments are not treated as grants.

Some grants are ignored as income (see p889) and others are taken into account. When calculating income from a grant, certain amounts can be disregarded.

If you are assessed as entitled to a parental or partner's contribution to your grant, it counts as income, whether or not it has been paid to you.[92] However, only the amount of contribution you actually receive counts if:

- for IS, you are a lone parent, a lone foster carer or a disabled student (see p876); or
- for JSA, you qualify for a disability premium (see p325); or
- for ESA, you are a lone parent or a full-time student who gets disability living allowance (DLA), child disability payment (CDP), personal independence payment (PIP) or adult disability payment (ADP).

Calculating grant income

Your grant income is apportioned:[93]

- if it is payable for your period of study (unless you are attending a sandwich course), over the number of benefit weeks in your period of study;
- if it is payable for a period other than your period of study, over the number of benefit weeks in the period for which the grant is payable.

In most cases, the former applies and your grant income is assessed over a period starting from the 'benefit week' which coincides with (or immediately follows) the first day of your 'period of study' (see below) and ending with the benefit week, the last day of which coincides with (or immediately precedes) the last day of your period of study. In this context, 'benefit week' means the week for which benefit is paid.[94]

This means your grant income is apportioned over the number of complete benefit weeks in your period of study. Any part weeks at the beginning or end of that period are ignored.

Period of study

'Period of study' means:[95]

– for a course of one year or less, from the start of the course to the last day of the course;

– for a course of more than one year, in the first and subsequent years (but not the final year), from the start of the course or the start of the year of the course to:

– if the grant is payable for a period of 12 months, the day before the start of the next year of the course; or

– in any other case, the day before the start of your normal summer vacation;

– in the final year of a course lasting more than one year, from the start of the final year of the course to the last day of the course.

Dependants' grants are taken into account over the same period as the student loan if you have a student loan or you are eligible for one.[96]

If you are attending a sandwich course, your grant income is taken into account over a different period. Any periods spent on placement or work experience in your period of study are excluded and your grant is apportioned over the remaining benefit weeks in your period of study. **Note:** this only applies if your grant is payable for your period of study. If your grant is payable for a different period, it is taken into account over the number of benefit weeks in the period for which it is payable.

Grant income that is ignored

The following grant income is ignored:[97]

- any allowance for tuition and examination fees;
- disabled students' allowance;
- any allowance to meet the cost of residential study away from your normal educational establishment during term time;
- any allowance for the cost of your normal home (away from college) but, for IS, JSA and ESA, only up to the amount of your rent that is not met by HB;
- any amount for a partner or child living abroad;
- for IS/JSA/ESA only, any amount intended to maintain a dependent child (unless you still have amounts for children included in your IS/JSA and do not get child tax credit);
- any amount for the childcare costs of a dependent child;
- any amount for the cost of books and equipment;
- any amount for travel costs related to course attendance;
- parents' learning allowance;
- Welsh government learning grant for further education students;
- special support payment in Wales;[98]
- if you have been required to make a contribution to your own grant (eg, because you have other income, such as maintenance), an amount equivalent to that contribution is disregarded.[99] In the case of a couple, the amount of any contribution that one member has been assessed to pay to her/his partner who is a student is disregarded from the non-student's income;[100]
- an education maintenance allowance, 16 to 19 bursary or similar payments, including a Care to Learn payment;[101]
- higher education bursary for care leavers in England.

Part 6: Special benefit rules
Chapter 41: Benefits for students
6. Student income and means-tested benefits

In addition to the above amounts, the following fixed sums are ignored.[102] These disregards apply only to the grant you receive for your period of study and not to any supplementary allowances you may be paid during the long vacation.[103]

- A fixed amount of £390 for books and equipment (2021/22 academic year). If your grant includes a specific amount to cover the cost of books and equipment, that amount is ignored in addition to this fixed amount.
- A fixed amount of £303 for the cost of travel (2021/22 academic year). If your grant includes a specific amount to cover the cost of travel expenses for attending your course, that amount is ignored in addition to this fixed amount. If your actual travel costs are higher than any sum specified in your grant for travel (which is ignored under the rules above) plus this fixed amount, the additional costs are not ignored and are taken into account.[104]

Note:
- If you also receive a student loan, the fixed amounts for books and equipment and for travel are not disregarded when calculating your grant income, but are disregarded from your loan income instead (see p891).
- For the purpose of these fixed amounts, the 2021/22 academic year began on 1 August 2021 if your period of study (see p888) began in August 2021. If your period of study began on or after 1 September 2021, the fixed sums apply from that date.

Loans

Student loans are treated as income, but certain amounts can be disregarded. **Note:** some supplementary allowances paid under the student loan provisions are paid as non-repayable grants and are treated as grant income (see p888).

Calculating income from a student loan

How your, or your partner's, student loan is treated depends on whether your course lasts for one year or less, or for a longer period (see p892 and p893).[105]

The maximum amount of available loan is taken into account as income, even if you do not apply for a loan or for the maximum amount.[106] If you get a postgraduate master's degree or doctoral degree loan in England or Wales, 30 per cent of the maximum is taken into account.[107] However, for ESA only, if you do not get a loan while you are taking time out because of ill health, there is no assumed loan taken into account.[108] The special support element in a maintenance loan for full-time undergraduate students in England is ignored as income[109] – you may need to get a statement from Student Finance England showing the breakdown of your loan entitlement.

You are treated as having a parental or partner's contribution to your loan and this is taken into account as income, whether or not it has been paid to you. However, only the amount of contribution you actually receive counts if:[110]

- for IS, you are a lone parent, a lone foster carer or a disabled student (see p876); *or*
- for JSA, you qualify for a disability premium (see p325); *or*
- for ESA, you are a full-time student who gets DLA, CDP, PIP or ADP (see p881).

A student loan for maintenance and a supplementary allowance paid to a student on a Postgraduate Certificate in Education course are treated in the same way as student loans and supplementary allowances for undergraduate students.

If you are on a health-related course funded by the NHS, only the lower maximum loan rate should be taken into account.

Loan income that is ignored

The following are ignored.

- Loans paid for tuition fees (known as a 'fee loan' or a 'fee contribution loan').[111]
- If you have been required to make a contribution to your own loan (eg, because you have other income, such as maintenance), an amount equivalent to that contribution is disregarded as income.[112]
- In the case of a couple, the amount of any contribution that one member has been assessed to pay to her/his partner who is a student is disregarded from the non-student's income.[113]

Also ignored is a fixed amount of:[114]

- £390 for the cost of books and equipment (2021/22 academic year); *and*
- £303 for the cost of travel (2021/22 academic year).

Note: for the purpose of the above fixed amounts, the 2021/22 academic year began on 1 August 2021 if your period of study (see p888) began in August 2021. If your period of study began on or after 1 September 2021, the fixed sums apply from that date.

£10 a week is ignored for each week in the period over which your loan income is taken into account (see below). This amount may overlap with other disregards applied to certain war pensions (see p421) and access funds (see p893). A combined maximum sum of £20 a week can be ignored.

The period over which loan income is taken into account

Loan income is apportioned over a period of 'benefit weeks'.

The first benefit week may fall before the start of your actual academic year and the last benefit week may fall either before or after the last day of your academic year (academic years vary between educational institutions). This may mean your benefit is recalculated several times depending on when your actual academic

Part 6: Special benefit rules
Chapter 41: Benefits for students
6. Student income and means-tested benefits

year falls in relation to the relevant benefit weeks. You must make a new claim (if you still can) or check that your entitlement is revised at these times.

Academic year

The rules give a definition of an 'academic year' for the purposes of calculating student loan income. This definition may be different from the actual academic year of the educational institution you attend. '**Academic year**' means a period of 12 months beginning on 1 January, 1 April, 1 July or 1 September according to whether your course begins in the winter, the spring, the summer or the autumn respectively. If you are required to begin attending your course during August or September and to continue attending through the autumn, the academic year of your course is treated as beginning in the autumn rather than summer – ie, from 1 September.[115]

If you are required to start attending your course in August, or your course is for less than one academic year, the period begins with the benefit week, the first day of which coincides with, or immediately follows, the first day of the course.[116]

If your academic year does not start on 1 September, your loan payable for that academic year is apportioned equally between the benefit weeks in the period beginning with the benefit week, the first day of which coincides with, or immediately follows, the first day of that academic year and ending with the benefit week, the last day of which coincides with, or immediately precedes, the last day of that academic year. Excluded from that are any benefit weeks falling entirely within the quarter during which, in the opinion of the decision maker, your longest vacation falls.[117]

Quarters

'**Quarter**' means one of the periods from 1 January to 31 March, 1 April to 30 June, 1 July to 31 August, or 1 September to 31 December.[118]

In the first, or only, year of your course, your loan income (calculated under the rules below) is ignored for each benefit week that falls before the start of your 'period of study' (the first day of the first term). This is because you cannot be treated as a student until you actually start your course.[119]

A course lasting for one academic year or less

Your loan is apportioned over the benefit weeks beginning with the benefit week, the first day of which coincides with or immediately follows the first day of the 'academic year' (or, if a course begins in August, from the first day of the first benefit week on or after the first day of the course) and ending with the benefit week, the last day of which coincides with or immediately follows the last day of the course.

A course lasting for more than one academic year

Unless it is your final year, your loan is apportioned over the period from the earlier of:

- the first day of the first benefit week in September; *or*
- the first benefit week, the first day of which coincides with or immediately follows the first day of the autumn term.

It is taken into account until the last day of the benefit week that coincides with or immediately precedes the last day of June.

Final year of a course

Your loan is taken into account over the period beginning with either:

- if the final academic year starts on 1 September, the benefit week, the first day of which coincides with or immediately follows the earlier of 1 September or the first day of the autumn term; *or*
- the benefit week, the first day of which coincides with or immediately follows the first day of the academic year.

It is taken into account until the benefit week, the last day of which coincides with, or immediately precedes, the last day of the course.

Income from other types of loan

Any financial support you receive in the form of a loan (other than a student loan), including a loan received from an overseas source, does not count as a student loan or a grant.[120] It is taken into account as 'other income' (see p419).

Discretionary funds and other payments

Access funds (which include the discretionary learner support funds available to some students in further education, any discretionary hardship funds offered by higher education institutions in England or Wales, the 16 to 19 bursary fund in England and discretionary funds in Scotland) are administered by colleges and universities.[121] Individual educational institutions may call all or part of these funds by other names – eg, access bursary, mature students' bursary and childcare support. Payments from access funds should be distinguished from payments with similar names from other sources – eg, hardship loans.

How a payment from access funds is treated depends on whether it is paid as a single lump sum, in instalments or to bridge the period before you start your course or receive a student loan payment.

A single lump-sum payment

A single lump-sum payment is treated as capital, but is disregarded for 52 weeks if the payment is intended for, and used for, any items, expenses or charges which you or your partner may incur (other than 'daily living expenses').[122] However, if

Part 6: Special benefit rules
Chapter 41: Benefits for students
6. Student income and means-tested benefits

the payment is intended for but not used for these items, expenses or charges, it is taken into account as capital immediately. A single lump-sum payment made for 'daily living expenses' counts as capital immediately.

> *Daily living expenses*
> **'Daily living expenses'** are:
> – food;
> – ordinary clothing or footwear – ie, for normal daily use, but not including school uniforms or any that are used solely for sporting activities;
> – household fuel;
> – for IS/JSA/ESA only, rent for which HB is payable;
> – for HB, your 'eligible rent', minus any non-dependant deductions;
> – for IS/JSA/ESA only, housing costs met by IS, income-based JSA or income-related ESA;
> – council tax;
> – water charges.

Payments made in instalments

Payments made in instalments are treated as income, but are disregarded in full.[123] However, if the payment is intended and used for daily living expenses, it is taken into account as income for each week it is intended to cover, except for the first £20 a week, which is disregarded. This amount may overlap with other disregards applied to certain war pensions (see p421) and student loans (see p891). A combined maximum sum of £20 a week can be ignored.

Payments before course starts or student loan received

A payment (whether paid as a single payment or in instalments) is ignored, even if it is for 'daily living expenses', if it is made:[124]
- on or after whichever is the earlier of 1 September or the first day of your course, if it is intended to bridge the period before you receive your student loan; *or*
- before the first day of your course, if it is made in anticipation of your becoming a student.

Other sources of income intended to cover study costs

If you receive a payment from any source other than a grant or student loan, which is intended to cover items or expenses that would be ignored when calculating grant income, the payment made from that other source for those items or expenses is also ignored.[125] You must show that the payment is necessary for you to be able to attend the course. Any sum paid which is not necessary (or is likely to exceed the sum necessary) for you to attend the course counts as income. For example, if your grant or student loan does not cover all your tuition fees, any money received from another source such as a parent, intended to make up the difference, is ignored as income. However, if the amount you receive is greater than is likely to be necessary to pay the difference, the amount above that sum counts as income.

Once you have completed your course

For IS/JSA/ESA only, any grant income, student loan, or assessed contribution made by a parent or spouse/civil partner as part of the loan or grant that you received, no longer counts as income once you have completed your course.[126] It should also be ignored as income for HB once you have completed the course.

Any student financial support you have left once you have completed your course counts as capital (see Chapter 22), as there are no provisions to disregard it under the rules about capital.

7. Giving up, changing or taking time out from your course

This section only applies to income support (IS), contribution-based and income-based jobseeker's allowance (JSA), income-related employment and support allowance (ESA) and housing benefit (HB). It does *not* apply if (for IS and JSA) you are (or were) in 'relevant education' (see p873 instead), or (for ESA) you are (or were) a 'qualifying young person' for child benefit purposes (see p881 and p882 instead). For the rules for universal credit, see p872.

Note: most people cannot make a new claim for IS, income-based JSA, income-related ESA or HB (see p23).

If you abandon your course or are dismissed from it, you can qualify for IS, JSA or income-related ESA from the day after that date, provided you satisfy the other rules for getting these benefits (see Chapters 11, 12 and 9). If you are on a sandwich course (see p875), or your course includes a compulsory or optional period on placement, you count as a full-time student during the sandwich or placement period, even if you have been unable to find a placement or your placement comes to an end prematurely.[127]

If you attend a course at an educational institution that provides training or instruction to enable you to take examinations set and marked by an entirely different and unconnected body (ie, a professional institution) and you abandon or take time out from it because you fail the examinations set by the other body (or you finish the course at the educational institution but fail the exams), you may be able to argue that you are not a student from the date you left the course at your educational institution, even if you intend to re-sit the examinations set by the other body at a later date.[128]

If you are taking time out from your course for any other reason and for however long a period, you cannot qualify for IS, JSA or income-related ESA

Part 6: Special benefit rules
Chapter 41: Benefits for students
7. Giving up, changing or taking time out from your course

during your period of absence,[129] except in the limited circumstances set out below (but if you are taking time out from a modular or similar course, see also p876).

You may retain entitlement to some student support on a statutory or discretionary basis – eg, through student loans or hardship funds. You should get specialist advice.

If you complete one course and start a different course, you are not treated as a student in any period between the courses.[130]

Changing from full-time to part-time attendance

If, for personal reasons, you have to change from full-time to part-time attendance on a 'traditional' full-time course, you may be able to argue that you have abandoned your full-time course and are registered on a part-time course and therefore that you are not a full-time student.[131]

If, because of exam failure or any other reason, you change to a different course, or your college requires you to change the level of course (eg, from A level to GCSE) and this involves a change from full-time to part-time study, argue that you are a part-time student.[132]

However, changing your attendance may affect your entitlement to any student support you may be receiving. Get advice on this before acting.

Time out to be a carer

If you are a full-time student and you have taken time out from your course to care for someone, you cannot qualify for IS, JSA or income-related ESA unless you are someone who can qualify while studying (see p876, p877 and p881). In some cases, you may be able to get carer's allowance (see p886).

You can qualify for JSA and HB, but not IS or income-related ESA, when your caring responsibilities have come to an end.[133] **Note:** the rules do not provide a definition of caring responsibilities or when they come to an end. You can then qualify for a maximum period of one year, provided you are not eligible for a student grant or loan during the period, until whichever is the earlier of:

- the day you rejoin your course; *or*
- the first day from which your educational institution has agreed you can rejoin your course.

Time out because of illness

If you are a full-time student and you have taken time out from your course because you are ill, you cannot qualify for income-related ESA unless you get disability living allowance, child disability payment, personal independence payment, adult disability payment or armed forces independence payment.

Once your illness has ended, you can qualify for JSA and HB. The rules are the same as for when caring responsibilities have ended (see above).

Time out because you are pregnant

If you are a full-time student and you have taken time out from your course because you are pregnant, you cannot qualify for IS, JSA or income-related ESA, unless you are someone who can qualify while studying (see p876, p877 and p881). Note:

- Check to see whether you qualify for statutory maternity pay or maternity allowance.
- Once your baby is born, you may then qualify for IS (eg, if you are a lone parent) or you or your partner may qualify for HB.

Calculating student income

Grants

For IS, income-based JSA and income-related ESA, if you cease to be a full-time student before your course finishes, any grant you have received is taken into account as if you were still a student (see p888) until the earliest of:[134]

- the date you repay the grant; *or*
- the last date of the academic term or vacation in which you ceased to be a full-time student; *or*
- if the grant is paid in instalments, the day before the date the next instalment would have been paid had you still been a full-time student.

For HB, it is not taken into account as if you were still a student.[135] Instead, it is taken into account until the grant provider asks you to repay it. Until then, it should be calculated over an appropriate period.[136] It could be argued that your grant should be taken into account as income only to the end of the period which your last instalment was meant to cover.

Loans

For income-related ESA, if you suspend attendance on your course because of illness or disability and this is confirmed in writing by the educational institution, you are not treated as having any part of a student loan which has not been paid to you.

If you abandon or are dismissed from your course before it finishes, there are special rules on how your student loan is treated for IS, income-based JSA, income-related ESA and HB.

If you abandon your course before you have received the final instalment of your student loan, it is taken into account using the formula:[137]

$$\frac{A - (B \times C)}{D}$$

A = the maximum amount of student loan available to you (see p890), including any amount paid as a grant intended to maintain your dependants, that you would have received had you remained a student until *the last day of the academic*

Part 6: Special benefit rules
Chapter 41: Benefits for students
7. Giving up, changing or taking time out from your course

term in which you abandoned or were dismissed from your course, less any disregards that apply (see p891). This amount is the 'relevant payment'. If, however, you were paid in two or more instalments in a quarter (eg, monthly, as is currently the case for Scottish students studying in Scotland), A = the relevant payment that you would have received, calculated in the same way except that it is the amount that you would have received had you remained a student up until *the day you abandoned or were dismissed from your course.*

B = the number of benefit weeks immediately following the benefit week which includes the first day of your academic year to the benefit week immediately before that which includes the day on which you abandoned or were dismissed from your course (for HB, calculate up until the week that includes the one in which you left the course).

C = the weekly amount of student loan for the academic year which would have been taken into account to calculate your benefit under the normal rules (see p890) but without applying the £10 a week disregard (see p891). This applies regardless of whether you were actually entitled to benefit before you abandoned or were dismissed from your course.

D = the number of benefit weeks beginning with the benefit week which includes the day on which you abandoned or were dismissed from your course and ending with the benefit week which includes the last day of the last 'quarter' for which your relevant payment (see A) would have been payable to you had you remained on your course, or to the day before which you would have been due your next loan payment, if earlier.

Example
Bhavna abandons her three-year degree course at a university outside London on 22 October 2021 during the first term of her second year. She is claiming HB. Her benefit week starts on a Monday. Her assumed maximum loan income (ignoring any special support element) would have been taken into account for 42 weeks (first complete benefit week in September to last complete benefit week in June).

Step one: calculate the relevant payment

Loan instalment paid for first term (33% x £6,801)	£2,244.33
less deduction for books and travel	£693.00
Total taken into account	**£1,551.33**

Step two: calculate the benefit weeks prior to
leaving the course

5 September 2021 to 23 October 2021	= 7 weeks

Step three: calculate maximum loan for the academic year

Maximum loan	£6,801
less deduction for books and travel	£693
Total loan	£6,108
Weekly amount	**= £145.43**
(£6,108 ÷ 42 weeks)	

Step four: calculate complete benefit weeks from the benefit week including the date of abandonment to the end of the benefit week including the end of the quarter

17 October 2021 to 1 January 2022   = 11 weeks

$$\frac{£1,551.33 - (7 \times 145.43)}{11} = £48.48$$

Therefore, £48.48 a week is taken into account from 17 October 2021 to 1 January 2022 (11 weeks) and nothing thereafter.

Note: this formula can result in a nil loan income figure depending on the exact date in your term that you abandon, or are dismissed from, your course.

If you voluntarily repay your student loan, for IS, income-based JSA and income-related ESA you are treated as still having that loan income calculated under the above rules.[138] However, for all the benefits, guidance to decision makers says you should not be treated as having any loan income if the Student Loans Company demands you repay the loan instalment immediately.[139]

Notes

1. Universal credit
1 s4(1)(d) WRA 2012
2 Reg 12 UC Regs
3 Reg 5 UC Regs
4 para H6035 ADM
5 Reg 12(4) UC Regs
6 Reg 13 UC Regs
7 Reg 13(1)(b), (2) and (3) UC Regs
8 Reg 14 UC Regs
9 Reg 3(2)(b) UC Regs
10 Reg 13(4) UC Regs
11 Reg 8(3) UC Regs
12 CIS/11766/1996
13 R(IS) 9/94
14 *NP v SSWP* [2009] UKUT 243 (AAC)
15 R(SB) 2/87
16 CIS/11441/1995
17 Reg 89 UC Regs
18 Reg 12(4) UC Regs
19 Reg 95(4) UC Regs
20 Regs 68-71 UC Regs
21 Reg 68(1) UC Regs
22 Reg 68(7) UC Regs
23 Reg 70 UC Regs
24 Reg 68(3) UC Regs
25 Reg 68(7) UC Regs
26 Reg 69(1A) UC Regs
27 para H6131 ADM
28 Reg 68(7) UC Regs
29 Reg 68(1) UC Regs
30 Reg 68(7) UC Regs
31 Reg 13(4) UC Regs
32 *RVS v SSWP* [2019] UKUT 102 (AAC)

2. Income support and jobseeker's allowance
33 s124(1)(d) SSCBA 1992; s1(2)(g) JSA 1995
34 Reg 54(4A) JSA Regs
35 **IS** Reg 12 IS Regs
JSA Reg 54 JSA Regs
36 **IS** Reg 4ZA(2) IS Regs
JSA Reg 15(a) JSA Regs
37 **IS** Reg 61(1), definition of 'student', IS Regs
JSA Reg 1(3), definition of 'student', JSA Regs

Part 6: Special benefit rules
Chapter 41: Benefits for students
Notes

38 **IS** Reg 2(1), definition of 'period of study', IS Regs
   JSA Reg 1(3A) JSA Regs
   HB Reg 53(2)(b) HB Regs
39 **IS** Reg 61(1), definition of 'last day of the course', IS Regs
   JSA Reg 130, definition of 'last day of the course', JSA Regs
   HB Reg 53(1), definition of 'last day of the course', HB Regs
40 Reg 4, definition of 'period of study', JSA Regs
41 **IS** Reg 61(1), definitions of 'full-time course of advanced education' and 'full-time course of study', IS Regs; Vol 6 Ch 30, para 30148 DMG
   JSA Reg 1(3), definition of 'full-time student', JSA Regs
   HB Reg 53(1), definition of 'full-time course of study', HB Regs
42 Vol 6 Ch 30, paras 30197-98 DMG
43 **IS** Reg 61, definitions of 'full-time course of advanced education' and 'full-time course of study', IS Regs; Vol 6 Ch 30, para 30149 DMG
   JSA Reg 1(3), definition of 'full-time student', JSA Regs
   HB Reg 53(1), definitions of 'full-time course of study' and 'higher education', HB Regs
44 **IS** Reg 61(1), definition of 'sandwich course', IS Regs
   JSA Reg 1(3), definition of 'sandwich course', JSA Regs
   HB Reg 53(1), definition of 'sandwich course', HB Regs
45 R(IS) 19/98
46 **IS** Reg 61(4) IS Regs
   JSA Reg 1(3C) JSA Regs
   HB Reg 53(4) HB Regs
47 **IS** Reg 61(2)(a) IS Regs
   JSA Reg 1(3A)(a) JSA Regs
   HB Reg 53(2)(a) HB Regs
48 **IS** Reg 61(3)(b) IS Regs
   JSA Reg 1(3B)(b) JSA Regs
   HB Reg 53(3)(b) HB Regs
49 **IS** Reg 61(3)(a) IS Regs
   JSA Reg 1(3B)(a) JSA Regs
   HB Reg 53(3)(a) HB Regs
50 R(IS) 15/98; R(IS) 7/99; CJSA/836/1998; R(IS)1/00; *Chief Adjudication Officer v Webber* [1997] 4 All ER 274
51 *RVS v SSWP* [2019] UKUT 102 (AAC)
52 R(SB) 40/83; R(SB) 41/83

53 **IS** Reg 61, definitions of 'full-time course of advanced education' and 'full-time course of study', IS Regs
   JSA Reg 1(3), definition of 'full-time student', JSA Regs
54 Reg 4ZA and Sch 1B IS Regs
55 Reg 15(2) and (3) JSA Regs
56 Reg 14(1)(a) JSA Regs
57 Reg 14(1)(k) JSA Regs
58 Reg 7(2) JSA(SAPOE) Regs
59 Regs 17A and 21A JSA Regs
60 CIS/152/1994; R(IS) 15/98; CJSA/836/1998; R(IS) 1/00
61 Reg 1(3), definition of 'part-time student', JSA Regs
62 Vol 4 Ch 21, para 21241 DMG
63 Vol 4 Ch 21, para 21242 DMG
64 Vol 4 Ch 21, para 21243 DMG
65 Vol 4 Ch 21, para 21244 DMG
66 Reg 11 JSA Regs
67 Reg 11(3) JSA Regs
68 Regs 2(1) and 61(1), definitions of 'student' and 'course of study', IS Regs

3. Employment and support allowance
69 Reg 32(2) and (3) ESA Regs
70 Sch 1 para 6(1)(g) WRA 2007; reg 18 ESA Regs
71 Reg 15 ESA Regs
72 Reg 14 ESA Regs
73 *RVS v SSWP* [2019] UKUT 102 (AAC)
74 Regs 14 and 33(2) ESA Regs

4. Housing benefit
75 There are no student rules in the HB(SPC) Regs.
76 Reg 56(2) HB Regs
77 Reg 55(1) HB Regs
78 Reg 55(2) HB Regs
79 Reg 57 HB Regs
80 Reg 8(1)(e) HB Regs
81 Reg 58 HB Regs
82 Reg 92(7) HB Regs

5. Other benefits
83 Reg 5 SS(ICA) Regs
84 *SSWP v Deane* [2010] EWCA Civ 699
85 Reg 5(2) SS(ICA) Regs
86 *SM v SSWP* [2016] UKUT 406 (AAC)
87 R(G) 2/02
88 Reg 45 JSA Regs 2013

6. Student income and means-tested benefits

89 **IS** Regs 2(1), definition of 'student', and 61(1), definition of 'course of study', IS Regs
    JSA Regs 1(3), definition of 'full-time student', and 130, definition of 'course of study', JSA Regs
    ESA Reg 131, definition of 'full-time student', ESA Regs
    HB Reg 53(1), definition of 'student' and 'course of study', HB Regs

90 Sch 5 para 4 HB Regs

91 **IS** Reg 61(1), definition of 'grant', IS Regs
    JSA Reg 130, definition of 'grant', JSA Regs
    ESA Reg 131(1), definition of 'grant', ESA Regs
    HB Reg 53(1), definition of 'grant', HB Regs

92 **IS** Reg 61(1), definition of 'grant income', IS Regs
    JSA Reg 130, definition of 'grant income', JSA Regs
    ESA Reg 131(1), definition of 'grant income', ESA Regs
    HB Reg 53(1), definition of 'grant income', HB Regs

93 **IS** Reg 62(3) IS Regs
    JSA Reg 131(4) JSA Regs
    ESA Reg 132(4) ESA Regs
    HB Reg 59(5) HB Regs

94 Sch 7 para 4 SS(C&P) Regs

95 **IS** Reg 61(1), definition of 'period of study', IS Regs
    JSA Reg 1(3), definition of 'period of study', JSA Regs
    ESA Reg 131(1), definition of 'period of study', ESA Regs
    HB Reg 53, definition of 'period of study', HB Regs

96 **IS** Reg 62(3B) IS Regs
    ESA Reg 132(6) ESA Regs
    HB Reg 59(7) HB Regs

97 **IS** Reg 62(2) and (2A) IS Regs
    JSA Reg 131(2) and (3) JSA Regs
    ESA Reg 132(2) and (3) ESA Regs
    HB Reg 59(2) and (3) HB Regs

98 **IS/JSA** Vol 6 Ch 30, para 30329 DMG
    ESA Vol 9 Ch 51, para 51951 DMG
    HB paras C2/2.170-73 GM

99 **IS** Reg 67A IS Regs
    JSA Reg 137A JSA Regs
    ESA Reg 141 ESA Regs
    HB Reg 67 HB Regs

100 **IS** Reg 67 IS Regs
    JSA Reg 137 JSA Regs
    ESA Reg 140 ESA Regs
    HB Reg 66 HB Regs

101 **IS** Schs 9 para 11 and 10 para 63 IS Regs
    JSA Schs 7 para 12 and 8 para 52 JSA Regs
    ESA Schs 8 para 13 and 9 para 52 ESA Regs
    HB Schs 5 para 11 and 6 para 51 HB Regs

102 **IS** Reg 62(2A) IS Regs
    JSA Reg 131(3) JSA Regs
    ESA Reg 132(3) ESA Regs
    HB Reg 59(3) HB Regs

103 CIS/91/1994

104 R(IS) 7/95

105 **IS** Reg 61(1), definition of 'student loan', IS Regs
    JSA Reg 130, definition of 'student loan', JSA Regs
    ESA Reg 131(1), definition of 'student loan', ESA Regs
    HB Reg 53(1), definition of 'student loan', HB Regs

106 **IS** Reg 66A(3) and (4) IS Regs
    JSA Reg 136(3) and (4) JSA Regs
    ESA Reg 137(4) and (5) ESA Regs
    HB Reg 64(3) and (4) HB Regs

107 **IS** Reg 66A (4A) IS Regs
    ESA Reg 137 (5A) ESA Regs
    HB Reg 64 (4A) HB Regs

108 Reg 137(4A) ESA Regs

109 **IS** Reg 66D IS Regs; Vol 6 Ch 30, para 30330 DMG
    ESA Reg 139A ESA Regs; para 51953 DMG
    JSA Reg 136C JSA Regs
    HB Reg 64B HB Regs

110 **IS** Reg 66A(4) IS Regs
    ESA Reg 137(5) ESA Regs
    JSA Reg 136(4) JSA Regs

111 **IS** Reg 66C IS Regs
    JSA Reg 136B JSA Regs
    ESA Reg 139 ESA Regs
    HB Reg 64A HB Regs

112 **IS** Reg 67A IS Regs
    JSA Reg 137A JSA Regs
    ESA Reg 141 ESA Regs
    HB Reg 67 HB Regs

113 **IS** Reg 67 IS Regs
    JSA Reg 137 JSA Regs
    ESA Reg 140 ESA Regs
    HB Reg 66 HB Regs

114 **IS** Reg 66A(2) and (5) IS Regs
    JSA Reg 136(2) and (5) JSA Regs
    ESA Reg 137(3) and (6) ESA Regs
    HB Reg 64(2) and (5) HB Regs

Part 6: Special benefit rules
Chapter 41: Benefits for students
Notes

115 **IS** Reg 61(1), definition of 'academic year', IS Regs
JSA Reg 130, definition of 'academic year', JSA Regs
ESA Reg 131(1), definition of 'academic year', ESA Regs
HB Reg 53(1), definition of 'academic year', HB Regs
116 **IS** Reg 66A(2)(a) IS Regs
JSA Reg 136(2)(a) JSA Regs
ESA Reg 137(3)(a) ESA Regs
HB Reg 64(2)(a) HB Regs
117 **IS** Reg 66A(2)(aa) IS Regs
JSA Reg 136(2)(aa) JSA Regs
ESA Reg 137(3)(b) ESA Regs
HB Reg 64(2)(b) HB Regs
118 **IS** Reg 66A(2)(aa) IS Regs
JSA Reg 136(2)(aa) JSA Regs
ESA Regs 104(6) and 137(3)(c) ESA Regs
HB Reg 64(2)(b) HB Regs
All The Education (Student Support) (No.2) Regulations 2008 No.1582
119 CIS/3734/2004
120 R(IS) 16/95
121 **IS** Reg 61(1), definition of 'access funds', IS Regs
JSA Reg 130, definition of 'access funds', JSA Regs
ESA Reg 131(1), definition of 'access funds', ESA Regs
HB Reg 53(1), definition of 'access funds', HB Regs
122 **IS** Reg 68(3) and (4) IS Regs
JSA Reg 138(3) and (4) JSA Regs
ESA Regs 2(1) and 142(3) ESA Regs
HB Regs 2(1) and 68(3) and (4) HB Regs
123 **IS** Reg 66B IS Regs
JSA Reg 136A JSA Regs
ESA Regs 2(1) and 138 ESA Regs
HB Regs 2(1) and 65 HB Regs
124 **IS** Reg 66B(4) IS Regs
JSA Reg 136A(4) JSA Regs
ESA Reg 138(4) ESA Regs
HB Reg 65(5) HB Regs
125 **IS** Reg 66(1) IS Regs
JSA Reg 135(1) JSA Regs
ESA Reg 136(1) ESA Regs
HB Reg 63 HB Regs
126 **IS** Sch 9 paras 13 and 61 IS Regs
JSA Sch 7 paras 14 and 59 JSA Regs
ESA Sch 8 paras 15 and 54 ESA Regs

7. Giving up, changing or taking time out from your course
127 CIS/368/1992; R(IS) 6/97
128 R(JSA) 2/02; CJSA/1965/2008
129 R(IS) 7/99

130 R(IS) 1/96
131 Vol 6 Ch 30, paras 30230-33 DMG; paras C2/2.41-42 GM
132 CIS/152/1994; R(IS) 15/98
133 **JSA** Reg 1(3D) and (3E) JSA Regs
HB Reg 56(6) and (7) HB Regs
134 **IS** Regs 29(2B) and 32(6A) IS Regs
JSA Regs 94(2B) and 97(7) JSA Regs
ESA Regs 91(4) and 94(7) ESA Regs
135 para C2/2.425 GM
136 *Leeves v Chief Adjudication Officer*, reported as R(IS) 5/99; reg 31(1) HB Regs
137 **IS** Reg 40(3A), (3AA), (3AAA) and (3AB) IS Regs
JSA Reg 103(5), (5ZA), (5AZA) and (5ZB) JSA Regs
ESA Reg 104(4)-(6) ESA Regs
HB Reg 40(7)-(9) HB Regs
138 Reg 6(6)(a) SS&CS(DA) Regs; CJSA/549/03
139 Vol 6 Ch 30, para 30470 DMG; para C2/2.421 GM

Chapter 42

• •

Benefits in hospital, care homes, prison and in other special circumstances

This chapter covers:
1. Hospital patients (below)
2. People in care homes and similar accommodation (p913)
3. Prisoners (p923)
4. 16/17 year old care leavers (p933)
5. People without accommodation (p935)

Key facts
- Your benefit entitlement may be affected if you (or your partner, child or non-dependant) go into hospital, a care home or prison. It may also be affected if you are without accommodation, or if you are aged 16 or 17 and were previously looked after by a local authority.
- Some benefits are not payable, or are payable at a reduced rate, either immediately or after a specified period.
- You should always notify the relevant benefit authority as soon as possible if any of the above circumstances apply, or cease to apply, to avoid being overpaid or underpaid.

1. Hospital patients

Some benefits are affected after you, your partner or child have been a patient in a hospital, or in an institution similiar to a hospital, for a period of time. In some cases, benefit is no longer paid. In other cases, it is paid at a reduced rate.

See p912 for information on paying for your normal home while you are a patient.

You can arrange for someone else to collect your benefit while you are a patient (see p1149). If you are unable to manage your affairs, someone else can act as your appointee (see p1135).

Part 6: Special benefit rules
Chapter 42: Benefits in hospital, care homes, prison and in other special circumstances
1. Hospital patients

Always inform the DWP, HM Revenue and Customs (HMRC), Social Security Scotland and/or the local authority as soon as you can if your benefits may be affected by the rules described below, to avoid being overpaid or underpaid.

Who counts as a patient

For benefits other than personal independence payment (PIP) and adult disability payment (ADP), you count as a 'patient' if you are being maintained free of charge while undergoing medical or other treatment as an inpatient in a hospital or 'similar institution'. The treatment must be provided and funded under NHS legislation, or in a hospital or similar institution which is maintained or administered by the Defence Council.[1] You do not count as a patient if you are getting treatment as a private patient, you are meeting the cost of your treatment in a private hospital or the local authority has organised the placement.[2]

For PIP and ADP, you count as a 'patient' if are undergoing medical or other treatment as an inpatient at a hospital or 'similar institution' and any of the costs of your treatment, accommodation and any related services are paid for 'out of public funds'. The costs count as being paid for 'out of public funds' where you are being provided with medical or other treatment under NHS legislation, or you are in a hospital or similar institution which is maintained or administered by the Defence Council. You do not count as a patient for PIP or ADP if you are getting treatment as a private patient or you are meeting the cost of your treatment in a private hospital.[3]

Definitions
'Hospitals' include all NHS hospitals, armed forces hospitals and special hospitals such as Broadmoor, Rampton and the State Hospital in Scotland. Prison hospital wings do not count as hospitals.[4]
A **'similar institution'** to a hospital is not defined in the law, but can include some care homes (see below), and rehabilitation units that provide medical or nursing care.[5]
'Medical or other treatment' is treatment by a doctor, dentist or professionally qualified or trained nurse, or by someone under the supervision of such a person.[6]

If you are in a care home and receiving medical or nursing care which is more than 'incidental and ancillary' to your other care needs, the NHS is responsible for meeting your care home costs in full. In this situation, you count as a patient. For PIP or ADP, if you are in a care home which is deemed to be a 'similar institution' to a hospital (ie, because you are provided with medical or nursing care), you count as a patient if the NHS is paying for any of your care, treatment, accommodation or related services.[7]

Note: if you are detained in hospital while serving a sentence of imprisonment under certain provisions, you may be treated as a prisoner rather than a patient for benefit purposes (see p928).

The days on which you count as a patient

You count as a patient from the day after the day you enter hospital (or a similar institution) up to and including:

- for attendance allowance (AA), disability living allowance (DLA), PIP and ADP, the day before the day you leave (unless, for PIP only, you go straight into a care home or prison, in which case you count as a patient until the day you leave hospital);[8] or
- for other benefits where the issue is relevant, the day you leave.[9]

Example

Hilda is claiming PIP and employment and support allowance (ESA). She is taken ill and admitted to hospital on 1 January. After successful treatment, she is discharged on 21 January.

For PIP purposes, she counts as a patient from 2 January up to and including 20 January = 19 days.

For ESA purposes, she counts as a patient from 2 January up to and including 21 January = 20 days.

Disability benefits

If you were under 18 when you went into hospital, you continue to be paid DLA, PIP, child disability payment (CDP) or ADP regardless of how long you are in hospital, even if you turn 18 while you are still a hospital inpatient.[10] This applies whether or not you were entitled to DLA, PIP, CDP or ADP when you went into hospital, so if you were under 18 when you became a patient, you can claim DLA, PIP, CDP or ADP while you are in hospital and if it is awarded, you will be paid it. If you are under 16 and were entitled to DLA when you went into hospital, you can continue to get DLA after the age of 16 (and have your DLA renewed) while you remain in hospital – you do not have to claim PIP.[11]

If you are aged 18 or over when you become a hospital patient, you are not paid AA, DLA, PIP or ADP after you have been a patient for 28 days.[12] Even if your payment of AA, DLA, PIP or ADP stops because of these rules, your *entitlement* continues. This means that payment can begin again following your discharge from hospital without your having to make a new claim. Payment of AA, DLA, PIP and ADP can be at a daily rate if you are expected to be readmitted within 28 days.[13]

There is a 28-day 'linking rule' which means that:[14]

- different periods spent as a patient that are separated by 28 days or less are linked together and treated as one period;
- periods spent as a resident in a care home (or, for PIP and ADP, as a prisoner) link with periods spent as a patient if they are 28 days or less apart.

Part 6: Special benefit rules
Chapter 42: Benefits in hospital, care homes, prison and in other special circumstances
1. Hospital patients

. . . .
. . . .

Example

Horace is claiming AA. He goes into hospital for an operation on 16 July and is discharged on 30 July. He counts as a patient from 17 July up to and including 29 July = 13 days. His AA is not affected by his stay in hospital.

Horace has to go back into hospital for further treatment on 10 August. He counts as a patient again from 11 August. As there are less than 28 days between his discharge and readmission, the two spells in hospital are linked. When he has been a patient for a further 15 days, he cannot be paid AA.

. . . .

Note:
- If you are terminally ill, you can be paid AA, DLA, CDP, PIP or ADP while you are in a hospice.[15] This applies unless the hospice is an NHS hospital. For AA, DLA and PIP, the DWP must have been informed in writing that you are terminally ill.
- If you are awarded AA, DLA, PIP or ADP while you are a patient aged 18 or over, payment cannot begin until you are discharged.[16]
- You can continue to be paid the mobility component of DLA while you are a patient if you have been a patient since 31 July 1995 (other than if you are detained under the Mental Health Act). You are paid at the lower rate (even if you would otherwise qualify for the higher rate). This transitional protection ends if you cease to be a patient for more than 28 consecutive days.[17]
- You continue to be exempt from the benefit cap (see p1156) even if you or your partner are no longer receiving AA, DLA, PIP or ADP after being a patient for 28 days.[18]

Carer's allowance

You no longer qualify for carer's allowance (CA) if the person you care for no longer receives AA, DLA, PIP or ADP – ie, if s/he is aged 18 or over and has been a patient for 28 days. If the person you care for is discharged and payment of AA, the DLA care component or the daily living component of PIP or ADP resumes, you should reclaim CA if you satisfy the rules for entitlement. Your claim can be backdated to the date from when AA, DLA PIP or ADP is payable again, provided you reclaim CA within three months of that date.[19]

A temporary break in caring does not necessarily affect your CA (see p547), including if you (or the person you care for) are a hospital patient. You can remain entitled to CA during a temporary break (or breaks) of up to four weeks in any period of 26 weeks. You can remain entitled to CA for up to 12 weeks if you or the person you care for has been in hospital for at least eight of those 12 weeks.[20] This can be useful if you (or the person you care for) are going in and out of hospital.

However, if the person you care for is 18 or over when s/he goes into hospital, has been a patient for 28 days and is therefore no longer receiving AA, DLA, PIP or ADP (see p905), your entitlement to CA ends, even though you have not yet had a temporary break of 12 weeks.

Universal credit

Your universal credit (UC) is not normally affected until you (or your partner or child) have been in hospital for more than six months. However, you are no longer entitled to a carer element if the AA, DLA, PIP or ADP of the person you care for stops because s/he is aged 18 or over when s/he goes into hospital and s/he has been in hospital for more than 28 days.[21] See p912 for information on paying for your usual home.

Single claimants

You can continue to get UC while you are in hospital. However, the housing costs element stops if your stay in hospital exceeds, or is expected to exceed, six months.[22] If you receive a loan from the DWP to help you with your mortgage interest, payments will stop if your stay in hospital exceeds, or is expected to exceed, six months.[23] **Note:** when calculating the six-month period, there is no 'linking rule' joining two or more periods in hospital.

Couples

You and your partner continue to count as a couple for UC while one of you is temporarily absent from the household, including when one of you is in hospital. You must continue to make a joint claim with your partner and UC is paid as usual. If the partner who is not in hospital is working, you may qualify for a childcare costs element (see p73). If the absence exceeds, or is expected to exceed, six months, you no longer count as a couple.[24] **Note:** when calculating the six-month period, there is no 'linking rule' joining two or more periods in hospital.

If you no longer count as a couple:
- you can no longer make a joint claim for UC;
- the calculation of your benefit no longer includes amounts for your partner;
- you should notify the DWP as you may both have to reclaim UC as single people.

Children

A child continues to be included in your UC claim while s/he is temporarily absent from your household because s/he is in hospital. However, s/he is no longer included in your claim if the absence exceeds, or is expected to exceed, six months.[25] **Note:** when calculating the six-month period, there is no 'linking rule' joining two or more periods in hospital.

Part 6: Special benefit rules
Chapter 42: Benefits in hospital, care homes, prison and in other special circumstances
1. Hospital patients

If your child is no longer included in your claim:

- the calculation of your benefit no longer includes amounts for her/him;
- your work allowance (see p40) and the work-related requirements you must meet may change (see Chapter 46).

Other means-tested benefits

If you are getting income support (IS), income-related ESA, housing benefit (HB) or pension credit (PC) when you go into hospital, these benefits can often continue, although the amount to which you are entitled might change (see below). See p907 for how UC is affected. See p912 for information on paying for your ususal home.

If your, or your partner's, disability benefit stops

If payment of your (or your partner's) AA, DLA or PIP/ADP stops because you (or your partner) are 18 or over when you (or your partner) go into hospital and you (or your partner) have been in hospital for 28 days, the severe disability premium included in your IS, income-based jobseeker's allowance (JSA), income-related ESA or HB or the severe disability addition in your PC is affected.

- If you are a single claimant, you are no longer entitled to the severe disability premium in your IS, income-based JSA, income-related ESA or HB, or to the PC severe disability addition.
- If you are a member of a couple, you (or your partner) are treated as getting AA, DLA or PIP/ADP if the only reason it is not being paid is because you (or s/he) are a patient. This means that you continue to get the severe disability premium/addition in your means-tested benefit. However, it is paid at the single rate instead of the couple rate.[26] For the purposes of entitlement to the severe disability premium/addition, it does not affect the rate if your carer or your partner's carer stops getting CA because you (or your partner) have been an inpatient for more than 28 days.[27]

Entitlement to the disability premium in IS, income-based JSA and HB, the enhanced disability premium in IS, income-based JSA, income-related ESA and HB, and the higher pensioner premium in IS and income-based JSA, are not affected when payment of AA, DLA or PIP/ADP stops after 28 days.[28] However, these premiums can be affected if you (or your partner) are a patient for 52 weeks (see p909).

For HB, if you are a member of a couple, a deduction for childcare charges can be made from earnings if one of you is in full-time paid work and the other is in hospital (see p416 and p458).

Note: for IS only, if you are only in hospital for part of the week and are entitled to PIP/ADP when you are not in hospital, you can be paid the severe disability and enhanced disability premiums when you are staying away from the hospital from the date the change occurs (or is expected to occur).[29]

If your carer's allowance stops

You no longer qualify for CA when payment of the AA, DLA, PIP or ADP of the person you are caring for stops. In this situation, the carer premium in your IS, income-based JSA, income-related ESA and HB or the carer addition in PC can continue to be paid for eight weeks after your entitlement to CA stops (see p334). After this, you are no longer entitled to a carer premium or addition. If your CA stops because *you* are a patient, the person you were caring for may become entitled to the severe disability premium or addition (see p330 for more information on the severe disability premium). If claiming CA was the only basis for your IS claim, eight weeks after your CA stops your IS will stop.[30]

Pension credit child amounts

If you get PC which includes an amount for a child (see p307), the amount for the child can continue while s/he is in hospital – providing the hospital stay is not expected to exceed, or has not exceeded, 52 weeks or, in exceptional circumstances, it is unlikely to be substantially more than 52 weeks.[31] There is no 'linking rule' in this provision. This means that if your child is discharged from hospital and is then readmitted, a new period as a patient starts.

If you have been in hospital for 52 weeks

You still count as a couple for IS, JSA, ESA, PC and HB while you and your partner are temporarily apart. However, you no longer count as a couple if you are likely to be separated for more than 52 weeks or, in exceptional circumstances (including a stay in hospital), not substantially more than 52 weeks.[32] If you no longer count as a couple, you are both treated as a single claimant (or lone parent) for these benefits.

If your child has been in hospital for more than 52 weeks, s/he may no longer count as living with you (see p311) and no longer be included in your claim.

Note:
- HB and help with your housing costs may no longer be payable once you have been away from home for 52 weeks – eg, if you live alone. For information about paying for your usual home while you are a patient, see p912.
- If you have a non-dependant living with you and s/he has been a patient for 52 weeks, non-dependant deductions made for her/him stop (see p913).

The rate of IS, income-based JSA or income-related ESA may be lower if you (or your partner) have been a patient for a continuous period of more than 52 weeks, because you are no longer entitled to certain premiums. You may have already lost the severe disability and carer premiums (see p908). The calculation of HB may also be affected if you are not 'passported' to the maximum amount.

There are no 'linking rules' with these provisions. This means that if you are discharged from hospital and are then readmitted, a new period as a patient starts and you can again be entitled to IS, income-based JSA, income-related ESA, PC or

Part 6: Special benefit rules
Chapter 42: Benefits in hospital, care homes, prison and in other special circumstances
1. Hospital patients

HB premiums at the rate you were getting before your admission to hospital. If you have completely lost your entitlement to IS, income-based JSA, income-related ESA or HB, you are likely to have to claim UC instead. See p21 for when you might have to claim UC.

Premiums and components: single claimants and lone parents

If you are a single claimant or a lone parent and you have been a patient for more than 52 weeks:[33]

- the disability premium is not included in your IS or income-based JSA and the enhanced disability premium is not included in your IS, income-based JSA or income-related ESA;
- the work-related activity component and the support component are not included in your income-related ESA.

Premiums and components: couples

If you are a member of a couple and:

- both you and your partner have been a patient for more than 52 weeks, but you still count as a couple:[34]
  - the higher pensioner premium and enhanced disability premium are not included in your IS, income-based JSA or income-related ESA. Note: the pensioner premium is included in your IS if your partner qualifies, or in your income-based JSA or income-related ESA if you or your partner qualify;
  - the disability premium is not included in your IS or income-based JSA;
  - the work-related activity component and the support component are not included in your income-related ESA;
- one of you has been a patient for more than 52 weeks, but you still count as a couple:
  - you are paid the normal rate of IS and income-based JSA, but without any premiums for the patient, other than the pensioner premium;[35]
  - you are paid the normal rate of income-related ESA. Premiums may be affected by changes to other benefits (see p909).[36]

Premiums: children

If you have a child and s/he is (or you are) a patient, s/he may no longer be included in your claim if s/he no longer counts as living with you (see p307). If this happens, you can no longer get allowances and premiums for her/him in your HB (and in your IS or income-based JSA, if still included). If s/he *is* still included in your claim:

- you continue to be entitled to the normal HB premiums, including the disabled child and enhanced disability premiums – these are not affected if you or your child have been a patient for more than 52 weeks;[37]

- if your child is the patient, you are no longer entitled to the disabled child premium and enhanced disability premium for her/him in IS and income-based JSA.[38]

Other benefits

Child benefit

Your entitlement to child benefit can be affected if your child is not living with you. However, periods of up to 84 days when your child is receiving inpatient treatment in a hospital or similar institution are ignored. If your child has been in hospital for 84 days or longer, you remain entitled to child benefit if:

- you are regularly incurring expenditure in respect of the child; or
- you are contributing at least the amount of child benefit to the cost of supporting the child.

See p567 for details of these rules.

Child tax credit

Child tax credit (CTC) remains payable for a child, provided s/he normally lives with you.[39] Guidance from HMRC says this means that the child 'regularly, usually, typically' lives with you, and that this allows for temporary absences.[40] You remain entitled to CTC if your child is in hospital on a temporary basis.

Contributory employment and support allowance

You are not entitled to a work-related activity or support component in your contributory ESA once you have been a patient for a continuous period of more than 52 weeks.[41]

Jobseeker's allowance

You cannot qualify for JSA if you have limited capability for work (see p987). You must also be available for, and actively seeking, work (see p1092). If you cannot satisfy these conditions because you are in hospital, you may need to claim a different benefit such as UC or ESA instead. You can continue to get JSA:[42]

- for up to 13 weeks during a period of sickness; or
- indefinitely, if you are absent from Great Britain for NHS hospital treatment.

In these circumstances, you are treated as not having limited capability for work and as satisfying the jobseeking requirements for JSA. See p690 for further information.

Winter fuel payment

You are not entitled to a winter fuel payment if you have been a patient for more than 52 weeks.[43]

Part 6: Special benefit rules
Chapter 42: Benefits in hospital, care homes, prison and in other special circumstances
1. Hospital patients

. . . .

Scottish child payment

If you are entitled to Scottish child payment for a child, you continue to get it while the child is in hospital or while you are in hospital, provided you continue to satisfy the normal conditions of entitlement (see p1729).

Paying for your usual home

The benefit you can get to help pay for your usual home may be affected while you, or your partner, child or non-dependant, are temporarily in hospital (whether as an NHS or private patient). **Note:** if you leave your home permanently, you are no longer entitled to benefit for it.

- You can get a UC housing costs element for up to six months, provided your absence from home does not exceed (or is not expected to exceed) six months (see p92).[44] If you are on UC and are getting a DWP loan to help pay your mortgage interest, payments stop if you have been absent for six months (or if your absence is likely to exceed six months).[45]

- You can get HB, or help with your housing costs (service charges and ground rent for owner-occupiers) in your IS, income-based JSA, income-related ESA or PC, provided you have not been absent (or are not likely to be absent) from home for more than 52 weeks or, in exceptional circumstances, not substantially longer than 52 weeks (see p181 and p354).[46] You can get HB or help with housing costs for a maximum of 52 weeks. If you are on IS, income-based JSA, income-related ESA or PC and you get a DWP loan to help with your mortgage interest, you can continue to get this provided you have not been absent (or are not likely to be absent) for more than 52 weeks or, in exceptional circumstances, not substantially longer than 52 weeks. You can continue to get the DWP loan for a maximum of 52 weeks.[47]

Note:
- Another person (eg, your partner) might be able to qualify for these benefits (or for the DWP loan to help pay mortgage interest – see p842) instead of you if s/he is (or can be treated as) liable to pay the rent or housing costs (see p86, p176 and p352).
- There are no 'linking rules' with these provisions. This means that if a new period as a patient starts, you can again be entitled to HB or an amount in your UC, IS, income-based JSA, income-related ESA or PC – eg, if you are discharged from hospital and then are readmitted.
- For HB, you can be treated as occupying, but temporarily absent from, a new dwelling, even if you have not yet stayed there, if you move your furniture and belongings in but cannot move in yourself – eg, because you have to go into hospital.[48]

Partners, children and non-dependants

If your partner, child or non-dependant is away from home because s/he is in hospital, this could affect the amount of your HB or housing costs paid with your UC, IS, income-based JSA, income-related ESA or PC. This could apply, for example, if s/he no longer counts as living with you or, for UC, s/he no longer counts as a member of your 'extended benefit unit' (see p95). Bear the following in mind.

- If you live in rented accommodation, you may no longer be allowed the same number of bedrooms under the size criteria (see p370, p378, p384 and p97) and your UC or HB may be reduced. For UC, this only applies if your partner, child or non-dependant is absent (or expected to be absent) from home for more than six months.[49]

- If your non-dependant is absent, check whether a deduction for housing costs contributions or a non-dependant deduction should still be made for her/him (see p198, p347 and p102).

2. People in care homes and similar accommodation

Most benefits are paid as normal if you live in a care home or similar type of accommodation. However, some benefits are no longer payable and some may be paid at a reduced rate. The benefits affected are covered from p914 to p921, but see p567 for how your child benefit could be affected if you or your child are resident in a care home.

Always inform the DWP, HM Revenue and Customs, Social Security Scotland (SSS) and/or the local authority promptly if your benefits may be affected by the rules described in this section, to avoid being overpaid or underpaid.

> *Care homes and similar accommodation*
>
> There is not sufficient space in this *Handbook* to cover all the different kinds of care homes and similar accommodation, and the funding arrangements for people living in them. The rules covered below mainly apply to homes which provide you with accommodation and personal and/or nursing care. They do not apply to other types of supported or sheltered accommodation, even if you are receiving personal care services from your local authority social services department (social work department in Scotland). Some homes are run by the NHS, some by local authorities and some are independent. If your care home is funded by the NHS, you may count as a 'patient' in a hospital or similar institution, in which case the rules on p903 apply to you. If you are in a local authority-funded or independent home, you may have to contribute part of the cost.

Part 6: Special benefit rules
Chapter 42: Benefits in hospital, care homes, prison and in other special circumstances
2. People in care homes and similar accommodation

Disability benefits

You cannot usually be paid the following benefits once you have been a resident in a care home for 28 days if any of the 'costs of any qualifying services' provided for you are met out of public or local funds:[50]

- attendance allowance (AA);
- care component of disability living allowance (DLA) or child disability payment (CDP);
- daily living component of personal independence payment (PIP) or adult disability payment (ADP).

Until then, AA, the DLA/CDP care component and the PIP/ADP daily living component are paid as normal. See p915 for exceptions to these rules.

Care homes, qualifying services and specified provisions

For these purposes, a '**care home**' is an establishment that provides you with accommodation as well as nursing or personal care.[51]

'**Qualifying services**' are the costs of accommodation, board and personal care.[52] For AA and DLA, the 'costs of any qualifying services' do *not* include the cost of:[53]

– domiciliary services (including personal care) provided in a private dwelling;

– improvements to, or furniture/equipment provided for, a private dwelling because of a disabled person's needs, or for a care home, for which a grant/payment was made out of public funds, except if the grant/payment is of a regular or repeated nature;

– social and recreational activities outside the care home;

– buying or running a motor vehicle used in connection with any qualifying service provided in the care home.

For AA, DLA and PIP, the 'qualifying services' only count as such if they are provided under 'specified provisions'. The '**specified provisions**' are:[54]

– Part III of the National Assistance Act 1948, sections 59 and 59A of the Social Work (Scotland) Act 1968, the Mental Health (Care and Treatment) (Scotland) Act 2003, the Community Care and Health (Scotland) Act 2002, the Mental Health Act 1983, section 57 of the Health and Social Care Act 2001, Part 1 of the Care Act 2014 and Part 4 of the Social Services and Well-being (Wales) Act 2014; *or*

– any other Acts relating to people with disabilities or (in the case of DLA and PIP only) young people, education or training – eg, in some special residential schools.

In most cases, a local authority pays for the services in a care home under one of these provisions, but it is always worth checking. Local authorities also have powers to provide accommodation under housing legislation and the Local Government Act 1972, in which case AA, DLA and PIP are not affected.[55] **Note:** the First-tier Tribunal can decide that your placement is being funded under a different legal power than the one the local authority has stated.[56]

Note:
- The mobility component of DLA, PIP, CDP and ADP, and armed forces independence payment are paid as normal however long you are a resident in a care home.
- If your entitlement to AA, the DLA/CDP care component or PIP/ADP daily living component begins while you are in a care home, you cannot be paid for days when you count as resident in the care home (including the first 28 days).[57]
- Entitlement to AA, DLA, CDP, PIP or ADP continues while you are in a care home, even after payment stops. This means that payment can begin again when you are no longer resident in a care home.
- You continue to be exempt from the benefit cap (see p1156), even if you or your partner or child are no longer receiving AA, DLA/CDP or PIP/ADP after being resident in a care home for 28 days.[58]
- If the NHS provides nursing services in a care home and your nursing needs are more than 'merely incidental and ancillary' to other care needs, you may be treated as a 'patient' for AA, DLA and PIP purposes (see p904).[59]
- If you think the DWP or SSS has refused payment of AA, DLA, CDP, PIP or ADP wrongly, you can appeal (see Chapters 57 and 80). You must apply for a mandatory reconsideration (or redetermination for CDP and ADP) first.

Exceptions

There are exceptions to the rules. You can continue to be paid AA, the DLA/CDP care component and the PIP/ADP daily living component after you have been resident in a care home for 28 days if:
- you are terminally ill and are in a hospice, provided the DWP has been informed that you are terminally ill. In most cases, the DWP must be informed in writing.[60] This applies unless the hospice is an NHS hospital; *or*
- for CDP, you are in a hospice;[61] *or*
- for ADP, you are in a hospice and you have a terminal illness;[62] *or*
- for DLA and PIP only, you are a student and the cost of your accommodation is wholly or partly met from a student grant or loan, or from a grant made to educational institutions under specified legislation;[63] *or*
- you are under 16 (for DLA and CDP) and being looked after by a local authority, or aged 16 or 17 (for DLA, CDP, PIP and ADP) and you are receiving services from your local authority because of your disability or health, but only if you have been placed by the local authority in a private dwelling with a family, a relative or some other suitable person;[64] *or*

Part 6: Special benefit rules
Chapter 42: Benefits in hospital, care homes, prison and in other special circumstances
2. People in care homes and similar accommodation

- for DLA, CDP, PIP and ADP, your accommodation is outside the UK and the costs of any qualifying services are being met by a local authority under specified legislation relating to education – eg, at the Higashi School;[65] *or*
- you are 'self-funding' (see below).

If you are self-funding

You can continue to be paid AA, the DLA/CDP care component and the PIP/ADP daily living component if you are meeting the whole cost of all the 'qualifying services' either from your own resources, or with the help of another person or a charity – known as 'self-funding'.[66] This applies whether you are in an independent or local authority home. **Note:** in Scotland, if you receive free personal care from the local authority, you do not count as self-funding.

You count as self-funding even if:

- you are claiming benefits, such as universal credit (UC), income support (IS), employment and support allowance (ESA), pension credit (PC), AA, DLA, CDP, PIP or ADP; *or*
- a local authority has arranged and contracted to pay for your placement, provided you are paying the whole cost of all the 'qualifying services'; *or*
- a local authority is temporarily funding your placement while you sell a property (eg, your former home), or if you have entered into what is known as a 'deferred payment agreement'. You must be liable and able to repay the local authority in full when the property is sold, or when payment under the deferred agreement falls due. This is known as 'retrospective self-funding'.[67]

Are you likely to become self-funding?

If you move into a care home and are initially receiving help with the fees from the local authority, the DWP should suspend payment of your AA, DLA or PIP if you are likely to become self-funding in the future – eg, if you are only getting local authority help while you sell your former home, or your capital is likely to increase above the limit of the local authority's means test. When you repay the local authority and become self-funding, payment can resume and any arrears can be paid to you. If the DWP terminated payment of your AA, DLA or PIP and refuses to pay you arrears when you become self-funding, you can argue that the decision to terminate payment should be revised on the grounds of 'official error'.[68] We expect this principle to apply to CDP and ADP.

Days on which you count as being resident in a care home

The general rule is that you do not count as resident in a care home on the day you enter and the day you leave.[69] However, if you are a patient in a hospital or similar institution (or, for PIP/ADP, a prisoner) and enter a care home, you count as a resident in the care home from:[70]

- for AA and DLA/CDP and ADP, the day you enter;
- for PIP, the day after the day you enter.

For AA and DLA, if you transfer from a care home to a hospital or similar institution, or for PIP, if you transfer from a care home to hospital, a similar institution or to prison, the last day you count as resident in a care home is the day on which you transfer. For ADP, you stop counting as a resident in a care home the day before you transfer to hospital, a similiar institution or prison. For CDP, if you transfer from a care home to prison, you stop counting as a resident in a care home the day before you transfer.[71]

There is a 28-day 'linking rule'. This means that different periods as a resident in a care home separated by 28 days or less link together for the purpose of calculating the 28 days when you can continue to be paid AA, the DLA/CDP care component or the PIP/ADP daily living component.[72] For AA, DLA and PIP, periods spent as a patient in a hospital or similar institution (or, for PIP only, as a prisoner) also count towards the 28-day limit on payment if they are separated by 28 days or less from periods when you are resident in a care home in the circumstances described above. A period in hospital if you were under 18 when you were admitted does not count.[73]

It can be important to plan periods of respite care in the light of the linking rules so that you can continue to be paid AA, the DLA/CDP care component or the PIP/ADP daily living component for as long as possible. This can also enable your carer to keep her/his carer's allowance (CA).

How other benefits are affected

If payment of AA, the DLA/CDP care component or the PIP/ADP daily living component stops, CA is affected in the same way as for hospital patients (see p905). The carer premium, paid with IS, income-based jobseeker's allowance (JSA), income-related ESA and housing benefit (HB), and the carer addition paid with PC, can continue to be paid for eight weeks after CA stops (see p334).[74] The UC carer element stops as soon as the relevant disability benefit stops because you no longer satisfy the conditions of entitlement for CA.[75]

Once payment of AA, the DLA care component or the PIP/ADP daily living component stops because you have been resident in a care home for 28 days, you are no longer entitled to the severe disability premium or addition paid with IS, income-based JSA, income-related ESA, HB and PC. In addition, you may no longer be entitled to the disability, enhanced disability or higher pensioner premium if the only reason you qualified was because you were receiving AA, DLA care component or PIP daily living component.

Note:
- For IS and ESA only, if you only live in a care home for part of the week and are entitled to DLA when you are staying elsewhere, you can be paid, for example, the severe disability and enhanced disability premiums when you are staying away from the care home from the date the change occurs (or is expected to occur).[76] For ESA, this also applies if you are entitled to PIP when you are staying elsewhere.

Part 6: Special benefit rules
Chapter 42: Benefits in hospital, care homes, prison and in other special circumstances
2. People in care homes and similar accommodation

- For ESA only, you qualify for the enhanced disability premium if you are getting the ESA support component, even if you are not receiving the DLA care component or PIP daily living component.
- If you are still being paid AA, DLA care component or PIP/ADP daily living component (eg, because you have not yet been in a care home for 28 days), you may be entitled to a severe disability premium, even if you were not before – eg, if you are no longer treated as living with a non-dependant or a partner.

Universal credit

You cannot get the UC housing costs element for the rent you pay to your care home.[77] If you are in a care home, the lower capital threshold for the tariff income rule remains £6,000 (see p139) unlike in benefits such as IS, income-based JSA, income-related ESA and HB for people under pension age, where the lower capital threshold increases if you are resident in a care home (see p920).

> ### Care home
> A **'care home'** means:[78]
> – a care home (a care home service in Scotland) as defined in section 3 of the Care Standards Act 2000, paragraph 2 of Schedule 12 to the Public Services Reform (Scotland) Act 2010 or Part I of the Regulation and Inspection of Social Care (Wales) Act 2016. If the home comes within the definition, it counts as a care home even if it also has some other function, such as an educational institution;[79]
> – an independent hospital (an independent healthcare service in Scotland) as defined in section 275 of the National Health Service Act 2006 (in England) other than a health service hospital, section 2 of the Care Standards Act 2000 (in Wales) or section 10F(1)(a) and (b) of the National Health Service (Scotland) Act 1978 (in Scotland).
> If you are not sure whether you live in a care home that falls within this definition, get advice.

Single claimants

You can continue to get UC while in a care home. The housing costs element for your normal home can continue if your stay in a care home is temporary. However, the housing costs element stops if your stay in a care home exceeds, or is expected to exceed, six months.[80] If your stay is temporary and you receive a loan from the DWP to help with your mortgage interest, payments stop if your stay in a care home exceeds, or is expected to exceed, six months.[81]

Couples

You and your partner continue to count as a couple while one of you is temporarily absent from the household, including when one of you is in a care home. You must continue to make a joint claim and UC is paid as normal. If the person who is not living in a care home is working, you may qualify for the childcare costs element (see p73). However, if the absence is permanent or it exceeds, or is likely to exceed, six months, you no longer count as a couple.[82] If you no longer count as a couple:

- you can no longer make a joint claim for UC;
- the calculation of your benefit no longer includes amounts for your partner;
- you may both need to reclaim UC as single claimants.

Children

A child continues to be included in your claim while s/he is temporarily absent from your household because s/he is in a care home. However, s/he is no longer included in your claim if the absence exceeds, or is expected to exceed, six months.[83] If your child is 'looked after' by the local authority (see p62) and living in a care home, then s/he will not longer be included in your claim, unless it is just for a period of respite.[84] If your child is no longer included in your claim:

- the calculation of your benefit no longer includes amounts for her/him;
- the work-related requirements you must meet may change (see Chapter 46).

Other means-tested benefits

How your IS, income-based JSA, income-related ESA, PC and HB are affected depends on whether you (or your partner or child) are temporarily or permanently living in a care home. If you are in a care home (on either basis), these benefits are generally calculated in the usual way, although if payment of your AA, DLA/CDP care component or PIP/ADP daily living component stops, you may no longer be entitled to certain premiums (see p917). For information about paying for your usual home, see p922.

For the definition of 'care home', see p918. The meaning is the same as for UC, except it also includes an Abbeyfield home.

Note:

- If you have a partner, you may no longer count as a couple if you (or your partner) are resident in a care home. If your child is resident in a care home, s/he may no longer be included in your claim (see p920).
- For PC, if you have an 'assessed income period' (see p267), it comes to an end if you do not have a partner and are provided with accommodation in a care home (other than in an Abbeyfield home) on a permanent basis. This means your income may be reassessed.[85]

Housing benefit for your care home

You cannot usually get HB for the rent you pay to your care home.[86] For these purposes, a care home does *not* include an Abbeyfield home. There are exceptions if you were entitled to HB for your care home when the rules changed at various times in the past and you have transitional protection.[87]

Part 6: Special benefit rules
Chapter 42: Benefits in hospital, care homes, prison and in other special circumstances
2. People in care homes and similar accommodation

Note: if you are living with an approved carer under the adult placement scheme, the normal conditions of entitlement to HB apply and you may be able to get HB.[88]

Tariff income from savings

For IS, income-based JSA, income-related ESA and, if you and your partner are under pension age, for HB, if you are permanently resident in a care home, the threshold for calculating your tariff income from any capital is increased to £10,000 (see p473), instead of £6,000. This also applies if you live in Polish resettlement accommodation (certain care homes for Polish people who came to the UK as refugees after the second world war). Some temporary absences from the care home or resettlement accommodation are ignored.[89] For HB, the £10,000 threshold is only relevant (and only applies) in the limited situations in which you can get HB while living in a care home. For PC (and for HB, if you or your partner are at least pension age), the threshold is always £10,000 (see p502).

6 Partners and children

- If you or your partner move into a care home permanently (for PC only, other than to an Abbeyfield home), you no longer count as a couple.[90] This also applies if you and your partner are both in care homes permanently, even if you are in the same home and the same room.[91] If you do not count as a couple, your benefit, and that of your partner, is calculated as if you were single claimants.
- If you or your partner move into a care home temporarily, you still count as a couple if you intend to live together again. This only applies if you are unlikely to be apart for more than 52 weeks or your time apart is longer than 52 weeks, but there are exceptional circumstances and the time apart is unlikely to be substantially longer than 52 weeks.[92] If you still count as a couple:
  - your PC and HB continue to be assessed under the normal rules. This means that, once the person in the care home stops getting AA, the DLA care component or the PIP/ADP daily living component, no severe disability premium (or additional amount) for either of you can be included in your applicable amount unless you can receive it on the basis that the person who is in the care home is severely sight impaired or blind (see p330);
  - your applicable amount for IS, income-based JSA and income-related ESA is calculated in a special way. You receive the amount for two single claimants if this is higher than the amount you receive as a couple. This can include the severe disability premium in respect of either or both of you, as if you were single claimants, even if you are not normally entitled to it at home.[93]

If child benefit stops because your child lives in a care home or is being looked after by a local authority, this may affect whether s/he is included in your claim (see p307). If your child is no longer included, you can no longer get a personal allowance and premiums for her/him in your HB (or your IS or income-based JSA, if amounts for your child are still included in these benefits – see p317). Entitlement to premiums for your child is also affected if s/he is no longer paid DLA/CDP or PIP/ADP.

Pension credit child amounts

If you get PC which includes an amount for a child (see p307) and s/he is in a care home, what happens to the child amount depends on whether the child is looked after by the local authority. If s/he is not looked after by the local authority, the amount for the child can continue while s/he is in a care home providing the stay is not expected to exceed, or has not exceeded, 52 weeks or, in exceptional circumstances, the stay is unlikely to be substantially more than 52 weeks.[94] The extra amount that you may get if the child has a disability (see p323) continues during a temporary absence even if her/his DLA, CDP or PIP has stopped being paid.[95] There is no 'linking rule' in this provision. This means that if the child comes home from a care home and then goes back in, a new period as a patient starts. If s/he is in a care home and counts as 'looked after' by the local authority, you no longer get the child amount in your PC, unless it is a 'planned short break' (respite).[96]

Social fund payments

Some social fund payments are affected if you are in a care home. You cannot get:
- a cold weather payment (see p791) if you are in a care home (see p913) or Polish resettlement accommodation, unless you are responsible for a child under five or you are getting child tax credit which includes a disabled child or severely disabled child element;[97]
- a winter fuel payment (see p792) if you are getting income-based JSA, income-related ESA or PC and are (and for a period have been) in a care home or Polish resettlement accommodation (see p793). If you are not getting one of these benefits, you are entitled to a winter fuel payment of £100 if you are aged between pension age and 79 and £150 if you are aged 80 or over.[98]

Child winter heating assistance

You remain entitled to the Scottish child winter heating assistance (see p1673) even if your child's DLA/CDP care component or PIP daily living component has stopped being paid because s/he has been in a care home for more than 28 days.[99]

Scottish child payment

If you are entitled to Scottish child payment for a child, you can continue to get it while the child is in a care home, or while you are in a care home, provided you continue to satisfy the conditions of entitlement (see p1729).

Part 6: Special benefit rules
Chapter 42: Benefits in hospital, care homes, prison and in other special circumstances
2. People in care homes and similar accommodation
. . . .

Paying for your usual home

The benefit you can get to help pay for your usual home may be affected while you, or your partner, child or non-dependant, are temporarily in a care home. **Note:** if you leave your home permanently (eg, you become a permanent resident in a care home), you are no longer entitled to benefit for it.

If you are temporarily away from home, you can qualify for:

- UC housing costs element for up to six months, provided your absence from home does not exceed (or is not expected to exceed) six months (see p92). If you are on UC and are getting a DWP loan to help pay your mortgage interest, payments stop if you have been absent for six months (or your absence is likely to exceed six months);[100]
- HB, or help with your housing costs (service charges and ground rent for owner-occupiers) in your IS, income-based JSA, income-related ESA or PC, for up to 52 weeks, provided your absence from home does not exceed (or is not likely to exceed) 52 weeks, you intend to return to your home and you do not sub-let it. In exceptional circumstances, the absence may be expected to be longer than 52 weeks, provided it is not likely to last substantially longer than 52 weeks. HB or housing costs are still only payable for a maximum of 52 weeks (see p181 and p354). If you are on IS, income-based JSA, income-related ESA or PC and you get a DWP loan to help with your mortgage interest, these same rules apply. The loan is still only payable for a maximum of 52 weeks.[101]

Note:
- Another person (eg, your partner) might be able to qualify for these benefits (or for the DWP loan to help with mortgage interest – see p842) instead of you if s/he is (or can be treated as) liable to pay the rent or housing costs (see p87, p176 and p352).
- There are no 'linking rules' with these provisions. This means that, if a new period in a care home starts, you can again be entitled to HB or an amount in your UC, IS, income-based JSA, income-related ESA or PC.
- For HB, you can be treated as occupying, but temporarily absent from, a new dwelling, even if you have not yet stayed there, if you move in your furniture and belongings but cannot move in yourself – eg, because you are in hospital or a care home[102] on a temporary basis.[103]
- There are special rules if you are a temporary resident in a care home for a trial period. If you intend to return home, you can get HB and help with your housing costs in your IS, income-based JSA, income-related ESA and PC for up to 13 weeks for each trial period (in different care homes) subject to an overall maximum of 52 weeks (see p181 and p354).[104] This does not apply to UC.

Partners, children and non-dependants

If your partner, child or non-dependant is away from home because s/he is in a care home, this could affect the amount of your HB or housing costs paid with your UC, IS, income-based JSA, income-related ESA or PC. This could apply, for example, if s/he no longer counts as living with you or, for UC, s/he no longer counts as a member of your 'extended benefit unit' (see p95). Bear the following in mind.

- If you live in rented accommodation, you may no longer be allowed the same number of bedrooms under the size criteria (see p370, p378, p384 and p97) and your UC or HB may be reduced. For UC, this only applies if your partner, child or non-dependant is absent (or expected to be absent) from home for more than six months.[105]

- If your non-dependant is absent, check whether a deduction for housing costs contributions or a non-dependant deduction should still be made for her/him (see p198, p347 and p102).

3. Prisoners

Most benefits are affected if you are a prisoner. Some are not payable, some are suspended and some are only payable for a temporary period. There are also issues to consider if you are given an alternative sentence to prison.

Always inform the DWP, HM Revenue and Customs, Social Security Scotland and/or the local authority as soon as you, or a member of your family, enter or leave prison to avoid any underpayment or overpayment of benefit. If you are being held on remand and are then sentenced, notify the benefit authorities as soon as you are remanded and again when you are sentenced.

Non-means-tested benefits

You are disqualified from getting most non-means-tested benefits while you are a prisoner. For statutory sick pay (SSP), statutory maternity pay (SMP), statutory adoption pay (SAP), statutory paternity pay (SPP), statutory shared parental pay (SSPP) and statutory parental bereavement pay (SPBP), see p924. For other non-means-tested benefits, see p924. In some cases, payment of your benefit is only suspended pending the outcome of your trial or sentencing (see p925). For benefits that are payable, see p925.

Prisoners

You count as a **'prisoner'** for **non-means-tested benefits** if you are in prison or detained in legal custody.[106] This includes if you are remanded in custody awaiting trial or sentencing as well as if you are serving a custodial sentence. You do not count as a prisoner if you are on bail or living in approved premises (eg, a bail or probation hostel), or if you are released on parole, temporary licence or under a home detention curfew (electronic tagging).

Part 6: Special benefit rules
Chapter 42: Benefits in hospital, care homes, prison and in other special circumstances
3. Prisoners

See p928 if you are detained in a hospital or similar institution as a person with a mental disorder.

Statutory sick, maternity, adoption, paternity and other parental pay

If you are a prisoner you:[107]

- are not entitled to SSP. If you are getting SSP, your entitlement ends;
- cannot be paid SMP or SPP. Even if you are then released from prison during the maternity or paternity pay period, you do not get SMP or SPP for the rest of that period. If you cannot be paid SMP, check whether you can be paid maternity allowance (MA) (see p708) instead on your release from prison;
- cannot be paid SAP, SSPP or SPBP for the time you are a prisoner, unless you are subsequently released without charge or after being found not guilty, or you are convicted but do not receive a custodial sentence. If one of these applies, you should receive arrears for the period you were detained and payment should also resume for any period of entitlement after your release.

6. Other non-means-tested benefits

If you are a prisoner, you cannot be paid attendance allowance (AA), bereavement benefits, disability living allowance (DLA), carer's allowance (CA), contributory employment and support allowance (ESA), incapacity benefit (IB), MA, reduced earnings allowance (REA), retirement allowance, retirement pensions or severe disablement allowance (SDA).[108] Pending trial or sentencing, these benefits are only suspended, which means that you may be owed arrears if you do not receive a prison sentence (see p925).

You are paid **personal independence payment** (PIP) or adult disability payment (ADP) for the first 28 days that you count as a prisoner, whatever the outcome of the proceedings against you.[109] However, this does not apply if you are awarded PIP or ADP while you are a prisoner, in which case you are not paid PIP or, if you are 18 or over, ADP until your release from prison.[110] If you are aged 16 or 17, ADP mobility component can be paid while you are in prison, including if you are awarded it after you become a prisoner.[111] There is a 'linking rule' for PIP which means that different periods spent as a prisoner separated by one year or less are linked together and treated as one period.[112] Periods spent in a care home or hospital are also linked with periods spent as a prisoner (see p905 and p916).

If you get child disability payment (CDP), you continue to be paid the care component for the first 28 days that you are a prisoner and you continue to be paid the mobility component during any period when you are a prisoner, including if it is awarded after you become a prisoner.[113]

You cannot be paid an **increase in CA or retirement pensions for your spouse or civil partner** if s/he is a prisoner.[114]

If you get 'new-style' jobseeker's allowance (JSA), you are unable to meet the work-related requirements for JSA while you are in prison. In addition, you are treated as not having met the work availability requirement if you are a prisoner on temporary release under specified provisions.[115] However, you may be able to satisfy the DWP that you should not have to meet a work search requirement during temporary police detention (legal custody in Scotland).

For non-means-tested benefits payable while you are a prisoner, see below.

Benefits that are suspended

If you are a remand prisoner awaiting trial or sentence, payment of contributory ESA, IB, SDA, AA, DLA, CA, MA, REA, retirement pensions, retirement allowance and bereavement benefits is suspended pending the outcome. An increase of CA or retirement pension for your spouse or civil partner is suspended if s/he is a remand prisoner. If you (or s/he) subsequently receive a sentence of imprisonment or detention (including a suspended sentence), you are not paid the benefits for the whole period you are (or s/he is) in prison.[116]

If you (or your spouse or civil partner) do not receive a sentence of imprisonment or detention, or your conviction is quashed, full arrears of any of the benefits that have been withheld are payable when you are released.[117] Arrears are only payable if the normal conditions of entitlement for benefit were met while you (or your spouse/civil partner) were a remand prisoner. For contributory ESA, you are treated as not having limited capability for work once you have been disqualified as a prisoner for six weeks.[118] This rule does not apply if contributory ESA is suspended and subsequently reinstated because you do not receive a custodial sentence, because you are not actually 'disqualified' in this situation.[119]

For the purpose of entitlement to an increase in your benefit for a spouse or civil partner, you should be treated as still 'residing with' her/him while s/he is in prison, unless your marriage/partnership has broken down and your separation is likely to be permanent.[120]

Benefits payable

You are entitled to **industrial injuries disablement benefit** (but not any of the increases on p677) for periods when you are a prisoner. However, you are not paid until you are released and you can only get a maximum of 12 months' arrears.[121] If you are in prison for more than a year, you should be paid for the 12-month period which gives you the most benefit.[122] You are entitled to full arrears for any period you were on remand, provided you are not subsequently sentenced to imprisonment or detention.[123]

You are entitled to **child benefit** and **guardian's allowance:**[124]
- while you are a prisoner. You must continue to be 'responsible' for the child (see p567). If you are in prison for some time, you may want to arrange for child benefit to be paid to the person looking after your child;
- while your child is a prisoner, but entitlement to child benefit usually ends after eight weeks.[125] There are exceptions to the rules (see p574). Full arrears are payable at the end of any period of remand if your child is not sentenced to

Part 6: Special benefit rules
Chapter 42: Benefits in hospital, care homes, prison and in other special circumstances
3. Prisoners

imprisonment or detention. Once entitlement to child benefit ends, entitlement to guardian's allowance in respect of the child also ends.

Note: if child benefit stops because your child is a prisoner, this may affect whether you can get an increase for her/him with your non-means-tested benefits, and personal allowances and premiums for her/him with your housing benefit (HB) (and income support (IS) or income-based JSA if these amounts are still included). For increases for a child, see the chapter in this *Handbook* about the benefit you are claiming. For IS and JSA, see p317.

Universal credit

If you are a single person and you become a prisoner (see below), you can get the housing costs element in your UC for up to six months. To be entitled, you must have been getting the housing costs element immediately before you were a prisoner, and certain other conditions apply (see p931).[126] You do not get any other elements of UC.[127]

> ### Prisoners
> You count as a '**prisoner**' if you are:[128]
> – detained in custody (eg, in prison or a young offenders' institution) awaiting trial or sentence (on remand) or following a sentence of imprisonment; *or*
> – on temporary release under specific provisions (this does not include parole licence).

If your partner or a child included in your claim is a prisoner, see below. If you have a non-dependant who is a prisoner, no deduction is made from your housing costs element (see p102), but you may no longer qualify for a bedroom for her/him after a period (see p100).[129]

Couples

If you are a member of a couple and one of you is a prisoner, or is serving a prison sentence while detained in hospital, the other partner can claim UC as a single claimant.[130] Provided you still count as a couple, your and your partner's income and capital are still assessed jointly, but your UC amount is that for a single person.[131] If the partner who is not a prisoner is working, you may qualify for a childcare costs element (see p73). In any case, if the absence from the household exceeds, or is expected to exceed, six months, you no longer count as a couple.[132] The amount of your housing costs element for your rent may be affected (see p932).

Children

If your child is a prisoner, s/he can no longer be included in your claim (see p61).[133] If your child is no longer included in your claim:

- the calculation of your benefit no longer includes amounts for her/him;
- the amount of your housing costs element for your rent may be affected (see p932);
- the work allowance which applies to you (see p40) and work-related requirements you must meet may change if, for example, you no longer have a dependent child living with you (see Chapter 46).

Other means-tested benefits

If you are a prisoner (see below):

- you cannot qualify for income-based JSA as you are unable to satisfy the jobseeking conditions;
- IS, income-related ESA and PC guarantee credit usually stop immediately. The only exception to this is if you get IS, income-related ESA or PC guarantee credit which includes an amount for housing costs (service charges and ground rent for owner-occupiers – see p343). In this situation, you can get the benefit for up to 52 weeks while you are detained in custody awaiting trial or sentence, but you only get your housing costs paid. If you have continued to be entitled to one of these benefits (because you get housing costs), it will stop once you have been sentenced;[134]
- you can continue to qualify for HB for a limited period (see p931);
- you cannot get any savings credit of PC.[135]

If you have a non-dependant who is a prisoner, no non-dependant deduction is made for her/him.[136] However, for HB you may no longer qualify for a bedroom for her/him after a period. See p198 and p347 for further information about non-dependant deductions.

For information about UC if you (or your partner or child) are a prisoner, see p926.

For IS, JSA, ESA, PC and HB, see p926 for when you count as a **'prisoner'**.[137]

You do not count as a prisoner if you are detained in hospital under specific mental health provisions (but see p928 if you received a prison sentence as a result of a criminal conviction). Check to see whether your benefit is affected by the special rules for hospital patients instead (see p908). In addition, you do not count as a prisoner if you are:

- released on licence or parole; *or*
- on bail or living in approved premises – eg, a bail or probation hostel; *or*
- released under a home detention curfew (electronic tagging).

Partners and children

If you have a partner and one of you is a prisoner:

- you no longer count as a couple for IS, income-based JSA, income-related ESA or PC;[138]

Part 6: Special benefit rules
Chapter 42: Benefits in hospital, care homes, prison and in other special circumstances
3. Prisoners

- you continue to count as a couple for HB, provided you intend to live together again and the prisoner is unlikely to be away for substantially longer than 52 weeks.[139] If the partner who is not a prisoner is working, s/he may be able to have childcare costs deducted from her/his earnings (see p416 and p458).[140]

If you no longer count as a couple, the partner who is *not* a prisoner may be able to claim benefit as a single person.

If child benefit stops because your child is a prisoner, s/he may no longer be included in your claim for HB (or IS or income-based JSA), in which case your entitlement to a personal allowance and premiums for her/him might be affected.

Child tax credit (CTC) continues to be paid for your child, unless s/he has been sentenced to more than four months in prison, in which case CTC stops and s/he no longer counts as a dependant for working tax credit (WTC).[141]

If you get PC which includes an amount for a child (see p307), the amount for the child stops if s/he becomes a prisoner.[142]

6 Social fund payments

You cannot get a winter fuel payment if you are serving a custodial sentence (see p793). You cannot get other social fund payments if you are not getting a qualifying benefit (see Chapter 37).[143]

If you are detained under mental health legislation

Special rules apply for non-means-tested benefits (other than contribution-based JSA, SSP, SMP, SAP, SPP, SSPP, CDP and ADP) and UC, IS, income-related ESA and PC if, although you received a prison sentence as a result of a criminal conviction, you are currently detained in a hospital or similar institution as a person with a mental disorder under sections 45A or 47 of the Mental Health Act 1983, section 59A of the Criminal Procedure (Scotland) Act 1995 or section 136 of the Mental Health (Care and Treatment) (Scotland) Act 2003. This applies if you are:[144]

- ordered to be detained in hospital by a court after you are convicted, where the court specifies a length of sentence; *or*
- sent to prison, but later transferred to hospital by order.

If this applies, although you are a hospital patient, you are treated as a prisoner for the above benefits, but only until you would have been entitled to be released under your original sentence or, if you are held under an indeterminate sentence (eg, you are a life prisoner), until your release is authorised.[145] After that, if you are still in hospital, your benefit might be affected under the rules that apply to hospital patients (see p903).

Note:
- The rules do not apply to JSA, but in this situation you are unable to satisfy the jobseeking conditions (or, if you come under the UC system, the work-related requirements).

- If you are detained in a hospital or similar institution under provisions other than those listed above (eg, you were convicted of a criminal offence but were ordered to be detained in hospital and were not given a prison sentence), you may be paid non-means-tested benefits, or you may qualify for UC, IS, income-related ESA or PC. Check whether your benefit is affected under the rules that apply to hospital patients (see p903).

Community sentences

If you have been given a community sentence that involves punishment or supervision in the community, you do not count as a prisoner. However, bear the following in mind.

- There might be a question about whether you satisfy the work-related requirements for UC or JSA. Guidance for UC and JSA suggests that any restrictions caused by a community sentence or order should be taken into account when setting a work search requirement.[146]
- If you undertake basic skills training and are treated as a full-time student, this may affect your entitlement to benefits (see Chapter 41).

If you are on bail or living in approved premises

Your non-means-tested benefits are paid as normal if you are on bail or living in approved premises (eg, a bail or probation hostel) or other accommodation as a condition of bail. However, special rules can apply for means-tested benefits.

For UC, you and your partner continue to count as a couple while one of you is temporarily absent from the household. You must continue to make a joint claim and UC is paid as normal. However, if the absence exceeds, or is expected to exceed, six months, you no longer count as a couple.[147] If you no longer count as a couple, you can no longer make a joint claim for UC and the calculation of your benefit no longer includes amounts for your partner. Each partner must make a claim for UC as a single person if appropriate.

For IS, income-based JSA, income-related ESA, PC and HB, if you have a partner and are temporarily separated because one of you is living away from home, you still count as a couple if you intend to live together again, but only if you are unlikely to be apart for more than 52 weeks or, in exceptional circumstances, not substantially longer than 52 weeks.[148] For IS, income-based JSA and income-related ESA only, if one of you is living in an approved bail or probation hostel, your applicable amount is calculated in a special way – at either the single rate for each of you added together or the couple rate, whichever is greater.[149]

If you are required to live away from home in an approved bail or probation hostel or another address that you are bailed to:

Part 6: Special benefit rules
Chapter 42: Benefits in hospital, care homes, prison and in other special circumstances
3. Prisoners

- you cannot get the UC housing costs element for the hostel.[150] You can get the housing costs element for your normal home for up to six months, provided you are not expected to be away for longer;[151]
- you cannot get HB for the rent you pay for the hostel;[152]
- you can continue to get HB and help with your housing costs in IS, income-based JSA, income-related ESA or PC for your normal home for up to 52 weeks, provided you intend to return home and you are unlikely to be away for longer than this (or, in exceptional circumstances, not substantially longer than this);[153]
- you can get a DWP loan for your mortgage interest on your normal home for up to six months (UC) or 52 weeks (other benefits), provided you are not expected to be away for longer than this and you continue to satisfy the other conditions of entitlement.[154]

If you are no longer entitled to the UC housing costs element or HB for your normal home (or the DWP loan to help with mortgage interest – see p842), these can be paid to another person if s/he is (or can be treated as) liable (see p86, p352 and p176).

Benefits on release

If you are **temporarily released** (on temporary licence), you no longer count as a prisoner for non-means-tested benefits. You still count as a prisoner for means-tested benefits (unless you are released on parole licence).

When you are **permanently released** from prison, you should claim any benefits to which you are entitled as soon as possible. The prison gives you a discharge form that can help you prove your identity. You may also be interviewed by a DWP liaison officer before you leave prison, who should point out which benefits you might be able to claim.

- As UC is generally paid in arrears, you may need to apply for a UC advance (see p1153).
- If you are at least 25 and are an offender who is subject to multi-agency risk management arrangements, you are exempt from the private sector rent restriction rules for single claimants under 35 (see p393).
- You may receive a discharge grant from the Prison Service, which counts as capital for IS, income-based JSA and income-related ESA purposes.[155] The rules do not say how it should be treated for UC, PC or HB.
- If you are released without being sentenced to imprisonment or detention, you should receive any arrears of your non-means-tested benefits that were suspended (see p925).
- If you are released following the quashing of a conviction, you are entitled to national insurance credits for the period you were imprisoned or detained (see p963).

Help with travelling expenses

The Help with Prison Visits scheme can help a partner or close relative (or another person if s/he is your only visitor) with the cost of visiting you in prison, or the cost of someone bringing your children to visit you. S/he must be getting 'qualifying income'.

Claim online at gov.uk/help-with-prison-visits or contact Help with Prison Visits, PO Box 17594, Birmingham B2 2QP (tel: 0300 063 2100). You can also email HelpwithPrisonVisits@justice.gov.uk.

Qualifying income
'**Qualifying income**' is UC, IS, income-based JSA, income-related ESA and PC, and health benefits on low-income grounds, as well as CTC or WTC. The WTC must include a disabled worker element, or you must be getting CTC and WTC. If your qualifying benefit is UC, you must have a monthly income of less than £1,250. If your qualifying income is tax credits, your annual income must be less than £17,474.

Paying for your usual home

The benefit you can get to help pay for your normal home may be affected while you, or your partner, child or non-dependant, are temporarily in prison. **Note:** if you leave your home permanently, you are no longer entitled to benefit for it.

Universal credit housing costs

If you are a prisoner, whether you are awaiting trial or sentence or are serving a custodial sentence, you can continue to qualify for a UC housing costs element for your normal home for up to six months.[156] However, you can only qualify following a sentence of imprisonment if you have not been sentenced to a term that is expected to go beyond the six-month period. The six-month period includes any time you have already been in prison before being sentenced – eg, if you were remanded in custody.[157] You can only get the housing costs element if you were entitled to it immediately before becoming a prisoner.[158] If you are on UC and get a DWP loan for your mortgage interest, payments may continue for up to six months, provided your absence is not expected to last for more than six months.[159]

The UC housing costs element (or the DWP loan to help with mortgage interest – see p842) can be paid to another person (eg, your partner) if s/he is (or can be treated as) liable to pay the rent or housing costs (see p87).

Housing benefit and other means-tested benefits

While you are detained in custody awaiting trial or sentence, you can get HB and help with your housing costs (service charges and ground rent for owner-occupiers) paid with IS, income-related ESA or PC for your normal home for up to

Part 6: Special benefit rules
Chapter 42: Benefits in hospital, care homes, prison and in other special circumstances
3. Prisoners

52 weeks, provided you intend to return home, you are unlikely to be away for longer than this (or, in exceptional circumstances, unlikely to be away for substantially longer than this) and you do not sub-let your home.[160]

If you get a DWP loan for your mortgage interest and you are on a benefit other than UC, payments may continue while you are detained in custody awaiting trial or sentence for up to 52 weeks, provided you intend to return home, you are unlikely to be away for longer than this (or in exceptional circumstances, unlikely to be away for substantially longer than this) and you do not sub-let your home.[161]

If you are serving a custodial sentence, you can get HB for up to 13 weeks, provided you are unlikely to be away from your normal home for longer than this – ie, you are serving a short sentence.[162] The 13 weeks run from the date you were first in prison and includes any time you spend in prison awaiting trial or sentence.[163] If you are serving a sentence of more than 13 weeks, you may still be entitled to HB, provided you are likely to spend no more than 13 weeks in prison – eg, you may be released early on a home detention curfew (electronic tagging).

If you are on temporary release under specific provisions, you continue to be treated as a prisoner.[164] This means that, even if you return home, you are still treated as if you are away from home.

In this situation, if you are a convicted prisoner, you are not entitled to IS, income-based JSA, income-related ESA or PC and cannot get help with your housing costs.

For HB, you are still treated as if you are away from home and these periods count towards the 13/52 weeks for which HB may be payable.[165]

When calculating how long you have been absent from home for HB, the day you go into prison is counted as a day of absence but the day you return home is not.[166]

Note:

- You should report any change in your circumstances as soon as possible – ie, when you are remanded in custody, begin a custodial sentence or are being released from custody.
- If you do not qualify for HB for 52 or 13 weeks under the rules described above, you may be able to continue to get HB for a former home for up to four benefit weeks if you are still liable to pay rent for it, and you could not reasonably have avoided this liability – eg, because your tenancy agreement required you to give notice.[167]
- HB and housing costs paid with IS, income-based JSA, income-related ESA or PC can be paid to another person (eg, your partner), if s/he is (or can be treated as) liable to pay the rent or housing costs (see p352, p86 and p176). There is a similar rule for mortgage interest loans.[168]

Partners, children and non-dependants

If your partner, child or non-dependant is away from home because s/he is in prison, this could affect the amount of your HB or housing costs paid with your

UC, IS, income-based JSA, income-related ESA or PC. This could apply, for example, if s/he no longer counts as living with you or, for UC, s/he no longer counts as a member of your 'extended benefit unit' (see p95). Bear the following in mind.

- If you live in rented accommodation, you may no longer be allowed the same number of bedrooms under the size criteria (see p370, p378, p384 and p97) and your UC or HB may be reduced. For UC, this only applies if your partner, child or non-dependant is absent (or expected to be absent) from home for more than six months.[169]
- If your non-dependant is absent, check whether a deduction for housing costs contributions or a non-dependant deduction should still be made for her/him (see p198, p347 and p102).

4. 16/17 year old care leavers

You cannot usually qualify for universal credit (UC) (or income support (IS), income-based jobseeker's allowance (JSA) or housing benefit (HB)) if you are aged 16 or 17 and count as a 'care leaver' for these purposes (although there are exceptions – see p935[170]). Entitlement to other benefits is not affected by being a care leaver.

Being a care leaver means that you were previously 'looked after' by the local authority and certain other conditions apply. Your local authority must assess and meet your needs for maintenance, accommodation and support. In addition, you cannot be treated as a child member of the family of a person claiming IS, income-based JSA, income-related employment and support allowance (ESA) or HB. So, for example, s/he cannot get allowances and premiums for you with her/his HB.[171]

Being looked after

Being **'looked after'** means, for example, that you were subject to a care, supervision or permanence order, or provided with accommodation by the local authority under specified legal provisions.

Note:

- If you are *currently* being looked after by a local authority:
  - for UC purposes, you generally cannot be treated as the responsibility of a person, so, for example, s/he cannot get child elements for you in her/his UC. However, there are exceptions to this (see p62);[172]
  - for pension credit (PC) purposes, you generally cannot be treated as the responsibility of a person, so, for example, s/he cannot get child elements for you in her/his PC. However, there are exceptions to this (see p309);[173]

Part 6: Special benefit rules
Chapter 42: Benefits in hospital, care homes, prison and in other special circumstances
4. 16/17 year old care leavers

- you cannot be included as a child in another person's claim for IS, income-based JSA, income-related ESA or HB if you are not living with her/him (see Chapter 16);
- a person cannot usually qualify for child benefit or child tax credit for you (see p570 and p275).

- If you are aged 16 or 17 and *currently* being looked after by a local authority, you cannot qualify for UC unless any of the exceptions on p935 apply.[174]
- Local DWP and social services offices should liaise to ensure any disputes about who is responsible for supporting you are quickly resolved. If you are refused both benefit and social services support, get specialist advice.

Who is excluded from universal credit

Unless one of the exceptions on p935 applies, you are excluded from UC as a care leaver if you are no longer looked after by the local authority, you are aged 16 or 17 and:[175]

- you were looked after by a local authority (and, in Scotland, were provided with accommodation) for at least 13 weeks (or, in Scotland, three months). The 13-week/three-month period must have started after your 14th birthday and, in England and Wales, ended after you turn 16. In Scotland, you must have been looked after and accommodated for at least three months since your 14th birthday and have been looked after, but not necessarily accommodated, by the local authority at or beyond your 16th birthday. The local authority must be obliged to provide you with aftercare services; *or*
- in Scotland, you are in a 'continuing care' placement under section 26A of the Children (Scotland) Act 1995, you were being looked after and accommodated for at least three months since your 14th birthday and were looked after, but not necessarily accommodated, by the local authority at or beyond your 16th birthday; *or*
- in England or Wales, you are not subject to a care order, but you were in hospital, or detained in a remand centre or a young offenders' or similar institution when you became 16 and, immediately before you were in hospital or detained, you were being looked after by a local authority (in Wales, accommodated) for at least 13 weeks since your 14th birthday.

The 13 weeks or three months do not have to be continuous. Some pre-planned short-term placements, after which you return to the care of your parent, or person acting as your parent, do not count towards the 13 weeks or three months. For UC, in Scotland, any period when you have been placed with a member of your family does not count towards the three months.[176]

Note: in England and Wales, you are not excluded from UC if you have been in a family placement (ie, living with your parent, someone with parental responsibility for you or someone who had a child arrangements order for you before you were looked after) for at least six months (unless the placement has broken down).[177]

Note: there are similar rules excluding 16/17-year-old care leavers from IS, income-based JSA and housing benefit, which now apply to few young people because of the roll-out of UC. See the 2021/22 edition of this *Handbook* for details.

Who is not excluded from universal credit

Even if you fall within the definition of care leaver, you can get UC if you (or your partner, if you have one) are responsible for a child or if you have limited capability for work.[178] However, you cannot get the housing costs element for your rent.[179]

5. People without accommodation

Entitlement to non-means-tested benefits, universal credit (UC) and pension credit (PC) is unaffected if you do not have accommodation. However, income support (IS), income-based jobseeker's allowance (JSA) and income-related employment and support allowance (ESA) may be paid at a reduced rate (see p936). If you do not have accommodation, you may have problems satisfying the jobseeking conditions for JSA or the claimant responsibilities for UC.

If you become homeless and have no money, you can apply for a budgeting advance or a short-term advance (see p51 and p1153). It is possible to get help at any time in an emergency. You may also be able to claim local welfare assistance (see p846).

If you are homeless, the local authority may have a duty to assist you with accommodation or advice. A child or young person may be entitled to help from social services.

Note:
- If you are at least 16, have been living in a homeless hostel for at least three months and have accepted rehabilitation or resettlement support, you are exempt from the private sector rent restriction rules in housing benefit and UC for single people under 35. The three-month period does not need to be continuous.[180]
- You can qualify for help with payments for a tent and its pitch (if that is your home) with IS, income-based JSA, income-related ESA and PC (see p344). You cannot get a UC housing costs element for rent payments you make for a tent or the site on which a tent stands.[181]

Jobseeking conditions and claimant responsibilities

Even if you are homeless, to qualify for UC (and contribution-based JSA and contributory ESA if you come under the UC system), you must accept a claimant

Part 6: Special benefit rules
Chapter 42: Benefits in hospital, care homes, prison and in other special circumstances
5. People without accommodation

commitment and, to avoid being sanctioned, meet your work-related requirements (see Chapter 46). To qualify for JSA if you do not come under the UC system, you must satisfy jobseeking conditions (see Chapter 48).

Being homeless may reduce your prospects of finding work, but personal circumstances that reduce your chances of being employed should not prevent you from getting UC or JSA. You can be available for work even if you do not have accommodation. However, it must be possible for you to be contacted at short notice in order to satisfy the requirement that you are willing and able to take up any job immediately, or after the amount of notice allowed (see p1034 and p1094).

Note:
- The fact that you are homeless should be taken into account when deciding whether you satisfy the work search requirements. UC guidance states that your work coach should carefully consider how homelessness and any other complex needs affect you and can tailor or temporarily switch off work search requirements.[182]
- If you come under the UC system, the DWP can agree deductions from your expected hours of work search for time you spend dealing with a domestic emergency or other temporary circumstances, which can include homelessness.[183] See p1032 for further information.

Income support, income-based jobseeker's allowance and income-related employment and support allowance

The amount of your IS, income-based JSA and income-related ESA may be lower than normal if you are a person 'without accommodation'.[184] You get the personal allowance for you (and your partner, if you have one) and any additional component in income-related ESA that you are entitled to, but do not get any premiums.[185] **Note:** there are no special rules about the amount of UC payable if you do not have accommodation.

Having no fixed address is *not* the same as being 'without accommodation'. If you have accommodation, but are staying in different places on different nights (eg, with different friends or relatives), your IS, income-based JSA or income-related ESA should be paid as normal.[186]

Accommodation
'**Accommodation**' is not defined in the rules and should be interpreted widely and flexibly. The DWP says that, to count as having accommodation, you must have 'an effective shelter from the elements which is capable of being heated, in which occupants can sit, lie down, cook and eat, and which is reasonably suited for continuous occupation. The site of the accommodation may alter from day to day, but it is still accommodation if the structure is habitable.'[187]

Examples include tents, caravans, mobile homes and other substantial shelters. The DWP is likely to say that cardboard boxes, bus shelters, sleeping bags and cars do not qualify.[188]

Note: if you are temporarily absent from the accommodation you normally occupy as your home, even if you are living a lifestyle as though you have no accommodation (eg, you are sleeping rough), you should be treated as having accommodation.[189]

Notes

1. Hospital patients

1 Reg 2(4) SS(HIP) Regs; reg 6 SS(AA) Regs; regs 8 and 12A SS(DLA) Regs
2 Vol 3 Ch 18, paras 18021 and 18059 DMG; R(DLA) 2/06
3 **PIP** s86(2) and (3) WRA 2012; reg 29(2) SS(PIP) Regs; para P3012 ADM
  ADP Reg 28 DAWAP(S) Regs
4 Vol 3 Ch 18, paras 18028-33 and 18041 DMG
5 *White v CAO, The Times,* 2 August 1993, reported as R(IS) 18/94; *Botchett v CAO, The Times,* 8 May 1996, 2 CCLR 121 (CA); *R v North and East Devon Health Authority ex parte Coughlan* [1999] 2 CCLR 285; R(DLA) 2/06
6 *SSWP v Slavin* [2011] EWCA Civ 1515, reported as [2012] AACR 30
7 Vol 3 Ch 18 paras 18060-63 DMG; s86(2) and (3) WRA 2012; reg 29(2) SS(PIP) Regs; para P3062 ADM; reg 28(4) DAWAP(S) Regs
8 **AA** Reg 6(2A) SS(AA) Regs
  DLA Regs 8(2A) and 12A(2A) SS(DLA) Regs
  PIP Reg 32(2) SS(PIP) Regs
  ADP Reg 31(2) DAWAP(S) Regs
9 Reg 2(5) SS(HIP) Regs
10 **DLA** Reg 8(2B) SS(DLA) Regs
  PIP Reg 29(3) SS(PIP) Regs
  CDP Reg 21 DACYP(S) Regs
  ADP Reg 28(1) DAWAP(S) Regs
11 Regs 2, 3(4A) and (5B) and 19 PIP(TP) Regs
12 **AA** Reg 8(4) SS(AA) Regs
  DLA Regs 10(6) and (7) and 12B(9A) and (12) SS(DLA) Regs
  PIP Reg 30(3) and (4) SS(PIP) Regs
  ADP Reg 28(2) DAWAP(S) Regs

13 **AA/DLA** Reg 25 SS(C&P) Regs
  PIP Reg 50 UC,PIP,JSA&ESA(C&P) Regs
  ADP Reg 34(3) DAWAP(S) Regs
14 **AA** Reg 8(2) SS(AA) Regs
  DLA Regs 10(5) and 12B(3) SS(DLA) Regs
  PIP Reg 32(4) and (5) SS(PIP) Regs
  ADP Regs 28(3)and 31(5) and (6) DAWAP(S) Regs
15 **AA** Reg 8(4) and (5) SS(AA) Regs
  DLA Regs 10(6) and (7) and 12B(9A) and (12) SS(DLA) Regs
  PIP Reg 30(3) and (4) SS(PIP) Regs
  ADP Reg 29 DAWAP(S) Regs
16 **AA** Reg 8(3) SS(AA) Regs
  DLA Regs 10(3) and 12B(2) SS(DLA) Regs
  PIP Reg 30(2) SS(PIP) Regs
  ADP Reg 32(2)(b) DAWAP(S) Regs
17 Regs 12B(4)-(6) and 12C SS(DLA) Regs
18 Reg 75F(1)(f) HB Regs; reg 83(1)(h) UC Regs
19 Reg 6(19)-(21) SS(C&P) Regs
20 Reg 4(2) SS(ICA) Regs
21 Regs 29(1) and 30 UC Regs
22 Sch 3 para 9 UC Regs
23 Sch 3 para 18 LMI Regs
24 s39 WRA 2012; reg 3(6) UC Regs
25 s10 WRA 2012; reg 4(7) UC Regs
26 **IS** Sch 2 paras 13(2)(b) and (3A)(a) and (c) and 15(5)(b) IS Regs
  JSA Sch 1 paras 15(2) and (5)(a) and (aa) and 20(6)(b) JSA Regs
  ESA Sch 4 paras 6(2)(b) and (5)(a) and (c) and 11(2(b) ESA Regs
  HB Sch 3 paras 14(2)(b) and (5)(a) and (c) and 20(6)(b) HB Regs; Sch 3 paras 6(2)(b) and (7)(a) and (c) and 12(b) HB(SPC) Regs
  PC Reg 6(5)(b) and Sch 1 paras 1(1)(b) and (2)(b) and (ba) SPC Regs

Part 6: Special benefit rules
Chapter 42: Benefits in hospital, care homes, prison and in other special circumstances
Notes

27 **IS** Sch 2 paras 13(2)(b) and (3A)(b) IS Regs
JSA Sch 1 paras 15(2) and (5)(b) JSA Regs
ESA Sch 4 paras 6(2)(b) and (5)(b) ESA Regs
HB Sch 3 paras 14(2)(b) and (5)(b) HB Regs; Sch 3 paras 6(2)(b) and (7)(b) HB(SPC) Regs
PC Reg 5(5)(b) SPC Regs

28 **IS** Sch 2 paras 12(1)(d) and 13A(1) IS Regs
JSA Sch 1 paras 14(1)(g)(ii) and 15A(1) JSA Regs
ESA Sch 4 para 7 ESA Regs
HB Sch 3 paras 13(1)(a)(iii) and 15(1) HB Regs; Sch 3 para 7 HB(SPC) Regs

29 Sch 3A para 3(i) SS&CS(DA) Regs

30 Sch 1B para 5 IS Regs

31 Reg 6 and Sch IIA para 6 SPC Regs

32 **IS** Reg 16(1) and (2) IS Regs
JSA Reg 78(1)-(2) JSA Regs
ESA Reg 156(1)-(3) ESA Regs
PC Reg 5(1)(a) SPC Regs
HB Reg 21(1) and (2) HB Regs; reg 21(1) and (2) HB(SPC) Regs

33 **IS** Reg 2(1), definition of 'long-term patient', and Sch 2 paras 11(2)(a) and 13A(2)(b) IS Regs
JSA Reg 1(3), definition of 'long-term patient', and Sch 1 paras 13(2)(a) and 15A(2)(b) JSA Regs
ESA Schs 4 para 7(2)(a) and 5 para 13 ESA Regs

34 **IS** Reg 2(1), definition of 'long-term patient', and Sch 2 paras 10(6), 11(2)(b) and 13A(2)(c) IS Regs
JSA Reg 1(3), definition of 'long-term patient', and Sch 1 paras 12(5)(b) and 20IA(2)(b) JSA Regs
ESA Schs 4 para 7(2)(b) and 5 para 13 ESA Regs

35 **IS** Reg 2(1), definition of 'long-term patient', and Sch 2 paras 10(6), 11(2)(c) and 13A(2)(d) IS Regs
JSA Reg 1(3), definition of 'long-term patient', and Sch 1 paras 12(5)(c), 13(2)(c), 15A(2)(c), 20F(5), 20(G)(a) and 20IA(2)(a) JSA Regs

36 Schs 4 paras 5, 6, 7, and 5 para 13 ESA Regs

37 Sch 3 paras 15(1) and 16(a) HB Regs; Sch 3 paras 7 and 8(a) HB(SPC) Regs

38 **IS** Reg 2(1), definition of 'long-term patient', and Sch 2 paras 13A(2)(a) and 14(2) IS Regs
JSA Reg 1(3), definition of 'long-term patient', and Sch 1 paras 15A(2)(a) and 16(2) JSA Regs

39 Reg 3 CTC Regs

40 TCTM 02202

41 Sch 5 para 13 ESA Regs; reg 63(1) ESA Regs 2013

42 Regs 46A(1), (3) and (3A) and 47 JSA Regs 2013; regs 55ZA(1), (3) and (3A) and 55A JSA Regs

43 Reg 3 SFWFP Regs

44 Sch 3 para 9 UC Regs

45 Sch 3 para 18 LMI Regs

46 **IS** Sch 3 para 3(11) IS Regs
JSA Sch 2 para 3(11) JSA Regs
ESA Sch 6 para 5(11) ESA Regs
PC Sch II para 4(11) SPC Regs
HB Reg 7(16) HB Regs; reg 7(16) HB(SPC) Regs

47 Sch 3 para 10 LMI Regs

48 R(H) 9/05

49 Sch 4 para 11 UC Regs

2. People in care homes and similar accommodation

50 **AA/DLA** ss67(2) and 72(8) SSCBA 1992; regs 7 and 8(1) SS(AA) Regs; regs 9 and 10(1) SS(DLA) Regs
PIP s85 WRA 2012; regs 28 and 30(1) SS(PIP) Regs
CDP Reg 17(2) DACYP(S) Regs
ADP Reg 27(2) DAWAP(S) Regs

51 ss67(3) and 72(9) SSCBA 1992; s85(3) WRA 2012; reg 2 DACYP(S) Regs; reg 2 DAWAP(S) Regs

52 **AA/DLA** ss67(4) and 72(10) SSCBA 1992
PIP s85(4) WRA 2012
CDP Reg 2 DACYP(S) Regs
ADP

53 Reg 7(3) SS(AA) Regs; reg 9(6) SS(DLA) Regs

54 **AA** Reg 7(2) SS(AA) Regs
DLA Reg 9(2) SS(DLA) Regs
PIP Reg 28(2)-(4) SS(PIP) Regs

55 CDLA/1465/1998; CDLA/2127/2000

56 CA/2985/1997

57 **AA** Reg 8(3) SS(AA) Regs
DLA Reg 10(3) SS(DLA) Regs
PIP Reg 30(2) SS(PIP) Regs
CDP Reg 20 DACYP(S) Regs
ADP Reg 32(1) and (2)(a) DAWAP(S) Regs

58 **UC** Reg 83(1)(h) UC Regs
HB Reg 75F(1)(f) HB Regs

Chapter 42

Benefits in hospital, care homes, prison and in other special circumstances

- -

59 R(DLA) 2/06
60 **AA** Reg 8(4) and (5) SS(AA) Regs
   DLA Reg 10(6) and (7) SS(DLA) Regs
   PIP Reg 30(3) SS(PIP) Regs
61 Reg 21 DACYP(S) Regs
62 Reg 29 DAWAP(S) Regs
63 **DLA** Reg 9(3) SS(DLA) Regs
   PIP Reg 28(2)(f) SS(PIP) Regs
64 **DLA** Reg 9(4)(a) and (b) and (5)
   SS(DLA) Regs
   PIP Reg 28(3)(a) and (4) SS(PIP) Regs
   CDP Reg 17(5) DACYP(S) Regs
   ADP Reg 27(5) DAWAP(S) Regs
65 **DLA** Reg 9(4)(c) SS(DLA) Regs
   PIP Reg 28(3)(b) SS(PIP) Regs
   CDP Reg 17(5)(b) DACYP(S) Regs
   ADP Reg 27(5)(b) DAWAP(S) Regs
66 **AA** Reg 8(6) SS(AA) Regs
   DLA Reg 10(8) SS(DLA) Regs
   PIP Reg 30(5) SS(PIP) Regs
   CDP Reg 17(4) DACYP(S) Regs
   ADP Reg 27(4) DAWAP(S) Regs
   Steane v CAO and Secretary of State, 24
   July 1996, reported as R(A) 3/96
67 R(A) 1/02; CA/3800/2006; *CAO v
   Creighton and Others*, 15 December
   1999 ([1999] NICA 13), reported as R 1/
   00 (AA); *SSWP v DA* [2009] UKUT 214
   (AAC)
68 *SSWP v JL (DLA)* [2011] UKUT 293 (AAC);
   Vol 10 Ch 61 para 61751 DMG; para
   P3049 ADM
69 **AA** Reg 7(4) SS(AA) Regs
   DLA Reg 9(7) SS(DLA) Regs
   PIP Reg 32(1) and (2) SS(PIP) Regs
   CDP Reg 19 DACYP(S) Regs
   ADP Reg 31 DAWAP(S) Regs
70 **AA** Reg 7(5) SS(AA) Regs
   DLA Reg 9(8) SS(DLA) Regs
   PIP Reg 32(3) SS(PIP) Regs
   CDP Reg 19(4) DACYP(S) Regs
   ADP Reg 31(5) DAWAP(S) Regs
71 **AA** Reg 7(6) SS(AA) Regs
   DLA Reg 9(9) SS(DLA) Regs
   PIP Reg 32(3) SS(PIP) Regs
   CDP Reg 19(5) DACYP(S) Regs
   ADP Reg 31(5) DAWAP(S) Regs
72 **AA** Reg 8(2) SS(AA) Regs
   DLA Reg 10(5) SS(DLA) Regs
   PIP Reg 32(4) SS(PIP) Regs
   CDP Reg 17(3) DACYP(S) Regs
   ADP Reg 27(3) DAWAP(S) Regs
73 **AA** Reg 8(2)(b) SS(AA) Regs
   DLA Reg 10(5)(b) SS(DLA) Regs
   PIP Reg 32(4) and (5) SS(PIP) Regs

74 **IS** Sch 2 para 14ZA IS Regs
   JSA Sch 1 para 17(3) JSA Regs
   ESA Sch 4 para 8(4) ESA Regs
   PC Sch 1 para 4 SPC Regs
   HB Sch 3 para 17(2) HB Regs; Sch 3 para
   9(2) HB(SPC) Regs
75 Regs 29(1) and 30 UC Regs
76 **IS** Sch 3A para 3(h) and (i) SS&CS(DA)
   Regs
   ESA Sch 3C para 3(f) and (g)
   SS&CS(DA) Regs
77 Sch 1 para 3(d) UC Regs
78 Sch 1 para 1 UC Regs
79 *SA v SSWP (IS)* [2010] UKUT 345 (AAC),
   reported as [2011] AACR 16
80 Sch 3 para 9 UC Regs
81 Sch 3 para 18 LMI Regs
82 s39 WRA 2012; reg 3(6) UC Regs
83 s10 WRA 2012; reg 4(7) UC Regs
84 Regs 4 and 4A UC Regs
85 Reg 12(c) SPC Regs
86 Reg 9(1)(k) HB Regs; reg 9(1)(k)
   HB(SPC) Regs
87 Sch 3 para 9 HB&CTB(CP) Regs
88 HB/CTB Circular A20/05
89 **IS** Reg 53(1A), (1B) and (1C) IS Regs
   JSA Reg 116(1A), (1B) and (1C) JSA Regs
   ESA Reg 118(2), (3) and (4) ESA Regs
   HB Reg 52(3)-(5), (8) and (9) HB Regs
90 **IS** Reg 16(3)(e) IS Regs
   JSA Reg 78(3)(d) JSA Regs
   ESA Reg 156(4)(d) ESA Regs
   PC Reg 5(1)(b) SPC Regs
   HB Reg 21(2) HB Regs; reg 21(2)
   HB(SPC) Regs
91 Appendix to CIS/4934/1997; CIS/4965/
   1997; CIS/5232/1997; CIS/3767/1997
92 **IS** Reg 16(1) and (2) IS Regs
   JSA Reg 78(1)-(2) JSA Regs
   ESA Reg 156(1)-(3) ESA Regs
   PC Reg 5(1)(a) SPC Regs
   HB Reg 21(1) and (2) HB Regs; reg
   21(1) and (2) HB(SPC) Regs
93 **IS** Sch 7 paras 9 and 10 IS Regs
   JSA Schs 5 paras 5 and 6 and 5A paras 4
   and 5 JSA Regs
   ESA Sch 5 paras 4 and 5 ESA Regs
   All CIS/1544/2001
94 Reg 6 and Sch IIA para 6 SPC Regs
95 Sch IIA para 9 SPC Regs
96 Sch IIA para 4 SPC Regs
97 Reg 1A(4) and (5) SFCWP Regs
98 Regs 1 and 2 SFWFP Regs
99 Reg 4(2) WHACYP(S) Regs
100 Sch 3 para 18(1) LMI Regs
101 Sch 3 para 10 LMI Regs
102 R(H) 9/05
103 R(H) 9/05

Part 6: Special benefit rules
Chapter 42: Benefits in hospital, care homes, prison and in other special circumstances
Notes

. . . .

104 **IS** Sch 3 para 3(8)-(12) IS Regs
JSA Sch 2 para 3(8)-(12) JSA Regs
ESA Sch 6 para 5(8)-(12) ESA Regs
PC Sch 2 para 4(8)-(12) SPC Regs
HB Reg 7(11)-(13), (16) and (17) HB
Regs; reg 7(11)-(13), (16) and (17)
HB(SPC) Regs
105 Sch 4 para 11 UC Regs

3. Prisoners

106 **ESA** s18(4)(b) WRA 2007
PIP s87 WRA 2012
Statutory payments Reg 3(1) and (2)
SSP Regs; reg 9 SMP Regs; regs 18(c)
and 27(1)(c) SPPSAP(G) Regs; regs 14
and 26 SSPP(G) Regs
Other benefits s113(1)(b) and Sch 9
para 1 SSCBA 1992; reg 2(9) and (10)
SS(GB) Regs; reg 10(2)(d) and Sch 2
para 7(b)(ii) SSB(Dep) Regs; R(S) 8/79
107 Reg 3(1) and (2) SSP Regs; reg 9 SMP
Regs; regs 18(c) and 27(1)(c) and (2)
SPPSAP(G) Regs; regs 14 and 26
SSPP(G) Regs; reg 9(1)(c) and (2)
SPBP(G) Regs
108 **ESA** s18(4)(b) WRA 2007; reg 160 ESA
Regs; reg 96 ESA Regs 2013
Other benefits s113(1)(b) SSCBA
1992; reg 2 SS(GB) Regs; s19 PA 2014;
regs 2 and 3 SP Regs
109 **PIP** s87 WRA 2012; reg 31(1) SS(PIP)
Regs
ADP Reg 30 DAWAP(S) Regs
110 **PIP** Reg 31(2) SS(PIP) Regs
ADP Reg 32(2)(c) DAWAP(S) Regs
111 Regs 3(3)(b) and 32(2)(c)(ii) DAWAP(S)
Regs
112 **PIP** Reg 32(1) and (5) SS(PIP) Regs
ADP Reg 30(4) DAWAP(S) Regs
113 Reg 18 DACYP(S) Regs
114 s113(1)(b) SSCBA 1992
115 Reg 13(1)(b) JSA Regs 2013
116 **ESA** Reg 160(1), (2) and (5)(c) ESA
Regs; reg 96(1), (2) and (6)(c) ESA Regs
2013
Other benefits Reg 2(2) and (8)(c)
SS(GB) Regs; reg 14 SS(ICA) Regs; s19
PA 2014; regs 2 and 3 SP Regs
All R(S) 1/71
117 **ESA** Reg 161 ESA Regs; reg 97 ESA Regs
2013
Other benefits Reg 3 SS(GB) Regs; reg
14 SS(ICA) Regs
118 Reg 159(1) ESA Regs; reg 95 ESA Regs
2013
119 Reg 160 ESA Regs; reg 96 ESA Regs
2013
120 CS/541/1950

121 Regs 2(6) and (7) and 3(1) SS(GB) Regs
122 Reg 2(7) SS(GB) Regs; Vol 3 Ch 12, para
12091 DMG
123 Reg 2(2) and (7) SS(GB) Regs
124 **CB** s113(1)(b) SSCBA 1992. Child
benefit is not in Parts 2-5 of that Act.
GA Reg 2(5) SS(GB) Regs
125 Sch 9 para 1(a) SSCBA 1992; regs 16
and 17 CB Regs
126 Reg 19 UC Regs
127 This is the policy intention as reflected in
ADM E3030 and 3040. Reg 19 UC Regs
states that 'entitlement to UC cannot
arise' where the claimant is a prisoner.
This wording suggests new claims to UC
are prevented, as opposed to existing
claims being affected.
128 Reg 2 UC Regs
129 Sch 4 paras 11 and 16(2)(h) UC Regs
130 Reg 3(3)(c) UC Regs
131 Regs 18, 22(3) and 36(3) UC Regs
132 s39 WRA 2012; reg 3(6) UC Regs
133 Reg 4(6)(b) UC Regs
134 **IS** Sch 1B para 22, Sch 3 para 3(11) and
(12) and Sch 7 para 8 IS Regs
ESA Schs 5 para 3 and 6 para 5(11) and
(12) ESA Regs
PC Reg 6(2)(a), (3), (6)(c), (7), (9) and
(10) SPC Regs
135 Reg 7(3) SPC Regs
136 **IS** Sch 3 para 18(7)(g) IS Regs
JSA Sch 2 para 17(7)(g) JSA Regs
ESA Sch 6 para 19(7)(g) ESA Regs
PC Sch 2 para 14(7)(e) SPC Regs
HB Reg 74(7)(f) HB Regs; reg 55(7)(f)
HB(SPC) Regs
137 **IS** Reg 21(3) IS Regs
JSA Reg 85(4) JSA Regs
ESA Reg 69(2) ESA Regs
PC Reg 1(2) SPC Regs
HB Reg 7(14) and (16)(c)(i) HB Regs;
reg 7(14) and (16)(c)(i) HB(SPC) Regs
138 **IS** Reg 16(3)(b) IS Regs
JSA Reg 78(3)(b) JSA Regs
ESA Reg 156(4) ESA Regs
PC Reg 5(1)(c)(ii) and (iii) SPC Regs
139 Reg 21(2) HB Regs; reg 21(2) HB(SPC)
Regs
140 Reg 28 HB Regs; reg 31 HB(SPC) Regs
141 Reg 3, Rule 4.1 Case C, CTC Regs; reg
2(2) WTC(EMR) Regs
142 Sch IIA para 5 SPC Regs
143 *Stewart v SSWP* [2011] EWCA Civ 907
decided that the exclusion of prisoners
from entitlement to a funeral expenses
payment did not breach the HRA 1998

144 **UC** Reg 19(1)(c) and (4) UC Regs
IS Reg 21(3ZA)-(3ZC) and Sch 7 para 2A IS Regs
ESA Regs 69(3)-(5) and 160(3)-(4A) and Sch 5 para 12 ESA Regs; reg 96(3)-(5) ESA Regs 2013
PC Reg 8 and Sch 3 para 2 SPC Regs
PIP Reg 31(3) and (4) SS(PIP) Regs
Other benefits Reg 2(3), (4) and (4A) SS(GB) Regs
All CSS/239/2007; *JB v SSWP (IS)* [2010] UKUT 263 (AAC)

145 **UC** Reg 19(1)(c) and (4) UC Regs
IS Reg 21(3ZA)-(3ZC) and Sch 7 para 2A IS Regs
ESA Regs 69(3)-(5) and 160(3)-(4A) and Sch 5 para 12 ESA Regs; reg 96(3)-(5) ESA Regs 2013
PC Reg 8 and Sch 3 para 2 SPC Regs
PIP Reg 31(3) and (4) SS(PIP) Regs
Other benefits Reg 2(3)-(4A) SS(GB) Regs
All CSS/239/2007; *JB v SSWP (IS)* [2010] UKUT 263 (AAC)

146 paras J3086 and R4086 ADM; Vol 4 Ch 21 para 21201 DMG

147 s39 WRA 2012; reg 3(6) UC Regs

148 **IS** Reg 16(2) IS Regs
JSA Reg 78(2) JSA Regs
ESA Reg 156(3) ESA Regs
PC Reg 5(1)(a) SPC Regs
HB Reg 21(1) and (2) HB Regs; reg 21(1) and (2) HB(SPC) Regs

149 **IS** Sch 7 para 9(a)(v) IS Regs
JSA Schs 5 para 5(a)(vi) and 5A para 4(a)(vi) JSA Regs
ESA Sch 5 para 4(a)(v) ESA Regs

150 Schs 1 paras 1 and 3(c) and 3 para 1(1) UC Regs

151 Sch 3 para 9 UC Regs

152 Reg 7(5) HB Regs; reg 7(5) HB(SPC) Regs

153 **IS** Sch 3 para 3(11)(c)(i) and (12) IS Regs
JSA Sch 2 para 2(11)(c)(i) and (12) JSA Regs
ESA Sch 6 para 5(11)(c)(i) and (12) ESA Regs
PC Sch 2 para 4(11)(c)(i) and (12) SPC Regs
HB Reg 7(16)(c)(i) and (17) HB Regs; reg 7(16)(c)(i) and (17) HB(SPC) Regs

154 Sch 3 paras 10(2)(c) and 18 LMI Regs

155 **IS** Reg 48(7) IS Regs
JSA Reg 110(7) JSA Regs
ESA Reg 112(6) ESA Regs

156 Reg 19(2) and (3) UC Regs

157 Reg 19(2)(b) UC Regs

158 Reg 19(2)(a) UC Regs

159 Sch 3 para 18 LMI Regs

160 **IS** Schs 1B para 22, 3 para 3(11) and (12) and 7 para 8 IS Regs
ESA Schs 5 para 3 and 6 para 5(11) and (12) ESA Regs
PC Reg 6(2)(a), (3), (6)(c), (7), (9) and (10) and Sch 2 para 4(11) and (12) SPC Regs
HB Reg 7(16)(c)(i) and (17) HB Regs; reg 7(16)(c)(i) and (17) HB(SPC) Regs

161 Sch 3 para 10(1) and (2) LMI Regs

162 Reg 7(13) HB Regs; reg 7(13) HB(SPC) Regs

163 CSH/499/2006

164 **UC** Reg 2(1) UC Regs
IS Reg 21(3) and Sch 7 para 8(a) IS Regs
JSA Reg 85(4) JSA Regs
ESA Reg 69(2) and Sch 5 para 3(a) ESA Regs
PC Regs 1(2) and 6 SPC Regs

165 Reg 7(14) and (15) HB Regs; reg 7(14) and (15) HB(SPC) Regs; R(IS) 17/93

166 *KdeS v Camden LB (HB)* [2011] UKUT 457 (AAC)

167 Reg 7(7) HB Regs; reg 7(7) HB(SPC) Regs; Ch A3, paras 3.430-32 GM

168 Sch 2 para 2 LMI Regs

169 Sch 4 para 11 UC Regs

4. 16/17 year old care leavers

170 **UC** Reg 8(1), (2) and (4) UC Regs
IS Reg 4ZA(3A) IS Regs
JSA Reg 57, definition of 'young person', JSA Regs
IS/JSA/HB ss6 and 8(6) C(LC)A 2000; C(LC)SSB(S) Regs

171 **IS** Reg 14(2)(c) IS Regs
JSA Reg 76(2)(d) JSA Regs
ESA Reg 2(1), definition of 'young person', ESA Regs
HB Reg 19(2)(c) HB Regs; reg 19(2)(c) HB(SPC) Regs

172 Regs 4(6)(a) and 4A UC Regs

173 Sch IIA para 4 SPC Regs

174 Reg 8(1) and (4) UC Regs

175 **UC** Reg 8(2) and (4) UC Regs

176 Reg 8(4)(b) UC Regs. 'Member of your family' is not defined. Arguably, the intention is to exclude periods of time when you are living with a person who has parental responsibilities for you.

177 Reg 3(5) and (6) CL(E) Regs; reg 4(4)-(6) C(LC)(W) Regs

178 Reg 8(1) and (2) UC Regs

179 Sch 4 para 4 UC Regs

Part 6: Special benefit rules
Chapter 42: Benefits in hospital, care homes, prison and in other special circumstances
Notes

• •

5. People without accommodation

180 **UC** Sch 4 para 29(4) UC Regs
HB Reg 2(1), definition of 'young
individual', HB Regs

181 Sch 1 paras 1 and 3(b) UC Regs

182 http://data.parliament.uk/
DepositedPapers/Files/DEP2021-0835/
074_Homelessness_and_at_
risk_of_Homelessness_V10-0.pdf

183 **UC** Reg 95(2) UC Regs
JSA Reg 12(2) and (3) JSA Regs 2013

184 This rule was challenged under the HRA
1998, but the court decided the rules
did not conflict with it: *R (RJM) v SSWP*
[2008] UKHL 63

185 **IS** Sch 7 para 6 IS Regs
JSA Schs 5 para 3 and 5A para 2 JSA
Regs
ESA Sch 5 para 1 ESA Regs

186 Vol 4 Ch 24, para 24157 and Vol 9 Ch
54, para 54157 DMG

187 Vol 4 Ch 24, paras 24158-59 and Vol 9
Ch 54, paras 54158-59 DMG

188 Vol 4 Ch 24, paras 24159-60 and Vol 9
Ch 54, paras 54159-60 DMG; R(IS) 23/
98

189 Vol 4 Ch 24, para 24162 and Vol 9 Ch
54, para 54162 DMG

6

Part 7

National Insurance, work and work-related rules

Chapter 43

National insurance contributions

This chapter covers:
1. National insurance contributions and contributory benefits (below)
2. Paid contributions (p946)
3. National insurance credits (p954)
4. Contribution conditions for benefits (p964)

This chapter explains the national insurance (NI) contribution rules relevant to contributory benefits. For details of the NI number requirement that applies to most benefits, see p1137.

Key facts
- Entitlement to contributory benefits, and sometimes the amount paid, depends on your national insurance (NI) contribution record. For some benefits, it depends on the contribution record of your spouse or civil partner, or your late spouse or civil partner.
- If you are employed or self-employed, you may be liable to pay NI contributions. If you are not liable to pay contributions, in some circumstances you can be awarded NI 'credits', or you may be able to pay contributions voluntarily.
- There are different types of NI contributions (called 'classes'). Not all classes of NI contributions or all types of NI credits count for all contributory benefits.
- NI contributions are collected by HM Revenue and Customs.

1. National insurance contributions and contributory benefits

Your national insurance (NI) contribution record is based on the NI contributions you have paid, or the NI credits you have received, for each tax year – ie, 6 April to 5 April.

Part 7: National Insurance, work and work-related rules
Chapter 43: National insurance contributions
2. Paid national insurance contributions

Benefits that have NI contribution conditions, known as '**contributory benefits**', are:

- contribution-based jobseeker's allowance;
- contributory employment and support allowance;
- bereavement support payment and widowed parent's allowance; *and*
- state pension and 'old' (ie, category A and B) retirement pensions.

Entitlement to contributory benefits normally depends on NI contribution conditions being met. For the detailed rules, see pp964–69.

In some circumstances, you may be liable to pay NI contributions. If you are not, in order to help you meet the contribution conditions for some contributory benefits, you may either be credited with earnings or with contributions, or you can choose to pay contributions. For details of NI 'credits', see p954.

Note: if you are self-employed, your entitlement to maternity allowance (MA) and the amount you receive may be affected by whether you have paid class 2 NI contributions (see p711). For you to qualify for MA on the basis that you help your spouse or civil partner with her/his self-employment, s/he must meet conditions relating to class 2 NI contributions (see p709).

How decisions are made

Most decisions on NI contributions are made by an officer of HM Revenue and Customs (HMRC). Appeals against such decisions can be decided by a HMRC review or a tribunal that considers tax appeals.[1] The process is similar to appealing against an HMRC decision on entitlement to a statutory payment (see p1394).

Decisions relating to entitlement to NI credits are made either by HMRC or the DWP, depending on the type of NI credit. If you disagree with a decision on your entitlement, you can apply for a revision or supersession (see Chapter 56), or appeal against it (see Chapter 57). You must apply for a mandatory reconsideration before you can appeal. Your appeal is decided by a social security tribunal.[2]

---

2. Paid national insurance contributions

There are seven different types ('classes') of paid national insurance (NI) contribution.[3] Classes 1, 2 and 3 can help you to qualify for contributory benefits, but only class 1 contributions count for *all* contributory benefits. Class 3A contributions, which could only be paid if you reached pension age before 6 April 2016, count towards entitlement to additional state pension (see p782 of the 2015/16 edition of this *Handbook* for details).

If you are an 'employed earner', you may be liable for class 1 contributions, depending on the amount you earn. If you are a 'self-employed earner', you are normally liable to pay class 2 contributions (and you may also be liable for class 4 contributions), unless your profits are low or you are exempt from payment. If you are not liable to pay contributions, you may choose to pay class 2 (if self-employed) or class 3 contributions voluntarily, known as 'voluntary contributions'.

Class of contribution	Payable by	Giving entitlement to
Class 1	Employed earners and their employers	All benefits with contribution conditions
Class 1A and 1B	Employers of employed earners	No benefits
Class 2	Self-employed earners	All benefits with contribution conditions, except contribution-based jobseeker's allowance (JSA)
Class 3	Voluntary contributors	State pension, category A and B retirement pensions and widowed parent's allowance
Class 3A	Voluntary contributors	An amount (a 'unit') of additional state pension
Class 4	Self-employed earners	No benefits

The rules about your age

- You are not liable for class 1 or 2 contributions if you are under 16 years old or over pension age (see p766).[4]
- You cannot pay class 3 contributions if you are under 16 (and sometimes if you are 17 or 18) or for the tax year in which you reach pension age or any subsequent tax year.[5]

Employed earners and self-employed earners

Your liability to pay class 1, 2 or 4 NI contributions depends on whether you are an employed or self-employed earner.[6] It is normally clear whether you are employed or self-employed. If there is a dispute, it usually concerns whether you are employed under a *contract of service* (in which case, you are an employee) or a *contract for services* (in which case, you are self-employed).[7] **Note:**

- To be an employed or self-employed earner, you must be 'gainfully employed'.
- Office holders, including people in elective office, who receive earnings are classed as employed earners. Office holders include judges, registrars of births, marriages and deaths and most company directors. (If you are a company director and pay yourself a wage from which class 1 NI contributions are deducted, this may help you to claim both statutory payments and contributory benefits. You will need to register as an employer.)

Part 7: National insurance, work and work-related rules
Chapter 43: National insurance contributions
2. Paid national insurance contributions

- Certain people are deemed to be employed earners. These include office cleaners, many agency workers and people employed by their spouse or civil partner for the purposes of their spouse's or civil partner's employment.[8]
- Examiners, moderators and invigilators are deemed to be self-employed.[9]
- If you have two or more jobs, it is possible to be both employed and self-employed.
- You do not have to pay NI contributions on earnings from certain kinds of employment – eg, if you are employed by your spouse or civil partner and it is not for the purpose of her/his employment, or if you are employed in your home by a close relative who lives with you and the job is not for a trade or business that is carried out there.[10]

More than one job

If you are employed as an employed earner in more than one job, the basic rule is that your liability to pay class 1 contributions is calculated for each job as if the other(s) did not exist, although the total you pay is subject to a maximum.[11] There are some exceptions – eg, if you have two different jobs for the same employer or employers who carry on business in association with each other. In this situation, to stop employers avoiding liability, earnings from these jobs are normally added together and your NI contributions are based on your total earnings.[12]

If you are self-employed and also have a job as an employed earner, you may be liable to pay both class 1 and class 2 contributions, subject to a maximum.[13]

Class 1 contributions

Class 1 contributions have two elements: primary contributions (paid by employed earners) and secondary contributions (paid by employers).[14]

The amount of primary class 1 contributions you pay depends on the amount you earn in relation to the upper and lower earnings limit for the tax year, and to the amount of that year's 'primary threshold'. See Appendix 6 for details of the earnings limits and the primary threshold.

If your earnings are equal to or below the primary threshold (£190–£242 from July – a week in 2022/23), you do not have to pay NI contributions on them. If they are between the lower earnings limit (£123 a week in 2022/23) and the primary threshold, you are treated as if you had paid class 1 NI contributions on those earnings.[15]

The rate of class 1 NI contributions has been increased by 1.25 per cent in 2022/23. If you earn more than the primary threshold, you are liable to pay class 1 contributions of 13.25 per cent of your earnings between the primary threshold and upper earnings limit (£967 a week in 2022/23), plus 3.25 per cent of the earnings you have above the upper earnings limit.[16] If you are a married woman or widow with reduced liability for contributions (see p950), you pay lower class 1 contributions.[17]

It is your employer's responsibility to deduct your contributions from your earnings and pay them with its own contributions to HM Revenue and Customs

(HMRC).[18] If your employer has failed to pay your contributions to HMRC, you are treated as though they had been paid, unless you have been negligent, or consented to or connived in that arrangement.[19]

Class 2 contributions

You must pay class 2 contributions for each week in a tax year in which you are a self-employed earner, unless your taxable profits in that year are below the 'small profits threshold' (or, in 2022/2023, between that and the 'lower profits limit' of £11,908) or you are exempt from payment. The small profits threshold for 2022/23 is £6,725. The main grounds for being exempt from payment are that you receive certain benefits – eg, maternity allowance (MA) or employment and support allowance (ESA) for the week to which the contribution relates, or carer's allowance for at least part of that week.[20]

Your liability for class 2 contributions is calculated annually after the end of the tax year using the income tax self-assessment procedure. They are payable with any income tax and class 4 contributions for which you are liable in the same year (but see below if you are claiming MA).[21]

Even if you are not liable to pay class 2 contributions, provided you are a self-employed earner, you may still choose to pay voluntary class 2 contributions to protect your NI contribution record (see p952).[22]

Class 2 contributions are payable at a flat rate.[23] The current and previous year's rates are:

2022/23	£3.15 a week
2021/22	£3.05 a week

Note:
- The self-assessment procedure was not used to collect class 2 contributions in tax years before 2015/16. For details, see the 2014/15 edition of this *Handbook*.
- Married women and widows with reduced liability for contributions (see p950) are not liable for class 2 contributions and cannot pay them voluntarily.[24]
- Volunteer development workers employed abroad and share fishermen pay class 2 contributions at special rates, which count towards contribution-based JSA, unlike other class 2 contributions.[25]

Class 2 contributions and maternity allowance

Payment of class 2 contributions becomes due on 31 January after the end of the tax year for which they are paid. You can voluntarily pay them early in order to increase your entitlement to MA (see p711), or your spouse or civil partner can pay early to enable you to qualify for MA on the basis that you help with her/his self-employment (see p709). In either situation, the contributions may be

Part 7: National Insurance, work and work-related rules
Chapter 43: National insurance contributions
2. Paid national insurance contributions

paid at any time from the week to which they relate. If you (or your spouse or civil partner) pay them early and are later assessed as liable to pay class 2 contributions for the same weeks under the self-assessment procedure, these voluntary contributions are converted to cover that liability, so you do not pay twice.[26]

If you employ yourself (eg, if you are a company director) and pay yourself a wage, you should check to see whether you are liable for class 1 contributions, as you may be able to claim statutory maternity pay instead.

Class 3 contributions

Payment of class 3 contributions is voluntary.[27] They only give entitlement to state pension, category A and B retirement pensions and widowed parent's allowance.[28] To help you decide whether to pay class 3 contributions, see p952.

Class 3 contributions are paid at a flat rate. The current and previous year's rates are:[29]

2022/23	£15.85 a week
2021/22	£15.40 a week

Class 3A contributions

Class 3A contributions were voluntary contributions for people who would reach pension age before April 2016. See the 2016/17 edition of this *Handbook*.

Pre-1975 contributions

The present contribution system was introduced on 6 April 1975. Between 5 July 1948 and 5 April 1975, class 1 contributions were paid by a 'flat-rate stamp' in the same way as class 2 and class 3 contributions.

Before 6 April 1975, contribution years were not the same as tax years, as they are now. Transitional arrangements in both 1948 and 1975 may have resulted in your having a contribution year that was not 12 months long, which may explain what would otherwise be anomalies in your contribution record.

Reduced liability for married women and widows

Women who were married or widowed on 6 April 1977 could choose to pay reduced class 1 or no class 2 contributions, provided they applied to do so before 12 May 1977.[30]

If you 'elected' to pay at this reduced rate, you can continue to do so until you either apply to pay the full rate again (called 'revoking an election') or until the right to pay reduced contributions is automatically lost.[31] These reduced-rate contributions do not help you build up entitlement to contributory benefits.

If you have paid reduced-rate NI contributions and reach pension age on or after 6 April 2016, see p769 for how your state pension may be calculated. If you reached pension age before 6 April 2016 and you do not qualify for a retirement pension based on your own contributions, you may qualify for a category B retirement pension instead. See Chapter 36 of the 2015/16 edition of this *Handbook* for details.

To pay the full rate again, complete the form in HMRC leaflet CF9 for married women or CF9A for widows (available from gov.uk/reduced-national-insurance-married-women).

Coming from abroad and going abroad

The rules on liability for NI contributions when you have come to the UK from abroad, or if you go abroad, are complex. In particular, the rules described below may not apply if you are covered by the European Union co-ordination rules (see p1647) or if you move from or to a country which has a reciprocal agreement with the UK (see p1546). In some circumstances, contributions paid in other countries count towards British benefits. In particular, this may apply if you have paid contributions in the European Economic Area (see p1643). You may also be entitled to benefits from other countries while you are in this country.

If you have come from abroad and are employed or self-employed in Great Britain, you may be liable for class 1 or 2 (and 4) contributions.[32] If you are self-employed but not liable to pay contributions, you may be able to pay class 2 contributions voluntarily. If you are not liable to pay contributions, you can choose to pay class 3 contributions if you are resident (see p1549) in Great Britain throughout the course of the tax year in respect of which you wish to pay contributions and, in some circumstances, even if you have not been resident for the whole tax year.[33]

If you are abroad working as an employee and your employer has a place of business in Britain, in some circumstances for the first year you must still pay class 1 contributions. If you are not liable, or are no longer liable, to pay class 1 contributions, it may be worth paying class 3 contributions (see p952).[34]

If you are self-employed outside Great Britain, you may pay class 2 contributions if you wish, provided you were employed or self-employed immediately before you left Britain and either:
- you have been resident in Great Britain for a continuous period of at least three years at some time in the past; *or*
- you have paid contributions producing an earnings factor of at least 52 times the lower earnings limit in each of three years in the past. Each set of 52 flat-rate contributions paid before April 1975 counts as satisfying that condition in respect of one year.[35]

Certain volunteer development workers who are employed abroad may also be allowed to pay class 2 contributions.[36]

Part 7: National Insurance, work and work-related rules
Chapter 43: National insurance contributions
2. Paid national insurance contributions

Normally, class 3 contributions may be paid while you are abroad if you satisfy either of the conditions which would allow you to pay class 2 contributions (but you do not need to have been employed or self-employed before you left Britain or while abroad). You may also pay them if you paid class 1 contributions for the first year you were employed abroad.[37]

For information on payment of NI contributions while abroad, see gov.uk/national-insurance-if-you-go-abroad or telephone the HMRC helpline (tel: 0300 200 3500 or from abroad: +44 191 203 7010; textphone: 0300 200 3519).

Northern Ireland and Isle of Man contributions count towards British benefits.

Improving your contribution record

If there are years for which you do not have a full contribution record, it may be beneficial to pay 'voluntary contributions': either voluntary class 2 contributions (if you are self-employed but not liable to pay class 2 contributions – see p949) or class 3 contributions (see p950). Before paying voluntary contributions in respect of a tax year, check whether you qualify for NI credits in that year. (In any event, you are not entitled to pay class 3 contributions if you would instead be entitled to class 3 credits – see p954.[38]) You can request an NI statement to check whether there are gaps in your contribution record by completing an online form at gov.uk or by telephoning or writing to the National Insurance Contributions and Employer Office, HM Revenue and Customs, BX9 1AN (tel: 0300 200 3500).

If it is more than 30 days before you reach pension age, you can also request a state pension statement to help you decide whether to pay voluntary contributions. You can do this online at gov.uk/check-state-pension, by telephoning the Future Pension Centre (tel: 0800 731 0175; textphone: 0800 731 0176; Relay UK and BSL video relay available) or by post using Form BR19 (available at gov.uk/check-state-pension). If you are within 30 days of pension age, contact the Pension Service for details of your state pension (tel: 0800 731 7898; textphone: 0800 731 7339; Relay UK and BSL video relay available).

Should you make voluntary contributions?

1. Both class 2 and 3 contributions may help you qualify for state pension, or qualify for a higher rate of state pension. Class 2 contributions also count for contributory ESA.

2. Class 2 contributions count for bereavement support payment; class 3 contributions and NI credits do not.

3. Both class 2 and 3 contributions count for widowed parent's allowance.

4. Voluntary contributions may be paid on behalf of a contributor after her/his death, provided they are paid no later than s/he would have been allowed to pay them.[39]

5. Consider the cost of paying voluntary contributions and compare this to the additional amount of benefit that might be awarded.

6. Class 2 and 3 contributions paid late do not always count for benefit purposes (see p953).

7. If you have overpaid contributions for a particular year, or have paid voluntary contributions in error, you may be able to get a refund.

8. Get advice before paying voluntary contributions for years in which you have paid contributions abroad. In some cases, these can count towards British benefits (see p951).

9. If in doubt about paying the contributions, get advice.

Late payment of contributions

Payments of class 1, 2 or 3 NI contributions are considered late if they are paid after the date on which they are due to be paid.

If you are liable for class 1 contributions, your employer is responsible for paying them to HMRC. If your employer failed to pay these or has paid them late, you are treated as if the contributions had been paid (usually on the date they were due to be paid), unless you have been negligent or consented to, or connived in, the failure to pay.[40]

Class 2 contributions (including voluntary class 2 contributions) are due on 31 January after the end of the tax year for which they are paid. Class 3 contributions are due 42 days after the end of the tax year for which they are paid.[41]

Contributions paid after these dates normally cannot help you to qualify for contributory benefits for any period before you pay them. They can usually only count towards your benefit entitlement for the period from the date they have been paid if:[42]

- for class 1 contributions, they were paid by the end of the second tax year after the tax year for which the contributions are paid; or
- for class 2 or 3 contributions, they are paid by the end of the sixth tax year after the tax year in which you are liable to pay them or, if they are voluntary contributions, in which you are entitled to pay them (although special rules apply if you make late payments of class 2 contributions through PAYE (pay as you earn)); or
- for class 3 contributions (for any tax year in which, for at least six months, you were a full-time apprentice, in full-time education or training or a prisoner, and for the year before and after such a year in which you met this condition but for less than six months), they are paid by the end of the sixth complete tax year after the end of a period of education, apprenticeship or imprisonment.

Even if paid within these time limits, class 2 contributions paid late cannot count for the second contribution condition for contribution-based JSA and contributory ESA until six weeks after they have been paid.[43] This also applies to class 1 contributions which are paid after the start of the relevant benefit year, unless they can be treated as paid earlier in the circumstances described above.

In limited circumstances, contributions paid after the above time limits can still count for benefit purposes.[44] For example, if you reach pension age on or after

Part 7: National Insurance, work and work-related rules
Chapter 43: National insurance contributions
3. National insurance credits

6 April 2016, you have until 5 April 2023 to pay voluntary contributions for any of the tax years from 2006/07 to 2015/16.[45]

3. **National insurance credits**

In some circumstances, you can be 'credited' with earnings (sometimes known as class 1 credits) or with class 3 contributions. 'Credits' can help you satisfy:
* the second contribution condition for benefits with two contribution conditions – ie, contribution-based jobseeker's allowance (JSA), contributory employment and support allowance (ESA) and, if your spouse or civil partner died before 6 April 2017, widowed parent's allowance; *and*
* the contribution conditions for retirement pensions (see below).

Not all types of credits count for all these contributory benefits, although many class 1 credits do. Class 3 credits count for widowed parent's allowance and state pension. They also count for category A and B retirement pensions.

Note:
* You can only receive sufficient credits in any tax year to meet the contribution condition for that year.[46]
* Some credits are awarded automatically; others you must claim. To help you decide whether to claim credits or to see whether you have been awarded credits, you can check your national insurance (NI) contribution record at gov.uk/check-national-insurance-record or you can apply for a statement of your NI record at tax.service.gov.uk/shortforms/form/NIStatement or by telephoning the number below.
* Credits cannot help you to satisfy the first contribution condition for benefits with two contribution conditions, or to qualify for bereavement support payment, which has a single contribution condition.
* If you are a married woman with reduced liability for contributions (see p950), you can only qualify for credits for universal credit (UC) (see p957), for certain parents and carers (see p957), for family members providing childcare (see p959), for official error (see below), starting credits (but see p960) or credits following bereavement (see p962). You are not entitled to other types of credits.
* Some people were credited with earnings for the tax years from 1993/94 to 2007/08 following an official error arising from discrepancies between the DWP and HM Revenue and Customs (HMRC) computer systems.[47] These credits were awarded automatically. See the 2009/10 edition of this *Handbook*.

Enquiries about credits can be made to the NI helpline (tel: 0300 200 3500; textphone: 0300 200 3519), or by writing to HMRC (see p952).

Retirement pensions and credits

If you reach pension age on or after 6 April 2016, you may qualify for state pension. If you reached pension age before this date, you may qualify for category A or B retirement pension.

Most types of credits (including class 3 credits) can help you meet the contribution conditions for these benefits, and help determine the amount you receive.

For transitional rate state pension (see p768), most kinds of credits for tax years before 6 April 2016 can be taken into account when calculating your 'starting amount'.

Credits for unemployment

These credits can help you meet the contribution conditions for all contributory benefits (see p945), except bereavement support payment.

If you are entitled to UC and do not receive any JSA, these credits do not apply. However, you can get credits for UC (see p957).

You can be credited with earnings equal to the lower earnings limit for either:[48]

- each complete week (ie, the seven days from Sunday to Saturday) for which you receive JSA (or for which you would have received JSA but for the loss of benefit for benefit offences rules – see p1239); *or*
- each complete week in which you are not entitled to UC (to be entitled, you normally must have claimed it) but for which you satisfy, or can be treated as satisfying, the following qualifying conditions for JSA – ie, you:
  - are not engaged in full-time paid work (see p974); *and*
  - are not in relevant education (see p873); *and*
  - do not have limited capability for work (see Chapter 45); *and*
  - are under pension age; *and*
  - are either available for and actively seeking work (see p1093 and p1101) or, if you come under the UC system, satisfy the work search and work availability requirements (see p1030 and p1034), or you would have satisfied the availability and actively seeking work requirements or the work search and work availability requirements in that week but for having limited capability for work (see p690) or being incapable of work for part of the week.

You may also qualify for credits for weeks before 29 October 2013 in which you would have satisfied the above conditions for JSA but were treated as being in full-time paid work because you received a compensation payment. See pp885–86 of the 2013/14 edition of this *Handbook* for details.

Credits for unemployment are awarded automatically if you get JSA. Otherwise, you must apply in writing to Jobcentre Plus, either on the first day for which you are claiming them or within a reasonable period of time after that. You must

Part 7: National Insurance, work and work-related rules
Chapter 43: National insurance contributions
3. National insurance credits

provide the DWP with the evidence it requires to show that you satisfy the conditions. Even if you are not entitled to JSA, it can be important to continue to 'sign on' at the Jobcentre Plus office in order to get credits for unemployment and protect your right to contributory benefits.

However, you do not get credits for weeks in which:[49]

- you would not have been entitled to JSA (whether or not you actually claimed it) because you are involved in a trade dispute; *or*
- your JSA is reduced (or not paid) because you have been sanctioned. See p1058 and p1116 for the circumstances when this may apply; *or*
- you are receiving hardship payments of income-based or joint-claim JSA (see p1184); *or*
- you are a 16/17 year old receiving JSA severe hardship payments.

Credits for limited capability for work or incapacity for work

These credits can help you meet the contribution conditions for all contributory benefits, except bereavement support payment.

You can be credited with earnings equal to the lower earnings limit for each complete week during which you either:[50]

- are entitled to statutory sick pay (SSP); *or*
- have limited capability for work; *or*
- would have had limited capability for work for contributory ESA, had you been entitled to it (even if the reason you are not entitled to contributory ESA is because of the 365-day limit – see p640) or would have had limited capability for work had you claimed ESA or maternity allowance (MA) in time; *or*
- were incapable of work or could be treated as such, or you would have been had you made a claim for incapacity benefit (IB) or MA. For information on incapacity for work, see p683 of the 2013/14 edition of this *Handbook*.

You cannot qualify for these credits for weeks in which you are entitled to UC (you must have claimed it), unless you are also entitled to ESA, SSP, MA, IB or severe disablement allowance in those weeks. You also cannot qualify for these credits for days on which you were treated as not having limited capability for work (see p992) or not being incapable of work (or days on which you would have been, had you otherwise been entitled to ESA or IB).

These credits are awarded automatically if you get ESA or MA. You can apply for ESA, even if you are not entitled to the benefit, and maintain a 'credits only' claim for limited capability for work (but see p22 on coming under the UC system as a result of claiming ESA). To apply for credits on the basis that you get SSP, write to HMRC (see p952). In other circumstances, you must apply to Jobcentre Plus. Unless the credits are awarded automatically, you must apply for them before the end of the benefit year (ie, by the first Saturday in January – see p965) following the tax year in which you are entitled to the credit. This time limit can be extended if it is considered reasonable to do so, given your circumstances.

Credits for universal credit

These credits can help you meet the contribution conditions for widowed parent's allowance and state pension. They also count for category A and B retirement pensions. They are awarded automatically.

If you are entitled to UC for at least part of a week, you can be credited with a class 3 contribution for that week.[51]

If you are not entitled to UC because your income and/or capital is too high and you are looking for work or have limited capability for work, you should consider making a 'credits only' claim for JSA (see p955) or ESA (see p956).

Credits for certain parents and carers

These credits can help you meet the contribution conditions for widowed parent's allowance and state pension. They also count for category A and B retirement pensions.

You can be credited with a class 3 contribution for each week which falls after 6 April 2010 if:

- for any part of the week, you are awarded child benefit for a child under the age of 12;[52] *or*
- you reside with someone who, for any part of the week, is awarded child benefit for a child aged under 12 and:
  - you share responsibility with that person for a child under 12; *and*
  - in the tax year to which the credit relates, the person awarded child benefit has paid or been credited with NI contributions with an earnings factor of more than 52 times that year's lower earnings limit (see Appendix 6). In calculating this, any credits s/he gets on the basis of the child benefit award are ignored.[53]

Note: in this situation, for weeks from 6 April 2016, the rules on when you qualify for a class 3 credit for state pension are different and indicate only that you must be the partner of someone who gets child benefit for a child, you must reside with your partner and you both must share the responsibility for the child. The rules do not expressly state that the child must be under 12 (although your partner still must have paid, or been credited with, sufficient NI contributions);[54] *or*

- in that week you are caring for someone for at least 20 hours, or for more than one person for a total of at least 20 hours and:[55]
  - the person(s) for whom you care is entitled to a qualifying benefit (see p958); *or*
  - the decision maker considers that the level of care provided is appropriate.

You can continue to qualify for these credits for 12 weeks after the week in which you stop satisfying this condition – this allows you to have breaks in caring of up to 12 weeks without losing credits; *or*

Part 7: National Insurance, work and work-related rules
Chapter 43: National insurance contributions
3. National insurance credits

- in that week you satisfy the conditions for carers who may qualify for income support (IS) described on p235 (the rules do not state that you must get IS to qualify for credits in this situation);[56] *or*
- for any part of the week, you are an approved foster parent or foster carer (including a kinship carer in Scotland);[57] *or*
- the week falls in the 12 weeks:[58]
  - before the date you become entitled to carer's allowance (CA); *or*
  - following the week in which you stop being entitled to CA (unless you already qualify for credits for CA for that week – see p960).

Qualifying benefit

A '**qualifying benefit**' includes the daily living components of personal independence payment and adult disability payment, attendance allowance, the middle or highest rate of disability living allowance care component, child disability payment care component, armed forces independence payment, constant attendance allowance in respect of an industrial or war disablement and certain payments under the Pneumoconiosis, Byssinosis and Miscellaneous Diseases Benefit Scheme or Workmen's Compensation (Supplementation) Scheme.[59]

Unless you are entitled on the basis that you are awarded child benefit for a child under 12, in most circumstances you must be ordinarily resident in Great Britain and not in prison or in legal custody to qualify for these credits.[60]

If you get child benefit, IS or CA, the credits are awarded automatically. If you qualify because you are caring for someone for at least 20 hours, apply to the DWP using a carer's credit application form (Form CC1). Otherwise apply to HMRC on Form CF411A. Both forms are available at gov.uk. Your application must be received before the end of the tax year following the tax year to which the credits relate. This time limit can be extended if the DWP or HMRC considers it reasonable in the circumstances.[61]

Note: you can qualify for these credits on the basis of an award of child benefit even if you (or the person with whom you reside) have elected not to receive the child benefit because of the high-income child benefit charge (see p582).

Credits for home responsibilities protection

Home responsibilities protection, which helped a contributor satisfy the contribution conditions for widowed parent's allowance and category A or B retirement pension, was abolished on 6 April 2010 and was replaced with NI credits for certain parents and carers (see p957). For further details, see p973 of the 2021/22 edition of this *Handbook*.

Credits for family members providing childcare

If you do not qualify for credits as a parent or a carer (see p957), these credits can help you meet the contribution conditions for widowed parent's allowance and state pension. They also count for category A retirement pension if you reached pension age on or after 6 April 2012 and for category B retirement pension in certain circumstances. See the 2015/16 edition of this *Handbook* for details.

From 6 April 2011, you can be credited with a class 3 contribution for each week during which you provide childcare for a child aged under 12, if:[62]

- you are a specified 'family member' of the child (you do not need to be a blood relative and many ex-family members count – see below); *and*
- someone has been awarded child benefit for the child for that week and, in the tax year in which that falls, her/his contribution record is sufficient for the year to count as a qualifying year for state pension (see p969). In calculating this, any credits s/he gets on the grounds of receiving child benefit for a child under 12 are ignored; *and*
- you are ordinarily resident in Great Britain (see p1550).

There is no set number of hours for which you must care for the child to qualify. Only one person can qualify for these credits for a particular week for the same child(ren) covered by a child benefit award. The credits are in respect of the child benefit award, and not per child. However, if childcare is shared, it may be possible for someone else to get credits for different weeks in a tax year.

You must apply to HMRC for these credits after the end of the tax year in question. There is no time limit for claiming.[63] Use Form CA9176 (for specified adult childcare credits), available at gov.uk.

Note: if you satisfy the qualifying conditions, you can still get these credits, even if the person entitled to child benefit elects not to receive it because of the high-income child benefit charge (see p582).

Family member

You count as a **'family member'** if you are:[64]

– the child's parent (from 6 April 2016 for state pension only, if you are her/his non-resident parent, but see p957 if you reside together), grandparent, great- or great-great-grandparent, sibling, aunt or uncle (including if you are an adopted, step- or half-sibling of the child or of the child's parent);

– a spouse or civil partner, or former spouse or civil partner, of any of the above relatives, or her/his son or daughter;

– a partner or former partner of any of the above (including, for instance, a former partner of a former spouse of one of the above relatives), or her/his son or daughter;

– the child's niece, nephew or first cousin;

– a spouse, civil partner or partner (or former spouse, civil partner or partner) of the child's first cousin.

A 'partner' is someone with whom the relative lives as if they were married or civil partners.

Part 7: National Insurance, work and work-related rules
Chapter 43: National insurance contributions
3. National insurance credits

Credits for carer's allowance

These credits can help you meet the contribution conditions for all contributory benefits, except bereavement support payment. They are awarded automatically.

You can be credited with earnings equal to the lower earnings limit for each week in which you receive CA (see Chapter 26), or would receive it but for the loss of benefit for benefit offences rules (see p1239).[65] You also receive credits if the only reason why you do not receive CA is because you are receiving widowed parent's allowance, bereavement allowance or a widow's benefit instead. **Note:** this does not apply to bereavement support payment, as you receive both CA and bereavement support payment at the same time.

If you are caring for someone but are not entitled to these credits, you may qualify for credits for certain carers (see p957).

Starting credits

These credits can help you meet the contribution conditions for widowed parent's allowance. They also count for category A and B retirement pensions and for calculating the transitional rate of state pension (see p969). They are awarded automatically.

You can receive class 3 credits for the tax years in which you reach the age of 16, 17 and 18 if you would otherwise have had an insufficient contribution record for those years to count towards the contribution conditions for the above benefits.[66]

However, for category A and B retirement pensions (and for calculating the transitional rate of state pension), you could only qualify for these credits:

- for tax years falling before 6 April 2010; *and*
- if you had to make an application for an NI number to be allocated to you, if your application for an NI number was made before 6 April 2010.

No credits were made under this provision for years before 6 April 1975.

Education and training credits

For the purpose of qualifying for contribution-based JSA and contributory ESA, you can be credited with earnings equal to the lower earnings limit for either one of the two complete tax years that fall before the relevant benefit year (see p965) if:

- for any part of those tax years you were on:[67]
  - a course of full-time training, including training to acquire occupational or vocational skills (or, if you are disabled, a part-time course of at least 15 hours a week); *or*
  - a course of full-time education; *or*
  - an apprenticeship; *and*

- in the other tax year in which you must satisfy the second contribution condition for the benefit (see p966), you have an earnings factor of 50 times the lower earnings limit without relying on this provision; *and*
- you were at least 18 (or you reached 18) in the tax year in question; *and*
- you were under 21 when the course or apprenticeship started; *and*
- your course of education, training or apprenticeship has finished.

You can receive credits which count for all contributory benefits (except bereavement support payment) for each week in which you are undertaking a training course approved by a DWP decision maker if:[68]
- in that week you were not entitled to UC – but see p957 for credits if you were entitled to UC. To be entitled to UC, you normally must have claimed it; *and*
- the training is full time (or at least 15 hours a week if you are disabled) or it is an introductory course; *and*
- the training is not part of your job; *and*
- the training is intended to last for one year or less (except in certain circumstances, if it is a course for disabled people); *and*
- you were 18 or over at the beginning of the tax year in which the week falls.

If the course was arranged by Jobcentre Plus, you get the credits automatically. Otherwise, you must apply by writing to HMRC (see p952).

Credits for statutory maternity, adoption, additional paternity, shared parental and parental bereavement pay

These credits can help you meet the contribution conditions for all contributory benefits, except bereavement support payment.

You can be credited with earnings equal to the lower earnings limit for each week for which you receive statutory maternity pay, statutory adoption pay, statutory shared parental pay or statutory parental bereavement pay or for which you received additional statutory paternity pay.[69]

To apply for these credits, write to HMRC (see p952). Your application must be received before the end of the benefit year (see p965) following the tax year in which the week falls, but this time limit may be extended if reasonable to do so.

Credits for jury service

These credits can help you meet the contribution conditions for all contributory benefits, except bereavement support payment.

You are entitled to be credited with earnings equal to the lower earnings limit for each week after 6 April 1988 during which you spend at least part of the week on jury service, unless you are self-employed in that week.[70]

To apply for these credits, write to HMRC (see p952). Your application must be received before the end of the benefit year (see p965) following the tax year in which the week falls (or such further period as is reasonable).

Part 7: National Insurance, work and work-related rules
Chapter 43: National insurance contributions
3. National insurance credits

Credits following bereavement

These credits help you meet the contribution conditions for contribution-based JSA and contributory ESA. They are awarded automatically.

If you were entitled to bereavement payment, widowed parent's allowance or bereavement allowance, you can be credited with sufficient earnings for each year up to and including the one in which your entitlement to any of those benefits stopped, to enable you to satisfy the second contribution condition for contribution-based JSA or contributory ESA.[71]

For the purpose of satisfying the second contribution condition for contributory ESA, you are also entitled to credits for each year up to and including the one in which your entitlement to widow's allowance (abolished in April 1988) or widowed mother's allowance ended.[72]

Credits for tax credits

These credits are awarded automatically.

For each week for which you receive, for any part of the week, the disabled worker element or severe disability element in working tax credit (WTC), you are entitled to be credited with earnings equal to the lower earnings limit. These credits count for all contributory benefits, except bereavement support payment.[73]

Alternatively, for each week for which you are paid WTC (without the disabled worker element or the severe disability element), you are credited with earnings equal to the lower earnings limit to help you satisfy the contribution conditions for widowed parent's allowance and state pension. They also count for category A and B retirement pensions. In this case, if WTC was paid to you as a member of a couple but only one of you has earnings, the credits are awarded to that person. If you both have earnings, they are awarded to the person to whom WTC is paid.[74]

You can only qualify for either of these credits during any week in which you were:[75]

- employed and earning less than the lower earnings limit (see p948); *or*
- self-employed but not liable to pay class 2 contributions because your profits were below the small profits threshold (see p949) or you had a small earnings exception. (It is not possible to have a small earnings exception for tax years from 2015/16. See the 2014/15 edition of this *Handbook* for further details); *or*
- self-employed but exempt from paying class 2 contributions because you were getting a particular benefit (see p949). However, this does not apply for category A and B retirement pensions and only applies for state pension for weeks which fall in a tax year from 6 April 2016 (provided you did not qualify for the disabled worker or severe disability element in your WTC), otherwise it applies for state pension and the other benefits for weeks from 1 January 2017.

Credits for a quashed conviction

These credits can help you meet the contribution conditions for all contributory benefits, except bereavement support payment.

If you were imprisoned or detained in legal custody after being convicted of an offence, and that conviction has subsequently been quashed by the courts, you can be credited with earnings for each week during at least part of which you were imprisoned or detained.[76]

To apply for these credits, write to HMRC (see p952).

Credits for service families

These credits can help you meet the contribution conditions for all contributory benefits, except bereavement support payment.

From 6 April 2010, you can be credited with earnings equal to that year's lower earnings limit for each week during any part of which you were:[77]

- the spouse or civil partner of a member of the armed forces (or someone treated as such for the purpose of occupying accommodation); *and*
- accompanying, or were treated as accompanying, her/him on an assignment outside the UK.

You must usually apply for these class 1 credits on the approved form (Form MODCA1, available at gov.uk), once you have a confirmed date for the end of the overseas posting and before the end of the tax year following the tax year in which the overseas assignment ended. This time limit can be extended if it is reasonable, given your circumstances.

The decision maker has discretion to accept an application made before you receive confirmation of the end date of the overseas assignment. If your application is accepted, you can be awarded credits for the period before your application, but you must make a further application under these rules for credits for any subsequent period.

Alternatively, to help you meet the contribution conditions for state pension only, you can be credited with a class 3 contribution for each week in any tax year from 6 April 1975 in which, for at least part of the week, you meet the above conditions, provided the member of the armed forces you were accompanying had paid or been credited with sufficient NI contributions for that year to count as a qualifying year (see p969).[78] In this situation, you must normally apply for the credits on the approved form. There is an online form at gov.uk. Applications can only be made for a past period.

Note: in respect of years from 6 April 2010, claim the class 1 credits if you satisfy the conditions for them, as they count towards the contribution conditions for more benefits – the class 3 credits only count for state pension.

Part 7: National Insurance, work and work-related rules
Chapter 43: National insurance contributions
4. Contribution conditions for benefits

4. **Contribution conditions for benefits**

Entitlement to contributory benefits normally depends on the national insurance (NI) contribution conditions being met.

- **For state pension**, your entitlement is based on your own NI contribution record. However, in some cases, for the transitional rate of state pension, the amount you receive depends on the contribution record of your spouse or civil partner (or your late or former spouse or civil partner) (see p768).
- **For contribution-based jobseeker's allowance (JSA) and contributory employment and support allowance (ESA)**, your entitlement is based on your own NI contribution record (unless you qualify for contributory ESA without needing to satisfy the contribution conditions).
- **For bereavement support payment and widowed parent's allowance**, the relevant 'contributor' is your late spouse or civil partner.

You may be credited with earnings or contributions to fill gaps in your contribution record (see p954).

NI contributions normally cannot count for benefit purposes until after they have been paid (if they are paid late, see p953). However, in some circumstances, your entitlement to benefit, or the amount of benefit you are entitled to, may depend on class 2 or 3 contributions which you have not yet paid because the due date for their payment has not been reached (see p953). In this situation, provided you pay the contributions by the due date, they can be treated as having being paid earlier.[79] If you claimed benefit before paying the contributions, once you have paid them the earlier decision on your claim can be revised to take account of the contributions.[80] See p968 for details of this rule in relation to contribution-based JSA and contributory ESA. For other benefits, this may not apply if you are late in notifying HM Revenue and Customs (HMRC) of your self-employment.

If you reached pension age before 6 April 2016, see the 2015/16 edition of this *Handbook* for the contribution conditions for category A and B retirement pensions. The contribution conditions for bereavement payment, bereavement allowance, incapacity benefit and widow's pension are covered in previous editions of this *Handbook*.

It may be possible for you to rely on the contributions you have paid in other European Economic Area states to qualify for contributory benefits (see p1643).

If you are a woman who has paid reduced-rate NI contributions, see p769 for how your state pension is calculated.

Jobseeker's allowance and employment and support allowance

Contribution-based JSA and contributory ESA have two contribution conditions relating to the two complete tax years falling immediately before the 'relevant benefit year'. If you claim in 2022, you must satisfy the contribution conditions for the tax years 2019/20 and 2020/21.

Tax and relevant benefit years

A '**tax year**' runs from 6 April to 5 April the following year.

A '**benefit year**' is almost the same as a calendar year and runs from the first Sunday in January.[81]

The '**relevant benefit year**' is usually the calendar year during which you meet the entitlement conditions and submit a claim for contribution-based JSA or contributory ESA. However:

- for contribution-based JSA, if it is earlier than the year in which you make your claim, the relevant benefit year is the benefit year in which a period that is linked to the current jobseeking period began (see p689);
- for contributory ESA, if you otherwise would not meet the contribution conditions for contributory ESA, your relevant benefit year can be any benefit year which includes any part of your current period of limited capability for work (or any part of any period(s) of limited capability for work that can be linked to your current period – see p1018). **Note:** a period of limited capability for work cannot include a period that falls before the three-month time limit for backdating an ESA claim.[82]

When the contribution conditions do not apply

You can qualify for contributory ESA without having to satisfy the contribution conditions if[83] your contributory ESA ended because you had received it for 365 days in the circumstances described on p640, you continued to have (or be treated as having) limited capability for work after your entitlement ended and you now have, or are treated as having, limited capability for work-related activity (see p1004). In this situation, you can qualify for contributory ESA again without having to satisfy the contribution conditions. If you previously claimed incapacity benefit or severe disablement benefit, different rules may allow you to claim ESA without meeting the contributions conditions in the relevant year (see p980 of the 2021/22 edition of this *Handbook*).

The first condition: paid contributions

You must have paid, or regarding class 1 contributions be treated as having paid (see p948), at least 26 weeks' contributions on earnings at the lower earnings limit in one of the last two complete tax years immediately before the relevant benefit year.[84]

Lower earnings limits

2019/20	£118
2020/21	£120
2021/22	£120
2022/23	£123

Example

If Lexi makes a claim in 2022, she meets the first condition if she earned at least £118 a week for 26 weeks between 6 April 2019 and 5 April 2020, or at least £120 a week for 26 weeks between 6 April 2020 and 5 April 2021.

Part 7: National Insurance, work and work-related rules
Chapter 43: National insurance contributions
4. Contribution conditions for benefits

Note:
- The 26 weeks do not need to be consecutive, but must fall in a single tax year.
- For contribution-based JSA, only class 1 contributions count towards meeting this condition (unless you are a share fisherman or volunteer development worker, when special class 2 contributions also count). For ESA, both class 1 and class 2 contributions count.[85]

When the first condition is relaxed

In some situations, the first contribution condition is relaxed, so that sufficient contributions paid in *any* one tax year are enough to satisfy the condition, provided they were paid, or treated as paid (see p968), before the week for which you are claiming the benefit.

For contribution-based JSA and contributory ESA, this applies if you were entitled to credits for service families (see p963) in at least one week in the tax year before the relevant benefit year (see p965).[86]

For contributory ESA, it also applies if you:[87]
- were entitled to carer's allowance in the last complete tax year before the relevant benefit year (even if it was not paid because of the overlapping benefit rules – see p1151); *or*
- were entitled to NI credits for a quashed conviction at some time in any tax year before the relevant benefit year (or you would have been entitled to such credits had you claimed them); *or*
- were in full-time paid work (see p284) for more than two years immediately before your period of limited capability for work began and you were entitled to working tax credit which included a disabled worker or severe disability element (see p1420 and p1422).

The second condition: paid or credited contributions

You must have paid, or regarding class 1 contributions be treated as having paid (see p948), contributions or received NI credits on earnings of at least 50 times the lower earnings limit in each of the two complete tax years immediately before the relevant benefit year.[88]

* * *

Example

If Gabriel makes a claim in 2022, he meets the second condition if he paid (or is treated as having paid) contributions on total earnings of at least £5,900 (50 x £118) in 2019/20, and of at least £6,000 (50 x £120) in 2020/21.

* * *

Note:
- Only certain NI credits count towards meeting this condition – eg, credited class 3 contributions do not count (see pp954–63).

- To count, any paid contributions must be class 1 contributions (or special class 2 contributions – see p949) for contribution-based JSA, or class 1 or 2 contributions for contributory ESA.[89]
- For class 2 contributions, you must have paid at least 50 contributions in each of the two complete tax years – this condition cannot be satisfied by having reached this earnings level over fewer weeks.
- To satisfy this condition with NI credits, you must have been awarded them for at least 50 weeks during each of the two years.

The timing of your claim

In rare cases, it may be beneficial for you to delay a claim for contribution-based JSA so that you can draw on a different year's contribution record. This is because the years in which you must meet the contribution conditions depend on the benefit year in which your jobseeking period starts. So, for example, if your current jobseeking period is not linked to an earlier one (see p689) and you claim before 1 January 2023, you must meet the contribution conditions in the tax years 2019/20 and 2020/21, whereas if you claim on or after 1 January 2023, you must meet them in 2020/21 and 2021/22.

Any day for which you do not claim does not count as part of your jobseeking period (see p689),[90] so it is easy to postpone when that period begins. However, if you claim and are refused benefit because the contribution conditions are not satisfied, your jobseeking period will have started. You must then normally wait for more than 12 weeks to make a fresh claim. The 12-week gap breaks the jobseeking period.

The situation is different for contributory ESA. If your claim for contributory ESA is refused only on the grounds that you do not meet the contribution conditions, in some cases it can be worth making a later claim that falls in a different benefit year (see p965).

Example

Nita lives with her partner who works full time. Nita was self-employed and paid class 2 NI contributions throughout the tax years 2019/20 and 2020/21 (in the tax year 2018/19 she did not pay NI contributions or get NI credits). In December 2021, she became ill and claimed contributory ESA for the first time. The relevant benefit year was 2021 and the two complete tax years falling before that are 2018/19 and 2019/20. Having no contributions or credits for 2018/19, Nita was refused contributory ESA. If she claims again in the 2022 benefit year (which started on 2 January 2022), the contributions she paid in 2019/20 and 2020/21 are counted and she may qualify for contributory ESA. The rules allow 2022 to count as her relevant benefit year because part of her period of limited capability for work falls in that year.

Part 7: National Insurance, work and work-related rules
Chapter 43: National insurance contributions
4. Contribution conditions for benefits

Class 2 contributions treated as paid earlier

Since 6 April 2015, because the deadline for payment of class 2 contributions for a tax year is 31 January after the end of that year, your entitlement to contributory ESA (or contribution-based JSA on the basis of special class 2 contributions) may depend on class 2 contributions that are not yet due to be paid. If you claim benefit before paying the contributions, your claim may be refused because you do not meet the contribution conditions. You can choose to pay class 2 contributions early to try to avoid this problem – if you do, write to HMRC to ensure it knows the payment you are making is intended to be an early payment of class 2 contributions. Alternatively, provided you pay the contributions by 31 January, they can be treated as having been paid on an earlier date to enable you to qualify for contribution-based JSA or contributory ESA from a date before they were actually paid.[91]

Example

Eloise is self-employed and lives with her partner who works full time. Eloise becomes ill and unable to work on 8 January 2022 and claims ESA on the same day. Her relevant benefit year is 2022. The tax years in which she must have met the contribution conditions for contributory ESA are 2019/20 and 2020/21. Although she paid class 2 contributions for each week in 2019/20, her claim for contributory ESA is refused because she has not yet submitted her self-assessment tax return for 2020/21 and has not paid class 2 contributions for that tax year. On 29 January 2022, she submits her self-assessment return and pays class 2 contributions for 2020/21. She asks the DWP to reconsider the decision to refuse her contributory ESA. As Eloise paid her class 2 contributions by the due date (31 January 2022), they can be treated as having been paid before 8 January 2022. The earlier decision to refuse her claim is revised and she is awarded contributory ESA.

Bereavement support payment

To satisfy the contribution condition for bereavement support payment, your late spouse or civil partner must have paid NI contributions on earnings of at least 25 times that year's lower earnings limit – eg, £3,075 in 2022/23: 25 x £123.

This condition must be met in any one tax year in your late spouse's or civil partner's working life, but only class 1 or 2 NI contributions count (see p985 in the 2021/22 edition of this *Handbook* for the meaning of 'working life').[92]

If your spouse or civil partner died before 6 April 2017, you may be entitled to widowed parent's allowance (or may have been entitled to bereavement payment and bereavement allowance). For details of the contribution conditions for bereavement payment and bereavement allowance, see the 2017/18 edition of this *Handbook*.

Widowed parent's allowance

There are two contribution conditions for widowed parent's allowance. **Note:** you can only qualify for this benefit if your late spouse or civil partner died before 6 April 2017. See p984 of the 2021/22 edition of this *Handbook* for further details.

Retirement pensions

If you reached pension age before 6 April 2016, you are not entitled to state pension but may be entitled to category A or B retirement pension instead.[93] For the NI contribution conditions for category A and B retirement pensions, see the 2015/16 edition of this *Handbook*.

State pension

If you reach pension age on or after 6 April 2016 (ie, if you are a woman born on or after 6 April 1953 or a man born on or after 6 April 1951), you may be entitled to state pension (see Chapter 36).

Your entitlement to state pension and the amount you receive depends on the number of NI 'qualifying years' you have.

Qualifying years[94]

A **'qualifying year'** is a tax year in your working life in which you have paid class 1, 2 or 3 NI contributions or received NI credits which, in total, produced an earnings factor of at least 52 times that year's lower earnings limit – eg, £6,396 in 2022/23: 52 x £123. Most, but not all, kinds of NI credits can be counted. For tax years before 6 April 1978, contributions or credits must have been paid on earnings of at least 50 times that year's lower earnings limit for the year to count as a qualifying year.[95]

To qualify for state pension, you must have at least 10 qualifying years (but see below if you paid a reduced rate of NI contributions as a married woman).[96]

If one of your qualifying years is a tax year before 6 April 2016, your entitlement to state pension is calculated at the transitional rate (see below).[97]

Note:

- If you have paid reduced-rate NI contributions as a married woman or widow and your election to pay at a reduced rate was in force at the start of the 35-year period which ends in the tax year before you reach pension age, you do not need to have 10 qualifying years to qualify for state pension.[98] See p769 for how your entitlement is calculated.
- If your spouse or civil partner has died, you may qualify for an amount of state pension based on her/his contribution record. See p769 for details.

The transitional rate of state pension

If at least one of your qualifying years falls before 6 April 2016, your entitlement to state pension is assessed at the transitional rate. The amount you receive

Part 7: National Insurance, work and work-related rules
Chapter 43: National insurance contributions
Notes

depends on your 'starting amount'. Your starting amount is based on your contribution record up to 6 April 2016, and is the greater of either:[99]

- the weekly amount of basic category A retirement pension, additional state pension and graduated retirement benefit you would have qualified for had you reached pension age on 6 April 2016 and had the new state pension scheme not been introduced. See below for how your basic category A retirement pension is calculated and the 2015/16 edition of this *Handbook* for details of additional state pension and graduated retirement benefit; *or*
- the weekly amount of state pension you would be entitled to on 6 April 2016 if you reached pension age on that date, using the number of qualifying years you had up to that date (see p969). You are entitled to the full rate of state pension if you have at least 35 qualifying years in your working life. If you have less than 35 qualifying years (but at least 10), you build up one thirty-fifth of the full weekly rate of state pension for each of your qualifying years.

If you have been contracted out of the state second pension scheme, the above amounts are adjusted to reflect this.

See p768 for further details of how the transitional rate of state pension is calculated.

Note: if your spouse or civil partner has died, you may qualify for an inherited amount of state pension based on her/his contribution record (see p769).

Notes

1. **National insurance contributions and contributory benefits**
   1 s11 SSC(TF)A 1999; Part III SSC(DA) Regs; arts 6(c)(i) and 7 The First-tier Tribunal and Upper Tribunal (Chambers) Order 2010 No.2655
   2 Sch 3 para 17 SSA 1998; s17 SSC(TF)A 1999; arts 2-4 The National Insurance Contribution Credits (Transfer of Functions) Order 2009 No.1377

2. **Paid national insurance contributions**
   3 s1(2) SSCBA 1992
   4 ss6(1) and (3) and 11(7) SSCBA 1992
   5 s13 SSCBA 1992; regs 48(1) and 49(1)(f) and (2A)-(2C) SS(Con) Regs
   6 s2(1) SSCBA 1992

   7 *Ready Mix Concrete South East Ltd v Ministry of Pensions and National Insurance* [1968] 2 QB 497 (QBD); *Global Plant v Secretary of State for Health and Social Security* [1971] 3 All ER 385 (QBD)
   8 Sch 1 paras 1-5A SS(CatE) Regs; *ITV Services Ltd v HMRC* [2012] UKUT 47 (TCC)
   9 Sch 1 paras 6 SS(CatE) Regs
   10 Sch 1 paras 7-12 SS(CatE) Regs
   11 Regs 13, 14, 15 and 21 SS(Con) Regs
   12 Sch 1 para 1 SSCBA 1992; regs 13, 14, 15 and 21 SS(Con) Regs
   13 Reg 21 SS(Con) Regs
   14 ss6 and 7 SSCBA 1992
   15 ss6 and 6A SSCBA 1992

16 s8 SSCBA 1992
17 Reg 131 SS(Con) Regs
18 Sch 1 para 3 SSCBA 1992
19 Reg 60 SS(Con) Regs
20 s11 SSCBA 1992; reg 43 SS(Con) Regs
21 s11(5) SSCBA 1992
22 s11(6) SSCBA 1992; reg 43 SS(Con) Regs
23 s11(2) SSCBA 1992
24 Reg 127(1) SS(Con) Regs
25 Regs 125, 149, 151 and 152 SS(Con) Regs
26 Regs 1(2) and 90ZA SS(Con) Regs
27 s13 SSCBA 1992
28 s14 SSCBA 1992; reg 49 SS(Con) Regs
29 s13(1) SSCBA 1992
30 Reg 127 SS(Con) Regs
31 Regs 128(1) and 130 SS(Con) Regs
32 ss2(1), 6 and 11 SSCBA 1992; reg 145(1)(a), (c), (d) and (2) SS(Con) Regs
33 Reg 145(1)(c) and (e) SS(Con) Regs
34 Reg 146 SS(Con) Regs
35 Regs 147 and 148 SS(Con) Regs
36 Regs 149 and 151 SS(Con) Regs
37 Regs 146(2)(b), 147 and 148 SS(Con) Regs
38 s11(6) SSCBA 1992; regs 43(3), 48 and 49 SS(Con) Regs
39 Reg 62 SS(Con) Regs
40 Reg 60 SS(Con) Regs; reg 5 SS(CTCNIN) Regs
41 Reg 1(2) SS(CTCNIN) Regs
42 Reg 4 SS(CTCNIN) Regs; reg 48(3)(b) SS(Con) Regs
43 Reg 4(7) and (8) SS(CTCNIN) Regs
44 Regs 50 and 61 SS(Con) Regs; regs 4(11), 5A, 6, 6A and 6B SS(CTCNIN) Regs
45 Regs 50C and 61B SS(Con) Regs

3. National insurance credits
46 Reg 3 SS(Cr) Regs; reg 25(2) SP Regs
47 Regs 8D, 8E and 8F SS(Cr) Regs
48 Reg 8A SS(Cr) Regs; regs 26 and 29 SP Regs
49 Reg 8A(5) SS(Cr) Regs; regs 26 and 29 SP Regs
50 Reg 8B SS(Cr) Regs; regs 26 and 29 SP Regs
51 Reg 8G SS(Cr) Regs; regs 26 and 31 SP Regs
52 s23A(2) and (3)(a) SSCBA 1992; regs 27 and 34(1)(a) SP Regs
53 s23A(2) and (3)(c) SSCBA 1992; regs 2, 5(1)(a), 6 and 9 SS(CCPC) Regs; reg 27 SP Regs
54 Reg 34(1)(b) and (2)-(4) SP Regs
55 s23A(2) and (3)(c) SSCBA 1992; regs 5(1)(b) and 7(1)(c) SS(CCPC) Regs; regs 27, 37(1) and (2)(a) and 38(1)(c) SP Regs
56 s23A(2) and (3)(c) SSCBA 1992; reg 5(1)(c) SS(CCPC) Regs; reg 37(1) and (2)(b) SP Regs
57 s23A(2) and (3)(b) SSCBA 1992; reg 4 SS(CCPC) Regs; reg 36 SP Regs
58 Reg 7 SS(CCPC) Regs; reg 38(1)(a) and (b) and (2) SP Regs
59 Reg 2 SS(CCPC) Regs; reg 37(4) SP Regs
60 Reg 8 SS(CCPC) Regs; regs 34(2), 36(1) and 37(3) SP Regs
61 Regs 9-12 SS(CCPC) Regs; regs 34(2)(e), 36(3), 37(5) and (6) and 39(a) SP Regs
62 Reg 9F SS(Cr) Regs; reg 26 and 35 SP Regs
63 Reg 9F(8) SS(Cr) Regs; reg 39(b) SP Regs
64 Sch SS(Cr) Regs; reg 35(6)-(8) SP Regs
65 Reg 7A SS(Cr) Regs; regs 26 and 29 SP Regs
66 Reg 4 SS(Cr) Regs; reg 26 SP Regs
67 Reg 8 SS(Cr) Regs
68 Reg 7 SS(Cr) Regs; regs 26 and 29 SP Regs
69 Reg 9C SS(Cr) Regs; regs 26 and 29 SP Regs
70 Reg 9B SS(Cr) Regs; regs 26 and 29 SP Regs
71 Reg 8C SS(Cr) Regs
72 Reg 3(1)(b) SSB(MW&WSP) Regs
73 Reg 7B SS(Cr) Regs; regs 26 and 29 SP Regs
74 Reg 7C SS(Cr) Regs; regs 26 and 30 SP Regs
75 Regs 7B(2) and 7C(1) SS(Cr) Regs; regs 26, 29 and 30(1) SP Regs
76 Reg 9D SS(Cr) Regs; regs 26 and 29 SP Regs
77 Reg 9E SS(Cr) Regs; regs 26 and 29 SP Regs
78 Regs 28 and 33 SP Regs

4. Contribution conditions for benefits
79 Regs 7(1) and 7A SS(CTCNIN) Regs
80 Reg 3(8J) and (8K) SS&CS(DA) Regs
81 s21(6) SSCBA 1992; s2(4) JSA 1995; Sch 1 para 3 WRA 2007
82 Sch 1 para 3(1)(f) WRA 2007; regs 2(1) and 13 ESA Regs; regs 2 and 14 ESA Regs 2013
83 s1B WRA 2007; Sch 2 paras 2 and 15 ESA(TP)(EA)(No.2) Regs
84 **JSA** ss1(2)(d) and 2(1)(a) JSA 1995
   ESA Sch 1 para 1 WRA 2007

Part 7: National Insurance, work and work-related rules
Chapter 43: National insurance contributions
Notes

85 **JSA** ss1(2)(d) and 2 JSA 1995; regs 45A,
158 and 167 JSA Regs; regs 34, 69 and
75 JSA Regs 2013
ESA Sch 1 para 1 WRA 2007; reg 7 ESA
Regs; reg 8 ESA Regs 2013

86 Reg 45B JSA Regs; reg 8(2)(ca) ESA Regs;
reg 35 JSA Regs 2013; reg 9(2)(d) ESA
Regs 2013

87 Reg 8 ESA Regs; reg 9 ESA Regs 2013

88 **JSA** ss1(2)(d) and 2(1)(b) JSA 1995
ESA Sch 1 para 2 WRA 2007

89 s2 JSA 1995; Sch 1 para 2 WRA 2007;
regs 158 and 167 JSA Regs; regs 69 and
75 JSA Regs 2013

90 Reg 47(3)(a) JSA Regs; reg 37(2)(a) JSA
Regs 2013

91 Reg 7A SS(CTCNIN) Regs; reg 3(8E)
SS&CS(DA) Regs; reg 17(3)
UC,PIP,JSA&ESA(DA) Regs

92 s31 PA 2014

93 s1 PA 2014

94 s2(4) PA 2014

95 s4(4) and (5) PA 2014

96 Reg 13 SP Regs

97 s4(1)(c) PA 2014

98 s11(1) PA 2014

99 s5 and Sch 1 PA 2014

7

Chapter 44

. . . .

Work and benefits

This chapter covers:
1. The meanings of 'paid work', 'full-time paid work' and 'hours' (p974)
2. How work affects universal credit (p977)
3. How work affects other means-tested benefits (p977)
4. How work affects non-means-tested benefits (p981)
5. People involved in trade disputes (p982)

This chapter explains which benefits you can receive while you are in paid work. It also examines how benefits are affected when a partner, or somebody else living with you, works.

This chapter does not explain how earnings affect the calculation of benefits. For these rules, see the relevant chapter in this *Handbook* for each specific benefit.

This chapter does not cover the rules for tax credits (see Chapters 14 and 15).

Key facts
- You can qualify for universal credit if you or your partner are in paid work, with a limited exception for housing costs help for owner-occupiers.
- You cannot usually get income-based jobseeker's allowance if you or your partner are in full-time paid work.
- You cannot usually get income support if you or your partner are in full-time paid work.
- You cannot usually get income-related employment and support allowance if you are working, or if your partner is in full-time paid work.
- You can qualify for housing benefit and pension credit while working.
- Entitlement to some non-means-tested benefits is affected by work.
- Your benefits might be affected if you are (or a member of your household is) involved in a trade dispute.

Part 7: National Insurance, work and work-related rules
Chapter 44: Work and benefits
1. The meanings of 'paid work', 'full-time paid work' and 'hours'

1. The meanings of 'paid work', 'full-time paid work' and 'hours'

Universal credit

For universal credit (UC), 'paid work' means work for which you are paid, or which you do in expectation of payment, even if you never receive any. This applies both to employed earners and to self-employed people. Paid work does not include volunteering or pro-bono work for which you are not paid or are only paid expenses.[1] 'Full-time work' and 'hours' have not been defined for UC purposes.

Note: it is possible that caselaw relating to other benefits can be used to interpret the meanings of 'paid work' and 'hours' for UC, but this approach should be taken with care. Get advice if you are in doubt.

Other means-tested benefits

For means-tested benefits other than UC, the following meanings apply. Except where otherwise stated, these apply both for employed earners and self-employed people.

Paid work

'Paid work' is work for which you are paid, or which you do in expectation of payment, even if you never actually receive any.[2] Whether or not you are in 'paid work' should be decided at the time the work is done, not later with hindsight.[3] An expectation of payment needs to be realistic and not just a hope or desire to make money.[4] Payment includes payment in kind, such as meals, accommodation or produce.[5]

If you are self-employed, the DWP counts drawings from your business to meet living expenses (in cash or in kind) as payment for work, unless the drawings are from the business capital.[6] If you simply invest in a business and do not help to run it, you are not treated as self-employed.[7] If your business is not yet, or has stopped being, profitable, this might raise questions about whether you are really working in expectation of payment.[8]

Full-time paid work

'Full-time paid work', also called 'remunerative work', means different things for different benefits. These benefit-specific definitions are in sections 2 and 3 of this chapter.

Some general rules apply to income support (IS), income-based jobseeker's allowance (JSA) and income-related employment and support allowance (ESA). For these benefits, you, your partner and your non-dependant (or, for ESA, just your partner and non-dependant) are not be treated as being in full-time paid work if you (or s/he) are:[9]

- working on a training scheme and being paid a training allowance under specific provisions; *or*
- volunteering or working pro bono, other than for a relative, and receiving no payment or only expenses; *or*
- caring for someone who is staying with you but is not normally a member of your household, and receiving payments from a health authority, local authority, or voluntary organisation, or from the person concerned under section 26(3A) of the National Assistance Act 1948, for caring for her/him; *or*
- a foster carer (or, in Scotland only, a kinship carer) receiving a payment from a local authority or voluntary organisation for a child you are looking after; *or*
- working as a part-time firefighter, auxiliary coastguard, member of the Reserve Army or reserve forces, or member of a lifeboat crew; *or*
- performing duties as a local authority councillor; *or*
- engaged in an activity for which you receive, or expect to receive, an award from UK Sport and no other payment; *or*
- a student doing work in connection with your course;[10] *or*
- on maternity, adoption, paternity, shared parental or parental bereavement leave, or absent from work due to sickness, even if you normally work 16/24 hours or more each week.[11]

Hours

The hours you are classed as working include:
- all hours actually worked for (or in expectation of) payment; *and*
- hours from all jobs; *and*
- overtime that you do routinely.

For IS, JSA and income-related ESA only, paid lunch hours and breaks count towards your total hours.[12]

If you are self-employed, your hours include all those necessary to run your business. This includes time spent producing or selling goods, or providing services, for which you are paid, but can also include time spent on other tasks such as visiting potential customers, providing estimates, advertising, book-keeping, buying, cleaning and doing research.[13] The decision maker should accept your account of what is necessary to run your business unless there is a reason for doubt.[14] Note that some of the initial unpaid work necessary to set up a business might not count as hours of paid work.[15] During periods when you are not in work, or if you have ceased trading, you should not count as being in work.[16]

Fluctuating hours

If your (or your partner's or your non-dependant's) hours fluctuate, there are rules on how they should be averaged.

Part 7: National Insurance, work and work-related rules
Chapter 44: Work and benefits
1. The meanings of 'paid work', 'full-time paid work' and 'hours'

- **Regular pattern of work.** If there is a regular pattern of work (a 'work cycle'), the average hours worked throughout that cycle are used. For example, if you regularly work three weeks and then have one week off, your hours are averaged over the four-week period (the work cycle).[17] For weeks when you are on paid holiday, off sick, on maternity, adoption, paternity, shared parental or parental bereavement leave, or absent from work without a good reason, the hours you would otherwise have worked are included when calculating your average hours.[18]

- **If there is no regular patten of work.** If there is no recognisable work cycle, your hours are calculated using the average over the five weeks immediately before the date of claim (or supersession), or the average over a different period if this would give a more representative figure.[19] If you are self-employed, this may well be an accounting year.

- **No work pattern yet established.** This might be the case in a new job. In this instance, your hours are calculated as the number (or average number) of hours you are expected to work each week.[20] Once you have more evidence about your average hours, the decision can be revised or superseded.

- **Seasonal or term-time only work.** If your (or your partner's or non-dependant's) work is casual or intermittent, you can usually argue that your hours should only count during the period when you are actually working. For example, if you are a seasonal worker who only works in the summer, you can argue that you should not be treated as working the same hours throughout the rest of the year.[21]

  However, this might not be the case for IS, pension credit (PC) or housing benefit (HB) if you have a recognisable year-long work cycle, with periods when you do not work. In this situation, the average number of hours you work is calculated across your year-long work cycle. This figure determines whether you count as being in full-time paid work, even during your non-working, non-paid periods.[22] This is known as the 'term-time only' worker rule. It affects people who work in schools and colleges, and may also affect those doing other seasonal jobs.

Examples

Leo, a shop worker, works two 7.5 hour shifts each week, on Monday and Wednesday. Every three weeks he works two additional weekend shifts. These are also 7.5 hours each. Over his work cycle of three weeks, Leo therefore works a total of 60 hours. This means that his average working week is 20 hours.

Tina is a school meals worker. She works 22.5 hours a week, 38 weeks of the year. She gets four weeks' paid holiday, but otherwise is not paid when she is not working at the school. She wants to know if she can claim IS during the weeks of the year when she does not get paid. The term-time only rule applies, so Tina's average hours are calculated as follows:

22.5 hours x 38 weeks = 855 hours. 52 weeks – 4 weeks' paid holiday = 48 weeks. 855 hours divided by 48 weeks = 17.81 average hours a week.

Tina cannot get IS as her average weekly hours are too high.

See p981 for what these terms mean for non-means-tested benefits.

2. How work affects universal credit

You can qualify for universal credit (UC) whether or not you, your partner or anybody else in your household does paid work. This applies to employed earners and self-employed people.

However, any earnings might reduce your UC entitlement to nil. See Chapter 7 for how earned income affects the amount of your UC.

There are also some elements of UC which have eligibility rules based on work status.

- You cannot get the housing costs element of UC for payments you make as an owner-occupier if you or your partner have any earnings, no matter how low these are (see p83).
- You can usually only get the childcare costs element of UC if you are working, have an offer of work, or your work very recently ended (see p73).[23]

You are treated as being in work or receiving earned income if you are getting statutory sick pay, statutory maternity, adoption, paternity, shared parental or parental bereavement pay, or (for childcare costs only) maternity allowance.[24] See p974 for what else counts as paid work for UC.

Work can also affect deductions being made from your UC for third-party debts (see p1165). Certain deductions should stop when your earnings (or, if you have a partner, your combined earnings) equal or exceed your work allowance for three monthly assessment periods.

Work can determine whether your UC award will be subject to the benefit cap (see p1156).

3. How work affects other means-tested benefits

Except where otherwise stated, the rules in this section apply to both employed and self-employed people.

Note: having a non-dependant who is in full-time paid work does not affect your eligibility for the following benefits, but it might lead to higher non-

Part 7: National Insurance, work and work-related rules
Chapter 44: Work and benefits
3. How work affects other means-tested benefits

dependant deductions (see p349 and p200). For all of the following benefits, your non-dependant generally counts as being in full-time paid work if s/he works 16 hours or more a week.[25] See p975 for how hours are calculated.

Income support

You cannot usually get income support (IS) if you or your partner are in full-time paid work.[26] For IS, this generally means:
- you are working 16 hours or more a week;[27] *or*
- your partner is working 24 hours or more a week.[28]

See p975 for how hours are calculated. For IS, the 'term-time only' worker rule can apply (see p976).

You, your partner or your non-dependant can *also* be treated as in full-time paid work if you (or s/he) are:
- normally in full-time work, but currently on holiday and intending to resume work once the holiday is over.[29] You can argue that you only count as being on holiday if you are paid for it;[30] *or*
- absent from full-time paid work without a good reason;[31] *or*
- no longer in full-time paid work but still within the period covered by certain holiday pay or payments in lieu.[32] See also p408.

You, your partner or your non-dependant are *not* treated as being in full-time paid work if you (or s/he) are:
- in any of the categories on p974; *or*
- an unpaid carer for someone for whom it would be possible to qualify for IS as a carer (see p235); *or*
- working as a childminder in your (or her/his) own home;[33] *or*
- able to qualify for housing costs run-on (see p359).

Even if you are eligible for IS, any earnings might reduce your entitlement to nil. See Chapter 20 for how earned income affects the amount of your IS.

Jobseeker's allowance

You cannot usually get income-based jobseeker's allowance (JSA) if you or your partner are in full-time paid work.[34] For JSA, this generally means:[35]
- you are working 16 hours or more a week; *or*
- if you have a joint JSA claim, your partner is working 16 hours or more a week. You do not have to make a joint claim if your partner is working 16 or more hours a week;[36] *or*
- if you have a single JSA claim, your partner is working 24 hours or more a week.

See p975 for how hours are calculated. Hours spent as an unpaid carer for someone for whom it would be possible to qualify for IS as a carer are ignored.[37]

You, your partner or your non-dependant can *also* be treated as in full-time paid work if you (or s/he) are:

- absent from full-time paid work without a good reason;[38] *or*
- no longer in full-time paid work but still within the period covered by certain holiday pay or payments in lieu.[39] See also p408.

You, your partner or your non-dependant are *not* treated as being in full-time paid work if you (or s/he) are:

- in any of the categories on p974; *or*
- on work experience or participating in a specified scheme for helping people into work (see p1122).

Even if you are eligible for JSA, any earnings might reduce your entitlement to nil. See Chapter 20 for how earned income affects the amount of your JSA.

Employment and support allowance

You cannot usually get income-related employment and support allowance (ESA) if:

- you do any work (with some limited exceptions – see p1019);[40] *or*
- your partner does full-time paid work.

Your partner is generally classed as being in full-time paid work if s/he works 24 hours or more a week.[41] See p975 for how hours are calculated.

Your partner or your non-dependant can *also* be treated as being in full-time paid work if s/he:

- normally works full time, but is on holiday and intends to resume work once the holiday is over.[42] S/he can argue that s/he only counts as being on holiday if s/he is paid for it;[43] *or*
- is absent from full-time paid work without a good reason.[44]

You or your partner can also be treated as working if you have stopped work (in your partner's case, full-time paid work) but are still within the period covered by certain holiday pay or payments in lieu.[45] See also p408.

Your partner or your non-dependant is *not* treated as being in full-time paid work if s/he:

- falls into any of the categories on p974; *or*
- is an unpaid carer for someone for whom it would be possible to qualify for IS as a carer (see p235); *or*
- is working as a childminder in her/his own home.[46]

Even if you are eligible for income-related ESA, any earnings might reduce your entitlement to nil. See Chapter 20 for how earned income affects the amount of your ESA.

Part 7: National Insurance, work and work-related rules
Chapter 44: Work and benefits
3. How work affects other means-tested benefits

Pension credit

You can qualify for pension credit (PC) whether or not you, your partner, or anybody else in your household does paid work. However, any earnings might reduce your PC entitlement to nil. See Chapter 21 for how earned income affects the amount of your PC.

If a non-dependant counts as being in full-time paid work, this can affect non-dependant deductions from PC. Your non-dependant generally counts as being in full-time work when working 16 hours or more a week.[47] See p975 for how hours are calculated. For PC, the 'term-time only' worker rule can apply (see p976) and the calculation of hours does not include paid breaks like lunch or tea breaks.[48]

Your non-dependant can *also* be treated as in full-time paid work if s/he:[49]
- normally works full time, but is on holiday and intends to resume work once the holiday is over. S/he can argue that s/he only counts as being on holiday if s/he is paid for it;[50] *or*
- is absent from full-time paid work without a good reason.

Your non-dependant is *not* treated as being in full-time paid work if s/he:[51]
- is on maternity, paternity, shared parental, adoption or parental bereavement leave or is absent from work because of sickness; *or*
- gets income-based JSA, income-related ESA, or IS for more than three days in the relevant benefit week; *or*
- gets a sports award from UK Sport and no other payment.

Housing benefit

You can qualify for housing benefit (HB) whether or not you, your partner, or anybody else in your household does paid work.

However, work can affect the calculation of your HB. Work status determines whether you get an additional earnings disregard or childcare costs disregard, and can affect the rate of any non-dependant deductions (see p200, p415 and p458). Beyond this, any earnings might reduce your HB entitlement to nil. See Chapters 20 and 21 for how earned income affects the amount of your HB. See also p1159, which describes the effect that work can have on the benefit cap.

For HB, you, your partner or your non-dependant generally count as being in full-time work if you are working 16 hours or more a week.[52] See p975 for how hours are calculated. The 'term-time only' worker rule can apply (see p976).

You, your partner or your non-dependant can *also* be treated as in full-time paid work if you (or s/he) are:[53]
- normally in full-time work, but currently on holiday and intending to resume work once the holiday is over. You can argue that you only count as being on holiday if you are paid for it;[54] *or*
- absent from full-time paid work without a good reason.

You, your partner or your non-dependant are *not* treated as being in full-time paid work if you (or s/he) are:[55]

- on maternity, paternity, shared parental, adoption or parental bereavement leave or absent from work because of sickness. However, this rule does not apply for the purposes of the childcare costs disregard (see p416 and p458); *or*
- getting income-based JSA, income-related ESA, or IS for more than three days in the relevant benefit week; *or*
- getting a sports award from UK Sport and no other payment.

4. How work affects non-means-tested benefits

For the detailed rules for a specific benefit, see the relevant chapter in this *Handbook*.

Benefit	Work-related eligibility rules
Bereavement benefits (see Chapter 25)	For both bereavement support payment and widowed parent's allowance, the deceased partner must have either satisfied national insurance (NI) conditions or been an 'employed earner' who died as a result of industrial injury or disease. The surviving partner can be eligible for these benefits whether or not s/he works.
Carer's allowance (see Chapter 26)	You cannot qualify if you earn more than £132 each week (see p547 for how this is calculated). The person you care for can be in or out of work.
Child benefit (see Chapter 27)	You cannot claim for certain 16 to 19 year olds who do paid work for 24 hours or more a week (see p571).
Contributory ('new-style') employment and support allowance (see Chapter 30)	You cannot qualify while working,[56] with limited exceptions (see p1019).
Industrial injuries benefits (see Chapter 32)	You must have been an employed earner when you had an accident or contracted a disease.
Contribution-based ('new-style') jobseeker's allowance (JSA) (see Chapter 33)	You cannot qualify if you are in full-time paid work. The work rules for income-based JSA apply (see p978), except regarding your partner's work.

Part 7: National Insurance, work and work-related rules
Chapter 44: Work and benefits
5. People involved in trade disputes

Maternity allowance (see Chapter 34)	You must satisfy an employment condition in order to qualify (see p710).
Statutory sick pay (SSP) (see Chapter 39)	You are only eligible if you meet employment conditions (see p821). Self-employed people cannot claim SSP.
Statutory maternity, adoption, paternity, and other parental pay (see Chapter 38)	You are only eligible if you meet employment conditions (see pp797-808). Self-employed people do not qualify.

Whether you are an employed earner or self-employed also affects your NI contributions (see Chapter 43).

5. People involved in trade disputes

Note: trade dispute law is complex. If there is any doubt about whether you are involved in a trade dispute, get specialist employment advice.

Universal credit

For universal credit (UC), the definition of 'trade dispute' is the same as it is in employment law.[57] You remain entitled to UC if you are involved in a trade dispute, and remain eligible for advances if you meet the usual eligibility criteria. However, if you (or your partner) have withdrawn your labour in support of a trade dispute, you are treated as having the same earnings you would have otherwise. This applies unless your contract of employment has been terminated.[58] Any strike pay you receive (eg, from your trade union) does not count as income.[59] You should not be sanctioned for taking part in a trade dispute.[60]

Other means-tested benefits

For these benefits, a trade dispute means any dispute between fellow employees, or between employees and employers, connected with terms or conditions of employment, or the employment or non-employment of anyone.[61]

Income support and jobseeker's allowance

You can get income support (IS) while you are involved in a trade dispute.

You are not entitled to jobseeker's allowance (JSA), including hardship payments, for a week in which on any day you (or if you are a joint-claim couple, both of you) are involved in a trade dispute.[62] Weeks when you are not entitled to JSA do not count as part of your 'jobseeking period' (see p689) meaning that they do not count towards your 26-week entitlement to contribution-based JSA.[63]

. . . .

If you have a partner and only one of you is involved in a trade dispute, unless you are a joint-claim couple (see p247), the partner who is not involved can receive income-based JSA. If you are a joint-claim couple, you can both get income-based JSA.[64] The partner involved in the trade dispute does not have to satisfy the jobseeking conditions.

You should not be sanctioned on JSA for taking part in a trade dispute.[65]

For more on the special rules that apply to income-based JSA and IS, see Chapter 44 of the 2021/22 edition of this *Handbook*.

Income-related employment and support allowance, pension credit and housing benefit

There are no rules that reduce the amount of your income-related employment and support allowance (ESA), pension credit (PC) or housing benefit (HB) if you or your partner are involved in a trade dispute. However:

- For income-related ESA, your partner is treated as not being in full-time paid work if s/he is involved in a trade dispute and for the first 15 days following her/his return to work.[66]
- For HB, if your earnings are reduced due to a trade dispute, the local authority should take this into account.[67] Your earnings can be averaged over a different period than normal if this results in a more accurate estimate (see p440 and p467).
- For income-related ESA and PC, you can apply to have your award reassessed under the rules on variable earnings (see p438 and p467).

Non-dependants

Non-dependant deductions made from your IS, JSA, ESA or PC housing costs, and from HB, are usually higher if your non-dependant is in full-time paid work. However, if your non-dependant is involved in a trade dispute, this might mean that the non-dependant deduction should be reduced. See p200 and p349 for further information.

Benefits paid to you by your employer

Statutory sick pay

You can generally continue to qualify for statutory sick pay (SSP) if you were already entitled to it when a trade dispute began. You cannot qualify if you become incapable of work *during* a stoppage of work caused by a trade dispute, unless you can prove that you did not have a direct interest in the dispute on or before that date.[68] If you are disqualified from getting SSP on this basis, you are not entitled at any point during your period of sickness, even if the trade dispute ends. You may, however, qualify for ESA. 'Stoppage of work' and 'trade dispute' are not defined in the SSP rules. However, an overtime ban or working to grade does not count as a stoppage of work.[69]

Part 7: National Insurance, work and work-related rules
Chapter 44: Work and benefits
5. People involved in trade disputes

Statutory maternity, adoption, paternity, shared parental and parental bereavement pay

To qualify for these types of statutory parental pay, you must have been employed for a continuous period of at least 26 weeks ending on a specified date (see p804). Any week in which you are not working because of a trade dispute does not break your continuity of employment for this purpose. However, unless you can prove that at no time did you have a direct interest in the trade dispute:

- any such week does not count towards the total of 26 weeks' employment; *and*
- if you are dismissed during the stoppage of work, your continuity of employment ends on the day you stopped work.[70]

Tax credits

This chapter does not cover tax credits. See p290.

Social fund payments

Involvement in a trade dispute does not affect your entitlement to a DWP funeral expenses payment, cold weather payment or winter fuel payment, to a funeral support payment in Scotland, or to payments from the Scottish Welfare Fund. You cannot, however, qualify for a DWP budgeting loan if you or your partner are involved in a trade dispute.[71]

The rules about whether you count as being involved in a trade dispute are largely the same as for JSA (see p982).

You do not count as being involved in a trade dispute during a period when you are incapable of work, or from the sixth week before the week you are due to have a baby to the end of the seventh week after the week the baby is born.[72]

Sure Start and Best Start schemes

If you or your partner are involved in a trade dispute, your entitlement to a Sure Start maternity grant is not affected if your qualifying benefit is UC, income-related ESA or PC. However, if your qualifying benefit is IS or income-based JSA, you can only qualify for a Sure Start maternity grant if the trade dispute has been going on for at least six weeks when you claim a maternity grant.[73]

These restrictions do not apply to a Best Start pregnancy and baby payment in Scotland.

Notes

1. The meanings of 'paid work', 'full-time paid work' and 'hours'

1 Reg 2, definition of 'paid work,' UC Regs
2 R(IS) 5/95; *Fiore v CAO*, 20 June 1995; Vol 4 Ch 20, para 20210 DMG
3 *CAO v Ellis* [1995] (CA), reported as R(IS)22/95; CTC/626/2001
4 R(IS) 1/93
5 CFC/33/1993; R(FIS) 1/83
6 Vol 4 Ch 20, para 20238 DMG
7 CIS/649/1992
8 *CAO v Ellis* [1995] (CA), reported as R(IS)22/95; CIS/434/1994
9 **IS** Reg 6(1) and (5) IS Regs
JSA Reg 53(a)-(f) and (i)-(m) JSA Regs; reg 44 JSA Regs 2013
ESA Reg 43 and Sch 6 para 2(6) and (8) ESA Regs
10 R(FIS) 1/86; CDWA/1/1992
11 **IS** Reg 5(3A) IS Regs
JSA Reg 52(1) JSA Regs; reg 43(1) JSA Regs 2013
ESA Reg 43(3) and Sch 6 para 2(5) ESA Regs
12 **IS** Reg 5(7) IS Regs
JSA Reg 51(3)(a) JSA Regs; reg 42(3)(a) JSA Regs 2013
ESA Regs 42(2) and 45(9) and Sch 6 para 2(7) ESA Regs
13 Vol 4 Ch 20, para 20265 DMG; R(FIS) 6/85; *Kazantzis v CAO* [1999], reported as R(IS) 13/99
14 Vol 4 Ch 20, para 20267 DMG
15 *Kevin Smith v CAO* [1994] (CA), reported as R(IS) 21/95
16 R(JSA) 1/09; *GM v SSWP (JSA)* [2010] UKUT 221 (AAC), reported as [2012] AACR 9; *Saunderson v SSWP* [2012] ScotCS CSIH 10
17 **IS** Reg 5(2)(b)(i) IS Regs
JSA Reg 51(2)(b)(i) JSA Regs; reg 43(2)(b)(i) JSA Regs 2013
ESA Regs 42(2) and 45(8)(b)(i) and Sch 6 para 2(2)(a) ESA Regs
PC Sch 2 para 2(4) SPC Regs
HB Reg 6(2)(a) HB Regs; reg 6(2)(a) HB(SPC) Regs
18 R(JSA) 5/03
19 **IS** Reg 5(2)(b)(ii) IS Regs
JSA Reg 51(2)(b)(ii) JSA Regs; reg 42(2)(b)(ii) JSA Regs 2013
ESA Regs 42(2) and 45(8)(b)(ii) and Sch 6 para 2(2)(b) ESA Regs
PC Sch 2 para 2(2)(b) SPC Regs
HB Reg 6(2)(b) HB Regs; reg 6(2)(b) HB(SPC) Regs
All Para 20322 DMG; CFC/2963/2001; *NS v SSWP (IS)* [2015] UKUT 423 (AAC); Ch 115, para 15455 DMG
20 **IS** Reg 5(2)(a)
JSA Reg 51(2)(a) JSA Regs; reg 42(2)(a) JSA Regs 2013
ESA Regs 42(2) and 45(8)(a) and Sch 6 para 2(3) ESA Regs
PC Sch 2 para 2(4) SPC Regs
HB Reg 6(4) HB Regs; reg 6(4) HB(SPC) Regs
21 R(JSA)1/07; *Saunderson v SSWP* [2012] ScotCS CSIH 10
22 **IS** Regs 5(2)(b)(i) and 5(3B) IS Regs
PC Sch 2 para 2(3) SPC Regs
HB Reg 6(3) HB Regs; reg 6(3) HB(SPC) Regs
All *Stafford and Banks v CAO* [2001] UKHL 33, reported as R(IS) 15/01

2. How work affects universal credit

23 Reg 32 UC Regs
24 Regs 26(5), 32(2)(b) and 55 and Sch 5 para 4 UC Regs

3. How work affects other means-tested benefits

25 **IS** Regs 2(1) and 5 IS Regs
JSA Reg 51(1)(c) JSA Regs
ESA Sch 6 para 2(1) ESA Regs
PC Sch 2 para 2(1) SPC Regs
HB Reg 6(1) HB Regs; reg 6(1) HB(SPC) Regs
26 s124(1)(c) SSCBA 1992; s3(1)(e) JSA 1995; Sch 1 para 6(1)(f) WRA 2007
27 Reg 5 IS Regs
28 Reg 5(1A) IS Regs
29 Reg 5(3) IS Regs
30 R(JSA) 5/03; Vol 4 Ch 20, para 20309 DMG
31 Reg 5(3) IS Regs
32 Reg 5(5) and (5A) IS Regs

Part 7: National Insurance, work and work-related rules
Chapter 44: Work and benefits
Notes

● ●

33 Reg 6(1) and (5) IS Regs
34 s124(1)(c) SSCBA 1992; s3(1)(e) JSA 1995; Sch 1 para 6(1)(f) WRA 2007
35 Reg 51 JSA Regs; reg 42 JSA Regs 2013
36 Reg 3E(2)(g) JSA Regs
37 Reg 51(2)(b)(i) JSA Regs; reg 43(2)(b)(i) JSA Regs 2013
38 Reg 52(1) JSA Regs
39 Reg 52(3) and (3A) JSA Regs; reg 43(2) and (3) JSA Regs 2013
40 Sch 1 para 6(1)(e) WRA 2007; regs 40 and 41 ESA Regs; reg 37 ESA Regs 2013
41 Reg 42(1) ESA Regs
42 Reg 42(3) and Sch 6 para 2(4) ESA Regs
43 R(JSA) 5/03; Vol 4 Ch 20, para 20309 DMG
44 Reg 42(3) and Sch 6 para 2(4) ESA Regs
45 Regs 41(2) and (3) and 42(4) and (5) ESA Regs
46 Reg 6(1) and (5) IS Regs
47 Sch 2 para 2(1) SPC Regs
48 Vol 13 Ch 78 App 5, paras 21, 23 and 47 DMG
49 Sch 2 para 2(5) SPC Regs
50 R(JSA) 5/03; Vol 4 Ch 20, para 20309 DMG
51 Sch 2 para 2(6-8) SPC Regs
52 Reg 6(1) HB Regs; reg 6(1) HB(SPC) Regs
53 Reg 6(5) HB Regs; reg 6(5) HB(SPC) Regs
54 R(JSA) 5/03; Vol 4 Ch 20, para 20309 DMG
55 Reg 6(6-8) HB Regs; reg 6(6-8) HB(SPC) Regs

4. How work affects non-means-tested benefits
56 Reg 37, ESA Regs 2013

5. People involved in trade disputes
57 Reg 2, definition of 'trade dispute' (as defined in s244 of the Trade Union and Labour Relations (Consolidation) Act 1992), UC Regs
58 Reg 56 UC Regs
59 Reg 66 UC Regs
60 Reg 113(1) UC Regs
61 s126 SSCBA 1992; ss 14 and 35(1), definition of 'trade dispute,' JSA 1995
62 ss14, 15A and 35(1), definition of 'week', JSA 1995
63 Reg 47(3)(e) JSA Regs; reg 37(2)(d) JSA Regs 2013
64 ss15 and 15A JSA 1995; reg 3D and Sch A1 para 17 JSA Regs
65 Reg 28(1)(d) JSA Regs 2013
66 Reg 43(2)(b) ESA Regs

67 *R v HBRB LB Ealing ex parte Saville* [1986] HLR 349
68 Sch 11 paras 2(g) and 7 SSCBA 1992
69 R(SSP) 1/86
70 **SMP** Reg 13 SMP Regs
   SAP/SPP Reg 35 SPPSAP(G) Regs
   SSPP Reg 36 SSPP(G) Regs
   SPBP Reg 14 SPBP(G) Regs
71 SF Dir 8(1)(b); s14 JSA 1995
72 s126(1) and (2) SSCBA 1992; s14 JSA 1995; reg 171 JSA Regs; reg 3 SFM&FE Regs; SF Dir 8
73 Regs 3(1) and 6 SFM&FE Regs; s126 SSCBA 1992; s14 JSA 1995

Chapter 45

. . . .

Limited capability for work

This chapter covers:
1. The work capability assessment (below)
2. Challenging a decision (p1013)
3. Periods of limited capability for work (p1018)
4. Work you can do while claiming employment and support allowance (p1019)

Key facts

- If you are unable to work because of illness or disability, you may be entitled to benefit and national insurance credits on the basis of having 'limited capability for work'. The main benefits this affects are universal credit and employment and support allowance.
- Whether or not you have limited capability for work is assessed by a 'work capability assessment'. This also tests whether you have 'limited capability for work-related activity'. If so, you are not required to attend work-focused interviews or prepare to return to work, and are entitled to a higher amount of benefit.
- If you work, you may be regarded as not having limited capability for work or work-related activity.
- If you disagree with the decision about your limited capability for work or work-related activity, you can apply for a revision or supersession (see Chapter 56), or appeal against it (see Chapter 57).

---

1. The work capability assessment

The work capability assessment is a test used by the DWP to decide whether:
- you have 'limited capability for work' – ie, whether you can get benefit on the basis of being unable to work because of your health condition; *and*
- you have 'limited capability for work-related activity' – ie, whether your health condition is so severe that, in addition to not being able to work, you are not required to engage in activity such as attending interviews about looking for work or retraining.

Part 7: National Insurance, work and work-related rules
Chapter 45: Limited capability for work
1. The work capability assessment

The assessment is used to decide whether you can get extra amounts included in your universal credit (UC) and your work-related responsibilities if you come under the UC system. It is also used to decide your entitlement to employment and support allowance (ESA).

In addition, the work capability assessment is used to decide whether you are entitled to national insurance (NI) credits for limited capability for work (see Chapter 43) and whether you can still get a work-related activity component in your housing benefit (HB) (see p336). **Note:** this component was abolished for new claims from 3 April 2017. For NI credits and HB, whether you have limited capability for work is decided under the rules for ESA.

You satisfy the work capability assessment if you score sufficient points (see p994) or you do not but an exceptional circumstance applies (see p992). You also satisfy the test without actually undergoing the assessment if you are treated as having limited capability for work (see below). In some circumstances, you can be treated as not having limited capability for work even though you have passed the assessment (see p992).

Note: for UC, there are limited circumstances in which a work capability assessment may not be carried out. These are where you are treated as not having limited capability for work because you have previously failed the assessment (either for UC or 'new-style' ESA) or where you work and earn at or above a certain threshold, and no exceptions apply. See p992 for details.

Treated as having limited capability for work

You are automatically treated as having limited capability for work (without undergoing the work capability assessment) in certain circumstances. In other circumstances, you may be treated as having limited capability for work because of your health.[1]

Universal credit

You are automatically treated as having limited capability for work for UC if:

- you have already been assessed as having limited capability for work for 'new-style' ESA – ie, contributory ESA paid under the UC system;[2] *or*
- you are transferring to UC from ESA and you were assessed as having limited capability for work for ESA, or you were entitled to NI contribution credits for limited capability for work when you claimed UC.[3]

You are treated as having limited capability for work for UC because of your health if:[4]

- you are at least pension age (see p765) and get disability living allowance (DLA), personal independence payment (PIP) or adult disability payment (ADP); *or*
- you are terminally ill – ie, your death can reasonably be expected within 12 months; *or*

- you are receiving chemotherapy or radiotherapy treatment for cancer, recovering from such treatment or are likely to receive such treatment within six months from the date the DWP determines whether or not you pass the work capability assessment; *or*
- you have been given official notice not to work because of being in contact with an infectious disease; *or*
- you are an inpatient in hospital where you have been medically advised to stay for at least 24 hours, or are recovering from treatment as an inpatient (and the DWP is satisfied that your condition remains sufficiently serious), including if you are attending a residential programme of rehabilitation for drug or alcohol addiction; *or*
- you are receiving plasmapheresis, regular weekly treatment for haemodialysis for chronic renal failure, or regular weekly treatment for total parenteral nutrition for gross impairment of enteric function, or are recovering from such treatment; *or*
- you are pregnant and there is a serious risk to your health or your baby's health if you work.

Note: unlike for ESA (see p990), there is no UC rule that treats you as having limited capability for work while you are waiting for the work capability assessment to be carried out. However, the bullet points above might still apply to you in either of those situations.

Are you transferring to universal credit from employment and support allowance?

If you were getting ESA but then claim UC, you automatically have limited capability for work. However, the DWP may wrongly overlook this rule and insist that you have to be assessed again. If this affects you, do the following.

1. Point out the rule and insist that you should be treated as having limited capability for work for UC. If necessary, challenge the decision on your UC entitlement.

2. The DWP may say that it needs to check that you were getting ESA – complain if this is taking a long time. Ultimately, an unreasonably long delay might be challenged by judicial review (see p1410).

3. If you were getting the support component in your ESA, the limited capability for work-related activity element should be included in your UC from your first monthly assessment period.[5]

4. If you were getting the work-related activity component in your ESA, the limited capability for work element should be included in your UC from your first monthly assessment period.[6]

5. Remember that, despite these rules, the DWP can still apply the work capability assessment to you again.

Part 7: National Insurance, work and work-related rules
Chapter 45: Limited capability for work
1. The work capability assessment

Employment and support allowance

You are automatically treated as having limited capability for work for ESA if:[7]

- you are waiting for an assessment or (in some circumstances) an appeal (see p991); *or*
- you satisfy one of the eating and drinking descriptors for limited capability for work-related activity (see p1004); *or*
- you are entitled to statutory sick pay; *or*
- for income-related ESA only, you are in education, you are not a 'qualifying young person' (see p563) and you get income-related ESA because you receive DLA, PIP, ADP or armed forces independence payment;[8] *or*
- for contributory ESA only, you get UC and have been assessed as having limited capability for work for UC.[9]

You are treated as having limited capability for work because of your health for ESA if:[10]

- you are pregnant or have recently given birth, you are not entitled to maternity allowance (MA) or statutory maternity pay, you have a medical certificate giving the expected or actual date of birth, and you are within the period beginning with the first day of the sixth week before the expected week of childbirth (or the actual day of childbirth if earlier) and ending on the 14th day after you have the baby; *or*
- you are pregnant and entitled to MA; *or*
- you are pregnant and there is a serious risk to your health or your baby's health if you do not refrain from work; *or*
- you are terminally ill – ie, your death can reasonably be expected within 12 months; *or*
- you are receiving chemotherapy or radiotherapy treatment for cancer, recovering from such treatment or are likely to receive such treatment within six months from the date the DWP determines whether or not you pass the work capability assessment; *or*
- you have been given official notice not to work because of being in contact with an infectious disease; *or*
- you are an inpatient in hospital where you have been medically advised to stay for at least 24 hours, or are recovering from treatment as an inpatient (and the DWP is satisfied that your condition remains sufficiently serious), including if you are attending a residential programme of rehabilitation for drug or alcohol addiction; *or*
- you are receiving plasmapheresis, regular weekly treatment for haemodialysis for chronic renal failure, or regular weekly treatment for total parenteral nutrition for gross impairment of enteric function, or are recovering from such treatment. The DWP must be satisfied that you should continue to be treated as having limited capability for work. In the first week of such treatment, you must be receiving it or recovering from it for at least two days. You continue to

be treated as having limited capability for work if your treatment later goes down to one day a week. However, you cannot get income-related ESA in any week in which you work (apart from work you can do while claiming – see p1019), although you can claim contributory ESA for the days of treatment and recovery.[11]

If you are waiting for an assessment or you are appealing

You are treated as having limited capability for work if:[12]

- you are applying for ESA and have provided a current medical certificate, but the work capability assessment has not yet been carried out. You can get ESA while waiting for your assessment. However, this does not apply if you are reclaiming ESA after having failed the work capability assessment, unless your condition has significantly worsened or you have a new health condition. Your condition has significantly worsened if it is considered that you would now be likely to pass the work capability assessment;[13] *or*
- you are appealing against a decision that you have failed the work capability assessment (ie, you were found not to have limited capability for work) and you have submitted a medical certificate. However, unless your current claim for ESA was made before 30 March 2015, this only applies if:
  - this is the first time you have failed the work capability assessment; *or*
  - this the first time you have failed the work capability assessment since a previous decision that you satisfied it (see p1015); *or*
- you are reclaiming ESA and have provided a current medical certificate, after being treated as failing the work capability assessment because you failed to return the ESA50 questionnaire or failed to attend the medical. You can get ESA while waiting for your assessment. However, this only applies if:
  - you have now returned the questionnaire; *or*
  - it is more than six months since the decision treating you as not having limited capability for work; *or*
  - your condition has significantly worsened. Your condition has significantly worsened if it is considered that you would now be likely to pass the work capability assessment;[14] *or*
  - you have a new health condition.

Examples

Lowri had back pain and so applied for ESA, but failed the work capability assessment. Later, she develops depression and reclaims ESA, supplying a medical certificate. The DWP accepts that Lowri has a new condition, and so treats her as having limited capability for work and pays her ESA while a new work capability assessment is arranged.

Emmanuel claims ESA but fails the work capability assessment. He decides to apply for ESA again a month later. The DWP does not consider that Emmanuel's condition has

Part 7: National Insurance, work and work-related rules
Chapter 45: Limited capability for work
1. The work capability assessment

significantly worsened or that he has a new health condition, so he is not treated as having limited capability for work, and is not paid ESA before getting a decision on his new claim.

Exceptional circumstances

If you have been assessed under the work capability assessment but do not score sufficient points to have limited capability for work, you are treated as doing so for UC and ESA if:[15]

- you have an uncontrolled or uncontrollable life-threatening disease, and there is medical evidence to show this. There must be reasonable cause for the disease not to be controllable by a recognised therapeutic procedure; or
- because of your illness, there would be a substantial risk to the mental or physical health of any person were you to be found not to have limited capability for work. The 'substantial risk' is one that could arise from the sort of work you may be expected to do, or from the journey to or from work, although it is not necessary to go into the detail of individual job descriptions or potential jobseeker's agreements. The risk may also arise from the journey to or from a job interview or attendance at the Jobcentre.[16] However, this exceptional circumstance does not apply to you if the risk could be significantly reduced by reasonable adjustments in your workplace, or by your taking medication prescribed by your doctor.

Treated as not having limited capability for work

Universal credit

For UC, you are treated as *not* having limited capability for work if:[17]

- you have previously failed the work capability assessment, either for UC or for contributory ESA under the UC system ('new-style' ESA). The DWP does not reassess you unless the decision was made in ignorance of, or based on a mistake about, a material fact, or there has been a relevant change in your condition; or
- you do not return the UC50 questionnaire (see p1010), or you do not attend the medical (see p1011), and do not have good reason (see p1011) for this; or
- you work, none of the exceptions in the bullet points below apply and your earnings are at or above a certain threshold. This threshold is the level of earnings you would receive for 16 hours' work a week paid at the rate of the national minimum wage for people aged 23 and over, converted to a monthly amount – ie, in 2022/23 earnings at or above £658.66 a month.[18]

You can work and earn above this threshold without automatically being treated as not having limited capability for work if:

- you are entitled to attendance allowance (AA), DLA, child disability payment, PIP or ADP (but the DWP may apply the work capability assessment to you); or

- you have already been assessed as having limited capability for work or as having limited capability for work-related activity (see p1004) under the UC system (not for ESA outside the UC system) (but the DWP may reapply the work capability assessment to you); *or*
- you have been treated under the UC system as having limited capability for work, or for work-related activity, because of your health (see p988 and p1004), or because an exceptional circumstance applies (see p992). The DWP cannot apply or reapply the work capability assessment to you.

Are you transferring to universal credit from employment and support allowance?

If you were getting ESA and doing 'permitted work' (see p1020), but then claim UC, it is not clear whether the rules about work described above should apply to you. Bear in mind the following.

1. UC does not have a permitted work rule, but there is no general rule that prevents you from having limited capability for work if you are doing some work.

2. In many situations, your earnings from permitted work will be below the earnings threshold (see p922), you are getting PIP or DLA, or you are treated as having limited capability for work (or for work-related activity) because of your health or because an exceptional circumstance applies. In any of these situations, you are *not* automatically treated as not having limited capability for work.

3. In practice, it is understood that the DWP usually accepts that you have limited capability for work at the point you transfer to UC from ESA, but it may consider reapplying the work capability assessment to you.

Employment and support allowance

For ESA, you are treated as *not* having limited capability for work, even if you have been assessed as satisfying the work capability assessment, if you:

- do not return the ESA50 questionnaire (see p1010) or attend the medical (see p1011) while the work capability assessment applies to you, and you do not have good cause (see p1010 and p1012); *or*
- do any work, except certain work you can do while claiming (see p1019);[19] *or*
- are disqualified from receiving contributory ESA (even if you are not already entitled to it) for more than six weeks because you are a prisoner. If this applies, but you are entitled to income-related ESA (ie, pending trial, or sentence following conviction), you are only treated as not having limited capability for work after your entitlement has ended;[20] *or*
- attend a training course and receive a training allowance or premium, unless your ESA claim is for a period beginning after you stopped attending the course, or if the training allowance or premium was only for travelling or meal expenses;[21] *or*
- are (or were) a member of the armed forces and the day in question is a day of sickness absence from duty.[22]

Part 7: National Insurance, work and work-related rules
Chapter 45: Limited capability for work
1. The work capability assessment

Scoring points

The assessment does not take into account actual jobs, your education or training, or any language or literacy problems. It is a test of your ability to perform certain activities, taking account of a 'specific bodily disease or disablement' or a 'specific mental illness or disablement', and the direct results of medical treatment (from a registered doctor) for these.[23] There are two lists of activities: one physical (see below), one mental (see p1000). Under each activity, there is a further list of statements, called 'descriptors', which describe different levels of difficulty in carrying out the activity. Attached to each descriptor is a points score. You are awarded the highest scoring descriptor in each activity that applies to you.

For the physical activities, this takes into account your ability when wearing or using any aid, appliance or prosthesis that you normally wear or use, or any aid or appliance that you could reasonably be expected to wear or use.[24]

To score enough points to satisfy the test, you must score a total of 15 points or more. The points can be scored in one or more activities, and scores from the physical and mental activities can be combined. For example, you can score nine points in the physical test and six points in the mental test.

Good days and bad days, pain and tiredness

Generally, what counts is your capability as it is 'most of the time'. If you cannot repeat an activity without a reasonable degree of regularity, you should be considered unable to perform it. The following points apply.

- Your ability to perform an activity with some degree of repetition should be considered and a 'broad-brush' approach applied, rather than just a day-by-day approach.[25]
- A descriptor should apply to you if you cannot perform the activity most of the time. The severity of your condition, the frequency of your good and bad days and the unpredictability of the bad days are all relevant.[26]
- If you have long periods of remission, you may be considered capable of work during these periods. This depends on the severity of your condition and on the length of your periods of ill health and your periods of remission.[27]
- Pain, fatigue and the increasing difficulty you may have in performing an activity on a repeated basis compared with someone in good health should be taken into account.[28] 'Pain' may include nausea and dizziness.[29]
- Any risk to your health in performing an activity should be considered, particularly if carrying it out is against medical advice. If the risk is sufficiently serious, you may be considered incapable of the activity.[30]

Physical disabilities

To score points in the physical test, your incapacity must arise from a 'specific bodily disease or disablement'.[31]

Activity one: mobilising

Mobilising unaided by another person with or without a walking stick, manual wheelchair or other aid if such aid is normally used, or could reasonably be worn or used.

Descriptors   Points

a. Cannot, unaided by another person, either: 15

(i) mobilise more than 50 metres on level ground without stopping in order to avoid significant discomfort or exhaustion; *or*

(ii) repeatedly mobilise 50 metres within a reasonable timescale because of significant discomfort or exhaustion.

b. Cannot, unaided by another person, mount or descend two steps even with   9
the support of a handrail.

c. Cannot, unaided by another person, either: 9

(i) mobilise more than 100 metres on level ground without stopping in order to avoid significant discomfort or exhaustion; *or*

(ii) repeatedly mobilise 100 metres within a reasonable timescale because of significant discomfort or exhaustion.

d. Cannot, unaided by another person, either: 6

(i) mobilise more than 200 metres on level ground without stopping in order to avoid significant discomfort or exhaustion; *or*

(ii) repeatedly mobilise 200 metres within a reasonable timescale because of significant discomfort or exhaustion.

e. None of the above applies.   0

Your ability to use a walking stick or manual wheelchair (but not an electric one) or another aid can be taken into account if you normally use one or could 'reasonably' use one. Issues such as your ability to propel and handle a manual wheelchair, and whether one is medically suitable for you, should be taken into account.[32] Official guidance stresses the importance of considering things like fatigue and breathlessness.[33] **Note:** if descriptor 1(a) applies, you also have limited capability for work-related activity (see p1004).

Part 7: National Insurance, work and work-related rules
Chapter 45: Limited capability for work
1. The work capability assessment

Activity two: standing and sitting

Standing and sitting

Descriptors	Points
a. Cannot move between one seated position and another seated position located next to one another without receiving physical assistance from another person.	15
b. Cannot, for the majority of the time, remain at a work station, either: (i) standing unassisted by another person (even if free to move around); *or* (ii) sitting (even in an adjustable chair); *or* (iii) a combination of (i) and (ii), for more than 30 minutes, before needing to move away in order to avoid significant discomfort or exhaustion.	9
c. Cannot, for the majority of the time, remain at a work station: (i) standing unassisted by another person (even if free to move around); *or* (ii) sitting (even in an adjustable chair); *or* (iii) a combination of (i) and (ii), for more than an hour before needing to move away in order to avoid significant discomfort or exhaustion.	6
d. None of the above applies.	0

Official guidance says that in transferring from one seated position to another, it is reasonable to take into account a transfer board, but not something more specialised, such as a hoist. Your ability to stand does not require you to stand absolutely still, but you must have at least one hand free, so if you need two crutches to stand, this would not count as ability to stand.[34] **Note:** if descriptor 2(a) applies, you also have limited capability for work-related activity (see p1004).

Activity three: reaching

Reaching

Descriptors	Points
a. Cannot raise either arm as if to put something in the top pocket of a coat or jacket.	15
b. Cannot raise either arm to top of head as if to put on a hat.	9
c. Cannot raise either arm above head height as if to reach for something.	6
d. None of the above applies.	0

This activity is about your ability to reach with either arm above waist height. It is not a test of your ability to use your hands or fingers.[35] **Note:** if descriptor 3(a) applies, you also have limited capability for work-related activity (see p1004).

Activity four: picking up, moving and transferring things

Picking up and moving or transferring by the use of the upper body and arms

Descriptors	Points
a. Cannot pick up and move a 0.5 litre carton full of liquid.	15
b. Cannot pick up and move a one litre carton full of liquid.	9
c. Cannot transfer a light but bulky object such as an empty cardboard box.	6
d. None of the above applies.	0

This activity is about picking up and moving specified objects, but is not a test of your ability to carry them. Problems with your shoulders, neck or back, as well as with your arms, should be taken into account.[36] It may be that you can transfer a bulky cardboard box with just one arm, but this will depend on all the circumstances of your condition.[37] **Note:** if descriptor 4(a) applies, you also have limited capability for work-related activity (see p1004).

Activity five: manual dexterity

Manual dexterity

Descriptors	Points
a. Cannot press a button (such as a telephone keypad) with either hand or cannot turn the pages of a book with either hand.	15
b. Cannot pick up a £1 coin or equivalent with either hand.	15
c. Cannot use a pen or pencil to make a meaningful mark with either hand.	9
d. Cannot single-handedly use a suitable keyboard or mouse.	9
e. None of the above applies.	0

This activity is about your hand and wrist function with work-related tasks, such as using a keypad, or a computer keyboard or mouse. It is not a test of your computer literacy. A 'meaningful mark' can be something very simple such as a signature or tick.[38] Official guidance says that to score points for inability to use a suitable keyboard or mouse, you must be unable to use both the keyboard and mouse. However, there is a conflict in the caselaw about this, and you may be able to argue that your inability to use one of them means you should score points.[39] **Note:** if descriptor 5(a) applies, you also have limited capability for work-related activity (see p1004).

Part 7: National Insurance, work and work-related rules
Chapter 45: Limited capability for work
1. The work capability assessment

Activity six: making yourself understood

Making self understood though speaking, writing, typing, or other means which are normally or could reasonably be used, unaided by another person

Descriptors	Points
a. Cannot convey a simple message, such as the presence of a hazard.	15
b. Has significant difficulty conveying a simple message to strangers.	15
c. Has some difficulty conveying a simple message to strangers.	6
d. None of the above applies.	0

This activity is about expressing yourself so that you can be understood, but is not restricted to speech. Official guidance mentions brain injury, motor neurone disease, Parkinson's disease and stroke among possible relevant conditions. If you have communication problems arising from a panic disorder or chronic fatigue syndrome, the guidance suggests scoring points under the mental health assessment instead if your problems are 'purely due to mental health problems'.[40] **Note:** if descriptor 6(a) applies, you also have limited capability for work-related activity (see p1004).

Acitivity seven: understanding communication

Understanding communication by:
(i) verbal means (such as hearing or lip reading) alone;
(ii) non-verbal means (such as reading 16-point print or Braille) alone; *or*
(iii) a combination of (i) and (ii),
using any aid that is normally or could reasonably be used, unaided by another person.

Descriptors	Points
a. Cannot understand a simple message, such as the location of a fire escape, due to sensory impairment.	15
b. Has significant difficulty understanding a simple message from a stranger due to sensory impairment.	15
c. Has some difficulty understanding a simple message from a stranger due to sensory impairment.	6
d. None of the above applies.	0

You may score points in this activity if you have a hearing impairment, a visual impairment or both a hearing and a visual impairment that means you have problems understanding simple communication. Your ability is assessed taking account of things like hearing aids, Braille and large print communication. You may score points if you have problems in understanding either spoken or written communication – you do not need to have problems with both.[41] **Note:** if descriptor 7(a) applies, you also have limited capability for work-related activity (see p1004).

Activity eight: navigation and maintaining safety

Navigation and maintaining safety using a guide dog or other aid if either or both are normally or could reasonably be used.

Descriptors	Points
a. Unable to navigate around familiar surroundings, without being accompanied by another person, due to sensory impairment.	15
b. Cannot safely complete a potentially hazardous task such as crossing the road, without being accompanied by another person, due to sensory impairment.	15
c. Unable to navigate around unfamiliar surroundings, without being accompanied by another person, due to sensory impairment.	9
d. None of the above applies.	0

This is a test of your ability to get about safely, if you have a 'sensory impairment'. This usually means impaired sight or hearing, but could include impairment of other senses, or possibly if you have serious balance problems due to Meniere's disease.[42] Your ability is assessed taking into account your guide dog, or other aid if normally used or if it could reasonably be used. This means normally used by you or by people in your situation, acting reasonably in all the circumstances.[43] Official guidance says that you are not assessed as using a guide dog unless you actually have one, and that GPS devices are not considered.[44]

Activity nine: incontinence

Absence or loss of control while conscious leading to extensive evacuation of the bowel and/or bladder, other than enuresis (bedwetting), despite the wearing or use of any aids or adaptations which are normally or could reasonably be worn or used.

Descriptors	Points
a. At least once a month experiences:	15
(i) loss of control leading to extensive evacuation of the bowel and/or voiding of the bladder; or	
(ii) substantial leakage of the contents of a collecting device, sufficient to require cleaning and a change in clothing.	
b. The majority of the time is at risk of loss of control leading to extensive evacuation of the bowel and/or voiding of the bladder, sufficient to require cleaning and a change in clothing, if not able to reach a toilet quickly.	6
c. Neither of the above applies.	0

Part 7: National Insurance, work and work-related rules
Chapter 45: Limited capability for work
1. The work capability assessment

This activity is about managing incontinence. Because 'extensive' evacuation of the bowel or bladder is referred to, minor leakage or dribbling do not count. Incontinence that occurs while you are asleep or having a fit or seizure is not covered.[45] The test is meant to deal with issues of personal dignity, so if you have an incontinence problem and because of mobility problems you are unable to reach a toilet before you lose control, you score points, provided this is frequent enough.[46] **Note:** to be assessed as also having limited capability for work-related activity on this activity, you must lose control at least once a week (see p1004).

Activity 10: consciousness during waking moments

Consciousness during waking moments	
Descriptors	*Points*
a. At least once a week, has an involuntary episode of lost or altered consciousness resulting in significantly disrupted awareness or concentration.	15
b. At least once a month, has an involuntary episode of lost or altered consciousness resulting in significantly disrupted awareness or concentration.	6
c. Neither of the above applies.	0

This activity is about involuntary lost or altered consciousness that results in 'significantly disrupted awareness or concentration'. Because it is in the context of 'during waking moments', it is about problems that occur when you are normally awake. 'Altered' consciousness is regarded as a 'definite clouding of mental faculties resulting in loss of control of thoughts or action'.[47] Official guidance says that dizziness or vertigo are not relevant, unless it is in the context of an epileptic or similar seizure.[48]

Mental disabilities

To score points in the mental disabilities test, your incapacity must arise from a 'specific mental illness or disablement'.[49]

Activity 11: learning tasks

Learning tasks	
Descriptors	*Points*
a. Cannot learn how to complete a simple task, such as setting an alarm clock.	15
b. Cannot learn anything beyond a simple task, such as setting an alarm clock.	9
c. Cannot learn anything beyond a moderately complex task, such as the steps involved in operating a washing machine to clean clothes.	6
d. None of the above applies.	0

This is about your ability to learn new tasks – but note that the specified tasks are just examples. If you cannot repeat a task or have to be shown how to do it again, you have not learned it. Official guidance mentions learning disability, organic brain disorder including stroke and receptive dysphasia among possible relevant conditions.[50] **Note:** if descriptor 11(a) applies, you also have limited capability for work-related activity (see p1004).

Activity 12: awareness of everyday hazards

Awareness of everyday hazards (such as boiling water or sharp objects)

Descriptors	Points
a. Reduced awareness of everyday hazards leads to a significant risk of:	15
(i) injury to self or others; *or*	
(ii) damage to property or possessions,	
such that the claimant requires supervision for the majority of the time to maintain safety.	
b. Reduced awareness of everyday hazards leads to a significant risk of:	9
(i) injury to self or others; *or*	
(ii) damage to property or possessions,	
such that the claimant frequently requires supervision to maintain safety.	
c. Reduced awareness of everyday hazards leads to a significant risk of:	6
(i) injury to self or others; *or*	
(ii) damage to property or possessions,	
such that the claimant occasionally requires supervision to maintain safety.	
d. None of the above applies.	0

This activity is about your ability to recognise risks from common hazards, such as boiling water or sharp objects. A wide range of conditions could be relevant here: learning difficulties or conditions affecting concentration, including the detrimental effects of medication, or from brain injury or other neurological conditions affecting self-awareness. It may also apply if you have a severe depressive illness or a psychotic disorder and as a result of that have a significant reduction in your attention and concentration, although the official guidance says it is unlikely to apply to anxiety disorders.[51] **Note:** if descriptor 12(a) applies, you also have limited capability for work-related activity (see p1004).

Part 7: National Insurance, work and work-related rules
Chapter 45: Limited capability for work
1. The work capability assessment

Activity 13: initiating and completing personal action

Initiating and completing personal action (which means planning, organisation, problem solving, prioritising or switching tasks)

Descriptors	Points
a. Cannot, due to impaired mental function, reliably initiate or complete at least two sequential personal actions.	15
b. Cannot, due to impaired mental function, reliably initiate or complete at least two sequential personal actions for the majority of the time.	9
c. Frequently cannot, due to impaired mental function, reliably initiate or complete at least two sequential personal actions.	6
d. None of the above applies.	0

The 'personal action' is about planning, organisation, problem solving, prioritising and switching tasks. There is no definition of 'personal action' and a common sense approach should be taken, so it should include things like cooking, dressing, washing and brushing your teeth, planning a simple meal, and dealing with finances and appointments.[52] You must be able to carry out the personal action 'reliably'. In one case, someone with obsessive compulsive disorder who took an excessive amount of time to complete at least two actions was found not to be able to 'reliably' complete them.[53] **Note:** if descriptor 13(a) applies, you also have limited capability for work-related activity (see p1004).

Activity 14: coping with change

Coping with change

Descriptors	Points
a. Cannot cope with any change to the extent that day to day life cannot be managed.	15
b. Cannot cope with minor planned change (such as a pre-arranged change to the routine time scheduled for a lunch break), to the extent that, overall, day to day life is made significantly more difficult.	9
c. Cannot cope with minor unplanned change (such as the timing of an appointment on the day it is due to occur), to the extent that, overall, day to day life is made significantly more difficult.	6
d. None of the above applies.	0

Official guidance says that this activity is about your ability to deal with changes in routine. Possible relevant conditions include moderate/severe learning disability, autistic spectrum disorder, brain injury, obsessive compulsive disorder, severe anxiety or psychotic illness.[54] Inability to cope could be indicated by a number of responses, including stress reactions and the need for another person to intervene.[55] **Note:** if descriptor 14(a) applies, you also have limited capability for work-related activity (see p1004).

Activity 15: getting about

Getting about	
Descriptors	*Points*
a. Cannot get to any place outside the claimant's home with which the claimant is familiar.	15
b. Is unable to get to a specified place with which the claimant is familiar, without being accompanied by another person.	9
c. Is unable to get to a specified place with which the claimant is unfamiliar without being accompanied by another person.	6
d. None of the above applies.	0

This activity is about your ability to go out without being helped by someone else. It takes account of problems from conditions like learning difficulties, severe anxiety and agoraphobia, rather than physical health problems which are considered in Activities one and eight. Use of a mobile phone app should not be taken into account.[56]

Activity 16: coping with social engagement

Coping with social engagement due to cognitive impairment or mental disorder	
Descriptors	*Points*
a. Engagement in social contact is always precluded due to difficulty relating to others or significant distress experienced by the claimant.	15
b. Engagement in social contact with someone unfamiliar to the claimant is always precluded due to difficulty relating to others or significant distress experienced by the claimant.	9
c. Engagement in social contact with someone unfamiliar to the claimant is not possible for the majority of the time due to difficulty relating to others or significant distress experienced by the claimant.	6
d. None of the above applies.	0

The problems taken into account in this activity are those arising from 'cognitive impairment or mental disorder'. To score points, your social engagement must be restricted due to 'difficulty relating to others or significant distress'. Autism could be relevant here, but so could other conditions – eg, anxiety, depression and personality disorder. The activity is supposed to be a test of your ability to engage

Part 7: National Insurance, work and work-related rules
Chapter 45: Limited capability for work
1. The work capability assessment

with others in a working environment, so should not be limited to socialising, but should include things like reciprocity, give and take, initiation and response.[57] **Note:** if descriptor 16(a) applies, you also have limited capability for work-related activity (see below).

Acitivity 17: appropriateness of behaviour with other people

Appropriateness of behaviour with other people, due to cognitive impairment or mental disorder

Descriptors	Points
a. Has, on a daily basis, uncontrollable episodes of aggressive or disinhibited behaviour that would be unreasonable in any workplace.	15
b. Frequently has uncontrollable episodes of aggressive or disinhibited behaviour that would be unreasonable in any workplace.	15
c. Occasionally has uncontrollable episodes of aggressive or disinhibited behaviour that would be unreasonable in any workplace.	9
d. None of the above applies.	0

This activity considers problems due to 'cognitive impairment or mental disorder'. Merely being disinhibited or angry is not enough. Alcohol abuse, for example, does not count by itself, but if you are assessed as having alcohol (or drug) dependency, or a condition like autism or psychotic illness, the consequences for your behaviour may count.[58] All the descriptors look at whether you have 'uncontrollable episodes of aggressive or disinhibited behaviour which would be unreasonable in any workplace'. The behaviour could be physical but also verbal – eg, serious verbal aggression.[59] **Note:** if descriptor 17(a) applies, you also have limited capability for work-related activity (see below).

Limited capability for work-related activity

The work capability assessment includes an assessment of whether you have 'limited capability for work-related activity'. This is to decide whether your disability is so severe or your health is so poor that, in addition to not being able to work, you cannot be expected to do things like attend work-focused interviews or retraining. For UC, if you have limited capability for work-related activity, you are said to have 'limited capability for work and work-related activity'.[60]

The test decides whether you are entitled to a limited capability for work-related activity element in your UC (see p71) and whether you are in the 'support group' for ESA (see p636). If you have claimed HB as well as ESA, it is used to decide whether you are entitled to a support component in your HB (see p337).

You may automatically count as having limited capability for work-related activity, or you may be required to complete a questionnaire and/or attend a medical. If you do not return the questionnaire or take part in the medical and do not have 'good reason' ('good cause' for ESA), you are treated as not having limited capability for work-related activity.

When deciding whether you have good reason/good cause, the DWP must take into account:[61]

- whether you were outside Great Britain at the time you were notified;
- your state of health;
- the nature of any disability you have;
- any other matter it thinks appropriate.

Assessing limited capability for work-related activity

To have limited capability for work-related activity, your mental or physical condition must be such that one or more statements (or 'descriptors') describing a severe limitation in certain activities could be applied to you.

A descriptor applies if it applies to you for the majority of the time(s) you try to do the activity described. You are assessed wearing any prosthesis that you are normally fitted with or wear, and/or using any aid or appliance that you normally wear or use, or could reasonably be expected to wear or use.[62]

Some descriptors are about physical incapacity. To have them applied to you, your incapacity must arise from 'a specific bodily disease or disablement'. Other descriptors are about mental incapacity. To have them applied to you, your incapacity must arise from 'a specific mental illness or disablement'.[63]

The DWP may retest you to find out whether there has been a relevant change of circumstances, to see whether a previous finding was wrong or mistaken, or (for ESA only) if it is three months or more since your last test.[64]

You may be required to complete a questionnaire and/or attend a medical examination.

Activity	Descriptors
1. Mobilising unaided by another person with or without a walking stick, manual wheelchair or other aid if such aid is normally, or could reasonably be, worn or used.	Cannot either: (a) mobilise more than 50 metres on level ground without stopping in order to avoid significant discomfort or exhaustion; or (b) repeatedly mobilise 50 metres within a reasonable timescale because of significant discomfort or exhaustion.
2. Transferring from one seated position to another.	Cannot move between one seated position and another seated position located next to one another without receiving physical assistance from another person.

Part 7: National Insurance, work and work-related rules
Chapter 45: Limited capability for work
1. The work capability assessment

3. Reaching.	Cannot raise either arm as if to put something in the top pocket of a coat or jacket.
4. Picking up and moving or transferring by the use of the upper body and arms (excluding standing, sitting, bending or kneeling and all other activities specified in this Schedule).	Cannot pick up and move a 0.5 litre carton full of liquid.
5. Manual dexterity.	Cannot press a button (such as a telephone keypad) with either hand or cannot turn the pages of a book with either hand.
6. Making self understood through speaking, writing, typing, or other means which are normally, or could reasonably be, used unaided by another person.	Cannot convey a simple message, such as the presence of a hazard.
7. Understanding communication by: (i) verbal means (such as hearing or lip reading) alone; *or* (ii) non-verbal means (such as reading 16 point print or Braille) alone; *or* (iii) a combination of (i) and (ii), using any aid that is normally, or could reasonably be, used unaided by another person.	Cannot understand a simple message, such as the location of a fire escape, due to sensory impairment.
8. Absence or loss of control while conscious leading to extensive evacuation of the bowel and/or voiding of the bladder, other than enuresis (bed-wetting), despite the wearing or use of any aids or adaptations which are normally, or could reasonably be, worn or used.	At least once a week experiences: (a) loss of control leading to extensive evacuation of the bowel and/or voiding of the bladder; *or* (b) substantial leakage of the contents of a collecting device, sufficient to require the individual to clean themselves and change clothing.
9. Learning tasks.	Cannot learn how to complete a simple task, such as setting an alarm clock, due to cognitive impairment or mental disorder.

10. Awareness of hazard.	Reduced awareness of everyday hazards, due to cognitive impairment or mental disorder, leads to a significant risk of: (a) injury to self or others; or (b) damage to property or possessions, such that the claimant requires supervision for the majority of the time to maintain safety.
11. Initiating and completing personal action (which means planning, organisation, problem solving, prioritising or switching tasks).	Cannot, due to impaired mental function, reliably initiate or complete at least two sequential personal actions.
12. Coping with change.	Cannot cope with any change, due to cognitive impairment or mental disorder, to the extent that day to day life cannot be managed.
13. Coping with social engagement, due to cognitive impairment or mental disorder.	Engagement in social contact is always precluded due to difficulty relating to others or significant distress experienced by the claimant.
14. Appropriateness of behaviour with other people, due to cognitive impairment or mental disorder.	Has, on a daily basis, uncontrollable episodes of aggressive or disinhibited behaviour that would be unreasonable in any workplace.
15. Conveying food or drink to the mouth.	(a) Cannot convey food or drink to the claimant's own mouth without receiving physical assistance from someone else; or (b) Cannot convey food or drink to the claimant's own mouth without repeatedly stopping or experiencing breathlessness or severe discomfort; or (c) Cannot convey food or drink to the claimant's own mouth without receiving regular prompting given by someone else in the claimant's physical presence; or (d) Owing to a severe disorder of mood or behaviour, fails to convey food or drink to the claimant's own mouth without receiving: (i) physical assistance from someone else; or (ii) regular prompting given by someone else in the claimant's presence.

Part 7: National Insurance, work and work-related rules
Chapter 45: Limited capability for work
1. The work capability assessment

16. Chewing or swallowing food or drink.	(a) Cannot chew or swallow food or drink; *or*
	(b) Cannot chew or swallow food or drink without repeatedly stopping, experiencing breathlessness or severe discomfort; *or*
	(c) Cannot chew or swallow food or drink without repeatedly receiving regular prompting given by someone else in the claimant's presence; *or*
	(d) Owing to a severe disorder of mood or behaviour, fails to:
	(i) chew or swallow food or drink; *or*
	(ii) chew or swallow food or drink without regular prompting given by someone else in the claimant's presence.

7. Treated as having limited capability for work-related activity

You are treated as having limited capability for work-related activity because of your health if:[65]

- you have a terminal illness – ie, your death can reasonably be expected within 12 months; *or*
- you are receiving chemotherapy or radiotherapy treatment for cancer, or are recovering from that treatment, or you are likely to receive such treatment within six months from the date the DWP determines whether or not you have limited capability for work-related activity. In any of these circumstances, the DWP must be satisfied that you have limited capability for work-related activity. When deciding this, the decision maker should take into account the medical evidence to see if your cancer treatment has side effects which are likely to limit your ability to carry out work-related activity;[66] *or*
- because of a specific disease or disablement, there would be a substantial risk to your mental or physical health or to the mental or physical health of someone else if you were found not to have limited capability for work-related activity (if you appeal about this rule, the appeal tribunal should have a list of the types of work-related activity available in your area, indicating the most and least difficult, and which activities the DWP say that you can do without substantial risk[67]); *or*
- you are pregnant and there would be a serious risk of damage to your health or to your baby's health if you do not refrain from work-related activity and, for UC only, from work; *or*

• for UC only, you have reached pension age (see p257) and are entitled to AA, the highest rate of the DLA care component or the enhanced rate of the PIP/ADP daily living component.

Note that, apart from where you are terminally ill, qualifying under the rules above does not mean that the limited capability for work-related activity element is included in your UC straight away. See p71 for when it is included. In addition, for UC only, you are automatically treated as having limited capability for work-related activity if you are transferring to UC from ESA and you had, or were treated as having, limited capability for work-related activity for ESA – ie, you were entitled to the support component in your ESA.[68]

Are you transferring to universal credit from employment and support allowance?

If you were getting ESA and were assessed as having limited capability for work-related activity, but then claim UC, you automatically have limited capability for work-related activity. However, the DWP may wrongly overlook this rule and insist that you have to be assessed again. If this affects you, do the following.

1. Point out the rule and insist that you should be automatically treated as having limited capability for work-related activity for UC. If necessary, challenge the decision on your UC entitlement.

2. The DWP may say that it needs to check that you were getting ESA – complain if this is taking a long time. Ultimately, an unreasonably long delay might be challenged by judicial review (see p1410).

3. The limited capability for work-related activity element should be included in your UC from your first monthly assessment period.[69]

4. Remember that, despite these rules, the DWP can still apply the work capability assessment to you again.

The work capability assessment process

For UC, you are usually sent a questionnaire (UC50) to complete. You may also be required to take part in a medical assessment. However, a decision can be made without a questionnaire or a medical if it is considered that there is enough other information.[70] For ESA, information provided with your claim (including where required a medical certificate from your doctor) is considered. Unless you are treated as having limited capability for work (see p988), usually you are sent a questionnaire (ESA50) to complete. You may also be required to take part in a medical assessment. However, a decision can be made without a questionnaire or a medical if it is considered that there is enough other information.[71]

Medical assessments are carried out (by a doctor or other 'approved healthcare professional') on behalf of the DWP medical service by the Health Assessment

Part 7: National Insurance, work and work-related rules
Chapter 45: Limited capability for work
1. The work capability assessment

Advisory Service. For official information about the assessment, such as having an audio recording of your medical, using an interpreter and the location of assessment centres, see chdauk.co.uk. For advice about the questionnaire and medical, see below and p1011.

Face-to-face, telephone and video assessments
– During the coronavirus pandemic, face-to-face medical assessments were suspended during 2020 and much of 2021. Face-to-face assesments have begun to be reintroduced, but may still be carried out by telephone or video instead.
– If a telephone or video assessment is arranged, but you fail to attend or take part in it without good cause, as with a face-to-face assessment, you will be regarded as not having limited capability for work (see p1011).
– If a telephone or video assessment is not considered suitable for you, there may be a delay until a face-to-face assessment can be arranged. However, remember that a decision can be made without an assessment if there is enough other information.

As part of the work capability assessment, similar processes, including use of existing information and your UC50 or ESA50 questionnaire, apply to deciding whether you have limited capability for work-related activity.

There are no rules on how often you are reassessed. Usually, this is decided by the DWP medical service. If you are assessed as having limited capability for work-related activity (see p1004) and having a 'severe, lifelong' disability or condition and are 'unlikely to ever be able to move into work', you will not be reassessed.[72]

The questionnaire

Unless it is already accepted that you have limited capability for work, or you are treated as having limited capability for work, usually you are sent a questionnaire (UC50 or ESA50) to complete.

How do you complete the questionnaire?
1. Read the notes on the form before answering the questions. It may be helpful to draft your answers on a separate sheet of paper first.
2. If someone has to complete the questionnaire for you, or if you can only do so yourself slowly or with pain, explain this.
3. Make sure to list all your symptoms. If you have to appeal, the First-tier Tribunal may be less likely to believe you have symptoms if you did not mention them on the questionnaire. Ask someone who knows you well to check your answers.
4. If you have good and bad days, explain this. If possible, give a rough estimate of how often you could perform the activity and how often you could not.
5. Compare the draft of your answers with the list beginning on p994 and work out your score. Your answers should not be exaggerated, but check that you have not underestimated any of your problems and that you have given all the detail you can.

6. If you have any difficulties with English or with reading and writing, get independent help before you submit the form.

7. If someone has helped you fill out the form, include her/his details at the end where the form asks about this.

8. Always make a copy of your questionnaire with your answers before returning it.

You have four weeks from the date the questionnaire is sent to complete and return it. A reminder must be sent to you at least three weeks after the questionnaire was sent. You must then be given a further week from the date the reminder was sent to return the questionnaire. If you still do not return it in time, you are treated as not having limited capability for work, unless you can show that you had a good reason (for ESA, good cause) for not returning it on time.[73]

Good cause and good reason

When deciding whether you have '**good cause**', the DWP must consider all the circumstances, including whether you were outside Great Britain at the relevant time, your state of health and the nature of your disability.[74] There is no equivalent rule for deciding whether you have '**good reason**' for UC, but in practice the same sort of issues should be taken into account.

If you are late in completing and returning the questionnaire, do so as soon as you can and explain why you were late. If your benefit stops because you are considered not to have had good reason/cause, but you think you did, consider challenging the decision (see p1013). 'Complex needs' or 'safeguarding' procedures apply if you are considered to be 'vulnerable' – eg, if you have a serious mental health condition. These procedures are not a legal requirement, but involve extra checks before treating you as not having limited capability for work. If you think you are vulnerable, ask whether the procedures were considered, and seek advice. You should also make a fresh claim for benefit – but note that if you are not already under the UC system, a new claim for UC or ESA will bring you under the UC system (see p22). If the DWP decides that you did not have a good reason/cause, you can appeal (see Chapter 57).

On receiving your completed questionnaire, the DWP considers whether you should be treated as having limited capability for work or whether you clearly score enough points to satisfy the test. If neither of these apply, a medical examination is arranged.

Medical assessments

You may be required to attend and take part in a medical assessment as part of the work capability assessment. **Note:** face-to-face assessments are being reintroduced

Part 7: National Insurance, work and work-related rules
Chapter 45: Limited capability for work
1. The work capability assessment

in some cases, but you may be asked to take part in a telephone or video assessment instead (see p1009). Bear in mind the following.

- If you fail to attend and take part in a medical assessment without a good reason (for ESA, good cause), you are treated as not having limited capability for work.
- If you cannot attend or take part in the medical, contact your assessment centre immediately to explain why and ask for another appointment.
- If you have a face-to-face appointment but you are too ill to travel, ask to be examined at home.
- If you have a face-to-face medical, you can claim your travel expenses for going to the medical. If you have to attend by taxi or minicab, you cannot claim for your fares unless your assessment centre agrees to this before you travel.
- You can have a friend or adviser at the medical with you and they may take notes.
- The medical examiner takes into account the information on your questionnaire, what you tell her/him, and your appearance and behaviour during the assessment.

In order to complete the medical report, the medical examiner asks about your condition and assesses whether, in her/his opinion, you have limited capability for work. S/he considers your abilities in each of the specific areas of activity.

The medical examiner asks about your typical day and uses the information to assess your ability to perform the activities in the work capability assessment. Make sure to tell the examiner about things like good and bad days and what medication you are taking. S/he then completes a report (a UC85 or ESA85), indicating which descriptors s/he thinks apply to you, and sends it to the DWP.

Failing to attend a medical assessment

If you do not attend and take part in a medical examination without a good reason (good cause for ESA), you are treated as not having limited capability for work – ie, you fail the work capability assessment. You must have been sent notice of the date and time of the medical at least seven days beforehand, unless you agreed to accept less than this.[75]

Good reason and good cause

When deciding whether you have '**good cause**' for ESA, the DWP must consider all the circumstances, including those that apply to the questionnaire (see p1010). 'Good cause' may also include being too ill or distressed on the day of the medical, or wishing to be examined by someone of the same sex and this was not possible. In practice, the same sort of things should be taken into account when deciding whether you have '**good reason**' for UC.

If your benefit stops because you are considered not to have good reason/cause for failing to attend and take part in the medical, but you think you did, consider challenging the decision (see below). 'Complex needs', or 'safeguarding' procedures apply if you are considered to be 'vulnerable' – eg, if you have a serious mental health condition. These procedures are not a legal requirement, but involve extra checks before treating you as not having limited capability for work. If you think you are vulnerable, ask whether the procedures were considered, and seek advice. You should also make a fresh claim for benefit, but note that a new claim for UC or ESA will bring you under the UC system (see p22). If the DWP does not accept that you had good cause/reason, consider appealing (see Chapter 57).

The decision

The decision on whether or not you have limited capability for work is made by a DWP decision maker. The decision maker can disagree with the medical report, although in practice this is unusual. The medical examiner includes in the medical report a suggested date when the work capability assessment should be applied to you again in order to retest your capability. You cannot appeal about how often you are retested.

If the decision maker does not consider that you have limited capability for work, you may still be entitled to some UC if your claim was for UC. If your claim was for ESA, you are not entitled to ESA. If you have been getting ESA, your award is revised or superseded (see Chapter 56) and your benefit is stopped.

2. Challenging a decision

You can challenge a decision by applying for a revision or supersession (see Chapter 56), or by making an appeal (see Chapter 57). You must usually apply for a mandatory reconsideration before you can appeal. However, in an ESA case where you are challenging a decision that you do not have limited capability for work, if you would be entitled to get ESA while appealing (see p1015) then you can appeal straight away.[76]

Initially, the DWP makes a 'determination' on your limited capability for work.[77] The determination should then be incorporated into a decision about your entitlement to benefit or national insurance (NI) credits for limited capability for work. You only have a right of appeal once this is included in a decision.[78]

Appeals are considered by the First-tier Tribunal, which must include a medically qualified person (see p1329). The tribunal does not have to follow either the UC85 or ESA85 medical report or the DWP's decision.

When you appeal against a decision, the whole decision can be looked at again if it is considered right to do so. So the tribunal might decide to look at an aspect of the decision that you are happy with and do not want changed. This could

Part 7: National Insurance, work and work-related rules
Chapter 45: Limited capability for work
2. Challenging a decision

result in your losing some, or even all, of your entitlement. The tribunal should give you a warning if it wants to look at an aspect of the decision that you do not want changed.

Are you appealing?

1. Get advice from one of the organisations listed in Appendix 1.

2. Remember that there are only certain circumstances in which you can work and still be regarded as having limited capability for work (see p987). If you work while you are appealing, you may lose entitlement to benefit, even if you eventually win your appeal.

3. Request a copy of the medical evidence that the DWP holds on your file. If you appeal, a copy of the medical report should be included in the appeal papers that the DWP sends to you and HM Courts and Tribunals Service.

4. Request a hearing of your appeal (ie, rather than a decision just based on the papers). This will give the tribunal the opportunity to hear from you first hand about how your condition affects you, and what happened at the medical examination.

5. Discuss your limited capability for work with your own doctor. In practice, it can be very difficult to win an appeal if your GP or consultant does not support you.

6. Get medical evidence to support your appeal, if you can. This could be from your GP or your consultant, or from both. It is more helpful if this comments on the things at issue in your appeal rather than just setting out your diagnosis and treatment. Check whether your doctor insists on charging you.

7. If you cannot get medical evidence yourself, consider using previous medical reports if you passed the work capability assessment and getting evidence from other sources – eg, a community nurse or an occupational therapist. You could ask the tribunal to obtain further medical evidence, although in practice, it may refuse.[79]

8. The tribunal should make a decision based on all the evidence – medical and non-medical. If necessary, point out that it can prefer your own or your doctor's evidence to that of the medical examiner.[80]

9. DWP medical reports are in electronic form. These may have inconsistencies or errors in them. The tribunal must deal with any discrepancies and take these into account when considering the weight to be given to different sources of evidence.[81]

10. The tribunal cannot carry out its own examination of you.[82] However, be aware that it may observe your conduct in the room – eg, how you walk or sit.

11. Consider asking a person who lives with you or who knows you well to attend the hearing to describe the day-to-day problems you have.

12. Take a list of any medication you are taking to the hearing.

Getting benefit while challenging a decision

If you have claimed **universal credit** (UC), you can continue to get UC while your request for a mandatory reconsideration is being considered and while your appeal is pending.

If you have been refused **employment and support allowance (ESA)** because you have failed the work capability assessment, you cannot get ESA while your request for a mandatory reconsideration is being considered. However, if you would be able to get ESA while appealing (see below) then the requirement for you to have a mandatory reconsideration before you can appeal does not apply, so you can appeal straight away.[83] If you cannot get ESA, you may be able to get UC instead (see p1017). However, a claim for UC will bring you under the UC system (see p22). That will mean that you can no longer get income-related ESA (or other means-tested benefits or tax credits), even if your challenge of the ESA decision is successful.

If you submit a new claim for ESA or jobseeker's allowance (JSA) of any kind, you can no longer get income-related ESA or income-based JSA (except in very limited circumstances where you are prevented by law from claiming UC), even if your challenge to the refusal of your ESA is successful (see p22).

Once you have appealed, you may be able to get ESA while your appeal is pending (see below) – you do not need to make a new claim. This is usually the best option, if you are able to get ESA. You cannot get income-related ESA pending your appeal if you have claimed UC or JSA (income-based or contribution-based) and so have come under the UC system. Getting ESA pending your appeal does *not* mean that you come under the UC system, as it does not require a new claim to be made,[84] although there are cases where the DWP has wrongly said that it does involve a new claim.

Example

Syed was getting income-related ESA, but this stops when he fails the work capability assessment. Syed requests a mandatory reconsideration of the decision, and decides to claim JSA in the meantime. Syed is not prevented from claiming UC. As he has made a new claim for JSA, he now comes under the UC system. He cannot get income-based JSA and must claim UC instead.

Syed then appeals and gets UC while his ESA appeal is pending. Syed's appeal against the work capability assessment is eventually successful, but he remains on UC and does not go back to income-related ESA. If Syed had decided not to claim JSA, once he appealed he may have been able to get income-related ESA pending his appeal instead of having to claim UC.

Getting employment and support allowance while appealing

If you can appeal against a decision that you do not have limited capability for work for ESA and it is the first such decision you have had, or the first since a previous decision that you have limited capability for work, then once you have appealed and you have submitted a medical certificate, you can get ESA until the First-tier Tribunal makes its decision.[85] You cannot get ESA pending an appeal if

Part 7: National Insurance, work and work-related rules
Chapter 45: Limited capability for work
2. Challenging a decision

you are being *treated as* not having limited capability for work because you did not return the questionnaire or attend the medical (see p1010 and p1012).

Once you have appealed, the government has said that your ESA pending an appeal can cover the period when your request for a mandatory reconsideration was being considered.[86]

However, you cannot get ESA pending an appeal if the decision that you do not have limited capability for work is the second, or a subsequent, such decision you have had in a row and the decision you are appealing against is about a claim made on or after 30 March 2015.

Examples

Erin claims ESA in June 2022. She is found not to have limited capability for work – ie, she fails the work capability assessment. Erin would be entitled to ESA whle appealing (in her case, this is because it is the first time she has failed the work capability assessment), so she appeals straight away and sends in a medical certificate. Erin gets ESA pending the appeal.

Max claimed ESA in June 2021. He was found not to have limited capability for work (ie, he failed the work capability assessment), but he appealed and successfully challenged this and so he was paid ESA. In May 2022, Max has another work capability assessment, and fails it. Max would be entitled to ESA whle appealing, as although this is not the first time he has failed the work capability assessment, it is the first time since the tribunal decided that in fact he had passed it. But he decides to ask for a mandatory reconsideration of the new decision. Max cannot be paid ESA pending the mandatory reconsideration. After the mandatory reconsideration, which did not change the new decision, Max appeals again and sends in a medical certificate. Max gets ESA pending the appeal.

If you have limited capability for work, but are appealing about whether or not you should be put in the support group, you remain entitled to ESA while your request for a mandatory reconsideration is being considered and while your appeal is pending. However, the amount you are paid does not include the support component.

Note:
- To get ESA pending an appeal, you must continue to submit medical certificates. You do not need to make a new claim for ESA.[87]
- ESA pending an appeal does not include an additional component, although it can include any premiums and housing costs to which you are entitled.[88]
- You are treated as having limited capability for work while you are appealing, so the DWP does not usually assess you in this period. However, if you develop a new condition or your condition significantly worsens, the DWP can assess you again. If it determines that you have limited capability for work, you can get ESA in the normal way (including either of the additional components) from that point on. The First-tier Tribunal still considers your appeal for the

period up until then. Even if the DWP determines that you do not have limited capability for work, you remain entitled to ESA pending the appeal.[89]

- If your appeal is successful, the original decision about your limited capability for work is changed so that you are entitled to ESA. Your ESA continues in the normal way, and you can qualify for an additional component.

- If your appeal is successful but the DWP considers that your condition improved while the appeal was pending, it might decide that you do not have limited capability for work now.[90] You can appeal against this decision, and should be able to get ESA pending the appeal again.[91]

- If you lose your appeal, the original decision that you do not have limited capability for work is not changed. From the week after the week in which the First-tier Tribunal notifies the DWP of its decision, the DWP treats you as not having had limited capability for work while you were getting ESA pending your appeal.[92] Your entitlement to ESA therefore stops, although you keep the ESA that was paid to you pending the appeal. Although you can appeal against the decision to treat you as not having limited capability for work, the prospect of success is likely to be limited, as the rules allow the DWP to do this when you have lost your appeal.[93]

Getting jobseeker's allowance or income support while challenging a decision

If you submit a new claim for JSA (income-based or contribution-based), then you will come under the UC system, unless (in very limited circumstances) you are prevented by law from claiming UC (see p22). You cannot then get income-based JSA or income-related ESA, even if your challenge is successful.

You cannot make a new claim for income support, unless (in very limited circumstances) you are prevented by law from claiming UC (see p23).

Getting universal credit while challenging a decision

Generally, you can get UC while challenging a decision. If you make a new claim for UC, you come under the UC system (see p22) and you cannot get income-related ESA (or other means-tested benefits or tax credits) again.

You can get UC while you are waiting for your request for a mandatory reconsideration to be considered and once you have appealed. You may still be able to get contributory ESA or contribution-based JSA under the UC system. You may be subject to work-related requirements while you are appealing (see Chapter 46). If your challenge is successful, your UC can then include a limited capability for work element, if you can still get it, or a limited capability for work-related activity element if that applies.[94] If your challenge is unsuccessful, you may still be able to get UC, but will not be entitled to a limited capability for work or limited capability for work-related activity element.

Part 7: National Insurance, work and work-related rules
Chapter 45: Limited capability for work
3. Periods of limited capability for work

If your condition worsens

For UC, once there has been a decision that you do not have limited capability for work, there is no further work capability assessment, unless there is evidence to suggest that the decision was made in ignorance of, or based on a mistake about, a material fact, or there has been a relevant change in circumstances regarding your condition.[95]

For ESA, if your condition has significantly worsened since the decision, or you have a new condition, and you are not already getting ESA pending the appeal, you could make a new claim for ESA – but see the note below. In this situation, you should be treated as having limited capability for work until a new work capability assessment is carried out (see p988).

Note: if you make a new claim for ESA, you come under the UC system unless (in very limited circumstances) you are prevented from claiming UC (see p22). If you come under the UC system, you cannot get income-related ESA. You can get UC instead. You may still be able to get contributory ESA.

If you are already getting ESA pending the appeal, you could inform the DWP and ask it to make a determination on your limited capability for work. If the DWP thinks that you still fail the work capability assessment, your entitlement to ESA after the appeal has been decided could be affected, even if you win your appeal.

3. Periods of limited capability for work

A 'period of limited capability for work' for employment and support allowance (ESA) generally means a period in which you have, or are treated as having, limited capability for work. It does not include any period not covered by your claim for ESA.[96] However, see the linking rules below. There are no rules on periods of limited capability for work for universal credit.

Linking rules

Different periods of limited capability for work can be joined or 'linked' to form one continuous period for ESA. The effect is that you are treated as having had limited capability for work throughout the whole of the linked period. Different periods are linked if they are not more than 12 weeks apart.[97]

If periods of limited capability for work are linked, it means that:
- the question of whether or not you satisfy the national insurance contribution conditions for ESA may be decided at the beginning of the first period (see p964);[98]
- you do not have to serve further 'waiting days' (see p646) before becoming entitled to ESA because you have already served them;

- you may get one of the additional ESA components straight away, or once you have been reassessed as passing the work capability assessment;
- for the purposes of the rules on housing costs, certain linking rules apply (see p358).

4. Work you can do while claiming employment and support allowance

The general rule is that you cannot work and be entitled to employment and support allowance (ESA) at the same time.[99] With certain exceptions (see below), in any week in which you work (paid or unpaid), you are not entitled to ESA and you are automatically treated as not having limited capability for work, even if it has previously been decided that you do.[100]

However, you are only treated as not entitled to ESA on the actual days that you work, rather than the whole week, if you work:
- during the first week of your claim; or
- during the last week in which you had limited capability for work or were treated as having limited capability for work.[101]

It is arguable that work that is so minimal that it can be regarded as trivial or negligible should be ignored.[102]

You can do certain work without automatically being treated as not having limited capability for work. For how earnings from this may affect income-related ESA, see p413. **Note:** earnings under the 'permitted work' rules (see p1020) that are under the relevant earnings limit are ignored for ESA.

You can do the following:[103]
- work as a local councillor;
- work (for a maximum of one day or two half days a week) as a member of the First-tier Tribunal if you have been appointed because of your experience of disability issues;
- domestic work (eg, cooking and cleaning) in your own home;
- caring for a relative;
- caring for another person living with you under specific legislation relating to accommodating children or temporarily caring for someone else if you are paid for this;
- caring for someone provided with 'continuing care' by a local authority under section 26A of the Children (Scotland) Act 1995, where you get payments for that;
- work you do to protect someone or prevent serious damage to property or livestock during an emergency;

Part 7: National Insurance, work and work-related rules
Chapter 45: Limited capability for work
4. Work you can do while claiming employment and support allowance

- work done while receiving assistance in pursuing self-employment under section 2 of the Employment and Training Act 1973 or section 2 of the Enterprise and New Towns (Scotland) Act 1990 (test-trading);
- voluntary work that is not for a relative, provided the only payment you receive is to cover your reasonable expenses and it is considered reasonable for you to work free of charge;
- work done in the course of a work placement (unpaid work experience with an employer), approved in writing by the DWP before the placement starts;
- for contributory ESA, any work you do in a week in which you are treated as having limited capability for work because you are receiving plasmapheresis, regular weekly treatment for haemodialysis for chronic renal failure, regular weekly treatment for total parenteral nutrition, or are recovering from such treatment (see p990);[104]
- 'permitted work' (see below).

Relatives
A **'relative'** is a grandparent, grandchild, uncle, aunt, nephew, niece, and includes **'close relatives'** – ie, parent, parent-in-law, son, son-in-law, daughter, daughter-in-law, step-parent, stepson, stepdaughter, brother, sister, or the partner of any of these.

Note: you can work and still be entitled to universal credit (UC). However, if you earn more than a set monthly amount from work, you may be treated as not having limited capability for work or the DWP may reassess you (see p992). If you are doing permitted work for contributory ESA and also claiming UC, for UC your earnings from that work are treated in the same way as any other earnings from work (see p117).

Permitted work

'Permitted work' (sometimes called 'exempt' work) is work of any kind, which you can do while on ESA:[105]

- as part of a treatment programme done under medical supervision while you are in hospital or regularly attending hospital as an outpatient, provided you do not earn more than £152 a week; *or*
- for an unlimited period, provided you do not earn more than £20 a week. This is called the 'permitted work lower limit'; *or*
- for an unlimited period, provided you do not earn more than £152 a week and you are in 'supported work' (sometimes called 'supervised work'); *or*
- for an unlimited period, where you work on average fewer than 16 hours a week and in any week you do not earn more than £152 a week. This is called the 'permitted work higher limit'. For how your hours are calculated, see p975.

. . . .

Supported work

'**Supported work**' is work which is supervised by someone employed by a public or local authority, or by a voluntary organisation or community interest company, whose job it is to find work for people with disabilities. This could include work in a sheltered workshop or with help from social services. The DWP usually says that you need not have the person working alongside you, although the support should be ongoing and regular. Where possible, check in advance that the DWP agrees that the work counts as supported work.

. . . .

If your earnings in any week are higher than the relevant limit, you are not entitled to ESA for that week.[106] Your earnings are worked out for this purpose in the same way as for income-related ESA (see p405), except that only your own earnings count, not those of your partner. Only your earnings count, not any other kind of income.

Although there are no special rules, you must inform the DWP, in advance if possible, about any permitted work you do. The DWP asks you to complete Form PW1, available at gov.uk/government/publications/employment-and-support-allowance-permitted-work-form. If the particular activities you carry out in your work suggest that your limited capability for work might have changed, the DWP might reassess this.

Notes

. . . .

1. The work capability assessment

1 **UC** Reg 39 and Schs 8 and 9 UC Regs
  ESA Regs 20, 25 and 26 ESA Regs; regs 16, 22 and 26 ESA Regs 2013
2 Reg 39(1)(a) UC Regs
3 Regs 19(2) and 21(2) UC(TP) Regs
4 Reg 39(6) and Sch 8 UC Regs
5 Reg 19(4) UC(TP) Regs
6 Reg 19(2) UC(TP) Regs, with savings regarding pre-April 2017 as in the ESAUC(MA) Regs
7 Regs 20, 25 and 26 ESA Regs; regs 16, 22 and 26 ESA Regs 2013
8 Reg 33(2) ESA Regs
9 Reg 16(1)(h) ESA Regs 2013
10 Regs 20, 25, 26, 33 and 35 ESA Regs; regs 16, 21 and 22 ESA Regs 2013
11 Regs 26, 44 and 46 ESA Regs; regs 22, 38 and 40 ESA Regs 2013
12 Reg 30 ESA Regs; reg 26 ESA Regs 2013
13 *EI v SSWP (ESA)* [2016] UKUT 397 (AAC)
14 *EI v SSWP (ESA)* [2016] UKUT 397 (AAC)
15 **UC** Sch 8 paras 4 and 5 UC Regs
  ESA Reg 29 ESA Regs; reg 25 ESA Regs 2013
16 *Charlton v SSWP* [2009] EWCA Civ 42; *JW v SSWP* [2011] UKUT 416 (AAC); *ET v SSWP (UC)* [2021] UKUT 47 (AAC)
17 Regs 41, 43 and 44 UC Regs
18 Reg 41(2) and (3) UC Regs
19 Reg 44 ESA Regs; reg 37 ESA Regs 2013
20 Reg 159 ESA Regs; reg 95 ESA Regs 2013
21 Reg 32(2) and (3) ESA Regs; reg 27 2) and (3) ESA Regs 2013
22 Reg 32(1) ESA Regs; reg 27(1) ESA Regs 2013

Part 7: National Insurance, work and work-related rules
Chapter 45: Limited capability for work
Notes

23 **UC** Regs 39 and 42 UC Regs
ESA Reg 19 ESA Regs; reg 15 ESA Regs 2013
24 **UC** Reg 42(2) UC Regs
ESA Reg 19(4) ESA Regs; reg 15(4) ESA Regs 2013
25 *AF v SSWP (ESA)* [2011] UKUT 61 (AAC); *SAG v Department for Social Development (ESA)* [2011] NICom 171
26 CIB/14534/1996
27 CIB/2620/2000
28 CIB/14587/1996; CIB/14722/1996; CIB/13161/1996; CIB/13508/1996
29 CIB/14722/1996
30 CSIB/12/1996
31 **UC** Reg 39(4) UC Regs
ESA Reg 19(5) ESA Regs; reg 15(5) ESA Regs 2013
32 *SI v SSWP (ESA)* [2014] UKUT 308 (AAC), reported as [2015] AACR 5; *AR v SSWP (ESA)* [2013] UKUT 417 (AAC)
33 *WCA Handbook* para 3.2.2
34 *WCA Handbook* para 3.2.3
35 *WCA Handbook* para 3.2.4
36 *TO'B v SSWP (ESA)* [2011] UKUT 461 (AAC); *AG v SSWP (ESA)* [2018] UKUT 137 (AAC)
37 *KH v SSWP (ESA)* [2014] UKUT 455 (AAC)
38 *SSWP v LH (ESA)* [2017] UKUT 475 (AAC)
39 *WCA Handbook* para 3.2.6; *CL v SSWP (ESA)* [2013] UKUT 434 (AAC) holds that inability to use keyboard or a mouse is sufficient, *DG v SSWP (ESA)* [2014] UKUT 100 (AAC) holds that inability to use both is required
40 *WCA Handbook* para 3.2.8
41 *WCA Handbook* para 3.2.9
42 *SSWP v AI (rule 17) (ESA)* [2017] UKUT 346 (AAC)
43 CIB/14499/1996
44 *WCA Handbook* para 3.2.7
45 *WCA Handbook* 3.2.10
46 *EM v SSWP (ESA)* [2014] UKUT 34 (AAC)
47 *CB v SSWP (ESA)* [2015] UKUT 287 (AAC)
48 *WCA Handbook* para 3.2.11
49 **UC** Reg 39(4) UC Regs
ESA Reg 19(5) ESA Regs; reg 15(5) ESA Regs 2013
50 *WCA Handbook* para 3.5.2
51 *WCA Handbook* para 3.5.3
52 *MP v SSWP (ESA)* [2015] UKUT 458 (AAC); *WCA Handbook* para 3.5.4
53 *MW v SSWP (ESA)* [2014] UKUT 112 (AAC)
54 *WCA Handbook* para 3.5.5
55 *GV v SSWP (ESA)* [2013] UKUT 405 (AAC)

56 *WCA Handbook* para 3.5.6; *TM v SSWP (ESA)* [2018] UKUT 9 (AAC)
57 *JC v SSWP (ESA)* [2014] UKUT 352 (AAC), reported as [2015] AACR 6
58 *WCA Handbook* para 3.5.8; *DR v SSWP (ESA)* [2014] UKUT 188 (AAC); [2014] AACR 38
59 *WC v SSWP (ESA)* [2014] UKUT 363
60 Reg 40 UC Regs
61 Reg 39 ESA Regs; reg 36 ESA Regs 2013
62 **UC** Reg 42(2) UC Regs
ESA Reg 34(3) ESA Regs; reg 30(3) ESA Regs 2013
63 **UC** Reg 40(3) UC Regs
ESA Reg 34(6) ESA Regs; reg 30(6) ESA Regs 2013
64 **UC** Reg 41 UC Regs
ESA Reg 34 ESA Regs; reg 30 ESA Regs 2013
65 **UC** Sch 9 UC Regs
ESA Reg 35 ESA Regs; reg 31 ESA Regs 2013
66 paras 42050-52 and 42680 DMG
67 *KS v SSWP (UC)* [2021] UKUT 132 (AAC)
68 Reg 19(4) UC(TP) Regs
69 Reg 19(4) UC(TP) Regs
70 Regs 43 and 44 UC Regs
71 Regs 21 and 23 ESA Regs; regs 17 and 19 ESA Regs 2013
72 DWP, *Employment and Support Allowance and Universal Credit: changes to the work capability assessment from 29 September 2017*, September 2017
73 **UC** Reg 43 UC Regs
ESA Reg 22 ESA Regs; reg 18 ESA Regs 2013
74 Reg 24 ESA Regs; reg 18 ESA Regs 2013
75 **UC** Reg 44 UC Regs
ESA Reg 23 ESA Regs; reg 19 ESA Regs 2013

2. Challenging a decision
76 *R (Connor) v SSWP* [2020] EWHC 1999 (Admin); ADM Memo 21/20; DMG Memo 19/20
77 **UC** Reg 39 UC Regs
ESA Reg 19 ESA Regs; reg 15 ESA Regs 2013
78 Vol 1 Ch 6, para 06041 DMG
79 s20 SSA 1998; R(S) 3/84
80 CIB/407/1998; CIB/1149/1998; R(M) 1/93; CIB/3074/2003
81 CIB/511/2005
82 s20(3) SSA 1998
83 *R (Connor) v SSWP* [2020] EWHC 1999 (Admin); Official guidance in ADM 21/20 and DMG Memo 19/20
84 Reg 3(j) SS(C&P) Regs

85 Reg 30(1) and (3) ESA Regs; reg 26(1) and (3) ESA Regs 2013
86 House of Commons, *Hansard*, Written answers, 16 December 2013, col 486W
87 Reg 30(3) ESA Regs; reg 26(3) ESA Regs 2013; reg 3(j) SS(C&P) Regs; reg 7 UC,PIP,JSA&ESA(C&P) Regs
88 Reg 5(4) ESA Regs; reg 6(5) ESA Regs 2013 provides that the assessment phase applies, pending the First-tier Tribunal's decision
89 Reg 147A(2) and (4) ESA Regs; reg 87(2) and (4) ESA Regs 2013
90 Reg 147A(6) and (7) ESA Regs; reg 87(7) and (8) ESA Regs 2013
91 This is because the DWP will have made a determination that you do not have limited capability for work, and not merely treated you as not having limited capability for work, so reg 30(3) ESA Regs and reg 26(3) ESA Regs 2013 should apply
92 Reg 147A(5) ESA Regs; reg 87(5) ESA Regs 2013
93 Reg 3(j) SS(C&P) Regs; Memo DMG 33/10, para 52; reg 7 UC,PIP,JSA&ESA(C&P) Regs
94 Art 24 WRA(No.9)O
95 Reg 41(4) UC Regs

3. Periods of limited capability for work
96 Reg 2, definition of 'period of limited capability for work', ESA Regs
97 Regs 2 and 145 ESA Regs; regs 2 and 86 ESA Regs 2013
98 paras 1-3 Sch 1 WRA 2007

4. Work you can do while claiming employment and support allowance
99 Reg 40 ESA Regs; reg 37 ESA Regs 2013
100 Regs 40 and 44 ESA Regs; regs 37 and 38 ESA Regs 2013
101 Reg 40(4) ESA Regs; reg 37(4) ESA Regs 2013
102 CIB/5298/1997; CIB/6777/1999
103 Regs 40 and 45 ESA Regs; regs 37 and 39 ESA Regs 2013
104 Reg 46 ESA Regs; reg 40 ESA Regs 2013
105 Reg 45 ESA Regs; reg 39 ESA Regs 2013
106 Regs 40(1) and (2)(f) and 45 ESA Regs; regs 37(2)(f) and 39 ESA Regs 2013

Chapter 46

• •

Universal credit system work-related requirements

This chapter covers:
1. The claimant commitment (below)
2. The work-related requirements (p1027)
3. Which requirements apply (p1037)

This chapter covers your responsibilities if you come under the universal credit (UC) system (see p22), whether you are getting UC, jobseeker's allowance (JSA) or employment and support allowance (ESA). If you get JSA or ESA under the UC system, the DWP may refer to these as 'new style' JSA and ESA. If you do not come under the UC system, see Chapter 48.

Key facts
- If you come under the universal credit (UC) system, to qualify for UC, contribution-based jobseeker's allowance or contributory employment and support allowance, you must usually accept a 'claimant commitment'.
- You may have to meet some or all of the work-related requirements, which are conditions connected to finding work or getting ready to find work. These are: work-focused interviews, work preparation, work search and work availability.
- If you do not meet the work-related requirements which apply to you, you may be given a sanction. Your benefit is then paid at a reduced or nil rate. However, you may qualify for UC hardship payments (see Chapter 52).

1. The claimant commitment

A claimant commitment is a record of your responsibilities connected to your benefit award.[1] If you come under the universal credit (UC) system (see p22), you must usually accept a claimant commitment to qualify for UC, contribution-based jobseeker's allowance (JSA) and contributory employment and support allowance (ESA).[2] If you are claiming UC jointly with your partner, both of you must usually accept a claimant commitment.[3] If you are required to accept one and do not do so, you are not entitled to UC, JSA or ESA.

You *can* qualify for UC, contribution-based JSA or contributory ESA without accepting a claimant commitment if the DWP considers that you cannot accept one because you lack the capacity to do so, or there are exceptional circumstances which mean it would be unreasonable to expect you to accept one at the moment[4] – eg, you are likely to be in hospital for several weeks or there is a domestic emergency. For UC and contributory ESA, you do not have to accept a claimant commitment if you are terminally ill – ie, due to a progressive disease, your death can reasonably be expected within 12 months.[5] If you lack capacity, the DWP may refer your claim to see whether an appointee is needed (see p1135). Your appointee is not able to accept a claimant commitment on your behalf. If you already have an appointee, this does not automatically mean that you lack capacity, though it may indicate that you do.[6] The DWP should make a decision based on all the available evidence.[7]

A claimant commitment must include:[8]
- the work-related requirements you must meet (see p1037); *and*
- any other information the DWP thinks is appropriate to include.

Note:
- Specific work-related requirement actions may be stated elsewhere on your online journal – ie, not only in your commitments section. If so, it should always be made clear what you have to do and what are the consequences of not doing it.[9]
- Even if you do not have to meet any work-related requirements, your claimant commitment explains your other responsibilities – eg, to report changes in your circumstances.

Work coaches

Job centre staff who support and interview you if you are claiming benefits under the UC system are called '**work coaches**'. Your work coach draws up your claimant commitment and discusses your responsibilities with you. Decisions about what you have to do to meet your work-related responsibilities cannot be changed by a revision, supersession or an appeal, but you can negotiate, ask for a second opinion and/or a review or ask to speak to a manager. If necessary, you can complain. You may be interviewed over the telephone or in person at a job centre, and your work coach may also contact you via your online account.

Accepting your claimant commitment

You must accept the most up-to-date version of your claimant commitment using the method specified by the DWP. This could be online, by telephone or in

Part 7: National Insurance, work and work-related rules
Chapter 46: Universal credit system work-related requirements
1. The claimant commitment

writing.[10] Be sure to use the method specified or you may not count as accepting the claimant commitment. For example, even if you have attended a commitments meeting, you may still need to accept your claimant commitment via your online journal.

If no work-related requirements are to be imposed on you, or you only have to participate in work-focused interviews, your first claimant commitment is usually accepted as part of the normal claims process.[11] Otherwise, your claimant commitment is drawn up by your work coach for you to accept. Most claimants need to take part in a commitments meeting to discuss their circumstances. Ensure that you inform your work coach of any problems you may have in meeting the work-related requirements and that any limitations you are allowed (see p1035) are put on record.

Note:
• If you refuse to accept a claimant commitment, you should be offered up to seven days in which to reconsider so that your claim is not closed.[12]
• If you are not happy with your claimant commitment, you may be able to get it reviewed (see p1027).

If you accept your claimant commitment within the time the DWP has specified, you are usually treated as accepting it on the date of your claim (or any date to which your claim has been backdated).[13] If you are awarded UC or ESA without making a claim (see p44), you are treated as accepting it on the first day of the first assessment period (for UC) or the first benefit week (for ESA) of your benefit award. You can request a second opinion on whether the requirements in your commitment are reasonable before you accept them.[14]

The time within which you must accept your claimant commitment (including one that has been updated) can be extended, if:
• for UC and JSA, you ask the DWP to review any action that it has been proposed you take as a work search or work availability requirement, or whether there should be any limitations on these requirements;[15]
• for ESA, you ask for an extension.[16]

The DWP must be satisfied that your request is reasonable. Be careful not to miss any time limits specified by the DWP for accepting your claimant commitment as this may result in your claim being closed and any benefit terminating. Even if you are not happy with your claimant commitment, it may be better to agree to it and make it clear that you will comply. You can then ask for a review (see p1027).

Risk of 'claim closure' if you have not participated in a commitments meeting

Your claim can be closed because you have failed to attend or participate in a commitments meeting. If this happens, it is a decision that you are not entitled to benefit. You should contact the DWP as soon as possible to avoid your claim being refused in this way and explain any additional needs you have. Otherwise, your claim may be closed on the day after the appointment. If you have additional needs (eg, English is not your first language, or you have literacy difficulties or a disability), the DWP should help you to rebook your appointment.[17] The DWP may refer to this as 'complex needs'. Let them know about your circumstances if you think this should apply to you.[18] If your claim is closed, this is a refusal to award you benefit (eg, UC) and you can ask for a written explanation of the decision. You should be advised of your right to challenge the decision by mandatory reconsideration and appeal.[19] You should also consider submitting a new claim in the meantime.

Reviewing your claimant commitment

Your claimant commitment can be reviewed and updated as the DWP thinks fit.[20] This is done on an ongoing basis to record any changes to the expectations placed on you and the consequences for failing to comply with them. See p1026 for when the time for accepting your claimant commitment can be extended if you ask for a review.

Guidance suggests your claimant commitment should be reviewed after any change in your circumstances.[21] You can ask for your claimant commitment to be reviewed and updated at any time. While a review is being carried out, you should do everything possible to comply with the work-related requirements that are currently imposed on you and make it clear that you intend to do so. Keep a record of what you have done and any reasons you have for not being able to comply fully.

You cannot appeal a decision about your claimant commitment. If you think a decision is unreasonable, you can complain and continue to negotiate. See cpag.org.uk/jr for a pre-action template letter you may be able to use if the commitments are unreasonable for your circumstances.

2. The work-related requirements

If you come under the universal credit (UC) system (see p22), you may have to meet work-related requirements, sometimes even if you are in paid work.[22] There are some situations when no work-related requirements can be imposed on you (see p1039). See pp1037–52 for which (if any) requirements may apply.

If you do not meet the requirements, you continue to be entitled to benefit, but you may be given a sanction and your benefit may be paid at a reduced or nil rate (see Chapter 47). For information on avoiding a sanction, see p1058. **Note:** if

Part 7: National Insurance, work and work-related rules
Chapter 46: Universal credit system work-related requirements
2. The work-related requirements

you are entitled to UC and also to contribution-based jobseeker's allowance (JSA) or contributory employment and support allowance (ESA), you only need to meet one set of work-related requirements – those for UC.[23]

The work-related requirements are:
- work-focused interviews (see below); *and*
- work preparation (see p1029); *and*
- work search (UC and JSA only – see p1030); *and*
- work availability (UC and JSA only – see p1034).

Note: you may also have to attend other interviews connected to the work-related requirements while you are entitled to UC, contribution-based JSA or contributory ESA (see p1036).

Your work-related requirements and the specific actions you must take may be set out in your claimant commitment, or may be notified to you in some other way.[24] You should not be sanctioned if the DWP has not given you proper notification of a requirement which allows you to understand what you have to do and the consequences of not complying.[25]

7 Work-focused interviews

If a work-focused interview requirement is imposed on you, you must take part in one or more interviews relating to work or work preparation.[26] The main purpose of a work-focused interview is to make it more likely that you will find work (or more or better paid work if you are already working). You may also have to participate in other interviews for any purpose connected to the work-related requirements (see p1036).

If you have been referred to a work capability assessment in UC or ESA, you are usually required to have a 'health and work conversation' with your work coach first (see p987). The health and work conversation is a type of work-focused interview about the help you may need to get into work in the future. You do not need to have a health and work conversation in certain circumstances where it would not be appropriate – eg, if you have a terminal illness. The conversation can also be deferred – eg, because of medical treatment.

The DWP tells you how, when and where a work-focused interview is to take place. It should also tell you the reason for the interview, in basic terms, and the consequences of failing to participate.[27] If the DWP does not clarify the type of interview, and the consequences of non-compliance, you should not be sanctioned if you fail to attend or participate, as the DWP has not imposed a valid work-related requirement.[28]

There is no minimum or maximum frequency for work-focused interviews. A work-focused interview may:[29]
- assess your prospects for obtaining or remaining in work (and/or, for UC, more or better paid work);

- assist or encourage you to obtain or remain in work (and/or, for UC, more or better paid work);
- identify activities you can undertake and opportunities for training, education or rehabilitation that will make it more likely that you will obtain or remain in work (and/or, for UC, more or better paid work);
- for UC, determine whether you are in gainful self-employment (see p124) or whether you are in a 'start-up period' (see p125);
- identify current or future work opportunities that are relevant to you.

Note: during the coronavirus pandemic, and for other reasons, your interview may be carried out over the telephone or online, or it may be in person at a job centre. You do not have a choice about how the interview is carried out, but you should inform the DWP if you have any particular needs – eg, you have literacy difficulties, English is not your first language or you are disabled. You should be offered a home visit or telephone interviews, if appropriate. If you are unable to attend an interview for a specific reason such as working or a medical appointment you should let the DWP know, in writing if possible – eg, on your journal. If the DWP insists on an interview which is not appropriate (eg, because it is not accessible to you), you can complain.

Work preparation

If a work preparation requirement is imposed on you, you must take 'particular action' specified by the DWP that makes it more likely that you will obtain paid work, more paid work or better paid work.[30]

Particular action

'**Particular action**' can include attending a skills assessment, improving personal presentation, participating in training or in an employment programme, undertaking work experience or a work placement and developing a business plan.[31] At the time of writing, an example of work preparation is the Job Entry Targeted Support scheme (JETS), which you can be referred to after three months out of work. If you have limited capability for work, work preparation could include participating in a work-focused health-related assessment with a health professional to consider how you might be able to improve your capability for work. Voluntary employability support may also be available. The DWP must make it clear if you are required to participate in any work preparation activity, and explain the consequences if you fail to participate. Note: employment programmes provided by, or for, the Scottish government are voluntary and you cannot be sanctioned if you do not participate.

If you have a disability

If you have a disability or health condition that affects the work you can do, you may be able to get specialist support via the job centre. For further information,

Part 7: National Insurance, work and work-related rules
Chapter 46: Universal credit system work-related requirements
2. The work-related requirements

see gov.uk/looking-for-work-if-disabled. Your work-related requirements are not affected by getting specialist support, and your involvement can be voluntary, although your work coach may agree that it counts towards your work preparation. The Work and Health Programme (see p1122) is also available to disabled people (the DWP says this is voluntary unless you have been out of work and claiming unemployment benefits for two years[32]). In Scotland, there are voluntary programmes you can consider under the Fair Start Scotland scheme. You cannot be sanctioned if you fail to participate in an employment support scheme provided by, or for, the Scottish government.

Your health condition or disability should always be considered when deciding what you have to do as work preparation, including any adjustments you need.

If you are aged 16 to 24

If you are 16 to 24 years old, unemployed and must meet all the work-related requirements for UC (see p1047), you will agree one of three options with your work coach either at the beginning of your claim or when your work coach has got to know you (referred to by DWP as the 'Youth Offer'). At the time of writing, the options are the Youth Employment Programme, Youth Hubs or referral to a youth employability coach.[33] If you are referred to training to help you gain skills needed to find work (or more or better-paid work), this does not prevent you from receiving UC.[34] If you are referred to a job placement via the Kickstart Scheme and are offered a job,[35] then your UC will be affected by your earnings in the usual way (see p40).

The Youth Offer is a work preparation requirement. If your work preparation requirement is temporarily suspended, you should not be referred to a Youth Hub or youth employability coach.[36] If you choose to take part in employment support services provided by, or for, the Scottish government, these are voluntary and you cannot be sanctioned if you do not participate. However, your work coach may refer you to work preparation which is mandatory as part of the Youth Offer. You should be clearly informed of anything which is compulsory and the consequences of not taking part should be explained to you.

Work search

If a work search requirement is imposed on you, you are expected to take 'all reasonable action' (see p1031) to obtain paid work, more paid work or better paid work. You must also take any 'particular action' specified by the DWP.[37]

Particular action
'**Particular action**' can include carrying out work searches, applying for jobs, creating and maintaining an online profile, registering with an employment agency and seeking references.[38] The DWP can specify the amount of time you must spend doing any 'particular action'.

Note: if you are told to apply for a particular job vacancy, you are treated as failing to meet the work search requirement if you are offered an interview for the vacancy and do not participate.[39] The DWP must give you adequate notice of what you are required to do, and explain the consequences of failing to comply.

All reasonable action

In general, 'reasonable action' means you are expected to look for work, regardless of its type or the salary. However, certain limitations can apply to the work you are available for and seeking to do (see p1035).

To count as taking 'all reasonable action' to find paid work, more paid work or better paid work, you must take action that gives you the best prospects of obtaining work. If you are unemployed, this usually includes making job applications. You must normally spend a specified number of hours in each week seeking work – ie:[40]

- at least the weekly number of hours you are expected to work (your 'expected hours' – see below), minus any deductions the DWP allows (see p1032); or
- fewer hours than your 'expected hours', provided the DWP is satisfied that you have taken all reasonable action. For example, if you have been offered a job to start the following week, you may have completed all reasonable action despite having spent fewer than your expected hours on searching for work. Alternatively, you may have an unavoidable situation which has prevented you from spending more hours on your work search.[41] You should make sure the DWP is aware of any particular circumstances that affected your work search.

Your expected hours

You are normally expected to spend 35 hours a week looking for work (your 'expected hours'). However, a lower number of expected hours applies in some cases. This is the number that the DWP thinks is:[42]

- for UC, compatible with your caring responsibilities, if you are a 'responsible carer' (see p1041) of a child who has not yet reached compulsory school age – ie, aged three or four. The DWP says that the expectation is usually 16 hours a week, but it can be lower;[43]
- compatible with your child's normal school hours (including travelling time to and from school), if you are a 'responsible carer' (or, for JSA only, a 'responsible foster carer') for a child under 13. For UC, your child must have reached compulsory school age. The DWP says that the expectation is usually 25 hours a week, but it can be lower.[44] 'Responsible foster carer' is not defined, but it should apply if you are a 'responsible foster parent' (see p1042);
- compatible with your caring responsibilities, if you are a 'relevant carer', a 'responsible carer' (for UC, for a child aged 13 or over) or a 'responsible foster parent (see p1040 for the definitions), and the DWP is satisfied that you have

Part 7: National Insurance, work and work-related rules
Chapter 46: Universal credit system work-related requirements
2. The work-related requirements

reasonable prospects of obtaining paid work, more paid work or better paid work;
- reasonable in the light of your 'physical or mental impairment'.

A table showing the default expected hours for different groups is available in DWP guidance.[45] If you think that your expected hours are too high given your health, disability or caring responsibilities, you can negotiate with your work coach and ask for a review (see p1027). Make it clear that you will comply with your current hours if at all possible. You cannot appeal a decision about your expected hours of work search. If negotiation is unsuccessful, you can complain, but get advice first if possible. If negotiation and complaining are not successful, it may be appropriate to consider sending a judicial review pre-action letter (see p1383).[46] Keep a record of the requests you make to vary your expected hours (eg, by asking via your online journal and taking a screenshot), even if they are not changed.

The DWP can agree deductions from your expected hours of work search for time you spend:[47]
- carrying out paid work; *or*
- carrying out voluntary work. You can do as much voluntary work as you wish, but this can only ever count towards 50 per cent of your expected hours; *or*
- carrying out a work preparation requirement or 'voluntary work preparation' – ie, action that you agree with the DWP to take on a voluntary basis to make it more likely you will obtain paid work, more work or better paid work; *or*
- dealing with temporary childcare responsibilities, a domestic emergency, funeral arrangements or other temporary circumstances. You should not be sanctioned if you temporarily reduce your hours of work search because of this type of unavoidable circumstance,[48] but you should try to agree this with your work coach or inform the DWP as soon as possible. In some cases, your work coach could decide to suspend your work search requirement completely for a temporary period (see p1052).

Examples
Paige is getting contribution-based JSA. She is looking for shop work. To get relevant experience, she volunteers in a charity shop for 10 hours a week. Her expected hours are 35 hours a week. However, she need only spend 25 hours a week looking for work because the DWP agrees to deduct the 10 hours during which she is doing voluntary work.

Ade and Kevin are joint UC claimants. Ade spends a lot of time caring for Kevin who is on long-term sick leave but does not receive personal independence payment or disability living allowance. All of the work-related requirements are imposed on Ade. No work-related requirements are imposed on Kevin because he has limited capability for work-related activity. Ade counts as a 'relevant carer' (see p1041) and his expected hours are 16 hours a week (the hours the DWP is satisfied are compatible with his caring responsibilities). He is therefore meant to look for work for 16 hours a week.

Proving you are searching for work

Always keep careful records of the steps you take to find work or get more hours/pay. Your work coach should agree with you how you are going to evidence your work search, and the DWP may require you to verify what you have done.[49]

How do you prove you are searching for work?

1. Check your claimant commitment to ensure you understand what the DWP expects you to do each week. You must be able to give details of the action you have taken (eg, at an interview with your work coach), so it is extremely important that you keep a record of your attempts to get a job. However, the DWP should accept that it will not always be possible to provide evidence of your work search – eg, employers do not always respond and some of your work search may be done via face-to-face conversations which you cannot prove took place.[50]

2. Make a note every time you do anything that may count as work search. Include the dates and times, who you spoke to and what was said. You should do this online if you have been asked to do so as part of your UC journal.

3. Keep copies of any letters or emails you send, of any advertisements to which you reply and of any job applications you make. If you deliver your CV or a job application by hand, ask for a receipt as proof. Make notes of job searches you do online, including when you use the government's online 'Find a job' service. If your job search is mainly recorded online, take screenshots of relevant activity.

4. Tell the DWP if you have difficulty using a computer, or in reading or writing, or with the English language. You should still try to present proof of your work search – eg, by getting a friend or relative to help you compile your record of jobseeking steps. The DWP should consider what is reasonable for you in the light of all your circumstances and consider whether you need additional support.[51]

5. Sometimes your activities to seek work may be looked at more intensively than usual, possibly over several previous weeks, so ensure they are always sufficient. Do not rely on the fact that your activities have so far not been challenged by the job centre.

6. The 'Find a job' service shows the jobs that have been suggested for you and the jobs for which you have applied. The DWP may ask you to allow it to access your account to check on what you have been doing. Although using 'Find a job' is not a requirement of UC or JSA, if you do not use it the DWP may decide that you are not taking 'all reasonable action'.

7. If the DWP has suggested jobs that you have not applied for, your work coach may question whether you meet the work search requirement. It is therefore best to follow up suggestions and apply for jobs, even if you think they are not appropriate. If you do not meet the requirements of a job (eg, it requires a driving licence and you do not have one), you should point this out to your work coach and could also consider a complaint, but it is still best to apply to avoid a sanction.

Part 7: National Insurance, work and work-related rules
Chapter 46: Universal credit system work-related requirements
2. The work-related requirements

Work availability

If a work availability requirement is imposed on you, you must be able and willing immediately to:[52]
- take up paid work, more paid work or better paid work; *and*
- attend an interview in connection with obtaining paid work, more paid work or better paid work.

You may be able to limit the work you are available for and seeking to do. See p1035 for further information.

Note: for JSA, you are treated as *not* having met the work availability requirement if you are a prisoner on temporary release under specified provisions, so you cannot claim JSA (see p930).[53]

Able and willing to take up work or attend an interview immediately

You must usually be immediately willing and able to attend an interview offered to you in connection with obtaining paid work.[54] It must be lawful for you to work in Great Britain.[55] There must be nothing to prevent you from receiving offers of interviews or job offers (eg, because you are away from home for a short time), and nothing to prevent you from acting on them straight away, with the following exceptions. You are allowed:[56]
- **up to one week** to take up work if you are doing voluntary work, if the DWP is satisfied you need longer;
- **up to one month** to take up work if you are a 'responsible carer' or a 'relevant carer' (see p1041 for the definitions), if the DWP is satisfied you need longer, taking into account alternative care arrangements;
- **until after your notice period** has passed if you are working and you have a duty under employment law, or under the terms of your contract, to give your employer notice that you are leaving work.

In all the situations above, you can also be given **up to 48 hours' notice to attend an interview** in connection with obtaining work. If you cannot arrange to attend an interview because you are employed, you should argue that the law only requires you to attend an interview if you are able to do so.

Even if no work search requirement can be imposed on you for a period, you must still be able and willing to take up paid work or attend an interview immediately, once the circumstances that exempt you from the work search requirement no longer apply, and, in some cases, if the DWP thinks it is reasonable, *before* the circumstances that exempt you from looking for work no longer apply. See p1048 for periods of sickness and p1052 for other circumstances where no work search requirement can be imposed.

Holidays

You are not allowed a holiday from work search and work availability in UC or in JSA under the UC system. If you go away, you must make sure that you continue to meet your work-related requirements, including being contactable and being able to return to attend an interview or start a job. You should also make sure that you are aware of the rules on being away from your normal home for the housing element (see p92), and being away from Great Britain (see p1639), to avoid losing your UC.

Limitations on availability and search for work

You can limit the work you are available for and seeking to do, provided the DWP is satisfied that certain conditions apply. You can limit:[57]

- the type of work and rate of pay (see below);
- the number of hours a week, or the times, you can work (see below);
- the location of the work (see p1036).

You may be able to agree limits on your availability for either an indefinite or a limited period.

The type of work and rate of pay

You can limit the type of work and/or rate of pay in the following circumstances.[58]

- If you have previously done work of a particular type and/or at a particular rate of pay, you can limit your work search and availability to work of a similar type and/or rate of pay for up to four weeks from your date of claim (or, if you were exempt from work-related requirements while getting UC because you had sufficient earnings, from the date you cease paid work if this is later). The DWP must be satisfied that you still have a reasonable prospect of getting work despite the limitation. Ensure you understand when the period starts and ends.
- If you have a 'physical or mental impairment' that has a substantial adverse effect on your ability to do work of a particular type or in particular locations, you do not have to be available for or look for such work. You do not have to show that you have a reasonable prospect of getting work.

DWP guidance says that you can also limit the type of work you look for because of sincerely held beliefs – eg, on religious or conscientious grounds. However, you must show you have reasonable prospects of finding work despite the restriction.[59]

The number of hours

You are normally expected to search for work for at least 35 hours a week (see p1031 for the rules about your 'expected hours' of work search), but the work you have to look for will depend on your earnings from work. However, if you are a 'relevant carer' or a 'responsible carer' (see p1041 for the definitions), or you have a 'physical or mental impairment', your expected hours may be lower, and in this

Part 7: National Insurance, work and work-related rules
Chapter 46: Universal credit system work-related requirements
2. The work-related requirements

situation the hours you are expected to search for work and to be available for work are the same.[60]

There may be times when you have taken 'all reasonable action' (see p1031) to find work even though your hours of work search are lower than the expected number, providing you can show what you have done gives you the best prospects of finding work.[61]

The location of the work

You can limit the location of the work you must search for and be available to do.[62] However, in general, the following apply.

- You need only be available for, and to look for, work in locations that are no more than 90 minutes travel time from your home in either direction. When looking at travel time, the DWP should take into account the frequency of public transport and any disability or health condition you have, which may mean travelling independently takes you longer than it would do otherwise. Your ability to travel may also be affected by your caring responsibilities. In the case of responsible carers of young children, DWP guidance suggests that travel-to-work time should be proportionate to work search requirements – eg, reduced to 60 minutes each way if your expected hours are 16 a week.[63] As the responsible carer of a child, you can negotiate an even shorter expected travel time based on your circumstances if you can show that you still have a reasonable prospect of work.

- If you have a 'physical or mental impairment' that has a substantial adverse effect on your ability to do work in particular locations (eg, you cannot manage stairs), you do not have to be available for work or to look for work in those locations.

The effect of the rules on minimum working conditions

The rules about minimum working conditions (see Appendix 7) can affect your claim for UC or JSA if you are looking for work. You can insist that you are only available for work that meets these conditions (ie, that you will not accept a job if the terms do not comply with the legal requirements) – eg, if an employer is offering a job at less than the minimum wage. The DWP says that you can be sanctioned for failing to apply for a zero-hour contract, as these are not unlawful as long as the employer allows you to take work with other employers.[64] However, you should consider a complaint if you are told to apply for a job without guaranteed hours which is inappropriate for your circumstances – eg, because you have childcare responsibilities, and you may have good reason if you fail to apply for or accept such a job (see p1084)

Other interviews

The DWP can require you to participate in an interview for any purpose connected to any of the work-related requirements – ie, to:[65]

- impose a work-related requirement on you; *or*
- verify that you have complied with a work-related requirement; *or*
- assist you to comply with a work-related requirement.

At the interviews, you may be asked to provide evidence and information. You may also be asked to report any changes in your circumstances that are relevant to your work-related requirements and your compliance with them. You must be informed of an interview and made aware of the consequences of failing to attend and take part (you cannot be sanctioned for failing to attend or participate unless you received proper notification).[66] This can be provided in a written document (letter or claimant commitment), online (eg, via your UC journal), face to face, by text, by email or by telephone. The DWP should keep a record of how and when you were notified and what you were told in case there is a dispute about whether you were correctly informed.[67]

3. Which requirements apply

Many people must meet *all* the work-related requirements (see p1047). However:
- in some cases, no work-related requirements at all can be imposed on you (see p1039); *or*
- you may only have to meet a work-focused interview requirement (see p1045); *or*
- you may only have to meet a work-focused interview and a work preparation requirement (see p1046); *or*
- you may not have to meet a work search or a work availability requirement for a period (see p1048).

A tool to help you identify the correct level of conditionality is available on AskCPAG.

Note: if you are entitled to universal credit (UC) and also to contribution-based jobseeker's allowance (JSA) or contributory employment and support allowance (ESA), you only need to meet one set of work-related requirements – those for UC.[68]

Your work-related requirements depend on your circumstances. If you are responsible for a child, your work-related requirements usually depend on her/his age, and if you are in a couple, whether you are the 'responsible carer' (see p1041). You cannot appeal a decision about which work-related responsibilities apply to you, so if you think they are unreasonable, you should negotiate with your work coach and, if necessary, complain. Where negotiation and complaining are not successful, you could consider a judicial review pre-action letter (see p1383).[69] To avoid a sanction, make it clear that you will comply with your work-related responsibilities in the meantime. Keep a record of your attempts to negotiate and/

Part 7: National Insurance, work and work-related rules
Chapter 46: Universal credit system work-related requirements
3. Which requirements apply

or complain. If you are sanctioned, you can appeal this decision (see p1086) – eg, because your work-related requirements were not reasonable (see p1079). You must ask for a mandatory reconsideration first, but can do this at any time (there is no time limit for requesting a revision of sanction decisions).

Which work-related requirements apply?

Your circumstances	Work-related requirement
Sick or disabled (see p1042) Looking after a child(ren) under one or caring for someone with a disability (see p1040) Threat or history of domestic abuse (see p1039) On UC and earning a sufficient amount (see p1043) At least pension age (see p1044) In education (see p1044)	No work-related requirements. You do not have to look for work, be available for work or participate in activity or conversations about preparing for work or improving your skills. However, you must usually still agree a claimant commitment (see p1024), and you must report changes in your circumstances.
Looking after a child(ren) aged one On ESA as a lone parent with a child(ren) aged at least one but under three Foster parent or 'friend and family carer' for a child(ren) over one and under 16 (see p1045)	Work-focused interviews only (see p1045).
Looking after a child(ren) aged two (see p1046) Limited capability for work (see p1046)	Work preparation (see p1029) and work-focused interviews (see p1028).
All other claimants (see p1047)	All the work-related requirements apply if you are not in any of the above groups. This could include some people with responsibility for children aged three or over, some disabled people, some students and some people in work. Your expected hours of work search are up to your work coach but may depend on your circumstances, including the age of your children if you are a responsible carer (see p1031). However, you may be able to restrict your availability for work and the type of work you have to look for (see p1035).

Temporary circumstances

Even if you would usually have all work-related requirements, there may be temporary circumstances when the work search and work availability requirements do not apply to you, including if you are sick (see p1048), bereaved or have experienced domestic abuse (see p1049), are working (see p1050) and in other temporary circumstances (see p1051).

No work-related requirements

No work-related requirements *at all* can be imposed on you if:
* you have recently experienced domestic violence or abuse (see below); *or*
* for UC and contributory ESA (or if you are getting *both* contribution-based JSA *and* UC), you fit into a specified group – ie, you are:
  – looking after children or have other responsibilities (see p1040);
  – sick or disabled (see p1042);
  – for UC only, in work and earning enough (see p1043);
  – in other specified situations (see p1044).

If your situation changes so that you are covered by the above, any requirements that have already been imposed cease to have effect.[70]

Domestic violence or abuse

If you notify the DWP that you have experienced, or been threatened with, domestic violence or abuse from a person aged 16 or over who is your partner, your former partner or a family member, and you satisfy specified conditions, all work-related requirements that have been imposed on you cease to have effect for 13 consecutive weeks from the date of notification.[71] In addition, no new work-related requirements can be imposed on you during this period. For UC, if, but for the domestic abuse rules, you would have to meet all the work-related requirements and you are the 'responsible carer' of a child under 16 (see p1041), no work availability or work search requirements can be imposed for a further 13 consecutive weeks (ie, for 26 weeks in total), although you could be required to attend work-focused interviews and/or engage in work preparation after the first 13 weeks.[72]

You must satisfy all the following conditions.
* This rule must not have applied to you on any earlier occasion in the 12 months before you notify the DWP.
* The domestic abuse (or threat of domestic abuse) must have taken place within the six months before you notify the DWP.

Part 7: National Insurance, work and work-related rules
Chapter 46: Universal credit system work-related requirements
3. Which requirements apply

- When you notify the DWP, you must not be living at the same address as the person who was abusive or threatened you with abuse. However, if you are still at the same address, the DWP can consider suspending your work search and work availability on the grounds of a domestic emergency.[73]
- As soon as possible, and no later than one month after you notify the DWP, you must provide evidence from a person acting in an official capacity that shows that your circumstances are consistent with those of a person who has experienced, or been threatened with, domestic violence or abuse in the six months before you notified the DWP, and that you have made contact with the person acting in an official capacity about an incident that occurred in that six-month period.

Domestic violence or abuse[74]

'**Domestic abuse**' means any incident or incidents of physical or sexual abuse, violent or threatening behaviour, controlling behaviour, coercive behaviour, psychological, emotional, economic or other abuse, regardless of gender or sexuality. Economic abuse can include financial abuse and any abuse which has an adverse effect on you being able to acquire, use or maintain money or other property, or which has an adverse effect on you being able to obtain goods and services. The abuse may have been directed towards another person and still be an experience or threat of domestic abuse – eg, if your child has experienced abuse.

'**Partner**' for the purposes of domestic abuse only includes: your spouse/civil partner or former spouse/civil partner, someone you have agreed to marry or civilly partner (even if that agreement has terminated), someone who has, or used to have, a parental relationship in relation to a child at the same time as you (as a legal parent or with parental responsibility), or someone with whom you have had an intimate personal relationship. It does not matter if you have never lived with the partner/former partner.

'**Family member**' for these purposes means: father, mother, stepfather, stepmother, son, daughter, stepson, stepdaughter, grandmother, grandfather, grandson, granddaughter, brother, sister, uncle, aunt, niece, nephew, first cousin. It includes half siblings, aunts, cousins, nieces, nephew and cousins, and relatives via marriage or civil partnerhip (whether current or former).

A '**person acting in an official capacity**' means a healthcare professional, a police officer, a registered social worker, your employer or your trade union representative. It also means any public, voluntary or charitable body with which you have had direct contact in connection with domestic abuse.

Looking after children and other caring responsibilities

If you are getting UC or contributory ESA, no work-related requirements can be imposed on you if:[75]

- for UC, you are the 'responsible carer' (see p1041) of a child under one; *or*

- for ESA, you are not a member of a couple and you are responsible for a child under one – eg, you are a lone parent. The rules do not define when you count as responsible for a child; *or*
- you are the 'responsible foster parent' (see p1042) of a child under one; *or*
- you are an 'adopter' (see p1042) and it is not more than 12 months (for UC) or 52 weeks (for ESA) since your child was placed with you for adoption. You can elect for the 12 months (or 52 weeks) to start in the 14 days before your child was expected to be placed with you; *or*
- you are pregnant and there are 11 weeks or fewer before the week your baby is due; *or*
- you had a baby not more than 15 weeks ago (including if this was a stillbirth); *or*
- you have 'regular and substantial caring responsibilities for a severely disabled person' (see p1042); *or*
- you have caring responsibilities for one or more severely disabled people for at least 35 hours a week, but do not satisfy the qualifying conditions for carer's allowance (CA). For UC, this only applies if the DWP is satisfied that it is unreasonable for you to meet a work search requirement and a work availability requirement, even if these are limited.

Definitions
You are a **'responsible carer'**:[76]
- for UC, if you are a single person, or a member of a couple claiming as a single person, who is responsible for a child under 16 (see p307) – eg, you are a lone parent, or you claim as a single person because your partner does not meet the basic conditions of UC;
- for JSA and ESA, if you are the only person responsible for a child under 16.

If you are a member of a couple and you are joint claimants, you are a responsible carer for UC if you or your partner (for JSA and ESA, you *and* your partner) are responsible for a child under 16 and you and your partner have nominated you as being responsible for the child. Only one of you can be nominated. The nomination applies to all your children. It can only be changed once in the 12 months after the nomination or if there has been a change of circumstances which the DWP considers relevant. If the DWP does not allow you to change a nomination, get advice. You cannot appeal a decision about who is the responsible carer.

You are a **'relevant carer'** if:[77]
- you are the parent of a child, have caring responsibilities for her/him but are not the 'responsible carer'; *or*
- you have caring responsibilities for someone who has a 'physical or mental impairment' (and for JSA only, the impairment means s/he needs such care). However, if you care for a disabled person on attendance allowance (AA), disability living allowance (DLA), child disability payment (CDP), personal independence payment (PIP) or adult disability payment (ADP), you may have regular and substantial caring responsibilities (see below).

Part 7: National Insurance, work and work-related rules
Chapter 46: Universal credit system work-related requirements
3. Which requirements apply

You are a **'responsible foster parent'** if you are the child's only foster parent or, if you are a member of a couple who are both foster parents, you and your partner have nominated you as the 'responsible foster parent'.[78] Only one of you can be nominated. The nomination applies to all your children. It can only be changed once in the 12 months after the nomination or if there has been a relevant change of circumstances.

You are an **'adopter'** if you have been matched with a child by an adoption agency and you are, or are intended to be, the 'responsible carer' of the child.[79] This does not apply if you are the foster parent or a close relative of the child.

A person is **'severely disabled'** if s/he is someone to whom AA, the highest or middle rate of DLA/CDP care component, the daily living component of PIP, armed forces independence payment or constant attendance allowance under the industrial or war disablement schemes (see p678) is payable.[80] It is expected that if ADP daily living component is payable to a person, s/he will count as severely disabled.

You have **'regular and substantial caring responsibilities'** if you satisfy the qualifying conditions for CA (see Chapter 26), or you would do but for the fact that your earnings are higher than allowed for CA (currently £128 a week – see p547).[81] However, you must not receive any earnings at all from your caring responsibilities. You do not have to be getting CA. If you are not covered by these rules, you may still be a 'relevant carer', which may reduce your work-related requirements (see above and p1035).

Sick and disabled people

If you are getting UC or contributory ESA, no work-related requirements can be imposed on you if:[82]

- you have both limited capability for work and limited capability for work-related activity – ie, you are in the support group for ESA and/or have limited capability for work-related activity for UC (see Chapter 45); *or*
- you are entitled to ESA only, but it is paid at a nil rate – eg, because you are getting an occupational pension.

Do you have limited capability for work-related activity?

If you are on ESA and in the support group, or you were in the support group on ESA when you moved to UC, the same limited capability for work-related activity decision should be applied to your UC. You can be reassessed at any time, but if you have recently had a work capability assessment, you should point this out to your work coach. If you were told that you should not be reassessed after your last work capability assessment, but you are referred to be assessed again, consider making a complaint or contacting your MP.

You are earning enough

If you are getting UC, no work-related requirements at all can be imposed on you if you are:[83]

- a single claimant, or a member of a couple, and your own average monthly earnings are at least your individual earnings threshold (see below); *or*
- a member of a couple and your combined average monthly earnings are at least your joint earnings threshold (see below). No work-related requirements can be imposed on you even if you are not working but your partner earns enough to meet this threshold;[84] *or*
- self-employed and are treated as having a minimum earnings level (see p122); *or*
- an apprentice and your average monthly earnings are at least the amount you would be paid at the rate of the national minimum wage (see Appendix 7) for 30 hours work (or, if lower, for your weekly 'expected hours' – see p1031).

Your monthly earnings are calculated using your gross actual or estimated earned income in the current assessment period – ie, before income tax, national insurance (NI) contributions and pension contributions have been deducted.[85] If your earnings fluctuate, these are averaged over one cycle of work or, if there is no cycle, over three months or the period that enables the average to be worked out more accurately. The DWP can disregard earnings from employment that has ended if this enables it to determine your monthly earnings more accurately. This means that if you are no longer working and receive a final payment of wages, the DWP can decide that you must meet work-related requirements, but does not have to.

Note: usually, if you are getting UC and you or your partner earn a certain amount each month (excluding self-employed earnings) – called the 'administrative earnings threshold' – you are not expected to look for more work (see p1051). Other work-related requirements (eg, attending work-focused interviews) can be imposed on you. The DWP may refer to this as being in the 'light touch' regime. At the time of writing, the DWP has the power to select you for an 'in-work pilot scheme', but none are currently running. If you are selected, you must be informed, and you can then be required to look for more work or work that pays up to the thresholds below (called the 'conditionality earnings threshold').

Earnings thresholds

- **To work out your individual earnings threshold**, multiply the amount you would earn at the hourly rate of the national minimum wage by the relevant number of hours for you (see p1044). Multiply this amount by 52 and divide it by 12.[86]
- **To work out your joint earnings threshold if you are a member of a couple**, work out the sum of your and your partner's individual earnings thresholds

Part 7: National Insurance, work and work-related rules
Chapter 46: Universal credit system work-related requirements
3. Which requirements apply

and add these together.[87] However, if you are claiming as a single person (see p35), your joint earnings threshold is the sum of your individual threshold and the amount someone would be paid at the rate of the minimum wage for 35 hours work (multiplied by 52 and divided by 12).

Fractions of a pound are ignored.[88]

For your individual threshold, the relevant hours are:[89]

- 16 hours a week, but only if (even though you are exempt from any work-related requirements under this rule) you would otherwise be someone who only has to meet a work-focused interview requirement (see p1045) or a work-focused interview requirement and a work preparation requirement (see p1046); *or*
- the hours you are expected to work each week (your 'expected hours') – usually 35 a week. A lower number of hours can apply (see p1031).

Example

Tarik and Aarna are joint UC claimants in their 40s. They have three children, the youngest of whom is of compulsory school age and under 13. They agree that Aarna should be the 'responsible carer'. Tarik's 'expected hours' are 35 a week. The DWP has agreed that Aarna's 'expected hours' are 25 a week as these are compatible with their youngest child's school hours (see p1031).

Tarik works 30 hours a week and earns £1,800 a month.

35 hours x £9.50 = £332.50

£332.50 x 52 ÷ 12 = £1,440.83

His individual earnings threshold is therefore £1,440

Aarna works 15 hours a week and earns £780 a month.

25 hours x £9.50 = £237.50

£237.50 x 52 ÷ 12 = £1,029.17

Her individual earnings threshold is therefore £1,029

Their joint earnings threshold is therefore £1,440.83 + £1,029.17 = £2,470.

Their joint earnings (£2,580) exceed their joint earnings threshold. No work-related requirements can be imposed on either of them.

Other situations – pension age claimants and claimants in education

If you are getting UC or contributory ESA, no work-related requirements can be imposed on you if:[90]

- for UC, you are at least pension age. This is only relevant if you are a member of a couple and your partner is under pension age; *or*
- you are in full-time, non-advanced education or training and you have no parental support (see p37). For ESA, this also applies if you have been enrolled or accepted for the education or training. For both UC and ESA, you must be under 21, or be aged 21 and have reached that age while on the course; *or*

- for UC, you are eligible for UC while receiving education (see p869) and you have student income (see p871) for your course which is taken into account when calculating your UC. If your student income is a postgraduate master's degree loan, this only applies if your course is full time.

Work-focused interview requirement only

If you are in the work-focused interview 'regime', you are required to participate in interviews to discuss work and consider steps to prepare for it, but all action other than participating in the interviews is voluntary.

A work-focused interview requirement, and no other work-related requirements, can be imposed on you if you are getting UC or contributory ESA and:[91]

- for UC, you are the 'responsible carer' (see p1041) of a child aged one; or
- for ESA, you are a single person who is responsible for a child aged at least one but under three; or
- you are a foster parent, and you:
  - are the 'responsible foster parent' (see p1042) of a:
    - child aged at least one but under 16; or
    - qualifying young person (see p308). The DWP must be satisfied that s/he has care needs which make it unreasonable for you to have to meet a work search requirement or a work availability requirement even if these were limited (for UC), or a work preparation requirement (for ESA); or
  - are not the 'responsible foster parent' (see p1042) of a child under 16 or a qualifying young person, but the DWP is satisfied that the child or young person has care needs which make it unreasonable for you to have to meet a work search requirement or a work availability requirement even if these were limited (for UC), or a work preparation requirement (for ESA); or
  - do not have a child or qualifying young person placed with you currently, but intend to have one placed with you, and within the past eight weeks:
    - for UC, you have been in any of the situations described above applying to foster parents; or
    - for ESA, you have been the 'responsible foster parent' of a child aged at least one but under 16; or
- you have become a 'friend or family carer' (see p1046) for a child under 16 in the past 12 months, and you are her/his 'responsible carer' (see p1041).

Note: if your child is under one and you are the 'responsible foster parent', or for UC, the 'responsible carer', or for ESA, a single person who is responsible for the child, no work-related requirements can be imposed on you (see p1040).

Part 7: National Insurance, work and work-related rules
Chapter 46: Universal credit system work-related requirements
3. Which requirements apply

Friend or family carer [92]

You are a '**friend or family carer**' if you are responsible for a child under 16 but are not her/his parent or step-parent. You must be taking care of the child because:

– s/he has no parents, or has parents who are unable to care for her/him. For when you count as responsible for a child for UC, see p62. 'Responsible for a child' is not defined in the ESA rules; *or*

– it is likely that s/he would otherwise be looked after by a local authority because there are concerns about her/his welfare.

If you have been getting UC or ESA on the basis that you have to meet additional work-related requirements but you now fit into one of the groups above, any requirements previously imposed on you cease to apply.[93]

If you have young children, your work-focused interviews should be arranged taking childcare availability into account. You should be told that you can rearrange your interview if you have a good reason why you cannot attend – eg, childcare, social services or medical appointments.[94]

7 Work-focused interview and work preparation requirement only

If a work-focused interview requirement *and* a work preparation requirement (but no other work-related requirements) can be imposed on you, you are only expected to prepare for a move into paid work, more paid work or better paid work – eg, by participating in a training or employment scheme. You do not have to look for work or be available for work.

For UC, this requirement applies if you are the 'responsible carer' (see p1041) of a child aged two. It also applies if you are entitled to contributory ESA or UC and you have limited capability for work (see Chapter 45).[95] You do not automatically count as having limited capability for work until this has been decided in a work capability assessment (see p988 for some exceptions). If you are providing medical evidence (usually fit notes), guidance states that after 28 days you should be referred for a work capability assessment if this has not already been done.[96] Apart from the first 14 days (during which the DWP may have to suspend your work search and work availability requirement), the DWP has discretion about which work-related requirements to apply until you have a decision about your limited capability for work (see p1048). Any work search requirements must take your condition(s) into account. Your work coach may agree voluntary, tailored commitments with you during this time, but can still set mandatory commitments as well if appropriate. They must make clear what you have to do to avoid being sanctioned, and what is voluntary.

Do you have limited capability for work?

If you have a limited capability for work decision, make sure your work coach knows how your illness affects what you can do and ask her/him to use her/his discretion in deciding which requirements to impose on you. If you are on ESA and have been found to have limited capability for work, or you were on ESA or had NI credits for limited capability for work when you claimed UC, and there has been no subsequent decision finding you capable of work, that limited capability for work decision applies to your UC.[97] You may have to point this out to your work coach. Having a limited capability for work decision for ESA or NI credits does not prevent the DWP from referring you for another work capability assessment for UC, but if you have had a limited capability for work decision recently and it has been recommended that you should not be reassessed for some time (eg, by the health professional in her/his report to the DWP or by a tribunal), you should make sure your work coach is aware of this and consider making a complaint if you are referred again.

If you have limited capability for work, reasonable adjustments for your health needs must be offered when carrying out work-focused interviews (eg, offering telephone interviews where appropriate) and in determining what you should do to prepare for work. Your work coach may agree voluntary, tailored commitments with you which can allow you to test out certain activities without risking a sanction, but can still decide to set mandatory commitments as well.[98]

If you are the responsible carer of a child aged two, interviews must be accommodated around childcare availability and you should only be expected to carry out work preparation when another responsible adult is looking after your child(ren).[99]

Note:
- In some situations (eg, if you are in the ESA 'support group'), no work-related requirements at all can be imposed on you (see p1039).
- If you have been getting UC on the basis that you have to meet other work-related requirements, but you are now in one of the above groups, any requirements previously imposed cease to apply.[100]

All work-related requirements

If you do not come into any of the other work-related requirement groups (see p1038) and none of the temporary circumstances apply to you (see p1048), the DWP *must* impose a work search requirement and a work availability requirement on you for UC and JSA. It can also impose a work-focused interview requirement or a work preparation requirement, or both, and is likely to do so.[101] **Note:** if you are getting ESA, a work search and work availability requirement can *never* be imposed on you.

Consider negotiating with your work coach and complaining if necessary, if you think you should have been covered by any of the exceptions, but have been

Part 7: National Insurance, work and work-related rules
Chapter 46: Universal credit system work-related requirements
3. Which requirements apply

told you must meet all the requirements, or if your work-related requirements are unreasonable given your circumstances. You cannot appeal against your work-related requirements, but if negotiation and complaining fail, you could consider a judicial review pre-action letter (see p1383).[102] If you are given a sanction for failing to meet a requirement, you can appeal. You must apply for a mandatory reconsideration first, but there is no time limit on doing this (even if the sanction has now finished).

No work search or work availability requirement for a period

If you are getting UC or contribution-based JSA or both, a work search and a work availability requirement cannot be imposed on you for a period (but you may have to meet other work-related requirements) in a number of situations.

Note: for ESA, a work search or work availability requirement can *never* be imposed on you.

Sick and disabled people

If you are getting UC or contribution-based JSA, a work search requirement cannot be imposed on you for certain specified periods if you are unfit for work. This usually applies for a maximum of 14 days and no more than twice in any 12-month period.[103] For the first seven days, you must provide a declaration that you are unfit for work. For any further days, you must provide a fit note from your doctor (for UC only, this only applies if requested by the DWP). However, if you have previously failed a work capability assessment while under the UC system, or you have been treated as not having limited capability for work for UC because you failed to provide information or attend an assessment, the DWP can decide not to suspend your work search requirement. This should only apply if you are unfit for work because of the same condition (or substantially the same condition) and you are not being referred to a new work capability assessment.[104]

In several situations, the DWP has discretion whether or not to impose a work search requirement. This applies:[105]

- for UC, if you are unfit more than twice, or for longer than 14 days if the DWP thinks it would be unreasonable to require you to meet a work search requirement even if it were limited. This could apply, for example, if you are waiting for a work capability assessment. If it is not possible to meet even limited requirements, or your requirements do not reflect your condition, you should negotiate with your work coach and complain if necessary;
- for UC and JSA, if you have failed a previous work capability assessment or were treated as not having limited capability for work, and your medical evidence shows that you currently have the same, or substantially the same, condition as you had before those decisions were made. Even if the DWP does not refer you for a new work capability assessment, it can decide that it is unreasonable to require you to meet a limited work search requirement. However, it does not have to do so. This means that you can be expected to

meet a limited work search requirement even though you are unwell or disabled – eg, while you are appealing a work capability assessment outcome. You should negotiate with your work coach and complain if it is not possible for you to meet your requirements and/or it affects your health;

- for JSA, if you are allowed an 'extended period of sickness' of up to 13 weeks under the rules described on p692 and the DWP thinks it would be unreasonable to require you to meet a work search requirement. If you are sick for longer than 13 weeks, you can no longer claim JSA.

You must provide a fit note from your doctor. For UC only, this only applies if requested by the DWP after the first seven days of sickness.

For the purposes of the work availability requirement, you only need to be willing and able to take up work and attend an interview for UC when the above circumstances no longer apply or, for JSA, when the period of sickness has ended.[106] However, if the DWP thinks it is reasonable to require you to attend an interview, you must be able and willing to attend one before the period of sickness has ended.

You cannot appeal against your work-related requirements but if negotiation and complaining are not successful, you could consider a judicial review pre-action letter (see p1383). Keep a record of everything you do to try to change your work-related requirements and explain clearly why you cannot meet them if this is the case.

If you continue to provide fit notes for UC, guidance says that the DWP should refer you for a work capability assessment from day 29 of your sickness or declared disability, if it has not already done so.[107] While you are waiting for the assessment, your work coach may agree voluntary commitments with you, as well as any mandatory ones s/he thinks are appropriate. However, if you have previously failed a work capability assessment, the DWP cannot refer you to a further assessment unless there is evidence to suggest that there has been a relevant change of circumstances (eg, your condition has deteriorated), or the previous decision was made without being aware of the facts, or was based on a mistake about facts.[108] If you have failed a work capability assessment, the DWP should still take your condition into account when putting together your work-related requirements, and can take into account medical evidence to do so (this applies whether or not you are challenging the decision that you are capable of work).

Bereavement and domestic violence and abuse

If you are getting UC or contribution-based JSA, a work search requirement cannot be imposed on you if it is less than six months since the death of your partner or a child under 16 (or, for UC only, a 'qualifying young person').[109] You or your partner must have been responsible for the child or qualifying young person, or you must have been the child's parent. For when you count as responsible for a child for UC, see p62. 'Responsible for a child' is not defined in the JSA rules.

Part 7: National Insurance, work and work-related rules
Chapter 46: Universal credit system work-related requirements
3. Which requirements apply

For UC only, a work search requirement cannot be imposed on you if you are the 'responsible carer' of a child under 16 (see p1041 for who counts), and there has been a 'significant disruption' in your normal childcare responsibilities because in the last 24 months:[110]

- a parent, sister or brother, or a person who was the previous responsible carer, of the child has died; *or*
- any person who normally lived in the same accommodation as the child has died. The person does not have to have been a relative or carer. S/he must have being living in the accommodation at the time of her/his death, and must not be liable to make payments for the accommodation on a commercial basis; *or*
- the child has experienced, or witnessed, a violent or abusive incident. This does not apply if you are the perpetrator of that violence or abuse. Violence and abuse are not defined but incidents of physical or emotional, financial and other non-physical abuse should count, as long as this has significantly disrupted your childcare responsibilities. The violence or abuse does not have to happen within the child's home, and the perpetrator does not have to be a family member or anyone known to you or the child.

The suspension of the work search requirement can apply for one month in each of the four consecutive six-month periods after the event occurs, beginning on a date specified by the DWP after you have notified it of the circumstances, and provided that the DWP is satisfied that the circumstances apply.[111] If the death affecting the child is that of your partner or another child or of a qualifying young person and the rules described above apply, or if *you* have experienced domestic abuse and the rules on p1039 apply, the month runs at the same time as any period you have been allowed under those rules – ie, you do not get any extra time.

For the purposes of the work availability requirement, you only need to be willing and able to take up work and attend an interview once the circumstances no longer apply.[112]

You have sufficient earnings from employment

If you are getting UC, a work search requirement cannot be imposed on you, but you may have to meet other work-related requirements, if:[113]

- you are a single claimant and your employed earnings (see p118) are at least £355 a month (from April 2022); *or*
- you are in a couple and your joint employed earnings (see p118) are at least £567 a month (from April 2022).

Your gross earnings in the current assessment period are calculated or estimated before deductions for tax, national insurance or pension contributions. However, if your earnings fluctuate, they can be averaged over your cycle of work, over three months, or over any other period which will allow an accurate monthly average to be calculated.[114] The DWP can ignore earnings you receive from a job which has finished.

The DWP calls these earnings levels the 'administrative earnings threshold' and may refer to people as being in the 'light touch' regime.[115] The 'light touch' regime does not apply if you are selected to participate in an 'in-work pilot scheme' (a scheme testing which work-related requirements are likely to help you retain work or obtain more or better paid work if you have a job). If you are selected for a scheme, a work search requirement can be imposed on you, even if your monthly employed earnings are at least £355 or £567.[116] In this case, you continue to have a work search requirement until you reach the earnings threshold that applies to you (see p1043). You must be notified in writing (this includes electronic communication) if you are selected for the scheme. **Note:** at the time of writing, the DWP was not running an in-work pilot scheme, but had the power to do so until 19 February 2023.[117] See AskCPAG and CPAG's *Welfare Rights Bulletin* for updates.

Note: if your monthly earnings are above your individual or joint earnings threshold (the 'conditionality earnings threshold'), no work-related requirements can be imposed on you (see p1043), so this rule only applies if your monthly employed earnings are at least £355 or £567, but lower than your earnings threshold, and you have not been selected for an in-work pilot scheme.

Example
Jessie, aged 27, is working part time. Her gross pay is £870 a month. Under the UC rules, she is expected to work 35 hours a week. 35 x £9.50 = £332.50. £332.50 x 52 ÷ 12 = £1,440.83. Her individual earnings threshold is therefore £1,440. Although she is not exempt from all the work-related requirements, because her take-home pay is more than £355 a month, a work search requirement cannot be imposed on her. However, she can be required to participate in work-focused interviews and work preparation.

For the purposes of the work availability requirement, you only need to be willing and able to take up work and attend an interview once the circumstances no longer apply – ie, once your earnings reduce to below the relevant limit.[118]

Other temporary circumstances
If you are getting UC or contribution-based JSA, a work search requirement cannot be imposed on you if:[119]
- you are attending a court or tribunal as a witness or party to the proceedings; or
- you qualify for UC or JSA while you are temporarily absent from Great Britain (see p1631 and p1639) because you are:
  - for UC only, receiving, or taking your child under 16 (or your partner or a qualifying young person) for, medical treatment or convalescence or care; or

Part 7: National Insurance, work and work-related rules
Chapter 46: Universal credit system work-related requirements
3. Which requirements apply

- – for JSA only, attending a job interview; *or*
- – for JSA only, receiving, or taking your child under 16 for, medical treatment; *or*
- you are receiving and participating in a course of treatment for alcohol or drug addiction and have been for no more than six months; *or*
- you are under police protection while involved as a witness in a criminal investigation or proceedings; *or*
- for UC only, you are a prisoner (see p926); *or*
- for UC, you are carrying out a 'public duty'. This is not defined, but should include being on jury service, crewing a lifeboat or carrying out duties as a volunteer firefighter or special constable.[120] For JSA, see below.

For the purposes of the work availability requirement, you only need to be willing and able to take up work and attend an interview once the circumstances no longer apply.[121]

If the DWP is satisfied that it would be unreasonable for you to have to meet a work search requirement even if this were limited, a work search requirement cannot be imposed on you if:[122]

- for JSA only, you are carrying out a public duty; *or*
- you are carrying out a work preparation requirement (see p1029) or 'voluntary work preparation' – ie, action agreed with the DWP that makes it more likely that you will get paid work; *or*
- you have temporary childcare responsibilities; *or*
- there are other temporary circumstances. These could include anything that makes it unreasonable for you to have to seek work – eg, becoming homeless, caring for a relative, or a flood, fire or other disaster at your home. For UC, dealing with domestic emergencies and funeral arrangements are specifically included, but other situations may also make it unreasonable – eg, a child's exclusion from school.[123]

For the purposes of the work availability requirement, if you fall under the bullet points above, you only need to be willing and able to take up work and attend an interview when the circumstances no longer apply.[124] However, for UC, if the DWP thinks it is reasonable to require you to attend an interview and/or take up work, you must be able and willing to do so before the circumstances cease to apply. The DWP may decide that it is reasonable to require you to attend an interview, but not to require you to be willing and able to take up paid work immediately.

If any of the temporary circumstances apply to you, you should explain why you are not currently able to look for work and make sure that there is a record of your circumstances. You may be able to argue you should not be sanctioned if temporary circumstances applied and the DWP did not consider suspending your work search requirement.[125]

Notes

1. The claimant commitment

1 **UC** s14(1)WRA 2012
JSA s6A(1) JSA 1995
ESA s11A(1) WRA 2007
2 **UC** s4(1)(e) WRA 2012
JSA s1(2)(b) JSA 1995
ESA s1(3)(aa) WRA 2007
3 s3(2) WRA 2012
4 **UC** Reg 16 UC Regs
JSA Reg 8 JSA Regs 2013
ESA Reg 45 ESA Regs 2013
5 **UC** Reg 16(2) UC Regs
ESA Reg 45(2) ESA Regs
6 See also DWP, *Universal Credit Guidance*, 'Appointees Personal Acting Bodies and Corporate Acting Bodies', v9.0 and 'Claimant Commitment – Overview', v4.0, House of Commons library deposited papers, available at rightsnet.org.uk/universal-credit-guidance
7 para J1022 ADM
8 **UC** s14(4) WRA 2012
JSA s6A(4) JSA 1995
ESA s11A(4) WRA 2007
9 *JB v SSWP (UC)* [2018] UKUT 360 (AAC)
10 **UC** s14(5) WRA 2012; reg 15 UC Regs
JSA s6A(5) JSA 1995; reg 7 JSA Regs 2013
ESA s11A(5) WRA 2007; reg 44 ESA Regs 2013
11 para J1011 ADM
12 para J1010 ADM
13 **UC** Reg 15(1) and (2) UC Regs
JSA Reg 7(1) JSA Regs 2013
ESA Reg 44(1) and (2) ESA Regs 2013
14 DWP, *Universal Credit Guidance*, 'Claimant Commitment Not Accepted', v2.0, House of Commons library deposited papers, available at rightsnet.org.uk/universal-credit-guidance
15 **UC** Reg 15(3) UC Regs
JSA Reg 7(2) JSA Regs 2013
16 Reg 44(3) ESA Regs 2013
17 DWP, *Universal Credit Guidance*, 'Fail to Attend', v17.0, House of Commons deposited papers, available at rightsnet.org.uk/universal-credit-guidance

18 DWP, *Universal Credit Guidance*, 'Complex Needs Overview', v 17.0, House of Commons deposited papers, available at rightsnet.org.uk/universal-credit-guidance
19 You may be able to challenge the decision by arguing that you accepted your default claimant commitment when you made your UC claim and this has not yet been replaced by a personalised commitment, so the DWP cannot show that you do not meet the basic conditions of UC
20 **UC** s14(2) WRA 2012
JSA s6A(2) JSA 1995
ESA s11A(2) WRA 2007
21 DWP, *Universal Credit Guidance*, 'Claimant Commitment - Overview', v6.0, House of Commons library deposited papers, available at rightsnet.org.uk/universal-credit-guidance

2. The work-related requirements

22 **UC** s13 WRA 2012
JSA ss6 and 6F JSA 1995
ESA s11 WRA 2007
23 **JSA** Reg 5(2) JSA Regs 2013
ESA Reg 42(2) ESA Regs 2013
24 **UC** s24(4) WRA 2012
ESA s11H(4) WRA 2007
JSA s6H(4) JSA 1995
25 *JB v SSWP* [2018] UKUT 360 (AAC)
26 **UC** s15 WRA 2012
JSA s6B JSA 1995
ESA s11B WRA 2007
27 para J3031 ADM; failing to do this may mean no valid work-related requirement has been imposed, see *JB v SSWP (UC)* [2018] 360 (AAC)
28 *KG v Secretary of State for Work and Pensions (UC)* [2020] UKUT 307 (AAC)
29 **UC** Regs 87 and 93 UC Regs
JSA Reg 10 JSA Regs 2013
ESA Reg 46 ESA Regs 2013
30 **UC** s16(1) and (2) WRA 2012
JSA s6C(1) and (2) JSA 1995
ESA s11C(1) and (2) WRA 2007

Part 7: National Insurance, work and work-related rules
Chapter 46: Universal credit system work-related requirements
Notes

• •

31 **UC** s16(3)-(6) WRA 2012
 JSA s6C(3) JSA 1995
 ESA s11C(3)-(6) WRA 2007
32 See gov.uk/work-health-programme
33 See gov.uk/guidance/help-to-find-work-for-universal-credit-claimants-aged-18-to-24
34 Reg 12(1B) UC Regs
35 See gov.uk/government/collections/kickstart-scheme
36 DWP, *Universal Credit Guidance,* 'Youth Offer' v1.0, House of Commons deposited papers, available at rightsnet.org.uk/universal-credit-guidance
37 **UC** s17(1) WRA 2012
 JSA s6D(1) JSA 1995
38 **UC** s17(2) and (3) WRA 2012
 JSA s6D(2) and (3) JSA 1995
39 **UC** Reg 94 UC Regs
 JSA Reg 11 JSA Regs 2013
40 **UC** Reg 95(1) UC Regs
 JSA Reg 12(1) JSA Regs 2013
41 *RR v SSWP (UC)* [2017] UKUT 459 (AAC)
42 **UC** Reg 88 UC Regs
 JSA Reg 9 JSA Regs 2013
43 para J3058 ADM
44 para J3058 ADM
45 DWP, *Universal Credit Guidance,* 'Expected Hours', v5.0, House of Commons deposited papers, available at rightsnet.org.uk/universal-credit-guidance
46 cpag.org.uk/welfare-rights/judicial-review/judicial-review-pre-action-letters/claimant-commitment-uc
47 **UC** Reg 95(2)-(4) UC Regs
 JSA Regs 4(1) and 12(2) and (3) JSA Regs 2013
48 *RR v SSWP (UC)* [2017] UKUT 459 (AAC)
49 **UC** s23(3) WRA 2012
 JSA s6G(3) JSA 1995
 DWP, *Universal Credit Guidance,* 'Intensive Work Search Regime', v 19.0, House of Commons deposited papers, available at rightsnet.org.uk/universal-credit-guidance
50 para J3103 ADM
51 paras J3253-57 ADM
52 **UC** s18(1) and (2) WRA 2012; regs 87 and 96(1) UC Regs
 JSA s6E(1) and (2) JSA 1995; regs 3(7) and 13(1) JSA Regs 2013
53 Reg 13(1)(b) JSA Regs 2013
54 **UC** Reg 96(1) UC Regs 2013
 JSA Reg 13(1)(a) JSA Regs 2013
55 *Shaukat Ali v CAO,* Appendix to R(U) 1/85

56 **UC** Reg 96(2)-(5) UC Regs
 JSA Regs 2 and 13(2)-(5) JSA Regs 2013
57 **UC** s17(4) and (5) WRA 2012
 JSA s6D(4) and (5) JSA 1995
58 **UC** Reg 97(4)-(6) UC Regs
 JSA Reg 14(3) and (4) JSA Regs 2013
59 DWP, *Universal Credit Guidance,* 'Availability For Work', v6.0, House of Commons library deposited papers, available at rightsnet.org.uk/universal-credit-guidance
60 **UC** Reg 97(2) UC Regs
 JSA Reg 14(5) JSA Regs 2013
61 **UC** Reg 95 (1) UC Regs
 JSA Reg 12(1) JSA Regs 2013
62 **UC** Reg 97(3) and (6) UC Regs
 JSA Reg 14(2) and (4) JSA Regs 2013
63 DWP, *Universal Credit Guidance,* 'Intensive Work Search Regime', v19.0, House of Commons library deposited papers, available at rightsnet.org.uk/universal-credit-guidance
64 para K2301 ADM
65 **UC** s23 WRA 2012
 JSA s6G JSA 1995
 ESA s11G WRA 2007
66 para K1171 ADM; *JB v SSWP (UC)* [2018] UKUT 360 (AAC)
67 para J3001 ADM

3. **Which requirements apply**
68 **JSA** Reg 5(2) JSA Regs 2013
 ESA Reg 42(2) ESA Regs 2013
69 cpag.org.uk/welfare-rights/judicial-review/judicial-review-pre-action-letters/claimant-commitment-uc
70 **UC** s19(5) WRA 2012
 JSA Reg 15(1)(a) JSA Regs 2013
 ESA s11D(3) WRA 2007
71 **UC** Reg 98 UC Regs
 JSA Regs 5 and 15 JSA Regs 2013
 ESA Reg 49 ESA Regs 2013
72 Reg 98(1A) UC Regs
73 DWP, *Universal Credit Guidance,* 'Domestic Violence and Abuse' v 20.0, House of Commons library deposited papers, available at rightsnet.org.uk/universal-credit-guidance

7

74 The DWP is using the cross-governmental definition of domestic violence and abuse under the Domestic Abuse Act 2021. The UC and JSA regulations have not been amended at the time of writing. DWP, *Help available from the Department for Work and Pensions for people who are victims of domestic violence and abuse'*, updated 1 October 2021, available on gov.uk; ss1 and 2 Domestic Abuse Act 2021

75 **UC** s19(2)(b) and (c) WRA 2012; reg 89(1)(b), (c), (d) and (f) UC Regs
JSA Reg 5 JSA Regs 2013
ESA s11D(2)(b) and (c) WRA 2007; reg 47(1)(a), (b), (c), (f) and (g) ESA Regs 2013

76 **UC** s19(6) WRA 2012; reg 86 UC Regs
JSA Reg 4 JSA Regs 2013
ESA Reg 41 ESA Regs 2013

77 **UC** Reg 85 UC Regs
JSA Reg 4(1) JSA Regs 2013

78 **UC** Regs 85 and 86 UC Regs
JSA Reg 4 JSA Regs 2013
ESA Reg 41 ESA Regs 2013

79 **UC** Reg 89(3) UC Regs
ESA Reg 47(5) ESA Regs 2013

80 **UC** Reg 89(2) UC Regs
ESA Reg 47(5) ESA Regs 2013

81 **UC** Reg 30 UC Regs
ESA Reg 47(2) and (3) ESA Regs 2013

82 **UC** s19(2)(a) WRA 2012
ESA s11D(2)(a) WRA 2007; reg 47(1)(e) ESA Regs 2013

83 Reg 90 UC Regs

84 DWP, *Universal Credit Guidance,* 'Working Enough Regime', v7.0, House of Commons library deposited papers, available at rightsnet.org.uk/universal-credit-guidance

85 Reg 90(6) UC Regs
86 Reg 90(2) UC Regs
87 Reg 90(3) UC Regs
88 Reg 6(1A) UC Regs
89 Regs 88 and 90(2) UC Regs
90 **UC** s19 WRA 2012; reg 89(1)(a), (da) and (e) UC Regs
ESA s11D WRA 2007; reg 47(1)(d) ESA Regs 2013

91 **UC** s20 WRA 2012; reg 91 UC Regs
ESA s11E WRA 2007; reg 48 ESA Regs 2013

92 **UC** Reg 91(3) UC Regs
ESA Reg 48(3) ESA Regs 2013

93 **UC** s20(3) WRA 2012
ESA s11E(3) WRA 2007

94 DWP, *Universal Credit Guidance*, 'Work-focused Interview Regime', v7.0, House of Commons library deposited papers, available at rightsnet.org.uk/universal-credit-guidance

95 **UC** s21 WRA 2012
ESA s11F WRA 2007

96 DWP, *Universal Credit Guidance,* 'Health Conditions and Disabilities – day 1 to day 29', v12.0, House of Commons library deposited papers, available at rightsnet.org.uk/universal-credit-guidance

97 Regs 19 and 21 UC(TP) Regs; reg 39(1)(a) UC Regs

98 Letter to Stephen Timms MP from Chloe Smith, Minister for Disabled People, Health and Work, 25 October 2021

99 DWP, *Universal Credit Guidance,* 'Work Preparation Regime', v14.0, House of Commons library deposited papers, available at rightsnet.org.uk/universal-credit-guidance

100 s21(4) WRA 2012
101 **UC** s22 WRA 2012
JSA s6F JSA 1995

102 cpag.org.uk/welfare-rights/judicial-review/judicial-review-pre-action-letters/claimant-commitment-uc

103 **UC** Reg 99(1)(a) and (4) UC Regs
JSA Reg 16(1)(a) and (5) JSA Regs 2013

104 **UC** Reg 99(4ZA) and (4ZB) UC Regs
JSA Reg 16(5A) and (5B) JSA Regs 2013

105 **UC** Reg 99(5)(c) and (d) UC Regs
JSA Regs 16(5B) and 16A(1) and (2) JSA Regs 2013

106 **UC** Reg 99 (1)(b), (2B), (2C), (5A) and (5B) UC Regs
JSA Regs 16 (1)(b) and 16A(4)-(6) JSA Regs 2013

107 DWP, *Universal Credit Guidance*, 'Health Conditions and Disabilities – day 1 to day 29', v12.0, House of Commons library deposited papers, available at rightsnet.org.uk/universal-credit-guidance

108 Reg 41(4) UC Regs
109 **UC** Reg 99(1) and (3)(d) UC Regs
JSA Reg 16(3)(c) JSA Regs 2013

110 Reg 99(1) and (4A) UC Regs
111 Reg 99(4B) and (4C) UC Regs
112 **UC** Reg 99(1)(b) UC Regs
JSA Reg 16(1)(b) JSA Regs 2013

113 Regs 6(1A) and 99(1), (6) and (6A) UC Regs

114 Reg 2, definition of 'monthly earnings' and reg 90(6), UC Regs

Part 7: National Insurance, work and work-related rules
Chapter 46: Universal credit system work-related requirements
Notes

115 DWP, *Universal Credit Guidance,* 'Light Touch Regime', v9.0, House of Commons library deposited papers, available at rightsnet.org.uk/universal-credit-guidance
116 The Universal Credit (Work-Related Requirements) and In Work Pilot Scheme Amendment Regulations 2015 No.89, as amended by SI 2021/147
117 The Universal Credit (Work-Related Requirements) In Work Pilot Scheme (Extension) Order 2022 No.139
118 Reg 99(1)(b) UC Regs
119 **UC** Reg 99(1) and (3)(a)-(c) and (e)-(g) UC Regs
JSA Reg 16(1), (3)(a), (b), (d) and (e) and (4) JSA Regs 2013
120 para J3208 ADM
121 **UC** Reg 99(1)(b) UC Regs
JSA Reg 16(1)(b) JSA Regs 2013
122 **UC** Reg 99(2A) and (5)(a) and (b) UC Regs
JSA Reg 16(1) and (4) JSA Regs 2013
123 paras J3068-72 ADM
124 **UC** Reg 99(2B), (2C), (5A) and (5B) UC Regs
JSA Reg 16(1)(b) JSA Regs 2013
125 *RR v SSWP (UC)* [2017] UKUT 459 (AAC)

7

Chapter 47

• •

Universal credit system sanctions

This chapter covers:
1. When you can be sanctioned (p1058)
2. How your benefit is reduced (p1067)
3. The sanction period (p1072)
4. Good reasons for your actions (p1079)
5. Sanction decisions (p1085)
6. Challenging a sanction decision (p1086)

The rules on sanctions in this chapter apply if you come under the universal credit (UC) system, whether you are getting UC, jobseeker's allowance (JSA) or employment and support allowance (ESA) (see p22). If you get JSA or ESA under the UC system, the DWP may refer to these as 'new style' JSA and ESA. If you get JSA or ESA and you do not come under the UC system, see Chapter 49.

Key facts
- It is always better to avoid a sanction if you can. If a sanction decision is made, consider challenging it.
- If you are getting universal credit, jobseeker's allowance or employment and support allowance and you do not meet your work-related requirements, you may be given a sanction.
- If you are given a sanction, your benefit is paid at a reduced (or sometimes nil) rate for a period.
- Whether or not you can be sanctioned, and for how long, depends on what you have done, or failed to do, in relation to your work-related requirements.
- You may be able to avoid a sanction if you can show that you have a good reason for your actions.
- You may qualify for hardship payments if you have been given a sanction.
- You can apply for a revision or supersession (see Chapter 56), or appeal (see Chapter 57) against a sanction decision. You must apply for a mandatory reconsideration before you can appeal.

Part 7: National Insurance, work and work-related rules
Chapter 47: Universal credit system sanctions
1. When you can be sanctioned

1. **When you can be sanctioned**

You can be given a sanction if you do not meet the work-related requirements you have as a condition of getting universal credit (UC) and, if you come under the UC system (see p22), jobseeker's allowance (JSA) and employment and support allowance (ESA). See Chapter 46 for the work-related requirements.

You cannot be sanctioned if you do not have any work-related requirements, including if you are in the 'support group' for ESA (see p1039).

What can you do to avoid a sanction?

1. If you think that any work-related activity you are being asked to do is unreasonable, talk to your work coach about it. Explain why it is unreasonable – eg, because of your health or caring responsibilities. You should keep a record (a note of the date, time and what was said) of your attempts to negotiate with your work coach, as this could be important if you have to show you had a good reason at a later date. Unreasonable claimant commitments could, depending on the facts of your case, be the subject of judicial review (see Chapter 59). Further information about judicial review, and template letters for pre-action letters are available at cpag.org.uk/JR.

2. If there is a possibility that you will be given a sanction, make sure you give full details of your side of the story. Check all the relevant sections in this chapter to work out what information and evidence you should provide. Make sure the DWP is aware of any needs you have which could make it difficult for you to fulfil your work-related requirements.

3. If, to avoid being given a sanction, you must show you had a good reason for what you did or did not do, make sure you explain your reasons fully, and provide these in time. See pp1079–84 for what may (or may not) count.

4. If you left or were dismissed from a job and it appears there may have been misconduct or that you left voluntarily without a good reason, your former employer is asked for a statement. You should be given an adequate chance to comment on what it says. Your remarks may be passed to your employer for further comments. Make sure you explain why you disagree with an allegation of misconduct or why you had a good reason for leaving your job. If you are going to an employment tribunal (eg, to claim unfair dismissal), say so. Discuss your reply with whoever is advising you on this, as you may be asked questions at the employment tribunal hearing by your former employer about what you have said.

5. If you refused to apply for or accept a job, what the potential employer says might be taken into account. Make sure you explain what enquiries you made about the nature of the job, and your reasons for not applying for or accepting it. For example, if you assumed the employer would not make adjustments but you did not ask it about this, you may not have a good reason.

6. If you are taking part in a training scheme or employment programme, it will probably be the provider who raises doubts about your compliance or attendance. Before a sanction is imposed, you should be given an adequate chance to comment on any statements

made against you. Bear in mind that even if the scheme or programme provider is satisfied that you have done what was required of you, or that you had a good reason for failing to do so, the DWP may reach a different conclusion.

7. Information, queries or declarations you send to the DWP can be posted on your online journal, if you have one. If you are unable to post on your journal or do not have one, you should communicate with the DWP in any way accessible to you – eg, by telephone or in person. In any case, you should keep a record of all your interactions with the DWP, irrespective of how they take place – eg, by taking a screenshot of messages you post on your journal.

If you are given a sanction, your UC, JSA or ESA is paid at a reduced (or nil) rate during a set 'sanction period'. There are four levels of sanctions (see below). The amount of the benefit reduction and the length of the sanction period depend on which work-related requirement you have failed to meet. Some special rules apply to the length of the sanction period if you are aged 16 or 17.

If you are entitled to UC, the reduction in your benefit is applied to your UC, even if the sanction was in respect of your JSA or ESA claim. See p1071 for information about applying a sanction to another benefit if your circumstances change. The days in your sanction period count towards your days of entitlement to contribution-based JSA or contributory ESA, even if you are not actually paid any benefit. For example, if you are entitled to 365 days of contributory ESA and you are sanctioned for 14 days, in total you will only receive contributory ESA for 351 days.

Work-related requirement	Level of sanction
Failing to apply for or to accept paid work (UC and JSA only)	High
Ceasing paid work or losing pay for specified reasons (UC and JSA only)	High
Failing to be available for paid work or to take all reasonable action to get paid work (UC and JSA only)	Medium
Failing to meet a work-focused interview requirement (where other requirements also apply)	Low
Failing to meet a requirement connected to a work-related requirement	Low
Failing to meet a work preparation requirement	Low
Failing to take a particular action to get paid work (UC and JSA only)	Low
Failing to meet a work-related interview requirement (where no other requirements apply) (UC and ESA only)	Lowest

Part 7: National Insurance, work and work-related rules
Chapter 47: Universal credit system sanctions
1. When you can be sanctioned

We refer to things that can lead to a sanction (eg, leaving work voluntarily) as 'sanctionable actions'. The DWP may refer to the cause of a sanction as a 'sanctionable failure'.[1]

In some cases, you cannot be given a sanction if you can show you had a good reason for your actions (see p1079). You may be able to get UC hardship payments (including if you are getting JSA or ESA) if you have been sanctioned.

If you disagree with a sanction decision, see p1086 for information about challenging it.

Note: different rules apply if you have been given a sanction because of a benefit offence (see p1239).

High level sanctions

If you are getting UC or JSA, you can be given a high level sanction if you are in the 'all work-related requirements group' (see p1047) and you:[2]

- fail to apply for a particular vacancy or accept an offer of paid work without a good reason (see below); *or*
- cease paid work or lose pay voluntarily without a good reason or because of 'misconduct' (see p1061);
- fail to take part in a prescribed work placement. At the time of writing, the only prescribed scheme (Mandatory Work Activity) is closed, but other schemes may be prescribed in the future.

Failing to apply for or to accept paid work

You can be given a high level UC or JSA sanction if, without a good reason:[3]

- you are told to apply for a particular vacancy for paid work and you do not do so, or you fail to take up paid work when it is offered to you (see p1034). **Note:** if the vacancy was available because of a strike, you cannot be given a sanction;[4] *or*
- you failed to take up an offer of paid work before you claimed UC (or JSA). For UC, you must be subject to all the work-related requirements (see p1047) when you are awarded UC. For both UC and JSA, no reduction in your benefit can be made if the number of days between the date you failed to take up the offer and your date of claim for UC (or JSA) is more than the sanction period that would otherwise apply.[5]

- -

Paid work
'**Paid work**' for these purposes means work done for payment or for which you expect to be paid.[6]

- -

The DWP might treat you as having refused to apply for or accept paid work if you do not arrive on time, go to the wrong place, ask an employer for unreasonable conditions or behave in such a way as to put off a prospective employer.[7] It is not a 'good reason' to refuse paid work or fail to apply for it because you are not sure of the effect on your benefits.[8]

Note:

- You only have to be available for work and to look for work in locations that are no more than 90 minutes from your home.[9] You may find it difficult to show you have a good reason if your travel time is shorter than this, but if you have agreed (or tried to agree) a shorter travel to work time with your work coach, you should make this clear when you challenge the sanction (see p1036).

- You may be able to show that you have a good reason for refusing a job if you have previously done work of a particular type or at a particular rate of pay, you have been allowed to limit your work search to looking for work of a similar type or rate of pay (see p1035), and you refuse a job that does not meet these conditions.

- The DWP says that if you are getting UC and you refuse to accept a job with a zero-hour contract without a good reason, you can be given a sanction if the contract allows you to take up work with other employers that will lift your earnings above your individual earnings threshold (see p1043). However, you should not be given a sanction if the contract restricts your ability to increase your earnings with other employers.[10] Exclusivity clauses are unenforceable in law,[11] but DWP guidance suggests that such a requirement from a potential employer could mean you cannot be required to take up the job – eg, if the hours offered restrict your flexiblity to increase your earnings with other employers, you should not be sanctioned for refusing.[12] You are likely to be asked for proof that your employer would prevent you from doing other work, but a contract does not necessarily have to be in writing. If you are reluctant to take a zero-hour contract because of fluctuating earnings which would make it difficult for you to budget, make your work coach aware of this and get independent advice.

Ceasing paid work or losing pay

Unless any of the exceptions on p1062 apply, you can be given a high level UC or JSA sanction if you cease paid work or lose pay:[13]

- 'voluntarily' (see p1063) and without a good reason (see p1081). You have not left work voluntarily if there is a genuine redundancy situation or your contract of employment ends, even if you volunteer for redundancy (see p1063); *or*
- because of misconduct (see p1064). You can also be sanctioned if you are suspended from work for misconduct or if you resigned rather than be dismissed.[14]

For UC, you can be given a sanction on this ground even if you had no work-related requirements imposed on you at the time the event occurred because you

Part 7: National Insurance, work and work-related rules
Chapter 47: Universal credit system sanctions
1. When you can be sanctioned

were earning a sufficient amount (see p1043 for the earnings thresholds), provided your ceasing work or losing pay means you are now subject to all the work-related requirements. However, if you currently have no work search requirement because you are still earning enough to have this requirement removed and you have not been selected for an 'in-work pilot scheme' (see p1050), you cannot be sanctioned (see below).

For both UC and JSA, you can be given a sanction on this ground if you ceased the paid work or you lost pay before your claim for UC (or JSA). For UC, to be given a sanction on this ground, you must be subject to all the work-related requirements when you are awarded UC (see p1037). However, for both UC and JSA, no reduction in your benefit can be made if the number of days between the date you ceased work or lost pay and your date of claim for UC (or JSA) is more than the sanction period that would otherwise apply.[15]

If you are self-employed, you will not be sanctioned for giving up paid work or losing pay.[16] The DWP decides whether you are still gainfully self-employed, looking at all the circumstances – eg, whether a drop in income is part of your normal pattern of work.[17] If it decides that you are still self-employed, you may be treated as having more income than you actually earn (see p122). If you stop self-employment completely because of the application of this rule (the 'minimum income floor'), you should not be sanctioned.

For what may happen if you take retirement, see p1065.

Exceptions

For UC only, you cannot be given a sanction on this ground (even if you cease paid work or lose pay voluntarily or because of misconduct) if your monthly earnings (or, if you are a joint claimant, your joint monthly earnings) are still above the amount that means a work search requirement cannot be imposed on you at the present time (see p1050), unless you have been selected to take part in an 'in-work pilot scheme'. If you are in an in-work pilot scheme, you can be sanctioned for ceasing work or losing pay which takes your earnings below a higher amount (see p1043).[18]

For both UC and JSA, you cannot be given a sanction (even if you cease paid work or lose pay voluntarily) if:[19]

- you volunteer or accept your employer's proposal for redundancy (see p1063); *or*
- you are allowed to limit the number of hours you are available for work and are looking for work (see p1031), you take up paid work (or more hours of paid work) for more hours than that limit and you cease that paid work (or doing the higher hours) or lose pay within a trial period. 'Trial period' is not defined in the rules, but the DWP says it is a period of 56 days starting on the 29th day and ending on the 84th day on which you took up paid work (or more hours).[20] You can argue that anything that can reasonably be described as a trial period should count; *or*

- you ceased paid work or lost pay because of a strike; *or*
- you ceased paid work as a member of the regular or reserve armed forces, or lost pay in that capacity; *or*
- you have been laid off or kept on short-time work by your employer for at least four consecutive weeks (or for six weeks in a 13-week period). You must have applied for redundancy pay within a specified time.[21]

Leaving a job or losing pay voluntarily

If you are getting UC or JSA, you can be given a high level sanction if you leave your job or lose pay 'voluntarily' without a good reason (see p1081).

Voluntarily

'**Voluntarily**' is not defined in the rules, but the DWP says it means that you have brought the situation about by your own acts and of your own free will.[22] You have not left your employment (or lost pay) voluntarily if you had no choice in the matter or there is convincing evidence (eg, medical evidence from your GP) that you were not responsible for your actions. You have not lost pay voluntarily if your hours under a zero-hour contract are reduced because you worked for another employer to gain more hours.[23]

If you are thinking of reducing your hours for a good reason (eg, because of your caring responsibilities or health), speak to your work coach first and make a written record of your conversations. It is not clear whether you would be regarded as having lost pay voluntarily in this situation. You may be expected to explore other options first – eg, investigating the availability and costs of childcare.

You are likely to be treated as giving up your job voluntarily if:

- you resign giving notice. If you genuinely believed that your employer was about to end your employment or you were given the 'choice' of resignation or dismissal, you have not left your job voluntarily, but the DWP may then consider whether you lost your job through misconduct (see p1064);
- your employer gives you notice to end your employment but then cancels or suspends it, but you decide not to continue in the employment, if it is clear that you have a genuine choice to remain.[24] However, the circumstances may mean you have a 'good reason'.

You have *not* left your job voluntarily if:

- you volunteer, or accept your employer's proposal, for redundancy, even if you were offered, or could have applied for, alternative jobs with the same employer.[25] This only applies if there is a redundancy situation at your workplace – eg, if a whole factory or department is closing down or if there is a cut in the number of people needed to carry out certain tasks. **Note:** if you refuse other work, you might be sanctioned for another reason – eg, refusing employment or 'neglecting to avail' yourself of an opportunity of employment;

Part 7: National Insurance, work and work-related rules
Chapter 47: Universal credit system sanctions
1. When you can be sanctioned

- your employer ends your contract of employment.[26] If you left your job because your employer imposed a change in your terms or conditions without your agreement and the new terms are less favourable than before, you may be able to argue that you have not left voluntarily, or that you had a good reason for leaving.[27] However, a cut in pay is not a good reason to leave if your pay remains at or above the national minimum wage (see Appendix 7).

Misconduct

'Misconduct' is not defined in the rules. However, bear the following in mind.

- You are only guilty of misconduct if your actions or omissions are 'blameworthy'. You do not have to have done anything dishonest or deliberately wrong; serious carelessness or negligence may be enough.[28]
- Everyone makes mistakes or is inefficient from time to time. So, for example, if you are a naturally slow worker who, despite making every effort, cannot produce the output required by your employer, you are not guilty of misconduct even if the poor performance may justify your dismissal.
- The misconduct must have some connection with your employment but it does not have to take place during working hours to count. However, a sanction cannot be imposed if the actions or omissions took place before your employment began – eg, you gave inaccurate information about yourself when applying for the job.[29]

Some behaviour is clearly misconduct – eg, dishonesty (whether or not connected with your work) if it causes your employer to dismiss you because it no longer trusts you.[30] However, some behaviour is not necessarily misconduct.

- A refusal to carry out a reasonable instruction by an employer is not misconduct if you had a good reason or you refused because of a genuine misunderstanding.[31]
- You should not be treated as losing a job because of misconduct if you are dismissed for 'whistleblowing' – ie, for disclosing wrongful behaviour which it was in the public interest to disclose. However, if you have not reported the matter through the proper channels, you might be guilty of misconduct.[32]
- Bad timekeeping and failing to report in time that you are sick might amount to misconduct – eg, if you were persistently late or failed to report that you were sick on a number of occasions.
- Breaking rules covering personal conduct might amount to misconduct, depending on the seriousness of the breach. A breach of a trivial rule might not be misconduct.[33]
- Refusing to work overtime is misconduct if you were under a duty to work overtime when required and the request to do it was reasonable.

Although evidence from your employer is taken into account, the fact that it did not describe your actions as 'misconduct' does not guarantee that you will not be given a sanction.

If there is medical evidence that you had a mental illness and you were not responsible for your actions at the time of the alleged misconduct, the DWP decision maker should not impose a sanction.[34]

Whether misconduct caused the loss of employment or pay

Your misconduct need not be the only cause of the loss of your employment or pay, but it must be an immediate and substantial reason.[35] If your misconduct was not the real reason for your dismissal (eg, your employer used this as an excuse but really only wanted to reduce staff numbers), you should not be sanctioned.

If you believe that your dismissal was unreasonable or an overreaction on your employer's part, get advice to see whether you might have a case for unfair dismissal at an employment tribunal. You should tell the DWP if you are seeking advice and/or taking action against your employer.

If there was misconduct, the exact way in which you lost your employment is not important. You may be summarily dismissed, be dismissed with notice or resign as an alternative to possible dismissal.[36]

Relationship with unfair dismissal and other proceedings

Sometimes the same facts have to be considered by other bodies – eg, employment tribunals and the criminal courts. The questions and legal tests that other bodies use may not be the same as those which apply to benefits.

DWP decision makers, the First-tier Tribunal and employment tribunals are independent of each other; decisions by one are not binding on the other. This means:

- a finding by an employment tribunal that a dismissal was fair does not prevent the DWP decision maker or the First-tier Tribunal from concluding that you did not lose your job through misconduct;[37]
- although the First-tier Tribunal normally accepts a criminal conviction as proof that you have done what is alleged, it must go on to consider whether this was connected with your employment, whether it amounts to misconduct and whether the misconduct was the reason why you lost your employment;
- the DWP decision maker or the tribunal does not have to wait for the outcome of other proceedings before making a decision, but they are more likely to do so if there is a conflict of evidence.

Taking retirement

If you take retirement, you might be treated as having left your job voluntarily.[38] Under employment law, your employer cannot usually make you retire at any particular age, so taking retirement is something you do of your own choice. However, you might be able to show you have a good reason – eg, if you can show that the work was getting too much for you because of your age or your health. If you have retired early due to ill health you may need to submit sick notes at the

Part 7: National Insurance, work and work-related rules
Chapter 47: Universal credit system sanctions
1. When you can be sanctioned

beginning of your claim while you are waiting for a work capability assessment (see p1048).

Employers sometimes have special early retirement schemes allowing you to take your occupational pension at an earlier age than normal, often in order to deal with a redundancy situation. In this case, you come under the special rules about redundancy (see p1063). Employers often try to avoid using the word 'redundancy' and you may have to prove that a redundancy situation existed.

If you take early retirement under some other special scheme, you cannot show you have a good reason merely because your action was in your employer's interest.[39]

Medium level sanctions

If you are getting UC or JSA, you can be given a medium level sanction if you have a work search and/or work availability requirement (see p1047) and, without a good reason, you:[40]

- do not take all reasonable action to get paid work, more paid work or better paid work (see p1030); *or*
- are not available for work (see p1034).

You should keep detailed records of your work search and be able to prove what you have done to look for work (see p1033). If there are particular reasons why you cannot take your expected steps to seek work (eg, because of illness or caring responsibilities), or you think your work-related responsibilities are unreasonable for your circumstances, make you sure you tell the DWP as soon as possible and keep a record of this. For more tactics to avoid sanctions, see p1058.

Low level sanctions

If you are getting UC, JSA or ESA, you can be given a low level sanction if, without a good reason, you:[41]

- fail to meet a work-focused interview requirement (see p1028). **Note:** for UC and ESA, this does not apply if you are *only* required to meet a work-focused interview requirement and have no other work-related requirements. In this case, you can be given a lowest level sanction instead (see p1067); *or*
- fail to meet a requirement to participate in interviews, provide information or evidence, confirm your compliance (eg, by completing a task on your online 'to do' list) or report a change in your circumstances that is relevant to whether work-related requirements can be imposed on you or to your compliance with a work-related requirement; *or*
- fail to meet a work preparation requirement (see p1029) – eg, you refuse to do a community work placement or to go on a training scheme or employment programme. Failure to participate, even if you attend a work preparation activity, could also be a failure to meet a work preparation requirement – eg, if

you fail to confirm your identity without a good reason, this could be a failure to participate;[42] *or*

- for UC and JSA only, fail to take any particular action specified by the DWP to get paid work, more paid work or better paid work (see p1030).

For ESA, to be given a low level sanction, you must be someone who can be required to meet a work preparation requirement *and* a work-focused interview requirement (see p1046). For UC, you must be someone who can be required to meet all the work-related requirements, or to meet a work preparation requirement and a work-focused interview requirement.

A low level sanction should not be applied unless you have been notified clearly about what you have to do and the consequences of not complying.[43] Details of the specific appointment for a work-focused interview and its purpose (ie, the type of interview), including the date, time and place, as well as the consequences of failing to attend, must have been given to you.[44]

How quickly do you have to contact the DWP?

The rules do not specify a time within which you must contact the DWP to explain your reasons if you have failed to do any of the above. However, to avoid a sanction decision being made, you should contact the DWP as soon possible and provide as much information as you can to show you had a good reason. The DWP may contact you (this may be via your journal if you are on UC) and ask for additional information (see p1085), which you should provide if possible. If it was not clear what your work-related requirements were (eg, you did not realise you had to participate in an interview), make sure you state this and also consider making a complaint.

Lowest level sanctions

If you are getting UC or ESA, you can be given a lowest level sanction if you can only be required to meet a work-focused interview requirement (see p1045) and you fail to participate in a work-focused interview without a good reason.[45] Details of the interview and the consequences of failing to attend must have been given to you. If you fail to attend or to participate, contact the DWP as soon as possible to explain.

---

2. How your benefit is reduced

If you are given a sanction, your benefit is paid at a reduced (or nil) rate until the sanction period (see p1072) ends. The reduction for each universal credit (UC) assessment period or each benefit week for jobseeker's allowance (JSA) and employment and support allowance (ESA) is calculated as follows.[46]

Part 7: National Insurance, work and work-related rules
Chapter 47: Universal credit system sanctions
2. How your benefit is reduced

- **Step one:** take the number of days in the assessment period or benefit week (or, if lower, the total number of outstanding days in the sanction period). Deduct any days in the assessment period/benefit week for which the sanction period has been suspended because you have also been given a sanction for a benefit offence (see p1071).
- **Step two:** multiply the number of days in Step one by the relevant daily reduction rate. See below for UC, p1071 for JSA and p1069 for ESA.

For UC, the amount in Step two is adjusted so that it is not more than your standard allowance (see p65) or, if you are a joint claimant and only one of you has been sanctioned, so that it is not more than 50 per cent of your standard allowance. The reduction in your UC is made after the benefit cap has been applied, if relevant (see p1156).

Universal credit

For UC, the daily reduction rate is normally the amount of standard allowance that applies to you multiplied by 12 and divided by 365 (the 'high rate').[47] However, the daily reduction is 40 per cent of this amount (the 'low rate') if, at the end of the assessment period for which the reduction is being calculated:[48]
- you do not have to meet any work-related requirements (see p1039) because you:
  - are the responsible carer or responsible foster parent of a child under one;
  - are pregnant and there are 11 weeks or less before the week your baby is due;
  - had a baby not more than 15 weeks ago (including if the baby was stillborn);
  - are adopting a child and it is no more than 52 weeks since the child was placed with you; or
- you can only be required to meet a work-focused interview requirement (see p1045); or
- you are 16 or 17 years old.

If you are in a couple and are a joint claimant, the daily rate using the calculation above is divided by two.[49] If your partner is also given a sanction, the daily reduction rate that applies to her/him is also divided by two. The following chart shows the daily reduction rate for a couple if only one of you has been sanctioned.

The daily reduction rate is nil if, at the end of the assessment period for which the reduction is being calculated, you are someone who does not have to meet any work-related requirements because you have limited capability for work and work-related activity (see p1042).[50]

The daily reduction rates are rounded down to the nearest 10 pence.[51]

Daily reduction rates

	High rate £ per day	Low rate £ per day
Single		
Under 25	8.70	3.40
25 or over	11.00	4.40
Couple		
Both under 25	6.80	2.70
Either 25 or over	8.60	3.40

Note: you may still be entitled to some UC during the assessment period – ie, if you qualify for elements for children or any other elements, such as for childcare or housing costs. However, any deductions from benefit will still apply (see p1164).

Example

Teddy and his partner are both aged 35 and are getting UC as joint claimants. They live in rented accommodation. Teddy was given a 182-day high level sanction. There are 150 days outstanding in Teddy's sanction period. This month is a 30-day assessment period. His partner was not given a sanction.

Step one: the relevant number of days is 30, as this is lower than the number of outstanding days in Teddy's sanction period.

Step two: the daily rate is £8.60. The reduction is therefore 30 x £8.60 = £258

Fifty per cent of Teddy's standard allowance is £262.86 (£525.72 ÷ 2). This is higher than the reduction.

Teddy and his partner's UC is therefore reduced by £258 over the assessment period. They continue to get the amount to which they are entitled that exceeds £258, including the help they get with their rent.

Employment and support allowance

For ESA, the daily reduction rate is normally the weekly amount of ESA to which you are entitled (not including any component or premium(s)) multiplied by 52 and divided by 365, rounded down to the nearest 10 pence (the 'high rate').[52]

The daily reduction rate is 40 per cent of the amount as calculated above (the 'low rate') if, at the end of the benefit week for which the reduction is being calculated:[53]

- you are a lone parent responsible for a child under one or the responsible foster parent of a child under one (see p1042); *or*
- you are pregnant and there are 11 weeks or less before the week your baby is due; *or*

Part 7: National Insurance, work and work-related rules
Chapter 47: Universal credit system sanctions
2. How your benefit is reduced

- you had a baby not more than 15 weeks ago (including if the baby was stillborn); *or*
- you are adopting a child and it is no more than 52 weeks since the child was placed with you (see p1041); *or*
- you can only be required to meet a work-focused interview requirement (see p1045).

The daily reduction rate is nil if, at the end of the benefit week for which the reduction is being calculated, you do not have to meet any work-related requirements because you have limited capability for work and for work-related activity (see p1042).[54]

Note:

- The ESA work-related activity component was abolished for new claims from 3 April 2017. This means the impact of a sanction is greater for those who do not get the component. If this affects you, you may be able to apply for a higher hardship payment.
- If you are getting a reduced rate of ESA because you have been disqualified from receiving ESA for any of the reasons on p633 (eg, because of failure to accept treatment), the daily reduction rates are also reduced – ie, because your ESA entitlement is already reduced.

Daily reduction rates

	High rate	Low rate
	£ per day	£ per day
Entitled to main phase ESA	10.90	4.36
Under 25, not entitled to main phase ESA	8.60	3.44
25 or over, not entitled to main phase ESA	10.90	4.36

Example

Luisa, aged 30, claimed ESA recently. She is getting £77 a week ESA. She fails to participate in a work-focused interview, but participates three days later. She is given a low level sanction. Her total sanction period is nine days (see p1075): two days before she complies plus seven days = nine days.

For the first benefit week, the reduction is calculated as follows.

Step one: the relevant number of days is seven (the number of days in the benefit week).

Step two: 7 x £10.90 = £76.30

Luisa's ESA is reduced by £76.30 for one benefit week. She is paid the remainder (£0.70).

For the second benefit week, the reduction is calculated as follows.

Step one: the relevant number of days is two (the number of days in the sanction period still outstanding).
Step two: 2 x £10.90 = £21.80
Luisa's ESA for the week is reduced by £21.80. She is paid the remainder (£55.20). For the following weeks, she is paid as normal.

Jobseeker's allowance

For JSA, the daily reduction rate is the weekly amount of JSA to which you are entitled multiplied by 52 and divided by 365, rounded down to the nearest 10 pence.[55] The daily reduction rates are therefore as follows. If you are:
- under 25: £8.60;
- 25 or over: £10.90.

Example
Anais is a JSA claimant aged 24. She was given a seven-day low level sanction.
Step one: the relevant number of days is seven.
Step two: 7 x £8.60 = £60.20
Anais' JSA for the benefit week is reduced by £60.20. She is paid the remainder (£0.85). The following benefit week, she is paid the full rate of JSA (£61.05) because the sanction period has ended.

If your benefits change

- If you are given a UC sanction, your UC is being paid at a reduced rate when your entitlement ends, you still come under the UC system and you are entitled to JSA or ESA, the reduction is then made to your JSA or ESA.[56] The reduction is calculated as for JSA (see above) or ESA (see p1069) and is made for the remainder of the UC sanction period. Any days between the day your entitlement to UC ends and the day your entitlement to JSA or ESA starts are deducted from the period.
- If you are given a JSA or ESA sanction under the UC system and you become entitled to UC, the reduction is made to your UC instead of your JSA or ESA.[57] It is calculated as for UC (see p1068) and is made for the remainder of the JSA or ESA sanction period. If your award of JSA or ESA has ended, any days between the day your award of JSA or ESA ends and the day your award of UC starts are deducted from the period.

Special rules apply if you were given a sanction while entitled to JSA (or ESA) before you came under the UC system. In this case, if you are now entitled to:
- JSA (or ESA) under the UC system, but not UC, you are treated as if you were given a JSA (or ESA) sanction under the UC system;[58]

Part 7: National Insurance, work and work-related rules
Chapter 47: Universal credit system sanctions
3. The sanction period

- UC, you are treated as if you were given a UC sanction.[59]

In both cases, the reduction is made for the remainder of the former JSA (or ESA) sanction period, minus any days between the day your former JSA (or ESA) entitlement ended (if relevant) and your current UC, JSA or ESA entitlement starts.

3. **The sanction period**

Length of the sanction period

Sanctions can be given for various periods, depending on your work-related requirements, for universal credit (UC) or jobseeker's allowance (JSA) and employment and support allowance (ESA) under the UC system, and what you have done or failed to do. A sanction period may be longer if you have previously been sanctioned at the same level.

Sanction	Sanction period
High level sanctions (UC and JSA only)	91 or 182 days
Failing to apply for or to accept paid work	
Ceasing paid work or losing pay for specified reasons	
Medium level sanctions (UC and JSA only)	28 or 91 days
Failing to be available for paid work or to take all reasonable action to get paid work	
Low level sanctions (UC, JSA and ESA)	Until you comply with a requirement, plus a fixed period of seven, 14 or 28 days
Failing to meet a work-focused interview requirement (where other requirements also apply)	
Failing to meet a requirement connected to a work-related requirement	
Failing to meet a work preparation requirement	
Failing to take a particular action to get paid work (UC and JSA only)	
Lowest level sanctions (UC and ESA only)	Until you comply with a requirement
Failing to meet a work-related interview requirement (where no other requirements apply)	

High level sanctions

If you are given a high level sanction, it is usually imposed for 91 days. However, it is imposed for 182 days if you have previously had a 91-day high level sanction (see below).[60]

If you are given a high level UC sanction and you are 16 or 17 years old, a fixed sanction period is imposed for:[61]

- 14 days; or
- 28 days, if you have previously had a 14- or 28-day high level sanction.

Longer sanction periods if you have previously been sanctioned

You can be given a longer sanction period of 182 days (28 days if you are 16/17 years old) if you have previously had a high level sanction. For the longer sanction period to apply, your previous sanctionable action must have taken place at least 14 days, but less than 365 days, before your current sanctionable action. If you have already had more than one high level sanction, only the most recent one is considered when deciding the length of a new sanction.

The 365 days run from the date of the previous sanctionable action, not from the date of the decision imposing the previous sanction, which could be some time later. If the previous sanctionable action was within 14 days of the current one, the length of the new sanction period is the same as the previous one. If it was 365 days or more before the current one, the length of the new sanction period is the same as if you were given a sanction for the first time.

For JSA, a high level UC sanction, and for UC, a high level JSA sanction which has been applied to your UC, also counts for these purposes.[62]

Sanctions you received when you were getting JSA but not under the UC system also count.

Note: if you are given a longer sanction period, but later a previous sanction is removed (eg, by the First-tier Tribunal), ask the DWP decision maker to reduce the sanction period if relevant.[63] Appeal if s/he fails to do so. If you have already appealed against the later sanction, the tribunal should take this into account and ensure that if it upholds the later sanction decision, the sanction period is for 91 days.[64]

Reduced sanction periods

If you are given a high level sanction because you failed to accept paid work, ceased paid work or lost pay voluntarily or because of misconduct before the date of your claim, your sanction period is reduced to take account of days when you did not claim UC (or JSA). It is calculated as follows and is the shorter of the following.[65]

- **Step one:** if the job was only due to last for a limited period, work out the number of days starting with the day after the date of your current sanctionable action and ending on the day the paid work would have ended. 'Limited period' is not defined.

Part 7: National Insurance, work and work-related rules
Chapter 47: Universal credit system sanctions
3. The sanction period

- **Step two:** in any other case, work out the sanction period that would normally apply.
- **Step three:** reduce the amount in Step one or Step two, as relevant, by the number of days between the date of your current sanctionable action and your date of claim (see p46 and p699).

In practical terms, this means that if you claim UC (or JSA) after the job would have ended, or you delay your claim for UC (or JSA) long enough, your benefit is not paid at a reduced (or nil) rate.[66]

Example
Angela quits her job on 7 October. It was only due to last until 1 November. She claims JSA on 16 November. She is given a high level sanction for the first time, so a 91-day sanction period would normally apply. However, her job was only due to last for a limited period. The number of days from 8 October to 1 November is 25 days. The number of days between 7 October and 16 November is 39 days. Angela's sanction period is therefore reduced to nil and her JSA is not paid at a reduced rate.

Medium level sanctions

Medium level sanctions are usually imposed for 28 days. However, a medium level sanction is imposed for 91 days if you have previously had a 28-day or 91-day medium level sanction.[67]

If you are given a medium level UC sanction and you are 16 or 17 years old, a fixed sanction period applies of:[68]

- seven days; *or*
- 14 days, if you have previously had a seven- or 14-day medium level sanction.

Longer sanction periods if you have previously been sanctioned

You can be given a longer sanction period of 91 days (14 days if you are 16/17 years old) if you have previously had a medium level sanction.

For the longer sanction periods to apply, the previous sanctionable action must have taken place at least 14 days, but less than 365 days, before your current sanctionable action. The 365 days run from the date of the previous sanctionable action, not from the date of the decision imposing the previous sanction, which could be some time later. If you have already had more than one medium level sanction, only the most recent one is considered when deciding on the length of a new sanction.

If the previous sanctionable action was within 14 days of the current one, the length of the new sanction period is the same as the previous one. If it was 365 days or more before the current one, the length of the new sanction period is the same as if you were given a sanction for the first time.

For JSA, a medium level UC sanction also counts for these purposes. For UC, a medium level JSA sanction which was applied to your UC also counts for these purposes. If you were given a JSA sanction when you did not come under the UC system, and you are then given another sanction under the UC system, the previous sanctionable action can count when the new sanction period is determined.

If you are given a sanction but later a previous sanction is removed (eg, by the First-tier Tribunal), ask the DWP decision maker to reduce the sanction period if relevant. Appeal if s/he fails to do so. If you have already appealed against the later sanction, the tribunal should take the removal of the previous sanction into account and ensure that if it upholds the later sanction decision, the sanction period is for 28 days.

Low level sanctions

If you are given a low level UC, JSA or ESA sanction, it is imposed for a period made up of the period until you comply with the work-related requirement plus a fixed period as follows.

Step one: work out the number of days, starting on the date your sanctionable action took place and ending on the earliest of the following:[69]

- the day before the date you meet a 'compliance condition' (see below) specified by the DWP; *or*
- for UC and ESA, the day before the date you come into a category in which you no longer have to meet any work-related requirements (see p1039); *or*
- the day before the date you are no longer required to take particular action specified in a work preparation requirement; *or*
- the date your entitlement to UC (or JSA or ESA) ends. For UC, this does not apply if this is because you cease to be, or become, a member of a couple.

Compliance condition

A '**compliance condition**' is:[70]

– a condition that you stop a sanctionable action – eg, if you failed to participate in an employment programme, a condition that you must participate; *or*

– a condition relating to your future compliance with a work-related requirement (or a requirement connected to one) – eg, if you failed to attend a training scheme, a condition that you must attend and participate in an interview to discuss what training may be suitable.

The DWP should inform you of the consequences of not meeting the condition immediately.

Step two: work out the fixed sanction period.

- For UC if you are at least 18 years old, and for JSA or ESA, this is usually for seven days. However, the period is:[71]

Part 7: National Insurance, work and work-related rules
Chapter 47: Universal credit system sanctions
3. The sanction period

- 14 days, if you have previously had a seven-day low level sanction; *or*
- 28 days, if you have previously had a 14-day or 28-day low level sanction.
- For UC if you are 16 or 17 years old, this is for seven days, but only if you have been given a low level sanction previously (see below).[72] If you have not been given a low level sanction previously (or it is not taken into account – see below), there is no fixed period and your sanction lasts only until you meet the compliance condition.

Step three: add the number of days in Steps one and two together. This is your low level sanction period.

- -

What can you do to limit the length of a low level sanction period?
If the DWP does not make a decision to give you a sanction until some time after your sanctionable action, you might not have a compliance condition to meet until you are given the sanction. The DWP is still likely to say that your indefinite sanction period starts from the date your sanctionable action took place and runs until the start of the assessment period in which it is decided to give you the sanction. Try to argue that you have already complied with the condition before you were given the sanction – eg, if you are given a sanction because you failed to provide your CV on a specified date, but you provided one later. Provide any relevant information and evidence to prove you have already complied. You could also make a complaint about the time the DWP took to decide to give you a sanction (see Chapter 61). If there was any confusion about what you were required to do at the time of the sanctionable action and in the period before the DWP accepts that you complied with the condition, explain this when challenging the sanction and/or complaining.

- -

Longer sanction periods if you have previously been sanctioned

You can be given a longer sanction period if you have previously had a low level sanction. For the longer sanction periods to apply, the previous sanctionable action must have taken place at least 14 days, but less than 365 days, before your current sanctionable action. If you have already had more than one low level sanction, only the most recent one is considered when making a decision about the length of a new sanction.

The 365 days run from the date of the previous sanctionable action, not from the date of the decision imposing the previous sanction, which could be some time later. If the previous sanctionable action was within 14 days of the current one, the length of the new sanction period is the same as the previous one. If it was 365 days or more before the current one, the length of the new sanction period is the same as if you were given a sanction for the first time.

For UC, a low level JSA or ESA sanction that has been applied to your UC also counts for these purposes. For JSA, a low level UC or ESA sanction, and for ESA, a low level UC or JSA sanction, also count for these purposes.[73]

If you were given a JSA or ESA sanction when you did not come under the UC system and you are then given another sanction under the UC system, the previous sanctionable action can count when the new sanction period is determined.[74]

Note: if you are given a sanction but later a previous sanction is removed (eg, by the First-tier Tribunal), ask the DWP decision maker to reduce the sanction period if relevant.[75] Appeal if s/he fails to do so. If you have already appealed against the later sanction, the tribunal should take the removal of the previous sanction into account.[76]

Lowest level sanctions

If you are given a lowest level sanction, it can be imposed indefinitely. It is imposed for the number of days starting on the date your sanctionable action took place and only ends on the earliest of:[77]

- the day before the date you meet a 'compliance condition' specified by the DWP (see p1075 for the meaning). If it was not made clear to you what you had to do, or it was difficult to rearrange the work-focused interview, you should include that in your good reason when challenging the length of the sanction, and complain; *or*
- the day before the date you come into a category in which you no longer have to meet any work-related requirements (see p1039); *or*
- the date your entitlement to UC (or ESA) ends. For UC, this does not apply if this is because you cease to be, or become, a member of a couple.

When the sanction period starts and ends

For all levels of sanction, the sanction period starts:[78]

- for UC, on the first day of the assessment period in which the decision is made to give you a sanction or, if your UC was not reduced for the sanction during that period, from the first day of the next assessment period;
- for JSA, if you have not been paid any JSA for the benefit week in which the sanctionable action took place, on the first day of that benefit week, or if you have been paid for that week, the first day of the benefit week after the last benefit week for which you were paid JSA;
- for ESA, if you have not been paid any ESA for the benefit week in which the DWP decision maker decides you should be sanctioned, on the first day of that benefit week, or if you have been paid for that week, the first day of the benefit week after the last benefit week for which you were paid ESA.

However, if your benefit is already being paid at a reduced rate because of a previous sanction, it is not reduced for a new sanction until the previous reduction ends.

Once a sanction period has begun, it continues unbroken until the sanction period comes to an end.[79] This means, for example, that if you take a job for a

Part 7: National Insurance, work and work-related rules
Chapter 47: Universal credit system sanctions
3. The sanction period

short period but then claim UC (or JSA or ESA) again during the period of the sanction, although you are still caught by the sanction, this is only for any days still outstanding in the sanction period.

If your UC (or JSA or ESA) entitlement ends before the DWP decision maker has decided to give you a sanction, but the decision to do so is made when you are again entitled to the benefit, the decision is treated as having been made on the day before your previous entitlement ended.[80] So, in practice, the number of days between the two awards of benefit are deducted from the sanction period.

A sanction is suspended for any period during which you are sanctioned for a benefit offence (see p1239).[81]

If you have more than one sanction at the same time

Your sanction period is worked out for each sanction you are given. If more than one decision to sanction you is made at the same time, or you are sanctioned when your benefit is already reduced because of a sanction, the sanction periods run consecutively. If your benefit is already being paid at a reduced rate because of a previous sanction, it is not reduced for a new sanction until the previous reduction ends.[82]

The maximum outstanding sanction period for all sanctions is 1,095 days. So if a new sanction is imposed when you already have an existing sanction, the sanction period is adjusted to ensure that the outstanding period for all your sanctions will not go over the 1,095-day limit.[83]

When a sanction is terminated

All sanctions terminate and your benefit is no longer paid at a reduced (or nil) rate if, since the date of the most recent sanctionable action, you have been in paid work for (or for periods that total) at least six months (for UC) or 26 weeks (for JSA or ESA).[84] You count as being in paid work if:

- for UC, your monthly earnings during the six months are at least the amount of your individual earnings threshold (see p1043). This includes if you are treated as having a minimum level of self-employed earnings under the rules described on p122;
- for UC, you are someone who does not have to satisfy any work-related requirements for any of the reasons listed on p1039 and p1044 (other situations) and your monthly earnings during the six months are at least 16 times the minimum wage for a person of your age multiplied by 52 and divided by 12;
- for JSA, your weekly earnings are at least what you would earn for the number of hours you are expected to work (see p1031) at the minimum wage for a person of your age;
- for ESA, your weekly earnings are at least 16 times the minimum wage for a person of your age.

4. Good reasons for your actions

In a number of situations, a sanction cannot be imposed if you have a good reason for your actions. **'Good reason'** is not defined in the rules, but caselaw on sanctions in the universal credit (UC) system, as well as caselaw on 'good cause' and caselaw on 'good reason' for jobseeker's allowance (JSA) sanctions outside the UC system (see p1126), can be applied.[85] In addition, what may count as good reason is set out in guidance.[86] If you appeal against the sanction decision, the guidance is not binding on the First-tier Tribunal. It must make up its own mind about what counts as a good reason.

It is up to you to show you have a good reason, but the DWP decision maker should take all the circumstances into account.

How much time are you given to explain your good reasons?

You should always be given the opportunity to provide your reasons for what you did or did not do. You should be given sufficient time to explain your reasons and to provide relevant evidence. There are no specified time limits, but the DWP says you should be given at least five working days if the information is requested by post. You may be given less time than this if you can be contacted by telephone, face to face or by electronic means. The DWP says that you should be given more time if you have to get information or evidence from someone else, you have a representative, or you have a health condition or there are other temporary circumstances (eg, caring responsibilities) that prevent you from replying.[87] The time you are given should reflect your circumstances. If the time you are given seems unreasonable, you should mention this when you challenge the sanction decision and/or complain.

For ideas about what might count as a good reason, see below.

Circumstances that should be taken into account

The DWP decision maker should take all your circumstances into account when deciding whether you have a good reason for any sanctionable action. This should include the following.

- Any restrictions or limitations you have been allowed to place on your availability for work, including reductions to your expected hours of work (see p1031), or restrictions which should have been made if your circumstances had been fully taken into account.[88] You may have taken all 'reasonable action' given your circumstances at the time (see p1031). You do not necessarily have a good reason for refusing to apply for a job which does not meet your restrictions or limitations, but your restrictions are very significant factors to take into account.[89]

Part 7: National Insurance, work and work-related rules
Chapter 47: Universal credit system sanctions
4. Good reasons for your actions

- Any condition you have or any personal circumstances that suggest that a particular job or activity would be likely to cause you unreasonable physical or mental stress or significant harm to your health.
- A disease or physical/mental disability that affects your ability to work or to meet your work-related requirements, or which means your health (or the health of others) would have been at risk.
- You misunderstood what you had to do because of language, learning or literacy difficulties, or because you were misled by the DWP. Instructions about work preparation and work-related activity must be clear.[90] There must be notification of the work-related requirement and an explanation of the consequences of non-compliance.[91] Ignorance of the law may sometimes mean that you have a good reason, but you are expected to make reasonable enquiries of your work coach if you do not understand what you have to do.[92] If you do not know about a requirement (eg, you do not receive notification of a work-focused interview), you have good reason for not complying with it.[93] However, you are expected to check your UC online account, including messages on your journal, where reasonable. If you were unable to do this, you should explain why.
- You (or someone for whom you care) were attending a medical, dental or other important appointment which it would have been unreasonable to rearrange.
- You have experienced domestic violence or bullying or harassment.
- You have a sincerely held religious or conscientious objection.[94]
- Caring responsibilities that make it unreasonable for you to meet your work-related requirements or continue in work, including whether suitable childcare would have been (or was) reasonably available.[95] You are expected to consider available options for childcare and give reasons if you believe they are not suitable.
- You are homeless.[96] You may also be able to argue that your work coach should have suspended your work-related requirements during a period of homelessness.
- Any transport difficulties.
- Excessive travelling time involved, including where this is excessive because of your health or caring responsibilities (but see p1081 for when this does not count as a good reason).
- Unreasonably high expenses (eg, for childcare or travel) that were (or would be) unavoidable.[97]

Account should also be taken of any other factor that appears relevant. See, in particular, p1084 for when the terms of a job on offer break the law on minimum working conditions.

Note: there are situations where the work search requirement for UC and JSA should be suspended temporarily (see p1051). If this should have applied to you, you may not have to argue that you had a good reason for your actions. Instead, you should show why your work-related requirements were not reasonable at the time. You may still have been required to take part in work preparation (see p1029), but you may be able to argue that you have a good reason for failing to do so because of the same temporary circumstances.

When might you not have a good reason?

You may find it difficult to show that you have a good reason for failing to apply for, or accept, paid work on the grounds of distance if your travel time is shorter than 90 minutes. This is because you have to be available for work and to look for work in locations that are up to 90 minutes from your home.[98] However, there could be other factors such as childcare or high travelling expenses, which can be considered when deciding whether you had a good reason, and in some cases the DWP should consider whether a shorter travel to work time should be allowed (see p1036). Although not specified, it is probable that travel time of up to 90 minutes to attend work-related activity or an interview would also not be seen as a good reason, but all the other relevant factors (including childcare, expenses and the effect on your health) should be taken into account.

Leaving a job or reducing your hours

You may be able to show you have a good reason for leaving a job or reducing your hours in the following situations.

- Your chances of getting other employment, including self-employment, were good, there were strong reasons for leaving your job and you acted reasonably in doing so.[99]
- You genuinely did not know or were mistaken about the conditions of the job (eg, it was beyond your physical or mental capacity, or was harmful to your health), you gave it a fair trial before leaving and it was reasonable for you to leave when you did.[100]
- You left your job or reduced your hours for personal or domestic reasons – eg, to look after a sick relative.[101] Explain why you left your job before looking for, or getting, alternative employment. It could be helpful to show that you tried to negotiate an arrangement with your employer to resolve the problem – eg, for a reduction in your hours or time off work.
- You left your job to move with your partner who has taken a job elsewhere.[102] Relevant factors may include how important it was to your partner's career to move and how good your chances are of finding work in the new area.
- Your employer made a change in the terms and conditions of your employment that does not amount to your contract of employment ending. You are expected to use any grievance procedure first. In some situations (eg, with a zero-hour contract), a reduction in hours may be part of your contract of

Part 7: National Insurance, work and work-related rules
Chapter 47: Universal credit system sanctions
4. Good reasons for your actions

employment because your hours are not guaranteed. You should not be sanctioned if the reduction in hours is not voluntary (see p1063).

If you leave your job because your employer cuts your wages unilaterally, you might not be able to show you have a good reason. The DWP will not consider a cut unless it takes you below the national minimum wage (see Appendix 7), but a cut in wages may be a good reason if, for example, you are not given proper notice of an imposed change to your pay, or your work-related expenses are now an unreasonably high proportion of your pay. If you stay in your job, a cut in wages is a reduction in pay, but may not be voluntary (see p1063).

- You left your job because of a firm offer of alternative employment, but claimed benefit because the offer fell through. However, the DWP may say you do not have a good reason if the offer was cancelled before you left your previous employment or you changed your mind and did not take the new job and you could have stayed in the existing employment, or you did not ask your employer if you could stay.

The DWP decision maker should take into account:
- any caring responsibilities you have which made it unreasonable for you to stay in your job and whether suitable childcare was (or could have been) available; *and*
- any childcare expenses you had to pay as a result of being in the job, if they were an unreasonably high proportion of the income you received.

What should you do before you give up a job or reduce your hours?

1. Do everything possible to resolve problems before you give up your job. If the conditions of a job are poor, try to sort out any problems (eg, by raising them with your employer, or using any grievance procedure) rather than leaving immediately, and to look for another job seriously before giving one up. Keep a record of your negotiations with your employer. You may have difficulty showing you have a good reason if you do not do so.

2. Employers are required to provide certain minimum working conditions and pay the minimum wage. These could help to show that you have a good reason for giving up work. Point out that the intention of the Working Time Regulations 1998 is to protect the health and safety of workers, so conditions that do not comply with them should be regarded as unacceptable. Your employer should also comply with the Equality Act 2010 and make reasonable adjustments if you are disabled.

3. If you need to reduce your hours because of your health or caring responsibilities, make sure that you have a record of your request to your employer and any other adjustments you have asked for before the reduction in hours. You should try to negotiate with your employer rather than leaving the job, if possible.

4. You are likely to have difficulty showing you have a good reason for leaving a job or reducing your hours just because the pay is low (although your work-related expenses should be taken into account).[103] However, you can argue that this does not apply if you left your job because your employer refused to pay the national minimum wage.[104]

Leaving or failing to participate in work preparation or work-related activity

You should be given clear instructions about where you have to attend for work-related activity and the consequences of failing to participate. For example, if it is not clear that the activity is mandatory, or you do not understand what you are supposed to do and when, you may have a good reason for failing to participate. You may not have a good reason simply because you consider that the work preparation or work-related activity is not useful or not relevant to your needs, but you could consider complaining. You are likely not to have a good reason for failing to participate if you refuse to confirm your identity because of data protection concerns and you do not offer another acceptable form of evidence of identity.[105]

You may be able to show you have a good reason for leaving a particular work-related activity (eg, a training scheme or employment programme) or for failing to participate in work preparation or work-related activity (see p1079). The DWP decision maker should consider the following.

- Your continued participation would have put your health and safety, or that of others, at risk.
- The travelling time to or from the scheme or programme was excessive (although not listed as a good reason in guidance, this could relate to other good reasons such as your health).
- You had caring responsibilities, no one else was available to provide the care, and it was not practical to make other arrangements.
- Temporary circumstances made it difficult for you to participate – eg, you were attending court as a party to the proceedings, a witness or a juror, you were crewing or launching a lifeboat, or you were on duty as a part-time member of a fire brigade.
- You were arranging or attending the funeral of a close relative or a close friend.
- You had to deal with a domestic emergency.
- You were having structured alcohol or drug dependency treatment.

Note: there are temporary circumstances in which the work search requirement in UC should be lifted[106] and you may not be expected to be available for work (see p1052). However, you may still have been required to take part in work preparation. If this applied to you, you may be able to argue that your good reason relates to the same temporary circumstances, and/or that the temporary circumstances should have been taken into account in limiting the work preparation you were required to do.

Part 7: National Insurance, work and work-related rules
Chapter 47: Universal credit system sanctions
4. Good reasons for your actions

Refusing or failing to apply for a job

You may be able to show you have a good reason for refusing a job – eg:

- if the travelling time to or from the job was more than 90 minutes or more than the maximum travelling time agreed with your work coach;
- if you are within your 'permitted period' and have restricted the type of work for which you are available to your usual occupation or to at least your usual rate of pay, or both, and you refuse a job that does not meet these conditions;
- if you have been laid off or are on short-time working, have been accepted as available only for casual employment and you refuse to take some other type of work;[107]
- if you come under the rules that exempt you from having to be able to start work immediately, and you refuse to take a job which you would have to start immediately (see p1094).

You can be sanctioned for refusing to accept a job which does not have guaranteed hours (a zero-hour contract), but you should not be sanctioned if:[108]

- your employer reduces your hours because you have taken work with another employer in order to gain more hours of work (or arguably, because you look for other work); or
- the hours offered by your employer would restrict the opportunity for you to increase your paid work with other employers.

Note: you cannot be given a sanction if you refuse a job because it is vacant because of a trade dispute.[109]

What should you do before refusing or failing to apply for a job?

Employers are required to provide certain minimum working conditions and pay the minimum wage (see Appendix 7). Try to argue that you have a good reason for not applying for any job where the terms do not comply with the legal requirements. Make sure that this is the case, particularly where the Working Time Regulations 1998 are concerned, as there are many exceptions and opt-outs that might apply. If the terms offered break the rules about the limit on the number of hours in the average working week, the DWP may suggest that you agree to an 'individual opt-out'. Argue that this would be unreasonable, as the working time rules are intended to protect the health and safety of workers. The DWP accepts that you have a good reason for refusing a job if you do so because it does not pay at least the national minimum wage that applies to you.[110] However, you are unlikely to have a good reason simply because you are not sure of the effect of work and pay on your benefits.[111] You may not have a good reason for not applying for a job simply because you believe you are unlikely to be successful. You should ask your work coach to reconsider, explaining why you think you will not get the job and suggesting other actions you could take. You are especially unlikely to have a good reason if you have previously agreed to apply for the job and did not attempt to negotiate with your work coach.[112]

5. Sanction decisions

A DWP decision maker decides whether you should be given a sanction, often some time after the sanctionable action took place. Do not assume that because you have not yet been informed of any sanction, the DWP has decided not to sanction you.

You should be issued with notice, telling you that you have been given a sanction.[113] This information should either be sent in a letter or be posted on your universal credit (UC) online journal.

It is possible that you will not know you have been given a sanction until your benefit is paid at a reduced (or nil) rate. You should contact the DWP as soon as you are aware of the reduction in your benefit to find out what sanctionable action is involved, give a good reason, if possible, and comply with your work-related requirements if applicable. For example, with a low level sanction (which runs until you comply with the requirement), you must be given formal notification of the decision and then, in theory, you could comply on the same day – eg, if you fail to attend an appointment, you could telephone and remake the appointment on the same day.

If the sanction decision is made some time after the sanctionable action, you could complain as well as challenge the sanction decision. Your 'good reason' may be affected by whether your work-related requirements were made clear to you at the time of the sanctionable action. Any compliance condition you need to meet to stop a sanction period from increasing must also be made clear to you. This may be a different requirement if the original is no longer appropriate – eg, if you failed to attend a training day which is no longer available. If your work-related requirements or the compliance condition (see p1075) were not made clear, you should complain as well as challenge the sanction decision.

If you have complex needs (see below), you should be contacted by telephone (or another method which is accessible to you) about what led to the sanction and any good reason you may have, before the sanction decision is made.

Only a DWP decision maker can decide whether you have a good reason for the sanctionable action and whether a sanction should be applied. However, if an employment or training scheme provider requires you to do something on behalf of the DWP,[114] failure to comply may result in a sanction. If a provider alerts the DWP about a possible sanctionable action, the DWP should ask you, in writing, whether you have a good reason for what happened.

People who are vulnerable

If you have complex needs, special procedures apply before your case is referred for a sanction decision. 'Complex needs' procedures may apply if you are considered to be 'vulnerable'. This may be if you have a serious mental health condition, but can also apply if there is a language barrier, you have an addiction

Part 7: National Insurance, work and work-related rules
Chapter 47: Universal credit system sanctions
6. Challenging a sanction decision

or are homeless. These procedures involve extra checks before you are given a sanction, to make sure you understand your work-related requirements and to gather any reasons for what you did or did not do.

If you think that you are vulnerable because of your condition or situation, but have been given a sanction, ask whether the 'complex needs' procedures were considered, and seek advice. If you have a disability and the DWP does not follow these procedures (eg, it does not make sure that you were able to comply with your work-related requirements without your health being affected), this could be a breach of the Equality Act 2010 and be a ground for judicial review of the decision for discrimination (see p1381). If you have failed to comply with a work-related requirement, the DWP should check whether you have complex needs before referring your case for a sanction decision.[115] If you have a health condition which affects your ability to leave your home, at least two attempts should be made to make a home visit, and a sanction referral should not be considered unless the home visit and all other attempts to contact you have failed.[116] If the sanction decision is passed to a decision maker and the evidence shows the requirements were unreasonable at the time of your sanctionable action, the decision maker should accept that you had a good reason and return the case to the DWP for your requirements to be reduced.[117]

6. **Challenging a sanction decision**

If you are given a sanction, your benefit is paid at a reduced rate, often for a lengthy period. It is therefore always worth challenging a sanction decision.

You can challenge:
- the decision to give you a sanction, including:
  – whether you have lawfully been required to do something: whether you have been properly notified of any requirements and the consequences of not complying – eg, to attend an interview or participate in work-related activity. Your work-related requirements must have been made clear to you,[118] and you should also make it clear if you considered your requirements to be unreasonable given your circumstances;
  – whether you failed to do something, or did something, as alleged by the DWP;
  – whether you have a good reason (see p1079) for what you did or did not do;
- the length of the sanction period – eg, if there is a dispute about the number of times you have been sanctioned, or you are challenging a previous decision to give you a sanction.

You should also consider complaining if the actions of the DWP contributed to the sanction and/or the length of the sanction – eg, if your work-related requirements were not made clear to you, or you did not get notification until some time after the sanctionable action, which made it difficult for you to comply and end the sanction period. You can apply for a revision or appeal against a sanction decision in the usual way (see Chapters 56 and 57).

If you have been given a sanction more than once, you should challenge *all* the decisions if possible. Apply for a mandatory reconsideration of all the sanction decisions, asking for the time limit for doing so to be extended if relevant. If you are not sure about the number or length of the sanctions, ask the DWP to clarify what decisions have been made.

If a previous sanction is removed (eg, by a decision maker or the First-tier Tribunal), the sanction period for a later sanction of the same type can be reduced.[119] If you have appealed against the later sanction, the tribunal should take the removal of the previous sanction into account.[120]

You must apply for a mandatory reconsideration before you can appeal. You can ask for a sanction decision to be revised, even if it was made a long time ago, as universal credit (UC) sanctions, and jobseeker's allowance and employment and support allowance sanctions under the UC system, can be revised at any time (see p1267).

You must be given written notice of the sanction decision, setting out your appeal rights.[121] Although notification of sanction decisions is meant to happen automatically when the sanction is applied to your benefit, this does not always happen. If you were given a sanction but did not receive written notice of the decision, get advice. You may still be able to ask for a mandatory reconsideration and then appeal, even if the decision was made a long time ago.

If you have received a decision letter with a postal address, you can send your request for a mandatory reconsideration to the address on the letter and/or hand it in to the job centre (if possible, do both). If you are a UC claimant, you can state that you want a mandatory reconsideration on your online journal, if you have one. However, it is advisable to follow this up by telephone and in writing if possible – eg, you may not be able to upload all the evidence you want to send via your journal. Ensure that your request for a mandatory reconsideration is acknowledged and keep a copy of your application (including a screenshot if you request the mandatory reconsideration via your journal). Even if you post it on your journal, provide a copy to the job centre as soon as possible, making a note of the date and time that you do so. If you do not have an online journal, you can request a mandatory reconsideration by telephone or in writing. You should make it clear that you are formally requesting a mandatory reconsideration and keep proof of your request.

You should apply for a revision of *all* outstanding sanction decisions made against you, including those which will not be applied until your existing sanction period is over. If you decide to appeal once you have a mandatory reconsideration notice (see p1299), you can ask for related sanction decisions to be considered in the same appeal hearing.

Part 7: National Insurance, work and work-related rules
Chapter 47: Universal credit system sanctions
Notes

* *

* *

How can you increase your chances of getting a decision changed?

1. An appeal to the First-tier Tribunal gives you a chance to challenge the DWP's version of events, including the evidence it is using from your former employer or a work-related activity scheme provider. You should ask the DWP for all the information and documents that were used in the process of making the sanction decision. If the DWP does not provide these, the tribunal can be asked to direct it to do so (see p1318). As you must request a mandatory reconsideration first, any information you can supply to the DWP at that point is useful, in case you can get the decision changed quickly. If a mandatory reconsideration is refused, you can still use the same arguments at an appeal.

2. Attend the appeal hearing if you can. Explain your case fully and, if relevant, the good reasons for what you did or failed to do (see p1079), including any factors relating to your own situation and/or how the sanction was notified to you.

3. Provide as much evidence as you can to support your case – eg, medical evidence or evidence about your caring responsibilities. The tribunal can allow witnesses (eg, family members or former work colleagues) to give evidence on your behalf.

Note: if you do not attend the appeal hearing and further evidence or information about you is submitted by the DWP, the tribunal should consider an adjournment to allow you to attend, or to respond to the information/evidence.

7

* *

Notes

* *

1. When you can be sanctioned

1 **UC** Reg 100(1) UC Regs
   JSA Reg 17 JSA Regs 2013
   ESA Reg 50 ESA Regs 2013
2 **UC** s26 WRA 2012; reg 114 UC Regs
   JSA s6J JSA 1995; reg 29 JSA Regs 2013
3 **UC** s26(2)(b) and (c) and (4)(a) WRA 2012
   JSA s6J(2)(b) and (c) and (3)(a) JSA 1995
4 **UC** Reg 113(1)(a) UC Regs
   JSA Reg 28(1)(a) JSA Regs 2013
5 **UC** Reg 113(1)(e) UC Regs
   JSA Reg 28(1)(c) JSA Regs
6 R(IS) 5/95; *Fiory v CAO*, 20 June 1995
7 para K3057 ADM
8 *S v SSWP* [2017] UKUT 477 (AAC)
9 **UC** Reg 97(3) UC Regs
   JSA Reg 14(2) JSA Regs 2013
10 paras K3271-75 ADM
11 s27A Small Business, Enterprise and Employment Act 2015
12 para K2301 ADM
13 **UC** s26(2)(d), (3) and (4) WRA 2012
   JSA s6J(2)(d) and (3) JSA 1995
14 R(U) 10/71; R(U) 2/76
15 **UC** Reg 113(1)(e) UC Regs
   JSA Reg 28(1)(c) JSA Regs 2013
16 para K2224 ADM
17 para H4055 ADM
18 Reg 113(1)(g) UC Regs
19 **UC** Reg 113(1)(b)-(d) and (f) and (2) UC Regs
   JSA Reg 28(1)(b) and (d)-(f) and (2) JSA Regs 2013
20 para K3213 ADM
21 s148 Employment Rights Act 1996
22 para K3203 ADM
23 para K2031 ADM
24 para K3236 ADM

25 **UC** Reg 113(1)(f) UC Regs
   JSA Reg 28(1)(f) and (2) JSA Regs 2013
26 R(U) 25/52
27 para K2241 ADM
28 R(U) 8/57, para 6
29 R(U) 26/56; R(U) 1/58
30 R(U) 10/53
31 R(U) 14/56
32 *AA v SSWP (JSA)* [2012] UKUT 100
   (AAC), reported as [2012] AACR 42
33 R(U) 24/56
34 K3073 ADM
35 R(U) 1/57; R(U) 14/57; CU/34/1992
36 R(U) 2/76
37 R(U) 2/74
38 R(U) 26/51; R(U) 20/64; R(U) 4/70; R(U)
   1/81
39 R(U) 3/81
40 **UC** s27 WRA 2012; reg 103(1) UC Regs
   JSA s6K JSA 1995; reg 17 JSA Regs 2013
41 **UC** s27 WRA 2012; reg 104(1) UC Regs
   JSA s6K JSA 1995; reg 17 JSA Regs 2013
   ESA s11J WRA 2007; reg 50 ESA Regs
   2013
42 *CS v SSWP (JSA)* [2019] UKUT 218 (AAC)
43 *JB v SSWP* [2018] UKUT 360 (AAC)
44 paras K1181-82 ADM
45 **UC** s27 WRA 2012; reg 105 UC Regs
   ESA s11J WRA 2007; reg 50 ESA Regs
   2013

2. How your benefit is reduced

46 **UC** Regs 101(5) and 110 UC Regs
   JSA Regs 17 and 26 JSA Regs 2013
   ESA Regs 50 and 58 ESA Regs 2013
47 Reg 111(1) UC Regs
48 Reg 111(2) UC Regs
49 Reg 111(5) UC Regs
50 Reg 111(3) UC Regs
51 Reg 111(4) UC Regs
52 Reg 59 ESA Regs 2013
53 Reg 60(1) ESA Regs 2013
54 Reg 60(2) ESA Regs 2013
55 Reg 27 JSA Regs 2013
56 **JSA** Reg 30 JSA Regs 2013
   ESA Reg 61 ESA Regs 2013
57 **UC** Reg 112 and Sch 11 paras 1 and 2
   UC Regs
   JSA Reg 6 JSA Regs 2013
   ESA Reg 43 ESA Regs 2013
58 Arts 14, 15, 17 and 18 WRA(No.9)O
59 Regs 30 and 32 UC(TP) Regs

3. The sanction period

60 Reg 102(2)(a) UC Regs
61 Reg 102(2)(b) UC Regs
62 **UC** Sch 11 para 3 UC Regs
   JSA Reg 19 JSA Regs 2013

63 Reg 14 UC,PIP,JSA&ESA(DA) Regs
64 CJSA/2375/2000
65 **UC** Reg 102(4) and (5) UC Regs
   JSA Regs 17 and 19(3) JSA Regs 2013
66 **UC** Reg 113(1)(e) UC Regs
   JSA Reg 28(1)(c) JSA Regs 2013
67 **UC** Regs 103(2)(a) and 112 and Sch 11
   para 3 UC Regs
   JSA Reg 20 JSA Regs 2013
68 Reg 103(2)(b) UC Regs
69 **UC** Reg 104(2)(a) and (3)(a) UC Regs
   JSA Reg 21(2) JSA Regs 2013
   ESA Reg 52(a) ESA Regs 2013
70 **UC** s27(6) and (7) WRA 2012
   JSA s6K(6) and (7) JSA 1995
   ESA s11J(5) and (6) WRA 2007
71 **UC** Regs 104(2)(b) and 112 and Sch 11
   para 3 UC Regs
   JSA Reg 21(3) JSA Regs 2013
   ESA Reg 52(b) ESA Regs 2013
72 Reg 104(3)(b) UC Regs
73 **UC** Sch 11 para 3 UC Regs
   JSA Reg 21 JSA Regs 2013
   ESA Regs 50 and 52 ESA Regs 2013
74 Regs 31 and 33 UC(TP) Regs; arts 16-19
   WRA(No.9)O
75 Reg 14 UC,PIP,JSA&ESA(DA) Regs
76 CJSA/2375/2000
77 **UC** Reg 105(2) UC Regs
   ESA Reg 53 ESA Regs 2013
78 **UC** Reg 106 UC Regs
   JSA Reg 22 JSA Regs 2013
   ESA Reg 54 ESA Regs 2013
79 **UC** Reg 107(1) UC Regs
   JSA Reg 23(1) JSA Regs 2013
   ESA Reg 55(1) ESA Regs 2013
80 **UC** Reg 107(2) UC Regs
   JSA Reg 23(2) and (3) JSA Regs 2013
   ESA Reg 55(2) and (3) ESA Regs 2013
81 **UC** Reg 108 UC Regs
   JSA Reg 24 JSA Regs 2013
   ESA Reg 56 ESA Regs 2013
82 **UC** Reg 106(c) UC Regs
   JSA Reg 22(c) JSA Regs 2013
   ESA Reg 54(c) ESA Regs 2013
83 **UC** Reg 101(1)-(3) UC Regs
   JSA Reg 18(1)-(3) JSA Regs 2013
   ESA Reg 51(1)-(3) ESA Regs 2013
84 **UC** Reg 109 UC Regs
   JSA Reg 25 JSA Regs 2013
   ESA Reg 57 ESA Regs 2013

4. Good reasons for your actions

85 *S v SSWP* [2017] UKUT 477 (AAC)
86 Ch K2 ADM
87 paras K2011-14 ADM
88 *RR v SSWP* [2017] UKUT 459 (AAC)

Part 7: National Insurance, work and work-related rules
Chapter 47: Universal credit system sanctions
Notes

89 *HS v SSWP* [2009] UKUT 177 (AAC), reported as [2010] AACR 10
90 *SSWP v DC (JSA)* [2017] UKUT 464
91 *JB v SSWP* [2018] UKUT 360 (AAC)
92 *S v SSWP* [2017] UKUT 477 (AAC)
93 *SP v SSWP* [2018] UKUT 227
94 R(JSA) 7/03 discusses the meaning of 'conscientious objection' in this context
95 para K2142 ADM
96 paras K2091-95 ADM
97 para K2157 ADM
98 **UC** Reg 97(3) UC Regs
   JSA Reg 14(2) JSA Regs 2013
99 R(U) 4/73
100 R(U) 3/73
101 R(U) 14/52
102 R(U) 19/52; R(U) 4/87; CJSA/2507/2005
103 para K2157 ADM
104 para K2238 ADM
105 *CS v SSWP (JSA)* [2019] UKUT 218 (AAC)
106 Reg 99(3) UC Regs
107 paras K2175-76 ADM
108 para K2301 ADM
109 **UC** Reg 113(1)(a) UC Regs
   JSA reg 28(1)(a) JSA Regs 2013
110 para K2213 ADM
111 *S v SSWP* [2017] UKUT 477 (AAC)
112 *KB v SSWP (UC)* [2019] UKUT 408 (AAC)

5. Sanction decisions
113 Reg 51 UC,PIP,JSA&ESA(DA) Regs
114 s29 WRA 2012
115 para J3257 ADM
116 DWP, *Universal Credit Guidance,* Home Visits, House of Commons library deposited papers, available at rightsnet.org.uk/universal-credit-guidance
117 paras K2054-58 ADM

6. Challenging a sanction decision
118 *JB v SSWP (UC)* [2018] UKUT 360 (AAC)
119 Reg 14 UC,PIP,JSA&ESA(DA) Regs
120 CJSA/2375/2000
121 Reg 51 UC,PIP,JSA&ESA(DA) Regs

Chapter 48

Claimant responsibilities: other benefits

This chapter covers:
1. The jobseeking conditions for jobseeker's allowance outside the universal credit system (p1092)
2. Work-focused interviews for other benefits (p1110)
3. Work-related activity for income support and employment and support allowance (p1111)

This chapter covers the work-related responsibilities you, and in some cases your partner, may have in order to get income support (IS), jobseeker's allowance (JSA) and employment and support allowance (ESA). The DWP may refer to JSA and ESA outside the universal credit (UC) system as 'old style' JSA and ESA. If you come under the UC system (see p22), including if you are claiming contribution-based JSA or contributory ESA under the UC system ('new style' JSA or ESA), the rules in this chapter do not apply to you. See Chapter 46 instead.

Key facts
- To qualify for jobseeker's allowance (JSA) outside the universal credit (UC) system, you must usually satisfy jobseeking conditions.
- If you do not meet the jobseeking conditions, your JSA may end and you may be given a sanction if you reclaim JSA under the UC system or UC. This means your JSA or UC is paid at a reduced or nil rate. However, you may qualify for hardship payments.
- You and your partner may have to take part in work-focused interviews for income support (IS), JSA (as the partner of the claimant) or employment and support allowance (ESA) outside the UC system.
- Some claimants of IS or ESA may be required to undertake work-related activity.
- If you do not take part in work-focused interviews or undertake work-related activity and you cannot show a good cause, you may be given a sanction.
- If you disagree with a decision that you are not entitled to benefit and/or to impose a sanction, you can apply for a revision or a supersession (see Chapter 56) or appeal against the decision (see Chapter 57). You must apply for a mandatory reconsideration before you can appeal.

Part 7: National Insurance, work and work-related rules
Chapter 48: Claimant responsibilities: other benefits
1. The jobseeking conditions for jobseeker's allowance outside the universal credit system

1. The jobseeking conditions for jobseeker's allowance outside the universal credit system

To qualify for jobseeker's allowance (JSA) if you do not come under the universal credit (UC) system (ie, income-based jobseeker's allowance), you must usually satisfy three jobseeking conditions. You must:

- be (or be treated as) available for work; *and*
- be (or be treated as) actively seeking work; *and*
- have (or be treated as having) a current jobseeker's agreement with the DWP. In practice, the job centre calls this a claimant commitment.

You can also be required to attend a scheme for assisting people to obtain employment (see p1093).[1]

There are special rules if:

- you are a lone parent (see p1094);
- you have experienced or been threatened with domestic abuse (see p1096);
- you have a disability (see p1102);
- you are a laid-off or short-time worker. For more information, see pp1085–86 of the 2019/20 edition of this *Handbook;*
- you are in full-time training or study, or, in limited circumstances, you are participating in a specified scheme for assisting people to obtain employment. For more information, see pp1086–88 of the 2019/20 edition of this *Handbook*.

If you do not satisfy the jobseeking conditions, or there is doubt about whether you do, you may be able to get hardship payments (see Chapter 52).

Work coaches

The Jobcentre Plus staff who support and interview people seeking work are usually called **'work coaches'**. For JSA outside the UC system, their legal title is employment officers. They are sometimes also called personal advisers. An employment officer means an officer of the Secretary of State for Work and Pensions, or someone officially designated as an employment officer by her/him.[2] The job of a work coach is to agree with you the steps you will take to get back to work, keep a check on those steps, offer practical help and advice, and notify you of job vacancies. You cannot apply for a revision or supersession, or appeal, against decisions made by your work coach – eg, decisions about what you must do to look for work. A decision that you are not entitled to JSA, or a decision to sanction you, is made by a DWP decision maker. You can ask for these decisions to be changed by a revision and appeal.

Schemes for assisting people to obtain employment

If you are participating in a specified scheme for assisting people to obtain employment (eg, the Work and Health Programme, see p1122), you usually have to be available for work and actively seek work as well as attend the scheme. If you have been directed to attend, you can be sanctioned if you do not participate. You must be told in writing that you are required to participate, when the scheme starts, what you have to do and what will happen if you fail to participate. Even if you do not think the scheme is reasonable activity for you (eg, because of your work experience), it may still be reasonable if it will provide recent evidence of good attendance and dealing with people in the workplace, and you have been out of work for a long time.

You do not have to actively seek work if you are establishing a business with the help of a government scheme called New Enterprise Allowance (only available to existing participants).

In some limited circumstances (if you are a full-time student or you have very recently been released from detention), you do not have to be available for work or actively seek work while participating in a scheme. For more information, see p1087 of the 2019/20 edition of this *Handbook*.

Available for work

To qualify for JSA, you must be available for work. The general rule is that to be available for work you must be:[3]

- 'willing and able' to take up work 'immediately' (see p1094); *and*
- available at any time of the day and on any day of the week; *and*
- prepared to take a job that would involve working for *at least* 40 hours a week; *and*
- prepared to work for *less than* 40 hours a week if required to do so. In practice, this means that you must be prepared to work part time.

However, you may be able to place restrictions on your availability for work (see p1098), such as the type of work or the days and times you are available.

In some circumstances:

- you do not have to be available for work if you are getting a training allowance or if you are participating in a specified scheme for assisting people to obtain employment (see above);
- you can be treated as being available for work even if you are not (see p1095);
- you can qualify for joint-claim JSA even if you or your partner (but not both of you) are not available for work (see p247).

Your availability for work will have been considered at an initial interview when you first claimed JSA (see p698). Your jobseeker's agreement (called a 'claimant commitment' by the DWP) contains details of the particular days and times that

Part 7: National Insurance, work and work-related rules
Chapter 48: Claimant responsibilities: other benefits
1. The jobseeking conditions for jobseeker's allowance outside the universal credit system

you are available for work (your 'pattern of availability') as well as any other restrictions you may place on your availability.

Note:

- The DWP can decide that you are not available for work without having to show that you have turned down a job – eg, based on your statements or conduct.[4] However, the fact that you turn down a job does not necessarily mean that you are not available.
- If your entitlement to JSA ends because you have not complied with the requirement to be available for work, you may be given a sanction if you claim JSA again under the UC sytem or UC (see p1071).
- If you are not available or treated as being available for work, or there is a doubt about whether you meet the conditions, payment of benefit may stop, be reduced or be suspended, but you may be able to get hardship payments (see Chapter 52).

If you are a lone parent or have temporary additional childcare responsibilities

If you are a lone parent and have childcare responsibilities, you must be available for work to qualify for JSA. This also applies in general (whether you are a lone parent or not) if you are looking after children under 16, even during the school holidays. However, some special rules can apply which may treat you as available for work, allow you to restrict your availability or give you more time to take up a job. For more information, see p1089 and p1091 of the 2019/20 edition of this *Handbook*.

Willing and able to take up work immediately

Being *willing* to work is essentially a test of your attitude – your desire and willingness to work. What you do in practice to display this willingness is usually dealt with under the rules for actively seeking work.

You must be prepared to take up work as an employed person – being only available for self-employment is not sufficient.[5] However, this means that you do not count as being unavailable for work if you refuse to work as a self-employed person.

In order to be *able* to work, it must be lawful for you to work in Great Britain.[6] Your immigration status may affect this – eg, if a condition of your entry is that you do not work. In addition, there must be nothing to prevent you from receiving job offers (eg, because you are away from home for more than a short time) and nothing to prevent you from acting on them straight away – eg, because you have other commitments that you cannot easily abandon.

Being able to take up work *immediately* means that you must usually be able to start work without any delay, with little more than the time needed to get washed and dressed and have breakfast.[7] You can be allowed more time than this in some situations.

When you are allowed more time

You do not have to be available for work immediately in the following situations. You only need to be available for work:

- **on one week's notice** if you are doing voluntary work or have caring responsibilities (see below for what counts).[8] You must be willing and able to attend a job interview on **48 hours' notice**. However, if you have caring responsibilities for a child under 16 and you can show these make it unreasonable for you to take up a job or attend an interview within these periods, you only have to be available on **28 days' notice** and be willing and able to attend an interview on **seven days' notice**;

- **on 24 hours' notice** if you are providing a paid or unpaid service (other than if you are doing voluntary work or have caring responsibilities).[9] This can include services you provide for family or friends on a non-commercial basis, such as giving someone a regular lift to work in your car.[10] However, it does not include things you do as part of your everyday parental responsibility for children over 16 – eg, taking them to school or college. It could include activities that are of service to the community in general – eg, offenders working in the community as part of their punishment and tribunal members;

- **after your notice period** has passed if you are working part time. This applies if you have a duty to give your employer notice that you are leaving work under employment law.[11] If under the terms of your contract you must give longer notice, argue that the longer notice period should apply.

Note: if the DWP agrees that you are only available to work at certain times (see p1099), you are not required to be able to take up employment at times when you are not available.[12] However, you must be willing and able to take up the offer as soon as you reach the next period in your pattern of availability (the days and times you are available).

Definitions[13]

'**Voluntary work**' is work which is done for a charity or other not-for-profit organisation or for anyone other than your partner or a child who is included in your claim, for which you receive no payment other than for your reasonable expenses.

'**Caring responsibilities**' means responsibility for looking after someone over pension age, someone who needs care because of her/his mental or physical condition, or someone under 16 who is a member of your household or a close relative (see p312 for the meaning of household and p353 for the meaning of close relative). This applies even if you share the responsibilities with someone – eg, with your partner.

Treated as available for work

Even if you are not actually available for work, you can be treated as if you are for periods during your claim. You must still satisfy the other conditions of

Part 7: National Insurance, work and work-related rules
Chapter 48: Claimant responsibilities: other benefits
1. The jobseeking conditions for jobseeker's allowance outside the universal credit system

entitlement to JSA. The rules which treat you as available for work cover lone parents, some people looking after a child under 16, people undertaking certain studying and training, people doing certain community activities and those affected by bereavement and other domestic emergencies. For more information on being treated as available for work in these situations, see pp1091–94 of the 2019/20 edition of this *Handbook*.

In addition, you can be treated as available for work during some periods of temporary absence from Great Britain, if you are affected by domestic violence or abuse, during certain periods of sickness (see p691) and in some other situations (see below).

Temporary absence from Great Britain

You are treated as being available for work when you are temporarily absent from Great Britain and you are:[14]

- taking a child who is included in your claim (see p307) abroad temporarily for specified medical treatment (for a maximum of eight weeks);[15] *or*
- attending a job interview (for a maximum of seven days). You must tell your work coach in advance and confirm it in writing if required to do so; *or*
- a member of a couple and the pensioner, enhanced pensioner, higher pensioner, disability or severe disability premium is being paid for your partner (see Chapter 17) and you are both away from Great Britain (for a maximum of four weeks); *or*
- abroad for the purpose of getting NHS hospital treatment (see p693); *or*
- a member of a joint-claim couple on the date of your claim and, on the day your partner makes the claim for JSA, you are:
  - in Northern Ireland (for a maximum of four weeks) but only if you are unlikely to be away for more than 52 weeks; *or*
  - attending a job interview (for a maximum of seven days).

Domestic violence or abuse

If you notify the DWP that you have experienced, or been threatened with, domestic violence or abuse (see p1039), you can be treated as being available for work for up to four weeks from the date of notification.[16] This only applies if you are not living at the same address as the person and if the domestic abuse (or threat) took place within the 26 weeks before you notified the DWP.

The four-week period is extended to 13 weeks if you provide relevant evidence during the four weeks from a person acting in an official capacity. You can only be treated as available for work under this rule once in any 12-month period.

Other situations when you can be treated as available for work

As well as the situations listed on p1095, you are treated as being available for work:[17]

- during temporary police detention (legal custody in Scotland) of up to 96 hours, but not if you come within the definition of 'prisoner' (see p927);[18]
- during a two-week (see p691) or extended (see p692) period of sickness, or if you are temporarily absent from Great Britain for the purpose of getting NHS hospital treatment (see p693);
- during any part week at the end of your claim.

Treated as unavailable for work

Even if you are (or can be treated as) available for work, you are nevertheless treated as unavailable for work if:[19]

- you are a full-time student (see p874). **Note:** there are exceptions;
- you are on temporary release from prison;
- you are receiving maternity allowance or statutory maternity pay;
- you are on adoption, paternity, shared parental or parental bereavement leave.

Unavailable for part of a week

On occasion, you might be unavailable for work for a short period during a benefit week – eg, because you are away from home.

If this happens and you have put restrictions on the times that you are available (see p1099):[20]

- your JSA is not affected if the period during which you are not available comes entirely outside the particular days and times that you are available for work (your 'pattern of availability'); *or*
- you lose JSA for the whole of that benefit week if all or part of the period during which you are not available comes within your pattern of availability.

If you have not put any restrictions on the times you are available, you may lose benefit for that week because you are not available to take up work immediately.[21] For this reason, it is best to avoid signing a jobseeker's agreement with totally unrestricted times that you are available.

If you are arrested and held by the police for a short time but then released, you can be treated as being available for work for up to 96 hours while you are detained.

If you are doing voluntary work and have placed restrictions on the total number of hours you are available to work (see p1099), any voluntary work you do (see p1095 for what counts) within your pattern of availability must be ignored when deciding whether you are available, provided you are willing and able to rearrange the voluntary work with:[22]

- one week's notice, in order to take up any job whose hours fall within your pattern of availability;
- 48 hours' notice, to attend an interview in connection with an opportunity for work at a time that falls within your pattern of availability.

There is a similar rule in certain cases if you are a part-time student (see p878).

Part 7: National Insurance, work and work-related rules
Chapter 48: Claimant responsibilities: other benefits
1. The jobseeking conditions for jobseeker's allowance outside the universal credit system

Restrictions on availability for work

You can restrict your availability for work *in any way* if the restrictions are reasonable in light of your physical or mental condition and, in some cases, if you have specified caring responsibilities for a child under 16 (see below). Otherwise, if you can prove that you still have a reasonable prospect of securing employment (see below), you can place some restrictions on the work you are available to do. These are:[23]

- the type of work for which you are available (see p1099);
- the number of hours, days and times you are available (see p1099);
- the terms and conditions of employment for which you are available (see p1100);
- the location of the job (see p1100).

Any restrictions are entered in your jobseeker's agreement. If you and your work coach have not agreed in advance that there are certain types of work which you cannot, or are unwilling to, do, it may prove difficult to justify not being available for it in the future.

A reasonable prospect of securing employment

You must usually show that you have a 'reasonable prospect' of securing employment, despite any restrictions you are allowed to place on your availability. This does not apply if you can restrict your availability in any way (see below), or if you are a lone parent who can restrict your availability to your child's normal school hours (see p1099).[24] When considering restrictions, your work coach should consider all the relevant evidence, including your skills and experience and the type of vacancies available.[25] Negotiating restrictions on your availability can help to avoid a sanction, but it is important not to be too restrictive if this is likely to limit your reasonable prospect of finding work.

Restricting your availability in any way

You can restrict your availability for work in any way if:[26]

- the restrictions are reasonable in light of your physical or mental condition; *or*
- you have caring responsibilities for a child under 16 and you are the subject of a parenting order or have entered into a parenting contract in respect of the child under specific provisions.

You can restrict anything about the work, including the type, hours, location and terms and conditions. If the restrictions you impose are reasonable in light of your physical or mental condition, or the terms of the order or contract, you do not have to show that you have reasonable prospects of securing employment. For example, it may be reasonable to refuse to consider work which requires travel away from home because of your caring responsibilities for a child who needs supervision under the terms of a parenting order.

To restrict your availability because of your physical or mental condition, you usually need to provide medical evidence. If you have not already done so, you may want to consider whether you have limited capability for work (see p987) and can claim a different benefit (ESA and/or UC). However, get advice before doing so as you may end up worse off on UC. Remember that being capable of work is a condition of JSA, but just because you are disabled or have a long-term condition does not mean you have limited capability for work.

The type of work

The general rule is that you must be available for any type of employment, but you are allowed to place restrictions on the sort of jobs for which you are available, provided you have a reasonable prospect of securing employment if this is required (see p1098).[27] In addition, special rules allow you to make restrictions:

- if you are a laid-off or short-time worker;
- because of a sincerely held religious belief or conscientious objection.

Religious belief or conscientious objection

You do not have to be available for work that offends a sincerely held religious belief or a sincere conscientious objection – eg, a job in a company associated with live animal exports if you have a conscientious objection to these.[28] You must still have reasonable prospects of securing employment despite those restrictions and any other restrictions you may have imposed (see p1098).[29]

The number of hours, days and times

You can restrict the total number of hours you are available, provided you are available for at least 40 hours a week and:[30]

- you have agreed with your work coach the particular days and times that you are available for work (a 'pattern of availability') and this has been recorded in your jobseeker's agreement; *and*
- you still have reasonable prospects of securing employment despite the restrictions (see p1098) and they do not *considerably* reduce your prospects of securing employment.

You are allowed to restrict the total number of hours you are available to less than 40 in some situations if you are a lone parent or if you have caring responsibilities. You may also be allowed to restrict your availability in any way, including the number of hours, if you have a physical or mental condition (see p1098).

Note: you must be prepared to work for the maximum number of hours for which you are available, but you must also be prepared to accept jobs that offer fewer hours than you would wish.

If you are a lone parent

If you are a lone parent and you have a child under 13 included in your claim (see p307), you only need to be available for work during her/his normal school

Part 7: National Insurance, work and work-related rules
Chapter 48: Claimant responsibilities: other benefits
1. The jobseeking conditions for jobseeker's allowance outside the universal credit system

hours.[31] You do not have to show that you still have reasonable prospects of securing employment. You may be able to restrict your total hours further depending on how your caring responsibilities affect your availability. The DWP says you cannot restrict your availability to school hours during school holidays[32] but, as a person with caring responsibilities, you may be able to restrict your hours in other ways and/or look only for temporary work.

Caring responsibilities

If you have caring responsibilities (see p1095), you can restrict the total hours you are available for work to less than 40 hours a week if:[33]

- you are available for employment for at least 16 hours a week and for as many hours as your caring responsibilities permit, taking into account relevant factors, including the particular hours and days you spend caring, whether your caring responsibilities are shared with someone else, and the age and physical and mental condition of the person for whom you care; *and*
- you have a reasonable chance of securing employment (see p1098) despite the restricted hours. You do not have to show you have a reasonable chance if you have caring responsibilities for a child under 16 and your work coach considers that you would not satisfy the condition because of the type and number of job vacancies within travelling distance.

If you are a carer and you cannot be available for work for at least 16 hours a week, you may be able to claim UC, depending on your circumstances, the circumstances of the person you care for and how much time you spend caring. You should get advice before claiming a different benefit as, if you claim UC, you cannot return to JSA outside the UC system.

The terms and conditions of employment

You can put restrictions on the terms and conditions of employment for which you are available, provided you can show that you still have reasonable prospects of securing employment despite those restrictions and any other restrictions you may have imposed (see p1098).[34]

The rules about minimum working conditions (see Appendix 7) can affect your claim for JSA. The DWP should not object to your placing a restriction on your availability for work – ie, that you will not accept a job if the terms do not comply with the legal requirements, such as if an employer is offering a job at less than the national minimum wage.

Note: the DWP says you should *not* be told to apply for jobs that include a zero-hour contract or an 'employee shareholder contract' and that you should not be given a sanction if you refuse or fail to apply for, or to accept, such a vacancy.[35]

The location of the job

You can put restrictions on the localities within which you are available for work, provided you can show that you still have reasonable prospects of securing employment in the selected areas (see p1098).[36] Your travel-to-work time may also be a factor, especially if it is combined with caring responsibilities or physical or mental conditions that limit your travel.

Actively seeking work

To qualify for JSA, you must actively seek work. In some cases you:

- do not have to actively seek work if you are participating in a specified scheme to obtain employment or you are getting a training allowance (see p1095);
- can be treated as if you are actively seeking work even if you are not (see p1102);
- can qualify for joint-claim JSA even if you or your partner (but not both of you) are not actively seeking work (see p247).

Note: if your entitlement to JSA ends because you failed to comply with the requirement to actively seek work, you may be given a sanction if you claim 'new style' JSA under the UC system or UC (see p1071).

What you must do

To count as actively seeking work, you must do the following.

- In each benefit week (and part week at the beginning of your claim) you must take such 'steps' as you can reasonably be expected to have to take in order to have the best prospects of securing employment in Great Britain.[37]
- You are expected to take a minimum of three steps, unless taking fewer steps is all that is reasonable.[38] **Note:** it is possible that, in some weeks, there may be no steps that you could reasonably be expected to take.[39] On the other hand, the minimum number of steps may not be enough to show you have done what can reasonably be expected.

Your jobseeker's agreement (called a 'claimant commitment' by the DWP) records what steps you have agreed to take to find work. Your work coach is likely to suggest that you take considerably more than three steps each week. Bear in mind that by signing the agreement you are accepting that it is reasonable for you to take the number of steps specified. Unspecified steps are unlikely to be accepted as reasonable.[40] In the event of a dispute, point out if you felt you had no option but to agree to what was proposed. Any changes to your jobseeker's agreement should be recorded (see p1106).

Your work coach is likely to look at whether or not you have kept to your jobseeker's agreement in deciding whether you are actively seeking work.[41] S/he will review the steps you have taken at your regular interview. You do not necessarily have to take all the steps in your jobseeker's agreement each week to prove you are actively seeking work: the test is what you did, not what you did not do.[42] However, if there is a dispute, the DWP decision maker is likely to say that what is in your jobseeker's agreement is a good indication of what you could

Part 7: National Insurance, work and work-related rules
Chapter 48: Claimant responsibilities: other benefits
1. The jobseeking conditions for jobseeker's allowance outside the universal credit system

reasonably have been expected to do. Your work coach will expect you to spend a considerable amount of time looking for work and, unless there are specific reasons, will expect seeking work to take up the same amount of time as a full-time job. It is your responsibility to show that you are actively seeking work based on steps you have taken, even if you consider that you are not receiving adequate support from the job centre.[43] If a DWP decision maker decides that you are not actively seeking work, your entitlement to JSA ends. If you then claim JSA under the UC system or UC, you can be given a sanction (see p1071).

For more information on showing that you have taken sufficient 'steps' and what steps are reasonable, see pp1101–03 of the 2019/20 edition of this *Handbook*.

If you have a disability

If you have a disability or health condition that affects the work you can do, you may be able to get specialist support to help you get into work. For further information, contact Jobcentre Plus. Make sure you are clear about what is voluntary, and what you have agreed to do as part of your jobseeking conditions.

Treated as actively seeking work

Even if you are not actively seeking work, you can be treated as if you are.
- If you are attending a 'qualifying course' with the approval of your work coach and are treated as being available for work (see p1095), you are also treated as actively seeking work.[44] If this is in any week that falls entirely in a vacation, you must take such steps as can reasonably be expected in order to have the best prospects of securing temporary employment.
- You are allowed two weeks (longer in some circumstances) during which time you are regarded as actively seeking work while away from home (see p1103).

Other situations in which you can be treated as actively seeking work generally mirror those where you are treated as being available for work and have the same maximum lengths (see p1095).[45] In most cases, you are only considered to be actively seeking work if the situation affects you for at least three days in the 'benefit week' (see p438 for the definition). However, you are treated as actively seeking work in any week:[46]
- in which you are allowed an extended period of sickness under the rules described on p692. However, this does not apply if it would be reasonable for you to take steps to seek employment in that week, and you have not taken such steps;
- which is part of a period in which you are taking active steps to set yourself up as self-employed under a scheme to assist people to do so (for up to eight weeks). This can only apply once in any period of entitlement to JSA. The scheme must be provided or funded by a specified government agency. **Note:**

if you are participating in New Enterprise Allowance (only available to existing participants), you do not have to actively seek work;[47]
- in which you spend at least three days on a government-sponsored employment or training course or programme for which you are not paid a training allowance. This does not apply if you are participating in work experience.

You are *not* treated as actively seeking work just because you have caring responsibilities for a child under 16 and are looking after her/him during the school holidays or at a time when s/he is excluded from school, although you may be treated as being available for work. For more information, see p1091 of the 2019/20 edition of this *Handbook*.

Holidays and other absences from home

While you are on JSA, you can be treated as actively seeking work while away from home – eg, on holiday.[48] You still must be available for work, so you are expected to give an assurance that you are willing and able to cut your absence short if notified of a job. In any 12-month period, you can be away from home for up to:[49]
- three weeks, if during each week you spend at least three days on an Outward Bound course; *or*
- if you are blind, two weeks, plus up to four other weeks spent attending training in the use of guide dogs for at least three days a week; *or*
- two weeks, in any other case.

If you are away for longer than this and so cannot be treated as actively seeking work, you must show that you are looking for work while you are away.

You must usually be in Great Britain to qualify for JSA. To check whether you can get JSA while temporarily away, see p1631, and whether you can be treated as available for work, see p1096.

What should you do before you go away?

1. Inform your work coach before you go away from home, even if you will be in Great Britain. You can be required to give notice in writing.[50] Make sure you keep a record of your notification.

2. You must be available for work and be able to receive information about job offers. You must therefore provide details of how you can be contacted or how you plan to contact your work coach while you are away.[51]

3. Check with your Jobcentre Plus office when you are next expected to have an appointment with your work coach ('sign on') once you return home (see p1107). If you do not attend or participate (including if the appointment is by telephone) when you are supposed to, you may lose benefit for the whole of the period you were away unless you can show you had a good reason for failing to sign on (see p1109).

Part 7: National Insurance, work and work-related rules
Chapter 48: Claimant responsibilities: other benefits
1. The jobseeking conditions for jobseeker's allowance outside the universal credit system

The jobseeker's agreement (claimant commitment)

To qualify for JSA, you must agree and sign a 'jobseeker's agreement'.[52] This enables your work coach to monitor and direct your search for a job and gives you a chance to put any agreed restrictions on your availability for work on record. **Note:** the DWP calls your jobseeker's agreement a 'claimant commitment'. However, the rules are not the same as for claimant commitments under the UC system. If you are claiming JSA under the UC system, see Chapter 46.

While you are on JSA, your agreement may be reviewed (see p1106).

Note: In some cases, you can qualify for joint-claim JSA even if you or your partner (but not both of you) do not have a current jobseeker's agreement (see p247).

What is in the jobseeker's agreement

A jobseeker's agreement must contain specific information, such as your name and the date of the agreement. It must also include:[53]

- the type of job you are going to actively seek. If you are allowed to place restrictions on the type of work for which you are available, these are entered in a separate box;[54] *and*
- the total number of hours that you are available for work each week (unless you say that you are prepared to work at any time), with a breakdown of what hours you are available each day. This is known as your 'pattern of availability'. For information on restricting the number of hours and the times for which you are available, see p1099; *and*
- how quickly you must be available for work (see p1094), and other restrictions you are placing on the work for which you are available – eg, the level of pay or the distance you are prepared to travel; *and*
- the steps you are to take to seek work or to improve your chances of work – eg, preparing a CV, registering on job websites and attending relevant courses; *and*
- a statement of your right to have a proposed jobseeker's agreement referred to a decision maker (see p1105) who can decide whether it is reasonable, and to apply for a revision or supersession or appeal against her/his decision if you and your work coach cannot agree on what should be in the agreement.

It also advises you to keep a record of what you do to find work and states that if you do not do enough, your JSA might be affected.

Your jobseeker's agreement is not binding on you or the DWP;[55] there is no automatic penalty if you fail to keep it.[56] However, the contents of the agreement and whether you have abided by it are important evidence if there is a dispute about whether you are available for or actively seeking work, and also if you are accused of refusing a suitable job offer.[57] If you have done everything in your jobseeker's agreement, try to argue that you should not be accused of not being available for or actively seeking work.[58]

Do you think your jobseeker's agreement is unreasonable?

You may think that what your jobseeker's agreement says you are expected to do to find work is unreasonable – eg, you are expected to take too many steps, or you are expected to be available for work for too many hours or at unreasonable times. You may consider that specific steps are unreasonable for you. However, whether something is unreasonable depends on all the circumstances,[59] including what other steps you are taking to find work. You can ask for your jobseeker's agreement to be referred to a decision maker. However, you risk losing benefit if you refuse to sign it. Rather than refusing to sign the jobseeker's agreement proposed by your work coach, it may be better to sign it and then write to the DWP saying that you would like it changed (see p1106). You should not lose JSA, provided you comply with the original agreement while the variation is being considered. It is important to make it clear that you intend to do so. If your agreement is revised, unless you can show it is unreasonable, it is better to comply with it (and make it clear that you are doing so) even if you want to seek a further change. Broad statements that you will do everything you can to seek employment may not be reasonable by themselves, and you can be expected to give details of what you have done to find employment.[60]

Disputes about a jobseeker's agreement

You and your work coach may disagree about what should be in your jobseeker's agreement. Your work coach is not allowed to sign your jobseeker's agreement unless s/he is satisfied that you will qualify as being available for and actively seeking work if you comply with its terms.[61] If s/he thinks you are placing unreasonable restrictions on your availability for work, or that the steps you propose to take to actively seek work are not sufficient, s/he will not sign an agreement based on your proposals. In this situation:[62]

- the work coach may refer a proposed jobseeker's agreement (including one proposed by you) to a decision maker; *or*
- if you ask your work coach to do so, s/he *must* refer a proposed agreement to a decision maker immediately.

You can apply for hardship payments while you are waiting for the decision (see p1185). However, you risk losing benefit if you refuse to sign the agreement while it is being considered. For more information about what happens when a jobseeker's agreement is referred to a decision maker, see p1108 of the 2019/20 edition of this *Handbook*.

If you are unhappy with a decision about your jobseeker's agreement, you can ask for a revision or appeal (see Chapters 56 and 57). You must apply for a mandatory reconsideration before you can appeal.

Part 7: National Insurance, work and work-related rules
Chapter 48: Claimant responsibilities: other benefits
1. The jobseeking conditions for jobseeker's allowance outside the universal credit system

Changing your jobseeker's agreement

The terms of your jobseeker's agreement can be changed by agreement between you and your work coach. Any change must be in writing and signed by both of you.[63] This can be in electronic form and can be signed by an electronic signature.[64]

Both you and your work coach can propose changes at any time. Put your proposals in writing (keeping a copy) and explain how they give you a reasonable chance of finding a job. If the work coach changes your jobseeker's agreement, you should consider what it requires and if it is reasonable for you to comply with it (see p1105).[65] Bear in mind that if you do not agree to it, your JSA may end.

A work coach cannot agree to a change unless s/he considers that the terms mean that you satisfy the jobseeking conditions.[66] If you and the work coach:

- agree the proposed changes, you must be given a copy of the new jobseeker's agreement;[67]
- do not agree the proposed changes, these can be referred to a decision maker.[68] They *must* be referred to a decision maker if you request this. For more information on what happens when changes to a jobseeker's agreement are referred to a decision maker, see pp1109–10 of the 2019/20 edition of this *Handbook*.

If you are unhappy with a decision maker's decision, you can request a revision or appeal (see Chapters 56 and 57). You must apply for a mandatory reconsideration before you can appeal.

Interviews and 'signing on'

While you are getting JSA, you (or both of you if you are a joint-claim couple) must normally participate in regular interviews and may be asked to sign a declaration ('sign on') regularly.[69] This is to enable the DWP to check that you have satisfied the jobseeking conditions and that you continue to qualify for JSA. You can be required to provide information and evidence about your circumstances, your availability for work and how you have been actively seeking work.[70] You can be notified of the manner, time and place of an interview by telephone, post or electronic means.[71] If you:

- fail to participate in an interview, your entitlement to JSA may end (see p1108) or you may be given a sanction;
- fail to sign on, your entitlement to JSA may end (see p1109).

Note: interviews may be carried out on the telephone or online, rather than face to face in a job centre.

Travel expenses

Your travel expenses to and from the Jobcentre Plus office to participate in interviews and to 'sign on' are generally not reimbursed. If travelling to sign on is causing you hardship, ask whether you can sign on by post, or have your interviews over the telephone or online.

Signing on

At your regular interview, you may be asked to sign a declaration (known as 'signing on') that:[72]

- you have been available for and actively seeking work or could be treated as if you were. You may be asked for evidence that you continue to meet these conditions; *and*
- there has been no change in your circumstances that might affect the amount of, or your right to, JSA (other than those you may have already notified to the DWP).

If you fail to sign on, your entitlement to JSA can end (see p1109) or you may be given a sanction under the rules that apply to interviews (see p1121).

Generally, you are told you must attend interviews and sign on every two weeks, but it can be more or less frequently.

You may be required to sign on or attend interviews more frequently in certain circumstances – eg, if your work coach thinks you need more help to find work, if you are suspected of not meeting the jobseeking conditions or of fraud, or if you have no fixed abode. Because decisions about how often you have to sign on are made by your work coach, you cannot appeal. However, you can ask for the frequency to be altered – eg, if your circumstances change or the cost of travel causes hardship. It is always best to continue to sign on as required by the DWP, even if your JSA is stopped, so that you can be paid arrears if the decision is changed.[73] If you are struggling to sign on as frequently as required (eg, because of travel costs or disability), discuss this with your work coach.

Signing on by post

The DWP may allow you to sign on by post – eg, if you live a long way from the Jobcentre Plus office, or the cost of travel to the job centre causes you hardship, or you have a disability which restricts your mobility. Even so:

- if required, you must attend, and participate in, any further interviews, and you are likely to be required to participate in telephone interviews;
- if required, you must send a signed declaration and show that you are available for and actively seeking work. If this is not received at the time specified by the DWP, your entitlement to JSA ends, unless you can show a good reason for the delay (see p1109). You may be able to make a fresh claim for contribution-based JSA but you cannot make a fresh claim for income-based JSA, and your JSA claim will bring you under the UC system (see p22).

Part 7: National Insurance, work and work-related rules
Chapter 48: Claimant responsibilities: other benefits
1. The jobseeking conditions for jobseeker's allowance outside the universal credit system

Further interviews

If you remain unemployed for a period of time, you must participate in a number of additional interviews. If you fail to do so, your entitlement to JSA can end (see p1109) or you can be given a sanction.

Some interviews take place at set intervals. However, you can be required to participate in an interview at any time – eg, if your work coach thinks you need more help with your search for work or there is a question about whether you fulfil the jobseeking conditions.

You may be asked to agree to a change of your jobseeker's agreement (see p1106) to record any change in the type of work for which you are looking or the steps you will take to find it.

When your entitlement to jobseeker's allowance ends

Your entitlement to JSA can end if:

- you fail to 'sign on' on the day you were notified to do so (see p1109). However, it does not end if you contact the Jobcentre Plus office within five working days of your failure and show you had a 'good reason';[74] *or*
- you fail to participate in an interview when you are required to do so (see p1109). However, it does not end if you contact the Jobcentre Plus office within five working days of your failure.[75] You may instead be given a sanction if you cannot show you had a 'good reason' (see p1126).

Ensure that you contact the Jobcentre Plus office within five working days of your failure to participate in an interview or to sign on. Explain why you have a good reason – eg, if you did not receive notice that you were supposed to attend, or genuinely misunderstood when you were supposed to attend.

What should you do if your entitlement ends?

1. If a decision is made to stop your entitlement, ask for the decision to be revised, or appeal against it. You must apply for a mandatory reconsideration before you can appeal.

2. You may be able to make a fresh claim for contribution-based JSA but you cannot make a fresh claim for income-based JSA, and your JSA claim will bring you under the UC system (see p22). For your work-related responsibilities on JSA under the UC system (which the DWP may call 'new style' JSA), see Chapter 46. You cannot return to JSA outside the UC system, and any benefit you get as a result of challenging the decision to terminate your JSA will only run until the date of your new claim. For this reason, you should get advice before making a new claim to check how likely it is that your original benefit can be reinstated.

3. If you have missed signing on or attending an interview, ask the Jobcentre Plus office to accept the information about your search for work that is available on your 'Find a job' account, or any other information that you would have provided on your signing-on day or at your appointment. If this is accepted, the decision maker should revise the decision that stopped your benefit so that you are at least paid up to the date you did not sign on.[76]

Failure to sign on

Your entitlement to JSA can end if you do not provide a signed declaration on the day you were notified to do so, unless you can show a good reason within five working days of your failure.[77] You must be given five days before a decision is made to end your entitlement.[78] 'Good reason' is not defined in the rules, but for information about what may count, see p1126. See above for how you can minimise your loss. **Note:** your signing-on day is usually a day you are required to attend an interview with your work coach. If that is the case then you may instead lose your entitlement or be given a sanction under the rules about participating in interviews – ie, if you failed to sign on because you did not show up at the Jobcentre Plus office for your interview.[79] You may be able to make a fresh claim for contribution-based JSA but you cannot make a fresh claim for income-based JSA, and your JSA claim will bring you under the UC system (see p22).

If you failed to sign on, the date on which your entitlement to JSA ends is the earliest of:[80]

- the day after the last day for which you have provided information or evidence that shows you continue to be entitled to JSA – eg, at your most recent interview. In many cases, this is the day after the last day on which you signed on. Ask the Jobcentre Plus office to accept the information that you would have provided on your signing-on day. If this is accepted, you can be paid up to the day you did not sign on;[81] *or*
- the day on which you should have signed on.

The effect of this is that, if you fail to sign on, you may lose JSA for the full period for which you would have been paid had you signed on at the right time. In addition, you may have to claim JSA under the UC system or UC instead.

Failure to participate in an interview

Your entitlement to JSA can end if you do not participate in an interview when you are required to do so – eg, if you are late for or miss the appointment, or you turn up but refuse to answer questions. Notification of interviews can be sent or given in writing, by telephone or by electronic means.[82] If you did not receive confirmation, you should argue that you were not properly notified. The law assumes that if a letter has been addressed correctly and full postage paid, it will be received, so if you do not receive postal notification, you will need to give good reasons why this happened – eg, there are problems receiving post at your address.[83]

If you are notified that you must participate in an interview on a specified date, unless you contact your work coach within five working days (see p1110), your entitlement to JSA ends if you fail to participate in the interview:[84]

- at the right time – eg, you attend on the right day, but are late. This only applies if, when you failed to participate in an interview on a previous occasion, the DWP gave or sent you a written notice warning you that, if you fail to

Part 7: National Insurance, work and work-related rules
Chapter 48: Claimant responsibilities: other benefits
2. Work-focused interviews for other benefits

participate the next time you are required to do so, your entitlement to JSA could cease or you could be given a sanction. **Note:** if you failed to sign on because you were late for the interview, you may instead lose your entitlement under the rules about failing to sign on (see p1109). Under those rules, you do not have to have been given a warning; *or*

- on the right day. You do not have to have been given a warning.

Your entitlement to JSA can only end if you do not contact the work coach within five working days of the date you failed to participate in an interview.[85] You must be given five days before a decision is made to end your entitlement.[86] **Note:** you may be given a sanction if you cannot show a good reason (see Chapter 49).

If you contact the work coach more than five days from the date you failed to participate in an interview, your entitlement to JSA ends. You may be able to make a fresh claim for contribution-based JSA but you cannot make a fresh claim for income-based JSA, and your JSA claim will bring you under the UC system (see p22). The date on which your entitlement to JSA ends is the earliest of:[87]

- the day after the last day for which you have provided information that shows you continue to be entitled to JSA – eg, at your most recent interview. In many cases, this means the day after the last day on which you signed on. Ask the Jobcentre Plus office to accept the information that you would have provided at the interview. If this is accepted, you can be paid up to the day you did not participate in the interview;[88] *or*
- the day on which you should have participated in an interview.

Note: if the requirement to attend or participate in an interview is for a training or employment scheme or programme, your entitlement does not end, but you can be given a sanction under other rules (see p1116).[89]

2. **Work-focused interviews for other benefits**

If you are getting certain specified benefits, you (or, in some cases, your partner) can be required to take part in work-focused interviews. Claimants who are not required to attend an interview can still take part in the schemes on a voluntary basis. Interviews may be held throughout the time you are on benefits, but can be waived or deferred if they are not appropriate or unlikely to be helpful.

At the interview, job opportunities, education, training and rehabilitation are discussed. There is no requirement to take action based on the discussions.

There are currently a number of ways you can be required to take part in work-focused interviews:

- interviews for employment and support allowance (ESA) if you are in the work-related activity group (see p638).You may also have to attend a 'work and health conversation' with a Jobcentre Plus work coach;

- interviews for income support (IS) claimants, regardless of why you are on IS, and including some lone parents;
- interviews for the partners of people entitled to IS, income-based jobseeker's allowance or income-related ESA.

Some exemptions apply, including lone parents responsible for a child under one.[90] You also do not have to have an interview as the partner of a claimant if you or your partner are responsible for a child under one.[91] If you are claiming joint claim JSA (see p247), interviews for partners do not apply as the jobseeking conditions apply to both you and your partner (see p1092).

You may be required to take part in interviews by decision makers at the DWP or by advisers contracted by the DWP – eg, as part of the Work and Health Programme (see p1122).[92] If you (or your partner) do not take part, you could be given a sanction and your benefit could then be paid at a reduced rate. Taking part involves attending the interview, participating in discussions, and may involve completing an action plan. You do not have to look for work. There is no right of appeal about work-focused interviews, but you can complain. Reasonable adjustments must be made if you have a disability. For further details of the interviews, including exemptions, see Chapter 48 of the 2021/2 edition of this *Handbook*.

---

3. Work-related activity for income support and employment and support allowance

Unless you are exempt, you may be required to undertake some 'work-related activity'. If the DWP decides that you are required to do so, you must be notified properly in a written action plan which is given to you, telling you what you have to do.[93] Any requirement must be reasonable, taking into account your circumstances.[94] You may be required to undertake work-related activity if you are required to take part in work-focused interviews and you are entitled to:[95]

- income support (IS), the only reason you are entitled is because you are a lone parent and you do not have any children under three; *or*
- employment and support allowance (ESA). **Note:** you are exempt from the requirement to take part in work-focused interviews if you have, or are treated as having, limited capability for work-related activity – ie, you are in the 'support group' (see p637).

You may be required to undertake the work-related activity by decision makers at the DWP as well as by advisers contracted by the DWP – eg, in the Work and Health Programme (see p1122).[96] If the DWP refers you to a scheme, the scheme manager decides what, if any, work-related activity you are required to undertake.

Part 7: National Insurance, work and work-related rules
Chapter 48: Claimant responsibilities: other benefits
3. Work-related activity for income support and employment and support allowance

If you fail to take part in work-related activity without good cause, you may be given a sanction. However, this does not apply to employment support schemes delivered by or for the Scottish government (eg, as part of Fair Start Scotland), which are voluntary (you cannot be sanctioned for failing to participate).

The main features are as follows.

- 'Work-related activity' is activity that makes it more likely that you will get a job or remain in work.[97] The exact activity is at the discretion of your work coach. For ESA, it specifically includes work experience and work placements. However, the DWP says you cannot be required to undertake work experience as an ESA claimant; this is voluntary.[98] So if you do not undertake work experience, you should *not* be given a sanction.
- You cannot be required to apply for a job or undertake work (as an employee or otherwise).[99] If you are put under pressure to do so, get advice.
- For ESA, you cannot be required to undergo medical treatment.[100]
- All work-related activity must be recorded in an 'action plan', which must be in writing and specify the activity you are required to undertake.[101] You must be given a copy. An action plan must be reconsidered if you request it, and a written decision issued following the request.[102]
- A requirement about the time when, or by which, you must undertake work-related activity can be lifted if the DWP considers it would be (or would have been) unreasonable.[103]

For IS, you can restrict the times you are required to be available to undertake work-related activity, but you must be available during your child's normal school hours, or during periods in which you have entrusted someone over 18 to supervise your child on a temporary basis (other than for healthcare) – eg, a babysitter or member of your family.[104] For ESA, if you are the lone parent of a child under 13, you can only be required to undertake work-related activity during your child's normal school hours.[105]

Exemptions

You cannot be required to undertake work-related activity if:[106]

- you are a lone parent who is responsible for a child under three who is a member of your household (see p309 and p311); *or*
- you are exempt from the requirement to take part in work-focused interviews; *or*
- for IS, as well as being a lone parent, you come within any of the other groups of people who can claim IS (see p233); *or*
- for ESA, you are entitled to carer's allowance, or your ESA includes a carer premium (p334).

Notes

1. **The jobseeking conditions for jobseeker's allowance outside the universal credit system**
   1 s17A JSA 1995
   2 ss9(1) and 35(1) JSA 1995
   3 s6(1) JSA 1995; reg 6 JSA Regs
   4 R(U) 44/53
   5 s6(1) and (9) JSA 1995
   6 *Shaukat Ali v CAO*, appendix to R(U) 1/85
   7 *Secretary of State for Social Security v David*, 15 December 2000, reported as R(JSA) 3/01
   8 Regs 4 and 5(1)-(1B) and (6) JSA Regs
   9 Reg 5(2) JSA Regs
   10 CU/96/1994
   11 Reg 5(3) JSA Regs
   12 Reg 5(4) JSA Regs
   13 Reg 4 JSA Regs
   14 Reg 14(1)(c), (m), (n), (nn), (p) and (q) JSA Regs
   15 Reg 14(4) JSA Regs
   16 Reg 14A JSA Regs
   17 Reg 14(1)(h), (i), (j), (l), (o) and (s) JSA Regs
   18 CJSA/5944/1999
   19 Reg 15 JSA Regs
   20 Reg 7(3) JSA Regs
   21 *Secretary of State for Social Security v David*, 15 December 2000, reported as R(JSA) 3/01
   22 Reg 12 JSA Regs
   23 s6(2) and (3) JSA 1995; regs 6, 7, 8, 13 and 13A JSA Regs
   24 Reg 10 JSA Regs
   25 Reg 10(1) JSA Regs
   26 Reg 13(3) and (3A) JSA Regs
   27 Reg 8 JSA Regs
   28 Vol 4 Ch 21, para 21451 DMG
   29 Reg 13(2) JSA Regs
   30 Reg 7 JSA Regs
   31 Reg 13A JSA Regs
   32 Vol 4 Ch 21, para 21454 DMG
   33 Regs 4 and 13(4)-(7) JSA Regs
   34 Reg 8 JSA Regs
   35 Vol 6 Ch 34, paras 34415-18 and 34335-38 DMG
   36 Reg 8 JSA Regs

37 s7(1) JSA 1995; *GP v SSWP (JSA)* [2015] UKUT 476 (AAC), reported as [2016] AACR 14
38 Reg 18(1) JSA Regs
39 CJSA/2162/2001
40 *RL v SSWP (JSA)* [2018] UKUT 177 (AAC)
41 *R (Smith) v SSWP (JSA)* [2015] EWHC 2284 (Admin)
42 CJSA/1814/2007
43 *PC v SSWP (JSA)* [2016] UKUT 277 (AAC)
44 Reg 21A JSA Regs
45 Regs 19 and 21B JSA Regs
46 Regs 1(3) and 19(1)(lzl), (q) and (r) and (3) JSA Regs
47 Reg 7 JSA(SAPOE) Regs
48 Reg 19(1)(p) JSA Regs
49 Reg 19(2) JSA Regs
50 Reg 19(1)(p) JSA Regs
51 R(U) 4/66
52 s1(2)(b) JSA 1995
53 s9(1) JSA 1995; reg 31 JSA Regs
54 *HS v SSWP (JSA)* [2009] UKUT 177 (AAC), reported as [2010] AACR 10
55 *RL v SSWP (JSA)* [2017] UKUT 282 (AAC)
56 CJSA/1814/2007
57 *R (Smith) v SSWP (JSA)* [2015] EWHC 2284 (Admin)
58 CJSA/2162/2001
59 *PG v SSWP (JSA)* [2017] UKUT 388 (AAC); *CH v SSWP (JSA) (No.2)* [2018] UKUT 320 (AAC)
60 *RL v SSWP (JSA)* [2018] UKUT 177 (AAC)
61 s9(5) JSA 1995
62 s9(6) JSA 1995
63 s10(1) and (2) JSA 1995
64 s10(2A) JSA 1995
65 *PG v SSWP (JSA)* [2017] UKUT 388 (AAC)
66 s10(4) JSA 1995
67 s10(3) JSA 1995
68 s10(5) JSA 1995
69 s8 JSA 1995; regs 23 and 23A JSA Regs
70 Reg 24(1)-(5A) JSA Regs; *RL v SSWP (JSA)* [2017] UKUT 282 (AAC)
71 Regs 23 and 23A JSA Regs
72 s8 JSA 1995; regs 24(6) and (10) and 65A JSA Regs
73 CJSA/1080/2002; *GM v SSWP (JSA)* [2014] UKUT 57 (AAC)
74 Regs 25(1)(c) and 27 JSA Regs
75 Reg 25(1)(a) JSA Regs

Part 7: National Insurance, work and work-related rules
Chapter 48: Claimant responsibilities: other benefits
Notes

76 R(JSA) 2/04
77 Regs 25(1)(c) and (1A) and 27 JSA Regs;
   SSWP v Michael Ferguson [2003] EWCA
   Civ 536, reported as R(JSA) 6/03
78 *DL v SSWP (JSA)* [2013] UKUT 295 (AAC)
79 R(JSA) 2/04
80 Reg 26 JSA Regs; *SSWP v Michael
   Ferguson* [2003] EWCA Civ 536,
   reported as R(JSA) 6/03; R(JSA) 2/04
81 R(JSA) 2/04
82 Regs 23 and 23A JSA Regs
83 Regs 23 and 23A JSA Regs; s7
   Interpretation Act 1978; R(JSA) 1/04
84 s8(2) JSA 1995; reg 25(1)(a) and (b) and
   (1A) JSA Regs
85 Reg 25(1)(a) and (b)(iii) JSA Regs
86 *DL v SSWP (JSA)* [2013] UKUT 295 (AAC)
87 Reg 26 JSA Regs; *SSWP v Michael
   Ferguson* [2003] EWCA Civ 536,
   reported as R(JSA) 6/03; R(JSA) 2/04
88 R(JSA) 2/04
89 Reg 25(1A) JSA Regs

2. Work-focused interviews for other benefits

90 **ESA** Reg 54(2) ESA Regs
   IS Reg 4 SS(WFILP) Regs; s2A(2A)(b)
   SSAA 1992; reg 8(4) SS(JPI) Regs
91 Reg 7 SS(JPIP) Regs
92 **ESA** Reg 62 ESA Regs
   Other benefits Reg 3(1) SS(JPI) Regs;
   reg 2(1) SS(WFILP) Regs; reg 3(1)
   SS(JPIP) Regs; reg 5 SS(IBWFI) Regs

3. Work-related activity for income support and employment and support allowance

93 **IS** Reg 3 IS(WRA) Regs
   ESA Reg 5 ESA(WRA) Regs
94 **IS** Reg 2(3)(a) IS(WRA) Regs
   ESA Reg 3(4)(a) ESA(WRA) Regs
95 **IS** s2D SSAA 1992; reg 2 IS(WRA) Regs
   ESA s13 WRA 2007; reg 3 ESA(WRA)
   Regs
96 **IS** Reg 11 IS(WRA) Regs
   ESA Reg 9 ESA(WRA) Regs
97 **IS** s2D(9)(d) SSAA 1992
   ESA s13(7) and (8) WRA 2007
98 Vol 9 Ch 53, para 53073 DMG
99 **IS** Reg 2(3)(b) IS(WRA) Regs
   ESA Reg 3(4)(b)(i) ESA(WRA) Regs
100 Reg 3(4)(b)(ii) ESA(WRA) Regs
101 **IS** Reg 3 IS(WRA) Regs
   ESA Reg 5 ESA(WRA) Regs

102 **IS** Reg 5 IS(WRA) Regs
   ESA Reg 7 ESA(WRA) Regs
103 **IS** Reg 4 IS(WRA) Regs
   ESA Reg 6 ESA(WRA) Regs
104 Reg 10 IS(WRA) Regs
105 Reg 3(5) ESA(WRA) Regs
106 **IS** Reg 2(2) IS(WRA) Regs
   ESA Reg 3(2) ESA(WRA) Regs

Chapter 49

Sanctions: other benefits

This chapter covers:
1. Jobseeker's allowance (p1116)
2. Other benefit sanctions (p1127)
3. Sanction decisions (p1127)
4. Challenging a sanction decision (p1128)

This chapter covers the sanction rules if you do not come under the universal credit (UC) system. The DWP may refer to jobseeker's allowance (JSA) and employment and support allowance (ESA) outside the UC system as 'old style' JSA and 'old style' ESA. Information on sanctions if you come under the UC system is in Chapter 47.

7

Key facts

- It is always advisable to avoid a sanction if you can. If a sanction decision is made, consider challenging it.
- If you are getting jobseeker's allowance (JSA), you can be given a sanction if you do not meet certain work-related requirements – eg, if you fail to participate in interviews, you leave work voluntarily or because of misconduct, you do not accept a job or a place on a training scheme or employment programme, or you are found not to be available for work or actively seeking work.
- You can be given a sanction if you are getting income support (IS) or employment and support allowance (ESA) and you do not take part in work-focused interviews or work-related activity. If your partner is entitled to IS, income-based JSA or income-related ESA, you can be sanctioned if s/he does not take part in work-focused interviews.
- You may be able to avoid a sanction if you can show that you have a good reason or good cause for your actions.
- If you are given a sanction, your benefit is paid at a reduced (or nil) rate for a period.
- You may qualify for hardship payments if you have been given a sanction.
- You can apply for a revision or supersession (see Chapter 56), or appeal (see Chapter 57) against a sanction decision. You must apply for a mandatory reconsideration before you can appeal.

Part 7: National Insurance, work and work-related rules
Chapter 49: Sanctions: other benefits
1. Jobseeker's allowance

1. **Jobseeker's allowance**

If you get jobseeker's allowance (JSA) and you do not come under the universal credit (UC) system, you can be given a sanction if you do not meet your jobseeking conditions. If you come under the UC system and are getting contribution-based JSA, different rules apply (see Chapter 47).

If you are given a sanction, your JSA is paid at a reduced (or nil) rate. There are high level sanctions (see p1117), low level sanctions (see p1121) and sanctions if you are found not to be available for work or to be actively seeking work (also known as 'intermediate level' sanctions – see p1120). The amount of the benefit reduction and the length of your sanction period depends on your situation (see below). If you are given a sanction, you might be able to get hardship payments (see p1184).

Note: we refer to things that can lead to your being given a sanction as 'sanctionable actions'. The DWP may call these 'sanctionable failures'.[1]

Jobseeking requirement	Sanction period
High level sanctions	13 or 26 weeks
Losing a job because of misconduct (see p1117)	
Leaving a job voluntarily (see p1117)	
Refusing or failing to apply for or accept a job (see p1117)	
'Neglecting to avail' yourself of a job opportunity (see p1118)	
Intermediate level sanctions	Four or 13 weeks
Found not to be available for or actively seeking work (see p1120)	
Low level sanctions	Four or 13 weeks
Failing to participate in interviews (see p1121)	
Failing to participate in a specified scheme for assisting people to obtain employment (see p1122)	
Other training scheme or employment programme sanctions (see p1123)	
Failing to carry out a jobseeker's direction (see p1124)	

Note:
- The days in your sanction period count towards your 182 days of entitlement to contribution-based JSA (see p696), even if you are not actually paid any benefit.
- If you disagree that you should be given a sanction or disagree with the sanction period, you can challenge the decision (see p1128).
- For housing benefit (HB) purposes, if you satisfy the conditions for entitlement to income-based JSA, you are treated as being on it even if you are not being

paid it because of a sanction.[2] In this situation, the local authority should *not* end your entitlement to HB. You remain entitled to maximum HB.

Different rules apply if you have been given a sanction because of a benefit offence (see p1239).

High level sanctions

You can be given a high level sanction if you:[3]
- lose a job because of 'misconduct' (see p1128–30 of the 2018/19 edition of this *Handbook*); *or*
- leave a job voluntarily without a good reason (see p1130 the 2018/19 edition of this *Handbook*); *or*
- refuse or fail to apply for, or accept, a job without a good reason (see below); *or*
- 'neglect to avail' yourself of a job without a good reason (see p1118).

A **'job'** for these purposes does not include employment while participating in an employment programme (see p1122) or self-employment.[4] When considering whether you should be given a sanction, the decision maker should only look at your last employment preceding your claim and your subsequent actions.[5]

Refusing or failing to apply for, or to accept, a job

You can be given a high level sanction if you are informed of a job vacancy by your work coach (including someone officially designated as an employment officer, who may not work for the DWP – see p1092), and you refuse or fail to apply for the job or to accept it when it is offered to you.[6] This does not apply if you can show you have a good reason (see p1126).

To be sanctioned, you must have been informed of a job vacancy by a work coach. You can try to argue that this does not include an appointment with a recruitment agency.[7] You may be informed verbally, in writing or by other means – eg, by text or email. No sanction should be imposed if you did not receive the notification. The DWP says you should be clearly informed of the specific vacancy, what you are expected to do and by when, and the consequence of failing to comply.[8]

If you are informed of a vacancy and are unsure about what your financial situation would be, get advice about the amount of financial help you would get if you took the job, including in-work benefits, passported benefits and free childcare. However, it may be difficult to show you have a good reason for refusing a job because of your income or the rate of pay. It is best to apply for jobs, even if you think they are not appropriate, to avoid the risk of losing your benefit.

Note:
- The decision maker cannot give you this sanction if the job was vacant because of a stoppage of work caused by a trade dispute.[9]

Part 7: National Insurance, work and work-related rules
Chapter 49: Sanctions: other benefits
1. Jobseeker's allowance

- The DWP says you should *not* be told to apply for jobs that have a 'zero-hour contract' or an 'employee shareholder contract' and that you should *not* be given a sanction if you refuse or fail to apply for, or to accept, such a vacancy.[10]
- You can be expected to apply for and accept temporary work. You cannot escape a sanction on the grounds that a job is temporary.
- If you repeatedly fail to take jobs that are offered to you, a decision maker may also decide that you are not available for or actively seeking work and end your entitlement to JSA altogether. You may then be sanctioned when you claim JSA again (see p1120).

The DWP may treat you as having refused to apply for or accept a job if you behave in any way which means you lose a job opportunity or an offer of employment is withdrawn – eg, you do not arrive on time for an interview or go to the wrong place without a good reason.[11]

'Neglecting to avail' yourself of a job

You can be given a high level sanction if you fail to take up a reasonable opportunity of employment without a good reason (see p1126).[12] This is called 'neglecting to avail' yourself of a job. You do not have to be informed of a vacancy by a work coach for this sanction to apply.

In practice, this sanction usually only applies where the opportunity for employment is with your current or former employer – eg, if you do not return to work with a former employer after what was originally intended to be a temporary break, such as maternity leave, or you refuse an offer of alternative employment in a redundancy situation. However, it may be applied more generally.[13]

The DWP is likely to give a sanction if, for example, you knew you had a reasonable chance of getting the job and did not take the necessary steps to get it. However, it cannot give a sanction if:

- the job was vacant because of a stoppage of work caused by a trade dispute;[14] *or*
- the 'opportunity' is for further work with an employer you have been working for during a trial period.

Trial periods

In certain circumstances, you may take a job for a trial period and leave it without the risk of being sanctioned for leaving voluntarily or for 'neglecting to avail' yourself of a reasonable opportunity of employment.[15] You can only use these rules if you are claiming JSA outside the UC system after leaving a job within the trial period rules. For more information, see the p1133 of the 2018/19 edition of this *Handbook*.

Length of the sanction period

If you are given a high level sanction, it is usually imposed for 13 weeks. However, it can be imposed for 26 weeks if you have been given a high level sanction previously (but see below) for a sanctionable action of yours (not your partner's).[16]

For the 26-week sanction period to apply, the most recent previous sanctionable action must have taken place at least two weeks, but less than 52 weeks, before your current sanctionable action. The 52 weeks run from the date of the previous sanctionable action, not from the date of the decision imposing the previous sanction, which could be some time later. If the most recent previous sanctionable action was within two weeks of the current one, the length of the new sanction is the same as the previous one. If it was 52 weeks or more before the current one, the length of the new sanction period is the same as if you were given a sanction for the first time.

Losing a job because of misconduct (see p1117), leaving a job voluntarily (see p1117) and 'neglecting to avail' yourself of a job (see p1118) *before* your date of claim (see p699) do not count as sanctionable actions for the purpose of working out whether a 26-week sanction period should be applied.[17]

For when your sanction period could be reduced, see below. For what happens if you stop claiming JSA, see p1127.

Note: if you are given a 26-week sanction but later a previous sanction is removed (eg, by the First-tier Tribunal), ask a decision maker to reduce the sanction period if relevant.[18] If s/he fails to do so, appeal. If you have already appealed against the later sanction, the tribunal should take the removal of the previous sanction into account.[19]

When sanction periods can be reduced after leaving work

If you are sanctioned because, before the day you claim JSA, you lost a job because of misconduct, you left a job voluntarily or you 'neglected to avail' yourself of a job (see p1118):[20]

- if the job was only due to last for a 'limited period' that ends on or before the end of the sanction period that would normally apply, the sanction period ends on the day the job would have ended, and is reduced by the number of days between the date of the sanctionable action and your date of claim (see p699). A 'limited period' is a specific length of time that is either fixed or which can be ascertained before it begins by reference to some relevant circumstance;[21] *or*
- in other cases, the sanction period that would normally apply is reduced to take account of days on which you did not claim JSA – ie, by the number of days between the date of the sanctionable action and your date of claim.

In practical terms, this means that if you claim JSA after the job would have ended, your benefit is not paid at a reduced (or nil) rate.[22]

When the sanction period starts

The sanction period normally starts on the first day of the benefit week (see p438) after the last benefit week for which you were paid JSA.[23] However, if you have not

Part 7: National Insurance, work and work-related rules
Chapter 49: Sanctions: other benefits
1. Jobseeker's allowance

been paid any JSA since the sanctionable action, the sanction period starts on the first day of the benefit week in which it took place.

Intermediate level sanctions

If you were previously entitled to JSA outside the UC system and that entitlement ended because you (or, if you are a member of a joint-claim couple, your partner or both of you) did not comply with the requirement to be available for or to be actively seeking work, you could be given an intermediate level sanction if you were able to make a new claim for JSA outside the UC system. However, a new claim for JSA now means that you come under the UC system (see p22).[24] For when an intermediate level sanction could not be applied even when you could make a new claim for JSA outside the UC system, see Chapter 49 of the 2020/21 edition of this *Handbook*.

Length of the sanction period

If you are given an intermediate level sanction because a previous entitlement to JSA ended when you (or if you are a member of a joint-claim couple, your partner) were found not to be available for work or to be actively seeking work, it is normally imposed for:[25]
- four weeks if entitlement has only ended once for this reason; *or*
- 13 weeks, if entitlement has ended two or more times for this reason and the most recent time is at least two weeks, but less than 52 weeks, since the time before. If the most recent previous sanctionable action was within two weeks of the current one, the length of the new sanction is the same as the previous one. If it was 52 weeks or more before the current one, the length of the new sanction period is the same as if you were given a sanction for the first time.

Any period that is more than 13 weeks since your (or your partner's) entitlement to JSA ended cannot be included in the sanction period.[26] For when your sanction period could be reduced, see below. For what happens if you stop claiming JSA, see p1127.

Note: if you are given a 13-week sanction but later the previous sanction is removed (eg, by the First-tier Tribunal), ask a decision maker to reduce the sanction period if relevant.[27] If s/he fails to do so, appeal. If you have already appealed against the later sanction, the tribunal should take the removal of the previous sanction into account.[28]

Reduced sanction periods

The four- or 13-week sanction period is reduced by the number days on which you were not paid JSA. This is the number of days starting on the first day of the benefit week (see p438) following the benefit week in which you were last paid JSA on your previous claim and ending with the day before your date of claim (see p699), or if your JSA was suspended because there was a question about whether you were available for or actively seeking work, the date the suspension ends.[29]

When the sanction period starts

The sanction period starts on your date of claim (see p699) or, if your JSA was suspended because there was a question about whether you were available for or actively seeking work, on the date the suspension ends.[30]

Low level sanctions

You can be given a low level sanction if you:[31]
- fail to participate in an interview without a good reason (see below); *or*
- fail to participate in a specified scheme for assisting people to obtain employment without a good reason (see p1122); *or*
- refuse or fail to apply for or to accept, give up, fail to attend or 'neglect to avail' yourself of a place on a training scheme or employment programme without a good reason (see p1123); *or*
- lose a place on a training scheme or employment programme through misconduct (see p1123); *or*
- refuse or fail to carry out a jobseeker's direction without a good reason (see p1124).

Failure to participate in an interview

You can be given a low level sanction if you are given a notice by your work coach (see p1092) that you must participate in an interview on a specified date and you fail to do so without a good reason (see p1126). Notice can be given in writing, by telephone or by electronic means.[32] This applies if you fail to participate:[33]
- at the right time – eg, you attend on the right day but are late. There must have been a previous occasion in which you failed to participate in an interview at the right time and the work coach must have given or sent you a written notice warning you that, if you failed to participate at the right time the next time you were required to do so, your entitlement to JSA could cease or you could be sanctioned; *or*
- on the right day.

To avoid being given a sanction on this ground, you must contact the work coach within five working days and show you had a good reason for your failure.
Note:
- In some cases, if you fail to participate in an interview, your entitlement to JSA could instead end (see p1109) – ie, if you do not contact the work coach within five working days. If this happens, you may not be able to reclaim JSA outside the UC system.
- If you attend and participate in an interview but do not 'sign on', your entitlement to JSA could end (see p1109).

Part 7: National Insurance, work and work-related rules
Chapter 49: Sanctions: other benefits
1. Jobseeker's allowance

Schemes for assisting people to obtain employment

You can be given a low level sanction if you fail to participate in a specified scheme for assisting people to obtain employment (see below for which schemes) without a good reason (see p1126).[34] For other training scheme and employment programme low level sanctions, see p1123.

You must be given notice in writing.[35] The notice must give you specified information, including the day on which your participation will begin, what you must do to participate and the consequences of failing to do so. The hours, where you are to participate and the likely nature of the tasks you will be expected to do should be included. You cannot simply be told that you must carry out any activities required by the scheme provider.

You may be able to argue that before a notice requiring you to participate is given, you should be provided with enough information about the scheme and the criteria for being placed on it to enable you to make informed and meaningful representations on why you should not be required to participate.[36] You should also be able to make such representations about any activity you are required to undertake once you have been required to participate. Your conduct is relevant to your participation in a scheme, not just attendance. A refusal to confirm your identity to the scheme provider due to data protection concerns, for example, could be a failure to participate if you do not offer to confirm it in another way.[37]

If you were not given proper notice, including if you did not receive notice (eg, because it was sent to the wrong address), or the notice is not sufficiently clear, you can argue that you cannot be given a sanction if you failed to participate in the scheme.[38] **Note:** scheme providers can notify you that you are required to participate in a particular scheme, but they cannot decide to give you a sanction if you do not do so. Only a DWP decision maker can do this.[39] Designated employment officers (see p1092) working for scheme providers can also direct you to apply for or accept jobs, but only a DWP decision maker can make a high level sanction decision in relation to a failure to apply for or accept these jobs.

Specified schemes [40]
The Work and Health Programme: this scheme is compulsory for long-term (24 months or more) unemployed claimants in England and Wales. It provides support and activities for up to 456 days to assist claimants to obtain and retain employment. Activity and support must be considered reasonable in your circumstances, in the view of the provider. Some claimants may be on the programme on a voluntary basis – eg, disabled people. If this applies to you, you cannot be sanctioned for failing to participate.
Skills Conditionality: skills training.
The sector-based work academy: up to six weeks of pre-employment training, a work experience placement for an agreed period and a guaranteed job interview or support in the application process. **Note:** the DWP says that it is voluntary to agree to participate in this scheme, but if you agree, it can be compulsory to attend the training element and job interview and you can be given a sanction if you fail to do so.[41] However, sanctions should

not be given for failing to take part in the work experience except in cases of misconduct.

New Enterprise Allowance: self-employment support (only available to existing participants). **Note:** if you are claiming JSA or employment and support allowance (ESA), your partner can also join this scheme.

Full-time Training Flexibility: training for 16 to 30 hours a week for those on JSA continuously for at least 26 weeks.

Schemes may be added to or deleted from the above list, so get advice if you are in doubt about whether a scheme is specified. Remember that even if a scheme is not specified, other sanction rules may apply (see below).

Restart Scheme: intensive employment support for those in England and Wales who have been unemployed for nine months or more.

If you have completed a specified scheme and are still claiming JSA, you may be expected to undertake other activities in order to improve your job prospects. You can be given a low level sanction for failing to participate in an interview (see p1121) or failing to carry out a jobseeker's direction (see p1124). You may be expected to attend the job centre every day, participate in unpaid community work placements or attend intensive support and training.

Other training scheme and employment programme sanctions

You can be given a low level sanction in connection with 'training schemes' or 'employment programmes' if you:[42]

- lose your place because of 'misconduct'. See p1128–30 of the 2018/19 edition of this *Handbook* for information on misconduct; *or*
- give up or fail to attend without a good reason (see p1126). You might be treated as failing to attend if you have been absent without authorisation, even if the absence is only for one day, or if you arrive late and are not allowed to attend;[43] *or*
- are informed by a work coach of a place and you refuse or fail to apply for, or to accept, it without a good reason. See the information in the section about refusing or failing to apply for or accept a job on p1117. References to an employer should be read as references to your scheme or programme provider; *or*
- 'neglect to avail' yourself of a reasonable opportunity of a place without a good reason.

Training schemes and employment programmes

A **'training scheme'** is any scheme or course designed to help you gain skills, knowledge or experience that will make it more likely that you will obtain work, or be able to do so.[44]

An **'employment programme'** is any programme or scheme designed to assist you to prepare for, or move into, work.[45]

Part 7: National Insurance, work and work-related rules
Chapter 49: Sanctions: other benefits
1. Jobseeker's allowance

If you refuse to start a scheme or programme or if you fail to attend or leave a scheme or programme without a good reason, you can be given a sanction under these rules. If it is a specified scheme for assisting people to obtain employment, once you have begun, you may be given a sanction if you fail to participate in it (see p1122).

Note:

- Training schemes and work experience placements do not count as 'remunerative work'.[46]
- You may not have a good reason for failing to participate or refusing to accept a place because of your previous work experience if this was some time ago.[47]
- You may be offered voluntary work experience or work placements via the job centre. If you decide to participate, you will have a good reason for leaving, unless you leave as a result of misconduct after you have been informed in writing of the requirement to behave appropriately in the workplace.[48]

Jobseeker's direction sanctions

You can be given a low level sanction if you refuse or fail to carry out a jobseeker's direction, without a good reason (see p1126).[49]

A '**jobseeker's direction**' is a direction given by your work coach aimed at assisting you to find a job or increase your chances of employment.[50]

A jobseeker's direction must be reasonable. It would not be reasonable, for example, if it would not help you find a job or increase your chances of being employed, was at odds with your sincere conscientious or religious beliefs or if it might unlawfully discriminate against you on grounds such as gender, disability, religion or nationality.

Any jobseeker's direction must be relevant to *your* needs and to the circumstances of the local labour market. If your work coach accepts that a jobseeker's direction was unreasonable, or could not be carried out in the time required, s/he cancels it.

A jobseeker's direction might, for example, direct you to apply for a specific job vacancy, to use the government's 'Find a job' website, to attend a training or employment scheme, or to improve your appearance or behaviour in order to present yourself better to potential employers. You can be given an opportunity to take the action voluntarily before any direction is given. It must be clear that you are being given a jobseeker's direction.[51]

A jobseeker's direction can be given at any time and more than once. It states the time within which you are expected to comply with it, and checks are made to ensure that you have done so. Each refusal to carry out a direction could result in your being sanctioned.

Note: you cannot appeal against a work coach's decision to issue a jobseeker's direction. However, if you are sanctioned for failing to carry one out, you can challenge this on the basis that the direction that led to the sanction was not given to you, was not reasonable, or that you did not fail to carry it out or you have a good reason for not carrying it out.[52]

Length of the sanction period

If you are given a low level sanction, it is imposed for:[53]

* four weeks; or
* 13 weeks, if you have been given one or more of this type of low level sanction for a sanctionable action of yours (not your partner's), the most recent of which took place at least two weeks, but less than 52 weeks, before your current sanctionable action. If the most recent previous sanctionable action was within two weeks of the current one, the length of the new sanction is the same as the previous one. If it was 52 weeks or more before the current one, the length of the new sanction period is the same as if you were given a sanction for the first time.

The 52 weeks run from the date of the previous sanctionable action, not from the date of the decision imposing the previous sanction, which could be some time later.

For what happens if you stop claiming JSA, see p1127.

If you are given a 13-week sanction but later the previous sanction is removed (eg, by the First-tier Tribunal), ask a decision maker to reduce the sanction period if relevant.[54] If s/he fails to do so, appeal. If you have already appealed against the later sanction, the tribunal should take the removal of the previous sanction into account.[55]

When the sanction period starts

The sanction period normally starts on the first day of the benefit week after the last benefit week (see p438) for which you were paid JSA.[56] However, if you have not been paid any JSA since the sanctionable action, the sanction period starts on the first day of the benefit week in which it took place.

How your jobseeker's allowance is reduced

JSA is paid at a reduced (or nil) rate during the sanction period.[57]

If you are a:

* single person, a member of a couple (other than a joint-claim couple) or a member of a joint-claim couple and both of you are given a sanction, your JSA is reduced by 100 per cent of the amount of JSA that is payable to you – ie, you are not paid any JSA during the sanction period; or
* member of a joint-claim couple and only one of you is given a sanction, your JSA is paid at the rate of:
  - contribution-based JSA, if the person who has not been given a sanction qualifies for it; or
  - hardship payments, if you and your partner qualify (see p1184); or

Part 7: National Insurance, work and work-related rules
Chapter 49: Sanctions: other benefits
1. Jobseeker's allowance

– in any other case, income-based JSA calculated as if the person who has not been given the sanction is a single person. However, any income or capital either of you have is taken into account in the calculation.

In this situation, the joint-claim JSA is paid to the person who has not been given a sanction.[58]

If your JSA is paid at a reduced (or nil) rate, you might be able to get hardship payments (see p1184). You may be able to claim other benefits, but be aware that a sanction from JSA outside the UC system will carry over if you claim UC or contribution-based JSA under the UC system (see p1071).

If you are given more than one sanction

No benefit reduction can be made for a new sanction for any days when your JSA is already being paid at a reduced (or nil) rate because of a previous sanction.[59] If you are a member of a joint-claim couple, this only applies if both the new and the previous sanctions are as a result of a sanctionable action by the same member of the couple. Because of the rules for when a sanction period starts, this means that if you are given more than one sanction for the same period, the sanctions effectively overlap – ie, run concurrently.[60]

Good reasons for your actions

In a number of situations, you cannot be given a sanction if you have a good reason for your actions. 'Good reason' is not defined in the rules, but what may count is set out in guidance.[61] If you appeal against the sanction decision, the guidance is not binding on the First-tier Tribunal. It must make up its own mind about what counts as a good reason.

It is up to you to show you have a good reason, but the DWP decision maker should take all the circumstances into account. The factors that may mean you have a good reason depend on the sanction.

For good reasons that may be relevant to leaving a job, see p1142 of the 2018/19 edition of this *Handbook*.

How much time are you given to explain your good reasons?
You should be given the opportunity to explain your reasons and to provide relevant evidence. For example, if the DWP thinks you have lost a job because of your misconduct, you should be given a chance to comment on any statements made by your employer.[62] If you fail to participate in an interview (see p1121), you must be given at least five working days. However, in all cases, the sooner you give your reasons, the more likely you are to avoid a sanction. If there are circumstances which prevent you giving your reasons immediately, you should explain these – eg, you have to get evidence from someone else. If you are sanctioned, you can request a mandatory reconsideration of a sanction decision and then appeal if necessary.

If you stop claiming jobseeker's allowance

If you stop claiming JSA before the end of your sanction period, a new claim for JSA will bring you under the UC system (see p22). If you claim UC or JSA under the UC system, the JSA sanction can be applied to JSA/UC under the UC system – see p1071.

2. Other benefit sanctions

You can also be sanctioned if you are getting income support (IS) or employment and support allowance (ESA) not paid under the universal credit (UC) system. If you come under the UC system (see p22), different rules apply (see Chapter 47).

You can be given a sanction if, without 'good cause':

- you (or, in some cases, your partner) fail to take part in a work-focused interview; or
- you fail to take part in work-related activity when required to do so while entitled to ESA or IS. For IS, this only applies if the only reason you are on IS is because you are a lone parent and if you do not have any children under three.

You should be given at least five days to show you have good cause before any decision to impose a sanction is made.[63] For more detail about these sanctions, see Chapter 49 of the 2021/22 edition of this *Handbook*.

3. Sanction decisions

A DWP decision maker decides whether you should be given a sanction, often some time after the 'sanctionable action' took place. Do not assume that because you have not yet been informed of any sanction, the DWP has decided not to sanction you. If a sanction decision is made, you should consider challenging it.

You should be issued with a notice, telling you that you have been given a sanction automatically. This means that you should know you have been given a sanction before your benefit is paid at a reduced (or nil) rate and you have a chance to contact the DWP urgently if a mistake has been made.

'Complex needs' or 'safeguarding' procedures apply if you are considered to be 'vulnerable' – eg, if you have a serious mental health condition. These procedures are not a legal requirement, but involve extra checks before you are given a sanction. If you think that you are vulnerable because of your condition but have been given a sanction, ask whether the complex needs or safeguarding procedures have been considered and seek advice. You could argue that the same sort of procedures and guidance used in universal credit for people who are vulnerable should apply (see p1085).

Part 7: National Insurance, work and work-related rules
Chapter 49: Sanctions: other benefits
4. Challenging a sanction decision

4. Challenging a sanction decision

If you are given a sanction, your benefit is paid at a reduced rate, often for a lengthy period. It is therefore always worth challenging a sanction decision. You can apply for a revision or appeal against it in the usual way.

You must apply for a mandatory reconsideration before you can appeal. You should apply within the time limit for an 'any grounds' revision if you can (see p1301). Ask for the time limit to be extended if your application is late. In some cases, there is no time limit for applying for a mandatory reconsideration – ie, if you can show grounds for an 'any time' revision (see p1265). See p1267 for the specific situations in which a sanction decision can be revised at any time.

You must be given written notice of the sanction decision, setting out your appeal rights.[64] Although notification of sanction decisions is meant to happen automatically, this does not always happen. If you were given a sanction but did not receive written notice of the decision, get advice. You may still be able to ask for a mandatory reconsideration and then appeal, even if the decision was made a long time ago. If possible, you should hand in your application for a revision to the job centre office to ensure it is received as soon as possible, but you should also post it to the address on your sanction decision letter. You can also request a revision by telephone, though it is a good idea to follow this up in writing. Keep a copy of your application. If your mandatory reconsideration is not successful, but you still believe the sanction decision is wrong, it is often worth appealing as this provides an independent assessment of events.

Sanction decisions you can challenge

You can challenge:
- the decision to give you a sanction – eg:
  - whether you failed to do something or did what it is alleged you did;
  - whether you have been properly notified of any requirements and the consequences of non-compliance – eg, to attend an interview or participate in a scheme;
  - for jobseeker's allowance, if you are given a sanction for failing to carry out a jobseeker's direction, whether the jobseeker's direction was reasonable;
  - whether you have a good reason (see p1126) or good cause (for what you did or did not do);
- the length of the sanction period – eg, if there is a dispute about the number of times you have been sanctioned, or you are challenging a previous decision to give you a sanction.

If you have been given a sanction more than once, you should challenge *all* the decisions if possible. Apply for a mandatory reconsideration of all the sanction decisions, asking for the time limit for doing so to be extended if relevant.

If a previous sanction is removed (eg, by a DWP decision maker or the First-tier Tribunal), the sanction period for a later sanction should be reduced.[65] If you have appealed against the later sanction, the tribunal should take the removal of the previous sanction into account.[66]

Notes

1. **Jobseeker's allowance**
1　Reg 75(5) JSA Regs
2　Reg 2(3)(a) HB Regs
3　s19(2) JSA 1995
4　Reg 75(4) JSA Regs
5　CJSA/3304/1999
6　s19(2)(c) JSA 1995
7　*MT v SSWP (JSA)* [2016] UKUT 72 (AAC)
8　Vol 6 Ch 34, para 34729 DMG
9　s20(1) JSA 1995
10　Vol 6 Ch 34, paras 34415-18, 34335-38 and 34743 DMG
11　Vol 6 Ch 34, para 34732 DMG; CJSA/ 2082/2002; CJSA/2692/1999
12　s19(2)(d) JSA 1995
13　*MT v SSWP (JSA)* [2016] UKUT 72 (AAC)
14　s20(1) JSA 1995
15　s20(3) JSA 1995
16　Reg 69(1) and (2) JSA Regs
17　Reg 69(3) JSA Regs
18　Reg 3(6) SS&CS(DA) Regs
19　CJSA/2375/2000
20　Reg 69(4) JSA Regs
21　Reg 69(5) JSA Regs
22　Reg 70A(1) JSA Regs
23　Reg 69(6) JSA Regs
24　s19B JSA 1995; reg 69B JSA Regs
25　Reg 69B(6) JSA Regs
26　s19B(5) JSA 1995
27　Reg 3(6) SS&CS(DA) Regs
28　CJSA/2375/2000
29　Reg 69B(7) JSA Regs
30　Reg 69B(8) JSA Regs
31　s19A(2) JSA 1995
32　Regs 23 and 23A JSA Regs
33　s19A(2)(a) JSA 1995; reg 70A(2)-(4) JSA Regs
34　s19A(2)(b) JSA 1995
35　Reg 5 JSA(SAPOE) Regs
36　*R (Reilly and Another) v SSWP* [2013] UKSC 68, reported as [2014] AACR 9; *SSWP v TJ (JSA)* [2015] UKUT 56 (AAC). *SSWP v TJ* was appealed in *Reilly and Hewstone and Jeffrey & Bevan v SSWP* [2016] EWCA Civ 413 and the court upheld this aspect of the decision.
37　*CS v SSWP (JSA)* [2019] UKUT 218 (AAC)
38　*PL v SSWP (JSA)* [2013] UKUT 227 (AAC); *DD v SSWP (JSA)* [2015] UKUT 318 (AAC); *SSWP v DC (JSA)* [2017] UKUT 464 (AAC)
39　Reg 17 JSA(SAPOE) Regs
40　Reg 3 JSA(SAPOE) Regs
41　Vol 6 Ch 34, para 34852 DMG
42　s19A(2)(d)-(g) JSA 1995
43　R(JSA) 2/06
44　Reg 75(1)(b) JSA Regs
45　Reg 75(1)(a) JSA Regs
46　*AW v SSWP* [2016] UKUT 387 (AAC)
47　*AW v SSWP* [2016] UKUT 387 (AAC)
48　s17A JSA 1995; reg 5 JSA(SAPOE) Regs; para 34954 DMG
49　s19A(2)(c) JSA 1995
50　s19A(11) JSA 1995
51　*DM v SSWP (JSA)* [2015] UKUT 67 (AAC)
52　*SA v SSWP (JSA)* [2015] UKUT 454 (AAC)
53　Reg 69A(1) and (2) JSA Regs
54　Reg 3(6) SS&CS(DA) Regs
55　CJSA/2375/2000
56　Reg 69A(3) JSA Regs
57　ss19(1), 19A(1) and 19B(1)-(3) JSA 1995; reg 70 JSA Regs
58　ss19(7), 19A(10) and 19B(8) JSA 1995
59　Reg 70(2) JSA Regs
60　Regs 69(6), 69A(3) and 69B(8) JSA Regs
61　Vol 6 Ch 34, paras 34200-503 DMG
62　Vol 6 Ch 34, para 34571 DMG

Part 7: National Insurance, work and work-related rules
Chapter 49: Sanctions: other benefits
Notes

● ●

2. Other benefit sanctions
  63 *DL v SSWP (JSA)* [2013] UKUT 295 (AAC)

4. Challenging a sanction decision
  64 Regs 3ZA and 28 SS&CS(DA) Regs
  65 Reg 3(6) SS&CS(DA) Regs
  66 CJSA/2375/2000

7

Part 8

Claiming benefits and getting paid

Chapter 50

Claims

This chapter covers:
1. Making a claim (below)
2. Who should claim (p1135)
3. Information to support your claim (p1136)
4. The date of your claim (p1141)

This chapter covers the general rules on claims and backdating. See the chapter about the benefit you are claiming for the specific rules about that benefit. This chapter does not cover the rules for tax credits (see Chapter 64), the Scottish benefits (see Chapter 79), statutory sick pay (see Chapter 39), statutory maternity, adoption, paternity, shared parental and parental bereavement pay (see Chapter 38), social fund budgeting loans (see p778), health benefits (see Chapter 31), the other payments in Chapter 40 or discretionary housing payments (see Chapter 29). Generally, the rules for housing benefit (HB) are not covered (see Chapter 10), although the national insurance number requirement described in this chapter also applies to HB.

Key facts
- To be entitled to a benefit, you must usually make a claim for it.
- Depending on the benefit, you may be able to claim by telephone, online, on a paper claim form or in person.
- You must usually provide your national insurance number and any other evidence considered reasonable.
- Once you have made a valid claim, a decision must be made by a decision maker at the DWP or HM Revenue and Customs (see Chapter 55).

1. Making a claim

In most cases, to be entitled to benefit, you must make a claim for it.[1] If you cannot claim for yourself, an 'appointee' can claim on your behalf (see p1135).

Note: it is not usually possible to make a new claim for income support (IS), income-based jobseekers allowance (JSA) and income-related employment and

Part 8: Claiming benefits and getting paid
Chapter 50: Claims
1. Making a claim

support allowance (ESA). See p23 for exceptions and, for the rules on claiming in the exceptional situations, see the 2020/21 edition of this *Handbook*. See p173 for the limited circumstances when you can make a new claim for housing benefit (HB). New claims for contribution-based JSA and contributory ESA under the universal credit (UC) system can still be made (see p25). The DWP may refer to these as 'new-style' JSA and ESA

How to make a claim

Each benefit has its own rules for how to make a claim. See the chapter in this *Handbook* about the benefit you want to claim. You may be able to claim in writing, including online, or by telephone. You may also have to attend an interview to complete your claim, or be sent a written statement to sign and return.

Is making a claim impractical or impossible for you?

If starting a claim is difficult for you, explain this and ask to claim in a different way. For example:

– if speaking in English is difficult, an interpreter can be arranged;
– another person may be able to telephone on your behalf, especially if you are there to help;
– if you cannot claim online, you may be able to claim by telephone;
– if you cannot claim by telephone or online, a face-to-face interview could take place at a local Jobcentre Plus office;
– a home visit could be arranged;
– you may be able to claim in person at an 'alternative office' (see below);
– except for UC, a claim form could be completed and sent.

Alternative offices

The DWP has made arrangements to enable you to get help to claim some benefits at an 'alternative office'. You can claim carer's allowance, disability living allowance, pension credit and retirement pension at an alternative office. If you are over pension age (see p765), you can also claim attendance allowance, bereavement benefits and winter fuel payment at these offices.[2]

Alternative offices[3]

'Alternative offices' may include designated DWP offices, designated local authority housing benefit offices and some English county councils. Also included are some local advice centres. If you want to claim at an alternative office, ask whether it has been designated to accept your claim.

Amending or withdrawing your claim

You can amend your claim at any time before a decision is made by contacting the office handling it.[4] In some circumstances, your claim may be treated as having been amended from the date it was originally made. For example, if you claimed ESA but did not request that it be backdated, you can amend your claim to include this and your request should be treated as having been made at the date of your claim. However, if you amend your claim to say that your circumstances have changed since you claimed (eg, a partner has moved in with you), this amendment would only take effect from the date the change happened (in this example, the date s/he moved in).

You can withdraw your claim at any time before a decision is made by contacting the office handling it.[5] Notice to withdraw your claim takes effect from the day it is received.

You can also amend or withdraw your claim online if you do so in an approved way.[6]

Note: a claim for UC affects any existing claims you have for the benefits and tax credits which UC replaces (see p21). Withdrawing your claim for UC before a decision is made on it will not enable you to continue to get the benefits and tax credits you previously claimed. Get advice before claiming UC if you already receive benefits and/or tax credits.

For other benefits, you can also withdraw your claim by telephoning the DWP or HMRC office handling it.

In practice, where a claim for a benefit has already been decided and awarded, you can ask for the award to end (sometimes called 'withdrawing an award'). Your award should then be superseded and brought to an end (see p1274), as you should not be forced to continue receiving benefit when you have indicated that you no longer wish to do so.[7]

2. Who should claim

The general rule is that a claim must be made by you, the claimant. For most means-tested benefits, although you usually receive an extra amount because you have a partner, your partner is not a claimant and does not have to make the claim with you. The chapters on individual benefits explain who must make the claim for each benefit.

Appointees

Someone else (eg, a friend or relative, or a solicitor or the representative of an organisation) can be authorised to act on your behalf if s/he is aged at least 18 and you cannot claim for yourself – eg, if you have a mental illness or a learning disability.[8] S/he is called an 'appointee'. The appointee takes on your rights and

Part 8: Claiming benefits and getting paid
Chapter 50: Claims
3. Information to support your claim

responsibilities as a claimant – eg, s/he can make claims for benefit on your behalf, and must notify changes in your circumstances. S/he signs claim forms and other statements on your behalf, and if s/he receives the benefit on your behalf must spend the benefit in your best interests. If benefit is overpaid, the appointee may be responsible for repaying it. Normally, the appointeeship applies from the date of the appointment, but if someone acts on your behalf and later becomes your appointee, these actions can be validated in retrospect.[9]

To apply to be made an appointee, the potential appointee should contact the helpline for the benefit in question – eg, for attendance allowance (AA), the AA helpline. The DWP arranges for someone to visit to assess if an appointee is needed for you, and to make sure s/he is a suitable appointee. The application form (Form BF56) can be completed by the visiting officer during the assessment. If the DWP agrees with the application, it will send Form BF57 to the appointee, confirming her/his appointment. The appointment is effective from this time.

Only one person at any one time can be an appointee for a claimant's DWP benefits.

The appointment continues until you are clearly able to manage your affairs or the appointee no longer wishes, or is no longer able, to act for you (s/he should contact the DWP straight away and inform it of this). It can also be stopped if the appointee is not acting properly.

If you are an appointee for a claimant who dies, you should reapply for appointee status to settle any outstanding benefit matters.[10] An executor of a will can pursue an outstanding claim or appeal on behalf of a claimant who has died, even if the decision was made before probate is granted.[11]

If someone is your appointee for housing benefit purposes, the DWP can make her/him an appointee for other benefits without a written application if s/he agrees to this.[12]

If no one has been appointed to act for you and another person purports to make a claim on your behalf because you are unable to act then that claim may still be valid and can be awarded.[13]

3. **Information to support your claim**

When you claim benefit, you must:
- satisfy the national insurance (NI) number requirement (see p1137); *and*
- prove your identity, if required (see p1138); *and*
- provide sufficient information to ensure your claim is valid (see p1138).

If you claim in the right way (see p1134) and satisfy the above criteria, you have made a 'valid claim'. It is important that you make a valid claim as it affects your 'date of claim' (see p1141).

If your claim is accepted as valid, it is then referred to a decision maker to decide whether you are entitled to benefit (see Chapter 55).

Note: even if your claim is accepted as valid, you can be asked for additional information and evidence before a decision is made on it (see p1140).

If your claim is not accepted as valid, you should be given a decision saying so. You can ask for a mandatory reconsideration of the decision, and then appeal if the decision is not changed (see p1299).[14]

The national insurance number requirement

To be entitled to benefit, you must usually satisfy the NI number requirement by:[15]

- providing an NI number and information or evidence showing it is yours; *or*
- providing evidence or information to enable your NI number to be traced, if you do not know it; *or*
- applying for an NI number if you do not have one and providing sufficient information and evidence to allow one to be allocated. This does not necessarily mean that you must be allocated an NI number. In general, you have done enough if you have supplied all the information that you could reasonably have been expected to with your application.[16]

If you are claiming a means-tested benefit, your partner must usually also satisfy the NI number requirement (but see p1138 for who is exempt).[17] This also applies if you are getting benefit and your partner has started living with you and so your benefit award must be superseded.[18]

Note:

- Contrary to the law described above, the current DWP policy is that you must actually have an NI number before you can be awarded benefit, particularly universal credit (UC) and personal independence payment (PIP). This is being challenged by judicial review.[19] HMRC takes a similar approach to child benefit. Instead, DWP/HMRC uses internal procedures which are supposed to ensure that an NI number is allocated to you before your first benefit payment is due. Although this can work, in practice, it has resulted in delays in some cases. For more information, including what you can do if there is a delay or if the DWP does not let you make a claim at all, see the article in CPAG's *Welfare Rights Bulletin 282* (June 2021), and cpag.org.uk/jr-letters/ni.
- If you do not need to make a claim for the benefit (eg, in some circumstances for retirement pension), the NI number requirement should not apply.
- If you cannot satisfy the NI number requirement straight away, you may be able to ask for a short-term advance of benefit (see p1153).
- If you are refused benefit because you do not satisfy the NI number requirement, you can ask for a mandatory reconsideration of the decision, and then appeal if the decision is not changed (see p1299).[20]

Part 8: Claiming benefits and getting paid
Chapter 50: Claims
3. Information to support your claim

Who is exempt

You are exempt from the NI number requirement if the benefit is:

- disability living allowance (DLA) and you are under 16;[21] *or*
- housing benefit (HB) and you live in a hostel.[22]

If a child (including a qualifying young person – see p563) is included in your claim for UC or HB, s/he is exempt from the NI number requirement.[23] If you are claiming a means-tested benefit as a couple and your partner is a 'person subject to immigration control', s/he could be exempt from the NI number requirement in some situations (see p1537).

Proof of identity

You may be asked to produce further documents or evidence that prove your identity. If you are claiming for your partner, you must also prove her/his identity.

You can prove your identity with a passport, a biometric residence card, a permanent residence card, an identity card issued by a European Economic Area state, a certificate of naturalisation as a British citizen or a letter from the Home Office. You could also produce your birth certificate, driving licence, a travel pass with a photograph, a local council rent card or tenancy agreement, or even paid fuel or telephone bills.

Provide details of any other people who can confirm what you have stated – eg, your solicitor or other legal representative or official organisation.

You should not be refused benefit simply because you do not have a document, especially if it is unreasonable for you to have or obtain it. Ask the decision maker to make a decision on your claim. You can ask for a mandatory reconsideration of the decision, and then appeal if the decision is not changed (see p1299).

In some cases, the available evidence that you are who you say you are may not be accepted. Some claimants may have particular difficulty getting evidence. Ask for an explanation of exactly what is required and why. Complain if you consider any requests for information are unreasonable (see Chapter 61). If you think you have experienced discrimination, get advice – eg, from the Equality Advisory and Support Service.[24]

Providing sufficient information

Before making a decision on whether you are entitled to benefit, the decision maker can ask you to provide further information or evidence to support your claim, including proof of your identity. You must provide sufficient information to ensure your claim is valid.

You must normally attend an interview for a jobseeker's allowance (JSA) claim to be valid (see p698).

For other benefits, or for JSA if you do not have to attend an interview, if you claimed by telephone, in writing or online, see p1139.

Note: if you claim UC, you may be required to agree your claimant commitment at an interview (see p1024).

Claims by telephone

A claim made by telephone is valid if you provide all the information needed during the telephone call. If you do not do this, your claim is 'defective'. You are given a chance to remedy the defect.[25] For employment and support allowance (ESA) and pension credit only, you must also approve a written statement of your circumstances if asked to.[26]

For other benefits, if you supply the necessary information within a month of the date you are first notified of the defect, your claim is treated as having been made when you first notified your intention to claim. The decision maker can extend this one-month period if s/he thinks it is reasonable.[27]

Claims in writing or online

If you initially made your claim in writing or online on the approved form, it is valid if it is completed in accordance with the instructions on the form. If you do not do this, your claim is defective. You should be given a chance to remedy the defect.[28] If you supply the necessary information within one month of the date you are first notified of the defect, your claim is treated as having been made when it was first received. The decision maker can extend this one-month period if s/he thinks it is reasonable.[29]

Note: if you claim online, the system may not allow you to submit a claim if essential information is not entered. Without the required information it is generally not possible to make a claim for UC, as the system will not accept it. If your claim for UC is not accepted, you should complete your claim the same day if possible to avoid losing benefit. For other benefits, you should try to claim in another way as soon as you can, otherwise you may lose benefit.[30]

To be valid, written claims for JSA, ESA and PIP *must* be made on an approved form.[31] For other benefits, any letter or other written communication may be treated as being a valid claim for benefit.[32] In practice, if you make a written claim that is not on the approved form, you are likely to be sent it to complete. If you properly complete and return the form within one month (or longer, if the decision maker considers it reasonable) of its being sent to you, you count as having made a valid claim on the date of your first letter or other written communication.[33]

Written claims for employment and support allowance and jobseeker's allowance

A written claim for ESA and JSA is not valid unless you:[34]
- claim on the approved form; *and*
- complete the claim form according to the instructions; *and*
- produce all the information and evidence required by the form (the 'evidence requirement').

Part 8: Claiming benefits and getting paid
Chapter 50: Claims
3. Information to support your claim

If you do not meet the evidence requirement, the DWP must notify you that your claim is defective. If you complete the form and return it within one month, along with any necessary information or evidence, your claim is treated as having been made on the date you first notified your intention to claim.[35]

If you cannot complete the form or provide the required information or evidence, tell the office handling your claim as soon as possible. Ideally, explain your circumstances on the claim form or by telephoning the office. You can provide supporting letters – eg, from a social worker or a solicitor. If the DWP exempts you from the evidence requirement, it might:

- help you to fill in the form or give you longer to complete it; *or*
- collect evidence or information on your behalf; *or*
- tell you that you do not have to provide the information.

Further information to support your claim

Even if your claim has been accepted as valid, you may still be required to provide additional documentation and evidence.[36] Provided you have made a valid claim, your date of claim should not be affected if you fail to do so.[37]

You must provide the information or evidence within one month of the request, or within seven days of the request for JSA. A decision maker can allow longer than this if it is reasonable. If you do not provide the information, adverse conclusions are likely to be drawn and your claim decided on that basis. In some circumstances, decisions must be made in a certain way if the required information is not available (see p1250).

It is best to send evidence and documents to the office handling your claim. For some benefits, an 'alternative office' (see p1134) may also be able to accept evidence and documents. If a local authority has used information on your claim for HB and has passed it to the DWP because it is relevant to your claim for another benefit, in most cases the DWP must use that information without checking it further.[38]

If you must travel to provide the evidence, you may be able to claim your travelling expenses.[39]

If you are asked to provide evidence which you do not have, ask what other evidence would be acceptable. Ask what is required and why, and complain (see Chapter 61) if you think any requests for information are unreasonable. Ask for a decision to be made on your claim. You can appeal against this decision (see Chapter 57).[40] You must request a mandatory reconsideration first.

Contacting the benefit office

1. Writing to the DWP or HMRC is the best way to have your case dealt with. It ensures there is a record of what you said and enables you to cover all the points you want to make. If you are claiming UC, you can contact the DWP by writing in your UC journal.

2. Always keep a copy of the letters, forms and other documents you send, as well as copies of those sent to you. Take screenshots of corresponsence on your UC journal. This may help you or your adviser to challenge decisions.

3. It is often necessary to telephone the DWP or HMRC. If you do this, make a note of the date, the name and location of the person you spoke with and what is said. If the information is important, follow up the call with a letter confirming what was said.

4. If you need to visit an office (eg, because your case cannot be dealt with by telephone) and you cannot get there (eg, because of your age, health or a disability), an officer may be able to make a home visit. If you are refused a visit and are not satisfied with the reason you are given, ask to speak to a supervisor or the customer services manager.

If your claim involves medical issues, you may have to provide evidence in the form of a questionnaire. In most cases, the decision maker can refer you to a 'healthcare professional' or, for PIP only, a 'health professional' for an examination and/or a report. If you fail to have an examination and are not accepted as having 'good cause' or 'good reason', your claim will be decided against you.[41] See the chapter in this *Handbook* about the benefit that you have claimed for more details.

Healthcare and health professionals

A **'healthcare professional'** is a registered medical practitioner (eg, a doctor), registered nurse, or registered occupational therapist or physiotherapist, or for DLA mobility component for a severe visual impairment only, a registered optometrist or orthoptist.[42]

The rules for who counts as a **'health professional'** for PIP are not set out in regulations. Guidance states that paramedics are included, along with doctors, registered nurses, occupational therapists and physiotherapists.[43]

4. The date of your claim

Usually, your date of claim is the date on which a valid claim (see p1136) is received by the DWP or HM Revenue and Customs (HMRC). Once a decision is made that you are entitled to benefit, the date from when it is awarded, and the date from when you are paid, is determined by the date of claim. Check the relevant chapter for the specific rules about the date of claim for that benefit and the date from when you are paid.

The date of claim is earlier than the date a valid claim is made if:

- your claim is 'backdated' (see p1142);
- the claim you made for one benefit is treated as a claim for a different benefit instead (see p1144).

Part 8: Claiming benefits and getting paid
Chapter 50: Claims
4. The date of your claim

In some situations, you may be able to claim a benefit in advance. See the relevant chapter for the specific rules on the benefit you want to claim.

Backdating your claim

In general, you should claim benefit as soon as you think you qualify. There are strict time limits for making a claim.[44] If you miss the time limit, you may be able to have your claim backdated. If you want your claim to be backdated, you must ask for this to happen, otherwise (except for bereavement support payment) it is not considered.[45] If you satisfy the conditions for getting benefit, it should be paid from your date of claim, even if backdating is refused. If backdating is refused, you can ask for a mandatory reconsideration of the decision, and then appeal if the decision is not changed. Payment should not be held up because you are challenging a decision on backdating.

If you have not asked for backdating, but you want it to be considered, you should ask for your claim to be amended to include backdating *before* a decision on it is made (see p1135). If a decision has been made on your claim, the DWP or local authority may say that in order to have a request for backdating considered, you must make a new claim for the past period and that your request for backdating runs from when you make this new claim.

The rules for backdating are different, depending on your circumstances and the benefit you have claimed.

- For the universal credit (UC) backdating rules, see p47.
- Claims for attendance allowance (AA), disability living allowance (DLA) and personal independence payment (PIP) can never be backdated.[46]
- Claims for some benefits can be backdated without special reasons (see below).
- Claims for jobseeker's allowance (JSA) can only be backdated in limited circumstances (see p700).
- The backdating period is longer for some benefits if you are reclaiming following an award of a 'qualifying benefit' (see p1143).
- Special rules apply if you are reclaiming backdated JSA after your JSA stopped when you failed to attend an interview or sign on (see p1109).

If you are prevented from receiving backdated benefit because of an error of the DWP or, in child benefit and guardian's allowance cases, HMRC, write and request compensation (see p1403). The intervention of an MP or the Ombudsman (see p1408) may help.

Benefits that can be backdated without special reasons

Claims for some benefits can be backdated for up to three months, regardless of the reason why you did not claim earlier. State pension can be backdated for up to 12 months without needing to have special reasons.[47] If you want benefit for a period before the date you make your claim, you must show that you would have qualified for the benefit had you claimed at the time. The benefits that can be backdated without special reasons are:

- bereavement support payment (see p538);
- carer's allowance (CA) (see p555);
- child benefit and guardian's allowance (see p578);
- employment and support allowance (ESA) (see p644);
- industrial injuries benefits (see p682);
- maternity allowance (MA) (see p718);
- pension credit (PC) (see p264);
- state pension (see p774).

There are exceptions to the rules.

- The time limit for claiming bereavement support payment can be extended in some cases – eg, when you did not know your partner had died (see p539).
- If you are claiming backdated child benefit or guardian's allowance after being awarded refugee status, see p1540.
- If you miss the time limit to claim disablement benefit for occupational deafness or occupational asthma (see p670), you may lose your right to benefit altogether.

Backdating after an award of a qualifying benefit

If your claim for benefit is refused, it can be backdated if you reclaim it after an award of a 'qualifying benefit'.

Note:

- More generous rules apply for CA (see p555).
- Different rules apply for Sure Start maternity grants and funeral expenses payments (see p785).
- This rule does not apply to backdating claims for 'new style' JSA (see p22), or to claims for UC and ESA.

Qualifying benefit

A **'qualifying benefit'** is any benefit (except PIP) awarded to you or someone else, which gives you entitlement to another benefit, or makes another benefit payable at a higher rate. PIP is only a qualifying benefit in relation to backdating entitlement to CA.[48] If you will *only* qualify for a means-tested benefit if you are awarded PIP, you should claim it immediately and ask the DWP not to decide your claim until your PIP claim has been decided. You should also get specialist advice.

You can get backdating if:[49]

- your original claim (eg, for PC) is refused; *and*
- you, or your partner or dependent child, claimed a qualifying benefit (eg, AA for your partner) no later than 10 working days after your original claim; *and*

Part 8: Claiming benefits and getting paid
Chapter 50: Claims
4. The date of your claim

- the qualifying benefit is awarded; *and*
- you make a further claim (eg, for PC) within three months of the decision awarding the qualifying benefit and are now entitled to the award of the original benefit.

In these circumstances, benefit is backdated to the date of your original claim or the date on which the qualifying benefit was first paid, whichever is later.

Note:

- The qualifying benefit rule also applies if the claim for the qualifying benefit was originally refused, but later awarded after a revision, supersession or appeal.[50]
- If you lost entitlement to benefit (eg, CA), or payment of it stopped because the award of a qualifying benefit (eg, DLA) was terminated or reduced, your benefit is backdated if you reclaim within three months of the reinstatement of the qualifying benefit.[51]
- If you lost entitlement to your benefit because AA or DLA stopped being paid because the person entitled was in hospital, a care home or other special accommodation, your benefit is backdated if you reclaim it within three months of payment of AA or DLA restarting.[52] **Note:** this rule does not apply when PIP stops in these circumstances.

If you are already entitled to UC, IS, JSA, ESA, PC or housing benefit, you might get a higher rate once you, a family member or a non-dependant qualifies for another benefit. See p1287 for backdating additional benefit in this situation.

If you claim the wrong benefit

If you claim one benefit when you are entitled to another benefit, your claim can sometimes be treated as a claim for that other benefit. This can be a way round the strict rules about your date of claim and backdating, as your claim for the benefit you should have claimed is treated as having been made on the date you claimed the wrong benefit.

A claim for:[53]

- ESA can be treated as a claim for MA and vice versa;
- bereavement benefits (but not bereavement support payment) can be treated as a claim for state pension and vice versa;
- bereavement support payment can be treated as a claim for other bereavement benefits and vice versa;
- IS can be treated as a claim for CA;
- AA, DLA or an increase in disablement pension for constant attendance (see p677) can be treated as a claim for any of the others;
- PIP can be treated as a claim for either DLA or AA and vice versa, but only if it appears that you are not entitled to the benefit that you actually claimed;
- child benefit can be treated as a claim for guardian's allowance and vice versa.

Note:
- The decision maker does not have to accept your claim for one benefit as a claim for another. You cannot appeal if this is refused. You can request a revision (see p1261) but your only remedy if the decision maker refuses to change the decision is to seek a judicial review (see p1377).[54]
- For all benefits, except UC, JSA, ESA and PIP, there is a general power to treat any written document as a claim for benefit, which could arguably include if you filled in the wrong claim form.[55]
- For some benefits, although you cannot be treated as having claimed the right benefit, there are special rules about the date your claim is treated as having been made if you first claimed the wrong benefit and later claim the right one when your claim is refused. For more details, see 'The date of your claim' in the chapter of this *Handbook* about the benefit you should have claimed.
- If you claimed the wrong benefit as a result of incorrect information given to you by an employee of the DWP or HMRC and the above rules cannot help you, see p1403 for information about how to ask for compensation.

Notes

1. Making a claim
1 s1(1) SSAA 1992
2 Regs 4(6A)-(6CC), 4D and 4H SS(C&P) Regs
3 Regs 4(6B), 4D(3A) and (4) and 4H(3) SS(C&P) Regs
4 **UC/PIP/JSA&ESA under UC** Reg 30 UC,PIP,JSA&ESA(C&P) Regs
 CB/GA Reg 8 CB&GA(Admin) Regs
 Other benefits Reg 5(1) and (1A) SS(C&P) Regs
5 **UC/PIP/JSA&ESA under UC** Reg 31 UC,PIP,JSA&ESA(C&P) Regs
 CB/GA Reg 9 CB&GA(Admin) Regs
 Other benefits Reg 5(2) SS(C&P) Regs
6 **UC/PIP/JSA&ESA under UC** Reg 2 and Sch 2 UC,PIP,JSA&ESA(C&P) Regs
 CB/GA Reg 2 and Sch 2 CB&GA(Admin) Regs
 Other benefits Reg 4ZC and Sch 9ZC SS(C&P) Regs
7 CJSA/3979/1999; CJSA/1332/2001; CDLA/1589/2005

2. Who should claim
8 **UC/PIP/JSA&ESA under UC** Reg 57 UC,PIP,JSA&ESA(C&P) Regs
 CB/GA Reg 28 CB&GA(Admin) Regs
 Other benefits Reg 33 SS(C&P) Regs
9 R(SB) 5/90
10 CIS/642/1994
11 CIS/379/1992
12 **UC/PIP/JSA&ESA under UC** Reg 57(6) UC,PIP,JSA&ESA(C&P) Regs
 Other benefits Reg 33(1A) SS(C&P) Regs
13 R(SB) 9/84(T)

3. Information to support your claim
14 Sch 2 SS&CS(DA) Regs, Sch 3 UC,PIP,JSA&ESA(DA) Regs and Sch 2 CB&GA(DA) Regs do not include such decisions in the list of decisions against which there is no right of appeal
15 **CB/GA** s13(1A) and (1B) SSAA 1992
 Other benefits s1(1A) and (1B) SSAA 1992
16 CH/4085/2007
17 s1(1A) SSAA 1992

18 *SSWP v Wilson* [2006] EWCA Civ 882, reported as R(H) 7/06
19 Upper Tribunal file reference UA-2021-000580-JR
20 CH/1231/2004; CH/4085/2007
21 Reg 1A SS(DLA) Regs
22 Reg 4(a) HB Regs; reg 4(a) HB(SPC) Regs
23 **UC** Reg 5 UC,PIP,JSA&ESA(C&P) Regs
   HB Reg 4(b) HB Regs; reg 4(b) HB(SPC) Regs
24 equalityadvisoryservice.com; telephone 0808 800 0082 (textphone: 0808 800 0084)
25 **UC/PIP/JSA&ESA under UC** Regs 8(4) and (5), 11(4) and (5), 13 and 23 UC,PIP,JSA&ESA(C&P) Regs
   Other benefits Regs 4(11)-(13), 4D(6A)-(6E) and 4G SS(C&P) Regs
26 **ESA under UC** Reg 13(2) UC,PIP,JSA&ESA(C&P) Regs
   Other benefits Reg 4D(6B) SS(C&P) Regs
27 **UC/PIP/JSA&ESA under UC** Regs 8(5) and (6), 11(5) and (6), 13(4) and (5) and 23(3) and (4) UC,PIP,JSA&ESA(C&P) Regs
   Other benefits Regs 4(7) and (13), 4D(6D) and (6E) SS(C&P) Regs
28 **UC/PIP/JSA&ESA under UC** Regs 8(3), 11(3), 15(2) and 21(3) UC,PIP,JSA&ESA(C&P) Regs
   CB/GA Reg 10 CB&GA(Admin) Regs
   Other benefits Regs 4 (7) and (8), 4D(2) and 4H(2) SS(C&P) Regs
29 **UC/PIP/JSA&ESA under UC** Regs 8(5) and (6), 11(5) and (6), 15(3) and (4) and 21(4) and (5) UC,PIP,JSA&ESA(C&P) Regs
   CB/GA Reg 10 CB&GA(Admin) Regs
   Other benefits Regs 4(7)(b), 4D (10) and (11) SS(C&P) Regs
30 *CW v SSWP (JSA)* [2016] UKUT 114 (AAC)
31 **UC/PIP/JSA&ESA under UC** Regs 8(1), 11(1)(a), 15(1) and 21(1) UC,PIP,JSA&ESA(C&P) Regs
32 **CB/GA** Reg 5 CB&GA(Admin) Regs
   Other benefits Regs 4(1) and 4D(2) SS(C&P) Regs
33 **CB/GA** Reg 10 CB&GA(Admin) Regs
   Other benefits Reg 4(7ZA) SS(C&P) Regs
34 Regs 15 and 21 UC,PIP,JSA(C&P) Regs; ADM A2069 and 2085
35 Regs 15(3) and (4) and 21(4) and (5) UC,PIP,JSA(C&P) Regs

36 **UC/PIP&ESA under UC** Reg 37 UC,PIP,JSA&ESA(C&P) Regs
   JSA Reg 31 JSA Regs 2013
   CB/GA Reg 7 CB&GA(Admin) Regs
   Other benefits Reg 7 SS(C&P) Regs
37 R(IS) 4/93; CIS/51/2007; *MS v SSWP (JSA)* [2016] UKUT 206 (AAC)
38 The Social Security (Claims and Information) Regulations 2007 No.2911
39 ss180 and 180A SSAA 1992
40 CIS/51/2007
41 **PIP** s80 WRA 2012
   ESA ss8-9 WRA 2007
   IIDB Reg 12(3) SS&CS(DA) Regs; s19 SSA 1998
   Other benefits s19 SSA 1998
42 s39(1) SSA 1998; reg 3 SS(DLA)A Regs
43 PIP AG, p122

4. **The date of your claim**
44 **UC/PIP/JSA&ESA under UC** Regs 26-29 UC,PIP,JSA&ESA(C&P) Regs
   CB/GA Reg 6 CB&GA(Admin) Regs
   Other benefits Reg 19 and Sch 4 SS(C&P) Regs
45 This is sometimes said to be based on R(SB) 9/84
46 ss65(4) and 76 SSCBA 1992; reg 27 UC,PIP,JSA&ESA(C&P) Regs
47 **ESA under UC** Reg 28 UC,PIP,JSA&ESA(C&P) Regs
   CB/GA Reg 6 CB&GA(Admin) Regs
   Other benefits Reg 19(1)-(3B) and Sch 4 SS(C&P) Regs
48 Reg 6(22) SS(C&P) Regs. PIP does not count for the general rule, as it is not defined as a 'relevant benefit' for the purpose of this regulation.
49 Reg 6(16)-(26) SS(C&P) Regs
50 Reg 6(26) SS(C&P) Regs
51 Reg 6(19) SS(C&P) Regs
52 Reg 6(19)-(21A) SS(C&P) Regs
53 **UC/PIP/JSA&ESA under UC** Reg 25 UC,PIP,JSA&ESA(C&P) Regs
   CB/GA Reg 11 CB&GA(Admin) Regs
   Other benefits Reg 9 and Sch 1 SS(C&P) Regs
54 **UC/PIP/JSA&ESA under UC** Sch 3 para 1(b) UC,PIP,JSA&ESA(DA) Regs
   CB/GA Sch 2 para 6(d) CB&GA(DA) Regs
   Other benefits Sch 2 para 5(g) SS&CS(DA) Regs
   See also R(A) 3/81
55 **CB/GA** Reg 5(1)(b) CB&GA(Admin) Regs
   Other benefits Regs 4(1) and 4D(2) SS(C&P) Regs

Chapter 51

∙ ∙

Getting paid

This chapter covers:

This chapter covers the general rules for most benefits. See the chapter about the benefit you are getting for the specific rules about that benefit. This chapter does not cover the rules for Scottish benefits (see Chapter 79 and the chapter about the benefit you are claiming), statutory sick pay (see Chapter 39), statutory maternity, adoption, paternity, shared parental and parental bereavement pay (see Chapter 38), social fund payments (see Chapter 37), the health benefits in Chapter 31, the other types of financial help in Chapter 40 or discretionary housing payments (see Chapter 29). For information about payment of tax credits, see Chapter 64.

Key facts

- The DWP, local authority or HM Revenue and Customs (HMRC) decides how benefit is paid to you. There is no right of appeal.
- You are usually paid by direct credit transfer into a bank or similar account.
- If your claim or payment of your benefit is delayed, you may be able to get an advance payment.
- A benefit cap may restrict the total amount of benefit you receive.
- You must report certain changes in your circumstances.
- Deductions can be made from your benefit. In certain circumstances, payment of your benefit can be suspended. In addition, your benefit might not be paid, or might be paid at a reduced rate, as a result of a sanction or a penalty.

Part 8: Claiming benefits and getting paid
Chapter 51: Getting paid
2. How and when you are paid

1. **Who is paid**

Payment is usually made direct to you, but there are some circumstances when payments can be made to other people or organisations on your behalf.

- If you are unable to manage your own money or if you die, your benefit is paid to a person appointed to act on your behalf – called an 'appointee' (see p1135).[1]
- You can choose to have universal credit (UC), child benefit, guardian's allowance or joint-claim jobseeker's allowance (JSA) paid to your partner.
- Your benefit (except housing benefit (HB)) can be paid to someone else if it is in the interests of you or your partner, or any children for whom you are getting benefit.[2] This includes paying your UC housing costs for rent to someone who then makes payments to your landlord.
- Your HB can be paid direct to your landlord (or the person to whom you pay rent) on your behalf in certain circumstances (see p214). Your UC housing costs for rent are not paid direct to your landlord, unless the DWP thinks the 'alternative payment arrangements' should apply. If you live in Scotland, you can request direct payment (see p50).
- Deductions can be made from certain benefits (usually UC, income support, JSA, employment and support allowance or pension credit) for certain payments to be made to someone else on your behalf (see p1164).[3]

2. **How and when you are paid**

The DWP or HM Revenue and Customs (HMRC) decides how and when your benefit is paid. There is no right of appeal about this. For how and when housing benefit is paid, see p213.

Note:

- You are usually paid by direct credit transfer into a bank or similar account.
- If you cannot open or manage an account, payment can sometimes be made by the payment exception service (see p1150). Child benefit and guardian's allowance can be paid by a payment voucher (see p1150).
- You can check your universal credit (UC) payments online. If you are unable to do this, ask the DWP for help in accessing your online journal. It may be possible to do this by telephone, or possibly in person at a Jobcentre Plus office.
- If you are entitled to arrears of benefit, but it is considered necessary to pay them in instalments in order to protect your interests, then if you (in a joint claim for UC, both you and your partner) agree, you are paid your arrears in instalments.[4]

Direct payment

You are usually paid by direct credit transfer into a bank account, building society account or similar account (including, if you already have one, a post office card account, and some credit union accounts). This is called 'direct payment'. If this is not suitable for you, you may be able to get your DWP benefit paid by the payment exception service (see p1150), or your child benefit or guardian's allowance paid by voucher (see p1150). **Note:** the DWP and HMRC prefer you to have a bank account or building society account, and will encourage you to move to one of these or a similar account. Some people still have a post office card account for benefit payments, but use of these is being phased out. HMRC stopped paying into these accounts from 30 November 2021. Benefit payments to post office card accounts by the DWP will stop by November 2022. The DWP has said that those who cannot open a different type of account or provide details of a new account will be able to get paid by the payment exception service instead (see p1150).[5] There is a DWP customer service centre for notifying new accounts or queries about closure of post office card accounts (telephone 0800 085 7133; textphone 0800 085 7146).

Your benefit is paid into an account nominated by you or by your appointee.[6]

If you experience difficulty accessing your money as a result of these arrangements, complain to the DWP or HMRC (see Chapter 61). You could also contact your MP (see p1408).

If someone collects your benefit for you

It should be possible, if necessary, to arrange for someone else to be able to access your account in order to collect your benefit for you. Ask your bank or building society about this. If you use a post office card account, a second card can be issued to the person who collects your benefit.

If you lose your card or forget your PIN

If you lose your bank card or forget your PIN, contact the bank and ask for a replacement card or new PIN to be issued as soon as possible.

If you lose your post office card account card, call 0800 389 2101. If you forget your PIN, call the customer service helpline on 0345 722 3344 (typetalk: 0345 722 3355). You should get a replacement card or PIN within four working days.

If you cannot access your benefit while waiting for a new card or PIN, contact the office that pays your benefit for advice.

If all else fails, you may be able to get a payment from your local authority while the problem is sorted out (see p846). If you cannot get access to your benefit, and the DWP or HMRC refuses to remedy the situation, get advice (see Appendix 1).

Part 8: Claiming benefits and getting paid
Chapter 51: Getting paid
2. How and when you are paid

Payment by the payment exception service or voucher

If you cannot open or manage an account, your DWP benefits are paid by the government's payment exception service at a PayPoint outlet. The DWP sends you an information pack about the payment exception service and identifies two PayPoint outlets near your home which you could use. To withdraw your benefit at the PayPoint outlet, you must produce your payment service card, or text message or emailed voucher from the payment exception service, a memorable date agreed with the DWP and proof of your identity. The voucher is valid for 30 days. If you do not use it in time, ask the DWP to reissue it. If someone regularly gets your benefit for you, s/he can be issued with a payment service card. See gov.uk/payment-exception-service for more information.

If you lose your payment service card, contact the office that pays your benefit. Your card will be blocked and you will be sent a new one. You may be sent a voucher or text message to get your benefit in the meantime. In an emergency, you may be given a telephone number to call for a reference number which will enable you to get your benefit.

If you cannot open or manage an account, HMRC may pay your child benefit or guardian's allowance by issuing you with a Post Office Payout voucher. This can be cashed at a post office, using a code and reference number which HMRC sends you. The local authority may arrange to pay your housing benefit by another method, including by cheque.

When you are paid

When and how often your benefit is paid depends on the benefit you have claimed.[7] You are sometimes paid in advance and sometimes in arrears. Some benefits have specific paydays. For others, the day you are paid depends on your national insurance (NI) number. See the chapter for the benefit you are claiming.

Last two numbers of your NI number	Day of payment
00–19	Monday
20–39	Tuesday
40–59	Wednesday
60–79	Thursday
80–99	Friday

Missing payments

If you are entitled to benefit, you must be paid it.[8] If your benefit is not paid into your account, your payment service card does not allow you to collect your benefit or you are not issued with a voucher, the DWP or HMRC must rectify this.

If there is a long delay, the DWP or HMRC may say that your entitlement to payment is lost 12 months after the date it was due to be paid into your account. However, this should not apply if you have not been paid.[9] If necessary, get advice (see Appendix 1).

Emergencies

If you have lost all your money or there has been a crisis, it is possible to get help at any time. Your local police station should have a contact number for DWP staff on call outside normal office hours.

If you are unable to contact the DWP, or it does not help, you may be able to get a payment from your local authority in a crisis (see p846). The police station should have a contact number.

If you need money urgently, you should provide as much information as you can to support your claim. It may help if you can get an advice agency or third party (eg, a health visitor, social worker, doctor or MP) to support you.

3. Overlapping benefits

Sometimes you cannot be paid more than one non-means-tested benefit in full at the same time. This is because of the overlapping benefit rules. These may also apply if:

- more than one person is claiming an increase for the same child or adult (see p1153);
- you are getting child benefit, guardian's allowance or an increase in your non-means-tested benefit for your child (see p1153);
- you are entitled to an increase in your non-means-tested benefit for an adult who is getting one or more of certain benefits her/himself (see p1153).

Disability living allowance (DLA) care component, the daily living component of personal independence payment (PIP) and of adult disability payment (ADP), attendance allowance (AA) and armed forces independence payment overlap with (ie, are reduced by) constant attendance allowance.[10] Otherwise AA, DLA, PIP, disablement benefit (see p676), reduced earnings allowance (see p678) and retirement allowance (see p680) can be received in addition to any of the other benefits described in this *Handbook* – eg, you can receive employment and support allowance (ESA), both components of PIP and disablement benefit at the same time.

Earnings-replacement benefits

Some benefits compensate you for your inability to work because of unemployment, sickness, pregnancy or old age. These are 'earnings-replacement'

benefits. You cannot usually receive more than one of the following earnings-replacement benefits at the same time.
- Contributory benefits:
  - contribution-based jobseeker's allowance;
  - contributory ESA;
  - maternity allowance (which counts as contributory for the purposes of this rule);
  - retirement pension;
  - widow's pension;
  - widowed parent's allowance.
- Non-contributory benefits:
  - severe disablement allowance;
  - carer's allowance (CA).

If more than one of the earnings-replacement benefits listed above is payable to you, the following applies.[11]
- A contributory benefit is paid in preference to a non-contributory benefit. This is then topped up by any balance of a non-contributory benefit due.
- If the above bullet point does not apply, weekly benefits are paid and topped up by any balance of a daily benefit (unless you make an application to receive the daily benefit in full). See the chapter in this *Handbook* about the benefit you are claiming to see if it is a daily or a weekly benefit.
- If neither of the above bullet points apply, the highest rate benefit is paid or, if the rates are the same, one benefit is paid.

Retirement pensions

You cannot usually get more than one retirement pension at a time.[12] However, there are special rules if you are married or in a civil partnership and at least one of you reached pension age after 6 April 1979, or you are a surviving spouse or civil partner entitled to both an old category A and an old category B retirement pension (see Chapter 36 of the 2015/16 edition of this *Handbook*), and your category A pension would be paid at a reduced rate because you have not paid sufficient contributions (see p969). In this situation, your basic category A pension is increased by whichever is less of either:[13]
- the amount of the shortfall between your category A pension and the full category A pension of £141.85; *or*
- the amount of your category B pension.

You are also entitled to an additional pension on your own contribution record and one on that of your spouse or civil partner up to the maximum additional pension a person could theoretically receive on one contribution record.[14]

Additional pensions under the old additional state pension scheme and graduated retirement benefit do not overlap with non-means-tested benefits.

However, if two or more such benefits are payable with an additional pension and graduated retirement benefit, the benefits are calculated as if the additional pension or graduated retirement benefit is part of the benefit, and the overlapping benefit rule is then applied to the benefits.[15] For more information about additional state pension and graduated retirement benefit, see Chapter 36 of the 2015/16 edition of this *Handbook*.

There are exceptions to this rule if you are a category B retirement pensioner whose own contribution record would entitle you to a category A retirement pension. See p278 of the 2008/09 edition of this *Handbook*. Also, an additional pension paid with widow's pension (see p536) overlaps with the new state pension (see p764).[16]

An age addition paid with retirement pension overlaps with another age addition.[17]

Increases in non-means-tested benefits for adults

An increase in a non-means-tested benefit for an adult overlaps with certain earnings-replacement benefits (see p1151) or training allowances which are payable to that adult – eg, an increase of retirement pension for your partner is not paid if s/he is being paid CA in her/his own right.[18] If the increase is less than or equal to the benefit payable to the adult, the increase is not paid. If the increase is greater than the basic benefit, you get the difference. This does not apply if the adult is not residing with you and is employed by you to care for a child.

Increases in non-means-tested benefits for children

Only one person can receive child benefit or an increase in a non-means-tested benefit for the same child.

The standard rate of child benefit (see p574) does not overlap with any other benefit. However, if you receive the higher amount payable for your eldest child (see p574), any other non-means-tested benefit for the same child (except DLA, PIP and guardian's allowance) or increase paid for the same child is reduced by £3.70.[19] All increases for children overlap with guardian's allowance and are reduced by the amount of guardian's allowance you get for the child.[20]

4. Advance payments

If you are waiting for a decision on your claim or you are waiting to be paid and you are in 'financial need', you may be able to get an advance loan of your benefit.[21] This is called a 'short-term advance' of benefit or, for universal credit (UC), a 'universal credit advance'. You must repay the advance by deductions from future payments of your benefit, but you are not charged interest.

Financial need

'Financial need' means that because you have not received your benefit, there is a serious risk of damage to the health or safety of you or a member of your family. 'Family' means your partner and any children for whom you or your partner are responsible (see p567).[22]

You may be in financial need in various circumstances – eg, if you have no money for food or for your gas or electricity meter, or during a 'waiting period' that applies before you are entitled to benefit, or while you are waiting for an increase in benefit after a change in your circumstances. For UC, if you have transferred from any of the legacy benefits (see p21) in the last month, the DWP treats you as being in financial need.[23]

You can get an advance payment of most benefits. See p1155 for the exceptions. **Note:** the rules on advance payments described here do not apply to the Scottish benefits (see Chapter 72).

If you are in financial need because you are waiting for a decision on your claim, you may be able to get an advance payment if the decision maker considers it likely that you are entitled to the benefit and:

- you have made a claim, but the claim has not yet been decided; *or*
- you are not required to make a claim for the benefit, but you have not yet been awarded it.

If you are in financial need because you are waiting to be paid, you may be able to get an advance payment if you have been awarded the benefit and:

- you are waiting for your first payment; *or*
- you have received your first payment, but it was for a shorter period than subsequent payments will be paid for, and you are waiting for your next payment; *or*
- you have had a change of circumstances which increases your entitlement, but your benefit has not yet been increased and paid to you; *or*
- you are entitled to a payment but it is 'impracticable' to pay all or some of it on the date on which it is due.

Note:

- You can request an advance payment at your local Jobcentre Plus office, or use the telephone number for the specific benefit at gov.uk/short-term-benefit-advance. For UC, the DWP encourages you to apply using your journal or via your Jobcentre Plus work coach. If you need help, telephone the UC helpline on 0800 328 5644 (textphone: 0800 328 1344; Relay UK and BSL video relay are available).
- There are no rules on how much a short-term advance should be. The DWP considers how much you have asked for, how much you can afford to repay and what your benefit entitlement will be. For UC, you can get up to 100 per

cent of your estimated award within five days of requesting an advance – but in urgent cases payment can be made faster, including on the same day as your request.

- The DWP says that you must ask for a UC advance no later than three working days before the end of your monthly assessment period (see p38), unless you are claiming within a month of coming off a legacy benefit.
- You are usually contacted about your application on the day you apply or early the next day. If you are to be offered an advance payment, you are asked to accept the amount and the repayment terms. You should explain any problems with this. If you do not accept the offer, you are not given the advance.
- There is no right of appeal against a refusal to award an advance payment.[24] You can ask the DWP to reconsider the decision, but after that the only legal remedy is judicial review (see Chapter 59). You could contact your MP to see whether s/he can help to get the decision reconsidered (see p1408). You may be able to get help in a crisis from your local authority (see p846). You could also try using the emergency service (see p1151).
- You must be notified of your liability to repay the advance.[25] Advances of benefit paid outside the UC system are recovered by deductions from subsequent payments of your benefit. Usually, the DWP wants to recover the advance within 12 weeks, at no more than 25 per cent of your benefit. If you need longer to repay, tell the DWP and explain why. You can ask the DWP to reconsider the decision about repayment, and (for benefits other than UC) if you remain unhappy you can can appeal.[26]
- The DWP usually wants to recover a UC advance within 24 months. Arguably, the correct rate of recovery is either 15 per cent or, if you have earnings, 25 per cent of your standard allowance.[27] However, note that when you apply for an advance, if you tell the DWP that you will refuse to repay at the specified rate, it may decide not to offer you an advance in the first place, and you will not be able to appeal. If you need longer to repay, tell the DWP and explain why.
- You cannot appeal against the decision about the repayment of an advance of UC, including the rate of recovery. You can ask the DWP to reconsider the decision, but after that the only legal remedy is judicial review.[28]

Benefits for which you cannot get a short-term advance

You cannot get a short-term advance of:[29]
- housing benefit (HB). If your HB is delayed and you are a private or housing association tenant, you might be able to get an interim payment known as a 'payment on account' (see p220);
- attendance allowance, disability living allowance and personal independence payment;
- child benefit or guardian's allowance (but see p580);
- statutory sick, maternity, adoption, paternity, shared parental or parental bereavement pay.

Part 8: Claiming benefits and getting paid
Chapter 51: Getting paid
5. The benefit cap

5. **The benefit cap**

The 'benefit cap' may limit the total amount of benefit you can be paid.[30] If the total amount of your benefits is capped, the cap is applied:

- by reducing the amount of your universal credit (UC) (see p1158); *or*
- by reducing the amount of your working-age housing benefit (HB) (see p1159). The cap is not applied through your HB if you are the HB claimant and you are also getting UC.[31]

See p1158 and p1159 for the 'specified' benefits that are taken into account when deciding whether the cap applies.

There are a number of situations when the benefit cap does not apply, or when it is not applied immediately (see below).

You can appeal (see Chapter 57) against having the benefit cap applied through your HB.[32] There is no right of appeal against a decision to apply the benefit cap through UC. Instead, you must ask for a revision or a supersession (see Chapter 56).

When the benefit cap does not apply

The benefit cap does not apply if:

- you are not getting UC or not getting working-age HB (see p187); *or*
- you or your partner are working and get working tax credit (WTC – see below); *or*
- you or your partner (or, in some cases, your child) are entitled to one of the disability or carer benefits listed on p1158; *or*
- it would be applied through your UC, you and/or your partner work and your combined earnings are high enough (see below).

In addition, if you or your partner have been working recently, there may be a 'grace period' during which the cap does not apply.

If you get a relatively high amount of HB, the cap is especially likely to apply. If the amount of your HB decreases (eg, because you move to cheaper accommodation), this may mean that the cap no longer applies.

Work-related exceptions

If the benefit cap should be applied through your UC, it is not applied if:[33]

- you or your partner have net monthly earnings from employed or self-employed work of at least £658 in your UC monthly assessment period (see p117 for what counts as earnings, and p135 if the only reason you do not earn enough to meet this earnings rule is because you are paid four-weekly or otherwise not on a monthly basis). Your partner's earnings are added to yours; *or*
- you are within a nine-month 'grace period'.

Grace period for universal credit

The benefit cap is not applied through your UC for a 'grace period' of nine consecutive months, if:[34]

- your earnings (or your and your partner's combined earnings) from employed or self-employed work are now less than £658 a month (ie, the adult national minimum wage for 16 hours a week converted to a monthly amount) but, immediately before the first day on which this applies, they had been at least £658 a month (or, if different, the adult national minimum wage for a 16 hour week that applied at that time, converted to a monthly amount) in each of the preceding 12 months; *or*
- before your current period of entitlement to UC, you stopped paid employed or self-employed work and, before you stopped work, your earnings (or your and your partner's combined earnings) had been at least £658 a month (or, if different, the adult national minimum wage for a 16 hour week that applied at that time, converted to a monthly amount) in each of the preceding 12 months.

The grace period begins on the most recent day on which either condition applies. Note that it does not matter if you are no longer part of a couple with your then partner – your now ex-partner's earnings in the grace period should be taken into account.

For how earnings from work are calculated for UC, see Chapter 7.

Although not explicitly stated in the UC rules, it is arguable that you count as still in work while on maternity, adoption, paternity, shared parental or parental bereavement leave, or while receiving statutory sick pay (SSP). If you are in this position, get advice.

Grace period for housing benefit

If the benefit cap should be applied through your working-age HB, it is not applied if:[35]

- you (or your partner) are entitled to WTC. This includes if you have claimed WTC but have a nil award because of your income (see p1462); *or*
- you are within a 39-week 'grace period' after finishing work.

The benefit cap is not applied through your HB for a 'grace period' of 39 weeks if:[36]

- you or your partner were previously in work (either employed or self-employed) for at least 50 weeks out of the 52 weeks before the last day of work; *and*
- in that 50 weeks, the person in work was not entitled to income support (IS), jobseeker's allowance (JSA) or employment and support allowance (ESA).

The grace period begins on the day after the last day of work. Note that it does not matter if you are no longer part of a couple with your then partner – your now ex-partner's earnings in the grace period should be taken into account.

Part 8: Claiming benefits and getting paid
Chapter 51: Getting paid
5. The benefit cap

You count as still in work while on maternity, adoption, paternity, shared parental or parental bereavement leave, or while receiving SSP.[37]

Benefits for disabled people and carers

The benefit cap does not apply if you or your partner get:[38]

- UC that includes the limited capability for work-related activity element; *or*
- ESA that includes the support component; *or*
- carer's allowance, guardian's allowance or UC that includes the carer element; *or*
- attendance allowance (including where it is not paid because of being in hospital or a care home); *or*
- disability living allowance, child disability payment, personal independence payment, adult disability payment or armed forces independence payment. This exemption also applies if the person entitled is a child for whom you or your partner are responsible. The exemption continues while the person entitled is not paid benefit while s/he is in hospital or a care home; *or*
- industrial injuries disablement benefit, reduced earnings allowance or retirement allowance; *or*
- a war pension, or a guaranteed income payment or survivor's guaranteed income payment under the Armed Forces Compensation Scheme (including where it is not paid because of being in hospital or a care home).

When the benefit cap applies

The benefit cap only applies if:

- you get UC or you get working-age HB (see p187); *and*
- none of the exceptions apply (see p1156); *and*
- the total amount of certain specified benefits you (and your partner, if you are a member of a couple) receive is above a certain level.

When calculating the amount of benefit you receive, the general rule is that your full benefit entitlement is taken into account. Deductions for repayment of overpayments, payments to third parties, council tax debts, fines and sanctions are generally ignored (but see p1159 for some exceptions if the cap is applied through your HB and you get child tax credit (CTC) or widowed parent's allowance).[39]

If you get universal credit

The cap applies once your (and, if you are in a couple, your partner's) monthly entitlement to specified benefits exceeds a certain amount. The amount is:

- if you live outside Greater London: £1,116.67 a month (£257.69 a week) if you are single, or £1,666.67 a month (£384.62 a week) if you are a couple or a lone parent; *or*

- if you live in Greater London: £1,284.17 a month (£296.35 a week) if you are single, or £1,916.67 a month (£442.31 a week) if you are a couple or a lone parent.

Your benefit payments are converted into monthly amounts for this calculation.

Specified benefits for UC
If you get UC, the **'specified benefits'** taken into account for the benefit cap are:[40]
- UC;
- JSA;
- ESA, if neither you nor your partner are in the support group (ESA is not taken into account while you are disqualified from receiving it);
- child benefit;
- maternity allowance (MA);
- widowed parent's allowance;
- widow's pension.

If you get housing benefit
The cap applies once your (and, if you are in a couple, your partner's) weekly entitlement to specified benefits exceeds a certain amount. The amount is:
- if you live outside Greater London: £257.69 a week if you are single, or £384.62 a week if you are a couple or a lone parent; or
- if you live in Greater London: £296.35 a week if you are single, or £442.31 a week if you are a couple or a lone parent.

Specified benefits for HB
If you get working-age HB, the **'specified benefits'** taken into account for the benefit cap are:[41]
- IS;
- JSA;
- ESA, if neither you nor your partner are in the support group (ESA is not taken into account while you are disqualified from receiving it);
- HB, except for 'specified accommodation'. This means: 'exempt accommodation' (see p387) or accommodation provided by a housing association, charity, voluntary organisation or English county council to meet your need for care, support or supervision; temporary accommodation provided by one of these bodies or a local authority because you have left home because of domestic abuse; or a local authority hostel where you get care, support or supervision;
- child benefit;
- incapacity benefit;
- MA;
- severe disablement allowance;

Part 8: Claiming benefits and getting paid
Chapter 51: Getting paid
6. Change of circumstances after you claim

- widowed parent's allowance (after the £15 disregard);
- widow's pension;
- CTC (but if you are repaying an overpayment from the previous tax year, the amount of CTC taken into account is reduced by the amount deducted for the repayment).

The local authority does not have to decide whether or not to apply the cap, unless it is told by the DWP that it may apply in your case or that you have had a change in your benefit entitlement. However, it can decide to apply the cap on the basis of information or evidence suggesting that it should do so.[42]

How the benefit cap is applied

If the cap is applied through your UC, the DWP reduces your UC by the amount by which the total amount of the specified benefits you receive exceeds the cap. However, if you are entitled to the childcare costs element in your UC (see p73) and this is more than the amount by which your specified benefits exceeds the cap (the 'excess'), your UC is not reduced. If it is not more than the excess, your UC is reduced, but the excess is reduced by your childcare costs element before the reduction is applied.[43]

If the cap is applied through your HB, the local authority reduces your HB by the amount by which the total amount of the specified benefits you receive exceeds the cap. You must be left with at least 50 pence a week HB, so that you can still access discretionary housing payments (see Chapter 29) and other passported payments.[44]

6. Change of circumstances after you claim

You have a duty to report certain changes in your circumstances. The DWP or HM Revenue and Customs (HMRC) should inform you of the main kinds of changes that you must report, but might not list them all. It is also your duty to report *any* change in your circumstances that you might reasonably be expected to know might affect your right to, the amount of, or the payment of, your benefit.[45] For the changes of circumstances that apply to housing benefit, see pp220–23.

You must notify changes promptly to the DWP or HMRC office handling your claim. Check the information sent to you about your benefit award, but get advice if you are in doubt. The rules say that the office handling your claim for child benefit or guardian's allowance includes the HMRC Child Benefit Office (PO Box 1, Newcastle Upon Tyne NE88 1AA), or any office specified by HMRC.

You must notify the changes in writing or by telephone.[46] It is best to notify changes in writing so that you have a record of what you have reported. If you report a change by telephone, note the time and date of your call, the name of the person you spoke with, and confirm what was said in writing. Keep a copy of any letters you send and take screenshots if reporting online. If you give the original to an officer, ask her/him to stamp your copy to confirm s/he has received the original.

There are additional ways you can report a change of circumstances.

- For child benefit and guardian's allowance, you may be able to report the change in person,[47] either at the HMRC Child Benefit Office or another office specified by HMRC. However, it is always better to do so in writing.
- Except for child benefit and guardian's allowance, if the change is a death, there is a special rule (sometimes called 'Tell Us Once'). For information, see gov.uk/after-a-death/organisations-you-need-to-contact-and-tell-us-once. You can also report a birth or a death in person at a local authority (and, in England, a county council) office specified for that purpose. If the change is a death, you can notify it by telephone to the DWP if a number has been specified for that purpose.[48]

Note:
- If you do not promptly report a change which you have a duty to notify, any resulting overpayment may be recoverable from you (see Chapter 53).
- If you are considered to have acted 'knowingly' or dishonestly, you may also be guilty of an offence, which may lead to prosecution or a benefit penalty. Even if you have not committed an offence, a civil penalty may be applied (see Chapter 54).

7. When payments can be suspended

Payment of part or all of your benefit can be suspended in certain circumstances. This means that the suspended benefit is not paid to you.

Suspension while an appeal is pending

Your benefit can be suspended if the DWP, the local authority or HM Revenue and Customs (HMRC) is appealing (or considering an appeal) against:[49]
- a decision of the First-tier Tribunal, Upper Tribunal or court to award you benefit; or
- a decision of the Upper Tribunal or court about someone else's case if the issue in the appeal could affect your claim. For housing benefit (HB) only, the other case must also be about an HB issue.

The DWP, the local authority or HMRC must give you written notice that it intends to request the statement of reasons from the First-tier Tribunal, or that it intends to apply for leave to appeal, or to appeal. It must do this as soon as is 'reasonably practicable'.[50]

Part 8: Claiming benefits and getting paid
Chapter 51: Getting paid
7. When payments can be suspended

The decision maker must then do one of these things within the usual time limits for doing so (see Chapters 57 and 58).

If s/he does not, the suspended benefit must be paid to you.[51] The suspended benefit must also be paid to you if the decision maker withdraws an application for leave to appeal, withdraws the appeal or is refused leave to appeal and cannot renew the application for leave to appeal.

Suspension for not providing information and evidence

You can be required to supply information or evidence if the decision maker needs this to determine whether your award of benefit should be revised or superseded (see p1261 and p1274).[52]

Payment of your benefit can be suspended if you do not provide the information and evidence.[53]

You must be notified in writing if the decision maker wants you to provide information or evidence. Within 14 days, or seven days for contribution-based jobseeker's allowance (JSA) if you come under the universal credit (UC) system (see p22), or one month for child benefit, guardian's allowance and HB, of being sent the request, you must:

- supply the information or evidence.[54] You can be given more time than this if you satisfy the decision maker that this is necessary; or
- satisfy the decision maker that the information does not exist or you cannot obtain it.[55]

If the decision maker has not already done so, your benefit can be suspended if you do not provide the information or evidence within the relevant time limit.[56] See below for whether your entitlement to benefit can be terminated.

Suspension for not taking part in a medical examination

Most benefits can be suspended if you do not take part in a medical examination on two consecutive occasions without 'good cause'.[57] This applies if:

- the decision maker is looking at whether you should still be getting a benefit (or whether you are getting it at the correct rate); or
- you apply for a revision or a supersession and the decision maker thinks a medical examination is necessary in order to make a decision.

This rule does not apply if the issue is whether you have limited capability for work. For information on these medicals and the consequences of failing to take part in them, see p1011. It also does not apply to personal independence payment. However, if you do not take part in a medical, the DWP may still suspend your benefit because of a doubt about your entitlement.

Suspension in other circumstances

Your benefit can also be suspended in various other circumstances, including if:[58]

- a question has arisen about your entitlement, or if the DWP, HMRC or the local authority thinks you are being, or have been, overpaid;[59]
- you have been getting JSA and a question has arisen about whether you are meeting your jobseeking conditions. Your JSA must be suspended until this matter is resolved. **Note:** this does not apply to contribution-based JSA if you come under the UC system (see p22).[60]

Challenging decisions to suspend benefit

You cannot appeal to the First-tier Tribunal against the decision to suspend your benefit. The only ways to change the decision are to negotiate to get your benefit reinstated or to challenge the decision by judicial review (see Chapter 59). You could also ask for an advance payment of benefit (see p1153). Get advice.

The decision maker may be willing to continue to pay your benefit, or at least some of it, if you can show that you will experience hardship otherwise. If you receive a letter telling you that your benefit has been suspended, reply and explain how the suspension affects you and ask for it to be reconsidered. It may be wise to get advice first (see Appendix 1).

8. **When your entitlement is terminated**

Your entitlement to benefit can be terminated if:

- your benefit was suspended in full, you are then required to provide information or evidence to determine whether the decision awarding you benefit should be revised or superseded, and you fail to do so within one month of the request;[61] or
- your benefit was suspended in full because you did not provide information or evidence required to determine whether the decision awarding you benefit should be revised or superseded and it is more than one month since your benefit was suspended.[62]

The termination of your entitlement to benefit takes effect from the date payment was suspended (or an earlier date if you ceased to be entitled for another reason).[63]

Your entitlement to most benefits may also be terminated if you do not take part in a medical examination and it is more than one month since your benefit was suspended on this ground.[64]

If you disagree with a decision to terminate your benefit, you can ask for a revision (see p1261) and then appeal (see Chapter 57).

Part 8: Claiming benefits and getting paid
Chapter 51: Getting paid
9. Deductions and payments to third parties

9. **Deductions and payments to third parties**

Your benefit is usually paid direct to you, but there are some circumstances when money can be deducted and paid to another person (a third party) on your behalf.

What deductions can be made

Amounts can be deducted from your benefit to pay third parties for:[65]
- housing costs (see p1165); *and*
- rent arrears (see p1166); *and*
- fuel (see p1167); *and*
- water charges (p1168); *and*
- council tax arrears (see p1168); *and*
- child support maintenance (see p1168); *and*
- other payments – eg, loan repayments, fines and other charges (see p1169).

Note: in addition to the above deductions to third parties, you may also have deductions to the DWP or HM Revenue and Customs (HMRC) made to recover budgeting loans from the social fund (see p781), overpayments (see p1208) or regarding fraud and penalties (Chapter 54). Your benefit may also be reduced if you have been sanctioned (see Chapters 47 and 49) or because the DWP is recovering a hardship payment (see Chapter 52).

From which benefits can deductions be made

Deductions for payments to third parties are usually made from UC, income support (IS), income-based jobseeker's allowance (JSA), income-related employment and support allowance (ESA) and pension credit (PC). In some circumstances, they can also be made from contribution-based JSA and contributory ESA (see below).

Deductions can only be made from other benefits to repay eligible loans (see p1169) and child support maintenance that you owe (see p1168).

Deductions from contribution-based jobseeker's allowance and contributory employment and support allowance

Deductions to third parties can be made from your contribution-based JSA or your contributory ESA for the payments listed above if you have an 'underlying entitlement' to income-based JSA or income-related ESA – ie, if you were not entitled to contribution-based JSA or contributory ESA, you would be entitled to income-based JSA or income-related ESA at the same rate.[66]

Deductions can also be made from contribution-based JSA and contributory ESA for council tax arrears and for fines, even if you have no underlying entitlement to income-based JSA or income-related ESA.

When deductions can be made

Deductions and direct payments to third parties can only be made if you or your partner are liable to make the payments.[67] Deductions should only be made if there is evidence that you are liable – eg, the bill is in your or your partner's name.

Your consent is required before direct payments (including for arrears) are made for fuel costs and water charges from your UC if the total amount deducted for these payments exceeds 25 per cent of your UC standard allowance and child elements (see Chapter 5).[68]

Otherwise, the DWP can make deductions from your UC without your consent.

Your written consent is required before deductions for tax credit overpayments and self-assessment tax debts can be made from your IS, income-based JSA, income-related ESA or PC. Your consent is also required before deductions are made for rent arrears, service charges for fuel and water, fuel costs (including arrears), water charges (including arrears) and repayment of integration loans if:[69]

- you (or your partner) do not get child tax credit (CTC) and the total to be deducted for these payments exceeds 25 per cent of your family's applicable amount (see Chapter 17) or, in the case of PC, 25 per cent of your minimum guarantee (see p259); *or*
- you (or your partner) get CTC, and the total to be deducted for these payments exceeds 25 per cent of the total sum of your CTC and child benefit plus your family's applicable amount (see Chapter 17) (or, in the case of PC, your minimum guarantee) (see p259).

The DWP can make deductions from these benefits without your consent if they are made for:

- council tax arrears;
- fines;
- current housing costs;
- nursing home charges or hostel charges not included in housing benefit (HB).

The deductions

Deductions to third parties are made before you receive your regular benefit payment. If you want to have deductions made to help you clear any arrears or debts, ask the DWP office dealing with your claim. If you disagree with a decision about deductions, you can challenge it by applying for a mandatory reconsideration (see p1299) and then by appealing (see Chapter 57).

Housing costs

Deductions can only be made for the housing costs that can be included in your benefit – this does not include rent payments. For which housing costs can be included, see p82 for UC (in effect, just service charges, as deductions for rent payments cannot be made) and p344 for other benefits. For the amount of the

Part 8: Claiming benefits and getting paid
Chapter 51: Getting paid
9. Deductions and payments to third parties

deductions, see p1170. If you are in rent arrears, see below for the separate deductions which can be made.[70]

To have deductions made from your UC, you must be in arrears with your service charges. Your earnings (or if you are claiming jointly with your partner, your combined earnings) must also be below the UC work allowance that applies to you (see p40). If your earnings (or combined earnings) are equal to, or exceed, the work allowance for three monthly assessment periods, the deduction must stop.

If your current IS, income-based JSA, income-related ESA or PC includes amounts for housing costs and you are in arrears (excluding payments for ground rent or rent charge payments, unless paid with your service charges or for a tent[71]), deductions can be made from your IS, JSA, ESA or PC to clear the debt and to meet current payments. Deductions are made if it would be 'in the interests' of you or your family to do so. In England and Wales, if collection of your arrears is suspended under a breathing space debt respite scheme, deductions for payment of current costs can still be made.[72]

You only qualify for direct deductions from IS, income-based JSA, income-related ESA and PC if you owe more than half of the annual total of the relevant housing cost. This condition can be waived if it is in the 'overriding interests' of you or your family that deductions start as soon as possible – eg, repossession of your home is imminent.[73]

Rent arrears

Deductions can be made from your UC for rent arrears if you are in debt with your rent (including water, service and other charges included in it), if:[74]

- you are entitled to UC housing costs for rent payments or occupy 'exempt' accommodation' and get HB for that (p387); *and*
- you occupy the accommodation to which the rent applies; *and*
- your earnings (or if you make a joint claim with your partner, your combined earnings) for the previous UC monthly assessment period (see p38) are below the level of the work allowance that applies to you (see p40). If your earnings (or joint earnings) equal or exceed the work allowance for three monthly assessment periods, the deduction must stop.

The DWP can make a monthly deduction from your UC equivalent to between 10 and 20 per cent of the standard allowance (see p65) that applies in your case and pay it to your landlord. The DWP should take your circumstances into account in deciding how much the deduction will be.

If you are in arrears with your rent while on **HB**, or are £100 or more in arrears of hostel payments, an amount can be deducted from your **IS, income-based JSA, income-related ESA or PC** and paid direct to your landlord. This can also apply if (in England and Wales) you are in approved premises under section 13 of the

Offender Management Act 2007 and have built up arrears of service charges rather than rent arrears.[75] For the amount of the deductions, see p1170.

Rent arrears do not include the amount of any non-dependant deductions (see p198), but can cover any water charges or service charges payable with your rent and not met by HB. Fuel charges included in your rent cannot be covered by direct deductions if they change more than twice a year.

To qualify for direct deductions for rent arrears, your arrears must be equal to at least four times your full weekly rent. If you have not paid your full rent for eight weeks or more, direct deductions can be made automatically if your landlord asks the DWP to make them.[76] If your arrears relate to a shorter period, deductions can only be made if it is in the overriding interests of your family to do so.[77] In either case, the decision maker must be satisfied that you are in rent arrears. Even if you are, you can ask her/him not to make direct deductions – eg, if you are claiming compensation from your landlord because of the state of repair of your home.[78] Once your arrears are paid off, direct payments can continue for any fuel and water charges included in your rent.[79]

Fuel

If you are in debt with your mains gas or electricity, the DWP can make deductions from your benefit and pay it to the supplier. This is sometimes called 'Fuel Direct'.

For UC, it can deduct a monthly amount equal to 5 per cent of your standard allowance (see p65), plus an additional amount that the DWP considers to be equal to the average monthly fuel costs, except if you are paying for that by other means – eg, a prepayment meter.[80]

If you are in debt for any gas or electricity (including reconnection or disconnection charges), deductions can be made from your UC if your earnings (or, if you are claiming jointly with your partner, your combined earnings) for the previous monthly UC assessment period (see p38) are below the level of the work allowance that applies in your case (see p40).[81] If your earnings equal or exceed the work allowance for three monthly assessment periods, the deduction must stop.

For IS, income-based JSA, income-related ESA and PC, an amount can be deducted each week and paid to the fuel company in instalments – usually once a quarter.[82] For the amount of the deduction, see p1170. Deductions can be made if:[83]

- the amount you owe is £77 or more (including reconnection or disconnection charges if you have been disconnected); *and*
- you continue to need the fuel supply; *and*
- it is in your, or your family's, interests to have deductions made.

An amount is deducted for the fuel you use each week (your current consumption) as well as for the arrears you owe. The amount deducted for current consumption is whatever is necessary to meet your current weekly fuel costs. This is adjusted if

Part 8: Claiming benefits and getting paid
Chapter 51: Getting paid
9. Deductions and payments to third parties

the cost increases or decreases. Deductions for current consumption can be continued after the debt has been cleared.[84] In England and Wales, if collection of your arrears is suspended under a breathing space debt respite scheme, deductions for payment of current costs can still be made.[85]

See CPAG's *Fuel Rights Handbook* for help if you have fuel debts.

Water charges

If you are in debt with charges for water and sewerage (including reconnection charges), deductions may be made from your UC if your earnings (or, if you are claiming jointly with your partner, your combined earnings) for the previous monthly UC assessment period (see p38) are below the level of the work allowance that applies in your case (see p40). If your earnings equal or exceed the work allowance for three monthly assessment periods, the deduction must stop.

The DWP can make a deduction from your UC and pay it to the water company. It can deduct a monthly amount equal to 5 per cent of your standard allowance (see p65), plus an additional amount that the DWP considers necessary to meet your continuing monthly water costs.

If you are in debt with charges for water and sewerage, direct deductions can be made from your **IS, income-based JSA, income-related ESA and PC**.[86] Debt includes any disconnection, reconnection and legal charges. For the amount of the deductions, see p1170. If you pay your landlord for water with your rent, deductions are made under the arrangements for rent arrears (see p1166).[87] In England and Wales, if collection of your arrears is suspended under a breathing space debt respite scheme, deductions for payment of current costs can still be made.[88]

Deductions can be made if you failed to budget and it is in the interests of you or your family to make deductions.[89] If you are in debt to two water companies, you can only have a deduction for arrears made to one at a time. Your debts for water charges should be cleared before your debts for sewerage costs, but the amount paid for current consumption can include both water and sewerage charges.[90]

Council tax arrears

Deductions for council tax arrears can be made from UC, IS, JSA, ESA or PC if the local authority gets a liability order from a magistrates' court (in Scotland, a summary warrant or decree from a sheriff court) and applies to the DWP for recovery to be made in this way.[91] Deductions can be made for arrears and any unpaid costs or penalties imposed. For the amount of the deductions, see p1170. See CPAG's *Council Tax Handbook* for help if you have council tax arrears.

Child support maintenance

Some child support maintenance is paid under the official child support scheme (often referred to as the '2012 rules' scheme) operated by the DWP through the

Child Maintenance Service whereby deductions from a non-resident parent's benefit can be made to enforce payment. For full details of child support maintenance, see CPAG's *Child Support Handbook*.

If you are liable to pay child support maintenance under the official scheme at the flat rate, a deduction of £8.40 a week (this includes the addition of the DWP 'collect and pay' service) can be made from your:[92]

- UC (at a rate of £36.40 a month), IS, income-based JSA, income-related ESA or PC, including if your partner is liable;
- carer's allowance (CA);
- contributory ESA;
- industrial injuries benefit;
- contribution-based JSA;
- retirement pension;
- war widow's or war disablement pension;
- widowed parent's allowance;
- widow's pension;
- training allowance.

The whole of the child support may be deducted from the above benefits.[93] If more than one partner in a couple or polygamous marriage is liable to pay child support maintenance at the flat rate, it is deducted from any UC, IS, income-based JSA, income-related ESA or PC they jointly receive, with the deduction paid equally. So, for example, if both partners in a couple are liable for child support at a flat rate of £8.40, they each pay £4.20.

A deduction of £8.40 a week can also be made from any of the above benefits for any arrears of child support. Deductions for arrears can only be made if there are no deductions for ongoing child support liablity being made. Once a person's ongoing liability for child support ends (eg, when the youngest or only child for whom they are paying child support is no longer a qualifying child), a deduction of £8.40 can continue to be made towards any arrears due.

If you come under the UC system (see p22), a deduction for arrears can be made from your UC, or contribution-based JSA or contributory ESA. The deduction for arrears in all cases is £8.40 a week (£36.40 a month).[94]

Other deductions

Other deductions can be made from your benefit for the following.

- **Court fines.** Magistrates' courts (any court in Scotland) can apply to the DWP for a fine, costs or compensation order to be deducted from your UC, IS, JSA, ESA or PC.[95]
- **Eligible loans.** Deductions can be made from your UC, IS, JSA, ESA or PC and (if necessary) your retirement pension or CA towards repaying 'eligible' loans if you have not kept up with the repayments.[96] 'Eligible loans' are loans made

Part 8: Claiming benefits and getting paid
Chapter 51: Getting paid
9. Deductions and payments to third parties

by certain not-for-profit lenders, such as community development financial institutions, credit unions and charities, but do not include business loans.

- **Integration loans.** Deductions can be made to repay an integration loan – ie, loans paid to refugees and people granted humanitarian protection and their dependants. Deductions can be made from your UC, IS, JSA, ESA or PC.[97]
- **Tax credit overpayments and self-assessment tax debts.** Deductions can be made from your IS, JSA, ESA or PC to repay these. The deduction is paid to HMRC. Your written consent is required.[98] Deductions can also be made from your UC (or contributory ESA or contribution-based JSA paid under the UC system – ie, where you are no longer getting tax credits and have come under the UC system). The overpayment is treated as a UC overpayment. Your consent is not required.[99]
- **Residential accommodation charges.** Deductions can be made from your IS, JSA, ESA or PC (not UC) to meet your accommodation charges if you have failed to budget for them and it is considered to be in your interests for deductions to be made.[100]
- **Hostel payments.** If you (or your partner) live in a hostel or (in England and Wales) approved premises under section 13 of the Offender Management Act 2007, you have claimed HB to meet your accommodation costs and your payments cover fuel, meals, water charges, laundry and/or cleaning of your room, part of your IS, JSA, ESA or PC (not UC) can be paid direct to the hostel for these items.[101]

How much can be deducted

Deductions from universal credit

If deductions to third parties are made from your UC, in most cases they are made at a fixed rate of 5 per cent of your standard allowance (see p65), with the following exceptions.

- Deductions for child support maintenance are made at a flat rate of £8.40 a week (£36.40 a month) for ongoing liability or £8.40 a week (£36.40 a month) for arrears.
- Deductions for rent arrears are made at a rate of at least 10 per cent but not more than 20 per cent of your standard allowance.
- Deductions for court fines are made at a rate of 5 per cent of your standard allowance.[102]

In practice, deductions of any kind from your UC do not usually exceed 25 per cent of your standard allowance (see p65). For how this limit applies if you have more than one deduction, see p1171. Third-party deductions cannot leave you with less than one pence of UC.[103]

Deductions from other means-tested benefits

If deductions to third parties are made from your **IS, income-based JSA, income-related ESA or PC**, the maximum deductions are shown below.

Type of arrears	Deduction for arrears	Deduction for ongoing cost
Housing costs	£3.85 for each housing debt (maximum of £11.55)	Current weekly cost
Rent arrears and hostel payments	£3.85	Nil (met by UC or HB)
Residential accommodation charges	Nil	The accommodation allowance (for those in local authority homes); all but £27 of your IS, JSA, ESA or PC (for those in private or voluntary homes)
Hostel payments	Nil	Weekly amount assessed by local authority
Fuel	£3.85 for each fuel debt (maximum of £7.70 payable)	Estimated amount of current consumption
Water charges	£3.85 (adjusted every 26 weeks)	Estimated costs
Council tax arrears	£3.85	Nil
Fines	Nil	£5 (lower amount £3.85)
Repayment of eligible loans	Nil	£3.85
Repayment of integration loans	Nil	£3.85
Child support maintenance	£8.40	£8.40
Repayment of tax credit overpayments and self-assessment tax debts	Nil	Maximum £11.55

More than one deduction

More than one deduction can be made from your **UC**. No more than three of the following deductions for third parties may be made from UC at any one time,[104] and you must be left with at least one pence of UC:[105]

- housing costs;
- rent arrears;
- fuel debts;
- water charges;

Part 8: Claiming benefits and getting paid
Chapter 51: Getting paid
9. Deductions and payments to third parties

- repayment of eligible loans;
- repayment of integration loans;
- council tax arrears;
- fines, costs and compensation orders.

The total amount payable for fuel debts and water charges combined cannot exceed an amount equal to 25 per cent of your standard allowance plus any child elements to which you are entitled (see Chapter 5) without your consent.[106]

In practice, the DWP does not usually deduct more than 25 per cent of your standard allowance (see p65).[107] This maximum applies to the total of most deductions from your UC, not just those for third parties. The total includes all those mentioned in the priority between deductions rules (see below), as well as those for sanctions (see Chapter 47), benefit offences (p1239) and to recover most overpayments of UC, JSA or ESA and advances of UC. If the total deductions would exceed 25 per cent of your standard allowance, then the deductions mentioned in the priority between deductions rules are reduced (using the priority rules – see below). However, deductions for ongoing costs (as opposed to arrears) of fuel or water charges are ignored when calculating the total. Deductions of more than the limit may still be made for housing costs, rent arrears or fuel debts, if the DWP considers it would be in your best interests.[108]

More than one third-party deduction can be made from your **IS, income-based JSA, income-related ESA and PC**. You must be left with at least 10 pence of benefit.[109] If you are also having an overpayment recovered from your benefit, having agreed to pay a penalty, admitted fraud or been found guilty of fraud (see p1228), the total amount of the deductions cannot exceed £30.80 a week.[110] Otherwise, if you are having an overpayment recovered from your benefit, the deductions for third parties described in this chapter should have priority – ie, they are applied first.[111]

Note: for IS, income-based JSA, income-related ESA and PC:
- deductions for the total of housing costs, rent arrears, fuel arrears, water arrears, council tax arrears, court fines and repayment of integration loans cannot exceed £11.55 a week;[112] *and*
- if the combined cost of deductions for arrears and current consumption for fuel, rent, water charges, housing costs arrears and repayment of integration loans is more than 25 per cent of a certain limit, the deductions cannot be made without your consent. If you (or your partner) do not get CTC, this limit is your total applicable amount (see p316) or, for PC, your minimum guarantee (see p259) before housing costs. If you (or your partner) get CTC, this limit is increased by the amount of child benefit and CTC paid to you.

Priority between deductions

For **UC**, an order of priority applies if your UC is 'insufficient' to meet all the deductions. Your award of UC is 'insufficient' if the total amount of deductions

would be more than 40 per cent of the standard allowance that applies to you (see p65). The following deductions are paid in the following order of priority:[113]
- housing costs;
- rent arrears (and related charges), if the amount of the deduction is 10 per cent of your standard allowance;
- fuel;
- council tax arrears;
- fines;
- water charges;
- repayment of social fund payments;
- recovery of hardship payments;
- penalties instead of prosecution for benefit offences;
- recovery of overpayments of benefits or tax credits caused by fraud;
- civil penalties;
- recovery of overpayments of benefits or tax credits not caused by fraud;
- repayment of integration loans;
- repayment of eligible loans;
- rent arrears (and related charges), if the amount of the deduction is more than 10 per cent of your standard allowance.

For IS, income-based JSA, income-related ESA and PC, if you have more debts or current charges than can be met from your benefit (see p1170), the following deductions are paid in the following order of priority:[114]
- housing costs;
- rent arrears (and related charges);
- fuel charges;
- water charges;
- council tax arrears;
- unpaid fines, costs and compensation orders;
- repayment of integration loans;
- repayment of eligible loans;
- repayment of tax credit overpayments and self-assessment tax debts.

Deductions for child support are always payable.

If you owe both gas and electricity arrears, the DWP chooses which one to pay first, depending on your circumstances.[115]

If you have been overpaid benefit or given a social fund loan, you may also have to repay these through deductions from your benefit.[116] Argue that these deductions should take a lower priority than the deductions set out above.

Part 8: Claiming benefits and getting paid
Chapter 51: Getting paid
10. Recovery of benefits from compensation payments

10. **Recovery of benefits from compensation payments**

If you are seeking compensation from someone (the 'defendant') through the courts (eg, because you have been unfairly dismissed or because you have had a personal injury), you might be awarded damages to compensate you for your loss. However if, as the result of a defendant's action, you have had to claim benefit, the amount of damages awarded is reduced by the amount of benefit you received.

Employment cases

In an employment case such as wrongful or unfair dismissal, your claim for compensation for loss of earnings may be reduced by the amount of benefit (eg, jobseeker's allowance (JSA)) you receive.[117] Get specialist employment law advice. Also, the DWP is able to recover payments of JSA, income support (IS) or income-related employment and support allowance (ESA) from your employer by deductions from your compensation if it is an unfair dismissal or protective award case dealt with in an employment tribunal. In such cases, the DWP sends a 'recoupment notice' to the employer, and a copy to you, setting out the benefit to be deducted before the compensation is paid to you. You may give notice to the DWP that you do not accept the amount recouped within 21 days of the recoupment notice (or longer if allowed), and can appeal to the First-tier Tribunal against the decision that the DWP makes in response.[118]

Personal injury cases

If you are paid compensation for an accident, injury or disease after 6 October 1997, those compensating you can reduce the amount paid to you when you have received benefit in respect of the same loss. They must then pay the money back to the Compensation Recovery Unit (CRU), which is part of the DWP. It does not matter whether the payment is voluntary, with or without legal proceedings, or by order of a court. A reduction is not made if the compensation is paid for pain and suffering, because benefits are not paid for this.

The CRU can only recover the benefit in the right-hand column of the table on p1175, and only if you were paid it as a consequence of the accident, injury or disease.

Note: the CRU can also recover, under a similar scheme with its own rules, certain lump-sum payments made by the DWP to you or a dependant.[119] The lump-sum payments that can be recovered are those made by the DWP for lung diseases under the Pneumoconiosis etc. (Workers' Compensation) Act 1979 (or as compensation if you have had a claim under that Act rejected) or payments under the Diffuse Mesothelioma Payment Scheme.

A guide to the procedures, *Recovery of Benefits and Lump Sum Payments and NHS Charges: technical guidance*, is available at gov.uk/government/collections/cru.

Which benefits can be recovered

All benefits paid to you 'in consequence' of the injury or disease from which you have suffered during the 'relevant period' are recoverable.

The relevant period

The **'relevant period'** is usually the period of five years from the day:[120]
- after the day of your accident or injury if you are claiming compensation for an accident or injury; *or*
- you first claimed a recoverable benefit because of the disease if you are claiming compensation in respect of a disease.

The relevant period ends if those compensating you make a final payment of compensation or an agreement is made under which compensation already paid is accepted as being in final payment.[121]

Before you are paid compensation, those compensating you must apply to the DWP for a 'certificate of recoverable benefits'.[122] This tells them which benefits are recoverable. Those compensating you become liable to pay the DWP for the total amount of recoverable benefit 14 days after the certificate is issued.[123] It is the compensator's obligation, not yours, and so if the compensator fails to pay, the CRU cannot pursue you for the money. The compensator remains liable even if it fails to apply for a certificate.[124]

Offsetting against your compensation

Before the compensator pays your compensation, it can deduct the recoverable benefits paid during the relevant period from certain types of compensation.[125]

Compensation	Recoverable benefits
Loss of earnings	Universal credit, disablement benefit, ESA, incapacity benefit, IS, invalidity allowance, invalidity pension, JSA, reduced earnings allowance, severe disablement allowance, sickness benefit, statutory sick pay (paid before 6 April 1994), unemployment benefit, unemployability supplement
Cost of care	Attendance allowance, disability living allowance (DLA) care component, disablement benefit paid for constant attendance (see p678) or exceptionally severe disablement (see p678), personal independence payment (PIP) daily living component
Loss of mobility	Mobility allowance, DLA mobility component, PIP mobility component

Part 8: Claiming benefits and getting paid
Chapter 51: Getting paid
10. Recovery of benefits from compensation payments

Example

Kenny receives a £30,000 compensation payment consisting of £15,000 for loss of earnings, £5,000 for pain and suffering, and £10,000 for the cost of care. By the time the award is made, he has received £20,000 of ESA and £5,000 of PIP daily living component. The award for loss of earnings is reduced to nil. Kenny receives the full award for pain and suffering, but his award for the cost of care is reduced by £5,000. The compensator is liable to pay the DWP recoverable benefits of £25,000, and pays Kenny a net award of £10,000 (£5,000 pain and suffering, plus £5,000 care).

Any compensation reduced by this method is treated as being paid to you. Those compensating you must give you a statement showing how the payment has been calculated, even if the recovery of benefits reduces a particular type of compensation to nil. If the recoverable benefit exceeds the compensation paid to you for a particular loss, those compensating you still have to pay the balance to the DWP.

Exempt payments

The recovery rules apply to all claims, no matter how small. However, certain compensation payments are exempt.[126] These include:
- contractual sick pay and redundancy payments;
- payments under the Fatal Accidents Act 1996, the Vaccine Damage Payments Act 1979 and the NHS industrial injury scheme;
- payments under the Pneumoconiosis Compensation Scheme and certain payments for loss of hearing;
- criminal injuries compensation and certain disaster/emergency relief funds – eg, the London Bombings Relief Charitable Fund;
- payments from insurance companies from policies agreed before the accident;
- payments from certain trusts – eg, an approved scheme regarding infected blood such as the Macfarlane Trust or Eileen Trust and the Thalidomide Trust.

Challenging a recovery decision

A decision maker may look at a certificate of recoverable benefit again (this is called a review) if s/he is satisfied that there was an error in its preparation, or that it recovers too much benefit, or that the person who applied for the certificate supplied incorrect or insufficient information, as a result of which the amount of benefit recovered is less than it should be.[127] You and those compensating you can both appeal to the First-tier Tribunal (see Chapter 57) against the certificate, but not until the compensation payment has been made and the benefit paid back to the DWP.[128] Also, the person appealing must apply for a review before s/he can appeal. It is best to apply for a review as soon as possible, but there is no absolute time limit.[129] Further appeals can be made to the Upper Tribunal in the usual way (see Chapter 58).[130]

Notes

1. Who is paid
1 **UC/PIP/JSA&ESA under UC** Regs 57 and 58 UC,PIP,JSA&ESA(C&P) Regs
   HB Reg 94(2) HB Regs; reg 75(2) HB(SPC) Regs
   CB/GA Regs 27 and 28 CB&GA(Admin) Regs
   Other benefits Regs 30 and 33 SS(C&P) Regs
2 **UC/PIP/JSA&ESA under UC** Reg 58 UC,PIP,JSA&ESA(C&P) Regs
   CB/GA Reg 34 CB&GA(Admin) Regs
   Other benefits Reg 34(1) and (2) SS(C&P) Regs
3 **UC/PIP/JSA&ESA under UC** Reg 60 UC,PIP,JSA&ESA(C&P) Regs
   Other benefits Reg 35 SS(C&P) Regs

2. How and when you are paid
4 Reg 21ZA SS(C&P) Regs; regs 47(6A), 48, 51 and 52 UC,PIP,JSA&ESA(C&P) Regs
5 DWP, *Touchbase*, 19 February 2021
6 **UC/PIP/JSA&ESA under UC** Reg 46 UC,PIP,JSA&ESA(C&P) Regs
   CB/GA Reg 16 CB&GA(Admin) Regs
   Other benefits Reg 21 SS(C&P) Regs
7 **UC/PIP/JSA&ESA under UC** Reg 51 UC,PIP,JSA&ESA(C&P) Regs
   CB/GA Regs 16-20 CB&GA(Admin) Regs
   Other benefits Regs 22-26C SS(C&P) Regs
8 **UC/PIP/JSA&ESA under UC** Reg 45 UC,PIP,JSA&ESA(C&P) Regs
   HB Reg 91 HB Regs; reg 72 HB(SPC) Regs
   CB/GA Reg 18 CB&GA(Admin) Regs
   Other benefits Reg 20 SS(C&P) Regs
9 **UC/PIP/JSA&ESA under UC** Reg 55 UC,PIP,JSA&ESA(C&P) Regs
   CB/GA Reg 25 CB&GA(Admin) Regs
   Other benefits Reg 38(1)(bb) SS(C&P) Regs
   All CDLA/2609/2002 commented on the way a similar rule applied to payment by giro/order book

3. Overlapping benefits
10 Reg 6 SS(OB) Regs; for ADP, reg 34(4) DAWAP(S) Regs
11 Reg 4(5) SS(OB) Regs
12 s43(1) SSCBA 1992; s1 PA 2014; reg 4(5) SS(OB) Regs
13 ss51A and 52(2) SSCBA 1992
14 s16(1), (2) and (6) SSCBA 1992; reg 2 SS(MAP) Regs
15 Reg 4(2)(f) and (4) SS(OB) Regs
16 Reg 4(4A) SS(OB) Regs
17 Reg 4(3) SS(OB) Regs
18 Reg 10 SS(OB) Regs
19 Reg 8 SS(OB) Regs
20 Reg 7 SS(OB) Regs

4. Advance payments
21 Regs 5 and 6 SS(PAB) Regs
22 Reg 7 SS(PAB) Regs
23 Reg 17 UC(TP) Regs does not refer to 'financial need' in this situation.
24 **UC/PIP/JSA&ESA under UC** Sch 3 para 14 UC,PIP,JSA&ESA(DA) Regs
    Other benefits Sch 2 para 20A SS&CS(DA) Regs
25 Reg 8 SS(PAB) Regs
26 Advances under the UC system are recovered under regs 3, 10 and 11 SS(OR) Regs, and there is no right of appeal about recovery under those rules. For other advances, Sch 2 para 20A SS&CS(DA) Regs allows a right of appeal against decisions on deductions under reg 10 SS(PAB) Regs.
27 Arguably, recovery of UC advances are subject to the rates in reg 11 SS(OR) Regs.
28 Advances under the UC system are recovered under regs 3, 10 and 11 SS(OR) Regs, and there is no right of appeal about recovery under those rules.
29 Reg 3, definition of 'benefit', SS(PAB) Regs

5. The benefit cap
30 ss96 and 97 WRA 2012
31 Reg 75(1)(g) HB Regs

32 Under Sch 2 para 8A SSA 1998 there is no right of appeal for UC, but at the time of writing the relevant rule for HB appeals at Sch 7 para 6 CSPSSA 2000 had not been amended.
33 Reg 82(1) UC Regs
34 Reg 82(2) UC Regs
35 Reg 75E HB Regs; HB Circular A15/2013
36 Reg 75E(3) HB Regs
37 Reg 75E(4) HB Regs
38 Reg 75F HB Regs; reg 83 UC Regs
39 Reg 75C HB Regs; reg 80 UC Regs
40 s96(5A) WRA 2012; reg 79 UC Regs
41 s96(5A) WRA 2012; regs 75A, 75C and 75G HB Regs
42 Reg 75B HB Regs
43 Reg 81 UC Regs
44 Reg 75D HB Regs

6. Change of circumstances after you claim
45 **UC/PIP/JSA&ESA under UC** Reg 38 UC,PIP,JSA&ESA(C&P) Regs
   JSA Reg 24 JSA Regs
   CB/GA Reg 23 CB&GA(Admin) Regs
   Other benefits Reg 32 SS(C&P) Regs
46 **UC/PIP/JSA&ESA under UC** Reg 38(5) UC,PIP,JSA&ESA(C&P) Regs
   JSA Reg 24(7) JSA Regs
   JSA and other benefits Regs 2, 3 and 5 SS(NCC) Regs, which apply for fraud, allow notification by telephone (unless it is specifically required to be in writing).
   Other benefits Reg 32(1B) SS(C&P) Regs
47 Reg 23(5) CB&GA(Admin) Regs
48 **UC/PIP/JSA&ESA under UC** Reg 39 UC,PIP,JSA&ESA(C&P) Regs
   JSA Reg 24 JSA Regs
   Other benefits Reg 32ZZA SS(C&P) Regs

7. When payments can be suspended
49 **UC/PIP/JSA&ESA under UC** Reg 44(2)(b) and (c) UC,PIP,JSA&ESA(DA) Regs
   HB Reg 11(2)(b) HB&CTB(DA) Regs
   CB/GA Sch 7 para 13(2) CSPSSA 2000
   Other benefits s21(2)(c) and (d) SSA 1998; reg 16(3)(b) SS&CS(DA) Regs
50 **UC/PIP/JSA&ESA under UC** Reg 44(5) UC,PIP,JSA&ESA(DA) Regs
   HB Reg 11(3) HB&CTB(DA) Regs
   CB/GA Reg 18(4) and (5) CB&GA(DA) Regs
   Other benefits Reg 16(4) SS&CS(DA) Regs

51 **UC/PIP/JSA&ESA under UC** Reg 46(c) UC,PIP,JSA&ESA(DA) Regs
   HB Reg 12(1)(b) HB&CTB(DA) Regs
   CB/GA Reg 21 CB&GA(DA) Regs
   Other benefits Reg 20(2) and (3) SS&CS(DA) Regs
52 **UC/PIP/JSA&ESA under UC** Reg 38(2) UC,PIP,JSA&ESA(C&P) Regs; reg 45 UC,PIP,JSA&ESA(DA) Regs
   HB Reg 86(1) HB Regs; reg 67(1) HB(SPC) Regs
   CB/GA Reg 23 CB&GA(Admin) Regs
   Other benefits Reg 32(1) SS(C&P) Regs
53 **UC/PIP/JSA&ESA under UC** Reg 45(6) UC,PIP,JSA&ESA(DA) Regs
   HB Reg 13 HB&CTB(DA) Regs
   CB/GA Reg 19 CB&GA(DA) Regs
   Other benefits Reg 17(2) SS&CS(DA) Regs
54 **UC/PIP/JSA&ESA under UC** Reg 45(4)(a) UC,PIP,JSA&ESA(DA) Regs
   HB Reg 13(4)(a) HB&CTB(DA) Regs
   CB/GA Reg 19(2) CB&GA(DA) Regs
   Other benefits Reg 17(4)(a) SS&CS(DA) Regs
55 **UC/PIP/JSA&ESA under UC** Reg 45(4)(b) UC,PIP,JSA&ESA(DA) Regs
   HB Reg 13(4)(b) HB&CTB(DA) Regs
   CB/GA Reg 19(2)(b) CB&GA(DA) Regs
   Other benefits Reg 17(4)(b) SS&CS(DA) Regs
56 **UC/PIP/JSA&ESA under UC** Reg 45(6) UC,PIP,JSA&ESA(DA) Regs
   HB Reg 13(4) HB&CTB(DA) Regs
   CB/GA Reg 19(5) CB&GA(DA) Regs
   Other benefits Reg 17(5) SS&CS(DA) Regs
57 s24 SSA 1998; reg 19(2) SS&CS(DA) Regs
58 **HB** Sch 7 para 13(2)(a) CSPSSA 2000
   CB/GA Reg 18(2) CB&GA(DA) Regs
   Other benefits ss21(2)(a) and (b), 22 and 24 SSA 1998
59 **UC/PIP/JSA&ESA under UC** Reg 44(2)(a)(i) and (iii) UC,PIP,JSA&ESA(DA) Regs
   HB Reg 11(2)(a)(i) and (c) HB&CTB(DA) Regs
   CB/GA Reg 18(2)(a) and (c) CB&GA(DA) Regs
   Other benefits Reg 16(3)(a)(i) and (iii) SS&CS(DA) Regs
60 Reg 16(2) SS&CS(DA) Regs; reg 44(2) UC,PIP,JSA&ESA(C&P) Regs does not include this provision.

8

107 The legal limit is actually 40 per cent.
Sch 6 para 4 UC,PIP,JSA&ESA(C&P)
Regs; 'Universal credit: debt and
deductions that can be taken from
payment', DWP guidance, at gov.uk/
guidance/universal-credit-debt-and-
deductions-that-can-be-taken-from-
payments; HM Treasury, *Budget 2021*, 3
March 2021

108 Sch 6 para 4 UC,PIP,JSA&ESA(C&P)
Regs

109 Sch 9 para 2(2) SS(C&P) Regs

110 Reg 16(5ZA) SS(PAOR) Regs

111 Reg 16(5ZB) SS(PAOR) Regs

112 Sch 9 para 8(1) SS(C&P) Regs

113 Sch 6 para 5 UC,PIP,JSA&ESA(C&P)
Regs

114 Sch 9 para 9 SS(C&P) Regs

115 Reg 4 CC(DIS) Regs; reg 8 CT(DIS) Regs

116 Regs 15 and 16 SS(PAOR) Regs; reg 3
SF(RDB) Regs

10. Recovery of benefits from compensation payments

117 *Nabi v British Leyland (UK) Ltd* [1980] 1
WLR 529 (CA)

118 The Employment Protection
(Recoupment of Jobseeker's Allowance
and Income Support) Regulations 1996
No.2349

119 The Social Security (Recovery of
Benefits) (Lump Sum Payments)
Regulations 2008 No.1596

120 s3 SS(RB)A 1997

121 s3(4) SS(RB)A 1997

122 s4 SS(RB)A 1997

123 s6(4) SS(RB)A 1997

124 s7 SS(RB)A 1997

125 s8 and Sch 2 SS(RB)A 1997

126 s1 and Sch 1 SS(RB)A 1997; reg 2 SS(RB)
Regs

127 s10 SS(RB)A 1997; reg 9 SS&CS(DA)
Regs

128 ss11 and 12 SS(RB)A 1997

129 s11(2A) SS(RB)A 1997; reg 9ZB
SS&CS(DA) Regs. Neither provide a
time limit for review. See the official
guidance at gov.uk/government/
publications/repaying-compensation-
to-dwp-what-to-do-if-you-think-our-
decision-is-wrong.

130 s13 SS(RB)A 1997; reg 13 SS(RB)App
Regs

Chapter 52

· ·

Hardship payments

This chapter covers:
1. Hardship payments of universal credit (below)
2. Hardship payments of jobseeker's allowance (p1184)
3. Hardship payments of employment and support allowance (p1187)
4. Deciding hardship (p1187)
5. Applying for hardship payments (p1190)
6. Getting paid (p1191)
7. Challenging a hardship payment decision (p1191)
8. Tax, other benefits and the benefit cap (p1191)

Key facts
- Hardship payments are reduced-rate payments of universal credit (UC), jobseeker's allowance (JSA) and employment and support allowance (ESA) that are made in limited circumstances, including if you have been sanctioned.
- To get them, you or your partner or children must be experiencing hardship. For JSA, you might need to be in a 'vulnerable group'.
- You must apply for hardship payments and to keep getting them, you may need to demonstrate on a regular basis that you are experiencing hardship.
- You must usually pay back hardship payments of UC. You do not have to pay back hardship payments of JSA or ESA.

---

1. Hardship payments of universal credit

You may be able to get hardship payments of universal credit (UC) if your UC is being paid at a reduced or nil rate because you have been given a sanction or because you have committed a benefit offence. You must usually pay back hardship payments of UC (see p1184). Hardship payments of UC are not made automatically. You must apply for them (see p1190).

Note: if your 'new-style' contribution-based jobseeker's allowance (JSA) or contributory employment and support allowance (ESA) is paid at a reduced or nil rate and you experience hardship, you may qualify for hardship payments of UC.[1]

Part 8: Claiming benefits and getting paid
Chapter 52: Hardship payments
1. Hardship payments of universal credit

When you can get hardship payments

Universal credit reduced because of a sanction

You can get hardship payments of UC if:[2]

- you are 18 or over and are given a sanction (or your partner is 18 or over and has been given a sanction); *and*
- as a result, your UC has been paid at a reduced or nil rate using the 'high rate' daily reduction (see p1068); *and*
- you (or your partner) apply for hardship payments in the approved manner, or in a way that the DWP accepts is sufficient, and provide any information or evidence required by the DWP; *and*
- you (and your partner) accept that the hardship payments are recoverable; *and*
- the DWP is satisfied that you (and your partner) have met all the work-related requirements that were in force in the seven days before you applied for hardship payments; *and*
- the DWP is satisfied that you (and your partner) are experiencing hardship (see p1188); *and*
- for low level sanctions only, you (or your partner, or both of you if both of you have been given a sanction) have complied with any condition specified by the DWP – eg, you have now taken part in a work-focused interview or have agreed to attend training.

Universal credit reduced because of a benefit offence

If your UC has been reduced because of a benefit offence (see p1239), you can qualify for hardship payments of UC if:[3]

- you (and your partner) meet all the conditions of entitlement to UC; *and*
- you (and your partner) apply for hardship payments in the approved manner, or in a way that the DWP accepts is sufficient, and provide any information or evidence required by the DWP; *and*
- you (and your partner) accept that the hardship payments are recoverable; *and*
- the DWP is satisfied that you (and your partner) are experiencing hardship (see p1188).

Note: you can qualify under the benefit offences rules even if you (or your partner) are aged 16 or 17.

Hardship payment periods

Each hardship payment is paid at a daily rate for a period described as the 'hardship period'. This starts on the date you satisfy all the conditions for getting a hardship payment, including having made an application. This date can be no earlier than the normal payday for the first assessment period in respect of which you are paid reduced UC.[4] Backdating is not available.

The hardship payment normally ends the day before your next normal UC payday, but if this would make the hardship period less than eight days long, it ends on the payday for the following assessment period or, if sooner, the last day in respect of which your UC is paid at a reduced or nil rate.[5]

How do you ensure you get maximum hardship payments?

You must apply for hardship payments of UC for each assessment period in which you need one. To ensure you get the maximum amount, make your first application on the first payday when you receive a reduced amount of UC, and submit a new application every payday until your UC is no longer being reduced. Apply on your 'normal' payday even if your UC is actually paid on a different day. Remember that backdating is not available.

The amount of hardship payments

The amount of hardship payments is worked out as follows.[6]

- **Step one:** determine the amount of the reduction made from your UC for the sanction (see p1068) or the benefit offence (see p1240) in the assessment period before the one in which you apply for hardship payments. Note that the reduction takes effect from the first day of the assessment period in which the sanction or benefit offence decision was made (see p1077).
- **Step two:** multiply the amount in Step one by 12 and divide by 365. Take 60 per cent of this amount, rounding to the nearest penny.
- **Step three:** multiply the amount in Step two by the number of days for which hardship payments can be made to you .

Example

Calvin is a single claimant aged 40. His normal UC payday is the 3rd of the month. He was given a 91-day medium level sanction on 17 September, in a 30-day assessment period. When his UC starts to be paid at a reduced rate, he applies and qualifies for a hardship payment on 7 October. He therefore gets a hardship payment for the period starting on 7 October and ending on 2 November (27 days).

Step one: the relevant amount is £330 (£11 daily reduction x 30 days).

Step two: £330 x 12 ÷ 365 x 60% = £6.51

Step three: Calvin can be paid hardship payments for 27 days.

£6.51 x 27 days = £175.76

Calvin's hardship payment for that assessment period is £175.76. He gets this in addition to any UC he can be paid – eg, if he qualifies for a housing costs element.

If still experiencing hardship, Calvin should apply for another hardship payment on the day he gets his next payment of UC (ie, 3 November) to maximise his hardship payments.

Part 8: Claiming benefits and getting paid
Chapter 52: Hardship payments
2. Hardship payments of jobseeker's allowance

Recovery of hardship payments

You must usually pay back hardship payments of UC.[7] However:

- the DWP *has a discretion not to recover* all or part of a hardship payment.[8] This is not affected by the fact that, at the application stage, you were required to accept that the payment was recoverable. You can ask the DWP not to recover your hardship payment – eg, if this would cause you to be in hardship again. Advice about the DWP's discretion not to recover hardship payments is similar to that which applies regarding recovery of overpayments (see p1208); *and*
- hardship payments are *not* recoverable during any assessment period in which you have sufficient monthly earnings (see below); *and*
- hardship payments *stop* being recoverable (ie, are 'written off') if, since the last day on which your UC was paid at a reduced or nil rate, you have had sufficient monthly earnings (combined earnings, if you are a joint claimant) for a single period of, or periods that total, six months.[9]

You are classed as having sufficient monthly earnings if you (or, if you are a joint claimant, you and your partner) do not have to meet any work-related requirements:

- because your earnings (your combined earnings if you are a joint claimant) are the same as, or above, your earnings threshold (see p1043); *or*
- for any of the other reasons listed on p1039 and p1044 (other situations).
  In this case, your monthly earnings (your combined monthly earnings if you are a joint claimant) must be at least 16 times the minimum hourly wage for a person of your age (or your partner's age if s/he is younger than you) multiplied by 52 and divided by 12.[10]

Hardship payments can normally only be recovered from the person to whom they were paid. However, if you are a joint claimant, an amount paid to your partner can be treated as paid to you, and vice versa.[11]

All the methods used to recover overpayments described on p1209 can be used to recover hardship payments.[12] Recovery rates for hardship payments from ongoing UC are the same as for the recovery of overpayments of UC (see p1210). These are the maximum rates of recovery, which can be reduced if you can show that you cannot afford them.

2. Hardship payments of jobseeker's allowance

If you currently receive **income-based** jobseeker's allowance (JSA) and it is being paid at a reduced or nil rate or has been suspended, you may be able to get hardship payments of JSA. You do not have to pay them back.[13] Hardship payments of JSA are not made automatically. You must apply for them (see p1190). If you receive **'new-style' contribution-based** JSA, see p1181.

When you can get hardship payments

You can qualify for hardship payments of income-based JSA:
- if it is not clear that you satisfy the jobseeking conditions (see below); *or*
- if you do not satisfy the jobseeking conditions and you are in a vulnerable group (see below); *or*
- if your JSA has been reduced because of a sanction (see p1186); *or*
- in some cases, if you have committed a benefit offence (see p1186).

You cannot qualify for hardship payments if you (or your partner) are in one of the specific groups of people who can claim income support (see p233) – eg, a lone parent with a child under five.[14] **Note:** if you are unable to claim hardship payments because you are in one of these specific groups, you may be able to claim UC instead. However, if you claim UC, you cannot return to JSA once the sanction period ends.

If, after getting hardship payments, you are awarded full income-based JSA for the same period, it is reduced by the amount of the hardship payments you received.[15]

If it is not clear whether you satisfy the jobseeking conditions

If your JSA is suspended because there is doubt about whether you (or if you are a member of a joint-claim couple, you or your partner) satisfy the 'jobseeking conditions' (see p1092), you can get hardship payments until the DWP makes a decision, provided you satisfy the other conditions for getting income-based JSA.[16] If you are a member of a joint-claim couple, both of you must satisfy these conditions (or one of you, if the other is in an exempt group). The rules are different if you are in a vulnerable group (see below).

You cannot start getting hardship payments until the 15th day of the suspension.[17] If you are subject to successive 14-day suspensions (eg, at each signing-on day, your work coach doubts that you have taken sufficient steps to find work) and so never reach the 15th day of any suspension period, get advice, as this might be unlawful.

If you do not satisfy the jobseeking conditions and you are in a vulnerable group

You might qualify for hardship payments if the DWP decides that you (or if you are a member of a joint-claim couple, you or your partner) do not satisfy the jobseeking conditions and you are (or s/he is) in a 'vulnerable group' (see p1189). However, you cannot qualify if you (or, if you are a joint-claim couple, either of you) are treated as unavailable for work for one of the reasons listed on p1097.[18]

Your hardship payments start from whichever is latest:[19]
- the date the DWP decides you are in a vulnerable group; *or*

Part 8: Claiming benefits and getting paid
Chapter 52: Hardship payments
2. Hardship payments of jobseeker's allowance

- if your JSA is suspended, the date that the suspension begins; *or*
- the date the DWP decides that you do not satisfy the 'jobseeking conditions'. You (or if you are a member of a joint-claim couple, both of you) must continue to satisfy the other conditions for getting income-based JSA.

Jobseeker's allowance is reduced because of a sanction

If you are given a sanction (see p1116), you can qualify for hardship payments.[20]

If you are in a vulnerable group (see p1189), you get hardship payments from the first day of the period when JSA is not paid.

If you are not in a vulnerable group, you cannot get hardship payments until the 15th day of the period. The DWP says that if during a sanction period another sanction is imposed for a different reason, you cannot get hardship payments for the first 14 days of the period of the new sanction.[21] If this happens, you should appeal and argue this is wrong.

Hardship payments continue until the end of the sanction period, provided you satisfy the other conditions for getting income-based JSA. If you are a member of a joint-claim couple, both of you must satisfy these conditions unless one of you is exempt.

Jobseeker's allowance is reduced because of a benefit offence

If you have committed a benefit offence, your benefit may be paid at a reduced rate (see p1239). If you are not entitled to a reduced payment of benefit, you may be able to get a hardship payment. If you are in a vulnerable group (see p1189), you get hardship payments from the first day of the period when JSA is not paid. **Note:** this does not apply if the only reason you would be considered 'vulnerable' is because you or your partner are homeless or because your (or your partner's) functional capacity is limited by a 'mental illness without physical impairment'.[22] If you are not in a vulnerable group, you cannot get hardship payments until the 15th day of the period. Hardship payments continue until the end of the reduction period, provided you satisfy the other conditions for getting income-based JSA. If you are a member of a joint-claim couple, both of you must satisfy these conditions unless one of you is exempt.

The amount of hardship payments

To calculate your weekly amount of hardship payment, your personal allowance, premiums and housing costs are added together as for income-based JSA. The usual disregards for capital and income are applied to give your 'applicable amount'. Your hardship payment will normally be your applicable amount minus:[23]

- 40 per cent of the personal allowance for a single person of your age, if you are single; *or*
- 40 per cent of the personal allowance for a single person aged 25 or over, if you are a member of a couple.

The reduction is only 20 per cent if you or your partner, or a child included in your claim (see p307), are pregnant or 'seriously ill' (not defined). In all cases, the reduction is rounded to the nearest five pence.

3. Hardship payments of employment and support allowance

You may be able to get hardship payments of **income-related** employment and support allowance (ESA) if you are already getting income-related ESA and it is being paid at a reduced or nil rate because you have been given a sanction or because you have committed a benefit offence.[24] The DWP must be satisfied that you will suffer hardship as a result.[25] You must satisfy the rules for entitlement to income-related ESA (see Chapter 9). The weekly amount of hardship payments is a percentage of the personal allowance for main-phase ESA.[26] You do not have to pay these hardship payments back. Hardship payments of ESA are not made automatically. You must apply for them (see p1190).

For more detail about the rules for hardship payments of income-related ESA, see the 2021/22 edition of this *Handbook*.

Note: different hardship rules apply if you could be disqualified from getting ESA (eg, because you have limited capability for work through your own misconduct, or you have failed to accept treatment without 'good cause'), but you are experiencing hardship (see p633).

Note: if you receive '**new-style' contributory** ESA, see p1181.

4. Deciding hardship

When you apply for hardship payments, explain anything that is causing you hardship, or which makes it more likely that you will experience hardship. This includes health, disability, pregnancy and any needs you, your partner and children have.

Hardship

'**Hardship**' is not defined in the rules. For jobseeker's allowance (JSA) and employment and support allowance (ESA), the DWP says that it means 'severe suffering' or 'a lack of the necessities of life'.[27] For universal credit (UC), hardship should be decided by looking at whether you can cover your immediate, basic and essential needs for accommodation, heating, food and hygiene.[28]

When deciding whether or not you are experiencing hardship, the DWP must consider certain things. For UC, see below; for JSA, see p1189; and for ESA, see p1190. If your claim is refused, consider applying for a revision or appealing (see Chapters 56 and 57).

In all cases, the DWP looks at the resources available to you.

- The DWP normally takes into account income and capital that is disregarded when calculating your benefit – eg, personal independence payment (PIP), disability living allowance (DLA) and savings below £6,000.
- You should only be treated as having resources that are likely to be actually available to you. For example, if you have savings in a bank account but they are subject to a notice period for withdrawal, you should not be treated as having this capital until you can access it. You may be expected to ask your family for help, and investigate sources of free help, but you are not expected to rely on charity.
- You should not be treated as having resources if these are only available on credit, or you would have to sell any of your possessions.

Universal credit

The DWP only considers you to be in hardship if both the following apply.[29]

- Because your UC has been reduced as a result of a sanction using the 'high rate' daily reduction (see p1068) or because you have committed a benefit offence (see p1240), you (and your partner) cannot meet your immediate and most basic and essential needs, or those of a child or qualifying young person for whom you (or your partner) are responsible (see p309). '**Needs**' means needs for accommodation, heating, food and hygiene – eg, products to keep you and your home clean, or nappies for your baby. In considering whether you can meet these needs, the DWP will consider the other resources available to you not including child benefit.[30]
- You (and your partner) have made every effort to get alternative sources of financial support (eg, from your family) and to stop incurring any expenditure not related to your basic and essential needs. The DWP says that this does not mean that you must stop spending money on things you need to help you look for work, such as a telephone and internet access, or things you need to maintain your child(ren)'s access to education.[31] The DWP must consider what is reasonable in your case, but you should not be required to sell or pawn anything (other than stocks and shares), find cheaper accommodation, take out credit or incur certain financial penalties – eg, for cancelling a gym membership.[32] The DWP should not force you to request or accept help from charities if you choose not to do so, but may expect you to investigate and consider what help might be available.[33]

The DWP recognises some people as being more likely to suffer hardship – eg, parents, carers and people who are seriously ill.[34]

Jobseeker's allowance

For JSA, you cannot get hardship payments unless the DWP is satisfied that you are in a 'vulnerable group' or that you or your partner would experience hardship if payments were not made.[35] In some situations, you can only get hardship payments if you are in a vulnerable group (see p1185).

When deciding whether or not you would experience hardship, the DWP must consider the following.[36]

- Whether you or your partner, or a child included in your claim (see p307), qualify for a disability premium or the disabled child element (lower or higher rate) of child tax credit (CTC).
- The resources likely to be available to you or your partner, or a child included in your claim, if no hardship payments are made, how far these fall short of your reduced applicable amount (see p1186) and the length of time this is likely to be the case. Also included are any resources that may be available from others in your household. CTC and child benefit cannot be taken into account.[37] See p1188 for what resources might be taken into account.
- Whether there is a 'substantial risk' that you, your partner or a child included in your claim would be without essential items (including food, clothes, heating and accommodation) or whether they would be available at considerably reduced levels and, if so, for how long.

Vulnerable groups

You are in a vulnerable group if any of the following apply.[38]

- You or your partner are **pregnant** and would experience hardship if no payment were made.
- You or your partner are **responsible for a child** who would experience hardship if no payment were made. See p309 for when you count as responsible for a child. **Note:** if you are a lone parent and are responsible for a child under five, you cannot claim hardship payments (see p1185).
- Your income-based JSA includes a **disability premium** for you or your partner, or would include one if your claim were to succeed, and the person for whom the premium is paid would experience hardship if no payment were made.
- You or your partner have a **chronic medical condition** and as a result your (or your partner's) functional capacity is 'limited or restricted by physical or mental impairment', and the DWP is satisfied that:
  – it has lasted or is likely to last for at least 26 weeks; *and*
  – if no payment were made, the health of the person with the condition would decline further than that of a 'normal healthy adult' within the next two weeks and the person would experience hardship.
- You or your partner:
  – are, for a considerable portion of the week, **caring for someone** who:

Part 8: Claiming benefits and getting paid
Chapter 52: Hardship payments
5. Applying for hardship payments

- is getting attendance allowance (AA), the highest or middle rate of the care component of DLA or child disability payment (CDP), either rate of the daily living component of PIP or adult disability payment (ADP), or armed forces independence payment. If the person has claimed one of these benefits, you count as being in a vulnerable group for up to 26 weeks from the date of the claim or until the claim is decided, whichever is first; *or*

- has been awarded AA, the highest or middle rate of DLA/CDP care component, the daily living component of PIP/ADP or armed forces independence payment but it is not yet in payment; *and*

- would not be able to continue caring if no hardship payment were made. You do not have to show that the person you are caring for would experience hardship.

This rule does not apply if the person who is being cared for lives in a care home, an Abbeyfield home or an independent hospital.[39]

- You (or if you are a joint-claim couple, at least one of you) are under 21 at the date of your hardship statement (see below) and within the last three years were **being looked after by the local authority** (see p933), were someone the local authority had a duty to keep in touch with, or you qualified for advice and assistance from the local authority.[40] **Note:** the law does not cover local authorities in Scotland, but in practice it is the DWP's intention that this rule does cover you in Scotland.

- You or your partner are **homeless.**

Employment and support allowance

See p1187. For more detail about the rules on deciding hardship for ESA, see the 2021/22 edition of this *Handbook*.

---

5. Applying for hardship payments

Hardship payments are not made automatically. You must apply for them in the approved manner, or in such other form as the DWP accepts is sufficient. Check with the Jobcentre Plus office, the universal credit (UC) helpline or post an enquiry in your online journal about how you should apply. You must provide information and evidence if the DWP says it is required.[41] For jobseeker's allowance (JSA), the DWP requires a written declaration called a 'hardship statement'.

Although you cannot get JSA or employment and support allowance (ESA) hardship payments until you have made your application, there is no general rule to prevent you from getting these backdated. You cannot get a UC hardship payment backdated (see p1182).

Note:
- For UC, you must make a fresh application for hardship payments in each assessment period. See p1182 for when you can apply and how to ensure maximum payments.
- For JSA, while you are getting hardship payments, you (or if you are a joint-claim couple, one of you) must normally make a 'hardship declaration' at the Jobcentre Plus office each time you sign on to confirm that you are still in hardship.[42]

6. Getting paid

The general rules on getting paid are covered in Chapter 51. Hardship payments of universal credit should be made as quickly as possible, once the application has been allowed. Where practical, this should be on the day the application is accepted.[43] Hardship payments of jobseeker's allowance (JSA) and employment and support allowance (ESA) are made on the day that your JSA or ESA would normally be paid.

7. Challenging a hardship payment decision

If you are refused hardship payments, you can appeal to the First-tier Tribunal (see Chapter 57). You must apply for a mandatory reconsideration first. Ask for a written statement of reasons for the decision if this has not already been provided (see p1256).

Remember to tell the DWP if your circumstances worsen while you are applying for a reconsideration or appealing. Ask it to consider whether hardship payments can now be paid based on your new circumstances.

If you are unhappy with a decision about the recovery of a universal credit hardship payment, see p1184.

8. Tax, other benefits and the benefit cap

Tax

Hardship payments of jobseeker's allowance (JSA) are taxable in the same way as income-based JSA (see p253). Hardship payments of universal credit (UC) and employment and support allowance (ESA) are not taxable.

The benefit cap

In some cases, there is a limit on the total amount of specified benefits you can receive (a 'benefit cap'). Hardship payments of UC, JSA and ESA count towards this total amount, although in JSA and ESA cases the benefit cap only applies if you are getting housing benefit (HB). See p1156 for further information.

Passported benefits

Hardship payments are a type of UC, income-based JSA and income-related ESA and so you are still entitled to passported benefits, such as help with health costs, in the usual way.

Whether or not you are getting hardship payments, payment of your HB should not be affected if you have been given a sanction. If it is, contact the local authority immediately. You may also be entitled to a council tax reduction from your local authority (see p836).

Notes

1. Hardship payments of universal credit
1 Reg 112 and Sch 11 UC Regs
2 s28 WRA 2012; reg 116(1) UC Regs
3 Regs 16D(1) and (2)(a) and 16E(a)-(c) SS(LB) Regs
4 Regs 117(1)(a) and 118 UC Regs; regs 16F(a)(i) and 16G SS(LB) Regs; paras L1142 and L1146 ADM
5 Reg 117(1)(b) and (2) UC Regs; reg 16F(a)(ii) and (b) SS(LB) Regs
6 Regs 6 and 118 UC Regs; reg 16G SS(LB) Regs
7 s71ZH(1)(a) and (e) SSAA 1992; s28(2)(f) WRA 2012; reg 119 UC Regs; reg 16H SS(LB) Regs
8 s71ZH(1)(a) SSAA 1992; DWP, *Benefit Overpayment Recovery Guide*, paras 5.83 and 8.1
9 Reg 119 UC Regs
10 Reg 119(2)(c) UC Regs
11 s71ZH(4) SSAA 1992
12 s71ZH(5) SSAA 1992

2. Hardship payments of jobseeker's allowance
13 s71ZH(1)(b)-(d) SSAA 1992; s19C(2)(f) JSA 1995 came into force on 19 June 2017, but there are currently no regulations providing for the recovery of JSA hardship payments
14 Regs 140(3) and 146A(3) JSA Regs
15 Regs 146 and 146H JSA Regs; reg 5(2) Cases 1 and 2 SS(PAOR) Regs
16 Regs 141(5), 142(3), 146C(5) and 146D(3) JSA Regs
17 Regs 141(3), 142(2) and (4), 146C(3), and 146D(2) and (4) JSA Regs
18 Regs 141(4) and 146C(4) JSA Regs
19 Regs 141 and 146C JSA Regs
20 Regs 141(6), 142(5), 146C(6) and 146D(5) JSA Regs
21 Vol 6 Ch 35, para 35304 DMG
22 Regs 5-16 SS(LB) Regs
23 Regs 145 and 146G JSA Regs

8

Chapter 53

Overpayments

This chapter covers:
1. Introduction (below)
2. Overpayments that are always recoverable (p1196)
3. Overpayments that are sometimes recoverable (p1199)
4. Recovery of overpaid benefit (p1208)
5. Overpayments of housing benefit (p1214)

For overpayments of tax credits, see Chapter 65. For overpayments of Scottish benefits, see Chapter 79.

References in this chapter to HM Revenue and Customs apply to overpayments of child benefit and guardian's allowance.

Key facts

- If you are paid more benefit than you are entitled to, this is called an overpayment.
- If you are overpaid benefit under the universal credit system, you can always be required to repay it, regardless of how it was caused.
- In other situations, except for housing benefit (HB), the general rule is that you must repay the overpayment if it arose because you did not disclose something or you misrepresented something, regardless of whether this was your fault.
- All overpayments of HB must be repaid, except those caused by official error which you also could not have reasonably known were overpayments.
- The DWP, HM Revenue and Customs and local authorities have the discretion not to recover an overpayment in certain situations.

1. Introduction

An 'overpayment' occurs when you are paid more benefit than you should have been paid. If you are told that you must repay an overpayment, do the following.
- Use the relevant chapters in this *Handbook* to check whether or not you were entitled to some, or all, of the amount that the DWP, HM Revenue and Customs or local authority says is an overpayment. If you were entitled to

some, or all, of the amount, you should challenge the decision about your entitlement.

- If some, or all, of the amount should not have been paid, check whether:
  - for benefits other than housing benefit (HB), the overpayment is always recoverable (see p1196);
  - for benefits other than HB, the overpayment is sometimes recoverable, depending on the circumstances. Check whether all three conditions that allow the overpayment to be recovered are met, and also whether the overpayment can be reduced under the rules described on p1205;
  - the overpayment of HB is recoverable (see p1214). If so, check whether it can be recovered from you (p1218) and whether any amount can be offset against the sum claimed (see p1217).
- If you are not the person whose benefit was overpaid, check whether the overpayment can be recovered from you (see p1206 and p1218).
- Consider whether it is worth asking for the overpayment not to be recovered. For overpayments of HB, see p1219, and for other benefits, see p1208.
- If you must repay an overpayment, check that the method of recovery used is correct and whether you should ask for the money to be recovered in a different way. For overpayments of HB, see p1219, and for other benefits, see p1208.

Note:

- For benefits other than HB, if you are overpaid and this was because you made an incorrect statement or failed to provide information, you may also have to pay a penalty (p1229). If it is considered that an overpayment was made because of fraud, in addition to the overpayment being recovered, you may be prosecuted or given the option of paying a penalty instead of going to court. See Chapter 54 for further information.
- If an overpayment has been included in a debt relief order, it cannot be recovered.[1] Similarly, if you are subject to a bankruptcy order, any overpayment that is notified to you as recoverable before the order was made is not recoverable. However, once the order ceases to have effect, any overpayment caused by fraud becomes recoverable.
- If you live in England and Wales, recovery of your benefit overpayment is suspended for 60 days if you have been accepted onto the breathing space debt respite scheme. You must have sought debt advice from, and applied via, a professional debt adviser who is authorised by the Financial Conduct Authority, or a local authority where it provides debt advice to residents.[2]

Part 8: Claiming benefits and getting paid
Chapter 53: Overpayments
2. Overpayments that are always recoverable

2. Overpayments that are always recoverable

Except for overpayments of housing benefit (HB – see p1214), the DWP or HM Revenue and Customs (HMRC) can always recover the following overpayments.

- You come under the universal credit (UC) system (see p22) and you have been paid too much UC, contribution-based jobseeker's allowance (JSA) or contributory employment and support allowance (ESA).
- You have been paid too much income support (IS), income-based JSA, income-related ESA or pension credit (PC) because you were owed income that you have now received (see p1198).
- Too much mortgage interest was paid direct to your lender (see p1198).
- Too much benefit has been paid into your bank account by mistake (see p1199).

Although the above overpayments are always recoverable, you may still be able to argue that you were entitled to some, or all, of the amount, or that some or all of the overpayment does not fall into one of the above categories. The decision maker at the DWP or HMRC also has the discretion not to recover in certain circumstances (see p1208).

Overpayments if you come under the universal credit system

If you come under the UC system (see p22) and you are overpaid UC, contribution-based JSA or contributory ESA, the DWP can recover any amount of overpaid benefit, regardless of the cause of the overpayment.[3] See p1208 for how the overpayment can be recovered.

Note:
- In general, the DWP must first change the decision awarding you benefit before it can decide whether the overpayment can be recovered (see p1204).[4]
- You can appeal against a decision that you have been overpaid, or about the amount of an overpayment. You must request a mandatory reconsideration before you can appeal (see p1298). You cannot appeal against a decision to recover an overpayment.[5]
- You can ask the DWP to use its discretion not to recover the overpayment (see p1208).

The amount recovered

The amount recovered is the difference between what you received and the amount to which you were entitled after the decision awarding you benefit has been changed.[6] This amount can be reduced in the following circumstances.

Offsetting universal credit

If you were overpaid JSA or ESA, the amount that can be recovered may be reduced by the amount of any UC you could have received. For this to happen, you must have made a claim for UC. The overpaid amount is reduced by the amount of UC you would have got:[7]

- had you notified any change of circumstances that affected your JSA or ESA entitlement (other than a change of dwelling) to the DWP at the time it occurred; *or*
- had you not misrepresented or failed to disclose something before the award of JSA or ESA; *or*
- had a mistake by the decision maker not occurred.

You are overpaid universal credit because of a mistake about your capital

If you are overpaid UC because of a mistake about your savings for a period of more than three months, the amount that can be recovered is reduced to take into account the fact that you would have been spending your capital had you not been receiving UC.

At the end of each three-month period for which you have been overpaid, the amount of capital you are regarded as having is reduced by the amount of UC that you were overpaid in those three months.[8] The overpayment for the next three months is then calculated as if you had this reduced amount of capital.

You are overpaid because you moved home

If you are overpaid the housing element of UC because you moved home, but payments continued being made for your previous home, the decision maker may reduce the amount to be recovered by an amount equal to what you would have received in respect of your new home.[9]

S/he can only do this if the payments for your previous home are made to the same person as those for your new home.[10] If the decision maker reduces the amount to be recovered in this way, the reduction in the overpaid amount is treated as if it were paid in respect of your new home.[11]

From whom can an overpayment be recovered

An overpayment of UC, contribution-based JSA or contributory ESA is usually recoverable from the person to whom it was paid. However, it can be recovered from someone else in the following circumstances.[12]

- If the overpaid amount was paid to an appointee or to someone other than you because it was not in your interest to pay you directly (see p1148), the overpayment can also be recovered from you, the claimant.
- If an overpaid amount was paid to a third party under the rules about deductions and payments to third parties (see p1164), the amount is recoverable from you, the claimant. However, amounts paid to the third party in excess of the amounts allowed by those rules are only recoverable from the third party.
- If the overpaid amount includes an amount for housing costs paid to another person (eg, your landlord) and:

Part 8: Claiming benefits and getting paid
Chapter 53: Overpayments
2. Overpayments that are always recoverable

- the overpayment occurred because someone failed to disclose or misrepresented a material fact (see p1200 and p1204), it is recoverable from that person, not the person to whom it was paid;
- the overpayment occurred because you moved home, it is recoverable from you, as well as from the person to whom it was paid;
- the overpayment occurred because the payment exceeded the housing costs for which you are liable (eg, it was more than your rent), it is recoverable from the person to whom it was paid – eg, your landlord;
- the overpayment did not occur for any of the above three reasons, it is recoverable from you, the claimant, not the person to whom it was paid.

You were owed income that you have now received

If you are owed money while you are getting IS, income-based JSA, income-related ESA or PC, this may result in your being overpaid benefit. This is because when you receive the money you are owed, your income for benefit purposes is calculated afresh and you must repay any IS, income-based JSA, income-related ESA or PC to which you would not have been entitled had the money been paid on time.[13]

This rule applies to any income that affects the amount of IS, income-based JSA, income-related ESA or PC you get, including:[14]

- earnings;
- other social security benefits. **Note:** arrears of some benefits are treated as capital and ignored for 52 weeks (see Chapters 22 and 23);
- benefits paid by European Economic Area member states.[15]

If you are owed arrears of benefit, the DWP can reduce (or 'abate') those arrears before they are paid to you, if not doing so would mean that you have then been overpaid UC, IS, income-based JSA, income-related ESA or PC. If the arrears are not reduced and you are overpaid, the DWP can recover the overpayment from you.[16]

Note: you can appeal about whether an overpayment has occurred and how it has been calculated.[17] You must apply for a mandatory reconsideration before you can appeal (see p1299). You cannot appeal against the decision to recover any overpayment that has occurred, but you can ask the DWP to use its discretion not to recover it (see p1208).

See p1208 for how the overpayment can be recovered.

Too much mortgage interest has been paid to your lender

Before April 2018, if you were getting help with your housing costs in your IS, income-based JSA, income-related ESA or PC (see Chapter 18), your mortgage interest was usually paid direct to your lender. From April 2018, help with your mortage interest is no longer included in your IS, income-based JSA, income-related ESA or PC (or UC). You are offered a loan instead (see p839).

If it is decided that you were overpaid mortgage interest in the past, see p1239 of the 2018/19 edition of this *Handbook* for details of when it is recoverable.

Too much benefit has been credited to your account

Your benefit may be paid by direct credit transfer into a bank or building society account. If you are credited with too much money because of the direct credit transfer system itself, the excess can be recovered in certain circumstances.[18]

The overpayment can only be recovered if it was caused by the direct credit transfer system and:[19]

- you were notified in writing before you agreed to your benefit being paid into a bank or other account that any excess benefit could be recovered; *and*
- it has been certified that you were paid excess benefit because of the direct credit transfer system.

If the excess benefit cannot be recovered under the rules described above, it may be recoverable under the rules described below, or those for recovery following late payment of income (see p1198).

You can appeal to the First-tier Tribunal against a decision to recover excess benefit credited to your bank or other account.[20] You must apply for a mandatory reconsideration before you can appeal (see p1299).

Even if the overpayment is recoverable, you can ask the DWP or HMRC to use its discretion not to recover it (see p1208).

3. Overpayments that are sometimes recoverable

Except for the overpayments described on p1196 and overpayments of housing benefit (HB – see p1214), some overpayments can only be recovered if:[21]

- you failed to disclose, or you misrepresented, a 'relevant material fact' (see p1200) and this caused the overpayment (see p1204); *and*
- the decision awarding you benefit has been changed (see p1204).

If you have been overpaid and both the above conditions do not apply to the whole of the overpayment, only that part of the overpayment to which they all apply is recoverable from you. For example, if you were paid too much benefit over a two-year period, but you told the DWP about all the relevant facts after the

Part 8: Claiming benefits and getting paid
Chapter 53: Overpayments
3. Overpayments that are sometimes recoverable

first year, the overpayment made after this was not caused by your failure to disclose and is therefore not recoverable from you.

Example
Carl was receiving income support (IS) as a carer. The person he was caring for stopped getting personal independence payment (PIP) in 2019. Carl informed the DWP of this in 2020, but the DWP continued to pay Carl his IS until 2021. From 2020 onwards, this overpayment is not recoverable.

Note:
- Even if an overpayment can be recovered, in some situations amounts must be deducted from the recoverable sum (see p1205).
- This type of overpayment can sometimes be recovered from you, even if you are not the claimant (see p1206).
- You can appeal against a decision that the overpayment is recoverable from you (see p1207). You must apply for a mandatory reconsideration first (see p1299).
- Even if an overpayment is recoverable , you can ask the DWP or HM Revenue and Customs (HMRC) to use its discretion not to recover it (see p1208).

You failed to disclose, or you misrepresented, a material fact

For an overpayment to be recoverable, you must have:
- failed to disclose a relevant 'material fact' (see below); *or*
- misrepresented a relevant 'material fact' (see p1203).

A material fact
A **'material fact'** is one which influences how much benefit you should be paid.[22] Sometimes there can be a difference between your honest opinion and a material fact.[23] For example, a statement about the distance you can walk should be taken as your honest opinion of your ability, rather than as a statement of fact.[24] If the decision maker comes to a different conclusion about the facts, you can argue that an overpayment should not be recovered.[25]

Facts	Conclusions about the facts
You have arthritis	You have limited capability for work
A friend is sharing your flat	You are living together as spouses or civil partners
You have a bad back	Your mobility is severely restricted most of the time

Failure to disclose
You count as having failed to disclose a relevant material fact if:[26]
- you knew about a fact; *and*

8

- you had a legal duty to disclose that fact; *and*
- you did not comply with that legal duty.

Knowledge of a fact

If you did not know about a fact, including if it was a change in your circumstances, you have not 'failed' to disclose it.[27] You cannot fail to disclose something you did not know about unless:

- there was a reason why you should have been aware of it;[28] *or*
- it was reasonable for you to make enquiries, which would have revealed the information to you;[29] *or*
- you had been aware of it, but simply forgot.[30]

Legal duty to disclose

You have two different legal duties to disclose facts: a specific duty and a general duty.

You have a **specific duty** to disclose a fact that you know about and which is a type of fact that you have clearly been told by the DWP or HMRC that you must disclose – eg, in your benefit award letter or in the notes which accompanied it.[31]

You do not have a specific legal duty to disclose something unless the instruction is clear and there is no room for doubt about whether or not you are required to report it.[32]

If you were not clearly told that you must report a certain fact, this specific duty to disclose does not apply. If, despite there being a clear instruction to disclose a particular fact in a letter or accompanying notes, you are subsequently told by an officer of the DWP that you do not need to disclose this type of fact, this can mean that you no longer have a duty to disclose it.[33]

You also have a **general duty** to disclose any change in your circumstances since the decision awarding you benefit was made, if you could reasonably be expected to know that your benefit may be affected.[34]

What you can reasonably be expected to know depends on the details of your case. For example, if you were told by the DWP or a lawyer that your benefit would not be affected, or if you were too ill to have realised that it might be, it is arguable that you could not reasonably have been expected to have known that your benefit could be affected.[35] If there is no obvious connection between the fact and the overpaid benefit, argue that it was not reasonable for you to have known that your benefit might be affected.

Complying with your duty to disclose

Generally, to make a valid disclosure, you must tell the 'relevant office' in sufficiently clear terms so that the effect on your claim can be examined.

If you have a specific duty to disclose, the 'relevant office' is the one that handles the benefit you are claiming.[36] Arguably, you are entitled to assume that one office of the DWP knows about decisions of other offices within the DWP that

Part 8: Claiming benefits and getting paid
Chapter 53: Overpayments
3. Overpayments that are sometimes recoverable

affect your benefit claim. However, this is not the current law and you should disclose to the office handling your claim.[37] This may be a benefit delivery centre (eg, for pension credit (PC)) or a central office (eg, for PIP). For special rules on reporting a birth or death (sometimes called 'Tell Us Once'), see p1160.

If you have a general duty to disclose, the 'relevant office' is any DWP office or, in jobseeker's allowance (JSA) cases, a specified DWP office. However, it is always best to tell the office handling your claim if you can. For child benefit and guardian's allowance, you can disclose changes in your circumstances to the Child Benefit Office, or any office specified to you by HMRC.[38] Again, it is best to ensure that you tell the Child Benefit Office, as it administers your claim. You only count as having failed to disclose once the time by when it was reasonably practicable for you to have done so has passed – eg, if it was impossible for you to make the disclosure earlier than you did, you have not failed to comply with the general duty to disclose.

If the office already knew about the fact and you were aware it knew, it is strongly arguable that you have not failed to disclose.[39] Even if you were not aware that the office already knew, it may be possible to argue that its knowledge means that any failure on your part did not actually cause the overpayment (see p1204). This is especially so if the office would not have acted any differently, even if you had reported the fact to it.[40]

You can usually notify changes in writing or by telephone, but it is best to do so in writing.[41]

If you completed a form while giving information, whether you count as having failed to disclose depends not just on what you said on the form, but also on whether you gave the necessary information in another way.[42] If you do not complete a form correctly and give the relevant information in the wrong place, you have disclosed the facts.[43]

If you made a statement in person or by telephone, but the decision maker says there is no record of this, you should appeal and give as much information as possible about the circumstances in which the disclosure was made – eg, when you called, who you spoke to and what was said. A record of the telephone number called, if you have it, is likely to be helpful.

You should usually make the disclosure yourself, unless you have an appointee acting for you (see p1135).[44] If someone else discloses the fact on your behalf, it must be made to the correct office with your knowledge and you must believe that there is no need to repeat it yourself. If someone else makes the disclosure to an office not handling your claim, but s/he reasonably believes that the information will be passed to the correct office, this may count as disclosure.[45]

Once you have made a proper disclosure to the office handling your claim, you are not expected to repeat it.[46] However, if you give the information to a different office and subsequently become aware that it has not been acted on, you must take further steps to make a proper disclosure.[47] A short time may elapse before you can reasonably be expected to realise that the original information has not been acted on.[48]

Misrepresentation

Misrepresentation occurs if you have provided information that is inaccurate – eg, you gave a wrong answer to a specific question on the claim form. It does not apply if you have not given information, unless this was deliberately intended to mislead.[49] The following apply.

- It does not matter whether a reasonable person would also have given innaccurate information. No 'failure' on your part needs to be shown.[50]
- It does not matter if you honestly believed that the information you gave was correct – once it is shown to be incorrect, you have misrepresented it. However, you have not misrepresented if you added the phrase 'not to my knowledge' to your statement.[51]
- A written statement may be qualified by an oral one. If you fill in a form incorrectly but explain the situation to an officer when handing in the form, your explanation must be taken into account when deciding whether what is stated on the form is misrepresentation.[52] Similarly, if you give incorrect information in one document but correct information in another, there may not be a misrepresentation.[53] However, if you have declared a fact on a previous claim, but inadvertently give incorrect information on a later claim, you have misrepresented it. The decision maker is not required to check the information you gave on the earlier claim for you.[54]
- If you are incapable of managing your affairs, but nevertheless sign a claim form which is incorrectly completed, you cannot argue later that you were not capable of making a true representation of your circumstances.[55] However, it is arguable that benefit cannot be recovered from you if you:[56]
  - have a disability or you cannot read or write English very well; *and*
  - thought you were signing something different from what you were, or you did not understand the effect of your signature; *and*
  - took precautions to understand what you were signing – eg, you checked the form for accuracy before you signed it.[57]
- If you sign a declaration on a claim form that states, 'I declare that the information I have given is correct and complete', but you left out relevant information because you were unaware of it, this is not misrepresentation unless you knew (or ought reasonably to have known) the information was incomplete.[58]

Note:
- If you did not declare a fact because you were unaware of it, signing the declaration does not amount to a misrepresentation because all you are declaring is that you have correctly disclosed those facts *which were known to you*.[59]

Part 8: Claiming benefits and getting paid
Chapter 53: Overpayments
3. Overpayments that are sometimes recoverable

- If you were told by the DWP or HMRC that certain facts are irrelevant to your claim, signing the declaration cannot be a misrepresentation if you fail to disclose these facts.[60]
- If someone else disclosed a fact to an office not handling your claim but s/he reasonably believed it would be passed to the correct office, it may be that disclosure has been made, and therefore your signing the declaration does not amount to a misrepresentation.[61]

Your failure to disclose, or your misrepresentation, has caused the overpayment

An overpayment is only recoverable if it was caused by your failure to disclose (see p1200), or your misrepresenting (see p1203), a material fact (see p1200). **Note:** it is possible that if you have a duty to disclose a fact in respect of one benefit and you fail to do so, this could be regarded as the cause of an overpayment of another benefit.[62]

You may be able to argue that the overpayment was not caused by your failure to disclose or your misrepresentation.

- If the relevant office has been given the correct information to decide your claim by someone else, but does not act on it, you could argue that the overpayment did not arise because of your failure.[63] However, if one DWP office does not inform another about *other* changes in your circumstances (eg, an increase in your earnings), this does not prevent the overpayment resulting from your failure to disclose the information yourself to the second office.[64]
- If the relevant office has obtained information from another source that leads it to think you may be being overpaid but it does not suspend your benefit while it makes enquiries to establish this for certain, it is still possible that the cause of the overpayment is your failure to disclose or your misrepresentation.[65]
- If you have not disclosed a relevant fact to the relevant office and you then sign a declaration that you have reported the relevant facts (eg, when you sign on), this is a misrepresentation.
- If what you say on your claim form is obviously incorrect and the decision maker does not check this, the overpayment will have been caused by official error, not your misrepresentation, and it is not recoverable.[66]

The decision awarding you benefit has been changed

If the decision to award you benefit is considered to be incorrect, it must be changed before any overpayment can be recovered.[67] The only exception to this rule is when the circumstances of the overpayment mean that there is no decision that needs to be revised in order for an overpayment to exist – ie, if you were actually paid more than the amount the original decision awarded to you.[68]

A decision to change your benefit award is made by a decision maker, who then carries out a revision or a supersession (see p1261 and p1274). The new decision should state the new amount payable (if any).[69]

During the period when you were overpaid, there may have been more than one decision on your benefit award. Unless *all* these decisions are changed, *all* of the overpayment cannot be recovered.[70]

Note: in practice, there are therefore two decisions that must be made before an overpayment can be recovered from you: the decision that changes a previous decision about your benefit, and the decision that the overpayment is recoverable.[71] Both decisions may be included in one decision letter, but it must be clear that both have been made.[72] It is also possible that your benefit award has been changed, but you are not notified about this until you are also notified that the overpayment is recoverable.[73]

If the decision(s) about your benefit has not been changed and/or the new decision(s) has not been notified to you (or it appears that it may not have been), appeal to the First-tier Tribunal (see p1297) against the decision that the overpayment is recoverable. You must apply for a mandatory reconsideration first (see p1299).

The amount that is recovered

The amount of the overpayment is the difference between what you were paid and what you should have been paid.[74] Check that the amount of the overpayment is correct by:

- checking the period of the overpayment; *and*
- working out the total amount of benefit you were paid over the period; *and*
- establishing the correct amount of benefit you should have received during the period; *and*
- deducting this from the total amount of benefit you were paid.

No interest charges may be added to the amount of the overpayment.

The decision maker works out what you should have been paid using the information you originally gave her/him, plus any facts you misrepresented or did not disclose.

If you have been overpaid, the decision maker should deduct from the overpayment any universal credit (UC), IS, income-based JSA, income-related employment and support allowance (ESA) or PC to which you or your partner would have been entitled had benefit been paid correctly.[75]

If additional facts are needed to prove you were underpaid UC, IS, income-based JSA, ESA or PC, you cannot offset the underpayment of these benefits against the overpayment.[76] However, if you have been getting one of these benefits, you can ask the DWP to revise or supersede your award (see p1261 and p1274). It could then withhold any arrears owed to you to reduce the overpayment.

Part 8: Claiming benefits and getting paid
Chapter 53: Overpayments
3. Overpayments that are sometimes recoverable

If you were overpaid UC, IS, income-based JSA, income-related ESA or PC because you had too much capital, the overpayment is calculated taking account of the fact that, had you received no benefit, you would have had to use your capital to meet everyday expenses. For each 13-week period, the DWP assumes your capital is reduced by the amount of overpaid benefit.[77] This is known as the 'diminishing capital' rule. If your capital goes below the capital limit, any subsequent overpayment is not recoverable. However, if there are any increases or decreases in your actual capital during the overpayment period, these are also taken into account.[78]

Example
Denise received IS of £100 a week for a period of 30 weeks. She has capital of £20,000. After 13 weeks, the diminishing capital rule means that she is treated as having spent 13 x £100 = £1,300 and her capital is deemed to be £18,700. After a further 13 weeks, her capital is deemed to be £17,400.
After 26 weeks, Denise has paid £5,000 towards her credit card arrears after the credit card company threatened her with court proceedings. As long as obtaining benefit was not the significant purpose for making this payment (see p486), her capital is now deemed to be £12,400.

In addition to checking that the overpayment has been calculated correctly, you should claim any other benefits or tax credits to which you may be entitled and ask for these to be backdated (see p1142 for benefits and p1467 for tax credits) so you can repay the overpayment. Do not delay making the claims or you could lose out.

If you were overpaid a benefit which overlaps with another benefit you claimed but were not paid (see p1151), ask for a revision or supersession of that benefit and ask for it to be paid instead (see p1261).

If you were overpaid a benefit but, in fact, were entitled to another, check whether the claim for the benefit you were overpaid can be treated as a claim for the other (see p1144).

Example
Shaida should not have been receiving IS because her partner is in full-time paid work. However, she is caring for her aunt who is disabled and receiving attendance allowance. Shaida should ask the DWP to treat her claim for IS as a claim for carer's allowance (CA) and offset arrears of CA against the IS she has been overpaid.

From whom can an overpayment be recovered

An overpayment can be recovered from you if it was caused by your failing to disclose or your misrepresenting a material fact (see p1200).[79] The DWP or HMRC may argue that it can recover the overpayment from you, even if you are not the claimant or you were not paid the benefit. However, it is arguable that only a claimant, an 'appointee' or a person with power of attorney to whom the benefit was paid can fail to disclose a material fact.[80]

If you are an appointee (see p1135), the overpayment can be recovered from you or the claimant (or both of you), depending on your circumstances and the facts of the case – ie, which one of you misrepresented or failed to disclose a material fact. The DWP or HMRC should issue a decision that deals with both your liabilities.[81] However:

- if the overpaid benefit has not been given to the claimant, the overpayment cannot be recovered from her/him, unless s/he contributed to the misrepresentation or s/he did not disclose a material fact;
- the overpayment cannot be recovered from you if you used 'due care and diligence' in making any statements that led to the overpayment.

Whether the overpayment can be recovered from you if you have **power of attorney** depends on whether the benefit was paid to you. If benefit was paid to you on behalf of the claimant, the overpayment is recoverable from you in the same way as from appointees.[82] If benefit was not paid to you, it cannot be recovered from you.[83]

An overpayment can be recovered from a claimant's estate if s/he dies.[84] Recovery can only begin after either probate or letters of administration have been granted.[85]

Challenging an overpayment decision

If you disagree that an overpayment has been made, or that an overpayment can be recovered (ie, because the required conditions are not met) or with the amount to be recovered (ie, because you were entitled to some, or all, of the payments), you can appeal. You must ask for a mandatory reconsideration first.

If you have missed the time limit for a mandatory reconsideration (see p1301), you can apply for a supersession and then appeal against any refusal to supersede.[86]

The First-tier Tribunal can consider whether you were entitled to some, or all, of the money (the amount of the overpayment), as well as whether the overpayment is recoverable from you on the basis that it was caused by your failure to disclose or misrepresentation. Both issues can also be considered, even if you have only challenged the decision about whether the overpayment is recoverable (and not the decision about your entitlement to benefit during the period of overpayment).[87]

Do not pay back any of the money until your appeal has been decided. If you do so and then successfully appeal, the DWP or HMRC should reimburse you. If it does not, you may be entitled to recover the money in court proceedings because

Part 8: Claiming benefits and getting paid
Chapter 53: Overpayments
4. Recovery of overpaid benefit

you repaid the money on the basis of a mistake. Write to the DWP or HMRC and explain that you do not intend to repay any of the money until your appeal has been decided. Official guidance says that, except for overpayments of UC, recovery of overpaid benefit should be suspended while you are challenging the decision about the overpayment.[88] If the DWP or HMRC is already making deductions from your benefit (see p1209 and p1211), ask it to stop doing so straight away.

Note: even if the tribunal decides that an overpayment is recoverable, the decision maker has the discretion not to recover, so it can still be worth asking for it not to be recovered.

4. Recovery of overpaid benefit

Note: this section does *not* apply to recovery of overpayments of housing benefit (HB – see p1214).

If an overpayment can be recovered (see p1196 and p1199), the DWP or HM Revenue and Customs (HMRC) must decide whether to recover it and, if so, the method to use. The recovery method depends on the type of overpayment. If you come under the universal credit (UC) system and have been overpaid UC, contribution-based jobseeker's allowance (JSA) or contributory employment and support allowance (ESA), see p1209. For all other overpayments, see p1211.

Note: except when seeking to recover overpaid benefit through the courts, there is no time limit within which the DWP or HMRC must begin recovery action. See CPAG's *Debt Advice Handbook* for more information about recovery and enforcement methods. In England and Wales, recovery of your overpayment can be suspended for 60 days under the breathing space scheme (see p1195).

The discretion not to recover

Even if an overpayment is recoverable, the DWP and HMRC have the discretion not to recover all or part of it. The DWP has two policies that set out the situations when recovery is not made.
- Guidance for overpayments of UC, contribution-based JSA and contributory ESA if you come under the UC system (see p1196) used to state that the DWP can use its discretion not to recover an overpayment if it would cause you hardship.[89] Although this guidance has been withdrawn, the discretion should still apply. You can also ask the DWP not to recover if the reason you were overpaid was because of a mistake on the part of the DWP.[90]
- Guidance for all other overpayments emphasises that it is only in exceptional cases that recovery is not pursued.[91] However, the DWP and HMRC can use their discretion to decide not to recover the overpayment, particularly if you

acted in good faith and recovery would cause you hardship or be detrimental to your health or the health of your family.

If you agree to repay the overpayment or you do not ask for recovery not to be made, in almost all cases the DWP or HMRC recovers the overpayment from you. If an overpayment is recoverable from you, but repaying it is difficult or you think there is a reason why recovery should not take place, contact the DWP or HMRC debt management section. The details should be on the letters you receive about the overpayment. Each case is decided on its merits. You should emphasise that you acted in good faith, point out any misleading advice you received (particularly from the DWP or HMRC) and how repaying would cause you hardship. To demonstrate hardship on financial grounds, you must usually provide full income and expenditure details for you and your family. In attempting to get the DWP or HMRC to exercise their discretion, it may be helpful to get the help of your MP.

If the DWP or HMRC refuses to use its discretion not to recover, you cannot appeal against this decision. Your only possible legal recourse is judicial review (see Chapter 59). For information about judicial review and some tools regarding judicial review challenges about overpayment recovery, see cpag.org.uk/jr. The First-tier Tribunal cannot 'write off' part of the overpayment, even if there are mitigating circumstances. It can only decide whether it is recoverable and, if so, how much is repayable.

If you have been underpaid in the past but cannot now get arrears (eg, because of the rules on backdating – see p1142), ask the DWP or HMRC to reduce the amount to be recovered by this sum if it will not write it off altogether.

Methods of recovery: universal credit system

This section applies to the recovery of overpayments of UC, and of contribution-based JSA or contributory ESA if you come under the UC system (see p1196).

Note: the methods of recovery described in this section can also be used to collect or recover court costs incurred in recovering overpayments, advance payments of UC (see p1153), budgeting advances of UC (see p51), hardship payments of UC (see p1181), financial penalties for benefit offences (see p1236), civil penalties for incorrect statements (see p1229) and overpayments of tax credits if the debt has been transferred to the DWP (see p1491).

Deductions from benefit

Overpayments of UC, and contribution-based JSA or contributory ESA if you come under the UC system, can be recovered through deductions from all the benefits in this *Handbook* except income support (IS), HB, social fund payments, child benefit and guardian's allowance.[92]

Part 8: Claiming benefits and getting paid
Chapter 53: Overpayments
4. Recovery of overpaid benefit

Maximum deductions from universal credit

Note: the maximum amounts below apply to *all* overpayments being recovered by deductions from your UC – eg, an overpayment of IS that occurred before you came under the UC *system*.[93]

If an overpayment is being recovered from your UC, the regulations provide that the maximum amount that can be deducted each month is 40 per cent of the appropriate UC standard allowance.[94] However, in practice, deductions are at either 25 or 15 per cent of the appropriate UC standard allowance.[95] This means that in practice the maximum monthly deduction is the:

- 25 per cent rate (if you have some earned income or if you or your partner are found guilty of an offence, or have accepted a caution or agreed to pay a penalty in connection with the overpayment (see p1228), or if UC hardship payments are being recovered):
  – £66.33 if you are single and under 25;
  – £83.73 if you are single and 25 or over;
  – £104.11 if you and your partner are both under 25;
  – £131.43 if you or your partner are 25 or over; *or*
- 15 per cent rate (in all other cases):
  – £39.80 if you are single and under 25;
  – £50.24 if you are single and 25 or over;
  – £62.47 if you and your partner are both under 25;
  – £78.86 if you or your partner are 25 or over.

You must be left with at least one penny of UC each month after the deduction.[96] The above maximum amounts do not apply if:

- you are being paid arrears of UC (other than if they are as a result of payments being restored following a suspension of your benefit), so the whole of the arrears can be used to recover an overpayment;[97] *or*
- the overpayment is of UC housing costs to cover rent and it is being recovered from someone else – eg, your landlord.[98]

Maximum deductions from jobseeker's allowance or employment and support allowance

The maximum weekly deduction that can be made to recover an overpayment from your contribution-based JSA is an amount equal to 40 per cent of your JSA.[99]

The maximum weekly deduction that can be made to recover an overpayment from your contributory ESA is 40 per cent of the basic allowance that applies to you (see p634).[100]

In both cases, if the 40 per cent figure is not a multiple of five pence, the amount is rounded up to the next highest multiple of five pence.

Maximum deductions from pension credit

The maximum weekly amount that can be deducted from pension credit (PC) to repay an overpayment under these rules (ie, if you were overpaid under the UC system but are now getting PC) is:[101]

- £19.35 if the overpayment is one for which you were found guilty of an offence, you were cautioned or you agreed to pay a penalty as an alternative to prosecution; *or*
- £11.60 in all other cases.

You must be left with at least 10 pence of PC after any deductions.

Deductions from earnings

Overpayments can be recovered by your employer deducting amounts from your wages or salary.[102] The rules are the same as those outlined on p1212.

Recovery through the courts

The rules for recovering overpayments through the courts are similar to those for the recovery of HB (see p1221).[103]

Methods of recovery: other benefits

This section applies to all recoverable overpayments, except overpayments of UC, and contribution-based JSA or contributory ESA if you come under the UC system. For these, see p1209.

Deductions from benefit

If you have a recoverable overpayment of benefit and you are now getting UC, the overpayment can be transferred to your UC claim and treated as an overpayment of UC. It is then recovered under the rules for UC (see p1209).

Recoverable overpayments can usually be repaid through deductions from most of the benefits in this *Handbook*. There are some exceptions.

- Overpayments of child benefit and guardian's allowance can be recovered by deductions from either of these benefits,[104] but overpayments of other benefits cannot be deducted from them.[105]
- No deductions can be made from HB, except for HB or council tax benefit overpayments.[106]

Deductions can only be made from the benefit of the person who must repay the overpayment. However, if you are a member of a couple, overpayments of IS, income-based JSA, income-related ESA and PC can be recovered from benefits either of you receive, provided you are still a couple at the date of the deduction.[107]

Overpayments can also be recovered from arrears of benefit you are owed, except arrears of a benefit that has been suspended (see p1161).[108]

Part 8: Claiming benefits and getting paid
Chapter 53: Overpayments
4. Recovery of overpaid benefit

If an overpayment of IS, income-based JSA, income-related ESA or PC occurred because of a duplication of payment, the DWP usually deducts it from the arrears owing to you.[109] However, if it does not do so, you can still be asked to repay it even if you have spent the money.

Note: overpaid benefit cannot be recovered by making deductions from tax credits.

Maximum deductions

The maximum weekly amounts that can be deducted from **IS, income-based JSA, contribution-based JSA** (if you would be entitled to income-based JSA at the same rate), **income-related ESA, contributory ESA** (if you would be entitled to income-related ESA at the same rate) and **PC** are:[110]

- £30.80 if you have agreed to pay a penalty (see p1236), admitted fraud or been found guilty of fraud; *or*
- £11.55 in any other case.

The deduction can be increased by half of any:[111]

- £5, £10 or £20 earnings disregard (see p413); *or*
- charitable income paid on a regular basis subject to a disregard (see p425); *or*
- benefit subject to a £10 disregard (see p413).

If you have been overpaid contribution-based JSA but are not entitled to income-based JSA, the maximum deduction is one-third of the personal allowance for someone of your age (see p318).[112]

The above amounts are maximum amounts. You might be able to persuade the DWP to deduct less. If other deductions are also being made from your benefit, see p1171 for the total maximum amount that can be deducted.

If an overpayment is being recovered from a benefit other than IS, income-based JSA, income-related ESA or PC, the rules limiting the maximum payment that can be deducted do not apply. See p1210 if the overpayment is being recovered from your UC.[113] The DWP usually wants to deduct one-third of your weekly benefit. However, you can argue that your rate of repayment should be less than this.

Deductions from earnings

If you work for an organisation with 10 or more employees, an overpayment can be recovered by your employer deducting amounts from your earnings.[114] If this happens, you and your employer should be sent a notice setting out that deductions from your earnings are to be made and the rules for calculating how much to deduct.[115] You must inform the DWP if you leave your employment and you must give the DWP details of any new employment.[116] Failure to notify the DWP of these is a criminal offence.[117] Your employer should inform you, in writing, of how much the deductions are and how they were calculated no later than the day on which you are given a payment which has had a deduction made from it (or, if that is impractical, no later than the following payday).[118]

The maximum that can be deducted each week is worked out as a percentage of your net earnings – ie, earnings after income tax, class 1 national insurance contributions and pension contributions have been deducted.[119] The maximum is higher if you have been found guilty of an offence.[120]

Maximum deductions from earnings

Net monthly earnings (if paid monthly)	Net weekly earnings (if paid weekly)	Deduction	Deduction if found guilty of an offence
Less than £430	£100 or less	Nil	5%
£430.01 to £690	£100.01 to £160	3%	6%
£690.01 to £950	£160.01 to £220	5%	10%
£950.01 to £1,160	£220.01 to £270	7%	14%
£1,160.01 to £1,615	£270.01 to £375	11%	22%
£1,615.01 to £2,240	£375.01 to £520	15%	30%
£2,240.01 or over	£520.01 or over	20%	40%

If you would be left with less than 60 per cent of your net earnings after the deductions (eg, because amounts are being deducted from your wages or salary for other things), the deduction should be reduced so that you are left with 60 per cent of your net earnings.[121] There are rules on the order of priority in which deductions should be made (see p1172).[122] **Note:** the decision maker can reduce the amount to be deducted below the above percentages by issuing a new notice to your employer with the reduced amount.[123]

Recovery through the courts

Recoverable overpayments of benefit may be recovered by enforcement proceedings in the County Court in England or Wales or the sheriff court in Scotland (but see below regarding use of the common law).[124] The DWP or HMRC may use these proceedings to recover a recoverable overpayment if you are no longer claiming benefit.

Once there is a decision from a decision maker, the First-tier Tribunal or Upper Tribunal, the court must enforce it, unless you persuade it to delay enforcement (known as a 'stay of execution') while you appeal against the relevant decision. If you are in this situation, get advice.

Note: recovery action through the courts in England and Wales must be taken within six years of the decision to recover or, if later, any written acknowledgement of the overpayment or voluntary repayment.[125] In Scotland, the DWP regards the time limit as being 20 years from the date of the decision to recover (or, if there was no such decision, five years from the decision that there was an overpayment).[126] Get advice about how these limits apply to you.

Part 8: Claiming benefits and getting paid
Chapter 53: Overpayments
5. Overpayments of housing benefit

Can the DWP rely on common law?
The DWP cannot recover benefit overpayments using the 'common law'. This means that if an overpayment is not recoverable under the rules described in this chapter (see p1199) because, for example, it was not caused by misrepresentation or a failure to disclose, then it cannot instead reclaim it (using the common law) through the courts.[127]

5. **Overpayments of housing benefit**

An 'overpayment' is an amount of housing benefit (HB) which has been paid and which the local authority decides you were not entitled to under the HB rules.[128] Being 'paid' includes payment to you, your landlord or someone else, including HB credited to your local authority rent account (see p213).[129]

If you have been overpaid income support (IS), income-based jobseeker's allowance (JSA) or income-related employment and support allowance (ESA), you may also have been overpaid HB. This is because your automatic passport to maximum HB ceases when you are no longer entitled to these benefits. If you are in this situation, inform the local authority. Although it cannot change the decision about your other benefit, the local authority should still go on to make its own decision on your entitlement to HB.

Note:
- Council tax benefit (CTB) was abolished on 1 April 2013. The rules on calculating the amount and the recoverability of overpayments of CTB were similar to those for HB. For further details, see p1094 of the 2012/13 edition of this *Handbook*.
- In England and Wales, recovery of your overpayment can be suspended for 60 days under the breathing space debt respite scheme (see p1194).

Overpayments that are always recoverable

An overpayment of HB is always recoverable if:
- it is the result of the local authority's overestimating your HB when making a payment on account (see p220). When the local authority decides how much HB you should get, it must recover any excess you were paid from future HB payments.[130] However, if you stop getting HB before the local authority decides, the overpayment can only be recovered under the other rules (see p1215); *or*
- it is a future payment that has been credited to your rent account. In this case, the overpayment can be recovered even if it was made as a result of an 'official error'.[131] If an overpayment of HB caused by an official error has been credited to your account for a *past* period, see p1215.

Overpayments that are not recoverable

An overpayment that is not covered by either of the bullet points above is not recoverable if you can show that:[132]

- it was caused by an 'official error' (see below); *and*
- no 'relevant person' contributed to making the official error (see p1216); *and*
- no 'relevant person' could reasonably have been expected to realise that an overpayment was being made (see p1216).

Overpayments to which all these criteria apply are sometimes referred to as 'official error' overpayments.

Was the overpayment caused by an official error?

For the overpayment not to be recoverable, it must have been caused by an 'official error'. **Note:** the official error does not have to be the sole cause of the overpayment, but if the substantial cause of the overpayment was something that you did or failed to do, the overpayment is likely to be recoverable.[133]

An 'official error' is a mistake (either an act or omission) by:[134]

- the local authority responsible for HB; *or*
- an officer of the authority; *or*
- a person acting for that authority – eg, an employee of a contractor providing HB services; *or*
- an officer of the DWP or HM Revenue and Customs (HMRC) acting as such.

Examples of 'official error' include the following.

- A mistake made by the local authority in calculating your entitlement.
- A failure by the local authority to reduce your HB when you inform it of a change of circumstances. It is always best to notify changes in writing to the office you have been told to report changes to, and keep a copy. If you have reported a move into work to the DWP by telephone under the arrangements where it passes this on to the local authority (see p220) and have provided all the information and evidence needed, any overpayment that occurs is due to official error. However, if you did not provide all that was needed, the local authority does not treat any overpayment as official error.[135]
- Using a claim form that does not ask a question relevant to your entitlement. Whether or not this counts as an official error depends on the particular facts of your case. Leaving out a particular question is more likely to be an official error if the information omitted is likely to be relevant in a large number of cases, and if it is reasonable for the question to have been asked.[136]
- A failure by another department of the local authority to pass on details of a change of circumstances when it promised to do so. This is an official error because the definition does not require the mistake to be made by the HB office. If you have not been given a particular office to report a change to, you may have fulfilled your duty by reporting the change to any local authority

Part 8: Claiming benefits and getting paid
Chapter 53: Overpayments
5. Overpayments of housing benefit

office, and there may be an official error if that office fails to pass it to the HB office.[137]

- A mistake made by the DWP in calculating your entitlement to IS, income-based JSA or income-related ESA which results in an incorrect calculation of your entitlement to HB. However, it is not an official error if the local authority failed to check your entitlement with the DWP, unless it has information that shows the award is wrong or fraudulent.[138]
- A failure by the DWP to pass on information to the local authority.[139]
- Incorrect advice given to you by an officer of the local authority, the DWP or HMRC, provided s/he is acting as an officer at the time (rather than as a friend giving you informal advice).

The list above is not exhaustive.

Did a relevant person contribute to making the offical error?

Even if the overpayment was caused by an official error, if a 'relevant person' contributed to that mistake being made, the overpayment can still be recovered.

Relevant person

A '**relevant person**' is:

– the HB claimant; *or*

– a person acting on the claimant's behalf, either because the claimant is unable to deal with her/his affairs or because the claimant has asked the authority in writing to deal with the other person on her/his behalf; *or*

– a person to whom the payment was made, including a different person acting on the claimant's behalf or a landlord.

The relevant person must have caused the *error*, not the overpayment.[140]

The local authority might say that it only needs to show that *any* relevant person caused the official error, but it does not have to pursue that person for the overpayment.[141] If a relevant person caused the official error, the overpayment is recoverable. However, you may still be able to argue that it is not recoverable from you – eg, it was caused by a failure to disclose a relevant fact, but it was not you who failed to disclose. See p1218 for information about from whom overpayments can be recovered.

Did a relevant person realise that an overpayment was being made?

Even if the official error was not caused by a relevant person, an overpayment is still recoverable if any relevant person knew, or ought reasonably to have known, that an overpayment had been made. The test is whether or not you could reasonably have been be expected to *know* (not merely suspect) that an overpayment had occurred. Much depends on what could reasonably have been expected of you given the information available to you, in particular the extent to which the local authority advised you about the scheme, your duties and obligations (especially your duty to notify changes of circumstances).[142] For example, in one case it was held that although the local authority's letter about entitlement showed that an official error had been made, the complexity of the letter and the claimant's circumstances were such that he coud not reasonably be expected to have known that he was being overpaid.[143]

If you or another relevant person could only have realised that there was an overpayment at some point during the period of the overpayment, the overpayment is only recoverable from that date.

The amount that is recovered

Check the amount of an overpayment to ensure the local authority has calculated it correctly. The local authority should distinguish between parts of an overpayment that are recoverable and those that are not. To calculate the amount of the overpayment, it should:

- determine the period over which you have been paid too much benefit; *and*
- identify the period(s) over which it is entitled to recover; *and*
- work out the total amount of HB you were paid over the period(s) during which it can recover; *and*
- work out the correct amount of HB you should have received during the period(s) of the overpayment. The local authority must award you the amount of HB you (or your partner) would have received if it had been aware of your true circumstances. If necessary, it should ask you for any required information or evidence to do this. However, the local authority does not include a change of your address when doing this;[144] *and*
- deduct the HB you should have been paid from what you were paid.[145]

The local authority must not add any interest charges to the amount of the overpayment.[146]

Deductions from the overpayment

As well as any amount of HB which you should have been paid, the local authority must consider deducting other amounts from the overpayment (this is known as 'offsetting'). These are:

- if you are a council tenant, extra rent paid into your rent account. If you have been getting HB during the overpayment period and, for some reason, have paid more into your rent account than you should have paid according to your original (incorrect) benefit assessment, the extra rent you have paid can be deducted from any overpayment made during that period. The local authority might not apply this rule if you paid extra rent to repay rent arrears;[147]
- reductions under the 'diminishing capital rule'.

Part 8: Claiming benefits and getting paid
Chapter 53: Overpayments
5. Overpayments of housing benefit

No other amounts can be deducted.

If you were overpaid HB because you had too much capital, the overpayment is calculated taking into account the fact that, had you received no HB, you would have used your capital. This is known as the **'diminishing capital rule'**. It only applies if you were overpaid for more than 13 weeks and either:[148]

- the overpayment was caused by a misrepresentation of, or a failure to disclose, the amount of your capital (see p1200); *or*
- the overpayment was caused by an error (other than an 'official error' – see p1215) about your capital (or that of a member of your family).

For each 13-week period, the local authority assumes that your capital is reduced by the amount of overpaid HB.[149]

From whom can an overpayment be recovered

The general rule is that a recoverable overpayment can be recovered from the person to whom it was paid – eg, a landlord.[150] However, this does not apply if someone else misrepresented or failed to disclose a material fact, or if someone else should have realised that there was an overpayment at the time.

An overpayment can be recovered from someone other than the person to whom it was paid, including the claimant, if:[151]

- the overpayment was caused by misrepresentation or failure to disclose a material fact (see p1199). In this case, it can be recovered from the person who misrepresented or failed to disclose the fact, but not the person to whom the payment was made; *or*
- the overpayment was caused by an official error (see p1215) and the claimant (or someone acting on the claimant's behalf) or any other person to whom the HB was paid could reasonably have been expected to realise that there was an overpayment at the time. In this case, it can be recovered from whoever should have realised, but not the person to whom it was paid; *or*
- neither of the above two bullet points apply, in which case the overpayment is also recoverable from the claimant. If you are the claimant, the overpayment may be recovered from you, as well as the person to whom it was paid.

If you are the claimant and the overpayment is recoverable from you, no matter how it was caused, the local authority can also recover the overpayment by deducting any HB paid to your partner, provided you were a couple both at the time of the overpayment and when the deduction is made.[152]

If you think you have been wrongly chosen under these rules (eg, because you did not fail to disclose a material fact), you can appeal to the First-tier Tribunal. However, if the overpayment can be recovered from you under these rules, you cannot appeal simply because you think the local authority should recover from another person instead.[153]

If the person from whom recovery is being sought dies, the local authority may consider recovering any outstanding overpayment from her/his estate.[154]

Methods of recovery

A local authority can decide how much, if any, of a recoverable overpayment it will recover (but see p220 if the overpayment was of a payment on account).[155] This is similar to the discretion that the DWP and HMRC have to recover overpayments (see p1208).

If the local authority decides to recover, it can ask for the whole amount or recover it by instalments. When an overpayment is recovered from your landlord, note how this affects your liability to pay rent (see p1223). Overpayments of HB can be recovered:

- from payments of HB (see below);
- from other benefits (see p1220);
- by adjusting your rent account if you are a local authority tenant (see p1221);
- by your employer deducting amounts from your wages or salary (see p1221);
- through the courts (see p1221).

The methods used and the rates of recovery should be consistent between groups of claimants. For example, council tenants should not be required to repay an overpayment in a lump sum if private tenants can repay by instalments.

Note: except when seeking to recover overpaid benefit through the courts, there is no time limit within which a local authority must begin recovery action.

Deductions from housing benefit

A local authority can recover an overpayment by deducting amounts from HB payable to any person from whom an overpayment can be recovered (see p1206).[156] As well as yourself, this could be your partner or your landlord. Deductions can be made from both future payments of HB and any arrears that are owing.

If you have moved home, the local authority may be able to recover an overpayment of HB from your previous home by adjusting the HB paid at your new home. It can decide to do this if:[157]

- the overpayment occurred after you moved, and occurred because you were no longer living at your previous home; *and*
- the same local authority that paid you the overpayment is paying your HB at your new home.

In these circumstances, the local authority can deduct all the weekly HB owing to you for your new home to recover the overpayment, for however many weeks you were overpaid at your previous home.

Part 8: Claiming benefits and getting paid
Chapter 53: Overpayments
5. Overpayments of housing benefit

Deductions from your partner's housing benefit

If you were the claimant and the overpayment, no matter how it was caused, is recoverable from you, the local authority can also recover it by deductions from any HB later awarded to your partner, provided you were a couple at both the time of the overpayment and when the deduction is made.[158]

Deductions from your landlord's housing benefit

The local authority may recover the overpayment from:

- HB paid to your landlord if s/he is claiming HB her/himself;[159] *or*
- HB paid direct to your landlord on your behalf.[160] The notification of the overpayment (see p1222) should make it clear from whom the authority is recovering; *or*
- HB paid direct to your landlord on behalf of other claimants.[161]

When HB is recovered from a landlord in this way, there are special rules on how this affects your liability to pay rent (see p1223).

Maximum deductions

The maximum weekly amount that can be deducted is £19.25 if you have agreed to pay a penalty (see p1236), admitted fraud or been found guilty of fraud, or £11.55 in any other case.[162]

The rate of recovery can be increased by up to half of any amount of earned income which is disregarded as income in the calculation of your HB (see p413 and p456).[163] Amounts of income disregarded for childcare costs cannot be used to increase the rate of recovery in this way.

However, you can argue that the rate will cause you hardship and a lesser amount should be recovered instead. You must be left with at least 50 pence of HB per week.[164]

Deductions from other benefits

The local authority can ask the DWP to recover an overpayment of HB by making deductions from most of the benefits in this *Handbook* (except guardian's allowance and, arguably, child benefit).[165] If the overpayment is recoverable from your partner (see p1218), it can be recovered by deductions from her/his universal credit (UC), IS, income-based JSA, income-related ESA, pension credit or personal independence payment.

An overpayment can also be recovered from any benefits paid to your landlord in her/his own right.[166]

Deductions can only be made if:[167]

- a recoverable overpayment has been made as a result of a misrepresentation of, or failure to disclose (see p1200), a material fact by you, on your behalf or by or on behalf of another person to whom HB has been paid; *and*
- the local authority is unable to recover that overpayment from any HB; *and*

8

- the person who is to repay the overpayment is receiving a sufficient amount of at least one of the relevant benefits to allow deductions to be made.

Except for UC (see p1210), there are no rules limiting the maximum amount that can be deducted. However, you can argue that your rate of repayment should be reasonable. If you are on IS, income-based JSA or income-related ESA, argue that the weekly maximums for these benefits should apply (see p1212). Ask the DWP to use its discretion to reduce the amounts if the deductions will cause you hardship.

If deductions stop because you are no longer entitled to a particular benefit, or the amount to which you are entitled is insufficient for deductions to be made, the DWP notifies the local authority which, once again, becomes responsible for any further recovery action.

Adjusting your rent account

If you are a local authority tenant, the local authority can recover an overpayment by adding it as a debt to your rent account. If a local authority recovers overpaid HB in this way, the overpayment should be separately identified and you should be informed that the amount being recovered does not represent rent arrears.[168]

If the local authority is seeking to evict you because you have rent arrears, you should get advice. It cannot argue you owe it rent arrears if you have only been overpaid HB. Local authorities are reminded in DWP guidance that overpayments of HB paid to their own tenants are not rent arrears and should not be treated as such.[169]

An overpayment cannot be recovered in this way if you have a private or housing association landlord. However, an overpayment can be recovered from your landlord (see p1220). If the local authority recovers from your landlord, you might count as being in rent arrears (see p1203).

Deductions from earnings

The local authority can order your employer to deduct amounts from your (but not your partner's) wages or salary in order to recover the overpayment.[170] The rules for this are explained on p1212.

Court action

If a local authority cannot use any of the methods of recovery listed on p1219 and you cannot agree on repayments, it can try to recover the money you owe through the County Court (sheriff court in Scotland) if it thinks you can afford to make repayments. It should not start proceedings until your time for challenging the decision has passed.

A local authority should not use court proceedings to recover an overpayment if it has not followed the correct procedure (see p1213) – eg, if it has not issued the correct notification.[171]

Part 8: Claiming benefits and getting paid
Chapter 53: Overpayments
5. Overpayments of housing benefit

A local authority can:

- sue you for the debt created by the overpayment. If the correct procedure has not been followed, you can use this as a defence.[172] You may also be able to claim compensation in certain circumstances. However, you cannot say that you should have received more HB;[173] *or*
- use the special rules to register the overpayment as a debt which can then be recovered using a court procedure.[174] Get advice if you think the local authority is not entitled to do this.

Note: recovery action through the courts in England and Wales must be taken within six years of the decision to recover or, if later, any written acknowledgement of the overpayment or voluntary repayment.[175] In Scotland, the DWP regards the time limit as being 20 years from the date of the decision to recover (or, if there was no such decision, five years from the decision that there was an overpayment). Get advice about how these limits apply to your case.[176]

If the local authority is successful in its court proceedings against you, you may have to pay legal costs and interest, as well as the overpayment. Remember that court procedures often require you to take action within a very short period of time. If the local authority is threatening to use court proceedings, get advice.

Notification of an overpayment

If the local authority decides that a recoverable overpayment has occurred, it must write to the person from whom repayment is being sought (see p1218) within 14 days if possible, notifying her/him of this.[177]

This notification must state:[178]

- that there is an overpayment which is legally recoverable; *and*
- the reason why there is a recoverable overpayment; *and*
- the amount of the recoverable overpayment; *and*
- how the amount of the overpayment was calculated; *and*
- the benefit weeks to which the overpayment relates; *and*
- if recovery is to be made from future benefit, the amount of the deductions; *and*
- if recovery is to be made from your landlord by deductions from someone else's HB, your identity and the claimant from whose HB the deduction will be made;[179] *and*
- your right to ask for a further written explanation of any of the decisions the local authority has made about the overpayment, how you can do this and the time limit for doing so; *and*
- that you have a right to ask the local authority to reconsider any of the decisions it has made about the overpayment, how you can do this and the time limit for doing so.

It may also include any other relevant matters.

Guidance states that the local authority should issue a single notification to all relevant parties (eg, landlord and tenant) saying from whom the overpayment is recoverable and from whom it is not.[180]

If you write and ask the local authority for a more detailed written explanation of any of the decisions it has made about an overpayment, it must send you this within 14 days or, if this is not reasonably practicable, as soon as possible.[181]

If a notification sent to you is a clear decision that there is an overpayment which is recoverable from you, but does not contain all the matters above, it is only valid if the omissions do not put you at a disadvantage.[182] If, for example, it does not set out your right to apply for a revision so that you do not do so until it is too late, you have been put at a disadvantage and so can argue that the overpayment is not recoverable. However, if the decision is not about recoverability and is only about the fact that you have been overpaid, you can argue that there is no decision saying that you must repay the overpayment.[183]

No recovery should be sought until after you have been notified and the one-month time period for asking for a revision or appealing has passed.[184]

The effect of recovery from your landlord

If you are a private or housing association tenant, an overpayment of HB recovered from your landlord (see p1220) could mean that s/he tries to obtain money from you. The landlord could argue that you are in rent arrears as a result and could seek possession of your home.

Whether or not HB was paid direct to your landlord, s/he may still try to argue that, even if you owe no rent, you nevertheless owe a debt under common law. This is probably not correct. If s/he threatens to sue you, get advice straight away.

If you are a local authority tenant, these rules do not apply. However, the local authority can recover an overpayment of HB by making deductions from your rent account (see p1220).

If overpaid HB was paid direct to your landlord, the following rules apply.

- If the local authority recovers the overpayment from your landlord by making deductions from direct payments of other tenants' HB (see p1219), the other tenants are treated as having paid the amount of the deduction towards their rent.[185]

- If the local authority recovers the overpayment from your landlord by making deductions from direct payments of your HB, you are treated as having paid the amount of the deduction towards your rent if your landlord is convicted of an offence or agrees to pay a penalty (see p1236) in relation to that overpayment.[186] If the local authority decides to recover under this rule, it must notify both your landlord and you that you are to be treated as having paid your rent.[187]

In these situations, your landlord cannot argue that you are in arrears of rent. It is also much easier to argue that your landlord cannot sue you under common law for a debt.

Challenging an overpayment decision

You can apply for a revision or appeal (see Chapters 56 and 57) if you want to dispute:

- the decision that you have been overpaid HB;
- the amount of the overpayment;
- the decision that it can be recovered;
- that the overpayment is to be recovered from you under the rules set out on p1218.

Do not pay back any of the money until your challenge has been dealt with. Local authority guidance states that overpayments should not be recovered while under appeal.[188] If the local authority is already making deductions from your HB (see p1217) or deductions are being made from your other benefits (see p1220), ask it to stop this straight away.

Notes

1. Introduction
1 *SSWP v Payne and Another* [2011] UKSC 60
2 Official advice via gov.uk/government/ publications/debt-respite-scheme- breathing-space-guidance

2. Overpayments that are always recoverable
3 s71ZB(1) SSAA 1992; art 5(3A) WRA(No.8)O
4 s71ZB(3) SSAA 1992
5 *LP v SSWP* [2018] UKUT 332 (AAC)
6 Reg 16 SS(OR) Regs
7 Reg 8(3) SS(OR) Regs
8 Reg 7 SS(OR) Regs
9 Reg 9(1)(a) and (b) and (2) SS(OR) Regs
10 Reg 9(1)(c) SS(OR) Regs
11 Reg 9(3) SS(OR) Regs
12 Reg 4 SS(OR) Regs
13 s74 SSAA 1992
14 Reg 7(1) SS(PAOR) Regs
15 R(SB) 3/91
16 s74(2) and (4) SSAA 1992
17 See, for example, the appeals in R(SB) 28/85 and R(IS) 6/02

18 s71(4) SSAA 1992; reg 11 SS(PAOR) Regs; reg 35 CB&GA(Admin) Regs
19 Reg 11 SS(PAOR) Regs; reg 35 CB&GA(Admin) Regs
20 Sch 2 para 20(d) SS&CS(DA) Regs

3. Overpayments that are sometimes recoverable
21 s71(1) and (5A) SSAA 1992; R(SB) 34/83
22 R(SB) 2/92
23 CDLA/5803/1999
24 CDLA/1823/2004
25 R(S) 4/86; R(I) 3/75
26 *B v SSWP* [2005] EWCA Civ 929, reported as R(IS) 9/06. The effect of the decision is that recovery is under reg 32 SS(C&P) Regs and, presumably, under the equivalent rules in reg 24 JSA Regs and reg 23 CB&GA(Admin) Regs.
27 R(SB) 21/82
28 R(SB) 54/83; CSB/296/1985
29 CG/160/1999
30 R(SB) 21/82
31 Reg 32(1A) SS(C&P) Regs; reg 24(1)- (5A) JSA Regs; reg 38(3) UC,PIP,JSA&ESA(C&P) Regs

32 *Hooper v SSWP* [2007] EWCA Civ 495, reported as R(IB) 4/07. See also official guidance in Memo DMG 26/07.
33 R(A) 2/06
34 Reg 32(1B) SS(C&P) Regs; reg 24(7) JSA Regs; reg 38(4) UC,PIP,JSA&ESA(C&P) Regs
35 *DG v SSWP* [2009] UKUT 120 (AAC)
36 R(SB) 15/87; *Hinchy v SSWP* [2005] UKHL 16, reported as R(IS) 7/05
37 *SK v Department for Communities (ESA)* [2020] NICom 73. This Northern Ireland Commissioners decision found that developments in the computerisation of DWP administration mean that the decision of the House of Lords in *Hinchy v SSWP* [2005] UKHL 16 should no longer be followed. The decision is not binding authority in Great Britain, but may be persuasive.
38 Reg 23(5) CB&GA(Admin) Regs
39 *LH v SSWP (RP)* [2017] UKUT 249 (AAC)
40 CG/5631/1999; CIS/1887/2002; *WA v SSWP* [2009] UKUT 132 (AAC); *GJ v SSWP (IS)* [2010] UKUT 107 (AAC)
41 Reg 32(1B) SS(C&P) Regs requires notification in writing or by telephone, unless the DWP specifically requires otherwise
42 R(SB) 18/85
43 CWSB/2/1985
44 R(SB) 15/87
45 CDLA/6336/1999
46 R(SB) 15/87; CIS/3529/2008
47 R(SB) 54/83
48 CSB/393/1985
49 CIS/5117/1998
50 R(SB) 9/85
51 *Jones and Sharples v CAO* [1994] 1 All ER 225 (CA); R(SB) 9/85
52 R(SB) 18/85
53 R(SB) 2/91
54 R(SB) 3/90
55 *Sheriff v CAO* [1995] (CA), reported as R(IS) 14/96
56 CG/4494/1999 suggests the principle may apply in social security; R(IS) 4/06 is more doubtful, but does not rule it out
57 CIS/3846/2001
58 *Jones and Sharples v CAO* [1994] 1 All ER 225 (CA); *Franklin v CAO* [1995] (CA); CIS/674/1994; CIS/583/1994; CIS/674/1994
59 *Franklin v CAO* [1995] (CA)
60 CIS/583/1994
61 CDLA/6336/1999
62 *TM v SSWP (ESA)* [2015] UKUT 109 (AAC)

63 CIS/159/1990; CS/11700/1996; CSIS/7/1994; CG/5631/1999; *GJ v SSWP (IS)* [2010] UKUT 107 (AAC)
64 *Duggan v CAO* [1989] (CA); CG/662/1998; CG/4494/1999; *Hinchy v SSWP* [2003] EWCA Civ 138
65 *JM v SSWP (IS)* [2011] UKUT 15 (AAC)
66 CIS/222/1991
67 s71(5A) SSAA 1992; CIS/3228/2003; R(IS) 13/05. See CPC/3743/2006 for when not all the overpayment period has been covered by the change of the award.
68 Reg 12 SS(PAOR) Regs
69 CIS/3228/2003
70 CSIS/45/1990
71 R(SB) 7/91
72 *LL v SSWP* [2013] UKUT 208 (AAC)
73 This was the case in *Hamilton v Department for Social Development* [2010] NICA 46, but it is clear from *SSWP v AD (IS)* [2011] UKUT 184 (AAC) that whether this is the case depends on the specific decision-making history in your case
74 R(SB) 20/84; R(SB) 24/87
75 Reg 13(1)(b) and (1A) SS(PAOR) Regs
76 *Commock v CAO*, reported as an appendix to R(SB) 6/90; CSIS/8/1995
77 Reg 14 SS(PAOR) Regs
78 CIS/5825/1999
79 s71(3) SSAA 1992
80 *B v SSWP* [2005] EWCA Civ 929, reported as R(IS) 9/06, which says that overpayments for failure to disclose are recoverable because of a breach of duty by a claimant of reg 32 SS(C&P) Regs; CIS/1996/2006; CIS/2125/2006; *PA v SSWP (DLA)* [2016] UKUT 428 (AAC)
81 R(IS) 5/03. This tribunal of commissioners' decision was intended to resolve the conflict between the earlier CIS/332/1993 and R(IS) 5/00, and preferred the latter.
82 *PA v SSWP (DLA)* [2016] UKUT 428 (AAC)
83 CA/1014/1999; CSDLA/1282/2001
84 *Secretary of State for Social Services v Solly* [1974] 3 All ER 922; R(SB) 21/82
85 CIS/1423/1997
86 *PA v SSWP (DLA)* [2016] UKUT 428 (AAC)
87 *MC v SSWP (IS)* [2015] UKUT 600 (AAC)
88 DWP, *Benefit Overpayment Recovery Guide*, Chapter 4

4. Recovery of overpaid benefit

89 gov.uk/government/publications/what-happens-if-you-are-overpaid-universal-credit-jobseekers-allowance-or-employment-and-support-allowance. At the time of writing, this guidance remains withdrawn.

90 When the Welfare Reform Bill (which introduced these rules) was being debated, the minister said it was the intention not to recover many overpayments which had been caused by official error – see House of Commons, *Hansard*, 19 May 2011, col 1019

91 DWP, *Benefit Overpayment Recovery Guide,* available at gov.uk

92 Reg 10 SS(OR) Regs

93 Reg 16(7A) and (7B) SS(PAOR) Regs

94 Reg 11 SS(OR) Regs

95 DWP, *Benefit Overpayment Recovery Guide,* April 2021

96 Reg 11(7) SS(OR) Regs

97 Reg 11(8) SS(OR) Regs

98 Reg 11(9) SS(OR) Regs

99 Reg 12 SS(OR) Regs

100 Reg 13 SS(OR) Regs

101 Reg 14 SS(OR) Regs. The maximum recoverable weekly amounts stated in this rule are calculated as percentages of a monthly figure of UC. It is assumed that these are converted to weekly figures.

102 Reg 29A SS(PAOR) Regs

103 s71ZE SSAA 1992

104 Reg 42A CB&GA(Admin) Regs

105 Reg 16(1) and (2) SS(PAOR) Regs

106 Regs 15 and 16 SS(PAOR) Regs

107 Reg 17 SS(PAOR) Regs

108 Reg 16(3) SS(PAOR) Regs

109 s74(2)(b) SSAA 1992

110 Reg 16(4), (4A), (5) and (6) SS(PAOR) Regs

111 Reg 16(6) SS(PAOR) Regs

112 Reg 16(5A) SS(PAOR) Regs

113 Reg 16(7A) and (7B) SS(PAOR) Regs

114 Reg 18 SS(OR) Regs

115 Reg 19 SS(OR) Regs

116 Reg 23 SS(OR) Regs

117 Reg 30 SS(OR) Regs

118 Reg 21 SS(OR) Regs

119 Reg 20(3) SS(OR) Regs

120 Reg 20(3A)-(3B) SS(OR) Regs

121 Regs 17(1) and 20(7) SS(OR) Regs

122 Reg 29 SS(OR) Regs

123 Reg 25 SS(OR) Regs

124 s71(10) SSAA 1992

125 s9(1) Limitation Act 1980

126 DWP, *Benefit Overpayment Recovery Guide,* based on the provisions of the Prescription and Limitation (Scotland) Act 1973, available at gov.uk

127 *CPAG v SSWP* [2010] UKSC 54, upholding the decision of the Court of Appeal in *CPAG, R (on the application of) v SSWP* [2009] EWCA Civ 1058. The DWP's Overpayment Recovery Guide still states that it can use common law principles for recovering 'overprovisioning' overpayments. This guidance is not in accordance with the law.

5. Overpayments of housing benefit

128 Reg 99 HB Regs; reg 80 HB(SPC) Regs

129 Reg 99 HB Regs; reg 80 HB(SPC) Regs

130 Reg 93(3) HB Regs; reg 74(3) HB(SPC) Regs

131 Reg 100(4) HB Regs; reg 81(4) HB(SPC) Regs

132 Reg 100(2) HB Regs; reg 81(2) HB(SPC) Regs

133 *Duggan v CAO* [1989] (CA); *R on the application of Sier v Cambridge CC* [2001] EWCA Civ 1523; CH/571/2003; CH/3761/2005

134 Reg 100(3) HB Regs; reg 81(3) HB(SPC) Regs

135 HB/CTB Circular A23/2009

136 *MB v Christchurch BC (HB)* [2014] UKUT 201 (AAC), reported as [2014] AACR 39

137 CH/2567/2007; HB/CTB Circular A15/2009

138 CH/571/2003; CH/5485/2002

139 CH/939/2004; see also *R on the application of Sier v Cambridge CC* [2001] EWCA Civ 1523; CH/3761/2005

140 *R on the application of Sier v Cambridge CC* [2001] EWCA Civ 1523

141 *Warwick DC v Freeman* [1994] 27 HLR 616 (CA); CH/4918/2003

142 *R v Liverpool City Council ex parte Griffiths* [1990] 22 HLR 312; CH/2554/2002; CH/2567/2007

143 *DP v East Dorset DC (HB)* [2020] UKUT 270 (AAC)

144 Reg 104 HB Regs; reg 85 HB(SPC) Regs; *Adan v LB Hounslow and SSWP* [2004] EWCA Civ 101, reported as R(H) 5/04; CH/4943/2001; HB/CTB Circular A13/2006; *JM v LB Tower Hamlets* [2015] UKUT 460 (AAC)

145 Reg 104(1) HB Regs; reg 85 HB(SPC) Regs

146 *R v Kensington and Chelsea RBC ex parte Brandt* [1995] 28 HLR 528 (QBD), at 537

147 Reg 104(3) HB Regs; reg 85(3) HB(SPC) Regs
148 Reg 103 HB Regs; reg 84 HB(SPC) Regs
149 Reg 103(1)(a) and (b) HB Regs; reg 84(1)(a) and (b) HB(SPC) Regs
150 s75(3)(a) SSAA 1992
151 Reg 101(2) HB Regs; reg 82(2) HB(SPC) Regs
152 Reg 102(1ZA) HB Regs; reg 83(1ZA) HB(SPC) Regs
153 R(H) 6/06
154 DWP, *Housing Benefit Overpayments Guide*, paras 4.43(k) and 4.210-89, available at gov.uk;
NSP v Stoke on Trent City Council and AT [2020] UKUT 311 (AAC). This makes clear that a claimant is always a second respondent in an appeal made by a landlord.
155 s75(1) SSAA 1992
156 Reg 102 HB Regs; reg 83 HB(SPC) Regs; s75 SSAA 1992
157 Reg 104A HB Regs; reg 85A HB(SPC) Regs
158 Reg 102(1ZA) HB Regs; reg 83(1ZA) HB(SPC) Regs
159 s75(5)(a) SSAA 1992; reg 106 HB Regs; reg 87 HB(SPC) Regs
160 s75(5)(b) SSAA 1992; reg 106 HB Regs; reg 87 HB(SPC) Regs
161 s75(5)(c) SSAA 1992; reg 106 HB Regs; reg 87 HB(SPC) Regs
162 Reg 102 HB Regs; reg 83 HB(SPC) Regs; HB/CTB Circular A42/00
163 Reg 102(4) HB Regs; reg 83(4) HB(SPC) Regs
164 Reg 102(5) HB Regs; reg 83(5) HB(SPC) Regs
165 Reg 105(1)(a) HB Regs
166 s75(5)(a) SSAA 1992; reg 106 HB Regs; reg 87 HB(SPC) Regs
167 Regs 102 and 105 HB Regs; regs 83 and 86 HB(SPC) Regs
168 *R v Haringey LBC ex parte Azad Ayub* [1992] 25 HLR 566 (QBD)
169 DWP, *Housing Benefit Overpayments Guide*, para 4.90
170 Reg 106A HB Regs; reg 87A HB(SPC) Regs; *LA Welfare Direct Bulletin* 9/2019
171 *Warwick DC v Freeman* [1994] 27 HLR 616 (CA)
172 *Warwick DC v Freeman* [1994] 27 HLR 616 (CA)
173 *Plymouth CC v Gigg* [1997] 30 HLR 284 (CA)
174 s75(7) SSAA 1992
175 s9(1) Limitation Act 1980
176 DWP, *Benefit Overpayment Recovery Guide*, based on the provisions of the Prescription and Limitation (Scotland) Act 1973, available at gov.uk
177 Reg 90(1)(b) HB Regs; reg 71(1)(b) HB(SPC) Regs
178 Sch 9 paras 2, 3, 6 and 15 HB Regs; Sch 8 paras 2, 3, 6 and 15 HB(SPC) Regs; para A7.222 GM
179 Sch 9 para 15(2) HB Regs; Sch 8 para 15(2) HB(SPC) Regs
180 HB/CTB Circular A13/2006
181 Reg 90(4) HB Regs; reg 71(4) HB(SPC) Regs
182 *Haringey LBC v Awaritefe* [1999] 32 HLR 517 (CA)
183 CH/1395/2006
184 DWP, *Housing Benefit Overpayments Guide*, Part 4, paras 4.240-42, available at gov.uk
185 s75(6) SSAA 1992
186 s75(6) SSAA 1992; reg 107 HB Regs; reg 88 HB(SPC) Regs
187 Reg 107(3) HB Regs; reg 88(3) HB(SPC) Regs
188 DWP, *Housing Benefit Overpayments Guide*, Part 4, paras 4.240-42, available at gov.uk

8

Chapter 54

Fraud and penalties

This chapter covers:
1. Civil penalties (p1229)
2. Investigations (p1230)
3. Prosecution of offences (p1234)
4. Administrative penalties for benefit offences (p1236)
5. Sanctions for benefit offences (p1239)

This chapter covers the rules on fraud for benefits administered by the DWP, housing benefit, child benefit and guardian's allowance. For tax credits and fraud, see Chapter 66. For the rules on the Scottish benefits and fraud, see Chapter 79. This chapter does not cover the rules for statutory sick, maternity, adoption, paternity, shared parental and parental bereavement pay.

8 Key facts

- When you claim benefit, you must give correct and complete information to the DWP, HM Revenue and Customs or the local authority. You might commit an offence if you deliberately mislead the agency dealing with your claim.
- You must report changes in your circumstances that could affect your entitlement. You may commit an offence if you do not notify the relevant office of changes promptly.
- Even if you are not suspected of an offence, you may get a fine (known as a 'civil penalty') if you provide incorrect information and you are considered to have acted negligently, or if you have not notified a change of circumstances promptly and do not have a reasonable excuse.
- If it is believed that you have committed fraud, you may be prosecuted. Alternatively, you may be given the option of paying an administrative penalty. Your benefit could be suspended or you could be given a sanction, even if you are not prosecuted.
- If you are suspected or accused of fraud, get advice before taking any action or making any statements.

1. Civil penalties

Even if you are not considered to have acted fraudulently, you can be given a civil penalty if you or someone acting on your behalf have acted carelessly in relation to your claim or award.

Civil penalties are different from the 'administrative penalties' imposed for benefit offences (see p1236). You cannot be given a civil penalty if you have been charged in connection with, or accepted a formal caution for, the same benefit offence, or have received a notice about an administrative penalty for that offence.

A civil penalty of £50 *may* be given if:[1]

- you 'negligently' make an incorrect statement or representation, or negligently give incorrect information or evidence, about a claim for or an award of a benefit, and you do not take 'reasonable steps' to correct the error; *or*
- you do not provide information or evidence, or you fail to notify a 'relevant change of circumstances', and you do not have a 'reasonable excuse'; *and*
- your negligence or failure results in your being overpaid benefit of more than £65.[2] The overpayment period must start on or after 1 October 2012.

Even if the DWP decides you fit the criteria above, imposing a civil penalty on you is still at its discretion and both your circumstances and the circumstances that led to the overpayment should be considered before one is imposed.[3]

Definitions

A **'relevant change of circumstances'** is one that affects entitlement to benefit.[4]

'Reasonable excuse' means something that would have caused a reasonable person of a similar age and experience to act as you did.[5] Your state of health and the information which you received or might have obtained may be relevant, as may any advice you have received.[6]

Other terms used are not defined in the legislation but the DWP has produced guidance on the meaning of the following.[7]

'Negligently' is acting carelessly, not paying attention to, or disregarding the importance of, anything that needs to be done in relation to your claim. It is more than a simple mistake.

'Reasonable steps' is doing something which is sensible or practicable to correct an error.

The penalty is added to the overpayment and recovered in the same way (see p1209 for overpayments under the universal credit system, p1219 for housing benefit overpayments and p1211 for all other overpayments).[8] If you are claiming jointly with your partner and the penalty is for negligently making or giving incorrect statements, representations, information or evidence, it can be

Part 8: Claiming benefits and getting paid
Chapter 54: Fraud and penalties
2. Investigations

recovered from your partner instead of you, unless s/he was not (and could not reasonably be expected to be) aware of the error.

You can appeal against the imposition of a civil penalty (see Chapter 57)[9] – eg, you can argue that you did not behave negligently or that you had a 'reasonable excuse' for not declaring a change in your circumstances. **Note:** you may also want to consider appealing the overpayment decision (see Chapter 53).

2. **Investigations**

Investigation of suspected benefit fraud covered by this chapter is carried out by the DWP's Counter Fraud, Compliance and Debt Directorate. It does not have to tell you straight away about any enquiries it is making. It usually waits until it has collected more information and then asks you to attend an interview.

Collecting information

There are special rules allowing the release of information to the DWP from:
- HM Revenue and Customs (HMRC);[10]
- government departments – eg, on issues about passports, immigration, emigration, nationality and prisoners;[11]
- the Registration Service – eg, about age, death, marriage and civil partnership;[12]
- local authorities.[13]

Local authorities may also be supplied with information held by the DWP or HMRC, and may share information with other local authorities.[14]

Local authorities, HMRC and the DWP can require information about redirected post and have undelivered social security post returned to them.[15]

All information acquired is confidential to the bodies concerned with the administration of benefit, including private companies contracted to carry out such functions. Unauthorised disclosure of this information is a criminal offence.[16]

Are you unhappy about the use of your personal information?
The Data Protection Act 2018 restricts the use of personal data held about you. If a local authority, the DWP or HMRC makes a request for information which you think is inappropriate or unreasonable, refer the matter to the Information Commissioner (see ico.org.uk).

Powers of investigation

As 'authorised officers', fraud investigators have certain powers to obtain information.[17] '**Authorised officers'** can be:

- officials of any government department (not just the DWP); *or*
- employees of local authorities carrying out housing benefit (HB) functions; *or*
- employees of organisations that perform contracted-out HB functions.

Authorised officers should use a code of practice when obtaining information.[18] Information that is the subject of 'legal privilege' (ie, confidential communication between a legal adviser and her/his client) cannot be requested.[19]

Authorised officers have powers to enter, at a reasonable time, premises which they have reasonable grounds for suspecting are:[20]

- a person's place of employment; *or*
- where a trade or business is carried out or documents relating to it are kept; *or*
- where a personal or occupational pension scheme is administered or documents relating to it are kept; *or*
- where someone operating a compensatory scheme for an industrial accident or disease may be found; *or*
- where a person on whose behalf a compensatory payment for an industrial accident or disease has been made may be found.

The above may include someone's home. The authorised officer must show a certificate of appointment if asked for it. S/he can question anyone on the premises and require, if reasonable, any documents or copies of documents.

Authorised officers cannot come into your home without your permission (except if you run a business from your home) and they cannot detain you. They cannot make you give information or answer questions in such a way as to confess that you, or your partner, are guilty of an offence.[21]

Authorised officers may access certain electronic records, including those kept by:[22]

- any bank or person whose business is providing credit to the public – eg, credit card companies and building societies;
- the Director of National Savings;
- any insurer;
- any credit reference agency;
- any money transfer service;
- any utility or telephone company;
- any educational institution;
- the Student Loans Company.

All fraud investigators can use surveillance to investigate social security fraud – eg, observing people entering or leaving premises. Any surveillance must be authorised by an officer of the appropriate level.

Fraud investigators in England and Wales are bound by codes of practice under the Police and Criminal Evidence Act 1984.[23] In Scotland, fraud investigators must work to the common law principle of the 'test of fairness'. If these are

Part 8: Claiming benefits and getting paid
Chapter 54: Fraud and penalties
2. Investigations

breached, this may restrict the use of evidence they have obtained.[24] If you think the officers have acted unfairly, get advice.

Interviews under caution

If you are suspected of fraud, fraud investigators should carry out a formal interview, known as an 'interview under caution'. You should receive reasonable advance notification in writing (uploaded to your journal if you are claiming universal credit) of around 10 to 15 days informing you specifically that you must attend an interview under caution. You may receive a reminder telephone call before the interview confirming your attendance and to check whether any special arrangements are needed.[25] Note that an interview under caution is not the same as other types of interviews conducted by the DWP, such as 'compliance interviews', which are not fraud related.

You should always be cautioned before the interview. If the fraud officer fails to do so, the interview may not be admissible in court. If you do not understand the caution, its meaning should be explained to you. If you appear unable to understand the significance of the interview or the questions being put to you (eg, due to incapacity or a learning disability), you should be asked if you want someone to assist or attend with you (such as a relative, other 'appropriate adult' or solicitor) and the interview may be suspended if you do.[26]

You do not have to answer any questions put to you, but if you do not answer questions, this might be taken as a sign of guilt. If you decide not to answer questions, you could instead prepare a written statement to give to the investigators.

You might not be told why the interview is happening. If you have not been informed of the purpose of the interview, it may be inadmissible as evidence in court.

The interview is normally recorded and you can request a copy. A transcript is produced for use at any trial or appeal hearing.

If you have extra travel costs to attend the interview, these should be reimbursed. If you need someone to accompany you because you are vulnerable (eg, you are under 18, have a learning disability or other complex needs), her/his travel expenses can also be reimbursed.

Are you suspected of fraud?

1. If you think fraud officers may interview you, get advice before you attend the interview. Free legal advice may be available from a solicitor.

2. Take someone (eg, a solicitor, adviser or friend) to the interview with you. Although s/he cannot speak for you, s/he can support you and take notes. A solicitor can advise you during the interview, ask for clarification of questions and challenge improper questioning.

3. Try to remain calm and listen carefully to the questions you are asked. If you do not understand anything, ask for clarification. You must answer the questions yourself. Think carefully about the implications of the answers you give.

4. If you think you can explain why the situation has arisen, you should mention it at the interview, as any explanation you give later is less likely to be believed if you are prosecuted.[27] If you can explain matters, your benefit is less likely to be taken away.

5. Do not confess to something that you did not do just to finish the interview or to prevent your benefit from being stopped.

6. Consider making a complaint (see Chapter 61) if you feel the interview was not conducted fairly or you were treated in a way which failed to take into account issues such as disability.

The effect of a fraud investigation on your benefit

If the DWP, HMRC or local authority has doubts about your entitlement to benefit, other processes may also be applied at the same time as a fraud investigation.

- Your benefit may be suspended (see p1161) – eg, if there are doubts about your entitlement or if there is a possibility that you are being overpaid.
- You may be asked to provide additional information and evidence. If you do not do so within a specified time limit, your award can be terminated (see p1163). If you still believe that you are entitled to benefit, make a new claim.

If a fraud investigation is taking a long time to complete, your benefit may be suspended for a long time. However, the DWP, HMRC or local authority should not withhold your benefit indefinitely without making a decision on whether or not you are entitled to it. Complain if you think an investigation is taking too long (see Chapter 61). If that brings no results, seek legal advice about forcing the DWP, HMRC or local authority to make a decision (see p1410).

The decision on whether you should be prosecuted is separate from a decision to recover any overpayment of benefit (see Chapter 53). The two processes are independent and have different tests. Therefore:

- a decision or appeal on your claim does not have to be delayed while you wait for the outcome of a criminal prosecution;[28]
- a court fine does not prevent recovery of an overpayment. However, if you have to make payments under a compensation order made by a court to the DWP, HMRC or local authority, it cannot also recover that amount as an overpayment.[29]

Acquittal in a fraud case does not necessarily mean that the decision on your benefit entitlement was wrong. Whatever the result of an investigation or prosecution, it may take longer to assess your future claims because your circumstances may be checked more thoroughly. Complain if it takes too long

Part 8: Claiming benefits and getting paid
Chapter 54: Fraud and penalties
3. Prosecution of offences

(see Chapter 61). You should not be prevented from making a fresh claim during a fraud investigation if your circumstances change. You can also apply for an advance payment (see p1153) or help from a local welfare assistance scheme (see p846).

3. Prosecution of offences

Benefit offences can broadly be divided into two categories, based on the severity of the penalty you can be given.

- Making false representations in order to claim benefit is the less serious of the benefit offences (see below).
- Making dishonest representations in order to claim benefit is the more serious benefit offence (see p1235).

In the most serious cases in England and Wales, you may instead be charged with the criminal offences of theft or fraud, and in Scotland, with common law offences.[30] These offences carry more severe penalties.

If found guilty, you can be fined or imprisoned, or both. Any fine that you have to pay is in addition to any recoverable overpayment (see Chapter 53). You can also be given a sanction for a period (see p1239).

In England and Wales, DWP and HM Revenue and Customs (HMRC) prosecutions are carried out by the Crown Prosecution Service, which also conducts prosecutions on behalf of many local authorities. In Scotland, prosecutions are conducted by the Crown Office and Procurator Fiscal Service.

False representations

You commit the offence of making false representations if you:[31]

- make a statement which you know to be false or give information or produce documents that you know to be false (or knowingly cause or allow someone else to do so) in order to claim a benefit or payment for yourself or someone else, or for any other purpose relating to the benefit rules. It does not have to be shown that you intended to obtain benefit to which you were not entitled;[32] *or*
- fail to notify the DWP, HMRC or local authority promptly of a change of circumstances which you know affects your entitlement to benefit or another payment. This also applies to appointees and other third parties receiving benefit on your behalf, and landlords receiving direct payments of housing benefit. You count as notifying a change promptly if you do so as soon as reasonably practicable after the change occurs; *or*
- cause or allow another person to fail to notify a change of circumstances to the DWP, HMRC or local authority promptly which you know affects her/his entitlement to benefit or other payment.

For an offence to have been committed, you must have acted 'knowingly'. You do not 'know' something if you are merely careless about whether or not something is true, or if you fail to find out.[33] You have not committed an offence if you do not notify a change of circumstances that did not affect your entitlement to benefit or if there was already no entitlement to benefit.[34] To have acted 'knowingly', you must have been made aware of where any change must be reported and the manner in which it must be reported.[35]

The maximum penalty for these offences is a £5,000 fine or three months in prison, or both.[36]

Duty to report a change in circumstances

The rules on fraud and your duty to report a change of circumstances are different to those outlined on p1160. For fraud purposes, you only commit an offence if you do not report promptly a change that you *know* affects your benefit. However, to avoid potential allegations of fraud or prosecution, you should report *all* changes promptly. It is always advisable to report the change in a way that allows you to show that you have done so – eg, if in writing, date and retain a copy or get a receipt, keep records of telephone calls and take screenshots if reporting online. For more information about reporting changes of circumstances, see p1160.

Duties of advisers and other third parties

If you are an adviser, you are not under a duty to notify the DWP, HMRC or local authority about a claimant's change of circumstances, provided you have fully advised her/him of the law and her/his requirement to notify changes in her/his circumstances and provide truthful information. In order to commit an offence of allowing or causing someone to fail to notify a change of circumstances, or knowingly allowing or causing someone to give false information, there must be some sort of implied permission given to the person to not report the change or to give false information.[37] You do not 'allow' someone to do something unless you can stop them doing it.[38] You should do nothing to help facilitate a misrepresentation or failure to notify a change of circumstances – eg, help to complete a claim or review form which you know is inaccurate. If you – as an adviser – know that a claimant is being overpaid, you should make sure you advise her/him of her/his duty to notify the relevant benefit authority of the overpayment and you should do nothing that facilitates the overpayment continuing.

Dishonest representations

You commit the offence of making dishonest representations if you make any of the false representations on p1234 in order to claim benefit and you act dishonestly ('knowingly' in Scotland) in doing so.[39] This means that you did something that most people would consider dishonest and that you must have known it was dishonest.[40]

Part 8: Claiming benefits and getting paid
Chapter 54: Fraud and penalties
4. Administrative penalties for benefit offences

The maximum penalty if you are convicted in a magistrates' court (sheriff court in Scotland) is a £5,000 fine or six months in prison (12 months in Scotland), or both.[41] If you are convicted in the Crown Court (High Court in Scotland), you can receive an unlimited fine or up to seven years in prison, or both.[42]

Prosecutions

Not all cases in which there is evidence to justify a prosecution are taken to court. Instead, you may be given the chance to pay an 'administrative penalty' (see p1237). In some cases, no action is taken at all. The factors taken into account include the strength of the evidence, the amount of benefit involved, whether an offence was planned and your personal circumstances. The decision about whether or not to prosecute is normally taken by the Crown Prosecution Service or Crown Office and Procurator Fiscal Service. **Note:** you may be given a sanction, even if you are not prosecuted (see p1239).

There are time limits for bringing a prosecution for making false representations in order to claim benefit (see p1234). A prosecution must be started either within three months of the date the DWP, HMRC or local authority (or, in Scotland, the Crown Office and Procurator Fiscal Service) thinks it has sufficient evidence to prosecute you, or within 12 months of the date you committed the offence, whichever is later.[43]

There are no time limits for bringing a prosecution for making dishonest representations in order to claim benefit (see p1235).

Are you being prosecuted?

If you are being prosecuted, get advice. You may be entitled to free legal help from a solicitor and representation in court. Check carefully that the Counter Fraud, Compliance and Debt Directorate is able to prove all the parts of the offence with which you are charged. Do not plead guilty until you have obtained advice. You should also get specialist welfare rights advice about challenging any overpayment decision and whether it is recoverable separately, as the solicitor helping with any fraud allegations may not be a welfare rights specialist.

4. Administrative penalties for benefit offences

The Counter Fraud, Compliance and Debt Directorate (CFCD) may offer you the option of paying an administrative penalty under civil law instead of being prosecuted for a benefit offence under criminal law. These administrative penalties are not the same as the civil penalties described on p1229. You can still be sanctioned if you accept an administrative penalty (see p1239).

The amount of the penalty depends on when the offence was committed.

- For offences committed wholly after 7 May 2012, the penalty is 50 per cent of any amount overpaid, subject to a minimum of £350 even if you were not actually overpaid, and:[44]
  - a maximum of £2,000 if committed partly or wholly before 1 April 2015; *or*
  - a maximum of £5,000 if committed wholly after 31 March 2015.
- For offences committed partly or wholly before 8 May 2012, the amount of the penalty is 30 per cent of the overpayment.

The overpayment must have been caused by an offence you committed on or after 18 December 1997.[45]

The penalty is added to any overpayment of benefit and is recoverable in the same way (see p1209 for overpayments under the universal credit system, p1219 for housing benefit overpayments and p1211 for all other overpayments).[46]

The option of paying a penalty

You can be offered the option of paying a penalty if:[47]

- an overpayment has been found to be recoverable from you, or, for offences committed wholly after 7 May 2012, would have been if an award had been made. The DWP, HMRC or local authority must have revised or superseded your award of benefit and issued a decision that any overpayment is recoverable (see Chapter 53); *and*
- the overpayment was due to an act or omission on your part. This must have occurred on or after 18 December 1997;[48] *and*
- there are grounds for prosecuting you for an offence relating to the overpayment.

The CFCD issues you with a notice setting out how the scheme works, how to agree to pay a penalty and how to withdraw your agreement.[49] If you are not issued with a proper notice, it may not be possible to enforce the penalty.

The notice is sent with an invitation to an interview to discuss accepting the penalty. The interview is only about whether to offer you a penalty. The interview should not be carried out by an officer who was present during the interview under caution (see p1232).[50] You cannot use it to add to or alter any statement you made about the alleged offence in an interview under caution. If you are unable to decide whether or not to accept the penalty at the interview, you can ask for up to five days to make up your mind, provided the DWP considers the request reasonable in your circumstances.[51]

What happens if you accept a penalty?[52]

1. If you agree to pay a penalty, you cannot be prosecuted for any offence relating to the overpayment. However, you can still be prosecuted in the future if you commit another offence or one relating to a different overpayment.

Part 8: Claiming benefits and getting paid
Chapter 54: Fraud and penalties
4. Administrative penalties for benefit offences

2. If it is found on revision, supersession or appeal that the overpayment is *not due or not recoverable*, any penalty you have paid must be repaid to you. This does not change the fact that you have agreed to pay a penalty in exchange for immunity from prosecution, so you still cannot be prosecuted for the offence.

3. If *the amount of the overpayment is changed* following a revision, supersession or appeal, the agreement is cancelled, so you lose your immunity from prosecution, and any penalty you have paid must be repaid to you. However, if you make a fresh agreement to accept a penalty, you are again immune from prosecution and the amount of penalty you have already paid can be offset against the new penalty rather than being repaid to you.

If you do not accept the penalty, the CFCD *may* pass the case to the Crown Prosecution Service or Crown Office and Procurator Fiscal Service to consider whether to prosecute you.

Changing your mind

If you agree to pay a penalty, you can change your mind, provided you notify the CFCD within 14 days (28 days for offences committed partly or wholly before 8 May 2012) in the manner it specifies.[53] If you change your mind after the end of this period, there is no right of appeal against the imposition of the penalty, but you can complain (see Chapter 61) if you think you should not have been offered a penalty – eg, if it turns out there was insufficient evidence to prosecute you. Note that if any overpayment is later found not to be due or recoverable, any penalty you have already paid must be repaid to you but you remain immune from prosecution for the same offence. If you decide not to accept the penalty, you lose your immunity from prosecution. If you have already paid any part of it, this must be refunded to you.

Should you agree to pay a penalty?

1. Get advice and consider your options carefully.

2. If you are not prosecuted, your case does not go to court and you cannot get a prison sentence.

3. If you accept a penalty, you may still be given a sanction (see p1239).

4. You may be invited to pay a penalty when there is insufficient evidence to prosecute you. The fraud officer can only recommend that your case be considered for prosecution. The Crown Prosecution Service, Crown Office and Procurator Fiscal Service or local authority legal department decides whether or not to prosecute (see p1234). You are not automatically prosecuted if you refuse to accept a penalty.

5. If you are prosecuted and found guilty, the court might offer you a caution or community service rather than a fine. On the other hand, you could get a large fine or even a prison sentence.

6. A penalty may be a substantial amount of money. For minor offences, the amount of a fine imposed by the court could be less.

5. **Sanctions for benefit offences**

If you get certain benefits, known as 'sanctionable benefits' (see p1240), you can be sanctioned if:[54]
- you are convicted of one or more benefit offences in a set of proceedings; *or*
- you agree to pay an administrative penalty for a benefit offence instead of being prosecuted (see p1236).

If you are sanctioned, your benefit is not paid or sometimes paid at a reduced rate (see p1240).

Note: these sanctions are different to those imposed for failing to comply with work-related requirements described in Chapters 47 and 49.

Under what is sometimes referred to as the 'one-strike rule' (because it can apply after just one offence), a conviction is not always required as your benefit can be sanctioned by just agreeing to pay an administrative penalty for an offence.

If you are convicted of a benefit offence and have already committed an earlier offence(s), a longer sanction may be imposed under the 'two-strikes rule' instead. This applies if:[55]
- you are convicted of one or more benefit offences in the current set of proceedings; *and*
- within five years of the date you *committed* any of the current offences, you committed an earlier benefit offence, including an offence for which you accepted an administrative penalty or caution; *and*
- the current offence has not been previously treated as a current offence, and the earlier offence has not been previously treated as an earlier offence, under the two-strikes rule in relation to a reduction of your benefits, a joint claim for jobseeker's allowance (JSA) or a family member's benefit under these sanction rules.

Note: the DWP no longer offers cautions for offences committed wholly or partly after 1 April 2012. The DWP may offer administrative penalties instead. For more details about DWP cautions, see the 2012/13 edition of this *Handbook*. However, an 'administrative caution' may still be recommended in exceptional circumstances by the Crown Prosecution Service or Crown Office and Procurator Fiscal Service as an alternative to prosecution.

The benefit offence(s) must have been committed after 1 April 2010 (for the one-strike rule) or on or after 1 April 2002 (for the two-strikes rule) and be:[56]
- in connection with a 'disqualifying' benefit (see below); *or*
- to attempt, conspire or aid the committing of a benefit offence.

Disqualifying benefits [57]
All social security benefits and tax credits are **'disqualifying benefits'** for the purposes listed above, except statutory sick pay, statutory maternity pay, statutory adoption pay, statutory paternity pay and maternity allowance.

Part 8: Claiming benefits and getting paid
Chapter 54: Fraud and penalties
5. Sanctions for benefit offences

Sanctionable benefits

'Sanctionable benefits' are :[58]
- universal credit (UC);
- employment and support allowance (ESA);
- housing benefit (HB);
- income support (IS);
- JSA (joint-claim JSA is not a 'sanctionable benefit' but can still be removed or reduced);[59]
- pension credit (PC);
- bereavement benefits (except bereavement support payment);
- carer's allowance;
- industrial injuries benefits (except constant attendance and exceptionally severe disablement allowances);
- war pensions (except constant attendance allowance, exceptionally severe disablement allowance and mobility supplement).

Under separate rules, you lose your working tax credit (WTC) if you have committed a benefit offence on or after 5 April 2012 (see p1242).

Payment of any other benefits cannot, therefore, be stopped or reduced under these rules.

The sanctions

Usually, sanctionable benefits are not paid during a sanction period (see p1241). In some cases, however, your benefit may be paid at a reduced rate.
- UC is usually reduced by the rate of your UC standard allowance calculated on a daily basis. This is the same amount as when a sanction for failing to meet your work-related requirements applies (see p1068).[60] However, the 'low rate' only applies if you are subject to no work-related requirements because you are a responsible carer or foster parent for a child under the age of one, an adopter or are pregnant, and the 'high rate' still applies if you are subject to no work-related requirements only because you have been found to have limited capability for work and work-related activity. Only half of the applicable rate is applied to individual joint claimants.
  If your UC is reduced, you may be able to get hardship payments in the same way as when you are sanctioned for not meeting your claimant responsibilities, except that 16/17 year olds *can* get hardship payments in these circumstances (see p1181).[61]
- **IS, income-based JSA, joint-claim JSA, PC and HB** are usually reduced by 40 per cent of the appropriate personal allowance for a single person of your age (see p318), or 20 per cent if you or a member of your family are pregnant or seriously ill.[62] However:

- if you are a member of a joint-claim JSA couple (see p247), one of you is sanctioned for a benefit offence and the other is not subject to *any* type of sanction (including the sanctions described in Chapter 49), JSA is paid at the rate of:[63]
  - contribution-based JSA, if the person who has not been sanctioned qualifies for it; *or*
  - hardship payments, if you and your partner qualify (see p1186);[64] *or*
  - in any other case, income-based JSA calculated as if the partner who has not been sanctioned were a single person. However, both your and your partner's income and capital are taken into account;
- if you are a member of a joint-claim JSA couple, one or both of you are sanctioned for a benefit offence *and* either both of you are also sanctioned under the rules described in Chapter 49 *or* one of you would qualify for IS, JSA is not paid. However, you may still qualify for hardship payments under the rules described on p1186;[65]
- if you are claiming income-based JSA in any circumstances other than those of a joint-claim couple as described in the bullet points above, you are not paid at the reduced rate unless you qualify under rules which are the same as those that apply for JSA hardship payments as described on p1186.[66] If you are also sanctioned under the rules described in Chapter 49, you do not qualify for a reduced rate of JSA under these rules but can still qualify under the rules in Chapter 52;
- HB is unaffected if you or a member of your family are entitled to IS, income-based JSA, income-related ESA or PC during the sanction period.[67]
- **Income-related ESA** is reduced by 100 per cent of the appropriate personal allowance for a single person of your age (see p318), or 40 per cent if you or a member of your family are subject to no work-related requirements, or 20 per cent if you or a member of your family are pregnant or seriously ill.[68] You may be able to get hardship payments if your income-related ESA is reduced in this way (see p1187).

The sanction period

For benefit offences committed wholly after 31 March 2013, the following sanction periods apply.[69]

The sanction period is **three years** if:
- you are convicted for serious fraud or conspiracy to defraud; *or*
- the overpayment is at least £50,000; *or*
- you are given a sentence of at least a year; *or*
- the offence is committed over a period of at least two years.

The sanction period under the one-strike rule (see p1239) is **13 weeks** if you are convicted in less serious cases and **four weeks** if you pay an administrative penalty (see p1236).

Part 8: Claiming benefits and getting paid
Chapter 54: Fraud and penalties
Notes

Sanction periods under the two-strikes rule (see p1239) are **26 weeks** (except where three years applies as above) or **three years** if the earlier offence is within five years of a previous one.

For benefit offences committed partly or wholly before 1 April 2013, the sanction period is four weeks under the one strike rule or 13 weeks under the two strike rule.[70]

The sanction period starts at least 28 days after the determination that a restriction on payment of benefits should apply.[71]

Note: sanctions under these rules prevent payment of a benefit during the sanction period, not entitlement, which ensures the link between benefits and other entitlements (eg, free school lunches and free prescriptions) remains.[72] However, a minimal 10 pence a week entitlement to IS, PC and income-related ESA remains in place while you are sanctioned.[73]

Loss of working tax credit for a benefit offence

You are disqualified from being paid WTC for a set period of time if you have committed a benefit offence.[74] You do not need to have been convicted.

You are disqualified from WTC if:
- you commit a benefit offence concerning a 'disqualifying benefit' (see p1239) on or after 5 April 2012; *and*
- you would be entitled to WTC if it were not for this rule, either as a single person or as part of a joint claim. If you have a joint claim, but only one of you is disqualified from WTC, WTC remains payable, but the amount is reduced by 50 per cent.[75]

The 'one-strike' and 'two-strikes' rules and the definition of a sanctionable offence that apply to sanctionable benefits (see p1239) apply. The sanction periods are the same as those for benefit offences commited wholly after 31 March 2013 on p1241.

You are not disqualified from receiving child tax credit under this rule.

Notes

1. Civil penalties
1 ss115C-115D SSAA 1992; SS(CP) Regs
2 Vol 3 Ch 9, para 09420 DMG; Ch D1 para D1271 ADM

3 *VT v SSWP (IS)* [2016] UKUT 178 (AAC), reported as [2016] AACR 42; *CT v SSWP (ESA)* [2021] UKUT 6 (AAC)
4 s115D(6) SSAA 1992

5   *VT v SSWP (IS)* [2016] UKUT 178 (AAC),
    reported as [2016] AACR 42
6   *JP v SSWP* [2017] UKUT 505 (AAC); *CT v
    SSWP (ESA)* [2021] UKUT 6 (AAC)
7   Vol 3 Ch 9, paras 09425-29 DMG; Ch
    D1 paras D1276-80 ADM
8   Reg 15 SS(PAOR) Regs; reg 3 SS(OR)
    Regs
9   *VT v SSWP (IS)* [2016] UKUT 178 (AAC),
    reported as [2016] AACR 42

2. Investigating benefit claims
10 s127 WRA 2012
11 s122B SSAA 1992
12 ss124, 124A, 124B and 125 SSAA 1992
13 ss122D and 122E SSAA 1992
14 ss122C and 122E SSAA 1992
15 ss182A and 182B SSAA 1992
16 s123 and Sch 4 SSAA 1992
17 ss109A, 109B and 109C SSAA 1992
18 s3 SSFA 2001; DWP, *Code of Practice on
    Obtaining Information*, November 2016,
    available at gov.uk
19 s109B(5)(b) SSAA 1992
20 s109C SSAA 1992
21 ss109B(5) and 109C(6) SSAA 1992
22 ss109BA and 109B(2A) SSAA 1992
23 s67(9) PACEA 1984
24 s78(1) PACEA 1984; *DHSS v McKee*
    [1995] 6 *Bulletin of NI Law* 17 (NI Crown
    Court)
25 DWP, *Fraud Investigations: staff guide
    part 1*, May 2019, p511, 'Planning the
    interview' available at gov.uk
26 DWP, *Fraud Investigations: staff guide
    part 1*, *May 2019*, p521-22, paras 74-
    76, available at gov.uk
27 s34 CJPOA 1994
28 *Mote v SSWP and Chichester DC* [2007]
    EWCA Civ 1324, reported as R(IS) 4/08
29 CIS/683/1994; *KP v RB of Kensington and
    Chelsea* [2014] UKUT 393 (AAC)

3. Prosecution of offences
30 *Osinuga v Director of Public Prosecution*
    [1997] 30 HLR 853
31 s112(1)-(1F) SSAA 1992
32 *Clear v Smith* [1981] 1 WLR 399
33 *Taylor's Central Garages v Roper* [1951]
    115 JPR 445
34 *R v Passmore* [2007] EWCA Crim 2053; *R
    v Laku* [2008] EWCA Crim 1745
35 *Coventry City Council v Vassell* [2011]
    EWHC 1542 (Admin)
36 s112(2) SSAA 1992; s122 Sentencing
    Act 2020; s225 Criminal Procedure
    (Scotland) Act 1995
37 *R v Chainey* [1914] 1 KB 137 at 142 (DC)

38 *R v Tilley* [2009] EWCA Crim 1426
39 s111A SSAA 1992
40 *R v Ghosh* [1982] EWCA Crim 2
41 s111A(3)(a) SSAA 1992; s122
    Sentencing Act 2020; s225 Criminal
    Procedure (Scotland) Act 1995; s45
    Criminal Proceedings etc (Reform)
    (Scotland) Act 2007
42 s111A(3)(b) SSAA 1992
43 s116(2), (2A) and (7) SSAA 1992;
    Bennett v SSWP [2012] EWHC 371
    (Admin)

4. Administrative penalties for benefit
offences
44 s115A(3)-(3A) SSAA 1992
45 s25(7) SSA(F)A 1997; art 2(1)(b)
    SSA(F)AO No.5
46 s115A(4)(a) SSAA 1992
47 s115A(1)-(1A) SSAA 1992
48 s25(7) SSA(F)A 1997; art 2(1)(b)
    SSA(F)AO No.5
49 s115A(2) SSAA 1992
50 DWP, *Fraud Investigations: staff guide
    part 1*, May 2019, 'Officers who may
    issue the Administrative Penalty notice
    and interview people' para 6, available
    at gov.uk
51 DWP, *Fraud Investigations: staff guide
    part 1*, May 2019, pp76-77, 'Additional
    time allowed to consider Administrative
    Penalty Offer advising the person of the
    conditions' paras 6-12, available at
    gov.uk
52 ss115A(4)(b), (6) and (7) SSAA 1992
53 s115A(5) SSAA 1992

5. Sanctions for benefit offences
54 s6B(1) SSFA 2001
55 s7(1) SSFA 2001
56 ss6B(13) and 7(8), definition of 'benefit
    offence', SSFA 2001
57 s6A(1), definition of 'disqualifying
    benefit', SSFA 2001; reg 19A, definition
    of 'disqualifying benefit', SS(LB) Regs
58 s6A(1), definition of 'sanctionable
    benefit', SSFA 2001; reg 19 SS(LB) Regs
59 s8 SSFA 2001
60 Reg 3ZB SS(LB) Regs
61 Regs 16D-16H SS(LB) Regs
62 ss6B, 7, 8 and 9 SSFA 2001; regs 3, 3A,
    5-10, 17 and 18 SS(LB) Regs
63 Regs 4 and 11-13 SS(LB) Regs
64 Regs 11-16 SS(LB) Regs. These are
    hardship payments under the loss of
    benefit rules but the qualifying
    conditions are the same as those
    described in Chapter 52.

8

Part 8: Claiming benefits and getting paid
Chapter 54: Fraud and penalties
Notes

65 Reg 11(4) SS(LB) Regs excludes joint-claim JSA couples with both partners sanctioned under the rules described in Chapter 49, or if one is entitled to IS, from hardship payments under the loss of benefit rules, but this does not prevent them from qualifying under the hardship payment rules in Chapter 52.

66 ss7(2) and (4) and 8(2) and (4) SSFA 2001; regs 5-8 and 10 SS(LB) Regs

67 Reg 18 SS(LB) Regs

68 Reg 3ZA SS(LB) Regs

69 ss6B(11A), (13) and (14), and 7(1A), (6A) and (8) SSFA 2001; paras B2002 and B2201 ADM

70 ss6B(11A) and (14) and 7(6) and (8) SSFA 2001 prior to amendments brought into force on 1 April 2013 by art 6(4)(c) SI 2013/358; paras B2002 and B2201 ADM

71 ss6B(11) and 7(6) SSFA 2001; reg 1A and 2 SS(LB) Regs

72 ss6B(4) and (5) and 7(1) SSFA 2001

73 Regs 3(2), 3ZA(4) and 3A(3) SS(LB) Regs

74 ss36A-36C TCA 2002

75 Reg 3 The Loss of Tax Credits Regulations 2013 No.715

Part 9

· ·

Getting a benefit decision changed

Chapter 55

● ●

Decisions

This chapter covers:
1. When a decision must be made (below)
2. Decisions on claims (p1253)
3. Decisions on other issues (p1254)
4. Delays in getting a decision (p1255)
5. Information about decisions (p1255)

This chapter covers the rules for decisions about benefits (including housing benefit), the social fund payments in Chapter 37 (except budgeting loans) and decisions about DWP loans for mortgage interest (see p839). It does not cover the rules for Scottish benefits (see Chapter 79), statutory payments (see Chapter 60) or the health benefits in Chapter 31.

References in this chapter to HM Revenue and Customs (HMRC) only apply to decisions about child benefit and guardian's allowance. HMRC also makes decisions about tax credits. For the rules for tax credits, see Chapter 64.

Key facts
- The benefits system is a 'decision-based system', so decisions about your benefit must be made and notified to you in many situations.
- Decisions are needed to create awards of benefit and set the amounts and dates of those awards.
- Decisions are also needed to decide if you have been overpaid.
- Decisions should be made within a reasonable time.
- You should be notified of decisions which carry a right of appeal.

---

1. When a decision must be made

The benefits system is a 'decision-based system'.[1] This means that there must be a formal and identifiable decision on questions such as:
- whether, and when, a valid claim for benefit has been made;
- when you submit a valid claim for benefit, whether or not you are entitled to an award of that benefit;

Part 9: Getting a benefit decision changed
Chapter 55: Decisions
1. When a decision must be made

- the date from which your award should start;
- the amount you should be awarded;
- whether amounts to which you are entitled can be paid;
- whether you need to repay an overpayment.

Decisions are made by decision makers in the agency that deals with that particular benefit (see below). In order to make a decision, the decision maker must first determine the facts of your case and then establish which rules apply to someone in your situation (see below). This might involve deciding other issues as part of coming to a full decision. Sometimes, the decision maker is bound to accept the ruling of another body on a particular issue (see p1251). There can only ever be a single decision in respect of your entitlement to benefit on a particular day (see p1250). In making initial decisions, the decision maker must consider the situation at the time of her/his decision (see p1253).

Who makes decisions

Decisions about most benefits are made by officers of the DWP. Decisions about child benefit and guardian's allowance are made by officers of HM Revenue and Customs (HMRC). Decisions about housing benefit (HB) are made by officers at the local authority. In this *Handbook*, we refer to all these officers as '**decision makers**'.

The DWP refers to personal independence payment (PIP) decision makers as 'case managers', although their role is the same.

Decisions about whether you have limited capability for work or are terminally ill for benefit purposes are made by the DWP, even if the main benefit decision is made by another authority – eg, the local authority for your housing benefit.[2]

You may have to attend your local Jobcentre Plus office to discuss your jobseeking conditions or claimant responsibilities (see Chapters 46 and 48). In practice, the person you meet is extremely unlikely to be a decision maker, although s/he may make recommendations to the decision maker – eg, about whether your benefit should be sanctioned.

How decisions are made

In order to make a decision about your benefit, a decision maker first needs to know the facts of your case. To do this, the decision maker should consider the evidence and decide what that evidence shows is more likely to be the situation than not.

A decision maker can take account of what you say and accept that as evidence, even if you do not have other evidence confirming this is the case. If there is a range of evidence about a particular point which could lead to different conclusions, the decision maker has to weigh the evidence and decide what facts it establishes overall.

Once the decision maker has decided what facts the evidence establishes, s/he considers what those facts mean for your entitlement to benefit. S/he does this by looking at the benefit entitlement rules for someone in your situation.

It is helpful to think about a decision as made up of a number of building blocks (sometimes called 'determinations'). For example, a decision that you are entitled to universal credit (UC) could be based on determinations that:

- you made a valid claim for UC on a particular date; *and*
- you are in Great Britain because you are habitually resident and have a right to reside; *and*
- you are aged 35; *and*
- you are not subject to immigration control; *and*
- you are not in education; *and*
- you do not have too much income or capital.

These determinations do not themselves have legal force and affect your entitlement to UC until they are incorporate into an 'outcome decision' about whether or not you are entitled to UC. As your right to challenge a decision (see p1253) attaches to a decision and not a determination, if you disagree with the individual determinations, you can challenge them when they are incorporated into a decision which is notified to you.[3]

Guidance used by decision makers

To help in understanding the benefit entitlement rules, a decision maker may look at guidance. This guidance is an explanation of the law made by the government for use by decision makers. The guidance is therefore not itself the law but simply the government's view of what the law means. If the explanation of the law in the guidance helps establish your entitlement, you can refer to it. However, if the guidance indicates you are not entitled, you can argue that it does not properly reflect the law where that is the case. The following are the most commonly used bits of guidance.

– *Decision Makers' Guide: staff guide.*[4] For DWP decision makers on all DWP benefits except those covered by the *Advice for Decision Making: staff guide.*

– *Advice for Decision Making: staff guide.* For DWP decision makers on UC, PIP, contribution-based jobseeker's allowance (JSA) and contributory employment and support allowance (ESA) for people who come under the UC system.[5]

– *Universal Credit Guidance.* Operational guidance for DWP decision makers on all aspects of UC.[6]

– *Personal Independence Payment Assessment Guide.* This is for assessment providers[7] and comes in several parts. It should be read with the assessment provider's own guidance, where it exists.[8] See also the *Personal Independence Payment Handbook,* aimed at claimants and advisers.[9]

– *Work Capability Assessment Handbook.* For healthcare professionals who carry out work capability assessments.[10]

Part 9: Getting a benefit decision changed
Chapter 55: Decisions
1. When a decision must be made

– *Housing Benefit Guidance Manual.*[11] See also housing benefit bulletins and urgent bulletins and the *Discretionary Housing Payment Guidance Manual.*[12] Local authorities also have their own guidance.

Decisions made with limited information

The decision maker can make a decision in certain circumstances, even if s/he is waiting for you to provide more evidence or information.

A decision is always made on the basis that the evidence or information needed is adverse to you if:[13]

- for income support (IS) and JSA only, it is needed to decide:
  - whether you should be paid benefit (or less benefit) because you (or a member of your family) are involved in a trade dispute (see p982). This does not apply to JSA if you come under the UC system (see p22); *or*
  - whether you are in relevant education (see p873);
- for IS, ESA, pension credit (PC) and social fund payments only, it is needed to decide whether you are entitled to a severe disability premium (additional amount for PC).

In both of these cases, if you request an 'any grounds' revision (see p1262) and provide the missing information, the decision can be revised to take account of it.

Special rules apply if, when you claim your retirement pension, you have not yet elected whether to take a lump sum or an increased pension (for state pension, this must be because your late partner deferred claiming her/his pension). The decision maker can choose whether or not to decide your claim immediately. If s/he does make a decision on your claim, for state pension s/he *may* revise it when you make the election, and for category A or B retirement pension, s/he *must* revise it when you make the election (see p1270).[14]

For PIP, if you are in a care home and evidence or information is required to decide whether the cost of your accommodation will be met from local or public funds, if the decision maker makes 'reasonable enquiries', s/he can make a decision on the evidence or information s/he has.[15]

For UC, if further evidence or information is needed to decide whether you qualify for a DWP loan to help with your mortgage interest (see p839), the decision maker has discretion to make a decision.[16] If you are entitled to IS, ESA or PC, the decision maker can also make a decision on the basis of the evidence or information s/he already has.[17]

In all of these cases, if you request an any grounds revision (see p1262) and provide the missing information, the decision can be revised to take account of it.

Decisions are final

Decisions about benefits are final in the sense that once a decision has been made about your entitlement to a particular benefit for a particular day, then there cannot be another decision about your entitlement on that day.[18] If this were not the case, there would be a question about which of the two decisions was the correct one.

Example

Eunice claims PIP on 10 June. Her claim is refused on 20 August. She appeals. While she is waiting for that appeal to be dealt with, she makes a new, second claim for PIP on 7 September. On 11 October, PIP is awarded at the standard rate starting from 7 September. When the tribunal comes to deal with Eunice's appeal, it cannot award PIP for any date after 6 September as the decision on the second PIP claim is final. If Eunice is not happy with the decision on her second claim, she must also challenge that decision.

This means that if you think there is something wrong with your entitlement to a particular benefit on a particular day, you need to get the decision which deals with that benefit for that day changed (see p1253). Similarly, it means that if a decision maker thinks there is something wrong with your entitlement on a particular day, s/he cannot simply make a completely new decision about this. Instead, s/he needs to change the decision that applies to that day.

Decisions made by a different decision maker

There are some situations in which the decision maker who is making the decision about a benefit you have claimed, or for which you have an award, is not the one who decides a particular issue. These include:
- for HB, decisions about whether you have income or capital when you get UC, IS, income-related ESA, income-based JSA or PC (see below);
- for HB and tax credits, decisions about limited capability for work (see p1252);
- decisions about national insurance (NI) contributions (see p1252).

Housing benefit decisions on income and capital where you get certain benefits

If you get UC, IS, income-related ESA, income-based JSA or PC (although not if you get the savings credit of PC only), all of your income and capital is ignored when calculating HB entitlement.[19]

The HB decision maker should not therefore consider your income or capital. There are two exceptions to this rule.
- If the decision maker has evidence about your income and capital that has not already been considered by the DWP decision maker which raises doubt about whether your benefit award is correct, s/he may inform the DWP. The decision maker can suspend your HB while s/he waits to see if the DWP makes a new decision (see p1163).

Part 9: Getting a benefit decision changed
Chapter 55: Decisions
1. When a decision must be made

- If the decision maker has strong and clear evidence you are fraudulently concealing evidence from the DWP about your income and capital, s/he can make her/his own decision on the issue.[20]

Decisions about limited capability for work

Only a DWP decision maker can decide whether you have limited capability for work, and her/his decision is binding for decision makers for other benefits and tax credits.[21]

Decisions about national insurance contributions

Certain questions about NI contributions and employment are dealt with by a special procedure – eg:[22]

- whether you were an 'employed earner' for the purposes of paying contributions or entitlement to industrial injuries disablement benefit; or
- whether you were liable to pay a particular class of contributions or have paid contributions for a particular period; or
- the amount of contributions you were liable to pay.

These matters are referred to HMRC for a decision, which is then binding on the decision maker.[23] The decision maker can continue to deal with other aspects of your claim, but can defer making a decision on it. The decision maker should also refer matters to HMRC if s/he decides your claim on the basis of facts which do not appear to be disputed (eg, if it appears you do not satisfy the contribution conditions for a benefit), but you apply for a revision or supersession, or appeal against the decision because you dispute the facts – eg, you think your contribution record is wrong.

When HMRC makes a decision, you can appeal against it.[24] The appeals process is similar to appealing against an HMRC decision on your entitlement to statutory payments (see Chapter 60).

The First-tier Tribunal can also require the DWP to refer matters that are HMRC's responsibility, but which are relevant to a benefit appeal, to HMRC for a decision.[25] The DWP may revise the decision on your claim as a result. If not, the matter goes back to the tribunal.

Note: the decision maker can make arrangements for HMRC to decide whether you can be credited with earnings or contributions.[26] You can appeal against these decisions in the same way as against DWP decisions. You must first request a mandatory reconsideration (see p1299).

Correcting a decision

Unless the benefit is child benefit or guardian's allowance, if the decision maker makes an accidental error in her/his decision (eg, a typing error or a miscalculation in the arithmetic), this can be corrected.[27] You must be sent or given written notice of the correction as soon as is practicable. To see how the time limit for applying for an 'any grounds' revision of the decision can be extended when a decision has been corrected, see p1263.

If you disagree with a decision maker's decision

If you think a decision is wrong, you may be able to:
- apply for a revision of the decision (see p1261); or
- apply for a supersession of the decision (see p1274).

In most cases, you also have the right to appeal to the First-tier Tribunal (see Chapter 57). Usually, it is required ('mandatory') that you have first applied for the decision to be reconsidered in a revision and that a decision has been made on that – hence a revision is often also called a 'mandatory reconsideration' (see p1299).

The time limit for applying for what is known as an 'any grounds' revision is strict – normally only one month from the date on the decision letter (see p1263).

2. Decisions on claims

Once you have made a valid claim for benefit (see p1138), your claim is referred to a decision maker to decide whether you are entitled. A decision maker must normally make a decision on the claim,[28] but may sometimes withhold making a decision if there is a 'test case' pending (see p1290).

Before making a decision, the decision maker may request further information (see p1140). If there is a question about the facts of your claim that needs special expertise, the decision maker can get assistance from experts.[29]

Once a valid claim has been made, it is not possible for a decision maker to refuse to make a decision on the claim.[30] Sometimes, decision makers say that they have 'closed' a claim – eg, because after claiming universal credit (UC), you did not book or attend an interview to establish your identity. There is no power allowing them to do this – a decision to 'close' a claim is in fact a decision to say that you are not entitled, and booking an interview is not a condition of entitlement to UC.[31] You can appeal against such a decision (usually, after mandatory reconsideration is refused). Your appeal should succeed, provided you met the conditions of entitlement – ie, the fact you did not attend the interview or provide requested information should not matter if you can now prove the facts which the intereview or information was supposed to give you a chance to establish.

Circumstances at time of decision

When deciding a claim for benefit, the decision maker must consider your circumstances at the date s/he is making the decision. The decision maker cannot

Part 9: Getting a benefit decision changed
Chapter 55: Decisions
3. Decisions on other issues

later change a decision to take account of new circumstances which did not exist at the time of the decision.

That means that if your claim for benefit was refused and you want to have new circumstances taken into account, you must make a new claim for benefit.[32]

Example
Franklin had capital worth £17,750 when he made a claim for UC. His claim was refused on the basis that he had too much capital. He now has capital worth £12,000. He must make a new claim to allow the decision maker to take into account his new circumstances.

If your circumstances have changed between when you made your claim for benefit and when your claim is decided, the decision maker should decide whether you met the conditions of entitlement on each of the days between when you made the claim and when it is decided. For example, if you claimed contributory ESA but your health improved and you commenced work for over 16 hours a week before the claim was decided, then the decision should award you ESA for the period from the date of claim to the day before you started work. Similarly, if you did not meet the rules for entitlement when you made your claim but you start to meet them before the claim is decided, the decision can award you benefit from the day you started to meet the rules for entitlement.[33]

Once a decision has been made about a claim for benefit, that claim ceases to exist.[34] If the decision was that you were entitled and you have an *award* of benefit, quite often this is still called a 'claim', but strictly speaking that is wrong.

3. **Decisions on other issues**

In addition to decisions about whether to make an award of benefit where a claim has been made, decisions are needed about other issues. These include decisions about:

- whether an overpayment is recoverable (see p1194);
- whether an overpayment should be recovered (see p1208);
- whether you have to pay a penalty (see p1229);
- whether you are entitled to hardship payments (see p1181);
- whether you can get an advance payment (see p1153);
- whether deductions should be made from your payment (see p1164);
- whether payment of benefit under an award should be suspended (see p1161);
- whether payment under an award should cease because you are in hospital or a care home (see p903);
- what work-related requirements apply to your universal credit award (see p1037).

4. Delays in getting a decision

New claims can take several weeks or more to process (or longer for claimants from abroad). The DWP no longer publishes official targets, but all claims should be dealt with as soon as is reasonably practicable.[35]

Is there a delay?

1. If you have been waiting a long time for a decision, check that your claim has been received. If it has not, if possible send a copy or claim again, and refer to the claim you made earlier.

2. If the decision maker denies receiving your claim, claim again and ask for backdating and refer to your previous claim. If the decision maker makes a decision that your award only starts from when the second claim was received, you can challenge that decision and argue that you made the earlier claim. In an appeal, the tribunal can accept that an earlier claim was made.

3. If your claim has been received but not dealt with, ask why. Complain if you are not satisfied with the explanation for the delay (see Chapter 61). If the claim is not decided within a reasonable time, it might be possible to send a letter before action for judicial review (see p1377).

4. If a decision cannot be made on your claim straight away, ask the office to make a short-term advance of benefit if these are payable for the benefit you have claimed (see p1153), or an interim payment of child benefit or guardian's allowance (see p580).

5. You may be able to claim a means-tested benefit or, for housing benefit, a payment on account while a decision is being made on your claim for a non-means-tested benefit. The amount paid may be deducted from arrears of the other benefit(s) you subsequently receive, or you may be asked to repay the amount (see p1198).

6. You may be able to get help from your local authority for any short-term needs in a crisis (see p846).

5. Information about decisions

You must be given written notice of a decision against which you can appeal (see p1303 for which decisions). This is usually called a '**decision notice**'. You must be informed of:[36]

- your right to appeal against the decision; *and*
- your right to a written statement of reasons for the decision, if this is not already included (see p1256).

For benefits other than housing benefit, you are also told that you must apply for a mandatory reconsideration before you can appeal against the decision (see p1299).

Part 9: Getting a benefit decision changed
Chapter 55: Decisions
5. Information about decisions

If a decision has not been notified to you, then it may not have legal effect.[37] That could mean that other decisions which depend on that decision cannot be enforced. For example, if a decision reducing your entitlement for a past period was not notified to you, then a subsequent decision that the resultant overpayment was recoverable is invalid.[38]

Explanations

Sometimes the decision maker may claim that you must ask for an explanation before you can apply for a revision or a supersession, or to appeal. This is wrong. Although you can ask for an explanation of any decision, you do not have to do so before you challenge the decision. If you want an explanation, contact the office that made the decision.

At the end of the explanation, you should be asked whether you are happy with the decision. If you are not happy, say so. The decision maker should then advise you about your right to apply for a revision (see p1261). S/he may refer to this as a dispute or a mandatory reconsideration.

Explanations are usually given orally. You may also have the right to request a written statement of reasons for a decision (see below) if it is one against which you can appeal.

The time limit for applying for a revision is very strict. It runs from the date you are sent or are given the decision with which you disagree (*not* the date of the explanation) and can only be extended in limited circumstances (see p1263). Therefore, ensure you apply for a revision within the time limit, even if the decision has not yet been explained to you.

Written reasons

You may want to see the reasons for a decision in writing. You only have a right to a written statement of reasons for a decision if this has not already been provided with the decision and it is a decision against which you can appeal. You must ask for the written statement of reasons within one month of the date of the notification of the decision. The decision maker must then provide the statement within 14 days, or as soon as practicable afterwards.[39]

Note: the time limit to apply for a revision is extended if you ask for a written statement of reasons, but only if this has not already been provided. See p1263 for further information.

Month

'**Month**' means a complete calendar month running from the day after the day you were sent or given a decision.[40] For example, a decision sent on 22 July has a time limit that expires at the end of 22 August.

A dispute could arise about whether a decision notice already includes an explanation of the reasons for the decision. Sometimes that should be clear because the decision notice will state that you can ask for a written explanation – that indicates the DWP does not think such an explanation has already been given. You may believe that a written statement of reasons has not been included with your decision or is inadequate, but the DWP, HMRC or local authority could disagree. In these cases, the decision maker is likely to argue that your time limit for applying for a revision cannot be extended.

If you are in any doubt, you should assume that the time limit for applying for a revision has *not* been extended. If you miss the time limit in this situation, argue that the rules that allow a late application for a revision apply (see p1264). You may also be able to apply for a revision if you have specific grounds (see p1265).

Notes

1. When a decision must be made

1 *AW v SSWP (JSA)* [2013] UKUT 99 (AAC); CA/1020/2007
2 **UC/PIP/JSA&ESA under UC** Reg 40 UC,PIP,JSA&ESA(DA) Regs
Other benefits Reg 11 SS&CS(DA) Regs
3 CIB/2338/2000, paras 19-25
4 gov.uk/government/collections/ decision-makers-guide-staff-guide
5 gov.uk/government/publications/ advice-for-decision-making-staff-guide
6 Available at rightsnet.org.uk/universal-credit-guidance
7 gov.uk/government/publications/ personal-independence-payment-assessment-guide-for-assessment-providers
8 For Independent Assessment Services (Atos), see mypipassessment.co.uk. For Capita, see capita-pip.co.uk/en/ assessment-process.html
9 gov.uk/government/publications/ personal-independence-payment-fact-sheets
10 gov.uk/government/publications/work-capability-assessment-handbook-for-healthcare-professionals

11 gov.uk/guidance/housing-benefit-information-guidance-and-good-practice-for-local-authority-staff#housing-benefit-and-council-tax-benefit-manual
12 gov.uk/government/collections/ housing-benefit-for-local-authorities-bulletins; gov.uk/government/ publications/housing-benefit-urgent-bulletins-2019; gov.uk/government/ publications/discretionary-housing-payments-guidance-manual
13 **UC/PIP&ESA under UC** Reg 39 UC,PIP,JSA&ESA(DA) Regs
Other benefits Regs 13(2) and (3) and 15 SS&CS(DA) Regs
14 Regs 13A and 13B SS&CS(DA) Regs
15 Reg 39(5) UC,PIP,JSA&ESA(DA) Regs
16 Reg 39(4) UC,PIP,JSA&ESA(DA) Regs
17 Reg 13(1) SS&CS(DA) Regs
18 s17 SSA 1998
19 Sch 4 para 12 and Sch 6 para 5 HB Regs; regs 25-26 HB(SPC) Regs
20 *DF v LB Waltham Forest (HB)* [2017] UKUT 161 (AAC)
21 Reg 11 SS&CS(DA) Regs; reg 40(3) UC,PIP,JSA,ESA(DA) Regs
22 s8 SSC(TF)A 1999

23 s10A SSA 1998; reg 42
    UC,PIP,JSA&ESA(DA) Regs; reg 11A
    SS&CS(DA) Regs
24 s11 SSC(TF)A 1999
25 s24A SSA 1998; reg 43
    UC,PIP,JSA&ESA(DA) Regs; reg 38A
    SS&CS(DA) Regs
26 s17 SSC(TF)A 1999; Sch 3 para 17 SSA
    1998; National Insurance Contribution
    Credits (Transfer of Functions) Order
    2009 No.1377
27 **UC/PIP/JSA&ESA under UC** Reg 38
    UC,PIP,JSA&ESA(DA) Regs
    Other benefits Reg 9A SS&CS(DA)
    Regs

2. Decisions on claims
28 R(SB) 29/83; CIS/807/1992; R(H) 3/05
29 s11(2) SSA 1998
30 R(H) 3/05
31 *PP v SSWP (UC)* [2020] UKUT 109 (AAC)
32 s8(2)(b) SSA 1998
33 *SSWP v KK (JSA)* [2019] UKUT 313 (AAC)
34 s8(2)(a) SSA 1998

4. Delays in getting a decision
35 *R (C and W) v SSWP and Zacchaeus 2000
    Trust* [2015] EWHC 1607 (Admin)

5. Information about decisions
36 **UC/PIP/JSA&ESA under UC** Reg 51
    UC,PIP,JSA&ESA(DA) Regs
    CB/GA Reg 26(1) CB&GA(DA) Regs
    Other benefits Reg 28(1) SS&CS(DA)
    Regs
37 *R (Anufrijeva) v SSHD* [2003] UKHL 26
38 *SM v SSWP (SPC)* [2017] UKUT 336
    (AAC)
39 **UC/PIP/JSA&ESA under UC** Regs 3
    and 51 UC,PIP,JSA&ESA(DA) Regs
    CB/GA Regs 3 and 26(1)(b) and (2)
    CB&GA(DA) Regs
    Other benefits Regs 2 and 28(1)(b)
    and (2) SS&CS(DA) Regs
40 R(IB) 4/02

Chapter 56

• •

Revisions and supersessions

This chapter covers:
1. Getting a decision changed (below)
2. Revisions (p1261)
3. Supersessions (p1274)
4. Revisions and supersessions after a 'qualifying benefit' award (p1287)
5. The 'anti-test case rule' (p1289)

This chapter covers the rules for benefits, the social fund payments in Chapter 37 (except budgeting loans) and decisions about DWP loans for mortgage interest (see p839). It does not cover the rules for Scottish benefits (see Chapter 79), statutory payments (see Chapter 60) or the health benefits in Chapter 31.

References in this chapter to HM Revenue and Customs (HMRC) only apply to decisions about child benefit and guardian's allowance. HMRC also makes decisions about tax credits. For the rules for tax credits, see Chapter 67.

Key facts

- If a decision is wrong or no longer correct, it can be changed by a new decision – called either a 'revision' or a 'supersession'.
- You can apply for a revision or a supersession, or the DWP, local authority or HM Revenue and Customs can carry out one because it wants to change your award.
- In some cases, you do not need to show any grounds for a revision, but you must ask for one within a set time limit. In other cases, you can ask for a revision at any time, but you must show there are specific grounds.
- The date on which a revision or a supersession takes effect determines the date from when you are paid arrears if you are entitled to more benefit, or the date from when you have overpaid if you are entitled to less benefit.

---

1. Getting a decision changed

The DWP, the local authority and HM Revenue and Customs (HMRC) make many decisions about your entitlement to benefits (see Chapter 55). Once a decision

Part 9: Getting a benefit decision changed
Chapter 56: Revisions and supersessions
1. Getting a decision changed

has been made, it can only be changed by a further decision.[1] These further decisions are called revisions (see pp1261–74) and supersessions (see pp1274–87).

To get more information about a decision, ask for an explanation or a written statement of reasons if this has not already been provided (see p1256).

In many cases, decisions can also be changed by appealing to the First-tier Tribunal (see Chapter 57). However, you must apply for a mandatory reconsideration before you can appeal (see p1299), unless the benefit is housing benefit (HB) or, in some cases, employment and support allowance (ESA). A 'mandatory reconsideration' is simply another name for a revision – the term is used because the decision maker must have considered whether or not to revise the decision before an appeal can be made.

You can apply for a revision or a supersession of a decision that you cannot appeal (see p1304 for some examples). If such a decision is not changed following your application, you may be able to apply for a judicial review (see Chapter 59).

Note: it is important that you keep within any time limit (see p1263 for revisions and p1305 for appeals).

Revisions and supersessions

Revisions and supersessions are both ways of changing a decision about your benefit entitlement.

- A **revision** is the way of changing a decision that was wrong at the time it was made – ie, the decision maker wrongly refused to award you benefit, or awarded you an incorrect amount – eg, because s/he thought you had savings which you did not have. A revision takes effect from the date the original decision took effect.
- A **supersession** is usually the way of changing a decision which was correct at the time it was originally made, but which has subsequently become wrong – eg, because your circumstances have now changed and you no longer meet a condition of entitlement. A supersession does not take effect from the date the original decision took effect – it takes effect from a later date.

You can apply for a revision or a supersession and the decision maker at the DWP, local authority or HMRC can also initiate one.

Note: you must apply for a revision within a certain time (unless one of the specific grounds allowing revisions to be carried out at any time apply). If you miss the time limit or you do not have specific grounds, it may be possible to get a decision that was wrong when it was originally made changed via a supersession. However, as you generally get less arrears of benefit after a supersession, make sure you apply within the time allowed if you can.

In some cases, if the decision maker is reducing or removing your entitlement, it may be in your interests to argue that this can only be done by carrying out a supersession, rather than a revision.

The risks of applying for a revision or supersession

Following a revision or a supersession, the original decision may remain the same – ie, your application for a revision or supersession is refused. It may also be revised or superseded so as to either increase *or* decrease the amount of your benefit, or to take away your entitlement altogether.

You may apply for a revision or supersession in the hope that your benefit will be increased, but the outcome could be that you get less benefit, and you could be required to repay an overpayment (see Chapter 54). This is because (although s/he does not have to do so) the decision maker can consider issues that are not raised in your application for a revision or supersession.[2] Therefore, before you apply for a revision or supersession consider whether it is possible that less or no benefit could be awarded for all, or some, of the period in question. If you apply for a revision or supersession and the decision maker makes a decision which is less advantageous to you than the original decision, s/he must show that there was a specific ground to do so and that the outcome of the revision or supersession is related to that ground. However, this does not apply if the decision maker starts taking action to revise the decision within a month of the original decision having been made. In this case, s/he can make an 'any grounds' revision (see p1262).[3]

2. Revisions

If you think a decision is wrong, you can apply for a revision.[4] The decision maker must then look at the decision again to see whether it can be changed. The DWP, the local authority and HM Revenue and Customs (HMRC) often refer to your request as a 'dispute' or a 'request for a reconsideration'.

Mandatory reconsideration

You must apply for a a decision to be looked at again by way of a revision before you can appeal against it (see p1299), unless the benefit is housing benefit (HB) or is employment and support allowance (ESA) and you would have a right to get ESA while appealing against the decision (see p1013). This revision is called a 'mandatory reconsideration'. You do not have to use this term when applying for the decision to be looked at again, but in practice it is helpful if you do. When the DWP or HMRC deals with your application, it looks at its decision again – ie, it considers whether to carry out a revision. The rules and advice on revisions in this chapter therefore apply when you apply for a mandatory reconsideration. Once the DWP or HMRC has considered your application, it issues a mandatory reconsideration notice (see p1301). You are required to provide this notice when you appeal to the First-tier Tribunal.

Part 9: Getting a benefit decision changed
Chapter 56: Revisions and supersessions
2. Revisions

When a decision can be revised

A decision can be revised either following your request for a revision or because the decision maker decides to carry out a revision.[5] There are two types of revision.

- 'Any grounds' revisions. You (or the decision maker) do not have to show that specific grounds apply (see below), but you (or the decision maker) must apply or start the process within a strict time limit (see p1265 for the time limit that applies to the decision maker and p1263 for the time limit that applies to you).
- 'Any time' revisions. You (or the decision maker) must show that one of the specific permitted grounds exists (see p1265). If this is the case, the decision can be revised, even if it was made a long time ago.

Decisions of the First-tier (or Upper) Tribunal cannot be revised. In some cases, these decisions can be superseded. Otherwise, they can only be changed by appealing further to the Upper Tribunal or a court (see Chapter 58).

'Any grounds' revisions

If action to get a decision changed is started within a specific time limit, the decision can be changed on 'any grounds'. This means that it can be changed simply because a new decision maker takes a different view of the same evidence.

The time limits for getting a decision changed by a revision on 'any grounds' are different depending on whether:

- you are applying for a decision to be revised (see p1263); *or*
- the revision is started by the decision maker (see p1265).

A revision on 'any grounds' is a completely fresh look at the decision. The decision maker can do any or all of the following:

- simply form a different opinion about the same evidence – eg, the first decision maker may have decided that the money in your bank account belonged to you and so meant you had too much capital to qualify for benefit, but the new decision maker might accept your explanation that the money belonged to someone else;
- take into account any new evidence which shows what your circumstances were at the time of the original decision – eg, you have a new medical report, showing that you have limited capability for work;
- take into account any omissions in the information you gave at the time – eg, if you failed to mention in your claim for universal credit (UC) that you had housing costs;
- correct any misunderstanding of the law which affected the previous decision – eg, by accepting you do not need to receive child benefit for a child in order to count as responsible for her/him for the purposes of UC.

A decision maker can only revise a decision on any grounds on the basis of your circumstances at the time:[6]

- the decision took effect; *or*
- in the case of advance awards for benefits other than HB, the decision was made.

If your circumstances have since changed, make a fresh claim in a case where you have no current award, or ask for a supersession where you have an ongoing award (see p1274) instead.

Note: if you apply for an 'any grounds' revision of a decision about ESA, attendance allowance (AA), disability living allowance (DLA) or personal independence payment (PIP) because you (or the person on whose behalf you are claiming) are terminally ill, you must state this explicitly.[7] If you do not do so, the decision maker cannot revise the decision on this ground.

Time limit for applying for an 'any grounds' revision

You must apply for an 'any grounds' revision:

- **in the case of a Sure Start maternity grant or a social fund funeral expenses payment**, within one month of the date you were sent or given the decision or, if later, within the time limit for claiming the payment (see p784 and p790);[8]
- **in the case of a cold weather payment or a winter fuel payment**, within one month of the date you were notified of the decision. For these purposes, you are generally assumed to have been notified seven days after the decision was made, but there are exceptions;[9]
- **in the case of HB**, within one month of the date you were sent or given the decision.[10] If a written statement of reasons has not already been included with the decision, days from the date your request for the statement is received by the local authority to the date on which it is provided to you are ignored when calculating the one month;[11]
- **in all other cases:**[12]
  - within one month of the date you were sent or given the decision; *or*
  - within one month and 14 days of the date you were sent or given the decision, if you requested a written statement of reasons (see p1256) and it is provided within the month; *or*
  - within 14 days of a written statement of reasons being provided, if you requested one within one month of the date you were sent or given the decision, but it is not provided within that one-month period.

For benefits (other than a Sure Start maternity grant or a social fund funeral expenses payment, child benefit or guardian's allowance), if an accidental error in a decision has been corrected (see p1252), any day falling before the day on which the correction is notified to you is ignored when calculating the one-month period.[13]

Part 9: Getting a benefit decision changed
Chapter 56: Revisions and supersessions
2. Revisions

Late requests

You can apply for an 'any grounds' revision outside the time limit in limited circumstances, provided this is within an absolute time limit.

The absolute time limit

In most cases, you must apply for an 'any grounds' revision within **13 months** of the date you were notified of the decision.[14]

If you requested a written statement of reasons (see p1256):

– for HB, days from the date you requested the statement to the date on which it was provided are ignored when calculating the 13 months; *or*

– for other benefits, if the statement of reasons is provided within one month of the date you were notified of the decision, the 13 months are extended by 14 days. If it is provided during a period later than one month after that date, the 13 months are extended by 14 days, plus the number of days in that period.

In all cases, for a late request for an 'any grounds' revision to be accepted:[15]

* your application must contain:
  – sufficient details about the decision with which you disagree for it to be identified. Say which benefit you are disagreeing about and the date the DWP, the local authority or HMRC sent you the decision; *and*
  – a summary of your reasons for applying late; *and*
* you must show that:
  – it is reasonable to grant your application; *and*
  – there are special circumstances which mean that it was not practicable for you to apply for a revision within the time limit. Any special circumstances can count. The longer you have delayed applying for a revision, the more compelling these must be.

In addition, for child benefit, guardian's allowance and HB:[16]

* you must show that your application has merit – ie, that there is a prospect the decision can be changed if time is extended; *and*
* when deciding whether it is reasonable to grant your application, the decision maker cannot take account of the fact that:
  – a court or the Upper Tribunal has interpreted the law in a different way than previously understood and applied;
  – you (or anyone acting for you) misunderstood or were unaware of the relevant law, including the time limits for applying for a revision.

If your late request for an 'any grounds' revision is refused, you cannot appeal against that refusal.[17] However:

* for benefits other than HB, or ESA where you would have a right to payment of ESA pending appeal, you may still be able to appeal against the original

decision. Under the rules on mandatory reconsiderations, you only have a right of appeal against a decision if the decision maker has considered whether to revise it. If you applied for an 'any grounds' revision within the absolute time limit, by refusing to accept that time should be extended, the decision maker *has* considered whether to revise the decision, so you can appeal.[18] If you have missed the absolute time limit for an 'any grounds' revision, you only have a right of appeal if you can show that one of the specific grounds for a revision applied. In practice, decision makers at the DWP rarely refuse to accept a late request for a revision made within the absolute time limit;

- for HB, or ESA where you would have a right to payment of ESA pending appeal, you may be able to make a late appeal against the original decision. A late appeal must be admitted if the decision maker does not object or if the First-tier Tribunal thinks it is fair and just to do so. It is more likely that you will have your request for a late appeal accepted than your request for an 'any grounds' revision accepted;
- where you are making a late application, it is also worth considering whether you can argue that some earlier contact you had with the decision maker could have been considered as a request for a revision. This may enable you to argue that your application is not late at all.

Time limit for decision makers

For benefits other than HB, the decision maker can revise a decision her/himself on any grounds provided s/he starts action within one month of the date you are sent or given a decision.[19] For HB, a decision maker can also decide to revise a decision her/himself, but only if, within one month of the date you are sent or given it, s/he has information which shows that there was a mistake about the facts of your case or the decision was made in ignorance of relevant facts.[20]

If these conditions are not met, the decision maker can only carry out a revision if there are specific grounds.

'Any time' revisions

A revision can be carried out at any time (even years after the original decision was made) in specific situations. So, if you can show there are specific grounds, you can apply for a revision at any time. The decision maker at the DWP, local authority or HMRC can also carry out a revision at any time if s/he thinks one of the specific grounds exists. If a decision maker refuses to consider an 'any time' revision, see p1273.

In practice, if you apply for a revision (including a mandatory reconsideration) and it is within one month of your being sent or given the decision, the DWP, the local authority or HMRC treats your application as one for an 'any grounds' revision (see p1262). If your application is late and reasons for lateness are not accepted, the decision maker should go on to consider whether any of the specific grounds exist to allow an 'any time' revision.

Part 9: Getting a benefit decision changed
Chapter 56: Revisions and supersessions
2. Revisions

There are a number of grounds for an 'any time' revision. The main ones are where there has been:

- an official error (see below);
- a sanction decision (see p1267);
- an award of a 'qualifying benefit' (see p1268);
- an appeal against a decision (see p1268);
- a mistake about or ignorance of facts (see p1269).

Some other specific grounds are summarised on p1270.

Official error

A decision can be revised at any time if there was an official error.[21]

For child benefit and guardian's allowance, it means an error made by an officer of HMRC or a person employed by someone providing services to HMRC.[22]

For benefits, other than child benefit and guardian's allowance, this means:[23]

- an error made by an officer of the DWP or HMRC; *or*
- for HB only, errors made by the local authority or by a person authorised to carry out any function of the local authority or provide HB-related services; *or*
- other than for HB, errors made by a person employed by someone providing services to the DWP; *or*
- other than for HB, PIP, UC and, if you come under the UC system (see p22), contribution-based jobseeker's allowance (JSA) and contributory ESA, errors made by an employee of a local authority (or an employee of a person acting on behalf of, or providing services to, a local authority).

Note:

- If the error is that the decision maker got the law wrong, this does not count as an official error if this is only shown to be the case because of a later decision from the Upper Tribunal or a court.[24] If a legal mistake was made in your case that was only later shown to be a legal mistake because of a subsequent decision in another case, you could make a fresh claim (or apply for a supersession), and the 'anti-test case rule' could apply (see p1289).
- The mere fact that a decision needs to be changed does not mean that there has been an official error. For example, a decision that you have failed the work capability assessment might be changed because of new evidence, or a different view is taken of the same evidence, but that does not in itself mean that there was an official error.
- If someone else (eg, you, your partner or your representative) caused or contributed to the error, it does not count as an official error.[25] This includes if the way your claim form was completed contributed to the error.[26]

Official error: examples

The following can count as official errors.

Getting the law wrong (unless this is only established by a subsequent Upper Tribunal or court decision in another case).

The decision maker (or local authority) had specific evidence which s/he failed to take into account, even though it was relevant. You should argue that this applies even if the evidence does not conclusively prove your entitlement, so long as it raised a strong possibility that you were entitled.

The DWP, the local authority or HMRC had documentary or other written evidence of your entitlement, but failed to give it to the decision maker dealing with your claim when the earlier decision was made.

No reasonable decision maker having established the facts could have made the decision that was made.[27]

The decision maker failed to ask you about something that was relevant to the decision and which was reasonably obvious would need to be asked in order to be able to ensure the decision was correct.[28]

Sanction decisions

A decision can be revised at any time if:[29]

- for UC and JSA, and, if you come under the UC system, ESA, it is a decision to give you a sanction for any reason; *or*
- you do not come under the UC system and it is a decision to give you a sanction because:
  - you (or in some cases your partner) failed to take part in a work-focused interview without good cause. This only applies if the decision contained an error and, for ESA only, if you did not materially contribute to the error; *or*
  - for ESA and income support (IS) only, you failed to undertake work-related activity without good cause. This only applies if the decision contained an error to which you did not materially contribute.

This means that you can apply for a revision (including a mandatory reconsideration) even if the decision to give you a sanction was made a long time ago. This is useful if you did not realise you could challenge the decision at the time it was made and, for example, you can show you had good cause or a good reason for your actions, or you did not do (or fail to do) what is alleged. If you have been given a sanction more than once, you should apply for a revision of all the decisions if possible and then appeal if you do not get all that you want. If you are applying for a mandatory reconsideration before you can appeal (see p1299), make this clear in your application. See p1086 and p1128 for further information about challenging a sanction decision.

Note: for JSA if you do not come under the UC system, a decision can also be revised at any time to begin a sanction on the grounds that you were previously

Part 9: Getting a benefit decision changed
Chapter 56: Revisions and supersessions
2. Revisions

entitled to JSA and that entitlement ended because you were found not to be available for or actively seeking work (see p1120).[30] In practice, this means that if you are awarded and paid JSA while a decision maker considers whether you should be sanctioned, the sanction applies from the date you were awarded JSA.

Awards of a 'qualifying benefit'

A decision can be revised at any time if:

- you are awarded a benefit (eg, UC, IS, income-based JSA, income-related ESA, pension credit (PC) or HB) and, for a period which includes the date that award took effect, you (or your partner, or a child included in your claim – see p307) are awarded another benefit or an increase in its rate. This can work to your advantage if the other benefit is a 'qualifying benefit' (eg, DLA or carer's allowance – see p1287);[31] *or*
- for IS, JSA, ESA and PC only, if you have a non-dependant living with you (see p330) and, since you were awarded IS, income-based JSA, income-related ESA or PC, your non-dependant has been awarded a qualifying benefit (see p1287) for a period that includes the date your award took effect and this means that you are now entitled to a severe disability premium (for IS, JSA or ESA) or a severe disability addition (for PC).[32]

A decision to end your entitlement to HB because your (or your partner's or child's) qualifying benefit ceases can also be revised at any time. This only applies if the qualifying benefit is later reinstated following a revision, supersession or appeal.[33]

See p1287 for further information. If you are only entitled to a benefit once a qualifying benefit is awarded, see p210 and p1143.

A decision that has been appealed

If you appealed against a decision, and you:

- appealed within the time limit or were allowed a late appeal (see p1305 and p1306) and the appeal has not yet been determined, a decision maker can look at the decision again and revise it.[34] This includes if the First-tier Tribunal has adjourned the hearing or if the Upper Tribunal has sent a case back to the First-tier Tribunal to make a new decision. This enables the decision maker to take new information that has come to light in the appeal process into account. **Note:** your appeal could lapse if a decision maker revises the decision, even if you do not get everything you want (see p1316); *or*
- make a fresh claim or request a supersession when your circumstances change (see p1334) and, as a result, a new decision about your entitlement is made, a decision maker can revise the new decision once your appeal has been decided. This only applies if you appealed against a decision to the First-tier Tribunal (or, for HB only, to the Upper Tribunal or a court) and:[35]
  - a fresh claim is decided or the decision is superseded before your appeal is determined; *and*

- the appeal is then determined; *and*
- the decision maker would have made her/his decision differently had s/he been aware of the appeal decision at the time her/his decision was made.

Mistake about or ignorance of facts

A decision can be revised at any time if there was a mistake about the facts of your case or the decision was made in ignorance of relevant facts, provided, as a result of the mistake or ignorance about the facts, the decision was more favourable to you than it would have been – eg, you were awarded too much benefit.[36] If you have been overpaid, the decision maker may seek to recover the overpayment (see Chapter 53). Because this specific ground only arises when the decision was more generous to you than it would have been without the mistake or ignorance about a fact, in practice this ground is only used when a decision maker wants to revise a decision. **Note:** there must have been a mistake about or ignorance of facts, not conclusions or opinions about the facts. See p1200 for some examples.

For AA, DLA and for ESA not paid under the UC system, the rules are different if there was a mistake about, or ignorance of, facts relating to a 'disability determination' or a 'limited capability for work determination'.[37] In this case, it must be shown that, at the time the decision that you were entitled to a benefit (eg, DLA or ESA) was made, you knew, or could reasonably have been expected to know, about the fact and that it was relevant to your benefit. Otherwise, a decision cannot be revised on this ground and you will not have been overpaid benefit, although there may be grounds for a supersession.

Disability and limited capability for work determinations[38]

A **'disability determination'** is a decision about whether you satisfy the disability conditions for AA or DLA, are disabled for the purposes of severe disablement allowance, or whether the existence or extent of your disablement is sufficient for you to be entitled to industrial injuries disablement benefit or to be paid at the same rate as that paid immediately before the decision. It does *not* include decisions about PIP.

A **'limited capability for work determination'** is a decision about whether you have, or can be treated as having, limited capability for work under any of the first six bullet points on p990 or because you get the support component on the basis that you meet one of the eating and drinking descriptors in the test for limited capability for work-related activity (see Appendix 4).

If the mistake about or ignorance of facts means you should be entitled to *more* benefit:

- a decision can be superseded on this ground (see p1277);
- a decision can be revised if you are in time to apply for an 'any grounds' revision (see p1262).

Part 9: Getting a benefit decision changed
Chapter 56: Revisions and supersessions
2. Revisions

Other grounds for an any time revision

There are many other situations when a decision maker can carry out a revision at any time. This includes if the decision is one against which you have no right of appeal (see p1304 for which decisions).[39]

Other decisions that can be revised at any time include a decision:
- to reduce your UC or your HB under the benefit cap rules (see p1156);[40]
- to end your entitlement to contributory ESA because you have been receiving it for 365 days, but it is subsequently found that you had, or can be treated as having had, limited capability for work-related activity before your entitlement ended;[41]
- to refuse you PIP because you are resident in a care home and the costs of any qualifying services (see p914) provided for you are met by public funds, the decision was made with incomplete evidence (see p1250) and, after the decision, any of the costs of the qualifying services are recovered from you;[42]
- to treat you as not satisfying the disability conditions for the daily living component or the mobility component of PIP because you did not return your questionnaire or you failed to participate in your assessment consultation. However, this only applies if the decision was made because of an error to which you did not contribute;[43]
- to increase the amount of rent used for the housing costs element (for UC) or your maximum rent (for HB) because of a rent officer's redetermination, or because a local housing allowance rate or broad rental market area has been amended because of a rent officer's error;[44]
- about state pension (or an 'old' retirement pension), PC or HB, where you or your partner deferred claiming a pension, then changed your option from a higher pension to a lump sum (or, for state pension and retirement pension only, vice versa);[45]
- to award ESA following a period of your being treated as in an extended period of sickness for JSA of 13 weeks. This allows the component to be added to your ESA award from the date of claim.[46]

Note: the list above is not exhaustive. There are a number of other decisions that can be revised at any time.[47]

How to apply for a revision

For UC, you can apply for a revision by requesting this on your online journal – this gives you a record you can access, proving you have made the request. If you also need to submit evidence, speak to your work coach or telephone the UC helpline and ask for a facility to enable you to upload the relevant documents. You do not have to apply for a revision online. You can also telephone or send a letter by post or take a written request to the job centre. It is always worth telephoning the UC helpline after you have submitted an application, either via your journal or in writing, to confirm that it is being dealt with as a request for revision.

For HB, you must apply for a revision (including a late application) in writing.[48]

For benefits other than HB, you do not have to apply for a revision in writing, although it is always best to do so. This ensures that the decision maker understands that you are asking for one, not just seeking an explanation or complaining about the rules.

In all cases, it is worth checking that an application sent by post has been received and is being dealt with appropriately.

When establishing whether an 'any grounds' revision is made within the time limit (see p1263), your application counts as having been received on the day it arrives at an 'appropriate office'.[49] **Note:** if you are applying for a mandatory reconsideration before you can appeal (see p1299), make this clear in your application (although the law does not say you must use this term, it is helpful if you do).

The appropriate office

The '**appropriate office**' is the office specified on the notice of the decision with which you disagree or, for JSA if you do not come under the UC system (see p22), the office where you have to sign on.[50] If you are a person who is, or would be, required to attend a work-focused interview as a condition of getting benefit, the Jobcentre Plus office is also an appropriate office in respect of decisions for benefits other than child benefit, guardian's allowance, HB, PIP and if you come under the UC system, JSA, ESA and UC.

A decision maker does not have to consider any issues other than those raised in your application.[51] To ensure the decision maker considers everything you want her/him to, you should:
- make it clear what sort of revision you are applying for. Show how you meet the specific grounds for an 'any time' revision or the time limit for an 'any grounds' revision; *and*
- set out all the points about the decision with which you disagree; *and*
- provide any information or evidence that supports your case. This includes, for example, medical evidence from a GP, consultant or other health worker if this is relevant. If the benefit is AA, DLA or PIP, evidence or information from your carer or a diary of your walking, supervision or care needs over a period may be useful. The decision maker may ask you for further information or evidence (see p1272).

The DWP, the local authority or HMRC can treat an application for a supersession as an application for a revision and vice versa.[52] In addition, any correspondence in which you make it clear that you are unhappy with a decision and want it changed, even if you do not use the term 'revision' or 'mandatory reconsideration',

Part 9: Getting a benefit decision changed
Chapter 56: Revisions and supersessions
2. Revisions

should be treated as a request for a revision. For example, a claim for benefit accompanied by a request for it to be backdated to the date a previous award ended can be treated as an application for a revision of the decision to end that previous award.[53] In general, if looking at your correspondence the only way you could be given what you want is by a supersession or revision of a particular decision, then that correspondence should be treated as the appropriate application.[54] Although you do not have to use the correct terminology, doing so ensures that there can be no doubt about what you are asking for.

How do you get evidence of previous decisions to support your application?

1. If the decision you are trying to get changed was made a long time ago, it can be difficult to identify the grounds. You can obtain information held by the DWP, the local authority or HMRC by making a 'subject access request' under the Data Protection Act 2018. See the Information Commissioner's website at ico.org.uk for details.

2. In some cases, the DWP, the local authority or HMRC may say it has destroyed old papers relating to your claim. Ask whether your papers have simply been archived, rather than destroyed. You can try to argue that missing papers should be presumed to contain information that is favourable to your case. However, this is unlikely to be accepted unless you can show that the papers should have been retained because they could have been relevant to any potential appeal, or that they were destroyed deliberately to thwart your case.[55]

Providing further evidence and information

The decision maker can ask you for more evidence or information if s/he thinks this is needed to consider all the issues raised by your application for a revision.[56] You must provide this within one month of the request.[57] The decision maker can allow longer. If you do not provide the information, your application is decided on the basis of the information and evidence the decision maker already has. If this happens and as a result the decision is unfavourable to you, if you later appeal, the evidence or information should be taken into account. The DWP can also ask you to have a medical examination – eg, if the decision concerns whether you have limited capability for work.

Note: in some cases, if you fail to provide information in a specified time period or have a medical examination, payment of your benefit could be suspended, which may lead to your entitlement being terminated (see p1162).

Similar rules allow the decision maker to ask for evidence or information if you apply for a supersession (although in UC cases the time limit to provide the information is within 14 days).[58]

When a revision takes effect

The date a revision takes effect is important. This is the date from when you are paid arrears if you are entitled to more benefit, or from when you have been overpaid if you are entitled to less benefit. In all cases, a revision takes effect from:

- the date the decision being revised took (or would have taken) effect[59] – eg, your date of claim if you are challenging a decision on a claim; *or*
- the correct date, if the date on which the decision being revised took effect was found to be wrong.[60]

It is important to make it clear that you want payment for the past period. You may get less backdating if the 'anti-test case rule' applies (see p1289).

Note: if a decision is revised on the grounds that there was a mistake about, or ignorance of, facts relating to a 'disability determination' or a 'limited capability for work determination' in the circumstances described on p1269, if the benefit is a qualifying benefit for another benefit (see p1287) and the revision means your entitlement to the other benefit is affected, the decision about the other benefit takes effect on the same date.[61]

Challenging a revision

If the original decision is one against which you have a right of appeal (see p1303), you can appeal to the First-tier Tribunal against that decision *as revised*. If the decision maker refuses to revise a decision, you can appeal against the original decision *as made*. In both cases, the appeal is against the original decision. You must be notified in writing of whether the decision maker has revised the decision or whether s/he has refused to revise it. For UC, the written notification can be given on your online journal. For benefits other than HB, if you applied for a mandatory reconsideration, this is called a 'mandatory reconsideration notice' (see p1301).

The time limit for appealing (see p1305) depends on the benefit involved and whether it was an 'any grounds' or an 'any time' revision.[62]

For HB, the time limit for appealing runs from the date:

- you were sent or given notification of the revision or the refusal to carry out an 'any grounds' revision and your application for a revision was made within the time limit (or a late application was accepted);
- of the original decision if a decision maker has refused to do an 'any time' revision – eg, because s/he does not accept that an official error was made.[63]

If the decision maker refuses to do an 'any grounds' revision because your application was late and s/he did not accept your reasons for why it was late, arguably the time runs from the date you are notified that the revision is not to be considered. However, it is arguable that this is wrong and the time runs from the

Part 9: Getting a benefit decision changed
Chapter 56: Revisions and supersessions
3. Supersessions

date of the notice of the original decision. If you are in this situation, try to appeal within 13 months of the original decision.

If the time for appealing runs from the date of the original decision, you may be able to apply for a judicial review (see Chapter 59) of the refusal to carry out an 'any time' revision or the refusal to accept your reasons for applying late for an 'any grounds' revision. Alternatively, you may be able to make a late appeal (see p1306). If you want to appeal against the original HB decision, the time limit runs from the date you were sent or given notice of it, so if you are outside the absolute time limit, you cannot appeal.

For benefits other than HB, the time for appealing runs from the date you were sent or given notification of the revision/refusal to revise. The only exception to this is if you were seeking an 'any time' revision, you were notified of the original decision more than 13 months ago and your application for a revision is refused. In this case, you can appeal if the tribunal accepts that the decision could have been revised as there was a specific ground.[64] **Note:** in this case, it is not clear whether your application needs to clearly raise a specific ground for an any time revision or whether it is sufficient that a ground for an any time revision was available. Get advice if this affects you.

3. **Supersessions**

A decision that is wrong or which is no longer correct can be changed by a supersession, but there must be grounds to do so.[65] The most common ground for a supersession is that your circumstances have changed since the decision was made.

You can apply for a supersession even if the decision was made a long time ago, but the arrears of benefit you are paid can be limited (see p1279 for when a supersession takes effect). It is usually better to apply for a revision or appeal.

When a decision can be superseded

You can ask for a decision maker's decision (and in some cases a First-tier Tribunal's or an Upper Tribunal's decision) to be superseded or the decision maker can decide to do this her/himself.[66] There must be grounds for a supersession. There are many grounds for supersession. The main ones are:
- where the decision maker has obtained a new medical report and the decision is about limited capability for work or work related activity for universal credit (UC) or employment and support allowance (ESA), or is about the disability conditions for personal independence payment (PIP) (see p1275);
- a change of circumstances (see p1275);
- mistakes about or ignorance of facts (see p1277);
- where a decision is legally wrong (see p1277);
- after a qualifying benefit has been awarded (see p1278).

Some other grounds for a supersession are summarised on p1278.

Note: if a decision could be revised, it cannot be superseded unless there are grounds for a supersession that are not covered by the revision rules.[67]

New medical reports from a healthcare professional and capability for work and disability conditions

A decision maker's or a tribunal's decision can be superseded if it is a decision to award you UC, ESA or national insurance (NI) credits on the basis that you have, or are treated as having, limited capability for work (see Chapter 45), or it is a decision to award you PIP on the basis that you satisfy one of the disability conditions. The decision can be superseded if:

- since the decision was made:[68]
  - a healthcare professional (see p1141 for who counts) or, for PIP and ESA under the UC system, an 'other person' approved by the Secretary of State, has provided medical evidence – eg, on your capability for work (or on whether you satisfy the disability conditions for PIP); *or*
  - the decision maker has decided that you can be treated as having limited capability for work (or, for UC, for work and work-related activity) under specified provisions.

The rules therefore allow the decision maker to consider your entitlement to UC, ESA, NI credits or PIP without identifying a specific change of circumstances.[69] The rate of benefit may be increased or reduced, or your entitlement may end. However, your entitlement should *only* end if s/he decides on the basis of the evidence that you no longer have limited capability for work, or no longer satisfy the conditions for PIP.[70]

If you have told the decision maker that your condition has not improved since your last assessment or you have a variable condition, argue that reference should be made to earlier assessments and decisions on your claim;[71] *or*

- it is a decision to award you PIP and there has been a determination that, because you did not return your questionnaire or you failed to participate in your assessment consultation, you do not satisfy the disability conditions for the daily living component or the mobility component.[72]

Change of circumstances

A decision maker's or a tribunal's decision can be superseded if:[73]
- your circumstances have changed since it had effect; *or*
- in the case of advance awards (other than for housing benefit (HB)), your circumstances have changed since it was made; *or*
- it is anticipated that your circumstances will change.

There must be a relevant change of circumstances (see p1276).

Part 9: Getting a benefit decision changed
Chapter 56: Revisions and supersessions
3. Supersessions

Note:

- The decision maker may say that a change of circumstances you have reported is a change that could not possibly result in a supersession and so refuse to consider a supersession. If this happens, see p1286.

- If there is doubt about whether a change of circumstances has occurred (eg, whether your medical condition has improved or worsened), it is necessary to compare the circumstances as they were at the time the decision took effect with the circumstances as they were at the time the supersession would take effect.[74]

- Some changes in your capability for work or the effects of your disability are dealt with under different rules (see p1275).

Relevant changes of circumstances

The change must be what is known as a 'relevant change of circumstances' – ie, it must mean that the original decision (eg, to award you benefit) may no longer be correct. What is relevant can depend on the benefit. Examples include changes in your income or your medical or physical condition, moving home or being absent from home, becoming or ceasing to be a member of a couple, or having a child or a child leaving home. Bear the following in mind.

- An amendment to the law counts as a relevant change of circumstances, but a decision of a court or the Upper Tribunal that the law has been wrongly interpreted does not.[75]

- Although a new medical opinion does not count, a new medical report following an examination may provide evidence of a relevant change.[76] **Note:** a new medical report might mean there is a separate ground for a supersession (see p1275).

- If you have a fixed-term award of attendance allowance (AA), disability living allowance (DLA) or PIP, a change in how long it is likely you will continue to meet the conditions of entitlement is a change of circumstances (effectively allowing you to seek a supersession on this ground in order to say the award should be for a longer period).[77]

- Becoming terminally ill counts for UC, ESA, AA, DLA and PIP, but you or the person claiming on your behalf must state explicitly that you are terminally ill in the supersession application.[78]

Change of circumstances after benefit is refused

If you were correctly refused benefit but your circumstances are now different, you *cannot* seek a supersession on the grounds of a change of circumstances. You must instead make a fresh claim (unless you are seeking a supersession because there has been a 'recrudescence' of a prescribed disease – see p672).[79] Even if you are appealing against the decision refusing or stopping your benefit, make a fresh claim when your circumstances change, and appeal if you are still refused. You could lose out if you do not do so, because the tribunal cannot take a change of circumstances into account if it happens after the decision with which you disagree (see p1334).

Mistake about or ignorance of facts

A decision maker's or a tribunal's decision can be superseded if there was a mistake about the facts of your case or if it was made in ignorance of relevant facts. However, in the case of a decision maker's decision, this only applies if:[80]

* for HB, a revision on the same ground cannot be done. **Note:** the local authority can revise a decision if, within one month of your being sent or given it, it has information that shows that there was a mistake about the facts of your case or the decision was made in ignorance of relevant facts;[81] *or*
* for other benefits, the time limit for applying for an 'any grounds' revision (or any longer period allowed) has passed (see p1263) or, if the decision maker decides to do a supersession her/himself, it is more than one month since you were sent or given the decision.

In practice, this ground for supersession generally only applies if, as a result of a mistake or ignorance about the facts, a decision was less favourable to you than it would have been (eg, you were awarded too little benefit) and you have missed the time limit for applying for an 'any grounds' revision. If a decision is more favourable to you than it would have been (ie, you were being overpaid), a decision maker can initiate an 'any time' revision (see p1269).

Note:
* There must have been a mistake about the facts or the decision maker (or the tribunal) must not have had all the facts, but it does not matter how the mistake came about or whether you could have produced evidence sooner than you did or failed to give the information on your claim form.
* The mistake or ignorance must be in respect of facts, not conclusions or opinions about the facts.[82] See p1200 for some examples.
* Sometimes it is possible to argue that the decision maker's mistake was an 'official error' (see p1266). If so, an 'any time' revision on this ground may be possible. If superseding the decision would give you an increased award, this is the better option, as full arrears of benefit are payable.

Decisions that are legally wrong

A decision maker's decision can be superseded if it was legally wrong (known as an error of law)[83] and:

* for HB, a revision on the same basis cannot be done; *or*
* for other benefits, the time limit for seeking an 'any grounds' revision (or any longer period allowed) has passed (see p1263) or, if the decision maker decides to carry out a supersession her/himself, it is more than one month since you were sent or given the decision.

Part 9: Getting a benefit decision changed
Chapter 56: Revisions and supersessions
3. Supersessions

In many cases, if there has been an error of law, an 'any time' revision on the basis of official error is also possible (see p1266). If the new decision is to your advantage, a revision is the better option, as full arrears of benefit are payable.

Note: if a decision of the First-tier or Upper Tribunal is legally wrong, this is not a ground that allows it to be changed by a supersession (it can only be changed by appealing against it).

Awards of qualifying benefits

A decision maker's or a tribunal's decision awarding you benefit can be superseded if:

- you are awarded the benefit (eg, income support (IS), ESA or HB) but, from a later date than the entitlement began, you or your partner (or a child included in your claim – see p307) are awarded another benefit or an increase in its rate. This can work to your advantage if the other benefit is a 'qualifying benefit' (eg, DLA, PIP or carer's allowance – CA) (see p1287);[84] *or*
- for IS, income-based jobseeker's allowance (JSA), income-related ESA and pension credit (PC) only, if you have a non-dependant living with you (see p332) and since you were awarded the benefit, your non-dependant has been awarded a qualifying benefit (see p1287) for a period beginning after the date your award took effect, and this means that you are now entitled to a severe disability premium (for IS, JSA or ESA) or a severe disability addition (for PC).[85]

See p1287 for further information. If you are only entitled to a benefit once a qualifying benefit is awarded, see p210 and p1143.

Other grounds for supersession

There are other situations when a decision can be superseded, including if the decision is one against which you have no right of appeal (see p1304).[86] Other decisions that can be superseded include those:

- where the amount of rent for the purposes of the housing costs element (for UC) or your maximum rent (for HB) decreases because of a rent officer's redetermination. **Note:** for HB, a decrease in your maximum rent because a local housing allowance rate or a broad rental market area has been amended due to a rent officer's error is a change of circumstances;[87]
- which reduced your HB under the benefit cap rules (see p1156), or increased or reduced the reduction;[88]
- about PC and HB, where you or your partner deferred claiming a retirement pension or a state pension and you are paid a lump sum or repay it because you change your option to a pension increase;[89]
- of the First-tier or Upper Tribunal made while a test case was pending, where the test case is eventually decided in your favour (see p1324).[90]

The list above is not exhaustive. Other decisions can be superseded.[91]

How to apply for a supersession

For **HB**, you must apply for a supersession in writing.[92] **For benefits other than HB**, you do not have to apply for a supersession in writing, although it is always best to do so. This ensures that the decision maker understands that you are asking for one, not just seeking an explanation or complaining about the rules. For **UC**, in practice the DWP may refuse to deal with an application for a supersession unless you have indicated that there is a 'change of circumstances' on your online journal. **Note:** the date of your application for a supersession may be before this – eg, if at an earlier date you wrote about the change on your journal.

The application counts as received when received at an appropriate office. This is the same as for revisions (see p1271).

A notification of a change in circumstances can be treated as an application for a supersession, so if you are reporting a change of circumstances, check that your application is received. The date of receipt is important as it can affect the date from when your benefit is changed.

When you apply for a supersession, include any information and evidence that supports your case and that may enable the decision maker to change the decision in your favour. For how to get evidence and for providing further information, see p1272. The issues are the same as for revisions. **Note:**

- The DWP, the local authority or HMRC can treat an application for a supersession as an application for a revision and vice versa.[93]
- A claim for benefit or a question about your entitlement can be treated as an application for a supersession.[94]

When a supersession takes effect

If a decision is superseded, the date the new decision (the supersession) takes effect is important. This is the date from when you are paid arrears if you are entitled to more benefit, or the date from when you have been overpaid if you are entitled to less benefit. It is important to make it clear that you want payment for a past period. For how the 'anti-test case rule' may affect the amount of backdated benefit you can receive, see p1289.

The general rule

There is a general rule that applies in many cases. This is that if a decision is superseded, the new decision takes effect from:[95]

- the date you applied for the supersession; *or*
- if the decision maker decides to carry out a supersession on her/his own initiative, the date the decision is made.

There are many exceptions when the general rule does not apply. For these, the date a supersession takes effect depends on the ground for the supersession. For

Part 9: Getting a benefit decision changed
Chapter 56: Revisions and supersessions
3. Supersessions

the exceptions, see below and the chapter in this *Handbook* about the benefit you are claiming.

New medical reports and disability/limited capability for work decisions

Where the benefit is UC, ESA or PIP and the ground for supersession is that the decision maker has received medical evidence from a healthcare professional (see p1275), the supersession takes effect as follows.

- For UC:[96]
  - where it is the first decision about whether you have limited capability for work and work related activity and a waiting period applies (see p71), from the start of the assessment period after the waiting period;
  - in any other case, from the start of the assessment period in which the decision is made, or from the start of the assessment period in which you first asked to be reassessed.
- For ESA:
  - where it is the first decision about whether you have limited capabilty for work given in respect of that award, from the start of the 14th week of entitlement (or earlier if your award is linked to an earlier award – in which case the supersession takes effect from the date on which your combined entitlement has lasted 14 weeks) (see p635);[97]
  - where it is not the first decision, from the date of decision,[98] or from the date you asked to be reassessed, if the reassessment took place at your request.[99]
- For PIP, from the date of the decision.[100]

The decision maker may obtain a new medical report which suggests that you do not meet the relevant disability/capability test which you had previously been accepted as meeting. Where this happens, the question which arises is whether this is because your circumstances have changed (ie, an improvement in your health) or simply because the new report gives a different opinion from a previous one. The question is important because, if your circumstances have changed, the supersession could be on the grounds of a change of circumstances rather than on the grounds of receipt of a new medical report. A supersession on the grounds of a change of circumstances takes effect from different dates to supersessions following receipt of a medical report (see p1275).

Changes in your circumstances

If the ground for supersession is a change in your circumstances, when the supersession takes effect usually depends on whether or not it is advantageous to you. There are also some special rules that apply in particular situations, including the following.

- For benefits other than UC, child benefit and guardian's allowance, if there has been a change in the legislation that affects your benefit, the supersession takes effect from the date the legislation takes effect (for UC, the change takes effect from the start of the next assessment period unless the legislation took effect on the first day of an assessment period).[101]

- For IS, income-based JSA, income-related ESA and PC, if your carer (or your partner's carer) has stopped being paid CA, the supersession takes effect from the day after the last day for which CA was paid, provided this was to someone other than you or your partner. This means that if you are now entitled to the severe disability premium in your IS, income-based JSA or income-related ESA or the severe disability addition in your PC, your award can be increased from when the carer stopped getting CA for looking after you (or your partner).[102]
- For ESA and UC, if the change is that you are terminally ill (you must state this in the application for a supersession), the supersession takes effect, for ESA, from the date you became terminally ill and, for UC, from the first day of the assessment period in which you became terminally ill.[103]

If a supersession is not advantageous

If the decision maker decides to carry out a supersession her/himself or you apply for a supersession and it is *not advantageous* to you, the supersession usually takes effect from:

- for UC, the start of the assessment period in which the change takes place or is expected to take place. There is an exception if the decision is one you were required to notify and is about limited capability for work;[104]
- if you come under the UC system (see p22), for contribution-based JSA and contributory ESA, the start of the benefit week in which the change takes place or is expected to take place.[105] There is an exception if the decision is one you were required to notify and is about limited capability for work;
- for HB, the Monday after the week in which the change occurs.[106] For the exceptions to this rule, see p223;
- for PIP, the date on which the change takes place or is expected to take place.[107] There is an exception if the change is one you were required to notify and relates to the disability conditions for PIP;
- for other benefits, the date of the change of circumstances.[108] There is an exception if the change is one you were required to notify and relates to a disability or limited capability for work determination.

Note: if a supersession is not advantageous to you, you may have been overpaid. The DWP, the local authority or HMRC may seek to recover the overpayment.

Disability and limited capability for work

Different rules apply if the decision is *not advantageous* to you, it concerns a change you were required to notify and it related to:

- if you come under the UC system, limited capability for work; *or*

Part 9: Getting a benefit decision changed
Chapter 56: Revisions and supersessions
3. Supersessions

- if you do not come under the UC system, a disability or limited capability for work determination (see p1269 for what counts); *or*
- the disability conditions for PIP.

In this case, if you (or the person being paid the benefit) failed to notify the change when you knew that you should have, or could reasonably be expected to have known that you should have, the supersession takes effect from the date you (or the person being paid the benefit) ought to have notified the change.[109] However, if you (or the person being paid) could not have reasonably been expected to know that you should have reported the change, the supersession usually takes effect from:[110]

- for UC, the start of the assessment period in which the DWP makes the decision; *or*
- for ESA if you come under the UC system and PIP, the date you applied for the supersession, or if the decision maker decides to do a supersession on her/his own, the date the decision is made; *or*
- for other benefits, from the date on which the supersession decision is made.

So if your condition is found to have improved in the past, and you could not have been expected to report this, you will not have been overpaid, or be expected to repay any overpayment.

Note: if you do not come under the UC system, the benefit is a 'qualifying benefit' (see p1287 for what counts) and the supersession means your entitlement to another benefit is affected, the decision about the other benefit takes effect on the same date.[111]

If a supersession is advantageous

If the supersession is *advantageous* to you, when it takes effect depends on whether the decision maker initiated the supersession, or you applied for one.

If the decision maker initiated a supersession, it usually takes effect from:

- for UC, the start of the assessment period in which s/he first took action with a view to carrying out a supersession;[112]
- for HB, the Monday after the week in which the change occurs.[113] However, if the change is one you are required to notify to the local authority (other than, if you get PC and the rate of this changes as described in the first bullet point on p223), you must have notified the local authority of the change within one month of the change.[114] For further information on when changes in circumstances take effect and exceptions to this rule, see p222;
- for AA, DLA and PIP, the date on which s/he first took action with a view to carrying out a supersession;[115]
- for other benefits, the start of the benefit week in which s/he first took action with a view to carrying out a supersession.[116]

If you apply for the supersession, it usually takes effect from:
- for UC, the start of the assessment period in which the change takes place or is expected to take place. You must have notified the DWP of the change within that assessment period;[117]
- for JSA and ESA if you come under the UC system (see p22), the start of the benefit week in which the change takes place or is expected to take place. You must have notified the DWP of the change within one month of the change;[118]
- for HB, the Monday after the week in which the change occurs.[119] However, if the change is one you are required to notify to the local authority (other than if you get PC – see the note on p223), you must have notified the local authority of the change within one month of the change;[120]
- for PIP, the date the change takes place, or is expected to take place. You must notify the DWP of the change within one month of the change.[121] However, if the change means you are now entitled to a higher rate of benefit, the supersession takes effect from the day you satisfy the conditions of entitlement for that rate (this includes the 'required period condition' – see p742).[122] In this case, you must have notified the DWP within one month of satisfying the conditions of entitlement;
- for AA or DLA, if the change:[123]
  - means you are now entitled to a higher rate of benefit, the day you satisfy the conditions of entitlement to that rate (this includes the qualifying period condition – see p518, p587 and p594). You must have notified the DWP of the change within one month of doing so;
  - makes a difference to whether benefit is payable to you (eg, you leave hospital or a care home), the day of the change. You must have notified the DWP of the change within one month of the change;
- for other benefits, from the date the change takes place, or is expected to take place. You must have notified the DWP (or HMRC) of the change within one month of the change.[124] There are exceptions to this rule for IS and PC and, if you do not come under the UC system, JSA and ESA.[125]

The one-month periods can be extended (see below). If your application for an extension is refused, see p1284 for when the supersession takes effect.

Late notification of a change of circumstances

If the supersession is *advantageous* to you and you fail to notify a change within the one-month periods above (or, for UC, within the assessment period), you can apply for an extension of time in limited circumstances, to a **maximum of 13 months**.[126] Your application must contain:[127]
- details of the relevant change of circumstances; *and*
- the reasons why you failed to notify the change in time. You must show that:
  - it is reasonable to grant your request; *and*

Part 9: Getting a benefit decision changed
Chapter 56: Revisions and supersessions
3. Supersessions

- the change of circumstances is relevant to the decision you want changed; *and*
- there are special circumstances that mean it was not practicable for you to notify the change within the time limit. The longer you have delayed, the more compelling the special circumstances must be.

When deciding whether it is reasonable to grant your application, the decision maker cannot take account of the fact that:[128]

- a court or the Upper Tribunal has interpreted the law in a different way than was previously understood and applied;
- you (or anyone acting for you) misunderstood or were unaware of the relevant law, including the time limits for applying for a supersession.

If your application for an extension of time is refused, or your application was made outside the maximum time limit, arrears are limited. The supersession takes effect:

- for UC, from the start of the assessment period in which you notified the change;[129] *or*
- for AA or DLA, from the date you applied for the supersession;[130] *or*
- for IS, JSA, ESA and PC:[131]
  - if you are paid in arrears, from the start of the benefit week in which you notified the change; *or*
  - if you are paid in advance and you notified the change on the first day of the benefit week, from that day. Otherwise it takes effect from the start of the benefit week following the week in which you notified the change; *or*
- for HB, usually from the Monday after the date when you notified the change (see p222);[132] *or*
- for other benefits, from the date you notified the change.[133]

Mistake about or ignorance of facts

If there has been a mistake about or ignorance of facts, the general rule on p1279 usually applies. So even if you are entitled to more benefit, arrears are limited. There are exceptions.

Exceptions to the general rule

If the First-tier or Upper Tribunal made a decision in ignorance of relevant facts or made a mistake about the facts and, as a result, it was more *advantageous* to you than it would otherwise have been (eg, you have been overpaid benefit), the supersession takes effect:[134]

- for UC and ESA if you come under the UC system (see p22), from the start of the assessment period (for UC) or the start of the benefit week (for ESA) in which the tribunal's decision took effect; *or*
- for other benefits, from the date the tribunal's decision took effect.

However, the First-tier or Upper Tribunal decision is only superseded from this earlier date if you knew, or you could reasonably have been expected to know, the fact in question and that it was relevant to the decision and:[135]

- the decision related to a disability determination (see p1269); *or*
- it is a decision about your limited capability for work or whether you can be treated as having limited capability for work.

If you did not know (or could not be expected to know), the general rule on p1279 applies.

For HB, if a decision maker's decision was made in ignorance of facts or there was a mistake about the facts and the new decision is *advantageous* to you, the supersession takes effect from the start of the benefit week in which:[136]

- you applied for the supersession; *or*
- if you did not apply for a supersession, the local authority first had sufficient information to show that the original decision was made in ignorance of, or based on a mistake about, the facts.

The list above is not exhaustive. There are other exceptions.[137]

Awards of qualifying benefits

If you are entitled to a benefit at a higher rate because you (or your partner, your child or a non-dependant) were awarded a qualifying benefit (see p1287 for what counts), the supersession takes effect on the date of entitlement to the qualifying benefit or to an increase in its rate. For IS, JSA, ESA and PC only, if you had a non-dependant living with you while you were waiting for a decision on your claim for a qualifying benefit, your IS, JSA, ESA or PC award can be superseded to include a severe disability premium (additional amount with PC) from the date the non-dependant can be ignored (or ceased to live with you). See pp1287–89 for further information.

Test cases

If a decision about your benefit is being superseded because of a decision by the Upper Tribunal or a court in another case (a 'test case'), the supersession is effective from the date of the tribunal's or court's decision, even if you did not realise it was relevant to your case until some time later.[138] This could help you get considerable arrears of benefit. For the special rule for the period before the date the test case is decided, see p1289.

If, while an appeal against the initial decision in a test case was pending:

- for benefits other than HB, a decision was made on your claim for benefit or to make a revision or a supersession, but your benefit was suspended, and if the test case is eventually decided against you (in whole or in part), the supersession takes effect from the date the earlier decision took effect;[139]

Part 9: Getting a benefit decision changed
Chapter 56: Revisions and supersessions
3. Supersessions

- you appealed to the First-tier or Upper Tribunal, it determined your appeal as if the test case had been decided in the way most unfavourable to you and the test case eventually goes in your favour (see p1324), the supersession takes effect from the date it would have taken effect had the tribunal made its decision in accordance with the decision in the test case.[140] For UC, the date is the start of the assessment period (for IS, JSA, ESA and PC, the start of the benefit week) in which it would have taken effect had the tribunal made its decision in accordance with the decision in the test case.[141]

Other grounds for supersession

There are a large number of other exceptions to the general rule on p1279. These include if:

- your rent for the purposes of the housing costs element (for UC) or your maximum rent (for HB) has decreased because of a rent officer's redetermination;[142]
- for PC and HB, you or your partner deferred claiming a retirement pension or state pension and you are paid a lump sum or change your option to a pension increase;[143]
- entitlement to a benefit depends on your NI contribution record, and the decision needed to be changed because additional contributions have been added to the record.[144]

The list above is not exhaustive. There are many other exceptions to the general rule.[145]

Challenging a supersession

Following your application for a supersession, or a decision maker initiating a supersession, a new decision is issued in writing. If you do not get all that you wanted, you can apply for a revision of the new decision. If the decision is one against which you have a right of appeal (see p1303), you can appeal to the First-tier Tribunal. Unless the benefit is HB, or is ESA and the decision is that you do not have limited capability for work and would be one where you would get ESA while you are appealing (see p1015), you must apply for a mandatory reconsideration first (see p1299). If you have a right of appeal against the decision, you must be told about this.

If the decision maker has said there are no grounds for a supersession, you must show why there are, and say what you think the new decision should be. If the decision maker has conducted a supersession, but you do not agree that s/he had grounds for this, you should explain why.

If a decision maker refuses to consider a supersession

When you apply for a supersession, a decision maker must make a decision if your application contains a ground for supersession that is potentially relevant to the amount of benefit you can be paid or the length of time you can be paid it. There are two possibilities.

- The decision maker agrees that there is a reason to change your award. For example, you are claiming HB and notify the decision maker that your non-dependant has moved out and so you are entitled to more benefit. In this situation, the decision maker carries out a supersession.
- The decision maker does not think there is a reason to change your award. For example, you are getting the standard rate of the PIP daily living component, feel your condition has deteriorated and want to claim the enhanced rate instead. However, the decision maker thinks you do not qualify for the enhanced rate. In this situation, the decision maker issues a decision refusing to carry out a supersession.

In either situation, you can apply for a revision of the decision maker's decision or appeal against it.[146] Unless the benefit is HB, you must apply for a mandatory reconsideration before you can appeal (see p1299).

The only situations in which a decision maker does not have to make a decision are if an application has not been made properly and therefore cannot possibly lead to a supersession, or if an application is clearly not on a potentially relevant ground or is otherwise misconceived. In these cases, there is no decision against which you can seek a revision or appeal, but you may be able to apply for a judicial review (see p1377).

---

4. Revisions and supersessions after a 'qualifying benefit' award

Some of the rules for revisions and supersessions can help you if you (or your partner, your child or a non-dependant) become entitled to a 'qualifying benefit'.

Qualifying benefits
A '**qualifying benefit**' is, in general, any benefit which gives you entitlement to another benefit, or makes another benefit payable at a higher rate.

For example, the rules can help if there was a delay in assessing your entitlement to a qualifying benefit (eg, attendance allowance (AA), disability living allowance (DLA), personal independence payment (PIP), carer's allowance (CA) or child benefit) and so:

- you did not get an element in your universal credit (UC), a disability- or carer-related premium in your means-tested benefit or an additional amount in your pension credit (PC), or allowances for your children. For income support (IS),

Part 9: Getting a benefit decision changed
Chapter 56: Revisions and supersessions
4. Revisions and supersessions after a 'qualifying benefit' award

jobseeker's allowance (JSA), employment and support allowance (ESA) and PC only, this includes where there are delays in assessing your non-dependant's entitlement to a qualifying benefit (see p1289); *or*

- a non-dependant deduction was made from your means-tested benefit.

Note: these rules can help you get arrears of benefit, even if the qualifying benefit was awarded some time ago, and you did not report the change in your circumstances at the time.[147]

Do you have to be entitled to a means-tested benefit?

You can only apply for a revision or supersession on this ground if you are already entitled to UC, IS, JSA, ESA, PC or housing benefit (HB).[148] It is therefore essential to make a claim, if you are not prevented from doing so by the introduction of UC, at the same time as the claim for a qualifying benefit. If you only qualify for one of these when the qualifying benefit is awarded, see p1289.

You or a family member are awarded a qualifying benefit or an increased rate

If you, or your partner or a child included in your claim (see p307), are awarded a qualifying benefit, or are awarded an increase in its rate (eg, you were getting the standard rate of the daily living component of PIP and are awarded the enhanced rate of that component), and arrears of the qualifying benefit are payable, your award of UC, IS, JSA, ESA, PC or HB can be increased on revision or supersession and arrears paid for the same length of time.[149] This applies if:

- you are now entitled to premiums/components/elements/additional amounts or, if the qualifying benefit is child benefit, to allowances or premiums for your children paid with your benefit; *or*
- no non-dependant deduction, or for UC, a deduction for housing costs contributions, should now be made from your means-tested benefit because you or your partner are now entitled to a qualifying benefit – eg, AA, the care component of DLA or the daily living component of PIP.

Note: for IS, JSA, ESA and PC only, if you had a non-dependant living with you while you were waiting for a decision on your claim for a qualifying benefit, your IS, JSA, ESA or PC award can be superseded to include the severe disability premium (or additional amount), from the date s/he can be ignored (or from the date s/he ceased to reside with you) if this is after the date from which the qualifying benefit is payable.[150]

Example

Jamal has been getting income-related ESA and HB for three years. His ESA does not include any premiums and, because his uncle lives with him and his partner, Mia, a non-dependant deduction is being made from his HB. He claims PIP and Mia claims CA on 15 July. Six months later, Jamal is awarded the enhanced rate of the daily living component of PIP and Mia is awarded CA, both payable from 15 July. Jamal is now entitled to the enhanced disability and carer premiums in his ESA and a non-dependant deduction should not be made from his HB. His ESA and HB awards are superseded and he is paid arrears, backdated to 15 July.

Your non-dependant is awarded a qualifying benefit or an increased rate

For IS, JSA, ESA and PC only, if you have a non-dependant (see p347) living with you and, but for this, a severe disability premium (or additional amount for PC) would be paid, your award of IS, income-based JSA, income-related ESA or PC can be increased on revision or supersession to include this premium (or additional amount) from the date the non-dependant is awarded a qualifying benefit.[151]

You only qualify when the qualifying benefit is awarded

If you make an unsuccessful claim for a benefit, and only qualify when the qualifying benefit is awarded, you should make a second claim as soon as you hear about the qualifying benefit. See p1143 for further information.

If you only qualify for HB when the qualifying benefit is awarded, see p210. If you lose benefit because of the way the rules operate, ask the local authority for compensation.

If you only claim for the first time *after* you hear about the qualifying benefit, you can only qualify for backdated benefit under the normal backdating rules. See Chapter 50 and the chapter about the benefit you are claiming.

See p555 for a similar rule that helps you get extra backdated CA when the person for whom you care becomes entitled to a qualifying benefit.

5. The 'anti-test case rule'

A special rule applies when a case is going through the appeals system that will determine a point of social security law (a 'test case'), which can affect how the decision on that point in the test case is applied in your case.

The rule applies if the Upper Tribunal or a court decides in an appeal that a decision maker in a different case (the test case) has made an error of law (see p1357), and you make a claim, or apply for a revision or a supersession (either before or after the test case decision). In this situation, your decision maker must

Part 9: Getting a benefit decision changed
Chapter 56: Revisions and supersessions
5. The 'anti-test case rule'

decide any part of your claim (or revision or supersession) which relates to the period before the test case decision as if the decision that was under appeal in the test case had been found by the tribunal or court not to have been wrong.[152] **Note:**
- The anti-test case rule only applies if the test case is the first authoritative decision on the issue, and not merely a later decision confirming an earlier decision.[153]
- The test case decision only has to be disregarded for the period before it was made if it found the decision maker to have been wrong, not if it found her/him to be right.

For housing benefit (HB), you can avoid the anti-test case rule by appealing rather than seeking a revision or supersession if the rules allow you to do so.

What happens while a test case is pending

If an appeal (a test case) is pending against a decision of the Upper Tribunal or a court, the decision maker can postpone making a decision on your claim or request for a supersession or revision.[154] The decision maker can only do this if s/he thinks that a possible result of the test case is that you will have no entitlement to benefit. This prevents you appealing until a decision is made in the test case. If the decision is postponed, once a decision has been made in the test case, the decision maker makes the decision in your case.[155]

If you would be entitled to benefit even if the test case were decided against you, the decision maker can make a decision on the assumption that the test case has been decided in the way that is most unfavourable to you.[156] However, this means that you can at least be paid something while you wait for the result of the test case. Then, if the decision in the test case is in your favour, the decision maker revises her/his decision. **Note:**
- If you already have a decision in your favour, the decision maker can suspend payment of your benefit (see p1161).
- If you have already appealed to the First-tier Tribunal, see p1324.

Notes

1. **Getting a decision changed**
   1 **HB** Sch 7 para 11 CSPSSA 2000
     Other benefits s17 SSA 1998
   2 **HB** Sch 7 paras 3(2) and 4(3) CSPSSA
     2000
     Other benefits ss9(2) and 10(2) SSA
     1998
   3 *Wood v SSWP* [2003] EWCA Civ 53

2. **Revisions**
   4 **HB** Sch 7 para 3 CSPSSA 2000
     Other benefits s9 SSA 1998
   5 **UC/PIP/JSA&ESA under UC** s9(1) SSA
     1998; regs 5 and 8 UC,PIP,JSA&ESA(DA)
     Regs
     HB Sch 7 para 3(1) CSPSSA 2000; reg 4
     HB&CTB(DA) Regs
     CB/GA s9(1) SSA 1998; regs 5, 8, 10
     and 11 CB&GA(DA) Regs
     Other benefits s9(1) SSA 1998; reg 3
     SS&CS(DA) Regs
   6 **UC/PIP/JSA&ESA under UC** Reg
     5(2)(a) UC,PIP,JSA&ESA(DA) Regs
     HB Reg 4(10) HB&CTB(DA) Regs
     CB/GA Reg 5(3) CB&GA(DA) Regs
     Other benefits Reg 3(9)(a)
     SS&CS(DA) Regs
   7 **UC/PIP/JSA&ESA under UC** Reg
     5(2)(c) UC,PIP,JSA&ESA(DA) Regs
     Other benefits Reg 3(9)(b) and (c)
     SS&CS(DA) Regs
   8 Reg 3(3) SS&CS(DA) Regs
   9 Regs 1(3), definition of 'date of
     notification', and 3(1)(b) SS&CS(DA)
     Regs
   10 Regs 2 and 4(1)(a) HB&CTB(DA) Regs
   11 Reg 4(4) HB&CTB(DA) Regs
   12 **UC/PIP/JSA&ESA under UC** Regs 2,
     3(2) and 5(1)(b) UC,PIP,JSA&ESA(DA)
     Regs
     CB/GA Regs 3 and 5(2)(b) CB&GA(DA)
     Regs
     Other benefits Regs 1(3), 2(b) and
     3(1)(b) SS&CS(DA) Regs
   13 **UC/PIP/JSA&ESA under UC** Reg
     38(4) UC,PIP,JSA&ESA(DA) Regs
     HB Reg 10A(3) HB&CTB(DA) Regs
     Other benefits Reg 9A(3) SS&CS(DA)
     Regs

14 **UC/PIP/JSA&ESA under UC** Reg 6
     UC,PIP,JSA&ESA(DA) Regs
     HB Regs 4(4) and 5(3)(b) HB&CTB(DA)
     Regs
     CB/GA Reg 6(3)(c) CB&GA(DA) Regs
     Other benefits Reg 4 SS&CS(DA) Regs
   15 **UC/PIP/JSA&ESA under UC** Reg 6(3)-
     (6) UC,PIP,JSA&ESA(DA) Regs
     HB Reg 5(3)(a), (4) and (6)
     HB&CTB(DA) Regs
     CB/GA Reg 6(3)(a) and (b), (4) and (5)
     CB&GA(DA) Regs
     Other benefits Reg 4(3)(a), (4) and (5)
     SS&CS(DA) Regs
   16 **HB** Reg 5(4)(b) and (5) HB&CTB(DA)
     Regs
     CB/GA Reg 6(4)(b) and (6)
     CB&GA(DA) Regs
     Other benefits Reg 4(4)(b) and (6)
     SS&CS(DA) Regs
   17 R(TC) 1/05
   18 *R(CJ) and SG v SSWP (ESA)* [2017] UKUT
     324 (AAC); DMG 03013; ADM A3015
   19 **UC/PIP/JSA&ESA under UC** Reg
     5(1)(a) UC,PIP,JSA&ESA(DA) Regs
     CB/GA Reg 5(2)(a) CB&GA(DA) Regs
     Other benefits Reg 3(1)(a)
     SS&CS(DA) Regs
   20 Reg 4(1)(b) HB&CTB(DA) Regs
   21 **UC/PIP/JSA&ESA under UC** Regs 8
     and 9(a) UC,PIP,JSA&ESA(DA) Regs
     HB Reg 4(2)(a) HB&CTB(DA) Regs
     CB/GA Reg 10(2)(a) CB&GA(DA) Regs
     Other benefits Reg 3(5)(a)
     SS&CS(DA) Regs
   22 Reg 10(3) CB&GA(DA) Regs
   23 **UC/PIP/JSA&ESA under UC** Reg 2
     UC,PIP,JSA&ESA(DA) Regs
     HB Reg 1(2) HB&CTB(DA) Regs
     Other benefits Reg 1(3) SS&CS(DA)
     Regs
   24 **UC/PIP/JSA&ESA under UC** Reg 2
     UC,PIP,JSA&ESA(DA) Regs
     HB Reg 1(2) HB&CTB(DA) Regs
     CB/GA Reg 10(3) CB&GA(DA) Regs
     Other benefits Reg 1(3) SS&CS(DA)
     Regs

9

Part 9: Getting a benefit decision changed
Chapter 56: Revisions and supersessions
Notes
• •

25 **UC/PIP/JSA&ESA under UC** Reg 2
UC,PIP,JSA&ESA(DA) Regs
HB Reg 1(2) HB&CTB(DA) Regs
CB/GA Reg 10(3) CB&GA(DA) Regs
Other benefits Reg 1(3) SS&CS(DA)
Regs
26 CDLA/393/2006
27 CDLA/1707/2005
28 *R (Smith) v SSWP* [2018] UKUT 270
(AAC)
29 **UC/JSA&ESA under UC** Reg 14(1)(a)-
(c) UC,PIP,JSA&ESA(DA) Regs
Other benefits Reg 3(5C), (6), (6A)
and (7CD) SS&CS(DA) Regs
30 Reg 3(6B) SS&CS(DA) Regs
31 **UC/PIP/JSA&ESA under UC** Regs 8
and 12 UC,PIP,JSA&ESA(DA) Regs
HB Reg 4(7B) HB&CTB(DA) Regs
CB/GA Reg 11 CB&GA(DA) Regs
Other benefits Reg 3(7) SS&CS(DA)
Regs
32 Reg 3(7ZA) SS&CS(DA) Regs
33 Reg 4(7C) HB&CTB(DA) Regs
34 **UC/PIP/JSA&ESA under UC** Regs 8
and 11(1) UC,PIP,JSA&ESA(DA) Regs
HB Reg 4(1)(c) HB&CTB(DA) Regs
CB/GA Reg 8(2) CB&GA(DA) Regs
Other benefits Reg 3(4A) SS&CS(DA)
Regs
35 **UC/PIP/JSA&ESA under UC** Regs 8
and 11(2) UC,PIP,JSA&ESA(DA) Regs
HB Reg 4(7) HB&CTB(DA) Regs
CB/GA Reg 8(3) CB&GA(DA) Regs
Other benefits Reg 3(5A) SS&CS(DA)
Regs
36 **UC/PIP/JSA&ESA under UC** Regs 8
and 9(b) UC,PIP,JSA&ESA(DA) Regs
HB Reg 4(2)(b) HB&CTB(DA) Regs
CB/GA Reg 10(2)(b) CB&GA(DA) Regs
Other benefits Reg 3(5)(b) and (d)
SS&CS(DA) Regs
37 Regs 3(5)(c)and 7A(1) SS&CS(DA) Regs
38 Reg 7A SS&CS(DA) Regs
39 **UC/PIP/JSA&ESA under UC** Regs 8
and 10 UC,PIP,JSA&ESA(DA) Regs
HB Reg 4(6) HB&CTB(DA) Regs
CB/GA Reg 9 CB&GA(DA) Regs
Other benefits Reg 3(8) SS&CS(DA)
Regs
40 **UC/PIP/JSA&ESA under UC** Regs 8
and 19(1) UC,PIP,JSA&ESA(DA) Regs
HB Reg 4(7H) HB&CTB(DA) Regs
41 **UC/PIP/JSA&ESA under UC** Reg
15(5) UC,PIP,JSA&ESA(DA) Regs
Other benefits Reg 3(5I) SS&CS(DA)
Regs
42 Regs 8 and 18(2) UC,PIP,JSA&ESA(DA)
Regs

43 Regs 8 and 18(3) UC,PIP,JSA&ESA(DA)
Regs
44 **UC/PIP/JSA&ESA under UC** Regs 8
and 19(2) UC,PIP,JSA&ESA(DA) Regs
HB Reg 4(3) HB&CTB(DA) Regs; reg
18A(1) and (3) HB Regs; reg 18A(1) and
(3) HB(SPC) Regs
45 **State pension** Reg 3(7DB) SS&CS(DA)
Regs
RP Reg 3(7E) SS&CS(DA) Regs
PC Reg 3(7D) and (7DA) SS&CS(DA)
Regs
HB Reg 4(7D) and (7DA) HB&CTB(DA)
Regs
46 Reg 3(5J) SS&CS(DA) Regs; reg 15(4A)
UC,PIP,JSA&ESA(DA) Regs
47 **UC/PIP/JSA&ESA under UC** Regs 8,
13, 15(2)-(4) and (4A), 16, 17 and 18(1)
UC,PIP,JSA&ESA(DA) Regs
HB Reg 4(7A) and (7DB) HB&CTB(DA)
Regs
Other benefits Reg 3(5D)-(5H), (7A),
(7EA), (7EB), (8B)-(8K) SS&CS(DA) Regs
48 Regs 4(8) and 5(2) HB&CTB(DA) Regs
49 **UC/PIP/JSA&ESA under UC** Reg
5(1)(b) UC,PIP,JSA&ESA(DA) Regs
CB/GA Reg 5(1)(b) CB&GA(DA) Regs
Other benefits Reg 3(1)(b)
SS&CS(DA) Regs
50 **UC/PIP/JSA&ESA under UC** Reg 2
UC,PIP,JSA&ESA(DA) Regs
HB Reg 4(8) HB&CTB(DA) Regs
CB/GA Reg 2(1), definition of
'appropriate office', CB&GA(DA) Regs
Other benefits Reg 3(11) SS&CS(DA)
Regs
51 **HB** Sch 7 paras 3(2) and 4(3) CSPSSA
2000
Other benefits ss9(2) and 10(2) SSA
1998
52 **UC/PIP/JSA&ESA under UC** Regs
20(1) and 33(1) UC,PIP,JSA&ESA(DA)
Regs
HB Regs 4(9) and 7(6) HB&CTB(DA)
Regs
CB/GA Regs 7(1) and 14(1)
CB&GA(DA) Regs
Other benefits Regs 3(10) and 6(5)
SS&CS(DA) Regs
53 R(JSA) 2/04
54 *WO'C v SSWP and JW* [2020] UKUT 34
(AAC) paras 70-71- although this
judgment concerns applications to
tribunals the same principles should
apply to applications to the decision
maker
55 R(IS) 11/92; *SSWP v TJ (JSA)* [2015]
UKUT 56 (AAC), paras 213-15

9

Part 9: Getting a benefit decision changed
Chapter 56: Revisions and supersessions
Notes

84 **UC/PIP/JSA&ESA under UC** Reg 23 UC,PIP,JSA&ESA(DA) Regs. For these benefits, although this counts as a change of circumstances, it takes effect differently to most such changes.
HB Reg 7(2)(i) HB&CTB(DA) Regs
CB/GA Reg 13(2)(e) CB&GA(DA) Regs
Other benefits Reg 6(2)(e) SS&CS(DA) Regs

85 Reg 6(2)(ee) SS&CS(DA) Regs

86 **UC/PIP/JSA&ESA under UC** Reg 25 UC,PIP,JSA&ESA(DA) Regs
HB Reg 7(2)(e) HB&CTB(DA) Regs
CB/GA Reg 13(2)(d) CB&GA(DA) Regs
Other benefits Reg 6(2)(d) SS&CS(DA) Regs

87 **UC** Reg 30 UC,PIP,JSA&ESA(DA) Regs
HB Reg 7(2)(c) HB&CTB(DA) Regs; reg 18A(2) HB Regs; reg 18A(2) HB(SPC) Regs

88 Reg 7(2)(r) HB&CTB(DA) Regs

89 **PC** Reg 6(2)(o) and (oa) SS&CS(DA) Regs
HB Reg 7(2)(j), (ja) and (jb) HB&CTB(DA) Regs

90 **UC/PIP/JSA &ESA under UC** Reg 31(b) UC,PIP,JSA&ESA(DA) Regs
HB Reg 7(2)(d)(ii) HB&CTB(DA) Regs
CB/GA Reg 13(2)(c)(ii) CB&GA(DA) Regs
Other benefits Reg 6(2)(c)(ii) SS&CS(DA) Regs

91 **UC/PIP/JSA&ESA under UC** Regs 27, 28 and 29 UC,PIP,JSA&ESA(DA) Regs
HB Regs 7(2)(g), (h), (q), (r) and (s) and 7A(2) and (3) HB&CTB(DA) Regs
Other benefits Reg 6(2)(f), (fa), (h), (j), (k), (p), (q), (s), (sa), (t) and (u) SS&CS(DA) Regs

92 Reg 7(7) HB&CTB(DA) Regs

93 **UC/PIP/JSA&ESA under UC** Regs 20(1) and 33(1) UC,PIP,JSA&ESA(DA) Regs
HB Regs 4(9) and 7(6) HB&CTB(DA) Regs
CB/GA Regs 7(1) and 14(1) CB&GA(DA) Regs
Other benefits Regs 3(10) and 6(5) SS&CS(DA) Regs

94 R(I) 50/56

95 **HB** Sch 7 para 4(5) CSPSSA 2000
Other benefits s10(5) SSA 1998

96 Reg 35(9) UC,PIP,JSA&ESA(DA) Regs

97 Reg 7(38) and (40) SS&CS(DA) Regs; reg 35(7) and (8) UC,PIP,JSA&ESA(DA) Regs

98 s10(5) SSA 1998

99 Reg 7(39) SS&CS(DA) Regs; reg 35(6) UC,PIP,JSA&ESA(DA) Regs

100 s10(5) SSA 1998

101 **UC/PIP/JSA&ESA under UC** Reg 35(1) and Sch 1 paras 32 and 33 UC,PIP,JSA&ESA(DA) Regs
HB Reg 8(10) HB&CTB(DA) Regs
Other benefits Reg 7(9)(a)(ii), (30) and (30A) SS&CS(DA) Regs

102 Reg 7(2)(bc) SS&CS(DA) Regs

103 **UC/PIP/JSA&ESA under UC** Reg 35(1) and Sch 1 paras 9 and 28 UC,PIP,JSA&ESA(DA) Regs
Other benefits Reg 7(2)(be) SS&CS(DA) Regs

104 Sch 1 para 20 UC,PIP,JSA&ESA(DA) Regs

105 Sch 1 para 1 UC,PIP,JSA&ESA(DA) Regs

106 Reg 8(2) HB&CTB(DA) Regs

107 Sch 1 para 12 UC,PIP,JSA&ESA(DA) Regs

108 **AA/DLA** Reg 7(2)(c)(iv) SS&CS(DA) Regs
CB/GA Reg 16(5) CB&GA(DA) Regs
Other benefits Reg 7(2)(c)(v) SS&CS(DA) Regs

109 **UC/PIP/JSA/ESA under UC** Sch 1 paras 7, 8, 11, 16, 17, 19, 23, 24 and 30 UC,PIP,JSA&ESA(DA) Regs
Other benefits Regs 7(2)(c)(ii) and 7A(1) SS&CS(DA) Regs

110 **UC/PIP/JSA&ESA under UC** s10(5) SSA 1998; Sch 1 paras 2, 13 and 25 UC,PIP,JSA&ESA(DA) Regs
Other benefits s10(5) SSA 1998 as none of the other heads of reg 7(2)(c) SS&CS(DA) Regs apply

111 Reg 7A(2) SS&CS(DA) Regs

112 Sch 1 para 29 UC,PIP,JSA&ESA(DA) Regs

113 Reg 8(2) HB&CTB(DA) Regs

114 Reg 8(3) HB&CTB(DA) Regs

115 **AA/DLA** Reg 7(9)(a) SS&CS(DA) Regs
PIP Sch 1 para 18 UC,PIP,JSA&ESA(DA) Regs

116 **JSA&ESA under UC** Sch 1 para 10 UC,PIP,JSA&ESA(DA) Regs
CB/GA Reg 16(4) CB&GA(DA) Regs
Other benefits Reg 7(2)(bb) SS&CS(DA) Regs

117 Sch 1 paras 20 and 21 UC,PIP,JSA&ESA(DA) Regs

118 Sch 1 paras 1 and 6 UC,PIP,JSA&ESA(DA) Regs

119 Reg 8(2) HB&CTB(DA) Regs

120 Reg 8(3) HB&CTB(DA) Regs

121 Sch 1 paras 12 and 14 UC,PIP,JSA&ESA(DA) Regs

122 Sch 1 para 15 UC,PIP,JSA&ESA(DA) Regs

123 Reg 7(9) SS&CS(DA) Regs; *SSWP v DA* [2009] UKUT 214 (AAC)

124 **CB/GA** Reg 16(3)(a) CB&GA(DA) Regs
Other benefits Reg 7(2)(a)
SS&CS(DA) Regs
125 Schs 3A, 3B and 3C SS&CS(DA) Regs
126 **UC/PIP/JSA&ESA under UC** Reg 36
UC,PIP,JSA&ESA(DA) Regs
HB Reg 9 HB&CTB(DA) Regs
CB/GA Reg 17 CB&GA(DA) Regs
Other benefits Reg 8 SS&CS(DA) Regs
127 **UC/PIP/JSA&ESA under UC** Reg
36(3)-(7) UC,PIP,JSA&ESA(DA) Regs
HB Reg 9(2)-(4) HB&CTB(DA) Regs
CB/GA Reg 17(3)-(5) CB&GA(DA) Regs
Other benefits Reg 8(3)-(5)
SS&CS(DA) Regs
128 **UC/PIP/JSA&ESA under UC** Reg
36(7) UC,PIP,JSA&ESA(DA) Regs
HB Reg 9(5) HB&CTB(DA) Regs
CB/GA Reg 17(6) CB&GA(DA) Regs
Other benefits Reg 8(6) SS&CS(DA)
Regs
129 Sch 1 para 21 UC,PIP,JSA&ESA(DA) Regs
130 Reg 7(9)(d) SS&CS(DA) Regs
131 Reg 7(2)(b)(i) and (ii) SS&CS(DA) Regs;
Sch 1 para 6 UC,PIP,JSA&ESA(DA) Regs
132 Reg 8(3) HB&CTB(DA) Regs; reg 79(1)
HB Regs; reg 59(1) HB(SPC) Regs
133 **UC/PIP/JSA&ESA under UC** Sch 1
para 14 UC,PIP,JSA&ESA(DA) Regs
CB/GA Reg 16(3)(b) CB&GA(DA) Regs
Other benefits Reg 7(2)(b)(iii)
SS&CS(DA) Regs
134 **UC/PIP/JSA&ESA under UC** Reg
37(1)-(3) UC,PIP,JSA&ESA(DA) Regs
HB Reg 8(7) HB&CTB(DA) Regs
CB/GA Reg 16(7) CB&GA(DA) Regs
Other benefits Reg 7(5) SS&CS(DA)
Regs
135 **UC/ESA** Regs 2 and 37(1) and (3)
UC,PIP,JSA&ESA(DA) Regs
Other benefits Reg 7(5) and Sch 3C
para 8 SS&CS(DA) Regs
136 Reg 8(4) HB&CTB(DA) Regs
137 **UC/PIP/JSA&ESA under UC** Reg
35(2)-(4) UC,PIP,JSA&ESA(DA) Regs
Other benefits Reg 16(2) SS(C&P)
Regs; Schs 3A para 12, 3B para 7, and
3C para 9 SS&CS(DA) Regs
138 **UC/PIP/JSA&ESA under UC** Reg
35(5) UC,PIP,JSA&ESA(DA) Regs
HB Reg 8(8) HB&CTB(DA) Regs
CB/GA Reg 16(9) CB&GA(DA) Regs
Other benefits Reg 7(6) SS&CS(DA)
Regs
All *MP v SSWP (DLA)* [2010] UKUT 130
(AAC)

139 **UC/PIP/JSA&ESA under UC** Reg
37(5) and (6) UC,PIP,JSA&ESA(DA) Regs
CB/GA Reg 16(9A) CB&GA(DA) Regs
Other benefits Reg 7(6A) SS&CS(DA)
Regs
140 **HB** Reg 8(11) HB&CTB(DA) Regs
CB/GA Reg 16(8) CB&GA(DA) Regs
PIP Reg 37(4)(a) UC,PIP,JSA&ESA(DA)
Regs
Other benefits Reg 7(33) SS&CS(DA)
Regs
141 **UC/PIP/JSA&ESA under UC** Reg
37(4)(b) and (c) UC,PIP,JSA&ESA(DA)
Regs
Other benefits Schs 3A para 12, 3B
para 7, and 3C para 8 SS&CS(DA) Regs
142 **UC** Reg 35(14) UC,PIP,JSA&ESA(DA)
Regs
HB Reg 8(2) and (6) HB&CTB(DA) Regs
143 **PC** Reg 7(7A) SS&CS(DA) Regs
HB Reg 8(14A) HB&CTB(DA) Regs
144 Reg 35(13) UC,PIP,JSA&ESA(DA) Regs;
reg 7(8A) SS&CS(DA) Regs
145 **UC/PIP/JSA&ESA under UC** Reg
35(10)-(12) UC,PIP,JSA&ESA(DA) Regs
HB Reg 8(6A), (9), (14D), (14E), (14F),
(14G) and (15) HB&CTB(DA) Regs
Other benefits Reg 7(8), (8ZA), (11),
(12A)-(12G), (24), (25), (28), (29),
(29A)-(29C), (34)-(37) and (41)-(43)
SS&CS(DA) Regs
146 *Wood v SSWP* [2003] EWCA Civ 53,
reported as R(DLA) 1/03

4. Revisions and supersessions after a 'qualifying benefit' award

147 *HR v Wakefield DC* [2009] UKUT 72
(AAC); *OL v SSWP (ESA)* [2018] UKUT
135 (AAC)
148 **IS/JSA/ESA/PC/UC** s8(2) SSA 1998
HB Sch 7 para 2 CSPSSA 2000
149 **UC/PIP/JSA&ESA under UC** Regs 12
and 23 and Sch 1 para 31
UC,PIP,JSA&ESA(DA) Regs
IS/JSA/ESA/PC Regs 3(7), 6(2)(e) and
7(7) SS&CS(DA) Regs
HB Regs 4(7B) and (7C), 7(2)(i) and
8(14) HB&CTB(DA) Regs; CIS/1178/
2001
All *BB v SSWP (ESA)* [2017] UKUT 280
(AAC)
150 Reg 7(7)(b) SS&CS(DA) Regs
151 Regs 3(7ZA), 6(2)(ee) and 7(7)
SS&CS(DA) Regs

Part 9: Getting a benefit decision changed
Chapter 56: Revisions and supersessions
Notes

5. **The 'anti-test case rule'**
152 **HB** Sch 7 para 18 CSPSSA 2000
   Other benefits s27 SSA 1998
   All *CAO and Another v Bate* [1996] 2 All
   ER 790 (HL)
153 R(FC) 3/98; R(I) 1/03
154 **HB** Sch 7 para 16 CSPSSA 2000
   Other benefits s25 SSA 1998
155 **HB** Sch 7 para 18(2) CSPSSA 2000
   Other benefits s27(2) SSA 1998
156 **UC/PIP/JSA&ESA under UC** s25(3)
   and (4) SSA 1998; reg 53
   UC,PIP,JSA&ESA(DA) Regs
   HB Sch 7 para 16(3) and (4) CSPSSA
   2000; reg 15 HB&CTB(DA) Regs
   CB/GA s25(3) and (4) SSA 1998; reg 22
   CB&GA(DA) Regs
   Other benefits s25(3) and (4) SSA
   1998; reg 21 SS&CS(DA) Regs

Chapter 57

Appealing to the First-tier Tribunal

This chapter covers:
1. Before you appeal (p1298)
2. How to appeal (p1304)
3. After you submit your appeal (p1312)
4. How the tribunal makes its decision (p1325)
5. Preparing your appeal (p1336)
6. The tribunal's decision (p1345)

This chapter covers the rules for appeals to the First-tier Tribunal about benefits, the social fund payments in Chapter 37 (except budgeting loans), decisions about DWP loans for mortgage interest (see p839) and national insurance credits. It does *not* cover the rules for statutory payments (see Chapter 60), the health benefits in Chapter 31 or the Scottish benefits (see Chapter 80).

References in this chapter to HM Revenue and Customs only apply to decisions about child benefit and guardian's allowance. For information about appeals about tax credits, see Chapter 67.

Key facts
- If you disagree with certain decisions made by the DWP, the local authority or HM Revenue and Customs, you can appeal to the First-tier Tribunal.
- For benefits other than housing benefit, you must usually apply for a mandatory reconsideration before you can appeal.
- There is an absolute time limit for appealing.
- Appeals can take time. You may need to make a fresh claim for benefit or seek a supersession while you are waiting for your appeal to be heard.
- The tribunal can allow or reject your appeal, and replace the decision about which you appealed with any decision it thinks is right. This could be more or less favourable to you.
- If your appeal is unsuccessful, you may be able to appeal to the Upper Tribunal.

Part 9: Getting a benefit decision changed
Chapter 57: Appealing to the First-tier Tribunal
1. Before you appeal

1. Before you appeal

You can appeal against some decisions of the DWP, the local authority or HM Revenue and Customs (HMRC). Appeals are dealt with in the Social Entitlement Chamber of the First-tier Tribunal (Social Security and Child Support) – referred to as the First-tier Tribunal in this *Handbook* (except in Chapter 60). Appeals are dealt with by a judge (and, in some cases, members) assigned to the First-tier Tribunal. The administration of the work of all tribunals is the responsibility of HM Courts and Tribunals Service (HMCTS), part of the Ministry of Justice. HMCTS officials deal with the day-to-day work of the First-tier Tribunal through a network of regional offices. See p1313 for who may deal with your appeal.

Before you appeal, you should do the following.

- Make sure you have sufficient information about the decision you are unhappy about. You can ask for a written statement of reasons if this has not already been provided (see p1256).
- Check whether you must apply for a mandatory reconsideration before you can appeal and apply within the time limit if relevant (see p1299).
- Check whether you would be better off applying for a revision or supersession instead of appealing (see below).
- In some cases, you should get advice before you appeal. If you apply for a mandatory reconsideration, the DWP or HMRC looks at your case afresh. So does the First-tier Tribunal when you appeal. There is a risk you could lose benefit. For example, if your appeal is about a benefit that can be paid at different rates (eg, personal independence payment (PIP)), the rate could go down. If you are appealing about an overpayment, the amount could increase.

Revision, supersession or appeal?

1. Unless the benefit is housing benefit (HB), you must usually apply for a mandatory reconsideration before you can appeal (see p1299).

2. For HB, if you are not yet sure if you want to appeal it can be worth applying for a revision before you appeal. You get two bites at the cherry, because if your application for a revision is turned down, you can still appeal against the original decision.

3. There is no time limit for applying for certain revisions ('any time revisions') but you must show specific grounds (see p1265). You can ask for an 'any time' revision even if the time limit for applying for what is known as an 'any grounds' revision or appealing has expired. However, you might not be able to appeal against a refusal to do an 'any time' revision (see p1273).

4. In most cases, there is no time limit for applying for a supersession – eg, if there has been a mistake about the facts or if a test case is decided in your favour but you do not become aware of this until some time later. However, you generally get less arrears of benefit if you apply for a supersession. See pp1279–86 for when a supersession takes effect.

5. If the 'anti-test case' rule applies to you (see p1289), and all that you did before the test case was decided was apply for a revision or a supersession, the arrears of benefit you get could be limited. This is not the case if you appealed.

Mandatory reconsideration

Before you can appeal you must usually ask for the decision you are unhappy with to be looked at again – ie, you must apply for a mandatory reconsideration. If you must apply for a mandatory reconsideration, the officer reconsidering the decision must then consider whether to revise the decision.

You do *not* have to apply for a mandatory reconsideration if:

- the benefit is HB; *or*
- your appeal concerns an employment and support allowance (ESA) decision that you do not have limited capability for work and you would qualify for payment of ESA pending an appeal against that decision (see p1015). You can appeal direct to the First-tier Tribunal without having to apply for a mandatory reconsideration first;[1] *or*
- the DWP does not tell you that you need to apply for a mandatory reconsideration before you can appeal. You can appeal direct to the First-tier Tribunal without having to apply for a mandatory reconsideration first.[2]

When you must apply for a mandatory reconsideration

You must apply for a mandatory reconsideration before you can appeal against a decision in the following situations. You can only appeal if:

- for child benefit and guardian's allowance, you have applied for a mandatory reconsideration and HMRC has decided not to revise the decision. Note: if it revises the decision, you can appeal against the original decision, as revised;[3]
- for other benefits (other than HB), you have been notified properly, in writing, that you must apply for a revision before you can appeal (the DWP uses the term 'mandatory reconsideration'), you have done so, and the DWP has considered your application. This includes if it refuses your application because it was late.[4] You have only been notified properly if the decision notice (see p1255) includes a statement that you only have a right of appeal if the DWP has considered an application for a revision of the decision. The notice must also inform you of the time limit for applying for an 'any grounds' revision (see p1263) and that you can ask for a statement of reasons for the decision (if one has not been included) within one month of being notified of the decision (see p1256).

There are tools for generating mandatory reconsideration letters on AskCPAG.

Bear in mind that it is the First-tier Tribunal that decides whether you have a right of appeal, *not* the DWP or HMRC. However, the easiest way to prove to the tribunal that you have a right of appeal is to apply for a mandatory reconsideration

Part 9: Getting a benefit decision changed
Chapter 57: Appealing to the First-tier Tribunal
1. Before you appeal

and send the tribunal the 'mandatory reconsideration notice' that you are given by the DWP or HMRC (see p1301).

Has the DWP notified you properly?

If the DWP does not notify you properly (this is only likely to happen in limited cases), you do *not* have to apply for a mandatory reconsideration before you can appeal, although it may be better to do so.[5] If you have not applied for a mandatory reconsideration, make it clear on your appeal form that you have *not* been notified properly and provide proof.

Time limits for applying for a mandatory reconsideration

When you apply for a mandatory reconsideration, you are applying for a revision. There are two types of revision: 'any grounds' revisions (p1262) and 'any time' revisions (see p1265). If you are disputing a decision that was made:

- recently, it is always best to apply for an 'any grounds' revision. You must do so within a strict time limit. In most cases, you must apply within **one month** of being sent or given the decision (see p1263). If you can show there are special circumstances, you can apply outside this limit so long as you do so within the absolute time limit (usually 13 months – see p1264);
- some time ago, and you have missed the time limits for an 'any grounds' revision, you need to apply for an 'any time' revision. You must show grounds (see p1265) – eg, that there has been an official error.

If you miss the time limit for an 'any grounds' revision

If the decision maker refuses to accept your application for a mandatory reconsideration because you missed the one-month time limit for an 'any grounds' revision, but you have applied within the absolute time limit, the decision maker has considered whether to revise the decision so you have a right to appeal.[6] The DWP says the decision maker should make a decision refusing to revise and issue you with a mandatory reconsideration notice.[7]

Note: if the decision maker:[8]

- refuses to consider your application for an 'any grounds' revision because it was made outside the absolute time limit for doing so (see p1263), s/he should go on to consider whether there are grounds for an 'any time' revision;
- decides there are no grounds for a revision, s/he should consider whether to do a supersession.

In both cases, you should argue that the decision maker has considered whether to revise the decision and that you now have a right of appeal.

An application for an 'any time' revision can count as an application for a mandatory reconsideration even if you apply outside the time limit for an 'any grounds' revision.[9] If the DWP says your application does not count, appeal to the First-tier Tribunal and point out that the DWP has considered whether to revise the decision, so you have satisfied the mandatory reconsideration rules and have a right to appeal.

Applying for a mandatory reconsideration

It is always best to apply for a mandatory reconsideration in writing (on a form or by letter), although you can apply by telephone. If you are appealing about universal credit (UC), you can apply on your online journal. In all cases, make it clear that you are applying for a mandatory reconsideration.

Forms

For child benefit and guardian's allowance, use Form CH24A available at gov.uk/government/publications/child-benefit-and-guardians-allowance-appeal-form.

For other benefits, use Form CRMR1 available at gov.uk/government/publications/challenge-a-decision-made-by-the-department-for-work-and-pensions-dwp.

Explain why you disagree with the decision and provide any additional information and evidence that supports your case. It is important to follow up your application to ensure that it has been received.

Note:

• If you sent or delivered your appeal to the First-tier Tribunal when you should have applied for a mandatory reconsideration first, the tribunal may say your appeal is not valid and return it to you to resolve the issue. If you do not do so, it can 'strike out' your appeal (see p1321).

• If you sent your appeal to the DWP or direct to the tribunal before first applying for a mandatory reconsideration, the DWP can (but does not have to) treat your appeal as an application for a mandatory reconsideration.[10] If the DWP does not do this, apply for a mandatory reconsideration as soon as possible, explaining why your application is late if relevant. Although there is no equivalent rule for child benefit and guardian's allowance, there is nothing to prevent HMRC from treating an appeal as an application for a mandatory reconsideration.

The mandatory reconsideration notice

The DWP or HMRC gives or sends you a mandatory reconsideration notice telling you the result of your application. This notice is proof that the DWP or HMRC has accepted and considered your application. If you are still unhappy with the decision, you can then appeal to the First-tier Tribunal. You must send a copy of the notice to the tribunal when you appeal.[11] Although the tribunal can waive this requirement, this is discretionary and it may instead 'strike out' your appeal (see p1321).[12] **Note:** the tribunal *cannot* waive the requirement to apply for a mandatory reconsideration.

Part 9: Getting a benefit decision changed
Chapter 57: Appealing to the First-tier Tribunal
1. Before you appeal

What if you do not have a mandatory reconsideration notice?

If you have applied for a mandatory reconsideration, but have not been sent or given a mandatory reconsideration notice, try to provide the tribunal with as much evidence as you can that you did apply, and that the DWP or HMRC has considered your application. Provide a copy of your application along with proof you posted or delivered it, if possible. For UC, if you applied via your journal, take and provide a screenshot. Also provide copies of any correspondence, notes of telephone calls or personal contact with the DWP or HMRC since you made the application.

Who can appeal

If you are **appealing about a benefit other than HB**, you have a right to appeal if you are:[13]

- a claimant; *or*
- an appointee claiming on someone's behalf (see p1135); *or*
- claiming attendance allowance, disability living allowance or PIP on behalf of someone who is terminally ill, even if this is without her/his knowledge; *or*
- a person from whom an overpayment of a benefit or one of the regulated social fund payments in Chapter 37 (other than a budgeting loan) or a duplication of payment of UC, pension credit, income support, income-based jobseeker's allowance (JSA) or income-related ESA can be recovered (see Chapter 53). This is the case even if you were not the person who claimed the benefit that was overpaid;[14] *or*
- someone from whom a short-term or budgeting advance, or hardship payments, can be recovered; *or*
- the partner of a claimant, if the decision concerns whether you failed to take part in a work-focused interview without good cause;[15] *or*
- a person appointed by the DWP or HMRC to make a benefit claim for, or proceed with a claim made by, someone who has died.

If you are **appealing about HB**, you have a right to appeal if you are a person affected by the decision – ie, your rights, duties or obligations are affected by the decision, and you are:[16]

- a claimant; *or*
- someone acting for a claimant who is unable to act for her/himself – eg, an appointee (see p206); *or*
- someone from whom the local authority decides an overpayment can be recovered (including a landlord or agent);[17] *or*
- a landlord or agent, if the decision concerns whether or not to make a direct payment of HB to you; *or*
- a person appointed by the local authority to proceed with the appeal.

Decisions you can appeal

You can appeal to the First-tier Tribunal against most decisions taken by the Secretary of State for Work and Pensions (the DWP), a local authority officer or an officer of HMRC (known as decision makers – see p1248).[18] Unless the benefit is HB, you must usually apply for a mandatory reconsideration before you can appeal (see p1299). You can appeal against an original decision or a decision made after a supersession. You cannot appeal against a decision to do a revision (or not to do a revision), but you can appeal against the original decision, as revised.

Has the decision maker refused to make a decision?

If a decision maker refuses to make a decision on your claim, this effectively prevents you having the right to appeal. You should remind the decision maker that s/he *must* make a decision on every valid claim.[19] Even if the decision maker does not accept that a claim made on the correct claim form is valid, you should be given a decision saying so. You can then appeal and ask the tribunal to decide whether your claim is valid.[20] If a decision maker refuses to consider your application for a supersession, see p1286.

Note: a decision maker can sometimes postpone making a decision if there is a test case pending (see p1290).

You must be given a written notice of any decision that you can appeal.[21] This:
* must give you information about your right to appeal and your right to request a written statement of reasons for it if this has not been included; *and*
* for benefits other than HB, child benefit and guardian's allowance, normally includes information about applying for a mandatory reconsideration before you can appeal.

Examples of decisions you can appeal

Whether you are entitled to a benefit.

Whether an overpayment is recoverable (unless you come under the UC system and it is an overpayment of UC, contribution-based JSA or contributory ESA), and the amount of an overpayment.

Whether to impose a civil penalty (see p1229).[22]

Whether your claim has been validly made or can be backdated.

Whether benefit is payable under the overlapping benefit rules.[23]

Whether you should be given a sanction, and whether you had good cause or a good reason for your actions or your failure to take action.

Whether you have limited capability for work or limited capability for work-related activity.

Whether you satisfy the habitual residence test.

Whether you satisfy the disability conditions for benefit.

Whether you can be paid hardship payments.

Part 9: Getting a benefit decision changed
Chapter 57: Appealing to the First-tier Tribunal
2. How to appeal

Whether your award of contributory ESA should end because you have been paid it for 365 days (see p640).[24]

Whether you are available for, or actively seeking, work.

Whether a jobseeker's agreement is reasonable or you had a good reason for refusing or failing to carry out a jobseeker's direction.

Decisions you cannot appeal

You cannot appeal against some decisions.[25] You *can* ask for an 'any time' revision or a supersession of a decision about which you do not have a right of appeal, whatever your reason for thinking it is wrong.[26] However, if the decision maker refuses to revise or supersede such a decision, your only legal remedy is to apply for a judicial review (see Chapter 59).

Examples of decisions you cannot appeal

Who should be the claimant when a couple is unable to decide.

Who should be entitled to child benefit when two people whose claims have equal priority cannot agree.

Whether a claim for one benefit can be treated as a claim for (or in addition to) another benefit.

Whether to demand recovery of an overpayment, and the amount of weekly deductions.

Whether to suspend payment of benefit.

Whether to appoint a person as an appointee (see p1135).

Whether to make a short-term advance, a budgeting advance or a payment on account.

How much benefits are increased (uprated) every year.[27]

2. How to appeal

You must appeal in writing. This is known as a **'notice of appeal'**. Unless it is an appeal about housing benefit (HB), you must usually apply for a mandatory reconsideration before you can appeal (see p1299).

Can you submit your appeal online?

You can submit appeals about benefits (other than HB, child benefit or guardian's allowance) online at gov.uk/appeal-benefit-decision.

You must appeal within a strict time limit (see p1305). See p1309 to find out what information your notice of appeal must contain to ensure your appeal is valid.

If you are *not* submitting your appeal online, you should use the appropriate form wherever possible. If you do not use the appropriate form, your appeal must be accepted as valid if it is in writing and includes all the information required (see p1309).

Appeal forms

For HB, use the form approved by your local authority.[28]

For other benefits (other than child benefit and guardian's allowance), use form SSCS1 in the leaflet *Appeal a social security benefits decision (Notice of Appeal)*.

For child benefit and guardian's allowance, use the appeal form (SSCS5) in the leaflet *Notice of Appeal Against a Decision of HM Revenue and Customs*.

All the forms are available from gov.uk.

If you want the First-tier Tribunal to deal with your appeal quickly (to do what is known as expedite your appeal), make this clear when you appeal, explaining why your case is urgent. For HB, because you have to send or deliver your notice of appeal to the local authority, you could write to the tribunal, asking it to intervene. For further information, see the article 'Expediting UC appeals' on p8 of CPAG's *Welfare Rights Bulletin* 278.

Where to send your written appeal

If you are not submitting your appeal online, you must send or deliver it:
- for HB, to the local authority office that sent you the decision.[29] It passes your appeal to the First-tier Tribunal;
- for other benefits, direct to the First-tier Tribunal at the appeal centre, sometimes referred to as 'direct lodgement'. The addresses to use are on the appeal forms. The appeal centre checks whether your appeal is valid and, if so, passes it to the appropriate regional office.[30]

The time limit for appealing

The time limit for appealing depends on whether or not you had to apply for a mandatory reconsideration before you could appeal. If you miss the time limit, it can be extended (see p1306), but there is an absolute time limit within which you must appeal (see p1308).

If you had to apply for a mandatory reconsideration

If you had to apply for a mandatory reconsideration before you could appeal (see p1299), your appeal, including all the information described on p1309, must

Part 9: Getting a benefit decision changed
Chapter 57: Appealing to the First-tier Tribunal
2. How to appeal

arrive at the First-tier Tribunal appeal centre within one month after you are sent the mandatory reconsideration notice (see p1301).[31]

> *Month*
> 'Month' means a complete calendar month running from the day after the day you have been sent or given a decision.[32] For example, a decision sent on 25 July has an appeal time limit that expires at the end of 25 August.
> When calculating time, if something has to be done by a certain day, it must be done by 5pm that day. If a time limit ends on a day other than a working day, you have until the end of the next working day to meet the time limit.[33] A 'working day' is any day other than Saturday, Sunday, Christmas Day, Good Friday or a bank holiday.

If you did not have to apply for a mandatory reconsideration

If you did not have to apply for a mandatory reconsideration (this generally only applies to HB), your appeal, including all the information described on p1309, must arrive at the relevant office (for HB, this is the office that sent you the decision and for other benefits, this is the First-tier Tribunal appeal centre) by the latest of the following:[34]

- one month after the date the written decision was sent to you; *or*
- if you ask for a written statement of reasons within one month of being given notice of the decision (if one has not already been given to you – see p1256), 14 days after the latest of:
  - the end of that month – ie, if the written statement of reasons is provided within the one-month period, you get one month plus 14 days to appeal; *or*
  - the date the written statement of reasons is provided.

If you applied for a revision before you appealed and the decision maker revises the decision, but you still want to appeal because you did not get all you want, the one-month time limit runs from the date you are sent the new decision.[35] If you applied for an 'any grounds' revision and the decision maker refused to do a revision, you must appeal no later than one month after the date you are sent notice of the refusal.[36]

If the decision maker refuses to do an 'any time' revision and says you cannot appeal, you should appeal against the original decision within the time limit (if this has not already passed). If this is not possible, get advice.

If you miss the time limit

If you miss the time limit for appealing, your appeal is still treated as made in time if neither the decision maker nor any other person with a right of appeal against the decision (or anyone who has been added as a party to the appeal – eg, the other parent if you are disputing who counts as responsible for your child) does not object.[37] Often, the DWP or HM Revenue and Customs (HMRC) does not object. However, for benefits other than HB, the tribunal can look at the issue of lateness even if the decision maker (or party to the appeal) has not raised an objection. **Note:** for HB appeals only, there are special rules that set out when the decision maker can treat your appeal as made in time and so should not object.

If the decision maker (or other person) *does* object, the tribunal can still extend your time limit.[38] There is no guarantee that it will do so, so keep within the time limit wherever possible. There is an absolute time limit for appealing after which you cannot appeal (see p1308).

In addition to the information you must provide on your appeal form (see p1309), you must include the reasons why your appeal is late.[39] The tribunal can extend the time limit for appealing if this will enable it to deal with your appeal fairly and justly, so give details of any special circumstances that mean this would be the case. See p1308 for some ideas about what may be relevant.

Note:

- The First-tier Tribunal decides whether your appeal has been made within the time limit, *not* the DWP, the local authority or HMRC. If you think there may be a dispute about whether your appeal has been made in time, explain why you think it was when you appeal.
- If you miss the time limit and the First-tier Tribunal does not extend it, you can appeal to the Upper Tribunal against the First-tier Tribunal's decision.[40]
- The tribunal can also shorten time limits, but should only do this if this will enable it to deal with your appeal fairly and justly.

Housing benefit appeals

A decision maker can treat your HB appeal as made in time if it is in the 'interests of justice'.[41] For these purposes, it is *not* in the interests of justice unless it was not practicable for you to appeal in time because:[42]

- your partner or a dependant died or had a serious illness; *or*
- the person who appealed died or had a serious illness; *or*
- you are not resident in the UK; *or*
- normal postal services were disrupted; *or*
- there are other special circumstances that are 'wholly exceptional'. The longer you have delayed appealing, the more compelling these must be.[43]

When deciding whether it is in the interests of justice, account cannot be taken of the fact that:[44]

- a court or the Upper Tribunal has interpreted the law in a different way than was previously understood and applied; *or*
- you (or anyone acting for you) misunderstood or were unaware of the relevant law, including the time limits for appealing.

If the decision maker objects to your appeal being treated as made within the time limit, s/he must refer it to the First-tier Tribunal immediately.[45] The tribunal then decides whether your time limit can be extended.

Part 9: Getting a benefit decision changed
Chapter 57: Appealing to the First-tier Tribunal
2. How to appeal

Why your time limit should be extended

Your reasons and circumstances need to show it would be fair and just to extend your time limit for appealing. What may or may not be such a reason or circumstance cannot be defined in advance, but the following are all relevant.

- **The reasons for the delay.** Explain these as clearly and as fully as possible. Do not worry if some or all of the delay is your fault. Any explanation is better than none at all. Even if you knew the time limit, but simply ignored it, it may be possible to say something favourable. Say if things have been difficult at home or you were confused by the rules or just assumed that the DWP (or the local authority or HMRC) was the expert and had got it right until, for example, you were advised otherwise or read an article in a newspaper. Reasons for the delay could include the fact that:
  - you did not receive the decision;
  - you made a reasonable mistake in calculating the time limit;
  - you posted your appeal in time, but it went astray in the post;
  - you were ill;
  - a mistake was made by your advisers. It should not make any difference that you might be able to sue them for negligence;
  - you were given wrong advice or otherwise misled by the DWP (or the local authority or HMRC) – eg, you were discouraged from appealing by a decision maker who advised you incorrectly that an appeal would be doomed to fail. If you lose money because you are refused a late appeal, consider claiming compensation (see p1403).
- **The length of the delay.** The usual approach is that time limits have to be kept to, and there has to be good reason for not doing so. Short delays are likely to be easier to justify than long delays, but a good reason is still needed.
- **The merits of your appeal.** The more likely your appeal is to succeed, the greater the injustice in refusing to extend the time limit. A strong case is particularly useful if there has been a very long delay and a time limit is usually extended where there has been a 'clear error', which would have long-term continuing effects unless corrected.[46]
- **The amount of money at stake.** Even if there has been no clear error, a time limit may be extended if there is a lot of money at stake.[47]
- **A decision in a test case.** A decision in a test case, establishing that an earlier decision was incorrect, can amount to a reason to extend a time limit, in some circumstances.[48]

The absolute time limit for appealing

You cannot appeal if it is more than 12 months after the date your time limit for appealing expired.[49] **Note:** in very exceptional circumstances (eg, if you did not receive notice of the decision you want to appeal), you can argue that the tribunal should waive the absolute time limit and allow you to appeal if this is absolutely necessary to protect your right to a fair hearing under human rights law.[50]

However, this is unlikely to apply unless you have done all that you could to appeal in time.

For HB, if the decision maker thinks your appeal has been made outside the absolute time limit, s/he must refer it to the First-tier Tribunal immediately.[51] The tribunal decides whether your appeal has been made in time, not the local authority.

If the First-tier Tribunal decides that you cannot appeal because your appeal was made outside the absolute time limit, but you think it was made in time, or it refuses to waive the absolute time limit, you can appeal to the Upper Tribunal against the decision.[52]

Making sure your appeal is valid

The First-tier Tribunal decides whether your appeal is valid, *not* the DWP, the local authority or HMRC. For your appeal to be valid:

- you must provide all the information required. **Note:** even if you do not use the correct appeal form, your appeal can still be valid; *and*
- if you submit your appeal other than online, you must sign your notice of appeal.[53] However, if you have provided written notice that you have appointed a representative, s/he can sign it on your behalf. If your solicitor signs on your behalf, it should be accepted that s/he is authorised to do so;[54] *and*
- your notice of appeal must be in English or Welsh.

The information you must provide

You must provide:[55]

- your name and address and that of your representative, if you have one; *and*
- the address where documents can be sent or delivered – eg, to you or your representative; *and*
- if you are appealing about HB, details about the decision with which you disagree, sufficient for it to be identified; *and*
- if you are appealing about benefits other than HB:
  - the name and address of any other person who has a right of appeal against the decision; *and*
  - a copy of the mandatory reconsideration notice (see p1301) or, if you did not have to apply for a mandatory reconsideration before the appeal, a copy of the decision you want to appeal. **Note:** if you were not given written notice that you had to apply for a mandatory reconsideration before you could appeal, state this clearly on the appeal form and enclose a copy of the decision notice as proof; *and*
  - any statement of reasons for the decision that you have; *and*
  - any documents in support of your appeal that you have not already supplied to the decision maker; *and*

Part 9: Getting a benefit decision changed
Chapter 57: Appealing to the First-tier Tribunal
2. How to appeal

- a summary of your reasons for believing the decision is wrong (your grounds for appeal). Do not simply say you think the decision is wrong, but explain why.

It is also helpful to include information and evidence that supports your appeal because a decision maker may look at the decision again before the appeal hearing and might revise it.

Examples of grounds for appeal

'The decision says I have been overpaid housing benefit because I failed to disclose that my wife had started working part time, but I wrote to the local authority as soon as she started work and told it what her take-home pay would be.'

'The DWP says I am not entitled to a housing costs element for my rent in my universal credit because my tenancy agreement is contrived. It says this is because I am paying rent to a relative. My landlord is my aunt, but she owns a number of properties that she lets commercially, including the one she lets to me.'

'HMRC says I should not get child benefit for my son because he left school in June. This decision is wrong because my son stayed on at school to do his A levels.'

'You say I cannot get personal independence payment daily living component. This decision is wrong because you have not taken into account the amount of help I need because of my incontinence problems.'

If you had to apply for a mandatory reconsideration before you could appeal and the DWP or HMRC only provided a mandatory reconsideration notice after a long delay, this may put you at a disadvantage – eg, if it is now difficult to obtain evidence to support your appeal. Point out if you think this improves the DWP's or HMRC's chances, or reduces your chances, of winning your appeal. The tribunal should then consider if it can do something to remedy the situation.[56]

If you are appealing about HB and do not provide sufficient information

If you are appealing about HB and you do not include the information required, the local authority can ask you to provide the information you left out.[57] If you used an appeal form, this is returned to you to complete. Be sure to provide the information within the time allowed, otherwise you may not have made your appeal within the time limit.

Your time limit for appealing (see p1305) is extended by:[58]

- 14 days from the date your appeal form is returned to you for completion, if the completed form is received back within 14 days; *or*
- 14 days from the date you are asked for further information, if you provide this within 14 days of the request; *or*
- the length of time you are given to complete the form or provide information, if this is longer than 14 days.

If you do not complete the form properly or provide the information required in time, your appeal, along with any relevant documents and evidence, is forwarded to the First-tier Tribunal by the local authority. It then considers whether your appeal is valid and can go ahead.[59] **Note:** if you complete and return the form or provide the information:

- after the expiry of the time limit, but before your appeal is forwarded to the tribunal, the local authority should accept that your appeal is valid and then consider whether to object to it being treated as made in time (see p1306);[60]
- before the tribunal makes a decision, any further details you provide must be taken into account.[61]

If your appeal is not accepted as valid, try to make a fresh appeal, giving reasons why your appeal is late if relevant.

If you are appealing about other benefits and do not provide sufficient information

If you are appealing about benefits other than HB and you do not include the information or documents (including the mandatory reconsideration notice) required, the tribunal clerk (see p1313) can waive the requirement, or require you to provide what you left out and then 'strike out' your appeal (see p1321) if you fail to do so.[62] You can ask the tribunal to reconsider the clerk's decision. You must apply in writing within 14 days after the date you are sent notice of the decision.[63] The tribunal can give you longer, but there is no guarantee of this, so keep within the time limit wherever possible. If your appeal is struck out, it can be reinstated by the clerk – eg, if you later provide the mandatory reconsideration notice (see p1321).

If you had to (and did) apply for a mandatory reconsideration before you could appeal, but you have not been sent or given a mandatory reconsideration notice, see p1302.

Representatives

You can have a representative to help you with your appeal and to be with you at the hearing.[64] S/he can explain the procedures, present your case to the tribunal and ensure it is aware of all the relevant issues and the law. Bear in mind that, even if you have a representative, you may have to answer questions from the tribunal. Your representative is not normally allowed to answer for you.

You must provide the tribunal with written notice of your representative's name and address or s/he must do this on your behalf – eg, on the appeal form or in a letter.[65]

This does not apply for HB if you provide this notice to the local authority before your appeal is forwarded to the tribunal. If your representative is providing the notice, unless s/he is a solicitor, s/he should also provide an authorisation signed by you.

Part 9: Getting a benefit decision changed
Chapter 57: Appealing to the First-tier Tribunal
3. After you submit your appeal

Once you have given notice that you have a representative, s/he is presumed to be acting for you unless you (or your representative) give notice in writing that this is no longer the case.[66] Your representative must be sent any documents required to be sent to you. These then do not have to be sent to you.[67] However, do not presume this always happens. If you receive documents, check that your representative has also received them.

Even if you have not previously notified the tribunal that you have a representative, someone can attend the hearing with you (eg, a friend or relative) and act as one, or assist you at the hearing, if the tribunal agrees.[68]

Meeting the costs

You do not have to pay a fee to appeal to the First-tier Tribunal, nor do you have to pay the DWP's, local authority 's or HMRC's costs.[69]

Free legal help with your appeal is available in limited cases.

- In England and Wales, you cannot get free legal help to cover preparatory work, such as obtaining medical reports and writing submissions. However, if you have a solicitor acting for you in an industrial injury or personal injury claim, s/he may have medical and other reports and evidence which you can use for your benefit appeal. In Scotland, you may be able to get free legal help for preparatory work.
- You cannot *normally* get free legal help from a lawyer to cover representation at a hearing. In England and Wales, you may be able to get this in very exceptional cases, if it is necessary to make these services available to you because a failure to do so would be a breach of your human rights or your retained rights under European Union law.[70]

If you are not eligible for free advice and assistance, or you want to be represented by a lawyer at a hearing, you are likely to have to pay. However, you may be able to get free help from a law centre, advice centre or Citizens Advice. There are a number of agencies that can advise you and help you prepare your case, and even represent you (see Appendix 1). Remember that many non-lawyer advisers know more about social security law than lawyers, and their advice and representation is usually free.

3. After you submit your appeal

If you submit your appeal direct to the First-tier Tribunal, it sends a copy to the DWP or HM Revenue and Customs (HMRC). In all cases, the DWP, the local authority or HMRC prepares its case – known as the 'decision maker's response' (see p1314). For housing benefit (HB) appeals, you are sent an enquiry form (see p1314) to complete and return to the tribunal. **Note:** you may find that your appeal is not dealt with if there is a test case or a lead case pending that deals with the same issues (see p1324).

How can you track the progress of your appeal?

You can receive email and text message updates and manage your appeal online. To ensure this happens, telephone 0300 123 1142, Monday to Friday, 8am to 8pm. You then get regular updates on the progress of your appeal – eg, notices reminding you to send evidence or confirming evidence you sent to the tribunal office has been received, and reminding you of your hearing date.

Who deals with your appeal

Any of the following may be be involved with your appeal at some time.

- **A judge.** S/he is always legally qualified. As well as hearing and making the decision on your appeal, s/he carries out various other functions – eg, s/he decides whether you have made your appeal in time, and whether to extend a time limit or to issue directions.
- **A member of the First-tier Tribunal.** S/he could be a doctor, a person with experience of disability or an accountant. S/he hears and makes the decision on your appeal with the judge.
- **An expert.** If your appeal involves issues that require specialist expertise, an expert (the tribunal may call her/him an 'assessor') may be used.[71] If s/he provides a written report, it should be sent to every party involved in the appeal. The expert cannot take part in making the decision on your appeal.
- **A registrar** (s/he must be legally qualified) or a **tribunal caseworker** (s/he must be appropriately trained). They can carry out any of the functions of the First-tier Tribunal, under the supervision of a judge, and can make all the decisions a judge can make other than the final decision on your appeal.[72]
- **A clerk to the First-tier Tribunal.** S/he can carry out specified functions, including waiving a requirement for you to provide information with your notice of appeal, requiring you to provide information and in some cases striking out your appeal (see p1321). S/he attends the appeal hearing in an administrative capacity – eg, to pay expenses. S/he cannot take part in making the decision on your appeal and should not express any views on the case.[73]

To see who hears and makes the decision on your appeal, see p1329.

Note: you must be given 14 days to ask a judge to reconsider a registrar's, a tribunal caseworker's or a clerk's decision.[74] You must apply in writing within 14 days after the date you are sent notice of the decision.[75] The tribunal can give you longer, but there is no guarantee of this, so keep within the time limit wherever possible.

Part 9: Getting a benefit decision changed
Chapter 57: Appealing to the First-tier Tribunal
3. After you submit your appeal

The enquiry form

In some cases, the First-tier Tribunal sends you a questionnaire (called an enquiry form). For appeals about:

- a benefit other than HB, if you submit your appeal direct to the First-tier Tribunal, you are unlikely to be sent an enquiry form if you have already provided this information on your appeal form. However, if you did not use an appeal form (eg, you appealed by letter), you *are* sent an enquiry form;
- HB, you are sent an enquiry form when the First-tier Tribunal receives your appeal papers from the local authority.

The enquiry form asks you whether you want a hearing and, if so, when you and your representative (if you have one) are available to attend. If you want a hearing, you must state this. It is always best to opt for a hearing. You should always consult your representative before completing and returning the enquiry form.

Return the enquiry form within 14 days. If you do not return it in time, the tribunal can 'strike out' your appeal (see p1321) or automatically deal with your appeal based on the papers only. However, you are entitled to receive a ruling on the merits of your appeal, so it should only be struck out on this ground in exceptional cases.[76] For information about decisions based on the papers only and about hearings, see p1326 and p1327.

The decision maker's response

The DWP, the local authority or HMRC must prepare a bundle of papers relevant to your appeal (called the 'decision maker's response') and forward this to the First-tier Tribunal:

- for HB, as soon as reasonably practicable. An ombudsman has said the local authority should forward an appeal to the First-tier Tribunal within 28 days;[77]
- for other benefits, within 28 days of receiving the notice of appeal.[78]

Both you and your representative (if any) are normally sent a copy.[79] However, check with your representative as this might not always happen.[80]

If the decision maker opposes your appeal, the response must include any reasons for this that are not in the documents the First-tier Tribunal has already been given.[81] It must refer to the law on which the decision was based and explain the legal basis on which the decision was made in a way that enables the tribunal to ensure that you are able to participate fully in the appeal.[82] The decision maker must also provide:[83]

- a copy of any written record of, and statement of reasons for, the decision with which you disagree, if you did not send these with your appeal form; *and*
- copies of all documents s/he has that may be relevant, unless the tribunal directs otherwise. The decision maker should treat as relevant anything that the tribunal might rely on to make findings about the facts, irrespective of

what s/he considers to be relevant.[84] If the information in the documents is not in a form that can be understood by you and the tribunal (eg, screen shots that use DWP codes), the decision maker should provide an explanation or translation.[85] If the tribunal thinks that the decision maker may have other relevant evidence, it can direct her/him to produce this. If your appeal involves a medical issue or one about your disability:

- any recent medical reports there have been in connection with your claim are usually included; *and*
- if the decision you are appealing followed from a report by a healthcare professional (eg, your benefit was reduced or stopped following such a report), that report should be included; *and*
- for HB appeals only, a copy of your appeal form (or letter) along with all the documents you provided with it and, unless already provided to the First-tier Tribunal, the name and address of your representative.

Read through the whole response carefully to find out the case being made against you. Be sure to take it with you to the hearing.

Has your appeal been held up by the decision maker?

You cannot usually bypass the normal procedures. However, note the following.

1. Although you cannot usually expect the First-tier Tribunal to deal with your appeal before the decision maker has had a chance to prepare her/his response, it is free to allow matters to be handled differently if circumstances require it.[86]

2. Ask the tribunal to require the decision maker to provide documents, information and evidence by a specified date (make a direction – see p1318), or make a direction setting a hearing date.[87]

3. If you are appealing about HB and the decision maker does not forward your appeal within a reasonable period, forward a copy of it to the First-tier Tribunal yourself and proceed as above.

Note: in some circumstances, the tribunal can bar the decision maker from taking any further part in the appeal (see p1322), in which case your appeal could be decided without a response being made. However, it can lift the bar if the response is eventually received.

Providing additional information

Make sure that everything you want to say in support of your appeal has been put in writing and that there are no other documents and evidence that you would like the tribunal to see. See p1336 for help with preparing your appeal. **Note:**

- It is always good to provide a written submission and additional evidence or information to support your appeal (known as a 'reply') – eg, independent medical evidence or supporting statements from witnesses.
- You (or your representative) must provide your reply within one month after the date you are sent the decision maker's response.[88] The tribunal can give

Part 9: Getting a benefit decision changed
Chapter 57: Appealing to the First-tier Tribunal
3. After you submit your appeal

you longer (or shorter) than one month.[89] There is no guarantee that you will be given longer, so keep within the time limit wherever possible.

Do you intend to send a reply to the decision maker's response?
Tribunal staff often want to fix a hearing date, or arrange for a decision to be made based on the papers only, as soon as they can after the decision maker's response has been received. As a result, they sometimes overlook the need to allow you one month to reply.[90] To avoid this happening, inform the tribunal office that you intend to send a reply as soon as possible after you receive the response.

Note: your reply and any further documents and submissions that are sent to the tribunal by you (or the DWP, local authority or HMRC) are added to the decision maker's response forming what is known as the 'appeal bundle'.

At this stage, your appeal is likely to be considered ready for a hearing or for the tribunal to make its decision based on the papers only (see p1325). The tribunal may issue directions (see p1318) requiring you (or the DWP, the local authority or HMRC) to provide a submission, further information or documents within a specific period. You (or the decision maker) can also ask it to issue directions. If you are given a direction, it is important that you comply with it. If you do not, your appeal can be struck out (see p1321).

When your appeal can lapse

After you appeal, a decision maker may look at the decision you are appealing about again and revise it – eg, on the basis of any facts, information or evidence you provided with your appeal form. This is the case, even if the decision maker had already considered a revision when you applied for a mandatory reconsideration. If the decision maker revises the decision, your appeal could lapse, even if you do not get everything you want, and you have to appeal again.[91]

Your appeal lapses if the revised decision is more advantageous to you than the original decision – eg, the decision:[92]
- awards you benefit at a higher rate or for a longer period; *or*
- lifts a refusal or disqualification of benefit or a sanction (in whole or in part); *or*
- reverses a decision to pay benefit to a third party (see p1164); *or*
- means you gain financially from the revised decision; *or*
- says an overpayment of benefit is not recoverable or that less should be recovered.

Note: the DWP says you should be contacted by a decision maker to see if you would still want to appeal if the decision were revised to your advantage. You should be told that you will have a right of appeal against that decision as revised. If you would still want to appeal (eg, because the new decision does not give you all that the tribunal could award), it says it should still revise the decision if that is what you want it to do.[93] You should be given enough time to decide and should *not* be put under pressure to agree to the decision being revised. If you have a representative, s/he should be contacted before you.

If a decision is:

- revised and is:
  - to your advantage, your appeal lapses, but you can make a fresh appeal against the revised decision – eg, if you did not get all you wanted. You do not have to apply for another mandatory reconsideration before you can appeal in this situation.[94] Your time limit for appealing (see p1305) runs from the date the revised decision is sent to you;[95]
  - not to your advantage, your appeal must go ahead, but against the decision in its revised form.[96] You have one month from the date the decision is sent or given to you to make further representations.[97] At the end of that period (or earlier if you agree in writing), your appeal proceeds unless the decision is revised again and is now more advantageous to you;[98]
- not revised, your appeal must go ahead against the original decision. If the decision maker contacted you to see if you would still want to appeal if the decision were revised to your advantage, you can argue that the tribunal should take the decision maker's proposal as the starting point for its considerations.[99]

Note: if the First-tier Tribunal decides that your appeal has lapsed, you can appeal against that decision to the Upper Tribunal. However, it is better, if you can, to make a fresh appeal against the original decision.

What the First-tier Tribunal can do

There are procedural rules that the First-tier Tribunal must follow when dealing with your appeal. Whenever the tribunal considers using these rules it should do so in a way that enables the case to be dealt with fairly and justly (known as the 'overriding objective').[100] This includes avoiding delay (provided the issues can be considered properly), avoiding unnecessary formality, seeking flexibility in the proceedings and ensuring that all the parties can participate fully. You, the DWP, the local authority and HMRC must help the First-tier Tribunal further this objective and co-operate with it. This involves ensuring, as far as possible, that your case is ready by the time of the hearing.[101]

The First-tier Tribunal can:[102]

- extend or shorten any time limits (see p1318); *and*
- issue directions (see p1318); *and*
- postpone or adjourn your appeal hearing (see p1319); *and*
- 'strike out' your appeal (see p1321); *and*
- bar the decision maker or another party to the appeal from taking part (see p1322); *and*

Part 9: Getting a benefit decision changed
Chapter 57: Appealing to the First-tier Tribunal
3. After you submit your appeal

- summon witnesses to attend a hearing, answer questions or produce documents. If someone fails to comply, the First-tier Tribunal can refer the matter to the Upper Tribunal. The Upper Tribunal can punish the person for contempt of court.[103] **Note:** you cannot be required to give evidence or produce any document that you could not be compelled to give by a court;[104] *and*
- suspend the effect of its decision while any application for permission to appeal, or any appeal against or review of that decision, is outstanding.[105]

Note: the rules for what the Upper Tribunal can do are generally the same as for the First-tier Tribunal. The endnotes in this section therefore also refer to Upper Tribunal rules where relevant.

Extending or shortening time limits

Time limits can be extended or shortened.[106]

The tribunal can shorten your and the DWP's, the local authority's or HMRC's time limits if it thinks that delay should be avoided, provided the issues can be considered properly.[107] You might want to ask for the DWP's (or the local authority's or HMRC's) time limits (eg, to comply with a direction) to be shortened if your situation is urgent or your circumstances are exceptional.

If you know that you are going to miss (or have missed) a time limit, you should ask for it to be extended by the tribunal. Always ask in writing for a time limit to be extended and apply in advance if you can. Give the reasons why you are going to be (or are) late in meeting the time limit, as well as any special circumstances which mean your time limit should be extended so that your appeal can be dealt with fairly and justly. **Note:**

- The tribunal does not have to extend any particular time limit, so there is no guarantee that you will be given more time. Keep within the time limits wherever possible.
- For the rules about extending your time limit for appealing, see p1306. For some ideas about what may count as a good reason for a late appeal, see p1308.

Directions

In the course of your appeal, the First-tier Tribunal can issue directions – eg, requiring you (or the DWP, the local authority or HMRC) to provide a submission, further information or documents, or requiring you or a presenting officer (see p1329) to attend a hearing.[108] The tribunal can decide to issue directions on its own initiative. You or the decision maker can also apply to the tribunal to ask it to issue directions. This can be useful, for example, if you are having trouble getting documents or information from the decision maker. You can apply in writing, or orally at the hearing.[109] In either case, you must give reasons for your application.

The tribunal must send you and the decision maker (and anyone affected by the direction) notice of any direction it issues, unless it thinks there is a good reason not to do so.[110] You can challenge a direction (eg, if you think insufficient time has been given to comply with it) by applying for another direction to amend, suspend or set aside the first one.[111]

If you are given a direction, it is important that you comply with it. If you fail to comply with a requirement or a direction, the tribunal can take any action it thinks is 'just' – eg, it can:[112]

- waive the requirement; or
- require you to remedy the failure; or
- strike out your appeal (see p1321); or
- conclude that any information or evidence required was adverse to you.[113] However, it should not use this as a way to punish you. It should only decide information or evidence was adverse to you if it is probable that the reason it was not provided was that it did not exist or would harm your case.[114] The tribunal should not decide information or evidence was adverse to you because you refuse your consent to disclose your medical records, but you may have more difficulty proving your case.[115]

The tribunal can also take the above action if it is the DWP, the local authority or HMRC that is given a direction. The tribunal can also bar the DWP, the local authority or HMRC from taking further part in your appeal (see p1322).

If you miss the deadline in a direction, try to provide what has been requested as soon as possible. The tribunal may still consider the information or evidence – eg, if you provide it at the hearing.[116] However, remember that it can decide *not* to consider evidence if it is late or if it would otherwise be unfair to do so.[117]

Postponements and adjournments

The First-tier Tribunal can postpone or adjourn a hearing.[118] The decision can be made by the judge. However, if the issue arises at a hearing and the panel comprises more than one member, the judge should consult the other member(s).[119] The decision must be recorded properly. **Note:** if a hearing is postponed or adjourned, this does not mean that you cannot get another postponement or adjournment if you need one – eg, if there is a good reason why the next hearing should not take place. The tribunal making the decision to postpone or adjourn should therefore not tie the hands of the next tribunal by directing it to proceed when the appeal is listed again.[120] The next tribunal must consider any further application for a postponement or adjournment on its merits, although the fact that there has been a previous one is something it can take into account.

Postponements and adjournments

The decision to postpone a hearing to a different date takes place before the hearing starts. The decision can be made by a judge alone. The decision to adjourn a hearing, so it is heard at a later date, takes place at the hearing. The decision must be made by the tribunal as a whole.

Part 9: Getting a benefit decision changed
Chapter 57: Appealing to the First-tier Tribunal
3. After you submit your appeal

Remember that if you do not attend a hearing, the tribunal can decide not to adjourn the hearing and hear the appeal without you (see p1327).[121] Your appeal is less likely to succeed if you do not attend.

Your case might be postponed or adjourned if there is a test case or lead case pending which deals with the same issues as your appeal (see p1324).

Getting a hearing postponed

If the hearing date you are given is inconvenient or you want more time to prepare your case, you can ask for the hearing to be postponed to another date. You should apply in writing to the First-tier Tribunal before the hearing date, as soon as you decide you want a postponement, giving your reasons. Make it clear that you do not want the hearing to go ahead in your absence. If you have not provided enough information about why you want your appeal to be postponed (eg, you simply say you have an appointment, but not that it is an important medical appointment), the clerk to the tribunal should ask you for more information rather than simply referring your request for a decision.[122]

Bear the following in mind.

- Do not presume that a postponement will be granted. Telephone before the hearing is due to take place to check whether it has been agreed. Be ready to attend the hearing if it goes ahead. Your representative should warn you that your application might not be successful.[123]
- The judge conducting the hearing should consider whether it should be adjourned, even if you have been refused a postponement.[124]
- The tribunal can postpone your hearing even if this is not requested.

Getting a hearing adjourned

If a hearing is under way, or the tribunal is considering its decision on the papers only, the tribunal can adjourn – eg, if you or the DWP, the local authority or HMRC ask for an adjournment or if the First-tier Tribunal thinks this is the best course – eg, if more evidence is required or you need time to consider the law. You should consider asking for an adjournment if the tribunal says it is going to consider whether you should get a lower rate of benefit than you are getting currently, to allow you to prepare your case and make representations. If you no longer want to pursue your appeal, you may be able to withdraw it (see p1323).

The tribunal should consider the benefit of an adjournment, why you (or the DWP, the local authority or HMRC) are not ready to go ahead and what the impact would be on the other party and the tribunal system.[125] This is the case even if you have not asked for an adjournment. It should adjourn a hearing:

- if you are not there and:
  - there is doubt about whether you received notice of the hearing;[126] *or*
  - information you provided that is relevant to the decision (eg, your reply to the work capability assessment questionnaire) was missing from the appeal papers so there was not enough evidence to make your case clear;[127] *or*

- if you have advised it that you cannot attend, have a good reason for not attending and have asked for another hearing date;[128] *or*
- if you are unable to attend the hearing (eg, you are in prison or hospital), but your evidence could play an important part in its reaching a decision;[129] *or*
- if you want to be represented at the hearing, but your representative is not available on the date it has been listed and has made a reasonable request for a postponement. Your representative should explain why s/he cannot attend and why no one else can represent you instead;[130] *or*
- if you need to get a representative – eg, because you have mental health problems or the decision with which you disagree concerns a large overpayment;[131] *or*
- to enable you to get additional evidence which you could not until then have reasonably been expected to realise was needed.[132]

If a hearing is not postponed or adjourned

If the tribunal does not postpone or adjourn the hearing and makes a decision with which you disagree, in limited circumstances you can apply for the decision to be 'set aside' (see p1348). Alternatively, you may be able to appeal to the Upper Tribunal against the First-tier Tribunal's final decision on the grounds that its refusal to postpone or adjourn the hearing was an error of law.

When your appeal can be struck out

If you fail to comply with a direction, or in a limited number of other circumstances, your appeal can be 'struck out', in whole or in part. This cancels your appeal, or part of your appeal, and it does not go ahead. If your appeal is struck out because you failed to comply with a direction, see below for when you can get your appeal reinstated.

If you fail to comply with a direction

If you fail to comply with a direction given to you by the tribunal – eg, you do not provide required information or documents:[133]

- your appeal is struck out automatically if you were notified in the direction that a failure to comply *would* lead to your appeal being struck out; *or*
- there is discretion to strike out your appeal if you were notified in the direction that a failure to comply with it *could* lead to your appeal being struck out. In this case, before deciding to do so, the tribunal should consider carefully why the direction was given and whether it can still make a fair and just decision – eg, without the information you were supposed to provide.[134]

Can your appeal be reinstated?

If your appeal is struck out because you failed to comply with a direction, you can apply for your appeal to be reinstated.[135] You must apply in writing. Your application must be received by the tribunal within one month of your being sent notice that your appeal was

Part 9: Getting a benefit decision changed
Chapter 57: Appealing to the First-tier Tribunal
3. After you submit your appeal

struck out. It can give you longer (or shorter) than one month. There is no guarantee that you will be given longer, so keep within the time limit wherever possible. Explain why you think your appeal should not have been struck out – eg, why you think you *did* comply with the direction, or why you were unable to do so or to comply in time.

Other circumstances

Your appeal *must* be struck out if the tribunal does not have 'jurisdiction' to deal with it – eg, you do not have a right to appeal against the decision or you have appealed to the wrong tribunal.[136]

In addition, there is *discretion* to strike out your appeal if:[137]

- you failed to co-operate with the tribunal to such an extent that it cannot deal with your appeal fairly and justly; *or*
- the tribunal considers your appeal has no reasonable prospect of success. It should only do so if the result of the appeal is clear and incontestable. It should generally not do so if the facts of the case are in dispute.[138]

In all cases, you must be given an opportunity to comment. You should always take this opportunity and explain why you think your appeal should not be struck out – eg, why you had a good reason for failing to co-operate or why you think you have a chance of winning your appeal.

Although you cannot apply for your appeal to be reinstated, you may be able to challenge the decision to strike it out.

Challenging a decision to strike out your appeal

If the tribunal strikes out your appeal or refuses to reinstate your appeal after it has been struck out, you may be able to make a fresh appeal against the decision maker's decision.[139] See p1305 for the time limit for doing so. Otherwise, you can appeal to the Upper Tribunal against the decision to strike out your appeal or to refuse to reinstate it.[140]

Being barred from taking part in an appeal

The decision maker and any person (other than you) who is taking part in the appeal because s/he has a right of appeal against the decision you are challenging (see p1302) or s/he has been added as a party to the appeal by the tribunal (eg, the other parent if you are disputing who counts as responsible for your child) can be barred from taking further part in the appeal in the same circumstances in which your appeal can be struck out.[141] In practice, this is likely to apply mainly if the decision maker (or other person with a right of appeal):

- fails to comply with a direction; *or*
- fails to co-operate with the tribunal to such an extent that it cannot deal with your appeal fairly and justly.

The decision maker (or other person) can apply for the bar to be lifted in the same circumstances in which you can apply for an appeal to be reinstated (see p1321). If the bar is not lifted, the tribunal does not have to consider any response or other submission made by her/him.[142] It can decide any or all of the issues against her/him and can deal with her/his case more briefly than would otherwise be required. However, the decision maker (or person) still has a right of appeal against the tribunal's decision and a right to apply for a statement of reasons for the decision.[143]

Withdrawing an appeal

If you change your mind about appealing, you can withdraw your appeal.[144]

- If you are appealing about HB and your appeal has not yet been passed to the First-tier Tribunal, write to the local authority office dealing with your appeal, saying that you do not wish your appeal to go ahead. Your representative can write on your behalf.
- In any other case (ie, once your appeal is lodged with the tribunal), you can withdraw your appeal:
  - by sending or giving written notice to the tribunal. You can withdraw your appeal before the tribunal makes its decision – eg, before a hearing takes place, or if a hearing has taken place but was adjourned without the tribunal reaching a decision. The withdrawal takes effect immediately. Usually, you do not need the tribunal's agreement to withdraw in this way, but in limited cases it may notify you that you can only do so if it agrees;[145] or
  - at a hearing, but only if the tribunal agrees. The withdrawal takes effect when it agrees.

The tribunal must notify you and any other party that the withdrawal of the appeal has taken effect.

If you tell the tribunal that you want to withdraw your appeal before the hearing (eg, you telephone the tribunal office), but then you fail to confirm this in writing, the tribunal clerk can waive the requirement to provide written notice.[146] You can ask the tribunal to reconsider the clerk's decision – eg, if you did not send written notice because you changed your mind and no longer wanted to withdraw your appeal. You must apply in writing within 14 days after the date you are sent notice of the decision.[147] The tribunal can give you longer (or shorter) than this. There is no guarantee you will be given longer, so keep within the time limit wherever possible.

If you withdraw your appeal but then decide that you want it to go ahead, you can apply for it to be reinstated.[148] The other parties can also apply for your appeal to be reinstated. The application must be in writing and it must be received by the tribunal within one month after the earliest of the following:

- the date the applicant was sent notice that the withdrawal of your appeal had taken effect; or

Part 9: Getting a benefit decision changed
Chapter 57: Appealing to the First-tier Tribunal
3. After you submit your appeal

- if your appeal was withdrawn at a hearing and the applicant was present at the hearing when this happened, the date of the hearing.

The tribunal can give you longer (or shorter) than one month. There is no guarantee that you will be given longer, so keep within the time limit wherever possible.

Note: you can only withdraw your appeal, or apply for the appeal to be reinstated, once – ie, if your appeal is reinstated, you cannot withdraw it again.[149]

Consent orders

If all the parties to the appeal agree what the solution to your dispute should be, you can ask the tribunal judge to make a 'consent order' and to make any other appropriate provision you have agreed.[150] This procedure is only likely to be of use if you are effectively giving up your appeal, but the DWP, the local authority or HMRC promises you something in return for this. The First-tier Tribunal only deals with your appeal in this way if it considers it appropriate. It may simply make a decision on your appeal in the usual way.

If a consent order is made, there does not have to be a hearing and no reasons for the order need to be given. Get independent advice *before* agreeing to a consent order.

Test cases and lead cases

Sometimes appeals to the First-tier Tribunal are made by more than one person about the same issues of fact or law. When this happens, appeals dealing with the same issues may be delayed until a decision has been made in a test case or a lead case.

Test cases

If a case is pending against a decision of the Upper Tribunal or a court that deals with issues raised in your case (a 'test case'), the DWP, the local authority or HMRC can suspend payment of your benefit (see p1161) or even postpone making a decision about your claim (see p1290), pending the outcome of the appeal in the test case. In addition, for benefits other than HB, if a test case is pending and you have already appealed to the First-tier Tribunal (your appeal is then known as a 'look alike' case), the decision maker can serve notice requiring the First-tier Tribunal in *your* appeal:[151]

- not to make a decision and to refer your case back to her/him; *or*
- to deal with your appeal by either:
  - postponing making a decision until the test case is decided. Once a decision has been made in the test case, the decision is made on your appeal; *or*
  - deciding your appeal as if the test case had been decided in the way most unfavourable to you, but only if this is in your interests. If this happens, and

the test case eventually goes in your favour, the decision maker has to make a new decision superseding the tribunal's decision in the light of the decision in the test case.[152]

Lead cases

If appeals are made to the First-tier Tribunal by more than one person about the same issues of fact or law (eg, a number of appeals about service charges from tenants in the same block of flats), one or more of the appeals can be specified as a 'lead case'. The tribunal can then postpone making a decision on all the other related appeals.[153]

The tribunal can also order that when it makes its decision in the lead cases(s), the decision applies to (and is binding on) all the other related appeals. You must be sent a copy of the decision.

If your appeal is not the lead case, you can apply to the tribunal for a direction that the decision does not apply to, and is not binding on, your appeal. You must apply in writing within one month after the date you are sent a copy of the decision. The tribunal can give you longer (or shorter) than this. There is no guarantee that you will be given longer, so keep within the time limit wherever possible.

---

4. How the tribunal makes its decision

The First-tier Tribunal makes its decision either:
- at a hearing held in person or remotely – eg, by telephone or video link;[154] *or*
- on the papers only by looking at what you said on your appeal form, any evidence or other information you provided and the decision maker's response.

You can tell the tribunal the type of hearing you prefer on the appeal form or enquiry form. Your appeal *must* be dealt with at a hearing, unless:[155]
- both you and the DWP, the local authority or HM Revenue and Customs (HMRC) have consented (or both of you have not objected) to the appeal being dealt with on the papers only. **Note:** if you (or the DWP, local authority or HMRC) state you want a hearing, there must be one; *and*
- the First-tier Tribunal considers that it can decide the matter without a hearing. The tribunal must consider whether this is in the interests of justice, particularly if it is not clear whether you consented to your appeal being decided on the papers only.[156] It should explain this in its statement of reasons.

If you want a hearing, state this on the appeal form or the enquiry form (see p1314). Otherwise, the tribunal presumes that you do not object to your appeal being dealt with on the papers only. **Note:** if you consent to (or do not object to)

Part 9: Getting a benefit decision changed
Chapter 57: Appealing to the First-tier Tribunal
4. How the tribunal makes its decision

your appeal being dealt with on the papers only, the tribunal should not draw adverse conclusions about your reasons for this.[157]

During the coronavirus pandemic, temporary rules allow tribunals to decide cases without a hearing, even if you (or the DWP, local authority or HMRC) have asked for one. The First-tier Tribunal can decide to make its decision without a hearing (including a remote hearing) if the matter is urgent, it is not reasonably practicable and it is in the interests of justice to do so.[158] Alternatively, the tribunal may offer you a hearing by telephone or video link, rather than in person. For further information, see the article 'Unappealing tribunals and coronavirus?' on AskCPAG.

Should you opt for a hearing?

You may not want to attend a hearing – eg, because you are worried about speaking for yourself or about the cost or difficulty in attending. Get advice before you decide what to do. Bear the following in mind.

1. You are more likely to win your appeal if you attend a hearing, particularly if it concerns a medical issue or your disability, or if the facts of your case are in dispute.

2. If you attend a hearing, you can explain your side of the story.

3. Unlike with hearings in a court, hearings in the First-tier Tribunal are meant to be informal. For example, you do not have to stand when the judge enters and only rarely do you have to swear an oath.

4. The tribunal must consider how to assist child, vulnerable adult and sensitive witnesses (see p1328).

5. You can have a representative at the hearing (see p1311) and your chances of winning are likely to be higher if you do.[159] You can also take a friend, relative or adviser with you for support.

5. The First-tier Tribunal aims to provide a qualified interpreter if you need one.

7. You, an interpreter and any witnesses may be able to get expenses paid. You can claim for travel, meals, loss of earnings and childcare costs.[160]

8. If you or your representative cannot attend a hearing at a particular venue (eg, because of a disability), a hearing might be arranged at an alternative venue, or you might be able to participate via video link or telephone (see p1328).[161]

Decisions based on the papers only

If there is not a hearing, the tribunal makes its decision in your absence and you are then notified of its decision.

If you want your appeal to be dealt with based on the papers only, send the tribunal your arguments about your appeal in writing and any information and evidence you can get to support it (called a 'reply') as soon as possible. See p1336 for help with preparing your appeal. Write to the tribunal to let it know you intend to send a reply and state how long it may take to do so.

You must provide your reply within one month after the date you were sent the decision maker's response.[162] If you need longer than this, ask for an extension before the month has expired. However, if a decision is made on the papers only before the month is up and you could (and would) have provided further evidence within that period, you can challenge the tribunal's decision on the ground that it made an error of law.[163]

Can there be a hearing if you do not opt for one?

1. Even if you do not opt for a hearing, one could still take place. This could happen, for example, if the other party wants a hearing or the tribunal decides there should be one because it can only deal with your appeal fairly and justly by having one – eg, it needs to ask you questions about the facts of your case. It could also happen if, while it is considering what to decide on the papers only, it is uncertain whether or not anyone has asked for a hearing, or if the tribunal suspects that you did not opt for a hearing due to a misunderstanding.[164]

2. If you get unexpected notice of a hearing, contact the tribunal to check the reasons for this. You should attend the hearing.

3. If you do not opt for a hearing but then decide you want one, you may be able to change your mind. You must tell the tribunal before it makes its decision.

Hearings

You must be given reasonable notice of a hearing – at least 14 days' notice, unless you agree to less notice than this or there are urgent or exceptional circumstances.[165] If your hearing takes place in person, this is at an appeal venue in your area. If you are unable to attend a hearing at a venue, see p1328.

If you have not been given the correct notice (you can argue that this includes the decision maker's response as well as the time and date of the hearing[166]), you can object to the hearing going ahead. If the tribunal decides to proceed with the hearing, attend and explain why your case will be prejudiced (eg, you did not have adequate time to prepare it) and ask for an adjournment (see p1320).

Can a hearing go ahead without you?

The tribunal can go ahead with a hearing even if you are not there if:[167]

– it is satisfied that you were notified of the hearing, or that reasonable steps have been taken to notify you. However, it does not normally have to find out why you have not attended – eg, by getting the clerk to the tribunal to telephone you.[168] It *should* attempt to contact you (eg, if your case is complex or your evidence is needed to allow the tribunal to decide your appeal fairly) if this would ensure, so far as is practicable, that you are able to participate fully in the proceedings;[169] *and*

Part 9: Getting a benefit decision changed
Chapter 57: Appealing to the First-tier Tribunal
4. How the tribunal makes its decision

– it thinks that it is in the interests of justice. It should always consider the alternative of adjourning the hearing to give you another opportunity to attend (see p1320).

The tribunal should only go ahead with the hearing if it considers that it has sufficient evidence to decide the appeal fairly.[170] **Note:** if the panel hearing your appeal comprises more than one member, the decision whether or not to go ahead with the hearing should be made by all of the members, not just by the judge alone.[171]

If you turn up late, after the tribunal has decided to proceed in your absence, it should still consider whether to allow you to participate, and whether it should adjourn the hearing to give you another opportunity to attend.[172]

An appeal is heard in public unless the tribunal thinks it should be in private.[173] If you want your hearing to be in private, ask for this to be considered. In practice, it is extremely rare for members of the public to attend.

The tribunal can postpone or adjourn a hearing (see p1319).

Child, vulnerable adult and sensitive witnesses

The First-tier Tribunal must consider how to assist any children under 18, vulnerable adults (eg, people aged 18 or over who are mentally or physically disabled or are appealing about personal independence payment or the work capability assessment) and 'sensitive witnesses' to give evidence.[174] This includes allowing them to give evidence by telephone, video link or other means, or appointing someone with special expertise to help the person give evidence and adopting a less robust style of questioning. You are a 'sensitive witness' if the quality of evidence you give is likely to be diminished because of your fear or distress in connection with giving evidence. If you are a child, vulnerable adult or sensitive witness, and you need special arrangements to be made, you or your representative should let the tribunal know as soon as possible in advance of the hearing. The tribunal should make a note in its record of proceedings that it has considered how to assist you.

Ways to participate in a hearing

If you are unable to attend a hearing at a venue, you may be able to participate in a 'remote hearing' via telephone or video link.[175] If you did not opt for a hearing, the tribunal should take note of any reasons that you give for this choice. If these suggest that you might be happy to give your evidence by telephone, the tribunal should consider adjourning the hearing to give you an opportunity to ask for a telephone hearing.[176]

Alternative venues

Most appeal venues have access for disabled people, and the First-tier Tribunal may meet the cost of special transport to get there. It may also arrange the hearing at another venue – eg, a hotel meeting room near where you live. However, if you are unable to attend a hearing at any of the venues, in rare cases it is possible to hold the hearing in your home (known as a 'domiciliary hearing'), although the tribunal may say this is not necessary if you can use special transport.[177] Include a letter from your doctor with your request for a domiciliary hearing, confirming that you are unable to travel at all – eg, even by private ambulance. Explain why it would not be an adequate solution for you to give your evidence by telephone. You can appeal against a decision to refuse you a domiciliary hearing.[178] Alternatively, if the refusal meant that the way your appeal was dealt with was unfair, you may be able to appeal to the Upper Tribunal.[179]

At the hearing

Any of the following may be present at your appeal hearing.
- A **judge** (see p1313). S/he always acts as the chair of the hearing.
- A **member of the First-tier Tribunal** (see p1313). To see which members hear and decide your appeal, see below.
- An **expert** (see p1313). S/he cannot take part in making the decision.
- A **tribunal clerk** (see p1313). S/he cannot take part in making the decision.

A **presenting officer** may be present to represent the decision maker. S/he explains the reasons for the decision, but is not there to defend it at all costs and may provide information which helps your case. Presenting officers often only attend if an appeal is considered complicated. The tribunal can issue a direction requiring a presenting officer to attend the hearing.

The judge and up to two other members hear and decide your appeal. A record of what is said at the hearing is kept. This is either notes made by the judge or an audio recording.

You can have a **representative** with you at the hearing.[180] S/he can explain the procedures, present your case and ensure that the tribunal is aware of all the relevant issues and the law. If you have one, see p1311 for the notice you must send or give to the tribunal. You can also be accompanied by someone at the hearing – eg, a friend or relative. The tribunal can give permission for her/him to act as your representative or assist you in presenting your case.[181]

The First-tier Tribunal aims to provide a qualified **interpreter** if you need one. If you do, tell it in advance of the hearing. If an official interpreter is not available, on rare occasions, it might allow a relative to act as your interpreter if s/he understands that s/he should simply translate accurately and give your answers in your own words, without comment or explanation.[182]

The judge and members

Those who decide a particular kind of appeal are as follows.[183]
- A **judge, a doctor and a person with experience of disability** decide attendance allowance (AA), disability living allowance (DLA) and personal independence payment (PIP) appeals.

Part 9: Getting a benefit decision changed
Chapter 57: Appealing to the First-tier Tribunal
4. How the tribunal makes its decision

However, if your appeal only raises issues of law, a judge hears your appeal (or a judge and a member whose experience and qualifications are needed to make the decision).

- **A judge and a doctor** decide appeals:
  - about whether you have limited capability for work under the work capability assessment or have limited capability for work-related activity; *and*
  - about industrial injuries benefits or severe disablement allowance (SDA).

  However, if your appeal only raises issues of law, a judge hears your appeal (or a judge and a member whose experience and qualifications are needed to make the decision).[184]
- **A judge** decides all other appeals on her/his own.

Unless your appeal is about AA, DLA or PIP, an additional judge can be included in specified cases, an accountant may be included (if the examination of financial accounts is required) or there can be an additional doctor (if there are complex medical issues). However, there can never be more than three deciding an appeal.

If the group deciding your appeal is comprised incorrectly, you can appeal to the Upper Tribunal and argue that this was an error of law.[185]

Note:
- If your appeal is meant to be heard by two or more members but some of these are absent, the hearing can still go ahead, but only if you and the DWP, or the local authority or HMRC, agree.[186]
- If you have both a DLA (or PIP) and an employment and support allowance appeal, they should be heard completely separately, by entirely different members.[187]
- If your appeal is only partly heard by a judge and at least one member, the group deciding your appeal at a new hearing should generally be the same, or completely different.[188]
- You cannot argue that a doctor should not decide your appeal even if s/he regularly provides medical reports about benefit claimants to the DWP.[189]
- You can argue that the tribunal should not rely on evidence from a DWP doctor with whom any of the members hearing your appeal sit at other times. This depends on how often and how recently this has happened.[190]

Procedure at the hearing

At the hearing, there are no strict rules of procedure. The judge decides how it is conducted.[191] The tribunal's overriding objective is that your appeal be dealt with fairly and justly.[192] This includes ensuring that you are able to participate fully.

What happens at a hearing?

1. The judge should introduce everyone present.

2. The judge (and member(s)) often starts by asking you (and the presenting officer) questions. Even if you have a representative, you are usually expected to give your own evidence (see p1344). Be prepared for some searching questions.

3. The presenting officer may be asked to summarise the decision maker's case.

4. You should be given the opportunity to explain your case. It is the tribunal's job to help you to say everything you want by putting you at your ease and asking the right questions. If you think there are mistakes in the papers, point them out. You can call witnesses and ask questions of the presenting officer's witnesses. If you forget to say something when it is your turn to speak, do not hesitate to add it at the end of the hearing. See p1336 for help with preparing your appeal.

5. The tribunal considers all the facts, evidence and law before it makes a decision. It should not bargain with you by 'offering' to allow part of your appeal if you agree to drop other parts – eg, by offering you one component of PIP if you agree not to argue for the other.[193]

Appeals about disability or limited capability for work

If your appeal concerns your disability or your limited capability for work, the tribunal considers all the medical and other relevant evidence, and tries to draw out the evidence about your disabilities, listening to all you have to say with the help of questioning from the doctor member(s). The doctor member is there to help the tribunal understand the medical evidence and provide medical information. However, s/he should not give her/his clinical opinion.[194] The evidence may confirm the opinions expressed in medical reports with which you disagree, or it may support your view. See p1343 for information about medical evidence. Consider the following.

- Tell the tribunal how your disability or limited capability for work affects you at work or in your daily life at home. You should be completely straightforward, neither underplaying nor overplaying your symptoms. If you feel better on some days than others, explain how and how often, and say whether you are being seen on a good day or a bad day.

- The tribunal should not restrict itself to accepting the medical evidence about you given in written reports.[195] If there is conflict between what is said in a report and what you have said in writing (eg, on your claim form), it should not accept the evidence in the report without first listening to what you have to say about how your condition affects you.[196] Ensure that you explain any

Part 9: Getting a benefit decision changed
Chapter 57: Appealing to the First-tier Tribunal
4. How the tribunal makes its decision

inconsistencies. The tribunal should be particularly careful not to accept automatically the findings in medical reports produced with the assistance of a computer programme.[197]

Can the tribunal take its observations of you into account?

The tribunal may observe your abilities and behaviour at the hearing and take these into account when making its decision – eg, if your appeal concerns your ability to walk, but it cannot subject you to a walking test.[198] It should not attach undue weight to its observations[199] and you should usually be given the opportunity to comment on them.[200] Remind the tribunal that what it sees may only be relevant to your physical or mental condition on that day and not in general.[201] Tell it, for instance, whether you have just taken medication or have been resting for some time in the waiting area. **Note:** the tribunal can use information about walking distances it obtains itself – eg, from Google Maps. However, the evidence should be presented to you so that you can comment on, or refute, it.[202]

Medical examination at the hearing

The tribunal cannot usually carry out physical examinations.[203] Studying x-ray evidence does not count as a physical examination, so you can ask the tribunal to consider this.[204]

It *can* carry out a physical examination if your appeal relates to the assessment of your disablement for SDA or industrial injuries disablement benefit, or whether you have a prescribed disease or injury.[205] It should let you know during the hearing if it thinks a physical examination is not necessary so you can make representations.[206]

You are examined by the medical member(s) of the tribunal.[207] You can have someone with you as a chaperone or if, for instance, you need help undressing. Make sure you tell the medical member(s) if you are in pain or discomfort. It is also a good idea to provide a full list of any medicines you are taking. After the examination, you should be invited to make further representations to the tribunal if you wish.

Referral for a medical report

The tribunal can refer you to a healthcare professional approved by the DWP (see p1141) for a medical examination and report if your appeal concerns:[208]

- whether you are entitled to AA, DLA or PIP, the appropriate rate of benefit or the period for which you are entitled; *or*
- whether you are entitled to SDA; *or*
- whether you have limited capability for work or for work-related activity; *or*
- the extent of your disablement for SDA or industrial injuries disablement benefit purposes; *or*

- whether you have a loss of faculty as a result of an industrial accident (see p672).

The tribunal can specify the type of healthcare professional to whom you should be referred.[209] The medical examination may take place in your home or at a DWP medical examination centre. **Note:** athough you cannot be compelled to undergo a medical examination, the tribunal may draw negative conclusions if you refuse.

A report or medical notes may also be requested from your GP or other medical adviser with your permission.

The written decision to adjourn for a report should make clear why the tribunal adjourned and what sort of medical evidence is being sought.

What the tribunal considers

The tribunal's job is to decide whether the decision you are appealing about was correct. It must look at the law and issues afresh, taking into account any new evidence or information you (and the DWP, the local authority or HMRC) provide. The tribunal considers all the evidence.[210] It should decide your appeal in an investigative way, but the members should generally not make their own enquiries into the facts of your case before the hearing.[211] **Note:**

- You (or the DWP, the local authority or HMRC) can raise an issue at the hearing.[212] However, the tribunal might then adjourn to give the other side a chance to address the point.
- The tribunal should consider an issue if it is in the appeal papers or in any representations you make, or if the evidence should lead it to believe it is relevant to your appeal, even if your representative has not made a submission on the issue.[213] It has the discretion to (ie, it does not have to) consider issues that are 'not raised by' your appeal.[214] **Note:**
  - You do not necessarily have to raise an issue with the tribunal for it to be something it should consider, even if you have a representative, but the issue must be one which in some way obviously demands attention – eg, from evidence included in the appeal papers.[215] Even if you say that you do not want an issue to be considered, the tribunal can still exercise its discretion to consider it.[216] However, if you have a representative, the tribunal may decide not to investigate matters that s/he does not raise on your behalf or that s/he says s/he does not want to be considered.[217]
  - The tribunal can consider issues even if no one has raised them.[218] It should use its discretion fairly.

Are you appealing about a disability benefit?
If you are appealing because you were not awarded one component of DLA or PIP when you are in receipt of the other, or you ask for a higher rate of DLA, PIP or AA than you are already getting, the tribunal does not have to consider issues which are not the subject of

Part 9: Getting a benefit decision changed
Chapter 57: Appealing to the First-tier Tribunal
4. How the tribunal makes its decision

your appeal. However, it may decide to consider both components of DLA or PIP, or to consider whether you should get a lower rate of DLA, PIP or AA than you are already getting. **Note:**
– You should be given warning of this, and a chance to prepare your case properly and make representations or to consider withdrawing your appeal.[219]
– Ask for the hearing to be adjourned if you need time or want someone to advise or represent you.
– If your appeal is being dealt with on the basis of the papers only, you should be given the opportunity to attend a hearing or to withdraw your appeal.[220]
– You should be given an explanation of why the tribunal decided to use its discretion in this way in the statement of reasons for its decision.[221]

If you are concerned about what might happen in your appeal, you may be able to withdraw it (see p1323). You need permission if you ask to withdraw your appeal at the hearing, or if you are notified that you can only withdraw your appeal if the tribunal agrees. **Note:** the DWP (or the local authority or HMRC) can apply for your appeal to be reinstated (see p1323).

Appeals involving revisions and supersessions

If your appeal involves a revision or a supersession decision, the tribunal can make any decision that the decision maker could have taken.[222] This includes where the decision maker carried out a supersession:
- but failed to state the grounds or to identify the correct grounds for doing so; *or*
- when s/he should have conducted a revision (and, in some cases, vice versa).

In addition, the tribunal can decide that an 'any time' revision should be done where no decision has been made on the matter by a decision maker (either to revise the decision or refuse to do so) – ie, if you are appealing because the decision maker refused to carry out a supersession.[223]

If there are errors in the decision, argue that the tribunal should correct the decision. However, it can adjourn the hearing, point out the errors to the decision maker and invite the decision maker to reconsider, rather than making any corrections itself.[224]

Changes of circumstances after the decision under appeal

When the tribunal deals with your appeal, it considers whether the decision with which you disagree was correct for the period up to and including the date it was made. If your circumstances change after the decision, it cannot take this into account.[225]

Any evidence you get after the decision with which you disagree could still be relevant to your appeal. If the evidence relates to the period before the decision you are disputing was made, or to a past event that was relevant to the decision, it must be taken into account.[226] In some situations, events that happen after the date of a decision can throw light on the situation at or before that date, in which case evidence of such events may also be taken into account – eg, if the tribunal needs to decide whether an improvement in your health was likely to happen.

What you should do if your circumstances change

As a general rule, you should consider making a fresh claim (or seeking a supersession) every time your circumstances change, and appeal if you are unhappy with the subsequent decision, particularly if your appeal is about:

- whether you have limited capability for work, have limited capability for work-related activity or qualify for AA, DLA or PIP, or the rate of AA, DLA or PIP to which you are entitled and your condition has worsened; *or*
- whether you satisfy the 'habitual residence test' (see p1550); *or*
- how much income or capital you have, and this changes.

If you wait until the tribunal makes its decision and this goes against you, you could lose out. You can only get arrears from the date your circumstances changed if a fresh claim (or the effect of a supersession) can be backdated. This is only possible in limited circumstances.

> #### Example
> Jing has been getting PIP mobility component. A decision maker decides his condition has improved so stops his PIP. He appeals. While waiting for his appeal hearing, his condition deteriorates, he makes a fresh claim and is awarded PIP mobility component. When the tribunal hears his appeal against the original decision, it upholds the decision maker's decision. However, because Jing made a fresh claim when his circumstances changed, he has not lost out.

If you make a fresh claim (or seek a supersession), you can ask the decision maker to wait until your appeal has been determined before making a decision. However, if the decision maker decides the fresh claim (or supersession) and you disagree with the decision:

- you can appeal against the new decision. All the appeals may be heard together by the tribunal, but it may be better for them to be heard separately;[227] *or*
- whether or not you appeal against the new decision, you can ask the decision maker to revise it once your first appeal is determined (see p1268).

> #### Example
> Leonard claims pension credit (PC) but the decision maker says he does not satisfy the habitual residence test and refuses his claim. He appeals against the decision and makes a fresh claim for PC on 9 May 2022. The new claim is refused. Leonard wins his appeal.

Part 9: Getting a benefit decision changed
Chapter 57: Appealing to the First-tier Tribunal
5. Preparing your appeal

Because there has been a fresh decision on his entitlement, the tribunal can only award PC up to 9 May 2022. However, the decision maker does an 'any time' revision and awards PC from that date as well.

5. Preparing your appeal

Preparing for your appeal to be heard by the First-tier Tribunal is important, even if you do not opt for a hearing. Appeals to the First-tier Tribunal are taken on many issues – disputes about facts or the law, or both. You usually need to think about both the facts and the law because they are connected. Consider the legal tests the decision maker says you have not met carefully and decide which of these to argue s/he got wrong.

How should you prepare your appeal?

1. Check the law – ie, work out the law that applies in your case (the relevant legal tests) using the information in this *Handbook*. Consider whether the decision maker has correctly set out and understood the legal tests that are relevant in your case. If you think the decision maker has misunderstood or misstated the law think about how to explain why as clearly as possible.

2. Sort out the facts (see p1341) – ie, work out the evidence you need to provide to show that you satisfy the relevant legal tests.

3. Prepare a submission (a 'reply') to send to the tribunal that sets out the legal tests and the evidence that shows you satisfy them. Always send any detailed submissions, medical reports and other evidence in time, before the hearing.

4. If you are attending a hearing, think about how best to present your case to the tribunal (see p1344).

Checking the law

If you know what the law says, you know what facts you have to prove and what evidence you need to provide to the tribunal. The primary sources of social security law are statute law and caselaw decided by the Upper Tribunal and courts. Both types are important. The statute law sets out the rules; caselaw explains what the statute law means (ie, it interprets it) and explains how the rules should be applied.

It is easy to find both statute law and caselaw, once you know what you are looking for. The endnotes in this *Handbook* point you in the right direction. There are also a number of books that explain the law and refer you to relevant legislation and cases (see Appendix 2).

Look carefully at the decision maker's response (see p1314), as this refers to the statute law and caselaw which s/he thinks is relevant. The DWP, the local authority or HMRC does not always get the law right and you should emphasise a point that it has overlooked or got wrong.

Statute law

Statute law comprises Acts of Parliament and regulations (and rules for procedure in the First-tier Tribunal and Upper Tribunal). The Acts set out the main framework and allow regulations and rules covering the details to be made. These regulations and rules are known as statutory instruments. The legislation is often amended, so you must confirm that what you are referring to is up to date.

The best way to look up the relevant statute law is in one of the annotated volumes of legislation listed in Appendix 2. Acts, regulations and rules are also available at legislation.gov.uk and amended versions are usually available.

Guidance

Benefit law is complicated and the staff who administer benefits are issued with guidance manuals and circulars. The DWP, the local authority, HMRC and the First-tier and Upper Tribunals are only bound by what the law says, not by the guidance. Nevertheless, it is sometimes useful to check the guidance. See Appendix 2 for a list of what is available.

European legislation

European Union (EU) law continued to apply during the transition period that began when the UK left the EU and ended on 31 December 2020. 'EU co-ordination rules' can apply since the end of the transition period. See Chapter 71 for information about changes due to the UK leaving the European Union.

Human rights

The Human Rights Act 1998 incorporates into UK law most of the Articles of the European Convention on Human Rights. All legislation must be applied, *so far as it is possible to do so*, in a way which is compatible with this Convention.[228] If a provision of secondary legislation (eg, a regulation), even as so interpreted, results in a breach of Convention rights (eg, it is discriminatory), a tribunal must disapply it, unless it is prevented from doing so by a provision in primary legislation.[229] A tribunal does not have the power to disapply primary legislation and, unlike the courts, it does not have any power to make a declaration of incompatibility.

The First-tier Tribunal must take into account any relevant caselaw of the European Court of Human Rights (ECtHR), but if there is a conflict between a UK court and the ECtHR, the decision of the UK court should generally be followed.[230]

The Convention Articles most likely to be relevant in social security cases are:
- Article 6(1): right to a fair hearing before an independent and impartial tribunal;

Part 9: Getting a benefit decision changed
Chapter 57: Appealing to the First-tier Tribunal
5. Preparing your appeal

- Article 8: right to respect for private and family life;
- Article 1 of the First Protocol: right to protection of property;
- Article 14: prohibition of discrimination.

If your case involves a Human Rights Act argument, get specialist advice.

Caselaw

The decision maker's response often refers to decisions of the Upper Tribunal and the courts (known as 'caselaw'). You should also use caselaw to support your appeal if possible. To help you decide which cases to use, see p1340.

Before 3 November 2008, decisions now made by the Upper Tribunal were made by social security commissioners.

Identifying Upper Tribunal and commissioners' decisions

All Upper Tribunal decisions have file numbers – eg, CDLA/2195/2008.
- The last numbers indicate the year in which the appeal was lodged.
- The letters after the 'C' indicate the benefit involved in the decision. An extra 'S' after the 'C' denotes a Scottish case, as in CSIB/721/2004.

Upper Tribunal decisions that are published on the official websites (see p1341) are given a 'citation number' (sometimes called a 'neutral citation'). Then, when citing a case the case name (in italics) is combined with the neutral citation like this: *JP v SSWP (ESA)* [2016] UKUT 48 (AAC).
- First, the parties to the appeal are identified. The benefit claimant is identified by initials. The first name (or initials) is the party who appealed and the second is the other party. **Note:** 'SSWP' stands for Secretary of State for Work and Pensions – ie, the DWP.
- Next is the year the decision was given (in square brackets) and the letters 'UKUT' (meaning United Kingdom Upper Tribunal).
- The final number is the appeal number.
- Since 2010, letters to indicate the type of benefit involved in the decision are usually included in the case name before the neutral citation.

The most important Upper Tribunal decisions are chosen to be reported and are given a new number. All reported decisions:
- from 1951 to 2010 begin with an 'R' – eg, CU/255/1984 became R(U) 3/86. The following letter(s) denote(s) the type of benefit. The last numbers indicate the year in which the decision was published;
- from 2010 begin with the citation number. This is followed by the year the decision is reported (in square brackets), then the letters AACR (meaning Administrative Appeals Chamber Reports) and the reported decision number. In this *Handbook*, a reported decision is shown as follows: eg, *Torbay BC v RF (HB)* [2010] UKUT 7 (AAC), reported as [2010] AACR 26.

Identifying court decisions

Court decisions are identified by the names of the parties involved in the appeal. The first name is usually the party who has appealed and the second name is the other party. In judicial review cases, the case citation begins with 'R', which stands for 'Regina' (the Queen).

Examples of court decisions

Hockenjos v Secretary of State for Social Security [2004] EWCA Civ 1749, 21 December 2004 is a decision of the England and Wales Court of Appeal Civil Division.

R v South Tyneside MBC ex parte Tooley [1997] QBD and *R (Reynolds) v Secretary of State for Work and Pensions* [2002] EWHC Admin 426 are decisions of the England and Wales High Court, formerly known as the Queen's Bench Division and now as the Administrative Court, following applications for judicial review.

Saunderson v SSWP [2012] CSIH 10 is a decision of the Court of Session Inner House in Scotland.

Identifying decisions of the Court of Justice of the European Union

The Court of Justice of the European Union (CJEU) ensures that European law is interpreted and applied in the same way across the EU. Its cases include those that decide one or more questions that have been referred by a national court where there is doubt as to how an EU law should be interpreted. The CJEU also decides cases brought by the European Commission, or another member state, against the failure of a member state to comply with EU law. Decisions are identified by the names of the parties involved. The first name is usually the party who has brought the case, and the second name is the other party in that case. These names are then followed by a unique reference number and the year that the case was decided.

Examples of decisions of the Court of Justice of the European Union

Gusa v Minister for Social Protection, C-442/16 [2017]

Commission of the European Communities v Kingdom of Belgium, C-408/03 [2006]

Precedent

When the Upper Tribunal or a court decides an appeal, the decision sets a precedent, which a decision maker or the First-tier Tribunal deciding a similar case *must* follow.[231] What that means is that the First-tier Tribunal must apply the interpretation of the law or procedural rule that the Upper Tribunal or court decided applied to the facts of the case before it. Unreported decisions must be followed in the same way as reported ones.[232] **Note:** commissioners' decisions also set a precedent.

Part 9: Getting a benefit decision changed
Chapter 57: Appealing to the First-tier Tribunal
5. Preparing your appeal

If there is an irreconcilable conflict between two or more decisions, the First-tier Tribunal has to choose which decision to follow.[233]

- It normally follows a reported decision of the Upper Tribunal (or a commissioner) in preference to an unreported one.
- It must follow an Upper Tribunal decision made by a three-judge panel (or the decision of a tribunal of commissioners) in preference to a decision of a single judge (or commissioner).
- Decisions of the Supreme Court, House of Lords, the Court of Appeal or the Court of Session (or the Court of Justice of the European Union) take precedence over all decisions of the Upper Tribunal (and commissioners).[234] **Note:** from the end of the transition period that began when the UK left the EU and ended on 31 December 2020, the Courts are not generally bound by retained EU caselaw. However, they *are* bound by retained EU caselaw if there is UK caselaw after the transition period that modifies or applies that caselaw, which is binding on the court.[235]

The Upper Tribunal has more freedom than the First-tier Tribunal.

- It does not have to follow an Upper Tribunal decision made by a single judge (or the decision of a single commissioner) if satisfied that the earlier decision was wrong.[236]
- It follows an Upper Tribunal decision made by a three-judge panel (and the decision of a tribunal of commissioners) unless there are compelling reasons not to. If the judge thinks it may be wrong, s/he can ask the President of the Administrative Appeals Chamber for the case to be transferred to another three-judge panel in the Upper Tribunal to reconsider the point.
- If an appeal is heard by a three-judge panel in the Upper Tribunal, the panel does not have to follow the decision of another similarly comprised panel (or tribunal of commissioners), but usually does so.[237]

Which cases to use

Caselaw can seem less precise than statute law, and frequently cases seem to contradict each other. Very often there are small differences in the facts of the cases, which justify the different results. To find cases relevant to your own, use the endnotes in this *Handbook* or the references to cases in the publications listed in Appendix 2. Bear the following in mind.

- Find cases where the facts are similar to yours. If cases appear to be against you, look at the facts of those cases carefully and see whether any differences justify a different decision in your case (known as 'distinguishing' cases). One distinction may simply be that what seemed reasonable in the 1950s does not seem fair in the 2020s.[238]
- Ensure that the caselaw is still relevant to the decision you are appealing – ie, check whether there have been amendments to the statute law since the caselaw was decided.

- Check the decisions referred to in the decision maker's response (see p1314). Think of arguments why the decisions should not apply in your case. Sometimes the response relies on only part of a decision and fails to mention another part which is more favourable to you.

Obtaining Upper Tribunal, commissioners' and court decisions

Many **Upper Tribunal decisions** made from January 2016 are available at gov.uk/administrative-appeals-tribunal-decisions. Many of the Upper Tribunal and commissioners' decisions made before January 2016 are available at administrativeappeals.decisions.tribunals.gov.uk/Aspx/default.aspx. Some decisions are also available at bailii.org/databases.html and an archive of older decisions is at rightsnet.org.uk. You can also get decisions from the Upper Tribunal Offices (see gov.uk/courts-tribunals/upper-tribunal-administrative-appeals-chamber for the addresses).

Reported decisions are published from time to time in bound volumes, which are sometimes available in law libraries. The bound volumes of decisions from 2010 onwards are called Administrative Appeals Chamber Reports and contain reports of social security cases as well as those from other jurisdictions.

Summaries of important Upper Tribunal and court decisions are published in CPAG's *Welfare Rights Bulletin*. However, use the full decision, not just the summary, at the appeal hearing.

If an unreported decision is to be used at a hearing in the First-tier Tribunal by the DWP, the local authority or HMRC, a copy should be supplied to you. Similarly, if you wish to use one, you should supply copies to everyone, preferably by sending one to the tribunal in advance of the hearing.

Many **court decisions** are available online. See, for example, judiciary.uk/judgments, scotcourts.gov.uk and supremecourt.uk/decided-cases/index.html. Also, a useful link to court decisions is at bailii.org/databases.html.

Sorting out the facts

It is important to provide evidence that shows that the facts in your case mean you satisfy the relevant legal tests if the decision maker has disputed that this is the case. You are likely to know more than anyone else about the facts of your case. Your key task is to pass your knowledge on to the tribunal. It rehears your case completely, so fresh evidence and arguments can be put by either side.

How do you ensure the tribunal has all the facts?

1. Check through the appeal papers carefully to work out what evidence the decision maker used in support of the decision. This helps you decide what evidence you need to win your case.

2. Study the decision maker's evidence and think about your arguments – eg, to show how the decision maker may have got the wrong impression.

Part 9: Getting a benefit decision changed
Chapter 57: Appealing to the First-tier Tribunal
5. Preparing your appeal

3. Gather evidence and information to back up your arguments. Send it to the tribunal as soon as possible before your hearing. Otherwise, it might decide to adjourn your hearing (see p1319) or even decide not to take the evidence or information into account.[239] The tribunal sends a copy to the DWP, the local authority or HM Revenue and Customs (HMRC), which might then decide to support your appeal.

4. Ask any witnesses who support your case to attend the hearing.

The tribunal can issue directions (see p1318) on how you (or the DWP, the local authority or HMRC) should provide evidence and submissions or on how witnesses should give evidence – eg, orally at a hearing, or by making a written submission or a witness statement within a set period of time.[240] It can accept evidence from you (or the DWP, the local authority or HMRC) even if it was not available to a previous decision maker.[241]

Evidence includes:

- written evidence – any documents you (or the DWP, the local authority or HMRC) provide, including medical evidence (see below and p1343); *and*
- filmed evidence (see p1343); *and.*
- oral evidence – what you (and any witnesses or others) actually say at the hearing (see p1344). The tribunal cannot dismiss oral evidence without a proper explanation of why it has done so.[242]

Written evidence

Written evidence includes letters, medical and other reports, wage slips, bank statements, birth certificates and anything else that helps prove the facts. If, for example, the DWP says you failed to disclose an increase in your earnings and you have been overpaid, you could explain how and when you did so. It is even better to produce a copy of the letter you sent informing the decision maker of the change, or a letter you received confirming you reported the change or if you telephoned the DWP (or the local authority or HMRC) to report the change on a specific day, an itemised telephone bill confirming that you called on that day.

It is not unknown for the DWP, HMRC or the local authority to fail to include copies of relevant documents in the decision maker's response. Check the response carefully and submit copies of any missing documents to the tribunal as soon as you can. If you do not have copies, insist that the decision maker provides these. The tribunal can issue a direction requiring the decision maker to do so (see p1318).

Is the person who provided written evidence absent from the hearing?

1. Argue that the tribunal should not place any weight on the written evidence of someone who is not at the hearing as you have not had the opportunity to question her/him.

2. The tribunal should not place weight on the written evidence of an interviewing officer if you are disputing the interview, or an investigating officer if you are disputing what s/he

heard or saw if the officer is not at the hearing. However, the tribunal may still decide that there is no reason to doubt the truth of the officer's written statement.

3. The evidence of an anonymous witness cannot be relied on without the consent of the tribunal, and consent should only be given in exceptional circumstances.[243]

Medical evidence

You can ask your doctor to provide medical evidence, or ask an advice agency to write to your doctor. Your doctor may charge for such evidence, but an advice agency or solicitor might be able to get a report free. Your medical evidence should deal with the points in dispute and also with the dates relevant to the decision with which you disagree. If your doctor does not know about the effect of your disability on your everyday life, tell her/him about it and ask her/him to confirm that this is consistent with the degree of your disability. Your evidence, or that of a friend or relative, may also be of use.

If you obtain a medical report, send it to the tribunal in advance of the hearing, with a copy of the letter to your doctor as this helps to show that s/he is expressing her/his own opinion about your case. You could also ask your doctor to supply a copy of her/his notes about you over the last few years.

Note: the tribunal can refer you for an examination and obtain a report if it thinks this is necessary (see p1332). If the lack of medical evidence is causing you difficulties at the hearing, remind the tribunal of its power to obtain one.

Do you disagree with the medical evidence?

1. If the DWP has a report from your GP's surgery which is provided by a doctor you do not usually see, point this out to the tribunal. In all cases if the evidence is unfavourable, point out how long the doctor has known you and what s/he knows about your day-to-day living activities or walking ability. If a doctor does not know you (or know you well) or know how you are affected by your condition, this should be taken into account.

2. If a medical report is provided by a healthcare professional, tell the tribunal about any relevant issues with the examination – eg, if you were not examined or were only given a very short examination, if you were not allowed to explain how you are affected by your condition properly, or if the person examining you has not recorded your answers to her/his questions correctly. Try to point out anything in the content of the report that confirms what you say.

3. Argue that the tribunal should not rely on evidence from a DWP doctor who also sits as a tribunal member with whom any of the members hearing your appeal sit at other times. This depends on how often and on how recently this has happened.[244]

Filmed evidence

The DWP, the local authority or HMRC might use evidence filmed during the course of an investigation – eg, if you are appealing about entitlement to

Part 9: Getting a benefit decision changed
Chapter 57: Appealing to the First-tier Tribunal
5. Preparing your appeal

employment and support allowance (ESA), disability living allowance or personal independence payment (PIP). You cannot prevent it doing so.[245] The tribunal should always find out if the surveillance was properly authorised. If it was not authorised, argue that any evidence obtained should be ignored.

You must be given time to view and consider the evidence in advance of the hearing. You should be allowed to be present when the tribunal views it and must be given the opportunity to comment on the issues and evidence.[246] If relevant, insist that the person who did the filming be called as a witness. If the filming was only intermittent and if filming in the intervening periods would have provided evidence favourable to you, point this out to the tribunal.

Oral evidence

You, the presenting officer and witnesses can give your oral evidence at the hearing. You are usually expected to give your own oral evidence at the hearing, if you can. Your representative is generally not allowed to give this for you. However, s/he can assist the tribunal in gathering evidence from you (eg, by asking you questions)[247] and can give her/his *own* evidence based on her/his observations, or factual evidence within her/his own knowledge.[248]

If s/he is at the hearing, the presenting officer can put forward arguments as to why s/he thinks the tribunal should confirm that the DWP's, the local authority's or HMRC's decision was correct. However, s/he is not necessarily the person who actually made the decision on your claim.

You or the DWP, the local authority or HMRC can call witnesses to give evidence, but the tribunal can limit the number.[249] The tribunal can refuse to hear witnesses who are not relevant, but it should always be fair to you and generally allow witnesses to speak, even if it looks like they may have nothing useful to say.[250] The tribunal itself can summon witnesses.[251]

Hearsay evidence

If you, your representative, the presenting officer or witnesses report what other people have said, this is known as 'hearsay evidence'. The tribunal must carefully weigh up its value, given that the person who originally made the statement is not present at the hearing.[252]

Unless the presenting officer is giving her/his own evidence (eg, because s/he was directly involved in the decision on your claim), any factual statements s/he makes are hearsay evidence, but the tribunal might not doubt the accuracy of the evidence.[253]

Presenting your case at the hearing

Each case is different and hearings are informal, so there is no set pattern for presenting cases. If you want to make a presentation on your appeal, make this clear to the First-tier Tribunal as soon as possible – eg, before the hearing starts, because the tribunal often expects to go straight into asking you questions. This is the way hearings are commonly conducted.

How should you present your case?

1. You can use a written submission at the hearing and read directly from it. However, the tribunal usually asks questions, so be prepared to talk about your case without the script.

2. Make it clear at the start what you think the outcome of the appeal should be and why – eg, what rate of PIP you think you qualify for, or which ESA descriptors you think you satisfy, or that your claim for housing benefit should be backdated.

3. Tell the tribunal which parts of the decision maker's response you dispute and the parts with which you agree.

4. Set out the facts and call any witnesses before turning to legal arguments.

5. It is the tribunal's job to help you to say everything you want by putting you at your ease and asking the right questions. However, you must also be prepared for some searching questions. If you forget to say something when it is your turn to speak, do not hesitate to add it at the end of the hearing.

6. The tribunal's decision

You may be told the tribunal's decision at the hearing and you are given a **decision notice** confirming it. If it is not given at the hearing or you opted for a paper hearing, the decision notice is sent to you later. It may include a summary of the tribunal's reasons for its decision. You *must* be informed of:[254]

- your right to request a statement of reasons for the decision (see p1346); *and*
- the conditions for appealing to the Upper Tribunal, including the time limit for doing so.

Note:

- If the tribunal is unable to come to a unanimous decision, it makes a majority decision. The judge has the casting vote.[255] However, if the tribunal consists of two members and there is complete disagreement about the facts, the judge should not use her/his casting vote, but instead should adjourn the appeal to be heard by different tribunal members.[256]
- A decision can be corrected, superseded, reviewed or set aside (see p1347). You, or the DWP, the local authority or HM Revenue and Customs (HMRC) can also appeal against it to the Upper Tribunal.

Record of proceedings

A record of the tribunal proceedings is made by the judge that indicates the evidence taken and submissions made, as well as any procedural applications.[257]

Part 9: Getting a benefit decision changed
Chapter 57: Appealing to the First-tier Tribunal
6. The tribunal's decision

This could be a recording of the hearing or a written record.[258] If you are considering an appeal to the Upper Tribunal, it is a good idea to get a copy. If you foresee disputes about what happened at the hearing, keep your own notes. **Note:** during the coronavirus pandemic, the hearing must be recorded, if practicable, if the hearing, or part of it, is held in private. If you apply, you can have access to the recording with the consent of the tribunal.[259]

The record is kept by the tribunal for six months from the date of its decision or for six months from various other specific dates, including the date you are sent written reasons for its decision. So, if you applied for a statement of reasons for the decision, the record of proceedings should not be destroyed until six months after the statement has been provided.[260]

You can request a copy of the record of proceedings. You must do so in writing within the relevant six-month period. Bear in mind that if you request it after the six-month period, the record may have been destroyed. You can apply for a typed copy of a written record – eg, if the written copy is difficult to read, but the tribunal may refuse to provide one. However, if you appeal to the Upper Tribunal, you can ask an Upper Tribunal judge to make a direction that a typed version is to be prepared.

The statement of reasons

The First-tier Tribunal may give the reasons for its decision at the hearing, or give or send you a written statement of reasons, prepared by the judge.[261] If you are not provided with a written statement of reasons, you have a right to apply for one.[262] **Note:** the judge may say that the decision notice (see p1345) is to stand as the written statement of reasons, so check it carefully.

You must generally have a statement of reasons if you want to appeal to the Upper Tribunal. You must show that the First-tier Tribunal made a mistake about the law (an 'error of law' – see p1357) and it may be difficult to do so without a statement of reasons.

Your request for a statement of reasons must be:[263]
- in writing; *and*
- received by the First-tier Tribunal within one month (see p1306) of your being sent or given its decision notice. It can give you longer (or shorter) than this.[264] There is no guarantee that you will be given longer, so keep within the time limit wherever possible.

The written statement of reasons must then be sent to you within one month or as soon as it is reasonably practicable after that.[265] There are, however, often long delays.

Note:
- If you mistakenly ask the First-tier Tribunal for permission to appeal to the Upper Tribunal instead of asking for a statement of reasons, it should treat this as a request for a statement of reasons.[266]

- If the judge refuses wrongly to provide a statement of reasons, you may have grounds for appeal to the Upper Tribunal.[267]
- If there is a long delay in getting a statement of reasons, you could apply for permission to appeal to the Upper Tribunal. The Upper Tribunal can require the First-tier Tribunal to provide reasons for its decision.[268]

The DWP, the local authority or HMRC can also ask for a statement of reasons. If this happens, it usually means it is considering appealing to the Upper Tribunal.

If you win your appeal

If you win your appeal, the DWP, local authority or HMRC should carry out the First-tier Tribunal's decision straight away. It can do this on the basis of the decision notice (see p1345). However, if the DWP, the local authority or HMRC:

- disagrees with the decision, it might consider appealing against it to the Upper Tribunal. In this case, you are not normally paid while it decides what to do. See p1161 for what the DWP, the local authority or HMRC must do before it can suspend payment of your benefit. If the DWP, local authority or HMRC decides to appeal, you are not normally paid until the Upper Tribunal decides the case.[269] However, you can ask the DWP, the local authority or HMRC to pay you if you are in financial hardship;
- applies for permission to appeal to the Upper Tribunal, the First-tier Tribunal may be able to suspend the effect of its decision until the application is determined (by either tribunal), and then until any review of, or appeal against, the decision is determined.[270]

The First-tier Tribunal can also suspend the effect of its decision if *you* apply for permission to appeal to the Upper Tribunal.

If you disagree with the tribunal's decision

If you disagree with the First-tier Tribunal's decision, you cannot simply ask it to look at the decision again – eg, if you have additional evidence. However:

- if the decision contains a clerical mistake or other accidental slip or omission, this can be corrected by the tribunal. This only applies if it is a genuine error such as a typing or spelling mistake or a mathematical miscalculation, not an error of law on an important issue in your appeal. **Note:** the tribunal cannot use this rule to amend or add to its reasons for the decision, but can amend these if it reviews its decision (see p1364);[271]
- the decision can be superseded by the DWP, the local authority or HMRC, if there are grounds (see p1274), though arrears can be limited. However, if the tribunal made a mistake about the law, you must appeal to the Upper Tribunal;
- you (or the DWP, the local authority or HMRC) can appeal to the Upper Tribunal against the decision (see Chapter 58);

Part 9: Getting a benefit decision changed
Chapter 57: Appealing to the First-tier Tribunal
6. The tribunal's decision

- if you (or the DWP, the local authority or HMRC) seek permission to appeal to the Upper Tribunal against a decision, the First-tier Tribunal can review it (see p1364);
- the decision can be set aside, which means the decision is cancelled and your appeal is heard again.

If you are considering an appeal to the Upper Tribunal, ask for the First-tier Tribunal's statement of reasons (if one has not yet been provided) within the one-month time limit (see p1346), even if you are first going to apply for the decision to be set aside.

Setting aside a decision on procedural grounds

A First-tier Tribunal decision can only be set aside on procedural grounds if the judge thinks it is 'in the interests of justice' to do so and:[272]
- you, your representative or the DWP, the local authority or HMRC:
  - were not sent, or did not receive, appeal papers or other relevant documents at an appropriate time – eg, in sufficient time before the hearing; *or*
  - were not present at the hearing. However, if you (or they) chose not to attend, it might not be 'in the interests of justice' to set the decision aside; *or*
- the tribunal was not sent appeal papers or other relevant documents at an appropriate time – eg, in sufficient time before the hearing; *or*
- there was some other procedural irregularity.

The tribunal cannot set aside a decision unless an application to set aside the decision is made.[273]

You must apply in writing to the First-tier Tribunal. The application must be received no later than one month after the date you are sent the decision notice (see p1345).[274] The tribunal can give you longer (or shorter) than this.[275] There is no guarantee that you will be given longer, so keep within the time limit wherever possible. The rules do not say what the time limit is if you are given the decision notice at the hearing but you should apply within the time limit above to protect your position.

Note:
- Applications are normally decided without a hearing.[276] Make sure you give a full explanation of your reasons when you apply.
- If you could not attend your hearing (eg, because you were ill), provide evidence of this – eg, a note from your doctor. If your application is late, explain the reasons for this.
- If the decision is set aside, your appeal is heard again and a new decision is made. You should be given the opportunity to ask for a hearing, even if your appeal was originally decided based on the papers only.[277]

- If a decision is wrongly set aside (eg, the tribunal decides to set aside the decision although no application for a set aside has been made), any subsequent rehearing by the First-tier Tribunal is invalid.[278]

In some circumstances, a decision can also be set aside by agreement.

If the decision is not set aside
If the First-tier Tribunal refuses to set aside a decision, you can appeal to the Upper Tribunal against the refusal.[279] You can often argue that the circumstances you mentioned in your application for a set aside also show that the tribunal made a mistake about the law. So it might be better to try to appeal to the Upper Tribunal against the original decision *and* the refusal. If your application for the First-tier Tribunal's decision to be set aside is refused, the time limit for applying for permission to appeal to the Upper Tribunal can run from the date you are sent notice of this.[280] However, this only applies if you applied for the decision to be set aside within the one-month time limit (or any longer period allowed by the First-tier Tribunal).

Note: the First-tier Tribunal can treat your application for a decision to be set aside as an application for permission to appeal to the Upper Tribunal, or as an application for a correction of the decision.[281]

Setting aside a decision by agreement
The First-tier Tribunal must set aside a decision if an application is made for permission to appeal against it to the Upper Tribunal, and you and the DWP, the local authority or HMRC agree that the First-tier Tribunal made a mistake about the law (an 'error of law' – see p1357).[282] Bear in mind that the First-tier Tribunal does not send copies of applications for permission to appeal to the other party. If you think that the DWP, the local authority or HMRC might agree that the tribunal made an error of law, you should send it a copy of your application. However, there is no guarantee that it will take any action on this.

Part 9: Getting a benefit decision changed
Chapter 57: Appealing to the First-tier Tribunal
Notes

Notes

1. Before you appeal

1 *R (Connor) v SSWP* [2020] EWHC 1999 (Admin)
2 *PP v SSWP (UC)* [2020] UKUT 109 (AAC)
3 s12(1), (2) and (3D) SSA 1998
4 s12(2)(b) and (3A)-(3C) SSA 1998; reg 3ZA SS&CS(DA) Regs; reg 7 UC,PIP,JSA&ESA(DA) Regs
5 *PP v SSWP (UC)* [2020] UKUT 109 (AAC)
6 *R (CJ) and SG v SSWP (ESA)* [2017] UKUT 324 (AAC), reported as [2018] AACR 5
7 Memo DMG 5/19; Memo ADM 8/19
8 Memo DMG 5/19; Memo ADM 8/19
9 *PH and SM v SSWP* [2018] UKUT 404 (AAC)
10 **UC/PIP/JSA&ESA under UC** Reg 7(5) UC,PIP,JSA&ESA(DA) Regs
   Other benefits Reg 3ZA(5) SS&CS(DA) Regs
11 r22(4)(a) TP(FT) Rules
12 r7 TP(FT) Rules
13 **UC/PIP/JSA&ESA under UC** Reg 49 UC,PIP,JSA&ESA(DA) Regs
   CB/GA Reg 24 CB&GA(DA) Regs
   Other benefits Reg 25 SS&CS(DA) Regs
   All s12 SSA 1998
14 s12(4) SSA 1998
15 Reg 14 SS(JPIP) Regs
16 Sch 7 para 6(3) and (6) CSPSSA 2000; regs 3 and 21 HB&CTB(DA) Regs; *Wirral MBC v Salisbury Independent Living Ltd* [2012] EWCA Civ 84, reported as [2012] AACR 37
17 R(H) 3/04; R(H) 10/07
18 **UC/PIP/JSA&ESA under UC** s12 and Schs 2 and 3 SSA 1998; reg 50(1) and Sch 2 UC,PIP,JSA&ESA(DA) Regs
   HB Sch 7 para 6 CSPSSA 2000
   CB/GA s12 and Schs 2 and 3 SSA 1998; reg 25(2) CB&GA(DA) Regs
   Other benefits s12 and Schs 2 and 3 SSA 1998; reg 26 SS&CS(DA) Regs
19 R(SB) 29/83; R(SB) 12/89; CIS/807/1992; R(H) 3/05
20 R(IS) 6/04

21 **UC/PIP/JSA&ESA under UC** Regs 7(3) and 51 UC,PIP,JSA&ESA(DA) Regs
   HB Reg 10 HB&CTB(DA) Regs
   CB/GA Reg 26 CB&GA(DA) Regs
   Other benefits Regs 3ZA and 28 SS&CS(DA) Regs
22 *VT v SSWP (IS)* [2016] UKUT 178 (AAC), reported as [2016] AACR 42
23 *SSWP v Adams* [2003] EWCA Civ 796, reported as R(G) 1/03
24 *MC and JH v SSWP (ESA)* [2014] UKUT 125 (AAC), reported as [2014] AACR 35
25 **UC/PIP/JSA&ESA under UC** Sch 2 SSA 1998; reg 50(2) and Sch 3 UC,PIP,JSA&ESA(DA) Regs
   HB Sch 7 para 6(2) CSPSSA 2000; reg 16 and Sch HB&CTB(DA) Regs
   CB/GA Sch 2 SSA 1998; reg 25 and Sch 2 CB&GA(DA) Regs
   Other benefits Sch 2 SSA 1998; reg 27 and Sch 2 SS&CS(DA) Regs
26 **UC/PIP/JSA&ESA under UC** Regs 10 and 25 UC,PIP,JSA&ESA(DA) Regs
   HB Regs 4(6) and 7(2)(e) HB&CTB(DA) Regs
   CA/GA Regs 9 and 13(2)(d) CB&GA(DA) Regs
   Other benefits Regs 3(8) and 6(2)(d) SS&CG(DA) Regs
27 *RL v SSWP (JSA)* [2017] UKUT 282 (AAC)

2. How to appeal

28 Reg 20(1) HB&CTB(DA) Regs
29 Reg 20(1) HB&CTB(DA) Regs; r23 TP(FT) Rules
30 r22 TP(FT) Rules
31 r22(2)(d)(i) TP(FT) Rules
32 R(IB) 4/02; *SSWP v SC (SF)* [2013] UKUT 607 (AAC)
33 r12 TP(FT) Rules
34 **HB** r23(2)(a)(i) and (ii) TP(FT) Rules
   Other benefits r22(2)(d)(ii) and Sch 1 para 5(a) and (b) TP(FT) Rules
   All r12 TP(FT) Rules
35 s9(5) SSA 1998; Sch 7 para 3(5) CSPSSA 2000
36 r23(2)(a)(iii) and Sch 1 para 5(c) TP(FT) Rules
37 rr22(8)(a) and 23(4) and (5) TP(FT) Rules

Part 9: Getting a benefit decision changed
Chapter 57: Appealing to the First-tier Tribunal
Notes

• •

93 Vol 1 Ch 6, paras 6160-83 DMG; paras A5159-5161 ADM; 'Latest offers – PIP appeals', *Welfare Rights Bulletin* 284, October 2021, p6

94 *AI v SSWP (PIP)* [2019] UKUT 103 (AAC); para 4 Memo DMG 20/13

95 **HB** Sch 7 para 3(5) CSPSSA 2000; r23(2) TP(FT) Rules
Other benefits s9(5) SSA 1998; Sch 1 para 5 TP(FT) Rules

96 **UC/PIP/JSA&ESA under UC** Reg 52(2) UC,PIP,JSA&ESA(DA) Regs
HB Reg 17(3) HB&CTB(DA) Regs
CB/GA Reg 27(2) CB&GA(DA) Regs
Other benefits Reg 30(3) SS&CS(DA) Regs

97 **UC/PIP/JSA&ESA under UC** Reg 52(3) UC,PIP,JSA&ESA(DA) Regs
HB Reg 17(4) HB&CTB(DA) Regs
CB/GA Reg 27(3) CB&GA(DA) Regs
Other benefits Reg 30(4) SS&CS(DA) Regs

98 **UC/PIP/JSA&ESA under UC** Reg 52(4) UC,PIP,JSA&ESA(DA) Regs
HB Reg 17(5) HB&CTB(DA) Regs
CB/GA Reg 27(4) CB&GA(DA) Regs
Other benefits Reg 30(5) SS&CS(DA) Regs

99 *DO v SSWP (PIP)* [2021] UKUT 121 (AAC)

100 r2 TP(FT) Rules; r2 TP(UT) Rules

101 *MA v SSWP* [2009] UKUT 211 (AAC)

102 rr5, 6, 8, 15 and 16 TP(FT) Rules; rr5-7, 8, 15 and 16 TP(UT) Rules

103 s25 TCEA 2007; r7(3) TP(FT) Rules; r7(3) and (4) TP(UT) Rules; *MD v SSWP (Enforcement Reference)* [2010] UKUT 202 (AAC), reported as [2011] AACR 5; *CB v Suffolk CC (Enforcement Reference)* [2010] UKUT 413 (AAC), reported as [2011] AACR 22

104 r16(3) TP(FT) Rules; r16(3) TP(UT) Rules

105 r5(3)(l) TP(FT) Rules; r5(3)(l) and (m) TP(UT) Rules

106 r5(3)(a) TP(FT) Rules; r5(3)(a) TP(UT) Rules

107 r2(2)(e) TP(FT) Rules; r2(2)(e) TP(UT) Rules

108 rr5, 6 and 15 TP(FT) Rules; rr5, 6 and 15 TP(UT) Rules; *SR v Bristol CC* [2008] UKUT 7 (AAC)

109 r6(2) and (3) TP(FT) Rules; r6(2) and (3) TP(UT) Rules

110 r6(4) TP(FT) Rules; r5(4) TP(UT) Rules

111 r6(5) TP(FT) Rules; r6(5) TP(UT) Rules

112 r7 TP(FT) Rules; r7 TP(UT) Rules

113 R(H) 3/05; CCS/3757/2004

114 *SSWP v HS (JSA)* [2016] UKUT 272 (AAC), reported as [2017] AACR 29

115 *AP v SSWP (ESA)* [2017] UKUT 304 (AAC)

116 CIB/4253/2004

117 r15(2)(b) TP(FT) Rules; r15(2)(b) TP(UT) Rules

118 r5(3)(h) TP(FT) Rules; r5(3)(h) TP(UT) Rules; *MA v SSWP* [2009] UKUT 211 (AAC); Practice Statement: *Composition of Tribunals in Social Security and Child Support Cases in the Social Entitlement Chamber on or after 1 August 2013*, 31 July 2013, para 10

119 *GC v SSWP (ESA)* [2012] UKUT 60 (AAC)

120 *LJT v SSWP (PIP)* [2019] UKUT 21 (AAC)

121 r31 TP(FT) Rules; r38 TP(UT) Rules

122 *BV v SSWP (PIP)* [2018] UKUT 444 (AAC)

123 CDLA/1290/2004

124 CDLA/3680/1997; *JC v SSWP (PIP)* [2018] UKUT 110 (AAC)

125 *MA v SSWP* [2009] UKUT 211 (AAC)

126 CDLA/5413/1999

127 *CB v SSWP (ESA)* [2020] UKUT 15 (AAC)

128 CIS/566/1991; CS/99/1993

129 CIS/2292/2000; *DC v SSWP (ESA)* [2015] UKUT 150 (AAC)

130 CIS/6002/1997; *R v Social Security Commissioner ex parte Angora Bibi* [2000] unreported (HC); CIB/1009/2004; CIB/2058/2004

131 CIS/3338/2001; *DC v SSWP* [2014] UKUT 218 (AAC)

132 *MH v Pembrokeshire (HB)* [2010] UKUT 28 (AAC)

133 r8(1), (3)(a) and (5) TP(FT) Rules; r8(1), (3)(a) and (5) TP(UT) Rules

134 *DTM v Kettering BC (CTB)* [2013] UKUT 625 (AAC)

135 r8(5) and (6) TP(FT) Rules; r8(5) and (6) TP(UT) Rules

136 r8(2) and (4) TP(FT) Rules; r8(2) and (4) TP(UT) Rules

137 r8(3)(b) and (c) and (4) TP(FT) Rules; r8(3)(b) TP(UT) Rules

138 *AW v IC and Blackpool CC* [2013] UKUT 30 (AAC)

139 R(IS) 5/94

140 *LS v Lambeth LB (HB)* [2010] UKUT 461 (AAC), reported as [2011] AACR 27

141 rr1(3), definition of 'respondent', and 8(7) TP(FT) Rules; rr1(3), definition of 'respondent', and 8(7) TP(UT) Rules

142 r8(8) TP(FT) Rules; r8(8) TP(UT) Rules

143 *ZB v SSWP (CSM)* [2013] UKUT 367 (AAC); *SL v SSWP and KL (CSM)* [2014] UKUT 128 (AAC); *CW v SSWP and Another (CSM)* [2014] UKUT 290 (AAC)

144 **HB** Reg 20(9) HB&CTB(DA) Regs; r17 TP(FT) Rules
Other benefits r17 TP(FT) Rules
All *WM v SSWP (DLA)* [2015] UKUT 642 (AAC)
145 *PD v SSWP (PIP)* [2021] UKUT 172
146 rr4 and 7(2)(a) TP(FT) Rules; Practice Statement: *Delegation of Functions to Staff in Relation to the Social Entitlement Chamber of the First-tier Tribunal on or after 1 October 2014*, 18 September, paras 3 and 4
147 r4(3) TP(FT) Rules
148 r17(4) and (5) TP(FT) Rules
149 *FI v (1) SSWP (2) MC (CSM)* [2020] UKUT 173 (AAC)
150 r32 TP(FT) Rules; r39 TP(UT) Rules
151 s26 SSA 1998
152 s26(5) SSA 1998
153 rr5(3)(b) and 18 TP(FT) Rules

4. How the tribunal makes its decision

154 r1(3) TP(FT) Rules
155 r21(2) and 27(1) TP(FT) Rules; *MH v Pembrokeshire CC (HB)* [2010] UKUT 28 (AAC); *AT v SSWP (ESA)* [2010] UKUT 430 (AAC); *MM v SSWP (ESA)* [2011] UKUT 334 (AAC)
156 *RA v SSWP (II)* [2021] UKUT 148 (AAC)
157 *JS v Wirral MBC (HB)* [2021] UKUT 219 (AAC)
158 s55(b) and Sch 25 para 2 CA 2020; r5A TP(FT) Rules
159 r11 TP(FT) Rules
160 r21 TP(FT) Rules
161 r1 TP(FT) Rules, definition of 'hearing'
162 r24(6) and (7) TP(FT) Rules
163 *MP v SSWP (DLA)* [2010] UKUT 103 (AAC)
164 r5(3)(f) TP(FT) Rules; *DT v SSWP (UC)* [2019] UKUT 268 (AAC)
165 r29 TP(FT) Rules
166 CH/3594/2002
167 r31 TP(FT) Rules; *WT v SSWP (DLA)* [2011] UKUT 93 (AAC)
168 *PS v SSWP (ESA)* [2017] UKUT 55 (AAC)
169 *KD v SSWP (ESA and IS) and KD and HMRC (TC)* [2020] UKUT 9 (AAC)
170 *LR v SSWP (ESA)* [2017] UKUT 412 (AAC)
171 *RK v SSWP (ESA)* [2018] UKUT 436 (AAC)
172 *AK v HMRC (TC)* [2016] UKUT 98 (AAC)
173 r30 TP(FT) Rules

174 Practice Direction: *Child, Vulnerable Adult and Sensitive Witnesses*, 30 October 2008; *SW v SSWP (DLA)* [2015] UKUT 319 (AAC); *LO'L v SSWP (ESA)* [2016] UKUT 10 (AAC), reported as [2016] AACR 31; *RT v SSWP (PIP)* [2019] UKUT 207 (AAC), reported as [2020] AACR 4; *JE v SSWP (PIP)* [2020] UKUT 17 (AAC)
175 r1(3) TP(FT) Rules, definition of 'hearing'
176 *LO'L v SSWP (ESA)* [2016] UKUT 10 (AAC), reported as [2016] AACR 31
177 *KO v SSWP (ESA)* [2013] UKUT 544 (AAC); *LS v SSWP (DLA)* [2015] UKUT 638 (AAC); *DB v SSWP (DLA)* [2016] UKUT 205 (AAC)
178 *LS v Lambeth LB (HB)* [2010] UKUT 461 (AAC), reported as [2011] AACR 27
179 CIB/2751/2002; CDLA/1350/2004
180 r11 TP(FT) Rules; CIB/1009/2004; CIB/2058/2004
181 r11(7) and (8) TP(FT) Rules
182 *ZO v SSWP (IB)* [2010] UKUT 143 (AAC); *AS v SSWP (ESA)* [2019] UKUT 261 (AAC)
183 r2 The First-tier Tribunal and Upper Tribunal (Composition of Tribunal) Order 2008 No.2835; Practice Statement: *Composition of Tribunals in Social Security and Child Support Cases in the Social Entitlement Chamber on or after 1 August 2013*, 31 July 2013
184 *CH v SSWP (ESA)* [2017] UKUT 6 (AAC)
185 *MB and Others v SSWP (ESA & DLA)* [2013] UKUT 111 (AAC), reported as [2014] AACR 1
186 Sch 4 para 15(6) TCEA 2007; *SB v SSWP (DLA)* [2013] UKUT 531 (AAC); *PF v SSWP (ESA)* [2015] UKUT 553 (AAC)
187 *PJ v SSWP (ESA)* [2011] UKUT 224 (AAC); *MB and Others v SSWP (ESA & DLA)* [2013] UKUT 111 (AAC), reported as [2014] AACR 1
188 R(U) 3/88; *JH v SSWP and MH* [2016] UKUT 158 (AAC); *SW v SSWP (ESA)* [2019] UKUT 415 (AAC)
189 *Gillies v SSWP* [2006] UKHL 2, reported as R(DLA) 5/06
190 *SSWP v Cunningham* [2004] ScotCS 211, reported as R(DLA) 7/04; R(DLA) 3/07
191 Practice Statement: *Composition of Tribunals in Social Security and Child Support Cases in the Social Entitlement Chamber on or after 1 August 2013*, 31 July 2013, para 12
192 r2 TP(FT) Rules
193 CSDLA/606/2003
194 *PM v SSWP (PIP)* [2017] UKUT 154 (AAC)
195 CM/527/1992; CIB/3074/2003
196 CIB/5586/1999

Part 9: Getting a benefit decision changed
Chapter 57: Appealing to the First-tier Tribunal
Notes

- -

197 CIB/476/2005; CIB/511/2005
198 r25(4) TP(FT) Rules
199 R(DLA) 1/95, qualified by CM/2/1994;
    GL v SSWP [2008] UKUT 36 (AAC)
200 ID v SSWP (PIP) [2015] UKUT 692 (AAC);
    KMN v SSWP (PIP) [2019] UKUT 42
    (AAC)
201 R(DLA) 8/06
202 HI v SSWP [2014] UKUT 238 (AAC)
203 s20(3) SSA 1998
204 R(IB) 2/06
205 s20(3) SSA 1998; r25(2) TP(FT) Rules;
    R(DLA) 5/03
206 CI/3384/2006
207 Practice Statement: Composition of
    Tribunals in Social Security and Child
    Support Cases in the Social Entitlement
    Chamber on or after 1 August 2013, 31
    July 2013, para 14
208 ss20(2) and 39 SSA 1998; r25(3) and
    Sch 2 TP(FT) Rules; SSWP v DB (PIP)
    [2016] UKUT 212 (AAC)
209 s20(2A) SSA 1998
210 CDLA/2014/2004
211 GL v SSWP [2008] UKUT 36 (AAC); HI v
    SSWP [2014] UKUT 238 (AAC)
212 CH/1229/2002
213 Mongan v Department for Social
    Development [2005] NICA 16, reported
    as R3/05 (DLA); KN v SSWP (ESA) [2021]
    UKUT 155 (AAC)
214 **HB** Sch 7 para 6(9)(a) CSPSSA 2000
    Other benefits s12(8)(a) SSA 1998
    All DT v SSWP (PIP) [2020] UKUT 156
    (AAC)
215 Mooney v SSWP [2004] SLT 1141,
    reported as R(DLA) 5/04; Mongan v
    Department for Social Development
    [2005] NICA 16, reported as R3/05
    (DLA); SSWP v Hooper [2007] EWCA Civ
    495, reported as R(IB) 4/07; KKL v SSWP
    (CPIP) [2018] UKUT 17 (AAC)
216 KKL v SSWP (CPIP) [2018] UKUT 17
    (AAC)
217 CSDLA/336/2000; CSIB/160/2000;
    R(H) 1/02
218 CH/1229/2002; R(IB) 2/04; AP-H v SSWP
    (DLA) [2010] UKUT 183 (AAC)
219 CI/531/2000; CDLA/1000/2001; CH/
    1229/2002; R(IB) 2/04; CDLA/884/
    2008; ET v SSWP (PIP) [2017] UKUT 478
    (AAC); LJ v SSWP (PIP) [2017] UKUT 455
    (AAC)
220 CDLA/4184/2004
221 R(IB) 2/04
222 R(IB) 2/04; CH/3009/2002
223 CDLA/1707/2005
224 R(IB) 2/04; R(IB) 7/04; CIS/1675/2004

225 **HB** Sch 7 para 6(9)(b) CSPSSA 2000
    Other benefits s12(8)(b) SSA 1998;
    R(DLA) 4/05
226 R(DLA) 2/01; R(DLA) 3/01; CJSA/2375/
    2000; KK v Liverpool City Council (HB)
    [2020] UKUT 80 (AAC)
227 R(SB) 4/85

5. Preparing your appeal
228 s3(1) HRA 1998
229 RR v SSWP [2019] UKSC 52
230 Leeds City Council v Price [2006] UKHL 10
231 R(I) 12/75; Dorset Healthcare Trust v MH
    [2009] UKUT 4 (AAC); CT v SSWP (ESA)
    [2021] UKUT 131 (AAC)
232 R(SB) 22/86
233 R(I) 12/75; Dorset Healthcare Trust v MH
    [2009] UKUT 4 (AAC)
234 CSBO v Leary, reported as R(SB) 6/85;
    see generally CS/140/1991
235 The European Union (Withdrawal) Act
    2018 (Relevant Court) (Retained EU
    Case Law) Regulations 2020 No.1525
236 R(G) 3/62; R(U) 4/88
237 R(U) 4/88
238 Nancollas v Insurance Officer [1985] 1 All
    ER 833 (CA), reported as R(I) 7/85
239 r15(2) TP(FT) Rules
240 r15(1)(e) and (f) TP(FT) Rules
241 r15(2) TP(FT) Rules
242 R(SB) 33/85; R(SB) 12/89
243 JM v SSWP [2012] UKUT 472 (AAC)
244 SSWP v Cunningham [2004] ScotCS 211,
    reported as R(DLA) 7/04; R(DLA) 3/07
245 R(DLA) 4/02; CIS/1481/2006; DG v
    SSWP (DLA) [2011] UKUT 14 (AAC); BS v
    SSWP (DLA) [2016] UKUT 73 (AAC),
    reported as [2016] AACR 32; TD v SSWP
    (PIP) [2020] UKUT 283 (AAC)
246 AF v SSWP (DLA) (No.2) [2017] UKUT
    366 (AAC)
247 CIB/2058/2004
248 r11(5) TP(FT) Rules; CDLA/1138/2003;
    CDLA/2462/2003; SK v SSWP (ESA)
    [2014] UKUT 141 (AAC)
249 r15(1)(d) TP(FT) Rules; CDLA/2014/
    2004
250 R(SB) 6/82
251 r16 TP(FT) Rules
252 CIS/4901/2002
253 Walsall MBC v PL [2009] UKUT 27 (AAC)

6. The tribunal's decision
254 r33 TP(FT) Rules
255 Art 8 First-tier Tribunal and Upper
    Tribunal (Composition of Tribunal)
    Order 2008 No.2835

9

256 PF (Nigeria) v Secretary of State for the
Home Department [2015] EWCA Civ
251, reported as 1 WLR 5235
257 Practice Statement, Record of
Proceedings in Social Security and Child
Support Cases in the Social Entitlement
Chamber on or after 3 November 2008,
30 October 2008
258 MK v SSWP (CI) [2014] UKUT 323 (AAC)
259 s29ZA(2)(b) TCEA 2007; r30A TP(FT)
Rules
260 DT v SSWP [2015] UKUT 509 (AAC)
261 r34(2) TP(FT) Rules
262 r34(3) TP(FT) Rules; CCS/1664/2001
263 r34(4) TP(FT) Rules; CIB/3937/2000
264 r5(3)(a) TP(FT) Rules
265 r34(5) TP(FT) Rules
266 r38(7)(a) TP(FT) Rules
267 RU v SSWP (ESA) [2014] UKUT 532 (AAC)
268 r5(3)(n) TP(UT) Rules
269 **UC/PIP/JSA&ESA under UC** s21 SSA
1998; reg 44 UC,PIP,JSA&ESA(DA) Regs
HB Sch 7 para 13 CSPSSA 2000; reg 11
HB&CTB(DA) Regs
CB/GA s21 SSA 1998; reg 18
CB&GA(DA) Regs
Other benefits s21 SSA 1998; reg 16
SS&CS(DA) Regs
270 r5(3)(l) TP(FT) Rules
271 r36 TP(FT) Rules; CI/3887/1999;
CSDLA/168/2008; AS v SSWP (ESA)
[2011] UKUT 159 (AAC)
272 r37(1) and (2) TP(FT) Rules
273 MA v SSWP (PIP) [2020] UKUT 2 (AAC)
274 r37(3) TP(FT) Rules
275 r5(3)(a) TP(FT) Rules
276 r27(2) TP(FT) Rules; CSB/172/1990
277 CIB/4193/2003
278 CI/79/1990; CIS/373/1994; MA v SSWP
(PIP) [2020] UKUT 2 (AAC)
279 LS v Lambeth LB (HB) [2010] UKUT 461
(AAC), reported as [2011] AACR 27
280 r38(3) and (4) TP(FT) Rules
281 r41 TP(FT) Rules
282 **HB** Sch 7 para 7(3) and (4) CSPSSA
2000
Other benefits s13(3) and (4) SSA
1998

9

Chapter 58

Appealing to the Upper Tribunal and the courts

This chapter covers:
1. Appealing to the Upper Tribunal (below)
2. How to appeal to the Upper Tribunal (p1360)
3. After you get permission to appeal (p1366)
4. Hearings (p1369)
5. The decision (p1370)
6. Appealing to the Court of Appeal or Court of Session (p1372)

This chapter does *not* cover the rules for appeals to the Upper Tribunal for Scotland about the Scottish social security benefits (see Chapter 80).

Key facts

- If your appeal to the First-tier Tribunal is unsuccessful, you may be able to appeal to the Upper Tribunal, but only if the First-tier Tribunal made a legal mistake (an error of law). You must first get permission to appeal from the First-tier or Upper Tribunal.
- If your Upper Tribunal appeal is unsuccessful, you may be able to appeal to the Court of Appeal or the Court of Session.
- The DWP, local authority and HM Revenue and Customs can also appeal to the Upper Tribunal or the courts.
- There are strict time limits for appealing. They can sometimes be extended.
- Appeals can take time. If your circumstances change while you are waiting for your appeal to be heard, you may need to make a fresh claim for benefit or request a supersession.

1. Appealing to the Upper Tribunal

You have a right of appeal against any First-tier Tribunal decision (except an excluded decision – see p1357) to the Administrative Appeals Chamber of the Upper Tribunal.[1] Your appeal is dealt with by a judge (or judges). HM Courts and

Tribunals Service (HMCTS) is responsible for the administration of the tribunal's work.

Excluded decisions[2]

'Excluded decisions' are certain decisions taken by the First-tier Tribunal when it considers a review (see p1364) – ie, decisions:

– to review, or not to review, an earlier decision;
– to take no action, or not to take any particular action, in the light of a review of an earlier decision;
– to set aside an earlier decision on review (the decision that is set aside is also excluded);
– to refer, or not to refer, a matter to the Upper Tribunal.

You can only appeal to the Upper Tribunal if the First-tier Tribunal made a legal mistake – ie, an 'error of law' (see below).[3] You must first apply for, and obtain, permission to appeal and there is a strict time limit for applying (see p1363 and p1366). The DWP, the local authority and HM Revenue and Customs (HMRC) have the same appeal rights as you.

If you have evidence not known by the First-tier Tribunal, you may be able to ask the DWP, the local authority or HMRC for a supersession of the tribunal's decision on the grounds that there was a mistake about or ignorance of the facts (see p1277). You can do this while you are waiting for your appeal to be heard. Bear in mind that the amount of arrears you can get with a supersession is usually limited, so you need to continue with your appeal at the same time.

Note:

- If a decision in a test case is pending that deals with issues raised in your appeal, the Upper Tribunal may delay your appeal. For when the decision maker can serve a notice requiring the tribunal to delay your appeal, see p1324 – the rules are the same as for the First-tier Tribunal.
- Some Upper Tribunal decisions can be made by legally qualified HMCTS staff (called 'registrars').[4] You can ask an Upper Tribunal judge to reconsider a registrar's decision. You must apply in writing within 14 days after the date you are sent notice of the decision. The tribunal can give you longer (or shorter) than this. There is no guarantee you will be given longer, so keep within the time limit wherever possible.

Error of law

An 'error of law' is a legal mistake. The error must have made a difference to the outcome of the appeal. The First-tier Tribunal made an error of law in the following situations.[5]

- The tribunal got the law wrong or misinterpreted it – eg, it misunderstood the particular benefit rule concerned. **Note:** if the tribunal gives the reasons for its

Part 9: Getting a benefit decision changed
Chapter 58: Appealing to the Upper Tribunal and the courts
1. Appealing to the Upper Tribunal

decision in its decision notice (see p1345) and these indicate that it did not apply the law correctly, the decision notice is likely to be a more reliable statement of its reasons than a later conflicting explanation in a statement of reasons.[6]

- The tribunal gave you a physical examination when it was not permitted to do so (see p1332) and based its decision on evidence obtained from this.[7]
- There were errors due to unfairness in how the appeal was decided (see below).
- The tribunal made errors about the facts (see p1359) – ie, it failed to make proper findings of fact or did not make use of those findings correctly in coming to its decision.
- The tribunal did not provide adequate reasons for its decision (see p1360).

What if a different tribunal would have made a different decision?

The First-tier Tribunal has not made an error of law simply because a different First-tier Tribunal (or the Upper Tribunal) might have reached a different conclusion.[8] An appeal to the Upper Tribunal is *not* another opportunity for you to argue about the facts of the case.[9]

Errors due to unfairness in how the appeal was decided

The First-tier Tribunal made an error of law if there were procedural or other irregularities that could make a material difference to the outcome or fairness of the proceedings. That could occur due to a breach of the principles of natural justice or a failure to follow a procedural rule, Practice Statement or Practice Direction. Examples of procedural unfairness include if:

- you have not been given the opportunity to present your case;
- there has been bias in the conduct of your case.

Not given the opportunity to present the case

The First-tier Tribunal made an error of law if you have not been given the opportunity to present your case – eg:

- a hearing was requested but one did not take place;[10]
- you did not get notice of the hearing through no fault of your own and so you lost the appeal without having had a chance to put your case properly, even if you could have applied for the tribunal's decision to be set aside instead;[11]
- you did not receive the decision maker's response or did not receive it in sufficient time before the hearing, or you did not receive advance notice of documentary evidence that you had not seen before, and were not given an opportunity to read it properly;[12]
- the tribunal failed to properly consider and explain why it felt it was fair to proceed to determine the appeal without a hearing, or in your absence. Even if you did not ask for a hearing, the tribunal still needs to consider whether it is fair to proceed without one;[13]

- the tribunal failed to include you as a party to the appeal when it should have been obvious that you had an interest in the outcome of the case – eg, in your child's other parent's appeal if there is a dispute about who should receive child benefit;[14]
- the tribunal failed to act on a request for an interpreter and, as a result, it was unable to understand your evidence correctly;[15]
- you are not allowed to call witnesses who are likely to be able to give relevant evidence to support you;
- the standard of interpretation was not adequate and the tribunal did not take appropriate action;[16]
- the tribunal made a decision without a hearing, based on the papers only, that was more unfavourable to you than the one you had appealed – eg, it removed your entitlement to benefit without warning you or giving you the chance to make representations.[17]

Bias in the conduct of the case

The First-tier Tribunal made an error of law if there has been bias in the conduct of your case. That is, the circumstances would lead a fair minded and informed observer to conclude that there was a real possibility that one or more of the tribunal members regarded a party with favour or disfavour – eg:

- the person presenting the DWP case (the presenting officer) is allowed to be in the room with the tribunal members without you;[18]
- the way the tribunal conducted your case made it look like it had already made up its mind before the hearing commenced;
- the tribunal pressurises you into giving up your right to a fair hearing – eg, it bargains with you by 'offering' you one component of personal independence payment if you agree not to argue for the other. **Note:** if you decide to carry on with the appeal and the tribunal decides not to award the component 'offered', it should warn you before the hearing ends to allow you to consider this and make representations. This should be recorded in the statement of reasons for its decision.[19]

Errors about the facts

The First-tier Tribunal made an error of law if:

- there is no evidence to support its decision; *or*
- when making its conclusions from the facts, it took things into account which it should not have, or refused or failed to take things into account which it should have (see p1333). However, the tribunal has not necessarily made an error of law if it fails to take account of evidence that was not before it at the hearing – ie, evidence only produced when your appeal is before the Upper Tribunal; *or*

Part 9: Getting a benefit decision changed
Chapter 58: Appealing to the Upper Tribunal and the courts
2. How to appeal to the Upper Tribunal

- the facts are inconsistent with the decision – eg, the tribunal accepted that a man and a woman live in separate households, but then decided that they are living together as a married couple;[20] or
- it does not give proper findings of fact. The tribunal must show there are sufficient facts to support its decision.[21] It can rely on the summary of the facts given in the decision maker's response (see p1314), provided these are not in dispute and they cover all the relevant issues.[22] If you and the DWP, the local authority or HMRC disagree about the facts, the tribunal must explain which version it prefers and why. It should refer to the main evidence on which it has relied. However, it is not necessarily an error of law if it does not mention every item of evidence put forward. The tribunal should give an adequate explanation of why it rejected any piece of evidence as untrue;[23] or
- it made a mistake about a fact that would have made a difference to the outcome of your appeal, there was unfairness as a result, and the fact could have been established by objective and uncontentious evidence. This only applies if you and your adviser were not responsible for the mistake.[24]

Inadequate reasons for the decision

The First-tier Tribunal made an error of law if it does not provide adequate reasons for its decision.[25] The tribunal must not simply say what its decision is; it must give sufficient reasons so that you can see why it reached the conclusion it did. If the summary of the reasons given in the decision notice are inconsistent with those given in its written statement of reasons, this is an error of law.[26] If a delay in writing the reasons indicates that they are unreliable as an accurate statement of the tribunal's reasoning, you can argue that the reasons are inadequate.[27]

Note: the tribunal does not have to give its reasons for refusing to adjourn an appeal hearing.[28] However, a refusal to adjourn may be so obviously unfair that it constitutes an error of law.

2. How to appeal to the Upper Tribunal

You must obtain permission to appeal to the Upper Tribunal.[29] This means you must show that the First-tier Tribunal has possibly made an error of law (see p1357) and you have the beginnings of a case. You must first apply to the First-tier Tribunal for permission. If it refuses (or rejects) your application, you can then apply for permission direct to the Upper Tribunal. There are strict time limits for applying for permission to appeal (see p1363 and p1366).

Note: because of the length of time you usually have to wait before your case is dealt with, you should make a fresh claim for benefit (or request a supersession) – eg, if your circumstances change. See p1334 for the advantages of doing this (the issues are similar to those for First-tier Tribunal appeals).

Representatives

You can have a representative to help you with your appeal.[30] S/he can explain the procedures, present your case and produce a written submission to ensure the Upper Tribunal is aware of all the relevant issues and the law. You must send or give the tribunal written notice of your representative's name and address, or s/he must do this on your behalf. Unless s/he is a solicitor or barrister, if your representative is providing the notice, s/he should also provide an authorisation signed by you.

Note:

- You must authorise your representative to act for you in your appeal to the Upper Tribunal, even if s/he acted for you in your appeal to the First-tier Tribunal and you authorised her/him at an earlier stage. Once you have given notice that you have a representative, s/he is presumed to be acting for you unless you give (or s/he gives) notice in writing that this is no longer the case.[31] Your representative must be sent any documents that are required to be sent to you; these then do not have to be sent to you.[32] However, do not assume that this always happens. If you receive documents, check that your representative has also received them;

- If you have not previously notified the tribunal that you have a representative, someone can attend a hearing with (or for) you and act as your representative and help you present your case, if the tribunal agrees.[33]

Can your representative or adviser get help with your appeal?

If you live in England or Wales, your representative, adviser or support worker may be able to get advice about, and assistance with, your appeal to the Upper Tribunal from CPAG under its Upper Tribunal Assistance Project. This can include advice on procedure and the merits of your case, as well as help making your application for permission to appeal. In some cases, CPAG may be able to provide representation. See cpag.org.uk/upper-tribunal-assistance-project for further information and an online referral form.

Meeting the costs of representation

Free legal help from a solicitor is available in limited cases. This is means tested. If you cannot qualify, you may be able to get free help from your local Citizens Advice office, law centre, welfare rights service or advice centre.

If you are resident in England or Wales, free legal help is available for advice and assistance with appealing to the Upper Tribunal, including applications for permission to appeal that are made direct to the Upper Tribunal, but you will only qualify for help from a lawyer to cover representation at a hearing in exceptional cases – if it is necessary to make these services available to you because a failure to do so would be a breach of your right to have legal representation as provided under human rights law or your retained enforceable European Union rights.[34]

Part 9: Getting a benefit decision changed
Chapter 58: Appealing to the Upper Tribunal and the courts
2. How to appeal to the Upper Tribunal

If you are resident in Scotland, free legal help is currently available for Upper Tribunal appeals, including for help preparing for appeals that will be decided at a hearing and those that will be decided on the papers only. If the Scottish Legal Aid Board approves and the Upper Tribunal is sitting in Scotland, you can get help with representation. The Board only gives approval if it is satisfied that your case is arguable, it is reasonable for representation to be made available and your case is too complex for you to be able to present it effectively yourself in person – eg, if there is likely to be procedural difficulty or a substantial question of law, if the evidence is complex, or if you may be unable to understand the proceedings or to state your own case because of a disability, your age or your knowledge of English.[35]

If you are granted funding for legal help, you must send a copy of the funding notice (in Scotland, the legal aid certificate) to the Upper Tribunal as soon as practicable.[36] You must also let the other parties involved in your appeal know that you have been granted funding.

Applying to the First-tier Tribunal for permission

You must apply for permission to appeal, in the first instance, to the First-tier Tribunal.[37] Before applying, you should obtain a statement of reasons for its decision (see p1346). If you do not have a statement of reasons, see p1363.

Your application for permission to appeal must:[38]
- be in writing; *and*
- contain:
  - details of your grounds for appeal (ie, the error(s) of law you think the tribunal made); *and*
  - sufficient information about the decision for it to be identified; *and*
  - if you are making a late application, your reasons for this; *and*
- state the result you are seeking – eg, that permission to appeal should be given and the Upper Tribunal should send the case back to the First-tier Tribunal for a new hearing.

Bear in mind that the person considering your application is often the same judge who decided your appeal, although this is not always the case.[39] Applications for permission to appeal are normally decided without a hearing, so make sure you give a full explanation of your grounds for appeal when you apply.[40]

The First-tier Tribunal must send you a record of its decision on your application as soon as practicable.[41] If your application is refused, reasons for the refusal must be provided, as well as notice of your right to make a fresh application to the Upper Tribunal for permission to appeal, along with information about how to apply, and the time limit for doing so. You should study the First-tier Tribunal's reasons for refusal carefully. Be prepared to rethink your arguments before applying to the Upper Tribunal.

If you, the DWP, the local authority or HM Revenue and Customs (HMRC) apply for permission to appeal to the Upper Tribunal, the First-tier Tribunal can review its decision (see p1364) or treat the application for permission to appeal as an application for the decision to be corrected or 'set aside'.[42] If you and the other party agree that the tribunal made an error of law, its decision *must* be set aside (see p1349).

If you do not have a statement of reasons

You may find it difficult to show that the First-tier Tribunal made an error of law if you do not have a statement of reasons for its decision. **Note:** if you do not have a statement of reasons because:[43]

- you did not apply for one, the First-tier Tribunal must treat your application for permission to appeal as an application for a statement of reasons. Once the statement of reasons is provided, unless the tribunal decides to give you permission to appeal, you must then apply for permission to appeal again;
- your application for one was refused when you missed the time limit (see p1346), the First-tier Tribunal can only allow your application for permission to appeal to go ahead ('admit' your application) if it thinks it is in the interests of justice.[44] If it admits your application, it then decides whether or not to give you permission. If it rejects your application (ie, refuses to admit it) or refuses to give you permission, you can still apply direct to the Upper Tribunal for permission.

Time limit for applying

Your application for permission to appeal must be received by the First-tier Tribunal no later than one month (see p1306 for the meaning) after the latest of the following dates – ie, the date you were sent:[45]

- the decision notice; *or*
- a written statement of reasons (see p1346) for the tribunal's decision; *or*
- notice that, following a review (see p1364), the reasons for the tribunal's decision were amended, or the decision was corrected; *or*
- notice that an application for the tribunal's decision to be set aside (see p1348) was unsuccessful, but only if that application was made within the time limit for applying for a set aside (or any longer period allowed).

The tribunal can extend (or shorten) your time limit.[46] There is no absolute time limit for applying, but the longer you delay, the harder it may be to show that the time limit should be extended. There is no guarantee that you will be given longer, so keep within the one-month time limit wherever possible. See p1308 for when it might be fair and just to extend your time limit.

If your time limit is not extended, the First-tier Tribunal must reject your application.[47] If your application is rejected, you can still apply direct to the Upper Tribunal for permission. However, the Upper Tribunal can only allow your

Part 9: Getting a benefit decision changed
Chapter 58: Appealing to the Upper Tribunal and the courts
2. How to appeal to the Upper Tribunal

application to go ahead ('admit' your application) if it considers it is in the interests of justice to do so.[48]

When the First-tier Tribunal can review its decision

When the First-tier Tribunal receives an application for permission to appeal to the Upper Tribunal, it must first consider whether or not to review its own decision.[49] It should not go on to consider the application until it has decided not to review its decision, or decided to review it but to take no action. However, if it does go on, that does not necessarily make its decision about permission invalid.[50] You do not have a right to apply for a review yourself, but if you do, your application can be treated as an application for permission to appeal.[51]

The First-tier Tribunal can only review a decision if it is satisfied that there is an error of law in it (see p1357).[52] If it decides to carry out a review, it should consider whether to give you and the decision maker an opportunity to comment. This means that if the DWP, local authority or HMRC has applied for permission to appeal, you have the chance to say why the decision should not be changed. If the tribunal *does* review the decision, it can:[53]

- correct any accidental errors in the decision or the record of the decision; *and*
- amend the reasons given for the decision – eg, if it considered matters, but inadvertently did not include them in the statement of reasons. However, the tribunal should not add reasons which were not part of its thinking at the time it made its decision;[54] *and*
- 'set aside' the decision. This means the decision is cancelled. The tribunal usually then directs a new tribunal to make a new decision. In rare circumstances, it makes a new decision itself at the same time as it reviews the decision. The tribunal also has the power to refer your appeal to the Upper Tribunal to make a decision, but this power is rarely used.

You must be notified in writing of the outcome of the review and your right of appeal (if any).[55] If the First-tier Tribunal has taken any action and you were not given an opportunity to comment before the review, you must also be notified that you can apply for the action to be cancelled and for the decision to be reviewed again.

If the First-tier Tribunal decides not to review its decision, or reviews it but takes no action, it must consider whether to give you permission to appeal to the Upper Tribunal against the decision.[56]

Applying to the Upper Tribunal for permission

Before you can apply to the Upper Tribunal for permission to appeal, you must first apply to the First-tier Tribunal.[57] If the First-tier Tribunal refuses you permission or rejects your application (eg, because it was late), you can then make a fresh application to the Upper Tribunal. You must apply in writing.

Forms

Use Form UT1 Application for permission and Notice of Appeal From First-tier Tribunal (Social Entitlement Chamber). This is available at gov.uk/government/collections/administrative-appeals-chamber-upper-tribunal-forms or from the regional office of HM Courts and Tribunals Service (HMCTS) or the Upper Tribunal Office (see gov.uk/courts-tribunals/upper-tribunal-administrative-appeals-chamber for the addresses).

Your application must include:[58]

- your name and address, the name and address of your representative (if any) and the address where documents can be sent or delivered. If you have an appointee, the appeal form asks for her/his details; *and*
- details of the decision you want to appeal (eg, the date of the decision) and the First-tier Tribunal reference number; *and*
- the grounds for your appeal – ie, the error(s) of law you think the First-tier Tribunal made; *and*
- if your application is late, a request for your time limit to be extended and the reasons why you are applying late; *and*
- whether you want your application to be dealt with at a hearing; *and*
- copies of the First-tier Tribunal's decision, its statement of reasons and the notice of its rejection or refusal of your application for permission. If your application to the First-tier Tribunal was rejected because it (or your application for a statement of reasons) was late, you must also include the reasons for the lateness.

The Upper Tribunal can waive any irregularities in your application in some cases.[59] If your application to the First-tier Tribunal for permission to appeal was rejected because it was late or your application for a statement of reasons was late, the Upper Tribunal can only allow your application for permission to appeal to go ahead ('admit' your application) if it thinks it is in the interests of justice to do so.[60] If your application is admitted, it then goes on to decide whether to give you permission to appeal.

The appeal form asks whether you want a hearing of your application.

What if you do not have a statement of reasons?

If you do not have a statement of reasons for the First-tier Tribunal's decision, you are not prevented from applying to the Upper Tribunal for permission to appeal. However, you must be able to show that the First-tier Tribunal made an error of law (see p1357) without it – eg, from what is said in the decision notice.[61] It is an error of law if the First-tier Tribunal fails to provide a statement of reasons where it has a duty to do so – eg, you apply for one in time, but the tribunal says your application was late and refuses to provide one.[62]

Part 9: Getting a benefit decision changed
Chapter 58: Appealing to the Upper Tribunal and the courts
3. After you get permission to appeal

The appeal form asks you to send your application by email if possible (to adminappeals@justice.gov.uk if your appeal was in England or Wales, or UTAACMailbox@justice.gov.uk if your appeal was in Scotland). You can also send your application to the Upper Tribunal office by post, fax or document exchange, or deliver it in person. The tribunal can also permit you to send it by other methods.[63]

The Upper Tribunal obtains the file of your appeal papers from the regional HMCTS office. It considers these as well as what you say in your application before reaching a decision. The DWP, local authority or HMRC normally plays no part in the procedure at this stage, although the tribunal sometimes asks it to make a submission in cases of particular difficulty. If this happens, you are given an opportunity to reply.

You are sent a written notice of the tribunal's decision on your application, usually including the reasons for the decision.[64] You cannot appeal against a refusal to admit your application to appeal or to give you permission to appeal, but you might be able to apply for the decision to be set aside (see p1371) or to a court for judicial review (see p1388).[65]

Time limit for applying

Your application for permission to appeal must be received by the Upper Tribunal no later than one month (see p1306) after the date the First-tier Tribunal's refusal (or rejection) was sent to you.[66] The Upper Tribunal can extend (or shorten) your time limit.[67] There is no guarantee that you will be given longer, so keep within the one-month time limit wherever possible.

The decision whether or not to allow a late appeal to the Upper Tribunal must be made bearing in mind the merits of the appeal and the consequences for you (and the DWP, the local authority or HMRC).[68] See p1308 for when it might be fair and just to extend your time limit. The issues are the same as for appeals to the First-tier Tribunal. If your time limit is not extended, the Upper Tribunal rejects your application to appeal and your appeal does not go ahead.

3. After you get permission to appeal

If you have been given permission to appeal by the First-tier Tribunal, you must send the Upper Tribunal:[69]

- a 'notice of appeal', so that it is received within one month after you are sent notice of the permission. You are sent Form UT1 Application for permission and Notice of Appeal From First-tier Tribunal (Social Entitlement Chamber) on which to do this; *and*
- if you are sending the notice of appeal late, a request for an extension of time and the reasons why your notice is late; *and*
- a copy of the notice that you have been given permission to appeal; *and*

- a copy of the First-tier Tribunal's decision and its statement of reasons (if you have one); *and*
- your details; *and*
- your reasons for appealing against the decision.

The Upper Tribunal can extend (or shorten) the time limit for receipt of your notice of appeal.[70] There is no guarantee that you will be given longer, so keep within the time limit wherever possible. See p1308 for when it might be fair and just to extend your time limit. The issues are the same as for appeals to the First-tier Tribunal. If your time limit is not extended, the Upper Tribunal rejects your appeal and it does not go ahead.

Note: if you have applied for permission to appeal direct to the Upper Tribunal on Form UT1, unless you are told otherwise, your application is treated as a notice of appeal. In this case, you do not need to send in another.[71]

What the Upper Tribunal can do

There are procedural rules that the Upper Tribunal must follow when dealing with your appeal. Whenever the Upper Tribunal is considering applying these procedural rules it must bear in mind the 'overriding objective' which is to enable it to deal with cases fairly and justly.[72] This includes avoiding delay (provided the issues can be considered properly), avoiding unnecessary formality, allowing flexibility in the proceedings and ensuring that all the parties can participate fully. You, the DWP, the local authority and HM Revenue and Customs (HMRC) must help the tribunal further the objective and co-operate with it. This involves ensuring, as far as possible, that your case is ready by the time of any hearing.[73] The rules are generally the same as for the First-tier Tribunal, so where relevant, these are referred to below.

The Upper Tribunal can do the following.[74]

- Extend or shorten any time limits (see p1318). For the rules about extending your time limit for applying for permission to appeal, see p1363 and p1366.
- Issue directions (see p1318).
- Postpone or adjourn your appeal hearing (see p1319).
- 'Strike out' an appeal (see p1321). Note: the Upper Tribunal does *not* have the discretion to strike out your appeal on the grounds that there is no reasonable prospect of success.
- Bar people from taking part in an appeal (see p1322). Note: *you* can be barred from taking part in an appeal to the Upper Tribunal if the other party appealed.
- Require the First-tier Tribunal to provide reasons for its decision, or other information or documents relating to its decision or the proceedings.[75]
- Summons witnesses to attend a hearing, answer questions and produce documents. If someone fails to comply, the tribunal can punish her/him for contempt of court.[76] Note: you cannot be required to give evidence or produce any document that you could not be compelled to give by a court.[77]

Part 9: Getting a benefit decision changed
Chapter 58: Appealing to the Upper Tribunal and the courts
3. After you get permission to appeal

- Suspend the effect of its decision while considering any application for permission to appeal against, or review of, that decision. It can also suspend the effect of a First-tier Tribunal decision while an application for permission to appeal against the decision is being considered, and pending that appeal being determined.[78]

Withdrawing an appeal

If you change your mind about appealing, you can withdraw your appeal.[79] However, once you have been given permission to appeal, you must have the Upper Tribunal's consent. You must give notice to the tribunal that you want to withdraw your appeal in writing or at a hearing.

Getting an appeal reinstated

If you withdraw your appeal but then decide that you want it to go ahead, you can apply for it to be reinstated.[80] You must apply in writing. Your application must be received by the Upper Tribunal within one month after the date it received written notice that you wanted to withdraw your appeal, or, if you withdraw your appeal at a hearing, within one month (see p1306) after the date of the hearing. The tribunal can give you longer (or shorter) than one month.[81] There is no guarantee that you will be given longer, so keep within the time limit wherever possible.

The written procedure

When permission to appeal has been given, the Upper Tribunal sends you a copy of the appeal file. This is the file that was used by the First-tier Tribunal plus any documents added since you first contacted the Upper Tribunal. You and the DWP, local authority or HMRC are asked for a response and are told the timetable for providing one.[82]

The decision maker is usually asked to provide a response first. DWP and HMRC responses are written by specialist staff working from national centres. They often take a different view than decision makers who have been involved previously and may even support your appeal.

You are given the chance to reply to the response and are usually given one month in which to do so, although the tribunal may extend (or shorten) the time limit.[83] There is no guarantee that you will be given longer, so keep within the time limit wherever possible. If you have nothing to add and do not want to reply at any stage, tell the tribunal.

If the decision maker supports your appeal, the tribunal may give its decision without reasons if you agree to this.[84]

Has the decision maker been given permission to appeal?

If you won your appeal at the First-tier Tribunal, the DWP, local authority or HMRC may have obtained permission to appeal to the Upper Tribunal. If so, you are asked to provide a response under the rules described above. It is very important to provide one. Consider the decision maker's arguments carefully and explain why you think the First-tier Tribunal did not make an error of law and why you think its decision was correct. Bear in mind that if the decision maker wins the appeal to the Upper Tribunal, the First-tier Tribunal's decision could be overturned and you could, for example, lose the benefit that it awarded to you, or have to repay an overpayment it said was not recoverable.

4. Hearings

The Upper Tribunal decides whether or not there should be a hearing of the appeal.[85] It must take your views, and those of the DWP, the local authority or HM Revenue and Customs (HMRC), into account. The form you are sent on which to provide your reply to the response (if you are bringing the appeal) or your response (if DWP, the local authority or HMRC is bringing the appeal) asks you whether you want a hearing and, if so, why. The tribunal can decide to hold a hearing, even if you have not asked for one. However, it normally only holds one if the case involves complicated issues of law that cannot easily be resolved by written arguments. If there is no hearing, the tribunal reaches a decision on the basis of the papers only – ie, the written responses and other documents provided.

Hearings can be in person or 'remote' hearings by telephone or video link.[86] You and your representative may be able to participate in the hearing via a video link such as Skype for Business or the HMCTS Cloud Video Platform – eg, if your disability makes it difficult for you to travel, or to avoid travel costs and time.

If the tribunal decides there should be a hearing, you must be given at least 14 days' notice, although you may get less notice than this if you agree, or your appeal is urgent or there are exceptional circumstances.[87]

Hearings are held on a regular basis in Cardiff, Edinburgh, London and Manchester, but can be held in other locations if necessary. You can claim for reimbursment of your travel costs and should be given a leaflet about this. A hearing closer to your home can be arranged in exceptional circumstances – eg, if you have difficulty travelling because of a disability. A judge decides whether or not to hold a local hearing based on, for example, medical evidence and why a local hearing is needed.

Usually, one judge hears your appeal. However, if there is a 'question of law of special difficulty', an important point of principle or practice, or it is otherwise appropriate, two or three judges may hear your appeal,[88] but the procedure is the same.

Part 9: Getting a benefit decision changed
Chapter 58: Appealing to the Upper Tribunal and the courts
5. The decision

Note:
- The tribunal may ask you to provide a summary of the arguments you are going to make (a 'skeleton argument') in advance of the hearing. If it does, you must provide one.[89] You should do this within the time you are allowed, and ensure it reaches the tribunal at least a week before the hearing.[90]
- The hearing is more formal than First-tier Tribunal hearings, but the judge lets you say everything you want to. Judges usually intervene a lot and ask questions, so be prepared to argue your case without your script.
- A full set of Upper Tribunal decisions and the statute law (see p1336) are available for your use.
- The decision maker is usually represented by a lawyer, so you should also consider obtaining representation – eg, from a solicitor, your local Citizens Advice or advice centre. See p1361 for meeting the costs of representation.

5. **The decision**

There are two stages to an Upper Tribunal decision.[91]
- **Stage one:** the tribunal decides whether the First-tier Tribunal made an error of law. If it decides that it did, the First-tier Tribunal's decision is normally 'set aside' and no longer has any effect. However, in some cases, the Upper Tribunal may decide that the error of law had no practical effect on the outcome of your appeal and so the decision does not have to be set aside.
- **Stage two:** if the First-tier Tribunal's decision is set aside, the Upper Tribunal decides how to deal with the case.
    - If it agrees that the First-tier Tribunal's decision was wrong, the case is often sent back to the First-tier Tribunal to hear your appeal again and make a new decision. The Upper Tribunal usually makes an order stating that the new tribunal should not include the judge or any of the members from the original appeal hearing and gives directions on how it should reconsider the issues. Note: at the new hearing, the First-tier Tribunal will not necessarily decide your appeal in your favour. However, you may be able to appeal to the Upper Tribunal again if there is another error of law.
    - If the Upper Tribunal thinks the First-tier Tribunal's statement of reasons for its decision contains all the material facts, or it has been able to make any necessary extra findings of fact, it may make the final decision. This might, or might not, be in your favour.

The Upper Tribunal's decision is usually given in writing, but may be given orally at the hearing.[92] You are normally not referred to by name in the decision.[93] Detailed reasons are given. You must be sent a decision notice as soon as is reasonably practicable, as well as notice of your right of appeal, how to appeal and the time limit for doing so. Decisions are often lengthy as they may need to explain difficult issues of law. So it may take time for the judge to prepare the decision. If there is undue delay, you can complain to the Adminstrative Appeals Chamber President.

If you disagree with the Upper Tribunal's decision

If you disagree with the Upper Tribunal's decision, you cannot simply ask it to look at the decision again – eg, if you have additional points to make. However, the following may be done.

- The tribunal may correct any clerical mistake or an accidental slip or omission in a decision or record of a decision.[94]
- The tribunal may 'set aside' its decision on procedural grounds – ie, how it handled your appeal.[95] If it sets aside a decision, this means the decision is cancelled. A decision can be set aside if the tribunal thinks it is in the interests of justice and:
  - you, your representative or the DWP, the local authority or HM Revenue and Customs (HMRC) were not sent papers or other documents relating to the proceedings, or did not receive them at an appropriate time, or the tribunal was not sent them at an appropriate time; *or*
  - you, your representative or the DWP, local authority or HMRC were not present at a hearing; *or*
  - there has been some other procedural irregularity in the proceedings in the Upper Tribunal.

  You must apply in writing for a decision to be set aside. Your application is dealt with by the judge who made the original decision. It must be received by the tribunal no later than one month after you were sent notice of the decision. The tribunal can extend (or shorten) this time limit. However, there is no guarantee that you will be given longer, so keep within the time limit wherever possible.[96] If you think the tribunal made a legal error, you must instead appeal to the Court of Appeal or Court of Session (see p1372) or, if relevant, apply for a judicial review (see Chapter 59).
- The decision can be superseded by the DWP, local authority or HMRC if there are grounds – eg, if there was a mistake about, or ignorance of, the facts (see p1274). However, if the tribunal made a mistake about the law, you must appeal to a court.
- You or the DWP, local authority or HMRC can appeal to the Court of Appeal (in Scotland, the Court of Session) – see p1372.
- If you (or the decision maker) seek permission to appeal to the Court of Appeal or Court of Session, the tribunal can review its decision (see p1373).

The Upper Tribunal can treat an application for a decision to be corrected, set aside or reviewed, or for permission to appeal against a decision, as an application for any other of these.[97]

Part 9: Getting a benefit decision changed
Chapter 58: Appealing to the Upper Tribunal and the courts
6. Appealing to the Court of Appeal or Court of Session

6. Appealing to the Court of Appeal or Court of Session

You have a right to appeal against an Upper Tribunal decision (except an excluded decision) to the Court of Appeal or, in Scotland, the Court of Session. You can only do this if the Upper Tribunal made an error of law (see p1357 for what may count) and you must first obtain permission to appeal.[98] The DWP, the local authority and HM Revenue and Customs (HMRC) have the same appeal rights as you.

> ### Excluded decisions
>
> 'Excluded decisions'[99] are decisions taken by the Upper Tribunal on an application for permission to appeal against a First-tier Tribunal decision and certain decisions taken when it considers a review (see p1373) – ie, decisions:
> – to review, or not to review, an earlier decision;
> – to take no action, or not to take any particular action, in the light of a review of an earlier decision;
> – to set aside an earlier decision on review (the decision that is set aside is also excluded).

Permission to appeal to the Court of Appeal or the Court of Session cannot be given unless the Upper Tribunal or the Court considers that the appeal would raise some important point of principle or practice or there is another compelling reason to hear the appeal.[100]

You should obtain advice before appealing. See p1374 for information about meeting the cost of going to court. Before making any application, get advice about whether you could be liable for the other side's costs as well as your own.

The procedure in the Court of Appeal and Court of Session is strict, formal and far less flexible than the procedure before the tribunals. The DWP, local authority or HMRC is represented by a solicitor and a barrister.

Note: in England and Wales, if the Upper Tribunal decision involves a point of law of general public importance, in exceptional cases, it can grant you a certificate that allows you to apply for permission to appeal direct to the Supreme Court, rather than appealing to the Court of Appeal first.[101]

Applying to the Upper Tribunal for permission

You must apply for permission to appeal, in the first instance, to the Upper Tribunal. Your application must:[102]
- be in writing; *and*
- contain sufficient information about the tribunal's decision for it to be identified; *and*

- state the error(s) of law you think the tribunal made. These must be identified clearly;[103] *and*
- if your application is late, include a request for an extension of time and the reasons why the application was not made in time; *and*
- state the result you are seeking – eg, what you think the tribunal's decision should have been.

You must be sent a record of the decision on your application as soon as practicable.[104] If your application is refused, you must also be sent a statement of reasons for the refusal and notice of your right to apply to the Court of Appeal or Court of Session for permission to appeal, along with information about how to apply and the time limit for doing so.

The time limit for applying

Your application must be received by the Upper Tribunal within three months after the date you were sent:[105]
- written notice of the decision; *or*
- notice that the reasons for the decision have been amended, or the decision has been corrected, following a review; *or*
- notice that an application for the tribunal's decision to be set aside was unsuccessful, but only if that application was made within the time limit for applying for a set-aside (or any longer period allowed).

The tribunal can extend (or shorten) your time limit for applying for permission to appeal to the Court of Appeal/Court of Session.[106] However, there is no guarantee that you will be given longer, so keep within the time limit wherever possible. If your time limit is not extended, the tribunal must refuse your application.[107]

When the Upper Tribunal can review its decision

The Upper Tribunal can review its own decision (other than an excluded decision – see p1372) if an application has been made for permission to appeal to the Court of Appeal or Court of Session.[108] You do not have a right to apply for a review yourself, but if you do, your application can be treated as an application for permission to appeal.[109]

The tribunal can review its decision if:[110]
- when it made the decision, it overlooked a legal provision, or a court or tribunal decision it was required to follow, which could have had a 'material effect' on the decision; *or*
- since the decision, a court has made a decision which the tribunal must follow. This only applies if the court's decision could have had a 'material effect' on the tribunal's decision had it been made at the time.

Part 9: Getting a benefit decision changed
Chapter 58: Appealing to the Upper Tribunal and the courts
6. Appealing to the Court of Appeal or Court of Session

If the tribunal *does* review the decision, it can:[111]
- correct accidental errors in the decision or the record of the decision; *and*
- amend the reasons given for the decision; *and*
- 'set aside' the decision. If it does this, it must make a new decision.

You must be notified in writing of the review outcome and your right of appeal (if any).[112] If the tribunal has taken any action and you were not given an opportunity to comment before the review, you must also be notified that you can apply for the outcome to be set aside and for the decision to be reviewed again.

If the tribunal does not review its decision, or reviews it but takes no action, it must consider whether to give you permission to appeal to the Court of Appeal or Court of Session.[113]

Applying to the court for permission

If the Upper Tribunal refuses you permission to appeal, you can make a fresh application to the Court of Appeal or Court of Session.[114] The tribunal's statement of reasons for the refusal must specify the relevant court.[115] It tells you the time limit for applying: this is very short, so you should lodge your application as soon as possible. You should seek advice *before* you make your application. Because the requirements and procedures are complicated, you should contact the relevant court to find out what you need to do, and when you need to serve notices on the relevant parties.

In England and Wales, the Court of Appeal considers your application for permission to appeal without a hearing. It can direct that there is a hearing, and must do so if it thinks your application cannot be determined fairly without one.[116] If it refuses you permission to appeal, you cannot appeal further or apply for a judicial review.

In Scotland, the procedure for appealing to the Court of Session is similar to that for England and Wales, but there are a number of differences. The Court of Session hears applications for permission to appeal at a hearing rather than making the decision simply by reading the papers. The application for permission and the appeal itself can be heard at the same time.

Meeting the cost of going to court

Free legal help from a solicitor is currently available for appeals on a point of law in the Supreme Court, the Court of Appeal and the Court of Session, and you should consider obtaining legal advice and representation for these. Free legal help is means tested. You usually have to pay court fees unless you are eligible for free legal help or you are exempt from paying court fees – eg, because of your financial circumstances. If you want to be represented by a lawyer and do not have free legal help, you also have to pay her/his fees and, if you lose your case, the other side's costs. Before making *any* application to a court, get advice about what the costs could be and how to protect yourself against having to pay the other side's costs.

Notes

1. Appealing to the Upper Tribunal

1 s11 TCEA 2007; *LS v Lambeth LB (HB)* [2010] UKUT 461 (AAC), reported as [2011] AACR 27
2 s11(5)(d) and (e) TCEA 2007
3 s11 TCEA 2007
4 r4 TP(UT) Rules; Practice Statement, *Delegation of Functions to Staff on or after 3 November 2008*, 30 October 2008
5 R(A) 1/72; R(SB) 11/83; R(IS) 11/99; R(I) 2/06; *R (Iran) v Secretary of State for the Home Department* [2005] EWCA Civ 982
6 CIS/2345/2001; CH/4065/2001
7 CDLA/433/1999
8 CDLA/1456/2002; R(H) 1/03
9 *Basildon DC v AM* [2009] UKUT 113 (AAC)
10 CDLA/3224/2001
11 CS/1939/1995; CDLA/5413/1999; CIB/303/1999
12 CH/3594/2002; *RC (Dec'd) v Maldon DC (HB)* [2012] UKUT 333 (AAC)
13 *LO'K v SSWP (ESA)* [2016] UKUT 10 (AAC), reported as [2016] AACR 31; *MS v SSWP (DLA and PIP)* [2021] UKUT 41 (AAC); *JS v Wirral MBC (HB)* [2021] UKUT 219 (AAC)
14 *GC v HMRC and DC (CHB)* [2018] UKUT 223 (AAC)
15 *DS v SSWP (ESA)* [2013] UKUT 572 (AAC)
16 CDLA/2748/2002
17 CDLA/1480/2006
18 *TA v LB of Islington (HB)* [2014] UKUT 71 (AAC)
19 CSDLA/606/2003; *KMN v SSWP (PIP)* [2019] UKUT 42 (AAC)
20 CDLA/7980/1995; CH/5221/2001; CH/396/2002; CIB/2977/2002
21 *ES v SSWP* [2009] UKUT 6 (AAC)
22 R(IS) 4/93
23 *JH v HMRC* [2015] UKUT 397 (AAC)
24 *R (Iran) v Secretary of State for the Home Department* [2005] EWCA Civ 982; *SM v SSWP (IIDB)* [2020] UKUT 287 (AAC)
25 R(DLA) 3/08; *SP v SSWP* [2009] UKUT 97 (AAC)
26 *LA v SSWP (ESA)* [2014] UKUT 482 (AAC)
27 CJSA/322/2001; R(IS) 5/04
28 *Carpenter v SSWP* [2003] EWCA Civ 33, reported as R(IB) 6/03

2. How to appeal to the Upper Tribunal

29 s11(3) TCEA 2007
30 r11 TP(UT) Rules; CIB/1009/2004; CIB/2058/2004
31 r11(4)(b) TP(UT) Rules
32 r11(4)(a) TP(UT) Rules; *MP v SSWP (DLA)* [2010] UKUT 103 (AAC)
33 r11(5) TP(UT) Rules
34 s10 Legal Aid, Sentencing and Punishment of Offenders Act 2012
35 Regs 5A(d) and 13 Advice and Assistance (Assistance by Way of Representation) (Scotland) Regulations 2003 No.179
36 r18 TP(UT) Rules
37 s11(4)(a) TCEA 2007; r21(2) TP(UT) Rules
38 r38(2), (5) and (6) TP(FT) Rules
39 Practice Statement, *Composition of Tribunals in Social Security and Child Support Cases in the Social Entitlement Chamber on or after 1 August 2013*, 31 July 2013, para 11
40 r27(2) TP(FT) Rules; CSB/172/1990
41 r39(3)-(5) TP(FT) Rules
42 r41 TP(FT) Rules
43 r38(7) TP(FT) Rules
44 *HP v SSWP (ESA)* [2014] UKUT 491 (AAC)
45 r38(3) and (4) TP(FT) Rules
46 r5(3)(a) TP(FT) Rules
47 r38(5) TP(FT) Rules
48 r21(7)(b) TP(UT) Rules
49 s9 TCEA 2007; r39(1) TP(FT) Rules
50 *GA v SSWP* [2017] UKUT 416 (AAC)
51 r41 TP(FT) Rules
52 r40(2) TP(FT) Rules
53 s9(4) and (5) TCEA 2007
54 *SE v SSWP* [2009] UKUT 163 (AAC); *AM v SSWP (IB)* [2009] UKUT 224 (AAC); *JS v SSWP* [2013] UKUT 100 (AAC), reported as [2013] AACR 30
55 r40(3) and (4) TP(FT) Rules; *SSWP v AM and Northumberland CC (HB)* [2015] UKUT 360 (AAC)
56 r39(2) TP(FT) Rules
57 s11(4)(a) TCEA 2007; r21(2) TP(UT) Rules
58 r21(4), (5), (6)(a) and (7) TP(UT) Rules; CSDLA/1207/2000
59 r7(1) and (2)(a) TP(UT) Rules

9

Part 9: Getting a benefit decision changed
Chapter 58: Appealing to the Upper Tribunal and the courts
Notes

60 r21(7)(b) TP(UT) Rules
61 R(IS) 11/99; CDLA/5793/1997
62 CCS/1664/2001
63 r13(1) TP(UT) Rules
64 r22(1) and (2) TP(UT) Rules
65 s13(8)(c) TCEA 2007
66 r21(3)(b) TP(UT) Rules
67 r5(3)(a) TP(UT) Rules
68 R(M) 1/87; *R (Birmingham City Council) v Birmingham County Court* [2009] EWHC 3329 (Admin), reported as [2010] 1 WLR 1287

3. **After you get permission to appeal**
69 r23 TP(UT) Rules
70 r5(3)(a) TP(UT) Rules
71 r22(2)(b) TP(UT) Rules
72 r2 TP(UT) Rules
73 *MA v SSWP* [2009] UKUT 211 (AAC)
74 rr5-7, 8, 15 and 16 TP(UT) Rules
75 r5(3)(n) TP(UT) Rules
76 s25 TCEA 2007
77 r16(3) TP(UT) Rules
78 r5(3)(l) and (m) TP(UT) Rules
79 r17 TP(UT) Rules
80 r17(4) and (5) TP(UT) Rules
81 r5(3)(a) TP(UT) Rules
82 rr24 and 25 TP(UT) Rules
83 rr5(3)(a) and 25(2) TP(UT) Rules
84 r40(3)(b) TP(UT) Rules

4. **Hearings**
85 r34 TP(UT) Rules
86 r1(3) TP(UT) Rules, definition of 'hearing'
87 r36 TP(UT) Rules
88 r3 The First-tier Tribunal and Upper Tribunal (Composition of Tribunal) Order 2008 No.2835; Practice Statement, *Composition of Tribunals in Relation to Matters that Fall to be Decided by the Administrative Appeals Chamber of the Upper Tribunal on or after 26th March 2014*, 26 March 2014
89 R(I) 1/03
90 R(IS) 2/08; *NA v SSWP (ESA)* [2018] UKUT 399 (AAC)

5. **The decision**
91 s12 TCEA 2007
92 r40 TP(UT) Rules
93 *Adams v SSWP and Green (CSM)* [2017] UKUT 9 (AAC), reported as [2017] AACR 28
94 r42 TP(UT) Rules
95 r43 TP(UT) Rules; *SK v SSWP* [2016] UKUT 529 (AAC), reported as [2017] AACR 25

96 r5(3)(a) TP(UT) Rules
97 r48 TP(UT) Rules

6. **Appealing to the Court of Appeal or Court of Session**
98 s13 TCEA 2007
99 s13(8)(c)-(e) TCEA 2007
100 s13(6) and (6A) TCEA 2007; Appeals from the Upper Tribunal to the Court of Appeal Order 2008 No.2834; r41.57 Rules of the Court of Session 1994
101 ss14A-14C TCEA 2007
102 r44(1), (6)(a) and (7) TP(UT) Rules
103 *Fryer-Kelsey v SSWP* [2005] EWCA Civ 511, reported as R(IB) 6/05
104 r45(3)-(5) TP(UT) Rules
105 r44(2), (3) and (5) TP(UT) Rules
106 r5(3)(a) TP(UT) Rules
107 r44(6) TP(UT) Rules
108 r46(1) TP(UT) Rules
109 r48 TP(UT) Rules
110 s10 TCEA 2007; r45(1) TP(UT) Rules
111 s10(4) and (5) TCEA 2007
112 r46(2) and (3) TP(UT) Rules
113 r45(2) TP(UT) Rules
114 s13(3)-(5) TCEA 2007
115 s13(11)-(13) TCEA 2007; r45(4)(b) TP(UT) Rules
116 r52.5 CPR

Chapter 59

· ·

Applying for judicial review

This chapter covers:

Key facts

- Judicial review may be appropriate when there is no other effective remedy available to you.
- Most judicial review proceedings must be started in the High Court in England and Wales, or Court of Session in Scotland, promptly and within three months of the decision you want to challenge.
- Judicial review of an Upper Tribunal decision to refuse permission to appeal from the First-tier Tribunal must be started within 16 days.
- In England and Wales, you must usually follow a judicial review pre-action protocol before going to court. The protocol does not apply in Scotland.
- Where judicial review is appropriate, a 'letter before action' sent by your representative will often resolve the problem without going to court. You can get advice from an advice agency; you do not need a solicitor to send a 'letter before action'.
- If you are thinking about going to court, get advice from a solicitor. Legal aid is available for judicial review under a public law legal aid contract.

1. The judicial review process

Judicial review is a form of legal challenge to the lawfulness of a decision, action or a failure to act (referred to as 'decisions' in this chapter). It is generally a challenge to the *way* in which a decision has been reached, rather than to the decision itself.

A claim for judicial review can be brought by an individual with a 'sufficient interest' in the decision (you will always have a sufficient interest in a decision

Part 9: Getting a benefit decision changed
Chapter 59: Applying for judicial review
1. The judicial review process

about your own benefit claim) or an organisation which has established standing in the courts – eg, CPAG.[1] A claim can only be brought against a decision of a 'public nature', which includes decisions of the DWP, HM Revenue and Customs or a local authority about benefit entitlement.

Judicial review is a 'remedy of last resort' and usually only available when you do not have an alternative remedy – eg, a right of appeal (see p1379).

A claim for judicial review relating to welfare benefits is usually brought in the High Court in England and Wales, or the Court of Session in Scotland (see p1386). Unlike tribunals, these courts have the power to make costs orders – ie, you can be ordered to pay the other side's costs as well as your own. If you are successful in a claim for judicial review, the court rarely substitutes its own view of what the correct decision is. It leaves it to the original decision maker to remake the decision, this time following the correct procedure.

In England and Wales, before you can apply for a judicial review in the High Court you must follow a 'pre-action protocol' (see p1383). This aims to avoid expensive litigation, and the majority of straightforward cases in which there has clearly been unlawfulness on the part of the decision maker are resolved at this stage. This protocol does not apply in Scotland, but it is good practice to avoid litigation and sending a 'letter before claim' can provide a way of doing so.

Judicial review can be used to challenge an Upper Tribunal decision to refuse permission to appeal against a First-tier Tribunal decision (see p1388), and occasionally to challenge First-tier Tribunal decisions in the Upper Tribunal (see p1387).

Note: get advice if you are considering a judicial review. You are unlikely to be successful without the help of a solicitor or welfare rights adviser and there are costs risks involved in starting a claim.

Time limit

In England and Wales, you must make your claim for judicial review in the High Court promptly and, in any event, no later than three months from the date the grounds to make the claim first arose – ie, the date of the decision you want to challenge.[2] The whole pre-action stage must be completed within the three-month time limit. The High Court may extend the time limit where there are good reasons for doing so.

In Scotland, you must apply to the Court of Session within three months of the decision you want to challenge (or a longer period that it considers equitable).[3] **Note:** it is good practice to send a 'letter before claim' to try to resolve the issue without going to court.

Note:
- If you want to challenge a delay or failure to make a decision, your time limit does not start to run until a decision has been received.

- If it is more than three months since the date of the decision you want to challenge, in some cases you can ask the decision maker to make a new decision and the three-month time limit will start again. For example, you may be able to request a mandatory reconsideration of the decision and on receipt of the mandatory reconsideration decision, challenge this 'promptly'.

To challenge a decision of the Upper Tribunal refusing you permission to appeal against a First-tier Tribunal decision, you must apply to the court no more than 16 days from the date on which the Upper Tribunal's decision was sent (see p1387).[4] You do not need to follow a pre-action protocol.

When to consider judicial review

Judicial review is only possible in limited circumstances.
- **If there is no right of appeal.** Judicial review is appropriate when there is no right of appeal and any other available remedies are not 'effective' (see below). There is no right of appeal against an increasing number of benefit decisions. These include discretionary decisions (eg, discretionary housing payments) and decisions which specifically exclude a right to appeal (eg, whether to split benefit payments between members of a couple or the amount offered to you as a benefit advance).[5]
- **If it is the last resort.** If there is another way of challenging a decision, you are expected to use it. This might include appealing to the First-tier or Upper Tribunal, complaining or using an Ombudsman service (see Chapter 61). If there is a right of appeal, or an internal dispute process (eg, within a local authority), you must use it. However, the alternative remedy must be both 'effective and appropriate'.[6] Using a complaints process or an Ombudsman will rarely be an effective alternative if a quick decision is needed. Even if you have a right of appeal, you may still be able to start the judicial review process with a 'letter before claim' (see p1383) if the appeal will not be effective or if is not appropriate. If this applies to you, ask for a mandatory reconsideration/ appeal and send a 'letter before claim' at the same time.

Is the appeal 'effective and appropriate'?

An appeal might not be effective and appropriate for a number of reasons.
- There is a need for speed. Your circumstances may mean that an appeal is not 'effective' because it will take too long – eg, if you are homeless and/or destitute, or if you are facing eviction for rent arrears and have no income for food or heating, and you have been refused benefits to which you are legally entitled.
- It is a matter of public importance. If you are an adviser, you may be aware of instances where decision makers have routinely misinterpreted or misapplied the law. Starting judicial review proceedings with a 'letter before claim' can improve future decision making, as well as resolving the issue for an individual claimant.

Part 9: Getting a benefit decision changed
Chapter 59: Applying for judicial review
2. Grounds for judicial review

– The remedy you are seeking is not available from an appeal – eg, you might want a change made to the decision makers' guidance, staff training or damages under the Human Rights Act.

---

2. Grounds for judicial review

The reasons for asking for a decision to be judicially reviewed are known as 'grounds for judicial review'. Common grounds for judicial review in welfare benefit cases include the following.

Failure to follow the law

The most common ground for judicial review is a failure to apply the law.[7] This is similar to one of the grounds for appeal (see p1357), so if there is a right of appeal, you must use it or explain why it is ineffective.

You can challenge a decision maker's failure to follow primary legislation (ie, Acts of Parliament), secondary legislation (ie, regulations) and caselaw.

Failure to make a decision or to make a decision within a reasonable time

Decision makers have a duty to consider all claims for benefit (whether new claims or revision/supersession requests) within a 'reasonable time'.[8] What counts as 'reasonable' depends on all the circumstances, including the impact on you and the complexity of the case. The coronavirus pandemic should be taken into account if you are considering whether or not there has been an unreasonable delay – eg, in referring you for a medical or work capability assessment.

Failure to exercise discretion

It is unlawful for decision makers to operate a 'blanket policy' when they have a discretion.[9] Examples of blanket policies include:
- the same decision being made in all cases in your area, regardless of individual factors;
- a local authority policy which has eligibility criteria for a benefit which is not provided for in the governing legislation and consequently restricts its ability to consider each application on a case-by-case basis.

Failure to take into account relevant evidence, or taking irrelevant evidence into account

You may have grounds for a judicial review if no account has been taken of relevant evidence or information (eg, medical evidence, proof of earnings or guidance) in reaching a decision. If the decision maker has made no reference to particular evidence or information you provided, nor explained why it has not been taken into account, this may indicate no account has been taken of it. You must be able to demonstrate how, had it been properly taken into account, a different decision would have been reached.[10]

Note: if the DWP or a tribunal fails to give *any* reasons for a decision (rather than failure to explain exclusion of particular evidence), the usual remedy is to appeal. For judicial review, failure to provide reasons primarily indicates 'failure to take account of relevant evidence' but you may also be able to argue that, as a matter of public law, you are entitled to know what was taken into account.

You may also have grounds for judicial review if the decision maker has taken irrelevant evidence or information into account – eg, if incorrect criteria have been used (such as length of residence for council tax reduction[11]).

Failure to make enquiries

You have a duty to provide information and evidence in connection with your benefit claim and the DWP, HM Revenue and Customs (HMRC) and local authority have a duty to make enquiries if information or evidence is available to them which is not available to you.[12]

Example

Pavlina left an abusive relationship and has no contact with her estranged spouse who is a European Economic Area worker. Both have pre-settled status under the EU Settlement Scheme. She could challenge the DWP's failure to seek information from HMRC to establish her right to reside based on her spouse's worker status.

Failure to follow guidance, or applying unlawful guidance

There is extensive guidance for decision makers to use when making decisions (see p1249). It is useful to identify what the guidance says, how it corresponds to the law, and whether it has been followed correctly.

- If the guidance corresponds to the law (eg, legislation and caselaw), but has not been followed in practice, the ground for judicial review is 'failure to follow the law and guidance'.
- If the guidance does not correspond to the law and has been followed in preference to the law to your detriment, your ground is 'failure to follow the law'. In addition to challenging the decision affecting you, you can request that the Secretary of State change the guidance that does not reflect the law.[13]

Discrimination and breach of human rights

Decision makers must comply with both the Equality Act 2010 and the Human Rights Act 1998, which provide duties not to discriminate directly or indirectly.

Part 9: Getting a benefit decision changed
Chapter 59: Applying for judicial review
2. Grounds for judicial review

The Equality Act can be useful where you can demonstrate that in failing to apply the law or guidance, the decision maker has discriminated against you because of your age, disability, gender reassignment, marriage or civil partnership, pregnancy or maternity, race, religion or belief, sex or sexual orientation – ie, the protected characteristics under the Act. Section 20 also imposes a duty on public authorities to make reasonable adjustments to avoid substantial disadvantage to disabled people; failure to make reasonable adjustments is a ground for judicial review. Equality Act arguments cannot be used in appeals before the tribunal[14] if the decision maker has breached the Equality Act when reaching a decision on your benefit entitlement. (**Note:** this does not prevent you from making a separate claim for discrimination in the county court.)

Article 14 of the European Convention on Human Rights (brought into UK law by the Human Rights Act) provides protection from discrimination in the enjoyment of the other rights set out in the Convention. Protocol 1, Article 1 provides a right to enjoy property peacefully, and welfare benefits are accepted as 'property' for these purposes.[15] Article 8 provides protection for private and family life and welfare benefits which are designed to facilitate or contribute to family life, supporting families with children, are likely to fall within the ambit of Article 8 for the purposes of Article 14.[16] The Human Rights Act provides broader protection from discrimination than the Equality Act as it makes it unlawful to discriminate on a wider range of grounds. Human Rights Act arguments can also be used at tribunal when you appeal a decision, but Human Rights Act damages cannot be awarded by the tribunal, unlike in judicial review.

Note:
- Brexit has no direct impact on the UK's obligations under the European Convention on Human Rights.
- The Human Rights Act can be used to challenge secondary legislation (regulations);[17] the Equality Act cannot.

Irrationality

Irrationality is also known as 'Wednesbury unreasonableness'. A decision is Wednesbury unreasonable if it is 'so unreasonable that no reasonable person, acting reasonably could have made it.'[18]

Unlike other grounds for judicial review, irrationality looks at the content of a decision rather than how the decision was made. You may be able to argue irrationality if, for example, the effect of a policy achieves an outcome which is opposed to its stated aim or if the effect of a policy disadvantages a group that it sets out to protect.[19]

3. The pre-action protocol

In England and Wales, before you can apply for judicial review in the High Court, you must usually use the pre-action protocol for judicial review.[20] In exceptional circumstances (eg, if the time limit is imminent or the matter is urgent), you do not have to comply, but you will have to explain the circumstances.

There are no court fees and no risk of having to pay the other side's costs during the pre-action stage. The only costs at this stage are any charges made by your adviser or solicitor (which may be eligible to be covered by legal help (a form of legal aid)). Failure to comply with the pre-action protocol can result in sanctions against the non-compliant party if the matter reaches the High Court, the costs of which are potentially high. The risk of costs if the matter reaches the High Court provides a strong incentive for both parties to comply with the pre-action protocol and to resolve the issue without court action.

The majority of cases where there is clear unlawfulness on the part of the decision maker are resolved at the pre-action stage. It is important to get advice before sending a pre-action letter, as it is only likely to be successful if sent on your behalf by a solicitor or advice agency.

Note:

- If your issue is not resolved at the pre-action stage, there is no requirement to pursue the matter to the next stage (ie, actual litigation) if you do not want to go to court.
- The pre-action protocol does not apply in Scotland, but it is good practice to try to avoid litigation and sending a 'letter before claim' as described in the pre-action protocol can provide a way of doing so.
- You do not need to use the pre-action protocol if you wish to challenge a decision of the Upper Tribunal refusing you permission to appeal against a First-tier Tribunal decision.[21]

The letter before claim

The pre-action protocol requires you (the 'claimant') to send a 'letter before claim' to the decision maker (the 'defendant') before initiating judicial review proceedings. The letter must contain:[22]

- the name and address of the 'defendant' – ie, the legal department of the DWP, HM Revenue and Customs (HMRC) or your local authority; *and*
- your full name and address; *and*
- your reference details – this will usually be your national insurance number, but could also be your housing benefit reference number, or any other reference which will assist the relevant benefit authority to identify you; *and*
- the name, address and reference details of your legal advisers (if any) or welfare rights adviser; *and*
- details of the matter being challenged; *and*

Part 9: Getting a benefit decision changed
Chapter 59: Applying for judicial review
3. The pre-action protocol

- details of any interested parties who need to be sent a copy of the paperwork. An 'interested party' is 'any person (other than the claimant and defendant) who is directly affected by the claim' or may be another government department – eg, HMRC (in benefit cases, there are usually no interested parties);[23] *and*
- a brief summary of the facts and relevant legal principles, the date and details of the decision being challenged, and why you consider it to be wrong; *and*
- details of the remedy you are seeking; *and*
- proposals for any alternative way of resolving the dispute. Both parties should consider whether alternative dispute resolution or using a complaints procedure would be more suitable than litigation. This is unlikely to be the case, but you must demonstrate that you have considered this; *and*
- details of any information sought from the benefits authority; *and*
- details of any relevant documents; *and*
- the address to be used for all the court documents. This will usually be the address of the advice agency or legal firm assisting you; *and*
- a proposed reply date. This will depend on the circumstances of your case; within 14 days is usually a reasonable time. The benefit authority should normally respond within 14 days, but may contact you for an extension. Failure to do so will be taken into account by the court and sanctions may be imposed if the matter proceeds to litigation.

The letter before claim should be sent to:
- DWP Legal Advisers, Government Legal Department, 2nd Floor, Caxton House, Tothill Street, London SW1H 9NA; email: legal.queries@dwp.gov.uk; *or*
- HMRC Solicitor's Office, South West Wing, Bush House, Strand, London WC2B 4RD; email: preactionletters@hmrc.gov.uk; *or*
- your local authority's legal department.

Note: it is acceptable to send your letter attached to an email. Include 'Pre-action Correspondence' in the subject header.

If you are writing on behalf of a client, you must include your client's signed form of authority to act.

'Letter before claim'
You can use the following structure. Ensure you include all the above required information.
Background facts
What are your circumstances? Give relevant details of your family, your health and housing.
What has happened? Include relevant dates.
What action has already been taken to try to resolve the dispute?
What has been the effect on you of the decision or action being challenged?

Legal background

What does the legislation say should have happened?

What does any caselaw say should have happened?

What does any guidance say should have happened?

How is this different to what, in fact, has happened – ie, to the decision/action you are challenging?

Grounds for judicial review

What are your reasons for requesting judicial review? These are your 'grounds for judicial review' (see p1380 and also p1357 – the grounds rules are similar to those when appealing to the Upper Tribunal).

Alternative remedies

If there is an alternative remedy, explain how you have exhausted it or justify why you are not using it.

Details of the action you expect the benefit agency to take

Explain what you are asking for. This will depend on your grounds for judicial review . If you have challenged the decision maker's failure to do something, your request will be for it to do that thing and might also include a request to improve future decision making. For example, you might want to ask:

– for your claim to be decided and paid without further delay (including from the date you first made your application);

– that the decision maker takes into account all the relevant evidence you supplied and exercises its discretion. For example, you could ask it to 'waive recovery of an overpayment' or 'reduce the level of the deductions from my benefit to [amount]';

– that the decision maker follows the law and its own guidance and awards you benefit from and including [date];

– for Human Rights Act damages;

– that staff guidance be issued and staff training provided to ensure all staff are aware of the discretion available to them and the relevant regulations and guidance;

– for guidance to be amended where it does not comply with the law.

CPAG has 'letters before claim' templates available at cpag.org.uk/welfare-rights/judicial-review/judicial-review-pre-action-letters. You can use these to challenge commonly occuring benefit problems where there is no effective alternative remedy. Ask an adviser or solicitor to send any of these templates on your behalf and note that edits are needed if you are in Scotland.

If you send a letter before claim and do not receive a reply within the time requested, contact the benefit authority's legal department to request a response without further delay. Point out that 14 days is considered a reasonable time by the judicial review pre-action protocol.

If you receive a response saying that 'judicial review is not appropriate', check whether the decision has, in fact, been changed by a revision. If so, and you are satisfied with this, no further action is needed.

Part 9: Getting a benefit decision changed
Chapter 59: Applying for judicial review
4. Judicial review in the High Court or Court of Session

If you receive a negative response that you do not think addresses your challenge and the decision has not been changed, you can:

- make further representations to the benefit authority's legal department; *or*
- drop the matter and take no further action; *or*
- refer the matter to a solicitor to issue judicial review proceedings in the High Court or Court of Session (making sure you are within the strict time limit).

4. Judicial review in the High Court or Court of Session

Judicial review in the High Court in England and Wales or Court of Session in Scotland is a means of challenging a decision where there is no effective alternative means for challenging the decision and, in England and Wales, you have exhausted the pre-action stage set out on p1383 (there is no pre-action protocol in Scotland). The grounds for your challenge are those in your pre-action correspondence (see p1383).

You cannot usually apply to the High Court/Court of Session for a judicial review if you have another way of resolving the problem (see p1379).

England and Wales

To start a claim for judicial review in the High Court of England and Wales, you have to submit Form N461 together with supporting documents and the court fee or a request for a fee remission. You may not have to pay some or all of your court fees if you get certain benefits or are on a low income and have little or no savings. Check whether you are eligible and apply online or download a form at gov.uk/get-help-with-court-fees.

Once your claim has been 'issued' by the court (ie, it has been allocated a court number and been stamped), send a copy of it and the supporting documents to the body whose decision you are challenging. It has 21 days to file with the court and send you an acknowledgement of service and a very basic defence to the claim ('summary grounds of defence').

Once a claim for judicial review is started in the courts, the process involves two stages. First, you must get High Court permission to apply for judicial review. Your application for permission is initially decided on the papers. If refused, you have the opportunity of renewing it at a hearing. If permission is refused at the hearing, you have a right of appeal to the Court of Appeal. Permission to apply for judicial review is only given if the case has reasonable prospects of success. If permission is granted (whether on the papers or at a renewed hearing), the second stage is a substantive hearing of the case.

You should always obtain legal advice from a solicitor or legal advice centre before starting judicial review proceedings as there are likely to be significant costs involved and it is important that your claim is presented clearly and cogently, particularly when the decision maker will be legally represented. However, legal aid is available for many judicial review cases, subject to conditions. Check whether you are eligible at gov.uk/legal-aid/eligibility.

If you are looking for a solicitor to pursue judicial review in the High Court, note that legal firms and law centres which undertake judicial review work often do so under a public law contract as there are very few welfare benefit legal aid contracts available. There is a map of legal firms which have confirmed they are able to consider referrals from advice agencies for judicial review litigation at cpag.org.uk/welfare-rights/judicial-review/map-solicitors – the majority hold public law legal aid contracts. Some city firms also take referrals on a pro bono basis if you are not eligible for legal aid or cannot obtain a legal aid solicitor.

A claim for judicial review can typically take between six and 12 months to go through all the High Court stages.

Scotland

The procedure is similar in Scotland, except there is no pre-action protocol. Court action for judicial review starts using a document known as a 'petition'.

You must obtain 'leave' (permission) from the court to bring a judicial review action. The court may grant permission where there is 'sufficient interest' in the subject matter and the application has a real prospect of success.

If permission is refused by the court, you have a right to a hearing before a different judge, as well as a further right of appeal to the Inner House of the Court of Session.[24]

For details of legal firms which have confirmed they are able to consider referrals from advice agencies for judicial review litigation, see cpag.org.uk/welfare-rights/judicial-review/map-solicitors.

5. Judicial review in the Upper Tribunal

Challenging a decision of the First-tier Tribunal

Occasionally, you can challenge a First-tier Tribunal decision by applying for a judicial review by the Upper Tribunal, though not usually if you have a right of appeal to the Upper Tribunal against the decision. You may need the services of a solicitor or legal advice centre to apply for a judicial review. Check what you might have to pay – you may qualify for free legal help.

Note: if you are in any doubt about whether you have a right of appeal against a decision you want to challenge, you can apply for both permission to appeal and for a judicial review. The Upper Tribunal decides which is the proper route.

Part 9: Getting a benefit decision changed
Chapter 59: Applying for judicial review
5. Judicial review in the Upper Tribunal

In England and Wales, you can apply for a judicial review of a First-tier Tribunal decision:

- against which you have no right of appeal to the Upper Tribunal, *and either*
- that was made under any of the First-tier Tribunal procedural rules; *or*
- is a decision to review (or not to review) a decision following an application for permission to appeal to the Upper Tribunal or a decision as to what action to take in the light of the review.[25]

You must first apply for permission in writing and must include specified information.[26] You can use Form JR1, available at gov.uk. You must apply promptly and your application must be received by the Upper Tribunal no later than three months after the date of the decision you want to challenge.[27] Provided you apply promptly, the time limit can be extended to:

- one month after the date you were sent written reasons for the First-tier Tribunal's decision; *or*
- one month after the date you were sent notice that an application to set aside the decision was unsuccessful, provided the application was made within the time limit for applying for a set-aside (or longer period allowed).

In Scotland, you can challenge a First-tier Tribunal decision by a judicial review if it is a procedural decision or ruling, including procedural omissions or oversights.[28] You cannot apply direct to the Upper Tribunal. You must first apply to the Court of Session. You must apply within three months of the decision you want to challenge (or a longer period that the Upper Tribunal considers equitable).[29] If specified conditions are satisfied, your case is transferred to the Upper Tribunal.[30] The Upper Tribunal then decides whether your application was made in time and whether to give you permission.[31]

Transferring judicial review cases to the Upper Tribunal

The High Court and the Court of Session can transfer judicial review claims to the Upper Tribunal.[32] It may be appropriate to request a transfer if you think your case would benefit from being decided by an Upper Tribunal judge experienced in social security law rather than a High Court/Court of Session judge.

Challenging refusal of permission to appeal to the Upper Tribunal

There is no right of appeal against a decision by the Upper Tribunal to refuse permission to appeal from the First-tier Tribunal. This type of decision can only be challenged by way of a judicial review. Judicial review is only available where:[33]

- the proposed appeal would raise an important point of principle; *or*
- there is another compelling reason for the court to hear the appeal.

The procedure is the same as issuing proceedings in the High Court or Court of Session (see p1386), except that the time limit is 16 days from the date the decision letter was sent[34] and you do not need to follow the pre-action protocol.

The government intends to remove the right to challenge Upper Tribunal decisions refusing permission to appeal from the First-tier Tribunal. However, until proposed legislation[35] is in force, it remains possible to do so.

Notes

1. The judicial review process
1 **EW** s31(3) Senior Courts Act 1981
  S s 27B(2)(a) Court of Session Act 1988
2 r54.5(1) CPR
3 s27A Court of Session Act 1988
4 r54.7A(3) CPR
5 For example Sch 3 UC, PIP,JSA&ESA (DA) Regs
6 *Glencore Energy UK Limited v Commissioners of HMRC* [2017] EWHC 1476 (Admin), para 42

2. Grounds for judicial review
7 For an example, see JR49 at cpag.org.uk/jr-letters/elements-uc
8 *R (C and W) v SSWP* [2015] EWHC 1607 (Admin), para 61
9 *R (S) v SSHD* [2007] EWCA Civ 546, para 50
10 For an example of use, see JR12 at cpag.org.uk/jr-letters/disputed-earnings-uc
11 *R (Winder and Others) v Sandwell MBC* [2014] EWHC 2617 (Admin)
12 *Kerr v Department for Social Development (Northern Ireland)* [2004] UKHL 23, para 62
13 For an example of a challenge to unlawful guidance, see JR33 at cpag.org.uk/jr-letters/deductions-uc
14 *JS v SSWP* (ESA)[2014] UKUT 428 (AAC), para 56; *TS (by TS) v SSWP(DLA)*; *EK (by MK) v SSWP (DLA)* [2020] UKUT 284 (AAC) (in relation to Public Sector Equality Duty)
15 *Stec v United Kingdom* [2006] 43 EHRR 47, para 53

16 For example, *R (SC, CB and 8 children) v SSWP* [2021] UKSC 26, para 41
17 For example, *RR v SSWP* [2019] UKSC 52, para 27
18 *Associated Provincial Picture Houses Ltd v Wednesbury Corporation* [1948] 1 KB 223
19 For example, *SSWP v Johnson, Woods, Barrett & Stewart* [2020] EWCA Civ788

3. The pre-action protocol
20 gov.uk/guidance/pre-action-protocol-for-judicial-review
21 r54.7A CPR
22 Annex A of the pre-action protocol for judicial review, gov.uk/guidance/pre-action-protocol-for-judicial-review
23 r54.1(f) CPR

4. Judicial review in the High Court or Court of Session
24 ss27B-27D Court of Session Act 1988

5. Judicial review in the Upper Tribunal
25 s18(6) TCEA 2007; Practice Direction (Upper Tribunal: Judicial Review Jurisdiction) [2009] 1WLR 327
26 r28(1) TP(UT) Rules
27 r28(2) and (3) TP(UT) Rules; *CICA v First-tier Tribunal and CB (CIC)* [2015] UKUT 371 (AAC)
28 ss20, 20A and 21 TCEA 2007; Act of Sederunt (Transfer of Judicial Review Applications from the Court of Session) 2008 No.357; *Currie, Petitioner* [2009] CSOH 145, reported as [2010] AACR 8
29 s27A Court of Session Act 1988
30 *EF v SSWP* [2009] UKUT 92 (AAC), reported as R(IB) 3/09

Part 9: Getting a benefit decision changed
Chapter 59: Applying for judicial review
Notes

31 s20A(2) TCEA 2007
32 s31A Senior Courts Act 1981; s20 TCEA
    2007
33 *R (Cart) v the Upper Tribunal and Others*
    [2011] UKSC 28; *Eba v Advocate General
    for Scotland* [2011] UKSC 29
34 r54 7A(3) CPR
35 Check the Judicial Review and Courts Bill
    status: https://bills.parliament.uk/bills/
    3035

Chapter 60

Challenging decisions on statutory payments

This chapter covers:
1. Notification of your employer's decision (p1392)
2. Involving HM Revenue and Customs (p1392)
3. Appealing against a decision (p1394)
4. Appeals to the Upper Tribunal (p1398)
5. Appeals to the courts (p1399)
6. Payment if your challenge is successful (p1399)

This chapter explains the rules for challenging decisions on entitlement to statutory payments. These rules do not apply to challenging decisions on other benefits (except some decisions on national insurance contributions – see p946).

In this chapter, when the term First-tier Tribunal is used, it means the First-tier Tribunal (Tax) and when the term Upper Tribunal is used, it means the Upper Tribunal (Tax and Chancery).

Key facts
- Your employer should make the initial decision on your entitlement to statutory sick pay, statutory maternity pay, statutory adoption pay, statutory paternity pay, statutory shared parental pay and statutory parental bereavement pay.
- If you disagree with your employer's decision, or your employer has failed to make a decision, you can ask HM Revenue and Customs (HMRC) to decide whether you are entitled.
- If you disagree with HMRC's decision on your entitlement, you can ask for it to be reviewed. If you are unhappy with the outcome of the review, you can appeal to the First-tier Tribunal.
- If you disagree with the First-tier Tribunal's decision, you may be able to appeal to the Upper Tribunal. If you disagree with the Upper Tribunal's decision, you may be able to appeal to a court.

Part 9: Getting a benefit decision changed
Chapter 60: Challenging decisions on statutory payments
2. Involving HM Revenue and Customs

1. **Notification of your employer's decision**

If you have taken the necessary steps to request statutory sick pay (SSP), statutory maternity pay (SMP), statutory adoption pay (SAP), statutory paternity pay (SPP), statutory shared parental pay (SSPP) or statutory parental bereavement pay (SPBP) from your employer (see Chapters 38 and 39), but your employer decides it is not liable to pay you, it should notify you of its decision within:[1]

- seven days for SSP or SMP (or, for SMP only, within 28 days of your giving notice of your maternity leave or your baby's birth, if this is earlier);
- 28 days for SAP, SPP, SSPP or SPBP.

This also applies to a former employer for SMP, SAP, SPP, SSPP and SPBP.

For SSP and SPBP, your employer should normally provide this information on Form SSP1 or SPBP1 respectively, or on its own computerised form if it contains the same information. For SMP, SAP and SPP, it is normally given on Form SMP1, SAP1 or SPP1 respectively. There is no official form for SSPP. If you have given your employer certain evidence to establish your entitlement, it should be returned to you – eg, Form MAT B1 for SMP.

2. **Involving HM Revenue and Customs**

If you disagree with your employer's decision on your entitlement to statutory sick pay (SSP), statutory maternity pay (SMP), statutory adoption pay (SAP), statutory paternity pay (SPP), statutory shared parental pay (SSPP) or statutory parental bereavement pay (SPBP), or if your employer has failed to make a decision, you can request that HM Revenue and Customs (HMRC) makes a formal decision on your entitlement.[2] You must do so within six months of the earliest date for which your entitlement is in dispute.[3]

Telephone HMRC's Statutory Payment Dispute Team to initiate your request on 0300 322 9422 (textphone: 0300 200 3212). You may be sent a form to use or HMRC may suggest you write a letter.

Forms

You should normally apply on Form SSP14 (for SSP), SMP14 (for SMP), SAP14 (for SAP), SPP14 (for SPP), ShPP14 (for SSPP) or SPBP14 (for SPBP), which can be obtained from, and returned to, HMRC's Statutory Payment Dispute Team, PT Operations NE England, HMRC, BX9 1AN.

On either the form or in your letter, you must provide details of the period for which your entitlement to SSP, SMP, SAP, SPP, SSPP or SPBP is at issue and the grounds on which your employer has refused payment, if you know them.[4]

If possible, you should also send a copy of Form SSP1, SMP1, SAP1, SPP1 or SPBP1 that your employer has given you, or the information your employer has given you about its decision on your entitlement to SSPP, and evidence of your entitlement – eg, a medical certificate (if you have been sick for more than seven days), Form MAT B1 or the 'matching certificate' from the adoption agency. However, do not delay your application if you do not have this information.

It can take some time to get a final decision on your entitlement, so consider whether there are other benefits which you can claim in the interim (see Chapter 1). However, if you claim employment and support allowance (ESA) while waiting for a decision on your entitlement to SSP, or maternity allowance (MA) while waiting for a decision on your entitlement to SMP, the DWP does not normally make a decision on your ESA/MA claim until HMRC has made a decision on your entitlement to SSP or SMP (because you do not qualify for ESA if you are entitled to SSP, nor for MA if you are entitled to SMP). For this reason, the DWP can request that HMRC makes a formal decision on your entitlement to SSP or SMP, if you have not already done so. If you would qualify for ESA or MA, do not delay claiming or you may lose out financially if the final decision is that you do not qualify for SSP or SMP.

Note: if you are thinking of challenging your employer's decision on your entitlement to a statutory payment, you should tell your employer that you intend to contact HMRC. Your employer can get advice on statutory payments from HMRC's Employers' Helpline: 0300 200 3200.

Requests for further information

HMRC may contact you and/or your partner for information, and can also require your employer to provide information relating to your entitlement – eg, the reasons for its decision. HMRC can impose a financial penalty on your employer if it fails to provide the information. If your employer fails to comply with requests for information, press HMRC to make its own decision on your entitlement.

HMRC can also impose a financial penalty on you for not providing information or documents that you have been reasonably required to provide to decide your entitlement.[5] However, this is only likely to happen if HMRC believes that you have acted fraudulently or have been negligent.

HM Revenue and Customs' decision

In order to resolve your dispute, HMRC may send both you and your employer a written opinion on your entitlement before it issues a formal decision on your application. It may give you a deadline before which both you and your employer can object to its written opinion before it issues a formal decision.

The formal decision is legally binding on your employer. If HMRC decides you are entitled to be paid by your employer (and your employer does not appeal), it

Part 9: Getting a benefit decision changed
Chapter 60: Challenging decisions on statutory payments
3. Appealing against a decision

should pay you on or before your first payday after the 30-day appeal time limit (see below) expires.[6]

Varying or superseding a decision

HMRC can change its own decision by varying or superseding it.[7] It can **vary** its decision if it now believes that the decision was wrong at the time it was made. It must tell you and your employer of the new decision in writing. The new decision takes effect from the date that the original decision would have had effect if the reason for the variation had been known. If you or your employer have appealed against a decision, HMRC may vary that decision at any time before the appeal is determined.

HMRC can **supersede** an earlier decision if it has become incorrect for any reason – eg, if your circumstances have changed. The new decision takes effect from the date of your change of circumstances.

If HMRC varies or supersedes an earlier decision, either you or your employer can appeal against the new decision.

3. Appealing against a decision

Both you and your employer can appeal against a decision made by HM Revenue and Customs (HMRC).[8]

Your appeal should be made in writing to HMRC and include your reasons for appealing.[9] Send your appeal to the Statutory Payment Dispute Team, PT Operations, NE England, HMRC, BX9 1AN. You have a choice about how your appeal is dealt with (see below).

Time limit for appealing

Your appeal should reach HMRC within 30 days of the date on which HMRC made its formal decision.[10] This time limit may be extended by HMRC if the reason you are late is considered reasonable.[11] If HMRC does not accept your late appeal, you can apply to the First-tier Tribunal for permission to appeal late, by giving reasons for lateness (see p1397). However, you cannot be certain that a late appeal will be accepted, so it is preferable to keep within the time limit.

Choosing how your appeal is dealt with

You can choose whether you would like your appeal to be decided by the First-tier Tribunal or by HMRC conducting a review. To make this choice, in addition to sending your written appeal to HMRC, you should notify:[12]

- the tribunal in writing that you want it to consider your appeal (see p1397); *or*

- HMRC in writing that you want it to conduct a review. (If HMRC conducts a review and you disagree with its decision, you can still apply to the tribunal for a decision on your appeal, provided you apply within the time limits below.)

If, having made your appeal, you do not ask either the tribunal to consider your appeal or HMRC to review its decision, HMRC should write to you, offering to review its decision (called an 'HMRC-initiated review' in this chapter). Before HMRC initiates a review, it may try to settle the appeal (see below). However, until HMRC has issued a notification offering you a review, you can still notify the tribunal that you want it to decide your appeal or inform HMRC yourself that you want it to conduct a review.

Settling or withdrawing your appeal

HMRC can try to settle your appeal at any time before the determination of the appeal. If, before the appeal is decided, you reach an agreement with HMRC (or if an agreement is reached between your employer and HMRC, if your employer has appealed), the matter is treated as settled by agreement and the appeal lapses.[13]

You can withdraw your appeal at any time before it is decided by notifying HMRC and your employer that you wish to do so. Your employer and HMRC have 30 days to object and, if no objection is made, your appeal will lapse.[14]

Review by HM Revenue and Customs

Initial view on entitlement

If you have asked for your appeal to be decided by an HMRC review, or if HMRC has initiated a review, HMRC first informs you of its 'initial view on your entitlement'.

If you have requested an HMRC review, HMRC should send you its initial view on your entitlement within 30 days, beginning with the date it receives your written request for a review, although it can send it later than this if it is reasonable.[15] The same rules apply if it is your employer who has initiated the review.

If HMRC has initiated the review, HMRC should send its initial view on your entitlement with its offer of a review.[16] You then have 30 days, starting on the date of HMRC's letter, to inform in writing:[17]

- HMRC, that you want it to conduct the review (see p1396); *or*
- the First-tier Tribunal, that you want it to decide your appeal (see p1397). In some circumstances, the tribunal can consider your appeal even if you apply after the 30-day time limit (see p1397).

If HMRC has initiated the review but you neither accept the offer of a review nor notify the tribunal that you want it to consider your appeal within the above time limit, HMRC proceeds as if you have agreed to its initial view on your entitlement

Part 9: Getting a benefit decision changed
Chapter 60: Challenging decisions on statutory payments
3. Appealing against a decision

and treats the matter as settled by agreement. Notification of this should be sent to you and your employer, and your appeal lapses.[18]

The review

After HMRC has issued its initial view on your entitlement (and, for HMRC-initiated reviews, provided you have accepted HMRC's offer of a review), a review is carried out by an HMRC decision maker who was not involved in making the original decision.

If you disagree with HMRC's initial view, it is important to write to explain why. The decision maker must consider any information you provide, if you provide it at a stage that gives her/him a reasonable opportunity to do so.[19]

HMRC should notify you of its review decision and the reasons for it within 45 days beginning with the date it:[20]

- notified you of its initial view of the matter, if you requested the review; *or*
- received your acceptance of its offer of a review, if HMRC initiated the review.

In either case, these time limits can be changed if you agree.

If HMRC does not notify you of its review decision within this time limit, its decision is taken to be the same as its initial view on your entitlement and HMRC must inform you of this.[21]

If you do not agree with the review decision

If you or your employer do not agree with HMRC's review decision, you may notify the First-tier Tribunal that you want it to consider your appeal. The time limit for doing so is 30 days, beginning with the date of either:[22]

- HMRC's letter notifying you of its review decision; *or*
- if HMRC did not notify you of its review decision within the time limit, the date of its letter telling you it has adopted its initial view on your entitlement as its decision.

In the latter situation, you can appeal before receiving HMRC's letter, provided your appeal is made after the expiry of the time limit for making the review decision.

If you do not notify the tribunal within the time limit, your appeal can only be considered if the tribunal gives permission (see p1397).[23]

Alternative dispute resolution

If either you or your employer have notified the First-tier Tribunal that you want it to consider your appeal, HMRC may invite you to apply for alternative dispute resolution. If alternative dispute resolution is suggested before this, do not delay notifying the tribunal of your appeal, as the time limits for notifying the tribunal are not put on hold while you consider or take part in alternative dispute resolution. If alternative dispute resolution is used, an HMRC officer who has not been involved in the decision acts as a mediator to try to resolve the dispute. If you reach an agreement, you and your employer are sent written confirmation and, if it is different from HMRC's earlier decision on your entitlement, HMRC may vary its earlier decision (see p1394). For alternative dispute resolution to be used, both you and your employer must agree to it. If you are offered alternative dispute resolution, get advice.

Appeals to the First-tier Tribunal

You can request that the First-tier Tribunal considers your appeal if:[24]
- you have appealed against HMRC's original decision on your entitlement and want your appeal to be decided by the tribunal, rather than by an HMRC review (see p1394); *or*
- you have appealed and HMRC has initiated a review (see p1395). Rather than accept the offer of a review, you can notify the tribunal that you want it to decide your appeal. See p1395 for the time limits for notifying the tribunal, and below if you miss the time limit; *or*
- your appeal against HMRC's original decision has been decided by an HMRC review and you disagree with the decision, or if HMRC has not notified you of its review decision within the time limits; *or*
- you missed the time limit for appealing against HMRC's original decision on your entitlement and HMRC does not agree to accept your late appeal (but see below).

Notifying the First-tier Tribunal

If you want the First-tier Tribunal to consider your appeal, you must notify it in writing or submit the appeal online. See p1395 for the time limit for doing so. Your written notice must contain certain information, including the details of the decision you are appealing against, the result you want and your grounds for appealing. If you miss the time limit, you must also ask for permission to make a late application and explain why your request is late.[25]

Use Form T240 'Notice of Appeal (tax)', available from gov.uk or telephone 0300 123 1024. You can appeal at gov.uk/tax-tribunal/appeal-to-tribunal. You must include a copy of the written record of the decision you are appealing against and any statement giving the reasons for that decision (eg, the notification HMRC sent informing you of its decision), unless you do not have this information and cannot reasonably obtain it.

Note: when completing Form T240, be aware that statutory payments are described as 'direct taxes' by HMRC.

Missed time limits

If you miss the relevant time limit for notifying the First-tier Tribunal that you want it to determine your appeal or the time limit for appealing against HMRC's original decision on your entitlement (and HMRC does not agree to accept your

Part 9: Getting a benefit decision changed
Chapter 60: Challenging decisions on statutory payments
4. Appeals to the Upper Tribunal

late appeal), you can still ask the First-tier Tribunal to consider your appeal. It may give its permission for the time limit to be extended. Although there are no specific rules about when the time limit can be extended,[26] the overriding objective of the rules is to enable tribunals to deal with cases fairly and justly.[27] Whether the First-tier Tribunal extends the time limit depends on the circumstances, so give detailed reasons why your appeal is late. As you cannot be certain of success, it is essential to keep within the time limits if you can.

How the First-tier Tribunal decides your case

The First-tier Tribunal allocates your case to be considered in one of four ways.[28] Further details of the procedures are in leaflet T242 *Making an Appeal: explanatory leaflet*, available from gov.uk.

The tribunal can confirm HMRC's decision or change it.[29] It must send you a notice informing you of its decision, which may include its full written findings and the reasons for its decision.[30] If you disagree with the tribunal's decision, you may be able to appeal against it to the Upper Tribunal (see below).

In certain circumstances, you can apply for the First-tier Tribunal's decision to be 'set aside' (there is a time limit for doing so), or the tribunal can correct its own decision.[31] The tribunal can also review its decision if you have applied for permission to appeal to the Upper Tribunal and it considers there was an error of law in the decision.[32]

4. **Appeals to the Upper Tribunal**

You and your employer can appeal to the Upper Tribunal (Tax and Chancery Chamber) against a decision of the First-tier Tribunal, but only on the grounds that the First-tier Tribunal has made a legal mistake – an 'error of law' (see p1357).[33] The rules for making an appeal are almost the same as those for making an appeal to the Upper Tribunal (Administrative Appeals Chamber) described in Chapter 58, although there are differences in the procedure for lodging an appeal and in the time limit for applying. You must first apply to the First-tier Tribunal (Tax) for permission to appeal. Your application must normally be received no later than 56 days after the latest of the dates listed on p1363 (usually the date the tribunal sent you its full written reasons for the decision). In some circumstances, the First-tier Tribunal can give permission for you to appeal later than this.[34] Use Form T247 to apply to the First-tier Tribunal for permission to appeal to the Upper Tribunal (available from gov.uk).

If you have not been sent the First-tier Tribunal's full written findings and reasons, you must obtain these before applying for permission to appeal. Write to the First-tier Tribunal to request these – your request must be received within 28 days of the date it sent you its decision notice. In some circumstances, this time limit can be extended.[35] If the First-tier Tribunal gives permission for you to appeal, you must submit a 'notice of appeal' and certain other information to the Upper Tribunal within the time limit. For details, see p1366. Use Form FTC1 available from gov.uk.

If the First-tier Tribunal refuses permission for you to appeal or only gives permission on limited grounds, you can apply to the Upper Tribunal for permission. Use Form FTC1. See p1366 for the time limits for applying.[36] If, without a hearing, the Upper Tribunal refuses you permission to appeal or to appeal late, or gives permission to appeal subject to conditions or on limited grounds, you can apply for this decision to be reconsidered at a hearing. An application to do so must be made in writing and be received by the Upper Tribunal within 14 days of the date it sent you notice of its decision, although the Upper Tribunal has discretion to extend this time limit.[37] The Upper Tribunal has the power to make an order for costs (expenses in Scotland), so before making any application get advice about whether you could be liable for costs if you lose your case.

5. Appeals to the courts

You and your employer can appeal against the decision of the Upper Tribunal to the Court of Appeal (the Court of Session in Scotland) if the tribunal made an 'error of law' – ie, it interpreted the law incorrectly.[38]

You must apply for permission to appeal, which is only granted if certain conditions are met (see p1372). Your application should normally be made to the Upper Tribunal within one month of the date it sent you written reasons for its decision. This time limit can be extended with the tribunal's permission.[39] See p1372 for further details on appealing to the courts.

6. Payment if your challenge is successful

If it is decided that your employer should pay you a statutory payment, your employer should pay you within a certain time limit. If your employer has appealed or is within the time limit for doing so, it does not have to pay you until a final decision is given on appeal, or until the time limit for the appeal or a further appeal has passed. If no appeal against the decision has been made (or if the matter has been finally determined), your employer should pay you on or before the first payday after:[40]

- the day the employer is notified that the appeal has been finally determined; or
- the day the employer receives notification that leave to appeal has been refused, and there is no further opportunity to apply for leave; or

Part 9: Getting a benefit decision changed
Chapter 60: Challenging decisions on statutory payments
Notes

• in any other case, the day the time limit for appeal expires.

If, because of your employer's payroll methods, it is not practical for you to be paid by that payday, your employer should pay you on or before your next payday after this date. If you are not otherwise due to be paid (eg, because you are no longer employed by that employer), then the time limits for paying you should be met by the first day on which you would have been paid (or if not practicable, by the following payday).

If your employer does not pay

If your employer does not pay you within the time limit, HM Revenue and Customs (HMRC) should pay you (although HMRC states it will first contact your employer to try to get it to pay).[41] Write to HMRC's Statutory Payment Dispute Team (see p1392) asking for payment. This applies even if your employer is insolvent, but only for payment owed for the period before the date of insolvency. For any period that falls after the date of insolvency, HMRC, rather than your employer, is automatically liable to pay you any statutory payment for which you are eligible.[42]

Notes

1. Notification of your employer's decision
1 **SSP** s130 SSAA 1992; reg 15 SSP Regs
   SMP s132 SSAA 1992; reg 25A SMP Regs
   SPP/SAP Reg 11 SPPSAP(A) Regs
   SSPP Regs 2(2) and 11 SSPP(A) Regs
   SPBP Regs 2 and 11 SPBP(A) Regs

2. Involving HM Revenue and Customs
2 s8 SSC(TF)A 1999
3 **SSP/SMP** Reg 3 SSP&SMP(D) Regs
   SPP/SAP Reg 13 SPPSAP(A) Regs
   SSPP Reg 13 SSPP(A) Regs
   SPBP Reg 13 SPBP(A) Regs
4 **SSP/SMP** Reg 3 SSP&SMP(D) Regs
   SPP/SAP Reg 13 SPPSAP(A) Regs
   SSPP Reg 13 SSPP(A) Regs
   SPBP Reg 13 SPBP(A) Regs

5 **SSP/SMP** s113A SSAA 1992
   SPP/SAP/SSPP/SPBP s11(1) and (2) Employment Act 2002
6 **SSP** Reg 9 SSP Regs
   SMP Reg 29 SMP Regs
   SPP/SAP Reg 42 SPPSAP(G) Regs
   SSPP Reg 44 SSPP(G) Regs
   SPBP Reg 24 SPBP(G) Regs
7 s10 SSC(TF)A 1999; regs 5 and 6 SSC(DA) Regs

3. Appealing against a decision
8 s11(2)(a) SSC(TF)A 1999
9 s12 SSC(TF)A 1999
10 s12(1) SSC(TF)A 1999
11 s49 TMA 1970; reg 9 SSC(DA) Regs
12 ss49A, 49B, 49D and 49I TMA 1970; reg 7 SSC(DA) Regs
13 s49A(4) TMA 1970; reg 11 SSC(DA) Regs
14 Reg 11(5) SSC(DA) Regs

9

Chapter 61

Complaints

This chapter covers:
1. Grounds for a complaint (below)
2. Compensation payments (p1403)
3. Complaining about the DWP (p1403)
4. Complaining about HM Revenue and Customs (p1405)
5. Complaining about a local authority (p1407)
6. Complaining about HM Courts and Tribunals Service (p1407)
7. Using your MP (p1408)
8. Complaining to the Ombudsman (p1408)
9. Legal action (p1410)

This chapter covers the rules for making complaints about benefits administered by the DWP and HM Revenue and Customs. It also covers the rules for making complaints about housing benefit and HM Courts and Tribunal Service. See Chapter 79 for how to make a complaint about a Scottish social security benefit.

Key facts
- You can complain about any government or local authority department, and anyone contracted to provide a service on its behalf.
- Your complaint can be about a delay in dealing with your claim, poor administration, the behaviour of staff, or the way in which a particular policy or practice has impacted on you.
- It is best to put your complaint in writing, even if you have to start the process by telephone.
- If your complaint is not resolved satisfactorily, you may be able to escalate your complaint to the Independent Case Examiner, the Adjudicator or an Ombudsman.

1. Grounds for a complaint

If you are unhappy with your treatment by a government or local authority department, or someone providing a service on its behalf, you can complain.

Your complaint can be about any issue concerning how your claim has been handled or how you have been treated. This includes matters such as delays, discourtesy, poor administration, the behaviour of staff, bad advice, or the way in which a particular department's policy or practice impacts on you. You can also ask for compensation for any loss you incur related to your complaint (see below).

If you disagree with a decision about your benefit or tax credit entitlement, see Chapters 56, 57 and 67 instead.

2. Compensation payments

You should expect prompt, courteous and efficient service from staff dealing with your claim. If you are unhappy with the way your claim has been administered, you can ask for compensation. Compensation payments are discretionary.

The DWP, HM Revenue and Customs (HMRC) and local authorities sometimes pay compensation if you can show that you have lost out through their error or delay and the loss cannot be made good by a revision, supersession or appeal (see Chapters 56, 57 and 67) or by backdating your claim. For instance, if you did not claim carer's allowance because you were misled by the DWP and you could not have the benefit backdated for more than three months, you can claim compensation. You may also receive 'consolatory payments' if you are considered to have experienced injustice, hardship or distress.

The DWP should automatically consider whether compensation should be paid if you are owed arrears of benefit, but you should still write to your local DWP office and ask. If you do not get a sympathetic response, ask your MP (see p1408) to write on your behalf or to take up your case with the social security minister.

The DWP uses a guide, *Financial Redress for Maladministration*, to help it decide when and how much compensation (known as 'extra-statutory' or ex gratia payments) should be paid.[1] HMRC's *Complaints and Remedy Guidance* sets out when it makes 'financial redress'.[2]

You should ask for a payment equal to the money you have lost. You can also ask for additional amounts to cover interest on arrears and any extra expenses you had, and to compensate you for any injustice, hardship or distress experienced because of the mistake. If your loss was as a clear result of incorrect advice or negligence on the part of the agency, you may be able to bring a court action for damages. Get legal advice promptly if this is the case.

3. Complaining about the DWP

The DWP has a complaints procedure that applies to all its agencies including:
* the Pension Service;

Part 9: Getting a benefit decision changed
Chapter 61: Complaints
3. Complaining about the DWP

- Jobcentre Plus;
- Debt Management;
- the Disability Service Centre.

The DWP does not deal with complaints about contracted providers – eg, those carrying out medical assessments on its behalf. To complain about a contracted provider, use its own internal complaints procedure. If you are still not satisfied, you can complain to the Independent Case Examiner (see below) and then the Parliamentary and Health Service Ombudsman (see p1409).

You can find information about standards and complaints on the DWP website.[3]

For universal credit (UC) and jobseeker's allowance complaints only, the DWP has an online complaints service: makeacomplaint.dwp.gov.uk. Otherwise you should start your complaint by using the contact details provided in any correspondence about the matter you want to complain about. If you do not have contact details, check the 'Who to contact' section at gov.uk/government/organisations/department-for-work-pensions/about/complaints-procedure.

If after you receive the DWP's initial response you are still unhappy, you can ask that your complaint be passed to the DWP's dedicated Complaints Handling Team. It should deal with your complaint within 15 days or let you know if it is going to take longer.

If you remain unhappy after getting the Complaints Handling Team's final response, you can complain to the Independent Case Examiner.

9 Complaining to the Independent Case Examiner

The Independent Case Examiner (ICE) deals with complaints about DWP agencies and its contracted providers.

ICE's role is to consider whether there has been maladministration. It cannot deal with matters of law or cases that are subject to judicial review or other legal procedures (other than appeals).

You can only make a complaint to ICE if you have already completed the complaints procedure of the particular agency concerned. This usually means that you have had a final response to your complaint. A complaint should be made to ICE no later than six months after the final response.

Complaints to ICE can be made by email to ice@dwp.gov.uk, in writing to PO Box 209, Bootle L20 7WA or by telephone on 0800 414 8529. Text and video relay services are also available: see gov.uk/government/organisations/independent-case-examiner. An appointed representative can act on your behalf if you provide written consent. You must provide all relevant information, including the final response to your complaint from the agency you are complaining about.

ICE should tell you within two weeks if it can accept your complaint. If accepted, ICE then attempts to resolve the complaint within eight weeks by mediating an agreement between you and the agency concerned. If this fails, ICE calls for all the relevant information from the parties and the case is then allocated to an investigation case manager who attempts to settle the complaint by agreeing actions to address the issues, usually within 15 weeks of the case being allocated. If this is not possible, the investigation case manager reports the details of her/his investigation to the ICE who will make a finding and any recommendations on how the complaint should be resolved within 20 weeks of the case being allocated to the investigation case manager. If you remain unhappy, you can ask ICE to review its decision if you have new evidence or can show an error in the report, or ask your MP to consider referring your complaint to the Parliamentary and Health Service Ombudsman (see p1409).

If you are unhappy with the way ICE dealt with your case, use its own complaints process.

Is it worth complaining?

ICE's 2021 annual report shows that it resolved, settled or investigated 1,778 cases in 2020/21 (187 about UC), 343 of which were resolved or settled without investigation. Of the cases investigated, 58 per cent were partially or fully upheld, but in UC cases this rises to 64 per cent. ICE recommendations include apologies, corrective action and financial redress. This shows that in 2020/21, you were likely to get a satisfactory outcome in around seven out of 10 cases but in UC cases this rose to nearly eight out of 10 cases. Note that for cases investigated but not upheld, these include complaints that had 'merit' but all necessary action to resolve the matter had already been taken prior to referral.

4. Complaining about HM Revenue and Customs

You can complain about how HM Revenue and Customs (HMRC) has dealt with your tax credit, child benefit or guardian's allowance claim, or with your national insurance credits or contributions. You can do this online if you have, or set up, a Government Gateway account, by telephone or in writing to HMRC (see gov.uk/complain-about-hmrc). If you want to dispute the recovery of a tax credit overpayment, HMRC has a different process you need to follow (see p1485).

If you are not happy with the initial response ('first tier review'), ask HMRC to review your complaint. The review ('second tier review') should be carried out by a different customer service adviser, who will give you HMRC's final reply to your complaint.

If you are not happy with HMRC's final reply, you can ask the Adjudicator to look into it.

Part 9: Getting a benefit decision changed
Chapter 61: Complaints
4. Complaining about HM Revenue and Customs

Complaining to the Adjudicator

The Adjudicator deals with complaints about HMRC and is similar in nature to the Independent Case Examiner (see p1404). The Adjudicator only investigates a complaint if you have already completed the HMRC internal complaints procedure. You cannot complain direct to the Adjudicator about an HMRC-contracted service provider; you must complain via HMRC first. A complaint should be made within six months of the final response from HMRC.

A complaint to the Adjudicator should be made in writing or using the form available at gov.uk/guidance/contact-the-adjudicators-office. If you have problems, you can telephone the Adjudicator's Office on 0300 057 1111. You can appoint someone to act on your behalf by completing a form available from the Adjudicator's Office website. You must provide the final response to your complaint from HMRC.

Complaints can be made about delays, inappropriate staff behaviour, misleading advice, the application of discretion, or any other form of maladministration. The Adjudicator cannot investigate disputes about matters of law. If the complaint is accepted, the Adjudicator investigates the complaint by reviewing the information you have sent, carrying out further enquiries and reaching a decision about whether HMRC did anything wrong. A formal written decision including any recommendations is then sent to you. Recommedations can include 'redress payments'. HMRC should follow the Adjudicator's recommendations in all but exceptional circumstances.

If you are unhappy with the Adjudicator's response, ask your MP to put your complaint to the Parliamentary and Health Service Ombudsman (see p1409). As well as looking at your complaint about HMRC, the Ombudsman may also look into the way in which the Adjudicator has investigated your complaint. Further information about the Adjudicator can be found at gov.uk/government/organisations/the-adjudicator-s-office.

Is it worth complaining?

The Adjudicator's 2021 annual report does not break down the complaints investigated by subject – eg, tax credits or other matters handled by HMRC. Of the 1,266 complaints about HMRC investigated in 2020/21, just over 24 per cent were partially or fully upheld, compared to 35 per cent, rising to just over 46 per cent in tax credit cases, in 2019/20. The report notes that this decrease 'is mainly due to' coronavirus-related cases about policy decisions outside the Adjudicator's remit. The report highlights examples of tax credit overpayment disputes upheld and where HMRC was not at fault for closing tax credit awards due to a universal credit claim made based on information from other departments.

5. Complaining about a local authority

If you are unhappy about the actions of your local authority or someone providing services on its behalf and wish to make a complaint, ask for a copy of its complaints policy. Local authorities are required to have an effective complaints procedure, which should be made available to the public. If you are unable to obtain the policy, write to the supervisor of the person dealing with your claim, making it clear why you are dissatisfied. Not being able to obtain a copy of the complaints procedure can form part of your complaint. If you do not receive a satisfactory reply, complain to the principal officer. Send a copy of the letter to your ward councillor and to the councillor who chairs the relevant local authority committee – local authority officers are always accountable to the councillors. If this does not produce results, or if the delay is causing you hardship, consider a complaint to the Ombudsman (see p1409) or legal action (see p1410).

Government departments also monitor local authorities, so you could contact your MP or write to the relevant minister – eg, the Secretary of State for Work and Pensions.

6. Complaining about HM Courts and Tribunals Service

Complaints about the administration of your appeal

If you are dissatisfied with the administration of your appeal, complain to HM Courts and Tribunals Service (HMCTS). You can raise a complaint in person with any member of staff at the court or tribunal. Alternatively, you can write, telephone or email the court or tribunal directly (see find-court-tribunal.service.gov.uk/search-option), or complain about HMCTS online at complain-about-a-court-or-tribunal.form.service.justice.gov.uk. You should receive a response to your complaint within 10 working days. If you are not happy with the response, you can ask that your complaint be reviewed. You should receive a response again within 10 working days.

If you think the matter has still not been resolved satisfactorily, ask the Customer Investigation Team to carry out a further review (the senior manager who dealt with your complaint should give you contact details). The Customer Investigation Team aims to respond within 15 days.

If you are still dissatisfied, you can complain to the Parliamentary and Health Service Ombudsman (see p1409).

HMCTS's complaints procedure is at gov.uk/government/organisations/hm-courts-and-tribunals-service/about/complaints-procedure.

Part 9: Getting a benefit decision changed
Chapter 61: Complaints
8. Complaining to the Ombudsman

Complaints about the conduct of tribunal members

If you are unhappy about the way in which you were treated by a tribunal judge or member (eg, s/he was rude or racist), raise the matter initially by writing to the relevant tribunal president within three months of the incident. The name of the appropriate president is at judicialconduct.judiciary.gov.uk/contact-a-tribunal-president.

If your complaint is about the conduct of a tribunal president, complain to the Judicial Conduct Investigations Office (complaints.judicialconduct.gov.uk).

If you are not happy with the response to your complaint about a tribunal judge, member or president, you can complain to the Judicial Appointments and Conduct Ombudsman (see gov.uk/guidance/judicial-conduct-complain-to-the-ombudsman). The Ombudsman's decision is final.

7. **Using your MP**

If you are not satisfied with the response from the officers to whom you have complained, you may wish to take up the matter with your MP. Your MP may also be able to help if you are getting no response to your complaint.

To find out who your MP is and how to contact her/him, call the House of Commons Enquiry Service on 0800 112 4272 (Freephone) or 020 7219 4272, or go to members.parliament.uk/constituencies.

Your MP will probably want to write to the benefit authority for an explanation of what has happened. If you want to make a complaint to the Ombudsman, you must usually do so through your MP. This does not apply if you are complaining about a local authority or tribunal members.

8. **Complaining to the Ombudsman**

The role of the Ombudsman is to investigate complaints of maladministration by government departments, including avoidable delays, failure to advise about appeal rights or refusal to answer reasonable questions or respond to correspondence, discourtesy, racism or sexism. The Parliamentary and Health Service Ombudsman (PHSO) deals with complaints about central government departments, and the Local Government and Social Care Ombudsman (in England) or the Public Services Ombudsman (in Scotland and Wales) handles complaints about local government.

Should you ask for compensation first?

It is probably better to pursue a compensation payment before making a complaint to the Ombudsman. This is because, if the Ombudsman does not uphold your complaint, the benefit authority is unlikely to compensate you. Wherever possible, get and keep receipts for expenses such as postage, telephone calls, travel and professional advice to help prove the cost of any delay or maladministration.

The Ombudsman does not usually investigate a complaint unless you have exhausted the internal complaints procedure. However, if the authority is not acting on your complaint, or there are unreasonable delays, this delay may form part of your complaint. The time limit for lodging a complaint with the Ombudsman is normally 12 months from the date you were notified of the matter complained about. However, a delay in bringing a complaint does not necessarily prevent a complaint being investigated if there are good reasons for the delay.

The Ombudsman can look at documents on your claim held by benefit authorities. You may be interviewed to check any facts. The Ombudsman can recommend financial redress if you have been unfairly treated or experienced a loss as a result of the maladministration.

A public body, such as the DWP or a local authority, is expected to follow the recommendations of an independent complaints service such as the Independent Case Examiner or the Adjudicator unless there are good reasons not to. If it has failed to do so, you may have grounds to complain to the Ombudsman and, in some circumstances, may have grounds for a judicial review (see p1377).

The Parliamentary and Health Service Ombudsman

The PHSO deals with complaints about all central government departments. This includes the DWP, HM Revenue and Customs, HM Courts and Tribunals Service and any agencies carrying out functions on behalf of these departments. 'Complain for change' on the PHSO website provides information to encourage people to complain about government departments and particularly those from under-represented groups by providing Easy Read information and some translated materials: ombudsman.org.uk/making-complaint/before-you-come-to-us/complain-change.

To make a complaint, you contact your MP, who then refers the complaint to the PHSO. See p1408 for how to contact your MP. Remember, the PHSO can only investigate complaints of maladministration and not complaints about entitlement, which should be dealt with by the First-tier Tribunal (see p1297).

The Local Government and Social Care Ombudsman/Public Services Ombudsman

If you have complained to your local authority but you are not satisfied with the outcome, you can apply to the Local Government and Social Care Ombudsman (in England) or the Public Services Ombudsman (in Wales and Scotland). The Ombudsman can investigate any cases of maladministration by local authorities, but not matters of entitlement, which are dealt with by the First-tier Tribunal (see p1297).

You usually complain to the Ombudsman by completing an online form, but you may also be able to start a complaint by post or by telephone (in England, see lgo.org.uk/make-a-complaint or call 0300 061 0614; in Wales, see ombudsman.wales/complaints or call 0300 790 0203; in Scotland, see spso.org.uk/making-complaint or call 0800 377 7330). The Ombudsman may take up to 12 months to complete its investigation but straightforward cases can be dealt with more quickly. A complaint may make the authority review its procedures, which could benefit other claimants.

If you are unhappy with the way in which the Ombudsman has dealt with your complaint, you can ask that it be reviewed internally or take legal action.

9. **Legal action**

In some circumstances, you may have grounds for judicial review against a benefit authority – eg, if it refuses to process your claim or has made a decision against which you have no right of appeal. For further information, see Chapter 59.

You cannot sue a benefit authority for negligence in the way it decides your claim.[4] However, you can seek compensation through the courts if there has been:
- 'misadvice' – ie, if an employee of a benefit authority or HM Courts and Tribunals Service gives wrong advice which leads to financial loss for you; *or*
- unpaid benefit – ie, if your benefit claim has been determined, but you have not been paid; *or*
- discrimination, victimisation or harassment under the Equality Act 2010 or a breach of human rights (see p1381).

Although it is possible to seek compensation through the courts, it should not be your first course of action and should only be considered after getting legal advice.

Notes

2. **Compensation payments**
   1 gov.uk/government/publications/
      compensation-for-poor-service-a-guide-
      for-dwp-staff
   2 gov.uk/hmrc-internal-manuals/
      complaints-and-remedy-guidance

3. **Complaining about the DWP**
   3 gov.uk/government/organisations/
      department-for-work-pensions/about/
      complaints-procedure

9. **Legal action**
   4 *Jones v Department of Employment*
      [1989] QB 1

Part 10

General rules for tax credits

Chapter 62

. . . .

Tax credit amounts

This chapter covers:
1. The relevant period (below)
2. The maximum amount of child tax credit (p1414)
3. The maximum amount of working tax credit (p1419)
4. How to calculate the amount of tax credits (p1427)
5. Change of circumstances (p1432)

Key facts
- The amount of tax credits to which you are entitled depends on your family circumstances and your income.
- There are no limits on the amount of savings or other capital you can have.
- If you get income support (IS), income-based jobseeker's allowance (JSA), income-related employment and support allowance (ESA) or pension credit (PC), you automatically get the maximum amount of tax credits that you could receive.
- If you do not get IS, income-based JSA, income-related ESA or PC, you may get less than your tax credits maximum amount, depending on your income level.
- Your child tax credit maximum amount depends on how many children you have, and whether any child in your family has a disability.
- Your working tax credit maximum amount depends on whether you are single with no dependants, a lone parent or a member of a couple, the hours you work, whether you (or your partner) are disabled, and whether you have eligible childcare costs.

10

---

1. **The relevant period**

The amount of tax credits you can get is based on your entitlement during a 'relevant period'. Tax credit awards are calculated using a maximum annual amount that you could receive.
- Your award is usually calculated on the basis that you will be entitled to tax credits for the whole tax year (6 April to 5 April), and your relevant period is therefore one year.[1] Your annual entitlement is calculated and then paid to you over the course of that year.

Part 10: General rules for tax credits
Chapter 62: Tax credit amounts
2. The maximum amount of child tax credit

- If your circumstances change in the course of the year, and your award is amended, a new relevant period begins – calculated on the basis that it will end at the end of the tax year.[2] In both cases, you are entitled to tax credits for less than a year, so only a proportion of the annual amount can be paid.

In order to work out your maximum amount of tax credits exactly, therefore, you must know the length of your relevant period.

Relevant period

A **'relevant period'** for child tax credit (CTC) is the number of days in a period of an award during which your maximum amount remains the same.[3]

A **'relevant period'** for working tax credit (WTC) is the number of days in a period during which the elements making up your maximum amount of tax credit (apart from the childcare element) remain the same and your average weekly childcare charge does not change by £10 or more or reduce to nil.[4]

If you are entitled to both CTC and WTC, a **'relevant period'** is one during which both of the above conditions are satisfied.[5]

2. **The maximum amount of child tax credit**

Calculate the maximum amount of child tax credit (CTC) you can get by adding together the 'elements' that apply to you.[6] The amount of each element is set at an annual rate. To convert the annual rate to a daily rate, divide it by the number of days in the tax year (365 in 2022/23) and round up to the nearest penny. To calculate entitlement, multiply the daily rate of each element by the number of days in the relevant period. The effect of this is that entitlement in a whole year is always slightly higher than the annual rates listed below – eg, for the family element, £547.50 in 2022/23 (£1.50 x 365). If you are entitled to CTC for a period of less than a year, or if your entitlement changes part way through the year, the amount of each of these elements is adjusted so that the correct proportion of your annual maximum amount is paid.[7] How entitlement is calculated when entitlement changes part way through a tax year is explained on p1432. If your child is disabled, s/he may qualify for a disabled child element.

Element	Annual rate	Daily rate
Family element	£545	£1.50
Child element	£2,935	£8.05
Disabled child element		
– lower rate	£3,545	£9.72
– higher rate for a severely disabled child	£4,975	£13.64

Family element

One family element (£545 annual rate) is payable if you are responsible for a child or young person born before 6 April 2017.[8] The family element is not payable in claims that only include children born on or after 6 April 2017. If you are getting CTC for a child born on or after 6 April 2017, without the family element, and then become responsible for another child born before 6 April 2017, the family element is added from the date you became responsible for the older child. If you are responsible for a child born before 6 April 2017, the family element is still payable. You do not have to have been entitled to CTC before 6 April 2017. Only one family element is payable, regardless of how many children you have.

Child element

You get a child element (£2,935 annual rate) for each child or young person you are responsible for (see p273). However, it is not payable for a child born on or after 6 April 2017, if you have two or more other children already included in your CTC award (unless an exception applies – see p1416).[9] This is known as the 'two-child limit' (see below). You get a child element for each child born before 6 April 2017. You do not have to have been entitled to CTC before 6 April 2017.

The two-child limit

You cannot get a child element for a child born on or after 6 April 2017 if you already have two or more other children included in your award, unless an exception applies. You can always get an element for a child born before 6 April 2017.

When establishing the number of children you have for this purpose, a child who is covered by the first two exceptions on p1416 (ie, you have adopted her/him or s/he is living with you under a 'non-parental caring arrangement') is ignored.

So you can get an element for:

- any child born before 6 April 2017; *and*
- a child born on or after 6 April 2017 who is not counted as your third or subsequent child; *and*
- a third or subsequent child born on or after 6 April 2017 to whom an exception applies.

Examples

Amy has four children. Three were born before 6 April 2017, and one was born on 6 May 2017. No exceptions apply to the children. Amy gets three child elements for the three children born before 6 April 2017.

Jim and his partner have three children. Two were born before 6 April 2017 and are Jim's nephews, who have been living with them for several years under a child arrangements

Part 10: General rules for tax credits
Chapter 62: Tax credit amounts
2. The maximum amount of child tax credit

order. The other child was born on 6 May 2017. They are entitled to three child elements
for all three children. An element is included for the two older children because they were
born before 6 April 2017. Because Jim's nephews do not count for the purposes of the
two-child limit, an element is also included for the child born on 6 May 2017.

The order of children (ie, whether a child is the first, second, third or subsequent child) is determined by allocating each child a date:

- if you or your partner are the child's parent, the child's date of birth; *or*
- in any other case, the date you/your partner became responsible for her/him.

The child with the earliest allocated date is usually the 'first child', and so on. However, if the date for two or more children is the same, the order of children must be decided to ensure you receive the highest number of child elements.

The child element can become payable for a third child to whom the two-child limit would apply when an older child leaves the household (as you are no longer responsible for her/him) or when a young person leaves education (as s/he no longer qualifies). In these situations, you should report the change as soon as possible so that you continue to get the maximum two child elements. You should always notify the Tax Credit Office of the birth of a third or subsequent child so that the child element can become payable if there is a change, and because other elements for disabled children (see p1418) and childcare costs in working tax credit (see p1422) remain payable.

Exceptions

The 'two-child limit' does not apply to the following children.[10]

- A child born in a multiple birth, other than the first born if you already have two or more children. So, if you have:
  - no older children, you get the child element for all children in a multiple birth;
  - one older child, you get the child element for all children in a multiple birth;
  - two or more older children, you get the child element for all but one of the children in a multiple birth.
- A child living with you under a 'non-parental caring arrangement' – ie:
  - a child whose parent is a child or qualifying young person for whom you are responsible; *or*
  - where the child is living with you on a long-term basis because s/he is unable to live with her/his parents and you are caring for her/him as a family member or friend. You or your partner must not be the child's parent or step-parent and you must:
    - be named in a child arrangements order under section 8 of the Children Act 1989 or a residence order under Article 8 of the Children (Northern Ireland) Order 1995 as a person with whom the child is to live; *or*

- be the appointed or special guardian, or be entitled to guardian's allowance, for the child; *or*
- have a kinship care order under section 72(1) of the Children and Young People (Scotland) Act 2014, or parental responsibilities or rights under section 80 of the Adoption and Children (Scotland) Act 2007 for the child; *or*
- continue to be responsible for the child if any of the above bullet points applied immediately before the child's 16th birthday; *or*
- be caring for the child because otherwise it is likely s/he would be taken into the care of the local authority. You must provide evidence from a social worker (see gov.uk/government/publications/support-for-a-child-who-is-informally-living-with-you).

- A child who is being adopted by you from local authority care or who has been placed with you for adoption. This exception does *not* apply if:
  - you or your partner were the child's step-parent immediately before the adoption;
  - you or your partner have been the child's parent (other than by adoption) at any other time;
  - the child is being adopted directly from abroad.

- A child who is likely to have been conceived as a result of rape, or in a controlling or coercive relationship ('non-consensual conception'). You must not be living at the same address as the alleged perpetrator for this exception to apply, even though you might have been living with the alleged perpetrator at the time of conception. A controlling or coercive relationship includes behaviour that causes you to fear, on at least two occasions, that violence will be used against you, or that causes you serious alarm or distress which has a substantial adverse effect on your day-to-day activities. You must provide evidence from an 'approved person' that you have had contact with her/him or another approved person about the rape or relationship. A list of 'approved persons' is in official guidance and includes healthcare professionals, social workers and approved organisations such as specialist rape charities.[11] Third-party evidence is not required if there has been a conviction for rape or coercive, controlling behaviour in the UK, or for a similar offence abroad, or if you have been awarded criminal injuries compensation after a sexual offence, physical abuse or mental injury, and it is likely that the offence or injury resulted in the conception. You can be treated as having provided evidence if you have already provided it to the DWP for universal credit, income support or jobseeker's allowance purposes.

If you are the step-parent of the child but are no longer part of a couple with the child's parent, the exception can continue to apply if you have continuously been entitled to CTC and responsible for the child. Get advice.[12]

Part 10: General rules for tax credits
Chapter 62: Tax credit amounts
2. The maximum amount of child tax credit

Disabled child element (lower rate)

You get a disabled child element at the lower rate (£3,545 annual rate) for each child you are responsible for who gets disability living allowance (DLA) or child disability payment (CDP), or young person who gets personal independence payment (PIP), adult disability payment (ADP) or armed forces independence payment, or who is certified as blind or severely sight impaired by a consultant ophthalmologist, or was certified in the last 28 weeks. If your child qualifies for the higher rate for a severely disabled child, this is payable instead of the lower rate. The element still applies if DLA, CDP, PIP or ADP has stopped because your child or young person is in hospital.[13] It is paid in addition to the child element for that child. You can get the disabled child element for a third or subsequent child born on or after 6 April 2017 who is disabled, even if you are not getting a child element for her/him.[14] If you were getting CTC in 2016/17 and your child was entitled to DLA or PIP, but you were not getting a disabled child element, the government announced that it would pay the element even if you had not notifed HMRC of the DLA/PIP award.[15]

Higher rate for a severely disabled child

You get the disabled child element at the higher rate for a severely disabled child (£4,975 annual rate) for each child you are responsible for who gets the DLA care component highest rate or the higher rate of the CDP care component, or young person who gets the PIP daily living component enhanced rate, ADP care component highest rate or armed forces independence payment. The element still applies if DLA, CDP, PIP or ADP has stopped because your child or young person is in hospital.[16] It is paid in addition to the child element for that child. It is paid instead of the disabled child element lower rate for that child. You can get the higher rate for a third or subsequent child born on or after 6 April 2017, even if you are not getting a child element for her/him. If you were getting CTC in 2016/17 and your child was entitled to DLA highest care component or PIP enhanced daily living component, but you were not getting the higher rate for a severely disabled child, the government announced that it would pay the element even if you had not notified HMRC of the DLA/PIP award, or a change in the award.[17]

The higher rate for a severely disabled child may be referred to as the 'severely disabled child element' on tax credit award notices.

10

3. **The maximum amount of working tax credit**

Calculate the maximum amount of working tax credit (WTC) you get by adding together the 'elements' that apply to you.[18] The amount of each element, except the childcare element, is set at an annual rate. To convert the annual rate to a daily rate, divide it by the number of days in the tax year (365 in 2022/23) and round up to the nearest penny. To calculate entitlement, multiply the daily rate of each element by the number of days in the relevant period. The effect of this is that entitlement in a whole year is always slightly higher than the annual rates listed below – eg, for the lone parent or couple element, £2,127.95 in 2022/23 (£5.83 x 365). The amount of the childcare element is set using your average *weekly* childcare costs.[19] See p1422 for how your childcare element is calculated.

If you are entitled to WTC for a period of less than a year, or if your entitlement changes part way through the year, the amount of the elements is adjusted so that the correct proportion of your annual maximum amount is paid.[20] See p1432 for how your entitlement is calculated when it changes part way through a tax year.

Element	Annual rate	Daily rate
Basic element	£2,070	£5.68
Lone parent element	£2,125	£5.83
Couple element	£2,125	£5.83
30-hour element	£860	£2.36
Disabled worker element	£3,345	£9.17
Severe disability element	£1,445	£3.96
Childcare element: see p1422.		

Basic element

One basic element (£2,070 annual rate) is paid with each award of WTC. To be entitled to this element, you must be engaged in 'qualifying remunerative work' (see p284).[21] Unless you qualify for the basic element of WTC, you cannot qualify for any of the other elements.[22]

Lone parent element

You get the lone parent element (£2,125 annual rate) if you claim as a single person and are responsible for a child or qualifying young person.[23]

Couple element

You get the couple element (£2,125 annual rate) if you are a couple making a joint claim (see p1459).[24] If you are not responsible for a child or qualifying young

Part 10: General rules for tax credits
Chapter 62: Tax credit amounts
3. The maximum amount of working tax credit

person, you cannot get it if your partner is serving a prison sentence of more than 12 months or is a 'person subject to immigration control' (see p1524), but you must still make a joint claim.[25] You can only have one couple element included in your maximum amount.[26] For when you count as a couple, see p1460.

30-hour element

You get a 30-hour element (£860 annual rate) if you are:[27]
* a single claimant who works for at least 30 hours a week; *or*
* making a joint claim and either or both of you work for at least 30 hours a week; *or*
* making a joint claim, responsible for a child or qualifying young person and:
  – you are both working; *and*
  – one of you works at least 16 hours a week; *and*
  – your joint hours of work total at least 30 hours a week.

You can only have one 30-hour element included in your maximum amount.[28] The 30-hour element is only included during periods in which you are treated as being in work (see p288) if you qualified for it before the period began.

Disabled worker element

You get a disabled worker element (£3,345 annual rate) if you:[29]
* work at least 16 hours a week; *and*
* have a disability which puts you at a disadvantage in getting a job; *and*
* receive, or have recently received, a qualifying benefit for sickness or disability.

If you are claiming as a couple, at least one of you must satisfy all these conditions – ie, it is not payable if only you are working and your partner is disabled.

If both you and your partner meet all these conditions, two disabled worker elements can be paid.[30]

Having 'a disability which puts you at a disadvantage in getting a job' means you must meet any one of the conditions listed in Appendix 3.[31] For initial claims only (ie, no entitlement to the disabled worker element in the preceding two years), this can include undergoing a period of rehabilitation as a result of an illness or accident, but only for the remainder of the tax year in which you claim.

In order to count as receiving a 'qualifying benefit', you must satisfy one of the following conditions. A disabled worker element can be included in calculating your maximum amount in a new claim or added to an existing tax credit award at any time during the tax year if your award is revised (see p1432). You must:
* for at least one day in the 182 days immediately preceding the date your award is calculated or revised, have been in receipt of:
  – incapacity benefit (IB) at the long-term or short-term higher rate; *or*
  – severe disablement allowance (SDA); *or*

- employment and support allowance (ESA) for at least 28 weeks (including linked periods); *or*
- credits for limited capability for work following time limiting of contributory ESA, for at least 28 weeks (including periods on ESA and linked periods); *or*
- ESA or credits (as above), together with IB, SDA or statutory sick pay (SSP) for at least 28 weeks (including linked periods); *or*

- for at least one day in the 182 days immediately preceding the date your award is calculated or revised, have been in receipt of a disability premium paid for you with income support (IS), income-based jobseeker's allowance (JSA) or housing benefit (HB), or a higher pensioner premium with IS or JSA; *or*
- have received for at least 140 days forming a single period of incapacity for work (see p823) or limited capability for work (see Chapter 45) (the last of which must have fallen within 56 days of the date your award is calculated or revised) SSP, occupational sick pay, ESA or credits for limited capability for work for a period of 20 weeks; *and*
  - have a disability at the date of the claim which is likely to last for at least six months (or for the rest of your life if your death is expected within that time); *and*
  - have gross earnings that are less than they were before the disability began by at least the greater of 20 per cent and £15 a week; *or*
- have undertaken 'training for work' for at least one day in the 56 days immediately preceding the date your award is calculated or revised *and* were receiving one of the benefits or credits listed in the first bullet point above within the 56 days before that training started. 'Training for work' means training provided under the Employment and Training Act 1973, or, in Scotland, the Enterprise and New Towns (Scotland) Act 1990, or training which you attend for 16 hours or more a week if its primary purpose is teaching occupational or vocational skills;[32] *or*
- get disability living allowance (DLA), personal independence payment (PIP), adult disability payment (ADP), attendance allowance (AA), armed forces independence payment or a mobility supplement or constant attendance allowance payable with a war pension or industrial injuries disablement benefit (IIDB). If your qualifying benefit stops or is not payable (eg, because you are in hospital), you are no longer entitled to the disability element on these grounds;[33] *or*
- have an invalid carriage or similar vehicle; *or*
- have been entitled to WTC with the disabled worker element under one of the above first four bullet points and still have a disability which puts you at a disadvantage in getting a job (see Appendix 3). In this case, you can continue to be entitled to the disabled worker element indefinitely. **Note:** this does not apply if you previously only qualified through DLA or PIP, but if you were getting HB with a disability premium, you can remain entitled even though DLA or PIP has stopped.[34]

Part 10: General rules for tax credits
Chapter 62: Tax credit amounts
3. The maximum amount of working tax credit

Renewals or linked claims

If you renew or make a further claim for WTC within 56 days of the day your previous award ended, *and* in that earlier claim you qualified for the disabled worker element under any of the first four bullet points above, you are treated as though you still meet those conditions and can continue to get this element in your new award. You must also still have a disability which puts you at a disadvantage in getting a job (see Appendix 3 – for renewals and new claims within two years of a previous entitlement to the disabled worker element, this must be under Part 1[35]). You can benefit from this rule as long as you are still entitled to child tax credit (CTC), which allows you to make a further claim for WTC.

You can still benefit from this rule if your income was too high for you to get any WTC within the previous 56 days, provided your WTC maximum amount would have included the disabled worker element on one of the above grounds.[36]

Severe disability element

You get a severe disability element (£1,445 annual rate) if you get the highest rate of the care component of DLA, the enhanced rate of the daily living component of PIP, higher rate of the daily living component of ADP, the higher rate of AA, or armed forces independence payment (including if payment of these has been suspended because you are in hospital).[37] It can be paid in addition to the disabled worker element. If you have a partner who meets this condition, a severe disability element can be included for her/him, whether or not s/he is in work.

If both you and your partner meet the condition, two severe disability elements can be paid.[38]

Childcare element

Your maximum amount of WTC can include a childcare element to help meet the cost of 'relevant childcare' (see p1424).[39] This element is 70 per cent of your actual childcare costs of up to £175 a week for one child or £300 a week for two or more children – ie, up to £122.50 or £210 a week.[40]

To get the childcare element of WTC, you or your partner must be 'responsible for' at least one child.[41] You can include childcare costs for a third or subsequent child born on or after 6 April 2017, even if you do not get the child element for her/him because of the 'two-child limit' (see p1415). You do not have to be the child's parent. 'Responsible for' has the same meaning for WTC as it does for CTC (see p273).[42]

The childcare element is part of the maximum WTC calculation and cannot be claimed on its own or as part of CTC.[43]

You must be:[44]

- a lone parent working at least 16 hours a week; *or*

- a member of a couple and:
  - you are both working at least 16 hours a week; *or*
  - one of you is working at least 16 hours a week, and the other is incapacitated (see below), entitled to carer's allowance (including an underlying entitlement) or is in hospital or in prison (serving a sentence or remanded in custody).

You are still entitled to the childcare element during periods throughout which you are treated as being in work for WTC purposes – eg, during the first 39 weeks of maternity leave or the four-week run-on period (see p288).[45]

Incapacitated

You or your partner are treated as being '**incapacitated**' if you (or your partner, if s/he is the one who is not working):[46]

- get IB or SDA; *or*
- have been getting contributory ESA for at least 28 weeks; *or*
- get contributory ESA after a period on SSP, which adds up to at least 28 weeks, provided you satisfied the national insurance contribution conditions for contributory ESA (the 28 weeks can have been in one period or in periods that can be linked together); *or*
- get contributory ESA after being transferred from IB or SDA; *or*
- are entitled to credits for limited capability for work only because your contributory ESA has stopped after 52 weeks; *or*
- get AA, DLA, PIP, ADP or armed forces independence payment (or an equivalent award paid as an increase under the war pensions or industrial injuries disablement scheme), or would get it but for the fact that you are in hospital; *or*
- get IIDB with constant attendance allowance; *or*
- have an award of HB which includes a disability premium or a childcare earnings disregard, because the non-working member of the couple is incapacitated; *or*
- were treated as incapacitated solely on the basis of being paid council tax benefit on 31 March 2013 that included a disability premium because the non-working member of the couple was incapacitated, but only if your entitlement to WTC remains continuous from 1 April 2013; *or*
- have an invalid carriage or similar vehicle; *or*
- get an equivalent benefit from a European Economic Area (EEA) country.[47]

10

You can claim the childcare element for a new baby as well as for any other children for whom you are responsible while you are on statutory maternity, adoption, paternity, shared parental or parental bereavement leave (for the first 39 weeks only), or while you are paid maternity allowance. See p288 for these and other situations when you are treated as being in full-time work.

Part 10: General rules for tax credits
Chapter 62: Tax credit amounts
3. The maximum amount of working tax credit

Relevant childcare charges can be for any child in your family up to the last day of the week in which 1 September falls, following the child's 15th birthday or her/his 16th birthday if s/he qualifies for the disabled child element (see p1418).[48]

You can only include the charges that you pay for childcare that is being provided. If you get childcare vouchers from your employer, your WTC cannot include the childcare element for the amount covered by the voucher.

You cannot get the childcare element for free early years' entitlement (see p854) or for charges in respect of the child's compulsory education or, in England, for childcare during school hours for a child of compulsory school age. If you have made an agreement for the provision of future childcare, you can include charges which you will pay and you can notify HM Revenue and Customs (HMRC) of the charges up to a week in advance.[49]

You cannot get tax-free childcare (see p856) and tax credits at the same time, and your entire tax credit claim will end if you apply for tax-free childcare payments.[50]

Relevant childcare

In England, in order to be 'relevant childcare', the childcare must be:[51]
- provided by a childcare provider correctly registered by Ofsted; *or*
- provided by a childminder who is registered with a childminder agency registered with Ofsted; *or*
- provided to a child who is three or four years old by a school under the direction of the school's governing body (or equivalent) on school premises or premises that may be inspected as part of an inspection of the school by the Chief Inspector; *or*
- out-of-school-hours childcare or supervised activity-based childcare provided for a child aged between five and 15 years (16 if disabled) by a school on the school premises or premises that may be inspected as part of an inspection of the school by the Chief Inspector; *or*
- provided for a child by a person registered with the Care Quality Commission as a service provider in relation to the regulated activity of personal care; *or*
- provided by a foster parent who is also registered with Ofsted, but not in respect of the child who is being fostered by that foster parent.

In Wales, in order to be 'relevant childcare', the childcare must be:[52]
- provided by a childcare provider registered by the Care Inspectorate Wales; *or*
- provided by an approved foster parent, who is providing daycare or childminding for a child aged eight or over, but not for a child who is being fostered by that foster parent. If the child is under eight, the foster parent must also be registered by the Care Inspectorate Wales; *or*
- out-of-school-hours childcare provided by a school on the school premises or by a local authority; *or*

- provided in the child's home by a person approved under the Tax Credits (Approval of Child Care Providers) (Wales) Scheme 2007 or, if several children are being looked after, in one of the children's homes; *or*
- provided by a domiciliary worker or nurse from an agency registered under the Regulation and Inspection of Social Care (Wales) Act 2016 in the child's home.

In Scotland, in order to be 'relevant childcare', the childcare must be:[53]
- provided by a childcare provider registered by the Care Inspectorate; *or*
- in an out-of-school-hours childcare club registered by the Care Inspectorate; *or*
- provided in the child's home by, or introduced through, a childcare agency, sitter service or nanny agency registered by the Care Inspectorate.

If you are a member of the armed forces or a civil servant working for the Ministry of Defence in another country, you can include childcare costs approved by the Department for Education.[54] If you use a childcare provider in an EEA country, you can include childcare costs approved under that country's equivalent registration scheme.[55]

You cannot get help with the costs of childcare provided in your own home if that care is provided by a relative of your child.

'**Relative**' means parent, grandparent, aunt or uncle, brother or sister, whether related by blood, marriage, civil partnership or 'affinity'.[56] By 'affinity', we understand that HMRC means people related through a partner, rather than a spouse or civil partner. For example, if childcare is provided in your home by your partner's mother, she is related to the child by affinity, even if your partner is not the child's parent, and so you cannot claim for the cost of paying her.

You can claim help with the costs of childcare provided by a relative away from your home, but s/he must also be a registered or approved childminder. In practice, it is unlikely that a childminder would be able to remain registered for long if only looking after a child to whom s/he was related – contact the relevant agency for advice in this situation. If approved under the Tax Credits (Approval of Child Care Providers) (Wales) Scheme 2007, s/he must also care for at least one other child who is not related to her/him.[57]

The amount of the childcare element

Step one: work out your relevant period
Add up the number of days in your relevant period (see p1413). If you are making or renewing a claim for tax credits for a new tax year, your award is usually based on entitlement at the same rate for a whole tax year, and your relevant period is one year. The tax year 2022/23 has 365 days.

Step two: calculate your relevant childcare charge
Your 'relevant childcare charge' is your average weekly charge. The way in which your average weekly charge is calculated depends on whether you pay for

Part 10: General rules for tax credits
Chapter 62: Tax credit amounts
3. The maximum amount of working tax credit

childcare weekly, monthly or at some other interval, and on whether the amount you pay varies over time.[58]

- If you pay for childcare on a weekly basis and the charge is a fixed weekly amount, add together the charges in the most recent four weeks before the claim and divide by four.

- If you pay for childcare on a weekly basis, have paid for childcare for at least 52 weeks and the charge varies over time, add together the charges in the last 52 weeks and divide by 52.

- If you pay on a monthly basis and the charge is a fixed monthly amount, multiply that monthly amount by 12 and divide the total by 52.

- If you pay on a monthly basis and the charge varies from month to month, add together the charges for the last 12 months and divide the total by 52.

- If there is insufficient information for HMRC to establish your average weekly charge by any of the above methods, the charge is calculated on the basis of information you provide about your childcare costs, using any method which, in its opinion, is reasonable.

- If you have entered into an agreement to pay for childcare that will be provided during the period of your award, your average weekly childcare costs are calculated on the basis of your own written estimate of these. In practice, you provide this estimate on your tax credit claim form and annual review.

- If you are only paying childcare costs for a fixed period (eg, over the summer holidays), your relevant childcare charge can be averaged and paid over that period rather than over the whole year.

When you have calculated your average weekly childcare charges by one of these methods, round up the figure to the nearest whole pound. This is the figure that you should notify to HMRC. If this weekly amount is less than the maximum of £175 a week for one child, or £300 a week for two or more children, your actual childcare costs are used, as in Step three. If your actual childcare costs are more than these limits, the maximum amounts are used, as in Step four. There is no minimum amount of childcare charges that can be included.

Step three: calculate your actual childcare costs for the relevant period
The weekly amount from Step two is converted to an amount covering your relevant period. Multiply the weekly charge by 52 to calculate the annual amount. Divide this figure by the number of days in the current tax year to find the daily rate, and then multiply this daily rate by the number of days in your relevant period. This gives your childcare costs for the relevant period. There is no rounding up or down for actual childcare costs at this stage.[59]

Step four: calculate your maximum eligible childcare costs for the relevant period

Divide the maximum eligible weekly amounts by seven and round up to the nearest penny to find the daily rate. Multiply this by the number of days in the relevant period.

Maximum childcare costs	Weekly rate	Daily rate
One child	£175	£25.00
Two or more children	£300	£42.86

Step five: calculate the childcare element for the relevant period

Take the lower of the two figures from Steps three and four, and calculate 70 per cent of that figure. Round up the amount to the nearest penny. This gives your childcare element for the relevant period.

Example

Tracy, a lone parent with two children aged two and six, pays a fixed amount of £200 every week in eligible childcare costs for her two children. Her childcare element for the whole of the tax year is calculated as follows.

Step one: work out her relevant period

Tracy's relevant period is one year (365 days).

Step two: calculate her relevant childcare charge

Her relevant childcare charge is £200 a week for two children. This is below the maximum of £300 a week, so her actual childcare costs are used.

Step three: calculate her actual childcare costs for the relevant period

£200 x 52 = £10,400

(£10,400 ÷ 365) x 365 = £10,400

Step four is not necessary because actual childcare costs are below the maximum.

Step five: calculate the childcare element for the relevant period

Childcare element is 70% x £10,400 = £7,280

Tracy's childcare element for the relevant period (here, one whole tax year) is £7,280.

4. **How to calculate the amount of tax credits**

If you get certain benefits

If you or your partner get income support (IS), income-based jobseeker's allowance (JSA), income-related employment and support allowance (ESA) or pension credit (PC), you are automatically entitled to the maximum amount of child tax credit (CTC) or working tax credit (WTC). **Note:** this does not apply to WTC during the four-week 'run-on' period after stopping work (see p289).[60] You calculate the

Part 10: General rules for tax credits
Chapter 62: Tax credit amounts
4. How to calculate the amount of tax credits

maximum amount by adding together the elements of each tax credit for which you qualify over your relevant period, as described on pp1414–1427. Your maximum amount is not subject to any reduction during the period you are getting IS, income-based JSA, income-related ESA or PC, regardless of your income in the rest of the current or previous tax year (but see Chapter 65 if an overpayment is being recovered from your award).

If you do not get certain benefits

If you or your partner do *not* get IS, income-based JSA, income-related ESA or PC, your entitlement is worked out as described below.

Step one: work out your relevant period

Add up the number of days in your relevant period (see p1413). If you are making a claim for tax credits at the beginning of a new tax year, your award is based on entitlement at the same rate for a whole tax year, and your relevant period is one year. The tax year 2022/23 has 365 days.

Step two: calculate your maximum entitlement for the relevant period

Identify the different elements of each tax credit for which you are eligible. Take each element's daily rate (see pxxi), apart from the childcare element of WTC.

Multiply this daily rate by the number of days in the relevant period. Add the adjusted amounts of each element together. Next, calculate your childcare element for the relevant period as described on p1425.

Add the childcare element for the relevant period to the other elements for the relevant period to find your maximum entitlement for the relevant period.

Step three: work out your relevant income

The income used in the tax credit calculation is called your 'relevant income' (see Chapter 63).

HM Revenue and Customs (HMRC) begins by using your previous tax year's income to calculate your award for the current year. To finalise your entitlement at the end of the tax year, it requires details of your income in the year that has just ended (the current year's income) and compares this with the previous year's income. If your income has not changed, the current year's income is used. If your income has changed by a disregarded amount or less, your entitlement is still based on the previous year's income. If your income has changed by more than a disregarded amount, your entitlement is based on the current year's income after the disregard. Your relevant income is calculated as follows.[61]

- If your current year's income is more than your previous year's income and the difference is not more than £2,500, your previous year's income is used.
- If your current year's income is more than your previous year's income and the difference is more than £2,500, your current year's income minus £2,500 is used.

- If your current year's income is less than your previous year's income and the difference is not more than £2,500, your previous year's income is used.
- If your current year's income is less than your previous year's income and the difference is more than £2,500, your current year's income plus £2,500 is used.

Divide this income by the number of days in the tax year to which your claim for tax credits relates (365 in 2022/23) to find the daily rate, then multiply this by the number of days in the relevant period. Round down this amount to the nearest penny. This is your income in the relevant period. See p1436 for more on relevant income, including if your tax credit award is finalised during the year because you become entitled to universal credit.

Step four: compare your income with the threshold
Find the annual threshold that applies to you.
- If you are entitled to WTC only, the annual threshold is £6,770.
- If you are entitled to WTC *and* CTC, the annual threshold is £6,770.
- If you are entitled to CTC only, the annual threshold is £17,005.

Divide the threshold that applies to you by the number of days in the current tax year (no rounding at this stage), then multiply this figure by the number of days in the relevant period. Round up this amount to the nearest penny. This figure is your threshold for the relevant period.

Step five: calculate tax credit entitlement for the relevant period
- If your income is less than the threshold that applies to you, you get the maximum amount of tax credit(s).
- If your income is greater than the threshold that applies to you, subtract the threshold figure from your relevant income to find your excess income. Calculate 41 per cent of this excess income and round down to the nearest penny. Finally, reduce your maximum amount of tax credit(s) by this amount.
- The different elements of your maximum tax credit taper away in a set order.
  - First, the elements of WTC, except for the childcare element, are reduced.
  - Second, the childcare element is reduced.
  - Third, the child elements of CTC plus any disabled child elements for your children are reduced.
  - Finally, the family element is reduced.

If you get CTC only, or WTC only, and the calculation results in entitlement of less than £26, no tax credit award is made. If you get both CTC and WTC and the total entitlement is less than £26, no award is made.[62]

To find out the amount of your weekly payment, divide the above total by the number of days in your relevant period to find the daily rate and then multiply

Part 10: General rules for tax credits
Chapter 62: Tax credit amounts
4. How to calculate the amount of tax credits

this daily rate by seven. If your tax credit is paid four-weekly, multiply the daily rate by 28 to calculate the amount of your payments.

Example

Tracy, a lone parent with two children aged two and six, has been getting tax credits for several years. During 2021/22, she worked 20 hours a week and earned £8.91 an hour gross. During the tax year 2022/23, she expects to continue to work the same hours, with a rise in pay to £9.50 an hour.

Step one: work out the relevant period

Tracy's relevant period is 365 days in 2022/23.

Step two: calculate her maximum entitlement for the relevant period

		Daily rate	x 365
CTC	Family element	£1.50	£547.50
	Child element for two-year-old child	£8.05	£2,938.25
	Child element for six-year-old child	£8.05	£2,938.25
WTC	Basic element	£5.68	£2,073.20
	Lone parent element	£5.83	£2,127.95
	Childcare element		£7,280.00
Maximum amount of tax credits			**£17,905.15**

Step three: work out her relevant income

In 2021/22, Tracy earned £9,291.85 ((£8.91 x 20 hours) ÷ 7 days) x 365 (rounded down to the nearest penny).

She continues at the same hours, with a small rise in pay during 2022/23.

In 2022/23, she expects to earn £9,907.14 ((£9.50 x 20 hours) ÷ 7 days) x 365 (rounded down to the nearest penny).

During the year in which tax credits are paid (2022/23), as the increase is below the disregard, her income for the year 2021/22 is used.

Tracy's income for the relevant period is therefore:

(£9,291.85 ÷ 365) x 365 = £9,291.85 (rounded down to the nearest penny)

Step four: compare her income with the threshold for the relevant period

As Tracy is eligible for both WTC and CTC, her annual threshold figure is £6,770.

The threshold for the relevant period is therefore:

(£6,770 ÷ 365) x 365 = £6,770 (rounded up to the nearest penny)

Step five: calculate tax credit entitlement for the relevant period

Tracy has excess income of £2,521.85 (£9,291.85 income — threshold figure of £6,770).

Apply the taper of 41 per cent to this excess income:

41% x £2,521.85 = £1,033.95 (rounded down to the nearest penny)

Tracy's maximum tax credit (£17,905.15) is reduced by this amount. Her total tax credit entitlement is:

£17,905.15 – £1,033.95 = £16,871.20

The reduction is first applied to the elements of her WTC, apart from the childcare element.

Tracy's tax credit entitlement for the tax year 2022/23 is:

WTC (not including childcare element)	£3,167.20
Childcare element	£7,280.00
CTC	£6,424.00
Total tax credits	**£16,871.20**

Tax credits are paid weekly or four-weekly. To find the approximate weekly rate of payment, this figure is divided by 365 (the number of days in Tracy's relevant period) and multiplied by 7.

(£16,871.20 ÷ 365) x 7 = £323.56

Calculating the amount of tax credits: a quick way

For a rough projection of an award, you can use the annual rates as follows.

Step one: calculate maximum tax credits

Add together the annual rates of CTC and WTC elements to which you are entitled. For the childcare element, multiply 70 per cent of the weekly cost by 52 to give an annual amount.

Step two: work out relevant income

This is either your income in the previous tax year, or an estimate of your current year's income after a disregard, if it has increased or decreased by more than the disregarded amounts (see p1428).

Step three: compare income with threshold

The threshold is £6,770 if you are eligible for WTC only, or to WTC and CTC. The threshold is £17,005 if you are eligible for CTC only – ie, you are not working sufficient hours to qualify for WTC.

If your income is below the threshold, the maximum tax credit in Step one is payable.

If your income is above the threshold, the difference is used for Step four.

Step four: work out tax credits payable

The maximum amount of tax credits in Step one is reduced by 41 per cent of your income above the threshold in Step three. This gives an annual figure for a complete tax year, which can be misleading as circumstances may change. It may be more helpful to divide by 52 to give a weekly income figure.

Note: a new calculation must be made if your circumstances change or if your income goes up or down by more than you estimated.

Part 10: General rules for tax credits
Chapter 62: Tax credit amounts
5. Change of circumstances

* *

Example

As in the previous examples, Tracy is a lone parent with two children, working 20 hours a week at the minimum wage, paying £200 a week for childcare.

Step one: calculate maximum tax credits

Maximum CTC = £545 (family element) + £5,870 (2 x £2,935 child element) = £6,415

Maximum WTC = £2,070 (basic element) + £2,125 (lone parent element) + £7,280 (childcare element £200 x 70% x 52 weeks) = £11,475

Total = £17,890

Step two: work out relevant income

Relevant income = £9,266.40 (£8.91 x 20 x 52 weeks in 2021/22)

Step three: compare income with threshold

£9,266.40 (income) – £6,770 (threshold) = £2,496.40. The 41% taper is applied to this.

Step four: work out tax credits payable

£17,890 (maximum tax credits) – £1,023.52 (£2,496.40 x 41%) = £16,866.48 tax credits payable for complete tax year = £324.35 a week.

* *

5. **Change of circumstances**

There are different ways in which a change in your circumstances can affect your entitlement to tax credits.

- If your circumstances change and affect your maximum entitlement, a new relevant period begins – eg, if a disability benefit which gives entitlement to a disability element is awarded to you or someone included in your award, this changes your tax credit maximum amount and starts a new relevant period.
- Other changes, such as becoming single or part of a couple, bring your award to an end. You usually have to claim universal credit (UC) instead.
- Changes in income do not affect your maximum entitlement and do not bring your existing award to an end, but can affect the amount of tax credit which is payable to you – eg, if your existing award has been based on your current tax year's income and you have a significant rise in your income during that tax year, you may be overpaid tax credit, unless you report the change at once, enabling your award to be recalculated.

See p1470 for more information about how these changes affect your award.

In any of these circumstances, your tax credit award must be recalculated. Work through Steps one to five on pp1428–1429, for each relevant period.

Example

Tracy claims disability living allowance (DLA) for her six-year-old child; the middle rate of the care component is awarded from day 201 of tax year 2022/23. She therefore has two relevant periods during this tax year: the first is 200 days, and the second, from the date her daughter is awarded DLA, is 165 days. Two calculations must be done.

The first calculation

Step one: work out the relevant period

Tracy's relevant period is 200 days without the disabled child element.

Step two: calculate maximum entitlement for the relevant period

		Daily rate	x 200
CTC	Family element	£1.50	£300
	Child element for two-year-old child	£8.05	£1,610
	Child element for four-year-old child	£8.05	£1,610
WTC	Basic element	£5.68	£1,136
	Lone parent element	£5.83	£1,166
	Childcare element		£3,989.05
Maximum tax credits			**£9,811.05**

Step three: work out her relevant income

Relevant income is (£9,291.85 ÷ 365) x 200 = £5,091.42 (rounded down to the nearest penny)

Step four: compare her income with the threshold for the relevant period

Threshold for the relevant period is (£6,770 ÷ 365) x 200 = £3,709.59 (rounded up to the nearest penny)

Step five: calculate tax credit entitlement for the relevant period

Tracy has excess income of £1,381.83 (income £5,091.42 minus threshold £3,709.59).
41% x £1,381.83 = £566.55 (rounded down to the nearest penny)
Maximum tax credit £9,811.05 reduced by £566.55 = £9,244.50.
Tracy's tax credit entitlement for the first relevant period of 200 days is £9,244.50.

The second calculation

Step one: work out the relevant period

Tracy's relevant period is 165 days with the disabled child element.

Step two: calculate maximum entitlement for the relevant period

		Daily rate	x 165
CTC	Family element	£1.50	£247.50
	Child element for two-year-old child	£8.05	£1,328.25
	Child element for six-year-old child	£8.05	£1,328.25
	Disabled child element (lower rate)	£9.72	£1,603.80
WTC	Basic element	£5.68	£937.20
	Lone parent element	£5.83	£961.95
	Childcare element		£3,290.96
Maximum tax credits			**£9,697.91**

10

Part 10: General rules for tax credits
Chapter 62: Tax credit amounts
5. Change of circumstances

Step three: work out her relevant income
Relevant income is (£9,291.85 ÷ 365) x 165 = £4,200.42 (rounded down to the nearest penny)
Step four: compare her income with the threshold for the relevant period
Threshold for the relevant period is (£6,770 ÷ 365) x 165 = £3,060.42 (rounded up to the nearest penny)
Step five: calculate tax credit entitlement for the relevant period
Tracy has excess income of £1,140 (income £4,200.42 minus threshold £3,060.42).
41% x £1,140 = £467.40 (rounded down to the nearest penny)
Maximum tax credit £9,697.91 reduced by £467.40 = £9,230.51
Tracy's tax credit entitlement for the second relevant period of 165 days is £9,230.51.

The final amount of tax credits if you claim universal credit

If your tax credits claim is finalised during the year (see p1479) because you claim or become entitled to UC, your income is treated differently. This may happen if you become part of a couple with someone who is already getting UC, or if you make a claim for UC. In this situation, your part-year income up to the date you become entitled to UC is required. Your income in the part year is divided by the number of days in that part year, and then multiplied by the number of days in the tax year (365) to find your 'notional current year income'. This figure is then compared with your income in the previous year. If your notional current year income in 2022/23 has increased or decreased compared to 2021/22 by more than £2,500, your notional current year income is used, after applying the disregard. Your notional current year income is divided by 365 and then multiplied by the number of days in the relevant period and rounded down to the nearest penny to find your income in the relevant period.[63] See p1439 for more information.

Notes

1. **The relevant period**
   1 s5(1) TCA 2002
   2 s5(2) TCA 2002
   3 Reg 8(2) TC(ITDR) Regs
   4 Reg 7(2) TC(ITDR) Regs
   5 Reg 8(2) TC(ITDR) Regs

2. **The maximum amount of child tax credit**
   6 Reg 7 CTC Regs
   7 Regs 7 and 8 TC(ITDR) Regs
   8 s13 WRWA 2016
   9 s13 WRWA 2016
   10 Regs 9-13 CTC Regs
   11 See gov.uk/government/publications/
      support-for-a-child-conceived-without-
      your-consent/approved-third-party-
      professionals-who-can-complete-
      these-forms
   12 Reg 14 CTC Regs
   13 Reg 8(1) and (2) CTC Regs
   14 s13(3) WRWA 2016
   15 Autumn Statement 2016
   16 Reg 8(1) and (3) CTC Regs
   17 Autumn Statement 2016; HMRC email
      to CPAG, 18 December 2018

3. **The maximum amount of working tax credit**
   18 Reg 20 WTC(EMR) Regs
   19 Reg 15 WTC(EMR) Regs
   20 Regs 7 and 8 TC(ITDR) Regs
   21 Reg 4 WTC(EMR) Regs
   22 Reg 3(2) WTC(EMR) Regs
   23 Reg 12 WTC(EMR) Regs
   24 Reg 11(1) WTC(EMR) Regs
   25 Reg 11 WTC(EMR) Regs
   26 Reg 3 WTC(EMR) Regs
   27 Reg 10 WTC(EMR) Regs
   28 Reg 3 WTC(EMR) Regs
   29 Reg 9 WTC(EMR) Regs
   30 Reg 3(3) WTC(EMR) Regs
   31 For further guidance on the terms used,
      see TCM 0122060
   32 Reg 9B WTC(EMR) Regs
   33 R(TC) 1/06
   34 HMRC, Helpsheet TC956, *How to Qualify
      for the Disability Element of Tax Credits*,
      October 2020, p4; *PW v HMRC (TC)*
      [2018] UKUT 12 (AAC)

   35 Reg 9A WTC(EMR) Regs
   36 Reg 9(8) WTC(EMR) Regs
   37 Reg 17 WTC(EMR) Regs
   38 Reg 3(3) WTC(EMR) Regs
   39 Regs 3 and 13 WTC(EMR) Regs
   40 Reg 20(3) WTC(EMR) Regs
   41 Reg 14(1) WTC(EMR) Regs
   42 Reg 14(1) WTC(EMR) Regs
   43 Reg 20 WTC(EMR) Regs
   44 Reg 13(1) WTC(EMR) Regs
   45 Regs 5-8 WTC(EMR) Regs; Explanatory
      Memorandum to The Working Tax
      Credit (Entitlement and Maximum Rate)
      (Amendment) Regulations 2009
      No.1829
   46 Reg 13(4) WTC(EMR) Regs
   47 *AS v HMRC (TC)* [2017] UKUT 361 (AAC)
   48 Reg 14(3) WTC(EMR) Regs
   49 Reg 14(6) WTC(EMR) Regs; reg 27(2A)
      and (5B) TC(CN) Regs
   50 s30 Childcare Payments Act 2014
   51 Reg 14(2) WTC(EMR) Regs; see also
      HMRC leaflet WTC5, *Working Tax Credit:
      help with the costs of childcare*
   52 Reg 14(2)(f) WTC(EMR) Regs
   53 Reg 14(2)(b) WTC(EMR) Regs
   54 Reg 14(2)(d)(i) WTC(EMR) Regs
   55 Reg 14(2)(d)(ii) WTC(EMR) Regs
   56 Reg 14(1A)(a) and (1B)(a) WTC(EMR)
      Regs
   57 Reg 14(1A)(d) WTC(EMR) Regs
   58 Reg 15 WTC(EMR) Regs
   59 Reg 7(3) TC(ITDR) Regs, steps 7-10

4. **How to calculate the amount of tax credits**
   60 ss7(2) and 13 TCA 2002; reg 4 TC(ITDR)
      Regs
   61 s7(3) TCA 2002; reg 5 TC(ITDR) Regs
   62 Reg 9 TC(ITDR) Regs

5. **Change of circumstances**
   63 Reg 12A and Sch UC(TP) Regs, as
      amended by UC(TP)(A) Regs

10

Chapter 63

· ·

Income: tax credits

This chapter covers:
1. Relevant income (below)
2. Whose income counts (p1440)
3. What income counts (p1440)
4. Notional income (p1454)

Key facts

- The amount of tax credits to which you are entitled depends on how much income you have.
- In general, most taxable income is taken into account and non-taxable income is ignored, but there are exceptions.
- The assessment is usually based on income for a full tax year, 6 April to 5 April.
- The amount to which you are entitled changes if your income increases or decreases by more than £2,500 in the current year compared with the previous year.
- Your savings or other capital are not taken into account, and you are eligible for tax credits whatever the level of your capital. However, interest and other income earned from savings or capital do count.

10

---

1. Relevant income

Tax credits are calculated using your 'relevant income'.

- If your income has not changed by more than £2,500, your relevant income is your income in the complete tax year before your claim (the previous year's income).
- If your income has changed by more than £2,500, your relevant income is your income in the complete tax year of your claim (the current year's income) after a disregard has been applied.
- If your tax credits award ended because you claimed universal credit (UC), your relevant income is determined by comparing your previous year's income with your income in the part of the year up to the date your entitlement to tax credits stops (the part-year income) spread over the full year. If this has

changed by more than £2,500, your relevant income is the part-year income, after a disregard has been applied.

The tax credit assessment is based on income over a full tax year (6 April to 5 April) except during a time when you are getting income support (IS), income-based jobseeker's allowance (JSA), income-related employment and support allowance (ESA) or pension credit (PC). If the tax credit award only runs for part of the year, the full year's income is reduced on a pro rata basis (see p1428), unless your tax credit claim has ended because you are entitled to UC.

Note: while you are on IS, income-based JSA, income-related ESA or PC, you are entitled to maximum tax credits, so the level of your income in the previous or current year does not matter. When your benefit stops, the tax credit award is again based on your relevant income.

Previous year's income

Tax credit awards are initially based on your income in the tax year before the year of the award. This is referred to as the 'previous year's income'. So, for a tax credit award made from 6 April 2022, the previous year is 2021/22. Your tax credit entitlement is finalised at the end of the year by comparing this figure with your income in the year of the award (the current year's income). Your income can increase or decrease by up to £2,500 compared with the previous year without it affecting your final entitlement in the current year. If your income has not changed by more than £2,500, your final tax credit entitlement is still based on the previous year's income. Changes of less than £2,500 do not affect your award until the following year.

If HM Revenue and Customs (HMRC) does not receive any information about a change in your income, your award continues to be based on the previous year's income until the end of the tax year.

Current year's income

Your final tax credit entitlement is based on a comparison of your income in the previous year with your income in the year of the award (the current year's income). So, for a tax credits award made from 6 April 2022, the current year is 2022/23. An annual amount for a complete tax year is required, which you may not know for certain until the end of the tax year, but you can provide an estimate during the year. At the end of each tax year, HMRC finalises your entitlement by comparing your previous year's income with your current year's income, and applying a disregard of £2,500 for an increase or decrease in income. This process is called the 'annual review'.

If your income in the current year (2022/23):[1]

- has not changed since the previous year, the current year's income is used;
- has decreased by £2,500 or less, the previous year's income is used;

Part 10: General rules for tax credits
Chapter 63: Income: tax credits
1. Relevant income

- has decreased by more than £2,500, the current year's income plus £2,500 is used;
- has increased by £2,500 or less, the previous year's income is used;
- has increased by more than £2,500, the current year's income minus £2,500 is used.

If you tell HMRC during the year about an increase in income of more than £2,500 compared with the previous year, your award can be revised based on an estimate of the current year's income less a disregard of £2,500. This is advisable if you want to reduce the risk of overpayments at the end of the year.

If you expect your income in the current year to decrease by more than £2,500 compared with the previous year, tell HMRC. It may adjust your award, basing it on your estimate plus £2,500. Tell HMRC quickly if you later think your estimate was too low so it can readjust your award. If you do not, you could end up with an overpayment. HMRC may also use a figure for your earnings it obtains via 'real-time information' from your employer for PAYE (pay as you earn) tax purposes.

You can telephone the Tax Credit Helpline or write to the Tax Credit Office with details of your current year's income. There is no form to complete. Make sure you provide full details of *all* your (and your partner's) relevant income for the current year. At the end of the year, HMRC carries out an annual review and you are usually required to declare your income for the year just ended.

Examples

From 6 April 2021 to 5 April 2022, Aliyah worked part time and earned a total of £8,000. Since then, she has increased her hours and expects to earn £12,500 in the current year of the award, from 6 April 2022 to 5 April 2023. Her tax credit award is initially based on income of £8,000. Because her income is expected to increase by £4,500 in the current year (ie, above the £2,500 disregard), her final entitlement is based on an income of £10,000 (£12,500 – £2,500). She should report this change during the year to avoid an overpayment.

From 6 April 2021 to 5 April 2022, Marsha and Bill, who are claiming as a couple, had a total income of £27,000. In the current year of the award, from 6 April 2022 to 5 April 2023, Marsha stops work and they expect to earn £11,000 between them. Their tax credit award is initially based on the previous year's income of £27,000. Because their income is expected to decrease by £16,000 in the current year (£27,000 – £11,000), their final entitlement is based on income of £13,500 (£11,000 + £2,500). For the next year, 6 April 2023 to 5 April 2024, if they are still getting tax credits, their award will initially be based on an income of £11,000.

Part-year income

If your tax credit award has ended because you have claimed or become entitled to UC, your income for part of that year is used. This allows your tax credits claim to be finalised during the year, so that you do not get an annual review at the end of the tax year (see p1479). This can happen if you become a couple with someone who is entitled to UC or if you make a claim for UC. HMRC may decide to wait until the end of the year to finalise an award, if it decides it is not practical to do so during the year.[2]

If your tax credit award is finalised during the tax year because you claim UC, you are asked to provide details of your income in the earlier part of the year, up to the date you become entitled to UC. Your income from 6 April to the date your tax credit award ends is divided by the number of days in that part of the year, and multiplied by the number of days in the tax year (365 in 2022/23), then rounded down to the nearest pound. This is referred to as 'notional current year income' in the legislation.[3] The result is compared with your 2021/22 income, applying the disregard of £2,500 for an increase or decrease.

Example

From 6 April 2021 to 5 April 2022, Freya received tax credits as a lone parent working 16 hours a week at £12 an hour, with an income of £9,984. From 6 April 2022 to 12 October 2022, she continues to claim tax credits as a lone parent in the same job, although she takes on extra shifts, working 28 hours a week. On 13 October 2022 she moves in with her partner, Sam, who is getting UC. Freya's tax credit claim ends and Sam's UC claim becomes a joint claim. HMRC asks Freya to provide details of her earnings from 6 April 2022 to 12 October 2022, a period of 190 days. She calculates the gross taxable amount she has earned in this period, including the extra shifts, which she works out as £9,072. HMRC takes this figure, divides it by 190 and multiplies it by 365, then rounds down to the nearest pound, which works out as £17,427. As this exceeds Freya's 2021/22 income by more than £2,500, the notional current year's income after applying the disregard is £14,927. This is the relevant income for the final tax credits assessment (see p1428, Step 3). There is no reassessment at the end of the tax year, even though she earns much less in the latter part of the year.

Estimating income

There are no special rules for how to estimate income. Using, for instance, payslips and benefit award letters, work out how much income you have already received in the current year and estimate how much you will receive for the remainder of the year. Tax credits are always worked out using annual income (unless you claim UC – see p1479), so you must include all income received or estimated for the whole tax year, 6 April to 5 April, even if you are asking for an award to be adjusted part way through the year.

Part 10: General rules for tax credits
Chapter 63: Income: tax credits
3. What income counts

If you are self-employed, HMRC's self-assessment helpline (tel: 0300 200 3310; textphone: 0300 200 3319) can advise you how to work out your business profits. You must estimate your profits for the accounting period that ends in the current tax year. This might be different from your current earnings, particularly if your accounting year end is early in the tax year.

You should always make it clear that you are using an estimate. There is a box to tick on the annual declaration to do this. If you provide an estimate in response to an annual declaration, you must be notified that this is to be treated as your actual income unless you rectify your estimate by a specified date, which must be at least 30 days after the notice and no later than 31 January.[4]

2. **Whose income counts**

If you are a member of a couple (see p1460), your partner's income is added to yours.[5] Otherwise, only your own income counts.

If you were previously getting tax credits as a couple, but you are now a single claimant, only your individual income in the previous and current year counts in your new single tax credits award, not that of your former partner. In your old award as a couple, your joint income in the previous and current year counts – ie, including the remainder of the tax year after you stopped being a couple.[6] The income in the complete tax year is used and then apportioned on a pro rata basis for the period of the claim (see p1428).

If you were a single claimant but are now in a couple, your joint income in the previous and current year counts in the new joint claim, even if you were not in a couple in the previous year.[7]

Children's income

Children's income is ignored. However, if you have transferred money under a trust to your child and tax rules treat that income as still belonging to you, it may also be treated as yours for tax credits.[8]

3. **What income counts**

In general, taxable social security benefits are taken into account, and gross earnings (before tax and national insurance (NI)) and business profits are taken into account less your pension contributions. Most other income, such as pensions and interest on savings, is added together and is only taken into account if the total is more than £300 a year. The rules specify what income must be taken into account and what is disregarded. Although based on income tax rules, there are some differences for tax credits.

If you have a special exemption from income tax, your income is calculated as though you were liable for tax.[9] Foreign military personnel, officials of international organisations or consular staff may have such an exemption.

Types of income

The sources of your income fall into certain categories and within each category certain amounts can be disregarded. There is also a general list of income that is disregarded (see p1451).

The income taken into account in the tax credits assessment is worked out as follows.[10]

Add together your income, or your joint income if you are a couple, from the following categories:
- social security benefits (see p1442);
- income from employment (see p1443);
- taxable profits from self-employment (see p1446);
- student income (see p1447);
- miscellaneous income (see p1447).

Add together your income, or your joint income if you are a couple, from:
- pension income (see p1448);
- income from investments (see p1449);
- income from property (see p1450);
- foreign income (see p1450);
- notional income (see p1454).

If the total income in the last group of five categories is £300 or less, it is ignored completely. Otherwise, deduct £300 and add the remainder to your income from the first group of five categories. **Note:** couples share one £300 disregard.[11]

This gives you the total income that is taken into account – subject to any disregards (see p1451).

Example

Carl and Ellie renew their claim for child tax credit (CTC) and working tax credit (WTC) from April 2022. HM Revenue and Customs (HMRC) assesses their claim on their joint income for the year 6 April 2021 to 5 April 2022. In 2021/22, Ellie earned £13,500 before tax and NI contributions. Carl received contributory employment and support allowance (ESA) totalling £4,700 and a £500 occupational pension. Income taken into account is:

Employment income = £13,500

ESA = £4,700

Occupational pension = £200 (ie, £500 *minus* £300 disregard)

Total income = £18,400

Part 10: General rules for tax credits
Chapter 63: Income: tax credits
3. What income counts

Benefits

Generally, benefits are taken into account if they are taxable, and ignored if they are not.

Disregarded benefits

The following benefits are disregarded:[12]
- adult disability payment in Scotland;
- armed forces independence payment;
- attendance allowance;
- bereavement support payment;
- Best Start grants and Best Start foods in Scotland;
- carer's allowance (CA) supplement in Scotland;
- child benefit;
- child disability payment in Scotland;
- Christmas bonus;
- disability living allowance;
- discretionary housing payments;
- free school meal payments by cash or voucher;
- funeral support payment in Scotland;
- guardian's allowance;
- Healthy Start vouchers and vitamins, or payments in lieu of vouchers;
- housing benefit (HB);
- income support (IS), except to strikers;
- income-based jobseeker's allowance (JSA) (even though this is taxable);
- income-related ESA, including a transitional addition;[13]
- industrial injuries benefit (except industrial death benefit);
- job start payment in Scotland;
- maternity allowance;
- pension credit;[14]
- personal independence payment;
- Scottish child payment;
- Scottish Welfare Fund payments;[15]
- severe disablement allowance;
- short-term assistance in Scotland;
- short-term lower rate incapacity benefit (IB);
- social fund payments;
- tax-free childcare payments;[16]
- transitional long-term IB (paid if you transferred from invalidity benefit in 1995);
- universal credit (UC);[17]
- winter heating assistance or child winter heating assistance in Scotland;
- young carer grant in Scotland;

- any payment to compensate for the loss of IS, JSA or HB;
- increases for a child[18] or adult[19] paid with any of the above.

Tax credits themselves are disregarded, as are the £500 one-off coronavirus payments for people on WTC. Local welfare assistance scheme payments are not specifically disregarded, but they are not taxable so do not count as income. Statutory sick pay (SSP), statutory maternity pay (SMP), statutory adoption pay (SAP), statutory paternity pay (SPP), statutory shared parental pay (SSPP) and statutory parental bereavement pay (SPBP) are treated as employment income (see below). Retirement pensions, widowed mother's allowance, widowed parent's allowance, widow's pension, industrial death benefit and war pensions are treated as pension income (see p1448).

Benefits taken into account

Any benefits not in the list above are taken into account in full. These include:
- CA;
- contribution-based JSA;[20]
- contributory ESA, including a transitional addition;
- long-term IB (except the non-taxable transitional long-term IB – see above);
- increases for a child or adult (even if not taxable) paid with any of the above.

It is the amount of benefit payable that is taken into account. Arrears of benefit or any ex gratia payment in connection with a benefit are taken into account as income for the year in which the payment of arrears is made.[21]

Each year the DWP should give you a statement of the taxable benefits you received in the previous tax year. You can ask the local benefit office for a replacement if you did not get one. If you get any increase for a child paid with CA or IB (or widowed mother's or widowed parent's allowance), this is not included in the statement but is taken into account as income, so you should declare it for tax credits purposes.

Employment income

For tax credits, it is your 'gross' taxable pay that is taken into account.[22] This means your pay before any income tax or NI contributions are deducted, but after pension contributions are deducted.

Income counts whether received in the UK or elsewhere, unless it has been classed as not taxable because it cannot be transferred to or realised in the UK.[23]

What counts as employment income

'Employment income' means the following income received in the tax year:[24]
- any earnings from an office or employment, including:[25]
  - wages and overtime pay;
  - furlough pay;

Part 10: General rules for tax credits
Chapter 63: Income: tax credits
3. What income counts

> - holiday pay and occupational sick pay;
> - bonuses and commission (including tips or gratuities);
> - 'benefits in kind' – ie, goods or assets that can be converted into money, such as gifts of drink, clothes and fuel;
> - payments made on your behalf – eg, rent paid by your employer direct to your landlord;
> - earnings from work you can do while claiming ESA ('permitted work' – see p1020);

- taxable expenses (see below for expenses that do not count as earnings);[26]
- any taxable cash voucher, non-cash voucher or credit token – eg, company credit card.[27] Vouchers spent on allowable expenses are ignored;[28]
- taxable payments in connection with the termination of your employment or with a change in your duties or wages, including non-statutory and statutory redundancy payments, pay in lieu of notice and employment tribunal awards for unfair dismissal. With the exception of pay in lieu of notice (except in some cases involving damages for breach of contract or practice),[29] the first £30,000 of the total of such payments is ignored;[30]
- SSP;[31]
- SMP, SAP, SPP, SSPP and SPBP above £100 a week. The first £100 a week is ignored;[32]
- strike pay from your trade union (even though this is non-taxable);[33]
- the cash equivalent of the benefit of a company car for private use and car fuel benefits.[34] Other expenses in connection with the car are ignored.[35] If you enter into a salary sacrifice arrangement for a company car on or after 6 April 2017, the amount included as earnings is the higher of the amount given up or the cash equivalent benefit of the car, unless it is an 'ultra-low emissions vehicle', in which case it is the cash equivalent benefit that counts.[36] However, if you are a disabled employee with an adapted or automatic company car, the car is exempt from income tax and ignored for tax credits;[37]
- payments for agreeing to restrict your future conduct or activities;[38]
- taxable income from an employee share scheme;[39]
- payment for work done while sentenced or on remand in prison;[40]
- the amount of earnings given up under a salary sacrifice scheme which is not tax exempt, or the cash equivalent of the benefit, whichever is higher.[41]

The taxable value of goods and vouchers is shown on Form P11D, given to you by your employer at the end of the tax year.

Payments not counted as earnings

Some payments do not count as earnings and are disregarded in the tax credits assessment. Payments from your employer that are not taxable generally do not count as income for tax credits.

Note: if you use a salary sacrifice arrangement, the taxable income figure should be used, so the exemption or value of the benefit is the same for tax credits and income tax purposes.[42] The following payments are ignored (provided they are exempt from income tax):[43]

- expenses incurred 'wholly, exclusively and necessarily' in the course of your employment.[44] Note: if you are a volunteer with a charity or voluntary organisation, all your expenses are ignored.[45] However, any that are taxable are taken into account – eg, a 'round-sum' expense allowance payable irrespective of how you might spend it;[46]
- certain other expenses – eg, for removal benefits, cars or transport for disabled employees, travel and subsistence, mileage allowance, car parking expenses, tax-free mobile phone and fixed deductions for repairing and maintaining work tools;[47]
- non-taxable vouchers, benefits or credit tokens, such as for recreational facilities, subsidised meals, transport, entertainment or hospitality;[48]
- small gifts or vouchers from third parties, not made in recognition of particular services (not exceeding £250 in total);[49]
- tax-free cycles and equipment under Cyclescheme;[50]
- homeworkers' additional household expenses;[51]
- childcare vouchers or credit tokens for 'relevant childcare' (see p1424);[52]
- tax-free awards under a staff suggestion scheme;[53]
- certain professional fees – eg, to approved professional bodies, for indemnity insurance or registration;[54]
- any charity payments under a payroll giving scheme;[55]
- payment for work-related training, individual learning account training and retraining expenses when leaving employment;[56]
- certain discretionary payments made by the DWP to help you into work (but in-work payments made by a third-party provider, including non-cash items such as clothing or travelcards, are not exempt from income tax and are likely to be treated as employment income);[57]
- tax-free benefits and payments under PAYE (pay as you earn) settlement agreements and special arrangements;[58]
- tax-exempt bonus payments of up to £3,600 paid to employees, or former employees, by an employee ownership trust;[59]
- the amount given up under certain salary sacrifice arrangements which are tax exempt, including for benefits listed above and for independent pension advice, counselling and other outplacement services;[60]
- the first £30,000 of payments to compensate for the termination of your employment or a change in your duties or wages.[61]

10

Part 10: General rules for tax credits
Chapter 63: Income: tax credits
3. What income counts

Some groups of workers have special income tax exemptions. The following are ignored as earnings for tax credits:

- certain armed forces' allowances – eg, for travel to and from leave, food, accommodation, certain operational allowances, council tax relief, continuity of education and reserve forces' training;[62]
- free coal to miners, or former miners, or cash in lieu;[63]
- if you are an actor or performer, the tax-free amount of agents' fees;[64]
- expenses for mainland transfers for offshore oil and gas workers;[65]
- Crown employees' foreign service allowance;[66]
- expenses of a minister of religion, including a rent deduction;[67]
- European Commission daily subsistence allowance to seconded national experts.[68]

Deduct pension contributions

Deduct any contributions you make to a personal or occupational pension approved by HMRC.[69]

If you pay contributions through your employer, your P60 or P45 should show your wages after the contributions have been deducted, so there is no further deduction to make.

If you pay the pension contributions direct, deduct the gross annual contributions. Because tax relief is given on personal pension contributions, your actual contributions are less than the gross amount included in the pension plan. It is the higher gross amount that you should deduct from your employment income. Your pension provider should supply you with annual statements of contributions received.

If you have no income from employment but are still making pension contributions, deduct the contributions from any other income you may have.

Income from self-employment

Your taxable profits from any 'trade', 'profession' or 'vocation' are taken into account for the relevant year.[70] Payments under the Self-Employment Income Support Scheme and other coronavirus-related support for the self-employed count as your income for self-assessment of income tax, so do not need to be counted again separately for tax credits.[71] Your profits for tax credits should usually be the same as declared for income tax purposes, but there are some differences, such as coronavirus self-isolation payments which are taxable but disregarded as income for tax credits. If you have a business partner, it is taxable profits from your share of the business income that count.[72] This includes trading outside the UK. It also includes profits from renting out property if this is conducted as a business. (If property income comes from a 'trade', income counts without the £300 disregard that would otherwise apply to such income.) If renting property is not conducted as a business, see p1450. You may be asked to provide evidence that your self-emploment is organised and regular, on a commercial basis, with a view to making a profit.

Payments under the New Enterprise Allowance scheme to help you start a new business are not counted as income for working out your trading profits.[73] Taxable profits are shown on your tax return for the relevant year. You should deduct allowable business expenses from the annual turnover to arrive at a profit figure. HMRC's self-assessment helpline (tel: 0300 200 3310; textphone: 0300 200 3319) should be able to give advice. See also p1439.

Business losses

If your business is run on a commercial basis and has made a loss, your income is nil for that tax year unless you have other income that counts in the assessment. If you do have other income, you should deduct the amount of the loss from that income (from joint income if you are claiming as a couple).[74] If you do not have enough income to offset the full amount, any left over can be carried forward and deducted from profits of the same trade in the next and later tax years.

Deductions from self-employment

Deduct the gross amount of personal pension contributions (see p1446) and any gift aid donation to charity (see p1453).

Student income

The following income is taken into account:[75]
* adult dependants' grant;
* in Scotland, lone parents' grant;
* professional and career development loans, but only any amount applied for or paid in respect of living expenses for the period supported by the loan.[76]

All other kinds of student support are disregarded, including student loans, childcare grants, discretionary grants and hardship funds.

Note: unlike most means-tested benefits, becoming a student does not affect your entitlement to WTC and CTC. Provided you satisfy the eligibility rules, you can continue to qualify.

Miscellaneous income

Any income that does not fit into any of the other nine categories on p1441 is taken into account if it is taxable under the HMRC 'sweep-up' provisions in Part 5 of the Income Tax (Trading and Other Income) Act 2005.[77] This includes copyright royalties if your writing does not amount to a trade or profession.

Part 10: General rules for tax credits
Chapter 63: Income: tax credits
3. What income counts

Pension income

Pension income taken into account

The following pension income is taken into account. The first £300 a year is ignored from the total of your pension and any income from savings, investments, property or foreign or notional income.

- **State retirement pensions and graduated retirement benefit.**[78] (The Christmas bonus and winter fuel payment are ignored.) HMRC says that, as well as your pension, it takes into account any additional state pension, and any increase for an adult or child paid with your pension.[79] Include as income any lump sum to which you become entitled through deferring your state pension.
- **Personal and occupational pensions.**[80] It is the gross amount before tax is deducted that counts. Your pension provider should give you a certificate each year showing how much pension was paid and how much tax deducted. If you retired because of work-related illness or disability caused by injury on duty, only count the amount of pension that you would have been paid if you had retired on non-work-related ill-health grounds. Any extra amount paid is ignored.[81] Tax-free lump sums paid under a personal pension scheme, retirement annuity contract or tax-exempt pension scheme are ignored completely.[82] If you have the option of taking a lump sum from a pension because you are aged 55 or over, the tax-free amount (usually up to 25 per cent of the total value of the pension pot) is ignored, but other payments count as income. If you choose not to take an income or lump sum from a personal or occupational pension, regardless of your age, this cannot be counted as notional income (see p1454). If you cash in a small pension or the fund is too small to pay a pension, the lump sum you get counts. If you get a winding-up lump sum when your occupational pension scheme winds up, this counts.
- **Widow's pension, widowed mother's and widowed parent's allowance**, including any increases for a child or adult dependant.[83]
- **Industrial death benefit.**[84]
- **Survivor's guaranteed income payment and child's payment** under the Armed Forces Compensation Scheme.[85]

Pension income disregarded

Ignore the following **war pensions:**[86]
- war disablement pension, including constant attendance allowance and mobility supplement;
- annuity or additional pension to holders of the Victoria Cross, George Cross and certain other medals;
- wounds, injury or disablement pensions to members of the armed forces – eg, guaranteed income payment;
- war widow's and widower's pensions;

- death in service pensions for service in the armed forces. If the death in service pension is overlapped by another pension, ignore an equivalent amount from the other pension.

Investment income

There is no capital limit in the tax credit assessment as there is with means-tested benefits. The value of your savings is ignored completely. However, taxable *income* from savings and investments is taken into account. For example, the amount of savings in a bank account is ignored, but the interest on those savings is taken into account.

Investment income is taken into account as described below. The first £300 a year is ignored from the total of your investment income and any income from pensions or property, or foreign or notional income.

Investment income taken into account

Take into account the following amounts before tax is deducted:[87]

- interest on invested money, including outside the UK – eg, interest on savings in a bank account;
- dividends from shares of a company resident in the UK (including the tax credit payable by the company with the dividend);
- income from government stocks and bonds;
- taxable payments from a life assurance policy, life annuity contract or capital redemption policy;
- discounts on securities – ie, the profit from trading in securities such as government stocks and bonds;
- interest, annuity or other annual payment payable as a charge on a property or as a reservation out of it;
- income from trusts, settlements and estates of someone who has died, as shown on certificate R185, which the trustees or administrators should have given you;
- interest arising from a debt owed to you.

Investment income disregarded

Certain investment income is disregarded:

- interest, a dividend or bonus from an individual savings account (ISA);[88]
- government bonus payments into a lifetime ISA or a help-to-save account;[89]
- interest under a certified save as you earn (SAYE) scheme;[90]
- income from savings certificates;[91]
- tax-exempt annual payments made by an individual in the UK not for commercial reasons – eg, from a covenant;[92]
- winnings from betting, pools, lotteries and games with prizes;[93]
- certain compensation payments to second world war victims;[94]

Part 10: General rules for tax credits
Chapter 63: Income: tax credits
3. What income counts

- tax-free periodical payments of damages for personal injury, disease or death awarded through a court, out-of-court settlement or agreement, and interest on such damages;[95]
- periodical payments from the Thalidomide Trust;[96]
- annuity payments under a Criminal Injuries Compensation Scheme award;[97]
- interest on the first £30,000 of a home income plan loan taken out before 9 March 1999 to buy a life annuity;[98]
- interest on compensation to a child under 18 for the loss of a parent;[99]
- payments from the variant Creutzfeldt-Jakob disease government-funded trust, the Macfarlane Trusts, Independent Living Funds and the Eileen Trust. These are disregarded for the lifetime of the disabled person or a partner who receives the payment or inherits from the estate, or for two years if paid to or inherited by a parent;[100]
- tax-exempt capital element of a purchased life annuity;[101]
- tax-exempt health and employment insurance payments (eg, permanent health insurance or employment protection policies) or immediate-needs annuity payments.[102]

Property income

The capital value of property is ignored, but rental income is taken into account unless this is exempt from tax under the 'rent-a-room' scheme.[103] This scheme allows you to rent furnished accommodation in your own home, earning up to £7,500 a year tax free.[104]

If you are not covered by the 'rent-a-room' scheme (eg, you rent out a property that you do not live in yourself), you can deduct expenses wholly and exclusively incurred in running the property – eg, repairs, water charges, insurance premiums and mortgage interest (but not capital repayments of a mortgage).[105] This may be different from how the property is treated for tax purposes.

The first £300 a year is ignored from the total of your property income and any pensions, investment income, foreign or notional income.

If you rent out property as a business (eg, you run a hotel or guesthouse), count this as income from self-employment (see p1446).[106]

Income from property outside the UK counts as 'foreign income'.

Income from outside the UK

Although earnings from abroad are taken into account in the same way as UK earnings, other 'foreign income' (eg, from pensions, property or investments) is taken into account subject to the following rules.[107]

The following are disregarded:[108]
- a banking charge or commission for converting currency to sterling;[109]
- social security payments from outside the UK that are equivalent to tax-free UK benefits (see p1442);

- certain pensions or compensation for victims of persecution during the second world war;
- tax-free lump-sum payments under an overseas pension scheme;
- personal injury damages from a court outside the UK;
- certain education allowances payable to workers in the public sector of some countries outside the UK;
- property losses in one tax year that can be offset against property income in the following year;[110]
- maintenance payments;
- income that you are prevented from transferring to the UK by law or by the government of the country where the income arises or because you cannot get foreign currency in that country. Other income that remains abroad is counted.[111]

The first £300 a year is disregarded from the total of your foreign income and any pensions, investment, property or notional income.

Income from outside the UK is still taken into account even if you would normally have tax relief on that income in the UK to avoid double taxation in both countries (such income is treated as though it were taxable in the UK in the normal way).[112]

Converting currency

If your income is in another currency, HMRC expects you to convert it to sterling using an average of the exchange rates over 12 months ending on 31 March for the tax year in which the income is paid.[113] These rates are published on gov.uk/government/collections/exchange-rates-for-customs-and-vat. If your tax credit award is based on an estimate of the current year's income, the rate of conversion is adjusted once the exchange rate average is available at the end of the tax year.

General income disregards

All of the following income is disregarded in the tax credit assessment.[114]

Employment and training programmes

Ignore the following income:

- travelling expenses, a living-away-from-home allowance and a training grant if you are participating in training under section 2 of the Employment and Training Act 1973 or, in Scotland, under section 2 of the Enterprise and New Towns (Scotland) Act 1990, or attending a course at an employment rehabilitation centre (where these are not taxable as profits);[115]
- if you are aged 25 or over and getting JSA while on a 'qualifying course', a discretionary payment to help meet your special needs;[116]

Part 10: General rules for tax credits
Chapter 63: Income: tax credits
3. What income counts

- a payment to a disabled person under section 2 of the Employment and Training Act 1973 or section 15 of the Disabled Persons (Employment) Act 1944 to assist disabled people to get or keep employment;[117]
- education maintenance allowance;[118]
- certain DWP payments from former employment programmes. Payments from Work and Health Programme providers are not specifically disregarded and are likely to be treated as employment income.[119]

See also p1446 for other disregarded payments.

Maintenance

Any maintenance you receive from an ex-partner, or that your partner receives from her/his ex-partner, is ignored, whether it is paid under a court order or not. Any maintenance for a child or qualifying young person which you receive from her/his other parent (if the parent is not currently your partner) is also ignored.[120]

If you *pay* maintenance, you cannot deduct this from income.

Payments for fostering, kinship care, adult placements and adoption

If you foster a child placed with you by a local authority or independent fostering provider, or you are a kinship carer of a looked-after child, all your income from foster care or kinship care (eg, the fostering allowance or kinship care allowance) is ignored, provided the annual amount is no more than £10,000 plus £200 a week for each child under 11 and £250 a week for each child aged 11 or over. If your fostering income is over this limit, only the taxable amount is taken into account – ie, the amount above this limit or the actual net profit.[121] **Note:** a foster child or looked-after child may not count as a member of your family for tax credits, so you may not get CTC for her/him (see p275).

The disregard of £10,000 a year plus £250 a week for each adult (the tax-free amount known as 'qualifying care receipts') also applies to payments for adult placement/'shared lives' schemes, or 'staying put' care for care leavers.[122] You may qualify for WTC as self-employed (see p292) if you are receiving a payment as a foster carer, kinship carer or adult placement/shared lives carer, even if your income is nil after applying the disregard.[123]

An adoption allowance,[124] or special guardianship payment, for a child who is a member of your household is ignored completely. For a child who lives with you under a residence order, a residence order allowance and any payments made by a local authority under section 17 of the Children Act 1989 or, in Scotland, under section 22 of the Children (Scotland) Act 1995 or section 50 of the Children Act 1975 are ignored.[125]

Other income

The following is ignored from your income:
- cash payments or vouchers in lieu of free school meals;[126]

- emergency volunteer leave payments under the Coronavirus Act 2020;[127]
- payments from the NHS and Social Care Coronavirus Life Assurance Scheme 2020 (these are payments of capital so do not affect tax credits);[128]
- self-isolation support payments;[129]
- COVID-19 Household Support fund payments, including winter grant and local support scheme payments, Discretionary Assistance Fund payments in Wales, and Scottish child payment bridging payments in Scotland ;[130]
- any contribution you make to an approved personal or occupational pension scheme (see p1446);[131]
- payments for fares to hospital or to assist prison visits;[132]
- community care direct payments;[133]
- payments under the Supporting People programme;[134]
- adult placement or 'shared lives' payments which are tax exempt ('qualifying care receipts');[135]
- asylum support payments or vouchers for a former asylum seeker or dependant;[136]
- trade union provident benefits – eg, sickness or accident benefit or funeral payment;[137]
- payment for expenses incurred if you are an unpaid volunteer with a charity or voluntary organisation;[138]
- jury or witness payments, if this is not compensation for loss of earnings or loss of benefit;[139]
- a payment for someone you are caring for temporarily made to you by a health authority, local authority, voluntary organisation, clinical commissioning group, NHS England, or by the person her/himself under the local authority's financial assessment. This disregard only applies if the payment would be tax free under HMRC's 'rent-a-room' scheme (see p1450);[140]
- any payment under an insurance policy taken out to insure against the risk of being unable to maintain mortgage repayments or other payments on a loan secured on your home. However, any payment you get above the amount you use to maintain the repayments, plus the premiums on that policy or buildings insurance premiums required as a condition of the mortgage, count as your income;[141]
- any payment under an insurance policy taken out to insure against the risk of being unable to maintain repayments under a hire purchase, regulated or conditional sale agreement. However, any payment above the amount you use to maintain the repayments and the premiums on that policy counts as your income;[142]
- the gross amount of any 'gift aid' donation to charity;[143]
- a sports award for anything other than living expenses. Living expenses count as your income. Ignore parts of the award for dietary supplements and living-away-from-home accommodation costs;[144]

10

Part 10: General rules for tax credits
Chapter 63: Income: tax credits
4. Notional income

- any payment made under, or in connection with, the Home Office Windrush Compensation Scheme (interest on such a payment is disregarded for 52 weeks from the date you receive it);[145]
- any payment in connection with the Scottish Child Abuse Inquiry;[146]
- any payment made by the National Emergencies Trust;[147]
- victims' payment made in respect of a Troubles-related incident;[148]
- any payment made by the Scottish government to support women affected by mesh implant surgery;[149]
- any payment under the Homes for Ukraine Scheme.[150]

4. **Notional income**

Sometimes you are treated as though you have income that you do not actually have. This is called '**notional income**'.[151] There are four kinds of notional income.

- **Income you have deprived yourself of to get, or increase, tax credits.**[152] See p487 for details of when this rule might affect you (the basic rules are similar to those that apply to deprivation of capital for benefits).
- **Income that you have failed to apply for.** You are treated as having income that would become available to you if you applied for it.[153] This does not include:
  - income under a trust set up from a personal injury payment;
  - income from a personal pension scheme, regardless of your age;
  - interest on damages awarded through the courts for personal injury;
  - a rehabilitation allowance;
  - state pension;
  - category A or B retirement pension;
  - graduated retirement benefit;
  - shared additional pension.
- **Cheap or unpaid labour.** If you work or provide a service for less than the going rate, you are treated as getting a reasonable rate for the job if the person has the means to pay.[154] This does not affect you if you are a volunteer and it is reasonable for you to provide your services free of charge. Nor does it apply if you are on an approved employment or training programme.

  Sometimes carers looking after disabled people have been expected to charge the person they care for under a similar provision affecting means-tested benefits. If you are in this position, see p436 for more details.
- **Income treated as yours under certain tax avoidance provisions or where tax law treats capital as income.** It also counts as your income for tax credits, although there is a difference to income tax provisions for a claimant who receives property income through an estate rather than directly.[155]

Notes

1. Relevant income

1   s7(3) TCA 2002; reg 5 TC(ITDR) Regs
2   Reg 12A(3) UC(TP) Regs
3   s7(4A) TCA 2002, as added by reg 12A and Sch UC(TP) Regs
4   s17(8) TCA 2002; reg 33 TC(CN) Regs

2. Whose income counts

5   s7(5) TCA 2002
6   *PD v HMRC (TC)* [2010] UKUT 159 (AAC)
7   R(TC) 1/08
8   Reg 14(2)(b)(vii) TC(DCI) Regs

3. What income counts

9   Reg 3(6) TC(DCI) Regs
10 Reg 3(1) TC(DCI) Regs
11 Reg 3(1) Step 1 TC(DCI) Regs
12 Reg 7(3) Table 3 and reg 19 Table 6 TC(DCI) Regs
13 A transitional addition is part of the ESA applicable amount under reg 67(1)(d) ESA Regs, inserted by Sch 2 para 52 ESA(TP)(EA)(No.2) Regs
14 Pension credit paid under SPCA 2002 is, by definition, not counted as social security income under reg 7(1) TC(DCI) Regs
15 Scottish Welfare Fund payments are paid under the Welfare Funds (Scotland) Act 2015 so cannot count as social security income under reg 7 TC(DCI) Regs
16 s66 Childcare Payments Act 2014
17 Reg 7(1) TC(DCI) Regs (UC is paid under WRA 2012)
18 Reg 7(4) TC(DCI) Regs
19 The regulations do not mention the treatment of increases for adults. However, these are non-taxable if paid with a non-taxable benefit and the intention is that tax credits follow suit. See HMRC, *Employment Income Manual*, para 76102.
20 s674 IT(EP)A 2003
21 Reg 7(1)(c) and (d) TC(DCI) Regs; TCM 0120040
22 Reg 4 TC(DCI) Regs
23 Reg 3(3)-(5) TC(DCI) Regs
24 Reg 4 TC(DCI) Regs
25 Regs 2(2) and 4(1)(a) TC(DCI) Regs; HMRC, *Employment Income Manual*, para 00520
26 Reg 4(1)(b) TC(DCI) Regs
27 Reg 4(1)(c)-(e) TC(DCI) Regs
28 ss362-63 IT(EP)A 2003; reg 4(4) Table 1 para 11D and (5) TC(DCI) Regs
29 HMRC, *Employment Income Manual*, paras 12975-79
30 Reg 4(1)(f) TC(DCI) Regs; see also TCTM 04111
31 Reg 4(1)(g) TC(DCI) Regs
32 Reg 4(1)(h) TC(DCI) Regs
33 Reg 4(1)(k) TC(DCI) Regs
34 Reg 4(1)(i) TC(DCI) Regs
35 Reg 4(4) Table 1 paras 14B, 14C and 14D TC(DCI) Regs
36 Reg 4(1)(ia) TC(DCI) Regs
37 Reg 4(4) Table 1 para 2B TC(DCI) Regs
38 Reg 4(1)(j) TC(DCI) Regs
39 Reg 4(1)(l) TC(DCI) Regs
40 Reg 4(1)(m) TC(DCI) Regs; reg 4(2)(g) WTC(EMR) Regs
41 Reg 4(6)-(10) TC (DCI) Regs
42 Explanatory Memorandum to The Tax Credits (Definition and Calculation of Income) (Amendment) Regulations 2017 No.396
43 Reg 4(4) TC(DCI) Regs; for a full list, see TCTM 04200-04229
44 Reg 4(5) TC(DCI) Regs; s336 IT(EP)A 2003
45 Reg 19 Table 7 para 1 TC(DCI) Regs
46 Reg 4(1)(b) TC(DCI) Regs; HMRC, *Employment Income Manual*, para 05100
47 Regs 4(4) Table 1 paras 1, 2A, 2C, 4, 6, 11F and 13, and 4(5) TC(DCI) Regs
48 Reg 4(4) Table 1 paras 5, 11D and 11E TC(DCI) Regs
49 Reg 4(4) Table 1 para 14 TC(DCI) Regs
50 Reg 4(4) Table 1 para 11D TC(DCI) Regs; ss244 and 266 IT(EP)A 2003
51 Reg 4(4) Table 1 para 17 TC(DCI) Regs
52 Reg 4(4) Table 1 para 15 TC(DCI) Regs
53 Reg 4(4) Table 1 para 12 TC(DCI) Regs
54 Regs 4(4) Table 1 para 21 and 4(5) TC(DCI) Regs; ss343 and 346 IT(EP)A 2003
55 Reg 4(5) TC(DCI) Regs; s713 IT(EP)A 2003

Part 10: General rules for tax credits
Chapter 63: Income: tax credits
Notes

56 Reg 4(4) Table 1 paras 11C and 18 TC(DCI) Regs
57 Reg 4(4) Table 1 para 16 TC(DCI) Regs; DWP, *Provider Guidance, Generic Guidance,* Ch13
58 Reg 4(4) Table 1 para 20 TC(DCI) Regs
59 Reg 4(4) Table 1 para 22 TC(DCI) Regs
60 Reg 4(6), (8) and (9) TC(DCI) Regs
61 Reg 4(1)(f) TC(DCI) Regs; see also TCTM 04111
62 Reg 4(4) Table 1 paras 3, 3A, 3B, 3C and 7 TC(DCI) Regs
63 Regs 4(4) Table 1 para 9 and 5(2) Table 2 para 11 TC(DCI) Regs
64 Reg 4(5) TC(DCI) Regs; s352 IT(EP)A 2003
65 Reg 4(4) Table 1 para 11A TC(DCI) Regs
66 Reg 4(4) Table 1 para 11B TC(DCI) Regs
67 Reg 4(5) TC(DCI) Regs; s351 IT(EP)A 2003
68 Reg 4(4) Table 1 para 11 TC(DCI) Regs
69 Reg 3(7)(c) TC(DCI) Regs
70 Reg 6(a) TC(DCI) Regs
71 Para 7.3, Explanatory Memorandum to The Tax Credits (Coronavirus Miscellaneous Amendments) (No.2) Regs 2020 No.941
72 Reg 6(b) TC(DCI) Regs
73 HMRC, *Business Income Manual,* para 40401
74 Reg 3(1) Step 4 TC(DCI) Regs
75 Reg 8 TC(DCI) Regs
76 Reg 19(c) Table 8 para 2 TC(DCI) Regs
77 Reg 18 TC(DCI) Regs
78 Reg 5(1)(a) TC(DCI) Regs
79 TCTM 04301; HMRC, *Employment Income Manual,* para 76102
80 Reg 5(1)(b)-(o) TC(DCI) Regs
81 Reg 5(2) Table 2 para 9 TC(DCI) Regs
82 Reg 5(2) Table 2 para 10 TC(DCI) Regs
83 Reg 5(1)(a) TC(DCI) Regs
84 Reg 5(1)(a) TC(DCI) Regs
85 Reg 5(1)(b) TC(DCI) Regs; HMRC, *Employment Income Manual,* para 74306
86 Reg 5(2) Table 2 paras 1-8 TC(DCI) Regs
87 Reg 10(1) TC(DCI) Regs
88 Reg 10(2)(a) Table 4 para 1(a) and (b) TC(DCI) Regs
89 Reg 10(2)(a) Table 4 para 15 TC(DCI) Regs
90 Reg 10(2)(a) Table 4 para 3 TC(DCI) Regs
91 Reg 10(2)(c) TC(DCI) Regs
92 Reg 10(2)(e) TC(DCI) Regs
93 Reg 10(2)(a) Table 4 para 4 TC(DCI) Regs
94 Reg 10(2)(a) Table 4 paras 5-7 TC(DCI) Regs

95 Reg 10(2)(a) Table 4 para 8 TC(DCI) Regs (a lump-sum payment of personal injury compensation or damages is not taxable under s51(2) Taxation of Chargeable Gains Act 1992)
96 TCTM 04608
97 Reg 10(2)(a) Table 4 para 9 TC(DCI) Regs
98 Reg 10(2)(a) Table 4 para 10 TC(DCI) Regs
99 Reg 10(2)(a) Table 4 para 11 TC(DCI) Regs
100 Reg 10(2)(b) Table 5 TC(DCI) Regs
101 Reg 10(2)(a) Table 4 para 12 TC(DCI) Regs
102 Reg 10(2)(a) Table 4 para 13 TC(DCI) Regs; TCTM 04612
103 Reg 11 TC(DCI) Regs
104 Income Tax (Limit for Rent-a-Room Relief) Order 2015 No.1539; see HMRC, Helpsheet HS223, *Rent-a-Room Scheme*
105 TCTM 04006; HMRC, *Property Income Manual,* paras 2020-40 and 2105
106 TCTM 04006
107 Reg 12(1) TC(DCI) Regs
108 Reg 12(3) TC(DCI) Regs
109 Reg 3(7)(a) TC(DCI) Regs
110 Reg 12(4) TC(DCI) Regs
111 Reg 3(3) TC(DCI) Regs
112 Reg 3(5A) TC(DCI) Regs
113 Reg 3(6A) TC(DCI) Regs
114 Reg 19 TC(DCI) Regs
115 Reg 19 Table 7 para 2(a)-(c) TC(DCI) Regs
116 Reg 19 Table 8 para 1 TC(DCI) Regs
117 Reg 19 Table 6 para 2 TC(DCI) Regs
118 Reg 19 Table 6 para 5 TC(DCI) Regs
119 Reg 19 Table 6 para 3 TC(DCI) Regs; DWP, *Provider Guidance, Generic Guidance,* Chapter 13
120 Reg 19 Table 6 para 10 TC(DCI) Regs
121 Reg 19 Table 6 para 9 TC(DCI) Regs
122 Reg 19 Table 6 para 9 TC(DCI) Regs; The Qualifying Care Relief (Specified Social Care Schemes) Order 2011 No.712; s806A IT(TOI)A 2005
123 TCTM 02440
124 Reg 19 Table 6 para 11(a) TC(DCI) Regs
125 Reg 19 Table 6 para 11(a) and (b) TC(DCI) Regs
126 Reg 19 Table 6 para 34 TC(DCI) Regs
127 Reg 19 Table 6 para 35 TC(DCI) Regs
128 Para 7.7, Explanatory Memorandum to The Tax Credits (Coronavirus Miscellaneous Amendments) (No.2) Regs 2020 No.941
129 Reg 19 Table 6 para 37 TC(DCI) Regs

10

Chapter 64

Claims, decisions and getting paid: tax credits

This chapter covers:
1. Who can get tax credits (p1459)
2. How and when to make a claim (p1462)
3. Decisions (p1466)
4. Backdating your claim (p1467)
5. Getting paid (p1467)
6. Change of circumstances (p1470)
7. Annual reviews (p1475)
8. Contacting HM Revenue and Customs (p1479)

Key facts

- You cannot usually make a new claim for tax credits.
- Tax credits are administered and paid by HM Revenue and Customs' Tax Credit Office.
- Tax credits are dealt with differently from social security benefits. Tax credits are dealt with over a tax year, using annual income, and entitlement is finalised at the end of the tax year.
- Your tax credits may be affected by changes in your circumstances or income.
- Tax credit claims are finalised between April and July each year. This annual review also acts as a renewal claim for the new tax year.
- If you claim universal credit (UC), your entitlement to tax credits ends.

Moving to universal credit

The 'managed migration' transfer process started in January 2022, under which you are told by the DWP that your tax credits will end and are invited to claim UC. See p29 for further information, and AskCPAG and CPAG's *Welfare Rights Bulletin* for updates

1. Who can get tax credits

You must be at least 16 years old to be entitled to tax credits.[1] You must meet the qualifying conditions for child tax credit (CTC – see p271) or working tax credit (WTC – see p284). You can be entitled to either tax credit or both. You must not be a universal credit (UC) claimant (see p1471). If you are already getting tax credits and you claim UC, your tax credits will stop.[2]

If you are a member of a married couple or registered civil partnership, or live with someone as if you are married, you get tax credits jointly with your partner. This is known as a 'joint claim' and 'joint award', based on your and your partner's circumstances and income.[3] HM Revenue and Customs (HMRC) has the discretion to treat a claim by one member of a couple as having also been made by the other, but usually only uses this power to accept renewal claims by telephone.[4] See p1460 for when you are treated as a couple.

If you are not part of a couple, you have a single claim and single award, solely based on your circumstances and income.

If you made a joint claim and are no longer in a couple, or if you made a single claim and are now in a couple, your entitlement ends and cannot be renewed.[5] You must usually make a new claim for UC instead.[6] You should tell the Tax Credit Office as soon as possible. If you do not, you could be overpaid. You could also be given a financial penalty if you fail to notify the change within one month (see p1470).[7]

Who can make a new claim for tax credits

You can only make a new claim for tax credits if any of the following apply.[8]
- You already have an award of one type of tax credit and you become entitled to the other one – eg, if you are already getting CTC, you can start to get WTC. This is treated as a change in circumstances and a new claim is not required.
- You had an award of a tax credit in 2021/22 and are making a claim for the same tax credit for 2022/23. This includes renewals, but could also apply in other situations. It does not apply if you have already renewed your claim and then attempt to reclaim later in the year after a gap in entitlement.[9]
- You are prevented from claiming UC because you (or if you are in a couple, you and your partner) are in a category from which it has been decided not to accept claims for UC.
- You are a refugee who applied for asylum in the UK on or before 31 January 2019, and you claim CTC within one month of being granted refugee status (see p1540).[10]

10

Part 10: General rules for tax credits
Chapter 64: Claims, decisions and getting paid: tax credits
1. Who can get tax credits

Couples

You and your partner count as a 'couple' if you are:[11]
- married or registered civil partners, unless you are separated and this is under a court order or is likely to be permanent; *or*
- not married or registered civil partners, but are living together as if you are.[12]

Note: if you are entitled to tax credits and become part of a couple with someone who is entitled to UC (see p22), your tax credit award ends and you are treated as making a joint UC claim.[13]

Married couples and civil partners

You have a joint tax credits award with your partner if you are married to her/him or you are registered as civil partners. You still count as a couple for tax credits purposes if you are married or are registered civil partners and are still in a relationship but are not living together – eg, because of work or housing reasons. You continue to count as a couple while you and your partner are temporarily separated. It does not matter how long the temporary separation lasts (but see p1461 if you or your partner go abroad).

If you and your partner are permanently separated or are separated under a court order, your joint tax credit award ends and you will usually have to claim UC instead. This is the case even if you are still living under the same roof and whether or not you are taking steps to divorce your partner or dissolve your civil partnership.[14] The test is whether you are 'separated in circumstances in which the separation is likely to be permanent' and this depends on your (and your partner's) intentions, and should also take into account the context of cultural attitudes to separation and divorce.[15] The focus is on the state of the relationship, not exclusively whether you are living in the 'same household', which differs from the rule for means-tested benefits (see p303).[16] If you are having a trial separation and there is at least a 50 per cent chance of reconciliation, HMRC is likely to say you still count as a couple.[17]

Special rules apply if you are a member of a polygamous unit.[18]

Living together as a couple

You must claim tax credits jointly with your partner if you are living together as if you are married or in a registered civil partnership. In determining whether or not you count as living together as a couple, HMRC is likely to consider the same factors as the DWP does for means-tested benefits.[19] See p304 and p307 for more information.

If you and your partner stop living together, your joint tax credits award ends and you will usually have to claim UC instead. However, if you and your partner are only temporarily living apart (eg, one of you is in hospital or in respite care), you may still be treated as a couple.

Note: HMRC often applies too narrow an interpretation of the test. For example, there is no rule that says that if your partner stays with you for three nights or more a week you are *automatically* to be treated as a couple living together.

Challenging a living together decision

If you get tax credits as a single person, HMRC may investigate your award if it suspects that you are living with a partner (see Chapter 66). HMRC may ask you for information or evidence and may suspend payments if you have not responded by the specified date (you must be given at least 30 days). If it decides that you are not entitled as a single person, you can request a mandatory reconsideration and, if you are unhappy with the outcome, appeal against such a decision (but not against a suspension of payments) (see Chapter 67). **Note:** HMRC often relies on information it obtains from credit reference agencies, but such information on its own is unlikely to be sufficient. In the event of an appeal, HMRC must usually produce all the evidence it used to make the decision.[20] HMRC sometimes makes standard requests for a list of evidence, including a legal separation order and utility bills showing the alleged partner's address is elsewhere. However, if you explain why such evidence does not exist or is not available to you, the fact that you cannot provide it should not go against you when making a decision.[21]

If you think a decision about whether or not you count as a couple is wrong and it affects your tax credits, consider requesting a mandatory reconsideration and then appealing. It is possible that the DWP, the local authority and HMRC might reach different conclusions about whether you are a couple. If so, appeal *all* the decisions with which you disagree.

Couples and residence rules

If you or your partner go abroad, either permanently or for more than a set period of time, and cannot be treated as being in the UK (see p1638), you cease to satisfy the residence conditions. In this case, you must terminate your joint tax credits claim. If you do not do so, you may be given a financial penalty (see p1498). The person still in the UK will usually have to claim UC instead.

If your partner does not have a right to reside in the UK (see p1557), s/he is treated as not being present in the UK for CTC, so you can get CTC as a single person.[22] The requirement to have a right to reside only applies to CTC, not WTC. In some cases, HMRC may treat you as a single claimant for CTC and joint claimants for WTC. It is advisable to ensure that HMRC is fully aware of your circumstances.

You can get tax credits as a couple even though your partner is a 'person subject to immigration control' (see p1524) and would not be able to get tax credits in her/his own right.[23]

Part 10: General rules for tax credits
Chapter 64: Claims, decisions and getting paid: tax credits
2. How and when to make a claim

Appointees

The following people can act on your behalf if you are unable to manage your claim yourself:[24]

- a receiver appointed by the Court of Protection with power to make a claim for tax credits on your behalf; *or*
- in Scotland, a tutor, curator or other guardian acting or appointed in terms of the law who is administering your estate; *or*
- a person who is your 'appointee' (see p1135) for social security purposes; *or*
- if none of the above applies, a person aged 18 or over who applies to HMRC in writing to act on your behalf and is appointed by HMRC in that capacity – see gov.uk/getting-help-with-your-tax-credits-claim/appointees.

---

2. **How and when to make a claim**

You can only make a new claim for tax credits in limited circumstances (see p1459). You must usually claim tax credits by telephone. You have no entitlement to tax credits unless you make a claim.[25] You claim both child tax credit (CTC) and working tax credit (WTC) together. HM Revenue and Customs (HMRC) has discretion to accept an application made by other means, but in practice this rarely happens.[26] HMRC no longer issues claim forms.

You claim by contacting the Tax Credit Helpline (see p1479).

The Tax Credit Helpline may also ask you questions about your identity and eligibility for tax credits.

Note: the date of your claim is the date of your telephone call if you provide sufficient information as accepted by HMRC. Your claim can be backdated in certain circumstances (see p1467).

If you are renewing a claim, this may be done by telephone, online or automatically in specific cases (see p1465).

When to claim

You should claim tax credits as soon as you think you are eligible. You cannot make a claim for tax credits in advance of the tax year for which you are claiming.[27] The general rule is that a claim for tax credits runs from the date it is received by the Tax Credit Office until the end of the tax year in which the claim is made.[28]

If you were entitled to tax credits before the date your claim is received by the Tax Credit Office, your claim can be backdated for up to 31 days. Backdating of WTC is possible for a longer period if you are entitled to a disabled worker element and only become entitled to WTC following an award of a qualifying benefit (see p1467).

Once a claim for tax credits has been made, it can be renewed at the end of that tax year (see p1465).

Should you renew a nil award?[29]

Tax credits are always based on annual income. HMRC bases the initial award on your (and your partner's) *previous* tax year's income (see p1437). If your income in the previous year was too high to qualify for tax credits, but you think your income in the current year may be substantially lower and you will qualify (eg, if you are self-employed with a fluctuating income, or your income is going to fall because your work is seasonal, you are going on maternity leave or you might be made redundant), you may have a 'nil award'.[30] This means that you are eligible for tax credits and your claim is in the system, but you are currently not paid anything because your previous year's income was too high. This protects your position because, once your current year's income is known, HMRC can amend the nil award to make a payment for the whole period of your claim. The nil award can be amended during the year or at the end of the tax year, and the new award runs from your original date of claim (or the date to which your claim was backdated).

Information to support your claim

You must provide all the information required by HMRC, unless HMRC decides otherwise.[31] If you do not supply all the requested information, a decision may be delayed, or HMRC may decide to 'reject' your claim as not validly made. You can appeal against a decision to reject a claim that is not made in an accepted manner or does not contain all the required information.[32] If you need advice about the information required, contact the helpline (see p1479).

National insurance number requirement

Your claim must include the following for each person:[33]

- your (and your partner's if you are claiming as a couple) national insurance (NI) number plus information or evidence establishing that the number is yours (or your partner's); *or*
- information or evidence to enable HMRC to find your (and your partner's) NI number; *or*
- an application for an NI number, with the necessary evidence or information to allow one to be allocated (this does not necessarily mean that you must actually be allocated an NI number).

You do not need to meet the above NI number requirement if HMRC believes you have a reasonable excuse.[34] 'Reasonable excuse' is not defined, but HMRC says it varies from case to case and discretion must be used fairly.[35] You can appeal against a decision that you do not have a reasonable excuse for not meeting the NI number requirement.[36] If someone has not been given an NI number, you can argue this is a reasonable excuse.

Part 10: General rules for tax credits
Chapter 64: Claims, decisions and getting paid: tax credits
2. How and when to make a claim

If you or your partner are a 'person subject to immigration control' (see p1524), see p1538 for the NI number requirement and p1529 for how tax credits are affected by your immigration status.

Child benefit reference number

You may be asked for the child benefit reference number for any child(ren) for whom you are claiming. You do not have to provide one if you do not have one. There is no legal requirement to claim child benefit in order to be entitled to CTC. If you do not have a child benefit reference number (eg, because you are waiting for your child benefit claim to be processed), do not delay claiming CTC. Child benefit can be backdated for three months, but CTC can only be backdated for 31 days, and it usually takes longer than this for a child benefit claim to be made and processed. HMRC has confirmed that tax credit claims will not be rejected because the child benefit reference number is missing.[37]

If you do not have a child benefit reference number, it may take longer to confirm the identity of the child, and that you are responsible for her/him. However, the tax credit award will still be made from the date of claim, with up to 31 days' backdating. As long as your tax credit claim is received within 31 days of the date of birth of a new baby, or the date you became responsible for a child, it will be awarded from that date, even if it takes longer than this to process.

Income

If you are receiving income support, income-based jobseeker's allowance (JSA), income-related employment and support allowance (ESA) or pension credit when you claim tax credits, you must confirm this. You do not need to provide any other income details.[38] HMRC expects you to know which type of JSA or ESA you are getting.[39]

Otherwise, when you make a claim for tax credits, you must provide a figure for your income during the previous tax year. If you are part of a couple and making a joint claim, your award is based on your joint income during the previous tax year. This applies even in situations in which you may not have been living as a couple in the previous year, so income before the relationship began still counts as joint income.[40] For what counts as income, see Chapter 63.

If you think that your current tax year's income is going to be substantially different from the previous tax year's income, you must still provide details of your previous tax year's income. When HMRC makes a decision on your claim, you are sent an award notice informing you how to notify it of your estimated income for the current year. You can also request that your award be adjusted at any time during the year of the award. Where appropriate, HMRC adjusts your award of tax credits, using your estimated figure of your current year's income (see p1437).

If you worked as an employee throughout the previous tax year, your P60 for that year has details of your taxable income. If you received any payments in kind from your employer, you should have details of these on Form P11D, which your employer should give you. If you were self-employed throughout the previous tax year, you can use your tax return as the basis for your taxable income. If you were in receipt of taxable social security benefits, you should be able to get a statement of taxable benefit income from the DWP.

Bank account details

You are required to provide details of a bank, building society or other account into which the tax credits can be paid. This is because entitlement depends on having a bank or other account.[41] See p1468 if you do not have an account.

Further information and evidence

HMRC might need further information or evidence before making a decision on your claim or renewal or when considering whether to revise a decision. The information or evidence can be required from you or from your employer or childcare provider. If material is required, HMRC gives notice to provide it within a specified time limit. In all cases, this must be at least 30 days.[42] The basic rule is that you can be required to provide any further information or evidence that HMRC considers necessary. If you do not provide the material requested, your claim should be decided on the information available and you might be refused tax credits. If you provide incorrect information or fail to comply with requirements to provide information or evidence, you may be given a financial penalty or, if you are considered to have acted fraudulently, a fine or imprisonment, or both (see Chapter 66).

Renewing your award

From 6 April each year, HMRC reviews all tax credit awards (see p1475). This annual review, and your response, is also your renewal claim for the new tax year. If you were entitled to either tax credit in 2021/22, you can make a renewal claim for 2022/23.[43] Tax credits continue to be paid on a provisional basis during the annual review (see p1469).

Withdrawing your award

If you no longer wish to receive tax credits, you can withdraw your claim during the annual review (see p1475). However, if you have been receiving 'provisional payments' (see p1469) since the start of the new tax year, these become overpayments if there is no renewal claim. If you have a nil award because your income is too high for an award to be made, HMRC seeks to withdraw your claim. HMRC writes to you at least 35 days before the annual review to notify you that your claim will not be renewed unless you respond within 30 days that you want your claim to continue.[44] Renewing a nil award protects your future entitlement and may prove valuable if income drops unexpectedly later in the year.[45]

Part 10: General rules for tax credits
Chapter 64: Claims, decisions and getting paid: tax credits
3. Decisions

3. **Decisions**

Once you have made a valid claim for tax credits (see p1462), HM Revenue and Customs (HMRC) must make a decision on whether you are entitled to either of the tax credits and, if so, at what rate.[46] HMRC must decide your entitlement to both child tax credit and working tax credit. HMRC may first require you, or your partner if you are making a joint claim, to provide any information or evidence that it needs to make a decision.[47]

You can amend, either verbally or in writing, the details you provided when making your claim at any time until HMRC makes its initial decision and your date of claim will remain the same.[48]

An '**initial decision**' is made at the start of your claim or renewal, and is based on an estimate of your tax credit award for the whole year (6 April to 5 April). You are notified of the initial decision in an award notice (Form TC602). You are asked to check the details on your award notice using a checklist (Form TC602(SN)). Contact the Tax Credit Office if any of the details shown on the award notice are wrong or have changed. If you do not and an overpayment results, HMRC may expect you to pay it back (see p1486).

You must be notified of the initial decision. The notice must include the date on which it is given and your right to request a mandatory reconsideration, and subsequent right to appeal.[49] If you had already claimed tax credits in the previous year, your initial decision for the coming year may be included in the annual review (see p1475).[50]

A '**revised decision**' may be made during the tax year – eg, following certain changes of circumstances (see p1470). Decisions can be revised at any time during the tax year, and as many times as is required. Each revised decision is notified on a tax credits award notice (Form TC602).

A '**final decision**' is made after the end of the tax year, as part of the annual review (see p1478). It is based on your circumstances during the year and is the decision that confirms what your entitlement actually was. You are sent a tax credits award notice (Form TC602). A final decision can only be changed in limited circumstances (see p1508).

Unless the decision on your award is changed after a revision, mandatory reconsideration or appeal, the initial decision and the final decision are the only decisions on your claim that you receive.

If you think an initial decision, revised decision or final decision is wrong, you can request a mandatory reconsideration and then appeal (see Chapter 67).

4. **Backdating your claim**

In general, your claim for a tax credit can be backdated for up to 31 days (but see below), provided you satisfied the rules of entitlement throughout the 31-day period.[51] This cannot include a period in which you were entitled to universal credit (UC), or when you were receiving tax-free childcare payments (see p856), unless you were registered for tax-free childcare but no payments were made from your tax-free childcare account and the account has now been closed.

It is best to ask for your claim to be backdated to when you think your entitlement began (subject to the 31-day limit), either in writing or in a subsequent telephone call. You do not need to give any reasons.

A renewal claim can be backdated for a longer period, depending on when you make your annual declaration (see p1476).

If you were entitled to tax credits but no payment was made because you did not provide sufficient details of an account into which payments could be made and you subsequently provide the necessary details, payment can be backdated for up to three months from the date you supply the information, (but no more than 31 days before the date you claimed).[52]

A new claim for working tax credit (WTC) can be backdated for more than 31 days if you have a disability and you have been waiting to hear about a disability benefit. If your claim includes the disabled worker element (see p1420) and you claim within 31 days of being awarded a qualifying disability benefit (usually personal independence payment (PIP)), your WTC claim can be backdated to the date from which your PIP was awarded, provided you were working at least 16 hours throughout the period and did not qualify for WTC without the award of the disability benefit, including because your income was too high.[53]

A new claim for child tax credit (CTC) cannot be backdated for more than 31 days, even if a disability benefit has been awarded for the child. If you have an existing award of WTC or CTC and want to be awarded the disability or severe disability elements following an award of a qualifying disability benefit, see p1472.

See p1540 for backdating if you are granted refugee status.

10

5. **Getting paid**

Who is paid

If you have a joint award, child tax credit (CTC) and the childcare element of working tax credit (WTC) are paid into the account of the 'main carer' of the child(ren), as nominated when you claim.[54] The **'main carer'** can be either you or your partner, depending on who you both agree should be paid. If both live at the same address and either you do not identify who should be paid, or you cannot

Part 10: General rules for tax credits
Chapter 64: Claims, decisions and getting paid: tax credits
5. Getting paid

agree, HM Revenue and Customs (HMRC) decides. If you and your partner are not currently living at the same address or one of you is temporarily absent, HMRC decides which of you will be paid. If the main carer changes following an award of tax credits, HMRC can make the payments to that person instead if it considers it reasonable.

If you have a joint award of WTC and one of you is working, the payment (apart from any amount for childcare) is made to the person who is in paid work (see p284). If you are both in paid work, you can decide who will receive the payment. If you cannot agree, HMRC decides. If you both agree who should be paid, write to the Tax Credit Office requesting that payment be made to that person.[55]

If you make a joint claim and your partner dies, you receive any outstanding amount of tax credits that would have been paid to you and your partner up to the date of death, after which you must usually claim universal credit instead.[56]

If an appointee (see p1135) is acting on your behalf, payment is normally made to her/him.[57]

How and when payments are made

HMRC makes payments of tax credits by direct credit transfer into a bank, building society or credit union account.[58] Use of post office card accounts for tax credits and child benefit is being phased out by 5 April 2022. The government says it will use an alternative 'Post Office Payout' voucher service for those unable to open a 'mainstream account'.[59] You can request that the payments be made into your account every week or every four weeks, but HMRC has the discretion to make payments weekly or four-weekly as it sees fit. CTC and the childcare element of WTC must be paid at the same time and at the same intervals.[60] Generally, tax credits payments are made in arrears.[61]

If you are entitled to less than £2 tax credits a week, your award may be paid as a single lump sum for the year, payable at such time as HMRC considers appropriate.[62]

If it is not considered appropriate for payments to be made into an account, HMRC can decide on the manner and timing of payment by other means, such as by Post Office Payout voucher (but it no longer issues cheques).[63]

If you do not provide account details, HMRC should write to you, requesting that you supply the information within four weeks, after which your payments may be postponed.[64] If you then require an authority from HMRC to open an account, you have three weeks from the date it supplies you with this to provide details of your account. If you do not provide details of an account within three months of your payments being postponed (or by the end of the relevant tax year if this is earlier), your entitlement may cease from the date payments were postponed. These periods can be extended if there are exceptional circumstances or you have a 'reasonable excuse' for not being able to provide the details within the time limits.[65]

If you lose your bank account card or forget your PIN, see p1149.

Payments of tax credits may be reduced if an overpayment is being recovered. See Chapter 65 for more information.

Urgent payments

There is no provision in the tax credits legislation for payments to be made before a decision has been made on entitlement. However, once a decision has been made to award tax credits, there is official guidance on making payments urgently when requested. Urgent payments should be made if you or your child are experiencing hardship, especially in cases of domestic violence, identity fraud or immediate risk of eviction. These payments are referred to in the *Tax Credits Manual* as 'manual payments', 'interim payments' and 'user-requested payments'. Payment can be made by the next day into an account.[66]

When payment is postponed or suspended

Payment of tax credits may be postponed or suspended if:[67]
- you have failed to provide correct account details (see p1465); *or*
- you have failed to respond to a request for information or evidence by a specified date (see p1465); *or*
- you are receiving 'provisional payments' (see below); *or*
- there is an appeal pending against a decision of the First-tier Tribunal, Upper Tribunal or a court either in your case or in another case that might affect your award (including if HMRC is considering whether to make a further appeal or request a statement of reasons).

If your income drops during the year, your tax credits may be increased and you may appear to be due some arrears of tax credits for the earlier part of the year. HMRC refers to this as a 'potential payment', and it may be held back until the end of the year when your final income is known. If the underpayment is confirmed at the end of the tax year, it must be paid to you.[68]

Provisional payments

Your claim is renewed by the annual review process from April to July, during which time your tax credits may continue to be paid on a provisional basis.[69]

Provisional payments can be made while you are waiting to renew your claim and have not had a final decision on the previous year. Provisional payments can also continue if you have renewed your claim but not yet received an initial decision on the new tax year. Provisional payments are discretionary and can be made, adjusted or suspended without a formal decision being made, but you may

10

Part 10: General rules for tax credits
Chapter 64: Claims, decisions and getting paid: tax credits
6. Change of circumstances

receive a letter which is referred to as a 'statement like an award notice' (Form TC602(J)).[70]

If HMRC does not have up-to-date income details, these payments are based on the assumption that your income for the tax year just ended increased in line with average earnings.[71] If your income increased by more than this, you may be overpaid until the review is complete. Therefore, it is best to provide details of your income as soon as possible and not wait for the annual review. If you withdraw or fail to renew your claim, any provisional payments since the start of the year will become an overpayment because there is no claim for the new tax year.

6. **Change of circumstances**

Changes in your family circumstances, childcare charges or income during your award may lead to changes in your tax credit entitlement. If changes do affect your entitlement, this can be altered either soon after the change has occurred, or at the end of the year when the final decision is made and HM Revenue and Customs (HMRC) makes a final check on your details. Certain changes must be notified to the Tax Credit Office within one month or you may incur a penalty. You should report other changes which increase your entitlement within one month of the date of change, for your increased award to be backdated for up to one month.

Changes that must be notified

Some changes must be notified to the Tax Credit Office within one month of the date of the change or the date you became aware of the change, if this was later. The notification must be 'given' to the appropriate office (see p1475).[72] If you do not do this, you may receive a penalty decision notice (see p1498).

If you have any of the following changes in your circumstances, the way your tax credits are calculated changes.[73] Either your entitlement to tax credits ceases or a new 'relevant period' starts from the date the change is treated as having taken effect. A new relevant period means that a new calculation of your tax credit entitlement is made. See p1413 for more on the relevant period and details of the calculation.

You must notify the Tax Credit Office within one month if:[74]
- you were claiming as a single person but are now part of a couple. Your tax credit entitlement comes to an end from the date the change occurred, and you must usually claim universal credit (UC) instead;
- you were claiming as a couple but are no longer part of that couple. Your entitlement comes to an end from the date the change occurred, and you must usually claim UC instead;

- you or your partner leave the UK permanently or for more than eight weeks (12 if due to illness or bereavement) and cannot be treated as being in the UK (see p1638). Entitlement comes to an end and you must usually claim UC instead;
- for child tax credit (CTC) only, you lose your right to reside in the UK (see p1557);
- there has been a decrease of £10 a week or more over four consecutive weeks in your or your partner's average weekly childcare charge (as calculated on p1425) or the childcare costs have stopped. This change takes effect on the day after the four consecutive weeks. If you have been awarded childcare costs for a fixed period that was known when the costs were awarded, the change takes effect from the week following the end of the period of the award, instead of the usual four-week period;[75]
- you or your partner stop normally working at least 16 or 30 hours a week (see p284 for rules about work). You can still count as being in work in some situations – eg, in some cases of illness or maternity, or during the four-week run-on of working tax credit (WTC) (see p289).[76] For a couple, you do not need to report a change in which partner is working, provided this does not affect your entitlement or maximum rate;[77]
- you are a couple with children, and you and your partner stop normally working a combined total of 24 or 30 hours a week;
- you or your partner cease to be responsible for one or more of your children (see p273 for when you count as responsible);
- a child for whom you or your partner are responsible dies (see p272 for who counts as a child);
- a child for whom you or your partner are responsible stops counting as a child or qualifying young person, other than by reaching age 20 (see p272 for who counts as a child). You must notify the Tax Credit Office within one month of the date the change actually occurred, rather than when you became aware of the change.

Changes that terminate your tax credits award

Your tax credit award automatically terminates in the following situations.
- You become a UC claimant. This may happen if you make a claim for UC or become part of a couple with someone who is already entitled to UC. The DWP issues a 'stop notice' to HMRC, notifying it that you have claimed and meet the basic conditions for UC.[78] Your tax credit award is terminated, even if you do not receive any UC because your income or capital is too high. If you withdraw your UC claim before the stop notice is issued, your tax credits should not be terminated.[79] Your tax credits claim usually ends on the day before your entitlement to UC begins. However, if you become part of a couple with a UC claimant, your new joint UC claim begins from the start of your

Part 10: General rules for tax credits
Chapter 64: Claims, decisions and getting paid: tax credits
6. Change of circumstances

partner's assessment period in which you became a couple.[80] In this case, you are still entitled to tax credits up to the actual date you became a couple.[81]

- You apply for, and are entitled to, tax-free childcare payments (see p856). Check whether you will be better off on tax-free childcare before applying. This is only likely to be the case if you are entitled to a small amount of tax credits. Your entire tax credits claim, not just the childcare element, ends on the day before your entitlement period for tax-free childcare begins.[82]

Changes that affect your maximum entitlement

In addition to the changes outlined above, other changes in your circumstances can also affect your entitlement to tax credits. Some changes can be notified up to a week in advance (see p1475). However, most changes which *increase* your entitlement are only backdated for a maximum of one month from the time that you notify the Tax Credit Office of the change (except a change that affects your entitlement to one of the disability elements – see below).[83] Delaying notifying these changes can lead to an underpayment.

Changes that *decrease* your entitlement always take effect from the date of change, irrespective of when you notify the Tax Credit Office. Delaying notifying these changes can therefore lead to an underpayment or overpayment, so tell the Tax Credit Office as soon as possible. Overpayments are usually recovered from you (see Chapter 65).

The changes in your circumstances that affect your entitlement include if:

- you have a new baby, or another child joins your family (you should still report this change even if you may be affected by the two-child limit – see p1415);
- your child is staying on in full-time, non-advanced education after 31 August following his/her 16th birthday (HMRC considers this to be a change, as the default position is that CTC will stop unless you notify it of this);
- you or your partner start normally working at least 16, 24 or 30 hours a week;
- your childcare costs increase by £10 or more a week for at least four weeks in a row. The change takes effect from the first week in which your costs increase.[84] You can report an increase of £10 or more a week as soon as one occurs, provided you expect it to last for at least four weeks. For how your childcare costs are calculated, see p1425.

Backdating your entitlement to a disabled worker, severe disability or disabled child element

The disabled worker and severe disability elements of WTC can be backdated for more than one month if you notify the Tax Credit Office that you have been awarded a qualifying disability benefit (usually personal independence payment (PIP)), within one month of that award being made.[85] The elements can be backdated to the date from which the disability benefit was awarded. This includes after an appeal or supersession from a previous tax year. If the award means that you become entitled to WTC for the first time, see p1467.

A similar rule applies to CTC entitlement. If a child for whom you are responsible is awarded disability living allowance (DLA) or child disability payment (CDP), or a young person is awarded PIP, adult disability payment (ADP) or armed forces independence payment, you are entitled to the disabled child element. If the child is awarded the DLA care component at the highest rate, CDP highest rate care component, the enhanced rate of the PIP daily living component, ADP care component highest rate or armed forces independence payment, you are entitled to the higher rate for a severely disabled child in your CTC award. The elements can be backdated for more than one month, to the date from which DLA, CDP, PIP or ADP was awarded, if you notify the Tax Credit Office of the award of DLA, CDP, PIP or ADP within one month of the decision.[86] This includes after an appeal or supersession from a previous tax year.

You should report changes to a qualifying disability benefit, as failure to do so may result in an underpayment or overpayment. However, as it is not listed as a change that you are legally obliged to report, you cannot be given a penalty for failing to report a change in entitlement to a disability benefit during a tax year (but if you fail to notice it is incorrectly recorded in your circumstances at the annual review, you could be given a penalty for a false declaration).[87]

If you or your child have been awarded a qualifying disability benefit for a period when you were on tax credits, you can still get arrears of tax credits, even if you are no longer getting tax credits. You should notify HMRC within one month of the disability benefit decision and request a review (see p1514).

Changes in income

The initial decision on your award of tax credit is usually based on your previous year's income. Your award can be changed to reflect:

- an expected fall in your annual income of more than £2,500 compared with the previous year; *or*
- an expected rise in your annual income of more than £2,500 compared with the previous year.

You are not required to report a change in income during the year and a penalty cannot be imposed on you if you fail to do so, unless it is a formal request for information (see p1497). However, it is often worth reporting a change when it occurs, to avoid overpayments or underpayments. HMRC may use 'real-time information' on wages obtained from your employer for tax purposes. HMRC always requires a figure for your annual income in the complete tax year, so be careful to keep an in-year estimate accurate and up to date.

If you expect your annual income to fall by more than £2,500

- If you notify the Tax Credit Office of an estimated decrease in your annual income of more than £2,500 during the year, your tax credit payments may be increased. However, the first £2,500 of the decrease is disregarded, so it is only

10

Part 10: General rules for tax credits
Chapter 64: Claims, decisions and getting paid: tax credits
6. Change of circumstances

any decrease over that amount which makes a difference. HMRC adds £2,500 onto the current year's income and bases your award on the result. For example, if your 2021/22 income was £10,000 and your 2022/23 income is £6,000, your tax credits award for 2022/23 is based on £8,500.[88]

- An increase in tax credits means that if you get housing benefit (HB), the amount could be reduced because tax credits count as income.
- At the end of the year, it may be that your income did not fall as you predicted and, as a result, you have been overpaid tax credits, which you may have to repay. For example, if your 2021/22 income was £9,000 and you ask for your tax credits to be based on an estimate that your 2022/23 income will be £6,000 but, at the end of 2022/23, your actual income is £8,000, your tax credit award should not have been increased and you will have been overpaid.
- HB takes into account the amount of tax credits you actually *receive*. If you have been overpaid tax credits, HB is *not* increased for the period during which you should have received a lower amount of tax credits. Not only will you usually have to repay the overpaid tax credits, you may have lost out on the additional HB which you would have been able to claim had you been receiving a lower award of tax credits.
- If the Tax Credit Office is not aware of a fall in income of more than £2,500 during the year, your tax credit entitlement is not adjusted until the final decision at the end of the year. In this instance, you will have been underpaid tax credits for the year, and this should be paid to you as a lump sum. This lump sum counts as capital for HB and is ignored for 52 weeks after you have received it.[89] You will not, therefore, have been overpaid HB as a result of receiving these arrears and you will not have been overpaid or lost out on tax credits.

If you expect your annual income to rise by more than £2,500

- If you notify the Tax Credit Office that you expect your income to increase by more than £2,500 during the year, your tax credit award is decreased. This may mean that you prevent an overpayment of tax credits building up further during the year (see Chapter 65). Your HB (if you are entitled to any) can then be increased to take account of the lower award of tax credits.
- If the Tax Credit Office is not aware of an expected rise in your income during the year, you keep being paid the 'extra' tax credits during the year and will incur an overpayment. The overpaid tax credits are usually recoverable from you by reducing the amount of tax credits you are paid in the following year, in which case your HB in that year is likely to increase.
- There is no penalty for incurring an overpayment of tax credits on the basis of an increase in income.
- If you have overestimated your income, and it does not rise as expected, you may have been underpaid tax credits and you can receive a lump sum at the end of the year.

Notifying changes of circumstances

You can notify any changes in your circumstances by telephone, in writing or online through a government gateway account. The notification must be given to any office specified in writing by HMRC – eg, the Tax Credit Office address on your award notice.[90] This could include the government's 'Tell Us Once' service following a death.

If you notified the DWP or another part of HMRC of a change which affects your tax credit entitlement and this was not passed on and resulted in an underpayment or overpayment, you should raise this in *any* dispute (see p1485). In practice, to be safe, you should ensure that the Tax Credit Office has been informed. HMRC encourages claimants to telephone the Tax Credits Helpline (see p1479) with queries or to report a change. However, it is advisable to confirm the notification in writing to the Tax Credit Office and to keep a copy so you have a record of what you have said and when you said it.

Notification must be given by the person who claimed the tax credit. In joint claim cases, it can be given by either member of the couple.[91]

Some changes of circumstances can be notified up to a week in advance. These are if:[92]

- you have accepted an offer of work and expect to start work within seven days;
- you have arranged childcare and will incur childcare costs during the current tax year;
- your weekly childcare costs are going to change by £10 a week or more.

You can also notify HMRC in advance if you expect your child to stay on in full-time, non-advanced education or approved training from 1 September after her/his 16th birthday.[93]

You can amend the notification at any time before the initial award is revised, in which case the amended notification is taken as being notified at the time that your original notification was sent.[94]

If you notify a change of circumstances, HMRC should send you a new award notice (if the change affected your award) within 30 days.[95] If you do not receive one within 30 days, HMRC's leaflet asks you to call the Tax Credits Helpline again. However, provided you can prove the original notification was made, it is HMRC's responsibility to act on the information provided (see p1486).

7. Annual reviews

The annual review is the process by which HM Revenue and Customs (HMRC) finalises your entitlement for the year that has just ended, and makes an initial decision on your award for the year that has just begun. By responding to the annual review, you renew your claim for tax credits for the new tax year.

Part 10: General rules for tax credits
Chapter 64: Claims, decisions and getting paid: tax credits
7. Annual reviews

If you had an award of tax credits for the tax year 2021/22, HMRC should write to you between April and July 2022 enclosing an annual review form (Form TC603R). This is referred to in the legislation as the 'final notice'.[96]

If you had more than one award for tax credits during the previous tax year (eg, because of a gap in eligibility), you receive a separate annual review form and annual declaration form, if required, for each award. If you are sent more than one set of forms covering different awards, check and reply to each separately, even if they ask for the same information.

If you are sent an annual review form, but not an annual declaration form, you are asked to check that all the details about your award for the previous year are correct and to notify the Tax Credit Office of any changes in your circumstances. You are then deemed to have confirmed that all the details in the form are correct.[97] The final decision on the award for 2021/22 and an initial decision on the award for 2022/23 are as set out on the annual review form and you do not receive another notice of the final decision when it is made on or after 31 July. However, always check the form and the notes accompanying it carefully to see whether you need to return the forms or report a change or error.

If the details on the forms sent to you about your award and income are not correct and you fail to reply within the time allowed, you may not receive the correct amount of tax credits. If you are overpaid as a result, you may have to repay the overpayment. If you fail to notify certain changes of circumstances promptly, you may be given a penalty (see p1498).

If your tax credit award ends because you become entitled to universal credit (UC), see p1479.

Automatic renewal

If you have been receiving income support, income-based jobseeker's allowance, income-related employment and support allowance or pension credit throughout 2021/22 and are still getting one of those benefits, the annual review may tell you that your award will be renewed automatically on the information shown on the notice, unless you report a change or error. This automatic renewal process may also apply if HMRC uses 'real-time information' on earnings provided by your employer for PAYE (pay as you earn) purposes, but you must still check that this is correct. In other cases, you may also receive an annual declaration form (Form TC603D).

The annual declaration

You may receive an annual declaration form (Form TC603D) that asks for details of your income in the previous tax year. You must also tell the Tax Credit Office of any changes in your personal circumstances that are different from those set out in the annual review form.

If you are sent an annual declaration form, you must always respond to it on or before the date specified – usually 31 July, unless it was issued after 1 July, in which case you must be given at least 30 days to respond. If you are returning the annual declaration form by post, this is the date by which it must be received by the Tax Credit Office.

Responses must usually be on a form provided by HMRC (Form TC603RD). Alternatively, you can call the Tax Credit Helpline (see p1479) or renew your award online at gov.uk/manage-your-tax-credits. If you are unable to respond to the annual declaration (eg, because of illness), responses can be accepted from receivers and people who are appointees for tax credit or benefit purposes.[98]

If you respond in writing but do not use the annual declaration form, HMRC has discretion whether or not to accept it.[99]

If you do not respond to the annual declaration, your tax credit payments will stop, you may have to repay any tax credits paid since 6 April and you may have to pay a penalty.

For a joint award, one member of a couple can make the declaration by telephone or online on behalf of her/his partner; if it is in writing, both partners must sign it.[100] If a couple separate during the renewal period, a declaration by one partner allows the claim to be renewed up to the date of separation.[101] Both members of a separated couple are expected to make signed declarations for the previous year to allow the award for that year to be finalised. However, if only one signs the declaration, the award can be finalised, based on the information held by HMRC about the other member.[102]

If you do not know your total income for the period in question, do not delay making your annual declaration. Instead, provide an estimate and send details of your actual income as soon as you can. The annual declaration form allows for this, and there is a box to tick to show that you have given an estimate. You must provide your actual income figure by a second deadline, usually 31 January at the latest. The annual declaration form notifies you that if you do not do so, you are treated as having declared that your final income was as estimated, and your estimate is used to finalise your entitlement.[103]

Responding to the annual declaration, if required, is how your award is renewed for the new tax year, and failure to meet the deadline can mean that you lose out on tax credits. Unless you are single and are now part of a couple or you were in a couple and are now single, the following apply.

- If you make your annual declaration by the 31 July deadline, your renewal claim is backdated to 6 April 2022.[104]
- If you do not make your annual declaration by 31 July, HMRC sends you a notice that your payments of tax credits have ceased. If you make your annual declaration within 30 days following the date on this notice, your renewal claim is backdated to 6 April 2022.[105]
- If neither of the above applies, but you make your annual declaration by 31 January 2023 and have 'good cause' for making a late declaration, your renewal

10

Part 10: General rules for tax credits
Chapter 64: Claims, decisions and getting paid: tax credits
7. Annual reviews

claim is backdated to 6 April 2022.[106] 'Good cause' is not defined, but HMRC says it will look at each case on its individual merits. It will consider whether you were not able to complete the form because of exceptional circumstances and could not make arrangements for someone else to handle your affairs.[107]

- If you make your annual declaration late without good cause, or after 31 January in any case, arguably this can still be treated as a new claim and it can only be backdated for 31 days.[108] You will have to argue that this can be treated as a new claim for tax credits because the wording of the renewal provision still applies to you (see p1459).

Note: if you are not accepted as having good cause for making a late declaration, you should request a mandatory reconsideration, and then appeal to the First-tier Tribunal if you are unhappy with the outcome.[109] Remember that your late declaration should be treated as a new claim in any case.

The final decision

After the annual review has been completed, HMRC must make a final decision on whether you were entitled to tax credits for the tax year in question and, if so, the amount of your entitlement for that year.[110] The final decision can, therefore, establish that:

- the initial decision was correct and you received the right amount;
- you were underpaid tax credits;
- you were overpaid tax credits.

If you are underpaid tax credits, HMRC must pay you, usually in a lump sum.[111] If you are overpaid, HMRC asks you to pay back the overpayment (see Chapter 65).

If you do not agree that you have been overpaid, it is important that you request a mandatory reconsideration of the lower award notified to you in the final decision.

HMRC aims to deal with your review within eight weeks of receiving your declaration.[112] If you did not have an annual declaration form to complete, the final decision is as set out in your annual review form (unless, having read your annual review form, you find that you have a change of circumstances to report, in which case HMRC sends you details of your new award after it has dealt with the reported change). If your annual review told you what the final decision will be, and when it will be made, and you do not report any changes, the final decision can be made without further notification.[113] Any other decision must be notified to you in writing, stating the date on which it is made and including details of your right to request a mandatory reconsideration and your subsequent right of appeal.[114] If a decision does not include these details, it is 'defective' and the time limit for requesting a mandatory reconsideration does not start to run.[115]

A final decision must not be made before you have been given the chance to respond to the annual review and/or make your annual declaration on or before the deadline (usually 31 July). Once you have made your annual declaration, HMRC may make a final decision before the deadline. However, you can still change your declaration by the deadline, in which case HMRC may revise the final decision.[116] If you do not make your annual declaration by the deadline, the final decision can be made after that date, based on the information held by HMRC at that time.[117] If you have given an estimate, HMRC may make a final decision, but can revise it if you give details of your actual income by the second deadline (usually 31 January).

HMRC also sends you an initial decision notice (Form TC602), setting out your award for the tax year 2022/23.

Note: if your tax credit award ends because you become entitled to UC, the final decision may be made during the tax year.

In-year finalisation

If your tax credits award ends because you become entitled to UC, your tax credits award is finalised during the year, rather than at the end of the tax year.[118] This may happen if you become part of a couple with someone who is already entitled to UC, or if you make a claim for UC. HMRC may decide to wait until the end of the tax year to finalise an award if it decides it is not practical to do so during the year. If in-year finalisation applies, you do not get another annual review at the end of the year. You are asked to confirm or declare your income up to the date that your tax credits award ended, and your award is based on part-year income (see p1439). If you do not know your exact income, you can provide an estimate within 30 days. However, your estimated part-year income is used to finalise your award and you are not given an opportunity to rectify the estimate later.[119] If you disagree with the final decision following in-year finalisation for any reason, including the income figure used, you can request a mandatory reconsideration and, if you are unhappy with the outcome, appeal (see Chapter 67).

10

---

8. **Contacting HM Revenue and Customs**

You can telephone the Tax Credit Helpline (tel: 0345 300 3900; Relay UK available). Be ready to give your name, address and national insurance (NI) number. Always keep a note of the date and time of your call, with a brief note of what is said and, if possible, the name and title of the person you speak to. HM Revenue and Customs (HMRC) aims to record all calls, but a small number may not be recorded because of technical difficulties.[120] In the event of a dispute, you can request the recording of your call. If the recording is not available, and you can show that you made a call on a certain date, HMRC has agreed that you should be given the benefit of the doubt about what was said.[121]

Part 10: General rules for tax credits
Chapter 64: Claims, decisions and getting paid: tax credits
8. Contacting HM Revenue and Customs

It is best to follow up your call with a letter confirming the information you have provided and the advice given. Write to the Tax Credit Office at the address on the award notice and include your name, address, NI number and the date. Always keep a copy of your letter. If you are requesting a mandatory reconsideration, appealing, disputing recovery of an overpayment or making a complaint, it is best to use the relevant form or put it in writing. HMRC has an online service (gov.uk/manage-your-tax-credits) to check details of your claim and report changes of circumstances. HMRC's policy is to retain images of claim forms, documents and recordings of telephone calls for five years plus the tax year or from the date of the last decision on that claim, but it is advisable to keep your own record and letters received from HMRC.[122]

There is also a separate intermediaries line for use by approved advice agencies (see gov.uk/getting-help-with-your-tax-credits-claim/authorisation) and exclusive hotline for use by MPs' offices, which in some cases can get quicker results.

If things go wrong

If a decision is wrong, you can request a mandatory reconsideration and, if you are unhappy with the outcome, appeal against it (see Chapter 67). If you are given wrong advice by an employee of HMRC, you may be able to seek compensation either through the internal complaints procedure (see p1405) or judicial review. If you are given wrong information by HMRC or the DWP which led to an overpayment, this may be grounds for its recovery to be waived (see p1485). Official guidance states that in some cases, if HMRC has given you incorrect advice in the past, it may be bound by it if applying the correct legal position retrospectively would cause you real harm or loss and be so unfair as to constitute an abuse of power.[123]

If your claim has been received but not dealt with, ask why. If you are not satisfied with the explanation, make a complaint to HMRC (see p1405). You can also complain if, for example, you have been treated badly or your case has been mishandled. In some cases, you can seek a judicial review (see Chapter 59). If you are unhappy with the way HMRC handles your complaint, you can take it to the Adjudicator's Office and, if still unhappy, ask your MP to take it to the Parliamentary and Health Service Ombudsman (see p1408). It is not possible to sue HMRC for negligence in the way your award is decided.[124]

Notes

1. **Who can get tax credits**
   1 s3(3) TCA 2002
   2 Reg 8 UC(TP) Regs; *HMRC v LD (TC)* [2018] UKUT 306 (AAC)
   3 s3(3)(a) and (8) TCA 2002
   4 Reg 13(3) TC(CN) Regs
   5 *HMRC v ED (TC) [2021] UKUT 195 (AAC)*
   6 s3(4) TCA 2002; regs 5 and 6 UC(TP) Regs; *W v HMRC (TC)* [2020] UKUT 239 (AAC)
   7 s32(3) TCA 2002; reg 21(2)(a) TC(CN) Regs
   8 Art 7(1), (2), (5) and (6) WRA(No.23)O
   9 *HMRC v RS (CTC)* [2021] UKUT 310 (AAC)
   10 R (on the application of) DK v HMRC and SSWP; [2022] EWCA Civ 120
   11 s3(5A) TCA 2002
   12 s48(2) TCA 2002. Tax credits legislation has not been amended to reflect same-sex marriage. HMRC says this is not necessary because the legal interpretation of a married couple is changed via Sch 3 M(SSC)A 2013 and s4 Marriage and Civil Partnership (Scotland) Act 2014.
   13 Regs 5 and 6 UC(TP) Regs; reg 9(8) UC,PIP,JSA&ESA(C&P) Regs
   14 *HMRC v PD (TC)* [2012] UKUT 230 (AAC)
   15 s3(5A)(a)(ii) and (c)(ii) TCA 2002; *UA v HMRC (TC)* [2019] UKUT 113 (AAC)
   16 *DG v HMRC (TC)* [2013] UKUT 631 (AAC)
   17 R(TC) 2/06
   18 TC(PM) Regs
   19 *Crake and Butterworth v SBC* [1982] 1 All ER 498; R(SB) 17/81; CTC/3864/2004
   20 *TM v HMRC (TC)* [2013] UKUT 444 (AAC); *NI v HMRC (TC)* [2015] UKUT 490 (AAC)
   21 *SS v HMRC (TC)* [2014] UKUT 383 (AAC)
   22 Reg 3(5) and (6) TC(R) Regs
   23 Reg 3(2) TC(Imm) Regs; reg 11(4) WTC(EMR) Regs
   24 Regs 17 and 18 TC(CN) Regs

2. **How and when to make a claim**
   25 s3(1) TCA 2002
   26 Reg 5(2) TC(CN) Regs
   27 Reg 9 TC(CN) Regs

   28 s5(2) TCA 2002; reg 4 TC(CN) Regs
   29 See 'If you know your income will go down' at gov.uk/claim-tax-credits/when-to-claim
   30 s14(3) TCA 2002
   31 Reg 5(3) TC(CN) Regs
   32 *CI v HMRC (TC)* [2014] UKUT 158 (AAC), which rejects the decision saying there is no such right in *ZM and AB v HMRC (TC)* [2013] UKUT 547 (AAC)
   33 Reg 5(4) TC(CN) Regs
   34 Reg 5(6) TC(CN) Regs
   35 TCTM 06110
   36 *CI v HMRC (TC)* [2014] UKUT 158 (AAC), which rejects the decision saying there is no such right in *ZM and AB v HMRC (TC)* [2013] UKUT 547 (AAC)
   37 HMRC reply to CPAG email, 11 April 2012
   38 s7(2) TCA 2002; Form TC600, Part 5; reg 4 TC(ITDR) Regs
   39 HMRC leaflet WTC8, *Child Tax Credit and Working Tax Credit: why overpayments happen*, pp5-6
   40 s7(5)(a) TCA 2002; R(TC) 1/08
   41 Reg 14 TC(PC) Regs
   42 ss14, 15, 16, 17, 18, 19 and 22 TCA 2002; regs 30-33 TC(CN) Regs
   43 Art 7(6) WRA(No.23)O
   44 Reg 12(8) TC(CN) Regs
   45 s14(3) TCA 2002

3. **Decisions**
   46 s14(1) TCA 2002
   47 s14(2) TCA 2002
   48 Regs 5 and 6 TC(CN) Regs
   49 s23 TCA 2002
   50 s23(3) TCA 2002

4. **Backdating your claim**
   51 Reg 7 TC(CN) Regs
   52 Reg 14(2) TC(PC) Regs
   53 Reg 8 TC(CN) Regs; *MMB v HMRC (TC)* [2014] UKUT 221 (AAC)

5. **Getting paid**
   54 Reg 3 TC(PC) Regs
   55 Reg 4 TC(PC) Regs
   56 Reg 5 TC(PC) Regs
   57 Reg 6 TC(PC) Regs

10

Part 10: General rules for tax credits
Chapter 64: Claims, decisions and getting paid: tax credits
Notes

58 Reg 13(1) TC(PC) Regs
59 Letter from Guy Opperman MP, Minister for Pensions, to Stephen Timms MP, 13 December 2021 available at committees.parliament.uk/ publications/8332/documents/84747/ default/
60 Reg 8(2), (2A) and (2B) TC(PC) Regs
61 TCTM 08102
62 Reg 10 TC(PC) Regs
63 Regs 9 and 13 TC(PC) Regs
64 Reg 11(2A) TC(PC) Regs
65 Reg 14(3) and (4A)-(4E) TC(PC) Regs; TCM 0212200
66 TCM 0212160
67 Reg 11 TC(PC) Regs; HMRC leaflet WTC/FS9, *Tax Credits: suspension of payments*
68 Reg 12(3) TC(PC) Regs; s30 TCA 2002
69 s24(4) TCA 2002; reg 7 TC(PC) Regs
70 TCTM 09490
71 Na 12(4) TC(PC) Regs

6. Change of circumstances
72 ss6(3) and 32(3) TCA 2002; regs 2, 21 and 22 TC(CN) Regs
73 Regs 7(2) and 8(2) TC(ITDR) Regs
74 Regs 21(2) and 21A TC(CN) Regs
75 Reg 16(5) WTC(EMR) Regs
76 gov.uk/government/news/tax-credits-customers-will-continue-to-receive-payments-even-if-working-fewer-hours-due-to-covid-19
77 *JL v HMRC (TC)* [2013] UKUT 325 (AAC)
78 *HMRC v LH* [2018] UKUT 306 (AAC)
79 *HMRC v AB* [2021] UKUT 209 (AAC)
80 Reg 21(3B) UC Regs
81 Regs 5, 7 and 12A UC(TP) Regs
82 s30 Childcare Payments Act 2014
83 Regs 20 and 25 TC(CN) Regs
84 Reg 16(5)(a) WTC(EMR) Regs
85 Reg 26 and 26B TC(CN) Regs
86 Reg 26A TC(CN) Regs
87 Reg 21 TC(CN) Regs
88 s7(3)(d) TCA 2002; reg 5(b) TC(ITDR) Regs
89 Sch 6(9) HB Regs
90 Regs 2 and 22 TC(CN) Regs
91 Reg 23 TC(CN) Regs
92 Reg 27 TC(CN) Regs
93 Reg 27(2B) TC(CN) Regs
94 Reg 24 TC (CN) Regs
95 HMRC leaflet COP26, *What Happens If We've Paid You Too Much Tax Credits?*

7. Annual reviews
96 s17(1) TCA 2002
97 s17(2)(b) and (6)(b) TCA 2002

98 Regs 34-36 TC(CN) Regs
99 *SG v HMRC (TC)* [2011] UKUT 199 (AAC)
100 Reg 34 TC(CN) Regs
101 Reg 13 TC (CN) Regs
102 s18(3) TCA 2002
103 s17(8) TCA 2002; reg 33(b) TC(CN) Regs
104 Reg 11(3)(a) TC(CN) Regs
105 Reg 11(3)(b) TC(CN) Regs
106 Reg 11(3)(c) TC(CN) Regs
107 TCM 0136160
108 Reg 11(3)(d) TC(CN) Regs; Art 7 WRA(No.23)O
109 *SG v HMRC (TC)* [2011] UKUT 199 (AAC), in particular para 84
110 s18 TCA 2002
111 s30 TCA 2002
112 HMRC leaflet TC603RD, *Renew Your Tax Credits Now*
113 s23(3) TCA 2002
114 s23(2) TCA 2002
115 *NA v HMRC (TC)* [2016] UKUT 404 (AAC), para 11
116 s18(5) TCA 2002
117 s18(8) TCA 2002
118 Reg 12A UC(TP) Regs, as amended by UC(TP)(A) Regs
119 Sch para 2 UC(TP) Regs, as amended by UC(TP)(A) Regs; HMRC leaflet TC603URD, *Ending Your Tax Credits Award Because of a Claim for Universal Credit*

8. Contacting HM Revenue and Customs
120 Response to a Freedom of Information request, 12 January 2009
121 HMRC Benefits and Credits Consultation Group minutes, 4 December 2008
122 *AG v HMRC (TC)* [2013] UKUT 530 (AAC)
123 Adjudicator's Office, *Annual Report 2019*, p11; HMRC's *Admin Law Manual* (ADML1300)
124 *Jones v Department of Employment* [1989] QB 1 (CA)

Chapter 65

Overpayments of tax credits

This chapter covers:
1. What is an overpayment of tax credits (below)
2. Disputing recovery (p1485)
3. Recovery of overpayments (p1489)
4. Interest on overpayments (p1494)

Key facts

- The rules on the recovery of tax credit overpayments are different from those that apply to most social security benefits.
- All tax credit overpayments are recoverable, however they are caused, but HM Revenue and Customs (HMRC) has the discretion to decide whether or not to do so.
- There are rules on the amount that may be recovered and guidance on the way in which HMRC should recover an overpayment.
- There is no right to request a mandatory reconsideration by HMRC or appeal to an independent tribunal about a decision on whether or not to recover an overpayment of tax credits. However, you can ask HMRC to look at it again and use its discretion not to recover (known as a 'dispute').
- If you do not agree that you were overpaid, you can request a mandatory reconsideration by HMRC of the decision on your entitlement and appeal to an independent tribunal.

1. What is an overpayment of tax credits

The main rules on overpayments are the same for child tax credit (CTC) and working tax credit (WTC).[1] If you (and your partner if you are making a joint claim) are paid more tax credits for a tax year than you are entitled to, the extra amount is regarded as an overpayment.

HM Revenue and Customs (HMRC) can decide to adjust your award during the year of your current tax credit award to prevent an overpayment building up (an 'in-year overpayment') and/or recover all or some of the overpayment from you after the end of the tax year (an 'end-of-year overpayment').

Part 10: General rules for tax credits
Chapter 65: Overpayments of tax credits
1. What is an overpayment of tax credits

Note: you cannot request a mandatory reconsideration by HMRC or appeal to the First-tier Tribunal against the decision to recover the overpayment. However, you can ask HMRC to use its discretion not to recover. This is referred to as a 'dispute'.

If you do not accept that you received more tax credits than you should have (ie, you were not overpaid because you were correctly entitled to some or all of the amount that HMRC says was an overpayment), you can request a mandatory reconsideration of the decision on your entitlement by HMRC. If you are unhappy with the outcome, you can appeal to the tribunal (see Chapter 67). If your challenge is successful and the decision on your tax credit entitlement is changed, there is no overpayment (or a lower amount of overpayment) to be recovered.

When an overpayment occurs

The most likely causes of an overpayment are the following.
- Your income falls or rises by more than £2,500 (see p1473) in the current year, compared with the previous tax year.[2]
- You did not tell the Tax Credit Office in time about a change of circumstances, or the change was not acted on (see p1470).
- The information you gave the Tax Credit Office was incorrect, or inaccurately recorded.
- None of the above applies, but an overpayment occurred anyway because of the way the rules on income and changes in circumstances work.

In-year overpayments

In-year overpayments arise during the year of your current tax credit award. Decisions on in-year overpayments can be made during the course of the tax year concerned in the following circumstances.[3]
- If HMRC thinks there is likely to be an overpayment, it can adjust the award (or an award of another tax credit) to reduce or wipe out the overpayment. This may mean that your award is reduced for the rest of the year.
- If an award is terminated on the grounds that you did not satisfy the basic conditions of entitlement, HMRC may decide that the amount already paid to you, or some of it, is to be regarded as an overpayment. The basic conditions of entitlement are, for CTC, that you are responsible for a child (see p272) and, for WTC, that you are engaged in full-time work (see p284).

End-of-year overpayments

End-of-year overpayments are overpayments that are identified after the end of the tax year concerned – ie, after your award for that year has been finalised. HMRC can decide that there has been an end-of-year overpayment when it makes:[4]
- a final decision (see p1478);

- an enquiry decision (see p1509);
- a decision on discovery (see p1509).

Notification of overpayments

HMRC must change the decision on your entitlement and notify you of the new decision.[5] **Note:** you have the right to request a mandatory reconsideration by HMRC and then appeal against any decision about your entitlement (see p1511). If you think that the new decision is wrong and that you have not been overpaid as much as HMRC says, or that you have not been overpaid at all, request a mandatory reconsideration. If you are unhappy with the outcome, appeal to the First-tier Tribunal.

You may only find out about an in-year overpayment when HMRC writes to you to say that your entitlement has changed and your payment has been adjusted. If HMRC intends to recover an end-of-year overpayment from you, it must also give you notice of that, how much it is and how it is to be recovered from you. It usually does this at the same time as it writes to you about the final decision on your entitlement for the tax year. **Note:** you cannot request a mandatory reconsideration or appeal against the decision to recover an overpayment.[6]

2. **Disputing recovery**

You cannot request a mandatory reconsideration by HM Revenue and Customs (HMRC) or appeal to the First-tier Tribunal against the decision to recover the overpayment. However, you can ask HMRC to look again at its decision again and use its discretion to recover. This is referred to as a 'dispute'.

You should dispute recovery if you accept that you received more tax credits than you were correctly entitled to, but you do not think you should have to pay back the money. To dispute recovery, complete Form TC846, which can be completed online or downloaded at gov.uk/government/publications/tax-credits-overpayment-tc846 (or contact the Tax Credit Helpline for a copy) or write to the Tax Credit Office. Recovery of the overpayment usually begins immediately and is not suspended during the dispute, although if your dispute is successful, the amount already recovered is refunded to you.[7] There is no legal time limit for disputing recovery, but HMRC expects you to do so within three months of notification of the overpayment or of the outcome of a mandatory reconsideration or an appeal deciding that you have been overpaid.[8] HMRC says it will consider exceptions to this if you could not reasonably have been expected to act within three months – eg, if you were in hospital. It is arguable that a late dispute should also be allowed if you have been waiting for an explanation of the

Part 10: General rules for tax credits
Chapter 65: Overpayments of tax credits
2. Disputing recovery

overpayment. HMRC has discretion on this, but if it applies the time limit too rigidly, this may be unlawful.

What should you do?

1. If you do not agree that you have been overpaid and you think you were entitled to all, or part, of the amount of tax credit you received, request a mandatory reconsideration by HMRC of the decision on your entitlement that gave rise to the alleged overpayment, using Form WTC/AP. If you are unhappy with the outcome, you can appeal to the First-tier Tribunal on Form SSCS5. Recovery of the overpayment is suspended during the mandatory reconsideration and appeal process.

2. If you have been overpaid because your claim should have ended, but you would have been entitled to some, or all, of the amount you received if you had claimed correctly, ask for the overpayment to be reduced by offsetting your notional entitlement (see p1487).

3. If you accept that you were overpaid, but you do not think you should have to repay some, or all, of the money because you met your responsibilities and some (or all) of the overpayment was caused by an HMRC error, dispute the decision to recover, using Form TC846. If there were exceptional circumstances that meant you were unable to meet your responsibilities, tell HMRC about this on the form. The dispute is an internal HMRC process and recovery continues during the dispute. HMRC says that you can only dispute recovery once, unless you provide new information within 30 days of being notified of the outcome of the dispute (or later, in exceptional circumstances).

4. If you cannot afford to repay the money, ask for the rate of recovery to be reduced, or for recovery to be written off altogether on hardship grounds. Form TC846 does not allow you to raise this in the dispute, so raise this separately via the Tax Credit Helpline or in writing to the address on your notice to pay.

5. If you have mental health problems and recovery may cause you distress, supply evidence in writing and ask for the overpayment to be written off in line with HMRC guidance.

6. If you are still unhappy with the decision to recover, consider applying for a judicial review or making a complaint.

The responsibilities test

The way in which HMRC uses its discretion whether or not to recover tax credit overpayments is set out in its leaflet *What Happens If We've Paid You Too Much Tax Credits?* (COP26), which is used if you dispute recovery. If an overpayment has been caused by a mistake or failure to act by HMRC (ie, it has not met its responsibilities), it may decide not to recover all or part of the overpayment.

However, for the overpayment not to be recovered, you must also show that you have acted correctly in relation to your claim for tax credits – ie, you have met your responsibilities. Your 'responsibilities' are not defined in the law, only in guidance.

If HMRC thinks it has met all its responsibilities but you have not met all of yours, it normally recovers the overpayment. If it thinks that both itself and you have failed to meet responsibilities, it looks at the circumstances and may write off part of the overpayment. An overpayment can still occur even though both you and HMRC have met these responsibilities, in which case HMRC is still likely to seek recovery.

HMRC regards its responsibilities as:
- giving you correct advice based on your information;
- accurately recording your information and paying the correct amount;
- putting right mistakes you tell it about and sending you a corrected award notice;
- accurately recording your notification of changes in your circumstances;
- sending you a new award notice within 30 days of having all the necessary information.

HMRC regards your responsibilities as:
- providing accurate, complete and up-to-date information;
- reporting changes of circumstances throughout the year;
- using the checklist (TC602(SN)) sent with your award notice to tell it if anything is wrong or incomplete;
- checking that your payments match the amount given on the award notice;
- reporting any errors on your award notice, normally within one month.

Note: if there were exceptional circumstances (eg, illness) which meant that you were unable to meet your responsibilities at the time, explain this and HMRC may write off the overpayment. HMRC must take into account your circumstances and your ability to comply.[9] Remember that it is best to dispute the decision to recover the overpayment on Form TC846, and attach additional pages if necessary.

Reducing the overpayment

HMRC may reduce ('offset') the amount of the overpayment by the amount of any tax credit to which you would have been entitled had you claimed correctly – ie, by your 'notional entitlement'. This process is referred to in HMRC guidance as 'offsetting notional entitlement' and is applied if the overpayment was caused by:[10]
- your ceasing to count as a single claimant and becoming part of a couple (you need details of your partner's income); *or*
- your ceasing to count as part of a couple and claiming instead as a single claimant.

Previous guidance stated that a new claim for tax credits must be made in order to calculate notional entitlement. However, it is generally no longer possible to

Part 10: General rules for tax credits
Chapter 65: Overpayments of tax credits
2. Disputing recovery

make a new claim for tax credits and you usually have to claim universal credit (UC) (see p1459). Instead, you should provide HMRC with all the information that would have been needed for a new tax credits claim following the change in your status, so that your notional entitlement can be calculated up to the date that you claimed UC. HMRC says that offsetting your notional entitlement will be applied in all cases to any overpayment which has occurred as a result of a change in single/couple status in the current year, regardless of why you did not notify the change.[11] For previous years, HMRC says that notional entitlement will be applied unless there is evidence of fraudulent behaviour that has resulted in financial gain.[12]

HMRC says that it will proactively identify such cases but, as this cannot be guaranteed, you should contact it yourself if you think you may benefit from offsetting. If your claim was incorrect from the start, or you made a false statement, notional entitlement can still be applied, but in such cases HMRC may consider imposing a penalty or prosecution. Notional entitlement should not be withheld as a consequence of late or non-reporting of a change of circumstances.[13]

Although the guidance only refers to single person/couple claims, you should request that the amount of the overpayment is offset in other circumstances – eg, if you were overpaid because you left the UK for more than the permitted period but you would have been entitled to tax credits on your return. In some cases, a refusal by HMRC to offset may be challenged by judicial review in the courts. Get further advice if you are affected.

Hardship and mental health

Hardship is not defined, but HMRC leaflet *What Happens If We've Paid You Too Much Tax Credits?* (COP26) refers to financial hardship in terms of family circumstances that lead to extra living costs, such as looking after someone who is chronically ill or disabled, and an inability to pay for essential living expenses such as rent, gas or electricity. In cases of hardship, HMRC may put recovery on hold, extend the period over which the overpayment is repaid, partially remit or, in exceptional circumstances, write off the overpayment altogether. Other guidance suggests that consideration should also be given to reducing or writing off your overpayment if you have no means to repay, no assets and recovery would cause hardship.[14]

The guidance also states that if you have a mental health problem, HMRC should deal with your case carefully and sympathetically to avoid causing you distress. It may require a letter from a healthcare professional or mental health social worker explaining the nature of your illness, prognosis and prospects for recovery. If your mental health problem existed at the time the overpayment occurred, this may be considered to be exceptional circumstances and so HMRC should consider writing off the overpayment. If you have a mental health problem at the time the overpayment is being recovered, HMRC may decide not to continue with the recovery.[15]

The guidance on hardship and mental health applies whether you are repaying directly or by deductions from an ongoing award, but it may not be commonly known to all helpline staff.

There is a special payment helpline (tel: 0345 302 1429; textphone: 0345 300 3909) to discuss hardship. You may also write, with a financial statement, to the HMRC office dealing with repayment. See CPAG's *Debt Advice Handbook* for help preparing a financial statement. You should *not* use Form TC846 (see p1492) if you want more time to repay. If you remain unhappy with the decision, see p1486 for what you can do.

Taking your dispute further

If HMRC has considered your dispute and you still think you should not have to pay back an overpayment, you can ask HMRC to review its decision, provided you give new information within 30 days (or later in exceptional circumstances). HMRC says that you can only do this once.[16]

The only legal way to challenge a decision on recovering an overpayment (ie, either after a dispute or an attempt to negotiate repayment) is by judicial review in the courts. Usually, this is only possible in extreme cases – eg, if HMRC insists on your repaying an overpayment that was clearly caused by an error or failure on its part, you met all your responsibilities and it is urgent that HMRC changes its decision. See judicial review template JR83 'Failure to exercise discretion not to recover an overpayment where official error and financial hardship' at cpag.org.uk/jr-letters/tax-credits . For more about judicial review, see Chapter 59.

The only other way of persuading HMRC to change its mind is by making a complaint. You first need to use HMRC's own complaints procedure. If you remain dissatisfied, you can complain to the Adjudicator's Office and then to the Parliamentary and Health Service Ombudsman via your MP. Both can recommend action and order financial compensation, but are likely to take time to complete their investigations. You may wish to involve your MP at an earlier stage of your complaint, as this can produce quicker results. See Chapter 61 for details about making a complaint.

3. Recovery of overpayments

HM Revenue and Customs (HMRC) can recover either all or part of any overpayment.[17] It usually recovers the overpayment by:

- adjusting (ie, reducing) your current award; *or*
- transferring the debt to the DWP to recover from you; *or*
- requiring you to repay the overpayment.

Note: although all overpayments are legally recoverable, HMRC can use its discretion not to recover and you can dispute recovery (see p1485).

Part 10: General rules for tax credits
Chapter 65: Overpayments of tax credits
3. Recovery of overpayments

You must be given notice that you must repay an end-of-year overpayment. The notice must also say how much the overpayment is, and how it is to be recovered from you.[18]

HMRC usually begins recovery immediately after it notifies you of the overpayment. It does not ask you whether recovering an overpayment will cause you hardship or if you think it should not be recovered from you. It is therefore important to contact the Tax Credit Office if you do not think the overpayment should be recovered. HMRC refers to this as a 'dispute' (see p1485). Recovery is not suspended during the dispute process, but if the dispute is found in your favour, the amount already recovered is refunded to you.[19]

Note: if you do not agree that you have been overpaid, request a mandatory reconsideration by HMRC of the decision about your entitlement and, if you are unhappy with the outcome, appeal to the First-tier Tribunal (see Chapter 67). Recovery is suspended during the mandatory reconsideration and appeal process.[20]

Overpayments and award notices

If you have been overpaid, you should be sent an award notice outlining the revised decision on your entitlement. Award notices can be very complicated. You should also be sent a checklist (Form TC602(SN)) with information used in the calculation, for you to check. You can request an award calculation notice (Form TC647) from HMRC, which gives more details about how your payment has been worked out. If it is still unclear, write to the Tax Credit Office (its address is at the top of the award notice) requesting an individual explanation. However, do not delay sending in your dispute form while you are waiting for the explanation, as a dispute should usually be made within three months. You can send further details once you have received the full explanation.

If you still do not receive a satisfactory response, consider taking up the matter with your MP or making a complaint (see Chapter 61).

From whom can an overpayment be recovered

In-year overpayments are recovered from you by reducing the ongoing tax credit award. An end-of-year overpayment can be recovered from the person(s) to whom the tax credit award was made. This means:[21]

- if you made a claim as a single person, the overpayment can be recovered from you;
- if you made a joint claim with your partner, the overpayment can be recovered from one or both of you. If you have separated from your partner, HMRC's practice is first to ask you both to repay the overpayment equally. If you wish, you and your ex-partner may agree to pay different amounts. Although HMRC has the power to ask one person to repay the whole amount, guidance states that usually each person is asked to repay a maximum of half the overpayment,

unless one partner has acted fraudulently or negligently and the other is seen to be an 'innocent partner'.[22]

How the overpayment is recovered

You must be notified of the new decision on your entitlement.[23] For end-of-year overpayments, HMRC must notify you (and your partner, if it is a joint overpayment) of the amount to be repaid, and how the overpayment is to be repaid.[24] Tax credit overpayments are treated as unpaid tax debts. If the debt is transferred to the DWP (see the third bullet point below), all methods of recovery used by the DWP may apply.[25]

HMRC can require you to repay:[26]

- by deductions from ongoing payments of any tax credit (see below). This is HMRC's preferred method of repayment. The amount that is deducted is usually limited;
- direct to HMRC. You should receive a notice showing the full amount to be repaid. You are offered a standard repayment period of 12 monthly instalments, although up to 10 years may be negotiated;
- by transferring the debt to the DWP to make deductions from universal credit (UC) or certain other benefits (see p1209 – your overpayment is treated as an overpayment of UC). This can happen without your agreement, but you must be notified. The debt should not be transferred to DWP while there is an outstanding dispute about recovery, or ongoing mandatory reconsideration or appeal about the decision that gave rise to the overpayment;[27]
- with your agreement, by deductions from certain benefits paid by the DWP (see p1169). Note that if HMRC transfers the debt to the DWP to recover, this method can be used without your agreement;[28]
- with your agreement, via pay as you earn (PAYE) by altering your tax code to allow deductions from your wages. Note that if HMRC transfers the debt to the DWP to recover, this method can be used without your agreement;[29]
- by deduction from your bank account, in some cases, or court action (see p1493).[30]

Deductions from ongoing awards

HMRC can adjust your tax credit payments so that you receive less money and so, in effect, repay the overpayment. It only does this if you or your partner have previously been overpaid either as single claimants or as part of the same couple. It does not recover an overpayment in this way if you or your partner have previously been overpaid in a joint award with a different partner. You should be notified of the amount being deducted. There is a maximum amount by which HMRC can reduce your tax credit award to recover an end-of-year overpayment:[31]

- 10 per cent of the award if you are receiving the maximum tax credits to which you could be entitled – ie, with no reduction for income;

Part 10: General rules for tax credits
Chapter 65: Overpayments of tax credits
3. Recovery of overpayments

- 100 per cent of the award if you receive only the family element of child tax credit (CTC);
- 50 per cent of the award if your income is over £20,000 (this is the figure being treated at the time as your actual current year's income);
- 25 per cent of the award if none of the above apply.

Note: these are maximum amounts, although HMRC applies them automatically. If you accept that you should repay but cannot afford to repay at the above rates, ask HMRC to accept repayment at a lower rate. You may need to show why it would cause you hardship (see p1486) to pay at the maximum rate.

The maximum amounts only apply to end-of-year overpayments. For an in-year overpayment, HMRC may stop or reduce your ongoing payments by more than the above limits, so that you only receive your estimated remaining entitlement (if any) for the rest of the year.[32] HMRC says that this is to prevent a further overpayment building up, but you can request hardship payments if this leaves you unable to meet your basic living expenses.

HMRC considers adjusting recovery or making payments on hardship grounds if requested.[33] In-year recovery is adjusted to the limits used for end-of-year recovery if you are accepted as being in hardship, or the amount you get may be increased further in exceptional cases.[34] You may be asked to provide details of your income and expenditure. In urgent cases, HMRC says a decision on adjusting payments due to hardship should be made within two working days.[35]

Revised notices of overpayments, changing the method of recovery, can be issued at any time.[36]

Direct payment to HM Revenue and Customs

If you are no longer entitled to tax credits, or you were overpaid as part of a couple and you have now separated, you must repay your overpayment by direct payment to HMRC. HMRC suspends direct recovery if you are already repaying another overpayment (at the 10, 25 or 50 per cent rate described above) through your current tax credit award – but you may need to ask for this.[37] The notice to pay (Form TC610) asks you to contact HMRC to pay in full or negotiate repayment. If the overpayment has not been repaid and you have not contacted HMRC within 42 days, a reminder letter is sent, followed by a more strongly worded warning letter. If you fail to respond to this letter, HMRC may use a debt collection agency or start legal proceedings to recover the debt.

Other methods of recovery

HMRC may ask the DWP to recover tax credit overpayments by deduction from specified benefits with your written consent (see p1169).[38] However, HMRC has begun the process of transferring old tax credits debt to the DWP to recover as if it were an overpayment of UC, which can be recovered without your consent through deductions from UC or other benefits, or by any other methods of recovery available to the DWP (see p1209).[39] HMRC may recover tax credit overpayments from your wages via PAYE, but only with your agreement.[40]

HMRC may recover tax credit debts direct from bank and building society accounts and individual savings accounts (ISAs). In England and Wales, it can only do so if the debt is £1,000 or more, and you must usually be left with a minimum of £5,000 in your account or accounts.[41] HMRC guidance includes safeguards, including a guaranteed face-to-face visit, before this method is used and there is a right of appeal to the County Court.[42] In Scotland, it can apply for bank arrestment under a 'summary warrant'.

If HMRC cannot recover by any other methods, or you do not respond to requests for recovery, it may consider taking legal action. Further action will follow if HMRC considers that you are refusing to repay, or neglecting to keep to an agreement to repay. All the circumstances are taken into account before taking such action, but HMRC may:

- take enforcement proceedings to take control of your goods (England and Wales) or seize and sell your possessions (Scotland). Unless you let HMRC officials or agents into your property, they cannot enter your home and take control of/seize your personal possessions without a warrant from the court; *or*
- take court action against you, including bankruptcy proceedings.

Note: recovery action through the courts in England and Wales must be taken within six years of the decision that there has been an overpayment, or, if later, any written acknowledgement of the overpayment or voluntary repayment.[43] In Scotland, HMRC regards the time limit for court action as being five years from the last effective action.[44]

For more on the recovery of debts, see CPAG's *Debt Advice Handbook*.

Negotiating repayment

If you have difficulty repaying, HMRC may agree to your repaying the overpayment over a longer period than normal by making an instalment plan. In cases of hardship, or if your mental health is a factor (see p1486), the overpayment may be written off. Contact the Tax Credit Payment Helpline on 0345 302 1429 (textphone: 0345 300 3909), or write to HMRC at the address on the notice to pay, or complete Form TC1133 online using a government gateway account. Usually, you are asked to pay something straight away, and the rest over a later period. HMRC takes into account all the relevant circumstances, including your income, savings, other debts and outgoings. You must show how the repayments will cause you hardship by providing evidence of your income and expenditure and showing, for example, how you will be unable to meet your essential living expenses, or providing evidence of your mental health problems.

10

Part 10: General rules for tax credits
Chapter 65: Overpayments of tax credits
4. Interest on overpayments

4. **Interest on overpayments**

Interest may be added to an overpayment being recovered from you (and/or your partner, if you have a joint claim) if HM Revenue and Customs (HMRC) considers that the overpayment is due to 'fraud or neglect' on the part of you (and/or your partner).[45]

Interest is added 30 days after whichever of the following dates apply:[46]

- if you (or your partner) were treated during the tax year concerned as being overpaid as a result of your award being terminated because you did not satisfy the basic conditions of entitlement (see p1484), the date of the decision terminating the award; *or*
- if the above did not apply, the date in the final notice that you were given to confirm your actual income for the tax year.

When added to the overpayment, the interest is treated as if it were part of the overpayment. This means that it is subject to the same rules as the overpayment itself.[47]

The amount of interest added to the penalty is 6.5 per cent a year or, if it is different from the average lending rate of the main banks, the bank lending rate plus 2.5 per cent.[48]

You can request a mandatory reconsideration of the decision to add interest to an overpayment and, if you are still unhappy, appeal (see Chapter 67). For example, you might wish to argue that you did not act fraudulently or negligently, or that the amount of the interest is wrong. You (and/or your partner, if s/he is subject to the decision) must be given notice of a decision adding interest to an overpayment. The notice must be dated and include details of your right to request a mandatory reconsideration of the decision.[49]

10

Notes

1. What is an overpayment of tax credits
1 s28 TCA 2002
2 Reg 5 TC(ITDR) Regs
3 s28(5) and (6) TCA 2002
4 s28(1) TCA 2002
5 s23 TCA 2002
6 ss29(1) and (2) and 38 TCA 2002

2. Disputing recovery
7 HMRC leaflet COP26, *What Happens If We've Paid You Too Much Tax Credits?*
8 HMRC leaflet COP26, *What Happens If We've Paid You Too Much Tax Credits?*
9 Adjudicator's Office, *Annual Report 2014*, p20
10 *Pre-Budget Report 2009*; TCM 0228220; HMRC leaflet COP26, *What Happens If We've Paid You Too Much Tax Credits?*
11 Benefits and Credits Consultation Group email, 16 February 2017
12 HMRC email to CPAG, 1 August 2018
13 Adjudicator's Office, *Annual Report 2017*, p17
14 HMRC, *Debt Management and Banking Manual*, 555090
15 HMRC, *Debt Management and Banking Manual*, 555600
16 HMRC leaflet COP26, *What Happens If We've Paid You Too Much Tax Credits?*

3. Recovery of overpayments
17 s28(1) TCA 2002
18 ss28(1) and 29 TCA 2002
19 HMRC leaflet COP26, *What Happens If We've Paid You Too Much Tax Credits?*
20 HMRC leaflet COP26, *What Happens If We've Paid You Too Much Tax Credits?*
21 s28(3) and (4) TCA 2002
22 HMRC leaflet COP 26, *What Happens If We've Paid You Too Much Tax Credits?*; CCM 8290
23 s23 TCA 2002
24 s29 TCA 2002
25 The Tax Credits (Exercise of Functions) Order 2014 No.3280; The Tax Credits (Exercise of Functions in relation to Northern Ireland and Notices for Recovery of Tax Credit Overpayments) Order 2017 No.781
26 s29(3)-(5) TCA 2002

27 s28(1)(b) TCA 2002; reg 12 UC(TP) Regs; The Tax Credits (Exercise of Functions in relation to Northern Ireland and Notices for Recovery of Tax Credit Overpayments) Order 2017 No.781; para 7.4, government response to the Public Accounts Committee, March 2018
28 Sch 9(7E) SS(C&P) Regs
29 s29(5) TCA 2002
30 Sch 8 Finance (No.2) Act 2015
31 Reg 12A TC(PC) Regs; HMRC leaflet COP26, *What Happens If We've Paid You Too Much Tax Credits?*
32 *Autumn Statement 2013*, para 1.317
33 HMRC leaflet COP26, *What Happens If We've Paid You Too Much Tax Credits?*
34 TCM 0214120
35 Benefits and Credits Consultation Group, email 27 November 2016
36 s29(2) TCA 2002
37 HMRC leaflet COP26, *What Happens If We've Paid You Too Much Tax Credits?*
38 Sch 9(7E)(3) SS(C&P) Regs
39 s28(1)(b) TCA 2002; reg 12 UC(TP) Regs; The Tax Credits (Exercise of Functions) Order 2014 No.3280 and The Tax Credits (Exercise of Functions in relation to Northern Ireland and Notices for Recovery of Tax Credit Overpayments) Order 2017 No.781
40 Reg 4 Income Tax (Pay As You Earn) (Amendment No.4) Regulations 2014 No.2689
41 Sch 8 Finance (No.2) Act 2015
42 *Autumn Statement 2014*, para 2.165
43 s9(1) Limitation Act 1980
44 HMRC, *Debt Management and Banking Manual*, 595080

4. Interest on overpayments
45 s37(1) TCA 2002
46 s37(2)-(3) TCA 2002
47 s37(6) TCA 2002
48 Reg 4 TC(IR) Regs
49 ss37(4) and 38(1)(d) TCA 2002

10

Chapter 66

Investigations, penalties and fraud: tax credits

This chapter covers:
1. Investigating awards (below)
2. Penalties (p1498)
3. Prosecution for fraud (p1502)

Key facts

- HM Revenue and Customs has wide powers to investigate your tax credits award and require information from you.
- In certain circumstances, including if you supply incorrect information or do not comply with other requirements, a financial penalty may be imposed.
- If you are considered to have acted fraudulently, you may be prosecuted and fined or imprisoned, or both.

1. Investigating awards

HM Revenue and Customs (HMRC) can require you to supply information and evidence to help it check whether your award is correct. HMRC refers to investigations into the accuracy of awards as 'examinations' and 'enquiries'. Examinations are carried out on some awards *during* the year in order to check that they are correct. Enquiries may be carried out *after* the year concerned to check that you were paid the correct amount. More serious investigations into fraud may also be carried out.

HMRC might ask you to provide things like bank statements or your rent book. You can appoint someone else to deal with HMRC on your behalf – eg, an adviser, accountant or a relative. HMRC requires a signed letter from you confirming this is what you want (or use Form TC689 at gov.uk/government/publications/tax-credits-and-child-benefit-allow-someone-else-to-act-for-you-tc689). However, you are still treated as responsible for the information provided.

HMRC does not currently undertake face-to-face meetings with tax credit claimants as part of a routine examination or enquiry.

Not all examinations or enquiries are fraud investigations. Fraud investigations tend only to happen in the more serious cases and, in such cases, HMRC has additional powers (see p1498).

Examinations

During the tax year of your award, HMRC may telephone or write to you requiring information or evidence.[1] Normally, it writes to you to say that it is examining your award, but this is not a legal requirement. There is no limit on the number of examinations that can take place during the same tax year. If the examination is started while you are already receiving tax credits, usually you continue to be paid while the examination is being carried out. Payments can only be suspended in specific circumstances (see p1469). An examination may end without a new decision but you should be notified that it has been completed.[2] See p1506 for more information on decisions made following an examination.

You cannot stop an examination taking place, but if you are unhappy with the way you are being treated, you can make a complaint (see p1405).

Enquiries

After your tax credit award is finalised at the end of the tax year, HMRC may carry out an enquiry into the award. It may request further information or evidence in connection with your award. An enquiry can only be opened within one year of the final decision, and only once in respect of a tax year. HMRC must notify you in writing that it is opening an enquiry. When it has completed the enquiry, it must make a decision on your entitlement.[3] See p1509 for more details about decisions made following an enquiry.

You can apply to HMRC to complete its enquiry by making a decision on your tax credit entitlement for the year in question. If HMRC wishes to continue with the enquiry, it passes your request to the First-tier Tribunal, which must give a direction that the enquiry is completed unless it is is satisfied that there are reasonable grounds for it to continue.[4] If you are unhappy with the decision following the enquiry, you can request a mandatory reconsideration and then appeal.

Powers to seek information

HMRC can require you (and/or your partner if you have a joint award) to provide information or evidence during the tax year if it believes your award may be wrong (for an examination). It can also require information or evidence after your award has been finalised (for an enquiry).

It can also do this if it is necessary for a revision during an award or a final notice and final decision (see p1478).[5] You must be given at least 30 days to provide the information.[6] HMRC does not have to suspect you of fraud in order to require information or evidence from you.

Part 10: General rules for tax credits
Chapter 66: Investigations, penalties and fraud: tax credits
2. Penalties

It is important that you co-operate with requests for information or evidence as far as you can. Even though you may not be the subject of a fraud investigation, HMRC might suspend your payments or apply for a financial penalty if you refuse to supply information and evidence. If the information or evidence is not available, explain why.

HMRC can also require your employer or childcare provider to provide information. They must be given at least 30 days to do so. If they are subject to these requirements, they can also be subject to penalties (see below). They can be required to provide information and evidence relating to your award or for the purpose of a revision during an award or an enquiry (see p1505).[7]

If fraud is suspected

If you are suspected of fraud, HMRC may undertake an investigation to consider whether or not to give you a financial penalty (see below). In serious cases, it undertakes a criminal investigation with a view to prosecution (see p1502). Fraud investigations in serious cases may be carried out by an HMRC criminal investigation officer and may be linked to investigations by other sections of HMRC, or by the DWP and local authorities. You are usually told why your award is being investigated and that you can seek legal advice from someone who can attend any interview with you. It is advisable to get legal advice as quickly as possible (eg, from a solicitor) if you are being investigated. You are likely to be interviewed under caution (see p1232).

In addition to the powers described above and in Chapter 54, HMRC has specific powers when investigating fraud.[8] If HMRC has 'reasonable grounds' for suspecting serious fraud, a court can make an order requiring you (or any other person) to provide documents containing relevant evidence within a specified time. Falsifying, concealing, destroying or disposing of the documents is an offence.[9]

2. **Penalties**

You can be given a financial penalty if you have:[10]
- fraudulently or negligently made an incorrect statement or declaration, or supplied incorrect information or evidence; *or*
- failed to comply with requirements.

These penalties are civil penalties. You do not have to be prosecuted for a criminal offence. If you do not think a penalty should be imposed (eg, because you had a reasonable excuse for not declaring a change in circumstances or you could not obtain the information asked for), tell HM Revenue and Customs (HMRC). You must be notified of the penalty, including the date of the decision and your right to request a mandatory reconsideration and subsequent appeal (see p1514).[11] A penalty cannot be imposed more than one year after an enquiry decision, or more than one year after the end of the enquiry window (see p1509), whichever is later.[12]

In certain circumstances, these rules can also apply in the same way to your employer or your childcare provider (see p1497).

Incorrect statements and information

HMRC can impose a penalty of up to £3,000 on you if you have acted fraudulently or negligently and you have:[13]
- made an incorrect statement or declaration in connection with an award, a notification of a change of circumstances (see p1470) or in a response to a final notice (see p1478); *or*
- given incorrect information or evidence in connection with an initial decision (see p1466), a requirement to provide information or evidence during the course of your award, a revision during an award (see p1506), a final decision (see p1478) or an enquiry (see p1509).

There is no definition of 'negligence' but, in practice, HMRC considers what you could reasonably be expected to have known and how careful you were.[14]

Penalties for incorrect statements and information

The maximum penalty is £3,000, although HMRC need not impose the maximum. For a deliberate and wrong new claim, the penalties are set at £600 for the first time, £1,000 for a second wrong new claim and £1,500 for further claims. For a deliberate and wrong declaration in the course of an award, HMRC sets penalties at 30 per cent of the amount over-claimed for a first incorrect declaration, 50 per cent for a second incorrect declaration, or 100 per cent for a third, subject to the £3,000 maximum.[15] The decision maker must consider whether there are any aggravating or mitigating factors, and that the maximum penalty is reserved for the worst offences.[16] The penalty is payable 30 days after the date you were notified of it.[17] The amount of the penalty may be increased by the addition of interest (see p1501).

If you are a member of a joint-claim couple (see p1459), a penalty may be imposed on both you and your partner. However, a penalty cannot be imposed on you if you are an 'innocent partner' – ie, if you were not, and could not reasonably have been expected to have been, aware that your partner had fraudulently or negligently made an incorrect statement or provided incorrect information or evidence.[18] In this case, the penalty is imposed solely on your partner. However, even if a penalty is imposed, or partly imposed, on you and your partner, the total penalty for the same incorrect statement cannot amount to more than £3,000.

Part 10: General rules for tax credits
Chapter 66: Investigations, penalties and fraud: tax credits
2. Penalties

If you are acting for someone else and you fraudulently or negligently make an incorrect statement, the penalty applies to you as well as that person.[19]

Failing to comply

A financial penalty of up to £300 (it does not have to be the maximum) may be imposed for:[20]

- failing to provide information or evidence requested by HMRC by a specified date in connection with an initial claim (see p1466), a revision during an award (see p1506), a final decision (see p1478) or for an enquiry (see p1509). HMRC cannot impose such a penalty itself, but may start proceedings in the First-tier Tribunal to do so;[21] or
- failing to comply with a requirement to declare your circumstances or income by a specified date in your annual review (see p1475). HMRC can impose such a penalty itself, but you have the right to request a mandatory reconsideration and then appeal;[22] or
- failing to notify a specified change of circumstances within one month of the change or of the date you became aware of the change, if that is later.[23] HMRC can impose such a penalty itself, but you have the right to request a mandatory reconsideration and then appeal. The specified changes are listed on p1470.

A penalty is not imposed if you had a 'reasonable excuse' for not telling HMRC about the change. Tell HMRC if you think this applies. However, HMRC does not accept the fact that you did not know you had to inform it as a reasonable excuse.[24]

Penalties for failing to comply

The maximum penalty for failing to comply is £300. If the penalty is for failing to comply with a request to provide information or evidence, or for failing to comply with a requirement to declare circumstances or income by the date specified in the annual review, there may be a further daily penalty of up to £60 a day for each day you continue to fail to comply. You must be notified of the penalty, including the date on which it is given, and your right to a mandatory reconsideration. The penalty is payable 30 days after the date you were notified of it.[25] The amount of the penalty may be increased by the addition of interest (see p1501).

However, if the penalty is for failing to comply with a request to provide information or evidence, HMRC cannot apply the penalty itself. Instead, it must write to HM Courts and Tribunals Service, which then summons you to the First-tier Tribunal, which decides whether the penalty should be applied.[26] You can appeal against the tribunal's decision to the Upper Tribunal (see p1519).

A penalty cannot be imposed after you have provided the information or evidence requested.[27] You have not failed to provide information or evidence if you did so within any time that HMRC has allowed you to, or if you had a 'reasonable excuse' for the failure, or if, having had a reasonable excuse, you later provided the information or evidence without unreasonable delay.[28]

If you are a member of a couple and a £300 penalty has been imposed for failing to comply with a requirement about a final notice or for failing to report the specified change of circumstances, the total of that penalty applied to either or both of you is a maximum of £300 for each failure.[29]

Interest added to penalties

HMRC may apply interest to a penalty, even if you are not considered to have acted fraudulently or negligently – ie, if the penalty is for failing to comply. The amount of the interest becomes part of the penalty and is recoverable in the same way as the penalty itself.[30]

The amount of interest added to the penalty is 6.5 per cent a year or, if that is different from the average lending rate of the main banks, the bank lending rate plus 2.5 per cent.[31]

You can appeal against the penalty itself and the amount of the penalty. However, there is no right of appeal about the addition of interest to a penalty (although there is a right of appeal if interest has been added to an overpayment – see p1511).[32]

Recovery of penalties

HMRC has discretion about whether to impose a penalty and, subject to the maximum amounts, the amount. Also, although the penalty itself can only be altered on appeal, HMRC has discretion about whether to insist that you pay all or some of it.[33] If you tried your best to fulfil all your obligations, or if the penalty would cause you hardship, tell HMRC and ask it to use its discretion not to recover all or some of the amount.

If you have not paid or made an arrangement to pay, HMRC may take enforcement proceedings, including court action against you to recover the amount owed. **Note:** some enforcement proceedings do not require court action. See CPAG's *Debt Advice Handbook* for more information.

Challenging a penalty

You can tell HMRC that you disagree with the penalty and/or the addition of interest to it – eg, when it contacts you to tell you that you are liable for a penalty. In some cases, it may warn you about a possible penalty before a formal decision is made. It can remove the penalty and/or the interest.

Once a formal decision has been made, you can request a mandatory reconsideration and then appeal, including against the amount of the penalty, but not against any addition of interest (see Chapter 67).

Note: be aware that, subject to the maximum, the tribunal considering your appeal can increase, as well as decrease, the amount of the penalty.

Part 10: General rules for tax credits
Chapter 66: Investigations, penalties and fraud: tax credits
3. Prosecution for fraud

For more information on mandatory reconsiderations and appeals, see p1511, and for more on penalty appeals, see p1514.

Have you been given a penalty?
1. Explain to HMRC why you think a penalty should not be imposed – eg, if you acted with reasonable care or had a reasonable excuse for failing to report a change in circumstances.
2. If you get a decision imposing a penalty, you can request a mandatory reconsideration and then appeal. Remember that if the penalty is for failing to provide information requested by HMRC, it can only be imposed by a First-tier Tribunal and you have a right of appeal to the Upper Tribunal against this decision.
3. If you accept that a penalty can be imposed, you can still negotiate with HMRC about the amount. You could argue that the maximum amount should not be imposed in your case – eg, because you acted innocently and to the best of your knowledge or abilities.
4. If HMRC has used its discretion to mitigate or waive a penalty, check whether this means that a new decision on the penalty will be issued. If a decision is not issued, you may lose your right to challenge the penalty.

3. **Prosecution for fraud**

You are regarded as having committed the offence of fraud if you knowingly take part in fraudulent activity in order to get a tax credit for you or anyone else.[34] If you are prosecuted and then convicted by a court, you are liable to be fined or imprisoned, or both.

Will you be prosecuted?

Whether or not you will be prosecuted is a discretionary decision. Not all cases of fraud end in prosecution. HM Revenue and Customs (HMRC) may investigate your award under civil investigation procedures – ie, without a view to prosecuting you, but with a view to charging a penalty (see p1498). You are usually told about this. However, this does not mean that HMRC cannot change its mind and decide to refer you to the Crown Prosecution Service (the Crown Office and Procurator Fiscal Service in Scotland) for prosecution.

The factors that it may take into account are likely to include the strength of the evidence, the amount of tax credits involved, whether an offence was planned and your personal circumstances.

Official HMRC policy indicates that criminal investigations are more likely if:[35]
- there is organised or systematic fraud, including conspiracy;
- false statements are made or false documents given during a civil investigation;
- deliberate concealment, deception, conspiracy or corruption is suspected;
- false or forged documents have been used;

- you have committed previous offences or there is a repeated course of unlawful conduct or previous civil action;
- there is a link to suspected wider criminality.

This is not a complete list and, ultimately, everything depends on the circumstances of your case.

What should you do if you are prosecuted?
1. The most important thing to do is to get advice. You may be entitled to legal help and have a solicitor or barrister represent you in court.
2. Check carefully that HMRC can prove all the parts of the offence with which you are charged. Do not plead guilty until you have obtained advice.

Fines and imprisonment

If a court convicts you of fraud in connection with tax credits and:[36]
- you are convicted in a moderately serious case (summary procedure), usually in a magistrates' court (sheriff court in Scotland), you can be given a maximum of six months' imprisonment or a fine of an unlimited amount in England and Wales (or in Scotland, a maximum fine of £10,000), or both; *or*
- you are convicted in a very serious case (on indictment), usually in the Crown Court (High Court in Scotland), you can be given a maximum of seven years' imprisonment or a fine of an unlimited amount, or both.

Future changes
At some point, the rules on fines and imprisonment will change as follows.[37]
If your offence is in connection with no more than £20,000 of tax credits, you may be tried only under summary procedure in the magistrates' court (sheriff court in Scotland). If you are convicted, you are liable to a maximum of 51 weeks' (England and Wales) or six months' (Scotland) imprisonment, or a fine of an unlimited amount in England and Wales (or in Scotland, a maximum fine of £10,000).
If the offence is in connection with more than £20,000 of tax credits, you may be tried either under summary procedure or on indictment in either the magistrates' court (sheriff court in Scotland) or the Crown Court (High Court in Scotland). If you are convicted under summary procedure, you are liable to a maximum of 12 months' imprisonment or a fine of an unlimited amount in England and Wales (or in Scotland, a maximum fine of £10,000), or both. If you are convicted on indictment, you are liable to a maximum of seven years' imprisonment or a fine of an unlimited amount, or both.
See AskCPAG and CPAG's *Welfare Rights Bulletin* for updates.

10

Part 10: General rules for tax credits
Chapter 66: Investigations, penalties and fraud: tax credits
Notes

Loss of benefit

If you have committed an offence in connection with working tax credit (WTC) or child tax credit, you can be sanctioned or disqualified from certain other benefits (see p1240). If you have committed an offence in connection with tax credits or other benefits, you can be disqualified from receiving WTC (see p1242).

Notes

1. Investigating awards
1 ss14(2) and 16(3) TCA 2002
2 Sch 2 TCA 2002; HMRC leaflet WTC7, *Tax Credits Penalties: what happens at the end of a tax credits check,* available at gov.uk
3 s19(3) and (8) TCA 2002
4 ss19(9) and (10) and 63(3) TCA 2002
5 ss14(2), 15(2), 16(3), 18(10), 19(2) and 22 TCA 2002
6 Reg 32 TC(CN) Regs
7 ss14(2)(b), 15(2)(b), 16(3)(b) and 19(2)(b) TCA 2002; regs 30 and 31 TC(CN) Regs
8 s36 TCA 2002
9 s20BB TMA 1970, as applied by s36 TCA 2002

2. Penalties
10 ss31 and 32 TCA 2002
11 Sch 2 TCA 2002; HMRC leaflet WTC7, *Tax Credits Penalties: what happens at the end of a tax credits check,* available at gov.uk
12 Sch 2 para 6 TCA 2002
13 s31 TCA 2002
14 HMRC leaflet WTC7, *Tax Credits Penalties: what happens at the end of a tax credits check,* available at gov.uk
15 HMRC leaflet WTC7, *Tax Credits Penalties: what happens at the end of a tax credits check,* available at gov.uk
16 *SP v HMRC* [2016] UKUT 238 (AAC), reported as [2016] AACR 46
17 Sch 2 para 1 TCA 2002; HMRC leaflet WTC7, *Tax Credits Penalties: what happens at the end of a tax credits check,* available at gov.uk
18 s31(3) TCA 2002

19 s31(5) TCA 2002
20 s32 TCA 2002
21 s32(1)(a) and Sch 2 paras 1 and 3 TCA 2002
22 s32(1)(b) TCA 2002
23 ss3(4) and (7), 6(3) and 32(3) TCA 2002; reg 21(2) TC(CN) Regs
24 s32(5)(b) TCA 2002; CCM 10170
25 Sch 2 para 1 TCA 2002
26 Sch 2 paras 1 and 3 TCA 2002; CCM 10220
27 s32(4) TCA 2002
28 s32(5) TCA 2002
29 s32(6) TCA 2002
30 s37(5) and (6) TCA 2002
31 Reg 4 TC(IR) Regs
32 ss37(5)-(6) and 38 TCA 2002
33 Sch 2 paras 1 and 5 TCA 2002

3. Prosecution for fraud
34 s35(1) TCA 2002
35 HMRC criminal investigation policy, available at gov.uk
36 s35(2) TCA 2002
37 s124 WRA 2012. At the time of writing, there was no commencement order.

Chapter 67

Getting a tax credit decision changed

This chapter covers:
1. Revisions (below)
2. Mandatory reconsiderations (p1511)
3. Appealing to the First-tier Tribunal (p1515)
4. Appealing to the Upper Tribunal (p1519)
5. Appealing to the Court of Appeal or Court of Session (p1519)

Tax credit appeals are heard by the First-tier Tribunal Social Entitlement Chamber, which also deals with social security benefits. Chapters 57 and 58 cover appeals about benefit decisions. This chapter refers you to these when the tax credit rules are the same as the benefit rules.

Key facts
- Decisions on your tax credit entitlement can be changed by a revision by HM Revenue and Customs, provided certain grounds are met.
- If you think a decision is wrong, you can ask for it to be looked at again (reviewed). This is called a mandatory reconsideration.
- A decision can be changed if you have been awarded a disability benefit.
- If you are unhappy with the outcome of a mandatory reconsideration, you can appeal to an independent tribunal – the First-tier Tribunal.
- There are strict time limits for carrying out a revision, applying for a mandatory reconsideration and appealing.

10

1. Revisions

A decision may be revised by HM Revenue and Customs (HMRC). How a revision is made depends on whether the decision with which you disagree is:
- an 'initial decision' on a claim or renewal (see p1506); *or*
- a 'final decision' after the tax year has ended following an annual review (see p1508); *or*
- a decision of the First-tier Tribunal (see p1518).

Part 10: General rules for tax credits
Chapter 67: Getting a tax credit decision changed
1. Revisions

The revision process is used when HMRC uses its power to change a decision – eg, after notification of a change of circumstances. If *you* disagree with a decision, including a revised decision, you should request a mandatory reconsideration and then appeal.

Revising an initial decision during an award

When you claim or renew a tax credit, HMRC must decide whether to make an award and the rate at which to award it.[1] This is called an 'initial decision'. If you disagree with it, you can request a mandatory reconsideration and then appeal (see p1511).

The initial decision can be revised if:

- your circumstances have changed so that you should get an additional or higher element (see below); *or*
- HMRC has reasonable grounds for believing that you are entitled to a different rate of tax credit or that you are not entitled to a tax credit at all (see p1507); *or*
- there has been an official error (see p1508).

If your claim has been turned down altogether or your award has been terminated, you cannot ask for the decision to be revised, unless it is on grounds of official error. Instead, you should usually request a mandatory reconsideration within 30 days if you want the decision to be changed.

If your income in the previous year is too high to qualify for a tax credit, but you satisfy the other qualifying conditions, you are awarded a tax credit at a nil rate. This nil-rate award can be revised if your income is estimated to be lower in the current year.[2]

An initial decision can also be changed if you or your child have been awarded a disability benefit (see p1514).

Your circumstances have changed

If you notify the Tax Credit Office that your circumstances have changed so that you should now get an element that you were not previously getting, HMRC must decide whether to amend your award and, if so, how.[3] For example, if you report that you have started to pay childcare costs, your working tax credit (WTC) award can be revised to include the childcare element. HMRC may request further information or evidence before making a revised decision.

If you notify the Tax Credit Office of the change within one month, the increase in your award can be fully backdated.[4] There are specific rules on backdating if your award is recalculated following a change in childcare charges or childcare provided (see p1472) or if you have been awarded a disability benefit (see p1472).

The increase in your award cannot be backdated for more than one month before the date you notify HMRC of the change, except if the change is that you have been awarded a disability benefit (see p1472).

If you disagree with a revised decision, you can request a mandatory reconsideration and then appeal to the First-tier Tribunal (see p1511). A revised decision may be revised as many times as necessary, either following another change, if HMRC has 'reasonable grounds' for believing your entitlement has changed (see below), or because of an official error (see p1510).

Reasonable grounds for believing your entitlement has changed

HMRC can amend or terminate an award if it has 'reasonable grounds' for believing that you are:[5]
- entitled to a different rate of tax credit; *or*
- not entitled to WTC or not entitled to child tax credit.

This could happen, for example, because you tell the Tax Credit Office about a change in your income or because incorrect information was used to decide your claim. It could also happen following an examination into your award (see p1497).

If the rate of tax credit is changed, HMRC revises your award, taking into account any change in circumstances from the date it arose unless:
- it is a change that increases your entitlement to tax credit elements, which can only be backdated for up to one month (see p1506); *or*
- your childcare charges decrease by £10 a week or more. In this case, there is a four-week 'run-on' at the same rate before the award is reduced (see p1470);[6] *or*
- there is a four-week 'run-on' because you stop work or reduce your hours below 16, 24 or 30 a week (see p289).

Decisions can only be revised in this way during the period of the award, not after an award has been terminated, nor after a final decision has been made.[7]

Example

Martha provides an estimate of her income for the current year. This has decreased by more than £2,500 compared with the previous year's income on which her award was based. The initial decision can be revised and her award recalculated based on the current year's income plus £2,500. The estimate she provides must be sufficient to give HMRC reasonable grounds for believing that her entitlement should change.

HMRC is not obliged to revise your award, even when there are grounds. It could leave the changes to be dealt with at the annual review – eg, if it is late in the year and the change is minor.[8]

If you disagree with the revised decision, you can request a mandatory reconsideration and then appeal (see p1511). The burden of proof is on HMRC to set out the reasonable grounds for its decision and the evidence used to support it.[9]

Part 10: General rules for tax credits
Chapter 67: Getting a tax credit decision changed
1. Revisions

Official error

An initial decision can be revised in your favour if it is incorrect because of an official error (see p1510).[10]

Revising a final decision

After 5 April, HMRC carries out the annual review (see p1475) for the year just ended and makes a final decision on your entitlement for that year. It sends you an annual review form which details the circumstances on which the award was based and usually an annual declaration form, giving your income for the tax year just passed.

If HMRC sends you an annual declaration form, you must complete and return it by the deadline given (31 July in most cases). HMRC finalises your entitlement for the year just passed. A final decision is conclusive unless it is changed on mandatory reconsideration or appeal, or in the following circumstances.

- If you change your statement about your income or circumstances before the deadline, the final decision can be changed (see below).
- Once a final decision is made, there is a period during which HMRC can open an enquiry into your entitlement (see p1509). This is known as a 'revision on enquiry'.
- Outside the period of enquiry, a final decision can be revised on 'discovery' of certain information about your tax liability or in relation to fraud or neglect (see p1509). This is known as a 'revision on discovery'.
- A final decision can be revised in your favour because of an official error (see p1510).

A final decision can also be changed if you or your child have been awarded a disability benefit (see p1514).

Changing your statement

If you reply to the annual review notice but then wish to change your statement, you may do so. If it is on or before the deadline given in the notice for replying (31 July in most cases), but HMRC has already made a final decision, the final decision may be revised.[11]

If HMRC only had an estimate of your income for the current year (eg, because you are self-employed and have not yet finalised your accounts), you have a later deadline (usually 31 January) by which to give details of your actual income for that year. If you do so, HMRC must make a new final decision.[12] It can revise the new decision if you change your statement on or before the later deadline.[13] If you do not give further details of actual income, HMRC must nevertheless make a new final decision once the later deadline is passed.

'Revision on enquiry'

HMRC does not need any particular grounds to open an enquiry into your entitlement, and some awards are selected for enquiry at random.[14] It must begin its enquiry by giving you written notice. An enquiry can only be opened for a particular tax year after the final decision for that year has been made, and within a limited period of time. This is known as the 'enquiry window'. It begins immediately after the final decision and ends a year after the deadline by when you had to reply to the annual review notice, or a year after the later deadline for self-employed people and others to supply actual income details if only an estimate was provided.[15] If you are required to submit an income tax return, the enquiry must begin by the day your tax return becomes final.

When the enquiry is completed, HMRC makes a fresh decision on whether you are entitled and how much the award should be. There is no time limit in which HMRC should conclude an enquiry, but you can apply to the First-tier Tribunal for a direction to bring the enquiry to an end.[16]

Only one enquiry into entitlement can be conducted for any one tax year.[17] For more details, see p1497.

If you disagree with the decision, you can ask for a mandatory reconsideration and then appeal (see p1511). It can also be revised if it is incorrect because of an official error (see p1510).[18] HMRC can also revise an enquiry decision by a 'revision on discovery'.

'Revision on discovery'

'Discovery' is a power to revise your entitlement in earlier years. If it is too late to 'enquire' into your entitlement, HMRC can still revise a final decision in specific circumstances. A final decision or an enquiry decision may be revised within five years if HMRC has 'reasonable grounds' for believing that your tax credit entitlement is wrong:

- because of a revision of your income tax liability. The revision of your tax credit entitlement must take place within a year of your income tax liability being revised;[19] *or*
- because of fraud or neglect.[20] The fraud or neglect may be on your part, or your partner's if it is a joint claim, or on the part of anyone acting for you (see p1462). Your tax credit entitlement in a tax year cannot be revised on this ground after five years from the end of the tax year – eg, a tax credit award for 2016/17 (or earlier) cannot be revised after 5 April 2022.[21]

There is nothing to stop HMRC going through this process more than once.[22] If a final decision, enquiry decision or discovery decision has been revised because of an official error, this can be further revised in this way.[23]

If you disagree with a discovery decision, or do not think HMRC has shown grounds to revise using this power, you can request a mandatory reconsideration

Part 10: General rules for tax credits
Chapter 67: Getting a tax credit decision changed
1. Revisions

and then appeal (see p1511). Alternatively, the decision may be revised if it is incorrect because of an official error.

Official error

An initial decision, final decision, enquiry decision or discovery decision can be revised in your favour if it is incorrect because of an official error.[24] The decision can be revised at any time up to five years after the date of the decision. An official error can include opening an enquiry (see p1509) without notice, and it is arguable that there is an official error if you have not been given the opportunity to contribute to an enquiry.[25]

> *Official error*
>
> **'Official error'** means an error relating to a tax credit made by an HMRC or DWP officer or a person providing tax credit services for them. If you, or someone acting for you, contributed to the error, it is *not* an official error. An error of law can be an official error, but not if it is only shown to be an error of law because of a later Upper Tribunal or court decision.

How to request a revision

If your circumstances change, there are rules on how HMRC should be notified (see p1475). In other cases, there are no set rules to follow. If you disagree with a decision, you should usually request a mandatory reconsideration, then appeal if you are unhappy with the outcome rather than ask HMRC to use one of its powers to revise a decision. If you are outside the absolute time limit for a mandatory reconsideration or appeal and want a decision to be revised on grounds of official error, you should request this in writing. If HMRC refuses to revise a decision on official error grounds, it is arguable that you have a right of appeal against this decision.[26]

Keep a copy of any letter you send to HMRC. If you call the Tax Credit Helpline, keep a log of your calls: the date and time you made the call, the name of the person you spoke with, the information provided and what was agreed.

What happens after you request a revision

Before making its decision, HMRC may ask you to provide more information or evidence if it needs this to help with the decision.[27] HMRC may contact your employer or childcare provider if it also needs information from them.[28]

It is important that you respond to a request for information by the date given in the letter. If you do not provide the required information, HMRC may take proceedings to the First-tier Tribunal to impose a penalty of up to £300, and if you still do not comply, a further daily penalty of up to £60 a day could be imposed. See p1498 for how these penalties are applied.

10

HMRC must give notice of the decision to you, and to your partner if it is a joint claim. This must include details of your right to appeal.[29]

2. **Mandatory reconsiderations**

HM Revenue and Customs (HMRC) must carry out a review if you have made a valid request for one, and it must notify you of the outcome. You must be notified of the outcome of the review before you can appeal. A review is known as a 'mandatory reconsideration', and applies to all tax credit decisions made on or after 6 April 2014.[30]

Who can request a mandatory reconsideration

The following people can request a mandatory reconsideration:[31]
- you, the tax credit claimant. For joint claimants, only one partner needs to make the request;
- for decisions about penalties, the person subject to the penalty;
- an appointee, if you are unable to make the request yourself (see p1462). If you do not have an appointee, the person (who must be 18 or over) who is to act on your behalf should write to HMRC asking to be appointed;
- another person with the power to make a tax credit claim for you – ie, a receiver appointed by the Court of Protection, a judicial factor or guardian.

The law does not specify who can request a mandatory reconsideration, but Form WTC/AP (see p1513) requires a signature from the tax credit claimant or appointee. It also asks whether you are getting help from a representative, and requires your signature to authorise that person to act for you. You may be able to argue that your representative has the right to request a mandatory reconsideration on your behalf with your prior signed authority, but it may be simpler to ensure you sign the request where possible. HMRC does not accept photocopied signatures.

Which decisions can be reconsidered

You can request a mandatory reconsideration of:[32]
- an initial decision;
- a final decision;
- a revised decision (after a change in circumstances, on reasonable grounds or for official error);
- an enquiry decision;
- a discovery decision;
- a decision imposing a penalty;
- a decision charging interest on an overpayment.

10

Part 10: General rules for tax credits
Chapter 67: Getting a tax credit decision changed
2. Mandatory reconsiderations

Caselaw has established that there is a right to have a mandatory reconsideration and then appeal against the following decisions (but, in practice, HMRC may not accept this):

- a decision to reject a claim that is not made on the approved form, or that does not contain all the information requested on the form, including the national insurance (NI) number requirement (see p1463);[33]
- a decision that you do not have good cause for making a late annual declaration (see p1476);[34]
- a refusal to revise a decision on the grounds of official error (see p1510);[35]
- a decision contained in a 'statement like an award notice' (see p1469);[36]
- a decision to terminate your tax credit award because you are a universal credit claimant or have applied for tax-free childcare (the termination decision may be contained within the final decision on your tax credits) (see p1471);[37]
- a refusal to extend the time limit to request a mandatory reconsideration (see p1513).[38] In this case, you should appeal to the First-tier Tribunal, citing caselaw and asking it to decide whether to accept reasons for the late request and, if the time is extended, to decide your appeal.

In these situations, you should request a mandatory reconsideration, quoting the relevant caselaw. If HMRC refuses to carry out a mandatory reconsideration, you should ask for confirmation of this in writing and then appeal to the First-tier Tribunal on Form SSCS5, asking it to decide whether you have a right of appeal.

Which decisions cannot be reconsidered

You cannot request a mandatory reconsideration or appeal against:
- a decision to recover all or part of an overpayment (see below);
- a decision about the rate or method of recovery of an overpayment;
- a decision to postpone payments (see p1469);
- a decision to open an enquiry into your entitlement (but you can apply to the tribunal for a direction to bring an enquiry to an end – see p1497).

Decisions to recover overpayments

There is a different process if you want to dispute a decision to recover an overpayment – ie, if you accept that you were overpaid, but do not think you should have to repay any money. If HMRC decides you have been overpaid tax credits, it can recover all or part of them at its discretion, and you cannot request a mandatory reconsideration or appeal against this decision. You can, however, request a mandatory reconsideration of the decision on your entitlement – ie, if you do not agree that you were overpaid, or disagree with the amount. In some cases, HMRC may use its discretion not to recover an overpayment, or to reduce the amount – eg, if recovery would cause hardship (see p1488). Complain to HMRC if you are unhappy with the way your award has been handled. If your complaint is not resolved to your satisfaction, you can ask the Adjudicator to look into it (see p1405). See Chapter 65 for more information on tax credit overpayments.

How to request a mandatory reconsideration

A mandatory reconsideration must be requested in writing and must identify you (eg, your name and NI number) and the decision in question. It is advisable to use Form WTC/AP, *What To Do If You Think Your Child Tax Credit Or Working Tax Credit Is Wrong,* available as an online form or to print off and post at gov.uk/government/publications/child-tax-credit-and-working-tax-credit-appeal-form. If you telephone HMRC to ask for a decision to be reconsidered, this is not a formal request for a mandatory reconsideration. You must still put your request in writing. If your representative requests the mandatory reconsideration on your behalf, your signed authority should be included.

Time limit

Unless the rule about reviews following an award of a disability benefit applies (see p1514), your request for a mandatory reconsideration must be received by HMRC within 30 days of the date given on the decision letter.[39]

You may not get a separate initial or final decision notice if the annual review notice states what the decision will be and the date on which it will be made – usually 31 July. This may apply if your claim has been automatically renewed. In this case, your request for a mandatory reconsideration must be received within 30 days of the date specified as the date on which the decision is made on the annual review notice – eg, by 30 August if the decision date is given as 31 July.

If you or your child have been awarded a disability benefit, your request for a mandatory reconsideration must be received by HMRC within one month of the decision awarding you or your child a disability benefit (see p1514).

10

Late requests

If your request for a mandatory reconsideration is received by HMRC outside the time limit, you must explain why it is late. HMRC may accept a late request within 13 months of the original decision if it is satisfied that there were special circumstances that meant it was not practical for you to meet the time limit. HMRC must also be satisfied that it is reasonable, given all the circumstances, to accept the late request. The longer the delay, the more compelling the reasons must be.[40] Reasons that may be acceptable are if:

- you, your partner or dependant had a serious illness, or has died; *or*
- you are not resident in the UK; *or*
- there has been a disruption in normal postal services.

This list is not exhaustive and other reasons for lateness may be accepted.

Part 10: General rules for tax credits
Chapter 67: Getting a tax credit decision changed
2. Mandatory reconsiderations

If your application to extend the time limit is refused, an Upper Tribunal decison has held that you do have a right to appeal, and the First-tier Tribunal decides whether or not to extend time.[41]

Review following an award of a disability benefit

A tax credits decision can be reviewed at any time if you (or your partner or child) have been awarded a disability benefit that affects your entitlement in that tax year. You must request a review (also known as a mandatory reconsideration) within one month of the date of the decision on the disability benefit.[42] This applies to any tax credits decision, including an initial decision or a revised decision during the tax year, or a final decision after the tax year has ended, and any decision that has been revised on enquiry, discovery or official error grounds, or has been decided on mandatory reconsideration or appeal. A tax credits decision can be reviewed in this way even if you are no longer getting tax credits. If the decision is changed and you become entitled to tax credits for a previous year following the award of a disability benefit, your entitlement to tax credits can be renewed for subsequent years, for as long as you continue to meet the entitlement conditions and have not claimed universal credit.

A request for a review of a tax credits decision following an award of a disability benefit does not have to be in writing, and can be made by telephone to the Tax Credits Helpline.

A disability benefit includes any of the benefits or credits that affect entitlement to the disabled worker element, severe disability element (see p1420) or disabled child element (see p1418). The decision on the disability benefit could be following a mandatory reconsideration or appeal, and arguably includes a change in the rate to which you are entitled.

HMRC must review the decision as soon as is reasonable, and may request further information or evidence (see p1515). The sole purpose of the review is to consider whether the decision should be changed as a result of the award of the disability benefit. You must be notified of the outcome of the review and you then have a right of appeal against the new decision.

Penalty decisions

You can request a mandatory reconsideration of most decisions to impose a penalty. HMRC can impose a penalty for making incorrect statements, failing to report a required change of circumstances or failing to comply with the annual review. You can request a mandatory reconsideration in the normal way, then appeal to the First-tier Tribunal if necessary.[43]

However, if you fail to comply with a request for information or evidence, HMRC cannot decide to impose a penalty of up to £300 itself, but must take 'proceedings' to the First-tier Tribunal. You have an opportunity to attend a hearing where the tribunal decides whether or not you should be given a penalty.

You can then appeal to the Upper Tribunal.[44] Unlike most appeals to the Upper Tribunal, you do not need to show that there has been an 'error of law'.[45] The usual time limits and procedures for applying for permission to appeal apply. For information on penalties, see p1498.

After you request a mandatory reconsideration

If a written request is received within the time limit, or a late request is accepted, HMRC must carry out a mandatory reconsideration of the decision in question. The mandatory reconsideration must be carried out as soon as is reasonably practical, and HMRC's stated target is 42 days.[46] If you are still waiting for the outcome of a mandatory reconsideration by the time the final decision is made (usually 31 July) (see p1478), you should also request a mandatory reconsideration against the final decision, because your mandatory reconsideration or appeal against the in-year decision lapses.[47] If your annual review told you what the final decision would be and when it would be made, you may not get another notice, but you should still request a mandatory reconsideration within 30 days of the date you were told it would be made (usually 31 July).

HMRC may request further information or evidence from you. This must be in writing and specify a date by when it should be provided. If you do not provide the information or evidence by the date specified, HMRC may proceed with the mandatory reconsideration. New information or evidence does not have to be provided as a pre-condition for a mandatory reconsideration.

A penalty cannot be imposed on you for failing to provide information or evidence requested in connection with a mandatory reconsideration.

HMRC must issue a 'mandatory reconsideration notice', containing sufficient information for you to understand the outcome, details of any change to the decision and the reasons for its conclusion. The outcome must be one of the following.[48]

- The decision is upheld. There is no change to the original decision with which you disagree, and you have the right of appeal.
- The decision is varied. In this case, the original decision is changed. If the decision is changed in your favour but you still disagree with part of it, you can appeal against the decision as varied. You do not have to go through the mandatory reconsideration process again.
- The decision is cancelled. You are left in the position you were in before the decision was made. There does not appear to be a right of appeal in this situation, as this would be against a decision that has been cancelled.

3. Appealing to the First-tier Tribunal

You can only appeal against a tax credits decision after a mandatory reconsideration has been carried out and the outcome has been notified to you in

Part 10: General rules for tax credits
Chapter 67: Getting a tax credit decision changed
3. Appealing to the First-tier Tribunal

writing. Tax credit appeals are heard by the same First-tier Tribunal that deals with social security benefits, which is administered by HM Courts and Tribunals Service (HMCTS).[49] Many of the rules are the same as those for social security benefits (see Chapter 57). This chapter refers you to Chapter 57 where the tax credit rules are the same as the benefit rules.

Who can appeal

The following people have the right of appeal:[50]
- you, the tax credit claimant. For joint claimants, both or either of you can make the appeal. If only one appeals, the First-tier Tribunal decision still applies to both, provided you are both given the right to a hearing;[51]
- for appeals about penalties, the person subject to the penalty;
- an appointee, if you are unable to appeal yourself (see p1462). If you do not have an appointee, the person (who must be 18 or over) who is to act on your behalf in the appeal should write to HM Revenue and Customs (HMRC) asking to be appointed;
- another person with the power to make a tax credit claim for you – ie, a receiver appointed by the Court of Protection, a judicial factor or guardian.[52]

The tribunal rules state that you must sign the appeal, but also state that you can appoint a representative who can do anything that you are required to do, except sign a witness statement. Your representative may sign the appeal on your behalf with your signed consent, but it may be simpler to ensure you sign the appeal yourself if possible.[53]

How to appeal

You should appeal on the appropriate form – Form SSCS5 (*Notice Of Appeal Against A Decision Of HM Revenue and Customs*), which must be signed by you or by your representative. If your representative signs the appeal, s/he must send your signed authority to act on your behalf. Enclose a copy of the mandatory reconsideration notice and send Form SSCS5 to HMCTS. Alternatively, you can write a letter. You must include:
- a copy of the mandatory reconsideration notice; *and*
- your signature (on the appeal request itself, or on a signed authority for your representative to act on your behalf); *and*
- your name and address; *and*
- the name and address of your representative, if you have one; *and*
- the grounds for appeal – ie, the reasons why you disagree with the decision.

Time limit
Your appeal must be received by HMCTS within one month of the date on the mandatory reconsideration notice.[54]

Late appeals

If your appeal is received outside the one-month time limit but within the absolute time limit of 13 months, it is accepted, provided HMRC does not object and unless the First-tier Tribunal directs otherwise. If HMRC objects, the tribunal can still accept your appeal if it is in the interest of justice.[55] In very exceptional circumstances (eg, if you did not receive notice of the decision you want to appeal), you can argue that the tribunal has the discretion to allow you to appeal outside the absolute time limit.[56] However, this is unlikely to apply unless you have done all you could to appeal in time.

What happens after you appeal

HMRC must prepare its response (a submission) within 28 days of receiving notice of your appeal from the tribunal.[57] This should include the law used to make its decision, and all relevant information and evidence.[58]

Settling the appeal

HMRC may want to settle the appeal without going to the tribunal. You can point out to HMRC where you think its decision is wrong and supply information or arguments you want it to consider. Even though HMRC has already had the opportunity to reconsider its decision, once you have lodged your appeal it may offer you terms on which to settle the appeal. Your appeal can only be settled with your consent. If you do not agree, the appeal must proceed to the tribunal.

If you are asked to settle the appeal, check first whether the proposed agreement gives you everything to which you think you are entitled. Get advice if you are not sure whether or not to agree. If in doubt, continue with the appeal. If you agree to settle, HMRC must write to you setting out the terms of the agreement – eg, giving you a new amount. Your appeal then lapses unless you write to HMRC within 30 days of the date of the written notice of agreement saying you have changed your mind and wish to proceed with your appeal.[59]

If your appeal has not been heard by the end of the year

If your appeal has not been heard by the time you get HMRC's final decision on your entitlement at the end of the year, request another mandatory reconsideration and appeal against the final decision. This is because an appeal against an in-year decision lapses once a final decision is made on that year.[60]

Withdrawing an appeal

You can ask to withdraw the appeal if you decide not to go ahead with it. See p1323 for details of withdrawing and reinstating an appeal if you change your mind.

Part 10: General rules for tax credits
Chapter 67: Getting a tax credit decision changed
3. Appealing to the First-tier Tribunal

When your appeal can be struck out

Your appeal may be 'struck out' before the hearing in certain circumstances. The rules are the same as those for benefits (see p1321). Your appeal may be struck out if it was against an in-year decision and a final decision has since been made on the same year.[61]

The hearing

The tribunal holds a hearing if you have asked for one. Otherwise, there is a paper hearing in your absence (see p1325). For information on asking for the hearing to be postponed or adjourned to a later date, see p1319. The tax credit rules are the same as those for benefits, except that there are no special 'test case' provisions for tax credits that can block your appeal or affect its outcome (although payment can be postponed while there is an appeal pending in another case that could affect your own award).[62] The rules on 'lead cases' described on p1325 also apply to tax credits.

Procedures for tax credit appeals

There are procedural rules that the tribunal must follow when dealing with your appeal. See pp1329–1349 and pp1317–1324 for details. The tax credit rules are the same, with the following exceptions.

- **Medical examinations.** The tribunal cannot refer you to a doctor for a medical examination.[63] However, if your appeal concerns a disability question, it may be important to get your own medical evidence (see p1343).
- **Change in circumstances after you appeal.** The rules apply to tax credits in the same way as they do to benefits except:
  - wherever Chapter 57 refers to 'supersession', read 'revision' for tax credits;
  - if you reclaim or ask for a revision because of a change in circumstances after you appeal, there is no specific provision for a decision maker to revisit her/his decision on that claim or revision once the appeal has been heard on the grounds that s/he would have made a different decision had s/he known what the tribunal's decision would be.
- **After the hearing.** If HMRC is considering appealing to the Upper Tribunal, you are normally not paid until the Upper Tribunal decides the case. HMRC can postpone payment in these circumstances, without notifying you of its intention.[64]
- **If you disagree with the First-tier Tribunal's decision.** The decision cannot be superseded (because supersessions do not apply to tax credits), but it can be revised in any of the ways described in this chapter except for official error (see p1505).

  If the First-tier Tribunal made an error of law, you can appeal to the Upper Tribunal as you can in benefit appeals. For tax credits, HMRC is not prevented

10

from revising the First-tier Tribunal's decision on 'reasonable grounds', which could also include an error of law (if it is still within the tax year of the award).
- **When a decision can be set aside.** If you appeal to the Upper Tribunal, there is no provision obliging the First-tier Tribunal to set aside the decision if both you and HMRC agree that the First-tier Tribunal made an error of law.[65]

4. Appealing to the Upper Tribunal

You can appeal to the Upper Tribunal against a decision of the First-tier Tribunal if the First-tier Tribunal made an error of law. In some penalty appeals, you can also appeal about the amount of the penalty (see p1514), without having to show an error of law.

Chapter 58 explains what an error of law is and how to appeal (see p1357). The rules for tax credits are the same as those for benefits, except that if you disagree with the Upper Tribunal decision, it cannot be superseded but it can be revised in any of the ways described on p1505, except because of an official error.

5. Appealing to the Court of Appeal or Court of Session

You can appeal to the Court of Appeal (in England and Wales) or to the Court of Session (in Scotland) against a decision of the Upper Tribunal, but only if there has been an error of law (see Chapter 58).

10

Notes

1. Revisions
1   s14(1) TCA 2002
2   s14(3) TCA 2002
3   s15(1) TCA 2002
4   Reg 25 TC(CN) Regs; reg 16(5)(a) WTC(EMR) Regs
5   s16(1) TCA 2002
6   Reg 16(5)(b) WTC(EMR) Regs
7   s16(1) TCA 2002
8   CTC/2662/2005; CTC/3981/2005
9   *SB v HMRC (TC)* [2014] UKUT 543 (AAC); *NI v HMRC (TC)* [2015] UKUT 490 (AAC)
10   s21 TCA 2002
11   s18(5) TCA 2002
12   s18(6) TCA 2002
13   s18(9) TCA 2002
14   s19(1) TCA 2002
15   s19(4) TCA 2002
16   s19(9) TCA 2002
17   s19(11) TCA 2002

Part 10: General rules for tax credits
Chapter 67: Getting a tax credit decision changed
Notes

18 s21 TCA 2002
19 s20(1) and (3) TCA 2002
20 s20(4) TCA 2002
21 s20(5) TCA 2002
22 s20(6)(a) TCA 2002
23 s20(6)(b) TCA 2002
24 s21 TCA 2002; reg 3 TC(OE) Regs
25 *JI v HMRC (TC)* [2013] UKUT 199 (AAC), para 53
26 *JI v HMRC (TC)* [2013] UKUT 199 (AAC), para 50
27 ss15(2)(b), 16(3)(b) and 19(2)(b) TCA 2002
28 Regs 30 and 31 TC(CN) Regs
29 s23 TCA 2002

2. Mandatory reconsiderations
30 Footnote to art 2 The Tax Credits, Child Benefit and Guardian's Allowance Reviews and Appeals Order 2014 No.886
31 See HMRC leaflet WTC/AP, *What To Do If You Think Your Child Tax Credit Or Working Tax Credit Is Wrong*
32 s38 TCA 2002
33 *CI v HMRC (TC)* [2014] UKUT 158 (AAC) held that there is a right of appeal, but this disagrees with the earlier *ZM and AB v HMRC (TC)* [2013] UKUT 547 (AAC), which held there there is no such right
34 *SG v HMRC (TC)* [2011] UKUT 199 (AAC)
35 *JI v HMRC (TC)* [2013] UKUT 199 (AAC), para 50
36 *TM v HMRC (TC)* [2016] UKUT 512 (AAC), but see also *DG v HMRC (TC)* [2016] UKUT 505 (AAC)
37 *HMRC v LH (TC)* [2016] UKUT 306 (AAC); *HMRC v AB (TC)* [2016] UKUT 209
38 CTC/886/2021
39 ss23(2) and 39(1) TCA 2002
40 s21A TCA 2002
41 CTC/886/2021 *AB v HMRC* [2021]
42 s21C TCA 2002
43 s38 TCA 2002
44 s63 and Sch 2 para 4(1) TCA 2002
45 Sch 2 para 4(1) TCA 2002; see also *SP v HMRC (No.2)* [2017] UKUT 329 (AAC)
46 David Gauke MP, Exchequer Secretary to the Treasury, Eighth Delegated Legislation Committee, 26 March 2014
47 *LS and RS v HMRC* [2017] UKUT 257 (AAC)
48 s21A(3) TCA 2002

3. Appealing to the First-tier Tribunal
49 s63(2) TCA 2002
50 s12 SSA 1998, as applied by reg 4 TC(A) Regs under the power in s63(8) TCA 2002
51 CTC/2612/2005
52 Reg 3 TC(A)(No.2) Regs
53 rr11 and 22 TP(FT) Rules
54 r22(2)(d)(i) TP(FT) Rules
55 rr2 and 5(3)(a) TP(FT) Rules
56 *KK v Sheffield City Council (CTB)* [2015] UKUT 367 (AAC)
57 r24(1)(c) TP(FT) Rules
58 *CS v HMRC (TC)* [2015] UKUT 407 (AAC)
59 s54 TMA 1970, as applied by The Tax Credits (Settlement of Appeals) Regulations 2014 No.1933
60 *LS and RS v HMRC (TC)* [2016] UKUT 257 (AAC)
61 *LS and RS v HMRC (TC)* [2017] UKUT 257 (AAC)
62 Reg 11 TC(PC) Regs
63 The power to refer to a doctor in s20 SSA 1998 does not apply to tax credits
64 Reg 11 TC(PC) Regs
65 s13(3) SSA 1998, as applied by reg 5(2) TC(A) Regs under the power in s63(8) TCA 2002

10

Part 11

Immigration and residence rules for benefits and tax credits

Part I.1

Immigration and residence
rules for benefits and tax
credits

Chapter 68

Coming from abroad: immigration status

This chapter covers:
1. Immigration status (below)
2. Benefits and tax credits affected by immigration status (p1529)
3. Partners and children (p1533)
4. National insurance numbers and contributions (p1537)
5. Asylum seekers and refugees (p1538)

The rules in this chapter can apply if you, your partner and child are *not* all British or Irish citizens. Since the end of the transition period that followed the UK leaving the European Union (11pm on 31 December 2020), the immigration status restrictions on benefits can extend to European Economic Area (EEA) as well as non-EEA nationals. In all cases, you must satisfy the residence and presence requirements in Chapter 69.

Key facts
- Your immigration status may mean that you are not entitled to some benefits and tax credits, although there are limited exceptions.
- The immigration status of your partner can affect the amount you are paid.
- If your partner's or child's leave in the UK is subject to a 'no recourse to public funds' condition, your claim could affect her/his right to remain in the UK.

11

1. Immigration status

It is important to know your immigration status, and that of anyone included in your claim, before making a claim for a benefit or tax credit. This is because it affects your right to benefits and tax credits and also because being paid an increased amount for someone included in your claim can affect her/his right to remain in the UK if her/his leave is subject to the condition that s/he has 'no recourse to public funds'. If you are unsure about your immigration status, you should obtain specialist advice from your local law centre, Citizens Advice or

Part 11: Immigration and residence rules for benefits and tax credits
Chapter 68: Coming from abroad: immigration status
1. Immigration status

other immigration advice provider registered with the Office of the Immigration Services Commissioner (OISC): gov.uk/find-an-immigration-adviser.

Who is a 'person subject to immigration control'

Most people, apart from British citizens, are subject to immigration control. However, for benefit and tax credit purposes, the term 'person subject to immigration control' has the specific meaning given below. It is this meaning that is referred to when the phrase 'person subject to immigration control' is used in this *Handbook*.

You are defined as a **'person subject to immigration control'** if you:[1]
- require leave to enter or remain in the UK, but do not have it (see p1526); *or*
- have leave to enter or remain subject to the condition that you do not have 'recourse to public funds' (see p1527); *or*
- have leave to enter or remain given as a result of a maintenance undertaking (see p1528); *or*
- have leave to enter or remain solely because you are appealing a decision to refuse to vary your previous leave (see p1529).

If you are defined as a person subject to immigration control, you are excluded from many benefits and tax credits (see p1529). There are, however, some limited exempt groups (see p1530, p1531 and p1533).

Note:
- You cannot be a person subject to immigration control if you are a **British or Irish citizen**. British and Irish citizens never require leave to enter or remain in the UK.
- If you are a **European Economic Area (EEA) national** (see p1644 for a list of EEA states), you need to check whether you are defined as a 'person subject to immigration control' for any period since the end of the transition period (11pm on 31 December 2020). Before this date, the definition only applied to non-EEA nationals, and this limitation continues to apply while you are in one of the first three protected groups. You are also *not* a 'person subject to immigration control' while the fourth protected group applies.
- If you are a **non-EEA national**, you are not defined as a 'person subject to immigration control' while you are in one of the protected groups, *and* you have a free movement right to reside.
- If you have leave to enter or remain in the UK under the European Union Settlement Scheme (EUSS – see p1563), you are not defined as a 'person subject to immigration control' for the duration of that leave. For the reasons why the fourth bullet point of the definition is very unlikely to apply, see p1529.

Protected groups who can have free movement rights

If you have a European free movement right to reside in the UK, you do not require leave to enter or remain and are therefore not defined as a 'person subject to immigration control'. However, since the end of the transition period (11pm on 31 December 2020), whether you are an EEA or non-EEA national, you can only have a free movement right to reside while you are in one of the protected groups listed below.

If you are a **non-EEA national**, you do not require leave to enter or remain in the UK if:

- you are in one of the protected groups below; *and*
- you currently have a free movement right to reside (see p1568).

If both the above points apply, you do not require leave to enter or remain, and you cannot be refused benefit on the basis of your immigration status even if, for example, you have leave that is subject to a condition that you do not have recourse to public funds, or which has been given as a result of a maintenance undertaking. Conditions attached to any leave you have been given do not have any effect while you have a free movement right to reside under the EEA Regulations.[2] As a non-EEA national, the free movement residence rights you may have include being a 'family member' (see p1583) of an EEA national who has a relevant free movement right to reside (eg, as a worker – see p1576), or having a permanent right to reside (see p1591), or having a derivative right to reside (see p1589). **Note:** if you have a derivative right to reside as the primary carer of a British citizen in the UK because this is necessary for her/him to continue to reside within the EU (known as a 'Zambrano carer'),[3] in most cases, this does not entitle you to any benefits that require a right to reside (see p1557), but you can still be entitled to other benefits that do not require a right to reside – eg, personal independence payment (PIP) and carer's allowance (CA).[4]

If you are an **EEA national**, you are not defined as 'person subject to immigration control' while you are in one of the protected groups below *whether or not* you currently have a free movement right to reside. For periods when one of the first three groups below applies, this is because transitional rules limit the definition of 'person subject to immigration control' to only non-EEA nationals.[5] For periods when the fourth group below applies, your protections arise from the Withdrawal Agreements, and are confirmed in guidance.

You are in a protected group:[6]

- **(between 31 December 2020 and 30 June 2021)** if on 31 December 2020 you had a free movement right to reside, and you did not, during that period, have leave under the EUSS; *or*
- **(beyond 30 June 2021)** if you were in the group above and by 30 June 2021 you applied for leave under EUSS and that application (or appeal against a refusal) has not been finally determined, withdrawn or abandoned; *or*
- **(between 31 December 2020 and 30 June 2021)** if you were defined as the 'relevant family member' of a person who on 31 December 2020 had a free

Part 11: Immigration and residence rules for benefits and tax credits
Chapter 68: Coming from abroad: immigration status
1. Immigration status

movement right to reside and you did not, during that period, have leave under the EUSS; *or*

- from the date you make a valid application for leave under the EUSS, if that application (or appeal against a refusal) has not been finally determined, withdrawn or abandoned. DWP guidance states you should be accepted as in this group once you have received a certificate of application (see p1565).[7]

Note: you are also in a protected group if you have pre-settled status, but that is not listed above since this status by itself means you are not defined as a 'person subject to immigration control'.

For further details, including on extra-statutory benefit payments beyond 30 June 2021 if you had not applied to the EUSS, the definition of 'relevant family member', and when you can be *treated as* having had a free movement right to reside on 31 December 2020 despite being absent from the UK on that date, see p1566.

You require leave to enter or remain but do not have it

You are a 'person subject to immigration control' if you require leave to enter or remain but do not have it,[8] *unless* you are an EEA national and in one of the protected groups listed on p1525.

You require leave to enter or remain in the UK *unless* you are:
- a British or Irish citizen or person with the right of abode; *or*
- an EEA national in the UK as a frontier worker (from 1 July 2021, you will need to hold a valid frontier worker permit) (see p1595);[9] *or*
- in a protected group listed above *and,* if you are a non-EEA national, you have a free movement right to reside.

Examples of when you require leave to enter or remain but do not have it include if you:
- are an asylum seeker on immigration bail (see p1538);
- have overstayed your limited leave to enter or remain. **Note:** if you apply for further leave on the same or a different basis before your current leave expires, your leave is extended from the date it would have expired until your application is decided or withdrawn. While your leave is extended in this way, you are not someone who requires leave and does not have it;[10]
- have entered the UK without immigration leave, and since then have not obtained leave to remain and you do not have a pending application (or appeal against a refusal) to the EUSS;
- are subject to a deportation order.

Note:
- If you came to live in the UK before 1973 and you are, or were, a Commonwealth citizen, or you came before August 1988 and you are now

11

British or have a right of abode or indefinite leave, you may be entitled to compensation from the Windrush Compensation Scheme if you experienced losses, including loss of benefits, due to a lack of documentary evidence of your status.[11] Payments under this scheme are disregarded as income or capital for all the means-tested benefits, since 1 January 2022.[12] For ealier periods, DWP guidance states that payments under this scheme, or the previous Windrush Exceptional Payments scheme, should be disregarded for all means-tested benefits 'on an extra-statutory basis'.[13] The council tax reduction regulations also disregard these payments as income and capital. Also, interest on payments made under the scheme are ignored as income for tax credits for 52 weeks.[14]

• There are close links between the benefit authorities and the Home Office. Making a claim for benefit could alert the immigration authorities to your presence and status in the UK. Get specialist immigration advice before claiming benefits if you are unsure about your immigration status.

Your leave has a 'no recourse to public funds' condition

You are a 'person subject to immigration control' if you have leave to enter or remain in the UK that is subject to the condition that you do not have recourse to 'public funds'.[15]

Most people admitted to the UK with time-limited leave, such as spouses/civil partners, students or visitors, are given limited leave to stay which is subject to the condition they do not have recourse to public funds.

Public funds

'**Public funds**' are defined in the Immigration Rules as:[16]

– attendance allowance;
– CA;
– child benefit;
– child tax credit;
– council tax benefit (now abolished);
– council tax reduction;
– disability living allowance;
– income-related employment and support allowance;
– homelessness assistance and housing provided under specific provisions;
– housing benefit (HB);
– income support;
– income-based jobseeker's allowance;
– local welfare assistance (except the Discretionary Assistance Fund for Wales);
– pension credit;
– PIP;
– severe disablement allowance;

11

Part 11: Immigration and residence rules for benefits and tax credits
Chapter 68: Coming from abroad: immigration status
1. Immigration status

- social fund payments;
- universal credit;
- working tax credit.

Only the benefits, tax credits and assistance listed in the Immigration Rules are public funds. Therefore, if you get any other benefit or other assistance, you are not in breach of the no recourse to public funds condition.

If you have recourse to public funds when your leave prohibits you from doing so, you have breached a condition of your leave. This may affect your right to remain in the UK: you could be liable to be deported, have further leave refused and/or be prosecuted for committing a criminal offence.[17]

If your leave is subject to a no recourse to public funds condition, you are defined as a 'person subject to immigration control' and (unless you are within an exempt group – see pp1530–33) you are not entitled to the benefits and tax credits defined as public funds. However, if you *are* within an exempt group, you can claim and receive that public fund benefit (other than council tax reduction), as you are not regarded as having recourse to public funds under the Immigration Rules.[18]

You are regarded as having recourse to public funds if someone else's benefit is increased because of your presence – eg, if the amount of your partner's HB is greater because you are included in her/his claim. If this happens, you have breached the condition not to have recourse to public funds. Obtain specialist immigration advice before making a claim.

Your leave was given as a result of a maintenance undertaking

If your leave to enter or remain was given as a result of a maintenance undertaking, you are a 'person subject to immigration control'.[19] For example, if an elderly relative is seeking to join family in the UK, it is usual to require a maintenance undertaking.

Maintenance undertaking

A '**maintenance undertaking**' means a written undertaking given by another person under the Immigration Rules to be responsible for your maintenance and accommodation.[20] There are specific Home Office forms on which an undertaking can be given. However, no official form need be used, provided the undertaking is sufficiently formal and definite.[21] The document must contain a promise or agreement that the other person will maintain and accommodate you in the future. If it merely contains a statement about her/his present abilities and intentions, it does not amount to an undertaking.[22]

Your leave is considered to be 'as a result of a maintenance undertaking' if this was a factor in granting it. It does not need to have been the only, or even a major, factor.[23] However, if the maintenance undertaking was not relevant to your being granted leave, its existence does not make you a person subject to immigration control. If you are in doubt about whether you have leave given as a result of an undertaking, get specialist immigration advice.

You are appealing a refusal to vary your previous leave

If you have leave solely because you have appealed against a decision to refuse an application to vary the leave you previously had, you are a 'person subject to immigration control'.[24]

Example

Sayf is an Iraqi national who has been granted two and a half years' discretionary leave. Just before this expires, he applies for a further period of discretionary leave, and his original leave is extended while that application is pending. His application is refused and he immediately appeals against this decision. His previous discretionary leave is extended further while the appeal is pending, but he is now a 'person subject to immigration control'.

Note: this is currently unlikely to apply if you have pre-settled status because this is granted for five years and, as this type of leave only began to be granted in August 2018, the earliest it could expire for anyone is in August 2023. Furthermore, if you have leave solely because you requested an appeal against, or administrative review of, a refusal of leave under the EUSS, it is arguable that this does not bring you within the definition of 'person subject to immigration control'.[25] Get specialist advice.

2. Benefits and tax credits affected by immigration status

The general rule is that if you are defined as a 'person subject to immigration control' (see p1524), you are excluded from council tax reduction[26] and the following benefits and tax credits:[27]

- adult disability payment (ADP – in Scotland);[28]
- attendance allowance (AA);
- carer's allowance (CA);
- child benefit;
- child disability payment (CDP – in Scotland);[29]
- child tax credit (CTC);

Part 11: Immigration and residence rules for benefits and tax credits
Chapter 68: Coming from abroad: immigration status
2. Benefits and tax credits affected by immigration status

- disability living allowance (DLA);
- funeral support payment (in Scotland);[30]
- income-related employment and support allowance (ESA);
- ESA in youth;[31]
- housing benefit (HB);
- incapacity benefit (IB) for incapacity in youth;[32]
- income support (IS);
- income-based jobseeker's allowance (JSA);
- pension credit (PC);
- personal independence payment (PIP);
- severe disablement allowance (SDA);
- social fund payments;
- universal credit (UC);
- working tax credit (WTC).

However, there are limited exceptions when some people subject to immigration control can claim means-tested benefits (see below), some can claim disability, carers' and child benefits (see p1531) and some can claim tax credits (see p1533).

A person subject to immigration control is only excluded from the above benefits and tax credits and can therefore claim any other benefit. For example, if you have paid sufficient national insurance (NI) contributions, you can claim any of the contributory benefits – eg, retirement pensions, contribution-based JSA and contributory ESA. You can also claim benefits that depend on employment – eg, maternity allowance (MA), industrial injuries benefits or statutory payments.

Exempt groups

Means-tested benefits

If you are in any of the exempt groups below, being a 'person subject to immigration control' does not exclude you from entitlement to the following means-tested benefits:[33]

- UC;
- IS;
- income-based JSA;
- income-related ESA;
- PC;
- HB.

You are not excluded if:

- (except UC from 1 January 2021, unless your claim began before that date[34]) you are a national of North Macedonia, Turkey[35] or any of the European Economic Area (EEA) countries (except Bulgaria, Liechtenstein, Lithuania, Romania or Slovenia) and you are lawfully present – eg, during a period in which you have leave to enter or remain in the UK (you are very unlikely to be assisted by this exemption if you are an asylum seeker because although you are lawfully present, you still need a right to reside for each of these benefits – see p1557[36]). The countries listed have each ratified either the European Convention on Social and Medical Assistance or the European Social Charter (1961). **Note:** if you receive a means-tested benefit because this exempt group applies to you, the Home Office does not regard you as having recourse to public funds.[37] If this exempt group applies, you are also not excluded from council tax reduction, although receiving it *does* count as having recourse to public funds and so breaches any no recourse to public funds condition attached to your leave;[38]

- you have leave to enter or remain given as a result of a maintenance undertaking and have been resident in the UK for at least five years (beginning on either the date you entered the UK or when the maintenance undertaking was signed, whichever is later). If there are gaps in your residence as a result of your going to live for a period in another country, the periods of residence in the UK can be added together to make the five years.[39] However, depending on your circumstances, you may not have ceased to be resident during the short periods of absence, and each absence must be considered individually (see p1549);[40]

- you have leave to enter or remain given as a result of a maintenance undertaking and the person (or, if more than one, all the people) who gave the undertaking has died.

Social fund and other payments

If you are defined as a 'person subject to immigration control', this does not exclude you from entitlement to:

- social fund payments *if* you are in any of the exempt categories for means-tested (see above) or disability, carers' and child benefits (see below);[41] *or*
- funeral support payments *if* you are in any of the exempt categories for disability, carers' and child benefits (see below);[42] *or*
- Best Start grants.

However, you must meet the other conditions of entitlement, including (except for Best Start grants if you are under 20, and winter fuel payments) being in receipt of a qualifying benefit.

Disability, carers' and child benefits

If you are in any of the exempt groups below, being a person subject to immigration control does not exclude you from getting the following non-means-tested, non-contributory benefits:[43]

- ADP;
- AA;
- CA;

Part 11: Immigration and residence rules for benefits and tax credits
Chapter 68: Coming from abroad: immigration status
2. Benefits and tax credits affected by immigration status

- child benefit;
- CDP;
- DLA;
- ESA in youth;
- funeral support payment in Scotland;
- IB for incapacity in youth;
- PIP;
- SDA.

You are not excluded if:
- you have leave to enter or remain given as a result of a maintenance undertaking;
- you are a national of Albania (for child benefit only[44]), Morocco, San Marino, Tunisia or Turkey (or Algeria if you made you claim before 1 January 2021,[45] and potentially in the future as engagement continues to reach a new agreement with Algeria[46]) and either you are currently lawfully working (see below) in Great Britain, or you have ceased to be lawfully working in Great Britain for a reason such as pregnancy, childcare, illness or accident, or because you have reached retirement age;[47]
- you are living with a member of your family (see p1652) who is covered by the above bullet point;
- in very limited circumstances, covered in CPAG's *Benefits for Migrants Handbook,* you are a member of an EEA national's family;[48]
- for DLA, PIP, AA and child benefit only, you are covered by a reciprocal agreement. At the time of writing, only Denmark and Germany (and, for claims made before 1 January 2021 only, Norway) had agreements in relation to AA and DLA and no agreements had been amended to include PIP. For child benefit, check whether you are covered by the agreements with Austria, Barbados, Belgium, Canada, Denmark, Finland, France, Germany, Israel, Mauritius, New Zealand, Norway (only for claims made before 1 January 2021), Portugal, Spain and Sweden or former the Yugoslavia (Bosnia-Herzegovina, Croatia, Kosovo, North Macedonia, Montenegro, Serbia and Slovenia[49]). See p1546 for more information about reciprocal agreements.

Lawfully working

You should be accepted as **'lawfully working'** if you have been insured (by paying, or being credited with, NI contributions),[50] and any work you have done has not breached any conditions attached to your leave. If you are an asylum seeker, you should be accepted as lawfully working if you have permission to work from the Home Office.

Tax credits

If you are a 'person subject to immigration control', this does not exclude you from getting CTC or WTC in the following circumstances.[51]

- You have leave to enter or remain given as a result of a maintenance undertaking and you have been resident in the UK for at least five years (beginning on either the date you entered the UK or when the maintenance undertaking was signed, whichever is later).
- You have leave to enter or remain given as a result of a maintenance undertaking and the person (or, if more than one, all the people) who gave the undertaking has died.
- For CTC only, you are a national of Albania,[52] Morocco, San Marino, Tunisia or Turkey (or Algeria if you made you claim before 1 January 2021), and either you are lawfully working in the UK, or you have ceased lawfully working for a reason such as pregnancy, childcare, illness or accident, or because you have reached retirement age.[53]
- For WTC only, you are a national of an EEA state (except Bulgaria, Liechtenstein, Lithuania, Romania or Slovenia), or North Macedonia or Turkey and you are lawfully present in the UK – eg, during a period in which you have leave to enter or remain in the UK.

If you are a person subject to immigration control, but your partner is not (or s/he comes into one of the above groups), you can get tax credits on the basis of a joint claim (see p1536).

3. **Partners and children**

Some benefits and tax credits have special rules that apply if any partner or child who lives with you is subject to immigration control. These rules vary, so check the rules for the relevant benefit or tax credit.

11

Means-tested benefits

Universal credit

If you live with your partner and claim universal credit (UC), you are generally required to make a joint claim. If your partner is a 'person subject to immigration control' and is not in one of the exempt groups who can get UC (see p1530), your joint claim is treated as a claim for UC as a single person and:[54]

- your award is based on the maximum amount for a single person;[55] *and*
- your partner does not have to accept a claimant commitment or comply with any work-related requirements because s/he is not a claimant;[56] *and*
- your partner's income and capital are taken into account (see p35);[57] *and*

Part 11: Immigration and residence rules for benefits and tax credits
Chapter 68: Coming from abroad: immigration status
3. Partners and children

- your partner is not classed as a 'non-dependant' and therefore no 'housing costs contribution' (see p102) is made from your UC;[58] *and*
- if you are under 35, your partner does not prevent your rent being restricted to the one-bedroom shared accommodation rate (see p105);[59] *and*
- if you have a child, your partner does not affect your being her/his 'responsible carer' (see p1040) – eg, to determine your work-related requirements;[60] *and*
- the couple rate of the earnings threshold applies for determining when no work-related requirements apply to you (see p1043), and in calculating any self-employed 'minimum income floor' that may apply if you are self-employed (note the 'minimum income floor' does not apply to your partner if s/he is self-employed) (see p122).[61]

Other than in the two potential exceptions below, the claims described above do not include additional amounts for your partner. Therefore, if her/his leave is subject to a 'no recourse to public funds' condition, your claim for UC does not breach this condition because it does not result in your receiving increased public funds as a result of her/his presence (see p1527). If your UC claim includes a housing costs element, other than in the potential exception below, this will not be higher as a result of your partner's presence, as s/he is not a claimant and is therefore ignored in the housing costs calculation.[62]

The first potential exception arises if you and your partner are joint tenants, as then the amount of rent used to calculate your housing costs element includes your partner's share (see p103 and p109). If this results in an additional amount of UC housing costs element being paid, this will breach any no recourse to public funds condition attached to your partner's leave. The only scenario that CPAG is aware of in which this can arise is if you and your partner are joint tenants with one or more other joint tenants. The second potential exception is if you are entitled to the childcare element due to both you and your partner working (or being treated as working), and the amount of the childcare element is greater due to the amount of work done by your partner *and* not fully offset by the amount of earned income from your partner's work taken into account.[63] Obtain specialist immigration advice before claiming UC including a housing costs or childcare element if you have concerns about breaching a no recourse to public funds condition.

Note: if you have reached pension age and your partner is under pension age, but is not entitled to UC because s/he is a 'person subject to immigration control', your claim is *not* treated as a single claim for UC. Instead, you must claim pension credit (PC) and housing benefit (HB) and you are treated as a single person for each of these claims (for HB, see p174).[64]

If you are entitled to UC, any child you are responsible for is included in your claim, regardless of the child's immigration status. However, if the child's leave is subject to a no recourse to public funds condition, receiving UC amounts for her/

him will breach that condition and could affect her/his right to remain in the UK (see p1527). Obtain specialist immigration advice before making a claim.

Income support, income-based jobseeker's allowance and income-related employment and support allowance

If your partner is a 'person subject to immigration control' (see p1524), s/he is included in your claim for income support (IS), income-based jobseeker's allowance (JSA), including if you are a joint-claim couple, or income-related employment and support allowance (ESA). However, you are only paid a personal allowance at the single person's rate, unless s/he is in one of the exempt groups of people who can get the means-tested benefits listed on p1530, in which case, you are paid at the couple rate.[65]

In all cases, your partner is still treated as part of your household and part of your claim. Therefore, her/his work, income and capital can all affect your benefit entitlement. Her/his presence means you cannot be entitled to IS as a lone parent (see p233) and may mean you are not entitled to a severe disability premium (see p330).

Premiums are payable if either you or your partner satisfy the qualifying conditions (see p323) and should be paid at the couple rate.

Note: if your partner's leave to enter or remain in the UK is subject to a no recourse to public funds condition, receiving an additional (or a couple rate of a) premium for her/him can be regarded as having additional recourse to public funds and affect her/his right to remain in the UK (see p1527). Obtain specialist immigration advice before claiming the benefit that would result in the premium being paid.

Pension credit

If your partner is a 'person subject to immigration control' (whether or not s/he is in one of the exempt groups listed on p1530), s/he is treated as not being part of your household.[66] This means that you are paid as a single person and your partner's income and capital do not affect your claim. Your partner's presence may mean you cannot get the additional amount for severe disability as the DWP treats her/him as 'normally residing with' you for this purpose, unless an exemption applies (see p330).[67]

If you are entitled to PC, any child you are responsible for is included in your claim, regardless of the child's immigration status. However, if the child's leave is subject to a no recourse to public funds condition, receipt of PC amounts for her/him will breach that condition and can affect her/his right to remain in the UK (see p1527). Obtain specialist immigration advice before making a claim.

Housing benefit

If your partner and/or child for whom you are responsible is a 'person subject to immigration control', this does not affect the amount you are paid. Unless the

Part 11: Immigration and residence rules for benefits and tax credits
Chapter 68: Coming from abroad: immigration status
3. Partners and children

exception below applies, your partner is included in your claim and your applicable amount includes the couple rate of the personal allowance and any premiums to which either of you are entitled.

Similarly, your child is included in your claim and your applicable amount includes a personal allowance for each child (subject to the 'two-child limit' – see p322), together with any premiums for which s/he qualifies.

Therefore, if your partner's and/or child's leave is subject to a no recourse to public funds condition, a claim for HB can result in additional public funds being paid as a result of her/his presence. This can affect her/his right to remain in the UK (see p1527). Obtain specialist immigration advice before making a claim.

The only **exception** is if you have reached pension age and your partner is under pension age, but you cannot make a joint claim for UC because s/he is a 'person subject to immigration control', and not covered by an exempt group (see p1533). You are treated as single for your HB (and PC) claim (see p174).[68]

Non-means-tested benefits

Non-means-tested benefits include both contributory benefits (based on your national insurance (NI) contribution record) and non-contributory benefits.

Your immigration status, and that of your partner or child, does not affect your entitlement to either contributory benefits (eg, contributory ESA) or benefits based on current or past employment – eg, maternity allowance and statutory payments.

Your entitlement to non-contributory benefits is affected by your immigration status if you are the claimant, but is not affected by the immigration status of any partner or child included in your claim. Therefore, for **child benefit**, if you are not a 'person subject to immigration control', or you are but you are in one of the exempt groups (see p1531), you can claim for any child for whom you are responsible, regardless of the child's immigration status. However, if the child's leave is subject to a no recourse to public funds condition, receiving child benefit for her/him may be regarded as recourse and could affect her/his right to remain in the UK. Obtain specialist immigration advice before making a claim.

Similarly, if your child is not a person subject to immigration control, or s/he is but is in one of the exempt groups on p1531, s/he can claim **disability living allowance**, or, in Scotland, **child disability payment**, even if *you* are a person subject to immigration control.

Tax credits

If your partner is a 'person subject to immigration control' and you are not (or you are, but you are in one of the exempt groups on p1533), your joint claim for tax credits (see p1459) is treated as if your partner were *not* subject to immigration control.[69] However, unless you or your partner are responsible for a child, or your partner is a national of an EEA country (except Bulgaria, Liechtenstein, Lithuania,

Romania or Slovenia), North Macedonia or Turkey and lawfully present in the UK, your working tax credit (WTC) does not include the couple element.[70]

There are no immigration status conditions for children, so your child tax credit (CTC) and/or WTC includes amounts for any child for whom you are responsible (subject to the 'two-child limit' – see p1415).

If your partner's leave is subject to the condition that s/he does not have recourse to public funds, s/he is *not* regarded as having recourse by receiving tax credits on the basis of a joint claim as described above. Therefore, the claim does not breach that condition. If such a joint claim includes a child whose leave is subject to the condition that s/he does not have recourse to public funds, any tax credits awarded in respect of that child are also not regarded as recourse to public funds.[71]

If your claim for CTC or WTC is *not* a joint claim as described above (ie, one partner is a person subject to immigration control) and it includes an amount for a child whose leave is subject to a no recourse to public funds condition, this may be regarded as recourse and could affect her/his right to remain in the UK. Obtain specialist immigration advice if this could apply.

4. **National insurance numbers and contributions**

Exemption from the national insurance number requirement

In general, the national insurance (NI) number requirement (see p1137) applies, regardless of immigration status, to you and any partner included in your claim (even if you are not going to get any extra benefit for her/him because s/he is a 'person subject to immigration control' – see p1533).

However, if you are the benefit claimant, your partner does not have to satisfy the NI number requirement if:[72]

- s/he is a 'person subject to immigration control' because s/he requires leave to enter or remain in the UK, but does not have it (see p1526); *and*
- s/he has not previously been given an NI number.

You may still be asked for information about an NI number application for your partner, even though s/he is exempt, but a refusal to allocate an NI number does not prevent you from being entitled to benefits or tax credits, or council tax reduction.

Note: this exemption is not relevant to universal credit (UC) because you do not need an NI number to *make* a claim for UC and the DWP only requests it later. If your partner is a 'person subject to immigration control', your joint claim is

Part 11: Immigration and residence rules for benefits and tax credits
Chapter 68: Coming from abroad: immigration status
5. Asylum seekers and refugees

treated as a claim for UC by you as a single person (see p1533) and therefore your partner is not a claimant and does not need an NI number.[73]

Tax credits

The NI number requirement for tax credits is similar to the requirement for benefits (and includes the above exemption for partners who require leave but do not have it).[74]

In addition, the NI number requirement does not apply if the Tax Credit Office is satisfied that you (and/or your partner if it is a joint claim) have a 'reasonable excuse' for not complying with the requirement – eg, if you are unable to prove your identity because the Home Office has all your documents and you can prove this – eg, with a letter from your solicitor.[75]

If your claim was refused because you have not satisfied the NI number requirement, you can appeal on the grounds that either your partner is exempt or you had a 'reasonable excuse'.[76] You must apply for a mandatory reconsideration before you can appeal.

National insurance contributions

If you have worked and paid contributions in a European Economic Area country and you are covered by the European Union co-ordination rules (see p1647), these can be taken into account when working out your entitlement to UK contributory benefits (under the 'aggregation principle' – see p1659). Similar rules apply if you have worked and paid contributions in a country with which the UK has a reciprocal agreement (see p1546).[77] You may also be able to make up a shortfall in your contribution record by making voluntary contributions (see p950). Get advice to check whether this is worth doing. Being a 'person subject to immigration control' (see p1529) does not exclude you from any of the contributory benefits.

11 | 5. **Asylum seekers and refugees**

Asylum seekers

You are referred to as an 'asylum seeker' while you are waiting for a Home Office decision on an application for refugee status. If you are seeking asylum in the UK, you generally come within the definition of a 'person subject to immigration control' as someone who requires leave, but does not have it (see p1526). You are therefore excluded from the social security benefits listed on p1529 unless you are in one of the exempt groups on pp1530–33.

If benefit can be paid for you because, for example, you are in an exempt group or because your partner can include you in her/his claim, this does not affect your asylum application. You can receive any benefit defined as a 'public fund' (see p1527) because asylum seekers are *not* subject to a 'no recourse to public funds' condition.

If you are excluded from social security benefits because you are a 'person subject to immigration control', you may be entitled to alternative forms of state support. If you are destitute, you may be eligible for asylum support from the Home Office. **Note:** asylum support is not taken into account as income for universal credit (UC). It is only disregarded for income support (IS), income-based jobseeker's allowance (JSA) and income-related employment and support allowance (ESA) if it is 'income in kind'. If your partner claims housing benefit (HB), asylum support is taken into account as income unless your partner is 'passported' onto maximum HB due to receiving UC, IS, income-based JSA, income-related ESA or pension credit.[78]

However, any benefit your partner receives is taken into account as income when calculating your asylum support, unless you can show it would not reasonably be available to you – eg, if s/he receives a disability benefit.

If you are not eligible for asylum support or benefits, you may be able to get assistance from your local authority under one or more of the community care provisions, particularly if you have additional needs as a result of your age, sickness or disability. If you have children, or you are a child, you may be eligible for support under the Children Act 1989 or Children (Scotland) Act 1995. Get independent legal advice about what you are entitled to, if possible before you apply, and always if you are refused.

For more about asylum support, see CPAG's *Benefits for Migrants Handbook*.

Refugee and other leave granted after an asylum application

If, following your asylum application, you are granted leave that is not subject to a condition that you do not have recourse to public funds (eg, refugee leave or humanitarian protection), you are no longer a 'person subject to immigration control'. During this period of leave, you can claim all benefits, provided you meet the usual rules of entitlement. If you are granted leave that *is* subject to a condition that you do not have recourse to public funds, you *are* defined as a 'person subject to immigration control' and you are excluded from the benefits listed on p1529, unless you are in an exempt group (see pp1530–33).

If you are granted refugee leave or humanitarian protection, you can be joined by certain family members under family reunion provisions. A family member who is given leave to enter or remain in the UK under these provisions is not a 'person subject to immigration control' during her/his period of leave and can claim all benefits, provided s/he meets the usual rules of entitlement. In Scotland, you can also claim a Scottish Welfare Fund family reunion crisis grant from your local authority if your family members have been granted permission to join you in this way. Contact the British Red Cross if you want help to apply for this grant.

Part 11: Immigration and residence rules for benefits and tax credits
Chapter 68: Coming from abroad: immigration status
5. Asylum seekers and refugees

If you (or the family member you have joined) have refugee leave or humanitarian protection, or you have come from Afghanistan and been granted leave under one of the relocation or resettlement schemes, you do not need to satisfy the past presence test for the disability and carers' benefits (see p1602).

If you are granted refugee leave, humanitarian protection or discretionary leave, or you have come from Afghanistan and been granted leave under a specified relocation or resettlement scheme, you are exempt from the habitual residence test (see p1553) and exempt from the requirement to have lived in the UK for three months for child benefit and child tax credit (see p1548).

If you are granted refugee leave or humanitarian protection, you are *not* excluded from a Sure Start maternity grant (or, in Scotland, you should not get a lower Best Start grant) on the basis that you already have a child under 16 who was a member of your family before you came to the UK (see p782 and p1700).[79]

Backdating child benefit, guardian's allowance and tax credits

If you have been granted refugee leave, or leave as an unaccompanied child relocated from Europe (known as 'section 67 leave'), you can claim child benefit, guardian's allowance and, in limited circumstances, tax credits and have them backdated to the date of your asylum application.[80] If you made more than one asylum application, these benefits can be backdated to the date of the first, provided the basis of the applications remained the same. If refugee leave was only granted as a result of later events, these benefits will only be backdated to the date of the asylum application made since they occurred.[81]

You must claim backdated child benefit and guardian's allowance within three months, and tax credits within one month, of receiving the Home Office letter granting you leave.[82] If the Home Office letter is sent to a solicitor acting for you, the three- or one-month period starts from the date your solicitor receives the letter.[83]

You can only claim backdated tax credits if you applied for asylum on or before 31 January 2019 (the final day that a claim for tax credits could be made before UC was introduced). To ensure you claim within the one-month deadline, claim by telephone and provide all information required on the claim form. For a copy of the claim form, the steps to follow to make your claim, and details of current legal challenges, see cpag.org.uk/welfare-rights/resources/test-case/retrospective-child-tax-credits-newly-recognised-refugees.

If you have received any asylum support for essential living needs this reduces your tax credits over that period and often completely cancels out entitlement.[84] Child benefit and guardian's allowance are not reduced by any asylum support you may have received.

Note: there is no provision to pay backdated UC.

Integration loans

If you (or someone upon whom you are dependent) are granted refugee leave or humanitarian protection and you are aged 18 or over, you may be eligible for an integration loan.[85] This is a discretionary loan of at least £100, paid for expenses associated with your integration into UK society, including for employment, education and housing. Applications are made online[86] and are decided by the Home Office. For more information, see CPAG's *Benefits for Migrants Handbook*.

Before applying for, or in addition to, an integration loan, you may want to consider accessing help from your local welfare assistance scheme (see p846) or applying for other financial help (see p859).

Notes

1. Immigration status

1 s115(9) IAA 1999
2 Reg 43 and Sch 3 para 1 I(EEA) Regs; paras C1050 and C2012 ADM; Vol 2 Ch 7 Part 1, para 070838 DMG
3 *Zambrano*, C-34/09 [2011]; *Dereci and Others*, C-256/11 [2011]; reg 16(1) and (5) I(EEA) Regs
4 See, for example, *DM v SSWP (PIP)* [2019] UKUT 26 (AAC)
5 Regs 3(4)-(6), 4(2) and (5)-(8) and 12(1)(i) CR(ADTP) Regs; DMG Memos 26/20 paras 36,37 and 41, 6/21 and 7/21; ADM Memos 30/20 paras 36, 37 and 41, 7/21 and 8/21
6 Regs 3(4)-(6), 4(2) and (5)-(8) CR(ADTP) Regs; Art 18(3) WA 2019; Art 17(3) UK-EFTA; Art 16(3) UK-Swiss Agreement
7 HB Circular A10/2021, paras 11 and 12; DMG Memo 10/21, para 8; ADM Memo 19/21, para 8
8 s115(9)(a) IAA 1999
9 Regs 1(2)(b) and (4), 5 and 6 CR(FW) Regs; DMG Memo 29/20, paras 45 and 49; ADM Memo 33/20, paras 45 and 49
10 s3C IA 1971; Vol 2 para 073202 DMG; paras C1679 and C2017 ADM
11 gov.uk/guidance/windrush-compensation-scheme
12 The Social Security (Income and Capital Disregards) (Amendment) Regulations 2021 No 1405; DMG Memo 15/21; ADM Memo 21/21
13 HB Adjudication Circular A8/2019, paras 13-14
14 Regs 10(2)(f) and 19 (table 6, para 23) TC(DCI) Regs
15 s115(9)(b) IAA 1999
16 para 6.2, notes under 'public funds' definition, IR
17 s24(1)(b)(ii) IA 1971
18 para 6.2, notes under 'public funds' definition, IR
19 s115(9)(c) IAA 1999
20 s115(10) IAA 1999
21 *R (Begum) v Social Security Commissioner* [2003] EWHC 3380 (Admin)
22 *Ahmed v SSWP* [2005] EWCA Civ 535
23 CIS/3508/2001; see also *SJ v SSWP (SPC)* [2015] UKUT 505 (AAC), reported as [2016] AACR 17

Part 11: Immigration and residence rules for benefits and tax credits
Chapter 68: Coming from abroad: immigration status
Notes

24 s115(9)(d) IAA 1999 referred to Sch 4
    para 17 IAA 1999, which was repealed
    by Sch 9 para 1 NIAA 2002. It has been
    held that the reference should be read as
    if to s3C(1) and (2)(b) and (c) IA 1971
    (as s17(2) Interpretation Act 1978
    applies) – *EE v City of Cardiff (HB)* [2018]
    UKUT 418 (AAC).

25 s3C(2)(ca) and (cb) IA 1971 was only
    inserted from 31 January 2020, and
    s3C(2)(d) IA 1971 from 20 October
    2014, so the reasoning of *EE v City of
    Cardiff (HB)* [2018] UKUT 418 (AAC)
    does not apply.

2. Benefits and tax credits affected by immigration status

26 Reg 13 CTRS(PR)E Regs; reg 19
    CTR(SPC)S Regs; reg 19 CTR(S) Regs;
    reg 29 CTRSPR(W) Regs; Sch para 20
    CTRS(DS)W Regs
27 s115 IAA 1999; s42 TCA 2002; reg 3
    TC(Imm) Regs
28 Reg 15(1)(c) DAWAP(S) Regs
29 Reg 5(1)(c) DACYP(S) Regs
30 Reg 9(5) FEA(S) Regs
31 Reg 11(1)(b) ESA Regs; reg 12(1)(b) ESA
    Regs 2013
32 Reg 16(1)(b) SS(IB) Regs
33 Reg 2(1) and Part 1 of Sch SS(IA)CA
    Regs; para C1060 ADM; Vol 2, para
    070835 DMG; ADM Memo,29/20,
    paras 36-41; DMG Memo 25/20, paras
    41-46
34 Regs 1(2) and 2(2)(a) SSCBCTC(A) Regs
35 Confirmed in *OD v SSWP (JSA)* [2015]
    UKUT 438 (AAC)
36 *Szoma v SSWP* [2005] UKHL 64,
    reported as R(IS) 2/06; *Yesiloz v LB
    Camden and Another* [2009] EWCA Civ
    415. These decisions about temporary
    admission are likely to apply equally to
    immigration bail.
37 para 6.2, notes under 'public funds'
    definition, IR
38 Reg 13(1A) CTRS(PR)E Regs; reg 19(2)
    CTR(S) Regs; reg 19(2) CTR(SPC)S Regs;
    reg 29(2) CTRSPR(W) Regs; Sch para
    20(2) CTRS(DS)W Regs; para 6A IR. CTR
    Regs are not included in the regulations
    referred to in para 6B IR, which
    disregards claims made as a result of
    exemptions.
39 R(IS) 2/02
40 CPC/1005/2005
41 Reg 2 SS(IA)CA Regs
42 Reg 9(5) FEA(S) Regs

43 **All** Reg 2(2), (3) and (4)(b) and Sch Part
    II SS(IA)CA Regs; Vol 2, paras 070836-37
    DMG; para 10140 CBTM; ADM Memo
    29/20, paras 35 and 41(2) and (3);
    DMG Memo 25/20, paras 40 and 46(2)
    and (3)
    ADP Reg 15(5) DAWAP(S) Regs
    AA Reg 2(1)(a)(ib) SS(AA) Regs
    CA Reg 9(1)(ia) SS(ICA) Regs
    CDP Reg 5(5A) DACYP(S) Regs
    DLA Reg 2(1)(a)(ib) SS(DLA) Regs
    ESA Reg 11(1)(b) and (3) ESA Regs; reg
    12(1)(b) and (3) ESA Regs 2013
    FSP Reg 9(5) FEA(S) Regs
    IB Reg 16(1)(b) and (5) SS(IB) Regs
    PIP Reg 16(d)(ii) SS(PIP) Regs
    SDA Reg 3(a)(ib) SS(SDA) Regs
    YCG Reg 7(7) CA(YCG)(S) Regs
44 para 10140 CBTM
45 Reg 1(3) SSCBCTC(A) Regs
46 para 7.2 Explanatory Memo to
    SSCBCTC(A) Regs; gov.uk/guidance/uk-
    trade-agreements-with-non-eu-
    countries
47 *Krid v Caisse Nationale d'Assurance
    Vieillesse des Travailleurs Salariés
    (CNAVTS)*, C-103/94 [1995], para 26
48 *JFP v DSD (DLA)* [2012] NICom 267,
    which declined to follow the more
    restrictive approach of CDLA/708/2007.
    However, see also *MS v SSWP (DLA)*
    [2016] UKUT 42 (AAC). See also para
    10140 CBTM.
49 The Family Allowances, National
    Insurance and Industrial Injuries
    (Yugoslavia) Order 1958 No.1263
50 *Sürül v Bundesanstalt für Arbeit*, C-262/
    96 [1999]
51 Reg 3 TC(Imm) Regs; TCTM 02105,
    02107 (North Macedonia instead of
    Croatia should be listed) and 02108
52 TCTM para 02108
53 *Krid v Caisse Nationale d'Assurance
    Vieillesse des Travailleurs Salariés
    (CNAVTS)*, C-103/94 [1995], para 26

3. Partners and children

54 ss3 and 4(1)(c) and (2) WRA 2012; reg
    3(3) UC Regs; reg 9(1)
    UC,PIP,JSA&ESA(C&P) Regs
55 Regs 3(3) and 36(3) UC Regs
56 ss3 and 4(1)(e) WRA 2012; reg 3(3) UC
    Regs; reg 9(1) UC,PIP,JSA&ESA(C&P)
    Regs
57 Regs 3(3), 18(2) and 22(3) UC Regs
58 Sch 4 para 9(2)(b) UC Regs
59 Sch 4 paras 27 and 28 UC Regs
60 s 19(6) WRA 2012; reg 86 UC Regs

11

. . . .

61 s39 WRA 2012; regs 62(1), (3) and (4) and 90(3) UC Regs; para H4077 ADM
62 S/he must be a claimant to be defined as a joint renter or joint owner-occupier: Schs 4 para 1 and 5 para 1 UC Regs.
63 Regs 32(1)(b) and 34 UC Regs
64 Art 7(1), (2)(a) and (b) and (3)(b) WRA(No.31)O; HB Circular A9/2019, paras 15-17; Vol 13, Ch 77, paras 77035 note 2, 77150-51 and 77160 DMG
65 **IS** Reg 21(3) and Sch 7 para 16A IS Regs
   JSA Reg 85(4) and Sch 5 para 13A JSA Regs
   ESA Reg 69 and Sch 5 para 10 ESA Regs
66 Reg 5(1)(h) SPC Regs
67 Sch 1 paras 1(1)(a)(ii) and 2 SPC Regs; Vol 13, para 78946 DMG
68 Art 7(1),(2)(a) and (b) and (3)(b) WRA(No.31)O; HB Circular A9/2019, paras 15-17
69 Reg 3(2) TC(Imm) Regs
70 Reg 11(4) and (5) WTC(EMR) Regs
71 para 6.2, notes under 'public funds' definition, IR. The TC(Imm) Regs are made under s42 TCA 2002.

80 **CB/GA** Reg 6(2)(d) and (e) CB&GA(Admin) Regs
   TC Regs 3(4)-(10) and 4 TC(Imm) Regs
81 *FK v HMRC* [2009] UKUT 134 (AAC); CBTM10140
82 **CB/GA** Reg 6(2)(d) and (e) CB&GA(Admin) Regs
   TC Reg 3(5) TC(Imm) Regs
83 *Tkachuk v SSWP* [2007] EWCA Civ 515; CIS/3797/2003
84 Reg 3(9) TC(Imm) Regs; CTC/3692/2008
85 s13 Asylum and Immigration (Treatment of Claimants, etc) Act 2004; The Integration Loans for Refugees and Others Regulations 2007 No.1598
86 gov.uk/refugee-integration-loan

4. National insurance numbers and contributions

72 **IS** Reg 2A IS Regs
   JSA Reg 2A JSA Regs
   ESA Reg 2A ESA Regs
   PC Reg 1A SPC Regs
   HB Reg 4(c) HB Regs; reg 4(c) HB(SPC) Regs
   Bereavement benefits and retirement pensions Reg 1A(c) SS(WB&RP) Regs
   TC Reg 5(8) TC(CN) Regs
73 paras A2153-54 ADM
74 Reg 5 TC(CN) Regs
75 Reg 5(6) TC(CN) Regs
76 *ZM and AB v HMRC (TC)* [2013] UKUT 547 (AAC); *CI v HMRC (TC)* [2014] UKUT 158 (AAC); but see also *HMRC v ED (TC)* [2021] UKUT 195 (AAC)
77 Under orders made in powers conferred by s179 SSAA 1992.

5. Asylum seekers and refugees

78 **UC** Reg 66 UC Regs
   IS Sch 9 para 21 IS Regs
   JSA Sch 7 para 22 JSA Regs
   ESA Sch 8 para 22 ESA Regs
   HB Sch 5 para 23 HB Regs
79 *SK and LL v SSWP* [2020] UKUT 145 (AAC); paras L2070 and L2076 ADM

11

Chapter 69

Coming from abroad: residence rules

This chapter covers:
1. Introduction (p1545)
2. The different residence and presence tests (p1547)
3. Habitual residence (p1550)
4. Right to reside (p1557)
5. Who has a right to reside (p1561)
6. Rules for specific benefits and tax credits (p1596)

This chapter describes the residence and presence rules that affect your entitlement while you are in Great Britain. If you go abroad, see Chapter 70.

If you (and your partner and child) are not a British or Irish citizen, before using this chapter check Chapter 68 to see if your (or her/his) immigration status means you (or s/he) are excluded from benefits as a 'person subject to immigration control'.

Key facts
- Different types of residence conditions apply to many benefits and tax credits. These are: **residence**, **ordinary residence**, **right to reside** and **habitual residence**.
- Entitlement to most benefits and tax credits also depends on your being **present** in Great Britain or the UK.
- Some benefits require you to have been present for a certain period of time (known as **past presence**) or to have been **living in** the UK or common travel area for three months prior to your claim.
- The rules on residence and presence vary between different benefits and tax credits. If you satisfy the conditions for one, it does not mean you satisfy the conditions for another.

11

1. Introduction

Many benefits have residence and/or presence conditions. The rules vary between different benefits and tax credits. Whether you meet the conditions can depend on your nationality, your immigration status, how long you have been in Great Britain (or, depending on the benefit, Scotland or the UK), whether you are in a protected group that can have a free movement right of residence, and whether you are covered by the European Union (EU) co-ordination rules.

Although many presence and residence rules refer to Great Britain rather than the UK, there is a reciprocal agreement between Britain and Northern Ireland, which means that, in general, you can satisfy the residence conditions if you move between Great Britain and Northern Ireland.

There are residence conditions for the following benefits and tax credits:

- adult disability payment (in Scotland) (see p1601);
- attendance allowance (see p1601);
- Best Start grant (in Scotland) (see p1608);
- bereavement support payment (see p1598);
- carer's allowance (see p1601);
- child benefit (see p1599);
- child disability payment (in Scotland) (see p1601);
- child tax credit (see p1609);
- child winter heating allowance (in Scotland) (see p1609);
- disability living allowance (see p1601);
- contributory employment and support allowance (ESA) in youth (see p1601);
- income-related ESA (see p1596);
- funeral expenses payment (see p1608);
- funeral support payment (in Scotland) (see p1608);
- guardian's allowance (see p1600);
- housing benefit (see p1596);
- incapacity benefit in youth (see p1601);
- income support (see p1596);
- income-based jobseeker's allowance (JSA) (see p1596);
- pension credit (see p1596);
- personal independence payment (see p1601);
- category D retirement pension (see p1607);
- Scottish child payment (in Scotland) (see p1600);
- severe disablement allowance (see p1601);
- Sure Start maternity grant (see p1608);
- universal credit (see p1596);
- winter fuel payment (see p1609);
- working tax credit (see p1609);
- young carer grant (in Scotland) (see p1601).

11

Part 11: Immigration and residence rules for benefits and tax credits
Chapter 69: Coming from abroad: residence rules
1. Introduction

Council tax reduction also has residence conditions (see p1596).

Contributory benefits, such as contribution-based JSA, contributory ESA and retirement pensions (except category D), as well as the employment-related benefits (maternity allowance and industrial injuries benefits) do not have residence conditions. However, they have presence requirements, which mean that if you go abroad, some benefits cease and others are not increased unless exceptions apply (see Chapter 70). Industrial injuries benefits also have conditions related to your presence in Great Britain at the time you had your accident or contracted your disease. There are no residence or presence requirements for statutory sick pay, statutory maternity pay, statutory adoption pay, statutory paternity pay, statutory shared parental pay and statutory parental bereavement pay paid by your employer.

Which rules apply

The UK benefits and tax credits legislation contains rules about the residence and presence conditions that you must satisfy to be entitled to certain benefits. These rules are set out in this chapter.

If you are a European Economic Area (EEA) national and you began residing in the UK before 31 December 2020, or you are the family member of such an EEA national, you may be in one of the protected groups that can use **free movement residence rights** (see p1566) to satisfy the right to reside requirement for benefits that have it (see p1557).

If you are covered by the **EU co-ordination rules** (see p1647), these can help you to satisfy, or disapply, residence or presence conditions and so be entitled to benefits in the UK (eg, by enabling you to count periods of residence in an EEA state to satisfy the past presence requirements – see p1547), but they can also prevent you from claiming a UK benefit – eg, if the UK is not the 'competent state' to pay that benefit (see p1656).

In general, if you are covered by the EU co-ordination rules, these apply in preference to the provisions of a reciprocal agreement.

Reciprocal agreements exist between the UK and some other countries that can assist in similar ways to the EU co-ordination rules.

Reciprocal agreements with the UK

EEA states: Austria, Belgium, Croatia, Cyprus, Denmark, Finland, France, Germany, Iceland, Ireland, Italy, Luxembourg, Malta, Netherlands, Norway, Portugal, Slovenia, Spain and Sweden. In general, the reciprocal agreement applies if the EU co-ordination rules do not apply.

Non-EEA states: Barbados, Bermuda, Bosnia-Herzegovina, Canada, Chile, Guernsey, Isle of Man, Israel, Jamaica, Jersey, Kosova, North Macedonia, Mauritius, Montenegro, New Zealand, Philippines, Serbia, Switzerland, Turkey and the United States of America.

There are also reciprocal agreements between Great Britain and Northern Ireland.

. . . .

> There are also other agreements with Albania, Morocco, San Marino, Tunisia and Turkey and, until 1 January 2021, with Algeria.

. . . .

The scope of the agreements differs greatly, in terms of the people covered, the benefits covered and the provisions made. It is therefore crucial to check the individual agreement. You can find the agreements at legislation.gov.uk – search under the relevant country and check for subsequent amendments.

---

2. **The different residence and presence tests**

The presence and residence conditions you are required to satisfy vary between the different benefits and tax credits. You may be required to satisfy tests for your:

- presence (see below);
- past presence (see below);
- 'living in' for three months (see p1548);
- residence (see p1549);
- ordinary residence (see p1550);
- habitual residence (see p1550);
- right to reside (see p1557).

Presence

You must usually be present in Great Britain (UK for tax credits, common travel area for child disability payment (CDP) and adult disability payment (ADP)) at the time you make your benefit or tax credit claim, and continue to be present. There are specific rules that allow you to be treated as present during temporary absences (see Chapter 70). If you are covered by the European Union (EU) co-ordination rules (see p1647), these can also mean that you do not need to be present. See the rules for the relevant benefits and tax credits starting on p1596 and p1622.

Being present means being physically present in Great Britain (or the UK or common travel area). For the benefit authority to disqualify you because you were absent, it must show that you were absent throughout that day (see p1621).

Past presence

The following benefits require that, in addition to being present at the time you make your claim, you must also have been present in Great Britain (common travel area for CDP) for a period of time before you become entitled:

- ADP;
- attendance allowance;
- carer's allowance (CA);

Part 11: Immigration and residence rules for benefits and tax credits
Chapter 69: Coming from abroad: residence rules
2. The different residence and presence tests

- CDP;
- disability living allowance;
- personal independence payment.

If you are covered by the EU co-ordination rules (see p1647), these may exempt you from this requirement, or help you to satisfy it more quickly (see p1602).

For details of the past presence test, including exceptions, see p1601.

'Living in' for three months

There is a requirement to have been living for the past three months in:
- the UK, for **child benefit and child tax credit (CTC)** (see below);[1] *or*
- the common travel area (the UK, Ireland, the Channel Islands and the Isle of Man) in order to satisfy the habitual residence test for **income-based jobseeker's allowance (JSA)** (for exceptions, see the 2019/20 edition of this *Handbook* or CPAG's *Benefits for Migrants Handbook*).[2]

The phrase 'living in' is not defined in the regulations and should therefore have its ordinary, everyday meaning. It does not have the same meaning as 'presence' and you may satisfy this condition despite having been temporarily absent.

When deciding whether your absence means you ceased living in the common travel area/UK, the following factors are relevant:[3]
- the reasons for, and the intended and actual length of, your absence;
- the duration and connectedness (including your family ties, education, work, bank account, GP and accommodation) of your previous residence in the common travel area/UK;
- whether you maintained any of these connections, particularly your accommodation, while you were gone and the nature of your accommodation abroad.

See p1622 for more information about temporary absences. For child benefit and CTC only, also check whether you are exempt from this requirement (see below).

If you are covered by the EU co-ordination rules (see p1647) and have moved to the UK from a European Economic Area (EEA) country, you may be able to use certain periods of residence there to satisfy this condition (under the 'aggregation principle' – see p1659).

Child benefit and child tax credit

To be treated as present in Great Britain for child benefit and present in the UK for CTC, you must have been living in the UK for the three months before your first day of entitlement.[4] This requirement does not apply if you:[5]
- are an EEA national and a 'worker' in the UK (see p1576), including if you have retained that status;

- are an EEA national and a 'self-employed person' in the UK (see p1577), including if you have retained that status;
- are an EEA national and would be in either of the above two groups if you had pre-settled status (and were therefore in a protected group – see p1566);
- are a non-EEA national who would be classed as a 'worker' or 'self-employed person' if you were an EEA national with pre-settled status;
- are a family member (see p1583) of someone in any of the three bullets above;
- are a refugee;
- have humanitarian protection;
- (from 15 September 2021, child benefit only) have leave granted by virtue of the Afghan Relocations and Assistance Policy, or the scheme for locally employed staff in Afghanistan, or the Afghan Citizens Resettlement Scheme, or having left Afghanistan in connection with the collapse of the Afghan government on 15 August 2021;
- (from 22 March 2022, child benefit only) were living in Ukraine immediately before 1 January 2022 and you left in connection with the Russian invasion on 24 February 2022;
- were granted leave as an unaccompanied child relocated from Europe (known as 'section 67 leave');
- have leave under the displaced persons provisions;
- have leave granted outside the Immigration Rules with no restriction on accessing public funds;
- have leave to remain in the UK pending an application for indefinite leave to remain as a victim of domestic violence;
- have been deported or otherwise legally removed from another country to the UK;[6]
- are returning to the UK after a period working abroad and, other than for the last three months of your absence, you were paying UK class 1 or class 2 national insurance contributions;
- are returning to the UK after an absence of less than 52 weeks, and either:
  - before departing the UK you were ordinarily resident for three months; *or*
  - you were covered by the rules that treat you as present during a temporary absence for eight or 12 weeks during payment of child benefit or CTC.

Residence

The requirement to be simply 'resident', rather than 'ordinarily resident' or 'habitually resident', is only a condition for a category D retirement pension (see p1607), child winter heating assistance in Scotland (see p1609), carer's allowance supplement in Scotland (see p1601), and universal credit payment options in Scotland (see p1671). However, it is a necessary part of being ordinarily resident (see p1550) or habitually resident (see p1550). Residence is more than mere physical presence in a country and you can be resident without being present – eg, if you are away on holiday. You are usually resident in the country in which

Part 11: Immigration and residence rules for benefits and tax credits
Chapter 69: Coming from abroad: residence rules
3. Habitual residence

you have your home for the time being. You can remain resident during a temporary absence, depending on your circumstances, including the length of your absence, your intentions to return, your accommodation, and where your family and your personal belongings are.[7]

Note: you must be 'living in' England or Wales for a funeral expenses payment (see p1608) and a Sure Start maternity grant (see p1608), a phrase which is not defined (see p1548) and is arguably very similar to 'resident'.

Ordinary residence

The benefits and tax credits that have an ordinary residence requirement are:
- ADP (in Scotland);
- bereavement support payment;
- Best Start grant (in Scotland);
- child benefit;
- CDP (in Scotland);
- CTC;
- employment and support allowance in youth;
- funeral support payment (in Scotland);
- incapacity benefit in youth;
- category D retirement pension;
- Scottish child payment (in Scotland)
- severe disablement allowance;
- social fund funeral expenses payment and winter fuel payment;
- working tax credit;
- young carer grant (in Scotland).

The term 'ordinary residence' is not defined in the legislation, and caselaw has confirmed that the words should have their natural and ordinary meaning.[8] You are ordinarily resident in a country if you are living there for a settled purpose for the time being (whether for a short or long duration).[9] The Upper Tribunal has held that the residence must be lawful.[10] There are some exceptions to the requirement to be ordinarily resident, and if you are covered by the EU co-ordination rules, these may assist you in satisfying it (see pp1596–1611). In practice, claims are rarely refused on the basis of ordinary residence.

3. **Habitual residence**

The requirement to be habitually resident applies to:[11]
- adult disability payment (ADP – in Scotland);
- attendance allowance (AA);
- Best Start grant (in Scotland – only in limited circumstances);

- carer's allowance (CA);
- child disability payment (CDP – in Scotland);
- disability living allowance (DLA);
- housing benefit (HB);
- income support (IS);
- income-based jobseeker's allowance (JSA);
- income-related employment and support allowance (ESA);
- pension credit (PC);
- personal independence payment (PIP);
- universal credit (UC);
- young carer grant (in Scotland).

To be entitled to one of these benefits, you must be habitually resident in the **'common travel area'** (ie, the UK, Ireland, the Channel Islands and the Isle of Man) or, for a Best Start grant or a young carer grant, the UK, the Channel Islands, Isle of Man or the European Economic Area (EEA), or be exempt from the requirement (see p1553).

Note:
- You are also excluded from council tax reduction if you do not satisfy (and are not exempt from) the habitual residence test (see below).[12] See CPAG's *Benefits for Migrants Handbook* for details.
- If you are habitually resident in an EEA country or Switzerland, you may be entitled to a winter fuel payment from the social fund without being ordinarily resident in Great Britain, or child winter heating assistance without being resident in Scotland (see p1609).

The habitual residence test

To satisfy the habitual residence test for **AA, CA, DLA, CDP, PIP and ADP**, you must be 'habitually resident in fact' in the common travel area (however, the area required is different if you are covered by the main EU co-ordination rules – see p1602).

To satisfy the habitual residence test for a **young carer grant**, you must be 'habitually resident in fact' in the UK, Channel Islands, Isle of Man, Switzerland or the EEA.

For a **Best Start grant**, the habitual residence test only applies if you are aged under 20 and neither you nor your partner receive a qualifying benefit. You must be 'habitually resident in fact' in the UK, Channel Islands or Isle of Man, or, if you have leave under the EU Settlement Scheme (EUSS) or a specified free movement residence right, the EEA (see p1608).

To satisfy the habitual residence test for **UC, IS, income-based JSA, income-related ESA, PC and HB**, you must:
- be 'habitually resident in fact' in the common travel area; *and*

Part 11: Immigration and residence rules for benefits and tax credits
Chapter 69: Coming from abroad: residence rules
3. Habitual residence

- have a right to reside in the common travel area (see p1557); *and*
- for income-based JSA only, have been living in the common travel area for the past three months (see p1548).

For details on establishing that you are 'habitually resident in fact', see p1555.

Some groups of people are exempt from the habitual residence test (see p1553). If you are in one of these groups, your residence should not be examined further and, provided you meet the other conditions of entitlement, you are eligible for benefit. Whether or not you are exempt is not always considered, so if you come into one of these groups, make it clear to the DWP or local authority that you are exempt, if you might not otherwise be accepted as habitually resident (eg, if you only recently arrived in the common travel area).

The habitual residence test applies to the benefit claimant.

If you are making a joint claim for UC, both you and your partner must satisfy, or be exempt from, the test. If your partner fails the test, your joint claim is treated as a claim for UC as a single person and your UC award is based on the maximum amount for a single person, but your partner's income and capital are taken into account (see p1597).[13] For other means-tested benefits, if you are the claimant and you satisfy (or are exempt from) the habitual residence test, whether or not your partner satisfies it does not affect your entitlement, unless you are a joint-claim couple for JSA. In this case, if you satisfy the test, but your partner does not, you are entitled to JSA without your partner making a joint claim with you and you are paid as a couple (see p247).

If you fail the habitual residence test

If you fail the habitual residence test, you are not paid any benefit.
- For UC and PC, you are treated as not present in Great Britain.[14]
- For IS, income-based JSA, income-related ESA and HB, you are classed as a 'person from abroad'. This means for IS, income-based JSA and income-related ESA, you have an applicable amount of nil,[15] and for HB, you are treated as not liable for rent.[16]
- For AA, CA, DLA, CDP, PIP and ADP, young carer grant and Best Start grant, you have failed to meet the prescribed residence requirements.[17]

Have you failed the habitual residence test?

1. If you are refused benefit because you have failed the habitual residence test, consider challenging this decision (see Chapters 56, 57 and 80). You may want to contact a local advice agency for help with this.

2. The decision maker must consider whether you satisfied the habitual residence test on your date of claim and on any subsequent date until the date of her/his decision.[18]

3. While challenging the decision, you should make a further claim. If this is refused, also challenge that decision and claim again and so on. This is because when the decision refusing your initial claim is looked at again, the decision maker (or First-tier Tribunal)

cannot take account of things that have changed since the decision was made. So, if the decision maker considers that you were not habitually resident at the time benefit was originally refused, but you are now (eg, because you have been resident for an appreciable period of time), s/he cannot take this into account when looking again at the previous decision in your case. However, s/he can take it into account if sufficient residence had been completed by the date of the decision on your second, or subsequent, claim. Sometimes, the benefit authorities say that you cannot make another claim while your appeal (or request to have the first decision looked at again) is pending. This is wrong and you should, with the help of an adviser if possible, insist on making a further claim.

4. Check whether you are exempt from the habitual residence test (see below).

5. Establish which part of the test the decision maker considers you have failed.

6. If you have claimed a means-tested benefit and the decision maker considers you do not have a right to reside, use the section in this chapter starting on p1561 to check the ways in which you can have a right to reside.

7. If you made a joint claim for UC and the decision maker found that you failed the habitual residence test but your partner satisfied it, your joint claim is treated as a claim by your partner as a single person (see p1597). S/he can continue to be paid UC while you challenge the decision on your entitlement.

8. If you have been receiving IS, HB, child tax credit (CTC) and/or working tax credit (WTC) and you make a claim for UC which the DWP refuses on the basis that you fail the habitual residence test, it has been accepted, particularly for HB, that this does *not* terminate your award and you could continue to receive benefit while challenging the refusal of your UC claim. This is because the regulations state these four benefits only end if you have claimed UC *and* the DWP is satisfied that you meet the first four basic conditions for UC, including the condition to 'be in Great Britain' (see p35).[19] However, a recent Upper Tribunal decision held that this condition should be understood without reference to the regulations which treat you as not 'in Great Britain' if you fail the habitual residence test. Arguably this is wrong and may be reconsidered in a future case. See AskCPAG and CPAG's *Welfare Rights Bulletin* for updates.[20]

9. If you can claim HB, the local authority must make its own decision and not just follow the DWP's decision that you have failed the habitual residence test.

10. Although the onus of proof is on the benefit authorities to establish that you are *not* habitually resident,[21] produce as much evidence as possible to show that you *are*. All decisions should be made on the balance of probabilities.[22]

Who is exempt from the habitual residence test

You are exempt from the habitual residence test for **means-tested benefits** if you:[23]

- are a refugee; *or*
- have humanitarian protection; *or*
- have leave granted outside the Immigration Rules (including discretionary leave or desitutional domestic violence consession leave); *or*

Part 11: Immigration and residence rules for benefits and tax credits
Chapter 69: Coming from abroad: residence rules
3. Habitual residence

- (from 15 September 2021) have leave granted by virtue of the Afghan Relocations and Assistance Policy (ARAP), or the scheme for locally employed staff in Afghanistan (LES Scheme), or the Afghan Citizens Resettlement Scheme, or (other than for Best Start Grant and young carer grant) you left Afghanistan in connection with the collapse of the Afghan government on 15 August 2021;[24] *or*
- have been deported, expelled or legally removed from another country to the UK and you are not a 'person subject to immigration control' (see p1524); *or*
- (from 22 March 2022) were living in Ukraine immediately before 1 January 2022 and you left in connection with the Russian invasion of 24 February 2022, and you have leave, or a right of abode, in the UK (including if you are British); *or*
- are an EEA national and a 'worker' (see p1576), including if you have retained this status; *or*
- are an EEA national and a 'self-employed person' (see p1577), including if you have retained this status; *or*
- are a family member (see p1583), other than an 'extended family member', of someone in either of the above two bullet points; *or*
- are an EEA national and a frontier worker (see p1595); *or*
- have pre-settled status (see p1563) and you are a family member, other than an 'extended family member', of someone in the above bullet point; *or*
- have pre-settled status, and you are a family member, other than an extended family member, of a 'relevant person of Northern Ireland' (see p1558) and s/he *would be* a worker or self-employed person *if* s/he were are an EEA national; *or*
- are an EEA national with a permanent right of residence as a retired or permanently incapacitated worker or self-employed person, or you are a family member of such a person (see p1594); *or*
- (for income-related ESA only) are being transferred from an award of IS which was transitionally protected from the requirement to have a right to reside (see p1560); *or*
- (for HB only) receive IS, income-related ESA, PC or (if you have a right to reside other than one that is excluded for HB – see p1557) income-based JSA.

For a young carer grant, you are exempt from the requirement to be habitually resident if you are in one of the first six bullet points listed above.[25]

For a Best Start grant, you are exempt from the requirement to be habitually resident if you or your partner get a qualifying benefit (see p1697) or you are in one of the first six bullet points listed above.[26]

For AA, CA, DLA, CDP, PIP and ADP, you are only exempt from the requirement to be habitually resident if you:[27]

- (from 15 September 2021) have leave in the UK granted by virtue of ARAP or the LES Scheme or discretionary leave as the dependant of a person with leave under either of these two schemes, or leave granted under the Afghan Citizens

Resettlement Scheme. **Note:** you are also exempt from the past presence requirement (see p1602);[28] *or*

- (from 22 March 2022) you left Ukraine and are in the sixth point bullet above, or (and, for CDP and ADP, this applied from 9 February 2022) you have refugee status or humanitarian protection or have leave as the dependent family member of either. **Note:** you are also exempt from the past presence requirement; *or*
- are abroad in your capacity as a serving member of HM forces (or, for CDP or ADP, a civil servant, and immediately prior to the start of either employment you satisfied the residence and presence conditions), or are living with someone who is abroad as a serving member of the forces (or civil servant) and you are the spouse, civil partner (or for CDP or ADP, living together as if married/civil partners), son, stepson, daughter, stepdaughter (or, for CDP or ADP, a child in the care of), or (except for CDP) father, stepfather, mother, stepmother mother-in-law or father-in-law of that person. **Note:** you are also treated as present for the purpose of the presence and past presence requirements (and, for CDP and ADP, treated as ordinarily resident and exempt from the past presence test) (see p1625).

Establishing you are 'habitually resident in fact'

You are required to be habitually resident in the **'common travel area'** (ie, the UK, Ireland, Channel Islands and the Isle of Man) for all the benefits that have this requirement, with only three exceptions.

- **For a young carer grant**, you must be habitually resident in the common travel area or Switzerland or an EEA country.
- **For a Best Start grant**, if you are aged under 20 and you or your partner are not getting a qualifying benefit, you must be habitually resident in the UK, Channel Islands, Isle of Man, or, if you have leave (pre-settled or settled status) under the EUSS or a specified free movement residence right, the EEA.
- **For AA, CA, the care component of DLA/CDP or the daily living component of PIP/ADP**, if you are covered by the EU co-ordination rules and have a genuine and sufficient link to the UK, you must be habitually resident in either Great Britain (for CDP and ADP, the UK and a genuine and sufficient link is not required) (see p1602) or an EEA country or Switzerland, or, for CDP and ADP, Gibraltar (for CDP and ADP, your genuine and sufficient link must be to Scotland) (see p1626).

There is no definition of 'habitual residence' in the legislation. However, there is a considerable amount of caselaw on its meaning, and from this certain principles have emerged.

- There is no comprehensive list of factors that are relevant, so all the facts of your situation should be considered.[29]
- To be habitually resident, you must be resident (see p1549). It is not enough merely to intend to reside in the future.[30]

11

Part 11: Immigration and residence rules for benefits and tax credits
Chapter 69: Coming from abroad: residence rules
3. Habitual residence

- You must have a settled intention to reside in the relevant area. It does not need to be permanent; it is enough if you intend to make the relevant area your home for the time being.[31] You must provide evidence of your intention, including your reasons for moving there, the strength of your ties (or your 'centre of interest') and the viability of your residence. Factors that could be relevant include arranging or seeking employment, education or training, joining and/or bringing your family, obtaining, if you are eligible, leave under the EUSS (see p1563), arranging accommodation, bringing possessions, registering with a doctor, joining clubs and associations, and breaking ties with the place of your previous residence. The viability of your continued residence, although a relevant factor, is not an additional requirement.[32]

- In most cases, you must have an 'appreciable period' of actual residence. How long this period must be is not fixed and depends on your circumstances.[33] The DWP or local authority must not set a standard period of time for which all claimants must be resident before they can become habitually resident, and any such policy should be challenged by judicial review (see p1377). There is a large amount of caselaw on what constitutes an appreciable period of residence. Periods of between one and three months are frequently cited,[34] but no general rule can be derived from any one case and your appreciable period may be longer or shorter.[35] The stronger your settled intention to make your home in the common travel area for the time being, the shorter your period of actual residence needs to be before you can be accepted as habitually resident (and vice versa).[36]

  You may not need an appreciable period of actual residence, or the period may be very short, if you are:

  – a returning resident. This applies if you have been habitually resident in the relevant area previously, you left in circumstances which meant you ceased to be habitually resident and you then return to live in the area again. The decision on how long a period of residence you need to have in order to resume your previous habitual residence depends on the circumstances in which you left, your links with the relevant area while you were away and the circumstances of your return.[37] You can be found to be habitually resident on the day of your return;

  – covered by the EU co-ordination rules (see p1647) and are claiming income-based JSA, income-related ESA, PC or the mobility component of DLA, CDP, PIP or ADP (since these are special non-contributory benefits – see p1655). If this applies, you cannot be denied benefit solely because your period of residence is considered to be too short. Your period of residence is one of the factors that should be taken into account in assessing habitual residence, but it is not an absolute requirement and may be outweighed by other factors.[38]

- A temporary absence, such as a holiday, should not mean that you cease to be habitually resident. This should be accepted if you have a definite date of return[39] or you are abroad for a temporary reason such as a Voluntary Service Overseas placement.[40]

- When deciding whether you are habitually resident, the DWP or local authority must consider the whole period from your date of claim down to the date the decision is made, since at some point during this period you may have become resident for an appreciable period and your entitlement would begin from that date.[41]

---

4. Right to reside

The right to reside requirement applies to:
- universal credit (UC); *and*
- income support (IS); *and*
- income-based jobseeker's allowance (JSA); *and*
- income-related employment and support allowance (ESA); *and*
- pension credit (PC); *and*
- housing benefit (HB); *and*
- child benefit; *and*
- child tax credit (CTC).

You are also excluded from council tax reduction if you do not have a right to reside.[42] See CPAG's *Benefits for Migrants Handbook* for details.

Means-tested benefits

You must have a right to reside in the **common travel area** (ie, the UK, Ireland, the Channel Islands and the Isle of Man) in order to satisfy the habitual residence test for UC, IS, income-based JSA, income-related ESA, PC and HB. If you (or your partner, for UC) do not satisfy the habitual residence test because you do not have a right to reside, see p1552.

The type of residence right you need

Any right of residence in the common travel area enables you to satisfy the right to reside requirement for each of the means-tested benefits unless your *only* right of residence is:[43]

- pre-settled status (limited leave granted under the European Union Settlement Scheme – EUSS) – see p1558; *or*
- limited leave to enter as the holder of an EUSS family permit or travel permit (see p1564). However, check whether you are in a protected group that can have a free movement right to reside (eg, if you have made a valid application for leave under the EUSS, which is pending – see p1566), and if you have such a free movement right (see p1568); *or*

Part 11: Immigration and residence rules for benefits and tax credits
Chapter 69: Coming from abroad: residence rules
4. Right to reside

- as a European Economic Area (EEA) national with an initial right of residence during your first three months in the UK (see p1573); *or*
- as a family member of the above; *or*
- as the primary carer of a British citizen who is dependent on you and would have to leave the EU if you left the UK (see p1589);[44] *or*
- (except for income-based JSA) as an EEA jobseeker; *or*
- (except for income-based JSA) as a family member of an EEA jobseeker. **Note:** this exclusion does not apply if you are a former family member of a jobseeker and have retained your right to reside – eg, following the departure of the jobseeker from the UK (see p1587).[45]

Pre-settled status

If you have pre-settled status (limited leave granted under the EUSS – see p1563), this leave by itself will not satisfy the right to reside requirement because the regulations for each of the means-tested benefits list pre-settled status as an excluded right to reside.[46] However, work through the steps below to check whether your other circumstances mean you can satisfy this requirement.

Step 1: are you an Irish citizen? If you are, your citizenship satisfies the right to reside requirement, and this is not altered by your having pre-settled status (see p1562).

Step 2: do you have a free movement right to reside? Having pre-settled status means you are in one of the protected groups (see p1566) that can have a free movement right to reside (see p1568), and if you have such a right to reside, other than one listed above, you satisfy the right to reside requirement for the means-tested benefit(s) you want to claim.

Step 3: were you living in Ukraine immediately before 1 January 2022 and left due to the Russian invasion of 24 February 2022 *or* **are you the family member of a frontier worker** (see p1595)? If either applies, you are exempt from the habitual residence test for each of the means-tested benefits (see p1553).

Step 4: are you the family member (see p1583) of a 'relevant person of Northern Ireland', other than an extended family member, who *would* have a free movement right to reside under the EEA Regulations, other than one listed above, *if* s/he were are an EEA national? If this applies, the regulations for each of the means-tested benefits do not exclude you.[47]

A **'relevant person of Northern Ireland'** is defined as a British, or Irish, citizen who was born in Northern Ireland and at the time of her/his birth at least one of her/his parents was a British, or Irish, citizen, or had the right to reside in Northern Ireland without time limit.[48]

Step 5: if you have pre-settled status, but no other non-excluded right to reside, your pre-settled status does not satisfy the right to reside requirement because it is specifically excluded. The Court of Justice of the European Union (CJEU) held that this exclusion of pre-settled status as a qualifying right to reside for UC in Northern Ireland is not unlawfully discriminatory.[49] Although the

Court of Appeal had previously reached the opposite decision in relation to the exclusion within the UC regulations in Great Britain,[50] the DWP's appeal against that judgment was allowed by the Supreme Court in December 2021, because the question was held to have already been answered definitively by the CJEU.[51]

If you are at risk of destitution as a result of being excluded from a means-tested benefit, it may be arguable that this is unlawful based on either or both of the following arguments.

- If this breaches rights you arguably have under the EU Charter of Fundamental Rights. This argument is based on the CJEU judgment finding that because an EU citizen who is lawfully resident in the UK on the basis of having pre-settled status is within the scope of EU law, s/he can rely on the EU Charter of Fundamental Rights. Consequently, the benefit authority cannot refuse a benefit such as UC without first checking that refusal does not violate the specific rights under the charter: to live in dignified conditions, to private and family life and to have the best interests of the child considered.[52] This argument requires demonstrating that there is no alternative state support that both is available and would mean your fundamental charter rights are not breached. Alternative state support in most circumstances means local authority support, such as under the Children Act 1989 (in Scotland, the Children (Scotland) Act 1995). Although the CJEU judgment concerned a UC claim made before the end of the transition period (31 December 2020), it may be arguable that it applies beyond the end of 2020 if you are an EU citizen with pre-settled status since you are covered by the Withdawal Agreement, which must be applied in accordance with EU law principles including those contained in the Charter.[53]
- If this unlawfully discriminates against you under the Human Rights Act 1998. This argument is based on comparing your circumstance of being excluded from benefits during a period of limited leave granted under the EUSS, with a person excluded from benefits during a period of limited leave granted subject to a no recourse to public funds condition due to this condition meaning s/he is defined as a 'person subject to immigration control' (see p1524). The difference is that, in the latter circumstance, the person *may* be able to apply to have the condition lifted in circumstances which include being destitute or at risk of destitution.

11

Both of the above arguments are legally complex. If your claim has been refused and you need to rely on one of these arguments, challenge the refusal, get advice and ask your adviser to contact CPAG.

For links to the judgments and the latest advice on possible arguments, see cpag.org.uk/welfare-rights/legal-test-cases/current-test-cases/eu-pre-settled-status.

Part 11: Immigration and residence rules for benefits and tax credits
Chapter 69: Coming from abroad: residence rules
4. Right to reside

If you have been receiving benefits since April 2004

You do not need a right to reside to be entitled to any of the means-tested benefits, except UC, if you have been receiving any combination of IS, income-based JSA, PC, HB, income-related ESA (since 31 October 2011 and including periods linked by the 12-week linking rule – see p1018) or council tax benefit (until it was abolished from 1 April 2013) *continuously* since 30 April 2004. This transitional protection means you do not need a right to reside in order to continue to receive that benefit or if you make a new claim for one of these benefits, provided the periods of entitlement have been continuous since 30 April 2004.[54]

Example

Delphine is French. She came to the UK in 2003 with her baby and claimed IS as a lone parent while living with friends. In 2008, she had another child, moved into a rented flat and made a new claim for HB. In 2012, her partner moved in and so her IS stopped, but she continued to get HB. In 2016, her partner moved out and she claimed income-related ESA as she had several health problems.

Delphine has not needed a right to reside for any of these benefit claims because she has been receiving one of the five benefits on each day since 30 April 2004. However, if Delphine were to claim UC, because UC is not covered by this transitional protection, she would not be entitled unless she had a right to reside. If Delphine obtained settled status under the EUSS (see p1563), this would give her a right to reside and she could then be entitled to UC.

Child benefit and child tax credit

If you (and your partner for CTC) do not have a right to reside in the UK, you are treated as not present in Great Britain for child benefit and CTC and therefore are not entitled to these benefits.[55]

If you are claiming CTC and you (or your partner, if it is a joint claim) lose your (or her/his) right to reside, this is a change of circumstances that you must notify to HM Revenue and Customs (HMRC) within one month (see p1470). If your partner lost her/his right to reside, unless you can make a single claim for CTC (see p1459), you may be entitled to claim UC as a single person.

The right to reside requirement was introduced on 1 May 2004. You do not need a right to reside to continue to receive child benefit or CTC if you have been receiving it since before this date.

The type of residence right you need

Any right of residence in the UK enables you to satisfy the requirement for child benefit and CTC, unless your *only* right of residence is:[56]
- pre-settled status (limited leave granted under the EUSS – see p1563), but see below for exceptions and an argument that this exclusion is unlawful; *or*

- limited leave to enter as the holder of an EUSS family permit or travel permit (see p1564). However, check whether you are in a protected group that can have a free movement right to reside (see p1566) and whether you have such a free movement right (see p1568); *or*
- as the primary carer of a British citizen who is dependent on you and would have to leave the EU if you left the UK (see p1589).[57] However, you are not excluded on this basis if you are a national of Morocco, San Marino, Tunisia or Turkey (or Algeria if your claim began before 1 January 2021) and working in the UK, as you are covered by agreements that override this exclusion (see p1531).[58] To date, all other legal challenges to this exclusion have failed.[59]

If you have **pre-settled status**, this leave by itself will not satisfy the right to reside requirement. However, work through the steps below to check whether your other circumstances mean you can satisfy this requirement.

Step 1: are you an Irish citizen? If you are, your citizenship satisfies the right to reside requirement, and this is not altered by your having pre-settled status.

Step 2: do you have a free movement right to reside? Having pre-settled status means you are in one of the protected groups (see p1566) that can have a free movement right to reside (see p1568), and if you have such a right to reside, other than the one in the last bullet point above, this satisfies the right to reside requirement for child benefit and CTC.

Step 3: are you the family member (see p1583), other than an extended family member, of a 'relevant person of Northern Ireland' (see p1558) who *would* have a free movement right to reside under the EEA Regulations (see p1568) *if* s/he were are an EEA national? If this applies, the regulations for child benefit and CTC do not exclude you on the basis of your pre-settled status.[60]

Step 4: if you have pre-settled status but no other non-excluded right to reside, the child benefit and CTC regulations exclude this right to reside. The exclusion of pre-settled status has been held not to be unlawfully discriminatory for means-tested benefits. For details and possible arguments that may also apply to CTC, and, in exceptional circumstances, to child benefit, see 'Step 5' on p1558. Those arguments are unlikely to assist you to access child benefit because it is not a subsistence benefit, and is unlikely to significantly affect your risk of destitution.

Note: if you are not entitled to child benefit for a child living with you, someone else who contributes to the cost of that child may be able to claim child benefit instead (see p568).

---

5. **Who has a right to reside**

Whether or not you have a right to reside can depend on your nationality, immigration status and the circumstances of you and your family members. You may have more than one right of residence, or you may not have any.

Part 11: Immigration and residence rules for benefits and tax credits
Chapter 69: Coming from abroad: residence rules
5. Who has a right to reside

Any residence right is sufficient to satisfy the right to reside requirement, unless it is specifically excluded for the benefit you want to claim (see p1557 and p1560).

You have a right to reside if you are:
- a British citizen, or an Irish citizen or a Commonwealth citizen with a right of abode; *or*
- within a period of leave to enter or remain in the UK granted under UK immigration law. However, if you have limited leave which is subject to a 'no recourse to public funds' condition, or indefinite leave granted as the result of a maintenance undertaking, or you only have leave solely because you are appealing a decision to refuse to vary your previous leave, you are defined as a 'person subject to immigration control' (see p1524) and therefore excluded from benefits on that basis unless you are in an exempt group (see p1529); *or*
- in one of the protected groups who can have a European free movement right to reside (see p1566) *and* you have a free movement right to reside (see p1568).

British and Irish citizens

If you are a **British citizen**, including if you also hold another nationality, you have an automatic right to reside in the UK. If you are the family member of a British citizen, see p1586. If you are the primary carer of a British citizen, see p1589.

If you are an **Irish citizen**, you have an automatic right to reside in the UK and do not require leave to enter or remain in the UK (unless you are subject to a deportation or exclusion order).[61] You are not required to obtain leave under the European Union Settlement Scheme (EUSS – see p1563), but you can if you began residing in the UK before 31 December 2020 and you wish to do so.

If you are the **family member of an Irish citizen** in the UK, your free movement residence rights as a family member depend on the Irish citizen having a relevant right to reside in the same way as family members of other European Economic Area (EEA) nationals (see p1583). If you do not already have leave, you need to apply for leave under the EUSS (see p1563).

Changes due to the UK leaving the European Union

The UK left the EU on 31 January 2020, but the European free movement rights described in this chapter, continued to apply in the UK during the transition period. At the end of this transition period, free movement rights were, in general, ended within UK law. However, if you are within a protected group (see p1566), you can potentially have a free movement right and use this for the purpose of claiming benefits.

Transition period

The transition period (also called the 'implementation period') was the period from the UK leaving the EU at 11pm on 31 January 2020 to 11pm on 31 December 2020.[62]

During the transition period, in general, EU legislation and caselaw, and all EU-derived law (eg, the EEA Regulations), continued to have effect just as it did before the UK left the EU.[63]

During the transition period, all references to the EU or EEA were treated as if they included references to the UK, and references to an EEA national or EU citizen were treated as if they included references to a UK national. However, note that British citizens only had European free movement residence rights in limited circumstances (see p1586).[64]

If you are an EEA national who was already living in the UK by the end of the transition period, or the family member of such an EEA national, to continue living lawfully in the UK, you need to obtain leave under the EUSS. For details and the relevance for claiming benefits that require a right to reside, see below.

If you are an EEA national arriving after the end of the transition period, unless you are joining your family member who is an EEA national living in the UK before that period ended, you will need leave to enter or remain in the UK under the same rules as non-EEA nationals. Your benefit entitlements will depend primarily on your immigration status, and whether you are defined as a 'person subject to immigration control' (see p1524) and, if you are, whether you are covered by an exempt group for the benefit you want to claim (see p1530 onwards).

Note: the UK leaving the EU also affects the EU co-ordination rules (see p1645).

Settled and pre-settled status

The EU Settlement Scheme (EUSS) is set out in the Immigration Rules.[65]

To be eligible for leave under the EUSS, you must be an EEA national who began residing in the UK before the end of the transition period (see above), or the family member of such an EEA national, or have been residing in the UK with a derivative right to reside (see p1589) before the end of the transition period.

Although, in general, the deadline for applications to the EUSS was 30 June 2021:[66]

- you can apply after this date if you have 'reasonable grounds' for missing this deadline. If you are eligible for leave, but have not yet applied, get urgent immigration advice;
- the deadline can be different in specific circumstances. For example, if you have come to the UK since 1 April 2021 to join your EEA national family member who was already living in the UK by the end of the transition period, and you entered with an EUSS family permit or EUSS travel permit (see p1564), you should generally apply to the EUSS within three months of arriving. Get immigration advice about your individual situation.

Part 11: Immigration and residence rules for benefits and tax credits
Chapter 69: Coming from abroad: residence rules
5. Who has a right to reside

You may be eligible for:
- **settled status (indefinite leave under the EUSS)** if you can show you have been residing in the UK:
  - for five years as an EEA national, or family member (see p1583) of an EEA national or with a derivative right to reside (see p1589). Certain gaps abroad are disregarded (these are the same as those disregarded for acquiring permanent residence – see p1592); *or*
  - for less than five years and you satisfy the conditions for obtaining permanent residence in less than five years (see p1594); *or*
- **pre-settled status (limited leave for five years)** if you:
  - began residing in the UK before the end of the transition period as an EEA national, or family member of an EEA national, or with a derivative right to reside, but your residence in the UK has been less than five years; *or*
  - have come to the UK to join an EEA national who was your family member at the end of the transition period, and remains your family member.

Before your pre-settled status expires, you need to apply for settled status once you can show you have resided in the UK for five years, as above.
Note: if you are an EEA national, your residence in the UK does not have to have been with a right to reside – actual residency is sufficient.

If you are joining an EEA national who was living in the UK before 31 December 2020, and who was your family member on that date and continues to be, you may have entered the UK with leave to enter as a holder of an **EUSS family permit** or **EUSS travel permit**. Once you are in the UK, you need to apply for leave under the EUSS, generally within three months.

If you are an Irish citizen or you have indefinite leave to remain in the UK, you do not need to obtain settled or pre-settled status, but you can do so if you are eligible.

If you are the family member of an Irish citizen, and you do not have leave on another basis, you need to obtain leave under the EUSS.

You lose your settled status if you are outside the UK for more than five years.

If you have been granted leave under the EUSS, this does not automatically give anyone defined as your family member a right to reside, but s/he may be eligible to make her/his own application to the EUSS.

It is particularly important to get immigration advice before applying for leave under the EUSS if you are a non-EEA national, or you entered the UK with leave that was not granted under the EUSS, or you have a criminal conviction, or you have been subject to a deportation, exclusion or removal decision, or to check whether there may be other types of leave you can apply for, or for guidance on what is a 'reasonable ground' to apply after the deadline. You should also get advice if your application is refused, or if you have lived in the UK for at least five years but have only been granted pre-settled status, or if you are having difficulty proving your residence in the UK.

11

Benefit entitlement

If you have **settled status** (indefinite leave granted under the EUSS), you have a right to reside that satisfies the right to reside requirement of all benefits that have this requirement.[67]

If you have **pre-settled status** (limited leave granted under the EUSS), this is an excluded right to reside for all benefits with that requirement. However, having pre-settled status means you are in a protected group that can have a free movement right to reside (see p1566).

If you have **limited leave to enter as the holder of a valid EUSS family permit or travel permit**, these residence rights are excluded for all benefits that require a right to reside. However, check whether you are in a protected group that can have a free movement right to reside (see p1566).

If you have made a valid application for leave under the EUSS, and your application (or appeal against a refusal) is pending, you may be in a protected group that can have a free movement right to reside (see p1566).

For further details of the type of right to reside you need, including potential arguments if you have pre-settled status, but no qualifying free movement right to reside, see p1557 for means-tested benefits and p1560 for child benefit and CTC.

If you have either settled status or pre-settled status, or you have limited leave to enter as the holder of a valid EUSS family permit or travel permit, you are *not* defined as a 'person subject to immigration control' (see p1524), and therefore not excluded from any benefits on this basis, *unless*, possibly, you have that leave solely because you are appealing a refusal to vary your leave (see p1529).

Evidence of your status

If you are granted settled or pre-settled status, or leave to enter on the basis that you hold an EUSS family or travel permit, in most cases you are not issued with a physical document (unless, for example, you are a non-EEA national family member of an EEA national and did not already have a biometric residence card when you applied). Instead, you confirm your settled or pre-settled status by accessing your online profile, and the DWP may ask you to do this at a job centre. You can get a 'share code' to allow others, including the DWP, HM Revenue and Customs (HMRC) or local authority, to view your status online.[68]

If you are unable to provide the benefit authority with a share code, you can provide a copy of the Home Office document emailed to you when you were granted leave under the EUSS. Although this is not proof of status by itself, the decision maker should accept this as supporting evidence and can then verify your status directly with the Home Office or by you attending a job centre and showing your online profile.

If you have applied to the EUSS and your application is pending, your online status shows a certificate of application. Providing the benefit authority with a share code enables the decision maker to view this. If you are unable to provide a

Part 11: Immigration and residence rules for benefits and tax credits
Chapter 69: Coming from abroad: residence rules
5. Who has a right to reside

share code, you can provide the benefit authority with a copy of the email acknowledging your application and the decision maker can verify your application with the Home Office.

Protected groups who can have European free movement residence rights

Since the end of the transition period (11pm on 31 December 2020), you can only have a free movement right to reside if you are in one of the protected groups below. If you are, the EEA Regulations continue to be available to you, for the purpose of claiming benefits, despite their having been revoked more generally as part of the ending of free movement rights within UK law at the end of the transition period.

If you need a free movement right to reside to claim a benefit that requires you to have a right to reside, you need to check whether:

- you are in one of the four protected groups below; *and*
- you have a free movement right to reside (see the checklist on p1568), other than one that is excluded for the benefit you want to claim (see p1557).

You are in a protected group:[69]

- while you have **pre-settled status** (limited leave granted under the EUSS – see p1563); *or*
- **(between 31 December 2020 and 30 June 2021)** if, on 31 December 2020, you had a free movement right to reside (see notes below for when you can be *treated as* having this) and you did not, during that period, have leave under the EUSS; *or*
- **(beyond 30 June 2021)** if you were in the group above and by 30 June 2021 you applied for leave under the EUSS and that application (or appeal against a refusal) has not been finally determined, withdrawn or abandoned. See also second bullet point in note below; *or*
- **(between 31 December 2020 and 30 June 2021)** if you were defined as the 'relevant family member' (see 1567) of a person who, on 31 December 2020, had a free movement right to reside and you did not, during that period, have leave under the EUSS; *or*
- **from the date you make a valid application for leave under the EUSS after 30 June 2021**, if that application (or appeal against a refusal) has not been finally determined, withdrawn or abandoned. DWP guidance states you should be accepted as in this group once you have received a certificate of application (see p1565).[70] See second bullet point in the note below.

Note:

- If you were receiving benefits on 30 June 2021, are eligible to apply to the EUSS, but you did not apply by that date, you ceased to be in either the second or fourth protected group under the regulations from 1 July 2021. However, the DWP's policy was to continue to pay benefits on an extra-statutory basis for a limited period. The policy was to contact claimants in this situation, but from November 2021 if you still had not applied to the EUSS, and you do not have an alternative qualifying immigration status, your benefit could be suspended. If you then apply to the EUSS your benefit should be reinstated, but if you do not your benefit will be terminated. You should be contacted by the benefit authorities before your benefit is supended or terminated and if there are reasons why you cannot apply to the EUSS within any stated time limit (usually one month), explain this to the benefit authorities and get urgent advice. The DWP policy is to allow extra time if you are vulnerable.

- Once you have made a valid application to the EUSS, whether before 30 June 2021 or, if you have 'reasonable grounds' for not applying by that date, after, it may be arguable that you are in a protected group, even if you did not have a free movement right to reside on 31 December 2020. The Home Office guidance appears to confirm this and DWP guidance is unclear. It may be arguable that this protection is provided directly by the Withdrawal Agreements. If your benefit is refused because you did not have a free movement right to reside on 31 December 2020, challenge the refusal and get specialist advice.[71]

- You can be *treated* as having had a free movement right to reside on 31 December 2020, if you previously had a free movement right to reside in the UK and on that date you were absent from the UK, but your absence was in circumstances that did not break your continuity of residence – eg, if that absence, together with any other absences in the last 12-month period, were less than six months in total (see p1592).[72]

- If you previously had a permanent right to reside in the UK and since then you lost this right to reside due to being absent from the UK for more than two years, you are *treated as* having a permanent right to reside on 31 December 2020 if on that date you had been absent from the UK for a period of more than two, but less than five years, and immediately before leaving the UK you had a permanent right to reside in the UK.[73]

- You cannot be defined as a 'person subject to immigration control' if you are an EEA national while the second, third or fourth protected group applies, even if you do not have a free movement right to reside (see p1525),[74] or, arguably, while the fifth group applies (see second bullet point under this note).

- If you are in the second or third protected group, note that the free movement right to reside you had on 31 December 2020 can be the same as, or different from, the free movement right to reside that you have when you claim benefits.

You were a **'relevant family member'** of a person ('P') if:[75]
- on 31 December 2020, you were a 'family member' (see p1583) of P but you only arrived in the UK after that date (but by 30 June 2021); *or*

Part 11: Immigration and residence rules for benefits and tax credits
Chapter 69: Coming from abroad: residence rules
5. Who has a right to reside

- on 31 December 2020, you were an 'extended family member' of P (see p1585) and either:
  - you were *treated as* P's 'family member' because you held a valid residence document, issued under the EEA Regulations, on that date (see p1570), but you only arrived in the UK after that date (but by 30 June 2021); *or*
  - on 31 December 2020, you were P's durable partner (but were not treated as P's 'family member' because you did *not* hold a valid residence document issued under the EEA Regulations on that date); *or*
  - you were issued with a valid residence document under the EEA Regulations *after* 31 December 2020 (but by 30 June 2021); *or*
- you are the spouse or civil partner of P and P is a Swiss national; *or*
- you are P's child and either:
  - the other parent is in the second or fourth of the protected groups, or has leave granted under the EUSS, or is a British citizen; *or*
  - you were born or adopted after 31 December 2020 and P is either an EEA or Swiss national living in the UK (or a British citizen living in an EEA state or Switzerland), with a right to reside in that state, since before 31 December 2020, and P has sole or joint custody of you.[76]

European free movement rights: checklist

Since the end of the transition period (11pm on 31 December 2020), you can only have a free movement right to reside if you are in one of the **protected groups** above.

Unless you have pre-settled status (limited leave granted under the EUSS), whether you are in a protected group may depend on you (or the person that you are a 'relevant family member' of for the period 31 December 2020 to 30 June 2021) having had (or being treated as having had during particular absences – see above) a free movement right to reside on 31 December 2020.

You can work through the following checklist to see if you had a free movement right to reside on 31 December 2020, as well as to check whether you have a free movement right to reside when you claim benefit.

Note: the free movement right to reside that you had on 31 December 2020 does *not* need to be the same free movement right to reside that subsequently enables you to claim benefit.

In relation to the relevant time (see above):

- **Option one:** (only relevant for periods before 1 April 2021) are you an EEA national who began residing in the UK in the last three months of 2020, or were you the family member of such an EEA national? For details of this **initial right to reside**, see p1573.
- **Option two:** are you an EEA national with a right to reside as a '**qualified person**'[77] – ie, are you an EEA national in the UK as a:
  - jobseeker (see p1574);

- worker (see p1576), including if you have retained this status (see p1578);
- self-employed person (see p1577), including if you have retained this status (see p1578);
- self-sufficient person (see p1582);
- student (see p1583).
- **Option three:** are you a **'family member'** (see p1583) of an EEA national covered in Options two or four? If so, you have a right to reside whether or not you are an EEA national yourself.
- **Option four:** do you have a permanent right of residence (see p1591)? This is normally after five years of 'legal residence', which can include periods with a right to reside under Options one, two and three (see p1593).
- **Option five:** do you have a 'derivative' right to reside through someone else's right to reside, but not as her/his family member? This covers certain children and carers (see p1589).

Note:
- If you have been granted settled status (indefinite leave to remain granted under the EUSS – see p1563), you have a right to reside for all benefits that have this requirement and so you do not need to also show you have any free movement rights. However, note that your settled status does *not* confer a right to reside on your family member(s) (see p1583).
- If you are a Croatian, A2 or A8 national (see p1571), or a family member of a Croatian, A2 or A8 national, needing to rely on past periods of residence, check whether additional restrictions applied (see p1572).
- You can have more than one right to reside at a time.[78] For example, you may be both a self-employed person and also the family member of someone with a permanent right of residence.
- In very limited circumstances, if you do not satisfy all the requirements for a particular free movmement right to reside, it may be possible to argue that you should still have such a right by applying principles that have been accepted in other cases. In particular, if it is necessary for someone else's rights not to be infringed or if it would be 'proportionate' in your circumstances. See CPAG's *Benefits for Migrants Handbook*.

Main legal sources of free movement residence rights

Although the UK left the EU on 31 January 2020, European free movement rights continued to apply in the UK until the end of the transition period (11pm on 31 December 2020).

At the end of the transition period, EU law was converted into UK law, and together with EU-derived law, continues to apply in the UK as it did on 31 December 2020.[79] However, from this date, this retained law could be amended or revoked and, in general free movement legislation, including the EEA Regulations, was revoked with immediate effect. However, the Withdrawal Agreements provide protections for EEA nationals already living

Part 11: Immigration and residence rules for benefits and tax credits
Chapter 69: Coming from abroad: residence rules
5. Who has a right to reside

in the UK, and British citizens living in EEA states, before the end of the transition period, and the family members of each.[80] New UK regulations were intended to reproduce these protections, but where they fail to do so, the Withdrawal Agreements have direct effect in the UK. If you are in one of the protected groups (see p1566), the EEA Regulations continue to be available to you, and must continue to be interpreted in accance with EU legislation and Court of Justice of the EU (CJEU) caselaw (as of 31 December 2020), which the EEA Regulations are intended to implement (see below).[81] Only the highest courts (the Court of Appeal and Supreme Court and equivalent-level courts) may depart from CJEU caselaw.[82] The Withdrawal Agreements must also be interpreted in accordance with EU legislation, including the Treaty on the Functioning of the EU (TFEU), and caselaw.[83] Questions about the interpretation of the Withdrawal Agreement protections can be referred to the CJEU for up to eight years from the end of the transition period.[84]

The main EU legislation that continues to be relevant in determining European free movement residence rights comes from EU treaties, in particular the **TFEU** and, for Norway, Iceland and Liechtenstein, **the EEA Agreement.** However, the details of residence rights are set out in **EU Directive 2004/38.** This sets out most of the situations in which an EEA national or her/his family member has a right to reside in the UK. This came into force from 30 April 2006 and was extended to cover nationals of Norway, Iceland and Liechtenstein from 1 March 2009.[85] Swiss nationals and their family members are covered by a separate agreement, which provides similar rights.[86] EU Regulation 492/2011 is also significant for certain derivative residence rights (see p1589).

The Immigration (European Economic Area) Regulations 2016 (called '**the EEA Regulations**' in this *Handbook*) apply to all EEA nationals and Swiss nationals (but not British citizens – see p1562).[87] These give similar rights of residence to those contained in the above EU Directive and should be interpreted in accordance with it and other EU legislation and caselaw on free movement residence rights. The current EEA Regulations replaced the previous, very similar, EEA Regulations 2006, from 1 February 2017.[88] **Note:** the EEA Regulations were, in general, revoked from the end of the transition period. However, they continue to be available if you are in a protected group listed on p1566 while one of those groups applies.

Residence documents

To be in one of the protected groups that can have a free movement right to reside, other than for periods before 1 July 2021, you need to either have pre-settled status or have made a valid application for leave under the EUSS and that application (or appeal against a refusal) must still be pending. For details on how to prove either, see p1565.

The only circumstance when you need a residence document issued under the EEA Regulations in order to have a European free movement right to reside is if you are an 'extended family member' (see p1585), when, to be *treated as* a 'family member', you need a family permit, registration certificate or residence card, which remains in force.[89] If you had any other free movement right to reside, although you could, until the end of the transition period, apply for the residence documents listed below, they were not necessary. A residence document does not, in itself, give you a right to reside – eg, if your right to reside ceases.[90]

You could be issued with the following residence documents if you applied before the end of the transition period or you applied by 30 June 2021 if the exception for a family permit applied to you.

- **A registration certificate** if you were an EEA national with a right of residence provided under the EEA Regulations.[91]
- **A residence card** if you were a non-EEA national and you had a right to reside as the family member of an EEA national who had either a right to reside as a 'qualified person' (see p1568) or a permanent right of residence.[92]
- **A derivative residence card** if you had a derivative right to reside (see p1589).[93]
- **A document certifying a permanent right of residence** if you were an EEA national with a permanent right of residence, or a **permanent residence card** if you were a non-EEA national with a permanent right of residence.[94]
- **A residence document** issued, or treated as issued, under previous regulations. These are treated as if they were issued under the current EEA Regulations.[95]
- **An EEA family permit** for entry to the UK if you were a family member of an EEA national with a free movement right of residence in the UK and either:[96]
  - you applied before the end of the transition period; *or*
  - you applied by 30 June 2021 and you were in a protected group that could continue to have a free movement right to reside at the time (for details of these protections including their duration, see p1566). After 31 December 2020, you could only be issued with an EEA family permit as an 'extended family member' if you were the EEA national's partner in a durable relationship.

Note: if you have obtained one of the above residence documents it should be accepted as remaining in force if it has not yet expired. If it has expired, it may be arguable that you should continue to be treated as a 'family member' due to protections under the Withdrawal Agreements. If your benefit claim is refused because it is not accepted that your residence document remains in force, challenge the decision and get specialist advice. See also CPAG's *Benefits for Migrants Handbook* for details.

Croatian, A2 and A8 nationals

Since the end of the transition period (11pm on 31 December 2020), you can only have a free movement right to reside while you are in one of the protected groups (see p1566). If you are in one of the protected groups, or for a period before the end of the transition period, your free movement residence rights could be affected by additional restrictions that previously applied to nationals of the countries listed below.

Part 11: Immigration and residence rules for benefits and tax credits
Chapter 69: Coming from abroad: residence rules
5. Who has a right to reside

Croatia, A2 and A8 states
Croatia joined the EU on 1 July 2013.
Restrictions applied until 30 June 2018.
The A2 states are: Bulgaria and Romania.
These states joined the EU on 1 January 2007.
Restrictions applied until 31 December 2013.
The A8 states are: Czech Republic, Estonia, Hungary, Latvia, Lithuania, Poland, Slovakia and Slovenia.
These states joined the EU on 1 May 2004.
Restrictions applied until 30 April 2009 (see below).

The treaties under which the above 'accession' states joined the EU allowed existing member states, including, at the relevant dates, the UK, to restrict accession state nationals' access to their labour markets and their residence rights as workers and jobseekers. The duration of these restrictions was limited to five years from the date the states joined the EU, but could be extended for a further two years if certain conditions were met. The UK government imposed the restrictions for five years and then extended the A8 and A2 restrictions for the additional two-year period. However, this extension of the A8 restrictions from 1 May 2009 to 30 April 2011 was held to be unlawful. This means that A8 nationals were *not* subject to restrictions during that two-year period.[97]

Restrictions on employment and residence rights

Although the restrictions on Croatian, A2 and A8 nationals ended some years ago, the restrictions remain relevant if they affect your current free movement rights. In particular, these restrictions can be relevant if you are seeking to establish either:

- permanent residence if you, or your family member whose free movement residence rights you need to rely on, are a Croatian, A2 or A8 national; *or*
- a derivative right to reside as the primary carer of a child (in education), of a Croatian, A2 or A8 national who worked during the period of restrictions.

If you are a Croatian or an A2 national, and were not in circumstances that meant you were exempt from the restrictions (see p1573), during the period of restrictions, there were restrictions on your employment and residence rights. Before taking up employment, you were required to obtain an 'accession worker authorisation document' (in most cases, an accession worker registration certificate, specifying the employer you could work for), and then work in accordance with it.[98] Your residence rights were restricted as follows.[99]

- You did not have a right to reside as a jobseeker.
- You were only defined as a 'worker' if you had an accession worker authorisation document and were working in accordance with it.

11

- You could not retain your worker status when you stopped work in the ways other workers could (see p1578).

If you are an A8 national, and were not in circumstances that meant you were exempt from the restrictions (see below), during the period of restrictions, there were restrictions on your employment and residence rights. You had to work for an 'authorised employer', which broadly meant you had to register each job you took with the Worker Registration Scheme within the first month (you were defined as working for an 'authorised employer' during the first month of employment or in certain other limited circumstances).[100] Your residence rights were restricted as follows.[101]

- You did not have a right to reside as a jobseeker.
- You were only defined as a 'worker' if you were working for an 'authorised employer'.
- You could not retain your worker status when you stopped work in the ways other workers could (see p1578). However, if you lost your job within the first month of employment, you could retain your status in those ways, but only until the end of the month.[102]

If you are a Croatian, A2 or A8 national you were **exempt from the restrictions**, in specific circumstances. These included once you had been employed for 12 months, without breaks of more than 30 days (in total), either before the start of the period of restrictions, or during it if your work was in accordance with those restrictions.

For further details on the restrictions, including lists of all the exempt groups, see the 2021/22 edition of this *Handbook* or CPAG's *Benefits for Migrants Handbook*.

The restrictions do not affect other residence rights you may have, or had, as an EEA national (eg, as a self-employed or self-sufficient person)[103] or other rights you may have under EU law.

Initial right of residence

If you are an EEA national and arrived in the UK before the end of transition period (11pm on 31 December 2020), you had an initial right of residence for the first three months of your stay in the UK, provided you had a valid identity card or passport and were not an unreasonable burden on the social assistance system of the UK.

If you were a family member (see p1583) of an EEA national who had this initial right of residence (even if you are not an EEA national), you had a right to reside, provided you had a valid passport and were not an unreasonable burden on the social assistance system of the UK.[104]

Although these residence rights did not satisfy the right to reside requirement for any of the means-tested benefits at the time:

Part 11: Immigration and residence rules for benefits and tax credits
Chapter 69: Coming from abroad: residence rules
5. Who has a right to reside

- either can count towards meeting the five years' residence required for permanent residency (see p1591);[105] *and*
- if you had this initial right of residence on 31 December 2020, it may mean you are, or were, in a protected group that can have other free movement rights. For further details, including the duration of these protections, see p1566.

Jobseekers

Since the end of the transition period (11pm on 31 December 2020), you can only have a free movement right to reside, including as a jobseeker (or family member of a jobseeker), while you are in one of the protected groups that can have these rights (see p1566).

If you *are* in one of the protected groups, or for a period before the end of the transition period, you have a right to reside as a jobseeker if you are an EEA national and:[106]

- you are in the UK and you provide evidence that you are seeking employment and have a 'genuine chance of being engaged'. **Note:** (under the EEA Regulations only) after 91 days this evidence must be compelling (see below), but note the CJEU recently held that a jobseeker cannot be required to show a 'genuine chance of being engaged' until after a 'reasonable period' which could be six months;[107] *and*
- (very rarely required by the benefit authorities) you entered the UK in order to seek employment, or (EEA Regulations only) you are present in the UK seeking employment immediately after having a right to reside as a worker (except if you retained worker status while involuntarily unemployed – see p1579), a student or self-sufficient person.

There is no time limit on how long you can have a right to reside as a jobseeker. It continues for as long as you continue to satisfy the above requirements (but see below).[108]

If you are a Croatian, A2 or A8 national who was subject to restrictions, you did not have a right to reside as a jobseeker during the period of those restrictions (see p1571).[109]

Providing evidence

To have a right to reside as a jobseeker, you must provide evidence that you are seeking employment. The EEA Regulations also require you to provide evidence of having a genuine chance of being engaged.[110] However, the CJEU recently held that a jobseeker cannot be required to show a 'genuine chance of being engaged' until after a 'reasonable period' which could be six months.[111]

The most straightforward way of demonstrating that you are a jobseeker is to 'sign on' for contribution-based jobseeker's allowance (JSA) or national insurance (NI) credits on the basis of unemployment, and provide evidence that you are available for work and actively seeking work (see p1093 and p1101) or that you satisfy the work search and work availability requirements (see p1047) if you come under the universal credit (UC) system (see p22). There would only be a few unusual circumstances in which you would satisfy these conditions and not be accepted as having a genuine chance of being engaged.[112] However, it is not necessary to claim or receive JSA if you can provide evidence that you are seeking employment and, although arguably not required, have a genuine chance of being engaged in another way.[113]

Under the EEA Regulations, the evidence that you are looking for work and have a genuine chance of being engaged must be 'compelling':[114]

- to continue to have a right to reside as a jobseeker for more than 91 days, or from the start of your period of residence as a jobseeker (unless you have since been absent from the UK for a period of at least 12 months) if you previously had a right to reside as a jobseeker for a total of 91 days or you previously retained worker or self-employed status while involuntarily unemployed (see p1579) for at least six months; *and*
- since then you have had an absence from the UK. **Note:** the benefit authorities have not been enforcing this requirement, except in very occasional cases.

The requirement for your evidence to be compelling is known as the 'genuine prospects of work test'. The introduction of UC has reduced the relevance of this test for benefit claimants who are jobseekers (as this right to reside does not satisfy the requirement for UC – see p1557). The 'genuine prospects of work test' can only be applied to you if you have no other non-excluded right to reside other than as a jobseeker. If this happens (eg, while you are claiming child benefit), check it has been applied at the right time and see the *Benefits for Migrants Handbook*.

Benefit entitlement

If you have a right to reside as a jobseeker and this is your only right to reside:

- it does not satisfy the right to reside requirement for UC, income support (IS), income-related employment and support allowance (ESA), pension credit (PC) or housng benefit (HB);
- it does satisfy the right to reside requirement for child benefit, child tax credit (CTC) and income-based JSA. Note, for each of these benefits, unless you are in an exempt group, you must also have been living in the UK for the past three months (see p1548);
- it can count towards meeting the five years' residence requirement for permanent residency (see p1591);
- if you had a right to reside as a jobseeker (or family member of a jobseeker) on 31 December 2020, this can mean that you are, or were, in a protected group that can have *other* free movement rights. For further details, including the duration of these protections, see p1566.

Part 11: Immigration and residence rules for benefits and tax credits
Chapter 69: Coming from abroad: residence rules
5. Who has a right to reside

Workers

Since the end of the transition period (11pm on 31 December 2020), you can only have a free movement right to reside, including as a worker, while you are in one of the protected groups that can have these rights (see p1566).

If you *are* in one of the protected groups, or for a period before the end of the transition period, you have a right to reside as a 'worker' if you are an EEA national and:[115]

- you are in an employment relationship. This means you must:[116]
  - provide services; *and*
  - work in return for remuneration; *and*
  - work under the direction of another person; *and*
- the work you do entails activities that are 'genuine and effective', rather than 'marginal and ancillary'.

* * *

Is your work genuine and effective?

When deciding whether your work is genuine and effective, all relevant factors must be taken into account, including the following.

1. The duration of the employment. The longer the period of time your employment lasts, the more likely it is that you have established worker status. However, in specific cases, two weeks has been held to be sufficient to establish worker status.[117]

2. The number of hours worked. There is no minimum threshold. Someone working 10 hours a week was held to be a worker,[118] as was an au pair working 13 hours a week for a modest wage plus board and lodging.[119] The European Court of Justice held that 5.5 hours' work is potentially capable of making someone a worker.[120]

3. The level of your earnings. There must be some remuneration (although it can be in kind, such as board and lodgings[121]), and voluntary work does not result in worker status.[122] Provided the work done is genuine and effective, earnings that are so low that you need to subsidise them with benefits do not prevent you from being a worker.[123]

4. The regularity of the work. The more regular and less erratic the work, the more likely it is that worker status will be established. It is possible to be a worker while undertaking work through an agency,[124] or while working 'cash in hand' without tax and NI being deducted.[125]

* * *

Although guidance to decision makers advises that someone is automatically a worker if s/he has been earning, on average, a 'minimum income threshold' (£190 a week or £823 per month in 2022/23) for three months, it confirms that, in all other cases, an individual assessment must be made, taking the above factors into account.[126]

Note: if you are a Croatian or A2 national who, during the period of restrictions, was subject to those restrictions, you only count as a 'worker' if you had an accession worker authorisation document and worked in accordance with it.

Similarly, if you were an A8 national who, during the period of restrictions, was subject to those restrictions, you only counted as a 'worker' if you were working for an 'authorised employer' (see p1573). For details of the periods of these restrictions and who is affected, see p1571.

You only **cease to be a worker** when the employment relationship ends. While you are still under a contract of employment, you continue to be a worker. Consequently, you are still a worker if you are a woman on maternity leave (including unpaid maternity leave),[127] or if you are on holiday leave or sick leave (including if it is unpaid),[128] or during periods when you have been furloughed.

If you have ceased to be a worker, you may retain your worker status in certain circumstances (see p1578).

If you have a right to reside as a 'worker' in the UK, this satisfies the right to reside requirement for all the benefits that have this requirement and you are exempt from the habitual residence test (see p1553) and you are exempt from the requirement to have been living in the UK for the past three months for child benefit and CTC (see p1548).

If you were a worker on 31 December 2020, this can mean you are, or were, in a protected group that can have free movement rights. For further details, including the duration of these protections, see p1566.

Note: if you are an EEA national and on 31 December 2020, and continuously since then, you have been working in the UK while 'not primarily resident in the UK', you may have rights as a 'frontier worker' (see p1595). These rights include being exempt from the habitual residence test for means-tested benefits (see p1553).

Self-employed people

Since the end of the transition period (11pm on 31 December 2020), you can only have a free movement right to reside, including as a self-employed person, while you are in one of the protected groups that can have these rights (see p1566).

If you *are* in one of the protected groups, or for a period before the end of the transition period, you have a right to reside as a self-employed person if you are an EEA national and you provide services in return for remuneration, but not under the direction of another person.[129] The work you do must entail activities that are 'genuine and effective' rather than 'marginal and ancillary' (see p1576).[130]

You count as being self-employed when you are established in the UK in order to pursue self-employed activity.[131] You must provide evidence of the steps you have taken or the ways in which you have set yourself up as self-employed.[132] It helps if you have registered with HMRC as self-employed. However, if you have not registered, this does not necessarily mean you cannot be accepted as self-employed.[133]

If you are a Croatian, A2 or A8 national and during the periods of restrictions (see p1571), you were self-employed, you had the same rights as other EEA nationals; no additional restrictions applied.

11

Part 11: Immigration and residence rules for benefits and tax credits
Chapter 69: Coming from abroad: residence rules
5. Who has a right to reside

If you stop working, you do not necessarily **cease to be self-employed**. You may be in a temporary lull, and it is accepted that you can continue to be self-employed during such times, depending on your particular circumstances and the evidence you provide – eg, the amount of work you have, any steps you are taking to develop your business or find new work, and your marketing and business administration. Account must also be taken of your motives and intentions.[134]

You can continue to be self-employed if you stop work for a period of maternity leave, but intend to return to self-employment afterwards (see p1581).[135]

If you have ceased to be self-employed, you may be able to retain your self-employed status in certain circumstances (see below).

If you have a right to reside as a 'self-employed person' in the UK, this satisfies the right to reside requirement for all the benefits that have this requirement and you are exempt from the habitual residence test (see p1553) and you are exempt from the requirement to have been living in the UK for the past three months for child benefit and CTC (see p1548).

If you were a self-employed person on 31 December 2020, this can mean you are, or were, in a protected group that can have free movement rights. For further details, including the duration of these protections, see p1566.

Note: if you are an EEA national and on 31 December 2020, and continuously since then, you have been self-employed in the UK while 'not primarily resident in the UK', you may have rights as a 'frontier worker' (see p1595). These rights include being exempt from the habitual residence test for means-tested benefits (see p1553).

Retaining worker or self-employed status

Since the end of the transition period (11pm on 31 December 2020), you can only have a free movement right to reside, including retained worker or self-employed status, while you are in one of the protected groups that can have these rights (see p1566).

If you *are* in one of the protected groups, or for a period before the end of the transition period, you can retain the status of 'worker' or 'self-employed', even though you are no longer working, if:[136]
- you are involuntarily unemployed and registered as a jobseeker (see p1579); *or*
- you are temporarily unable to work because of an illness or accident (see p1580); *or*
- you are undertaking vocational training (see p1581);
- you are unable to work because you are in the late stages of pregnancy or you have just given birth (see p1581).[137]

Before considering whether you have retained your worker or self-employed status, check whether you have ceased to be a worker (see p1577) or self-employed (see p1578). For example, if you are off work on unpaid sick leave but you can return to your job when you are better, you are still a worker and so you do not need to argue that you have retained your worker status.

If you have retained worker or self-employed status, this satisfies the right to reside requirement for all the benefits that have this requirement and you are exempt from the habitual residence test (see p1553) and you are exempt from the requirement to have been living in the UK for the past three months for child benefit and CTC (see p1548).

If you had retained worker or self-employed status on 31 December 2020, this can mean you are, or were, in a protected group that can have free movement rights. For further details, including the duration of these protections, see p1566.

Note: if you are a Croatian, A2 or A8 national who, during the relevant period of restrictions, was subject to those restrictions, you could not retain your worker status in the ways described in this section, unless you are an A8 national and you stopped working during the first month of employment. In this case, you could retain your worker status in the ways described in this section for the remainder of that month.[138] There were no restrictions on retaining self-employed status for Croatian, A2 or A8 nationals. For details of the restriction periods and who they affect, see p1571.

You are involuntarily unemployed and registered as a jobseeker

Under EU Directive 2004/38, you retain your status as a worker or self-employed person if you:[139]

- are recorded as involuntarily unemployed (see p1580); *and*
- have registered yourself as a jobseeker with the relevant employment office; *and*
- provide evidence that you are seeking employment (or, to retain self-employed status, seeking either employment or self-employment).

The EEA Regulations also contain requirements that are rarely enforced by the benefit authorities. These are that:[140]

- after six months, the evidence referred to in the last bullet point above must be 'compelling'. Until 31 December 2020, the regulations also required that you provide evidence of having a 'genuine chance of being engaged', and that, after six months, this had to be 'compelling' (known as the 'Genuine Prospects of Work' test). However, the Upper Tribunal held that this requirement was unlawful in February 2020.[141] You can rely on this judgment for periods before the regulations were amended. Guidance confirms that 'Genuine Prospects of Work' tests should no longer be carried out if you are retaining your worker or self-employed status due to involuntary unemployment;[142]
- you must have entered the UK in order to seek employment (or self-employment if you are retaining self-employed status); *and*

11

Part 11: Immigration and residence rules for benefits and tax credits
Chapter 69: Coming from abroad: residence rules
5. Who has a right to reside

- you must be in the UK seeking employment (and self-employment if you are retaining self-employed status) immediately after having a right to reside as a student or a self-sufficient person or a worker, other than if you retained your worker status on this basis (or a self-employed person, other than if you retained your self-employed status on this basis).

You are '**involuntarily unemployed**' if you are seeking, and are available to take up, employment (or self-employment, to retain your status as a self-employed person). This depends on your remaining in the labour market. The circumstances in which you left your last job, or ceased your self-employment, are just one factor in determining this, and your actions and circumstances since ceasing work must also be taken into account.[143]

The best way to register as a jobseeker is to claim UC and/or JSA, and show that you continue to satisfy the work search and work availability requirements (or the requirements to be available for and actively seeking work for JSA), even if you are not entitled to benefit.[144] If you are claiming a benefit that does not require you to look for work, you can satisfy the requirement to register as a jobseeker (and thereby retain your worker status) if you declare to the job centre that you are looking for work before your claim is determined, and provide evidence of seeking work.[145] If there was a gap between your ceasing work and registering as a jobseeker, see p1581.

If you were employed or self-employed for less than a year, the EEA Regulations limit the period during which you can retain your worker or self-employed status while registered as a jobseeker to a maximum of six months.[146] The EU Directive allows you to retain worker status for no less than six months.[147]

If you were employed or self-employed for more than a year (not necessarily in one continuous job), you can retain your worker or self-employed status on this basis indefinitely, unless there is an event that indicates you have withdrawn from the labour market entirely.[148]

11 You are temporarily unable to work because of an illness or accident

To retain your worker or self-employed status on this basis, your inability to work must be temporary. This simply means not permanent.[149] This can apply if you have a permanent health condition that fluctuates and causes temporary periods when you are unable to work.[150] You are considered to be temporarily unable to work if there is a realistic prospect of your being able to work again in the foreseeable future.[151] You do not need to have claimed ESA or another benefit on the grounds of inability to work, nor do you need to pass the test of limited capability for work. The test is a factual one of whether you are unable to do the work you were doing or, if it follows a period in which you were seeking work, the sort of work you were seeking.[152] Your inability to work must be caused by an illness or accident which *you* have – eg, you are not covered if you are unable to work because you are looking after a child who is ill.[153]

If you are permanently incapable of work, you may have a permanent right to reside (see p1594).

If you are unable to work because of pregnancy, see below.

You are undertaking vocational training

You retain your worker or self-employed status if you are undertaking a vocational training course. Unless you are involuntarily unemployed, the training must be related to your previous employment. If it is not, you must be accepted as being 'involuntarily unemployed'. You should be accepted as 'involuntarily unemployed' if there is no employment available to you that is reasonably equivalent to your last employment.[154]

Pregnancy and childbirth

If you have established worker or self-employed status and you are now not working because of late pregnancy or childbirth, you may still count as a worker or self-employed person, or you may be able to retain your worker or self-employed status.

You do not cease to be a worker while you are still under a contract of employment, so you are still a worker while on maternity leave, whether or not it is paid. This also applied to Croatian, A2 and A8 nationals who established worker status during the periods of restrictions (see p1572).[155]

You can continue to be a self-employed person if you stop work for a period of maternity leave, but intend to resume your self-employment.[156]

You can retain your worker or self-employed status if you have a pregnancy-related illness that prevents you from working (see p1580).[157]

You can retain worker or self-employed status if you gave up work (or seeking work, if you retained your worker or self-employed status while involuntarily unemployed – see p1579) because of the physical constraints of the late stages of pregnancy or the aftermath of childbirth, provided you intend to start work again (or start seeking work and thereby retain your worker status while involuntarily unemployed) within a 'reasonable period' after giving birth.[158] Other than in unusual cases, 52 weeks is a 'reasonable period' and the period will usually start 11 weeks before the due date.[159]

If you were retaining worker or self-employed status on this basis on 31 December 2020, and the benefit authority does not accept that you are in a protected group (see p1566) because the EEA Regulations do not include this as a basis to retain status, challenge the decision and get specialist advice. It is strongly arguable this right to reside does bring you within a protected group – see CPAG's *Benefits for Migrants Handbook* for details.

Moving between groups and gaps

You can retain your worker or self-employed status if you are in one of the groups on p1578 and continue to do so if you move into another category.[160] For

11

Part 11: Immigration and residence rules for benefits and tax credits
Chapter 69: Coming from abroad: residence rules
5. Who has a right to reside

example, you may have been involuntarily unemployed and registered as a jobseeker, then you became ill and were temporarily unable to work, and then you got better and started vocational training. You retain your worker or self-employed status throughout.

You may be able to retain your worker or self-employed status if there is a gap between your ceasing work and registering as a jobseeker with the DWP.[161] If the delay is more than a few days, all your circumstances, including the reasons for the gap and what you did during it, should be considered to establish whether there was undue delay[162] and whether you withdrew from the labour market during that period.[163] Arguably, you should also be able to retain your worker or self-employed status if there is a gap between your ceasing work and being temporarily unable to work because of illness or an accident, since there is no requirement for the illness or accident to be the reason for your ceasing work. You should also still retain your worker or self-employed status during a short gap between two different circumstances applying, provided you remain in the labour market during that time.

Self-sufficient people and students

Since the end of the transition period (11pm on 31 December 2020), you can only have a free movement right to reside, including as a self-sufficient person or student, while you are in one of the protected groups that can have these rights (see p1566).

If you *are* in one of the protected groups, or for a period before the end of the transition period, you have a right to reside as a self-sufficient person if you are an EEA national and you, and any family members whose right to reside depends on their being your family member, have:[164]

- sufficient resources not to become an unreasonable burden on the social assistance system of the UK during your period of residence;[165] *and*
- comprehensive sickness insurance.

The UK government cannot set a fixed amount that is regarded as 'sufficient resources' and must take account of your personal situation.[166] You have **'sufficient resources'** if they:[167]

- exceed the maximum level you (and your family) can have to be eligible for 'social assistance' (see p1583); *or*
- do not exceed that level, but the decision maker considers that you still have sufficient resources, taking into account your (and your family's) personal situation.

The 'maximum level' is the equivalent of your means-tested benefit applicable amount, including any premiums. Your resources also include your accommodation, so if your resources are more than your applicable amount plus your rent, or if friends or family provide you with free and stable accommodation, they should be 'sufficient'.[168]

You cannot automatically be regarded as not self-sufficient just because you make a claim for a means-tested benefit. All your circumstances, including the likely duration of your claim, must be assessed to determine whether or not your benefit claim makes you an unreasonable burden on the social assistance system of the UK.[169]

The source of the resources does not matter.[170] However, you cannot rely on your earnings from employment in the UK to give you self-sufficient status.[171] Check instead whether the employment gives you 'worker' status (see p1576). You can, however, rely on the earnings of your non-EEA national spouse/civil partner, or if you are a child, the earnings of your non-EEA parent (even if derived from employment that is unlawful due to a lack of residence card and work permit[172]).

The requirement to have **comprehensive sickness insurance** cover is satisfied if you have private health insurance.[173] It is also satisfied if the UK can be reimbursed by another state for any NHS costs you incur while in the UK. This usually applies if you are covered by the EU co-ordination rules (see p1647) and another state continues to be your 'competent state' (see p1656) after you come to the UK.[174] In March 2022, the CJEU held that this requirement was satisfied by being affiliated to the UK's system of health insurance offered free by the NHS.[175]

If you were a self-sufficient person (or student) on 31 December 2020, this can mean you are, or were, in a protected group that can have free movement rights. For further details, including the duration of these protections, see p1566.

Students

You have a free movement right to reside as a student if you are an EEA national and you:[176]
- are enrolled as a student in a government-accredited college; *and*
- provide an assurance that you have sufficient resources for you, and any family members whose right to reside depends on their being your family member, not to become a burden on the UK social assistance system during your intended period of residence (see above); *and*
- together with any family members who do not have an independent right to reside, have comprehensive sickness insurance (see above).

Family members

Since the end of the transition period (11pm on 31 December 2020), you can only have a free movement right to reside, including as a family member of an EEA national with a relevant free movement residence right (ie, one listed in the next paragraph), while you are in one of the protected groups that can have these rights (see p1566).

11

Part 11: Immigration and residence rules for benefits and tax credits
Chapter 69: Coming from abroad: residence rules
5. Who has a right to reside

If you *are* in one of the protected groups, or for a period before the end of the transition period, you have a right to reside if you are a 'family member' of an EEA national who has a free movement right to reside in the UK as a 'qualified person' (see p1568), or a permanent right to reside (see p1591) or an initial right to reside (see p1573). This applies whether or not you are an EEA national yourself. You have a right to reside for as long as you are in a protected group, the EEA national has a right to reside and you remain her/his family member.

Family members[177]

You are a **'family member'** if you are the EEA national's:
– spouse or civil partner; *or*
– child, grandchild or great-grandchild, or the child, grandchild or great-grandchild of the EEA national's spouse/civil partner, and you are under 21; *or*
– child, grandchild or great-grandchild, or the child, grandchild or great-grandchild of the EEA national's spouse/civil partner, and you are her/his dependant; *or*
– parent, grandparent or great-grandparent, or the parent, grandparent or great-grandparent of the EEA national's spouse/civil partner, and you are her/his dependant.

You remain a spouse or civil partner even if you are separated. You only cease to be a spouse or civil partner on divorce or dissolution of the civil partnership.[178]

'Dependence' is not defined in the legislation, but caselaw has established a number of principles.[179] To be dependent, you must receive support from the other person. The support must be 'material', although not necessarily financial, and must contribute towards your basic necessities. It does not need to be your only source of support. Translation, emotional and social support do not count.[180] It is irrelevant if there are alternative sources of support, including employment, available.[181]

If you only became dependent on the EEA national in the UK, this does not prevent you from being classed as a family member, unless you are an 'extended family member' (see p1585), in which case you must have already been dependent (or a member of her/his household) in the country you have come from.[182]

Note:
- If you are the family member of a person who has settled status their indefinite leave does not confer any rights on you. However, if s/he is an EEA national in circumstances that mean s/he *would* have a right to reside in the UK as a qualified person or a permanent right to reside, other than for the fact of not being in one of the protected groups, the benefit authorities accept this *does* confer a right to reside on you provided *you* are in a protected group. If this is not accepted, challenge the refusal and get advice to argue that the Withdrawal Agreements protect your rights in this situation.
- If you are not covered by the definition above, check whether you can be *treated as* a family member if you are an 'extended family member' *and* you

have a relevant residence document issued under the EEA Regulations (see below).

- If on 31 December 2020 you were a family member of an EEA national with a free movement right to reside, this can mean you are, or were, in a protected group that can have free movement rights. For further details, including the duration of these protections, see p1566.

- The definition of 'relevant family member' (see p1567), which could be relevant for determining whether you wre in a protected group between 31 December 2020 and 30 June 2021, is wider than the definition of family member given above. It was mainly relevant for family members arriving in the UK during that period (as well as durable partners without a residence document) because if, on 31 December 2020, you were in the UK as a family member of an EEA national with a relevant right to reside, you had your own free movement right to reside on 31 December 2020 that meant you were in a protected group at least until 30 June 2021.

- If your only right to reside is as a family member of an EEA national who has a right to reside as a jobseeker, this does not enable you to satisfy the right to reside requirement for UC, IS, income-related ESA, PC and HB, but does satisfy the right to reside requirement for child benefit and CTC (see p1557).

Are you unable to prove your right to reside?

If you are relying on your family member for your right to reside and you cannot prove what s/he is, or was, doing (eg, if you have separated from your spouse and have no evidence that s/he is a worker), ask the DWP, HMRC or local authority to investigate this – eg, by using the database of NI contributions to establish that your spouse is a worker. Provide information about your spouse to enable it to do so. If it is refused and you appeal, you can ask the First-tier Tribunal to issue a direction (see p1318) to the DWP, HMRC or local authority to make these investigations and argue that otherwise it has not shown that you do not have a right to reside.[183]

Extended family members

If you are not defined as a family member under the definition above, but you have a partner or relative in the UK who is an EEA national, you can be *treated as* her/his family member if you are her/his 'extended family member' and you have been issued with an EEA family permit, a registration certificate or a residence card, which remains in force.[184] Although you can no longer apply for these residence documents if you have already obtained one, it should be accepted as remaining in force if it has not yet expired (see p1570).

Part 11: Immigration and residence rules for benefits and tax credits
Chapter 69: Coming from abroad: residence rules
5. Who has a right to reside

Extended family member

You are an **'extended family member'** of an EEA national if s/he is your:[185]

– partner and you are in a durable relationship with her/him (or you are the child, under 18, of the partner); *or*

– non-adoptive legal guardian (under the laws of the country in which the guardianship order was granted), you are under 18, dependent on her/him and have lived with her/him since s/he became your legal guardian; *or*

– relative; *and*

– you meet the requirements of the Immigration Rules (other than those relating to entry clearance) for indefinite leave as her/his dependent relative; *or*

– you have serious health problems that require her/his (or her/his spouse's or civil partner's) care; *or*

– you previously were dependent on her/him, or were a member of her/his household, in a country other than the UK and you are accompanying her/him to, or wish to join her/him in, the UK, or you have joined her/him in the UK and continue to be dependent on her/him or to be a member of her/his household.[186]

Family members of British citizens

British citizens do not automatically give residence rights to their family members.

However, if you are a family member (including an extended family member with the relevant residence document) of a British citizen, you have a free movement right to reside under EU law if:[187]

- s/he is residing, or immediately before returning to the UK, did reside with a right to reside as a worker, self-employed person, self-sufficient person or self-sufficient student, or a permanent right to reside, in an EEA state; *and*

- you resided with the British citizen as her/his family member in that EEA state, your family life was created or strengthened there, and your joint residence in that EEA state was 'genuine' (see below).

On returning to the UK together, the British citizen confers free movement residence rights on you. Since 31 December 2020, the EEA Regulations *treat* the British person as satisfying any requirement to be a 'qualified person' (see p1568) on her/his return to the UK.[188] For periods before this, you can rely on caselaw that confirmed the British person does not need to undertake economic activity on return to the UK in order for her/his family member to have a right to reside.[189]

The EEA Regulations list the following as relevant to whether your residence in the EEA state is, or was, genuine:[190]

- the length of joint residence there;
- the nature and quality of the joint accommodation there and whether it was her/his principal residence;
- the degree of your and the British citizen's integration;
- whether it was your first lawful residence in the EU.

These factors go beyond the findings of the CJEU which, when considering whether residence is 'genuine', focused on whether it enabled the creation or strengthening of family life in that state and whether the conditions for the relevant residence rights were satisfied.[191]

The EEA Regulations exclude you from having a right to reside on this basis if the purpose of your residence in the EEA state was to circumvent the immigration laws.[192]

Family members of dual citizens

If you are the family member of a British citizen who also has citizenship of an EEA country, you can have a right to reside in the same circumstances as if you were the family member of an EEA national, provided that before acquiring British citizenship s/he had a free movement right to reside as either a 'qualified person' (see p1568) or a permanent right to reside (see p1591). The British citizen must have moved to the UK and resided as an EEA national with a right to reside as a 'qualified person' or with a permanent right to reside at the time s/he acquired British citizenship. If s/he currently has a right to reside as a qualified person, s/he must have had such a right continuously since acquiring British citizenship.[193]

A dual British/EEA national does not have rights under EU law if s/he has lived all her/his life in the UK. In this case, you cannot derive any rights from her/him.[194]

Former family members who retain their right to reside

In general, if you are the family member of an EEA national who has a right to reside, you lose your right to reside if s/he ceases to be your family member or to have a right to reside. However, there are some exceptions which mean you can retain your right to reside if the EEA national dies or leaves the UK, or if your marriage or civil partnership ends. These rights are in EU Directive 2004/38, but they are not exactly reproduced in the UK's EEA Regulations. The benefit authorities accept the rights set out in the EEA Regulations (listed below), but do not always accept those in the Directive (listed on p1588). If you only have a right to reside under the Directive and are refused benefit, you should challenge the decision and get specialist advice.

You retain your right to reside under the EEA Regulations if you are in one of the protected groups (see p1566) that can have a free movement right to reside after 31 December 2020, or for a period before that date, if you are a family member of an EEA national who is a 'qualified person' (see p1568) or a person with a permanent right to reside (see p1591) and:[195]

- the EEA national dies and you are:
  - not an EEA national, but if you were, you would be a worker, or a self-employed or self-sufficient person (or you are the family member of such a non-EEA national), and you resided in the UK with a right to reside under the EEA Regulations for at least a year immediately before s/he died; or

Part 11: Immigration and residence rules for benefits and tax credits
Chapter 69: Coming from abroad: residence rules
5. Who has a right to reside

　　　　– her/his child or grandchild (or the child or grandchild of her/his spouse or
　　　　civil partner) and you were in education (see p1591) immediately before
　　　　her/his death and you remain in education; *or*
　　　– the parent with custody of a child in the previous bullet point; *or*
　• the EEA national leaves the UK and you are:
　　　– her/his child or grandchild (or the child or grandchild of her/his spouse or
　　　　civil partner) and you were in education (see p1591) immediately before
　　　　s/he left the UK and you remain in education; *or*
　　　– the parent with custody of a child in the previous bullet point; *or*
　• your marriage or civil partnership to the EEA national is terminated, and s/he
　　was a qualified person or had a permanent right to reside at least until the
　　termination proceedings began,[196] and you are not an EEA national, but if you
　　were, you would be a worker, or a self-employed or self-sufficient person (or
　　you are the family member of such a non-EEA national), and you were residing
　　in the UK with a right to reside under the regulations at the date of the
　　termination and:
　　　– prior to the termination, the marriage/civil partnership had lasted for at
　　　　least three years with you both residing in the UK for at least one of those
　　　　years; *or*
　　　– you have custody of the EEA national's child; *or*
　　　– you have a right of access to the EEA national's child, which a court has said
　　　　must take place in the UK; *or*
　　　– your continued right of residence in the UK is warranted by particularly
　　　　difficult circumstances, such as your (or another family member's) being
　　　　subject to domestic violence during the period of the marriage/civil
　　　　partnership.

You have a right to reside on this basis for as long as the conditions apply to
you,[197] until you can acquire a permanent right of residence (see p1591).[198]

You should retain your right to reside under EU Directive 2004/38 if you
are a family member of an EEA national who has a right to reside as a worker, or as
a self-employed or self-sufficient person or a student and:
　• the EEA national dies and you have lived in the UK as her/his family member
　　for at least a year before her/his death and you are a non-EEA national;[199] *or*
　• the EEA national leaves the UK and you are:[200]
　　　– her/his child or grandchild and in education; *or*
　　　– the parent with custody of a child in the previous bullet point in education;
　　　　or
　• your marriage or civil partnership to the EEA national is terminated and s/he
　　had her/his right to reside at least until the termination proceedings began,[201]
　　you are a non-EEA national, and:[202]
　　　– prior to the commencement of the termination (which must occur while the
　　　　EEA national is in the UK[203]), the marriage/civil partnership had lasted for at

least three years with you both residing in the UK for at least one of those years; *or*

- you have custody of the EEA national's child; *or*
- you have a right of access to the EEA national's child, which a court has said must take place in the UK; *or*
- your continued right of residence in the UK is warranted by particularly difficult circumstances, such as your being subject to domestic abuse during the period of the marriage/civil partnership. Your rights are not retained in this way if your spouse or civil partner left the UK before the termination proceedings began.[204]

Note:

- It may be arguable that if you are an EEA national, you can retain your right to reside in each of the three circumstances above without needing to satisfy any other conditions.[205] However, two Upper Tribunal decisions have rejected this interpretation, taking the view that the provisions in the Directive just confirm that any independent residence rights that an EEA national may have had are not affected by the above changes.[206] It is arguable that these parts of each decision are not legally binding as each case failed on other grounds, but they will be persuasive until further caselaw decides the issue.

- Periods when you have retained your right to reside under the EU Directive in one of the ways above are not sufficient on their own to enable you to acquire permanent residence after five years (see p1591), because you are also required to show that you are a worker, or a self-employed or self-sufficient person, or you are the family member of such a person.[207]

Derivative right to reside

Since the end of the transition period (11pm on 31 December 2020), you can only have a free movement right to reside, including a derivative right to reside, while you are in one of the protected groups that can have these rights (see p1566).

If you *are* in one of the protected groups, or for a period before the end of the transition period, you may have a right to reside based on someone else's right to reside, without being her/his family member. The EEA Regulations list these as 'derivative' rights of residence. If the EEA Regulations interpret the rights more narrowly than EU caselaw, you can rely directly on the caselaw (see p1569).

You have a 'derivative' right to reside if (EEA Regulations only, you are not an 'exempt person' – see p1590 – and) you are:[208]

- the child (or stepchild[209]) of an EEA national who was a 'worker' in the UK (see p1576) while you were living in the UK, and you are currently in education;[210] *or*
- the primary carer of a child in the above bullet point and the child would be unable to continue her/his education in the UK if you left the UK;[211] *or*

Part 11: Immigration and residence rules for benefits and tax credits
Chapter 69: Coming from abroad: residence rules
5. Who has a right to reside

- the primary carer of a self-sufficient (see p1582) child who is an EEA national, who would be unable to remain in the UK if you left the UK;[212] *or*
- the primary carer of a British citizen residing in the UK who would be unable to reside in the UK or any EEA state if you left the UK (known as a 'Zambrano carer'),[213] aged under 18 and your primary carer is covered by either the second, third or fourth bullet points above and s/he would be prevented from residing in the UK if you left the UK, and you do not have leave to enter or remain in the UK (other than under the EUSS – see p1563); *or*
- (not in the EEA Regulations) the primary carer of a child with a permanent right to reside, who would be unable to remain in the UK if you left the UK.[214]

You are a child's primary carer if s/he is dependent on you, taking into account all the circumstances, including her/his best interests.[215] You can have a right to reside as the primary carer if you share equally the responsibility for the child's care with someone else. If this applies, the consequences of your being required to leave the UK are considered on the basis that both you and the other carer left the UK.[216]

The EEA Regulations exclude you from having a derivative right to reside if you are defined as an **'exempt person'**, and included within this definition is if you have a right to reside under any other provision of the EEA Regulations.[217] This exclusion is unlawful. If you are an EEA national and have been refused UC (or another means-tested benefit) on the basis that you have a right to reside under the EEA Regulations as a jobseeker (which does not satisfy the right to reside requirement for UC) and are therefore an 'exempt person', challenge this decision. Firstly, if you do not have to satisfy the work search and availability requirements (see p1037), argue that you are not a jobseeker. Secondly, or if you *are* required to seek work, you will need to argue that this exclusion is unlawful as it is contrary to the EU law which the regulation is intended to implement and this was recently confirmed by the CJEU in relation to a similar exclusion in German legislation.[218] See CPAG's *Benefits for Migrants Handbook* for further details of this argument.

Note:

- If your only right of residence is as the primary carer of a dependent British citizen who would otherwise have to leave the whole of the EEA, you do not satisfy the right to reside requirement for any means-tested benefits (see p1557) and only satisfy it for child benefit and CTC if you are a national of Morocco, San Marino, Tunisia, Turkey or, for claims made before 1 January 2021, Algeria and working in the UK (see p1560).
- Periods with any of the above derivative rights to reside do not count towards the period of residence required for acquiring a permanent right to reside (see p1591).

Child in education

To have a right to reside as a worker's child in education and as a primary carer of a worker's child in education, there must have been a common period when the child was in the UK and the parent (or step-parent[219]) was a worker in the UK. The child need not have entered education while the parent (or step-parent) was a worker.[220]

These rights also apply if the worker was an A8 national working during the period of restrictions (see p1571) for an 'authorised employer' (see p1573), even if it was for less than 12 months.[221] As the first month of work would have always been for an authorised employer, the A8 national's child who was in the UK during that first month of work and who is now in education can also have these rights.[222] These rights also apply in the same way if the worker was a Croatian or an A2 national working in accordance with her/his worker authorisation document during the period of restrictions.

Your right to reside as a primary carer of a worker's child in education ends when the child reaches 18, unless s/he continues to need your presence and care in order to be able to pursue and complete her/his education.[223]

Education

'**Education**' excludes nursery education, but includes education before the compulsory school age if it is equivalent to that received at or after compulsory school age – eg, education received by a child under five in a school reception class.[224]

If you are the primary carer of a pre-school-age child of a worker,[225] or of a child of a self-employed EEA national,[226] you are not accepted as deriving a right to reside from that child. However, it may be arguable that the Withdrawal Agreements provide a right to reside to the child of a self-employed EEA national in education, and her/his primary carer.[227] The DWP accepts this if the parent had been a frontier worker in the UK on the basis of being a self-employed person (or worker) (see p1595).[228]

People with a permanent right of residence

Since the end of the transition period (11pm on 31 December 2020), you can only have a free movement right to reside, including a permanent right to reside, while you are in one of the protected groups that can have these rights (see p1566).

If you *are* in one of the protected groups, or for a period before the end of the transition period, you can have a permanent right of residence if you have 'resided legally' (see p1593) in the UK for a 'continuous period of five years' (see p1592) or in limited circumstances after a shorter period (see p1594).[229] Once you have this permanent right of residence, you satisfy the right to reside requirement for all benefits that have that requirement.[230]

Part 11: Immigration and residence rules for benefits and tax credits
Chapter 69: Coming from abroad: residence rules
5. Who has a right to reside

Once acquired, you only lose your permanent right of residence if you are absent from the UK for more than two consecutive years.[231] However:

- for the purpose of being in a protected group that can have a free movement right to reside, you are *treated* as having permanent right to reside on 31 December 2020 if you had lost a previously acquired permanent right to reside due to being absent for more than two years, but your absence on that date was less than five years.[232] For details of the protected groups, including their duration, see p1566;
- in exceptional circumstances, your residence rights can be revoked or cancelled on grounds of public policy, public security or public health.[233]

Note: you should check whether you can obtain settled status (indefinite leave granted under the EUSS), based on either five years' residence in the UK (whether or not you had a right to reside during that time), or satisfying the requirements for permanent residence in less than five years (see p1594). From the date you are granted this leave, it will satisfy the right to reside requirement for all benefits that require it. For more information on settled status, see p1563.

A continuous period of five years

When calculating whether you have 'five years' continuous residence', temporary absences from the UK do not affect the continuity of your residence (and you can count the time spent abroad as part of your five years[234]) if:[235]

- they are not more than a total of six months a year; *or*
- they comprise one absence of up to 12 consecutive months for important reasons, such as pregnancy and childbirth, serious illness, study or vocational training, or a posting abroad; *or*
- they are for compulsory military service.

Note: if one of the absences above applied to you on 31 December 2020, you are *treated as* residing in the UK for the purpose of determining whether you are or were in a protected group that can have a free movement right to reside. For details of these protections, including their duration, see p1566.[236]

If you have a gap during which you remain in the UK, but do not have a free movement right to reside, it may be possible to argue it does not break your continuity of residence. Guidance to decision makers states that cumulative gaps of up to 30 days in any one year do not break your continuity of residence if they are between two periods when you have different residence rights, but not if they separate two periods when you have the same residence right.[237] Refer to this guidance if it is helpful, but remember it is not legally binding.

In most other circumstances, continuous residence during which you are 'residing legally' is required for the whole five years.[238] For details of how to argue that some periods of residence when you are not 'residing legally' do not interrupt your 'continuity of residence', provided the total period of 'residing legally' is at least five years, see the *Benefits for Migrants Handbook*.[239]

If you are removed from the UK or subject to a deportation or expulsion order[240] or, if you spend time in prison in circumstances that mean your integration in the UK has been broken,[241] this interrupts the continuity of your residence and you cannot count this time towards your five years.

What counts as 'resided legally'

You have 'resided legally' in any period during which you had a right of residence as a:

- worker (see p1576) (including if you retain your worker status – see p1578); *or*
- self-employed person (see p1577) (including if you retain your self-employed status – see p1578); *or*
- self-sufficient person (see p1582); *or*
- student (see p1583); *or*
- jobseeker (see p1574) since 30 April 2006 (see below); *or*
- person with an initial right of residence since 30 April 2006 (see below); *or*
- family member (see p1583) of any of the above.

If you have a continuous period of five years' residence on the basis of one or more of the above, you have a right of permanent residence under both the EEA Regulations and (other than an initial right of residence or as a jobseeker, or family member of either) EU Directive 2004/38.

The **EEA Regulations** allow you to count continuous residence 'in accordance with these regulations' (or in accordance with previous regulations), other than with a 'derivative right to reside' (see p1589).[242] This includes periods since 30 April 2006 when you had an initial right to reside or a right to reside as a jobseeker (or family member of either).[243] However, if you have pre-settled status (and are therefore in a protected group – see p1566), the EEA Regulations are amended to simply require you to have resided 'lawfully', which could include periods when you had pre-settled status but did not also have a free movement right to reside.[244]

Under **EU Directive 2004/38**, you must have 'resided legally for a continuous period of five years'.[245] This means that you must have had a residence right under the Directive or under any of the earlier EU legislation that it replaced.[246] This covers all the groups listed above, except for jobseekers and their family members.

You are not counted as having 'resided legally' during periods when your right to reside was as the primary carer of either a worker's child in education or a self-sufficient child,[247] or when your right of residence was only in accordance with UK law – eg, a period during which you had leave to remain under the Immigration Rules.[248]

If you are an A8, A2 or a Croatian national, you count as having 'resided legally' during periods before your state joined the EU if you would have come into one of the groups above (other than a jobseeker), or you would have resided

Part 11: Immigration and residence rules for benefits and tax credits
Chapter 69: Coming from abroad: residence rules
5. Who has a right to reside

in accordance with the EEA Regulations were it not for the fact that you were not an EU national at that time.[249] Once your state joined the EU, the periods when you count as having resided legally are as above, except they were subject to the additional restrictions for A8, A2 and Croatian nationals (see p1572).

Family members

If you are the family member (including extended family member with the relevant residence document[250]) (see p1583) of a person with a permanent right of residence, you have a right to reside for as long as you remain a family member and continue to be in a protected group that can have free movement residence rights.[251] After five years of being the family member of an EEA national with a permanent right of residence, you acquire a permanent right of residence yourself. You can also add periods as a family member of a person with a permanent right of residence to other periods when you count as 'residing legally' (see p1593) to make up your five years, and so acquire a permanent right of residence.[252]

Permanent residence in less than five years

If you are in one of the protected groups (see p1566), or for a period before the end of the transition period, you can, in the circumstances listed below, acquire a permanent right of residence before five years.[253] If so, you are exempt from the habitual residence test (see p1553).

- You were a worker (see p1576) or self-employed person (see p1577) in the UK, but have now stopped working in the UK and:
  - at the time you stopped working, you had reached pension age or (workers only) taken early retirement and:
    - your spouse or civil partner is a British citizen (or s/he lost that nationality by marrying you); *or*
    - you worked in the UK for the preceding year and resided (whether or not you had a right to reside[254]) in the UK continuously for more than three years; *or*
  - you stopped working as a result of a permanent incapacity (this means it is not a temporary incapacity (see p1580), but it may follow temporary incapacity – see the note below[255]) and:
    - your spouse or civil partner is a British citizen (or s/he lost that nationality by marrying you); *or*
    - you have resided (whether or not you had a right to reside[256]) in the UK continuously for more than two years (under the EEA Regulations only, immediately before you stopped working); *or*
    - the incapacity was because of an accident at work or occupational disease that resulted in benefit entitlement (eg, industrial injuries disablement benefit); *or*
  - you are a worker or self-employed in an EEA country while residing in the UK and returning, as a rule, at least once a week, following (under the EEA

Regulations only, immediately following) three years of continuous employment or self-employment and residence in the UK.

- You are the family member of a worker or self-employed person in any of the above bullet points and both of you are residing in the UK.[257] **Note:** the EEA Regulations require that you had a right to reside on the basis of being her/his family member at the point s/he ceased working.[258]

- You are the family member of a worker or self-employed person who died while still working and who did not acquire a permanent right of residence in one of the above ways and:
  - s/he had lived in the UK for two years; or
  - the death resulted from an accident at work or an occupational disease; or
  - you lost your UK nationality as a result of marrying her/him.

Note:
- You can count as periods of employment any period in which you were not working because of illness or accident, or some reason not of your own making, or periods of involuntary unemployment while registered as a jobseeker (it is arguable that the restriction in the EEA Regulations of this last group to workers is unlawful following the CJEU confirming that self-employed people can also retain status on this basis – see p1578).[259]

- The Upper Tribunal has held that no restrictions were imposed on A8 nationals in order to limit their rights to permanent residence in under five years.[260]

Frontier workers

You may have rights as a frontier worker in the UK if you are an EEA national and on 31 December 2020, and continuously since then, you have been 'not primarily resident in the UK', and either:[261]

- a worker in the UK (see p1576); or
- a self-employed person in the UK (see p1577); or
- you have retained your worker or self-employed status (see p1578).

You are treated as **'not primarily resident in the UK'** if you have either:[262]

- been present in the UK for less than 180 days in the last 12 months; or
- returned to your country of residence at least once in the last six months, or at least twice in the last 12 months, unless there are exceptional reasons for you not doing so.

The rights that you have as a frontier worker include rights to means-tested benefits without nationality-based discrimination.[263] Consequently, if you are a frontier worker, or if you have pre-settled status (limited leave granted under the EUSS) and you are a family member of a frontier worker, you are exempt from the habitual residence test for all means-tested benefits (see p1553). **Note:** you still have to satisfy all the other conditions of entitlement, including the requirement

11

Part 11: Immigration and residence rules for benefits and tax credits
Chapter 69: Coming from abroad: residence rules
6. Rules for specific benefits and tax credits

to be present in Great Britain (other than for specified temporary absences – see Chapter 70).[264]

If you are the child of a frontier worker, you and your primary carer have a right to reside in the UK in order for you to complete your education. These rights are similar to the derivative residence rights that the child of a worker in education, and her/his primary carer, can have, but note that they can apply whether the frontier worker was a worker or self-employed (see p1589).[265]

Note: until 30 March 2022, separate regulations prevented you from claiming UC, if you were (or, for a joint claim, you and your partner were both) a frontier worker. For the purpose of this exclusion, 'frontier worker' was defined as a person 'in Great Britain' for the purpose of UC,[266] but who does not reside in the UK (other than a Crown servant or member of the forces posted overseas) (see p23).[267] If you were excluded from claiming UC on this basis, you may have been able to make new claim for the legacy benefits (see p23).

---

6. **Rules for specific benefits and tax credits**

This section explains the residence and presence rules for each benefit. It includes which residence and presence tests apply and how you may be assisted by the European Union (EU) co-ordination rules.

For the rules on being paid while you are abroad, see Chapter 70.

Universal credit and other means-tested benefits

To be entitled to universal credit (UC), income support (IS), income-based jobseeker's allowance (JSA), income-related employment and support allowance (ESA), pension credit (PC) and housing benefit (HB), you (and your partner, for UC) must:

- be present in Great Britain (although for HB see below) (see p1547);[268] *and*
- be habitually resident (see p1550), including having a right to reside (see p1557) and, for income-based JSA only, have been living for the past three months (see p1548) in the 'common travel area' – ie, the UK, Ireland, the Channel Islands and the Isle of Man (unless you are exempt – see p1553).[269]

In certain circumstances, the rules treat you as being present in Great Britain during a temporary absence, so you can continue to receive these benefits while you are abroad for limited periods (see Chapter 70).

For UC, if your partner fails the habitual residence test, your joint claim is treated as a claim for UC as a single person (see p1597).

To be entitled to the carer element in your UC (see p73), you must satisfy the past presence test as it applies to carer's allowance (CA) (see p1601).

If you are receiving HB, IS, child tax credit (CTC) or working tax credit (WTC) and claim UC, and the DWP decides you do not satisfy the above residence or presence tests, this does *not* terminate your existing award of any of these four benefits (see p1553, point 8).

For HB, although being present in Great Britain is not a condition of entitlement, going abroad can still affect your entitlement due to the rules on occupying your home (see p1628).

Council tax reduction requires you to be habitually resident, including having a right to reside, in the common travel area (unless you are exempt). For details, see CPAG's *Benefits for Migrant's Handbook*.

Note: if you are moving, or have moved, to Great Britain from Northern Ireland or vice versa and are claiming income-related ESA, see p1604.

Couples claiming universal credit

If you live with your partner and claim UC, you are generally required to make a joint claim, and you and your partner must both satisfy, or be exempt from, the habitual residence test. If your partner fails the habitual residence test, your joint claim is treated as a claim for UC as a single person and:[270]

- the maximum amount of UC is that for a single person;[271]
- your partner does not have to accept a claimant commitment or comply with any work-related requirements because s/he is not a claimant;[272]
- your partner's income and capital are taken into account (see p35);[273]
- your partner is not classed as a 'non-dependant' and therefore no 'housing costs contribution' (see p102) is made from your UC due to her/him living with you;[274] *and*
- if you are under 35, your partner does not prevent your rent being restricted to the one-bedroom shared accommodation rate (see p105);[275] *and*
- if you have a child, your partner does not affect you being her/his 'responsible carer' (see p1040), to determine your work-related requirements;[276]
- the couple rate of the earnings threshold applies for determining when no work-related requirements apply to you (see p1043) and in calculating any self-employed 'minimum income floor' that may apply if you are self-employed (note that the 'minimum income floor' does not apply to your partner if s/he is self-employed) (see p122).[277]

Note: if you have reached pension age and your partner is under pension age but is not entitled to UC because s/he fails the habitual residence test, your claim is *not* treated as a single claim for UC. Instead, you must claim PC and HB and you are treated as a single person for each of these claims.[278]

If your partner is abroad

If you have a partner who is abroad, you may continue to receive benefit that includes an amount for her/him for a limited period if you are only temporarily living apart. The rules vary between the benefits (see Chapter 70).

Part 11: Immigration and residence rules for benefits and tax credits
Chapter 69: Coming from abroad: residence rules
6. Rules for specific benefits and tax credits

If these rules do not apply, or at the end of the limited period, or before then if her/his absence means s/he is no longer habitually resident in the common travel area:

- you cease to be entitled to UC as joint claimants. You must notify the DWP and your award is then based on the maximum amount for a single person, but your partner's income and capital are taken into account (for details, see p1597), *until* you have been, or you expect to be, apart for six months (as then you cease to be treated as a couple).[279] Once you cease to be treated as a couple, you are treated as having claimed as a single person (see p44).[280] However, if you are of pension age, but your partner is under pension age, see p1640;
- your applicable amount for IS, income-based JSA, income-related ESA, PC and HB no longer includes an amount for your partner. However, your partner's capital, income and work are still taken into account when working out how much benefit you get. This is because s/he is still treated as being part of your household, despite temporarily living away from you, unless you are in any of the situations listed on p306.[281]

Where questions of 'intention' are involved (eg, when deciding whether you or your partner intend to resume living with your family), the intention must be 'unqualified'. This means it must not depend on a factor over which you have no control – eg, the right of entry to the UK being granted by the Home Office,[282] or the offer of a suitable job.[283]

If your child is abroad

If you have a child who is abroad, your benefit entitlement could be affected if s/he ceases to be treated as part of your household (see p311).[284]

If your child is abroad, s/he is only included in your applicable amount for UC, IS, income-based JSA and PC for a limited period, and her/his absence can also affect your HB (see Chapter 70).

11 Bereavement benefits

You must be ordinarily resident (see p1550) in Great Britain on the date your spouse or civil partner died to be entitled to bereavement support payment.[285]

You do not need to satisfy any residence or presence rules to be entitled to widowed parent's allowance.

European Union co-ordination rules

If you are covered by any of the EU co-ordination rules (see p1647) and the UK is your 'competent state' (see p1656):[286]

- you can, if necessary, rely on national insurance (NI) contributions paid by your late spouse/civil partner in European Economic Area (EEA) states (EU states if relying on the UK-EU Protocol, or Ireland if you are relying on the UK-

Ireland Convention) to calculate your entitlement to bereavement benefits (under the 'aggregation principle' – see p1659); *and*

- for bereavement support payment, the requirement to be ordinarily resident in Great Britain on the date your spouse or civil partner died does not apply if you were resident in an EEA/EU state or Ireland on that date.

Reciprocal agreements

If you are covered by a reciprocal agreement (see p1546), these can assist in similar ways to the EU co-ordination rules in respect of the relevant country. If the agreement treats you as being present in the UK while in the other country and you were ordinarily resident in that country on the date your spouse or civil partner died, you are treated as ordinarily resident in Great Britain on that date.[287] Guidance lists the relevant countries.[288]

Child benefit, Scottish child payment and guardian's allowance

Child benefit

To be entitled to child benefit, you and your child(ren) must be present in Great Britain (see p1547).[289]

To be treated as present, you (but not your child/ren) must also:[290]

- be ordinarily resident in the UK (see p1550); *and*
- have a right to reside in the UK (see p1560), unless your current claim began before 1 May 2004; *and*
- have been living in the UK for the three months prior to your date of claim (unless you are exempt – see p1548).

You are treated as present if you are:[291]

- a Crown servant posted overseas and:
  - you are, or immediately before your posting abroad you were, ordinarily resident in the UK; *or*
  - immediately before your posting, you were in the UK in connection with that posting; *or*
- the partner of a Crown servant posted overseas and in the same country as her/him or temporarily absent from that country under the same exceptions that enable child benefit to continue during a temporary absence from Great Britain (see p1623).

You are treated as ordinarily resident if you are in the UK as a result of your being deported or legally removed from another country.[292]

You and/or your child can be treated as present for limited periods during a temporary absence (see p1623).

While you are treated as present, you continue to satisfy that condition of entitlement. This means that you can continue to receive child benefit if it is

Part 11: Immigration and residence rules for benefits and tax credits
Chapter 69: Coming from abroad: residence rules
6. Rules for specific benefits and tax credits

already being paid and you can also make a fresh claim during your, or your child's, absence. If you, or your child, spend longer abroad than the permitted periods, you (or s/he) cease to satisfy the presence condition and your entitlement to child benefit ends. **Note:** if you or your child are treated as being present, you must satisfy all the other conditions of entitlement including, if your child is not living with you, contributing to the costs of that child (see p568).

Scottish child payment

To be entitled to a Scottish child payment, you must be ordinarily resident (see p1550) in Scotland.[293]

Guardian's allowance

Entitlement to guardian's allowance depends on entitlement to child benefit, so you must meet the conditions for child benefit on p1599.

In addition, at least one of the child's parents must have:[294]
- been born in the UK or an EEA country; *or*
- at some time after reaching the age of 16, spent a total of 52 weeks in any two-year period in Great Britain.

In order to satisfy the second condition above, you are treated as being present in Great Britain during any absence abroad which is due to your employment as a serving member of HM forces, an aircraft worker, mariner or continental shelf worker.

European Union co-ordination rules

If the main EU co-ordination rules, or, for situations involving the UK and Ireland only, the UK-Ireland Convention, apply to you (see p1647), you may be able to:
- use certain periods of residence in one or more EEA countries (Ireland, if relying on the Convention) to satisfy the child benefit requirement to have been living in the UK for the past three months under the 'aggregation principle' (see p1659);
- be paid child benefit and guardian's allowance for a child who is resident in an EEA country (Ireland, if relying on the Convention) without her/his needing to satisfy the rules on temporary absences, provided you satisfy all the other conditions of entitlement, including contributing to the costs of the child (see p568). These rules can apply as these benefits are classed as 'family benefits' (see p1661);
- use time spent in one or more EEA states (Ireland, if relying on the Convention) to satisfy the requirement for guardian's allowance to have spent 52 weeks in any two-year period in Great Britain (under the 'aggregation principle' – see p1659). It may also be arguable that this condition should not apply if you have a 'genuine and sufficient link to the UK' (see p1602).[295]

Note:
- Scottish child payment has been categorised as a special non-contributory benefit (see p1655) and therefore the middle bullet above does not apply to it.
- The UK-EU Protocol cannot assist in the above ways as it does not cover family benefits.

Disability benefits and carer's allowance

To be entitled to attendance allowance (AA), disability living allowance (DLA), child disability payment (CDP), personal independence payment (PIP), adult disability payment (ADP) and CA you must:[296]
- be present in Great Britain (the common travel area for CDP and ADP) at the time of your claim; *and*
- have been present in Great Britain (the common travel area for CDP and ADP) for at least 104 weeks in the last 156 weeks (26 weeks in the last 52 for DLA, CDP and ADP, and see note on CA below) (the 'past presence test'). See immediately below if you are a child, and see further below for exemptions; *and*
- be habitually resident in the common travel area (see p1550, but also the exemptions below); *and*
- (CDP and ADP only) be ordinarily resident in Scotland.

The past presence test if you are claiming CDP or, if you are aged three to 16, DLA, is 26 weeks in the last 52 weeks.[297] This is reduced to 13 weeks for a **baby** under six months old claiming either CDP or DLA, and this requirement then continues to apply until the baby's first birthday. If the child becomes entitled to DLA at between six and 36 months, the past presence test is 26 weeks in the last 156 weeks.[298]

Note:
- (For CA only) it is arguable the past presence test must be aligned with that of DLA if you are caring for a child awarded DLA after being present for 26 weeks in the last 52. For details and a template letter, see cpag.org.uk/welfare-rights/legal-test-cases/disability-living-allowance-2-year-past-presence-test.
- (For CDP or ADP only) if you do not satisfy the past presence test (or other residence and presence requirements), but will within 13 weeks, your claim may be treated as an advance claim from the date you satisfy this requirement.[299]

To be entitled to the **carer's allowance supplement**, you must be in receipt of CA and resident (see p1549) in Scotland on the qualifying date (see p553).[300]

To qualify for a **young carer grant**, on the day of your application you must be:[301]
- ordinarily resident in Scotland; *and*
- habitually resident in the UK, Channel Islands, Isle of Man, Switzerland or the EEA (see p1551) or be exempt from this requirement (see p1553).

11

Part 11: Immigration and residence rules for benefits and tax credits
Chapter 69: Coming from abroad: residence rules
6. Rules for specific benefits and tax credits

For ESA in youth, incapacity benefit (IB) in youth and severe disablement allowance (SDA), see the 2017/18 edition of this *Handbook*.[302]

When you can be treated as present

You are treated as being present during certain absences (see p1625). Any period when you are treated as present can be counted to satisfy both the presence and the past presence tests.

Exemptions from habitual residence and past presence test

For AA, DLA, CDP, PIP, ADP and CA the past presence test does not apply (and for the last four bullet points below, the habitual residence test also does not apply – for the third bullet point this is since 22 March 2022, but since 9 February 2022 for CDP and ADP) if you:[303]

- (except CA) are terminally ill;
- (ADP and CDP only) are an aircraft worker, mariner or continental shelf worker;
- have refugee leave or humanitarian protection (or you have leave as the dependent family member of someone who has such leave);
- (since 22 March 2022) were living in the Ukraine immediately before 1 January 2022 and you left in connection with the Russian invasion of 24 February 2022, and you have leave, or a right of abode, in the UK (including if you are British);
- (since 15 September 2021) have leave by virtue of the Afghan Relocations and Assistance Policy (ARAP), or the scheme for locally employed staff in Afghanistan (LES Scheme), or discretionary leave as the dependant of a person with leave under either, or leave granted under the Afghan Citizens Resettlement Scheme;[304] *or*
- (for ADP and CDP only) are abroad as a serving member of the armed forces, or as a civil servant, provided you satisfied the residence and presence requirements (other than the past presence test), immediately prior to the start of this employment outside the common travel area, or you are living with someone who is abroad as a serving member of the armed forces or civil servant, and s/he is your spouse, civil partner (or living together as if you were either), or son, stepson, daughter, stepdaughter, or child in their care, or, other than for CDP, father, stepfather, father-in-law, mother, stepmother or mother-in-law. You are also treated as ordinarily resident for ADP and CDP.

For AA, DLA, PIP and CA, you are exempt from the habitual residence test, and treated as present in Great Britain if you are abroad as a serving member of the armed forces, or are living with someone who is abroad as a serving member of the armed forces and s/he is your spouse, civil partner, son, stepson, daughter, stepdaughter, or father, stepfather, father-in-law, mother, stepmother or mother-in-law.[305]

European Union co-ordination rules

The EU co-ordination rules can help you to be entitled to AA, DLA, CDP, PIP, ADP and CA more quickly in the UK.

The past presence test does not apply to AA, DLA, CDP, PIP, ADP and CA if:[306]
- you are habitually resident in Great Britain (in the UK, for CDP and ADP); *and*
- you are covered by the main co-ordination rules (or, for CDP and ADP only, the agreement with Gibraltar) (see p1647); *and*
- the UK is your competent state to pay that category of benefit (see below and p1656);
- (other than CDP or ADP) you can demonstrate 'a genuine and sufficient link' to the UK (see below).

If you are covered by the main co-ordination rules (see p1647) or for situations involving the UK and Ireland only you are covered by the UK-Ireland Convention, you may be able to count certain periods of residence in one or more EEA states to satisfy the past presence test for these benefits (under the 'aggregation principle' – see p1659).[307] **Note:** you can use the aggregation principle of the main co-ordination rules if you are covered by either the Withdrawal Agreement protections (see p1647) or, if these do not, or no longer apply, the *partial* Withdrawal Agreement protections (see p1649).

If you are covered by the main co-ordination rules or, for situations involving the UK and Ireland only, the UK-Ireland Convention, or, for ADP and CDP only, the agreement with Gibraltar, and if the UK is your competent state (see below), you may (other than for the mobility components) be able to make a new claim or continue to be paid when you are habitually resident in an EEA state (Ireland, if relying on the UK-Ireland Convention, Gibraltar if relying on the agreemnt with Gibraltar), if you have a 'genuine and sufficient link' to the UK (to Scotland for Scottish benefits) (see p1604 and p1626).

Note: if you are covered by the main co-ordination rules, you cannot be entitled to AA, DLA care component, PIP daily living component, CA, CA supplement or young carer grant, unless the UK is the **'competent state'** to pay that category of benefit.[308] The requirement for the UK to be the competent state applies to CDP and ADP if you are relying on the main co-ordination rules, or agreement with Gibraltar, to disapply the past presence test. This requirement also applies for payment to the care component of CDP, the daily living component of ADP, CA supplement or young carer grant while you are habitually resident in an EEA country if covered by the main co-ordination rules, or in Gibraltar if you are covered by the agreement with Gibraltar, and in Ireland if you are covered by the UK-Ireland Convention.[309]

The UK might not be your competent state if you (or your family member who brings you within the co-ordination rules) receive a contributory benefit (classed as a 'pension') from an EEA state (Ireland, if relying on the Convention).[310] For details on the competent state, see p1656.

The UK-EU Protocol does not cover these disability and carers' benefits (see p1652).[311]

11

Part 11: Immigration and residence rules for benefits and tax credits
Chapter 69: Coming from abroad: residence rules
6. Rules for specific benefits and tax credits

Do you have a genuine and sufficient link?

Factors that are relevant when demonstrating that you have a 'genuine and sufficient link to the UK' (not to the 'UK social security system' as specified in the regulations[312]) (for Scottish benefits, see the note below) can include:[313]

– whether you have worked in the UK;

– whether you have spent a significant part of your life in the UK;

– whether you have been present in the UK for a reasonable period;

– whether you are receiving a UK contributory benefit;

– evidence of your motives, intentions and expectations;

– the benefit you are claiming, and if you are claiming a disability benefit, whether your carer would be entitled to CA;

– the duration of your presence in Great Britain;

– whether you are dependent on a family member who has worked in the UK and/or who receives a UK contributory benefit. 'Family member' in this context is not limited to people covered by the definition of 'member of the family' in the co-ordination rules (see p1652), and can, for example, include your sister.[314]

Note: the requirement to demonstrate a 'genuine and sufficient link to Scotland', for specific elements of the residence and presence requirements for CDP and ADP, child winter heating assistance, CA supplement and young carer grant, must be interpreted in a way that is consistent with the caselaw referred to above, but in relation to Scotland.

Contributory employment and support allowance

To be entitled to contributory ESA, you must be in Great Britain.[315] The rules on when you can be paid during a temporary absence are in Chapter 70. There are no residence conditions, except for contributory ESA in youth (see the 2017/18 edition of this *Handbook* or CPAG's *Benefits for Migrants Handbook*).

European Union co-ordination rules

If you are covered by any of the EU co-ordination rules (see p1647) and the UK is your 'competent state' (see p1656), you can, if necessary, rely on NI contributions paid in one or more EEA states (EU, if relying on the UK-EU Protocol, or Ireland, if relying on the UK-Ireland Convention) to entitle you to contributory ESA in the UK (under the 'aggregation principle' – see p1659).

You may also be able to 'export' (ie, continue to receive) a 'sickness' or (unless you are only covered by the UK-EU Protocol) 'invalidity' benefit from an EEA/EU state/Ireland (see p1660).

Reciprocal agreements

If you have lived and worked in a country with which the UK has a reciprocal agreement (see p1546), you may be able to count periods of insurance paid in that country towards your entitlement to contributory ESA in the UK.

If you have moved from Northern Ireland to Great Britain (or vice versa), reciprocal arrangements mean your ESA (both income-related and contributory) should be paid at the same rate.[316] For further details, see CPAG's *Benefits for Migrants Handbook*.

Industrial injuries benefits

To be entitled to any of the industrial injuries benefits, you must have:
- been in Great Britain when the accident at work happened;[317] *or*
- been engaged in Great Britain in the employment that caused the disease (even if you have also been engaged outside Great Britain in that employment);[318] *or*
- been paying UK class 1 or class 2 NI contributions when the accident at work happened or you contracted the disease. Benefit is not payable until you return to Great Britain.[319]

There are exceptions, which mean that you can qualify for benefit in respect of an accident that happens, or a disease that is contracted, outside Great Britain while you are:[320]
- employed as a mariner or aircraft worker; *or*
- employed as an apprentice pilot on board a ship or vessel; *or*
- on board an aircraft on a test flight starting in Great Britain in the course of your employment.

In these cases, there are also more generous rules for defining when accidents arise 'out of and in the course of' your employment, and for complying with time limits under benefit rules.[321]

European Union co-ordination rules

If you are covered by any of the EU co-ordination rules (see p1647) and the UK is your 'competent state' (see p1656), you can, if necessary, rely on periods of employment and NI paid in one or more EEA states (EU states, if relying on the UK-EU Protocol or Ireland, if relying on the UK-Ireland Convention) in order to qualify for industrial injuries benefits in the UK (under the 'aggregation principle' – see p1659).

If you have an accident while travelling abroad in a member state, this can be deemed to have occurred in the state liable to pay industrial injuries benefits.[322] If you have worked in two or more member states in a job that gave you a prescribed industrial disease, you get benefit from the state in which you last did work that, by its nature, is likely to cause that disease and which recognises that disease under its industrial injuries scheme.[323]

Part 11: Immigration and residence rules for benefits and tax credits
Chapter 69: Coming from abroad: residence rules
6. Rules for specific benefits and tax credits

Contribution-based jobseeker's allowance

To be entitled to contribution-based JSA, you must be in Great Britain.[324] The rules on when you can be paid during a temporary absence are covered in Chapter 70. There are no residence conditions.

European Union co-ordination rules

In most cases, if you are covered by any of the EU co-ordination rules (see p1647), you may be able to count NI contributions paid in one or more EEA states to entitle you to contribution-based JSA in the UK (under the 'aggregation principle'). However, this is usually only possible if your most recent period of paying, or being credited with, contributions was in the UK (see p1659).[325]

If you are covered by the main co-ordination rules, you have been working in an EEA state and are coming to, or returning to, the UK to look for work, you may be able to obtain, before you leave, a U2 form authorising you to export your unemployment benefit from that EEA state. If you are covered by the UK-Ireland Convention and have been working in Ireland, you may be able to export your Irish unemployment benefit. In either situation, you can continue to receive that unemployment benefit for up to three months if:[326]

- you were getting it immediately before coming to the UK; *and*
- you have been registered as available for work for four weeks (or less, if that state's rules allow) in the other state; *and*
- you claim JSA within seven days after you were last registered in the other member state; *and*
- you satisfy the relevant jobseeking requirements for JSA.

The three months can be extended to a maximum of six months if the state from which you are claiming the unemployment benefit agrees.[327]

You cannot 'export' unemployment benefit under the UK-EU Protocol.[328]

Reciprocal agreements

If you have lived and worked in a country with which the UK has a reciprocal agreement (see p1546), you may be able to count periods of insurance paid in that country towards your entitlement to contribution-based JSA. If you are covered by the agreements between Great Britain and Northern Ireland, you can be treated as in Great Britain if you go to Northern Ireland (see p1631).

Maternity allowance

Entitlement to maternity allowance (MA) is based on past employment, generally in Great Britain.[329] There are no residence requirements. However, in general you are disqualified if you are absent from Great Britain.[330] See p1634 for the rules allowing you to be paid during a temporary absence.

European Union co-ordination rules

If any of the EU co-ordination rules apply to you (see p1647) and the UK is your 'competent state' (see p1656), you can, if necessary, rely on periods of employment or self-employment in one or more EEA states (EU states, if relying on the UK-EU Protocol, or Ireland, if relying on the UK-Ireland Convention) in order to qualify for MA in the UK (under the 'aggregation principle' – see p1659). You may also be able to 'export' (ie, continue to receive) a maternity or paternity benefit from an EEA state (or EU/Ireland) (see p1660).

Retirement pensions

Retirement pensions, other than category D retirement pension, do not have any residence or presence entitlement conditions. They can be paid without a time limit, whether or not you are present in Great Britain. However, going abroad can mean you are not paid the annual uprating, can be relevant to decisions on deferring your retirement and can prevent you from 'de-retiring' while you are abroad (see p1636).[331]

To be entitled to a category D retirement pension, you must have been:[332]

- resident in Great Britain for at least 10 years in any continuous period of 20 years ending on or after your 80th birthday; *and*
- ordinarily resident (see p1550) in Great Britain on either:
  - your 80th birthday; *or*
  - the date on which you claimed category D pension, if later.

European Union co-ordination rules

If you are covered by any of the EU co-ordination rules (see p1647) and the UK is your 'competent state' (see p1656), you can, if necessary, rely on NI contributions paid, or for category D retirement pension certain periods of residence completed, in EEA states (Ireland, if relying on the UK-Ireland Convention) to calculate your entitlement to retirement pensions in the UK (under the 'aggregation principle' – see p1659). However, your award may be made in proportions that reflect the proportion of years of contributions paid, or periods of residence completed, in the UK and other member states, out of the total years of contributions paid or periods of residence completed in all states.[333] **Note:** the UK-EU Protocol does not apply to Iceland, Norway, Liechtenstein or Switzerland, but the main co-ordination rules on aggregating NI contributions for entitlement to, and uprating of, UK retirement pensions continue to apply even if you are not covered by the Withdrawal Agreement protections.[334] Also note new agreements co-ordinating pensions with these four countries may be agreed in future (see p1636).

The requirement to be ordinarily resident for a category D retirement pension may not apply to you if you can show that you have a 'genuine and sufficient link to the UK' (see p1604).[335]

You may also be able to 'export' (ie, continue to receive) an old age pension from an EEA state (see p1660).

Part 11: Immigration and residence rules for benefits and tax credits
Chapter 69: Coming from abroad: residence rules
6. Rules for specific benefits and tax credits

Reciprocal agreements

If you have lived and worked in a country with which the UK has a reciprocal agreement (see p1546), you may be able to count periods of residence or insurance paid in that country towards your UK retirement pension entitlement.

Social fund and other payments

Funeral payments

To qualify for a **funeral support payment** in Scotland, you must be ordinarily resident in Scotland on the date you make your application.[336]

To qualify for a **funeral expenses payment** from the social fund, you must live in England or Wales.[337]

To qualify for either a **funeral expenses payment** or a **funeral support payment**:

- the person who has died must have been ordinarily resident (see p1550) in the UK at the date of death (this does not apply in Scotland if s/he was a stillborn child);[338] *and*
- the funeral must usually take place in the UK. However, it can take place in any EEA state or the UK if you or your partner are:[339]
  - an EEA national with a right to reside as a worker (see p1576) or self-employed (see p1577), including if you have retained either status (see p1578); *or*
  - a family member of one of the above (see p1583); *or*
  - an EEA national with a permanent right of residence acquired in less than five years (see p1594); *or*
  - (funeral support payment only) have limited leave (pre-settled status) or indefinite leave (settled status) granted under the EUSS (see p1563); *or*
  - arguably, a person with any other free movement right of residence in the UK. For further details, see CPAG's *Benefits for Migrants Handbook*.[340]

To qualify for a **children's funeral fund payment** in England, the funeral must take place in England for a child aged under 18 or stillborn. There are no residence (or immigration status) requirements.[341] To qualify for a children's funeral payment in Wales, the family home must be in Wales.[342]

Maternity grant payments

To qualify for a **Sure Start maternity grant** from the social fund, you must live in England or Wales.[343]

To qualify for a **Best Start grant**, you must be ordinarily resident (see p1550) in Scotland.[344] In addition, if neither you nor your partner receive a qualifying benefit (see p1697), but you qualify for a grant because you are aged under 20 (see p1700):[345]

- you must be habitually resident in the UK, Channel Islands or Isle of Man; *or*

- you or your partner must be habitually resident in the EEA or Switzerland *and* have a right to reside in the UK either as a 'qualified person' (see p1568) or a family member (see p1583) (other than an extended family member) of a qualified person or EEA national with a permanent right to reside (see p1591), or have limited leave (pre-settled status) or indefinite leave (settled status) under the EUSS (see p1563); *or*
- you must be exempt from this habitual residence test (see p1553).

Winter fuel payments

To qualify for a **winter fuel payment**, you must be ordinarily resident (see p1550) in Great Britain on any day in the qualifying week (see p792).[346]

To qualify for **child winter heating assistance** if you are under 19 and in receipt of the higher rate of the DLA/CDP care component or enhanced rate of the PIP/ADP daily living component, on any day in the qualifying week (see p1673) you must be:[347]

- resident (see p1549) in Scotland; *or*
- habitually resident (see p1550) in an EEA state (other than Cyprus, France, Greece, Malta, Portugal or Spain) *and* have a 'genuine and sufficient link' to Scotland (see p1604).

European Union co-ordination rules

You are not required to be ordinarily resident in Great Britain in order to be entitled to a **winter fuel payment** if, on any day in the qualifying week, you are:[348]

- covered by either the Withdrawal Agreement protections (see p1647) or the UK-Ireland Convention (see p1650); *and*
- habitually resident in Switzerland or an EEA country (other than Cyprus, France, Gibraltar, Greece, Malta, Portugal or Spain); *and*
- can demonstrate a 'genuine and sufficient link' to the UK (see p1603).

Winter fuel payments are not covered by the UK-EU Protocol or, other than to overcome the requirement to be ordinarily resident in Great Britain as above, the UK-Ireland Convention.[349]

Tax credits

To be entitled to **child tax credit** (CTC), you (and your partner, if you have made a joint claim) must:[350]

- be present in the UK (see p1547); *and*
- be ordinarily resident in the UK (see p1550); *and*
- have a right to reside in the UK (see p1561), unless you have been receiving CTC since before 1 May 2004; *and*
- have been living in the UK for the three months prior to your date of claim (unless you are exempt – see p1548).

Part 11: Immigration and residence rules for benefits and tax credits
Chapter 69: Coming from abroad: residence rules
6. Rules for specific benefits and tax credits

To be entitled to **working tax credit** (WTC), you (and your partner, if you have made a joint claim) must be:[351]

- present in the UK (see p1547); *and*
- ordinarily resident in the UK (see p1550).

There are limited exceptions for Crown servants posted overseas, and exceptions from the requirement to be ordinarily resident (although, in practice, claims are rarely refused on the latter basis).[352]

For the rules on when you can be treated as present, and can therefore either continue to receive tax credits (or make a fresh claim if you are in one of the groups on p1459), see p1638.

Being absent (except when you are treated as being present), ceasing to be ordinarily resident or losing your right to reside are all changes that you must notify to HM Revenue and Customs (HMRC) within one month. If you do not, HMRC may recover any overpaid tax credits (see Chapter 65) and impose a penalty (see Chapter 66).

Couples

If you are a member of a couple and have made a joint tax credit claim, both of you must satisfy the residence requirements. Your entitlement to tax credits as a couple ends if HMRC considers that you and your partner have separated and this is likely to be permanent,[353] or if either you or your partner:

- are abroad for longer than a permitted temporary absence (see p1638); *or*
- (for CTC only) lose the right to reside; *or*
- cease to be ordinarily resident.

If your entitlement to tax credits as a couple ends, you and/or your partner may be entitled to UC (or may be able to make a single claim for tax credits if you are in one of the groups on p1459).

If you receive tax credits on the basis of a single claim, but then your partner returns to the UK or becomes ordinarily resident or acquires a right to reside, you cease to be entitled to tax credits. You may then be entitled to UC (or may be able to make a joint claim for tax credits if you are in one of the groups on p1459).

If you or your partner are abroad (even during a period while being treated as present) and you (or s/he) were the only partner in full-time work, you may lose entitlement to WTC if the requirement to be in full-time work is no longer satisfied (see p284).

You have a duty to notify HMRC of any of the above changes within one month (see p1470). If you fail to do so, HMRC may recover any overpaid tax credits (see Chapter 65) and impose a penalty (see Chapter 66).

European Union co-ordination rules

If you are covered by the main EU co-ordination rules or, for situations involving the UK and Ireland only, the UK-Ireland Convention (see p1647), you may be

Chapter 69

Coming from abroad: residence rules

able to be paid CTC for a partner or child who is resident in an EEA country (see p1661). WTC is not covered by any of the EU co-ordination rules (see p1652) and so if your partner is in an EEA state, *you* can be entitled to CTC on the basis of a joint CTC claim, but entitled to WTC on the basis of a single WTC claim.[354]

Notes

2. The different residence and presence tests

1 **CB** Reg 23(5) CB Regs
   CTC Reg 3(6) TC(R) Regs
2 Reg 85A(2) JSA Regs
3 *AEKM v Department for Communities (JSA)* [2016] NICom 80, paras 21, 46-48 and 61; *TC v SSWP (JSA)* [2017] UKUT 222 (AAC); Vol 2, para 072996 DMG; TCTM 02035; CBTM 10025
4 **CB** Reg 23(5) CB Regs
   CTC Reg 3(6) TC(R) Regs
5 **CB** Reg 23(6) CB Regs
   CTC Reg 3(7) TC(R) Regs
6 **CB** Reg 23(3) CB Regs
   CTC Reg 3(3) TC(R) Regs
7 R(IS) 6/96, para 19; R(P) 2/67; CPC/1035/2005; see also *TC v SSWP (JSA)* [2017] UKUT 222 (AAC)
8 R(M) 1/85
9 *R v Barnet LBC ex parte Shah* [1983] 2 AC 309; *GC v HMRC (TC)* [2014] UKUT 251 (AAC); *Arthur v HMRC* [2017] EWCA Civ 1756, paras 16, 31 and 32
10 *MS v SSWP (DLA)* [2016] UKUT 42 (AAC)

3. Habitual residence

11 **UC** Reg 9 UC Regs
   IS Regs 21 and 21AA IS Regs
   JSA Regs 85 and 85A JSA Regs
   ESA Regs 69 and 70 ESA Regs
   PC Reg 2 SPC Regs
   HB Reg 10 HB Regs; reg 10 HB(SPC) Regs
   AA Reg 2(1)(a)(i) SS(AA) Regs
   DLA Reg 2(1)(a)(i) SS(DLA) Regs
   CDP Reg 5(1)(b) DACYP(S) Regs
   PIP Reg 16(c) SS(PIP) Regs
   ADP Reg 15(1)(b) DAWAP(S) Regs
   CA Reg 9(1)(a) SS(ICA) Regs
12 Reg 12 CTRS(PR)E Regs; reg 16 CTR(SPC)S Regs; reg 16 CTR(S) Regs; reg 28 CTRSPR(W) Regs; Sch para 19 CTRS(DS)W Regs
13 Regs 3(3), 18(2), 22(3) and 36(3) UC Regs; reg 9(1) UC,PIP,JSA&ESA(C&P) Regs
14 **UC** Reg 9 UC Regs
   PC Reg 2 SPC Regs
15 **IS** Regs 21 and 21AA and Sch 7 para 17 IS Regs
   JSA Regs 85 and 85A and Sch 5 para 14 JSA Regs
   ESA Regs 69 and 70 and Sch 5 para 11 ESA Regs
16 Reg 10(1) HB Regs; reg 10(1) HB(SPC) Regs
17 **AA** s35(1) SSA 1975; reg 2(1) SS(AA) Regs
   DLA s71(6) SSCBA 1992; reg 2(1) SS(DLA) Regs
   CDP reg 5(1)(b) DACYP(S) Regs
   PIP s77(3) WRA 2012; reg 16 SS(PIP) Regs
   ADP Reg 15(1)(b) DAWAP(S) Regs
   CA s70(2) SSCBA 1992; reg 9(1) SS(ICA) Regs
   YCG regs 3 and 8 CA(YCG)(S) Regs
   BSG Sch 1 paras 1(c) and 4 EYA(BSG)(S) Regs
18 See, for example, *GE v SSWP (ESA)* [2017] UKUT 145 (AAC), reported as [2017] AACR 34, paras 52-58, and *SSWP v KK (JSA)* [2019] UKUT 313 (AAC), para 8
19 Reg 8 UC(TP) Regs
20 *SK v HMRC and SSWP* [2022] UKUT 10 (AAC); see also different view taken in *HMRC v AB* [2021] UKUT 209 (AAC)
21 R(IS) 6/96

Part 11: Immigration and residence rules for benefits and tax credits
Chapter 69: Coming from abroad: residence rules
Notes

◦ ◦

22 Confirmed in para A1340 ADM and Vol 1 Ch 1, para 01343 DMG
23 **UC** Reg 9(4) UC Regs
  IS Reg 21AA(4) IS Regs
  JSA Reg 85A(4) JSA Regs
  ESA Reg 70(4) ESA Regs
  PC Reg 2(4) SPC Regs
  HB Reg 10(3B) HB Regs
24 see ADM Memo 14/21 and DMG Memo 11/21
25 Reg 8(2) CA(YCG)(S) Regs
26 Sch 2 para 4(1)(b) and (2) EYA(BSG)(S) Regs
27 **AA** Regs 2(2) and (3A), and 2C SS(AA) Regs
  DLA Regs 2(2) and (3A), and 2C SS(DLA) Regs
  CDP Reg 5(6)-(7) and (10A)-(11) DACYP(S) Regs
  PIP Regs 19, 20 and 23A SS(PIP) Regs
  ADP Regs 15(7)-(8) and 17 DAWAP(S) Regs
  CA Regs 9(3) and 9C SS(ICA) Regs
28 See also ADM Memo 14/21 and DMG Memo 11/21
29 R(IS) 6/96, paras 17 and 20; CIS/13498/96, para 17
30 CIS/15927/1996
31 *R v Barnet LBC ex parte Shah* [1983] 2 AC 309, para 344; CIS/13498/1996
32 R(IS) 2/00; CIS/4474/2003
33 *Nessa v Chief Adjudication Officer* [1999] UKHL 41
34 CIS/4474/2003
35 CIS/1972/2003
36 CIS/1304/97; CJSA/5394/98
37 CIS/1304/1997; CJSA/5394/1998
38 Art 70 EU Reg 883/04; Art 10a EU Reg 1408/71; *Swaddling v Adjudication Officer*, C-90/97 [1999]
39 CIS/12703/1996
40 *KS v SSWP (SPC)* [2010] UKUT 156 (AAC); see also *TC v SSWP (JSA)* [2017] UKUT 222 (AAC)
41 R(IS) 2/00; CIS/11481/1995

4. Right to reside

42 Reg 12 CTRS(PR)E Regs; reg 16 CTR(SPC)S Regs; reg 16 CTR(S) Regs; reg 28 CTRSPR(W) Regs; Sch para 19 CTRS(DS)W Regs
43 **UC** Reg 9(3) UC Regs
  IS Reg 21AA(2) and (3) IS Regs
  JSA Reg 85A(2) and (3) JSA Regs
  ESA Reg 70(2) and (3) ESA Regs
  PC Reg 2(2) and (3) SPC Regs
  HB Reg 10(3) and (3A) HB Regs; reg 10(3) and (4) HB(SPC) Regs

44 To date all legal challenges to this exclusion have failed – most recently, *R (on the application of HC) v SSWP and Others* [2017] UKSC 73.
45 *Slezak v SSWP* [2017] CSIH 4, reported as [2017] AACR 21
46 **UC** Reg 9(3)(c)(i) UC Regs
  IS Reg 21AA(3A)(a) IS Regs
  JSA Reg 85A(3A)(a) JSA Regs
  ESA Reg 70(3A)(a) ESA Regs
  PC Reg 2(3A)(a) SPC Regs
  HB Reg 10(3AA)(a) HB Regs; reg 10(4ZA)(a)HB(SPC) Regs
47 **UC** Reg 9(3A) UC Regs
  IS Reg 21AA(3B) IS Regs
  JSA Reg 85A(3B) JSA Regs
  ESA Reg 70(3B) ESA Regs
  PC Reg 2(3B) SPC Regs
  HB Reg 10(3AB) HB Regs; reg 10(4ZB) HB(SPC) Regs, confirmed in ADM Memo 19/20 and DMG Memo 17/20
48 Appendix EU, Annex 1, IR; see also ADM Memo 19/20, para 10, and DMG Memo 17/20, para 10
49 *CG v Department for Communities NI*, C-709/20 [2021]
50 *Fratila and Tanase v SSWP* [2020] EWCA Civ 1741
51 *Fratila and Tanase v SSWP* [2021] UKSC 53
52 *CG v Department for Communities NI*, C-709/20 [2021], paras 84-93; Arts 1, 7 and 24 EU Charter of Fundamental Rights
53 Arts 2 and 4 WA 2019
54 Reg 6 SS(HR)A Regs; reg 11 SS(PA)A Regs; see also *AP v SSWP (IS)* [2018] UKUT 307 (AAC)
55 **CB** Reg 23(4) CB Regs
  TC Reg 3(5) TC(R) Regs
56 **CB** Reg 23(4) CB Regs
  CTC Reg 3(5) TC(R) Regs
57 **CB** Reg 23(4) CB Regs
  TC Reg 3(5) TC(R) Regs
58 **CB** Regs 1(3) and 23(4)(b) and (4A) CB Regs
  CTC Reg 3(5)(b)(ii) and (5A) and (12) TC(R) Regs
  HMRC v HEH and SSWP (TC and CHB) [2018] UKUT 237 (AAC)
59 Most recently, *R (on the application of HC) v SSWP and others* [2017] UKSC 73
60 **CB** Regs 1(3) and 23(4B) CB Regs
  TC Reg 3(5B) and (11) TC(R) Regs

5. **Who has a right to reside**

61 s3ZA IA 1971

62 Arts 2(e), 126 and 127 WA 2019; ss1A, 1B, 8A and Sch 2 Part 1A EU(W)A 2018

63 ss1A-1B EU(W)A 2018

64 s1B(3)(d) and (e) EU(W)A 2018

65 Appendices EU and EU (Family Permit) IR

66 Reg 2 CR(ADTP) Regs; articles of the Withdrawal Agreements listed

67 Confirmed in para C1871 ADM; Vol 2 Part 3 Ch7 para 073491 DMG; HB Circular A7/2019, para 9

68 gov.uk/view-prove-immigration-status

69 Regs 3 and 4 CR(ADTP) Regs; reg 83 and Sch 4 paras 1-4 ISSC(CSTTP) Regs; ADM Memo 29/20, paras 24 and 87-114; DMG Memo 25/20, paras 23-35 and 92-119; ADM Memo 30/20; DMG Memo 26/20

70 Home Office, *Public Funds: migrant access to public funds, including social housing, homelessness assistance and social care* (version 18), 20 August 2021, p30; HB Circular A10/2021, paras 8, 11 and 12; DMG Memo 10/21, paras 8 and 9; ADM Memo 19/21, paras 8 and 9

71 Home Office, *Public Funds: migrant access to public funds, including social housing, homelessness assistance and social care* (version 18), 20 August 2021, p30; HB Circular A10/2021, paras 8-13; DMG Memo 10/21; ADM Memo 19/21

72 Reg 3(5)(b) and 4(6)(c) CR(ADTP) Regs; reg 3 I(EEA) Regs

73 Regs 3(5)(c) and 4(5)(d) CR(ADTP) Regs

74 Regs 3(4)-(6), 4(2) and (5)-(8) and 12(1)(i) CR(ADTP) Regs

75 Regs 3(6) CR(ADTP) Regs; ADM Memo 30/20, para 9; DMG Memo 26/20, para 9

76 Reg 3(6)(g)(iii) and (iv) CR(ADTP) Regs; provisions of the Withdrawal Agreements cited

77 Regs 6 and 14(1) I(EEA) Regs. The same groups are covered in Arts 7 and 14 EU Dir 2004/38 but the term 'qualified person' is not used in the Directive.

78 *SSWP v JB (JSA)* [2011] UKUT 96 (AAC)

79 ss2-5 EU(W)2018

80 Part 2 WA 2019; Part 2 UK-EFTA; UK-Swiss Agreement

81 For a helpful discussion, see *Geci (EEA Regs: transitional provisions, appeal rights) Albania* [2021] UKUT 285 (IAC)

82 s6 EU(W)A 2018; The European Union (Withdrawal) Act 2018 (Relevant Court) (Retained EU Case Law) Regulations 2020 No.1525

83 Arts 2 and 4 WA 2019; Arts 2 and 4 UK-EFTA; Art 4 UK-Swiss Agreement

84 Art 158 WA 2019

85 Decision of the EEA Joint Committee No.158/2007

86 Swiss nationals: *Agreement between the European Community and its Member States, of the one part, and the Swiss Confederation, of the other, on the Free Movement of Persons*, 21 June 1999, Cmd 5639. In force from 1 June 2002.

87 Reg 2(1) I(EEA) Regs

88 Reg 1 I(EEA) Regs – except reg 9, which was replaced from 25 November 2016

89 Reg 7(3) I(EEA) Regs; para C1738 ADM; Vol 2 Ch 7, para 073294 DMG

90 *SSWP v Dias*, C-325/09 [2011]; *EM and KN v SSWP* [2009] UKUT 44 (AAC); *MD v SSWP (SPC)* [2016] UKUT 319 (AAC); regs 17(8), 18(7), 19(4) and 20(5) I(EEA) Regs

91 Reg 17 I(EEA) Regs; Sch 3 para 3(3) ISSC(CSTTP) Regs

92 Reg 18 I(EEA) Regs; Sch 3 para 3(4) ISSC(CSTTP) Regs

93 Reg 20 I(EEA) Regs; Sch 3 para 3(6) ISSC(CSTTP) Regs

94 Reg 19 I(EEA) Regs; Sch 3 para 3(5) ISSC(CSTTP) Regs

95 Reg 45 and Sch 6 para 2 I(EEA) Regs; reg 10 CR(ADTP) Regs

96 Reg 12 I(EEA) Regs; regs 3(4)-(6), 4(2) and (5)-(8) and 6(b) CR(ADTP) Regs; Sch 3 para 3(1) and (2) ISSC(CSTTP) Regs

97 *SSWP v Gubeladze* [2019] UKSC 31; see also DMG Memo 11/19 and ADM Memo 14/19 and *AM v SSWP (ESA)* [2019] UKUT 215 (AAC)

98 **Croatia** Reg 8 AC(IWA) Regs
A2 Reg 9 A(IWA) Regs

99 **Croatia** Regs 4 and 5 AC(IWA) Regs
A2 Reg 6 A(IWA) Regs

100 Reg 7 A(IWR) Regs

101 Reg 5 A(IWR) Regs

102 The CJEU held that this restriction was lawful: *Prefeta v SSWP*, C-618/16 [2018]

103 CIS/1042/2008; *SSWP v JB* [2011] UKUT 96 (AAC)

104 Reg 13(2) and (3) I(EEA) Regs; Art 6(2) EU Dir 2004/38

105 *GE v SSWP (ESA)* [2017] UKUT 145 (AAC), reported as [2017] AACR 34

106 Art 45 TFEU; Arts 14 and 24 EU Dir 2004/38; reg 6 I(EEA) Regs

107 *GMA v État belge*, C-710/19 [2020]

108 *The Queen v Immigration Appeal Tribunal, ex parte Antonissen*, C-292/89 [1991]

11

Part 11: Immigration and residence rules for benefits and tax credits
Chapter 69: Coming from abroad: residence rules
Notes

109 **Croatia** Reg 5 AC(IWA) Regs
A2 Reg 6 A(IWA) Regs
A8 Regs 4(2) and (4) and 5(2) A(IWR)
Regs

110 *The Queen v Immigration Appeal
Tribunal, ex parte Antonissen,* C-292/89
[1991]

111 *GMA v État belge,* C-710/19 [2020]

112 R(IS) 8/08

113 *GE v SSWP (ESA)* [2017] UKUT 145
(AAC), reported as [2017] AACR 34,
para 46; see also *Cardiff CC v HM (HB)*
[2019] UKUT 271 (AAC), paras 6 and 18,
and *SSWP v KK (JSA)* [2019] UKUT 313
(AAC), para 9

114 Reg 6(1) and (7)-(10) I(EEA) Regs

115 Regs 6(1) and 14 I(EEA) Regs; Arts 7(1)
and 14 EU Dir 2004/38

116 *Lawrie-Blum v Land Baden-Württemberg,*
C-66/85 [1986]

117 *Barry v LB Southwark* [2008] EWCA Civ
1440; *Tarola v Minister for Social
Protection,* C-483/17 [2019]

118 *Rinner-Kühn v FWW Spezial-
Gebäudereinigung GmbH and Co. KG,*
171/88 [1989]

119 R(IS) 12/98

120 *Genc v Land Berlin,* C-14/09 [2010]

121 *Steymann v Staatssecretaris van Justitie,*
196/87 [1988]

122 CIS/1837/2006; CIS/868/2008

123 *Kempf v Staatssecretaris van Justitie,* C-
139/85 [1986]; *Bettray v Staatssecretaris
van Justitie,* C-344/87 [1989]; *Genc v
Land Berlin,* C-14/09 [2010]

124 CIS/1502/2007

125 *JA v SSWP (ESA)* [2012] UKUT 122 (AAC),
cited with approval in *EP v SSWP (JSA)*
[2016] UKUT 445 (AAC), para 21

126 Vol 2, paras 073038-40 DMG; paras
C1487-89 ADM; HB A3/2014, para 15;
*Child Benefit and Child Tax Credit: right to
reside establishing whether an EEA
national is/was a worker or a self-
employed person under EU law,* para 7; *RF
v LB Lambeth* [2019] UKUT 52 (AAC)

127 CIS/4237/2007

128 *BS v SSWP* [2009] UKUT 16 (AAC)

129 Regs 4(1)(b), 6(1) and 14 I(EEA) Regs;
Arts 7(1) and 14 EU Dir 2004/38

130 *Jany and Others v Staatssecretaris van
Justitie,* C-268/99 [2001]

131 Reg 4(1)(b) I(EEA) Regs

132 R(IS) 6/00, para 31

133 *TG v SSWP* [2009] UKUT 58 (AAC)

134 *SSWP v JS (IS)* [2010] UKUT 240 (AAC)

135 CIS/1042/2008; *HMRC v GP* [2017]
UKUT 11 (AAC)

136 Art 7(3) EU Dir 2004/38; *Gusa v Minister
for Social Protection (Ireland),* C-442/16
[2017]; reg 6 I(EEA) Regs

137 *Saint Prix v SSWP,* C-507/12 [2014];
HMRC v Dakneviciute, C-544/18 [2019];
see also ADM Memo 21/19 and DMG
Memo 17/19

138 Reg 5(4) A(IWR) Regs; reg 7A(4) I(EEA)
Regs 2006, as saved by reg 45 and Sch 4
para 2 I(EEA) Regs

139 Art 7(3)(b) and (c) EU Dir 2004/38; *Gusa
v Minister for Social Protection (Ireland),*
C-442/16 [2017]

140 Reg 6(2)-(10) I(EEA) Regs

141 *KH v Bury MBC and SSWP* [2020] UKUT
50 (AAC), especially paras 39-44 and 67

142 paras C1302 and C1403-4 ADM; DMG
Memo 27/20 paras 11 and 14

143 CH/3314/2005, para 11; *SSWP v MK*
[2013] UKUT 163 (AAC); *SB v SSWP (UC)*
[2019] UKUT 219 (AAC), paras 8-13

144 See, for example, *SSWP v WN (rule 17)*
[2018] UKUT 268 (AAC)

145 *SSWP v Elmi* [2011] EWCA Civ 1403

146 Reg 6(2)(c), (3), (4)(c), (4A), (4B), (4C),
(5) and (6) I(EEA) Regs

147 Art 7(3)(c) EU Dir 2004/38; see, for
example, *Tarola v Minister for Social
Protection,* C-483/17 [2019] and *SB v
SSWP (UC)* [2019] UKUT 219 (AAC)

148 Art 7(3)(b) EU Dir 2004/38; reg 6(2)(b),
(4)(b), (4B), (4C), and (5)-(7) I(EEA)
Regs; *SSWP v MM* [2015] UKUT 128
(AAC), para 54; see also *KH v Bury MBC
and SSWP* [2020] UKUT 50 (AAC), paras
40-41

149 *SSHD v FB* [2010] UKUT 447 (IAC); *LM v
HMRC (CHB)* [2016] UKUT 389 (AAC);
SSWP v LM (ESA) (Interim decision)
[2017] UKUT 485 (AAC), paras 31-34

150 CIS/3890/2005

151 *De Brito v SSHD* [2012] EWCA Civ 709;
Konodyba v RB of K&C [2012] EWCA Civ
982; *Samin v SSHD* [2012] EWCA Civ
1468; *SSWP v LM (ESA) (Interim decision)*
[2017] UKUT 485(AAC), paras 31-34;
see also *BL v SSWP (ESA)* [2019] UKUT
364 (AAC), paras 20-23

152 CIS/4304/2007; *HK v SSWP* [2017]
UKUT 421 (AAC), paras 4-6 and 8

153 CIS/3182/2005

154 *SSWP v EM* [2009] UKUT 146 (AAC); see
also *OB v SSWP (ESA)* [2017] UKUT 255
(AAC), para 32

155 CIS/4237/2007

156 CIS/1042/2008; *HMRC v GP* [2017]
UKUT 11 (AAC); see also *HMRC v HD
(CHB) (Second interim decision)* [2018]
UKUT 148 (AAC), paras 2 and 3

11

157 CIS/731/2007
158 *Saint Prix v SSWP*, C-507/12 [2014]; *HMRC v Dakneviciute*, C-544/18 [2019]; *SSWP v SFF and others* [2015] UKUT 502 (AAC), reported as [2016] AACR 16
159 *SSWP v SFF and others* [2015] UKUT 502 (AAC), reported as [2016] AACR 16; *Weldemichael and Another v SSHD* [2015] UKUT 540 (IAC)
160 CIS/4304/2007; *SSWP v IR* [2009] UKUT 11 (AAC); *SSWP v SFF and others* [2015] UKUT 502 (AAC), para 40
161 CIS/1934/2006
162 *SSWP v MK* [2013] UKUT 163 (AAC); *VP v SSWP (JSA)* [2014] UKUT 32 (AAC), paras 56-61; *SSWP v MM* [2015] UKUT 128 (AAC), paras 47-52; *SSWP v LM (ESA) (Interim decision)* [2017] UKUT 485 (AAC), para 23
163 *SSWP v IR* [2009] UKUT 11 (AAC)
164 Art 7(1) EU Dir 2004/38; regs 4(1)(c) and (2)-(4), 6(1) and 14(1) I(EEA) Regs
165 *Pensionsversicherungsanstalt v Brey*, C-140/12 [2013], paras 54-57
166 Art 8(4) EU Dir 2004/38
167 Reg 4(4) I(EEA) Regs
168 *SG v Tameside MBC (HB)* [2010] UKUT 243 (AAC)
169 *Pensionsversicherungsanstalt v Brey*, C-140/12 [2013]; *AMS v SSWP (PC) (Final Decision)* [2017] UKUT 381 (AAC), reported as [2018] AACR 27; *AS v SSWP (UC)* [2018] UKUT 260 (AAC), para 43
170 *Commission of the European Communities v Kingdom of Belgium*, C-408/03 [2006]; *Zhu and Chen v SSHD*, C-200/02 [2004]; *Alokpa v Ministre du Travail, de l'Emploi et de l'Immigration*, C-86/12 [2013], para 27
171 *VP v SSWP (JSA)* [2014] UKUT 32 (AAC), reported as [2017] AACR 25, paras 88-97
172 *Singh and Others v Minister of Justice and Equality*, C-218/14 [2015]; *Bajratari v SSHD*, C-93/18 [2019]
173 *W (China) and Another v SSHD* [2006] EWCA Civ 1494
174 *SG v Tameside MBC (HB)* [2010] UKUT 243 (AAC); *SSWP v GS (PC)* [2016] UKUT 394 (AAC), reported as [2017] AACR 7
175 *VI v HMRC* C-247[2022], paras 66–70
176 Art 7(1) EU Dir 2004/38; regs 4(1)(d) and (2)-(4), 6(1) and 14(1) I(EEA) Regs
177 Art 2(2) EU Dir 2004/38; reg 7(1) I(EEA) Regs
178 *Diatta v Land Berlin*, 267/83 [1985]
179 CIS/2100/2007, which considers the findings of *Centre Public d'Aide Sociale de Courcelles v Lebon*, C-316/85 [1987]; *Zhu and Chen v SSHD*, C-200/02 [2004]; and *Jia v Migrationsverket*, C-1/05 [2007]
180 *SSWP v MF (SPC)* [2018] UKUT 179 (AAC)
181 *Reyes v Migrationsverket* C-423/12 [2014]; *Centre Public d'Aide Sociale de Courcelles v Lebon*, C-316/85 [1987]; *ECO v Lim (EEA dependency)* [2013] UKUT 437 (IAC)
182 *Pedro v SSWP* [2009] EWCA Civ 1358; *Jia v Migrationsverket*, C-1/05 [2007]; *SSHD v Rahman and Others*, C-83/11 [2012]; *Oboh and Others v SSHD* [2013] EWCA Civ 1525
183 *Kerr v DSDNI* [2004] UKHL 23, paras 62-69; para A1405 ADM; ADM Memo 30/20, para 42; DMG Memo 26/20, para 42; Sch 2 para 5(3) Data Protection Act 2018
184 Reg 7(3) I(EEA) Regs; CPC/3588/2006; *SS v SSWP (ESA)* [2010] UKUT 8 (AAC); *SSWP v LZ (SPC)* [2014] UKUT 147 (AAC); *Macastena v SSHD* [2018] EWCA Civ 1558; *SSHD v Aibangbee* [2019] EWCA Civ 339; *MW v SSWP (UC)* [2019] UKUT 184; *AM v SSWP and CC Swansea Council* [2019] UKUT 361 (AAC), paras 19-21; para C1738 ADM; Vol 2 Ch 7, para 073294 DMG
185 Reg 8 I(EEA) Regs. Most of these groups are covered in Art 3 EU Dir 2004/38, but the term is not used.
186 See also *AA (Algeria) v SSHD* [2014] EWCA Civ 1741; *Dauhoo (EEA Regs – Reg 8(2)) v SSHD* [2012] UKUT 79 (IAC); *Chowdhury v SSHD* [2021] EWCA Civ 1220; *Begum v SSHD* [2021] EWCA Civ 1878
187 Regs 1, 7(4) and 9 I(EEA) Regs since 1 February 2017 and reg 4 and Sch 5 I(EEA) Regs for the prior period from 25 November 2016; Art 21(1) TFEU; *R v IAT et Surinder Singh ex parte SSHD*, C-370/90 [1992]; *O and B v Minister voor Immigratie, Integratie en Asiel*, C-456/12 [2014]; *Coman v Inspectoratul General pentru Imigrari*, C-673/16 [2018]; *SSHD v Banger*, C-89/17 [2018]
188 Reg 5(h) CR(ADTP) Regs; Sch 3 para 6(h) and Sch 4 para 4(h) ISSC(CSTTP) Regs

11

Part 11: Immigration and residence rules for benefits and tax credits
Chapter 69: Coming from abroad: residence rules
Notes

189 *Minister voor Vreemdelingenzaken en Integratie v Eind*, C-291/05 [2007], para 45; *HK v SSWP (PC)* [2020] UKUT 33 (AAC). For an additional summary of *Eind*, see *B v SSWP* [2017] UKUT 472 (AAC), paras 33-39. See also DMG Memo 21/20 and ADM Memo 24/20

190 Reg 9(4) I(EEA) Regs; *ZA (Reg 9 EEA Regs; abuse of rights) Afganistan* [2019] UKUT 281 (IAC)

191 *O and B v Minister voor Immigratie, Intergratie en Asiel*, C-456/12 [2014], especially paras 51-56; see also *ZA (Reg 9 EEA Regs; abuse of rights) Afghanistan* [2019] UKUT 281 (IAC), para 75; *VW v SSWP (PC)* [2014] UKUT 573 (AAC)

192 Reg 9(4) I(EEA) Regs

193 Regs 2(1) (see definition of 'EEA national') and 9A I(EEA) Regs; reg 3 I(EEA)A Regs 2018; reg 5(I) CR(ADTP) Regs; Sch 4 para 4(i) ISSC(CSTTP) Regs; *Lounes v SSHD*, C-165/16 [2017]; Art 21(1) TFEU; *AS v SSWP (UC)* [2018] UKUT 260 (AAC); *Kovacevic (British Citizen – Art 21 TFEU) Croatia* [2018] UKUT 273 (IAC); *ODS v SSWP (UC)* [2019] UKUT 192 (AAC)

194 *McCarthy v SSHD*, C-434-09 [2011]

195 Reg 10 I(EEA) Regs

196 *Baigazieva v SSHD* [2018] EWCA Civ 1088

197 Reg 14(3) I(EEA) Regs

198 Reg 10(8) and (9) I(EEA) Regs; *MK v SSWP (ESA)* [2020] 235 (AAC), para 11

199 Art 12 EU Dir 2004/38

200 Art 12(3) EU Dir 2004/38

201 *Baigazieva v SSHD* [2018] EWCA Civ 1088

202 Art 13 EU Dir 2004/38

203 *Singh and Others v Minister of Justice and Equality*, C-218/14 [2015]

204 *SSHD v NA*, C-115/15 [2016]

205 Arts 12(1) and 13(1) EU Dir 2004/38

206 *JP v SSWP (ESA)* [2018] UKUT 161 (AAC), paras 12-21; *GA v SSWP (SPC)* [2018] UKUT 172 (AAC), paras 27-44

207 Arts 12, 13 and 18 EU Dir 2004/38

208 Reg 16 I(EEA) Regs

209 *Baumbast and R v SSHD*, C-413/99 [2002], para 57; *IP v SSWP (IS)* [2015] UKUT 691 (AAC)

210 See also *LB Harrow v Ibrahim and SSHD*, C-310/08 [2010] ECR I-01065; *Teixeira v LB Lambeth and SSHD*, C-480/08 [2010]; *GBC Echternach and A Moritz v Minister van Onderwijs en Wetenschappen*, joined cases C-389/87 and C-390/87 [1989] ECR 00723; *Baumbast and R v SSHD*, C-413/99 [2002]

211 See also *LB Harrow v Ibrahim and SSHD*, C-310/08 [2010]; *Teixeira v LB Lambeth and SSHD*, C-480/08 [2010]; *GBC Echternach and A Moritz v Minister van Onderwijs en Wetenschappen*, joined cases C-389/87 and C-390/87 [1989]; *Baumbast and R v SSHD*, C-413/99 [2002]

212 See also *Zhu and Chen v SSHD*, C-200/02 [2004]; *SSHD v NA*, C-115/15 [2016]

213 See also *Zambrano v ONEm*, C-34/09 [2011]; *Dereci and Others v Bundesministerium für Inneres*, C-256/11 [2011]; see also *DM v SSWP (PIP)* [2019] UKUT 26 (AAC)

214 *FE v HMRC (CHB)* [2022] UKUT 4 (AAC); *VI v HMRC* C-247/20 [2022]

215 *Chavez-Vilchez v Raad van bestuur van de Sociale verzekeringsbank* C-133/15 [2017] and caselaw cited

216 Reg 16(8)-(11) I(EEA) Regs. See also *MA v DSD (JSA)* [2011] NICom 205

217 Reg 16(7)(c) I(EEA) Regs

218 Art 10 EU Reg 492/2011 (before 1 June 2012, Art 12 EC Reg 1612/68 had identical terms); *MA v Department for Social Development (JSA)* [2011] NICom 205, para 13; see also comment in *HK v SSWP* [2017] UKUT 421 (AAC), para 10, which was cited in support in *AV v SSWP (UC)* CUC 1190/2019, paras 6-10; *JD v Jobcenter Krefeld* C-181/19 [2020], especially paras 64, 71 and 79; see also *Fratila and Tanase v SSWP* [2020] EWCA Civ 1741, especially paras 42-55

219 *Baumbast and R v SSHD*, C-413/99 [2002], para 57; *IP v SSWP (IS)* [2015] UKUT 691 (AAC)

220 *Teixeira v LB Lambeth and SSHD*, C-480/08 [2010], para 74; *Bolton MBC v HY (HB)* [2018] UKUT 103 (AAC) and caselaw cited

221 *SSWP v JS (IS)* [2010] UKUT 347 (AAC)

222 *DJ v SSWP* [2013] UKUT 113 (AAC)

223 *Teixeira v LB Lambeth and SSHD*, C-480/08 [2010], para 87; see also *Alarape and Tijani v SSHD*, C-529/11 [2013]

224 Reg 16(7(a) I(EEA) Regs; DMG Memo 24/16, para 15; see also CIS/3960/2007; *Shabani v SSHD* [2013] UKUT 315 (IAC)

225 *AM v SSWP and CC Swansea Council* [2019] UKUT 361 (AAC), paras 49-64

226 Joined cases of *Czop* (C-147/11) and *Punakova* (C-148/11) [2012]; *Hrabkova v SSWP* [2017] EWCA Civ 794 – permission to appeal to UKSC refused

227 Arts 24(1)(h) and (2) and 25(1)(b) and (2) WA 2019; Arts 23(1)(h) and (2) and 24(1)(b) and (2) UK-EFTA

228 ADM Memo 33/20, para 53; DMG
Memo, 29/20 para 53

229 Arts 16 and 17 EU Dir 2004/38; regs 5
and 15 I(EEA) Regs

230 See, for example, *MW v SSWP (UC)*
[2019] UKUT 184

231 Art 16(4) EU Dir 2004/38; reg 15(3)
I(EEA) Regs - note that the words 'only'
and 'consecutive' were removed from
these regulations from 1 February 2017,
but EU law has not changed and should
be followed.

232 Regs 3(5)(c) and 4(6)(d) CR(ADTP) Regs

233 Part 4 I(EEA) Regs

234 *Idezuna v SSHD* [2011] UKUT 474 (IAC);
Babajanov v SSHD [2013] UKUT 513
(IAC)

235 Art 16(3) EU Dir 2004/38; reg 3 I(EEA)
Regs

236 Regs 3(5)(b) and 4(6)(c) CR(ADTP)
Regs; reg 3 I(EEA) Regs

237 Vol 2 paras 073433-35 DMG; paras
C1812-14 ADM

238 *SSHD v Ojo* [2015] EWCA Civ 1301, para
20; *Cardiff City Council v HM (HB)* [2019]
UKUT 271(AAC)

239 *OB v SSWP (ESA)* [2017] UKUT 255
(AAC), paras 29-30 and 34; endorsed in
AP v SSWP (IS) [2018] UKUT 307 (AAC),
paras 15-18

240 Reg 3(3) I(EEA) Regs

241 Reg 3(1), (3)(a) and (4) I(EEA) Regs; Art
28(3) EU Dir 2004/38; *Onuekwere v
SSHD*, C-378/12 [2014]; *SSHD v Viscu*
[2019] EWCA Civ 1052 and caselaw
cited

242 Reg 15(1) and (2) I(EEA) Regs; Sch 6
para 8 I(EEA) Regs

243 Regs 6(1)(a), 7, 13, 14(1) and (2), 15(1)
and Sch 6 para 8 I(EEA) Regs; *GE v SSWP
(ESA)* [2017] UKUT 145 (AAC), reported
as [2017] AACR 34; Vol 2, para 073428
DMG; para C1807 ADM

244 Sch 4 para 4(m) ISSC(CSTTP) Regs

245 Art 16(1) EU Dir 2004/38

246 *SSWP v Taous Lassal*, C-162/09 [2010];
SSWP v Dias, C-325/09 [2011]

247 *Oakafor and Others v SSHD* [2011] EWCA
Civ 499; *Alarape and Tijani v SSHD*, C-
529/11 [2013]; *Bee and Another v SSHD*
[2013] UKUT 83 (IAC)

248 *Ziolkowski* (C-425/10) and *Szeja* (C-425/
10) *v Land Berlin* [2011]

249 *Ziolkowski* (C-425/10) and *Szeja* (C-425/
10) *v Land Berlin* [2011]; Sch 6 para 8(3)
I(EEA) Regs

250 See, for example, *MW v SSWP (UC)*
[2019] UKUT 184 (AAC)

251 Reg 14(2) I(EEA) Regs

252 Regs 14(2) and 15(1)(a) and (b) I(EEA)
Regs

253 Regs 5 and 15 I(EEA) Regs; Art 17 EU Dir
2004/38

254 *SSWP v Gubeladze* [2019] UKSC 31

255 *De Brito v SSHD* [2012] EWCA Civ 709

256 *SSWP v Gubeladze* [2019] UKSC 31;
SSWP v NZ (ESA) (Final decision) [2019]
UKUT 250 (AAC)

257 Art 17(3) EU Dir 2004/38; *PM (EEA –
spouse – 'residing with') Turkey* [2011]
UKUT 89 (IAC)

258 Reg 15(1)(d) I(EEA) Regs

259 Art 17(1) EU Dir 2004/38; reg 5(7)
I(EEA) Regs

260 Art 17(1) EU Dir 2004/38; regs 5(7) and
6(2), and Sch 4 para 2 I(EEA) Regs,
preserving regs 7A(3) and 7B(4) I(EEA)
Regs 2006; *NZ v SSWP (ESA) (Third
interim decision)* [2017] UKUT 360
(AAC); see also *SSWP v NZ (ESA) (Final
decision)* [2019] UKUT 250 (AAC)

261 Regs 3 and 4 CR(FW) Regs; Arts 45 and
49 TFEU; Arts 24 and 25 WA 2019; Arts
23 and 24 UK-EFTA; Arts 20 and 23 UK-
Swiss Agreement; ADM Memo 33/20;
DMG Memo 29/20

262 Regs 3(3) CR(FW) Regs

263 Arts 24 and 25 WA 2019; Arts 23 and 24
UK-EFTA; Arts 20 and 23 UK:Swiss
Agreement; Arts 45 and 49 TFEU; EU
Reg 492/2011

264 ADM Memo 33/20 para 51; DMG
Memo 29/20, para 51

265 Arts 24(1)(h) and (2) and 25(1)(b) and
(2) WA 2019; Arts 23(1)(h) and (2) and
24(1)(b) and (2) UK-EFTA; EU Reg 492/
2011; ADM Memo 33/20, para 35 and
53; DMG Memo 29/20, para 35 and 53

266 s4(1)(c) WRA 2012

267 Arts 1(3) and 4(11) WRA(No.32)O

6. Rules for specific benefits and tax credits

268 **UC** s4(1)(c) WRA 2012
IS s124(1) SSCBA 1992
JSA s1(2)(i) JSA 1995
ESA s1(3)(d) WRA 2007
PC s1(2)(a) SPCA 2002

269 **UC** Reg 9 UC Regs
IS Regs 21-21AA IS Regs
JSA Regs 85-85A JSA Regs
ESA Regs 69-70 ESA Regs
HB Reg 10 HB Regs; reg 10 HB(SPC)
Regs
PC Reg 2 SPC Regs

270 ss3 and 4(1)(c) and (2) WRA 2012; regs
3(3) and 9 UC Regs

271 Regs 3(3) and 36(3) UC Regs

Part 11: Immigration and residence rules for benefits and tax credits
Chapter 69: Coming from abroad: residence rules
Notes

272 ss3 and 4(1)(e) WRA 2012; reg 3(3) UC Regs; reg 9(1) UC,PIP,JSA&ESA(C&P) Regs
273 Regs 3(3), 18(2) and 22(3) UC Regs
274 Sch 4 para 9(2)(b) UC Regs
275 Sch 4 paras 27 and 28 UC Regs
276 s 19(6) WRA 2012; reg 86 UC Regs
277 s39 WRA 2012; Regs 62(1),(3) and (4) and 90(3) UC Regs
278 Art 7(1) and (2)(a) and (b) and (3)(b) WRA(No.31)O; HB Circular A9/2019, paras 15-17; Vol 13 ch 77, paras 77035 note 2, 77150-51 and 77160 DMG
279 s39 WRA 2012; Regs 3, 18(2), 22(3) and 36(3) UC Regs; reg 9(1) UC,PIP,JSA&ESA(C&P) Regs
280 Reg 9(6) UC,PIP,JSA&ESA(C&P) Regs
281 **IS** Reg 16 IS Regs
JSA Reg 78 JSA Regs
ESA Reg 156 ESA Regs
PC Reg 5 SPC Regs
HB Reg 21 HB Regs; reg 21 HB(SPC) Regs
282 CIS/508/1992; CIS/13805/1996
283 CIS/484/1993
284 **UC** Reg 4(7) UC Regs
IS Reg 16 IS Regs
JSA Reg 78 JSA Regs
ESA Reg 156 ESA Regs
PC Reg 5 SPC Regs
HB Reg 21 HB Regs; reg 21 HB(SPC) Regs
285 s30(1) PA 2014
286 Arts 5, 6, 7, 42 and 43 EU Reg 883/04; Arts 5, 6, 7 and 43 UK-IC; Arts SSC 6, 7, 8, 37 and 38 UK-EUP
287 Sch 1 para 4 The Social Security (Reciprocal Agreements) Order 2017 No.159; Vol 2 Ch 7 Part 6, para 077080-83 DMG
288 Vol 2 Ch 7 Part 6, para 077110-24 DMG
289 s146 SSCBA 1992
290 Reg 23 CB Regs
291 Regs 23, 30 and 31 CB Regs
292 Reg 23(3) CB Regs
293 Regs 18(d) and 19(2)(c) SCP Regs
294 Reg 9 GA(Gen) Regs
295 *Stewart v SSWP*, C-503/09 [2011]
296 **AA** Reg 2 SS(AA) Regs
DLA Reg 2 SS(DLA) Regs
PIP Reg 16 SS(PIP) Regs
ADP Reg 15 DAWAP(S) Regs
CA Reg 9 SS(ICA) Regs
CDP Reg 5 DACYP(S) Regs
297 *TS and EK v SSWP (DLA)* [2020] UKUT 284 (AAC), reported as [2021] AACR 4; DMG Memo 8/21; reg 5(1)(e) DACYP(S) Regs

298 Reg 2(6) and (7) SS(DLA) Regs; reg 5(1)(e), (2) and (3) DACYP(S) Regs
299 Regs 5(9) and 24 DACYP(S) Regs; reg 35 DAWAP(S) Regs
300 s81 SS(S)A 2018
301 Reg 8 CA(YCG)(S) Regs
302 **ESA** Reg 11 ESA Regs; reg 12 ESA Regs 2013
IB Reg 16 SS(IB) Regs
SDA Reg 3 SS(SDA) Regs
303 **AA** Regs 2(3) and 2C SS(AA) Regs
DLA Regs 2(4) and 2C SS(DLA) Regs
CDP Reg 5(6), (7), (8), (10), (10A) and (11) DACYP(S) Regs
PIP Regs 21 and 23A SS(PIP) Regs
ADP Regs 15(6)-(8), 17, 18, 21 DAWAP(S) Regs
CA Reg 9C SS(ICA) Regs
304 See also ADM Memo 14/21 and DMG Memo 11/21
305 **AA** Reg 2(2) and (3A) SS(AA) Regs
DLA Reg 2(2) and (3A) SS(DLA) Regs
PIP Reg 19 and 20 SS(PIP) Regs
CA Reg 9(3) SS(ICA) Regs
306 **AA** Reg 2A SS(AA) Regs
DLA Reg 2A SS(DLA) Regs
CDP Reg 8 DACYP(S) Regs
PIP Reg 22 SS(PIP) Regs
ADP Reg 19 DAWAP(S) Regs
CA Reg 9A SS(ICA) Regs
307 Art 6 and Annex XI UK entry para 2 EU Reg 883/04; *SSWP v MM and BK v SSWP* [2016] UKUT 547 (AAC), reported as [2019] AACR 21; Art 6 UK-IC
308 ss65(7), 70(4A) and 72(7B) SSCBA 1992; s84 WRA 2012; s81 SS(S)A 2018; reg 8 CA(YCG)(S) Regs; Art 16 UK-IC
309 **CDP** Reg 5(4), 8 and 9 DACYP(S) Regs
ADP Reg 15(3), 19 and 20 DAWAP(S) Regs
CAS s81(2A) and (9)-(15) SS(S)A 2018
YCG Reg 8(3)-(10) CA(YCG)(S) Regs
310 Arts 23-32 EU Reg 883/04; Art 20 UK-IC
311 SSC3(4) and SSC-1 Part 2 UK-EUP
312 *Kavanagh and Another v SSWP* [2019] EWCA Civ 272, para 68 – see also para 32: the DWP dropped this part of its appeal against *SSWP v MM and BK v SSWP* [2016] UKUT 547 (AAC), reported as [2019] AACR 21, paras 28-31.
313 *Stewart v SSWP*, C-503/09 [2011]; *Kavanagh and Another v SSWP* [2019] EWCA Civ 272; *SSWP v JG (IS)* [2013] UKUT 298 (AAC); *SSWP v Garland* [2014] EWCA Civ 1550. See also ADM Memo 11/19 and DMG Memo 8/19
314 *PB v SSWP (DLA)* [2016] UKUT 280 (AAC)
315 ss1(3)(d) and 18(4)(a) WRA 2007
316 SS(NIRA) Regs; SS(GBRA)NI Regs

317 s94(5) SSCBA 1992
318 Reg 14 SS(IIPD) Regs
319 Reg 10C(5) and (6) SSB(PA) Regs
320 Reg 2 SS(II)(AB) Regs; reg 2 SS(II)(MB) Regs
321 Regs 3, 4, 6 and 8 SS(II)(MB) Regs; regs 3 and 6 SS(II)(AB) Regs
322 Art 5 EU Reg 883/04; Art 5 UK-IC; Art SSC 6 UK-EUP
323 Art 38 EU Reg 883/04; Art 36 EU Reg 987/09; *SSWP v OF (by MF) (II)* UKUT [2011] 448 (AAC); Art SSC 33 UK-EUP
324 s1(2)(i) JSA 1995
325 Art 61(2) EU Reg 883/04; Art 21(1) and (2) UK-IC; Art SSC 56 UK-EUP
326 Art 64 EU Reg 883/04; Arts 7 and 21 UK-IC
327 Art 64(3) EU Reg 883/04; Art 21(4(c) UK-IC
328 Art 3(1) and (4) and 8 UK-EUP
329 s2(1) and s35(1) SSCBA 1992. For exceptions, see the Social Security (Maternity Allowance) (Work Abroad) Regulations 1987 No.417; Vol 2 Ch 7, paras 075570-73 DMG
330 s113(1) SSCBA 1992
331 s113 SSCBA 1992; reg 4(1) SSB(PA) Regs
332 Reg 10 SS(WB&RP) Regs
333 Arts 51, 52 and 58 EU Reg 883/04; eg, Vol 2, paras 075771 and 076060-64 DMG; Arts 25 and 26 UK-IC; Arts SSC 45, 46 and 47 UK-EUP
334 Regs 5 and 9 The Social Security Co-ordination (Revocation of Retained Direct EU Legislation and Related Amendments) (EU Exit) Regulations 2020 No.1508
335 *Stewart v SSWP*, C-503/09 [2011]; *SSWP v Garland* [2014] EWCA Civ 1550, paras 14 and 28
336 Reg 9(1) FEA(S) Regs
337 Reg 7(9A) SFM&FE Regs
338 Reg 7(5) SFM&FE Regs; reg 9(2)(a) and (6) FEA(S) Regs
339 Reg 7(9) and (10) SFM&FE Regs; reg 9(2)(b) and (3) FEA(S) Regs
340 *John O'Flynn v Adjudication Officer*, C-237/94 [1996]; R(IS) 4/98; Art 24 EU Dir 2004/38
341 The Social Fund (Children's Funeral Fund for England) Regulations 2019 No.1064
342 gov.wales/child-funeral-and-other-related-costs-information
343 Reg 5(6) SFM&FE Regs
344 Sch 2 para 4(1)(a), Sch 3 para 3(1)(a) and Sch 4 para 4(1)(a) EYA(BSG)(S) Regs

345 Sch 2 para 4(1)(b) and (2), Sch 3 para 3(1)(b) and (2) and Sch 4 para 4(1)(b) and(2) EYA(BSG)(S) Regs
346 Reg 2 SFWFP Regs
347 Reg 4(1)(c) and Sch WHACYP(S) Regs
348 Reg 2 SFWFP Regs
349 Art SSC 3(4) UK-EUP; Art 3 UK-IC
350 s3(3) TCA 2002; reg 3(1) and (5) TC(R) Regs
351 s3(3) TCA 2002; reg 3(1) TC(R) Regs; *GC v HMRC (TC)* [2014] UKUT 251 (AAC) contains a useful discussion of these requirements
352 Reg 3 TC(R) Regs
353 s3(5A) TCA 2002
354 CCM 20090, 20160 and 20170; TCTM 09374 and 09376

11

Chapter 70

Going abroad

This chapter covers:
1. The rules on getting paid abroad (below)
2. Rules for specific benefits and tax credits (see p1622)

Key facts
- Most benefits and tax credits are affected if you, or your partner or child, go abroad.
- In certain circumstances, you can continue to receive benefit for a set number of weeks while you are away for a temporary period.
- You may be entitled to receive UK benefits for a longer (or indefinite) period if you go to a European Economic Area country.

1. **The rules on getting paid abroad**

Most benefits and tax credits are affected if you, or your partner or child, go abroad. Some can always be paid abroad, some can only be paid in certain circumstances and for limited periods, and some have rules affecting the amount that can be paid if you are abroad.

Your entitlement abroad depends on:
- the benefit or tax credit you are claiming (see p1622);
- the reason why you are going abroad;
- whether your absence is temporary or permanent;
- the length of time you intend to be abroad;
- the country you are going to;
- whether you are covered by any of the European Union (EU) co-ordination rules;
- whether you are covered by a reciprocal agreement.

Which rules apply

The UK benefit and tax credit legislation contains rules about how your absence affects your entitlement (see p1621). If these allow your entitlement to continue when you are abroad, you do not need to check the other rules.

The **EU co-ordination rules** may apply if you are going to a European Economic Area (EEA) country. The rules can enable you to be paid your benefits for longer than would be the case under UK law, or to continue to be paid for a family member who has moved to an EEA country. Since the end of the post-Brexit transition period (11pm on 31 December 2020), you need to check which co-ordination rules you are covered by (see p1647). The main co-ordination rules provide the greatest protections, the UK-Ireland Convention has similar rules but only if you (or your family member) are going to Ireland, and the new UK-EU Protocol has the fewest protections, covers the fewest benefits and only applies to EU (not EEA) member countries. See p1644 for a list of EU and EEA countries, see pp1622–40 for information on individual benefits and see Chapter 71 for further information on the co-ordination rules.

Reciprocal agreements exist between the UK and some other countries, and can assist in similar ways to the EU co-ordination rules. In general, these only apply if the EU co-ordination rules do not assist you. Great Britain and Northern Ireland also have reciprocal agreements. See p1546 for the countries with agreements and see CPAG's *Benefits for Migrants Handbook* for more information on how they can assist.

UK law

Ordinary residence

You must be 'ordinarily resident' in Great Britain (the UK, for child benefit and tax credits, and Scotland for most Scottish benefits) in order to receive some benefits and tax credits (see p1550). If, by going abroad, you cease to be ordinarily resident, your entitlement stops. However, if your absence abroad is temporary and you intend to return to Great Britain (or the UK or Scotland), your ordinary residence is not usually affected.[1] In practice, it is very rare that ceasing to be ordinarily resident is the reason why your entitlement ends when you go abroad. It is more likely that your entitlement ends simply because you are absent (see below). If you receive a decision that your entitlement to a benefit or tax credit has ended because you have ceased to be ordinarily resident, challenge the decision and get specialist advice.

Presence and absence

Most benefits require you to be **present** in Great Britain (the UK for tax credits, and the common travel area for child disability payment (CDP) and adult disability payment (ADP)). There are rules that allow you to be treated as present and therefore still entitled to the benefit or tax credit in specified circumstances during a temporary absence. Some benefits also have a rule that disqualifies you from entitlement if you are **absent** from Great Britain. There are specified exemptions to this rule for each benefit.

'**Presence**' means being physically present in Great Britain (or the UK or common travel area) and '**absence**' means not being physically present. You

Part 11: Immigration and residence rules for benefits and tax credits
Chapter 70: Going abroad
2. Rules for specific benefits and tax credits

count as present on the day you arrive or return from an absence. In general, you also count as present on the day you go abroad.[2] However, for housing benefit, the day of departure counts as your first day of absence from Great Britain.[3]

Temporary absence

In specified circumstances, you can be treated as present, and therefore entitled to benefit, during a temporary absence.

For tax credits, attendance allowance (AA), disability living allowance (DLA), CDP, personal independence payment (PIP), ADP and (for your, not the child's, absence) child benefit, you are defined as being temporarily absent from Great Britain (the UK for tax credits, and the common travel area for CDP and ADP), if, at the beginning of the period of absence, you are unlikely to be absent for more than 52 weeks.[4]

For all other benefits, temporary absence is not defined and you must demonstrate that your absence will be temporary.[5] Provide full details of why you are going abroad, how long you intend to be away, and what you intend to do while abroad. **Note:** although your intentions are relevant, they are not decisive.[6] If your circumstances change while you are abroad (eg, you go abroad for one reason and decide to stay abroad for a different purpose), your absence may no longer be regarded as temporary.[7] Although there is no set period for a temporary absence (except for tax credits, child benefit, AA, DLA, CDP, PIP and ADP), as a general rule absences of more than 12 months are not considered to be temporary unless there are exceptional circumstances.[8] If the purpose of the trip abroad is obviously temporary (eg, for a holiday, to visit friends or relatives or for a particular course of medical treatment) and you buy a return ticket, your absence should be viewed as temporary.

2. **Rules for specific benefits and tax credits**

Bereavement benefits

In general, bereavement benefits are payable while you are abroad. However, your benefit is not uprated each year if you have ceased to be ordinarily resident in Great Britain on the day before the annual uprating takes place,[9] unless you have gone to a European Economic Area (EEA) country and you are covered by the European Union (EU) co-ordination rules or can rely on a reciprocal agreement (see p1599).

If you were abroad on the date your spouse or civil partner died, you are only entitled to a bereavement support payment if, despite your absence, you were ordinarily resident in Great Britain on that date (see p1598), or the EU co-ordination rules apply or a reciprocal agreement applies.

European Union co-ordination rules

If you are covered by any of the EU co-ordination rules (see p1647) and the UK is your 'competent state' (see p1656):[10]

- and you go to stay or live in an EEA country (or EU country if relying on the UK-EU Protocol, or Ireland if relying on the UK-Ireland Convention), you can be paid your bereavement support payment or widowed parent's allowance for as long as you would receive them if you remained in Great Britain, including any annual uprating. See p1660 for more information on exporting benefits; *and*
- for bereavement support payment, if the UK is your 'competent state' (see p1656), the requirement to be ordinarily resident in Great Britain on the date your spouse or civil partner died does not apply if you were resident in an EEA country (or EU or Ireland) on that date.

Child benefit, Scottish child payment and guardian's allowance

Child benefit

You and your child can be treated as being present in Great Britain during a temporary absence (see p1622).

Provided you are ordinarily resident (see p1550), you continue to be entitled to child benefit for:[11]

- **the first eight weeks**; *or*
- **the first 12 weeks** of any period of absence, or any extension to that period, which is in connection with:
  - the treatment of an illness or disability of you, your partner, a child for whom you are responsible, or another relative of you or your partner; *or*
  - the death of your partner, a child or qualifying young person for whom you or your partner are responsible, or another relative of you or your partner.

Relative

'**Relative**' means brother, sister, parent, grandparent, great-grandparent, child, grandchild or great-grandchild.[12]

Your child is treated as being present during a temporary absence for:[13]

- the first 12 weeks; *or*
- any period during which s/he is absent for the specific purpose of being treated for an illness or disability which began before her/his absence began; *or*
- any period when s/he is in Northern Ireland; *or*
- any period during which s/he is absent because s/he is:
  - receiving full-time education at a school or college in an EEA country or in Switzerland; *or*

Part 11: Immigration and residence rules for benefits and tax credits
Chapter 70: Going abroad
2. Rules for specific benefits and tax credits

- engaged in an educational exchange or visit made with the written approval of the school or college which s/he normally attends; *or*
- a child who normally lives with a Crown servant posted overseas who is either in the same country as her/him or is absent from that country for one of the reasons in the above two bullet points.[14]

If a child is born outside the UK during the eight- or 12-week period in which you could be treated as being present in Great Britain, s/he is treated as being in the UK for up to 12 weeks from the start of your absence.[15]

While you and your child are present, or treated as present, you can continue to receive child benefit that was already in payment and can also make a fresh claim during your, or her/his, absence.

Scottish child payment

You cease to be entitled to a Scottish child payment the week after you cease to be ordinarily resident in Scotland (see p1550).[16]

Guardian's allowance

Entitlement to guardian's allowance depends on entitlement to child benefit, so you can be paid guardian's allowance abroad for the same period as child benefit.

However, your guardian's allowance is not uprated each year if you have ceased to be ordinarily resident in Great Britain on the day before the annual uprating takes place,[17] unless you have gone to an EEA country and you are covered by the EU co-ordination rules or you can rely on a reciprocal agreement.

European Union co-ordination rules

If you are covered by the main EU co-ordination rules or the UK-Ireland Convention (see p1647):

- you can be paid child benefit and guardian's allowance for a child resident in an EEA country (Ireland, if you are relying on the Convention). S/he does not have to be in education; *and/or*
- you can be paid child benefit and guardian's allowance, and your benefit uprated, if you go to stay or live in an EEA country (Ireland, if you are relying on the Convention) *if* the UK continues to be your competent state (see p1656).

Child benefit and guardian's allowance are categorised under the main EU co-ordination rules, and listed under the UK-Ireland Convention, as 'family benefits' (see p1661).

Scottish child payment has been categorised as a special non-contributory benefit (see p1655) so the above rules do not apply.

The UK-EU Protocol does not cover family benefits.

· ·

Disability benefits and carer's allowance

You can be treated as present in Great Britain (or in the common travel area, for child disability payment (CDP) and adult disability payment (ADP)), and therefore continue to be entitled to (or make a new claim for,[18] or count the period towards the past presence required for) attendance allowance (AA), disability living allowance (DLA), CDP, personal independence payment (PIP), ADP or carer's allowance (CA), during an absence abroad:[19]

- (except CA) for the first **13 weeks** of a 'temporary absence' (see p1622); *or*
- (except CA) for the first **26 weeks** of a 'temporary absence' (see p1622) if the absence is solely in connection with medical treatment for your illness or disability that began before you left Great Britain (common travel area, for CDP and ADP); *or*
- (for CA only) for up to **four weeks** if your absence is, and was when it began, for a temporary purpose and does not exceed four weeks. If you are not accompanied by the person for whom you are caring, you must satisfy the rules that entitle you to CA during a break from caring (see p547); *or*
- (for CA only) if your absence is temporary and is for the specific purpose of caring for someone who is also absent from Great Britain and who continues to receive AA, DLA care component paid at the highest or middle rate, the daily living component of PIP, armed forces independence payment or constant attendance allowance; *or*
- if you are an aircraft worker, mariner or continental shelf worker (for ADP and CDP, you are also treated as satisfying the past presence test); *or*
- (for AA, DLA, PIP and CA) while you are a serving member of the armed forces or are living with someone who is abroad as a serving member of the armed forces and s/he is your spouse, civil partner, son, stepson, daughter, stepdaughter, or father, stepfather, father-in-law, mother, stepmother or mother-in-law; *or*
- (for CDP or ADP) while you are a serving member of the armed forces or, a civil servant, and immediately prior to the start of either employment outside the common travel area you satisfied the residence and presence conditions (other than the past presence test), or are living with someone who is abroad as a serving member of the forces or civil servant, and you are the spouse, civil partner, or living together as if you were either, or son, stepson, daughter, stepdaughter, or a child in the care of, or, other than for CDP, father, stepfather, mother, stepmother mother-in-law or father-in-law of that person. See also note below.

Note: you must also continue to be habitually resident (see p1550), *except* if either of the last two bullet points applies, when you are *treated as* being habitually resident, and if the last bullet point applies you are also *treated as* ordinarily resident for CDP and ADP, and, for ADP only, also treated as satisfying the past presence test (see p1602).

Part 11: Immigration and residence rules for benefits and tax credits
Chapter 70: Going abroad
2. Rules for specific benefits and tax credits

If your entitlement to PIP ended because you went abroad and the rules above did not apply for the whole period you were away, and you return to Great Britain within 12 months, a new claim for PIP can be assessed on the basis of the information held about your last claim if your needs have not changed. The DWP refers to this as a 'rapid reclaim'.[20]

If you are aged under 19, in receipt of the higher rate DLA/CDP care component or enhanced rate of the PIP/ADP daily living component, and have a 'genuine and sufficient link' to Scotland while habitually resident in specific EEA countries, you may qualify for child winter heating assistance (see p1609).

Entitlement to CDP and ADP ends after 13 weeks of you ceasing to be ordinarily resident in Scotland if you move to another part of the UK (or, for CDP only, if notification is given within 13 weeks of that date, after 13 weeks of that notification). If you move to Scotland, your DLA or PIP continues until a decision is made on your entitlement to CDP or ADP, which is then awarded without a claim being required (see p1718, p1692 and p1762).[21]

You can continue to be paid an increase in your CA for your spouse/civil partner or dependent adult while s/he is abroad, provided you continue to be entitled to CA and reside with her/him. **Note:** you can be treated as residing together during a temporary absence from each other.[22]

European Union co-ordination rules

If you move to an EEA country and are covered by the main EU co-ordination rules (or, for CDP and ADP, the UK-Ireland Convention or the agreement between the UK and Gibraltar[23]) (see p1647), you can continue to be paid (or make a new claim for) AA, the care component of DLA/CDP, the daily living component of PIP/ADP and CA without having to satisfy the presence, past presence and habitual residence (and for CDP/ADP, the ordinary residence) tests (see p1601) if:[24]

- you are habitually resident in an EEA country or Switzerland (Ireland if relying on the UK-Ireland Convention, or for CDP or ADP only, Gibraltar if relying on the agreement with Gibraltar); *and*
- you can demonstrate a 'genuine and sufficient link' to the UK (to Scotland for CDP and ADP) (see p1604).

You can continue to be paid for as long as the UK continues to be your 'competent state' (see p1656).[25]

You can make a new claim (including for a backdated period if you would have been entitled if these rules been in force at the time) for carer's allowance supplement or young carer grant without needing to be resident or ordinarily resident in Scotland if:[26]

- you have a 'genuine and sufficient link' to Scotland (see p1604); *and*
- the UK is your 'competent state' to pay this benefit; *and*

- you are either:
  - resident in an EEA state and covered by the main EU co-ordination rules (see p1649); *or*
  - resident in Ireland and covered by the UK-Ireland Convention (see p1650); *or*
  - resident in Gibraltar and covered by the agreement between the UK and Gibraltar.[27]

You can only be paid the mobility components of DLA, CDP, PIP and ADP while you are resident in the UK, because each is classed (or, for ADP, treated as, until it is classed) as a 'special non-contributory benefit' under the main co-ordination rules.[28] The UK-Ireland Convention does not cover mobility components.

Disability and carers' benefits are not covered by the UK-EU Protocol at all.

If you receive CA while in the UK and the main EU co-ordination rules apply to you, you may be able to continue to be paid an addition for an adult or child who goes to stay or live in an EEA country. See p1661 for more information.

Employment and support allowance

You cannot normally get employment and support allowance (ESA) if you are not in Great Britain.[29] However, provided you meet the other conditions of entitlement, if you were entitled to ESA immediately before leaving Great Britain and are temporarily absent, you can continue to be entitled:[30]

- **indefinitely** if:
  - your absence is for NHS treatment at a hospital or other institution outside Great Britain; *or*
  - you are living with your spouse, civil partner, son, stepson, daughter, stepdaughter, father, father-in-law, stepfather, mother, mother-in-law or stepmother who is a serving member of the armed forces; *or*
- **for the first four weeks**, if your absence is unlikely to exceed 52 weeks; *or*
- **for the first 26 weeks**, if your absence is unlikely to exceed 52 weeks and is solely in connection with arrangements made to treat:
  - your disease or disablement which is directly related to your limited capability for work which began before you left Great Britain; *or*
  - the disease or disablement of a dependent child who you are accompanying.

The treatment must be carried out by, or under the supervision of, a person qualified to provide medical treatment, physiotherapy or similar treatment.

If you are going to Northern Ireland from Great Britain (or vice versa), see p1604.

Note: there are also rules on when you can get housing costs in your income-related ESA if you are temporarily absent from your home (see p354).

Part 11: Immigration and residence rules for benefits and tax credits
Chapter 70: Going abroad
2. Rules for specific benefits and tax credits

If your partner is abroad

If you are the claimant and you stay in Great Britain, your income-related ESA includes an amount for your partner for:[31]

- the first four weeks s/he is abroad; or
- the first 26 weeks if s/he is accompanying a child abroad for treatment in line with the 26-week rule above.

If both you and your partner are abroad, your income-related ESA includes an amount for your partner for the first 26 weeks if both of you are accompanying a child abroad for treatment in line with the 26-week rule above.[32]

After this four- or 26-week period, your benefit is reduced because your applicable amount is calculated as if you have no partner. However, your partner is still treated as being part of your household, and therefore her/his work, income and capital affect your income-related ESA entitlement, unless you are no longer treated as a couple (see p306).[33]

European Union co-ordination rules

If you are covered by any of the co-ordination rules (see p1647) and the UK is your 'competent state' (see p1656), you can, if you go to live in an EEA country (EU if relying on the UK-EU Protocol, and Ireland if relying on the UK-Ireland Convention), continue to be paid contributory ESA.[34] However, if you are only covered by the UK-EU Protocol, you can only continue to be paid contributory ESA if you are able to argue it is a 'sickness', rather than an 'invalidity', benefit, and this may only be accepted during either the assessment phase or during the first year of the award (see p1653).

If the UK continues to pay your contributory ESA while you are resident in an EEA (or EU) country (or Ireland), the DWP continues to assess your limited capability for work and your limited capability for work-related activity. However, any checks and medicals take place in the state in which you live and the reports are sent to the DWP.[35]

None of the co-ordination rules assist you to be paid income-related ESA abroad, and you can only be paid abroad under the UK rules on p1627.

Housing benefit

You cannot normally get housing benefit (HB) if you are not in Great Britain due to the requirements for you to be occupying your home.[36] However, provided you meet the other conditions of entitlement, HB can be paid when you are temporarily absent from Great Britain for:[37]

- **up to four weeks**, if your absence is not expected to exceed this; or
- **up to eight weeks**, if your absence is not expected to exceed that and is in connection with the death of your partner, your child or qualifying young person who normally lives with you or your (or her/his) close relative and the

local authority considers it unreasonable for you to return to Great Britain within four weeks; *or*

- **up to 26 weeks**, if your absence is not expected to exceed this and it is solely in connection with your (or your partner's or child's or qualifying young person's) medical treatment, or medically approved convalescence.

Note:
- The periods for which you can continue to be entitled to HB while you are absent abroad are shorter than if you were absent from your home but remain in Great Britain (see p181).
- The period of absence starts on the day you leave Great Britain.[38]
- DWP guidance states your HB can continue if you are unable to return from abroad within the periods above due to coronavirus pandemic travel restrictions, although there has been no change to the regulations.[39]
- If you are (or you are a family member of) an EEA national with a right to reside in the UK and go abroad to an EEA country, it is arguable that the shorter period for which you can be entitled while abroad is discriminatory under EU law and should not apply (see p1658).[40]

If your partner or child is abroad

Whether or not you have amounts included in your HB for your partner or child who is abroad depends on whether s/he is treated as part of your household (see p306 and p311). The amount of HB you are entitled to may also depend on whether s/he is treated as occupying the home (see p181).[41]

European Union co-ordination rules

HB is not covered by any of the EU co-ordination rules. These rules cannot assist you and, if you go to an EEA country, you can only be paid under the UK rules above.

Income support

You cannot normally get income support (IS) if you are not in Great Britain.[42] However, IS can be paid when you are temporarily absent from Great Britain, provided you meet the other conditions of entitlement:[43]

- **indefinitely** if your absence is for NHS treatment at a hospital or other institution outside Great Britain; *or*
- **during the first four weeks** of your absence, if it is unlikely to exceed 52 weeks and:
  - you are in Northern Ireland; *or*
  - you and your partner are both abroad and s/he satisfies the conditions for one of the pensioner premiums, the disability premium or the severe disability premium (see p323); *or*

Part 11: Immigration and residence rules for benefits and tax credits
Chapter 70: Going abroad
2. Rules for specific benefits and tax credits

- you are enititled to statutory sick pay (SSP) and are abroad for the sole purpose of receiving treatment (see below) for the incapacity that entitles you to SSP; *or*
- you have been continuously entitled to SSP for 364 days before you go abroad (or for 196 days if you are terminally ill or receiving the highest rate of DLA/CDP care component, the enhanced rate of the daily living component of PIP/ADP, or armed forces independence payment). Two or more periods of entitlement to SSP are treated as continuous if the break between them is not more than 56 days each time; *or*
- you are not in one of the following groups of people who can claim IS (see p233):
  - a person in 'relevant education'; *or*
  - involved in a trade dispute, or have returned to work for 15 days or less following the dispute; *or*
  - entitled to SSP (other than in the situations above); *or*
- **during the first eight weeks** of your absence, if it is unlikely to exceed 52 weeks and is solely in connection with arrangements made for the treatment of a disease or disablement of a child or qualifying young person. The child or young person must be a member of your family (see p307).

'Treatment' must be carried out by, or under the supervision of, a person qualified to provide medical treatment, physiotherapy or similar treatment.

Note: there are also rules on when you can get housing costs in your IS if you are temporarily absent from your home (see p354).

If your partner is abroad

If you are the IS claimant and you stay in Great Britain, your IS applicable amount includes an amount for your partner who is abroad for:[44]
- the first four weeks; *or*
- the first eight weeks if s/he meets the conditions of the eight-week rule above.

If both you and your partner are abroad, your IS includes amounts for your partner for the first eight weeks if you both meet the conditions of the eight-week rule above.[45]

After this four- or eight-week period, your benefit is reduced because your applicable amount is calculated as if you have no partner. However, your partner is still treated as being part of your household and therefore her/his work, income and capital affect your IS entitlement, unless you are no longer treated as a couple (see p306).[46]

If your child is abroad

If you were getting an amount in your IS for your child before s/he went abroad, you can continue to be paid for her/him for:[47]

- the first four weeks; *or*
- the first eight weeks, if s/he meets the conditions of the eight-week rule above.

European Union co-ordination rules
IS is not covered by any of the EU co-ordination rules. These rules cannot assist you, and if you go to an EEA country, you can only be paid under the UK rules above.

Industrial injuries benefits
Disablement benefit and retirement allowance are not affected if you go abroad.[48]

Constant attendance allowance and exceptionally severe disablement allowance are payable for the first six months of a temporary absence, or a longer period that the DWP may allow.[49]

Reduced earnings allowance (REA) can be paid while you are temporarily absent abroad for the first three months, or longer if the DWP allows, if:[50]
- your absence from Great Britain is *not* in connection with employment, trade or business; *and*
- your claim was made before you left Great Britain; *and*
- you were entitled to REA before going abroad.

Note: REA has now been abolished. If you break your claim, you may no longer be eligible for benefit.

European Union co-ordination rules
Industrial injuries benefits, except retirement allowance, are classed as 'benefits for accidents at work and occupational diseases' under each of the EU co-ordination rules (see p1653). If you are covered by these rules (see p1647) and you go to stay or live in an EEA country (EU if relying on the UK/EU Protocol, or Ireland if relying on the UK-Ireland Convention), you can be paid industrial injuries benefits without any time limit and they are fully uprated each year. See p1660 for more details.

Jobseeker's allowance
You cannot normally get jobseeker's allowance (JSA) if you are not in Great Britain.[51] However, provided you meet the other conditions of entitlement, JSA can be paid when you are temporarily absent:[52]
- **indefinitely**, if you are entitled to JSA immediately before leaving Great Britain and your absence is for NHS treatment at a hospital or other institution outside Great Britain; *or*
- **for up to four weeks**, if you are entitled to JSA immediately before leaving Great Britain and:
  - your absence is unlikely to exceed 52 weeks, you continue to satisfy the conditions of entitlement and you are in Northern Ireland. **Note:** the

Part 11: Immigration and residence rules for benefits and tax credits
Chapter 70: Going abroad
2. Rules for specific benefits and tax credits

reciprocal agreements between Great Britain and Northern Ireland can mean that after four weeks, the administration of your claim transfers to Northern Ireland – you do not need to make a new claim;[53] *or*

– (except if you come under the universal credit (UC) system – see p22) the absence is unlikely to exceed 52 weeks, you continue to satisfy the conditions of entitlement and your partner is also abroad with you and satisfies the conditions for one of the pensioner premiums, the disability premium or the severe disability premium (see p323); *or*

– (except if you come under the UC system) you get a training allowance;[54] *or*

- **for up to eight weeks,** if you are entitled to JSA immediately before leaving Great Britain and your absence is unlikely to exceed 52 weeks and is solely in connection with arrangements made to treat a disease or disablement of a child or qualifying young person. The treatment must be carried out by, or under the supervision of, a person qualified to provide medical treatment, physiotherapy or similar treatment and the child or young person must be a member of your family (see p307); *or*
- **for an absence of up to seven days,** if you are attending a job interview and you notified your work coach before you left (in writing if required). On your return, you must satisfy her/him that you attended the interview as stated; *or*
- **for an absence of up to 15 days,** to train as a member of the reserve forces.

You can be treated as being available for work and actively seeking work or, if you come under the UC system (see p22), you are exempt from the work search requirement and are treated as 'able and willing immediately to take up work' during certain temporary absences abroad. These are similar to, but more limited than, those listed above (see p1096, p1103 and p1051).[55]

Note: there are also rules on when you can get housing costs in your income-based JSA if you are temporarily absent from your home (see p354).

Joint-claim jobseeker's allowance if your partner is abroad

If you are a joint-claim couple (see p247) and your partner is temporarily absent from Great Britain **on the date you make your claim,** you are paid as a couple for:[56]

- **an absence of up to seven days,** if your partner is attending a job interview;
- **up to four weeks,** if your partner is:
  - in Northern Ireland and the absence is unlikely to exceed 52 weeks; *or*
  - getting a training allowance in the circumstances above.

If you are a joint-claim couple and your partner goes abroad **after you claimed JSA,** and her/his absence is for NHS treatment at a hospital or other institution outside Great Britain, you continue to be paid as a couple for up to four weeks.[57]

After this seven-day/four-week period, your JSA is reduced because your applicable amount is calculated as if you have no partner.[58] However, your partner is still treated as part of your household if s/he is abroad for treatment in the circumstances above. Therefore, her/his work, income and capital affects your joint-claim JSA entitlement, unless s/he ceases to be treated as part of your household for another reason (see p306).[59]

Income-based jobseeker's allowance if your partner is abroad

If you are the income-based JSA claimant and you stay in Great Britain, your applicable amount includes an amount for your partner while s/he is abroad for:[60]

- **the first four weeks** of a temporary absence; *or*
- **the first eight weeks** if your partner meets the conditions of the eight-week rule on p1632.

If both you and your partner are abroad, your applicable amount includes an amount for your partner for the first eight weeks if both of you meet the conditions of the eight-week rule on p1632.[61]

After this four- or eight-week period, your benefit is reduced because your applicable amount is calculated as if you have no partner. However, your partner is still treated as being part of your household, and therefore her/his work, income and capital affect your income-based JSA entitlement unless you are no longer treated as a couple (see p306).[62]

Income-based jobseeker's allowance if your child is abroad

If you were getting JSA for your child before s/he went abroad, you can continue to be paid for her/him for:[63]

- **the first four weeks**; *or*
- **the first eight weeks** if your child meets the conditions of the eight-week rule on p1632.

European Union co-ordination rules

Contribution-based JSA is classed as an 'unemployment benefit' under each of the EU co-ordination rules (see p1653). However, the UK-EU Protocol does not provide for unemployment benefits to be 'exported'.[64]

If you are covered by the main co-ordination rules or the UK-Ireland Convention (see p1647) and the UK is your 'competent state' (see p1656), you can continue to be paid contribution-based JSA for up to three months if:[65]

- you satisfied the conditions for contribution-based JSA for at least four weeks before you left the UK, unless the DWP authorised you to go abroad before then; *and*
- you register as unemployed in the EEA state you go to (Ireland, if relying on the UK-Ireland Convention) within seven days and comply with its procedures.

None of the co-ordination rules can assist you to be paid income-based JSA abroad. You can only be paid income-based JSA abroad under the UK rules on p1631.

11

Part 11: Immigration and residence rules for benefits and tax credits
Chapter 70: Going abroad
2. Rules for specific benefits and tax credits

Maternity allowance, incapacity benefit and severe disablement allowance

If you are temporarily absent from Great Britain, you can continue to be paid maternity allowance (MA), incapacity benefit (IB) and severe disablement allowance (SDA) if:[66]

- you are receiving AA, DLA, PIP or armed forces independence payment (see p1625); or
- the DWP agrees. You can then receive the benefit for the first 26 weeks of your temporary absence; or
- you are the spouse, civil partner, son, stepson, daughter, stepdaughter, father, stepfather, father-in-law, mother, stepmother or mother-in-law of a serving member of the armed forces, and you are abroad only because you are living with her/him.

In addition:
- when you left Great Britain, you must have been continuously incapable of work for six months and have been continuously incapable since your departure; or
- your absence from Great Britain must be for the specific purpose of being treated for an incapacity which began before you left Great Britain; or
- for IB only, the incapacity for work is the result of a personal injury caused by an accident at work (see p666) and your absence from Great Britain is for the specific purpose of receiving treatment for it.

If you are due to have a medical examination, this can be arranged abroad.
Note: most IB and SDA claims have been transferred to ESA (see p640). If you lose entitlement to IB or SDA by going abroad, you are not entitled to contributory ESA on your return if you do not satisfy the contribution conditions at that time.

You can continue to be paid an increase for your spouse/civil partner or dependent adult in your IB or SDA while s/he is abroad if you are entitled to IB/SDA and you are residing with her/him. You can be treated as residing together during a temporary absence from each other.[67]

European Union co-ordination rules

If you are covered by any of the EU co-ordination rules (see p1647) and the UK is your 'competent state' for the payment of this benefit (see p1656), you can be paid MA if you go to stay or live in an EEA country (EU if relying on the UK-EU Protocol, or Ireland if relying on the Convention), as MA is classed as a 'maternity benefit' under the EU co-ordination rules (see p1653).[68]

If you are covered by the main co-ordination rules, you can continue to be paid your IB and SDA, including any uprating, if you go to live in an EEA country, as both are classed as 'invalidity benefits' under these rules (see p1653). The UK continues to determine your incapacity for work, but any checks and medicals take place in the country in which you are living and the reports are then sent to the paying state.[69] If you remain in the UK, you may be able to continue to be paid an increase in your IB or SDA for an adult or child if s/he goes to stay or live in an EEA country (see p1661).

See p1660 for more details on exporting benefits.

Pension credit

You cannot normally get pension credit (PC) if you are not in Great Britain.[70] However, provided you meet the other conditions of entitlement, PC can be paid when you are temporarily absent from Great Britain for:[71]

- **up to four weeks**, if your absence is not expected to exceed this; *or*
- **up to eight weeks**, if your absence is not expected to exceed that and is in connection with the death of your partner, your child or qualifying young person who normally lived with you or your (or her/his) close relative and the DWP considers it unreasonable for you to return to Great Britain within four weeks; *or*
- **up to 26 weeks**, if your absence is not expected to exceed this and it is solely in connection with your (or your partner's or child's or qualifying young person's) medical treatment, or medically approved convalescence.

'**Qualifying young person**' is defined as it is for UC (see p61) but someone getting UC, IS, JSA or ESA is not a qualifying young person.[72]

'**Close relative**' is defined as it is for UC (see p89).[73]

Note: there are also rules on when you can receive housing costs in your PC if you are temporarily absent from your home (see p354).

If your partner is abroad

If you are entitled to PC and your partner is abroad, your PC only includes an amount for her/him if s/he is covered by the rules above.[74] After this, s/he is not treated as being part of your household and you are paid as a single person. Your partner can also stop being treated as part of your household in the circumstances on p306.[75] **Note:** if your partner is under pension age and ceases to be treated as part of your household, when s/he returns your entitlement to PC ends but you may instead be able to claim UC, although not if, for example, s/he fails the habitual residence test, in which case you would continue to be entitled to PC (and HB) as a single person (see p257).

If your child is abroad

You are treated as not responsible for your child or qualifying young person, and therefore not entitled to an amount for her/him within your PC, if s/he is temporarily absent from Great Britain for more than:[76]

- **four weeks**, if her/his absence is not expected to exceed this; *or*

Part 11: Immigration and residence rules for benefits and tax credits
Chapter 70: Going abroad
2. Rules for specific benefits and tax credits

- **eight weeks**, if her/his absence is not expected to exceed this and is in connection with the death of your partner, a child or qualifying young person who normally lives with you, a close relative of hers/his, yours or your partner's, and the DWP considers it unreasonable for her/him to return to Great Britain within four weeks; *or*
- **up to 26 weeks**, if her/his absence is not expected to exceed this and it is solely in connection with her/his or your or your partner's medical treatment, or medically approved convalescence.

European Union co-ordination rules

None of the EU co-ordination rules assist you to be paid PC abroad.

You can only be paid PC abroad under the UK rules on p1635.

Retirement pension

All retirement pensions are payable without time limit while you are abroad.[77] However, unless you have gone to an EEA country and you are covered by the EU co-ordination rules or you can rely on a reciprocal agreement, if you are not ordinarily resident (see p1550) in Great Britain:[78]

- on the day before the annual uprating takes place, your benefit is not uprated each year;
- for state pension only, when you claim a pension that you have deferred, the upratings that occurred while you were abroad are ignored when calculating both the deferral increase and rate payable;
- for 'old' retirement pensions only, you cannot stop claiming your pension ('de-retire') in order to accrue a deferral payment.[79]

Although category D retirement pension is payable if you are abroad, you must meet the residence requirements at the date you claim, see p1607.

You can continue to be paid an increase in your category A retirement pension for your spouse/civil partner or dependent adult while s/he is abroad if you are entitled to the pension and residing with her/him.[80] You can be treated as residing together during a temporary absence from each other.[81]

European Union co-ordination rules

Retirement pensions are classed as 'old age benefits' under each of the EU co-ordination rules (see p1653). If you are covered by these rules (see p1647), the UK is your 'competent state' (see p1656) and you go to stay or live in an EEA country (Ireland, if relying on the UK-Ireland Convention):

- you can continue to be paid your retirement pension without time limit, including your annual uprating;
- you can opt to stop claiming your pension ('de-retire') in order to accrue a deferral payment while living in an EEA country (Ireland, if relying on the Convention).

Note: if you are relying on the UK-EU Protocol, note that this does not cover Iceland, Norway, Liechtenstein or Switzerland. Bilateral agreements that cover retirement pensions have been made with Switzerland and Norway and the UK government continues to seek a new co-ordination agreement on retirement pensions with all EEA states. In addition, the main co-ordination rules on aggregating national insurance (NI) contributions for entitlement to, and uprating of, UK retirement pensions continue to apply even if you are not covered by the Withdrawal Agreement protections.[82]

If you are covered by the main EU co-ordination rules and you remain in the UK, you may be able to continue to be paid an increase for an adult or child if s/he goes to stay or live in an EEA country (see p1661).

Reciprocal agreements

If you are covered by a reciprocal agreement (see p1546) that provides for uprating, you can be paid your pension at the same rate as if you were still in the UK, including your annual uprating. **Note:** the agreements with Canada and New Zealand, and the former agreement with Australia, do not provide for uprating.

Statutory payments

There are no presence or residence rules for SSP, statutory maternity pay (SMP), statutory adoption pay (SAP), statutory paternity pay (SPP), statutory shared parental pay (SSPP) and statutory parental bereavement pay (SPBP). You remain entitled to these benefits if you go abroad, provided you meet the normal rules of entitlement, including those relating to being an employee (see Chapters 38 and 39).[83]

Although you are generally required to be employed in Great Britain to count as an 'employee', you count as an employee even while employed abroad in certain circumstances, including if:[84]

- your employer is required to pay secondary class 1 NI contributions for you; *or*
- you are a continental shelf worker or, in certain circumstances, an aircraft worker or mariner; *or*
- you are employed in an EEA country and, had you been employed in Great Britain, you would have been considered an employee, and the UK is the competent state under the EU co-ordination rules (see p1656).

Your employer is not required to pay you SSP, SMP, SAP, SPP, SSPP or SPBP if:[85]

- your employer is not required by law to pay employer's class 1 NI contributions (even if those contributions are in fact made) because, at the time they become payable, your employer:
  – is not resident or present in Great Britain; *and*
  – has (or is treated as having) no place of business in Great Britain; *or*

Part 11: Immigration and residence rules for benefits and tax credits
Chapter 70: Going abroad
2. Rules for specific benefits and tax credits

- because of an international treaty or convention, your employer is exempt from the Social Security Acts or those Acts are not enforceable against your employer.

European Union co-ordination rules

It has always been arguable that SSP is a 'sickness benefit' and SMP, SAP, SPP, SSPP and SPBP are 'maternity/paternity benefits', and recent guidance lists them as such under each of the co-ordination rules (see p1653).[86] However, the absence of residence and presence requirements for these benefits means you can generally be paid these benefits if you go abroad without needing to rely on co-ordination rules.

The UK-Ireland Convention prevents these benefits being paid at the same time as Irish sickness, invalidity, maternity or paternity benefits.[87]

Tax credits

Provided you are ordinarily resident, you can be treated as present and therefore entitled to child tax credit (CTC) and working tax credit (WTC) during a 'temporary absence' (see p1622) for:[88]

- **the first eight weeks**; *or*
- **the first 12 weeks** of any period of absence, or any extension to this period of absence, which is in connection with:
  - treating an illness or disability of you, your partner, a child for whom you are responsible, or another relative of either you or your partner; *or*
  - the death of your partner, a child or qualifying young person for whom you or your partner are responsible, or another relative of you or your partner.

Relative
'**Relative**' means brother, sister, parent, grandparent, grandchild, great-grandparent or child.[89]

You are also treated as present if you are:[90]

- a Crown servant posted overseas and:
  - you are, or immediately before your posting abroad you were, ordinarily resident in the UK; *or*
  - immediately before your posting you were in the UK in connection with that posting; *or*
- the partner of a Crown servant posted overseas and in the same country as her/ him or temporarily absent from that country under the same exceptions that enable tax credits to continue during a temporary absence from Great Britain.

While you are treated as present in any of the above ways, you can continue to get any tax credits that are already in payment, renew your award and, if you are getting CTC or WTC, make a new claim for the other (see p1459) during your absence.

If you (or your partner, if you have a joint claim) spend longer abroad than the permitted periods, you cease to satisfy the presence condition and your tax credit entitlement ends. If you do not notify this to HM Revenue and Customs within one month (see p1470), you may be overpaid (see Chapter 65) and could be given a penalty (see Chapter 66). On your return to the UK, in most cases you will be unable to claim tax credits, but may be able to claim UC (see p1459).

See p1610 for considerations if you are making a joint claim as a couple.

European Union co-ordination rules

CTC is classed as a 'family benefit' under the main EU co-ordination rules and the UK-Ireland Convention. If you are covered by these rules (see p1647), you can, if you satisfy the other conditions (including that the child is 'normally living with' you), be paid CTC:

- for a child resident in an EEA country; *and/or*
- if you are an EEA national and you go to stay or live in an EEA country.

See p1661 for more details.

WTC is not covered by any of the EU co-ordination rules (see p1652). This means that the EU co-ordination rules cannot assist you and, if you (or your partner) go to an EEA country, you can only be paid under the UK rules above.

Universal credit

You cannot normally be paid UC if you (and your partner, if it is a joint claim) are not in Great Britain.[91] However, provided you were entitled immediately before the period of absence and you continue to meet the other conditions of entitlement, UC can be paid when you are temporarily absent from Great Britain for:[92]

- **one month**, if your absence is not expected to exceed, and does not exceed, one month; *or*
- **two months**, if your absence is in connection with the death of your partner or child, or a 'close relative' (see p89) of yours or of your partner or child, and it would be unreasonable for you to return to Great Britain within the first month; *or*
- **six months**, if your absence is not expected to exceed, and does not exceed, six months and you are a mariner or continental shelf worker; *or*
- **six months**, if your absence is not expected to exceed, and does not exceed, six months and is solely in connection with the medically approved care, convalescence or treatment of you, your partner or child. If this applies to you, you are automatically exempt from the work search requirement and also treated as 'able and willing immediately to take up work' during your absence (see p1048).[93]

Part 11: Immigration and residence rules for benefits and tax credits
Chapter 70: Going abroad
2. Rules for specific benefits and tax credits

Note:
- Since 24 July 2020, periods of temporary absence in Northern Ireland are ignored due to reciprocal arrangements between Great Britain and Northern Ireland treating periods of presence and residence (and also employment) in one territory as having the same effect on UC as if it had occurred in the other territory.[94]
- To be entitled to the carer element in your UC while you are abroad, you must satisfy the rules for CA (see p1625).

If your partner is abroad

If you have a joint claim for UC and you both go abroad, UC continues to be paid while both of you meet one of the above conditions. If you both remain abroad for longer than the relevant period, your entitlement ends.

If you stay in Great Britain while your partner is abroad, her/his absence does not affect your entitlement during the one-, two- or six-month period if one of the above circumstances applies to her/him. After this time, unless your partner is in Northern Ireland (see the note above), you cease to be entitled as joint claimants and must claim as a single person. However, if you have been, and expect to be, apart for less than six months, although your award is based on the maximum amount for a single person, your partner's income and capital are taken into account until you have been (or expect to be) apart for six months, when you then stop being treated as a couple.[95]

If you are of pension age, but your partner is under pension age, once her/his absence exceeds the periods above, your joint claim for UC is treated as a claim by you as a single person. However, as a single person you are not entitled to UC once you have reached pension age and therefore your entitlement to UC ends. From this date, you can claim PC and HB and you are treated as a single person for each of these claims.[96]

For further details on couples claiming UC if one partner does not satisfy the residence or presence rules, see p1597.

If your child is abroad

If your child is abroad, you are treated as no longer responsible for her/him if her/his absence abroad is, or is expected to be, longer than the one-, two- or six-month period allowed in the circumstances above (the circumstances must apply to your child).[97]

European Union co-ordination rules

The DWP considers UC not to be a social security benefit under any of the EU co-ordination rules (see p1653). This means that the EU co-ordination rules cannot assist you and, if you go to an EEA country, you can only be paid under the UK rules above.

Notes

1. The rules on getting paid abroad

1 *R v Barnet LBC ex parte Shah* [1983] 2 AC 309 (HL), Lord Scarman at p342D; see also *GC v HMRC (TC)* [2014] UKUT 251 (AAC)
2 Vol 2 Part 1 Ch7, para 070642 DMG; para C1122 ADM
3 *Slough BC v PK* [2019] UKUT 128 (AAC)
4 **CB** Reg 24(2) CB Regs
   AA Reg 2(3C) SS(AA) Regs
   CDP Reg 7(2)(a) DACYP(S) Regs
   DLA Reg 2(3C) SS(DLA) Regs
   PIP Reg 17(2) SS(PIP) Regs
   TC Reg 4(2) TC(R) Regs
5 *Chief Adjudication Officer v Ahmed and Others*, 16 March 1994 (CA), reported as R(S) 1/96
6 *Chief Adjudication Officer v Ahmed and Others*, 16 March 1994 (CA), reported as R(S) 1/96
7 R(S) 1/85
8 R(U) 16/62

2. Rules for specific benefits and tax credits

9 Reg 5 SSB(PA) Regs
10 Arts 5, 7, 42 and 43 EU Reg 883/04
11 Reg 24 CB Regs
12 Reg 24(1) CB Regs
13 Reg 21 CB Regs
14 Reg 32 CB Regs
15 Reg 21(2) CB Regs
16 Reg 19 SCP Regs
17 Reg 5 SSB(PA) Regs
18 Confirmed in ADM Memo 9/20 and DMG Memo 12/20
19 **AA** Reg 2(2), (3B) and (3C) SS(AA) Regs
   DLA Reg 2(2), (3B) and (3C) SS(DLA) Regs
   PIP Regs 17-20 SS(PIP) Regs
   CA Reg 9(2) and (3) SS(ICA) Regs
   CDP Regs 5(6)-(8) and 7 DACYP(S) Regs
   ADP Regs 16, 17 and 18 DAWAP(S) Regs
20 House of Commons, *Hansard*, Written statement HCWS603, 20 April 2017, available at questions-statements.parliament.uk; confirmed by emails to CPAG, November 2020

21 **CDP** Regs 35 and 36 and Sch, Part 3 DACYP(S) Regs
   ADP Regs 52 and 53 and Sch 2, Part 3 DAWAP(S) Regs
22 Reg 13 SSB(PA) Regs; Sch 2 para 7 SSB(Dep) Regs; reg 2(4) SSB(PRT)Regs
23 The Family Allowances, National Insurance and Industrial Injuries (Gibraltar) Order 1974 No.555
24 **AA** Reg 2B SS(AA) Regs
   DLA Reg 2B SS(DLA) Regs
   CDP Regs 5(4)-(5) and 9 DACYP(S) Regs
   PIP Reg 23 SS(PIP) Regs
   ADP Regs 15(3)-(4) and 20 DAWAP(S) Regs
   CA Reg 9B SS(ICA) Regs
   All see also ADM Memos 9/20 and 17/20, and DMG Memos 12/20 and 16/20
25 **AA** s65(7) SSCBA 1992
   DLA s72(7B) SSCBA 1992
   CDP Reg 9(2)(a)(ii) DACYP(S) Regs
   PIP s84 WRA 2012
   ADP Reg 20(2)(ii) DAWAP(S) Regs
   CA s70(4A) SSCBA 1992
26 **CAS** s81(2A) and (9)-(15) SS(S)A 2018
   YCG Reg 8(3)-(10) CA(YCG)(S) Regs
27 The Family Allowances, National Insurance and Industrial Injuries (Gibraltar) Order 1974 No.555
28 *Bartlett and Others v SSWP*, C-537/09 [2011]; *SSWP v DS* [2019] UKUT 238 (AAC); Art 70 EU Reg 883/04; *Swaddling v AO*, C-90/97 [1999]
29 ss1(3)(d) and 18(4)(a) WRA 2007
30 Regs 151-55 ESA Regs; regs 88-92 ESA Regs 2013
31 Reg 156 and Sch 5 paras 6 and 7 ESA Regs
32 Reg 156 and Sch 5 para 7 ESA Regs
33 Reg 156 ESA Regs
34 Confirmed paras C4 and C4142-3 ADM
35 Arts 5, 46 and 82 EU Reg 883/04; Arts 27 and 46 EU Reg 987/2009; Art 59(7) UK-IC; Art SSC63 UK-EUP
36 s130(1)(a) SSCBA 1992
37 Reg 7 HB Regs; reg 7 HB(SPC) Regs
38 *Slough BC v PK* [2019] UKUT 128 (AAC)
39 LA Welfare Direct 6/2020, updated 5 November 2020

11

- -

40 Art 18 TFEU; Art 24 EU Dir 2004/38; *O'Flynn v Adjudication Officer*, C-237/94 [1996]; R(IS) 4/98
41 Regs 7 and 21 HB Regs; regs 7 and 21 HB(SPC) Regs
42 s124(1) SSCBA 1992
43 Reg 4 IS Regs
44 Reg 21 and Sch 7 paras 11 and 11A IS Regs
45 Reg 21 and Sch 7 para 11A IS Regs
46 Reg 16 IS Regs
47 Reg 16(5) IS Regs
48 Reg 9(3) SSB(PA) Regs
49 Reg 9(4) SSB(PA) Regs
50 Reg 9(5) SSB(PA) Regs
51 s1(2)(i) JSA 1995
52 s21 and Sch 1 para 11 JSA 1995; reg 50 JSA Regs; reg 41 JSA Regs 2013
53 Sch para 2 SS(NIRA) Regs; Sch para 2 SS(GBRA)NI Regs
54 Regs 50(4) and 170 JSA Regs
55 Regs 14 and 19 JSA Regs; reg 16 JSA Regs 2013
56 Regs 3E(1) and (2)(c), 50(6B), 86C and 170 and Sch 5A para 7 JSA Regs; Vol 4, paras 24146-49 DMG
57 Regs 3E(1) and (2)(c), 50(6B) and 86C JSA Regs
58 Regs 50(6B) and 78(1A) and (3)(c) and Sch 5A para 7 JSA Regs
59 Reg 78 JSA Regs
60 Reg 85 and Sch 5 paras 10 and 11 JSA Regs
61 Reg 85 and Sch 5 para 11 JSA Regs
62 Reg 78 JSA Regs
63 Reg 78(5) JSA Regs
64 Arts SSC3(1) and (4) and SSC8 UK-EUP
65 Art 64 EU Reg 883/04; Arts 7 and 21 UK-IC
66 Reg 2 SSB(PA) Regs
67 Reg 13 SSB(PA) Regs; reg 14 SS(IB-ID) Regs; reg 2(4) SSB(PRT) Regs
68 Arts 7 and 21 EU Reg 883/04; Art 7 UK-IC; Art SSC8 UK-EUP
69 Arts 5 and 46 EU Reg 883/04; Art 87 EU Reg 987/2009
70 s1(2)(a) SPCA 2002
71 Reg 3 SPC Regs
72 Reg 4A SPC Regs
73 Reg 1 SPC Regs
74 Reg 5 SPC Regs
75 Reg 5 SPC Regs
76 Sch 2IIA para 7 SPC Regs; DMG Memo 14/18, paras 21-24
77 s113 SSCBA 1992; reg 4(1) SSB(PA) Regs
78 Regs 4(3) and 5 SSB(PA) Regs; ss18 and 20 PA 2014; regs 21-23 SP Regs

79 Reg 6 SSB(PA) Regs
80 Reg 2(4) SSB(PRT) Regs
81 Reg 13 SSB(PA) Regs; reg 10 SSB(Dep) Regs
82 Regs 5 and 9 The Social Security Co-ordination (Revocation of Retained Direct EU Legislation and Related Amendments) (EU Exit) Regulations 2020 No.1508
83 **SSP** Reg 10 SSP(MAPA) Regs
   SMP Reg 2A SMP(PAM) Regs
   SAP/SPP Reg 4 SPPSAP(PAM) Regs
   SSPP Reg 6 SSPP(PAM) Regs
   SPBP Reg 6 SPBP(PAM) Regs
84 **SSP** s163(1) SSCBA 1992; reg 16 SSP Regs; regs 5-10 SSP(MAPA) Regs
   SMP s171(1) SSCBA 1992; regs 2, 2A, 5, 7 and 8 SMP(PAM) Regs
   SAP/SPP ss171ZJ(2)-(3) and 171ZS(2)-(3) SSCBA 1992; regs 3, 4, 8 and 9 SPPSAP(PAM) Regs
   SSPP s171ZZ4(2) SSCBA 1992; regs 5, 6, 7, 9, 10 SSPP(PAM) Regs
   SPBP ss171ZZ14(20-(3) SSCBA 1992; regs 5-10 SPBP(PAM) Regs
85 **SSP** Reg 16(2) SSP Regs
   SMP Reg 3 SMP(PAM) Regs; reg 17(3) SMP Regs
   SAP/SPP Reg 2 SPPSAP(PAM) Regs; reg 32(3) SPPSAP(G) Regs; reg 24(4) ASPP(G) Regs
   SSPP Reg 33(5) SSPP(G) Regs; reg 4 SSPP(PAM) Regs
   SPBP Reg 4 SPBP(PAM) Regs
86 DWPWAG, Fig 4 in contrast to Vol 2 para 070153 DMG
87 Arts 16 and 17 UK-IC
88 Reg 4 TC(R) Regs
89 Reg 2(1) TC(R) Regs
90 Regs 3, 5 and 6 TC(R) Regs
91 ss3 and 4(1)(c) WRA 2012
92 Reg 11 UC Regs
93 Reg 99(1)-(3) UC Regs
94 Sch para 2 The Universal Credit (Northern Ireland Reciprocal Arrangements) Regulations 2020 No.677; see also ADM Memo 18/20, para 3
95 Regs 3, 18, 22 and 36 UC Regs
96 Art 7(1), (2)(a) and (b) and (3)(b) WRA(No.31)O; HB Circular A9/2019, paras 15-17; Vol 13 Ch 77, paras 77035 note 2, 77150-51 and 77160 DMG
97 Reg 4(7) UC Regs

Chapter 71

European Union co-ordination rules

This chapter covers:
1. Introduction (below)
2. Who is covered (p1647)
3. Which benefits are covered (p1652)
4. Principles of co-ordination (p1656)
5. Family benefits (p1661)

Key facts

- If your circumstances involve more than one European Economic Area (EEA) state (or the UK and an EEA state), your benefit entitlements may be affected by the European Union (EU) co-ordination rules.
- The EU co-ordination rules are most relevant when you have moved to the UK from an EEA country or vice versa.
- This *Handbook* uses the phrase 'EU co-ordination rules' to refer to four sets of co-ordination rules, which can apply since the end of the post-Brexit transition period (11pm on 31 December 2020). They provide similar social security rights and require similar conditions to be met, but differ in terms of who, which countries, and which benefits, each covers, and the ways they can affect entitlements.

11

1. Introduction

The phrase 'EU co-ordination rules' is used in this *Handbook* to refer to four different pieces, or collections, of legislation, which provide broadly similar social security rights, and require broadly similar conditions to be met. However, the rules contain important differences, in terms of who, which European countries and which benefits, are covered by each, and the ways they affect benefit entitlements. These differences, and how to determine which rules apply to you, are both covered in this chapter.

Part 11: Immigration and residence rules for benefits and tax credits
Chapter 71: European Union co-ordination rules
1. Introduction

. . . .

The co-ordination rules can affect whether you qualify for benefits in the UK. In most cases, they make it easier to satisfy the UK rules – eg, by enabling you to count periods of residence, insurance and employment in a European Economic Area (EEA) country to meet the conditions of entitlement for a UK benefit. However, in limited circumstances, the co-ordination rules can prevent you from claiming a UK benefit if, for example, the UK is not the competent state to pay that type of benefit. The co-ordination rules can also help you to be paid a UK benefit while you are abroad in a EEA country for longer than you would be able to under UK law alone.

Overview

The original aim of the European Union (EU) co-ordination rules was to secure and promote European free movement by co-ordinating the social security systems within the EEA to ensure that those covered do not lose out on social security protection simply because they move to another member state. Although the UK left the EU, and free movement to and from the UK has been ended, the co-ordination rules that now apply continue this co-ordinating aim, but in more limited ways (see p1645).

. . . .

Member states of the European Union

Austria	Estonia	Italy	Portugal
Belgium	Finland	Latvia	Romania
Bulgaria	France	Lithuania	Slovakia
Croatia	Germany	Luxembourg	Slovenia
Cyprus	Greece	Malta	Spain
Czech Republic	Hungary	The Netherlands	Sweden
Denmark	Ireland	Poland	

Member states of the European Economic Area

The EEA consists of the EU countries plus Iceland, Liechtenstein and Norway.

Agreements with Switzerland mean that, in general, Swiss nationals are treated the same as EEA nationals. Any references to EEA nationals, therefore, also include Swiss nationals, and any references to EEA countries, include Switzerland.[1]

Note: during the transition period and since then if you are covered by the Withdrawal Agreement protections, references within the EU co-ordination rules to EU or EEA member states were treated as if the UK continued to be a member state, and references to EU or EEA nationals were treated as if they included references to British citizens.

. . . .

The phrase '**member state**', when used in the context of the co-ordination rules in this *Handbook* means those states covered by the specific rules being referred to. The main co-ordination rules and the old co-ordination rules cover the UK, all

EEA states plus Switzerland, the UK-EU Protocol covers the UK and EU states, and the UK-Ireland Convention is a bilateral agreement between the UK and Ireland only.

EU law, including the co-ordination rules, applies beyond the actual territory of the EEA states to territories 'for whose external relations a member state is responsible'.[2]

Changes due to the UK leaving the European Union

The UK left the EU on 31 January 2020 and this was followed by a transition period, which ended at 11pm on 31 December 2020. During this transition period, the main EU co-ordination rules, and the European caselaw that has interpreted their meaning, together with other parts of EU law relating to European free movement, continued to apply to the UK as if it was still an EEA state, and to British citizens, as if they were still EU or EEA citizens.[3]

From the end of the transition period, in general, the EU co-ordination rules ceased to apply within UK law. However, the Withdrawal Agreements provide protections for people in certain situations to be able to continue to use these co-ordination rules (see p1647). For those not covered by these protections, a new UK-EU Protocol on Social Security may apply. In addition, a new UK-Ireland Convention on Social Security came into force from the end of the transition period, providing broadly the same level of co-ordination as under the main co-ordination rules, but just between those two countries.

From the end of the transition period, there are four sets of co-ordination rules that may apply.

- **The main co-ordination rules** can continue for EEA nationals and British citizens (and family members of either) covered by the Withdrawal Agreement protections. In broad terms, these protections may apply if on 31 December 2020 your situation involved both an EEA state and the UK – eg, if on that date you were an EEA national living and working in the UK or a British citizen living and working in an EEA state. For those who remain covered by the main co-ordination rules, they apply as if the UK were still a member of the EEA.

- **The old co-ordination rules** can apply in limited circumstances, mainly for non-EEA (and non-British) nationals covered by the Withdrawal Agreement protections.

- **The UK-EU Protocol on Social Security** provides more limited social security co-ordination, between the UK and EU countires, after the end of the transition period for those not covered by the Withdrawal Agreement protections.

- **The UK-Ireland Convention on Social Security** broadly reproduces the principles and effects of the main co-ordination rules, but only between the UK and Ireland for specified benefits of each country, after the end of the transition period.

11

Part 11: Immigration and residence rules for benefits and tax credits
Chapter 71: European Union co-ordination rules
1. Introduction

For details on who is covered by each of the four sets of rules, see p1647. For details of the benefits covered by each of the sets of rules, see p1652.

Note: the UK leaving the EU also affects residence rights (see p1562).

How to check if the co-ordination rules apply

To check whether and how the co-ordination rules apply to you, work through the following steps.

- **Step one:** check whether you are covered by the Withdrawal Agreement protections (see p1647).
- **Step two:** check which, if any, of the four sets of co-ordination rules listed on p1645 you are covered by. If you are covered by the Withdrawal Agreement protections, this is likely to be the main co-ordination rules (see p1649), but could be the old co-ordination rules (see p1650). If you are not covered by the Withdrawal Agreement protections, check whether you are covered by the UK-EU Protocol (see p1651). If your situation only involves the UK and Ireland, check whether you are (as well or instead) covered by the UK-Ireland Protocol (see p1650).
- **Step three:** check whether the particular benefit you want to claim is covered by the co-ordination rules, and into which category it falls (see p1652).
- **Step four:** check which state is the 'competent state' to pay the benefit you are claiming (see p1656).
- **Step five:** check the principle you want to apply – see below for a list.
- **Step six:** check how that principle can affect your entitlement to an individual benefit while you are in the UK: in Chapter 69 for your entitlement in the UK, or in Chapter 70 if you want to be paid when you or a member of your family are in an EEA country.

The co-ordination rules are complex and this chapter only provides an overview. For more information, see CPAG's *Benefits for Migrants Handbook*.

The co-ordination principles

The following principles are contained in the main co-ordination rules in relation to the EEA and UK states, in the UK-EU Protocol in relation to the EU and UK, and in the UK-Ireland Convention in relation to Ireland and the UK.

- **The single state principle.** You can generally, at any one time, only claim a particular category of benefit from one member state, referred to as the 'competent state' (see p1656).
- **Equal treatment of people.** Discrimination on nationality grounds in terms of access to, the rate of and payment of the benefits covered is prohibited (see p1658).

- **Equal treatment of benefits, income, facts or events.** If receipt of a benefit or a fact or an event has a legal consequence in one member state, this must be recognised in the same way by other member states (see p1658).
- **Aggregation.** Periods of residence, insurance and employment in any member state can be used towards entitlement to benefit in another (see p1659).
- **Exportability of certain benefits.** You can continue to be paid certain benefits if you go to another member state (see p1660).
- **Administrative co-operation.** Member states undertake to co-operate in the administration of the co-ordination rules.

The main co-ordination rules succeed, but do not repeal, the previous set of rules (referred to in this *Handbook* as the 'old co-ordination rules'). See p1650 for who is covered by the old rules.

2. Who is covered

This *Handbook* refers to you being 'covered by the co-ordination rules' if you are covered by one of the four sets of rules that co-ordinate the social security systems throughout the European Economic Area (EEA) and UK. It can be important to identify which, if any, you are covered by as some of the specific provisions are different. Check which rules apply by working through the following steps.

- **Step 1:** are you covered by the **Withdrawal Agreement protections** below? These mean the **main co-ordination rules** are potentially available to you, so you next need to check whether you are covered by the main co-ordination rules (see p1649). The Withdrawal Agreement protections can also mean that the **old co-ordination rules** are available to you (see p1650).
- **Step 2:** are you covered by the **UK-Ireland Convention**? This can apply if you are (or you are a member of the family of) an Irish or British citizen, or a refugee and live in either Ireland or the UK (see p1650).
- **Step 3:** are you covered by the **UK-EU Protocol**? This can apply if you have only moved between the UK and the EU since the end of 2020 or if, for another reason, the other co-ordination rules do not apply (see p1651).

Note: if more than one set of rules appears to apply to you, in general, you are covered by the main co-ordination rules (exceptions to this are noted when they arise). However, if you are covered by both the main co-ordination rules and the UK-Ireland Convention, you can rely on whichever is the more generous.[4]

Withdrawal Agreement protections

Since the end of the transition period (11pm on 31 December 2020), you can only be covered by the main co-ordination rules (or, in limited circumstances, the old

Part 11: Immigration and residence rules for benefits and tax credits
Chapter 71: European Union co-ordination rules
2. Who is covered

co-ordination rules) if you covered by the Withdrawal Agreement protections. **Note:** this phrase refers to the protections under each of the three Withdrawal Agreements between the UK and EU, the UK and European Free Trade Association (EFTA) countries (Iceland, Liechtenstein and Norway), and the UK and Switzerland).

You have Withdrawal Agreement protections if, at the end of the transition period (ie, on 31 December 2020), you were:[5]

- an EEA national 'subject to the legislation' (see p1651) of the UK – eg, a Polish national working in the UK; *or*
- a UK national 'subject to the legislation' of an EEA state; *or*
- an EEA national 'subject to the legislation' of an EEA state while residing in the UK – eg, a French national living in the UK receiving a French social security benefit; *or*
- a UK national 'subject to the legislation' of the UK while residing in an EEA state; *or*
- a refugee or stateless person residing in the UK or an EEA state and 'subject to the legislation' of the UK or an EEA state; *or*
- a member of the family (see p1652) or survivor of one of the above; *or*
- (other than under the EFTA or Swiss Agreements) a non-EEA national covered by the old co-ordination rules (see p1650) and legally resident in, and 'subject to the legislation' of, the UK or an EEA state; *or*
- if none of the above apply, you are an EEA national with a European free movement right to reside in the UK (see p1568) or a UK national with an EU free movement right to reside in an EEA state; *or*
- a family member (see p1583) of a person in the group immediately above.

Note: if one or more of the above groups applies to you, the main co-ordination rules (or, in limited circumstances, the old co-ordination rules – see p1650) are potentially available to you. You therefore need to *also* check whether you are covered by the main co-ordination rules (see p1649).

The **Withdrawal Agreement protections continue to apply** for as long as:

- (if you are covered by one of the last two bullet points) you continue to have a free movement right to reside, or a right to work, as an EEA national in the UK, or a British citizen in an EEA country, or you continue to be a family member of a person who does;[6] *or*
- (if you are covered by one of the first seven bullet points) you continue, 'without interruption', to be in one of the situations listed[7] – eg, you continue to be an EEA national residing and working or claiming social security benefits in the UK or a British citizen residing and working or claiming social security benefits in an EEA country. Until new caselaw is established on the meaning of an 'interruption' to your situation, it may be relevant to refer to the caselaw on the meaning of the 'relevant situation remains unchanged', which can

determine when the main co-ordination rules apply in place of the old (see p1650).

If you are not, or no longer, covered by the Withdrawal Agreement protections, check if you are covered by the partial Withdrawal Agreement protections, which only enable limited use of the main co-ordination rules.

Partial Withdrawal Agreement protections

If you are not covered by the Withdrawal Agreement protections, partial Withdrawal Agreement protections can enable you to use limited aspects of the main co-ordination rules.

The '**aggregation principle**' (see p1659) of the main co-ordination rules can be available to you if you are not, or no longer, covered by the Withdrawal Agreement protections, and *before* the end of the transition period (31 December 2020), you were:[8]

- an EEA national 'subject to the legislation' (see p1651) of the UK (and, for example, you are currently residing in an EEA state); *or*
- a UK national 'subject to the legislation' of an EEA state (and, for example, you are currently residing in the UK); *or*
- a refugee or stateless person living in an EEA state and 'subject to the legislation' of the UK or living in the UK and 'subject to the legislation' of an EEA state; *or*
- (other than under the EFTA or Swiss agreements) a non-EEA national covered by the old co-ordination rules (see p1650), 'subject to the legislation' of the UK and are currently legally resident in an EEA state, or 'subject to the legislation' of an EEA state and are currently legally resident in the UK; *or*
- a member of the family (see p1652) or survivor of one of the above categories.

If this applies, you may be able to add together periods of residence, insurance or employment/self-employment completed in one or more EEA states or the UK to satisfy the requirements for a particular benefit, completed both before or after the end of the transition period. If, as a result, you receive attendance allowance (AA), personal independence payment (PIP)/adult disability payment (ADP) daily living component, disability living allowance (DLA)/child disability payment (CDP) care component or carer's allowance (CA), you are also subject to the requirement that the UK be the competent state to pay this benefit (see p1656).[9]

You may be able to continue to receive **family benefits** for family members living in another member state, if you are not, or or are no longer, covered by the Withdrawal Agreement protections, in limited circumstances – see p1661.

Who is covered by the main co-ordination rules

In order to be covered by the main co-ordination rules, you must come within the Withdrawal Agreement protections (see p1647) *and* come within the '**personal scope**' of the main co-ordination rules.

Part 11: Immigration and residence rules for benefits and tax credits
Chapter 71: European Union co-ordination rules
2. Who is covered

You are within the personal scope of the main co-ordination rules if you are:[10]

- residing in the UK or an EEA country and you have been 'subject to the legislation of one or more member states' (see p1651) and you are:
  - an EEA national; *or*
  - a British citizen; *or*
  - a refugee; *or*
  - a stateless person; *or*
- a member of the family (see p1652) or a 'survivor' of one of the above (in the UK, a widow, widower or surviving civil partner).

In addition, for the main co-ordination rules to apply, your situation must involve the UK and one or more EEA states, or at least two EEA states. This usually means that you must have moved between an EEA country and the UK (or another EEA country), or you live in one and work in another, or you live in one and are the national of another.[11]

When the old co-ordination rules apply

The main co-ordination rules[12] replaced, but did not repeal, the old co-ordination rules.[13] The old co-ordination rules can only apply to you if you are covered by the Withdrawal Agreement protections (see p1647). They may apply if you are a non-EEA (and non-British) national (other than a refugee or member of the family of an EEA or British citizen who is covered by the main rules), legally resident in an EEA country or the UK. They may also continue to apply to you if you have already been relying on them to receive your benefit since before June 2012, and your 'relevant situation remains unchanged'.[14]

As very few claims are now covered by the old co-ordination rules, this *Handbook* does not cover them. For more information on when the old co-ordination rules apply, see CPAG's *Benefits for Migrants Handbook* and, for the old rules, see the 2012/13 edition of this *Handbook*.

Who is covered by the UK-Ireland Convention

You are covered by the UK-Ireland Convention on Social Security if you come within the range of people to whom it applies. This is known as the 'personal scope' of this Convention. In addition, your situation must involve both the UK and Ireland. This generally means that you have moved between the two states, or you live in one and work in the other, or you live in one and are the national of another.

You are within the 'personal scope' of the UK-Ireland Convention on Social Security if:[15]

- you are:
  - an Irish citizen; *or*
  - a British citizen; *or*

- a refugee; *or*
- a stateless person,

residing in the UK or Ireland and you are or, have been, 'subject to the legislation of' the UK or Ireland (see below); *or*
- you are a member of the family (see p1652) or a survivor of someone covered in the above bullet point. 'Survivor' is defined as a surviving spouse or civil partner or child to whom a survivor's benefit or death grant is payable under Irish or (not including for a child) UK legislation.[16]

Note: if you are covered by both the UK-Ireland Convention and the main co-ordination rules (which would require you to be covered by the Withdrawal Agreement protections), you can rely on whichever is the more generous.[17]

Who is covered by the UK-EU Protocol

You are covered by the UK-EU Protocol if you are, or have been, 'subject to the legislation of' (see below) the UK or an EU state, or you are the 'member of the family' (see p1652) or survivor (not defined) of someone who has.[18] In addition, your situation must involve either the UK and one or more EU states or at least two EU states. This generally means that you must have moved between an EU state and the UK (or another EU state), or you live in one and work in another, or you live in one but are the national of another.[19]

Note:
- You can be covered by the Protocol regardless of your nationality. The Protocol simply applies to 'persons, including stateless persons and refugees' who satisfy the above requirements.[20]
- The Protocol is between the UK and the EU. Unlike the main EU co-ordinaton rules, it does not extend to Iceland, Liechtenstein, Norway and Switzerland. Although the UK government has sought similar co-ordination provisions with these four states,[21] at the time of writing the only agreements in force were on a bilateral basis with Switzerland, and a limited agreement with Norway. For details, see CPAG's *Benefits for Migrants Handbook*.

Common terms

'Subject to the legislation'

The requirement that you (or the person you are a member of the family of) have been 'subject to a legislation of' one of the states to which the relevant co-ordination rules applies, is essential to being covered by those rules. The meaning of the phrase is broadly the same for each of the co-ordination rules, but may be narrower under the UK-EU Protocol.

Part 11: Immigration and residence rules for benefits and tax credits
Chapter 71: European Union co-ordination rules
3. Which benefits are covered

Subject to the legislation of

You have been '**subject to the legislation of**' a state if you have worked in and paid (or should have paid) national insurance contributions to, or received any social security or special non-contributory benefit (see below) from, that state. You may also be subject to the legislation if you are potentially eligible for any social security benefit or special non-contributory benefit.[22]

'**Legislation**' is defined as the legislation of each member state relating to the 'social security branches covered' (or under the UK-Ireland Convention, the benefits specified) in the relevant set of co-ordination rules.[23]

The 'social security benefits' include UK benefits that are intended to assist you in the event of one of the risks on p1653.

Member of the family

A member of the family of someone covered by the co-ordination rules can also rely on the rules that cover that person (which can vary depending on the rules they are covered by and the type of benefit claimed). **Note:** the consequences of being a member of someone's family are not always favourable – eg, if it changes which state is competent to pay your benefit (see p1656).

Members of the family

You are a '**member of the family**' of a person covered by the co-ordination rules if you are:[24]

– someone defined or recognised as a member of the family, or designated as a member of the household, by the legislation under which benefits are provided; *or*

– if the legislation under which benefits are provided does not distinguish between members of the family and other people to whom the legislation applies, the person's spouse or child either under the age of 'majority' (18 in England and Wales; 16 in Scotland) or older but dependent on the person covered.

If, under the legislation, you are only considered to be a member of the family or member of the household if you are living in the same household as the person, this condition is considered satisfied if you are mainly dependent on her/him.

For more details, see CPAG's *Benefits for Migrants Handbook*.

3. **Which benefits are covered**

The benefits to which the co-ordination rules apply are referred to as being within the '**material scope**' of the rules.

Social security benefits are categorised according to the risk against which they are designed to provide financial protection.

The main co-ordination rules and the UK-EU Protocol do not list the benefits that assist with each risk within the legislation, but each member state must provide a list to the European Union (EU).[25] The UK-Ireland Convention includes the benefits of each state that assist with each category of risk.[26] The categorisation of a benefit can be challenged, as ultimately it depends on its characteristics rather than on how an individual state lists it.

The table below lists the benefits that are accepted as categorised for each risk under the main co-ordination rules (with disputes noted), and the benefits listed in the UK-Ireland Convention. Under the UK-EU Protocol, benefit categorisation should follow that of the main co-ordination rules, unless the Protocol specifically provides otherwise.[27]

The UK-EU Protocol is the only set of rules that lists benefits that are *not* covered. The UK-EU Protocol does not apply to:[28]

- family benefits (see p1661); *and*
- long-term care benefits. These are listed as attendance allowance (AA), disability living allowance (DLA) care component, personal independence payment (PIP) daily living component, carer's allowance (CA), carer's allowance supplement and young carer grant.[29] Although child disability payment (CDP) and adult disability payment (ADP) are not listed, both are expected to be treated as long-term care benefits; *and*
- winter fuel or cold weather payments; *and*
- special non-contributory benefits (see p1655); *and*
- social and medical assistance (see p1656).

Social security benefits

Risk	UK benefit	UK benefit listed under UK-Ireland Convention
Sickness	AA	Contributory ESA in the assessment phase
	CA	
	Carer's allowance supplement	
	Young carer grant	
	Child winter heating assistance	
	DLA/CDP care component	
	PIP/ADP daily living component	
	Statutory sick pay	
	Contributory employment and support allowance (ESA) in the assessment phase or for the first 365 days (see below)	

Part 11: Immigration and residence rules for benefits and tax credits
Chapter 71: European Union co-ordination rules
3. Which benefits are covered

Long-term care benefits	Treated as sickness benefits[30]	AA
		DLA care component
		PIP daily living component
		CA
		(CDP care component and ADP daily living component expected to be treated as listed)
Maternity and paternity	Maternity allowance (MA)	MA
	Statutory maternity, adoption, paternity, shared parental and parental bereavement pay (see p1638)	
Invalidity	AA, DLA care and mobility component and CA if you were in receipt of benefit before 1 June 1992.	Contributory ESA after the assessment phase
	Long-term incapacity benefit	
	Severe disablement allowance	
	Contributory ESA after the assessment phase or after first 365 days (or arguably before – see below)	
Old age	State pension	State retirement pension
	Category A, B and D retirement pensions	
	Additional pension	
	Graduated retirement benefit	
	Winter fuel payments	
	Increments – eg, to pensions	
	Increases of retirement pension for an adult	
	Age addition in pensions	
Pre-retirement	None	None
Survivors	Bereavement benefits	Widowed mother's allowance
		Widow's pension
		Widowed parent's allowance
Death grants	Bereavement support payment	Bereavement support payment
Accidents at work and occupational diseases	Industrial injuries disablement benefit	Industrial injuries benefits
	Constant attendance allowance	
	Exceptionally severe disablement allowance	
	Reduced earnings allowance	

Unemployment	Contribution-based jobseeker's allowance (JSA)	Contribution-based JSA
Family benefits (see p1661)	Child benefit	Child benefit
	Child tax credit (CTC)	Guardian's allowance
	Increases in other benefits for an adult or a child	CTC
	Guardian's allowance	

Note:
- **Contributory ESA** under the main co-ordination rules is classed initially as a sickness benefit during either the assessment phase (older guidance[31]) or the first 365 days (recent guidance[32]) and then an invalidity benefit thereafter. Under the UK-EU Protocol, the recent guidance classes it as an invalidity benefit from the outset, which is significant as invalidity benefits cannot be exported under the UK-EU Protocol (see p1660).
- The DWP considers **universal credit** (UC) to be neither a social security benefit nor a special non-contributory benefit.[33] UC is listed as 'social assistance' in the UK-Ireland Convention (see p1656).

Disability and carers' benefits

Under **the main co-ordination rules**, AA, DLA/CDP care component, PIP/ADP daily living component, CA, carer's allowance supplement and young carer grant are categorised as sickness benefits.[34]

The mobility components of DLA, CDP, PIP and, it is expected ADP, are categorised as special non-contributory benefits (see below).

The **UK-Ireland Convention** categorises AA, DLA care component, PIP daily living component and CA as long-term care benefits, but then treats them in broadly the same way as sickness benefits are treated under the main co-ordination rules.[35] Although not listed under the Convention, the regulations for CDP, ADP, young carer grant and carer's allowance supplement enable you to make a new claim for either payment while resident in Ireland in certain circumstances if you are covered by the Convention (see p1626).[36]

The **UK-EU Protocol** states it does not cover AA, DLA care or mobility component, PIP daily living or mobility component, CA, carer's allowance supplement and young carer grant.[37] The similar characteristics of CDP and ADP mean they are also not covered by the Protocol.

Special non-contributory benefits

Under the **main EU co-ordination rules**, the UK government has only listed pension credit (PC), income-related ESA, income-based JSA and DLA mobility component as special non-contributory benefits.[38] However, the mobility component of PIP is also accepted as a special non-contributory benefit,[39] and the

Part 11: Immigration and residence rules for benefits and tax credits
Chapter 71: European Union co-ordination rules
4. Principles of co-ordination

mobility components of CDP and ADP are also treated as such. Scottish child payment, funeral support payment, Best Start grants and Best Start food payments have also been categorised as special non-contributory benefits.

Special non-contributory benefits can only be paid by, and under the legislation of, the state in which you are resident.[40] See p1657 for details of how residence is determined. However, although you cannot 'export' special non-contributory benefits, all the other co-ordination principles apply.[41]

Under the **UK-EU Protocol**, all the above benefits are listed as or, for CDP and ADP mobility components and Scottish child payment, treated as special non-contributory benefits. The Protocol states it does not apply at all to these benefits.[42]

The **UK-Ireland Convention** does not refer to special non-contributory benefits, but defines the three means-tested benefits as 'social assistance' (see below), and does not refer to the others at all.

Social and medical assistance

Under the **main co-ordination rules** and the **UK-EU Protocol**, benefits that are neither social security nor special non-contributory benefits are considered to be social assistance and are excluded from the co-ordination rules.[43] The UK does not specify which benefits it considers to be social assistance under either legislation. The Scottish government has categorised Job Start Payment as social assistance.

Under the **UK-Ireland Convention**, 'social assistance' is defined in relation to UK benefits as UC, PC, income support, income-related ESA and income-based JSA.[44] The only provisions made by the Convention for 'social assistance' relate to the recovery of overpayments from benefit paid by the other state.[45]

4. Principles of co-ordination

The single competent state

In general, under each of the co-ordination rules, you can only claim a particular category of benefit from one member state, and are only liable to pay national insurance (NI) contributions to one member state, at any one time. This is expressed as the general principle that you can only be subject to the legislation of a single member state.[46]

Note: the UK-Ireland Convention refers to 'competent party' rather than 'competent state', but the same principle applies.

The '**competent state**' is the one responsible for paying your benefit and to which you are liable to pay NI contributions.[47] In general, it is the state in which you are:[48]

- employed or self-employed (even if you are not currently earning enough to pay NI[49]); or

- a civil servant; *or*
- (other than for the UK-EU Protocol) resident while receiving an unemployment benefit under specific provisions;[50] *or*
- (other than for the UK-EU Protocol) a conscripted member of the armed forces or doing compulsory civilian service.

If none of the above apply, the competent state is the state in which you are 'resident' (see below).[51]

You are treated as still employed or self-employed if, as a result of that activity, you are receiving cash benefits (other than for the risks of old age, or accidents at work, or except under the UK-Ireland Convention, invalidity, sickness or being a survivor).[52]

There are exceptions to this general rule – eg, under the main co-ordination rules or the UK-Ireland Convention, in the payment of attendance allowance (AA), disability living allowance (DLA)/child disability payment (CDP) care component, personal independence payment (PIP)/adult disability payment (ADP) daily living component and carer's allowance (CA), if you (or the member of your family who brings you within the co-ordination rules) receive a 'pension' (which includes most contribution-based state benefits, not only retirement pensions from a European Economic Area (EEA) state other than the one in which you live (from Ireland or the UK, if relying on the UK-Ireland Convention), then the competent state will generally be the state that pays the pension.[53]

If the DWP decides that a member of your family affects your competent state (eg, because s/he works in another state), get specialist advice taking account of the developing caselaw.[54]

'**Residence**' means habitual residence.[55] If there is a difference of views between two states or institutions about where you are 'resident', they must agree where your centre of interest is, taking into account all your circumstances. If there is still a dispute, your intentions, especially the reasons why you moved, will be decisive in establishing where you are resident.[56]

If the state in which you claim benefit decides it is not the competent state to pay that category of benefit, it must pass your claim to the state it considers competent without delay. The date you submitted a claim (or appeal) to a state that is not competent is treated as your date of claim (or appeal) by the state that is competent.[57]

If two or more states take a different view on which is competent to pay a benefit, you can get provisional payments from your state of residence (or, for family benefits under the UK-Ireland Convention, the child's state of residence[58]), or (other than under the UK-Ireland Convention) if you are not resident in any, the state to which you first applied, while the issue is resolved.[59]

For further information on how the competent state is determined, including when exceptions apply, see CPAG's *Benefits for Migrants Handbook*.

Part 11: Immigration and residence rules for benefits and tax credits
Chapter 71: European Union co-ordination rules
4. Principles of co-ordination

When the competent state changes

If you are subject to the legislation of a member state, it continues to be your competent state until a change makes another state competent. The main changes are:[60]

- you start to work in another member state;[61] *or*
- in some circumstances, you move to an EEA state and become resident there.

Note: these general rules can be supplemented by other rules specific to the category of benefit being paid.[62] For example, if you start receiving a pension from an EEA state, this generally means that state becomes competent to pay most disability, carers' and family benefits (see CPAG's *Benefits for Migrants Handbook*).

In general, under each of the co-ordination rules, if you continue to be entitled to a UK benefit when you move to an EEA state, the UK remains the competent state for paying that benefit until either you become employed/self-employed in the other state or, in certain circumstances, you start to receive a benefit from it.[63] However, this can be affected by the category of benefit being claimed. For example, the Court of Appeal recently held that the UK ceased to be the competent state for child benefit when the claimant moved, with her child, to reside in Spain. Consequently, entitlement to child benefit ceased and this was not altered by the UK continuing to be the competent state for the child's DLA care component, which is a different category of benefit.[64]

Equal treatment

If you are covered by any of the co-ordination rules, you are entitled to the same benefits under the legislation of the competent state (see p1656) as a national of that state.[65] Equal treatment is one of the fundamental rights of EU law,[66] and the principle of non-discrimination prohibits discrimination based on your nationality. Both direct discrimination, and, if it cannot be justified as proportionate and in pursuit of a legitimate aim, indirect discrimination based on your nationality are prohibited.

The legal effects of facts or events, including receipt of a particular benefit or income, must also be treated equally.[67] A benefit paid by a member state is 'equivalent' to a benefit paid by another if they are comparable, taking account of the aim of each benefit and the legislation under which they are established. For example, a Polish benefit was accepted in one case as equivalent to the middle or higher rate of DLA care component and therefore entitled the claimant's carer to CA, and in a separate case as equivalent to AA and therefore entitled the claimant to a severe disability addition within her pension credit.[68] The Upper Tribunal has held that although this does not apply to the effects on working tax credit (WTC) (because WTC is not covered by the co-ordination rules – see p1652), other EU equal treatment provisions[69] mean that the WTC rules on entitlement to the childcare element must be interpreted so as to accept receipt of Dutch invalidity benefit as evidence of a claimant's incapacity.[70]

See CPAG's *Benefits for Migrants Handbook* for further information.

Aggregation

The principle of **'aggregation'** enables you to add together periods of insurance, residence or employment/self-employment completed under the legislation of one or more member states to satisfy the requirements of a benefit.[71] This may be necessary if your entitlement to benefit depends on your fulfilling a certain period of residence, employment or insurance. For example, if you want to claim a UK contribution-based benefit, such as contributory employment and support allowance, but you have not paid sufficient NI contributions in the UK, you can rely on contributions paid in one or more member states to satisfy the UK contribution rules. To be entitled to a UK benefit, the UK must be the competent state to pay the category of benefit you are claiming. The competent institution (eg, in the UK, the DWP and HM Revenue and Customs) must contact the institutions in the relevant state(s) to determine the periods completed under their legislation.[72] What constitutes a period of residence, employment or insurance is determined by the legislation of the state under which it took place.[73] **Note:** the Upper Tribunal has held that 'mere residence' in an EEA country cannot be aggregated under the main co-ordination rules to satisfy the past presence test in disability and carers' benefits.[74] Similarly, the UK-Ireland Convention requires you to have been 'insured' during periods of aggregated residence used to satisfy the past presence test when the disability or carers' benefit is paid by the UK while you reside in Ireland (see p1602).[75]

Example

Sancha is a Portuguese national who worked for many years in Portugal. She leaves her job in Portugal and moves to the UK. She works for two weeks before being made redundant. Sancha is expecting a baby in two months' time and claims maternity allowance (MA). She can be entitled to MA because the UK is her competent state and she can add her periods of employment in Portugal to her employment in the UK to satisfy the employment condition of having worked for 26 out of the last 66 weeks. **Note:** if Sancha had moved to and begun working in the UK before 31 December 2020, she would have been be covered by the main co-ordination rules and, if she moved after, she would be covered by the UK-EU Protocol, but the aggregation principle would apply in either case.

Note:

- In general, to rely on the main co-ordination rules you need to covered by the Withdrawal Agreement protections (see p1647). However, if you are not, or no longer, covered by these, you can use aggregation principle of the main co-

Part 11: Immigration and residence rules for benefits and tax credits
Chapter 71: European Union co-ordination rules
4. Principles of co-ordination

ordination rules if you are covered by the *partial* Withdrawal Agreement protections (see p1649). This is particularly important if you need to rely on aggregating past periods of residence to satisfy the past presence test for the disability and carers' benefits, because the UK-EU protocol does not cover these benefits. **Note:** if you receive benefit as a result of aggregating past periods of residence, the requirement for the UK to be the competent state applies, other than for the mobility components (see p1656).

- For unemployment benefits, your periods of insurance (or, if required for entitlement, employment or self-employment) can only be aggregated if you were last insured (or worked) in the state from which you claim. However, this additional condition does not apply if, during your last period of work, you resided in a state other than your competent state (eg, because you worked in another state) *and* you claim in that state where you still reside or have returned to.[76]

Exporting benefits

Each of the co-ordination rules allow you to 'export' certain benefits from one member state to another if you cease to be resident in the state in which your entitlement arose.

This means that certain benefits may not be reduced, modified, suspended, withdrawn or confiscated just because you go to live in a different member state.[77] The rules for exporting vary according to the benefit concerned: some are fully exportable, some may be exportable on a temporary basis, and some are not exportable at all.

Check the individual benefit rules in Chapter 70 to see whether the benefit can be exported. If it can, contact the office that pays your benefit well in advance, so that arrangements can be made to pay you in the state you are going to.

Under the **main co-ordination rules** and the **UK-Ireland Convention**, all benefits categorised as social security benefits are exportable, provided the UK remains the competent state for the payment of that benefit (see p1656). However, the **UK-EU Protocol** excludes invalidity and unemployment benefits from export provisions and does not cover family or long-term care benefits at all. See p1653 for a list of the UK benefits covered.

The following benefits can be exported indefinitely:
- old age benefits; *and*
- survivors' cash benefits; *and*
- pensions for accidents at work or occupational diseases; *and*
- (not under the UK-EU Protocol) invalidity benefits; *and*
- (not under the UK-EU Protocol) family benefits (see p1661); *and*
- death grants.

The following benefits can be exported for a limited period or subject to certain restrictions:

- (not under UK-EU Protocol) unemployment benefits;
- sickness, maternity and paternity benefits (although, in most cases, these are exportable in a similar way to the fully exportable benefits).

Special non-contributory benefits (see p1655) cannot be exported. Under the main co-ordination rules, they are paid only in the country in which you are resident.[78]

Overlapping benefit rules

A general principle of each of the co-ordination rules is that you should not use one period of compulsory insurance to obtain more than one benefit.[79] In general, you are only insured in one member state for any one period, so you cannot use insurance from that period to obtain entitlement to benefits of the same kind from two states. Usually, benefits are adjusted to ensure that either only one state pays the benefit, taking into account periods of insurance in other countries, or that the benefit is paid pro rata according to the lengths of the periods of insurance in different member countries.

In certain cases, however, you may be paid both the full level of a UK benefit and a proportion of a benefit from one or more member states, accrued as a result of having paid insurance contributions there. Member states are not allowed to apply provisions preventing the overlapping of their own benefits with those of other member states if it would reduce what you would have received from your years of contributions in the first state alone.[80]

5. Family benefits

Under the **main co-ordination rules,** family benefits in the UK include child benefit, child tax credit (CTC), guardian's allowance and child dependants' additions in other benefits. Scottish child payment has been categorised as a special non-contributory benefit (see p1655), so the rules below do not apply to it.

Under the **UK-Ireland Convention,** family benefits are listed as child benefit, CTC and guardian's allowance.[81]

The **UK-EU Protocol** does not apply to family benefits.

If you are covered by the **main co-ordination rules** (or, for situations involving only the UK and Ireland, you are covered by the **UK-Ireland Convention**), you can export family benefits and they are updated in the normal way, without any time limit, *provided* the competent state to pay your family benefits has not changed (see p1658).[82] You can also be paid for members of your family (see

Part 11: Immigration and residence rules for benefits and tax credits
Chapter 71: European Union co-ordination rules
5. Family benefits

p1652) living in a European Economic Area (EEA) state (under the UK-Ireland Convention, Ireland).[83] However, you must satisfy the other conditions for that benefit, including, for CTC, that the child is 'normally living with' you, and for child benefit, if the child is not living with you that you are contributing to the costs of that child at least the amount of child benefit that would be payable.[84]

Note: in general, to rely on the main co-ordination rules, you need to be covered by the Withdrawal Agreement protections (see p1647).[85] However, if these do not, or no longer, apply to you, you can continue to receive a family benefit that you were entitled to, as a result of the main co-ordination rules, on 31 December 2020 for a family member living in:[86]

- an EEA country while you were 'subject to the legislation of' (see p1651) the UK, if you are a British citizen (or refugee, or stateless person or non-EEA national legally resident in the UK); *or*
- the UK while you were 'subject to the legislation of' an EEA country, if you are an EEA national (or refugee, or stateless person or non-EEA national legally resident in that EEA country).

This is referred to in this *Handbook* as having partial Withdrawal Agreement protection (see p1649). If you cease to be entitled to the family benefit, or your entitlement ceases to be as a result of the main co-ordination rules, this partial Withdrawal Agreement protection ends.

Generally, you are entitled to receive family benefits from your competent state under the rules on p1656.[87] However, if you are receiving a pension, you claim family benefits from the state that is the competent state for paying your pension.[88]

To ensure that equivalent family benefits are not paid by more than one state in respect of the same family member for the same period, there are detailed rules to determine which state has priority to pay.[89] **Note:** these priority rules only need to be considered if there is an actual overlap of entitlement because claims have been made in more than one state (unless entitlement does not require a claim to have been made).[90] If the state with priority pays family benefits at a lower rate than a state with lower priority, the latter pays a 'top-up' to supplement the amount paid by the priority state. However, this top-up need not be paid for children residing in another state where entitlement to the family benefit is based on residence only (rather than on employment or receipt of a pension).[91] For further information on family benefits, including the priority rules, see CPAG's *Benefits for Migrants Handbook*.

Chapter 71

European Union co-ordination rules

Notes

11

Part 11: Immigration and residence rules for benefits and tax credits
Chapter 71: European Union co-ordination rules
Notes

41 Art 3(3) EU Reg 883/04; *Dano v Jobcenter Leipzig,* C-333/13 [2014], paras 46-55
42 Art SSC3(4)(a) and Annex SSC-1 Part 1(i) UK-EUP
43 Art 3(5) EU Reg 883/04; Art SSC3(4)(b) UK-EUP
44 Art1(1) UK-IC
45 Art 47 UK-IC

4. Principles of co-ordination
46 Art 11 EU Reg 883/04; Art 9 UK-IC; Art SSC10 UK-EUP
47 Art 1(q) and (s) EU Reg 883/04; Art SSC1(h) and (i) UK-EUP
48 Art 11 EU Reg 883/04; Art 9 UK-IC; Art SSC10 UK-EUP
49 *JS v SSWP* [2019] UKUT 239 (AAC); ADM Memo 1/20; DMG Memo 3/20
50 Art 65 EU Reg 883/04; Art 22 UK-IC
51 Art 11(3)(e) EU Reg 883/04; Art 9(4)(e) UK-IC; Art SSC10(3)(c) UK-EUP
52 Art 11(2) EU Reg 883/04; Art 9(2) and (3) UK-IC; Art SSC10(2) UK-EUP
53 Arts 23-32 EU Reg 883/04; Vol 2 Ch 7, Part 2 Appendix 3 DMG; Ch C2 Appendix 1 ADM; DMG Memo 16/20; ADM Memo 17/20; Art 20 UK-IC
54 *AM v SSWP* [2017] UKUT 26 (AAC); *AH v SSWP (DLA)* [2020] UKUT 53 (AAC) – appeal to CA awaiting hearing date, case ref: C3/2020/1399 *Harrington v SSWP;* but see *SSWP v TG (DLA)* [2019] UKUT 86 (AAC), paras 7-8 and 13-18; *GK v SSWP (CA)* [2019] UKUT 87 (AAC), paras 6-7 and 12-17 and pending cases: CSDLA/136/2017 and CSG/95/2017
55 Art 1(j) EU Reg 883/04; Art 1(1) UK-IC; Art SSC1(aa) UK-EUP
56 Art 11 EU Reg 987/2009; Annex SSC-7, Art SSCI.10 UK-EUP
57 **Main rules** Art 81 EU Reg 883/04; Art 2 EU Reg 987/2009; *SSWP v AK (AA)* [2015] UKUT 110 (AAC), reported as [2015] AACR 27; see also *MGL v SSWP (ESA)* [2018] UKUT 352 (AAC); Vol 2 Ch 7, Part 2 Appendix 4 DMG; Ch C2 Appendix 2 ADM
UK-IC Art 60
UK-EUP Art SSC62
58 Art 40(2) UK-IC
59 Art 6(2) and (3) EU Reg 987/2009; *SSWP v HR (AA)* [2014] UKUT 571 (AAC); *SSWP v Fileccia* [2017] EWCA Civ 1907; Vol 2 Ch 7, Part 2 Appendix 4 DMG; Ch C2 Appendix 2 ADM; Art 63(2) UK-IC; Annex SSC-7, Art SSCI.6 UK-EUP

60 Arts 11-16 EU Reg 883/04; Arts 9-13 UK-IC; Arts SSC10-13 UK-EUP
61 See, for example, *SSWP v MC (DLA)* [2019] UKUT 84 (AAC)
62 Title III EU Reg 883/04
63 See, for example, *Kuusijärvi v Riksförsäkringsverket,* C-275/96 [1998]; *HB v HMRC (CHB)* [2014] UKUT 554 (AAC); *SSWP v Tolley,* C-430/15 [2017]; see also *KR v SSWP (DLA)* [2019] UKUT 85 (AAC), reported as [2019] AACR 22
64 *Carrington v HMRC and SSWP* [2021] EWCA Civ 1724
65 Art 4 EU Reg 883/04; Art 4 UK-IC; Art SSC 5 UK-EUP
66 Art 18 TFEU; Art 24 EU Dir 2004/38; Art 7 EU Reg 492/2011
67 Art 5 EU Reg 883/04; Art 5 UK-IC; Art SSC 6 UK-EUP
68 CG/1346/2018; *HT v SSWP* [2020] UKUT 57 (AAC); DMG Memo 02/20
69 Art 7(1) and (2) EU Reg 492/11
70 *AS v HMRC* [2017] UKUT 361 (AAC), reported as [2018] AACR 14, resulting in the inclusion of reg 13(6)(K) in the WTC(EMR) Regs
71 Art 6 EU Reg 883/04; Art 6 UK-IC; Art SSC 7 UK-EUP
72 Art 12 EU Reg 987/2009
73 Arts 1(t)(u) and (v) and 6 EU Reg 883/04; *Decision H6 of 16 December 2010 of the Administrative Commission for the Co-ordination of Social Security Systems* [2011] OJ C-45/04; Art 6(2) UK-IC; Art SSC 7 UK-EUP
74 *SSWP v MM and BK v SSWP* [2016] UKUT 547 (AAC), reported as [2019] AACR 21 - note the appeal against this part of the decision was not pursued when it went to the Court of Appeal – *Kavanagh and Another v SSWP* [2019] EWCA Civ 272.
75 Art 19 UK-IC
76 Arts 61 and 65(5)(a) EU Reg 883/04; Art 21(1) and (2) UK-IC; Art SSC 56 UK-EUP
77 Art 7 EU Reg 883/04; Art 7 UK-IC; Art SSC8 UK-EUP
78 Art 70 EU Reg 883/04
79 Art 10 EU Reg 883/04; Arts 8 and 31-33 UK-IC; Arts SSC9 and SSC48-50 UK-EUP
80 *Teresa and Silvana Petroni v Office National des Pensions Pour Travailleurs Salariés (ONPTS), Bruxelles* 24-75 [1975]

5. Family benefits
81 Art 3(x) UK-IC
82 Art 67 EU Reg 883/04; *HB v HMRC (CHB)* [2014] UKUT 554 (AAC); *HMRC v Carrington* [2021] EWCA Civ 1724

83 Art 67 EU Reg 883/04; *HMRC v Ruas*
    [2010] EWCA Civ 291; *JL v HMRC (CHB)*
    [2017] UKUT 193 (AAC); Art 38 UK-IC
84 s143(1)(b) SSCBA 1992; s8 TCA 2002;
    reg 3(1) CTC Regs; *RI v HMRC (TC)*
    [2019] UKUT 306 (AAC); *RK v HMRC
    (CHB)* [2015] UKUT 357 (AAC), reported
    as [2016] AACR 4; *JL v HMRC (CHB)*
    [2017] UKUT 193 (AAC), paras 30-32
    and 49; *MZ v HMRC* [2020] UKUT 65
    (AAC)
85 TCTM para 02015; CBTM para 10015
86 Art 32(1)(d) WA 2019; Art 31(1)(d) UK-
    EFTA; Art 26a(1)(d) UK-Swiss
    Agreement; see also DWPWAG, Ch 1
    paras 87-95
87 *Bogatu v Minister for Social Protection*, C-
    322/17 [2019]
88 Art 67 EU Reg 883/04, second sentence;
    Art 38(2) UK-IC
89 Art 68 EU Reg 883/04; Art 39 UK-IC
90 *Bundesagentur für Arbeit – Familienkasse
    Sachsen v Trapkowski*, C-378/14 [2015];
    JL v HMRC (CHB) [2017] UKUT 193
    (AAC); see also *WC v HMRC (CF)* [2019]
    UKUT 289 (AAC) in paras 1, 8 and 9, but
    note this decision was set aside on other
    grounds in *Carrington v HMRC and SSWP*
    [2021] EWCA Civ 1724.
91 Art 68(2) EU Reg 833/04; Art 39(4) UK-
    IC

11

Part 12

Scottish social security benefits

Chapter 72

The Scottish social security system

This chapter covers:
1. Overview of the Scottish social security system (below)
2. How this part of the *Handbook* is organised (p1672)
3. Child winter heating assistance (p1673)

Key facts
- Responsibility for some benefits is devolved to the Scottish government.
- Several one-off grants and benefits for disabled people and carers will eventually be different in Scotland.
- Scottish child payment, child disability payment and several one-off payments, including child winter heating assistance, have already been introduced.
- From spring 2022, personal independence payment will start to be replaced by adult disability payment for new claims.
- Later in 2022, cold weather payments will be replaced in Scotland by low income winter heating assistance.
- Social Security Scotland (part of the Scottish government) administers and pays the 'Scottish benefits'.
- The rules about how to claim Scottish benefits and challenge decisions are different from the rules for the other benefits in this *Handbook*.
- The rules on some other payments, including the Scottish Welfare Fund and council tax reduction, are also different in Scotland, but these are *not* covered in this part of the *Handbook*.

12

1. Overview of the Scottish social security system

A number of new benefits are now delivered by Social Security Scotland (SSS). Some other DWP benefits will also be replaced by new benefits in the coming years. The way you apply for, and challenge decisions about, benefits delivered by SSS is different to the benefits they replace.

Part 12: Scottish social security benefits
Chapter 72: The Scottish social security system
1. Overview of the Scottish social security system

The Scottish government can also introduce new benefits in devolved areas, or top up benefits that are not devolved. Scottish child payment is a new benefit introduced using these powers.

The Scottish benefits

SSS administers and pays a number of benefits. The law refers to most of these benefits as coming under the 'Scottish social security system'.[1] In this *Handbook*, we refer to them as 'Scottish benefits'. There are common rules for most Scottish benefits about:[2]
- how a decision (known as a 'determination' – see p1754) about your entitlement is made and can be challenged; *and*
- when and how overpayments are recovered; *and*
- criminal offences.

The Scottish benefits that have already been introduced are:
- adult disability payment, which replaces personal independence payment, starting from March 2022 in some areas (see Chapter 73); *and*
- three Best Start grants (see Chapter 74); *and*
- child disability payment, which has replaced disability living allowance for children for new claims (see Chapter 75); *and*
- a child winter heating assistance payment (see p1673); *and*
- a funeral support payment (see Chapter 76); *and*
- Scottish child payment (see Chapter 77); *and*
- a young carer grant (see Chapter 78).

Note: some other benefits are also administered and paid by SSS or local authorities, and have different rules in Scotland, but *do not* come under the Scottish social security system, and so are not covered in this part of the *Handbook* (see p1672).

The following changes are expected to take place during 2022.
- Scottish child payment will be extended to children under 16 (see p1729).
- Cold weather payments will be replaced by low income winter heating assistance (see p1671).
- Industrial injuries benefits will be replaced by employment injury assistance.

Future changes

It is expected that the following benefits will eventually be replaced in Scotland. The common rules described in this part of the *Handbook* will apply to the new benefits. At the time of writing, dates for most of the changes have not been announced.[3]

– Carer's allowance (CA) will be replaced by carer's assistance (and if you care for more than one disabled child, your payment may be increased). This is expected to be the next new benefit to be introduced.

– Winter fuel payments will be replaced by winter heating assistance, possibly from winter 2024.

– Attendance allowance will be replaced by pension age disability payment.

The transfer of existing claimants to the new Scottish benefits is likely to begin soon after they are introduced. During the transitional period, some claimants will continue to get the existing benefits from the DWP and others will get the new Scottish benefits from SSS. See AskCPAG and CPAG's *Welfare Rights Bulletin* for updates.

Low income winter heating assistance

The plans for low income winter heating assistance are in draft form and may change. See AskCPAG and CPAG's *Welfare Rights Bulletin* for updates.

The Scottish government plans to introduce low income winter heating assistance from November 2022, replacing cold weather payments if you live in Scotland. The common rules in this part of the *Handbook* will apply to low income winter heating assistance.[4] At the time of writing, the Scottish government plans are as follows.[5]

- Low income winter heating assistance will have the same qualifying benefits as cold weather payments (see p791).
- Payment will *not* depend on there being a period of cold weather where you live.
- A single payment of £50 will be made during February 2023 to anyone who was receiving a qualifying benefit during the week of 19–25 September 2022.
- You will not have to claim low income winter heating assistance, it will be paid automatically.
- You will have 31 days to request a redetermination if you are told that you do not qualify and disagree with this.

Universal credit payment rules

Although universal credit (UC) is administered and paid by the DWP, the Scottish government has the power to change the UC payment arrangements and the amount of the housing costs element.[6] The common rules in this part of the *Handbook* do not apply to these arrangements.

- If you live in Scotland, you can request that your UC is paid twice monthly, and/or that the housing costs element is paid to your landlord, unless the DWP has already made a similar 'alternative payment arrangement' (see p48).
- In the future, members of a couple will be able to split their UC payment into two separate payments.[7]
- In the future, how the UC housing costs element is calculated will be changed in Scotland to abolish the 'bedroom tax' for social sector tenants.[8] For the current rules, see p107. If you are affected by the bedroom tax, you should apply for a discretionary housing payment from your local authority (see Chapter 29).

12

Part 12: Scottish social security benefits
Chapter 72: The Scottish social security system
2. Hos this part of the *Handbook* is organised

Benefits that do not come under the Scottish social security system

Some payments made by SSS, and any payments made by local authorities, are *not* part of the Scottish social security system. The information in this part of the *Handbook* does *not* cover the following devolved payments.[9]

- **Carer's allowance supplement.** This is a payment made twice a year by SSS to people getting CA who live in Scotland. See p553 for details. However, note that if you can claim a CA supplement because you are living in the European Economic Area and have a close link to Scotland (see p1626), the rules described in this part *do* apply.[10]
- **Best Start foods.** This smartcard scheme run by SSS is the Scottish equivalent of the Healthy Start scheme. See p850 for details.
- **Job start payment.** This payment from SSS has no equivalent in the rest of the UK. See p859 for details.
- **Benefits delivered by local authorities.** These include:
  - discretionary housing payments (see Chapter 29);
  - the Scottish Welfare Fund (see p846);
  - council tax reduction (see p836).

Severe disablement allowance is also devolved, but continues to be delivered by the DWP if you still get it. It will not be part of the Scottish social security system.

2. **How this part of the *Handbook* is organised**

This part contains information about individual benefits and the common rules for Scottish benefits that are part of the Scottish social security system (see p1670). For detailed information about how to use this *Handbook*, see Chapter 1.

Rules for individual Scottish benefits

For information about who can get the Scottish benefits, how to claim and how they are paid, see:
- Chapter 73 for adult disability payment;
- Chapter 74 for Best Start grants;
- Chapter 75 for child disability payment;
- p1673 for child winter heating assistance;
- Chapter 76 for funeral support payments;
- p1671 for low income winter heating assistance;
- Chapter 77 for Scottish child payment;
- Chapter 78 for young carer grants.

Common rules for all Scottish benefits

Chapters 79 and 80 describe the common rules about Scottish benefits. This information will also apply to those Scottish benefits expected to be introduced in future years (see p1670). See:
- Chapter 79 for claims, getting paid, overpayments, fraud and complaints;
- Chapter 80 for determinations of entitlement and how to challenge them, including appeals to the First-tier Tribunal.

3. Child winter heating assistance

Child winter heating assistance is an annual payment of £214.10 (winter 2022 rate) for some children and young people who are entitled to a disability benefit (child disability payment (CDP), disability living allowance (DLA), personal independence allowance (PIP) or adult disability payment (ADP)).[11]

Note: you claim disability benefits on behalf of a child under 16, and also for some young people who are 16 or over as an 'appointee' (see p1135 for DLA and PIP, and p1744 for CDP and ADP). In this section, 'you' also refers to a child you claim a disability benefit for.

Who can get a child winter heating assistance payment

You qualify for a child winter heating assistance payment if on at least one day during a qualifying week – which starts on the third Monday in September each year since 2020 (in 2022, 19–25 September):[12]
- you are under 19; *and*
- you are entitled to the highest rate of the CDP or DLA care component or the enhanced rate of the PIP or ADP daily living component (unless the entitlement is not paid as you are in prison that week – see p923); *and*
- you are either 'resident' in Scotland or exempt from this requirement (see p1609).

Claims and getting paid

If you are resident in Scotland and meet the qualifying conditions, you should be given a child winter heating assistance payment automatically, without making a claim. If you get DLA or PIP, this appears to depend on the DWP using a Scottish address for the award. When you become entitled to a disability benefit, you are entitled to child winter heating assistance for qualifying weeks in any previous years covered by your award.[13]

If you receive an award of a disability benefit for a qualifying week that has already passed, contact Social Security Scotland (SSS) and explain the situation. Ask for a determination of entitlement to be made for any previous years in which

Part 12: Scottish social security benefits
Chapter 72: The Scottish social security system
3. Child winter heating assistance

you now qualify for child winter heating assistance. If entitlement is not determined, you can complain (see p1750), or apply for a judicial review (see Chapter 59).[14]

If you need to make a claim (because you are not resident in the UK), you can claim:
- by telephone on 01382 931000; *or*
- in writing on the approved form. You can download the form from mygov.scot/child-winter-heating-assistance-for-children-who-no-longer-live-in-scotland. Send it to Child Winter Heating Assistance, PO Box 10317, Dundee DD1 9GR.

If you need to claim, you will be asked to provide information about your identity and link to Scotland (see p1604). You can also be asked to provide any other information that SSS needs to determine entitlement (even if you did not have to make a claim).[15] If you fail to provide such evidence within the time limit you are given to do so, a determination can be made that you are not entitled to child winter heating assistance.[16] Try to provide any evidence that you are asked for if you can, or explain why this is not possible.

Your entitlement to child winter heating assistance must be determined again if you:[17]
- were given a child winter heating assistance payment that you were not entitled to, due to an official error (even if you did not have to claim it); *or*
- were refused child winter heating assistance and are later awarded a qualifying disability benefit (see p1673) following an appeal; *or*
- were refused child winter heating assistance and this was due to an 'official error' (see p1759).

Payments of child winter heating assistance are normally made from the end of November onwards. If you do not have to claim child winter heating assistance, it is paid in the same way as your disability benefit award. If you have to make a claim, it is paid into the account that you nominate when you claim.

Tax, other benefits and the benefit cap

Child winter heating assistance payments are not taxable.[18]

Child winter heating assistance payments are not counted as income or capital (in some cases for 52 weeks from the date you receive the payment) for means-tested benefits and tax credits.[19]

Child winter heating assistance payments are not 'specified benefits' for the benefit cap (see p1156).

Notes

1. **Overview of the Scottish social security system**
   1 s23 SS(S)A 2018
   2 **SCP** Parts 3 and 4 SS(S)A 2018; SCP Regs
   Other benefits Parts 2 and 4 SS(S)A 2018
   3 Scottish Parliament Social Justice and Social Security Committee, *Official Report,* 23 September 2021, cols 2-4
   4 s30 SS(S)A 2018
   5 Scottish government, *Low Income Winter Heating Assistance (LIWHA): consultation,* 1 December 2021, available at gov.scot/publications/consultation-low-income-winter-heating-assistance-liwha
   6 ss29 and 30 SA 2016
   7 Scottish government, *Joint Ministerial Working Group on Welfare Minutes: December 2020,* published 19 July 2021, available at gov.scot/publications/joint-ministerial-working-group-on-welfare-minutes-december-2020
   8 Scottish government, *Social security policy: housing cost support,* available at gov.scot/policies/social-security/support-with-housing-costs
   9 s23 SS(S)A 2018
   10 s81(2A) SS(S)A 2018; Part 2 and Sch 2 of The Carer's Allowance Supplement and Young Carer Grants (Residence Requirements and Procedural Provisions) (EU Exit) (Scotland) Regulations 2020 No.475

3. **Child winter heating assistance**
   11 Reg 10 WHACYP(S) Regs
   12 s30 and Sch 4 SS(S)A 2018; regs 2 and 4 WHACYP(S) Regs
   13 Reg 5 WHACYP(S)
   14 s41(1) SS(S)A 2018 – you can only request redetermination of a determination, not of a failure to make a determination

   15 s54(1) SS(S)A 2018
   16 s54 SS(S)A 2018
   17 Regs 6-8 WHACYP(S) Regs
   18 While not yet explicitly exempted from being taxable by s677 IT(EP)A 2003, CWHA payments are not a 'taxable benefit' as defined by ss657 and 660 IT(EP)A 2003.
   19 **UC** Reg 66 and Sch 10 para 24 UC Regs
   IS Sch 10 para 78 IS Regs
   JSA Sch 8 para 71 JSA Regs
   ESA Sch 9 para 66 ESA Regs
   HB Sch 6 para 68 HB Regs; reg 29(1)(j)(xviih) and Sch 6 paras 21(2)(w) and 26K HB(SPC) Regs
   PC Reg 15 (1)(rg) and Sch 5 para 20(2)(x) SPC Regs
   WTC/CTC Reg 19 Table 6 para 31 TC(DCI) Regs
   While CWHA payments are not explicitly disregarded as income other than earnings for legacy working-age benefits, the Explanatory Memorandum to The Social Security (Scotland) Act 2018 (Young Carer Grants, Short-Term Assistance and Winter Heating Assistance) (Consequential Provision and Modifications) Order 2020 No.989 makes clear the draftsperson's view that they do not count as income.

12

Chapter 73

Adult disability payment

This chapter covers:
1. Who can get adult disability payment (below)
2. The rules about your age (p1682)
3. The amount of benefit (p1684)
4. Special benefit rules (p1684)
5. Claims and getting paid (p1686)
6. Tax, other benefits and the benefit cap (p1692)

Key facts
- Adult disability payment (ADP) is a new benefit for adults who live in Scotland with a disability or long-term health condition.
- ADP will replace personal independence payment (PIP) for new claims by September 2022. PIP claimants living in Scotland will be transferred to ADP.
- ADP has a daily living component and a mobility component. You can qualify for one or both components. Each component has two rates.
- ADP is a non-means-tested benefit.
- ADP is disregarded as income for means-tested benefits and tax credits and can be paid in addition to most other benefits.
- ADP is administered and paid by Social Security Scotland.
- If you disagree with a determination about ADP, you can request a redetermination and then appeal against it (see Chapter 80). You must request a redetermination before you can appeal.

1. Who can get adult disability payment

You can get adult disability payment (ADP) if you:[1]
- are not entitled to child disability payment (CDP), disability living allowance (DLA), personal independence payment (PIP), attendance allowance or armed forces independence payment (but see p1691 if you are being transferred to ADP, and p1685 if you are terminally ill); *and*
- meet the age rules (see p1682); *and*
- are not a 'person subject to immigration control' (see Chapter 68); *and*

- meet the residence conditions (see p1601); *and*
- unless you are terminally ill (see p1684):
  - you meet the disability conditions for the daily living component, the mobility component; *and*
  - you meet the required period condition (see p1681).

The disability conditions

Note: in most respects, the ADP disability conditions are identical to those for PIP. This section sets out the main ADP disability conditions and refers you to the information about PIP in Chapter 35 where the detailed rules are the same.

A points-based test is used to assess how your physical or mental condition (see p724) affects your ability to undertake specific daily living activities and mobility activities.[2] Each activity has a list of statements (called 'descriptors') which describe different difficulties with the activity or types of help you might need to manage it.

Each descriptor has a points score. You get points for one descriptor for each activity – the one which best describes the difficulties you have with it. If your difficulties with an activity fluctuate, or more than one descriptor in an activity applies to you, see p1678.

The points you score for each activity relevant to a component are added together. You qualify for a component at:[3]

- the standard rate if you score eight points or more; *or*
- the enhanced rate if you score 12 points or more.

How the adult disability payment assessment is different from the personal independence payment assessment

The following differences apply to every activity in the ADP assessment. In practice, your entitlement should still be the same is it would be if you had claimed PIP, as the changes either reflect existing PIP caselaw, or clarify the meaning of the regulations.

- There is a definition of 'needs' in the regulations to ensure that you are assessed as needing a type of help if you reasonably require it, even if it is not available or provided to you.[4] This reflects previous PIP caselaw.
- Where the PIP rules refer to 'C' or a 'claimant', the ADP regulations use 'individual'. This does not change how the assessment works.

PIP caselaw and ADP

Some of the information in the rest of this section explains how the ADP rules incorporate previous PIP caselaw (decisions made by the Upper Tribunal and the courts which say how the law must be applied) into the regulations. PIP caselaw which has *not* been incorporated into the ADP assessment is still likely to be persuasive in deciding your ADP entitlement. However, decision makers and tribunals are *not* bound to follow the PIP caselaw in every

Part 12: Scottish social security benefits
Chapter 73: Adult disability payment
1. Who can get adult disability payment

case. Seek advice if you need to challenge an ADP decision and either the PIP caselaw referenced in Chapter 35 has not been followed, or it has and you want to argue that it should not have been.

There is unlikely to be any ADP caselaw during the lifetime of this Handbook. But over time the ADP assessment criteria may be interpreted differently by courts and tribunals. See AskCPAG and CPAG's *Welfare Rights Bulletin* for updates.

Aids and appliances

For ADP, 'aid or appliance':[5]

'(a) means any object or device which–
(i) the individual needs to be able to perform an activity, and
(ii) improves, provides or replaces the individual's impaired physical or mental function,
(b) includes an object or device which a person without a disability might choose to use for the same function,
(c) in relation to managing toilet needs includes the use of incontinence pads, *and*
(d) includes a prosthesis,'

This new definition ensures that to score points for using an aid or appliance you must *need to* use it (rather than choosing to). It also makes it clear that aids and appliances can include things which are not designed for disabled people. This reflects previous PIP caselaw.

It appears that this definition is also intended to make clear that incontinence pads can *only* count as an aid or appliance for the managing toilet needs activity, and *not* for the other activities in the assessment. In other respects, the assessment of your ability to use an aid or appliance is likely to be the same as for PIP (see p725).

Can you carry out an activity?

To be awarded a descriptor (rather than a higher scoring one) you must be able to carry out the activity in that way safely, to an acceptable standard, repeatedly and within a reasonable time period.[6] The way in which this is assessed is the same as for PIP (see p740), but the rules are worded slightly differently, to reflect previous PIP caselaw.

- In deciding whether you can manage an activity 'safely', both the likelihood and severity of any harm must be considered.[7]
- In deciding whether you can manage an activity 'to an acceptable standard', the impact of carrying out the activity on you must be considered.[8]

Fluctuating conditions

For ADP, you satisfy a descriptor if it applies during some part of the day (midnight to midnight) unless you do so only for a 'minimal or fleeting' time.[9] To qualify, your needs must be expected to last for over 52 weeks at a particular level. The period over which your entitlement is assessed is a past period of 13 weeks (which can begin before you claim ADP) and a prospective period of 39 weeks (PIP uses three and nine months).[10] If you have a previous award of ADP, CDP, DLA or PIP the past period can sometimes be the last 13 weeks of that award (see p1682).

Other than these rules, how your entitlement is assessed if the effect of your condition fluctuates is the same as for PIP (see p741).

Differences in the wording of the daily living and mobility activities

Other than the differences from PIP that affect the whole ADP assessment (see p1677), there are *no* differences in the following daily living activities and so the information about PIP applies to ADP as well.[11]

- Activity 1: preparing food (see p726).
- Activity 8: reading and understanding signs, symbols and words (see p734).
- Activity 10: making budgeting decisions (see p736).

The following sections explain the differences in wording from the PIP rules in the other ADP activities.

Daily living activity 2: taking nutrition

It is expected that the points for this activity will be the same as for PIP (see p727). The definition of 'take nutrition' uses the words '*ingest* nutrition using a therapeutic source', where the PIP assessment uses '*take* nutrition…'.[12]

Daily living activity 3: managing therapy or monitoring a health condition

The definition of 'medication' for ADP includes medication prescribed or recommended by a 'health professional registered by the Health and Care Professions Council' who is *not* a doctor, nurse or pharmacist.[13] There is list of the other regulated professions on the Health and Care Professions Council website.[14] Note that this can only help you to score more points than for PIP if the professional (eg, a clinical psychologist) prescribes or recommends 'medication' (and not 'therapy').

The definitions of 'manage medication' and 'manage therapy' clarify that medication or therapy 'which improves the individual's symptoms or health' comes within the definition.[15] This reflects previous PIP caselaw.

The definitions of 'medication', 'monitor a health condition' and 'therapy' all use 'medical practitioner' where the PIP assessment uses 'doctor'.[16] In practice, this should make no difference.

Other than who can prescribe medication possibly allowing you to satisfy descriptor 3b, it is expected that the points you score for this activity will be the same as for PIP (see p728).

12

Part 12: Scottish social security benefits
Chapter 73: Adult disability payment
1. Who can get adult disability payment

Daily living activity 4: washing and bathing

It is expected that the points for this activity will be the same as for PIP (see p730). The wording of descriptor 4e is 'Needs assistance to be able to get in or out of *an unadapted* bath or shower.'[17] This reflects previous PIP caselaw.

Daily living activity 5: managing toilet needs or incontinence

It is expected that the points for this activity will be the same as for PIP (see p731). The definition of 'aid or appliance' in relation to this activity 'includes the use of incontinence pads'.[18] This reflects previous PIP caselaw.

Daily living activity 6: dressing and undressing

It is expected that the points for this activity will be the same as for PIP (see p732). The ADP assessment includes separate definitions of 'dress' and 'undress' (which are combined in the PIP assessment):[19]

- 'dress' includes put on socks and shoes; *and*
- 'undress' includes take off socks and shoes.

Daily living activity 7: communicating verbally

It is expected that the points for this activity will be the same as for PIP (see p733). In the ADP assessment, the wording of descriptor 7a is 'Can express and understand *basic and complex* verbal information unaided.'[20] The extra words appear to have been inserted for clarity.

The definitions of 'basic verbal information' and 'complex verbal information' contain extra words to the PIP definitions. Both add that the definition 'excludes information that is not communicated orally or received aurally' (ie, writing).[21] The definition does not make it completely clear that lip-reading cannot be taken into account, as this is still information that is 'communicated orally' (using the mouth), even though it is not 'received aurally'. However, previous PIP caselaw has held that ability to lip read should never be taken into account for this activity.

The definition of 'communication support' also contains extra words. The person providing support can be 'trained or experienced in communicating with *people in general, or the individual in particular...*'.[22] This reflects previous PIP caselaw.

Daily living activity 9: engaging socially with other people face to face

It is expected that the points for this activity will be the same as for PIP (see p735).

The title of the activity and all of the descriptors have an extra word inserted which is not in the PIP assessment. In each case they refer to your ability to 'engage *socially* with other people'.[23] This reflects previous PIP caselaw, which confirmed that the definition of 'engage socially' applies to this activity.

The definition of 'social support' also contains extra words. The person providing support can be 'trained or experienced in assisting *people in general, or the individual in particular...*'.[24] This reflects previous PIP caselaw.

Mobility activity 1: planning and following journeys

It is expected that the points for this activity will be the same as for PIP (see p737). The ADP regulations contain an extra definition that is not included in the PIP regulations. '"Follow the route of a journey" means for an individual to navigate and make their way along a planned route to a planned destination.'[25]

This appears to be intended to ensure that entitlement to points for this activity is assessed in accordance with previous PIP caselaw.

Descriptor 1b contains extra words. It reads: 'Needs *the prompting of another person* to be able to undertake any journey to avoid overwhelming psychological distress to the individual.'[26] It appears that the intention is to leave beyond doubt that reminders from something other than a person (eg, reminder notifications set up on a mobile phone) cannot allow you to satisfy this descriptor.

Mobility activity 2: moving around

It is expected that the points for this activity will be the same as for PIP (see p739). Descriptors 2c and 2d contain extra words that are not in the PIP descriptors. They clarify that to satisfy them, you must only be able to move 'no more than 50 metres *either aided or unaided*.'[27] This reflects previous PIP caselaw.

The required period condition

You meet the required period condition if you have satisfied the disability conditions throughout the 13 weeks immediately before the day on which you claim ADP, and are likely to continue to satisfy them for at least a further 39 weeks.[28] If you do not satisfy the required period condition when you claim, you can be awarded ADP as long as you satisfy it within 13 weeks of the date of your claim.[29] This rule effectively means that you must score enough points to qualify for ADP on the date you claim, but it does not matter how long your needs have lasted on that date, as long as they are expected to last for more than a year.

Note:
- If you previously got a disability benefit the 13 week part of the required period condition may be different (see p1682).
- To continue to satisfy the required period condition once you have been awarded ADP, your needs must be expected to last for at least a further 39 weeks.[30]

12

Example
Jethro was involved in a serious road traffic accident on 14 June. Before this he has no difficulty with daily living or mobility activities. As he already knew about ADP, he claims it the following day. The decision maker accepts that his needs are likely to last for over a year, and awards him ADP from 13 September.

Part 12: Scottish social security benefits
Chapter 73: Adult disability payment
2. The rules about your age

The required period condition if you previously got a disability benefit

If you had a previous award of a disability benefit you do not always need to have met the disability conditions for 13 weeks before you can be entitled to ADP. You can be awarded ADP immediately if your previous award:[31]

- was of ADP, CDP, PIP or DLA; *and*
- ended less than two years (one year, if you are over 66) before you claim ADP; *and*
- was of the same component(s) as your new award is (for the purpose of this rule, the DLA/CDP/PIP mobility component counts as the ADP mobility component and the DLA/CDP care component and PIP daily living component count as the ADP daily living component);[32] *and*
- was based on the same condition(s) as your new award would be, or a new condition that developed due to a previous one.

Your needs must also be expected to last for at least 39 weeks when you make your new ADP claim.[33]

---

2. **The rules about your age**

You must be aged 16 or over to be entitled to adult disability payment (ADP).[34] You can instead claim child disability payment (CDP) for a child under 16 (see Chapter 75).

The upper age limit for making a new claim for ADP is normally the day before you turn 66.[35] If you are 66 or over and do not get a disability benefit, you can instead claim attendance allowance (see Chapter 24). However, you can make a new claim for ADP after turning 66 if you had a previous award of ADP, disability living allowance (DLA) or personal independence payment (PIP) that ended less than a year before you claim, and you meet the other conditions above about your previous award.[36]

The upper age limit does not apply if you:[37]

- claimed ADP before turning 66; *or*
- are already entitled to ADP when you turn 66; *or*
- are being transferred from PIP to ADP as you do not have to make a claim (see p1691).

If you can claim ADP after you turn 66, or in some situations if your award changes after you turn 66, your entitlement to the mobility component is restricted (see p1683).

Future changes
The upper age limit to claim ADP will increase to 67 as pension age rises between 2026 and 2028 (see p766).

Mobility component for older people

If you are entitled to the mobility component when you turn 66, you continue to get it, provided you still meet the entitlement conditions. If your award later changes, see below.

New claims after you turn 66

If you can make a new ADP claim after turning 66 (see p1682), special rules restrict the rate of the mobility component you can be awarded. You can get:[38]

- the enhanced rate if you meet the entitlement conditions for it and you got the enhanced rate mobility component[39] in an award which ended less than one year before you claim; *or*
- the standard rate if you meet the entitlement conditions for it and you got either rate of the mobility component in an award which ended less than one year before you claim.

If your award changes after you turn 66

There are restrictions if your existing award of ADP includes the mobility component (or you got the ADP, PIP or DLA mobility component and it stopped less than a year before the date on which a new mobility component award would take effect) and is changed due to:[40]

- a change of circumstances (see p1761) that happened after you turned 66; *or*
- ignorance of a material fact (see p1763) that SSS became aware of after you turned 66; *or*
- receipt of medical evidence after you turn 66, unless the evidence is that you are terminally ill (see p1684) and is dated before you turned 66.

In the above situations, to be entitled to the mobility component at its previous rate, your entitlement must be due to substantially the same condition(s) as your previous mobility component award. You can move from the enhanced rate to the standard rate (even if your mobility needs result from a new condition). You cannot move from the standard rate to the enhanced rate or qualify for the first time.[41]

Note:

- There may be other reasons that your award is changed (see p1760). It is only if your award changes for one of the reasons above that your entitlement to the mobility component is restricted.
- The equivalent PIP rule restricts mobility component entitlement for *anyone* getting PIP who is 66 or over (see p744). The Scottish government's position is that the ADP rule has the same effect. At the time of writing, it is considering whether to amend the regulations to put this beyond doubt.[42] See AskCPAG and CPAG's *Welfare Rights Bulletin* for updates.

12

Part 12: Scottish social security benefits
Chapter 73: Adult disability payment
4. Special benefit rules

3. **The amount of benefit**

The daily living component of adult disability payment (ADP) is paid at one of two weekly rates:[43]
- the standard rate is £61.85;
- the enhanced rate is £92.40.

The mobility component of ADP is paid at one of two weekly rates:[44]
- the standard rate is £24.45;
- the enhanced rate is £64.50.

4. **Special benefit rules**

Special rules may apply if you:
- are terminally ill (see below);
- are subject to immigration control (see Chapter 68);
- have come from or are going abroad (see Chapters 69, 70 and 71);
- are in hospital or a hospice or living in a care home or other similar accommodation, or in prison or legal detention (see Chapter 42).

Terminal illness

If you are terminally ill, you are normally entitled to the enhanced rates of both components of adult disability payment (ADP).[45] However, if you become terminally ill after turning 66 your entitlement to the mobility component may be restricted (see p1683).[46]

If a child is terminally ill, s/he is entitled to the highest rate of the care component of child disability payment (CDP), and the higher rate of the mobility component from her/his third birthday.[47] In the rest of this section, 'you' includes a child you claim CDP for.

You are terminally ill if it is the judgement of a doctor or nurse, who is involved in your care or diagnosis and acting in a professional capacity, that you have a progressive disease that can reasonably be expected to cause your death.[48] Account must be taken of the guidance that is published by the Chief Medical Officer of Scotland.[49]

Claims if you are terminally ill

The process of claiming ADP and CDP is different if you are terminally ill. If you are terminally ill you need to provide either a DS1500 (see p747) or a Benefits Assistance under Special Rules in Scotland (BASRiS) form completed by a doctor or nurse.[50] You should get this as soon as possible, and also start your claim

. . . .

immediately and declare that you are terminally ill. When you do these things affects when your entitlement can begin (see below).

You can start your claim in any of the normal ways (see p1686 for ADP and p1714 for CDP). If you declare that you are terminally ill, you do not have to provide extra information about your care and mobility needs.

If you have a progressive disease but cannot get a DS1500 or BASRiS form, you do *not* meet the definition of being terminally ill. You can still be awarded benefit if you meet the normal disability conditions (see p1677 for ADP and p1706 for CDP).

Note:
- If you are terminally ill, someone else should be able to claim ADP or CDP on your behalf, if s/he informs you of this and you give consent for her/him to do so.
- If someone dies after getting a DS1500 or BASRiS form but before claiming ADP or CDP or telling SSS, it appears that you can make a claim or report the change on her/his behalf as an appointee (see p1744).[51] Because the benefit can be awarded from the date of the DS1500 or BASRiS form, it appears arguable that you can do this even if someone has already died. Seek specialist advice if SSS refuse to award ADP or CDP for a period before someone died in this situation.

When your entitlement starts if you are terminally ill

If you are terminally ill, your ADP or CDP entitlement on that basis can begin before you claim it or tell SSS that you are terminally ill. Your entitlement can *never* begin before the benefit was first introduced (21 March 2022 for ADP and 26 July 2021 for CDP). Subject to this limit, your entitlement under the terminal illness rules starts on the *earliest* of:[52]
- the day you claim ADP or CDP; *or*
- the day you informed SSS that you were terminally ill (if you already get ADP or CDP); *or*
- the date of your DS1500 or BASRiS form, if this is less than 26 weeks before you claimed or told SSS you were terminally ill.

If the DS1500 or BASRiS form is dated *more than* 26 weeks before than the date on which you claim or tell SSS you are terminally ill, a doctor or nurse must confirm you are still terminally ill. Your entitlement then starts 26 weeks before you claimed or told SSS you were terminally ill.[53]

When entitlement starts if you are terminally ill and transfer from another benefit

If you are terminally ill and transfer from disability living allowance (DLA) to CDP, you can be awarded CDP for a period during which you previously got DLA. See p1717 for when your CDP entitlement begins.

If you transfer from personal independence payment (PIP) to ADP and either you were already terminally ill under the PIP rules (see p745) or you provide a

Part 12: Scottish social security benefits
Chapter 73: Adult disability payment
5. Claims and getting paid

DS1500 or BASRiS form before you are transferred to ADP, your ADP entitlement begins on the *latest* of:[54]
- 21 March 2022; *or*
- the date of the DS1500 or BASRiS form; *or*
- one year before your ADP entitlement is determined.

At the time of writing, draft rules provide for the transfer from DLA to ADP. If you are terminally ill, the draft rules do not currently include the one-year time limit on when your ADP entitlement starts.[55] See AskCPAG and CPAG's *Welfare Rights Bulletin* for updates.

If you are now terminally ill, you can be awarded ADP for a period during which you previously got PIP, CDP, DLA, attendance allowance or armed forces independence payment.

Your entitlement for any period you got another benefit is the difference between your old award and your ADP award.[56]

5. **Claims and getting paid**

The general rules on claims and getting paid are covered in Chapter 79. This section explains the specific rules for adult disability payment (ADP).

Making a claim

Note: if you get child disability payment (CDP) and are aged 15–17, see p1712 for information to help you to decide whether to claim ADP.

Once ADP is introduced in an area (see p1687), you can start a claim:
- online at mygov.scot/adult-disability-payment/how-to-apply; *or*
- by telephoning 0800 182 2222 to request a paper claim form.

Forms

If you want to claim on a paper form, telephone Social Security Scotland (SSS) and ask them to send you the form. Send your completed form to Adult Disability Payment, PO Box 10324, Dundee, DD1 9GZ. You should be sent a prepaid envelope with the form.

Unless you are terminally ill (see p1684), your claim is made in two parts. If you appear to meet the entitlement conditions *other than the disability conditions* (see p1676), you must then complete the second part of the claim. You have eight weeks to complete the second part, from the date you started your claim (see p1687).

Note: you have *not* made a claim for ADP until you complete all of the required parts of your claim, and provide any required evidence to Social Security Scotland (SSS).

When you can claim adult disability payment in different areas

When ADP is introduced for new claims depends on the area in which you are 'resident'. The table below sets out when you can *first* claim ADP in different local authority areas.[57] If you cannot yet claim ADP, you can claim personal independence payment (PIP) instead (see Chapter 35).

Date	Local authority areas
21 March 2022	Dundee City, Perth and Kinross, Western Isles
20 June 2022	Angus, North Lanarkshire, South Lanarkshire
25 July 2022	Aberdeen City, Aberdeenshire, East Ayrshire, Fife, Moray, North Ayrshire, South Ayrshire
30 August 2022	All local authority areas in Scotland

Note:
- If you claimed PIP before 21 March 2022 and your claim has not yet been decided, you *cannot* be entitled to ADP even if you also claim it.[58]
- If you are already entitled to PIP, you do not need to claim ADP and will be transferred to it (see p1691).

Who should claim

You must normally make a claim for ADP yourself. In some situations, another person can claim ADP for you as your 'appointee' (see p1744).

Information to support your claim

In order to start your claim, you must provide SSS with your full name and date of birth. In practice, you are also asked questions about the residence and presence conditions at this point. SSS refers to this as 'Part 1' of your ADP claim.

Unless you are terminally ill (see p1684), you then have eight weeks to complete your claim by providing the rest of the required information (referred to as 'Part 2').[59] This eight-week period can be extended if there is 'good reason' for the delay.[60]

You should contact SSS and ask for an extension as soon as possible if you need more time to complete your claim. If SSS does not extend the period, your date of claim may be delayed (see p1689) or your entitlement to ADP may not be determined (see p1755).

12

Part 12: Scottish social security benefits
Chapter 73: Adult disability payment
5. Claims and getting paid

The required information

The information that you are required to provide as Part 2 of your claim relates to how your condition(s) affect your ability to manage the different daily living and mobility activities. You can provide this online if you started your claim online, or on a paper questionnaire form. You can ask SSS to help you complete the claim by telephoning 0800 182 2222.

The information requested is similar to a PIP questionnaire, but with more detailed questions about each daily living and mobility activity. You should complete Part 2 in the same way as a PIP questionnaire (see p748).

You may also be asked to provide supporting evidence.

Supporting evidence

Note: in practice, you should be able to ask SSS to get any required supporting evidence for you. However, you must give your permission for this to happen. So if you do not give permission, you may be asked to provide evidence yourself.

You can also be asked to provide evidence in support of your ADP claim.[61] If you do not provide any required supporting evidence within the time allowed to do so, you can be given a determination that you are not entitled to ADP.[62] If this happens, see below – the advice is the same as if you are refused ADP for failing to take part in an assessment.

You can provide supporting evidence even if you are not asked to do so. If you are not sure how useful a piece of supporting evidence is, check how closely it relates to the disability conditions (see p1677). Evidence confirming the severity of your condition (eg, details of your visual or hearing impairment), may also be useful.

Assessment consultations

If SSS believes it is needed to determine your entitlement, you can be asked to take part in an assessment.[63] SSS is likely to refer to this as a 'consultation'. You should be asked how you would prefer to be assessed.[64] A supporter (eg, a family member, friend or adviser) can take part in your assessment, including speaking on your behalf, unless this is considered unreasonable by SSS.[65]

It is expected that you will be able to ask for a consultation to be carried out by telephone, video call or face to face (in your home or somewhere else).

The advice about what to do at an assessment is similar to that for PIP (see p750). However, note that ADP assessments do not include any physical examination.

If you do not take part in an assessment

If you are not able to take part in an assessment, explain this to SSS as soon as possible and ask for it to be rearranged. Unless the assessment is rearranged or SSS decides it is no longer necessary, you may be given a determination that you are not entitled to ADP – simply because you did not take part in the assessment.[66]

If you are sent a determination that you are not entitled to ADP, you can request a redetermination (see p1755). It is arguable that a decision maker carrying out a redetermination or a First-tier Tribunal at appeal can make any determination that the original decision maker *could* have made, including ignoring your failure to take part in the assessment and determining your entitlement under the normal rules.[67] Seek specialist advice about how to present your case. You should also always make a new claim for ADP as well, in case your challenge is unsuccessful.

The date of your claim

When ADP is paid from is determined by the date of your claim. It is important to claim as soon as possible as ADP cannot be backdated unless you are terminally ill (see p1685).

The date of claim is the date you 'submit' your full name and date of birth to SSS, as long as you then provide the rest of the required information (see p1688). If you do not provide all of the required information within the time allowed, your date of claim is the date you eventually provide it.[68]

Note:
- You should try to complete all of Part 1 of your ADP claim immediately, as otherwise your date of claim may not be registered by SSS. If you cannot do this, you should provide at least your full name and date of birth. You can then request a redetermination if your claim starts later than the date you gave this information.[69]
- If you do not meet the entitlement conditions on the day you claim, you may be able to claim in advance (see below).
- There are different rules about the date of your claim if you get CDP or PIP and are transferring to ADP (see p1712 if you get CDP and p1691 if you get PIP).
- If your ADP claim is refused due to an 'official error', your entitlement must be determined again (see p1759). In this situation, your ADP starts from the date your previous claim was treated as made.

Backdating your claim

You cannot backdate a claim for ADP, unless you are terminally ill (see p1685).

If you might have qualified for ADP sooner but did not claim because you were given the wrong information or misled by SSS, you could complain and ask for compensation (see p1750).

Claiming in advance

You can make a claim for ADP up to 13 weeks before you satisfy:[70]
- the disability conditions (see p1677); *or*
- the required period condition (see p1681); *or*
- the residence rules (see p1601); *or*
- the age rules (see p1682).

The date of your claim is set as the date you meet all of the entitlement conditions.

12

Part 12: Scottish social security benefits
Chapter 73: Adult disability payment
5. Claims and getting paid

Getting paid

ADP is usually paid four weekly in arrears. If you are terminally ill you are instead paid weekly in advance.[71] Payment is made into the account you nominate when you claim.

Payment of your ADP can be made to another person for your benefit, if SSS considers this is appropriate.[72]

If you are entitled to ADP and on leave from a care home or residential educational establishment you can be paid at a daily rate.[73]

- For when your ADP payments can be suspended, see p1746.
- For when a deduction can be made from your ADP to recover an overpayment, see p1748.
- For when your ADP mobility component can be paid to Motability, see p1693.
- If you are overpaid ADP, you may have to repay it (see p1748).

Changes of circumstance

You must report any change you have been told to report to SSS.[74] A change of circumstances can include that your needs are no longer expected to last for 39 weeks at the same level, as you will no longer meet the required period condition (see p1681).

You should report any changes in your circumstances as soon as possible. You can report a change by telephone or in writing.[75] At the time of writing, SSS requires that changes reported in writing are reported using the official form. Check your most recent determination of entitlement carefully, as it should tell you how you must report a change.[76]

If you report a change that may affect the ADP entitlement conditions, SSS makes a new determination. For when the new determination takes effect, see p1760.

Before making a determination, SSS can ask you to provide further information.

Reviews of adult disability payment awards

If your determination of entitlement specifies a period after which your ADP award must be reviewed, a further determination must be made at the end of this period.[77] It is expected that if your condition is unlikely to change there will be at least five years between reviews, and your award will not be reviewed if you are terminally ill.

For when the new determination following a review takes effect, see p1761.

As part of the review, you are likely to be asked to provide further information.

Providing further information during an award

If it is reviewing your ADP award, or it thinks that your circumstances may have changed, SSS can ask you to provide further information. This information may be similar to that required when you make a new claim (see p1688).

If you do not provide the information within the time limit SSS sets you to do so, your ADP payments can be suspended (see p1746). If you think that you need more time to provide the information, contact SSS as soon as possible to request an extension.

Transfers to adult disability payment

If you get CDP or PIP, you will eventually transfer to ADP. If you get CDP, see p1712.

If you get PIP, you will be transferred to ADP automatically.

Note: at the time of writing, it is expected that if you live in Scotland and still get DLA, you will be automatically transferred to ADP, but the rules have not yet been finalised.[78] See AskCPAG and CPAG's *Welfare Rights Bulletin* for updates. Until this process begins, you should still claim PIP if you are told to do so (see p602).[79]

Moving from personal independence payment to adult disability payment

If you get PIP and live in Scotland (or abroad and have a genuine and sufficient link to Scotland – see p1604), you will be automatically transferred to ADP without having to make a claim. At the time of writing, it was expected that the transfer process will start from August 2022.[80] Until you are transferred, you should still report any changes of circumstances in relation to your PIP award (see p754). If your PIP award is ending, see p753.

If you get PIP and move to Scotland, see p1692.

Automatic transfers to adult disability payment

If you are being transferred to ADP, you will be notified of this in writing. The notification will tell you how long the process will take and that your PIP will end when your ADP starts.[81] If SSS later realises that you were wrongly sent a transfer notification or wants to extend the period allowed to transfer you to ADP, you are sent another notification about this.[82]

When will you be transferred to ADP?

Once the process of transferring PIP claimants to ADP begins in August 2022, it is expected that you will be transferred to ADP when your PIP award is due to be reviewed, or is coming to an end (see p753). If your PIP award runs out in less than six months and you have not been told that you are being transferred to ADP, contact SSS and ask when you will be transferred.

It is expected that you will also be transferred to ADP if you report a change of circumstances in relation to your PIP once the transfer process has begun.

12

Part 12: Scottish social security benefits
Chapter 73: Adult disability payment
6. Tax, other benefits and the benefit cap

Unless you are terminally ill (see p1684), you are awarded the same rate of ADP as your previous PIP award.[83] If you disagree with this, you can request a redetermination, or report a change of circumstances.

If you report a change of circumstances

If you have not yet been automatically transferred to ADP and you report a change of circumstances which the DWP does not take into account for your PIP award, you will be transferred to ADP.[84] You can also report a change during or after the automatic transfer from PIP to ADP.

Unless the change is that you are now terminally ill (see p1684), you are initially awarded ADP at the same rate as your PIP. SSS then makes a further determination of your entitlement as soon as possible.[85] The second determination takes effect:[86]

* if it increases your award, from:
  - the date of the change if you reported it within one month (or up to 13 months if you had a good reason for reporting the change late); *or*
  - the date you reported the change if the above bullet does not apply; *or*
* if it does not change or decreases your ADP award, from the date it is made.

If your award is higher, you can be awarded ADP for a period during which you got PIP under the rule above. You are paid the difference between your PIP award and the ADP award.[87]

If you get personal independence payment and move to Scotland

If you get PIP and move to Scotland from another part of the UK, SSS must make a determination of your entitlement to ADP.[88] In practice, your ADP entitlement may not be determined until the wider transfer from PIP to ADP begins in August 2022. Your ADP entitlement begins the day after your PIP award ends.[89]

Note: in this situation you are *not* automatically awarded ADP at the same rate as your PIP award.[90] If you are asked to provide extra information, you should do so. If you do not agree with the amount of your ADP award, you can request a redetermination (see p1755).

---

6. **Tax, other benefits and the benefit cap**

Tax

Adult disability payment (ADP) is not taxable.[91]

Other benefits and tax credits

ADP interacts with means-tested benefits and tax credits in the same way as personal independence payment (PIP) does (see p755).

Non-means-tested benefits

ADP is paid in addition to most other non-means-tested benefits. You cannot be entitled to both ADP and one of the benefits listed on p1676. Your payment of ADP may be reduced if you also get constant attendance allowance under the industrial injuries scheme (see p678) or a war pension mobility supplement (see p857).[92]

If you get the daily living component of ADP and someone regularly looks after you, s/he may be entitled to carer's allowance (CA) (see Chapter 26) and the carer element of universal credit (see p73). However, any severe disability premium/addition that you get stops if s/he gets CA or the carer element, so always get advice.

If you get the daily living component, a young person may be able to get a young carer grant for looking after you (see Chapter 78).

The benefit cap

In some cases, there is a limit on the total amount of specified benefits you can receive (a 'benefit cap'). ADP is not one of the specified benefits. The benefit cap does not apply if you, your partner or child get ADP (even it is not paid because the person entitled is in hospital or a care home). In other cases, it only applies if you are getting UC or HB. See p1156 for further information.

Passports and other sources of help

These are the same as for PIP (see p757).

Motability

Motability is a charity that runs a scheme to help you lease or buy a car, scooter or powered wheelchair. You are eligible if you get the enhanced rate of the ADP mobility component and have 12 months or more left to run on your award. Social Security Scotland may refer to this as the 'Accessible Vehicles and Equipment' scheme.

If you use the scheme, your ADP mobility component is paid direct to Motability.[93] You may also have to make extra payments. For further information, telephone 0300 456 4566 (textphone: 0300 037 0100) or see motability.co.uk. If you use British Sign Language, see motability.co.uk/contact/british-sign-language-service.

12

Part 12: Scottish social security benefits
Chapter 73: Adult disability payment
Notes

Notes

1. **Who can get adult disability payment**
1   s31 and Sch 5 SS(S)A 2018; regs 3 and 4 DAWAP(S) Regs
2   Regs 5-10 and Sch 1 DAWAP(S) Regs
3   Regs 8 and 9 DAWAP(S) Regs
4   Reg 2 DAWAP(S) Regs
5   Reg 2 DAWAP(S) Regs
6   Reg 7(2)(b) DAWAP(S) Regs
7   Reg 7(3)(a) DAWAP(S) Regs
8   Reg 7(3)(b) DAWAP(S) Regs
9   Reg 10(2) DAWAP(S) Regs
10 Regs 10, 13 and 14 DAWAP(S) Regs
11 Sch 1 Parts 1 and 2 DAWAP(S) Regs
12 Sch 1 Part 1 DAWAP(S) Regs
13 Sch 1 Part 1 DAWAP(S) Regs
14 hcpc-uk.org/about-us/who-we-regulate/the-professions
15 Sch 1 Part 1 DAWAP(S) Regs
16 Sch 1 Part 1 DAWAP(S) Regs
17 Sch 1 Part 2 DAWAP(S) Regs
18 Reg 2 DAWAP(S) Regs
19 Sch 1 Part 1 DAWAP(S) Regs
20 Sch 1 Part 2 DAWAP(S) Regs
21 Sch 1 Part 1 DAWAP(S) Regs
22 Sch 1 Part 1 DAWAP(S) Regs
23 Sch 1 Part 2 DAWAP(S) Regs
24 Sch 1 Part 1 DAWAP(S) Regs
25 Sch 1 Part 1 DAWAP(S) Regs
26 Sch 1 Part 3 DAWAP(S) Regs
27 Sch 1 Part 3 DAWAP(S) Regs
28 Regs 10(3), 11, 12 and 13 DAWAP(S) Regs
29 Reg 35(2) DAWAP(S) Regs
30 Reg 10(3)(b) DAWAP(S) Regs
31 Regs 10(3), 13, 14 and 23 DAWAP(S) Regs
32 Regs 14(5) and 23(7) DAWAP(S) Regs
33 Regs 10(3), 14(4) and 23(4) DAWAP(S) Regs

2. **The rules about your age**
34 Reg 22(1)(a) DAWAP(S) Regs
35 Reg 22(1)(b) and (2) DAWAP(S) Regs
36 Reg 23 DAWAP(S) Regs
37 Reg 24 DAWAP(S) Regs
38 Reg 23(5) and (6) DAWAP(S) Regs
39 It is expected that the DLA higher rate mobility component will be treated as the enhanced rate mobility component for the purpose of this rule

40 Reg 25 DAWAP(S) Regs
41 Reg 25(3) DAWAP(S) Regs. It is expected that the DLA higher rate mobility component will be treated as the enhanced rate mobility component for the purpose of this rule
42 Email from Scottish government to CPAG, 18 March 2022.

3. **The amount of benefit**
43 Reg 34(1) DAWAP(S) Regs
44 Reg 34(2) DAWAP(S) Regs

4. **Special benefit rules**
45 Reg 26(1) DAWAP(S) Regs
46 In this situation, you can argue that the restriction on your mobility component entitlement is unlawful as some people over 66 can get the mobility component and you must be given the maximum ADP possible - see Sch 5 para 12 SS(S)A 2018. Get specialist advice.
47 Reg 15(1) DACYP(S) Regs
48 **ADP** Reg 26(7) and (10) DAWAP(S) Regs
    CDP Reg 15(6) and (9) DACYP(S) Regs
    All s31(1)(b) and Sch 5 para 1(2)-(2D) SS(S)A 2018
49 **ADP** Reg 26(8) DAWAP(S) Regs
    CDP Reg 15(7) DACYP(S) Regs
    All Sch 5 para 1(3) SS(S)A 2018; SSS, *Chief Medical Officer's Guidance for Clinicians Completing a BASRiS Form*, 29 June 2021, available at socialsecurity.gov.scot/guidance-resources/guidance/chief-medical-officers-guidance-for-clinicians-completing-a-basris-form-for-terminal-illness
50 SSS, *Special Rules for Terminal Illness: frequently asked questions*, 28 June 2021, available at socialsecurity.gov.scot/guidance-resources/guidance/special-rules-for-terminal-illness-frequently-asked-questions
51 s85B(6) SS(S)A 2018
    If a child under 16 dies, a parent may still be able to act on her/his behalf without being formally made an appointee.

52 **ADP** Reg 26(4) and (5) DAWAP(S) Regs
  CDP Reg 15(3) and (4) DACYP(S) Regs
53 **ADP** Reg 26(6) DAWAP(S) Regs
  CDP Reg 15(5) DACYP(S) Regs
54 Sch 2 para 11(2) DAWAP(S) Regs
55 Reg 9(2)(b) of The Disability Assistance
  for Working Age People Transitional
  Provisions and Miscellaneous
  Amendment) (Scotland) Regulations
  2022 (draft), 14 February 2022,
  available at gov.scot/publications/
  disability-living-allowance-to-adult-
  disability-payment-case-transfer/pages/
  draft-regulations
56 Regs 26(11) and (12), 45(3) and Sch 2
  para 14(c) and (d) DAWAP(S) Regs
  At the time of writing, it is unclear how
  ADP and armed forces independence
  payment interact, and how it would be
  possible to claim ADP after being
  entitled to AA.

5. Claims and getting paid
57 Reg 64 and Sch 2 paras 5 and 6
  DAWAP(S) Regs
58 Reg 65 DAWAP(S) Regs
59 Reg 35(4) DAWAP(S) Regs
60 Reg 35(6) DAWAP(S) Regs
61 s54(1) SS(S)A 2018
62 s54(2) SS(S)A 2018
63 s14(a) SS(S)A 2018
64 s14(b) SS(S)A 2018
65 s59 SS(S)A 2018
66 s54(3) SS(S)A 2018
67 ss43 and 49 SS(S)A 2018
  As there has been a determination of
  your entitlement, any redetermination
  or appeal determination replaces it
  completely.
68 Reg 35(1) and (5) DAWAP(S) Regs
69 Reg 35(4) DAWAP(S) Regs. You can
  argue that by phoning SSS or providing
  this information online and saving your
  claim, you have 'submitted' it. Get
  specialist advice.
70 Reg 35(2) DAWAP(S) Regs
71 Reg 36 DAWAP(S) Regs
72 Reg 33(1) DAWAP(S) Regs
73 Reg 34(3) DAWAP(S) Regs
74 s56 SS(S)A 2018
75 Scottish government, *Adult Disability
  Payment – If your circumstances change*,
  18 February 2022, available at
  mygov.scot/adult-disability-payment-
  changes
76 s56(2)(b) SS(S)A 2018
77 Reg 47 DAWAP(S) Regs

78 The Disability Assistance for Working
  Age People (Transitional Provisions and
  Miscellaneous Amendment) (Scotland)
  Regulations 2022 (draft), 14 February
  2022, available at gov.scot/
  publications/disability-living-allowance-
  to-adult-disability-payment-case-
  transfer/pages/draft-regulations
79 Reg 20(2) and (4) of The Disability
  Assistance for Working Age People
  (Consequential and Miscellaneous
  Amendment and Transitional Provision)
  (Scotland) Regulations 2022 No.31
80 Scottish government, *Adult Disability
  Payment Launch Dates Announced*, 17
  December 2021, available at gov.scot/
  news/adult-disability-payment-launch-
  dates-announced
81 Sch 2 para 8 DAWAP(S) Regs
82 Sch 2 paras 8(3) and (4) and 9(6)(c)
  DAWAP(S) Regs
83 Sch 2 para 9(5) DAWAP(S) Regs
84 Sch 2 para 12(1)(a)(i) DAWAP(S) Regs.
  While nothing in the DAWAP(S) Regs
  requires you to immediately be
  transferred if you report a change of
  circumstances relevant to your PIP
  award, this appears to be the intention,
  once the transfer process has begun.
85 Sch 2 para 12(1)-(3) DAWAP(S) Regs
86 Sch 2 para 12(4) and (5) DAWAP(S)
  Regs
87 Sch 2 para 12(6) DAWAP(S) Regs
88 Reg 52(1) DAWAP(S) Regs
89 Reg 52(2) DAWAP(S) Regs
90 Reg 52 DAWAP(S) Regs contains no
  equivalent to the provision made for this
  in Sch 2 Part 3 DAWAP(S) Regs

6. Tax, other benefits and the benefit cap
91 While not yet explicitly exempted from
  being taxable by s677 IT(EP)A 2003,
  ADP is not a 'taxable benefit' as defined
  by ss657 and 660 IT(EP)A 2003.
92 Reg 34(4)-(6) DAWAP(S) Regs
93 Regs 55 and 56 DAWAP(S) Regs

12

Chapter 74

Best Start grants

This chapter covers:
1. Who can get a Best Start grant (below)
2. The rules about your age (p1700)
3. The amount of benefit (p1700)
4. Claims and getting paid (p1701)
5. Tax, other benefits and the benefit cap (p1703)

Key facts
- Best Start grants include a payment for women who are pregnant or who have recently given birth – called a **pregnancy and baby payment** – and amounts to help with the costs of young children – called an **early learning payment** and a **school-age payment**.
- Best Start grants are not means tested, but you must usually receive a means-tested benefit to qualify.
- You do not need to have paid national insurance contributions to qualify.
- Best Start grants are administered and paid by Social Security Scotland.
- If you disagree with a decision about a Best Start grant, you can request a redetermination and then appeal against it (see Chapter 80). You must request a redetermination before you can appeal.

1. Who can get a Best Start grant

You qualify for a Best Start grant if:[1]
- you or your partner are aged under 18. In some circumstances, 18/19 year olds can qualify (see p1700); *or*
- on the date of your application, you or your partner are receiving a qualifying benefit (see p1697).

You must also:
- claim within the time limit (see p1702); *and*
- be ordinarily resident in Scotland (see p1550); *and*
- be 'habitually resident' in the UK, Channel Islands or Isle of Man or, if you have leave under the European Union Settlement Scheme or a specified free

movement residence right, the European Economic Area. You do not need to meet this condition if you are receiving a qualifying benefit or you are exempt from it (see p1553).

In addition, you must meet the conditions for the pregnancy and baby payment below, the early learning payment (see p1698) or the school-age payment (see p1698).

Qualifying benefits

You qualify for a Best Start grant if you or your partner are getting one of the following:[2]
- universal credit (UC); *or*
- income-based jobseeker's allowance; *or*
- income-related employment and support allowance; *or*
- income support; *or*
- housing benefit; *or*
- pension credit (PC); *or*
- child tax credit (CTC); *or*
- working tax credit.

You must be getting UC in the assessment period that includes the date of your claim for a Best Start grant, or getting UC in the assessment period before that. For the other benefits, you must be getting the benefit on the date of your claim for a Best Start grant. See p1702 for when your claim is made or can be treated as made.

You must be getting one of the above qualifying benefits at a rate of more than £0 before any third-party deductions or sanctions are applied. You do not count as getting a qualifying benefit if it was paid in error, including an official error.[3]

Who can get a pregnancy and baby payment

In addition to the basic rules for a Best Start grant on p1696, to qualify for the pregnancy and baby payment:[4]
- either:
  - you (or your partner) must be (or have been) more than 24 weeks' pregnant, or you gave birth to a child before or during the 24th week of pregnancy; *or*
  - you (or your partner) have become responsible for a baby under the age of one and you (or your partner) are not the child's mother (see p1699); *and*
- you have not received, and are not due to receive, a Sure Start maternity grant (see p782) for the same child; *and*
- no other person has received, and is not due to receive, a Best Start grant pregnancy and baby payment or a Sure Start maternity grant (see p782) for the same child, unless:
  - you are responsible for the child on the date of your claim; *and*

12

Part 12: Scottish social security benefits
Chapter 74: Best Start grants
1. Who can get a Best Start grant

- you have not been that person's partner or dependant, and s/he has not been your or your partner's dependant, since that person claimed a payment or grant; *and*
- the child does not normally live with the person who has already received a payment or grant.

If your child dies, or is stillborn, after the 24th week of pregnancy, you are still entitled to the pregnancy and baby payment and do not have to pay it back.

You are not entitled to the pregnancy and baby payment if the child is living in a residential establishment (ie, a local authority-approved children's home) on the date of your claim.

Who can get an early learning payment

In addition to the basic rules for a Best Start grant on p1696, you qualify for the early learning payment if:[5]

- you or your partner are responsible for the child (see p1699) on the day you claim, which must be within the period from the child's second birthday to six months after the child's third birthday; *and*
- no other person has received, or is due to receive, an early learning payment for the child, unless:
  - you are responsible for the child on the date of your claim; *and*
  - you have not been that person's partner at any time since s/he applied for an early learning payment for the child; *and*
  - the child does not normally live with the person who has already received an early learning payment.

You are not entitled to the early learning payment if the child is living in a residential establishment (ie, a local authority-approved children's home) on the date of your claim. You can qualify for an early learning payment whether or not you have received a pregnancy and baby payment for the child. It does not matter whether your child is actually in early learning (eg, nursery, childcare or with a childminder) or not.

Who can get a school-age payment

In addition to the basic rules for a Best Start grant on p1696, you qualify for the school-age payment if:[6]

- you or your partner are responsible for a child (see p1699) born between 1 March 2017 and 28 February 2018 inclusive, and you claim from 1 June 2022 to 28 February 2023; *and*
- no other person has received, or is due to receive, a school-age payment for the child unless:
  - you are responsible for the child on the date of your claim; *and*

– you have not been that person's partner at any time since s/he claimed a school-age payment for the child; *and*
– the child does not normally live with the person who has already received a school-age payment.

You are not entitled to the school-age payment if the child is living in a residential establishment (ie, a local authority-approved children's home) on the date of your claim. You can qualify for a school-age payment whether or not you have received a pregnancy and baby payment or an early learning payment for the child. It does not matter whether your child has actually started school or not.

Responsible for a child

You count as responsible for a child if you meet any of the following conditions on the day you claim a Best Start grant.[7]
- The child is your dependant. S/he is your dependant if:
  – you are getting child benefit for her/him; *or*
  – you are getting CTC and s/he is included in your award (it does not matter if a child element is not payable because of the 'two-child limit'); *or*
  – you are getting UC and s/he is included in your award in the assessment period which includes the date of your Best Start grant claim, or the one before that (it does not matter if a child element is not payable because of the 'two-child limit'); *or*
  – you are getting a child amount for her/him in your PC.
- You are under 20, the parent of the child, you normally live with her/him, and you are a dependant in someone else's child benefit, CTC, UC or PC award (see p1700).
- You have been granted a parental order following a surrogate pregnancy.
- You have adopted the child under Scottish law, or the law of any other country or jurisdiction recognised under Scottish law.
- The child has been placed with you for adoption by an approved adoption agency in the UK.
- You are the appointed guardian of the child.
- You are an approved kinship carer for the child, and the child lives with you (exclusively or predominantly) under the terms of a kinship care order, or of an agreement with a local authority in the UK for a looked-after child.

Competing claims

If you and another person(s) claim a Best Start grant for the same child at the same time, Social Security Scotland (SSS) decides entitlement according to the following rules.[8]
- If only one person is responsible for the child for UC, CTC or PC, s/he is usually entitled.

Part 12: Scottish social security benefits
Chapter 74: Best Start grants
3. The amount of benefit

- If more than one person is responsible for the child for UC, CTC or PC, it depends on the circumstances of the child. This may happen if the competing claimants are members of the same couple, or if the DWP/HMRC is paying more than one person for the same child (even if this is by mistake).
- If one person is responsible for the child for UC, CTC or PC and the other competing claimant is an approved kinship carer (see p1730) for the child, it depends on the circumstances of the child.
- If no one is responsible for the child for UC, CTC or PC, the person getting child benefit is usually entitled, unless the other competing claimant is an approved kinship carer for the child.
- If the competing claimants are both kinship carers, and neither is responsible for the child for UC, CTC, PC or child benefit, the person whose claim is determined first is entitled.

If none of these apply, SSS must decide who has responsibility for the child taking into account the circumstances of the child, as set out in official guidance.

2. **The rules about your age**

There are no age limits for a Best Start grant. However, you qualify for a Best Start grant without being awarded a qualifying benefit if:[9]
- you are aged under 18 on the date of your claim; *or*
- you are aged 18 or 19 on the date of your claim, and you are the dependant of another person. You are a dependant of another person if:
  - s/he is getting child benefit for you; *or*
  - s/he is getting child tax credit and you are included as a 'qualifying young person' (see p272 for who counts) in the award (it does not matter if a child element is not payable because of the 'two-child limit'); *or*
  - s/he is getting universal credit and you are included as a 'qualifying young person' (see p61 for who counts) in the award in the assessment period which includes the date of your claim for a Best Start grant, or the one before that (it does not matter if a child element is not payable because of the 'two-child limit'); *or*
  - s/he is getting an amount in her/his pension credit for you; *or*
  - s/he is an approved kinship carer for you (see p1699).

3. **The amount of benefit**

The pregnancy and baby payment is £642.35 if there are no other children aged under 16 living in your household, or £321.20 if there is another child aged under

16 living in your household. You still get the £642.35 payment if the only other child(ren) in your household is:

- a parent of the child for whom a Best Start grant is being made; *or*
- a sibling of a parent of the child; *or*
- a child for whom you are not responsible; *or*
- a sibling born as a result of the same birth, but this only applies to one payment of £642.35 (see example below).

You should also still get the £642.35 payment if you have been granted refugee status or humanitarian protection (see p1539) and the only other child(ren) in your household was your responsibility before you fled to the UK.[10] There is a multiple pregnancy supplement of £321.20 if more than one child is born, or is to be born, as a result of the same pregnancy.

Example
Lauryn is pregnant with triplets. She has no other children living in her household. She is entitled to £642.35 for one child, £321.20 each for the other two children, and a multiple pregnancy supplement of £321.20. Her total best start grant is £1,605.95.

The early learning payment is £267.65 for each child.
The school-age payment is £267.65 for each child.

4. Claims and getting paid

The general rules on claims and getting paid are covered in Chapter 79. This section explains the specific rules that apply to Best Start grants.

Making a claim

You can claim a Best Start grant:

- online at mygov.scot/best-start-grant; *or*
- by telephone on 0800 182 2222; *or*
- in writing on the approved form; *or*
- if you are British Sign Language user, you can use the contactSCOTLAND app.

Forms
You can download the form from mygov.scot/best-start-grant-form or request it by telephone. Send your completed form to PO Box 10314, Dundee DD1 9GN – a prepaid envelope is available on request.

12

Part 12: Scottish social security benefits
Chapter 74: Best Start grants
4. Claims and getting paid

Information to support your claim

You do not need to send any evidence with your claim for a pregnancy and baby payment if you are getting a qualifying benefit and you have received a 'baby box' from the Scottish government. If you are aged 18 or 19 and not getting a qualifying benefit in your own right, you must send a letter from your school or college confirming the course you are on. If you have responsibility for a child under a legal order but the child is not included as your dependant in a benefit claim, you are asked to send a copy of the legal order.

You do not need to send any other evidence with your claim but it may be requested.

The date of your claim

You must usually claim a Best Start grant within a time limit (known as the 'application window'). This is:

* for the pregnancy and baby payment, between being 24 weeks pregnant and six months after the birth if you, or your partner or dependant, have been pregnant with the child, or if you have become responsible for a child in other circumstances, the day before her/his first birthday;
* for the early learning payment, from the child's second birthday to six months after her/his third birthday;
* for the school-age payment, from 1 June in the calendar year in which the child's fifth birthday falls (or if the child is born in January or February, the calendar year in which her/his fourth birthday falls), to the last day in February in the following year.

Until 1 April 2022 (although this may be extended to 1 October 2022), these time limits can be extended if they are not met due to the coronavirus pandemic.[11] Your claim is usually treated as having been made on the day it is received by Social Security Scotland (SSS). If you are not eligible on that date, but you would be eligible within 10 days, your claim can be treated as having been made up to 10 days later. If you are waiting for a backdated award of a qualifying benefit and you apply for a Best Start grant within 20 working days after the end of the application window, your claim can be treated as having been made on a day that falls within the application window.[12] If you were previously turned down for a Best Start grant but are awarded a qualifying benefit on appeal, which is backdated to include the date of your Best Start grant claim, a Best Start grant can be awarded without a new claim.[13]

If you claim the wrong payment

If you have claimed one type of payment (eg, a pregnancy and baby payment) and SSS finds that you will be entitled to a payment for another child (eg, a school-age payment for an older child) within 10 days, it can decide your entitlement without your having to make a claim.[14]

Getting paid

A Best Start grant is paid into the bank or other account you nominate when you make your claim. If you do not have an account, and have arranged for other benefits to be paid by the government's payment exception service (see p1150), the Best Start grant can be paid in the same way. Some, or all, of a Best Start grant payment can be made in a form other than money (eg, a voucher) if you accept an offer from SSS to receive it in this way. If you withdraw your agreement before the grant is given, it must be paid as money.

5. Tax, other benefits and the benefit cap

Tax, benefits and tax credits

Best Start grants are not taxable.[15]

They are not counted as income or capital for means-tested benefits or tax credits.[16] You cannot qualify for a Sure Start maternity grant if you have received a Best Start grant pregnancy and baby payment for the same child.[17]

The benefit cap

In some cases, there is a limit on the total amount of specified benefits you can receive (a 'benefit cap'). Best Start grant payments are not specified benefits. The benefit cap only applies if you are getting universal credit or housing benefit. See p1156 for further information.

Notes

1. Who can get a Best Start grant
1 EYA(BSG)(S) Regs
2 Regs 11 and 12 and Sch 2(1)(e) EYA(BSG)(S) Regs
3 Reg 12 EYA(BSG)(S) Regs
4 Sch 2 EYA(BSG)(S) Regs
5 Sch 3 EYA(BSG)(S) Regs
6 Sch 4 EYA(BSG)(S) Regs
7 Regs 9 and 10 EYA(BSG)(S) Regs
8 Sch 1(6) EYA(BSG)(S) Regs

2. The rules about your age
9 Sch 2(1)(iv) EYA(BSG)(S) Regs

3. The amount of benefit
10 *SK and LL v SSWP* [2020] UKUT 145 (AAC)

● ●

4. **Claims and getting paid**
11 s1 Coronavirus (Extension and Expiry)
    (Scotland) Act 2021
12 Regs 4 and 5 EYA(BSG)(S) Regs
13 Sch 1(5) EYA(BSG)(S) Regs
14 Sch 1(3) EYA(BSG)(S) Regs

5. **Tax, other benefits and the benefit cap**
15 s12 Finance Act 2019
16 The Social Security (Scotland) Act 2018
    (Best Start Grants) (Consequential
    Modifications and Saving) Order 2018
    No.1138
17 Reg 3A SFM&FE(G) Regs, as amended
    by the Social Security (Scotland) Act
    2018 (Best Start Grants) (Consequential
    Modifications and Saving) Order 2018
    No.1138

Chapter 75

Child disability payment

This chapter covers:

Key facts

- Child disability payment (CDP) is a benefit for children and young people in Scotland with disabilities or long-term health problems.
- It replaces disability living allowance for children and young people living in Scotland.
- CDP has a care component and a mobility component. You can qualify for one or both components. Each component has different rates.
- CDP is a non-means-tested benefit.
- You do not need to have paid national insurance contributions to get CDP.
- CDP is disregarded as income for means-tested benefits and tax credits and can be paid in addition to other benefits. It can also lead to increases in means-tested benefits.
- CDP is administered and paid by Social Security Scotland.
- If you disagree with a decision about CDP, you can request a redetermination and then appeal against it (see Chapter 80). You must request a redetermination before you can appeal.

12

Part 12: Scottish social security benefits
Chapter 75: Child disability payment
1. Who can get child disability payment

1. **Who can get child disability payment**

Child disability payment (CDP) is a benefit for children and young people in Scotland with a disability or long-term health problem.

In this chapter, the term 'child' refers to both a child under 16 for whom you are claiming, and a young person aged between 16 and 18 years old who may be entitled to CDP in her/his own right (see p1711). You can get CDP for a child if s/he:[1]

- meets the age rules (see p1711); *and*
- is not a 'person subject to immigration control' (see p1524); *and*
- meets the residence conditions (see p1601); *and*
- is not getting disability living allowance (DLA), personal independence payment (PIP), adult disability payment (ADP) or armed forces independence payment; *and*
- unless s/he is terminally ill:
  – satisfies the disability conditions for the care component (see below), the mobility component (see p1709) or both; *and*
  – has satisfied those conditions for that component throughout the 13 weeks immediately before the award begins and is likely to continue to satisfy them for the next 26 weeks.[2]

It is no longer possible to make a new claim for DLA for a child living in Scotland. If you claimed DLA before 22 November 2021, you will be transferred to CDP (see p1717).

Disability conditions for the care component

The care component is paid at one of three rates: lowest, middle or highest.

Note: a child under 16 must also satisfy the 'additional requirement' condition unless s/he is terminally ill or qualifies because s/he is getting renal dialysis (see p1707).[4]

A child can get the **lowest rate** care component if:[5]

- as a result of a physical or mental disability, s/he requires attention from another person for a significant portion of the day in connection with her/his bodily functions; *or*
- s/he is 16 or over and, as a result of a physical or mental disability, cannot prepare a cooked main meal for her/himself if s/he has the ingredients.

A child can get the **middle rate** care component if s/he:[6]

- satisfies one of the daytime conditions *or* one of the night-time conditions; *or*
- has renal dialysis in certain circumstances (see p1713).

A child can get the **highest rate** care component if s/he:[7]
- satisfies one of the daytime conditions *and* one of the night-time conditions; *or*
- has renal dialysis in certain circumstances (see p1713); *or*
- is terminally ill (see p1714).

The daytime conditions

The daytime conditions are that, as a result of a physical or mental disability, a child requires:[8]
- frequent attention throughout the day in connection with her/his bodily functions; *or*
- continual supervision throughout the day in order to avoid substantial danger to her/himself or others.

The night-time conditions

The night-time conditions are that, as a result of a physical or mental disability, a child requires:[9]
- prolonged or repeated attention from another person at night in connection with his/her bodily functions; *or*
- another person to be awake for a prolonged period or at frequent intervals at night to watch over the child in order to avoid substantial danger to her/himself or others.

Daytime and night-time

When daytime begins and ends depends on the ordinary routine of the child's household.[10] The definition looks at the household's rather than the child's routine. For example, help that is given after the child goes to bed but before the adults would normally go to bed, should not count towards satisfying the night-time conditions. See also p598 for the similar test in DLA.

The additional requirement condition

In addition to needing attention or supervision, the child must also have either:[11]
- attention or supervision requirements 'substantially in excess of the normal requirements' of a child of the same age; *or*
- substantial attention or supervision requirements which younger children in 'normal' physical and mental health may also have, but which children of the same age and in 'normal' physical and mental health would not have.

This extra test does not apply if you are claiming for a child who is terminally ill, a child who qualifies because they are getting renal dialysis, or a child who is aged 16 or over.

All young children need lots of help throughout the day. However, if a child needs substantially more help, or a different type of help, compared to the help

Part 12: Scottish social security benefits
Chapter 75: Child disability payment
1. Who can get child disability payment

normally required by a child of the same age, s/he should qualify. For a similiar test in DLA, see p595.

Definitions for the care component

Note: for CDP some of the terms used in the rules are defined in law. Some terms have been explained in caselaw for DLA. It is expected that terms that have been defined for DLA should mean the same for CDP. However, decision makers and tribunals are not bound to follow the DLA caselaw.

'**Attention**' means 'the provision of personal care, prompting or motivation in relation to bodily functions or assistance with communication needs'.[12] For a similar test in DLA, see p597.

'**Repeated attention**' is not defined. For DLA, this phrase means twice or more (see p600).[13]

'**Bodily function**' means 'the normal action of any organ of the body, including the brain, or of a number of organs acting together'.[14] For a similar test in DLA, see p597.

'**Frequent attention**' is not defined for CDP. For a similar test in DLA, see p599.

'**Frequent intervals**' is not defined for CDP. For a similar test in DLA, see p601.

CDP regulations do not define what it means for a child to be '**severely disabled, physically or mentally**'. For DLA, it has been established that 'severely disabled, physically or mentally' does not mean that the child needs to have a diagnosis of a specific medical condition (see p596). The same test should apply to CDP. There is no need to wait for a diagnosis before claiming.

'**Prolonged**' is not defined for CDP. For a similar test in DLA, see p600.

'**Require**' means 'reasonably require'.[15] For a similar test in DLA, see p596.

'**Significant portion of the day**' can be a single period or several periods during the day.[16] For DLA, it has been established that a 'significant portion of the day' should be taken to mean about an hour, but a shorter period could qualify (see p599).

'**Substantial danger**' is not defined for CDP. For a similar test in DLA, see p600.

'**Supervision**' means 'the precautionary or anticipatory presence of another person to monitor an individual's physical, mental or emotional health including monitoring for obstacles or dangerous places or situations'.[17] For a similar test in DLA, see p597.

'**Continual supervision**' is not defined for CDP, but for DLA has been found to mean less than 'continuous' supervision (see p600).

'**Watching over**' is not defined for CDP. For DLA, it has been found to mean that the person watching over has to be awake for a prolonged period or repeatedly at night (see p601).

Disability conditions for the mobility component

The mobility component is paid at one of two rates: higher or lower.

Note: a child cannot qualify for either rate of the mobility component unless s/he is 'able, from time to time, to benefit from assistance for movement'.[18] For a similar test in DLA, see p587.

The higher rate mobility component

A child can get the higher rate mobility component if s/he is aged three or over and:[19]

- s/he is unable, or virtually unable, to walk (see below); *or*
- the exertion required to walk would lead to a danger to the child's life or a serious deterioration in the child's health (for a similar test in DLA, see p590); *or*
- s/he has no legs or feet (regardless of the use of artificial limbs); *or*
- s/he is both blind and deaf and is 'unable, without the assistance of another person, to walk to any intended or required destination while out of doors' (see p1710); *or*
- s/he has a 'severe visual impairment' (see p1710); *or*
- s/he is terminally ill (see p1714); *or*
- s/he qualifies for the highest rate of the CDP care component and:
  - has a 'severe mental impairment' (see p1710); *and*
  - has 'severe behavioural difficulties' (see p1710).

Unable or virtually unable to walk

A child's inability or virtual inability to walk must be assessed taking account of her/his physical condition as a whole without regard to where the child lives.[20] For DLA, it has been found that there is no need for a diagnosed medical condition and that it does not matter if the original cause was mental, provided a current physical impairment affects the child's walking (see p588). Arguably, the same should apply to CDP.

A child should be considered unable to walk if s/he cannot move her/his body along by alternate, weight-bearing steps of the feet.[21]

When considering if a child is virtually unable to walk, the following must all be taken into account:[22]

- the speed; *and*
- the time taken; *and*
- the manner of walking; *and*
- the ability to cover distance (only the distance that can be walked without beginning to experience severe discomfort).

See p589 for the similar test in DLA.

A child's ability to walk should be considered taking into account any prosthesis or artificial aid s/he uses, or that would be suitable for her/him.[23]

12

Part 12: Scottish social security benefits
Chapter 75: Child disability payment
1. Who can get child disability payment

Both blind and deaf

A child is both blind and deaf if s/he:[24]

- has 100 per cent loss of vision; *and*
- at least 80 per cent hearing loss, even with the use of an artificial aid; *and*
- the effect of these combined means s/he is unable to get to any intended or required destination outdoors, without assistance from another person.

See p590 for a similar test in DLA.

Severe visual impairment

A child has a severe visual impairment if s/he meets the Visual Impairment Network for Children and Young People (VINCYP) definition of 'severe visual impairment'.[25]

The VINCYP definition of severe visual impairment for children is not clear. It seems that, in practice, the same criteria that applies to adults will be used. If it is not appropriate to apply adult visual acuity or field of vision criteria to the child, it applies if it is the opinion of a medical professional that s/he has a visual function equivalent to an adult with severe visual impairment ie, equivalent to vision of:[26]

- less than 3/60 with a full visual field; *or*
- between 3/60 and 6/60 with a severe reduction of field of vision, such as tunnel vision; *or*
- 6/60 or above but with a very reduced field of vision, especially if a lot of sight is missing in the lower part of the field.

Severe mental impairment

A child has a 'severe mental impairment' if s/he has a severe impairment of intelligence and social functioning. This must result from:[27]

- a state of arrested development due to a failure of her/his brain to grow or develop in the way normally expected; *or*
- a deficiency in the functionality of the brain due to its incomplete physical development.

'Severe impairment of intelligence and social functioning' is not defined for CDP. See p592 for the similar test in DLA.

Severe behavioural difficulties

A child has severe behavioural difficulties if s/he exhibits disruptive behaviour which:[28]

- is extreme; *and*
- regularly requires another person to intervene in order to prevent physical injury to her/himself or another person; *and*
- is so unpredictable that another person needs to be awake and watching over her/him while s/he is awake.

12

The disruptive behaviour does not need to be constant but should be regular. The child may exhibit severe behavioural difficulties if s/he shows aggression, or destructive behaviour, or behaves in a way that could be dangerous for her/him or another person. The intervention must be related 'to the provision of care and support of, or treatment provided to, the child.[29]

Note: as well as severe mental impairment and severe behavioural difficulties, the child must also be getting the highest rate care component to qualify for the higher rate mobility component on this basis.

The lower rate mobility component
A child can get the lower rate mobility component if s/he:[30]
- is aged five or over; *and*
- is able to walk; *and*
- as a result of physical or mental impairment, cannot move around outside, on unfamiliar routes, without requiring supervision or guidance from another person most of the time.

If the child is under 16, the guidance or supervision s/he requires must meet the additional requirement condition (see p1707).[31] See p592 for how the test applies to the DLA lower rate mobility component.

Definitions for the mobility component
'Supervision' means 'the precautionary or anticipatory presence of another person to monitor an individual's physical, mental or emotional health including monitoring for obstacles or dangerous places or situations'.[32] For a similar test in DLA, see p593.
'Guidance' means 'direction or leading by physical means or verbal suggestion or persuasion'.[33] For a similar test for DLA, see p593.

2. **The rules about your age**

The lower age limit for entitlement to begin is:[34]
- age three months for the care component (from birth if the child is terminally ill);
- age three for the higher rate mobility component;
- age five for the lower rate mobility component.

Payment can begin as soon as the child reaches this age if s/he meets the disability conditions for 13 weeks beforehand and you claimed during that time.[35]

The upper age limit for entitlement to begin is normally the day before the child's 16th birthday.[36]

Part 12: Scottish social security benefits
Chapter 75: Child disability payment
2. The rules about your age

Entitlement can begin later if your child is transferred from disability living allowance (DLA). If you have not claimed child disability payment (CDP) by then, and s/he does not get DLA (and is not terminally ill, see p1714), s/he can claim adult disability payment (ADP) from aged 16, if it is available in your area (see p1687) or personal independence payment (PIP) if it is not (see p722).

The upper age limit for CDP entitlement to end is normally the child's 18th birthday.[37]

However, it can continue until her/his 19th birthday if s/he:[38]

- claimed ADP before s/he turned 18; *or*
- moved to Scotland before turning 18 and was getting DLA immediately before moving; *or*
- is transferred from DLA to CDP (see p1717).

Moving to adult disability payment

A child who gets CDP must claim ADP before reaching 18 to ensure that the CDP does not stop. However, s/he can choose to claim ADP from as early as age 16.

Should you claim ADP early?

You should get specialist advice to help you and your child decide whether to claim ADP as soon as s/he is able to. The entitlement conditions for ADP are completely different, and s/he may not qualify for ADP at all or may qualify for a lower award. If ADP is awarded, the child's CDP will end.[39]

However, s/he may be better off claiming ADP – eg, if s/he does not have any night-time care needs but would be entitled to the enhanced rate of ADP daily living component. Use the information in Chapter 73 to work out the likely ADP entitlement, and compare this with her/his CDP award.

If s/he gets CDP highest rate care component and higher rate mobility component, that cannot be increased, so s/he would not gain anything from claiming ADP sooner than s/he needs to.

If s/he does claim ADP early, the new award normally starts from the date it is determined.[40] However, if the ADP award is higher than the CDP award, the first payment is increased by the amount that would have been paid if entitlement had started from the date of claim (see p1689).[41] If the ADP claim is refused, CDP entitlement continues until the child's 18th birthday (and s/he can try to claim ADP again later).[42]

If your child is terminally ill (see p1714), the CDP award should be automatically tranferred to ADP from age 18 (unless s/he asks for it to be transferred sooner or not transferred at all). If it is not automatically transferred, CDP entitlement continues indefinitely, as long as the child is still terminally ill.[43]

3. **The amount of benefit**

Child disability payment (CDP) mobility component is paid at one of two weekly rates:[44]
- the lower rate is £24.45;
- the higher rate is £64.50.

CDP care component is paid at one of three weekly rates:[45]
- the lowest rate is £24.45;
- the middle rate is £61.85;
- the highest rate is £92.40.

4. **Special benefit rules**

Special rules may apply to children who:
- have renal dialysis;
- are terminally ill;
- are subject to immigration control (see Chapter 68);
- have come from or are going abroad (see Chapters 69, 70, and 71);
- are living in a care home or similar accommodation, including some residential schools, or in a young offenders' institution or other form of detention (see Chapter 42).

Renal dialysis

If a child is getting renal dialysis, special rules may allow her/him to get the child disability payment (CDP) care component.[46] The child must have this treatment at least twice a week. The dialysis must normally be a type that requires the attendance or supervision of another person, or the child's particular needs must make it necessary to have another person there to provide the specific attention or supervision s/he requires.

If the renal dialysis takes place both by day and at night, the child is entitled to the highest rate care component. If the renal dialysis takes place either by day or at night, the child is entitled to the middle rate care component.[47]

It makes no difference whether the dialysis takes place in hospital or at home.

To qualify under these rules, the child must have been getting the treatment for 13 weeks before the date the award would begin and must be expected to continue for another 26 weeks from that date.[48]

Part 12: Scottish social security benefits
Chapter 75: Child disability payment
5. Claims and getting paid

Terminal illness

If a child is terminally ill, s/he is entitled to the highest rate care component and the higher rate mobility component. The care component can be paid from birth but the mobility component is not payable until the child is three years old.

A child is terminally ill if it is the judgement of a registered medical practitioner or a registered nurse, who is involved in the care or diagnosis of the child, that the child has a progressive disease that can reasonably be expected to cause her/his death.[49] When making such a judgement, account must be taken of the guidance that is published by the Chief Medical Officer of Scotland.[50] For information about the claim process, see p1684.

5. **Claims and getting paid**

The general rules on claims and getting paid are covered in Chapter 79. This section explains the specific rules that apply to child disability payment (CDP). If you are transferring from disability living allowance (DLA), there is no need to make a claim (see p1717).

Making a claim

You can start a claim for CDP:[51]
- online at mygov.scot/child-disability-payment/how-to-apply; *or*
- by telephone on 0800 182 2222; *or*
- by post on paper form which can be sent out; *or*
- in British Sign Language via the contactScotland app.

Claims for CDP are made in two parts.
- **Part 1** registers the claim. You can do this by telephone, in writing or online. You need to provide the name and date of birth of the child to register the claim.[52] In practice, Social Security Scotland (SSS) also asks for other information, such as contact details and the name of the adult with responsibility for the child, where you live and bank details. If you do this by telephone, you will be sent a paper form to complete.
- **Part 2** asks about the child's disability or health condition and how it affects them. This form should be returned in the prepaid envelope sent with the form to Social Security Scotland, PO Box 10301, Dundee DD1 9FW.

If you start your claim online, you need to set up an account with SSS. You can then complete both parts online.

You should return the form, or complete Part 2 if you claimed online, within six weeks of the date you completed Part 1, to protect your date of claim (see p1716).

Forms

You can request a paper form and prepaid envelope by telephoning SSS on 0800 182 2222, or writing to the address on p1714.

SSS's Local Delivery Team can also help with claims. You can book appointments with a local adviser by calling 0800 182 2222.

Who should claim

You can make a claim for CDP if you are a child's parent, or someone who has authority to act on behalf of the child (see p1745).

When s/he turns 16, a young person is normally expected to manage her/his own CDP claim. If the young person is unable to manage the claim, see p1744.

If a child is terminally ill, anyone can apply on her/his behalf as long as they have consent to do so from the parent or appointee.[53]

Information to support your claim

You have six weeks from starting a claim to complete the application process by providing the required information. The information you must provide for Part 2 of the claim relates to the care and mobility needs of the child. This can be provided online or in a paper form depending on whether you completed Part 1 online, by telephone or in writing.

Further information to support the claim should be provided where possible. For example, a letter from the child's GP, school or other health professional might help SSS to make a determination. Do not delay submitting part two of the claim while waiting for such letters. They can be provided later by post or online at mygov.scot. If you are not able to provide supporting information yourself you can ask SSS to gather this on your behalf. You are asked about this when completing Part 2. If you do not ask for help and SSS asks for a further piece of supporting information, the claim can arguably be rejected if you do not provide this.[54] If this happens, you should reapply as soon as possible and can also appeal that 'process decision' (see p1781). If you do not provide requested information within the period allowed, you may get a determination that you are not entitled to CDP.[55] You can ask for a redetermination of that decision (see p1755).

If the child is terminally ill, you need to provide a Benefits Assistance under Special Rules in Scotland (BASRiS) form completed by an appropriate healthcare professional (see p1684).

Part 12: Scottish social security benefits
Chapter 75: Child disability payment
5. Claims and getting paid

The date of your claim

CDP is usually paid from the date of your claim. This is normally the date you provide SSS with the child's full name and date of birth, Part 1 of the claim. You must provide Part 2 of the claim within six weeks of that date. The six-week period can be extended if you can show there is 'good reason' for the delay.[56] If anything is preventing you from submitting this, ask for more time as soon as possible.

Note: good reason could include such things as the child or adult's health issues, hospitalisation or recent bereavement.[57]

If you do not provide this information within six weeks and do not have a good reason, the date of claim is the date it is received.[58]

Backdating your claim

CDP cannot be backdated unless your child is terminally ill (see p1685).

Claiming in advance

A claim for CDP can be made before a child has satisfied the qualifying condition (see p1706) provided s/he will meet the condition within 13 weeks of making the claim. The date of claim is the date s/he meets the conditions.[59]

Getting paid

CDP is usually paid four-weekly in arrears. If the child is terminally ill (see p1714) you are paid weekly in advance.[60] If a child is entitled to CDP while on leave from a care home or residential school, you can be paid CDP at a daily rate.[61]

Payment is made to the parent or person with parental responsibilities who has made the claim on behalf of the child, or a person that SSS has appointed to act on the child's behalf (see p1744). When the child is 16, payment can be made direct to the child or to an appointee.

- For when CDP payments can be suspended, see p1746.
- For when a deduction can be made from CDP to recover an overpayment, see p1748.
- CDP mobility component can be paid to Motability, see similar rules for DLA on p621.
- If you are overpaid CDP, you may have to repay it (see p1747).
- For when you can be paid short-term assistance, see p1778.

Change of circumstances

You must tell SSS about any changes that you have been told to report.[62] This includes any change that could affect the amount of CDP that the child is entitled to. When you receive a determination notice telling you about the award you should be told what changes you need to report. It is advisable to report any changes, even if you are unsure if it is relevant. If you do not report a change that affects your entitlement you may miss out on extra payments or be overpaid and have to pay it back (see p1761).

Reviews of child disability payment awards

Once awarded, CDP continues to be paid until a new determination is made about entitlement. The award has no end date unless the child no longer satisfies the rules – eg, from her/his 18th birthday.[63] However, SSS may specify a review date in the determination notice when it plans to look at the award again and make a new determination.[64] SSS calls this a 'scheduled review'.

If a new determination reduces or ends your CDP, you may be entitled to short-term assistance if you are challenging that decision (see p1778).

For the review, SSS may request further supporting information to decide if the child's award is correct. It is important that you respond to such requests for information as failure to do so could lead to the benefit being suspended or later ended (see p1746).

If a child dies

An extra eight weeks of CDP is paid as a lump sum after a child dies.[65] Any payments of CDP already made for a period after the date of death are deducted from the lump sum.[66]

Moving from disability living allowance to child disability payment

If your child gets DLA and lives in Scotland (or abroad and has a close link to Scotland – see p1602), the DLA award will be automatically transferred to CDP without having to make a claim.[67] The transfer process started in October 2021 and all DLA awards are due to be transferred by 2023.[68] Until DLA is transferred, you should report any changes of circumstances to the DWP. If your child gets DLA and moves to Scotland, see p1718.

Automatic transfers to child disability payment

You should receive a letter telling you that your child's DLA is being transferred to CDP and how long the process will take. In most cases, SSS must make a determination that you will be paid CDP at the same rate as your DLA.[69] However, it could be higher if your child is:

- terminally ill (see p1714). CDP must include higher rate mobility (if s/he is aged 3 or over) component as well as highest rate care component; *or*
- severely visually impaired (see p1710) but did not get higher rate mobility component in the DLA award; *or*
- aged 16 or over and is now entitled to the care component, or to a higher rate, because s/he cannot prepare a cooked main meal or because the additional requirement condition no longer applies (see p1707).

12

Part 12: Scottish social security benefits
Chapter 75: Child disability payment
6. Tax, other benefits and the benefit cap

If you think your child should be entitled to a higher rate, you should contact SSS as soon as you can.

It is expected that most payments will be made on the same payment dates as the DLA award.[70]

You will be notified of the date of transfer when CDP entitlement starts and DLA ends.[71] If the CDP award is higher because the child is terminally ill, the difference between the higher CDP rate and the lower DLA rate can be paid from the date of clinical judgement, but no earlier than 26 weeks before the case transfer date. If it is higher for any of the other reasons in the bullet points on p1717, the difference can be backdated to the date the child met the conditions of entitlement (but not before the start of the transfer process on 11 October 2021).[72]

When the transfer is complete, any passporting entitlements now depend on getting CDP and not DLA (see below). Make sure you tell all the relevant departments – eg, the Carer's Allowance Unit, Tax Credit Office, the local authority or your universal credit journal.

Note: if a child who gets DLA has not yet been transferred to CDP, you should continue to report any changes in circumstances to the DWP and complete a DLA renewal form if her/his award is coming to an end. Although no new claims for DLA can generally be made in Scotland, renewal claims are still possible.[73] For more information about changes to your DLA, see p617 and for renewal claims, see p610.

If you get disability living allowance and move to Scotland

If your child gets DLA and moves to Scotland from another part of the UK, you should notify the DWP. The DWP will notify SSS, who will make a determination of the child's entitlement to CDP. There is no need for you to make a new claim. Entitlement to CDP begins the day after the DLA award ends.[74]

If your child gets CDP and moves from Scotland to another part of the UK, see p1762.

6. **Tax, other benefits and the benefit cap**

Tax

Child disability payment (CDP) is not taxable.[75]

Other benefits and tax credits

CDP interacts with means-tested and non-means-tested benefits, and passports you to the same sources of help, in the same way as disability living allowance (DLA) (see p618).

Non-means-tested benefits

CDP can be paid in addition to other non-means tested benefits, but you cannot get CDP while you are entitled to DLA, personal independence payment (PIP), adult independence payment (ADP) or armed forces independence payment.[76]

If you are regularly caring for a child who gets CDP middle or highest rate care component, you may be entitled to carer's allowance (CA) (see Chapter 26) and the carer element of universal credit (see p73).

For details of other additional amounts for carers, see p620.

A young person aged 16, 17 or 18 living in Scotland may be able to get a young carer grant for looking after a child who gets CDP middle or highest rate care component (see Chapter 78).

A child living in Scotland who gets the CDP highest rate care component can get a child winter heating assistance payment (see p1673).

The benefit cap

In some cases, the 'benefit cap' can limit the total amount of benefit you can be paid. CDP is not one of the specified benefits. The benefit cap does not apply if you, your partner or child get CDP (even it is not paid because the person entitled is in a care home).[77] In other cases, it only applies if you are getting UC or HB. For more information, see p1156.

Passports and other sources of help

If you are not entitled to CA, you may still be credited with class 3 national insurance contributions if you are caring for a child for at least 20 hours a week who gets CDP middle or highest rate care component (see p957).

You qualify for a Christmas bonus if you or your child get CDP at any rate. You may be entitled to council tax reduction if you have a low income.

If you get CDP mobility component, other sources of help are the same as those for DLA (see p620).

Notes

12

1. Who can get child disability payment
1 s31 and Sch 5 SS(S)A 2018; reg 3 DACYP(S) Regs
2 Regs 11(3), 12(6) and 13(10) DACYP(S) Regs
3 Reg 19 DACYP(CATP)(S) Regs
4 Reg 11(2) and (4) DACYP(S) Regs
5 Regs 11(1)(a) and (b) and 11(5)(c) DACYP(S) Regs
6 Regs 11(5)(b) and 16(3) DACYP(S) Regs
7 Regs 11(5)(a), 15(1)(a) and 16(4) DACYP(S) Regs

Part 12: Scottish social security benefits
Chapter 75: Child disability payment
Notes

● ●

8   Reg 11(1)(c) DACYP(S) Regs
9   Reg 11(1)(d) DACYP(S) Regs
10 Reg 11(6)(a) DACYP(S) Regs
11 Reg 11(2) DACYP(S) Regs
12 Reg 11(6)(b) DACYP(S) Regs
13 R(DLA) 5/05
14 Reg 2 DACYP(S) Regs
15 Reg 11(8) DACYP(S) Regs
16 Reg 11(1)(a) DACYP(S) Regs
17 Reg 11(7) DACYP(S) Regs
18 Reg 14 DACYP(S) Regs
19 Reg 13 DACYP(S) Regs
20 Reg 13(2)(a) DACYP(S) Regs
21 Because, arguably, R(M) 2/89, CDLA/
    97/2001 and *Sandhu v SSWP* [2010]
    EWCA Civ 962 apply.
22 Reg 13(2)(a) (ii) DACYP(S) Regs
23 Reg 13(3) DACYP(S) Regs
24 Reg 13(6) DACYP(S) Regs
25 Reg 13(2)(c) and (5) DACYP(S) Regs;
26 VINCYP, *Visual Impairment Care Bundle*,
    available at vincyp.scot.nhs.uk/wp-
    content/uploads/2021/06/NSD610-
    021.10-Care-Bundle.pdf; VINCYP, *Who
    Can be Certified as Sight Impaired?*
    available at vincyp.scot.nhs.uk/wp-
    content/uploads/2021/07/2021-07-15-
    Criteria-for-Certification-as-
    Sight-Impaired-V0.1.pdf; SSS, *Child
    disability payment DMG*, paras 61-66,
    available at socialsecurity.gov.scot/
    asset-storage/production/downloads/
    CDP-DMG-Higher-Rate-Mobility-
    Component.pdf
27 Reg 13(7) DACYP(S) Regs
28 Reg 13(8) DACYP(S) Regs
29 Reg 13(8)(b) and (9) DACYP(S) Regs
30 Reg 12 DACYP(S) Regs
31 Reg 12(2) and (3) DACYP(S) Regs
32 Reg 11(7) DACYP(S) Regs
33 Reg 12(7) DACYP(S) Regs

2. The rules about your age

34 Regs 4(1), 12(1) and 13(1) DACYP(S)
    Regs
35 Reg 24(2) DACYP(S) Regs
36 Reg 4(2) DACYP(S) Regs
37 Reg 4(1) DACYP(S) Regs
38 Reg 4(1B)(b) DACYP(S) Regs
39 Reg 10 DACYP(S) Regs
40 Reg 58(2) DAWAP(S) Regs
41 Reg 58(3) DAWAP(S) Regs
42 Reg 4(1) DACYP(S) Regs – being refused
    ADP does not affect your award of CDP
43 Reg 4(1B)(a)DACYP(S) Regs; reg 59
    DAWAP(S) Regs

3. The amount of benefit

44 Reg 23(2) DACYP(S) Regs
45 Reg 23(1) DACYP(S) Regs

4. Special benefit rules

46 Reg 16 (1) and (2) DACYP(S) Regs
47 Reg 16 (3) and (4) DACYP(S) Regs
48 Reg 16 (5) DACYP (S) Regs
49 Sch 5 para 1(2) SS(S)A 2018; reg 15 (6)
    DACYP(S) Regs
50 Sch 5 para 1(3) SS(S)A 2018; reg 15(7)
    DACYP(S) Regs

5. Claims and getting paid

51 mygov.scot/child-disability-payment/
    how-to-apply
52 Reg 24 (4) DACYP(S) Regs
53 SSS, *Who should apply*, available at
    mygov.scot/child-disability-payment/
    applicants
54 s38(1) SS(S)A 2018
55 s54(1) and (2) SS(S)A 2018
56 Reg 24(4) and (6) DACYP(S) Regs
57 SSS, *Child disability payment DMG*, paras
    20-23, available at
    socialsecurity.gov.scot/asset-storage/
    production/downloads/CDP-DMG-
    Applying-for-CDP.pdf
58 Reg 24(5) DACYP (S) Regs
59 Reg 24(2) DACYP(S) Regs
60 Reg 25 DACYP(S) Regs
61 Reg 23(3) DACYP(S) Regs
62 s56 SS(S)A 2018
63 Reg 26 DACYP(S) Regs
64 Reg 30 DACYP(S) Regs
65 Reg 23(7) DACYP(S) Regs
66 s69 and Sch 5 para 15 SS(S)(A) 2018
67 Sch para 9 DACYP(S) Regs
68 SSS, *Case Transfer Guide*, available at
    socialsecurity.gov.scot/guidance-
    resources/guidance/case-transfer-guide
69 Sch paras 9(4) and 11 DACYP(S) Regs
70 SSS, *Case Transfer Guide*, available at
    socialsecurity.gov.scot/guidance-
    resources/guidance/case-transfer-guide
71 Sch para 10 DACYP(S) Regs
72 Sch paras 9(2), 10(b), 11(3), 13(za) and
    (zb) DACYP(S) Regs. The intention is
    that any higher CDP award can overlap
    with DLA entitlement in this situation,
    but the law does not clearly allow this for
    backdated terminal illness awards.
73 Reg 19(2) DACYP(CATP)(S) Regs
74 Reg 35 DACYP(S) Regs

6. Tax, other benefits and the benefit cap

75 s677(1) IT(EP)A 2003
76 Reg 10 DACYP(S) Regs
77 Reg 75F HB Regs; reg 83 UC Regs

12

Funeral support payment

This chapter covers:
1. Who can get a funeral support payment (below)
2. The rules about your age (p1725)
3. The amount of benefit (p1725)
4. Claims and getting paid (p1726)
5. Tax, other benefits and the benefit cap (p1727)

Key facts
- A funeral support payment is a one-off payment to help with the costs of a funeral.
- A funeral support payment is not means tested, but you must receive a qualifying benefit to qualify.
- You do not need to have paid national insurance contributions to qualify.
- Funeral support payments are administered and paid by Social Security Scotland.
- If you disagree with a decision about a funeral support payment, you can request a redetermination and then appeal against it (see Chapter 80). You must request a redetermination before you can appeal.

1. Who can get a funeral support payment

You qualify for a funeral support payment if:[1]
- you are ordinarily resident in Scotland (see p1550);[2] *and*
- on the date of your claim, you or your partner are receiving a qualifying benefit (see p1722);[3] *and*
- you or your partner have accepted responsibility for the funeral and it is reasonable for you to do so (see p1722);[4] *and*
- the funeral takes place in the UK or, in certain circumstances, it takes place in any European Economic Area (EEA) country or Switzerland (see p1724);[5] *and*
- a funeral support payment or a social fund funeral expenses payment (see p784) has not already been paid in respect of the person who has died;[6] *and*
- the person who has died was ordinarily resident in the UK (see p1550);[7] *and*

12

Part 12: Scottish social security benefits
Chapter 76: Funeral support payment
1. Who can get a funeral support payment

- you are not a 'person subject to immigration control' (there are exceptions to this rule) – see p1524;[8] *and*
- you claim within the time limit (see p1726).[9]

It may be the funeral of a stillborn child, which means that the stillbirth occurs after the 24th week of pregnancy.[10]

If the person who has died was aged 18 or over, you cannot get a funeral support payment if her/his assets are sufficient to meet the cost of the funeral.[11] Assets include lump sums due to be paid as a result of an insurance policy, occupational pension scheme, burial club, prepaid funeral plan or similar scheme.[12]

Qualifying benefits

To qualify for a funeral support payment, you or your partner must be getting one of the following:[13]
- universal credit (UC); *or*
- income support; *or*
- income-based jobseeker's allowance; *or*
- income-related employment and support allowance; *or*
- housing benefit; *or*
- child tax credit; *or*
- working tax credit which includes the disabled worker or severe disability element; *or*
- pension credit.

You must be getting UC in the assessment period that includes the date of your claim for a funeral support payment, or have been getting UC in the assessment period before that.[14] For the other benefits, you must be getting the benefit on the date of your claim for a funeral support payment. See p1726 for when your claim is made, or can be treated as having been made.

You must be getting one of the above qualifying benefits at a rate of more than £0, before any third-party deductions or sanctions are applied.[15] You do not count as getting a qualifying benefit if it was paid in error, including an official error.[16]

Responsible for the funeral expenses

To qualify for a funeral support payment, you or your partner must have accepted responsibility for the costs of the funeral and it must be reasonable that you or your partner have accepted responsibility.[17]

In assessing whether it is reasonable that you or your partner have accepted responsibility, Social Security Scotland (SSS) must take into account whether the person who has died had a closer relative than you or your partner and any other

12

relevant factors. In deciding whether there is a closer relative, the following 'table of hierarchy' is used.[18]

Adult death	Child death
Spouse or civil partner	Parent or a person who had parental rights
Someone neither married to nor in a civil	and parental responsibilities for her/him
partnership with the person who died, but	(but not a local authority)
who had been living with her/him as if	Sister or brother
they were married for at least six months	Grandparent
(or if the person who died was in hospital	Aunt or uncle
immediately before her/his death, for at	Cousin
least six months before s/he was admitted	Niece or nephew
to hospital)	A long-standing friend
Child	
Parent	
Sister or brother	
Grandparent	
Aunt or uncle	
Cousin	
Niece or nephew	
A long-standing friend	

Usually, it will be reasonable for the person who has the closest family relationship to the person who has died to take responsibility for the funeral expenses, but there are other circumstances, such as estrangement, which may be relevant and may mean that you are entitled even if there is a closer family member. SSS guidance suggests that a spouse or civil partner should not be considered to be the closest relative where the couple were permanently separated, either by court order, verbal or written agreement or by desertion.[19] The guidance also highlights situations in which couples may have been living apart but were not permanently separated and should therefore still be considered to be the closest relative. The examples provided include couples living apart due to drug or alcohol misuse, work arrangements and care arrangements.

The guidance suggests that it *may* be reasonable for you to accept responsibility for the funeral even though there is a closer relative where:
- you were the carer of the person who has died; *or*
- you lived with the person who has died; *or*
- you had a close relationship with the person who has died; *or*
- you had looked after the person who has died since her/his childhood; *or*
- you had power of attorney for the person who has died, or were her/his legal guardian or appointee; *or*

12

Part 12: Scottish social security benefits
Chapter 76: Funeral support payment
1. Who can get a funeral support payment

- you are the parent, sibling, relative or friend of the person who has died; *or*
- no one else has accepted responsibility for the funeral.

The guidance also provides examples of reasons why the person who is the closest relative *may* not have been able to take responsibility for the funeral. These include:

- being estranged from or having had a grievance with the person who has died;
- drug or alcohol misuse;
- being too young or being in higher education;
- not being financially or emotionally capable of arranging the funeral;
- not being capable due to health, lifestyle or mental capacity;
- living too far away;
- currently serving in the armed forces;
- being under suspicion in the death of the person who has died.

If SSS decides that it was not reasonable for you to have accepted responsibility for the funeral, you can challenge this decision (see Chapter 80). It is advisable to point out the limited financial resources of the closer relative, as well as any other relevant factors such as whether the closer relative was estranged from the deceased. At an appeal, the First-tier Tribunal can take its own view, and is not bound by the guidance.

If there is another family member at the same level on the hierarchy, but no one above you, SSS should accept that it is reasonable for you to accept responsibility without looking at that other person's circumstances.[20]

If more than one person claims a funeral support payment, the application of the person who is the closest relative will be considered first. If s/he is entitled, the other person cannot be entitled.[21] If more than one person applies, they are equally close relatives to the person who died and they cannot decide whose claim should proceed, SSS decides which to consider first.[22]

European Economic Area nationals

You may be able to get a funeral support payment for a funeral that takes place in the EEA or Switzerland if:[23]

- you are in a 'protected group' (see p1566) *and*:
  - you are a 'worker', a self-employed person, or you retain that status; *or*
  - you are a family member of a worker, a self-employed person or someone who retains that status; *or*
  - you have a permanent right to reside in the UK; *or*
- you have limited or indefinite leave to remain in the UK granted under the EU settlement scheme – ie, you have pre-settled or settled status.

You must satisfy all the other rules for getting a funeral support payment.

12

2. The rules about your age

There are no age limits for funeral support payment. However, because you or your partner must be getting a qualifying benefit, this means that you or your partner must be aged 16 or over.

3. The amount of benefit

You are entitled to a funeral support payment to cover the cost of:[24]
- a burial plot;
- necessary burial fees and fees of digging a grave;
- cremation fees, including the cost of removing a pacemaker (restricted to £21.55 if not carried out by a doctor);
- any medical references and medical certificates, if required;
- documentation for the release of the assets of the person who has died;
- transport for the portion of journeys in excess of 80 kilometres, undertaken to:
  - transport the body within the UK to a funeral director's premises or to a place of rest;
  - transport the coffin and bearers in a hearse and the mourners in another vehicle from the funeral director's premises or place of rest to the funeral;
- one return journey undertaken to make arrangements for the funeral, which does not exceed the cost of a return journey from your home to the place of the burial or cremation.

In addition, you can get a payment of £1,070.60 towards any other funeral expenses, or £130.65 if the person was aged 18 or over when s/he died and had a prepaid funeral plan.

If the burial or cremation takes place in an area where the person who died was not ordinarily resident and the cost of the burial or cremation, including transport costs, are more than what the costs would otherwise have been, the funeral support payment does not cover the excess.[25]

Deductions from awards

If available to help meet the funeral costs, the following are deducted from the amount of the funeral support payment:[26]
- any assets of the person who died that are available without confirmation having been granted, or without probate or letters of administration; *and*
- an insurance policy, occupational pension scheme, burial club or similar arrangement; *and*
- a funeral grant paid by the government if the person who died was receiving a war disablement pension.

12

Part 12: Scottish social security benefits
Chapter 76: Funeral support payment
4. Claims and getting paid

Note:
- No deduction is made if the person who died was under 18.[27]
- No deduction is made in respect of arrears of social security benefits paid to th‹ deceased's estate.[28]

4. **Claims and getting paid**

The general rules on claims and getting paid are covered in Chapter 79. Thi‹ section explains the specific rules that apply to funeral support payment.

Making a claim

You can claim a funeral support payment:
- online at mygov.scot/funeral-support-payment; *or*
- by telephone on 0800 182 2222; *or*
- in writing on the approved form; *or*
- if you are British Sign Language user, you can use the contactSCOTLAND app‹

Forms

The form can be downloaded from mygov.scot/funeral-support-payment-17-or-under (if the person who has died was under 18) or mygov.scot/funeral-support-payment-over-18-form (if the person who has died was 18 or over) or requested by telephone. Send your completed form to Social Security Scotland, PO Box 10311, Dundee DD1 9GH.

Information to support your claim

You will need to provide details of the funeral director, if you are using one, an‹ details of any travel receipts or funeral bills you have already had. You are asked i you give permission for Social Security Scotland (SSS) to contact the funera‹ director to get further information.

The date of your claim

You can claim at any time from the date the person died until six months afte‹ the date of the funeral. SSS calls this the 'period for applications'.[29] The time cai be extended where it is not met due to the coronavirus pandemic.[30] If you ar‹ refused a funeral support payment because you are not getting a qualifying benefi and you later become entitled to a qualifying benefit, you can claim agaii provided you are still within this period. If you are waiting for a backdated awarc of a qualifying benefit, the benefit is awarded for at least one day that falls withii the period for applications and you claim within 20 days after the end of th‹ period for applications, your claim can be treated as having been made on a da‹

in the period for applications.[31] If you were previously turned down for a funeral support payment but are awarded a qualifying benefit on appeal, which is backdated to include the date on which your previous claim was refused, a funeral support payment can be considered again without your having to make a new claim.[32]

Getting paid

Usually, payment is made direct to the funeral director if the bill is still outstanding. If the bill has been paid, payment is usually made to you.

A funeral support payment can be recovered from the estate of the person who died.[33]

5. Tax, other benefits and the benefit cap

Tax, benefits and tax credits

Funeral support payments are not taxable.[34]

They are not counted as income or capital for other means-tested benefits or tax credits.

You cannot get a funeral support payment if you or anyone else has been awarded a social fund funeral expenses payment in respect of the person who died.[35]

The benefit cap

In some cases, there is a limit on the total amount of specified benefits you can receive (a 'benefit cap'). A funeral support payment is not a specified benefit. The benefit cap only applies if you are getting universal credit or housing benefit. See p1156 for further information.

12

Part 12: Scottish social security benefits
Chapter 76: Funeral support payment
Notes

Notes

1. Who can get a funeral support payment

1 Reg 3 FEA(S) Regs
2 Reg 9(1) FEA(S) Regs
3 Reg 10 FEA(S) Regs
4 Reg 7 FEA(S) Regs
5 Reg 9(2)(b) FEA(S) Regs
6 Reg 8(4) and (5) FEA(S) Regs
7 Reg 9(2)(a) FEA(S) Regs
8 Reg 9(5) FEA(S) Regs
9 Reg 5 FEA(S) Regs
10 Reg 2 FEA(S) Regs
11 Reg 11 FEA(S) Regs
12 Reg 11(3) FEA(S)Regs
13 Reg 10 FEA(S) Regs
14 Reg 10(4) FEA(S) Regs
15 Reg 10(2)(b) FEA(S) Regs
16 Reg 10(2)(a) FEA(S) Regs
17 Reg 7 FEA(S) Regs
18 Reg 7(2)(a) and (3) FEA(S) Regs
19 SSS guidance at socialsecurity.gov.scot/
guidance-resources/guidance/
eligibility-for-funeral-support-payment
20 Scottish government, *Funeral Expense Assistance Regulations: consultation*, May 2018
21 Reg 8(1), (2) and (4) FEA(S) Regs
22 Reg 8 (3) FEA(S) Regs
23 Reg 9(2)(b), (3) and (4) FEA(S) Regs

3. The amount of benefit

24 Reg 13 FEA(S) Regs
25 Reg 13(5) FEA(S) Regs
26 Reg 14 FEA(S) Regs
27 Reg 14(2) FEA(S) Regs
28 Regs 14(3) FEA(S) Regs

4. Claims and getting paid

29 Reg 5 FEA(S) Regs
30 s1 Coronavirus (Extension and Expiry) (Scotland) Act 2021. This provision is in force until end March 2022 and may be extended to end September 2022.
31 Reg 5(5) FEA(S) Regs
32 Reg 4(2) FEA(S) Regs
33 s70 SS(S)A 2018

5. Tax, other benefits and the benefit cap

34 s660 IT(EP)A 2003, as amended by s12 Finance Act 2009
35 Reg 8(5) FEA(S) Regs

Chapter 77

Scottish child payment

This chapter covers:
1. Who can get Scottish child payment (below)
2. The rules about your age (p1731)
3. The amount of benefit (p1732)
4. Claims and getting paid (p1732)
5. Tax, other benefits and the benefit cap (p1734)

Key facts
- Scottish child payment is a top-up benefit for lower income families in Scotland responsible for children under the age of six.
- Scottish child payment is not means-tested, but you must be receiving a means-tested benefit or tax credit to qualify.
- You do not have to have paid national insurance contributions to qualify.
- You can qualify for Scottish child payment whether you are in or out of work.
- Scottish child payment can be paid in addition to other benefits and tax credits, and does not count as income for means-tested benefits.
- Scottish child payment is administered and paid by Social Security Scotland.
- If you disagree with a determination about Scottish child payment, you can request a redetermination and then appeal against it (see Chapter 80). You must request a redetermination before you can appeal.

Future changes

Scottish child payment is expected to be extended to families with children under 16 by the end of 2022.[1] The payment is also expected to increase to £25. Scottish child payment bridging payments will be made to some families during 2022 (see p1735).

1. Who can get Scottish child payment

You qualify for Scottish child payment if:[2]
- you are reponsible for a child under the age of six; *and*
- you are entitled to a qualifying benefit; *and*
- you are ordinarily resident in Scotland (see p1550).

Part 12: Scottish social security benefits
Chapter 77: Scottish child payment
1. Who can get Scottish child payment

You must usually meet all the qualifying conditions on the date your claim is received.

In some circumstances, such as if you or the child are in hospital or detention or go abroad, your entitlement to Scottish child payment depends on whether you still count as responsible for the child (see below) and whether you are still entitled to a qualifying benefit (see p1731).

Responsible for a child

You must be responsible for the child on the date of your claim for Scottish child payment. You must continue to be responsible for the child for each week of entitlement to Scottish child payment. You count as responsible for a child if you meet either of the following conditions.[3]

- The child is your or your partner's dependant. S/he is a dependant if you are getting:
  - child benefit for her/him; *or*
  - universal credit (UC) and s/he is included in your award (it does not matter if a child element is not payable because of the 'two-child limit'); *or*
  - child tax credit (CTC) and s/he is included in your award (it does not matter if a child element is not payable because of the 'two-child limit'); *or*
  - a child amount for her/him in your pension credit (PC).
- You are an approved kinship carer for the child, and the child lives with you (exclusively or predominantly) under the terms of a kinship care order, or of an agreement between you and/or your partner and a local authority in the UK for a looked-after child. Note that if you are responsible for the child as a kinship carer, you must still be getting a qualifying benefit for yourself.

Competing claims

Only one person can receive Scottish child payment for a child. If you and another person(s) claim, or are treated as claiming (see p1732), and are both eligible for Scottish child payment for the same child, Social Security Scotland (SSS) decides entitlement according to the following rules.[4]

- If only one person is responsible for the child for UC, CTC or PC, s/he is usually entitled.
- If more than one person is responsible for the child for UC, CTC or PC, it depends on the circumstances of the child. This may happen if the competing claimants are members of the same couple, or if the DWP/HMRC is paying more than one person for the same child (even if this is by mistake).
- If one person is responsible for the child for UC, CTC or PC and the other competing claimant is an approved kinship carer (see above) for the child, it depends on the circumstances of the child.
- If no one is responsible for the child for UC, CTC or PC, the person getting child benefit is usually entitled, unless the other competing claimant is an approved kinship carer for the child.

12

- If the competing claimants are both kinship carers and neither is responsible for the child for UC/PC/CTC, the person whose claim is determined first is entitled.

If none of these apply, SSS must decide who has responsibility for the child taking into account the circumstances of the child, as set out in official guidance.

Qualifying benefits

To qualify for Scottish child payment, you or your partner must have been awarded:[5]
- UC; *or*
- income support; *or*
- income-based jobseeker's allowance; *or*
- income-related employment and support allowance; *or*
- CTC; *or*
- working tax credit; *or*
- PC.

You or your partner must be awarded a qualifying benefit for the date of your claim for Scottish child payment. Someone counts as your partner if you are part of a couple as defined for UC purposes (see p56), even if you get one of the other qualifying benefits.[6] If your claim for Scottish child payment is turned down because you are still waiting to hear about a qualifying benefit, it can be decided again if the qualifying benefit is later awarded for a period that includes the date of your claim for Scottish child payment (see p1733).

Your award of a qualifying benefit must continue for at least one day for each week of entitlement to Scottish child payment. You are still regarded as having been awarded a benefit if it has been reduced to nil because of a sanction or third-party deduction.[7] If the qualifying benefit has been awarded in error, you are not entitled to Scottish child payment.

2. The rules about your age

There is no minimum age for Scottish child payment, but you must be aged at least 16 in order to get any of the qualifying benefits. If you are responsible for a dependent child who has a child, you should also claim Scottish child payment for your dependant's child.

There is no upper age limit for the person who claims Scottish child payment. The child must be under the age of six. It is expected that this will be extended to under the age of 16 by the end of 2022.

Part 12: Scottish social security benefits
Chapter 77: Scottish child payment
4. Claims and getting paid

3. **The amount of benefit**

Scottish child payment is paid at a weekly rate of £20 for each child for whom you are responsible (see p1730).

4. **Claims and getting paid**

The general rules on claims and getting paid are covered in Chapter 79. This section explains the specific rules that apply to Scottish child payment.

Making a claim

You can claim Scottish child payment:
- online at mygov.scot/scottish-child-payment/how-to-apply; *or*
- by telephone on 0800 182 2222; *or*
- in writing on the approved form; *or*
- if you are British Sign Language user, you can us the contactSCOTLAND app.

Forms

You can download the form at mygov.scot/scottish-child-payment-forms or telephone and request it is sent to you. Send your completed form to Social Security Scotland, PO Box 27155 Glasgow G4 7DX – a prepaid envelope is available on request.

You can apply for a Best Start grant (see Chapter 74) and Best Start foods (see p850) at the same time.

If you are already getting Scottish child payment for one child and you tell Social Security Scotland (SSS) that you are responsible for another child, a determination of your entitlement for that child can be made without a new claim. Your entitlement starts on the date you notify that you are responsible for the child, or up to four weeks earlier if you were responsible for the child for the purposes of universal credit (UC), child tax credit (CTC) or pension credit (PC).[8]

You can be awarded Scottish child payment without making a new claim if you were getting Scottish child payment within the last 12 weeks, your entitlement ended due to a break in responsibility for the child or receipt of a qualifying benefit, and you have since become entitled again.[9] It is important to give the date on which you met the qualifying conditions again, so that your new entitlement starts on the date on which the change occurred. If the date of the change is not known, your claim is treated as made on the date SSS became aware of the change.

If someone else has claimed Scottish child payment for the same child, see p1730.

Information to support your claim

You do not usually need to provide any further information to support your claim if you are getting UC, CTC, PC or child benefit for the child. SSS checks with the DWP or HMRC that you are getting a qualifying benefit at an address in Scotland and that you are responsible for the child. If you do not get a benefit for the child, you have to provide evidence that you are a kinship carer to show that you are responsible for her/him. This could be a legal order or letter from your local authority. Your claim may be refused if the evidence requested is not provided.[10]

The date of your claim

Your claim is treated as made on the day it is received by SSS, provided it is properly completed.[11]

If you have claimed Scottish child payment and you are waiting to hear about a qualifying benefit, or a benefit showing you have responsibility for the child, the determination may be delayed until the outcome is known.

If you are refused Scottish child payment and you are later awarded a qualifying benefit, or a benefit showing you have responsibility for the child, which is backdated to include the date of your claim for Scottish child payment, your entitlement can be determined from that date without the need to make a new claim.[12]

If you have previously been turned down for Scottish child payment and this was due to an official error (see p1760), your entitlement can be determined again.[13]

Scottish child payment cannot usually be backdated. The date your claim is received is usually the date your award starts, and it cannot be treated as made on an earlier date, unless the reason for it not being made sooner is related to coronavirus.[14]

If you do not meet all the qualifying conditions on the date of your claim, but it is expected that you will meet them within 14 days, your claim can be treated as made up to 14 days later.[15]

The people included in your claim

You can only qualify for Scottish child payment for a child you are responsible for (see p1730). It does not matter if the child element of UC or CTC is not payable because of the 'two-child limit'. There is no limit on the number of children that you can get Scottish child payment for. If you are part of a couple, you claim as an individual and only one of you is entitled to Scottish child payment, but it can be you or your partner who gets the qualifying benefit.

Getting paid

Scottish child payment is payable weekly, starting on the day your claim is received. Payments are made every four weeks, in arrears, during the last week of

12

Part 12: Scottish social security benefits
Chapter 77: Scottish child payment
5. Tax, other benefits and the benefit cap

the four-week period, into your nominated account.[16] If you already get Scottish child payment for one child and become entitled to a payment for another child, the payment cycles will be aligned so that you will receive payments for all children at the same time.[17] The first payment for another child will include arrears for each week, or part of a week, from the date you are treated as claiming, up to the payment date.

Your Scottish child payment may be reduced if you have an outstanding overpayment of a Scottish benefit (see p1748).[18] You can request a redetermination of the reduced amount (see p1748). Your Scottish child payment may be suspended in some circumstances (see p1746). If SSS considers that the original decision was made incorrectly, resulting in an overpayment (see p1748), a new determination can be made, with effect from the date of your original claim.[19]

Change of circumstances

If you no longer meet the qualifying conditions, your entitlement to Scottish child payment ends from the week following the date on which you no longer qualify.[20] Your Scottish child payment entitlement can be determined again following a change of circumstances relating to the qualifying conditions – ie responsibility for the child, ordinary residence in Scotland and entitlement to qualifying benefits.[21] A new determination following a change of circumstances takes effect from the date of the change, or if this is not known, the date SSS became aware of the change. A new determination can be made on your Scottish child payment if SSS decides to pay someone else for the child instead, with effect from the date the other person's claim is determined.[22]

Your Scottish child payment ends from the week after the week in which the child's sixth birthday falls (it is expected that this will be extended to the 16th birthday by the end of 2022).[23]

5. **Tax, other benefits and the benefit cap**

Tax

Scottish child payment is not taxable.[24]

Means-tested benefits and tax credits

Scottish child payment does not count as income for means-tested benefits or tax credits.

The benefit cap

In some cases, there is a limit on the total amount of specified benefits you can receive (a 'benefit cap'). Scottish child payment does not count as a specified benefit. See p1156 for further information.

Passports and other sources of help

Scottish child payment does not directly help you qualify for any other benefits, but if you are entitled to Scottish child payment, you may also be entitled to:

- Scottish child payment bridging payment: four payments of £130 for each child (of any age) entitled to free school meals due to low income (see p851), paid automatically by your local authority at the start of the Easter, summer, October and Christmas holidays in 2022;
- a Best Start grant, depending on the age(s) of your child(ren) (see Chapter 74);
- Best Start foods, depending on the ages of your children and your other income or earnings (see p850);
- health benefits (see Chapter 31);
- education benefits such as a clothing grant (see p851);
- council tax reduction (see p836).

Notes

1 Scottish Budget, 2022/23

2. Who can get Scottish child payment
2 Reg 18 SCP Regs
3 Regs 9, 11 and 12 SCP Regs
4 Sch para 5 SCP Regs
5 Reg 14 SCP Regs
6 Reg 10 SCP Regs
7 Reg 15 SCP Regs

4. Claims and getting paid
8 Sch para 11 SCP Regs
9 Sch para 12 SCP Regs
10 s54(2) SS(S)A
11 Reg 5 SCP Regs
12 Sch para 8 SCP Regs
13 Sch para 6 SCP Regs
14 Sch para 35(2) SCP Regs
15 Sch para 1(2) SCP Regs
16 Reg 21 SCP Regs
17 Reg 21(3) and (4) SCP Regs
18 Sch para 31 SCP Regs
19 Sch para 7 SCP Regs
20 Reg 19 SCP Regs

21 Sch para 10 SCP Regs
22 Sch para 10 SCP Regs
23 Reg 19(2)(b) SCP Regs

5. Tax, other benefits and the benefit cap
24 Table B – PART 2, s677 Income Tax (Earnings and Pensions) Act 2003

12

Chapter 78

Young carer grants

This chapter covers:
1. Who can get a young carer grant (below)
2. The rules about your age (p1738)
3. The amount of benefit (p1738)
4. Claims and getting paid (p1738)
5. Tax, other benefits and the benefit cap (p1740)

Key facts
- A young carer grant is a payment for young people aged 16 to 18 who care, or have been caring, for someone with a disability.
- You must live in Scotland, or live outside the UK and have a close link to Scotland, to qualify.
- You can add together hours caring for different people, but they must all be getting a disability benefit at the right level.
- You can only get a young carer grant once a year.
- Young carer grants are not means tested.
- You can qualify for a young carer grant whether you are in or out of work.
- You do not need to have paid national insurance contributions to qualify.
- Young carer grants are administered and paid by Social Security Scotland.
- If you disagree with a decision about a young carer grant, you can request a redetermination and then appeal against it (see Chapter 80). You must request a redetermination before you can appeal.

1. Who can get a young carer grant

You qualify for a young carer grant if:[1]
- you are aged at least 16 and under 19 on the date you claim (but see p1738); *and*
- you have been caring for at least one person who gets a qualifying disability benefit (see p1737); *and*
- you spent sufficient hours caring during the 13-week 'qualifying period' (see p1738); *and*

- you are not entitled to carer's allowance (CA) and have not claimed CA (unless the claim has been refused) when you claim a young carer grant (but see p1740); and
- you are either ordinarily resident in Scotland (see p1550), or exempt from this requirement (see p1626); and
- you are habitually resident in the UK, Channel Islands, Isle of Man, European Economic Area or Switzerland, unless you are exempt (see p1553).

Note:
- You can get a young carer grant once a year. If you have previously received a young carer grant, claim again one year after the date of your last claim.[2]
- You can only get three young carer grants in total.[3]
- You cannot normally get a young carer grant if someone else has received one for someone that you care for within the past year (but see p1740).
- You should claim a young carer grant if you would meet all of the above conditions, but a person you care for claimed a disability benefit more than 13 weeks ago and has not yet been awarded it. Your claim may be refused, but if the disability benefit is later awarded, you can still get a young carer grant.
- Getting a young carer grant does not affect any benefits that a person you care for gets.

Qualifying benefits

The person or people you care for must get a qualifying disability benefit *throughout* the 13-week qualifying period (see p1738). The qualifying benefits are:[4]
- attendance allowance (AA);
- the highest or middle rate of disability living allowance care component;
- the highest or middle rate of child disability payment care component;
- either rate of the daily living component of personal independence payment;
- either rate of the daily living component of adult disability payment;
- armed forces independence payment;
- constant attendance allowance of £75.50 a week or more in respect of an industrial injury (see p678) or war disablement (see p857).

If the benefit is not paid for someone that you care for during part of the qualifying period (eg, if s/he is in a care home), you cannot count hours spent caring for her/him.[5]

If your claim for a young carer grant was refused because a person you care for was not receiving a qualifying disability benefit throughout the qualifying period, your entitlement must be determined again without you having to make another claim if:[6]
- that person is later awarded a qualifying benefit for the whole of the qualifying period; and

12

Part 12: Scottish social security benefits
Chapter 78: Young carer grants
4. Claims and getting paid

- no one else has been awarded a young carer grant for caring for her/him since you originally claimed.

The care you must provide

During the 13 weeks before your date of claim (see p1739) (the 'qualifying period'), you must have provided care for at least 208 hours, during at least 10 of those weeks.[7] If you care every week during the qualifying period, this is an average of 16 hours a week. The care you provide must involve activity that promotes the physical, mental or emotional wellbeing of the person you care for.[8] The regulations do not define what this means, but guidance suggests that it could include activities such as helping with personal care, dealing with bills, shopping or keeping someone company.[9]

You can add together hours of care you provide for up to three people, so long as they all got a qualifying benefit (see p1737) throughout the qualifying period. You must not be paid for the hours you spend caring, or provide the care as voluntary work.[10]

Example

Maddy, 17, cares for her grandmother (who gets AA) for about 20 hours a week. She has done so for the past year. Maddy also volunteers at a youth club for people with learning disabilities. Even though Maddy cannot count her voluntary work as hours of care, she can still get a young carer grant, as she spends enough time caring for her grandmother.

2. The rules about your age

You can get a young carer grant if you are aged at least 16 and are under 19 on the date of your claim (see p1739).[11] The upper age limit does not apply if your claim is late due to the coronavirus pandemic.[12]

3. The amount of benefit

A young carer grant is a single annual payment of £326.65.[13] The amount of a young carer grant normally increases every year, and depends on your date of claim (see p1739).[14]

4. Claims and getting paid

For the general rules on claims and getting paid, see Chapter 79. This section explains the specific rules that apply to young carer grants.

Making a claim

If you live in Scotland, you can claim a young carer grant:
- online at mygov.scot/young-carer-grant/how-to-apply; *or*
- by telephone on 0800 182 2222; *or*
- in writing on the approved form.

Note:
- If you do not have a bank account or you are claiming as someone else's appointee (see p1744), you cannot claim online.[15]
- If you live outside Scotland, you must either claim in writing on the approved form or by telephoning +44(0)1382 931000.[16]

* *

Forms

You can download the appropriate young carer grant form from mygov.scot/young-carer-grant-paper-form or request one by telephone. Send your completed form to Social Security Scotland, PO Box 10314, Dundee DD1 9GN.

* *

Information to support your claim

You are asked to confirm that each person you care for is aware that you are applying for a young carer grant and gives her/his permission for Social Security Scotland (SSS) to contact her/him or use her/his personal data. SSS also asks you for evidence of your identity and address after you have claimed. If you claim using the paper form, you can send this evidence, if you have it, with the form.

The date of your claim

Your claim is normally treated as made on the day it is received by SSS, provided it is properly completed.[17] If you could not claim before your 19th birthday due to the coronavirus pandemic, your claim can be treated as having been made when you were 18.[18] You must have been eligible for a young carer grant before you turned 19.

If your claim is refused as someone you care for does not get a qualifying benefit (see p1737), your entitlement must be determined again without you having to make another claim if s/he is later awarded a qualifying benefit and no one else has been awarded a young carer grant for caring for her/him since you originally claimed.[19] If your entitlement is determined again, the date of your claim is the same as it was for your original claim.

If you live outside the UK and meet the conditions on p1626, your young carer grant claim can be treated as having been made on any date between 22 July 2019 and 24 December 2020. There is no time limit to claim under this rule.[20]

12

Part 12: Scottish social security benefits
Chapter 78: Young carer grants
5. Tax, other benefits and the benefit cap

Getting paid

A young carer grant is paid into the bank or other account you nominate when you make your claim. If you do not have access to a bank account, you should claim by telephone and discuss how you want to receive your grant.

Some, or all, of a payment can be made in a form other than money (eg, a voucher) if you accept an offer from SSS to receive it in this way.[21] If you withdraw your agreement before you get the grant, it must be paid as money.

If someone else has claimed a young carer grant

If you and someone else care for the same person and you both claim a young carer grant, SSS decides which of you is entitled. The claim that was received first must be determined first.[22]

If someone else has received a young carer grant in respect of a person you care for within one year of the date of your claim (see p1739), you cannot get a young carer grant for caring for that person unless:[23]
- the other claimant has died; *or*
- SSS has decided that s/he should not have been paid a young carer grant.

5. **Tax, other benefits and the benefit cap**

Tax

Young carer grants are not taxable.[24]

Other benefits and tax credits

Young carer grants do not count as income or capital for means-tested benefits or tax credits.[25]

You cannot qualify for a young carer grant if you are entitled to carer's allowance (CA) on the date of your claim, or if you have claimed CA, unless your claim has been refused.[26]

Young carer grants and carer's allowance
– It does not matter if someone else gets CA or the carer element of universal credit (UC) for looking after someone that you care for. You can still get a young carer grant.
– If you care 35 hours a week or more for one person, you may be eligible for both CA and a young carer grant. Normally, you should claim a young carer grant first. As soon as you are awarded it, you can immediately claim CA and request backdating. It does not matter if you are later awarded CA for the date of your young carer grant claim. However, if your young carer grant takes a long time to be awarded, then in some situations you may lose out. Seek advice if you are unsure.
– If your CA stops (eg, if you start work or education), check whether you can get a young carer grant. Days on which you got CA can count as part of the 13-week qualifying period for a young carer grant (see p1738).

12

The benefit cap

In some cases, there is a limit on the total amount of specified benefits you can receive (a 'benefit cap'). A young carer grant is not a specified benefit. The benefit cap only applies if you are getting UC or housing benefit. See p1156 for further information.

Passports and other sources of help

If you are a young carer living in Scotland, you can get a package of support (whether or not you can get a young carer grant) from Young Scot. There is more information at young.scot.

You may be able to get help, support and services from your local authority – ask for a young carer's assessment.

If you are 18 or over and have a low income, you may be entitled to council tax reduction (see p836).

Notes

1. Who can get a young carer grant
1 s28 and Sch 2 SS(S)A 2018; Part 2 CA(YCG)(S) Regs
2 Reg 7(3) CA(YCG)(S) Regs
3 Reg 7(6) CA(YCG)(S) Regs
4 Reg 6 CA(YCG)(S) Regs; Sch para 15 DACYP(S) Regs
5 Reg 6(1) CA(YCG)(S) Regs
6 Reg 11 CA(YCG)(S) Regs
7 Reg 5(2) CA(YCG)(S) Regs
8 Reg 5(3) CA(YCG)(S) Regs
9 Social Security Scotland, *Eligibility for Young Carer Grant*, 13 November 2020, available at socialsecurity.gov.scot/ guidance-resources/guidance/ eligibility-for-young-carer-grant
10 Reg 5(4) CA(YCG)(S) Regs; reg 2 The Carers (Scotland) Act 2016 (Agreements of a Specified Kind) Regulations 2017 No.257 which ensures that kinship care payments from the local authority are not treated as payments for work.

2. The rules about your age
11 Reg 4(1) CA(YCG)(S) Regs
12 s52B SS(S)A 2018

3. The amount of benefit
13 Reg 12(1) CA(YCG)(S) Regs
14 s78 SS(S)A 2018

4. Claims and getting paid
15 Social Security Scotland, *Overview of Young Carer Grant*, 13 November 2020, available at socialsecurity.gov.scot/ guidance-resources/guidance/ overview-of-young-carer-grant
16 Scottish government, *Young Carer Grant: applying outside of Scotland*, 4 February 2021, available at mygov.scot/ young-carer-grant/applying-outside-of-scotland
17 Reg 4(3) CA(YCG)(S) Regs
18 s52B SS(S)A 2018
19 Reg 11 CA(YCG)(S) Regs
20 Reg 4(7) CA(YCG)(S) Regs
21 Reg 12(3) CA(YCG)(S) Regs
22 Reg 10 CA(YCG)(S) Regs
23 Reg 7(4) and (5) CA(YCG)(S) Regs

12

Part 12: Scottish social security benefits
Chapter 78: Young carer grants
Notes

5. Tax, other benefits and the benefit cap

24 s677 IT(EP)A 2003
25 **UC** Sch 10 para 23 UC Regs (but note
   that a young carer grant counts as
   capital if it is not spent within 52 weeks
   of receiving it)
   IS Sch 10 para 77 IS Regs
   JSA Sch 8 para 70 JSA Regs
   ESA Sch 9 para 65 ESA Regs
   HB Sch 6 para 67 HB Regs; Reg
   29(1)(j)(xviif) and Sch 6 paras 21(2)(u)
   and 26J HB(SPC) Regs
   PC Reg 15(1)(re) and Sch 5 para
   20(2)(v) SPC Regs
   WTC/CTC Reg 19 Table 6 para 29
   TC(DCI) Regs
26 Reg 7(1) and (2) CA(YCG)(S) Regs

Chapter 79

Claiming Scottish benefits and getting paid

This chapter covers:
1. Claims (below)
2. Getting paid (p1746)
3. Overpayments (p1747)
4. Fraud (p1749)
5. Complaints (p1750)

Key facts

- Scottish benefits are administered and paid by Social Security Scotland (SSS).
- To be entitled to a Scottish benefit, you must usually make a claim for it.
- Decisions on entitlement to Scottish benefits are called 'determinations'.
- You must give correct and complete information when you make your claim, and report any changes that could affect your entitlement.
- Some overpayments, called 'assistance given in error', are recoverable.
- If you are unhappy about the way you have been treated by SSS, you can complain.

1. Claims

In most cases, to be entitled to a Scottish benefit, you must make a claim for it.[1] Social Security Scotland (SSS) refers to claims as 'applications'. If you cannot claim for yourself, an 'appointee' (see p1744) can claim on your behalf.[2]

How to make a claim

Each Scottish benefit has its own rules for how to make a claim. See the chapter in this part of the *Handbook* about the benefit you want to claim. You may be able to claim in writing, online or by telephone.

If you do not claim in the correct way, SSS may reject your application. You have a right of appeal in this situation. This is called a 'process appeal' (see p1781).[3]

Part 12: Scottish social security benefits
Chapter 79: Claiming Scottish benefits and getting paid
1. Claims

You may be asked to provide further information before a decision (known as a 'determination') is made on your claim.[4] You should be given a specific period of time to respond to the request for more information. Try to provide any evidence that you are asked for if you can, or explain why this is not possible. If you fail to provide the required information within the time you are given to do so, SSS may determine that you are not entitled to the benefit you have claimed.[5] If this happens, you can ask for a redetermination of the decision that you are not entitled to the benefit you have claimed (see p1755).

SSS local delivery teams can help with claims for Scottish benefits. You can book an appointmnet with a local adviser by telephoning SSS on 0800 182 2222.

Withdrawing a claim

Once you have made a claim for a Scottish benefit you can withdraw your claim at any point before the determination is made, provided you do so in the way you are told to by SSS.[6]

Appointees

Someone aged 16 or over (eg, a relative or friend) can be authorised to act on your behalf if you cannot claim for yourself – eg, if you have a mental illness or a learning disability or if you are a child claiming a benefit such as child disability payment (CDP).[7] S/he is called an 'appointee'. The appointee takes on your rights and responsibilities as a claimant and receives payment of benefit.

If someone has died and there is no executor appointed to deal with the estate, another person can be appointed to deal with social security issues.[8]

It is planned that you will be able to ask the First-tier Tribunal to review certain decisions about appointeeship.[9]

Appointees for adults

If you are aged 16 or over, you may have an appointee if you are incapable within the meaning of the Adults with Incapacity (Scotland) Act 2000, with no guardian acting or appointed under that Act and no other person who has the power to act on your behalf and is willing to do so.[10] In appointing someone to act on your behalf, SSS must, if possible, take account of your wishes and feelings and the views of anyone else who appears to have an intest in your welfare or financial affairs.

It is planned that you may also have an appointee if you are *not* incapable within the meaning of the Adults with Incapacity (Scotland) Act 2000, but you have agreed to the appointment, and:
- you understand the effect of it; *and*
- you have not been subject to any undue influence in agreeing to the appointment; *and*
- the proposed appointee is suitable to act as an appointee.[11]

Appointees for children

If a child is claiming a benefit, such as CDP, a person aged 16 or over can be appointed to act on behalf of the child if there is no one who:[12]

- already has the authority to act on behalf of the child; *and*
- lives with, and has responsibility for, the child; *and*
- is willing to act on the child's behalf.

When deciding whether and who to appoint, SSS must, if practicable, take account of the child's views and also the views of any person who has parental rights or parental responsibilities for the child and anyone else who appears to have an interest in the child's welfare or financial affairs.[13]

Ending an appointeeship

An appointeeship may be ended at any time by SSS.[14]

Where the appointeeship relates to a child, the following people may request that it ends:[15]

- the child; *or*
- anyone with parental rights or parental responsibilities for the child; *or*
- anyone who has an interest in the child's welfare or financial affairs.

When making a decision about ending a child appointeeship, and where it is practical to do so, SSS must take into account the views of the people in the bullet points above.[16]

Where the appointeeship relates to an adult who is *not* incapable under the Adults with Incapacity (Scotland) Act 2000, SSS must end the appointeeship if you withdraw your agreement to it and must consider ending it if a request to do so is made by someone who appears to have an interest in your welfare or financial financial affairs.[17]

Where the appointeeship relates to an adult who *is* incapable under the Adults with Incapacity (Scotland) Act 2000, SSS must consider ending the appointeeship if a request to do so is made by you or by someone who has authority to act on your behalf or by someone who appears to have an interest in your welfare or financial affairs.[18] When making a decision about ending an appointeeship for an adult in this situation, SSS must, where it is practical to do so, take into account your wishes and feelings and the views of anyone who appears to have an interest in your welfare or financial affairs.[19]

Right to support

During the claim and assessment process, you can have someone with you to support you – eg, a support worker or advice worker.[20] This includes during any discussions with SSS and during any assessment you are asked to undertake. A supporter is allowed to make representations to SSS on your behalf.

12

Part 12: Scottish social security benefits
Chapter 79: Claiming Scottish benefits and getting paid
2. Getting paid

Right to advocacy

If you have any kind of disability, you have a right to be assisted by an independent advocate in any part of the claim or assessment process.[21] If you want to get help from an advocate, telephone SSS on 0800 182 2222 (Relay UK available or, if you are a BSL user, you can use the contactSCOTLAND app) and ask to be referred to the independent advocacy service. Although this service is funded by the Scottish government, it is independent of the government and of SSS. The independent advocacy service must follow service standards which are set out by the Scottish government.[22] You can have someone to support you (see p1745) as well as having an independent advocate.[23]

2. **Getting paid**

Once Social Security Scotland (SSS) has made a determination that you are entitled to benefit, you must be paid.[24] For details of how you are paid, see the chapter in this part of the *Handbook* about the benefit you have claimed.

Once you are receiving a Scottish benefit, you can ask for it to be stopped at any time.[25]

If you have an ongoing entitlement to a Scottish benefit, SSS will inform you about your responsibility to report any changes in your circumstances. You must be advised what changes you need to report and how to report them.[26] In some situations, failing to report a change of circumstances can constitute an offence (see p1749).[27]

Suspension of payments

When can payment be supended

Payment of Scottish benefits which are paid on an ongoing basis can be supended in certain cricumstances. Scottish child payment, child disability payment (CDP) and adult disability payment (ADP) may be suspended if:[28]

- SSS has asked you to provide information relating to your ongoing entitlement and you have failed to provide it withint the time allowed; *or*
- you have an appointee and either:
  - the appointee can no longer continue in that role; *or*
  - SSS suspects that you are at risk of financial abuse; *or*
- for CDP, you have reached 16 and SSS still has to make arrangements to pay CDP to you, as an adult, or to an appointee.

SSS must consider your financial circumstances before making a decision to suspend payment of your Scottish child payment, CDP or ADP.[29]

You must be notified of the decision to suspend your benefit, told the reasons for the suspension and what steps you can take that may end the suspension.[30]

Right to review

If your Scottish child payment, CDP or ADP is suspended you can ask SSS to look again at its decision. This is called a 'review'. SSS must complete the review within 31 days of receiving your request and must inform you of the outcome and the reasons for that outcome.[31]

When does the suspension end

Suspension of payment ends if:[32]

- you provide the information that SSS requires and SSS decides that your award of benefit can continue unchanged; *or*
- you do *not* provide the information that SSS required and a determination is made to end you entitlement; *or*
- if you have an appointee, that person is able to continue in that role, another person is appointed instead or SSS no longer has concerns that you are at risk of financial abuse; *or*
- SSS makes a 'determination without application' (see p1758) that:
  - you have been underpaid as a result of official error; *or*
  - you have been overpaid; *or*
  - you are no longer entitled to the benefit due to a change of circumstances; *or*
  - your benefit should be reduced to recover an overpayment or a decuction should stop; *or*
  - you are owed a backdated award of Scottish child payment; *or*
  - you are entitled to Scottish child payment for another child; *or*
  - another person is entitled to Scottish child payment for the child instead of you; *or*
  - your benefit should be reduced to recover an overpayment or a decuction should stop; *or*
  - for CDP/ADP, a 'specified period' of entitlement (see p1690 and p1717) has resulted in a determination that you are no longer entitled to CDP/ADP.
- SSS decides that it is appropriate to end the suspension. This includes having regard to your financial circumstances.

Payment after a benefit is suspended

If, when the suspension of benefit ends, you are still entitled to the benefit, SSS should immediately pay you the benefit that you have not received during the period of the suspension.[33]

12

3. Overpayments

If you are paid a Scottish benefit by mistake or you are paid more than you should have been, Social Security Scotland (SSS) calls this overpayment 'assistance given

Part 12: Scottish social security benefits
Chapter 79: Claiming Scottish benefits and getting paid
3. Overpayments

in error'. You may have to repay an overpayment, but only in certain circumstances.[34]

Overpayments that may be recoverable

Overpayments of Scottish benefits can be recovered from you if you were paid in error and the error was caused, or contributed to, by your:

- providing false or misleading information; or
- failing to report a change of circumstances which you were told you should report; or
- causing someone else to do either of the above.[35]

An overpayment can also be recovered from you if you could reasonably have been expected to notice the error.[36] When assessing this, the following are examples of what should be taken into account:[37]

- the amount of benefit paid to you, compared with your actual entitlement;
- any information given to you by SSS that might have alerted you to the fact that the award was wrong.

Other relevant matters can also be taken into account.

Recovery of overpayments

The amount recoverable is the amount of benefit you received less your actual entitlement (if any) had the error not taken place.[38]

Even if the overpayment is recoverable, SSS has the discretion not to recover it from you (eg, if recovery would cause you financial hardship) and also should use its discretion when considering the method of recovery.[39]

If an overpayment of a Scottish benefit is recoverable, SSS can recover it by making deductions from ongoing payments of Scottish child payment, child disability payment (CDP) and adult disability payment (ADP).[40] It is expected that this rule will apply to any other Scottish benefits which are paid on an ongoing basis, once they are introduced.[41]

The level of deductions should be reasonable, taking into acount your financial circumstances.[42] If you are unhappy with a decision about deductions for an overpayment from Scottish child payment, CDP or ADP you can challenge this by asking for a 'redetermination' and, if necessary, by appealing (see Chapter 80).[43]

If a Scottish benefit is paid in respect of a person following her/his death, it can be recovered from her/his estate.[44]

Challenging an overpayment determination

If you disagree with a determination about an overpayment, you can ask for a redetermination (see p1755). If you are still unhappy following the redetermination, you can appeal (see p1764). **Note:** a 'determination' has a specific legal meaning.[45] Some decisions made about overpayments (eg, that an overpayment is recoverable from you) may not constitute a determination and so you may not be able to challenge them using the redetermination and appeal process. In this situation, you should seek advice and consider making a complaint (see p1750), involving your MSP and/or considering judical review action (see Chapter 59). At the time of writing, this issue was under consultation and the situation may change. See AskCPAG and CPAG's *Welfare Rights Bulletin* for updates.

4. Fraud

The following are offences under the Social Security (Scotland) Act 2018.[46]
- Trying to obtain assistance by deceit. This means that you provide, or cause someone else to provide, misleading or false information with the intention of obtaining a Scottish benefit to which you would not otherwise be entitled.
- Without reasonable excuse, failing to notify a change of circumstances as soon as resonably practicable. This must be a change which you have a duty to notify and which you ought to have known would result in your entitlement stopping or being reduced. It is also an offence to cause another person to fail to notify a change of circumstances.

The possible penalties if you are convicted of fraud include a fine and/or imprisonment.[47]

Powers of investigation

An 'authorised officer' is authorised by Social Security Scotland (SSS) to carry out certain investigations into suspected fraud.[48] An authorised officer can require a person or body to provide information (including electronic records[49]) relevant to the fraud investigation.

The following organisations cannot be required to provide information, unless the information relates to the employment of a person by that organisation or to the nature of services provided by an individual to the organisation:[50]
- those whose main purpose is providing free advice or information on social security, housing or debt;
- law centres;
- voluntary organisations providing accommodation, support or advocacy services to people who have experienced domestic abuse;
- certain advocacy services.

Authorised officers can request permission to enter premises, but not if the premises are occupied as someone's home.[51] They can only enter and search

12

Part 12: Scottish social security benefits
Chapter 79: Claiming Scottish benefits and getting paid
5. Complaints

premises with the permission of the occupier or, if the premises are not occupied, of the owner.[52]

In the context of a fraud investigation, it is an offence to:[53]

- intentionally delay an authorised officer in her/his investigation;
- fail to comply with any requirement, without good reason;
- knowingly provide false or misleading material;
- destroy information with the intention of avoiding compliance.

The possible penalty for this type of offence is a fine.[54]

Interviews under caution

If you are suspected of fraud, SSS may invite you to take part in a formal interview, called an 'interview under caution'. Taking part in this interview is voluntary.[55] You should be sent a letter inviting you to attend and SSS should be flexible about where and when the interview takes place, taking account of any particular needs you have.[56] You should be cautioned before the interview starts. This means you should be told that you do not need to say anything and that anything you do say during the interview can be used in evidence in court if there is a criminal prosecution. The interview will be recorded and you are entitled to ask for a copy of the recording.[57] You can have someone with you at the interview for support – eg, a friend, relative, advocate, welfare rights worker or solicitor.[58] If it appears that, because of a disability, you are unable to understand the process or you are unable to communicate effectively, SSS must make arrangements to have a suitable person present at the interview to provide support.[59]

5. **Complaints**

If you are unhappy about the way you have been treated by Social Security Scotland (SSS), you can complain. Your complaint can be about any issue concerning how your claim has been handled or how you have been treated. This includes matters such as delays, discourtesy, poor administration, the behaviour of staff and bad advice.

You should complain by contacting SSS by telephone (0800 182 2222; Relay UK service available; if you are a British Sign Language user, you can use the contactSCOTLAND app); in writing (Social Security Scotland, PO Box 10304, Dundee DD1 9FZ) or online at socialsecurity.gov.scot/contact/feedback/how-to-make-a-complaint. SSS states that you should normally make your complaint within six months of the event you wish to complain about or of finding out that you have reason to complain.

SSS's complaints procedure has two stages.[60] In stage one, called 'frontline response', SSS states that it will give you a response within one to five working days unless there are exceptional circumstances. If you are unhappy with the response after stage one, you can ask for your complaint to be dealt with at stage two, which is called an 'investigation'. You should make your request for a stage two investigation within:

- six months of the event you wish to complain about; *or*
- two months of the stage one response, if this is later.

If your complaint requires investigation it can be dealt with directly at stage two, without needing to go through the initial stage one process. You can also request that your complaint is dealt with directly at stage two level. At stage two, SSS should acknowledge your complaint within three working days. SSS should attempt to resolve your complaint and, where it cannot resolve it, provide you with a full response, normally within 20 working days. If it takes longer than 20 working days, SSS should keep you updated about how long it will take.

The SSS charter states that staff will listen to complaints, learn and improve the service.[61]

If you are still unhappy after your complaint has been considered by SSS, you can complain to the Scottish Public Services Ombudsman. Usually, you must complain to the Ombudsman within 12 months of the event you are complaining about. Use the online complaint form at spso.org.uk/complain/form/start or telephone 0800 377 7330.

Notes

1. **Claims**
   1 **SCP** Sch para 1 SCP Regs
      Other benefits ss37 and 38 SS(S)A 2018
   2 ss85A and 85B SS(S)A 2018
   3 **SCP** Sch para 1(4) SCP Regs
      Other benefits s38(5) SS(S)A 2018
   4 **SCP** Sch para 25(1) SCP Regs
      Other benefits s54(1) SS(S)A 2018
   5 **SCP** Sch para 25(2) SCP Regs
      Other benefits s54(2) SS(S)A 2018
   6 **SCP** Sch para 2 SCP Regs
      Other benefits s39 SS(S)A 2018
   7 ss85A and 85B SS(S)A 2018
   8 s85B(6) SS(S)A 2018
   9 s85D SS(S)A 2018 (still to be commenced at time of writing)
   10 s85B(3)(b) and(7) SS(S)A 2018
   11 s85B(3)(a) and (4) SS(S)A 2018 (yet to be commenced)
   12 s85A SS(S)A 2018
   13 s85A(5C) SS(S)A 2018
   14 ss85A(6) and 85B(11) SS(S)A 2018
   15 s85A(5A) SS(S)A 2018
   16 s85A(5C) SS(S)A 2018
   17 s85B(12) SS(S)A 2018
   18 s85B(14) SS(S)A 2018
   19 s85B(16) SS(S)A 2018
   20 **SCP** Sch para 28 SCP Regs
      Other benefits s59 SS(S)A 2018
   21 s10 SS(S)A 2018

12

Part 12: Scottish social security benefits
Chapter 79: Claiming Scottish benefits and getting paid
Notes

22 Reg 2 SS(ASS)(S) Regs; Social Security
Advocacy Service Standards, available at
gov.scot/publications/social-security-
advocacy-service-standards
23 para 8 Social Security Advocacy Service
Standards, available at gov.scot/
publications/social-security-advocacy-
service-standards

2. **Getting paid**
24 **SCP** reg 17 SCP Regs
   Other benefits s24 SS(S)A 2018
25 **SCP** Reg 22 SCP Regs
   Other benefits s26 SS(S)A 2018
26 **SCP** Sch para 26 SCP Regs
   Other benefits s56 SS(S)A 2018
27 **SCP** Sch para 26(2)(c) SCP Regs
   Other benefits s56(2)(c) SS(S)A 2018
28 **SCP** Reg 19A SCP Regs
   CDP Reg 26A DACYP(S) Regs
   ADP Reg 38 DAWAP(S)Regs
29 **SCP** Reg 19B SCP Regs
   CDP Reg 26B DACYP(S) Regs
   ADP Reg 39 DAWAP(S) Regs
30 **SCP** Reg 19C SCP Regs
   CDP Reg 26C DACYP(S) Regs
   ADP Reg 40 DAWAP(S0 Regs
31 **SCP** Reg 19D SCP Regs
   CDP Reg 26D DACYP(S) Regs
   ADP Reg 41 DAWAP(S) Regs
32 **SCP** Reg 19E SCP Regs
   CDP Reg 26E DACYP(S) Regs
   ADP Reg 42 DAWAP(S) Regs
33 **SCP** Reg 19F SCP Regs
   CDP Reg 26F DACYP(S) Regs
   ADP Reg 43 DAWAP(S) Regs

3. **Overpayments**
34 **SCP** Sch paras 29 and 30 SCP Regs
   Other benefits ss63 and 64 SS(S)A
   2018
35 **SCP** Sch para 30(2) SCP Regs
   Other benefits s64(2) SS(S)A 2018
36 **SCP** Sch para 30(1)(b) SCP Regs
   Other benefits s64(1)(b) SS(S)A 2018
37 **SCP** Sch para 30(3) SCP Regs
   Other benefits s64(3) SS(S)A 2018
38 **SCP** Sch para 29(2) SCP Regs
   Other benefits s63(2) SS(S)A 2018
39 **SCP** Sch para 31(2) SCP Regs
   Other benefits s65 SS(S)A 2018
40 **SCP** Reg 20(3) SPC Regs
   CDP Reg 27 DACYP(S) Regs
   ADP Reg 44 DAWAP(S) Regs
41 Schs 2 para 10(b), 5 para 15(b), 7 para
   12(b) and 9 para 11(b) SS(S)A 2018

42 **SCP** Reg 20(3) and (4) SCP Regs
   CDP Reg 27(2) DACYP(S) Regs
   ADP Reg 44(2) DAWAP(S) Regs
43 **SCP** Sch paras 13, 14 and 19 SCP Regs
   CDP ss25, 41 and 45 SS(S)A 2018; reg
   34 DACYP(S) Regs
   ADP ss25, 41 and 45 SS(S)A 2018; reg
   51 DAWAP(S) Regs
44 **SCP** Sch para 33 SCP Regs
   Other benefits s69 SS(S)A 2018
45 **SCP** Reg 13 SCP Regs
   Other benefits s25 SS(S)A 2018

4. **Fraud**
46 ss71-73 and 80A SS(S)A 2018
47 ss71(3), 72(4), 73(4) and 80 SS(S)A
   2018
48 Regs 2 and 3 SSA(IO)(S) Regs
49 Regs 4 and 7 SSA(IO)(S) Regs
50 Regs 5 and 7 SSA(IO)(S) Regs
51 Reg 8(2) SSA(IO)(S) Regs
52 Reg 8(1) SSA(IO)(S) Regs
53 Reg 9 SSA(IO)(S) Regs
54 Reg 9 SSA(IO)(S) Regs
55 SSS, *Code of Practice for Investigations*,
   para 71
56 SSS, *Code of Practice for Investigations*,
   para 72
57 SSS, *Code of Practice for Investigations*,
   para 74
58 SSS, *Code of Practice for Investigations*,
   para 76
59 SSS, *Code of Practice for Investigations*,
   para 78

5. **Complaints**
60 SSS, *Complaints Handling Procedure*, April
   2021
61 SSS, *Our Charter*, p6

Chapter 80

Getting a determination changed

This chapter covers:

This chapter applies to the Scottish benefits listed on p1670. Part 9 of this *Handbook* explains the rules on decisions and appeals for other benefits. The information in this chapter only applies to carer's allowance supplement if you have to claim it because you live outside the UK.[1]

Key facts

- If you claim a Scottish benefit correctly, you must be given a 'determination' of your entitlement.
- If you disagree with a determination, you can ask Social Security Scotland (SSS) to remake it. This is called a 'redetermination'.
- In some other situations (eg, if your award may no longer be correct), your entitlement must be determined again.
- If you disagree with a redetermination, you can appeal to the First-tier Tribunal for Scotland Social Security Chamber.
- If the First-tier Tribunal applies the law wrongly, you can appeal to the Upper Tribunal for Scotland.
- If you are challenging a determination that reduces or stops your child disability payment or adult disability payment, you may be able to get short-term assistance. This stops your payments from reducing straight away.
- You can make a different kind of 'process appeal' if you claimed a Scottish benefit or requested a redetermination in the wrong way.
- There are strict time limits to request a redetermination and appeal.

12

Part 12: Scottish social security benefits
Chapter 80: Getting a determination changed
1. Determinations of entitlement

Time limits

For Scottish benefits, you are treated as receiving something sent to you by SSS or a Scottish tribunal by post or email 48 hours after it was sent, unless you can show you received it later.[2] In practice, this means that a time limit normally runs from two days (including weekends and bank holidays) after the date something was sent to you.

This rule *does not* apply if you are given a written decision by hand (eg, after a First-tier Tribunal hearing), and to some time limits to challenge tribunal decisions, which instead run from the date on which the decision is sent to you.[3]

1. **Determinations of entitlement**

If you claim a Scottish benefit in the correct way (see p1743), Social Security Scotland (SSS) must make a 'determination' of your entitlement and notify you of this in a way that gives you a record of it – eg, by letter.[4] The determination notice must tell you what the determination is, the reasons for it and about your right to challenge it by requesting a redetermination.

For adult disability payment, if you had an assessment, the determination notice tells you that you can request a copy of the assessment report (see p1688).[5]

If you do not get a determination after making a claim, see p1755.

Note: some Scottish benefits can be awarded without you having to claim them. See the chapter of this *Handbook* about the benefit to see whether it can be awarded without a claim.

Determinations of entitlement

A determination of your entitlement will include 'decisions' about:[6]
– whether you are eligible for the benefit; *and*
– if you are eligible, what form your entitlement should take (this may include reducing your payment to recover an overpayment – see p1748); *and*
– for ongoing benefits (ie, not one-off payments), what your entitlement will be in the future.

If you are refused a Scottish benefit which is a one-off payment for a particular event because you made your claim too soon (eg, if you claimed a pregnancy and baby payment when you were only 15 weeks pregnant), the determination notice must also tell you that you can make another claim.[7]

Note: separate rules allow you to claim ongoing benefits in advance (see the chapter of this *Handbook* about the benefit you are claiming for details).

If you disagree with a determination, you can challenge it by requesting a redetermination (see p1755). There is a time limit to do so. You must request a redetermination before you can appeal.

There are also situations in which SSS must determine your entitlement again, even if you are now too late to request a redetermination (see p1758).

If you do not get a determination after you make a claim

If there is a delay in getting a determination after you claim a Scottish benefit, contact SSS and check that it has received your claim. Make sure that you do not need to provide anything else before you can get a determination. If your claim has been properly made and you are unhappy with the delay, you can make a complaint (see p1750).

If you claim a benefit in the wrong way, or do not provide some evidence that you need to send with a claim, SSS does not have to make a determination.[8] You must be told if your claim will not be determined, and of your right to appeal against this 'process decision' (see p1781).[9] If this happens, you should also make another claim as soon as possible if you can.[10] There may be a time limit to make a claim. See the chapter of this *Handbook* about the benefit for details of how to claim and the time limit to do so.

2. Redeterminations

Any 'determination' of your entitlement to a Scottish benefit (see p1754) can be challenged by requesting a redetermination, if you disagree with it.[11]

If you request a redetermination, every aspect of the previous determination is considered again. If you have been awarded some benefit, the amount of it could be reduced as a result. You can make clear exactly what you disagree with, but there is no guarantee that the decision maker will not change other aspects of your entitlement. Seek advice if you have been awarded some benefit and are considering requesting a redetermination.

Has something changed since the date of the determination?

When Social Security Scotland (SSS) is redetermining your entitlement (or the First-tier Tribunal decides an appeal), the law arguably does not prevent it from taking into account changes that have happened since the previous determination was made.[12] At the time of writing, it is unclear how the lack of such a rule will be interpreted by the Upper Tribunal and the courts.

As the law is unclear, contact SSS and explain the situation if something changes after the date of the determination. You should also check if SSS is now required to a make a new determination of your entitlement as a result (see p1758). For grants and one-off payments, any changes must be to your circumstances *at the time you originally claimed*.

If you are not already receiving an ongoing payment of the benefit, you should make another claim, even if you have already requested a redetermination.[13] However, for

12

Part 12: Scottish social security benefits
Chapter 80: Getting a determination changed
2. Redeterminations

ongoing benefits, making a new claim will limit the effect of a tribunal's decision, if you later win your appeal.[14]

If you are now too late to make a new claim (or a new claim or increased award cannot be backdated), you can argue that SSS (or the tribunal) can still award you the benefit, even if the determination was correct at the time it was made. Seek expert advice about how to present your case.

Who can request a redetermination

You can request a redetermination if you claimed a Scottish benefit, are claiming as someone else's appointee (see p1744) or have legal authority to act for someone – eg, as a guardian or judicial factor, or the executor of someone who has died.[15]

How to request a redetermination

SSS decides how you must request a redetermination.[16] This is currently by:[17]
- completing the form sent to you with the determination of entitlement; *or*
- telephoning 0800 182 2222; *or*
- if you have hearing or speech difficulties, using Relay UK (18001 then 0300 244 4000); *or*
- if you use British Sigh Language, via the contactSCOTLAND app.

Note:
- You may have to request a redetermination differently for different Scottish benefits. Check your determination notice carefully to see what you must do.
- If your child disability payment (CDP) or adult disability payment (ADP) award has been reduced, you may be able to get short-term assistance while your redetermination request is being considered (see p1778).
- If you only agree with some aspects of the determination, make this clear in your redetermination request. However, other aspects of the determination may also be changed if you request a redetermination.

If you request a redetermination in the wrong way, SSS should inform you of this (and does not have to redetermine your entitlement).[18] You can appeal against this 'process decision' (see p1781). If you are still within the time limit to do so (see p1757), you should also request a redetermination in the correct way, as you cannot be sure that you will win your appeal.

For CDP, ADP, child winter heating assistance or short-term assistance, your request for a redetermination must be received by SSS within 42 days of you being notified of the determination.[19] For other Scottish benefits, the time limit is 31 days.[20] You are normally treated as being notified of the determination two days after it is sent to you (see p1754).

* *

Example
Fleur is refused a young carer grant. The determination letter is dated 1 July. She is treated as receiving it on 3 July. The time limit to request a redetermination is 31 days. Fleur's redetermination request must be received by SSS on or before 2 August.

* *

f you miss the time limit

If you miss the time limit above, but your redetermination request is received within a time limit of one year after you were notified of the determination, your entitlement is still redetermined if you have 'good reason' for not making the request sooner.[21] The one-year time limit can be extended if your good reason is related to coronavirus.[22] You should explain why your request is late.

* *

Good reason
The law does not define 'good reason' for missing a time limit. If you think that your request may arrive late, explain in detail why you did not make it sooner. Your reasons might include that:
– you were away from home and so did not receive the determination;
– you did not understand the determination, or what you had to do next;
– you were affected by illness (of yourself or someone you had to look after);
– you were waiting for further evidence (but do not wait until you get such evidence before requesting a redetermination, if this means that you might miss the time limit or you have already missed it);
– you have a condition which makes it hard for you to deal with letters.
Any other reasons that apply in your case may also be relevant, so include them as well.

* *

If SSS does not accept your reasons for missing the time limit, it does not redetermine your entitlement. You should be notified of this, and can then appeal against the 'process decision' not to redetermine your entitlement (see p1781).[23]

After you request a redetermination

Once you have made a valid request for a redetermination, SSS must redetermine your entitlement.[24] If you have additional evidence that shows why the determination was wrong, send a copy of it to SSS. If something has changed since the date of the determination, see p1755.

The time limit for a redetermination to be carried out

There is a time limit for SSS to redetermine your entitlement.[25] For CDP and ADP, this is 56 *calendar* days.[26] For other Scottish benefits, this is 16 *working* days.[27] The time limit normally runs from the day SSS receives your redetermination request.

Part 12: Scottish social security benefits
Chapter 80: Getting a determination changed
3. Other ways to get a determination changed

However, the time limit runs from the date SSS (or if you had to make a proces[s] appeal, the First-tier Tribunal) decides to accept your request if you:[28]

- requested a redetermination late; *or*
- made a redetermination request in the wrong form (except for Scottish chil[d] payment).

Working days

A 'working day' is any day other than a Saturday, Sunday or bank holiday.[29] A bank holiday is not the same as a public holiday, as public holidays may not be the same in different areas. There is a list of bank holidays at mygov.scot/scotland-bank-holidays.

If your entitlement is redetermined within the time limit above, you must be:[30]

- notified of the redetermination outcome; *and*
- given the reasons for it; *and*
- told that you can appeal if you disagree with it (see p1764); *and*
- sent an appeal form.

If your entitlement is *not* redetermined within the time limit, you must b[e] informed of this.[31] You then have the right to appeal to the First-tier Tribuna[l] against the original determination (see p1764).[32]

Note: if you are told that you can appeal because your redetermination reques[t] has not been dealt with in time, SSS can still redetermine your entitlement at [a] later date.[33] Even if you are told that you can wait for a redetermination befor[e] appealing, you should appeal within the 31-day time limit to do so. The time limit runs from the date that you are told that you have the right of appeal.

---

3. Other ways to get a determination changed

A 'determination without application' is the legal term for when your entitlemen[t] to a Scottish benefit must be determined *without* you making a claim. This coul[d] be because the original determination was wrong for a specific reason, or you ge[t] an ongoing benefit and something has changed.

'Determinations without application' are similar to certain types of 'revision' decisions and all 'supersession' decisions for other benefits (see Chapter 56).

Your entitlement must be determined again if you were refused a benefit, o[r] your award was too low, and:

- (except for young carer grants) this was due to an 'official error' (see p1759); *or*
- (except for child disability payment (CDP) and adult disability payment (ADP)[)] you have now been awarded a 'qualifying benefit' (see the chapter of thi[s] *Handbook* about the benefit you were refused).

Your entitlement must also be determined again if:
- you get CDP, ADP or Scottish child payment and your award may not be correct (see p1760 for CDP and ADP, and p1734 for Scottish child payment); *or*
- you get Scottish child payment, CDP or ADP and Social Security Scotland (SSS) makes or amends a deduction to recover an overpayment (see p1748); *or*
- you have been overpaid child winter heating assistance due to an official error (see p1673).

If you disagree with a determination made under any of these rules, you can request a redetermination (see p1755).

Note:
- If your entitlement must be determined again, there is no time limit to ask for this. However, in some situations your entitlement cannot be determined again if you have already requested a redetermination or appealed.
- For ongoing benefits, there are rules setting out when any change to your award takes effect, so you should explain the situation to SSS as soon as possible. For Scottish child payment, see p1734, and for ADP and CDP, see p1760.
- If you have been awarded a benefit and ask for a further determination, the new determination will completely replace any previous determination made for the same period or event.[34] So your benefit could decrease, even if you think it should increase. Seek advice if you get a benefit and are unsure what effect asking for another determination will have.

If you do not get a determination

SSS must normally determine your entitlement again if one of the situations on p1758 applies. The only exception is that in some cases another determination cannot be made if you have already requested a redetermination or appealed. See the section that is relevant to your situation for whether this restriction applies.

If you have asked for a further determination or reported a change and there is a delay, contact SSS and check whether it will make a new determination. If SSS does not make a new determination, you *cannot* request a redetermination.[35] Your only options are to complain (see p1750) or apply for a judicial review (see Chapter 59).

If there was an official error

If you were refused a Scottish benefit (except a young carer grant) or awarded less than you should have been, and SSS later establishes that this was due to an 'official error', it must make another determination.[36] The new determination normally takes effect from the same date as the previous determination did.[37] However, for ADP or CDP an earlier date can be set if it would be 'unjust' not to do so (see p1761).

Part 12: Scottish social security benefits
Chapter 80: Getting a determination changed
3. Other ways to get a determination changed

A new determination *cannot* be made under these rules (except for child winter heating assistance – see p1674) if you have requested a redetermination and your request is being considered, or if you have appealed against the determination.[3] If you have requested a redetermination or appealed, tell SSS or the First-tier Tribunal what the error was.[39] Any error can then arguably be corrected by the appeals process.

> **Official error**
>
> 'Official error' is a legal mistake made by someone acting on behalf of the Scottish Ministers (ie, SSS or another part of the Scottish government) or on behalf of a Minister of the Crown – ie, the DWP, HM Revenue and Customs or (for Best Start grants and funeral support payments) local authority staff processing a housing benefit claim.[40] However, a mistake is not an official error if it was 'materially contributed to' by anyone else. So, if you or someone helping you made a mistake, there is not an official error even if SSS also made a mistake.
>
> In practice, this is similar to the definition for other benefits (see p1266). However, a mistake in a determination can also arguably count as an official error even if it was only shown to be wrong by a later Upper Tribunal or court decision.[41]

If you realise that there has been an official error and have missed the time limit to request a redetermination (see p1757), tell SSS what it is and ask it for another determination. There is no time limit to do so. If SSS does not make a new determination and you cannot instead make a new claim for the benefit, see p1759.

If SSS makes a determination and you disagree with it, you can request a redetermination (see p1755).

If your disability benefit award may not be correct

If you are entitled to CDP or ADP, a determination of your entitlement must be made if:

- the award is reviewed at the end of the period specified in your previous determination (see p1761); *or*
- your award was too low due to an official error (see p1759); *or*
- there is a change in your circumstances that may affect your award (including if you are now terminally ill or the claimant has died) (see p1761); *or*
- your award was too high due to an 'error' in the last determination (see p1763); *or*
- the previous determination was made in ignorance of a 'material fact' (see p1763); *or*
- the amount of disability living allowance (DLA) or personal independence payment (PIP) you were entitled to before your award began changes (see p1764).

12

If you think that one of these situations applies, contact SSS and ask it for a determination. A further determination could increase or decrease your award. Seek advice if you are unsure of the risks. See the section about your situation for the date from which your award changes.

If SSS does not make a determination when you ask it to, see p1759.

Flexibility of when changes to your award take effect

In most situations, SSS can increase your entitlement from an earlier date than the rules provide for, or decrease it from a later date. This only applies if it would be 'unjust' not to do so.[42] When requesting a determination, make clear if you think that the normal rules are unfair, and ask for a different date to be set.

However, if SSS uses this flexiblity and you request a redetermination or appeal because you want your new entitlement to take effect from a date which is more generous, SSS or the First-tier Tribunal can do the opposite, and set a *less* favourable date. Seek advice about the risks if you want to challenge the effective date of a determination.

If your award is being reviewed

Your entitlement to CDP or ADP must be determined again at the end of the period (if any) specified in a determination notice.[43] For how CDP reviews are expected to work, see p1717. For how ADP reviews are expected to work, see p1690.

If your award is changed, the date from which your benefit changes depends on whether it increases or decreases (see p1762).

If your award is not changed, the new determination is likely to take effect from the date it is made.[44]

If you think that the new determination is wrong, you can request a redetermination (see p1755).

If there has been a change in your circumstances

Note: different rules apply if the change is that:
- you are no longer ordinarily resident in Scotland (see p1762); *or*
- you are now terminally ill (see p1685); *or*
- you reported a change during the process of being transferred from PIP to ADP (see p1692).

When you are awarded ADP or CDP, SSS writes to you and tells you what changes you need to report. In practice, even if you are unsure if a change is relevant, you should report it anyway. If you do not report a change that affects your entitlement, you may miss out if your award should increase, or be overpaid if your award should decrease.

12

Part 12: Scottish social security benefits
Chapter 80: Getting a determination changed
3. Other ways to get a determination changed

If you report a change that would possibly affect the amount of your benefit SSS must make another determination. If your award is changed, the date from which your benefit changes depends on whether it increases or decreases.

If your award is not changed after you report a change but you get a determination notice, you can request a redetermination.

If SSS does not make a new determination after you report a change, see p1759

When a determination following a change of circumstances takes effect

If your entitlement or payment is increased, the new determination takes effect from:

- if you reported the change:[45]
  - within one month of it happening (13 months if you had good reason for reporting the change late), the date of the change; or
  - outside the time limits above, the date you reported the change; or
- if the above rule does not apply, the date on which the new determination is made.[46]

Note: an earlier date can be set if it would be 'unjust' not to do so (see p1761).

If your award is decreased, or entitlement ends, the new determination takes effect from:

- if you knowingly fail to report a change that you had been told you had to report, or fail to report it as soon as is reasonably practicable, the date on which you should have reported the change;[47] or
- the date on which the new determination is made.[48]

Note: a later date can be set if it would be 'unjust' not to do so (see p1761).

When should you have reported a change that reduces your entitlement?

You should always report a change as soon as you realise that your benefit might be affected. If SSS decides that you have been overpaid because you reported a change late, check any letters that you have from SSS carefully to see when you ought to have reported it. If the instructions were not clear, you may be able to argue that you did not need to report it immediately (and so your entitlement decreases from a later date). This will depend on the wording of the letters and exactly what has changed.

Even if this does not apply, in some situations you can argue that it would be 'unjust' not to decrease your entitlement from a later date (see p1761).

If you have moved elsewhere in the UK

If you move out of Scotland to elsewhere in the UK, you will no longer be entitled to ADP or CDP as you are no longer 'ordinarily resident' in Scotland (see p1550).
Note:

- This rule does not apply if you go into hospital, residential care or prison elsewhere in the UK.[49] For how your benefit is affected in these situations, see Chapter 42.
- For how your benefit is affected if you have moved abroad (outside the UK), see p1625.

If you move elsewhere in the UK, your CDP entitlement ends:[50]
- if you tell SSS less than 13 weeks after you move, 13 weeks after you *tell SSS* about the move; *or*
- 13 weeks after you moved, if you tell SSS either before moving or 13 weeks or more after moving.

If you move elsewhere in the UK, your ADP entitlement ends 13 weeks after you move, whenever you inform SSS of the move.[51]

If your entitlement was too high due to an error

If your CDP or ADP award was too high due to an 'error', a new determination is made.[52] An error means that the previous determination was either wrong, or was based on incorrect information or an incorrect assumption (including if SSS failed to correct your award when it discovered an error).[53]

The new determination normally takes effect from the same date as the previous determination did.[54] However, a later date can be set if it would be 'unjust' not to do so (see p1761).

For whether any resulting overpayment is recoverable from you, see p1748.

Note: a new determination *cannot* be made under this rule if you have requested a redetermination or appealed against the previous determination.[55] SSS can instead reduce your award in a redetermination, or argue that the First-tier Tribunal should do so.

If the previous determination was made in ignorance of a material fact

If the previous CDP or ADP determination was made in ignorance of a 'material fact' which might have affected your entitlement, a new determination must be made.[56] A material fact is likely to mean the same as for other benefits (see p1277).

A determination under this rule that changes your entitlement normally takes effect from the date it is made.[57] However, an earlier date can be set if your entitlement increases, or a later date if it decreases, if it would be 'unjust' not to do so (see p1761).

Note:
- In practice, it is extremely unlikely that SSS will use this rule to decrease your entitlement, as it is likely to decide that any ignorance of a material fact also counts as an 'error', meaning that you have been overpaid (see above).
- If you are not too late to do so, request a redetermination (see p1755) if you realise that your award may be too low and the previous determination was made in ignorance of a material fact.

12

Part 12: Scottish social security benefits
Chapter 80: Getting a determination changed
4. Appealing to the First-tier Tribunal

- If you *are* too late to request a redetermination, think carefully about whether there has also been a change in your circumstances that should increase your award (see p1761), as a new determination based on a change of circumstance may increase your award from an earlier date.

If your previous disability benefit award changes

In some circumstances, your previous DLA or PIP award could be changed after you have transferred to CDP or ADP. For example, you might have appealed against a DLA decision and win your appeal after being transferred to CDP. If your DLA or PIP award alters, your entitlement to CDP or ADP must be determined again.[58] Your new award will normally be the same as the amended DLA or PIP award.

The determination always takes effect from the date your CDP or ADP award started.[59] You *cannot* argue that a different date should apply instead.

For how the transfer process works, see p1691 for ADP and p1717 for CDP.

4. Appealing to the First-tier Tribunal

You can only appeal against a determination of entitlement to a Scottish benefit after requesting a redetermination (see p1755).

Appeals about Scottish benefits are decided by the Social Security Chamber of the First-tier Tribunal for Scotland, part of the Scottish Courts and Tribunals Service. Some appeal rules for Scottish benefits are different from the rules for other benefits. This chapter refers you to Chapter 57 where the rules are the same.

Some of the terms used in the Scottish tribunal rules and the UK tribunal rules are different, but have the same meaning.

UK tribunal rules	Scottish tribunal rules
Direction	Order
Strike out a case	Dismiss a case
Stay proceedings	Sist proceedings
Summons	Citation
Judge	Legal member

Who can appeal

If you can request a redetermination (see p1756), you can make an appeal.

Note: for Scottish benefits, the rules do not explicitly allow your representative to make an appeal for you, so you should sign the appeal form yourself, even if you have a representative helping you to appeal.[60]

How to appeal

You must appeal in the way required by Social Security Scotland (SSS). An appeal form is sent to you with your redetermination notice or notice that the redetermination time limit has been missed.[61] The appeal form must be sent to SSS.[62]

SSS also currently allows an appeal to be submitted by telephone (0800 182 2222), giving details of your appeal.[63] If you have hearing or speech difficulties, you can submit an appeal via Relay UK (18001 and then 0300 244 4000) or, if you use British Sign Language, using the contactSCOTLAND-BSL app.[64]

Check what you must do to submit your appeal in the letter telling you about your right of appeal, as how you can appeal may change.

Note: if you are appealing against a determination that reduced your award of child disability payment (CDP) or adult disability payment (ADP), you may be able to get short-term assistance until your appeal is decided (see p1778).

Making sure your appeal is valid

Your appeal must be submitted in the required way (see above). To be valid, the appeal must give:[65]
- your name and address; *and*
- the name and address of your representative, if you have one (see p1311 – the rules are the same as for other benefits except that you must still be sent all relevant documents, even if you have a representative);[66] *and*
- a postal or email address where documents can be sent to you; *and*
- details of the determination you are challenging (the benefit name and date of the determination or redetermination); *and*
- why you disagree with the determination; *and*
- if your appeal is late (see below), the reasons why you did not appeal sooner.

If you cannot provide some of this information, you should still submit your appeal as soon as possible, and explain why it is incomplete. The First-tier Tribunal can waive these requirements,[67] but for the purposes of deciding whether your appeal is late (see below), you have not appealed until you provide all the above information (or the requirement is waived by the tribunal).[68]

The time limit to appeal

Your appeal must be received by SSS within **31 days** of you being notified of the redetermination (or that the redetermination time limit was missed).[69] You are normally treated as receiving a notification two days after it was sent (see p1754).

If you miss the time limit

If you miss the time limit above, but your appeal is received within a time limit of one year after you were notified of the redetermination (or that the

Part 12: Scottish social security benefits
Chapter 80: Getting a determination changed
4. Appealing to the First-tier Tribunal

redetermination time limit was missed), it can still be admitted.[70] The one-year time limit can be extended if your good reason is related to coronavirus.[71]

You must explain why your appeal is late. If the First-tier Tribunal accepts that you have good reason for not appealing in time, your appeal goes ahead, unless your good reason is *not* related to coronavirus and you have missed the one-year time limit. For some things that may count as good reason, see p1757.

After you appeal

As soon as it receives your appeal (even if you have missed the time limit), SSS must send it to the First-tier Tribunal, along with the information used to make the determination, and tell you that it has done so.[72] If your appeal is missing some of the required information or is late, the tribunal may ask for more information to decide whether or not your appeal should go ahead.

The response

Once the First-tier Tribunal decides that your appeal is valid, it informs you and SSS of this in writing.[73] SSS then has 31 days to produce a response to the appeal and send it to the tribunal.[74] See p1314 for the information included in the response (the rules are the same as for other benefits). The tribunal sends the response to you, and any representative you have.[75]

When you are sent the response you are also asked if you would like a hearing of your appeal. This is normally a good idea. See p1326, as the considerations are the same as for other benefits.

Providing additional information

You (or your representative) can make written comments or submit evidence in reply to the SSS response. You must do so within 31 days of receiving it.[76] You are treated as receiving the response two days after it was sent (see p1754).[77] You can ask for this time limit to be extended.[78] Your request should be made in writing explaining why you need more time to reply. See p1315 – the considerations are the same as for appeals about other benefits.

What the First-tier Tribunal can do

The powers of the First-tier Tribunal are similar to those for appeals about other benefits. Most of the information on pp1312–25 also applies to appeals about Scottish benefits. See, in particular, the information about what the First-tier Tribunal can do on p1317 – the powers are similar, although the terms used are sometimes different (see p1764).[79] The most important differences for appeals about Scottish benefits are the following.

- Your appeal does not lapse (not go ahead) if the decision maker makes a new determination before it is heard (see p1769).
- The First-tier Tribunal *cannot* dispose of your appeal with a consent order.[80]

- If you fail to attend a hearing as a witness or produce a document when ordered to do so by the tribunal, this is potentially a criminal offence, but it is dealt with by the courts, not the Upper Tribunal.[81]
- The First-tier Tribunal cannot designate a 'lead case' (although it can join your appeal with another one if it raises the same issues).[82]
- There are no special rules about 'test cases',[83] but note that the First-tier Tribunal can sometimes 'sist' (delay) your case – eg, if it decides to wait for the outcome of another appeal.

isting appeals

The tribunal can make an order sisting your appeal.[84] This means that it is not decided straight away. This power might be used, for example, to wait for the Upper Tribunal or a court to decide another case that raises similar issues to yours.

You can ask the First-tier Tribunal to make another order which sets aside the order sisting your case.[85] Your application must be in writing and give reasons. For example, it might be urgent that your appeal is heard as soon as possible, or you may be able to argue that the issues in your case are not exactly the same as those in another case. However, it can sometimes be to your advantage to wait for another case to be decided, so get advice.

When your appeal can be dismissed

Note: 'dismissing' an appeal about a Scottish benefit means the same as 'striking out' an appeal about another benefit. If the First-tier Tribunal dismisses your appeal, it does not decide whether the determination was correct.[86]

The only situation in which the First-tier Tribunal *must* dismiss your appeal is if it does not have jurisdiction to hear your case.[87] In this case, it can transfer your case to another court or tribunal that does have jurisdiction. You must be given an opportunity to argue that your appeal should not be dismissed.[88]

The First-tier Tribunal *may* dismiss all or part of your appeal if:[89]

- you fail to comply with an order which warned you that your appeal could be dismissed if you did not comply; *or*
- there is no possibility of you meeting the conditions of entitlement for the benefit your appeal is about; *or*
- you have failed to co-operate with the First-tier Tribunal to the extent that it cannot deal with your case fairly. In this case, you must be given an opportunity to argue that your appeal should not be dismissed.[90]

You must be notified in writing that your appeal has been dismissed.[91]

The rules also allow the First-tier Tribunal to bar SSS from taking any further part in the appeal if it fails to co-operate or to comply with an order. See p1322 – the rules are the same as for other benefits.[92]

Note: in addition to requesting that your appeal is reinstated, it is arguable that you can request a statement of reasons for the decision dismissing your appeal,

12

Part 12: Scottish social security benefits
Chapter 80: Getting a determination changed
4. Appealing to the First-tier Tribunal

and then appeal against it (see p1771).[93] Requesting a reinstatement does not sto
the time limits to take these actions from running.

Reinstating an appeal that was dismissed for failing to comply with an order

If your appeal has been dismissed because you failed to comply with an order, yo
can request that it is reinstated. Your request must be made in writing, givin
reasons why the appeal should be reinstated, and be received by the First-tie
Tribunal within 31 days of you being notified of the dismissal.[94] You are normall
treated as being notified two days after a notice is sent (see p1754).[95] The First-tie
Tribunal can change this deadline (including shortening it), so check the notic
of dismissal carefully, and try to request a reinstatement within the time limit o₁
the notice.

Your appeal is only reinstated if the First-tier Tribunal accepts that you hav
'good reason' for not complying with the order.[96] 'Good reason' is not defined
You should explain in detail why you did not comply with the order.

Withdrawing an appeal

You can withdraw your appeal if you decide not to go ahead with it. See p1323 fo
details of how to withdraw an appeal, including when you need the First-tie
Tribunal's permission, and reinstating an appeal if you change your mind. Th
rules are similar to those for other benefits,[97] except that if you (or SSS) ask fo
your appeal to be reinstated:

- the time limit to do so is different; *and*
- the appeal is only reinstated if there is 'good reason' to do so.

If you apply for reinstatement of a withdrawn appeal, the First-tier Tribunal mus
receive your application within 31 days of you being notified that your appeal ha
been withdrawn. You are treated as being notified:[98]

- if you withdrew your appeal at a hearing in person, on that day; *or*
- if the withdrawal was notified in writing, two days after it was sent to you.

The First-tier Tribunal can change this deadline (including shortening it), s₀
check the withdrawal notice carefully, and try to request a reinstatement withir
the time limit.[99]

....

'Good reason'

The First-tier Tribunal only reinstates your appeal if it is satisfied that you have 'good
reason'. **'Good reason'** is not defined. Some examples might be if:

– you did not realise that even though you have been awarded some benefit, you did not
   get everything you could have got if you had won your appeal;
– you thought you had no chance of success, but have since received expert advice and
   realised that you have a good case for your appeal;

– you have received evidence which shows that you meet the entitlement conditions (if so, send a copy of it with your request);

– you were anxious about going to an appeal hearing, but have now realised that you can take someone along to support you.

You should mention any other reasons why you think your appeal should be reinstated.

f there is a new determination after you appeal

In some situations, SSS may determine your entitlement to the same benefit again after you have already appealed – eg, for most Scottish benefits if you are later awarded a 'qualifying benefit' following an appeal (see the chapter of this *Handbook* about the benefit that you claimed for details). If this happens, tell the First-tier Tribunal about the determination. Your appeal should continue unless you withdraw it.[100]

If you made another claim for the same benefit as well as appealing and this is successful before your appeal is decided, your appeal should continue unless you withdraw it.

If you are in one of these situations, get advice about whether to withdraw your appeal or not. See p1768 for how to withdraw an appeal.

How your appeal is decided

The rules about when your appeal is decided at a hearing, and what you should do to try to prove your case are similar to those for other benefits.[101] See pp1325–45 for details. If you need to request a postponement or adjournment of a hearing, see p1319. If you (or your representative) have special requirements for a hearing or days when you are not available, contact the First-tier Tribunal and explain this as soon as possible. You can contact the tribunal by telephone (0141 302 5858) or email (sscadmin@scotcourtstribunals.gov.uk).

The following aspects of appeal hearings are different for Scottish benefits.

- You are asked if you want your appeal dealt with at a hearing when the tribunal sends you the response of SSS to your appeal.
- While there are no rules suspending appeal hearings during the coronavirus pandemic, at the time of writing, all First-tier Tribunal hearings were taking place by telephone.[102] Video link hearings may be introduced. See AskCPAG and CPAG's *Welfare Rights Bulletin* for updates.
- If there is no other way to achieve the same result, the First-tier Tribunal can arguably consider changes in your circumstances that have occurred since the determination that you are appealing against.
- The First-tier Tribunal can determine your entitlement, so may consider things which were not raised by your appeal.[103] In practice, it may focus on why you disagree with the determination, but you should be prepared for other questions.

12

Part 12: Scottish social security benefits
Chapter 80: Getting a determination changed
4. Appealing to the First-tier Tribunal

- The First-tier Tribunal cannot carry out a medical examination at a hearing.[10]
- In addition to a representative, you can also be accompanied by a 'supporter'.[1] If s/he wants to give evidence as a witness, you should tell the tribunal thi before the hearing starts. The First-tier Tribunal can order that your supporte is excluded from the hearing until s/he gives evidence.[106] If this happens, yo can still ask the tribunal to let your supporter be present – eg, if it would b harder for you to give evidence without her/him in the room.[107]

Note:
- There is unlikely to be much caselaw about Scottish benefits during the lifetim of this *Handbook*. Some caselaw about other benefits may be relevant. Ge advice about whether caselaw is relevant to your situation if you are unsure.
- If your appeal is about the impact of 'physical condition or mental health' o entitlement to CDP or ADP, the First-tier Tribunal consists of a legal member, doctor and a disability expert. In other cases, there is only a legal member.[108]

The tribunal's decision

The First-tier Tribunal's decision can either uphold the previous determinatio (and so refuse your appeal), or it can make its own determination of you entitlement.[109]

The ways in which you can be told about the First-tier Tribunal's decision ar the same as for other benefits (see p1345).[110] However, there are importan differences in what you can do if you do not agree with the decision.

Record of proceedings

First-tier Tribunal appeals must normally be recorded. If the recording equipmen fails, a written record of proceedings must be produced instead.[111] If you request statement of reasons as you disagree with the tribunal's decision (see p1771), it is good idea to request a copy of the record of proceedings too.

The statement of reasons

If you want to challenge the tribunal's decision, it is always best to request written statement of reasons (and the record of proceedings), unless the decisior notice says it is also a full written statement of reasons. The more information yo have about a decision, the easier it is to show that the tribunal has made an erro of law.

The rules about written statements of reasons are similar to other benefits (se p1346),[112] but with the following differences.
- Your request for a statement of reasons must be received by the First-tie Tribunal within 31 days of you being notified of a decision. The tribunal car amend the time limit (including shortening it), so check your decisior notice.[113] You are treated as being notified:[114]

- on the day of the hearing if you are given the decision (orally or in writing) that day; *or*
- two days after the date it was sent to you.

- If the decision notice says that it includes a written summary of the decision, you do not have to request a full statement of reasons before requesting permission to appeal.[115] **Note:** it is usually best to request a statement of reasons anyway.[116]

f you disagree with the tribunal's decision

If you disagree with the First-tier Tribunal's decision, you can challenge it if you can show that it made an error of law (see p1357 – the meaning is largely the same as for other benefits[117]). You should always request a written statement of reasons for the tribunal's decision, unless you already have one, to help you to identify possible errors of law.

There are two ways to challenge a decision. You can:

- request a review of the tribunal's decision (see p1772); *or*
- apply straight away for permission to appeal to the Upper Tribunal (see p1774).

Should you request a review or permission to appeal to the Upper Tribunal?

You can choose how to challenge the First-tier Tribunal decision. Bear in mind the following points when deciding what to do, and get advice if you are unsure.

1. A request for a review is treated as also being a request for permission to appeal, unless you ask for this not to happen. You are later given an opportunity to change your mind before that application proceeds.

2. The time limit to apply for a review is shorter (but the First-tier Tribunal can extend it).

3. A review is an extra stage in the process of challenging a decision, but it gives you another opportunity to argue that the First-tier Tribunal made an error of law.

4. If you apply for a review, there may be a hearing (which will normally be before the legal member of the same First-tier Tribunal that heard your appeal). You will need to successfully argue that s/he made an error of law in deciding your case.

5. If there is an obvious error of law, a review may get the First-tier Tribunal's decision changed more quickly.

6. If a decision is set aside at review and there will be a further First-tier Tribunal decision, any short-term assistance you were getting (see p1778) will start again.

7. If the First-tier Tribunal decides to change its decision on review, it make further findings about the facts of your case at a hearing to help it make a new decision.

8. If you appeal to the Upper Tribunal, its decision may affect future cases which are similar to yours, while a review has no effect on anyone else's appeal.

12

Part 12: Scottish social security benefits
Chapter 80: Getting a determination changed
4. Appealing to the First-tier Tribunal

Note:
- The First-tier Tribunal can correct any accidental errors or omissions in it decision.[118] This does not affect the time limit to challenge the decision.
- For appeals about Scottish benefits, you *cannot* request that the First-tie Tribunal sets aside its decision on procedural grounds. There is also no rul that its decision must be set aside if you request permission to appeal against i and you and SSS agree that the tribunal has made an error of law.
- The First-tier Tribunal's powers to review its own decisions are very differen for Scottish benefits than for other benefits. The information in Chapter 5: about reviews does *not* apply to decisions about Scottish benefits.
- The tribunal can suspend its decision if you (or SSS) are challenging it.[119]
- SSS can apply for a review of, or permission to appeal against, a First-tie Tribunal decision in the same way as you can. If SSS requests a review of tribunal decision and you also disagree with it, consider requesting permission to appeal to the Upper Tribunal.
- Decisions in 'process appeals' cannot be reviewed or appealed to the Uppe Tribunal (see p1781).

Requesting a review

If you think that the First-tier Tribunal has made an error of law, you can ask it t review its decision. Your request for a review must:[120]
- be made in writing; *and*
- be received by the First-tier Tribunal within 14 days of:
  - the date of the decision; *or*
  - the date the written statement of reasons was sent to you, if later; *and*
- identify what error of law the tribunal has made (see p1357).

Note: unless you ask for it not to be, your review request is also treated as being request for permission to appeal to the Upper Tribunal.[121] This means tha following the review decision, you may still be able to appeal to the Uppe Tribunal.

Once the decision is made on your review request, you are asked if you want t continue with a request for permission to appeal.[122] You should do so, unless yo now think that the First-tier Tribunal's decision is correct – eg, if the review decision has given you what you asked for when you originally appealed.

If Social Security Scotland requests a review

If SSS has requested a review of a First-tier Tribunal decision, consider requesting permission to appeal to the Upper Tribunal (see p1774) if you also disagree with i – eg, if your appeal was partially successful, but you were not awarded everything you asked for by the First-tier Tribunal. The time limit for you to reques permission to appeal continues to run during a review, which may take some time.[123] If the review does not change the First-tier Tribunal's decision, you canno

12

challenge the review decision.[124] So you could lose the opportunity to challenge the original tribunal decision by waiting for a review. You can ask the First-tier Tribunal to extend the time limit to request permission to appeal, but there is no guarantee of success.[125]

How the First-tier Tribunal carries out a review

If the First-tier Tribunal considers that a review application is 'without merit' (eg, if it does not identify any arguable errors of law), it is refused immediately. You must be told of the reasons for this.[126] Otherwise, the tribunal sends you (and SSS) a notice:[127]

- setting a time limit for you or SSS to respond to the review request; *and*
- asking for views about whether a hearing of the review is needed; *and*
- (if it considers it appropriate) giving its initial views on the request.

Even if you requested the review, you should respond to this notice if you want a hearing, if the First-tier Tribunal has given provisional views and you have comments in response, or if you are able to provide more detail about what error of law you think was made.

The First-tier Tribunal must arrange a hearing of the review, unless it decides this is not needed in the interests of justice.[128] **Note:** even if both you and SSS want a hearing, the tribunal does not have to agree to this. See p1326 for information about whether to request a hearing.

If it is practicable, the review is carried out by the legal member of the First-tier Tribunal who originally decided your appeal.[129]

Note: the First-tier Tribunal can review its decision even if neither party has requested a review.[130] The rules are unclear on the procedure for reviews in this situation. The First-tier Tribunal may either follow a procedure like that above, or simply decide the review straight away.

The review decision

The review decision must be sent to both you and SSS.[131] The tribunal can:[132]

- take no action; *or*
- correct any minor errors in the decision; *or*
- 'set aside' (cancel) the decision, and:
  - redecide the matter again itself; *or*
  - refer your case to the Upper Tribunal, which can redecide the matter; *or*
  - make an order – eg, for your case to be heard again by a different tribunal.

In redeciding your appeal, the First-tier Tribunal or Upper Tribunal can make further findings about the facts of your case.[133] If you attend a hearing of a review, you should be prepared to argue what new decision the tribunal should make.

12

Part 12: Scottish social security benefits
Chapter 80: Getting a determination changed
5. Appealing to the Upper Tribunal

If you disagree with a review decision

If you disagree with a review decision, you cannot request a further review, unless the First-tier Tribunal has 'set aside' (cancelled) its original decision.[134] If the decision was not set aside, you cannot challenge the review decision (but if you requested the review, your request may be treated as a request for permission to appeal to the Upper Tribunal). You may still be in time to apply for permission to appeal against the First-tier Tribunal's original decision if you have not done so.

If the decision is set aside and remade, and you do not agree with the new decision, you can request permission to appeal to the Upper Tribunal or request another review.[135] However, you cannot request a further written statement of reasons.[136]

5. **Appealing to the Upper Tribunal**

You can appeal to the Upper Tribunal for Scotland against a decision of the First-tier Tribunal if it made an 'error of law' (see p1357 – the rules about what counts as an error of law are the same as for other benefits). The rules for appeals about Scottish benefits are similar to other benefits, but some important differences are explained in this section.

How to appeal

Before you can appeal to the Upper Tribunal, you must request permission to appeal from the First-tier Tribunal. If the First-tier Tribunal refuses you permission, you can request permission from the Upper Tribunal (see p1775).

The rules about how to appeal to the Upper Tribunal are similar to those for other benefits. See p1360 for those rules.[137] There are differences in:

- the time limit to take action – this is generally 30 days, not one month; *and*
- the ways in which the First-tier Tribunal can respond to your application for permission to appeal; *and*
- the form you can use to apply to the Upper Tribunal (see p1776); *and*
- what you can do if the Upper Tribunal refuses you permission to appeal without a hearing (see p1776).

Applying to the First-tier Tribunal for permission

The process of applying to the First-tier Tribunal for permission to appeal is the same as that set out on p1362.[138] However, the time limit and the tribunal's possible responses to your request are different. In particular:

- the First-tier Tribunal is not required to consider reviewing its decision if you apply for permission to appeal (but can choose to do so).[139] If you want the First-tier Tribunal to review its decision, you should ask it to (see p1772);

- the rules do not require the First-tier Tribunal to treat your application as being for a written statement of reasons if you do not have one.[140] This makes it particularly important to check the tribunal decision notice, and apply for a written statement of reasons if you want to challenge it, unless the decision says that it includes full written reasons (see p1770).

Your application for permission to appeal must be received by the First-tier Tribunal within 30 days of:[141]

- the date the decision was sent or given to you, if:
  - you have not requested a written statement of reasons; *or*
  - a full statement of reasons was included in the decision notice; *or*
  - you were given the decision orally at a hearing and you requested a statement of reasons more than 14 days later;[142] *or*
- the date a written statement of reasons that you or Social Security Scotland (SSS) requested was sent to you (but see above); *or*
- if the decision was 'set aside' following a review, the date it was set aside.

This time limit can be extended by the First-tier Tribunal.[143] Keep within the time limit if possible, and if your application might be late, explain why this is. Unless the tribunal extends the time limit it must 'refuse to admit' a late application.[144] It appears that you then *cannot* apply for permission to appeal to the Upper Tribunal, so your only option is to apply for judicial review (see Chapter 59).[145] Seek specialist advice if your application for permission to appeal is not admitted.

If the First-tier Tribunal gives you permission to appeal

If the First-tier Tribunal gives you permission to appeal, you must appeal to the Upper Tribunal (you can use Form UTS-1 for this – see p1776) within 30 days of being notified that you have been given permission to appeal.[146] You are treated as receiving the notification two days after it was sent to you.[147]

Your notice of appeal must:[148]

- identify the First-tier Tribunal decision you are challenging; *and*
- identify the errors of law in the decision; *and*
- state whether you want a hearing of your appeal or not.

You must send any written decision and statement of reasons from the First-tier Tribunal with your appeal, as well as the notice of permission to appeal.[149]

If your appeal is late, you must request an extension of time, explain why it is late, and explain why it is in the interests of justice to extend the time limit.[150] Unless the Upper Tribunal extends the time limit, it cannot consider your appeal.[151]

Applying to the Upper Tribunal for permission

The rules about how to apply for permission to appeal to the Upper Tribunal are the same as those set out on p1364, except that the time limit to do so is 30 days

12

Part 12: Scottish social security benefits
Chapter 80: Getting a determination changed
5. Appealing to the Upper Tribunal

rather than one month.[152] The time limit runs from the date on which the First-tier Tribunal sent you its refusal of permission to appeal.

This time limit can be extended by the Upper Tribunal.[153] If your request is late, you must request an extension of time, explain why it is late, and explain why it is in the interests of justice to extend the time limit.[154] Unless the Upper Tribunal extends the time limit, it must refuse you permission to appeal.[155]

Forms

The Upper Tribunal for Scotland appeal form is form UTS-1, which you can download from scotcourts.gov.uk/the-courts/tribunal-locations/the-upper-tribunal-for-scotland. Post or deliver it to: Upper Tribunal for Scotland, Glasgow Tribunals Centre, 20 York Street, Glasgow G2 8GT.

If you are refused permission to appeal by the Upper Tribunal, you cannot request a review of this decision or appeal against it to the Court of Session.[156]

However, if the Upper Tribunal refused you permission to appeal (or gave permission to appeal on limited grounds) without a hearing, you can ask for a hearing to reconsider that decision. Your application must be made in writing and received by the Upper Tribunal within 14 days of you being notified of the Upper Tribunal's decision.[157] You are treated as receiving the notification two days after it was sent to you.[158] A different member of the Upper Tribunal then decides at a hearing whether to give you permission to appeal.[159]

If the Upper Tribunal gives you permission to appeal, your application is treated as being a notice of appeal.[160]

What the Upper Tribunal can do

The powers of the Upper Tribunal for Scotland when dealing with an appeal about a Scottish benefit are similar to the powers the Upper Tribunal has for other benefits (see pp1367–69),[161] but with the following differences.

- The time limits for responses and replies are normally 30 days, and run from two days after a document is sent.[162]
- Some of the terms used in the rules are different (see p1764).
- The Upper Tribunal has the same powers as the First-tier Tribunal to dismiss appeals (although an appeal cannot be dismissed on the ground that it is not possible for you to meet the entitlement rules) and to reinstate them (see p1767).[163]
- The rules on withdrawing appeals are similar to those for the First-tier Tribunal (see p1768), but you can ask to withdraw only part of your case.[164]
- If you fail to attend a hearing as a witness or produce a document when ordered to do so, this is potentially a criminal offence, but is dealt with by the courts not the Upper Tribunal.[165]

12

- The Upper Tribunal can specify one or more lead cases if several cases raise common or related issues. The cases that are not the lead case are 'sisted' (ie, delayed) until the common or related issues have been determined, although you can apply for an order allowing your appeal to continue (see p1767).[166]

Hearings

The rules about hearings of Upper Tribunal appeals are similar to those for other benefits (see p1369).[167] At the time of writing, all Upper Tribunal hearings were being carried out by telepone or video link.[168]

The decision

Upper Tribunal decisions are made in a similar way for Scottish benefits as for other benefits (see p1370).[169] If you disagree with the Upper Tribunal's decision, you can:
- request a review of it (see below); or
- request permission to appeal against it (see p1778).

Reviewing Upper Tribunal decisions

The Upper Tribunal can review its decision on its own initiative, or if you or SSS ask for a review. If you want a review, you must request this in writing within 14 days of the date of the decision, and give your reasons.[170] The Upper Tribunal must send an application for review to the other parties.[171]

The review must be decided as soon as reasonably practicable, and if possible by the same Upper Tribunal member(s) who made the decision.[172] The review decision must be sent to both you and SSS.[173] The Upper Tribunal can decide to:[174]
- take no action; or
- correct any minor errors in the decision; or
- set aside (ie, cancel) the decision and:
  - decide the matter itself (and make further findings of fact if needed);[175] or
  - make an order – eg, that there will be a hearing of your case.

If the Upper Tribunal makes a new decision, you can request permission to appeal to the Court of Session against the review decision.[176] If the Upper Tribunal does not set aside its decision, you can request permission to appeal against the original decision.[177] See p1778 for how to appeal to the Court of Session.

If the Upper Tribunal does not set aside its decision following a review, the deadline to request permission to appeal is extended by the time between the review application being made (or the Upper Tribunal deciding to review the decision) and the date you receive the review decision.[178] You are treated as receiving the decision two days after it is sent to you by post or email.[179]

12

Part 12: Scottish social security benefits
Chapter 80: Getting a determination changed
7. Short-term assistance

6. **Appealing to the Court of Session**

You can appeal against an Upper Tribunal decision to the Court of Session. Yo
can only appeal if the Upper Tribunal made an 'error of law', and the case als
raises an important point of principle or practice, or there are other compellin
reasons for the appeal to go ahead.[180] See p1372 for details – the rules are simila
to those for other benefits,[181] with the following exceptions.

- The time limit to request permission to appeal from the Upper Tribunal is 3
  days, and normally runs from the date on which the Upper Tribunal's decisio
  was sent to you (or, if later, the date a written statement of reasons for th
  decision was sent to you – but note that Upper Tribunal decisions usuall
  include full written reasons).[182]
- In addition to applying for permission to appeal, you can also request a revie
  of an Upper Tribunal decision about a Scottish benefit (see p1777).
- Your application for permission to appeal must explain the important point c
  principle or practice your appeal would raise, or what other compelling reaso
  there is to give you permission to appeal.[183]

7. **Short-term assistance**

If you are challenging a determination to reduce or stop your entitlement to chil
disability payment (CDP) or adult disability payment (ADP), you may be able t
get short-term assistance.[184]

Note: short-term assistance is *not* a qualifying benefit to allow someone wh
cares for you to get carer's allowance (CA), the carer element of universal credit c
a young carer grant. If you claim short-term assistance, your carer may not be abl
to later get one of these benefits for the period for which you got short-terr
assistance, even if your challenge is successful. If the amount of short-terr
assistance is the same as the CDP care component or ADP daily living componen
you are later awarded, you will not be paid the CDP/ADP component for tha
period.[185] Seek advice before claiming short-term assistance if you think that thi
may affect you.

Who can get short-term assistance

You can get short-term assistance if:[186]
- you were receiving ADP or CDP; *and*
- there has been a further determination that reduced or removed you
  entitlement; *and*
- that determination is 'under review'.

A determination is 'under review' if:[187]

- you have requested a redetermination and Social Security Scotland (SSS) is yet to redetermine your entitlement; *or*
- you have appealed to the First-tier Tribunal against the determination (including a late appeal, if the First-tier Tribunal is considering whether to admit it); *or*
- a First-tier Tribunal's determination about your appeal has been set aside following a review (see p1772), and a further determination will be made by the tribunal.

You are not eligible for short-term assistance if:[188]

- the claimant has died; *or*
- the determination is that the rules about your age for CDP are no longer satisfied (see p1711); *or*
- the determination ended your CDP entitlement and you now get ADP (even if your ADP award is lower than your CDP was); *or*
- you have moved to another part of the UK and are no longer entitled for that reason (see p1762 for when your benefit ends); *or*
- the determination under review is that you no longer meet the residence or presence conditions (see p1601).

If you are not paid a component as you are living in residential care, hospital or prison (see Chapter 42), you cannot get short-term assistance to replace the component(s) that are not paid.[189]

If you are refused short-term assistance and you think the determination is wrong, you can request a redetermination (see p1755). However, you *cannot* get short-term assistance while challenging a determination that you are not entitled to short-term assistance.[190]

The amount of benefit

The amount of short-term assistance is the difference between your previous payment prior to the determination that is under review, and your current payment (if any).[191]

Claims and getting paid

To get short-term assistance, you must claim it. At the time of writing, you can claim by ticking a box on the redetermination or appeal form saying that you want to receive short-term assistance, or requesting it if you make your challenge by telephone.[192]

Note:

- If you do not get a determination of your entitlement after claiming short-term assistance, see p1755.

Part 12: Scottish social security benefits
Chapter 80: Getting a determination changed
7. Short-term assistance

- If you do not claim short-term assistance when you challenge th
  determination but later change your mind, telephone SSS to make a claim o
  0800 182 2222.
- Even if you got short-term assistance while requesting a redetermination, yo
  must make a further claim for it when you appeal.
- You can be awarded short-term assistance without a further claim if:[193]
  - your process appeal against a refusal to accept a redetermination request i
    later allowed by the First-tier Tribunal; *or*
  - a First-tier Tribunal decision is set aside following a review.

The date of your claim

Short-term assistance begins on the date:[194]
- your redetermination request was made, if it is accepted; *or*
- your process appeal against the refusal to accept your redetermination reque
  was allowed; *or*
- you appealed; *or*
- the First-tier Tribunal's decision is set aside following a review.

Getting paid

Short-term assistance is paid in the same way as your previous award was. So an
deductions to recover an overpayment (see p1748) continue.

Short-term assistance ends when:[195]
- SSS redetermines your entitlement; *or*
- you tell SSS that you no longer want to receive CDP, ADP or short-term
  assistance; *or*
- the First-tier Tribunal decides your appeal; *or*
- the First-tier Tribunal refuses to admit your late appeal; *or*
- you withdraw your appeal.

Tax, other benefits and the benefit cap

Tax

Short-term assistance is not taxable.[196]

Means-tested benefits and tax credits

Short-term assistance is not taken into account as income when calculatin
means-tested benefits and tax credits, and is paid in addition to them.

Short-term assistance does not increase your entitlement to means-teste
benefits and tax credits in the way that CDP and ADP do. So any premiums o
elements that you got due to being awarded CDP or ADP will stop if you no longe
qualify for them. See the chapter(s) of this *Handbook* about the other benefits tha
you get for details.

Non-means-tested benefits

If your eventual CDP or ADP award following a redetermination or appeal is the same as or higher than your short-term assistance, any arrears are reduced by the short-term assistance that you were paid for the same period.[197] It appears that the intention is that if your new CDP or ADP award is *lower* than your short-term assistance, you will not also be paid CDP/ADP for the period you got short-term assistance, but the law is unclear.[198]

Short-term assistance is *not* a qualifying benefit to allow someone to get CA or a young carer grant for looking after you (see p1778).

The benefit cap

Short-term assistance is *not* a qualifying benefit for exemption from the benefit cap. Unless you are still entitled to some CDP or ADP, the benefit cap may apply if you or someone in your household gets universal credit or housing benefit (see p1156).

Passports and other sources of help

Any passported benefits you were getting from your local authority due to your entitlement to CDP or ADP should continue while you get short-term assistance. Contact your local authority to check if you are unsure.

---

3. Appealing about 'process decisions'

Social Security Scotland (SSS) may decide that you:
- claimed a benefit in the wrong way or did not send some required evidence with your claim;[199] *or*
- requested a redetermination in the wrong way;[200] *or*
- do not have good reason for requesting a redetermination late.[201]

These decisions are called 'process decisions'. They are *not* determinations of your benefit entitlement. You can appeal against process decisions, but some rules are different.[202] You do not have to request a redetermination before making a process appeal.

Note:
- If you did not claim a benefit in the correct way, you should reclaim it if it is not too late to do so, or provide any missing evidence. See the chapter about the benefit in this *Handbook* for the time limits to make a claim.
- If you asked for a redetermination in the wrong way, and it is not too late to do so, also make another redetermination request in the correct way (see p1756).
- In the first two situations, you can also complain about the fact that what you tried to do was not accepted by SSS (see p1750). However, you should always make a process appeal as well.

12

Part 12: Scottish social security benefits
Chapter 80: Getting a determination changed
8. Appealing about 'process decisions'

How to appeal against a process decision

You must appeal against a process decision direct to the First-tier Tribunal. To be valid, your appeal must be made in writing, and give the same information needed to make a valid appeal about a determination of entitlement (see p1765).[203]

Forms

You can download a form to appeal against a process decision from the First-tier Tribunal's website at socialsecuritychamber.scot/home/your-appeal/a-process-appeal. You do not have to use the form, but it will help to provide all the information for a valid appeal. You can email the appeal to sscadmin@scotcourtstribunals.gov.uk, or post it to Social Security Chamber, Scottish Courts and Tribunals Service, Glasgow Tribunals Centre, 20 York Street, Glasgow G2 8GT.

The time limit for appealing

Your appeal must reach the First-tier Tribunal within 31 days of you being told about the decision that you are appealing against.[204] You are normally treated as receiving a notification two days after it was sent to you (see p1754).[205]

If you miss the time limit to appeal against a process decision

If you miss the time limit, your appeal can be considered if it is received within an absolute time limit of one year after you were notified of the decision that you are appealing against.[206] The First-tier Tribunal can only consider a late appeal if it accepts that you have 'good reason' for not appealing sooner.[207]

You must explain why your appeal is late. If the First-tier Tribunal accepts that you have a good reason, your appeal goes ahead unless you missed the absolute time limit above. For what might count as 'good reason', see p1757.

What happens after you appeal

Once your appeal is received by the First-tier Tribunal, the process is similar to that for other appeals (see p1766). One difference is that there is no requirement for SSS to respond to your appeal, unless it is ordered to by the First-tier Tribunal.[208]

Decisions about process appeals

The First-tier Tribunal cannot determine your entitlement to benefit. If it allows your appeal, it must tell SSS to determine your claim (or redetermine it). If you disagree with the (re)determination, you can then challenge it.

In a process appeal, the First-tier Tribunal's decision is final. If you disagree with it, you cannot appeal to the Upper Tribunal and it cannot be reviewed.[209] Your only option is to apply for judicial review (see Chapter 59). If you are considering a judicial review, you should ask for a statement of reasons for the decision (see p1770),[210] as well as getting legal advice.

Notes

1 s81(2A) and (9)-(15) SS(S)A 2018; Part 2 and Sch 2 The Carer's Allowance Supplement and Young Carer Grants (Residence Requirements and Procedural Provisions) (EU Exit) (Scotland) Regulations 2020 No.475; reg 2(c) and rr1, 20B and 22(1)(c) FTT(S) Rules; reg 3(c) UT(S) Rules; reg 3(2)(c) FTTS(AFSSC) Regs
2 **SCP** Sch para 24 SCP Regs
Other benefits s62 SS(S)A 2018
All r1(2) FTT(S) Rules; r1(2) UT(S) Rules
3 Regs 2 and 3 ST(TL) Regs

Determinations of entitlement
4 **SCP** Sch paras 3(a) and 4 SCP Regs
Other benefits ss37 and 40 SS(S)A 2018
5 s60 SS(S)A 2018
6 **SCP** Reg 13(3) SCP Regs
Other benefits s50(1) SS(S)A 2018
Note: in the law the meanings of 'determination' and 'decision' are the opposite to their meaning for other benefits described in this *Handbook*.
7 s50(1)(d) and (2) SS(S)A 2018
8 **SCP** Sch para 1(3) SCP Regs
Other benefits s38(1) SS(S)A 2018
9 **SCP** Sch para 1(4) SCP Regs
Other benefits s38(5) SS(S)A 2018
10 s38(3) SS(S)A 2018 cannot prevent you from claiming again as there has been no determination of your entitlement

Redeterminations
11 **SCP** Sch para 14 SCP Regs
Other benefits s41 SS(S)A 2018
12 SS(S)A 2018 contains no provision equivalent to ss8(2)(b) and 12(8)(b) SSA 1998
13 For CDP, guidance states that changes that happened after the date of your claim *cannot* be considered if your claim was refused. See SSS, *CDP DMG Redeterminations*, 28 February 2022, available at socialsecurity.gov.scot/asset-storage/production/downloads/CDP-DMG-Redeterminations.pdf

14 This depends on whether the determinations of entitlement are in relation to the same period – see s27 SS(S)A 2018 and Reg 23 SCP Regs
15 **SCP** ss85A and 85B SS(S)A 2018; Sch para 14(1) SCP Regs
Other benefits ss41(1), 85A and 85B SS(S)A 2018
16 **SCP** Sch para 14(4) SCP Regs
Other benefits s41(2)(a) and (3) SS(S)A 2018
17 **ADP** *Adult Disability Payment: If you do not agree with the decision*, 21 March 2022
CDP *Child Disability Payment: If you do not agree with the decision*, 7 January 2022, available at mygov.scot/child-disability-payment/disagree-decision
Other benefits *If you do not agree with a benefit decision*, 5 May 2021, available at mygov.scot/if-you-do-not-agree-with-a-benefit-decision. Relay UK and contactSCOTLAND app confirmed as acceptable ways to request a redetermination for all benefits by email from Scottish government to CPAG, 8 February 2022.
18 **SCP** Sch para 14(5) SCP Regs
Other benefits s41(6) SS(S)A 2018
19 **ADP** Reg 54(1) (and Sch 2 para 1(8) for short-term assistance) DAWAP(S) Regs
CDP Reg 37(1) (and Sch para 1(5) for short-term assistance) DACYP(S) Regs
CWHA Reg 9(1) WHACYP(S) Regs
20 **BSG** Sch 1 para 1 EYA(BSG)(S) Regs
FSP Reg 6(1) FEA(S) Regs
SCP Sch para 14(2) SCP Regs
YCG Reg 9(1) CA(YCG)(S) Regs
21 **SCP** Sch para 14(3) SCP Regs
Other benefits s41(4)(b) SS(S)A 2018
22 **SCP** Sch para 34(1) SCP Regs
Other benefits s52A(1) SS(S)A 2018
23 **SCP** Sch para 15 SCP Regs
Other benefits s42 SS(S)A 2018
24 **SCP** Sch para 16(1) SCP Regs
Other benefits s43(1) SS(S)A 2018
25 **SCP** Sch para 16 SCP Regs
Other benefits s43(2) and (5) SS(S)A 2018

12

Part 12: Scottish social security benefits
Chapter 80: Getting a determination changed
Notes

· ·

26 **ADP** Reg 54(2) DAWAP(S) Regs
CDP Reg 37(2) DACYP(S) Regs
27 **BSG** Sch 1 para 2(1) EYA(BSG)(S) Regs
CWHA Reg 9(2) WHACYP(S) Regs
FSP Reg 6(2) FEA(S) Regs
SCP Sch para 16(2) SCP Regs
YCG Reg 9(2) CA(YCG)(S) Regs
28 **ADP** Reg 54(2)(b) and (c) DAWAP(S) Regs
BSG Sch 1 para 2(1)(b) and (c) EYA(BSG)(S) Regs
CDP Reg 37(2)(b) and (c) DACYP(S) Regs
CWHA Reg 9(2)(b) and (c) WHACYP(S) Regs
FSP Reg 6(2)(b) and (c) FEA(S) Regs
SCP Sch para 16(2)(b) SCP Regs
YCG Reg 9(2)(b) and (c) CA(YCG)(S) Regs
29 **BSG** Sch 1 para 2(2) EYA(BSG)(S) Regs
CWHA Reg 9(3) WHACYP(S) Regs
FSP Reg 2 FEA(S) Regs
SCP Reg 6 SCP Regs
YCG Reg 9(3) CA(YCG) Regs
30 **SCP** Sch para 17 SCP Regs
Other benefits s44 SS(S)A 2018
31 **SCP** Sch paras 16(3) and 18 SCP Regs
Other benefits ss43(3) and 45 SS(S)A 2018
32 **SCP** Sch para 19 SCP Regs
Other benefits s46 SS(S)A 2018
33 **SCP** Sch para 16(3) SCP Regs
Other benefits s43(3) SS(S)A 2018

3. **Other ways to get a determination changed**
34 **SCP** Reg 23 SCP Regs
Other benefits s27 SS(S)A 2018
35 s41(1) SS(S)A 2018
You can only request a redetermination of a determination, not of a failure to make a determination.
36 **ADP** Reg 49 DAWAP(S) Regs
BSG Sch 1 para 4 EYA(BSG)(S) Regs
CDP Reg 32 DACYP(S) Regs
CWHA Reg 6 WHACYP(S) Regs
FSP Reg 4(1) FEA(S) Regs
SCP Sch para 6 SCP Regs
If you are resident in Scotland, a more generous rule also applies for CWHA (reg 5 WHACYP(S) Regs), so there is no need to have previously been refused it or show that there was an official error
37 **ADP** Reg 45(1)(c) DAWAP(S) Regs
CDP Reg 28(1)(c) DACYP(S) Regs
SCP Sch para 6(3) SCP Regs
For one-off payments, there is no need for the rules to explicitly say this.

38 **ADP** Reg 49(1)(c) and (d) DAWAP(S) Regs
BSG Sch 1 para 4(1)(c) and (d) EYA(BSG)(S) Regs
CDP Regs 32(1)(c) and (d) DACYP(S) Regs
CWHA Reg 6 WHACYP(S) Regs – which does not prevent this rule from applying if you have challenged the refusal
FSP Reg 4(1)(c) and (d) FEA(S) Regs
SCP Sch para 6(1)(c) and (d) SCP Regs
39 Provided your appeal has not yet been decided, the correct situation can still arguably be taken into account as the SS(S)A 2018 contains no equivalent to s8(2)(b) SSA 1998
40 **ADP** Reg 49(3) DAWAP(S) Regs
BSG Sch 1 para 4(4) EYA(BSG)(S) Regs
CDP Reg 32(3) DACYP(S) Regs
CWHA Reg 6(2) WHACYP(S) Regs
FSP Reg 4(5) FEA(S) Regs
SCP Sch para 6(4) SCP Regs
While not explicitly excluded by the rule, local authority staff do not administer the qualifying benefits for Scottish child payment or have any role in ADP, CDP or CWHA decision making, so misadvice from the local authority will not count as an official error for these benefits.
41 For other benefits, this is specifically excluded from the definition of an 'official error' – see, for example, reg 1(3) SSCS(DA) Regs
42 **ADP** Regs 45(2) and 46(2) DWAP(S) Regs
CDP Regs 28(2) and 29(2) DACYP(S) Regs
43 **ADP** Reg 47 DAWAP(S) Regs
CDP Reg 30 DACYP(S) Regs
44 While the regulations do not actually specify a date, this is the default position for both increases and decreases.
45 **ADP** Reg 45(1)(b) DAWAP(S) Regs
CDP Reg 28(1)(b) DACYP(S) Regs
46 **ADP** Reg 45(1)(d) DAWAP(S) Regs
CDP Reg 28(1)(d) DACYP(S) Regs
47 **ADP** Reg 46(b)(i) DAWAP(S) Regs
CDP Reg 29(1)(b)(i) DACYP(S) Regs
48 **ADP** Reg 46(1)(b)(ii) and (d) DAWAP(S) Regs
CDP Reg 29(1)(b)(ii) and (d) DACYP(S) Regs
49 **ADP** Reg 53(2) DAWAP(S) Regs
CDP Reg 36(2) DACYP(S) Regs
50 Reg 36(4) DACYP(S) Regs
51 Reg 53(4) DAWAP(S) Regs

52 **ADP** Reg 50 DAWAP(S) Regs
CDP Reg 33 DACYP(S) Regs
53 **ADP** Reg 50(3) DAWAP(S) Regs
CDP Reg 33(3) DACYP(S) Regs
54 **ADP** Reg 46(1)(c) DAWAP(S) Regs
CDP Reg 29(1)(c) DACYP(S) Regs
55 **ADP** Reg 50(1)(c) and (d) DAWAP(S) Regs
CDP Reg 33(1)(c) and (d) DACYP(S) Regs
56 **ADP** Reg 48(a) DAWAP(S) Regs
CDP Reg 31(a) DACYP(S Regs
57 **ADP** 45(1)(d) and 46(1)(d) DAWAP(S) Regs
CDP Regs 28(1)(d) and 29(1)(d) DACYP(S) Regs
58 **ADP** Reg 48 (c) and (d) DAWAP(S) Regs
CDP Reg 31(c) and (d) DACYP(S) Regs
59 **ADP** Regs 45(1)(a) and 46(1)(a) DAWAP(S) Regs
CDP Regs 28(1)(a) and 29(1)(a) DACYP(S) Regs

Appealing to the First-tier Tribunal
60 There is no equivalent to r11(5) TP(FT) Rules in r9 FTT(S) Rules
61 **SCP** Sch paras 17(1)(b) and 18(1)(b) SCP Regs
Other benefits ss44(1)(b) and 45(1)(b) SS(S)A 2018
62 **SCP** Sch para 20(1) SCP Regs
Other benefits s47(1) SS(S)A 2018
63 Scottish government, *Appeal to a Tribunal about a Benefit Decision*, 5 May 2021, available at mygov.scot/appeal-to-a-tribunal-about-a-benefit-decision
64 **ADP** *Adult Disability Payment: If you do not agree with the decision*, 21 March 2022
CDP *Child Disability Payment: If you do not agree with the decision*, 7 January 2022, available at mygov.scot/child-disability-payment/disagree-decision
Other benefits Confirmed as an acceptable way to submit an appeal by email from Scottish government to CPAG, 8 February 2022.
65 **SCP** r20A(5) FTT(S) Rules
Other benefits r20(5) FTT(S) Rules
66 r9 FTT(S) Rules
67 r6 FTT(S) Rules
68 **SCP** Sch para 21(2)(b) SCP Regs
Other benefits s48(2)(b) SS(S)A 2018 Arguably, if a requirement is waived, your appeal should be treated as made on the date SSS received it.
69 **SCP** Sch para 21(1) SCP Regs
Other benefits s48 SS(S)A 2018

70 **SCP** Sch para 21(1) SCP Regs
Other benefits s48 SS(S)A 2018
71 **SCP** Sch para 34(2)-(4) SCP Regs
Other benefits s52A(2)-(4) SS(S)A 2018
72 **SCP** Sch para 20(2) and (3) SCP Regs; r20A(10) FTT(S) Rules
Other benefits s47(2) and (3) SS(S)A 2018; r20(10) FTT(S) Rules
73 r21(1) FTT(S) Rules
74 r21(2)-(4) FTT(S) Rules
75 rr9(3) and 21(5) FTT(S) Rules
76 r21(6) and (7) FTT(S) Rules
77 r1(2) FTT(S) Rules
78 r4(3)(a) FTT(S) Rules
79 rr4-19 FTT(S) Rules
80 The FTT(S) Rules contain no equivalent to r32 TP(FT) Rules
81 s67 T(S)A 2014; ST(ORP) Regs
82 r4(3)(b) FTT(S) Rules
83 SS(S)A 2018 contains no equivalent to s26 SSA 1998
84 r4(3)(j) FTT(S) Rules
85 r5(5) FTT(S) Rules
86 r7 FTT(S) Rules
87 r7(1) FTT(S) Rules
88 r7(3) FTT(S) Rules
89 r7(2) FTT(S) Rules
90 r7(3) FTT(S) Rules
91 r7(9) FTT(S) Rules
92 r7(7) and (8) FTT(S) Rules
93 The decision is not excluded from the possibility of appealing against it by the T(S)A 2014, so arguably the decision in *LS v Lambeth BC (HB)* [2010] UKUT 461, reported as [2011] AACR 27 applies to the FTT(S) Rules.
94 r7(5) and (6) FTT(S) Rules
95 r1(2) FTT(S) Rules
96 r7(4) FTT(S) Rules
97 r17 FTT(S) Rules
98 rr1(2) and 17(5) FTT(S) Rules
99 r4(3)(a) FTT(S) Rules
100 ss46 and 49 SS(S)A 2018 (and for Scottish child payment, Sch para 19 and 22 SCP Regs) still give the First-tier Tribunal the power to determine your entitlement in this situation, even though there has been another determination since you appealed.
101 rr23-27 FTT(S) Rules
102 First-tier Tribunal for Scotland Social Security Chamber, *Important Information – impact of COVID-19 pandemic*, 19 March 2020, available at socialsecuritychamber.scot
103 s49 SS(S)A 2018; reg 4 FTTS(AFSSC) Regs

12

Part 12: Scottish social security benefits
Chapter 80: Getting a determination changed
Notes

104 FTT(S) Rules contain no equivalent of r25 TP(FT) Rules
105 r10 FTT(S) Rules
106 r26(5) FTT(S) Rules
107 r5 FTT(S) Rules – this is technically a request for another order
108 Regs 2-4A First-tier Tribunal for Scotland Social Security Chamber and Upper Tribunal for Scotland (Composition) Regulations 2018 No.351
109 **SCP** Sch para 22 SCP Regs
Other benefits s49 SS(S)A 2018
110 r28 FTT(S) Rules
111 r19 FTT(S) Rules
112 r29 FTT(S) Rules
113 r4(3)(a) FTT(S) Rules
114 rr28 and 29(3) FTT(S) Rules – r1(2) FTT(S) Rules applies only to decisions sent to you by post or email
115 r28(3)(c) FTT(S) Rules
116 If you apply for permission to appeal, this is not treated as a request for full reasons, as there is no equivalent of r38(7) TP(FT) Rules in the FTT(S) Rules
117 For a discussion of errors of law in an Upper Tribunal for Scotland decision, see *Garret v Your Place Property Management Limited* [2020] UT 34
118 r32 FTT(S) Rules
119 r4(1)(l) FTT(S) Rules
120 r35(2) FTT(S) Rules
121 r36(1) FTT(S) Rules
122 r36(2) FTT(S) Rules
123 r35(8) FTT(S) Rules
124 ss44(1)(a), 51 and 52 T(S)A 2014
125 r33(3) FTT(S) Rules
If necessary, you can argue that *Aberdeen CC v LS* [2021] UT 1 suggests that the review process should not cause a delay that means you lose the right to challenge the decision. However, it is better to request permission to appeal within the time limit if you can.
126 r35(3) FTT(S) Rules
127 r35(4) FTT(S) Rules
128 r35(5) FTT(S) Rules
129 r35(6) FTT(S) Rules
130 s43(2)(a) T(S)A 2014
131 r35(7) FTT(S) Rules
132 s44 T(S)A 2014
133 s44(5) T(S)A 2014
134 s45 T(S)A 2014
135 ss 45(2)(b) and 52 T(S)A 2014
136 r29(5) FTT(S) Rules

5. Appealing to the Upper Tribunal
137 rr33 and 34 FTT(S) Rules; rr3 and 4 UT(S) Rules
138 rr33 and 34 FTT(S) Rules
139 s43(2)(a) T(S)A 2014
140 There is no equivalent of r38(7) TP(FT) Rules in the FTT(S) Rules.
141 Reg 2 ST(TL) Regs
142 If you requested a statement of reasons more than 14 days after the hearing, make sure that you request permission to appeal within 30 days, even if you do not have the statement of reasons yet.
143 r33(3) FTT(S) Rules
144 r33(3)(b) FTT(S) Rules
145 As your application has not been admitted, it appears that you will not be given the 'notice of refusal of permission to appeal' that you need to apply to the Upper Tribunal (see r3(1) and (3)(c) UT(S) Rules).
146 r4(1) UT(S) Rules
147 r1(2) UT(S) Rules
148 r4(2) UT(S) Rules
149 r4(3) UT(S) Rules
150 r4(5)(a) UT(S) Rules
151 r4(5)(b) UT(S) Rules
152 Reg 3 ST(TL) Regs
153 Reg 3(3) ST(TL) Regs
154 r3(4)(a) UT(S) Rules
155 r3(4)(b) UT(S) Rules
156 s55(2) T(S)A 2014
157 r3(6) UT(S) Rules
158 r1(2) UT(S) Rules
159 r3(7) UT(S) Rules
160 r3(8) UT(S) Rules
161 rr5-21 UT(S) Rules
162 rr1(2), 5(2) and 6(2) UT(S) Rules
163 r11 UT(S) Rules
While you must have good reason 'to apply for reinstatement', rather than for your failure to comply with an order, the intention appears to be the same.
164 r20 UT(S) Rules
165 s67 T(S)A 2014; ST(ORP) Regs
166 r8(3)(c) UT(S) Rules
167 rr22-26 UT(S) Rules
168 Email to CPAG from Upper Tribunal for Scotland, 13 January 2022
169 s47 T(S)A 2014; r27 UT(S) Rules
170 r28(2) UT(S) Rules
171 r28(3) UT(S) Rules
172 r28(4) UT(S) Rules
173 r28(5) UT(S) Rules
174 s44(1) and (4) T(S)A 2014
175 s44(5) T(S)A 2014
176 ss48(5)(b) and 52(2) T(S)A 2014

12

77 s52 T(S)A 2014 only excludes a review decision from having a right of appeal, not the original decision, if it was not set aside.
78 rr 1(1) and 28(6) UT(S) Rules
79 r1(2) UT(S) Rules

Appealing to the Court of Session
80 ss48 and 50 T(S)A 2014
81 ss48-55 T(S)A 2014; rr29-31 UT(S) Rules
82 Reg 2 ST(TL) Regs
83 r30(2)(c) UT(S) Rules

Short-term assistance
84 s36 and Sch 10 SS(S)A 2018
85 s70(2) SSCBA 1992 requires that a qualifying benefit is 'payable' to you for someone who cares for you to get CA. Sch para 4 DACYP(S) Regs and Sch 2 para 4 DAWAP(S) Regs appear to prevent payment of the ADP/CDP component if the short-term assistance award for the period was the same amount.
86 **ADP** Sch 2 para 1(1)(a) and (b) DAWAP(S) Regs
    CDP Sch para 1(1)(a) and (b) DACYP(S) Regs
87 **ADP** Sch 2 para 1(1)(b) and (2) DAWAP(S) Regs
    CDP Sch para 1(1)(b) and (1A) DACYP(S) Regs
    All Sch 10 para 1(2) SS(S)A 2018
88 **ADP** Sch 2 para 1(1)(c) and (5) DAWP(S) Regs
    CDP Sch para 1(1)(c) and (2) DACYP(S) Regs
89 **ADP** Sch 2 para 1(6) DAWP(S) Regs
    CDP Sch para 1(3) DACYP(S) Regs
90 Sch 10 para 1(1)(a) SS(S)A 2018
91 **ADP** Sch 2 para 2(1) DAWAP(S) Regs
    CDP Sch para 2(1) DACYP(S) Regs
92 Scottish government, *Short-term Assistance: how to apply*, 21 March 2022, available at mygov.scot/short-term-assistance/apply-short-term-assistance
93 **ADP** Sch 2 para 1(3) and (4) DAWAP(S) Regs
    CDP Sch para 1(1B) and (1C) DACYP(S) Regs
94 **ADP** Sch 2 para 1(7) DAWAP(S) Regs
    CDP Sch para 1(4) DACYP(S) Regs
95 **ADP** Sch 2 para 3 DAWAP(S) Regs
    CDP Sch para 3 DACYP(S) Regs
    All Sch 10 para 1(2)(a) SS(S)A 2018
96 s677(1) IT(EP)A 2003

197 **ADP** Sch 2 para 4 DAWAP(S) Regs
     CDP Sch para 4 (DACYP(S) Regs
198 Sch para 4 DACYP(S) Regs and Sch 2 para 4 DAWAP(S) Regs only apply if your eventual award is at 'the same rate or at a higher rate' than your short-term assistance.

8. **Appealing about 'process decisions'**
199 **SCP** Sch para 1(4) SCP Regs
     Other benefits s38(5) SS(S)A 2018
200 **SCP** Sch para 14(5) SCP Regs
     Other benefits s41(6) SS(S)A 2018
201 **SCP** Sch para 15 SCP Regs
     Other benefits s42 SS(S)A 2018
202 **SCP** Sch para 23 SCP Regs
     Other benefits s61 SS(S)A 2018
203 r22(4) FTT(S) Rules
204 **SCP** Sch para 23(2)(a) SCP Regs
     Other benefits s61(2)(a) SS(S)A 2018
205 **SCP** Sch para 24 SCP Regs
     Other benefits s62 SS(S)A 2018
206 **SCP** Sch para 23(2)(c) SCP Regs
     Other benefits s61(2)(c) SS(S)A 2018
207 **SCP** Sch para 23 (2)(b) and (3) SCP Regs
     Other benefits s61(2)(b) and (3) SS(S)A 2018
208 r21 FTT(S) Rules only applies to appeals against a determination of entitlement
209 **SCP** Sch para 23(4) and (5) SCP Regs
     Other benefits s61(4) and (5) SS(S)A 2018
210 The FTT(S) Rules do not prevent you from requesting a statement of reasons for a decision on a 'process appeal'.

Appendices

Appendix 1

Information and advice

Independent advice and representation

If you want advice or information on a benefit or tax credit issue, the following may be able to assist.

- Advicelocal (advicelocal.uk) has details of advice organisations in your area.
- Citizens Advice. You can find out where your local office is from the Citizens Advice website at citizensadvice.org.uk (England and Wales) or cas.org.uk (Scotland).
- Law centres. You can find your nearest law centre at lawcentres.org.uk.
- LawWorks (lawworks.org.uk) has details of local legal advice centres that give free advice.
- Housing association welfare rights services for tenants.
- Local authority welfare rights services.
- Local and national organisations for particular groups of claimants may offer help. For instance, there are unemployed centres, pensioners' groups and organisations for people with disabilities.

Advice from CPAG

Unfortunately, CPAG is unable to deal with enquiries directly from members of the public, but if you are an adviser you can phone or email for help with advising your client.

Advisers in England, Wales and Northern Ireland can call from 10am to 12pm and from 2pm to 4pm (Monday to Friday) on 020 7812 5231. Email advice is limited to enquiries that are specifically about universal credit, child benefit and tax credits. Our email address is advice@cpag.org.uk. For more information, see cpag.org.uk/advisers.

Advisers in Scotland can call from 10am to 4pm (Monday to Thursday) and from 10am to 12pm (Friday) on 0141 552 0552, or email advice@cpagscotland.org.uk.

CPAG's Upper Tribunal assistance project can provide help to advisers helping claimants challenge tribunal decisions. See cpag.org.uk/upper-tribunal-assistance-project. We also provide training and advice to support advisers to pursue judicial review remedies. See cpag.org.uk/jrproject.

The Survivors Welfare Advice Project is a free nationwide service run by CPAG. It advises professionals working with domestic abuse survivors on issues relating to their benefit claims and entitlement. See cpag.org.uk/swap.

CPAG takes on a small number of test cases each year. We focus on cases that have the potential to improve the lives of families with children in poverty. If you are an adviser and would like to refer a test case to us, please see cpag.org.uk/test-case-referrals.

Finding help online

Information about benefits and tax credits, including a selection of leaflets and forms, is available on the gov.uk website.

AskCPAG is an information and solutions platform for advisers, including digital version of this *Handbook* and other CPAG pblications, fully searchable and updated throughout the year. See AskCPAG.org.uk.

The *rightsnet* website (aimed at advisers) at rightsnet.org.uk provides information on new welfare rights legislation, caselaw and guidance. It also provides updates on developments in other areas of social welfare law and has discussion forum where advisers can discuss particular cases.

Most Acts and regulations can be found at legislation.gov.uk.

You can find commissioners' and Upper Tribunal decisions at gov.uk administrative-appeals-tribunal-decisions.

Appendix 2

Useful publications

1. Caselaw and legislation

The Law Relating to Social Security
All the legislation but without any commentary. Known as the 'Blue Book'. Available at lawvolumes.dwp.gov.uk and updated up until October 2015. Check also legislation.gov.uk.

Sweet and Mawell social security legislation with commentary:
Volume I: Non-Means-Tested Benefits and Employment and Support Allowance
Volume II: Universal Credit, State Pension Credit and the Social Fund
Volume III: Administration, Adjudication and the European Dimension
Volume IV: HMRC-administered Social Security Benefits and Scotland

CPAG's Housing Benefit and Council Tax Reduction Legislation. Legislation with commentary.

CPAG's Child Support: the legislation. Legislation with commentary.

2. Official guidance

Decision Makers' Guide: staff guide
gov.uk/government/collections/decision-makers-guide-staff-guide

Advice for Decision Making: staff guide
gov.uk/government/publications/advice-for-decision-making-staff-guide

Housing Benefit Guidance Manual
gov.uk/government/collections/housing-benefit-claims-processing-and-good-practice-for-local-authority-staff

Discretionary Housing Payments Guidance Manual
gov.uk/government/publications/discretionary-housing-payments-guidance-manual

Healthcare professionals: information from DWP
gov.uk/government/collections/healthcare-practitioners-guidance-and-information-from-dwp

Work Capability Assessment (WCA) Handbook: for healthcare professionals
gov.uk/government/publications/work-capability-assessment-handbook-for-healthcare-professionals

Tax Credits Technical Manual
hmrc.gov.uk/manuals/tctmanual

Budgeting Loan Guide
gov.uk/government/publications/budgeting-loan-guide-for-decision-makers-reviewing-officers-and-further-reviewing-officers

Personal Independence Payment (PIP) Assessment Guide for Assessment Providers
gov.uk/government/publications/personal-independence-payment-assessment-guide-for-assessment-providers

3. Leaflets
The DWP publishes many leaflets, available free from your local DWP or Jobcentre Plus office. To order DWP leaflets, or receive information about new leaflets, contact APS, Unit C, Orion Business Park, Bird Hall Lane, Cheadle Heath SK3 0RT, email: DWPCST@theapsgroup.com or complete the order form at gov.uk/government/publications/dwp-leaflets-order-form. Leaflets on housing benefit are available from your local council.

4. Periodicals
Welfare Rights Bulletin (CPAG, bi-monthly)
Available in print or online, this covers developments in social security law and updates this *Handbook* between editions. For more information, see cpag.org.uk/subscriptions.

Articles on social security can also be found in *Legal Action* (Legal Action Group), *Adviser* (Citizens Advice, available at medium.com/adviser) and the *Journal of Social Security Law* (Sweet & Maxwell).

5. Other publications
AskCPAG
The full text of the *Welfare Benefits and Tax Credits Handbook* online and updated throughout the year. See cpag.org.uk/subscriptions for details.

AskCPAG+
CPAG's full digital package which includes the full text of the *Welfare Benefits and Tax Credits Handbook* updated throughout the year, the *Welfare Rights Bulletin*, *Poverty* journal and decision-making tools and appeal letter generators. See cpag.org.uk/subscriptions for details.

CPAG guides
Universal Credit: what you need to know
Financial Help for Families: what you need to know (available free on AskCPAG)
Personal Independence Payment: what you need to know
Winning Your Benefit Appeal: what you need to know

Other CPAG handbooks
Benefits for Migrants Handbook (subscription available on AskCPAG)
Child Support Handbook
Council Tax Handbook
Debt Advice Handbook (available free on AskCPAG)
Fuel Rights Handbook
Student Support and Benefits Handbook (available free on AskCPAG)
Benefits for Students in Scotland Handbook (available free online at AskCPAG)
Children's Handbook Scotland (available free on AskCPAG)

Books from other publishers
Big Book of Mental Health, Tom Messere (subscription available on AskCPAG)
Disability Rights Handbook, Disability Rights UK (subscription available on AskCPAG)
Help with Housing Costs Vol 1: Guide to universal credit and council tax rebates, Shelter
Help with Housing Costs Vol 2: Guide to housing benefit, Shelter

For CPAG publications and most of those in Sections 1 and 5 contact:
CPAG, 30 Micawber Street, London N1 7TB (tel: 020 7837 7979, email: bookorders@cpag.org.uk). Order from cpag.org.uk/shop.

Appendix 3

Disability which puts a person at a disadvantage in getting a job

Schedule 1 Regulation 9(1) to the Working Tax Credit (Entitlement and Maximum Rate) Regulations 2002

PART 1

1. When standing he cannot keep his balance unless he continually holds onto something.

2. Using any crutches, walking frame, walking stick, prosthesis or similar walking aid which he habitually uses, he cannot walk a continuous distance of 100 metres along level ground without stopping or without suffering severe pain.

3. He can use neither of his hands behind his back as in the process of putting on a jacket or of tucking a shirt into trousers.

4. He can extend neither of his arms in front of him so as to shake hands with another person without difficulty.

5. He can put neither of his hands up to his head without difficulty so as to put on a hat.

6. Due to lack of manual dexterity he cannot, with one hand, pick up a coin which is not more than $2\frac{1}{2}$ centimetres in diameter.

7. He is not able to use his hands or arms to pick up a full jug of 1 litre capacity and pour from it into a cup, without difficulty.

8. He can turn neither of his hands sideways through 180 degrees.

9. He is certified as severely sight impaired or blind by a consultant ophthalmologist.

10. He cannot see to read 16 point print at a distance greater than 20 centimetres, if appropriate, wearing the glasses he normally uses.

11. He cannot hear a telephone ring when he is in the same room as the telephone, if appropriate, using a hearing aid he normally uses.

12. In a quiet room he has difficulty in hearing what someone talking in a loud voice at a distance of 2 metres says, if appropriate, using a hearing aid he normally uses.

13. People who know him well have difficulty in understanding what he says.

14. When a person he knows well speaks to him, he has difficulty in understanding what that person says.

15. At least once a year during waking hours he is in a coma or has a fit in which he loses consciousness.

16. He has a mental illness for which he receives regular treatment under the supervision of a medically qualified person.

17. Due to mental disability he is often confused or forgetful.

18. He cannot do the simplest addition and subtraction.

19. Due to mental disability he strikes people or damages property or is unable to form normal social relationships.

20. He cannot normally sustain an 8 hour working day or a five day working week due to a medical condition or intermittent or continuous severe pain.

PART 2 (INITIAL CLAIMS ONLY)

21. As a result of an illness or accident he is undergoing a period of habilitation or rehabilitation.

Appendix 4

Prescribed degrees of disablement

Schedule 2 to the Social Security (General Benefit) Regulations 1982 SI No.1408

Description of injury	Degree of disablement %
1 Loss of both hands or amputation at higher sites	100
2 Loss of a hand and a foot	100
3 Double amputation through leg or thigh, or amputation through leg or thigh on one side and loss of other foot	100
4 Loss of sight to such an extent as to render the claimant unable to perform any work for which eyesight is essential	100
5 Very severe facial disfiguration	100
6 Absolute deafness	100
7 Forequarter or hindquarter amputation	100
Amputation cases – upper limbs (either arm)	
8 Amputation through shoulder joint	90
9 Amputation below shoulder with stump less than 20.5 cm from tip of acromion	80
10 Amputation from 20.5 cm from tip of acromion to less than 11.5 cm below tip of olecranon	70
11 Loss of a hand or of the thumb and 4 fingers of 1 hand or amputation from 11.5 cm below tip of olecranon	60
12 Loss of thumb	30
13 Loss of thumb and its metacarpal bone	40
14 Loss of 4 fingers of 1 hand	50
15 Loss of 3 fingers of 1 hand	30
16 Loss of 2 fingers of 1 hand	20
17 Loss of terminal phalanx of thumb	20

Amputation cases – lower limbs

18 Amputation of both feet resulting in end-bearing stumps	90
19 Amputation through both feet proximal to the metatarso-phalangeal joint	80
20 Loss of all toes to both feet through the metatarso-phalangeal joint	40
21 Loss of all toes of both feet proximal to the proximal inter-phalangeal joint	30
22 Loss of all toes of both feet distal to the proximal inter-phalangeal joint	20
23 Amputation at hip	90
24 Amputation below hip with stump not exceeding 13 cm in length measured from tip of great trochanter	80
25 Amputation below hip and above knee with stump exceeding 13 cm in length measured from tip of great trochanter, or at knee not resulting in end-bearing stump	70
26 Amputation at knee resulting in end-bearing stump or below knee with stump not exceeding 9 cm	60
27 Amputation below knee with stump exceeding 9 cm but not exceeding 13 cm	50
28 Amputation below knee with stump exceeding 13 cm	40
29 Amputation of 1 foot resulting in end-bearing stump	30
30 Amputation through 1 foot proximal to the metatarso-phalangeal joint	30
31 Loss of all toes of 1 foot through the metatarso-phalangeal joint	20

Other injuries

32 Loss of 1 eye, without complications, the other being normal	40
33 Loss of vision of 1 eye, without complications or disfigurement of the eyeball, the other being normal	30

Loss of fingers of right or left hand

Index finger:

34 Whole	14
35 2 phalanges	11
36 1 phalanx	9
37 Guillotine amputation of tip without loss of bone	5

Middle finger:

38 Whole	12
39 2 phalanges	9
40 1 phalanx	7
41 Guillotine amputation of tip without loss of bone	4

A

Ring or little finger:

42 Whole   7

43 2 phalanges   6

44 1 phalanx   5

45 Guillotine amputation of tip without loss of bone   2

Loss of toes of right or left foot

Great toe:

46 Through metatarso-phalangeal joint   14

47 Part, with some loss of bone   3

Any other toe:

48 Through metatarso-phalangeal joint   3

49 Part, with some loss of bone   1

2 toes of 1 foot, excluding great toe:

50 Through metatarso-phalangeal joint   5

51 Part, with some loss of bone   2

3 toes of 1 foot, excluding great toe:

52 Through metatarso-phalangeal joint   6

53 Part, with some loss of bone   3

4 toes of 1 foot, excluding great toe:

54 Through metatarso-phalangeal joint   9

55 Part, with some loss of bone   3

The degree of disablement due to occupational deafness is assessed using tables and a formula to be found in reg 34 and Sch 3 Social Security (Industrial Injuries) (Prescribed Diseases) Regulations 1985, as amended.

Appendix 5

Prescribed industrial diseases

Part I of Schedule 1 to the Social Security (Industrial Injuries) Prescribed Diseases) Regulations 1985 as amended

Prescribed disease or injury	Occupation
A – Conditions due to physical agents	Any occupation involving:
A1 Leukaemia (other than chronic lymphatic leukaemia) or primary cancer of the bone, bladder, breast, colon, liver, lung, ovary, stomach testis or thyroid.	Exposure to ionising radiation where the dose is sufficient to double the condition.
A2 Cataract.	Frequent or prolonged exposure to radiation from red-hot or white-hot material.
A3 (a) Dysbarism, including decompression sickness and barotrauma; (b) Osteonecrosis	Subjection to compressed or rarified air or from molten or red-hot material.
A4 Task-specific focal dystonia of the hand or forearm.	Prolonged periods of handwriting, typing or other repetitive movements of the fingers, hand or arm.
A5 Subcutaneous cellulitis of the hand.	Manual labour causing severe or prolonged friction or pressure on the hand.
A6 Bursitis or subcutaneous cellulites arising at or about the knee due to severe or prolonged external friction or pressure at or about the knee.	Manual labour causing severe or prolonged external friction or pressure at or about the knee.
A7 Bursitis or subcutaneous cellulites arising at or about the elbow due to severe or prolonged external friction or pressure at or about the elbow (beat elbow).	Manual labour causing severe or prolonged external friction or pressure at or about the elbow.
A8 Traumatic inflammation of the tendons of the hand or forearm, or of the associated tendon sheaths.	Manual labour, or frequent or repeated movements of the hand or wrist.

Prescribed disease or injury	Occupation
A10 Sensorineural hearing loss amounting to at least 50dB in each ear, being the average of hearing losses at 1, 2 and 3 kHz frequencies, and being due in the case of at least one ear to occupational noise (occupational deafness).	Any occupation involving the use of, or work wholly or mainly in the immediate vicinity of the use of, a:

(a) band saw, circular saw or cutting disc to cut metal in the metal founding or forging industries, circular saw to cut products in the manufacture of steel, powered (other than hand powered) grinding tool on metal (other than sheet metal or plate metal), pneumatic percussive tool on metal, pressurised air arc tool to gouge metal, burner or torch to cut or dress steel based products, skid transfer bank, knock out and shake out grid in a foundry, machine (other than a power press machine) to forge metal including a machine used to drop stamp metal by means of closed or open dies or drop hammers, machine to cut or shape or clean metal nails, or plasma spray gun to spray molten metal;

(b) pneumatic percussive tool to drill rock in a quarry, on stone in a quarry works, used underground, for mining coal, for sinking a shaft, or for tunnelling in civil engineering works;

(c) vibrating metal moulding box in the concrete products industry, or circular saw to cut concrete masonry blocks;

(d) machine in the manufacture of textiles for weaving man-made or natural fibres (including mineral fibres), high speed false twisting of fibres, or the mechanical cleaning of bobbins;

(e) multi-cutter moulding machine on wood, planing machine on wood, automatic or semi-automatic lathe on wood, multiple cross-cut machine on wood, automatic shaping machine on wood, double-end tenoning machine on wood, vertical spindle moulding machine (including a high speed routing machine) on wood, edge banding machine on wood, bandsawing machine (with a blade width of not less than 75 millimetres) on wood including one operated by moving the blade towards the material being cut, or chain saw on wood;

(f) jet of water (or a mixture of water and abrasive material) at a pressure above 680 bar, or jet channelling process to burn stone in a quarry;

Prescribed disease or injury	Occupation
	(g) machine in a ship's engine room, or gas turbine for performance testing on a test bed, installation testing of a replacement engine in an aircraft, or acceptance testing of an Armed Service fixed wing combat aircraft;
	(h) machine in the manufacture of glass containers or hollow ware for automatic moulding, automatic blow moulding, or automatic glass pressing and forming;
	(i) spinning machine using compressed air to produce glass wool or mineral wool;
	(j) continuous glass toughening furnace;
	(k) firearm by a police firearms training officer;
	(l) shot-blaster to carry abrasives in air for cleaning.
A11(a) Intense blanching of the skin, with a sharp demarcation line between affected and non-affected skin, where the blanching is cold-induced, episodic, occurs throughout the year and affects the skin of the distal with the middle and proximal phalanges, or distal with the middle phalanx (or in the case of a thumb the distal with the proximal phalanx), of–	(a) The use of hand-held chain saws on wood; *or*
(i) in the case of a person with 5 fingers (including thumb) on one hand, any 3 of those fingers, or	(b) the use of hand-held rotary tools in grinding or in the sanding or polishing of metal, or the holding of material being ground, or metal being sanded or polished by rotary tools; *or*
(ii) in the case of a person with only 4 such fingers, any 2 of those fingers, or	(c) the use of hand-held percussive metal-working tools, or the holding of metal being worked upon by percussive tools, in riveting, caulking, chipping, hammering, fettling or swaging; *or*
(iii) in the case of a person with less than 4 such fingers, any one of them or, as the case may be, the one remaining finger, where none of the person's fingers was subject to any degree of cold-induced, episodic blanching of the skin prior to the person's employment in an occupation described in the second column in relation to this paragraph, or	(d) the use of hand-held powered percussive drills or hand-held powered percussive hammers in mining, quarrying, demolition, or on roads or footpaths, including road construction; *or*
	(e) the holding of material being worked upon by pounding machines in shoe manufacture.

Prescribed disease or injury	Occupation
(b) significant, demonstrable reduction in both sensory perception and manipulative dexterity with continuous numbness or continuous tingling all present at the same time in the distal phalanx of any finger (including thumb) where none of the person's fingers was subject to any degree of reduction in sensory perception, manipulative dexterity, numbness or tingling prior to the person's employment in an occupation described in the second column in relation to this paragraph, where the symptoms in paragraph (a) or paragraph (b) were caused by vibration.	
A12 Carpal tunnel syndrome.	(a) The use, at the time the symptoms first develop, of hand-held powered tools whose internal parts vibrate so as to transmit that vibration to the hand; *or* (b) repeated palmar flexion and dorsiflexion of the wrist for at least 20 hours per week for a period or periods amounting in aggregate to at least 12 months in the 24 months prior to the onset of the symptoms, where 'repeated' means once or more often in every 30 seconds.
A13 Osteoarthritis of the hip.	Work in agriculture as a farmer or farm worker for a period of, or periods which amount in aggregate to, 10 years or more.

A14 Osteoarthritis of the knee.	Work underground in a coal mine for a period of, or periods which amount in aggregate to, at least 10 years in any one or more of the following occupations:
	(a) before 1 January 1986 as a coal miner; *or*
	(b) on or after 1 Januray 1986 as a–
	  (i) face worker working on a non-mechanised coal face;*
	  (ii) development worker;
	  (iii) face-salvage worker;
	  (iv) conveyor belt cleaner; *or*
	  (v) conveyor belt attendant.
	*'A non-mechanised coal face' means a coal face without either powered roof supports or a power loader machine which simultaneously cuts and loads the coal or without both.
	Work wholly or mainly fitting or laying carpets or other floors (other than concrete floors) for a period of, or periods which amount in aggregate to, 20 years or more.

A

Prescribed disease or injury	Occupation
A15 Dupuytren's contracture of the hand resulting in fixed flexion deformity of one or more inter-phalangeal joints of one or more of the digits.	Any occupation involving the use of hand-held powered tools whose internal parts vibrate so as to transmit that vibration to the hand (but excluding those tools which are solely powered by hand) where: (a) the use of those tools amounts to a period or periods in aggregate of at least 10 years; (b) within that period or those periods, the use of those tools amounts to at least 2 hours per day for 3 or more days per week; *and* (c) the onset of the disease fell within the period or periods of use specified in this paragraph.
B – Conditions due to biological agents **B1** (a) Cutaneous anthrax; (b) Pulmonary anthrax.	Any occupation involving: (a) Contact with anthrax spores, including contact with animals infected by anthrax; *or* (b) handling, loading, unloading or transport of animals of a type susceptible to infection with anthrax or of the products or residues of such animals.
B2 Glanders.	Contact with equine animals or their carcasses.
B3 Infection by leptospira.	(a) Work in places which are, or are liable to be, infested by rats, field mice or voles, or other small mammals; *or* (b) work at dog kennels or the care or handling of dogs; *or* (c) contact with bovine animals or pigs or their meat products.
B4 (a) Cutaneous larva migrans; (b) Iron deficiency anaemia caused by gastrointestinal infection by hookwork.	Contact with a source of ankylostomiasis.
B5 Tuberculosis.	Contact with a source of tuberculous while undertaking– (a) work in a hospital, mortuary in which post mortems are conducted, or laboratory; *or.* (b) work in any other workplace.
B6 Extrinsic allergic alveolitis.	Exposure to moulds or fungal spores or heterologous proteins or any other biological substance that causes extrinsic allergic alveolitis by reason of employment in: (a) agriculture, horticulture, forestry, cultivation of edible fungi or malt-working; *or* (b) loading or unloading or handling in storage mouldy vegetable matter or edible fungi; *or* (c) caring for or handling birds; *or* (d) handling bagasse; *or* (e) work involving exposure to metalworking fluids mist; *or* (f) any other workplace.

Prescribed disease or injury	Occupation
B7 Infection by organisms of the genus brucella.	Contact with: (a) animals infected by brucella, or their carcasses or parts thereof, or their untreated products; *or* (b) laboratory specimens or vaccines of, or containing, brucella.
B8 (a) Infection by hepatitis A virus.	Contact with raw sewage.
(b) Infection by hepatitis B or C virus.	Contact with: (a) human blood or human blood products; *or* (b) any other source of hepatitis B or C virus.
B9 Infection by Streptococcus suis.	Contact with pigs infected by Streptococcus suis, or with the carcasses, products or residues of pigs so infected.
B10 (a) Avian chlamydiosis.	Contact with birds infected with chlamydia psittaci, or with the remains or untreated products of such birds.
(b) Ovine chlamydiosis.	Contact with sheep infected with chlamydia psittaci, or with the remains or untreated products of such sheep.
B11 Q fever.	Contact with animals, their remains or their untreated products.
B12 Orf.	Contact with sheep, goats or with the carcasses of sheep or goats.
B13 Hydatidosis.	Contact with dogs.
B14 Lyme disease.	Exposure to deer or other mammals of a type liable to harbour ticks harbouring Borrelia bacteria.
B15 Anaphylaxis.	Contact with products made with natural rubber latex.
C – Conditions due to chemical agents	Any occupation involving:
C1 (a) Anaemia with a haemoglobin concentration of 9g/dl or less, and a blood film showing punctate basophilia. (b) Peripheral neuropathy. (c) Central nervous system toxicity.	The use or handling of, or exposure to the fumes, dust or vapour of, lead or a compound of lead, or a substance containing lead.
C2 Central nervous system toxicity characterised by parkinsonism.	The use or handling of, or exposure to the fumes, dust or vapour of, manganese or a compound of manganese, or a substance containing manganese.
C3 (a) Phossy Jaw.	Work involving the use or handling of, or exposure to, white phosphorus.
(b) Peripheral polyneuropathy with pyramidal involvement of the central nervous system, caused by organic compounds of phosphorus which inhibit the enzyme neuropathy target esterase.	Work involving the use or handling of, or exposure to, organic compounds of phosphorus.
C4 Primary carcinoma of the bronchus or lung.	Exposure to the fumes, dust or vapour of arsenic, a compound of arsenic or a substance containing arsenic.
C5 (a) Central nervous system toxicity characterised by tremor and neuropsychiatric disease.	Exposure to mercury or inorganic compounds of mercury for a period of, or periods which amount in aggregate to, 10 years or more.

Prescribed disease or injury	Occupation
(b) Central nervous system toxicity characterised by combined cerebellar and cortical degeneration.	Exposure to methylmercury.
C6 Peripheral neuropathy.	The use or handling of, or exposure to carbon disulphide (also called carbon disulfide).
C7 Acute non-lymphatic leukaemia.	Exposure to benzene.
C12 (a) Peripheral neuropathy.	Exposure to methyl bromide (also called
(b) Central nervous system toxicity.	bromomethane).
C13 Cirrhosis of the liver.	Exposure to chlorinated naphthalene.
C16 (a) Neurotoxicity.	Exposure to the dust of gonioma kamassi.
(b) Cardiotoxicity.	
C17 Chronic beryllium disease.	Inhalation of beryllium or a compound of beryllium.
C18 Emphysema.	Inhalation of cadmium fumes for a period of, or periods which amount in aggregate to, 20 years or more.
C19 (a) Peripheral neuropath.	Exposure to acrylamide.
(b) Central nervous system toxicity.	
C20 Dystrophy of the cornea (including ulceration of the corneal surface) of the eye.	Exposure to quinone or hydroquinone.
C21 Primary carcinoma of the skin.	Exposure to arsenic or arsenic compounds, tar, pitch, bitumen, mineral oil (including paraffin) or soot.
C22 (a) Primary carcinoma of the mucous membrane of the nose or paranasal sinuses.	Work before 1950 in the refining of nickel involving exposure to oxides, sulphides or water-soluble compounds of nickel.
(b) Primary carcinoma of a bronchus or lung.	(a) The manufacture of 1-naphtylamine, 2-
C23 Primary neoplasm of the epithelial lining of the urinary tract (renal pelvis, ureter, bladder and urethra), including papilloma carcinoma-in-situ and invasive carcinoma.	naphthylamine, benzidine, auramine, magenta or 4 aminobiphenyl (also called biphenyl-4-ylamine);
	(b) work in the process of manufacturing methylenebis-orthochloroanile (also called MbOCA) for a period of, or periods which amount in aggregate to, 12 months or more;
	(c) exposure to 2-naphtylamine, benzidine, 4-aminobiphenyl (also called MbOCA) for a period of, or periods which amount in aggregate to, 12 months or more;
	(d) exposure to orthotoluidine, 4-chloro-2-methylaniline or salts of those compounds; *or*
	(e) exposure for a period of, or periods which amount in aggregate to, 5 years or more, to coal tar pitch volatiles produced in aluminium smelting involving the Sodeberg process (that is to say, the method of producing aluminium by electrolysis in which the anode consists of a paste of petroleum coke and mineral oil which is baked in situ).

Prescribed disease or injury	Occupation
C24 (a) Angiosarcoma of the liver. (b) Osteolysis of the terminal phalanges of the fingers. (c) Sclerodermatous thickening of the skin of the hand. (d) Liver fibrosis, due to exposure to vinyl chloride monomer.	Exposure to vinyl chloride monomer in the manufacture of polyvinyl chloride.
C24A Raynaud's phenomenon due to exposure to vinyl chloride monomer.	Exposure to vinyl chloride monomer in the manufacture of polyvinyl chloride before 1st January 1984.
C25 Vitiligo.	The use or handling of, or exposure to, para-tertiary-butylphenol (also called 4-tert-butylphenol), para-tertiary-butylcatechol (also called 4-tert-butylcatechol), para-amyl-phenol (also called p-pentyl phenol isomers), hydroquinone monobenzyl ether of hydroquinone (also called 4-benzyloxyphenol), mono-benzyl ether of hydroquinone (also called 4-benzyloxyphenol), or mono-butyl ether of hydroquinone (also called 4-butoxyphenol).
C26 (a) Liver toxicity. (b) Kidney toxicity.	The use of or handling of, or exposure to, carbon tetrachloride (also called tetrachloromethane).
C27 Liver toxicity.	The use of or handling of, or exposure to the fumes of, or vapour containing, trichloromethane (also called chloroform).
C29 Peripheral neuropathy.	The use of or handling of, or exposure to, n-hexane or n-butyl methyl ketone.
C30 (a) Dermatitis. (b) Ulceration of the mucous membrane or the epidermis.	The use or handling of, or exposure to, chromic acid, chromates or dichromates.
C31 Bronchiolitis obliterans.	The use or handling of, or exposure to, diacetyl (also called butanedione or 2,3-butanedione) in the manufacture of– (a) diacetyl; or (b) food favouring containing diacetyl; or (c) food to which food flavouring containing diacetyl is added.
C32 Carcinoma of the nasal cavity or associated air sinuses (nasal carcinoma).	(a) The manufacture of inorganic chromates; or (b) work in hexavalent chrome plating.
C33 Chloracne	Exposure to substances known as chloracnegans.
C34 Extrinsic allergic alveolitis	Exposure to airborne isocyanates; or to another chemical substance that causes extrinsic allergic alveolitis.
D – Miscellaneous conditions	Occupation involving:

Prescribed disease or injury	Occupation
D1 Pneumoconiosis.	[Occupations specified in reg 2(b) of, and Part II of Schedule 1 to, the Social Security (Industrial Injuries) (Prescribed Diseases) Regulations 1985 which are too numerous to set out here. They are all occupations involving exposure to dust, such as mining, quarrying, sand blasting, grinding, making china or earthenware, boiler-sealing and other work involving the use of stone, asbestos, etc.]
D2 Byssinosis.	Work in any room where any process up to and including the weaving process is performed in a factory in which the spinning or manipulation of raw or waste cotton or of flax, or the weaving of cotton or flax, is carried on.
D3 Diffuse mesothelioma (primary neoplasm of the mesothelium of the pleura or of the pericardium or of the peritoneum).	Exposure to asbestos, asbestos dust or any admixture of asbestos at a level above that commonly found in the environment at large.
D4 Allergic rhinitis which is due to exposure to any of the following agents: (a) isocyanates; (b) platinum salts; (c) fumes or dusts arising from the manufacture, transport or use of hardening agents (including epoxy resin curing agents) based on phthalic anhydride, tetrachlorophthalic anhydride, trimellitic anhydride or triethylenetetramine; (d) fumes arising from the use of rosin as a soldering flux; (e) proteolytic enzymes; (f) animals including insects and other anthropods used for the purposes of research or education or in laboratories; (g) dusts arising from the sowing, cultivation, harvesting, drying, handling, milling, transport or storage of barley, oats, rye, wheat or maize, or the handling, milling, transport or storage of meal or flour made therefrom; (h) antibiotics; (i) cimetidine; (j) wood dust; (k) ispaghula; (l) castor bean dust; (m) ipecacuanha; (n) azodice-bonamide;	Exposure to any of the agents set out in column 1 of this paragraph.

A

Prescribed disease or injury	Occupation
(o) animals including insects and other arthropods or their larval forms, used for the purposes of pest control or fruit cultivation, or the larval forms of animals used for the purposes of research, education or in laboratories;	
(p) glutaraldehyde;	
(q) persulphate salts or henna;	
(r) crustaceans or fish or products arising from these in the food processing industry;	
(s) reactive dyes;	
(t) soya bean;	
(u) tea dust;	
(v) green coffee bean dust;	
(w) fumes from stainless steel welding;	
(x) products made with natural rubber latex.	
D5 Non-infective dermatitis of external origin (excluding dermatitis due to ionising particles or electro-magnetic radiant heat).	Exposure to dust, liquid or vapour or any other external agent except chromic acid, chromates or bi-chromates capable of irritating the skin (including friction or heat but excluding ionising particles or electromagnetic radiations other than radiant heat).
D6 Carcinoma of the nasal cavity or associated air sinuses (nasal carcinoma).	(a) Attendance for work at a workplace where wooden goods or products made wholly or partially of wood are manufactured or repaired; *or*
	(b) attendance for work in a building used for the manufacture of footwear or components of footwear made wholly or partly of leather or fibre board; *or*
	(c) attendance for work at a place used wholly or mainly for the repair of footwear made wholly or partly of leather or fibre board; *or*
	(d) exposure to wood dust in the course of the machine processing of wood.
D7 Asthma which is due to exposure to any of the following agents:	Exposure to any of the agents set out in column 1 of this paragraph.
(a) isocyanates;	
(b) platinum salts;	
(c) fumes or dusts arising from the manufacture, transport or use of hardening agents (including epoxy resin curing agents) based on phthalic anhydride, tetrachlorophthalic anhydride, trimellitic anhydride or triethylenetetramine;	
(d) fumes arising from the use of rosin as a soldering flux;	
(e) proteolytic enzymes;	
(f) animals including insects and other anthropods used for the purposes of research or education or in laboratories;	

Prescribed disease or injury	Occupation
(g) dusts arising from the sowing, cultivation, harvesting, drying, handling, milling, transport or storage of barley, oats, rye, wheat or maize, or the handling, milling, transport or storage of meal or flour made therefrom;	
(h) antibiotics;	
(i) cimetidine;	
(j) wood dust;	
(k) ispaghula;	
(l) castor bean dust;	
(m) ipecacuanha;	
(n) azodicarbonamide;	
(o) animals including insects and other arthropods or their larval forms, used for the purposes of pest control or fruit cultivation, or the larval forms of animals used for the purposes of research, education or in laboratories;	
(p) glutaraldehyde;	
(q) persulphate salts or henna;	
(r) crustaceans or fish or products arising from these in the food processing industry;	
(s) reactive dyes;	
(t) soya bean;	
(u) tea dust;	
(v) green coffee bean dust;	
(w) fumes from stainless steel welding;	
(wa) products made with natural rubber latex;	
(x) any other sensitising agent (occupational asthma).	
D8 Primary carcinoma of the lung where there is accompanying evidence of asbestosis.	(a) The working or handling of asbestos or any admixture of asbestos; or (b) the manufacture or repair of asbestos textiles or other articles containing or composed of asbestos; or (c) the cleaning of any machinery or plant used in any of the foregoing operations and of any chambers, fixtures and appliances for the collection of asbestos dust; or (d) substantial exposure to the dust arising from any of the foregoing operations.

Prescribed disease or injury	Occupation
D8A Primary carcinoma of the lung.	Exposure to asbestos in the course of– (a) the manufacture of asbestos textiles; *or* (b) spraying asbestos; *or* (c) asbestos insulation work; *or* (d) applying or removing materials containing asbestos in the course of shipbuilding, where all or any of the exposure occurs before 1st January 1975, for a period of, or periods which amount in aggregate to, five years or more, or otherwise, for a period of, or periods which amount in aggregate to, ten years or more.
D9 Unilateral or bilateral diffuse pleural thickening.	(a) The working or handling of asbestos; or any admixture of asbestos; *or* (b) the manufacture or repair of asbestos textiles or other articles containing or composed of asbestos; *or* (c) the cleaning of any machinery or plant used in any of the foregoing operations and appliances for the collection of asbestos dust; *or* (d) substantial exposure to the dust arising from any of the foregoing operations.

D10 Primary carcinoma of the lung.	(a) Work underground in a tin mine; *or*
	(b) exposure to bis(chloromethyl) ether produced during the manufacture of chloromethyl methyl ether; *or*
	(c) exposure to zinc chromate, calcium chromate or strontium chromate in their pure forms; *or*
	(d) employment wholly or mainly as a coke oven worker–
	  (i) for a period of, or periods which amount in aggregate to, 15 years or more;
	  (ii) in top oven work, for a period of, or periods which amount in aggregate to, 5 years or more; *or*
	  (iii) in a combination of top oven work and other coke oven work for a total aggregate period of 15 years or more, where one year working in top oven work is treated as equivalent to 3 years in other coke oven work.

A

Prescribed disease or injury	Occupation
D11 Primary carcinoma of the lung where there is accompanying evidence of silicosis.	Exposure to silica dust in the course of: (a) the manufacture of glass or pottery; (b) tunnelling in or quarrying sandstone or granite; (c) mining metal ores; (d) slate quarrying or the manufacture of artefacts from slate; (e) mining clay; (f) using silicous materials as abrasives; (g) cutting stone; (h) stone masonry; *or* (i) work in a foundry.
D12 Except in the circumstances specified in regulation 2(d): chronic obstructive pulmonary disease, where there is evidence of a forced expiratory volume in one second (measured from the position of maximum inspiration with the claimant making maximum effort) which is: (i) at least one litre below the appropriate mean value predicted, obtained from the following prediction formulae which give the mean values predicted in litres: For a man, where the measurement is made without back-extrapolation, (3.62 x Height in metres) – (0.031 x Age in years) – 1.41; or, where the measurement is made with back-extrapolation, (3.71 x Height in metres) – (0.032 x Age in years) – 1.44. For a woman, where the measurement is made without back-extrapolation, (3.29 x Height in metres) – (0.029 x Age in years) – 1.42; or where the measurement is made with back-extrapolation, (3.37 x Height in metres) – (0.030 x Age in years) – 1.46; *or* (ii) less than one litre. The value of the litre in (i) and (ii) shall be construed as fixed and shall not vary by virtue of any treatment or treatments.	Exposure to coal dust (whether before or after 5th July 1948) by reason of working– (a) underground in a coal mine for a period or periods amounting in aggregate to at least 20 years; (b) on the surface of a coal mine as a screen worker for a period or periods amounting in aggregate to at least 40 years before 1st January 1983; *or* (c) both underground in a coal mine, and on the surface as a screen worker before 1st January 1983, where 2 years working as a surface screen worker is equivalent to 1 year working underground, amounting in aggregate to at least the equivalent of 20 years underground. Any such period or periods shall include a period or periods of incapacity while engaged in such an occupation.
D13 Primary cacinoma of the nasopharynx	Exposure to wood dust in the course of the processing of wood or the manufacture or repair of wood products, for a period or periods which amount in aggregate to at least 10 years.

Appendix 6

Upper and lower earnings limits

Year	Lower earnings limit £	Primary threshold £	Upper earnings limit £
1992/93	54		405
1993/94	56		420
1994/95	57		430
1995/96	58		440
1996/97	61		455
1997/98	62		465
1998/99	64		485
1999/00	66		500
2000/01	67	76	535
2001/02	72	87	575
2002/03	75	89	585
2003/04	77	89	595
2004/05	79	91	610
2005/06	82	94	630
2006/07	84	97	645
2007/08	87	100	670
2008/09	90	105	770
2009/10	95	110	844
2010/11	97	110	844
2011/12	102	139	817
2012/13	107	146	817
2013/14	109	149	797
2014/15	111	153	805
2015/16	112	155	815
2016/17	112	155	827
2017/18	113	157	866
2018/19	116	162	892
2019/20	118	166	962
2020/21	120	183	962
2021/22	120	184	967
2022/23	123	190 (242 from 6 July 2022)	967

Appendix 7

Minimum working conditions

Employers are required to provide certain minimum working conditions. These rules are relevant to the universal credit and jobseeker's allowance rules about sanctions and being available for and looking for work. A brief summary of the rules follows.

The Working Time Regulations

These regulations are designed to protect the health and safety of workers. The main rules are:

- a limit on the hours in the average working week;
- minimum annual holiday entitlement;
- entitlement to breaks from work (both daily breaks and a longer break once a week) and to rest periods while at work;
- special protection for night workers.

This *Handbook* cannot cover the detailed rules nor the complicated system of exceptions to them. Get specialist advice if you think your employer is breaking these rules.

The National Minimum Wage Act

This Act provides that the minimum hourly rate of pay in any job should be:

- if you are aged 23 or over, £9.50. The government calls this the 'national living wage';
- if you are aged 21–22, £9.18;
- if you are aged 18–20, £6.83;
- if you are aged 16 or 17, £4.81;
- if you are in the first year of employment or are under 19, and you are employed under a contract of apprenticeship (or treated as if you are), £4.81.

Appendix 8

Statutory payments for a birth and maternity allowance

Baby is expected during the week beginning Sunday	Latest start date of employment for SMP	15th week before the EWC begins Sunday+	Earliest week for SMP or MA begins Sunday++	66-week test period for MA begins Sunday
4.4.21	4.7.20	20.12.20	17.1.21	29.12.19
11.4.21	11.7.20	27.12.20	24.1.21	5.1.20
18.4.21	18.7.20	3.1.21	31.1.21	12.1.20
25.4.21	25.7.20	10.1.21	7.2.21	19.1.20
2.5.21	1.8.20	17.1.21	14.2.21	26.1.20
9.5.21	8.8.20	24.1.21	21.2.21	2.2.20
16.5.21	15.8.20	31.1.21	28.2.21	9.2.20
23.5.21	22.8.20	7.2.21	7.3.21	16.2.20
30.5.21	29.8.20	14.2.21	14.3.21	23.2.20
6.6.21	5.9.20	21.2.21	21.3.21	1.3.20
13.6.21	12.9.20	28.2.21	28.3.21	8.3.20
20.6.21	19.9.20	7.3.21	4.4.21	15.3.20
27.6.21	26.9.20	14.3.21	11.4.21	22.3.20
4.7.21	3.10.20	21.3.21	18.4.21	29.3.20
11.7.21	10.10.20	28.3.21	25.4.21	5.4.20
18.7.21	17.10.20	4.4.21	2.5.21	12.4.20
25.7.21	24.10.20	11.4.21	9.5.21	19.4.20
1.8.21	31.10.20	18.4.21	16.5.21	26.4.20
8.8.21	7.11.20	25.4.21	23.5.21	3.5.20
15.8.21	14.11.20	2.5.21	30.5.21	10.5.20
22.8.21	21.11.20	9.5.21	6.6.21	17.5.20
29.8.21	28.11.20	16.5.21	13.6.21	24.5.20
5.9.21	5.12.20.	23.5.21	20.6.21	31.5.20
12.9.21	12.12.20	30.5.21	27.6.21	7.6.20
19.9.21	19.12.20	6.6.21	4.7.21	14.6.20
26.9.21	26.12.20	13.6.21	11.7.21	21.6.20
3.10.21	2.1.21	20.6.21	18.7.21	28.6.20
10.10.21	9.1.21	27.6.21	25.7.21	5.7.20

Appendix 8: Statutory payments for a birth and maternity allowance

Baby is expected during the week beginning Sunday	Latest start date of employment for SMP	15th week before the EWC begins Sunday+	Earliest week for SMP or MA begins Sunday++	66-week test period for MA begins Sunday
17.10.21	16.1.21	4.7.21	1.8.21	12.7.20
24.10.21	23.1.21	11.7.21	8.8.21	19.7.20
31.10.21	30.1.21	18.7.21	15.8.21	26.7.20
7.11.21	6.2.21	25.7.21	22.8.21	2.8.20
14.11.21	13.2.21	1.8.21	29.8.21	9.8.20
21.11.21	20.2.21	8.8.21	5.9.21	16.8.20
28.11.21	27.2.21	15.8.21	12.9.21	23.8.20
5.12.21	6.3.21	22.8.21	19.9.21	30.8.20
12.12.21	13.3.21	29.8.21	26.9.21	6.9.20
19.12.21	20.3.21	5.9.21	3.10.21	13.9.20
26.12.21	27.3.21	12.9.21	10.10.21	20.9.20
2.1.22	3.4.21	19.9.21	17.10.21	27.9.20
9.1.22	10.4.21	26.9.21	24.10.21	4.10.20
16.1.22	17.4.21	3.10.21	31.10.21	11.10.20
23.1.22	24.4.21	10.10.21	7.11.21	18.10.20
30.1.22	1.5.21	17.10.21	14.11.21	25.10.20
6.2.22	8.5.21	24.10.21	21.11.21	1.11.20
13.2.22	15.5.21	31.10.21	28.11.21	8.11.20
20.2.22	22.5.21	7.11.21	5.12.21	15.11.20
27.2.22	29.5.21	14.11.21	12.12.21	22.11.20
6.3.22	5.6.21	21.11.21	19.12.21	29.11.20
13.3.22	12.6.21	28.11.21	26.12.21	6.12.20
20.3.22	19.6.21	5.12.21	2.1.22	13.12.20
27.3.22	26.6.21	12.12.21	9.1.22	20.12.20
3.4.22	3.7.21	19.12.21	16.1.22	27.12.20
10.4.22	10.7.21	26.12.21	23.1.22	3.1.21
17.4.22	17.7.21	2.1.22	30.1.22	10.1.21
24.4.22	24.7.21	9.1.22	6.2.22	17.1.21
1.5.22	31.7.21	16.1.22	13.2.22	24.1.21
8.5.22	7.8.21	23.1.22	20.2.22	31.1.21
15.5.22	14.8.21	30.1.22	27.2.22	7.2.21
22.5.22	21.8.21	6.2.22	6.3.22	14.2.21
29.5.22	28.8.21	13.2.22	13.3.22	21.2.21
5.6.22	4.9.21	20.2.22	20.3.22	28.2.21
12.6.22	11.9.21	27.2.22	27.3.22	7.3.21
19.6.22	18.9.21	6.3.22	3.4.22	14.3.21
26.6.22	25.9.21	13.3.22	10.4.22	21.3.21
3.7.22	2.10.21	20.3.22	17.4.22	28.3.21
10.7.22	9.10.21	27.3.22	24.4.22	4.4.21
17.7.22	16.10.21	3.4.22	1.5.22	11.4.21
24.7.22	23.10.21	10.4.22	8.5.22	18.4.21

Baby is expected during the week beginning Sunday	Latest start date of employment for SMP	15th week before the EWC begins Sunday+	Earliest week for SMP or MA begins Sunday++	66-week test period for MA begins Sunday
31.7.22	30.10.21	17.4.22	15.5.22	25.4.21
7.8.22	6.11.21	24.4.22	22.5.22	2.5.21
14.8.22	13.11.21	1.5.22	29.5.22	9.5.21
21.8.22	20.11.21	8.5.22	5.6.22	16.5.21
28.8.22	27.11.21	15.5.22	12.6.22	23.5.21
4.9.22	4.12.21	22.5.22	19.6.22	30.5.21
11.9.22	11.12.21	29.5.22	26.6.22	6.6.21
18.9.22	18.12.21	5.6.22	3.7.22	13.6.21
25.9.22	25.12.21	12.6.22	10.7.22	20.6.21
2.10.22	1.1.22	19.6.22	17.7.22	27.6.21
9.10.22	8.1.22	26.6.22	24.7.22	4.7.21
16.10.22	15.1.22	3.7.22	31.7.22	11.7.21
23.10.22	22.1.22	10.7.22	7.8.22	18.7.21
30.10.22	29.1.22	17.7.22	14.8.22	25.7.21
6.11.22	5.2.22	24.7.22	21.8.22	1.8.21
13.11.22	12.2.22	31.7.22	28.8.22	8.8.21
20.11.22	19.2.22	7.8.22	4.9.22	15.8.21
27.11.22	26.2.22	14.8.22	11.9.22	22.8.21
4.12.22	5.3.22	21.8.22	18.9.22	29.8.21
11.12.22	12.3.22	28.8.22	25.9.22	5.9.21
18.12.22	19.3.22	4.9.22	2.10.22	12.9.21
25.12.22	26.3.22	11.9.22	9.10.22	19.9.21
1.1.23	2.4.22	18.9.22	16.10.22	26.9.21
8.1.23	9.4.22	25.9.22	23.10.22	3.10.21
15.1.23	16.4.22	2.10.22	30.10.22	10.10.21
22.1.23	23.4.22	9.10.22	6.11.22	17.10.21
29.1.23	30.4.22	16.10.22	13.11.22	24.10.21
5.2.23	7.5.22	23.10.22	20.11.22	31.10.21
12.2.23	14.5.22	30.10.22	27.11.22	7.11.21
19.2.23	21.5.22	6.11.22	4.12.22	14.11.21
26.2.23	28.5.22	13.11.22	11.12.22	21.11.21
5.3.23	4.6.22	20.11.22	18.12.22	28.11.21
12.3.23	11.6.22	27.11.22	25.12.22	5.12.21
19.3.23	18.6.22	4.12.22	1.1.23	12.12.21
26.3.23	25.6.22	11.12.22	8.1.23	19.12.21
2.4.23	2.7.22	18.12.22	15.1.23	26.12.21
9.4.23	9.7.22	25.12.22	22.1.23	2.1.22
16.4.23	16.7.22	1.1.23	29.1.23	9.1.22
23.4.23	23.7.22	8.1.23	5.2.23	16.1.22
30.4.23	30.7.22	15.1.23	12.2.23	23.1.22
7.5.23	6.8.22	22.1.23	19.2.23	30.1.22

A

Baby is expected during the week beginning Sunday	Latest start date of employment for SMP	15th week before the EWC begins Sunday+	Earliest week for SMP or MA begins Sunday++	66-week test period for MA begins Sunday
14.5.23	13.8.22	29.1.23	26.2.23	6.2.22
21.5.23	20.8.22	5.2.23	5.3.23	13.2.22
28.5.23	27.8.22	12.2.23	12.3.23	20.2.22
4.6.23	3.9.22	19.2.23	19.3.23	27.2.22
11.6.23	10.9.22	26.2.23	26.3.23	6.3.22
18.6.23	17.9.22	5.3.23	2.4.23	13.3.22
25.6.23	24.9.22	12.3.23	9.4.23	20.3.22
2.7.23	1.10.22	19.3.23	16.4.23	27.3.22
9.7.23	8.10.22	26.3.23	23.4.23	3.4.22
16.7.23	15.10.22	2.4.23	30.4.23	10.4.22
23.7.23	22.10.22	9.4.23	7.5.23	17.4.22
30.7.23	29.10.22	16.4.23	14.5.23	24.4.22
6.8.23	5.11.22	23.4.23	21.5.23	1.5.22
13.8.23	12.11.22	30.4.23	28.5.23	8.5.22
20.8.23	19.11.22	7.5.23	4.6.23	15.5.22
27.8.23	26.11.22	14.5.23	11.6.23	22.5.22
3.9.23	3.12.22	21.5.23	18.6.23	29.5.22
10.9.23	10.12.22	28.5.23	25.6.23	5.6.22
17.9.23	17.12.22	4.6.23	2.7.23	12.6.22
24.9.23	24.12.22	11.6.23	9.7.23	19.6.22
1.10.23	31.12.22	18.6.23	16.7.23	26.6.22
8.10.23	7.1.23	25.6.23	23.7.23	3.7.22
15.10.23	14.1.23	2.7.23	30.7.23	10.7.22
22.10.23	21.1.23	9.7.23	6.8.23	17.7.22
29.10.23	28.1.23	16.7.23	13.8.23	24.7.22
5.11.23	4.2.23	23.7.23	20.8.23	31.7.22
12.11.23	11.2.23	30.7.23	27.8.23	7.8.22
19.11.23	18.2.23	6.8.23	3.9.23	14.8.22
26.11.23	25.2.23	13.8.23	10.9.23	21.8.22
3.12.23	4.3.23	20.8.23	17.9.23	28.8.22
10.12.23	11.3.23	27.8.23	24.9.23	4.9.22
17.12.23	18.3.23	3.9.23	1.10.23	11.9.22
24.12.23	25.3.23	10.9.23	8.10.23	18.9.22
31.12.23	1.4.23	17.9.23	15.10.23	25.9.22

+ EWC is the expected week of childbirth. The 15th week before the EWC is relevant to the continuous employment rule and the earnings condition for SMP, SPP and SSPP. See Chapter 38.

++ This is the 11th week before the baby is due (unless your baby is born earlier. See Chapters 34 and 38 for possible exceptions).

Appendix 9

Abbreviations used in the notes

AAC	Administrative Appeals Chamber
AACR	Administrative Appeals Chamber Reports
AC	Appeal Cases
All ER	All England Law Reports
Art(s)	Article(s)
BSG	Best Start grant
CA	Court of Appeal
CC	County Council
CCLR	Community Care Law Reports
Ch	chapter
CJEU	Court of Justice of the European Union
CLY	Current Law Year Book
col	column
CPR	Civil Procedure Rules
CS	Court of Session
CSIH	Court of Session, Inner House
CSOH	Court of Session, Outer House
CWHA	child winter heating assistance
DC	Divisional Court
Dir	Directive
E	England
ECJ	European Court of Justice
ECR	European Court Reports
ECtHR	European Court of Human Rights
EEA	European Economic Area
EEC	European Economic Community
EU	European Union
EWCA Civ	England and Wales Court of Appeal (Civil Division)
EWCA Crim	England and Wales Court of Appeal (Criminal Division)
EWHC	England and Wales High Court
FLR	Family Law Reports
FSP	funeral support payment
HC	High Court
HL	House of Lords
HLR	Housing Law Reports
IAC	Immigration and Asylum Chamber
ICR	Industrial Cases Reports
IR	Immigration Rules
JPR	Justice of the Peace Reports
KB	King's Bench
LB	London Borough
LC	Lands Chamber
MBC	Metropolitan Borough Council
NICA	Northern Ireland Court of Appeal
NICom	Northern Ireland Social Security Commissioner
OJ	Official Journal of the European Union
para(s)	paragraph(s)

QB	Queen's Bench Reports	SSWP	Secretary of State for Work and Pensions
QBD	Queen's Bench Division		
r(r)	rule(s)	TCC	Tax and Chancery Chamber
Reg(s)	Regulation(s)	UKHL	United Kingdom House of Lords
s(s)	section(s)		
SC	Supreme Court	UKSC	United Kingdom Supreme Court
Sch(s)	Schedule(s)		
SCLR	Scottish Civil Law Reports	UKUT	United Kingdom Upper Tribunal
ScotCS	Scottish Court of Session		
SCP	Scottish child payment	Vol	volume
SLT	Scots Law Times	W	Wales
SSAC	Social Security Advisory Committee	WLR	Weekly Law Reports
		YCG	young carer grant

Acts of Parliament

C(LC)A 2000	Children (Leaving Care) Act 2000
CA 2020	Coronavirus Act 2020
CJPOA 1994	Criminal Justice and Public Order Act 1994
CMOPA 2008	Child Maintenance and Other Payments Act 2008
CSA 1991	Child Support Act 1991
CSPSSA 2000	Child Support, Pensions and Social Security Act 2000
ETA 1973	Employment and Training Act 1973
EU(W)A 2018	European Union (Withdrawal) Act 2018
GRA 2004	Gender Recognition Act 2004
HRA 1998	Human Rights Act 1998
IA 1971	Immigration Act 1971
IA 1988	Immigration Act 1988
IAA 1999	Immigration and Asylum Act 1999
IT(EP)A 2003	Income Tax (Earnings and Pensions) Act 2003
ITT(OI)A 2005	Income Tax (Trading and Other Income) Act 2005
LGFA 1992	Local Government Finance Act 1992
JSA 1995	Jobseekers Act 1995
M(SSC)A 2013	Marriage (Same Sex Couples) Act 2013
MCA 1973	Matrimonial Causes Act 1973
NHSA 2006	National Health Service Act 2006
NHS(S)A 1978	National Health Service (Scotland) Act 1978
NHS(W)A 2006	National Health Service (Wales) Act 2006
NIAA 2002	Nationality, Immigration and Asylum Act 2002
PA 1995	Pensions Act 1995
PA 2014	Pensions Act 2014
PACEA 1984	Police and Criminal Evidence Act 1984
SPCA 2002	State Pension Credit Act 2002

A

SA 1998	Scotland Act 1998
SA 2016	Scotland Act 2016
SS(RB)A 1997	Social Security (Recovery of Benefits) Act 1997
SS(S)A 2018	Social Security (Scotland) Act 2018
SSA 1998	Social Security Act 1998
SSA(F)A 1997	Social Security Administration (Fraud) Act 1997
SSAA 1992	Social Security Administration Act 1992
SSC(TF)A 1999	Social Security Contributions (Transfer of Functions) Act 1999
SSCBA 1992	Social Security Contributions and Benefits Act 1992
SSFA 2001	Social Security Fraud Act 2001
T(S)A 2014	Tribunals (Scotland) Act 2014
TCA 2002	Tax Credits Act 2002
TCEA 2007	Tribunals, Courts and Enforcement Act 2007
TMA 1970	Taxes Management Act 1970
WRA 2007	Welfare Reform Act 2007
WRA 2012	Welfare Reform Act 2012
WRWA 2016	Welfare Reform and Work Act 2016

Regulations and other statutory instruments

Each set of regulations has a statutory instrument (SI) number and a date. You can find them all at legislation.gov.uk.

A(IWA) Regs	The Accession (Immigration and Worker Authorisation) Regulations 2006 No.3317
A(IWR) Regs	The Accession (Immigration and Worker Registration) Regulations 2004 No.1219
AC(IWA) Regs	The Accession of Croatia (Immigration and Worker Authorisation) Regulations 2013 No.1460
ASPP(G) Regs	The Additional Statutory Paternity Pay (General) Regulations 2010 No.1056
BSP Regs	The Bereavement Support Payment Regulations 2017 No.410
C(LC)SSB Regs	The Children (Leaving Care) Social Security Benefits Regulations 2001 No.3074
C(LC)SSB(S) Regs	The Children (Leaving Care) Social Security Benefits (Scotland) Regulations 2004 No.747
C(LC)(W) Regs	The Children (Leaving Care) (Wales) Regulations 2001 No.2189 (W151)
CA(YCG)(S) Regs	The Carer's Assistance (Young Carer Grants) (Scotland) Regulations 2019 No.324
CB Regs	The Child Benefit (General) Regulations 2006 No.223

CB(R) Regs	The Child Benefit (Rates) Regulations 2006 No.965
CB&GA(AA) Regs	The Child Benefit and Guardian's Allowance (Administrative Arrangements) Regulations 2003 No.494
CB&GA(Admin) Regs	The Child Benefit and Guardian's Allowance (Administration) Regulations 2003 No.492
CB&GA(DA) Regs	The Child Benefit and Guardian's Allowance (Decisions and Appeals) Regulations 2003 No.916
CC(DIS) Regs	The Community Charges (Deductions from Income Support) (No.2) Regulations 1990 No.545
CL(E) Regs	The Care Leavers (England) Regulations 2010 No.2571
CPP&CR(E) Regs	The Care Planning, Placement and Case Review (England) Regulations 2010 No.959
CR(ADTP) Regs	The Citizens' Rights (Application Deadline and Temporary Protection) (EU Exit) Regulations 2020 No.1209
CR(FW) Regs	The Citizens' Rights (Frontier Workers) (EU Exit) Regulations 2020 No.1213
CS(MCSC) Regs	The Child Support (Maintenance Calculations and Special Cases) Regulations 2000 No.2001/155
CT(DIS) Regs	The Council Tax (Deductions from Income Support) Regulations 1993 No.494
CTC Regs	The Child Tax Credit Regulations 2002 No.2007
CTR(S) Regs	The Council Tax Reduction (Scotland) Regulations 2021 No.249
CTR(SPC)S Regs	The Council Tax Reduction (State Pension Credit) (Scotland) Regulations 2012 No.319
CTRS(DS)E Regs	The Council Tax Reduction Schemes (Default Scheme) (England) Regulations 2012 No.2886
CTRS(DS)W Regs	The Council Tax Reduction Schemes (Default Scheme) (Wales) Regulations 2013 No.3035 (W303)
CTRS(PR)E Regs	The Council Tax Reduction Schemes (Prescribed Requirements) (England) Regulations 2012 No.2885
CTRSPR(W) Regs	The Council Tax Reduction Schemes and Prescribed Requirements (Wales) Regulations 2013 No.3029 (W316)
DACYP(S) Regs	The Disability Assistance for Children and Young People (Scotland) Regulations 2021 No.174
DAWAP(S) Regs	The Disability Assistance for Working Age People (Scotland) Regulations 2022 No.54
DFA Regs	Discretionary Financial Assistance Regulations 2001 No.1167

ESA Regs	The Employment and Support Allowance Regulations 2008 No.794
ESA Regs 2013	The Employment and Support Allowance Regulations 2013 No.379
ESA(TP) Regs	The Employment and Support Allowance (Transitional Provisions) Regulations 2008 No.795
ESA(TP)(EA)(No.2) Regs	The Employment and Support Allowance (Transitional Provisions, Housing Benefit and Council Tax Benefit) (Existing Awards) (No.2) Regulations 2010 No.1907
ESA(WRA) Regs	The Employment and Support Allowance (Work-Related Activity) Regulations 2011 No.1349
ESAUC(MA) Regs	The Employment and Support Allowance and Universal Credit (Miscellaneous Amendments and Transitional and Savings Provisions) Regulations 2017 No.204
EYA(BSG)(S) Regs	The Early Years Assistance (Best Start Grants) (Scotland) Regulations 2018 No.370
F(DIS) Regs	The Fines (Deductions from Income Support) Regulations 1992 No.2182
FEA(S) Regs	The Funeral Expense Assistance (Scotland) Regulations 2019 No.292
FTTS(AFSSC) Regs	The First-tier Tribunal for Scotland (Allocation of Functions to the Social Security Chamber) Regulations 2018 No.350
FTT(S) Rules	Schedule to The First-tier Tribunal for Scotland Social Security Chamber (Procedure) Regulations 2018 No.273
GA(Gen) Regs	The Guardian's Allowance (General) Regulations 2003 No.495
HB Regs	The Housing Benefit Regulations 2006 No.213
HB(HR)A Regs	The Housing Benefit (Habitual Residence) Amendment Regulations 2014 No.539
HB(SPC) Regs	The Housing Benefit (Persons who have Attained the Qualifying Age for State Pension Credit) Regulations 2006 No.214
HB&CTB(CP) Regs	The Housing Benefit and Council Tax Benefit (Consquential Provisions) Regulations 2006 No.217
HB&CTB(DA) Regs	The Housing Benefit and Council Tax Benefit (Decisions and Appeals) Regulations 2001 No.1002
HB&CTB(WPD) Regs	The Housing Benefit and Council Tax Benefit (War Pension Disregards) Regulations 2007 No.1619
HSS(DHSF)(W) Regs	The Healthy Start Scheme (Description of Healthy Start Food) (Wales) Regulations 2006 No.3108
HSS&WF(A) Regs	The Healthy Start Scheme and Welfare Food (Amendment) Regulations 2005 No.3262

I(EEA) Regs	The Immigration (European Economic Area) Regulations 2016 No.1052
I(EEA) Regs 2006	The Immigration (European Economic Area) Regulations 2006 No.1003
I(EEA)A Regs 2012	The Immigration (European Economic Area) (Amendment) Regulations 2012 No.1547
IIB(ETSC) Regs	The Industrial Injuries Benefit (Employment Training Schemes and Courses) Regulations 2013 No.2540
IS Regs	The Income Support (General) Regulations 1987 No.1967
IS(JSACA) Regs	The Income Support (General) (Jobseeker's Allowance Consequential Amendments) Regulations 1996 No.206
IS(WRA) Regs	The Income Support (Work-Related Activity) and Miscellaneous Amendments Regulations 2014 No.1097
ISSC(CSTTP) Regs	The Immigration and Social Security Co-ordination (EU Withdrawal) Act 2020 (Consequential, Saving, Transitional and Transitory Provisions) (EU Exit) Regulations 2020 No.1309
JSA Regs	The Jobseeker's Allowance Regulations 1996 No.207
JSA Regs 2013	The Jobseeker's Allowance Regulations 2013 No.378
JSA(HR)A Regs	The Jobseeker's Allowance (Habitual Residence) Amendment Regulations 2013 No.3196
JSA(SAPOE) Regs	The Jobseeker's Allowance (Schemes for Assisting Persons to Obtain Employment) Regulations 2013 No.276
LMI Regs	The Loans for Mortgage Interest Regulations 2017 No.725
MA(C) Regs	The Maternity Allowance (Curtailment) Regulations 2014 No.3053
NHS(CDA) Regs	The National Health Service (Charges for Drugs and Appliances) Regulations 2015 No.570
NHS(DC) Regs	The National Health Service (Dental Charges) Regulations 2005 No.3477
NHS(DC)(S) Regs	The National Health Service (Dental Charges) (Scotland) Regulations 2003 No.158
NHS(DC)(W) Regs	The National Health Service (Dental Charges) (Wales) Regulations 2006 No.491
NHS(FP&CDA)(S) Regs	The National Health Service (Free Prescriptions and Charges for Drugs and Appliances) (Scotland) Regulations 2011 No.55
NHS(FP&CDA)(W) Regs	The National Health Service (Free Prescriptions and Charges for Drugs and Appliances) (Wales) Regulations 2007 No.121

NHS(GOS) Regs	The National Health Service (General Ophthalmic Services) Regulations 1986 No.975
NHS(OCP) Regs	The National Health Service (Optical Charges and Payments) Regulations 1997 No.818
NHS(OCP) Regs 2013	The National Health Service (Optical Charges and Payments) Regulations 2013 No.461
NHS(OCP)(S) Regs	The National Health Service (Optical Charges and Payments) (Scotland) Regulations 1998 No.642
NHS(TERC) Regs	The National Health Service (Travelling Expenses and Remission of Charges) Regulations 2003 No.2382
NHS(TERC)(S) Regs	The National Health Service (Travelling Expenses and Remission of Charges) (Scotland) (No.2) Regulations 2003 No.460
NHS(TERC)(W) Regs	The National Health Service (Travelling Expenses and Remission of Charges Regulations) (Wales) 2007 No.1104
PAL Regs	The Paternity and Adoption Leave Regulations 2002 No.2788
PIP(TP) Regs	The Personal Independence Payment (Transitional Provisions) Regulations 2013 No.387
POS Regs	The Primary Ophthalmic Services Regulations 2008 No.1186
RO(HBF)O	The Rent Officers (Housing Benefit Functions) Order 1997 No.1984
RO(HBF)(S)O	The Rent Officers (Housing Benefit Functions) (Scotland) Order 1997 No.144
RO(UCF)O	The Rent Officers (Universal Credit Functions) Order 2013 No.382
SCP Regs	The Scottish Child Payment Regulations 2020 No.351
SF(AM) Regs	The Social Fund (Budgeting Loans) (Applications and Miscellaneous Provisions) Regulations 2015 No.1411
SF(AR) Regs	The Social Fund (Application for Review) Regulations 1988 No.34
SF(RDB) Regs	The Social Fund (Recovery by Deductions from Benefits) Regulations 1988 No.35
SFCWP Regs	The Social Fund Cold Weather Payments (General) Regulations 1988 No.1724
SFM&FE Regs	The Social Fund Maternity and Funeral Expenses (General) Regulations 2005 No.3061
SFWFP Regs	The Social Fund Winter Fuel Payment Regulations 2000 No.729
SMP Regs	The Statutory Maternity Pay (General) Regulations 1986 No.1960

SMP(ME) Regs	The Statutory Maternity Pay (Medical Evidence) Regulations 1987 No.235
SMP(PAM) Regs	The Statutory Maternity Pay (Persons Abroad and Mariners) Regulations 1987 No.418
SMP&SAP(C) Regs	The Statutory Maternity Pay and Statutory Adoption Pay (Curtailment) Regulations 2014 No.3054
SMPSS(MA) Regs	The Statutory Maternity Pay, Social Security (Maternity Allowance) and Social Security (Overlapping Benefits) (Amendment) Regulations 2006 No.2379
SP Regs	The State Pension Regulations 2015 No.173
SPBP(A) Regs	The Statutory Parental Bereavement Pay (Administration) Regulations 2020 No.246
SPBP(G) Regs	The Statutory Parental Bereavement Pay (General) Regulations 2020 No.233
SPBP(PAM) Regs	The Statutory Parental Bereavement Pay (Persons Abroad and Mariners) Regulations 2020 No.252
SPC Regs	The State Pension Credit Regulations 2002 No.1792
SPC(CTMP) Regs	The State Pension Credit (Consequential, Transitional and Miscellaneous Provisions) Regulations 2002 No.3019
SPP(A)&SAP(AO)(No.2) Regs	The Statutory Paternity Pay (Adoption) and Statutory Adoption Pay (Adoptions from Overseas) (No.2) Regulations 2003 No.1194
SPPSAP(A) Regs	The Statutory Paternity Pay and Statutory Adoption Pay (Administration) Regulations 2002 No.2820
SPPSAP(G) Regs	The Statutory Paternity Pay and Statutory Adoption Pay (General) Regulations 2002 No.2822
SPPSAP(PAM) Regs	The Statutory Paternity Pay and Statutory Adoption Pay (Persons Abroad and Mariners) Regulations 2002 No.2821
SPPSAP(POPA) Regs	The Statutory Paternity Pay and Statutory Adoption Pay (Parental Orders and Prospective Adopters) Regulations 2014 No.2934
SPPSAP(WR) Regs	The Statutory Paternity Pay and Statutory Adoption Pay (Weekly Rates) Regulations 2002 No.2818
SSA(IO)(S) Regs	Social Security Assistance (Investigation of Offences) (Scotland) Regulations 2020 SSI 2020 No.11
SS(AA) Regs	The Social Security (Attendance Allowance) Regulations 1991 No.2740
SS(C)(FM) Regs	The Social Security (Coronavirus) (Further Measures) Regulations 2020 No.371
SS(C)(P) Regs	The Social Security (Coronavirus) (Prisoners) Regulations 2020 No.409

A

SS(CatE) Regs	The Social Security (Categorisation of Earners) Regulations 1978 No.1689
SS(CCPC) Regs	Social Security (Contribution Credits for Parents and Carers) Regulations 2010 No.19
SS(Con) Regs	The Social Security (Contributions) Regulations 2001 No.1004
SS(C&P) Regs	The Social Security (Claims and Payments) Regulations 1987 No.1968
SS(CP)Regs	The Social Security (Civil Penalties) Regulations 2012 No.1990
SS(Cr) Regs	The Social Security (Credits) Regulations 1975 No.556
SS(CTCNIN)Regs	The Social Security (Crediting and Treatment of Contributions, and National Insurance Numbers) Regulations 2001 No.769
SS(DLA) Regs	The Social Security (Disability Living Allowance) Regulations 1991 No.2890
SS(DLA)A Regs	Social Security (Disability Living Allowance) (Amendment) Regulations 2010 No.1651
SS(DLA,AA&CA)(A) Regs	The Social Security (Disability Living Allowance, Attendance Allowance and Carer's Allowance) (Amendment) Regulations 2013 No.389
SS(EEEIIP) Regs	The Social Security (Employed Earners' Employment for Industrial Injuries Purposes) Regulations 1975 No.467
SS(EF) Regs	The Social Security (Earnings Factor) Regulations 1979 No.676
SS(GB) Regs	The Social Security (General Benefits) Regulations 1982 No.1408
SS(GBRA)NI Regs	The Social Security (Great Britain Reciprocal Arrangements) Regulations (Northern Ireland) 2016 No.149
SS(HIP) Regs	The Social Security (Hospital In-Patients) Regulations 2005 No.3360
SS(HR)A Regs	The Social Security (Habitual Residence) Amendment Regulations 2004 No.1232
SS(IA)CA Regs	The Social Security (Immigration and Asylum) Consequential Amendments Regulations 2000 No.636
SS(IB) Regs	The Social Security (Incapacity Benefit) Regulations 1994 No.2946
SS(IB)(T) Regs	The Social Security (Incapacity Benefit) (Transitional) Regulations 1995 No.310
SS(IB-ID) Regs	The Social Security (Incapacity Benefit – Increases for Dependants) Regulations 1994 No.2945

A

SS(IBWFI) Regs	The Social Security (Incapacity Benefit Work-focused Interviews) Regulations 2008 No.2928
SS(ICA) Regs	The Social Security (Invalid Care Allowance) Regulations 1976 No.409
SS(II)(AB) Regs	The Social Security (Industrial Injuries) (Airmen's Benefits) Regulations 1975 No.469
SS(II)(MB) Regs	The Social Security (Industrial Injuries) (Mariners' Benefits) Regulations 1975 No.470
SS(II)(REA) Regs	The Social Security (Industrial Injuries) (Reduced Earnings Allowance and Transitional) Regulations 1987 No.415
SS(II&D)MP Regs	The Social Security (Industrial Injuries and Diseases) Miscellaneous Provisions Regulations 1986 No.1561
SS(IIPD) Regs	The Social Security (Industrial Injuries) (Prescribed Diseases) Regulations 1985 No.967
SS(IIPD)(A) Regs	The Social Security (Industrial Injuries) (Prescribed Diseases) Amendment Regulations 2017 No.232
SS(JPI) Regs	The Social Security (Jobcentre Plus Interviews) Regulations 2002 No.1703
SS(JPIP) Regs	Social Security (Jobcentre Plus Interviews for Partners) Regulations 2003 No.1886
SS(LB) Regs	The Social Security (Loss of Benefit) Regulations 2001 No.4022
SS(MAP) Regs	The Social Security (Maximum Additional Pension) Regulations 1978 No.949
SS(MatA) Regs	The Social Security (Maternity Allowance) Regulations 1987 No.416
SS(MatA)(E) Regs	The Social Security (Maternity Allowance) (Earnings) Regulations 2000 No.688
SS(MatA)(WA) Regs	The Social Security (Maternity Allowance) (Work Abroad) Regulations 1987 No.417
SS(ME) Regs	The Social Security (Medical Evidence) Regulations 1976 No.615
SS(NCC) Regs	The Social Security (Notification of Change of Circumstances) Regulations 2001 No.3252
SS(NIRA) Regs	The Social Security (Northern Ireland Reciprocal Arrangements) Regulations 2016 No.287
SS(OB) Regs	The Social Security (Overlapping Benefits) Regulations 1979 No.597
SS(OR) Regs	The Social Security (Overpayments and Recovery) Regulations 2013 No.384
SS(PA)A Regs	Social Security (Persons from Abroad) Amendment Regulations 2006 No.1026

A

SS(PAB) Regs	The Social Security (Payments on Account of Benefit) Regulations 2013 No.383
SS(PAOR) Regs	The Social Security (Payments on Account, Overpayments and Recovery) Regulations 1988 No.664
SS(PFA)MA Regs	The Social Security (Persons From Abroad) Miscellaneous Amendment Regulations 1996 No.30
SS(PIP) Regs	The Social Security (Personal Independence Payment) Regulations 2013 No.377
SS(RB) Regs	The Social Security (Recovery of Benefits) Regulations 1997 No.2205
SS(RB)App Regs	The Social Security (Recovery of Benefits) (Appeals) Regulations 1997 No.2237
SS(SDA) Regs	The Social Security (Severe Disablement Allowances) Regulations 1984 No.1303
SS(WB&RP) Regs	The Social Security (Widow's Benefit and Retirement Pensions) Regulations 1979 No.642
SS(WBRP&OB)(T) Regs	The Social Security (Widow's Benefit, Retirement Pensions and Other Benefits) (Transitional) Regulations 1979 No.643
SS(WFILP) Regs	The Social Security (Work-focused Interviews for Lone Parents) and Miscellaneous Amendments Regulations 2000 No.1926
SS(WTCCTC)(CA) Regs	The Social Security (Working Tax Credit and Child Tax Credit) (Consequential Amendments) Regulations 2003 No.455
SSA(F)AO No.5	The Social Security Administration (Fraud) Act 1997 (Commencement No.5) Order 1997 No.2766
SSA(IO)(S)Regs	The Social Security Assistance (Investigation of Offences) (Scotland) Regulations 2020 No.11
SSB(CE) Regs	The Social Security Benefit (Computation of Earnings) Regulations 1996 No.2745
SSB(Dep) Regs	The Social Security Benefit (Dependency) Regulations 1977 No.343
SSB(MW&WSP) Regs	The Social Security (Benefit) (Married Women and Widows Special Provisions) Regulations 1974 No.2010
SSB(PA) Regs	The Social Security Benefit (Persons Abroad) Regulations 1975 No.563
SSB(PRT) Regs	The Social Security Benefit (Persons Residing Together) Regulations 1977 No.956
SSC(DA) Regs	The Social Security Contributions (Decisions and Appeals) Regulations 1999 No.1027

SSCBA(AAO) Regs	The Social Security Contributions and Benefits Act 1992 (Application of Parts 12ZA and 12ZB to Adoptions from Overseas) Regulations 2003 No.499
SSCBA(APOC) Regs	The Social Security Contributions and Benefits Act 1992 (Application of Parts 12ZA, 12ZB and 12ZC to Parental Order Cases) Regulations 2014 No.2866
SCBCTC(A) Regs	The Social Security, Child Benefit and Child Tax Credit (Amendment) (EU Exit) Regulations 2020 No.1505
SS&CS(DA) Regs	The Social Security and Child Support (Decisions and Appeals) Regulations 1999 No.991
SSFA(PM) Regs	The Social Security and Family Allowances (Polygamous Marriages) Regulations 1975 No.561
SSP Regs	The Statutory Sick Pay (General) Regulations 1982 No.894
SSP(MAPA) Regs	The Statutory Sick Pay (Mariners, Airmen and Persons Abroad) Regulations 1982 No.1349
SSP(ME) Regs	The Statutory Sick Pay (Medical Evidence) Regulations 1985 No.1604
SSPP(A) Regs	The Statutory Shared Parental Pay (Administration) Regulations 2014 No.2929
SSPP(G) Regs	The Statutory Shared Parental Pay (General) Regulations 2014 No.3051
SSPP(PAM) Regs	The Statutory Shared Parental Pay (Persons Abroad and Mariners) Regulations 2014 No.3134
SSPP(POC) Regs	The Statutory Shared Parental Pay (Parental Order Cases) Regulations 2014 No.3097
SSP&SMP(D) Regs	The Statutory Sick Pay and Statutory Maternity Pay (Decisions) Regulations 1999 No.776
ST(ORP) Regs	The Scottish Tribunals (Offences in Relation to Proceedings) Regulations 2016 No.342
ST(TL) Regs	The Scottish Tribunals (Time Limits) Regulations 2016 No.231
TC(A) Regs	The Tax Credits (Appeals) Regulations 2002 No.2926
TC(A)(No.2) Regs	The Tax Credits (Appeals) (No.2) Regulations 2002 No.3196
TC(CN) Regs	The Tax Credits (Claims and Notifications) Regulations 2002 No.2014
TC(DCI) Regs	The Tax Credits (Definition and Calculation of Income) Regulations 2002 No.2006
TC(Imm) Regs	The Tax Credits (Immigration) Regulations 2003 No.653
TC(IR) Regs	The Tax Credits (Interest Rate) Regulations 2003 No.123

TC(ITDR) Regs	The Tax Credits (Income Thresholds and Determination of Rates) Regulations 2002 No.2008
TC(OE) Regs	The Tax Credits (Official Error) Regulations 2003 No.692
TC(PC) Regs	The Tax Credits (Payments by the Commissioners) Regulations 2002 No.2173
TC(PM) Regs	The Tax Credits (Polygamous Marriages) Regulations 2003 No.742
TC(R) Regs	The Tax Credits (Residence) Regulations 2003 No.654
TCA(No.3)O	The Tax Credits Act 2002 (Commencement No.3 and Transitional Provisions and Savings) Order 2003
TCA(TP)O	The Tax Credits Act 2002 (Transitional Provisions) Order 2010 No.644
TP(FT) Rules	The Tribunal Procedure (First-tier Tribunal) (Social Entitlement Chamber) Rules 2008 No.2685
TP(FT)(TC) Rules	The Tribunal Procedure (First-tier Tribunal) (Tax Chamber) Rules 2009 No.273
TP(UT) Rules	The Tribunal Procedure (Upper Tribunal) Rules 2008 No.2698
UC Regs	The Universal Credit Regulations 2013 No.376
UC(ERSO) Regs	The Universal Credit (Energy Rebate Scheme Disregard) Regulations 2022 No.257
UC(MMP&MA) Regs	The Universal Credit (Managed Migration Pilot and Miscellaneous Amendments) Regulations 2019 No.115
UC(TP) Regs	The Universal Credit (Transitional Provisions) Regulations 2014 No.1230
UC(TP)(A) Regs	The Universal Credit (Transitional Provisions) (Amendment) Regulations 2014 No.1626
UC,PIP,JSA&ESA(C&P) Regs	The Universal Credit, Personal Independence Payment, Jobseeker's Allowance and Employment and Support Allowance (Claims and Payments) Regulations 2013 No.380
UC,PIP,JSA&ESA(DA) Regs	The Universal Credit, Personal Independence Payment, Jobseeker's Allowance and Employment and Support Allowance (Decisions and Appeals) Regulations 2013 No.381
UT(S) Rules	Schedule to The Upper Tribunal for Scotland (Social Security Rules of Procedure) Regulations 2018 No. 274
VP Regs	The Victims' Payments Regulations 2020 No.103
WF Regs	The Welfare Food Regulations 1996 No.1434
WF(BSF)(S) Regs	The Welfare Foods (Best Start Foods) (Scotland) Regulations 2019 No.193

WHACYP(S) Regs	The Winter Heating Assistance for Children and Young People (Scotland) Regulations 2020 No.352
WRA(No.8)O	The Welfare Reform Act 2012 (Commencement No.8 and Savings and Transitional Provisions) Order 2013 No.358
WRA(No.9)O	The Welfare Reform Act 2012 (Commencement No.9 and Transitional and Transitory Provisions and Commencement No.8 and Savings and Transitional Provisions (Amendment)) Order 2013 No.983
WRA(No.11)O	The Welfare Reform Act 2012 (Commencement No.11 and Transitional and Transitory Provisions and Commencement No.9 and Transitional and Transitory Provisions (Amendment)) Order 2013 No.1511
WRA(No.21)O	The Welfare Reform Act 2012 (Commencement and Transitional and Transitory Provisions) Order 2015 No.33
WRA(No.23)O	The Welfare Reform Act 2012 (Commencement No.23 and Transitional and Transitory Provisions) Order 2015 No.634
WRA(No.31)O	The Welfare Reform Act 2012 (Commencement No.31 and Savings and Transitional Provisions and Commencement No.21 and 23 and Transitional and Transitory Provisions (Amendment)) Order 2019 No.37
WRA(No.32)O	The Welfare Reform Act 2012 (Commencement No.32 and Savings and Transitional Provisions) Order 2019 No.167
WTC(EMR) Regs	The Working Tax Credit (Entitlement and Maximum Rate) Regulations 2002 No.2005

Other information

ADM	*Advice for Decision Making*, vols A1-V8
BLG	*Social Fund Budgeting Loan Guide*
CBTM	*Child Benefit Technical Manual*
CCM	*Claimant Compliance Manual* (HMRC guidance on investigation of tax credit claims)
DMG	*Decision Makers' Guide*, vols 1-14
DWPWAG	*Guidance relating to the UK's operational implementation of the social security coordination provisions of Part 2 of the EU Withdrawal Agreement: Citizens' Rights*, 29 November 2021
GM	*Housing Benefit/Council Tax Benefit Guidance Manual*
PIP AG	*PIP Assessment Guide*, 30 September 2019
SF Dir	*Social Fund Directive*
TCM	*Tax Credits Manual*
TCTM	Tax Credits Technical Manual
TFEU	The Treaty on the Functioning of the European Union
UK-EFTA	Agreement on arrangements between Iceland, Liechtenstein, Norway and the UK following the withdrawal of the UK from the EU, the EEA Agreement and other agreements
UK-EUP	Trade and cooperation agreement between the EU and (1) the European Atomic Energy Community and (2) the UK
UK-IC	Convention on social security between the UK and Ireland
UK-Swiss	Agreement between the UK and the Swiss Confederation on Citizens' Rights following the withdrawal of the UK from the EU and the Free Movement of Persons Agreement
WA 2019	*Agreement on the withdrawal of the United Kingdom of Great Britain and Northern Ireland from the European Union and the European Atomic Energy Community*, 19 October 2019

A

ndex

1835

ow to use this Index

ecause the *Handbook* is divided into separate sections covering the different benefits, many
ntries in the index have several references, each to a different section. Where this occurs, we
se the following abbreviations to show to which benefit each reference relates.

A	Attendance allowance	JSA	Jobseeker's allowance
DP	Adult disability payment	MA	Maternity allowance
A	Carer's allowance	NI	National insurance
DP	Child disability payment	PC	Pension credit
-ESA	Contributory employment and support allowance	PIP	Personal independence payment
		SAP	Statutory adoption pay
-JSA	Contribution-based jobseeker's allowance	SDA	Severe disablement allowance
		SMP	Statutory maternity pay
TC	Child tax credit	SPBP	Statutory parental bereavement pay
LA	Disability living allowance		
SA	Employment and support allowance	SPP	Statutory paternity pay
B	Housing benefit	SSP	Statutory sick pay
B	Incapacity benefit	SSPP	Statutory shared parental pay
DB	Industrial injuries disablement benefit	UC	Universal credit
		WTC	Working tax credit
S	Income support		
-ESA	Income-related employment and support allowance		
-JSA	Income-based jobseeker's allowance		

:ntries against the bold headings direct you to the general information on the subject, or
vhere the subject is covered most fully. Sub-entries are listed alphabetically and direct you to
pecific aspects of the subject.

offical errors 1403
payments exempt from recovery of
benefits 1176
personal injuries
UC 130
recovery of benefits from compensation
1174
special compensation schemes
means-tested benefits over pension
age 509
means-tested benefits under pension
age 484
UC 148
Compensation Recovery Unit 1174
compensation schemes
treatment of payments
means-tested benefits over pension
age 509
means-tested benefits under pension
age 484
UC 148
complaints 1402
about DWP 1403
about HM Courts and Tribunals Service
1407
about HMRC 1405
WTC/CTC 1480
about local authority administration
HB 1407
about Social Security Scotland 1750
grounds 1402
to councillor
HB 1407
to Independent Case Examiner 1404
to MP 1408
to Ombudsman 1408
HB 1409
components 336
ADP 1677
hospital patients 910
PIP 723
rates 338
support component
C-ESA 636
HB 337
I-ESA 337
work-related activity component 337
ESA 637
comprehensive sickness insurance 1583
conscientious objection
available for work rule
JSA 1099
good reason for refusing a job
UC 1080
jobseeker's direction 1124
constant attendance allowance 678
armed services 857
interchange of claims 1144

overlapping benefits 1151
treatment as income
means-tested benefits over pension
age 459
means-tested benefits under pension
age 420
contact lenses
vouchers 658
contaminated blood products
treatment of compensation payments
means-tested benefits over pension
age 509
means-tested benefits under pension
age 425, 485
UC 131, 149
continuous employment
SMP/SAP/SPP/SSPP/SPBP 803
contributory benefits 945
contribution conditions 964
cooking test
ADP 1679
PIP 726
coronavirus
AA
delay in claiming 523
renewal claims 523
appeal hearings
decisions without a hearing 1326
record of proceedings 1346
Best Start grants
time limits for claiming 1702
funeral support payment
time limits for claiming 1726
incapable of work
SSP 822, 826
judicial review
grounds for review 1380
limited capability for work
C-JSA 691
ESA 990
UC 989
MA
earnings 711
medical assessments 1010
work capability assessment process 1010
work-focused interview 1029
WTC 290
young carer grant
age rules 1738
date of claim 1739
Coronavirus Job Retention Scheme
payments treated as earnings
WTC/CTC 1443
council tax
arrears paid by deductions from benefit
1168
discretionary housing payments 627
discretionary reduction of bill 836

- -